The MIT Encyclopedia
of the Cognitive Sciences

The MIT Encyclopedia
of the Cognitive Sciences

EDITED BY

Robert A. Wilson and

Frank C. Keil

A Bradford Book

The MIT Press
Cambridge, Massachusetts
London, England

Library of Congress Cataloging-in-Publication Data

The MIT encyclopedia of the cognitive sciences / edited by Robert A. Wilson, Frank C. Keil.
      p.   cm.
    "A Bradford book."
    Includes bibliographical references and index.
    ISBN 0-262-73124-X (pbk. : alk. paper)
    1. Cognitive science—Encyclopedias I. Wilson, Robert A. (Robert Andrew) II. Keil, Frank C., 1952– .
    BF311.M556   1999
    153'.03—dc21   99-11115
                                               CIP

To the memory of Henry Bradford Stanton (a.k.a "Harry the hat"), 1921–1997, and to his wife Betty upon her retirement, after twenty-one years with Bradford Books. Harry and Betty were its cofounders and a major force in their own right in the flowering and cross-fertilization of the interdisciplinary cognitive sciences.

Contents

List of Entries

Preface

The *MIT Encyclopedia of the Cognitive Sciences* (*MITECS* to its friends) has been four years in the making from conception to publication. It consists of 471 concise articles, nearly all of which include useful lists of references and further readings, preceded by six longer introductory essays written by the volume's advisory editors. We see *MITECS* as being of use to students and scholars across the various disciplines that contribute to the cognitive sciences, including psychology, neuroscience, linguistics, philosophy, anthropology and the social sciences more generally, evolutionary biology, education, computer science, artificial intelligence, and ethology.

Although we prefer to let the volume speak largely for itself, it may help to provide some brief details about the aims and development of the project. One of the chief motivations for this undertaking was the sense that, despite a number of excellent works that overlapped with the ambit of cognitive science as it was traditionally conceived, there was no single work that adequately represented the full range of concepts, methods, and results derived and deployed in cognitive science over the last twenty-five years.

Second, each of the various cognitive sciences differs in its focus and orientation; in addition, these have changed over time and will continue to do so in the future. We see *MITECS* as aiming to represent the scope of this diversity, and as conveying a sense of both the history and future of the cognitive sciences.

Finally, we wanted, through discussions with authors and as a result of editorial review, to highlight links across the various cognitive sciences so that readers from one discipline might gain a greater insight into relevant work in other fields. *MITECS* represents far more than an alphabetic list of topics in the cognitive sciences; it captures a good deal of the structure of the whole enterprise at this point in time, the ways in which ideas are linked together across topics and disciplines, as well as the ways in which authors from very different disciplines converge and diverge in their approaches to very similar topics. As one looks through the encyclopedia as a whole, one takes a journey through a rich and multidimensional landscape of interconnected ideas. Categorization is rarely just that, especially in the sciences. Ideas and patterns are related to one another, and the grounds for categorizations are often embedded in complex theoretical and empirical patterns. *MITECS* illustrates the richness and intricacy of this process and the immense value of cognitive science approaches to many questions about the mind.

All three of the motivations for *MITECS* were instrumental in the internal organization of the project. The core of *MITECS* is the 471 articles themselves, which were assigned to one of six fields that constitute the foundation of the cognitive sciences. One or two advisory editors oversaw the articles in each of these fields and contributed the introductory essays. The fields and the corresponding advisory editors are

Philosophy (Robert A. Wilson)
Psychology (Keith J. Holyoak)
Neurosciences (Thomas D. Albright and Helen J. Neville)
Computational Intelligence (Michael I. Jordan and Stuart Russell)
Linguistics and Language (Gennaro Chierchia)
Culture, Cognition, and Evolution (Dan Sperber and Lawrence Hirschfeld)

These editors advised us regarding both the topics and authors for the articles and assisted in overseeing the review process for each. Considered collectively, the articles represent much of the diversity to be found in the corresponding fields and indicate much of what has been, is, and might be of value for those thinking about cognition from one or another interdisciplinary perspective.

Each introduction has two broad goals. The first is to provide a road map through *MITECS* to the articles in the corresponding section. Because of the arbitrariness of assigning some articles to one section rather than another, and because of the interdisciplinary vision guiding the volume, the introductions mention not only the articles in the corresponding section but also others from overlapping fields. The second goal is to provide a perspective on the nature of the corresponding discipline or disciplines, particularly with respect to the cognitive sciences. Each introduction should stand as a useful overview of the field it represents. We also made it clear to the editors that their introductions did not have to be completely neutral and could clearly express their own unique perspectives. The result is a vibrant and engaging series of essays.

We have been fortunate in being able to enlist many of the world's leading authorities as authors of the articles. Our directions to contributors were to write articles that are both representative of their topic and accessible to advanced undergraduates and graduate students in the field. The review process involved assigning two reviewers to each article, one an expert from within the same field, the other an outsider from another field represented in *MITECS*; nearly all reviewers were themselves contributors to *MITECS*. In addition, every article was read by at least one of the general editors. Articles that did not seem quite right to either or both of us or to our reviewers were sometimes referred to the advisory editors. One might think that with such short articles (most being between 1,000 and 1,500 words in length), the multiple levels of review were unnecessary, but the selectivity that this brevity necessitated made such a review process all the more worthwhile. Relatedly, as more than one contributor noted in explaining his own tardiness: "This article would have been written sooner if it hadn't been so short!".

Of course the content of the articles will be the chief source of their value to the reader, but given the imposed conciseness, an important part of their value is the guide that their references and further readings provide to the relevant literature. In addition, each article contains cross-references, indicated in SMALL CAPITALS, to related articles and a short list of "see also" cross-references at the end of the article. Responsibility for these cross-references lies ultimately with one of us (RAW), though we are thankful to those authors who took the time to suggest cross-references for their own articles.

We envisioned that many scholars would use *MITECS* as a frequent, perhaps even daily, tool in their research and have designed the references, readings, and cross-references with that use in mind. The electronic version will allow users to download relevant references into their bibliography databases along with considerable cross-classification information to aid future searches. Both of us are surprised at the extent to which we have already come to rely on drafts of articles in *MITECS* for these purposes in our own scholarly pursuits.

In the long list of people to thank, we begin with the contributors themselves, from whom we have learned much, both from their articles and their reviews of the articles of others, and to whom readers owe their first debt. Without the expertise of the advisory editors there is little chance that we would have arrived at a comprehensive range of topics or managed to identify and recruit many of the authors who have contributed to *MITECS*. And without their willingness to take on the chore of responding to our whims and fancies over a three-year period, and to write the section introductions, *MITECS* would have fallen short of its goals. Thanks Tom, Gennaro, Larry, Keith, Mike, Helen, Stuart, and Dan. At The MIT Press, we thank Amy Brand for her leadership and persistence, her able assistants Ed Sprague and Ben Bruening for their tech-know-how and hard work, and Sandra Minkkinen for editorial oversight of the process.

Rob Wilson thanks his coterie of research assistants: Patricia Ambrose and Peter Piegaze while he was at Queen's University; and Aaron Sklar, Keith Krueger, and Peter Asaro since he has been at the University of Illinois. His work on *MITECS* was supported, in part, by SSHRC Individual Three-Year Grant #410-96-0497, and a UIUC Campus Research Board Grant. Frank Keil thanks Cornell University for internal funds that were used to help support this project.

Philosophy

Robert A. Wilson

The areas of philosophy that contribute to and draw on the cognitive sciences are various; they include the philosophy of mind, science, and language; formal and philosophical logic; and traditional metaphysics and epistemology. The most direct connections hold between the philosophy of mind and the cognitive sciences, and it is with classical issues in the philosophy of mind that I begin this introduction (section 1). I then briefly chart the move from the rise of materialism as the dominant response to one of these classic issues, the mind-body problem, to the idea of a science of the mind. I do so by discussing the early attempts by introspectionists and behaviorists to study the mind (section 2). Here I focus on several problems with a philosophical flavor that arise for these views, problems that continue to lurk backstage in the theater of contemporary cognitive science.

Between these early attempts at a science of the mind and today's efforts lie two general, influential philosophical traditions, ordinary language philosophy and logical positivism. In order to bring out, by contrast, what is distinctive about the contemporary naturalism integral to philosophical contributions to the cognitive sciences, I sketch the approach to the mind in these traditions (section 3). And before getting to contemporary naturalism itself I take a quick look at the philosophy of science, in light of the legacy of positivism (section 4).

In sections 5 through 7 I get, at last, to the mind in cognitive science proper. Section 5 discusses the conceptions of mind that have dominated the contemporary cognitive sciences, particularly that which forms part of what is sometimes called "classic" cognitive science and that of its connectionist rival. Sections 6 and 7 explore two specific clusters of topics that have been the focus of philosophical discussion of the mind over the last 20 years or so, folk psychology and mental content. The final sections gesture briefly at the interplay between the cognitive sciences and logic (section 8) and biology (section 9).

1 Three Classic Philosophical Issues About the Mind

i. The Mental-Physical Relation

The relation between the mental and the physical is the deepest and most recurrent classic philosophical topic in the philosophy of mind, one very much alive today. In due course, we will come to see why this topic is so persistent and pervasive in thinking about the mind. But to convey something of the topic's historical significance let us begin with a classic expression of the puzzling nature of the relation between the mental and the physical, the MIND-BODY PROBLEM.

This problem is most famously associated with RENÉ DESCARTES, the preeminent figure of philosophy and science in the first half of the seventeenth century. Descartes combined a thorough-going mechanistic theory of nature with a *dualistic* theory of the nature of human beings that is still, in general terms, the most widespread view held by ordinary people outside the hallowed halls of academia. Although nature, including that of the human body, is material and thus completely governed by basic principles of mechanics, human beings are special in that they are composed both of material and nonmaterial or mental stuff, and so are not so governed. In Descartes's own terms, people are essentially a combination of mental substances (minds) and material substances (bodies). This is Descartes's *dualism*. To put it in more common-sense terms, people have both a mind and a body.

Although dualism is often presented as a possible solution to the mind-body problem, a possible position that one might adopt in explaining how the mental and physical are related, it serves better as a way to bring out why there is a "problem" here at all. For if the mind is one type of thing, and the body is another, how do these two

types of things interact? To put it differently, if the mind really is a nonmaterial substance, lacking physical properties such as spatial location and shape, how can it be
both the cause of effects in the material world—like making bodies move—and itself
be causally affected by that world—as when a thumb slammed with a hammer (bodily
cause) causes one to feel pain (mental effect)? This problem of causation between
mind and body has been thought to pose a largely unanswered problem for Cartesian
dualism.

It would be a mistake, however, to assume that the mind-body problem in its most
general form is simply a consequence of dualism. For the general question as to how
the mental is related to the physical arises squarely for those convinced that some version of materialism or PHYSICALISM must be true of the mind. In fact, in the next section, I will suggest that one reason for the resilience and relevance of the mind-body
problem has been the *rise* of materialism over the last fifty years.

Materialists hold that all that exists is material or physical in nature. Minds, then,
are somehow or other composed of arrangements of physical stuff. There have been
various ways in which the "somehow or other" has been cashed out by physicalists,
but even the view that has come closest to being a consensus view among contemporary materialists—that the mind *supervenes* on the body—remains problematic. Even
once one adopts materialism, the task of articulating the relationship between the
mental and the physical remains, because even physical minds have special properties,
like intentionality and consciousness, that require further explanation. Simply pro-
claiming that the mind is not made out of distinctly mental substance, but is material
like the rest of the world, does little to explain the features of the mind that seem to be
distinctively if not uniquely features of physical minds.

ii. The Structure of the Mind and Knowledge

Another historically important cluster of topics in the philosophy of mind concerns
what is in a mind. What, if anything, is distinctive of the mind, and how is the mind
structured? Here I focus on two dimensions to this issue.

One dimension stems from the RATIONALISM VS. EMPIRICISM debate that reached a
high point in the seventeenth and eighteenth centuries. Rationalism and empiricism
are views of the nature of human knowledge. Broadly speaking, empiricists hold that
all of our knowledge derives from our sensory, experiential, or empirical interaction
with the world. Rationalists, by contrast, hold the negation of this, that there is some
knowledge that does not derive from experience.

Since at least our paradigms of knowledge—of our immediate environments, of
common physical objects, of scientific kinds—seem obviously to be based on sense
experience, empiricism has significant intuitive appeal. Rationalism, by contrast,
seems to require further motivation: minimally, a list of knowables that represent a
prima facie challenge to the empiricist's global claim about the foundations of knowledge. Classic rationalists, such as Descartes, Leibniz, Spinoza, and perhaps more contentiously KANT, included knowledge of God, substance, and abstract ideas (such as
that of a triangle, as opposed to ideas of particular triangles). Empiricists over the last
three hundred years or so have either claimed that there was nothing to know in such
cases, or sought to provide the corresponding empiricist account of how we could
know such things from experience.

The different views of the sources of knowledge held by rationalists and empiricists
have been accompanied by correspondingly different views of the mind, and it is not
hard to see why. If one is an empiricist and so holds, roughly, that there is nothing in
the mind that is not first in the senses, then there is a fairly literal sense in which *ideas,*
found in the mind, are complexes that derive from *impressions* in the senses. This in
turn suggests that the processes that constitute cognition are themselves elaborations
of those that constitute perception, that is, that cognition and perception differ only in
degree, not kind. The most commonly postulated mechanisms governing these processes are *association* and *similarity,* from Hume's laws of association to feature-
extraction in contemporary connectionist networks. Thus, the mind tends to be viewed
by empiricists as a *domain-general* device, in that the principles that govern its opera-

tion are constant across various types and levels of cognition, with the common empirical basis for all knowledge providing the basis for parsimony here.

By contrast, in denying that all knowledge derives from the senses, rationalists are faced with the question of what other sources there are for knowledge. The most natural candidate is the mind itself, and for this reason rationalism goes hand in hand with NATIVISM about both the source of human knowledge and the structure of the human mind. If some ideas are innate (and so do not need to be derived from experience), then it follows that the mind already has a relatively rich, inherent structure, one that in turn limits the malleability of the mind in light of experience. As mentioned, classic rationalists made the claim that certain ideas or CONCEPTS were innate, a claim occasionally made by contemporary nativists—most notably Jerry Fodor (1975) in his claim that *all* concepts are innate. However, contemporary nativism is more often expressed as the view that certain implicit knowledge that we have or principles that govern how the mind works—most notoriously, linguistic knowledge and principles—are innate, and so not learned. And because the types of knowledge that one can have may be endlessly heterogeneous, rationalists tend to view the mind as a *domain-specific* device, as one made up of systems whose governing principles are very different. It should thus be no surprise that the historical debate between rationalists and empiricists has been revisited in contemporary discussions of the INNATENESS OF LANGUAGE, the MODULARITY OF MIND, and CONNECTIONISM.

A second dimension to the issue of the structure of the mind concerns the place of CONSCIOUSNESS among mental phenomena. From WILLIAM JAMES's influential analysis of the phenomenology of the stream of consciousness in his *The Principles of Psychology* (1890) to the renaissance that consciousness has experienced in the last ten years (if publication frenzies are anything to go by), consciousness has been thought to be the most puzzling of mental phenomena. There is now almost universal agreement that conscious mental states are a part of the mind. But how large and how important a part? Consciousness has sometimes been thought to exhaust the mental, a view often attributed to Descartes. The idea here is that everything mental is, in some sense, conscious or available to consciousness. (A version of the latter of these ideas has been recently expressed in John Searle's [1992: 156] *connection principle*: "all unconscious intentional states are in principle accessible to consciousness.")

There are two challenges to the view that everything mental is conscious or even available to consciousness. The first is posed by the *unconscious*. SIGMUND FREUD's extension of our common-sense attributions of belief and desire, our folk psychology, to the realm of the unconscious played and continues to play a central role in PSYCHOANALYSIS. The second arises from the conception of cognition as information processing that has been and remains focal in contemporary cognitive science, because such information processing is mostly *not* available to consciousness. If cognition so conceived is mental, then most mental processing is not available to consciousness.

iii. The First- and Third-Person Perspectives

Occupying center stage with the mind-body problem in traditional philosophy of mind is the *problem of other minds,* a problem that, unlike the mind-body problem, has all but disappeared from philosophical contributions to the cognitive sciences. The problem is often stated in terms of a contrast between the relatively secure way in which I "directly" know about the existence of *my own* mental states, and the far more epistemically risky way in which I must infer the existence of the mental states of others. Thus, although I can know about my own mental states simply by introspection and self-directed reflection, because this way of finding out about mental states is peculiarly first-person, I need some other type of evidence to draw conclusions about the mental states of others. Naturally, an agent's behavior is a guide to what mental states he or she is in, but there seems to be an epistemic gap between this sort of evidence and the attribution of the corresponding mental states that does not exist in the case of self-ascription. Thus the problem of other minds is chiefly an *epistemological* problem, sometimes expressed as a form of skepticism about the justification that we have for attributing mental states to others.

There are two reasons for the waning attention to the problem of other minds *qua problem* that derive from recent philosophical thought sensitive to empirical work in the cognitive sciences. First, research on introspection and SELF-KNOWLEDGE has raised questions about how "direct" our knowledge of our own mental states and of the SELF is, and so called into question traditional conceptions of first-person knowledge of mentality. Second, explorations of the THEORY OF MIND, ANIMAL COMMUNICATION, and SOCIAL PLAY BEHAVIOR have begun to examine and assess the sorts of attribution of mental states that are actually justified in empirical studies, suggesting that third-person knowledge of mental states is not as limited as has been thought. Considered together, this research hints that the contrast between first- and third-person knowledge of the mental is not as stark as the problem of other minds seems to intimate.

Still, there is something distinctive about the first-person perspective, and it is in part as an acknowledgment of this, to return to an earlier point, that consciousness has become a hot topic in the cognitive sciences of the 1990s. For whatever else we say about consciousness, it seems tied ineliminably to the first-person perspective. It is a state or condition that has an irreducibly *subjective* component, something with an essence to be experienced, and which presupposes the existence of a subject of that experience. Whether this implies that there are QUALIA that resist complete characterization in materialist terms, or other limitations to a science of the mind, remain questions of debate.

See also ANIMAL COMMUNICATION; CONCEPTS; CONNECTIONISM, PHILOSOPHICAL ISSUES; CONSCIOUSNESS; CONSCIOUSNESS, NEUROBIOLOGY OF; DESCARTES, RENÉ; FREUD, SIGMUND; INNATENESS OF LANGUAGE; JAMES, WILLIAM; KANT, IMMANUEL; MIND-BODY PROBLEM; MODULARITY OF MIND; NATIVISM; NATIVISM, HISTORY OF; PHYSICALISM; PSYCHOANALYSIS, CONTEMPORARY VIEWS; PSYCHOANALYSIS, HISTORY OF; QUALIA; RATIONALISM VS. EMPIRICISM; SELF; SELF-KNOWLEDGE; SOCIAL PLAY BEHAVIOR; THEORY OF MIND

2   From Materialism to Mental Science

In raising issue *i.*, the mental-physical relation, in the previous section, I implied that materialism was the dominant ontological view of the mind in contemporary philosophy of mind. I also suggested that, if anything, general convergence on this issue has intensified interest in the mind-body problem. For example, consider the large and lively debate over whether contemporary forms of materialism are compatible with genuine MENTAL CAUSATION, or, alternatively, whether they commit one to EPIPHENOMENALISM about the mental (Kim 1993; Heil and Mele 1993; Yablo 1992). Likewise, consider the fact that despite the dominance of materialism, some philosophers maintain that there remains an EXPLANATORY GAP between mental phenomena such as consciousness and any physical story that we are likely to get about the workings of the brain (Levine 1983; cf. Chalmers 1996). Both of these issues, very much alive in contemporary philosophy of mind and cognitive science, concern the mind-body problem, even if they are not always identified in such old-fashioned terms.

I also noted that a healthy interest in the first-person perspective persists within this general materialist framework. By taking a quick look at the two major initial attempts to develop a systematic, scientific understanding of the mind—late nineteenth-century introspectionism and early twentieth-century behaviorism—I want to elaborate on these two points and bring them together.

Introspectionism was widely held to fall prey to a problem known as the *problem of the homunculus*. Here I argue that behaviorism, too, is subject to a variation on this very problem, and that both versions of this problem continue to nag at contemporary sciences of the mind.

Students of the history of psychology are familiar with the claim that the roots of contemporary psychology can be dated from 1879, with the founding of the first experimental laboratory devoted to psychology by WILHELM WUNDT in Leipzig, Germany. As an *experimental* laboratory, Wundt's laboratory relied on the techniques introduced and refined in physiology and psychophysics over the preceding fifty years by HELMHOLTZ, Weber, and Fechner that paid particular attention to the report of SEN-SATIONS. What distinguished Wundt's as a laboratory of *psychology* was his focus on the data reported in consciousness via the first-person perspective; psychology was to be the science of immediate experience and its most basic constituents. Yet we should remind ourselves of how restricted this conception of psychology was, particularly relative to contemporary views of the subject.

First, Wundt distinguished between mere INTROSPECTION, first-person reports of the sort that could arise in the everyday course of events, and experimentally manipulable self-observation of the sort that could only be triggered in an experimental context. Although Wundt is often thought of as the founder of an introspectionist methodology that led to a promiscuous psychological ontology, in disallowing mere introspection as an appropriate method for a science of the mind he shared at least the sort of restrictive conception of psychology with *both* his physiological predecessors and his later behaviorist critics.

Second, Wundt thought that the vast majority of ordinary thought and cognition was *not* amenable to acceptable first-person analysis, and so lay beyond the reach of a scientific psychology. Wundt thought, for example, that belief, language, personality, and SOCIAL COGNITION could be studied systematically only by detailing the cultural mores, art, and religion of whole societies (hence his four-volume *Völkerpsychologie* of 1900–1909). These studies belonged to the humanities (*Geisteswissenshaften*) rather than the experimental sciences (*Naturwissenschaften*), and were undertaken by anthropologists inspired by Wundt, such as BRONISLAW MALINOWSKI.

Wundt himself took one of his early contributions to be a solution of the mind-body problem, for that is what the data derived from the application of the experimental method to distinctly psychological phenomena gave one: correlations between the mental and the physical that indicated how the two were systematically related. The discovery of psychophysical laws of this sort showed how the mental was related to the physical. Yet with the expansion of the domain of the mental amenable to experimental investigation over the last 150 years, the mind-body problem has taken on a more acute form: just how do we get all that mind-dust from merely material mechanics? And it is here that the problem of the homunculus arises for introspectionist psychology after Wundt.

The problem, put in modern guise, is this. Suppose that one introspects, say, in order to determine the location of a certain feature (a cabin, for example) on a map that one has attempted to memorize (Kosslyn 1980). Such introspection is typically reported in terms of exploring a mental image with one's *mind's eye*. Yet we hardly want our psychological story to end there, because it posits a process (introspection) and a processor (the mind's eye) that themselves cry out for further explanation. The problem of the homunculus is the problem of leaving undischarged homunculi ("little men" or their equivalents) in one's *explanantia,* and it persists as we consider an elaboration on our initial introspective report. For example, one might well report forming a mental image of the map, and then scanning around the various features of the map, zooming in on them to discern more clearly what they are to see if any of them is the sought-after cabin. To take this introspective report seriously as a guide to the underlying psychological mechanisms would be to posit, minimally, an *imager* (to form the initial image), a *scanner* (to guide your mind's eye around the image), and a *zoomer* (to adjust the relative sizes of the features on the map). But here again we face the problem of the homunculus, because such "mechanisms" themselves require further psychological decomposition.

To be faced with the problem of the homunculus, of course, is not the same as to succumb to it. We might distinguish two understandings of just what the "problem" is here. First, the problem of the homunculus could be viewed as a problem specifically for introspectionist views of psychology, a problem that was never successfully met and that was principally responsible for the abandonment of introspectionism. As such, the problem motivated BEHAVIORISM in psychology. Second, the problem of the homunculus might simply be thought of as a challenge that *any* view that posits internal mental states must respond to: to show how to discharge all of the homunculi introduced in a way that is acceptably materialistic. So construed, the problem remains one that has been with us more recently, in disputes over the psychological reality of various forms of GENERATIVE GRAMMAR (e.g., Stabler 1983); in the nativism that has been extremely influential in post-Piagetian accounts of COGNITIVE DEVELOPMENT (Spelke 1990; cf. Elman et al. 1996); and in debates over the significance of MENTAL ROTATION and the nature of IMAGERY (Kosslyn 1994; cf. Pylyshyn 1984: ch.8).

With Wundt's own restrictive conception of psychology and the problem of the homunculus in mind, it is with some irony that we can view the rise and fall of behaviorism as the dominant paradigm for psychology subsequent to the introspectionism that Wundt founded. For here was a view so deeply indebted to materialism and the imperative to explore psychological claims only by reference to what was acceptably experimental that, in effect, in its purest form it appeared to do away with the distinctively mental altogether! That is, because objectively observable behavioral responses to objectively measurable stimuli are all that could be rigorously explored, experimental psychological investigations would need to be significantly curtailed, relative to those of introspectionists such as Wundt and Titchener. As J. B. Watson said in his early, influential "Psychology as the Behaviorist Views It" in 1913, "Psychology as behavior will, after all, have to neglect but few of the really essential problems with which psychology as an introspective science now concerns itself. In all probability even this residue of problems may be phrased in such a way that refined methods in behavior (which certainly must come) will lead to their solution" (p. 177).

Behaviorism brought with it not simply a global conception of psychology but specific methodologies, such as CONDITIONING, and a focus on phenomena, such as that of LEARNING, that have been explored in depth since the rise of behaviorism. Rather than concentrate on these sorts of contribution to the interdisciplinary sciences of the mind that behaviorists have made, I want to focus on the central problem that faced behaviorism as a research program for reshaping psychology.

One of the common points shared by behaviorists in their philosophical and psychological guises was a commitment to an *operational* view of psychological concepts and thus a suspicion of any reliance on concepts that could not be operationally characterized. Construed as a view of scientific *definition* (as it was by philosophers), operationalism is the view that scientific terms must be defined in terms of observable and measurable operations that one can perform. Thus, an operational definition of "length," as applied to ordinary objects, might be: "the measure we obtain by laying a standard measuring rod or rods along the body of the object." Construed as a view of scientific *methodology* (as it was by psychologists), operationalism claims that the subject matter of the sciences should be objectively observable and measurable, by itself a view without much content.

The real bite of the insistence on operational definitions and methodology for psychology came via the application of operationalism to unobservables, for the various feelings, sensations, and other internal states reported by introspection, themselves unobservable, proved difficult to operationalize adequately. Notoriously, the introspective reports from various psychological laboratories produced different listings of the basic feelings and sensations that made up consciousness, and the lack of agreement here generated skepticism about the reliability of introspection as a method for revealing the structure of the mind. In psychology, this led to a focus on behavior, rather than consciousness, and to its exploration through observable stimulus and response: hence, behaviorism. But I want to suggest that this reliance on operationalism itself created a version of the problem of the homunculus for behaviorism. This point can be made in two ways, each of which offers a reinterpretation of a standard criticism of behaviorism. The first of these criticisms is usually called "philosophical behaviorism," the attempt to provide conceptual analyses of mental state terms exclusively in terms of behavior; the second is "psychological behaviorism," the research program of studying objective and observable behavior, rather than subjective and unobservable inner mental episodes.

First, as Geach (1957: chap. 4) pointed out with respect to belief, behaviorist analyses of individual folk psychological states are bound to fail, because it is only in concert with many other propositional attitudes that any given such attitude has behavioral effects. Thus, to take a simple example, we might characterize the belief that it is raining as the tendency to utter "yes" when asked, "Do you believe that it is raining?" But one reason this would be inadequate is that one will engage in this verbal behavior only if one *wants* to answer truthfully, and only if one *hears* and *understands* the question asked, where each of the italicized terms above refers to some other mental state. Because the problem recurs in *every* putative analysis, this implies that a behavioristically acceptable construal of folk psychology is not possible. This point would seem to generalize beyond folk psychology to representational psychology more generally.

So, in explicitly attempting to do without internal mental representations, behaviorists themselves are left with mental states that must simply be assumed. Here we are not far from those undischarged homunculi that were the bane of introspectionists, especially once we recognize that the metaphorical talk of "homunculi" refers precisely to internal mental states and processes that themselves are not further explained.

Second, as Chomsky (1959: esp. p. 54) emphasized in his review of Skinner's *Verbal Behavior*, systematic attempts to operationalize psychological language invariably smuggle in a reference to the very mental processes they are trying to do without. At the most general level, the behavior of interest to the linguist, Skinner's "verbal behavior," is difficult to characterize adequately without at least an implicit reference to the sorts of psychological mechanism that generate it. For example, linguists are not interested in mere noises that have the same physical properties—"harbor" may be pronounced so that its first syllable has the same acoustic properties as an exasperated grunt—but in parts of speech that are taxonomized at least partially in terms of the surrounding mental economy of the speaker or listener.

The same seems true for *all* of the processes introduced by behaviorists—for example, stimulus control, reinforcement, conditioning—insofar as they are used to characterize complex, human behavior that has a natural psychological description (making a decision, reasoning, conducting a conversation, issuing a threat). What marks off their instances as behaviors *of the same kind* is not exclusively their physical or behavioral similarity, but, in part, the common, internal psychological processes that generate them, and that they in turn generate. Hence, the irony: behaviorists, themselves motivated by the idea of reforming psychology so as to generalize about objective, observable behavior and so avoid the problem of the homunculus, are faced with undischarged homunculi, that is, irreducibly mental processes, in their very own alternative to introspectionism.

The two versions of the problem of the homunculus are still with us as a Scylla and Charybdis for contemporary cognitive scientists to steer between. On the one hand, theorists need to avoid building the very cognitive abilities that they wish to explain into the models and theories they construct. On the other, in attempting to side-step this problem they also run the risk of masking the ways in which their "objective" taxonomic categories presuppose further internal psychological description of precisely the sort that gives rise to the problem of the homunculus in the first place.

See also BEHAVIORISM; COGNITIVE DEVELOPMENT; CONDITIONING; EPIPHENOMENALISM; EXPLANATORY GAP; GENERATIVE GRAMMAR; HELMHOLTZ, HERMANN; IMAGERY; INTROSPECTION; LEARNING; MALINOWSKI, BRONISLAW; MENTAL CAUSATION; MENTAL ROTATION; SENSATIONS; SOCIAL COGNITION; SOCIAL COGNITION IN ANIMALS; WUNDT, WILHELM

3   A Detour Before the Naturalistic Turn

Given the state of philosophy and psychology in the early 1950s, it is surprising that within twenty-five years there would be a thriving and well-focused interdisciplinary unit of study, cognitive science, to which the two are central. As we have seen, psychology was dominated by behaviorist approaches that were largely skeptical of positing internal mental states as part of a serious, scientific psychology. And Anglo-American philosophy featured two distinct trends, each of which made philosophy more insular with respect to other disciplines, and each of which served to reinforce the behaviorist orientation of psychology.

First, ordinary language philosophy, particularly in Great Britain under the influence of Ludwig Wittgenstein and J. L. Austin, demarcated distinctly philosophical problems as soluble (or dissoluble) chiefly by reference to what one would ordinarily say, and tended to see philosophical views of the past and present as the result of confusions in how philosophers and others come to use words that generally have a clear sense in their ordinary contexts. This approach to philosophical issues in the post-war period has recently been referred to by Marjorie Grene (1995: 55) as the "Bertie Wooster season in philosophy," a characterization I suspect would seem apt to many philosophers of mind interested in contemporary cognitive science (and in P. G. Wodehouse). Let me illustrate how this approach to philosophy served to isolate the philosophy of mind from the sciences of the mind with perhaps the two most influential examples pertaining to the mind in the ordinary language tradition.

In *The Concept of Mind,* Gilbert Ryle (1949: 17) attacked a view of the mind that he referred to as "Descartes' Myth" and "the dogma of the Ghost in the Machine"—basically, dualism—largely through a repeated application of the objection that dualism consisted of an extended *category mistake*: it "represents the facts of mental life as if they belonged to one logical type or category . . . when they actually belong to another." Descartes' Myth represented a category mistake because in supposing that there was a special, inner theater on which mental life is played out, it treated the "facts of mental life" as belonging to a special category of facts, when they were simply facts about how people can, do, and would behave in certain circumstances. Ryle set about showing that for the range of mental concepts that were held to refer to private, internal mental episodes or events according to Descartes' Myth—intelligence, the will, emotion, self-knowledge, sensation, and imagination—an appeal to what one would ordinarily say both shows the dogma of the Ghost in the Machine to be false, and points to a positive account of the mind that was behaviorist in orientation. To convey why Ryle's influential views here turned philosophy of mind away from science rather than towards it, consider the opening sentences of *The Concept of Mind*: "This book offers what may with reservations be described as a theory of the mind. But it does not give new information about minds. We possess already a wealth of information about minds, information which is neither derived from, nor upset by, the arguments of philosophers. The philosophical arguments which constitute this book are intended not to increase what we know about minds, but to rectify the logical geography of the knowledge which we already possess" (Ryle 1949: 9). The "we" here refers to ordinary folk, and the philosopher's task in articulating a theory of mind is to draw on what we already know about the mind, rather than on arcane, philosophical views or on specialized, scientific knowledge.

The second example is Norman Malcolm's *Dreaming,* which, like *The Concept of Mind,* framed the critique it wished to deliver as an attack on a Cartesian view of the mind. Malcolm's (1959: 4) target was the view that "dreams are the activity of the mind during sleep," and associated talk of DREAMING as involving various mental acts, such as remembering, imagining, judging, thinking, and reasoning. Malcolm argued that such dream-talk, whether it be part of commonsense reflection on dreaming (How long do dreams last?; Can you work out problems in your dreams?) or a contribution to more systematic empirical research on dreaming, was a confusion arising from the failure to attend to the proper "logic" of our ordinary talk about dreaming. Malcolm's argument proceeded by appealing to how one would *use* various expressions and sentences that contained the word "dreaming." (In looking back at Malcolm's book, it is striking that nearly every one of the eighteen short chapters begins with a paragraph about words and what one would say with or about them.)

Malcolm's central point was that there was no way to *verify* any given claim about such mental activity occurring while one was asleep, because the commonsense criteria for the application of such concepts were incompatible with saying that a person was asleep or dreaming. And because there was no way to tell whether various attributions of mental states to a sleeping person were correct, such attributions were meaningless. These claims not only could be made without an appeal to any empirical details about dreaming or SLEEP, but implied that the whole enterprise of investigating dreaming empirically itself represented some sort of *logical* muddle.

Malcolm's point became more general than one simply about dreaming (or the word "dreaming"). As he said in a preface to a later work, written after "the notion that thoughts, ideas, memories, sensations, and so on 'code into' or 'map onto' neural firing patterns in the brain" had become commonplace: "I believe that a study of our psychological concepts can show that [such] psycho-physical isomorphism is not a coherent assumption" (Malcolm 1971: x). Like Ryle's straightening of the logical geography of our knowledge of minds, Malcolm's appeal to the study of our psychological concepts could be conducted without any knowledge gleaned from psychological science (cf. Griffiths 1997: chap. 2 on the emotions).

Quite distinct from the ordinary language tradition was a second general perspective that served to make philosophical contributions to the study of the mind "distinctive" from those of science. This was logical positivism or empiricism, which developed in Europe in the 1920s and flourished in the United States through the 1930s and 1940s with the immigration to the United States of many of its leading members, including Rudolph Carnap, Hans Reichenbach, Herbert Feigl, and Carl Hempel. The logical empiricists were called "empiricists" because they held that it was via the senses and observation that we came to know about the world, deploying this empiricism with the logical techniques that had been developed by Gottlob Frege, Bertrand Russell, and Alfred Whitehead. Like empiricists in general, the logical positivists viewed the sciences as the paradigmatic repository of knowledge, and they were largely responsible for the rise of philosophy of science as a distinct subdiscipline within philosophy.

As part of their reflection on science they articulated and defended the doctrine of the UNITY OF SCIENCE, the idea that the sciences are, in some sense, essentially unified, and their empiricism led them to appeal to PARSIMONY AND SIMPLICITY as grounds for both theory choice within science and for preferring theories that were ontological Scrooges. This empiricism came with a focus on *what could be verified,* and with it scepticism about traditional metaphysical notions, such as God, CAUSATION, and essences, whose instances could not be verified by an appeal to the data of sense experience. This emphasis on verification was encapsulated in the verification theory of meaning, which held that the meaning of a sentence was its method of verification, implying that sentences without any such method were *meaningless.* In psychology, this fueled skepticism about the existence of internal mental representations and states (whose existence could not be objectively verified), and offered further philosophical backing for behaviorism.

In contrast to the ordinary language philosophers (many of whom would have been professionally embarrassed to have been caught knowing anything about science), the positivists held that philosophy was to be informed about and sensitive to the results of science. The distinctive task of the philosopher, however, was not simply to describe scientific practice, but to offer a *rational reconstruction* of it, one that made clear the logical structure of science. Although the term "*rational reconstruction*" was used first by Carnap in his 1928 book *The Logical Construction of the World,* quite a general epistemological tract, the technique to which it referred came to be applied especially to scientific concepts and theories.

This played out in the frequent appeal to the distinction between the *context of discovery* and the *context of justification,* drawn as such by Reichenbach in *Experience and Prediction* (1938) but with a longer history in the German tradition. To consider an aspect of a scientific view in the context of discovery was essentially to raise psychological, sociological, or historical questions about how that view originated, was developed, or came to be accepted or rejected. But properly philosophical explorations of science were to be conducted in the context of justification, raising questions and making claims about the logical structure of science and the concepts it used. Rational reconstruction was the chief way of divorcing the relevant scientific theory from its mere context of discovery.

A story involving Feigl and Carnap nicely illustrates the divorce between philosophy and science within positivism. In the late 1950s, Feigl visited the University of California, Los Angeles, to give a talk to the Department of Philosophy, of which Carnap was a member. Feigl's talk was aimed at showing that a form of physicalism, the mind-brain identity theory, faced an empirical problem, since science had little, if anything, to say about the "raw feel" of consciousness, the WHAT-IT'S-LIKE of experience. During the question period, Carnap raised his hand, and was called on by Feigl. "Your claim that current neurophysiology tells us nothing about raw feels is wrong! You have overlooked the discovery of alpha-waves in the brain," exclaimed Carnap. Feigl, who was familiar with what he thought was the relevant science, looked puzzled: "Alpha-waves? What are they?" Carnap replied: "My dear Herbert. You tell me what raw feels are, and I will tell you what alpha-waves are."

Of the multiple readings that this story invites (whose common denominator is surely Carnap's savviness and wit), consider those that take Carnap's riposte to imply that he thought that one could defend materialism by, effectively, making up the science to fit whatever phenomena critics could rustle up. A rather extreme form of rational reconstruction, but it suggests one way in which the positivist approach to psychology could be just as a priori and so divorced from empirical practice as that of Ryle and Malcolm.

See also CAUSATION; DREAMING; PARSIMONY AND SIMPLICITY; SLEEP; UNITY OF SCIENCE; WHAT-IT'S-LIKE

4   The Philosophy of Science

The philosophy of science is integral to the cognitive sciences in a number of ways. We have already seen that positivists held views about the overall structure of science and the grounds for theory choice in science that had implications for psychology. Here I focus on three functions that the philosophy of science plays vis-à-vis the cognitive sciences: it provides a perspective on the place of psychology among the sciences; it raises questions about what any science can tell us about the world; and it explores the nature of knowledge and how it is known. I take these in turn.

One classic way in which the sciences were viewed as being unified, according to the positivists, was via reduction. REDUCTIONISM, in this context, is the view that intuitively "higher-level" sciences can be reduced, in some sense, to "lower-level" sciences. Thus, to begin with the case perhaps of most interest to MITECS readers, psychology was held to be reducible in principle to biology, biology to chemistry, chemistry to physics. This sort of reduction presupposed the existence of *bridge laws,* laws that exhaustively characterized the concepts of any higher-level science, and the generalizations stated using them, in terms of those concepts and generalizations at the next level down. And because reduction was construed as relating theories of one science to those of another, the advocacy of reductionism went hand-in-hand with a view of EXPLANATION that gave lower-level sciences at least a usurpatory power over their higher-level derivatives.

This view of the structure of science was opposed to EMERGENTISM, the view that the properties studied by higher-level sciences, such as psychology, were not mere aggregates of properties studied by lower-level sciences, and thus could not be completely understood in terms of them. Both emergentism and this form of reductionism were typically cast in terms of the relationship between laws in higher- and lower-level sciences, thus presupposing that there were, in the psychological case, PSYCHOLOGICAL LAWS in the first place. One well-known position that denies this assumption is Donald Davidson's ANOMALOUS MONISM, which claims that while mental states *are* strictly identical with physical states, our descriptions of them as mental states are neither definitionally nor nomologically reducible to descriptions of them as physical states. This view is usually expressed as denying the possibility of the bridge laws required for the reduction of psychology to biology.

Corresponding to the emphasis on scientific laws in views of the relations between the sciences is the idea that these laws state relations between NATURAL KINDS. The idea of a natural kind is that of a type or kind of thing that exists in the world itself, rather than a kind or grouping that exists because of our ways of perceiving, thinking about, or interacting with the world. Paradigms of natural kinds are biological kinds—species, such as the domestic cat (*Felis domesticus*)—and chemical kinds—such as silver (Ag) and gold (Au). Natural kinds can be contrasted with *artifactual* kinds (such as chairs), whose members are artifacts that share common functions or purposes relative to human needs or designs; with *conventional* kinds (such as marriage vows), whose members share some sort of conventionally determined property; and from purely arbitrary groupings of objects, whose members have nothing significant in common save that they belong to the category. Views of what natural kinds are, of how extensively science traffics in them, and of how we should characterize the notion of a natural kind vis-à-vis other metaphysic notions, such as essence, intrinsic property, and causal power, all remain topics of debate in contemporary philosophy of science (e.g., van Fraassen 1989; Wilson 1999).

There is an intuitive connection between the claims that there are natural kinds, and that the sciences strive to identify them, and *scientific realism,* the view that the entities in mature sciences, whether they are observable or not, exist and our theories about them are at least approximately true. For realists hold that the sciences strive to "carve nature at its joints," and natural kinds are the pre-existing joints that one's scientific carving tries to find. The REALISM AND ANTIREALISM issue is, of course, more complicated than suggested by the view that scientific realists think there are natural kinds, and antirealists deny this—not least because there are a number of ways to deny either this realist claim or to diminish its significance. But such a perspective provides one starting point for thinking about the different views one might have of the relationship between science and reality.

Apart from raising issues concerning the relationships between psychology and other sciences and their respective objects of study, and questions about the relation between science and reality, the philosophy of science is also relevant to the cognitive sciences as a branch of epistemology or the theory of knowledge, studying a particular type of knowledge, scientific knowledge. A central notion in the general theory of knowledge is JUSTIFICATION, because being justified in what we believe is at least one thing that distinguishes knowledge from mere belief or a lucky guess. Since scientific knowledge is a paradigm of knowledge, views of justification have often been developed with scientific knowledge in mind.

The question of what it is for an individual to have a justified belief, however, has remained contentious in the theory of knowledge. Justified beliefs are those that we are entitled to hold, ones for which we have reasons, but how should we understand such entitlement and such reasons? One dichotomy here is between *internalists* about justification, who hold that having justified belief exclusively concerns facts that are "internal" to the believer, facts about his or her internal cognitive economy; and *externalists* about justification, who deny this. A second dichotomy is between *naturalists,* who hold that what cognitive states are justified may depend on facts about cognizers or about the world beyond cognizers that are uncovered by empirical science; and *rationalists,* who hold that justification is determined by the relations between one's cognitive states that the agent herself is in a special position to know about. Clearly part of what is at issue between internalists and externalists, as well as between naturalists and rationalists, is the role of the first-person perspective in accounts of justification and thus knowledge (see also Goldman 1997).

These positions about justification raise some general questions about the relationship between EPISTEMOLOGY AND COGNITION, and interact with views of the importance of first- and third-person perspectives on cognition itself. They also suggest different views of RATIONAL AGENCY, of what it is to be an agent who acts on the basis of justified beliefs. Many traditional views of rationality imply that cognizers have LOGICAL OMNISCIENCE, that is, that they believe all the logical consequences of their beliefs. Since clearly we are not logically omniscient, there is a question of how to modify one's account of rationality to avoid this result.

See also ANOMALOUS MONISM; EMERGENTISM; EPISTEMOLOGY AND COGNITION; EXPLANATION; JUSTIFICATION; LOGICAL OMNISCIENCE, PROBLEM OF; NATURAL KINDS; PSYCHOLOGICAL LAWS; RATIONAL AGENCY; REALISM AND ANTIREALISM; REDUCTIONISM

5   The Mind in Cognitive Science

At the outset, I said that the relation between the mental and physical remains the central, general issue in contemporary, materialist philosophy of mind. In section 2, we saw that the behaviorist critiques of Cartesian views of the mind and behaviorism themselves introduced a dilemma that derived from the problem of the homunculus that any mental science would seem to face. And in section 3 I suggested how a vibrant skepticism about the scientific status of a distinctively psychological science and philosophy's contribution to it was sustained by two dominant philosophical perspectives. It is time to bring these three points together as we move to explore the view of the mind that constituted the core of the developing field of cognitive science in the 1970s, what is sometimes called *classic* cognitive science, as well as its successors.

If we were to pose questions central to each of these three issues—the mental-physical relation, the problem of the homunculus, and the possibility of a genuinely cognitive science, they might be:

a. What is the relation between the mental and the physical?
b. How can psychology avoid the problem of the homunculus?
c. What makes a genuinely *mental* science possible?

Strikingly, these questions received standard answers, in the form of three "isms," from the nascent naturalistic perspective in the philosophy of mind that accompanied the rise of classic cognitive science. (The answers, so you don't have to peek ahead, are, respectively, functionalism, computationalism, and representationalism.)

The answer to (a) is FUNCTIONALISM, the view, baldly put, that mental states are functional states. Functionalists hold that what really matters to the identity of types of mental states is not what their instances are made of, but how those instances are causally arranged: what causes them, and what they, in turn, cause. Functionalism represents a view of the mental-physical relation that is compatible with materialism or physicalism because even if it is the functional or causal *role* that makes a mental state the state it is, every *occupant* of any particular role could be physical. The role-occupant distinction, introduced explicitly by Armstrong (1968) and implicitly in Lewis (1966), has been central to most formulations of functionalism.

A classic example of something that is functionally identified or individuated is *money:* it's not what it's made of (paper, gold, plastic) that makes something money but, rather, the causal role that it plays in some broader economic system. Recognizing this fact about money is not to give up on the idea that money is material or physical. Even though material composition is not what determines whether something is money, every instance of money is material or physical: dollar bills and checks are made of paper and ink, coins are made of metal, even money that is stored solely as a string of digits in your bank account has *some* physical composition. There are at least two related reasons why functionalism *about the mind* has been an attractive view to philosophers working in the cognitive sciences.

The first is that functionalism at least appears to support the AUTONOMY OF PSYCHOLOGY, for it claims that even if, as a matter of fact, our psychological states are realized in states of our brains, their status as *psychological* states lies in their functional organization, which can be abstracted from this particular material stuff. This is a *nonreductive* view of psychology. If functionalism is true, then there will be distinctively psychological natural kinds that cross-cut the kinds that are determined by a creature's material composition. In the context of materialism, functionalism suggests that creatures with very different material organizations could not only have mental states, but have *the same kinds* of mental states. Thus functionalism makes sense of comparative psychological or neurological investigations across species.

The second is that functionalism allows for *nonbiological* forms of intelligence and mentality. That is, because it is the "form" not the "matter" that determines psychological kinds, there could be entirely artifactual creatures, such as robots or computers, with mental states, provided that they have the right functional organization. This idea has been central to traditional artificial intelligence (AI), where one ideal has been to create programs with a functional organization that not only allows them to behave in some crude way like intelligent agents but to do so in a way that instantiates at least some aspects of intelligence itself.

Both of these ideas have been criticized as part of attacks on functionalism. For example, Paul and Patricia Churchland (1981) have argued that the "autonomy" of psychology that one gains from functionalism can be a cover for the emptiness of the science itself, and Jaegwon Kim (1993) has argued against the coherence of the nonreductive forms of materialism usually taken to be implied by functionalism. Additionally, functionalism and AI are the targets of John Searle's much-discussed CHINESE ROOM ARGUMENT.

Consider (c), the question of what makes a distinctively mental science possible. Although functionalism gives one sort of answer to this in its basis for a defense of the autonomy (and so distinctness) of psychology, because there are more functional kinds than those in psychology (assuming functionalism), this answer does not explain what is distinctively *psychological* about psychology. A better answer to this question is *representationalism,* also known as the representational theory of mind. This is the view that mental states are relations between the bearers of those states and internal mental representations. Representationalism answers (c) by viewing psychology as the science concerned with the forms these mental representations can take, the ways in which they can be manipulated, and how they interact with one another in mediating between perceptual input and behavioral output.

A traditional version of representationalism, one cast in terms of Ideas, themselves often conceptualized as images, was held by the British empiricists John Locke, George Berkeley, and DAVID HUME. A form of representationalism, the LANGUAGE OF THOUGHT (LOT) hypothesis, has more recently been articulated and defended by Jerry Fodor (1975, 1981, 1987, 1994). The LOT hypothesis is the claim that we are able to cognize in virtue of having a mental language, *mentalese,* whose symbols are combined systematically by syntactic rules to form more complex units, such as thoughts. Because these mental symbols are intentional or representational (they are about things), the states that they compose are representational; mental states inherit their intentionality from their constituent mental representations.

Fodor himself has been particularly exercised to use the language of thought hypothesis to chalk out a place for the PROPOSITIONAL ATTITUDES and our folk psychology within the developing sciences of the mind. Not all proponents of the representational theory of mind, however, agree with Fodor's view that the system of representation underlying thought is a *language,* nor with his defense of folk psychology. But even forms of representationalism that are less committal than Fodor's own provide an answer to the question of what is distinctive about psychology: psychology is not mere neuroscience because it traffics in a range of mental representations and posits internal processes that operate on these representations.

Representationalism, particularly in Fodoresque versions that see the language of thought hypothesis as forming the foundations for a defense of both cognitive psychology and our commonsense folk psychology, has been challenged within cognitive science by the rise of connectionism in psychology and NEURAL NETWORKS within computer science. Connectionist models of psychological processing might be taken as an existence proof that one does not need to assume what is sometimes called the RULES AND REPRESENTATIONS approach to understand cognitive functions: the language of thought hypothesis is no longer "the only game in town."

Connectionist COGNITIVE MODELING of psychological processing, such as that of the formation of past tense (Rumelhart and McClelland 1986), face recognition (Cottrell and Metcalfe 1991), and VISUAL WORD RECOGNITION (Seidenberg and McClelland 1989), typically does not posit discrete, decomposable representations that are concatenated through the rules of some language of thought. Rather, connectionists posit a COGNITIVE ARCHITECTURE made up of simple neuron-like nodes, with activity being propagated across the units proportional to the weights of the connection strength between them. Knowledge lies not in the nodes themselves but in the values of the weights connecting nodes. There seems to be nothing of a propositional form within such connectionist networks, no place for the internal sentences that are the objects of folk psychological states and other subpersonal psychological states posited in accounts of (for example) memory and reasoning.

The tempting idea that "classicists" accept, and connectionists reject, representationalism is too simple, one whose implausibility is revealed once one shifts one's focus from folk psychology and the propositional attitudes to cognition more generally. Even when research in classical cognitive science—for example, that on KNOWLEDGE-BASED SYSTEMS and on BAYESIAN NETWORKS—is cast in terms of "beliefs" that a system has, the connection between "beliefs" and the beliefs of folk psychology has been underexplored. More importantly, the notion of representation itself has not been abandoned across-the-board by connectionists, some of whom have sought to salvage and adapt the notion of mental representation, as suggested by the continuing debate over DISTRIBUTED VS. LOCAL REPRESENTATION and the exploration of sub-symbolic forms of representation within connectionism (see Boden 1990; Haugeland 1997; Smolensky 1994).

What perhaps better distinguishes classic and connectionist cognitive science here is not the issue of whether some form of representationalism is true, but whether the question to which it is an answer needs answering at all. In classical cognitive science, what makes the idea of a genuinely *mental* science possible is the idea that psychology describes representation crunching. But in starting with the idea that neural representation occurs from single neurons up through circuits to modules and more nebulous, distributed neural systems, connectionists are less likely to think that psychology offers a distinctive level of explanation that deserves some identifying characterization. This rejection of question (c) is clearest, I think, in related DYNAMIC APPROACHES TO COGNITION, since such approaches investigate psychological states as dynamic systems that need not posit distinctly *mental* representations. (As with connectionist theorizing about cognition, dynamic approaches encompass a variety of views of mental representation and its place in the study of the mind that make representationalism itself a live issue within such approaches; see Haugeland 1991; van Gelder 1998.)

Finally, consider (b), the question of how to avoid the problem of the homunculus in the sciences of the mind. In classic cognitive science, the answer to (b) is *computationalism,* the view that mental states are computational, an answer which integrates and strengthens functionalist materialism and representationalism as answers to our previous two questions. It does so in the *way* in which it provides a more precise characterization of the nature of the functional or causal relations that exist between mental states: these are *computational relations between mental representations*. The traditional way to spell this out is the COMPUTATIONAL THEORY OF MIND, according to which the mind is a digital computer, a device that stores symbolic representations and performs operations on them in accord with *syntactic* rules, rules that attend only to the "form" of these symbols. This view of computationalism has been challenged not only by relatively technical objections (such as that based on the FRAME PROBLEM), but also by the development of neural networks and models of SITUATED COGNITION AND LEARNING, where (at least some) informational load is shifted from internal codes to organism-environment interactions (cf. Ballard et al. 1997).

The computational theory of mind avoids the problem of the homunculus because digital computers that exhibit some intelligence exist, and they do not contain undischarged homunculi. Thus, if *we* are fancy versions of such computers, then we can understand our intelligent capacities without positing undischarged homunculi. The way this works in computers is by having a series of programs and languages, each compiled by the one beneath it, with the most basic language directly implemented in the hardware of the machine. We avoid an endless series of homunculi because the capacities that are posited at any given level are typically simpler and more numerous than those posited at any higher level, with the lowest levels specifying instructions to perform actions that require no intelligence at all. This strategy of FUNCTIONAL DECOMPOSITION solves the problem of the homunculus if we are digital computers, assuming that it solves it for digital computers.

Like representationalism, computationalism has sometimes been thought to have been superseded by either (or both) the connectionist revolution of the 1980s, or the

Decade of the Brain (the 1990s). But as with proclamations of the death of representationalism, this notice of the death of computationalism is premature. In part this is because the object of criticism is a specific version of computationalism, not computationalism per se (cf. representationalism), and in part it is because neural networks and the neural systems in the head they model are both themselves typically claimed to be computational in some sense. It is surprisingly difficult to find an answer within the cognitive science community to the question of whether there is a univocal notion of COMPUTATION that underlies the various different computational approaches to cognition on offer. The various types of AUTOMATA postulated in the 1930s and 1940s—particularly TURING machines and the "neurons" of MCCULLOCH and PITTS, which form the intellectual foundations, respectively, for the computational theory of mind and contemporary neural network theory—have an interwoven history, and many of the initial putative differences between classical and connectionist cognitive science have faded into the background as research in artificial intelligence and cognitive modeling has increasingly melded the insights of each approach into more sophisticated hybrid models of cognition (cf. Ballard 1997).

While dynamicists (e.g., Port and van Gelder 1995) have sometimes been touted as providing a noncomputational alternative to both classic and connectionist cognitive science (e.g., Thelen 1995: 70), as with claims about the nonrepresentational stance of such approaches, such a characterization is not well founded (see Clark 1997, 1998). More generally, the relationship between dynamical approaches to both classical and connectionist views remains a topic for further discussion (cf. van Gelder and Port 1995; Horgan and Tienson 1996; and Giunti 1997).

See also AUTOMATA; AUTONOMY OF PSYCHOLOGY; BAYESIAN NETWORKS; CHINESE ROOM ARGUMENT; COGNITIVE ARCHITECTURE; COGNITIVE MODELING, CONNECTIONIST; COGNITIVE MODELING, SYMBOLIC; COMPUTATION; COMPUTATIONAL THEORY OF MIND; DISTRIBUTED VS. LOCAL REPRESENTATION; DYNAMIC APPROACHES TO COGNITION; FRAME PROBLEM; FUNCTIONAL DECOMPOSITION; FUNCTIONALISM; HUME, DAVID; KNOWLEDGE-BASED SYSTEMS; LANGUAGE OF THOUGHT; MCCULLOCH, WARREN S.; NEURAL NETWORKS; PITTS, WALTER; PROPOSITIONAL ATTITUDES; RULES AND REPRESENTATIONS; SITUATED COGNITION AND LEARNING; TURING, ALAN; VISUAL WORD RECOGNITION

6   A Focus on Folk Psychology

Much recent philosophical thinking about the mind and cognitive science remains preoccupied with the three traditional philosophical issues I identified in the first section: the mental-physical relation, the structure of the mind, and the first-person perspective. All three issues arise in one of the most absorbing discussions over the last twenty years, that over the nature, status, and future of what has been variously called commonsense psychology, the propositional attitudes, or FOLK PSYCHOLOGY.

The term *folk psychology* was coined by Daniel Dennett (1981) to refer to the systematic knowledge that we "folk" employ in explaining one another's thoughts, feelings, and behavior; the idea goes back to Sellars's Myth of Jones in "Empiricism and the Philosophy of Mind" (1956). We all naturally and without explicit instruction engage in psychological explanation by attributing beliefs, desires, hopes, thoughts, memories, and emotions to one another. These patterns of folk psychological explanation are "folk" as opposed to "scientific" since they require no special training and are manifest in everyday predictive and explanatory practice; and genuinely "psychological" because they posit the existence of various states or properties that seem to be paradigmatically mental in nature. To engage in folk psychological explanation is, in Dennett's (1987) terms, to adopt the INTENTIONAL STANCE.

Perhaps the central issue about folk psychology concerns its relationship to the developing cognitive sciences. ELIMINATIVE MATERIALISM, or eliminativism, is the view that folk psychology will find no place in any of the sciences that could be called "cognitive" in orientation; rather, the fortune of folk psychology will be like that of many other folk views of the world that have found themselves permanently out of step with scientific approaches to the phenomena they purport to explain, such as folk views of medicine, disease, and witchcraft.

Eliminativism is sometimes motivated by adherence to reductionism (including the thesis of EXTENSIONALITY) and the ideal of the unity of science, together with the recognition that the propositional attitudes have features that set them off in kind from the types of entity that exist in other sciences. For example, they are intentional or representational, and attributing them to individuals seems to depend on factors beyond the boundary of those individuals, as the TWIN EARTH arguments suggest. These arguments and others point to a prima facie conflict between folk psychology and INDIVIDUALISM (or *internalism*) in psychology (see Wilson 1995). The apparent conflict between folk psychology and individualism has provided one of the motivations for developing accounts of NARROW CONTENT, content that depends solely on an individual's intrinsic, physical properties. (The dependence here has usually been understood in terms of the technical notion of SUPERVENIENCE; see Horgan 1993.)

There is a spin on this general motivation for eliminative materialism that appeals more directly to the issue of the how the mind is structured. The claim here is that whether folk psychology is defensible will turn in large part on how compatible its ontology—its list of what we find in a folk psychological mind—is with the developing ontology of the cognitive sciences. With respect to classical cognitive science, with its endorsement of both the representational and computational theories of mind, folk psychology is on relatively solid ground here. It posits representational states, such as belief and desire, and it is relatively easy to see how the causal relations between such states could be modeled computationally. But connectionist models of the mind, with what representation there is lying in patterns of activity rather than in explicit representations like propositions, seem to leave less room in the structure of the mind for folk psychology.

Finally, the issue of the place of the first-person perspective arises with respect to folk psychology when we ask how people deploy folk psychology. That is, what sort of psychological machinery do we folk employ in engaging in folk psychological explanation? This issue has been the topic of the SIMULATION VS. THEORY-THEORY debate, with proponents of the simulation view holding, roughly, a "first-person first" account of how folk psychology works, and theory-theory proponents viewing folk psychology as essentially a third-person predictive and explanatory tool. Two recent volumes by Davies and Stone (1995a, 1995b) have added to the literature on this debate, which has developmental and moral aspects, including implications for MORAL PSYCHOLOGY.

See also ELIMINATIVE MATERIALISM; EXTENSIONALITY, THESIS OF; FOLK PSYCHOLOGY; INDIVIDUALISM; INTENTIONAL STANCE; MORAL PSYCHOLOGY; NARROW CONTENT; SIMULATION VS. THEORY-THEORY; SUPERVENIENCE; TWIN EARTH

7   *Exploring Mental Content*

Although BRENTANO's claim that INTENTIONALITY is the "mark of the mental" is problematic and has few adherents today, intentionality has been one of the flagship topics in philosophical discussion of the mental, and so at least a sort of mark of that discussion. Just what the puzzle about intentionality is and what one might say about it are topics I want to explore in more detail here.

To say that something is intentional is just to say that it is *about something,* or that it *refers to something.* In this sense, statements of fact are paradigmatically intentional, since they are about how things are in the world. Similarly, a highway sign with a picture of a gas pump on it is intentional because it conveys the information that there is gas station ahead at an exit: it is, in some sense, about that state of affairs.

The beginning of chapter 4 of Jerry Fodor's *Psychosemantics* provides one lively expression of the problem with intentionality:

I suppose that sooner or later the physicists will complete the catalogue they've been compiling of the ultimate and irreducible properties of things. When they do, the likes of *spin, charm,* and *charge* will perhaps appear upon their list. But *aboutness* surely won't; intentionality simply doesn't go that deep. It's hard to see, in face of this consideration, how one can be a Realist about intentionality without also being, to some extent or other, a Reductionist. If the semantic and the intentional are real properties of things, it must be in virtue of their identity with (or maybe of their supervenience on?) properties that are themselves *neither* intentional *nor* semantic. If aboutness is real, it must be really something else. (p. 97, emphases in original)

Although there is much that one could take issue with in this passage, my reason for introducing it here is not to critique it but to try to capture some of the worries about intentionality that bubble up from it.

The most general of these concerns the *basis* of intentionality in the natural order: given that only special parts of the world (like our minds) have intentional properties, what is it about those things that gives them (and not other things) intentionality? Since not only mental phenomena are intentional (for example, spoken and written natural language and systems of signs and codes are as well), one might think that a natural way to approach this question would be as follows. Consider all of the various sorts of "merely material" things that at least seem to have intentional properties. Then proceed to articulate why each of them is intentional, either taking the high road of specifying something like the "essence of intentionality"—something that all and only things with intentional properties have—or taking the low road of doing so for each phenomenon, allowing these accounts to vary across disparate intentional phenomena.

Very few philosophers have explored the problem of intentionality in this way. I think this is chiefly because they do not view all things with intentional properties as having been created equally. A common assumption is that even if lots of the nonmental world is intentional, its intentionality is *derived,* in some sense, from the intentionality of the mental. So, to take a classic example, the sentences we utter and write are intentional all right (they are about things). But their intentionality derives from that of the corresponding thoughts that are their causal antecedents. To take another often-touted example, computers often produce intentional output (even photocopiers can do this), but whatever intentionality lies in such output is not inherent to the machines that produce it but is derivative, ultimately, from the mental states of those who design, program, and use them and their products. Thus, there has been a focus on mental states as a sort of paradigm of intentional state, and a subsequent narrowing of the sorts of intentional phenomena discussed. Two points are perhaps worth making briefly in this regard.

First, the assumption that not all things with intentional properties are created equally is typically shared even by those who have not focused almost exclusively on mental states as paradigms of intentional states, but on languages and other public and conventional forms of representation (e.g., Horst 1996). It is just that their paradigm is different.

Second, even when mental states *have* been taken as a paradigm here, those interested in developing a "psychosemantics"—an account of the basis for the semantics of psychological states—have often turned to decidedly nonmental systems of representation in order to theorize about the intentionality of the mental. This focus on what we might think of as *proto-intentionality* has been prominent within both Fred Dretske's (1981) informational semantics and the biosemantic approach pioneered by Ruth Millikan (1984, 1993).

The idea common to such views is to get clear about the grounds of simple forms of intentionality before scaling up to the case of the intentionality of human minds, an instance of a research strategy that has driven work in the cognitive sciences from early work in artificial intelligence on KNOWLEDGE REPRESENTATION and cognitive modeling through to contemporary work in COMPUTATIONAL NEUROSCIENCE. Exploring simplified or more basic intentional systems in the hope of gaining some insight into the more full-blown case of the intentionality of human minds runs the risk, of course, of focusing on cases that leave out precisely that which is crucial to full-blown intentionality. Some (for example, Searle 1992) would claim that consciousness and phenomenology are such features.

As I hinted at in my discussion of the mind in cognitive science in section 5, construed one way the puzzle about the grounds of intentionality has a general answer in the hypothesis of computationalism. But there is a deeper problem about the grounds of intentionality concerning *just how* at least some mental stuff could be about other stuff in the world, and computationalism is of little help here. Computationalism does not even pretend to answer the question of what it is about specific mental states (say, my belief that trees often have leaves) that gives them the content that they have—for example, that makes them *about trees*. Even if we *were* complicated Turing machines, what would it be about *my* Turing machine table that implies that I have the belief that trees often have leaves? Talking about the correspondence between the semantic and syntactic properties that symbol structures in computational systems have, and of how the former are "inherited" from the latter is well and good. But it leaves open the "just how" question, and so fails to address what I am here calling the deeper problem about the grounds of intentionality. This problem is explored in the article on MENTAL REPRESENTATION, and particular proposals for a psychosemantics can be found in those on INFORMATIONAL SEMANTICS and FUNCTIONAL ROLE SEMANTICS.

It would be remiss in exploring mental content to fail to mention that much thought about intentionality has been propelled by work in the philosophy of language: on INDEXICALS AND DEMONSTRATIVES, on theories of REFERENCE and the propositional attitudes, and on the idea of RADICAL INTERPRETATION. Here I will restrict myself to some brief comments on theories of reference, which have occupied center stage in the philosophy of language for much of the last thirty years.

One of the central goals of theories of reference has been to explain in virtue of what parts of sentences of natural languages refer to the things they refer to. What makes the name "Miranda" refer to my daughter? In virtue of what does the plural noun "dogs" refer to dogs? Such questions have a striking similarity to my above expression of the central puzzle concerning intentionality. In fact, the application of causal theories of reference (Putnam 1975, Kripke 1980) developed principally for natural languages has played a central role in disputes in the philosophy of mind that concern intentionality, including those over individualism, narrow content, and the role of Twin Earth arguments in thinking about intentionality. In particular, applying them not to the meaning of natural language terms but to the content of thought is one way to reach the conclusion that *mental* content does not supervene on an individual's physical properties, that is, that mental content is not individualistic.

GOTTLOB FREGE is a classic source for contrasting descriptivist theories of reference, according to which natural language reference is, in some sense, mediated by a speaker's descriptions of the object or property to which she refers. Moreover, Frege's notion of sense and the distinction between SENSE AND REFERENCE are often invoked in support of the claim that there is much to MEANING—linguistic or mental—that goes beyond the merely referential. Frege is also one of the founders of modern logic, and it is to the role of logic in the cognitive sciences that I now turn.

See also BRENTANO, FRANZ; COMPUTATIONAL NEUROSCIENCE; FREGE, GOTTLOB; FUNCTIONAL ROLE SEMANTICS; INDEXICALS AND DEMONSTRATIVES; INFORMATIONAL SEMANTICS; INTENTIONALITY; KNOWLEDGE REPRESENTATION; MEANING; MENTAL REPRESENTATION; RADICAL INTERPRETATION; REFERENCE, THEORIES OF; SENSE AND REFERENCE

8   *Logic and the Sciences of the Mind*

Although INDUCTION, like deduction, involves drawing inferences on the basis of one or more premises, it is *deductive* inference that has been the focus in LOGIC, what is often simply referred to as "formal logic" in departments of philosophy and linguistics. The idea that it is possible to abstract away from deductive arguments given in natural language that differ in the content of their premises and conclusions goes back at least to Aristotle in the fourth century B.C. Hence the term "Aristotelian syllogisms" to refer to a range of argument forms containing premises and conclusions that begin with the words "every" or "all," "some," and "no." This abstraction makes it possible to talk about argument *forms* that are valid and invalid, and allows one to describe two arguments as being of the same *logical* form. To take a simple example, we know that any argument of the form:

All A are B.
No B are C.

No A are C.

is *formally* valid, where the emphasis here serves to highlight reference to the preservation of truth from premises to conclusion, that is, the validity, solely in virtue of the forms of the individual sentences, together with the form their arrangement constitutes. Whatever plural noun phrases we substitute for "A," "B," and "C," the resulting natural language argument will be valid: if the two premises are true, the conclusion must also be true. The same general point applies to arguments that are formally *invalid*, which makes it possible to talk about formal *fallacies*, that is, inferences that are invalid because of the forms they instantiate.

Given the age of the general idea of LOGICAL FORM, what is perhaps surprising is that it is only in the late nineteenth century that the notion was developed so as to apply to a wide range of natural language constructions through the development of the *propositional* and *predicate* logics. And it is only in the late twentieth century that the notion of logical form comes to be appropriated within linguistics in the study of SYNTAX. I focus here on the developments in logic.

Central to propositional logic (sometimes called "sentential logic") is the idea of a propositional or sentential *operator,* a symbol that acts as a function on propositions or sentences. The paradigmatic propositional operators are symbols for negation ("~"), conjunction ("&"), disjunction ("v"), and conditional ("→"). And with the development of formal languages containing these symbols comes an ability to represent a richer range of formally valid arguments, such as that manifest in the following thought:

> If Sally invites Tom, then either he will say "no," or cancel his game with Bill. But there's no way he'd turn Sally down. So I guess if she invites him, he'll cancel with Bill.

In predicate or quantificational logic, we are able to represent not simply the relations between propositions, as we can in propositional logic, but also the structure within propositions themselves through the introduction of QUANTIFIERS and the terms and predicates that they bind. One of the historically more important applications of predicate logic has been its widespread use in linguistics, philosophical logic, and the philosophy of language to formally represent increasingly larger parts of natural languages, including not just simple subjects and predicates, but adverbial constructions, tense, indexicals, and attributive adjectives (for example, see Sainsbury 1991).

These fundamental developments in logical theory have had perhaps the most widespread and pervasive effect on the foundations of the cognitive sciences of *any* contributions from philosophy or mathematics. They also form the basis for much contemporary work across the cognitive sciences: in linguistic semantics (e.g., through MODAL LOGIC, in the use of POSSIBLE WORLDS SEMANTICS to model fragments of natural language, and in work on BINDING); in metalogic (e.g., on FORMAL SYSTEMS and results such as the CHURCH-TURING THESIS and GÖDEL'S THEOREMS); and in artificial intelligence (e.g., on LOGICAL REASONING SYSTEMS, TEMPORAL REASONING, and METAREASONING).

Despite their technical payoff, the relevance of these developments in logical theory for thinking more directly about DEDUCTIVE REASONING in human beings is, ironically, less clear. Psychological work on human reasoning, including that on JUDGMENT HEURISTICS, CAUSAL REASONING, and MENTAL MODELS, points to ways in which human reasoning may be governed by structures very different from those developed in formal logic, though this remains an area of continuing debate and discussion.

See also BINDING THEORY; CAUSAL REASONING; CHURCH-TURING THESIS; DEDUCTIVE REASONING; FORMAL SYSTEMS, PROPERTIES OF; GÖDEL'S THEOREMS; INDUCTION; JUDGMENT HEURISTICS; LOGIC; LOGICAL FORM IN LINGUISTICS; LOGICAL FORM, ORIGINS OF; LOGICAL REASONING SYSTEMS; MENTAL MODELS; METAREASONING;

MODAL LOGIC; POSSIBLE WORLDS SEMANTICS; QUANTIFIERS; SYNTAX; TEMPORAL REASONING

9   Two Ways to Get Biological

By the late nineteenth century, both evolutionary theory and the physiological study of mental capacities were firmly entrenched. Despite this, these two paths to a biological view of cognition have only recently been re-explored in sufficient depth to warrant the claim that contemporary cognitive science incorporates a truly biological perspective on the mind. The neurobiological path, laid down by the tradition of physiological psychology that developed from the mid-nineteenth century, is certainly the better traveled of the two. The recent widening of this path by those dissatisfied with the distinctly nonbiological approaches adopted within traditional artificial intelligence has, as we saw in our discussion of computationalism, raised new questions about COMPUTATION AND THE BRAIN, the traditional computational theory of the mind, and the rules and representations approach to understanding the mind. The evolutionary path, by contrast, has been taken only occasionally and half-heartedly over the last 140 years. I want to concentrate not only on why but on the ways in which evolutionary theory is relevant to contemporary interdisciplinary work on the mind.

The theory of EVOLUTION makes a claim about the *patterns* that we find in the biological world—they are patterns of *descent*—and a claim about the predominant cause of those patterns—they are caused by the mechanism of natural selection. None of the recent debates concerning evolutionary theory—from challenges to the focus on ADAPTATION AND ADAPTATIONISM in Gould and Lewontin (1979) to more recent work on SELF-ORGANIZING SYSTEMS and ARTIFICIAL LIFE—challenges the substantial core of the theory of evolution (cf. Kauffman 1993, 1995; Depew and Weber 1995). The vast majority of those working in the cognitive sciences both accept the theory of evolution and so think that a large number of traits that organisms possess are adaptations to evolutionary forces, such as natural selection. Yet until the last ten years, the scattered pleas to apply evolutionary theory to the mind (such as those of Ghiselin 1969 and Richards 1987) have come largely from those outside of the psychological and behavioral sciences.

Within the last ten years, however, a distinctive EVOLUTIONARY PSYCHOLOGY has developed as a research program, beginning in Leda Cosmides's (1989) work on human reasoning and the Wason selection task, and represented in the collection of papers *The Adapted Mind* (Barkow, Cosmides, and Tooby 1992) and, more recently and at a more popular level, by Steven Pinker's *How the Mind Works* (1997). Evolutionary psychologists view the mind as a set of "Darwinian algorithms" designed by natural selection to solve adaptive problems faced by our hunter-gatherer ancestors. The claim is that this basic Darwinian insight can and should guide research into the cognitive architecture of the mind, since the task is one of discovering and understanding the *design* of the human mind, in all its complexity. Yet there has been more than an inertial resistance to viewing evolution as central to the scientific study of human cognition.

One reason is that evolutionary theory in general is seen as answering different questions than those at the core of the cognitive sciences. In terms of the well-known distinction between *proximal* and *ultimate* causes, appeals to evolutionary theory primarily allow one to specify the latter, and cognitive scientists are chiefly interested in the former: they are interested in the *how* rather than the *why* of the mind. Or to put it more precisely, central to cognitive science is an understanding of the *mechanisms* that govern cognition, not the various histories—evolutionary or not—that produced these mechanisms. This general perception of the concerns of evolutionary theory and the contrasting conception of cognitive science, have both been challenged by evolutionary psychologists. The same general challenges have been issued by those who think that the relations between ETHICS AND EVOLUTION and those between cognition and CULTURAL EVOLUTION have not received their due in contemporary cognitive science.

Yet despite the skepticism about this direct application of evolutionary theory to human cognition, its implicit application is inherent in the traditional interest in the minds of *other* animals, from *aplysia* to (nonhuman) apes. ANIMAL NAVIGATION, PRIMATE LANGUAGE, and CONDITIONING AND THE BRAIN, while certainly topics of interest in their own right, gain some added value from what their investigation can tell us about *human* minds and brains. This presupposes something like the following: that there are natural kinds in psychology that transcend species boundaries, such that there is a general way of exploring how a cognitive capacity is structured, independent of the particular species of organism in which it is instantiated (cf. functionalism). Largely on the basis of research with non-human animals, we know enough now to say, with a high degree of certainty, things like this: that the CEREBELLUM is the central brain structure involved in MOTOR LEARNING, and that the LIMBIC SYSTEM plays the same role with respect to at least some EMOTIONS.

This is by way of returning to (and concluding with) the neuroscientific path to biologizing the mind, and the three classic philosophical issues about the mind with which we began. As I hope this introduction has suggested, despite the distinctively philosophical edge to all three issues—the mental-physical relation, the structure of the mind, and the first-person perspective—discussion of each of them is elucidated and enriched by the interdisciplinary perspectives provided by empirical work in the cognitive sciences. It is not only a priori arguments but complexities revealed by empirical work (e.g., on the neurobiology of consciousness, or ATTENTION and animal and human brains) that show the paucity of the traditional philosophical "isms" (dualism, behaviorism, type-type physicalism) with respect to the mental-physical relation. It is not simply general, philosophical arguments against nativism or against empiricism about the structure of the mind that reveal limitations to the global versions of these views, but ongoing work on MODULARITY AND LANGUAGE, on cognitive architecture, and on the innateness of language. And thought about introspection and self-knowledge, to take two topics that arise when one reflects on the first-person perspective on the mind, is both enriched by and contributes to empirical work on BLINDSIGHT, the theory of mind, and METAREPRESENTATION. With some luck, philosophers increasingly sensitive to empirical data about the mind will have paved a two-way street that encourages psychologists, linguists, neuroscientists, computer scientists, social scientists and evolutionary theorists to venture more frequently and more surely into philosophy.

See also ADAPTATION AND ADAPTATIONISM; ANIMAL NAVIGATION; ARTIFICIAL LIFE; ATTENTION IN THE ANIMAL BRAIN; ATTENTION IN THE HUMAN BRAIN; BLINDSIGHT; CEREBELLUM; COMPUTATION AND THE BRAIN; CONDITIONING AND THE BRAIN; CULTURAL EVOLUTION; EMOTIONS; ETHICS AND EVOLUTION; EVOLUTION; EVOLUTIONARY PSYCHOLOGY; LIMBIC SYSTEM; METAREPRESENTATION; MODULARITY AND LANGUAGE; MOTOR LEARNING; PRIMATE LANGUAGE; SELF-ORGANIZING SYSTEMS

Acknowledgments

I would like to thank Kay Bock, Bill Brewer, Alvin Goldman, John Heil, Greg Murphy, Stewart Saunders, Larry Shapiro, Sydney Shoemaker, Tim van Gelder, and Steve Wagner, as well as the PNP Group at Washington University, St. Louis, for taking time out to provide some feedback on earlier versions of this introduction. I guess the remaining idiosyncrasies and mistakes are mine.

References

Armstrong, D. M. (1968). *A Materialist Theory of the Mind.* London: Routledge and Kegan Paul.
Ballard, D. (1997). *An Introduction to Natural Computation.* Cambridge, MA: MIT Press.
Ballard, D., M. Hayhoe, P. Pook, and R. Rao. (1997). Deictic codes for the embodiment of cognition. *Behavioral and Brain Sciences* 20: 723–767.
Barkow, J. H., L. Cosmides, and J. Tooby, Eds. (1992). *The Adapted Mind.* New York: Oxford University Press.
Boden, M., Ed. (1990). *The Philosophy of Artificial Intelligence.* Oxford: Oxford University Press.
Carnap, R. (1928). *The Logical Construction of the World.* Translated by R. George (1967). Berkeley: University of California Press.
Chalmers, D. (1996). *The Conscious Mind: In Search of a Fundamental Theory.* New York: Oxford University Press.

Chomsky, N. (1959). Review of B. F. Skinner's *Verbal Behavior. Language* 35 : 26–58.

Churchland, P. M. (1979). *Scientific Realism and the Plasticity of Mind.* New York: Cambridge University Press.

Churchland, P. M., and P. S. Churchland. (1981). Functionalism, qualia, and intentionality. *Philosophical Topics* 12: 121–145.

Clark, A. (1997). *Being There: Putting Brain, Body, and World Together Again.* Cambridge, MA: MIT Press.

Clark, A. (1998). Twisted tales: Causal complexity and cognitive scientific explanation. *Minds and Machines* 8: 79–99.

Cosmides, L. (1989). The logic of social exchange: Has natural selection shaped how humans reason? Studies with the Wason Selection Task. *Cognition* 31: 187–276.

Cottrell, G., and J. Metcalfe. (1991). EMPATH: Face, Emotion, and Gender Recognition Using Holons. In R. Lippman, J. Moody, and D. Touretzky, Eds., *Advances in Neural Information Processing Systems,* vol. 3. San Mateo, CA: Morgan Kaufmann.

Davies, M., and T. Stone, Eds. (1995a). *Folk Psychology: The Theory of Mind Debate.* Oxford: Blackwell.

Davies, M., and T. Stone, Eds. (1995b). *Mental Simulation: Evaluations and Applications.* Oxford: Blackwell.

Dennett, D. C. (1981). Three kinds of intentional psychology. Reprinted in his 1987.

Dennett, D. C. (1987). *The Intentional Stance.* Cambridge, MA: MIT Press.

Depew, D., and B. Weber. (1995). *Darwinism Evolving: Systems Dynamics and the Genealogy of Natural Selection.* Cambridge, MA: MIT Press.

Dretske, F. (1981). *Knowledge and the Flow of Information.* Cambridge, MA: MIT Press.

Elman, J., E. Bates, M. Johnson, A. Karmiloff-Smith, D. Parisi, and K. Plunkett, Eds. (1996). *Rethinking Innateness.* Cambridge, MA: MIT Press.

Fodor, J. A. (1975). *The Language of Thought.* Cambridge, MA: Harvard University Press.

Fodor, J. A. (1981). *Representations: Philosophical Essays on the Foundations of Cognitive Science.* Sussex: Harvester Press.

Fodor, J. A. (1987). *Psychosemantics: The Problem of Meaning in the Philosophy of Mind.* Cambridge, MA: MIT Press.

Fodor, J. A. (1994). *The Elm and the Expert.* Cambridge, MA: MIT Press.

Geach, P. (1957). *Mental Acts.* London: Routledge and Kegan Paul.

Ghiselin, M. (1969). *The Triumph of the Darwinian Method.* Berkeley: University of California Press.

Giunti, M. (1997). *Computation, Dynamics, and Cognition.* New York: Oxford University Press.

Goldman, A. (1997). Science, Publicity, and Consciousness. *Philosophy of Science* 64: 525–545.

Gould, S. J., and R. C. Lewontin. (1979). The spandrels of San Marco and the panglossian paradigm: A critique of the adaptationist programme. Reprinted in E. Sober, Ed., *Conceptual Issues in Evolutionary Biology,* 2nd ed. (1993.) Cambridge, MA: MIT Press.

Grene, M. (1995). *A Philosophical Testament.* Chicago: Open Court.

Griffiths, P. E. (1997). *What Emotions Really Are.* Chicago: University of Chicago Press.

Haugeland, J. (1991). Representational genera. In W. Ramsey and S. Stich, Eds., *Philosophy and Connectionist Theory.* Hillsdale, NJ: Erlbaum.

Haugeland, J., Ed. (1997). *Mind Design 2: Philosophy, Psychology, and Artificial Intelligence.* Cambridge, MA: MIT Press.

Heil, J., and A. Mele, Eds. (1993). *Mental Causation.* Oxford: Clarendon Press.

Horgan, T. (1993). From supervenience to superdupervenience: Meeting the demands of a material world. *Mind* 102: 555–586.

Horgan, T., and J. Tienson. (1996). *Connectionism and the Philosophy of Psychology.* Cambridge, MA: MIT Press.

Horst, S. (1996). *Symbols, Computation, and Intentionality.* Berkeley: University of California Press.

James, W. (1890). *The Principles of Psychology.* 2 vol. Dover reprint (1950). New York: Dover.

Kauffman, S. (1993). *The Origins of Order.* New York: Oxford University Press.

Kauffman, S. (1995). *At Home in the Universe.* New York: Oxford University Press.

Kim, J. (1993). *Supervenience and Mind.* New York: Cambridge University Press.

Kosslyn, S. (1980). *Image and Mind.* Cambridge, MA: Harvard University Press.

Kosslyn, S. (1994). *Image and Brain.* Cambridge, MA: MIT Press.

Kripke, S. (1980). *Naming and Necessity.* Cambridge, MA: Harvard University Press.

Levine, J. (1983). Materialism and qualia: The explanatory gap. *Pacific Philosophical Quarterly* 64: 354–361.

Lewis, D. K. (1966). An argument for the identity theory. *Journal of Philosophy* 63: 17–25.

Malcolm, N. (1959). *Dreaming.* London: Routledge and Kegan Paul.

Malcolm, N. (1971). *Problems of Mind: Descartes to Wittgenstein.* New York: Harper and Row.

Millikan, R. G. (1984). *Language, Thought, and Other Biological Categories.* Cambridge, MA: MIT Press.

Millikan, R. G. (1993). *White Queen Psychology and Other Essays for Alice.* Cambridge, MA: MIT Press.

Pinker, S. (1997). *How the Mind Works.* New York: Norton.

Port, R., and T. van Gelder, Eds. (1995). *Mind as Motion: Explorations in the Dynamics of Cognition.* Cambridge, MA: MIT Press.

Putnam, H. (1975). The meaning of "meaning." Reprinted in *Mind, Language, and Reality: Collected Papers,* vol. 2. Cambridge: Cambridge University Press.

Pylyshyn, Z. (1984). *Computation and Cognition.* Cambridge, MA: MIT Press.

Reichenbach, H. (1938). *Experience and Prediction.* Chicago: University of Chicago Press.

Richards, R. (1987). *Darwin and the Emergence of Evolutionary Theories of Mind and Behavior.* Chicago: University of Chicago Press.

Rumelhart, D., and J. McClelland. (1986). On Learning the Past Tenses of English Verbs. In J. McClelland, D. Rumelhart, and the PDP Research Group, Eds., *Parallel Distributed Processing,* vol. 2. Cambridge, MA: MIT Press.

Ryle, G. (1949). *The Concept of Mind.* New York: Penguin.

Sainsbury, M. (1991). *Logical Forms.* New York: Blackwell.

Searle, J. (1992). *The Rediscovery of the Mind.* Cambridge, MA: MIT Press.

Seidenberg, M. S., and J. L. McClelland. (1989). A distributed, developmental model of visual word recognition and naming. *Psychological Review* 96: 523–568.

Sellars, W. (1956). Empiricism and the philosophy of mind. In H. Feigl and M. Scriven, Eds., *Minnesota Studies in the Philosophy of Science,* vol. 1. Minneapolis: University of Minnesota Press.

Skinner, B. F. (1957). *Verbal Behavior.* New York: Appleton-Century-Crofts.

Smolensky, P. (1994). Computational models of mind. In S. Guttenplan, Ed., *A Companion to the Philosophy of Mind.* Cambridge, MA: Blackwell.

Spelke, E. (1990). Principles of object perception. *Cognitive Science* 14: 29–56.

Stabler, E. (1983). How are grammars represented? *Behavioral and Brain Sciences* 6: 391–420.

Thelen, E. (1995). Time-scale dynamics and the development of an embodied cognition. In R. Port and T. van Gelder, Eds., *Mind as Motion: Explorations in the Dynamics of Cognition.* Cambridge, MA: MIT Press.

van Fraassen, B. (1989). *Laws and Symmetry.* New York: Oxford University Press.

van Gelder, T. J. (1998). The dynamical hypothesis in cognitive science. *Behavioral and Brain Sciences* 21: 1–14.

van Gelder, T., and R. Port. (1995). It's about time: An overview of the dynamical approach to cognition. In R. Port and T. van Gelder, Eds., *Mind as Motion: Explorations in the Dynamics of Cognition.* Cambridge, MA: MIT Press.

Watson, J. B. (1913). Psychology as the behaviorist views it. *Psychological Review* 20: 158–177.

Wilson, R. A. (1995). *Cartesian Psychology and Physical Minds: Individualism and the Sciences of the Mind.* New York: Cambridge University Press.

Wilson, R. A., Ed. (1999). *Species: New Interdisciplinary Essays.* Cambridge, MA: MIT Press.

Wundt, W. (1900–1909). *Völkerpsychologie.* Leipzig: W. Engelmann.

Yablo, S. (1992). Mental causation. *Philosophical Review* 101: 245–280.

Psychology

Keith J. Holyoak

Psychology is the science that investigates the representation and processing of information by complex organisms. Many animal species are capable of taking in information about their environment, forming internal representations of it, and manipulating these representations to select and execute actions. In addition, many animals are able to adapt to their environments by means of learning that can take place within the lifespan of an individual organism. Intelligent information processing implies the ability to acquire and process information about the environment in order to select actions that are likely to achieve the fundamental goals of survival and propagation. Animals have evolved a system of capabilities that collectively provide them with the ability to process information. They have sensory systems such as TASTE and HAPTIC PERCEPTION (touch), which provide information about the immediate environment with which the individual is in direct contact; proprioception, which provides information about an animal's own bodily states; and SMELL, AUDITION, and VISION, which provide information about more distant aspects of the environment. Animals are capable of directed, self-generated motion, including EYE MOVEMENTS and other motoric behaviors such as MANIPULATION AND GRASPING, which radically increase their ability to pick up sensory information and also to act upon their environments.

The central focus of psychology concerns the information processing that intervenes between sensory inputs and motoric outputs. The most complex forms of intelligence, observed in birds and mammals, and particularly primates (especially great apes and humans) require theories that deal with the machinery of thought and inner experience. These animals have minds and EMOTIONS; their sensory inputs are interpreted to create perceptions of the external world, guided in part by selective ATTENTION; some of the products of perception are stored in MEMORY, and may in turn influence subsequent perception. Intellectually sophisticated animals perform DECISION MAKING and PROBLEM SOLVING, and in the case of humans engage in LANGUAGE AND COMMUNICATION. Experience coupled with innate constraints results in a process of COGNITIVE DEVELOPMENT as the infant becomes an adult, and also leads to LEARNING over the lifespan, so that the individual is able to adapt to its environment within a vastly shorter time scale than that required for evolutionary change. Humans are capable of the most complex and most domain-general forms of information processing of all species; for this reason (and because those who study psychology are humans), most of psychology aims directly or indirectly to understand the nature of human information processing and INTELLIGENCE. The most general characteristics of the human system for information processing are described as the COGNITIVE ARCHITECTURE.

See also ATTENTION; AUDITION; COGNITIVE ARCHITECTURE; COGNITIVE DEVELOPMENT; DECISION MAKING; EMOTIONS; EYE MOVEMENTS AND VISUAL ATTENTION; HAPTIC PERCEPTION; INTELLIGENCE; LANGUAGE AND COMMUNICATION; LEARNING; MANIPULATION AND GRASPING; MEMORY; PROBLEM SOLVING; SMELL; TASTE; VISION

1 The Place of Psychology within Cognitive Science

As the science of the representation and processing of information by organisms, psychology (particularly cognitive psychology) forms part of the core of cognitive science. Cognitive science research conducted in other disciplines generally has actual or potential implications for psychology. Not all research on intelligent information processing is relevant to psychology. Some work in artificial intelligence, for example, is based on representations and algorithms with no apparent connection to biological intelligence. Even though such work may be highly successful at achieving high levels of competence on cognitive tasks, it does not fall within the scope of cognitive science. For example, the Deep Blue II program that defeated the human CHESS champion Gary Kasparov is an example of an outstanding artificial-intelligence program that has little or no apparent psychological relevance, and hence would not be considered to be part of cognitive science. In contrast, work on adaptive PRODUCTION SYSTEMS and NEURAL NETWORKS, much of which is conducted by computer scientists, often has implications for psychology. Similarly, a great deal of work in such allied disciplines as neuroscience, linguistics, anthropology, and philosophy has psychological implications. At the same time, work in psychology often has important implications for research in other disciplines. For example, research in PSYCHOLINGUISTICS has influenced developments in linguistics, and research in PSYCHOPHYSICS has guided neurophysiological research on the substrates of sensation and perception.

In terms of MARR's tripartite division of levels of analysis (computational theory, representation and algorithm, and hardware implementation), work in psychology tends to concentrate on the middle level, emphasizing how information is represented and processed by humans and other animals. Although there are many important exceptions, psychologists generally aim to develop process models that specify more than the input-output functions that govern cognition (for example, also specifying timing relations among intervening mental processes), while abstracting away from the detailed neural underpinnings of behavior. Nonetheless, most psychologists do not insist in any strict sense on the AUTONOMY OF PSYCHOLOGY, but rather focus on important interconnections with allied disciplines that comprise cognitive science. Contemporary psychology at the information-processing level is influenced by research in neuroscience that investigates the neural basis for cognition and emotion, by work on representations and algorithms in the fields of artificial intelligence and neural networks, and by work in social sciences such as anthropology that places the psychology of individuals within its cultural context. Research on the psychology of language (e.g., COMPUTATIONAL PSYCHOLINGUISTICS and LANGUAGE AND THOUGHT) is influenced by the formal analyses of language developed in linguistics. Many areas of psychology make close contact with classical issues in philosophy, especially in EPISTEMOLOGY (e.g., CAUSAL REASONING; INDUCTION; CONCEPTS).

The field of psychology has several major subdivisions, which have varying degrees of connection to cognitive science. Cognitive psychology deals directly with the representation and processing of information, with greatest emphasis on cognition in adult humans; the majority of the psychology entries that appear in this volume reflect work in this area. Developmental psychology deals with the changes in cognitive, social, and emotional functioning that occur over the lifespan of humans and other animals (see in particular COGNITIVE DEVELOPMENT, PERCEPTUAL DEVELOPMENT, and INFANT COGNITION). Social psychology investigates the cognitive and emotional factors involved in interactions between people, especially in small groups. One subarea of social psychology, SOCIAL COGNITION, is directly concerned with the manner in which people understand the minds, emotions, and behavior of themselves and others (see also THEORY OF MIND; INTERSUBJECTIVITY). Personality psychology deals primarily with motivational and emotional aspects of human experience (see FREUD for discussion of the ideas of the famous progenitor of this area of psychology), and clinical psychology deals with applied issues related to mental health. COMPARATIVE PSYCHOLOGY investigates the commonalities and differences in cognition and behavior between different animal species (see PRIMATE COGNITION; ANIMAL NAVIGATION; CONDITIONING; and MOTIVATION), and behavioral neuroscience provides the interface between research on molar cognition and behavior and their underlying neural substrate.

See also ANIMAL NAVIGATION; ANIMAL NAVIGATION, NEURAL NETWORKS; AUTONOMY OF PSYCHOLOGY; CAUSAL REASONING; CHESS, PSYCHOLOGY OF; COGNITIVE DEVELOPMENT; COMPARATIVE PSYCHOLOGY; COMPUTATIONAL PSYCHOLINGUISTICS; CONCEPTS; CONDITIONING; EPISTEMOLOGY AND COGNITION; INDUCTION; INFANT COGNITION; INTERSUBJECTIVITY; LANGUAGE AND THOUGHT; MARR, DAVID; MOTIVATION; NEURAL NETWORKS; PERCEPTUAL DEVELOPMENT; PRIMATE COGNITION; PRODUCTION SYSTEMS; PSYCHOLINGUISTICS; PSYCHOPHYSICS; SOCIAL COGNITION; SOCIAL COGNITION IN ANIMALS; THEORY OF MIND

2   *Capsule History of Psychology*

Until the middle of the nineteenth century the nature of the mind was solely the concern of philosophers. Indeed, there are a number of reasons why some have argued that the scientific investigation of the mind may prove to be an impossible undertaking. One objection is that thoughts cannot be measured; and without measurement, science cannot even begin. A second objection is to question how humans could objectively study their own thought processes, given the fact that science itself depends on human thinking. A final objection is that our mental life is incredibly complex and bound up with the further complexities of human social interactions; perhaps cognition is simply too complex to permit successful scientific investigation.

Despite these reasons for skepticism, scientific psychology emerged as a discipline separate from philosophy in the second half of the nineteenth century. A science depends on systematic empirical methods for collecting observations and on theories that interpret these observations. Beginning around 1850, a number of individuals, often trained in philosophy, physics, physiology, or neurology, began to provide these crucial elements.

The anatomist Ernst Heinrich Weber and the physicist and philosopher Gustav Fechner measured the relations between objective changes in physical stimuli, such as brightness or weight, and subjective changes in the internal sensations the stimuli generate. The crucial finding of Weber and Fechner was that subjective differences were not simply equivalent to objective differences. Rather, it turned out that for many dimensions, the magnitude of change required to make a subjective difference ("just noticeable difference," or "jnd") increased as overall intensity increased, often following an approximately logarithmic function, known as the Weber-Fechner Law. Weber and Fechner's contribution to cognitive psychology was much more general than identifying the law that links their names. They convincingly demonstrated that, contrary to the claim that thought is inherently impossible to measure, it is in fact possible to measure mental concepts, such as the degree of sensation produced by a stimulus. Fechner called this new field of psychological measurement PSYCHOPHYSICS: the interface of psychology and physics, of the mental and the physical.

A further foundational issue concerns the speed of human thought. In the nineteenth century, many believed that thought was either instantaneous or else so fast that it could never be measured. But HERMANN VON HELMHOLTZ, a physicist and physiologist, succeeded in measuring the speed at which signals are conducted through the nervous system. He first experimented on frogs by applying an electric current to the top of a frog's leg and measuring the time it took the muscle at the end to twitch in response. Later he used a similar technique with humans, touching various parts of a person's body and measuring the time taken to press a button in response. The response time increased with the distance of the stimulus (i.e., the point of the touch) from the finger that pressed the button, in proportion to the length of the neural path over which the signal had to travel. Helmholtz's estimate of the speed of nerve signals was close to modern estimates—roughly 100 meters per second for large nerve fibers. This transmission rate is surprisingly slow—vastly slower than the speed of electricity through a wire. Because our brains are composed of neurons, our thoughts cannot be generated any faster than the speed at which neurons communicate with each other. It follows that the speed of thought is neither instantaneous nor immeasurable.

Helmholtz also pioneered the experimental study of vision, formulating a theory of color vision that remains highly influential today. He argued forcefully against the commonsensical idea that perception is simply a matter of somehow "copying" sensory input into the brain. Rather, he pointed out that even the most basic aspects of perception require major acts of construction by the nervous system. For example, it is possible for two different objects—a large object far away, and a small object nearby—to create precisely the same image on the retinas of a viewer's eyes. Yet normally the viewer will correctly perceive the one object as being larger, but further away, than the other. The brain somehow manages to unconsciously perform some basic geometrical calculations. The brain, Helmholtz argued, must construct this unified view by a process of "unconscious inference"—a process akin to reasoning without awareness.

Helmholtz's insight was that the "reality" we perceive is not simply a copy of the external world, but rather the product of the constructive activities of the brain.

Another philosopher, HERMANN EBBINGHAUS, who was influenced by Fechner's ideas about psychophysical measurements, developed experimental methods tailored to the study of human memory. Using himself as a subject, Ebbinghaus studied memory for nonsense syllables—consonant-vowel-consonant combinations, such as "zad," "bim," and "sif." He measured how long it took to commit lists of nonsense syllables to memory, the effects of repetition on how well he could remember the syllables later, and the rate of forgetting as a function of the passage of time. Ebbinghaus made several fundamental discoveries about memory, including the typical form of the "forgetting curve"—the gradual, negatively accelerated decline in the proportion of items that can be recalled as a function of time. Like Weber, Fechner, and Helmholtz, Ebbinghaus provided evidence that it is indeed possible to measure mental phenomena by objective experimental procedures.

Many key ideas about possible components of cognition were systematically presented by the American philosopher WILLIAM JAMES in the first great psychology textbook, *Principles of Psychology,* published in 1890. His monumental work included topics that remain central in psychology, including brain function, perception, attention, voluntary movement, habit, memory, reasoning, the SELF, and hypnosis. James discussed the nature of "will," or mental effort, which remains one of the basic aspects of attention. He also drew a distinction between different memory systems: *primary* memory, which roughly corresponds to the current contents of consciousness, and *secondary* memory, which comprises the vast store of knowledge of which we are not conscious at any single time, yet continually draw upon. Primary memory is closely related to what we now term *active, short-term,* or WORKING MEMORY, while secondary memory corresponds to what is usually called *long-term* memory.

James emphasized the *adaptive* nature of cognition: the fact that perception, memory, and reasoning operate not simply for their own sake, but to allow us to survive and prosper in our physical and social world. Humans evolved as organisms skilled in tool use and in social organization, and it is possible (albeit a matter of controversy) that much of our cognitive apparatus evolved to serve these basic functions (see EVOLUTIONARY PSYCHOLOGY). Thus, human cognition involves intricate systems for MOTOR CONTROL and MOTOR LEARNING; the capacity to understand that other people have minds, with intentions and goals that may lead them to help or hinder us; and the ability to recognize and remember individual persons and their characteristics. Furthermore, James (1890:8) recognized that the hallmark of an intelligent being is its ability to link ends with means—to select actions that will achieve goals: "The pursuance of future ends and the choice of means for their attainment are thus the mark and criterion of the presence of mentality in a phenomenon." This view of goal-directed thinking continues to serve as the foundation of modern work on PROBLEM SOLVING, as reflected in the views of theorists such as ALAN NEWELL and Herbert Simon.

Another pioneer of psychology was Sigmund Freud, the founder of psychoanalysis, whose theoretical ideas about cognition and consciousness anticipated many key aspects of the modern conception of cognition. Freud attacked the idea that the "self" has some special status as a unitary entity that somehow governs our thought and action. Modern cognitive psychologists also reject (though for different reasons) explanations of intelligent behavior that depend upon postulating a "homunculus"—that is, an internal mental entity endowed with all the intelligence we are trying to explain. Behavior is viewed not as the product of a unitary self or homunculus, but as the joint product of multiple interacting subsystems. Freud argued that the "ego"—the information-processing system that modulates various motivational forces—is not a unitary entity, but rather a complex system that includes attentional bottlenecks, multiple memory stores, and different ways of representing information (e.g., language, imagery, and physiognomic codes, or "body language"). Furthermore, as Freud also emphasized, much of information processing takes place at an unconscious level. We are aware of only a small portion of our overall mental life, a tip of the cognitive iceberg. For example, operating beneath the level of awareness are attentional "gates" that open or close to selectively attend to portions of the information that reaches our senses, memory stores that hold information for very brief periods of time, and inaccessible memories that we carry with us always but might never retrieve for years at a time.

Given the breadth and depth of the contributions of the nineteenth-century pioneers to what would eventually become cognitive science, it is ironic that early in the twentieth century the study of cognition went into a steep decline. Particularly in the United States, psychology in the first half of the century came to be dominated by BEHAVIORISM, an approach characterized by the rejection of theories that depended on "mentalistic" concepts such as goals, intentions, or plans. The decline of cognitive psychology was in part due to the fact that a great deal of psychological research had moved away from the objective measurement techniques developed by Fechner, Helmholtz, Ebbinghaus, and others, and instead gave primacy to the method of INTROSPECTION, promoted by WILHELM WUNDT, in which trained observers analyzed their own thought processes as they performed various cognitive tasks. Not surprisingly, given what is now known about how expectancies influence the way we think, introspectionists tended to find themselves thinking in more or less the manner to which they were theoretically predisposed. For example, researchers who believed thinking always depended on IMAGERY usually found themselves imaging, whereas those who did not subscribe to such a theory were far more likely to report "imageless thought."

The apparent subjectivity and inconstancy of the introspective method encouraged charges that all cognitive theories (rather than simply the method itself, as might seem more reasonable) were "unscientific." Cognitive theories were overshadowed by the behaviorist theories of such leading figures as John Watson, Edward Thorndike, Clark Hull, and B. F. Skinner. Although there were major differences among the behaviorists in the degree to which they actually avoided explanations based on assumptions about unobservable mental states (e.g., Hull postulated such states rather freely, whereas Watson was adamant that they were scientifically illicit), none supported the range of cognitive ideas advanced in the nineteenth century.

Cognitive psychology did not simply die out during the era of behaviorism. Working within the behaviorist tradition, Edward Tolman pursued such cognitive issues as how animals represented spatial information internally as COGNITIVE MAPS of their environment. European psychologists were far less captivated with behaviorism than were Americans. In England, Sir FREDERICK BARTLETT analyzed the systematic distortions that people exhibit when trying to remember stories about unfamiliar events, and introduced the concept of "schema" (see SCHEMATA) as a mental representation that captures the systematic structural relations in categories of experience. In Soviet Russia, the neuropsychologist Aleksandr LURIA provided a detailed portrait of links between cognitive functions and the operation of specific regions of the brain. Another Russian, LEV VYGOTSKY, developed a sociohistorical approach to cognitive development that emphasized the way in which development is constructed through social interaction, cultural practices, and the internalization of cognitive tools. Vygotsky emphasized social interaction through language in the development of children's concepts. The Swiss psychologist JEAN PIAGET spent decades refining a theory of cognitive development. Piaget's theory emphasizes milestones in the child's development including decentration, the ability to perform operations on concrete objects, and finally the ability to perform operations on thoughts and beliefs. Given its emphasis on logical thought, Piaget's theory is closely related to SCIENTIFIC THINKING AND ITS DEVELOPMENT.

In addition, the great German tradition in psychology, which had produced so many of the nineteenth-century pioneers, gave rise to a new cognitive movement in the early twentieth century: GESTALT PSYCHOLOGY. The German word *Gestalt* translates roughly as "form," and the Gestalt psychologists emphasized that the whole form is something different from the mere sum of its parts, due to emergent properties that arise as new relations are created. Gestalt psychology was in some ways an extension of Helmholtz's constructivist ideas, and the greatest contributions of this intellectual movement were in the area of GESTALT PERCEPTION. Where the behaviorists insisted that psychology was simply the study of how objective stimuli come to elicit objective responses, the Gestaltists pointed to simple demonstrations casting doubt on the idea that "objective" stimuli—that is, stimuli perceived in a way that can be described strictly in terms of the sensory input—even exist. Figure 1 illustrates a famous Gestalt example of the constructive nature of perception, the ambiguous Necker cube. Although this figure is simply a flat line drawing, we immediately perceive it as a three-dimensional cube. Moreover, if you look carefully, you will see that the figure can actually be seen as either of two different three-dimensional cubes. The same objective stimulus—the two-dimensional line drawing—gives rise to two distinct three-dimensional perceptions.

Although many of the major contributions by key Gestalt figures such as Max Wertheimer were in the area of perception, their central ideas were extended to memory and problem solving as well, through the work of people such as Wolfgang Köhler and Karl Duncker. Indeed, one of the central tenets of Gestalt psychology was that high-level thinking is based on principles similar to those that govern basic perception. As we do in everyday language, Gestalt psychologists spoke of suddenly "seeing" the solution to a problem, often after "looking at it" in a different way and achieving a new "insight." In all the areas in which they worked, the Gestalt idea of "a whole different from the sum of parts" was based on the fundamental fact that organized configurations are based not simply on individual elements, but also on the relations between those elements. Just as H_2O is not simply two hydrogen atoms and one oxygen atom, but also a particular spatial organization of these elements into a configuration that makes a molecule of water, so too "squareness" is more than four lines: it crucially depends on the way the lines are related to one another to make four right angles. Furthermore, relations can take on a "life of their own," separable from any particular set of elements. For example, we can take a tune, move it to a different key so that all the notes are changed, and still immediately recognize it as the "same" tune as long as the relations among the notes are preserved. A focus on relations calls attention to the centrality of the BINDING PROBLEM, which involves the issue of how elements are systematically organized to fill relational roles. Modern work on such topics as ANALOGY and SIMILARITY emphasizes the crucial role of relations in cognition.

Modern cognitive psychology emerged in the second half of this century. The "cognitive revolution" of the 1950s and 1960s involved not only psychology but also the allied disciplines that now contribute to cognitive science. In the 1940s the Canadian psychologist DONALD HEBB began to draw connections between cognitive processes and neural mechanisms, anticipating modern cognitive neuroscience. During World War II, many experimental psychologists (including JAMES GIBSON) were confronted with such pressing military problems as finding ways to select good pilots and train radar operators, and it turned out that the then-dominant stimulus-response theories simply had little to offer in the way of solutions. More detailed process models of human information processing were needed. After the war, DONALD BROADBENT in England developed the first such detailed model of attention. Even more importantly, Broadbent helped develop and popularize a wide range of experimental tasks in which an observer's attention is carefully controlled by having him or her perform some task, such as listening to a taped message for a particular word, and then precisely measuring how quickly responses can be made and what can be remembered. In the United States, William K. Estes added to the mathematical tools available for theory building and data analysis, and Saul Sternberg developed a method for decomposing reaction times into component processes using a simple recognition task.

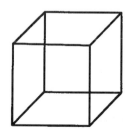

Figure 1.

Meanwhile, the birth of computer science provided further conceptual tools. Strict behaviorists had denounced models of internal mental processes as unscientific. However, the modern digital computer provided a clear example of a device that took inputs, fed them through a complex series of internal procedures, and then produced outputs. As well as providing concrete examples of what an information-processing device could be, computers made possible the beginnings of artificial intelligence—the construction of computer programs designed to perform tasks that require intelligence, such as playing chess, understanding stories, or diagnosing diseases. Herbert Simon (1978 Nobel Laureate in Economics) and Allan Newell were leaders in building close ties between artificial intelligence and the new cognitive psychology. It was also recognized that actual computers represent only a small class of a much larger set of theoretically possible computing devices, which had been described back in the 1940s by the brilliant mathematician ALAN TURING. Indeed, it was now possible to view the brain itself as a biological computer, and to use various real and possible computing devices as models of human cognition. Another key influence on modern cognitive psychology came from the field of linguistics. In the late 1950s work by the young linguist Noam Chomsky radically changed conceptions of the nature of human language by demonstrating that language could not be learned or understood by merely associating adjacent words, but rather required computations on abstract structures that existed in the minds of the speaker and listener.

The collective impact of this work in the mid-twentieth century was to provide a seminal idea that became the foundation of cognitive psychology and also cognitive science in general: the COMPUTATIONAL THEORY OF MIND, according to which human cognition is based on mental procedures that operate on abstract mental representations. The nature of the COGNITIVE ARCHITECTURE has been controversial, including proposals such as PRODUCTION SYSTEMS and NEURAL NETWORKS. In particular, there has been disagreement as to whether procedures and representations are inherently separable or whether procedures actually embody representations, and whether some mental representations are abstract and amodal, rather than tied to specific perceptual systems. Nonetheless, the basic conception of biological information processing as some form of computation continues to guide psychological theories of the representation and processing of information.

See also ANALOGY; BARTLETT, FREDERICK; BEHAVIORISM; BINDING PROBLEM; BROADBENT, DONALD; COGNITIVE ARCHITECTURE; COGNITIVE MAPS; COMPUTATIONAL THEORY OF MIND; EBBINGHAUS, HERMANN; EVOLUTIONARY PSYCHOLOGY; GESTALT PERCEPTION; GESTALT PSYCHOLOGY; GIBSON, JAMES; HEBB, DONALD; HELMHOLTZ, HERMANN VON; IMAGERY; INTROSPECTION; JAMES, WILLIAM; LURIA, ALEXSANDR ROMANOVICH; MOTOR CONTROL; MOTOR LEARNING; NEURAL NETWORKS; NEWELL, ALAN; PIAGET, JEAN; PROBLEM SOLVING; PRODUCTION SYSTEMS; PSYCHOPHYSICS; SCHEMATA; SCIENTIFIC THINKING AND ITS DEVELOPMENT; SELF; SIMILARITY; TURING, ALAN; VYGOTSKY, LEV; WORKING MEMORY; WUNDT, WILHELM

3   The Science of Information Processing

In broad strokes, an intelligent organism operates in a perception-action cycle (Neisser 1967), taking in sensory information from the environment, performing internal computations on it, and using the results of the computation to guide the selection and execution of goal-directed actions. The initial sensory input is provided by separate sensory systems, including smell, taste, haptic perception, and audition. The most sophisticated sensory system in primates is vision (see MID-LEVEL VISION; HIGH-LEVEL VISION), which includes complex specialized subsystems for DEPTH PERCEPTION, SHAPE PERCEPTION, LIGHTNESS PERCEPTION, and COLOR VISION.

The interpretation of sensory inputs begins with FEATURE DETECTORS that respond selectively to relatively elementary aspects of the stimulus (e.g., lines at specific orientations in the visual field, or phonetic cues in an acoustic speech signal). Some basic properties of the visual system result in systematic misperceptions, or ILLUSIONS. TOP-DOWN PROCESSING IN VISION serves to integrate the local visual input with the broader context in which it occurs, including prior knowledge stored in memory. Theorists working in the tradition of Gibson emphasize that a great deal of visual information may be provided by higher-order features that become available to a perceiver moving freely in a natural environment, rather than passively viewing a static image (see ECOLOGICAL PSYCHOLOGY). In their natural context, both perception and action are guided by the AFFORDANCES of the environment: properties of objects that enable certain uses (e.g., the elongated shape of a stick may afford striking an object otherwise out of reach).

Across all the sensory systems, psychophysics methods are used to investigate the quantitative functions relating physical inputs received by sensory systems to subjective experience (e.g., the relation between luminance and perceived brightness, or between physical and subjective weight). SIGNAL DETECTION THEORY provides a statistical method for measuring how accurately observers can distinguish a signal from noise under conditions of uncertainty (i.e., with limited viewing time or highly similar alternatives) in a way that separates the signal strength received from possible response bias. In addition to perceiving sensory information about objects at locations in space, animals perceive and record information about time (see TIME IN THE MIND).

Knowledge about both space and time must be integrated to provide the capability for animal and HUMAN NAVIGATION in the environment. Humans and other animals are capable of forming sophisticated representations of spatial relations integrated as COGNITIVE MAPS. Some more central mental representations appear to be closely tied to perceptual systems. Humans use various forms of imagery based on visual, auditory and other perceptual systems to perform internal mental processes such as MENTAL ROTATION. The close connection between PICTORIAL ART AND VISION also reflects the links between perceptual systems and more abstract cognition.

A fundamental property of biological information processing is that it is capacity-limited and therefore necessarily selective. Beginning with the seminal work of Broadbent, a great deal of work in cognitive psychology has focused on the role of attention in guiding information processing. Attention operates selectively to determine what information is received by the senses, as in the case of EYE MOVEMENTS AND VISUAL ATTENTION, and also operates to direct more central information processing, including the operation of memory. The degree to which information requires active attention or memory resources varies, decreasing with the AUTOMATICITY of the required processing.

Modern conceptions of memory maintain some version of William James's basic distinction between primary and secondary memory. Primary memory is now usually called WORKING MEMORY, which is itself subdivided into multiple stores involving specific forms of representation, especially phonological and visuospatial codes. Working memory also includes a central executive, which provides attentional resources for strategic management of the cognitive processes involved in problem solving and other varieties of deliberative thought. Secondary or long-term memory is also viewed as involving distinct subsystems, particularly EPISODIC VS. SEMANTIC MEMORY. Each of these subsystems appears to be specialized to perform one of the two basic functions of long-term memory. One function is to store individuated representations of "what happened when" in specific contexts (episodic memory); a second function is to extract and store generalized representations of "the usual kind of thing" (semantic memory). Another key distinction, related to different types of memory measures, is between IMPLICIT VS. EXPLICIT MEMORY. In explicit tests (typically recall or recognition tests), the person is aware of the requirement to access memory. In contrast, implicit tests (such as completing a word stem, or generating instances of a category) make no reference to any particular memory episode. Nonetheless, the influence of prior experiences may be revealed by the priming of particular responses (e.g., if the word "crocus" has recently been studied, the person is more likely to generate "crocus" when asked to list flowers, even if they do not explicitly remember having studied the word). There is evidence that implicit and explicit knowledge are based on separable neural systems. In particular, forms of amnesia caused by damage to the hippocampus and related structures typically impair explicit memory for episodes, but not implicit memory as revealed by priming measures.

A striking part of human cognition is the ability to speak and comprehend language. The psychological study of language, or psycholinguistics, has a close relationship to work in linguistics and on LANGUAGE ACQUISITION. The complex formal properties of language, together with its apparent ease of acquisition by very young children, have made it the focus of debates about the extent and nature of NATIVISM in cognition. COMPUTATIONAL PSYCHOLINGUISTICS is concerned with modeling the complex processes involved in language use. In modern cultures that have achieved LITERACY with the introduction of written forms of language, the process of READING lies at the interface of psycholinguistics, perception, and memory retrieval. The intimate relationship between language and thought, and between language and human concepts, is widely recognized but still poorly understood. The use of METAPHOR in language is related to other symbolic processes in human cognition, particularly ANALOGY and CATEGORIZATION.

One of the most fundamental aspects of biological intelligence is the capacity to adaptively alter behavior. It has been clear at least from the time of William James that the adaptiveness of human behavior and the ability to achieve EXPERTISE in diverse domains is not generally the direct product of innate predispositions, but rather the result of adaptive problem solving and LEARNING SYSTEMS that operate over the lifespan. Both production systems and neural networks provide computational models of some aspects of learning, although no model has captured anything like the full range of human learning capacities. Humans as well as some other animals are able to learn by IMITATION, for example, translating visual information about the behavior of others into motor routines that allow the observer/imitator to produce comparable behavior. Many animal species are able to acquire expectancies about the environment and the consequences of the individual's actions on the basis of CONDITIONING, which enables learning of contingencies among events and actions.

Conditioning appears to be a primitive form of causal induction, the process by which humans and other animals learn about the cause-effect structure of the world. Both causal knowledge and similarity relations contribute to the process of categorization, which leads to the development of categories and concepts that serve to organize knowledge. People act as if they assume the external appearances of category members are caused by hidden (and often unknown) internal properties (e.g., the appearance of an individual dog may be attributed to its internal biology), an assumption sometimes termed psychological ESSENTIALISM.

There are important developmental influences that lead to CONCEPTUAL CHANGE over childhood. These developmental aspects of cognition are particularly important in understanding SCIENTIFIC THINKING AND ITS DEVELOPMENT. Without formal schooling, children and adults arrive at systematic beliefs that comprise NAIVE MATHEMATICS and NAIVE PHYSICS. Some of these beliefs provide the foundations for learning mathematics and physics in formal EDUCATION, but some are misconceptions that can impede learning these topics in school (see also AI AND EDUCATION). Young children are prone to ANIMISM, attributing properties of people and other animals to plants and nonliving things. Rather than being an aberrant form of early thought, animism may be an early manifestation of the use of ANALOGY to make inferences and learn new cognitive structures. Analogy is the process used to find systematic structural correspondences between a familiar, well-understood situation and an unfamiliar, poorly understood one, and then using the correspondences to draw plausible inferences about the less familiar case. Analogy, along with hypothesis testing and evaluation of competing explanations, plays a role in the discovery of new regularities and theories in science.

In its more complex forms, learning is intimately connected to thinking and reasoning. Humans are not only able to think, but also to think *about* their own cognitive processes, resulting in METACOGNITION. They can also form higher-level representations, termed METAREPRESENTATION. There are major individual differences in intelligence as assessed by tasks that require abstract thinking. Similarly, people differ in their CREATIVITY in finding solutions to problems. Various neural disorders, such as forms of MENTAL RETARDATION and AUTISM, can impair or radically alter normal thinking abilities. Some aspects of thinking are vulnerable to disruption in later life due to the links between AGING AND COGNITION.

Until the last few decades, the psychology of DEDUCTIVE REASONING was dominated by the view that human thinking is governed by formal rules akin to those used in LOGIC. Although some theorists continue to argue for a role for formal, content-free rules in reasoning, others have focused on the importance of content-specific rules. For example, people appear to have specialized procedures for reasoning about broad classes of pragmatically important tasks, such as understanding social relations or causal relations among events. Such pragmatic reasoning schemas (Cheng and Holyoak 1985) enable people to derive useful inferences in contexts related to important types of recurring goals. In addition, both deductive and inductive inferences may sometimes be made using various types of MENTAL MODELS, in which specific possible cases are represented and manipulated (see also CASE-BASED REASONING AND ANALOGY).

Much of human inference depends not on deduction, but on inductive PROBABILISTIC REASONING under conditions of UNCERTAINTY. Work by researchers such as AMOS TVERSKY and Daniel Kahneman has shown that everyday inductive reasoning and decision making is often based on simple JUDGMENT HEURISTICS related to ease of memory retrieval (the *availability* heuristic) and degree of similarity (the *representativeness* heuristic). Although judgment heuristics are often able to produce fast and accurate responses, they can sometimes lead to errors of prediction (e.g., conflating the subjective ease of remembering instances of a class of events with their objective frequency in the world).

More generally, the impressive power of human information processing has apparent limits. People all too often take actions that will not achieve their intended ends, and pursue short-term goals that defeat their own long-term interests. Some of these mistakes arise from motivational biases, and others from computational limitations that constrain human attention, memory, and reasoning processes. Although human cognition is fundamentally adaptive, we have no reason to suppose that "all's for the best in this best of all possible minds."

See also AFFORDANCES; AGING AND COGNITION; AI AND EDUCATION; ANALOGY; ANIMISM; AUTISM; AUTOMATICITY; CASE-BASED REASONING AND ANALOGY; CATEGORIZATION; COGNITIVE MAPS; COLOR VISION; CONCEPTUAL CHANGE; CONDITIONING; CREATIVITY; DEDUCTIVE REASONING; DEPTH PERCEPTION; ECOLOGICAL PSYCHOLOGY; EDUCATION; EPISODIC VS. SEMANTIC MEMORY; ESSENTIALISM; EXPERTISE; EYE MOVEMENTS AND VISUAL ATTENTION; FEATURE DETECTORS; HIGH-LEVEL VISION; HUMAN NAVIGATION; ILLUSIONS; IMITATION; IMPLICIT VS. EXPLICIT MEMORY; JUDGMENT HEURISTICS; LANGUAGE ACQUISITION; LEARNING SYSTEMS; LIGHTNESS PERCEPTION; LITERACY; LOGIC; MENTAL MODELS; MENTAL RETARDATION; MENTAL ROTATION; METACOGNITION; METAPHOR; METAREPRESENTATION; MID-LEVEL VISION; NAIVE MATHEMATICS; NAIVE PHYSICS; NATIVISM; PICTORIAL ART AND VISION; PROBABILISTIC REASONING; READING; SCIENTIFIC THINKING AND ITS DEVELOPMENT; SHAPE PERCEPTION; SIGNAL DETECTION THEORY; TIME IN THE MIND; TOP-DOWN PROCESSING IN VISION; TVERSKY, AMOS; UNCERTAINTY; WORKING MEMORY

References

Cheng, P. W., and K. J. Holyoak. (1985). Pragmatic reasoning schemas. *Cognitive Psychology* 17: 391–394.
James, W. (1890). *The Principles of Psychology.* New York: Dover.
Neisser, U. (1967). *Cognitive Psychology.* Englewood Cliffs, NJ: Prentice-Hall.

Further Readings

Anderson, J. R. (1995). *Cognitive Psychology and Its Implications.* 4th ed. San Francisco: W. H. Freeman.
Baddeley, A. D. (1997). *Human Memory: Theory and Practice.* 2nd ed. Hove, Sussex: Psychology Press.
Evans, J., S. E. Newstead, and R. M. J. Byrne. (1993). *Human Reasoning.* Mahwah, NJ: Erlbaum.
Gallistel, C. R. (1990). *The Organization of Learning.* Cambridge, MA: MIT Press.
Gazzaniga, M. S. (1995). *The Cognitive Neurosciences.* Cambridge, MA: MIT Press.
Gibson, J. J. (1979). *The Ecological Approach to Visual Perception.* Boston: Houghton-Mifflin.
Gregory, R. L. (1997). *Eye and Brain: The Psychology of Seeing.* 5th ed. Princeton, NJ: Princeton University Press.

Holyoak, K. J., and P. Thagard. (1995). *Mental Leaps: Analogy in Creative Thought.* Cambridge, MA: MIT Press.

James, W. (1890). *Principles of Psychology.* New York: Dover.

Kahneman, D., P. Slovic, and A. Tversky. (1982). *Judgments Under Uncertainty: Heuristics and Biases.* New York: Cambridge University Press.

Keil, F. C. (1989). *Concepts, Kinds, and Cognitive Development.* Cambridge, MA: MIT Press.

Kosslyn, S. M. (1994). *Image and Brain: The Resolution of the Imagery Debate.* Cambridge, MA: MIT Press.

Newell, A., and H. A. Simon. (1972.) *Human Problem Solving.* Englewood Cliffs, NJ: Prentice-Hall.

Pashler, H. (1997). *The Psychology of Attention.* Cambridge, MA: MIT Press.

Pinker, S. (1994). *The Language Instinct.* New York: William Morrow.

Reisberg, D. (1997). *Cognition: Exploring the Science of the Mind.* New York: Norton.

Rumelhart, D. E., J. L. McClelland, and PDP Research Group. (1986). *Parallel Distributed Processing: Explorations in the Microstructure of Cognition.* 2 vols. Cambridge, MA: MIT Press.

Smith, E. E., and D. L. Medin. (1981). *Categories and Concepts.* Cambridge, MA: Harvard University Press.

Sperber, D., D. Premack, and A. J. Premack. (1995). *Causal Cognition: A Multidisciplinary Debate.* Oxford: Clarendon Press.

Tarpy, R. M. (1997). *Contemporary Learning Theory and Research.* New York: McGraw Hill.

Tomasello, M., and J. Call. (1997). *Primate Cognition.* New York: Oxford University Press.

Neurosciences

Thomas D. Albright and Helen J. Neville

1   Cognitive Neuroscience

The term alone suggests a field of study that is pregnant and full of promise. It is a large field of study, uniting concepts and techniques from many disciplines, and its boundaries are rangy and often loosely defined. At the heart of cognitive neuroscience, however, lies the fundamental question of knowledge and its representation by the brain—a relationship characterized not inappropriately by WILLIAM JAMES (1842–1910) as "the most mysterious thing in the world" (James 1890 vol. 1, 216). Cognitive neuroscience is thus a science of information processing. Viewed as such, one can identify key experimental questions and classical areas of study: How is information acquired (sensation), interpreted to confer meaning (perception and recognition), stored or modified (learning and memory), used to ruminate (thinking and consciousness), to predict the future state of the environment and the consequences of action (decision making), to guide behavior (motor control), and to communicate (language)? These questions are, of course, foundational in cognitive science generally, and it is instructive to consider what distinguishes cognitive neuroscience from cognitive science and psychology, on the one hand, and the larger field of neuroscience, on the other.

The former distinction is perhaps the fuzzier, depending heavily as it does upon how one defines cognitive science. A neurobiologist might adopt the progressive (or naive) view that the workings of the brain are the subject matter of both, and the distinction is therefore moot. But this view evidently has not prevailed (witness the fact that neuroscience is but one of the subdivisions of this volume); indeed the field of cognitive science was founded upon and continues to press the distinction between software (the content of cognition) and hardware (the physical stuff, for example, the brain) upon which cognitive processes are implemented. Much has been written on this topic, and one who pokes at the distinction too hard is likely to unshelve as much dusty political discourse as true science. In any case, for present purposes, we will consider both the biological hardware and the extent to which it constrains the software, and in doing so we will discuss answers to the questions of cognitive science that are rooted in the elements of biological systems.

The relationship between cognitive neuroscience and the umbrella of modern neuroscience is more straightforward and less embattled. While the former is clearly a subdivision of the latter, the questions of cognitive neuroscience lie at the root of much of neuroscience's turf. Where distinctions are often made, they arise from the fact that cognitive neuroscience is a functional neuroscience—particular structures and signals of the nervous system are of interest inasmuch as they can be used to explain cognitive functions.

There being many levels of explanation in biological systems—ranging from cellular and molecular events to complex behavior—a key challenge of the field of cognitive neuroscience has been to identify the relationships between different levels and the train of causality. In certain limited domains, this challenge has met with spectacular success; in others, it is clear that the relevant concepts have only begun to take shape and the necessary experimental tools are far behind. Using examples drawn from well-developed areas of research, such as vision, memory, and language, we illustrate concepts, experimental approaches, and general principles that have emerged—and, more specifically, how the work has answered many of the information processing questions identified above. Our contemporary view of cognitive neuroscience owes much to the heights attained by our predecessors; to appreciate the state of this field fully, it is useful to begin with a consideration of how we reached this vantage point.

See also JAMES, WILLIAM

2   Origins of Cognitive Neuroscience

Legend has it that the term "cognitive neuroscience" was coined by George A. Miller—the father of modern cognitive psychology—in the late 1970s over cocktails with Michael Gazzaniga at the Rockefeller University Faculty Club. That engaging tidbit of folklore nevertheless belies the ancient history of this pursuit. Indeed, identification of the biological structures and events that account for our ability to acquire, store, and utilize knowledge of the world was one of the earliest goals of empirical science. The emergence of the interdisciplinary field of cognitive neuroscience that we know today, which lies squarely at the heart of twentieth-century neuroscience, can thus be traced from a common stream in antiquity, with many tributaries converging in time as new concepts and techniques have evolved (Boring 1950).

Localization of Function

The focal point of the earliest debates on the subject—and a topic that has remained a centerpiece of cognitive neuroscience to the present day—is localization of the material source of psychological functions. With Aristotle as a notable exception (he thought the heart more important), scholars of antiquity rightly identified the brain as the seat of intellect. Relatively little effort was made to localize *specific* mental functions to *particular* brain regions until the latter part of the eighteenth century, when the anatomist Franz Josef Gall (1758–1828) unleashed the science of phrenology. Although flawed in its premises, and touted by charlatans, phrenology focused attention on the CEREBRAL CORTEX and brought the topic of localization of function to the forefront of an emerging nineteenth century physiology and psychology of mind (Zola-Morgan 1995). The subsequent HISTORY OF CORTICAL LOCALIZATION of function (Gross 1994a) is filled with colorful figures and weighty confrontations between localizationists and functional holists (antilocalizationists). Among the longest shadows is that cast by PAUL BROCA (1824–1880), who in 1861 reported that damage to a "speech center" in the left frontal lobe resulted in loss of speech function, and was thus responsible for the first widely cited evidence for localization of function in the cerebral cortex. An important development of a quite different nature came in the form of the Bell-Magendie law, discovered independently in the early nineteenth century by the physiologists Sir Charles Bell (1774–1842) and François Magendie (1783–1855). This law identified the fact that sensory and motor nerve fibers course through different roots (dorsal and ventral, respectively) of the spinal cord. Although far from the heavily contested turf of the cerebral cortex, the concept of nerve specificity paved the way for the publication in 1838 by Johannes Muller (1801–1858) of the law of specific nerve energies, which included among its principles the proposal that nerves carrying different types of sensory information terminate in distinct brain loci, perhaps in the cerebral cortex.

Persuasive though the accumulated evidence seemed at the dawn of the twentieth century, the debate between localizationists and antilocalizationists raged on for another three decades. By this time the chief experimental tool had become the "lesion method," through which the functions of specific brain regions are inferred from the behavioral or psychological consequences of loss of the tissue in question (either by clinical causes or deliberate experimental intervention). A central player during this period was the psychologist KARL SPENCER LASHLEY (1890–1958)—often inaccurately characterized as professing strong antilocalizationist beliefs, but best known for the concept of equipotentiality and the law of mass action of brain function. Lashley's descendants include several generations of flag bearers for the localizationist front—Carlyle Jacobsen, John Fulton, Karl Pribram, Mortimer Mishkin, Lawrence Weiskrantz, and Charles Gross, among others—who established footholds for our present understanding of the cognitive functions of the frontal and temporal lobes.

These later efforts to localize cognitive functions using the lesion method were complemented by studies of the effects of electrical stimulation of the human brain on psychological states. The use of stimulation as a probe for cognitive function followed its more pragmatic application as a functional brain mapping procedure executed in preparation for surgical treatment of intractable epilepsy. The neurosurgeon WILDER PENFIELD (1891–1976) pioneered this approach in the 1930s at the legendary Montreal Neurological Institute and, with colleagues Herbert Jasper and Brenda Milner, subsequently began to identify specific cortical substrates of language, memory, emotion, and perception.

The years of the mid-twentieth century were quarrelsome times for the expanding field of psychology, which up until that time had provided a home for much of the work on localization of brain function. It was from this fractious environment, with inspiration from the many successful experimental applications of the lesion method and a growing link to wartime clinical populations, that the field of neuropsychology emerged—and with it the wagons were drawn up around the first science explicitly devoted to the relationship between brain and cognitive function. Early practitioners included the great Russian neuropsychologist ALEKSANDR ROMANOVICH LURIA (1902–1977) and the American behavioral neurologist NORMAN GESCHWIND (1926–1984), both of whom promoted the localizationist cause with human case studies and focused attention on the role of connections between functionally specific brain regions. Also among the legendary figures of the early days of neuropsychology was HANS-LUKAS TEUBER (1916–1977). Renowned scientifically for his systematization of clinical neuropsychology, Teuber is perhaps best remembered for having laid the cradle of modern cognitive neuroscience in the 1960s MIT Psychology Department, through his inspired recruitment of an interdisciplinary faculty with a common interest in brain structure and function, and its relationship to complex behavior (Gross 1994b).

See also BROCA, PAUL; CEREBRAL CORTEX; CORTICAL LOCALIZATION, HISTORY OF; GESCHWIND, NORMAN; LASHLEY, KARL SPENCER; LURIA, ALEXANDER ROMANOVICH; PENFIELD, WILDER; TEUBER, HANS-LUKAS

Neuron Doctrine

Although the earliest antecedents of modern cognitive neuroscience focused by necessity on the macroscopic relationship between brain and psychological function, the last 50 years have seen a shift of focus, with major emphasis placed upon local neuronal circuits and the causal link between the activity of individual cells and behavior. The payoff has been astonishing, but one often takes for granted the resolution of much hotly debated turf. The debates in question focused on the elemental units of nervous system structure and function. We accept these matter-of-factly to be specialized cells known as NEURONS, but prior to the development of techniques to visualize cellular processes, their existence was mere conjecture. Thus the two opposing views of the nineteenth century were reticular theory, which held that the tissue of the brain was composed of a vast anastomosing reticulum, and neuron theory, which postulated neurons as differentiated cell types and the fundamental unit of nervous system function. The ideological chasm between these camps ran deep and wide, reinforced by ties to functional holism in the case of reticular theory, and localizationism in the case of neuron theory. The deadlock broke in 1873 when CAMILLO GOLGI (1843–1926) introduced a method for selective staining of individual neurons using silver nitrate, which permitted their visualization for the first time. (Though this event followed the discovery of the microscope by approximately two centuries, it was the Golgi method's complete staining of a minority of neurons that enabled them to be distinguished from one another.) In consequence, the neuron doctrine was cast, and a grand stage was set for studies of differential cellular morphology, patterns of connectivity between different brain regions, biochemical analysis, and, ultimately, electrophysiological characterization of the behavior of individual neurons, their synaptic interactions, and relationship to cognition.

Undisputedly, the most creative and prolific applicant of the Golgi technique was the Spanish anatomist SANTIAGO RAMÓN Y CAJAL (1852–1934), who used this new method to characterize the fine structure of the nervous system in exquisite detail. Cajal's efforts yielded a wealth of data pointing to the existence of discrete neuronal elements. He soon emerged as a leading proponent of the neuron doctrine and subsequently shared the 1906 Nobel Prize in physiology and medicine with Camillo Golgi. (Ironically, Golgi held vociferously to the reticular theory throughout his career.)

Discovery of the existence of independent neurons led naturally to investigations of their means of communication. The fine-scale stereotyped contacts between neurons were evident to Ramón y Cajal, but it was Sir Charles Scott Sherrington (1857–1952) who, at the turn of the century, applied the term "synapses" to label them. The transmission of information across synapses by chemical means was demonstrated experimentally by Otto Loewi (1873–1961) in 1921. The next several decades saw an explosion of research on the nature of chemical synaptic transmission, including the discovery of countless putative NEUROTRANSMITTERS and their mechanisms of action through receptor activation, as well as a host of revelations regarding the molecular events that are responsible for and consequences of neurotransmitter release. These findings have provided a rich foundation for our present understanding of how neurons compute and store information about the world (see COMPUTING IN SINGLE NEURONS).

The ability to label neurons facilitated two other noteworthy developments bearing on the functional organization of the brain: (1) cytoarchitectonics, which is the use of coherent regional patterns of cellular morphology in the cerebral cortex to identify candidates for functional specificity; and (2) neuroanatomical tract tracing, by which the patterns of connections between and within different brain regions are established. The practice of cytoarchitectonics began at the turn of the century and its utility was espoused most effectively by the anatomists Oscar Vogt (1870–1950), Cecile Vogt (1875–1962), and Korbinian Brodmann (1868–1918). Cytoarchitectonics never fully achieved the functional parcellation that it promised, but clear histological differences across the cerebral cortex, such as those distinguishing primary visual and motor cortices from surrounding tissues, added considerable reinforcement to the localizationist camp.

By contrast, the tracing of neuronal connections between different regions of the brain, which became possible in the late nineteenth century with the development of a variety of specialized histological staining techniques, has been an indispensable source of knowledge regarding the flow of information through the brain and the hierarchy of processing stages. Recent years have seen the emergence of some remarkable new methods for tracing individual neuronal processes and for identifying the physiological efficacy of specific anatomical connections (Callaway 1998), the value of which is evidenced most beautifully by studies of the CELL TYPES AND CONNECTIONS IN THE VISUAL CORTEX.

The neuron doctrine also paved the way for an understanding of the information represented by neurons via their electrical properties, which has become a cornerstone of cognitive neuroscience in the latter half of the twentieth century. The electrical nature of nervous tissue was well known (yet highly debated) by the beginning of the nineteenth century, following advancement of the theory of "animal electricity" by Luigi Galvani (1737–1798) in 1791. Subsequent work by Emil du Bois-Reymond (1818–1896), Carlo Matteucci (1811–1862), and HERMANN LUDWIG FERDINAND VON HELMHOLTZ (1821–1894) established the spreading nature of electrical potentials in nervous tissue (nerve conduction), the role of the nerve membrane in maintaining and propagating an electrical charge ("wave of negativity"), and the velocity of nervous conduction. It was in the 1920s that Lord Edgar Douglas Adrian (1889–1977), using new cathode ray tube and amplification technology, developed the means to record "action potentials" from single neurons. Through this means, Adrian discovered the "all-or-nothing property" of nerve conduction via action potentials and demonstrated that action potential *frequency* is the currency of information transfer by neurons. Because of the fundamental importance of these discoveries, Adrian shared the 1932 Nobel Prize in physiology and medicine with Sherrington. Not long afterward, the Finnish physiologist Ragnar Granit developed techniques for recording neuronal activity using electrodes placed on the surface of the skin (Granit discovered the electroretinogram, or ERG, which reflects large-scale neuronal activity in the RETINA). These techniques became the foundation for non-invasive measurements of brain activity (see ELECTROPHYSIOLOGY, ELECTRIC AND MAGNETIC EVOKED FIELDS), which have played a central role in human cognitive neuroscience over the past 50 years.

With technology for SINGLE-NEURON RECORDING and large-scale electrophysiology safely in hand, the mid-twentieth century saw a rapid proliferation of studies of physiological response properties in the central nervous system. Sensory processing and motor control emerged as natural targets for investigation, and major emphasis was placed on understanding (1) the topographic mapping of the sensory or motor field onto central target zones (such as the retinotopic mapping in primary visual cortex), and (2) the specific sensory or motor events associated with changes in frequency of action potentials. Although some of the earliest and most elegant research was directed at the peripheral auditory system—culminating with Georg von Bekesy's (1889–1972) physical model of cochlear function and an understanding of its influence on AUDITORY PHYSIOLOGY—it is the visual system that has become the model for physiological investigations of information processing by neurons.

The great era of single-neuron studies of visual processing began in the 1930s with the work of Haldan Keffer Hartline (1903–1983), whose recordings from the eye of the horseshoe crab (*Limulus*) led to the discovery of neurons that respond when stimulated by light and detect differences in the patterns of illumination (i.e., contrast; Hartline, Wagner, and MacNichol 1952). It was for this revolutionary advance that Hartline became a corecipient of the 1967 Nobel Prize in physiology and medicine (together with Ragnar Granit and George Wald). Single-neuron studies of the mammalian visual system followed in the 1950s, with the work of Steven Kuffler (1913–1980) and Horace Barlow, who recorded from retinal ganglion cells. This research led to the development of the concept of the center-surround receptive field and highlighted the key role of spatial contrast detection in early vision (Kuffler 1953). Subsequent experiments by Barlow and Jerome Lettvin, among others, led to the discovery of neuronal FEATURE DETECTORS for behaviorally significant sensory inputs. This set the stage for the seminal work of David Hubel and Torsten Wiesel, whose physiological investigations of visual cortex, beginning in the late 1950s, profoundly shaped our understanding of the relationship between neuronal and sensory events (Hubel and Wiesel 1977).

See also AUDITORY PHYSIOLOGY; CAJAL, SANTIAGO RAMÓN Y; COMPUTING IN SINGLE NEURONS; ELECTROPHYSIOLOGY, ELECTRIC AND MAGNETIC EVOKED FIELDS; FEATURE DETECTORS; GOLGI, CAMILLO; HELMHOLTZ, HERMANN LUDWIG FERDINAND VON; NEURON; NEUROTRANSMITTERS; RETINA; SINGLE-NEURON RECORDING; VISUAL CORTEX, CELL TYPES AND CONNECTIONS IN

Sensation, Association, Perception, and Meaning

The rise of neuroscience from its fledgling origins in the nineteenth century was paralleled by the growth of experimental psychology and its embracement of sensation and perception as primary subject matter. The origins of experimental psychology as a scientific discipline coincided, in turn, with the convergence and refinement of views on the nature of the difference between sensation and perception. These views, which began to take their modern shape with the concept of "associationism" in the empiricist philosophy of John Locke (1632–1704), served to focus attention on the extraction of meaning from sensory events and, not surprisingly, lie at the core of much twentieth century cognitive neuroscience.

The proposition that things perceived cannot reflect directly the material of the external world, but rather depend upon the states of the sense organs and the intermediary nerves, is as old as rational empiricism itself. Locke's contribution to this topic was simply that *meaning*—knowledge of the world, functional relations between sensations, nee *perception*—is born from an association of "ideas," of which sensation was the primary source. The concept was developed further by George Berkeley (1685–1753) in his "theory of objects," according to which a sensation has meaning—that is, a reference to an external material source—only via the context of its relationship to other sensations. This associationism was a principal undercurrent of Scottish and English philosophy for the next two centuries, the concepts refined and the debate further fueled by the writings of James Mill and, most particularly, John Stuart Mill. It was the latter who defined the "laws of association" between elemental sensations, and offered the useful dictum that perception is the belief in the "permanent possibilities of sensation." By so doing, Mill bridged the gulf between the ephemeral quality of sensations and the permanence of objects and our experience of them: it is the link between present sensations and those known to be possible (from past experience) that allows us to perceive the enduring structural and relational qualities of the external world.

In the mid-nineteenth century the banner of associationism was passed from philosophy of mind to the emerging German school of experimental psychology, which numbered among its masters Gustav Fechner (1801–1887), Helmholtz, WILHELM WUNDT (1832–1920), and the English-American disciple of that tradition Edward Titchener (1867–1927). Fechner's principal contribution in this domain was the introduction of a systematic scientific methodology to a topic that had before that been solely the province of philosophers and a target of introspection. Fechner's *Elements of Psychophysics,* published in 1860, founded an "exact science of the functional relationship . . . between body and mind," based on the assumption that the relationship between brain and perception could be measured experimentally as the relationship between a stimulus and the sensation it gives rise to. PSYCHOPHYSICS thus provided the new nineteenth-century psychology with tools of a rigorous science and has subsequently become a mainstay of modern cognitive neuroscience. It was during this move toward quantification and systematization that Helmholtz upheld the prevailing associationist view of objects as sensations bound together through experience and memory, and he advanced the concept of *unconscious inference* to account for the attribution of perceptions to specific environmental causes. Wundt pressed further with the objectification and deconstruction of psychological reality by spelling out the concept—implicit in the manifestoes of his associationist predecessors—of elementism. Although Wundt surely believed that the meaning of sensory events lay in the relationship between them, elementism held that any complex association of sensations—any perception—was reducible to the sensory elements themselves. Titchener echoed the Wundtian view and elaborated upon the critical role of context in the associative extraction of meaning from sensation.

It was largely in response to this doctrine of elementism, its spreading influence, and its corrupt reductionistic account of perceptual experience that GESTALT PSYCHOLOGY was born in the late nineteenth century. In simplest terms, the Gestalt theorists, led by the venerable trio of Max Wertheimer (1880–1943), Wolfgang Kohler (1887–1967), and Kurt Koffka (1886–1941), insisted—and backed up their insistence with innumerable compelling demonstrations—that our phenomenal experience of objects, which includes an appreciation of their meanings and functions, is not generally reducible to a set of elemental sensations and the relationships between them. Moreover, rather than accepting the received wisdom that perception amounts to an inference about the world drawn from the associations between sensations, the Gestalt theorists held the converse to be true: perception is native experience and efforts to identify the underlying sensory elements are necessarily inferential (Koffka 1935). In spite of other flaws and peculiarities of the broad-ranging Gestalt psychology, this holistic view of perception, its distinction from sensation, and the nature of meaning, has become a central theme of modern cognitive neuroscience.

At the time the early associationist doctrine was being formed, there emerged a physiological counterpart in the form of Johannes Muller's (1801–1858) law of specific nerve energies, which gave rise in turn to the concept of specific fiber energies, and, ultimately, our twentieth-century receptive fields and feature detectors. Muller's law followed, intellectually as well as temporally, the Bell-Magendie law of distinct sensory and motor spinal roots, which set a precedent for the concept of specificity of nerve action. Muller's law was published in his 1838 *Handbook of Physiology* and consisted of several principles, those most familiar being the specificity of the sensory information (Muller identified five kinds) carried by different nerves and the specificity of the site of termination in the brain (a principle warmly embraced by functional localizationists of the era). For present discussion, the essential principle is that "the immediate objects of the perception of our senses are merely particular states induced in the nerves, and felt as sensations either by the nerves themselves or by the sensorium" (Boring 1950). Muller thus sidestepped the ancient problem of the mind's access to the external world by observing that all it can hope to access is the state of its sensory nerves. Accordingly, perception of the external world is a consequence of the stable relationship between external stimuli and nerve activation, and—tailing the associationist philosophers—meaning is granted by the associative interactions between nerves carrying different types of information. The concept was elaborated further by Helmholtz and others to address the different submodalities (e.g., color vs. visual distance) and qualities (e.g., red vs. green) of information carried by different fibers, and is a tenet of contemporary sensory neurobiology and cognitive neuroscience. The further implications of associationism for an understanding of the neuronal basis of perception—or, more precisely, of functional knowledge of the world—are profound and, as we shall see, many of the nineteenth-century debates on the topic are being replayed in the courts of modern single-neuron physiology.

See also GESTALT PSYCHOLOGY; PSYCHOPHYSICS; WUNDT, WILHELM

3   Cognitive Neuroscience Today

And so it was from these ancient but rapidly converging lines of inquiry, with the blush still on the cheek of a young cognitive science, that the modern era of cognitive neuroscience began. The field continues to ride a groundswell of optimism borne by new experimental tools and concepts—particularly single-cell electrophysiology, functional brain imaging, molecular genetic manipulations, and neuronal computation—and the access they have offered to neuronal operations underlying cognition. The current state of the field and its promise of riches untapped can be summarized through a survey of the processes involved in the acquisition, storage, and use of information by the nervous system: sensation, perception, decision formation, motor control, memory, language, emotions, and consciousness.

Sensation

We acquire knowledge of the world through our senses. Not surprisingly, sensory processes are among the most thoroughly studied in cognitive neuroscience. Systematic explorations of these processes originated in two domains. The first consisted of investigations of the physical nature of the sensory stimuli in question, such as the wave nature of light and sound. Sir Isaac Newton's (1642–1727) *Optiks* is an exemplar of this approach. The second involved studies of the anatomy of the peripheral sense organs, with attention given to the manner in which anatomical features prepared the physical stimulus for sensory transduction. Von Bekesy's beautiful studies of the structural features of the cochlea and the relation of those features to the neuronal frequency coding of sound is a classic example (for which he was awarded the 1961 Nobel Prize in physiology and medicine). Our present understanding of the neuronal bases of sensation was further enabled by three major developments: (1) establishment of the neuron doctrine, with attendant anatomical and physiological studies of neurons; (2) systematization of behavioral studies of sensation, made possible through the development of psychophysics; and (3) advancement of sophisticated theories of neuronal function, as embodied by the discipline of COMPUTATIONAL NEUROSCIENCE. For a variety of reasons, vision has emerged as the model for studies of sensory processing, although many fundamental principles of sensory processing are conserved across modalities.

Initial acquisition of information about the world, by all sensory modalities, begins with a process known as transduction, by which forms of physical energy (e.g., photons) alter the electrical state of a sensory neuron. In the case of vision, phototransduction occurs in the RETINA, which is a specialized sheet-like neural network with a regular repeating structure. In addition to its role in transduction, the retina also functions in the initial detection of spatial and temporal contrast (Enroth-Cugell and Robson 1966; Kaplan and Shapley 1986) and contains specialized neurons that subserve

COLOR VISION (see also COLOR, NEUROPHYSIOLOGY OF). The outputs of the retina are carried by a variety of ganglion cell types to several distinct termination sites in the central nervous system. One of the largest projections forms the "geniculostriate" pathway, which is known to be critical for normal visual function in primates. This pathway ascends to the cerebral cortex by way of the lateral geniculate nucleus of the THALAMUS.

The cerebral cortex itself has been a major focus of study during the past forty years of vision research (and sensory research of all types). The entry point for ascending visual information is via primary visual cortex, otherwise known as striate cortex or area V1, which lies on the posterior pole (the occipital lobe) of the cerebral cortex in primates. The pioneering studies of V1 by Hubel and Wiesel (1977) established the form in which visual information is represented by the activity of single neurons and the spatial arrangement of these representations within the cortical mantle ("functional architecture"). With the development of increasingly sophisticated techniques, our understanding of cortical VISUAL ANATOMY AND PHYSIOLOGY, and their relationships to sensory experience, has been refined considerably. Several general principles have emerged:

Receptive Field   This is an operationally defined attribute of a sensory neuron, originally offered by the physiologist Haldan Keffer Hartline, which refers to the portion of the sensory field that, when stimulated, elicits a change in the electrical state of the cell. More generally, the receptive field is a characterization of the filter properties of a sensory neuron, which are commonly multidimensional and include selectivity for parameters such as spatial position, intensity, and frequency of the physical stimulus. Receptive field characteristics thus contribute to an understanding of the information represented by the brain, and are often cited as evidence for the role of a neuron in specific perceptual and cognitive functions.

Contrast Detection   The elemental sensory operation, that is, one carried out by all receptive fields—is detection of spatial or temporal variation in the incoming signal. It goes without saying that if there are no environmental changes over space and time, then nothing in the input is worthy of detection. Indeed, under such constant conditions sensory neurons quickly adapt. The result is a demonstrable loss of sensation—such as "snow blindness"—that occurs even though there may be energy continually impinging on the receptor surface. On the other hand, contrast along some sensory dimension indicates a change in the environment, which may in turn be a call for action. All sensory modalities have evolved mechanisms for detection of such changes.

Topographic Organization   Representation of spatial patterns of activation within a sensory field is a key feature of visual, auditory, and tactile senses, which serves the behavioral goals of locomotor navigation and object recognition. Such representations are achieved for these modalities, in part, by topographically organized neuronal maps. In the visual system, for example, the retinal projection onto the lateral geniculate nucleus of the thalamus possesses a high degree of spatial order, such that neurons with spatially adjacent receptive fields lie adjacent to one another in the brain. Similar visuotopic maps are seen in primary visual cortex and in several successively higher levels of processing (e.g., Gattass, Sousa, and Covey 1985). These maps are commonly distorted relative to the sensory field, such that, in the case of vision, the numbers of neurons representing the central portion of the visual field greatly exceed those representing the visual periphery. These variations in "magnification factor" coincide with (and presumably underlie) variations in the observer's resolving power and sensitivity.

Modular and Columnar Organization   The proposal that COLUMNS AND MODULES form the basis for functional organization in the sensory neocortex is a natural extension of the nineteenth-century concept of localization of function. The 1970s and 1980s saw a dramatic rise in the use of electrophysiological and anatomical tools to subdivide sensory cortices—particularly visual cortex—into distinct functional modules. At the present time, evidence indicates that the visual cortex of monkeys is composed of over thirty such regions, including the well-known and heavily studied areas V1, V2, V3, V4, MT, and IT, as well as some rather more obscure and equivocal designations (Felleman and Van Essen 1991). These efforts to reveal order in heterogeneity have been reinforced by the appealing computational view (e.g., Marr 1982) that larger operations (such as seeing) can be subdivided and assigned to dedicated task-specific modules (such as ones devoted to visual motion or color processing, for example). The latter argument also dovetails nicely with the nineteenth-century concept of elementism, the coincidence of which inspired a fevered effort to identify visual areas that process specific sensory "elements." Although this view appears to be supported by physiological evidence for specialized response properties in some visual areas—such as a preponderance of motion-sensitive neurons in area MT (Albright 1993) and color-sensitive neurons in area V4 (Schein and Desimone 1990)—the truth is that very little is yet known of the unique contributions of most other cortical visual areas.

Modular organization of sensory cortex also occurs at a finer spatial scale, in the form of regional variations in neuronal response properties and anatomical connections, which are commonly referred to as columns, patches, blobs, and stripes. The existence of a column-like anatomical substructure in the cerebral cortex has been known since the early twentieth century, following the work of Ramón y Cajal, Constantin von Economo (1876–1931), and Rafael Lorente de Nó. It was the latter who first suggested that this characteristic structure may have some functional significance (Lorento de Nó 1938). The concept of modular functional organization was later expanded upon by the physiologist Vernon B. Mountcastle (1957), who obtained the first evidence for columnar function through his investigations of the primate somatosensory system, and offered this as a general principle of cortical organization. The most well known examples of modular organization of the sort predicted by Mountcastle are the columnar systems for contour orientation and ocular dominance discovered in primary visual cortex in the 1960s by David Hubel and Torsten Wiesel (1968). Additional evidence for functional columns and for the veracity of Mountcastle's dictum has come from studies of higher visual areas, such as area MT (Albright, Desimone, and Gross 1984) and the inferior temporal cortex (Tanaka 1997). Other investigations have demonstrated that modular representations are not limited to strict columnar forms (Born and Tootell 1993; Livingstone and Hubel 1984) and can exist as relatively large cortical zones in which there is a common feature to the neuronal representation of sensory information (such as clusters of cells that exhibit a greater degree of selectivity for color, for example).

The high incidence of columnar structures leads one to wonder why they exist. One line of argument, implicit in Mountcastle's original hypothesis, is based on the need for adequate "coverage"—that is, nesting the representation of one variable (such as preferred orientation of a visual contour) across changes in another (such as the topographic representation of the visual field)—which makes good computational sense and has received considerable empirical support (Hubel and Wiesel 1977). Other arguments include those based on developmental constraints (Swindale 1980; Miller 1994; Goodhill 1997) and computational advantages afforded by representation of sensory features in a regular periodic structure (see COMPUTATIONAL NEUROANATOMY; Schwartz 1980).

Hierarchical Processing   A consistent organizational feature of sensory systems is the presence of multiple hierarchically organized processing stages, through which incoming sensory information is represented in increasingly complex or abstract forms. The existence of multiple stages has been demonstrated by anatomical studies, and the nature of the representation at each stage has commonly been revealed through electrophysiological analysis of sensory response properties. As we have seen for the visual system, the first stage of processing beyond transduction of the physical stimulus is one in which a simple abstraction of light intensity is rendered, namely a representation of luminance contrast. Likewise, the outcome of processing in primary visual cortex is, in part, a representation of image contours—formed, it is believed, by a convergence of inputs from contrast-detecting neurons at earlier stages (Hubel and Wiesel 1962). At successively higher stages of processing, information is combined to form representations of even greater complexity, such that, for example, at the pinnacle of the pathway for visual pattern processing—a visual area known as inferior temporal (IT) cortex—individual neurons encode complex, behaviorally significant objects, such as faces (see FACE RECOGNITION).

Parallel Processing   In addition to multiple serial processing stages, the visual system is known to be organized in parallel streams. Incoming information of different types is channeled through a variety of VISUAL PROCESSING STREAMS, such that the output of each serves a unique function. This type of channeling occurs on several scales, the grossest of which is manifested as multiple retinal projections (typically six) to different brain regions. As we have noted, it is the geniculostriate projection that serves pattern vision in mammals. The similarly massive retinal projection to the midbrain superior colliculus (the "tectofugal" pathway) is known to play a role in orienting responses, OCULOMOTOR CONTROL, and MULTISENSORY INTEGRATION. Other pathways include a retinal projection to the hypothalamus, which contributes to the entrainment of circadian rhythms by natural light cycles.

Finer scale channeling of visual information is also known to exist, particularly in the case of the geniculostriate pathway (Shapley 1990). Both anatomical and physiological evidence (Perry, Oehler, and Cowey 1984; Kaplan and Shapley 1986) from early stages of visual processing support the existence of at least three subdivisions of this pathway, known as parvocellular, magnocellular, and the more recently identified koniocellular (Hendry and Yoshioka 1994). Each of these subdivisions is known to convey a unique spectrum of retinal image information and to maintain that information in a largely segregated form at least as far into the system as primary visual cortex (Livingstone and Hubel 1988).

Beyond V1, the ascending anatomical projections fall into two distinct streams, one of which descends ventrally into the temporal lobe, while the other courses dorsally to the parietal lobe. Analyses of the behavioral effects of lesions, as well as electrophysiological studies of neuronal response properties, have led to the hypothesis (Ungerleider and Mishkin 1982) that the ventral stream represents information about form and the properties of visual surfaces (such as their color or TEXTURE)— and is thus termed the "what" pathway—while the dorsal stream represents information regarding motion, distance, and the spatial relations between environmental surfaces—the so-called "where" pathway. The precise relationship, if any, between the early-stage channels (magno, parvo, and konio) and these higher cortical streams has been a rich source of debate and controversy over the past decade, and the answers remain far from clear (Livingstone and Hubel 1988; Merigan and Maunsell 1993).

See also COLOR, NEUROPHYSIOLOGY OF; COLOR VISION; COLUMNS AND MODULES; COMPUTATIONAL NEUROANATOMY; COMPUTATIONAL NEUROSCIENCE; FACE RECOGNITION; MULTISENSORY INTEGRATION; OCULOMOTOR CONTROL; RETINA; TEXTURE; THALAMUS; VISUAL ANATOMY AND PHYSIOLOGY; VISUAL PROCESSING STREAMS

Perception

Perception reflects the ability to derive meaning from sensory experience, in the form of information about structure and causality in the perceiver's environment, and of the sort necessary to guide behavior. Operationally, we can distinguish sensation from perception by the nature of the internal representations: the former encode the physical properties of the proximal sensory stimulus (the retinal image, in the case of vision), and the latter reflect the world that likely gave rise to the sensory stimulus (the visual scene). Because the mapping between sensory and perceptual events is never unique—multiple scenes can cause the same retinal image—perception is necessarily an inference about the probable causes of sensation.

As we have seen, the standard approach to understanding the information represented by sensory neurons, which has evolved over the past fifty years, is to measure the correlation between a feature of the neuronal response (typically magnitude) and some physical parameter of a sensory stimulus (such as the wavelength of light or the orientation of a contour). Because the perceptual interpretation of a sensory event is necessarily context-dependent, this approach alone is capable of revealing little, if anything, about the relationship between neuronal events and perceptual state. There are, however, some basic variations on this approach that have led to increased understanding of the neuronal bases of perception.

Experimental Approaches to the Neuronal Bases of Perception

Origins of a Neuron Doctrine for Perceptual Psychology   The first strategy involves evaluation of neuronal responses to visual stimuli that consist of complex objects of behavioral significance. The logic behind this approach is that if neurons are found to be selective for such stimuli, they may be best viewed as representing something of perceptual meaning rather than merely coincidentally selective for the collection of sensory features. The early studies of "bug detectors" in the frog visual system by Lettvin and colleagues (Lettvin, Maturana, MCCULLOCH, and PITTS 1959) exemplify this approach and have led to fully articulated views on the subject, including the concept of the "gnostic unit" advanced by Jerzy Konorski (1967) and the "cardinal cell" hypothesis from Barlow's (1972) classic "Neuron Doctrine for Perceptual Psychology." Additional evidence in support of this concept came from the work of Charles Gross in the 1960s and 1970s, in the extraordinary form of cortical cells selective for faces and hands (Gross, Bender, and Rocha-Miranda 1969; Desimone et al. 1984). Although the suggestion that perceptual experience may be rooted in the activity of single neurons or small neuronal ensembles has been decried, in part, on the grounds that the number of possible percepts greatly exceeds the number of available neurons, and is often ridiculed as the "grandmother-cell" hypothesis, the evidence supporting neuronal representations for visual patterns of paramount behavioral significance, such as faces, is now considerable (Desimone 1991; Rolls 1992).

Although a step in the right direction, the problem with this general approach is that it relies heavily upon assumptions about how the represented information is used. If a cell is activated by a face, and only a face, then it seems likely that the cell contributes directly to the perceptually meaningful experience of face recognition rather than simply representing a collection of sensory features (Desimone et al. 1984). To some, that distinction is unsatisfactorily vague, and it is, in any case, impossible to prove that a cell *only* responds to a face. An alternative approach that has proved quite successful in recent years is one in which an effort is made to directly relate neuronal and perceptual events.

Neuronal Discriminability Predicts Perceptual Discriminability   In the last quarter of the twentieth century, the marriage of single-neuron recording with visual psychophysics has yielded one of the dominant experimental paradigms of cognitive neuroscience, through which it has become possible to explain behavioral performance on a perceptual task in terms of the discriminative capacity of sensory neurons. The earliest effort of this type was a study of tactile discrimination conducted by Vernon Mountcastle in the 1960s (Mountcastle et al. 1967). In this study, thresholds for behavioral discrimination performance were directly compared to neuronal thresholds for the same stimulus set. A later study by Tolhurst, Movshon, and Dean (1983) introduced techniques from SIGNAL DETECTION THEORY that allowed more rigorous quantification of the discriminative capacity of neurons and thus facilitated neuronal-perceptual comparisons. Several other studies over the past ten years have significantly advanced this cause (e.g., Dobkins and Albright 1995), but the most direct approach has been that adopted by William Newsome and colleagues (e.g., Newsome, Britten, and Movshon 1989). In this paradigm, behavioral and neuronal events are measured simultaneously in response to a sensory stimulus, yielding by brute force some of the strongest evidence to date for neural substrates of perceptual discriminability.

Decoupling Sensation and Perception A somewhat subtler approach has been forged by exploiting the natural ambiguity between sensory events and perceptual experience (see ILLUSIONS). This ambiguity is manifested in two general forms: (1) single sensory events that elicit multiple distinct percepts, a phenomenon commonly known as "perceptual metastability," and (2) multiple sensory events—"sensory synonyms"—that elicit the same perceptual state. Both of these situations, which are ubiquitous in normal experience, afford opportunities to experimentally decouple sensation and perception.

The first form of sensory-perceptual ambiguity (perceptual metastability) is a natural consequence of the indeterminate mapping between a sensory signal and the physical events that gave rise to it. A classic and familiar example is the Necker Cube, in which the three-dimensional interpretation—the observer's inference about visual scene structure—periodically reverses despite the fact that the retinal image remains unchanged. Logothetis and colleagues (Logothetis and Schall 1989) have used a form of perceptual metastability known as binocular rivalry to demonstrate the existence of classes of cortical neurons that parallel changes in perceptual state in the face of constant retinal inputs.

The second type of sensory-perceptual ambiguity, in which multiple sensory images give rise to the same percept, is perhaps the more common. Such effects are termed perceptual constancies, and they reflect efforts by sensory systems to reconstruct behaviorally significant attributes of the world in the face of variation along irrelevant sensory dimensions. Size constancy—the invariance of perceived size of an object across different retinal sizes—and brightness or color constancy—the invariance of perceived reflectance or color of a surface in the presence of illumination changes—are classic examples. These perceptual constancies suggest an underlying neuronal invariance across specific image changes. Several examples of neuronal constancies have been reported, including invariant representations of direction of motion and shape across different cues for form (Albright 1992; Sary et al. 1995).

Contextual Influences on Perception and its Neuronal Bases One of the most promising new approaches to the neuronal bases of perception is founded on the use of contextual manipulations to influence the perceptual interpretation of an image feature. As we have seen, the contextual dependence of perception is scarcely a new finding, but contextual manipulations have been explicitly avoided in traditional physiological approaches to sensory coding. As a consequence, most existing data do not reveal whether and to what extent the neuronal representation of an image feature is context dependent. Gene Stoner, Thomas Albright, and colleagues have pioneered the use of contextual manipulations in studies of the neuronal basis of the PERCEPTION OF MOTION (e.g., Stoner and Albright 1992, 1993). The results of these studies demonstrate that context can alter neuronal filter properties in a manner that predictably parallels its influence on perception.

Stages of Perceptual Representation
Several lines of evidence suggest that there may be multiple steps along the path to extracting meaning from sensory signals. These steps are best illustrated by examples drawn from studies of visual processing. Sensation itself is commonly identified with "early" or "low-level vision." Additional steps are as follows.

Mid-Level Vision This step involves a reconstruction of the spatial relationships between environmental surfaces. It is implicit in the accounts of the perceptual psychologist JAMES JEROME GIBSON (1904–1979), present in the computational approach of DAVID MARR (1945–1980), and encompassed by what has recently come to be known as MID-LEVEL VISION. Essential features of this processing stage include a dependence upon proximal sensory context to establish surface relationships (see SURFACE PERCEPTION) and a relative lack of dependence upon prior experience. By establishing environmental STRUCTURE FROM VISUAL INFORMATION SOURCES, mid-level vision thus invests sensory events with some measure of meaning. A clear example of this type of visual processing is found in the phenomenon of perceptual TRANS-PARENCY (Metelli 1974) and the related topic of LIGHTNESS PERCEPTION. Physiological studies of the response properties of neurons at mid-levels of the cortical hierarchy have yielded results consistent with a mid-level representation (e.g., Stoner and Albright 1992).

High-Level Vision   HIGH-LEVEL VISION is a loosely defined processing stage, but one that includes a broad leap in the assignment of meaning to sensory events—namely identification and classification on the basis of previous experience with the world. It is through this process that recognition of objects occurs (see OBJECT RECOGNITION, HUMAN NEUROPSYCHOLOGY; OBJECT RECOGNITION, ANIMAL STUDIES; and VISUAL OBJECT RECOGNITION, AI), as well as assignment of affect and semantic categorization. This stage thus constitutes a bridge between sensory processing and MEMORY. Physiological and neuropsychological studies of the primate temporal lobe have demonstrated an essential contribution of this region to object recognition (Gross 1973; Gross et al. 1985).

See also GIBSON, JAMES JEROME; HIGH-LEVEL VISION; ILLUSIONS; LIGHTNESS PERCEPTION; MARR, DAVID; MCCULLOCH, WARREN S.; MEMORY; MID-LEVEL VISION; MOTION, PERCEPTION OF; OBJECT RECOGNITION, ANIMAL STUDIES; OBJECT RECOGNITION, HUMAN NEUROPSYCHOLOGY; PITTS, WALTER; SIGNAL DETECTION THEORY; STRUCTURE FROM VISUAL INFORMATION SOURCES; SURFACE PERCEPTION; TRANSPARENCY; VISUAL OBJECT RECOGNITION, AI

Sensory-Perceptual Plasticity

The processes by which information is acquired and interpreted by the brain are modifiable throughout life and on many time scales. Although plasticity of the sort that occurs during brain development and that which underlies changes in the sensitivity of mature sensory systems may arise from similar mechanisms, it is convenient to consider them separately.

Developmental Changes
The development of the mammalian nervous system is a complex, multistaged process that extends from embryogenesis through early postnatal life. This process begins with determination of the fate of precursor cells such that a subset becomes neurons. This is followed by cell division and proliferation, and by differentiation of cells into different types of neurons. The patterned brain then begins to take shape as cells migrate to destinations appropriate for their assigned functions. Finally, neurons begin to extend processes and to make synaptic connections with one another. These connections are sculpted and pruned over a lengthy postnatal period. A central tenet of modern neuroscience is that these final stages of NEURAL DEVELOPMENT correspond to specific stages of COGNITIVE DEVELOPMENT. These stages are known as "critical periods," and they are characterized by an extraordinary degree of plasticity in the formation of connections and cognitive functions.

Although critical periods for development are known to exist for a wide range of cognitive functions such as sensory processing, motor control, and language, they have been studied most intensively in the context of the mammalian visual system. These studies have included investigations of the timing, necessary conditions for, and mechanisms of (1) PERCEPTUAL DEVELOPMENT (e.g., Teller 1997), (2) formation of appropriate anatomical connections (e.g., Katz and Shatz 1996), and (3) neuronal representations of sensory stimuli (e.g., Hubel, Wiesel, and LeVay 1977). The general view that has emerged is that the newborn brain possesses a considerable degree of order, but that sensory experience is *essential* during critical periods to maintain that order and to fine-tune it to achieve optimal performance in adulthood. These principles obviously have profound implications for clinical practice and social policy. Efforts to further understand the cellular mechanisms of developmental plasticity, their relevance to other facets of cognitive function, the relative contributions of genes and experience, and routes of clinical intervention, are all among the most important topics for the future of cognitive neuroscience.

Dynamic Control of Sensitivity in the Mature Brain
Mature sensory systems have limited information processing capacities. An exciting area of research in recent years has been that addressing the conditions under which processing capacity is dynamically reallocated, resulting in fluctuations in sensitivity to sensory stimuli. The characteristics of sensitivity changes are many and varied, but all serve to optimize acquisition of information in a world in which environmental features and behavioral goals are constantly in flux. The form of these changes may be broad in scope or highly stimulus-specific and task-dependent. Changes may be nearly instantaneous, or they may come about gradually through exposure to specific environmental features. Finally, sensitivity changes differ greatly in the degree to which they are influenced by stored information about the environment and the degree to which they are under voluntary control.

Studies of the visual system reveal at least three types of sensitivity changes represented by the phenomena of (1) contrast gain control, (2) attention, and (3) perceptual learning. All can be viewed as recalibration of incoming signals to compensate for changes in the environment, the fidelity of signal detection (such as that associated with normal aging or trauma to the sensory periphery), and behavioral goals.

Generally speaking, neuronal gain control is the process by which the sensitivity of a neuron (or neural system) to its inputs is dynamically controlled. In that sense, all of the forms of adult plasticity discussed below are examples of gain control, although they have different dynamics and serve different functions.

Contrast Gain Control   A well-studied example of gain control is the invariance of perceptual sensitivity to the features of the visual world over an enormous range of lighting conditions. Evidence indicates that the limited dynamic range of responsivity of individual neurons in visual cortex is adjusted in an illumination-dependent manner (Shapley and Victor 1979), the consequence of which is a neuronal invariance that can account for the sensory invariance. It has been suggested that this scaling of neuronal sensitivity as a function of lighting conditions may be achieved by response "normalization," in which the output of a cortical neuron is effectively divided by the pooled activity of a large number of other cells of the same type (Carandini, Heeger, and Movshon 1997).

Attention   Visual ATTENTION is, by definition, a rapidly occurring change in visual sensitivity that is selective for a specific location in space or specific stimulus features. The stimulus and mnemonic factors that influence attentional allocation have been studied for over a century (James 1890), and the underlying brain structures and events are beginning to be understood (Desimone and Duncan 1995). Much of our understanding comes from analysis of ATTENTION IN THE HUMAN BRAIN—particularly the effects of cortical lesions, which can selectively interfere with attentional allocation (VISUAL NEGLECT), and through electrical and magnetic recording (ERP, MEG) and imaging studies—POSITRON EMISSION TOMOGRAPHY (PET) and functional MAGNETIC RESONANCE IMAGING (fMRI). In addition, studies of ATTENTION IN THE ANIMAL BRAIN have revealed that attentional shifts are correlated with changes in the sensitivity of single neurons to sensory stimuli (Moran and Desimone 1985; Bushnell, Goldberg, and Robinson 1981; see also AUDITORY ATTENTION). Although attentional phenomena differ from contrast gain control in that they can be influenced by feedback WORKING MEMORY as well as feedforward (sensory) signals, attentional effects can also be characterized as an expansion of the dynamic range of sensitivity, but in a manner that is selective for the attended stimuli.

Perceptual Learning   Both contrast gain control and visual attention are rapidly occurring and short-lived sensitivity changes. Other experiments have targeted neuronal events that parallel visual sensitivity changes occurring over a longer time scale, such as those associated with the phenomenon of perceptual learning. Perceptual learning refers to improvements in discriminability along any of a variety of sensory dimensions that come with practice. Although it has long been known that the sensitivity of the visual system is refined in this manner during critical periods of neuronal development, recent experiments have provided tantalizing evidence of improvements in the sensitivity of neurons at early stages of processing, which parallel perceptual learning in adults (Recanzone, Schreiner, and Merzenich 1993; Gilbert 1996).

See also ATTENTION; ATTENTION IN THE ANIMAL BRAIN; ATTENTION IN THE HUMAN BRAIN; AUDITORY ATTENTION; COGNITIVE DEVELOPMENT; MAGNETIC RESONANCE IMAGING; NEURAL DEVELOPMENT; PERCEPTUAL DEVELOPMENT; POSITRON EMISSION TOMOGRAPHY; VISUAL NEGLECT; WORKING MEMORY; WORKING MEMORY, NEURAL BASIS OF

Forming a Decision to Act

The meaning of many sensations can be found solely in their symbolic and experience-dependent mapping onto actions (e.g., green = go, red = stop). These mappings are commonly many-to-one or one-to-many (a whistle and a green light can both be signals to "go"; conversely, a whistle may be either a signal to "go" or a call to attention, depending upon the context). The selection of a particular action from those possible at any point in time is thus a context-dependent transition between sensory processing and motor control. This transition is commonly termed the decision stage, and it has become a focus of recent electrophysiological studies of the cerebral cortex (e.g., Shadlen and Newsome 1996). Because of the nonunique mappings, neurons involved in making such decisions should be distinguishable from those representing sensory events by a tendency to generalize across specific features of the sensory signal. Similarly, the representation of the neuronal decision should be distinguishable from a motor control signal by generalization across specific motor actions. In addition, the strength of the neuronal decision signal should increase with duration of exposure to the sensory stimulus (integration time), in parallel with increasing decision confidence on the part of the observer. New data in support of some of these predictions suggests that this may be a valuable new paradigm for accessing the neuronal substrates of internal cognitive states, and for bridging studies of sensory or perceptual processing, memory, and motor control.

Motor Control

Incoming sensory information ultimately leads to action, and actions, in turn, are often initiated in order to acquire additional sensory information. Although MOTOR CONTROL systems have often been studied in relative isolation from sensory processes, this sensory-motor loop suggests that they are best viewed as different phases of a processing continuum. This integrated view, which seeks to understand how the nature of sensory representations influences movements, and vice-versa, is rapidly gaining acceptance. The oculomotor control system has become the model for the study of motor processes at behavioral and neuronal levels.

Important research topics that have emerged from consideration of the transition from sensory processing to motor control include (1) the process by which representations of space (see SPATIAL PERCEPTION) are transformed from the coordinate system of the sensory field (e.g., retinal space) to a coordinate system for action (e.g., Graziano and Gross 1998) and (2) the processes by which the neuronal links between sensation and action are modifiable (Raymond, Lisberger, and Mauk 1996), as needed to permit MOTOR LEARNING and to compensate for degenerative sensory changes or structural changes in the motor apparatus.

The brain structures involved in motor control include portions of the cerebral cortex, which are thought to contribute to fine voluntary motor control, as well as the BASAL GANGLIA and CEREBELLUM, which play important roles in motor learning; the superior colliculus, which is involved in sensorimotor integration, orienting responses, and oculomotor control; and a variety of brainstem motor nuclei, which convey motor signals to the appropriate effectors.

See also BASAL GANGLIA; CEREBELLUM; MOTOR CONTROL; MOTOR LEARNING; SPATIAL PERCEPTION

Learning and Memory

Studies of the neuronal mechanisms that enable information about the world to be stored and retrieved for later use have a long and rich history—being, as they were, a central part of the agenda of the early functional localizationists—and now lie at the core of our modern cognitive neuroscience. Indeed, memory serves as the linchpin that binds and shapes nearly every aspect of information processing by brains, including perception, decision making, motor control, emotion, and consciousness. Memory also exists in various forms, which have been classified on the basis of their relation to other cognitive functions, the degree to which they are explicitly encoded and available for use in a broad range of contexts, and their longevity. (We have already considered some forms of nonexplicit memory, such as those associated with perceptual and motor learning.) Taxonomies based upon these criteria have been reviewed in detail elsewhere (e.g., Squire, Knowlton, and Musen 1993). The phenomenological and functional differences among different forms of memory suggest the existence of a variety of different brain substrates. Localization of these substrates is a major goal of modern cognitive neuroscience. Research is also clarifying the mechanisms underlying the oft-noted role of affective or emotional responses in memory consolidation (see MEMORY STORAGE, MODULATION OF; AMYGDALA, PRIMATE), and the loss of memory that occurs with aging (see AGING, MEMORY, AND THE BRAIN).

Three current approaches (broadly defined and overlapping) to memory are among the most promising for the future of cognitive neuroscience: (1) neuropsychological and neurophysiological studies of the neuronal substrates of explicit memory in primates, (2) studies of the relationship between phenomena of synaptic facilitation or depression and behavioral manifestations of learning and memory, and (3) molecular genetic studies that enable highly selective disruption of cellular structures and events thought to be involved in learning and memory.

Brain Substrates of Explicit Memory in Primates

The current approach to this topic has its origins in the early studies of Karl Lashley and colleagues, in which the lesion method was used to infer the contributions of specific brain regions to a variety of cognitive functions, including memory. The field took a giant step forward in the 1950s with the discovery by Brenda Milner and colleagues of the devastating effects of damage to the human temporal lobe—particularly the HIPPOCAMPUS—on human memory formation (see MEMORY, HUMAN NEUROPSYCHOLOGY). Following that discovery, Mortimer Mishkin and colleagues began to use the lesion technique to develop an animal model of amnesia. More recently, using a similar approach, Stuart Zola, Larry Squire, and colleagues have further localized the neuronal substrates of memory consolidation in the primate temporal lobe (see MEMORY, ANIMAL STUDIES).

Electrophysiological studies of the contributions of individual cortical neurons to memory began in the 1970s with the work of Charles Gross and Joaquin Fuster. The logic behind this approach is that by examining neuronal responses of an animal engaged in a standard memory task (e.g., match-to-sample: determine whether a sample stimulus corresponds to a previously viewed cue stimulus), one can distinguish the components of the response that reflect memory from those that are sensory in nature. Subsequent electrophysiological studies by Robert Desimone and Patricia Goldman-Rakic, among others, have provided some of the strongest evidence for single-cell substrates of working memory in the primate temporal and frontal lobes. These traditional approaches to explicit memory formation in primates are now being complemented by brain imaging studies in humans.

Do Synaptic Changes Mediate Memory Formation?

The phenomenon of LONG-TERM POTENTIATION (LTP), originally discovered in the 1970s—and the related phenomenon of long-term depression—consists of physiologically measurable changes in the strength of synaptic connections between neurons.

LTP is commonly produced in the laboratory by coincident activation of pre- and post-synaptic neurons, in a manner consistent with the predictions of DONALD O. HEBB (1904–1985), and it is often dependent upon activation of the postsynaptic NMDA glutamate receptor. Because a change in synaptic efficacy could, in principle, underlie behavioral manifestations of learning and memory, and because LTP is commonly seen in brain structures that have been implicated in memory formation (such as the hippocampus, cerebellum, and cerebral cortex) by other evidence, it is considered a likely mechanism for memory formation. Attempts to test that hypothesis have led to one of the most exciting new approaches to memory.

From Genes to Behavior: A Molecular Genetic Approach to Memory
The knowledge that the NMDA receptor is responsible for many forms of LTP, in conjunction with the hypothesis that LTP underlies memory formation, led to the prediction that memory formation should be disrupted by elimination of NMDA receptors. The latter can be accomplished in mice by engineering genetic mutations that selectively knock out the NMDA receptor, although this technique has been problematic because it has been difficult to constrain the effects to specific brain regions and over specific periods of time. Matthew Wilson and Susumu Tonegawa have recently overcome these obstacles by production of a knockout in which NMDA receptors are disrupted only in a subregion of the hippocampus (the CA1 layer), and only after the brain has matured. In accordance with the NMDA-mediated synaptic plasticity hypothesis, these animals were deficient on both behavioral and physiological assays of memory formation (Tonegawa et al. 1996). Further developments along these lines will surely involve the ability to selectively disrupt action potential generation in specific cell populations, as well as genetic manipulations in other animals (such as monkeys).

See also AGING, MEMORY, AND THE BRAIN; AMYGDALA, PRIMATE; HEBB, DONALD O.; HIPPOCAMPUS; LONG-TERM POTENTIATION; MEMORY, ANIMAL STUDIES; MEMORY, HUMAN NEUROPSYCHOLOGY; MEMORY STORAGE, MODULATION OF

Language

One of the first cognitive functions to be characterized from a biological perspective was language. Nineteenth-century physicians, including Broca, observed the effects of damage to different brain regions and described the asymmetrical roles of the left and right hemispheres in language production and comprehension (see HEMISPHERIC SPECIALIZATION; APHASIA; LANGUAGE, NEURAL BASIS OF). Investigators since then have discovered that different aspects of language, including the PHONOLOGY, SYNTAX, and LEXICON, each rely on different and specific neural structures (see PHONOLOGY, NEURAL BASIS OF; GRAMMAR, NEURAL BASIS OF; LEXICON, NEURAL BASIS OF). Modern neuroimaging techniques, including ERPs, PET, and fMRI, have confirmed the role of the classically defined language areas and point to the contribution of several other areas as well. Such studies have also identified "modality neutral" areas that are active when language is processed through any modality: auditory, written, and even sign language (see SIGN LANGUAGE AND THE BRAIN). Studies describing the effects of lesions on language can identify neural tissue that is necessary and sufficient for processing. An important additional perspective can be obtained from neuroimaging studies of healthy neural tissue, which can reveal all the activity associated with language production and comprehension. Taken together the currently available evidence reveals a strong bias for areas within the left hemisphere to mediate language if learned early in childhood, independently of its form or modality. However, the nature of the language learned and the age of acquisition have effects on the configuration of the language systems of the brain (see BILINGUALISM AND THE BRAIN).

Developmental disorders of language (see LANGUAGE IMPAIRMENT, DEVELOPMENTAL; DYSLEXIA) can occur in isolation or in association with other disorders and can result from deficits within any of the several different skills that are central to the perception and modulation of language.

See also APHASIA; BILINGUALISM AND THE BRAIN; DYSLEXIA; GRAMMAR, NEURAL BASIS OF; HEMISPHERIC SPECIALIZATION; LANGUAGE, NEURAL BASIS OF; LANGUAGE IMPAIRMENT, DEVELOPMENTAL; LEXICON; LEXICON, NEURAL BASIS OF; PHONOLOGY; PHONOLOGY, NEURAL BASIS OF; SIGN LANGUAGE AND THE BRAIN; SYNTAX

Consciousness

Rediscovery of the phenomena of perception and memory without awareness has renewed research and debate on issues concerning the neural basis of CONSCIOUSNESS (see CONSCIOUSNESS, NEUROBIOLOGY OF). Some patients with cortical lesions that have rendered them blind can nonetheless indicate (by nonverbal methods) accurate perception of stimuli presented to the blind portion of the visual field (see BLINDSIGHT). Similarly, some patients who report no memory for specific training events nonetheless demonstrate normal learning of those skills.

Systematic study of visual consciousness employing several neuroimaging tools within human and nonhuman primates is being conducted to determine whether consciousness emerges as a property of a large collection of interacting neurons or whether it arises as a function of unique neuronal characteristics possessed by some neurons or by an activity pattern temporarily occurring within a subset of neurons (see BINDING BY NEURAL SYNCHRONY).

Powerful insights into systems and cellular and molecular events critical in cognition and awareness, judgment and action have come from human and animal studies of SLEEP and DREAMING. Distinct neuromodulatory effects of cholenergic and aminergic systems permit the panoply of conscious cognitive processing, evaluation, and planning during waking states and decouple cognition, emotional, and mnemonic functions during sleep. Detailed knowledge of the neurobiology of sleep and dreaming presents an important opportunity for future studies of cognition and consciousness.

See also BINDING BY NEURAL SYNCHRONY; BLINDSIGHT; CONSCIOUSNESS; CONSCIOUSNESS, NEUROBIOLOGY OF; DREAMING; SLEEP

Emotions

Closely related to questions about consciousness are issues of EMOTIONS and feelings that have, until very recently, been ignored in cognitive science. Emotions sit at the interface between incoming events and preparation to respond, however, and recent studies have placed the study of emotion more centrally in the field. Animal models have provided detailed anatomical and physiological descriptions of fear responses (Armony and LeDoux 1997) and highlight the role of the amygdala and LIMBIC SYSTEM as well as different inputs to this system (see EMOTION AND THE ANIMAL BRAIN). Studies of human patients suggest specific roles for different neural systems in the perception of potentially emotional stimuli (Adolphs et al. 1994; Hamann et al. 1996), in their appraisal, and in organizing appropriate responses to them (see EMOTION AND THE HUMAN BRAIN; PAIN). An important area for future research is to characterize the neurochemistry of emotions. The multiple physiological responses to real or imagined threats (i.e., STRESS) have been elucidated in both animal and human studies. Several of the systems most affected by stress play central roles in emotional and cognitive functions (see NEUROENDOCRINOLOGY). Early pre- and postnatal experiences play a significant role in shaping the activity of these systems and in their rate of aging. The profound role of the stress-related hormones on memory-related brain structures, including the hippocampus, and their role in regulating neural damage following strokes and seizures and in aging, make them a central object for future research in cognitive neuroscience (see AGING AND COGNITION).

See also AGING AND COGNITION; EMOTION AND THE ANIMAL BRAIN; EMOTION AND THE HUMAN BRAIN; EMOTIONS; LIMBIC SYSTEM; NEUROENDOCRINOLOGY; PAIN; STRESS

4   Cognitive Neuroscience: A Promise for the Future

A glance at the neuroscience entries for this volume reveals that we are amassing detailed knowledge of the highly specialized neural systems that mediate different and specific cognitive functions. Many questions remain unanswered, however, and the applications of new experimental techniques have often raised more questions than they have answered. But such are the expansion pains of a thriving science.

Among the major research goals of the next century will be to elucidate how these highly differentiated cognitive systems arise in ontogeny, the degree to which they are maturationally constrained, and the nature and the timing of the role of input from the environment in NEURAL DEVELOPMENT. This is an area where research has just begun. It is evident that there exist strong genetic constraints on the overall patterning of different domains within the developing nervous system. Moreover, the same class of genes specify the rough segmentation of the nervous systems of both vertebrates and invertebrates. However, the information required to specify the fine differentiation and connectivity within the cortex exceeds that available in the genome. Instead, a process of selective stabilization of transiently redundant connections permits individual differences in activity and experience to organize developing cortical systems. Some brain circuits display redundant connectivity and pruning under experience only during a limited time period in development ("critical period"). These time periods are different for different species and for different functional brain systems within a species. Other brain circuits retain the ability to change under external stimulation throughout life, and this capability, which now appears more ubiquitous and long lasting than initially imagined, is surely a substrate for adult learning, recovery of function after brain damage, and PHANTOM LIMB phenomena (see also AUDITORY PLASTICITY; NEURAL PLASTICITY). A major challenge for future generations of cognitive neuroscientists will be to characterize and account for the markedly different extents and timecourses of biological constraints and experience-dependent modifiability of the developing human brain.

Though the pursuit may be ancient, consider these the halcyon days of cognitive neuroscience. As we cross the threshold of the millenium, look closely as the last veil begins to fall. And bear in mind that if cognitive neuroscience fulfills its grand promise, later editions of this volume may contain a section on history, into which all of the nonneuro cognitive science discussion will be swept.

See also AUDITORY PLASTICITY; NEURAL DEVELOPMENT; NEURAL PLASTICITY; PHANTOM LIMB

References

Adolphs, R., D. Tranel, H. Damasio, and A. Damasio. (1994). Impaired recognition of emotion in facial expressions following bilateral damage to the human amygdala. *Nature* 372: 669–672.

Albright, T. D. (1992). Form-cue invariant motion processing in primate visual cortex. *Science* 255: 1141–1143.

Albright, T. D. (1993). Cortical processing of visual motion. In J. Wallman and F. A. Miles, Eds., *Visual Motion and its Use in the Stabilization of Gaze*. Amsterdam: Elsevier.

Albright, T. D., R. Desimone, and C. G. Gross. (1984). Columnar organization of directionally selective cells in visual area MT of the macaque. *Journal of Neurophysiology* 51: 16–31.

Armony, J. L., and J. E. LeDoux. (1997). How the brain processes emotional information. *Annals of the New York Academy of Sciences* 821: 259–270.

Barlow, H. B. (1972). Single units and sensation: A neuron doctrine for perceptual psychology? *Perception* 1: 371–394.

Boring, E. G. (1950). *A History of Experimental Psychology,* 2nd ed. R. M. Elliott, Ed. New Jersey: Prentice-Hall.

Born, R. T., and R. B. Tootell. (1993). Segregation of global and local motion processing in primate middle temporal visual area. *Nature* 357: 497–499.

Bushnell, M. C., M. E. Goldberg, and D. L. Robinson. (1981). Behavioral enhancement of visual responses in monkey cerebral cortex. 1. Modulation in posterior parietal cortex related to selective visual attention. *Journal of Neurophysiology* 46(4): 755–772.

Callaway, E. M. (1998). Local circuits in primary visual cortex of the macaque monkey. *Annual Review of Neuroscience* 21: 47–74.

Carandini, M., D. J. Heeger, and J. A. Movshon. (1997). Linearity and normalization in simple cells of the macaque primary visual cortex. *Journal of Neuroscience* 17(21): 8621–8644.

Desimone, R. (1991). Face-selective cells in the temporal cortex of monkeys. *Journal of Cognitive Neuroscience* 3: 1–7.

Desimone, R., T. D. Albright, C. G. Gross, and C. J. Bruce. (1984). Stimulus selective properties of inferior temporal neurons in the macaque. *Journal of Neuroscience* 8: 2051–2062.

Desimone, R., and J. Duncan. (1995). Neural mechanisms of selective visual attention. *Annual Review of Neuroscience* 18: 193–222.

Dobkins, K. R., and T. D. Albright. (1995). Behavioral and neural effects of chromatic isoluminance in the primate visual motion system. *Visual Neuroscience* 12: 321–332.

Enroth-Cugell, C., and J. G. Robson. (1966). The contrast sensitivity of retinal ganglion cells of the cat. *Journal of Physiology (London)* 187: 517–552.

Felleman, D. J., and D. C. Van Essen. (1991). Distributed hierarchical processing in the primate cerebral cortex. *Cerebral Cortex* 1: 1–47.

Gattass, R., A. P. B. Sousa, and E. Cowey. (1985). Cortical visual areas of the macaque: Possible substrates for pattern recognition mechanisms. In C. Chagas, R. Gattass, and C. Gross, Eds., *Pattern Recognition Mechanisms*. Vatican City: Pontifica Academia Scientiarum, pp. 1–17.

Gilbert, C. D. (1996). Learning and receptive field plasticity. *Proceedings of the National Academy of Sciences USA* 93: 10546–10547.

Goodhill, G. J. (1997). Stimulating issues in cortical map development. *Trends in Neurosciences* 20: 375–376.

Graziano, M. S., and C. G. Gross. (1998). Spatial maps for the control of movement. *Current Opinion in Neurobiology* 8: 195–201.

Gross, C. G. (1973). Visual functions of inferotemporal cortex. In H. Autrum, R. Jung, W. Lowenstein, D. McKay, and H.-L. Teuber, Eds., *Handbook of Sensory Physiology*, vol. 7, 3B. Berlin: Springer.

Gross, C. G. (1994a). How inferior temporal cortex became a visual area. *Cerebral Cortex* 5: 455–469.

Gross, C. G. (1994b). Hans-Lukas Teuber: A tribute. *Cerebral Cortex* 4: 451–454.

Gross, C. G. (1998). *Brain, Vision, Memory: Tales in the History of Neuroscience*. Cambridge, MA: MIT Press.

Gross, C. G., D. B. Bender, and C. E. Rocha-Miranda. (1969). Visual receptive fields of neurons in inferotemporal cortex of the monkey. *Science* 166: 1303–1306.

Gross, C. G., R. Desimone, T. D. Albright, and E. L. Schwartz. (1985). Inferior temporal cortex and pattern recognition. In C. Chagas, Ed., *Study Group on Pattern Recognition Mechanisms*. Vatican City: Pontifica Academia Scientiarum, pp. 179–200.

Hamann, S. B., L. Stefanacci, L. R. Squire, R. Adolphs, D. Tranel, H. Damasio, and A. Damasio. (1996). Recognizing facial emotion [letter]. *Nature* 379(6565): 497.

Hartline, H. K., H. G. Wagner, and E. F. MacNichol, Jr. (1952). The peripheral origin of nervous activity in the visual system. *Cold Spring Harbor Symposium on Quantitative Biology* 17: 125–141.

Hendry, S. H., and T. Yoshioka. (1994). A neurochemically distinct third channel in the macaque dorsal lateral geniculate nucleus. *Science* 264(5158): 575–577.

Hubel, D. H., and T. N. Wiesel. (1962). Receptive fields, binocular interaction and functional architecture in the cat's visual cortex. *Journal of Physiology* 160: 106–154.

Hubel, D. H., and T. N. Wiesel. (1968). Receptive fields and functional architecture of monkey striate cortex. *Journal of Physiology* 195: 215–243.

Hubel, D. H., and T. N. Wiesel. (1977). Ferrier lecture. Functional architecture of macaque monkey visual cortex. *Proceedings of the Royal Society of London, Series B, Biological Sciences* 198(1130): 1–59.

Hubel, D. H., T. N. Wiesel, and S. LeVay. (1977). Plasticity of ocular dominance columns in monkey striate cortex. *Philosophical Transactions of the Royal Society of London, Series B, Biological Sciences* 278: 377–409.

James, W. (1890). *The Principles of Psychology*, vol. 1. New York: Dover.

Kaplan, E., and R. M. Shapley. (1986). The primate retina contains two types of ganglion cells, with high and low contrast sensitivity. *Proceedings of the National Academy of Sciences of the USA* 83(8): 2755–2757.

Katz, L. C., and C. J. Shatz. (1996). Synaptic activity and the construction of cortical circuits. *Science* 274: 1133–1138.

Koffka, K. (1935). *Principles of Gestalt Psychology*. New York: Harcourt, Brace.

Konorski, J. (1967). *Integrative Activity of the Brain*. Chicago: University of Chicago Press.

Kuffler, S. W. (1953). Discharge patterns and functional organization of the mammalian retina. *Journal of Neurophysiology* 16: 37–68.

Lettvin, J. Y., H. R. Maturana, W. S. McCulloch, and W. H. Pitts. (1959). What the frog's eye tells the frog's brain. *Proceedings of the Institute of Radio Engineers* 47: 1940–1951.

Livingstone, M. S., and D. H. Hubel. (1984). Anatomy and physiology of a color system in the primate visual cortex. *Journal of Neuroscience* 4: 309–356.

Livingstone, M. S., and D. H. Hubel. (1988). Segregation of form, color, movement, and depth: Anatomy, physiology, and perception. *Science* 240: 740–749.

Logothetis, N. K., and J. D. Schall. (1989). Neuronal correlates of subjective visual perception. *Science* 245: 761–763.

Lorento de Nó, R. (1938). Cerebral cortex: Architecture, intracortical connections, motor projections. In J. F. Fulton, Ed., *Physiology of the Nervous System*. New York: Oxford University Press, pp. 291–339.

Marr, D. (1982). *Vision: A Computational Investigation into the Human Representation and Processing of Visual Information.* San Francisco: W. H. Freeman.

Merigan, W. H., and J. H. Maunsell. (1993). How parallel are the primate visual pathways? *Annual Review of Neuroscience* 16: 369–402.

Metelli, F. (1974). The perception of transparency. *Scientific American* 230(4): 90–98.

Miller, K. D. (1994). A model for the development of simple cell receptive fields and the ordered arrangement of orientation columns through activity-dependent competition between ON- and OFF-center inputs. *Journal of Neuroscience* 14: 409–441.

Moran, J., and R. Desimone. (1985). Selective attention gates visual processing in the extrastriate cortex. *Science* 229(4715): 782–784.

Mountcastle, V. B. (1957). Modality and topographic properties of single neurons of cat's somatic sensory cortex. *Journal of Neurophysiology* 20: 408–434.

Mountcastle, V. B., W. H. Talbot, I. Darian-Smith, and H. H. Kornhuber. (1967). Neural basis of the sense of flutter-vibration. *Science* 155(762): 597–600.

Newsome, W. T., K. H. Britten, and J. A. Movshon. (1989). Neuronal correlates of a perceptual decision. *Nature* 341: 52–54.

Perry, V. H., R. Oehler, and A. Cowey. (1984). Retinal ganglion cells that project to the dorsal lateral geniculate nucleus in the macaque monkey. *Neuroscience* 12(4): 1101–1123.

Raymond, J. L., S. G. Lisberger, and M. D. Mauk. (1996). The cerebellum: A neuronal learning machine? *Science* 272: 1126–1131.

Recanzone, G. H., C. E. Schreiner, and M. M. Merzenich. (1993). Plasticity in the frequency representation of primary auditory cortex following discrimination training in adult owl monkeys. *Journal of Neuroscience* 13: 87–103.

Rolls, E. T. (1992). Neurophysiological mechanisms underlying face processing within and beyond the temporal cortical visual areas. In V. Bruce, A. Cowey, W. W. Ellis, and D. I. Perrett, Eds., *Processing the Facial Image.* Oxford: Clarendon Press, pp. 11–21.

Sary, G., R. Vogels, G. Kovacs, and G. A. Orban. (1995). Responses of monkey inferior temporal neurons to luminance-, motion-, and texture-defined gratings. *Journal of Neurophysiology* 73: 1341–1354.

Schein, S. J., and R. Desimone. (1990). Spectral properties of V4 neurons in the macaque. *Journal of Neuroscience* 10: 3369–3389.

Schwartz, E. L. (1980). Computational anatomy and functional architecture of striate cortex: A spatial mapping approach to perceptual coding. *Vision Research* 20: 645–669.

Shadlen, M. N., and W. T. Newsome. (1996). Motion perception: Seeing and deciding. *Proceedings of the National Academy of Sciences* 93: 628–633.

Shapley, R. (1990). Visual sensitivity and parallel retinocortical channels. *Annual Review of Psychology* 41: 635–658.

Shapley, R. M., and J. D. Victor. (1979). Nonlinear spatial summation and the contrast gain control of cat retinal ganglion cells. *Journal of Physiology (London)* 290: 141–161.

Squire, L. R., B. Knowlton, and G. Musen. (1993). The structure and organization of memory. *Annual Review of Psychology* 44: 453–495.

Stoner, G. R., and T. D. Albright. (1992). Neural correlates of perceptual motion coherence. *Nature* 358: 412–414.

Stoner, G. R., and T. D. Albright. (1993). Image segmentation cues in motion processing: Implications for modularity in vision. *Journal of Cognitive Neuroscience* 5: 129–149.

Swindale, N. V. (1980). A model for the formation of ocular dominance stripes. *Proceedings of the Royal Society of London Series B, Biological Sciences* 208(1171): 243–264.

Tanaka, K. (1997). Columnar organization in the inferotemporal cortex. *Cerebral Cortex* 12: 469–498.

Teller, D. Y. (1997). First glances: The vision of infants. The Friedenwald lecture. *Investigative Ophthalmology and Visual Science* 38: 2183–2203.

Tolhurst, D. J., J. A. Movshon, and A. F. Dean. (1983). The statistical reliability of signals in single neurons in cat and monkey visual cortex. *Vision Research* 23(8): 775–785.

Tonegawa, S., J. Z. Tsien, T. J. McHugh, P. Huerta, K. I. Blum, and M. A. Wilson. (1996). Hippocampal CA1-region-restricted knockout of NMDAR1 gene disrupts synaptic plasticity, place fields, and spatial learning. *Cold Spring Harbor Symposium on Quantitative Biology* 61: 225–238.

Ungerleider, L. G., and M. Mishkin. (1982). Two cortical visual systems. In D. J. Ingle, M. A. Goodale, and R. J. W. Mansfield, Eds., *Analysis of Visual Behavior.* Cambridge, MA: MIT Press, pp. 549–586.

Zola-Morgan, S. (1995). Localization of brain function: The legacy of Franz Joseph Gall. *Annual Review of Neuroscience* 18: 359–383.

Further Readings

Churchland, P. S., and T. J. Sejnowski. (1992). *The Computational Brain.* Cambridge, MA: MIT Press.

Cohen, N. J., and H. Eichenbaum. (1993). *Memory, Amnesia, and the Hippocampal System.* Cambridge, MA: MIT Press.

Dowling, J. E. (1987). *The Retina: An Approachable Part of the Brain.* Cambridge, MA: Belknap Press of Harvard University Press.

Finger, S. (1994). *Origins of Neuroscience: A History of Explorations into Brain Function.* New York: Oxford University Press.

Gazzaniga, M. S. (1995). *The Cognitive Neurosciences.* Cambridge, MA: MIT Press.

Gibson, J. J. (1966). *The Senses Considered as Perceptual Systems.* Boston: Houghton Mifflin.

Heilman, E. M., and E. Valenstein. (1985). *Clinical Neuropsychology,* 2nd ed. New York: Oxford University Press.

Helmholtz, H. von. (1924). *Physiological Optics.* English translation by J. P. C. Southall for the Optical Society of America from the 3rd German ed., *Handbuch der Physiologischen Optik* (1909). Hamburg: Voss.

Kanizsa, G. (1979). *Organization in Vision.* New York: Praeger.

Kosslyn, S. M. (1994). *Image and Brain.* Cambridge, MA: MIT Press.

LeDoux, J. E. (1996). *The Emotional Brain: The Mysterious Underpinnings of Emotional Life.* New York: Simon & Schuster.

Milner, A. D., and M. A. Goodale. (1995). *The Visual Brain in Action.* New York: Oxford University Press.

Penfield, W. (1975). *The Mystery of the Mind.* New Jersey: Princeton University Press.

Posner, M. L. (1989). *Foundations of Cognitive Science.* Cambridge, MA: MIT Press.

Squire, L. R. (1987). *Memory and Brain.* New York: Oxford University Press.

Weiskrantz, L. (1997). *Consciousness Lost and Found.* New York: Oxford University Press.

Computational Intelligence

Michael I. Jordan and Stuart Russell

There are two complementary views of artificial intelligence (AI): one as an engineering discipline concerned with the creation of intelligent machines, the other as an empirical science concerned with the computational modeling of human intelligence. When the field was young, these two views were seldom distinguished. Since then, a substantial divide has opened up, with the former view dominating modern AI and the latter view characterizing much of modern cognitive science. For this reason, we have adopted the more neutral term "computational intelligence" as the title of this article—both communities are attacking the problem of understanding intelligence in computational terms.

It is our belief that the differences between the engineering models and the cognitively inspired models are small compared to the vast gulf in competence between these models and human levels of intelligence. For humans are, to a first approximation, *intelligent*; they can perceive, act, learn, reason, and communicate *successfully* despite the enormous difficulty of these tasks. Indeed, we expect that as further progress is made in trying to emulate this success, the engineering and cognitive models will become more similar. Already, the traditionally antagonistic "connectionist" and "symbolic" camps are finding common ground, particularly in their understanding of reasoning under uncertainty and learning. This sort of cross-fertilization was a central aspect of the early vision of cognitive science as an interdisciplinary enterprise.

1 Machines and Cognition

The conceptual precursors of AI can be traced back many centuries. LOGIC, the formal theory of deductive reasoning, was studied in ancient Greece, as were ALGORITHMS for mathematical computations. In the late seventeenth century, Wilhelm Leibniz actually constructed simple "conceptual calculators," but their representational and combinatorial powers were far too limited. In the nineteenth century, Charles Babbage designed (but did not build) a device capable of universal computation, and his collaborator Ada Lovelace speculated that the machine might one day be programmed to play chess or compose music. Fundamental work by ALAN TURING in the 1930s formalized the notion of universal computation; the famous CHURCH-TURING THESIS proposed that all sufficiently powerful computing devices were essentially identical in the sense that any one device could emulate the operations of any other. From here it was a small step to the bold hypothesis that human cognition was a form of COMPUTATION in exactly this sense, and could therefore be emulated by computers.

By this time, neurophysiology had already established that the brain consisted largely of a vast interconnected network of NEURONS that used some form of electrical signalling mechanism. The first mathematical model relating computation and the brain appeared in a seminal paper entitled "A logical calculus of the ideas immanent in nervous activity," by WARREN MCCULLOCH and WALTER PITTS (1943). The paper proposed an abstract model of neurons as linear threshold units—logical "gates" that output a signal if the weighted sum of their inputs exceeds a threshold value (see COMPUTING IN SINGLE NEURONS). It was shown that a network of such gates could represent any logical function, and, with suitable delay components to implement memory, would be capable of universal computation. Together with HEBB's model of learning in networks of neurons, this work can be seen as a precursor of modern NEURAL NETWORKS and connectionist cognitive modeling. Its stress on the representation of logical concepts by neurons also provided impetus to the "logicist" view of AI.

The emergence of AI proper as a recognizable field required the availability of usable computers; this resulted from the wartime efforts led by Turing in Britain and by JOHN VON NEUMANN in the United States. It also required a banner to be raised;

this was done with relish by Turing's (1950) paper "Computing Machinery and Intelligence," wherein an operational definition for intelligence was proposed (the Turing test) and many future developments were sketched out.

One should not underestimate the level of controversy surrounding AI's initial phase. The popular press was only too ready to ascribe intelligence to the new "electronic super-brains," but many academics refused to contemplate the idea of intelligent computers. In his 1950 paper, Turing went to great lengths to catalogue and refute many of their objections. Ironically, one objection already voiced by Kurt Gödel, and repeated up to the present day in various forms, rested on the ideas of incompleteness and undecidability in formal systems to which Turing himself had contributed (see GÖDEL'S THEOREMS and FORMAL SYSTEMS, PROPERTIES OF). Other objectors denied the possibility of CONSCIOUSNESS in computers, and with it the possibility of intelligence. Turing explicitly sought to separate the two, focusing on the objective question of intelligent *behavior* while admitting that consciousness might remain a mystery—as indeed it has.

The next step in the emergence of AI was the formation of a research community; this was achieved at the 1956 Dartmouth meeting convened by John McCarthy. Perhaps the most advanced work presented at this meeting was that of ALLEN NEWELL and Herb Simon, whose program of research in symbolic cognitive modeling was one of the principal influences on cognitive psychology and information-processing psychology. Newell and Simon's IPL languages were the first symbolic programming languages and among the first high-level languages of any kind. McCarthy's LISP language, developed slightly later, soon became the standard programming language of the AI community and in many ways remains unsurpassed even today.

Contemporaneous developments in other fields also led to a dramatic increase in the precision and complexity of the models that could be proposed and analyzed. In linguistics, for example, work by Chomsky (1957) on formal grammars opened up new avenues for the mathematical modeling of mental structures. NORBERT WIENER developed the field of cybernetics (see CONTROL THEORY and MOTOR CONTROL) to provide mathematical tools for the analysis and synthesis of physical control systems. The theory of optimal control in particular has many parallels with the theory of rational agents (see below), but within this tradition no model of internal representation was ever developed.

As might be expected from so young a field with so broad a mandate that draws on so many traditions, the history of AI has been marked by substantial changes in fashion and opinion. Its early days might be described as the "Look, Ma, no hands!" era, when the emphasis was on showing a doubting world that computers *could* play chess, learn, see, and do all the other things thought to be impossible. A wide variety of methods was tried, ranging from general-purpose symbolic problem solvers to simple neural networks. By the late 1960s, a number of practical and theoretical setbacks had convinced most AI researchers that there would be no simple "magic bullet." The general-purpose methods that had initially seemed so promising came to be called *weak methods* because their reliance on extensive combinatorial search and first-principles knowledge could not overcome the complexity barriers that were, by that time, seen as unavoidable. The 1970s saw the rise of an alternative approach based on the application of large amounts of domain-specific knowledge, expressed in forms that were close enough to the explicit solution as to require little additional computation. Ed Feigenbaum's gnomic dictum, "Knowledge is power," was the watchword of the boom in industrial and commercial application of *expert systems* in the early 1980s.

When the first generation of expert system technology turned out to be too fragile for widespread use, a so-called AI Winter set in—government funding of AI and public perception of its promise both withered in the late 1980s. At the same time, a revival of interest in neural network approaches led to the same kind of optimism as had characterized "traditional" AI in the early 1980s. Since that time, substantial progress has been made in a number of areas within AI, leading to renewed commercial interest in fields such as *data mining* (applied machine learning) and a new wave of expert system technology based on probabilistic inference. The 1990s may in fact come to be seen as the decade of probability. Besides expert systems, the so-called

Bayesian approach (named after the Reverend Thomas Bayes, eighteenth-century author of the fundamental rule for probabilistic reasoning) has led to new methods in planning, natural language understanding, and learning. Indeed, it seems likely that work on the latter topic will lead to a reconciliation of symbolic and connectionist views of intelligence.

See also ALGORITHM; CHURCH-TURING THESIS; COMPUTATION; COMPUTING IN SINGLE NEURONS; CONTROL THEORY; GÖDEL'S THEOREMS; FORMAL SYSTEMS, PROPERTIES OF; HEBB, DONALD O.; LOGIC; MCCULLOCH, WARREN; MOTOR CONTROL; NEURAL NETWORKS; NEURON; NEWELL, ALLEN; PITTS, WALTER; TURING, ALAN; VON NEUMANN, JOHN; WIENER, NORBERT

2   Artificial Intelligence: What's the Problem?

The consensus apparent in modern textbooks (Russell and Norvig 1995; Poole, Mackworth, and Goebel 1997; Nilsson 1998) is that AI is about the design of intelligent *agents*. An agent is an entity that can be understood as perceiving and acting on its environment. An agent is *rational* to the extent that its actions can be expected to achieve its goals, given the information available from its perceptual processes. Whereas the Turing test defined only an informal notion of intelligence as emulation of humans, the theory of RATIONAL AGENCY (see also RATIONAL CHOICE THEORY) provides a first pass at a *formal specification* for intelligent agents, with the possibility of a constructive theory to satisfy this specification. Although the last section of this introduction argues that this specification needs a radical rethinking, the idea of RATIONAL DECISION MAKING has nonetheless been the foundation for most of the current research trends in AI.

The focus on AI as the design of intelligent agents is a fairly recent preoccupation. Until the mid-1980s, most research in "core AI" (that is, AI excluding the areas of robotics and computer vision) concentrated on isolated reasoning tasks, the inputs of which were provided by humans and the outputs of which were interpreted by humans. Mathematical theorem-proving systems, English question-answering systems, and medical expert systems all had this flavor—none of them took actions in any meaningful sense. The so-called situated movement in AI (see SITUATEDNESS/ EMBEDDEDNESS) stressed the point that reasoning is not an end in itself, but serves the purpose of enabling the selection of actions that will affect the reasoner's environment in desirable ways. Thus, reasoning always occurs in a specific context for specific goals. By removing context and taking responsibility for action selection, AI researchers were in danger of defining a subtask that, although useful, actually had no role in the design of a complete intelligent system. For example, some early medical expert systems were constructed in such a way as to accept as input a complete list of symptoms and to output the most likely diagnosis. This might seem like a useful tool, but it ignores several key aspects of medicine: the crucial role of hypothesis-directed *gathering* of information, the very complex task of interpreting sensory data to obtain suggestive and uncertain indicators of symptoms, and the overriding goal of *curing* the patient, which may involve treatments aimed at less likely but potentially dangerous conditions rather than more likely but harmless ones. A second example occurred in robotics. Much research was done on motion planning under the assumption that the locations and shapes of all objects in the environment were known exactly; yet no feasible vision system can, or should, be designed to obtain this information.

When one thinks about building intelligent agents, it quickly becomes obvious that the task environment in which the agent will operate is a primary determiner of the appropriate design. For example, if all relevant aspects of the environment are immediately available to the agent's perceptual apparatus—as, for example, when playing backgammon—then the environment is said to be *fully observable* and the agent need maintain no internal model of the world at all. Backgammon is also *discrete* as opposed to *continuous*—that is, there is a finite set of distinct backgammon board states, whereas tennis, say, requires real-valued variables and changes continuously over time. Backgammon is *stochastic* as opposed to *deterministic*, because it includes dice rolls and unpredictable opponents; hence an agent may need to make contingency plans for many possible outcomes. Backgammon, unlike tennis, is also *static* rather than *dynamic*, in that nothing much happens while the agent is deciding what move to make. Finally, the "physical laws" of the backgammon universe—what the legal moves are and what effect they have—are known rather than unknown. These distinctions alone (and there are many more) define thirty-two substantially different kinds of task environment. This variety of tasks, rather than any true conceptual differences, may be responsible for the variety of computational approaches to intelligence that, on the surface, seem so philosophically incompatible.

See also RATIONAL AGENCY; RATIONAL CHOICE THEORY; RATIONAL DECISION MAKING; SITUATEDNESS/EMBEDDEDNESS

3   Architectures of Cognition

Any computational theory of intelligence must propose, at least implicitly, an INTELLIGENT AGENT ARCHITECTURE. Such an architecture defines the underlying organization of the cognitive processes comprising intelligence, and forms the computational substrate upon which domain-specific capabilities are built. For example, an architecture may provide a generic capability for learning the "physical laws" of the environment, for combining inputs from multiple sensors, or for deliberating about actions by envisioning and evaluating their effects.

There is, as yet, no satisfactory theory that defines the range of possible architectures for intelligent systems, or identifies the optimal architecture for a given task environment, or provides a reasonable specification of what is required for an architecture to support "general-purpose" intelligence, either in machines or humans. Some researchers see the observed variety of intelligent behaviors as a consequence of the operation of a unified, general-purpose problem-solving architecture (Newell 1990). Others propose a functional division of the architecture with modules for perception, learning, reasoning, communication, locomotion, and so on (see MODULARITY OF MIND). Evidence from neuroscience (for example, lesion studies) is often interpreted as showing that the brain is divided into areas, each of which performs some function in this sense; yet the functional descriptions (e.g., "language," "face recognition," etc.) are often subjective and informal and the nature of the connections among the components remains obscure. In the absence of deeper theory, such generalizations from scanty evidence must remain highly suspect. That is, the basic organizational principles of intelligence are still up for grabs.

Proposed architectures vary along a number of dimensions. Perhaps the most commonly cited distinction is between "symbolic" and "connectionist" approaches. These approaches are often thought to be based on fundamentally irreconcilable philosophical foundations. We will argue that, to a large extent, they are complementary; where comparable, they form a continuum.

Roughly speaking, a *symbol* is an object, part of the internal state of an agent, that has two properties: it can be compared to other symbols to test for equality, and it can be combined with other symbols to form *symbol structures*. The symbolic approach to AI, in its purest form, is embodied in the physical symbol system (PSS) hypothesis (Newell and Simon 1972), which proposes that algorithmic manipulation of symbol structures is necessary and sufficient for general intelligence (see also COMPUTATIONAL THEORY OF MIND.)

The PSS hypothesis, if taken to its extreme, is identical to the view that cognition can be understood as COMPUTATION. Symbol systems can emulate any Turing machine; in particular, they can carry out finite-precision numerical operations and thereby implement neural networks. Most AI researchers interpret the PSS hypothesis more narrowly, ruling out primitive numerical quantities that are manipulated as *magnitudes* rather than simply tested for (in)equality. The Soar architecture (Newell 1990), which uses PROBLEM SOLVING as its underlying formalism, is the most well developed instantiation of the pure symbolic approach to cognition (see COGNITIVE MODELING, SYMBOLIC).

The symbolic tradition also encompasses approaches to AI that are based on logic. The symbols in the logical languages are used to represent objects and relations among objects, and symbol structures called *sentences* are used to represent facts that the agent knows. Sentences are manipulated according to certain rules to generate new sentences that follow logically from the original sentences. The details of logical agent design are given in the section on knowledge-based systems; what is relevant here is the use of symbol structures as direct representations of the world. For example, if the agent sees John sitting on the fence, it might construct an internal representation from symbols that represent John, the fence, and the sitting-on relation. If Mary is on the fence instead, the symbol structure would be the same except for the use of a symbol for Mary instead of John.

This kind of compositionality of representations is characteristic of symbolic approaches. A more restricted kind of compositionality can occur even in much simpler systems. For example, in the network of logical gates proposed by McCulloch and Pitts, we might have a neuron J that is "on" whenever the agent sees John on the fence; and another neuron M that is "on" when Mary is on the fence. Then the proposition "either John or Mary is on the fence" can be represented by a neuron that is connected to J and M with the appropriate connection strengths. We call this kind of representation *propositional*, because the fundamental elements are propositions rather than symbols, denoting objects and relations. In the words of McCulloch and Pitts (1943), the state of a neuron was conceived of as "factually equivalent to a proposition which proposed its adequate stimulus." We will also extend the standard sense of "propositional" to cover neural networks comprised of neurons with continuous real-valued activations, rather than the 1/0 activations in the original McCulloch-Pitts threshold neurons.

It is clear that, in this sense, the raw sensory data available to an agent are propositional. For example, the elements of visual perception are "pixels" whose propositional content is, for example, "this area of my retina is receiving bright red light." This observation leads to the first difficulty for the symbolic approach: how to move from sensory data to symbolic representations. This so-called symbol grounding problem has been deemed insoluble by some philosophers (see CONCEPTS), thereby dooming the symbolic approach to oblivion. On the other hand, existence proofs of its solubility abound. For example, Shakey, the first substantial robotics project in AI, used symbolic (logical) reasoning for its deliberations, but interacted with the world quite happily (albeit slowly) through video cameras and wheels (see Raphael 1976).

A related problem for purely symbolic approaches is that sensory information about the physical world is usually thought of as numerical—light intensities, forces, strains, frequencies, and so on. Thus, there must at least be a layer of nonsymbolic computation between the real world and the realm of pure symbols. Neither the theory nor the practice of symbolic AI argues against the existence of such a layer, but its existence does open up the possibility that some substantial part of cognition occurs therein without ever reaching the symbolic level.

A deeper problem for the narrow PSS hypothesis is UNCERTAINTY—the unavoidable fact that unreliable and partial sensory information, combined with unreliable and partial theories of how the world works, must leave an agent with some doubt as to the truth of virtually all propositions of interest. For example, the stock market may soon recover this week's losses, or it may not. Whether to buy, sell, or hold depends on one's assessment of the prospects. Similarly, a person spotted across a crowded, smoky night club may or may not be an old friend. Whether to wave in greeting depends on how certain one is (and on one's sensitivity to embarrassment due to waving at complete strangers). Although many decisions under uncertainty can be made without reference to numerical degrees of belief (Wellman 1990), one has a lingering sense that degrees of belief in propositions may be a fundamental component of our mental representations. Accounts of such phenomena based on probability theory are now widely accepted within AI as an *augmentation* of the purely symbolic view; in particular, probabilistic models are a natural generalization of the logical approach. Recent work has also shown that some connectionist representations (e.g., Boltzmann machines) are essentially identical to probabilistic network models developed in AI (see NEURAL NETWORKS).

The three issues raised in the preceding paragraphs—sensorimotor connections to the external world, handling real-valued inputs and outputs, and robust handling of noisy and uncertain information—are primary motivations for the connectionist approach to cognition. (The existence of networks of neurons in the brain is obviously another.) Neural network models show promise for many low-level tasks such as visual pattern recognition and speech recognition. The most obvious drawback of the connectionist approach is the difficulty of envisaging a means to model higher levels of cognition (see BINDING PROBLEM and COGNITIVE MODELING, CONNECTIONIST), particularly when compared to the ability of symbol systems to generate an unbounded variety of structures from a finite set of symbols (see COMPOSITIONALITY). Some solutions have been proposed (see, for example, BINDING BY NEURAL SYNCHRONY); these solutions provide a plausible neural *implementation* of symbolic models of cognition, rather than an *alternative*.

Another problem for connectionist and other propositional approaches is the modeling of *temporally extended* behavior. Unless the external environment is completely observable by the agent's sensors, such behavior requires the agent to maintain some internal state information that reflects properties of the external world that are not directly observable. In the symbolic or logical approach, sentences such as "My car is parked at the corner of Columbus and Union" can be stored in "working memory" or in a "temporal knowledge base" and updated as appropriate. In connectionist models, internal states require the use of RECURRENT NETWORKS, which are as yet poorly understood.

In summary, the symbolic and connectionist approaches seem not antithetical but complementary—connectionist models may handle low-level cognition and may (or rather *must*, in some form) provide a substrate for higher-level symbolic processes. Probabilistic approaches to representation and reasoning may unify the symbolic and connectionist traditions. It seems that the more relevant distinction is between propositional and more expressive forms of representation.

Related to the symbolic-connectionist debate is the distinction between *deliberative* and *reactive* models of cognition. Most AI researchers view intelligent behavior as resulting, at least in part, from deliberation over possible courses of action based on the agent's knowledge of the world and of the expected results of its actions. This seems self-evident to the average person in the street, but it has always been a controversial hypothesis—according to BEHAVIORISM, it is meaningless. With the development of KNOWLEDGE-BASED SYSTEMS, starting from the famous "Advice Taker" paper by McCarthy (1958), the deliberative model could be put to the test. The core of a knowledge-based agent is the knowledge base and its associated reasoning procedures; the rest of the design follows straightforwardly. First, we need some way of acquiring the necessary knowledge. This could be from experience through MACHINE LEARNING methods, from humans and books through NATURAL LANGUAGE PROCESSING, by direct programming, or through perceptual processes such as MACHINE VISION. Given knowledge of its environment and of its objectives, an agent can reason that certain actions will achieve those objectives and should be executed. At this point, if we are dealing with a physical environment, robotics takes over, handling the mechanical and geometric aspects of motion and manipulation.

The following sections deal with each of these areas in turn. It should be noted, however, that the story in the preceding paragraph is a gross idealization. It is, in fact, close to the view caricatured as good old-fashioned AI (GOFAI) by John Haugeland (1985) and Hubert Dreyfus (1992). In the five decades since Turing's paper, AI researchers have discovered that attaining real competence is not so simple—the principle barrier being COMPUTATIONAL COMPLEXITY. The idea of *reactive systems* (see also AUTOMATA) is to implement direct mappings from perception to action that avoid the expensive intermediate steps of representation and reasoning. This observation was made within the first month of the Shakey project (Raphael 1976) and given new life in the field of BEHAVIOR-BASED ROBOTICS (Brooks 1991). Direct mappings of this kind can be learned from experience or can be compiled from the results of deliberation within a knowledge-based architecture (see EXPLANATION-BASED LEARNING). Most current models propose a *hybrid* agent design incorporating a variety of decision-making mechanisms, perhaps with capabilities for METAREASONING to control and integrate these mechanisms. Some have even proposed that intelligent systems should be constructed from large numbers of separate agents, each with percepts, actions, and goals of its own (Minsky 1986)—much as a nation's economy is made up of lots of separate humans. The theory of MULTIAGENT SYSTEMS explains how, in some cases, the goals of the whole agent can be achieved even when each sub-agent pursues its own ends.

See also AUTOMATA; BEHAVIORISM; BEHAVIOR-BASED ROBOTICS; BINDING BY NEURAL SYNCHRONY; BINDING PROBLEM; COGNITIVE MODELING, CONNECTIONIST; COGNITIVE MODELING, SYMBOLIC; COMPOSITIONALITY; COMPUTATION; COMPUTATIONAL COMPLEXITY; COMPUTATIONAL THEORY OF MIND; CONCEPTS; EXPLANATION-BASED LEARNING; INTELLIGENT AGENT ARCHITECTURE; KNOWLEDGE-BASED SYSTEMS; MACHINE LEARNING; MACHINE VISION; METAREASONING; MODULARITY OF MIND; MULTIAGENT SYSTEMS; NATURAL LANGUAGE PROCESSING; NEURAL NETWORKS; PROBLEM SOLVING; RECURRENT NETWORKS; UNCERTAINTY

4   Knowledge-Based Systems

The *procedural-declarative controversy*, which raged in AI through most of the 1970s, was about which way to build AI systems (see, for example, Boden 1977). The procedural view held that systems could be constructed by encoding expertise in domain-specific algorithms—for example, a procedure for diagnosing migraines by asking specific sequences of questions. The declarative view, on the other hand, held that systems should be *knowledge-based*, that is, composed from domain-specific *knowledge*—for example, the symptoms typically associated with various ailments—combined with a general-purpose reasoning system. The procedural view stressed efficiency, whereas the declarative view stressed the fact that the overall internal representation can be decomposed into separate *sentences*, each of which has an identifiable meaning. Advocates of knowledge-based systems often cited the following advantages:

Ease of construction: knowledge-based systems can be constructed simply by encoding domain knowledge extracted from an expert; the system builder need not construct and encode a *solution* to the problems in the domain.

Flexibility: the same knowledge can be used to answer a variety of questions and as a component in a variety of systems; the same reasoning mechanism can be used for all domains.

Modularity: each piece of knowledge can be identified, encoded, and debugged independently of the other pieces.

Learnability: various learning methods exist that can be used to extract the required knowledge from data, whereas it is very hard to construct programs by automatic means.

Explainability: a knowledge-based system can *explain* its decisions by reference to the explicit knowledge it contains.

With arguments such as these, the declarative view prevailed and led to the boom in expert systems in the late 1970s and early 1980s.

Unfortunately for the field, the early knowledge-based systems were seldom equal to the challenges of the real world, and since then there has been a great deal of research to remedy these failings. The area of KNOWLEDGE REPRESENTATION deals with methods for encoding knowledge in a form that can be processed by a computer to derive consequences. Formal logic is used in various forms to represent definite knowledge. To handle areas where definite knowledge is not available (for example, medical diagnosis), methods have been developed for representation and reasoning under uncertainty, including the extension of logic to so-called NONMONOTONIC LOGICS. All knowledge representation systems need some process for KNOWLEDGE ACQUISITION, and much has been done to automate this process through better interface tools, machine learning methods, and, most recently, extraction from natural language texts. Finally, substantial progress has been made on the question of the computational complexity of reasoning.

See also KNOWLEDGE ACQUISITION; KNOWLEDGE REPRESENTATION; NONMONO-
TONIC LOGICS

5   *Logical Representation and Reasoning*

Logical reasoning is appropriate when the available knowledge is definite. McCarthy's (1958) "Advice Taker" paper proposed first-order logic (FOL) as a formal language for the representation of commonsense knowledge in AI systems. FOL has sufficient expressive power for most purposes, including the representation of objects, relations among objects, and universally quantified statements about sets of objects.

Thanks to work by a long line of philosophers and mathematicians, who were also interested in a formal language for representing general (as well as mathematical) knowledge, FOL came with a well-defined syntax and semantics, as well as the powerful guarantee of *completeness:* there exists a computational procedure such that, if the answer to a question is entailed by the available knowledge, then the procedure will find that answer (see GÖDEL'S THEOREMS). More expressive languages than FOL generally do not allow completeness—roughly put, there exist theorems in these languages that cannot be proved.

The first complete logical reasoning system for FOL, the resolution method, was devised by Robinson (1965). An intense period of activity followed in which LOGICAL REASONING SYSTEMS were applied to mathematics, automatic programming, planning, and general-knowledge question answering. Theorem-proving systems for full FOL have proved new theorems in mathematics and have found widespread application in areas such as program verification, which spun off from mainstream AI in the early 1970s.

Despite these early successes, AI researchers soon realized that the computational complexity of general-purpose reasoning with full FOL is prohibitive; such systems could not scale up to handle large knowledge bases. A great deal of attention has therefore been given to more restricted languages. *Database systems*, which have long been distinct from AI, are essentially logical question-answering systems the knowledge bases of which are restricted to very simple sentences about specific objects. *Propositional* languages avoid objects altogether, representing the world by the discrete values of a fixed set of propositional variables and by logical combinations thereof. (Most neural network models fall into this category also.) Propositional reasoning methods based on CONSTRAINT SATISFACTION and GREEDY LOCAL SEARCH have been very successful in real-world applications, but the restricted expressive power of propositional languages severely limits their scope. Much closer to the expressive power of FOL are the languages used in LOGIC PROGRAMMING. Although still allowing most kinds of knowledge to be expressed very naturally, logic programming systems such as Prolog provide much more efficient reasoning and can work with extremely large knowledge bases.

Reasoning systems must have content with which to reason. Researchers in knowledge representation study methods for codifying and reasoning with particular kinds of knowledge. For example, McCarthy (1963) proposed the SITUATION CALCULUS as a way to represent states of the world and the effects of actions within first-order logic. Early versions of the situation calculus suffered from the infamous FRAME PROBLEM—the apparent need to specify sentences in the knowledge base for all the *noneffects* of actions. Some philosophers see the frame problem as evidence of the impossibility of the formal, knowledge-based approach to AI, but simple technical advances have resolved the original issues.

Situation calculus is perhaps the simplest form of TEMPORAL REASONING; other formalisms have been developed that provide substantially more general frameworks for handling time and extended events. Reasoning about knowledge itself is important particularly when dealing with other agents, and is usually handled by MODAL LOGIC, an extension of FOL. Other topics studied include reasoning about ownership and transactions, reasoning about substances (as distinct from objects), and reasoning about physical representations of information. A general *ontology*—literally, a description of existence—ties all these areas together into a unified taxonomic hierarchy of categories. FRAME-BASED SYSTEMS are often used to represent such hierarchies, and use specialized reasoning methods based on *inheritance* of properties in the hierarchy.

See also CONSTRAINT SATISFACTION; FRAME PROBLEM; FRAME-BASED SYSTEMS; GÖDEL'S THEOREMS; GREEDY LOCAL SEARCH; LOGIC PROGRAMMING; LOGICAL REASONING SYSTEMS; MODAL LOGIC; SITUATION CALCULUS; TEMPORAL REASONING

6   *Logical Decision Making*

An agent's job is to make *decisions*, that is, to commit to particular actions. The connection between logical reasoning and decision making is simple: the agent must conclude, based on its knowledge, that a certain action is best. In philosophy, this is known as *practical reasoning*. There are many routes to such conclusions. The simplest leads to a reactive system using *condition-action rules* of the form "If P then do A." Somewhat more complex reasoning is required when the agent has explicitly represented *goals*. A goal "G" is a description of a desired state of affairs—for example, one might have the goal "On vacation in the Seychelles." The *practical syllogism*, first expounded by Aristotle, says that if G is a goal, and A achieves G, then A should be done. Obviously, this rule is open to many objections: it does not specify which of many eligible As should be done, nor does it account for possibly disastrous side-effects of A. Nonetheless, it underlies most forms of decision making in the logical context.

Often, there will be no single action A that achieves the goal G, but a solution may exist in the form of a *sequence* of actions. Finding such a sequence is called PROBLEM SOLVING, where the word "problem" refers to a task defined by a set of actions, an initial state, a goal, and a set of reachable states. Much of the early cognitive modeling work of Newell and Simon (1972) focused on problem solving, which was seen as a quintessentially intelligent activity. A great deal of research has been done on efficient algorithms for problem solving in the areas of HEURISTIC SEARCH and GAME-PLAYING SYSTEMS. The "cognitive structure" of such systems is very simple, and problem-solving competence is often achieved by means of searching through huge numbers of possibilities. For example, the Deep Blue chess program, which defeated human world champion Gary Kasparov, often examined over a billion positions prior to each move. Human competence is not thought to involve such computations (see CHESS, PSYCHOLOGY OF).

Most problem-solving algorithms treat the states of the world as atomic—that is, the internal structure of the state representation is not accessible to the algorithm as it considers the possible sequences of actions. This fails to take advantage of two very important sources of power for intelligent systems: the ability to *decompose* complex problems into subproblems and the ability to identify relevant actions from explicit goal descriptions. For example, an intelligent system should be able decompose the goal "have groceries and a clean car" into the subgoals "have groceries" and "have a clean car." Furthermore, it should immediately consider buying groceries and washing the car. Most search algorithms, on the other hand, may consider a variety of action sequences—sitting down, standing up, going to sleep, and so on—before happening on some actions that are relevant.

In principle, a logical reasoning system using McCarthy's situation calculus can generate the kinds of reasoning behaviors necessary for decomposing complex goals and selecting relevant actions. For reasons of computational efficiency, however, special-purpose PLANNING systems have been developed, originating with the STRIPS planner used by Shakey the Robot (Fikes and Nilsson 1971). Modern planners have been applied to logistical problems that are, in some cases, too complex for humans to handle effectively.

See also CHESS, PSYCHOLOGY OF; GAME-PLAYING SYSTEMS; HEURISTIC SEARCH; PLANNING; PROBLEM-SOLVING

7   *Representation and Reasoning under Uncertainty*

In many areas to which one might wish to apply knowledge-based systems, the available knowledge is far from definite. For example, a person who experiences recurrent headaches may suffer from migraines or a brain tumor. A logical reasoning system can represent this sort of disjunctive information, but cannot represent or reason with the belief that migraine is a *more likely* explanation. Such reasoning is obviously essential for diagnosis, and has turned out to be central for expert systems in almost all areas. The theory of *probability* (see PROBABILITY, FOUNDATIONS OF) is now widely accepted as the basic calculus for reasoning under uncertainty (but see FUZZY LOGIC for a complementary view). Questions remain as to whether it is a good model for human reasoning (see TVERSKY and PROBABILISTIC REASONING), but within AI many of the computational and representational problems that deterred early researchers have been resolved. The adoption of a probabilistic approach has also created rich connections with statistics and control theory.

Standard probability theory views the world as comprised of a set of interrelated random variables the values of which are initially unknown. Knowledge comes in the form of *prior* probability distributions over the possible assignments of values to subsets of the random variables. Then, when evidence is obtained about the values of some of the variables, inference algorithms can infer *posterior* probabilities for the remaining unknown variables. Early attempts to use probabilistic reasoning in AI came up against complexity barriers very soon, because the number of probabilities that make up the prior probability distribution can grow exponentially in the number of variables considered.

Starting in the early 1980s, researchers in AI, decision analysis, and statistics developed what are now known as BAYESIAN NETWORKS (Pearl 1988). These networks give structure to probabilistic knowledge bases by expressing *conditional independence* relationships among the variables. For example, given the actual temperature, the temperature measurements of two thermometers are independent. In this way, Bayesian networks capture our intuitive notions of the causal structure of the domain of application. In most cases, the number of probabilities that must be specified in a Bayesian network grows only linearly with the number of variables. Such systems can therefore handle quite large problems, and applications are very widespread. Moreover, methods exist for *learning* Bayesian networks from raw data (see BAYESIAN LEARNING), making them a natural bridge between the symbolic and neural-network approaches to AI.

In earlier sections, we have stressed the importance of the distinction between propositional and first-order languages. So far, probability theory has been limited to essentially propositional representations; this prevents its application to the more complex forms of cognition addressed by first-order methods. The attempt to unify probability theory and first-order logic, two of the most fundamental developments in the history of mathematics and philosophy, is among the more important topics in current AI research.

See also BAYESIAN LEARNING; BAYESIAN NETWORKS; FUZZY LOGIC; PROBABILISTIC REASONING; PROBABILITY, FOUNDATIONS OF; TVERSKY, AMOS

8   Decision Making under Uncertainty

Just as logical reasoning is connected to action through goals, probabilistic reasoning is connected to action through *utilities*, which describe an agent's preferences for some states over others. It is a fundamental result of UTILITY THEORY (see also RATIONAL CHOICE THEORY) that an agent whose preferences obey certain rationality constraints, such as transitivity, can be modeled as possessing a *utility function* that assigns a numerical value to each possible state. Furthermore, RATIONAL DECISION MAKING consists of selecting an action to maximize the expected utility of outcome states. An agent that makes rational decisions will, on average, do better than an agent that does not—at least as far as satisfying its own preferences is concerned.

In addition to their fundamental contributions to utility theory, von Neumann and Morgenstern (1944) also developed GAME THEORY to handle the case where the environment contains other agents, which must be modeled as independent utility maximizers. In some game-theoretic situations, it can be shown that optimal behavior must be *randomized*. Additional complexities arise when dealing with so-called *sequential* decision problems, which are analogous to planning problems in the logical case. DYNAMIC PROGRAMMING algorithms, developed in the field of operations research, can generate optimal behavior for such problems. (See also the discussion of REIN-FORCEMENT LEARNING in segment 12—Learning.)

In a sense, the theory of rational decision making provides a zeroth-order theory of intelligence, because it provides an operational definition of what an agent *ought* to do in any situation. Virtually every problem an agent faces, including such problems as how to gather information and how to update its beliefs given that information, can be formulated within the theory and, in principle, solved. What the theory ignores is the question of complexity, which we discuss in the final section of this introduction.

See also DYNAMIC PROGRAMMING; GAME THEORY; RATIONAL CHOICE THEORY; RATIONAL DECISION MAKING; REINFORCEMENT LEARNING; UTILITY THEORY

9   Learning

LEARNING has been a central aspect of AI from its earliest days. It is immediately apparent that learning is a vital characteristic of any intelligent system that has to deal with changing environments. Learning may also be the only way in which complex and competent systems can be constructed—a proposal stated clearly by Turing (1950), who devoted a quarter of his paper to the topic. Perhaps the first major public success for AI was Arthur Samuel's (1959) checker-playing system, which learned to play checkers to a level far superior to its creator's abilities and attracted substantial television coverage. State-of-the-art systems in almost all areas of AI now use learning to avoid the need for the system designer to have to anticipate and provide knowledge to handle every possible contingency. In some cases, for example speech recognition, humans are simply incapable of providing the necessary knowledge accurately.

The discipline of machine learning has become perhaps the largest subfield of AI as well as a meeting point between AI and various other engineering disciplines concerned with the design of autonomous, robust systems. An enormous variety of learning systems has been studied in the AI literature, but once superficial differences are stripped away, there seem to be a few core principles at work. To reveal these principles it helps to classify a given learning system along a number of dimensions: (1) the type of feedback available, (2) the component of the agent to be improved, (3) how that component is represented, and (4) the role of prior knowledge. It is also important to be aware that there is a tradeoff between learning and inference and different systems rely more on one than on the other.

The type of feedback available is perhaps the most useful categorizer of learning algorithms. Broadly speaking, learning algorithms fall into the categories of *supervised learning, unsupervised learning*, and *reinforcement learning*. Supervised learning algorithms (see, e.g., DECISION TREES and SUPERVISED LEARNING IN MULTILAYER NEURAL NETWORKS) require that a target output is available for every input, an assumption that is natural in some situations (e.g., categorization problems with labeled data, imitation problems, and prediction problems, in which the present can be used as a target for a prediction based on the past). UNSUPERVISED LEARNING algorithms simply find structure in an ensemble of data, whether or not this structure is useful for a particular classification or prediction (examples include clustering algorithms, dimensionality-reducing algorithms, and algorithms that find independent components). REINFORCEMENT LEARNING algorithms require an evaluation signal that gives some measure of progress without necessarily providing an example of correct behavior. Reinforcement learning research has had a particular focus on temporal learning problems, in which the evaluation arrives after a sequence of responses.

The different components of an agent generally have different kinds of representational and inferential requirements. Sensory and motor systems must interface with the physical world and therefore generally require continuous representations and smooth input-output behavior. In such situations, neural networks have provided a useful class of architectures, as have probabilistic systems such as HIDDEN MARKOV MODELS and Bayesian networks. The latter models also are generally characterized by a clear propositional semantics, and as such have been exploited for elementary cognitive processing. Decision trees are also propositional systems that are appropriate for simple cognitive tasks. There are variants of decision trees that utilize continuous representations, and these have close links with neural networks, as well as variants of decision trees that utilize relational machinery, making a connection with INDUCTIVE LOGIC PROGRAMMING. The latter class of architecture provides the full power of first-order logic and the capability of learning complex symbolic theories.

Prior knowledge is an important component of essentially all modern learning architectures, particularly so in architectures that involve expressive representations. Indeed, the spirit of inductive logic programming is to use the power of logical inference to bootstrap background knowledge and to interpret new data in the light of that knowledge. This approach is carried to what is perhaps its (logical) extreme in the case of EXPLANATION-BASED LEARNING (EBL), in which the system uses its current theory to *explain* a new observation, and extracts from that explanation a useful rule for future use. EBL can be viewed as a form of generalized caching, also called *speedup learning*. CASE-BASED REASONING AND ANALOGY provides an alternate route to the same end through the solution of problems by reference to previous experience instead of first principles.

Underlying all research on learning is a version of the general problem of INDUCTION; in particular, on what basis can we expect that a system that performs well on past "training" data should also perform well on future "test" data? The theory of learning (see COMPUTATIONAL LEARNING THEORY and STATISTICAL LEARNING THEORY) attacks this problem by assuming that the data provided to a learner is obtained from a fixed but unknown probability distribution. The theory yields a notion of *sample complexity*, which quantifies the amount of data that a learner must see in order to expect—with high probability—to perform (nearly) as well in the future as in the past. The theory also provides support for the intuitive notion of Ockham's razor—the idea that if a simple hypothesis performs as well as a complex hypothesis, one should prefer the simple hypothesis (see PARSIMONY AND SIMPLICITY).

General ideas from probability theory in the form of Bayesian learning, as well as related ideas from INFORMATION THEORY in the form of the MINIMUM DESCRIPTION LENGTH approach provide a link between learning theory and learning practice. In particular, Bayesian learning, which views learning as the updating of probabilistic beliefs in hypotheses given evidence, naturally embodies a form of Ockham's razor. Bayesian methods have been applied to neural networks, Bayesian networks, decision trees, and many other learning architectures.

We have seen that learning has strong relationships to knowledge representation and to the study of uncertainty. There are also important connections between learning and search. In particular, most learning algorithms involve some form of search through the hypothesis space to find hypotheses that are consistent (or nearly so) with the data and with prior expectations. Standard heuristic search algorithms are often invoked—either explicitly or implicitly—to perform this search. EVOLUTIONARY COMPUTATION also treats learning as a search process, in which the "hypothesis" is an entire agent, and learning takes place by "mutation" and "natural selection" of agents that perform well (see also ARTIFICIAL LIFE). There are also interesting links between learning and planning; in particular, it is possible to view reinforcement learning as a form of "on-line" planning.

Finally, it is worth noting that learning has been a particularly successful branch of AI research in terms of its applications to real-world problems in specific fields; see for example the articles on PATTERN RECOGNITION AND FEEDFORWARD NETWORKS, STATISTICAL TECHNIQUES IN NATURAL LANGUAGE PROCESSING, VISION AND LEARNING, and ROBOTICS AND LEARNING.

See also ARTIFICIAL LIFE; CASE-BASED REASONING AND ANALOGY; COMPUTATIONAL LEARNING THEORY; DECISION TREES; EVOLUTIONARY COMPUTATION; HIDDEN MARKOV MODELS; INDUCTION; INDUCTIVE LOGIC PROGRAMMING; INFORMATION THEORY; MINIMUM DESCRIPTION LENGTH; PARSIMONY AND SIMPLICITY; PATTERN RECOGNITION AND FEEDFORWARD NETWORKS; ROBOTICS AND LEARNING; STATISTICAL LEARNING THEORY; STATISTICAL TECHNIQUES IN NATURAL LANGUAGE PROCESSING;

SUPERVISED LEARNING IN MULTILAYER NEURAL NETWORKS; UNSUPERVISED LEARNING; VISION AND LEARNING

10 Language

NATURAL LANGUAGE PROCESSING, or NLP—the ability to perceive, understand, and generate language—is an essential part of HUMAN-COMPUTER INTERACTION as well as the most obvious task to be solved in passing the Turing test. As with logical reasoning, AI researchers have benefited from a pre-existing intellectual tradition. The field of linguistics (see also LINGUISTICS, PHILOSOPHICAL ISSUES) has produced formal notions of SYNTAX and SEMANTICS, the view of utterances as *speech acts,* and very careful philosophical analyses of the meanings of various constructs in natural language. The field of COMPUTATIONAL LINGUISTICS has grown up since the 1960s as a fertile union of ideas from AI, cognitive science, and linguistics.

As soon as programs were written to process natural language, it became obvious that the problem was much harder than had been anticipated. In the United States substantial effort was devoted to Russian-English translation from 1957 onward, but in 1966 a government report concluded that "there has been no machine translation of general scientific text, and none is in immediate prospect." Successful MACHINE TRANSLATION appeared to require an *understanding* of the content of the text; the barriers included massive ambiguity (both syntactic and semantic), a huge variety of word senses, and the vast numbers of idiosyncratic ways of using words to convey meanings. Overcoming these barriers seems to require the use of large amounts of commonsense knowledge and the ability to reason with it—in other words, solving a large fraction of the AI problem. For this reason, Robert Wilensky has described natural language processing as an "AI-complete" problem (see also MODULARITY AND LANGUAGE).

Research in NLP has uncovered a great deal of new information about language. There is a better appreciation of the *actual* syntax of natural language—as opposed to the vastly oversimplified models that held sway before computational investigation was possible. Several new families of FORMAL GRAMMARS have been proposed as a result. In the area of semantics, dozens of interesting phenomena have surfaced—for example, the surprising range of semantic relationships in noun-noun pairs such as "alligator shoes" and "baby shoes." In the area of DISCOURSE understanding, researchers have found that grammaticality is sometimes thrown out of the window, leading some to propose that grammar itself is not a useful construct for NLP.

One consequence of the richness of natural language is that it is very difficult to build by hand a system capable of handling anything close to the full range of phenomena. Most systems constructed prior to the 1990s functioned only in predefined and highly circumscribed domains. Stimulated in part by the availability of large online text corpora, the use of STATISTICAL TECHNIQUES IN NATURAL LANGUAGE PROCESSING has created something of a revolution. Instead of building complex grammars by hand, these techniques train very large but very simple probabilistic grammars and semantic models from millions of words of text. These techniques have reached the point where they can be usefully applied to extract information from general newspaper articles.

Few researchers expect simple probability models to yield human-level understanding. On the other hand, the view of language entailed by this approach—that the text is a form of *evidence* from which higher-level facts can be inferred by a process of probabilistic inference—may prove crucial for further progress in NLP. A probabilistic framework allows the smooth integration of the multiple "cues" required for NLP, such as syntax, semantics, discourse conventions, and prior expectations.

In contrast to the general problem of natural language understanding, the problem of SPEECH RECOGNITION IN MACHINES may be feasible without recourse to general knowledge and reasoning capabilities. The statistical approach was taken much earlier in the speech field, beginning in the mid-1970s. Together with improvements in the signal processing methods used to extract acoustic features, this has led to steady improvements in performance, to the point where commercial systems can handle dictated speech with over 95 percent accuracy. The combination of speech recognition and SPEECH SYNTHESIS (see also NATURAL LANGUAGE GENERATION) promises to make interaction with computers much more natural for humans. Unfortunately, accuracy rates for natural dialogue seldom exceed 75 percent; possibly, speech systems will have to rely on knowledge-based expectations and real understanding to make further progress.

See also COMPUTATIONAL LINGUISTICS; DISCOURSE; FORMAL GRAMMARS; HUMAN-COMPUTER INTERACTION; LINGUISTICS, PHILOSOPHICAL ISSUES; MACHINE TRANSLATION; MODULARITY AND LANGUAGE; NATURAL LANGUAGE GENERATION; NATURAL LANGUAGE PROCESSING; SEMANTICS; SPEECH RECOGNITION IN MACHINES; SPEECH SYNTHESIS; STATISTICAL TECHNIQUES IN NATURAL LANGUAGE PROCESSING; SYNTAX

11   Vision

The study of vision presents a number of advantages—visual processing systems are present across a wide variety of species, they are reasonably accessible experimentally (psychophysically, neuropsychologically, and neurophysiologically), and a wide variety of artificial imaging systems are available that are sufficiently similar to their natural counterparts so as to make research in machine vision highly relevant to research in natural vision. An integrated view of the problem has emerged, linking research in COMPUTATIONAL VISION, which is concerned with the development of explicit theories of human and animal vision, with MACHINE VISION, which is concerned with the development of an engineering science of vision.

Computational approaches to vision, including the influential theoretical framework of MARR, generally involve a succession of processes that begin with localized numeric operations on images (so-called early vision) and proceed toward the high-level abstractions thought to be involved in OBJECT RECOGNITION. The current view is that the interpretation of complex scenes involves inference in both the bottom-up and top-down directions (see also TOP-DOWN PROCESSING IN VISION).

High-level object recognition is not the only purpose of vision. Representations at intermediate levels can also be an end unto themselves, directly subserving control processes of orienting, locomotion, reaching, and grasping. Visual analysis at all levels can be viewed as a process of recovering aspects of the visual scene from its projection onto a 2-D image. Visual properties such as shape and TEXTURE behave in lawful ways under the geometry of perspective projection, and understanding this geometry has been a focus of research. Related geometrical issues have been studied in STEREO AND MOTION PERCEPTION, where the issue of finding correspondences between multiple images also arises. In all of these cases, localized spatial and temporal cues are generally highly ambiguous with respect to the aspects of the scene from which they arise, and algorithms that recover such aspects generally involve some form of spatial or temporal integration.

It is also important to prevent integrative processes from wrongly smoothing across discontinuities that correspond to visually meaningful boundaries. Thus, visual processing also requires segmentation. Various algorithms have been studied for the segmentation of image data. Again, an understanding of projective geometry has been a guide for the development of such algorithms. Integration and segmentation are also required at higher levels of visual processing, where more abstract principles (such as those studied by GESTALT PSYCHOLOGY; see GESTALT PERCEPTION) are needed to group visual elements.

Finally, in many cases the goal of visual processing is to detect or recognize objects in the visual scene. A number of difficult issues arise in VISUAL OBJECT RECOGNITION, including the issue of what kinds of features should be used (2-D or 3-D, edge-based or filter-based), how to deal with missing features (e.g., due to occlusion or shadows), how to represent flexible objects (such as humans), and how to deal with variations in pose and lighting. Methods based on learning (cf. VISION AND LEARNING) have played an increasingly important role in addressing some of these issues.

See also COMPUTATIONAL VISION; GESTALT PERCEPTION; GESTALT PSYCHOLOGY; MARR, DAVID; OBJECT RECOGNITION, ANIMAL STUDIES; OBJECT RECOGNITION, HUMAN

NEUROPSYCHOLOGY; STEREO AND MOTION PERCEPTION; TEXTURE; TOP-DOWN PROCESSING IN VISION; VISION AND LEARNING; VISUAL OBJECT RECOGNITION, AI

12   Robotics

Robotics is the control of physical effectors to achieve physical tasks such as navigation and assembly of complex objects. Effectors include grippers and arms to perform MANIPULATION AND GRASPING and wheels and legs for MOBILE ROBOTS and WALKING AND RUNNING MACHINES.

The need to interact directly with a physical environment, which is generally only partially known and partially controllable, brings certain issues to the fore in robotics that are often skirted in other areas in AI. One important set of issues arises from the fact that environments are generally dynamical systems, characterizable by a large (perhaps infinite) collection of real-valued state variables, whose values are not generally directly observable by the robot (i.e., they are "hidden"). The presence of the robot control algorithm itself as a feedback loop in the environment introduces additional dynamics. The robot designer must be concerned with the issue of *stability* in such a situation. Achieving stability not only prevents disasters but it also simplifies the dynamics, providing a degree of predictability that is essential for the success of planning algorithms.

Stability is a key issue in manipulation and grasping, where the robot must impart a distributed pattern of forces and torques to an object so as to maintain a desired position and orientation in the presence of external disturbances (such as gravity). Research has tended to focus on static stability (ignoring the dynamics of the grasped object). Static stability is also of concern in the design of walking and running robots, although rather more pertinent is the problem of dynamic stability, in which a moving robot is stabilized by taking advantage of its inertial dynamics.

Another important set of issues in robotics has to do with uncertainty. Robots are generally equipped with a limited set of sensors and these sensors are generally noisy and inherently ambiguous. To a certain extent the issue is the same as that treated in the preceding discussion of vision, and the solutions, involving algorithms for integration and smoothing, are often essentially the same. In robotics, however, the sensory analysis is generally used to subserve a control law and the exigencies of feedback control introduce new problems (cf. CONTROL THEORY). Processing time must be held to a minimum and the system must focus on obtaining only that information needed for control. These objectives can be difficult to meet, and recent research in robotics has focused on minimizing the need for feedback, designing sequences of control actions that are guaranteed to bring objects into desired positions and orientations regardless of the initial conditions.

Uncertainty is due not only to noisy sensors and hidden states, but also to ignorance about the structure of the environment. Many robot systems actively model the environment, using system identification techniques from control theory, as well as more general supervised and unsupervised methods from machine learning. Specialized representations are often used to represent obstacles ("configuration space") and location in space (graphs and grids). Probabilistic approaches are often used to explicitly represent and manipulate uncertainty within these formalisms.

In classical robotic control methodology, the system attempts to recover as much of the state of the environment as possible, operates on the internal representation of the state using general planning and reasoning algorithms, and chooses a sequence of control actions to implement the selected plan. The sheer complexity of designing this kind of architecture has led researchers to investigate simpler architectures that make do with minimal internal state. BEHAVIOR-BASED ROBOTICS approaches the problem via an interacting set of elemental processes called "behaviors," each of which is a simplified control law relating sensations and actions. REINFORCEMENT LEARNING has provided algorithms that utilize simplified evaluation signals to guide a search for improved laws; over time these algorithms approach the optimal plans that are derived (with more computational effort) from explicit planning algorithms (see ROBOTICS AND LEARNING).

See also BEHAVIOR-BASED ROBOTICS; CONTROL THEORY; MANIPULATION AND GRASPING; MOBILE ROBOTS; REINFORCEMENT LEARNING; ROBOTICS AND LEARNING; WALKING AND RUNNING MACHINES

13   Complexity, Rationality, and Intelligence

We have observed at several points in this introduction that COMPUTATIONAL COMPLEXITY is a major problem for intelligent agents. To the extent that they can be analyzed, most of the problems of perceiving, learning, reasoning, and decision making are believed to have a worst-case complexity that is at least exponential in the size of the problem description. Exponential complexity means that, for example, a problem of size 100 would take 10 billion years to solve on the fastest available computers. Given that humans face much larger problems than this all the time—we receive as input several billion bytes of information every second—one wonders how we manage at all.

Of course, there are a number of mitigating factors: an intelligent agent must deal largely with the typical case, not the worst case, and accumulated experience with similar problems can greatly reduce the difficulty of new problems. The fact remains, however, that humans cannot even come close to achieving perfectly rational behavior—most of us do fairly poorly even on problems such as chess, which is an *infinitesimal* subset of the real world. What, then, is the right thing for an agent to do, if it cannot possibly compute the right thing to do?

In practical applications of AI, one possibility is to restrict the allowable set of problems to those that are efficiently soluble. For example, deductive database systems use restricted subsets of logic that allow for polynomial-time inference. Such research has given us a much deeper understanding of the sources of complexity in reasoning, but does not seem directly applicable to the problem of general intelligence. Somehow, we must face up to the inevitable compromises that must be made in the quality of decisions that an intelligent agent can make. Descriptive theories of such compromises—for example, Herbert Simon's work on *satisficing*—appeared soon after the development of formal theories of rationality. Normative theories of BOUNDED RATIONALITY address the question at the end of the preceding paragraph by examining what is achievable with fixed computational resources. One promising approach is to devote some of those resources to METAREASONING (see also METACOGNITION), that is, reasoning about what reasoning to do. The technique of EXPLANATION-BASED LEARNING (a formalization of the common psychological concept of *chunking* or *knowledge compilation*) helps an agent cope with complexity by caching efficient solutions to common problems. Reinforcement learning methods enable an agent to learn effective (if not perfect) behaviors in complex environments without the need for extended problem-solving computations.

What is interesting about all these aspects of intelligence is that without the need for effective use of limited computational resources, they make no sense. That is, computational complexity may be responsible for many, perhaps most, of the aspects of cognition that make intelligence an interesting subject of study. In contrast, the cognitive structure of an infinitely powerful computational device could be very straightforward indeed.

See also BOUNDED RATIONALITY; EXPLANATION-BASED LEARNING; METACOGNITION; METAREASONING

14   Additional Sources

Early AI work is covered in Feigenbaum and Feldman's (1963) *Computers and Thought,* Minsky's (1968) *Semantic Information Processing,* and the *Machine Intelligence* series edited by Donald Michie. A large number of influential papers are collected in *Readings in Artificial Intelligence* (Webber and Nilsson 1981). Early papers on neural networks are collected in *Neurocomputing* (Anderson and Rosenfeld 1988). The *Encyclopedia of AI* (Shapiro 1992) contains survey articles on almost every topic in AI. The four-volume *Handbook of Artificial Intelligence* (Barr and Feigenbaum

1981) contains descriptions of almost every major AI system published before 1981. Standard texts on AI include *Artificial Intelligence: A Modern Approach* (Russell and Norvig 1995) and *Artificial Intelligence: A New Synthesis* (Nilsson 1998). Historical surveys include Kurzweil (1990) and Crevier (1993).

The most recent work appears in the proceedings of the major AI conferences: the biennial International Joint Conference on AI (IJCAI); the annual National Conference on AI, more often known as AAAI after its sponsoring organization; and the European Conference on AI (ECAI). The major journals for general AI are *Artificial Intelligence, Computational Intelligence,* the IEEE *Transactions on Pattern Analysis and Machine Intelligence,* and the electronic *Journal of Artificial Intelligence Research.* There are also many journals devoted to specific areas, some of which are listed in the relevant articles. The main professional societies for AI are the American Association for Artificial Intelligence (AAAI), the ACM Special Interest Group in Artificial Intelligence (SIGART), and the Society for Artificial Intelligence and Simulation of Behaviour (AISB). AAAI's *AI Magazine* and the *SIGART Bulletin* contain many topical and tutorial articles as well as announcements of conferences and workshops.

References

Anderson, J. A., and E. Rosenfeld, Eds. (1988). *Neurocomputing: Foundations of Research.* Cambridge, MA: MIT Press.

Barr, A., P. R. Cohen, and E. A. Feigenbaum, Eds. (1989). *The Handbook of Artificial Intelligence,* vol. 4. Reading, MA: Addison-Wesley.

Barr, A., and E. A. Feigenbaum, Eds. (1981). *The Handbook of Artificial Intelligence*, vol. 1. Stanford and Los Altos, CA: HeurisTech Press and Kaufmann.

Barr, A., and E. A. Feigenbaum, Eds. (1982). *The Handbook of Artificial Intelligence*, vol. 2. Stanford and Los Altos, CA: HeurisTech Press and Kaufmann.

Boden, M. A. (1977). *Artificial Intelligence and Natural Man.* New York: Basic Books.

Brooks, R. A. (1991). Intelligence without representation. *Artificial Intelligence* 47(1–3): 139–159.

Chomsky, N. (1957). *Syntactic Structures.* The Hague: Mouton.

Cohen, P. R., and E. A. Feigenbaum, Eds. (1982). *The Handbook of Artificial Intelligence,* vol. 3. Stanford and Los Altos, CA: HeurisTech Press and Kaufmann.

Crevier, D. (1993). *AI: The Tumultuous History of the Search for Artificial Intelligence.* New York: Basic Books.

Dreyfus, H. L. (1992). *What Computers Still Can't Do: A Critique of Artificial Reason.* Cambridge, MA: MIT Press.

Feigenbaum, E. A., and J. Feldman, Eds. (1963). *Computers and Thought.* New York: McGraw-Hill.

Fikes, R. E., and N. J. Nilsson. (1971). STRIPS: A new approach to the application of theorem proving to problem solving. *Artificial Intelligence* 2(3–4): 189–208.

Haugeland, J., Ed. (1985). *Artificial Intelligence: The Very Idea.* Cambridge, MA: MIT Press.

Kurzweil, R. (1990). *The Age of Intelligent Machines.* Cambridge, MA: MIT Press.

McCarthy, J. (1958). Programs with common sense. *Proceedings of the Symposium on Mechanisation of Thought Processes,* vol. 1. London: Her Majesty's Stationery Office, pp. 77–84.

McCarthy, J. (1963). Situations, actions, and causal laws. Memo 2. Stanford, CA: Stanford University Artificial Intelligence Project.

McCulloch, W. S., and W. Pitts. (1943). A logical calculus of the ideas immanent in nervous activity. *Bulletin of Mathematical Biophysics* 5: 115–137.

Minsky, M. L., Ed. (1968). *Semantic Information Processing.* Cambridge, MA: MIT Press.

Minsky, M. L. (1986). *The Society of Mind.* New York: Simon & Schuster.

Newell, A. (1990). *Unified Theories of Cognition.* Cambridge, MA: Harvard University Press.

Newell, A., and H. A. Simon. (1972). *Human Problem Solving.* Englewood Cliffs, NJ: Prentice-Hall.

Nilsson, N. J. (1998). *Artificial Intelligence: A New Synthesis.* San Mateo, CA: Morgan Kaufmann.

Pearl, J. (1988). *Probabilistic Reasoning in Intelligent Systems: Networks of Plausible Inference.* San Mateo, CA: Morgan Kaufmann.

Poole, D., A. Mackworth, and R. Goebel. (1997). *Computational Intelligence: A Logical Approach.* Oxford: Oxford University Press.

Raphael, B. (1976). *The Thinking Computer: Mind Inside Matter.* New York: W. H. Freeman.

Robinson, J. A. (1965). A machine-oriented logic based on the resolution principle. *Journal of the Association for Computing Machinery* 12: 23–41.

Russell, S. J., and P. Norvig. (1995). *Artificial Intelligence: A Modern Approach.* Englewood Cliffs, NJ: Prentice-Hall.

Samuel, A. L. (1959). Some studies in machine learning using the game of checkers. *IBM Journal of Research and Development* 3(3): 210–229.

Shapiro, S. C., Ed. (1992). *Encyclopedia of Artificial Intelligence.* 2nd ed. New York: Wiley.

Turing, A. M. (1950). Computing machinery and intelligence. *Mind* 59: 433–460.

Von Neumann, J., and O. Morgenstern. (1944). *Theory of Games and Economic Behavior.* 1st ed., Princeton, NJ: Princeton University Press.

Webber, B. L., and N. J. Nilsson, Eds. (1981). *Readings in Artificial Intelligence.* San Mateo, CA: Morgan Kaufmann.

Wellman, M. P. (1990). Fundamental concepts of qualitative probabilistic networks. *Artificial Intelligence* 44(3): 257–303.

Linguistics and Language

Gennaro Chierchia

1   Language and Cognition

Why is the study of language central to cognition? The answer lies in the key properties of language as they manifest themselves in the way speakers use it. The best way to get a sense of the centrality of language in understanding cognitive phenomena is through some examples. In the rest of this introduction I illustrate some features of language that display surprising regularities. Among the many ways in which an efficient communication code could be designed, natural languages seem to choose quite peculiar ones. The question is why. We consider some of the answers that modern linguistics gives to this question, which lead us into a scenic (if necessarily brief) tour of its main problematics. In particular, section 2 is devoted to language structure and its main articulations. Section 3 is devoted to language use, its interplay with language structure, and the various disciplines that deal with these matters. We then close, in section 4, with a few short remarks on the place of linguistics within cognitive science.

Languages are made of words. How many words do we know? This is something that can be estimated quite accurately (see Pinker 1994: 149 ff.). To set a base line, consider that Shakespeare in his works uses roughly 15,000 different words. One would think that the vocabulary of, say, a high school student, is considerably poorer. Instead, it turns out that a high school senior reliably understands roughly 45,000 words out of a lexicon of 88,500 unrelated words. It might be worth mentioning how one arrives at this estimate. One samples randomly the target corpus of words and performs simple comprehension tests on the sample. The results are then statistically projected to the whole corpus. Now, the size of the vocabulary of a high school senior entails that from when the child starts learning words at a few months of age until the age of eighteen, he or she must be learning roughly a word every hour and half when awake. We are talking here of learning arbitrary associations of sound patterns with meanings. Compare this with the effort it takes to learn an even short poem by heart, or the names of a handful of basketball players. The contrast is striking. We get to understand 45,000 words with incomparably less effort, to the point of not even being aware of it. This makes no sense without the assumption that our mind must be especially equipped with something, a cognitive device of some sort, that makes us so successful at the task of learning words. This cognitive device must be quite specialized for such a task, as we are not as good at learning poems or the names of basketball players (cf. WORD MEANING, ACQUISITION OF)

The world of sounds that make up words is similarly complex. We all find the sounds of our native language easy to distinguish. For example, to a native English speaker the i-sounds in "leave" and "live" are clearly different. And unless that person is in especially unfavorable conditions, he or she will not take one for the other. To a native English speaker, the difficulty that an Italian learning English (as an adult) encounters in mastering such distinctions looks a bit mysterious. Italians take revenge when English speakers try to learn the contrast between words like "*fato*" 'fate' vs. "*fatto*" 'fact.' The only difference between them is that the t-sound in *fatto* sounds to the Italian speaker slightly longer or tenser, a contrast that is difficult for a speaker of English to master. These observations are quite commonplace. The important point, however, is that a child exposed to the speech sounds of *any* language picks them up effortlessly. The clicks of Zulu (sounds similar to the "tsk-tsk" of disapproval) or the implosive sounds of Sindhi, spoken in India and Pakistan (sounds produced by sucking in air, rather than ejecting it—see ARTICULATION) are not harder for the child to acquire than the occlusives of English. Adults, in contrast, often fail to learn to produce sounds not in their native repertoire. Figuring out the banking laws or the foods of a different culture is generally much easier. One would like to understand why.

Behind its daily almost quaint appearance, language seems to host many remarkable regularities of the sort just illustrated. Here is yet another example taken from a different domain, that of pronouns and ANAPHORA. Consider the following sentence:

(1) John promised Bill to wash him.

Any native speaker of English will agree that the pronoun "him" in (1) can refer to "Bill" (the object—see GRAMMATICAL RELATIONS), but there is no way it can refer to "John" (the subject). If we want a pronoun that refers to "John" in a sentence like (1), we have to use a reflexive:

(2) John promised Bill to wash himself.

The reflexive "himself" in (2) refers to "John." It cannot refer to "Bill." Compare now (1) with (3):

(3) John persuaded Bill to wash him

Here "him" can refer to the *subject*, but not to the object. If we want a pronoun to refer to "Bill" we have to use

(4) John persuaded Bill to wash himself.

The reflexive "himself" in (4) must refer to the object. It cannot refer to the subject. By comparing (1) and (2) with (3) and (4), we see that the way pronouns work with verbs like "promise" appears to be the opposite of verbs like "persuade." Yet the structure of these sentences appears to be identical. There must be a form of specialized, unconscious knowledge we have that makes us say "Yes, 'him' can refer to the subject in (1) but not in (3)." A very peculiar intuition we have grown to have.

What is common to these different aspects of language is the fact that our linguistic behavior reveals striking and complex regularities. This is true throughout the languages of the worlds. In fact the TYPOLOGY of the world's languages reveals significant universal tendencies. For example, the patterns of word order are quite limited. The most common basic orders of the major sentence constituents are subject-verb-object (abbreviated as SVO) and SOV. Patterns in which the object precedes the subject are quite rare. Another language universal one might mention is that all languages have ways of using clauses to modify nouns (as in "the boy that you just met," where the relative clause "that you just met" modifies the noun "boy"). Now structural properties of this sort are not only common to all known spoken languages but in fact can be found even in SIGN LANGUAGES, that is, visual-gestural languages typically in use in populations with impaired verbal abilities (e.g., the deaf). It seems plausible to maintain that universal tendencies in language are grounded in the way we are; this must be so for speaking is a cognitive capacity, that capacity in virtue of which we say that we "know" our native language. We exercise such capacity in using language. A term often used in this connection is "linguistic competence." The way we put such competence to use in interacting with our environment and with each other is called "performance."

The necessity to hypothesize a linguistic competence can be seen also from another point of view. Language is a dynamic phenomenon, dynamic in many senses. It changes across time and space (cf. LANGUAGE VARIATION AND CHANGE). It varies along social and gender dimensions (cf. LANGUAGE AND GENDER; LANGUAGE AND CULTURE). It also varies in sometimes seemingly idiosyncratic ways from speaker to speaker. Another important aspect of the dynamic character of language is the fact that a speaker can produce and understand an indefinite number of sentences, while having finite cognitive resources (memory, attention span, etc.). How is this possible? We must assume that this happens by analogy with the way we, say, add two numbers we have never added before. We can do it because we have mastered a combinatorial device, an ALGORITHM. But the algorithm for adding we have learned through explicit training. The one for speaking appears to grow spontaneously in the child. Such an algorithm is constitutive of our linguistic competence.

The fact that linguistic competence does not develop through explicit training can be construed as an argument in favor of viewing it as a part of our genetic endowment (cf. INNATENESS OF LANGUAGE). This becomes all the more plausible if one considers how specialized the knowledge of a language is and how quickly it develops in the child. In a way, the child should be in a situation analogous to that of somebody who is trying to break the mysteries of an unknown communication code. Such a code could have in principle very different features from that of a human language. It might lack a distinction between subjects and objects. Or it might lack the one between nouns and verbs. Many languages of practical use (e.g., many programming languages) are designed just that way. The range of possible communication systems is huge and highly differentiated. This is part of the reason why cracking a secret code is very hard—as hard as learning an unfamiliar language as an adult. Yet the child does it without effort and without formal training. This seems hard to make sense of without assuming that, in some way, the child knows what to look for and knows what properties of natural speech he or she should attend to in order to figure out its grammar. This argument, based on the observation that language learning constitutes a specialized skill acquired quickly through minimal input, is known as the POVERTY OF THE STIMULUS ARGUMENT. It suggests that linguistic competence is a relatively autonomous computational device that is part of the biological endowment of humans and guides them through the acquisition of language. This is one of the planks of what has come to be known as GENERATIVE GRAMMAR, a research program started in the late 1950s by Noam Chomsky, which has proven to be quite successful and influential.

It might be useful to contrast this view with another one that a priori might be regarded as equally plausible (see CONNECTIONIST APPROACHES TO LANGUAGE). Humans seem to be endowed with a powerful all-purpose computational device that is very good at extracting regularities from the environment. Given that, one might hypothesize that language is learned the way we learn any kind of algorithm: through trial and error. All that language learning amounts to is simply applying our high-level computational apparatus to linguistic input. According to this view, the child acquires language similarly to how she learns, say, doing division, the main difference being in the nature of the input. Learning division is of course riddled with all sorts of mistakes that the child goes through (typical ones involve keeping track of rests, misprocessing partial results, etc.). Consider, in this connection, the pattern of pronominalization in sentences (1) through (4). If we learn languages the way we learn division, the child ought to make mistakes in figuring out what can act as the antecedent of a reflexive and what cannot. In recent years there has been extensive empirical investigation of the behavior of pronominal elements in child language (see BINDING THEORY; SYNTAX, ACQUISITION OF; SEMANTICS, ACQUISITION OF). And this was not what was found. The evidence goes in the opposite direction. As soon as reflexives and nonreflexive pronouns make their appearance in the child's speech, they appear to be used in an adult-like manner (cf. Crain and McKee 1985; Chien and Wexler 1990; Grodzinsky and Reinhart 1993).

Many of the ideas we find in generative grammar have antecedents throughout the history of thought (cf. LINGUISTICS, PHILOSOPHICAL ISSUES). One finds important debates on the "conventional" versus "natural" origins of language already among the presocratic philosophers. And many ancient grammarians came up with quite sophisticated analyses of key phenomena. For example the Indian grammarian Panini (fourth to third century B.C.) proposed an analysis of argument structure in terms of THEMATIC ROLES (like *agent, patient,* etc.), quite close in spirit to current proposals. The scientific study of language had a great impulse in the nineteenth century, when the historical links among the languages of the Indo-European family, at least in their general setup, were unraveled. A further fundamental development in our century was the structuralist approach, that is the attempt to characterize in explicit terms language structure as it manifests itself in sound patterns and in distributional patterns. The structuralist movement started out in Europe, thanks to F. DE SAUSSURE and the Prague School (which included among it protagonists N. Trubeckoj and R. JAKOBSON) and developed, then, in somewhat different forms, in the United States through the work of L. BLOOMFIELD, E. SAPIR, Z. Harris (who was Chomsky's teacher), and others. Structuralism, besides leaving us with an accurate description of many important linguistic phenomena, constituted the breeding ground for a host of concepts (like "morpheme," "phoneme," etc.)

that have been taken up and developed further within the generative tradition. It is against this general background that recent developments should be assessed.

See also ALGORITHM; ANAPHORA; ARTICULATION; BINDING THEORY; BLOOMFIELD, LEONARD; CONNECTIONIST APPROACHES TO LANGUAGE; GENERATIVE GRAMMAR; GRAMMATICAL RELATIONS; INNATENESS OF LANGUAGE; JAKOBSON, ROMAN; LANGUAGE AND CULTURE; LANGUAGE AND GENDER; LANGUAGE VARIATION AND CHANGE; LINGUISTICS, PHILOSOPHICAL ISSUES; POVERTY OF THE STIMULUS ARGUMENTS; SAPIR, EDWARD; SAUSSURE, FERDINAND DE; SEMANTICS, ACQUISITION OF; SIGN LANGUAGES; SYNTAX, ACQUISITION OF; THEMATIC ROLES; TYPOLOGY; WORD MEANING, ACQUISITION OF

2   Language Structure

Our linguistic competence is made up of several components (or "modules," see MODULARITY AND LANGUAGE) that reflect the various facets of language, going from speech sounds to meaning. In this section we will review the main ones in a necessarily highly abbreviated from. Language can be thought of as a LEXICON and combinatiorial apparatus. The lexicon is constituted by the inventory of words (or morphemes) through which sentences and phrases are built up. The combinatorial apparatus is the set of rules and principles that enable us to put words together in well-formed strings, and to pronounce and interpret such strings. What we will see, as we go through the main branches of linguistics, is how the combinatorial machinery operates throughout the various components of grammar. Meanwhile, here is a rough road map of major modules that deal with language structure.

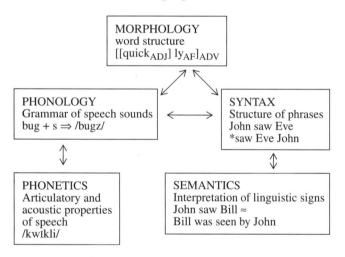

See also LEXICON; MODULARITY AND LANGUAGE

Words and Sounds

We already saw that the number of words we know is quite remarkable. But what do we mean by a "word"? Consider the verb "walk" and its past tense "walked." Are these two different words? And how about "walk" versus "walker"? We can clearly detect some inner regular components to words like "walked" namely the stem "walk" (which is identical to the infinitival form) and the ending "-ed," which signals "past." These components are called "morphemes;" they constitute the smallest elements with an identifiable meaning we can recognize in a word. The internal structure of words is the object of the branch of linguistics known as MORPHOLOGY. Just like sentences are formed by putting words together, so words themselves are formed by putting together morphemes. Within the word, that is, as well as between words, we see a combinatorial machinery at work. English has a fairly simple morphological structure. Languages like Chinese have even greater morphological simplicity, while languages like Turkish or Japanese have a very rich morphological structure. POLYSYNTHETIC LANGUAGES are perhaps the most extreme cases of morphological complexity. The following, for example, is a single word of Mohawk, a polysynthetic North American Indian language (Baker 1996: 22):

(5) *ni-mic-tomi-maka*
    first person-second person-money-give
    'I'll give you the money.'

Another aspect of morphology is compounding, which enables one to form complex words by "glomming" them together. This strategy is quite productive in English, for example, *blackboard, blackboard design, blackboard design school*, and so on. Compounds can be distinguished from phrases on the basis of a variety of converging criteria. For example, the main stress on compounds like "blackboard" is on "black," while in the phrase "black board" it is on "board" (cf. STRESS, LINGUISTIC; METER AND POETRY). Moreover syntax treats compounds as units that cannot be separated by syntactic rules. Through morphological derivation and compounding the structure of the lexicon becomes quite rich.

So what is a word? At one level, it is what is stored in our mental lexicon and has to be memorized as such (a listeme). This is the sense in which we know 45,000 (unrelated) words. At another, it is what enters as a unit into syntactic processes. In this second sense (but not in the first) "walk" and "walked" count as two words. Words are formed by composing together smaller meaningful units (the morphemes) through specific rules and principles.

Morphemes are, in turn, constituted by sound units. Actually, speech forms a continuum not immediately analyzable into discrete units. When exposed to an unfamiliar language, we can not tell where, for example, the word boundaries are, and we have difficulty in identifying the sounds that are not in our native inventory. Yet speakers classify their speech sound stream into units, the phonemes. PHONETICS studies speech sounds from an acoustic and articulatory point of view. Among other things, it provides an alphabet to notate all of the sounds of the world's languages. PHONOLOGY studies how the range of speech sounds are exploited by the grammars of different languages and the universal laws of the grammar of sounds. For example, we know from phonetics that back vowels (produced by lifting the rear of the tongue towards the palate) can be rounded (as in "hot") or unrounded (as in "but") and that this is so also for front vowels (produced by lifting the tongue toward the front of the vocal tact). The i-sound in "feet" is a high, front, unrounded vowel; the sound of the corresponding German word "füsse" is also pronounced raising the tongue towards the front, but is rounded. If a language has rounded front vowels it also has rounded back vowels. To illustrate, Italian has back rounded vowels, but lacks altogether unrounded back vowels. English has both rounded and unrounded back vowels. Both English and Italian lack front rounded vowels. German and French, in contrast, have them. But there is no language that has in its sound inventory front rounded vowels without also having back rounded ones. This is the form that constraints on possible systems of phonemes often take.

As noted in section 1, the type of sounds one finds in the world's languages appear to be very varied. Some languages may have relatively small sound inventories constituted by a dozen phonemes (as, for example, Polynesian); others have quite large ones with about 140 units (Khoisan). And there are of course intermediate cases. One of the most important linguistic discoveries of this century has been that all of the wide variety of phonemes we observe can be described in terms of a small universal set of DISTINCTIVE FEATURES (i.e., properties like "front," "rounded," "voiced," etc.). For example, /p/ and /b/ (bilabial stops) have the same feature composition except for the fact that the former is voiceless (produced without vibration of the vocal cords) while the latter is voiced. By the same token, the phoneme /k/, as in "bake," and the final sound of the German word "Bach" are alike, except in one feature. In the former the air flux is completely interrupted (the sound is a *stop*) by lifting the back of the tongue up to the rear of the palate, while in the latter a small passage is left which results in a turbulent continuous sound (a *fricative,* notated in the phonetic alphabet as /x/). So all phonemes can be analyzed as feature structures.

There is also evidence that features are not just a convenient way to classify phonemes but are actually part of the implicit knowledge that speakers have of their language. One famous experiment that provides evidence of this kind has to do with English plurals. In simplified terms, plurals are formed by adding a voiced alveolar fricative /z/ after a voiced sound (e.g., fad[z]) and its voiceless counterpart /s/ after a voiceless one (e.g., fat[s]). This is a form of *assimilation,* a very common phonological process (see PHONOLOGICAL RULES AND PROCESSES). If a monolingual English speaker is asked to form the plural of a word ending in a phoneme that is not part of his or her native inventory and has never been encountered before, that speaker will follow the rule just described; for example, the plural of the word "Bach" will be [baxs] not [baxz]. This means that in forming the plural speakers are actually accessing the featural make up of the phonemes and analyzing phonemes into voiced verus voiceless sets. They have not just memorized after which sounds /s/ goes and after which /z/ goes (see Akmajian et al. 1990: chapter 3 and references therein).

Thus we see that even within sound units we find smaller elements, the distinctive features, combined according to certain principles. Features, organized in phonemes, are manipulated by rule systems. Phonemes are in turn structured into larger prosodic constituents (see PROSODY AND INTONATION), which constitute the domains over which stress and TONE are determined. On the whole we see that the world of speech sounds is extremely rich in structure and its study has reached a level of remarkable theoretical sophistication (for recent important developments, see OPTIMALITY THEORY).

See also DISTINCTIVE FEATURES; METER AND POETRY; MORPHOLOGY; OPTIMALITY THEORY; PHONETICS; PHONOLOGICAL RULES AND PROCESSES; PHONOLOGY; POLYSYNTHETIC LANGUAGES; PROSODY AND INTONATION; STRESS, LINGUISTIC; TONE

Phrases

The area where we perhaps most clearly see the power of the combinatorial machinery that operates in language is SYNTAX, the study of how words are composed into phrases. In constructing sentences, we don't merely put words into certain sequences, we actually build up a structure. Here is a simple illustration.

English is an SVO language, whose basic word order in simple sentences is the one in (6a).

(6) a. Kim saw Lee
     b. *saw Lee Kim   b'. Ha visto Lee Kim (Italian)
     c. *Kim Lee saw   c'. Kim-ga Lee-o mita (Japanese)

Alternative orders, such as those in (6b–c), are ungrammatical in English. They are grammatical in other languages; thus (6b'), the word-by-word Italian translation of (6b), is grammatical in Italian; and so is (6c'), the Japanese translation of (6c). A priori, the words in (6a) could be put together in a number of different ways, which can be represented by the following tree diagrams:

(7) a.

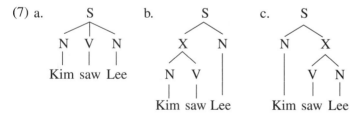

where: S = sentence, N = noun

The structure in (7a) simply says that "Kim," "Lee," and "saw" are put together all at once and that one cannot recognize any subunit within the clause. Structure (7b) says that there is a subunit within the clause constituted by the subject plus the verb; (7c) that the phrasing actually puts together the verb plus the object. The right analysis for English turns out to be (7c), where the verb and the object form a unit, a constituent called the verb phrase (VP), whose "center," or, in technical terms, whose "head" is the verb. Interestingly, such an analysis turns out to be right also for Japanese and Italian, and, it seems, universally. In all languages, the verb and the object form a unit.

There are various ways of seeing that it must be so. A simple one is the following: languages have proforms that is elements that lack an inherent meaning and get their semantic value from a linguistic antecedent (or, in some cases, the extralinguistic context). Personal pronouns like "he" or "him" are a typical example:

(8) A tall boy came in. Paul greeted him warmly.

Here the antecedent of "him" is most naturally construed as "a tall boy". "Him" is a noun phrase (NP), that is, it has the same behavior as things like "Kim" or "a tall boy," which can act as its antecedent. Now English, as many other languages, also has proforms that clearly stand for V+object sequences:

(9) Kim saw Lee. Mary swears that Paul did too

"Did" in (9) is understood as "saw Kim." This means that the antecedent of "did" in (9) is the verb+object sequence of the previous sentence. This makes sense if we assume that such sequences form a unit, the VP (just like "a tall boy" forms an NP).

Notice that English does not have a proform that stands for the subject plus a transitive verb. There is no construction of the following sort:

(10) Kim saw Lee. Mary swears that PROed John too.
    [meaning: "Mary swears that **Kim saw** John too"]

The hypothetical element "PROed" would be an overt morpheme standing for a subject+transitive verb sequence. From a logical point of view, a verb+subject proform doesn't look any more complex than a verb+object proform. From a practical point of view, such a proform could be as useful and as effective for communication as the proform "did." Yet there is nothing like "PROed," and not just in English. In no known language does such a proform appear. This makes sense if we assume that proforms must be constituents of some kind and that verb + object (in whatever order they come) forms a constituent. If, instead, the structure of the clause were (7a) there would be no reason to expect such asymmetry. And if the structure were (7b), we *would* expect proforms such as "PROed" to be attested.

A particularly interesting case is constituted by VSO languages, such as Irish, Breton, and many African languages, etc. Here is an Irish example (Chung and McCloskey 1987: 218):

(11) Ni olan   se bainne ariamh
     Neg drink-PRES.   he milk   ever
     He never drinks milk.

In this type of language the V surfaces next to the subject, separated from the object. If simple linear adjacency is what counts, one might well expect to find in some language of this form a verbal proform that stands for the verb plus the subject. Yet no VSO language has such a proform. This peculiar insistence on banning a potentially useful item even where one would expect it to be readily available can be understood if we assume that VSO structures are obtained by moving the verbal head out of a canonical VP as indicated in what follows:

(12)

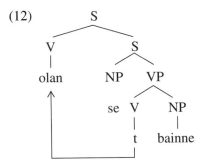

The process through which (11) is derived is called HEAD MOVEMENT and is analogous to what one observes in English alternations of the following kind:

(13) a. Kim has seen Lee.
　　 b. Has Kim seen Lee?

In English, yes-no questions are formed by fronting the auxiliary. This process that applies in English to questions applies in Irish more generally, and is what yields the main difference in basic word order between these languages (see Chung and McCloskey 1987 for evidence and references).

Summing up, there is evidence that in sentences like (6a) the verb and the object are tied together by an invisible knot. This abstract structure in constituents manifests itself in a number of phenomena, of which we have discussed one: the existence of VP pro-forms, in contrast with the absence of subject+verb proforms. The latter appears to be a universal property of languages and constitutes evidence in favor of the universality of the VP. Along the way, we have also seen how languages can vary and what mechanisms can be responsible for such variations (cf. X-BAR THEORY). Generally speaking, words are put together into larger phrases by a computational device that builds up structures on the basis of relatively simple principles (like: "put a head next to its complement" or "move a head to the front of the clause"). Aspects of this computational device are universal and are responsible for the general architecture that all languages share; others can vary (in a limited way) and are responsible for the final form of particular languages.

There is converging evidence that confirms the psychological reality of constituent structure, that is, the idea that speakers unconsciously assign a structure in constituents to sequences of words. A famous case that shows this is a series of experiments known as the "click" experiments (cf. Fodor, Bever, and Garret 1974). In these experiments, subjects were presented with a sentence through a headphone. At some stage during this process a click sound was produced in the headphone and subjects were then asked at which point of the presentation the click occurred. If the click occurred at major constituent breaks (such as the one between the subject and the VP) the subjects were accurate in recalling when it occurred. If, however, the click occurred within a constituent, subjects would make systematic mistakes in recalling the event. They would overwhelmingly displace the click to the closest constituent break. This behavior would be hard to explain if constituent structure were not actually computed by subjects in processing a sentence (see Clark and Clark 1977 for further discussion).

Thus, looking at the syntax of languages we discover a rich structure that reveals fundamental properties of the computational device that the speaker must be endowed with in order to be able to speak (and understand). There are significant disagreements as to the specifics of how these computational devices are structured. Some frameworks for syntactic analysis (e.g., CATEGORIAL GRAMMAR; HEAD-DRIVEN PHRASE STRUCTURE GRAMMAR; LEXICAL FUNCTIONAL GRAMMAR) emphasize the role of the lexicon in driving syntactic computations. Others, like MINIMALISM, put their emphasis on the economical design of the principles governing how sentences are built up (see also OPTIMALITY THEORY). Other kinds of disagreement concern the choice of primitives (e.g., RELATIONAL GRAMMAR and COGNITIVE LINGUISTICS). In spite of the liveliness of the debate and of the range of controversy, most, maybe all of these frameworks share a lot. For one thing, key empirical generalizations and discoveries can be translated from one framework to the next. For example, all frameworks encode a notion of constituency and ways of fleshing out the notion of "relation at a distance" (such as the one we have described above as head movement). All frameworks assign to grammar a universal structural core and dimensions along which particular languages may vary. Finally, all major modern frameworks share certain basic methodological tenets of formal explicitness, aimed at providing mathematical models of grammar (cf. FORMAL GRAMMARS).

See also CATEGORIAL GRAMMAR; COGNITIVE LINGUISTICS; FORMAL GRAMMARS; HEAD-DRIVEN PHRASE STRUCTURE GRAMMAR; HEAD MOVEMENT; LEXICAL FUNCTIONAL GRAMMAR; MINIMALISM; RELATIONAL GRAMMAR; SYNTAX; X-BAR THEORY

Interfaces

Syntax interacts directly with all other major components of grammar. First, it draws from the lexicon the words to be put into phrases. The lexical properties of words (e.g.

whether they are verbs or nouns, whether and how many complements they need, etc.) will affect the kind of syntactic structures that a particular selection of words can enter into. For example, a sentence like "John cries Bill" is ungrammatical because "cry" is intransitive and takes no complement. Second, syntax feeds into phonology. At some point of the syntactic derivation we get the words in the order that we want to pronounce them. And third, syntax provides the input to semantic interpretation.

To illustrate these interfaces further, consider the following set of sentences:

(14) a. John ignores that Mary saw who.
    b. John ignores who Mary saw t.
    c. who does John ignore that Mary saw t.

Here we have three kinds of interrogative structures. Sentence (14a) is not acceptable as a genuine question. It is only acceptable as an "echo" question, for example in reaction to an utterance of the form "John ignores that Mary saw so and so" where we do not understand who "so and so" is. Sentence (14b) contains an embedded question. In it, the *wh*-pronoun appears in place of the complementizer "that;" in other terms, in (14b), the pronoun "who" has been dislocated to the beginning of the embedded clause and "t" marks the site that it was moved from. Finally, sentence (14c), with the *wh*-pronoun moved to the beginning, constitutes a canonical matrix question (see WH-MOVEMENT). Now, the interpretations of (14b) and (14c) can be given roughly as follows:

(15) a. John ignores (the answer to the question) for which x Mary saw x.
    b. (tell me the answer to the question) for which x John ignores that Mary saw x.

The interpretations in (15) are quite close in form to the overt structures of (14b) and (14c) respectively, while the "echo" question (14a) is interpreted roughly as (15b), modulo the special contexts to which it is limited. Thus it seems that the structure of English (non-echo) questions reflects quite closely its interpretation. *Wh*-pronouns are interpreted as question-forming operators. To make sense of such operators we need to know their scope (i.e., what is being asked). English marks the scope of *wh*-operators by putting them at the beginning of the clause on which they operate: the embedded clause in (14b), the matrix one in (14c). Now, it is quite telling to compare this with what happens in other languages. A particularly interesting case is that of Chinese (see, in particular, Huang 1982; Cheng 1991) where there is no visible *wh*-movement. Chinese only has the equivalent of (14a) (Huang 1992).

(16) Zhangsan xian-zhidao [Lisi kanjian shei]
Zhangsan ignores [Lisi see who]

Sentence (16) in Chinese is ambiguous. It can either be interpreted as (15b) or as (15c). One way of making sense of this situation is along the following lines. *Wh*-pronouns must be assigned scope to be interpreted. One of the strategies that grammar makes available is placing the *wh*-pronoun at the beginning of the clause on which it operates. English uses such a strategy overtly. First the *wh*-word is fronted, then the result is fed to phonology (and hence pronounced) and to semantics (and hence interpreted). In Chinese, instead, one feeds to phonology the base structure (16); *then wh*-movement applies, as a step toward the computation of meaning. This gives rise to two abstract structures corresponding to (14b) and (14c) respectively:

(17) a. Zhangsan xian-zhidao shei [Lisi kanjian t]
    b. shei Zhangsan xian-zhidao [Lisi kanjian t]

The structures in (17) are what is fed to semantic interpretation. The process just sketched can be schematized as follows:

(18) John ignores [Mary saw who]   Zhangsan ignores [Lisi saw who]

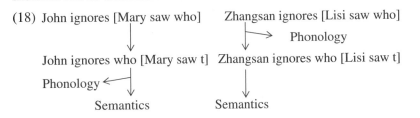

In rough terms, in Chinese one utters the sentence in its basic form (which is semantically ambiguous—see AMBIGUITY) then one does scoping mentally. In English, one first applies scoping (i.e., one marks what is being asked), then utters the result. This way of looking at things enables us to see question formation in languages as diverse as English and Chinese in terms of a uniform mechanism. The only difference lies in the level at which scoping applies. Scope marking takes place overtly in English (i.e., before the chosen sequence of words is pronounced). In Chinese, by contrast, it takes place covertly (i.e., after having pronounced the base form). This is why sentence (16) is ambiguous in Chinese.

There are other elements that need to be assigned a scope in order to be interpreted. A prime case is constituted by quantified NPs like "a student" or "every advisor" (see QUANTIFIERS). Consider (19):

(19) Kim introduced a new student to every advisor.

This sentence has roughly the following two interpretations:

(20) a. There is a student such that Kim introduced him to every advisor.
       b. Every advisor is such that Kim introduced a (possibly different) student to him.

With the help of variables, these interpretation can also be expressed as follows:

(21) a. There is some new student y such that for every advisor x, Kim introduced y to x.
       b. For every advisor x, there is some new student y such that Kim introduced y to x.

Now we have just seen that natural language marks scope in questions by overt or covert movement. If we assume that this is the strategy generally made available to us by grammar, then we are led to conclude that also in cases like (19) scope must be marked via movement. That is, in order to interpret (19), we must determine the scope of the quantifiers by putting them at the beginning of the clause they operate on. For (19), this can be done in two ways:

(22) a. [a new student$_i$ every advisor$_j$ [Kim introduced t$_i$ to t$_j$]]
       b. [every advisor$_j$ a new student$_i$ [Kim introduced t$_i$ to t$_j$]]

Both (22a) and (22b) are obtained out of (19). In (22a) we move "a new student" over "every advisor." In (22b) we do the opposite. These structures correspond to the interpretations in (21a) and (21b), respectively. In a more standard logical notation, they would be expressed as follows:

(23) a. [$\exists x_i$ x_i a new student][$\forall$ x_j x_j an advisor] [Kim introduces x_i to x_j]
       b. [$\forall$ x_j x_j an advisor] [$\exists x_i$ x_i a new student] [Kim introduces x_i to x_j]

So in the interpretation of sentences with quantified NPs, we apply scoping to such NPs. Scoping of quantifiers in English is a covert movement, part of the mental computation of MEANING, much like scoping of *wh*-words in Chinese. The result of scoping (i.e., the structures in [22], which are isomorphic to [23]) is what gets semantically interpreted and is called LOGICAL FORM.

What I just sketched in very rough terms constitutes one of several views currently being pursued. Much work has been devoted to the study of scope phenomena, in several frameworks. Such study has led to a considerable body of novel empirical generalizations. Some important principles that govern the behavior of scope in natural language have been identified (though we are far from a definitive understanding). Phenomena related to scope play an important role at the SYNTAX-SEMANTICS INTERFACE. In particular, according to the hypothesis sketched previously, surface syntactic representations are mapped onto an abstract syntactic structure as a first step toward being interpreted. Such an abstract structure, logical form, provides an explicit representation of scope, anaphoric links, and the relevant lexical information. These are all key factors in determining meaning. The hypothesis of a logical form onto which syntactic structure is mapped fits well with the idea that we are endowed with a LANGUAGE OF

THOUGHT, as our main medium for storing and retrieving information, reasoning, and so on. The reason why this is so is fairly apparent. Empirical features of languages lead linguists to detect the existence of a covert level of representation with the properties that the proponents of the language of thought hypothesis have argued for on the basis of independent considerations. It is highly tempting to speculate that logical form actually *is* the language of thought. This idea needs, of course, to be fleshed out much more. I put it forth here in this "naive" form as an illustration of the potential of interaction between linguistics and other disciplines that deal with cognition.

See also AMBIGUITY; LANGUAGE OF THOUGHT; LOGICAL FORM, ORIGINS OF; LOGICAL FORM IN LINGUISTICS; MEANING; QUANTIFIERS; SYNTAX-SEMANTICS INTERFACE; WH-MOVEMENT

Meaning

What is meaning? What is it to interpret a symbolic structure of some kind? This is one of the hardest question across the whole history of thought and lies right at the center of the study of cognition. The particular form it takes within the picture we have so far is: How is logical form interpreted? A consideration that constrains the range of possible answers to these questions is that our knowledge of meaning enables us to interpret an indefinite number of sentences, including ones we have never encountered before. To explain this we must assume, it seems, that the interpretation procedure is compositional (see COMPOSITIONALITY). Given the syntactic structure to be interpreted, we start out by retrieving the meaning of words (or morphemes). Because the core of the lexicon is finite, we can memorize and store the meaning of the lexical entries. Then each mode of composing words together into phrases (i.e., each configuration in a syntactic analysis tree) corresponds to a mode of composing meanings. Thus, cycling through syntactic structure we arrive eventually at the meaning of the sentence. In general, meanings of complex structures are composed by putting together word (or morpheme) meanings through a finite set of semantic operations that are systematically linked to syntactic configurations. This accounts, in principle, for our capacity of understanding a potential infinity of sentences, in spite of the limits of our cognitive capacities.

Figuring out what operations we use for putting together word meanings is one of the main task of SEMANTICS. To address it, one must say what the output of such operations is. For example, what is it that we get when we compose the meaning of the NP "Pavarotti" with the meaning of the VP "sings 'La Boheme' well"? More generally, what is the meaning of complex phrases and, in particular, what is the meaning of clauses? Although there is disagreement here (as on other important topics) on the ultimate correct answer, there is agreement on what it is that such an answer must afford us. In particular, to have the information that Pavarotti sings "La Boheme" well is to have also the following kind of information:

(24) a. Someone sings "La Boheme" well.
    b. Not everyone sings "La Boheme" poorly.
    c. It is not the case that nobody sings "La Boheme" well.

Barring performance errors or specific pathologies, we do not expect to find a competent speaker of English who sincerely affirms that Pavarotti sings "La Boheme" well and simultaneously denies that someone does (or denies any of the sentences in [24]). So sentence meaning must be something in virtue of which we can compute how the information associated with the sentence in question is related to the information of other sentences. Our knowledge of sentence meaning enables us to place sentences within a complex network of semantic relationships with other sentences.

The relation between a sentence like "Pavarotti sings well" and "someone sings well" (or any of the sentences in [24]), is called "entailment". Its standard definition involves the concept of truth: A sentence A entails a sentence B if and only if whenever A is true, then B must also be true. This means that if we understand under what conditions a sentence is true, we also understand what its entailments are. Considerations such as these have lead to a program of semantic analysis based on truth conditions.

The task of the semantic component of grammar is viewed as that of recursively spelling out the truth conditions of sentences (via their logical form). The truth conditions of simple sentences like "Pavarotti sings" are given in terms of the reference of the words involved (cf. REFERENCE, THEORIES OF). Thus "Pavarotti sings" is true (in a certain moment t) if Pavarotti is in fact the agent of an action of singing (at t). Truth conditions of complex sentences (like "Pavarotti sings or Domingo sings") involve figuring out the contributions to truth conditions of words like "or." According to this program, giving the semantics of the logical form of natural language sentences is closely related to the way we figure out the semantics of any logical system.

Entailment, though not the only kind of important semantic relation, is certainly at the heart of a net of key phenomena. Consider for example the following pair:

(25) a. At least two students who read a book on linguistics by Chomsky were in the audience.
 b. At least two students who read a book by Chomsky were in the audience.

Clearly, (25a) entails (25b). It cannot be the case that (25a) is true while simultaneously (25b) is false. We simply know this a priori. And it is perfectly general: if "at least two As B" is the case and if the Cs form a superset of the As (as the books by Chomsky are a superset of the books on linguistics by Chomsky), then "at least two Cs B" must also be the case. This must be part of what "at least two" means. For "at most two" the opposite is the case:

(26) a. At most two students who read a book on linguistics by Chomsky were in the audience.
 b. At most two students who read a book by Chomsky were in the audience.

Here, (26a) does not entail (26b). It can well be the case that no more than two students read a book on linguistics by Chomsky, but more than two read books (on, say, politics) by Chomsky. What happens is that (26b) entails (26a). That is, if (26b) is the case, then (26a) cannot be false. Now there must be something in our head that enables us to converge on these judgments. That something must be constitutive of our knowledge of the meaning of the sentences in (25) and (26). Notice that our entailment judgment need not be immediate. To see that in fact (26b) entails (26a) requires some reflection. Yet any normal speaker of English will eventually converge in judging that in any situation in which (26b) is true, (26a) has also got to be.

The relevance of entailment for natural language is one of the main discoveries of modern semantics. I will illustrate it in what follows with one famous example, having to do with the distributional properties of words like "any" (cf. Ladusaw 1979, 1992 and references therein). A word like "any" has two main uses. The first is exemplified in (27a):

(27) a.   You may pick any apple.
 b.   A: Can I talk to John or is he busy with students now?
 c.   B: No, wait. *He is talking to any student.
 c'.   B: No, wait. He is talking to every student.
 c".   B: Go ahead. He isn't talking to any student right now.

The use exemplified by (27a) is called free choice "any." It has a universal interpretation: sentence (27a) says that for every apple x, you are allowed to pick x. This kind of "any" seems to require a special modality of some kind (see e.g., Dayal 1998 and references therein). Such a requirement is brought out by the strangeness of sentences like (27c) (the asterisk indicates deviance), which, in the context of (27b), clearly describes an ongoing happening with no special modality attached. Free choice "any" seems incompatible with a plain descriptive mode (and contrasts in this with "every;" cf. [27c']). The other use of "any" is illustrated by (27c"). Even though this sentence, understood as a reply to (27b), reports on an ongoing happening, it is perfectly grammatical. What seems to play a crucial role is the presence of negation. Nonfree choice "any" seems to require a negative context of some kind and is therefore called a *negative polarity item*. It is part of a family of expressions that includes, for example, things like "ever" or "give a damn":

(28) a. *John gives a damn about linguistics.
    b. John doesn't give a damn about linguistics.
    c. *For a long time John ever ate chicken.
    d. For a long time, John didn't ever eat chicken.

In English the free choice and the negative polarity senses of "any" are expressed by the same morphemes. But in many languages (e.g., most Romance languages) they are expressed by different words (for example, in Italian free choice "any" translates as "*qualunque,*" and negative polarity "any" translates as "*alcuno*"). Thus, while the two senses might well be related, it is useful to keep them apart in investigating the behavior of "any." In what follows, we will concentrate on negative polarity "any" (and thus the reader is asked to abstract away from imagining the following examples in contexts that would make the free choice interpretation possible).

The main puzzle in the behavior of words like "any" is understanding what exactly constitutes a "negative" context. Consider for example the following set of sentences:

(29) a. *Yesterday John read any book.
    b. Yesterday John didn't read any book.
    c. *A student who read any book by Chomsky will want to miss his talk.
    d. No student who read any book by Chomsky will want to miss his talk.

In cases such as these, we can rely on morphology: we actually see there the negative morpheme "no" or some of its morphological derivatives. But what about the following cases?

(30) a. *At least two students who read any book by Chomsky were in the audience.
    b. At most two students who read any book by Chomsky were in the audience.

In (30b), where "any" is acceptable, there is no negative morpheme or morphological derivative thereof. This might prompt us to look for a different way of defining the notion of negative context, maybe a semantic one. Here is a possibility: A logical property of negation is that of licensing entailments from sets to their subsets. Consider for example the days in which John read a book by Chomsky. They must be subsets of the days in which he read. This is reflected in the fact that (31a) entails (31b):

(31) a. It is not the case that yesterday John read a book.
    b. It is not the case that yesterday John read a book by Chomsky.

In (30) the entailment goes from a set (the set of days in which John read book) to its subsets (e.g., the set of days in which John read a book by Chomsky). Now this seems to be precisely what sentential negation, negative determiners like "no" and determiners like "at most n" have in common: they all license inferences from sets to subsets thereof. We have already seen that "at most" has precisely this property. To test whether our hypothesis is indeed correct and fully general, we should find something seemingly utterly "non-negative," which, however, has the property of licensing entailments from sets to subsets. The determiner "every" gives us what we need. Such a determiner does not appear to be in any reasonable sense "negative," yet, within a noun phrase headed by "every," the entailment clearly goes from sets to subsets:

(32) a. Every employee who smokes will be terminated.
    b. Every employee who smokes cigars will be terminated.

If (32a) is true, then (32b) must also be. And the set of cigar smokers is clearly a subset of the set of smokers. If "any" wants to be in an environment with these entailment properties, then it should be grammatical within an NP headed by "every." This is indeed so:

(33) Every student who read any book by Chomsky will want to come to his talk.

So the principle governing the distribution of "any" seems to be:

(34) "any" must occur in a context that licenses entailments from sets to their subsets.

Notice that within the VP in sentences like (32), the entailment to subsets does not hold.

(35) a. Every employee smokes.
   b. Every employee smokes cigars.

Sentence (35a) does not entail sentence (35b); in fact the opposite is the case. And sure enough, within the VP "any" is not licensed (I give also a sentence with "at most n" for contrast):

(36) a. *Every student came to any talk by Chomsky.
   b.   At most two students came to any talk by Chomsky.

Surely no one explicitly taught us these facts. No one taught us that "any" is acceptable within an NP headed by "every," but not within a VP of which an "every"-headed NP is subject. Yet we come to have convergent intuitions on these matters. Again, something in our mental endowment must be responsible for such judgments. What is peculiar to the case at hand is that the overt distribution of a class of morphemes like "any" appears to be sensitive to the entailment properties of their context. In particular, it appears to be sensitive to a specific logical property, that of licensing inferences from sets to subsets, which "no," "at most n" and "every" share with sentential negation. It is worth noting that most languages have negative polarity items and their properties tend to be the same as "any," with minimal variations (corresponding to degrees of "strength" of negativity). This illustrates how there are specific architectural features of grammar that cannot be accounted for without a semantic theory of entailment for natural language. And it is difficult to see how to build such a theory without resorting to a compositional assignment of truth conditions to syntactic structures (or something that enables to derive the same effects—cf. DYNAMIC SEMANTICS). The case of negative polarity is by no means isolated. Many other phenomena could be used to illustrate this point (e.g. FOCUS; TENSE AND ASPECT). But the illustration just given will have to suffice for our present purposes. It is an old idea that we understand each other because our language, in spite of its VAGUENESS, has a logic. Now this idea is no longer just an intriguing hypothesis. The question on the table is no more whether this is true. The question is what the exact syntactic and semantic properties of this logic are.

See also COMPOSITIONALITY; DYNAMIC SEMANTICS; FOCUS; REFERENCE, THEORIES OF; SEMANTICS; TENSE AND ASPECT; VAGUENESS

3   Language Use

Ultimately, the goal of a theory of language is to explain how language is used in concrete communicative situations. So far we have formulated the hypothesis that at the basis of linguistic behavior there is a competence constituted by blocks of rules or systems of principles, responsible for sound structure, morphological structure, and so on. Each block constitutes a major *module* of our linguistic competence, which can in turn be articulated into further submodules. These rule systems are then put to use by the speakers in speech acts. In doing so, the linguistic systems interact in complex ways with other aspects of our cognitive apparatus as well as with features of the environment. We now turn to a consideration of these dimensions.

Language in Context

The study of the interaction of grammar with the CONTEXT of use is called PRAGMATICS. Pragmatics looks at sentences within both the extralinguistic situation and the DISCOURSE of which it is part. For example, one aspect of pragmatics is the study of INDEXICALS AND DEMONSTRATIVES (like "I," "here," "now," etc.) whose meaning is fixed by the grammar but whose reference varies with the context. Another important area is the study of PRESUPPOSITION, that is, what is taken for granted in uttering a sentence. Consider the difference between (37a) and (37b):

(37) a. John ate the cake.
   b. It is John that ate the cake.

How do they differ? Sentence (37a) entails that someone ate a cake. Sentence (37b), instead, *takes it for granted* that someone did and asserts that that someone is John. Thus, there are grammatical constructs such as clefting, exemplified in (37b), that appear to be specially linked to presupposition. Just like we have systematic intuitions about entailments, we do about presuppositions and how they are passed from simple sentences to more complex ones.

Yet another aspect of pragmatics is the study of how we virtually always go beyond what is literally said. In ordinary conversational exchanges, one and the same sentence, for example, "the dog is outside," can acquire the *illocutionary force* of a command ("go get it"), of a request ("can you bring it in?"), of an insult ("you are a servant; do your duty"), or can assume all sort of metaphorical or ironical colorings, and so on, depending on what the situation is, what is known to the illocutionary agents, and so on. A breakthrough in the study of these phenomena is due to the work of P. GRICE. Grice put on solid grounds the commonsense distinction between literal meaning, that is, the interpretation we assign to sentences in virtue of rules of grammar and linguistic conventions, and what is conveyed or *implicated*, as Grice puts it, beyond the literal meaning. Grice developed a theory of IMPLICATURE based on the idea that in our use of grammar we are guided by certain general conversational norms to which we spontaneously tend to conform. Such norms instruct us to be cooperative, truthful, orderly, and relevant (cf. RELEVANCE AND RELEVANCE THEORY). These are norms that can be ignored or even flouted. By exploiting both the norms and their violations systematically, thanks to the interaction of literal meaning and mutually shared information present in the context, the speaker can put the hearer in the position of inferring his communicative intentions (i.e., what is implicated). Some aspects of pragmatics (e.g., the study of deixis or presupposition) appear to involve grammar-specific rule systems, others, such as implicature, more general cognitive abilities. All of them appear to be rule governed.

See also CONTEXT AND POINT OF VIEW; DISCOURSE; GRICE, PAUL; IMPLICATURE; INDEXICALS AND DEMONSTRATIVES; PRAGMATICS; PRESUPPOSITION; RELEVANCE AND RELEVANCE THEORY

Language in Flux

Use of language is an important factor in language variation. Certain forms of variation tend to be a constant and relatively stable part of our behavior. We all master a number of registers and styles; often a plurality of grammatical norms are present in the same speakers, as in the case of bilinguals. Such coexisting norms affect one another in interesting ways (see CODESWITCHING). These phenomena, as well as pragmatically induced deviations from a given grammatical norm, can also result in actual changes in the prevailing grammar. Speakers' creative uses can bring innovations about that become part of grammar. On a larger scale, languages enter in contact through a variety of historical events and social dynamics, again resulting in changes. Some such changes come about in a relatively abrupt manner and involve simultaneously many aspects of grammar. A case often quoted in this connection is the great vowel shift which radically changed the vowel space of English toward the end of the Middle English period. The important point is that the dynamic of linguistic change seems to take place within the boundaries of Universal Grammar as charted through synchronic theory (cf. LINGUISTIC UNIVERSALS AND UNIVERSAL GRAMMAR). In fact, it was precisely the discovery of the regularity of change (e.g., Grimm's laws) that led to the discovery of linguistic structure.

A particularly interesting vantage point on linguistic change is provided by the study of CREOLES (Bickerton 1975, 1981). Unlike most languages that evolve from a common ancestor (sometimes a hypothesized protolanguage, as in the case of the Indoeuropean family), Creoles arise from communities of speakers that *do not* share a native language. A typical situation is that of slaves or workers brought together by a dominating group that develop an impoverished quasi-language (a *pidgin*) in order to communicate with one another. Such quasi-languages typically have a small vocabulary drawn from several sources (the language of the dominating group or the native languages of the speakers), no fixed word order, no inflection. The process of creolization takes place when such a language starts having its own native speakers, that is, speakers born to the relevant groups that start using the quasi-language of their parents as a native language. What typically happens is that all of a sudden the characteristics of a full-blown natural language come into being (morphological markers for agreement, case endings, modals, tense, grammaticized strategies for focusing, etc.). This process, which in a few lucky cases has been documented, takes place very rapidly, perhaps even within a single generation. This has led Bickerton to formulate an extremely interesting hypothesis, that of a "bioprogram," that is, a species-specific acquisition device, part of our genetic endowment, that supplies the necessary grammatical apparatus even when such an apparatus is not present in the input. This raises the question of how such a bioprogram has evolved in our species, a topic that has been at the center of much speculation (see EVOLUTION OF LANGUAGE). A much debated issue is the extent to which language has evolved through natural selection, in the ways complex organs like the eye have. Although not much is yet known or agreed upon on this score, progress in the understanding of our cognitive abilities and of the neurological basis of language is constant and is likely to lead to a better understanding of language evolution (also through comparisons of the communication systems of other species; see ANIMAL COMMUNICATION; PRIMATE LANGUAGE).

See also ANIMAL COMMUNICATION; CODESWITCHING; CREOLES; EVOLUTION OF LANGUAGE; LINGUISTIC UNIVERSALS AND UNIVERSAL GRAMMAR; PRIMATE LANGUAGE

Language in the Mind

The cognitive turn in linguistics has brought together in a particularly fruitful manner the study of grammar with the study of the psychological processes at its basis on the one hand and the study of other forms of cognition on the other. PSYCHOLINGUISTICS deals with how language is acquired (cf. LANGUAGE ACQUISITION) and processed in its everyday uses (cf. NATURAL LANGUAGE PROCESSING; SENTENCE PROCESSING). It also deals with language pathology, such as APHASIA and various kinds of developmental impairments (see LANGUAGE IMPAIRMENT, DEVELOPMENTAL).

With regard to acquisition, the available evidence points consistently in one direction. The kind of implicit knowledge at the basis of our linguistic behavior appears to be fairly specialized. Among all the possible ways to communicate and all the possible structures that a system of signs can have, those that are actualized in the languages of the world appear to be fairly specific. Languages exploit only some of the logically conceivable (and humanly possible) sound patterns, morphological markings, and syntactic and semantic devices. Here we could give just a taste of how remarkable the properties of natural languages are. And it is not obvious how such properties, so peculiar among possible semiotic systems, can be accounted for in terms of, say, pragmatic effectiveness or social conventions or cultural inventiveness (cf. SEMIOTICS AND COGNITION). In spite of this, the child masters the structures of her language without apparent effort or explicit training, and on the basis of an often very limited and impoverished input. This is clamorously so in the case of creolization, but it applies to a significant degree also to "normal" learning. An extensive literature documents this claim in all the relevant domains (see WORD MEANING, ACQUISITION OF; PHONOLOGY, ACQUISITION OF; SYNTAX, ACQUISITION OF; SEMANTICS, ACQUISITION OF). It appears that language "grows into the child," to put it in Chomsky's terms; or that the child "invents" it, to put it in Pinker's words. These considerations could not but set the debate on NATIVISM on a new and exciting standing. At the center of intense investigations there is the hypothesis that a specialized form of knowledge, Universal Grammar, is part of the genetic endowment of our species, and thus constitutes the initial state for the language learner. The key to learning, then, consists in fixing what Universal Grammar leaves open (see PARAMETER SETTING APPROACHES TO ACQUISITION, CREOLIZATION AND DIACHRONY). On the one hand, this involves setting the parameters of variation, the "switches" made available by Universal Grammar. On the other hand, it also involves exploiting, for various purposes such as segmenting the stream of sound into words, generalized statistical abilities that we also seem to have (see Saffran, Aslin, and Newport 1996). The interesting problem is determining what device we use in what domain of LEARNING. The empirical investigation of child language proceeds in interaction with the study of the formal conditions under which acquisition is possible, which has also proven to be a useful tool in investigating these issues (cf. ACQUISITION, FORMAL THEORIES OF).

Turning now to processing, planning a sentence, building it up, and uttering it requires a remarkable amount of cognitive work (see LANGUAGE PRODUCTION). The same applies to going from the continuous stream of speech sounds (or, in the case of sign languages, gestures) to syntactic structure and from there to meaning (cf. PROSODY AND INTONATION, PROCESSING ISSUES; SPEECH PERCEPTION; SPOKEN WORD RECOGNITION; VISUAL WORD RECOGNITION). The measure of the difficulty of this task can in part be seen by how partial our progress is in programming machines to accomplish related tasks such as going from sounds to written words, or to analyze an actual text, even on a limited scale (cf. COMPUTATIONAL LINGUISTICS; COMPUTATIONAL LEXICONS). The actual use of sentences in an integrated discourse is an extremely complex set of phenomena. Although we are far from understanding it completely, significant discoveries have been made in the last decades, also thanks to the advances in linguistic theory. I will illustrate it with one well known issue in sentence processing.

As is well known, the recursive character of natural language syntax enables us to construct sentences of indefinite length and complexity:

(38) a. The boy saw the dog.
   b. The boy saw the dog that bit the cat.
   c. The boy saw the dog that bit the cat that ate the mouse.
   d. The boy saw the dog that bit the cat that ate the mouse that stole the cheese.

In sentence (38b), the object is modified by a relative clause. In (38c) the object of the first relative clause is modified by another relative clause. And we can keep doing that. The results are not particularly hard to process. Now, subjects can also be modified by relative clauses:

(39) The boy that the teacher called on saw the dog.

But try now modifying the subject of the relative clause. Here is what we get:

(40) The boy that the teacher that the principal hates called on saw the dog.

Sentence (40) is hard to grasp. It is formed through the same grammatical devices we used in building (39). Yet the decrease in intelligibility from (39) to (40) is quite dramatic. Only after taking the time to look at it carefully can we see that (40) makes sense. Adding a further layer of modification in the most embedded relative clause in (40) would make it virtually impossible to process. So there is an asymmetry between adding modifiers to the right (in English, the recursive side) and adding it to the center of a clause (*center embedding*). The phenomenon is very general. What makes it particularly interesting is that the oddity, if it can be called such, of sentences like (40) does not seem to be due to the violation of any known grammatical constraint. It must be linked to how we parse sentences, that is, how we attach to them a syntactic analysis as a prerequisite to semantic interpretation. Many theories of sentence processing address this issue in interesting ways. The phenomenon of center embedding illustrates well how related but autonomous devices (in this case, the design of grammar vis a vis the architecture of the parser) interact in determining our behavior.

See also ACQUISITION, FORMAL THEORIES OF; APHASIA; COMPUTATIONAL LEXICONS; COMPUTATIONAL LINGUISTICS; LANGUAGE ACQUISITION; LANGUAGE PRODUCTION, LEARNING; NATIVISM; NATURAL LANGUAGE PROCESSING; PARAMETER-SETTING APPROACHES TO ACQUISITION, CREOLIZATION, AND DIACHRONY; PHONOLOGY, ACQUISITION OF; PROSODY AND INTONATION, PROCESSING ISSUES; PSYCHOLINGUISTICS; SEMANTICS, ACQUISITION OF; SEMIOTICS AND COGNITION; SENTENCE PROCESSING; SPEECH PERCEPTION; SPOKEN WORD RECOGNITION; SYNTAX, ACQUISITION OF; VISUAL WORD RECOGNITION; WORD MEANING, ACQUISITION OF

4   Concluding Remarks

Language is important for many fairly obvious and widely known reasons. It can be put to an enormous range of uses; it is the main tool through which our thought gets expressed and our modes of reasoning become manifest. Its pathologies reveal important aspects of the functioning of the brain (cf. LANGUAGE, NEURAL BASIS OF); its use in HUMAN-COMPUTER INTERACTION is ever more a necessity (cf. SPEECH RECOGNITION IN MACHINES; SPEECH SYNTHESIS). These are all well established motivations for studying it. Yet, one of the most interesting things about language is in a way independent of them. What makes the study of language particularly exciting is the identification of regularities and the discovery of the laws that determine them. Often unexpectedly, we detect in our behavior, in our linguistic judgments or through experimentation, a pattern, a regularity. Typically, such regularities present themselves as intricate, they concern exotic data that are hidden in remote corners of our linguistic practice. Why do we have such solid intuitions about such exotic aspects of, say, the functioning of pronouns or the distribution of negative polarity items? How can we have acquired such intuitions? With luck, we discover that at the basis of these intricacies there are some relative simple (if fairly abstract) principles. Because speaking is a cognitive ability, whatever principles are responsible for the relevant pattern of behavior must be somehow implemented or realized in our head. Hence, they must grow in us, will be subject to pathologies, and so on. The cognitive turn in linguistics, through the advent of the generative paradigm, has not thrown away traditional linguistic inquiry. Linguists still collect and classify facts about the languages of the world, but in a new spirit (with arguably fairly old roots)—that of seeking out the mental mechanisms responsible for linguistic facts. Hypotheses on the nature of such mechanisms in turn lead to new empirical discoveries, make us see things we had previously missed, and so on through a new cycle. In full awareness of the limits of our current knowledge and of the disputes that cross the field, it seems impossible to deny that progress over the last 40 years has been quite remarkable. For one thing, we just know more facts (facts not documented in traditional grammars) about more languages. For another thing, the degree of theoretical sophistication is high, I believe higher than it ever was. Not only for the degree of formalization (which, in a field traditionally so prone to bad philosophizing, has its importance), but mainly for the interesting ways in which arrays of complex properties get reduced to ultimately simple axioms. Finally, the cross-disciplinary interaction on language is also a measure of the level the field is at. Abstract modeling of linguistic structure leads quite directly to psychological experimentation and to neurophysiological study and vice versa (see, e.g., GRAMMAR, NEURAL BASIS OF; LEXICON, NEURAL BASIS OF; BILINGUALISM AND THE BRAIN). As Chomsky puts it, language appears to be the first form of higher cognitive capacity that is beginning to yield. We have barely begun to reap the fruits of this fact for the study of cognition in general.

See also BILINGUALISM AND THE BRAIN; GRAMMAR, NEURAL BASIS OF; HUMAN-COMPUTER INTERACTION; LANGUAGE, NEURAL BASIS OF; LEXICON, NEURAL BASIS OF; SPEECH RECOGNITION IN MACHINES; SPEECH SYNTHESIS

References

Akmajian, A., R. Demers, A. Farmer, and R. Harnish. (1990). *Linguistics. An Introduction to Language and Communication.* 4th ed. Cambridge, MA: MIT Press.

Baker, M. (1996). *The Polysynthesis Parameter.* Oxford: Oxford University Press.

Bickerton, D. (1975). *The Dynamics of a Creole System.* Cambridge: Cambridge University Press.

Bickerton, D. (1981). *Roots of Language.* Ann Arbor, MI: Karoma.

Chien, Y.-C., and K. Wexler. (1990). Children's knowledge of locality conditions in binding as evidence for the modularity of syntax and pragmatics. *Language Acquisition* 1: 225–295.

Crain, S., and C. McKee. (1985). The acquisition of structural restrictions on anaphora. In S. Berman, J. Choe, and J. McDonough, Eds., *Proceedings of the Eastern States Conference on Linguistics.* Ithaca, NY: Cornell University Linguistic Publications.

Clark, H., and E. Clark. (1977). *The Psychology of Language.* New York: Harcourt Brace Jovanovich.

Cheng, L. (1991). *On the Typology of Wh-Questions.* Ph.D. diss., MIT. Distributed by MIT Working Papers in Linguistics.

Chung, S., and J. McCloskey. (1987). Government, barriers and small clauses in Modern Irish. *Linguistic Inquiry* 18: 173–238.

Dayal, V. (1998). *Any* as inherent modal. *Linguistics and Philosophy*.

Fodor, J. A., T. Bever, and M. Garrett. (1974). *The Psychology of Language.* New York: McGraw-Hill.

Grodzinsky, Y., and T. Reinhart. (1993). The innateness of binding and coreference. *Linguistic Inquiry* 24: 69–101.

Huang, J. (1982). *Grammatical Relations in Chinese.* Ph.D. diss., MIT. Distributed by MIT Working Papers in Linguistics.

Ladusaw, W. (1979). *Polarity Sensitivity as Inherent Scope Relation.* Ph.D. diss., University of Texas, Austin. Distributed by IULC, Bloomington, Indiana (1980).

Ladusaw, W. (1992). Expressing negation. *SALT II.* Ithaca, NY: Cornell Linguistic Circle.

Pinker, S. (1994). *The Language Instinct.* New York: William Morrow.

Saffran, J., R. Aslin, and E. Newport. (1996). Statistical learning by 8-month-old infants. *Science* 274: 1926–1928.

Further Readings

Aronoff, M. (1976). *Word Formation in Generative Grammar.* Cambridge, MA: MIT Press.

Atkinson, M. (1992). *Children's Syntax.* Oxford: Blackwell.

Brent, M. R. (1997). *Computational Approaches to Language Acquisition.* Cambridge, MA: MIT Press.

Chierchia, G., and S. McConnell-Ginet. (1990). *Meaning and Grammar. An Introduction to Semantics.* Cambridge, MA: MIT Press.

Chomsky, N. (1981). *Lectures on Government and Binding.* Dordrecht: Foris.

Chomsky, N. (1987). *Language and Problems of Knowledge: The Managua Lectures.* Cambridge, MA: MIT Press.

Chomsky, N. (1995). *The Minimalist Program.* Cambridge, MA: MIT Press.

Chomsky, N., and M. Halle. (1968). *The Sound Pattern of English.* New York: Harper and Row.

Elman, J. L., E. A. Bates, M. H. Johnson, A. Karmiloff-Smith, D. Parisi, and K. Plunkett. (1996). *Rethinking Innateness: A Connectionist Perspective on Development.* Cambridge, MA: MIT Press.

Gleitman, L., and B. Landau, Eds. (1994). *The Acquisition of the Lexicon.* Cambridge, MA: MIT Press.

Haegeman, L. (1990). *An Introduction to Government and Binding Theory.* 2nd ed. Oxford: Blackwell.

Hauser, M. D. (1996). *The Evolution of Communication.* Cambridge, MA: MIT Press.

Jusczyk, P. W. (1997). *The Discovery of Spoken Language.* Cambridge, MA: MIT Press.

Kenstowicz, M., and C. Kisseberth. (1979). *Generative Phonology: Description and Theory.* New York: Academic Press.

Ladefoged, P. (1982). *A Course in Phonetics.* 2nd ed. New York: Harcourt Brace Jovanovich.

Levinson, S. (1983). *Pragmatics.* Cambridge: Cambridge University Press.

Lightfoot, D. (1991). *How to Set Parameters: Arguments from Language Change.* Cambridge, MA: MIT Press.

Ludlow, P., Ed. (1997). *Readings in the Philosophy of Language.* Cambridge, MA: MIT Press.

Osherson, D., and H. Lasnik. (1981). *Language: An Invitation to Cognitive Science.* Cambridge, MA: MIT Press.

Stevens, K. N. (1998). *Acoustic Phonetics.* Cambridge, MA: MIT Press.

Culture, Cognition, and Evolution

Dan Sperber and Lawrence Hirschfeld

Most work in the cognitive sciences focuses on the manner in which an individual device—be it a mind, a brain, or a computer—processes various kinds of information. Cognitive psychology in particular is primarily concerned with individual thought and behavior. Individuals however belong to populations. This is true in two quite different senses. Individual organisms are members of species and share a genome and most phenotypic traits with the other members of the same species. Organisms essentially have the cognitive capacities characteristic of their species, with relatively superficial individual variations. In social species, individuals are also members of groups. An important part of their cognitive activity is directed toward other members of the group with whom they cooperate and compete. Among humans in particular, social life is richly cultural. Sociality and culture are made possible by cognitive capacities, contribute to the ontogenetic and phylogenetic development of these capacities, and provide specific inputs to cognitive processes.

Although population-level phenomena influence the development and implementation of cognition at the individual level, relevant research on these phenomena has not been systematically integrated within the cognitive sciences. In good part, this is due to the fact that these issues are approached by scholars from a wide range of disciplines, working within quite different research traditions. To the extent that researchers rely on methodological and theoretical practices that are sometimes difficult to harmonize (e.g., controlled laboratory versus naturalistic observations), the influence of these insights across disciplines and traditions of research is often unduly limited, even on scholars working on similar problems. Moreover, one of the basic notions that should bring together these researchers, the very notion of culture, is developed in radically different ways, and is, if anything, a source of profound disagreements.

The whole area reviewed in this chapter is fraught with polemics and misunderstandings. No one can claim an ecumenical point of view or even a thorough competence. We try to be fair to the many traditions of research we consider and to highlight those that seem to us most important or promising. We are very aware of the fact that the whole area could be reviewed no less fairly but from a different vantage point, yielding a significantly different picture. We hope, at least, to give some sense of the relevance of the issues, of the difficulty involved in studying them, and of the creativity of scholars who have attempted to do so.

To better appreciate the combined importance of work on population-level phenomena, we sort relevant research into three categories:

1. Cognition in a comparative and evolutionary perspective
2. Culture in an evolutionary and cognitive perspective
3. Cognition in an ecological, social, and cultural perspective

1 Cognition in a Comparative and Evolutionary Perspective

Humans spontaneously attribute to nonhuman animals mental states similar to their own, such as desires and beliefs. Nevertheless, it has been commonplace, grounded in Western religion and philosophy, to think of humans as radically different from other species, and as being unique in having a true mind and soul. Charles Darwin's theory of EVOLUTION based on natural selection challenged this classical dichotomy between "man and beast." In the controversies that erupted, anecdotal examples of animal intelligence were used by DARWIN and his followers to question the discontinuity between humans and other species. Since that time, the study of animal behavior has been pursued by zoologists working on specific species and using more and more rigorous methods of observation. However, until recently, and with some notable exceptions such as the pioneering work of Wolfgang Köhler on chimpanzees (see GESTALT PSY-CHOLOGY), zoological observation had little impact on psychology.

Psychologists too were influenced by Darwin and espoused, in an even more radical form, the idea that fundamentally there is no difference between the psychology of humans and that of other animals. Drawing in particular on the work of Edward Thorndike and Ivan Pavlov on CONDITIONING, behaviorists developed the view that a single set of laws govern LEARNING in all animals. Whereas naturalists insisted that animal psychology was richer and more human-like than was generally recognized, behaviorist psychologists insisted that human psychology was poorer and much more animal-like than we would like to believe. In this perspective, the psychology of cats, rats, and pigeons was worth studying in order, not to understand better these individual species, but to discover universal psychological laws that apply to humans as well, in particular laws of learning. COMPARATIVE PSYCHOLOGY developed in this behavioristic tradition. It made significant contributions to the methodology of the experimental study of animal behavior, but it has come under heavy criticism for its neglect of what is now called ECOLOGICAL VALIDITY and for its narrow focus on quantitative rather than qualitative differences in performance across species. This lack of interest in natural ecologies or species-specific psychological adaptations, in fact, is profoundly anti-Darwinian.

For behaviorists, behavior is very much under the control of forces acting on the organism from without, such as external stimulations, as opposed to internal forces such as instincts. After 1940, biologically inspired students of animal behavior, under the influence of Konrad Lorenz, Karl von Frisch, and Niko Tinbergen, and under the label of ETHOLOGY, drew attention to the importance of instincts and species-specific "fixed action patterns." In the ongoing debate on innate versus acquired components of behavior, they stressed the innate side in a way that stirred much controversy, especially when Lorenz, in his book *On Aggression* (1966), argued that humans have strong innate dispositions to aggressive behavior. More innovatively, ethologists made clear that instinct and learning are not to be thought of as antithetic forces: various learning processes (such as "imprinting" or birds' learning of songs) are guided by an instinct to seek specific information in order to develop specific competencies.

By stressing the importance of species-specific psychological mechanisms, ethologists have shown every species (not just humans) to be, to some interesting extent, psychologically unique. This does not address the commonsense and philosophical interest (linked to the issue of the rights of animals) in the commonalties between human and other animals' psyche. Do other animals think? How intelligent are they? Do they have conscious experiences? Under the influence of Donald Griffin, researchers in COGNITIVE ETHOLOGY have tried to answer these questions (typically in the positive) by studying animals, preferably in their natural environment, through observation complemented by experimentation. This has meant accepting some of what more laboratory-oriented psychologists disparagingly call "anecdotal evidence" and has led to methodological controversies.

Work on PRIMATE COGNITION has been of special importance for obvious reasons: nonhuman primates are humans' closest relatives. The search for similarities between humans and other animals begins, quite appropriately, with apes and monkeys. Moreover, because these similarities are then linked to close phylogenetic relationships, they help situate human cognition in its evolutionary context. This phylogenetic approach has been popularized in works such as Desmond Morris's *The Naked Ape*. There have been more scientifically important efforts to link work on apes and on humans. For instance, the study of naïve psychology in humans owes its label, THEORY OF MIND, and part of its inspiration to Premack and Woodruff's famous article "Does the chimpanzee have a theory of mind?" (1978). As the long history of the study of apes' linguistic capacities illustrate, however, excessive focalization on continuities with the human case can, in the end, be counterproductive (see PRIMATE LANGUAGE). Primate psychology is rich and complex, and highly interesting in its own right.

Different species rely to different degrees and in diverse ways on their psychological capacities. Some types of behavior provide immediate evidence of highly specialized cognitive and motor abilities. ECHOLOCATION found in bats and in marine mammals is a striking example. A whole range of other examples of behavior based on specialized abilities is provided by various forms of ANIMAL COMMUNICATION. Communicating animals use a great variety of behaviors (e.g., vocal sounds, electric discharges, "dances," facial expressions) that rely on diverse sensory modalities, as signals conveying some informational content. These signals can be used altruistically to inform, or selfishly to manipulate. Emitting, receiving, and interpreting these signals rely on species-specific abilities. Only in the human case has it been suggested— in keeping with the notion of a radical dichotomy between humans and other animals—that the species' general intelligence provides all the cognitive capacities needed for verbal communication. This view of human linguistic competence has been strongly challenged, under the influence of Noam Chomsky, by modern approaches to LANGUAGE ACQUISITION.

Important aspects of animal psychology are manifested in social behavior. In many mammals and birds, for instance, animals recognize one another individually and have different types of interactions with different members of their group. These relationships are determined not only by the memory of past interactions, but also by kinship relations and hierarchical relationships within the group (see DOMINANCE IN ANIMAL SOCIAL GROUPS). All this presupposes the ability to discriminate individuals and, more abstractly, types of social relationships. In the case of primates, it has been hypothesized that their sophisticated cognitive processes are adaptations to their social rather than their natural environment. The MACHIAVELLIAN INTELLIGENCE HYPOTHESIS, so christened by Richard Byrne and Andrew Whiten (1988), offers an explanation not only of primate intelligence, but also of their ability to enter into strategic interactions with one another, an ability hyperdeveloped in humans, of course.

Many social abilities have fairly obvious functions and it is unsurprising, from a Darwinian point of view, that they should have evolved. (The adaptive value of SOCIAL PLAY BEHAVIOR is less evident and has given rise to interesting debates.) On the other hand, explaining the very existence of social life presents a major challenge to Darwinian theorizing, a challenge that has been at the center of important recent developments in evolutionary theory and in the relationship between the biological, the psychological, and the social sciences.

Social life implies COOPERATION AND COMPETITION. Competition among organisms plays a central role in classical Darwinism, and is therefore not at all puzzling; but the very existence of cooperation is harder to accommodate in a Darwinian framework. Of course, cooperation can be advantageous to the cooperators. Once cooperation is established, however, it seems that it would invariably be even more advantageous for any would-be cooperator to "defect," be a "free-rider," and benefit from the cooperative behavior of others without incurring the cost of being cooperative itself (a problem known in GAME THEORY and RATIONAL CHOICE THEORY as the "prisoner's dilemma"). Given this, it is surprising that cooperative behavior should ever stabilize in the evolution of a population subject to natural selection.

The puzzle presented by the existence of various forms of cooperation or ALTRUISM in living species has been resolved by W. D. Hamilton's (1964) work on kin selection and R. Trivers's (1971) work on reciprocal altruism. A gene for altruism causing an individual to pay a cost, or even to sacrifice itself for the benefit of his kin may thereby increase the number of copies of this gene in the next generation, not through the descendents of the self-sacrificing individual (who may thereby lose its chance of reproducing at all), but through the descendents of the altruist's kin who are likely to carry the very same gene. Even between unrelated individuals, ongoing reciprocal behavior may not only be advantageous to both, but, under some conditions, may be more advantageous than defecting. This may in particular be so if there are cheater-detection mechanisms that make cheating a costly choice. It is thus possible to predict, in some cases with remarkable precision, under which circumstances kin selection or reciprocal altruism are likely to evolve.

The study of such cases has been one of the achievements of SOCIOBIOLOGY. In general sociobiologists aim at explaining behavior, and in particular social behavior, on the assumption that natural selection favors behaviors of an organism that tends to maximize the reproductive success of its genes. Sociobiology, especially as expounded in E. O. Wilson's book *Sociobiology: The New Synthesis* (1975) and in his *On Human Nature* (1978), has been the object of intense controversy. Although some social scientists have espoused a sociobiological approach, the majority have denounced the extension of sociobiological models to the study of human behavior as reductionist and naïve. Sociobiology has had less of an impact, whether positive or negative, on the cognitive sciences. This can probably be explained by the fact that sociobiologists relate behavior directly to biological fitness and are not primarily concerned with the psychological mechanisms that govern behavior.

It is through the development of EVOLUTIONARY PSYCHOLOGY that, in recent years, evolutionary theory has had an important impact on cognitive psychology (Barkow, Cosmides, and Tooby 1992). Unlike sociobiology, evolutionary psychology focuses on what Cosmides and Tooby (1987) have described as the "missing link" (missing, that is, from sociobiological accounts) between genes and behavior, namely the mind. Evolutionary psychologists view the mind as an organized set of mental devices, each having evolved as an adaptation to some specific challenge presented by the ancestral environment. There is, however, some confusion of labels, with some sociobiologists now claiming evolutionary psychology as a subdiscipline or even describing themselves as evolutionary psychologists.

This perspective may help discover discrete mental mechanisms, the existence of which is predicted by evolutionary considerations and may help explain the structure and function of known mental mechanisms. As an example of the first type of contribution, the evolutionary psychology of SEXUAL ATTRACTION has produced strong evidence of the existence of a special purpose adaptation for assessing the attractiveness of potential mates that uses subtle cues such as facial symmetry and waist-to-hips ratio (Symons 1979; Buss 1994). As an example of the second type of contribution, Steven Pinker has argued in *The Language Instinct* (1994) that the language faculty is an evolved adaptation, many aspects of which are best explained in evolutionary terms. Both types of contribution have stirred intense controversies.

Evolutionary psychology has important implications for the study of culture, significantly different from those of sociobiology. Sociobiologists tend to assume that the behaviors of humans in cultural environments are adaptive. They seek therefore to demonstrate the adaptiveness of cultural patterns of behavior and see such demonstrations as explanations of these cultural patterns. Evolutionary psychologists, on the other hand, consider that evolved adaptations, though of course adaptive in the ancestral environment in which they evolved, need not be equally adaptive in a later cultural environment. Slowly evolving adaptations may have neutral or even maladaptive behavioral effects in a rapidly changing cultural environment.

For instance, the evolved disposition to automatically pay attention to sudden loud noises was of adaptive value in the ancestral environment where such noises were rare and very often a sign of danger. This disposition has become a source of distraction, annoyance, and even pathology in a modern urban environment where such noises are extremely common, but a reliable sign of danger only in specific circumstances, such as when crossing a street. This disposition to pay attention to sudden loud noises is also culturally exploited in a way that is unlikely to significantly affect biological fitness, as when gongs, bells, or hand-clapping are used as conventional signals, or when musicians derive special effect from percussion instruments. Such nonadaptive effects of evolved adaptations may be of great cultural significance.

See also ALTRUISM; ANIMAL COMMUNICATION; COGNITIVE ETHOLOGY; COMPARATIVE PSYCHOLOGY; CONDITIONING; COOPERATION AND COMPETITION; DARWIN, CHARLES; DOMINANCE IN ANIMAL SOCIAL GROUPS; ECHOLOCATION; ECOLOGICAL VALIDITY; ETHOLOGY; EVOLUTION; EVOLUTIONARY PSYCHOLOGY; GAME THEORY; GESTALT PSYCHOLOGY; LANGUAGE ACQUISITION; LEARNING; MACHIAVELLIAN INTELLIGENCE HYPOTHESIS; PRIMATE COGNITION; PRIMATE LANGUAGE; RATIONAL CHOICE THEORY; SEXUAL ATTRACTION, EVOLUTIONARY PSYCHOLOGY OF; SOCIAL PLAY BEHAVIOR; SOCIOBIOLOGY

2   Culture in an Evolutionary and Cognitive Perspective

There are many species of social animals. In some of these species, social groups may share and maintain behaviorally transmitted information over generations. Examples of this are songs specific to local populations of some bird species or nut-cracking techniques among West African chimpanzees. Such populations can be said to have a "culture," even if in a very rudimentary form. Among human ancestors, the archaeological record shows the existence of tools from which the existence of a rudimentary technical culture can be inferred, for some two million years (see TECHNOLOGY AND HUMAN EVOLUTION), but the existence of complex cultures with rich CULTURAL SYMBOLISM manifested through ritual and art is well evidenced only in the last 40,000 years. COGNITIVE ARCHAEOLOGY aims in particular at explaining this sudden explosion of culture and at relating it to its cognitive causes and effects.

The study of culture is of relevance to cognitive science for two major reasons. The first is that the very existence of culture, for an essential part, is both an effect and a manifestation of human cognitive abilities. The second reason is that the human societies of today culturally frame every aspect of human life, and, in particular, of cognitive activity. This is true of all societies studied by anthropologists, from New Guinea to Silicon Valley. Human cognition takes place in a social and cultural context. It uses tools provided by culture: words, concepts, beliefs, books, microscopes and computers. Moreover, a great deal of cognition is about social and cultural phenomena.

Thus two possible perspectives, a cognitive perspective on culture and a cultural perspective on cognition, are both legitimate and should be complementary. Too often, however, these two perspectives are adopted by scholars with different training, very different theoretical commitments, and therefore a limited willingness and ability to interact fruitfully. In this section, we engage the first, cognitive perspective on culture and in the next the second, cultural perspective on cognition, trying to highlight both the difficulties and opportunities for greater integration.

Let us first underscore two points of general agreement: the recognition of cultural variety, and that of "psychic unity." The existence of extraordinary cultural variety, well documented by historians and ethnographers, is universally acknowledged. The full extent of this variety is more contentious. For instance, although some would deny the very existence of interesting HUMAN UNIVERSALS in matters cultural, others have worked at documenting them in detail (Brown 1991). Until the early twentieth century, this cultural variation was often attributed to supposed biological variation among human populations. Coupled with the idea of progress, this yielded the view that, as biological endowment progressed, so did cultural endowment, and that some populations (typically Christian whites) were biologically and culturally superior. This view was never universally embraced. Adolf Bastian and Edward Tylor, two of the founders of anthropology in the nineteenth century, insisted on the "psychic unity" of humankind. FRANZ BOAS, one of the founders of American anthropology, in a resolute challenge to scientific racism, argued that human cultural variations are learned and not inherited. Today, with a few undistinguished exceptions, it is generally agreed among cognitive and social scientists that cultural variation is the effect, not of biological variation, but of a common biological, and more specifically cognitive endowment that, given different historical and ecological conditions, makes this variability possible.

No one doubts that the biologically evolved capacities of humans play a role in their social and cultural life. For instance, humans are omnivorous and, sure enough, their diet varies greatly, both within and across cultures. Or to take another example, humans have poorly developed skills for tree climbing, and, not surprisingly, few human communities are tree-dwelling. But what are the human *cognitive* capacities actually relevant to understanding cultural variability and other social phenomena, and in which manner are they relevant?

In the social sciences, it has long been a standard assumption that human learning abilities are general and can be applied in the same way to any empirical domain, and that reasoning abilities are equally general and can be brought to bear on any problem, whatever its content. The human mind, so conceived, is viewed as the basis for an extra somatic adaptation—culture—that has fundamentally changed the relationship between humans and their environment. Culture permits humans to transcend physical and cognitive limitations through the development and use of acquired skills and artifacts. Thus, humans can fly, scale trees, echolocate, and perform advanced mathematical calculus despite the fact that humans are not equipped with wings, claws, natural sonars, or advanced calculus abilities. Cultural adaptations trump cognitive ones in the sense that cultural skills and artifacts can achieve outcomes unpredicted by human cognitive architecture.

Many social scientists have concluded from this that psychology is essentially irrelevant to the social sciences and to the study of culture in particular. It is, however, possible to think of the mind as a relatively homogeneous general-purpose intelligence, and still attribute to it some interesting role in the shaping of culture. For instance, Lucien Lévy-Bruhl assumed that there was a primitive mentality obeying specific intellectual laws and shaping religious and magical beliefs. BRONISLAW MALINOWSKI sought to explain such beliefs, and culture in general, as a response to biological and psychological needs. CLAUDE LÉVI-STRAUSS explicitly tried to explain culture in terms of the structure of the human mind. He developed the idea that simple cognitive dispositions such as a preference for hierarchical classifications or for binary oppositions played an important role in shaping complex social systems such as kinship and complex cultural representations such as myth.

Most research done under the label COGNITIVE ANTHROPOLOGY (reviewed in D'Andrade 1995) accepts the idea that the human mind applies the same categorization and inference procedures to all cognitive domains. Early work in this field concentrated on classification and drew its conceptual tools more from semantics and semiotics (see SEMIOTICS AND COGNITION) than from a cognitive psychology (which, at the time, was in its infancy). More recently, building on Shank and Abelson's idea of scripts, cognitive anthropologists have begun to propose that larger knowledge structures—"cultural schema" or "cultural models"—guide action and belief, in part by activating other related cultural SCHEMATA or models, and as a whole encapsulate tenets of cultural belief. Some of this work has drawn on recent work on FIGURATIVE LANGUAGE, in particular, on METAPHOR (Lakoff and Johnson 1980; Lakoff 1987; Lakoff and Turner 1989) and has focused on cultural models structured in metaphorical terms (see METAPHOR AND CULTURE).

In an extended analysis, Quinn (1987), for instance, identifies a number of interconnecting metaphors for marriage in contemporary North America: marriage is enduring, marriage is mutually beneficial, marriage is unknown at the outset, marriage is difficult, marriage is effortful, marriage is joint, marriage may succeed or fail, marriage is risky. These conjoined metaphors—which together constitute a cultural model—in turn contain within them assumptions derived from models of other everyday domains: the folk physics of difficult activities, the folk social psychology of voluntary relationships, the folk theory of probability, and the folk psychology of human needs. Through this embedding, cultural schema or models provide a continuity and coherency in a given culture's systems of belief. Schema- and model-based analyses are intended to bridge psychological representations and cultural representations. They also provide a basis for relating MOTIVATION AND CULTURE. Not surprisingly, CONNECTIONISM, seen as a way to model the mind without attributing to it much internal structure, is now popular in this tradition of cognitive anthropology (Strauss and Quinn 1998).

Still, it is possible to acknowledge that culture has made the human condition profoundly different from that of any other animal species, and yet to question the image of the human mind as a general-purpose learning and problem-solving device. It is possible also to acknowledge the richness and diversity of human culture and yet to doubt that the role of human-evolved cognitive capacities has been merely to enable the development of culture and possibly shape the form of cultural representations, without exerting any influence on their contents. It is possible, in other terms, to reconcile the social sciences' awareness of the importance of culture with the cognitive sciences' growing awareness of the biological grounded complexity of the human mind.

For example, cognitive scientists have increasingly challenged the image of the human mind as essentially a general intelligence. Arguments and evidence from evolutionary theory, developmental psychology, linguistics, and one approach in cognitive anthropology render plausible a different picture. It is being argued that many human cognitive abilities are not domain-general but specialized to handle specific tasks or domains. This approach (described either under the rubric of MODULARITY or DOMAIN SPECIFICITY) seeks to investigate the nature and scope of these specific abilities, their evolutionary origin, their role in cognitive development, and their effect on culture.

The most important domain-specific abilities are evolved adaptations and are at work in every culture, though often with different effects. Some other domain-specific abilities are cases of socially developed, painstakingly acquired EXPERTISE, such as chess (see CHESS, PSYCHOLOGY OF), that is specific to some cultures. The relationship between evolved adaptations and acquired expertise has not been much studied but is of great interest, in particular for the articulation of the cognitive and the cultural perspective. For instance, writing—which is so important to cognitive and cultural development (see WRITING SYSTEMS and LITERACY)—is a form of expertise, although it has become so common that we may not immediately think of it as such. It would be of the utmost interest to find out to what extent this expertise is grounded in specific psychomotor evolved adaptations.

The first domain-specific mechanisms to be acknowledged in the cognitive literature were input modules and submodules (see Fodor 1982). Typical examples are linked to specific perceptual modality. They include devices that detect edges, surfaces, and whole objects in processing visual information; face recognition devices; and speech parsing devices; abilities to link specific outcomes (such as nausea and vomiting but not electric shock) to specific stimuli (such as eating but not light) through rapid, often single trial, learning.

More recently, there has been a growing body of evidence suggesting that central (i.e., conceptual) mechanisms, as well as input-output processes, may be domain-specific. It has been argued, for instance, that the ability to interpret human action in terms of beliefs and desires is governed by a naive psychology, a domain-specific ability, often referred to as THEORY OF MIND; that the capacity to partition and explain living things in terms of biological principles like growth, inheritance, and bodily function is similarly governed by a FOLK BIOLOGY; and that the capacity to form consistent predictions about the integrity and movements of inert objects is governed by a NAIVE PHYSICS. These devices are described as providing the basis for competencies that children use to think about complex phenomena in a coherent manner using abstract causal principles. Cultural competencies in these domains are seen as grounded in these genetically determined domain-specific dispositions, though they may involve some degree of CONCEPTUAL CHANGE.

The study of folk biology provides a good example of how different views of the mind yield different accounts of cultural knowledge. A great deal of work in classical cognitive anthropology has been devoted to the study of folk classification of plants and animals (Berlin, Breedlove, and Raven 1973; Berlin 1992; Ellen 1993). This work assumed that the difference in organization between these biological classifications and classifications of say, artifacts or kinship relations had to do with differences in the objects classified and that otherwise the mind approached these domains in exactly the same way. Scott Atran's (1990) cognitive anthropological work, drawing on developmental work such as that of Keil (1979), developed the view that folk-biological knowledge was based on a domain-specific approach to living things characterized by specific patterns of CATEGORIZATION and inference. This yields testable predictions regarding both the acquisition pattern and the cultural variability of folk biology. It predicts, for instance, that from the start (rather than through a lengthy learning process) children will classify animals and artifacts in quite different ways, will reason about them quite differently, and will do so in similar ways across cultures. Many of these predictions seem to be borne out (see Medin and Atran 1999).

Generally, each domain-specific competence represents a knowledge structure that identifies and interprets a class of phenomena assumed to share certain properties and hence be of a distinct and general type. Each such knowledge structure provides the basis for a stable response to a set of recurring and complex cognitive or practical challenges. These responses involve largely unconscious dedicated perceptual, retrieval, and inferential processes. Evolutionary psychology interprets these domain-specific competencies as evolved adaptations to specific problems faced by our ancestral populations.

At first, there might seem to be a tension between the recognition of these evolved domain-specific competencies and the recognition of cultural variety. Genetically determined adaptations seem to imply a level of rigidity in cognitive performance that is contradicted by the extraordinary diversity of human achievements. In some domain, a relative degree of rigidity may exist. For example, the spontaneous expectations of not only infants but also adults about the unity, boundaries, and persistence of physical objects may be based on a rather rigid naïve physics. It is highly probable that these expectations vary little across populations, although at present hardly any research speaks to this possibility, which thus remains an open empirical question. After all, evidence does exist suggesting that other nonconscious perceptual processes, such as susceptibility to visual illusions, do vary across populations (Herskovits, Campbell, and Segall 1969).

Generally, however, it is a mistake to equate domain-specificity and rigidity. A genetically determined cognitive disposition may express itself in different ways (or not express itself at all) depending on the environmental conditions. For instance, even in a case such as fear of snakes and other predators, where a convincing argument can be made for the existence, in many species, of evolved mechanisms that trigger an appropriate self-protection response, the danger cues and the fear are not necessarily directly linked. Marks and Nesse (1994: 255), following Mineka et al. (1984), describe such a case in which fear does not emerge instinctively but only after a specific sort of learning experience: "Rhesus monkeys are born without snake fear. Enduring fear develops after a few observations of another rhesus monkey taking fright at a snake . . . Likewise, a fawn is not born with fear of a wolf, but lifelong panic is conditioned by seeing its mother flee just once from a wolf."

Thus, even low-level effects like primordial fears develop out of interactions between prepotentials for discriminating certain environmental conditions, a preparedness to fast learning, and actual environmental inputs. In general, domain-specific competencies emerge only after the competence's initial state comes into contact with a specific environment, and, in some cases, with displays of the competence by older conspecifics. As the environmental inputs vary so does the outcome (within certain limits, of course). This is obviously the case with higher-level conceptual dispositions: It goes without saying, for instance, that even if there is a domain-specific disposition to classify animals in the same way, local faunas differ, and so does people's involvement with this fauna.

There is another and deeper reason why domain-specific abilities are not just compatible with cultural diversity, but may even contribute to explaining it (see Sperber 1996: chap. 6). A domain-specific competence processes information that meets specific input conditions. Normally, these input conditions are satisfied by information belonging to the proper domain of the competence. For instance, the face recognition mechanism accepts as inputs visual patterns that in a natural environment are almost exclusively produced by actual faces. Humans, however, are not just receivers of information, they are also massive producers of information that they use (or seek to use) to influence one another in many ways, and for many different purposes. *A reliable way to get the attention of others is to produce information that meets the input conditions of their domain-specific competencies.* For instance, in a human cultural environment, the face recognition mechanism is stimulated not just by natural faces, but also by pictures of faces, by masks, and by actual faces with their features highlighted or hidden by means of make-up. The effectiveness of these typically cultural artifacts is in part to be explained by the fact that they rely on and exploit a natural disposition.

Although the natural inputs of a natural cognitive disposition may not vary greatly across environments, different cultures may produce widely different artificial inputs that, nevertheless, meet the input conditions of the same natural competence. Hence not all societies have cosmetic make-up, pictures of faces, or masks, and those that do exhibit a remarkable level of diversity in these artifacts. But to explain the very existence of these artifacts and the range of their variability, it is important to understand that they all rely on the same natural mechanism. In the same way, the postulation of a domain-specific competence suggests the existence of a diversified range of possible exploitations of this competence. Of course these exploitations can also be enhancements: portraitists and make-up technicians contribute to culturally differentiated and enhanced capacities for face recognition (and aesthetic appraisal).

Let us give three more illustrations of the relationship between a domain-specific competence and a cultural domain: *color classification, mathematics, and social classifications.*

Different languages deploy different systems of COLOR CATEGORIZATION, segmenting the color spectrum in dramatically different ways. Some languages have only two basic color terms (e.g., Dani). Other languages (e.g., English) have a rich and varied color vocabulary with eleven basic color terms (and many nonbasic color terms that denote subcategories such as *crimson* or apply to specific objects such as *a bay horse*). Prior to Berlin and Kay's (1969) now classic study, these color naming differences were accepted as evidence for the LINGUISTIC RELATIVITY HYPOTHESIS, the doctrine that different modes of linguistic representation reflect different modes of thought. Thus, speakers of languages with two-term color vocabularies were seen as conceptualizing the world in this limited fashion.

Berlin and Kay found that although the boundaries of color terms vary across languages, the focal point of each color category (e.g., that point in the array of reds that is the reddest of red) remains the same no matter how the color spectrum is segmented linguistically. There are, they argued, eleven such focal points, and therefore eleven possible basic color terms. Although there are over two thousand possible subsets of these eleven terms, only twenty-two of these subsets are ever encountered. Moreover, the sequence in which color terms enter a language is tightly constrained. Further research has led to minor revisions but ample confirmation of these findings. Here, then, we have a case where the evolved ability to discriminate colors both grounds culturally specific basic color vocabularies and constrains their variability. Further work by Kay and Kempton (1988) showed that linguistic classification could have some marginal effect on nonverbal classification of color. Nevertheless, once the paradigm example of linguistic relativity, the case of color classification, is now the paradigm illustration of the interplay between cognitive universals and cultural variations, variations that are genuine, but much less dramatic than was once thought.

Naive mathematics provides another instance of the relationship between a domain-specific competence and cultural variation. It has been shown that human infants and some other animals can distinguish collections of objects according to the (small) number of elements in the collection. They also expect changes in the number of objects to occur in accordance with elementary arithmetic principles. All cultures of the world provide some system for counting (verbal and/or gestural), and people in all cultures are capable of performing some rudimentary addition or subtraction, even without the benefit of schooling. This suggests that humans are endowed with an evolved adaptation that can be called naive mathematics. Counting systems do vary from culture to culture. Some, like that of the Oksapmin of New Guinea, are extremely rudimentary, without base structure, and allow counting only up to some small number. Others are more sophisticated and allow, through combination of a few morphemes, the expression of any positive integer. These counting systems, drawing on the morpho-syntactic resources of language, provide powerful cultural tools for the use and enhancement of the naive mathematical ability. Cultural differences in counting largely reflect the degree of linguistic enhancement of this universal ability.

There are mathematical activities that go beyond this intuitive counting ability. Their development varies considerably and in different directions across cultures. Concepts such as the zero, negative numbers, rational numbers, and variables; techniques such as written arithmetical operations; and artifacts such as multiplication tables, abacus, rulers, or calculators help develop mathematics far beyond its intuitive basis. Some of these concepts and tools are relatively easy to learn and use, others require painstaking study in an educational setting. From a cognitive point of view, explaining these cultural developments and differences must include, among other things, an account of the cognitive resources they mobilize. For instance, given human cognitive dispositions, mathematical ideas and skills that are more intuitive, more easily grasped, and readily accepted should have a wider and more stable distribution and a stronger impact on most people's thinking and practice (see NUMERACY AND CULTURE).

NAIVE SOCIOLOGY provides a third example of the relationship between a domain-specific cognitive disposition and a varying cultural domain. According to the standard view, children learn and think about all human groupings in much the same way: they overwhelmingly attend to surface differences in forming categories and they interpret these categories virtually only in terms of these superficial features. Of course, knowledge of all social categories is not acquired at the same time. Children sort people by gender before they sort them by political party affiliation. The standard explanation is that children learn to pick out social groups that are visibly distinct and culturally salient earlier than they learn about other, less visually marked, groups.

Recent research suggests that surface differences determine neither the development of categories nor their interpretation (Hirschfeld 1996). In North America and Europe one of the earliest-emerging social concepts is "race." Surprisingly, given the adult belief that the physical correlates of "race" are extremely attention demanding, the child's initial concept of "race" contains little perceptual information. Three-year-olds, for instance, recognize that "blacks" represent an important social grouping long before they learn which physical features are associated with being "black." What little visual information they have is often inaccurate and idiosyncratic; thus, when one young child was asked to describe what made a particular person black, he responded that his teeth were longer. (Ramsey 1987.) Another set of studies suggests that even quite young children possess a deep and theory-like understanding of "race" (but not other similar groupings), expecting "race" to be a fundamental, inherited, and immutable aspect of an individual—that is, they expect it to be biological (Hirschfeld 1995).

Conceptual development of this sort—in which specific concepts are acquired in a singular fashion and contain information far beyond what experience affords—are plausibly the output of a domain-specific disposition. Since the disappearance of the Neanderthals, humans are no longer divided into subspecies or races, and the very idea of "race" appeared only relatively recently in human history. So, although there may well exist an evolved domain-specific disposition that guides learning about social groupings, it is very unlikely that it would have evolved with the function of guiding learning about "race." As noted previously, however, many cultural artifacts meet a device's input conditions despite the fact that they did not figure in the evolutionary environment that gave rise to the device. "Race" might well be a case in point.

As many have argued, "race" was initially a cultural creation linked to colonial and other overseas encounters with peoples whose physical appearance was markedly different from Europeans. The modern concept of "race" has lost some of this historic specificity and is generally (mis)interpreted as a "natural" system for partitioning humans into distinct kinds. That this modern concept has stabilized and been sustained over time owes as much to cognitive as cultural factors (Hirschfeld 1996). On the one hand, it is sustainable because a domain-specific disposition guides children to spontaneously adopt specific social representations, and "race" satisfies the input conditions of this disposition. On the other hand, it varies across cultures because each cultural environment guides children to a specific range of possible groupings. These possibilities, in turn, reflect the specific historical contexts in which colonial and other overseas encounters occurred. It is worth bearing in mind that "race" is not the only cultural domain that is "naturalized" because it resonates with an evolved disposition. It is plausible that children in South Asia, guided by the same domain-specific disposition but in another cultural context, find "caste" more biological than "race." Similarly, children in some East-African societies may find "age-grades" more biological than either "race" or "caste." In all such cases, the fact that certain social categories are more readily learned contributes to the social and cultural stability of these categories.

The cases of color classification, mathematics, and naïve sociology illustrate a fairly direct relationship between a domain-specific ability and a cultural domain grounded in this ability, enhancing it, and possibly biasing it. Not all cultural domains correspond in this simple way to a single underlying domain-specific competence. For instance, are RELIGIOUS IDEAS AND PRACTICES grounded in a distinct competence, the domain of which would be supernatural phenomena? This is difficult to accept from the point of view of a naturalistic cognitive science. Supernatural phenomena cannot be assumed to have been part of the environment in which human psychological adaptations evolved. Of course, it is conceivable that a disposition to form false or unevidenced beliefs of a certain tenor would be adaptive and might have evolved. Thus Malinowski and many other anthropologists have argued that religious beliefs serve a social function. Nemeroff and Rozin (1994) have argued that much of MAGIC AND SUPERSTITION is based on intuitive ideas of contagion that have clear adaptive value. Another possibility is that domain-specific competencies are extended beyond their domain, in virtue of similarity relationships. Thus, Carey (1985) and Inagaki and Hatano (1987) have argued that ANIMISM results from an overextension of naïve psychology.

The cultural prevalence of religious and magical beliefs may also be accounted for in terms of a domain-specific cognitive architecture without assuming that there is a domain-specific disposition to religious or magical beliefs (see Sperber 1975, 1996; Boyer 1990, 1994). Religious beliefs typically have a strong relationship with the principles of naïve physics, biology, psychology, and sociology. This relationship, however, is one of head-on contradiction. These are beliefs about creatures capable of being simultaneously in several places, of belonging to several species or of changing from one species to another, or of reading minds and seeing scenes distant in time or space. Apart from these striking departures from intuitive knowledge, however, the appearance and behavior of these supernatural beings is what intuition would expect of natural beings. Religious representations, as argued by Boyer (1994), are sustainable to the extent that a balance between counterintuitive and intuitive qualities is reached. A supernatural being with too few unexpected qualities is not attention demanding and thus not memorable. One with too many unexpected qualities is too information rich to be memorable (see MEMORY). Thus, religious beliefs can be seen as parasitical on domain-specific competencies that they both exploit and challenge.

So far in this section, we have illustrated how evolutionary and cognitive perspectives can contribute to our understanding of specific cultural phenomena. They can also contribute to our understanding of the very phenomenon of culture. Until recently, the evolutionary and the cognitive approaches to the characterization of culture were very different and unrelated. In more recent developments, they have converged to a significant degree.

From an evolutionary point of view, there are two processes to consider and articulate: the biological evolution of the human species, and the CULTURAL EVOLUTION of human groups. There is unquestionably a certain degree of coevolution between genes and culture (see Boyd and Richerson 1985; William Durham 1991). But, given the very different rates of biological and cultural evolution—the latter being much more rapid than the former—the importance of cultural evolution to biological evolution, or equivalently its autonomy, is hard to assess.

Sociobiologists (e.g., Lumsden and Wilson 1981) tend to see cultural evolution as being very closely controlled by biological evolution and cultural traits as being selected in virtue of their biological functionality. Other biologists such as Cavalli-Sforza and Feldman (1981) and Richard Dawkins (1976, 1982) have argued that cultural evolution is a truly autonomous evolutionary process where a form of Darwinian selection operates on cultural traits, favoring the traits that are more capable of generating replicas of themselves (whether or not they contribute to the reproductive success of their carriers). Neither of these evolutionary approaches gives much place to cognitive mechanisms, the existence of which is treated as a background condition for the more or less autonomous selection of cultural traits. Both evolutionary approaches view culture as a pool of traits (mental representations, practices, or artifacts) present in a population.

From a cognitive point of view, it is tempting to think of culture as an ensemble of representations (classifications, schemas, models, competencies), the possession of which makes an individual a member of a cultural group. In early cognitive anthropology, culture was often compared to a language, with a copy of it in the mind of every culturally competent member of the group. Since then, it has been generally recognized that cultures are much less integrated than languages and tolerate a much greater degree of interindividual variation (see CULTURAL CONSENSUS THEORY and CULTURAL VARIATION). Moreover, with the recent insistence on the role of artifacts in cognitive processes (see COGNITIVE ARTIFACTS), it has become common to acknowledge the cultural character of these artifacts: culture is not just in the mind. Still, in a standard cognitive anthropological perspective, culture is first and foremost something in the mind of every individual. The fact that culture is a population-scale phenomenon is of course acknowledged, but plays only a trivial role in explanation.

Some recent work integrates the evolutionary and cognitive perspectives. Sperber (1985, 1996) has argued for an "epidemiological" approach to culture. According to this approach, cultural facts are not mental facts but distributions of causally linked mental and public facts in a human population. More specifically, chains of interaction—of communication in particular—may distribute similar mental representations and similar public productions (such as behaviors and artifacts) throughout a population. Types of mental representations and public productions that are stabilized through such causal chains are, in fact, what we recognize as cultural.

To help explain why some items stabilize and become cultural (when the vast majority of mental representations and public productions have no recognizable descendants), it is suggested that domain-specific evolved dispositions act as receptors and tend to fix specific kinds of contents. Many cultural representations stabilize because they resonate with domain-specific principles. Because such representations tend to be rapidly and solidly acquired, they are relatively inured to disruptions in the process of their transmission. Hence the epidemiological approach to culture dovetails with evolutionary psychology (see Tooby and Cosmides 1992) and with much recent work in developmental psychology, which has highlighted the role of innate preparedness and domain-specificity in learning (Hirschfeld and Gelman 1994; Sperber, Premack, and Premack 1995).

Children are not just the passive receptors of cultural forms. Given their cognitive dispositions, they spontaneously adopt certain cultural representations and accept others only through institutional support such as that provided by schools. The greater the dependence on institutional support, the greater the cultural lability and variability. Other inputs, children reject or transform. A compelling example is provided by the case of CREOLES. When colonial, commercial, and other forces bring populations together in linguistically unfamiliar contexts a common result is the emergence of a pidgin, a cobbled language of which no individual is a native speaker. Sometimes, children are raised in a pidgin. When pidgin utterances are the input of the language acquisition process, a creole, that is a natural and fully elaborated language, is the output. Children literally transform the contingent and incomplete cultural form into a noncontingent and fully articulated form. This happens because children are equipped with an evolved device for acquiring language (Bickerton 1990).

Cultural forms stabilize because they are attention-grabbing, memorable, and sustainable with respect to relevant domain-specific devices. Of course, representations are also selected for in virtue of being present in any particular cultural environment. Domain-specific devices cannot attend to, act on, or elaborate representations that the organism does not come into contact with. For the development of culture, a cultural environment, a product of human history, is as necessary as a cognitive equipment, a product of biological evolution.

See also ANIMISM; BOAS, FRANZ; CATEGORIZATION; CHESS, PSYCHOLOGY OF; COGNITIVE ANTHROPOLOGY; COGNITIVE ARCHAEOLOGY; COGNITIVE ARTIFACTS; COLOR CATEGORIZATION; CONCEPTUAL CHANGE; CONNECTIONISM, PHILOSOPHICAL ISSUES OF; CREOLES; CULTURAL CONSENSUS THEORY; CULTURAL EVOLUTION; CULTURAL

SYMBOLISM; CULTURAL VARIATION; DOMAIN SPECIFICITY; EXPERTISE; FIGURATIVE LANGUAGE; FOLK BIOLOGY; HUMAN UNIVERSALS; LÉVI-STRAUSS, CLAUDE; LINGUISTIC RELATIVITY HYPOTHESIS; LITERACY; MAGIC AND SUPERSTITION; MALINOWSKI, BRONISLAW; MEMORY; METAPHOR; METAPHOR AND CULTURE; MODULARITY OF MIND; MOTIVATION AND CULTURE; NAIVE MATHEMATICS; NAIVE PHYSICS; NAIVE SOCIOLOGY; NUMERACY AND CULTURE; RELIGIOUS IDEAS AND PRACTICES; SCHEMATA; SEMIOTICS AND COGNITION; TECHNOLOGY AND HUMAN EVOLUTION; THEORY OF MIND; WRITING SYSTEMS

3 Cognition in an Ecological, Social, and Cultural Perspective

Ordinary cognitive activity does not take place in a fixed experimental setting where the information available is strictly limited and controlled, but in a complex, information-rich, ever-changing environment. In social species, conspecifics occupy a salient place in this environment, and much of the individual-environment interaction is, in fact, interaction with other individuals. In the human case, moreover, the environment is densely furnished with cultural objects and events most of which have, at least in part, the function of producing cognitive effects.

In most experimental psychology this ecological, social, and cultural dimension of human cognition is bracketed out. This practice has drawn strong criticisms, both from differently oriented psychologists and from social scientists. Clearly, there are good grounds for these criticisms. How damning they are remains contentious. After all, all research programs, even the most holistic ones, cannot but idealize their objects by abstracting away from many dimensions of reality. In each case, the issue is whether the idealization highlights a genuinely automous level about which interesting generalizations can be discovered, or whether it merely creates an artificial pseudodomain the study of which does not effectively contribute to the knowledge of the real world. Be that as it may, in the debate between standard and more ecologically oriented approaches to cognition, there is no doubt that the latter have raised essential questions and developed a variety of interesting answers. It is to these positive contributions that we now turn.

Issues of ecological validity arise not just when the social and cultural dimension of cognition is deployed, but at all levels of cognition. As argued by ECOLOGICAL PSYCHOLOGY, even the perceptions of an individual organism should be understood in ecological terms. Based on the work of J. J. GIBSON, ecological psychology relates perception not to "stimuli" but to the layout of the environment, to the possibilities it opens for action (the AFFORDANCES), and to the perceiver's own situation and motion in the environment. When the environment considered is social and cultural, there are further grounds to rethink even more basic tenets of cognitive science, particularly the notion that the individual mind is *the* site of cognitive processes. This is what recent work on SITUATED COGNITION AND LEARNING and on SITUATEDNESS/EMBEDDEDNESS has been doing.

Many of the issues described today in terms of situated cognition were raised in the pioneering work of the Russian psychologist LEV VYGOTSKY (1896–1934), whose work was introduced to English readers in the 1970s (see Wertsch 1985b). Vygotsky saw cognitive activity as being social as well as mental. He stressed the importance of cultural tools for cognition. His insight that historical, cultural, and institutional contexts condition learning by identifying and extending the child's capacities animates several ecological approaches in psychology. Writing in the first half of the twentieth century, Vygotsky was not aiming at an explicit modeling of the processes he discussed, nor were the first studies inspired by his work in the 1970s and 1980s (see Wertsch 1985a). Some of the more recent work about situated cognition, though inspired by Vygotsky, does involve modeling of cognitive processes, which means, of course, departing from Vygotsky's original conceptual framework.

To what extent is cognition in a social and cultural environment still an individual process? Regarding cognition in a social environment, James Wertsch raises the issue with a telling anecdote about helping his daughter remember where she left her shoes. When she was unable to remember, he began to pose questions that directed her recall until she "remembered" where they were. Wertsch asks who remembered in this case: he didn't since he had no prior information about the shoes' location, nor did his daughter because she was unable to recall their location without his intervention. Regarding cognition in an environment containing cultural artifacts, a striking example is provided by Edwin Hutchins (1995), who has demonstrated how the cognitive processes involved in flying a plane do not take place just in the pilot's head but are distributed throughout the cockpit, in the members of the crew, the control panel, and the manuals.

This interpenetration of processes internal and external to the individual can be studied in technologically rich environment such as that provided in HUMAN-COMPUTER INTERACTION, and also in more mundane circumstances such as finding one's way with the help of a map (see HUMAN NAVIGATION), or shopping at the supermarket where the arrangement of the shelves serves as a kind of shopping list (Lave et al. 1984). This type of research is being applied in COGNITIVE ERGONOMICS, which helps design technologies, organizations, and learning environments in a way informed by cognitive science.

The study of cultural tools and the form of cognitive activity they foster is of importance for the historical and anthropological study of culture. It is an old commonplace to contrast societies with and without writing systems. As Lévi-Strauss (1971) suggested, the very structure of oral narratives reflects an optimal form for memory unaided by external inscriptions. More recent work (e.g., Goody 1977, 1987; Rubin 1995; Bloch 1998) has attempted to elaborate and in part rethink this contrast by looking at the cognitive implications of orality and writing and of other systems for displaying information in the environment (see ARTIFACTS AND CIVILIZATION). EDUCATION too has been approached in a Vygotskyan perspective, as a collaborative enterprise between teacher and learner using a specially designed environment with ad hoc props. Education is thus described at a level intermediary between individual cognitive development and cultural transmission, thus linking and perhaps locking together the psychological and the cultural level (Bruner 1996).

From the point of view of the epidemiological approach to culture evoked in the preceding section, the situated cognition approach is quite congenial. The epidemiological approach insists on the fact that the causal chains of cultural distribution are complex cognitive *and* ecological processes that extend over time and across populations. This, however, dedramatizes the contrast between a more individualistic and a more situated description of cognitive processes (see INDIVIDUALISM). Consider a situated process such as a teacher-learner interaction, or the whole cockpit of a plane doing the piloting. These processes are not wholly autonomous. The teacher is a link in a wider process of transmission using a battery of artifacts, and the learner is likely to become a link, possibly of another kind, in the same process. Their interaction cannot be fully explained by abstracting away from this wider context. Similarly, the cockpit is far from being fully autonomous. It is linked to air control on the ground, through it to other aircrafts, but also, in time, to the engineering process that designed the plane, to the educational process that trained the pilot, and so on. Of course, both the teacher-learner interaction and the cockpit have enough autonomy to deserve being considered and studied on their own. But then so do the individual cognitive processes of the teacher, the learner, the pilot, and so on at a lower level, and the complex institutional networks in which all this take place at a higher level. Cognitive cultural causal chains extend indefinitely in all directions. Various sections of these chains of different size and structure are worth studying on their own.

The study of psychological processes in their social context is traditionally the province of *social psychology* (see Ross and Nisbett 1991; Gilbert, Fiske, and Lindzey 1998). The contribution of this rich discipline to the cognitive sciences can be read in two ways. On the one hand, it can be pointed out that, at a time where mainstream psychologists were behaviorists and not interested in contentful cognitive processes, social psychologists were studying beliefs, opinions, prejudices, influence, motivation, or attitudes (e.g., Allport 1954). On the other hand, it could be argued that the interest of social psychologists for these mental phenomena is generally quite different from that of cognitive scientists. The goals of social psychologists have typically been to identify trends and their causal factors, rather than mechanisms and their parts, so that most of social psychology has never been "cognitive" in this strong sense. In the practice of standard cognitive psychology too, it is quite often the case that a trend, a tendency, a disposition is identified well before the underlying mechanisms are considered.

Many of the phenomena identified by social psychologists could be further investigated in a more standardly cognitive way, and, more and more often, they are. For instance, according Festinger's (1957) theory of cognitive DISSONANCE, people are emotionally averse to cognitive inconsistencies and seek to reduce them. Festinger investigated various ways in which such dissonances arise (in decision making or in forced compliance, for instance), and how they can be dealt with. Recently, computational models of dissonance have been developed using artificial neural networks and relating dissonance to other psychological phenomena such as analogical reasoning. ATTRIBUTION THEORY, inspired by Heider (1958) and Kelley (1972), investigates causal judgments (see CAUSAL REASONING), and in particular interpretations of people's behavior. Specific patterns have been identified, such as Ross's (1977) "fundamental attribution error" (i.e., the tendency to overestimate personality traits and underestimate the situation in the causing of behavior). As in the case of dissonance, there has been a growing interest for modeling the inferential processes involved in these attributions (e.g. Cheng and Novick 1992). STEREOTYPING of social categories, another typical topic of social psychology, is also approached in a more cognitive way by focusing on information processing and knowledge structures.

The domain of social psychology where the influence of cognitive science is the most manifest is that of SOCIAL COGNITION (Fiske and Taylor 1991), that is the cognition of social life, sometimes extended to cognition as shaped by social life. Social cognition so understood is the very subject matter of social psychology, or at least its central part (leaving out emotion), but the reference to *cognition*, rather than to psychology generally, signals the intent to join forces with mainstream cognitive psychology. With the development of the domain-specificity approach, however, social cognition so understood may be too broad an area. For instance, it does not distinguish between naïve psychology and naïve sociology, when the trend may be rather toward distinguishing even more fine-grained mechanisms.

One issue that has always been central to social psychology and that has become important in cognitive science only later is rationality. Social judgment exhibits blatant cases of irrationality, and their study by social psychologists (see Nisbett and Ross 1980) has contributed to the development of the study of reasoning in general (see JUDGMENT HEURISTICS; CAUSAL REASONING; PROBABILITIC REASONING; DEDUCTIVE REASONING). One area of social life where rationality plays a special role is economics. It is within economics that RATIONAL CHOICE THEORY was initially developed (see also RATIONAL DECISION MAKING). The actual behavior of economic agents, however, does not fully conform to the normative theory. Drawing in particular on the work of Kahneman and TVERSKY (see Kahneman, Slovic, and Tversky 1982), experimental and behavioral economists explore and try to model the actual behavior of economic agents (see ECONOMICS AND COGNITIVE SCIENCE). In principle, economics should provide a paradigmatic case of fruitful interaction between the social and the cognitive sciences. The economic domain is quite specific, however, and it is an open question to know to what extent the cognitive approach to this area, based as it is on an abstract normative theory of rationality, can serve as a model in other areas (but see Becker 1976).

From the points of view of evolutionary psychology and situated cognition, it is tempting to adopt an alternative approach by developing a notion of evolutionarily grounded BOUNDED RATIONALITY as a criterion for evaluating the manner in which human inferential mechanisms perform their functions. Such a criterion would involve not just considerations of epistemic reliability, but also of processing speed and cost. In this perspective, evolutionary psychologists have investigated how reasoning abilities may be adjusted to specific problems and domains, and how they may privilege information available in ordinary environments (see Cosmides and Tooby 1992; Gigerenzer and Goldstein 1996; Gigerenzer and Hoffrage 1995).

We now turn to anthropological research on the role of culture in cognitive and more generally mental processes. It is hardly controversial that cultural factors enable, constrain, and channel the development of certain cognitive outcomes. Some cultural environments inhibit normal cognitive development (e.g., inequitable distributions of cultural resources underlie uneven performance on standardized tests). Other cultural environments promote the elaboration of complex knowledge structures such as modern science by providing the appropriate artifactual and institutional support. In fact, it takes little more than a trip abroad to appreciate that our abilities to make the best use of the natural and artifactual environment and to interpret the behaviors of others is culture-bound.

The social sciences, and anthropology in particular, tend to approach the relationship between culture and mind in a much more radical way. Quite commonly the claim made is not just that cultural factors affect mental activity, it is that the human mind is socially and culturally constituted. This could be understood as meaning just that human mental processes use at every moment and in every activity cultural tools, language to begin with, and also schemas, models, expertises, and values. This, surely, is correct, and makes human minds very complex and special. What is generally meant goes well beyond this triviality, however, and is part of an antinaturalistic approach common in the social sciences. On this view, there may be brains but there are no minds in nature, and, anyhow, there is no human nature. Minds are not natural systems informed and transformed by culture, they are made by culture, and differently so by different cultures. From this point of view, naturalistic psychology, at least when it deals with true mental functions, with thinking in particular, is a Western ethnocentric pseudoscience. Piaget's study of the acculturation of Swiss children is mistaken for the study of a universal human cognitive development; the study of American college students reasoning on laboratory tasks is mistaken for that of human (ir)rationality, and so on.

Such culturalism—in this extreme or in more hedged forms—goes together with a specific view of culture. We saw in the last section how cognitive anthropology puts culture essentially in the mind and how evolutionary and epidemiological approaches treat culture in terms of population-wide distributions of individual mental and artifactual phenomena. These are naturalistic views of culture, with little following in the social sciences. Much more characteristic are the influential views of the anthropologist Clifford Geertz. He writes: "The concept of culture I espouse is essentially a semiotic one. Believing, with Max Weber, that man is an animal suspended in webs of significance he himself has spun, I take culture to be those webs, and the analysis of it to be therefore not an experimental science in search of law but an interpretive one in search of meaning" (Geertz 1973: 5). Attacking cognitive anthropology for placing culture in the mind, and drawing on Wittgenstein's dismissal of the idea of a private meaning, Geertz (1973: 12) insists that "culture is public because meaning is."

This understanding of the notion of culture goes together with a strong individuation of individual cultures (comparable to the individuation of languages), each seen as a separate system of meanings. Cultures so understood are viewed as being not just different environments, but, literally, different worlds, differing from each other in arbitrary ways. This view, known as CULTURAL RELATIVISM, is, except in very watered-down versions, difficult to reconcile with any naturalistic approach to cognitive development. Given that the initial inputs to cognitive development are just myriad stimulations of nerve endings, the process of extracting from these inputs the objective regularities of a relatively stable world is already hard enough to explain. If, in fact, even the world in which cognitive development takes place is not given, if the child can draw neither from expectable environmental regularities nor from internal preparedness to deal with just these regularities, then the process is a pure mystery. It is a sign of the lack of concern for psychological issues that this mystery seems never to have worried defenders of cultural relativism.

In one area, anthropological linguistics, cultural relativism has guided positive research programs that continue to this day. The linguist and anthropologist Edward SAPIR and the linguist Whorf developed the thesis of linguistic relativity (the "Sapir-Whorf hypothesis") according to which lexical and grammatical categories of language determine the way the world is perceived and conceptualized, and each language is at the root of a different worldview (see also LANGUAGE AND COMMUNICATION). On this view, human cognition can be understood only through analysis of the linguistic and cultural structures that support it. The classical example is Whorf's treatment of the Hopi notion of time. Noting that the Hopi language "contains no words, grammatical forms, construction or expressions that refer directly to what we call 'time,' or to the past, or future, or to enduring or lasting," he concluded that the Hopi have "no general notion or intuition of time as a smooth flowing continuum" (Whorf 1956: 57). Subsequent research (see Brown 1991 for a review) tended to show that this radical linguistic relativity is not supported by closer analysis. However, less radical versions of linguistic relativity can be sustained (Lucy 1992; Gumperz and Levinson 1996). Recent comparative work on LANGUAGE AND CULTURE has been carried out with the methods of cognitive psycholinguistics at the Max Planck Institute for Psycholinguistics in Nijmegen. It has, in particular, gathered impressive evidence of the fact that the manner in which different languages encode spatial coordinates strongly affects people's conceptualization of spatial relations and movements (see Levinson 1996).

The standard anthropological characterization of cultures as relatively bounded, homogeneous, and coherent entities has repeatedly been challenged (e.g., Leach 1954; Fried 1975). The idea of discrete tribes each with its own culture was a colonial administrator's dream—a dream they forced on people—before being an anthropologist's presupposition. In fact, different flows of cultural information—linguistic, religious, technological—have different boundaries, or, quite often, do not even have proper boundaries, just zones of greater of lesser intensities. From an epidemiological point of view, of course, these ongoing cultural flows and the fuzziness of cultural boundaries are just what one should expect. From such a point of view, the notion of *a* culture should not have more of a theoretical status than that of a region in geography. Culture is best seen not as a thing, but as a property that representations, practices, and artifacts possess to the extent that they are caused by population-wide distribution processes.

It is the standard notion of a culture as an integrated whole that has guided most anthropological research bearing, directly or indirectly, on psychological issues. Much early anthropology, notably in North America, focused on the social and cultural correlates of psychological phenomena. A major and influential program of research, pioneered by Margaret Mead and Ruth Benedict, and lasting well after World War II, examined the relationship between personality and culture. The "personality and culture" school adapted the language of psychopathology to describe and analyze cultural phenomena. Still, the thrust of this approach was an abiding skepticism about psychological claims. Relying on ethnographic data, scholars assessed and critiqued universalist claims about the mind. Both Mead and Malinowski drew considerable attention from their challenges to several of Freud's generalizations about human nature, particularly claims about the development of sexuality. Ultimately the appeal of the culture and personality school waned in part as national character studies began more to resemble national stereotypes than cultural analysis, but also in part because the approach increasingly identified the sociocultural level with the psychological level, a move that made most anthropologists uncomfortable.

Much anthropological research, although deliberately apsychological, is nevertheless of genuine cognitive interest in that it investigates knowledge structures, from specific notions to ideological systems. For example, much work has been devoted to examining different notions of person across cultures. In contrast to work in psychology that tends to take the person as a fundamental and invariant concept (see, e.g., Miller and Johnson-Laird 1976), anthropologists challenge the assumption that a person implies a bounded and unique sense of individuality and self. Rather the person is a socially situated concept that can only be understood from the perspective of social and cultural relations (Mauss 1985; Geertz 1973). For instance, Lutz (1988) argues that the Ifaluk of Melanesia do not conceive of emotions as something occurring with an individual person, but as a relation between several individuals in which the emotion exists independent of (and outside) the psyche of any one person. The notion of persons as unique self-oriented entities, in its turn, has been analyzed as arising from the specific cultural and political-economic environments of North America and Europe (Bellah et al. 1985). Like all relativist ideas, these views are controversial. Notice, however, that, unlike the claim that the mind itself is a cultural product, the claim that the person, or the SELF, is socially and culturally constituted is compatible with a naturalistic cognitive science, and has been defended from a naturalistic point of view, for instance by Dennett (1991).

Standard anthropological evidence for the cultural character and variability of notions like "person" consists of cultural narratives and expression of conventional wisdom. More recently, however, researchers in social psychology, CULTURAL PSY-CHOLOGY and ETHNOPSYCHOLOGY have used innovative experimental methods to support ethnographic findings (see Markus and Kityama 1991; Shweder 1991). Shweder and colleagues have made important contributions (in both method and theory) toward integrating ethnographic and experimental approaches. Work on moral development, especially the way culture may fundamentally shape it, has been influential (Shweder, Mahapatra, and Miller 1990; see also Turiel 1983 for a carefully crafted and persuasive challenge to the antiuniversalist point of view).

See also AFFORDANCES; ARTIFACTS AND CIVILIZATION; ATTRIBUTION THEORY; BOUNDED RATIONALITY; CAUSAL REASONING; COGNITIVE ERGONOMICS; CULTURAL PSYCHOLOGY; CULTURAL RELATIVISM; DEDUCTIVE REASONING; DISSONANCE; ECO-LOGICAL PSYCHOLOGY; ECONOMICS AND COGNITIVE SCIENCE; EDUCATION; ETHNOP-SYCHOLOGY; GIBSON, J. J.; HUMAN NAVIGATION; HUMAN-COMPUTER INTERACTION; INDIVIDUALISM; JUDGMENT HEURISTICS; LANGUAGE AND COMMUNICATION; LAN-GUAGE AND CULTURE; PROBABILISTIC REASONING; RATIONAL CHOICE THEORY; RATIONAL DECISION MAKING; SAPIR, EDWARD; SELF; SITUATED COGNITION AND LEARNING; SITUATEDNESS/EMBEDDEDNESS; SOCIAL COGNITION IN ANIMALS; STEREO-TYPING; TVERSKY; VYGOTSKY, LEV

Conclusion

The various strains of research rapidly reviewed in this last section—the Vygotskian, the social-psychological and the anthropological—are extremely fragmented, diverse, and embattled. This should not obscure the fact that they all deal with important and difficult issues, and provide extremely valuable insights. It is encouraging to observe that, in all these approaches, there is a growing concern for explicit theorizing and sound experimental testing. More generally, it seems obvious to us that the various perspectives we have considered in this chapter should be closely articulated, and we have attempted to highlight the works that particularly contribute to this articulation. We are still far from the day when the biological, the cognitive, and the social sciences will develop a common conceptual framework and a common agenda to deal with the major issues that they share.

References

Allport, G. (1954). *The Nature of Prejudice.* Reading, MA: Addison-Wesley.

Atran, S. (1990). *Cognitive Foundation of Natural History.* New York: Cambridge University Press.

Barkow, J., L. Cosmides, and J. Tooby. (1992). *The Adapted Mind: Evolutionary Psychology and the Generation of Culture.* New York: Oxford University Press.

Becker, G. (1976). *The Economic Approach to Human Behavior.* Chicago: University of Chicago Press.

Bellah, R., R. Madsen, W. Sullivan, A. Swidler, and S. Tipton. (1985). *Habits of the Heart: Individualism and Commitment in American Life.* Berkeley: University of California Press.

Berlin, B. (1992). *Ethnobiological Classification: Principles of Categorization of Plants and Animals in Traditional Societies.* Princeton: Princeton University Press.

Berlin, B., D. Breedlove, and P. Raven. (1973). General principles of classification and nomenclature in folk biology. *American Anthropologist* 75: 214–242.

Berlin, B., and P. Kay. (1969). *Basic Color Terms: Their Universality and Growth.* Berkeley: University of California Press.

Bickerton, D. (1990). *Language and Species.* Chicago: University of Chicago Press.

Bloch, M. (1998). *How We Think They Think: Anthropological Approaches to Cognition, Memory, and Literacy.* Boulder: Westview Press.

Boyd, R., and P. Richerson. (1985). *Culture and the Evolutionary Process.* Chicago: University of Chicago Press.

Boyer, P. (1990). *Tradition as Truth and Communication.* New York: Cambridge University Press.

Boyer, P. (1994). *The Naturalness of Religious Ideas: Outline of a Cognitive Theory of Religion.* Los Angeles: University of California Press.

Brown, D. (1991). *Human Universals.* New York: McGraw-Hill.

Bruner, J. (1996). *The Culture of Education.* Cambridge, MA: Harvard University Press.

Buss, D. (1994). *The Evolution Of Desire: Strategies Of Human Mating.* New York: Basic Books.

Byrne, R., and A. Whiten. (1988). *Machiavellian Intelligence: Social Expertise and the Evolution of Intellect in Monkeys, Apes, and Humans.* New York: Oxford University Press.

Carey, S. (1985). *Conceptual Change in Childhood.* Cambridge, MA: MIT Press.

Cavalli-Sforza, L. L., and M. W. Feldman. (1981). *Cultural Transmission and Evolution: A Quantitative Approach.* Princeton: Princeton University Press.

Cheng, P. W., and L. R. Novick. (1992). Covariation in natural causal induction. *Psychological Review* 99: 595–602.

Cosmides, L., and J. Tooby. (1987). From evolution to behavior: Evolutionary psychology as the missing link. In J. Dupré, Ed., *The Latest on the Best: Essays on Evolution and Optimality.* Cambridge, MA: MIT Press.

Cosmides, L., and J. Tooby. (1992). Cognitive adaptations for social exchange. In J. Barkow, L. Cosmides, and J. Tooby, Eds., *The Adapted Mind: Evolutionary Psychology and the Generation of Culture.* New York: Oxford University Press.

D'Andrade, R. (1995). *The Development of Cognitive Anthropology.* New York: Cambridge University Press.

Dawkins, R. (1976). *The Selfish Gene.* New York: Oxford University Press.

Dawkins, R. (1982). *The Extended Phenotype.* San Francisco: W. H. Freeman.

Dennett, D. (1991). *Consciousness Explained.* Boston: Little, Brown.

Durham, W. (1991). *Coevolution: Genes, Cultures, and Human Diversity.* Stanford: Stanford University Press.

Ellen, R. (1993). *The Cultural Relations of Classification.* Cambridge: Cambridge University Press.

Festinger, L. (1957). *A Theory of Cognitive Dissonance.* Palo Alto: Stanford University Press.

Fiske, S., and S. Taylor. (1991). *Social Cognition.* New York: McGraw-Hill.

Fodor, J. (1982). *The Modularity of Mind.* Cambridge, MA: MIT Press.

Fried, M. (1975). *The Notion of Tribe.* Menlo Park: Cummings.

Geertz, C. (1973). *The Interpretation of Cultures.* New York: Basic Books.

Gigerenzer, G., and D. G. Goldstein. (1996). Reasoning the fast and frugal way: Models of bounded rationality. *Psychological Review* 103: 650–669.

Gigerenzer, G., and U. Hoffrage. (1995). How to improve Bayesian reasoning without instruction: Frequency formats. *Psychological Review* 102: 684–704.

Gilbert, D. T., S. T. Fiske, and G. Lindzey, Eds. (1998). *The Handbook of Social Psychology.* 4th ed. New York: McGraw-Hill.

Goody, J. (1977). *The Domestication of the Savage Mind.* Cambridge: Cambridge University Press.

Goody, J. (1987). *The Interface between the Written and the Oral.* Cambridge: Cambridge University Press.

Gumperz, J., and S. Levinson. (1996). *Rethinking Linguistic Relativity.* New York: Cambridge University Press.

Hamilton, W. D. (1964). The genetical theory of social behaviour. *Journal of Theoretical Biology* 7: 1–52.

Heider, F. (1958). *The Psychology of Interpersonal Relations.* New York: Wiley.

Herskovits, M., D. Campbell, and M. Segall. (1969). *A Cross-Cultural Study of Perception.* Indianapolis: Bobbs-Merrill.

Hirschfeld, L. (1995). Do children have a theory of race? *Cognition* 54: 209–252.

Hirschfeld, L. (1996). *Race in the Making: Cognition, Culture, and the Child's Construction of Human Kinds.* Cambridge, MA: MIT Press.

Hirschfeld, L., and S. Gelman. (1994). *Mapping the Mind: Domain-specificity in Cognition and Culture.* New York: Cambridge University Press.

Hutchins, E. (1995). How a cockpit remembers its speed. *Cognitive Science* 19: 265–288.

Inagaki, K., and G. Hatano. (1987). Young children's spontaneous personification and analogy. *Child Development* 58: 1013–1020.

Kahneman, D., P. Slovic, and A. Tversky. (1982). *Judgment under Uncertainty: Heuristics and Biases.* Cambridge: Cambridge University Press.

Kay, P., and W. M. Kempton. (1988). What is the Sapir-Whorf Hypothesis? *American Anthropologist* 86: 65–79.

Keil, F. (1979). *Semantic and Conceptual Development: An Ontological Perspective.* Cambridge, MA: Harvard University Press.

Kelley, H. (1972). Attribution in social interaction. In E. Jones, D. Kanouse, H. Kelley, R. Nisbett, S. Valins, and B. Weiner, Eds., *Attribution: Perceiving the Causes of Behavior.* Morristown, PA: General Learning Press.

Lakoff, G. (1987). *Women, Fire, and Dangerous Things: What Categories Reveal about the Mind.* Chicago: Chicago University Press.

Lakoff, G., and M. Johnson. (1980). *Metaphors We Live By.* Chicago: University of Chicago Press.

Lakoff, G., and M. Turner. (1989). *More Than Cool Reason: A Field Guide to Poetic Metaphor.* Chicago: University of Chicago Press.

Lave, J., M. Murtaugh, and O. de la Rocha. (1984). The dialectic of arithmetic in grocery shopping. In B. Rogoff and J. Lave, Eds., *Everyday Cognition: Its Development in Social Context.* Cambridge, MA: Harvard University Press.

Leach, E. (1954). *Political Systems of Highland Burma: A Study of Kachin Social Structure.* Cambridge, MA: Harvard University Press.

Levinson, S. (1996). Language and space. *Annual Review of Anthropology* 25: 353–382. Palo Alto: Academic Press.

Lévi-Strauss, C. (1971). *L'homme nu.* Paris: Plon.

Levy-Bruhl, L. (1922). *La Mentalité Primitive.* Paris: Libraire Felix Alcan.

Lorenz, K. (1966). *On Aggression.* Translated by M. K. Wilson. New York: Harcourt, Brace and World.

Lucy, J. (1992). *Language Diversity and Thought.* New York: Cambridge University Press.

Lumsden, C., and E. Wilson. (1981). *Genes, Minds, and Culture.* Cambridge, MA: Harvard University Press.

Lutz, C. (1988). *Unnatural Emotions: Everyday Sentiments on a Micronesian Atoll and Their Challenge to Western Theory.* Chicago: University of Chicago Press.

Marks, I., and R. Nesse. (1994). Fear and fitness: An evolutionary analysis of anxiety disorders. *Ethology and Sociobiology* 15: 247–261.

Markus, H., and S. Kityama. (1991). Culture and self: Implications for cognition, emotion, and motivation. *Psychological Review* 98: 224–253.

Mauss, M. (1985). A category of the human mind: The notion of person; the notion of self. In M. Carrithers, S. Collins, and S. Lukes, Eds., *The Category of Person.* New York: Cambridge University Press.

Medin, D., and S. Atran. (1999). *Folk Biology.* Cambridge, MA: MIT Press.

Miller, G., and P. Johnson-Laird. (1976). *Language and Perception.* New York: Cambridge University Press.

Mineka, S., M. Davidson, M. Cook, and R. Keir. (1984). Observational conditioning of snake fear in rhesus monkeys. *Journal of Abnormal Psychology* 93: 355–372.

Nemeroff, C., and P. Rozin. (1994). The contagion concept in adult thinking in the United States: Transmission of germs and interpersonal influence. *Ethos* 22: 158–186.

Nisbett, R., and L. Ross. (1980). *Human Inference: Strategies and Shortcomings of Social Judgment.* Englewoods Cliffs, NJ: Prentice-Hall.

Pinker, S. (1994). *The Language Instinct.* New York: William Morrow.

Premack, D., and G. Woodruff. (1978). Does the chimpanzee have a theory of mind? *Behavioral and Brain Sciences* 1: 516–526.

Quinn, N. (1987). Convergent evidence for a cultural model of American marriage. In D. Holland and N. Quinn, Eds., *Cultural Models in Language and Thought.* New York: Cambridge University Press.

Ramsey, P. (1987). Young children's thinking about ethnic differences. In J. Phinney and M. Rotheram, Eds., *Children's Ethnic Socialization.* Newbury Park, CA: Sage.

Ross, L. (1977). The intuitive psychologist and his shortcomings: Distortions in the attribution process. In L. Berkowitz, Ed., *Advances in Experimental and Social Psychology*, vol. 10. New York: Academic Press.

Ross, L., and R. Nisbett. (1991). *The Person and the Situation: Perspectives of Social Psychology.* Philadelphia: Temple University Press.

Rubin, D. (1995). *Memory in Oral Traditions.* New York: Oxford University Press.

Shweder, R. (1991). *Thinking Through Cultures: Expeditions in Cultural Psychology.* Cambridge, MA: Harvard University Press.

Shweder, R., A. Mahapatra, and J. Miller. (1990). Culture and moral development. In J. Kagan and S. Lamb, Eds., *The Emergence of Morality in Young Children.* Chicago: University of Chicago Press.

Sperber, D. (1975). *Rethinking Symbolism.* New York: Cambridge University Press.

Sperber, D. (1985). Anthropology and psychology: Towards an epidemiology of representations. *Man* 20: 73–89.

Sperber, D. (1996). *Explaining Culture: A Naturalistic Approach.* London: Blackwell.

Sperber, D., D. Premack, and A. Premack, Eds. (1995). *Causal Cognition.* Oxford: Oxford University Press.

Strauss, C., and N. Quinn. (1998). *A Cognitive Theory of Cultural Meaning.* New York: Cambridge University Press.

Symons, D. (1979). *The Evolution of Human Sexuality.* New York: Oxford University Press.

Tooby, J., and L. Cosmides. (1992). The psychological foundations of culture. In J. Barkow, L. Cosmides, and J. Tooby, Eds., *The Adapted Mind: Evolutionary Psychology and the Generation of Culture.* New York: Oxford University Press.

Trivers, R. L. (1971). The evolution of reciprocal altruism. *Quarterly Review of Biology* 46: 35–57.

Turiel, E. (1983). *The Development of Social Knowledge: Morality and Convention.* New York: Cambridge University Press.

Wertsch, J. (1985a). *Culture, Communication, and Cognition: Vygotskian Perspectives.* New York: Cambridge University Press.

Wertsch, J. (1985b). *Vygotsky and the Social Formation of the Mind.* Cambridge, MA: Harvard University Press.

Whorf, B. (1956). *Language, Thought, and Reality: Selected Writings of Benjamin Lee Whorf.* J. Carroll, Ed. New York: Free Press.

Wilson, E. O. (1975). *Sociobiology: The New Synthesis.* Cambridge, MA: Belknap Press of Harvard University Press.

Wilson, E. O. (1978). *On Human Nature.* Cambridge, MA: Harvard University Press.

Further Readings

Barrett, J., and F. Keil. (1996). Conceptualizing a nonnatural entity: Anthromorphism in God concepts. *Cognitive Psychology* 31: 219–247.

Boas, F. (1911). *The Mind of Primitive Man.* New York: Macmillan.

Bock, P. (1994). *Handbook of Psychological Anthropology.* Westport, CT: Greenwood Press.

Bogdan, R. J. (1997). *Interpreting Minds: The Evolution of a Practice.* Cambridge, MA: MIT Press.

Boster, J. (1985). Requiem for the omniscient informant: There's life in the old girl yet. In J. Dougherty, Ed., *Directions in Cognitive Anthropology.* Urbana: University of Illinois Press.

Boyer, P., Ed. (1993). *Cognitive Aspects of Religious Symbolism.* Cambridge, MA: Cambridge University Press.

Bronfenbrenner, U. (1979). *The Ecology of Human Development.* Cambridge, MA: Harvard University Press.

Bruner, J. (1990). *Acts of Meaning.* Cambridge: Harvard University Press.

Bullock, M. (1985). Animism in childhood thinking: A new look at an old question. *Developmental Psychology* 21: 217–225.

Carey, D., and E. Spelke. (1994). Doman-specific knowledge and conceptual change. In L. Hirschfeld and S. Gelman, Eds., *Mapping the Mind: Domain-Specificity in Cognition and Culture.* New York: Cambridge University Press.

Cole, M. (1996). *Cultural Psychology: A Once and Future Discipline.* Cambridge, MA: Harvard University Press.

D'Andrade, R. (1981). The cultural part of cognition. *Cognitive Science* 5: 179–195.

Dehaene, S. (1997). *The Number Sense: How the Mind Creates Mathematics.* New York: Oxford University Press.

Donald, M. (1991). *Origins of the Modern Mind.* Cambridge, MA: Harvard University Press.

Dougherty, J. (1985). *Directions in Cognitive Anthropology.* Urbana: University of Illinois Press.

Fiske, A. (1992). *The Four Elementary Forms of Sociality: Framework for a Unified Theory of Social Relations.* New York: Free Press.

Gallistel, C. (1990). *The Organization of Learning.* Cambridge, MA: MIT Press.

Gallistel, C., and R. Gelman. (1992). Preverbal and verbal counting and computation. Special issues: Numerical cognition. *Cognition* 44: 43–74.

Gelman, R., E. Spelke, and E. Meck. (1983). What preschoolers know about animate and inanimate objects. In D. Rogers and J. Sloboda, Eds., *The Acquisition of Symbolic Skills.* New York: Plenum.

Goodenough, W. (1981). *Culture, Language, and Society.* Menlo Park: Benjamin/Cummings.

Gumperz, J., and S. Levinson. (1996). *Rethinking Linguistic Relativity.* New York: Cambridge University Press.

Hamilton, D. (1981). *Cognitive Processes in Stereotypes and Stereotyping.* Hillsdale, NJ: Erlbaum.

Holland, D., and N. Quinn. (1987). *Cultural Models in Language and Thought.* Cambridge: Cambridge University Press.

Hutchins, E. (1995). *Cognition in the Wild.* Cambridge, MA: MIT Press.

Ingold, T. (1986). *Evolution and Social Life.* New York: Cambridge University Press.

Jones, E., and R. Nisbett. (1972). The actor and the observer: Divergent perceptions of the causes of behavior. In E. Jones, D. Kanouse, H. Kelly, R. Nisbett, S. Valins, B. Weiner, Eds., *Attribution: Perceiving the Causes of Behavior.* Morristown: General Learning Press.

Karmiloff-Smith, A. (1992). *Beyond Modularity: A Developmental Perspective on Cognitive Science.* Cambridge: MIT Press.

Lave, J. (1988). *Cognition in Practice: Mind, Mathematics, and Culture in Everyday Life.* New York: Cambridge University Press.

Lawson, E. T., and R. McCauley. (1990). *Rethinking Religion.* Cambridge: Cambridge University Press

Lévi-Strauss, C. (1966). *The Savage Mind.* Chicago: University of Chicago Press.

Liberman, P. (1984). *The Biology and Evolution of Language.* Cambridg, MAe: Harvard University Press.

Marler, P. (1991). The instinct to learn. In S. Carey and R. Gelman, Eds., *The Epigenesis of Mind: Essays on Biology and Cognition.* Hillsdale, NJ: Erlbaum.

McCloskey, M., A. Washburn, and L. Felch. (1983). Intuitive physics: The straight-down belief and its origin. *Journal of Experimental Psychology: Learning, Memory, and Cognition* 9: 636–649.

Nisbett, R., and D. Cohen. (1995). *The Culture of Honor: The Psychology of Violence in the South.* Boulder: Westview Press.

Norman, D. (1987). *The Psychology of Everyday Things.* Reading: Addison-Wesley.

Olson, D. (1994). *The World on Paper.* New York: Cambridge University Press.

Pinker, S. (1994). *The Language Instinct.* New York: Penguin Books.

Premack, D., and A. Premack. (1983). *The Mind of an Ape.* New York: Norton.

Rogoff, B., and J. Lave. (1984). *Everyday Cognition: Its Development in Social Contexts.* Cambridge, MA: Harvard University Press.

Romney, A., S. Weller, and W. Batchelder. (1986). Culture as consensus: A theory of culture and accuracy. *American Anthropologist* 88: 313–338.

Rozin, P., and J. Schull. (1988). The adaptive-evolutionary point of view in experimental psychology. In R. Atkinson, R. Herrnstein, G. Lindzey, and R. Luce, Eds., *Steven's Handbook of Experimental Psychology.* New York: Wiley.

Sapir, E. (1949). *The Selected Writings of Edward Sapir in Language, Culture and Personality.* D. Mandelbaum, Ed. Berkeley: University of California Press.

Saxe, G. (1985). Developing forms of arithmetic operations among the Oksapmin of Papua New Guinea. *Journal of Educational Psychology* 77: 503–513.

Saxe, G. (1991). *Culture and Cognitive Development: Studies in Mathematical Understanding.* Hillsdale, NJ: Erlbaum.

Scribner, S., and M. Cole. (1981). *The Psychology of Literacy.* Cambridge, MA: Harvard University Press.

Shore, B. (1996). *Culture in Mind: Cognition, Culture and the Problem of Meaning.* New York: Oxford University Press.

Shweder, R., and R. LeVine. (1987). *Culture Theory: Essays on Mind, Self, and Emotion.* New York: Cambridge University Press.

Slobin, D. (1985). *The Crosslinguistic Study of Language Acquisition,* vols. 1 and 2. Hillsdale, NJ: Erlbaum.

Spears, R., P. Oakes, N. Ellemars, and S. Haslam. (1997). *The Social Psychology of Stereotyping and Group Life.* Cambridge: Blackwell.

Spiro, M. (1986). Cultural relativism and the future of anthropology. *Cultural Anthropology* 1: 259–286.

Stigler, J., R. Shweder, and G. Herdt. (1989). *Cultural Psychology: The Chicago Symposia on Culture and Development.* New York: Cambridge University Press.

Suchman, L. (1987). *Plans and Situated Action.* New York: Cambridge University Press.

Tomasello, M., A. Kruger, and H. Ratner. (1993). Cultural learning. *Behavioral and Brain Sciences* 16: 495–552.

Tyler, S. (1969). *Cognitive Anthropology.* New York: Holt, Rinehart, and Winston.

Vygotsky, L. (1986). *Thought and Language.* Cambridge, MA: MIT Press.

Wagner, D. (1994). *Literacy, Culture, and Development.* New York: Cambridge University Press.

Aboutness

See INTENTIONALITY; NARROW CONTENT; REFERENCE, THEORIES OF

Acquisition, Formal Theories of

A formal theory of language acquisition (FTLA) can be defined as a mathematical investigation of the learnability properties of the class of human languages. Every FTLA can therefore be seen as an application of COMPUTATIONAL LEARNING THEORY to the problem of LANGUAGE ACQUISITION, one of the core problems of LEARNING (see also LEARNING SYSTEMS).

The need for FTLAs stems from one of the standard assumptions of linguistics: A successful theory must prove that the grammars proposed by linguists not only account for all linguistic data (descriptive adequacy) but also are the kind of objects that can be acquired on the kind of data and with the kind of cognitive resources that are typical of human language learning (explanatory adequacy).

In order to be properly stated, every FTLA requires four distinct components:

1. A formal characterization of the class L of languages to be learned (see FORMAL GRAMMARS)
2. A formal characterization of the criterion of success C
3. A formal characterization of the class of algorithms A that one is willing to consider as possible learners
4. An explicit characterization M of how linguistic information is presented to the learner.

Given this characterization, every FTLA consists of either a proof that there is at least a learner in A that successfully acquires every language in L when success is defined as in C and data are presented as prescribed by M (a *positive* result) or a proof that there is at least a language in L that no learner in A can successfully acquire according to C and M (a *negative* result).

Although the importance of a positive result (typically the presentation of a model shown as the proof of the existence of a learning algorithm with the desired properties) is obvious, it must not be overlooked that negative results can be just as useful. In fact, as explained earlier, such results can be used to eliminate whole classes of theories that are descriptively but not explanatorily adequate.

Most recent FTLAs assume that, in human language learning, M consists of unordered and simple positive evidence. This assumption rests on twenty years of research in developmental psycholinguistics (reviewed in Marcus 1993), pointing to the conclusion that children receive a largely grammatical set of simple sentences from their target language with very little or no reliable instruction on what sentences are ungrammatical.

The criterion of success C that has been most commonly adopted is *identification in the limit* (Gold 1967): a learner is successful if and only if, for every language in L, it *eventually* stabilizes on a grammar that is equivalent to that of all the other speakers of that language (i.e., it yields the same grammaticality judgments and assigns to sentences the same meanings). Identification in the limit, however, can be argued to be too strict and too liberal a criterion at the same time. The criterion is too strict because the evolution of languages over time (see LANGUAGE VARIATION AND CHANGE) would appear to be problematic, barring language contact, if each generation acquired *exactly* the language of the previous one, as required by the criterion of identification in the limit. The criterion is too weak because children appear to learn their target language(s) in a very short time, whereas identification in the limit considers successful any learner that *eventually* stabilizes on a correct grammar, however long this might take.

These considerations seem to recommend as a plausible alternative the PAC criterion (Probably Approximately Correct; Valian 1984): a learner is successful if and only if, for every language in L, it is very likely (but not certain) to produce a grammar that is very close (but not necessarily equivalent) to the target grammar and do so not in the limit but in a very short time, measured as a function of how close it gets and how likely it is to do so (see COMPUTATIONAL LEARNING THEORY). As an element of a FTLA, however, the PAC criterion is not without problems of its own. For example, if the error of a conjecture with respect to a target language is measured as the probability of the environment in which the language is exhibited, presenting a string that the conjecture misclassifies, then the assumption that children only receive positive evidence has as a consequence that their conjectures have error zero even if they overgeneralize. In this respect, PAC would appear to be too weak a criterion because, empirically, human learners do not appear to overgeneralize in this fashion.

The L and the A components have traditionally been the locus of the most important differences among alternative FTLAs. Common restrictions on A include memory limitations, smoothness (successive hypotheses must not be very different from one another), continuity (every hypothesis is a possible adult grammar), maturation (some possible adult grammars cannot be part of the child's early hypotheses), and so on. A principled investigation of the effects of such restrictions on identification in the limit can be found in Jain et al. (forthcoming). At the time of writing, however, developmental psycholinguists have not reached the kind of consensus on A that was reached on M.

As for the L component, it must be noted that no existing FTLA is based on a formal definition of the class of human languages quite simply because such a definition is currently unavailable. Indeed, some have even argued against the scientific relevance of formally defining a language as a set of strings (Chomsky 1986). In practice, although ultimately an FTLA would have to explain the child's ability to learn *every* aspect of a target language, most existing FTLAs have respected the division of labor that is traditional in linguistics, so that there now are formal theories of the acquisition of SYNTAX, acquisition of PHONOLOGY and acquisition of word meaning.

Within the domain of syntax, for example, several very broad results have been established with respect to classes of languages generated by formal grammars. Positive learnability results have been established for the class of languages generated by suitably restricted Transformational Grammars (Wexler and Culicover 1980), the class generated by rigid CATEGORIAL GRAMMARS (Kanazawa 1994), and the class generated by a recently introduced formalism based on Chomsky's MINIMALISM (Stabler 1997).

It is an open question whether this division of labor can be recommended. Indeed, several *nonformal* theories have advocated one form or other of *bootstrapping,* the view that the acquisition of any one of these domains aids and must be aided by the acquisition of the other domains (see Pinker 1987; Gleitman 1990; Mazuka 1996 for *semantic, syntactic,* and *prosodic bootstrapping* respectively).

Many current FTLAs try to sidestep the problem of the unavailability of a formal characterization of L in two ways, either by explicitly modeling only the fragments of their intended domain (syntax, phonology, SEMANTICS) for which a formal grammar is available or by providing a meta-analysis of the learnability properties of *every* class of languages that can be generated, assuming various kinds of innate restrictions on the possible range of variation of human languages (as dictated, for example, by POVERTY OF THE STIMULUS ARGUMENTS; see also LINGUISTIC UNIVERSALS and INNATENESS OF LANGUAGE). Most such meta-analyses are based either on the Principles and Parameters Hypothesis (Chomsky 1981) or on OPTIMALITY THEORY (Prince and Smolensky 1993). For reviews of such analyses, see Bertolo (forthcoming) and Tesar and Smolensky (forthcoming), respectively. It is instructive to note that exactly the same kind of meta-analysis can be achieved also in connectionist models (see NEURAL NETWORKS and CONNECTIONIST APPROACHES TO LANGUAGE) when certain principled restrictions are imposed on their architecture (Kremer 1996).

—*Stefano Bertolo*

References

Bertolo, S., Ed. (Forthcoming). *Principles and Parameters and Learnability.* Cambridge: Cambridge University Press.

Chomsky, N. (1981). *Lectures on Government and Binding.* Dordrecht: Foris.

Chomsky, N. (1986). *Knowledge of Language: Its Nature, Origins and Use.* New York: Praeger.

Gleitman, L. (1990). The structural sources of verb meaning. *Language Acquisition* 1(1): 3–55.

Gold, M. E. (1967). Language identification in the limit. *Information and Control* 10: 447–474.

Jain, S., D. Osherson, J. Royer, and A. Sharma. (Forthcoming). *Systems That Learn.* 2nd ed. Cambridge, MA: MIT Press.

Kanazawa, M. (1994). *Learnable Classes of Categorial Grammars.* Ph.D. diss., Stanford University.

Kremer, S. (1996). *A Theory of Grammatical Induction in the Connectionist Paradigm.* Ph.D. diss., University of Alberta.

Marcus, G. (1993). Negative evidence in language acquisition. *Cognition* 46(1): 53–85.

Mazuka, R. (1996). Can a grammatical parameter be set before the first word? Prosodic contributions to early setting of a grammatical parameter. In J. L. Morgan and K. Demuth, Eds., *Signal to Syntax: Bootstrapping from Speech to Grammar in Early Acquisition.* Hillsdale, NJ: Erlbaum, pp. 313–330.

Pinker, S. (1987). The bootstrapping problem in language acquisition. In B. MacWhinney, Ed., *Mechanisms of Language Acquisition.* Hillsdale, NJ: Erlbaum, pp. 399–441.

Prince, A., and P. Smolensky. (1993). *Optimality Theory: Constraint Interaction in Generative Grammar.* Technical Report, Center for Cognitive Science, Rutgers University, New Brunswick, NJ.

Stabler, E. (1997). Acquiring and Parsing Languages with Movement. Unpublished manuscript, University of California, Los Angeles.

Tesar, B., and P. Smolensky. (Forthcoming). The learnability of Optimality Theory: an algorithm and some complexity results. *Linguistic Inquiry.*

Valiant, L. G. (1984). A theory of the learnable. *Communications of the ACM* 27: 1134–1142.

Wexler, K., and P. W. Culicover. (1980). *Formal Principles of Language Acquisition.* Cambridge, MA: MIT Press.

Further Readings

Berwick, R. (1985). *The Acquisition of Syntactic Knowledge.* Cambridge, MA: MIT Press.

Bertolo, S. (1995). Maturation and learnability in parametric systems. *Language Acquisition* 4(4): 277–318.

Brent, M. R. (1996). Advances in the computational study of language acquisition. *Cognition* 61: 1–38.

Clark, R. (1992). The selection of syntactic knowledge. *Language Acquisition* 2(2): 83–149.

Clark, R., and I. Roberts. (1993). A computational model of language learnability and language change. *Linguistic Inquiry* 24(2): 299–345.

Clark, R. (1993). Finitude, boundedness and complexity. Learnability and the study of first language acquisition. In B. Lust, G. Hermon, and J. Kornfilt, Eds., *Syntactic Theory and First Language Acquisition: Cross Linguistic Perspectives.* Hillsdale, NJ: Erlbaum, pp. 473–489.

Clark, R. (1996a). *Complexity and the Induction of Tree Adjoining Grammars.* TechReport IRCS-96-14, University of Pennsylvania.

Clark, R. (1996b). *Learning First Order Quantifier Denotations. An Essay in Semantic Learnability.* TechReport IRCS-96-19, University of Pennsylvania.

Dresher, E., and J. Kaye. (1990). A computational learning model for metrical phonology. *Cognition* 34: 137–195.

Fodor, J. (Forthcoming). Unambiguous triggers. *Linguistic Inquiry.*

Frank, R., and S. Kapur. (1996). On the use of triggers in parameter setting. *Linguistic Inquiry* 27(4): 623–660.

Gibson, E., and K. Wexler. (1994). Triggers. *Linguistic Inquiry* 25(3): 407–454.

Niyogi, P., and R. Berwick. (1995). *The Logical Problem of Language Change.* A.I. Memo no. 1516, MIT.

Niyogi, P., and R. Berwick. (1996). A language learning model for finite parameter spaces. *Cognition* 61: 161–193.

Osherson, D., and S. Weinstein. (1984). Natural languages. *Cognition* 12(2): 1–23.

Osherson, D., M. Stob, and S. Weinstein. (1986). *Systems that Learn.* Cambridge, MA: MIT Press.

Osherson, D., D. de Jongh, E. Martin, and S. Weinstein. (1997). Formal learning theory. In J. van Benthem and A. ter Meulen, Eds., *Handbook of Logic and Language.* Amsterdam: North Holland, pp. 737–775.

Pinker, S. (1979). Formal models of language learning. *Cognition* 7: 217–283.

Pinker, S. (1984). *Language Learnability and Language Development*. Cambridge, MA: Harvard University Press.

Wacholder, N. (1995). *Acquiring Syntactic Generalizations from Positive Evidence: An HPSG Model*. Ph.D. diss., City University of New York.

Wexler, K., and R. Manzini. (1987). Parameters and learnability in binding theory. In T. Roeper and E. Williams, Eds., *Parameter Setting*. Dordrecht: Reidel.

Wu, A. (1994). *The Spell-Out Parameters: A Minimalist Approach to Syntax*. Ph.D. diss., University of California, Los Angeles.

Acquisition of Language

See INNATENESS OF LANGUAGE; LANGUAGE ACQUISITION

Acquisition of Phonology

See PHONOLOGY, ACQUISITION OF

Acquisition of Semantics

See SEMANTICS, ACQUISITION OF

Acquisition of Syntax

See SYNTAX, ACQUISITION OF

Action

See EPIPHENOMENALISM; MOTOR CONTROL; MOTOR LEARNING; WALKING AND RUNNING MACHINES

Adaptation and Adaptationism

In current usage a biological adaptation is a trait whose form can be explained by natural selection. The blink reflex, for example, exists because organisms with the reflex were fitter than organisms without this adaptation to protect the eyes. Biological adaptation must be distinguished from physiological adaptation. The fact that human beings can form calluses when their skin is subjected to friction is probably a biological adaptation, but the particular callus caused by my hedge-trimmers is not. The location and form of this particular callus cannot be explained by the differential reproduction of heritable variants, that is, by natural selection. *Adaptation* is still used in its nonevolutionary sense in disciplines such as exercise physiology. An *adaptive trait* is one that currently contributes to the fitness of an organism. The ability to read is highly adaptive, but is unlikely to be an adaptation. Reading is probably a side effect of other, more ancient cognitive abilities. There are also adaptations that are no longer adaptive. The human

appendix is a vestigial trait—a trace of an earlier process of adaptation.

Some authors distinguish adaptations from exaptations (Gould and Vrba 1982). A trait is an exaptation if it is an adaptation for one purpose but is now used for a different purpose. It is unlikely that feathers evolved from scales because they helped the ancestors of birds to fly better. It is thought that they evolved as insulation and were only later exapted for flight. Other authors doubt the value of the exaptation concept (Griffiths 1992; Reeve and Sherman 1993). The importance of the concept of adaptation in biology is that it explains many traits of the organisms we see around us. It explains not only how traits first arose but also why they persisted and why they are still here. If we want to understand why there are so many feathers in the world, their later use in flight is as relevant as their earlier use in thermoregulation.

The adaptation concept underwrites the continuing use of teleology in biology, something that distinguishes life sciences from the physical sciences (Allen, Bekoff, and Lauder 1997). Adaptations have biological purposes or functions—the tasks for which they are adaptations. Hemoglobin is meant to carry oxygen to the tissues. It is not meant to stain the carpet at murder scenes, although it does this just as reliably. Some authors use the term teleonomy to distinguish adaptive purposes from earlier concepts of natural purpose. The fact that the adaptation concept can create naturalistic distinctions between function and malfunction or normal and abnormal has made it of the first interest to cognitive science. Several authors have used the adaptation concept in analyses of INTENTIONALITY.

To identify an adaptation it is necessary to determine the selective forces responsible for the origins and/or maintenance of a trait. This requires understanding the relationship between organism and environment, something more onerous than is typically recognized (Brandon 1990). Some biologists think this task so onerous that we will frequently be unable to determine whether traits are adaptations and for what (Gould and Lewontin 1978; Reeve and Sherman 1993). Others argue that we can successfully engage in both reverse engineering—inferring the adaptive origins of observed traits—and adaptive thinking—inferring what adaptations will be produced in a particular environment (Dennett 1995; Dawkins 1996). Many advocates of EVOLUTIONARY PSYCHOLOGY believe that adaptive thinking about the human mind has heuristic value for those who wish to know how the mind is structured (Cosmides, Tooby, and Barkow 1992).

Adaptationism is the name given by critics to what they see as the misuse of the adaptation concept. Steve Orzack and Elliot Sober (1994) distinguish three views about adaptation: first, that adaptation is ubiquitous, meaning that most traits are subject to natural selection; second, that adaptation is important: a "censored" model that deliberately left out the effects of natural selection would make seriously mistaken predictions about evolution; and third, that adaptation is optimal: a model censored of all evolutionary mechanisms except natural selection could predict evolution accurately. Most biologists accept that natural selection is ubiquitous and important. In Orzack and Sober's view the distinctive feature of adaptationism is the thesis that organisms are frequently optimal. They argue that the adaptationist thesis should be empirically tested rather than assumed. Other authors, however, argue that adaptationism is not an empirical thesis, but a methodological one. Optimality concepts provide a well defined goal which it is equally illuminating to see organisms reach or to fall short of. Building models that yield the observed phenotype as an optimum is the best way to identify all sorts of factors acting in the evolutionary process (Maynard-Smith 1978).

There are several strands to antiadaptationism. One is the claim that many adaptive explanations have been accepted on insufficient evidence. Adaptationists claim that the complexity and functionality of traits is sufficient to establish both that they are adaptations and what they are adaptations for (Williams 1966). Antiadaptationists argue that adaptive scenarios do not receive confirmation merely from being qualitatively consistent with the observed trait. Some are also unsatisfied with quantitative fit between an adaptive model and the observed trait when the variables used to obtain this fit cannot be independently tested (Gray 1987). Many antiadaptationists stress the need to use quantitative comparative tests. Independently derived evolutionary trees can be used to test whether the distribution of a trait in a group of species or populations is consistent with the adaptive hypothesis (Brooks and McLennan 1991; Harvey and Pagel 1991). Other strands of antiadaptationism are concerned with broader questions about what biology should be trying to explain. Biology might focus on explaining why selection is offered a certain range of alternatives rather than explaining why a particular alternative is chosen. This would require greater attention to developmental biology (Smith 1992; Amundson 1994; Goodwin 1994). Another antiadaptationist theme is the importance of history. The outcome of an episode of selection reflects the resources the organism brings with it from the past, as well as the "problem" posed by the environment (Schank and Wimsatt 1986; Griffiths 1996). Finally, antiadaptationists have questioned whether the environment contains adaptive problems that can be characterized independently of the organisms that confront them (Lewontin 1982; Lewontin 1983).

See also ALTRUISM; EVOLUTION; SEXUAL ATTRACTION, EVOLUTIONARY PSYCHOLOGY OF; SOCIOBIOLOGY

—*Paul Griffiths*

References

Allen, C., M. Bekoff, and G. V. Lauder, Eds. (1997). *Nature's Purposes: Analyses of Function and Design in Biology.* Cambridge, MA: MIT Press.

Amundson, R. (1994). Two concepts of constraint: adaptationism and the challenge from developmental biology. *Philosophy of Science* 61(4): 556–578.

Brandon, R. (1990). *Adaptation and Environment.* Princeton: Princeton University Press.

Brooks, D. R., and D. A. McLennan. (1991). *Phylogeny, Ecology and Behavior.* Chicago: University of Chicago Press.

Cosmides, L., J. Tooby, and J. H. Barkow. (1992). Introduction: evolutionary psychology and conceptual integration. In J. H. Barkow, L. Cosmides, and J. Tooby, Eds., *The Adapted Mind: Evolutionary Psychology and the Generation of Culture.* Oxford: Oxford University Press, pp. 3–15.

Dawkins, R. (1996). *Climbing Mount Improbable.* London: Viking.

Dennett, D. C. (1995). *Darwin's Dangerous Idea.* New York: Simon and Schuster.

Goodwin, B. C. (1994). *How the Leopard Changed its Spots: The Evolution of Complexity.* New York: Charles Scribner and Sons.

Gould, J. A., and E. S. Vrba. (1982). Exaptation—a missing term in science of form. *Paleobiology* 8: 4–15.

Gould, S. J., and R. Lewontin. (1978). The Spandrels of San Marco and the Panglossian Paradigm: a critique of the adaptationist programme. *Proceedings of the Royal Society of London* 205: 581–598.

Gray, R. D. (1987). Faith and foraging: a critique of the "paradigm argument from design." In A. C. Kamil, J. R. Krebs and H. R. Pulliam, Eds., *Foraging Behavior.* New York: Plenum Press, pp. 69–140.

Griffiths, P. E. (1992). Adaptive explanation and the concept of a vestige. In P. E. Griffiths, Ed., *Essays on Philosophy of Biology.* Dordrecht: Kluwer, pp. 111–131.

Griffiths, P. E. (1996). The historical turn in the study of adaptation. *British Journal for the Philosophy of Science* 47(4): 511–532.

Harvey, P. H., and M. D. Pagel. (1991). *The Comparative Method in Evolutionary Biology.* Oxford: Oxford University Press.

Lewontin, R. C. (1982). Organism and environment. In H. Plotkin, Ed., *Learning, Development, Culture.* New York: Wiley, pp. 151–170.

Lewontin, R. C. (1983). The organism as the subject and object of evolution. *Scientia* 118: 65–82.

Maynard Smith, J. (1978). Optimisation theory in evolution. *Annual Review of Ecology and Systematics* 9: 31–56.

Orzack, S. E., and E. Sober. (1994). Optimality models and the test of adaptationism. *American Naturalist* 143: 361–380.

Reeve, H. K., and P. W. Sherman. (1993). Adaptation and the goals of evolutionary research. *Quarterly Review of Biology* 68 (1): 1–32.

Schank, J. C., and W. C. Wimsatt. (1986). Generative entrenchment and evolution. *Proceedings of the Philosophy of Science Association.* Vol 2: 33–60.

Smith, K. C. (1992). Neo-rationalism versus neo-Darwinism: integrating development and evolution. *Biology and Philosophy* 7: 431–452.

Williams, G. C. (1966). *Adaptation and Natural Selection.* Princeton: Princeton University Press.

Affordances

The term *affordance* was coined by JAMES JEROME GIBSON to describe the reciprocal relationship between an animal and its environment, and it subsequently became the central concept of his view of psychology, the *ecological* approach (Gibson 1979; Reed 1996; see ECOLOGICAL PSYCHOLOGY). An affordance is a resource or support that the environment offers an animal; the animal in turn must possess the capabilities to perceive it and to use it. "The affordances of the environment are what it offers animals, what it provides or furnishes, for good or ill" (Gibson 1977). Examples of affordances include surfaces that provide support, objects that can be manipulated, substances that can be eaten, climatic events that afford being frozen, like a blizzard, or being warmed, like a fire, and other animals that afford interactions of all kinds. The properties of these affordances must be specified in stimulus information. Even if an animal possesses the appropriate attributes and equipment, it may need to learn to detect the information and to perfect the activities that make the affordance useful—or perilous if unheeded. An affordance, once detected, is meaningful and has value for the animal. It is nevertheless objective, inasmuch as it refers to physical properties of the animal's niche (environmental constraints) and to its bodily dimensions and capacities. An affordance thus exists, whether it is perceived or used or not. It may be detected and used without explicit awareness of doing so.

Affordances vary for diverse animals, depending on the animal's evolutionary niche and on the stage of its development. Surfaces and substances that afford use or are dangerous for humans may be irrelevant for a flying or swimming species, and substances that afford eating by an adult of the species may not be appropriate for a member in a larval stage. The reciprocal relationship between the environmental niche and a certain kind of animal has been dubbed the "animal-environment fit."

Utilization of an affordance implies a second reciprocal relationship between perception and action. Perception provides the information for action, and action generates consequences that inform perception. This information may be proprioceptive, letting the animal know how its body is performing; but information is also exteroceptive, reflecting the way the animal has changed the environmental context with respect to the affordance. Perceiving this relationship allows adaptive control of action and hence the possibility of controlling environmental change.

It is the functioning and description of the animal-environment encounter that is at the heart of research on affordances. Research has addressed three principal questions:

1. Do human adults actually perceive affordances in terms of task constraints and bodily requirements? The reality of perceptual detection of an animal-environment fit has been verified in experiments on adult humans passing through an aperture, reaching for objects with their own limbs or tools, judging appropriate stair heights for climbing, chair heights for sitting, and so forth. J. J. Gibson said that "to perceive the world is to coperceive oneself." In that case, actors should perceive their own body dimensions and powers in relation to the requirements of the relevant environmental resource or support. Warren and Whang (1987) investigated adults' judgments of aperture widths relative to their own body dimensions. Both wide- and narrow-shouldered adults rotated their shoulders when doorways were less than 1.3 times their own shoulder width. Scaling of the environment in terms of the natural yardstick of eye-height (Mark 1987; Warren 1984) has also been demonstrated.

2. Can stimulus information specifying an affordance be described and measured? Can controlled actions of an animal preparing for and acting on an affordance be observed and measured? Gibson (1950) paved the way for this research by describing the optic flow field created by one's own locomotion when flying a plane. The specification by optical stimulus information of the time for a moving ani-

mal to contact a surface or a target object was described by Lee (1980), who showed that such information for an observer approaching a surface could be expressed as a constant, τ. The information is used in controlling locomotion during braking and imminent collision by humans (Lee 1976) and by other animals (Lee and Reddish 1981; Lee, Reddish, and Rand 1991). Effective information for heading (the direction in which one is going) has been described by Warren (1995) in terms of the global radial structure of the velocity field of a layout one is moving toward.

Research on the action systems called into play and their controllability in utilizing an affordance has been the subject of study for reaching, standing upright, locomotion, steering, and so on. (Warren 1995). The control of reaching and grasping by infants presented with objects of diverse sizes shows accommodation of action to the object's size and shape by hand shaping, use of one or both arms, and so forth (see Bertenthal and Clifton 1997 for many details). Research of the specification of the affordance in stimulus information, and on control of action in realizing the affordance, converges in demonstrating that behavior is prospective (planned and intentional) and that stimulus information permits this anticipatory feature.

3. How do affordances develop cognitively and behaviorally? Developmental studies of affordances, especially during the first year, abound (Adolph, Eppler, and Gibson 1993). The behavior of crawling infants on a visual cliff (Gibson and Walk 1960) suggests that even infants perceive the affordances of a surface of support and avoid traversal of an apparent drop at an edge. Subsequent research has shown that duration of crawling experience is significantly related to dependable avoidance of the cliff, supporting other research demonstrating that LEARNING plays a role in detecting and responding effectively to many affordances, at least in humans. Development of action systems and increased postural control instigate the emergence of new affordance-related behavior. Babies begin to pay ATTENTION to objects and make exploratory reaches toward them as posture gradually enables reaching out and making contact with their surfaces (Eppler 1995).

As an infant learns about the constraints involved in the use of some affordance, learning may at first be relatively domain specific. Research by Adolph (1997) on traversal of sloping surfaces by crawling infants demonstrates that learning which slopes are traversable and strategies for successful traversal of them is not transferred automatically to traversal of the same slopes when the infant first begins upright locomotion. New learning is required to control the action system for walking and to assess the safety of the degree of slope. Learning about affordances is a kind of perceptual learning, entailing detection of both proprioceptive and exteroceptive information. The learning process involves exploratory activity, observation of consequences, and selection for an affordance fit and for economy of both specifying information and action.

The concept of affordance is central to a view of psychology that is neither mentalism nor stimulus-response BEHAVIORISM, focusing instead on how an animal interacts with its environment. Furthermore, the concept implies neither nativism nor empiricism. Rather, genetic constraints characteristic of any particular animal instigate exploratory activity that culminates in learning what its environment affords for it.

See also COGNITIVE ARTIFACTS; DOMAIN-SPECIFICITY; HUMAN NAVIGATION; INFANT COGNITION; PERCEPTUAL DEVELOPMENT; SITUATEDNESS/EMBEDDEDNESS

—*Eleanor J. Gibson, Karen Adolph, and Marion Eppler*

References

Adolph, K. E. (1997). *Learning in the Development of Infant Locomotion.* Monographs of the Society for Research in Child Development.

Adolph, K. E., M. A. Eppler, and E. J. Gibson. (1993). Development of perception of affordances. In C. Rovee-Collier and L. P. Lipsitt, Eds., *Advances in Infancy Research.* Norwood, NJ: Ablex Publishing Co., pp. 51–98.

Bertenthal, B. I., and R. Clifton. (1997). Perception and action. In D. Kuhn and R. Siegler, Eds., *Handbook of Child Psychology* Vol. 2. New York: Wiley.

Eppler, M. A. (1995). Development of manipulatory skills and deployment of attention. *Infant Behavior and Development* 18: 391–404.

Gibson, E. J., and R. D. Walk. (1960). The "visual cliff." *Scientific American* 202: 64–71.

Gibson, J. J. (1950). *The Perception of the Visual World.* Boston: Houghton Mifflin.

Gibson, J. J. (1977). The theory of affordances. In R. Shaw and J. Bransford, Eds., *Perceiving, Acting and Knowing.* New York: Wiley, pp. 67–82.

Gibson, J. J. (1979). *The Ecological Approach to Visual Perception.* Boston: Houghton Mifflin.

Lee, D. N. (1976). A theory of visual control of braking based on information about time-to-collision. *Perception* 5: 437–459.

Lee, D. N. (1980). The optic flow field: the foundation of vision. *Philosophical Transactions of the Royal Society* B290: 169–179.

Lee, D. N., and P. E. Reddish. (1981). Plummeting gannets: paradigm of ecological optics. *Nature* 293: 293–294.

Lee, D. N., P. E. Reddish, and D. T. Rand. (1991). Aerial docking by hummingbirds. *Naturwissenschafften* 78: 526–527.

Mark, L. S. (1987). Eyeheight-scaled information about affordances: a study of sitting and stair climbing. *Journal of Experimental Psychology: Human Perception and Performance* 13: 683–703.

Reed, E. (1996). *Encountering the World.* New York: Oxford University Press.

Warren, W. H., Jr. (1984). Perceiving affordances: visual guidance of stair climbing. *Journal of Experimental Psychology: Human Perception and Performance* 10: 683–703.

Warren, W. H., Jr. (1995). Self-motion: visual perception and visual control. In W. Epstein and S. Rogers, Eds., *Perception of Space and Motion.* New York: Academic Press, pp. 263–325.

Warren, W. H., Jr., and S. C. Whang. (1987). Visual guidance of walking through apertures: body-scaled information for affordances. *Journal of Experimental Psychology: Human Perception and Performance* 13: 371–383.

Agency

See INTELLIGENT AGENT ARCHITECTURE; RATIONAL AGENCY

Aging and Cognition

Any discussion of the relations between aging and cognition must acknowledge a distinction between two types of cognition that are sometimes referred to as *fluid* and *crystallized* cognitive abilities (Cattell 1972) or INTELLIGENCE. Fluid abilities include various measures of reasoning (including both CAUSAL REASONING and DEDUCTIVE REASONING), MEMORY, and spatial performance, and can be characterized as reflecting the efficiency of processing at the time of assessment. In contrast, crystallized abilities are evaluated with measures of word meanings, general information, and other forms of knowledge, and tend to reflect the accumulated products of processing carried out in the past.

The distinction between these two types of abilities is important because the relations of age are quite different for the two forms of cognition. That is, performance on crystallized measures tends to remain stable, or possibly even increase slightly, across most of the adult years, whereas increased age is associated with decreases in many measures of fluid cognition. In large cross-sectional studies age-related declines in fluid abilities are often noticeable as early as the decade of the thirties, and the magnitude of the difference across a range from twenty to seventy years of age is frequently one to two standard deviation units. Although the average trends can be quite large, it is also important to point out that individual differences are substantial because chronological age by itself seldom accounts for more than 20 to 30 percent of the total variance in the scores.

The vast majority of the research in the area of aging and cognition has focused on fluid abilities. There appear to be two primary reasons for this emphasis. First, many researchers probably believe that explanations are clearly needed to account for the differences that have been reported (as in fluid abilities), but that a lack of a difference (as in crystallized abilities) does not necessarily require an explanation. And second, because fluid abilities are assumed to reflect the individual's current status, they are often considered to be of greater clinical and practical significance than crystallized abilities that are assumed to represent the highest level the individual achieved at an earlier stage in his or her life.

Both distal and proximal interpretations of the age-related decline in fluid cognitive abilities have been proposed. Distal interpretations focus on factors from earlier periods in the individual's life that may have contributed to his or her level of performance at the current time. Examples are speculations that the age-related declines are attributable to historical changes in the quantity or quality of education, or to various unspecified cultural characteristics that affect cognitive performance. In fact, comparisons of the scores of soldiers in World War II with the norms from World War I (Tuddenham 1948), and a variety of time-lag comparisons reported by Flynn (1987), suggest that the average level of cognitive ability has been improving across successive generations. However, the factors responsible for these improvements have not yet been identified (see Neisser 1997), and questions still remain about the implications of the positive time-lag effects for the interpretation of cross-sectional age differences in cognitive functioning (see

Salthouse 1991). Hypotheses based on differential patterns of activity and the phenomenon of disuse can also be classified as distal because they postulate that an individual's current level of performance is at least partially affected by the nature and amount of activities in which he or she has engaged over a period of years. Although experientially based interpretations are very popular among the general public (as exemplified in the cliché "Use it or lose it") and among many researchers, there is still little convincing evidence for this interpretation. In particular, it has been surprisingly difficult to find evidence of interactions of age and quality or quantity of experience on measures of fluid cognitive abilities that would be consistent with the view that age-related declines are minimized or eliminated among individuals with extensive amounts of relevant experience.

Proximal interpretations of age-related differences in cognitive functioning emphasize characteristics of processing at the time of assessment that are associated with the observed levels of cognitive performance. Among the proximal factors that have been investigated in recent years are differences in the choice or effectiveness of particular strategies, differences in the efficiency of specific processing components, and alterations in the quantity of some type of processing resource (such as WORKING MEMORY, ATTENTION, or processing speed), presumed to be required for many different types of cognitive tasks. Hypotheses based on speculations about the neuroanatomical substrates of cognitive functioning (such as dopamine deficiencies or frontal lobe impairments) might also be classified as proximal because they have primarily focused on linking age-related changes in biological and cognitive characteristics, and not in speculating about the origins of either of those differences. However, not all neurobiological mechanisms are necessarily proximal because some may operate to affect the susceptibility of structures or processes to changes that occur at some time in the future.

A fundamental issue relevant to almost all proximal interpretations concerns the number of distinct influences that are contributing to age-related differences in cognitive functioning. Moderate to large age-related differences have been reported on a wide variety of cognitive variables, and recent research (e.g., Salthouse 1996) indicates that only a relatively small proportion of the age-related effects on a given variable are independent of the age-related effects on other cognitive variables. Findings such as these raise the possibility that a fairly small number of independent causal factors may be responsible for the age-related differences observed in many variables reflecting fluid aspects of cognition. However, there is still little consensus regarding the identity of those factors or the mechanisms by which they exert their influence.

See also AGING AND MEMORY; COGNITIVE DEVELOPMENT; EXPERTISE; INFANT COGNITION; WORD MEANING, ACQUISITION OF

—Timothy Salthouse

References

Cattell, R. B. (1972). *Abilities: Their Structure, Growth, and Action.* Boston: Houghton Mifflin.
Flynn, J. R. (1987). Massive IQ gains in 14 nations: what IQ tests really measure. *Psychological Bulletin* 101: 171–191.
Neisser, U. (1997). Rising scores on intelligence tests. *American Scientist* 85: 440–447.
Salthouse, T. A. (1991). *Theoretical Perspectives on Cognitive Aging.* Mahwah, NJ: Erlbaum.
Salthouse, T. A. (1996). Constraints on theories of cognitive aging. *Psychonomic Bulletin and Review* 3: 287–299.
Tuddenham, R. D. (1948). Soldier intelligence in World Wars I and II. *American Psychologist* 3: 54–56.

Further Readings

Blanchard-Fields, F., and T. M. Hess. (1996). *Perspectives on Cognitive Change in Adulthood and Aging.* New York: McGraw-Hill.
Craik, F. I. M., and T. A. Salthouse. (1992). *Handbook of Aging and Cognition.* Mahwah, NJ: Erlbaum.

Aging, Memory, and the Brain

Memory is not a unitary function but instead encompasses a variety of dissociable processes mediated by distinct brain systems. *Explicit* or *declarative* memory refers to the conscious recollection of facts and events, and is known to critically depend on a system of anatomically related structures that includes the HIPPOCAMPUS and adjacent cortical regions in the medial temporal lobe. This domain of function contrasts with a broad class of memory processes involving the tuning or biasing of behavior as a result of experience. A distinguishing feature of these *implicit* or *nondeclarative* forms of memory is that they do not rely on conscious access to information about the episodes that produced learning. Thus, implicit memory proceeds normally independent of the medial temporal lobe structures damaged in amnesia. Although many important issues remain to be resolved concerning the organization of multiple memory systems in the brain, this background of information has enabled substantial progress toward defining the neural basis of age-related cognitive decline.

Traditionally, moderate neuron death, distributed diffusely across multiple brain regions, was thought to be an inevitable consequence of aging. Seminal studies by Brody (1955) supported this view, indicating neuron loss progresses gradually throughout life, totaling more than 50 percent in many cortical areas by age ninety-five (Brody 1955, 1970). Although not all regions of the brain seemed to be affected to the same degree, significant decreases in cell number were reported for both primary sensory and associational areas of cortex. Thus, the concept emerged from early observations that diffusely distributed neuron death might account for many of the cognitive impairments observed during aging (Coleman and Flood 1987).

In recent years, the application of new and improved methods for estimating cell number has prompted substantial revision in traditional views on age-related neuron loss. A primary advantage of these modern stereological techniques, relative to more traditional approaches, is that they are specifically designed to yield estimates of total neuron number in a region of interest, providing an unambiguous measure for examining potential neuron loss with age (West 1993a). Stereological tools have been most widely applied in recent studies to reevaluate the effects of age on neuron number in the hippocampus. In addition to the known importance of this structure for normal explicit memory, early research using older methods suggested that the hippocampus is especially susceptible to age-related cell death, and that this effect is most pronounced among aged subjects with documented deficits in hippocampal-dependent learning and memory (Issa et al. 1990; Meaney et al. 1988). The surprising conclusion from investigations using stereological techniques, however, is that the total number of principal neurons (i.e., the granule cells of the dentate gyrus, and pyramidal neurons in the CA3 and CA1 fields) is entirely preserved in the aged hippocampus. Parallel results have been observed in all species examined, including rats, monkeys and humans (Peters et al. 1996; Rapp 1995; Rapp and Gallagher 1996; Rasmussen et al. 1996; West 1993b). Moreover, hippocampal neuron number remains normal even among aged individuals with pronounced learning and memory deficits indicative of hippocampal dysfunction (Peters et al. 1996; Rapp 1995; Rapp and Gallagher 1996; Rasmussen et al. 1996). Contrary to traditional views, these findings indicate that hippocampal cell death is not an inevitable consequence of aging, and that age-related learning and memory impairment does not require the presence of frank neuronal degeneration.

Quantitative data on neuron number in aging are not yet available for all of the brain systems known to participate in LEARNING and MEMORY. However, like the hippocampus, a variety of other cortical regions also appear to maintain a normal complement of neurons during non-pathological aging. This includes dorsolateral aspects of the prefrontal cortex that participate in processing spatiotemporal attributes of memory (Peters et al. 1994), and unimodal visual areas implicated in certain forms of implicit memory function (Peters, Nigro, and McNally 1997). By contrast, aging is accompanied by substantial subcortical cell loss, particularly among neurochemically specific classes of neurons that originate ascending projections to widespread regions of the cortex. Acetylcholine containing neurons in the basal forebrain have been studied intensively in this regard, based partly on the observation that this system is the site of profound degeneration in pathological disorders of aging such as Alzheimer's disease. A milder degree of cholinergic cell loss is also seen during normal aging, affecting cell groups that project to the hippocampus, AMYGDALA, and neocortex (Armstrong et al. 1993; de Lacalle, Iraizoz, and Ma Gonzalo 1991; Fischer et al. 1991; Stroessner-Johnson, Rapp, and Amaral 1992). Information processing functions mediated by these target regions might be substantially disrupted as a consequence of cholinergic degeneration, and, indeed, significant correlations have been documented between the magnitude of cell loss and behavioral impairment in aged individuals (Fischer et al. 1991). Together with changes in other neurochemically specific projection systems, subcortical contributions to cognitive aging may be substantial. These findings also highlight the concept that neuron loss during normal aging appears to preferentially affect subcortical brain structures, sparing many cortical regions. Defining the cell biological mechanisms that confer this regional vulnerability or protection remains a significant challenge.

Research on the neuroanatomy of cognitive aging has also examined the possibility that changes in connectivity might contribute to age-related deficits in learning and memory supported by the hippocampus. The entorhinal cortex originates a major source of cortical input to the hippocampus, projecting via the perforant path to synapse on the distal dendrites of the dentate gyrus granule cells, in outer portions of the molecular layer. Proximal dendrites of the granule cells, in contrast, receive an intrinsic hippocampal input arising from neurons in the hilar region of the dentate gyrus. This strict laminar segregation, comprised of nonoverlapping inputs of known origin, provides an attractive model for exploring potential age-related changes in hippocampal connectivity. Ultrastructural studies, for example, have demonstrated that a morphologically distinct subset of synapses is depleted in the dentate gyrus molecular layer during aging in the rat (Geinisman et al. 1992). Moreover, the magnitude of this loss in the termination zone of the entorhinal cortex is greatest among aged subjects with documented deficits on tasks sensitive to hippocampal damage, and in older animals that display impaired cellular plasticity in the hippocampus (de Toledo-Morrell, Geinisman, and Morrell 1988; Geinisman, de Toledo-Morrell, and Morrell 1986).

The same circuitry has been examined in the aged monkey using confocal laser microscopy to quantify the density of N-methyl-D-aspartate (NMDA) and non-NMDA receptor subunits. Aged monkeys display a substantial reduction in NMDA receptor labeling that is anatomically restricted to outer portions of the molecular layer that receive entorhinal cortical input (Gazzaley et al. 1996). The density of non-NMDA receptor subunits is largely preserved. Although the impact of this change on cognitive function has not been evaluated directly, the findings are significant because NMDA receptor activity is known to play a critical role in cellular mechanisms of hippocampal plasticity (i.e., LTP). Thus, a testable prediction derived from these observations is that the status of hippocampal-dependent learning and memory may vary as a function of the magnitude of NMDA receptor alteration in the aged monkey. Studies of this sort, combining behavioral and neurobiological assessment in the same individuals, are a prominent focus of current research on normal aging.

A solid background of evidence now exists concerning the nature, severity and distribution of structural alterations in the aged brain. The mechanisms responsible for these changes, however, are only poorly understood. Molecular biological techniques are increasingly being brought to bear on this issue, revealing a broad profile of age-related effects with significant implications for cell structure and function (Sugaya et al. 1996). Although incorporating these findings within a neuropsychological framework will undoubtedly prove challenging, current progress suggests that molecular, neural-systems, and behavioral levels of analysis may soon converge on a more unified understanding of normal cognitive aging.

See also AGING AND COGNITION; IMPLICIT VS. EXPLICIT MEMORY; LONG-TERM POTENTIATION; WORKING MEMORY, NEURAL BASIS OF

—*Peter Rapp*

References

Armstrong, D. M., R. Sheffield, G. Buzsaki, K. Chen, L. B. Hersh, B. Nearing, and F. H. Gage. (1993). Morphologic alterations of choline acetyltransferase-positive neurons in the basal forebrain of aged behaviorally characterized Fisher 344 rats. *Neurobiology of Aging* 14: 457–470.

Brody, H. (1955). Organization of the cerebral cortex. III. A study of aging in the human cerebral cortex. *Journal of Comparative Neurology* 102: 511–556.

Brody, H. (1970). Structural changes in the aging nervous system. *Interdisciplinary Topics in Gerontology* 7: 9–21.

Coleman, P. D., and D. G. Flood. (1987). Neuron numbers and dendritic extent in normal aging and Alzheimer's disease. *Neurobiology of Aging* 8(6): 521–545.

de Lacalle, S., I. Iraizoz, and L. Ma Gonzalo. (1991). Differential changes in cell size and number in topographic subdivisions of human basal nucleus in normal aging. *Neuroscience* 43(2/3): 445–456.

de Toledo-Morrell, L., Y. Geinisman, and F. Morrell. (1988). Individual differences in hippocampal synaptic plasticity as a function of aging: Behavioral, electrophysiological and morphological evidence. *Neural Plasticity: A Lifespan Approach*. Alan R. Liss, Inc., pp. 283–328.

Fischer, W., K. S. Chen, F. H. Gage, and A. Björklund. (1991). Progressive decline in spatial learning and integrity of forebrain cholinergic neurons in rats during aging. *Neurobiology of Aging* 13: 9–23.

Gazzaley, A. H., S. J. Siegel, J. H. Kordower, E. J. Mufson, and J. H. Morrison. (1996). Circuit-specific alterations of N-methyl-D-aspartate receptor subunit 1 in the dentate gyrus of aged monkeys. *Proceedings of the National Academy of Science, USA* 93: 3121–3125.

Geinisman, Y., L. de Toledo-Morrell, and F. Morrell. (1986). Loss of perforated synapses in the dentate gyrus: morphological substrate of memory deficit in aged rats. *Proceedings of the National Academy of Science USA* 83: 3027–3031.

Geinisman, Y., L. de Toledo-Morrell, F. Morrell, I. S. Persina, and M. Rossi. (1992). Age-related loss of axospinous synapses formed by two afferent systems in the rat dentate gyrus as revealed by the unbiased stereological dissector technique. *Hippocampus* 2: 437–444.

Issa, A. M., W. Rowe, S. Gauthier, and M. J. Meaney. (1990). Hypothalamic-pituitary-adrenal activity in aged, cognitively impaired and cognitively unimpaired rats. *Journal of Neuroscience* 10(10): 3247–3254.

Meaney, M. J., D. H. Aitken, C. van Berkel, S. Bhatnagar, and R. M. Sapolsky. (1988). Effect of neonatal handling on age-related impairments associated with the hippocampus. *Science* 239: 766–768.

Peters, A., D. Leahy, M. B. Moss, and K. J. McNally. (1994). The effects of aging on area 46 of the frontal cortex of the rhesus monkey. *Cerebral Cortex* 4(6): 621–635.

Peters, A., N. J. Nigro, and K. J. McNally. (1997). A further evaluation of the effect of age on striate cortex of the rhesus monkey. *Neurobiology of Aging* 18: 29–36.

Peters, A., D. L. Rosene, M. B. Moss, T. L. Kemper, C. R. Abraham, J. Tigges, and M. S. Albert. (1996). Neurobiological bases of age-related cognitive decline in the rhesus monkey. *Journal of Neuropathology and Experimental Neurology* 55: 861–874.

Rapp, P. R. (1995). Cognitive neuroscience perspectives on aging in nonhuman primates. In T. Nakajima and T. Ono, Eds., *Emotion, Memory and Behavior*. Tokyo: Japan Scientific Societies Press, pp 197–211.

Rapp, P. R., and M. Gallagher. (1996). Preserved neuron number in the hippocampus of aged rats with spatial learning deficits. *Proceedings of the National Academy of Science, USA* 93: 9926–9930.

Rasmussen, T., T. Schliemann, J. C. Sorensen, J. Zimmer and M. J. West. (1996). Memory impaired aged rats: no loss of principal hippocampal and subicular neurons. *Neurobiology of Aging* 17(1): 143–147.

Stroessner-Johnson, H. M., P. R. Rapp, and D. G. Amaral. (1992). Cholinergic cell loss and hypertrophy in the medial septal nucleus of the behaviorally characterized aged rhesus monkey. *Journal of Neuroscience* 12(5): 1936–1944.

Sugaya, K., M. Chouinard, R. Greene, M. Robbins, D. Personett, C. Kent, M. Gallagher, and M. McKinney. (1996). Molecular indices of neuronal and glial plasticity in the hippocampal formation in a rodent model of age-induced spatial learning impairment. *Journal of Neuroscience* 16(10): 3427–3443.

West, M. J. (1993a). New stereological methods for counting neurons. *Neurobiology of Aging* 14: 275–285.

West, M. J. (1993b). Regionally specific loss of neurons in the aging human hippocampus. *Neurobiology of Aging* 14: 287–293.

Further Readings

Barnes, C. A. (1990). Animal models of age-related cognitive decline. In F. Boller and J. Grafman, Eds., *Handbook of Neuropsychology*, vol. 4. Amsterdam: Elsevier Science Publishers B.V., pp. 169–196.

Barnes, C. A. (1994). Normal aging: regionally specific changes in hippocampal synaptic transmission. *Trends in Neuroscience* 17(1): 13–18.

Gallagher, M., and P. R. Rapp. (1997). The use of animal models to study the effects of aging on cognition. *Annual Review of Psychology* 339–370.

Grady, C. L., A. R. McIntosh, B. Horwitz, J. Ma. Maisog, L. G. Ungerleider, M. J. Mentis, P. Pietrini, M. B. Schapiro, and J. V. Haxby. (1995). Age-related reductions in human recognition memory due to impaired encoding. *Science* 269: 218–221.

Salthouse, T. A. (1991). *Theoretical Perspectives on Cognitive Aging*. Hillsdale, NJ: Erlbaum.

Schacter, D. L., C. R. Savage, N. M. Alpert, S. L. Rauch, and M. S. Albert. (1996). The role of hippocampus and frontal cortex in age-related memory changes: a PET study. *NeuroReport* 11: 1165–1169.

AI

See INTRODUCTION: COMPUTATIONAL INTELLIGENCE; AI AND EDUCATION; COGNITIVE MODELING, SYMBOLIC

AI and Education

Perhaps computers could educate our children as well as the best human tutors. This dream has inspired decades of work in cognitive science. The first generation of computer tutoring systems (called Computer Aided Instruction or Computer Based Instruction) were essentially hypertext. They mostly just presented material, asked multiple-choice questions, and branched to further presentations depending on the student's answer (Dick and Carey 1990).

The next generation of tutoring systems (called Intelligent CAI or Intelligent Tutoring Systems) were based on building knowledge of the subject matter into the computer. There were two types. One coached students as they worked complex, multiminute problems, such as troubleshooting an electronic circuit or writing a computer program. The other type attempted to carry on a Socratic dialog with students. The latter proved to be very difficult, in part due to the problem of understanding unconstrained natural language (see NATURAL LANGUAGE PROCESSING). Few Socratic tutors have been built. Coached practice systems, however, have enjoyed a long and productive history.

A coached practice system usually contains four basic components:

1. An environment in which the student works on complex tasks. For instance, it might be a simulated piece of electronic equipment that the student tries to troubleshoot.
2. An expert system that can solve the tasks that the student works on (see KNOWLEDGE-BASED SYSTEMS).
3. A student modeling module that compares the student's behavior to the expert system's behavior in order to both recognize the student's current plan for solving the problem and determine what pieces of knowledge the student is probably using.
4. A pedagogical module that suggests tasks to be solved, responds to the students' requests for help and points out mistakes. Such responses and suggestions are based on the tutoring system's model of the student's knowledge and plans.

Any of these components may utilize AI technology. For instance, the environment might contain a sophisticated simulation or an intelligent agent (see INTELLIGENT AGENT ARCHITECTURE), such as a simulated student (called co-learners) or a wily opponent. The student modeling module's job includes such classic AI problems as plan recognition and uncertain reasoning (see UNCERTAINTY). The pedagogical module's job includes monitoring an instructional plan and adapting it as new information about the student's competence is observed. Despite the immense potential complexity, many intelligent tutoring systems have been built, and some are in regular use in schools, industry, and the military.

Although intelligent tutoring systems are perhaps the most popular use of AI in education, there are other applications as well. A common practice is to build an environment without the surrounding expert system, student modeling module, or pedagogical module. The environment enables student activities that stimulate learning and may be impossible to conduct in the real world. For instance, an environment might allow students to conduct simulated physics experiments on worlds where gravity is reduced, absent, or even negative. Such environments are called interactive learning environments or microworlds. A new trend is to use networking to allow several students to work together in the same environment. Like intelligent tutoring systems, many intelligent environments have been built and used for real educational and training needs.

Other applications of AI in education include (1) using AI planning technology to design instruction; (2) using student modeling techniques to assess students' knowledge on the basis of their performance on complex tasks, a welcome alternative to the ubiquitous multiple-choice test; and (3) using AI techniques to construct interesting simulated worlds (often called "microworlds") that allow students to discover important domain principles.

Cognitive studies are particularly important in developing AI applications to education. Developing the expert module of a tutoring system requires studying experts as they solve problems in order to understand and formalize their knowledge (see KNOWLEDGE ACQUISITION). Developing an effective pedagogical module requires understanding how students learn so that the tutor's comments will prompt students to construct their own understanding of the subject matter. An overly critical or didactic tutor may do more harm than good. A good first step in developing an application is to study the behavior of expert human tutors in order to see how they increase the motivation and learning of students.

However, AI applications often repay their debt to empirical cognitive science by contributing results of their own. It is becoming common to conduct rigorous evaluations of the educational effectiveness of AI-based applications. The evaluations sometimes contrast two or more versions of the same system. Such controlled experiments often shed light on important cognitive issues.

At this writing, there are no current textbooks on AI and education. Wenger (1987) and Polson and Richardson (1988) cover the fundamental concepts and the early systems. Recent work generally appears first in the proceedings of the AI and Education conference (e.g., Greer 1995) or the Intelligent Tutoring Systems conference (e.g., Frasson, Gauthier, and Lesgold 1996). Popular journals for this work include *The International Journal of AI and Education* (http://cbl.leeds.ac.uk/ijaied/), *The Journal of the Learning Sciences* (Erlbaum) and *Interactive Learning Environments* (Ablex).

See also EDUCATION; HUMAN-COMPUTER INTERACTION; READING

—*Kurt VanLehn*

References

Dick, W., and S. Carey. (1990). *The Systematic Design of Instruction.* 3rd ed. New York: Scott-Foresman.

Frasson, C., G. Gauthier, and A. Lesgold, Eds. (1996). *Intelligent Tutoring Systems: Third International Conference, ITS96.* New York: Springer.

Greer, J., Ed. (1995). *Proceedings of AI-Ed 95.* Charlottesville, NC: Association for the Advancement of Computing in Education.

Polson, M. C., and J. J. Richardson. (1988). *Foundations of Intelligent Tutoring Systems.* Hillsdale, NJ: Erlbaum.

Wenger, E. (1987). *Artificial Intelligence and Tutoring Systems.* San Mateo, CA: Morgan Kaufmann.

Algorithm   11

Algorithm

An *algorithm* is a recipe, method, or technique for doing something. The essential feature of an algorithm is that it is made up of a *finite* set of rules or operations that are unambiguous and simple to follow (computer scientists use technical terms for these two properties: *definite* and *effective,* respectively). It is obvious from this definition that the notion of an algorithm is somewhat imprecise, a feature it shares with all foundational mathematical ideas—for instance, the idea of a set. This imprecision arises because being unambiguous and simple are relative, context-dependent terms. However, usually algorithms are thought of as recipes, methods, or techniques for getting *computers* to do something, and when restricted to computers, the term "algorithm" becomes more precise, because then "unambiguous and simple to follow" means "a computer can do it." The connection with computers is not necessary, however. If a person equipped only with pencil and paper can complete the operations, then the operations constitute an algorithm.

A famous example of an algorithm (dating back at least to Euclid) is finding the greatest common divisor (GCD) of two numbers, m and n.

Step 1. Given two positive integers, set m to be the larger of the two; set n to be the smaller of the two.
Step 2. Divide m by n. Save the remainder as r.
Step 3. If $r = 0$, then halt; the GCD is n.
Step 4. Otherwise, set m to the old value of n, and set n to the value of r. Then go to step 2.

A tax form is also a relatively good example of an algorithm because it is finite and the instructions for completing it are mechanically and finitely completable (at least that is the intention). The recipe for cowboy chocolate cake (with two mugs of coffee) is not really an algorithm because its description is not definite enough (how much is a mug of coffee?). Of course, all computer programs are algorithms.

It should also be noted that algorithms are by no means restricted to numbers. For example, alphabetizing a list of words is also an algorithm. And, one interpretation of the computational hypothesis of the mind is that thinking itself is an algorithm—or perhaps better, the result of many algorithms working simultaneously.

Now to flesh out the definition. An algorithm is an unambiguous, precise, list of simple operations applied mechanically and systematically to a set of tokens or objects (e.g., configurations of chess pieces, numbers, cake ingredients, etc.). The initial state of the tokens is the input; the final state is the output. The operations correspond to *state transitions* where the states are the configuration of the tokens, which changes as operations are applied to them. Almost everything in sight is assumed to be finite: the list of operations itself is finite (there might be a larger but still finite set from which the operations are drawn) and each token is itself finite (or, more generally, a finitely determinable element in the set). Usually, the input, output, and intermediate sets of tokens are also finite, but this does not have to be the case, at least in theory; indeed these sets can be continuous (see Blum, Shub, and Smale 1989). An algorithm describes a process that the tokens participate in. This process (a computation) is either in a certain state or it is not, it may either go to a certain next state from its current state or it may not, and any transition taken is finite. (One way to relax this definition is to allow the state transitions to be probabilistic, but that doesn't affect their finiteness.)

And finally, in more technical parlance, an algorithm is an *intensional* definition of a special kind of function— namely a *computable* function. The intensional definition contrasts with the *extensional* definition of a computable function, which is just the set of the function's inputs and outputs. Hence, an algorithm describes *how* the function is computed, rather than merely *what* the function is. The connection with computable functions is crucial. A function F is computable if and only if it is describable as an algorithm. The relationship between the extensional definition of F and an intensional definition of it is interesting. There is one extensional definition of F, but there are an infinite number of intensional definitions of it, hence there are an infinite number of algorithms for every extensionally-described computable function F. (Proof: you can always construct a new, longer algorithm by adding instructions that essentially do nothing. Of course, usually we seek the *canonical* algorithm—the shortest and most efficient one.)

A computable function is a function whose inputs and outputs can be produced by a Turing machine. Church's thesis states that *all* the computable functions can be computed by a Turing machine (see CHURCH-TURING THESIS). The best way to understand Church's thesis is to say that Turing computability exhausts the notion of computability. Importantly, not all functions are computable, so not all functions are algorithmically describable (this was a profound discovery, first proved by TURING 1936; Church 1936a; and Kleene 1936; it and related results are among the greatest achievements of twentieth-century mathematics).

Sometimes algorithms are simply equated with Turing machines. The definition given here is logically prior to the notion of a Turing machine. This latter notion is intended to formally capture the former. Gödel (1931; 1934), among his other achievements, was the first to do this, to link a formal definition with an intuitive one: he identified a formally defined class of functions, the recursive functions, with the functions that are computable, that is, with the functions for which algorithms can be written.

This completes the definition of "algorithm." There are a few loose ends to tie up, and connections to be made. First, mathematicians and computer scientists sometimes sharply restrict the definition of "algorithm." They take the definition of "algorithm" given here, and use it to define the notion of an *effective procedure.* Then they define an algorithm as an effective procedure that always halts or terminates (not all procedures or computer programs do terminate—sometimes on purpose, sometimes accidentally).

Second, in common parlance, an algorithm is a recipe for *telling* a computer what to do. But this definition does more harm than good because it obliterates the crucial notion of a virtual machine, while it subtly reinforces the idea that a homunculus of some sort is doing all the work, and this in turn can reinforce the idea of a "ghost in the machine" in the COMPUTATIONAL THEORY OF MIND. So this folk definition should be avoided when precision is needed. Another problem with the folk definition is that it does not do justice the profundity of the notion of an algorithm as a description of a *process*. It is fair to regard algorithms as being as crucial to mathematics as sets. A set is a collection of objects. An intentional definition of a set describes all and only the objects in the set. An algorithm describes a collection of objects that does something. It would be impossible to overstate the importance of this move from statics to dynamics.

Third, the connection between algorithms and COMPUTATION is quite tight. Indeed, some mathematicians regard algorithms as abstract descriptions of computing devices. When implemented on a standard computer, such descriptions cease to be abstract and become real computing devices known as *virtual machines* (virtual does not mean not real, here). A virtual machine is the machine that does what the algorithm specifies. A virtual machine exists at some level higher than the machine on which the algorithm is implemented. For example: a word processor is a virtual machine that exists on top of the hardware machine on which it is implemented. The notion of a virtual machine is very important to cognitive science because it allows us to partition the study of the mind into levels, with neurochemistry at the bottom (or near the bottom) and cognitive psychology near the top. At each level, different methods and technical vocabularies are used. One of the crucial facts about virtual machines is that no one machine is more important than the rest. So it is with the brain and the rest of the nervous system that make up thinking things. Theories at all levels are going to be needed if we are to completely and truly understand the mind.

See also COMPUTATION AND THE BRAIN; FORMAL SYSTEMS, PROPERTIES OF

—Eric Dietrich

References

Blum, L., M. Shub, and S. Smale. (1989). On a theory of computation and complexity over the real numbers: NP-completeness, recursive functions, and universal machines. *Bulletin of the American Mathematical Society* 21 (1): 1–46.

Church, A. (1936a). A note on the entscheidungsproblem. *Journal of Symbolic Logic* 1: 40–41, 101–102.

Gödel, K. (1931). On formally undecidable propositions of Principia Mathematica and related systems I. *Monatschefte für Mathematick und Physik* 38: 173–198. (Reprinted in J. Heijenoort, Ed., (1967), *From Frege to Gödel.* Cambridge, MA: Harvard University Press, pp. 592–617.)

Gödel, K. (1934/1965). On undecidable propositions of formal mathematical systems. In M. Davis, Ed., *The Undecidable.* New York: Raven Press, pp. 41–71.

Kleene, S. C. (1936). General recursive functions of natural numbers. *Mathematishe Annelen* 112: 727–742.

Turing, A. (1936). On computable numbers with an application to the entscheidungsproblem. *Proceedings of the London Mathematical Society* series 2, 42: 230–265 and 43: 544–546.

Further Readings

Church, A. (1936b). An unsolvable problem of elementary number theory. *American Journal of Mathematics* 58: 345–363.

Dietrich, E. (1994). Thinking computers and the problem of intentionality. In E. Dietrich, Ed., *Thinking Computers and Virtual Persons: Essays on the Intentionality of Machines.* San Diego: Academic Press, pp. 3–34.

Fields, C. (1989). Consequences of nonclassical measurement for the algorithmic description of continuous dynamical systems. *Journal of Experimental and Theoretical Artificial Intelligence* 1: 171–189.

Knuth, D. (1973). *The Art of Computer Programming,* vol. 1: *Fundamental Algorithms.* Reading, MA: Addison-Wesley.

Rogers, H. (1967). *The Theory of Recursive Functions and Effective Computability.* New York: McGraw-Hill.

A-Life

See ARTIFICIAL LIFE; EVOLUTIONARY COMPUTATION

Altruism

In biology, *altruism* has a purely descriptive economic meaning: the active donation of resources to one or more individuals at cost to the donor. Moral values or conscious motivations are not implied, and the ideas are as applicable to plants as to animals. Four evolutionary causes of altruism will be considered here: kin selection, reciprocation, manipulation, and group selection. Each implies demonstrably different patterns for what individuals donate what resources to whom and under what circumstances and may suggest different motivational and emotional experiences by both donor and recipient.

It may seem that Darwinian EVOLUTION, directed by natural selection, could never favor altruism. Any avoidable activity that imposes a cost, always measured as reduced reproductive fitness, would be eliminated in evolution. This view is too simple. Natural selection should minimize costs whenever possible, but successful reproduction always requires donation of resources to offspring, at least by females putting nutrients into eggs. A closer look shows that offspring are important to natural selection only because they bear their parents' genes, but this is true of all relatives. From the perspective of genetics and natural selection, the survival and reproduction of any relative are partly equivalent to one's own survival and reproduction. So there must be an evolutionary force of *kin selection* that favors altruism between associated relatives.

Kin selection, first clearly formulated by Hamilton (1964), can be defined as selection among individuals for the adaptive use of cues indicative of kinship. The products of mitotic cell division are exactly similar genetically, and their special physical contact is reliable evidence of full kinship. This accounts for the subservence of somatic cells in a multicellular organism to the reproductive interests of the germ cells. Kin selection also accounts for the generally benign relations among young animals in the same nest. Such early proximity is often a cue indicative of close kinship. Nestmates are often full sibs, with a genetic relationship of 0.50. They could also be half sibs if the mother mated with more than one male. They may not be related at all if one or more eggs were deposited by females other than the apparent mother. Such nest parasites are often of the same species in birds, but some species, such as the European cuckoo and the American cowbird, reproduce exclusively by parasitizing other species. Their young's competition with nest mates has not been tempered by kin selection, and this accounts for their lethal eviction of the offspring of the parasitized pair. Many sorts of cues other than early proximity can be used to assess kinship, such as the odors used by mammals and insects to recognize relatives and make genetically appropriate adjustments in altruism. The classic work on mechanisms of kin recognition is Fletcher and Michener (1987); see Slater (1994) for a critical updating.

In the insect order Hymenoptera (ants, bees, and wasps), a male has only one chromosome set, from an unfertilized egg of his mother, and his sperm are all exactly the same genetically. So his offspring by a given female have a relationship of 0.75 to one another. This factor has been used to explain the multiple independent instances, in this insect order, of the evolution of sterile worker castes that are entirely female. These workers derive greater genetic success by helping their mothers produce sisters than they would by producing their own offspring, which would have only a 0.50 genetic similarity. These special relationships are not found in termites (order Isoptera) and, as expected, both males and females form the termite worker castes.

Reciprocity is another evolutionary factor that can favor altruism. The basic theory was introduced by Trivers (1971) and refined by Axelrod and Hamilton (1980). One organism has a net gain by helping another if the other reciprocates with benefits (simultaneous or delayed) that balance the donor's cost. Cleaning symbiosis between a large fish and a small one of a different species may provide simultaneous reciprocal benefits: the large fish gets rid of parasites; the small one gets food. This reciprocation implies that the small fish is more valuable as a cleaner to the large fish than it would be as food. Reciprocity is a pervasive factor in the socioeconomic lives of many species, especially our own. It requires safeguards, often in the form of evolved adaptations for the detection of cheating (Wright 1994).

Manipulation is another source of altruism. The donation results from actual or implied threat or deception by the recipient. In any social hierarchy, individuals of lower rank will often yield to the higher by abandoning a food item or possible mate, thereby donating the coveted resource to the dominant individual. Deception often works between species: a snapper may donate its body to an anglerfish that tempts it with its lure; some orchids have flowers that resemble females of an insect species, so that deceived males donate time and energy transporting pollen with no payoff to themselves. The nest parasitism discussed above is another example. Our own donations of money or labor or blood to public appeals can be considered manipulation of donors by those who make the appeals.

Group selection is another possibility. Individuals may donate resources as a group-level adaptation, which evolu-

tion can favor by operating at the level of competing groups rather than their competing members. A group of individuals that aid each other may prevail over a more individually selfish group. A difficulty here is that if selfishness is advantageous within a group, that group is expected to evolve a higher level of individual selfishness, no matter what the effect on group survival. The original concept of group selection focused on separate populations within a species (Wynne-Edwards 1962; Wade 1996). This idea has few adherents, because of the paucity of apparent population-level adaptations (Williams 1996: 51–53), because altruistic populations are readily subverted by the immigration of selfish individuals, and because the low rate of proliferation and extinction of populations, compared to the reproduction and death of individuals, would make selection among populations a relatively weak force.

More recently attention has been given to selection among temporary social groupings or *trait groups* (Wilson 1980), such as fish schools or flocks of birds. Trait groups with more benign and cooperative members may feed more efficiently and avoid predators more effectively. The more selfish individuals still thrive best within each group, and the evolutionary result reflects the relative strengths of selection within and between groups. In human history, groups with more cooperative relations among members must often have prevailed in conflicts with groups of more consistently self-seeking individuals (Wilson and Sober 1994). The resulting greater prevalence of human altruism would be more likely to result from culturally transmitted than genetic differences. It should be noted that any form of group selection can only produce modifications that benefit the sorts of groups among which selection takes place. It need not produce benefits for whole species or more inclusive groups.

A given instance of altruistic behavior may, of course, result from more than one of these four evolutionary causes. Genealogical relatives are especially likely to indulge in both reciprocation and manipulation. If reproductive processes result in stable associations of relatives, these kin-groups are inevitably subject to natural selection. The most extreme examples of altruism, those of social insects, probably resulted from the operation of all the factors discussed here, and social insect colonies may aptly be termed superorganisms (Seeley 1989). Excellent detailed discussions of altruism in the animal kingdom and in human evolution, and of the history of thought on these topics, are available (Ridley 1996; Wright 1994).

See also ADAPTATION AND ADAPTATIONISM; CULTURAL EVOLUTION; DARWIN

—*George C. Williams*

References

Axelrod, R., and W. D. Hamilton. (1980). The evolution of cooperation. *Science* 211: 1390–1396.

Fletcher, D. J. C., and C. D. Michener. (1987). *Kin Recognition in Animals.* New York: Wiley-Interscience.

Hamilton, W. D. (1964). The genetical theory of social behaviour, parts 1 and 2. *Journal of Theoretical Biology* 7:1–52.

Ridley, M. (1996). *The Origins of Virtue.* New York: Viking Press.

Seeley, T. D. (1989). The honey bee as a superorganism. *American Scientist* 77: 546–553.

Slater, P. J. B. (1994). Kinship and altruism. In P. J. B. Slater and T. R. Halliday, Eds., *Behavior and Evolution*. Cambridge University Press.

Trivers, R. L. (1971). The evolution of reciprocal altruism. *Quarterly Review of Biology* 46: 35–57.

Wade, M. J. (1996). Adaptation in subdivided populations: kin selection and interdemic selection. In M. R. Rose and G. V. Lauder (Eds.), *Adaptation*. San Diego: Academic Press.

Williams, G. C. (1996). *Plan and Purpose in Nature*. London: Weidenfeld and Nicholson.

Wilson, D. S. (1980). *Natural Selection of Populations and Communities*. Boston: Benjamin/Cummings.

Wilson, D. S., and E. Sober. (1994). Re-introducing group selection to the human behavioral sciences. *Behavioral and Brain Sciences* 17: 585–654.

Wright, R. (1994). *The Moral Animal: Why We Are the Way We Are*. Vintage Books.

Wynne-Edwards, V. C. (1961). *Animal Dispersion in Relation to Social Behavior*. London: Oliver and Boyd.

Ambiguity

A linguistic unit is said to be ambiguous when it is associated with more than one MEANING. The term is normally reserved for cases where the same linguistic form has clearly differentiated meanings that can be associated with distinct linguistic representations. Ambiguity is thus distinguished from general indeterminacy or lack of specificity.

Ambiguity has played an important role in developing theories of syntactic and semantic structure, and it has been the primary empirical testbed for developing and evaluating models of real-time language processing. Within artificial intelligence and COMPUTATIONAL LINGUISTICS, ambiguity is considered one of the central problems to be solved in developing language understanding systems (Allen 1995).

Lexical ambiguity occurs when a word has multiple independent meanings. "Bank" in the sentence "Jeremy went to the *bank*" could denote a riverbank or a financial institution. Ambiguous words may differ in syntactic category as well as meaning (e.g., "rose," "watch," and "patient"). True lexical ambiguity is typically distinguished from polysemy (e.g., "the N.Y. Times" as in this morning's edition of the newspaper versus the company that publishes the newspaper) or from vagueness (e.g., "cut" as in "cut the lawn" or "cut the cloth"), though the boundaries can be fuzzy.

Syntactic ambiguities arise when a sequence of unambiguous words reflects more than one possible syntactic relationship underlying the words in the sentence, as in:

(1) a. The company hires smart women and men.
    b. The burglar threatened the student with the knife.

In (1a), the ambiguity lies in whether the adjective *smart* modifies (provides information about) both *women* and *men* resulting in a practice not to hire unintelligent people of either sex, or whether *smart* modifies *women* only. In (1b), the phrase *with the knife* could be used to describe the manner in which the burglar threatened the student, or to indicate which student was threatened. Chomsky (1957) used

similar ambiguities to argue for the necessity of abstract syntactic structure.

The different underlying relationships in ambiguous sentences can frequently be observed directly by manipulating the form of the ambiguous sentence. When the order of the string *smart women and men* is reversed to *men and smart women,* the sentence can only be understood as involving modification of *women* but not *men.* When the adverb *wildly* is inserted before *with the knife,* only the reading in which the burglar is using the knife remains possible.

In its most technical sense, the term ambiguity is used to describe only those situations in which a surface linguistic form corresponds to more than one linguistic representation. In lexical ambiguities, one surface phonetic form has multiple independent lexical representations. For syntactic ambiguities, one surface string has different underlying syntactic structures. A subtler and more controversial example is the phenomenon of *scope ambiguity,* exemplified in:

(2) a. Some woman tolerates every man.
    b. John doesn't think the King of France is bald.

In (2a), the sentence can be understood as referring to a single woman who tolerates each and every man, or alternatively, it can mean that every man is tolerated by at least one woman (not necessarily the same one). Sentence (2b) can mean either that John believes that the King of France is not bald, or that John does not hold the particular belief that the King of France is bald. It is difficult to find clear syntactic tests for scope ambiguities that would demonstrate different underlying structures. For instance, reversing the order of *some woman* and *every man* does not eliminate the ambiguity (although it may affect the bias towards one reading):

(3) Every man is tolerated by some woman.

May (1977) argues that sentences such as (2) reflect different underlying structures at a level of linguistic representation corresponding to the LOGICAL FORM of a sentence. Subsequently, much of the linguistic literature has considered scope ambiguities as genuine ambiguities.

A broader notion of ambiguity includes a pervasive ambiguity type that involves not multiple possible structures, but rather, multiple associations between linguistic expressions and specific entities in the world. The sentence in (4) is an example of *referential ambiguity:*

(4) Mark told Christopher that he had passed the exam.

The ambiguity resides in the understanding of the pronoun *he,* which could refer to either Mark, Christopher, or some other salient entity under discussion.

Language processing necessarily involves ambiguity resolution because even unambiguous words and sentences are briefly ambiguous as linguistic input is presented to the processing system. Local ambiguities arise in spoken language because speech unfolds over time and in written language because text is processed in successive eye fixations (cf. Tanenhaus and Trueswell 1995).

The sentence in (5) illustrates how globally unambiguous sentences may contain local ambiguities.

(5) *The pupil spotted* by the proctor was expelled.

The pupil is the object of a relative clause. However, the underlined sequence is also consistent with *the pupil* being the subject of a main clause, as in "*The pupil spotted* the proctor." The ambiguity arises because the morphological form "-ed" is used for both the simple past and for the passive participle, illustrating the interdependence of ambiguity at multiple levels.

Laboratory studies have established that multiple senses of words typically become activated in memory with rapid resolution based on frequency and context. For example, when "pupil" is heard or read, both the "eye part" and the "student" senses become briefly active (Simpson 1984). Similarly, "elevator," "elegant," and "eloquent" are briefly activated as the unambiguous word "elephant" is heard because they are consistent with the initial phonemic sequence "eluh" (Marslen-Wilson 1987).

Syntactic ambiguities exhibit consistent preferences. Readers and listeners experience processing difficulty and sometimes a conscious feeling of confusion when the sentence becomes inconsistent with the preferred structure. The example in (6), from Bever (1970), is a classic example of a so-called garden-path, illustrating that the main clause is the preferred structure for the main clause/relative clause ambiguity.

(6) The raft floated down the river sank.

(7) The land mine buried in the sand exploded.

In (5), resolution in favor of the relative clause does not cause conscious confusion. Nonetheless, processing difficulty at *by the proctor* can be observed using sensitive measures, for instance the duration of eye-fixations in reading. Theoretical explanations for syntactic preferences can be roughly divided into structural and constraint-based approaches. In structural theories, principles defined over syntactic configurations determine an initial structure, which is then evaluated, and if necessary, revised. Different principles may apply for different classes of ambiguities (e.g., Frazier 1987). In constraint-based theories, preferences arise because a conspiracy of probabilistic constraints, many of them lexically based, temporarily make the ultimately incorrect interpretation the more likely one (MacDonald, Pearlmutter, and Seidenberg 1994; Tanenhaus and Trueswell 1995). The example in (7) illustrates a sentence with the same structure as (6) in which the probabilistic constraints initially favor the relative clause because "buried" is typically used as a passive participle without an agent, and land mines are more typically themes than agents of burying events. Whether or not constraint-based systems can provide a unified account of ambiguity resolution in language using general principles that hold across other perceptual domains remains a central unresolved issue.

See also FIGURATIVE LANGUAGE; LEXICON; NATURAL LANGUAGE PROCESSING; PSYCHOLINGUISTICS; SPOKEN WORD RECOGNITION; SYNTAX

—*Michael K. Tanenhaus and Julie C. Sedivy*

References

Allen, J. (1995). *Natural Language Understanding*. Redwood City, CA: Benjamin/Cummings.

Bever, T. (1970). The cognitive basis for linguistic structures. In J. R. Hayes, Ed., *Cognition and the Development of Language*. New York: Wiley.

Chomsky, N. (1957). *Syntactic Structures*. The Hague: Mouton.

Frazier, L. (1987). Sentence processing: a tutorial review. In M. Coltheart, Ed., *Attention and Performance XII: The Psychology of Reading*. London: Erlbaum.

MacDonald, M., N. Pearlmutter, and M. Seidenberg. (1994). Lexical nature of syntactic ambiguity resolution. *Psychological Review* 4: 676–703.

Marlsen-Wilson, W. D. (1987). Functional parallelism in spoken word recognition. *Cognition* 25:71–102.

May, R. (1977). *The Grammar of Quantification*. Ph.D. diss., MIT. Distributed by the Indiana University Linguistics Club, Bloomington.

Pritchett, B. (1992). *Grammatical Competence and Parsing Performance*. Chicago: University of Chicago Press.

Simpson, G. (1984). Lexical ambiguity and its role in models of word recognition. *Psychological Bulletin* 96: 316–340.

Small, S., G. Cottrell, and M. Tanenhaus, Eds. (1988). *Lexical Ambiguity Resolution: Perspectives from Psycholinguistics, Neuropsychology, and Artificial Intelligence*. San Mateo, CA: Morgan Kaufmann Publishers.

Tanenhaus, M., and J. Trueswell. (1995). Sentence comprehension. In J. Miller and P. Eimas, Eds., *Handbook of Cognition and Perception*. New York: Academic Press.

Zwicky, A., and J. Sadock. (1975). Ambiguity tests and how to fail them. In J. Kimball, Ed., *Syntax and Semantics, vol. 4*. New York: Academic Press.

Amygdala, Primate

For more than one century there has been evidence that the amygdala is involved in emotional behavior. Experimental lesion studies in monkeys demonstrated that large temporal lobe lesions that included the amygdala resulted in dramatic postoperative changes in behavior, including flattened affect, visual agnosia, hyperorality, and hypersexuality (Brown and Schaefer 1888; Klüver and Bucy 1938). Similar behaviors have also been observed in humans with large temporal lobe lesions that include the amygdala (Terzian and Dalle Ore 1955). The amygdala was more formally linked to emotional behavior in 1949, when Paul MacLean expanded Papez's notion of the LIMBIC SYSTEM to include this region, based on neuroanatomical criteria. Over the past several decades, converging results of neuroanatomical, behavioral, and physiological studies in macaque monkeys along with neuropsychological and neuroimaging studies in humans have firmly established a role for the amygdala in emotional processing. However, a number of important questions remain regarding the nature and specificity of this role. In addition, the amygdala has also been linked to social behavior but these data will not be reviewed here. In this article, a brief neuroanatomical review will be followed by a survey of two areas of particularly active research involving the primate amygdala: expression of emotional behavior and the recognition of facial emotion.

The unique neuroanatomical profile of the amygdala illustrates why this structure has been referred to as the "sensory gateway to the emotions" (Aggleton and Mishkin 1986). The amygdala comprises at least thirteen distinct nuclei, each with a rich pattern of intrinsic connections. As to extrinsic connections, the amygdala is directly interconnected with unimodal and polymodal sensory cortical areas as well as with subcortical structures such as the basal forebrain, THALAMUS, hypothalamus, striatum, and brainstem areas. Thus, the amygdala is centrally positioned to receive convergent cortical and thalamic sensory information and subsequently to direct the appropriate survival-oriented response via its brainstem and hypothalamic projections. Moreover, the significant neuroanatomical connections between the amygdala and nearby medial temporal lobe regions involved in MEMORY may provide the substrate for the enhancing effect of emotional arousal on memory, as demonstrated by a significant body of animal and human studies (McGaugh et al. 1995; Cahill et al. 1995).

Experimental lesions that target the amygdala have produced many of the behaviors that were originally described after the large lesions of Klüver and Bucy and Brown and Schaefer (Weiskrantz 1956; Aggleton, Burton, and Passingham 1980; Zola-Morgan et al. 1991). However, due to methodological difficulties, these lesions typically have included inadvertent cortical and/or fiber damage; thus, interpretations of amygdala function based on these classic studies alone must be made with caution. Highly circumscribed amygdala lesions can now be produced using the neurotoxic lesion technique, and results from these studies indicate a role for the amygdala in temperament and oral exploration (Amaral et al. 1997), food preferences (Murray, Gaffan, and Flint 1996), and in the devaluation of a food reward after selective satiation (Malkova, Gaffan, and Murray 1997).

Interestingly, the behavioral changes observed after neurotoxic amygdala lesions are much less profound than those that were reported using more traditional (i.e., less discrete) lesion techniques. The perirhinal cortex, known to be important for memory (Zola-Morgan et al. 1989), lies adjacent to the amygdala, and these two regions are strongly neuroanatomically interconnected (Stefanacci, Suzuki, and Amaral 1996). It has been suggested that the amygdala and the perirhinal cortex may have some shared roles in emotional behavior (Iwai et al. 1990; Stefanacci, Suzuki, and Amaral 1996). Thus, it is possible that dramatic emotional changes may occur only after lesions that include both of these regions.

Recent studies in humans have explored the role of the amygdala in the recognition of facial emotion and of the recognition of fear in particular (see EMOTION AND THE HUMAN BRAIN). Taken together, the evidence is not entirely supportive. On the positive side, one study reported that a patient with relatively discrete, bilateral amygdala damage as determined by MAGNETIC RESONANCE IMAGING (MRI) was impaired at recognizing fear in facial expressions (Adolphs et al. 1994). A second patient who has partial bilateral amygdala damage, determined by MRI, was similarly impaired (Calder et al. 1996) and was also impaired in recognizing fear and anger in the auditory domain (Scott et al. 1997). However, this patient also has more general facial and auditory processing impairments (Young et al. 1996; Scott et al. 1997).

Functional neuroimaging data provide additional support for the notion that the amygdala is preferentially involved in the recognition of fearful versus happy faces (Morris et al. 1996). However, the results from other studies are not consistent with this notion. First, recognition of facial emotion, including fear, may occur even in the absence of the amygdala (Hamann et al. 1996). Second, single neurons in the human amygdala respond to particular facial expressions but do not respond exclusively to fearful expressions (Fried, MacDonald, and Wilson 1997). In monkeys, there is a population of amygdala neurons that respond selectively to faces (Leonard et al. 1985), but there is little or no evidence to support the idea that these neurons respond selectively to fearful expressions. Finally, functional magnetic resonance imaging (fMRI) has revealed increased activation in the amygdala in response to both happy and fearful faces (Breiter et al. 1996).

To conclude, studies in monkeys and humans over the past several decades have reinforced the long-held view, supported by findings in other species (see EMOTION AND THE ANIMAL BRAIN), that the amygdala has an important role in emotional function. New experimental approaches, such as functional neuroimaging and the use of highly selective lesion techniques, hold promise for an exciting new era of progress that builds on this work.

See also EMOTIONS; FACE RECOGNITION; OBJECT RECOGNITION, HUMAN NEUROPSYCHOLOGY

—*Lisa Stefanacci*

References

Adolphs, R., D. Tranel, H. Damasio, and A. Damasio. (1994). Impaired recognition of emotion in facial expressions following bilateral damage to the human amygdala. *Nature* 372: 669–672.

Aggleton, J. P., and M. Mishkin. (1986). The amygdala: sensory gateway to the emotions. In R. Plutchik and H. Kellerman, Eds., *Emotion: Theory, Research, and Experience.* New York: Academic Press, Inc. pp. 281–298.

Aggleton, J. P. (1985). A description of intra-amygdaloid connections in old world monkeys. *Exp. Brain Res* 57: 390–399.

Aggleton, J. P., M. J. Burton, and R. E. Passingham. (1980). Cortical and subcortical afferents to the amygdala of the rhesus monkey (*Macaca Mulatta*). *Brain Res* 190: 347–368.

Amaral, D., J. P. Capitanio, C. J. Machado, W. A. Mason, and S. P. Mendoza. (1997). The role of the amygdaloid complex in rhesus monkey social behavior. *Soc. Neurosci. Abstr* 23: 570.

Breiter, H. C., N. L. Etcoff, P. J. Whalen, W. A. Kennedy, S. L. Rauch, R. L. Buckner, M. M. Strauss, S. E. Human, and B. R. Rosen. (1996). Response and habituation of the human amygdala during visual processing of facial expression. *Neuron* 17: 875–887.

Brown, S., and E. A. Schaefer. (1888). An investigation into the functions of the occipital and temporal lobes of the monkey's brain. *Philos. Trans. R. Soc. Lond. B* 179: 303–327.

Cahill, L., R. Babinsky, H. J. Markowitsch, and J. L. McGaugh. (1995). The amygdala and emotional memory. *Nature* 377: 295–296.

Calder, A. J., A. W. Young, D. Rowland, D. I. Perrett, J. R. Hodges, and N. L. Etcoff. (1996). Facial emotion recognition after bilateral amygdala damage: differentially severe impairment of fear. *Cognitive Neuropsychology* 13(5): 699–745.

Fried, I., K. A. MacDonald, and C. L. Wilson. (1997). Single neuron activity in human hippocampus and amygdala during recognition of faces and objects. *Neuron* 18: 753–765.

Hamann, S. B., L. Stefanacci, L. R. Squire, R. Adolphs, D. Tranel, H. Damasio, and A. Damasio. (1996). Recognizing facial emotion. *Nature* 379: 497.

Iwai, E., M. Yukie, J. Watanabe, K. Hikosaka, H. Suyama, and S. Ishikawa. (1990). A role of amygdala in visual perception and cognition in macaque monkeys (*Macaca fuscata* and *Macaca mulatta*). *Toholu J. Exp. Med* 161: 95–120.

Klüver, H., and P. C. Bucy. (1938). An analysis of certain effects of bilateral temporal lobectomy in the rhesus monkey, with special reference to "psychic blindness." *J. Psych* 5: 33–54.

Leonard, C. M., E. T. Rolls, F. A. W. Wilson, and G. C. Baylis. (1985). Neurons in the amygdala of the monkey with responses selective for faces. *Behavioral Brain Research* 15: 159–176.

Malkova, L., D. Gaffan, and E. A. Murray. (1997). Excitotoxic lesions of the amygdala fail to produce impairment in visual learning for auditory secondary reinforcement but interfere with reinforcer devaluation effects in rhesus monkeys. *J. Neuroscience* 17: 6011–6020.

McGaugh, J. L., L. Cahill, M. B. Parent, M. H. Mesches, K. Coleman-Mesches, and J. A. Salinas. (1995). Involvement of the amygdala in the regulation of memory storage. In J. L. McGaugh, F. Bermudez-Rattoni, and R. A. Prado Alcala, Eds., *Plasticity in the Central Nervous System—Learning and Memory*. Hillsdale, NJ: Erlbaum.

Morris, J. S., C. D. Frith, D. I. Perrett, D. Rowland, A. W. Yound, A. J. Calder, and R. J. Dolan. (1996). A differential neural response in the human amygdala to fearful and happy facial expressions. *Nature* 812–815.

Murray, E. A., E. A. Gaffan, and R. W. Flint, Jr. (1996). Anterior rhinal cortex and the amygdala: dissociation of their contributions to memory and food preference in rhesus monkeys. *Behav. Neurosci* 110: 30–42.

Scott, S. K., A. W. Young, A. J. Calder, D. J. Hellawell, M. P. Aggleton, and M. Johnson. (1997). Impaired auditory recognition of fear and anger following bilateral amygdala lesions. *Nature* 385: 254–257.

Stefanacci, L., W. A. Suzuki, and D. G. Amaral. (1996). Organization of connections between the amygdaloid complex and the perirhinal and parahippocampal cortices: an anterograde and retrograde tracing study in the monkey. *J. Comp. Neurol* 375: 552–582.

Terzian, H., and G. Dalle Ore. (1955). Syndrome of Kluver and Bucy, reproduced in man by bilateral removal of the temporal lobes. *Neurology* 5: 373–380.

Weiskrantz, L. (1956). Behavioral changes associated with ablation of the amygdaloid complex in monkeys. *J. Comp. Physio. Psych* 49: 381–391.

Young, A. W., D. J. Hellawell, C. Van de Wal, and M. Johnson. (1996). Facial expression processing after amygdalotomy. *Neuropsychologia* 34(1): 31–39.

Zola-Morgan, S., L. Squire, P. Alvarez-Royo, and R. P. Clower. (1991). Independence of memory functions and emotional behavior: separate contributions of the hippocampal formation and the amygdala. *Hippocampus* 1: 207–220.

Zola-Morgan, S., L. R. Squire, D. G. Amaral, and W. A. Suzuki. (1989). Lesions of perirhinal and parahippocampal cortex that spare the amygdala and hippocampal formation produce severe memory impairment. *J. Neurosci* 9: 4355–4370.

Further Readings

Amaral, D. G., J. L. Price, A. Pitkanen, and S. T. Carmichael. (1992). Anatomical organization of the primate amygdaloid complex. In J. Aggleton, Ed., *The Amygdala: Neurobiological Aspects of Emotion, Memory, and Mental Dysfunction*. New York: Wiley-Liss, pp. 1–66.

Gallagher, M., and A. A. Chiba. (1996). The amygdala and emotion. *Curr. Opin. Neurobio* 6: 221–227.

Kling, A. S., and L. A. Brothers. (1992). The amygdala and social behavior. In J. Aggleton, Ed., *The Amygdala: Neurobiological Aspects of Emotion, Memory, and Mental Dysfunction*. New York: Wiley-Liss, pp. 353–377.

Analogy

Analogy is (1) similarity in which the same relations hold between different domains or systems; (2) inference that if two things agree in certain respects then they probably agree in others. These two senses are related, as discussed below.

Analogy is important in cognitive science for several reasons. It is central in the study of LEARNING and discovery. Analogies permit transfer across different CONCEPTS, situations, or domains and are used to explain new topics. Once learned, they can serve as MENTAL MODELS for understanding a new domain (Halford 1993). For example, people often use analogies with water flow when reasoning about electricity (Gentner and Gentner 1983). Analogies are often used in PROBLEM SOLVING and inductive reasoning because they can capture significant parallels across different situations. Beyond these mundane uses, analogy is a key mechanism in CREATIVITY and scientific discovery. For example, Johannes Kepler used an analogy with light to hypothesize that the planets are moved by an invisible force from the sun. In studies of microbiology laboratories, Dunbar (1995) found that analogies are both frequent and important in the discovery process.

Analogy is also used in communication and persuasion. For example, President Bush analogized the Persian Gulf crisis to the events preceding World War II, comparing Saddam Hussein to Hitler, Spellman and Holyoak 1992). The invited inference was that the United States should defend Kuwait and Saudi Arabia against Iraq, just as the Allies defended Europe against Nazi Germany. On a larger scale, conceptual metaphors such as "weighing the evidence" and "balancing the pros and cons" can be viewed as large-scale conventionalized analogies (see COGNITIVE LINGUISTICS). Finally, analogy and its relative, SIMILARITY, are important because they participate in many other cognitive processes. For example, exemplar-based theories of conceptual structure and CASE-BASED REASONING models in artificial intelligence assume that much of human categorization and reasoning is based on analogies between the current situation and prior situations (cf. JUDGMENT HEURISTICS).

The central focus of analogy research is on the mapping process by which people understand one situation in terms of another. Current accounts distinguish the following subprocesses: *mapping,* that is, *aligning* the representational structures of the two cases and projecting inferences; and *evaluation* of the analogy and its inferences. These first two are signature phenomena of analogy. Two further processes that can occur are *adaptation* or *rerepresentation* of one or both analogs to improve the match and abstraction of the structure common to both analogs. We first discuss these core processes, roughly in the order in which they occur during normal processing. Then we will take up the issue of analogical *retrieval,* the processes by which people are spontaneously reminded of past similar or analogous examples from long-term memory.

In analogical *mapping,* a familiar situation—the base or source analog—is used as a model for making inferences about an unfamiliar situation—the target analog. According to Gentner's *structure-mapping* theory (1983), the mapping process includes a *structural alignment* between two represented situations and the *projection of inferences* from one to the other. The alignment must be *structurally consistent,* that is, there must be a one-to-one correspondence between the mapped elements in the base and target, and the arguments of corresponding predicates must also correspond (*parallel connectivity*). Given this alignment, candidate inferences are drawn from the base to the target via a kind of structural completion. A further assumption is the *systematicity principle:* a system of relations connected by higher-order constraining relations such as causal relations is more salient in analogy than an equal number of independent matches. Systematicity links the two classic senses of analogy, for if analogical similarity is modeled as common relational structure, then a base domain that possesses a richly linked system of connected relations will yield candidate inferences by completing the connected structure in the target (Bowdle and Gentner 1997).

Another important psychological approach to analogical mapping is offered by Holyoak (1985), who emphasized the role of pragmatics in problem solving by analogy—how current goals and context guide the interpretation of an analogy. Holyoak defined analogy as similarity with respect to a goal, and suggested that mapping processes are oriented toward attainment of goal states. Holyoak and Thagard (1989) combined this pragmatic focus with the assumption of structural consistency and developed a multiconstraint approach to analogy in which similarity, structural parallelism, and pragmatic factors interact to produce an interpretation.

Through *rerepresentation* or *adaptation,* the representation of one or both analogs is altered to improve the match. Although central to conceptual change, this aspect of analogy remains relatively unexplored. And through *schema abstraction,* which retains the common system representing the interpretation of an analogy for later use, analogy can promote the formation of new relational categories and abstract rules.

Evaluation is the process by which we judge the acceptability of an analogy. At least three criteria seem to be involved: structural soundness—whether the alignment and the projected inferences are structurally consistent; factual validity of the candidate inferences—because analogy is not a deductive mechanism, this is not guaranteed and must be checked separately; and finally, in problem-solving situations, goal-relevance—the reasoner must ask whether the analogical inferences are also relevant to current goals. A lively arena of current research centers on exactly how and when these criteria are invoked in the analogical mapping process.

As discussed above, processing an analogy typically results in a common schema. Accounts of how *cognitive*

simulation occurs fall into two classes: projection-first models, in which the schema is derived from the base and mapped to the target; and alignment-first models, in which the abstract schema is assumed to arise out of the analogical mapping process. Most current cognitive simulations take the latter approach. For example, the structure-mapping engine (SME) of Falkenhainer, Forbus, and Gentner (1989), when given two potential analogs, proceeds at first rather blindly, finding all possible local matches between elements of the base and target. Next it combines these into structurally consistent kernels, and finally it combines the kernels into the two or three largest and deepest matches of connected systems, which represent possible interpretations of the analogy. Based on this alignment, it projects candidate inferences—by hypothesizing that other propositions connected to the common system in the base may also hold in the target. The analogical constraint-mapping engine (ACME) of Holyoak and Thagard (1989) uses a similar local-to-global algorithm, but differs in that it is a multiconstraint, winner-take-all connectionist system, with soft constraints of structural consistency, semantic similarity, and pragmatic bindings. Although the multiconstraint system permits a highly flexible mapping process, it often arrives at structurally inconsistent mappings, whose candidate inferences are indeterminate. Markman (1997) found that this kind of indeterminacy was rarely experienced by people solving analogies. Other variants of the local-to-global algorithm are Hofstadter and Mitchell's Copycat system (1994) for perceptual analogies and Keane's incremental analogy machine (IAM; 1990), which adds matches incrementally in order to model effects of processing order. In contrast to alignment-first models, in which inferences are made after the two representations are aligned, projection-first models find or derive an abstraction in the base and then project it to the target (e.g., Greiner 1988). Although alignment-first models are more suitable for modeling the generation of new abstractions, projection-first models may be apt for modeling conventional analogy and metaphor.

Finally, analogy has proved challenging to subsymbolic connectionist approaches. A strong case can be made that analogical processing requires structured representations and structure-sensitive processing algorithms. An interesting recent "symbolic connectionist" model, Hummel and Holyoak's LISA (1997), combines such structured symbolic techniques with distributed concept representations.

Thus far, our focus has been on how analogy is processed once it is present. But to model the use of analogy and similarity in real-life learning and reasoning we must also understand how people think of analogies; that is, how they *retrieve* potential analogs from long-term memory. There is considerable evidence that similarity-based *retrieval* is driven more by surface similarity and less by structural similarity than is the mapping process. For example, Gick and Holyoak (1980; 1983) showed that people often fail to access potentially useful analogs. People who saw an analogous story prior to being given a very difficult thought problem were three times as likely to solve the problem as those who did not (30 percent vs. 10 percent). Impressive as this is, the majority of subjects nonetheless failed to benefit from the analogy. However, when the nonsolvers were given the hint to think back to the prior story, the solution rate again tripled, to about 80–90 percent. Because no new information was given about the story, we can infer that subjects had retained its meaning, but failed to think of it when reading the problem. The similarity match between the story and the problem, though sufficient to carry out the mapping once both analogs were present in working memory, did not lead to spontaneous retrieval. This is an example of the inert knowledge problem in transfer, a central concern in EDUCATION.

Not only do people fail to retrieve analogies, but they are often reminded of prior surface-similar cases, even when they know that these matches are of little use in reasoning (Gentner, Rattermann, and Forbus 1993). This relative lack of spontaneous analogical transfer and predominance of surface remindings is seen in problem solving (Ross 1987) and may result in part from overly concrete representations (Bassok, Wu, and Olseth 1995).

Computational models of similarity-based retrieval have taken two main approaches. One class of models aims to capture the phenomena of human memory retrieval, including both strengths and weaknesses. For example, analog retrieval by constraint satisfaction (ARCS; Thagard et al. 1990) and Many are called/but few are chosen (MAC/FAC; Forbus, Gentner, and Law 1995) both assume that retrieval is strongly influenced by surface similarity and by structural similarity, goal relevance, or both. In contrast, most case-based reasoning (CBR) models aim for optimality, focusing on how to organize memory such that relevant cases are retrieved when needed.

Theories of analogy have been extended to other kinds of similarity, such as METAPHOR and mundane literal similarity. There is evidence that computing a literal similarity match involves the same process of structural alignment as does analogy (Gentner and Markman 1997). Current computational models like ACME and SME use the same processing algorithms for similarity as for analogy.

The investigation of analogy has been characterized by unusually fruitful interdisciplinary convergence. Important contributions have come from philosophy, notably Hesse's analysis (1966) of analogical models in science, and from artificial intelligence (AI), beginning with Winston's research (1982), which laid out computational strategies applicable to human processing. Recent research that combines psychological investigations and computational modeling has advanced our knowledge of how people align representational structures and compute further inferences over them. Theories of analogy and structural similarity have been successfully applied to areas such as CATEGORIZATION, DECISION MAKING, and children's learning. At the same time, cross-species comparisons have suggested that analogy may be especially well developed in human beings. These results have broadened our view of the role of structural similarity in human thought.

See also CONSTRAINT SATISFACTION; FIGURATIVE LANGUAGE; LANGUAGE AND COMMUNICATION; METAPHOR AND CULTURE; SCHEMATA

—Dedre Gentner

References

Bassok, M., L. Wu, and K. L. Olseth. (1995). Judging a book by its cover: Interpretative effects of content on problem solving transfer. *Memory and Cognition* 23: 354–367.

Bowdle, B., and D. Gentner. (1997). Informativity and asymmetry in comparisons. *Cognitive Psychology* 34: 244–286.

Dunbar, K. (1995). How scientists really reason: scientific reasoning in real-world laboratories. In R. J. Sternberg and J. E. Davidson, Eds., *The Nature of Insight*. Cambridge, MA: MIT Press, pp. 365–395.

Falkenhainer, B., K. D. Forbus, and D. Gentner. (1989). The structure-mapping engine: An algorithm and examples. *Artificial Intelligence* 41: 1–63.

Forbus, K. D., D. Gentner, and K. Law. (1995). MAC/FAC: A model of similarity-based retrieval. *Cognitive Science* 19: 141–205.

Gentner, D. (1983). Structure-mapping: A theoretical framework for analogy. *Cognitive Science* 7: 155–170.

Gentner, D., and D. R. Gentner. (1983). Flowing waters or teeming crowds: Mental models of electricity. In D. Gentner and A. L. Stevens, Eds., *Mental Models*. Hillsdale, NJ: Erlbaum, pp. 99–129.

Gentner, D., and A. B. Markman. (1997). Structure-mapping in analogy and similarity. *American Psychologist* 52: 45–56.

Gentner, D., M. J. Rattermann, and K. D. Forbus. (1993). The roles of similarity in transfer: Separating retrievability from inferential soundness. *Cognitive Psychology* 25: 524–575.

Gick, M. L., and K. J. Holyoak. (1980). Analogical problem solving. *Cognitive Psychology* 12: 306–355.

Gick, M. L., and K. J. Holyoak. (1983). Schema induction and analogical transfer. *Cognitive Psychology* 15: 1–38.

Greiner, R. (1988). Learning by understanding analogies. *Artificial Intelligence* 35: 81–125.

Halford, G. S. (1993). *Children's Understanding: The Development of Mental Models*. Hillsdale, NJ: Erlbaum.

Hesse, M. B. (1966). *Models and Analogies in Science*. Notre Dame, IN. University of Notre Dame Press.

Hofstadter, D. R., and M. Mitchell. (1994). The Copycat project: A model of mental fluidity and analogy-making. In K. J. Holyoak and J. A. Barnden, Eds., *Advances in Connectionist and Neural Computation Theory*, vol. 2, *Analogical Connections*. Norwood, NJ: Ablex, pp. 31–112.

Holyoak, K. J. (1985). The pragmatics of analogical transfer. In G. H. Bower, Ed., *The Psychology of Learning and Motivation*, vol. 19. New York: Academic Press, pp. 59–87.

Holyoak, K. J., and P. R. Thagard. (1989). Analogical mapping by constraint satisfaction. *Cognitive Science* 13: 295–355.

Hummel, J. E., and K. J. Holyoak. (1997). Distributed representations of structure: A theory of analogical access and mapping. *Psychological Review* 104: 427–466.

Keane, M. T. (1990). Incremental analogising: Theory and model. In K. J. Gilhooly, M. T. G. Keane, R. H. Logie, and G. Erdos, Eds., *Lines of Thinking*, vol. 1. Chichester, England: Wiley.

Markman, A. B. (1997). Constraints on analogical inference. *Cognitive Science* 21(4): 373–418.

Ross, B. H. (1987). This is like that: The use of earlier problems and the separation of similarity effects. *Journal of Experimental Psychology: Learning, Memory, and Cognition* 13: 629–639.

Spellman, B. A., and K. J. Holyoak. (1992). If Saddam is Hitler then who is George Bush? Analogical mapping between systems of social roles. *Journal of Personality and Social Psychology* 62: 913–933.

Thagard, P., K. J. Holyoak, G. Nelson, and D. Gochfeld. (1990). Analog retrieval by constraint satisfaction. *Artificial Intelligence* 46: 259–310.

Winston, P. H. (1982). Learning new principles from precedents and exercises. *Artificial Intelligence* 19: 321–350.

Further Readings

Gentner, D., and A. B. Markman. (1995). Analogy-based reasoning in connectionism. In M. A. Arbib, Ed., *The Handbook of Brain Theory and Neural Networks.* Cambridge, MA: MIT Press, pp. 91–93.

Gentner, D., and J. Medina. (1998). Similarity and the development of rules. *Cognition* 65: 263–297.

Goswami, U. (1982). *Analogical Reasoning in Children.* Hillsdale, NJ: Erlbaum.

Holyoak, K. J., and P. R. Thagard. (1995). *Mental Leaps: Analogy in Creative Thought.* Cambridge, MA: MIT Press.

Keane, M. T. (1988). *Analogical Problem Solving.* Chichester, England: Ellis Horwood, and New York: Wiley.

Kolodner, J. L. (1993). *Case-Based Reasoning.* San Mateo, CA: Kaufmann.

Medin, D. L., R. L. Goldstone, and D. Gentner. (1993). Respects for similarity. *Psychological Review* 100: 254–278.

Nersessian, N. J. (1992). How do scientists think? Capturing the dynamics of conceptual change in science. In R. N. Giere, and H. Feigl, Eds., *Minnesota Studies in the Philosophy of Science.* Minneapolis: University of Minnesota Press, pp. 3–44.

Reeves, L. M., and R. W. Weisberg. (1994). The role of content and abstract information in analogical transfer. *Psychological Bulletin* 115: 381–400.

Schank, R. C., A. Kass, and C. K. Riesbeck, Eds. (1994). *Inside Case-Based Explanation.* Hillsdale, NJ: Erlbaum.

Anaphora

The term *anaphora* is used most commonly in theoretical linguistics to denote any case where two nominal expressions are assigned the same referential value or range. Discussion here focuses on noun phrase (NP) anaphora with pronouns (see BINDING THEORY for an explanation of the types of expressions commonly designated "anaphors," e.g., reflexive pronouns).

Pronouns are commonly viewed as variables. Thus, (1b) corresponds to (2), where the predicate contains a free variable. This means that until the pronoun is assigned a value, the predicate is an open property (does not form a set). There are two distinct procedures for pronoun resolution: *binding* and *covaluation*. In binding, the variable gets bound by the λ-operator, as in (3a), where the predicate is closed, denoting the set of individuals who think they have the flu, and where the sentence asserts that Lili is in this set.

(1) a. Lucie didn't show up today.
    b. Lili thinks she's got the flu.

(2) Lili (λx (x thinks z has got the flu))

(3) a. *Binding:* Lili (λx (x thinks x has got the flu))
    b. *Covaluation:* Lili (λx (x thinks z has got the flu) & z = Lucie)

In covaluation, the free variable is assigned a value from the DISCOURSE storage, as in (3b). An assumption standard since the 1980s is that, while processing sentences in context, we build an inventory of discourse entities, which can

further serve as antecedents of anaphoric expressions (Heim 1982; McCawley 1979; Prince 1981). Suppose (1b) is uttered in the context of (1a). We have stored an entry for *Lucie,* and when the pronoun *she* is encountered, it can be assigned this value. In theory-neutral terms, this assignment is represented in (3b), where *Lucie* is a discourse entry, and the pronoun is covalued with this entry.

The actual resolution of anaphora is governed by discourse strategies. Ariel (1990) argues that pronouns look for the most accessible antecedent, and discourse topics are always the most accessible. For example, (3b) is the most likely anaphora resolution for (1b) in the context of (1a), since *Lucie* is the discourse topic that will make this minimal context coherent.

Given the two procedures, it turns out that if *Lili* is identified as the antecedent of the pronoun in (1b), the sentence has, in fact, two anaphora construals. Since *Lili* is also in the discourse storage, (1b) can have, along with (3a), the covaluation construal (4).

(4) Lili (λx (x thinks z has got the flu) & z = Lili)

(5) Lili thinks she has got the flu, and Max does too.

Though (3a) and (4) are equivalent, it was discovered in the 1970s that there are contexts in which these sentences display a real representational ambiguity (Keenan 1971). For example, assuming that *she* is *Lili,* the elliptic second conjunct of (5) can mean either that Max thinks that Lili has the flu, or that Max himself has it. The first is obtained if the elided predicate is construed as in (4), and the second if it is the predicate of (3a).

Let us adopt here the technical definitions in (6). ((6a) differs from the definition used in the syntactic binding theory). In (3a), then, *Lucie* binds the pronoun; in (4), they are covalued.

(6) a. <u>Binding:</u> α binds β iff α is an argument of a λ-predicate whose operator binds β.
    b. <u>Coevaluation:</u> α and β are covalued iff neither binds the other and they are assigned the same value.

Covaluation is not restricted to referential discourse-entities—a pronoun can be covalued also with a bound variable. Indeed, Heim (1998) showed that covaluation-binding ambiguity can show up also in quantified contexts. In (7a), the variable *x* (*she*) binds the pronoun *her.* But in (7b) *her* is covalued with *x*.

(7) Every wife thinks that only she respects her husband.
    a. <u>Binding:</u> Every wife (λx (x thinks that [only x (λy(y respects y's husband))]))
    b. <u>Covaluation:</u> Every wife (λx (x thinks that [only x (λy(y respects x's husband))]))

In many contexts the two construals will be equivalent, but the presence of *only* enables their disambiguation here: (7a) entails that every wife thinks that other wives do not respect their husbands, while (7b) entails that every wife thinks other wives do not respect her husband. This is so, because the property attributed only to *x* in (7a) is respecting one's own husband, while in (7b) it is respecting *x*'s husband.

The binding interpretation of pronouns is restricted by syntactic properties of the derivation (see BINDING THEORY).

A question that has been debated is whether there are also syntactic restrictions on their covaluation interpretation. On the factual side, under certain syntactic configurations, covaluation is not allowed. For example, in (9), binding is independently excluded. The NP Lucie is not in a configuration to bind the pronoun (since it is not the argument of a λ-predicate containing the pronoun). Suppose, however, that (9) is uttered in the context of (8), so that Lucie is in the discourse storage. The question is what prevents the covaluation construal in (10) for (9) (# marks an excluded interpretation). It cannot be just the fact that the pronoun precedes the antecedent. For example, in (11), the preceding pronoun can be covalued with Max.

(8) Can we go to the bar without Lucie?

(9) She said we should invite Lucie.

(10) #She (λx x said we should invite Lucie) & she = Lucie)

(11) a. The woman next to him kissed Max.
     b. The woman next to him (λx (x kissed Max) & him = Max)

In the 1970s, it was assumed that there is a syntactic restriction blocking such an interpretation (Langacker 1966; Lasnik 1976). Reinhart (1976) formulated it as the requirement that a pronoun cannot be covalued with a full NP it c-commands, which became known as Chomsky's "condition C" (1981). (In (11), the pronoun does not c-command Max.) Another formulation in logical syntax terms was proposed by Keenan (1974): The reference of an argument must be determinable independently of its predicate.

The empirical problem with these restrictions is that, as shown in Evans (1980), there are systematic contexts in which they can be violated. Reinhart (1983) argued that this is possible whenever covaluation is not equivalent to binding.

(12) [Who is the man with the gray hat?] He is Ralph Smith.
     a. He (λx (x is Ralph Smith) & he = Ralph Smith)
     b. He (λx (x is x) & he = Ralph Smith)

(13) Only he (himself) still thinks that Max is a genius.
     a. Only he (λx (x thinks Max is a genius) & he = Max)
     b. Only Max (λx (x thinks x is a genius)

In (12), it is not easy to imagine a construal of the truth conditions that would not include covaluation of the pronoun with Ralph Smith. But this covaluation violates condition C, as does (13). In both cases, however, the covaluation reading (a) is clearly distinct from the bound reading (b). (12b) is a tautology, whereas (12a) is not. (13a) attributes a different property only to Max from what (13b) does. Believing oneself to be a genius may be true of many people, but what (13) attributes only to Max is believing Max to be a genius (13a).

The alternative (proposed by Reinhart 1983) is that covaluation is not governed by syntax, but by a discourse strategy that takes into account the options open for the syntax in generating the given derivation. The underlying assumption is that variable binding is a more efficient way to obtain anaphora than covaluation. So whenever the syntactic configuration allows, in principle, variable binding, obtaining an equivalent anaphora-interpretation through covaluation is excluded. Given a structure like (9), variable binding could be derived, with a different placement of Lucie and her, as in Lucie said we should invite her. The result would be equivalent to the covaluation construal (10) (for (9)). Hence, (10) is excluded. In (11a), no placement of he and Max could enable variable binding, so the covaluation in (11b) is the only option for anaphora. When a variable binding alternative exists, but it is not equivalent to covaluation, covaluation is permitted, as in (12)–(13).

A relevant question is why variable binding is more efficient than covaluation. One answer, developed in Levinson (1987), is purely pragmatic and derives this from the Gricean maxims of quantity and manner. The other, developed in Fox (1998), is based on the notion of semantic processing: variable binding is less costly since it enables immediate closure of open properties, while covaluation requires that the property is stored open until we find an antecedent for the variable.

The optimality account for the covaluation restriction entails a much greater computational complexity than the syntactic approach (condition C), since it requires constructing and comparing two interpretations for one derivation. This is among the reasons why covaluation is still a matter of theoretical debate. Nevertheless, evidence that such complexity is indeed involved in computing sentences like (10) comes from the acquisition of anaphora. Many studies (e.g., Wexler and Chien 1991) report that children have much greater difficulties in ruling out illicit covaluation than in violations of the syntactic restrictions on variable binding. Grodzinsky and Reinhart (1993) argue that this is because their working memory is not yet sufficiently developed to carry such complex computation.

See also PRAGMATICS; SEMANTICS; SENTENCE PROCESSING; SYNTAX-SEMANTICS INTERFACE

—*Tanya Reinhart*

References

Ariel, M. (1990). *Accessing Noun Phrase Antecedents.* London and New York: Routledge.

Chomsky, N. (1981). *Lectures on Government and Binding.* Dordrecht: Foris.

Evans, G. (1980). Pronouns. *Linguistic Inquiry* 11: 337–362.

Fox, D. (1998). Locality in variable binding. In P. Barbosa et al., Eds., *Is the Best Good Enough?* Cambridge, MA: MIT Press and MITWPL.

Grodzinsky, Y., and T. Reinhart. (1993). The innateness of binding and coreference. *Linguistic Inquiry.*

Heim, I. (1982). File change semantics and the familiarity theory of definiteness. In R. Bauerle et al., Eds., *Meaning, Use and the Interpretation of Language.* Berlin and New York: de Gruyter, pp. 164–189.

Heim, I. (1998). Anaphora and semantic interpretation: A reinterpretation of Reinhart's approach. In U. Sauerland and O. Percus, Eds., *The Interpretative Tract, MIT Working Papers in Linguistics,* vol. 25. Cambridge, MA: MITWPL.

Keenan, E. (1971). Names, quantifiers and a solution to the sloppy identity problem. *Papers in Linguistics* 4(2).

Keenan, E. (1974). The functional principle: Generalizing the notion "subject of." In M. LaGaly, R. Fox, and A. Bruck, Eds.,

Papers from the Tenth Regional Meeting of the Chicago Linguistic Society. Chicago: Chicago Linguistic Society.

Langacker, R. (1966). On pronominalization and the chain of command. In W. Reibel and S. Schane, Eds., *Modern Studies in English.* Englewood Cliffs, NJ: Prentice Hall.

Lasnik, H. (1976). Remarks on coreference. *Linguistic Analysis* 2(1).

Levinson, S. C. (1987). Pragmatics and the grammar of anaphora. *Journal of Linguistics* 23: 379–434.

McCawley, J. (1979). Presuppositions and discourse structure. In C. K. Oh and D. A. Dinneen, Eds., *Presuppositions. Syntax and Semantics,* vol. 11. New York: Academic Press.

Prince, E. (1981). Towards a taxonomy of given-new information. In P. Cole, Ed., *Radical Pragmatics.* New York: Academic Press, pp. 233–255.

Reinhart, T. (1976). *The Syntactic Domain of Anaphora.* Ph.D. diss., MIT.

Reinhart, T. (1983). *Anaphora and Semantic Interpretation.* Croom-Helm and Chicago University Press.

Wexler, K., and Y. C. Chien. (1991). Children's knowledge of locality conditions on binding as evidence for the modularity of syntax and pragmatics. *Language Acquisition* 1: 225–295.

Animal Cognition

See ANIMAL NAVIGATION; COMPARATIVE PSYCHOLOGY; PRIMATE COGNITION; SOCIAL PLAY BEHAVIOR

Animal Communication

Fireflies flash, moths spray pheromones, bees dance, fish emit electric pulses, lizards drop dewlaps, frogs croak, birds sing, bats chirp, lions roar, monkeys grunt, apes grimace, and humans speak. These systems of communication, irrespective of sensory modality, are designed to mediate a flow of information between sender and receiver (Hauser 1996).

Early ethologists argued that signals are designed to proffer information to receptive companions, usually of their own species (Tinbergen 1951; Hinde 1981; Smith 1969). When a bird or a monkey gives a "hawk call," for example, this conveys information about a kind of danger. And when a redwing blackbird reveals its red epaulette during territorial disputes, it is conveying information about aggressive intent. Analyses of aggressive interactions, however, revealed only weak correlations between performance of certain displays and the probability of attack as opposed to retreat, leaving the outcome relatively unpredictable (Caryl 1979). Thus, while information transfer is basic to all communication, it is unclear how best to characterize the information exchange, particularly because animals do not always tell the truth.

In contradistinction to the ethologists, a new breed of animal behaviorist—the behavioral ecologists—proposed an alternative approach based on an economic cost-benefit analysis. The general argument was made in two moves: (1) selection favors behavioral adaptations that maximize gene propagation; and (2) information exchange cannot be the entire function of communication because it would be easy for a mutant strategy to invade by providing dishonest information about the probability of subsequent actions. This places a premium on recognizing honest signals. Zahavi (1975) suggested a mechanism for this, using the following recipe: signals are honest, if and only if they are costly to produce relative to the signaler's current condition and if the capacity to produce honest signals is heritable. Consider the anti predator stotting displays of ungulates—an energetically expensive rigid-legged leap. In Thompson's gazelle, only males in good physical condition stot, and stotting males are more likely to escape cheetah attacks than those who do not.

Departing slightly from Zahavi, behavioral ecologists Krebs and Dawkins (1984) proposed that signals are designed not to inform but to manipulate. In response to such manipulation, selection favors skeptical receivers determined to discriminate truths from falsehoods. Such manipulative signaling evolves in situations of resource competition, including access to mates, parental care, and limited food supplies. In cases where sender and receiver must cooperate to achieve a common goal, however, selection favors signals that facilitate the flow of information among cooperators. Thus signals designed to manipulate tend to be loud and costly to produce (yelling, crying with tears), whereas signals designed for cooperation tend to be quiet, subtle, and cheap (whispers).

Turning to ecological constraints, early workers suggested that signal structure was conventional and arbitrary. More in-depth analyses, however, revealed that the physical structure of many signals is closely related to the functions served (Green and Marler 1979; Marler 1955). Thus, several avian and mammalian species use calls for mobbing predators that are loud, short, repetitive, and broad band. Such sounds attract attention and facilitate sound localization. In contrast, alarm calls used to warn companions of an approaching hawk are soft, high-pitched whistles, covering a narrow frequency range, only audible at close range and hard to locate (Marler 1955; Klump and Shalter 1984). The species-typical environment places additional constraints on the detectability of signals and the efficiency of transmission in long-distance communication, selecting for the optimal time of day and sound frequency window (Marten, Quine, and Marler 1977; Morton 1975; Wiley and Richards 1978). To coordinate the movements of groups who are out of sight, elephants and whales use very low frequency sounds that circumvent obstacles and carry over long distances. In contrast, sounds with high frequency and short wavelengths, such as some alarm calls and the biosonar signals used by bats and dolphins for obstacle avoidance and prey capture, attenuate rapidly.

The design of some signals reflects a conflict between natural and sexual selection pressures (Endler 1993). An elegant example is the advertisement call of the male *Tungara* frog (Ryan and Rand 1993). In its most complete form, one or more introductory whines are followed by chucks. Because females are attracted to the chucks, males who produce these sounds have higher mating success. But because frog-eating bats can localize chucks more readily than whines, frogs producing chucks are more likely to be eaten. They compromise by giving more whines than chucks until a female comes by. There are many such cases in which signal design is closely related to function, reflecting a tightly stitched tapestry of factors that include the sender's production capabilities, habitat structure, climate, time of day, competitors for signal space, the spatiotemporal distribution of intended recipients, and the pressures of predation and mate choice.

When signals are produced or perceived, complex processing by the sense organs and the central nervous system is engaged. Songbirds have a set of interconnected forebrain nuclei specialized for song learning and production. Nuclei vary widely in size between the sexes, between species and even between individuals of the same sex, though there are significant exceptions to these generalizations. Variations appear to correlate, not only with the commitment to singing behavior, but also with the size of the song repertoire (Arnold 1992; Nottebohm 1989). Some aspects of song learning are analogous to those documented for human speech, including involvement of particular brain areas, local dialects, categorical perception, innate learning preferences, and a motor theory-like system for coordinating articulatory production and feature perception (Nelson and Marler 1989).

For most animals, the acoustic morphology of the vocal repertoire appears to be innately specified, with experience playing little to no role in altering call structure during development. In contrast, the ontogeny of call usage and comprehension is stongly influenced by experience in several nonhuman primates, and possibly in some birds (Cheney and Seyfarth 1990; Hauser 1996; Marler 1991), with benefits accruing to individuals that can learn to use call types and subtypes in new ways. Generally speaking, however, the number of discrete signals in animal repertoires seems to be limited (Green and Marler 1979; Moynihan 1970), although reliable repertoire estimates are hard to come by, especially when signals intergrade extensively. Explosive expansion of the repertoire becomes possible if elements of the repertoire can be recombined into new, meaningful utterances, as they are in human speech.

Empirical studies documenting the decomposability of speech into smaller units, themselves meaningless, prepared the groundwork for the Chomskyan revolution in linguistics. The human brain takes our repertoire of phonemes and recombines them into an infinite variety of utterances with distinct meanings. There is no known case of animals using this combinatorial mechanism. Some birds create large learned song repertoires by recombination, but like human music, birdsongs are primarily affective signals, lacking the kind of referential meaning that has been attributed to primate vocalizations and chicken calls. Thus it appears that the songbirds' repertoire expansion serves more to alleviate habituation than to enrich meaning. The same is almost certainly true of animals with innate repertoires that engage in a more limited degree of recombination, although some researchers have reported evidence of syntactical organization (Hailman et al. 1987). More detailed analyses of the production and perception of vocal signals are required before we can reach any comprehensive conclusions on the developmental plasticity of animal communication systems.

At least one bird (the domestic chicken) and a few primates (ring-tailed lemurs, rhesus and diana monkeys, vervets) produce vocalizations that are functionally referential, telling others about specific objects and events (food, predators). Use of such calls is often contingent on the presence and nature of a social audience (e.g., allies or enemies). Vocalizing animals will, for example, withhold alarm calling in response to a predator if no audience is present, and in other cases, will use vocalizations to actively falsify information (Cheney and Seyfarth 1990; Evans and Marler 1991; Marler, Karakashian, and Gyger 1991; reviewed in Hauser 1996). While there is no evidence that animal signals are guided by awareness of beliefs, desires, and intentions, essential to human linguistic behavior (see PRIMATE COGNITION), there is a clear need for researchers in call semantics and cognition to work closely together to elucidate the mental states of animals while communicating.

See also COMPARATIVE PSYCHOLOGY; DISTINCTIVE FEATURES; ETHOLOGY; LANGUAGE AND COMMUNICATION; PHONOLOGY; PRIMATE LANGUAGE; SOCIAL COGNITION IN ANIMALS; SOCIAL PLAY BEHAVIOR

— *Marc Hauser and Peter Marler*

References

Arnold, A. P. (1992). Developmental plasticity in neural circuits controlling birdsong: Sexual differentiation and the neural basis of learning. *Journal of Neurobiology* 23: 1506–1528.

Caryl, P. G. (1979). Communication by agonistic displays: What can games theory contribute to ethology? *Behaviour* 68: 136–169.

Cheney, D. L., and R. M. Seyfarth. (1990). *How Monkeys See the World: Inside the Mind of Another Species.* Chicago: Chicago University Press.

Endler, J. (1993). Some general comments on the evolution and design of animal communication systems. *Proceedings of the Royal Society, London* 340: 215–225.

Evans, C. S., and P. Marler. (1991). On the use of video images as social stimuli in birds: Audience effects on alarm calling. *Animal Behaviour* 41: 17–26.

Green, S., and P. Marler. (1979). The analysis of animal communication. In P. Marler and J. Vandenbergh, Eds., *Handbook of Behavioral Neurobiology,* vol. 3, *Social Behavior and Communication.* New York: Plenum Press, pp. 73–158.

Hailman, J. P., M. S. Ficken, and R. W. Ficken. (1987). Constraints on the structure of combinatorial "chick-a-dee" calls. *Ethology* 75: 62–80.

Hauser, M. D. (1996). *The Evolution of Communication.* Cambridge, MA: MIT Press.

Hinde, R. A. (1981). Animal signals: Ethological and games-theory approaches are not incompatible. *Animal Behaviour* 29: 535–542.

Klump, G. M., and M. D. Shalter. (1984). Acoustic behaviour of birds and mammals in the predator context: 1. Factors affecting the structure of alarm signals. 2. The functional significance and evolution of alarm signals. *Zeitschrift für Tierpsychologie* 66: 189–226.

Krebs, J. R., and R. Dawkins. (1984). Animal signals: Mind-reading and manipulation. In J.R. Krebs and N.B. Davies, Eds., *Behavioural Ecology: an Evolutionary Approach.* Sunderland, MA: Sinauer Associates Inc., pp. 380–402.

Marler, P. (1955). Characteristics of some animal calls. *Nature* 176: 6–7.

Marler, P. (1991). Differences in behavioural development in closely related species: Birdsong. In P. Bateson, Ed., *The Development and Integration of Behaviour.* Cambridge: Cambridge University Press, pp. 41–70.

Marler, P., S. Karakashian, and M. Gyger. (1991). Do animals have the option of withholding signals when communication is inappropriate? The audience effect. In C. Ristau, Ed., *Cognitive Ethology: The Minds of Other Animals.* Hillsdale, NJ: Erlbaum, pp. 135–186.

Marten, K., D. B. Quine, and P. Marler. (1977). Sound transmission and its significance for animal vocalization. 2. Tropical habitats. *Behavioral Ecology and Sociobiology* 2: 291–302.

Morton, E. S. (1975). Ecological sources of selection on avian sounds. *American Naturalist* 109: 17–34.

Moynihan, M. (1970). The control, suppression, decay, disappearance, and replacement of displays. *Journal of Theoretical Biology* 29: 85–112.

Nelson, D. A., and P. Marler. (1989). Categorical perception of a natural stimulus continuum: Birdsong. *Science* 244: 976–978.

Nottebohm, F. (1989). From bird song to neurogenesis. *Scientific American* 260(2): 74–79.

Ryan, M. J., and A. S. Rand. (1993). Phylogenetic patterns of behavioral mate recognition systems in the *Physalaemus pustulosus* species group (Anura: Leptodactylidae): The role of ancestral and derived characters and sensory exploitation. In D. Lees and D. Edwards, Eds., *Evolutionary Patterns and Processes.* London: Academic Press, pp. 251–267.

Smith, W. J. (1969). Messages of vertebrate communication. *Science* 165: 145–150.

Tinbergen, N. (1952). Derived activities: Their causation, biological significance, origin and emancipation during evolution. *Quarterly Review of Biology* 27: 1–32.

Wiley, R. H., and D. G. Richards. (1978). Physical constraints on acoustic communication in the atmosphere: Implications for the evolution of animal vocalizations. *Behavioral Ecology and Sociobiology* 3: 69–94.

Zahavi, A. (1975). Mate selection: a selection for a handicap. *Journal of Theoretical Biology* 53: 205–214.

Further Readings

Andersson, M. (1982). Female choice selects for extreme tail length in a widowbird. *Nature* 299: 818–820.

Andersson, M. (1994). *Sexual Selection.* Princeton, NJ: Princeton University Press.

Brenowitz, E. A., and A. P. Arnold. (1986). Interspecific comparisons of the size of neural song control regions and song complexity in duetting birds: Evolutionary implications. *The Journal of Neuroscience* 6: 2875–2879.

Brown, C., and P. Waser. (1988). Environmental influences on the structure of primate vocalizations. In D. Todt, P. Goedeking, and D. Symmes, Eds., *Primate Vocal Communication.* Berlin: Springer, pp. 51–68.

Cheney, D. L., and R. M. Seyfarth. (1988). Assessment of meaning and the detection of unreliable signals by vervet monkeys. *Animal Behaviour* 36: 477–486.

Cleveland, J., and C. T. Snowdon. (1981). The complex vocal repertoire of the adult cotton-top tamarin, *Saguinus oedipus oedipus. Zeitschrift für Tierpsychologie* 58: 231–270.

DeVoogd, T. J., J. R. Krebs, S. D. Healy, and A. Purvis. (1993). Relations between song repertoire size and the volume of brain nuclei related to song: Comparative evolutionary analyses amongst oscine birds. *Proceedings of the Royal Society, London* 254: 75–82.

Endler, J. A. (1987). Predation, light intensity, and courtship behaviour in *Poecilia reticulata. Animal Behaviour* 35: 1376–1385.

FitzGibbon, C. D., and J. W. Fanshawe. (1988). Stotting in Thompson's gazelles: An honest signal of condition. *Behavioral Ecology and Sociobiology* 23: 69–74.

Hauser, M. D., and P. Marler. (1993). Food-associated calls in rhesus macaques (*Macaca mulatta*). 1. Socioecological factors influencing call production. *Behavioral Ecology* 4: 194–205.

Klump, G. M., E. Kretzschmar, and E. Curio. (1986). The hearing of an avian predator and its avian prey. *Behavioral Ecology and Sociobiology* 18: 317–323.

Langbauer, W. R., Jr., K. Payne, R. Charif, E. Rapaport, and F. Osborn. (1991). African elephants respond to distant playbacks of low-frequency conspecific calls. *Journal of Experimental Biology* 157: 35–46.

Marler, P. (1961). The logical analysis of animal communication. *Journal of Theoretical Biology* 1: 295–317.

Marler, P. (1976). Social organization, communication and graded signals: The chimpanzee and the gorilla. In P. P. G. Bateson and R. A. Hinde, Eds., *Growing Points in Ethology.* Cambridge: Cambridge University Press, pp. 239–280.

Marler, P. (1978). Primate vocalizations: Affective or symbolic? In G. Bourne, Ed., *Progress in Ape Research.* New York: Academic Press, pp. 85–96.

Marler, P. (1984). Song learning: Innate species differences in the learning process. In P. Marler and H. S. Terrace, Eds., *The Biology of Learning.* Berlin: Springer, pp. 289–309.

Marler, P., A. Dufty, and R. Pickert. (1986). Vocal communication in the domestic chicken: 2. Is a sender sensitive to the presence and nature of a receiver? *Animal Behaviour* 34: 194–198.

Nordeen, E. J., and K. W. Nordeen. (1990). Neurogenesis and sensitive periods in avian song learning. *Trends in Neurosciences* 13: 31–36.

Nottebohm, F. (1981). A brain for all seasons: Cyclical anatomical changes in song control nuclei of the canary brain. *Science* 214: 1368–1370.

Robinson, J. G. (1979). An analysis of the organization of vocal communication in the titi monkey, *Callicebus moloch. Zeitschrift für Tierpsychologie* 49: 381–405.

Robinson, J. G. (1984). Syntactic structures in the vocalizations of wedge-capped capuchin monkeys, *Cebus nigrivittatus. Behaviour* 90: 46–79.

Ryan, M. J., and A. S. Rand. (1995). Female responses to ancestral advertisement calls in *Tungara* frogs. *Science* 269: 390–392.

Ryan, M. J., and W. Wilczynski. (1988). Coevolution of sender and receiver: Effect on local mate preference in cricket frogs. *Science* 240: 1786–1788.

Seyfarth, R. M., and D. L. Cheney. (1997). Some general features of vocal development in nonhuman primates. In C. T. Snowdon and M. Hausberger, Eds., *Social Influences on Vocal Development.* Cambridge: Cambridge University Press, pp. 249–273.

Suga, N. (1988). Auditory neuroethology and speech processing: Complex sound processing by combination-sensitive neurons. In G. M. Edelman, W. E. Gall, and W. M. Cowan, Eds., *Auditory Function.* New York: Wiley-Liss Press, pp. 679–720.

Williams, H., and F. Nottebohm. (1985). Auditory responses in avian vocal motor neurons: A motor theory for song perception in birds. *Science* 229: 279–282.

Animal Navigation

Animal navigation is similar to conventional (formalized) navigation in at least three basic ways. First, it relies heavily on *dead reckoning,* the continual updating of position by summing successive small *displacements* (changes in position). In the limit (as the differences between successive positions are made arbitrarily small), this process is equivalent to obtaining the position vector by integrating the velocity vector with respect to time, which is why the process is also called *path integration* (see Gallistel 1990, chap. 4, for review of literature).

Second, it only occasionally *takes a fix,* that is, establishes position and *heading* (orientation) on a map using perceived distances and directions from mapped features of the terrain. While it is necessary from time to time to correct the inevitable cumulative error in dead reckoning, animals, like human navigators, often invert the process in the intervals between fixes, using their reckoned position and heading on their map to estimate their relation to surrounding features. In doing so, they appear to ignore the current testimony of their senses. Thus, when the dimensions of a familiar maze are altered, a rat moving rapidly through it collides with walls that come too soon, and turns into a wall where it expects an opening (Carr and Watson 1908). Indeed, it runs right over the pile of food that is its goal when it encounters that pile much sooner than expected (Stoltz and Lott 1964). Bats threading their way through obstacle courses bring their wings together over their head to squeeze through a gap that is no longer so narrow as to require this maneuver (Neuweiler and Möhres 1967).

And third, it places relatively minor reliance on *beacon navigation,* the following of sensory cues from a goal or its immediate surroundings. Animals of widely diverse species locate a goal by the goal's position relative to the general framework provided by the mapped terrain (see Gallistel 1990, chap. 5, for review), not by the sensory characteristics of the goal or its immediate surroundings. Indeed, when the two are placed in conflict, the animal goes to the place having the correct position in the larger framework, not to the place having the correct sensory characteristics. For example, if a chimpanzee sees food hidden in one of two differently colored containers whose positions are then surreptitiously interchanged, the chimpanzee searches for the food in the container at the correct location rather than in the one with the correct color (Tinkelpaugh 1932). In human toddlers, position also takes precedence over the characteristics of the container. When a toddler is misoriented within a rectangular room, it ignores the container in which it saw a toy hidden, but which it now mistakenly takes to be in the wrong location. It looks instead in an altogether different container, which it takes to be in the correct location, even though the child demonstrably remembers the appearance of the container in which it saw the toy hidden (Hermer and Spelke 1996).

The sensory cues from the goal itself appear to control approach behavior only in the final approach to the goal, and even then, only when the goal is in approximately the correct location. The same is true for the nearby landmarks with respect to which an animal more precisely locates its goal. It uses them as aids to locating its goal only if they occupy approximately the correct place in the larger framework. Bees readily learn to search for food on one side of a landmark in one location but on the opposite side of the identical landmark placed in a different location (Collett and Kelber 1988). In effect, location confers identity, rather than vice versa. A container or landmark with the wrong properties in the right place is taken to be the correct container or landmark, while a container or landmark with the correct properties in the wrong place is taken to be a different container or different landmark.

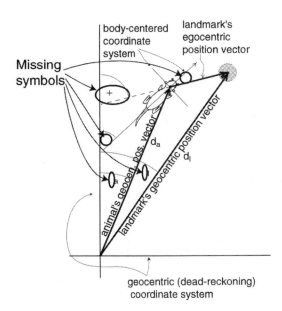

Figure 1. Conversion of egocentric position coordinates to a common geocentric framework. The egocentric position vector of the landmark, with angle β (bearing of landmark) and magnitude d_1 is first rotated so that it has angle $\eta + \beta$ (heading plus bearing), then added to the geocentric position vector of the animal (with compass angle γ_a and magnitude d_a), producing the geocentric position vector for the landmark (with compass angle γ_1 and magnitude d_1). (Slightly modified from figure 1 in Gallistel and Cramer 1996. Used by permission of the authors and publisher.)

From the above, it is clear that COGNITIVE MAPS are a critical component in animal navigation, just as conventional maps are in conventional navigation. A cognitive map is a representation of the layout of the environment. Its properties and the process by which it is constructed are questions of basic importance. These cognitive maps are known to be *Euclidean, sense-preserving* representations of the environment, that is, they encode the metric relations (distances and angles) and the sense relation (right versus left). This is most readily demonstrated by showing an animal the location of a hidden goal within a featureless rectangular room, then inertially disorienting the animal (by slow rotation in the dark) before allowing it to search for the goal. Animals of diverse species search principally at the correct location and its rotational equivalent, for example, in the correct corner and the corner diagonally opposite to it (Cheng 1986; Hermer and Spelke 1996; Margules and Gallistel 1988). They rarely look elsewhere, for example, in the other two corners. To distinguish between the diagonals of a rectangle, however, they must record both metric relations and sense relations on their map of the rectangular room. The short wall is on the left for one diagonal, regardless of which way one faces along that diagonal, but on the right for the other diagonal. If an animal could not distinguish walls based on their length (a metric relationship), or on which was to the left and which to the right (a sense relationship), then it could not distinguish between the diagonals of a rectangle.

Until recently, there were no suggestions about how animals might construct a Euclidean map of their environment. They only perceive small portions of it at any one time, so how can they perceive the relations between these portions? Recently, it has been suggested that the dead reckoning process is the key to the construction of the map (Gallistel 1990; Gallistel and Cramer 1996; McNaughton et al. 1996) because it specifies the Euclidean relationship between different points of view within a *geocentric framework,* a system of coordinates anchored to the earth, as opposed to an *egocentric framework,* a system of coordinates anchored to the animal's body (egocentric position vector in figure). Rotating the egocentric position vector by the animal's heading (its orientation in the geocentric framework) and adding the rotated vector to the geocentric position vector provided by the dead reckoning process carries the representation of the perceived portion of the environment into a common geocentric positional framework (landmark's geocentric position vector in figure). This method of map construction, in which the animal's dead reckoning automatically represents its position on its cognitive map, tells us much about how the animal perceives the shape of its environment.

See also ANIMAL NAVIGATION, NEURAL NETWORKS; COGNITIVE ARTIFACTS; HUMAN NAVIGATION

—*C. Randy Gallistel*

References

Carr, H., and J. B. Watson. (1908). Orientation of the white rat. *Journal of Comparative Neurology and Psychology* 18: 27–44.

Cheng, K. (1986). A purely geometric module in the rat's spatial representation. *Cognition* 23: 149–178.

Collett, T. S., and A. Kelber. (1988). The retrieval of visuo-spatial memories by honeybees. *Journal of Comparative Physiology,* series A 163: 145–150.

Gallistel, C. R. (1990). *The Organization of Learning.* Cambridge, MA: MIT Press.

Gallistel, C. R., and A. E. Cramer. (1996). Computations on metric maps in mammals: Getting oriented and choosing a multi-destination route. *Journal of Experimental Biology* 199: 211–217.

Hermer, L., and E. Spelke. (1996). Modularity and development: The case of spatial reorientation. *Cognition* 61: 195–232.

Margules, J., and C. R. Gallistel. (1988). Heading in the rat: Determination by environmental shape. *Animal Learning and Behavior* 16: 404–410.

McNaughton, B. L., C. A. Barnes, J. L. Gerrard, K. Gothard, M. W. Jung, J. J. Knierim, H. Kudrimoti, Y. Qin, W. E. Skaggs, M. Suster, and K. L. Weaver. (1996). Deciphering the hippocampal polyglot: The hippocampus as a path integration system. *Journal of Experimental Biology* 199: 173–185.

Neuweiler, G., and F. P. Möhres. (1967). Die Rolle des Ortgedächtnisses bei der Orientierung der Grossblatt-Fledermaus *Megaderma lyra. Zeitschrift für vergleichende Physiologie* 57: 147–171.

Stoltz, S. P., and D. F. Lott. (1964). Establishment in rats of a persistent response producing net loss of reinforcement. *Journal of Comparative and Physiological Psychology* 57: 147–149.

Tinkelpaugh, O. L. (1932). Multiple delayed reaction with chimpanzee and monkeys. *Journal of Comparative Psychology* 13: 207–243.

Animal Navigation, Neural Networks

Animals show a remarkable ability to navigate through their environment. For example, many animals must cover large regions of the local terrain in search of a goal (food, mates, etc.), and then must be able to return immediately and safely to their nesting spot. From one occasion to the next, animals seem to use varied, novel trajectories to make these searches, and may enter entirely new territory during part of the search. Nonetheless, on obtaining the goal, they are typically able to calculate a direct route to return to their home base.

For many species, this ANIMAL NAVIGATION is thought to be based on two general abilities. The first, called "dead reckoning" (or "path integration"), uses information about the animal's own movements through space to keep track of current position and directional heading, in relation to an abstract representation of the overall environment. The second, landmark-based orientation, uses familiar environmental landmarks to establish current position, relative to familiar terrain.

Over the last few decades, some insight has been gained about how NEURAL NETWORKS in the mammalian brain might work to provide the basis for these abilities. In particular, two specialized types of cells have been observed to possess relevant spatial signals in the brains of navigating rats.

"Place cells," originally discovered in the rat HIPPOCAMPUS (O'Keefe and Dostrovsky 1971), fire whenever the animal is in one specific part of the environment. Each place cell has its own, unique region of firing. As the animal travels through the environment, these cells seem to form a maplike representation, with each location represented by neural activity in a specific set of place cells.

Remarkably, these cells also seem to use the two general abilities mentioned above: dead reckoning and landmark-based orientation. Evidence that place cells use landmarks to establish the place-specific firing patterns came from early studies in which familiar landmarks were moved (e.g., O'Keefe and Conway 1978; Muller and Kubie 1987). For example, in one experiment (Muller and Kubie 1987), rats foraged in a large, cylindrical apparatus, equipped with a single, white cue card on its otherwise uniformly gray wall. When this single orienting landmark was moved to a different location on the wall, this caused an equal rotation of the place cell firing fields. Evidence that the cells can also use dead reckoning, however, was obtained from studies in which the landmarks were removed entirely (e.g., Muller and Kubie 1987; O'Keefe and Speakman 1987). In this case, the place cells were often able to maintain their firing patterns, so that they continued to fire in the same location, as the animal made repeated, winding trajectories through the environment. It was reasoned that this ability must be based on a dead reckoning process because in the absence of orienting landmarks, the only ongoing information about current position would have to be based on the animal's own movements through space. Further support for the dead reckoning (path integration) process came from a study in which artificial movement-related information was given directly to the animal while it navigated (Sharp et al. 1995). Animals foraged in a cylinder with black and white stripes, of uniform width.

Both activation of the vestibular system (indicating that the animal had moved through space), or rotation of the vertical stripes (as would happen due to the animal's own movement in relation to the stripes) could sometimes "update" the place cell firing fields, so that they shifted the location of their fields, as though the animal had actually moved in the way suggested by the vestibular or optic flow input. Thus movement-related inputs directly influence the positional setting of the hippocampal place cells.

The second type of navigation-related cells, known as "head direction cells" (Taube, Muller, and Ranck 1990a), complement the place cells by signaling the animal's current directional heading, regardless of its location. Each head direction cell fires whenever the animal is facing one particular direction (over an approximately 90 degree range). Each has its own, unique, directional preference, so that each direction the animal faces is represented by activity in a particular subset of head direction cells. These cells were initially discovered in the postsubiculum (a brain region closely related to the hippocampus), and have since been discovered in several other anatomically related brain regions.

Although it might be thought that these directional cells derive a constant, earth-based orientation from geomagnetic cues, this seems not to be the case. Rather, like place cells (and the animal's own navigational behavior), head direction cells seem to use both landmark orientation and dead reckoning (Taube, Muller, and Ranck 1990b). For example, in a familiar environment, these cells will rotate the preferred direction when familiar landmarks are rotated, using the landmarks to get a "fix" on the animal's current directional heading. When, however, all familiar landmarks are removed, the cells retain the animal's previously established directional preference. And, again like place cells, head direction cells use both vestibular and optic flow information to update their locational setting (Blair and Sharp 1996).

Theoretical models have been developed to simulate the spatial firing properties of these cells (e.g., Blair 1996; McNaughton et al. 1995; Skaggs et al. 1995; Redish, Elga, and Touretzky 1997; Samsonovich and McNaughton 1997). Most of these models begin with the idea that the place and head direction cells are respectively linked together to form stable attractor networks that can stabilize into a unitary representation any one of the possible places or directions. For example, in the head direction cell system, cells representing similar directional headings are linked together through predominantly excitatory connections, while cells representing different directional headings are linked through inhibitory connections. This reflects the basic phenomenon that, at any one time, cells within one particular portion of the directional range (e.g., 0 to 90 degrees) will be active, while all other head direction cells will be silent. Thus the stable attractor network, left on its own, will always settle into a representation of one particular direction (place). To reflect the finding that place and head direction cells can be "set" by environmental landmarks, most models equip the cells with sensory inputs that can influence which particular place or direction is represented. To reflect the finding that the navigation system can also be updated by movement related information, most models also incorporate an additional layer of cells (in some other, as yet unidentified brain

region) that combines place or head direction information, along with movement-related cues, to feed back onto the place or head direction cells, permitting them to choose a new locational or directional setting in response to movement.

While these complementary place and directional representations are thought to guide the animal's overall navigational behavior (see O'Keefe and Nadel 1978), the mechanism is not yet clear.

See also COGNITIVE MAPS; COMPUTATION AND THE BRAIN; HUMAN NAVIGATION; SPATIAL PERCEPTION

—*Patricia E. Sharp*

References

Blair, H. T. (1996). A thalamocortical circuit for computing directional heading in the rat. In D. S. Touretzky, M. C. Mozer, and M. E. Hasselmo, Eds., *Advances in Neural Information Processing,* vol. 8, Cambridge, MA: MIT Press.

Blair, H. T., and P. E. Sharp. (1996). Visual and vestibular influences on head direction cells in the anterior thalamus of the rat. *Behavioral Neuroscience* 110: 1–18.

McNaughton, B. L., C. A. Barnes, J. L. Gerrard, K. Gothard, M. W. Jung, J. J. Knierim, H. Kudrimoti, Y. Quin, W. E. Skaggs, M. Suster, and K. L. Weaver. (1995). Deciphering the hippocampal polyglot: The hippocampus as a path integration system. *Journal of Experimental Biology* 199: 173–185.

Muller, R. U., and J. L. Kubie. (1987). The effects of changes in the environment on the spatial firing of hippocampal complex-spike cells. *Journal of Neuroscience* 7: 1951–1968.

O'Keefe, J., and D. H. Conway. (1978). Hippocampal place units in the freely moving rat: Why they fire where they fire. *Experimental Brain Research* 31: 573–590.

O'Keefe, J., and J. Dostrovsky. (1971). The hippocampus as a spatial map: Preliminary evidence from unit activity in the freely moving rat. *Brain Research* 34: 171–175.

O'Keefe, J., and L. Nadel. (1978). *The Hippocampus as a Cognitive Map.* New York: Oxford.

O'Keefe, J., and A. Speakman. (1987). Single unit activity in the rat hippocampus during a spatial task. *Experimental Brain Research* 68: 1–27.

Redish, A. D., A. N. Elga, and D. S. Touretzky. (1997). A coupled attractor model of the rodent head direction system. *Network* 7: 671–686.

Samsonovich, A., and B. L. McNaughton. (1997). Path integration and cognitive mapping in a continuous attractor neural network model. *Journal of Neuroscience* 17: 5900–5920.

Sharp, P. E., H. T. Blair, D. Etkin, and D. B. Tzanetos. (1995). Influences of vestibular and visual motion information on the spatial firing patterns of hippocampal place cells. *Journal of Neuroscience* 15: 173–189.

Skaggs, W. E., J. J. Knierim, H. S. Kudrimoti, and B. L. McNaughton. (1995). A model of the neural basis of the rat's sense of direction. In G. Tesauro, D. S. Touretzky, and T. K. Lean, Eds., *Advances in Neural Information Processing Systems,* vol. 7, Cambridge, MA: MIT Press.

Taube, J. S., R. U. Muller, and J. B. Ranck, Jr. (1990a). Head direction cells recorded from the postsubiculum in freely moving rats: 1. Description and quantitative analysis. *Journal of Neuroscience* 10: 420–435.

Taube, J. S., R. U. Muller, and J. B. Ranck, Jr. (1990b). Head direction cells recorded from the postsubiculum in freely moving rats: 2. Effects of environmental manipulations. *Journal of Neuroscience* 10: 436–447.

Further Readings

Blair, H. T., and P. E. Sharp. (1995a). Anticipatory firing of anterior thalamic head direction cells: Evidence for a thalamocortical circuit that computes head direction in the rat. *Journal of Neuroscience* 15: 6260–6270.

Brown, M. A., and P. E. Sharp. (1995b). Simulation of spatial learning in the Morris water maze by a neural network model of the hippocampal formation and nucleus accumbens. *Hippocampus* 5: 189–197.

Chen, L. L., L. H. Lin, C. A. Barnes, and B. L. McNaughton. (1994). Head direction cells in the rat posterior cortex: 2. Contributions of visual and idiothetic information to the directional firing. *Experimental Brain Research* 101: 24–34.

Chen, L. L., L. H. Lin, E. J. Green, C. A. Barnes, and B. L. McNaughton. (1994). Head direction cells in the rat posterior cortex: 1. Anatomical distribution and behavioral modulation. *Experimental Brain Research* 101: 8–23.

Foster, T. C., C. A. Castro, and B. L. McNaughton. (1989). Spatial selectivity of rat hippocampal neurons: Dependence on preparedness for movement. *Science* 244: 1580–1582.

Gallistel, C. R. (1990). *The Organization of Learning*. Cambridge, MA: MIT.

Goodridge, J. P., and J. S. Taube. (1995). Preferential use of the landmark navigational system by head direction cells. *Behavioral Neuroscience* 109: 49–61.

Gothard, K. M., K. M. Skaggs, K. M. Moore, and B. L. McNaughton. (1996). Binding of hippocampal CA1 neural activity to multiple reference frames in a landmark-based navigation task. *Journal of Neuroscience* 16: 823–835.

McNaughton, B. L. (1989). Neural mechanisms for spatial computation and information storage. In L. A. Nadel, P. Cooper, P. Culicover, and R. Harnish, Eds., *Neural Connections and Mental Computations*, Cambridge, MA: MIT Press, pp. 285–349.

McNaughton, B. L., L. L. Chen, and E. J. Markus. (1991). "Dead reckoning," landmark learning, and the sense of direction: a neurophysiological and computational hypothesis. *Journal of Cognitive Neuroscience* 3: 190–201.

Mizumori, S. J. Y., and J. D. Williams. (1993). Directionally selective mnemonic properties of neurons in the laterodorsal nucleus of the thalamus of rats. *Journal of Neuroscience* 13: 4015–4028.

Muller, R. U., J. L. Kubie, and J. B. Ranck, Jr. (1987). Spatial firing patterns of hippocampal complex-spike cells in a fixed environment. *Journal of Neuroscience* 7: 1935–1950.

O'Keefe, J., and N. Burgess. (1996). Geometric determinants of the place fields of hippocampal neurons. *Nature* 381: 425–428.

Quirk, G. J., R. U. Muller, and J. L. Kubie. (1990). The firing of hippocampal place cells in the dark depends on the rat's recent experience. *Journal of Neuroscience* 10: 2008–2017.

Sharp, P. E., R. U. Muller, and J. L. Kubie. (1990). Firing properties of hippocampal neurons in a visually-symmetrical stimulus environment: Contributions of multiple sensory cues and mnemonic processes. *Journal of Neuroscience* 10: 3093–3105.

Taube, J. S. (1995). Head direction cells recorded in the anterior thalamic nuclei of freely moving rats. *Journal of Neuroscience* 15: 70–86.

Taube, J. S., and H. L. Burton. (1995). Head direction cell activity monitored in a novel environment and in a cue conflict situation. *Journal of Neurophysiology* 74: 1953–1971.

Taube, J. S., J. P. Goodridge, E. J. Golub, P. A. Dudchenko, and R. W. Stackman. (1996). Processing the head direction cell signal: A review and commentary. *Brain Research Bulletin* 40: 0–10.

Touretzky, D. S., and A. D. Redish. (1996). A theory of rodent navigation based on interacting representations of space. *Hippocampus* 6: 247–270.

Wiener, S. I. (1993). Spatial and behavioral correlates of striatal neurons in rats performing a self-initiated navigation task. *Journal of Neuroscience* 13: 3802–3817.

Wiener, S. I., V. Kurshunov, R. Garcia, and A. Berthoz. (1995). Inertial, substratal, and landmark cue control of hippocampal place cell activity. *European Journal of Neuroscience* 7: 2206–2219.

Zhang, K. (1996). Representation of spatial orientation by the intrinsic dynamics of the head direction cell ensemble: A theory. *Journal of Neuroscience* 16: 2112–2126.

Animism

Animism means labeling inanimate objects as living, attributing characteristics of animate objects (typically humans) to inanimate objects, and making predictions or explanations about inanimate objects based on knowledge about animate objects (again usually represented by human beings). *Anthropomorphism* or *personification* means the extension of human attributes and behaviors to any nonhumans. Thus animistic reasoning can be regarded as personification of an inanimate object. In both cases, assigning mental states (desires, beliefs, and consciousness) to inanimate objects, including extraterrestrial entities (e.g., the sun) and geographical parts (e.g., a mountain), provides the most impressive example ("The sun is hot because it wants to keep people warm").

The term *animism* was introduced by English anthropologists to describe mentalities of indigenous people living in small, self-sufficient communities. Although such usage was severely criticized by Lévy-Bruhl (1910), the term became popular among behavioral scientists, as PIAGET (1926) used it to characterize young children's thinking. Piaget and his followers (e.g., Laurendeau and Pinard 1962) took animistic and personifying tendencies as signs of immaturity, as reflecting the fact that young children have not yet learned to differentiate between animate and inanimate objects or between humans and nonhumans. Chiefly because of methodological differences, a large number of studies on child animism inspired by Piaget, conducted in the 1950s and early 1960s, obtained conflicting results as to the frequency of animistic responses (Richards and Siegler 1984), but the results were discussed only within the Piagetian framework.

Since the 1980s, studies of young children's biological understanding or naive biology have shed new light on child animism. A number of investigators have shown that even young children possess the knowledge needed to differentiate between humans, typical nonhuman animate objects, and inanimate ones (see COGNITIVE DEVELOPMENT). For example, Gelman, Spelke, and Meck (1983) found that even three-year-olds can almost always correctly attribute the presence or absence of animal properties to familiar animals and nonliving things. Simons and Keil (1995) demonstrated that young children can distinguish between natural and artificial constituent parts of their bodies even when they do not know specifics about them. Young children may even assume that each animal and plant has its underlying essential nature (Gelman, Coley, and Gottfried 1994; see also ESSENTIALISM).

Then why do young children, even when they are intellectually serious, make animistic or personifying remarks fairly often, although not so often as Piaget claimed? What functions does the mode of reasoning behind animistic or personifying errors have? Both Carey (1985) and Inagaki and Hatano (1987) propose that, though young children are able to classify entities into ontological categories, when they have to infer an object's unknown attributes or reactions, the children apply their knowledge about human beings to other animate objects or even to inanimate objects. This is probably because they do not have rich categorical knowledge, and thus have to rely on ANALOGY in inferences. Because they are intimately familiar with humans, although necessarily novices in most other domains, they can most profitably use their knowledge about humans as a source analogue for making analogies.

Inagaki and Hatano (1987) propose that animistic or personifying tendencies of young children are products of their active minds and basically adaptive natures. Young children's personification or person analogies may lead them to accurate predictions for animate objects phylogenetically similar to humans. It can also provide justification for a variety of experiences, sometimes even with phylogenetically less similar objects, such as trees or flowers. Young children may have learned these heuristic values through their prior contacts with a variety of animate objects. The analogies young children make may involve structurally inaccurate mapping (e.g., mapping the relation between humans and food to that between plants and water), and induce biased reasoning (neglect of the roles of nutrients in the soil and photosynthesis). Although young children may carry analogy beyond its proper limits, and produce false inferences, they can generate "educated guesses" by analogies, relying on their only familiar source analogue of a person (Holyoak and Thagard 1995). Animistic errors and overattribution of human characteristics to nonhuman animate objects should therefore be regarded as accidental by-products of this reasoning process. Because their personification is subject to a variety of constraints, such as checking the plausibility of the inference against what is known about the target, it does not produce many personifying errors, except for assigning mental states to nonhumans.

How can we explain animistic thinking among indigenous adults? According to Atran (forthcoming), in cultures throughout the world it is common to classify all entities into four ontological categories (humans, nonhuman animals, plants, and nonliving things, including artifacts), and to arrange animals and plants hierarchically and more or less accurately because such taxonomies are products of the human mind's natural classification scheme (see also FOLK BIOLOGY). Because indigenous people generally possess rich knowledge about major animals and plants in their ecological niche, their animistic and personifying remarks cannot result from having to rely on the person analogy, except for poorly understood nonnatural entities like God (Barrett and Keil 1996). Such remarks seem to be products of cultural beliefs, acquired through discourse about a specific class of entities. Mead's early observation (1932) that children in the Manus tribes were less animistic than adults lends support to this conjecture. Animistic or personifying explanations are widespread, but they are more about the metaphysical or imaginative universe than about the real world (Atran 1990). Even contemporary Japanese culture, outside the science classroom does not consider it a silly idea that large, old inanimate entities (e.g., giant rocks, mountains) have CONSCIOUSNESS.

See also CONCEPTUAL CHANGE; CULTURAL EVOLUTION; CULTURAL SYMBOLISM; CULTURAL VARIATION; MAGIC AND SUPERSTITION; NATIVISM

—*Giyoo Hatano*

References

Atran, S. (1990). *Cognitive Foundations of Natural History.* Cambridge: Cambridge University Press.

Atran, S. (Forthcoming). Folk biology and the anthropology of science: Cognitive universals and cultural particulars. *Brain and Behavioral Sciences.*

Barrett, J. L., and F. C. Keil. (1996). Conceptualizing a nonnatural entity: Anthropomorphism in God concepts. *Cognitive Psychology* 31: 219–247.

Carey, S. (1985). *Conceptual Change in Childhood.* Cambridge, MA: MIT Press.

Gelman, R., E. Spelke, and E. Meck. (1983). What preschoolers know about animate and inanimate objects. In D. Rogers and J. A. Sloboda, Eds., *The Acquisition of Symbolic Skills.* New York: Plenum Press, pp. 297–326.

Gelman, S. A., J. Coley, and G. M. Gottfried. (1994). Essentialist beliefs in children: The acquisition of concepts and theories. In L. A. Hirschfeld and S. A. Gelman, Eds., *Mapping the Mind: Domain Specificity in Cognition and Culture.* Hillsdale, NJ: Erlbaum, pp. 341–365.

Holyoak, K. J., and P. Thagard. (1995). *Mental Leaps.* Cambridge, MA: MIT Press.

Inagaki, K., and G. Hatano. (1987). Young children's spontaneous personification as analogy. *Child Development* 58: 1013–1020.

Laurendeau, M., and A. Pinard. (1962). *Causal Thinking in the Child: A Genetic and Experimental Approach.* New York: International Universities Press.

Lévy-Bruhl, L. (1910). *How Natives Think.* Translated by Princeton: Princeton University Press, 1985. Originally published as *Les fonctions mentales dans les sociétés inférieures.* Paris: Alcan.

Mead, M. (1932). An investigation of the thought of primitive children with special reference to animism. *Journal of the Royal Anthropological Institute* 62: 173–190.

Piaget, J. (1926). *The Child's Conception of the World.* Translated by Totowa, NJ: Rowman and Allanheld, 1960. Originally published as *La représentation du monde chez l'enfant.* Paris: Presses Universitaires de France.

Richards, D. D., and R. S. Siegler. (1984). The effects of task requirements on children's life judgments. *Child Development* 55: 1687–1696.

Simons, D. J., and F. C. Keil. (1995). An abstract to concrete shift in the development of biological thought: The inside story. *Cognition* 56: 129–163.

Further Readings

Bullock, M. (1985). Animism in childhood thinking: A new look at an old question. *Developmental Psychology* 21: 217–225.

Dennis, W. (1953). Animistic thinking among college and university students. *Scientific Monthly* 76: 247–249.

Dolgin, K. G., and D. A. Behrend. (1984). Children's knowledge about animates and inanimates. *Child Development* 55: 1646–1650.

Inagaki, K. (1989). Developmental shift in biological inference processes: From similarity-based to category-based attribution. *Human Development* 32: 79–87.

Looft, W. R., and W. H. Bartz. (1969). Animism revived. *Psychological Bulletin* 71: 1–19.

Massey, C. M., and R. Gelman. (1988). Preschoolers' ability to decide whether a photographed unfamiliar object can move itself. *Developmental Psychology* 24: 307–317.

Anomalous Monism

Anomalous monism is the thesis that mental entities (objects and events) are identical with physical entities, but under their mental descriptions mental entities are neither definitionally nor nomologically reducible to the vocabulary of physics. If we think of views of the relation between the mental and the physical as distinguished, first, by whether or not mental entities are identical with physical entities, and, second, divided by whether or not there are strict psychophysical laws, we get a fourfold classification: (1) *nomological monism,* which says there are strict correlating laws, and that the correlated entities are identical (this is often called materialism); (2) *nomological dualism* (interactionism, parallelism, epiphenomenalism); (3) *anomalous dualism,* which holds there are no laws correlating the mental and the physical, and the substances are discrete (Cartesianism); and (4) *anomalous monism,* which allows only one class of entities, but denies the possibility of definitional and nomological reduction. It is claimed that anomalous monism is the answer to the MIND-BODY PROBLEM, and that it follows from certain premises, the main ones being:

1. All mental events are causally related to physical events. For example, changes in PROPOSITIONAL ATTITUDES such as beliefs and desires cause agents to act, and actions cause changes in the physical world. Events in the physical world often cause us to alter our beliefs, intentions and desires.
2. If two events are related as cause and effect, there is a strict law under which they may be subsumed. This means that cause and effect have descriptions that instantiate a strict law. A strict law is one that makes no use of open-ended escape clauses such as "other things being equal." Such laws must belong to a closed system: whatever can affect the system must be included in it.
3. There are no strict psychophysical laws (laws connecting or identifying mental events under their mental descriptions with physical events under their physical descriptions). From this premise and the fact that events described in psychological terms do not belong to a closed system, it follows that there are no strict PSYCHO-LOGICAL LAWS; psychological laws, if carefully stated, must always contain ceteris paribus clauses.

Take an arbitrary mental event *M*. By (1), it is causally connected with some physical event *P*. By (2), there must be a strict law connecting *M* and *P*; but by (3), that law cannot be a psychophysical law. Because only physics aims to provide a closed system governed by strict laws, the law connecting *M* and *P* must be a physical law. But then *M* must have a physical description—it must be a physical event.

(The term "anomalous monism" and the argument were introduced in Davidson 1970.)

The three premises are not equally plausible. (1) is obvious. (2) has seemed true to many philosophers; HUME and KANT are examples, though their reasons for holding it were very different (Davidson 1995). It has been questioned by others (Anscombe 1971; Cartwright 1983). A defense of (2) would begin by observing that physics is defined by the aim of discovering or devising a vocabulary (which among other things determines what counts as an event) which allows the formulation of a closed system of laws. The chief argument for the nomological and definitional irreducibility of mental concepts to physical is that mental concepts, insofar as they involve the propositional attitudes, are normative, while the concepts of a developed physics are not. This is because propositions are logically related to one another, which places a normative constraint on the correct attribution of attitudes: since an attitude is in part identified by its logical relations, the pattern of attitudes in an individual must exhibit a large degree of coherence. This does not mean that people may not be irrational, but the possibility of irrationality depends on a background of rationality (Davidson 1991).

(3) rules out two forms of REDUCTIONISM: reduction of the mental to the physical by explicit definition of mental predicates in physical terms (some forms of behaviorism suggest such a program), and reduction by way of strict bridging laws—laws that connect mental with physical properties. (1)–(3) do, however, entail ontological reduction, because they imply that mental entities do not add to the physical furniture of the world. The result is ontological monism coupled with conceptual dualism. (Compare Spinoza's metaphysics.) Anomalous monism is consistent with the thesis that psychological properties or predicates are supervenient on physical properties or predicates, in this sense of SUPERVENIENCE: a property *M* is supervenient on a set of properties *P* if and only if *M* distinguishes no entities not distinguishable by the properties in *P* (there are other definitions of supervenience).

A widely accepted criticism of anomalous monism is that it makes MENTAL CAUSATION irrelevant because it is the physical properties of events that do the causing (Kim 1993). The short reply is that it is events, not properties, that are causes and effects (Davidson 1993). If events described in physical terms are effective, and they are identical with those same events described in psychological terms, then the latter must also be causally effective. The vocabularies of physics and of psychology are irreducibly different ways of describing and explaining events, but one does not rule out, or supercede, the other.

See also AUTONOMY OF PSYCHOLOGY; ELIMINATIVE MATERIALISM; PHYSICALISM; RADICAL INTERPRETATION

—*Donald Davidso*

References

Anscombe, G. E. M. (1971). *Causality and Determination.* Cambridge: Cambridge University Press.

Cartwright, N. (1983). *How the Laws of Physics Lie.* Oxford: Oxford University Press.

Davidson, D. (1980). Mental events. In D. Davidson, *Essays on Actions and Events.* Oxford: Oxford University Press.

Davidson, D. (1991). Three varieties of knowledge. In A. Phillips Griffiths, Ed., *A. J. Ayer: Memorial Essays.* Royal Institute of Philosophy Supplement, vol. 30. Cambridge: Cambridge University Press.

Davidson, D. (1993). Thinking causes. In J. Heil and A. Mele, Eds., *Mental Causation.* Oxford: Oxford University Press.

Davidson, D. (1995). Laws and cause. *Dialectica* 49: 263–279.

Kim, J. (1993). Can supervenience and "non-strict laws" save anomalous monism? In J. Heil and A. Mele, Eds., *Mental Causation.* Oxford: Oxford University Press.

Anthropology

See INTRODUCTION: CULTURE, COGNITION, AND EVOLUTION; COGNITIVE ANTHROPOLOGY; CULTURAL RELATIVISM; ETHNOPSYCHOLOGY

Antirealism

See REALISM AND ANTIREALISM

Aphasia

Aphasia (acquired aphasia) is a disorder of communication caused by brain damage. The acquired aphasias constitute a family of disruptions to comprehension and production of language in both oral and written form. Much of the history of aphasia has been (and continues to be) concerned with attempts to characterize the natural organization of language as revealed by the selective manner in which language breaks down under focal brain damage.

The history of the field has precursors in the very earliest recordings of medicine, but largely achieved modern form with the work of Paul BROCA (1861) and Carl Wernicke (1874). From this clinical work, two generalizations concerning the brain-language relationship were derived that have become canonical in the field. First, it was documented that lesions to areas in the left, but not right, cerebral hemisphere standardly result in language disruption (leading to the concept of unilateral cerebral dominance for language; e.g., Broca 1865). Second, within the left hemisphere, lesions to different areas result in reliably different patterns of language loss (e.g., Wernicke 1874).

Thus, damage to what has become known as Broca's area, in the lower portion of the left frontal lobe (more particularly, the opercular and triangular parts of the inferior frontal gyrus, including the foot of the third frontal convolution, and extending into subcortical white matter), produces clinical observations of difficulty in articulation and production of speech with relative (but not complete) sparing of comprehension, resulting in what has come to be called Broca's aphasia. Patients with damage to this area produce little (or at least labored) speech, which is poorly articulated and telegraphic, involving omission of so-called function or closed-class words (articles, auxiliaries, etc.). Their speech relies heavily on nouns, and (to a far smaller degree) verbs. Their written communication follows this same production-comprehension dissociation, with impaired writing but often less severe disturbance to reading. Because Broca's area lies next to motor areas for muscular control of speech (lips, palate, vocal chords, jaw), early assumptions were that Broca's area was a center for the encoding of articulated speech.

Wernicke's aphasia, by contrast, results from damage to the posterior region of the left hemisphere, specifically in the areas adjacent to the primary auditory cortex on the posterior portion of the superior left temporal gyrus. Patients with Wernicke's aphasia produce speech that is fluent, effortless, and rapid (hence the term *fluent aphasia*). The content of their productions, however, is remarkably "empty" and filled with inappropriate word use (verbal paraphasias). Importantly, patients with Wernicke's aphasia demonstrate a profound comprehension deficit—often even at the single word level. Both writing and (particularly) READING are standardly highly impaired.

The discovery of a link between these two distinct types of language disruption and two distinct brain areas led to neuroanatomical-connectionist models of brain organization for language (Wernicke 1874; Lichtheim 1884), which, in one form or another, have been pervasive through to the later twentieth century (e.g., GESCHWIND 1979). These models attempted to capture and predict the wide variety of language deficits that had been reported throughout the literature in terms of "disconnection" syndromes. Thus, for example, the early Wernicke-Lichtheim connectionist model easily represented the fact that damage to the arcuate fasciculus (which roughly connects Wernicke's to Broca's area) leads to the inability to repeat language, a syndrome that was termed *conduction aphasia*. (For a complete review of aphasic syndromes, see Goodglass 1993.)

Early versions of such models were modality-based, viewing Broca's and Wernicke's areas as essentially motor and sensory language areas, respectively. Broca's area was considered primarily responsible for the encoding of articulatory form for production (speaking), and Wernicke's area was considered primarily responsible for the organization of language perception (listening/understanding).

However, these connectionist/associationist approaches were criticized nearly from their inception as oversimplifications that did not capture the cognitive and conceptual complexity of the behavioral disruptions found in even the "classic" (Broca's and Wernicke's) aphasias (e.g., Jackson 1878; Head 1926; Pick 1931; Goldstein 1948; Luria 1966). Such criticisms led to changes in the postulated nature of the "nodes" underlying anatomical-connectionist models (or to nonconnectionist characterizations entirely), with movement toward more linguistically and cognitively relevant characterizations.

Zurif, Caramazza, and Myerson (1972) were major modern proponents of this movement, with empirical demonstrations of an "overarching agrammatism" underlying the deficit in many instances of Broca's aphasia. They demonstrated that not only was production in these patients "agrammatic," but that comprehension also suffered from a disruption to the comprehension of structural relationships, particularly when closed-class function words were critical to interpretation or when disambiguating semantic information was unavailable.

Similarly, a modality-overarching difficulty in semantical interpretation was claimed for patients with damage to Wernicke's area. In the early versions of this "linguistic-relevance" approach to aphasia, the loci of damage were described in terms of "loss of knowledge" (e.g., loss of syntactic rules). However the claim of knowledge-loss proved empirically difficult to sustain, whereas descriptions in terms of disruptions to the processing (access, integration) of linguistically relevant representations (words, SYNTAX, SEMANTICS) was empirically demonstrable. In support of such modality-independent descriptions of aphasia, this same distribution of deficits has been shown in languages that do not rely on the auditory/oral modality. Studies of SIGN LANGUAGES (a visuospatial, nonauditory language) in deaf signers have demonstrated that left-hemisphere damage results in marked impairment to sign language abilities, but right hemisphere damage does not (despite the fact that such damage disrupts non-language spatial and cognitive abilities). Further, syntactic versus semantic sign-language disruptions have been shown to pattern neuroanatomically with the language problems accompanying damage to Broca's and Wernicke's areas, respectively (Bellugi, Poizner, and Klima 1989).

In all, much work has demonstrated that characterizations of the functional commitment of brain architecture to language as revealed via the aphasias requires explicit consideration of the abstract, modality-neutral functional architecture (syntax, etc.) of language.

The use of behavioral techniques that examine language processing as it takes place in real time (online techniques; e.g., Swinney et al. 1996) have recently served to further detail the brain-language relationships seen in aphasia. This work has demonstrated disruptions to functional systems underlying language at finely detailed levels of linguistic processing/analysis, even providing a basis for the argument that some disruptions underlying "classic" syndromes may represent, at least partially, disruptions to elemental processing resources that are recruited by the language system (MEMORY, ATTENTION, access, etc.). With the details provided by these temporally fine-grained examinations of aphasias and by modern brain imaging, the apparent lack of homogeneity of the language disruptions found in aphasic syndromes (including the many putative aphasic syndromes not associated with Broca's or Wernicke's areas) appears on course to being better understood. It has led, on one hand, to increasing examination of individual cases of aphasia for determination of "new" aspects of the brain-language relationship (and, to more cautious claims about group/syndrome patterns), and on the other hand, to new models of language, based increasingly on verifiable language behaviors as revealed by "anomalous" aphasic cases.

See also GRAMMAR, NEURAL BASIS OF; HEMISPHERIC SPECIALIZATION; LANGUAGE IMPAIRMENT, DEVELOPMENTAL; LANGUAGE, NEURAL BASIS OF; SENTENCE PROCESSING

—*David A. Swinney*

References

Bellugi, U., H. Poizner, and E. Klima. (1989). Language, modality and the brain. *Trends in Neurosciences* 12(10): 380–388.

Broca, P. (1961). Perte de la parole. Ramollissement chronique et destruction partielle du lobe anterieur gauche du cerveau. *Bulletin de la Societe d'Anthropologie* 2: 235.

Broca, P. (1865). Sur la faculte du langage articule. *Bulletin de la Societe d'Anthropologie* 6: 337–393.

Geschwind, N. (1979). Specializations of the human brain. *Scientific American* September: 180–201.

Goodglass, H. (1993). *Understanding Aphasia.* San Diego: Academic Press.

Head, H. (1926). *Aphasia and Kindred Disorders of Speech.* New York: Macmillan.

Jackson, J. H. (1878). On affections of speech from disease of the brain. *Brain* 1: 304–330.

Lichtheim, O. (1984). On aphasia. *Brain* 7: 443–484.

Luria, A. R. (1966). *Higher Cortical Functions in Man.* New York: Basic Books.

Swinney, D., E. B. Zurif, P. Prather, and T. Love. (1996). Neurological distribution of processing resources underlying language comprehension. *Journal of Cognitive Neuroscience* 8(2): 174–184.

Wernicke, C. (1874). *Der aphasische Symptomenkomplex.* Breslau: Cohn und Weigert. Republished as: The aphasia symptom complex: A psychological study on an anatomical basis. In *Wernicke's Works on Aphasia.* The Hague: Mouton.

Zurif, E., A. Caramazza, and R. Myerson. (1972). Grammatical judgments of agrammatic aphasics. *Neuropsychologia* 10: 405–417.

Further Readings

Bellugi, U., and G. Hickok. (1994). Clues to the neurobiology of language. In Broadwell, Ed., *Neuroscience, Memory and Language.* Washington: Library of Congress.

Goldstein, K. (1948). *Language and Language Disturbances.* New York: Grune and Stratton.

Goodglass, H., and E. Kaplan. (1972). *The Assessment of Aphasia and Related Disorders.* Philadelphia: Lea and Febiger.

Jackson, J. H. (1915). Reprints of some Hughlings Jacksons papers on affections of speech. *Brain* 38: 28–190.

Jakobson, R. (1956). Two aspects of language and two types of aphasic disturbances. In R. Jakobson and M. Halle, Eds., *Fundamentals of Language.* The Hague: Mouton.

Marie, P. (1906). Revision de la question de l'aphasie: La troisieme circonvolution frontale gauche ne jose aucun role special dans la fonction du langage. *Semaine Medicale* 26: 241.

Pick, A. (1931). Aphasie. In O. Bumke and O. Foerster, Eds., *Handbuch der normalen und pathologischen Physiologie,* vol. 15, Berlin: Springer, pp. 1416–1524.

Sarno, M. T., Ed. (1981). *Acquired Aphasia.* New York: Academic Press.

Schwartz, M., M. Linebarger, and E. Saffran. (1985). The status of the syntactic deficit theory of agrammatism. In M. L. Kean, Ed., *Agrammatism.* Orlando: Academic Press.

Swinney, D., E. B. Zurif, and J. Nicol. (1989). The effects of focal brain damage on sentence processing: An examination of the neurological organization of a mental module. *Journal of Cognitive Neuroscience* 1: 25–37.

Zurif, E. B., and D. Swinney. (1994). The neuropsychology of language. In *Handbook of Psycholinguistics.* San Diego: Academic Press.

Archaeology

See ARTIFACTS AND CIVILIZATION; COGNITIVE ARCHAEOLOGY; TECHNOLOGY AND HUMAN EVOLUTION

Architecture

See COGNITIVE ARCHITECTURE

Art

See PICTORIAL ART AND VISION

Articulation

Articulation means movement. In speech, articulation is the process by which speech sounds are formed. The articulators are the movable speech organs, including the tongue, lips, jaw, velum, and pharynx. These organs, together with related tissues, comprise the *vocal tract,* or the resonating cavities of speech production that extend from the larynx (voice box) to the lips or nostrils. Human speech production is accomplished by the coordination of muscular actions in the respiratory, laryngeal, and vocal tract systems. Typically, the word *articulation* refers to the functions of the vocal tract, but speech production requires the action of all three systems. A full account of speech production would go beyond articulation to include such topics as intonation and emotional expression. Essentially, articulation is the means by which speech is formed to express language (see LANGUAGE PRODUCTION and LANGUAGE AND COMMUNICATION).

Articulation is a suitable topic for cognitive science for several reasons, but especially because it is (1) arguably the most precisely performed of human movements, (2) a serial behavior of exceptional complexity, (3) the most natural means of language expression in all communities except people with impairments of hearing, and (4) a uniquely human behavior linked to a variety of other accomplishments.

Ordinary conversational speech is produced at rates of five to ten syllables per second, or about twenty to thirty phonemes (sound units that distinguish words) per second. Individual speech sounds therefore have an average duration of approximately fifty milliseconds. This rapid rate has been emphasized in studies of speech perception because no other sound sequence can be perceived at comparable rates of presentation (Liberman et al. 1967). The rapid rate is impressive also from the perspective of production and the motor control processes it entails. Each sound must be uttered in the correct sequence, and each, in turn, requires the precise timing of the movements that distinguish it from other sounds. Although a given sound can be prototypically defined by its associated movements (e.g., closure of the lips and laryngeal vibrations for the *b* in *boy*), the actual pattern of movements varies with other sounds in the sequence to be produced (the phonetic context). Generally, articulatory movements overlap one another and can be mutually adjusted. At any one instant, the articulators may appear to be simultaneously adjusted to the requirements of two or more sounds. For example, the *s* sound in the word *stew* is typically produced with lip rounding, but the *s* sound in the word *stay* is not. The reason for this difference is that the *s* sound in the word *stew* anticipates the lip rounding required

for the forthcoming rounded vowel. This phenomenon is called *coarticulation* and has been one of the most challenging issues in speech production theory. Coarticulation is not restricted to immediately adjacent sounds and may, in fact, extend over several segments and even cross syllable and word boundaries. The complex overlapping of articulatory movements has been the subject of considerable research, as summarized by Fowler and Saltzman (1993) and by Kent and Minifie (1977). Coarticulation is an obstacle to segmentation, or the demarcation of speech behavior into discrete units such as phonemes and words.

With the exception of SIGN LANGUAGES used by people who are deaf, speech is the primary means of communication in all human communities. Speech is therefore closely related to language (and to the auditory perception of language) and is often the only means by which a particular language can be studied, because the majority of the world's languages do not have a written form. Speech appears to be unique to humans (see ANIMAL COMMUNICATION). Because speech is harnessed to language, it is difficult or impossible to gain a deep understanding of speech apart from its linguistic service. As Fujimura (1990) observed, "While speech signals convey information other than linguistic codes, and the boundary between linguistic and extra- or paralinguistic issues may not be clearcut, there is no question that the primary goal of speech research is to understand the relation of the units and organization of linguistic forms to the properties of speech signals uttered and perceived under varying circumstances" (p. 244). The output of the phonological component of the grammar has often been assumed as the input to the system that regulates speech production (see PHONETICS and PHONOLOGY).

Because the speech signal is perishable, expression and perception of its serial order are essential to communication by speech. In his classic paper, LASHLEY (1951) considered speech as exemplary of the problem of serial order in human behavior. He proposed three mechanisms for the control of seriation: determining tendency (the idea to be expressed), activation of the selected units (meaning that they are primed for use but not yet serially ordered), and the schema of order (or the syntax of the act that finally yields a serial ordering of the intended utterance). Lashley's insights illuminate some of the major cognitive dimensions of articulation, and Lashley's ideas resonate in contemporary studies of speech. One area in particular is the study of sequencing errors (e.g., substitutions, deletions, and exchanges of segments) in both normal and pathological speech. These errors have attracted careful study because of the belief that the mistakes in the motor output of speech can reveal the underlying organization of speech behavior. Large corpora of speech errors have been collected and analyzed in attempts to discover the structures of speech organization (Fromkin 1980). But this is only part of the problem of serial order in speech. It is also necessary to understand how individual movements are coordinated to meet the needs of intelligibility while being energetically efficient (Kelso, Saltzman, and Tuller 1986; MacNeilage 1970).

A number of laboratory techniques have been developed to study speech production. The two major methodologies are physiologic and acoustic. Physiological methods are diverse because no single method is suited to study the different structures and motor systems involved in speech. Among the methods used are electromyography, aerodynamics, various kinds of movement transduction, X-ray, and photoelectrical techniques (Stone 1997). Of these, X-ray techniques have provided the most direct information, but, to avoid the hazards of X-ray exposure, investigators are using alternative methods such as the use of miniature magnetometers. Acoustic studies offer the advantages of economy, convenience, and a focus on the physical signal that mediates between speaker and listener. Acoustic methods are limited to some degree because of uncertainties in inferring articulatory actions from the acoustic patterns of speech (Fant 1970), but acoustic analysis has been a primary source of information on articulation and its relation to speech perception (Fujimura and Erickson 1997, Stevens 1997).

Among the most influential theories or models of articulation have been stage models, dynamic systems, and connectionist networks. In stage models, information is successively processed in serially or hierarchically structured components (Meyer and Gordon 1985). Dynamic systems theories seek solutions in terms of task-dependent biomechanical properties (Kelso, Saltzman, and Tuller 1986). Connectionist networks employ massively parallel architectures that are trained with various kinds of input information (Jordan 1991). Significant progress has been made in the computer simulation of articulation, beginning in the 1960s (Henke 1966) and extending to contemporary efforts that combine various knowledge structures and control strategies (Saltzman and Munhall 1989, Guenther 1995, Wilhelms-Tricarico 1996). This work is relevant both to the understanding of how humans produce speech and to the development of articulatory speech synthesizers (*see* SPEECH SYNTHESIS).

A major construct of recent theorizing about speech articulation is the *gesture,* defined as an abstract characterization of an individual movement (e.g., closure of the lips). It has been proposed that gestures for individual articulators are combined in a motor score that specifies the movements for a particular phonetic sequence. A particularly appealing property of the gesture is its potential as a construct in phonology (Browman and Goldstein 1986), speech production (Saltzman and Munhall 1989), SPEECH PERCEPTION (Fowler 1986), and speech development in children (Goodell and Studdert-Kennedy 1993).

See also PHONOLOGY, ACQUISITION OF; PHONOLOGY, NEURAL BASIS OF; SPEECH RECOGNITION IN MACHINES

—*Raymond D. Kent*

References

Browman, C., and L. Goldstein. (1986). Towards an articulatory phonology. In C. Ewan and J. Anderson, Eds., *Phonology Yearbook* 3, pp. 219–252. Cambridge: Cambridge University Press.

Fowler, C. A. (1986). An event approach to the study of speech perception from a direct-realist perspective. *Journal of Phonetics* 14: 3–28.

Fowler, C. A., and E. Saltzman. (1993). Coordination and coarticulation in speech production. *Language and Speech* 36: 171–195.

Fromkin, V. A., Ed. (1980). *Errors in Linguistic Performance: Slips of the Tongue, Ear, Pen and Hand.* New York: Academic Press.

Fujimura, O., and D. Erickson. (1997). Acoustic phonetics. In W. J. Hardcastle and J. Laver, Eds., *Handbook of Phonetic Sciences,* pp. 65–115. Cambridge, MA: Blackwell.

Goodell, E. W., and M. Studdert-Kennedy. (1993). Acoustic evidence for the development of gestural coordination in the speech of 2-year-olds: a longitudinal study. *Journal of Speech and Hearing Research* 36: 707–727.

Guenther, F. H. (1995). Speech sound acquisition, coarticulation and rate effects in a neural network model of speech production. *Psychological Review* 102: 594–621.

Henke, W. L. (1966). *Dynamic Articulatory Model of Speech Production Using Computer Simulation.* Ph.D. diss., MIT.

Jordan, M. I. (1991). Serial order: a parallel distributed processing approach. In J. L. Elman and D. E. Rumelhart, Eds., *Advances in Connectionist Theory: Speech,* Hillsdale, NJ: Erlbaum, pp. 214–249.

Kelso, J. A. S., E. L. Saltzman, and B. Tuller. (1986). The dynamical perspective on speech production: data and theory. *Journal of Phonetics* 14: 29–59.

Kent, R. D., and F. D. Minifie. (1977). Coarticulation in recent speech production models. *Journal of Phonetics* 5: 115–133.

Lashley, K. (1951). The problem of serial order in behavior. In L. A. Jeffress, Ed., *Cerebral Mechanisms in Behavior,* pp. 506–528. New York: Wiley.

Liberman, A. M., F. S. Cooper, D. P. Shankweiler, and M. Studdert-Kennedy. (1970). Perception of the speech code. *Psychological Review* 74: 431–461.

Meyer, D. E., and P. C. Gordon. (1985). Speech production: motor programming of phonetic features. *Journal of Memory and Language* 24: 3–26.

MacNeilage, P. (1970). Motor control of serial ordering of speech. *Psychological Review* 77: 182–196.

Saltzman, E. L., and K. G. Munhall. (1989). A dynamical approach to gestural patterning in speech production. *Ecological Psychology* 1: 333–382.

Shattuck-Hufnagel, S. (1983). Sublexical units and suprasegmental structure in speech production planning. In P. MacNeilage, Ed., *The Production of Speech,* New York: Springer, pp. 109–136.

Stevens, K. N. (1997). Articulatory-acoustic-auditory relationships. In W. J. Hardcastle and J. Laver, Eds., *Handbook of Phonetic Sciences,* Cambridge, MA: Blackwell, pp. 462–506.

Stone, M. (1997). Laboratory techniques for investigating speech articulation. In W. J. Hardcastle and J. Laver, Eds., *Handbook of Phonetic Sciences,* Cambridge, MA: Blackwell, pp. 11-32.

Wilhelms-Tricarico, R. (1996). A biomechanical and physiologically-based vocal tract model and its control. *Journal of Phonetics* 24: 23–38.

Further Readings

Fant, G. (1980). The relations between area functions and the acoustic signal. *Phonetica* 37: 55–86.

Fujimura, O. (1990). Articulatory perspectives of speech organization. In W. J. Hardcastle and J. Laver, Eds., *Speech Production and Speech Modelling.* Dordrecht; Kluwer Academic Press, pp. 323-342.

Kent, R. D., S. G. Adams, and G. S. Turner. (1996). Models of speech production. In N. J. Lass, Ed., *Principles of Experimental Phonetics.* St. Louis: Mosby, pp. 3–45.

Levelt, W. J. M. (1989). *Speaking: From Intention to Articulation.* Cambridge, MA: MIT Press.

Kent, R. D., B. S. Atal, and J. L. Miller, Eds. (1991). *Papers in Speech Communication: Speech Production.* Woodbury, NY: Acoustical Society of America.

Lindblom, B. E. F., and J. E. F. Sundberg. (1971). Acoustical consequences of lip, tongue, jaw and larynx movement. *Journal of the Acoustical Society of America* 50: 1166–1179.

Lofqvist, A. (1997). Theories and models of speech production. In W. J. Hardcastle and J. Laver, Eds., *Handbook of Phonetic Sciences.* Cambridge, MA: Blackwell, pp. 405-426.

Mermelstein, P. (1973). Articulatory model of speech production. *Journal of the Acoustical Society of America* 53: 1070–1082.

Ohman, S. E. G. (1967). Numerical model of coarticulation. *Journal of the Acoustical Society of America* 41: 310–320.

Perkell, J. S. (1997). Articulatory processes. In W. J. Hardcastle and J. Laver, Eds., *Handbook of Phonetic Sciences.* Cambridge, MA: Blackwell, pp. 333-370.

Smith, A. (1992). The control of orofacial movements in speech. *Critical Reviews in Oral Biology and Medicine* 3: 233–267.

Stevens, K. N. (1989). On the quantal nature of speech. *Journal of Phonetics* 17: 3–46.

Artifacts

See ARTIFACTS AND CIVILIZATION; COGNITIVE ARTIFACTS; HUMAN NAVIGATION; TECHNOLOGY AND HUMAN EVOLUTION

Artifacts and Civilization

The development of civilization meant more than social and technological innovations. It required the acquisition of complex cognitive processes. In particular, the ability to manipulate data abstractly was key to the development of urban society. This is illustrated by the evolution of artifacts for counting and accounting associated with the rise of the very first civilization in Sumer, Mesopotamia, about 3300–3100 B.C. Here, the development of a system of clay tokens and its final transmutation into writing on clay tablets document the importance for an administration to process large amounts of information in ever greater abstraction (Schmandt-Besserat 1992). Tokens and economic clay tablets made it possible to

levy taxes and impose forced labor; in other words, they gave the temple institutional control over manpower and the production of real goods. The accumulation of wealth in the hands of a ruling priesthood bolstered the development of monumental architecture and the arts. More importantly, the temple economy fostered long distance trade and critical industries such as metallurgy (Moorey 1985). In turn, metal tools revolutionized crafts. For example, metal saws could cut wooden planks into circular shapes, allowing such inventions as the wheel (Littauer and Crauwel 1979). Metal weapons transformed warfare, leading to conquests far and near that could be administered with tokens and economic tablets (Algaze 1993). Finally, tokens and writing fostered new cognitive skills and thereby transformed the way people thought (Schmandt-Besserat 1996).

Starting with the beginning of agriculture ca. 8000 B.C., clay tokens of multiple shapes were used for counting and accounting goods. They were the first code or system for storing/communicating information: each token shape represented one unit of merchandise, for example, a cone and a sphere stood, respectively, for a small and a large measure of grain, and an ovoid for a jar of oil (figure 1). The tokens represent a first stage of abstraction. They translated daily-life commodities into miniature, mostly geometric counters, removing the data from its context and the knowledge from the knower. However, the clay counters represented plurality concretely, in one-to-one correspondence. Three jars of oil were shown by three ovoids, as in reality.

About 3500–3300 B.C., envelopes in the form of hollow clay balls were invented to keep in temple archives the tokens representing unfinished transactions (tax debts?). For convenience, the accountants indicated the tokens hidden inside the envelopes by impressing them on the outside. The two-dimensional markings standing for three-dimensional tokens represented a second step of abstraction. A third level of abstraction was reached ca. 3200–3100 B.C., when solid clay balls—tablets—did away with the actual tokens, only displaying the impressions. The impressed markings

Figure 1. Tokens held in an envelope from Susa, present-day Iran, ca. 3300 B.C. The large and small cones stood for large and small measures of grain and each of the lenticular disks represented a flock of animals (10?). The markings impressed on the outside of the envelope correspond to the tokens inside. Both tokens and

impressed markings represented units of goods concretely, in one-to-one correspondence. Published in Schmandt-Besserat, D. (1992), *Before Writing,* vol. 1. Austin: University of Texas Press, p. 126, fig. 73. Courtesy Musée du Louvre, Département des Antiquités Orientales.

still represented numbers of units of goods concretely, in one-to-one correspondence. Three jars of oil were shown by three impressions of the ovoid token. Each impressed marking therefore continued to fuse together the concept of the item counted (jar of oil) with that of number (one), without the possibility of dissociating them.

The fourth step, the abstraction of numbers, ca. 3100 B.C., coincided with pictography—signs in the shape of tokens but traced with a stylus, rather than impressed. These incised signs were never repeated in one-to-one correspondence. Numbers of jars of oil were shown by the sign for jar of oil preceded by numerals (figure 2). The symbols to express abstract numbers were not new. They were the former units of grain: the impression of a cone token that formerly was a small measure of grain stood for 1 and that of a sphere representing a large measure of grain was 10. When, finally, the concept of number was abstracted from that of the item counted, numerals and writing could evolve in separate ways. Abstract numerals grew to unprecedented large numbers, paving the way for mathematics and thereby providing a new grasp on reality (Justus 1996). Pictographs assumed a phonetic value in order to satisfy new administrative demands, namely, the personal names of recipients or donors of the stipulated goods. The syllables or words composing an individual's name were rendered in a rebus fashion. That is to say, a new type of pictographs no longer stood for the objects they pictured, but rather for the sound of the word they evoked. This fifth step in abstraction marked the final departure from the previous token system. The phonetic signs featured any possible items, such as the head of a man standing for the sound "*lu*" or that of a man's mouth that was read "*ka*." This further abstraction also marked the true takeoff of writing. The resulting syllabary was no longer restricted to economic record keeping but opened ca. 2900 B.C. to other fields of human endeavor. In sum, in Mesopotamia, the earliest civilization corresponded with the transmutation of an archaic token system of accounting into a script written on clay tablets. The metamorphosis meant far more than the reduction from a three- to a two-dimensional recording device. It signified step-by-step acquisition of new cognitive skills for processing data in greater abstraction.

Artifacts for counting and writing were also part and parcel of the rise of all subsequent Near Eastern civilizations. However, the cultures following in the wake of Sumer were spared some of the hurdles to abstract data manipulation. Elam, in present-day western Iran, the nearest neighbor to Mesopotamia, is the only exception where the stages from tokens to impressed markings on envelopes and tablets took place synchronically with Mesopotamia—no doubt because of the Sumerian domination of Elam ca. 3300–3200 B.C. But, when the Proto-Elamites created their own script ca. 3000 B.C., they borrowed simultaneously abstract numerals and phonetic signs (Hoyrup 1994). About 2500 B.C., the Indus Valley civilizations emulated their Sumerian trade partners by devising a script that had no links with the Mesopotamian-like tokens recovered in pre-Harappan sites (Possehl 1996). Crete probably adopted first the idea of tokens and then that of writing. This is suggested by the fact that Minoan clay counters in the shape of miniature vessels

Figure 2. Economic clay tablet showing an account of thirty-three jars of oil, from Godin Tepe, present-day Iran, ca. 3100 BC. The units of oil are no longer repeated in one-to-one correspondence, but the sign for a measure of oil is preceded by numerals. The circular sign stood for 10 and the wedge for 1. Published in Schmandt-Besserat, D. (1992), *Before Writing*, vol. 1. Austin: University of Texas Press, p. 192, fig. 115. Courtesy T. Cuyler Young, Jr.

seem unrelated to the following hieroglyphic, Linear A or B scripts used in the Aegean between 2200–1300 B.C. (Poursat 1994). Farther afield, Egypt, where the use of tokens is not clearly attested, produced ca. 3000 B.C. a full-blown system of writing based on the rebus principle, visibly imitating Sumer (Ray 1986). These examples imply that the multiple cognitive steps from concrete to abstract data manipulation occurred only once in the Near East. The Mesopotamian concrete tokens and abstract tablets loomed large over the process of civilization in the Old World. In fact, abstract accounting is probably a universal prerequisite for civilization. But this has to remain an hypothesis as long as the precursors of writing in China and the New World remain elusive.

See also COGNITIVE ARCHAEOLOGY; COGNITIVE ARTIFACTS; TECHNOLOGY AND HUMAN EVOLUTION

—*Denise Schmandt-Besserat*

References

Algaze, G. (1993). *The Uruk World System.* Chicago: University of Chicago Press.

Hoyrup, J. (1994). *In Measure, Number, and Weight.* Albany: State University of New York Press.

Justus, C. (1996). Numeracy and the Germanic upper decades. *Journal of Indo-European Studies* 23: 45–80.

Littauer, M. A., and J. H. Crauwel. (1979). Wheeled vehicles and ridden animals in the ancient Near East. In *Handbook der Orientalistik,* vol. 7. Leiden: E. J. Brill.

Moorey, P. R. S. (1985). *Materials and Manufacture in Ancient Mesopotamia.* Oxford: BAR International Series.

Possehl, G. L. (1996). *Indus Age: The Writing System.* Philadelphia: University of Pennsylvania Press.

Poursat, J.-C. (1994). Les systèmes primitifs de contabilité en Crète minoenne. In P. Ferioli, E. Fiandra, G.G. Fissore, and M. Frangipane, Eds., *Archives Before Writing.* Rome: Ministero per I beni Culturali e Ambientali Ufficio Centrale per I beni Archivisti, pp. 247–252.

Ray, J. D. (1986). The emergence of writing in Egypt. *World Archaeology* 17(3): 307–315.

Schmandt-Besserat, D. (1992). *Before Writing.* 2 vols. Austin: University of Texas Press.

Schmandt-Besserat, D. (1996). *How Writing Came About.* Austin: University of Texas Press.

Further Readings

Avrin, L. (1991). *Scribes, Script and Books.* Chicago: American Library Association.

Bowman, A. K., and G. Woolf. (1994). *Literacy and Power in the Ancient World.* Cambridge: Cambridge University Press.

Englund, R. K. (1994). Archaic administrative texts from Uruk. *Archaische Texte aus Uruk 5* Berlin: Gebr. Mann Verlag.

Ferioli, P., E. Fiandra, and G. G. Fissore, Eds. (1996). *Administration in Ancient Societies.* Rome: Ministero per I beni Culturali e Ambientali Ufficio Centrale per I beni Archivisti.

Ferioli, P., E. Fiandra, G. G. Fissore, and M. Frangipane, Eds. (1994). *Archives Before Writing.* Rome: Ministero per I beni Culturali e Ambientali Ufficio Centrale per I beni Archivisti.

Goody, J. (1977). *The Domestication of the Savage Mind.* Cambridge: Cambridge University Press.

Goody, J. (1986). *The Logic of Writing and the Organization of Society.* Cambridge: Cambridge University Press.

Goody, J. (1987). *The Interface Between the Written and the Oral.* Cambridge: Cambridge University Press.

Günther, H., Ed. (1994). *Schrift und Schriftlichkeit.* Berlin: Walter de Gruyter.

Heyer, P. (1988). *Communications and History, Theories of Media, Knowledge and Civilization.* New York: Greenwood Press.

Nissen, H. J., P. Damerow, and R. K. Englund. (1993). *Archaic Bookkeeping.* Chicago: University of Chicago Press.

Ong, W. J. (1982). *Orality and Literacy.* New York: Methuen.

Olson, D. R. (1994). *The World on Paper.* Cambridge: Cambridge University Press.

Rafoth, B. A., and D. L. Robin, Eds. (1988). *The Social Construction of Written Communication.* Norwood: Ablex.

Schousboe, K., and M. T. Larsen, Eds. (1989). *Literacy and Society.* Copenhagen: Akademisk Forlag.

Street, B. V. (1993). *Cross-Cultural Approaches to Literacy.* Cambridge: Cambridge University Press.

Wagner, D. A. (1994). *Literacy, Culture and Development.* Cambridge: Cambridge University Press.

Watt, W. C., Ed. (1994). *Writing Systems and Cognition.* Dordrecht: Kluwer Academic Publishers

Artificial Intelligence

See INTRODUCTION: AI AND EDUCATION; COGNITIVE MODELING, SYMBOLIC; COMPUTATIONAL INTELLIGENCE

Artificial Life

Artificial life (A-Life) uses informational concepts and computer modeling to study life in general, and terrestrial life in particular. It aims to explain particular vital phenomena, ranging from the origin of biochemical metabolisms to the coevolution of behavioral strategies, and also the abstract properties of life as such ("life as it could be").

It is thus a form of mathematical biology—albeit of a highly interdisciplinary type. Besides their presence in biology, especially ETHOLOGY and evolutionary theory, A-Life's research topics are studied also (for instance) in artificial intelligence, computational psychology, mathematics, physics, biochemistry, immunology, economics, philosophy, and anthropology.

A-Life was named by Christopher Langton in 1986 (Langton 1986 and 1989). Langton's term suggests (deliberately) that the aim of A-Life is to build new living things. However, not all A-Life scientists share this goal. Even fewer believe this could be done without providing some physical body and metabolism. Accordingly, some A-Life workers favor less philosophically provocative terms, such as "adaptive systems" or "animats" (real or simulated robots based on animals) (Meyer and Wilson 1991).

The claim that even virtual creatures in cyberspace could be genuinely alive is called strong A-Life, in analogy to strong AI. Most A-Lifers reject it (but see Langton 1989 and Ray 1994). Or rather, most reject the view that such creatures can be alive in just the same sense that biological organisms are, but allow that they are, or could be, alive to a lesser degree. Whether life does require material embodiment, and whether it is a matter of degree, are philosophically controversial questions. Proponents of *autopoiesis* (the continual self-production of an autonomous entity), for example, answer "Yes" to the first and "No" to the second (Maturana and Varela 1980). Others also answer the first question with a "Yes," but for different reasons (Harnad 1994). However, these philosophical questions do not need to be definitively answered for A-Life to progress, or be scientifically illuminating. Using artifacts to study life, even "life as it could be," is not the same as aiming to instantiate life artificially.

The theoretical focus of A-Life is the central feature of living things: self-organization. This involves the spontaneous EMERGENCE, and maintenance, of order out of an origin that is ordered to a lesser degree. (The lower level may, though need not, include random "noise.") Self-organization is not mere superficial change, but fundamental structural development. This development is spontaneous, or autonomous. That is, it results from the intrinsic character of the system (often in interaction with the environment), rather than being imposed on it by some external force or designer.

In SELF-ORGANIZING SYSTEMS, higher-level properties result from interactions between simpler ones. In living organisms, the relevant interactions include chemical diffusion, perception and communication, and processes of variation and natural selection. One core problem is the way in which self-organization and natural selection interact to produce biological order over time. Some work in A-Life suggests that whereas self-organization generates the fundamental order, natural selection (following on variation) weeds out the forms that are least well adapted to (least fit for) the environment in question (Kauffman 1993).

The higher-level properties in living organisms are very varied. They include universal characteristics of life (e.g., autonomy and evolution); distinct lifestyles (e.g., parasitism and symbiosis); particular behaviors (e.g., flocking, hunting, or evasion); widespread developmental processes (e.g., cell differentiation); and bodily morphology (e.g., branching patterns in plants, and the anatomy of sense organs or control mechanisms in animals).

A-Life studies all these biological phenomena on all these levels. A-Life simulations vary in their degree of abstractness or idealization. Some model specific behaviors or morphologies of particular living things, whereas others study very general questions, such as how different rates of mutation affect coevolution (Ray 1992). They vary also in their mode of modeling: some A-Life work concentrates on programs, displaying its creatures (if any) only as images on the VDU, while some builds (and/or evolves) physical robots. The wide range of A-Life research is exemplified in the journals *Artificial Life* and *Adaptive Behavior*, and in international (including European) conference proceedings of the same names. Brief overviews include Langton (1989) and Boden (1996, intro.). For popular introductions, see Emmeche (1994) and Levy (1992).

A-Life is closely related to—indeed, it forms part of—cognitive science in respect of its history, its methodology, and its philosophy.

Historically, it was pioneered (around the mid-twentieth century) by the founders of AI: Alan TURING and John VON NEUMANN. They both developed theoretical accounts of self-organization, showing how simple underlying processes could generate complex systems involving emergent order. Turing (1952) showed that interacting chemical diffusion gradients could produce higher-level (including periodic) structures from initially homogeneous tissue. Von Neumann, before the discovery of DNA or the genetic code, identified the abstract requirements for self-replication (Burks 1966). He even defined a universal replicator: a cellular automaton (CA) capable of copying any system, including itself. A CA is a computational "space" made up of many discrete cells; each cell can be in one of several states, and changes (or retains) its state according to specific—typically localistic—rules. Von Neumann also pointed out that copy errors could enable evolution, an idea that later led to the development of EVOLUTIONARY COMPUTATION (evolutionary programming, evolution strategies, genetic algorithms, etc.).

Even in relatively simple CAs, (some) high-level order may emerge only after many iterations of the relevant lower-level rules. Such cases require high-performance computing. Consequently, Turing's and von Neumann's A-Life ideas could be explored in depth only long after their deaths. Admittedly, CAs were studied by von Neumann's colleague Arthur Burks (1970) and his student John Holland, who pioneered genetic algorithms soon after CAs were defined (Holland 1975); and more people—John Conway (Gardner 1970), Steve Wolfram (1983 and 1986), Stuart Kauffman (1969 and 1971), and Langton (1984), among others—became interested in them soon afterward. But these early studies focused on theory rather than implementation. Moreover, they were unknown to most researchers in cognitive science. The field of A-Life achieved visibility in the early 1990s, largely thanks to Langton's initiative in organizing the first workshop on A-Life (in Los Alamos) in 1987.

Methodologically, A-Life shares its reliance on computer modeling with computational psychology and AI—especially connectionism, situated robotics, and genetic algorithms (evolutionary programming). These three AI approaches may be integrated in virtual or physical systems. For instance, some A-Life robots are controlled by evolved NEURAL NETWORKS, whose (initially random) connections specify "reflex" responses to specific environmental cues (e.g., Cliff, Harvey, and Husbands 1993).

A-Life's methodology differs from classical (symbolic) AI in many ways. It relies on bottom-up (not top-down) processing, local (not global) control, simple (not complex) rules, and emergent (not preprogrammed) behavior. Often, it models evolving or coevolving populations involving many thousands of individuals. It commonly attempts to model an entire creature, rather than some isolated module such as vision or problem-solving (e.g., Beer 1990). And it claims to avoid methods involving KNOWLEDGE REPRESENTATION and PLANNING, which play a crucial role in classical AI (Brooks 1991). The behavior of A-Life robots is the result of automatic responses to the contingencies of the environment, not preprogrammed sequences or internal plans. Each response typically involves only one body part (e.g., the third leg on the right), but their interaction generates "wholistic" behavior: the robot climbs the step, or follows the wall.

Philosophically, A-Life and AI are closely related. Indeed, if intelligence can emerge only in living things, then AI is in principle a subarea of A-Life. Nevertheless, some philosophical assumptions typical of classical AI are queried, even rejected, by most workers in A-Life. All the philosophical issues listed below are discussed in Boden 1996, especially the chapters by Bedau, Boden, Clark, Godfrey-Smith, Hendriks-Jansen, Langton, Pattee, Sober, and Wheeler; see also Clark (1997).

Much as AI highlights the problematic concept of intelligence, A-Life highlights the concept of life—for which no universally agreed definition exists. It also raises questions of "simulation versus realization" similar to those concerning strong AI. Problems in A-Life that are relevant also to the adequacy of FUNCTIONALISM as a philosophy for AI and cognitive science include the role of embodiment and/or environmental embeddedness in grounding cognition and INTENTIONALITY.

A-Life in general favors explanations in terms of emergence, whereas AI tends to favor explanation by functional decomposition. Moreover, many A-Life researchers seek explanations in terms of closely coupled dynamical systems, described by phase-space trajectories and differential equations rather than computation over representations. Although A-Life does avoid the detailed, "objective," world-modeling typical of classical AI, whether it manages to avoid internal representations entirely is disputed. Also in dispute is whether the "autonomy" of environmentally embedded A-Life systems can capture the hierarchical order and self-reflexiveness found in some human action (and partly modeled by classical AI). Many philosophers of A-Life justify their rejection of representations by criticizing the broadly Cartesian assumptions typical of classical, and most connectionist, AI. They draw instead on philosophical insights drawn from Continental philosophy, or phenomenology, sometimes using the concept of autopoiesis.

Besides its theoretical interest, A-Life has many technological applications. These include evolutionary computation for commercial problem solving, environmentally embedded robots for practical use, and computer animation for movies and computer games. The "Creatures" computer environment, for example, employs A-Life techniques to evolve individual creatures capable of interacting, and of learning from their "world" and the human user's "teaching."

See also ADAPTATION AND ADAPTATIONISM; EVOLUTION; DYNAMIC APPROACHES TO COGNITION; SITUATED COGNITION AND LEARNING; SITUATEDNESS/EMBEDDEDNESS

—*Margaret A. Boden*

References

Beer, R. D. (1990). *Intelligence as Adaptive Behavior: An Experiment in Computational Neuroethology.* New York: Academic Press.

Boden, M. A., Ed. (1996). *The Philosophy of Artificial Life.* Oxford: Oxford University Press.

Brooks, R. A. (1991). Intelligence without representation. *Artificial Intelligence* 47: 139-159.

Burks, A. W. (1966). *Theory of Self-Reproducing Automata.* Urbana: University of Illinois Press.

Burks, A. W. (1970). *Essays on Cellular Automata.* Urbana: University of Illinois Press.

Clark, A. J. (1997). *Being There: Putting Brain, Body, and World Together Again.* Cambridge, MA: MIT Press.

Cliff, D., I. Harvey, and P. Husbands. (1993). Explorations in evolutionary robotics. *Adaptive Behavior* 2: 71-108.

Emmeche, C. (1994). *The Garden in the Machine: The Emerging Science of Artificial Life.* Princeton: Princeton University Press.

Gardner, M. (1970). The fantastic combinations of John Conway's new solitaire game "Life." *Scientific American* 223(4): 120-123.

Harnad, S. (1994). Levels of functional equivalence in reverse bioengineering. *Artificial life* 1: 293-301.

Holland, J. H. (1975). *Adaptation in Natural and Artificial Systems.* Ann Arbor: University of Michigan Press.

Kauffman, S. A. (1969). Metabolic stability and epigenesis in randomly connected nets. *Journal of Theoretical Biology* 22: 437-467.

Kauffman, S. A. (1971). Cellular homeostasis, epigenesis, and replication in randomly aggregated macro-molecular systems. *Journal of Cybernetics* 1: 71-96.

Kauffman, S. A. (1992). *The Origins of Order: Self-Organization and Selection in Evolution.* Oxford: Oxford University Press.

Langton, C. G. (1984). Self-reproduction in cellular automata. *Physica D* 10: 135-144.

Langton, C. G. (1986). Studying artificial life with cellular automata. *Physica D* 22: 1120-1149.

Langton, C. G. (1989). Artificial life. In C. G. Langton, Ed., *Artificial Life: The Proceedings of an Interdisciplinary Workshop on the Synthesis and Simulation of Living Systems (held September 1987).* Redwood City, CA: Addison-Wesley, pp. 1-47. (Reprinted, with revisions, in M. A. Boden, Ed., *The Philosophy of Artificial Life.* Oxford: Oxford University Press, pp. 39-94.)

Levy, S. (1992). *Artificial Life: The Quest for a New Creation.* New York: Pantheon.

Maturana, H. R., and F. J. Varela. (1980). *Autopoiesis and Cognition: The Realization of the Living.* London: Reidel.

Meyer, J.-A., and S. W. Wilson, Eds. (1991). *From Animals to Animats: Proceedings of the First International Conference on Simulation of Adaptive Behavior.* Cambridge, MA: MIT Press.

Ray, T. S. (1992). An approach to the synthesis of life. In C. G. Langton, C. Taylor, J. D. Farmer, and S. Rasmussen, Eds., *Artificial Life II.* Redwood City, CA: Addison-Wesley, pp. 371-408. (Reprinted in M. A. Boden, Ed., *The Philosophy of Artificial Life.* Oxford: Oxford University Press, pp. 111-145.)

Ray, T. S. (1994). An evolutionary approach to synthetic biology: Zen and the art of creating life. *Artificial Life* 1: 179-210.

Turing, A. M. (1952). The chemical basis of morphogenesis. *Philosophical Transactions of the Royal Society: B* 237: 37-72.

Wolfram, S. (1983). Statistical mechanics of cellular automata. *Review of Modern Physics* 55: 601-644.

Wolfram, S. (1986). *Theory and Applications of Cellular Automata.* Singapore: World Scientific.

Aspect

See TENSE AND ASPECT

Attention

William JAMES once wrote, "Every one knows what attention is. It is the taking possession by the mind, in clear and vivid form, of one out of what seem several simultaneously possible objects or trains of thought. Focalization, concentration, of consciousness are of its essence. It implies withdrawal from some things in order to deal effectively with others" (James 1890: 403-404). The study of selectivity in information processing operations, of "withdrawal from some things in order to deal effectively with others," has its modern origins in the 1950s with BROADBENT's *Perception and Communication* (1958). Loosely speaking, much of this work may be taken as research into "attention," though problems of selective information processing of course need not be identical to James's first-person view of selective consciousness or awareness.

In fact many aspects of selectivity must contribute to the organization of any focused line of activity. At any given time, the person is actively pursuing some goals rather than others. Some actions rather than others bring those goals closer. Some parts rather than others of the sensory input are relevant and must be examined or monitored. The general state of alertness or drowsiness is also often considered an aspect of "attention." In *Perception and Communication*, a single selective device was used to handle many different phenomena: selective listening, loss of performance with long work periods, impairments by loud noise, and so forth. When the theory was updated in *Decision and Stress* (1971), data from many experimental tasks already required a substantially more complex approach, with a variety of distinct selective mechanisms. Modern work seeks to understand both separate aspects of processing selectivity and their relations.

Selective perception in a variety of modalities has been particularly well investigated. Experiments on selective listening in the 1950s dealt with people listening to two simultaneous speech messages. First, these experiments showed *limited capacity*: People were often unable to identify both messages at once. Second, they showed conditions for effective selectivity: People could identify one message and ignore the other providing the messages differed in simple physical characteristics such as location, loudness, or voice, but not when they differed only in content. Third, these experiments showed the striking consequences of efficient selection: A person listening to one message and ignoring another would subsequently be able to report only the crudest characteristics of the ignored message, for example, that it had changed from speech to a tone, but not whether it had been in a familiar or an unfamiliar language.

All three points have received much subsequent study. As an example of the many things learned regarding limited capacity, experiments with mixed visual and auditory stimuli show that the major limit on simultaneous perception is modality-specific: One visual and one auditory stimulus can be identified together much better than two stimuli in the same modality (Treisman and Davies 1973). Regarding the control of stimulus selection, experiments show the joint influence of top-down (task-driven) and bottom-up (stimulus-driven) considerations. Top-down influences are important when a person is specifically instructed to pay attention just to objects in a certain region of a visual display (selection by location), objects having a certain color or other property (selection by object feature), or objects of a certain category (e.g., letters rather than digits) (von Wright 1968). Selection by location (*spatial attention*) has been particularly well studied (Posner 1978). Irrespective of the task or instruction, however, stimulus factors such as intensity (Broadbent 1958) or sudden onset (Jonides and Yantis 1988) also contribute to the choice of which stimulus is processed. Long practice in considering a certain stimulus relevant or important will also favor its selection, as when one's own name attracts attention in a crowded room (Moray 1959). Regarding the results of efficient selection, finally, experiments have detailed what differs in the processing of attended and ignored stimuli. Often, very little can be explicitly remembered of stimuli a person was asked to ignore, even though those stimuli were perfectly audible or visible (Wolford and Morrison 1980). In contrast, indirect measures may suggest a good deal of hidden or unconscious processing; for example, an ignored word previously associated with shock may produce a galvanic skin response even while subjects fail to notice its occurrence (Corteen and Dunn 1974). The nature and duration of such implicit processing of unattended material remains a topic of active debate, for example, in the discussion of IMPLICIT VS. EXPLICIT MEMORY.

These studies reflect general questions that may be asked of any selective process. One is the question of *divided attention*, or how much can be done at once. Another is the question of *selective attention*, or how efficiently desired stimuli can be processed and unwanted stimuli ignored. Experiments measuring establishment of a new selective priority concern *attention setting and switching*. The complement to switching is *sustained attention*, or ability to maintain one fixed processing set over an extended time period.

The neurobiology of visual attention is a particularly active topic of current research. In the primate brain, visual information is distributed to a network of specialized cortical areas responsible for separate visual functions and dealing partially with separate visual dimensions such as shape, motion and color (Desimone and Ungerleider 1989). Taken together, these "visual areas" cover roughly the posterior third of the cerebral hemispheres. Recordings from single cells in several visual areas of the monkey show weak or suppressed responses to stimuli that the animal is set to ignore (Moran and Desimone 1985). Measurements of gross electrical activity in the human brain, and associated changes in local cerebral bloodflow, similarly suggest greater responses to attended than to unattended stimuli (Heinze et al. 1994). Damage to one side of the brain weakens the representation of stimuli on the opposite side of visual space. Such stimuli may be seen when they are presented alone, but pass undetected when there is concurrent input on the unimpaired side (Bender 1952). All these results suggest that concurrent visual inputs compete for representation in the network of visual areas (Desimone and Duncan 1995). Attended stimuli are strongly represented, while responses to unwanted stimuli are suppressed.

Complementary to selective perception is the selective activation of goals or components of an action plan. Here, too, errors reflect limited capacity, or difficulty organizing two lines of thought or action simultaneously. Everyday slips of action, such as driving to work instead of the store, or stirring coffee into the teapot, are especially likely when a person is preoccupied with other thoughts (Reason and Mycielska 1982). Practice is again a key consideration. Although it may be impossible to organize two unfamiliar activities at once, familiar behavior seems to occur automatically, leaving attention (in this sense) free for other concerns. Indeed, familiar actions may tend to occur "involuntarily," or when they are currently inappropriate. Again everyday action slips provide clear examples: taking a familiar route when intending to drive elsewhere, or taking out one's key on arrival at a friend's door (James 1890). A laboratory version is the Stroop effect: Naming the color of a written word suffers substantial interference from a tendency instead to read the word itself (Stroop 1935). Such results suggest a model in which conflicting action tendencies compete for activation. Practice increases an action's competitive strength.

Disorganized behavior and action slips occur commonly after damage to the frontal lobes of the brain (Luria 1966). Disorganization can take many forms: intrusive actions irrelevant to a current task, perseverative repetition of incorrect behavior, choices that seem ill-judged or bizarre. A major question is how action selection develops from the joint activity of multiple frontal lobe systems. A more detailed treatment is given in ATTENTION AND THE HUMAN BRAIN.

To some extent, certainly, it is appropriate to consider different aspects of "attention" as separate. To take one concrete example, it has been amply documented that there are many distinct forms of competition or interference between one line of activity and another. These include modality-specific perceptual competition, effector-specific response competition, and competition between similar internal representations (e.g., two spatial or two verbal representations; see Baddeley 1986); though there are also very general sources of interference even between very dissimilar tasks (Bourke, Duncan, and Nimmo-Smith 1996). Each aspect of competition reflects a distinct way in which the nervous system must select one set of mental operations over another.

At the same time, selectivities in multiple mental domains must surely be integrated to give coherent, purposive behaviour (Duncan 1996). It has often been proposed that some mental "executive" takes overall responsibility for coordinating mental activity (e.g., Baddeley 1986); for example, for ensuring that appropriate goals, actions, and perceptual inputs are all selected together. At least as attractive, perhaps, is an approach through self-organization. By analogy with "relaxation" models of many mental processes (McClelland and Rumelhart 1981), selected material in any one mental domain (e.g., active goals, perceptual inputs, material from memory) may support selection of related material in other domains. The description of top-down control given earlier, for example, implies that goals control perceptual selection; equally, however, active goals can always be overturned by novel perceptual input, as when a telephone rings or a friend passes by in the street. Whichever approach is taken, a central aspect of "attention" is this question of overall mental coordination.

See also CONSCIOUSNESS, NEUROBIOLOGY OF; EYE MOVEMENTS AND VISUAL ATTENTION; INTROSPECTION; MEMORY; NEURAL NETWORKS; SELF-KNOWLEDGE; TOP-DOWN PROCESSING IN VISION

—*John Duncan*

References

Baddeley, A. D. (1986). *Working Memory.* Oxford: Oxford University Press.

Bender, M. B. (1952). *Disorders in Perception.* Springfield, IL: Charles C. Thomas.

Bourke, P. A., J. Duncan, and I. Nimmo-Smith. (1996). A general factor involved in dual task performance decrement. *Quarterly Journal of Experimental Psychology* 49A: 525–545.

Broadbent, D. E. (1958). *Perception and Communication.* London: Pergamon.

Broadbent, D. E. (1971). *Decision and Stress.* London: Academic Press.

Corteen, R. S., and D. Dunn. (1974). Shock-associated words in a nonattended message: a test for momentary awareness. *Journal of Experimental Psychology* 102: 1143–1144.

Desimone, R., and L. G. Ungerleider. (1989). Neural mechanisms of visual processing in monkeys. In F. Boller and J. Grafman, Eds., *Handbook of Neuropsychology*, vol. 2. Amsterdam: Elsevier, pp. 267–299.

Desimone, R., and J. Duncan. (1995). Neural mechanisms of selective visual attention. *Annual Review of Neuroscience* 18: 193–222.

Duncan, J. (1996). Cooperating brain systems in selective perception and action. In T. Inui and J. L. McClelland, Eds., *Attention and Performance XVI.* Cambridge, MA: MIT Press, pp. 549–578.

Heinze, H. J., G. R. Mangun, W. Burchert, H. Hinrichs, M. Scholz, T. F. Munte, A. Gos, M. Scherg, S. Johannes, H. Hundeshagen, M. S. Gazzaniga, and S. A. Hillyard. (1994). Combined spatial and temporal imaging of brain activity during visual selective attention in humans. *Nature* 372: 543–546.

James, W. (1890). *The Principles of Psychology.* New York: Holt.

Jonides, J., and S. Yantis. (1988). Uniqueness of abrupt visual onset in capturing attention. *Perception and Psychophysics* 43: 346–354.

Luria, A. R. (1966). *Higher Cortical Functions in Man.* London: Tavistock.

McClelland, J. L., and D. E. Rumelhart. (1981). An interactive activation model of context effects in letter perception: Part 1. An account of basic findings. *Psychological Review* 88: 375–407.

Moran, J., and R. Desimone. (1985). Selective attention gates visual processing in the extratriate cortex. *Science* 229: 782–784.

Moray, N. (1959). Attention in dichotic listening: affective cues and the influence of instructions. *Quarterly Journal of Experimental Psychology* 11: 56–60.

Posner, M. I. (1978). *Chronometric Explorations of Mind.* Hillsdale, NJ: Erlbaum.

Reason, J., and K. Mycielska. (1982). *Absent-minded? The Psychology of Mental Lapses and Everyday Errors.* Englewood Cliffs, NJ: Prentice-Hall.

Stroop, J. R. (1935). Studies of interference in serial verbal reactions. *Journal of Experimental Psychology* 18: 643–662.

Treisman, A. M., and A. Davies. (1973). Divided attention to ear and eye. In S. Kornblum, Ed., *Attention and Performance IV.* London: Academic Press, pp. 101–117.

von Wright, J. M. (1968). Selection in visual immediate memory. *Quarterly Journal of Experimental Psychology* 20: 62–68.

Wolford, G., and F. Morrison. (1980). Processing of unattended visual information. *Memory and Cognition* 8: 521–527.

Further Readings

Allport, D. A. (1989). Visual attention. In M. I. Posner, Ed., *Foundations of Cognitive Science.* Cambridge, MA: MIT Press, pp. 631–682.

Norman, D. A., and T. Shallice. (1986). Attention to action: willed and automatic control of behavior. In R. J. Davidson, G. E. Schwartz, and D. Shapiro, Eds., *Consciousness and self-regulation. Advances in research and theory,* vol. 4. New York: Plenum, pp. 1–18.

Pashler, H. (1997). *The Psychology of Attention.* Cambridge, MA: MIT press.

Posner, M. I., and S. E. Petersen. (1990). The attention system of the human brain. *Annual Review of Neuroscience* 13: 25–42.

Attention in the Animal Brain

In most contexts ATTENTION refers to our ability to concentrate our perceptual experience on a selected portion of the available sensory information, and, in doing so, to achieve a clear and vivid impression of the environment. To evaluate something that seems as fundamentally introspective as attention, cognitive science research usually uses a measure of behavioral performance that is correlated with attention. To examine brain mechanisms of attention, the correlations are extended another level by measuring the activity of neurons during different 'attentive' behaviors. Although this article focuses exclusively on attentive processes in the visual system, attentive processing occurs within each sensory system (see AUDITORY ATTENTION) and more generally in most aspects of cognitive brain function. Our understanding of the neuronal correlates of attention comes principally from the study of the influence of attentive acts on visual processing as observed in animals. The selective aspects of attention are apparent in both of vision's principal functions, identifying objects and navigating with respect to objects and surfaces.

Attention is a dynamic process added on top of the passive elements of selection provided by the architecture of the visual system. For foveate animals, looking or navigating encompasses the set of actions necessary to find a desired goal and place it in foveal view. The selective aspects of attention within this context deal primarily with decisions about information in the peripheral field of view. Seeing or identifying objects encompasses a more detailed analysis of centrally available information. In this context the selective aspects of attention deal primarily with the delineation of objects and the integration of their parts that lead to their recognition (see OBJECT RECOGNITION, ANIMAL STUDIES).

Although the retinae encode a wide expanse of the visual environment, object analysis is not uniform across the visual field but instead is concentrated in a small zone called the field of focal attention (Neisser 1967). Under most circumstances this restricted zone has little to due with acuity limits set by the receptor density gradient in the retina but is due to an interference between objects generated by the density of the visual information. Focal attention encompasses the dynamic phenomena that enable us to isolate and examine objects under the conditions of interference. The selective aspect of attention raises an important question, namely, how many things can be attended to at one time? Interestingly, the answer varies, and depends at least in part on the level of analysis that is necessary to distinguish between the things that are present. What is clear is that the moment-to-moment analytic capacity of the visual system is surprisingly limited.

An examination of the physiology and anatomy of visual processes in animals, especially primates, provides us with key pieces of the attention puzzle. Visual information is dispersed from primary visual cortex through extrastriate cortex along two main routes. One leads ventrally toward anterior temporal cortex, the other dorsally into parietal association cortex. The ventral stream progression portrays a system devoted to object analysis, and in anterior temporal areas, represents a stage where sensory processes merge with systems associated with object recognition and memory (Gross 1992). The dorsal stream emphasizes the positions of surfaces and objects and in parietal areas represents a stage where the sensory and motor processes involved in the exploration of the surrounding space become intertwined (Mountcastle 1995). The different emphasis in information processing within parietal and temporal areas is also apparent with respect to the influences of attentional states. Both the sensitivity to visual stimuli and the effective receptive field size are more than doubled for parietal visual neurons during an attentive fixation task, whereas under similar conditions the receptive fields of inferior temporal cortical neurons are observed to collapse around a fixation target.

As visual processing progresses in both the dorsal and ventral streams, there is an accompanying expansion in the receptive field size of individual neurons and a corresponding convergence of information as an increasing number of objects fit within each receptive field. Despite the convergence, an inseparable mixture of information from different objects does not occur in part because of the competitive, winner-take-all nature of the convergence and in part because of attentive selection. Directing attention to a particular object alters the convergent balance in favor of the attended object and suppresses the neural response to other objects in the neuron's receptive field (Moran and Desimone 1985; Treue and Maunsell 1996).

Within the ventral stream and at progressively higher levels of object analysis, the competitive convergence of the system forces a narrowing of processing by selecting what information or which objects gain control of the neural activity. The connectivity of the visual system is not simply a feedforward system but a highly interconnected concurrent network. Whatever information wins the contention at one level is passed forward and backward and often laterally (Van Essen and DeYoe 1995). These factors heavily constrain the neural activity, limiting the activation of neurons at each subsequent level to a progressively restricted set of stimulus configurations. As increasingly higher levels of analytic abstraction are attained in the ventral stream, the receptive field convergence narrows the independence of parallel representations until in the anterior temporal lobe the neuronal receptive fields encompass essentially all of the central visual field. Because directing attention emphasizes the processing of the object(s) at the attended location, the act of attending both engages the ventral stream on the object(s) at that location and dampens out information from the remaining visual field (Chelazzi et al. 1993). These circumstances parallel the capacity limitation found in many forms in vision and may constitute the performance limiting factor. Capacity limits may vary depending upon the level of convergence in the cortical stream that must be reached before a discriminative decision about the set of observed objects can be achieved (Merigan, Nealey, and Maunsell 1993).

When attention is to be shifted to a new object, as we read the next word or reach for a cup or walk along a path, information must be obtained from the periphery as to the spatial layout of objects. The dorsal stream appears to provide this information. The convergence of information within the neuronal receptive fields generates sensitivity to large surfaces, their motion and boundaries and the positions of objects within them, without particular sensitivity to the nature of the objects themselves. The parietal visual system is especially sensitive to the relative motion of surfaces such as that generated during movement through the environment. An object to which attention is shifted is usually peripherally located with respect to the object currently undergoing perceptual analysis. For parietal cortical neurons, maintained attention on a particular object results in a heightened visual sensitivity across the visual field and, in contrast to the temporal stream, a suppressed sensitivity to objects currently at the locus of directed attention (Motter 1991).

The transition between sensory information and MOTOR CONTROL is subject to a clear capacity limitation—competition between potential target goals must be resolved to produce a coherent motor plan. When target goals are in different locations, spatially selective processing can be used to identify locations or objects that have been selected as target goals. In the period before a movement is made, the neural activity associated with the visual presence of the object at the target site evolves to differentiate the target object from other objects. This spatially selective change, consistent with an attentive selection process, has been observed in parietal cortex as well as the motor eye fields of frontal cortex and subcortical visuomotor areas such as the superior colliculus (Schall 1995).

How early in the visual system are attentive influences active? If attention effectively manipulates processing in the earliest stages of vision, then the visual experiences we have are in part built up from internal hypotheses about what we are seeing or what we want to see. Two sets of physiological observations suggest these important consequences of selective attention do occur. First, directed attention studies and studies requiring attentive selection of stimulus features have shown that the neural coding of objects can be completely dominated by top-down attentive demands as early as extrastriate cortex and can bias neuronal processing even in primary visual cortex. Second, after arriving in primary visual cortex, visual information spreads through the cortical systems within 60–80 msec. The effects of selective attention develop in parallel during the next 100 msec in extrastriate occipital, temporal, and parietal cortex and the frontal eye fields, making it not only difficult to pinpoint a single decision stage but also making it likely that a coherent solution across areas is reached by a settling of the network (Motter 1997).

The detailed physiological insights gained from animal studies complement the imaging studies of ATTENTION IN THE HUMAN BRAIN that have probed higher-order cognitive functions and attempted to identify the neural substrates of volitional aspects of attention. Together these sets of studies have provided new views of several classic phenomena in attention including capacity limitations and the temporal progression of selection.

See also ATTENTION IN THE HUMAN BRAIN; EYE MOVEMENTS AND VISUAL ATTENTION; VISUAL ANATOMY AND PHYSIOLOGY; VISUAL PROCESSING STREAMS

—*Brad Motter*

References

Chelazzi, L., E. K. Miller, J. Duncan, and R. Desimone. (1993). A neural basis for visual search in inferior temporal cortex. *Nature* 363: 345–347.

Gross, C. G. (1992). Representation of visual stimuli in inferior temporal cortex. *Philosophical Transactions of the Royal Society, London, Series B* 335: 3–10.

Merigan, W. H., and J. H. R. Maunsell. (1993). How parallel are the primate visual pathways? *Annual Review of Neuroscience* 16: 369–402.

Merigan, W. H., T. A. Nealey, and J. H. R. Maunsell. (1993). Visual effects of lesions of cortical area V2 in macaques. *Journal of Neuroscience* 13: 3180–3191.

Moran, J., and R. Desimone. (1985). Selective attention gate visual processing in the extrastriate cortex. *Science* 229: 782–784.

Motter, B. C. (1991). Beyond extrastriate cortex: the parietal visual system. In A. G. Leventhal, Ed., *Vision and Visual Dysfunction*, vol. 4, *The Neural Basis of Visual Function*. London: Macmillan, pp. 371–387.

Motter, B. C. (1998). Neurophysiology of visual attention. In R. Parasuraman, Ed., *The Attentive Brain*. Cambridge, MA: MIT Press.

Mountcastle, V. B. (1995). The parietal system and some higher brain functions. *Cerebral Cortex* 5: 377–390.

Neisser, U. (1967). *Cognitive Psychology*. New York: Appleton-Century-Crofts.

Schall, J. D. (1995). Neural basis of saccade target selection. *Reviews in the Neurosciences* 6: 63–85.

Treue, S., and J. H. R. Maunsell. (1996). Attentional modulation of visual motion processing in cortical areas MT and MST. *Nature* 382: 539–541.

Van Essen, D. C., and E. A. DeYoe. (1995). Concurrent processing in the primate visual cortex. In M.S. Gazzaniga, Ed., *The Cognitive Neurosciences*. Cambridge, MA: MIT Press, pp. 383–400.

Further Readings

Connor C. E., J. L. Gallant, D. C. Preddie, and D. C. Van Essen. (1996). Responses in area V4 depend on the spatial relationship between stimulus and attention. *Journal of Neurophysiology* 75: 1306–1308.

Corbetta, M., F. M. Miesin, S. Dobmeyer, G. L. Shulman, and S. E. Petersen (1991). Selective and divided attention during visual discriminations of shape, color and speed: functional anatomy by positron emission tomography. *Journal of Neuroscience* 11: 2382–2402.

Desimone, R., and J. Duncan. (1995). Neural mechanisms of selective visual attention. *Annual Review of Neuroscience* 18: 193–222.

Friedman-Hill, S. R., L. Robertson, and A. Treisman. (1995). Parietal contributions to visual feature binding: evidence from a patient with bilateral lesions. *Science* 269: 853– 855.

Haenny, P. E., J. H. R. Maunsell, and P. H. Schiller. (1988). State dependent activity in monkey visual cortex. II. Retinal and extraretinal factors in V4. *Experimental Brain Research* 69: 245–259.

Haxby, J., B. Horwitz, L. G. Ungerleider, J. Maisog, P. Pietrini, and C. Grady. (1994). The functional organization of human extra-striate cortex: a PET-rCBF study of selective attention to faces and locations. *Journal of Neuroscience* 14: 6336–6353.

Koch, C., and S. Ullman. (1985). Shifts in selective visual attention: towards the underlying neural circuitry. *Human Neurobiology* 4: 219–227.

Motter, B. C. (1994). Neural correlates of color and luminance feature selection in extrastriate area V4. *Journal of Neuroscience* 14: 2178–2189.

Olshausen B., C. Andersen, and D. C. Van Essen. (1993). A neural model of visual attention and invariant pattern recognition. *Journal of Neuroscience* 13: 4700–4719.

Petersen, S. E., P. T. Fox, M. I. Posner, M. Mintun, and M. E. Raichle. (1988). Positron emission tomographic studies of the cortical anatomy of single-word processing. *Nature* 331: 585–589.

Richmond, B. J., R. H. Wurtz, and T. Sato. (1983). Visual responses of inferior temporal neurons in the awake rhesus monkey. *Journal of Neurophysiology* 50: 1415–1432.

Robinson, D. L. (1993). Functional contributions of the primate pulvinar. *Progress in Brain Research* 95: 371–380.

Schiller, P. H., and K. Lee. (1991). The role of the primate extrastriate area V4 in vision. *Science* 251: 1251–1253.

Tsotsos, J. K., S. M. Culhane, W. Y. K. Wai, Y. Lai, N. Davis, and F. Nuflo. (1995). Modeling visual attention via selective tuning. *Artificial Intelligence* 78: 507–545.

Zipser, K., V. A. F. Lamme, and P. H. Schiller. (1996). Contextual modulation in primary visual cortex. *Journal of Neuroscience* 16: 7376–7389

Attention in the Human Brain

To illustrate what is meant by attention, consider the display in figure 1. Your ATTENTION may be drawn to the tilted T because it differs in such a striking way from the background. When one figure differs from the background by a

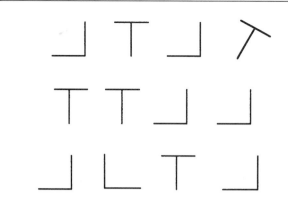

Figure 1.

single feature, it pops out and your attention is drawn to it. This is an example of attention driven by input. However, if you know that the target is an L you can guide your search among the stimuli with horizontal and vertical strokes. This is an example of the form of higher level voluntary control that is the subject of this section. Voluntary control is accompanied by the subjective feeling of selection between potential actions and is one of the most distinctive features of human experience. The interaction of top-down voluntary actions with bottom-up automatic processes, which is illustrated by figure 1, has interested researchers since the beginnings of psychology (James 1890; see WILLIAM JAMES).

One approach to the question of voluntary control is to argue that it is an illusion that arises out of the competitive activation of a large number of brain systems. What appears to be volition is the result of a complex network relaxing to a particular state. Although without denying the top-down component, this view stresses the bottom-up processes. A different view elaborated in this section is that there is a high-level executive attention network with its own anatomy that works to resolve competition and in the process gives rise to subjective feelings of cognitive control (Norman and Shallice 1986). This view emphasizes the top-down control.

The executive system participates in tasks that involve conflict between systems. This is a property one expects to find in a system that has as a major function inhibition of reflexive or bottom-up responses to external stimuli in order to allow autonomous action. A classical paradigm to study the inhibition of habitual responses is the Stroop task (Stroop 1935). In this task, subjects name the color of the ink of a word. Sometimes, the word is a color name (e.g., red) in a different ink color (e.g., blue). In those incongruent trials subjects automatically read "red" and have to inhibit this answer to respond "blue." Inhibition produces interference revealed by slow reaction times in the incongruent condition.

Is it possible to uncover the neural substrates of cognitive control? Imaging techniques developed in the last several years have yielded promising results (Toga and Mazziota 1996). An area in the medial surface of the frontal lobe, named the anterior cingulate gyrus, appears to be important for the inhibition of automatic response that is central to voluntary action. Five studies involving measurement of blood flow by POSITRON EMISSION TOMOGRAPHY (PET) in a Stroop task have shown activation of the anterior cingulate

in the incongruent condition when compared with the congruent condition (e.g., the noun blue displayed in blue color) or neutral (noncolor word; see Posner and DiGirolamo 1996 for a review).

Other tasks requiring inhibition of habitual responses also activate the anterior cingulate. For example, responding to a noun by generating an associated use produces more activation of the anterior cingulate than simply repeating the noun (Petersen et al. 1989). In the generate condition, the most familiar response (i.e., repeating the noun) needs to be repressed, to allow the expression of the verb. Classifying a noun into a category also produces cingulate activation related to the number of targets. This finding suggests that the anterior cingulate activation is due to special processing of the target rather than being necessary to make the classification, a result consistent with the idea of cognitive control. The cingulate has close connection to underlying subcortical areas in the BASAL GANGLIA (Houk 1995). These areas have also shown activity in some of the same tasks described above and play a role in the inhibition of reflexive motor responses. It seems likely they form part of the network subserving this form of voluntary control.

Goldberg and Bloom (1990) proposed a "dual premotor system hypothesis" of volitional movement. This theory, which attributes an executive function to the anterior cingulate and the supplementary motor area, was developed to explain the alien hand sign. The alien hand sign is the performance of apparently purposive movements that the patient fails to recognize as self-generated. The theory posits a lateral premotor system (LPS; Area 6), that organizes motor behavior in reaction to external stimulus, and a medial premotor system (MPS; anterior cingulate, supplementary motor area, and basal ganglia loops), which underlies intentional behavior. MPS underlies volitional movement by inhibiting the LPS. If a lesion occurs in MPS, LPS is released and obligatory dependence on external information emerges. The patient develops compulsive automatisms, which are not perceived as self-generated. The inhibitory effect of MPS over LPS during volitional movement resembles the inhibitory effect of MPS (i.e., anterior cingulate) over semantic networks during the Stroop task. The idea of alien rather than self control is also found in some forms of schizophrenia, a disorder that has also been shown to involve abnormalities in the anterior cingulate and basal ganglia (Benes 1993; Early 1994).

Cognitive studies have shown several forms of short term or WORKING MEMORY and considerable independence between them (Baddeley 1986). Recent imaging data show that verbal, spatial, and object memories involve separate anatomical areas (Smith and Jonides 1995). There is evidence that all forms of memory are interfaced to a common executive system that involves the same midline frontal anatomy described previously (Baddeley 1986; Posner and Raichle 1994).

PET studies have also shown that executive attention plays an important role in high level skills (Kosslyn 1994; Posner and Raichle 1994). Studies involving recording from scalp electrodes have provided some information on the time course of the activations found in PET studies during reading. Skills such as READING have a very strong dependence on rapid processing. A skilled reader fixates on a given word for only about 275 msec (Rayner and Sereno 1994). In generating the use of visual words, activation of the cingulate begins as early as 150 msec after input when blocks of trials in which subjects derive a word meaning alternate with blocks in which they read the word aloud (Snyder et al. 1995). The cingulate activation occurs whenever higher level supervisory control is needed to organize the mental response to the input. In the case of generating the use of a word, attention leads and probably is required for the activation of a network of areas that lead eventually to articulation of novel ideas associated with the input string. We see an early semantic analysis of the input word after 200 msec and development of associations to the input in frontal and parietal sites over the next second. Although it is possible to lay out a sequence of processing steps, they can be misleading. Because attention may occur rather early it is possible for subjects to reprogram the organization of these steps and thus to carry out a number of different instructions with the same brain network. Studies of the role of attention suggest that reorganization involves amplification of the operations that are attended in comparison to unattended operations. Increases in overall neuronal activity appear to produce faster speed and higher priority for the attended computations. As attention is released from high order activity during practice in the skill it becomes possible to improve the speed of performance by amplification of early processing steps.

Studies of mental arithmetic, visual IMAGERY, and other forms of skilled performance using neuroimaging methods seem to support many of the same principles that have been outlined above for word reading.

See also ATTENTION IN THE ANIMAL BRAIN; AUDITORY ATTENTION; ELECTROPHYSIOLOGY, ELECTRIC AND MAGNETIC FIELDS; EYE MOVEMENTS AND VISUAL ATTENTION; ILLUSIONS; MAGNETIC RESONANCE IMAGING; TOP-DOWN PROCESSING IN VISION; VISUAL WORD RECOGNITION

—Michael I. Posner and Diego Fernandez-Duque

References

Baddeley, A. (1986). *Working Memory.* Oxford: Oxford University Press.

Benes, F. M. (1993). Relationship of cingulate cortex to schizophrenia and other psychiatric disorders. In B. A. Vogt and M. Gabriel, Eds., *Neurobiology of Cingulate Cortex and Limbic Thalamus.* Boston: Birkhauser.

Early, T. S. (1994). Left globus pallidus hyperactivity and right-sided neglect in schizophrenia. In R. L. Cromwell and C. R. Snyder, Eds., *Schizophrenia: Origins, Processes, Treatment and Outcome.* New York: Oxford University Press, pp. 17–30.

Goldberg, G., and K. K. Bloom. (1990). The alien hand sign. *American Journal of Physical Medicine and Rehabilitation* 69(5): 228–238.

Houk, J. C. (1995). Information processing in modular circuits linking basal ganglia and cerebral cortex. In J. C. Houk, J. L. Davies, and D. G. Beiser, Eds., *Model of Information Processing in the Basal Ganglia.* Cambridge, MA: Bradford, pp. 3–10.

Kosslyn, S. M. (1994). *Image and Brain.* Cambridge, MA: MIT Press.

Norman, D. A., and T. Shallice. (1986). Attention to action: willed and automatic control of behavior. In R. J. Davidson, G. E. Schwartz, and D. Shapiro, Eds., *Consciousness and Self Regulation.* New York: Plenum, pp. 1–17.

Petersen, S. E., P. T. Fox, M. I. Posner, M. Mintun, and M. E. Raichle. (1989). Positron emission tomographic studies of the processing of single words. *Journal of Cognitive Neuroscience* 1: 153–170.

Posner, M. I., and G. J. DiGirolamo. (1998). Conflict, target detection and cognitive control. In R. Parasuraman, Ed., *The Attentive Brain.* Cambridge, MA: MIT Press.

Posner, M. I., and M. E. Raichle. (1994). *Images of Mind.* New York: Scientific American Library.

Rayner, K., and S. C. Sereno. (1994). Eye movements in reading: psycholinguistic studies. In M. A. Gernsbacher, Ed., *Handbook of Psycholinguistics.* New York: Academic Press, pp. 57–81.

Smith, E. E., and J. Jonides. (1995). Working memory in humans: neuropsychological evidence. In M. S. Gazzaniga, Ed., *The Cognitive Neurosciences.* Cambridge, MA: MIT Press, pp. 1009–1020.

Snyder, A. Z., Y. Abdullaev, M. I. Posner, and M. E. Raichle. (1995). Scalp electrical potentials reflect regional cerebral blood flow responses during processing of written words. *Proceedings of the National Academy of Sciences* 92: 1689–1693.

Stroop, J. R. (1935). Studies of interference in serial verbal reactions. *Journal of Experimental Psychology* 18: 643–662.

Toga, A. W., and J. C. Mazziotta, Eds. (1996). *Brain Mapping: The Methods.* New York: Academic Press.

Further Readings

Bisiach, E. (1992). Understanding consciousness: clues from unilateral neglect and related disorders. In A. D. Milner and M. D. Rugg (Eds.), *The Neuropsychology of Consciousness.* London: Academic Press, pp. 113–139.

Burgess, P. W., and T. Shallice. (1996). Response suppression, initiation and strategy use following frontal lobe lesions. *Neuropsychologia* 34: 263–273.

Chelazzi, L., E. K. Miller, J. Duncan, and R. Desimone. (1993). A neural basis for visual search in inferior temporal cortex. *Nature* 363: 345–347.

D'Esposito, M., J. A. Detre, D. C. Alsop, R. K. Shin, S. Atlas, and M. Grossman. (1995). The neural basis of the central executive system of working memory. *Nature* 378: 279–281.

Démonet, J. F., R. Wise, and R. S. J. Frackowiak. (1993). Language functions explored in normal subjects by positron emission tomography: a critical review. *Human Brain Mapping* 1: 39–47.

Graves, R. E., and B. S. Jones. (1992). Conscious visual perceptual awareness vs. non-conscious visual spatial localisation examined with normal subjects using possible analogues of blindsight and neglect. *Cognitive Neuropsychology* 9(6): 487–508.

Jonides, J. P. (1981). Voluntary versus automatic control over the mind's eye. In J. Long and A. Baddeley, Eds., *Attention and Performance IX.* Hillsdale, NJ: Erlbaum, pp. 187–204.

LaBerge, D. (1995). *Attentional Processing: The Brain's Art of Mindfulness.* Cambridge, MA: Harvard University Press.

Pardo, J. V., P. T. Fox, and M. E. Raichle. (1991). Localization of a human system for sustained attention by positron emission tomography. *Nature* 349(6304): 61–64.

Pardo, J. V., P. J. Pardo, K. W. Janer, and M. E. Raichle. (1990). The anterior cingulate cortex mediates processing selection in the Stroop attentional conflict paradigm. *Proceedings of National Academy of Science* 87: 256–259.

Posner, M. I., G. J. DiGirolamo, and D. Fernandez-Duque. (1997). Brain mechanisms of cognitive skills. *Consciousness and Cognition* 6: 267–290.

Rafal, R. D. (1994). Neglect. *Current Opinion in Neurobiology* 4: 231–236.

Stuss, D. T., T. Shallice, M. P. Alexander, and T. W. Picton. (1995). A multidisciplinary approach to anterior attention functions. In J. Grafman, K. J. Holyoak, and F. Boller, Eds., *Structure and Functions of the Human Prefrontal Cortex*. New York: New York Academy of Sciences.

Umiltà, C. (1988). Orienting of attention. In F. Boller and J. Grafman, Eds., *Handbook of Neuropsychology*. Amsterdam: Elsevier, pp. 175–192

Attribution Theory

Because humans are social animals, an individual's prospects for survival and success depend on the ability to understand, predict, and influence the behavior of other persons. Hence "people watching" is an essential human impulse. Yet it does not suffice to merely watch other people's overt actions; we strive to infer *why* people behave as they do. The psychological processes underlying these interpretations of the causes of behavior are studied in a subfield of social psychology known as attribution theory.

Although all proposed models of attribution assume that *accurate understanding* of the actual causes of behavior is a primary goal, models differ in assumptions about processing limitations that impede accuracy and about other human goals that interfere with accuracy. As in many areas of cognitive science, such as perception and DECISION MAKING, researchers often attempt to learn how the system works from where it fails, testing predictions about the errors that would arise from a process. One pattern of error is the tendency of observers to overestimate how much another's behavior is determined by the person's stable traits, a tendency first described by Ichheiser (1949) and formalized by Ross (1977) as "the fundamental attribution error" (FAE). Errors in attributing to stable dispositions (e.g., aptitudes, attitudes, and traits) have important consequences for the observer's subsequent expectancies, evaluations, and behavioral responses. For example, when a teacher attributes a student's failure to lack of intelligence (as opposed to a situational factor) this leads to reduced expectations of the student's future success, reduced liking of the student, and reduced teaching investment in the student. We will review theory and research on the FAE to illustrate how attribution theory has progressed.

The blueprint for attribution theory was Heider's (1958) GESTALT PERCEPTION analysis of interpersonal interaction. He argued that a person's response to a social situation is largely a function of how the person subjectively organizes the stimulus of a social situation, such as through attributions. Perhaps the most influential idea is that attributions are guided by *lay theories* such as the schema that achievement reflects both situational forces (environmental factors that facilitate or constrain the actor) and internal forces (the combination of effort and aptitude). Heider contended that the attributor, like a scientist, uses such theories in combination with his or her observations. However, the attributor errs because his or her observations are distorted by perceptual processes and, sometimes, emotional processes. For Heider, the FAE results from Gestalt perceptual processes that draw an observer's attention to the other person rather than to the situation surrounding the other person; that is, the person is "figural" against the "ground" of the situation.

A key development in research on the *perceptual* interpretation of the FAE was Jones and Nisbett's (1972) argument that although to an observer of action the person is figural, to the actor the situation is figural and hence self-attributions for behavior are less dispositional. The perceptual account of this *actor-observer difference* was supported by experiments that presented actors with the visual perspective on their behavior of an observer (by use of videotape) and found that their self-attributions became more dispositional (Storms 1973). Nevertheless, evidence also emerged for nonperceptual interpretations of why first-person explanations differ. An actor draws on different information—information about one's mental state while acting and about one's behavior in the past (see Eisen 1979).

A shift toward emphasis on *cognitive* mechanisms came in the research programs constructed on the foundation of Kelley's (1967 and 1972) models. Kelley's (1967) *covariation* model focused on cases where an uncertain or curious observer generates an attribution "bottom up" from the data provided by multiple instances of a behavior. Attributors induce the general locus of causation for a behavior by assessing how the behavior covaries with the actor, the situation, and the temporal occasion. For example, to interpret why Sue's date John is dancing by himself, one would consider whether a consensus of people at the party are dancing alone, whether dancing alone is something that Sue's dates have often done, and whether it is something that John has often done. In tests of the model, participants generally respond to summaries of covariation data roughly as predicted, with the exception that consensus information is under-weighted (McArthur 1972). Biases in INDUCTION have been interpreted in terms of "extra" information implicitly communicated to participants (see GRICE; Hilton and Slugoski 1985; McGill 1989) or in terms of "missing" information that participants lack (Cheng and Novick 1992). Of late, research on causal induction has merged with the field of CAUSAL REASONING.

To model more typical cases of attribution where people lack time and energy to work "bottom up," Kelley (1972) proposed that people interpret a single instance of behavior "top down" from a theory. For example, an attributor who applies the Multiple Sufficient Causes (MSC) schema follows the *discounting principle* that if one of two alternative causes is present then the other is less likely. Tests of this model, however, found that a dispositional attribution is not fully discounted by information about the presence of a sufficient situational cause for the behavior (Snyder and Jones 1974). This manifestation of the FAE was interpreted primarily in terms of human cognitive limitations that require the use of JUDGMENT HEURISTICS, such as anchoring, when making discounting inferences about a dispositional cause (Jones 1979).

To integrate insights about different mechanisms contributing to the FAE, researchers have proposed sequential *stage models*: An initial perception-like process traces an actor's behavior to a corresponding disposition, then a second inference-like process adjusts the initial attribution to account for any situational factors. Whereas the first stage is posited to be automatic, much like a perceptual module, the second stage requires effort and attention and hence takes place only if these are available—that is, if the attributor is not "cognitively busy." In support of a dual process model, experiments find that increasing participants' "busyness" results in more dispositional attributions (Gilbert, Pelham, and Krull 1988). However, it remains unclear whether the initial dispositional process is a perceptual module or merely a well-learned schematic inference.

Reacting against analyses of attribution as a decontextualized cognitive task, another recent theme is that attributions are markedly influenced by *goals* related to particular *social contexts*. The goal of assigning blame seems to accentuate the FAE (Shaver 1985). The goal of maintaining self-esteem leads people to dispositional attributions for successes but not failures (Snyder, Stephan, and Rosenfield 1976). The goal of making a good impression on an audience mitigates the FAE (Tetlock 1985). Studies of attributions in context have brought renewed attention to the important consequences of attribution, for example, the relation of dispositional attributions to sanctioning decisions (Carroll and Payne 1977). Applied research has found that self-serving styles of attribution not only protect an individual against clinical depression (Abrahamson, Seligman, and Teasdale 1978) but also contribute to achievement motivation and performance (Weiner 1985).

A current direction of attribution research involves closer attention to the *knowledge structures* that shape causal explanations. Explanations are constructed in order to cohere with the content knowledge triggered by observation of behavior, such as stereotypes and scripts (Read and Miller 1993). They are also constrained by frames for what constitutes an EXPLANATION in a given setting (Pennington and Hastie 1991). The guiding role of knowledge structures elucidates why the pattern of attribution errors differs across individuals, institutions, and cultures. Recent evidence points to individual differences (Dweck, Hong, and Chiu 1993) and cultural differences (Morris and Peng 1994) in the underlying causal schemas or lay theories that guide attribution. For example, findings that the FAE is stronger in Western, individualistic societies than in collectivist societies such as China seems to reflect different lay theories about the autonomy of individuals relative to social groups. Closer measurement of causal schemas and theories reveals that attribution errors previously interpreted in terms of processing limitations, such as the incomplete discounting of dispositions, reflect participants' knowledge structures rather than their inferential processes (Morris and Larrick 1995).

In sum, attribution theory has moved beyond the identification of errors like the FAE to an understanding of how they are produced by perceptual and cognitive limitations, by contextual goals, and by knowledge structures. As the story of research on the FAE phenomenon illustrates, attribution theory uncovers reciprocal relations between individual cognition, on one hand, and social and cultural contexts, on the other hand, and hence bridges the cognitive and social sciences.

See also ECONOMICS AND COGNITIVE SCIENCE; SCHEMATA; SOCIAL COGNITION

—*Michael W. Morris, Daniel Ames, and Eric Knowles*

References

Abramson, L. Y., M. E. P. Seligman, and J. Teasdale. (1978). Learned helplessness in humans: critique and reformulation. *Journal of Abnormal Psychology* 87: 49–74.

Carroll, J. S., and J. W. Payne. (1977). Crime seriousness, recidivism risk and causal attribution in judgments of prison terms by students and experts. *Journal of Applied Psychology* 62: 595–602.

Cheng, P. W., and L. R. Novick. (1992). Covariation in natural causal induction. *Psychological Review* 99: 365–382.

Dweck, C. S., Y. Hong, and C. Chiu. (1993). Implicit theories: individual differences in the likelihood and meaning of dispositional inference. *Personality and Social Psychology Bulletin* 19: 644–656.

Eisen, S. V. (1979). Actor-observer differences in information inference and causal attribution. *Journal of Personality and Social Psychology* 37: 261–272.

Gilbert, D. T., B. W. Pelham, and D. S. Krull. (1988). On cognitive busyness: when person perceivers meet persons perceived. *Journal of Personality and Social Psychology* 54: 733–740.

Heider, F. (1958). *The Psychology of Interpersonal Relations.* New York: Wiley.

Hilton, D. J., and B. R. Slugoski. (1985). Knowledge-based causal attribution: the abnormal conditions focus model. *Psychological Review* 93: 75–88.

Ichheiser, G. (1949). Misunderstandings in human relations. *American Journal of Sociology* 55: 150–170.

Jones, E. E. (1979). The rocky road from acts to dispositions. *American Psychologist* 34: 107–117.

Jones, E. E., and R. E. Nisbett. (1972). The actor and the observer: divergent perceptions of the causes of behavior. In E. E. Jones et al., Eds., *Attribution: Perceiving the Causes of Behavior.* Morristown, NJ: General Learning Press.

Kelley, H. H. (1967). Attribution theory in social psychology. In D. Levine, Ed., *Nebraska Symposium on Motivation.* Lincoln: University of Nebraska Press.

Kelley, H. H. (1972). Causal schemata and the attribution process. In E.E. Jones et al., Eds., *Attribution: Perceiving the Causes of Behavior.* Morristown, NJ: General Learning Press.

McArthur, L. Z. (1972). The how and what of why: some determinants and consequences of causal attributions. *Journal of Personality and Social Psychology* 22: 171–193.

Morris, M. W., and R. Larrick. (1995). When one cause casts doubt on another: a normative model of discounting in causal attribution. *Psychological Review* 102(2): 331–335.

Morris, M. W., and K. Peng. (1994). Culture and cause: American and Chinese attributions for social and physical events. *Journal of Personality and Social Psychology* 67: 949–971.

Pennington, N., and R. Hastie. (1991). A cognitive theory of juror decision making: the story model. *Cardozo Law Review* 13: 519–557.

Read, S. J., and L. C. Miller. (1993). Rapist or "regular guy": explanatory coherence in the construction of mental models of others. *Personality and Social Psychology Bulletin* 19: 526–540.

Ross, L. (1977). The intuitive psychologist and his shortcomings: distortions in the attribution process. In L. Berkowitz, Ed., *Advances in Experimental Social Psychology* vol. 10, New York: Academic Press, pp. 174–221.

Shaver, K. G. (1985). *The Attribution of Blame.* New York: Springer.

Snyder, M. L., and E. E. Jones. (1974). Attitude attribution when behavior is constrained. *Journal of Experimental Social Psychology* 10: 585–600.

Snyder, M. L., W. G. Stephan, and D. Rosenfield. (1976). Egotism and attribution. *Journal of Personality and Social Psychology* 33: 435–441.

Storms, M. D. (1973). Videotape and the attribution process: reversing actors' and observers' points of view. *Journal of Personality and Social Psychology* 27: 165–175.

Tetlock, P. E. (1985). Accountability: A social check on the fundamental attribution error. *Social Psychology Quarterly* 48: 227–236.

Weiner, B. (1985). An attributional theory of achievement motivation and emotion. *Psychological Review* 92: 548–573.

Further Readings

Gilbert, D. T., and P. S. Malone. (1995). The correspondence bias. *Psychological Bulletin* 117: 21–38.

Jones, E. E., D. E. Kannouse, H. H. Kelley, R. E. Nisbett, S. Valins, and B. Weiner, Eds. (1972). *Attribution: Perceiving the Causes of Behavior*. Morristown, NJ: General Learning Press.

Kunda, Z. (1987). Motivated inference: self-serving generation and evaluation of causal theories. *Journal of Personality and Social Psychology* 53: 636–647.

McArthur, L. Z., and R. M. Baron. (1983). Toward an ecological theory of social perception. *Psychological Review* 90: 215–238.

McGill, A. L. (1989). Context effects in judgments of causation. *Journal of Personality and Social Psychology* 57: 189–200.

Michotte, A. E. (1946). *La Perception de la Causalité*. Paris: J. Vrin. Published in English (1963) as *The Perception of Causality*. New York: Basic Books.

Nisbett, R. E., and L. Ross. (1980). *Human Inference: Strategies and Shortcomings of Social Judgment*. Englewood Cliffs, NJ: Prentice-Hall.

Read, S. J. (1987). Constructing causal scenarios: a knowledge structure approach to causal reasoning. *Journal of Personality and Social Psychology* 52: 288–302.

Regan, D. T., and J. Totten. (1975). Empathy and attribution: turning observers into actors. *Journal of Personality and Social Psychology* 32: 850–856.

Schank, R. C., and R. P. Abelson. (1977). *Scripts, Plans, Goals and Understanding*. Hillsdale, NJ: Erlbaum.

Winter, L., and J. S. Uleman. (1984). When are social judgments made? Evidence for the spontaneousness of trait inferences. *Journal of Personality and Social Psychology* 47: 237–252.

Audition

Audition refers to the perceptual experience associated with stimulation of the sense of hearing. For humans, the sense of hearing is stimulated by acoustical energy—sound waves—that enter the outer ear (pinna and external auditory meatus) and set into vibration the eardrum and the attached bones (ossicles) of the middle ear, which transfer the mechanical energy to the inner ear, the cochlea. The auditory system can also be stimulated by bone conduction (Tonndorf 1972) when the sound source causes the bones of the skull to vibrate (e.g., one's own voice may be heard by bone conduction). Mechanical energy is transduced into neural impulses within the cochlea through the stimulation of the sensory hair cells which synapse on the eighth cranial, or auditory, nerve. In addition to the ascending, or afferent, auditory pathway from the cochlea to the cortex, there is a descending, efferent, pathway from the brain to the cochlea, although the functional significance of the efferent pathway is not well understood at present (Brugge 1992). Immediately following stimulation, the auditory system may become less sensitive due to adapta-

tion or fatigue (Ward 1973), and prolonged high-intensity stimulation can damage the sensory process (noise-induced hearing loss; for a series of review articles, see *J. Acoust. Soc. Am.* 1991, vol. 90: 124–227).

The auditory system is organized tonotopically such that the frequency of a stimulating sound is mapped onto a location along the basilar membrane within the cochlea, providing a *place* code (cf. AUDITORY PHYSIOLOGY). For example, low-frequency tones lead to maximal displacement of the apical portion of the basilar membrane and high-frequency tones lead to maximal displacement of the basal portion of the basilar membrane. In addition, cells exhibit frequency selectivity throughout the auditory pathway (e.g., Pickles 1988). This tonotopic organization provides a basis for spectral analysis of sounds. Temporal aspects of the stimulus (waveform fine structure or envelope) are preserved in the pattern of activity of auditory nerve fibers (Kiang et al., 1965), providing a basis for the coding of synchronized activity both across frequency and across the two ears. The dual presence of place and timing cues is pervasive in models of auditory perception.

The percept associated with a particular sound might be described in a variety of ways, but descriptions in terms of pitch, loudness, timbre, and perceived spatial location are probably the most common (Blauert 1983; Yost 1994; Moore 1997). Pitch is most closely associated with sound frequency, or the fundamental frequency for complex periodic sounds; loudness is most closely associated with sound intensity; and timbre is most closely associated with the distribution of acoustic energy across frequency (i.e., the shape of the power spectrum). The perceived location of a sound in space (direction and distance) is based primarily on the comparison of the sound arriving at the two ears (binaural hearing) and the acoustical filtering associated with the presence of the head and pinnae. Each of these perceptual classifications also depends on other factors, particularly when complex, time-varying sounds are being considered.

The frequency range of human hearing extends from a few cycles per second (Hertz, abbreviated Hz) to about 20,000 Hz, although the upper limit of hearing decreases markedly with age (e.g., Weiss 1963; Stelmachowitcz et al. 1989). The intensity range of human hearing extends over many orders of magnitude depending on frequency; at 2–4 kHz, the range may be greater than twelve orders of magnitude (120 decibels, abbreviated dB).

Despite the wide dynamic range of human hearing, the auditory system is remarkably acute: the just-discriminable difference (JND) in frequency is as small as 0.2 percent (e.g., Wier, Jesteadt, and Green 1977) and in intensity is approximately one dB (e.g., Jesteadt, Wier, and Green 1977). Sensitivity to differences in sounds arriving at the two ears is perhaps even more remarkable: time delays as small as a few microseconds may be discerned (Klumpp and Eady 1956). Although behavioral estimates of the JND for intensity, frequency, etc., provide invaluable information regarding the basic properties of the human auditory system, it is important to keep in mind that estimates of JNDs depend on both sensory and nonsensory factors such as memory and attention (e.g., Harris 1952; Durlach and Braida 1969; Berliner and Durlach 1972; Howard et al. 1984).

The interference one sound causes in the reception of another sound is called masking. Masking has a peripheral component resulting from interfering/overlapping patterns of excitation in the auditory nerve (e.g., Greenwood 1961), and a central component due to uncertainty, sometimes called "informational masking" (Watson 1987; see also AUDITORY ATTENTION). In a classic experiment, Fletcher (1940) studied the masking of a tone by noise in order to evaluate the frequency selectivity of the human auditory system. To account for the obtained data, Fletcher proposed a "critical band" that likened the ear to a bandpass filter (or, to encompass the entire frequency range, a set of contiguous, overlapping bandpass filters). This proposed "auditory filter" is a theoretical construct that reflects frequency selectivity present in the auditory system, and, in one form or another, auditory filters comprise a first stage in models of the spectrotemporal (across frequency and time) analysis performed by the auditory system (e.g., Patterson and Moore 1986).

The separation of sound into multiple frequency channels is not sufficient to provide a solution to the problem of sound segregation. Sound waves from different sources simply add, meaning that the frequencies shared by two or more sounds are processed *en masse* at the periphery. In order to form distinct images, the energy at a single frequency must be appropriately parsed. The computations used to achieve sound segregation depend on the coherence/incoherence of sound onsets, the shared/unshared spatial location of the sound sources, differences in the harmonic structure of the sounds and other cues in the physical stimulus. Yost has proposed that the spectrotemporal and spatial-location analysis performed by the auditory system serves the purpose of sound source determination (Yost 1991) and allows the subsequent organization of sound images into an internal map of the acoustic environment (Bregman 1990).

Approximately 28 million people in the United States suffer from hearing loss, and a recent census indicated that deafness and other hearing impairments ranked 6th among chronic conditions reported (National Center for Health Statistics 1993). Among those aged sixty-five and older, deafness and other hearing impairments ranked third among chronic conditions. The assessment of function and non-medical remediation of hearing loss is typically performed by an audiologist, whereas the diagnosis and treatment of ear disease is performed by an otologist.

See also AUDITORY PLASTICITY; PHONOLOGY, ACQUISITION OF PSYCHOPHYSICS; SIGN LANGUAGE AND THE BRAIN; SPEECH PERCEPTION

—*Virginia M. Richards and Gerald D. Kidd, Jr.*

References

Berliner, J. E., and N. I. Durlach. (1972). Intensity perception IV. Resolution in roving-level discrimination. *J. Acoust. Soc. Am.* 53: 1270–1287.

Blauert, J. (1983). *Spatial Hearing.* Cambridge, MA: MIT Press.

Bregman, A. S. (1990). *Auditory Scene Analysis.* Cambridge, MA: MIT Press.

Brugge, J. F. (1992). An overview of central auditory processing. In A. N. Popper and R. R. Fay, Eds., *The Mammalian Auditory Pathway: Neurophysiology.* New York: Springer.

Durlach, N. I., and L. D. Braida. (1969). Intensity perception I, Preliminary theory of intensity resolution. *J. Acoust. Soc. Am.* 46: 372–383.

Fletcher, H. (1940). Auditory patterns. *Rev. Mod. Phys.* 12: 47–65.

Greenwood, D. D. (1961). Auditory masking and the critical band. *J. Acoust. Soc. Am.* 33: 484–502.

Harris, J. D. (1952). The decline of pitch discrimination with time. *J. Exp. Psych.* 43: 96–99.

Howard, J. H., A. J. O'Toole, R. Parasuraman, and K. B. Bennett. (1984). Pattern-directed attention in uncertain-frequency detection. *Percept. Psychophys.* 35: 256–264.

Jesteadt, W., C. C. Wier, and D. M. Green (1977). Intensity discrimination as a function of frequency and sensation level. *J. Acoust. Soc. Am.* 61: 169–177.

Kiang, N. Y-S., T. Watanabe, E. C. Thomas, and L. F. Clark. (1965). *Discharge Patterns of Single Fibers in the Cat's Auditory Nerve.* Cambridge, MA: MIT Press.

Klumpp, R., and H. Eady. (1956). Some measurements of interaural time differences thresholds. *J. Acoust. Soc. Am.* 28: 859–864.

Moore, B. C. J. (1997). *An Introduction to the Psychology of Hearing.* Fourth edition. London: Academic Press.

National Center for Health Statistics (1993). *Vital statistics: prevalence of selected chronic conditions: United States 1986–1988, Series 10.* Data from National Health survey #182, USHHS, PHS.

Patterson, R. A., and B. C. J. Moore. (1986). Auditory filters and excitation patterns as representations of frequency resolution. In B. C. J. Moore, Ed., *Frequency Selectivity in Hearing.* New York: Academic Press.

Pickles, J. O. (1988). *An Introduction to the Physiology of Hearing.* Second edition. London: Academic Press.

Stelmachowitcz, P. G., K. A. Beauchaine, A. Kalberer, and W. Jesteadt. (1989). Normative thresholds in the 8- to 20-kHz range as a function of age. *J. Acoust. Soc. Am.* 86: 1384–1391.

Tonndorf, J. (1972). Bone conduction. In J. V. Tobias, Ed., *Foundations of Modern Auditory Theory II.* New York: Academic Press.

Ward, W. D. (1973). Adaptation and Fatigue. In J. Jerger, Ed., *Modern Developments in Audiology.* New York: Academic Press.

Watson, C. S. (1987). Uncertainty, informational masking, and the capacity of immediate auditory memory. In W. A. Yost and C. S. Watson, Eds., *Auditory Processing of Complex Sounds.* Hillsdale, NJ: Erlbaum.

Weiss, A. D. (1963). Auditory perception in relation to age. In J. E. Birren, R. N. Butler, S. W. Greenhouse, L. Sokoloff, and M. Tarrow, Eds., *Human Aging: a Biological and Behavioral Study.* Bethesda: NIMH.

Wier, C. C., W. Jesteadt, and D. M. Green (1977). Frequency discrimination as a function of frequency and sensation level. *J. Acoust. Soc. Am.* 61: 178–184.

Yost, W. A. (1991). Auditory image perception and analysis. *Hear. Res.* 56: 8–18.

Yost, W. A. (1994). *Fundamentals of Hearing: An Introduction.* San Diego: Academic Press.

Further Readings

Gilkey, R. A., and T. R. Anderson. (1997). *Binaural and Spatial Hearing in Real and Virtual Environments.* Hillsdale, NJ: Erlbaum.

Green, D. M. (1988). *Profile Analysis: Auditory Intensity Discrimination.* Oxford: Oxford Science Publications.

Hamernik, R. P., D. Henderson, and R. Salvi. (1982). *New Perspectives on Noise-Induced Hearing Loss.* New York: Raven.

Hartmann, W. M. (1997). *Signals, Sound and Sensation*. Woodbury, NY: AIP Press.

NIH (1995). *NIH Consensus Development Conferences on Cochlear Implants in Adults and Children*. Bethesda: NIH.

Auditory Attention

Selective ATTENTION may be defined as a process by which the perception of certain stimuli in the environment is enhanced relative to other concurrent stimuli of lesser immediate priority. A classic auditory example of this phenomenon is the so-called cocktail party effect, wherein a person can selectively listen to one particular speaker while tuning out several other simultaneous conversations.

For many years, psychological theories of selective attention were traditionally divided between those advocating early levels of stimulus selection and those advocating late selection. Early selection theories held that there was an early filtering mechanism by which "channels" of irrelevant input could be attenuated or even rejected from further processing based on some simple physical attribute (BROADBENT 1970; Treisman 1969). In contrast, late selection theories held that all stimuli are processed to the same considerable detail, which generally meant through completion of perceptual analysis, before any selection due to attention took place (Deutsch and Deutsch 1963).

Various neurophysiological studies have attempted to shed light on both the validity of these theories and the neural mechanisms that underlie auditory attention. One possible neural mechanism for early stimulus selection would be the attenuation or gating of irrelevant input at the early levels of the sensory pathways by means of descending modulatory pathways (Hernandez-Peón, Scherrer, and Jouvet, 1956). For example, there is a descending pathway in the auditory system that parallels the ascending one all the way out to the cochlea (Brodal 1981), and direct electrical stimulation of this descending pathway at various levels, including auditory cortex, can inhibit the responses of the afferent auditory nerves to acoustic input. Other animal studies have indicated that stimulation of pathways from the frontal cortex and the mesencephalic reticular formation can modulate sensory transmission through the THALAMUS, thus providing another mechanism by which higher brain centers might modulate lower level processing during selective attention (Skinner and Yingling 1977). In addition, sensory processing activity in primary auditory CEREBRAL CORTEX or early auditory association cortices could conceivably be directly modulated by "descending" pathways from still higher cortical levels.

It has proven difficult, however, to demonstrate that any of these possible mechanisms for sensory modulation are actually used during auditory attention. Early animal studies purporting to show attenuation of irrelevant auditory input at the sensory periphery (Hernandez-Peón, Scherrer, and Jouvet 1956) were roundly criticized on methodological grounds (Worden 1966). Nevertheless, there have been animal studies providing evidence of some very early (i.e., brainstem-level) modulation of auditory processing as a function of attentional state or arousal (e.g., Oatman and Anderson 1977). In addition, Benson and Heinz (1978), studying single cells in monkey primary auditory cortex during a selective attention task (dichotic listening), reported relative enhancement of the responses to attended stimuli. Attending to sounds to perform sound localization vs. simple detection also has been shown to result in enhanced firing of units in auditory cortex (Benson, Heinz, and Goldstein 1981).

Auditory attention has been investigated extensively in humans using event-related potentials (ERPs) and event-related magnetic fields (ERFs). These recordings can noninvasively track with high temporal resolution the brain activity associated with different types of stimulus events. By analyzing changes in the ERPs or ERFs as a function of the direction of attention, one can make inferences about the timing, level of processing, and anatomical location of stimulus selection processes in the brain.

In an early seminal ERP study, Hillyard et al. (1973) implemented an experimental analog of the cocktail party effect and demonstrated differential processing of attended and unattended auditory stimuli at the level of the "N1" wave at ~100 msec poststimulus. More recent ERP studies furthering this approach have reported that focused auditory selective attention can affect stimulus processing as early as 20 msec poststimulus (the "P20-50" effect; Woldorff et al. 1987). Additional studies using ERPs (Woldorff and Hillyard 1991) and using ERFs and source-analysis modeling (Woldorff et al. 1993) indicated these electrophysiological attentional effects occurred in and around primary auditory cortex, had waveshapes that precisely took the form of an amplitude modulation of the early sensory-evoked components, and were colocalized with the sources of these sensory-evoked components. These results were interpreted as providing strong evidence for the existence of an attentionally modulated, sensory gain control of the auditory input channels at or before the initial stages of cortical processing, thereby providing strong support for early selection attentional theories that posit that stimulus input can be selected at levels considerably prior to the completion of perceptual analysis. Moreover, the very early onset latency of these attentional effects (20 ms) strongly suggests that this selection is probably accomplished by means of a top-down, preset biasing of the stimulus input channels.

On the other hand, reliable effects of attention on the earliest portion of the human auditory ERP reflecting auditory nerve and brainstem-level processing have generally not been found (Picton and Hillyard 1974), thus providing no evidence for peripheral filtering via the descending auditory pathway that terminates at the cochlea. Nevertheless, recent research measuring a different type of physiological response—otoacoustic cochlear emissions—has provided some evidence for such early filtering (Giard et al. 1991).

Additional evidence that attention can affect early auditory processing derives from studies of another ERP/ERF wave known as the mismatch negativity/mismatch field (MMN/MMF), which is elicited by deviant auditory stimuli in a series of identical stimuli. Because the MMN/MMF can be elicited in the absence of attention and by deviations in any of a number of auditory features, this wave was proposed to reflect a strong automaticity of the processing of auditory stimulus features (reviewed in Naatanen 1990 and 1992). Both the MMN (Woldorff et al. 1991) and the MMF (Woldorff et al. 1998), however, can also be modulated by attention, being greatly reduced when attention is strongly focused elsewhere, thus providing converging evidence that attention can influence early auditory sensory analysis. On the other hand, the elicitation of at least some MMN/MMF for many different feature deviations in a strongly ignored auditory channel has been interpreted as evidence that considerable feature analysis is still performed even for unattended auditory stimuli (Alho 1992). An intermediate view that may accommodate these findings is that various aspects of early auditory sensory processing and feature analysis may be "partially" or "weakly" automatic, occurring even in the absence of attention but still subject to top-down attentional modulation (Woldorff et al. 1991; Hackley 1993). Under this view, the very earliest stimulus processing (i.e., peripheral and brainstem levels) tends to be strongly automatic, but at the initial cortical levels there is a transition from strong to weak automaticity, wherein some amount of analysis is generally obligatory but is nevertheless modifiable by attention (reviewed in Hackley 1993).

There are also various slower-frequency, longer-latency ERP auditory attention effects that are not modulations of early sensory activity, but rather appear to reflect "endogenous," additional activations from both auditory and nonauditory association cortex (e.g., "processing negativity," target-related "N2b," "P300"). This type of activity occurs only or mainly for attended-channel stimuli or only for target stimuli within an attended channel and might reflect later selection, classification, or decision processes that also occur during auditory attention (reviewed in Alho 1992; Näätänen 1992). Attention to less discriminable features of auditory stimuli (Hansen and Hillyard 1983) or to a conjunction of auditory features (Woods et al. 1991) also produces longer-latency differential activation that may reflect later selection processes. In addition, there is a build-up of endogenous brain electrical activity (a "DC shift") as subjects begin to attend to a short stream of auditory stimuli (Hansen and Hillyard 1988), which could reflect some sort of initiation of the controlling executive function.

In contrast to electrophysiological studies, relatively few hemodynamically-based functional neuroimaging studies have been directed at studying auditory attention in humans. In a recent study using POSITRON EMISSION TOMOGRAPHY (PET), O'Leary et al. (1996) reported enhanced activity in the auditory cortex contralateral to the direction of attention during a dichotic listening task. PET studies have also shown that attention to different aspects of speech sounds (e.g., phonetics vs. pitch) can affect the relative activation of the two hemispheres (Zatorre, Evans, and Meyer 1992). In addition, functional MAGNETIC RESONANCE IMAGING has indicated that intermodal attention can modulate auditory cortical processing (Woodruff et al. 1996).

Most neurophysiological studies of auditory attention in humans have focused on the *effects* of attention on the processing of sounds in auditory cortical areas. Less work has been directed toward elucidating the neural structures and mechanisms that *control* auditory attention. Based on vari-ous hemodynamic imaging studies, the anterior cingulate is likely to be involved, as it is activated during a number of cognitive and/or executive functions (Posner et al. 1988). In addition, human lesion studies suggest the prefrontal cortex is important for modulating the activity in the ipsilateral auditory cortex during auditory attention (Knight et al. 1981). It may be that some of the slower-frequency, endogenous ERP auditory attention effects reflect the activation of these areas as they serve to modulate or otherwise control auditory processing. Whether these mechanisms actually employ thalamic gating, some other modulatory mechanism, or a combination, is not yet known.

See also ATTENTION IN THE ANIMAL BRAIN; ATTENTION IN THE HUMAN BRAIN; AUDITORY PHYSIOLOGY; AUDITORY PLASTICITY; ELECTROPHYSIOLOGY, ELECTRIC AND MAGNETIC EVOKED FIELDS; TOP-DOWN PROCESSING IN VISION

—Marty G. Woldorff

References

Alho, K. (1992). Selective attention in auditory processing as reflected in event-related brain potentials. *Psychophysiology* 29: 247–263.

Benson, D. A., and R. D. Heinz. (1978). Single-unit activity in the auditory cortex of monkeys selectively attending left vs. right ear stimuli. *Brain Research* 159: 307–320.

Benson, D. A., R. D. Heinz, and M. H. Goldstein, Jr. (1981). Single-unit activity in the auditory cortex actively localizing sound sources: spatial tuning and behavioral dependency. *Brain Research* 219: 249–267.

Broadbent, D. E. (1970). Stimulus set and response set: Two kinds of selective attention. In D. I. Mostofsky, Ed., *Attention: Contemporary Theory and Analysis*. New York: Appleton-Century-Crofts, pp. 51–60.

Brodal, A. (1981). *Neurological Anatomy*. New York: Oxford University Press.

Deutsch, J. A., and D. Deutsch. (1963). Attention: some theoretical considerations. *Psychological Review* 70: 80–90.

Giard, M. H., L. Collet, P. Bouchet, and J. Pernier. (1994). Auditory selective attention in the human cochlea. *Brain Research* 633: 353–356.

Hackley, S. A. (1993). An evaluation of the automaticity of sensory processing using event-related potentials and brain-stem reflexes. *Psychophysiology* 30: 415–428.

Hansen, J. C., and S. A. Hillyard. (1983). Selective attention to multidimensional auditory stimuli. *J. of Exp. Psychology: Human Perc. and Perf* 9: 1–18.

Hansen, J. C., and S. A. Hillyard. (1988). Temporal dynamics of human auditory selective attention. *Psychophysiology* 25: 316–329.

Hernandez-Peón, R., H. Scherrer, and M. Jouvet. (1956). Modification of electrical activity in the cochlear nucleus during attention in unanesthetized cats. *Science* 123: 331–332.

Hillyard, S. A., R. F. Hink, V. L. Schwent, and T. W. Picton. (1973). Electrical signs of selective attention in the human brain. *Science* 182: 177–179.

Knight, R. T., S. A. Hillyard, D. L. Woods, and H. J. Neville. (1981). The effects of frontal cortex lesions on event-related potentials during auditory selective attention. *Electroenceph. Clin. Neurophysiol.* 52: 571–582.

Naatanen, R. (1990). The role of attention in auditory information processing as revealed by event-related potentials and other brain measures of cognitive function. *Behavior and Brain Science* 13: 201–288.

Naatanen, R. (1992). *Attention and Brain Function.* Hillsdale, NJ: Erlbaum.

Oatman, L. C., and B. W. Anderson. (1977). Effects of visual attention on tone-burst evoked auditory potentials. *Experimental Neurology* 57: 200–211.

O'Leary, D. S., N. C. Andreasen, R. R. Hurtig, R. D. Hichwa, G. L. Watkins, L. L. B. Ponto, M. Rogers, and P. T. Kirchner. (1996). A positron emission tomography study of binaurally- and dichotically-presented stimuli: Effects of level of language and directed attention. *Brain and Language* 53: 20–39.

Picton, T. W., and S. A. Hillyard. (1974). Human auditory evoked potentials: II. Effects of attention. *Electroenceph. Clin. Neurophysiol* 36: 191–199.

Posner, M. I., S. E. Petersen, P. T. Fox, and M. E. Raichle. (1988). Localization of cognitive operations in the human brain. *Science* 240: 1627–1631.

Skinner, J. E., and C. D. Yingling. (1977). Central gating mechanisms that regulate event-related potentials and behavior. In J. E. Desmedt, Ed., *Attention, Voluntary Contraction and Event-Related Cerebral Potentials. Progress in Clinical Neurophysiology,* vol. 1. New York: S. Karger, pp. 30–69.

Treisman, A. (1969). Stategies and models of selective attention. *Psych. Review* 76: 282–299.

Woldorff, M. G., C. C. Gallen, S. A. Hampson, S. A. Hillyard, C. Pantev, D. Sobel, and F. E. Bloom. (1993). Modulation of early sensory processing in human auditory cortex during auditory selective attention. *Proc. Natl. Acad. Sci.* 90: 8722–8726.

Woldorff, M., S. A. Hackley, and S. A. Hillyard. (1991). The effects of channel-selective attention on the mismatch negativity wave elicited by deviant tones. *Psychophysiology* 28: 30–42.

Woldorff M., J. C. Hansen, and S. A. Hillyard. (1987). Evidence for effects of selective attention in the mid-latency range of the human auditory event-related potential. In R. Johnson, Jr., R. Parasuraman, and J. W. Rohrbaugh, Eds., *Current Trends in Event-Related Potential Research (EEGJ Suppl. 40).* Amsterdam: Elsevier, pp. 146–54.

Woldorff, M. G., and S. A. Hillyard. (1991). Modulation of early auditory processing during selective listening to rapidly presented tones. *Electroenceph. and Clin. Neurophysiology* 79: 170–191.

Woldorff, M. G., S. A. Hillyard, C. C. Gallen, S. A. Hampson, and F. E. Bloom. (1998). Magnetoencephalographic recordings demonstrate attentional modulation of mismatch-related neural activity in human auditory cortex. *Psychophysiology* 35: 283–292.

Woodruff, P. W., R. R. Benson, P. A. Bandetinni, K. K. Kwong, R. J. Howard, T. Talavage, J. Belliveua, and B. R. Rosen. (1996). Modulation of auditory and visual cortex by selective attention is modality-dependent. *Neuroreport* 7: 1909–1913.

Woods, D. L., K. Alho, and A. Algazi. (1991). Brain potential signs of feature processing during auditory selective attention. *Neuroreport* 2: 189–192.

Worden, F. G. (1966). Attention and auditory electrophysiology. In F. Stellar and J. M. Sprague, Eds., *Progress in Physiological Psychology.* New York: Academic Press, pp. 45–116.

Zatorre, R. J., A. C. Evans, and E. Meyer. (1992). Lateralization of phonetic and pitch discrimination in speech processing. *Science* 256: 846–849.

Further Readings

Alain, C., and D. L. Woods. (1994). Signal clustering modulates auditory cortical activity in humans. *Perception and Psychophysics* 56: 501–516.

Alho, K., K. Tottola, K. Reinikainen, M. Sams, and R. Naatanen. (1987). Brain mechanisms of selective listening reflected by event-related potentials. *Electroenceph. Clin. Neurophysiol.* 49: 458–470.

Arthur, D. L., P. S. Lewis, P. A. Medvick, and A. Flynn. (1991). A neuromagnetic study of selective auditory attention. *Electroenceph. Clin. Neurophysiol.* 78: 348–360.

Bregman, A. S. (1990). *Auditory Scene Analysis: The Perceptual Organization of Sound.* Cambridge, MA: MIT Press.

Hackley, S. A., M. Woldorff, and S. A. Hillyard. (1987). Combined use of microreflexes and event-related brain potentials as measures of auditory selective attention. *Psychophysiology* 24: 632–647.

Hackley, S. A., M. Woldorff, and S. A. Hillyard. (1990). Cross-modal selective attention effects on retinal, myogenic, brainstem and cerebral evoked potentials. *Psychophysiology* 27: 195–208.

Hansen, J. C., and S. A. Hillyard. (1980). Endogenous brain potentials associated with selective auditory attention. *Electroenceph. Clin. Neurophysiol.* 49: 277–290.

Johnston, W. A., and V. J. Dark. (1986). Selective attention. *Annual Rev. of Psychol.* 37: 43–75.

Okita, T. (1979). Event-related potentials and selective attention to auditory stimuli varying in pitch and localization. *Biological Psychology* 9: 271–284.

Rif, J., R. Hari, M. S. Hamalainen, and M. Sams. (1991). Auditory attention affects two different areas in the human supratemporal cortex. *Electroenceph. Clin. Neurophysiol* 79: 464–472.

Roland, P. E. (1982). Cortical regulation of selective attention in man: A regional blood flow study. *Journal of Neurophysiology* 48: 1059–1078.

Trejo, L. J., D. L. Ryan-Jones, and A. F. Kramer. (1995). Attentional modulation of the mismatch negativity elicited by frequency differences between binaurally presented tone bursts. *Psychophysiology* 32: 319–328.

Woods, D. L., K. Alho, and A. Algazi. (1994). Stages of auditory feature conjunction: an event-related brain potential study. *J. of Exper. Psychology: Human Perc. and Perf* 20: 81–94.

Auditory Physiology

The two main functions of hearing lie in auditory communication and in the localization of sounds. Auditory physiology tries to understand the perception, storage, and recognition of various types of sounds for both purposes in terms of neural activity patterns in the auditory pathways. The following article will try to analyze what auditory representations may have in common with other sensory systems, such as the visual system (see VISUAL ANATOMY AND PHYSIOLOGY), and what may be special about them.

Since the days of HELMHOLTZ (1885) the auditory system has been considered to function primarily as a frequency analyzer. According to von Békésy's work (1960), which was awarded the Nobel Prize in 1961, sound reaching the tympanic membrane generates a traveling wave along the basilar membrane in the cochlea of the inner ear. Depending on the frequency of the sound, the traveling wave achieves maximum amplitude in different locations. Thus frequency gets translated into a place code, with high frequencies represented near the base and low frequencies near the apex of the cochlea. Although the traveling wave has a rather broad peak, various synergistic resonance mechanisms assure effective stimulation of the cochlear hair cells at very precise locations.

Electrophysiological studies using tones of a single frequency (pure tones) led to a multitude of valuable data on the responses of neurons to such stimuli and to the recognition of tonotopic organization in the auditory pathways. Tonotopy, the neural representation of tones of best frequency in a topographic map, is analogous to retinotopy in the visual and somatotopy in the somatosensory system. The map is preserved by maintaining neighborhood relationships between best frequencies from the cochlea and auditory nerve through the initial stages of the central auditory system, such as cochlear nuclei, inferior colliculus and medial geniculate nucleus, to primary auditory cortex (A1; fig. 1). The standard assumption in pure-tone studies is that in order to understand stimulus coding at each subsequent level, one has to completely analyze the lower levels and then establish the transformations taking place from one level to the next (Kiang 1965). While this approach sounds logical, it assumes that the system is linear, which cannot always be taken for granted. Another problem that this theory has not solved is how information from different frequency channels gets integrated, that is, how complex sounds are analyzed by the auditory system.

The use of complex sound stimuli, therefore, is of the essence in the analysis of higher auditory pathways. This has been done successfully in a number of specialized systems, such as frogs, songbirds, owls, and bats. For all these species, a neuroethological approach has been adopted based on functional-behavioral data (Capranica 1972; see also ANIMAL COMMUNICATION, ECHOLOCATION, and ETHOLOGY). The same approach has been used only sparingly in higher mammals, including primates (Winter and Funkenstein 1973).

The neurophysiological basis in humans for processing complex sounds, such as speech (see SPEECH PERCEPTION), cannot be studied directly with invasive methods. Therefore, animal models (e.g., nonhuman primates) have to be used. The question then arises to what extent human speech sounds can be applied validly as stimuli for the study of neurons in a different species. From a biological-evolutionary vantage point, it is more meaningful to employ the types of complex sounds that are used for communication in those same species (see ANIMAL COMMUNICATION). In using conspecific vocalizations we can be confident that the central auditory system of the studied species must be capable of processing these calls. By contrast, human speech sounds may not be processed in the same way by that species.

When comparing human speech sounds with communication sound systems in other species it is plain to see that most systems have certain components in common, which are used as carriers of (semantic) information. Among these DISTINCTIVE FEATURES are segments of frequency changing over time (FM sweeps or "glides") and bandpass noise bursts with specific center frequencies and bandwidths (fig. 2). Such universal elements of auditory communication signals can be used as stimuli with a degree of complexity that is intermediate between the pure tones used in traditional auditory physiology and the whole signal whose representation one really wants to understand.

Psychophysical studies have indeed provided evidence for the existence of neural mechanisms tuned to the rate and direction of FM glides (Liberman et al. 1967, Kay 1982) as well as to specific bands of noise (Zwicker 1970). Neurophysiologically, neurons selective to the same parameters have been identified in the auditory cortex of various species. Most notably, a large proportion of FM selective neurons as well as neurons tuned to certain bandwidths have recently been found in the lateral belt areas of the superior temporal gyrus (STG) in rhesus monkeys (Rauschecker, Tian, and Hauser 1995). The posterior STG region has also been found to contain mechanisms selective for phoneme identification in humans, using functional neuroimaging techniques (see PHONOLOGY, NEURAL BASIS OF).

Many neurons in the lateral belt or STG region of rhesus monkeys (fig. 1B) also respond well and quite selectively to the monkey calls themselves. The question arises by what neural mechanisms such selectivity is generated. Studies in which monkey calls are dissected into their constituent elements (both in the spectral and temporal domains), and the elements are played to the neurons separately or in combination can provide an answer to this question (Rauschecker 1998). A sizable proportion of neurons in the STG (but not in A1) responds much better to the whole call than to any of the elements. These results are indicative of nonlinear summation in the frequency and time domain playing a crucial role in the generation of selectivity for specific types of calls. Coincidence detection in the time domain is perhaps the most important mechanism in shaping this selectivity. Temporal integration acts over several tens (or hundreds) of milliseconds, as most "syllables" in monkey calls (as well as in human speech) are of that duration.

There is some limited evidence for a columnar or patchy representation of specific types of monkey calls in the lateral belt areas. Rhesus calls can be subdivided into three coarse classes: tonal, harmonic, and noisy calls. Neurons responsive to one or another category are often found grouped together. It would be interesting to look for an orderly "phonetic map" of the constituent elements themselves, whereby interactions in two-dimensional arrays of time and frequency might be expected.

It is very likely that the lateral belt areas are not yet the ultimate stage in the processing of communication sounds. They may just present an intermediate stage, similar to V4 in the visual system, which also contains neurons selective for the size of visual stimuli. Such size selectivity is obviously of great importance for the encoding of visual patterns or objects, but the differentiation into neurons selective for even more specific patterns, such as faces, is not accomplished until an even higher processing stage, namely, the inferotemporal cortex (Desimone 1991; see also FACE RECOGNITION). In the auditory cortex, areas in the anterior or lateral parts of the STG or in the dorsal STS may be target areas for the exploration of call-specific neurons.

The second main task of hearing is to localize sound sources in space. Because the auditory periphery does not a priori possess a two-dimensional quality, as do the visual and somatosensory peripheries, auditory space has to be computed from attributes of sound that vary systematically with spatial location and are thus processed differentially by the

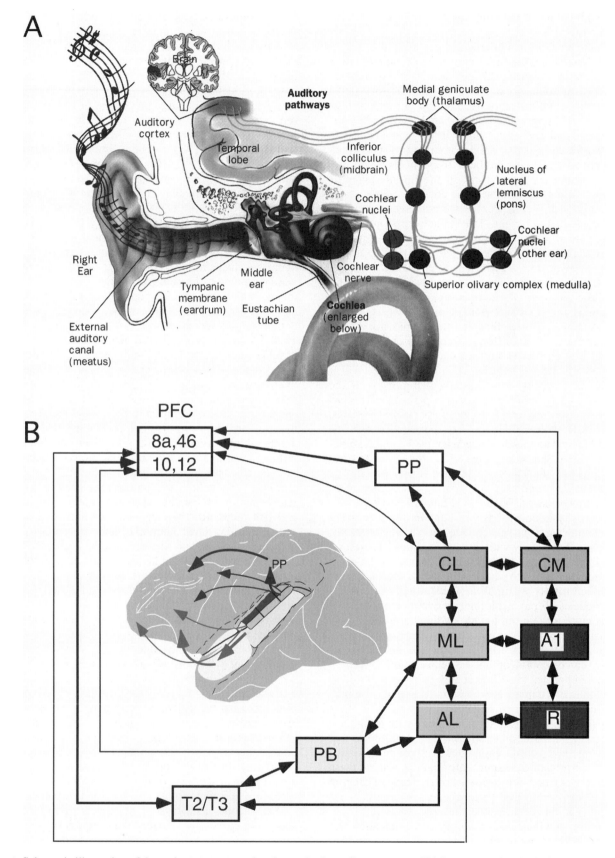

Figure 1. Schematic illustration of the major structures and pathways in the auditory system of higher mammals. (A) Pathways up to the level of primary auditory cortex (from *Journal of NIH Research* 9 [October 1997], with permission). (B) Cortical processing pathways in audition (from Rauschecker 1998b, *Current Opinion in Neurobiology* 8: 516–521, with permission).

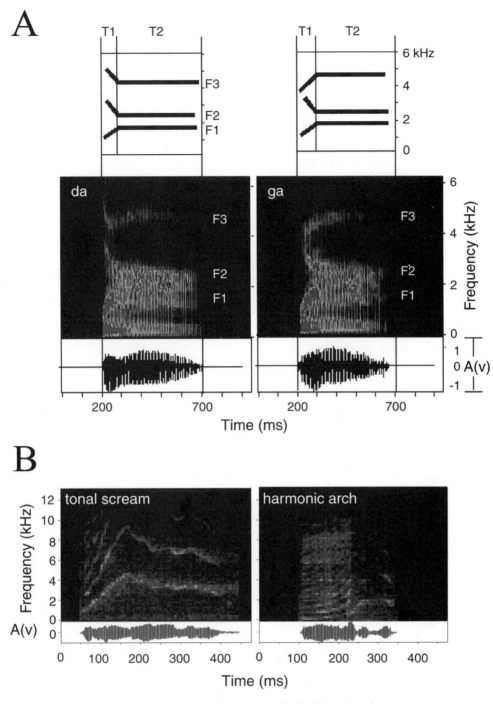

Figure 2. Sound spectrograms human speech samples (A) and monkey calls (B) illustrating the common occurrence of FM glides and band-pass noise bursts in vocalizations from both species.

central auditory system. This problem is logistically similar to the computation of 3-D information from two-dimensional sensory information in the visual system. Sound attributes most commonly assigned to spatial quality are differences between sound arriving at the two ears. Both the intensity and the time of arrival of sound originating from the same source differ when the sound source is located outside the median plane. Interaural time and intensity differences (ITD and IID, respectively) are registered and mapped already in areas of

the brainstem, such as the superior olivary complex (Irvine 1992). In addition, the spectral composition of sound arriving at the two ears varies with position due to the spectral filter characteristics of the external ears (pinnae) and the head. Even monaurally, specific spectral "fingerprints" can be assigned to spatial location, with attenuation of particular frequency bands ("spectral notches") varying systematically with azimuth or elevation (Blauert 1996). Neurons in the dorsal cochlear nuclei are tuned to such spectral notches and may thus be involved in extracting spatial information from complex sounds (Young et al. 1992).

The information computed by these lower brainstem structures is used by higher centers of the midbrain, such as the inferior and superior colliculi, to guide orienting movements toward sounds. For more "conscious" spatial perception in higher mammals, including humans, auditory cortex seems to be indispensable, as cortical lesions almost completely abolish the ability to judge the direction of sound in space. Neurons in the primary auditory cortex of cats show tuning to the spatial location of a sound presented in free field (Imig, Irons, and Samson 1990). Most recently, an area in the anterior ectosylvian sulcus (AES), which is part of the cat's parietal cortex, has been postulated to be crucially involved in sound localization (Korte and Rauschecker 1993, Middlebrooks et al. 1994). Functional neuroimaging studies in humans also demonstrate specific activation in the posterior parietal cortex of the right hemisphere by virtual auditory space stimuli (Rauschecker 1998a,b).

Both animal and human studies suggest, therefore, that information about auditory patterns or objects gets processed, among others, in the superior temporal gyrus (STG). By contrast, auditory spatial information seems to get processed in parietal regions of cortex (fig. 1B). This dual processing scheme is reminiscent of the visual pathways, where a ventral stream has been postulated for the processing of visual object information and a dorsal stream for the processing of visual space and motion (Mishkin, Ungerleider, and Macko 1983; see also VISUAL PROCESSING STREAMS).

See also AUDITION; AUDITORY PLASTICITY; AUDITORY ATTENTION; PHONOLOGY, NEURAL BASIS; SPEECH PERCEPTION; SINGLE-NEURON RECORDING

—*Josef P. Rauschecker*

References

Békésy, G. von. (1960). *Experiments in Hearing.* New York: McGraw-Hill.

Blauert, J. (1996). *Spatial Hearing.* 2d ed. Cambridge, MA: MIT Press.

Capranica, R. R. (1972). Why auditory neurophysiologists should be more interested in animal sound communication. *Physiologist* 15: 55–60.

Desimone, R. (1991). Face-selective cells in the temporal cortex of monkeys. *Journal of Cognitive Neuroscience* 3: 1–8.

Helmholtz, H. von. (1885). *On the Sensation of Tones.* Reprinted 1954. New York: Dover Publications.

Imig, T. J., W. A. Irons, and F. R. Samson. (1990). Single-unit selectivity to azimuthal direction and sound pressure level of noise bursts in cat high-frequency primary auditory cortex. *Journal of Neurophysiology* 63: 1448–1466.

Irvine, D. (1992). Auditory brainstem processing. In A. N. Popper and R. R. Fay, Eds., *The Mammalian Auditory Pathway: Neurophysiology.* New York: Springer, pp. 153–231.

Kay, R. H. (1982). Hearing of modulation in sounds. *Physiological Reviews* 62: 894–975.

Kiang, N. Y-S. (1965). Stimulus coding in the auditory nerve and cochlear nucleus. *Acta Otolaryngologica* 59: 186–200.

Korte, M., and J. P. Rauschecker. (1993). Auditory spatial tuning of cortical neurons is sharpened in cats with early blindness. *Journal of Neurophysiology* 70: 1717–1721.

Liberman, A. M., F. S. Cooper, D. P. Shankweiler, and M. Studdert-Kennedy. (1967). Perception of the speech code. *Psychological Review* 74: 431–461.

Middlebrooks, J. C., A. E. Clock, L. Xu, and D. M. Green. (1994). A panoramic code for sound location by cortical neurons. *Science* 264: 842–844.

Mishkin, M., L. G. Ungerleider, and K. A. Macko. (1983). Object vision and spatial vision: two cortical pathways. *Trends in Neurosciences* 6: 414–417.

Rauschecker, J. P. (1998a). Parallel processing in the auditory cortex of primates. *Audiology and Neurootology* 3: 86–103.

Rauschecker, J. P. (1998b). Cortical processing of complex sounds. *Current Opinion in Neurobiology* 8: 516–521.

Rauschecker, J. P., B. Tian, and M. Hauser. (1995). Processing of complex sounds in the macaque nonprimary auditory cortex. *Science* 268: 111–114.

Winter, P., and H. H. Funkenstein. (1973). The effects of species-specific vocalization on the discharge of auditory cortical cells in the awake squirrel monkey (Saimiri sciureus). *Experimental Brain Research* 18: 489–504.

Young, E. D., G. A. Spirou, J. J. Rice, and H. F. Voigt. (1992). Neural organization and responses to complex stimuli in the dorsal cochlear nucleus. *Philosophical Transactions of the Royal Society Lond B* 336(1278): 407–413.

Zwicker, E. (1970). Masking and psychological excitation as consequences of the ear's frequency analysis. In R. Plomp and G. F. Smoorenburg, Eds., *Frequency Analysis and Periodicity Detection in Hearing.* Leiden: Sijthoff, pp. 376–394.

Further Readings

Hauser, M. D. (1996). *The Evolution of Communication.* Cambridge, MA: MIT Press.

Kaas, J. H., and T. A. Hackett. (1998). Subdivisions of auditory cortex and levels of processing in primates. *Audiology Neurootology* 3: 73–85

Konishi, M., et al. (1998). Neurophysiological and anatomical substrates of sound localization in the owl. In Edelman, G. M., W. E. Gall, and W. M. Cowan, Eds., *Auditory Function: Neurobiological Bases of Hearing.* New York: Wiley, pp. 721–745.

Merzenich, M. M., and J. F. Brugge. (1973). Representation of the cochlear partition on the superior temporal plane of the macaque monkey. *Brain Research* 50: 275–296.

Morel, A., P. E. Garraghty, and J. H. Kaas. (1993). Tonotopic organization, architectonic fields, and connections of auditory cortex in macaque monkeys. *Journal of Comparative Neurology* 335: 437–459.

Pandya, D. N., and F. Sanides. (1972). Architectonic parcellation of the temporal operculum in rhesus monkey and its projection pattern. *Zeitschrift für Anatomie und Entwiklungs-Geschichte* 139: 127–161.

Peters, A., and E. G. Jones (1985). *Cerebral Cortex* vol. 4, *Association and Auditory Cortices.* New York: Plenum.

Rauschecker, J. P., and P. Marler. (1987). *Imprinting and Cortical Plasticity: Comparative Aspects of Sensitive Periods.* New York: Wiley.

Suga, N. (1992). Philosophy and stimulus design for neuroethology of complex-sound processing. *Phil Trans R Soc Lond* 336: 423–428.

Woolsey, C. M. (1982). *Cortical Sensory Organization.* vol. 3, *Multiple Auditory Areas.* New Jersey: Humana Press.

Auditory Plasticity

The perception of acoustic stimuli can be altered as a consequence of age, experience, and injury. A lasting change in either the perception of acoustic stimuli or in the responses of neurons to acoustic stimuli is known as auditory plasticity, a form of NEURAL PLASTICITY. This plasticity can be demonstrated at both the perceptual and neuronal levels through behavioral methods such as operant and classical CONDITIONING or by lesions of the auditory periphery both in the adult and during development. The plasticity of neuronal responses in the auditory system presumably reflects the ability of humans and animals to adjust their auditory perceptions to match the perceptual world around them as defined by the other sensory modalities, and to perceive the different acoustic-phonetic patterns of the native languages(s) learned during development (see Kuhl 1993).

There are several examples within the psychophysical literature where human subjects can improve their performance at making specific judgments of acoustic stimulus features over the course of several days to weeks, presumably due to changes in the cortical representation of the relevant stimulus parameters. For example, it has recently been shown that normal human subjects will improve their performance at a temporal processing task over the course of several days of training (Wright et al. 1997).

Training-induced changes in perceptual ability have recently been tested as a treatment strategy for children with language-based learning disabilities (cf. LANGUAGE IMPAIRMENT, DEVELOPMENTAL). It had been suggested that children with this type of learning disability are unable to determine the order of two rapidly presented sounds (Tallal and Piercy 1973). Recent studies have demonstrated that some children with this type of learning disability can make such discriminations following several weeks of practice (Merzenich et al. 1996), and these children also showed significant improvements in language comprehension (Tallal et al. 1996).

Several approaches in experimental animals have been employed to address the neuronal mechanisms that underlie auditory plasticity. Single auditory neurons have been shown to change their response properties following classical conditioning paradigms. As an example, SINGLE-NEURON RECORDING techniques define the response of a single neuron to a range of frequencies, and then a tone that was not optimal in exciting the neuron (the conditioned stimulus, CS) is paired with an unconditioned stimulus (US, e.g., a mild electrical shock). When the frequency response profile of the neuron is defined after conditioning, the response of the neuron to the conditioned tone can be much larger, in some cases to the point that the paired tone is now the best stimulus at exciting the neuron. These changes require a pairing of the CS and the US (Bakin and Weinberger 1990). This response plasticity has been demonstrated in both the auditory THALAMUS and auditory divisions of the CEREBRAL CORTEX (Ryugo and Weinberger 1978; Diamond and Weinberger 1986; Bakin and Weinberger 1990).

It has also been demonstrated that the modulatory neurotransmitter acetylcholine is an important contributor to this effect. If the acetylcholine receptor is blocked, there is no change in the response properties of the neurons (McKenna et al. 1989). Similarly, activation of the acetylcholine receptor produces a similar enhancement of the neuronal response to the conditioned stimulus (Metherate and Weinberger 1990).

A different experimental strategy is to observe the effects of the representation of frequencies across a wide region of the cerebral cortex. For example, if a limited region of the hair cells in the cochlea are destroyed, there is an expansion of the representation of the neighboring spared frequencies in the auditory cortex (Robertson and Irvine 1989; Rajan et al. 1993). These results indicate that the cerebral cortex is able to adjust the representation of different frequencies depending on the nature of the input. This same type of cortical reorganization probably occurs in normal humans during the progressive loss of high frequency hair cells in the cochlea with aging.

Cortical reorganization can also occur following a period of operant conditioning, where the perception of acoustic stimuli is improved over time, similar to the studies on human subjects described above. Monkeys trained at a frequency discrimination task show a continual improvement in performance during several weeks of daily training. After training, the area within the primary auditory cortex that is most sensitive to the trained frequencies is determined. This area of representation is the greatest in the monkeys trained to discriminate that frequency when compared to the representation of untrained monkeys. This occurs regardless of what particular frequency the monkey was trained to discriminate, but it occurs only at those trained frequencies, and no others. The cortical area of the representation of these trained and untrained frequencies is correlated with the behavioral ability (Recanzone, Schreiner, and Merzenich 1993). A further finding was that only animals that attended to and discriminated the acoustic stimuli showed any change in the cortical representations; monkeys stimulated in the same manner while engaged at an unrelated task had normal representations of the presented frequencies. Thus, stimulus relevance is important in both operant and classical conditioning paradigms.

Auditory plasticity also occurs during development, which has been investigated by taking advantage of the natural orienting behavior of barn owls. These birds can locate the source of a sound extremely accurately. Rearing young owls with optically displacing prisms results in a shift in the owl's perception of the source of an acoustic stimulus (Knudsen and Knudsen 1989). This shift can also be demonstrated electrophysiologically as an alignment of the visual and displaced auditory receptive fields of neurons in the optic tectum (Knudsen and Brainard 1991).

The converging neuronal data from experimental animals suggest that similar changes in response properties of cortical and subcortical neurons also occur in humans. The improvements in performance of human subjects in auditory discrimination tasks, the normal high frequency hearing loss during aging, the change from "language-general" to "language-specific" processing of phonetic information during language acquisition, and injuries to the cochlea or central auditory structures, are presumably resulting in changes in single neuron responses and in cortical and subcortical representations. It is quite likely that neuronal plasticity across other sensory modalities and other cognitive functions, particularly in the cerebral cortex, underlies the ability of humans and other mammals to adapt to a changing environment and acquire new skills and behaviors throughout life.

See also AUDITION; AUDITORY ATTENTION; CONDITIONING AND THE BRAIN; PHONOLOGY, NEURAL BASIS OF; SPEECH PERCEPTION

—Gregg Recanzone

References

Bakin, J. S., and N. M. Weinberger. (1990). Classical conditioning induces CS-specific receptive field plasticity in the auditory cortex of the guinea pig. *Brain Res.* 536: 271–286.

Diamond, D. M., and N. M. Weinberger. (1986). Classical conditioning rapidly induces specific changes in frequency receptive fields of single neurons in secondary and ventral ectosylvian auditory cortical fields. *Brain Res.* 372: 357–360.

Knudsen, E. I., and M. S. Brainard. (1991). Visual instruction of the neural map of auditory space in the developing optic tectum. *Science* 253: 85–87.

Knudsen, E. I., and P. F. Knudsen. (1989). Vision calibrates sound localization in developing barn owls. *J. Neurosci.* 9: 3306–3313.

Kuhl, P. K. (1993). Developmental speech perception: implications for models of language impairment. *Annal New York Acad. Sci.* 682: 248–263.

McKenna, T. M., J. H. Ashe, and N. M. Weinberger. (1989). Cholinergic modulation of frequency receptive fields in auditory cortex: 1. Frequency-specific effects of muscarinic agonists. *Synapse* 4: 30–43.

Merzenich, M. M., W. M. Jenkins, P. Johnston, C. Schreiner, S. L. Miller, and P. Tallal. (1996). Temporal processing deficits of language-learning impaired children ameliorated by training. *Science* 271: 77–81.

Metherate, R., and N. M. Weinberger. (1990). Cholinergic modulation of responses to single tones produces tone-specific receptive field alterations in cat auditory cortex. *Synapse* 6: 133–145.

Rajan, R., D. R. Irvine, L. Z. Wise, and P. Heil. (1993). Effect of unilateral partial cochlear lesions in adult cats on the representation of lesioned and unlesioned cochleas in primary auditory cortex. *J. Comp. Neurol.* 338: 17–49.

Recanzone, G. H., C. E. Schreiner, and M. M. Merzenich. (1993). Plasticity in the frequency representation of primary auditory cortex following discrimination training in adult owl monkeys. *Journal of Neuroscience* 13: 87–103.

Robertson, D., and D. R. Irvine. (1989). Plasticity of frequency organization in auditory cortex of guinea pigs with partial unilateral deafness. *J. Comp. Neurol.* 282: 456–471.

Ryugo, D. K., and N. M. Weinberger. (1978). Differential plasticity of morphologically distinct neuron populations in the medical geniculate body of the cat during classical conditioning. *Behav. Biol.* 22: 275–301.

Tallal, P., S. L. Miller, G. Bedi, G. Byma, X. Wang, S. S. Nagarajan, C. Schreiner, W. M. Jenkins, and M. M. Merzenich. (1996). Language comprehension in language-learning impaired children improved with acoustically modified speech. *Science* 271: 81–84.

Tallal, P., and M. Piercy. (1973). Defects of non-verbal auditory perception in children with developmental aphasia. *Nature* 241: 468–469.

Wright, B. A., D. V. Buonomano, H. W. Mahncke, and M. M. Merzenich. (1997). Learning and generalization of auditory temporal-interval discrimination in humans. *J. Neurosci.* 17: 3956–3963.

Further Readings

Knudsen, E. I. (1984). Synthesis of a neural map of auditory space in the owl. In G. M. Edelman, W. M. Cowan, and W. E. Gall, Eds., *Dynamic Aspects of Neocortical Function.* New York: Wiley, pp. 375–396.

Knudsen, E. I., and M. S. Brainard. (1995). Creating a unified representation of visual and auditory space in the brain. *Ann. Rev. Neurosci.* 18: 19–43.

Merzenich, M. M., C. Schreiner, W. Jenkins, and X. Wang. (1993). Neural mechanisms underlying temporal integration, segmentation, and input sequence representation: some implications for the origin of learning disabilities. *Annal New York Acad. Sci.* 682: 1–22.

Neville, H. J., S. A. Coffey, D. S. Lawson, A. Fischer, K. Emmorey, and U. Bellugi. (1997). Neural systems mediating American sign language: Effects of sensory experience and age of acquisition. *Brain and Language* 57: 285–308.

Recanzone, G. H. (1993). Dynamic changes in the functional organization of the cerebral cortex are correlated with changes in psychophysically measured perceptual acuity. *Biomed. Res.* 14, Suppl. 4: 61–69.

Weinberger, N. M. (1995). Dynamic regulation of receptive fields and maps in the adult sensory cortex. *Ann. Rev. Neurosci.* 18: 129–158.

Weinberger, N. M., J. H. Ashe, R. Metherate, T. M. McKenna, D. M. Diamond, and J. S. Bakin. (1990). Retuning auditory cortex by learning: A preliminary model of receptive field plasticity. *Concepts Neurosci.* 1: 91–131.

Autism

A developmental disorder of the brain, autism exists from birth and persists throughout life. The etiology of the disorder is still unknown, but is believed to be largely genetic, while different organic factors have been implicated in a substantial proportion of cases (for reviews see Ciaranello and Ciaranello 1995; Bailey, Phillips, and Rutter 1996). Autism was identified and labeled by Kanner (1943) and Asperger (1944).

The diagnosis of autism is based on behavioral criteria. The chief criteria as set out in ICD-10 (WHO 1992) and in DSM-IV (APA 1994) include: abnormalities of social interaction, abnormalities of verbal and nonverbal communication, and a restricted repertoire of interests and activities. Behavior suggestive of these impairments can already be discerned in infancy. A recent screening instrument, based on a cognitive account of autism, appears to be remarkably successful at eighteen months, involving failure of gaze monitoring, protodeclarative pointing, and pretend play (Baron-Cohen et al. 1996). These appear to be the first clear behavioral manifestations of the disorder. Contrary to popular belief, failure of bonding or attachment is not a distinguishing characteristic of autism.

The autistic spectrum refers to the wide individual variation of symptoms from mild to severe. Behavior not only varies with age and ability, but is also modified by a multitude of environmental factors. For this reason, one of the major problems with behaviorally defined developmental disorders is how to identify primary, associated, and secondary features. Three highly correlated features, namely characteristic impairments in socialization, communication, and imagination, were identified in a geographically defined population study (Wing and Gould 1979). These impairments appear to persist in development even though their outward manifestation is subject to change. For example, a socially aloof child may at a later age become socially interested and show "pestering" behavior; a child with initially little speech may become verbose with stilted, pedantic language. The triad of impairments appears to be a common denominator throughout a spectrum of autistic disorders (Wing 1996).

The prevalence of autistic disorder has been studied in a number of different countries, and is between 0.16 and 0.22 percent, taking into account the most recent estimates. Males predominate at approximately 3 to 1, and this ratio becomes more extreme with higher levels of ability. The prevalence of a milder variant of autism, Asperger syndrome, is estimated as between 0.3 and 0.7 percent of the general population on the basis of preliminary findings. These individuals are sometimes thought to be merely eccentric and may not be diagnosed until late childhood or even adulthood. Because they have fluent language and normal, if not superior verbal IQ, they can compensate to some extent for their problems in social communication.

MENTAL RETARDATION, a sign of congenital brain abnormality, is one of the most strongly associated features of autism; IQ is below 70 in about half the cases, and below 80 in three quarters. Epilepsy is present in about a third of individuals, while other neurological and neuropsychological signs are almost always detectable (for reviews see Gillberg and Coleman 1992). Postmortem brain studies have shown a number of abnormalities in cell structure in different parts of the brain, including temporal and parietal lobes, and in particular, limbic structures, as well as the CEREBELLUM. Findings indicate a curtailment of neuronal development at or before thirty weeks of gestation (Bauman and Kemper 1994). No consistent and specific structural or metabolic abnormalities have as yet been revealed, but overall brain volume and weight tend to be increased.

A genetic basis for autism is strongly indicated from twin and family studies favoring a multiplicative multilocus model of inheritance, perhaps involving only a small number of genes (reviewed by Bailey et al. 1995). There is evidence for a broader cognitive phenotype with normal intelligence and varying degrees of social and communication impairments which may be shared by family members. Other disorders of known biological origin, such as fragile X-syndrome, phenylketonuria, tuberous sclerosis, can lead to the clinical picture of autism in conjunction with severe mental retardation (Smalley, Asarnow, and Spence 1988). There is no known medical treatment. However, special education and treatment based on behavior management and modification often have beneficial effects (see chapters in Schopler and Mesibov 1995). Whatever the treatment, the developmental progress of children with autism is quite variable.

Cognitive explanations of the core features of autism provide a vital interface between brain and behavior. The proposal of a specific neurologically based problem in understanding minds was a significant step in this endeavor. The hypothesis that autistic children lack the intuitive understanding that people have mental states was originally tested with the Sally-Ann false belief paradigm (Baron-Cohen, Leslie, and Frith 1985). This impairment has been confirmed in a number of studies (see chapters in Baron-Cohen, Tager-Flusberg, and Cohen 1993) and has become known as the THEORY OF MIND deficit. Most individuals with autism fail to appreciate the role of mental states in the explanation and prediction of everyday behavior, including deception, joint attention, and those emotional states which depend on monitoring other people's attitudes, for example pride (Kasari et al. 1993). The brain basis for the critical cognitive ability that enables a theory of mind to develop has begun to be investigated by means of functional brain imaging (Fletcher et al. 1995; Happé et al. 1996). Other explanations of social communication impairments in autism have emphasized a primary emotional deficit in INTERSUBJECTIVITY (Hobson 1993).

The nonsocial features of autism, in particular those encompassed by the diagnostic sign *restricted repertoire of interests,* are currently tackled by two cognitive theories. The first proposes a deficit in executive functions. These include planning and initiation of action and impulse control, and are thought to depend on intact prefrontal cortex. Evidence for poor performance on many "frontal" tasks in autism is robust (Ozonoff, Pennington, and Rogers 1991; Pennington and Ozonoff 1996). For instance, individuals with autism often fail to inhibit prepotent responses and to shift response categories (Hughes, Russell, and Robbins 1994). Poor performance on these tasks appears to be related to stereotyped and perseverative behavior in everyday life. The site of brain abnormality need not necessarily be in prefrontal cortex, but could be at different points in a distributed system underlying executive functions, for example the dopamine system (Damasio and Maurer 1978).

A second cognitive theory that attempts to address islets of ability and special talents that are present in a significant proportion of autistic individuals is the theory of weak central coherence (Frith and Happé 1994). This theory proposes that the observed performance peaks in tests such as block design and embedded figures, and the *savant syndrome,* shown for instance in outstanding feats of memory or exceptional drawing, are due to a cognitive processing style that favors segmental over holistic processing. Some evidence exists that people with autism process information in an unusually piecemeal fashion (e.g., start a drawing from an unusual detail). Likewise, they fail to integrate information so as to derive contextually relevant meaning. For instance, when reading aloud "the dog was on a long lead," they may pronounce the word *lead* as *led.*

Clearly, the explanation of autism will only be complete when the necessary causal links have been traced between gene, brain, mind and behavior. This is as yet a task for the future.

See also COGNITIVE DEVELOPMENT; FOLK PSYCHOLOGY; MODULARITY OF MIND; NEUROTRANSMITTERS; PROPOSITIONAL ATTITUDES; SOCIAL COGNITION

—*Uta Frith*

References

American Psychiatric Association. (1994). *Diagnostic and Statistical Manual of Mental Disorders (DSM-IV).* Fourth edition. Washington, DC: American Psychiatric Association.

Asperger, H. (1944). "Autistic psychopathy" in childhood. In U. Frith, Ed., *Autism and Asperger Syndrome.* Translated and annotated by U. Frith. Cambridge: Cambridge University Press.

Bailey, A., A. Le Couteur, I. Gottesman, P. Bolton, E. Simonoff, E. Yuzda, and M. Rutter. (1995). Autism as a strongly genetic disorder: evidence from a British twin study. *Psychological Medicine* 25: 63–78.

Bailey, A. J., W. Phillips, and M. Rutter. (1996). Autism: integrating clinical, genetic, neuropsychological, and neurobiological perspectives. *Journal of Child Psychology and Psychiatry* 37: 89–126.

Baron-Cohen, S. (1995). *Mindblindness: An Essay on Autism and Theory of Mind.* Cambridge, MA: MIT Press.

Baron-Cohen, S., A. Cox, G. Baird, and J. Swettenham. (1996). Psychological markers in the detection of autism in infancy in a large population. *British Journal of Psychiatry* 168: 158–163.

Baron-Cohen, S., H. Tager-Flusberg, and D. J. Cohen, Eds. (1993). *Understanding Other Minds: Perspectives from Autism.* Oxford: Oxford University Press.

Baron-Cohen, S., A. Leslie, and U. Frith. (1985). Does the autistic child have a "theory of mind"? *Cognition* 21: 37–46.

Bauman, M., and T. Kemper, Eds. (1994). *The Neurobiology of Autism.* Baltimore: Johns Hopkins University Press.

Ciaranello, A. L., and R. D. Ciaranello. (1995). The neurobiology of infantile autism. *Annual Review of Neuroscience* 18: 101–128.

Damasio, A. R., and R. G. Maurer. (1978). A neurological model for childhood autism. *Archives of Neurology* 35: 777–786.

Fletcher, P. C., F. Happé, U. Frith, S. C. Baker, R. J. Dolan, R. S. J. Frackowiak, and C. D. Frith. (1995). Other minds in the brain: a functional imaging study of "theory of mind" in story comprehension. *Cognition* 57: 109–128.

Frith, U., and F. Happé. (1994). Autism: beyond "theory of mind." *Cognition* 50: 115–132.

Frith, U., J. Morton, and A. Leslie. (1991). The cognitive basis of a biological disorder. *Trends in Neuroscience* 14: 433–438.

Gillberg, C., and M. Coleman. (1992). *The Neurobiology of the Autistic Syndromes.* 2nd ed. London: Mac Keith Press.

Happé, F., S. Ehlers, P. Fletcher, U. Frith, M. Johansson, C. Gillberg, R. Dolan, R. Frackowiak, and C. Frith. (1996). "Theory of mind" in the brain. Evidence from a PET scan study of Asperger syndrome. *NeuroReport* 8: 197–201.

Hobson, R. P. J. (1993). *Autism and the Development of Mind.* Hove, Sussex: Erlbaum.

Hughes, C., J. Russell, and T. W. Robbins. (1994). Evidence for executive dysfunction in autism. *Neuropsychologia* 32: 477–492.

Kanner, L. (1943). Autistic disturbances of affective contact. *Nervous Child* 2: 217–250.

Kasari, C., M. D. Sigman, P. Baumgartner, and D. J. Stipek. (1993). Pride and mastery in children with autism. *Journal of Child Psychology and Psychiatry* 34: 353–362.

Ozonoff, S., B. F. Pennington, and S. J. Rogers. (1991). Executive function deficits in high-functioning autistic children: relationship to theory of mind. *Journal of Child Psychology and Psychiatry* 32: 1081–1106.

Pennington, B. F., and S. Ozonoff. (1996). Executive functions and developmental psychopathology. *Journal of Child Psychology and Psychiatry* 37: 51–87.

Schopler, E., and G. Mesibov, Eds. (1995). *Learning and Cognition in Autism.* New York: Plenum.

Smalley, S., R. Asarnow, and M. Spence. (1988). Autism and genetics: a decade of research. *Archives of General Psychiatry* 45: 953–961.

Wing, L. (1996). *The Autistic Spectrum. A Guide for Parents and Professionals.* London: Constable.

Wing, L., and J. Gould. (1979). Severe impairments of social interaction and associated abnormalities in children: epidemiology and classification. *Journal of Autism and Developmental Disorders* 9: 11–29.

World Health Organization. (1992). *The ICD-10 Classification of Mental and Behavioral Disorders.* Geneva: World Health Organization.

Further Readings

Frith, U. (1989). *Autism: Explaining the Enigma.* Oxford: Blackwell.

Happé, F. (1994). *Autism: An Introduction to Psychological Theory.* London: UCL Press.

Happé, F., and U. Frith. (1996). The neuropsychology of autism. *Brain* 119: 1377–1400.

Russell, J., Ed. (1998). *Autism as an Executive Disorder.* Oxford: Oxford University Press.

Sigman, M., and L. Capps. (1997). *Children with Autism. A Developmental Perspective.* Cambridge, MA: Harvard University Press.

Autocatalysis

See SELF-ORGANIZING SYSTEMS

Automata

An *automaton* (pl. *automata*) was originally anything with the power of self-movement, then, more specifically, a *machine* with the power of self-movement, especially a figure that simulated the motion of living beings. Perhaps the most impressive such automata were those of Jacques de Vaucanson (1709–1782), including a duck that ate and drank with realistic motions of head and throat, produced the sound of quacking, and could pick up cornmeal and swallow, digest, and excrete it.

People acting in a mechanical, nonspontaneous way came to be called automata, but this begs the very question for which cognitive science seeks a positive answer: "Is the working of the human mind reducible to information processing embodied in the workings of the human brain?" that is, is human spontaneity and intelligence a purely material phenomenon? René DESCARTES (1596–1650) saw the functioning of nonhuman animals, and much of human function, as being explainable in terms of the automata of his day but drew the line at cognitive function. However, whereas Descartes's view was based on clockwork and hydraulic automata, most cognitive science is based on a view of automata as "information processing machines" (though there is now a welcome increase of interest in *embodied automata*).

The present article describes key concepts of information processing automata from 1936 through 1956 (the year of publication of *Automata Studies* by Shannon and McCarthy), including Turing machines, finite automata, automata for formal languages, McCulloch-Pitts neural networks, and self-reproducing automata.

TURING (1936) and Post (1936) introduced what is now called a *Turing machine* (TM), consisting of a control box containing a finite program; an indefinitely extendable tape divided lengthwise into squares; and a device for scanning and then printing on one square of the tape at a time and subsequently moving the tape one square left or right or not at all. We start the machine with a finite sequence of symbols on the tape, and a program in the control box. The symbol scanned, and the instruction now being executed from the program, determine what new symbol is printed on the square, how the tape is moved, and what instruction is executed next.

We associate with a TM Z a numerical function f_Z by placing a number n encoded as a string $<n>$ on the tape and start Z scanning the leftmost square of $<n>$. If and when Z stops, we decode the result to obtain the number $f_Z(n)$. If Z never stops, we leave $f_Z(n)$ undefined. Just consider the program Z, which always moves right on its tape (new squares are added whenever needed), as an example of a machine that never stops computing, no matter what its input. More subtle machines might, for example, test to see whether n is prime and stop computing only if that is the case. (We can only associate f_Z with Z after we have chosen our encoding. Nonnumerical functions can be associated with a TM once we have a "straightforward" way of unambiguously coding the necessarily finite or countable input and output structures on the tape.)

Turing's Hypothesis (also called *Church's thesis*; see CHURCH-TURING THESIS) is that a function is effectively computable if and only if it is computable by some TM. This statement is informal, but each attempt to formalize the notion of effectiveness using finite "programs" has yielded procedures equivalent to those implementable by TMs (or a subclass thereof).

Because each TM is described by a finite list of instructions we may *effectively enumerate* the TMs as Z_1, Z_2, Z_3, . . .—given n we may effectively find Z_n, and given the list of instructions for Z, we may effectively find the n for which $Z = Z_n$. For example, we might list all the one-instruction programs first, then all those with two instructions, and so on, listing all programs of a given length in some suitable generalization of alphabetical order.

Turing showed that there is a *universal Turing Machine* that, given a coded description of Z_n on its tape as well as x, will proceed to compute $fz_n(x) = f_n(x)$, if it is defined. This is obvious if we accept Turing's hypothesis, for given n and x we find Z_n effectively, and then use it to compute $f_n(x)$, and so there should exist a TM to implement the effective procedure of going from the pair (n, x) to the value $f_n(x)$. More directly, we can program a Turing machine U that divides the data on its tape into two parts, that on the left providing the instructions for Z_n, and that on the right providing the string $x(t)$ on which Z_n would now be computing. U is programmed to place markers against the current instruction from Z_n and the currently scanned symbol of $x(t)$, and to move back and forth between instructions and data to simulate the effect of Z_n on x. For further details see Minsky (1967) and Arbib (1969), the second of which generalizes Turing machines to those that can work in parallel on multiple, possibly multidimensional tapes.

Is every function mapping natural numbers ($N = \{0, 1, 2, 3, . . .\}$) to natural numbers computable? Obviously not, for we have seen that the number of computable functions is countable, whereas the number of all functions is uncount-

able. To understand the latter claim, note that any real number between zero and one can be represented by an infinite decimal expansion $0.d_0d_1d_2d_3 . . . d_n . . .$ and thus as a function $f:N \to N$ with $f(n) = d_n$—and thus the uncountable set of these real numbers can be viewed as a subset of the set of all functions from N to N. However, the interest of computability theory is that there are "computationally interesting" functions that are not computable.

The following provides a simple example of an explicit proof of noncomputability. We define a *total* function h (i.e., $h(x)$ is defined for every x in N) as follows. Let $h(n) = n$ if f_n is itself total, while $h(n) = n_0$ if f_n is not total—where n_0 is a fixed choice of an integer for which f_{n_0} is a total computable function; h thus has the interesting property that a computable function f_n is total if and only if $n = h(m)$ for some m. h is certainly a well-defined total function, but is h a *computable* function? The answer is no. For if h were computable, then so too would be the function f defined by $f(n) = f_{h(n)}(n) + 1$, and f would also be total. Then f is total and computable, and so $f = f_{h(m)}$ for some m so that $f(m) = f_{h(m)}(m)$. But, by definition, $f(m) = f_{h(m)}(m) + 1$, a contradiction! This is one example of the many things undecidable by any effective procedure.

The most famous example—proved by an extension of the above proof—is that we cannot tell effectively for arbitrary (n, x) whether Z_n will stop computing for input x. Thus *the halting problem for TMs is unsolvable.*

Finite automata provide, essentially, the input-output behavior of the TM control box without regard for its interaction with the tape. A *finite automaton* is abstractly described as a quintuple $M = (X, Y, Q, \delta, \beta)$ where X, Y, and Q are finite sets of inputs, outputs, and states, and if at time t the automaton is in state q and receives input x, it will emit output $\beta(q)$ at time t, and then make the transition to state $\delta(q,x)$ at time $t + 1$.

Given this, we can view the control box of a Turing Machine as a finite automaton: let X be the set of tape symbols, Q the set of control-box instructions, and Y the set $X \times M$ of pairs (x, m) where x is symbol to be printed on the tape and m is a symbol for one of the three possible tape moves (left, right, or not at all).

Another special case of the finite automaton definition takes Y to be the set $\{0,1\}$—this is equivalent to dividing the set Q into the set F of designated *final* states for which $\beta(q) = 1$, and its complement—and then designates a specific state q_0 of Q to be the "initial state." In this case, interest focuses on the *language accepted* by M, namely the set of strings w consisting of a sequence of 0 or more elements of X (we use X^* to denote the set of such strings) with the property that if we start M in state q_0 and apply input sequence w, then M will end up in a state—denoted by $\delta^*(q_0,w)$—that belongs to F.

The above examples define two sets of "languages" (in the sense of subsets of X^*, i.e., strings on some specified alphabet): *finite-state languages* defined as those languages accepted by some finite automaton, and *recursively enumerable sets* that have many equivalent definitions, including "a set R is *recursively enumerable* if and only if there is a Turing machine Z such that Z halts computation on initial tape x if and only if x belongs to R." Without going into details and definitions here, it is interesting to note that two intermediate classes of formal languages—the context-free languages and the context-sensitive languages—have also been associated with classes of automata. The former are associated with *push-down automata* and the latter with *linear-bounded automata.* Discussion of the relation of these language classes to human language was a staple topic for discussion in the 1960s (Chomsky and Miller 1963; Chomsky 1963; Miller and Chomsky 1963), and Chomsky has subsequently defined a number of other systems of formal grammar to account for human language competence. However, much work in PSYCHOLINGUISTICS now focuses on the claim that adaptive networks provide a better model of language performance than does any system based on using some fixed automaton structure which embodies such a formal grammar (e.g., Seidenberg 1995).

McCulloch and Pitts (1943) modeled the neuron as a logic element, dividing time into units so small that in each time period at most one spike can be initiated in the axon of a given neuron, with output 1 or 0 coding whether or not the neuron "fires" (i.e., has a spike on its axon). Each connection from neuron i to neuron j has an attached *synaptic weight.* They also associate a *threshold* with each neuron, and assume exactly one unit of delay in the effect of all presynaptic inputs on the cell's output. A McCulloch-Pitts neuron (MP-neuron) fires just in case the weighted value of its inputs at that time reaches threshold.

Clearly, a network of MP-neurons functions like a finite automaton, as each neuron changes state synchronously on each tick of the time scale. Conversely, it was shown, though inscrutably, by McCulloch and Pitts that any finite automaton can be simulated by a suitable network of MP-neurons—providing formal "brains" for the TMs, which can carry out any effective procedure. Knowledge of these results inspired VON NEUMANN's logical design for digital computers with stored programs (von Neumann, Burks, and Goldstine 1947–48).

Intuitively, one has the idea that a construction machine must build a simpler machine. But in biological systems, the complexity of an offspring matches that of the parent; and evolution may yield increasing biological complexity. Von Neumann (1951) outlined the construction of an automaton A that, when furnished with the description of any other automaton M (composed from some suitable collection of elementary parts) would construct a copy of M. However, A is *not* self-reproducing: A, supplied with a copy of its own description, will build a copy of A *without* its own description. The passage from a *universal constructor* to a *self-reproducing automaton* was spelled out in von Neumann (1966) in which the "organism" is a pattern of activity in an unbounded array of identical finite automata, each with only twenty-nine states. This was one root of the study of *cellular automata.*

As embodied humans we have far richer interactions with the world than does a TM; our "computations" involve all of our bodies, not just our brains; and biological neurons are amazingly more subtle than MP-neurons (Arbib 1995, pp. 4–11). A TM might in principle be able to solve a given problem—but take far too long to solve it. Thus it is not enough that something be computable—it must be *tractable,* that is,

computable with available resources (Garey and Johnson 1979). Distributed computation may render tractable a problem that a serial TM would solve too slowly. When some people say "the brain is a computer," they talk as if the notion of "computer" were already settled. However, a human brain is built of hundreds of regions, each with millions of cells, each cell with tens of thousands of connections, each connection involving subtle neurochemical processes. To understand this is to push the theory of automata—and cognitive science—far beyond anything available today. Our concepts of automata will grow immensely over the coming decades as we better understand how the brain functions.

Arbib (1987) provides much further information on neural nets, finite automata, TMs, and automata that construct as well as compute, as well as a refutation of the claim that Gödel's Incompleteness theorem (see GÖDEL'S THEOREMS) sets limits to the intelligence of automata. Many articles in Arbib (1995) and in the present volume explore the theme of connectionist approaches to cognitive modeling (see COGNITIVE MODELING, CONNECTIONIST).

See also COMPUTATION; COMPUTATION AND THE BRAIN; COMPUTATIONAL COMPLEXITY; COMPUTATIONAL THEORY OF MIND; FORMAL GRAMMARS; VISUAL WORD RECOGNITION

—*Michael Arbib*

References

Arbib, M. A. (1969). *Theories of Abstract Automata.* Englewood Cliffs, NJ: Prentice-Hall.

Arbib, M. A. (1987). *Brains, Machines and Mathematics.* Second edition. New York: Springer.

Arbib, M. A., Ed. (1995). *The Handbook of Brain Theory and Neural Networks.* Cambridge, MA: MIT Press. (See pp. 4–11.)

Chomsky, N. (1963). Formal properties of grammars. In R. D. Luce, R. R. Bush, and E. Galanter, Eds., *Handbook of Mathematical Psychology,* vol. 2. New York: Wiley, pp. 323–418.

Chomsky, N., and G. A. Miller. (1963). Introduction to the formal analysis of natural languages. In R. D. Luce, R. R. Bush, and E. Galanter, Eds., *Handbook of Mathematical Psychology,* vol. 2. New York: Wiley, pp. 269–321.

Garey, M. R., and D. S. Johnson. (1979). *Computers and Intractability: A Guide to the Theory of NP-Completeness.* New York: W. H. Freeman.

McCulloch, W. S., and W. H. Pitts. (1943). A logical calculus of the ideas immanent in nervous activity. *Bull. Math. Biophys.* 5: 115–133.

Miller, G. A., and N. Chomsky. (1963). Finitary models of language users. In R. D. Luce, R. R. Bush, and E. Galanter, Eds., *Handbook of Mathematical Psychology,* vol. 2. New York: Wiley, pp. 419–491.

Minsky, M. L. (1967). *Computation: Finite and Infinite Machines.* Englewood Cliffs, NJ: Prentice-Hall.

Post, E. L. (1936). Finite combinatory processes—formulation I. *Journal of Symbolic Logic* 1: 103–105.

Seidenberg, M. (1995). Linguistic morphology. In M. A. Arbib, Ed., *The Handbook of Brain Theory and Neural Networks.* Cambridge, MA: MIT Press.

Shannon, C. E., and J. McCarthy, Eds. (1956). *Automata Studies.* Princeton: Princeton University Press.

Turing, A. M. (1936). On computable numbers. *Proc. London Math. Soc.* Ser. 2, 42: 230–265.

von Neumann, J. (1951). The general and logical theory of automata. In L. A. Jeffress, Ed., *Cerebral Mechanisms in Behaviour.* New York: Wiley.

von Neumann, J. (1966). *The Theory of Self-Reproducing Automata.* Edited and completed by Arthur W. Burks. Urbana: University of Illinois Press.

von Neumann, J., A. Burks, and H. H. Goldstine. (1947–48). *Planning and Coding of Problems for an Electronic Computing Instrument.* Institute for Advanced Study, Princeton. (Reprinted in von Neumann's *Collected Works* 5: 80–235.)

Automatic Processing

See AUTOMATICITY

Automaticity

Automaticity is a characteristic of cognitive processing in which practiced consistent component behaviors are performed rapidly, with minimal effort or with automatic allocation of attention to the processing of the stimulus. Most skilled behavior requires the development of automatic processes (e.g., walking, READING, driving, programming). Automatic processes generally develop slowly, with practice over hundreds of trials. An example of an automatic process for the skilled reader is encoding letter strings into their semantic meaning. As your eyes fixate on the word "red," a semantic code representing a color and an acoustic image of the phonemes /r/ /e/ /d/ are activated. Automatic processes may occur unintentionally, such as the refocusing of your ATTENTION when you hear your name used in a nearby conversation at a party. Automatic processing can release unintentional behaviors, such as automatic capture errors (e.g., walking out of an elevator when the doors open on an unintended floor).

Automaticity develops when there is a consistent mapping (CM) between the stimuli and responses at some stage of processing. For example, in a letter search task, a subject responds to a set of letters called the "target set" and ignores the "distracter set." If certain letter stimuli are consistently the target set, they will be attended and responded to whenever they occur. Automatic processing will develop with practice and the consistent target letters will attract attention and activate response processes. Automatic targets can be found rapidly in cluttered displays with little effort. Automaticity does not develop when stimuli have a varied mapping (VM) (e.g., when a letter that is a target on one trial is a distracter on the next).

Automatic processing (AP) is often contrasted with controlled or attentive processing. Controlled processing (CP) occurs early in practice, is maintained when there is a varied mapping, and is relatively slow and effortful.

Automatic processing shows seven qualitatively and quantitatively different processing characteristics relative to controlled processing. Automatic processing can be much faster than controlled processing (e.g., 2 ms per category for AP versus 200 ms for CP). Automatic processing is parallel across perceptual channels, memory comparisons, and across levels of processing, whereas controlled processing is serial. Automatic processing requires minimal effort, which enables multitask processing. Automatic processing is robust and highly reliable relative to controlled processing despite fatigue, exhaustion, and the effects of alcohol. On the other hand, automatic processing requires substantial consistent practice, typically hundreds of trials for a single task before accuracy is attained, whereas controlled processing often attains accuracy for a single task in a few trials. Subjects have reduced control of automatic processing, which attracts attention or elicits responses if task demands change relative to the subject's previous consistent training. Automatic processing produces less memory modification than controlled processing, which causes a stimulus to be processed without MEMORY of the processing (e.g., Did you lock the door when leaving the car?).

Models of automaticity seek to account for the characteristics noted above and, in particular, for the contrasts between automatic and controlled processing. They divide into two kinds: incremental learning and instance-based. In the incremental learning models (e.g., James 1890/1950; Laberge 1975; Schneider, Dumais, and Shiffrin 1984), the strength of association between the stimulus and a priority of the signal increases each time a positive stimulus-response sequence occurs. After a sufficient number of such events occur, the priority of the response is sufficient to result in an output of that stage of processing with the minimal need for attention. Stimuli not consistently attended to do not obtain a high priority, hence do not produce an automatic response. In contrast, the instance-based model of Logan (1992), for example, assumes that all instances are stored and the response time is determined by a parallel memory access in which the first retrieved instance determines the reaction time. In this model, the importance of consistency is due to response conflict between the instances slowing the response.

The concept of automaticity has been widely applied to many areas of psychology to interpret processing differences. In the area of attentional processing, it has been applied to interpret effects of processing speed, effort, visual search, and interference effects. In skill acquisition, it has been applied to interpret changes in performance with practice and the development of procedural knowledge. In the understanding of human error, it has been applied to understand unintended automatic behaviors such as capture errors and workload-related errors for controlled processing. In clinical disorders such as schizophrenia, difficulties in maintaining attention can result from too frequent or too few automatic attention shifts, and preservative behavior can result from automatic execution of component skills or lack of memory modification for automatic behaviors. In addictions such as smoking, a major obstacle in breaking a habit is the difficulty of inhibiting automatic behaviors linked to social contexts. In the aging literature, there is evidence that automatic and controlled behaviors may develop and decline differentially with age and that the aged may have more difficulty learning and altering automatic behaviors.

The concept of automatic processing has had a long history in cognitive psychology. The topic of automaticity was a major focus in WILLIAM JAMES's *Principles of Psychology* (1890/1950). In modern times, automatic processing has been an important issue in the attention literature (Posner and Snyder 1975; Schneider and Shiffrin 1977; Shiffrin 1988) and the skill acquisition literature (Laberge 1975), and the skill acquisition and memory literature (Anderson 1992; Schneider and Detweiler 1987; Logan 1992).

See also AGING AND COGNITION; ATTENTION IN THE HUMAN BRAIN; AUDITORY ATTENTION; EXPERTISE; EYE MOVEMENTS AND VISUAL ATTENTION; MOTOR CONTROL

—*Walter Schneider*

References

Anderson, J. R. (1992). Automaticity and the ACT theory. *American Journal of Psychology* 105: 165–180.

James, W. (1890/1950). *The Principles of Psychology,* vol. 1. Authorized edition. New York: Dover.

LaBerge, D. (1975). Acquisition of automatic processing in perceptual and associative learning. In P. M. A. Rabbit and S. Dornic, Eds., *Attention and Performance V.* New York: Academic Press.

Logan, G. D. (1992). Attention and preattention in theories of automaticity. *American Journal of Psychology* 105: 317–339.

Posner, M. I., and C. R. R. Snyder. (1975). Attention and cognitive control. In R. L. Solso, Ed., *Information Processing and Cognition: The Loyola Symposium.* Hillsdale, NJ: Erlbaum, pp 55–85.

Schneider, W., and M. Detweiler. (1987). A connectionist/control architecture for working memory. In G. H. Bower, Ed., *The Psychology of Learning and Motivation,* vol. 21. New York: Academic Press, pp. 54–119.

Schneider, W., S. T. Dumais, and R. M. Shiffrin. (1984). Automatic and control processing and attention. In R. Parasuraman, R. Davies, and R. J. Beatty, Eds., *Varieties of Attention.* New York: Academic Press, pp. 1–27.

Schneider, W., and R. M. Shiffrin. (1977). Automatic and controlled information processing in vision. In D. LaBerge and S. J. Samuels, Eds., *Basic Processes in Reading: Perception and Comprehension.* Hillsdale, NJ: Erlbaum, pp. 127–154.

Shiffrin, R. M. (1988). Attention. In R. C. Atkinson, R. J. Herrnstein, G. Lindzey, and R. D. Luce, Eds., *Steven's Handbook of Human Experimental Psychology,* vol. 2, *Learning and Cognition.* New York: Wiley, pp. 739–811.

Further Readings

Bargh, J. A. (1992). The ecology of automaticity: Toward establishing the conditions needed to produce automatic processing effects. *American Journal of Psychology* 105: 181–199.

Healy, A. F., D. W. Fendrich, R. J. Crutcher, W. T. Wittman, A. T. Gest, K. R. Ericcson, and L. E. Bourne, Jr. (1992). The long-term retention of skills. In A. F. Healy, S. M. Kosslyn, and R. M. Shiffrin, Eds., *From Learning Processes to Cognitive Processes: Essays in Honor of William K. Estes,* vol. 2. Hillsdale, NJ: Erlbaum, pp. 87–118.

Naatanen, R. (1992). *Attention and Brain Function.* Hillsdale, NJ: Erlbaum.

Neumann, O. (1984). Automatic processing: A review of recent findings and a plea for an old theory. In W. Prinz and A. F. Sanders, Eds., *Cognition and Motor Processes.* Berlin and Heidelberg: Springer–Verlag.

Norman, D. A., and D. G. Bobrow. (1975). On data-limited and resource-limited processes. *Cognitive Psychology* 7: 44–64.

Schneider, W., M. Pimm-Smith, and M. Worden. (1994). The neurobiology of attention and automaticity. *Current Opinion in Neurobiology* 4: 177–182.

Autonomy of Psychology

Psychology has been considered an autonomous science in at least two respects: its subject matter and its methods. To say that its subject matter is autonomous is to say that psychology deals with entities—properties, relations, states—that are not dealt with or not wholly explicable in terms of physical (or any other) science. Contrasted with this is the idea that psychology employs a characteristic method of explanation, which is not shared by the other sciences. I shall label the two senses of autonomy "metaphysical autonomy" and "explanatory autonomy."

Whether psychology as a science is autonomous in either sense is one of the philosophical questions surrounding the (somewhat vague) doctrine of "naturalism," which concerns itself with the extent to which the human mind can be brought under the aegis of natural science. In their contemporary form, these questions had their origin in the "new science" of the seventeenth century. Early materialists like Hobbes (1651) and La Mettrie (1748) rejected both explanatory and metaphysical autonomy: Mind is matter in motion, and the mind can be studied by the mathematical methods of the new science just as any matter can. But while materialism (and therefore the denial of metaphysical autonomy) had to wait until the nineteenth century before becoming widely accepted, the denial of explanatory autonomy remained a strong force in empiricist philosophy. HUME described his *Treatise of Human Nature* (1739–1740) as an "attempt to introduce the experimental method of reasoning into moral subjects"—where "moral" signifies "human." And subsequent criticism of Hume's views, notably by KANT and Reid, ensured that the question of naturalism—whether there can be a "science of man"—was one of the central questions of nineteenth–century philosophy, and a question that hovered over the emergence of psychology as an independent discipline (see Reed 1994).

In the twentieth century, much of the philosophical debate over the autonomy of psychology has been inspired by the logical positivists' discussions of the UNITY OF SCIENCE (see Carnap 1932–1933; Feigl 1981; Oppenheim and Putnam 1958). For the positivists, physical science had a special epistemological and ontological authority: The other sciences (including psychology) must have their claims about the world vindicated by being translated into the language of physics. This extreme REDUCTIONISM did not survive long after the decline of the positivist doctrines which generated it—and it cannot have helped prevent this decline that no positivist actually succeeded in translating any psychological claims into the language of physics. Thus even though positivism was a major influence on the rise of postwar PHYSICALISM, later physicalists tended to distinguish their metaphysical doctrines from the more extreme positivist claims. J. J. C. Smart (1959), for example, asserted that mental and physical properties are identical, but denied that the psychological language we use to describe these properties can be translated into physical language. This is not yet to concede psychology's explanatory autonomy. That psychology employs a different *language* does not mean it must employ a different explanatory *method*. And Smart's identity claim obviously implies the denial of psychology's metaphysical autonomy.

On the other hand, many philosophers think that the possibility of *multiple realization* forces us to accept the metaphysical autonomy of psychology. A property is multiply realized by underlying physical properties when not all of the instances of that property are instances of the same physical property. This is contrasted with property *identity,* where a brain property being identical with a mental property, for example, entails that all and only instances of the one property are instances of the other. Hilary Putnam (1975) argued influentially that there are good reasons for thinking that psychological properties are multiply realized by physical properties, on the grounds that psychological properties are *functional* properties of organisms—properties identified by the causal role they play in the organism's psychological organization (see FUNCTIONALISM).

This kind of functionalist approach implies a certain degree of metaphysical autonomy: Because psychological properties are multiply realized, it seems that they cannot be identical with physical properties of the brain (but contrast Lewis 1994). It does not, however, imply a Cartesian dualist account of the mind, because all these properties are properties of physical objects, and the physical still has a certain ontological priority, sometimes expressed by saying that everything *supervenes* on the physical (see SUPERVENIENCE and MIND-BODY PROBLEM). The picture that emerges is a "layered world": The properties of macroscopic objects are multiply realized by more microscopic properties, eventually arriving at the properties which are the subject matter of fundamental physics (see Fodor 1974; Owens 1989).

With the exception of some who hold to ELIMINATIVE MATERIALISM, who see the metaphysical autonomy of commonsense (or "folk") psychological categories as a reason for rejecting the entities psychology talks about, the "layered world" picture is a popular account of the relationship between the subject matters of the various sciences. But what impact does this picture have on the question of the explanatory autonomy of psychology? Here matters become a little complex. The "layered world" picture does suggest that the theories of the different levels of nature can be relatively independent. There is also room for different *styles* of explanation. Robert Cummins (1983) argues that psychological explanation does not conform to the "covering law" pattern of explanation employed in the physical sciences (where to explain a phenomenon is to show it to be an instance of a law of nature). And some influential views of the nature of computational psychology treat it as involving three different levels of EXPLANATION (see Marr 1982). But in general, nothing in the "layered world" picture prevents psychology from having a properly scientific status; it is still the *subject matter* (psychological properties and relations) of psychology that ultimately sets it apart from physics and the other sciences. In short, the "layered world" conception holds that psychological explanation has its autonomy in the sense that it does not need to be reduced to physical explanation, but nonetheless it is properly scientific.

This view can be contrasted with Davidson's (1970) view that there are features of our everyday psychological explanations that prevent these explanations from ever becoming scientific. Davidson argues that psychological explanations attributing PROPOSITIONAL ATTITUDES are governed by normative principles: In ascribing a propositional attitude to a person, we aim to make that person's thought and action as reasonable as possible (for related views, see McDowell 1985; Child 1994). In natural science, no comparable normative principles are employed. It is this dependence on the "constitutive ideal of rationality" that prevents a psychology purporting to deal with the propositional attitudes from ever becoming scientific—in the sense that physics is scientific. According to Davidson, decision theory is an attempt to systematize ordinary explanations of actions in terms of belief and desire, by employing quantitative measures of degrees of belief and desire. But because of the irreducibly normative element involved in propositional attitude explanation, decision theory can never be a natural science (for more on this subject, see Davidson 1995). Where the "layered world" picture typically combines a defense of metaphysical autonomy with an acceptance of the properly scientific (or potentially scientific) nature of all psychological explanation, Davidson's ANOMALOUS MONISM combines strong explanatory autonomy with an identity theory of mental and physical events.

See also BRENTANO; INTENTIONALITY; PSYCHOLOGICAL LAWS; RATIONALISM VS. EMPIRICISM

— *Tim Crane*

References

Carnap, R. (1932–1933). Psychology in physical language. *Erkenntnis* 3.

Child, W. (1994). *Causality, Interpretation and the Mind.* Oxford: Clarendon Press.

Cummins, R. (1983). *The Nature of Psychological Explanation.* Cambridge, MA: MIT Press.

Davidson, D. (1970). Mental events. In L. Foster and J. Swanson, Eds., *Experience and Theory.* London: Duckworth, pp. 79–101.

Davidson, D. (1995). Can there be a science of rationality? *International Journal of Philosophical Studies* 3.

Feigl, H. (1981). Physicalism, unity of science and the foundations of psychology. In Feigl, *Inquiries and Provocations.* Dordrecht: Reidel.

Fodor, J. (1974). Special sciences: The disunity of science as a working hypothesis. *Synthèse* 28.

Hobbes, T. (1651). *Leviathan.* Harmondsworth, England: Penguin Books, 1968.

Hume, D. (1739–1740). *A Treatise of Human Nature.* 2nd ed. Oxford: Clarendon Press, 1978.

La Mettrie, J. (1748). *Man the Machine.* Cambridge: Cambridge University Press, 1996.

Lewis, D. (1994). Reduction of mind. In S. Guttenplan, Ed., *A Companion to the Philosophy of Mind.* Oxford: Blackwell, pp. 412–431.

Marr, D. (1982). *Vision.* San Francisco: Freeman.

McDowell, J. (1985). Functionalism and anomalous monism. In E. LePore and B. Mclaughlin, Eds., *Actions and Events: Perspectives on the Philosophy of Donald Davidson.* Oxford: Blackwell.

Oppenheim, P., and H. Putnam. (1958). The unity of science as a working hypothesis. In H. Feigl and G. Maxwell, Eds., *Minnesota Studies in the Philosophy of Science.* Minneapolis: University of Minnesota Press.

Owens, D. (1989). Levels of explanation. *Mind* 98.

Putnam, H. (1975). The nature of mental states. In Putnam, *Philosophical Papers,* vol. 2. Cambridge: Cambridge University Press.

Reed, E. (1994). The separation of psychology from philosophy: Studies in the sciences of mind, 1815–1879. In S. Shanker, Ed., *Routledge History of Philosophy: The 19th Century.* London: Routledge.

Smart, J. J. C. (1959). Sensations and brain processes. *Philosophical Review* 68.

Autopoiesis

See SELF-ORGANIZING SYSTEMS

Backpropagation

See NEURAL NETWORKS; RECURRENT NETWORKS

Bartlett, Frederic Charles

Frederic C. Bartlett (1886–1969) was Britain's most outstanding psychologist between the World Wars. He was a cognitive psychologist long before the cognitive revolution of the 1960s. His three major contributions to current cognitive science are a methodological argument for the study of "ecologically valid" experimental tasks, a reconstructive approach to human memory, and the theoretical construct of the "schema" to represent generic knowledge.

Receiving a bachelor's degree in philosophy from the University of London (1909), Bartlett carried out additional undergraduate work in the moral sciences at Cambridge University (1914), where he later became director of the Cambridge Psychological Laboratory (1922) and was eventually appointed the first Professor of Experimental Psychology at Cambridge (1931). He was made Fellow of the Royal Society in 1932 and knighted in 1948.

Bartlett's unique position in the development of psychology derived in part from his multidisciplinary background. At London and also later at Cambridge, Bartlett was influenced by the philosophy of James Ward and George Stout (Bartlett 1936), who developed systems that were antiatomist and antiassociationist, as opposed to the traditional British empiricist view. At Cambridge, Bartlett's major intellectual influences were C. S. Myers and W. H. R. Rivers. Although both had been trained as physicians, Myers was an experimental psychologist and Rivers a cultural and physical anthropologist when Bartlett studied with them there. It was Myers who introduced Bartlett to German laboratory psychology with a particular focus on PSYCHOPHYSICS.

His work with Rivers had a strong impact on Bartlett's thinking. He published a number of books and papers devoted to social issues and the role of psychology in anthropological research (Harris and Zangwill 1973). The anthropological study of the conventionalization of human cultural artifacts over time served as a principal source of Bartlett's ideas about schemata. Recently social constructivists (Costall 1992) have argued that if psychology had followed Bartlett's early writings on these topics, the field would now be much more of a social-based discipline than it is.

As a young faculty member, Bartlett had extensive interactions with the neurologist Henry Head. While Bartlett never directly concerned himself with neurophysiological research (Broadbent 1970; Zangwill 1972), he provided intellectual support for a number of students who went on to become the first generation of British neuropsychologists (e.g., Oliver Zangwill, Brenda Milner). Bartlett's discussions with Henry Head about physiological "schemata" (used to account for aspects of human posture) was another important source of Bartlett's thinking on the psychological construct of "schema" (cf. Bartlett 1932).

Through a complex series of events that occurred late in his career, Bartlett had a direct hand in initiating the information-processing framework that is a major component of current cognitive science. During World War II, a brilliant young student named Kenneth Craik came to Cambridge to work with Bartlett. Craik carried out early work on control engineering and cybernetics, only to be killed in a bicycle accident the day before World War II ended. Bartlett was able to see the importance of Craik's approach and took over its development. Donald BROADBENT, in his autobiography (1980), notes that when he arrived at Cambridge after the war, he was exposed to a completely original point of view about how to analyze human behavior. Broadbent went on to develop the first information-processing box models of human behavior (cf. Weiskrantz 1994).

Bartlett worked on applied problems throughout his career, believing that in an effort to isolate and gain control of psychological processes, much laboratory research in psychology missed important phenomena that occurred in more natural settings. This argument for ECOLOGICAL VALIDITY (e.g., Neisser 1978) makes up an important subtheme in current cognitive science (see also ECOLOGICAL PSYCHOLOGY).

Bartlett's methodological preference for ecologically valid tasks led him to reject the traditional approach to the study of human memory that involved learning lists of nonsense syllables. In his book *Remembering* (1932), Bartlett reported a series of memory studies that used a broader range of material, including texts of folktales from Native American cultures. Bartlett focused not on the number of correct words recalled, but on the nature of the changes made in the recalls. He found that individuals recalling this type of material made inferences and other changes that led to a more concise and coherent story (conventionalization). Overall, Bartlett concluded that human memory is not a reproductive but a reconstructive process. Although Bartlett's approach made little impact on laboratory memory research at the time, with the advent of the cognitive revolution (e.g., Neisser 1967), his ideas became an integral part of the study of human MEMORY, and by the early 1980s, his book *Remembering* was the second most widely cited work in the area of human memory (White 1983).

To account for his memory data, Bartlett developed the concept of the "schema" (see SCHEMATA). He proposed that much of human knowledge consists of unconscious mental structures that capture the generic aspects of the world (cf. Brewer and Nakamura 1984). He argued that the changes he found in story recall could be accounted for by assuming that "schemata" operate on new incoming information to fill in gaps and rationalize the resulting memory representation. Bartlett's schema concept had little impact on memory research in his lifetime, and, in fact, at the time of his death, his own students considered it to have been a failure (Broadbent 1970; Zangwill 1972). However, the schema construct made an impressive comeback in the hands of computer scientist Marvin Minsky. In the early stages of the development of the field of artificial intelligence (AI), Minsky was concerned about the difficulty of designing computer models to exhibit human intelligence. He read Bartlett's 1932 book and concluded that humans were using top-down schema-based information to carry out many psychological tasks. In a famous paper, Minsky (1975) proposed the use of frames (i.e., schemata) to capture the needed top-down knowledge. In its new form, the schema construct has widely influenced psychological research on human memory (Brewer and Nakamura 1984) and the field of AI.

See also FRAME-BASED SYSTEMS; INFORMATION THEORY; MENTAL MODELS; TOP-DOWN PROCESSING IN VISION

— *William F. Brewer*

References

Bartlett, F. C. (1932). *Remembering*. Cambridge: Cambridge University Press.

Bartlett, F. C. (1936). Frederic Charles Bartlett. In C. Murchison, Ed., *A History of Psychology in Autobiography*, vol. 3. Worcester, MA: Clark University Press, pp. 39–52.

Brewer, W. F., and G. V. Nakamura. (1984). The nature and functions of schemas. In R. S. Wyer, Jr., and T. K. Srull, Eds., *Handbook of Social Cognition*, vol. 1. Hillsdale, NJ: Erlbaum, pp. 119–160.

Broadbent, D. E. (1970). Frederic Charles Bartlett. In *Biographical Memoirs of Fellows of the Royal Society*, vol. 16. London: Royal Society, pp. 1–13.

Broadbent, D. E. (1980). Donald E. Broadbent. In G. Lindzey, Ed., *A History of Psychology in Autobiography*, vol. 7. San Francisco: Freeman, pp. 39–73.

Costall, A. (1992). Why British psychology is not social: Frederic Bartlett's promotion of the new academic discipline. *Canadian Psychology* 33: 633–639.

Harris, A. D., and O. L. Zangwill. (1973). The writings of Sir Frederic Bartlett, C.B.E., F.R.S.: An annotated handlist. *British Journal of Psychology* 64: 493–510.

Minsky, M. (1975). A framework for representing knowledge. In P. H. Winston, Ed., *The Psychology of Computer Vision*. New York: McGraw-Hill, pp. 211–277.

Neisser, U. (1967). *Cognitive Psychology*. New York: Appleton-Century-Crofts.

Neisser, U. (1978). Memory: What are the important questions? In M. M. Gruneberg, P. E. Morris, and R. N. Sykes, Eds., *Practical Aspects of Memory*. London: Academic Press, pp. 3–14.

Weiskrantz, L. (1994). Donald Eric Broadbent. In *Biographical Memoirs of Fellows of the Royal Society*, vol. 40. London: Royal Society, pp. 33–42.

White, M. J. (1983). Prominent publications in cognitive psychology. *Memory and Cognition* 11: 423–427.

Zangwill, O. L. (1972). Remembering revisited. *Quarterly Journal of Experimental Psychology* 24: 123–138.

Basal Ganglia

The CEREBRAL CORTEX is massively interconnected with a large group of subcortical structures known as the "basal ganglia." In general, the basal ganglia can be described as a set of input structures that receive direct input from the cerebral cortex, and output structures that project back to the cerebral cortex via the THALAMUS. Thus a major feature of basal ganglia anatomy is their participation in multiple loops with the cerebral cortex, termed *cortico-basal ganglia-thalamo-cortical circuits* (see Alexander, DeLong, and Strick 1986, figure 1).

Although the term *basal ganglia* was first used to indicate the putamen and globus pallidus (Ringer 1879), it now refers to the striatum, globus pallidus, subthalamic nucleus (STN), and substantia nigra. The striatum has three subdivisions, the caudate, putamen, and ventral striatum, that together form the main input structures of the basal ganglia. The globus pallidus consists of an external segment (GPe) and an internal segment (GPi). The GPe and STN are thought to represent "intermediate" basal ganglia structures, although the STN also receives some direct cortical inputs. The substantia nigra comprises two major cell groups, the pars compacta (SNpc) and pars reticulata (SNpr). The SNpr and GPi are the major output structures of the basal ganglia.

There has been considerable progress in defining the intrinsic organization of basal ganglia circuits (see Parent and Hazrati 1995). Briefly, inputs from the cerebral cortex to the striatum use glutamate (GLU) as an excitatory neurotransmitter to synapse on medium-sized (12–20 μm) spiny stellate neurons, which are also the projection or output neurons of the striatum. Most of the cortical input terminates in striatal regions known as the "matrix," which contain high levels of acetylcholinesterase, the enzyme responsible for breaking down the neurotransmitter acetylcholine (Ragsdale and Graybiel 1981). Efferents from other cortical areas terminate in striatal regions termed "patches" or "striosomes," which have low levels of acetylcholinesterase. In addition to these differences in afferent input, the medium spiny stellate cells in the striosomes and matrix also have different efferent connections. Output cells in striosomes project to neurons in SNpc that produce the neurotransmitter dopamine. The axons of these SNpc cells project back to the striatum, where they release dopamine. The net effect of dopamine on striatal cells depends on the type of receptors present.

Output neurons in the matrix project to GPe, GPi, or SNpr. These striatal cells use the neurotransmitter gamma-aminobutyric acid (GABA) to inhibit their targets. The matrix cells projecting to GPi or SNpr express high levels of a neuropeptide called "substance P (SP)" and are excited by the action of dopamine on their D1 receptors. In contrast, matrix cells projecting to GPe express high levels of enkephalin (ENK) and are inhibited by the action of dopamine on their D2 receptors (figure 1).

Efferents from GPe project largely to the STN, GPi and SNpr and use GABA to inhibit their targets. Neurons in the STN project to GPi or SNpr where they use GLU to excite neurons in both structures (figure 1). There is also evidence

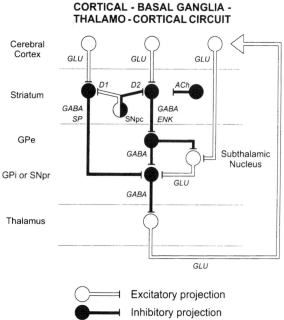

**CORTICAL - BASAL GANGLIA -
THALAMO - CORTICAL CIRCUIT**

Cerebral Cortex

Striatum

GPe

GPi or SNpr

Thalamus

⊸⊣ Excitatory projection

●━┨ Inhibitory projection

Figure 1.

for GPe projections to the reticular nucleus of the thalamus, but the significance of this projection is unknown.

Neurons in the GPi and SNpr are the principal outputs of the basal ganglia. These neurons innervate a specific set of thalamic nuclei and use GABA as an inhibitory transmitter. Output neurons in the thalamus that receive basal ganglia input use GLU as a neurotransmitter to excite their targets. Although some of these thalamic neurons project back to the striatum, and thus form a closed feedback loop with the basal ganglia, the major output from the basal ganglia is to thalamic neurons that in turn project to the cerebral cortex. This pathway forms the efferent limb of the cortico-basal ganglia-thalamocortical circuit. Output neurons in SNpr and GPi also project to brain stem nuclei such as the superior colliculus and pedunculopontine nucleus. The projection to the colliculus appears to play a role in the generation of eye and head movements. The function of the pedunculopontine projection is more obscure. Pedunculopontine neurons appear to largely project back upon SNpc, GPi, and STN.

Recently, there have been some dramatic changes in concepts about the function of basal ganglia loops with the cerebral cortex. These loops were thought to collect inputs from widespread cortical areas in the frontal, parietal, and temporal lobes and to "funnel" this information back to the primary motor cortex or other cortical motor areas for use in MOTOR CONTROL (Kemp and Powell 1971). New observations have led to the suggestion that basal ganglia loops are involved in a much more diverse range of behavior including MOTOR LEARNING and cognition. For example, Alexander, DeLong and Strick (1986) have proposed that basal ganglia output targeted at least five regions of the frontal lobe: two cortical areas concerned with skeletomotor and OCULOMOTOR CONTROL, and three regions of the prefrontal cortex involved in WORKING MEMORY, ATTENTION, and emotional behavior.

Subsequent experiments have supported this proposal and also suggested that basal ganglia-thalamocortical projections to the frontal lobe are topographically organized into discrete output channels (Hoover and Strick 1993; Middleton and Strick 1994). Furthermore, it is now apparent that basal ganglia output is directed to cortical areas outside the frontal lobe, including a region of the temporal lobe involved in visual processing (Middleton and Strick 1996a). Thus the anatomical substrate exists for basal ganglia output to influence multiple motor and nonmotor areas of the cerebral cortex. Consequently, current views of basal ganglia function emphasize the impact these subcortical nuclei may have on a broad spectrum of behavior.

Several lines of evidence implicate the basal ganglia in forms of "habit learning" that involve the creation of novel associations between stimuli and responses. For example, individuals with Parkinson's disease (PD) or Huntington's disease (HD) have been shown to be impaired in the performance of tasks that depend on habit learning (Knowlton, Mangels, and Squire 1996; Knowlton et al. 1996). Both PD and HD arise from the degeneration of specific cell groups in the basal ganglia (the SNpc and striatum, respectively). Interestingly, SINGLE-NEURON RECORDING studies in monkeys have shown that "tonically active neurons" in the striatum change their firing properties as an association is built between a specific sensory stimulus and an appropriate motor response (Aosaki et al. 1994). These neurons are thought to be large (50–60 μm) aspiny cholinergic interneurons. Similarly, some neurons in the SNpc are preferentially activated by appetitive rewards or stimuli that predict the occurrence of such rewards. Together, these striatal and nigral neurons may form part of the neural substrate underlying behavioral reinforcement (Schultz, Dayan, and Montague 1997).

Other forms of learning also appear to be influenced by the basal ganglia. Physiological studies have shown that portions of the striatum and pallidum are activated during the performance of tasks that require learning a sequence of movements (Jenkins et al. 1994; Mushiake and Strick 1995; Kermadi and Joseph 1995). Moreover, some patients with PD and HD are selectively impaired on motor learning tasks, but not on other forms of learning (Heindel et al. 1989). These observations suggest that the basal ganglia may play a critical role in what has been termed *procedural* or *motor-skill learning*.

There is also evidence to support the involvement of the basal ganglia in non-motor cognitive processes. First, some neurons in the basal ganglia display activity related to sensory and cognitive functions but not motor responses (Hikosaka and Wurtz 1983; Mushiake and Strick 1995; Brown, Desimone, and Mishkin 1996). Second, some individuals with PD and HD have striking cognitive and visual deficits, such as impaired recognition of faces and facial expressions, that actually precede the development of prominent motor symptoms (Jacobs, Shuren, and Heilman 1995a,b). Third, other patients with basal ganglia lesions exhibit profound cognitive, visual, and sensory disturbances. For example, lesions of the globus pallidus or SNpr have been reported to produce working memory deficits, obsessive-compulsive behavior, apathy, and visual hallucinations (Laplane et al.

1989; McKee et al. 1990). There is also growing evidence that alterations in the basal ganglia accompany disorders such as schizophrenia, depression, obsessive-compulsive disorder, Tourette's syndrome, AUTISM, and attention deficit disorder (for references, see Middleton and Strick 1996b; Castellanos et al. 1996). Finally, the current animal model of PD uses high doses of a neurotoxin called MPTP (1-methyl-4-phenyl-1,2,3,6-tetrahydropyridine) to reproduce the neuropathology and motor symptoms of this disorder with remarkable fidelity. However, chronic low-dose treatment of monkeys with this compound has been shown to cause cognitive and visual deficits, without gross motor impairments (Schneider and Pope-Coleman 1995).

Taken together, existing anatomical, physiological, and behavioral data suggest that the basal ganglia are not only involved in the control of movement, but also have the potential to influence diverse aspects of behavior. Future research will be needed to determine the full extent of the cerebral cortex influenced by basal ganglia output, the physiological consequences of this influence, and the functional operations performed by basal ganglia circuitry.

See also NEUROTRANSMITTERS

—*Peter L. Strick and Frank Middleton*

References

Alexander, G. E., M. R. DeLong, and P. L. Strick. (1986). Parallel organization of functionally segregated circuits linking basal ganglia and cortex. *Annual Review of Neuroscience* 9: 357–381.

Aosaki, T., H. Tsubokawa, A. Ishida, K. Watanabe, A. M. Graybiel, and M. Kimura. (1994). Responses of tonically active neurons in the primate's striatum undergo systematic changes during behavioral sensorimotor conditioning. *Journal of Neuroscience* 14: 3969-3984.

Brown, V. J., R. Desimone, and M. Mishkin. (1996). Responses of cells in the tail of the caudate nucleus during visual discrimination learning. *Journal of Neurophysiology* 74:1083–1094.

Castellanos, F. X., J. N. Giedd, W. L. Marsh, S. D. Hamburger, A. C. Vaituzis, D. P. Dickstein, S. E. Sarfatti, Y. C Vauss, J. W. Snell, N. Lange, D. Kaysen, A. L. Krain, G. F. Ritchie, J. C. Rajapakse, and J. L. Rapoport. (1996). Quantitative brain magnetic resonance imaging in attention deficit hyperactivity disorder. *Archives of General Psychiatry* 53: 607–616.

Heindel, W. C., D. P. Salmon, C. W. Shults, P. A. Walicke, and N. Butters. (1989). Neuropsychological evidence for multiple implicit memory systems: A comparison of Alzheimer's, Huntington's, and Parkinson's disease patients. *Journal of Neuroscience* 9: 582–587.

Hikosaka, O., and R. H. Wurtz. (1983). Visual and oculomotor functions of monkey substantia nigra pars reticulata: 1. Relation of visual and auditory responses to saccades. *Journal of Neurophysiology* 49: 1230–1253.

Hoover, J. E., and P. L. Strick. (1993). Multiple output channels in the basal ganglia. *Science* 259: 819–821.

Jacobs, D. H., J. Shuren, and K. M. Heilman. (1995a). Impaired perception of facial identity and facial affect in Huntington's disease. *Neurology* 45: 1217–1218.

Jacobs, D. H., J. Shuren, and K. M. Heilman. (1995b). Emotional facial imagery, perception, and expression in Parkinson's disease. *Neurology* 45: 1696–1702.

Jenkins, I. H., D. J. Brooks, P. D. Nixon, R. S. Frackowiak, and R. E. Passingham. (1994). Motor sequence learning: A study with positron-emission tomography. *Journal of Neuroscience* 14: 3775–3790.

Kemp, J. M., and T. P. S. Powell. (1971). The connexions of the striatum and globus pallidus: synthesis and speculation. *Philosophical Transactions of the Royal Society of London,* B262: 441–457.

Kermadi, I., and J. P. Joseph. (1995). Activity in the caudate nucleus of monkey during spatial sequencing. *Journal of Neurophysiology* 74: 911–933.

Knowlton, B. J., J. A. Mangels, and L. R. Squire. (1996). A neostriatal habit learning system in humans. *Science* 273: 1399–1402.

Knowlton, B. J., L. R. Squire, J. S. Paulsen, N. R. Swerdlow, M. Swenson, and N. Butters. (1996). Dissociations within nondeclarative memory in Huntington's disease. *Neuropsychology* 10: 538–548.

Laplane, D., M. Levasseur, B. Pillon, B. Dubois, M. Baulac, B. Mazoyer, S. Tran Dinh, G. Sette, F. Danze, and J. C. Baron. (1989). Obsessive-compulsive and other behavioural changes with bilateral basal ganglia lesions. *Brain* 112: 699–725.

McKee, A. C., D. N. Levine, N. W. Kowall, and E. P. Richardson. (1990). Peduncular hallucinosis associated with isolated infarction of the substantia nigra pars reticulata. *Annals of Neurology* 27: 500–504.

Middleton, F. A., and P. L. Strick. (1994). Anatomical evidence for cerebellar and basal ganglia involvement in higher cognitive function. *Science* 266: 458–461.

Middleton, F. A., and P. L. Strick. (1996a). The temporal lobe is a target of output from the basal ganglia. *Proceedings of the National Academy of Sciences, U.S.A.* 93: 8683–8687.

Middleton, F. A., and P.L. Strick. (1996b). Basal ganglia and cerebellar output influences non-motor function. *Molecular Psychiatry* 1: 429–433.

Mushiake, H., and P.L. Strick. (1995). Pallidal neuron activity during sequential arm movements. *Journal of Neurophysiology* 74: 2754–2758.

Parent, A., and L.-N. Hazrati. (1995). Functional anatomy of the basal ganglia: 1. The cortico-basal ganglia-thalamo-cortical loop. *Brain Research Reviews* 20: 91–127.

Ragsdale, C. W., and A. M. Graybiel. (1981). The fronto-striatal projection in the cat and monkey and its relationship to inhomogeneities established by acetylcholinesterase histochemistry. *Brain Research* 208: 259–266.

Ringer, S. (1879). Notes of a postmortem examination on a case of athetosis. *Practitioner* 23: 161.

Schneider, J. S., and A. Pope-Coleman. (1995). Cognitive deficits precede motor deficits in a slowly progressing model of parkinsonism in the monkey. *Neurodegeneration* 4: 245–255.

Schultz, W., P. Dayan, and P. R. Montague. (1997). A neural substrate of prediction and reward. *Science* 275: 1593–1599.

Further Readings

Albin, R. L., A. B. Young, and J. B. Penney. (1989). The functional anatomy of basal ganglia disorders. *Trends in Neuroscience* 12: 355-375.

Brown, L. L., J. S. Schneider, and T.I. Lidsky. (1997). Sensory and cognitive functions of the basal ganglia. *Current Opinion in Neurobiology* 7: 157–163.

Carpenter, M. B., K. Nakano, and R. Kim. (1976). Nigrothalamic projections in the monkey demonstrated by autoradiographic technics. *Journal of Comparative Neurology* 165: 401–416.

Cummings, J. L. (1993). Frontal-subcortical circuits and human behavior. *Archives of Neurology* 50: 873–880.

DeLong, M. R. (1990). Primate models of movement disorders. *Trends in Neuroscience* 13: 281–285.

DeVito, J. L., and M. E. Anderson. (1982). An autoradiographic study of efferent connections of the globus pallidus in *Macaca mulatta*. *Experimental Brain Research* 46: 107–117.

Divac, I., H. E. Rosvold, and M. K. Swarcbart. (1967). Behavioral effects of selective ablation of the caudate nucleus. *Journal of Comparative and Physiological Psychology* 63: 184–190.

Dubois, B., and B. Pillon. (1997). Cognitive deficits in Parkinson's disease. *Journal of Neurology* 244: 2–8.

Eblen, F., and A. M. Graybiel. (1995). Highly restricted origin of prefrontal cortical inputs to striosomes in the macaque monkey. *Journal of Neuroscience* 15: 5999–6013.

Gerfen, C. R. (1984). The neostriatal mosaic: Compartmentalization of corticostriatal input and striatonigral output systems. *Nature* 311: 461–464.

Goldman, P. S., and W. J. H. Nauta. (1977). An intricately patterned prefronto-caudate projection in the rhesus monkey. *Journal of Comparative Neurology* 171: 369–386.

Graybiel, A. M. (1995). Building action repertoires: Memory and learning functions of the basal ganglia. *Current Opinion in Neurobiology* 5: 733–741.

Ilinsky, I. A., M. Jouandet, and P. S. Goldman-Rakic. (1985). Organization of the nigrothalamocortical system in the rhesus monkey. *Journal of Comparative Neurology* 236: 315–330.

Kim, R., K. Nakano, A. Jayarman, and M. B. Carpenter. (1976). Projections of the globus pallidus and adjacent structures: An autoradiographic study in the monkey. *Journal of Comparative Neurology* 169: 263–290.

Lawrence, A. D., B. J. Sahakian, J. R. Hodges, A. E. Rosser, K. W. Lange, and T. W. Robbins. (1996). Executive and mnemonic functions in early Huntington's disease. *Brain* 119: 1633–1645.

Nauta, W. J. H., and W. R. Mehler. (1966). Projections of the lentiform nucleus in the monkey. *Brain Research* 1: 3–42.

Percheron, G., C. Francois, B. Talbi, J. Yelnik, and G. Fenelon. (1996). The primate motor thalamus. *Brain Research Reviews* 22: 93–181.

Pillon, B., S. Ertle, B. Deweer, M. Sarazin, Y. Agid, and B. Dubois. (1996). Memory for spatial location is affected in Parkinson's disease. *Neuropsychologica* 34: 77–85.

Saint-Cyr, J. A., L. G. Ungerleider, and R. Desimone. (1990). Organization of visual cortical inputs to the striatum and subsequent outputs to the pallido-nigral complex in the monkey. *Journal of Comparative Neurology* 298: 129–156.

Salmon, D. P., and N. Butters. (1995). Neurobiology of skill and habit learning. *Current Opinion in Neurobiology* 5: 184–190.

Schultz, W. (1997). Dopamine neurons and their role in reward mechanisms. *Current Opinion in Neurobiology* 7: 191–197.

Selemon, L. D., and P. S. Goldman-Rakic. (1985). Longitudinal topography and interdigitation of corticostriatal projections in the rhesus monkey. *Journal of Neuroscience* 5: 776–794.

Strub, R. L. (1989). Frontal lobe syndrome in a patient with bilateral globus pallidus lesions. *Archives of Neurology* 46: 1024–1027.

Taylor, A. E., and J. A. Saint-Cyr. (1995). The neuropsychology of Parkinson's disease. *Brain and Cognition* 23: 281–296.

Wise, S. P., E. A. Murray, and C. R. Gerfen. (1996). The frontal cortex-basal ganglia system in primates. *Critical Reviews in Neurobiology* 10: 317–356.

Bayesian Learning

The Bayesian approach views all model learning—whether of parameters, structure, or both—as the reduction of a user's UNCERTAINTY about the model given data. Furthermore, it encodes all uncertainty about model parameters and structure as probabilities.

Bayesian learning has two distinct advantages over classical learning. First, it combines prior knowledge and data, as opposed to classical learning, which does not explicitly incorporate user or prior knowledge, so that ad hoc methods are needed to combine knowledge and data (see also MACHINE LEARNING). Second, Bayesian learning methods have a built-in Occam's razor—there is no need to introduce external methods to avoid overfitting (see Heckerman 1995).

To illustrate with an example taken from Howard 1970, consider a common thumbtack—one with a round, flat head that can be found in most supermarkets. If we toss the thumbtack into the air, it will come to rest either on its point *(heads)* or on its head *(tails)*. Suppose we flip the thumbtack $N + 1$ times, making sure that the physical properties of the thumbtack and the conditions under which it is flipped remain stable over time. From the first N observations, we want to determine the probability of heads on the $(N + 1)$th toss.

In a classical analysis of this problem, we assert that there is some true probability of heads, which is unknown. We *estimate* this true probability from the N observations using criteria such as low bias and low variance. We then use this estimate as our probability for heads on the $(N + 1)$th toss. In the Bayesian approach, we also assert that there is some true probability of heads, but we encode our uncertainty about this true probability using the rules of probability to compute our probability for heads on the $(N + 1)$th toss.

To undertake a Bayesian analysis of this problem, we need some notation. We denote a variable by an uppercase letter (e.g., X, X_i, Θ), and the state or value of a corresponding variable by that same letter in lowercase (e.g., x, x_i, θ). We denote a set of variables by a boldface uppercase letter (e.g., $\mathbf{X}$, $\mathbf{X_i}$, $\mathbf{\Theta}$). We use a corresponding boldface lowercase letter (e.g., $\mathbf{x}$, $\mathbf{x_i}$, $\mathbf{\theta}$) to denote an assignment of state or value to each variable in a given set. We use $p(X = x \mid \xi)$, or $p(x \mid \xi)$ as a shorthand, to denote the probability that $X = x$ of a person with state of information ξ. We also use $p(x \mid \xi)$ to denote the probability distribution for X (both mass functions and density functions). Whether $p(x \mid \xi)$ refers to a probability, a probability density, or a probability distribution will be clear from context.

Returning to the thumbtack problem, we define Θ to be a variable whose values θ correspond to the possible true values of the probability of heads. We express the uncertainty about Θ using the probability density function $p(\theta \mid \xi)$. In addition, we use X_1 to denote the variable representing the outcome of the lth flip, $l = 1, \ldots, N + 1$, and $D = \{X_1 = x_1, \ldots, X_N = x_N\}$ to denote the set of our observations. Thus, in Bayesian terms, the thumbtack problem reduces to computing $p(x_{N+1} \mid D, \xi)$ from $p(\theta \mid \xi)$.

To do so, we first use Bayes's rule to obtain the probability distribution for Θ given D and background knowledge ξ:

$$p(\theta \mid D, \xi) = \frac{p(\theta \mid \xi) p(D \mid \theta, \xi)}{p(D \mid \xi)} \qquad (1)$$

where

$$p(D \mid \xi) = \int p(D \mid \theta, \xi) p(\theta \mid \xi) \, d\theta \qquad (2)$$

Next, we expand the *likelihood* $p(D|\theta, \xi)$. Both Bayesians and classical statisticians agree on this term. In particular, given the value of Θ, the observations in D are mutually independent, and the probability of heads (tails) on any one observation is θ $(1-\theta)$. Consequently, equation 1 becomes

$$p(\theta|D, \xi) = \frac{p(\theta|\xi)\theta^{h}(1-\theta)^{t}}{p(D|\xi)} \qquad (3)$$

where h and t are the number of heads and tails observed in D, respectively. The observations D represent a random sample from the binomial distribution parameterized by θ; the probability distributions $p(\theta \mid \xi)$ and $p(\theta \mid D, \xi)$ are commonly referred to as the "prior" and "posterior" for Θ, respectively; and the quantities h and t are said to be "sufficient statistics" for binomial sampling because they summarize the data sufficiently to compute the posterior from the prior.

To determine the probability that the $(N+1)$th toss of the thumbtack will come up heads, we use the expansion rule of probability to average over the possible values of Θ:

$$p(X_{N+1} = heads|D, \xi) \qquad (4)$$

$$= \int p(X_{N+1} = heads|(\theta, \xi)p(\theta|D, \xi)d\theta$$

$$= \int \theta p(\theta|D, \xi)d\theta \equiv E_{p(\theta|D, \xi)}(\theta)$$

where $E_{p(\theta|D, x)}(\theta)$ denotes the expectation of θ with respect to the distribution $p(\theta|D,\xi)$.

To complete the Bayesian analysis for this example, we need a method to assess the prior distribution for Θ. A common approach, usually adopted for convenience, is to assume that this distribution is a *beta distribution*:

$$p(\theta|\xi) = \text{Beta}(\theta|\alpha_h, \alpha_t) \equiv \qquad (5)$$

$$\frac{\Gamma(\alpha)}{\Gamma(\alpha_h)\Gamma(\alpha_t)}\theta^{\alpha_h - 1}(1-\theta)^{\alpha_t - 1}$$

where $\alpha_h > 0$ and $\alpha_t > 0$ are the parameters of the beta distribution, $\alpha = \alpha_h + \alpha_t$, and $\Gamma(\cdot)$ is the *gamma function* that satisfies $\Gamma(x+1) = x\Gamma(x)$ and $\Gamma(1) = 1$. The quantities α_h and α_t are often referred to as "hyperparameters" to distinguish them from the parameter θ. The hyperparameters α_h and α_t must be greater than zero so that the distribution can be normalized. Examples of beta distributions are shown in figure 1.

The beta prior is convenient for several reasons. By equation 3, the posterior distribution will also be a beta dis-

tribution:

$$p(\theta|D, \xi) \qquad (6)$$

$$= \frac{\Gamma(\alpha + N)}{\Gamma(\alpha_h + h)\Gamma(\alpha_t + t)}\theta^{\alpha_h + h - 1}(1-\theta)^{\alpha_t + t - 1}$$

$$= \text{Beta}(\theta|\alpha_h + h, \alpha_t + t)$$

We term the set of beta distributions a *conjugate family of distributions* for binomial sampling. Also, the expectation of θ with respect to this distribution has a simple form:

$$\int \theta \text{Beta}(\theta|\alpha_h, \alpha_t)d\theta = \frac{\alpha_h}{\alpha} \qquad (7)$$

Hence, given a beta prior, we have a simple expression for the probability of heads in the $(N+1)$th toss:

$$p(X_{N+1} = heads|D, \xi) = \frac{\alpha_h + h}{\alpha + N} \qquad (8)$$

Assuming $p(\theta|\xi)$ is a beta distribution, it can be assessed in a number of ways. For example, we can assess our probability for heads in the first toss of the thumbtack (e.g., using a probability wheel). Next, we can imagine having seen the outcomes of k flips, and reassess our probability for heads in the next toss. From equation 8, we have, for $k = 1$,

$$p(X_{N+1} = heads|\xi) = \frac{\alpha_h}{a_h + \alpha_t}$$

$$p(X_2 = heads|X_1 = heads, \varepsilon) = \frac{\alpha_2 + 1}{\alpha_h + \alpha_t + 1}$$

Given these probabilities, we can solve for α_h and α_t. This assessment technique is known as "the method of imagined future data." Other techniques for assessing beta distributions are discussed by Winkler (1967).

Although the beta prior is convenient, it is not accurate for some problems. For example, suppose we think that the thumbtack may have been purchased at a magic shop. In this case, a more appropriate prior may be a mixture of beta distributions—for example,

$$p(\theta|\xi)$$

$$= 0.4 \text{ Beta}(20, 1) + 0.4 \text{ Beta}(1, 20) + 0.2 \text{ Beta}(2, 2)$$

where 0.4 is our probability that the thumbtack is heavily weighted toward heads (tails). In effect, we have introduced an additional *hidden* or unobserved variable H, whose states correspond to the three possibilities: (1) thumbtack is biased toward heads, (2) thumbtack is biased toward tails, or (3) thumbtack is normal; and we have asserted that θ conditioned on each state of H is a beta distribution. In general, there are simple methods (e.g., the method of imagined future data) for determining whether or not a beta prior is an accurate reflection of one's beliefs. In those cases where the beta prior is inaccurate, an accurate prior can often be assessed by introducing additional hidden variables, as in this example.

So far, we have only considered observations drawn from a binomial distribution. To be more general, suppose our problem domain consists of variables $\mathbf{X} = (X_1, \ldots, X_n)$. In addition, suppose that we have some data $D = (x_1, \ldots, x_N)$,

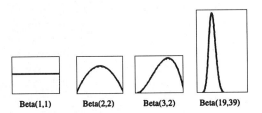

Beta(1,1)   Beta(2,2)   Beta(3,2)   Beta(19,39)

Figure 1. Several beta distributions.

which represent a random sample from some unknown (true) probability distribution for **X**. We assume that the unknown probability distribution can be encoded by some statistical model with structure **m** and parameters θ_m. Uncertain about the structure and parameters of the model, we take the Bayesian approach—we encode this uncertainty using probability. In particular, we define a discrete variable **M**, whose states **m** correspond to the possible true models, and encode our uncertainty about **M** with the probability distribution $p(\mathbf{m} \mid \xi)$. In addition, for each model structure **m**, we define a continuous vector-valued variable Θ_m, whose configurations θ_m correspond to the possible true parameters. We encode our uncertainty about Θ_m using the probability density function $p(\theta_m \mid \mathbf{m}, \xi)$.

Given random sample D, we compute the posterior distributions for each **m** and θ_m using Bayes's rule:

$$p(\mathbf{m}|D,\xi) = \frac{p(\mathbf{m}|\xi)p(D|\mathbf{m},\xi)}{\Sigma_{\mathbf{m}'}p(\mathbf{m}'|\xi)p(D|\mathbf{m}',\xi)} \qquad (9)$$

$$p(\theta_m|D,\mathbf{m},\xi) = \frac{p(\theta_m|\mathbf{m},\xi)p(D|\theta_m,\mathbf{m},\xi)}{p(D|\mathbf{m},\xi)} \qquad (10)$$

where

$$p(D|\mathbf{m},\xi)\int p(D|\theta_m,\mathbf{m},\xi)p(\theta_m|\mathbf{m},\xi)d\theta_m \qquad (11)$$

is the *marginal likelihood*. Given some hypothesis of interest, h, we determine the probability that h is true given data D by averaging over all possible models and their parameters according to the rules of probability:

$$p(h|D,\xi) = \sum_m p(\mathbf{m}|D,\xi)p(h|D,\mathbf{m},\xi) \qquad (12)$$

$$p(h|D,\mathbf{m},\xi) = \int p(h|\theta_m,\mathbf{m},\xi)p(\theta_m|D,\mathbf{m},\xi)d\theta_m \qquad (13)$$

For example, h may be the event that the next observation is x_{N+1}. In this situation, we obtain

$$p(x_{N+1}|D,\xi) \qquad (14)$$
$$= \sum_m p(\mathbf{m}|D,\xi)\int p(x_{N+1}|\theta_m,\mathbf{m},\xi)p(\theta_m|D,\mathbf{m},\xi)d\theta_m$$

where $p(\mathbf{x}_{N+1}|\theta_m,\mathbf{m},\xi)$ is the likelihood for the model. This approach is often referred to as "Bayesian model averaging." Note that no single model structure is learned. Instead, all possible models are weighted by their posterior probability.

Under certain conditions, the parameter posterior and marginal likelihood can be computed efficiently and in closed form. For example, such computation is possible when the likelihood is given by a BAYESIAN NETWORK (e.g., Heckerman 1998) and several other conditions are met. See Bernardo and Smith 1994, Lauritzen 1996, and Heckerman 1998 for a discussion.

When many model structures are possible, the sums in equations 9 and 12 can be intractable. In such situations, we can search for one or more model structures with large posterior probabilities, and use these models as if they were exhaustive—an approach known as "model selection." Examples of search methods applied to Bayesian networks are given by Heckerman, Geiger, and Chickering (1995) and Madigan et al. (1996).

See also HIDDEN MARKOV MODELS; PROBABILITY, FOUNDATIONS OF; PROBABILISTIC REASONING

—*David Heckerman*

References

Bernardo, J., and A. Smith. (1994). *Bayesian Theory*. New York: Wiley.

Heckerman, D. (1998). A tutorial on learning with Bayesian networks. In M. Jordan, Ed., *Learning in Graphical Models*. Kluwer, pp. 301–354

Heckerman, D., D. Geiger, and D. Chickering. (1995). Learning Bayesian networks: The combination of knowledge and statistical data. *Machine Learning* 20: 197–243.

Howard, R. (1970). Decision analysis: Perspectives on inference, decision, and experimentation. *Proceedings of the IEEE* 58: 632–643.

Lauritzen, S. (1996). *Graphical Models*. Oxford: Clarendon Press.

Madigan, D., A. Raftery, C. Volinsky, and J. Hoeting. (1996). Bayesian model averaging. *Proceedings of the AAAI Workshop on Integrating Multiple Learned Models*. Portland, OR.

Winkler, R. (1967). The assessment of prior distributions in Bayesian analysis. *American Statistical Association Journal* 62: 776–800.

Bayesian Networks

Bayesian networks were conceptualized in the late 1970s to model distributed processing in READING comprehension, where both semantical expectations and perceptual evidence must be combined to form a coherent interpretation. The ability to coordinate bidirectional inferences filled a void in EXPERT SYSTEMS technology of the early 1980s, and Bayesian networks have emerged as a general representation scheme for uncertain knowledge (Pearl 1988; Shafer and Pearl 1990; Heckerman, Mamdani, and Wellman 1995; Jensen 1996; Castillo, Gutierrez, and Hadi 1997).

Bayesian networks are directed acyclic graphs (DAGs) in which the nodes represent variables of interest (e.g., the temperature of a device, the gender of a patient, a feature of an object, the occurrence of an event) and the links represent informational or causal dependencies among the variables. The strength of a dependency is represented by conditional probabilities that are attached to each cluster of parent-child nodes in the network.

Figure 1 describes a simple yet typical Bayesian network: the causal relationships between the season of the year (X_1), whether rain falls (X_2) during the season, whether the sprinkler is on (X_3) during that season, whether the pavement would get wet (X_4), and whether the pavement would be slippery (X_5). Here the absence of a direct link between X_1 and X_5, for example, captures our understanding that the influence of seasonal variations on the slipperiness of the pavement is mediated by other conditions (e.g., wetness).

Figure 1. A Bayesian network representing causal influences among five variables.

As this example illustrates, a Bayesian network constitutes a model of the environment rather than, as in many other KNOWLEDGE REPRESENTATION schemes (e.g., rule-based systems and NEURAL NETWORKS), a model of the reasoning process. It simulates, in fact, the mechanisms that operate in the environment, and thus facilitates diverse modes of reasoning, including prediction, abduction, and control.

Prediction and abduction require an economical representation of a joint distribution over the variables involved. Bayesian networks achieve such economy by specifying, for each variable X_i, the conditional probabilities $P(x_i \mid pa_i)$ where pa_i is a set of predecessors (of X_i) that render X_i independent of all its other predecessors. Variables judged to be the direct causes of X_i satisfy this property, and these are depicted as the parents of X_i in the graph. Given this specification, the joint distribution is given by the product

$$P(x_1, \ldots, x_n) = \prod_i P(x_i \mid pa_i) \qquad (1)$$

from which all probabilistic queries (e.g., Find the most likely explanation for the evidence) can be answered coherently using probability calculus.

The first algorithms proposed for probabilistic calculations in Bayesian networks used message-passing architecture and were limited to trees (Pearl 1982; Kim and Pearl 1983). Each variable was assigned a simple processor and permitted to pass messages asynchronously with its neighbors until equilibrium was achieved. Techniques have since been developed to extend this tree propagation method to general networks. Among the most popular are Lauritzen and Spiegelhalter's (1988) method of join-tree propagation, and the method of cycle-cutset conditioning (see Pearl 1988, 204–210; Jensen 1996).

While inference in general networks is NP-hard, the COMPUTATIONAL COMPLEXITY for each of the methods cited above can be estimated prior to actual processing. When the estimates exceed reasonable bounds, an approximation method such as stochastic simulation (Pearl 1987; 1988, 210–223) can be used instead. Learning techniques have also been developed for systematically updating the conditional probabilities $P(x_i \mid pa_i)$ and the structure of the network, so as to match empirical data (see Spiegelhalter and Lauritzen 1990; Cooper and Herskovits 1990).

The most distinctive feature of Bayesian networks, stemming largely from their causal organization, is their ability to represent and respond to changing configurations. Any local reconfiguration of the mechanisms in the environment can be translated, with only minor modification, into an isomorphic reconfiguration of the network topology. For example, to represent a disabled sprinkler, we simply delete from the network all links incident to the node "Sprinkler." To represent the policy of turning the sprinkler off when it rains, we simply add a link between "Rain" and "Sprinkler" and revise $P(x_3 \mid x_1, x_2)$. This flexibility is often cited as the ingredient that marks the division between deliberative and reactive agents, and that enables deliberative agents to manage novel situations instantaneously, without requiring retraining or adaptation.

Organizing one's knowledge around stable causal mechanisms provides a basis for planning under UNCERTAINTY (Pearl 1996). Once we know the identity of the mechanism altered by the intervention and the nature of the alteration, the overall effect of an intervention can be predicted by modifying the corresponding factors in equation 1 and using the modified product to compute a new probability function. For example, to represent the action "turning the sprinkler ON" in the network of figure 1, we delete the link $X_1 \rightarrow X_3$ and fix the value of X_3 to ON. The resulting joint distribution on the remaining variables will be

$$P(x_1, x_2, x_4, x_5) \qquad (2)$$
$$= P(x_1)P(x_2 \mid x_1)P(x_4 \mid x_2, X_3 = \text{ON})P(x_5 \mid x_4)$$

Note the difference between the observation $X_3 = \text{ON}$, encoded by ordinary Bayesian conditioning, and the action $do(X_3 = \text{ON})$, encoded by conditioning a mutilated graph, with the link $X_1 \rightarrow X_3$ removed. This indeed mirrors the difference between seeing and doing: after observing that the sprinkler is ON, we wish to infer that the season is dry, that it probably did not rain, and so on; no such inferences should be drawn in evaluating the effects the contemplated action "turning the sprinkler ON."

One of the most exciting prospects in recent years has been the possibility of using Bayesian networks to discover causal structures in raw statistical data (Pearl and Verma 1991; Spirtes, Glymour, and Schienes 1993). Although any inference from association to CAUSATION is bound to be less reliable than one based on controlled experiment, we can still guarantee an aspect of reliability called "stability": Any alternative structure compatible with the data must be less stable than the structure inferred, which is to say, slight fluctuations in parameters will render that structure incompatible with the data. With this form of guarantee, the theory provides criteria for identifying genuine and spurious causes, with or without temporal information, and yields algorithms for recovering causal structures with hidden variables from empirical data.

In mundane decision making, beliefs are revised not by adjusting numerical probabilities but by tentatively accepting some sentences as "true for all practical purposes." Such sentences, called "plain beliefs," exhibit both logical and probabilistic character. As in classical LOGIC, they are propositional and deductively closed; as in probability, they are subject to retraction and to varying degrees of entrenchment. Bayesian networks can be adopted to model the dynamics of plain beliefs by replacing ordinary probabilities with nonstandard probabilities, that is, probabilities that are infinitesimally close to either zero or one (Goldszmidt and Pearl 1996).

Although Bayesian networks can model a wide spectrum of cognitive activity, their greatest strength is in CAUSAL REASONING, which in turn facilitates reasoning about actions, explanations, counterfactuals, and preferences. Such capabilities are not easily implemented in neural networks, whose strengths lie in quick adaptation of simple motor-visual functions.

Some questions arise: Does an architecture resembling that of Bayesian networks exist anywhere in the human brain? If not, how does the brain perform those cognitive functions at which Bayesian networks excel? A plausible answer to the second question is that fragmented structures of causal organizations are constantly being assembled on the fly, as needed, from a stock of functional building blocks. For example, the network of figure 1 may be assembled from several neural networks, one specializing in the experience surrounding seasons and rains, another in the properties of wet pavements, and so forth. Such specialized networks are probably stored permanently in some mental library, from which they are drawn and assembled into the structure shown in figure 1 only when a specific problem presents itself, for example, to determine whether an operating sprinkler could explain why a certain person slipped and broke a leg in the middle of a dry season.

Thus Bayesian networks are particularly useful in studying higher cognitive functions, where the problem of organizing and supervising large assemblies of specialized neural networks becomes important.

See also BAYESIAN LEARNING; PROBABILISTIC REASONING; PROBABILITY, FOUNDATIONS OF

—*Judea Pearl*

References

Castillo, E., J. M. Gutierrez, and A. S. Hadi. (1997). *Expert Systems and Probabilistic Network Models.* New York: Springer.

Cooper, G. F., and E. Herskovits. (1990). A Bayesian method for constructing Bayesian belief networks from databases. *Proceedings of the Conference on Uncertainty in AI,* pp. 86–94.

Goldszmidt, M., and J. Pearl. (1996). Qualitative probabilities for default reasoning, belief revision, and causal modeling. *Artificial Intelligence* 84(1–2): 57–112.

Heckerman, D., A. Mamdani, and M. P. Wellman, Guest Eds., (1995). Real-world applications of Bayesian networks. *Communications of the ACM* 38(3): 24–68.

Jensen, F. V. (1996). *An Introduction to Bayesian Networks.* New York: Springer.

Kim, J. H., and J. Pearl. (1983). A computational model for combined causal and diagnostic reasoning in inference systems. *Proceedings of IJCAI-83,* pp. 190–193. Karlsruhe, Germany.

Lauritzen, S. L., and D. J. Spiegelhalter. (1988). Local computations with probabilities on graphical structures and their application to expert systems. *Journal of the Royal Statistical Society Series B* 50(2): 157–224.

Pearl, J. (1982). Reverend Bayes on inference engines: A distributed hierarchical approach. *Proceedings of the AAAI National Conference on AI,* pp. 133–136. Pittsburgh.

Pearl, J. (1987). Evidential reasoning using stochastic simulation of causal models. *Artificial Intelligence* 32(2): 245–258.

Pearl, J. (1988). *Probabilistic Reasoning in Intelligent Systems.* San Mateo, CA: Morgan Kaufmann.

Pearl, J. (1996). Causation, action, and counterfactuals. In Y. Shoham, Ed., *Theoretical Aspects of Rationality and Knowledge: Proceedings of the Sixth Conference.* San Francisco: Morgan Kaufmann, pp. 51–73.

Pearl, J., and T. Verma. (1991). A theory of inferred causation. In J. A. Allen, R. Fikes, and E. Sandewall, Eds., *Principles of Knowledge Representation and Reasoning: Proceedings of the Second International Conference.* San Mateo, CA: Morgan Kaufmann, pp. 441–452.

Shafer, G., and J. Pearl, Eds. (1990). *Readings in Uncertain Reasoning.* San Mateo, CA: Morgan Kaufmann.

Spirtes, P., C. Glymour, and R. Schienes. (1993). *Causation, Prediction, and Search.* New York: Springer.

Spiegelhalter, D. J., and S. L. Lauritzen. (1990). Sequential updating of conditional probabilities on directed graphical structures. *Networks: An International Journal* 20(5): 579–605.

Behavior-Based Robotics

Behavior-based robotics (BBR) bridges the fields of artificial intelligence, engineering, and cognitive science. The behavior-based approach is a methodology for designing autonomous agents and robots; it is a type of INTELLIGENT AGENT ARCHITECTURE. Architectures supply structure and impose constraints on the way robot control problems are solved. The behavior-based methodology imposes a general, biologically inspired, bottom-up philosophy, allowing for a certain freedom of interpretation. Its goal is to develop methods for controlling artificial systems (usually physical robots, but also simulated robots and other autonomous software agents) and to use robotics to model and better understand biological systems (usually animals, ranging from insects to humans).

Behavior-based robotics controllers consist of a collection of behaviors that achieve and/or maintain goals. For example, "avoid-obstacles" maintains the goal of preventing collisions; "go-home" achieves the goal of reaching some home destination. Behaviors are implemented as control laws (sometimes similar to those used in CONTROL THEORY), either in software or hardware, as a processing element or a procedure. Each behavior can take inputs from the robot's sensors (e.g., camera, ultrasound, infrared, tactile) and/or from other behaviors in the system, and send outputs to the robot's effectors (e.g., wheels, grippers, arm, speech) and/or to other behaviors. Thus, a behavior-based controller is a structured network of interacting behaviors.

BBR is founded on subsumption architecture (Brooks 1986) and other work in reactive robotics (RR). RR achieves rapid real-time responses by embedding the robot's controller in a collection of preprogrammed, concurrent condition-action rules with minimal internal state (e.g., "if bumped, stop," "if stopped, back up"; Brooks and Connell 1986; Agre and Chapman 1987). Subsumption architecture provides a layered approach to assembling reactive rules into complete control systems from the bottom up. Rules, and layers of rules, are added incrementally; lower layers can function independently of the higher ones, and higher ones utilize the outputs of the lower ones, but do not override them. For example, "avoid-collision" at the lowest level, and "move-to-light" at a higher level, when combined, result in a robust light-chasing behavior; the higher-level rule never overrides the lower-level one, thus guaranteeing collision avoidance.

While robust, such reactive systems are limited by their lack of internal state; they are incapable of using internal representations and learning new behaviors. Behavior-based systems overcome this limitation because their underlying unit of representation, behaviors, can store state. The way state is represented and distributed in BBR is one of the sources of its novelty. Information is not centralized or centrally manipulated; instead, various forms of distributed representations are used, ranging from static table structures and networks to active, procedural processes implemented within the behavior networks.

In contrast to RR and BBR, both of which are structured and developed bottom-up, PLANNING-based deliberative control systems are top-down, and require the agent/robot to perform a sequence of processing sense-plan-act steps (e.g., "combine the sensory data into a map of the world, then use the planner to find a path in the map, then send steps of the plan to the robot's wheels"; Giralt, Chatila, and Vaisset 1983; Moravec and Elfes 1985; Laird and Rosenbloom 1990). Hybrid systems attempt a compromise between bottom-up and top-down by employing a reactive system for low-level control and a planner for high-level decision making (Firby 1987; Georgeoff and Lansky 1987; Arkin 1989; Payton 1990; Connell 1991). Often called "three-layer architectures," they separate the control system into three communicating but independent parts: (i) the planner, (ii) the reactive system, and (iii) the intermediate module, which reconciles the different time-scales and representations used by the other two and any conflicts between their outputs.

Behavior-based systems typically do not employ such a hierarchical division but are instead integrated through a homogeneous distributed representation. Like hybrid systems, they also provide both low-level control and high-level deliberation; the latter is performed by one or more distributed representations that compute over the other behaviors, often directly utilizing low-level behaviors and their outputs. The resulting system, built from the bottom-up, does not divide into differently represented and independent components as in hybrid systems, but instead constitutes an integrated computational behavior network. The power, elegance, and complexity of behavior-based systems all stem from the ways their constituent behaviors are defined and used.

Consequently, the organizational methodology of behavior-based systems differs from other control methods in its approach to modularity, the way in which the system is organized and subdivided into modules. Behavior-based philosophy mandates that the behaviors be relatively simple, added to the system incrementally, and not executed in a serial fashion. Subsets of behaviors are executed concurrently so that the system can exploit parallelism, both in the speed of computation and in the resulting dynamics that arise within the system itself (from the interaction among the behaviors) and with the environment (from the interaction of the behaviors with the external world). Behaviors can be designed at a variety of abstraction levels. In general they are higher than the robot's atomic actions (i.e., typically above "go-forward-by-a-small-increment," "turn-by-a-small-angle"), and they extend in time and space. Some implemented behaviors include: "go-home," "find-object," "get-recharged," "avoid-the-light," "aggregate-with-group," "pick-up-object," "find-landmark," etc. Because behaviors can be defined at different levels of abstraction and can represent various types of information, they are difficult to define precisely, but are also a rich medium for innovative interpretations.

Deciding what behavior to execute at a particular point in time is called *behavior arbitration,* and is one of the central design challenges of BBR. For simplicity, most implemented systems use a built-in, fixed priority for behaviors. More flexible solutions, which can be less computationally efficient and harder to analyze, are commonly based on computing some function of the behavior activation levels, such as a voting or activation spreading scheme (Maes 1989; Payton et al. 1992). Behavior-based systems are typically designed so the effects of the behaviors largely interact in the environment rather than internally through the system, taking advantage of the richness of interaction dynamics by exploiting the properties of SITUATEDNESS/EMBEDDEDNESS. These dynamics are sometimes called *emergent* behaviors because they *emerge* from the interactions and are not internally specified by the robot's program. Therefore, the internal behavior structure of a behavior-based system need not necessarily mirror its externally manifested behavior. For example, a robot that flocks with other robots may not have a specific internal "flocking" behavior; instead, its interaction with the environment and other robots may result in flocking, although its only behaviors may be "avoid collisions," "stay close to the group," and "keep going" (Matarić 1997).

Behavior-based robots have demonstrated various standard robotic capabilities, including obstacle avoidance, navigation, terrain mapping, following, chasing/pursuit, object manipulation, task division and cooperation, and learning maps, navigation and walking. They have also demonstrated some novel applications like large-scale group behaviors, including flocking, foraging, and soccer playing, and modeling insect and even human behavior (Agha and Bekey 1997; Webb 1994; Asada et al. 1994; Brooks and Stein 1994). Application domains have included MOBILE ROBOTS, underwater vehicles, space robotics, as well as robots capable of MANIPULATION AND GRASPING, and some WALKING AND RUNNING MACHINES.

Variations and adaptations of MACHINE LEARNING, and in particular REINFORCEMENT LEARNING, have been effectively applied to behavior-based robots, which have demonstrated learning to walk (Maes and Brooks 1990), navigate (Matarić 1992; Millan 1994), communicate (Yanco and Stein 1993), divide tasks (Parker 1993; Matarić 1997), behave socially (Matarić 1994), and even identify opponents and score goals in robot soccer (Asada et al. 1994). Methods from ARTIFICIAL LIFE, EVOLUTIONARY COMPUTATION, GENETIC ALGORITHMS, FUZZY LOGIC, VISION AND LEARNING, MULTIAGENT SYSTEMS, and many others continue to be actively explored and applied to behavior-based robots as their role in animal modeling and practical applications continues to develop.

—*Maja J. Matarić*

References

Agha, A., and G. Bekey. (1997). Phylogenetic and ontogenetic learning in a colony of interacting robots. *Autonomous Robots* 4(1).

Agre, P., and D. Chapman. (1987). Pengi: an implementation of a theory of activity. *Proceedings, Sixth National Conference of the American Association for Artificial Intelligence Conference.* Seattle, WA, pp. 268–272.

Arkin, R. (1989). Towards the unification of navigational planning and reactive control. *Proceedings, American Association for Artificial Intelligence Spring Symposium on Robot Navigation,* Palo Alto, CA, pp. 1–5.

Asada, M., E. Uchibe, S. Noda, S. Tawaratsumida, and K. Hosoda. (1994). Coordination of multiple behaviors acquired by a vision-based reinforcement learning. *Proceedings, IEEE/RSJ/GI International Conference on Intelligent Robots and Systems,* Munich, Germany.

Brooks, R. (1986). A robust layered control system for a mobile robot. *IEEE Journal of Robotics and Automation* RA-2 (April), pp. 14–23.

Brooks, R., and J. Connell. (1986). Asynchronous distributed control system for a mobile robot. *Proceedings, SPIE Intelligent Control and Adaptive Systems*, Cambridge, MA, pp. 77–84.

Brooks, R., and L. Stein. (1994). Building brains for bodies. *Autonomous Robots* 1 (1): 7–25.

Connell, J. (1991). SSS: a hybrid architecture applied to robot navigation. *Proceedings, International Conference on Robotics and Automation,* Nice, France, pp. 2719–2724.

Firby, J. (1987). An investigation into reactive planning in complex domains. *Proceedings, Sixth National Conference of the American Association for Artificial Intelligence Conference,* Seattle, WA, pp. 202–206.

Georgeoff, M., and A. Lansky. (1987). Reactive reasoning and planning. *Proceedings, Sixth National Conference of the American Association for Artificial Intelligence Conference,* Seattle, WA, pp. 677–682.

Giralt, G., R. Chatila, and M. Vaisset. (1983). An integrated navigation and motion control system for autonomous multisensory mobile robots. *Proceedings, First International Symposium on Robotics Research,* Cambridge, MA: MIT Press, pp. 191–214.

Laird, J., and P. Rosenbloom. (1990). An investigation into reactive planning in complex domains. *Proceedings, Ninth National Conference of the American Association for Artificial Intelligence Conference,* Cambridge, MA: MIT Press, pp. 1022–1029.

Maes, P. (1989). The dynamics of action selection. *Proceedings, International Joint Conference on Artificial Intelligence,* Detroit, MI, pp. 991–997.

Maes, P., and R. Brooks. (1990). Learning to coordinate behaviors. *Proceedings, Ninth National Conference of the American Association for Artificial Intelligence Conference,* Cambridge, MA: MIT Press, pp. 796–802.

Matarić, M. (1992). Integration of representation into goal-driven behavior-based robots. IEEE Transactions on Robotics and Automation 8 (3): 304–312.

Matarić, M. (1994). Learning to behave socially. In D. Cliff, P. Husbands, J-A. Meyer, and S. Wilson, Eds., *Proceedings, From Animals to Animats 3, Third International Conference on Simulation of Adaptive Behavior.* Cambridge, MA: MIT Press, pp. 453–462.

Matarić, M. (1997). Reinforcement learning in the multi-robot domain. *Autonomous Robots* 4 (1): 73–83.

Millan, J. (1994). Learning reactive sequences from basic reflexes. In D. Cliff, P. Husbands, J-A. Meyer, and S. Wilson, Eds., *Proceedings, From Animals to Animats 3, Third International Conference on Simulation of Adaptive Behavior.* Cambridge, MA: MIT Press, pp. 266–274.

Moravec, H., and A. Elfes. (1985). High resolution maps from wide angle sonar. *Proceedings, IEEE International Conference on Robotics and Automation,* St. Louis, MO.

Parker, L. (1993). Learning in cooperative robot teams. *Proceedings, International Joint Conference on Artificial Intelligence, Workshop on Dynamically Interacting Robots,* Chambery, France, pp. 12–23.

Payton, D. (1990). Internalized plans: a representation for action resources. In P. Maes, Ed., *Robotics and Autonomous Systems, Special Issue on Designing Autonomous Agents: Theory and Practice from Biology to Engineering and Back* 6 (1–2): 89–104.

Payton, D., D. Keirsey, D. Kimble, J. Krozel, and K. Rosenblatt. (1992). Do whatever works: a robust approach to fault-tolerant autonomous control. *Journal of Applied Intelligence* 3: 226–249.

Webb, B. (1994). Robotic experiments in cricket phonotaxis. *Proceedings of the Third International Conference on the Simulation of Adaptive Behavior.* Cambridge, MA: MIT Press.

Yanco, H., and L. Stein. (1993). An adaptive communication protocol for cooperating mobile robots. In D. Cliff, P. Husbands, J. A. Meyer, and S. Wilson, Eds., *Proceedings, From Animals to Animats 3, Third International Conference on Simulation of Adaptive Behavior.* Cambridge, MA: MIT Press, pp. 478–485.

Further Readings

Arkin, R. (1987). Motor schema based navigation for a mobile robot: an approach to programming by behavior. *IEEE International Conference on Robotics and Automatio.* Raleigh, NC, pp. 264–271.

Arkin, R. (1990). Integrating behavioral, perceptual and world knowledge in reactive navigation. In P. Maes, Ed., *Robotics and Autonomous Systems, Special Issue on Designing Autonomous Agents: Theory and Practice from Biology to Engineering and Back* 6 (1–2): 105–122.

Asada, M., E. Uchibe, and K. Hosoda. (1995). Agents that learn from other competitive agents. *Proceedings, Machine Learning Conference Workshop on Agents That Learn From Other Agents.*

Beer, R., H. Chiel, and L. Sterling. (1990). A biological perspective on autonomous agent design. In P. Maes, Ed., *Robotics and Autonomous Systems, Special Issue on Designing Autonomous Agents: Theory and Practice from Biology to Engineering and Back* 6 (1–2): 169–186.

Brooks, R. (1990). Elephants don't play chess. In P. Maes, Ed., *Robotics and Autonomous Systems, Special Issue on Designing Autonomous Agents: Theory and Practice from Biology to Engineering and Back* 6 (1–2): 3–16.

Brooks, A. (1991a). Intelligence without representation. *Artificial Intelligence* 47: 139–160.

Brooks, A. (1991b). Intelligence without reason. *Proceedings, International Joint Conference on Artificial Intelligence,* Sydney, Australia, Cambridge, MA: MIT Press.

Connell, J. (1990). *Minimalist Mobile Robotics: A Colony Architecture for an Artificial Creature.* Boston: Academic Press.

Connell, J., and S. Mahadevan. (1993). *Robot Learning.* Kluwer Academic Publishers.

Floreano, D., and F. Mondada. (1996). Evolution of homing navigation in a real mobile robot. *IEEE Transactions on Systems, Man, and Cybernetics.* Los Alamitos, CA: IEEE Press.

Grefenstette, J., and A. Schultz. (1994). An evolutionary approach to learning in robots. *Proceedings, Machine Learning Workshop on Robot Learning.* New Brunswick, NJ.

Jones, J., and A. Flynn. (1993). *Mobile Robots, Inspiration to Implementation.* Wellesley, MA: A. K. Peters, Ltd.

Kaelbling, L. (1993). *Learning in Embedded Systems*. Cambridge, MA: MIT Press.

Kaelbling, L., and S. Rosenschein. (1990). Action and planning in embedded agents. In P. Maes, Ed., *Robotics and Autonomous Systems, Special Issue on Designing Autonomous Agents: Theory and Practice from Biology to Engineering and Back* 6 (1–2): 35–48.

Maes, P. (1990). Situated agents can have goals. In P. Maes, Ed., *Robotics and Autonomous Systems, Special Issue on Designing Autonomous Agents: Theory and Practice from Biology to Engineering and Back* 6 (1–2)

Malcolm, C., and T. Smithers. (1990). Symbol grounding via a hybrid architecture in an autonomous assembly system. In P. Maes, Ed., *Robotics and Autonomous Systems, Special Issue on Designing Autonomous Agents: Theory and Practice from Biology to Engineering and Back* 6 (1–2): 145–168.

Marjanovic, M., B. Scassellati, and M. Williamson. (1996). Self-taught visually-guided pointing for a humanoid robot. In P. Maes, M. Matarić, J-A. Meyer, J. Pollack, and S. Wilson, Eds., *Proceedings, From Animals to Animats 4, Fourth International Conference on Simulation of Adaptive Behavior.* Cambridge, MA: MIT Press, pp. 35–44.

Matarić, M. (1990). Navigating with a rat brain: a neurobiologically-inspired model for robot spatial representation. In J-A. Meyer, and S. Wilson, Eds., *Proceedings, From Animals to Animats 1, First International Conference on Simulation of Adaptive Behavior.* Cambridge, MA: MIT Press, pp. 169–175.

Matarić, M. (1997). Behavior-based control: examples from navigation, learning, and group behavior. In Hexmoor, Horswill, and Kortenkamp, Eds., *Journal of Experimental and Theoretical Artificial Intelligence, Special Issue on Software Architectures for Physical Agents* 9 (2–3): 1997.

Nolfi, S., D. Floreano, O. Miglino, and F. Mondada. (1994). Now to evolve autonomous robots: different approaches in evolutionary robotics. In R. Brooks and P. Maes, Eds., *Proceedings, Artificial Life IV, the Fourth International Workshop on the Synthesis and Simulation of Living Systems.* Cambridge, MA: MIT Press, pp. 190–197.

Smithers, T. (1995). On quantitative performance measures of robot behaviour. In L. Steels, Ed., *The Biology and Technology of Intelligent Autonomous Agents.* Cambridge, MA: MIT Press, pp. 107–133.

Steels, L. (1994a). Emergent functionality of robot behavior through on-line evolution. In R. Brooks and P. Maes, Eds., *Proceedings, Artificial Life IV, the Fourth International Workshop on the Synthesis and Simulation of Living Systems.* Cambridge, MA: MIT Press, pp. 8–14.

Steels, L. (1994b). The artificial life roots of artificial intelligence. *Artificial Life* 1 (1).

Williamson, M. (1996). Postural primitives: interactive behavior for a humanoid robot arm. In P. Maes, M. Matarić, J. A. Meyer, J. Pollack, and S. Wilson, Eds., *Proceedings, From Animals to Animats 4, Fourth International Conference on Simulation of Adaptive Behavior.* Cambridge, MA: MIT Press, pp. 124–134.

Behaviorism

"Psychology is the Science of Mental Life, both of its phenomena and their conditions. The phenomena are such things as we call feelings, desires, cognitions, reasonings, decisions, and the like" (1890: 1). So said William JAMES in his *Principles of Psychology,* perhaps the most important and widely cited textbook in the history of psychology. James believed that psychology would have finished its job when it "ascertained the empirical correlation of the various sorts of thought or feeling with definite conditions of the brain" (1890: vi).

His own primary interest in conscious mental experience notwithstanding, James did predict that "the data assumed by psychology, like those assumed by physics and the other natural sciences, must some time be overhauled" (1890: vi). James did not, however, predict that only a few short years after publication of his *Principles,* just such a major overhaul would be in full swing. Nor did James foresee that the impact of this overhaul would be so revolutionary and controversial nearly a century later. *Behaviorism* is the name given to this dramatic shift away from psychology as the science of mental life and toward being the science of overt action.

John B. Watson is usually credited with beginning behaviorism; surely, his 1913 paper, "Psychology as the Behaviorist Views It," made the case for behaviorism in a most dramatic and forceful manner. But other scholars paved the way for behaviorism. Among them, H. S. Jennings, Watson's biologist colleague at Johns Hopkins University, more methodically and less polemically advocated a behavioristic approach for psychology in his 1906 book, *Behavior of the Lower Organisms.* Jennings's views on the science of psychology still serve as a fitting introduction to the premises and methods of behaviorism.

As did Watson, Jennings studied the behavior of nonhuman animals. Interest in nonhuman animals or even human infants poses very real limits on our readiest means for understanding the psychological phenomena of thinking and feeling: namely, INTROSPECTION, what Edward B. Titchener (1896) called the one distinctively psychological method. Without verbal report, how can we ever claim to have gained access to another organism's mental life? Indeed, just because we ask other people to report to us their private thoughts and feelings, why should we be sanguine that they are either willing or able to do so?

Jennings took a decidedly cautious stance concerning the private world of conscious thoughts and feelings. "The conscious aspect of behavior is undoubtedly most interesting. But we are unable to deal directly with this by the methods of observation and experiment. . . . Assertions regarding consciousness in animals, whether affirmative or negative, are not susceptible of verification" (1906: v). Contrary to the claims of their critics, most behaviorists, like Jennings, deny neither the existence nor the importance of CONSCIOUSNESS; rather, they hold that private data cannot be the subject of public science.

Having judged that the introspective investigation of consciousness is an unworkable methodology for objective science, Jennings offered a new alternative to a science of mental life—a science of overt action. "Apart from their relation to the problem of consciousness and its development, the objective processes in behavior are of the highest interest in themselves" (1906: v).

Jennings noted that behavior has historically been treated as the neglected stepsister of consciousness. The treatment of behavior as subsidiary to the problem of consciousness has tended to obscure the fact that in behavior we have the most marked and perhaps the most easily studied of the organic processes. Jennings observed that "in behavior we are dealing with actual objective processes (whether accompanied by consciousness or not), and we need a knowledge of the laws controlling them, of the same sort as our knowledge of the laws of metabolism" (1906: v). Discovering general laws of behavior—in both human and nonhuman animals—with the methods of natural science is the aim of a behavioristic psychology.

Jennings's consideration of nonhuman animal behavior (what we now call COMPARATIVE PSYCHOLOGY) was a key extension of psychological science, an extension that was effectively precluded through introspective investigation but was made possible by behavioristic study. This extension was controversial because it had important implications for our understanding of human behavior. "From a discussion of the behavior of the lower organisms in objective terms, compared with a discussion of the behavior of man in subjective terms, we get the impression of a complete discontinuity between the two" (1906: 329). Jennings believed that this dualistic view of human and nonhuman psychology offered centuries earlier by DESCARTES was stale and incorrect; a fresh and proper answer to the question of whether humans differed fundamentally from all other animals required examining their behavior from a common and objective vantage point. "Only by comparing the objective factors can we determine whether there is a continuity or a gulf between the behavior of lower and higher organisms (including man), for it is only these factors that we know" (1906: 329).

Based on that objective evidence, Jennings agreed with Charles DARWIN and his theory of EVOLUTION through natural selection that "there is no difference in kind, but a complete continuity between the behavior of lower and of higher organisms [including human beings]" (1906: 335). Indeed, many years of assiduous study convinced Jennings that, "if Amoeba were a large animal, so as to come within the everyday experience of human beings, its behavior would at once call forth the attribution to it of states of pleasure and pain, of hunger, desire, and the like, on precisely the same basis as we attribute these things to the dog" (1906: 336), however problematical for an objective psychology these anthropomorphic attributions of MOTIVATION and EMOTION might be.

Jennings's exhortation for us to limit our consideration of both human and nonhuman behavior to objective factors underscores the key imperative of behaviorism. "The ideal of most scientific men is to explain behavior in terms of matter and energy, so that the introduction of psychic implications is considered superfluous" (1906: 329). Mentalism was to play no part in this new psychological science of the twentieth century, although it is at the core of the current, but arguably (see Blumberg and Wasserman 1995) reactionary school of nonhuman animal behavior, COGNITIVE ETHOLOGY, founded by the biologist Donald R. Griffin (1976).

Critics of behaviorism nevertheless argue that excluding the realm of private experience from psychological science is misguided. Doesn't a behavioristic account omit most if not all of the truly interesting and important aspects of psychological functioning? No, said Jennings. What is advocated is simply an objective analysis of psychological processes. With remarkable sophistication and some thirty

years before Edward C. Tolman (1936) did so more prominently, Jennings urged the operationalization of psychological terms and phenomena so as to make their study completely objective and permit their exact experimental investigation—even in nonhuman animals and human infants. (Clark L. Hull 1952, B. F. Skinner 1945, and Kenneth W. Spence 1956 later developed behaviorism in very different ways to deal with ideation and thinking.)

Take, for example, one of James's favorite psychological notions—ATTENTION. For Jennings, attention is not a conscious mental state. Rather, "at the basis of *attention* lies objectively the phenomenon that the organism may react to only one stimulus even though other stimuli are present which would, if acting alone, likewise produce a response" (1906: 330). The organism can then be said to attend to the particular stimulus to which it responds. Or, take what to many is the hallmark of mental life—choice or DECISION MAKING. For Jennings, choice is not a conscious mental process. Instead, "*choice* is a term based objectively on the fact that the organism accepts or reacts positively to some things, while it rejects or reacts negatively or not at all to others" (1906: 330). In these and many other cases, Jennings explained that "we shall not attempt to take into consideration the scholastic definitions of the terms used, but shall judge them merely from the objective phenomena on which they are based" (1906: 329).

What then are the limits of a behavioristic approach to psychological phenomena? This key question has not yet been answered, but it has been vigorously debated. Watson believed that the matter would eventually be decided by experimental study. "As our methods become better developed it will be possible to undertake investigations of more and more complex forms of behavior. Problems which are now laid aside will again become imperative, but they can be viewed as they arise from a new angle and in more concrete settings" (1913: 175).

A case study for looking at psychological issues from a new angle and in a concrete setting is recent research into CATEGORIZATION and conceptualization by nonhuman animals. Building on powerful experimental methods pioneered by Skinner (1938) and his student Richard J. Herrnstein (1990), my colleagues and I have trained pigeons to categorize complex visual stimuli such as colored photographs and detailed line drawings into different classes, ranging from basic-level CONCEPTS (like cats, flowers, cars, and chairs), to superordinate concepts (like mammals, vegetables, vehicles, and furniture), to abstract concepts (like same versus different). In all three cases, the pigeons not only acquired the visual discriminations through reinforcement learning, but they also generalized those discriminations to completely novel stimuli (Wasserman 1995); such generalization is the hallmark of conceptualization. Additional extensions of behavioristic methods and analyses have been made to visual IMAGERY (Rilling and Neiworth 1987) and to the reporting of interoceptive stimuli induced by the administration of drugs (Lubinski and Thompson 1993). Here too, pigeons were taught with purely behavioral methods to engage in behaviors which, when performed by people, are conventionally considered to be the product of conscious mental states and processes. Behaviorists, like

Skinner, take a different tack and ask, Isn't it more productive and parsimonious to attribute these behaviors to the contingencies of reinforcement (which can be specified and experimentally manipulated) than to mental entities and psychic machinations (which cannot)?

Some firmly resist this maneuver and emphatically say no. Empirical demonstrations such as these have done little to convert behaviorism's most trenchant critics, such as Noam Chomsky (1959). These individuals argue that behaviorism is formally unable to explain complex human behavior, especially LANGUAGE AND COMMUNICATION.

These critics note, for instance, that human verbal behavior exhibits remarkable variability and temporal organization. They contend that CREATIVITY and grammar are properties of linguistic performance that are in principle beyond behavioristic explanation, and they instead argue that these properties of language uniquely implicate the operation of creative mental structures and processes. In response, behaviorists note that all behaviors—from the simplest acts like button pressing to the most complex like reciting poetry—involve intricate and changing topographies of performance. In fact, variability itself is a property of behavior that research (Eisenberger and Cameron 1996) has shown is modifiable through the systematic delivery of reinforcement and punishment, in much the same way as other properties of behavior like frequency, amplitude, and duration are conditioned by reinforcement contingencies. As to the temporal organization of behavior, even nonhuman animals like pigeons and monkeys have been taught to recognize and to produce structured sequences of stimuli and responses (Terrace 1993; Weisman et al. 1980). Such complex performances were again the result of elementary LEARNING processes brought about by familiar CONDITIONING techniques.

More famously and directly, Skinner offered a behavioristic account of human language in his 1957 book, *Verbal Behavior.*

Many theorists therefore conclude that behaviorism is the strongest alternative to a mentalistic account of human and nonhuman behavior. Far from being run out of business by the premature proclamations of their mentalistic critics, behaviorists have steadfastly proceeded with the task of experimentally analyzing many of the most complex and vexing problems of behavior using the most effective and current tools of natural science.

See also CONDITIONING AND THE BRAIN; ETHOLOGY; FUNCTIONALISM; LEARNING; NATIVISM, HISTORY OF

—*Edward Wasserman*

References

Blumberg, M. S., and E. A. Wasserman. (1995). Animal mind and the argument from design. *American Psychologist* 50: 133–144.

Chomsky, N. (1959). Review of B. F. Skinner's *Verbal Behavior.* *Language* 35: 26–58.

Eisenberger, R., and J. Cameron. (1996). Detrimental effects of reward: reality or myth? *American Psychologist* 51: 1153–1166.

Griffin, D. R. (1976). *The Question of Animal Awareness: Evolutionary Continuity of Mental Experience.* New York: The Rockefeller University Press.

Herrnstein, R. J. (1990). Levels of stimulus control: a functional approach. *Cognition* 37: 133–166.

Hull, C. L. (1952). *A Behavior System.* New Haven, CT: Yale University Press.

James, W. (1890, 1955). *The Principles of Psychology,* vol. 1. New York: Dover.

Jennings, H. S. (1906/1976). *Behavior of the Lower Organisms.* Bloomington: Indiana University Press.

Lubinski, D., and T. Thompson. (1993). Species and individual differences in communication based on private states. *Behavioral and Brain Sciences* 16: 627–680.

Rilling, M. E., and J. J. Neiworth. (1987). Theoretical and methodological considerations for the study of imagery in animals. *Learning and Motivation* 18: 57–79.

Skinner, B. F. (1938). *The Behavior of Organisms.* New York: Appleton-Century-Crofts.

Skinner, B. F. (1945). The operational analysis of psychological terms. *Psychological Review* 52: 270–277.

Skinner, B. F. (1957). *Verbal Behavior.* New York: Appleton-Century-Crofts.

Spence, K. W. (1956). *Behavior Theory and Conditioning.* New Haven, CT: Yale University Press.

Terrace, H. S. (1993). The phylogeny and ontogeny of serial memory: list learning by pigeons and monkeys. *Psychological Science* 4: 162–169.

Titchener, E. B. (1896). *An Outline of Psychology.* New York: Macmillan.

Tolman, E. C. (1936). Operational behaviorism and current trends in psychology. Paper included in the *Proceedings of the Twenty–fifth Anniversary Celebration of the Inauguration of Graduate Studies at the University of Southern California, 1936.* Reprinted in E. C. Tolman, Ed., *Behavior and Psychological Man: Essays in Motivation and Learning.* Berkeley: University of California Press, 1961/1966.

Wasserman, E. A. (1995). The conceptual abilities of pigeons. *American Scientist* 83: 246–255.

Watson, J. B. (1913). Psychology as the behaviorist views it. *Psychological Review* 20: 158–177.

Weisman, R. G., E. A. Wasserman, P. W. D. Dodd, and M. B. Larew. (1980). Representation and retention of two-event sequences in pigeons. *Journal of Experimental Psychology: Animal Behavior Processes* 6: 312–325.

Further Readings

Cook, R. G. (1993). The experimental analysis of cognition in animals. *Psychological Science* 4: 174–178.

Darwin, C. (1871/1920). *The Descent of Man; And Selection in Relation to Sex.* 2nd ed. New York: D. Appleton and Company.

Griffin, D. R. (1992). *Animal Minds.* Chicago: University of Chicago Press.

Honig, W. K., and J. G. Fetterman, Eds. (1992). *Cognitive Aspects of Stimulus Control.* Hillsdale, NJ: Erlbaum.

Hull, C. L. (1943). *Principles of Behavior.* New York: Appleton-Century-Crofts.

Hulse, S. H., H. Fowler, and W. K. Honig, Eds. (1978). *Cognitive Processes in Animal Behavior.* Hillsdale, NJ: Erlbaum.

Kennedy, J. S. (1992). *The New Anthropomorphism.* Cambridge: Cambridge University Press.

Lashley, K. S. (1923). The behaviorist interpretation of consciousness, II. *Psychological Review* 30: 329–353.

Mackenzie, B. D. (1977). *Behaviourism and the Limits of Scientific Method.* Atlantic Highlands, NJ: Humanities Press.

Mackintosh, N. J., Ed. (1994). *Animal Learning and Cognition.* San Diego, CA: Academic Press.

Nisbett, R. E., and T. D. Wilson. (1977). Telling more than we can know: verbal reports on mental processes. *Psychological Review* 84: 231–259.

Pavlov, I. P. (1927). *Conditioned Reflexes.* Oxford: Oxford University Press.

Rachlin, H. (1992). Teleological behaviorism. *American Psychologist* 47: 1371–1382.

Richelle, M. N. (1993). *B. F. Skinner: A Reappraisal.* Hillsdale, NJ: Erlbaum.

Ristau, C. A., Ed. (1991). *Cognitive Ethology: The Minds of Other Animals.* Hillsdale, NJ: Erlbaum.

Roitblat, H. L., T. G. Bever, and H. S. Terrace, eds. (1984). *Animal Cognition.* Hillsdale, NJ: Erlbaum.

Skinner, B. F. (1976). *About Behaviorism.* New York: Vintage.

Skinner, B. F. (1977). Why I am not a cognitive psychologist. *Behaviorism* 5: 1–10.

Sober, E. (1983). Mentalism and behaviorism in comparative psychology. In D. W. Rajecki, Ed., *Comparing Behavior: Studying Man Studying Animals.* Hillsdale, NJ: Erlbaum, pp. 113–142.

Spear, N. E., J. S. Miller, and J. A. Jagielo. (1990). Animal memory and learning. *Annual Review of Psychology* 41: 169–211.

Wasserman, E. A. (1993). Comparative cognition: beginning the second century of the study of animal intelligence. *Psychological Bulletin* 113: 211–228.

Wasserman, E. A. (1997). Animal cognition: past, present and future. *Journal of Experimental Psychology: Animal Behavior Processes* 23: 123–135.

Wasserman, E. A., and R. R. Miller. (1997). What's elementary about associative learning? *Annual Review of Psychology* 48: 573–607.

Weiskrantz, L., Ed. (1985). *Animal Intelligence.* New York: Oxford University Press.

Zuriff, G. E. (1985). *Behaviorism: A Conceptual Reconstruction.* New York: Columbia University Press.

Belief Networks

See BAYESIAN NETWORKS; PROBABILISTIC REASONING

Bilingualism and the Brain

In recent years, there has been growing interest in the cognitive neuroscience of bilingualism. The two central questions in this literature have been: (1) Does a bilingual speaker represent each language in different areas of the brain? (2) What effect does age of second language acquisition have on brain representation? These questions have been considered by using electrophysiological and functional neuroimaging measures as well as by looking at bilinguals who suffer strokes affecting the areas responsible for language processing in the brain. We will begin by considering the effects of age of acquisition before considering the localization of the first and second language in the brain.

What effects does age of second language acquisition have on brain representation? Researchers in cognitive science have considered whether there is a critical period for learning a language (*see also* LANGUAGE ACQUISITION). This topic is also of interest to those learning a second language. Specifically, investigators have inquired about the differences between early and late second language learners. Recent work using event-related potentials (ERP) supports

previous behavioral findings suggesting that second language learning is better in those who learn their second language early. Mclaughlin and Osterhout (1997) found that college students learning French progressively improve from chance to near-native performance on lexical decision (i.e., deciding if a letter string is a word or not); however, electrophysiological indices revealed sensitivity to French words after only a few weeks of instruction. An increased N400 (a waveform that indexes lexical-semantic processing) for words preceded by semantically unrelated words (coffee-dog) was found as the number of years of exposure to French increased, but it never approached the levels seen in native French speakers. Weber-Fox and Neville (1996) have found differences in the N400 to semantic violations, but only for those who learned a second language after the age of eleven. Changes in ERPs to grammatical violations, however, appeared even for those who learned their second language before the age of four. Perani et al. (1996), using POSITRON EMISSION TOMOGRAPHY (a measure of localized brain activity), have found that listening to passages in a first language results in an activation of areas that is not apparent in the second language for late second language learners (e.g., increased activation in the left and right temporal pole, the left inferior frontal gyrus, and the left inferior parietal lobe). Thus age of acquisition has an effect on electrophysiological measures of brain activity as well as on the neuroanatomical areas that are involved in second language processing.

Does a bilingual speaker represent each language in different areas of the brain? Researchers have long wondered whether cognitive functions are processed by separate areas of the brain (*see* CORTICAL LOCALIZATION, HISTORY OF). A similar question has been asked with respect to the cortical localization of the two languages in bilingual speakers. One way to answer this question is to look at the effects of brain lesions on the processing of a bilingual's two languages. Brain lesions that affect one language and not the other would lead to the conclusion that languages are represented in different areas of the brain. Indeed, there is evidence of different degrees of recovery in each language after a stroke (Junque, Vendrell and Vendrell 1995; Paradis 1977). Extreme cases have shown postoperative impairment in one language with spontaneous recovery after eight months (Paradis and Goldblum 1989). A more recent case has been used to suggest that there is a clear neuroanatomical dissociation between the languages (Gomez-Tortosa et al. 1995). Others, however, suggest that there are a number of other explanations for these data (see Paradis 1996 and Hines 1996 for further discussion).

The notion that bilinguals' two languages are represented in overlapping brain areas has also been supported with other methodologies. Ojemann and Whitaker (1978) found that electrical stimulation of certain areas in the cortex interrupted naming in both languages, whereas stimulation of other areas interrupted naming in only one language. More recent work using measures that look at activation as a measure of blood flow have come to similar conclusions. Klein et al. (1994), using PET, found that naming pictures in a second language vs. naming pictures in a first language resulted in activation in the putamen, a subcortical area that has been associated with phonological processing. Other studies have found that bilinguals show activity in left frontal areas of the brain for semantic and phonological analyses of words in both their languages (Klein et al. 1995; Wagner et al. 1996). Taken together these findings suggest that whereas naming in L2 involves activation in areas that are not involved in L1, lexical and semantic judgments of words activate mostly overlapping areas of the brain. Although there are some dissociations when surface tasks such as naming are used, these dissociations disappear when semantic tasks are used.

Having two linguistic systems that overlap presents an interesting challenge for theories of bilingual language processing. If these two languages are located on overlapping tissue, how do bilinguals manage to keep these languages from constantly interfering with each other? A recent study by Hernandez et al. (1997) was designed to look at this issue using functional MAGNETIC RESONANCE IMAGING (fMRI) for Spanish–English bilinguals. Participants were asked to name a picture in their first language, second language, or to alternate between each language on successive trials. Results revealed slower reaction times and an increase in the number of cross-language errors in the alternating condition relative to the single-language condition (Kohnert-Rice and Hernandez forthcoming). In the fMRI study, there was no difference when comparing activation for naming in the first and second language. However, activation in the prefrontal cortex increased significantly when participants were asked to alternate between languages. Thus it appears that the left prefrontal cortex may also act to reduce the amount of interference between languages (as indexed by slower reaction times and increased cross-language errors; *see also* WORKING MEMORY, NEURAL BASIS OF).

Languages can be represented across syntactic, phonological, orthographic, semantic, pragmatic, and DISCOURSE dimensions. These distinctions can vary depending on the two languages. For example, Chinese and English are very different orthographically and phonologically. However, some aspects of SYNTAX are very similar (e.g., the lack of morphological markers and the use of word order to indicate the agent of a sentence). Contrast this with Spanish and English, which are more similar orthographically but are very different in syntax in that the former uses a very large number of morphological markers. Despite the progress that has been made in addressing the relationship between bilingualism and brain representation, and although strides have been made in the PSYCHOLINGUISTICS and cognitive neuroscience of bilingualism, much work remains to be done. This research will necessarily involve behavior and the brain. Clearly the issue of bilingual brain bases involves both a rich multidimensional information space as well as a rich cerebral space. Understanding how the former maps onto the latter is a question that should keep researchers occupied into the next century and beyond.

See also ELECTROPHYSIOLOGY, ELECTRIC AND MAGNETIC EVOKED FIELDS; GRAMMAR, NEURAL BASIS OF; INNATENESS OF LANGUAGE; LANGUAGE, NEURAL BASIS OF; NEURAL PLASTICITY; NATURAL LANGUAGE PROCESSING

—*Arturo E. Hernandez and Elizabeth Bates*

References

Gomez-Tortosa, E., E. Martin, M. Gaviria, F. Charbel, and J. Ausman. (1995). Selective deficit of one language in a bilingual patient following surgery in the left perisylvian area. *Brain and Language* 48: 320–325.

Hernandez, A. E., A. Martinez, E. C. Wong, L. A. Frank, and R. B. Buxton. (1997). Neuroanatomical correlates of single- and dual-language picture naming in Spanish–English bilinguals. Poster presented at the fourth annual meeting of the Cognitive Neuroscience Society, Boston, MA.

Hines, T. M. (1996). Failure to demonstrate selective deficit in the native language following surgery in the left perisylvian area. *Brain and Language* 54: 168–169.

Junque, C., P. Vendrell, and J. Vendrell. (1995). Differential impairments and specific phenomena in 50 Catalan–Spanish bilingual aphasic patients. In M. Paradis, Ed., *Aspects of Bilingual Aphasia*. Oxford: Pergamon.

Klein, D., B. Milner, R. J. Zatorre, E. Meyer, and A. C. Evans. (1995). The neural substrates underlying word generation: a bilingual functional-imaging study. *Proceedings of the National Academy of Sciences of the United States of America* 92: 2899–2903.

Klein, D., R. J. Zatorre, B. Milner, E. Meyer, and A. C Evans. (1994). Left putaminal activation when speaking a second language: evidence from PET. *Neuroreport* 5: 2295–2297.

Kohnert-Rice, K. and A. E. Hernandez. (Forthcoming). Lexical retrieval and interference in Spanish–English bilinguals.

McLaughlin, J., and L. Osterhout. (1997). Event-related potentials reflect lexical acquisition in second language learners. Poster presented at the fourth annual meeting of the Cognitive Neuroscience Society, Boston, MA.

Ojemann, G. A., and A. A. Whitaker. (1978). The bilingual brain. *Archives of Neurology* 35: 409–412.

Paradis, M. (1977). Bilingualism and aphasia. In H. Whitaker and H. A. Whitaker, Eds., *Studies in Neurolinguistics,* vol. 3. New York: Academic Press, pp. 65–121.

Paradis, M. (1996). Selective deficit in one language is not a demonstration of different anatomical representation: comments on Gomez-Tortosa et al. (1995). *Brain and Language* 54: 170–173.

Paradis, M., and M. C. Goldblum. (1989). Selected crossed aphasia in a trilingual aphasic patient followed by reciprocal antagonism. *Brain and Language* 36: 62–75.

Perani, D., S. Dehaene, F. Grassi, L. Cohen, S. Cappa, E. Dupoux, F. Fazio, and J. Mehler. (1996). Brain processing of native and foreign languages. *Neuroreport* 7: 2439–2444.

Wagner, A. D., J. Illes, J. E. Desmond, C. J. Lee, G. H. Glover, and J. D. E. Gabrieli. (1996). A functional MRI study of semantic processing in bilinguals. *NeuroImage* 3: S465.

Webber-Fox, C., and H. J. Neville. (1996). Maturational constraints on functional specializations for language processing: ERP and behavioral evidence in bilingual speakers. *Journal of Cognitive Neuroscience* 8: 231–256.

Further Readings

Paradis, M. (1995). *Aspects of Bilingual Aphasia*. Oxford: Pergamon.

Binding by Neural Synchrony

Neuronal systems have to solve immensely complex combinatorial problems and require efficient binding mechanisms in order to generate representations of perceptual objects and movements. In the context of cognitive functions, combinatorial problems arise from the fact that perceptual objects are defined by a unique constellation of features, the diversity of possible constellations being virtually unlimited (cf. BINDING PROBLEM). Combinatorial problems of similar magnitude have to be solved for the acquisition and execution of motor acts. Although the elementary components of motor acts, the movements of individual muscle fibers, are limited in number, the spatial and temporal diversity of movements that can be composed by combining the elementary components in ever-changing constellations is again virtually infinite. In order to establish neuronal representations of perceptual objects and movements, the manifold relations among elementary sensory features and movement components have to be encoded in neural responses. This requires binding mechanisms that can cope efficiently with combinatorial complexity. Brains have acquired an extraordinary competence to solve such combinatorial problems, and it appears that this competence is a result of the evolution of the CEREBRAL CORTEX.

In the primary visual cortex of mammals, relations among the responses of retinal ganglion cells are evaluated and represented by having the output of selected arrays of ganglion cells converge in diverse combinations onto individual cortical neurons. Distributed signals are bound together by selective convergence of feed forward connections (Hubel and Wiesel 1962). This strategy is iterated in prestriate cortical areas in order to generate neurons that detect and represent more complex constellations of features including whole perceptual objects.

However, this strategy of binding features together by recombining input connections in ever-changing variations and representing relations explicitly by responses of specialized cells results in a combinatorial explosion of the number of required binding units. It has been proposed, therefore, that the cerebral cortex uses a second, complementary strategy, commonly called assembly coding, that permits utilization of the same set of neurons for the representation of different relations (Hebb 1949). Here, a particular constellation of features is represented by the joint and coordinated activity of a dynamically associated ensemble of cells, each of which represents explicitly only one of the more elementary features that characterize a particular perceptual object. Different objects can then be represented by recombining neurons tuned to more elementary features in various constellations (assemblies). For assembly coding, two constraints need to be met. First, a selection mechanism is required that permits dynamic, context dependent association of neurons into distinct, functionally coherent assemblies. Second, grouped responses must get labeled so that they can be distinguished by subsequent processing stages as components of one coherent representation and do not get confounded with other unrelated responses. Tagging responses as related is equivalent with raising their salience jointly and selectively, because this assures that they are processed and evaluated together at the subsequent processing stage. This can be achieved in three ways. First, nongrouped responses can be inhibited; second, the amplitude of the selected responses can be enhanced; and third, the selected cells can be made to discharge in precise temporal syn-

chrony. All three mechanisms enhance the relative impact of the grouped responses at the next higher processing level. Selecting responses by modulating discharge rates is common in labeled line coding where a particular cell always signals the same content. However, this strategy may not always be suited for the distinction of assemblies because it introduces ambiguities, reduces processing speed, and causes superposition problems (von der Malsburg 1981; Singer et al. 1997). Ambiguities could arise because discharge rates of feature-selective cells vary over a wide range as a function of the match between stimulus and receptive field properties; these modulations of response amplitude would not be distinguishable from those signalling the relatedness of responses. Processing speed would be reduced because rate coded assemblies need to be maintained for some time in order to be distinguishable. Finally, superposition problems arise, because rate coded assemblies cannot overlap in time within the same processing stage. If they did, it would be impossible to distinguish which of the enhanced responses belong to which assembly. Simultaneous maintenance of different assemblies over perceptual time scales is required, however, to represent composite objects.

Both the ambiguities and the temporal constraints can be overcome if the selection and labeling of responses is achieved through synchronization of individual discharges (Gray et al. 1989; Singer and Gray 1995). Synchronicity can be adjusted independently of rates, and so the signature of relatedness, if expressed through synchronization, is independent of rate fluctuations. Moreover, synchronization enhances only the salience of those discharges that are precisely synchronized and generate coincident synaptic potentials in target cells at the subsequent processing stage. Hence the selected event is the individual spike or a brief burst of spikes. Thus, the rate at which different assemblies can follow one another within the same neuronal network without getting confounded is much higher than with rate coding. It is only limited by the duration of the interval over which synaptic potentials summate effectively. If this interval is in the range of 10 or 20 ms, several different assemblies can alternate within preceptually relevant time windows.

If synchronization serves as a selection and binding mechanism, neurons must be sensitive to coincident input. Moreover, synchronization must occur rapidly and show a relation to perceptual phenomena.

Although the issue of *coincidence detection* is still controversial (König, Engel, and Singer 1996; Shadlen and Newsome 1994), evidence is increasing that neurons can evaluate temporal relations with precision among incoming activity (see e.g., Carr 1993). That cortical networks can handle temporally structured activity with high precision and low dispersion follows from the abundant evidence on the oscillatory patterning and precise synchronization of neuronal responses in the γ-frequency range (Singer and Gray 1995; König, Engel, and Singer 1996). Synchronization at such high frequencies is only possible if integration time constants are short. Precise synchronization over large distances is usually associated with an oscillatory patterning of responses in the β- and γ-frequency range, suggesting a causal relation (König, Engel, and Singer 1995). This oscillatory patterning is associated with strong inhibitory interactions (Traub et al. 1996), raising the possibility that the oscillations contribute to the shortening of integration time constants.

Simulations with spiking neurons reveal that networks of appropriately coupled units can undergo very rapid transitions from uncorrelated to synchronized states (Deppisch et al. 1993; Gerstner 1996). Rapid transitions from independent to synchronized firing are also observed in natural networks. In visual centers, it is not uncommon that neurons engage in synchronous activity, often with additional oscillatory patterning, at the very same time they increase their discharge rate in response to the light stimulus (Neuenschwander and Singer 1996; Gray et al. 1992). One mechanism is coordinated spontaneous activity that acts like a dynamic filter and causes a virtually instantaneous synchronization of the very first discharges of responses Fries et al. 1997b). The spatio-temporal patterns of these spontaneous fluctuations of excitability reflect the architecture and the actual functional state of intracortical association connections. Thus, grouping by synchronization can be extremely fast and still occur as a function of both the prewired associational dispositions and the current functional state of the cortical network.

Evidence indicates that the probability and strength of response synchronization reflects elementary Gestalt criteria such as continuity, proximity, similarity in the orientation domain, colinearity, and common fate (Gray et al. 1989; Engel, König, and Singer 1991; Engel et al. 1991; Freiwald, Kreiter, and Singer 1995; Kreiter and Singer 1996). Most importantly, the magnitude of synchronization exceeds that expected from stimulus-induced rate covariations of responses, indicating that it results from internal coordination of spike timing. Moreover, synchronization probability does not simply reflect anatomical connectivity but changes in a context-dependent way (Gray et al. 1989; Engel, König, and Singer 1991; Freiwald, Kreiter, and Singer 1995; Kreiter and Singer 1996), indicating that it is the result of a dynamic and context-dependent selection and grouping process. Most of the early experiments on response synchronization have been performed in anesthetized animals, but more recent evidence from cats and monkeys indicates that highly precise, internally generated synchrony occurs also in the awake brain, exhibits similar sensitivity to context (Kreiter and Singer 1996; Fries et al. 1997a; Gray and Viana Di Prisco 1997), and is especially pronounced when the EEG is desynchronized (Munk et al. 1996) and the animals are attentive (Roelfsema et al. 1997). Direct relations between response synchronization and perception have been found in cats who suffered from strabismic amblyopia, a developmental impairment of vision associated with suppression of the amblyopic eye, reduced visual acuity, and disturbed perceptual grouping (crowding) in this eye. Quite unexpectedly, the discharge rates of individual neurons in the primary visual cortex fail to reflect these deficits (see Roelfsema et al. 1994 for references). The only significant correlate of amblyopia is the drastically reduced ability of neurons driven by the amblyopic eye to synchronize their responses (Roelfsema et al. 1994), and this accounts well for the perceptual deficits: by reducing the salience of responses, disturbed synchronization could be responsible for the suppression of signals from the amblyopic eye, and by impairing binding, it could reduce visual acuity and cause crowding.

Another close correlation between response synchronization and perception has been found in experiments on binocular rivalry (Fries et al. 1997a). A highly significant correlation exists between changes in the strength of response synchronization in primary visual cortex and the outcome of rivalry. Cells mediating responses of the eye that won in interocular competition increased the synchronicity of their responses upon presentation of the rival stimulus to the other, losing eye, while the reverse was true for cells driven by the eye that became suppressed.

These results support the hypothesis that precise temporal relations between the discharges of spatially distributed neurons matter in cortical processing and that synchronization may be exploited to jointly raise the salience of the responses selected for further processing, that is, for the dynamic binding of distributed responses into coherent assemblies.

The example of rivalry also illustrates how synchronization and rate modulation depend on each other. The signals from the suppressed eye failed to induce tracking EYE MOVEMENTS, indicating that the vigorous but poorly synchronized responses in primary visual areas eventually failed to drive the neurons responsible for the execution of eye movements. Thus, changes of synchronicity result in changes of response amplitudes at subsequent processing stages. This convertibility provides the option to use both coding strategies in parallel in order to encode complementary information.

See also HIGH-LEVEL VISION; MID-LEVEL VISION; OCULO-MOTOR CONTROL

—*Wolf Singer*

References

Carr, C. E. (1993). Processing of temporal information in the brain. *Annu. Rev. Neurosci.* 16: 223–243.

Deppisch, J., H.-U. Bauer, T. B. Schillen, P. König, K. Pawelzik, and T. Geisel. (1993). Alternating oscillatory and stochastic states in a network of spiking neurons. *Network* 4: 243–257.

Engel, A. K., P. König, and W. Singer. (1991). Direct physiological evidence for scene segmentation by temporal coding. *Proc. Natl. Acad. Sci. USA* 88: 9136–9140.

Engel, A. K., A. K. Kreiter, P. König, and W. Singer. (1991). Synchronization of oscillatory neuronal responses between striate and extrastriate visual cortical areas of the cat. *Proc. Natl. Acad. Sci. USA* 88: 6048–6052.

Freiwald, W. A., A. K. Kreiter, and W. Singer. (1995). Stimulus dependent intercolumnar synchronization of single unit responses in cat area 17. *Neuroreport* 6: 2348–2352.

Fries, P., P. R. Roelfsema, A. K. Engel, P. König, and W. Singer. (1997a). Synchronization of oscillatory responses in visual cortex correlates with perception in interocular rivalry. *Proc. Natl. Acad. Sci. USA* 94: 12699–12704.

Fries, P., P. R. Roelfsema, W. Singer, and A. K. Engel. (1997b). Correlated variations of response latencies due to synchronous subthreshold membrane potential fluctuations in cat striate cortex. *Soc. Neurosci. Abstr.* 23: 1266.

Gerstner, W. (1996). Rapid phase locking in systems of pulse-coupled oscillators with delays. *Phys. Rev. Lett.* 76: 1755–1758.

Gray, C. M., A. K. Engel, P. König, and W. Singer. (1992). Synchronization of oscillatory neuronal responses in cat striate cortex—temporal properties. *Visual Neurosci.* 8: 337–347.

Gray, C. M., P. König, A. K. Engel, and W. Singer. (1989). Oscillatory responses in cat visual cortex exhibit inter-columnar synchronization which reflects global stimulus properties. *Nature* 338: 334–337.

Gray, C. M., and G. Viana Di Prisco. (1997). Stimulus-dependent neuronal oscillations and local synchronization in striate cortex of the alert cat. *J. Neurosci.* 17: 3239–3253.

Hebb, D. O. (1949). *The Organization of Behavior.* Wiley.

Hubel, D. H., and T. N. Wiesel. (1962). Receptive fields, binocular interaction and functional architecture in the cat's visual cortex. *J. Physiol. (Lond.)* 160: 106–154.

König, P., A. K. Engel, and W. Singer. (1995). Relation between oscillatory activity and long-range synchronization in cat visual cortex. *Proc. Natl. Acad. Sci. USA* 92: 290–294.

König, P., A. K. Engel, and W. Singer. (1996). Integrator or coincidence detector? The role of the cortical neuron revisited. *Trends Neurosci.* 19: 130–137.

Kreiter, A. K., and W. Singer. (1996). Stimulus-dependent synchronization of neuronal responses in the visual cortex of awake macaque monkey. *J. Neurosci.* 16: 2381–2396.

Munk, M. H. J., P. R. Roelfsema, P. König, A. K. Engel, and W. Singer. (1996). Role of reticular activation in the modulation of intracortical synchronization. *Science* 272: 271–274.

Neuenschwander, S., and W. Singer. (1996). Long-range synchronization of oscillatory light responses in the cat retina and lateral geniculate nucleus. *Nature* 379: 728–733.

Roelfsema, P. R., A. K. Engel, P. König, and W. Singer. (1997). Visuomotor integration is associated with zero time-lag synchronization among cortical areas. *Nature* 385: 157–161.

Roelfsema, P. R., P. König, A. K. Engel, R. Sireteanu, and W. Singer. (1994). Reduced synchronization in the visual cortex of cats with strabismic amblyopia. *Eur. J. Neurosci.* 6: 1645–1655.

Shadlen, M. N., and W. T. Newsome. (1994). Noise, neural codes and cortical organization. *Curr. Opin. Neurobiol.* 4: 569–579.

Singer, W., A. K. Engel, A. K. Kreiter, M. H. J. Munk, S. Neuenschwander, and P. R. Roelfsema. (1997). Neuronal assemblies: necessity, signature and detectability. *Trends Cognitive Sci.* 1(7): 252–261.

Singer, W., and C. M. Gray. (1995). Visual feature integration and the temporal correlation hypothesis. *Annu. Rev. Neurosci.* 18: 555–586.

Traub, R. D., M. A. Whittington, I. M. Stanford, and J. G. R. Jefferys. (1996). A mechanism for generation of long-range synchronous fast oscillations in the cortex. *Nature* 383: 621–624.

von der Malsburg, C. (1981). The correlation theory of brain function. *Internal Report 81-2* Max-Planck-Institute for Biophysical Chemistry. Reprinted 1994, in E. Domany, J. L. van Hemmen and K. Schulten, Eds., *Models of Neural Networks II.* Springer-Verlag, pp. 95–119.

Further Readings

Abeles, M. (1991). *Corticonics.* Cambridge: Cambridge University Press.

Abeles, M., Y. Prut, H. Bergman, and E. Vaadia. (1994). Synchronization in neuronal transmission and its importance for information processing. *Prog. Brain Res.* 102: 395–404.

Barlow, H. B. (1972). Single units and sensation: a neuron doctrine for perceptual psychology? *Perception* 1: 371–394.

Bauer, H.-U., and K. Pawelzik. (1993). Alternating oscillatory and stochastic dynamics in a model for a neuronal assembly. *Physica D.* 69: 380–393.

Braitenberg, V. (1978). Cell assemblies in the cerebral cortex. In R. Heim and G. Palm, Eds., *Architectonics of the Cerebral Cortex. Lecture Notes in Biomathematics 21, Theoretical Approaches in Complex Systems.* Springer-Verlag, pp. 171–188.

Edelman, G. M. (1987). *Neural Darwinism: The Theory of Neuronal Group Selection.* New York: Basic Books.

Engel, A. K., P. König, A. K. Kreiter, T. B. Schillen, and W. Singer. (1992). Temporal coding in the visual cortex: new vistas on integration in the nervous system. *Trends Neurosci.* 15: 218–226.

Frien, A., R. Eckhorn, R. Bauer, T. Woelbern, and H. Kehr. (1994). Stimulus-specific fast oscillations at zero phase between visual areas V1 and V2 of awake monkey. *Neuroreport* 5: 2273–2277.

Gerstein, G. L., and P. M. Gochin. (1992). Neuronal population coding and the elephant. In A. Aertsen and V. Braitenberg, Eds., *Information Processing in the Cortex, Experiments and Theory.* Springer-Verlag, pp. 139–173.

Gerstner, W., R. Kempter, J. L. van Hemmen, and H. Wagner. (1996). A neuronal learning rule for sub-millisecond temporal coding. *Nature* 383: 76–78.

Gerstner, W., and J. L. van Hemmen. (1993). Coherence and incoherence in a globally coupled ensemble of pulse-emitting units. *Phys. Rev. Lett.* 7: 312–315.

Hopfield, J. J., and A. V. M. Hertz. (1995). Rapid local synchronization of action potentials: toward computation with coupled integrate-and-fire neurons. *Proc. Natl. Acad. Sci. USA* 92: 6655–6662.

Jagadeesh, B., H. S. Wheat, and D. Ferster. (1993). Linearity of summation of synaptic potentials underlying direction selectivity in simple cells of the cat visual cortex. *Science* 262: 1901–1904.

Löwel, S., and W. Singer. (1992). Selection of intrinsic horizontal connections in the visual cortex by correlated neuronal activity. *Science* 255: 209–212.

Morgan, M. J., and E. Castet. (1995). Stereoscopic depth perception at high velocities. *Nature* 378: 380–383.

Palm, G. (1990). Cell assemblies as a guideline for brain research. *Concepts Neurosci.* 1: 133–147.

Phillips, W. A., and W. Singer. (1997). In search of common foundations for cortical computation. *Behav. Brain Sci.* 20(4): 657–722.

Schmidt, K., R. Goebel, S. Löwel, and W. Singer. (1997). The perceptual grouping criterion of colinearity is reflected by anisotropies of connections in the primary visual cortex. *Europ. J. Neurosci.* 9: 1083–1089.

Singer, W. (1993). Synchronization of cortical activity and its putative role in information processing and learning. *Annu. Rev. Physiol.* 55: 349–374.

Singer, W. (1995). Development and plasticity of cortical processing architectures. *Science* 270: 758–764.

Singer, W. (1996). Neuronal synchronization: a solution to the binding problem? In R. Llinas and P.S. Churchland, Eds., *The Mind-Brain Continuum. Sensory Processes.* Cambridge: MIT Press, pp. 100–130.

Singer, W., A. K. Engel, A. K. Kreiter, M. H. J. Munk, S. Neuenschwander, and P. R. Roelfsema. (1997). Neuronal assemblies: necessity, signature and detectability. *Trends in Cognitive Sciences* 1 (7): 252–261.

Softky, W. R. (1995). Simple codes versus efficient codes. *Curr. Opin. Neurobiol.* 5: 239–247.

Tallon-Baudry, C., O. Bertrand, C. Delpuech, and J. Pernier. (1996). Stimulus specificity of phase-locked and non-phase-locked 40 Hz visual responses in human. *J. Neurosci.* 16: 4240–4249.

Binding Problem

Binding is the problem of representing conjunctions of properties. It is a very general problem that applies to all types of KNOWLEDGE REPRESENTATION, from the most basic perceptual representations to the most complex cognitive representations. For example, to visually detect a vertical red line among vertical blue lines and diagonal red lines, one must visually bind each line's color to its orientation (see Treisman and Gelade 1980). Similarly, to understand the statement, "John believes that Mary's anger toward Bill stems from Bill's failure to keep their appointment," one must bind *John* to the agent role of *believes,* and the structure *Bill's failure to keep their appointment* to the patient role of *stems from* (see THEMATIC ROLES). Binding lies at the heart of the capacity for symbolic representation (cf. Fodor and Pylyshyn 1988; Hummel and Holyoak 1997).

A binding may be either *static* or *dynamic.* A static binding is a representational unit (such as a symbol or a node in a neural network) that stands for a specific conjunction of properties. For example, a neuron that responds to vertical red lines at location x, y in the visual field represents a static binding of *vertical, red,* and *location x, y.* Variants of this approach have been proposed in which bindings are coded as patterns of activation distributed over sets of units (rather than the activity of a single unit; e.g., Smolensky 1990). Although this approach to binding appears very different from the localist (one-unit-one-binding) approach, the two are equivalent in all important respects. In both cases, binding is carried in the units themselves, so different bindings of the same properties are represented by separate units. In a static binding, the capacity to represent how elements are bound together trades off against the capacity to represent the elements themselves (see Holyoak and Hummel forthcoming). In an extreme case, the units coding, say, red diagonal lines may not overlap at all with those representing red vertical lines.

Dynamic binding represents conjunctions of properties as bindings of units in the representation. That is, representational units are *tagged* with regard to whether they are bound together or not. For example, let red be represented by unit *R*, vertical by *V*, and diagonal by *D*, and let us denote a binding with the tag "+." A red diagonal would be represented as *R + D* and a red vertical as *R + V.* Dynamic binding permits a given unit (here, *R*) to participate in multiple bindings, and as a result (unlike static binding), it permits a representation to be isomorphic with the structure it represents (see Holyoak and Hummel forthcoming).

Dynamic binding permits greater representational flexibility than static binding, but it also has a number of properties that limit its usefulness. First, it is not obvious how to do dynamic binding in a neural (or connectionist) network. The most popular proposed binding tag is based on temporal synchrony: if two units are bound, then they fire in synchrony with one another; otherwise they fire out of synchrony (cf. Gray and Singer 1989; Hummel and Biederman 1992; Hummel and Holyoak 1997; Milner 1974; Shastri and Ajjanagadde 1993; von der Malsburg 1981). Although controversial (see Tovee and Rolls 1992), there is

evidence for this type of binding in biological nervous systems (see König and Engel 1995). A more important limitation of dynamic binding is that it is impractical as a basis for binding in long-term MEMORY. For example, we may remember where we parked our car last Tuesday, but it is unlikely that the neurons representing our car have been firing in synchrony with those representing our parking space continuously since then. (The memory might be coded by, say, synaptic links between those neurons, and those links may have been created at the time we parked the car, but such links do not constitute dynamic bindings in the sense discussed here; see Holyoak and Hummel forthcoming.) A third limitation of dynamic binding is that it requires more ATTENTION and WORKING MEMORY than static binding (see Hummel and Holyoak 1997; Stankiewicz, Hummel and Cooper 1998; Treisman and Gelade 1980; Treisman and Schmidt 1982). Although there is no theoretical limit on the number of conjunctive units (i.e., static bindings) that may be active at a given time, there are likely to be strong limits on the number of distinct tags available for dynamic binding. In the case of synchrony, for example, only a finite number of groups of neurons can be active and mutually out of synchrony with one another. Attention may serve, in part, to control the allocation of this finite dynamic binding resource (see Hummel and Stankiewicz 1996).

To the extent that a process exploits dynamic binding, it will profit from the isomorphism between its representations and the represented structures, but it will be demanding of processing resources (attention and working memory); to the extent that it binds properties statically, it will be free to operate in parallel with other processes (i.e., demanding few resources), but the resulting representations will not be isomorphic with the represented structures. These properties of static and dynamic binding have important implications for human perception and cognition. For example, these (and other) considerations led Hummel and Stankiewicz (1996) to predict that attended object images will visually prime both themselves and their left-right reflections, whereas ignored images will prime themselves but not their reflections. In brief, the reason is that dynamic binding (of features into object parts and object parts to spatial relations) is necessary to generate a left-right invariant structural description from an object's image (Hummel and Biederman 1992), and attention is necessary for dynamic binding (Treisman and Gelade 1980); attention should therefore be necessary for left-right invariant structural description. Stankiewicz, Hummel, and Cooper (1998) tested this prediction and the results were exactly as predicted. Apparently, the human visual system uses both static and dynamic codes for binding in the representation of object shape, and these separate codes manifest themselves, among other ways, as differing patterns of priming for attended and ignored object images. Similar tradeoffs between the strengths of static and dynamic binding are also apparent in aspects of human memory and thinking (cf. Hummel and Holyoak 1997).

See also BINDING BY NEURAL SYNCHRONY; BINDING THEORY; CONNECTIONISM, PHILOSOPHICAL ISSUES

— *John Hummel*

References

Fodor, J. A., and Z. W. Pylyshyn. (1988). Connectionism and cognitive architecture: a critical analysis. In S. Pinker and J. Mehler, Eds., *Connections and Symbols*. Cambridge, MA: MIT Press, pp. 3–71

Gray, C. M. and W. Singer. (1989). Stimulus specific neuronal oscillations in orientation columns of cat visual cortex. *Proceedings of the National Academy of Sciences USA* 86: 1698–1702.

Holyoak, K. J., and J. E. Hummel. (forthcoming). The proper treatment of symbols in connectionism. In E. Dietrich and A. Markman, Eds., *Cognitive Dynamics: Conceptual Change in Humans and Machines*. Cambridge, MA: MIT Press.

Hummel, J. E., and I. Biederman. (1992). Dynamic binding in a neural network for shape recognition. *Psychological Review* 99: 480–517

Hummel, J. E., and K. J. Holyoak. (1997). Distributed representations of structure: a theory of analogical access and mapping. *Psychological Review* 104: 427–466.

Hummel, J. E., and B. J. Stankiewicz. (1996). An architecture for rapid, hierarchical structural description. In T. Inui and J. McClelland, Eds., *Attention and Performance XVI: Information Integration in Perception and Communication*. Cambridge, MA: MIT Press, pp. 93–121.

König, P., and A. K. Engel. (1995). Correlated firing in sensory-motor systems. *Current Opinion in Neurobiology* 5: 511–519.

Milner, P. M. (1974). A model for visual shape recognition. *Psychological Review*. 81: 521–535.

Shastri, L., and V. Ajjanagadde. (1993). From simple associations to systematic reasoning: a connectionist representation of rules, variables and dynamic bindings. *Behavioral and Brain Sciences* 16: 417–494.

Smolensky, P. (1990). Tensor product variable binding and the representation of symbolic structures in connectionist systems. *Artificial Intelligence* 46: 159–216.

Stankiewicz, B. J., J. E. Hummel, and E. E. Cooper. (1998). The role of attention in priming for left–right reflections of object images: evidence for a dual representation of object shape. *Journal of Experimental Psychology: Human Perception and Performance* 24: 732–744.

Tovee, M. J., and E. T. Rolls. (1992). Oscillatory activity is not evident in the primate visual cortex with static stimuli. *NeuroReport* 3: 369–372.

Treisman, A., and G. Gelade. (1980). A feature integration theory of attention. *Cognitive Psychology* 12: 97–136.

Treisman, A. M., and H. Schmidt. (1982). Illusory conjunctions in the perception of objects. *Cognitive Psychology* 14: 107–141.

von der Malsburg, C. (1981). The correlation theory of brain function. *Internal Report 81–2*. Göttingen, Germany. Department of Neurobiology, Max-Plank-Institute for Biophysical Chemistry.

Further Readings

Gallistel, C. R. (1990). *The Organization of Learning*. Cambridge, MA: MIT Press.

Binding Theory

Binding theory is the branch of linguistic theory that explains the behavior of sentence-internal anaphora, which is labeled "bound anaphora" (see ANAPHORA). To illustrate the problem, the sentences in (1) each contain an anaphoric expression (*she, herself*), and a potential antecedent (*Lucie* or *Lili*).

(1) a. Lucie thought that Lili hurt her.
 b. Lucie thought that Lili hurt herself.
 c. *Lucie thought that herself hurt Lili.

The two anaphoric expressions have different anaphora options: In (1a), only *Lucie* can be the antecedent; in (1b), only *Lili;* in (1c), neither can. This pattern is universal. All languages have the two anaphoric types in (2), though not all have both anaphors. English does not have an SE anaphor; the Dravidian languages of India do not have a SELF anaphor; Germanic and many other languages have both.

(2) *Types of anaphoric expressions*
 Pronouns: *(she, her)*
 Anaphors:
 a. complex SELF anaphors (*herself*)
 b. SE (Simplex Expression) anaphors (*zich*, in Dutch)

The core restrictions on binding are most commonly believed to be purely syntactic. It is assumed that bound anaphora is possible only when the antecedent C-Commands the anaphoric expression. (Node A C-Commands node B iff the first branching node dominating A also dominates B; Reinhart 1976.) In (1b), *Lili* C-Commands *herself,* but in the illicit (1c), it does not.

The central problem, however, is the different distribution of the two anaphoric types. It was discovered in the seventies (Chomsky 1973) that the two anaphora types correspond to the two types of syntactic movement described below.

(3) *WH-movement:* Who$_i$ did you suggest that we invite t$_i$?

(4) *NP-movement*
 a. Felix$_i$ was invited t$_i$.
 b. Felix$_i$ seems [t$_i$ happy].

NP-movement is much more local than WH-MOVEMENT. Chomsky's empirical generalization rests on observing the relations between the moved NP and the trace left in its original position: in the syntactic domain in which a moved NP can bind its trace, an NP can bind an anaphor, but it cannot bind a pronoun, as illustrated in (5) and (6). Where an anaphor cannot be bound, NP movement is excluded as well, as in (7).

(5) a. Felix$_i$ was invited t$_i$
 b. Felix$_i$ invited himself$_i$
 c. *Felix$_i$ invited him$_i$

(6) a. Felix$_i$ was heard [t$_i$ singing]
 b. Felix$_i$ heard [himself$_i$ sing]
 c. Felix$_i$ hoorde [zich$_i$ zingen] (Dutch)
 d. *Felix$_i$ heard [him$_i$ sing]

(7) a. *Lucie$_i$ believes that we should elect herself$_i$
 b. *Lucie$_i$ is believed that we should elect t$_i$

In the early implementations of binding theory (Chomsky 1981), this was captured by defining NP-traces as anaphors. Thus, the restrictions on NP-movement were believed to follow from the binding conditions. Skipping the technical definition of a local domain, these are given in (8), where "bound" means coindexed with a C-Commanding NP.

(8) *Binding conditions*
Condition A: An anaphor must be bound in its local domain.
Condition B: A pronoun must be free in its local domain.

(5c) and (6d) violate condition B. (7a, b) and (1c) violate condition A. The others violate neither, hence are permitted.

Later developments in SYNTAX enabled a fuller understanding of what this generalization follows from. A crucial difference between WH-traces and NP-traces is that NP-traces cannot carry case. The conditions in (8) alone cannot explain why this should be so; what is required is an examination of the concept "argument." *An argument of some predicative head P is any constituent realizing a grammatical function of P (thematic role, case, or grammatical subject).* However, arguments can be more complex objects than just a single NP. In the passive sentence (5a), there is, in fact, just one argument, with two links. Arguments, then, need to be defined as chains: roughly, *An A(rgument)-chain is a sequence of (one or more) coindexed links satisfying C-Command, in a local domain* (skipping, again, the definition of the local domain, which requires that there are no "barriers" between any of the links).

If *A*-chains count as just one syntactic argument, they cannot contain two fully independent links. Specifically, coindexation that forms an *A*-chain must satisfy (9).

(9) *The A-chain condition*:
An *A*-chain must contain exactly one link that carries structural case (at the head of the chain).

Condition (9) is clearly satisfied in (5a) and (6a), where the trace gets no case. Turning to anaphoric expressions, Reinhart and Reuland (1993) argue that while pronouns are fully Case-marked arguments, anaphors, like NP-traces, are Case-defective. Consequently, it turns out that the binding conditions in (8) are just entailments of (9) (Fox 1993; Reinhart and Reuland 1993). If a pronoun is bound in the local domain, as in (5c) and (6d), an *A*-chain is formed. But since the chain contains two Case-marked links, (9) rules this out, as did condition *B* of (8). In all the other examples in (5) and (6), the *A*-chains satisfy (9), because they are tailed by a caseless link (NP-trace or anaphor). If an anaphor is not bound in the local domain, it forms an *A*-chain of its own. For example, in (7a) *Lucie* and *herself* are two distinct *A*-chains (i.e., two arguments, rather than one). The second violates (9), because it does not contain even one case. Hence, (9) filters out the derivation, as did condition *A* of (8). Condition *A*, then, is just a reflex of the requirement that arguments carry case, while condition *B* is the requirement that they do not carry more than one case, both currently stated in (9).

Recall that only arguments are required to have case. So (9) does not prevent an anaphor from occurring unbound in a nonargument position. For example, the only difference between (7) and (10) is that the anaphor in (10) is embedded in an argument, but is not an argument itself.

(7) *Lucie*$_i$ believes that we should elect herself$_i$.

(10) Lucie$_i$ believes that we should elect Max and herself$_i$.

Anaphors that are not part of a chain are commonly labeled "logophoric," and the question when they are preferred over pronouns is dependent on DISCOURSE—rather than syntax—conditions (Pollard and Sag 1992; Reinhart and Reuland 1993).

There is, however, an aspect of bound local anaphora that is not covered by (8) or (9). Regarding case, SE and SELF anaphors are alike. Nevertheless, while both can occur in (6c), repeated in (11), SE is excluded in (12), which does not follow from (9). The difference is that in (12) a reflexive predicate is formed, because the anaphor and *Max* are co-arguments. But in (11) the anaphor is the subject of the embedded predicate. The same contrast is found in many languages.

(11) Max$_i$ hoorde [zich$_i$/zichzelf$_i$ zingen] (Dutch)

(12) a. Max$_i$ hoorde zich$_i$.
b. Max$_i$ hoorde zichzelf$_i$. (Max heard himself.)

Reinhart and Reuland argue that, universally, the process of reflexivization requires morphological licensing. Thus, another principle is active here:

(13) *Reflexivity Condition*:
A reflexive predicate must be reflexive-marked.

A predicate can be reflexive-marked either on the argument, with a SELF anaphor, or on the predicate. (In the dravidian language Kannada, the reflexive morpheme *kol* is used on the verb.) Because *zich* is not a reflexive-marker, (12a) violates (13).

See also INDEXICALS AND DEMONSTRATIVES; GENERATIVE GRAMMAR; QUANTIFIERS; SEMANTICS; SYNTAX–SEMANTICS INTERFACE

—*Tanya Reinhart*

References

Chomsky, N. (1973). Conditions on transformations. In S. Anderson and P. Kiparsky, Eds., *A Festschrift for Morris Halle*. New York: Holt, Reinhart and Winston, pp. 232–286.

Chomsky, N. (1981). *Lectures on Government and Binding*. Dordrecht: Foris.

Fox, D. (1993). Chain and binding—a modification of Reinhart and Reuland's 'Reflexivity.' Ms., MIT, Cambridge, MA.

Pollard, C., and I. Sag. (1992). Anaphors in English and the scope of the binding theory. *Linguistic Inquiry* 23: 261–305.

Reinhart, T. (1976). *The Syntactic Domain of Anaphora*. Ph.D. diss., MIT, Cambridge, MA. Distributed by MIT Working Papers in Linguistics.

Reinhart, T., and E. Reuland. (1993). Reflexivity. *Linguistic Inquiry* 24: 657–720.

Further Readings

Barss, A. (1986). *Chains and Anaphoric Dependence*. Ph. D. diss., MIT, Cambridge, MA.

Chomsky, N. (1986). *Barriers*. Cambridge, MA: MIT Press.

Chomsky, N. (1986). *Knowledge of Language: Its Nature, Origin, and Use*. New York: Praeger.

Everaert, M. (1991). *The Syntax of Reflexivization*. Dordrecht: Foris

Hellan, L. (1988). *Anaphora in Norwegian and the Theory of Grammar*. Dordrecht: Foris.

Jayasseelan, K. A. (1996). Anaphors as pronouns. *Studia Linguistica* 50: 207–255.

Koster, J., and E. Reuland, Eds. (1991). *Long-Distance Anaphora*. Cambridge: Cambridge University Press.

Lasnik, H. (1989). *Essays on Anaphora*. Dordrecht: Kluwer.

Manzini, R., and K. Wexler. (1987). Parameters, binding theory and learnability. *Linguistic Inquiry* 18: 413–444.

Sigurjonsdottir, S., and N. Hyams. (1992). Reflexivization and logophoricity: evidence from the acquisition of Icelandic. *Language Acquisition* 2 (4): 359–413.

Williams, E. (1987). Implicit arguments, the binding theory and control. *Natural Language and Linguistic Theory* 5: 151–180.

Blindsight

In 1905, the Swiss neurologist L. Bard demonstrated residual visual functions, in particular an ability to locate a source of light, in cortically blind patients. The phenomenon was termed blindsight by Weiskrantz and colleagues (1974) and has been extensively studied both in human patients and in monkeys with lesions of the primary visual cortex (V1, striate cortex). The cortical blindness that results from the visual cortex's destruction or deafferentation is complete if the lesion destroys V1 in both hemispheres. The more common partial blindness (a field defect) always affects the contralesional visual hemifield. Its extent ("quadrantanopia," "hemianopia"), position ("to the left"), and density ("relative," "absolute") is perimetrically assessed. Density refers to the degree to which conscious vision is lost: in a relative defect, conscious vision is reduced and qualitatively altered; often, only fast-moving, high-contrast stimuli are seen (Riddoch 1917). In an absolute defect, no conscious vision remains.

Cortical blindness differs from blindness caused by complete destruction of the eye, the retina, or the optic nerve: the latter lesions destroy the visual input into the brain, while destruction of the striate cortex spares the retinofugal pathways that do not project (exclusively or at all) to this structure. These pathways form the extra-geniculo-striate cortical visual system that survives the effects of the V1-lesion and the ensuing degeneration of the lateral geniculate nucleus and the partial degeneration of the retinal ganglion cell layer. Physiological recordings in monkeys and functional neuroimaging in patients has shown that this system, which includes extrastriate visual cortical areas, remains visually responsive following inactivation or destruction of V1 (Bullier, Girard, and Salin 1993; Stoerig et al. 1997).

The discovery of residual visual functions that were demonstrable in patients who consistently claimed not to see the stimuli they nevertheless responded to (Pöppel, Frost, and Held 1973; Richards 1973; Weiskrantz et al. 1974) was met with a surprise that bordered on disbelief. It seemed inconceivable that human vision could be blind, nonphenomenal, and not introspectable. At the same time, the remaining visual responsivity of extensive parts of the visual system renders remaining visual functions likely to the point where one wonders how to explain that the subjects are blind.

These puzzling residual functions that have increasingly attracted attention from philosophers (e.g., Nelkin 1996; see consciousness) include neuroendocrine and reflexive responses that can even be demonstrated in unconscious (comatose) patients. In contrast, the nonreflexive responses that are the hallmark of blindsight are only found in conscious patients with cortical visual field defects. They have been uncovered with two types of approach that circumvent the blindness the patients experience. The first approach requires the patient to respond to a stimulus presented in the normal visual field, for instance by pressing a response key or by describing the stimulus. In part of the trials, unknown to the patient, the blind field is additionally stimulated. If the additional stimulus significantly alters the reaction time to the seen stimulus (Marzi et al. 1986), or if it alters its appearance, for instance by inducing perceptual completion (Torjussen 1976), implicit processing of the unseen stimulus has been demonstrated. The second type of approach requires the patients to respond directly to stimulation of the blind field. Commonly, forced-choice guessing paradigms are used, and the patients are asked to guess where a stimulus has been presented, whether one has been presented, or which one of a small number of possible stimuli has been presented. Saccadic and manual localization, detection, and discrimination of stimuli differing in dimensions ranging from speed and direction of motion to contrast, size, flux, spatial frequency, orientation, disparity, and wavelength have been demonstrated in this fashion (see Stoerig and Cowey 1997 for review). Whether a patient's performance is at chance level, moderately significant, or close to perfect depends on many variables. Among others they include (a) the stimulus properties: changes in on- and off-set characteristics, size, wavelength, adaptation level, and speed can all cause significant changes in performance (Barbur, Harlow, and Weiskrantz 1994); (b) the stimulus position: when the stimulus is stabilized using an eye-tracking device, at least in some patients stimuli are detectable at some positions and not at others (Fendrich, Wessinger, and Gazzaniga 1992); (c) the response: a spontaneous grasping response may yield better discriminability than a verbal one (Perenin and Rossetti 1996); (d) the training: performance in identical conditions may improve dramatically with practice (Stoerig and Cowey 1997); (e) the lesion: although a larger lesion does not simply imply less residual function (Sprague 1966), evidence from hemidecorticated patients indicates that at least the direct responses require extrastriate visual cortical mediation (King et al. 1996).

Monkeys with striate cortical ablation show very similar residual visual responses. In both humans and monkeys, compared to the corresponding retinal position in the normal hemifield, the residual sensitivity is reduced by 0.4–1.5 log units (Stoerig and Cowey 1997). It is important to note that detection based on straylight, determined with the stimulus positioned on the optic disc of normal observers or in the field defects of patients who are asked to respond by indicating whether they can notice light emanating from this area, requires stimulus intensities 2–3 log units above those needed in the normal field. Blindsight is thus considerably more sensitive and cannot be explained as an artifact of light scattered into the normal visual field (Stoerig and Cowey 1991). The relatively small loss in sensitivity that distinguishes blindsight from normal vision is remarkable in light of the patients' professed experience of blindness. Interestingly, hemianopic monkeys, when given the chance to indicate "no stimulus" in a signal detection paradigm, responded to stimuli they detected perfectly in a localization task as if they could not see them (Cowey and Stoerig 1995). This indicates that it may not just be the patients who deny seeing the stimuli and claim that they are only guessing, but that both species have blindsight: nonreflexive visual functions in response to stimuli that are not consciously seen.

That the visual functions that remain in absolute cortical blindness are indeed blind is one of the most intriguing aspects of the phenomenon. Like other implicit processes that have been described in patients with amnesia, achromatopsia, or prosopagnosia, they may help us understand which neuronal processes and structures mediate implicit as opposed to consciously represented processes. As ipsilesional as well as contralesional extrastriate cortical responsivity to visual stimulation remains in patients and monkeys with blindsight, it appears insufficient to generate the latter (Bullier, Girard, and Salin 1993; Stoerig et al. 1997). This hypothesis gains further support from a recent functional magnetic resonance imaging study that compared within the same patient with a relative hemianopia the activation patterns elicited with a consciously perceived fast moving stimulus and a slow moving one that the patient could only detect in an unaware mode: in both modes, extrastriate visual cortical areas were activated (Sahraie et al. 1997). Further exploration along these lines may help pin down the neuronal substrate(s) of conscious vision, and studies of what can and cannot be done on the basis of blind vision alone can throw some light on the function as well as the nature of conscious representations.

See also IMPLICIT VS. EXPLICIT MEMORY; QUALIA; SENSATIONS

—*Petra Stoerig*

References

Barbur, J. L., A. J. Harlow, and L. Weiskrantz. (1994). Spatial and temporal response properties of residual vision in a case of hemianopia. *Phil. Trans. R. Soc. Lond.* B 343: 157–166.

Bard, L. (1905). De la persistance des sensations lumineuses dans le champ aveugle des hemianopsiques. *La Semaine Medicale* 22: 253–255.

Bullier, J., P. Girard, and P.-A. Salin. (1993). The role of area 17 in the transfer of information to extrastriate visual cortex. In A. Peters and K. S. Rockland, Eds., *Cerebral Cortex.* New York: Plenum Press, pp. 301–330.

Cowey, A., and P. Stoerig. (1995). Blindsight in Monkeys. *Nature* 373: 247–249.

Fendrich, R., C. M. Wessinger, and M. S. Gazzaniga. (1992). Residual vision in a scotoma. Implications for blindsight. *Science* 258: 1489–1491.

King, S. M., P. Azzopardi, A. Cowey, J. Oxbury, and S. Oxbury. (1996). The role of light scatter in the residual visual sensitivity of patients with complete cerebral hemispherectomy. *Vis. Neurosci.* 13: 1–13.

Marzi, C. A., G. Tassinari, S. Aglioti, and L. Lutzemberger. (1986). Spatial summation across the vertical meridian in hemianopics: a test of blindsight. *Neuropsychologia* 30: 783–795.

Nelkin, N. (1996). *Consciousness and the Origins of Thought.* Cambridge: Cambridge University Press.

Perenin, M. T., and Y. Rossetti. (1996). Grasping without form discrimination in a hemianopic field. *NeuroReport* 7: 793–797.

Pöppel, E., D. Frost, and R. Held. (1973). Residual visual function after brain wounds involving the central visual pathways in man. *Nature* 243: 295–296.

Richards, W. (1973). Visual processing in scotomata. *Exp. Brain Res.* 17: 333–347.

Riddoch, G. (1917). Dissociation of visual perceptions due to occipital injuries, with especial reference to appreciation of movement. *Brain* 40: 15–57.

Sahraie, A., L. Weiskrantz, J. L. Barbur, A. Simmons, S. C. R. Williams, and M. J. Brammer. (1997). Pattern of neuronal activity associated with conscious and unconscious processing of visual signals. *Proc. Natl. Acad. Sci. USA* 94: 9406–9411.

Sprague, J. M. (1966). Interaction of cortex and superior colliculus in mediation of visually guided behavior in the cat. *Science* 153: 1544–1547.

Stoerig, P., and A. Cowey. (1991). Increment-threshold spectral sensitivity in blindsight. *Brain* 114: 1487–1512.

Stoerig, P., and A. Cowey. (1997). Blindsight in man and monkey. *Brain* 120: 120–145.

Stoerig, P., R. Goebel, L. Muckli, H. Hacker, and W. Singer. (1997). On the functional neuroanatomy of blindsight. *Soc. Neurosci. Abs.* 27: 845.

Torjussen, T. (1976). Residual function in cortically blind hemifields. *Scand. J. Psychol.* 17: 320–322.

Weiskrantz, L., E. K. Warrington, M. D. Sanders, and J. Marshall. (1974). Visual capacity in the hemianopic field following a restricted cortical ablation. *Brain* 97: 709–728.

Further Readings

Barbur, J. L., K. H. Ruddock, and V. A. Waterfield. (1980). Human visual responses in the absence of the geniculo-calcarine projection. *Brain* 103: 905–928.

Barbur, J. L., J. D. Watson, R. S. J. Frackowiak, and S. Zeki. (1993). Conscious visual perception without V1. *Brain* 116: 1293–1302.

Blythe, I. M., C. Kennard, and K. H. Ruddock. (1987). Residual vision in patients with retrogeniculate lesions of the visual pathways. *Brain* 110: 887–905.

Corbetta, M., C. A. Marzi, G. Tassinari, and S. Aglioti. (1990). Effectiveness of different task paradigms in revealing blindsight. *Brain* 113: 603–616.

Cowey, A., P. Stoerig, and V. H. Perry. (1989). Transneuronal retrograde degeneration of retinal ganglion cells after damage to striate cortex in macaque monkeys: selective loss of P(β) cells. *Neurosci.* 29: 65–80.

Czeisler, C. A., T. L. Shanahan, E. B. Klerman, H. Martens, D. J. Brotman, J. S. Emens, T. Klein, and J. F. Rizzo III. (1995). Suppression of melatonin secretion in some blind patients by exposure to bright light. *N. Engl. J. Med.* 322: 6–11.

Dineen, J., A. Hendrickson, and E. G. Keating. (1982). Alterations of retinal inputs following striate cortex removal in adult monkey. *Exp. Brain Res.* 47: 446–456.

Hackley, S. A., and L. N. Johnson. (1996). Distinct early and late subcomponents of the photic blink reflex. I. Response characteristics in patients with retrogeniculate lesions. *Psychophysiol.* 33: 239–251.

Heywood, C. A., A. Cowey, and F. Newcombe. (1991). Chromatic discrimination in a cortically colour blind observer. *Eur. J. Neurosci.* 3: 802–812.

Holmes, G. (1918). Disturbances of vision by cerebral lesions. *Brit. J. Opthalmol.* 2: 353–384.

Humphrey, N. K. (1974). Vision in a monkey without striate cortex: a case study. *Perception* 3: 241–255.

Humphrey, N. K. (1992). *A History of the Mind.* New York: Simon and Schuster.

Keane, J. R. (1979). Blinking to sudden illumination. A brain stem reflex present in neocortical death. *Arch. Neurol.* 36: 52–53.

Klüver, H. (1941). Visual functions after removal of the occipital lobes. *J. Psychol.* 11: 23–45.

Mohler, C. W., and R. H. Wurtz. (1977). Role of striate cortex and superior colliculus in the guidance of saccadic eye movements in monkeys. *J. Neurophysiol.* 40: 74–94.

Paillard, J., F. Michel, and G. Stelmach. (1983). Localization without content. A tactile analogue of 'blind sight'. *Arch. Neurol.* 40: 548–551.

Pasik, P., and T. Pasik. (1982). Visual functions in monkeys after total removal of visual cerebral cortex. *Contributions to Sensory Physiology* 7: 147–200.

Perenin, M. T., and M. Jeannerod. (1978). Visual function within the hemianopic field following early cerebral hemidecortication in man. I. Spatial localization. *Neuropsychologia* 16: 1–13.

Pöppel, E. (1986). Long-range colour-generating interactions across the retina. *Nature* 320: 523–525.

Riddoch, G. (1917). Dissociation of visual perceptions due to occipital injuries, with especial reference to appreciation of movement. *Brain* 40: 15–57.

Rodman, H. R., C. G. Gross, and T. D. Albright. (1989). Afferent basis of visual response properties in area MT of the macaque. I. Effects of striate cortex removal. *J. Neurosci.* 9: 2033–2050.

Rodman, H. R., C. G. Gross, and T. D. Albright. (1990). Afferent basis of visual response properties in area MT of the macaque. II. Effects of superior colliculus removal. *J. Neurosci.* 10: 1154–1164.

Sanders, M. D., E. K. Warrington, J. Marshall, and L. Weiskrantz. (1974). "Blindsight": vision in a field defect. *Lancet* 20 April, pp. 707–708.

Schacter, D. L. (1987). Implicit memory. History and current status. *J. Exp. Psychol.: Learn. Memory Cogn.* 13: 501–518.

Stoerig, P. (1996). Varieties of vision: from blind responses to conscious recognition. *Trends Neurosci.* 19: 401–406.

Stoerig, P., and A. Cowey. (1989). Wavelength sensitivity in blindsight. *Nature* 342: 916–918.

Stoeric, P., and A. Cowey. (1992). Wavelength discrimination in blindsight. *Brain* 115: 425–444.

Stoerig, P., M. Hübner, and E. Pöppel. (1985). Signal detection analysis of residual vision in a field defect due to a post-geniculate lesion. *Neuropsychologia* 23: 589–599.

Stoerig, P., J. Faubert, M. Ptito, V. Diaconu, and A. Ptito. (1996). No blindsight following hemidecortication in human subjects? *NeuroReport* 7: 1990–1994.

van Buren, J. M. (1963). Trans-synaptic retrograde degeneration in the visual system of primates. *J. Neurol. Neurosurg. Psychiatry* 34: 140–147.

Weiskrantz, L. (1986). *Blindsight: A Case Study and Implications.* Oxford: Oxford University Press.

Weiskrantz, L. (1990). Outlooks for blindsight: explicit methods for implicit processes. *Proc. R. Soc. Lond.* B 239: 247–278.

Weiskrantz, L., J. L. Barbur, and A. Sahraie. (1995). Parameters affecting conscious versus unconscious visual discrimination in a patient with damage to the visual cortex (V1). *Proc. Natl. Acad. Sci. USA* 92: 6122–6126.

Weller, R. E., and J. H. Kaas. (1989). Parameters affecting the loss of ganglion cells of the retina following ablations of striate cortex in primates. *Vis. Neurosci.* 3: 327–342.

Bloomfield, Leonard

Leonard Bloomfield (1887–1949) is, together with Edward Sapir, one of the two most prominent American linguists of the first half of the twentieth century. His book *Language* (Bloomfield 1933) was the standard introduction to linguistics for thirty years. Together with his students, particularly Bernard Bloch, Zellig Harris, and Charles Hockett, Bloomfield established the school of thought that has come to be known as American structural linguistics, which dominated the field until the rise of GENERATIVE GRAMMAR in the 1960s.

Throughout his career, Bloomfield was concerned with developing a general and comprehensive theory of language. His first formulation (Bloomfield 1914) embedded that theory within the conceptualist framework of Wilhelm Wundt. In the early 1920s, however, Bloomfield abandoned that in favor of a variety of BEHAVIORISM in which the theory of language took center stage: "The terminology in which at present we try to speak of human affairs—. . . 'consciousness,' 'mind,' 'perception,' 'ideas,' and so on— . . . will be discarded . . . and will be replaced . . . by terms in linguistics . . . . Non-linguists . . . constantly forget that a speaker is making noise, and credit him, instead, with the possession of impalpable 'ideas.' It remains for the linguist to show, in detail, that the speaker has no 'ideas' and that the noise is sufficient" (Bloomfield 1936: 322, 325; page numbers for Bloomfield's articles refer to their reprintings in Hockett 1970).

In repudiating the existence of all mentalist constructs, Bloomfield also repudiated the classical view that the structure of language reflects the structure of thought. For Bloomfield, the structure of language was the central object of linguistic study, and hence of cognitive science, had that term been popular in his day.

Bloomfield maintained that all linguistic structure could be determined by the application of analytic procedures starting with the smallest units that combine sound (or "vocal features") and meaning (or "stimulus-reaction features"), called *morphemes* (Bloomfield 1926: 130). Having shown how to identify morphemes, Bloomfield went on to show how to identify both smaller units (i.e., phonemes, defined as minimum units of "distinctive" vocal features) and larger ones (words, phrases, and sentences).

Bloomfield developed rich theories of both MORPHOLOGY and SYNTAX, much of which was carried over more or less intact into generative grammar. In morphology, Bloomfield paid careful attention to phonological alternations of various sorts, which led to the development of the modern theory of *morphophonemics* (see especially Bloomfield 1939). In syntax, he laid the foundations of the theory of constituent structure, including the rudiments of XBAR-THEORY (Bloomfield 1933: 194–195). Bloomfield generated so much enthusiasm for syntactic analysis that his students felt that they were doing syntax for the first time in the history of linguistics (Hockett 1968: 31).

Bloomfield did not develop his theory of semantics to the same extent as he did his theories of PHONOLOGY, morphology, and syntax, contenting himself primarily with naming the semantic contributions of various types of linguistic units.

For example, he called the semantic properties of morphemes "sememes," those of grammatical forms "episememes," etc. (Bloomfield 1933: 162, 166). Bloomfield contended that whereas the phonological properties of morphemes are analyzable into parts (namely phonemes), sememes are unanalyzable: "There is nothing in the structure of morphemes like *wolf, fox,* and *dog* to tell us the relation between their meanings; this is a problem for the zoölogist" (1933: 162). Toward the end of the heyday of American structural linguistics, however, this view was repudiated (Goodenough 1956; Lounsbury 1956), and the claim that there are submorphemic units of meaning was incorporated into early theories of generative grammar (Katz and Fodor 1963).

Bloomfield knew that for a behaviorist theory of meaning such as his own to be successful, it would have to account for the semantic properties of nonreferential linguistic forms such as the English words *not* and *and.* Bloomfield was aware of the difficulty of this task. His attempt at defining the word *not* is particularly revealing. After initially defining it as "the linguistic *inhibitor* [emphasis his] in our speech-community," he went on to write: "The utterance, in a phrase, of the word *not* produces a phrase such that simultaneous parallel response to both this phrase and the parallel phrase without *not* cannot be made" (Bloomfield 1935: 312). In short, what Bloomfield is attempting to do here is to reduce the logical law of contradiction to a statement about possible stimulus-response pairs.

However, such a reduction is not possible. No semantic theory that contains the law of contradiction as one of its principles is expressible in behaviorist terms. Ultimately, American structural linguistics failed not for its inadequacies in phonology, morphology, and syntax, but because behaviorism does not provide an adequate basis for the development of a semantic theory for natural languages.

See also DISTINCTIVE FEATURES; FUNCTIONAL ROLE SEMANTICS; MEANING; SAUSSURE

—D. Terence Langendoen

References

Bloomfield, L. (1914). *An Introduction to the Study of Language.* New York: Henry Holt.

Bloomfield, L. (1926). A set of postulates for the science of language. *Language* 2: 153–164. Reprinted in Hockett 1970, pp. 128–138.

Bloomfield, L. (1933). *Language.* New York: Henry Holt.

Bloomfield, L. (1935). Linguistic aspects of science. *Philosophy of Science* 2: 499–517. Reprinted in Hockett 1970, pp. 307–321.

Bloomfield, L. (1936). Language or ideas? *Language* 12: 89–95. Reprinted in Hockett 1970, pp. 322–328.

Bloomfield, L. (1939). Menomini morphophonemics. *Travaux du Cercle Linguistique de Prague* 8: 105–115. Reprinted in Hockett, 1970, pp. 351–362.

Goodenough, W. (1956). Componential analysis and the study of meaning. *Language* 32: 195–216.

Hockett, C. F. (1968). *The State of the Art.* The Hague: Mouton.

Hockett, C. F., Ed. (1970). *A Leonard Bloomfield Anthology.* Bloomington: Indiana University Press.

Katz, J. J., and J. F. Fodor. (1963). The structure of a semantic theory. *Language* 39: 170–210.

Lounsbury, F. (1956). A semantic analysis of Pawnee kinship usage. *Language* 32: 158–194.

Further Readings

Harris, Z. S. (1951). *Methods in Structural Linguistics.* Chicago: University of Chicago Press.

Joos, M., Ed. (1967). *Readings in Linguistics I.* Chicago: University of Chicago Press.

Matthews, P. H. (1993). *Grammatical Theory in the United States from Bloomfield to Chomsky.* Cambridge: Cambridge University Press.

Boas, Franz

Franz Boas (1858–1942) was the single most influential anthropologist in North America in the twentieth century. He immigrated to the United States from Germany in the 1880s, taught briefly at Clark University, then in 1896 took a position at Columbia University, where he remained for the rest of his career. He was trained originally in physics and geography, but by the time he came to this country his interests had already turned to anthropology.

He was a controversial figure almost from the start, in part because of his debates with the cultural evolutionists about the course of human history (*see* CULTURAL EVOLUTION). According to the evolutionists, the pattern of history is one of progress, whereby societies develop through stages of savagery, barbarism, and eventually civilization. In this view, progress is guided by human reason, and societies differ because some have achieved higher degrees of rationality and therefore have produced more perfect institutions than others. According to Boas, however, the dominant process of change is culture borrowing or diffusion. All societies invent only a small fraction of their cultural inventory, for they acquire most of their cultural material from other peoples nearby. The process of diffusion is a result not of reason but of historical accident, and each culture is a unique amalgamation of traits and has a unique historical past.

Boas's concept of culture changed radically in the context of these ideas about history, for he came to view culture as a body of patterns that people learn through interactions with the members of their society. People adhere to such patterns as hunting practices and marriage rules not because they recognize that these help to improve their lives, as the evolutionists thought, but because the members of society absorb the cultural forms of their social milieu. By this view, these historically variable patterns largely govern human behavior and thus are the most important component of the human character. Furthermore, most of culture is emotionally grounded and beyond the level of conscious awareness. Whereas the evolutionists assumed that people are consciously oriented by patterns of rationality and that reason itself is universal and not local—although different societies exhibit different degrees of it—from Boas's perspective people are oriented by a body of cultural patterns of which they are largely unaware. These include such features as linguistic rules, values, and assumptions about reality (*see* LANGUAGE AND CULTURE). These patterns are emotionally grounded in that people become attached to the ways of life they have learned and adhere to them regardless of rational or practical considerations.

Boas's thinking also had significant implications for the concept of race. People behave the way they do not because of differences in racial intelligence, but because of the cultural patterns they have learned through enculturation. Boas was an outspoken proponent of racial equality, and publication of his book *The Mind of Primitive Man* in 1911 was a major event in the development of modern racial thought. Furthermore, Boas's culture concept had important relativistic implications (*see* CULTURAL RELATIVISM). He proposed that values are historically conditioned, in the same way as pottery styles and marriage patterns, and consequently the standards that a person uses in judging other societies reflect the perspective that he or she has learned. Boas and his students developed a strong skepticism toward cross-cultural value judgments.

Boas's work was epistemologically innovative, and he elaborated an important version of cognitive relativism (*see* RATIONALISM VS. EMPIRICISM). In his view, human beings experience the world through such forms as linguistic patterns and cultural beliefs, and like all other aspects of culture these are influenced by the vicissitudes of history. Consequently, people experience the world differently according to the cultures in which they are raised. For example, the linguistic rules that a person learns have the capacity to lead that individual to mis-hear speech sounds that he or she is not accustomed to hearing, while the same person has no difficulty hearing minute differences between other speech sounds that are part of his or her native tongue. Thus this segment of experience is comprehended through a complex of unconscious linguistic forms, and speakers of different languages hear these sounds differently.

Yet in important respects Boas was not a relativist. For instance, while he argued that the speakers of different languages hear the same speech sounds differently, he also assumed that the trained linguist may discover this happening, for, with effort, it is possible to learn to hear sounds as they truly are. In a sense, the linguist is able to experience speech sounds outside of his or her own linguistic framework, and to avoid the cognitive distortions produced by culture. Boas held similar views about science. While reality is experienced through cultural beliefs, it is possible to move outside of those beliefs into a sphere of objective neutrality, or a space that is culture-free, in doing scientific research. Thus Boas's anthropological theory contained a version of cognitive relativism at one level but rejected it at another. Relativism applies when human beings think and perceive in terms of their learned, cultural frameworks, but it is possible for cognitive processes to operate outside of those frameworks as well.

See also CULTURAL VARIATION; HUMAN UNIVERSALS; SAPIR

—*Elvin Hatch*

References

Boas, F. (1911). *The Mind of Primitive Man.* New York: Macmillan.

Boas, F. (1928). *Anthropology and Modern Life.* New York: Norton.

Boas, F. (1940). *Race, Language and Culture.* New York: Macmillan.

Boas, F., Ed. (1938). *General Anthropology.* Boston: Heath.

Codere, H., Ed. (1966). *Kwakiutl Ethnography.* Chicago: University of Chicago Press.

Goldschmidt, W. (1959). *The Anthropology of Franz Boas: Essays on the Centennial of His Birth.* Menasha, WI: American Anthropological Association.

Hatch, E. (1973). Theories of Man and Culture. New York: Columbia University Press.

Holder, P. (1911, 1966). Introduction. In F. Boas, *Handbook of American Indian Languages.* Lincoln: University of Nebraska Press.

Jacknis, I. (1985). Franz Boas and exhibits: on the limitations of the museum method of anthropology. In G. W. Stocking, Jr., Ed., *Objects and Others: Essays on Museums and Material Culture.* Madison: University of Wisconsin Press.

Lowie, R. H. (1917, 1966). *Culture and Ethnology.* New York: Basic Books.

Rohner, R. P., and E. C. Rohner. (1969). *The Ethnography of Franz Boas.* Chicago: University of Chicago Press.

Stocking, G. W., Jr. (1968). *Race, Culture, and Evolution: Essays in the History of Anthropology.* New York: The Free Press.

Stocking, G. W., Jr. (1974). *The Shaping of American Anthropology: A Franz Boas Reader.* New York: Basic Books.

Stocking, G. W., Jr. (1992). *The Ethnographer's Magic and Other Essays in the History of Anthropology.* Madison: University of Wisconsin Press.

Stocking, G. W., Jr. (1996). *Volkgeist as Method and Ethic: Essays on Boasian Anthropology and the German Anthropological Tradition.* Madison: University of Wisconsin Press.

Boltzmann Machines

See RECURRENT NETWORKS

Bounded Rationality

Bounded rationality is rationality as exhibited by decision makers of limited abilities. The ideal of RATIONAL DECISION MAKING formalized in RATIONAL CHOICE THEORY, UTILITY THEORY, and the FOUNDATIONS OF PROBABILITY requires choosing so as to maximize a measure of expected utility that reflects a complete and consistent preference order and probability measure over all possible contingencies. This requirement appears too strong to permit accurate description of the behavior of realistic individual agents studied in economics, psychology, and artificial intelligence. Because rationality notions pervade approaches to so many other issues, finding more accurate theories of bounded rationality constitutes a central problem of these fields. Prospects appear poor for finding a single "right" theory of bounded rationality due to the many different ways of weakening the ideal requirements, some formal impossibility and tradeoff theorems, and the rich variety of psychological types observable in people, each with different strengths and limitations in reasoning abilities. Russell and Norvig's 1995 textbook provides a comprehensive survey of the roles of rationality and bounded rationality notions in artificial intelligence. Cherniak 1986 provides a philosophical introduction to the subject. Simon 1982 discusses numerous topics in economics; see Conlisk 1996 for a broad economic survey.

Studies in ECONOMICS AND COGNITIVE SCIENCE and of human DECISION MAKING document cases in which everyday and expert decision makers do not live up to the rational ideal (Kahneman, Slovic, and TVERSKY 1982; Machina 1987). The ideal maximization of expected utility implies a comprehensiveness at odds with observed failures to consider alternatives outside those suggested by the current situation. The ideal probability and utility distributions imply a degree of LOGICAL OMNISCIENCE that conflicts with observed inconsistencies in beliefs and valuations and with the frequent need to invent rationalizations and preferences to cover formerly unconceived circumstances. The theory of BAYESIAN LEARNING or conditionalization, commonly taken as the theory of belief change or learning appropriate to rational agents, conflicts with observed difficulties in assimilating new information, especially the resistance to changing cognitive habits.

Reconciling the ideal theory with views of decision makers as performing computations also poses problems. Conducting the required optimizations at human rates using standard computational mechanisms, or indeed any physical system, seems impossible to some. The seemingly enormous information content of the required probability and utility distributions may make computational representations infeasible, even using BAYESIAN NETWORKS or other relatively efficient representations.

The search for realistic theories of rational behavior began by relaxing optimality requirements. Simon (1955) formulated the theory of "satisficing," in which decision makers seek only to find alternatives that are satisfactory in the sense of meeting some threshold or "aspiration level" of utility. A more general exploration of the idea of meeting specific conditions rather than unbounded optimizations also stimulated work on PROBLEM SOLVING, which replaces expected utility maximization with acting to satisfy sets of goals, each of which may be achieved or not. Simon (1976) also emphasized the distinction between "substantive" and "procedural" rationality, concerning, respectively, rationality of the result and of the process by which the result was obtained, setting procedural rationality as a more feasible aim than substantive rationality. Good (1952, 1971) urged a related distinction in which "Type 1" rationality consists of the ordinary ideal notion, and "Type 2" rationality consists of making ideal decisions taking into account the cost of deliberation. The Simon and Good distinctions informed work in artificial intelligence on control of reasoning (Dean 1991), including explicit deliberation about the conduct of reasoning (Doyle 1980), economic decisions about reasoning (Horvitz 1987, Russell 1991), and iterative approximation schemes or "anytime algorithms" (Horvitz 1987, Dean and Boddy 1988) in which optimization attempts are repeated with increasing amounts of time, so as to provide an informed estimate of the optimal choice no matter when deliberation is terminated. Although reasoning about the course of reasoning may appear problematic, it can be organized to avoid crippling circularities (see METAREASONING), and admits theoretical reductions to nonreflective reasoning (Lipman 1991). One may also relax optimality by adjusting the scope of optimization as well as the process. Savage (1972) observed the practical need to formulate decisions in terms of "small worlds" abstracting the key elements, thus removing the most detailed alternatives from optimizations. The related "selective ratio-

nality" of Leibenstein (1980) and "bounded optimality" of Horvitz (1987) and Russell and Subramanian (1995) treat limitations stemming from optimization over circumscribed sets of alternatives.

Lessening informational requirements constitutes one important form of procedural rationality. Goal-directed problem solving and small world formulations do this directly by basing actions on highly incomplete preferences and probabilities. The extreme incompleteness of information represented by these approaches can prevent effective action, however, thus requiring means for filling in critical gaps in reasonable ways, including various JUDGMENT HEURISTICS based on representativeness or other factors (Kahneman, Slovic, and TVERSKY 1982). Assessing the expected value of information forms one general approach to filling these gaps. In this approach, one estimates the change in utility of the decision that would stem from filling specific information gaps, and then acts to fill the gaps offering the largest expected gains. These assessments may be made of policies as well as of specific actions. Applied to policies about how to reason, such assessments form a basis for the nonmonotonic or default reasoning methods appearing in virtually all practical inference systems (formalized as various NONMONOTONIC LOGICS and theories of belief revision) that fill routine gaps in rational and plausible ways. Even when expected deliberative utility motivates use of a nonmonotonic rule for adopting or abandoning assumptions, such rules typically do not involve probabilistic or preferential information directly, though they admit natural interpretations as either statements of extremely high probability (infinitesimally close to 1), in effect licensing reasoning about magnitudes of probabilities without requiring quantitative comparisons, or as expressions of preferences over beliefs and other mental states of the agent, in effect treating reasoning as seeking mental states that are Pareto optimal with respect to the rules (Doyle 1994). Nonmonotonic reasoning methods also augment BAYESIAN LEARNING (conditionalization) with direct changes of mind that suggest "conservative" approaches to reasoning that work through incremental adaptation to small changes, an approach seemingly more suited to exhibiting procedural rationality than the full and direct incorporation of new information called for by standard conditionalization.

Formal analogs of Arrow's impossibility theorem for social choice problems and multiattribute UTILITY THEORY limit the procedural rationality of approaches based on piecemeal representations of probability and preference information (Doyle and Wellman 1991). As such representations dominate practicable approaches, one expects any automatic method for handling inconsistencies amidst the probability and preference information to misbehave in some situations.

See also GAME THEORY; HEURISTIC SEARCH; LOGIC; RATIONAL AGENCY; STATISTICAL LEARNING THEORY; UNCERTAINTY

—*Jon Doyle*

References

Cherniak, C. (1986). *Minimal Rationality.* Cambridge, MA: MIT Press.
Conlisk, J. (1996). Why bounded rationality? *Journal of Economic Literature* 34: 669–700.

Dean, T. (1991). Decision-theoretic control of inference for time-critical applications. *International Journal of Intelligent Systems* 6 (4): 417–441.

Dean, T., and M. Boddy. (1988). An analysis of time-dependent planning. *Proceedings of the Seventh National Conference on Artificial Intelligence* pp. 49–54.

Doyle, J. (1980). A model for deliberation, action, and introspection. Technical Report AI-TR 58. Cambridge, MA: MIT Artificial Intelligence Laboratory.

Doyle, J. (1994). Reasoned assumptions and rational psychology. *Fundamenta Informaticae* 20 (1–3): 35–73.

Doyle, J., and M. P. Wellman. (1991). Impediments to universal preference-based default theories. *Artificial Intelligence* 49 (1–3): 97–128.

Good, I. J. (1952). Rational decisions. *Journal of the Royal Statistical Society* B, 14: 107–114.

Good, I. J. (1971). The probabilistic explication of information, evidence, surprise, causality, explanation, and utility. In V. P. Godambe and D. A. Sprott, Eds., *Foundations of Statistical Inference.* Toronto: Holt, Rinehart, and Winston, pp. 108–127.

Horvitz, E. J. (1987). Reasoning about beliefs and actions under computational resource constraints. *Proceedings of the Third AAAI Workshop on Uncertainty in Artificial Intelligence* pp. 429–444.

Kahneman, D., P. Slovic, and A. Tversky, Eds., (1982). *Judgment under Uncertainty: Heuristics and Biases.* Cambridge: Cambridge University Press.

Leibenstein, H. (1980). *Beyond Economic Man: A New Foundation for Microeconomics.* 2nd ed. Cambridge, MA: Harvard University Press.

Lipman, B. L. (1991). How to decide how to decide how to. . . : modeling limited rationality. *Econometrica* 59 (4): 1105–1125.

Machina, M. J. (1987). Choice under uncertainty: problems solved and unsolved. *Journal of Economic Perspectives* 1 (1): 121–154.

Russell, S. J. (1991). *Do the Right Thing: Studies in Limited Rationality.* Cambridge, MA: MIT Press.

Russell, S. J., and P. Norvig. (1995). *Artificial Intelligence: A Modern Approach.* Englewood Cliffs, NJ: Prentice-Hall.

Russell, S. J., and D. Subramanian. (1995). Provably bounded-optimal agents. *Journal of Artificial Intelligence Research* 2: 575–609.

Savage, L. J. (1972). The Foundations of Statistics. Second edition. New York: Dover Publications.

Simon, H. A. (1955). A behavioral model of rational choice. *Quarterly Journal of Economics* 69: 99–118.

Simon, H. A. (1976). From substantive to procedural rationality. In S. J. Latsis, Ed., *Method and Appraisal in Economics.* Cambridge: Cambridge University Press, pp. 129–148.

Simon, H. A. (1982). *Models of Bounded Rationality: Behavioral Economics and Business Organization,* vol. 2. Cambridge, MA: MIT Press.

Brain Mapping

See INTRODUCTION: NEUROSCIENCES; COMPUTATIONAL NEUROANATOMY; MAGNETIC RESONANCE IMAGING; POSITRON EMISSION TOMOGRAPHY

Brentano, Franz

Franz Brentano (1838–1917), German philosopher and psychologist, taught in the University of Vienna from 1874 to 1894. He is the author of *Psychology from an Empirical Standpoint* (first published in 1874), and is principally remembered for his formulation of the so-called Brentano thesis or doctrine of intentionality, according to which what is characteristic of mental phenomena is their INTENTIONALITY or the "mental inexistence of an object."

For Brentano, intentionality is to be understood in psychological (or in what might today be called methodologically solipsistic) terms. To say that a mental act is "directed toward an object" is to make an assertion about the interior structure or representational content of the act. Brentano's primary aim is to provide a taxonomy of the different kinds of basic constituents of mental life and of the different kinds of relations between them. Unlike more recent cognitive psychologists, Brentano takes as his main instrument in analyzing these basic constituents and relations not logic but a sophisticated ontological theory of part and whole, or "mereology." Where standard mereology is extensional, however, treating parts and wholes by analogy with Venn diagrams, Brentano's mereology is enriched by topological elements (Brentano 1987) and by a theory of the different sorts of dependence relations connecting parts together into unitary wholes of different sorts. A theory of "mereotopology" along these lines was first formalized by Husserl in 1901 in the third of his *Logical Investigations* (1970), and its application by Husserl to the categories of language led to the development of CATEGORIAL GRAMMAR in the work of Leśniewski and in Ajdukiewicz (1967).

The overarching context of all Brentano's writings is the psychology and ontology of Aristotle. Aristotle conceived perception and thought as processes whereby the mind abstracts sensory and intelligible forms from external substances. Impressed by the successes of corpuscularism in physics, Brentano had grown sceptical of the existence of any external substances corresponding to our everyday cognitive contents. He thus suspended belief in external substances but retained the Aristotelian view of cognition as a process of combining and separating forms within the mind. It is in these terms that we are to understand his view that "[e]very mental phenomenon includes something as object within itself" (1973).

Brentano distinguishes three sorts of ways in which a subject may be conscious of an object:

1. In presentation. Here the subject is conscious of the object or object-form, and has it before his mind, without taking up any position with regard to it, whether in sensory experience or via concepts.
2. In judgment. Here there is added to presentation one of two diametrically opposed modes of relating cognitively to the object: modes of acceptance and rejection or of belief and disbelief. Perception, for Brentano, is a combination of sensory presentation and positive judgment.
3. In phenomena of interest. Here there is added to presentation one of two diametrically opposed modes of relating conatively to the object: modes of positive and negative interest or of "love" and "hate." Judgment and interest are analogous in that there is a notion of correctness applying to each: the correctness of a judgment (its truth) serves as the objective basis of logic, the correctness of love and hate as the objective basis of ethics.

Brentano's theory of part and whole is presented in his *Descriptive Psychology* (1995). Many of the parts of consciousness are "separable" in the sense that one part can continue to exist even though another part has ceased to exist. Such separability may be either reciprocal—as in a case of simultaneous seeing and hearing—or one-sided—as in the relation of presentation and judgment, or of presentation and desire: a judgment or desire cannot as a matter of necessity exist without some underlying presentation of the object desired or believed to exist.

The relation of one-sided separability imposes upon consciousness a hierarchical order, with *ultimate* or *fundamental acts,* acts having no further separable parts, constituting the ground floor. Such basic elements are for Brentano always acts of sensation. Even among basic acts, however, we can still in a certain sense speak of further parts. Thus in a sensation of a blue patch we can distinguish a color determination and a spatial determination as "distinctional parts" that mutually pervade each other. Another sort of distinctional part is illustrated by considering what the sensation of a blue patch and the sensation of a yellow patch share in common: they share, Brentano holds, the form of coloredness as a logical part. Brentano's account of the range of different sorts of distinctional parts of cognitive phenomena, and especially of the tree structure hierarchies manifested by different families of logical parts, covers some of the ground surveyed by later studies of "ontological knowledge" (Keil 1979).

Brentano's students included not only Sigmund Freud and T. G. Masaryk, but also Edmund Husserl, Alexius Meinong, Christian von Ehrenfels, and Carl Stumpf. Each went on to establish schools of importance for the development of different branches of cognitive science within this century (Smith 1994). Husserl's disciples founded the so-called phenomenological movement; Meinong founded the Graz School of "Gegenstandstheorie" (ontology without existence assumptions); and it was students of Ehrenfels and Stumpf in Prague and Berlin who founded the school of GESTALT PSYCHOLOGY (the term "Gestalt" having been first used by Ehrenfels as a technical term of psychology in 1890; see Ehrenfels 1988; MacNamara and Boudewijnse 1995). The representatives of each of these schools and movements attempted to transform Brentano's psychological doctrine of intentionality into an ontological theory of how cognizing subjects are directed toward objects in the world. The influence of Brentano's philosophical ideas is alive today in the work of analytic philosophers such as Roderick Chisholm (1982), and it has been especially prominent in twentieth-century Polish logic and philosophy (Woleński and Simons 1989).

See also CONSCIOUSNESS; JAMES, WILLIAM; MENTAL REPRESENTATION

—*Barry Smith*

References

Ajdukiewicz, K. (1967). Syntactic connexion. In S. McCall, Ed., *Polish Logic 1920–1939.* Oxford: Clarendon Press, pp. 207–231.
Brentano, F. (1973). *Psychology from an Empirical Standpoint.* London: Routledge and Kegan Paul.
Brentano, F. (1987). *Philosophical Investigations on Space, Time and the Continuum.* London: Croom Helm.
Brentano, F. (1995). *Descriptive Psychology.* London: Routledge.
Chisholm, R. M. (1982). *Brentano and Meinong Studies.* Amsterdam: Rodopi.
Ehrenfels, C. von (1988). On "Gestalt Qualities." In B. Smith, Ed., *Foundations of Gestalt Theory.* Munich and Vienna: Philosophia, pp. 82–117.
Husserl, E. (1970). *Logical Investigations.* London: Routledge and Kegan Paul.
Keil, F. (1979). *Semantic and Conceptual Development. An Ontological Perspective.* Cambridge, MA: Harvard University Press.
MacNamara, J., and G.-J. Boudewijnse. (1995). Brentano's influence on Ehrenfels's theory of perceptual gestalts. *Journal for the Theory of Social Behaviour* 25: 401–418.
Smith, B. (1994). *Austrian Philosophy: The Legacy of Franz Brentano.* Chicago: Open Court.
Woleński, J., and P. M. Simons. (1989). De Veritate: Austro-Polish contributions to the theory of truth from Brentano to Tarski. In K. Szaniawski, Ed., *The Vienna Circle and the Lvov-Warsaw School.* Dordrecht: Kluwer, pp. 391–442.

Broadbent, Donald E.

After years of behaviorist denial of mental terms, DONALD HEBB (1949) admonished: "We all know that attention and set exist, so we had better get the skeleton out of the closet and see what can be done with it." Donald E. Broadbent (1926–1993), more than anyone, deserves the credit for shedding scientific light on this "skeleton." Through his own empirical contributions and his careful analyses of the findings of others, Broadbent demonstrated that experimental psychology could reveal the nature of cognitive processes. In his hands, an information processing approach to understanding ATTENTION, perception, MEMORY, and performance was exceptionally illuminating, and helped initiate and fuel the paradigm shift known as the "cognitive revolution."

Broadbent joined the Royal Air Force in 1944. Noting equipment poorly matched to the human pilot, the importance of practice, and the possibility of measuring individual differences, he envisaged a career in psychology. Under the leadership of Sir Frederic BARTLETT, the Psychology Department at Cambridge University was engaged in solving precisely the kind of real world problems that excited Broadbent. Upon graduation in 1949, Broadbent went straight into research as a staff member at the Medical Research Council's Applied Psychology Unit (APU) in Cambridge.

Broadbent's early research and thinking were strongly influenced by the APU's first two directors, Bartlett and Kenneth Craik. Bartlett (1932) emphasized that people were active, constructivist processors; Craik (1943) pioneered the use of engineering concepts (cybernetics) to explain human performance. At the time, communication theory (Shannon 1948), with its information metric and concept of a communication channel with a limited capacity for information transmission, was being applied to psychological phenomena. Broadbent induced the key principles of his "filter" theory from three basic findings on selective listening (e.g., Cherry 1953): (1) People are strictly limited in their ability to deal with multiple messages (sources of sensory information); (2) the ability to focus on one message while ignoring

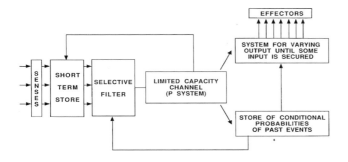

Figure 1. Broadbent's (1958) filter theory asserts that there exists a limited capacity stage of perception (P-system), that this stage is preceded by parallel analysis of simple stimulus features, and that access to the P-system is controlled by a selective filter. Short-term and long-term (store of conditional probabilities of past events) memory systems were postulated and integrated into the information processing system. (This figure is modeled on Broadbent 1958: 297.)

another, irrelevant one is greatly improved if the messages differ in a simple physical property such as location or pitch; and, (3) the consequence of focusing on one message is that the content of the ignored message is unreportable (though simple physical properties can be picked up).

These and other findings, and the theoretical framework Broadbent induced from them, were described in his first major work, *Perception and Communication* (1958). The information processing architecture of Broadbent's famous filter theory (fig. 1) quickly became the most influential model of human cognitive activity cast in information processing terms. Thirteen years later, when Broadbent published his second major work, *Decision and Stress* (1971), it was shown how the 1958 model needed modification: new mechanisms for selection (pigeon-holing and categorizing) that operated later in the processing sequence were added to filtering and an emphasis on the statistical nature of evidence accumulation and decision making was incorporated.

In light of their growing popularity it might be suggested that artificial NEURAL NETWORK models will replace the information processing approach. While acknowledging the value of models cashed out in neural network terms, Broadbent (1985) points out (cf. MARR 1982) that such models are at a different level of analysis (implementation) than information processing models (computation); the appropriate level depends on the nature of the problem to be solved. Considering the problem of designing human-machine systems for data-rich environments, Moray suggests an enduring role for models like Broadbent's: "Whatever the deep structure of attention may be, its surface performance is, in the vast majority of cases, well described by a single, limited capacity channel, which is switched discretely among the various inputs" (1993: 113).

Donald Broadbent was attracted to psychology because he believed that the application of psychological principles could benefit people. It is fitting, then, that in 1958 he was selected to direct the APU, which he did for sixteen years. During this time the APU—already widely respected— would become one of the world's preeminent facilities for

pure and applied psychological research. After this period of steadfast administrative service, Broadbent—who never held an academic appointment—stayed on the Medical Research Council's scientific staff while moving to Oxford. Although Broadbent is, and will continue to be, best known for his empirical and theoretical work on attention, his endorsement of applied psychology never waned. Thus, in contrast to an emphasis on the cognitive "hardware" implicit in his filter theory, Broadbent's belief in the importance of cognitive "software" (task variables and individual differences in strategy selection), led him to predict: "In the long run, psychology will, like computer science, become an ever-expanding exploration of the merits and disadvantages of alternative cognitive strategies" (1980: 69).

Broadbent (1980) was genuinely ambivalent about what he called "academic psychology," and although he recognized the importance of theory, unlike many of his contemporaries, he rejected the hypothetico-deductive approach as inefficient, advocating instead experiments whose results could discriminate between classes of theory (1958: 306) and generate a solid, empirical foundation (Broadbent 1973). In light of these attitudes, it is somewhat ironic that Broadbent would have such a great impact on academic psychology (wherein his theoretical language helped foster the cognitive revolution) and that his theory of attention would become the benchmark against which all subsequent theories are compared.

See also ATTENTION AND THE HUMAN BRAIN; BEHAVIOR- ISM; INFORMATION THEORY; SIGNAL DETECTION THEORY

—*Raymond M. Klein*

References

Bartlett, F. C. (1932). *Remembering.* Cambridge: Cambridge University Press.

Broadbent, D. E. (1958). *Perception and Communication.* Oxford: Pergamon.

Broadbent, D. E. (1971). *Decision and Stress.* London: Academic Press.

Broadbent, D. E. (1973). *In Defense of Empirical Psychology.* London: Methuen.

Broadbent, D. E. (1980). Donald E. Broadbent. In G. Lindzey, Ed., *A History of Psychology in Autobiography,* vol. 7. San Fransisco: W. H. Freeman, pp. 39–73.

Broadbent, D. E. (1985). A question of levels: comment on McClelland and Rumelhart. *Journal of Experimental Psychology: General* 114: 189–192.

Cherry, E. C. (1953). Some experiments on the recognition of speech, with one and with two ears. *Journal of the Acoustical Society of America* 26: 554–559.

Craik, K. J. W. (1943). *The Nature of Explanation.* Cambridge: Cambridge University Press.

Hebb, D. O. (1949). *The Organization of Behavior: A Neuropsychological Theory.* Wiley: New York.

Marr, D. (1982). *Vision.* San Fransisco: Freeman.

Moray, N. (1993). Designing for attention. In A. Baddeley and L. Weiskrantz, Eds., *Attention: Selection, Awareness and Control: A Tribute to Donald Broadbent.* New York: Oxford University Press.

Shannon, C. E. (1948). A mathematical theory of communication. *Bell System Technical Journal* 27: 379–423, 623–656.

Further Readings

Baddeley, A., and L. Weiskrantz, Eds. (1993). *Attention: Selection, Awareness and Control—A Tribute to Donald Broadbent.* New York: Oxford University Press.

Broadbent, D. E. (1961). *Behavior.* London: Eyre and Spottiswoode.

Broadbent, D. E. (1977). Levels, hierarchies and the locus of control. *Quarterly Journal of Experimental Psychology* 32: 109–118.

Duncan, J. (1996). Information and uncertainty in a cumulative science of behavior: 25 years after Broadbent's *Decision and Stress. American Journal of Psychology* 109: 617–625.

Klein, R. M. (1996). Attention: yesterday, today and tomorrow. Review of *Attention: Selection, Awareness and Control—A Tribute to Donald Broadbent. American Journal of Psychology* 109: 139–150.

Posner, M. I. (1972). After the revolution . . . What? Review of *Decision and Stress. Contemporary Psychology* 17: 185–187.

Posner, M. I. (1987). Forward. In D. E. Broadbent, *Perception and Communication.* Oxford University Press, pp. v–xi.

Broca, Paul

During the 1850s Paul Broca (1824–1880) became an important and respected member of the French scientific establishment, sufficient to overcome noteworthy political obstacles and to found the Société d'Anthropologie in 1859 and remain its secretary until his death (Schiller 1979). In a series of papers published between 1861 and 1866 employing the clinico-pathological correlation technique to analyze a loss of speech (aphemia), Broca persuaded a majority of his colleagues that there was a relatively circumscribed center, located in the posterior and inferior convolutions of the left frontal lobe, that was responsible for speech (*langage articulé*). His conclusions have been enshrined in the eponyms Broca's Area and Broca's APHASIA. Whether or not Broca's conclusions constituted a scientific discovery, and whether or not he merits priority in this matter, has been debated ever since (Moutier 1908; Souques 1928; Schiller 1979; Joynt and Benton 1964; Young 1970; Whitaker and Selnes 1975; Henderson 1986; Cubelli and Montagna 1994; Eling 1994; Whitaker 1996). What is not in doubt is that cognitive neuroscience irrevocably changed after the publication of Broca's papers; the cortical localization of language, and by implication other cognitive functions, was now a serious, testable scientific hypothesis.

Broca's sources of knowledge about brain, intelligence, and language functions included François Leuret and Louis P. Gratiolet (1839–1857) and Gratiolet (1854), in which the history of cerebral localization was well described. Gratiolet, a member of the anthropology society, argued from comparative anatomy the importance of the frontal lobes. Bouillaud, who had been influenced by Gall, argued for language localization in the frontal lobe on clinical evidence. Broca knew Bouillaud personally, had been to his house, and even had considered studying internal medicine with him (Schiller 1979: 172). In early 1861 meetings of the anthropology society, Auburtin led a discussion on the question of localizing mental functions to distinct parts of the brain, specifically on localizing speech to the frontal lobe.

Broca participated in that debate (1861a), and his April 1861 report noted the relevance of case Leborgne, alias "tan" (1861b). He chose the older, more prestigious anatomical society as the venue for publishing this case (1861c), stating his belief in cerebral localization in the convolutions, outlining his views regarding regional structural differences of the convolutions (prefiguring cytoarchitectonics) and suggesting that Leborgne's left frontal lesion and loss of speech furnished evidence in support of these views. Broca's second case of loss of speech, patient Lelong, was also published in the same bulletin (1861d); he expressed surprise that the lesion was in the same place as in the previous case—left posterior frontal lobe—and again noted the compatibility with the theory of localization.

The role of the left versus the right hemisphere in language officially arose in 1863 when Gustave Dax deposited for review a report that his father, Marc Dax, had presented to the Montpellier medical society in 1836. In this report the clinico-pathological correlations of forty cases of aphasia suggested that language function resided in the left hemisphere. While the existence of the 1836 Marc Dax mémoire is not absolutely proven, the version written by his son Gustave Dax existed on 24 March 1863, when it was deposited for review (it was published in 1865). The record also shows that Broca's own publication suggesting the special role of the left hemisphere did not appear until 2 April 1863. The priority issue, Dax or Broca, is ably discussed by Schiller (1979), Joynt and Benton (1964), and Cubelli and Montagna (1994); what is not in dispute is that by 1865 the lateralization of language had become an empirical question.

Broca's work was one more part of the ongoing debate on cerebral localization initiated by Gall and Bouillaud in the early nineteenth century; "What Broca seems to have contributed was a demonstration of this localization at a time when the scientific community was prepared to take the issue seriously" (Young 1970: 134–135). Less often appreciated is the fact that every component of Broca's analysis had been published before, between 1824 and 1849. In 1824, Alexander Hood, an obscure Scottish general practitioner who believed in phrenological doctrine, published a case of what would later be called Broca's Aphasia. Hood distinguished between the motor control of the vocal tract musculature, speech output control, and lexical-semantic representation, albeit not in those terms, and assigned each a different left frontal lobe locus. Bouillaud (1825), discussing cases presented earlier by Francois Lallemand, clearly presented classic clinico-pathological correlation techniques as applied to expressive language. Marc Dax observed (1836/1863) that Lallemand's case histories documented that aphasia-producing lesions were in the left hemisphere. The historical question is to explain why Paul Broca in the 1860s was suddenly able to focus neuroscience on brain localization and lateralization of language.

One must acknowledge that Gall's craniology (Spurzheim's phrenology) had stigmatized research on cerebral localization. The doctrine of (brain) symmetry, persuasively articulated by Xavier Bichat at the beginning of the century, posed a major theoretical hurdle. Jean-Pierre Flourens (1794–1867), an influential member of France's scientific establishment, opposed the cortical localization of cognitive functions. Finally, language was considered as verbal expression, as speech or as an output function primarily motoric in nature. What we today recognize as language comprehension fell under the rubric of intelligence or general intellectual functions. Much of the clinical evidence that had been marshaled against Bouillaud came from patients with posterior left hemisphere lesions who manifested aphasia; with no theoretical construct of language comprehension such data could only be interpreted as counter-evidence. The same arguments were offered against Broca, of course. It was the work of Theodor Meynert (1867), Henry Charlton Bastian (1869), and finally Carl Wernicke (1874) on disorders of comprehension that completed the model of language localization, thus setting the stage for the development of modern neurolinguistics and creating a historical niche for Paul Broca.

See also CORTICAL LOCALIZATION, HISTORY OF; HEMISPHERIC SPECIALIZATION; LANGUAGE, NEURAL BASIS OF

—*Harry A. Whitaker*

References

Bastian, C. (1869). On the various forms of loss of speech in cerebral disease. British and Foreign Medical and Surgical Review, January, p. 209, April, p. 470.

Bouillaud, J. B. (1825). Recherches cliniques propres à démontrer que la perte de la parole correspond à la lésion des lobules antérieurs du cerveau, et à confirmer l'opinion de M. Gall, sur le siège de l'organe du langage articulé. *Archives Générales de Médecine* tome VIII: 25–45.

Broca, P. (1861a). Sur le principe des localisations cérébrales. *Bulletin de la Société d'Anthropologie* tome II: 190–204.

Broca, P. (1861b). Perte de la parole, ramollissement chronique et destruction partielle du lobe antérieur gauche. [Sur le siège de la faculté du langage.] *Bulletin de la Société d'Anthropologie* tome II: 235–238.

Broca, P. (1861c). Remarques sur le siège de la faculté du langage articulé, suivies d'une observation d'aphémie. *Bulletin de la Société Anatomique* tome XXXVI: 330–357.

Broca, P. (1861d). Nouvelle observation d'aphémie produite par une lésion de la moitié postérieure des deuxième et troisième circonvolution frontales gauches. *Bulletin de la Société Anatomique* tome XXXVI: 398–407.

Broca, P. (1863). Localisations des fonctions cérébrales. Siège de la faculté du langage articulé. *Bulletin de la Société d'Anthropologie* tome IV: 200–208.

Broca, P. (1865). Du siège de la faculté du langage articulé dans l'hémisphère gauche du cerveau. *Bulletin de la Société d'Anthropologie* tome VI: 377–393.

Broca, P. (1866). Sur la faculté générale du langage, dans ses rapports avec la faculté du langage articulé. *Bulletin de la Société d'Anthropologie* deuxième série, tome I: 377–382.

Cubelli, R., and C. G. Montagna. (1994). A reappraisal of the controversy of Dax and Broca. *Journal of the History of the Neurosciences* 3: 1–12.

Dax, G. (1836/1863). Observations tendant à prouver la coincidence constante des dérangements de la parole avec une lésion de l'hémisphère gauche du cerveau. *C. R. hebdomadaire des séances Académie Science* tome LXI (23 mars): 534.

Dax, M. (1865). Lésions de la moitié gauche de l'encéphale coincidant avec l'oubli des signes de la pensée. *Gazette hebdomadaire médicale* deuxième série, tome II: 259–262.

Eling, P. (1994). Paul Broca (1824–1880). In P. Eling, Ed., *Reader in the History of Aphasia*. Amsterdam: John Benjamins, pp. 29–58.

Gratiolet, P. (1854). *Mémoire sur les Plis Cérébraux de l'Homme et des Primates*. Paris: Bertrand.

Henderson, V. W. (1986). Paul Broca's less heralded contributions to aphasia research. *Archives of Neurology* 43 (6): 609–612.

Hood, A. (1824). Case 4th—28 July 1824 (Mr. Hood's cases of injuries of the brain). *The Phrenological Journal and Miscellany* 2: 82–94.

Joynt, R. J., and A. L. Benton. (1964). The memoir of Marc Dax on aphasia. *Neurology* 14: 851–854.

Leuret, F., and P. Gratiolet. (1839–1857). *Anatomie Comparée du Système Nerveux Considéré dans Ses Rapports avec l'Intelligence*. 2 tomes. Paris: Didot.

Meynert, T. v. (1886). Ein Fall von Sprachstorung, anatomisch begründet. Medizinische Jahrbücher. Redigiert von C. Braun, A. Duchek, L. Schlager. XII. Band der Zeitschrift der K. K. Gesellschaft der Arzte in Wien. 22. Jahr: 152–189.

Moutier, F. (1908). *L'Aphasie de Broca*. Paris: Steinheil.

Schiller, Fr. (1979). *Paul Broca. Founder of French Anthropology, Explorer of the Brain*. Berkeley: University of California Press.

Souques, A. (1928). Quelques Cas d'Anarthrie de Pierre Marie. Aperçu historique sur la localisation du langage. *Revue Neurologique* 2: 319–368.

Wernicke, C. (1874). Der aphasische Symptomenkomplex: Eine psychologische Studie auf anatomischer Basis. Breslau: Max Cohn und Weigert.

Whitaker, H. A., and O. A. Selnes. (1975). Broca's area: a problem in brain-language relationships. *Linguistics* 154/155: 91–103.

Whitaker, H. A. (1996). Historical antecedents to Geschwind. In S.C. Schachter and O. Devinsky, Eds., *Behavioral Neurology and the Legacy of Norman Geschwind*. New York: Lippincott-Raven, pp. 63–69.

Young, R. M. (1970). *Mind, Brain and Adaptation in the Nineteenth Century. Cerebral Localization and its Biological Context from Gall to Ferrier*. Oxford: Clarendon Press.

Cajal, Santiago Ramón y

Santiago Ramón y Cajal (1852–1934) was one of the most outstanding neuroscientists of all time. He was born in Petil-la de Aragón, a small village in the north of Spain. He studied medicine in the Faculty of Medicine in Zaragoza. In 1883, Cajal was appointed in 1892 as chair of Descriptive and General Anatomy at the University of Valencia. In 1887, he moved to the University of Barcelona, where he was appointed to the chair of Histology and Pathological Anatomy. At the University of Madrid, where he remained until retirement, he was appointed to the chair of Histology and Pathological Anatomy. Dr. Cajal received numerous prizes, honorary degrees, and distinctions, among the most important being the 1906 Nobel Prize for physiology or medicine. To describe the work of Cajal is rather a difficult task, because, unlike other great scientists, he is not known for one discovery only, but for his many and important contributions to our knowledge of the organization of the nervous system. Those readers interested in his life should consult his autobiography (Cajal 1917), where there is also a brief description of his main discoveries and theoretical ideas.

The detailed study of the nervous system began in the middle of the last century. Before Cajal's discoveries, very little was known about the neuronal elements of the nervous system, and knowledge about the connections between its different parts was purely speculative. The origin of nerve fibers was a mystery, and it was speculated that they arose from the gray matter independently of the nerve cells (neurons). This lack of knowledge was due mainly to the fact that appropriate methods for visualizing neurons were not available; the early methods of staining only permitted the visualization of neuronal cell bodies, a small portion of their proximal processes, and some isolated and rather poorly stained fibers. It was in 1873 that the method of Camillo GOLGI (1843–1926) appeared; for the first time, neurons were readily observed in histological preparations with all their parts: soma, dendrites, and axon. Furthermore, Golgi-stained cells displayed the finest morphological details with an extraordinary elegance, which led to the characterization and classification of neurons, as well as to the study of their possible connections. In 1906 Golgi was awarded the Nobel Prize for physiology or medicine for discovering this technique. Cajal shared the Nobel Prize with Golgi in the same year, for his masterful interpretations of his preparations in which he applied the method of Golgi.

Cajal was not introduced to a scientific career under the direction of any scientist, as then usually occurred with most scientists, but rather he became a prominent neurohistologist on his own. The career of Cajal can be divided into three major phases (DeFelipe and Jones 1991).

The first phase extended from the beginning in 1877 until 1887, when he was introduced to Golgi's method. During this period he published a variety of histological and microbiological studies, but they were of little significance.

The second phase (1887–1903) was characterized by very productive research, in which he exploited the Golgi method in order to describe in detail almost every part of the central nervous system. These descriptions were so accurate that his classic book *Histologie* (Cajal 1909, 1911), in which these studies are summarized, is still a reference book in all neuroscience laboratories. Also, during the first few years of this second phase, Cajal found much evidence in favor of the neuron doctrine, which contrasted with the other more commonly accepted reticular theory. The neuron doctrine, the fundamental organizational and functional principle of the nervous system, states that the neuron is the anatomical, physiological, genetic, and metabolic unit of the nervous system, whereas for the reticular theory the nervous system consists of a diffuse nerve network formed by the anastomosing branches of nerve cell processes (either both dendritic and axonal, or only axonal), with the cell somata having mostly a nourishing role (for review, see Shepherd 1991; Jones 1994).

The third phase of Cajal's career began in 1903, with his discovery of the reduced silver nitrate method, and ended with his death in 1934; this period was devoted mainly to the investigation of traumatic degeneration and regeneration of the nervous system. He published numerous scientific papers about this subject that were of great relevance, and which were summarized in another classic book, *Degeneration and Regeneration* (Cajal 1913–1914). During this phase, Cajal also published some important papers on the structure of the RETINA and optic centers of invertebrates.

Interestingly, Golgi, as well as most neurologists, neuroanatomists, and neurohistologists of his time, was a fervent believer in the reticular theory of nerve continuity. However, for Cajal the neuron doctrine was crystal clear. Microphotography was not well developed at that time, and virtually the only way to illustrate observations was by means of drawings, which were open to skepticism (DeFelipe and Jones 1992). Some of Cajal's drawings were considered artistic interpretations rather than accurate copies of his preparations. Nevertheless, examination of Cajal's preparations, housed in the Cajal Museum at the Cajal Institute, proves the exactness of his drawings (DeFelipe and Jones 1988, 1992). Although Cajal had the same microscopes and produced similar histological preparations with comparable quality of staining as the majority of the neurohistologists of his time, he *saw* differently than they did. This was the genius of Cajal.

See also CORTICAL LOCALIZATION, HISTORY OF; NEURON

—*Javier DeFelipe*

References

Cajal, S. R. (1909, 1911). *Histologie du Système Nerveux de l'Homme et des Vertébrés*, L. Azoulay, trans. Paris: Maloine. Translated into English as *Histology of the Nervous System of Man and Vertebrates* (N. Swanson and L.W. Swanson, trans.). New York: Oxford University Press, 1995.

Cajal, S. R. (1913–1914). *Estudios sobre la Degeneración y Regeneración del Sistema Nervioso*. Madrid: Moya. Translated into English as *Degeneration and Regeneration of the Nervous System* (R. M. May, tran. and Ed.). London: Oxford University Press, 1928. Reprinted and edited with additional translations by J. DeFelipe and E. G. Jones (1991), *Cajal's Degeneration and Regeneration of the Nervous System*. New York: Oxford University Press.

Cajal, S. R. (1917). *Recuerdos de mi Vida, Vol. 2: Historia de mi Labor Científica*. Madrid: Moya. Translated into English as *Recollections of My Life* (E. H. Craigie and J. Cano, trans.). Philadelphia: American Philosophical Society, 1937. Reprinted, Cambridge, MA: MIT Press, 1989.

DeFelipe, J., and E. G. Jones. (1988) *Cajal on the Cerebral Cortex*. New York: Oxford University Press.

DeFelipe, J., and E. G. Jones. (1991). *Cajal's Degeneration and Regeneration of the Nervous System*. New York: Oxford University Press.

DeFelipe, J., and E. G. Jones. (1992). Santiago Ramón y Cajal and methods in neurohistology. *Trends in Neuroscience* 15: 237–246.

Jones, E. G. (1994). The neuron doctrine. *Journal of History of Neuroscience* 3: 3–20.

Shepherd, G. M. (1991). *Foundations of the Neuron Doctrine*. New York: Oxford University Press

Case-Based Reasoning and Analogy

Case-based reasoning (CBR) refers to a style of designing a system so that thought and action in a given situation are guided by a single distinctive prior case (precedent, prototype, exemplar, or episode). Historically and philosophically,

CBR exists as a reaction to rule-based reasoning: in CBR, the emphasis is on the case, not the rule.

CBR works with a set of past cases, a case base. CBR seeks to determine a "source case" relevant to a given "target case". All CBR systems separate their reasoning into two stages: (1) finding the appropriate source case (retrieving); and (2) determining the appropriate conclusions in the target case (revising/reusing). All CBR systems must have some way of augmenting their case base or learning new cases, even if this simply involves appending to a list of stored cases. Retrieval is described as finding the "most similar" past case or the "nearest neighbor"; this just begs the question of what is the appropriate similarity or distance metric.

To reason about an Italian automobile, consider past examples of automobiles. If the most similar retrieved case is a European automobile, this is a better source of information than a past example of an American automobile, all things being equal.

A set of cases might be viewed as a corpus from which rules could potentially be gleaned, but the appropriate generalizations of which have not yet been performed. In this view, CBR is a postponement of INDUCTION. The advantage of the raw cases, in this view, is that revision of the rule base can better be performed because the original cases remain available; they have not been discarded in favor of the rules that summarize them.

To guide deliberation in a situation, a case-based reasoner represents and transforms the rationale of a precedent or the etiology of a prior case. By hypothesis, a single case suffices for guidance if it is the appropriate case and it is transformed properly. In contrast, rule-based reasoners (e.g., EXPERT SYSTEMS and DEDUCTIVE REASONING) apply a rule to a situation with no transformation.

In both rule-based and case-based reasoning, managing the interaction of multiple sources of guidance is crucial. In CBR, different cases can suggest conflicting conclusions; in rule-based reasoning, several rules might conflict. In one, choose a case; in the other, choose a rule. Nonmonotonic reasoning is fundamentally concerned with both kinds of choice.

In practice, the separation of CBR from other forms of reasoning is imperfect. An interplay of rules and cases is unavoidable. A case can almost always be viewed as a compact representation of a set of rules. CBR is just one form of *extensional programming* (other examples are PATTERN RECOGNITION AND FEEDFORWARD NETWORKS, MACHINE LEARNING, and statistical learning) though CBR performs its generalizations on-line, while others preprocess their generalizations.

Nevertheless, CBR is a distinctly different paradigm. The emphasis is on the unique properties of each case, not the statistical properties of numerous cases. CBR differs from induction because induction derives its power from the aggregation of cases, from the attempt to represent what *tends* to make one case like or unlike another. CBR derives its power from the attempt to represent what *suffices* to make one case like or unlike another. CBR emphasizes the structural aspects of theory formation, not the statistical aspects of data.

Case-based reasoning is usually associated with work that has been called "scruffy": work that aims at the design of software systems and that takes its main themes and inspiration from psychology (e.g., Rosch and Lloyd 1978). Roger Schank (1982) imposes the view that case-based reasoning mimics human MEMORY. He refers to cases as "memories," retrieval of cases as "remindings," and representation of cases as "memory organization." Systems that owe their origin to this school of thought are considerable in scope and ability. There are case-based planners, case-based problem-solvers, case-based diagnosticians, case-based financial consultants, case-based approaches to learning (including EXPLANATION-BASED LEARNING), and case-based illuminations of search.

Research in this style tends to taxonomize issues and approaches. There are qualitative and quantitative metrics of similarity; there are approaches that seek to understand the causality underlying a case, and approaches that do not. The literature contains both a rich conceptual cartography and some of the most accessible polemics on the importance of a nonstatistical approach to the logging of past cases.

A good example of a case-based system is Katia Sycara's PERSUADER, which reasons about labor-management negotiations. It uses past agreements between similarly situated parties to suggest proposals that might succeed in the current negotiation. Past and present situations are compared on features such as wage rates and market competitiveness, and include structural models of how changing one feature affects another. Past agreements can be transformed according to the differences between past and present, possibly including numerically scaling the size of settlements.

Case-based reasoning moved to the center of AI when the logical issues of postponing rule formation were separated from the psychological issues of stuctural ANALOGY. Stuart Russell (1989) defined precisely the "logical problem of analogy" so that it could be studied with precision in the philosophical tradition. Russell proposed that there were relations between predicates, called "determinations," that would permit a single co-occurrence of P and Q to lead to the rule "if $P(x)$ then $Q(x)$." Thus, a person's nationality determines that person's language, but does not determine marital status. The logical formulation showed clearly what would be needed to formally justify analogy. Analogy is either presumptuous (thus, fallible, defeasible, or otherwise susceptible to discount and revision), or else it brings knowledge to bear that permits a single case to skew an entire (statistical) reference class. Like Nelson Goodman's (1972) paradox of "grue," which raises the question of justified projection with many cases, "determinations" raise the question of justified projection from a single case.

Kevin Ashley (1990) showed how cases are used in legal reasoning. Cases and precedents are fundamental to philosophy of law; AI and law have been equally concerned with the proper modeling of cases. Ashley noted that some features describing cases are inherently proplaintiff or pro–defendant. Understanding this distinction permits deeper comparisons of similarity. CBR appears in moral and legal philosophy under the name "casuistry."

Earlier researchers defended CBR by citing contemporary psychology. Ashley and Russell connected CBR to immense literatures that were historically concerned with the significance of the single case. Current work on CBR continues to revolve around these two foci: psychology-inspired themes for systems design, and the precise understanding of reasoning with the single case.

See also PROBABILITY, FOUNDATIONS OF; SIMILARITY; STATISTICAL LEARNING THEORY

—*Ronald Loui*

References

Ashley, K. (1990). *Modeling Legal Arguments: Reasoning with Cases and Hypotheticals.* Cambridge, MA: MIT Press.

Goodman, N. (1972). *Problems and Projects.* Indianapolis: Bobbs-Merrill.

Rosch, E., and B. Lloyd, Eds. (1978). *Cognition and Categorization.* Erlbaum.

Russell, S. (1989). *The Use of Knowledge in Analogy and Induction.* London: Pitman.

Schank, R. (1982). *Dynamic Memory: A Theory of Reminding and Learning in Computers and People.* Cambridge: Cambridge University Press.

Further Readings

Berman, D., and C. Hafner. (1991). Incorporating procedural context into a model of case-based legal reasoning. *Proc. Intl. Conf. on AI and Law* Oxford.

Berman, D., and C. Hafner. (1993). Representing teleological concepts in case-based legal reasoning: the missing link. *Proc. Intl. Conf. on AI and Law* Oxford.

Branting, K. (1991). Explanations with rules and structured cases. *International Journal of Man-Machine Studies* 34.

Burstein, M. (1985). *Learning by Reasoning from Multiple Analogies.* Ph.D. diss., Yale University.

Carbonell, J. (1981). A computational model of analogical problem-solving. *Proc. IJCAI* Vancouver.

Cohen, M., and E. Nagel. (1934). *An Introduction to Logic and Scientific Method.* Harcourt Brace.

Davies, T., and S. Russell. (1987). A logical approach to reasoning by analogy. *Proc. IJCAI* Milan.

DeJong, G. (1981). Generalizations based on explanations. *Proc. IJCAI* Vancouver.

Gardner, A. (1987). *An AI Approach to Legal Reasoning.* Cambridge, MA: MIT Press.

Gentner, D. (1983). Structure mapping: a theoretical framework for analogy. *Cognitive Science* 7.

Hammond, K. (1990). Case-based planning: a framework for planning from experience. *Cognitive Science* 14.

Hesse, M. (1966). *Models and Analogies in Science.* University of Notre Dame Press.

Keynes, J. (1957 [1908]). *A Treatise on Probability.* MacMillan.

Kolodner, J. (1993). *Case-Based Reasoning.* Morgan Kaufman.

Koton, P. (1988). *Using Experience in Learning and Problem Solving.* Ph.D. diss., MIT.

Leake, D., Ed. (1996). *Case-Based Reasoning: Experiences, Lessons, and Future Directions.* Cambridge, MA: MIT Press.

Loui, R. (1989). Analogical reasoning, defeasible reasoning, and the reference class. *Proc. Knowledge Representation and Reasoning* Toronto.

Loui, R., and J. Norman. (1995). Rationales and argument moves. *Artificial Intelligence and Law* 3.

Mitchell, T., R. Keller, and S. Kedar-Cabelli. (1986). Explanation-based generalization: a unifying view. *Machine Learning Journal* 1.

Raz, J. (1979). *The Authority of Law.* Oxford.

Riesbeck, C., and R. Schank. (1989). *Inside Case-Based Reasoning.* Erlbaum.

Skalak, D., and E. Rissland. (1992). Arguments and cases: an inevitable intertwining. *Artificial Intelligence and Law* 1.

Sunstein, C. (1996). *Legal Reasoning and Political Conflict.* Oxford.

Winston, P. (1980). Learning and reasoning by analogy. *Comm. ACM* 23.

Categorial Grammar

The term Categorial Grammar (CG) refers to a group of theories of natural language syntax and semantics in which the main responsibility for defining syntactic form is borne by the LEXICON. CG is therefore one of the oldest and purest examples of a class of lexicalized theories of grammar that also includes HEAD-DRIVEN PHRASE STRUCTURE GRAMMAR, LEXICAL FUNCTIONAL GRAMMAR, Tree-adjoining grammar, Montague grammar, RELATIONAL GRAMMAR, and certain recent versions of the Chomskean theory.

The various modern versions of CG are characterized by a much freer notion of derivational syntactic structure than is assumed under most other formal or generative theories of grammar. All forms of CG also follow Montague (1974) in sharing a strong commitment to the Principle of COMPOSITIONALITY—that is, to the assumption that syntax and interpretation are homomorphically related and may be derived in tandem. Significant contributions have been made by Categorial Grammarians to the study of SEMANTICS, SYNTAX, MORPHOLOGY, intonational phonology, COMPUTATIONAL LINGUISTICS, and human SENTENCE PROCESSING.

There have been two styles of formalizing the grammar of natural languages since the problem was first articulated in the 1950s. Chomsky (1957) and much subsequent work in GENERATIVE GRAMMAR begins by capturing the basic facts of English constituent order exemplified in (1) in a Context-free Phrase Structure grammar (CFPSG) or system of rewrite rules or "productions" like (2), which have their origin in early work in recursion theory by Post, among others.

(1) Dexter likes Warren.

(2) $S \rightarrow NP\ VP$
     $VP \rightarrow TV\ NP$
     $TV \rightarrow \{$ likes, sees, ... $\}$

Categorial Grammar (CG), together with its close cousin Dependency Grammar (which also originated in the 1950s, in work by Tesnière), stems from an alternative approach to the context-free grammar pioneered by Bar-Hillel (1953) and Lambeck (1958), with earlier antecedents in Ajdukiewicz (1935) and still earlier work by Husserl and Russell in category theory and the theory of types. Categorial Grammars capture the same information by associating a functional type or category with all grammatical entities. For example, all transitive verbs are associated via the lexicon with a category that can be written as follows:

(3) likes := $(S\backslash NP)/NP$

The notation here is the "result leftmost" notation according to which α/β and $\alpha\backslash\beta$ represent functions from β

into α, where the slash determines that the argument β is respectively to the right (/) or to the left (\) of the functor. Thus the transitive verb (3) is a functor over NPs to its right-yielding predicates, or functors over NPs to the left, which in turn yield *S*. (There are several other notations for categorial grammars, including the widely used "result on top" notation of Lambek 1958 and much subsequent work, according to which the above category is written *(NP\S)/NP*. The advantage of the present notation for cognitive scientists is that semantic type can be read in a consistent left-right order, regardless of directionality.)

In "pure" context-free CG, categories can combine via two general function application rules, which in the present notation are written as in (4), to yield derivations, written as in (5a), in which underlines indexed with right and left arrows indicate the application of the two rules.

(4) *Functional application*
  a. *X/Y   Y ⇒ X*
  b. *Y   X\Y ⇒ X*

(5) a. 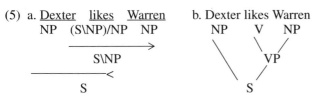   b. Dexter likes Warren

Such derivations are equivalent to traditional trees like (5b) in CFPSG. However, diagrams like (5a) should be thought of as derivations, delivering a compositional interpretation directly, rather than a purely syntactic structure. The identification of derivation with interpretation becomes important when we consider the extensions of CG that take it beyond weak equivalence with CFPSG.

A central problem for any theory of grammar is to capture the fact that elements of sentences that belong together at the level of semantics or interpretation may be separated by much intervening material in sentences, the most obvious example in English arising from the relative clause construction. All theories of grammar respond to this problem by adding something such as the transformationalists' WH-MOVEMENT, GPSG feature-passing, ATN HOLD registers, or whatever to a context-free core. Usually, such additions increase automata-theoretic power. To the extent that the constructions involved seem to be quite severely constrained, and that certain kinds of long-range dependencies seem to be universally prohibited, there is clearly some explanatory value in keeping such power to a minimum.

All of the generalizations of categorial grammar respond to this problem by adding various *type-driven combinatory operators* to pure CG. The many different proposals for how to do this fall under two quite distinct approaches. The first, *rule-based,* approach, pioneered by Lyons (1968), Bach (1976), and Dowty (1979), among other linguists, and by Lewis (1970) and Geach (1972), among philosophical logicians, starts from the pure CG of Bar-Hillel, and adds rules corresponding to simple operations over categories, such as "wrap" (or commutation of arguments), "type-raising," (which resembles the application of traditional nominative, accusative, etc. case to NPs, etc.) and functional composi-

tion. One possible derivation of a complex relative clause comes out as follows in one fairly typical version, "Combinatory" Categorial Grammar (CCG), discussed at length by the present author (see "Further Reading"), in which type-raising and composition are for historical reasons indicated by **T** and **B**, respectively.

(6)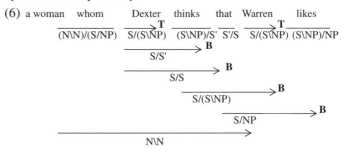

Notice that this analysis bears no resemblance to a traditional right-branching clause structure modified by structure-preserving movement transformations.

The alternative, *deductive,* style of Categorial Grammar, pioneered by van Benthem (1986) and Moortgat (1988), takes as its starting point Lambek's syntactic calculus. The Lambek system embodies a view of the categorial slash as a form of logical implication for which a number of axioms or inference rules define a proof theory. (For example, functional application corresponds to the familiar classical rule of *modus ponens* under this view). A number of further axioms give rise to a deductive calculus in which many but not all of the rules deployed by the alternative rule-based generalizations of CG are theorems. For example, the derivation (6) corresponds to a proof in the Lambek calculus using type-raising and composition as lemmas.

The differences between these approaches make themselves felt when the grammars in question are extended beyond the weak context-free power of the Lambek calculus and the combinatory rules that are theorems thereof, as they must be to capture natural language in an explanatory fashion. The problem is that almost any addition of axioms corresponding to the non-Lambek combinatory rules that have been proposed in the rule-based framework causes a collapse of the calculus into "permutation completeness"—that is, into a grammar that accepts all permutations of the words of any sentence it accepts. This forces the advocates of the Lambek calculus into the "multimodal" systems involving many distinct slashes encoding multiple notions of implication (Morrill 1994), and forces the advocates of rule-based systems to impose type restrictions on their rules. (Nevertheless, Joshi, Vijay-Shanker, and Weir 1991 show that certain rule-based CGs remain of low automata-theoretic power.)

These two styles of CG are reviewed and compared at length by Moortgat (1988) (with a deductive bias), and Wood (1993) (with a rule-based bias) (see Further Readings). To some extent the same biases are respectively exhibited in the selection made in two important collections of papers edited by Buszkowski, Marciszewski, and van Benthem (1988) and Oehrle, Bach, and Wheeler (1988) (see Further Readings), which include several of the papers cited here.

The differences are less important for the present purpose than the fact that all of these theories have the effect of engendering derivational structures that are much freer than traditional surface structures, while nonetheless guaranteeing that the nonstandard derivations deliver the same semantic interpretation as the standard ones. For example, because all of these theories allow the residue of relativization *Dexter thinks that Warren likes* in example (6) to be a derivational constituent of type *S/NP*, they also all allow a nonstandard analysis of the canonical sentence *Dexter thinks that Warren likes these flowers* in terms of an identically derived constituent followed by an object NP:

(7) [[Dexter thinks that Warren likes]$_{S/NP}$ [these flowers]$_{NP}$]$_S$

This is a surprising property, because it seems to flout all received opinion concerning the surface constituency of English sentences, suggesting that a structure in which objects—even embedded ones—dominate subjects is as valid as the standard one in which subjects dominate objects. The implication is that the BINDING THEORY (which must explain such facts as that in every language in the world you can say the equivalent of *Warren and Dexter shave each other* but not *Each other shave Dexter and Warren*) must be regarded as a property of semantic interpretation or LOGICAL FORM rather than of surface structure as such (cf. Dowty 1979; Szabolcsi 1989; Chierchia 1988; Hepple 1990; Jacobson 1992).

These proposals also imply that there are many semantically equivalent surface derivations for every traditional one, a problem that is sometimes misleadingly referred to as "spurious ambiguity," and which appears to make parsing more laborious. However, this problem can be eliminated using standard chart-parsing techniques with an equivalence check on Logical Forms associated with constituents, as proposed by Karttunen (1989) and other advocates of unification-based computational realizations of CG—see Carpenter 1997 for a review.

Flexible or combinatory Categorial Grammars of all kinds have real advantages for capturing a number of phenomena that are problematic for more traditional theories of grammar. For example, as soon as the analysis in (7) is admitted, we explain why similar fragments can behave like constituents for purposes of coordination:

(8) [[I dislike]$_{S/NP}$, but [Dexter thinks that Warren likes] $_{S/NP}$ [these flowers]$_{NP}$]$_S$

(Other even more spectacular coordinating nonstandard fragments are discussed in Dowty 1988.)

We also explain why intonation seems similarly able to treat such fragments as phrasal units in examples like the following, in which % marks an intonational boundary or break, and capitalization indicates STRESS (cf. Oehrle et al. 1985; Prevost 1995):

(9) [Q:] I know who YOU like, but who does DEXTER like?
    [A:] [DEXTER likes]$_{S/NP}$ % [WARREN]$_{NP}$

Moreover, the availability of semantic interpretations for such nonstandard constituents appears under certain plausible assumptions about the relation of the competence grammar to the processor to simplify the problem of explaining the availability to human sentence processors of semantic interpretations for fragments like *the flowers sent for*, as evidenced by the effect of this content in (b) below in eliminating the "garden-path" effect of the ambiguity in (a), discussed by Crain and Steedman (1985) and Altman (1988).

(10) a. The doctor sent for the patient died.
     b. The flowers sent for the patient died.

All of these phenomena imply that the extra structural ambiguity engendered by generalized categorial grammars is not "spurious," but a property of competence grammar itself.

See also MINIMALISM; PROSODY AND INTONATION; SYNTAX-SEMANTICS INTERFACE

—*Mark Steedman*

References

Ajdukiewicz, K. (1935). Die syntaktische Konnexitat. In S. McCall, Ed., *Polish Logic 1920–1939*. Oxford University Press, pp. 207–231. Translated from *Studia Philosophica* 1: 1–27.

Altmann, G. (1988). Ambiguity, parsing strategies, and computational models. *Language and Cognitive Processes* 3: 73–98.

Bach, E. (1976). An extension of classical transformational grammar. In *Problems in Linguistic Metatheory: Proceedings of the 1976 Conference at Michigan State University* 183–224.

Bar-Hillel, Y. (1953). A quasi-arithmetical notation for syntactic description. *Language* 29: 47–58.

Carpenter, R. (1997). *Type-Logical Semantics*. Cambridge, MA: MIT Press.

Chierchia, G. (1988). Aspects of a categorial theory of binding. In R. T. Oehrle, E. Bach, and D. Wheeler, Eds., *Categorial Grammars and Natural Language Structures*. (Proceedings of the Conference on Categorial Grammar, Tucson, AZ, June 1985.) Dordrecht: Reidel, pp. 153–98.

Chomsky, N. (1957). *Syntactic Structures*. The Hague: Mouton.

Crain, S., and M. Steedman. (1985). On not being led up the garden path: the use of context by the psychological parser. In L. Kartunnen, D. Dowty, and A. Zwicky, Eds., *Natural Language Parsing: Psychological, Computational and Theoretical Perspectives*. ACL Studies in Natural Language Processing. Cambridge: Cambridge University Press, pp. 320–358.

Dowty, D. (1979). Dative movement and Thomason's extensions of Montague Grammar. In S. Davis and M. Mithun, Eds., *Linguistics, Philosophy, and Montague Grammar*. Austin: University of Texas Press.

Dowty, D. (1988). Type-raising, functional composition, and nonconstituent coordination. In R. T. Oehrle, E. Bach, and D. Wheeler, Eds., *Categorial Grammars and Natural Language Structures*. Proceedings of the Conference on Categorial Grammar, Tucson, AZ, June 1985. Dordrecht: Reidel, pp. 153–198.

Geach, P. (1972). A program for syntax. In D. Davidson and G. Harman, Eds., *Semantics of Natural Language*. Dordrecht: Reidel, pp. 483–497.

Hepple, M. (1990). *The Grammar and Processing of Order and Dependency: A Categorial Aproach*. Ph.D. diss., University of Edinburgh.

Jacobson, P. (1992). The lexical entailment theory of control and the tough construction. In I. Sag and A. Szabolcsi, Eds., *Lexical Matters*. Chicago: CSLI/Chicago University Press, pp. 269–300.

Joshi, A., K. Vijay-Shanker, and D. Weir. (1991). The convergence of mildly context-sensitive formalisms. In P. Sells, S. Shieber, and T. Wasow, Eds., *Processing of Linguistic Structure.* Cambridge MA: MIT Press, pp. 31–81.

Karttunen, L. (1989). Radical lexicalism. In M. R. Baltin and A. S. Kroch, Eds., *Alternative Conceptions of Phrase Structure.* Chicago: University of Chicago Press.

Lambek, J. (1958). The mathematics of sentence structure. *American Mathematical Monthly* 65: 154–170.

Lewis, D. (1970). General semantics. *Synthese* 22: 18–67.

Lyons, J. (1968). *Introduction to Theoretical Linguistics.* Cambridge: Cambridge University Press.

Montague, R. (1974). *Formal philosophy: Papers of Richard Montague,* Richmond H. Thomason, Ed. New Haven: Yale University Press.

Moortgat, M. (1988). *Categorial Investigations.* Ph.D. diss., Universiteit van Amsterdam. (Published by Foris, 1989).

Morrill, G. (1994). *Type-Logical Grammar.* Dordrecht: Kluwer.

Oehrle, R. T. (1988). Multidimensional compositional functions as a basis for grammatical analysis. In R. T. Oehrle, E. Bach, and D. Wheeler, Eds., *Categorial Grammars and Natural Language Structures.* (Proceedings of the Conference on Categorial Grammar, Tucson, AZ, June 1985). Dordrecht: Reidel, pp. 349–390.

Prevost, S. (1995). *A Semantics of Contrast and Information Structure for Specifying Intonation in Spoken Language Generation.* Ph.D. diss., University of Pennsylvania, Philadelphia, PA.

Szabolcsi, A. (1989). Bound variables in syntax: are there any? In R. Bartsch, J. van Benthem, and P. van Emde Boas, Eds., *Semantics and Contextual Expression.* Dordrecht: Foris, pp. 295–318.

van Benthem, J. (1986). *Essays in Logical Semantics.* Dordrecht: Reidel.

Further Readings

Buszkowski, W., W. Marciszewski, and J. van Benthem, Eds. (1988). *Categorial Grammar.* Amsterdam: John Benjamins.

Moortgat, M. (1997). Categorial type logics. In J. van Benthem and A. ter Meulen, Eds., *Handbook of Logic and Language.* Amsterdam: North Holland, pp. 93–177.

Oehrle, R., E. Bach, and D. Wheeler. (1988). *Categorial Grammars and Natural Language Structures.* Dordrecht: Reidel.

Steedman, M. (1996). *Surface Structure and Interpretation.* Linguistic Inquiry Monograph 30. Cambridge MA: MIT Press.

Wood, M. M. (1993). *Categorial Grammar.* Routledge.

Categorization

Categorization, the process by which distinct entities are treated as equivalent, is one of the most fundamental and pervasive cognitive activities. It is fundamental because categorization permits us to understand and make predictions about objects and events in our world. People (necessarily) make use of only the tiniest fraction of the possible categorization schemes, but even a modest-sized set of entities can be grouped in a limitless number of ways. Therefore, a fundamental question is why we have the categories we have and not others. Further, what do our categorization schemes allow us to do that other schemes would not?

There has been a plethora of work on the structure of categories, mostly examining natural object categories (see Smith and Medin 1981; Rips 1990; Komatsu 1992 for

reviews). A powerful but controversial idea is that SIMILARITY is an organizing principle. Within this framework, there are important distinctions concerning just how similarity operates, but we will not be concerned with them here (see Medin 1989 for a review). Simply stated, this view suggests that we put things in the same categories because they are similar to each other. A robin and a hawk (both birds) seem obviously more similar than a robin and an elephant (not a bird); elephants are not birds because they are not sufficiently similar to them. A natural consequence of this similarity view is that the world is organized for us and our categories map onto this reality (e.g., Rosch and Mervis 1975).

Why is this notion that categories are defined by some "objective" similarity controversial? The main criticism has been that the notion of similarity is too unconstrained to be useful as an explanatory principle (Goodman 1972; Murphy and Medin 1985). Similarity is usually defined in terms of shared properties, but Goodman argued that any two things share an unlimited number of properties (e.g., robins and elephants can move, weigh more than an ounce, weigh more than two ounces, take up space, can be thought about, etc.). Given this apparent flexibility, it may be that we see things as similar *because* they belong to the same category and not vice versa. That is, maybe we can explain similarity in terms of categories.

An alternative to the similarity view of categorization is that *theories* provide conceptual coherence (Carey 1985; Keil 1989; Medin 1989; Rips 1989; Hirschfeld and Gelman 1994). The theory-based explanation of categorization is consistent with the idea that CONCEPTS are comprised of features or properties. By concept, we mean the mental representation of a category that presumably includes more than procedures for identifying or classifying. These explanations go beyond similarity models in arguing that underlying principles (often causal) determine which features are relevant and how they might be interrelated (Komatsu 1992; see also Billman and Knutson 1996).

In current cognitive science theorizing, similarity has a role to play but a limited one that, in many respects, changes its character. Researchers who focus on similarity (e.g., Nosofsky 1988) use models of selective feature weighting such that similarity is, in part, a byproduct of category learning. Other researchers derive a role for similarity from an analysis of how categories might be used to satisfy human goals such as in drawing inferences (e.g., Anderson 1991). Finally, investigators who argue that categories are organized around knowledge structures (e.g., Wisniewski and Medin 1994) allow theories to determine the very notion of what a feature is.

Is there a single set of principles that applies to all categories? Evidence suggests that there may be important differences among them. First of all, a great deal of attention has been directed to the hierarchical component of categories. Objects can be categorized at different levels of abstraction; for example, your pet Fido can be categorized as a living thing, an animal, a mammal, a dog, or a poodle. Work by Eleanor Rosch and her colleagues (Rosch et al. 1976; see Berlin, Breedlove, and Raven 1973 for related work in anthropology) has shown that one level in this hierarchy, dubbed the "basic level," seems to be psychologically privileged. In our example, *dog* would be a basic level term, and Rosch et al. found that a number of measures of privilege all converged on this level. The basic level is the level preferred in naming by adults, is the first learned by children, and is the level at which adults can categorize most rapidly. It may be that similarity plays a bigger role in categorization at the basic level than for more superordinate levels. Currently, investigators are actively pursuing issues such as whether the basic level might change with expertise (e.g., Tanaka and Taylor 1991) or vary across cultures (Berlin 1992; Coley, Medin, and Atran 1997). These questions bear on the respective roles of mind and world in categorization (variability with culture or expertise would tend to support the former).

Other researchers have attempted to extend this hierarchical structure to social categories (e.g., race, gender, occupation, etc.). There has been some work applying Rosch's measures of basic levels to the domains of person concepts and routine social events with moderate success (Cantor and Mischel 1979; Morris and Murphy 1990). Note, however, that many social categories are nonhierarchical and categories at the same level of abstractness may be overlapping rather than mutually exclusive. For example, a person can be categorized as a woman, an ethnic minority member, a millionaire, and a celebrity all at the same time. None of these categories are subordinate or superordinate to any other. This raises a new set of questions about which categories are activated in a given situation and how the corresponding concepts are updated with experience. There is even evidence that alternative social categories may compete and inhibit one another (Macrae, Bodenhausen, and Milne 1995). In short, there may be major differences between object and social categories (see Wattenmaker 1995 for a further example).

Goal-derived categories also differ from common taxonomic categories. Barsalou (1983, 1985) has shown that categories activated in the service of goals (e.g., things to take on a camping trip, things to eat when on a diet) may follow different processing principles. For instance, goodness of example for many object categories seems to be based on having typical properties (a robin is judged to be a very typical bird because it looks and acts like many other birds; ostriches are not typical for the opposite reason; see Rosch and Mervis 1975), but for goal-derived categories, goodness of example seems to be based on ideals or extremes. More specifically, the best example of a diet food is one with zero calories, even though zero may not be typical.

Still other researchers have suggested that categorization principles show DOMAIN SPECIFICITY. For example, some have suggested that biological categories constitute a distinct (and innate) domain and that people universally assume that biological categories have an underlying essence that makes things the way they are (Atran 1990). Domain-specificity is a topic that is currently receiving much attention (see chapters in Hirschfeld and Gelman 1994).

Categorization touches on many important applied and theoretical questions. How does the perception of social groups lead to stereotypes (see STEREOTYPING) and other forms of bias? What is the role of language in categorization and conceptual development? To what extent do people who categorize the same way also have the same concept? These are but a small sample of the fascinating issues associated with research on categorization.

See also ANALOGY; COLOR CLASSIFICATION; CONCEPTUAL CHANGE; FOLK BIOLOGY; NATIVISM; NATURAL KINDS

—Douglas L. Medin and Cynthia Aguilar

References

Anderson, J. R. (1991). The adaptive nature of human categorization. *Psychological Review* 98: 409–429.

Atran, S. (1990). *Cognitive Foundations of Natural History: Towards an Anthropology of Science.* Cambridge: Cambridge University Press.

Barsalou, L. W. (1983). Ad hoc categories. *Memory and Cognition* 11: 211–227.

Barsalou, L. W. (1985). Ideals, central tendency, and frequency of instantiation as determinants of graded structure of categories. *Journal of Experimental Psychology: Learning, Memory, and Cognition* 11: 629–654.

Berlin, B. (1992). *Ethnobiological Classification: Principles of Categorization of Plants and Animals in Traditional Societies.* Princeton, NJ: Princeton University Press.

Berlin, B., D. Breedlove, and P. Raven. (1973). General principles of classification and nomenclature in folk biology. *American Anthropologist* 74: 214–242.

Billman, D., and J. F. Knutson. (1996). Unsupervised concept learning and value systematicity: a complex whole aids learning the parts. *Journal of Experimental Psychology: Learning, Memory, and Cognition* 22: 539–555.

Cantor, N., and W. Mischel. (1979). Prototypes in person perception. In L. Berkowitz, Ed., *Advances in Experimental Social Psychology,* vol. 12. New York: Academic Press, pp. 3–52.

Carey, S. (1985). *Conceptual Change in Childhood.* Cambridge, MA: Bradford Books.

Coley, J. D., S. Atran, and D. L. Medin. (1997). Does rank have its privilege? Inductive inferences within folk biological taxonomies. *Cognition* 64: 73–112.

Goodman, N. (1972). Seven structures on similarity. In N. Goodman, Ed., *Problems and Projects.* New York: Bobbs-Merrill.

Hirschfeld, L. A., and S. A. Gelman, Eds. (1994). *Mapping the Mind: Domain Specificity in Cognition and Culture.* New York: Cambridge University Press.

Keil, F. C. (1989). *Concepts, Kinds and Cognitive Development.* Cambridge, MA: MIT Press.

Komatsu, L. K. (1992). Recent views of conceptual structure. *Psychological Bulletin* 112: 500–526.

Macrae, C. N., G.V. Bodenhausen, and A. B. Milne. (1996). The dissection of selection in person perception: inhibitory processes in social stereotyping. *Journal of Personality and Social Psychology.*

Medin, D. L. (1989). Concepts and conceptual structure. *American Psychologist* 44: 1469–1481.

Morris, M., and G. L. Murphy. (1990). Converging operations on a basic level in event taxonomies. *Memory and Cognition* 18: 107–418.

Murphy, G. L., and D. L. Medin. (1985). The role of theories in conceptual coherence. *Psychological Review* 92: 289–316.

Nosofsky, R. M. (1988). Similarity, frequency and category representations. *Journal of Experimental Psychology: Learning, Memory, and Cognition* 14: 54–65.

Rips, L. J. (1989). Similarity, typicality and categorization. In S. Vosniadou and A. Ortony, Eds., *Similarity and Analogical Reasoning.* Cambridge: Cambridge University Press.

Rips, L. J. (1990). Reasoning. *Annual Review in Psychology* 41: 321–353.

Rosch, E., and C. B. Mervis. (1975). Family resemblances: studies in the internal structure of categories. *Cognitive Psychology* 7: 573–605.

Rosch, E., C. B. Mervis, W. Gray, D. Johnson, and P. Boyes-Braem. (1976). Basic objects in natural categories. *Cognitive Psychology* 8: 573–605.

Smith, E., and D. L. Medin. (1981). *Categories and Concepts.* Cambridge, MA: Harvard University Press.

Tanaka, J. W., and M. Taylor. (1991). Object categories and expertise: is the basic level in the eye of the beholder? *Cognitive Psychology* 23: 457–482.

Tversky, A. (1977). Features of similarity. *Psychological Review* 84: 327–352.

Wattenmaker, W. D. (1995). Knowledge structures and linear separability: integrating information in object and social categorization. *Cognitive Psychology* 28: 274–328.

Wisniewski, E. J., and D. L. Medin. (1994). On the interaction of theory and data in concept learning. *Cognitive Science* 18: 221–281.

Causal Reasoning

Knowing that all pieces of butter have always melted when heated to 150°F, one would probably be willing to conclude that if the next solid piece of butter is heated to 150°F, it will melt. In contrast, knowing that all coins in Nelson Goodman's pockets, up to this point, were silver, one would be reluctant to conclude that if a copper coin were put in his pocket, it would become silver (examples adapted from Goodman 1954/1983). Why is it that one is willing to believe that heating causes butter to melt, but unwilling to believe that Goodman's pocket causes coins to be silver? These contrasting examples point to the kinds of questions that psychologists who study causal reasoning have asked and to the approaches taken in their answers. The central question is: What makes some sequences of events causal, thus licensing inference involving similar events, and other sequences noncausal?

The problem of causal INDUCTION as posed by David HUME (1739/1987) began with the observation that causal relations are neither deducible nor explicit in the reasoner's sensory input (where such input includes introspection as well as external sensory input). Given that sensory input is the ultimate source of all information that a reasoner has, it follows that all acquired causal relations must have been computed from (noncausal) sensory input in some way. A fundamental question therefore arises for such relations: How does a reasoner come to know that one thing, or type of thing, causes another? In other words, what is the mapping from observable events as input to causal relations as output?

The solution Hume (1739/1987) proposed is that causal relations are inferred from the spatial and temporal contiguity of the candidate cause c and the effect e, the temporal priority of c, and the constant conjunction between c and e. For the butter example, Hume's regularity approach might explain that one concludes that heating causes butter to melt from the fact that the heat is close to the butter, melting follows soon after heating, and whenever butter is heated to 150°F, its melting follows. Similarly, this approach might explain that one is reluctant to believe that Goodman's

pocket causes coins to be silver, because his pocket probably did not come into existence before the coins did. If his pocket did predate all the coins in it, however, Hume's solution would fail: the coins were close to his pocket and they were silver whenever they were in his pocket, including soon after they were in his pocket.

One approach to the psychology of causal inference inherited the problem posed by Hume and extended his *regularity* solution. A branch of this approach was adopted by Kelley's (1973) ANOVA model and subsequent variants of it in social psychology (e.g., Hilton and Slugoski 1986). To illustrate contemporary statistical variants of Hume's solution, consider the contrasting examples again. Cheng and Holyoak's (1995) model would explain that a reasoner concludes that heating causes butter to melt because heating occurs before melting and melting occurs more often when the butter is heated to 150°F than when it is not, when other plausible influences on melting such as the purity of the butter are controlled. In contrast, a reasoner does not conclude that Goodman's pocket causes coins to be silver because one knows of alternative causes of coins being silver that might be uncontrolled. For example, Goodman might have selectively kept only silver coins in his pocket, whereas there is no such selection for coins outside his pocket.

As these examples illustrate, the regularity approach requires specific knowledge about alternative causes. But how does such knowledge come about in the first place? Unless one first knows *all* alternative causes, normative inference regarding a candidate cause seems impossible. Yet such inferences occur everyday in science and daily life. For example, without assuming that one knows all the alternative causes of butter melting, it is nonetheless possible to feel convinced, after observing the heating and subsequent melting of butter, that heating causes butter to melt.

An independent branch of the regularity approach begun in Pavlovian CONDITIONING, culminating in Rescorla and Wagner's (1972) connectionist model and its variants, and has been adopted to apply to human causal reasoning (e.g., Dickinson, Shanks, and Evenden 1984). This branch modifies Hume's solution in a manner similar to the statistical approach, but in addition provides algorithms for computing causal output from observational input. These connectionist variants of the regularity approach explain a wide range of empirical findings but have their shortcomings, such as a failure to explain the causal analog of the extinction of conditioned inhibition (for reviews, see Cheng 1997; Miller, Barnet, and Grahame 1995). A common source of these shortcomings may be the inability of these variants to represent causal power as an explicit variable existing independently of its value (*see* BINDING PROBLEM).

A second approach rejects all regularity solutions, and claims to offer an alternative solution to causal inference: one infers a relation to be causal when one perceives or knows of a causal mechanism or causal power underlying the relation (e.g., Koslowski 1996; Michotte 1963; Shultz 1982; White 1995). Because *power* theorists do not explicitly define causal "power" or causal "mechanism," it is unclear whether heating, for example, qualifies as a causal mechanism for substances melting. Assuming that it does, then power theorists would predict that heating should be understood to cause butter to melt. In contrast, reasoners do not know of any mechanism involving Goodman's pocket that would cause coins to be silver, and therefore would not believe that his pocket causes coins to be silver. Power theorists attempt to refute the regularity view by demonstrating that knowledge regarding specific causal powers influence causal judgments.

To regularity theorists, it is unclear what question the power approach seeks to answer; that question, however, is definitely not the one posed by Hume (Cheng 1993). If it is "What kind of causal inference do people, including infants, typically make in their everyday life?" then the answer is that they often make inferences based on prior causal knowledge (e.g., previously acquired knowledge that heating causes substances to melt). Regularity theorists, however, have no objection to the use of prior causal knowledge, as long as not all of that knowledge is innate; the kind of evidence offered by power theorists is therefore compatible with the regularity view (Cheng 1993; see Morris and Larrick 1995 for an example of an application of prior causal knowledge using a statistical approach). If the power solution were to be regarded as an answer to Hume's problem, then it begs the question: How does acquired knowledge about the *causal* nature of mechanisms (e.g., heating as a cause of melting) come about? That is, how does a reasoner infer a *causal* mechanism from *noncausal* observations? The answer to this question (the same question that the regularity view attempts but fails to answer) is what ultimately explains why one believes that one relation is causal and another not.

In addition to their other problems, neither the regularity nor the power approach can explain the boundary conditions for causal inference (see Cheng 1997 for a review). For example, neither explains why controlling for alternative causes allows a regularity to imply causality.

A third approach to the psychology of causal inference inherited Hume's problem, but modified his regularity solution radically by adding a Kantian framework that assumes an a priori notion of causal power. This notion differs critically from the causal knowledge presupposed by traditional power theorists in that it is general rather than specific (see INFANT COGNITION for assumptions regarding specific causal knowledge). According to this approach, the reasoner innately postulates that there exist such things as causes that have the power to produce an effect and causes that have the power to prevent an effect, and determines whether a regularity is causal by attempting to generate it with such general possible powers. By integrating the two previous approaches, this new power approach claims to explain a wide range of findings regarding causal inference, overcoming many problems that cripple earlier approaches (Cheng 1997). The same basic approach has been adopted by computer scientists and philosophers in the last decade to study how it is possible in principle to draw inferences about causal networks from patterns of probabilities (BAYESIAN NETWORKS; Pearl 1995; Spirtes, Glymour, and Scheines 1993). Although psychological work has begun on aspects of causal networks (Busemeyer, McDaniel, and Byun 1997; Spellman 1997), how humans and other animal species infer causal networks remains to be investigated.

See also CAUSATION; CONCEPTS; DEDUCTIVE REASONING; EXPLANATION-BASED LEARNING;

—*Patricia Cheng*

References

Busemeyer, J., M. A. McDaniel, and E. Byun. (1997). Multiple input-output causal environments. *Cognitive Psychology* 32: 1–48.

Cheng, P. W. (1993). Separating causal laws from casual facts: pressing the limits of statistical relevance. In D. L. Medin, Ed., *The Psychology of Learning and Motivation, 30.* New York: Academic Press, pp. 215–264.

Cheng, P. W. (1997). From covariation to causation: a causal power theory. *Psychological Review* 104: 367–405.

Cheng, P. W., and K. J. Holyoak. (1995). Complex adaptive systems as intuitive statisticians: causality, contingency, and prediction. In H. L. Roitblat and J.-A. Meyer, Eds., *Comparative Approaches to Cognitive Science.* Cambridge, MA: MIT Press, pp. 271–302.

Dickinson, A., D. R. Shanks, and J. L. Evenden. (1984). Judgment of act-outcome contingency: the role of selective attribution. *Quarterly Journal of Experimental Psychology* 36A: 29–50.

Goodman, N. (1954/1983). *Fact, Fiction, and Forecast.* Fourth edition. Cambridge, MA: Harvard University Press.

Hilton, D. J., and B.R. Slugoski. (1986). Knowledge-based causal attribution: the abnormal conditions focus model. *Psychological Review* 93: 75–88.

Hume, D. (1739/1987). *A Treatise of Human Nature.* Second edition. Oxford: Clarendon Press.

Kant, I. (1781/1965). *Critique of Pure Reason.* London: Macmillan and Co.

Kelley, H. H. (1973). The processes of causal attribution. *American Psychologist* 28: 107–128.

Koslowski, B. (1996). *Theory and Evidence: The Development of Scientific Reasoning.* Cambridge, MA: MIT Press.

Michotte, A. E. (1946/1963). *The Perception of Causality.* New York: Basic Books.

Miller, R. R., R. C. Barnet, and N. J. Grahame. (1995). Assessment of the Rescorla-Wagner model. *Psychological Bulletin* 117: 363–386.

Morris, W. M., and R. Larrick. (1995). When one cause casts doubts on another: a normative analysis of discounting in causal attribution. *Psychological Review* 102: 331–355.

Pearl, J. (1995). Causal diagrams for experimental research, *Biometrika* 82(4): 669–710.

Rescorla, R. A., and A. R. Wagner. (1972). A theory of Pavlovian conditioning: variations in the effectiveness of reinforcement and nonreinforcement. In A. H. Black and W. F. Prokasy, Eds., *Classical Conditioning II: Current Theory and Research.* New York: Appleton-Century-Crofts, pp. 64–99.

Shultz, T. R. (1982). Rules of causal attribution. *Monographs of the Society for Research in Child Development* 47 (1).

Spellman, B. A. (1997). Crediting causality. *Journal of Experimental Psychology: General* 126: 1–26.

Spirtes, P., C. Glymour, and R. Scheines. (1993). *Causation, Prediction and Search.* New York: Springer-Verlag.

White, P. A. (1995). Use of prior beliefs in the assignment of causal roles: causal powers versus regularity-based accounts. *Memory and Cognition* 23: 243–254

Further Readings

Hart, H. L., and A. M. Honoré. (1959/1985). *Causation in the Law.* 2nd ed. Oxford: Oxford University Press.

Mackie, J. L. (1974). *The Cement of the Universe: A Study of Causation.* Oxford: Clarendon Press.

Shanks, D. R., K. J. Holyoak, and D. L. Medin, Eds. (1996). *The Psychology of Learning and Motivation,* vol. 34: *Causal Learning.* New York: Academic Press.

Sperber, D., D. Premack, and A. J. Premack, Eds. (1995). *Causal Cognition: A Multidisciplinary Debate.* New York: Oxford University Press.

Causation

Basic questions in the philosophy of causation fall into two main areas. First, there are central metaphysical questions concerning the nature of causation, such as the following: What are causal laws? What is it for two states of affairs to be causally related? Which are primary—causal relations between states of affairs, or causal laws? How are causal facts related to noncausal facts? How can one explain the formal properties of causation—such as irreflexivity, asymmetry, and transitivity? What is the ground of the direction of causation?

Second, there are issues concerning the epistemology of causation. Can causal relations be directly observed? How can the existence of causal laws be established? What statistical methods can be used to confirm causal hypotheses, and how can those methods be justified?

Such metaphysical and epistemological issues first came sharply into focus as a result of David Hume's penetrating scrutiny of causation, and the theses that he defended (Hume 1739–40, 1748). On the metaphysical side, HUME argued for the view that causal facts are reducible to noncausal facts, while, on the epistemological side, Hume argued that causal relations between events, rather than being directly observable, can only be known by establishing the existence of "constant conjunctions," or general laws.

The major metaphysical choice is between realist and reductionist approaches to causation. According to the latter, all causal facts are logically supervenient upon the totality of noncausal states of affairs. It is logically impossible, then, for two possible worlds to disagree with respect to some causal fact while agreeing completely with respect to all noncausal facts.

Reductionist approaches to causation have dominated the philosophical landscape since the time of Hume, and many different accounts have been advanced. Three types of approaches are, however, especially important. First, there are approaches that start out from the general notion of a law of nature, then define the ideas of necessary and sufficient nomological conditions, and, finally, employ the latter concepts to explain what it is for one state of affairs to cause another (Mackie 1965). Second, there are approaches that employ subjunctive conditionals in an attempt to give a counterfactual analysis of causation (Lewis 1973, 1979, 1986). Third, there are probabilistic approaches, where the central idea is that a cause must, in some way, make its effect more likely (Reichenbach 1956; Good 1961–62; Suppes 1970; Eells 1991; Mellor 1995).

Each of these three types of approaches faces difficulties specific to it. The attempt to analyze causation in terms of nomological conditions, for example, is hard pressed to provide any account of the direction of causation—a problem that quickly becomes evident when one notices that one state of affairs may be a nomologically sufficient condition for another either because the former is causally sufficient for the latter, or because, on the contrary, the latter is causally necessary for the former.

In the case of counterfactual approaches to causation, a crucial problem is that traditional analyses of subjunctive conditionals employ causal notions. Alternative accounts have been proposed, involving similarity relations over possible worlds. But these alternative accounts are exposed to decisive objections.

Finally, there are also specific problems for probabilistic accounts, two of which are especially important. First, probabilistic accounts have struggled to find an interpretation of their central claim—that causes must, in some way, make their effects more likely—that is not open to counterexamples. Second, probabilistic approaches to causation typically involve the very counterintuitive consequence that a completely deterministic world could not contain any causally related events (Tooley 1987).

There are also other objections, however—of a very serious sort—that tell against all reductionist approaches. First, one can show that some worlds with probabilistic laws may agree with respect to all causal laws and all noncausal facts, yet differ with respect to causal relations between events. So some causal facts not only are not logically supervenient upon the totality of noncausal states of affairs, they are not even supervenient upon the combination of that totality together with all causal laws (Carroll 1994; Tooley 1987).

Second, there are arguments showing that no reductionist approach to causation can account for the direction of causation. One problem, for example, is that very simple worlds containing causally related events may be devoid of all of the noncausal features upon which reductionist accounts rely to define the direction of causation—such as increasing entropy and the presence of open causal forks. Another problem is that, given deterministic laws of an appropriate sort—such as, for example, the laws of Newtonian physics—one can show that, corresponding to some worlds where a reductionist account assigns the correct direction to causation, there will be inverted worlds where the direction of causation is opposite to that specified by any reductionist account (Tooley 1990b).

Given these difficulties, it is natural to explore realist alternatives, and the most plausible form of realism involves viewing causation as a theoretical relation between states of affairs. The development of this type of approach, however, presupposed solutions to two problems that confronted realist interpretations of theories in general. First, there was the semantic problem of how one could even make sense of a realist interpretation of theoretical terms. Second, there was the epistemological problem of how one could justify any statement containing theoretical terms when those terms were interpreted as referring to unobservable states of affairs.

It is not surprising, then, that until those obstacles were surmounted, reductionist approaches to causation held sway. Now, however, satisfactory answers to the above problems are available. Thus, in the case of the semantical problem, one promising approach involves the use of existential quantification ranging over properties and relations to assign a realist interpretation to theoretical terms (Lewis 1970), while, as regards the epistemological problem, there is now widespread acceptance of a type of inductive reasoning—variously referred to as the method of hypothesis, abduction, hypothetico-deductive reasoning, and inference to the best explanation—that will allow one to justify theoretical claims realistically construed.

These philosophical developments have made it possible, then, to take seriously the idea that causation is a theoretical relation. To construct such an account, however, one needs to set out an analytically true theory of causation, and, at present, only one such theory has been worked out in any detail (Tooley 1987, 1990a). It seems likely, however, both that more theories will be proposed in the near future, and that, given the difficulties that reductionism faces, an account of the nature of causation along realist lines will turn out to be correct.

Some philosophers have maintained that causation is a basic and unanalyzable relation that is directly observable (Anscombe 1971; Fales 1990). That view, however, is exposed to some very serious objections (Tooley 1990a). Of these, one of the most important concerns the fact that causal beliefs are often established on the basis of statistical information—using methods that, especially within the social sciences, are very sophisticated. But if causation is a basic and unanalyzable relation, how can non-causal, statistical information possibly serve to establish causal hypotheses?

Recently, this question of how causal hypotheses can be established using statistical information has been the subject of intense investigation. The basic approach has been, first, to identify fundamental principles relating causation to probability. Two such principles that have been suggested as very important, for example, derive from the work of Hans Reichenbach (1949, 1956):

The Screening Off Principle: If A causes C only via B, then, given B, A and C are statistically independent.

The Common Cause Principle: If A and B are statistically dependent, and neither causes the other, then there is a common cause of A and B.

Then, second, one attempts to show that those principles can be used to justify algorithms that will enable one to move from information about statistical relationships to conclusions about causal relations (Glymour et al. 1987; Glymour, Spirtes, and Scheines 1991; Spirtes, Glymour, and Scheines 1993)

This is an interesting and important research program. In its present form, however, it suffers from certain defects. First, some of the principles employed are unsound. Reichenbach's common cause principle, for example, is shown to be false by the inverted worlds objection to causal reductionism mentioned above. Second, if reductionism is false, then it is a mistake to look for algorithms that will specify, for some set of statistical relationships, what the relevant causal relations must be, as given a realist view of causation, different causal relations may underlie a given set of statistical relationships. A sound algorithm, accordingly,

will generate only a probability distribution over possible causal relations.

The basic conclusion, in short, is that an investigation into the epistemology of causation cannot proceed in isolation from consideration of the metaphysics of causation, and if it turns out that a reductionist view of causation is untenable, then one needs to employ a realist account that connects causation to probability, and then isolate algorithms that can be justified on the basis of such an account.

See also CAUSAL REASONING; INDUCTION; MENTAL CAUSATION; REALISM AND ANTIREALISM; REDUCTIONISM; SUPERVENIENCE

—*Michael Tooley*

References

Anscombe, G. E. M. (1971). *Causality and Determination.* Cambridge: Cambridge University Press.

Carroll, J. W. (1994). *Laws of Nature.* Cambridge: Cambridge University Press.

Eells, E. (1991). *Probabilistic Causality.* Cambridge: Cambridge University Press.

Ehring, D. (1997). *Causation and Persistence.* New York: Oxford University Press.

Fales, E. (1990). *Causation and Universals.* London: Routledge.

Glymour, C., R. Scheines, P. Spirtes, and K. Kelly. (1987). *Discovering Causal Structure.* Orlando, FL: Academic Press.

Glymour, C., P. Spirtes, and R. Scheines. (1991). Causal inference. *Erkenntnis* 35: 151–189.

Good, I. J. (1961–62). A causal calculus I-II. *British Journal for the Philosophy of Science* 11: 305–318, 12: 43–51.

Hume, D. (1739–40). *A Treatise of Human Nature.* London: Millar.

Hume, D. (1748). *An Enquiry Concerning Human Understanding.* London: Millar.

Lewis, D. (1970). How to define theoretical terms. *Journal of Philosophy* 67: 427–446.

Lewis, D. (1973). Causation. *Journal of Philosophy* 70: 556–567. Reprinted, with postscripts, in *Philosophical Papers,* vol. 2. Oxford: Oxford University Press, 1986.

Lewis, D. (1979). Counterfactual dependence and time's arrow. *Noûs* 13: 455–476. Reprinted, with postscripts, in *Philosophical Papers,* vol. 2. Oxford: Oxford University Press, 1986.

Lewis, D. (1986). *Philosophical Papers, vol. 2.* Oxford: Oxford University Press.

Mackie, J. L. (1965). Causes and conditions. *American Philosophical Quarterly* 2: 245–264.

Mackie, J. L. (1974). *The Cement of the Universe.* Oxford: Oxford University Press.

Mellor, D. H. (1995). *The Facts of Causation.* London: Routledge.

Menzies, P. (1989). Probabilistic causation and causal processes: a critique of Lewis. *Philosophy of Science* 56: 642–663.

Reichenbach, H. (1949). *The Theory of Probability.* Berkeley: University of California Press.

Reichenbach, H. (1956). *The Direction of Time.* Berkeley: University of California Press.

Salmon, W. C. (1980). Probabilistic causality. *Pacific Philosophical Quarterly* 61: 50–74.

Salmon, Wesley C. (1984). *Scientific Explanation and the Causal Structure of the World.* Princeton, NJ: Princeton University Press.

Sosa, E., and M. Tooley, Eds. (1993). *Causation.* Oxford: Oxford University Press.

Spirtes, P., C. Glymour, and R. Scheines. (1993). *Causation, Prediction, and Search.* New York: Springer-Verlag.

Strawson, G. (1989). *The Secret Connexion: Causation, Realism, and David Hume.* Oxford: Oxford University Press.

Suppes, P. (1970). *A Probabilistic Theory of Causality.* Amsterdam: North-Holland Publishing Company.

Tooley, M. (1987). *Causation: A Realist Approach.* Oxford: Oxford University Press.

Tooley, M. (1990a). The nature of causation: a singularist account. In David Copp, Ed., *Canadian Philosophers. Canadian Journal of Philosophy* Supplement 16: 271–322.

Tooley, M. (1990b). Causation: reductionism versus realism. *Philosophy and Phenomenological Research* 50: 215–236.

Tooley, M. (1996). Causation. In Donald M. Borchert, Ed., *The Encyclopedia of Philosophy, Supplement.* New York: Simon and Schuster Macmillan, pp. 72–75.

von Wright, G. H. (1971). *Explanation and Understanding.* Ithaca, NY: Cornell University Press.

Woodward, J. (1992). Realism about laws. *Erkenntnis* 36: 181–218.

Cellular Automata

See AUTOMATA; VON NEUMANN, JOHN

Cerebellum

The cerebellum constitutes 10 to 15 percent of the entire brain weight, about 140 grams in humans. Rollando (1809; see Dow and Moruzzi 1958) was the first who, by observing motor disturbances in an animal with a lesioned cerebellum, related the cerebellum to movement. Careful analyses of the motor disturbances so induced led Flourens (1824; see Dow and Moruzzi 1958) to conclude that the cerebellum is neither an initiator nor an actuator, but instead serves as a coordinator of movements. An animal with a damaged cerebellum still initiates and executes movement, but only in a clumsy manner. Flourens (1842) and Luciani (1891; see Dow and Moruzzi 1958) observed that motor disturbances caused in an animal by a partial lesion of the cerebellum were gradually compensated for due to the functional plasticity of cerebellar tissues. According to the current knowledge cited below, this plasticity is an expression of a learning capability of the cerebellum, which normally plays a role in MOTOR LEARNING, as in the cases of practicing sports and acquiring skilled movements. Early in the twentieth century, neurologists defined the unique symptoms, such as dysmetria and motor incoordination, of cerebellar diseases. Based on these classic observations, it has been thought that the major function of the cerebellum is to enable us to learn to perform movements accurately and smoothly. The extensive studies that have been performed over the past four decades have facilitated the formulation of comprehensive views on the structure of the cerebellum, what processes occur there, and what roles it plays not only in bodily but also in cognitive functions, even though some of the views are still hypothetical.

The cerebellar cortex contains an elaborate neuronal circuit composed of five types of cells: Purkinje, basket, strellate, Golgi, and granule cells (fig. 1; Eccles, Ito, and Szentagothai 1967). With respect to their synaptic action, these cells are inhibitory except for the granule cells, which are excitatory. Afferent signals from various precer-

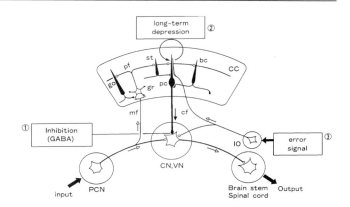

Figure 1. Neuronal circuitry of the cerebellum. CC, cerebellar cortex; pc, Purkinje cell; bc, basket cell; st, stellate cell; pf, parallel fiber; gr, granule cell; go, Golgi cell; mf, mossy fiber; cf, climbing fiber; IO, inferior olive; PCN, precerebellar nuclei; CN, cerebellar nuclei; VN, vestibular nuclei.

ebellar nuclei reach the cerebellar cortex and are relayed to the granule cells via mossy fibers, and to the dendrites of the Purkinje cells and other inhibitory cells via the axons of the granule cells, that is, parallel fibers. Afferent signals from the inferior olive in the medulla oblongata pass directly to the Purkinje cells via climbing fibers. L-glutamate is the neurotransmitter for the vast majority of mossy fibers and all granule cells, while GABA is the neurotransmitter for all inhibitory neurons.

The major signal flows in the cerebellum pass from the cells of origin for mossy fibers (PCN in fig. 1), granule cells (gr), and Purkinje cells (pc). Marr (1969), Albus (1971), and other theorists proposed that if climbing fiber signals modify granule cell-to-Purkinje cell synapses, the three-neuron structure would operate as a learning machine in the same way as the simple perceptron described by Rosenblatt (1962). It was a decade before long-term depression (LTD) was discovered to occur at parallel fiber-to-Purkinje cell synapses after conjunctive activation of these synapses together with climbing fiber-to-Purkinje cell synapses (Ito, Sakurai, and Tongroach 1982; Ito 1989). LTD occurs as a result of complex chemical processes involving a number of receptors and second messengers, eventually leading to the phosphorylation of glutamate receptors (Nakazawa et al. 1995).

The cerebellar cortex contains numerous small longitudinal microzones (Oscarsson 1976). Each microzone is paired with a small distinct group of neurons in a cerebellar or vestibular nucleus (CN, VN in fig. 1) to form a corticonuclear microcomplex that hereafter is referred to as a cerebellar chip or a chip (Ito 1984). In a cerebellar chip, input signals from various precerebellar nuclei activate the nuclear neurons that produce the output signals of the chip. This major signal path across a chip is attached with a sidepath through a microzone that receives input signals via mossy fibers and relays Purkinje cell signals to the nuclear neurons. Climbing fibers convey signals representing errors in the performance of the chip, as detected through various sensory pathways, which induce LTD in Purkinje cells. The LTD induction changes the signal flow through the microzone sidepath, thereby altering the signal flow across the chip. A cerebellar chip thus behaves as an adaptive unit in which input-output relationships are adaptively altered by error signals conveyed by climbing fibers.

The cerebellum is divided into the flocculonodular lobe and the corpus cerebelli, the latter being further divided into vermis, paravermis (intermediate part), and hemisphere. Cerebellar chips in the flocculonodular lobe, vermis, and paravermis are connected to the brain stem and spinal cord, and confer adaptiveness on reflexes (not only motor but also autonomic; for the vestibuloocular reflex, see Robinson 1976; Ito 1984; for eye-blink conditioned reflex, see Thompson 1987) and compound movements (for locomotion, see Yanagihara and Kondo 1996), which by themselves are stereotyped and nonadaptive. The role of the evolutionary old part of the cerebellum is therefore to ensure the adaptiveness of the spinal cord and brain stem control functions in order to enable animals to survive in ever-changing environments.

With respect to cerebral control functions, cerebellar chips appear to play a different role, that is, the formation of an internal model of a controller or a control object. If, while a chip and the system to be modeled are supplied with common input signals, differences in their output signals are returned to the chip as error signals, the chip will gradually assume dynamic characteristics equivalent to those of the system to be modeled.

Cerebellar chips located in the paravermis are connected to the cerebral motor cortex in such a way that these chips constitute a model that mimics the dynamics of the skeletomuscular system (Ito 1984). The motor cortex thus becomes capable of performing a learned movement with precision by referring to the model in the cerebellum and not to the skeletomuscular system. Dysmetria, the failure to perform a precise reaching movement without visual feedback, could be due to the loss of such internal models. Another possibility is that a chip located in the cerebellar hemisphere forms a model that acts as a controller in place of the motor cortex (Kawato, Furukawa, and Suzuki 1987; Shidara et al. 1995). Learned movements could then be controlled unconsciously, yet accurately, by the cerebellum. These two model systems, one eliminating the need for sensory feedback and the other awareness from learned voluntary movement control, appear to represent different phases of motor learning conducted in different cerebellar areas.

Based on the parallel development of the cerebral association cortex and cerebellar hemispheres in primates, Leiner, Leiner, and Dow (1986) suggested that the lateralmost part of the cerebellar hemisphere is involved in cognitive rather than motor functions. Thought may occur as a result of the prefrontal association cortex acting as a controller upon images, ideas, or concepts encoded in the parietolateral association cortex as a control object. During thought repetition, a cerebellar chip may form a model of the parietolateral cortex or the prefrontal cortex. A repeatedly learned thought may thus be performed quickly yet accurately even without reference to the consequences of the thought or without conscious attention. Evidence suggesting such roles of the cerebellum as this is accumulating from studies on the human cerebellum using noninvasive techniques (see Schmahmann 1997).

See also MOTOR CONTROL; MOTOR LEARNING

—*Masao Ito*

References

Albus, J. S. (1971). A theory of cerebellar function. *Mathematical Bioscience* 10: 25–61.

Dow, R. E., and G. Moruzzi. (1958). *The Physiology and Pathology of the Cerebellum.* Minneapolis: University of Minnesota Press.

Eccles J. C., M. Ito, and J. Szentagothai. (1967). *The Cerebellum as a Neuronal Machine.* New York: Springer-Verlag.

Ito, M. (1984). *The Cerebellum and Neural Control.* New York: Raven Press.

Ito, M. (1989). Long-term depression. *Annual Review of Neuroscience* 12: 85–102.

Ito, M. (1993). Movement and thought: identical control mechanisms by the cerebellum. *Trends in Neuroscience* 16: 448–450.

Ito, M., M. Sakurai, and P. Tongroach. (1982). Climbing fibre induced depression of both mossy fibre responsiveness and glutamate sensitivity of cerebellar Purkinje cells. *Journal of Physiology, London* 324: 113–134.

Kawato, M., K. Furukawa, and R. Suzuki. (1987). A hierarchical neuronal network model for control and learning of voluntary movement. *Biological Cybernetics* 57: 169–185.

Leiner, H. C., A. L. Leiner, and R. S. Dow. (1986). Does the cerebellum contribute to mental skill? *Behavioral Neuroscience* 100: 443–453.

Marr, D. (1969). A theory of cerebellar cortex. *Journal of Physiology, London* 202: 437–470.

Nakazawa, K., S. Mikawa, T. Hashikawa, and M. Ito. (1995). Transient and persistent phosphorylations of AMPA-type glutamate receptor subunits in cerebellar Purkinje cells. *Neuron* 1: 697–709.

Oscarsson, O. (1976). Spatial distribution of climbing and mossy fibre inputs into the cerebellar cortex. In O. Creutzfeldt, Ed., *Afferent and Intrinsic Organization of Laminated Structures in the Brain.* Berlin: Springer-Verlag, pp. 34–42.

Robinson, D. A. (1976). Adaptive gain control of vestibulo-ocular reflex by the cerebellum. *Journal of Neurophysiology* 39: 954–969.

Rosenblatt, F. (1962). *Principles of Neurodynamics: Perceptron and the Theory of Brain Mechanisms.* Washington, DC: Spartan Books.

Schmahmann, J. D. (1997). *The Cerebellum and Cognition.* San Diego: Academic Press.

Shidara, M., M. Kawano, H. Gomi, and M. Kawato. (1995). Inverse-dynamics encoding of eye movements by Purkinje cells in the cerebellum. *Nature* 365: 50–52.

Thompson, R. F. (1987). The neurobiology of learning and memory. *Science* 233: 941–947.

Yanagihara, D., and I. Kondo. (1996). Nitric oxide plays a key role in adaptive control of locomotion in cats. *Proceedings of the National Academy of Sciences, USA* 93: 13292–13297.

Further Readings

Palay, S. L., and V. Chan-Palay. (1974). *The Cerebellar Cortex.* New York: Springer-Verlag.

Cerebral Cortex

The cerebral cortex is a paired structure in the forebrain that is found only in mammals and that is largest (relative to body size) in humans (Herrick 1926; Jerison 1973). Its most distinctive anatomical features are (i) the very extensive internal connections between one part and another part, and

(ii) its arrangement as a six-layered sheet of cells, many of which cells are typical *pyramidal cells*. Although the crumpled, folded surface of this sheet is responsible for the very characteristic appearance of the brains of large mammals, the cortex of small mammals tends to be smooth and unfolded. Where folds occur, each fold, or *gyrus,* is about 1/2 cm in width (Sarnat and Netsky 1981).

Imagine the crumpled sheet expanded to form a pair of balloons with walls 2.5 mm thick, each balloon with a diameter of 18 cm and a surface area close to 1000 cm2. The pair weighs about 500 grams, contains about 2×10^{10} cells connecting with each other through some 1014 *synapses,* and through a total length of about 2×10^6 km of nerve fiber—more than five times the distance to the moon (Braitenberg and Schuz, 1991). The two balloons connect to each other through the *corpus callosum*, a massive tract of nerve fibers. Almost all the synapses and nerve fibers connect cortical neurons to each other, but it is of course the connections with the rest of the animal that allow the cortex to control the animal's highest behavior. The main connections are as follows.

The olfactory input from the nose probably represents the input to the primordial structure from which the cortex evolved. It goes directly to layer 1, the outermost layer, of a special region at the edge of the cortical sheet. Touch, hearing, and vision relay through *thalamic nuclei* that are situated near what would be the necks of the balloons, and these nuclei receive a large number of feedback connections from the cortical sheet as well as inputs from the sense organs. An important output pathway comes from the *motor area,* which is the region believed to be responsible for voluntary movement. The CEREBELLUM should be mentioned here because it is also concerned with the regulation and control of muscular movement; it has profuse connections to and from the cortex, and enlarged with it during evolution. It has recently become clear that it is concerned with some forms of CONDITIONING (Yeo, Hardiman, and Glickstein 1985; Thompson 1990).

The second set of pathways in and out of the cortex pass through two adjacent regions of modified cortical sheet called the *archicortex* and *paleocortex* that flank the six-layered *neocortex* (Sarnat and Netsky 1981). Paleocortex lies below the necks of the balloons and contains the *rhinencephalon* (nose brain), where smell information enters; it connects with other regions thought to be concerned with mood and EMOTION. Archicortex developed into the HIPPOCAMPUS, and is thought to be concerned with the laying down of memories. Like the paleocortex, it has connections with regions involved in mood, emotion, and endocrine control.

The words used to describe the higher mental capacities of animals with a large neocortex include CONSCIOUSNESS, *free will*, INTELLIGENCE, *adaptability*, and *insight,* but animals with much simpler brains learn well, so LEARNING should not be among these capacities (Macphail 1982). The comparative anatomists Herrick and Jerrison emphasize that neocortically dominated animals show evidence of having acquired extensive general knowledge about the world, but laboratory learning experiments are usually designed to prevent previously acquired knowledge from influencing results, and are therefore not good tests for stored general knowledge. The evidence for such knowledge is that cortically dominant animals take advantage of the enormously complicated associative structure of their environments, and this could come about in two ways. A species could have genetically determined mechanisms, acquired through evolutionary selection, for taking advantage of the regular features of the environment, or they could have learned through direct experience. It seems most likely that animals with a dominant neocortex have a combination of the two means—they have the best of both worlds by combining genetic and individual acquisition of knowledge about their environments (Barlow 1994).

Neuropsychologists who have studied the defects that result from damage and disease to the cerebral cortex emphasize localization of function (Phillips, Zeki, and Barlow 1984): cognitive functions are disrupted in a host of different ways that can, to some extent, be correlated with the locus of the damage and the known connections of the damaged part. But there can be considerable recovery of a function that has been lost in this way, particularly following damage in infancy or childhood: in the majority of adults the left hemisphere is absolutely necessary for speech and language, but these capacities can develop in the right hemisphere following total loss of the left hemisphere in childhood.

Neurophysiologists have recorded the activity of individual nerve cells in the cortical sheet. This work leads to the view that the cortex represents the sensory input and the animal is receiving, processes it for OBJECT RECOGNITION, and selects an appropriate motor output. Neurons in the *primary visual cortex* (also called *striate cortex* or *V1*) are selectively responsive to edge orientation, direction of MOTION, TEXTURE, COLOR, and disparity. These are the local properties of the image that, according to the laws of GESTALT PERCEPTION, lead to *segregation* of figure from ground. The neurons of V1 send their axons to adjacent *extra-striate visual cortex,* where the precise *topographic mapping* of the visual field found in V1 becomes less precise and information is collected together according to parameters (such as direction and velocity of motion) of the segregating features (Barlow 1981). These steps can account for the first stages of object recognition, but what happens at later stages is less clear.

Although there are considerable anatomical differences between the different parts of the cortical sheet, there are also great similarities, and its evolution as a whole prompts one to seek a similar function for it throughout. Here the trouble starts, for it is evident that comparative anatomists say it does one thing, neuropsychologists another, and neurophysiologists yet something else (Barlow 1994). These divergences result partly from the different spatial and time scales of the observations and experiments in different fields, for neurophysiology follows the activity of individual neurons from second to second, neuropsychologists are concerned with chronic, almost permanent defects resulting from damage to cortical areas containing several million cells, and behavioral observation is concerned with functions of the whole animal over intermediate periods of seconds and minutes. But the cells everywhere have an unusual and similar form, which suggests they have a common function; an attractive hypothesis is that this is *prediction.*and

Sense organs are slow, but an animal's competitive survival often depends upon speedy response; therefore, a representation that is up to the moment, or even ahead of the moment, would be of very great advantage. Prediction depends upon identifying a commonly occurring sequential pattern of events at an early stage in the sequence and assuming that the pattern will be completed. This requires knowledge of the spatio-temporal sequences that commonly occur, and the *critical* or *sensitive periods,* which neurophysiologists have studied in the visual cortex (Hubel and Wiesel 1970; Movshon and Van Sluyters 1981) but which are also known to occur in the development of other cognitive systems, may be periods when spatio-temporal sequences that occur commonly encourage the development of neurons with a selectivity of response to these patterns. If such *phase sequences,* as HEBB (1949) called them, were recognized by individual cells, one would have a computational unit that, with appropriate connections, would be of selective advantage in an enormous range of circumstances. The survival value of neurons with the power of prediction could have led to the explosive enlargement of the neocortex that culminated in the human brain.

See also ADAPTATION AND ADAPTATIONISM; CORTICAL LOCALIZATION, HISTORY OF; EVOLUTION; HEMISPHERIC SPECIALIZATION; NEURON

——*Horace Barlow*

References

Barlow, H. B. (1981). Critical limiting factors in the design of the eye and visual cortex. The Ferrier Lecture, 1980. *Proceedings of the Royal Society, London Series B* 212: 1–34.

Barlow, H. B. (1994). What is the computational goal of the neocortex? In C. Koch and J. Davis, Eds., *Large Scale Neuronal Theories of the Brain.* Cambridge, MA: MIT Press.

Braitenberg, V., and A. Schuz. (1991). *Anatomy of the Cortex: Statistics and Geometry.* Berlin: Springer-Verlag.

Hebb, D. O. (1949). *The Organisation of Behaviour.* New York: Wiley.

Herrick, C. J. (1926). *Brains of Rats and Men.* Chicago: University of Chicago Press.

Hubel, D. H., and T. N. Wiesel. (1970). The period of susceptibility to the physiological effects of unilateral eye closure in kittens. *Journal of Physiology* 206: 419–436.

Jerison, H. J. (1973). *Evolution of the Brain and Intelligence.* New York: Academic Press.

Macphail, E. (1982). *Brain and Intelligence in Vertebrates.* New York: Oxford University Press.

Movshon, J. A., and R. C. Van Sluyters. (1981). Visual neural development. *Annual Review of Psychology* 32: 477–522.

Phillips, C. G., S. Zeki, and H. B. Barlow. (1984). Localisation of function in the cerebral cortex. *Brain* 107: 327–361.

Sarnat, H. B., and M. G. Netsky. (1981). *Evolution of the Nervous System.* New York: Oxford University Press.

Thompson, R. F. (1990). Neural mechanisms of classical conditioning in mammals. *Philosophical Transactions of the Royal Society of London Series B* 329:171–178.

Yeo, C. H., M. J. Hardiman, and M. Glickstein. (1985). Classical conditioning of the nictitating membrane response of the rabbit (3 papers). *Experimental Brain Research* 60: 87–98; 99–113; 114–125.

Further Readings

Abeles, M. (1991). *Corticonics: Neural Circuits of the Cerebral Cortex.* Cambridge: Cambridge University Press.

Creuzfeldt, O. D. (1983). *Cortex cerebri: leistung, strukturelle und functionelle Organisation der Hirnrinde.* Berlin: Springer-Verlag. Translated by Mary Creuzfeldt et al. as "Cortex cerebri: performance, structural and functional organisation of the cortex," Gottingen 1993.

Jones, E. G., and A. Peters. (1985). *Cerebral Cortex.* Five volumes. New York: Plenum Press.

Martin, R. D. (1990). *Primate Origins and Evolution.* London: Chapman and Hall.

Cerebral Specialization

See HEMISPHERIC SPECIALIZATION

Chess, Psychology of

Historically, chess has been one of the leading fields in the study of EXPERTISE (see De Groot and Gobet 1996 and Holding 1985 for reviews). This popularity as a research domain is explained by the advantages that chess offers for studying cognitive processes: (i) a well-defined task; (ii) the presence of a quantitative scale to rank chess players (Elo 1978); and (iii) cross-fertilization with research on game-playing in computer science and artificial intelligence.

Many of the key chess concepts and mechanisms to be later developed in cognitive psychology were anticipated by Adriaan De Groot's book *Thought and Choice in Chess* (1946/1978). De Groot stressed the role of selective search, perception, and knowledge in expert chess playing. He also perfected two techniques that were to be often used in later research: recall of briefly presented material from the domain of expertise, and use of thinking-aloud protocols to study problem-solving behavior. His key empirical findings were that (i) world-class chess grandmasters do not search more, in number of positions considered and in depth of search, than weaker (but still expert) players; and (ii) grandmasters and masters can recall and replace positions (about two dozen pieces) presented for a few seconds almost perfectly, while weaker players can replace only a half dozen pieces.

De Groot's theoretical ideas, based on Otto Selz's psychology, were not as influential as his empirical techniques and results. It was only about twenty-five years later that chess research would produce a theory with a strong impact on the study of expertise and of cognitive psychology in general. In their chunking theory, Simon and Chase (1973) stressed the role of perception in skilled behavior, as did De Groot, but they added a set of elegant mechanisms. Their key idea was that expertise in chess requires acquiring a large collection of relatively small chunks (each at most six pieces) denoting typical patterns of pieces on the chess board. These chunks are accessed through a discrimination net and act as the conditions of a PRODUCTION SYSTEM: they evoke possible moves in this situation. In other respects, chess experts do not differ from less expert players: they have the same limits in memory (a short-term memory of about seven chunks) and learning rate (about eight seconds are required to learn a chunk). In chess, as well as in other domains, the chunking theory explains experts' remarkable memory by their ability to find more and larger chunks, and explains their selective search by the fact that chunks evoke potentially good actions. Some aspects of the theory were implemented in a computer program by Simon and Gilmartin (1973). Simulations with this program gave a good fit to the behavior of a strong amateur and led to the estimation that expertise requires the presence of a large number of chunks, approximately between 10,000 and 100,000.

A wealth of empirical data was gathered to test the chunking theory in various domains of expertise. In chess, five directions of research may be singled out as critical: importance of perception and pattern recognition, relative role of short-term and long-term memories, evidence for chunks, role of higher-level knowledge, and size of search.

Converging evidence indicates that perceptual, pattern-based cognition is critical in chess expertise. The most compelling data are that EYE MOVEMENTS during the first few seconds when examining a new chess position differ between experts and nonmasters (De Groot and Gobet 1996), and that masters still play at a high level in speed chess games where they have only five seconds per move on average, or in simultaneous games where their thinking time is reduced by the presence of several opponents (Gobet and Simon 1996).

Research on MEMORY has led to apparently contradictory conclusions. On the one hand, several experiments on the effect of interfering tasks (e.g., Charness 1976) have shown that two of Simon and Chase's (1973) assumptions—that storage into long-term memory is slow and that chunks are held in short-term memory—run into problems. This encouraged researchers such as Cooke et al. (1993) to emphasize the role of higher-level knowledge, already anticipated by De Groot (1946/1978). On the other hand, empirical evidence for chunks has also been mounting (e.g., Chi 1978; Gobet and Simon 1996; Saariluoma 1994).

Attempts to reconcile low-level and high-level types of encoding have recently been provided by the long-term WORKING MEMORY (LTWM) theory (Ericsson and Kintsch 1995) and by the template theory (Gobet and Simon 1996). LTWM proposes that experts build up both schema-based knowledge and domain-specific retrieval structures that rapidly encode the important elements of a problem. The template theory, based on the chunking theory and implemented as a computer program, proposes that chunks evolve into more complex data structures (templates), allowing some values to be encoded rapidly. Both theories also account for aspects of skilled perception and problem solving in chess.

Recent results indicate that stronger players search somewhat more broadly and deeply than weaker players (Charness 1981; Holding 1985), with an asymptote at high skill levels. In addition, the space searched remains small (thinking-aloud protocols indicate that grandmasters typically search no more than one hundred nodes in fifteen minutes). These results are compatible with a theory based on pattern recognition: chunks, which evoke moves or sequences of moves, make search more selective and allow better players to search more deeply.

While productive in its own terms, computer science research on chess (see GAME-PLAYING SYSTEMS) has had relatively little impact on the psychology of chess. The main advances have been the development of search techniques, which have culminated in the construction of DEEP BLUE, the first computer to have beaten a world champion in a match. More recently, chess has been a popular domain for testing MACHINE LEARNING techniques. Finally, attempts to use a production-system architecture (e.g., Wilkins 1980) have met with limited success in terms of the strength of the programs.

The key findings in chess research—selective search, pattern recognition, and memory for the domain material—have been shown to generalize to other domains of expertise. This augurs well for current interests in the field: integration of low- and high-level aspects of knowledge and unification of chess perception, memory, and problem-solving theories into a single theoretical framework.

See also COGNITIVE ARCHITECTURE; DOMAIN SPECIFICITY; HEURISTIC SEARCH; PROBLEM SOLVING

—*Fernand Gobet*

References

Charness, N. (1976). Memory for chess positions: resistance to interference. *Journal of Experimental Psychology: Human Learning and Memory* 2: 641–653.

Charness, N. (1981). Search in chess: age and skill differences. *Journal of Experimental Psychology: Human Perception and Performance* 2: 467–476.

Chi, M. T. H. (1978). Knowledge structures and memory development. In R. S. Siegler, Ed., *Children's Thinking: What Develops?* Hillsdale, NJ: Erlbaum, pp. 73–96.

Cooke, N. J., R. S. Atlas, D. M. Lane, and R. C. Berger. (1993). Role of high-level knowledge in memory for chess positions. *American Journal of Psychology* 106: 321–351.

de Groot, A. D. (1978). *Thought and Choice in Chess.* The Hague: Mouton Publishers.

de Groot, A. D., and F. Gobet. (1996). *Perception and memory in chess. Heuristics of the professional eye.* Assen: Van Gorcum.

Elo, A. (1978). *The Rating of Chess Players, Past and Present.* New York: Arco.

Ericsson, K. A., and W. Kintsch. (1995). Long-term working memory. *Psychological Review* 102: 211–245.

Gobet, F., and H. A. Simon. (1996). Templates in chess memory: a mechanism for recalling several boards. *Cognitive Psychology* 31: 1–40.

Holding, D. H. (1985). *The Psychology of Chess Skill.* Hillsdale, NJ: Erlbaum.

Saariluoma, P. (1994). Location coding in chess. *The Quarterly Journal of Experimental Psychology* 47A: 607–630.

Simon, H. A., and W. G. Chase. (1973). Skill in chess. *American Scientist* 61: 393–403.

Simon, H. A., and K. J. Gilmartin. (1973). A simulation of memory for chess positions. *Cognitive Psychology* 5: 29–46.

Wilkins, D. (1980). Using patterns and plans in chess. *Artificial Intelligence* 14: 165–203.

Further Readings

Binet, A. (1966). Mnemonic virtuosity: a study of chess players. *Genetic Psychology Monographs* 74: 127–162. (Translated fom the *Revue des Deux Mondes* (1893) 117: 826–859.)

Calderwood, B., G. A. Klein, and B. W. Crandall. (1988). Time pressure, skill, and move quality in chess. *American Journal of Psychology* 101: 481–493.

Charness, N. (1989). Expertise in chess and bridge. In D. Klahr and K. Kotovsky, Eds., *Complex Information Processing: The Impact of Herbert A. Simon.* Hillsdale, NJ: Erlbaum, pp. 183–208.

Chase, W. G., and H. A. Simon. (1973). Perception in chess. *Cognitive Psychology* 4: 55–81.

Frey, P. W., and P. Adesman. (1976). Recall memory for visually presented chess positions. *Memory and Cognition* 4: 541–547.

Freyhoff, H., H. Gruber, and A. Ziegler. (1992). Expertise and hierarchical knowledge representation in chess. *Psychological Research* 54: 32–37.

Fürnkranz, J. (1996). Machine learning in computer chess: the next generation. *International Computer Chess Association Journal* 19: 147–161.

Gobet, F., and H. A. Simon. (1996a). The roles of recognition processes and look-ahead search in time-constrained expert problem solving: evidence from grandmaster level chess. *Psychological Science* 7: 52–55.

Gobet, F., and H. A. Simon. (1996b). Recall of rapidly presented random chess positions is a function of skill. *Psychonomic Bulletin and Review* 3: 159–163.

Goldin, S. E. (1978). Effects of orienting tasks on recognition of chess positions. *American Journal of Psychology* 91: 659–671.

Hartston, W. R., and P. C. Wason. (1983). *The Psychology of Chess.* London: Batsford.

Newell, A., and H. A. Simon. (1972). *Human Problem Solving.* Englewood Cliffs, NJ: Prentice-Hall.

Pitrat, J. (1977). A chess combinations program which uses plans. *Artificial Intelligence* 8: 275–321.

Robbins, T. W., E. Anderson, D. R. Barker, A. C. Bradley, C. Fearnyhough, R. Henson, S. R. Hudson, and A. D. Baddeley. (1995). Working memory in chess. *Memory and Cognition* 24: 83–93.

Simon, H. A. (1979). *Models of Thought, vol. 1.* New Haven: Yale University Press.

Simon, H. A., and M. Barenfeld. (1969). Information processing analysis of perceptual processes in problem solving. *Psychological Review* 76: 473–483.

Chinese Room Argument

The Chinese room argument is a refutation of strong artificial intelligence. "Strong AI" is defined as the view that an appropriately programmed digital computer with the right inputs and outputs, one that satisfies the Turing test, would necessarily have a mind. The idea of Strong AI is that the implemented program by itself is constitutive of having a mind. "Weak AI" is defined as the view that the computer plays the same role in studying cognition as it does in any other discipline. It is a useful device for simulating and therefore studying mental processes, but the programmed computer does not automatically guarantee the presence of mental states in the computer. Weak AI is not criticized by the Chinese room argument.

The argument proceeds by the following thought experiment. Imagine a native English speaker, let's say a man, who knows no Chinese locked in a room full of boxes of Chinese symbols (a data base) together with a book of instructions for manipulating the symbols (the program). Imagine that people outside the room send in other Chinese symbols which, unknown to the person in the room, are questions in Chinese (the input). And imagine that by following the instructions in the program the man in the room is able to pass out Chinese symbols that are correct answers to the questions (the output). The program enables the person in the room to pass the Turing test for understanding Chinese, but he does not understand a word of Chinese.

The point of the argument is this: if the man in the room does not understand Chinese on the basis of implementing the appropriate program for understanding Chinese, then neither does any other digital computer solely on that basis because no computer, qua computer, has anything the man does not have.

The larger structure of the argument can be stated as a derivation from three premises.

1. Implemented programs are by definition purely formal or syntactical. (An implemented program, as carried out by the man in the Chinese room, for example, is defined purely in terms of formal or syntactical symbol manipulations. The notion "same implemented program" specifies an equivalence class defined purely in terms of syntactical manipulations, independent of the physics of their implementation.)
2. Minds have mental or semantic contents. (For example, in order to think or understand a language you have to have more than just the syntax, you have to associate some meaning, some thought content, with the words or signs.)
3. Syntax is not by itself sufficient for, nor constitutive of, semantics. (The purely formal, syntactically defined symbol manipulations don't by themselves guarantee the presence of any thought content going along with them.)

Conclusion: Implemented programs are not constitutive of minds. Strong AI is false.

Why does the man in the Chinese room not understand Chinese even though he can pass the Turing test for understanding Chinese? The answer is that he has only the formal syntax of the program and not the actual mental content or semantic content that is associated with the words of a language when a speaker understands that language. You can see this by contrasting the man in the Chinese room with the same man answering questions put to him in his native English. In both cases he passes the Turing test, but from his point of view there is a big difference. He understands the English and not the Chinese. In the Chinese case he is acting as a digital computer. In the English case he is acting as a normal competent speaker of English. This shows that the Turing test fails to distinguish real mental capacities from simulations of those capacities. Simulation is not duplication, but the Turing test cannot detect the difference.

There have been a number of attempts to answer this argument, all of them, in the view of this author, unsuccessful. Perhaps the most common is the systems reply: "While the man in the Chinese room does not understand Chinese, he is not the whole system. He is but the central processing unit, a simple cog in the large mechanism that includes room, books, etc. It is the whole room, the whole system, that understands Chinese, not the man."

The answer to the systems reply is that the man has no way to get from the SYNTAX to the SEMANTICS, but neither does the whole room. The whole room also has no way of attaching any thought content or mental content to the formal symbols. You can see this by imagining that the man internalizes the whole room. He memorizes the rulebook and the data base, he does all the calculations in his head, and he works outdoors. All the same, neither the man nor any subsystem in him has any way of attaching any meaning to the formal symbols.

The Chinese room has been widely misunderstood as attempting to show a lot of things it does not show.

1. The Chinese room does not show that "machines can't think." On the contrary, the brain is a machine and brains can think.
2. The Chinese room does not show that "computers can't think." On the contrary, something can be a computer and can think. If a computer is any machine capable of carrying out a computation, then all normal human beings are computers and they think. The Chinese room shows that COMPUTATION, as defined by Alan TURING and others as formal symbol manipulation, is not by itself constitutive of thinking.
3. The Chinese room does not show that only brains can think. We know that thinking is caused by neurobiological processes in the brain, but there is no logical obstacle to building a machine that could duplicate the causal powers of the brain to produce thought processes. The point, however, is that any such machine would have to be able to duplicate the specific causal powers of the brain to produce the biological process of thinking. The mere shuffling of formal symbols is not sufficient to guarantee these causal powers, as the Chinese room shows.

See also COMPUTATIONAL THEORY OF MIND; FUNCTIONALISM; INTENTIONALITY; MENTAL REPRESENTATION

—*John R. Searle*

Further Readings

Searle, J. R. (1980). Minds, brains and programs. *Behavioral and Brain Sciences*, vol. 3 (together with 27 peer commentaries and author's reply).

Chunking

See CHESS, PSYCHOLOGY OF; EXPLANATION-BASED LEARNING; FRAME-BASED SYSTEMS; METAREASONING

Church-Turing Thesis

Alonzo Church proposed at a meeting of the American Mathematical Society in April 1935, "that the notion of an effectively calculable function of positive integers should be identified with that of a recursive function." This proposal of identifying an informal notion, *effectively calculable function,* with a mathematically precise one, *recursive function,* has been called Church's thesis since Stephen Cole Kleene used that name in 1952. Alan TURING independently made a related proposal in 1936, Turing's thesis, suggesting the identification of effectively calculable functions with

functions whose values can be computed by a particular idealized computing device, a *Turing machine.* As the two mathematical notions are provably equivalent, the theses are "equivalent," and are jointly referred to as the Church-Turing thesis.

The reflective, partly philosophical and partly mathematical, work around and in support of the thesis concerns one of the fundamental notions of mathematical logic. Its proper understanding is crucial for making informed and reasoned judgments on the significance of limitative results—like GÖDEL'S THEOREMS or Church's theorem. The work is equally crucial for computer science, artificial intelligence, and cognitive psychology as it provides also for these subjects a basic theoretical notion. For example, the thesis is the cornerstone for Allen NEWELL's delimitation of the class of physical symbol systems, that is, universal machines with a particular architecture. Newell (1980) views this delimitation "as the most fundamental contribution of artificial intelligence and computer science to the joint enterprise of cognitive science." In a turn that had almost been taken by Turing (1948, 1950), Newell points to the basic role physical symbol systems have in the study of the human mind: "the hypothesis is that humans are instances of physical symbol systems, and, by virtue of this, mind enters into the physical universe . . . this hypothesis sets the terms on which we search for a scientific theory of mind." The restrictive "almost" in Turing's case is easily motivated: he viewed the precise mathematical notion as a crucial ingredient for the investigation of the mind (using computing machines to simulate aspects of the mind), but did not subscribe to a sweeping "mechanist" theory. It is precisely for an understanding of such—sometimes controversial—claims that the background for Church's and Turing's work has to be presented carefully. Detailed connections to investigations in cognitive science, programmatically indicated above, are at the heart of many contributions (cf. for example, COGNITIVE MODELING, COMPUTATIONAL LEARNING THEORY, and COMPUTATIONAL THEORY OF MIND).

The informal notion of an effectively calculable function, effective procedure, or algorithm had been used in nineteenth century mathematics and logic, when indicating that a class of problems is solvable in a "mechanical fashion" by following fixed elementary rules. Hilbert in 1904 already suggested taking formally presented theories as objects of mathematical study, and metamathematics has been pursued vigorously and systematically since the 1920s. In its pursuit concrete issues arose that required for their resolution a precise characterization of the class of effective procedures. Hilbert's *Entscheidungsproblem* (see Hilbert and Bernays 1939), the decision problem for first order logic, was one such issue. It was solved negatively—relative to the precise notion of recursiveness, respectively to Turing machine computability; though obtained independently by Church and Turing, this result is usually called Church's theorem. A second significant issue was the formulation of Gödel's Incompleteness theorems as applying to *all* formal theories (satisfying certain representability and derivability conditions). Gödel had established the theorems in his groundbreaking 1931 paper for specific formal systems like type theory of *Principia Mathematica* or Zermelo-Fraenkel set theory. The general formulation required a convincing characterization of "formality" (see FORMAL SYSTEMS).

According to Kleene (1981) and Rosser (1984), Church proposed in late 1933 the identification of effective calculability with λ-definability. That proposal was not published at the time, but in 1934 Church mentioned it in conversation to Gödel, who judged it to be "thoroughly unsatisfactory." In his subsequent Princeton Lectures Gödel defined the concept of a (general) recursive function using an equational calculus, but he was not convinced that all effectively calculable functions would fall under it. The proof of the equivalence between λ-definability and recursiveness (found by Church and Kleene in early 1935) led to Church's first published formulation of the thesis as quoted above; it was reiterated in Church's 1936 paper. Turing also introduced in 1936 his notion of computability by machines. Post's 1936 paper contains a model of computation that is strikingly similar to Turing's, but he did not provide any analysis in support of the generality of his model. On the contrary, he suggested considering the identification of effective calculability with his concept as a working hypothesis that should be verified by investigating ever wider formulations and reducing them to his basic formulation. The classical papers of Gödel, Church, Turing, Post, and Kleene are all reprinted in Davis 1965, and good historical accounts can be found in Davis 1982, Gandy 1988, and Sieg 1994.

Church (1936) presented one central reason for the proposed identification, namely that other plausible explications of the informal notion lead to mathematical concepts weaker than or equivalent to recursiveness. Two paradigmatic explications, calculability of a function *via algorithms* and *in a logic,* were considered by Church. In either case, the steps taken in determining function values have to be effective; if the effectiveness of steps is taken to mean recursiveness, then the function can be *proved* to be recursive. This requirement on steps in Church's argument corresponds to one of the "recursiveness conditions" formulated by Hilbert and Bernays (1939). That condition is used in their characterization of functions that are evaluated according to rules in a deductive formalism: it requires the proof predicate for a deductive formalism to be primitive recursive. Hilbert and Bernays show that all such "reckonable" functions are recursive and actually can be evaluated in a very restricted number theoretic formalism. Thus, in any formalism that satisfies the recursiveness conditions and contains this minimal number theoretic system, one can compute exactly the recursive functions. Recursiveness or computability consequently has, as Gödel emphasized, an absoluteness property not shared by other metamathematical notions like provability or definability; the latter notions depend on the formalism considered.

All such indirect and ultimately unsatisfactory considerations were bypassed by Turing. He focused directly on the fact that *human mechanical* calculability on symbolic configurations was the intended notion. Analyzing the processes that underlie such calculations (by a *computer*), Turing was led to certain boundedness and locality conditions. To start with, he demanded the immediate recognizability of symbolic configurations so that basic computation steps need not be further subdivided. This demand and the evident limitation of the computor's sensory apparatus motivate the conditions. Turing also required that the computor proceed deterministically. The above conditions, somewhat hidden in Turing's 1936 paper, are here formulated following Sieg (1994); first the *boundedness conditions:*

(*B.1*) There is a fixed bound for the number of symbolic configurations a computor can immediately recognize.

(*B.2*) There is a fixed bound for the number of a computor's internal states that need to be taken into account.

Because the behavior of the computor is uniquely determined by the finitely many combinations of symbolic configurations and internal states, he can carry out only finitely many different operations. These operations are restricted by the *locality conditions:*

(*L.1*) Only elements of observed configurations can be changed.

(*L.2*) The computor can shift his attention from one symbolic configuration to another only if the second is within a bounded distance from the first.

Thus, on closer inspection, Turing's thesis is seen as the result of a two-part analysis. The first part yields the above conditions and Turing's *central thesis,* that any mechanical procedure can be carried out by a computor satisfying these conditions. The second part argues that any number theoretic function calculable by such a computor is computable by a Turing machine. Both Church and Gödel found Turing's analysis convincing; indeed, Church wrote (1937) that Turing's notion makes "the identification with effectiveness in the ordinary (not explicitly defined) sense evident immediately." From a strictly mathematical point, the analysis leaves out important steps, and the claim that is actually established is the more modest one that Turing machines operating on strings can be simulated by machines operating on single letters; a way of generalizing Turing's argument is presented in Sieg and Byrnes (1996).

Two final remarks are in order. First, all the arguments for the thesis take for granted that the effective procedures are being carried out by human beings. Gandy, by contrast, analyzed in his 1980 paper *machine* computability; that notion crucially involves parallelism. Gandy's mathematical model nevertheless computes only recursive functions. Second, the effective procedures are taken to be mechanical, not general cognitive ones—as claimed by Webb and many others. Also, Gödel was wrong when asserting in a brief note from 1972 that Turing intended to show in his 1936 paper that "mental procedures cannot go beyond mechanical procedures." Turing, quite explicitly, had no such intentions; even after having been engaged in the issues surrounding machine intelligence, he emphasized in his 1953 paper that the precise concepts (recursiveness, Turing computability) are to capture the mechanical processes that can be carried out by human beings.

See also ALGORITHM; COMPUTATION; COMPUTATION AND THE BRAIN; LOGIC

—*Wilfried Sieg*

References

Church, A. (1935). An unsolvable problem of elementary number theory (abstract). *Bulletin of the Amer. Math. Soc.* 41: 332–333.

Church, A. (1936). An unsolvable problem of elementary number theory. *Amer. J. Math.* 58: 345–363.

Church, A. (1937). Review of Turing (1936). *J. Symbolic Logic* 2: 42–43.

Davis, M., Ed. (1965). *The Undecidable: Basic Papers on Undecidable Propositions, Unsolvable Problems and Computable Functions.* Raven Press.

Davis, M. (1982). Why Gödel didn't have Church's Thesis. *Information and Control* 54: 3–24.

Gandy, R. (1980). Church's Thesis and principles for mechanisms. In Barwise, Keisler, and Kunen, Eds., *The Kleene Symposium.* North-Holland, pp. 123–148.

Gandy, R. (1988). The confluence of ideas in 1936. In R. Herken, Ed., *The Universal Turing Machine.* Oxford University Press, pp. 55–111.

Gödel, K. (1931). Über formal unentscheidbare Sätze der Principia Mathematica und verwandter Systeme I. In *Collected Works I.* Oxford: Oxford University Press, 1986, pp. 144–195.

Gödel, K. (1934). On undecidable propositions of formal mathematical systems (Princeton Lectures). In *Collected Works I.* Oxford: Oxford University Press, 1986, pp. 346–369.

Gödel, K. (1972). A philosophical error in Turing's work. In *Collected Works II.* Oxford: Oxford University Press, 1986, pp. 306.

Gödel, K. (1986). *Collected Works.* Three volumes. S. Feferman et al., Eds. Oxford: Oxford University Press.

Hilbert, D., and P. Bernays. (1939). *Grundlagen der Mathematik,* vol. 2. Springer Verlag.

Kleene, S. (1952). *Introduction to Metamathematics.* Wolters-Noordhoff.

Kleene, S. (1981). Origins of recursive function theory. *Annals Hist. Computing* 3: 52–66.

Newell, A. (1980). Physical symbol systems. *Cognitive Science* 2: 135–184.

Post, E. (1936). Finite combinatory processes. Formulation 1. *J. Symbolic Logic* 1: 103–105.

Rosser, B. (1984). Highlights of the history of the lambda-calculus. *Annals Hist. Computing* 6: 337–349.

Sieg, W. (1994). Mechanical procedures and mathematical experience. In A. George, Ed., *Mathematics and Mind.* Oxford: Oxford University Press, pp. 71–117.

Sieg, W., and J. Byrnes. (1996). K-graph machines: generalizing Turing's machines and arguments. In P. Hájek, Ed., *Lecture Notes in Logic 6.* Springer Verlag, pp. 98–119.

Turing, A. (1936). On computable numbers, with an application to the Entscheidungsproblem. Reprinted in M. Davis, Ed., (1965), *The Undecidable: Basic Papers on Undecidable Propositions, Unsolvable Problems and Computable Functions.* Raven Press.

Turing, A. (1948). Intelligent Machinery. In D. C. Ince, Ed., *Collected Works of A. M. Turing: Mechanical Intelligence.* North-Holland, pp. 107–127.

Turing, A. (1950). Computing machinery and intelligence. *Mind* 59: 433–460.

Turing, A. (1953). Solvable and unsolvable problems. *Science News* 31: 7–23.

van Heijenoort, J. (1967). *From Frege to Gödel.* Cambridge, MA: Harvard University Press.

Webb, J. C. (1980). *Mechanism, Mentalism, and Metamathematics.* Reidel.

Webb, J. C. (1990). Introductory note to Gödel (1972). In *Collected Works II.* Oxford: Oxford University Press, 1986, pp. 292–304.

Further Readings

Hilbert, D., and W. Ackermann. (1928). *Grundzüge der theoretichen Logik.* Springer Verlag.

Mundici, D., and W. Sieg. (1995). Paper machines. *Philosophia Mathematica* 3: 5–30.

Post, E. (1947). Recursive unsolvability of a problem of Thue. *J. Symbolic Logic* 12: 1–11.

Sieg, W. (1997). Step by recursive step: Church's analysis of effective calculability. *Bulletin of Symbolic Logic* 3: 154–180.

Soare, R. (1996). Computability and recursion. *Bulletin of Symbolic Logic* 2: 284–321.

Civilization

See ARTIFACTS AND CIVILIZATION; TECHNOLOGY AND HUMAN EVOLUTION; WRITING SYSTEMS

Classification

See CATEGORIZATION; DECISION TREES; MACHINE LEARNING; NEURAL NETWORKS

Clustering

See UNSUPERVISED LEARNING

Codeswitching

Codeswitching (CS) is commonly defined as the alternating use of two or more codes in the same conversational event. The term was first employed to refer to the coexistence of more than one structural system in the speech of one individual by JAKOBSON, Fant, and Halle (1952), who use "code" in the abstract information theoretical sense. In later writings, "code" has come to be synonymous with "language" or "speech variety." Recent research on CS falls within two distinct traditions: the syntactic, providing insights into the linguistic principles that underlie the form that CS takes; and the pragmatic that relates linguistic form to function in everyday discourse.

Contrary to common assumptions, CS is most frequent among proficient multilinguals. CS may be intersentential or intrasentential, the latter exemplified in the English-Spanish utterance, "Codeswitching among fluent bilinguals *ha sido la fuente de numerosas investigaciones*" ("has been the source of numerous studies"), and the English-Japanese, "That's how you say it *nihongo de*" ("in Japanese"). The status of such intrasentential CS had been much in dispute: some linguists view it as indicative of imperfect language acquisition or interference. However, later studies reveal that intrasentential CS requires advanced competence in the syntactic systems involved. Particularly significant is the fact that intrasentential CS demonstrates grammatical regularities, reflecting underlying, unconscious principles that speakers rely on in distinguishing between permissible and unacceptable switches.

The notion of grammatical equivalence has played an important role in the syntactic analysis of CS. One early formalization is Poplack's (1980) "Equivalence Constraint," according to which codes will be switched at points where the surface structures of the languages map onto each other. This premise has been challenged by studies on CS in typologically dissimilar languages (Romaine 1989). More recently, researchers have introduced CS data into the discussion of universal grammar, as advanced in Chomsky's principles and parameters framework (Chomsky 1981, 1986), maintaining that the relevant constraints on CS should exploit syntactic distinctions and relations already extant in the grammar. This line of inquiry was initiated by Woolford (1983), who developed a generative model of CS. Since that time, investigations into the properly syntactic principles underlying CS patterns have grown significantly in number and scope: Di Sciullo, Muysken, and Singh (1986) propose the Government Constraint, invoking this syntactic-theoretical hierarchical relation in disallowing CS between certain elements in the sentence; Belazi, Rubin, and Toribio (1994) propose the Functional Head Constraint, a specific application of the general X-bar theoretical process of feature checking that holds between a functional head and its complement (see X-BAR THEORY); and McSwan (1997) demonstrates the proper role of CS constraints within Chomsky's (1993) Minimalist Program. The validity of the aforementioned works relating CS to grammatical competence is further corroborated by investigations focusing on the development of CS ability in children acquiring multiple languages simultaneously. Especially noteworthy are writings by Jürgen Meisel (1990, 1994), whose findings on the syntactic regularities underlying early CS provide theoretical insights obscured in the investigation of monolingual acquisition. These developments make clear that the study of CS has reached a dimension of inquiry that can be informed by, and at once contribute to, the continued advancement of syntactic theory.

Pragmatic approaches to CS deal with the relation between structure and function in everyday speech exchanges, and cover a wider, often more loosely defined range of switching phenomena. Talk is treated as discourse level intentional action, where actors communicate in the context of social groupings, be they speech communities, social, ethnic, professional, or other interest groups (Hymes 1967; Clark 1996), acting in pursuit of context-specific communicative ends (Grice 1989). The verbal resources of such human populations are described in terms of inherently variable linguistic repertoires (Labov 1972) that, depending on local circumstances, consist of either grammatically distinct languages or dialects, or styles of the same language (Gumperz 1964; Hymes 1967). The use of one or another of the available coexisting codes (languages, dialects, styles, or speaking genres) serves a variety of rhetorical functions, for example to engage the listener, to shift footing, to mitigate or strengthen a speech act, to mark reported speech, and to repair or clarify. In this way, language switching can be said to be functionally equivalent to style shifting in monolingual speech (Zentella 1997).

A common claim is that syntactic and pragmatic approaches complement each other, one dealing with struc-

ture and the other with function. In one widely accepted view, for any one speech event, specific codes count as appropriate while others are marked (Myers-Scotton 1993). CS is said to convey information by virtue of the fact that the markedness directly reflects societal values and ideologies. For example, "standard" speech varieties are said to convey authority because they are associated with official situations. But linguistic anthropologists criticize this approach on the grounds that it rests on a dichotomized view of structure and function that cannot account for situated understanding (Bourdieu 1991; Hanks 1995; Auer 1998). It is assumed that the signaling processes underlying interpretation involve both symbolic (i.e., denotational) and indexical signs, which communicate via conventionalized associations between sign and context (Lucy 1993; Silverstein 1993). In discourse, indexical signs function metapragmatically to evoke the mostly unverbalized contextual presuppositions on which assessments of communicative intent rest. CS functions as one of a class of indexical signs or contextualization cues (Gumperz 1992, 1996). Along with others of the same class (e.g., PROSODY AND INTONATION and rhythm), such signs are not lexically meaningful; they work by constructing the ground for situated interpretation. By way of example, consider the following exchange. A third grader, D, is having difficulty with the adjectival use of "surprising" in a workbook question about a story discussed in class: What surprising discovery does Molly make? His partner G makes several unsuccessful attempts to explain, but D remains unconvinced until G finally comes up with the paraphrase: "A discovery *que era* ["that was"] surprising discovery." Whereupon D finally produces the expression "surprising discovery" on his own. The switch here counts as an indexical cue that reframes the issue, so as to relate the new expression to what D already knows (Gumperz, Cook-Gumperz, and Szymanski 1998).

When seen in the perspective of practice, then, CS does not convey propositional meaning nor does it directly convey societal attitudes: CS affects the situated interpretive process by enabling participants to project particular interpretations that are then confirmed or disconfirmed by what happens in subsequent speech. What distinguishes CS from other metapragmatic signs is that it is always highly ideologized, so that the sequential analysis of the interactive process by which interpretations are agreed upon can be a highly sensitive index, not solely of grammatical knowledge, but also of shared, culturally specific knowledge.

See also BILINGUALISM AND THE BRAIN; MINIMALISM; PRAGMATICS; PRESUPPOSITION; RELEVANCE AND RELEVANCE THEORY; SYNTAX

—*John Gumperz and Almeida Jacqueline Toribio*

References

Auer, P., Ed. (1998). *Code-Switching in Conversation: Language, Interaction and Identity.* London: Routledge.

Belazi, H. M., E. J. Rubin, and A. J. Toribio. (1994). Code-switching and X-bar theory. *Linguistic Inquiry* 25 (2): 221–237.

Bourdieu, P. (1991). *Language and Symbolic Power.* Cambridge: Polity Press.

Chomsky, N. (1981). *Lectures on Government and Binding.* Dordrecht: Foris.

Chomsky, N. (1986). *Barriers.* Cambridge, MA: MIT Press.

Chomsky, N. (1993). A minimalist program for linguistic theory. In K. Hale and S. J. Keyser, Eds., *The View From Building 20: Essays in Linguistics in Honor of Sylvain Bromberger.* Cambridge, MA: MIT Press, pp. 1–52.

Clark, H. (1996). *Using Language.* Cambridge: Cambridge University Press.

Duran, R., Ed. (1988). *Latino Language and Communicative Behavior.* Norwood, NJ: ABLEX Publishing.

Di Sciullo, A. M., P. Muysken, and R. Singh. (1986). Government and code-mixing. *Journal of Linguistics* 22: 1–24.

Goffman, E. (1982). The interaction order. *American Sociological Review* 48: 1–17.

Grice, P. (1989). *Ways with Words.* Cambridge, MA: Harvard University Press.

Gumperz, J. (1964). Linguistic and social interaction in two communities. *American Anthropologist* 6: 137–153.

Gumperz, J. (1981). *Discourse Strategies.* Cambridge: Cambridge University Press.

Gumperz, J. (1992). Contextualization and understanding. In A. Duranti and C. Goodwin, Eds., *Rethinking Context.* Cambridge: Cambridge University Press, pp. 229–252.

Gumperz, J. (1996). The linguistic and cultural relativity of inference. In J. Gumperz and S. Levinson, Eds., *Rethinking Linguistic Relativity.* Cambridge: Cambridge University Press, pp. 374–406.

Gumperz, J. J., J. Cook-Gumperz, and M. Szymanski. (1998). *Collaborative Practice in Bilingual Learning.* Santa Barbara: CREDE Research Report, University of California.

Hanks, W. (1995). *Language and Communicative Practice.* Boulder, CO: Westview Press.

Heller, M., Ed. (1988). *Code-Switching: Anthropological and Sociolinguistic Perspectives.* The Hague: Mouton de Gruyter.

Hymes, D. (1967). Models of the interaction of language and social setting. *Journal of Social Issues* 23: 8–28.

Jakobson, R., G. M. Fant, and M. Halle. (1952). *Preliminaries to Speech Analysis: The Distinctive Features and Their Correlates.* Cambidge, MA: MIT Press.

Labov, W. (1972). *Sociolinguistic Patterns.* Philadelphia: University of Pennsylvania.

Lucy, J. (1993). Introduction. In J. Lucy, Ed., *Reflexive Language: Reported Speech and Metapragmatics.* Cambridge: Cambridge University Press, pp. 9–32.

McSwan, J. (1997). *A Minimalist Approach to Intrasentential Code Switching: Spanish-Nahuatl Bilingualism in Central Mexico.* Ph.D. diss., University of California, Los Angeles. Published as McSwan, J. (1999). *A Minimalist Approach to Intrasentential Code Switching.* New York: Garland Press.

Meisel, J. (1990). *Two First Languages: Early Grammatical Development in Bilingual Children.* Dordrecht: Foris.

Meisel, J. (1994). *Bilingual First Language Acquisition.* Amsterdam: John Benjamins Publishing Company.

Milroy, L., and P. Muysken, Eds. (1995). *One Speaker, Two Languages: Cross-Disciplinary Perspectives on Code-Switching.* Cambridge: Cambridge University Press.

Myers-Scotton, C. (1993). *Social Motivations of Code-Switching.* Oxford: Clarendon Press.

Poplack, S. (1980). Sometimes I'll start a sentence in English y termino en español: toward a typology of code-switching. *Linguistics* 18: 581–618.

Romaine, S. (1989). *Bilingualism.* Oxford: Blackwell.

Silverstein, M. (1993). Metapragmatic discourse and metapragmatic function. In J. Lucy, Ed., *Reflexive Language: Reported Speech and Metapragmatics.* Cambridge: Cambridge University Press, pp. 33–58.

Toribio, A. J., and E. J. Rubin. (1996). Code-switching in generative grammar. In A. Roca and J. Jensen, Eds., *Spanish in Contact: Issues in Bilingualism.* Sommerville, MA: Cascadilla Press, pp. 203–226.

Woolford, E. (1983). Bilingual code-switching and syntactic theory. *Linguistic Inquiry* 14: 520–536.

Zentella, A. C. (1997). *Growing Up Bilingual.* Malden, MA: Blackwell Publishers.

Cognition and Aging

See AGING AND COGNITION; AGING, MEMORY, AND THE BRAIN

Cognitive Anthropology

Cognitive anthropology is a unified subfield of cultural anthropology whose principal aim is to understand and describe how people in societies conceive and experience their world (Casson 1994).

The definition of culture that guides research in cognitive anthropology holds that culture is an idealized cognitive system—a system of knowledge, beliefs, and values—that exists in the minds of members of society. Culture is the mental equipment that society members use in orienting, transacting, discussing, defining, categorizing, and interpreting actual social behavior in their society.

Among the many research topics in cognitive anthropology, three are central: cultural models, cultural universals, and CULTURAL CONSENSUS. The first of these will be the focus here.

Cultural models, often termed schemata, are abstractions that represent conceptual knowledge. They are cognitive structures in memory that represent stereotypical concepts. Schemata structure our knowledge of objects and situations, events and actions, and sequences of events and actions. General aspects of concepts are represented at higher levels in schematic structures, and variables associated with specific elements are represented at lower levels.

Items in the LEXICON—words—and grammatical categories and rules are associated in memory with cultural models. Linguistic forms and cognitive schemata "activate" each other: linguistic forms bring schemata to mind, and schemata are expressed in linguistic forms. Virtually all research strategies exploit this relationship between LANGUAGE AND THOUGHT in studying conceptual knowledge and cognitive systems.

The cognitive model underlying commercial events in our culture, a much discussed schema (e.g., Casson 1994), can serve as an example. The [Commercial Event] schema has the variables [buyer], [seller], [money], [goods], and [exchange] (brackets here distinguish conceptual units from words). In this way, [buyer] is a person who possesses [money], the medium of exchange, and [seller] is a person who possesses [goods], the merchandise for sale; [exchange] is an interaction in which [buyer] gives [money] and gets [goods], while [seller] gives [goods] and gets [money]. An event is understood as a commercial transaction when persons, objects, and events in the environment are associated with appropriate schema variables.

A number of words—*buy, sell, pay, cost, worth, value, spend,* and *charge*—activate the [Commercial Event] schema. Each of these words selects particular aspects of the schema for highlighting or foregrounding, while leaving others in the background unexpressed. *Buy* focuses on the exchange from the buyer's perspective, and *sell* from the seller's perspective. *Cost* focuses on the money part of the money-goods relationship, and *value* and *worth* focus on the goods part of the relationship. *Pay* and *spend* focus on the buyer and the money part of the money-goods relationship, and *charge* focuses on the seller and the goods part of the money-goods relationship (Fillmore 1977).

Classification systems are complex cultural models structured by hierarchical embedding. Entities—objects, acts, and events—that are in fact different are grouped together in conceptual categories and regarded as equivalent. Semantic relationships among the categories define cognitive systems. Taxonomic hierarchies, or taxonomies, are classifications structured on the basis of the inclusion, or "kind of," relationship. Some categories included in the tree category, for example, are oak, pine, elm, spruce, poplar, walnut, and fir. Oak in turn includes white oak, post oak, pin oak, and many other kinds of oak.

Nontaxonomic classifications of various types are also hierarchically structured. Partonomic classifications are organized in terms of part-whole relationships. The family category, for example, has among its members (or parts) mother, son, and sister. Functional classifications are constructed on the basis of the instrumental, or "used for", relationship—a vehicle is any object that can be used for transportation, for example, car, bus, moped, or unicycle (Wierzbicka 1985).

Event scenarios are complex cultural models structured by horizontal linkages. Scenes in event schemata are linked in ordered sequences by way of causal relationships. The Yakan, a Philippine agricultural society living on Basilan Island in houses elevated on piles, have an event schemata specifying "how to enter a Yakan house." Social encounters are defined by the degree to which outsiders are able to negotiate penetration into households. An outsider progresses from "in the vicinity" of the house to "at" the house, from "below" the house to "on" the porch, from "outside" on the porch to "inside" the main room, and from the "foot zone" at the entrance door to the "head zone" opposite the door, which is the most private setting in the house (Frake 1975: 26–33).

Metaphorical cultural models are structured by conceptual METAPHORS. Abstract concepts that are not clearly delineated in experience, such as time, love, and ideas, are metaphorically structured, understood, and discussed in terms of other concepts that are more concrete in experience, such as money, travel, and foods (Lakoff and Johnson 1980). The metaphorical concept "embarrassment is exposure" is an example. The embarrassment schema is structured in terms of the exposure schema. The systematicity of the metaphor is reflected in everyday speech formulas, which are sources of insight into and evidence for the nature of the metaphor. Fixed-form expressions for "embarrass-ment is exposure" are evident in these sentences: "You really exposed yourself," "He felt the weight of everyone's eyes," "I felt naked," "I was caught with my pants down," and "I wanted to crawl under a rock" (Holland and Kipnis 1994: 320–322).

Cultural universals are systems of conceptual knowledge that occur in all societies. In studying cognitive commonalities, anthropologists assume a "limited relativist," or universalist, position, adopting a relativist view in recognizing differences in cognitive and cultural systems and a universalist position in emphasizing fundamental concepts and uniformities in these systems (Lounsbury 1969: 10).

Comparative color category research, for instance, has shown that basic color categories are organized around best examples, and that these focal colors are the same across individuals and languages (Berlin and Kay 1969). It has also established that there are exactly eleven of these universal color categories—[black], [white], [red], [green], [yellow], [blue], [brown], [purple], [orange], [pink] and [gray]—that they are encoded in a strict evolutionary sequence, and that these universals are determined largely by neurophysiological processes in human color perception (Kay, Berlin, and Merrifield 1991; see COLOR CLASSIFICATION).

Cultural consensus is concerned with individual variability in cultural knowledge and how the diversity of individual conceptual systems are organized in cultural systems. Consensus theory examines the patterns of agreement among group members about particular domains of cultural knowledge in order to determine the organization of cognitive diversity. It establishes both a "correct" version of cultural knowledge and patterns of cognitive diversity (Romney, Weller, and Batchelder 1986: 316).

The Aguaruna Jivaro, a forest tribe in northern Peru, for example, derive the majority of their sustenance from manioc plants. A study of Aguaruna manioc gardens discovered that, although individual Aguaruna vary widely in their naming of manioc plants, they nonetheless maintain a consensus model of manioc classification. Patterns of agreement reveal that individuals learn a single set of manioc categories with varying degrees of success: some individuals have greater cultural competence in manioc identification than others (Boster 1985: 185).

See also CATEGORIZATION; CULTURAL PSYCHOLOGY; CULTURAL RELATIVISM; CULTURAL VARIATION; HUMAN UNIVERSALS; LANGUAGE AND CULTURE; METAPHOR AND CULTURE; NATURAL KINDS

—*Ronald W. Casson*

References

Berlin, B., and P. Kay. (1969). *Basic Color Terms: Their Universality and Evolution.* Berkeley: University of California Press.

Boster, J. S. (1985). "Requiem for the Omniscient Informant": There's life in the old girl yet. In J. W. D. Dougherty, Ed., *Directions in Cognitive Anthropology.* Urbana: University of Illinois Press.

Casson, R. W. (1994). Cognitive anthropology. In P. K. Bock, Ed., *Handbook of Psychological Anthropology.* Westport, CT: Greenwood Press.

Fillmore, C. J. (1977). Topics in lexical semantics. In R. W. Cole, Ed., *Current Issues in Linguistic Theory.* Bloomington: Indiana University Press.

Frake, C. O. (1975). How to enter a Yakan house. In M. Sanches and B. Blount, Eds., *Sociocultural Dimensions of Language Use.* New York: Academic Press.

Holland, D., and A. Kipnis. (1994). Metaphors for embarrassment and stories of exposure: the not-so-egocentric self in American culture. *Ethos* 22: 316–342.

Kay, P., B. Berlin, and W. Merrifield. (1991). Biocultural implications of systems of color naming. *Journal of Linguistic Anthropology* 1: 12–25.

Lakoff, G., and M. Johnson. (1980). *Metaphors We Live By.* Chicago: University of Chicago Press.

Lounsbury, F. G. (1969). Language and culture. In S. Hook, Ed., *Language and Philosophy.* New York: New York University Press.

Romney, A. K., S. C. Weller, and W. H. Batchelder. (1986). Culture as consensus: a theory of culture and informant accuracy. *American Anthropologist* 88: 313–338.

Wierzbicka, A. (1985). *Lexicography and Conceptual Analysis.* Ann Arbor, MI: Karoma Publishers, Inc.

Further Readings

Alverson, H. (1994). *Semantics and Experience: Universal Metaphors of Time in English, Mandarin, Hindi, and Sesotho.* Baltimore, MD: Johns Hopkins University Press.

Berlin, B. (1992). *Ethnobiological Classification: Principles of Categorization of Plants and Animals in Traditional Societies.* Princeton, NJ: Princeton University Press.

Brown, C. H. (1984). *Language and Living Things: Uniformities in Folk Classification and Naming.* New Brunswick, NJ: Rutgers University Press.

Casson, R. W., Ed. (1981). *Language, Culture, and Cognition: Anthropological Perspectives.* New York: Macmillan.

D'Andrade, R. G. (1995). *The Development of Cognitive Anthropology.* New York: Cambridge University Press.

Dougherty, J. W. D., Ed. (1985). *Directions in Cognitive Anthropology.* Urbana: University of Illinois Press.

Frake, C. O. (1980). *Language and Cultural Description.* Stanford, CA: Stanford University Press.

Goodenough, W. H. (1981). *Culture, Language, and Society.* Second edition. Menlo Park, CA: Benjamin/Commings.

Hardin, C. L., and L. Maffi, Eds. (1997). *Color Categories in Thought and Language.* Cambridge: Cambridge University Press.

Holland, D., and N. Quinn, Eds. (1987). *Cultural Models in Language and Thought.* New York: Cambridge University Press.

Hunn, E. S. (1977). *Tzeltal Folk Zoology: The Classification of Discontinuities in Nature.* New York: Academic Press.

Kronenfeld, D. B. (1996). *Plastic Glasses and Church Fathers: Semantic Extension from the Ethnoscience Tradition.* New York: Oxford University Press.

Lakoff, G. (1987). *Women, Fire, and Dangerous Things.* Chicago: University of Chicago Press.

MacLaury, R. E. (1997). *Color and Cognition in Mesoamerica: Constructing Categories as Vantages.* Austin: University of Texas.

Scheffler, H. W., and F. G. Lounsbury. (1971). *A Study in Structural Semantics: The Siriono Kinship System.* Englewood Cliffs, NJ: Prentice-Hall.

Spradley, J. P., Ed. (1972). *Culture and Cognition: Rules, Maps, and Plans.* San Francisco: Freeman.

Tyler, S. A., Ed. (1969). *Cognitive Anthropology.* New York: Holt, Rinehart, and Winston.

Wallace, A. F. C. (1970). *Culture and Personality.* Second edition. New York: Random House.

Cognitive Archaeology

The term *cognitive archaeology* was introduced during the early 1980s to refer to studies of past societies in which explicit attention is paid to processes of human thought and symbolic behavior. As the archaeological record only consists of the material remains of past activities—artifacts, bones, pits, hearths, walls, buildings—there is no direct information about the types of belief systems or thought processes that existed within past minds. These must be inferred from those material remains. Cognitive archaeology attempts to do this, believing that appropriate interpretations of past material culture, the behavioral processes that created it, and long-term patterns of culture change evident from the archaeological record, such as the origin of agriculture and the development of state society, requires that those belief systems and processes of thought be reconstructed.

There is a diversity of approaches and studies that fall under the poorly defined umbrella of cognitive archaeology (see Renfrew et al. 1993). These can be grouped into three broad categories that we can term postprocessual archaeology, cognitive-processual archaeology, and evolutionary-cognitive archaeology. While these three categories differ in significant ways with regard to both form and content, they also share some overriding features. The first is that an understanding of human behavior and society, whether in the distant past or the present, requires explicit reference to human cognition—although there is limited agreement on quite what nature that reference should take. Second, that the study of past or present cognition cannot be divorced from the study of society in general—individuals are intimately woven together in shared frames of thought (Hodder, in Renfrew et al. 1993). Indeed, the study of past or present minds is hopelessly flawed unless it is integrated into a study of society, economy, technology, and environment. Third, that material culture is critical not only as an expression of human cognition, but also as a means to attain it.

Postprocessual studies, which began in the late 1970s, not only laid emphasis on the symbolic aspects of human behavior but also adopted a postmodernist agenda in which processes of hypothesis testing as a means of securing knowledge were replaced by hermeneutic interpretation (e.g., Hodder 1982, 1986). As such, these studies began as a reaction against what was perceived, largely correctly, as a crude functionalism that had come to dominate archaeological theory and attempted to provide a new academic agenda for the discipline, epitomized in a volume by Mike Shanks and Chris Tilley (1987) entitled *Re-constructing Archaeology.* While the critique of functionalism was warmly received and has had a long-lasting effect, it was soon recognized that the epistemology of relativism, the lack of explicit methodology, and the refusal to provide criteria to judge between competing interpretations constituted an appalling agenda for the discipline. Consequently, while such work was critical for the emergence of cognitive archaeology, it now plays only a marginal role within the discipline.

A contrasting type of cognitive archaeology has attempted to provide an equal emphasis on symbolic thought and ideology, but sought to do this within a scientific frame of reference in which claims about past beliefs and ways of thought can be objectively evaluated. As such, this archaeology has been characterized as a "cognitive-processual" archaeology by Colin Renfrew (Renfrew and Bahn 1991). This covers an extremely broad range of studies in which attention has been paid to ideology, religious thought, and cosmology (e.g., Flannery and Marcus 1983; Renfrew 1985; Renfrew and Zubrow 1993). Such studies argue that these aspects of human behavior and thought are as amenable to study as are the traditional subjects of archaeology, such as technology and subsistence, which leave more direct archaeological traces. Of course, when written records are available to supplement the archaeological evidence, reconstruction of past beliefs can be substantially developed (Flannery and Marcus, in Renfrew et al. 1993). One branch of this cognitive-processual archaeology has attempted to focus on processes of human DECISION-MAKING, and argued that explicit reference to individuals is required for adequate explanations of long-term cultural change. Perles (1992), for instance, has attempted to infer the cognitive processes of prehistoric flint knappers, while Mithen (1990) used computer simulations of individual decision making to examine the hunting behavior of prehistoric foragers. Another important feature has been an explicit concern with the process of cultural transmission. In such studies attempts have been made to understand how the processes of social learning are influenced by different forms of social organization (e.g., Mithen 1994; Shennan 1996). More generally, it is argued that the long-term patterns of culture change in the archaeological record, such as the introduction, spread, and then demise of particular artifact types (e.g., forms of axe head) can only be explained by understanding both the conscious and unconscious processes of social learning (Shennan 1989, 1991).

A third category of studies in cognitive archaeology, although one that could be subsumed within cognitive-processual archaeology, consists of those that are concerned with the EVOLUTION of the human mind and that can be referred to as an evolutionary-cognitive archaeology. As the archaeological record begins 2.5 million years ago with the first stone tools, it covers the period of brain enlargement and the evolution of modern forms of language and intelligence. While the fossil record can provide data about brain size, anatomical adaptations for speech, and brain morphology (through the study of endocasts), the archaeological record is an essential means to reconstruct the past thought and behavior of our ancestors, and the selective pressures for cognitive evolution. Consequently, studies of human fossils and artifacts need to be pursued in a very integrated fashion if we are to reconstruct the evolution of the human mind.

The last decade has seen very substantial developments in this area, although significant contributions had already been made by Wynn (1979, 1981). He attempted to infer the levels of intelligence of human ancestors from the form of early prehistoric stone tools by adopting a recapitualist posi-

tion and using the developmental stages proposed by PIAGET as models for stages of cognitive evolution. While there were other important attempts at inferring the mental characteristics of our extinct ancestors and relatives from their material culture, such as by Glynn Isaac (1986) and John Gowlett (1984), it was in fact a psychologist, Merlin Donald (1991), who was the first to propose a theory for cognitive evolution that made significant use of archaeological data in his book *Origins of the Modern Mind.*

His scenario, however, has been challenged by Mithen (1996a), who attempted to integrate current thought in EVOLUTIONARY PSYCHOLOGY with that in cognitive archaeology. As such, he argues that premodern humans (e.g., H. erectus, Neanderthals) had a domain-specific mentality and that this accounts for the particular character of their archaeological record. In his model, the origin of art, religious thought, and scientific thinking—all of which emerged rather dramatically about 30,000 years ago (70,000 years after anatomically modern humans appear in the fossil record)—arose from a new-found ability to integrate ways of thinking and types of knowledge that had been "trapped" in specific cognitive domains. It is evident that the remarkable development of culture in the past 30,000 years, and especially its cumulative character of knowledge (something that had been absent from all previous human cultures) is partly attributable to the disembodiment of mind into material culture. For example, the first art objects included those that extended memory from its biological basis in the brain to a material basis in terms of symbolic codes engraved on pieces of bone or in paintings on cave walls (e.g., Mithen 1988; Marshack 1991; D'Errico 1995). Depictions of imaginary beings are not simply reflections of mental representations, but are critical in allowing those representations to persist and to be transmitted to other individuals, perhaps across several generations (Mithen 1996b). In this regard, material culture plays an active role in formulating thought and transmitting ideas, and is not simply a passive reflection of these. Whether or not this particular scenario from evolutionary-cognitive archaeology has any merit remains to be seen. But it is one example of the major development of cognitive archaeology—in all of its guises—that has occurred during the last two decades. One must anticipate substantial future developments, especially if greater interdisciplinary research between archaeologists, biological anthropologists, and cognitive scientists can be achieved.

See also CULTURAL EVOLUTION; CULTURAL RELATIVISM; CULTURAL SYMBOLISM; DOMAIN SPECIFICITY; LANGUAGE AND CULTURE; TECHNOLOGY AND HUMAN EVOLUTION

—*Steven J. Mithen*

References

Donald, M. (1991). *Origins of the Modern Mind.* Cambridge, MA: Harvard University Press.

D'Errico, F. (1995). A new model and its implications for the origin of writing: the la Marche antler revisited. *Cambridge Archaeological Journal* 5: 163–206.

Flannery, K. V., and J. Marcus. (1983). *The Cloud People.* New York: Academic Press.

Gowlett, J. (1984). Mental abilities of early man: a look at some hard evidence. In R. Foley, Ed., *Hominid Evolution and Community Ecology*. London: Academic Press, pp. 167–192.

Hodder, I. (1986). *Reading the Past*. Cambridge: Cambridge University Press.

Hodder, I., Ed. (1982). *Symbolic and Structural Archaeology*. Cambridge: Cambridge University Press.

Isaac, G. (1986). Foundation stones: early artefacts as indicators of activities and abilities. In G. N. Bailey and P. Callow, Eds., *Stone Age Prehistory*. Cambridge: Cambridge University Press, pp. 221–241.

Marshack, A. (1991). The Tai plaque and calendrical notation in the Upper Palaeolithic. *Cambridge Archaeological Journal* 1: 25–61.

Mithen, S. (1988). Looking and learning: Upper Palaeolithic art and information gathering. *World Archaeology* 19: 297–327.

Mithen, S. (1990). *Thoughtful Foragers: A Study of Prehistoric Decision Making*. Cambridge: Cambridge University Press.

Mithen, S. (1994). Technology and society during the Middle Pleistocene. *Cambridge Archaeological Journal* 4: 3–33.

Mithen, S. (1996a). *The Prehistory of the Mind: A Search for the Origins of Art, Science and Religion*. London: Thames and Hudson.

Mithen, S. (1996b). The supernatural beings of prehistory: the cultural storage and transmission of religious ideas. In C. Scarre and C. Renfrew, Eds., *External Symbolic Storage*. Cambridge: McDonald Institute for Archaeological Research (forthcoming).

Perles, C. (1992). In search of lithic strategies: a cognitive approach to prehistoric chipped stone assemblages. In J-C. Gardin and C. S. Peebles, Eds., *Representations in Archaeology*. Bloomington: Indiana University Press, pp. 357–384.

Renfrew, C., (1985). *The Archaeology of Cult, the Sanctuary at Phylakopi*. London: Thames and Hudson.

Renfrew, C., and P. Bahn. (1991). *Archaeology: Theories, Methods and Practice*. London: Thames and Hudson.

Renfrew, C., C. S. Peebles, I. Hodder, B. Bender, K. V. Flannery, and J. Marcus. (1993). What is cognitive archaeology? *Cambridge Archaeological Journal* 3: 247–270.

Renfrew, C., and E. Zubrow, Eds. (1993). *The Ancient Mind*. Cambridge: Cambridge Univerity Press.

Shanks, M., and C. Tilley. (1987). *Re-Constructing Archaeology*. Cambridge: Cambridge University Press.

Shennan, S. J. (1989). Cultural transmission and cultural change. In S. E. van der Leeuw and R. Torrence, Eds., *What's New? A Closer Look at the Process of Innovation*. London: Unwin Hyman, pp. 330–346.

Shennan, S. J. (1991). Tradition, rationality and cultural transmission. In R. Preucel, Ed., *Processual and Postprocessual Archaeologies: Multiple Ways of Knowing the Past*. Carbondale: Center for Archaeological Investigations, Southern Illinois University at Carbondale, pp. 197–208.

Shennan, S. J. (1996). Social inequality and the transmission of cultural traditions in forager societies. In S. Shennan and J. Steele, Eds., *The Archaeology of Human Ancestry: Power, Sex and Tradition*. London: Routledge, pp. 365–379.

Wynn, T. (1979). The intelligence of later Acheulian hominids. *Man* 14: 371–391.

Wynn, T. (1981). The intelligence of Oldowan hominids. *Journal of Human Evolution* 10: 529–541.

Cognitive Architecture

Cognitive architecture refers to the design and organization of the mind. Theories of cognitive architecture strive to provide an exhaustive survey of cognitive systems, a description of the functions and capacities of each, and a blueprint to integrate the systems. Such theories are designed around a small set of principles of operation. Theories of cognitive architecture can be contrasted with other kinds of cognitive theories in providing a set of principles for constructing cognitive models, rather than a set of hypotheses to be empirically tested.

Theories of cognitive architecture can be roughly divided according to two legacies: those motivated by the digital computer and those based on an associative architecture. The currency of the first kind of architecture is information in the form of symbols; the currency of the second kind is activation that flows through a network of associative links. The most common digital computer architecture is called the VON NEUMANN architecture in recognition of the contributions of the mathematician John von Neumann to its development. The key idea, the stored-program technique, allows program and data to be stored together. The von Neumann architecture consists of a central processing unit, a memory unit, and input and output units. Information is input, stored, and transformed algorithmically to derive an output. The critical role played by this framework in the development of modern technology helped make the COMPUTATIONAL THEORY OF MIND seem viable. The framework has spawned three classes of theories of cognitive architecture, each encompassing several generations. The three classes are not mutually exclusive; they should be understood as taking different perspectives on cognitive organization that result in different performance models.

The original architecture of this type was a PRODUCTION SYSTEM. In this view, the mind consists of a working memory, a large set of production rules, and a set of precedence rules determining the order of firing of production rules. A production rule is a condition-action pair specifying actions to perform if certain conditions are met. The first general theory of this type was proposed by NEWELL, Simon, and Shaw (1958) and was called the General Problem Solver (GPS). The idea was that a production system incorporating a few simple heuristics could solve difficult problems in the same way that humans did. A descendant of this approach, SOAR (Newell 1990), elaborates the production system architecture by adding mechanisms for making decisions, for recursive application of operators to a hierarchy of goals and subgoals, and for learning of productions. The architecture has been applied to help understand a range of human performance from simple stimulus-response tasks, to typing, syllogistic reasoning, and more.

A second class of von Neumann-inspired cognitive architecture is the information processing theory. Unlike production systems, which posit a particular language of symbolic transformation, information processing theories posit a sequence of processing stages from input through encoding, memory storage and retrieval, to output. All such theories assume the critical components of a von Neumann architecture: a central executive to control the flow of information, one or more memories to retain information, sensory devices to input information, and an output device. The critical issues for such theories concern the nature and time course of processing at each stage. An early example of such a theory is Broadbent's (1958) model of ATTENTION, the imprint of which can be found on the "modal" information processing theory, whose central distinction is between short-term and long-term memory (e.g., Atkinson and Shiffrin 1968), and on later models of WORKING MEMORY.

The digital computer also inspired a class of cognitive architecture that emphasizes veridical representation of the structure of human knowledge. The computer model distinguishes program from data, and so the computer modeler has the option of putting most of the structure to be represented in the computer program or putting it in the data that the program operates on. Representational models do the latter; they use fairly sophisticated data structures to model organized knowledge. Theories of this type posit two memory stores: a working memory and a memory for structured data. Various kinds of structured data formats have been proposed, including frames (Minsky 1975), SCHEMATA (Rumelhart and Ortony 1977), and scripts (Schank and Abelson 1977), each specializing in the representation of different aspects of the world (objects, events, and action sequences, respectively). What the formats have in common is that they (i) represent "default" relations that normally hold, though not always; (ii) have variables, so that they can represent relations between abstract classes and not merely individuals; (iii) can embed one another (hierarchical organization); and (iv) are able to represent the world at multiple levels of abstraction.

The second type of cognitive architecture is associative. In contrast with models of the von Neumann type, which assume that processing involves serial, rule-governed operations on symbolic representations, associative models assume that processing is done by a large number of parallel operators and conforms to principles of similarity and contiguity. For example, an associative model of memory explains how remembering part of an event can cue retrieval of the rest of the event by claiming that an association between the two parts was constructed when the event was first encoded. Activation from the representation of the first part of the event flows to the representation of the second part through an associative connection. More generally, the first part of the event cues associative retrieval of the entire event (and thus the second part) by virtue of being similar to the entire event.

Associative models have a long history stretching back to Aristotle, who construed MEMORY and some reasoning processes in terms of associations between elementary sense images. More recent associative models are more promiscuous: different models assume associations between different entities, concepts themselves, or some more primitive set of elements out of which concepts are assumed to be constructed.

Such modern conceptions of associative cognitive architecture have two antecedents located in the history of cognitive science and two more immediate precursors. The first historical source is the foundational work on associative computation begun by MCCULLOCH and PITTS (1943) demonstrating the enormous computational power of populations of neurons and the ability of such systems to learn using simple algorithms. The second source is the application of associative models based on neurophysiology to psychology. An influential synthesis of these efforts was Hebb's

(1949) book, *The Organization of Behavior.* HEBB attempted to account for psychological phenomena using a theory of neural connections (cell assemblies) that could be neurophysiologically motivated, in part by appeal to large-scale cortical organization. Thus, brain architecture became a source of inspiration for cognitive architecture. Hebb's conception was especially successful as an account of perceptual learning. The two remaining antecedents involve technical achievements that led to a renewed focus on associative models in the 1980s. Earlier efforts to build associative devices resulted in machines that were severely limited in the kinds of distinctions they were able to make (they could only distinguish linearly separable patterns). This limitation was overcome by the introduction of a learning algorithm called "backpropagation of error" (Rumelhart, Hinton, and Williams 1986). The second critical technical achievement was a set of proofs, due in large part to Hopfield (e.g., 1982), that provided new ways of interpreting associative computation and brought new tools to bear on the study of associative networks. These proofs demonstrated that certain kinds of associative networks could be interpreted as optimizing mathematical functions. This insight gave theorists a tool to translate a problem that a person might face into an associative network. This greatly simplified the process of constructing associative models of cognitive tasks.

These achievements inspired renewed interest in associative architectures. In 1986, Rumelhart and McClelland published a pair of books on parallel, distributed processing that described a set of models of different cognitive systems (e.g., memory, perception, and language) based on common associative principles. The work lent credence to the claim that an integrated associative architecture could be developed.

Although a broad division between von Neumann and associative architectures helps to organize the various conceptions of mental organization that have been offered, it does an injustice to hybrid architectural proposals; that is, proposals that include von Neumann-style as well as associative components. Such alliances of processing systems seem necessary on both theoretical and empirical grounds (Sloman 1996). Only von Neumann components seem capable of manipulating variables in a way that matches human competence (*see* BINDING PROBLEM), yet associative components seem better able to capture the context-specificity of human judgment and performance as well as people's ability to deal with and integrate many pieces of information simultaneously. One important hybrid theory is ACT* (Anderson 1983). ACT* posits three memories: a production, a declarative, and a working memory, as well as processes that interrelate them. The architecture includes both a production system and an associative network. In this sense, ACT* is an early attempt to build an architecture that takes advantage of both von Neumann and associative principles. But integrating these very different attitudes in a principled and productive way is an ongoing challenge.

See also AUTOMATA; BROADBENT; COGNITIVE MODELING, CONNECTIONIST; COGNITIVE MODELING, SYMBOLIC; DISTRIBUTED VS. LOCAL REPRESENTATION

—*Steven Sloman*

References

Anderson, J. R. (1983). *The Architecture of Cognition.* Cambridge, MA: Harvard University Press.

Atkinson, R. C., and R. M. Shiffrin. (1968). Human memory: a proposed system and its control processes. In K. W. Spence and J. T. Spence, Eds., *The Psychology of Learning and Motivation: Advances in Research and Theory,* vol. 2. New York: Academic Press, pp. 89–195.

Broadbent, D. E. (1958). *Perception and Communication.* London: Pergamon Press.

Hebb, D. O. (1949). *The Organization of Behavior.* New York: Wiley.

Hopfield, J. J. (1982). Neural networks and physical systems with emergent collective computational abilities. *Proceedings of the National Academy of Sciences, USA* 79: 2554–2558.

McCulloch, W. S., and W. Pitts. (1943). A logical calculus of the ideas immanent in nervous activity. *Bulletin of Mathematical Biophysics* 5: 115–133.

Minsky, M. (1975). A framework for representing knowledge. In P. Winston, Ed., *The Psychology of Computer Vision.* New York: McGraw-Hill.

Newell, A. (1990). *Unified Theories of Cognition.* Cambridge: Harvard University Press.

Newell, A., H. A. Simon, and J. C. Shaw. (1958). Elements of a theory of human problem solving. *Psychological Review* 65: 151–166.

Rumelhart, D. E., and A. Ortony. (1977). The representation of knowledge in memory. In R. C. Anderson, R. J. Spiro, and W. E. Montague, Eds., *Schooling and the Acquisition of Knowledge.*

Rumelhart, D. E., G. E. Hinton, and R. J. Williams. (1986). Learning internal representations by error propagation. In D. E. Rumelhart, J. L. McClelland, and the PDP Research Group, Eds., *Parallel Distributed Processing, 1.* Cambridge, MA: MIT Press.

Schank, R. C., and R. Abelson. (1977). *Scripts, Plans, Goals, and Understanding.* Hillsdale, NJ: Erlbaum.

Sloman, S. A. (1996). The empirical case for two systems of reasoning. *Psychological Bulletin* 119: 3–22.

Further Readings

Newell, A., and H. A. Simon. (1972). *Human Problem Solving.* Englewood Cliffs, NJ: Prentice-Hall.

Hinton, G. E., and J. A. Anderson. (1989). *Parallel Models of Associative Memory.* Hillsdale, NJ: Erlbaum.

Pinker, S., and J. Mehler, Eds. (1988). *Connections and Symbols.* Cambridge, MA: MIT Press.

Rumelhart, D. E., J. L. McClelland, and the PDP Research Group, Eds. (1986). *Parallel Distributed Processing.* Cambridge, MA: MIT Press.

Smolensky, P. (1988). On the proper treatment of connectionism. *Behavioral and Brain Sciences* 11: 1–23.

Cognitive Artifacts

Cognitive artifacts are physical objects made by humans for the purpose of aiding, enhancing, or improving cognition. Examples of cognitive artifacts include a string tied around the finger as a reminder, a calendar, a shopping list, and a computer. In the modern world, many cognitive artifacts rely on LITERACY and numeracy skills. Lists of various kinds support not only MEMORY, but also reasoning about classification and comparison. Goody (1977) argues that the advent of WRITING SYSTEMS fundamentally transformed human cognition. Nonlinguistic inscriptions such as maps, charts, graphs, and tables enable the superimposition of representations of otherwise incommensurable items (Latour 1986). Tabular formats for data are at least three thousand years old (Ifrah 1987), and support reasoning about the coordination of differing category structures, types, and quantities of goods, for example.

People often engage in activities characterized by the incremental creation and use of cognitive artifacts. Doing place-value arithmetic amounts to successively producing artifact structure, examining it, and then producing more structure (Rumelhart et al. 1986). Everyday tasks such as cooking involve a continuous process of creating and using cognitive artifacts. Kirsh (1995) refers to the systematic creation and use of spatial structure in the placement of cooking implements and ingredients as the *intelligent use of space.* Here, the arrangement of artifacts is itself a cognitive artifact.

Norman (1993) relaxes the definition of cognitive artifacts to include mental as well as material elements. Rules of thumb, proverbs, mnemonics, and memorized procedures are clearly artifactual and play a similar role to objects in some cognitive processes (Shore 1996). Of course, material cognitive artifacts are only useful when they are brought into coordination with a corresponding mental element—the knowledge of how to use them.

The behaviors of other actors in a social setting can serve as cognitive artifacts. The work of VYGOTSKY (Vygotsky 1978, 1986; Wertsch 1985) on activity theory emphasizes the role of others in creating a "zone of proximal development" in which the learning child is capable of cognitive activities that it could not do alone. Activity theory takes words and concepts to be powerful psychological tools that organize thought and make higher level cognitive processes possible. In this view, language becomes the ultimate cognitive artifact system, and cognitive artifacts are absolutely fundamental to human consciousness and what it means to be human.

One of the principal findings of studies of SITUATED COGNITION AND LEARNING is that people make opportunistic use of structure. The *method of loci* in which an orator who must remember a speech associates elements of the speech with architectural features of the place where the speech is delivered is a well-known example. Lave, Murtaugh, and de la Rocha (1984) examined the way that shoppers made use of the structure of supermarkets. The layout of the supermarket itself with the orderly arrangement of items on the shelf is the ultimate icon of the shopping list. Regular shoppers develop routine trajectories through this space, thus creating a sequence of reminders of items to buy. Scribner (1984) documented the ways that dairy workers take advantage of the layouts of standard diary product cases in filling orders. Beach (1988) went to bartender's school and learned how to use the shapes of drink glasses and their placement on the bar to encode the drinks in a multiple drink order. Hutchins (1995b) showed how airline pilots take advantage of an incidental feature of the airspeed indicator to identify +/–5 knot deviations from target speeds by looking at the display in a particular way rather than by calculating. Frake (1985) showed how medieval sailors in northern Europe used the structure of the compass card to "see" the times of high and low tides at major ports. In each of these cases people use designed objects in ways that were not intended by the artifact's designers.

Sometimes even structures that are not made by humans play the same role as cognitive artifacts. Micronesian navigators can see the night sky as a 32-point compass that is used to express courses between islands (Gladwin 1970; Lewis 1972), and forms the foundation for a complex layered mental image that represents distance/rate/time problems in analog form (Hutchins and Hinton 1984; Hutchins 1995a). The Micronesian navigator uses the night sky in the same way that many manufactured navigational artifacts are used.

There is a continuum from the case in which a cognitive artifact is used as designed, to cases of cognitive uses of artifacts that were made for other purposes, to completely opportunistic uses of natural structure.

If one focuses on the products of cognitive activity, cognitive artifacts seem to amplify human abilities. A calculator seems to amplify my ability to do arithmetic, writing down something I want to remember seems to amplify my memory. Cole and Griffin (1980) point out that this is not quite correct. When I remember something by writing it down and reading it later, my memory has not been amplified. Rather, I am using a different set of functional skills to do the memory task. Cognitive artifacts are involved in a process of organizing functional skills into *functional systems.*

Computers are an especially interesting class of cognitive artifact. Their effects on cognition are in part produced via the reorganization of human cognitive functions, as is true of all other cognitive artifacts (Pea 1985). What sets computers apart is that they may also mimic certain aspects of human cognitive function. The complexity and power of the combination of these effects makes the study of HUMAN-COMPUTER INTERACTION both challenging and important.

While cognitive artifacts do not directly amplify or change cognitive abilities, there are side effects of artifact use. Functional skills that are frequently invoked in interaction with artifacts will tend to become highly developed, and those that are displaced by artifact use may atrophy.

Any particular cognitive artifact typically supports some tasks better than others. Some artifacts are tuned to very narrow contexts of use while others are quite general. The ones that are easy are easy because one can use very simple cognitive and perceptual routines in interaction with the technology in order to do the job (Norman 1987, 1993; Hutchins 1995a; Zhang 1992).

Cognitive artifacts are always embedded in larger sociocultural systems that organize the practices in which they are used. The utility of a cognitive artifact depends on other processes that create the conditions and exploit the consequences of its use. In culturally elaborated activities, partial solutions to frequently encountered problems are often crystallized in practices, in knowledge, in material artifacts, and in social arrangements.

Since artifacts require knowledge for use, the widespread presence of a technology affects what people know. Most members of Western society know how to read, use a telephone, drive a car, and so on. Conversely, the distribution of knowledge in a community constrains technology. If everyone already knows how to do something with a particular technology, an attempt to change or replace that technology may meet resistance because learning is expensive.

There is no widespread consensus on how to bound the category "cognitive artifacts." The prototypical cases seem clear, but the category is surrounded by gray areas consisting of mental and social artifacts, physical patterns that are not objects, and opportunistic practices. The cognitive artifact concept points not so much to a category of objects, as to a category of processes that produce cognitive effects by bringing functional skills into coordination with various kinds of structure.

See also ARTIFACTS AND CIVILIZATION; HUMAN NAVIGATION; SITUATEDNESS/EMBEDDEDNESS

—*Edwin Hutchins*

References

Beach, K. (1988). The role of external mnemonic symbols in acquiring an occupation. In M. M. Gruneberg, P. E. Morris, and R. N. Sykes, Eds., *Practical Aspects of Memory: Current Research and Issues,* vol. 1. New York: Wiley.

Cole, M., and P. Griffin. (1980). Cultural amplifiers reconsidered. In D. R. Olson, Ed., *The Social Foundations of Language and Thought.* New York: Norton, pp. 343–364.

Frake, C. (1985). Cognitive maps of time and tide among medieval seafarers. *Man* 20: 254–270.

Gladwin, T. (1970). *East is a Big Bird.* Cambridge, MA: Harvard University Press.

Goody, J. (1977). *The Domestication of the Savage Mind.* Cambridge: Cambridge University Press.

Hutchins, E. (1995a). *Cognition in the Wild.* Cambridge, MA: MIT Press.

Hutchins, E. (1995b). How a cockpit remembers its speeds. *Cognitive Science* 19: 265–288.

Hutchins, E., and G. E. Hinton. (1984). Why the islands move. *Perception* 13: 629–632.

Ifrah, G. (1987). *From One to Zero. A Universal History of Numbers.* Trans. L. Bair. New York: Penguin Books.

Kirsh, D. (1995). The intelligent use of space. *Artificial Intelligence* 72: 1–52.

Latour, B. (1986). Visualization and cognition: thinking with eyes and hands. *Knowledge and Society: Studies in the Sociology of Culture Past and Present* 6: 1–40.

Lave, J., M. Murtaugh, and O. de la Rocha. (1984). The dialectic of arithmetic in grocery shopping. In B. Rogoff and J. Lave, Eds., *Everyday Cognition: Its Development in Social Context.* Cambridge, MA: Harvard University Press, pp. 67–94.

Lewis, D. (1972). *We the Navigators.* Honolulu: University of Hawaii Press.

Norman, D. A. (1987). *The Psychology of Everyday Things.* New York: Basic Books.

Norman, D. A. (1993). *Things That Make Us Smart.* Reading, MA: Addison Wesley.

Pea, R. (1985). Beyond amplification: using computers to reorganize human mental functioning. *Educational Psychologist* 20: 167–182.

Rumelhart, D. E., P. Smolensky, J. L. McClelland, and G. E. Hinton. (1986). Schemata and sequential thought processes in PDP models. In J. L. McClelland, D. E. Rumelhart, and the PDP

Group, Eds., *Parallel Distributed Processing: Explorations in the Microstructure of Cognition.* vol. 2: *Psychological and Biological Models.* Cambridge, MA: MIT Press, pp. 7–57.

Scribner, S. (1984). Studying working intelligence. In B. Rogoff and J. Lave, Eds., *Everyday Cognition: Its Development in Social Context.* Cambridge, MA: Harvard University Press, pp. 9–40.

Shore, B. (1996). *Culture in Mind.* New York: Oxford University Press.

Vygotsky, L. S. (1978). *Mind and Society.* Cambridge, MA: Harvard University Press.

Vygotsky, L. S. (1986). *Thought and Language.* Cambridge, MA: MIT Press.

Wertsch, J. V. (1985). *Vygotsky and the Social Formation of Mind.* Cambridge, MA: Harvard University Press.

Zhang, J. (1992). *Distributed Representation: The Interaction Between Internal and External Information.* Tech. Rep. no. 9201. La Jolla: University of California, San Diego, Department of Cognitive Science.

Cognitive Development

Students of cognitive development ask how our young are able to acquire and use knowledge about the physical, social, cultural, and mental worlds. Questions of special interest include: what is known when; whether what is known facilitates or serves as a barrier to the accurate interpretation and learning of new knowledge; how knowledge development serves and interacts with problem-solving strategies; and the relationship between initial knowledge levels and ones achieved for everyday as opposed to expert use.

Several classes of theories share the premise that infants lack abstract representational abilities and therefore CONCEPTS. The infant mind to an associationist is a passive "blank slate"—upon which a wash of sensations emanating from the world is recorded as a result of the associative capacity. Stage theorists need not share the no innate knowledge assumption. Interestingly, however, PIAGET, Bruner, and VYGOTSKY do, although to them infants are able to participate actively in the construction of their own cognitive development. For Piaget, neonates spontaneously practice their reflexes, the effect being the differentiation of inborn reflexes into different sensory-motor schemes. Active use of these yields integrated action schemes, and thus novel ways to act on the environment (Piaget 1970). The information processing approach emphasizes the development of general processes like ATTENTION, short- and long-term memory, organization, and problem solving. The focus is on how learning and/or maturation overcome limits on information processing demands (Anderson 1995) and the development of successful PROBLEM SOLVING (Siegler 1997). Much attention is paid to how knowledge systems are acquired and circumvent these real-time limits on various processes. When it comes to the matter of what the newborn knows, the answer almost always is "nothing" (but see Mandler 1997). Thus, many cognitive development models are firmly grounded on associationist assumptions.

Reports of early conceptual competencies have encouraged the development of models that grant infants some knowledge to begin with. These include symbolic connectionist accounts that share much with associationist theories and modern instantiations of rationalism. In the latter case, humans are endowed with some innate ideas, modules, and/or domain-specific structures of mind. Possible candidates for innate endowments include implicit concepts about natural number, objects, and kinds of energy sources of animate and inanimate objects (Gelman and Williams 1997; Keil 1995; Pinker 1994). These kinds of models are learning models, ones built on the assumption that there is more than one learning mechanism. The idea is that there is a small set of domain-specific, computational learning devices—each with a unique structure and information processing system—that support and facilitate learning about the concepts of their domains. Gelman and Williams (1998) refer to these as skeletal-like, ready to assimilate and accommodate domain-relevant inputs, but very sketchy at first. Knowledge is not sitting in the head, ready to spring forth the moment the environment offers one bit of relevant data. But structures, no matter how nascent, function to support movement along a domain-relevant learning path by encouraging attention to and fostering storage of domain-relevant data.

For most associationist, stage, and information processing theorists, it takes a long time for newcomers to the world to develop concepts, because infants must first build up large memories of bits of sensory and response experiences; associate, connect, or integrate these in ways that represent things or events; associate, connect, or integrate the latter, and so on. The young mind's progress toward conceptual understandings is slow, from reliance on the sensory, on to use of perceptions, and eventually to developing the wherewithal to form abstract concepts and engage in intelligent problem solving. This common commitment to the traditional view that concepts develop from the concrete or perceptual to the abstract plays out differently depending on whether one is a stage theorist or not. For a non–stage theorist, the march to the abstract level of knowing is linear and cumulative. For a stage theorist, the progress usually involves movement through qualitatively different mental structures that can assimilate and use inputs in new ways. Many of the results of classification tasks used by Bruner, Piaget, and Vygotsky encourage the concrete-to-abstract characterization of cognitive development. Repeatedly, it is found that two- to six-year-olds do not use classification criteria in a consistent fashion. For example, when asked to put together objects that go together, one preschool child might make a train, another a long line of alternating colors, while another might focus on appearance as opposed to reality, and so on.

It is important to recognize that all theories of cognitive development grant infants some innate abilities. The abilities to receive punctate sensations of light, sound, or pressure, and so on, and form associations according to the laws of association (frequency and proximity) are foundational for associationists. Association between sensations and responses is the groundwork for knowledge of the world at a sensory and motor level. These in turn support knowledge acquisition at the perceptual level. Experiences at the perceptual level provide the opportunity for cross-modal associative learning and the eventual induction of abstract concepts that are not grounded on particular perceptual information. Although there are important differences in the foundational assumptions of the association and traditional stage accounts, their characterizations of an infant's initial world are more similar than not. For example, associations are not Piaget's fundamental units of cognition; sensori-motor schemes are. But to him, an infant's initial knowledge is limited to innate reflexes and is combined with an inclination to actively use and adapt these as a result of repeated interactions with objects. This eventually leads to the development of intercoordinated schemes and movement to action-based representations that take the infant from an out-of-sight, out-of-mind stage to internalized representations, the mental building blocks of a world of three-dimensional objects in a three-dimensional space.

Piaget's basic assumptions about the nature of the data that feed early development apply to other stage theorists. In general, what initially count as relevant inputs are simple motoric, sensory, or perceptual features. His emphasis is more on children's active participation in their own cognitive development. Bruner and Vygotsky concentrate more on how others help the young child develop coherent knowledge about their social, cultural, and historical environments. Still, all concur that initial "concepts" are sensori-motor or perceptual in form and content; these are variously labeled as graphic collections, preconcepts, complexes, pseudoconcepts, and chain concepts. Thus, whether the account of the origins of knowledge is rooted in an associationist, information processing, or stage theory, the assumption is that first-order sense data, for example sensations of colored light, sound, pressure, etc., serve as the foundation upon which knowledge is developed. Principles or structures that organize the representations of concepts are a considerably advanced accomplishment, taking hold somewhere between five and seven years of age.

Those who embrace more rationalist accounts assume that the mind starts out with much more than the ability to sense and form associations or schemas about sensations and reflexes. Beginning learners have some skeletal structures with which to actively engage the environment; domain-relevant inputs are those that can be brought together and mapped to the existing mental structure. Put differently, skeletal mental structures are attuned to information in the environment at the level of structural universals, not the level of surface characteristics. Thus the nature of relevant data, even for beginning learners, can be rather abstract. It need not be bits of sensation or concrete. Young learners can have abstract concepts.

We now know that preschool-age children appeal to invisible entities to explain contamination, invoke internal or invisible causal forces to explain why objects move and stop, reason about the contrast between the insides and outsides of unfamiliar animals, choose strategies that are remarkably well suited to arithmetic problems, pretend that the same empty cup is first a full cup and then an empty cup, etc. Five-month-old infants respond in ways consistent with the beliefs that one solid object cannot pass through another solid object; an inanimate object cannot propel itself; and that mechanical and biomechanical motion are very differ-

ent (see Wellman and S. Gelman 1997 for details and more examples).

With development, core knowledge systems can become extremely rich, whether or not formal schooling is available—so much so that the existing knowledge structure behaves like a barrier for learning new structures in the domain (Gelman 1993). For example, the intuitive belief that an inanimate object continues to move in a circle because it currently has such a trajectory is inconsistent with the theory of Newtonian mechanics. Yet the belief is held by many college students who have had physics courses. Similarly, our well-developed NAIVE MATHEMATICS, sometimes called "street mathematics" (Nunes, Schliemann, and Carraher 1993), makes it hard to learn school mathematics. In these cases, school lessons do not suffice to foster new understandings and kinds of expertise. Be they nativist or nonnativist in spirit, efforts to account for the course of cognitive development will have to incorporate this fact about the effect, or lack of effect, of experience on learning and concept acquisition

See also DOMAIN SPECIFICITY; INFANT COGNITION; MODULARITY OF MIND; NATIVISM; RATIONALISM VS. EMPIRICISM

—Rochel Gelman

References

Anderson, J. R. (1995). *Learning and Memory: An Integrated Approach.* New York: Wiley.

Gallistel, C. R., A. L. Brown, S. Carey, R. Gelman, and F. C. Keil. (1991). Lessons from animal learning for the study of cognitive development. In R. Gelman and S. Carey, Eds., *The Epigenesis of Mind: Essays on Biology and Cognition. The Jean Piaget Symposium Series.* Hillsdale, NJ: Erlbaum, pp. 3–36.

Gelman, R. (1993). A rational-constructivist account of early learning about numbers and objects. In D. Medin, Ed., *Learning and Motivation.* New York: Academic Press.

Gelman, R., and E. Williams. (1997). Enabling constraints on cognitive development. In D. Kuhn and R. Siegler, Eds., *Cognition, Perception and Language.* vol. 2. *Handbook of Child Psychology,* fifth ed. W. Damon, Ed. New York: Wiley.

Keil, F. C. (1995). The growth of causal understandings of natural kinds. In D. Sperber, D. Premack, and A. J. Premack, Eds., *Causal Cognition: A Multidisciplinary Debate. Symposia of the Fyssen Foundation.* New York: Clarendon Press/Oxford University Press, pp. 234–267.

Mandler, J. M. (1997). Representation. In D. Kuhn and R. Siegler, Eds., *Cognition, Perception and Language.* Vol. 2, *Handbook of Child Psychology,* 5th ed., W. Damon, Ed. New York: Wiley, pp. 255–308.

Nunes, T., A. D. Schliemann, and D. W. Carraher. (1993). *Street Mathematics and School Mathematics.* New York: Cambridge University Press.

Piaget, J. (1970). Piaget's theory. In P. H. Mussen, Ed., *Carmichael's Manual of Child Psychology.* New York: Wiley.

Pinker, S. (1994). *The Language Instinct.* New York: HarperCollins.

Siegler, R. S. (1997). *Emerging Minds: The Process of Change in Children's Thinking.* New York: Oxford University Press.

Wellman, H. M., and S. A. Gelman. (1997). Knowledge acquisition and foundational domains. In D. Kuhn and R. Siegler, Eds., *Cognition, Perception and Language.* Vol. 2, *Handbook of Child Psychology,* 5th ed., W. Damon, Ed. New York: Wiley, pp. 523–573.

Further Readings

Bruner, J. S., R. R. Olver, and P. M. Greenfield. (1966). *Studies in Cognitive Growth.* New York: Wiley.

Carey, S., and R. Gelman, Eds. (1991). *The Epigenesis of Mind: Essays on Biology and Cognition.* Hillsdale, NJ: Erlbaum.

Dehaene, S. (1997). *The Number Sense: How the Mind Creates Mathematics.* New York: Oxford University Press.

Gelman, R., and T. Au, Eds. (1996). *Cognitive and Perceptual Development.* vol. 12. *Handbook of Perception and Cognition.* E. Carterette and M. Friedman, Eds. Academic Press.

Karmiloff-Smith, A. (1992). *Beyond Modularity: A Developmental Perspective on Cognitive Science.* Cambridge, MA: MIT Press.

Simon, T. J., and G. S. Halford, Eds., *Developing Cognitive Competence: New Approaches to Process Modeling.* Hillsdale, NJ: Erlbaum.

Vygotsky, L. S. (1962). *Thought and Language.* Cambridge, MA: MIT Press.

Cognitive Dissonance

See DISSONANCE

Cognitive Ergonomics

Cognitive ergonomics is the study of cognition in the workplace with a view to design technologies, organizations, and learning environments. Cognitive ergonomics analyzes work in terms of cognitive representations and processes, and contributes to designing workplaces that elicit and support reliable, effective, and satisfactory cognitive processing. Cognitive ergonomics overlaps with related disciplines such as human factors, applied psychology, organizational studies, and HUMAN-COMPUTER INTERACTION.

The emergence of cognitive ergonomics as a unitary field of research and practice coincides with the rapid transformation of the workplace following the growth of complex technological environments and the widespread introduction of information technologies to automate work processes. The computerized workplace has generalized flexible and self-directed forms of work organization (Zuboff 1988; Winograd and Flores 1986). These transformations have raised a set of psychological, social, and technological issues: the development of competencies to master work processes through the new technology, the cognitive shift involved in the transition from controlling a process to monitoring automated systems (Bainbridge 1987; Sarter and Woods 1992), the acquisition of skills to use interactive tools, the transfer of knowledge and skills from the old to the new workplace. Technological innovation has also opened the possibility of improving human performance by aiding, expanding, and reorganizing human cognitive activities through the design of advanced tools, a challenge addressed by cognitive engineering and usability (Hollnagel and Woods 1983; Norman and Draper 1986; Nielsen 1993).

Cognitive ergonomics approaches these issues, on the one hand, by developing models of the knowledge structures and information-processing mechanisms that explain how individuals carry out their work tasks (doing PLANNING, PROBLEM SOLVING, DECISION-MAKING, using tools, and coordinating with other people); on the other, by developing methods for redefining the engineering process of workplace design. The two activities are tightly coupled because the integration of user needs and requirements in the design of systems and organizations is seen as the only possible answer for successful transformation of the workplace. User-centered design grounds the design process on general and domain-specific models of cognitive activity and is characterized by extensive investigation of user's goals, tasks, job characteristics, and by continual iterations of design and user testing of solutions. User-centered design encompasses a variety of methods to collect and analyze data about tasks and context of use, and of techniques to test and measure interactions between users and computer systems (Helander 1988).

General models of cognitive work-oriented activity have been developed to account for the complexity of human behaviors produced in work situations (Rasmussen 1986), to explain erroneous action (Norman 1981; Reason 1990), and to conceptualize human-computer interaction (Card, Moran, and Newell 1983; Norman and Draper 1986). Rasmussen's model of work activity distinguishes between automatic, automated, and deliberate behaviors, controlled respectively by skills, rules, and knowledge. Whereas skills and rules are activated in familiar situations, the elaboration of explicit understanding of the current situation and of a deliberate plan for action is necessary to deal with unfamiliar or unexpected situations. This framework has spurred several specific models of process control activities in, among others, fighter aircraft (Amalberti 1996), nuclear power plants (Woods, O'Brien, and Hanes 1987), steel plants (Hoc 1996), and surgical units (Cook and Woods 1994; De Keyser and Nyssen 1993).

The distinction between levels of cognitive control has also been the key to apprehend the reliability of the human component of the workplace. Reason's model (1990) of human error identifies slips and lapses caused respectively by ATTENTION and WORKING MEMORY failures at the skill-level of control; rule-based and knowledge-based mistakes caused by the selection/application of the wrong rule or by inadequate knowledge; and violations that account for intentional breaches of operational procedures.

Norman (1986) formulates a general model of human-computer interaction in terms of a cycle of execution and evaluation. The user translates goals into intentions and into action sequences compatible with physical variables, and evaluates the system state with respect to initial goals after perceiving and interpreting the system state. Bridging what Hutchins, Hollan, and Norman (1986) have named the *Gulf of Execution* and the *Gulf of Evaluation*, interaction can be facilitated by providing input and output functions for the user interface that match more closely the psychological needs of the user, building in AFFORDANCES that constrain the interpretation of the system state, and by providing coherent and clear design models that support users in building mental models of the system.

The bulk of the research in cognitive ergonomics has been carried out on domain-specific work processes. Viewed from an organizational perspective, work processes can be decomposed into sets of tasks, of which explicit descriptions exist in the form of procedures. Task analysis methods combine operational procedure analysis and interviews with experts to describe the cognitive requirements, i.e., demands on MEMORY, attention, understanding, and coordination for realizing each step of the task (Diaper 1989). Leplat (1981) points out the gap that exists between normative accounts of work and actual practice, and argues for activity analysis of work to be carried out in the field, using techniques derived from ethnography. Viewed from an activity perspective, work processes involve problem setting, problem solving, troubleshooting, and collaborating. Roth and Woods (1988) see the work process as problem solving and combine a conceptual analysis of what is required to solve the problem, in terms of EXPERTISE, CAUSAL REASONING, DEDUCTIVE REASONING, decision making, and resource management, with empirical observation of how agents solve the problem in practice. Their study provides options for better meeting the cognitive demands of the task and gives rise to proposals for the design and development of new information displays that enhance agents' ability to anticipate process behavior.

A new perspective on work is emerging from Hutchins's research on distributed cognition. Hutchins (1995) takes the work process as problem solving that is dealt with by the workplace as a whole: a culturally organized setting, comprising individuals, organizational roles, procedures, tools, and practices. The cognitive processes necessary to carry out tasks are distributed between cognitive agents and COGNITIVE ARTIFACTS. Hutchins (1991) shows, for instance, that aircraft are flown by a cockpit system that includes pilots, procedures, manuals, and instruments. This view, while keeping within the information processing paradigm of cognition, recognizes fully the social and cultural dimensions of the workplace, counteracting a tendency to overestimate the cognitive processes at the expense of environmental, organizational, and contextual factors.

See also AI AND EDUCATION; COGNITIVE ANTHROPOLOGY; HUMAN NAVIGATION

—*Francesco Cara*

References

Amalberti, R. (1996). *La Conduite des Systèmes à Risque.* Paris: Presses Universitaires de France.

Bainbridge, L. (1987). Ironies of automation. In J. Rasmussen, K. D. Duncan, and J. Leplat, Eds., *New Technology and Human Error.* Chichester: Wiley, pp. 271–284.

Card, S. K., T. P. Moran, and A. Newell. (1983). *The Psychology of Human-Computer Interaction.* Hillsdale, NJ: Erlbaum.

Carroll, J. M., Ed. (1991). *Designing Interaction: Psychology at the Human-Computer Interface.* New York: Cambridge University Press.

Cook, R. I., and D. D. Woods. (1994). Operating at the sharp end: the complexity of human error. In M. S. Bogner, Ed., *Human Error in Medicine.* Hillsdale, NJ: Erlbaum.

De Keyser, V., and A. S. Nyssen. (1993). Les erreurs humaines en anesthésie. *Le Travail Humain* 56: 243–266.

Diaper, D., Ed. (1989). *Task Analysis for Human-Computer Interaction.* New York: Wiley.

Helander, M., Ed. (1988). *Handbook of Human-Computer Interaction.* New York: Elsevier.

Hollnagel, E., and D. D. Woods. (1983). Cognitive systems engineering: new wine in new bottles. *International Journal of Man-Machine Studies* 18: 583–600.

Hoc, J. M. (1996). *Supervision et Contrôle de Processus: la Cognition en Situation Dynamique.* Grenoble: Presses Universitaires de Grenoble.

Hutchins, E. (1991). Distributed cognition in an airline cockpit. In Y. Engstrom and D. Middleton, Eds., *Communication and Cognition at Work.* New York: Cambridge University Press.

Hutchins, E. (1995). *Cognition in the Wild.* Cambridge, MA: MIT Press.

Hutchins, E., J. Hollan, and D. A. Norman. (1986). Direct Manipulation Interfaces. In D. A. Norman and S. Draper, Eds., *User Centered System Design: New Perspectives in Human-Computer Interaction.* Hillsdale, NJ: Erlbaum.

Leplat, J. (1981). Task analysis and activity analysis in field diagnosis. In J. Rasmussen and W. B. Rouse, Eds., *Human Detection and Diagnosis of Systems Failure.* New York: Plenum Press.

Nielsen, J. (1993). *Usability Engineering.* Boston, MA: Academic Press.

Norman, D. A. (1981). Categorization of action slips. *Psychological Review* 88: 1–15.

Norman, D. A. (1986). Cognitive engineering. In D. A. Norman and S. Draper, Eds., *User Centered System Design: New Perspectives in Human-Computer Interaction.* Hillsdale, NJ: Erlbaum.

Norman, D. A., and S. Draper, Eds. (1986). *User Centered System Design: New Perspectives in Human-Computer Interaction.* Hillsdale, NJ: Erlbaum.

Rasmussen, J. (1986). *Information Processing and Human-Machine Interaction.* Amsterdam: Elsevier.

Reason, J. (1990). *Human Error.* Cambridge: Cambridge University Press.

Roth, M., and D. D. Woods. (1988). Aiding human performance I: cognitive analysis. *Le Travail Humain* 51: 39–64.

Sarter, N., and D. D. Woods. (1992). Pilot interaction with cockpit automation: operational experiences with the Flight Management System. *International Journal of Aviation Psychology* 2: 303–321.

Winograd, T., and F. Flores. (1986). *Understanding Computers and Cognition: A New Foundation for Design.* Norwood, NJ: Ablex Corp.

Woods, D. D., J. O'Brien, and L. F. Hanes. (1987). Human factors' challenges in process-control: the case of nuclear power plants. In G. Salvendy, Ed., *Handbook of Human Factors/Ergonomics.* New York: Wiley.

Zuboff, S. (1988). *In the Age of the Smart Machine: The Future of Work and Power.* Basic Books.

Further Readings

Button, G., Ed. (1993). *Technology in Working Order.* London: Routledge.

Carroll, J. M. (1997). Human-computer interaction: psychology as a science of design. *Annual Review of Psychology* 48: 61–83.

Carroll, J. M., Ed. (1987). *Interfacing Thought: Cognitive Aspects of Human-Computer Interaction.* Cambridge: Cambridge University Press.

Engstrom, Y., and D. Middleton, Eds. (1991). *Communication and Cognition at Work.* New York: Cambridge University Press.

Gallagher, J., R. Krant, and C. Egido, Eds. (1990). *Intellectual Teamwork.* Hillsdale, NJ: Erlbaum.

Greenbaum, J., and M. Kying, Eds. (1991). *Design at Work: Cooperative Design of Computer Systems.* Hillsdale, NJ: Erlbaum.

Hollnagel, E., G. Mancini, and D. D. Woods, Eds. (1986). *Intelligent Decision Support in Process Environments*. New York: Springer-Verlag.

Norman, D. A. (1987). *The Psychology of Everyday Things*. Basic Books.

Norman, D. A. (1993). *Things that Make Us Smart*. Reading, MA: Addison-Wesley.

Shneiderman, B. (1982). *Designing the User Interface: Strategies for Effective Human-Computer Interaction*. Reading, MA: Addison-Wesley.

Suchman, L. A., Ed. (1995). Special section on representations of work. *Communications of ACM* 38: 33–68.

Woods, D. D., and M. Roth. (1988). Aiding human performance II: from cognitive analysis to support systems. *Le Travail Humain* 51: 139–159.

Cognitive Ethology

Cognitive ethology has been defined as the study of the mental experiences of animals, particularly in their natural environment, in the course of their daily lives. Data are derived from the observation of naturally occurring behavior as well as from experimental investigations conducted in the laboratory and in the field. By emphasizing naturally occurring behaviors, cognitive ethologists recognize that the problems faced in finding food and mates, rearing young, avoiding predators, creating shelters, and communicating and engaging in social interactions may require considerable cognitive skills, possibly more complex than and different from those usually examined in traditional psychological laboratory studies. The term "mental experiences" acknowledges that the mental capabilities of animals, in addition to unconscious mental processes, may also include conscious states. This affords the animals sensory experiences, pleasure and pain, the use of mental imagery, and involves at least simple intentional states such as wanting and believing.

Thus, broadly described, the subject of research in cognitive ethology includes any mental experiences and processes, including studies of habituation and sensitization, learning and memory, problem solving, perception, decision making, natural communication, and the artificial languages taught to apes, dolphins, and parrots (reviewed by Ristau and Robbins 1982; Ristau 1997). More narrowly defined, cognitive ethology emphasizes interest in possibly conscious animal mental experiences, particularly as occurring in communication and other social interactions and studies of intention. The field can also be construed as an ethological approach to cognition.

Although the field of cognitive ethology has roots in COMPARATIVE PSYCHOLOGY, ETHOLOGY, and studies of animal learning and memory, it traces its birth to the publication in 1976 of *The Question of Animal Awareness* by the biologist Donald Griffin (see also Griffin 1992).

What is the rationale for the field of cognitive ethology? As conceived by Griffin (1976), there are several reasons for considering that animals may think and be aware: (i) Argument from evolutionary continuity—animals share so many similarities in structure, process, and behavior with humans, why should we not expect them to share mental experience as well? (ii) Neurophysiological evidence—as far as can be determined, nonhuman animals share many neuroanatomical structures, including kinds of neurotransmitters, neurons, synaptic connections, and nerve impulses. We agree that humans are conscious, but, as yet, know of no special structure or process type that is responsible for consciousness or awareness, nor of any neurophysiological process that is uniquely human. (iii) Behavioral complexity and flexibility, particularly in the face of obstacles to the achievement of a goal, at least suggest that the organism may be thinking about alternative ways to behave. (iv) Communication as a window on animal minds—an animal's attention and response to the species' communicative signals—may suggest something of the mental experience and likely behaviors of the communicating organism.

Probably the most significant methodological characteristics of research in cognitive ethology is approximating important aspects of the natural conditions of the species under investigation and making very fine-grained analyses of behavior, usually necessitating videotaped data collection. Many experiments are conducted in the natural environment: (i) Ristau's (1991) studies of piping plovers' use of "injury feigning" in staged encounters with intruders. (ii) Observations of the social behavior of freely interacting organisms, for example Bekoff's (1995a) study of meta-communicative signals in play between two pet dogs. The dogs tended to use signals indicating "this is play" to initiate play bouts and after rough encounters possibly misinterpretable as aggressive (see SOCIAL PLAY BEHAVIOR). (iii) Structurally altered environmental space, for example Bekoff's (1995b) study of vigilance behavior as influenced by the geometry of birds' spatial arrangement at a feeder. Birds spent less time being vigilant for predators when perched in a circle and easily able to determine whether others were vigilant than when they were standing along a line so that such visibility was impossible. (iv) Acoustic playback of recorded species-typic communication signals, for example Seyfarth, Cheney, and Marler's (1980) playbacks to vervet monkeys. The vervets apparently can signal semantic information, not simply emotional states. The monkeys have distinct acoustic signals for a ground predator such as a leopard, a specific aerial predator, the martial eagle, and for snakes (see SOCIAL COGNITION IN ANIMALS).

Cognitive ethology studies differ in interpretation from more traditional approaches. Many ethologists and comparative psychologists have studied foraging behavior, but the cognitive ethologist is interested in different aspects of the data and draws different conclusions. The traditional ethologist might produce an ethogram of an individual animal's or species' behavior, namely a time budget of the various activities in which the animal(s) engage. A comparative psychologist might study the animals under laboratory conditions with strict stimulus control, striving to determine the stimuli apparently controlling the organism's behavior. In these various situations, the cognitive ethologists would be particularly interested in the cognitive capacities revealed, particularly as they might relate to problems encountered by the organism in its natural environment.

Cognitive ethological studies sometimes differ from other research in their scientific paradigm. A typical learning paradigm as used by experimental psychologists might test an animal's discriminative abilities and specificity, duration and stimulus control of memories, but the procedures rely on standard protocols with many trials. Learning over many trials is not the same capacity as intelligence, though it is necessary for intelligence. Intelligent behavior, of particular interest to cognitive ethologists, is most likely to be revealed when an organism encounters a novel problem, particularly one for which the organism is not specifically prepared by evolution. But one or few occurrences, at least in the past, have been pejoratively termed anecdotal and excluded from the scientific literature. Science can progress by including such observations, particularly from well-trained scientists who, with years of study, often have unique opportunities to observe animals in unusual circumstances. If possible, one attempts to design experiments that replicate the rare occurrence.

Since an organism's most interesting actions may not be predictable by the researcher, many investigations in cognitive ethology cannot proceed with predetermined checklists of behavior. Likewise the significance of given behaviors may not be apparent at the time of observation, but may later be understood in terms of a broader context, often extending over days, weeks, or years. These possibilities again require extensive use of video and careful notation of details. For example, a parent piping plover who hears an acoustic playback of a chick's screech and then searches unsuccessfully for the chick, sometimes next searches an area where a playback had been conducted days earlier (Ristau, pers. obs.).

A cognitive ethological approach is illustrated in experimental field studies of piping plovers' injury feigning or broken wing display (BWD), a behavior performed when an intruder/predator approaches the nest or young (Ristau 1991). The hypothesis to be evaluated was: The piping plover wants to lead the predator/intruder away from the nest/young. Alternatively, the use of BWDs might be viewed as the result of confusion or conflicting motivations or as a fixed action pattern with no voluntary control. Theories of how one might experimentally assess the plover's purpose drew inspiration from work such as that of the psychologist Tolman (1932), the philosopher Dennett (1983), and artificial intelligence researcher Boden (1983). Videotaped experiments were conducted on beaches where plovers nested. Human intruders approached the nest or young in directions unpredictable to the birds, so as to approximate the behavior of an actual predator. Questions asked were the following:

1. Is the bird's behavior appropriate to achieve the presumed goal? Specifically, does the plover move in a direction that would cause an intruder who was following to be further away from the nest/young? Answer: Yes. Furthermore, the plover displayed a behavior that might be expected if the bird were trying to attract the intruder's attention and thus was selective about where it displayed. The bird positioned itself before displaying, often even flying to a new location. Such new locations were closer to the intruder and usually closer to the center of the intruder's visual field/direction of movement as well.

2. Does a displaying bird monitor the intruder's behavior? Though difficult to determine exactly what the plover was monitoring, often in the midst of a display, the bird turned its head sharply back over its shoulder, eye toward the intruder.

3. Does the bird modify its behavior if its goal is not being achieved, specifically if the intruder does not follow the displaying bird? Again, yes. The plover reapproached the intruder or increased the intensity of its display if the intruder was not following, but did not do so if the intruder kept following the display.

Other experiments determined that the plover was sensitive to the direction of eye gaze of an intruder either toward or away from its nest. In others, the plover learned very rapidly to discriminate which intruders were dangerous, i.e., had approached closely to its nest, and which were not, those that had simply walked past the nest, rather far away.

The field of cognitive ethology has engendered considerable controversy (for example, see Mason 1976). Some experimental and comparative psychologists dissociate themselves from the endeavor and avoid use of mentalistic phrases such as "the organism wants to do X." However, in designing and interpreting the research, experimental psychologists have at least implicit assumptions about the needs and intentions of their animal subjects. The lab rat must *want* the food pellet and thus performs the experimenter's task to get it. In a test of CER (conditioned emotional responding), the rat inhibits bar pressing in the presence of a stimulus associated with shock. We are interested in the results only because we assume the rat is experiencing an emotional state related to human fear. Even the description of an organism's action contains implied attributions of intentions. Insofar as a rat is described as reaching *for* a pellet or walking *to* the water, a goal or motive is implied. To avoid the *for* or *to* makes the description a mere delineation of changes of position in space and loses the significance of the event. In similar vein, the experiments that studiously avoid mentalistic phrases, upon closer examination, entail assumptions about animal states and intentions.

One can only hope that the common concerns of the related disciplines will be recognized by researchers. It is probable that philosophers would find useful, directive constraints on their thinking from the data on animal cognition, and that the psychologists and biologists would better appreciate the contributions of philosophers that can help clarify concepts and reveal conceptual complexities in an experiment.

See also ANIMAL COMMUNICATION; ANIMAL NAVIGATION; CONDITIONING; EMOTION AND THE ANIMAL BRAIN; INTENTIONAL STANCE; INTENTIONALITY

—*Carolyn A. Ristau*

References

Bekoff, M. (1995a). Play signals as punctuation: the structure of social play in canids. *Behaviour* 132: 419–429.

Bekoff, M. (1995b). Vigilance, flock size, and flock geometry: information gathering by western evening grosbeaks (Aves, fringillidae). *Ethology* 99: 150–161.

Bekoff, M., and Jamieson, D., Ed. (1996). *Readings in Animal Cognition*. Cambridge, MA: MIT Press.

Boden, M. (1983). Artificial intelligence and animal psychology. *New Ideas in Psychology* 1: 11–33.

Dennett, D. C. (1983). Intentional systems in cognitive ethology: the panglossian paradigm defended. *Behavioral and Brain Sciences* 6: 343–390.

Dennett, D. C. (1996). *Kinds of Minds: Towards an Understanding of Consciousness.* New York: Basic Books.

Griffin, D. R. (1976). *The Question of Animal Awareness: Evolutionary Continuity of Mental Experience.* New York: Rockefeller University Press.

Griffin, D. R. (1992). *Animal Minds.* Chicago: University of Chicago Press.

Mason, W. (1976). Windows on other minds. Book review of *The Question of Animal Awareness* by Donald R. Griffin. *Science* 194: 930–931.

Ristau, C. A. (1991). Aspects of the cognitive ethology of an injury-feigning bird, the piping plover. In Ristau, C. A., Ed., *Cognitive Ethology: The Minds of Other Animals.* Hillside, NJ: Erlbaum, pp. 91–126.

Seyfarth, R. M., D. L. Cheney, and P. Marler. (1980). Vervet monkey alarm calls: evidence for predator classification and semantic communication. *Animal Behaviour* 28: 1070–1094.

Tolman, E. C. (1932). *Purposive Behavior in Animals and Men.* New York: Appleton-Century.

Further Readings

Allen, C., and M. Bekoff. (1997). *Species of Mind: The Philosophy and Biology of Cognitive Ethology.* Cambridge, MA: MIT Press.

Beer, C. (1992). Conceptual Issues in Cognitive Ethology. *Advances in the Study of Behavior* 21: 69–109.

Jamieson, D., and M. Bekoff. (1993). On aims and methods of cognitive ethology. *Philosophy of Science Association* 2: 110–124.

Lloyd, D. (1989). *Small Minds.* Cambridge, MA: MIT Press.

Ristau, C. A. (1997). Animal language and cognition research. In A. Lock and C. R. Peters, Eds., *The Handbook of Human Symbolic Evolution.* London: Oxford University Press, pp. 644–685.

Ristau, C. A., and D. Robbins. (1982). Language in the great apes: a critical review. In J. S. Rosenblatt, R. A. Hinde, C. Beer, and M.-C. Busnel, Eds., *Advances in the Study of Behavior,* vol. 12. New York: Academic Press, pp. 142–255.

Cognitive Linguistics

Cognitive linguistics is not a single theory but is rather best characterized as a paradigm within linguistics, subsuming a number of distinct theories and research programs. It is characterized by an emphasis on explicating the intimate interrelationship between language and other cognitive faculties. Cognitive linguistics began in the 1970s, and since the mid-1980s has expanded to include research across the full range of subject areas within linguistics: syntax, semantics, phonology, discourse, etc. The International Cognitive Linguistics Association holds bi-annual meetings and publishes the journal *Cognitive Linguistics.*

The various theoretical frameworks within the cognitive paradigm are to a large degree mutually compatible, differing most obviously in the kinds of phenomena they are designed to address. Construction grammar advances the hypothesis that grammatical constructions are linguistic units in their own right, and that the constructional templates in which verbs are embedded contribute to determining argument structure and MEANING (Goldberg 1995). Mental spaces theory (Fauconnier 1985) focuses on the subtle relationships among elements in the various mental models that speakers construct, relationships that underlie a vast array of semantic phenomena such as scope ambiguities, negation, counterfactuals, and opacity effects.

A number of cognitive linguists are exploring the central role of METAPHOR in SEMANTICS and cognition (Lakoff and Johnson 1980), while others focus on the specific relationships between general cognitive faculties and language (Talmy 1988). Though not self-identified as a cognitive theory, Chafe's (1994) information flow theory is certainly compatible with the cognitive linguistic paradigm, as it explores the relationship between DISCOURSE units and information units in mental processing.

Arguably the most comprehensive theoretical framework within this area is cognitive grammar (Langacker 1987, 1991). The goal of cognitive grammar is to develop a theory of grammar and meaning that is cognitively plausible and that adheres to a kind of theoretical austerity summed up in the content requirement (Langacker 1987): the only structures permitted in the grammar of a language are (1) phonological, semantic, or symbolic structures that actually occur in linguistic expressions (where a symbolic structure is a phonological structure paired with a semantic structure, essentially a Saussurean "sign"); (2) schemas for such structures, where a schema is a kind of pattern or template that a speaker acquires through exposure to multiple exemplars of the pattern; and (3) categorizing relationships among the elements in (1) and (2) (for example, categorizing the syllable /pap/ as an instantiation of the schematic pattern /CVC/).

While not all cognitive linguists adopt the content requirement specifically, the principle of eschewing highly abstract theoretical constructs is endorsed by the cognitive linguistic movement as a whole.

The published work in cognitive grammar has focused on developing a fundamental vocabulary for linguistic analysis in which grammatical constructs are defined in terms of semantic notions, which are themselves characterized in terms of cognitive abilities that are well attested even outside of the linguistic domain. Basic grammatical categories (noun, verb, subject, etc.) and constructions are given cognitive semantic characterizations, obviating the need for abstract syntactic features and representations.

The possibility of defining grammatical notions in semantic terms depends upon taking into account *construal.* Construal refers to the way in which a speaker mentally shapes and structures the semantic content of an expression: the relative prominence of elements, their schematicity or specificity, and the point of view adopted. Many grammatical distinctions that had been traditionally considered to be "meaningless" (i.e., lacking in stable semantic content) are found instead to be markers of subtle distinctions in construal. The subject/object distinction, for example, is defined as a linguistic correlate of the more general ability to perceive figure versus ground. Active and passive versions of the "same sentence" therefore do not mean the same thing, even if they have identical truth conditions; they differ in figure/ground organization. The semantic definitions of grammatical categories similarly rely upon construal, although the details would require a great deal more discussion.

There are several key principles uniting the various theories and approaches within the cognitive linguistic paradigm.

1. Conceptual (subjectivist) semantics. Meaning is characterized as conceptualization: The meaning of an expression is the concepts that are activated in the speaker or hearer's mind. In this view, meaning is characterized as involving a relationship between words and the mind, not directly between words and the world (cf. INDIVIDUALISM).

2. Encyclopedic as opposed to dictionary semantics (Haiman 1980). Words and larger expressions are viewed as entry points for accessing open-ended knowledge networks. Fully explicating the meaning of an expression frequently requires taking into account imagery (both visual and nonvisual), metaphorical associations, mental models, and folk understandings of the world. Thus, the meaning of a word is generally not capturable by means of a discrete dictionary-like definition.

3. Structured categories. Categories are not defined in terms of criterial-attribute models or membership determined by necessary and sufficient features (Lakoff 1987; Taylor 1989). Rather categories are organized around prototypes, family resemblances, and subjective relationships between items in the category.

4. Gradient grammaticality judgments. Grammaticality judgments involve a kind of categorization, inasmuch as a speaker judges an utterance to be a more or less acceptable exemplar of an established linguistic pattern. Grammaticality judgments are therefore gradient rather than binary, and depend upon subtleties of context and meaning as well as conformity to grammatical conventions. Cognitive linguists in general do not endorse the goal of writing a grammar that will generate all and only the grammatical sentences of a language (see GENERATIVE GRAMMAR), as the gradience, variability, and context-dependence of grammaticality judgments render such a goal unrealizable.

5. Intimate interrelationship of language and other cognitive faculties. Cognitive linguists search for analogues for linguistic phenomena in general cognition (hence the name "cognitive" linguistics). Findings from psychology about the nature of human CATEGORIZATION, ATTENTION, MEMORY, etc., are taken to inform linguistic theory directly.

6. The nonautonomy of syntax. SYNTAX is understood to be the conventional patterns by which sounds (or signs) convey meanings. Syntax therefore does not require its own special primitives and theoretical constructs. Grammatical knowledge is captured by positing conventionalized or "entrenched" symbolic patterns that speakers acquire through exposure to actually occurring expressions.

See also AMBIGUITY; FIGURATIVE LANGUAGE; LINGUISTIC UNIVERSALS AND UNIVERSAL GRAMMAR

—*Karen van Hoek*

References

Chafe, W. (1994). *Discourse, Consciousness and Time.* Chicago: University of Chicago Press.

Fauconnier, G. (1985). *Mental Spaces.* Cambridge, MA: MIT Press.

Goldberg, A. (1995). *Constructions.* Chicago: University of Chicago Press.

Haiman, J. (1980). Dictionaries and encyclopedias. *Lingua* 50: 329–357.

Lakoff, G. (1987). *Women, Fire and Dangerous Things.* Chicago: University of Chicago Press.

Lakoff, G., and M. Johnson. (1980). *Metaphors We Live By.* Chicago: University of Chicago Press.

Langacker, R. W. (1987). *Foundations of Cognitive Grammar,* vol. 1: *Theoretical Prerequisites.* Stanford: Stanford University Press.

Langacker, R. W. (1991). *Foundations of Cognitive Grammar,* vol. 2: *Descriptive Application.* Stanford: Stanford University Press.

Talmy, L. (1988). Force dynamics in language and cognition. *Cognitive Science* 12 (1): 49–100.

Taylor, J. (1989). *Linguistic Categorization: Prototypes in Linguistic Theory.* Oxford: Oxford University Press.

Cognitive Maps

Edward Tolman is credited with the introduction of the term *cognitive map,* using it in the title of his classic paper (1948). He described experiments in which rats were trained to follow a complex path involving numbers of turns and changes of direction to get to a food box. Subsequently in a test situation the trained path was blocked off and a variety of alternative paths provided. A large majority of the rats chose a path that headed very close to the true direct direction of the food box, and not one that was close to the original direction of the path on which they had been trained. On the basis of such data Tolman argued that the rat had "acquired not merely a strip-map . . . but, rather, a wider comprehensive map to the effect that the food was located in such and such a direction in the room" (p. 204).

This concept of cognitive map has elicited considerable interest over the years since. Tolman's results seem to imply that animals or humans go beyond the information given when they go directly to a goal after having learned an indirect path. That conclusion is strongest when the spatial cues marking the goal location are not visible from the starting position. Rieser, Guth, and Hill (1986) reported a compelling experimental example of such behavior. Blindfolded observers learned the layout of objects in a room. They were trained specifically, and only, to walk without vision from a home base to each of three locations. Naturally they were also able to point from home base to the three locations quickly and accurately without vision. Furthermore, when they walked to any one of the locations, still without vision, they could point as rapidly and almost as accurately to the other two locations as they had from home base. As with Tolman's rats these observers seemed to have acquired knowledge of many of the spatial relations in a complex spatial layout from direct experience with only a small subset of those relations. In that sense they had acquired a cognitive map. More generally, two different criteria are often used to attribute to people maplike organization of spatial knowledge. One, as in the previous example, is when spatial inferences about the direction and distances among locations can be made without direct experience. The other is when it is possible to take mentally a different perspective on an entire spatial layout. This can be done by imagining oneself in a different position with respect to a layout (Hintzman, Odell, and Arndt 1981).

From where do such cognitive maps arise? One answer involves the specific kinds of experience one has with the particular spatial layout in question. For example, Thorndyke and Hayes-Roth (1982) compared observers' organization of spatial knowledge after studying a map of a large building and after experience in actually navigating around the building. They found that map experience led to more accurate estimation of the straight line or Euclidean distances between locations and understandably to better map drawing, whereas actual locomotion around the building led to more accurate route distance estimation and to more accurate judgments of the actual direction of locations from station points within the building. A second answer involves the nature of one's experience with spatial layouts in general. Thus congenitally blind observers who have never had visual experience show less maplike organization of their spatial knowledge than do sighted ones (or at least take longer to develop such organization). Why might this be? One hypothesis (Rieser et al. 1995) is that sighted persons have prolonged experience with optical flow patterns as they move about during their lives. The information from this optical stimulation specifies how the distance and direction of locations with respect to the observer change as they move. Sighted persons use that knowledge to keep track of even out-of-sight locations as they move. Blind persons without the optical flow experience do not do this as well, and, of course, all their locomotion involves moving with respect to out-of-sight locations.

It seems clear that the absence of visual experience puts one at a disadvantage in developing cognitive maps of spatial layout. When is that visual experience important? The literature comparing early and late blinded observers in spatial perception and cognition tasks often reports better performance in the late blind (Warren 1984; Warren, Anooshian, and Bollinger 1973). However, the age boundaries are very fuzzy because the ages used vary from study to study and because the availability of blind participants of specific ages is rather limited. With sighted participants, maplike organization is evident at very early ages ranging from two years (Pick 1993) to six or seven years (Hazen, Lockman, and Pick 1978), depending on the situation.

Another kind of answer to the origin of maplike organization of spatial knowledge comes from the considerable research on underlying brain mechanisms. This research has been particularly concerned with where and how spatial information is represented in the brain and how, neurologically, orientation is maintained with respect to spatial layouts. Lesion studies and studies of single cell recording have been among the most informative. Many human brain damage studies have been concerned with VISUAL NEGLECT, a deficit in which part of a visual stimulus is ignored. Such deficits have often been associated with parietal lobe damage, and the neglect is of the visual space contralateral to the damage. This neglect apparently operates in memory as well as during perception. One example particularly relevant to cognitive mapping has been reported by Bisiach and Luzzatti (1978). Patients were asked to describe a familiar urban scene, when viewed from one end. They described it,

but ignored features on the left side. They were then asked to imagine viewing it from the other end. They now reported it including originally missing features that were now on the right side, omitting originally reported features now on the neglected left side.

A number of areas in the brain have been implicated in spatial information processing by SINGLE-NEURON RECORDING studies in animals. Besides the posterior parietal cortex, the HIPPOCAMPUS has been found to play a particularly important role. Indeed, O'keefe and Nadel (1978) authored a book entitled *The Hippocampus as Cognitive Map*. Early spatially relevant single cell recording research resulted in the exciting discovery of "place" cells. These cells fire selectively for particular locations in a spatial environment. However, place cells by themselves seem to reflect place recognition but not necessarily information about how to get from one place to another (especially if it is out of sight). An analysis by McNaughton, Knierim, and Wilson (1994) suggests a vector subtraction model that could solve the wayfinding problem. In their prototypic situation, a kind of detour behavior, an animal knows the distance and direction from its home to landmark A. On some occasion it finds itself at an unknown landmark C, from which A is visible but not its home. Their model suggests how hippocampus place cells in conjunction with distance and heading information are sufficient to generate a straight line path to its home. Heading information is potentially available from integration of vestibular stimulation, and there are a variety of visual sources for distance information.

Spatial analogies have frequently been attractive ways of describing nonspatial domains. Examples include kinship relations, bureaucratic organizations, statistical analyses, color perception, etc. An intriguing possibility is that our spatial thinking and the idea of cognitive maps can apply to other domains that are easily described in spatial terms. It is possible to think of cognitive maps of data bases—and indeed the term cognitive map is often being used more and more metaphorically. It is an empirical question with important practical and theoretical implications to know how well the underlying spatial cognition transfers to such nonspatial domains.

See also ANIMAL NAVIGATION; ANIMAL NAVIGATION, NEURAL NETWORKS; HUMAN NAVIGATION; SPATIAL PERCEPTION

—Herbert Pick, Jr.

References

Bisiach, E., and C. Luzzatti. (1978). Unilateral neglect of representational space. *Cortex* 14: 129–133.

Hazen, N. L., J. J. Lockman, and H. L. Pick, Jr. (1978). The development of children's representation of large–scale environments. *Child Development* 49: 623–636.

Hintzman, D. L., C. S. O'Dell, and D. R. Arndt. (1981). Orientation and cognitive maps. *Cognitive Psychology* 13: 149–206.

McNaughton, B. L., J. J. Knierman, and M. A. Wilson. (1994). Vector encoding and the vestibular foundations of spatial cognition: neurophysiological and computational mechanisms. In M. S. Gazzaniga, Ed., *The Cognitive Neurosciences*. Cambridge, MA: MIT Press.

O'keefe, J., and L. Nadel. (1978). *The Hippocampus as Cognitive Map*. Oxford: Oxford University Press.

Pick, H. L. Jr. (1993). Organization of spatial knowledge in children. In N. Eilan, R. McCarthy, and B. Brewer, Eds., *Spatial Representation*. Oxford: Blackwell Publishers, pp. 31–42.

Rieser, J. J., D. A. Guth, and E. W. Hill. (1988). Sensitivity to perspective structure while walking without vision. *Perception* 15: 173–188.

Rieser, J. J., H. L. Pick, Jr., D. H. Ashmead, and A. E. Garing. (1995). Calibration of human locomotion and models of perceptual–motor organization. *Journal of Experimental Psychology: Human Perception and Performance* 21: 480–497.

Samsonovitch, A., and B. L. McNaughton. (1997). Path integration and cognitive mapping in a continuous attractor neural network model. *Journal of Neuroscience* 17: 5900–5920.

Thorndyke, P. W., and B. Hayes-Roth. (1982). Differences in spatial knowledge acquired from maps and navigation. *Cognitive Psychology* 14: 560–589.

Tolman, E. C. (1948). Cognitive maps in rats and man. *Psychological Review* 55: 189–208.

Warren, D. H. (1984). *Blindness and Early Childhood Development*. New York: American Foundation for the Blind.

Warren, D. H., L. J. Anooshian, and J. G. Bollinger. (1973). Early vs. late blindness: the role of early vision in spatial behavior. *American Foundation for the Blind Research Bulletin* 26: 151–170.

Further Readings

Kitchin, R. M. (1994). Cognitive maps: what are they and why study them? *Journal of Environmental Psychology* 14: 1–19.

Siegel, A. W., and S. H. White. (1975). The development of spatial representation of large-scale environments. In H. W. Reese, Ed., *Advances in Child Development and Behavior*, vol 10. New York: Academic Press.

Cognitive Modeling, Connectionist

Connectionist cognitive modeling is an approach to understanding the mechanisms of human cognition through the use of simulated networks of simple, neuronlike processing units. Connectionist models are most often applied to what might be called natural cognitive tasks. These tasks include perceiving the world of objects and events and interpreting it for the purpose of organized behavior; retrieving contextually appropriate information from memory; perceiving and understanding language; and what might be called intuitive or implicit reasoning, in which an inference is derived or a solution to a problem is discovered without the explicit application of a predefined ALGORITHM. Because connectionist models capture cognition at a microstructural level, a more succinct characterization of a cognitive process—especially one that is temporally extended or involves explicit, verbal reasoning—can sometimes be given through the use of a more symbolic modeling framework. However, many connectionists hold that a connectionist microstructure underlies all aspects of human cognition, and a connectionist approach may well be necessary to capture the supreme achievements of human reasoning and problem solving, to the extent that such achievements arise from sudden insight, implicit reasoning, and/or imagining, as opposed to algorithmic derivation. See CONNECTIONISM, PHILOSOPHICAL ISSUES

Figure 1. A picture illustrating how a large number of very partial and ambiguous clues may lead to a perception of an object in a scene. Reprinted with permission from Figure 3-1 of Marr (1982).

for further discussion, and PROBLEM SOLVING and COGNITIVE MODELING, SYMBOLIC for other perspectives.

Connectionist models—often called parallel distributed processing models or NEURAL NETWORKS—begin with the assumption that natural cognition takes place through the interactions of large numbers of simple processing units. Inspiration for this approach comes from the fact that the brain appears to consist of vast numbers of such units—neurons. While connectionists often seek to capture putative principles of neural COMPUTATION in their models, the units in an actual connectionist simulation model should not generally be thought of as corresponding to individual neurons, because there are far fewer units in most simulations than neurons in the relevant brain regions, and because some of the properties of the units used may not be exactly neuron-like.

In connectionist systems, an active mental representation, such as a precept, is a pattern of activation over the set of processing units in the model. Processing takes place via the propagation of activation among the units, via weighted connections. The "knowledge" that governs processing consists of the values of the connection weights, and learning occurs through the gradual adaptation of the connection weights, which occur as a result of activity in the network, sometimes taken together with "error" signals, either in the form of a success or failure signal (cf. REINFORCEMENT LEARNING) or an explicit computation of the mismatch between obtained results and some "teaching" signal (cf., error correction learning, back propagation).

Perception

Perception is a highly context-dependent process. Individual stimulus elements may be highly ambiguous, but when considered in light of other elements present in the input, together with knowledge of patterns of co-occurrence of elements, there may be a single, best interpretation. Such is the case with the famous Dalmatian dog figure, shown in figure 1. An early connectionist model that captured the joint role of

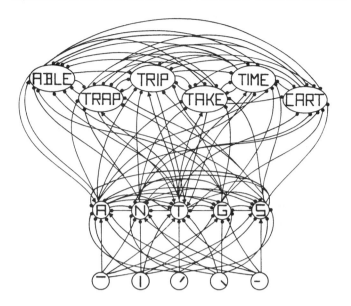

Figure 2. A fraction of the units and connections from the interactive activation model of visual word perception. Reprinted with permission from figure 3 of McClelland and Rumelhart 1981.

stimulus and context information in perception was the interactive activation model (McClelland and Rumelhart 1981). This model contained units for familiar words, for letters in each position within the words, and for features of letters in each position (fig. 2). Mutually consistent units had mutually excitatory connections (e.g., T unit for T in the first position had a mutually excitatory connection with the units for words beginning with T, such as *TIME, TAPE,* etc.). Mutually inconsistent units had mutually inhibitory connections (e.g., there can only be one letter per position, so the units for all of the letters in a given position are mutually inhibitory). Simulations of perception as occurring through the excitatory and inhibitory interactions among these units have led to a detailed account of a large body of psychological evidence on the role of context in letter perception. The interactive activation model further addresses the fact that perceptual enhancement also occurs for novel, wordlike stimuli such as *MAVE*. The presentation of an item like *MAVE* produces partial activation of a number of word units (such as *SAVE, GAVE, MAKE, MOVE,* etc.). Each of these provides a small amount of feedback support to the units for the letters it contains, with the outcome that the letters in items like *MAVE* receive almost as much feedback as letters in actual words. Stochastic versions of the interactive activation model overcome empirical shortcomings of the original version (McClelland 1991).

Other connectionist models have investigated issues in the perception of spoken language (McClelland and Elman 1986), in VISUAL OBJECT RECOGNITION, AI (Hummel and Biederman 1992), and in the interaction of perceptual and attentional processes (Phaf, van der Heijden, and Hudson 1990; Mozer 1987; Mozer and Behrmann 1990).

Memory and Learning

A fundamental assumption of connectionist models of MEMORY is that memory is inherently a constructive process, tak-

ing place through the interactions of simple processing units, just as in the case of perception. One can think of recall as a process of constructing a pattern of activation that is taken by the recaller to reflect not the present input to the senses, but some pattern previously experienced. Central to this view is the idea that recall is prone to a variety of influences that often help us fill in missing details but which are not always bound to fill in correct information. An early model of memory retrieval (McClelland 1981) showed how multiple items in memory can become partially activated, thereby filling in missing information, when memory is probed. The partial activation is based on similarity of the item in memory to the probe and to the information initially retrieved in response to the probe. Similarity based generalization appears to be ubiquitous, and it can often lead to correct inference, but this is far from guaranteed, and indeed subsequent work by Nystrom and McClelland (1992) showed how connectionist networks can lead to blend errors in recall. Connectionist models have also been applied productively to aspects of concept learning (Gluck and Bower 1988), prototype formation (Knapp and Anderson 1984; McClelland and Rumelhart 1985) and the acquisition of conceptual representations of concepts (Rumelhart and Todd 1993). A crucial aspect of this latter work is the demonstration that connectionist models trained with back propagation can learn what basis to use for representations of concepts, so that similarity based generalization can be based on deep or structural rather than superficial aspects of similarity (Hinton 1989; see McClelland 1994 for discussion).

Connectionist models also address the distinction between explicit and implicit memory. Implicit memory refers to an aftereffect of experience with an item in a task that does not require explicit reference to the prior occurrence of the item. These effects often occur without any recollection of one having previously seen the item. Connectionist models account for such findings in terms of the adjustments of the strengths of the connections among the units in networks responsible for processing the stimuli (McClelland and Rumelhart 1985; Becker et al. 1997). Explicit memory for recent events and experiences may be profoundly impaired in individuals who show normal implicit learning (Squire 1992), suggesting a special brain system may be required for the formation of new explicit memories. A number of connectionist models have been proposed in an effort to explain how and why these effects occur (Murre 1997; Alvarez and Squire 1994; McClelland, McNaughton, and O'Reilly 1995).

Language and Reading

Connectionist models have suggested a clear alternative to the notion that knowledge of language must be represented as a system of explicit (though inaccessible) rules, and have presented mechanisms of morphological inflection, spelling-sound conversion, and sentence processing and comprehension that account for important aspects of the psychological phenomena of language that have been ignored by traditional accounts. Key among the phenomena not captured by traditional, rule-based approaches have been the existence of quasi-regular structure, and the sensitivity of language behavior to varying degrees of frequency and consistency. While all approaches acknowledge the existence of exceptions, traditional approaches have failed to take account of the fact that the exceptions are far from a random list of completely arbitrary items. Exceptions to the regular past tense of English, for example, come in clusters that share phonological characteristics (e.g., weep-wept, sleep-slept, sweep-swept, creep-crept) and quite frequently have elements in common with the "regular" past tense (/d/ or /t/, like their "regular" counterparts). An early connectionist model of Rumelhart and McClelland (1986) showed that a network model that learned connection weights to generate the past tense of a word from its present tense could capture a number of aspects of the acquisition of the past tense. Critiques of aspects of this model (Pinker and Prince 1988; Lachter and Bever 1988) raised a number of objections, but subsequent modeling work (MacWhinney and Leinbach 1991; Plunkett and Marchman 1993) has addressed many of the criticisms. Debate still revolves around the need to assume that explicit, inaccessible rules arise at some point in the course of normal development (Pinker 1991). A similar debate has arisen in the domain of word reading (see Coltheart et al. 1993; Plaut et al. 1996).

Connectionist approaches have also been used to account for aspects of language comprehension and production. Connectionists suggest that language processing is a constraint-satisfaction process sensitive to semantic and contextual factors as well as syntactic constraints (Rumelhart 1977; McClelland 1987). Considerable evidence (Taraban and McClelland 1988; MacDonald, Pearlmutter, and Seidenberg 1994; Tanenhaus et al. 1995) now supports the constraint-satisfaction position, and a model that takes joint effects of content and sentence structure into account has been implemented (St. John and McClelland 1995). In production, evidence supporting a constraint-satisfaction approach to the generation of the sounds of a word has led to interactive connectionist models of word production (Dell 1986; Dell et al. forthcoming). Another, very important direction of connectionist work is the area of language centers on the learning of the grammatical structure of sentences in a class of connectionist networks known as the simple recurrent net (Elman 1990). Such networks could learn to become sensitive to long-distance dependencies characteristic of sentences with embedded clauses, suggesting that there may not be a need to posit explicit, inaccessible rules to account for human knowledge of syntax (Elman 1991; Servan-Schreiber, Cleeremans, and McClelland 1991; Rohde and Plaut forthcoming). However, existing models have been trained on very small "languages," and successes with larger language corpora, as well as demonstrations of sensitivity to additional aspects of syntax, are needed.

Reasoning and Problem Solving

While connectionist models have had considerable success in many areas of cognition, their full promise for addressing higher level aspects of cognition, such as reasoning and problem solving, remains to be fully realized. A number of papers point toward the prospect of connectionist models in these areas (Rumelhart et al. 1986; Rumelhart 1989) without full implementations, perhaps in part because higher level cognition often has a temporally extended character, not easily captured in a single settling of a network to an attractor state. Though there have been promising developments in the use of RECURRENT NETWORKS to model temporally extended aspects of cognition, many researchers have opted for "hybrid" models. These models often rely on external, more traditional modeling frameworks to assign units and connections so that appropriate constraint-satisfaction processes can then be carried out in the connectionist component. This approach has been used in the domain of analogical reasoning (Holyoak and Thagard 1989). A slightly different approach, suggested by Rumelhart (1989), assumes that concepts are represented by distributed patterns of activity that capture both their superficial and their deeper conceptual and relational features. Discovering an analogy then consists of activating the conceptual and relational features of the source concept, which may then settle to an attractor state consisting of an analog in another domain that shares these same deep features but differs in superficial details.

Many researchers in this area view the "binding problem" (the assignment of arbitrary content to a slot in a structural description) as a fundamental problem to be solved in the implementation of connectionist models of reasoning, and several solutions have been proposed (Smolensky, Legendre, and Miyata forthcoming; Shastri and Ajjanagadde 1993; Hummel and Holyoak 1997). However, networks can learn to create their own slots so that they can carry out natural inferences in familiar content areas (St. John 1992). Whether learning mechanisms can yield a general enough implementation to capture people's ability to reason in unfamiliar domains remains to be determined.

See also COMPUTATION AND THE BRAIN; COMPUTATIONAL THEORY OF MIND; CONNECTIONIST APPROACHES TO LANGUAGE; IMPLICIT VS. EXPLICIT MEMORY; RULES AND REPRESENTATIONS; VISUAL WORD RECOGNITION

— *James L. McClelland*

References

Alvarez, P., and L. R. Squire. (1994). Memory consolidation and the medial temporal lobe: a simple network model. *Proceedings of the National Academy of Sciences, USA* 91: 7041–7045.

Becker, S., M. Moscovitch, M. Behrmann, and S. Joordens. (1997). Long-term semantic priming: a computational account and empirical evidence. *Journal of Experimental Psychology: Learning, Memory, and Cognition* 23: 1059–1082.

Coltheart, M., B. Curtis, P. Atkins, and M. Haller. (1993). Models of reading aloud: dual-route and parallel-distributed-processing approaches. *Psychological Review* 100: 589–608.

Dell, G. S. (1986). A spreading-activation theory of retrieval in sentence production. *Psychological Review* 93: 283–321.

Dell, G. S., M. F. Schwartz, N. Martin, E. M. Saffran, and D. A. Gagnon. (forthcoming). Lexical access in normal and aphasic speakers.

Elman, J. L. (1990). Finding structure in time. *Cognitive Science* 14: 179–211.

Elman, J. L. (1991). Distributed representations, simple recurrent networks, and grammatical structure. *Machine Learning* 7: 194–220.

Gluck, M. A., and G. H. Bower. (1988). Evaluating an adaptive network model of human learning. *Journal of Memory and Language* 27: 166–195.

Hinton, G. E. (1989). Learning distributed representations of concepts. In R. G. M. Morris, Ed., *Parallel Distributed Processing: Implications for Psychology and Neurobiology.* Oxford, England: Clarendon Press, pp. 46–61.

Holyoak, K. J., and P. Thagard. (1989). Analogical mapping by constraint satisfaction. *Cognitive Science* 13: 295–356.

Hummel, J. E., and I. Biederman. (1992). Dynamic binding in a neural network for shape recognition. *Psychological Review* 99: 480–517.

Hummel, J. E., and K. J. Holyoak. (1997). Distributed representations of structure: a theory of analogical access and mapping. *Psychological Review* 104: 427–466.

Knapp, A., and J. A. Anderson. (1984). A signal averaging model for concept formation. *Journal of Experimental Psychology: Learning, Memory, and Cognition* 10: 617–637.

Lachter, J., and T. G. Bever. (1988). The relation between linguistic structure and theories of language learning: a constructive critique of some connectionist learning models. *Cognition* 28: 195–247.

MacDonald, M. C., N. J. Pearlmutter, and M. S. Seidenberg. (1994). The lexical nature of syntactic ambiguity resolution. *Psychological Review* 101: 676–703.

MacWhinney, B., and J. Leinbach. (1991). Implementations are not conceptualizations: revising the verb learning model. *Cognition* 40: 121–153.

Marr, D. (1982). *Vision.* W. H. Freeman.

McClelland, J. L. (1981). Retrieving general and specific information from stored knowledge of specifics. In *Proceedings of the Third Annual Conference of the Cognitive Science Society.* Berkeley, CA, pp. 170–172.

McClelland, J. L. (1987). The case for interactionism in language processing. In M. Coltheart, Ed., *Attention and Performance XII: The Psychology of Reading.* London: Erlbaum, pp. 1–36.

McClelland, J. L. (1991). Stochastic interactive activation and the effect of context on perception. *Cognitive Psychology* 23: 1–44.

McClelland, J. L. (1994). The interaction of nature and nurture in development: a parallel distributed processing perspective. In P. Bertelson, P. Eelen, and G. D'Ydewalle, Eds., *International Perspectives on Psychological Science,* vol. 1: *Leading Themes.* Hillsdale, NJ: Erlbaum, pp. 57–88.

McClelland, J. L., and J. L. Elman. (1986). The TRACE model of speech perception. *Cognitive Psychology* 18: 1–86.

McClelland, J. L., B. L. McNaughton, and R. C. O'Reilly. (1995). Why there are complementary learning systems in the hippocampus and neocortex: insights from the successes and failures of connectionist models of learning and memory. *Psychological Review* 102: 419–457.

McClelland, J. L., and D. E. Rumelhart. (1981). An interactive activation model of context effects in letter perception: Part 1: an account of basic findings. *Psychological Review* 88: 375–407.

McClelland, J. L., and D. E. Rumelhart. (1985). Distributed memory and the representation of general and specific information. *Journal of Experimental Psychology: General* 114: 159–188.

Mozer, M. C. (1987). Early parallel processing in reading: a connectionist approach. In M. Coltheart, Ed., *Attention and Performance XII: The Psychology of Reading.* London: Erlbaum, pp. 83–104.

Mozer, M. C., and M. Behrmann. (1990). On the interaction of selective attention and lexical knowledge: a connectionist account of neglect dyslexia. *Journal of Cognitive Neuroscience* 2: 96–123.

Murre, J. M. (1997). Implicit and explicit memory in amnesia: some explanations and predictions of the tracelink model. *Memory* 5: 213–232.

Nystrom, L. E., and J. L. McClelland. (1992). Trace synthesis in cued recall. *Journal of Memory and Language* 31: 591–614.

Phaf, R. H., A. H. C. van der Heijden, and P. T. W. Hudson. (1990). SLAM: A connectionist model for attention in visual selection tasks. *Cognitive Psychology* 22: 273–341.

Pinker, S. (1991). Rules of language. *Science* 253: 530.

Pinker, S., and A. Prince. (1988). On language and connectionism: analysis of a parallel distributed processing model of language acquisition. *Cognition* 28: 73–193.

Plaut, D. C., J. L. McClelland, M. S. Seidenberg, and K. E. Patterson. (1996). Understanding normal and impaired word reading: computational principles in quasi-regular domains. *Psychological Review* 103: 56–115.

Plunkett, K., and V. A. Marchman. (1993). From rote learning to system building: acquiring verb morphology in children and connectionist nets. *Cognition* 48: 21–69.

Rohde, D., and D. C. Plaut. (forthcoming). *Simple Recurrent Networks and Natural Language: How Important is Starting Small?* Pittsburgh, PA: Center for the Neural Basis of Cognition, Carnegie Mellon and the University of Pittsburgh.

Rumelhart, D. E. (1977). Toward an interactive model of reading. In S. Dornic, Ed., *Attention and Performance VI.* Hillsdale, NJ: Erlbaum.

Rumelhart, D. E. (1989). Toward a microstructural account of human reasoning. In S. Vosniadou and A. Ortony, Eds., *Similarity and Analogical Reasoning.* New York: Cambridge University Press, pp. 298–312.

Rumelhart, D. E., and J. L. McClelland. (1986). On learning the past tenses of English verbs. In J. L. McClelland, D. E. Rumelhart, and the PDP Research Group, Eds., *Parallel Distributed Processing: Explorations in the Microstructure of Cognition,* vol. 2. Cambridge, MA: MIT Press, pp. 216–271.

Rumelhart, D. E., P. Smolensky, J. L. McClelland, and G. E. Hinton. (1986). Schemata and sequential thought processes in PDP models. In J. L. McClelland, D. E. Rumelhart, and the PDP Research Group, Eds., *Parallel Distributed Processing: Explorations in the Microstructure of Cognition,* vol. 2. Cambridge, MA: MIT Press, pp. 7–57.

Rumelhart, D. E., and P. M. Todd. (1993). Learning and connectionist representations. In D. E. Meyer and S. Kornblum, Eds., *Attention and Performance XIV: Synergies in Experimental Psychology, Artificial Intelligence and Cognitive Neuroscience.* Cambridge, MA: MIT Press, pp. 3–30.

Servan-Schreiber, D., A. Cleeremans, and J. L. McClelland. (1991). Graded state machines: the representation of temporal contingencies in simple recurrent networks. *Machine Learning* 7: 161–193.

Shastri, L., and V. Ajjanagadde. (1993). From simple associations to systematic reasoning: a connectionist representation of rules, variables and dynamic bindings using temporal synchrony. *Behavioral and Brain Sciences* 16: 417–494.

Smolensky, P., G. Legendre, and Y. Miyata. (forthcoming). *Principles for an Integrated Connectionist/Symbolic Theory of Higher Cognition.* Hillsdale, NJ: Erlbaum. (Also available as *Technical Report CU-CS-600-92.* Boulder: Computer Science Department and Institute of Cognitive Science, University of Colorado at Boulder.)

Squire, L. R. (1992). Memory and the hippocampus: a synthesis from findings with rats, monkeys and humans. *Psychological Review* 99: 195–231.

St. John, M. F. (1992). The story gestalt: a model of knowledge-intensive processes in text comprehension. *Cognitive Science* 16: 271–306.

St. John, M. F., and J. L. McClelland. (1990). Learning and applying contextual constraints in sentence comprehension. *Artificial Intelligence* 46: 217–257.

Tanenhaus, M. K., M. J. Spivey-Knowlton, K. M. Eberhard, and J. C. Sedivy. (1995). Integration of visual and linguistic information in spoken language comprehension. *Science* 268: 1632–1634.

Taraban, R., and J. L. McClelland. (1988). Constituent attachment and thematic role assignment in sentence processing: influences of content-based expectations. *Journal of Memory and Language* 27: 597–632

Cognitive Modeling, Symbolic

Symbolic cognitive models are theories of human cognition that take the form of working computer programs. A cognitive model is intended to be an explanation of how some aspect of cognition is accomplished by a set of primitive computational processes. A model performs a specific cognitive task or class of tasks and produces behavior that constitutes a set of predictions that can be compared to data from human performance. Task domains that have received considerable attention include problem solving, language comprehension, memory tasks, and human-device interaction.

The scientific questions cognitive modeling seeks to answer belong to *cognitive psychology*, and the computational techniques are often drawn from *artificial intelligence*. Cognitive modeling differs from other forms of theorizing in psychology in its focus on functionality and computational completeness. Cognitive modeling produces both a theory of human behavior on a task and a computational artifact that performs the task.

The theoretical foundation of cognitive modeling is the idea that cognition is a kind of COMPUTATION (see also COMPUTATIONAL THEORY OF MIND). The claim is that what the mind does, in part, is perform cognitive tasks by computing. (This does not mean that the computer is a metaphor for the mind, or that the architectures of modern digital computers can give us insights into human mental architecture.) If this is the case, then it must be possible to explain cognition as a dynamic unfolding of computational processes. A cognitive model cast as a computer program is a precise description of what those processes are and how they develop over time to realize some task.

A cognitive model is considered to be a *symbolic* cognitive model if it has the properties of a symbolic system in the technical sense of Newell and Simon's (1976) physical symbol system hypothesis (PSSH). The PSSH provides a hypothesis about the necessary and sufficient conditions for a physical system to realize intelligence. It is a reformulation of Turing computation (see CHURCH-TURING THESIS) that identifies symbol processing as the key requirement for complex cognition. The requirement is that the system be capable of manipulating and composing symbols and symbol structures—physical patterns with associated processes that give the patterns the power to denote either external entities or other internal symbol structures (Newell 1980; Newell 1990; Pylyshyn 1989; Simon 1996). One of the distinguishing characteristics of symbols systems is that novel structures may be composed and interpreted, including structures that denote executable processes.

The extent to which symbolic processing is required for explaining cognition, and the extent to which *connectionist* models have symbolic properties, has been the topic of ongoing debates in cognitive science (Fodor and Pylyshyn 1988; Rumelhart 1989; Simon 1996; see COGNITIVE MODELING, CONNECTIONIST). Much of the debate has turned on the question of whether or not particular connectionist systems are able to compose and interpret novel structures. In particular, Fodor and Pylyshyn argue that any valid cognitive theory must have the properties of productivity and systematicity. Productivity refers to the ability to produce and entertain an unbounded set of novel propositions with finite means. Systematicity is most easily seen in linguistic processing, and refers to the intrinsic connection between our ability to produce and comprehend certain linguistic forms. For example, no speaker of English can understand the utterance "John loves the girl" without also being able to understand "the girl loves John," or any other utterance from the unbounded set of utterances of the form "X loves Y." Both productivity and systematicity point to the need to posit underlying abstract structures that can be freely composed, instantiated with novel items, and interpreted on the basis of their structure.

A variety of empirical constraints may be brought to bear on cognitive models. These include: basic *functionality* requirements (a model must actually perform the task to some approximation if it is to be veridical); data from *verbal protocols* of human subjects thinking aloud while PROBLEM SOLVING (these reveal intermediate cognitive steps that may be aligned with the model's behavior; Newell and Simon 1972; Ericsson and Simon 1984); *chronometric data* (such data can constrain a cognitive model once assumptions are made about the time course of the component computational processes; Newell 1990); *eye movement* data (eye fixation durations are a function of cognitive, as well as perceptual, complexity; Carpenter and Just 1987; Rayner 1977); *error patterns;* and data on *learning rates* and *transfer of cognitive skill* (such data constrain the increasing number of cognitive models that are able to change behavior over time; Singley and Anderson 1989).

Though the problem of under-constraining data is a universal issue in science, it is sometimes thought to be particularly acute in computational cognitive modeling, despite the variety of empirical constraints described above. There are two related sides to the problem. First, cognitive models are often seen as making many detailed commitments about aspects of processing for which no data distinguish among alternatives. Second, because of the universality of computational frameworks, an infinite number of programs can be created that mimic the desired behavior (Anderson 1978).

Theorists have responded to these problems in a variety of ways. One way is to adopt different levels of abstraction in the theoretical statements: in short, not all the details of the computer model are part of the theory. NEWELL (Newell 1990; Newell et al. 1991), MARR (1982), PYLYSHYN (1984) and others have developed frameworks for specifying systems at multiple levels of abstraction. The weakest possible correspondence between a model and human cognition is at the level of input/output: if the model only responds to functionality constraints, it is intended only as a sufficiency demonstration and formal task definition (Pylyshyn 1984, 1989). The strongest kind of correspondence requires that the model execute the same algorithm (take the same intermediate computational steps) as human processing. (No theoretical interpretation of a cognitive model, not even the strongest, depends on the hardware details of the host machine.)

An important method for precisely specifying the intended level of abstraction is the use of programming languages designed for cognitive modeling, such as PRODUCTION SYSTEMS. Production systems were introduced by Newell (1973) as a flexible model of the control structure of human cognition. The flow of processing is not controlled by a fixed program or procedure laid out in advance, as is the case in standard procedural programming languages. Instead, production systems posit a set of independent production rules (condition-action pairs) that may fire any time their conditions are satisfied. The flow of control is therefore determined at run time, and is a function of the dynamically evolving contents of the working memory that triggers the productions. A cognitive model written in a production system makes theoretical commitments at the level of the production rules, and defines a computationally complete system at that level. The particular underlying implementation (e.g., LISP or Java) is theoretically irrelevant.

A complementary approach to reducing theoretical degrees of freedom is to apply the same model with minimal variation to a wide range of tasks. Each new task is not an unrelated pool of data to be arbitrarily fitted with a new model or with new parameters. For example, a computational model of short-term memory that accounts for immediate serial recall should also apply, with minimal strategy variations, to free recall tasks and recognition tasks as well (Anderson and Matessa 1997).

Recent cognitive modeling research combines these approaches by building and working with cognitive architectures. A COGNITIVE ARCHITECTURE posits a fixed set of computational mechanisms and resources that putatively underlie a wide range of human cognition. As these cognitive architectures never correspond to the architectures of modern computers (for example, they may demand a higher degree of parallelism), the architectures must first be *emulated* on computers before cognitive models can be built within them for specific tasks. Such architectures, together with the variety of empirical constraints outlined above, place considerable constraint on task models.

Examples of the architectural approach include ACT-R (Anderson 1993), CAPS (Just and Carpenter 1992), SOAR (Newell 1990), EPAM (Feigenbaum and Simon 1984), and Epic (Meyer and Kieras 1997). (All are production systems, with the exception of EPAM.) These architectures have collectively been applied to a broad set of phenomena in cognitive psychology. For example, Anderson and colleagues (Anderson 1993; Singley and Anderson 1989) have demonstrated that a production rule analysis of cognitive skill, along with the learning mechanisms posited in the ACT architecture, provide detailed and explanatory accounts of a range of regularities in cognitive skill acquisition in complex domains such as learning to program LISP. ACT also provides accounts of many phenomena surrounding the recognition and recall of verbal material (e.g., the fan effect), and regularities in problem-solving strategies (Anderson 1993; Anderson and Lebiere forthcoming). EPAM is one of the earliest computational models in psychology and accounts for a significant body of data in the learning and high-level perception of verbal material. It has been compared in some detail to related connectionist accounts (Richman and Simon 1989). SOAR is a learning architecture that has been applied to domains ranging from rapid, immediate tasks such as typing and video game interaction (John, Vera and Newell 1994) to long stretches of problem-solving behavior (Newell 1990), building on the earlier analyses by Newell and Simon (1972). SOAR has also served as the foundation for a detailed theory of sentence processing, which models both the rapid on-line effects of semantics and context, as well as subtle effects of syntactic structure on processing difficulty across several typologically distinct languages (Lewis 1996, forthcoming). EPIC is a recent architecture that combines a parallel production system with models of peripheral and motor components, and accounts for a substantial body of data in the performance of dual cognitive tasks (Meyer and Kieras 1997). CAPS is a good example of recent efforts in symbolic modeling to account for individual differences in cognitive behavior. CAPS explains differences in language comprehension performance by appeal to differences in working memory capacity (Just and Carpenter 1992). Polk and Newell (1995) developed a constrained parametric model of individual differences in syllogistic reasoning that provides close fits to particular individuals by making different assumptions about the way they interpret certain linguistic forms (see also Johnson-Laird and Byrne 1991).

In short, modern symbolic cognitive modeling is characterized by detailed accounts of chronometric data and error patterns; explorations of the explanatory role of the same basic architectural components across a range of cognitive tasks; attempts to clearly distinguish the contributions of relatively fixed architecture and more plastic task strategies and background knowledge; and attempts to explicitly deal with the problem of theoretical degrees of freedom. The underlying goal of all these approaches is to produce more unified accounts of cognition explicitly embodied in computational mechanisms.

See also KNOWLEDGE-BASED SYSTEMS; KNOWLEDGE REPRESENTATION; RULES AND REPRESENTATIONS

—*Richard L. Lewis*

References

Anderson, J. R. (1978). Arguments concerning representations for mental imagery. *Psychological Review* 85: 249–277.

Anderson, J. R. (1993). *The Adaptive Character of Thought*. Hillsdale, NJ: Erlbaum.

Anderson, J. R., and M. Matessa. (1997). A production system theory of serial memory. *Psychological Review* 104(4): 728–748.

Anderson, J. R., and C. Lebeire. (Forthcoming). *ACT: Atomic Components of Thought*. Hillsdale, NJ: Erlbaum.

Ericcson, K. A., and H. A. Simon. (1984). *Protocol Analysis: Verbal Reports as Data*. Cambridge, MA: MIT Press.

Feigenbaum, E., and H. A. Simon. (1984). EPAM-like Models of Recognition and Learning. *Cognitive Science* 8:305–336.

Fodor, J. A., and Z. W. Pylyshyn. (1988). Connectionism and cognitive architecture: A critical analysis. *Cognition* 28:3–71.

John, B. E., A. H. Vera, and A. Newell. (1994). Toward real-time GOMS: A model of expert behavior in a highly interactive task. *Behavior and Information Technology* 13: 255–267.

Johnson-Laird, P. N., and R. M. J. Byrne. (1991). *Deduction.* Hillsdale, NJ: Erlbaum.

Just, M. A., and P. A. Carpenter. (1987). *The Psychology of Reading and Language Comprehension.* Boston: Allyn and Bacon.

Just, M. A., and P. A. Carpenter. (1992). A capacity theory of comprehension: Individual differences in working memory. *Psychological Review* 99 (1): 122–149.

Lewis, R. L. (1996). Interference in short-term memory: The magical number two (or three) in sentence processing. *Journal of Psycholinguistic Research.*

Lewis, R. L. (Forthcoming). *Cognitive and Computational Foundations of Sentence Processing.* Oxford: Oxford University Press.

Marr, D. (1982). *Vision.* New York: Freeman.

Meyer, D. E., and D. E. Kieras. (1997). A computational theory of executive cognitive processes and multiple-task performance: Part 1: basic mechanisms. *Psychological Review* 104(1): 3–65.

Newell, A. (1973). Production systems: models of control structures. In W. G. Chase, Ed., *Visual Information Processing.* San Diego, CA: Academic Press, pp. 463–526.

Newell, A. (1980). Physical symbol system. *Cognitive Science* 4; 135–183.

Newell, A. (1990). *Unified Theories of Cognition.* Cambridge, MA: Harvard University Press.

Newell, A., and H. A. Simon. (1972). *Human Problem Solving.* Englewood Cliffs, NJ: Prentice-Hall.

Newell, A., and H. A. Simon. (1976). Computer science as empirical inquiry: symbols and search. *Communications of the ACM* 19: 113–126.

Newell, A., G. Yost, J. E. Laird, P. S. Rosenbloom, and E. Altmann. (1991). Formulating the problem-space computational model. In R. F. Rashid, Ed., *CMU Computer Science: A 25th Anniversary Commemorative.* Reading, MA: Addison-Wesley.

Polk, T. A., and A. Newell. (1995). Deduction as verbal reasoning. *Psychological Review* 102 (3): 533–566.

Pylyshyn, Z. W. (1984). *Computation and Cognition.* Cambridge, MA: Bradford/MIT Press.

Pylyshyn, Z. W. (1989). Computing in cognitive science. In M. I. Posner, Ed., *Foundations of Cognitive Science.* Cambridge, MA: MIT Press.

Rayner, K. (1977). Visual attention in reading: eye movements reflect cognitive processes. *Memory and Cognition* 4: 443–448.

Richman, H. B., and H. A. Simon. (1989). Context effects in letter perception: comparison of two theories. *Psychological Review* 96 (3): 417–432.

Rumelhart, D. E. (1989). The architecture of mind: a connectionist approach. In M. I. Posner, Ed., *Foundations of Cognitive Science.* Cambridge, MA: MIT Press.

Simon, H. A. (1996). The patterned matter that is mind. In D. Steier and T. Mitchell, Eds., *Mind Matters: Contributions to Cognitive and Computer Science in Honor of Allen Newell.* Hillsdale, NJ: Erlbaum.

Singley, M. K., and J. R. Anderson. (1989). The transfer of cognitive skill. Cambridge, MA: Harvard University Press.

Color Categorization

Lexical color categorization consists of the division of color sensations into classes corresponding to the significata of the color words of a particular language. Perceptual color categorization consists of the division of the color sensations into classes by the perceptual processes of an organism—human or nonhuman, adult or neonate, possessed of knowledge of a language or not so possessed. Conflict among views on the relationship of lexical to perceptual color categorization has prevailed for over a century. Nineteenth-century classicists, anthropologists, and opthalmologists were aware that all languages do not reflect identical lexical classifications of color. The classicist (and statesman) William Gladstone concluded that differences in color lexicons reflect differences in perceptual abilities, for example, "that the organ of color and its impressions were but partially developed among the Greeks of the heroic age" (see Berlin and Kay 1969:135). The opthalmologist Hugo Magnus recognized that failure to distinguish colors lexically need not indicate inability to distinguish them perceptually (see Berlin and Kay 1969: 144ff). These and other late nineteenth-century scholars strongly tended to view differences in color lexicons in evolutionary terms.

In the 1920s, 1930s, and 1940s, Edward SAPIR (e.g., 1921: 219) and B. L. Whorf (e.g., 1956 [1940]: 212ff) rejected evolutionism for the doctrine of radical linguistic and cultural relativity. The favorite field for the empirical establishment and rhetorical defense of the relativist view, which became established doctrine in the 1950s and 1960s, was the lexicon of color. With respect to color categorization, there have been two major traditions of research stemming from the relativity thesis: a within-language, correlational line of research and a cross-language, descriptive one.

Early work in the former tradition (e.g., Brown and Lenneberg 1954; Lenneberg and Roberts 1956) is primarily concerned with establishing a correlation between a linguistic variable distinguishing colors (for example, how easy different colors are to name or how easy they are to communicate about) and a nonlinguistic cognitive variable over colors: memorability. Discovery of such a correlation was interpreted as support for the Sapir-Whorf view that linguistic categorization can influence nonlinguistic perception/cognition. In the 1950s and 1960s, such correlations were reported within English and, to a limited extent, in other languages (Stefflre, Castillo Vales, and Morley 1966). Because it was assumed at the time that the linguistic variable (codability or communication accuracy) would vary across languages, correlation between a linguistic and nonlinguistic variable within a single language (almost always English) was taken to validate the doctrine that the coding systems of different languages induce differences in the nonlinguistic cognition of their speakers. Eleanor Rosch (e.g., Heider 1972) challenged this assumption on the basis of the apparent universal lexical salience of certain "focal" colors (identified by Berlin and Kay 1969). Rosch showed that universal perceptual salience determines both the nonlinguistic and the linguistic variables of the correlational approach, thus undercutting the logic of this line of research. Rosch's view was criticized by Lucy and Shweder (1979), who also challenged her experimental procedure; Lucy and Shweder's experimental procedure was in turn challenged by Kay and Kempton (1984), who supported Rosch's view of the matter.

(Kay and Kempton, using a noncorrelational, cross-linguistic experimental procedure, showed that certain nonlinguistic color classification judgments may be influenced by the lexical classification of color in a language, while others are not so influenced, thus re-establishing limited Whorfian effects in the color domain.)

In the tradition of cross-language description, the studies of the 1950s and 1960s likewise reflected the dominance of radical linguistic relativism (Ray 1952; Conklin 1955; Gleason 1961: 4). These studies sought to discover and celebrate the differences among color lexicons. In 1969, using the original stimulus set of Lenneberg and Roberts (1956), Berlin and Kay compared the denotation of basic color terms in twenty languages and, based on these findings, examined descriptions of seventy-eight additional languages from the literature. They reported that there are universals in the semantics of color: the major color terms of all languages are focused on one of eleven landmark colors. Further, they postulated an evolutionary sequence for the development of color lexicons according to which black and white precede red, red precedes green and yellow, green and yellow precede blue, blue precedes brown, and brown precedes purple, pink, orange and gray. These results were challenged on experimental grounds, mostly by anthropologists (e.g., Hickerson 1971; Durbin 1972; Collier 1973), and largely embraced by psychologists (e.g., Brown 1976; Miller and Johnson-Laird 1976; Ratliff 1976). A number of field studies stimulated by Berlin and Kay tended to confirm the main lines of the universal and evolutionary theory, while leading to reconceptualization of the encoding sequence (Berlin and Berlin 1975; Kay 1975). Based on earlier, unpublished work of Chad K. McDaniel, which established the identity of some of the universal semantic foci of Berlin and Kay with the psychophysically determined unique hues (see also in this connection Miller and Johnson-Laird 1976: 342–355; Ratliff 1976; Zollinger 1979), Kay and McDaniel (1978) again reconceptualized the encoding sequence, introducing the notion of fuzzy set into a formal model of color lexicons, and emphasized the role in early systems of categories representing fuzzy unions of Hering primaries. Kay and McDaniel also related the universal semantics of color to the psychophysical and neurophysiological results of Russel De Valois and his associates (e.g., De Valois, Abramov, and Jacobs 1966).

Since 1978, two important surveys of color lexicons have been conducted, both supporting the two broad Berlin and Kay hypotheses of semantic universals and evolutionary sequence in the lexical encoding of colors: the World Color Survey (Kay et al. 1997) and the Mesoamerican Color Survey (MacLaury 1997). Relativist objection to the Berlin and Kay paradigm of research on color categorization has continued, emphasis shifting away from criticism of the rigor with which the Berlin and Kay procedures of mapping words to colors were applied toward challenging the legitimacy of any such procedures (e.g., Lucy 1997; Saunders and van Brake l997)

See also CATEGORIZATION; COLOR VISION; COLOR, NEUROPHYSIOLOGY OF; CULTURAL RELATIVISM; LINGUISTIC RELATIVITY

—Paul Kay

References

Berlin, B., and E. A. Berlin. (1975). Aguaruna color categories. *American Ethnologist* 2: 61–87.

Berlin, B., and P. Kay. (1969). *Basic Color Terms: Their Universality and Evolution.* Berkeley: University of California.

Brown, R. W. (1976). Reference. *Cognition* 4: 125–153.

Brown, R. W., and E. H. Lenneberg. (1954). A study of language and cognition. *Journal of Abnormal and Social Psychology* 49: 454–462.

Collier, G. A. (1973). Review of *Basic Color Terms. Language* 49: 245–248.

Conklin, H. C. (1955). Hanunóo color categories. *Southwestern Journal of Anthropology* 11: 339–344.

De Valois, R. L., I. Abramov, and G. H. Jacobs. (1966). Analysis of response patterns of LGN cells. *Journal of the Optical Society of America* 56: 966–977.

Durbin, M. (1972). Review of Basic Color Terms. *Semiotica* 6: 257–278.

Gleason, H. A. (1961). *An Introduction to Descriptive Linguistics.* New York: Holt, Rinehart and Winston.

Heider, E. R. (1972). Universals in color naming and memory. *Journal of Experimental Psychology* 93: 1–20.

Hickerson, N. (1971). Review of Basic Color Terms. *International Journal of American Linguistics* 37: 257–270.

Kay, P. (1975). Synchronic variability and diachronic change in basic color terms. *Language in Society* 4: 257–270.

Kay, P., B. Berlin, L. Maffi, and W. Merrifield. (1997). Color naming across languages. In C. L. Hardin and L. Maffi, Eds., *Color Categories in Thought and Language.* Cambridge: Cambridge University Press.

Kay, P., and W. M. Kempton. (1984). What is the Sapir-Whorf hypothesis? *American Anthropologist* 86: 65–79.

Kay, P., and C. K. McDaniel. (1978). The linguistic significance of the meanings of basic color terms. *Language* 54: 610–646.

Lenneberg, E. H., and J. M. Roberts. (1956). The language of experience: A study in methodology. *Memoir 13 of International Journal of American Linguistics.*

Lucy, J. A. (1997). The linguistics of color. In C. L. Hardin and L. Maffi, Eds., *Color Categories in Thought and Language.* Cambridge: Cambridge University Press.

Lucy, J. A., and R. A. Shweder. (1979). The effect of incidental conversation on memory for focal colors. *American Anthropologist* 90: 923–931.

MacLaury, R. E. (1997). *Color and Cognition in Mesoamerica: Constructing Categories as Vantages.* Austin: University of Texas Press.

Miller, G. A., and P. Johnson-Laird. (1976). *Language and Perception.* Cambridge, MA: Harvard University Press.

Ratliff, F. (1976). On the psychophysiological bases of universal color terms. *Proceedings of the American Philosophical Society* 120: 311–330.

Ray, V. (1952). Techniques and problems in the study of human color perception. *Southwestern Journal of Anthropology* 8: 251–259.

Sapir, E. (1921). *Language.* New York: Harcourt, Brace.

Saunders, B. A. C., and J. van Brakel. (1997). Are there non-trivial constraints on colour categorization? *Brain and Behavioral Sciences.*

Stefflre, V., V. Castillo Vales, and L. Morley. (1966). Language and cognition in Yucatan: A cross-cultural replication. *Journal of Personality and Social Psychology* 4: 112–115.

Whorf, B. L. (1956, 1940). Science and linguistics. In J. B. Carroll, Ed., *Language, Thought and Reality: The Collected Papers of Benjamin Lee Whorf.* Cambridge, MA: MIT Press. Originally published in *Technology Review* 42: 229–231, 247–248.

Zollinger, H. (1979). Correlations between the neurobiology of colour vision and the psycholinguistics of colour naming. *Experientia* 35: 1–8.

Further Readings

Berlin, B., P. Kay, and W. R. Merrifield. (1985). Color term evolution: recent evidence from the World Color Survey. Paper presented at the *84th Meeting of the American Anthropological Association*, Washington, D. C.

Bornstein, M. H. (1973a). The psychophysiological component of cultural difference in color naming and illusion susceptibility. *Behavioral Science Notes* 1: 41–101.

Bornstein, M. H. (1973b). Color vision and color naming: A psychophysiological hypothesis of cultural difference. *Psychological Bulletin* 80: 257–285.

Burnham, R. W., and J. R. Clark. (1955). A test of hue memory. *Journal of Applied Psychology* 39: 164–172.

Collier, G. A. (1976). Further evidence for universal color categories. *Language* 52: 884–890.

De Valois, R. L., and G. H. Jacobs. (1968). Primate color vision. *Science* 162: 533–540.

De Valois, R. L., H. C. Morgan, M. C. Polson, W. R. Mead, and E. M. Hull. (1974). Psychophysical studies of monkey vision. I: Macaque luminosity and color vision tests. *Vision Research* 14: 53–67.

Dougherty, J. W. D. (1975). *A Universalist Analysis of Variation and Change in Color Semantics.* Ph.D. diss., University of California, Berkeley.

Dougherty, J. W. D. (1977). Color categorization in West Futunese: variability and change. In B.G. Blount and M. Sanches, Eds., *Sociocultural Dimensions of Language Change.* New York: Plenum, pp. 133–148.

Hage, P., and K. Hawkes. (1975). Binumarin color categories. *Ethnology* 24: 287–300.

Hardin, C. L. (1988). *Color for Philosophers.* Indianapolis: Hackett.

Hardin, C. L., and L. Maffi, Eds. (1997). *Color Categories in Thought and Language.* Cambridge: Cambridge University Press.

Heider, E. R. (1972). Probabilities, sampling and the ethnographic method: The case of Dani colour names. *Man* 7: 448–466.

Heider, E. R., and D. C. Olivier. (1972). The structure of the color space for naming and memory in two languages. *Cognitive Psychology* 3: 337–354.

Kay, P., B. Berlin, and W. Merrifield. (1991). Biocultural implications of systems of color naming. *Journal of Linguistic Anthropology* 1: 12–25.

Kuschel, R., and T. Monberg. (1974). "We don't talk much about colour here": A study of colour semantics on Bellona Island. *Man* 9: 213–242.

Landar, H. J., S. M. Ervin, and A. E. Horrowitz. (1960). Navajo color categories. *Language* 36: 368–382.

Lenneberg, E. H. (1961). Color naming, color recognition, color discrimination: A reappraisal. *Perceptual and Motor Skills* 12: 375–382.

MacLaury, R. E. (1987). Coextensive semantic ranges: different names for distinct vantages of one category. *Papers from the 23rd Annual Meeting of the Chicago Linguistic Society, Part I,* 268–282.

Shepard, R. (1992). The perceptual organization of colors. In J. Barkow, L. Cosmides, and J. Tooby, Eds., *The Adapted Mind.* Oxford: Oxford University Press.

Zollinger, H. (1976). A linguistic approach to the cognition of colour vision. *Folia Linguistica* 9: 265–293.

Color, Neurophysiology of

Color vision is our ability to distinguish and classify lights of different spectral distributions. The first requirement of color vision is the presence in the RETINA of different photoreceptors with different spectral absorbances. The second requirement is the presence in the retina of postreceptoral neuronal mechanisms that process receptor outputs to produce suitable chromatic signals to be sent to the VISUAL CORTEX. The third requirement is a central mechanism that transforms the incoming chromatic signals into the color space within which the normal observer maps his sensations. A good deal is known of the neurophysiology and anatomy of the first two requirements, but very little is known of the third.

The visible range of light extends over a wavelength band from 400 to 700 nanometers (nm), from violet to red. Color vision has evolved in a number of species, including bees, fish, and birds, but among mammals only primates appear to use color as a major tool in their processing of visual scenes. Most natural colors, as opposed to those in the laboratory, are spectrally broad-band. There are many systems for specifying their spectral composition, ranging from simply the physical distribution across the spectrum, through industry standards based on descriptions of spectral mixtures as functions of three variables (for the three different photopigments in the human eye), to color spaces that attempt to reproduce the way in which we perceptually order colors (Wyszecki and Stiles 1982). For a cognitive psychologist, there are two different aspects of color vision: we are not only very good at distinguishing and classifying colors (under optimal conditions wavelength differences of just a few nanometers can be detected), but also color vision is very important in visual segmentation and OBJECT RECOGNITION.

Humans and Old World primates possess three different photoreceptor, or cone, types in the retina. A fourth type of photoreceptor, rods, is concerned with vision at low light levels and plays little role in color vision. The idea of three different cone types in human retina was derived from the empirical finding that any color can be matched by a mixture of three others. It was first proposed by Thomas Young in 1801, and taken up by Hermann von HELMHOLTZ later in the nineteenth century. The Young-Helmholtz theory came to be generally accepted, and the spectral absorbances of the three photopigments were determined through psychophysical measurements. However, it is only in recent years that it has become possible to directly demonstrate the presence of the three cones, either by measuring their spectral absorptions (Bowmaker 1991) or their electrical responses (Baylor, Nunn, and Schnapf 1987). The spectral absorbances peak close to 430, 535, and 565 nm, and preferred designations are short (S), middle (M), or long (L) wavelength cones, rather than color names such as blue, green, and red. It is important to realize that a single cone cannot deconfound intensity and wavelength; in order to distinguish colors, it is necessary to compare the outputs of two or more cone types.

There has been much recent interest in the molecular genetics of the photopigments in the cones, especially in the reason why about 10 percent of the male population suffer from some degree of red-green color deficiency (Mollon 1997). The amino acids in the photopigment molecule that are responsible for pigment spectral tuning have been identified. A change in just a single amino acid can be detectable in an individual's color matches; it is rare for such a small molecular change to give rise to a measurable behavioral effect.

The spectral absorbances of the photopigments are broad, and this means that the signals from the different cones are highly correlated, especially with the broad-band spectra of the natural environment. This correlation gives rise to redundancy in the pattern of cone signals, and so postreceptoral mechanisms in the retina add or subtract cone outputs to code spectral distributions more efficiently, before signals are passed up the optic tract to the CEREBRAL CORTEX (Buchsbaum and Gottschalk 1983). Again, the first suggestion of such mechanisms came in the nineteenth century, from Oswald Hering. He proposed that there were black-white, red-green, and blue-yellow opponent processes in human vision, based on the impossibility of conceiving of reddish-green or bluish-yellow hues, whereas reddish-yellow is an acceptable color. Red, green, blue, and yellow are called the unique hues; it is possible to pick a wavelength that is uniquely yellow, without a reddish or greenish component.

Three main VISUAL PROCESSING STREAMS leave the primate retina to reach the cortex via the lateral geniculate nucleus. Each of them is associated with a very specific retinal circuitry, with signals being added or subtracted very soon after they have left the cones (Lee and Dacey 1997). One carries summed signals of the M- and L-cones; it is thought to form the basis of a luminance channel of PSYCHOPHYSICS and is heavily involved in flicker and MOTION, PERCEPTION OF. It originates in a specific ganglion cell class, the parasol cells, and passes through the magnocellular layers of the lateral geniculate on the way to the cortex. A second channel carries the difference signal between the M- and L-cones, and forms the basis of a red-green detection channel of psychophysics. It begins in the midget ganglion cells of the retina and passes through the parvocellular layers of the lateral geniculate. The third channel carries the difference signal between the S-cones and a sum of the other two, and it is the basis of a blue-yellow detection mechanism. It begins in the small bistratified ganglion cells and passes through intercalated layers in the lateral geniculate. These red-green and blue-yellow mechanisms account well for our ability to detect small differences between colors. Neurophysiology and anatomy of these peripheral chromatic mechanisms have been established in some detail (Kaplan, Lee, and Shapley 1990; Lee 1996). It is thought that the S-cone and blue-yellow system is phylogenetically more ancient than the red-green one, and it is present in most mammals (Mollon 1991). Separate M- and L-cones and the red-green mechanism have evolved only in primates.

The lateral geniculate nucleus is not thought to substantially modify color signals from the retina, but what happens in the cerebral cortex is uncertain. It is possible to determine the spectral sensitivity of the opponent processes of Hering (Hurvich 1981), and it turns out that our perceptual color opponent space has different spectral properties compared to the cone difference signals that leave the retina, and that we use to distinguish small color differences. Put another way, the unique hues do not map directly onto the cone-opponent signals emanating from the retina. Transformation of retinal signals to produce our perceptual, opponent color space can be modeled (Valberg and Seim 1991; DeValois and DeValois 1993), but how this occurs neurophysiologically is unknown; it is even uncertain whether we should look for single cells in the cortex that code for Hering's opponent processes or unique hues, or whether these are an emergent property of the cortical cell network (Mollon and Jordan 1997).

It is generally thought that a high concentration of color-specific neurons are found in the cytochrome oxidase blobs in primary visual cortex (see Merigan and Maunsell 1993 for review). Some of these cells resemble retinal ganglion cells in their spectral properties; others do not (Lennie, Krauskopf, and Sclar 1990). These color-specific signals are then passed on to the temporal visual processing stream. Color signals do not seem to flow into the parietal visual processing stream, which has much to do with motion perception and is dominated by the magnocellular pathway.

Many cognitive aspects of COLOR VISION emerge at the cortical level. For example, so-called surface colors depend on the context in which they are seen; the color brown depends on a given spectral composition being set in a brighter surround. If the same spectral composition were viewed in a black surround, it would appear yellowish. The limited range of colors that can be seen in isolation, in a dark surround, are called aperture colors. Another important emergent feature is color constancy, our ability to correctly identify the color of objects despite wide changes in the spectral composition of illumination, which of course changes the spectral reflectance of light from a surface. Color constancy is not perfect, and is a complex function of the spectral and spatial characteristics of a scene (Pokorny, Shevell, and Smith 1991). It has been proposed that color constancy emerges in a secondary visual cortical area, V4 (Zeki 1980, 1983), but this remains controversial. Lastly, color also plays an important role in many higher order visual functions, such as SURFACE PERCEPTION or object identification. The neurophysiological correlates in the cortex of these higher order color vision functions are unknown, and are likely to be very difficult to ascertain. It seems probable that many of these functions are distributed through cortical neuronal networks, rather than existing as specific and well-defined chromatic channels, as in the retina.

See also COLOR CATEGORIZATION; ILLUSIONS; PHYSICALISM; QUALIA

—*Barry B. Lee*

References

Baylor, D. A., B. J. Nunn, and J. L. Schnapf. (1987). Spectral sensitivity of cones of the monkey Macaca Fascicularis. *Journal of Physiology* 390: 145–160.

Bowmaker, J. K. (1991). Visual pigments and color vision in primates. In A. Valberg and B. B. Lee, Eds., *From Pigments to Perception.* New York: Plenum, pp. 1–10.

Buchsbaum, G., and A. Gottschalk. (1983). Trichromacy, opponent colours coding and optimum colour information transmission in the retina. *Proceedings of the Royal Society of London B* 220: 89–113.

DeValois, R. L., and K. K. DeValois. (1993). A multi-stage color model. *Vision Research* 33: 1053–1065.

Hurvich, L. M. (1981). *Color Vision.* Sunderland, MA: Sinauer Associates.

Kaplan, E., B. B. Lee, and R. M. Shapley. (1990). New views of primate retinal function. *Progress in Retinal Research* 9: 273–336.

Lee, B. B. (1996). Receptive fields in primate retina. *Vision Research* 36: 631–644.

Lee, B. B., and D. M. Dacey. (1997). Structure and function in primate retina. In C.R. Cavonius, Ed., *Color Vision Deficiencies* XIII. Dordrecht, Holland: Kluwer, pp. 107–118.

Lennie, P., J. Krauskopf, and G. Sclar. (1990). Chromatic mechanisms in striate cortex of macaque. *Journal of Neuroscience* 10: 649–669.

Merigan, W. H., and J. H. R. Maunsell. (1993). How parallel are the primate visual pathways? *Annual Review of Neuroscience* 16: 369–402.

Mollon, J. D. (1991). Uses and evolutionary origins of primate color vision. In J. R. Cronly-Dillon and R. L. Gregory, Eds., *Evolution of the Eye and Visual System.* London: Macmillan, pp. 306–319.

Mollon, J. D. (1997). . . . aus dreyerly Arten von Membranen oder Molekülen: George Palmer's legacy. In C. R. Cavonius, Ed., *Color Vision Deficiencies* XIII. Dordrecht, Holland: Kluwer.

Mollon, J. D., and G. Jordan. (1997). On the nature of unique hues. In C. Dickinson, I. Murray, and D. Carden, Eds., *John Dalton's Colour Vision Legacy.* London: Taylor and Francis, pp. 381–392.

Pokorny, J., S. K. Shevell, and V. C. Smith. (1991). Colour appearance and colour constancy. In P. Gouras, Ed., *Vision and Visual Dysfunction,* vol. 6: *The Perception of Colour.* London: Macmillan, pp. 43–61.

Valberg, A., and T. Seim. (1991). On the physiological basis of higher color metrics. In A. Valberg and B. B. Lee, Eds., *From Pigments to Perception.* New York: Plenum, pp. 425–436.

Wyszecki, G., and W. S. Stiles. (1982). *Color Science—Concepts and Methods, Quantitative Data and Formulae.* Second edition. New York: Wiley.

Zeki, S. (1980). The representation of colors in the cerbral cortex. *Nature* 284: 412–418.

Zeki, S. (1983). Colour coding in the cerebral cortex: The reaction of cells in monkey visual cortex to wavelengths and colors. *Neuroscience* 9: 741–765.

Color Vision

Color vision is the ability to detect and analyze changes in the wavelength composition of light. As we admire a rainbow, we perceive different colors because the light varies in wavelength across the width of the bow.

An important goal of color science is to develop PSYCHOLOGICAL LAWS that allow prediction of color appearance from a physical description of stimuli. General laws have been elusive because the color appearance of a stimulus is strongly affected by the context in which it is seen. One well-known example is simultaneous color contrast. Color plates illustrating the color contrast can be found in most perception textbooks (e.g., Wandell 1995; Goldstein 1996; see also Evans 1948; Albers 1975; Wyszecki 1986).

In everyday use, we describe color appearance using simple color names, such as "red," "green," and "blue." There is good agreement across observers and cultures about the appropriate color name for most stimuli (see COLOR CATEGORIZATION). Technical and scientific use requires more precise terms. The purpose of a color order system is to connect physical descriptions of color stimuli with their appearance (see Derefeldt 1991; Wyszecki and Stiles 1982). Each color order system specifies a lexicon for color. Observers then scale (see PSYCHOPHYSICS) a large number of calibrated color stimuli using this lexicon, and from such data the relation between stimuli and names is determined. Examples of color order systems include the Munsell Book of Color and the Swedish Natural Color System (NCS). Note that color order systems do not address the problem of how context affects color appearance. Rather, each system specifies a particular configuration in which stimuli should be viewed if the system is to apply.

People are sensitive to wavelengths between 400 nanometers and 700 nanometers (nm); hence this region is called the visible spectrum. The chromatic properties of light are specified by how much energy the light contains at every wavelength in the visible spectrum. This specification is called the light's spectral power distribution. Color vision is mediated by three classes of cone photoreceptor. Each class of cones is characterized by its spectral sensitivity, which specifies how strongly that class responds to light energy at different wavelengths; the three classes of cones have their peak sensitivities in different regions of the visible spectrum, roughly at long (L), middle (M), and short (S) wavelengths. How the cones encode information about the spectral power distribution of light is discussed in RETINA and COLOR, NEUROPHYSIOLOGY OF (see also Wandell 1995).

Physically different lights can produce identical responses in all three classes of cones. Such lights, called metamers, are indistinguishable to the visual system (see Wyszecki and Stiles 1982; Brainard 1995). It is possible to construct metamers by choosing three primary lights and allowing an observer to mix them in various proportions. If the primaries are well chosen, essentially any other light can be matched through their mixture. This fact is known as the trichromacy of human color vision (see Wyszecki and Stiles 1982; Wandell 1995; Kaiser and Boynton 1996). Trichromacy facilitates most color reproduction technologies. Color television, for example, produces colors by mixing light emitted by just three phosphors, and color printers use only a small number of inks (see Hunt 1987).

Some people are color blind, usually because they lack one or more classes of cone. Individuals missing one class of cone are called dichromats. Consider a pair of lights which produce the same responses in the M- and S-cones but a different response in the L-cones. A normal trichromat will have no difficulty distinguishing the lights because of their different L-cone response. To a dichromat with no L-cones, however, the two lights will appear identical. Thus dichromats confuse lights that trichromats distinguish. In the most common forms of dichromacy, either the L- or M-cones are missing. This is often called red-green color blindness because of consequent confusions between reds and greens. Red-green dichromacy occurs more frequently in males (about 2% of Caucasian males) than females (about 0.03% of Caucasian females). The rate in females is lower because the genes that code the L- and M-cone photopigments are on the X-chromosome. There are other forms of color blindness and anomalous color vision (see Pokorny et al. 1979).

Different species code color differently. Many mammals are dichromats with correspondingly less acute color vision than most humans. In addition, for two species with the same number of cones, color vision can differ because the cones of each species have different spectral sensitivities. Bees, for example, are trichromatic but have cones sensitive to ultraviolet light (Menzel and Backhaus 1991). Thus bees are sensitive to differences in spectral power distributions that humans cannot perceive, and vice versa. Note that the color categories perceived by humans are unlikely to match those of other species. Behavioral studies indicate that humans and pigeons group regions of the visible spectrum quite differently (see Jacobs 1981).

A key idea about postreceptoral color vision is the idea that signals from the separate cone classes are compared in color opponent channels, one signaling redness and greenness and a second signaling blueness and yellowness (Wandell 1995; Kaiser and Boynton 1996). An informal observation that supports the idea of opponency is that we rarely experience a single stimulus as being simultaneously red and green or simultaneously blue and yellow. Quantitative behavioral and physiological evidence also supports the idea of color opponency.

Why is color vision useful? With some notable exceptions (e.g. rainbows and signal lights), we rarely use color to describe the properties of lights per se. Rather, color vision informs us about objects in the environment. First, color helps us distinguish objects from clutter: ripe fruit is easy to find because of color contrast between the fruit and leaves. Second, color tells us about the properties of objects: we avoid eating green bananas because their color provides a cue to their ripeness. Finally, color helps us identify objects: we find our car in a crowded parking lot because we know its color (for more extended discussions, see Jacobs 1981; Mollon 1989).

The spectral power distribution of the color signal reflected from an object to an observer depends on two physical factors. The first factor is the spectral power distribution of the illuminant incident on the object. This varies considerably over the course of a day, with weather conditions, and between natural and artificial illumination. The second factor is the object's surface reflectance function, which specifies, at each wavelength, what fraction of the incident illuminant is reflected. For color to be a reliable indicator about object properties and identity, the visual system must separate the influence of the illuminant on the color signal from the influence of the surface reflectance. To the extent that the human visual system does so, we say that it is color constant.

The problem of color constancy is analogous to the problem of lightness constancy (see LIGHTNESS PERCEPTION). More generally, color constancy embodies an ambiguity that is at the core of many perceptual problems: multiple physical configurations can produce the same image (see COMPUTATIONAL VISION). Human vision has long been believed to

exhibit approximate color constancy (e.g., Boring 1942; Evans 1948). Developing a quantitative account of human color constancy and understanding the computations that underlie it is an area of active current research (see Wandell 1995; Kaiser and Boynton 1996).

See also ILLUSIONS; PERCEPTUAL DEVELOPMENT; VISUAL ANATOMY; AND PHYSIOLOGY

—*David Brainard*

References

Albers, J. (1975). *Interaction of Color.* New Haven: Yale University Press.

Boring, E. G. (1942). *Sensation and Perception in the History of Experimental Psychology.* New York: D. Appleton Century.

Brainard, D. H. (1995). Colorimetry. In M. Bass, E. Van Stryland, and D. Williams, Eds., *Handbook of Optics: vol. 1. Fundamentals, Techniques, and Design,* Second edition. New York: McGraw-Hill, pp. 26.1–26.54.

Derefeldt, G. (1991). Colour appearance systems. In P. Gouras, Ed., *Vision and Visual Dysfunction,* vol. 6: *The Perception of Colour.* London, Macmillan, pp. 218–261.

Evans, R. M. (1948). *An Introduction to Color.* New York: Wiley.

Goldstein, E. B. (1996). *Sensation and Perception.* Pacific Grove, CA: Brooks/Cole Publishing Company.

Hunt, R. W. G. (1987). *The Reproduction of Colour.* Tolworth, England: Fountain Press.

Jacobs, G. H. (1981). *Comparative Color Vision.* New York: Academic Press.

Kaiser, P. K., and R. M. Boynton. (1996). *Human Color Vision.* Washington, DC: Optical Society of America.

Menzel, R., and W. Backhaus. (1991). Colour vision in insects. In P. Gouras, Ed., *Vision and Visual Dysfunction,* vol. 6: *The Perception of Color.* London: Macmillan, pp. 262–293.

Mollon, J. D. (1989). Tho' she kneel'd in that place where they grew. The uses and origins of primate color vision. *Journal of Experimental Biology* 146: 21–38.

Pokorny, J., V. C. Smith, G. Verriest, and A. J. L. G. Pinckers. (1979). *Congenital and Acquired Color Vision Defects.* New York: Grune and Stratton.

Wandell, B. A. (1995). *Foundations of Vision.* Sunderland, MA: Sinauer.

Wyszecki, G. (1986). Color appearance. In *Handbook of Perception and Human Performance.* New York, Wiley, 9.1–9.56.

Wyszecki, G., and W. S. Stiles. (1982). *Color Science—Concepts and Methods, Quantitative Data and Formulae.* New York: Wiley.

Columns and Modules

The CEREBRAL CORTEX sits atop the white matter of the brain, its 2 mm thickness subdivided into about six layers. Neurons with similar interests tend to cluster. Columns are usually subdivisions at the submillimeter scale, and modules are thought to occupy the intermediate millimeter scale, between maps and columns. Empirically, a column is simply a submillimeter region where many (but not all) neurons seem to have functional properties in common. They come in two sizes, with separate organizational principles. Minicolumns are about 23–65 μm across, and there are hundreds of them inside any given 0.4–1.0 mm macrocolumn.

Each cerebral hemisphere has about 52 "areas" distinguished on the basis of differences between the thickness of their layers; on average, a human cortical area is about half the size of a business card. Though area 17 seems to be a consistent functional unit, other areas prove to contain a half-dozen distinct physiological subdivisions ("maps") on the centimeter scale.

Both columns and modules may be regarded as the outcomes of a self-organizing tendency during development, patterns that emerge as surely as the hexagons of a honeycomb arise from the pounding of so many hemispherical bee's heads on the soft wax of tunnel walls. The hexagonal shape is an emergent property of such competition for territory; similar competition in the cortex may continue throughout adult life, maintaining a shifting mosaic of cortical columns.

A column functionally ties together all six layers. Layers *II* and *III* can usually be lumped together, as when one talks of the superficial pyramidal neurons. But layer *IV* has had to be repeatedly subdivided in the visual cortex (*IVa, IVb, IVcα, IVcβ*). Layer *IV* neurons send most of their outputs up to *II* and *III*. Some superficial neurons send messages down to *V* and *VI*, though their most prominent connections (either laterally in the layers or via U-fibers in white matter) are within their own layers. Layer *VI* sends messages back down to the THALAMUS via the white matter, while *V* sends signals to other deep and distant neural structures, sometimes even the spinal cord.

For any column of cortex, the bottom layers are like a subcortical outgoing mailbox, the middle layer like an inbox, and the superficial layers somewhat like an interoffice mailbox spanning the columns and reaching out to other cortical areas (Calvin and Ojemann 1994). Indeed, Diamond (1979) argues that the "motor cortex" isn't restricted to the motor strip but is the fifth layer of the entire cerebral cortex. That's because *V*, whatever the area, contains neurons that at some stage of development send their outputs down to the spinal cord, with copies to the brain stem, BASAL GANGLIA, and hypothalamus. Likewise the fourth layer everywhere is the "sensory cortex," and the second and third layers everywhere are the true "association cortex" in this view.

Minicolumns appear to be formed from dendritic bundles. Ramón y CAJAL saw connect-the-dots clusters of cell bodies, running from white matter to the cortical surface; these hair-thin columns are about 30 μm apart in human cortex. It now appears that a column is like a stalk of celery, a vertical bundle containing axons and apical dendrites from about 100 neurons (Peters and Yilmaz 1993) and their internal microcircuitry.

Macrocolumns may, in contrast, reflect an organization of the input wiring, for example, corticocortical terminations from different areas often terminate in interdigitating zones about the width of a thin pencil lead. In 1957, Mountcastle and his coworkers discovered a tendency for somatosensory strip neurons responsive to skin stimulation (hair, light touch) to alternate with those specializing in joint and muscle receptors about every 0.5 mm. It now appears that there is a mosaic organization of similar dimensions, the neurons within each macrocolumn (or "segregate") having a receptive field optimized for the same patch of body surface (Favorov and Kelly 1994).

Hubel and Wiesel, recording in monkey visual cortex, saw curtainlike clusters ("ocular dominance columns") that specialized in the left eye, with an adjacent cluster about 0.4 mm away specializing in the right eye. As seems appropriate for an outcome of self-organization, average size varies among individuals over 0.4–0.7 mm; those with smaller ocular dominance columns have more of them (Horton and Hocking 1996).

Orientation columns are of minicolumn dimensions, within which the neurons prefer lines and edges that are tilted about the same angle from the vertical; there are many such minicolumns specializing in various angles within an ocular dominance macrocolumn (Hubel and Wiesel 1977). The relationships between minicolumns and macrocolumns are best seen in VISUAL CORTEX, though it may be hazardous to generalize from this because ocular dominance columns themselves are less than universal; for instance, they are not a typical feature of New World monkeys.

Color blobs are clusters of COLOR-sensitive neurons in the cortex at macrocolumnar spacing but involving only neurons of the superficial layers and not extending throughout all cortical layers, as in a proper column. Recently, recurrent excitation in the superficial layers has been identified as a coordinating (and perhaps self-organizing) principle among distant minicolumns (Calvin 1995). The superficial pyramids send myelinated axons out of the cortical layers into the white matter; their eventual targets are typically the superficial layers of other cortical areas when of the "feedback" type; when "feedforward" they terminate in *IV* and deep *III*.

But superficial pyramidal neurons also send unmyelinated collaterals sideways, with an unusual patterning that suggests a columnar organizing principle. Like an express train that skips intermediate stops, the collateral axon travels a characteristic lateral distance without giving off any terminal branches; then it produces a tight terminal cluster (see fig. 5 in Gilbert 1993). The axon may continue for many millimeters, repeating such clusters about every 0.43 mm in primary visual cortex, 0.65 mm in the secondary visual areas, 0.73 mm in sensory strip, and 0.85 mm in motor cortex of monkeys (Lund, Yoshioka, and Levitt 1993). Because of this local standard for axon length, mutual re-excitation becomes probable among some cell pairs. Macrocolumns of similar emphasis are seen to be connected by such synchronizing excitation. Calvin (1996) argues that these express connections could implement a Darwinian copying competition among Hebbian cell-assemblies on the time scale of thought and action, providing one aspect of CONSCIOUSNESS.

Though COMPUTATIONAL NEUROANATOMY has proved more complex, it has been widely expected that cerebral cortex will turn out to have circuits which, in different cortical patches, are merely repeats of a standard "modular" pattern, something like modular kitchen cabinets. Columns, barrels, blobs, and stripes have all been called modules, and the term is loosely applied to any segmentation or repeated patchiness (Purves, Riddle, and LaMantia 1992) and to a wide range of functional or anatomical collectives. The best candidate for a true module was the "hypercolumn" (Hubel and Wiesel 1977): two adjacent ocular dominance columns, each containing a full set of orientation columns, suggested similar internal wiring, whatever the patch of visual field being represented. However, newer mapping techniques have shown that ocular dominance repeats are somewhat independent of orientation column repeats (Blasdel 1992), making adjacent hypercolumns internally nonidentical, that is, not iterated circuitry. Module remains a fuzzy term for anything larger than a macrocolumn but smaller than a map—though one increasingly sees it used as a trendy word denoting any cortical specialization, for example, modules as the foundation for "multiple intelligences."

See also CONSCIOUSNESS, NEUROBIOLOGY OF; NEURON; SELF-ORGANIZING SYSTEMS; VISUAL CORTEX, CELL TYPES AND CONNECTIONS IN; VISUAL PROCESSING STREAMS

—*William H. Calvin*

References

Bartfeld, E., and A. Grinvald. (1992). Relationships between orientation-preference pinwheels, cytochrome oxidase blobs, and ocular-dominance columns in primate striate cortex. *Proc. Natl. Acad. Sci. USA* 89: 11905–11909.

Blasdel, G. G. (1992). Orientation selectivity, preference, and continuity in monkey striate cortex. *J. Neurosci.* 12: 3139–3161.

Bullock, T. H. (1980). Reassessment of neural connectivity and its specification. In H. M. Pinsker and W. D. Willis, Jr., Eds., *Information Processing in the Nervous System.* New York: Raven Press, pp. 199–220.

Calvin, W. H. (1995). Cortical columns, modules, and Hebbian cell assemblies. In Michael A. Arbib, Ed., *The Handbook of Brain Theory and Neural Networks.* Cambridge, MA: Bradford Books/MIT Press, pp. 269–272.

Calvin, W. H. (1996). *The Cerebral Code: Thinking a Thought in the Mosaics of the Mind.* Cambridge, MA: MIT Press.

Calvin, W. H., and G. A. Ojemann. (1994). *Conversations with Neil's Brain: The Neural Nature of Thought and Language.* Reading, MA: Addison-Wesley.

Diamond, I. (1979). The subdivisions of neocortex: A proposal to revise the traditional view of sensory, motor, and association areas. In J. M. Sprague and A. N. Epstein, Eds., *Progress in Psychobiology and Physiological Psychology 8.* New York: Academic Press, pp. 1–43.

Favorov, O. V., and D. G. Kelly. (1994). Minicolumnar organization within somatosensory cortical segregates: I. Development of afferent connections. *Cerebral Cortex* 4: 408–427.

Gilbert, C. D. (1993). Circuitry, architecture, and functional dynamics of visual cortex. *Cerebral Cortex* 3: 373–386.

Goldman-Rakic, P. (1990). Parallel systems in the cerebral cortex: The topography of cognition. In M. A. Arbib and J. A. Robinson, Eds., *Natural and Artificial Parallel Computation.* Cambridge, MA: MIT Press, pp.155–176.

Horton, J. C., and D. R. Hocking. (1996). Intrinsic variability of ocular dominance column periodicity in normal macaque monkeys. *J. Neurosci.* 16 (22): 7228–7239.

Hubel, D. H., and T. N. Wiesel. (1977). Functional architecture of macaque visual cortex. *Proc. Roy. Soc. (London)* 198B: 1–59.

Katz, L. C., and E. M. Callaway. (1992). Development of local circuits in mammalian visual cortex. *Ann. Rev. Neurosci.* 15: 31–56.

Livingstone, M. S. (1996). Oscillatory firing and interneuronal correlations in squirrel monkey striate cortex. *J. Neurophysiol.* 75: 2467–2485.

Livingstone, M. S., and D. H. Hubel. (1988). Segregation of form, color, movement, and depth: Anatomy, physiology, and perception. *Science* 240: 740–749.

Lund, J. S., T. Yoshioka, and J. B. Levitt. (1993). Comparison of intrinsic connectivity in different areas of macaque monkey cerebral cortex. *Cerebral Cortex* 3: 148–162.

Mountcastle, V. B. (1979). An organizing principle for cerebral function: The unit module and the distributed system. In F. O. Schmitt and F. G. Worden, Eds., *The Neurosciences Fourth Study Program.* Cambridge, MA: MIT Press, pp. 21–42.

Peters, A., and E. Yilmaz. (1993). Neuronal organization in area 17 of cat visual cortex. *Cerebral Cortex* 3: 49–68.

Purves, D., D. R. Riddle, and A-S. LaMantia. (1992). Iterated patterns of brain circuitry (or how the cortex gets its spots). *Trends in the Neurosciences* 15: 362–368 (see letters in 16: 178–181).

Shaw, G. L., E. Harth, and A. B. Scheibel. (1982). Cooperativity in brain function: Assemblies of approximately 30 neurons. *Exp. Neurol.* 77: 324–358.

White, E. L. (1989). *Cortical Circuits.* Boston: Birkhauser.

Yuste, R., and D. Simons. (1996). Barrels in the desert: the Sde Boker workshop on neocortical circuits. *Neuron* 19: 231–237.

Communication

See ANIMAL COMMUNICATION; GRICE, H. PAUL; LANGUAGE AND COMMUNICATION

Comparative Psychology

The comparative study of animal and human cognition should be an important part of cognitive science. The field of comparative psychology, however, emerged from the paradigm of BEHAVIORISM and so has not contributed greatly toward this end. The reasons for this are telling and help to explicate the main directions of modern evolutionary thinking about behavior and cognition.

The general program of comparative psychology began with Charles DARWIN's *Origin of Species* (1859). Darwin believed that the comparative study of animal behavior and cognition was crucial both for reconstructing the phylogenies of extant species (behavioral comparisons thus supplementing morphological comparisons) and for situating the behavior and cognition of particular species, including humans, in their appropriate evolutionary contexts. Toward these ends, Darwin (1871, 1872) reported some informal comparisons between the behavior of humans and nonhuman animals, as did his disciples Spencer (1894), Hobhouse (1901), and Romanes (1882, 1883). The goal was thus clear: to shed light on human cognition through a study of its evolutionary roots as embodied in extant animal species.

Arising as a reaction to some of the anthropomorphic excesses of this tradition was behaviorism. During the early and middle parts of the century, researchers such as Watson, Thorndike, and Tolman espoused the view that the psychology of nonhuman animals was best studied not informally or anecdotally, but experimentally in the laboratory. Within this tradition, some psychologists became interested in comparing the learning skills of different animal species in a quantitative manner, and this procedure came to be known as comparative psychology. One especially well-known series of studies was summarized by Bitterman (1965), who compared several species of insect, fish, and mammal on such things as speed to learn a simple perceptual discrimination, speed to learn a reversal of contingencies, and other discrimination learning skills. An implicit assumption of much of this work was that just as morphology became ever more complex from insect to fish to mammals to humans, so behavior should show this same "progression" (see Rumbaugh 1970 and Roitblatt 1987 for more modern versions of this approach).

Comparative psychology came under attack from its inception by researchers who felt that studying animals outside of their natural ecologies, on experimental tasks for which they were not naturally adapted, was a futile, indeed a misguided, enterprise (e.g., Beach 1950; Hodos and Campbell 1969). They charged that studies such as Bitterman's smacked of a *scalae natura* in which some animals were "higher" or "more intelligent" than others, with, of course, humans atop the heap. That is, many of the comparative studies of learning implicitly assumed that nonhuman animals represented primitive steps on the way to humans as evolutionay *telos*. This contradicted the established Darwinian fact of treelike branching evolution in which no living species was a primitive version of any other living species, but rather each species was its own *telos*.

Another blow to comparative psychology came from experiments such as those of Garcia and Koelling (1966), which demonstrated that different species were evolutionarily prepared to learn qualitatively different things from their species-typical environments. More generally, many studies emanating from the traditions of ETHOLOGY and behavioral ecology at this same time demonstrated that different animal species were adapted to very different aspects of the environment and therefore that comparisons along any single behavioral dimension, such as learning or intelligence, were hopelessly simplistic and missed the essential richness of the behavioral ecology of organism-environment interactions (see Eibl-Eiblsfeldt 1970 for a review). Ethologists and behavioral ecologists were much less interested in finding general processes or principles that spanned all animal species than were comparative psychologists, and they were much less inclined to treat human beings as any kind of special species in the evolutionary scheme of things.

Today, most scientists who study animal behavior have incorporated the insights of the ethologists and behavioral ecologists into their thinking so that it would currently be difficult to locate any individuals who call themselves comparative psychologists in the classic meaning of the term (see Dewsbury 1984a, 1984b for a slightly different perspective). However, there does exist a journal called the *Journal of Comparative Psychology*, and many important studies of animal behavior are published there—mostly experimental studies of captive animals (as opposed to ethological studies, which are more often naturalistic). In contrast to the classic, behavioristic form of comparative psychology, modern comparative studies pay much more attention to the particular cognitive skills of particular species and how these are adapted to particular aspects of specific ecological niches. This enterprise is sometimes called COGNITIVE ETHOLOGY.

For these same reasons, modern comparative studies typically compare only species that are fairly closely related to one another phylogenetically—thus assuring at least some commonalities of ecology and adaptation based on their relatively short times as distinct species. As one example, in the modern study of primate cognition there are currently debates over possible differences between Old World monkeys and apes, whose common ancestor lived about 20 to 30 million years ago. Some researchers claim that monkeys live in an exclusively sensori-motor world of the here-and-now and that only apes have cognitive representations of a humanlike nature (Byrne 1995). Other researchers claim that all nonhuman primates cognitively represent their worlds for purposes of foraging and social interaction, but that only humans employ the forms of symbolic representation that depend on culture, intersubjectivity, and language (Tomasello and Call 1997). These kinds of theoretical debates and the research they generate employ the comparative method, but they do so in much more ecologically and evolutionarily sensitive ways than most of the debates and research in classical comparative psychology.

Comparative studies, in the broad sense of the term, are important for cognitive science in general because: (1) they document something of the range of cognitive skills that have evolved in the natural world and how these work; (2) they help to identify the functions for which particular cognitive skills have evolved, thus specifying an important dimension of their nature; and (3) they situate the cognition of particular species, including humans, in their appropriate evolutionary contexts, which speaks directly to such crucial questions as the ontogenetic mechanisms by which cognitive skills develop in individuals.

See also ADAPTATION AND ADAPTATIONISM; ECOLOGICAL VALIDITY; EVOLUTIONARY PSYCHOLOGY; PRIMATE COGNITION

—*Michael Tomasello*

References

Beach, F. (1950). The snark was a boojum. *American Psychologist* 5: 115–124.

Bitterman, M. (1965). Phyletic differences in learning. *American Psychologist* 20: 396–410.

Byrne, R. W. (1995). *The Thinking Ape.* Oxford: Oxford University Press.

Darwin, C. (1859). *On the Origin of Species by Means of Natural Selection.* London: John Murray.

Darwin, C. (1871). *The Descent of Man and Selection in Relation to Sex.* London: John Murray.

Darwin, C. (1872). *The Expression of Emotions in Man and Animals.* London: John Murray.

Dewsbury, D., Ed. (1984a). *Foundations of Comparative Psychology.* New York: Van Nostrand.

Dewsbury, D. (1984b). *Comparative Psychology in the Twentieth Century.* Stroudsburg, PA: Hutchinson Ross.

Eibl-Eibesfeldt, I. (1970). *Ethology: The Biology of Behavior.* New York: Holt, Rinehart, Winston.

Garcia, J., and R. Koelling. (1966). The relation of cue to consequent in avoidance learning. *Psychonomic Science* 4: 123–124.

Hobhouse, L. T. (1901). *Mind in Evolution.* London: Macmillan.

Hodos, W., and C. B. G. Campbell. (1969). Scala naturae: Why there is no theory in comparative psychology. *Psychological Review* 76: 337–350.

Roitblat, H. L. (1987). *Introduction to Comparative Cognition.* New York: W. H. Freeman and Company.

Romanes, G. J. (1882). *Animal Intelligence.* London: Kegan, Paul Trench and Co.

Romanes, G. J. (1883). *Mental Evolution in Animals.* London: Kegan, Paul Trench and Co.

Rumbaugh, D. M. (1970). Learning skills of anthropoids. In L. A. Rosenblum, Ed., *Primate Behavior: Developments in Field and Laboratory Research.* New York: Academic Press, pp. 1–70.

Spencer, H. (1894). *Principles of Psychology.* London: Macmillan.

Tomasello, M., and J. Call. (1997). *Primate Cognition.* Oxford University Press.

Competence/Performance Distinction

See INTRODUCTION: LINGUISTICS AND LANGUAGE; LINGUISTICS, PHILOSOPHICAL ISSUES; PARAMETER-SETTING APPROACHES TO ACQUISITION, CREOLIZATION, AND DIACHRONY

Competition

See COOPERATION AND COMPETITION; GAME THEORY

Competitive Learning

See UNSUPERVISED LEARNING

Compliant Control

See CONTROL THEORY; MANIPULATION AND GRASPING

Compositionality

Compositionality, a guiding principle in research on the SYNTAX-SEMANTICS INTERFACE of natural languages, is typically stated as follows: "The meaning of a complex expression is a function of the meanings of its immediate syntactic parts and the way in which they are combined." It says, for example, that the meaning of the sentence

$$_S [_{NP} \textit{Zuzana} [_{VP} [_V \textit{owns}] [_{NP} \textit{a schnauzer}]]],$$

where the commonly assumed syntactic structure is indicated by brackets, can be derived from the meanings of the NP *Zuzana* and the VP *owns a schnauzer,* and the fact that this NP and VP are combined to form a sentence. In turn, the meaning of *owns a schnauzer* can be derived from the meanings of *owns* and *a schnauzer* and the fact that they form a VP; hence, the principle of compositionality applies recursively. The principle is implicit in the work of Gottlob FREGE (1848–1920), and was explicitly assumed by Katz and Fodor (1963) and in the work of Richard Montague and his followers (cf. Dowty, Wall, and Peters 1981).

In some form, compositionality is a virtually necessary principle, given the fact that natural languages can express an infinity of meanings and can be learned by humans with finite resources. Essentially, humans have to learn the meanings of basic expressions, the words in the LEXICON (in the magnitude of 10^5), and the meaning effects of syntactic combinations (in the magnitude of 10^2; see SYNTAX). With that they are ready to understand an infinite number of syntactically well-formed expressions. Thus, compositionality is necessary if we see the language faculty, with Wilhelm von Humboldt, as making infinite use of finite means. But compositionality also embodies the claim that semantic interpretation is local, or modular. In order to find out what a (possibly complex) expression *A* means, we just have to look at *A,* and not at the context in which *A* occurs. In its strict version, this claim is clearly wrong, and defenders of compositionality have to account for the context sensitivity of intepretation in one way or other.

There are certain exceptions to compositionality in the form stated above. Idioms and compounds are syntactically complex but come with a meaning that cannot be derived from their parts, like *kick the bucket* or *blackbird.* They have to be learned just like basic words. But compositionality does allow for cases in which the resulting meaning is due to a syntactic construction, as in the comparative construction *The higher they rise, the deeper they fall.* Also, it allows for constructionally ambiguous expressions like *French teacher: French* can be combined with *teacher* as a modifier ("teacher from France"), or as an argument ("teacher of French"). Even though the constituents are arguably the same, the syntactic rules by which they are combined differ, a difference that incidentally shows up in stress (see STRESS, LINGUISTIC).

A hidden assumption in the formulation of the principle of compositionality is that the ways in which meanings are combined are, in some difficult-to-define sense, "natural." Even an idiom like *red herring* would be compositional if we allowed for unnatural interpretation rules like "The meaning of a complex noun consisting of an adjective and a noun is the set of objects that fall both under the meaning of the adjective and the meaning of the noun, except if the adjective is *red* and the noun is *herring,* in which case it may also denote something that distracts from the real issue." But often we need quite similar rules for apparently compositional expressions. For example, *red hair* seems to be compositional, but if we just work with the usual meaning of red (say, "of the color of blood"), then it would mean something like "hair of the color of blood." *Red hair* can mean that (think of a punk's hair dyed red), but typically is understood differently. Some researchers have questioned compositionality because of such context-dependent interpretations (cf. Langacker 1987). But a certain amount of context sensitivity can be built into the meaning of lexical items. For example, the context-sensitive interpretation of *red* can be given as: "When combined with a noun meaning N, it singles out those objects in N that appear closest to the color of blood for the human eye." This would identify ordinary red hair when combined with *hair.* Of course, prototypical red hair is not prototypically red; see Kamp and Partee (1995) for a discussion of compositionality and prototype theory.

Another type of context-sensitive expression that constitutes a potential problem for compositionality is pronouns. A sentence like *She owns a schnauzer* may mean different things in different contexts, depending on the antecedent of *she*. The common solution is to bring context into the formulation of the principle, usually by assuming that "meanings" are devices that change contexts by adding new information (as in models of DYNAMIC SEMANTICS, cf. Heim 1982; Groenendijk and Stokhof 1991). In general, compositionality has led to more refined ways of understanding MEANING (cf. e.g., FOCUS).

In the form stated above, compositionality imposes a homomorphism between syntactic structure and semantic interpretation: syntactic structure and semantic interpretation go hand in hand. This has led to a sophisticated analysis of the meaning of simple expressions. For example, while logic textbooks will give as a translation of *John and Mary came* a formula like $C(j) \land C(m)$, it is obvious that the structures of these expressions are quite different—the syntactic constituent *John and Mary* does not correspond to any constituent in the formula. But we can analyze *John and Mary* as a QUANTIFIER, $\lambda X[X(j) \land X(m)]$, that is applied to *came*, C, and thus gain a structure that is similar to the English sentence. On the other hand, compositionality may impose certain restrictions on syntactic structure. For example, it favors the analysis of relative clauses as noun modifiers, [*every* [*girl who came*]], over the analysis as NP modifiers [[*every girl*] [*who came*]], as only the first allows for a straightforward compositional interpretation (cf. von Stechow 1980).

Compositionality arguments became important in deciding between theories of interpretation. In general, semantic theories that work with a representation language that allows for unconstrained symbolic manipulation (such as Discourse Representation Theory—Kamp 1981; Dynamic Semantics, or Conceptual Semantics—Jackendoff 1990) give up the ideal of compositional interpretation. But typically, compositional reformulations of such analyses are possible.

See also DISCOURSE; SEMANTICS

—*Manfred Krifka*

References

Dowty, D., R. E. Wall, and S. Peters. (1981). *Introduction to Montague Semantics*. Dordrecht: Reidel.

Groenendijk, J., and M. Stokhof. (1991). Dynamic predicate logic. *Linguistics and Philosophy* 14: 39–100.

Heim, I. (1982). The Semantics of Definite and Indefinite Noun Phrases. Ph.D. diss., University of Massachusetts at Amherst. Published by Garland, New York, 1989.

Jackendoff, R. (1990). *Semantic Structures*. Cambridge, MA: MIT Press.

Janssen, T. M. V. (1993). Compositionality of meaning. In R. E. Asher, Ed., *The Encyclopedia of Language and Linguistics*. Oxford: Pergamon Press, pp. 650–656.

Janssen, T. M. V. (1997). Compositionality. In J. van Benthem and A. ter Meulen, Eds., *Handbook of Logic and Language*. Amsterdam: Elsevier.

Kamp, H. (1981). A theory of truth and semantic representation. In J. Groenendijk et al., Eds., *Formal Methods in the Study of Language*. Amsterdam: Mathematical Centre.

Kamp, H., and B. Partee. (1995). Protoype theory and compositionality. *Cognition* 57: 129–191.

Kamp, H., and U. Reyle. (1993). *From Discourse to Logic*. Dordrecht: Kluwer.

Katz, J., and J. Fodor. (1963). The structure of semantic theory. *Language* 39: 120–210.

Landman, F., and I. Moerdijk. (1983). Compositionality and the analysis of anaphora. *Linguistics and Philosophy* 6: 89–114.

Langacker, R. (1987). *Foundations of Cognitive Grammar*. Stanford, CA: Stanford University Press.

Partee, B. H. (1984). Compositionality. In F. Landman and F. Veltman, Eds., *Varieties of Formal Semantics*. Dordrecht: Foris.

Partee, B. H. (1995). Lexical semantics and compositionality. In L. R. Gleitman and M. Liberman, Eds., *Language. An Invitation to Cognitive Science*, vol. 1. Cambridge, MA: MIT Press, pp. 311–360.

von Stechow, A. (1980). Modification of noun phrases: A challenge for compositional semantics. *Theoretical Linguistics* 7: 57–110.

Computation

No idea in the history of studying mind has fueled such enthusiasm—or such criticism—as the idea that the mind is a computer. This idea, known as "cognitivism" (Haugeland 1981/1998) or the COMPUTATIONAL THEORY OF MIND, claims not merely that our minds, like the weather, can be modeled on a computer, but more strongly that, at an appropriate level of abstraction, we *are* computers.

Whether cognitivism is true—even what it means—depends on what computation is. One strategy for answering that question is to defer to practice: to take as computational whatever society *calls* computational. Cognitivism's central tenet, in such a view, would be the thesis that people share with computers whatever constitutive or essential property binds computers into a coherent class. From such a vantage point, a theory of computation would be *empirical*, subject to experimental evidence. That is, a theory of computation would succeed or fail to the extent that it was able to account for the machines that made Silicon Valley famous: the devices we design, build, sell, use, and maintain.

Within cognitive science, however, cognitivism is usually understood in a more specific, theory laden, way: as building in one or more substantive claims about the nature of computing. Of these, the most influential (especially in cognitive science and artificial intelligence) has been the claim that computers are *formal symbol manipulators* (i.e., actively embodied FORMAL SYSTEMS). In this three-part characterization, the term "symbol" is taken to refer to any causally efficacious internal token of a concept, name, word, idea, representation, image, data structure, or other ingredient that represents or carries information about something else (*see* INTENTIONALITY). The predicate "formal" is understood in two simultaneous ways: *positively*, as something like *shape, form*, or *syntax*, and *negatively*, as *independent of semantic properties*, such as reference or truth. *Manipulation* refers to the fact that computation is an active, embodied process—something that takes place in time. Together, they characterize computation as involving the active manipulation of semantic or intentional ingredients in a way that depends only on their formal properties. Given two data structures, for example, one encoding the fact that Socrates is a man, the other that all men are mortal, a computer (in this view) could draw the conclusion that Socrates is mortal *formally* (i.e., would honor what Fodor 1975 calls the "formality condition") if and only if it could do so by reacting to the form or shape of the implicated data structures, without regard to their truth, reference, or MEANING.

In spite of its historical importance, however, it turns out that the formal symbol manipulation construal of computing is only one of half a dozen different ideas at play in present-day intellectual discourse.

Among alternatives, most significant is the body of work carried on in theoretical computer science under the label *theory of computation*. This largely automata-theoretic conception is based on Turing's famous construction of a "Turing machine": a finite state controller able to read, write, and move sequentially back and forth along an infinitely long tape that is inscribed with a finite but indefinite number of tokens or marks. It is this Turing-based theory that explains the notion of a *universal computer* on which the CHURCH-TURING THESIS rests (that anything that can be done algorithmically at all can be done by a computer). Although the architecture of Turing machines is specific, Turing's original paper (1936/1965) introduced the now ubiquitous idea of *implementing* one (virtual) architecture on top of another, and so the Church-Turing thesis is not considered to be architecturally bound. The formal theory of Turing machines is relatively abstract, and used primarily for theoretical purposes: to show what can and cannot be computed, to demonstrate complexity results (how much work is required to solve certain classes of problems), to assign formal semantics to programming languages, etc. Turing machines have also figured in cognitive science at a more imaginative level, for example in the classic formulation of the Turing test: a proposal that a computer can be counted as intelligent if it is able to mimic a person answering a series of typed questions sufficiently well to fool an observer.

Because of their prominence in theoretical computer science, Turing machines are often thought to capture the essential nature of computing—even though, interestingly, they are not explicitly characterized in terms of either SYNTAX or formality. Nor do these two models, formal systems and Turing machines, exhaust extant ideas about the fundamental nature of computing. One popular third alternative is that computation is *information processing*—a broad intuition that can be broken down into a variety of subreadings, including syntactic or quantitative variants (*à la* Shannon, Kolmogorov, Chaitin, etc.), semantic versions (*à la* Dretske, Barwise and Perry, Halpern, Rosenschein, etc.), and historical or socio-technical readings, such as the notion of information that undergirds public conceptions of the Internet. Yet another idea is that the essence of being a computer is to be a *digital state machine*. In spite of various proofs of broad behavioral equivalence among these proposals, for purposes of cognitive science it is essential to recognize that these accounts are conceptually distinct. The notion of formal symbol manipulation makes implicit reference to both syntax and semantics, for example, whereas the notion of a digital machine does neither; the theory of Turing computa-

bility is primarily concerned with input-output behavior, whereas formal symbol manipulation focuses on internal mechanisms and ways of working. The proposals are distinct in extension as well, as continuous Turing machines can solve problems unsolvable by digital (discrete) computers; not all digital machines (such as Lincoln Log houses) are symbol manipulators; and information, especially in its semantic reading as a counterfactual-supporting correlation, seems unrestricted by the causal locality that constrains the notion of effectiveness implicit in Turing machines.

It is not only at the level of basic theory or model that computation affects cognitive science. Whatever their underlying theoretical status, it is undeniable that computers have had an unprecedented effect on the human lives that cognitive science studies—both technological (e-mail, electronic commerce, virtual reality, on-line communities, etc.) and intellectual (in artificial intelligence projects, attempts to fuse computation and quantum mechanics, and the like). It is not yet clear, however, how these higher level developments relate to technical debates within cognitive science itself. By far the majority of real-world systems are written in such high-level programming languages as Fortran, C++, and Java, for example. The total variety of software architectures built in such languages is staggering—including data and control structures of seemingly unlimited variety (parallel and serial, local and distributed, declarative and procedural, sentential and imagistic, etc.). To date, however, this architectural profusion has not been fully recognized within cognitive science. Internal to cognitive science, the label "computational" is often associated with one rather specific class of architectures: serial systems based on relatively fixed, symbolic, explicit, discrete, high-level representations, exemplified by axiomatic inference systems, KNOWLEDGE REPRESENTATION systems, KNOWLEDGE-BASED SYSTEMS, etc. (van Gelder 1995).

This classic symbolic architecture is defended, for example by Fodor and Pylyshyn (1988), because of its claimed superiority in dealing with the systematicity, productivity, and compositionality of high-level thought. Its very specificity, however, especially in contrast with the wide variety of architectures increasingly deployed in computational practice, seems responsible for a variety of self-described "non-" or even "anti-" computational movements that have sprung up in cognitive science over the last two decades: connectionist or neurally inspired architectures (see COGNITIVE MODELING, CONNECTIONIST and CONNECTIONISM, PHILOSOPHICAL ISSUES); DYNAMIC APPROACHES TO COGNITION; shifts in emphasis from computational models to cognitive neuroscience; embodied and situated architectures that exploit various forms of environmental context dependence (see SITUATEDNESS/EMBEDDEDNESS); so-called complex adaptive systems and models of ARTIFICIAL LIFE, motivated in part by such biological phenomena as random mutation and evolutionary selection; interactive or even merely reactive robotics, in the style of Brooks (1997), Agre and Chapman (1987); and other movements. These alternatives differ from the classical model along a number of dimensions: (i) they are more likely to be parallel than serial; (ii) their ingredient structures, particularly at the design stage, are unlikely to be assigned representational or semantic content; (iii) such content or interpretation as is ultimately assigned is typically based on use or experience rather than pure denotation or description, and to be "non-conceptual" in flavor, rather than "conceptualist" or "symbolic"; (iv) they are more likely to be used to model action, perception, navigation, motor control, bodily movement, and other forms of coupled engagement with the world, instead of the traditional emphasis on detached and even deductive ratiocination; (v) they are much more likely to be "real time," in the sense of requiring a close coupling between the temporality of the computational process and the temporality of the subject domain; and (vi) a higher priority is typically accorded to flexibility and the ability to cope with unexpected richness and environmental variation rather than to deep reasoning or purely deductive skills.

Taken collectively, these changes represent a sea change in theoretical orientation within cognitive science—often described in contrast with traditional "computational" approaches. Without a richer and more widely agreed upon theory of computation, however, able to account for the variety of real-world computing, it is unclear that these newly proposed systems should be counted as genuinely "noncomputational." No one would argue that these new proposals escape the COMPUTATIONAL COMPLEXITY limits established by computer science's core mathematical theory, for example. Nor can one deny that real-world computing systems are moving quickly in many of the same directions (toward parallelism, real-time interaction, etc.). Indeed, the evolutionary pace of real-world computing is so relentless that it seems a safe bet to suppose that, overall, society's understanding of "computation" will adapt, as necessary, to subsume all these recent developments within its ever-expanding scope.

See also ALGORITHM; COMPUTATION AND THE BRAIN; COMPUTATIONAL NEUROSCIENCE; CHINESE ROOM ARGUMENT; INFORMATION THEORY; TURING

—*Brian Cantwell Smith*

References

Agre, P., and D. Chapman. (1987). Pengi: An implementation of a theory of activity. In *The Proceedings of the Sixth National Conference on Artificial Intelligence*. American Association for Artificial Intelligence. Seattle: Morgan Kaufmann, pp. 268–272.

Barwise, J., and J. Perry. (1983). *Situations and Attitudes*. Cambridge, MA: MIT Press.

Brooks, R. A. (1997). Intelligence without representation. *Artificial Intelligence* 47: 139-159. In J. Haugeland, Ed., *Mind Design II: Philosophy, Psychology, Artificial Intelligence*. 2nd ed., revised and enlarged. Cambridge, MA: MIT Press, pp. 395–420.

Dretske, F. (1981). *Knowledge and the Flow of Information*. Cambridge, MA: MIT Press.

Fodor, J. (1975). *The Language of Thought*. Cambridge, MA: MIT Press.

Fodor, J., and Z. Pylyshyn. (1988). Connectionism and cognitive architecture: A critical analysis. In S. Pinker and J. Mehler, Eds., *Connections and Symbols*. Cambridge, MA: MIT Press, pp. 3–71.

Haugeland, J. (1981/1998). The nature and plausibility of cognitivism. *Behavioral and Brain Sciences* I: 215–226. Reprinted in J. Haugeland, Ed., *Having Thought: Essays in the Metaphysics of Mind*. Cambridge, MA: Harvard University Press, 1988, pp. 9–45.

Turing, A. M. (1936/1965). On computable numbers, with an application to the Entscheidungsproblem. *Proceedings of the London Mathematical Society* 2nd ser. 42: 230–265. Reprinted in M. Davis, Ed., *The Undecidable: Basic Papers on Undecidable Propositions, Unsolvable Problems and Computable Functions*. Hewlett, NY: Raven Press, 1965, pp. 116–154.

van Gelder, T. J. (1995). What might cognition be, if not computation? *Journal of Philosophy* 91: 345–381.

Computation and the Brain

Two very different insights motivate characterizing the brain as a computer. The first and more fundamental assumes that the defining function of nervous systems is *representational*; that is, brain states represent states of some other system—the outside world or the body itself—where transitions between states can be explained as computational operations on representations. The second insight derives from a domain of mathematical theory that defines computability in a highly abstract sense.

The mathematical approach is based on the idea of a Turing machine. Not an actual machine, the Turing machine is a conceptual way of saying that any well-defined function could be executed, step by step, according to simple "if you are in state P and have input Q then do R" rules, given enough time (maybe infinite time; see COMPUTATION). Insofar as the brain is a device whose input and output can be characterized in terms of some mathematical function— however complicated—then in that very abstract sense, it can be mimicked by a Turing machine. Because neurobiological data indicate that brains are indeed cause-effect machines, brains are, in this formal sense, equivalent to a Turing machine (see CHURCH-TURING THESIS). Significant though this result is mathematically, it reveals nothing specific about the nature of mind-brain representation and computation. It does not even imply that the best explanation of brain function will actually be in computational/representational terms. For in this abstract sense, livers, stomachs, and brains—not to mention sieves and the solar system—*all* compute. What is believed to make brains unique, however, is their evolved capacity to represent the brain's body and its world, and by virtue of computation, to produce coherent, adaptive motor behavior in real time. Precisely what properties enable brains to do this requires empirical, not just mathematical, investigation.

Broadly speaking, there are two main approaches to addressing the substantive question of how in fact brains represent and compute. One exploits the model of the familiar serial, digital computer, where representations are symbols, in somewhat the way sentences are symbols, and computations are formal rules (algorithms) that operate on symbols, rather like the way that "if-then" rules can be deployed in formal logic and circuit design. The second approach is rooted in neuroscience, drawing on data concerning how the cells of the brain (neurons) respond to outside signals such as light and sound, how they integrate signals to extract high-

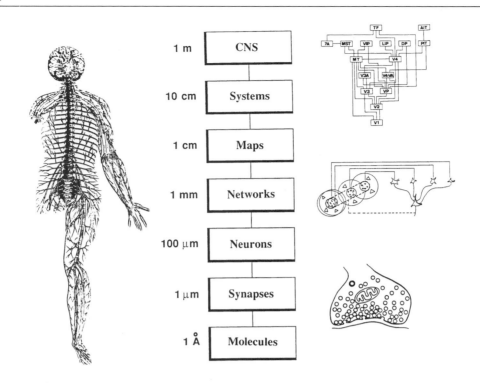

Figure 1. Diagram showing the major levels of organization of the nervous system.

order information, and how later stage neurons interact to yield decisions and motor commands. Although both approaches ultimately seek to reproduce input-output behavior, the first is more "top-down," relying heavily on computer science principles, whereas the second tends to be more "bottom-up," aiming to reflect relevant neurobiological constraints. A variety of terms are commonly used in distinguishing the two: algorithmic computation versus signal processing; classical artificial intelligence (AI) versus connectionism; AI modeling versus neural net modeling.

For some problems the two approaches can complement each other. There are, however, major differences in basic assumptions that result in quite different models and theoretical foci. A crucial difference concerns the idea of levels. In 1982, David MARR characterized three levels in nervous systems. That analysis became influential for thinking about computation. Based on working assumptions in computer science, Marr's proposal delineated (1) the computational level of *abstract problem analysis* wherein the task is decomposed according to plausible engineering principles; (2) the level of the ALGORITHM, specifying a formal procedure to perform the task, so that for a given input, the correct output results; and (3) the level of physical *implementation,* which is relevant to constructing a working device using a particular technology. An important aspect of Marr's view was the claim that a higher level question was independent of levels below it, and hence that problems of levels 1 and 2 could be addressed independently of considering details of the implementation (the neuronal architecture). Consequently, many projects in AI were undertaken on the expectation that the known parallel, analog, continuously adapting, "messy" architecture of the brain could be ignored as irrelevant to modeling mind/brain function.

Those who attacked problems of cognition from the perspective of neurobiology argued that the neural architecture imposes powerful constraints on the *nature* and *range* of computations that can be performed in real time. They suggested that implementation and computation were much more *inter*dependent than Marr's analysis presumed. For example a visual pattern recognition task can be performed in about 300 milliseconds (msec), but it takes about 5–10 msec for a neuron to receive, integrate, and propagate a signal to another neuron. This means that there is time for no more than about 20–30 neuronal steps from signal input to motor output. Because a serial model of the task would require many thousands of steps, the time constraints imply that the parallel architecture of the brain is critical, not irrelevant.

Marr's tripartite division itself was challenged on grounds that nervous systems display not a single level of "implementation," but many levels of structured organization, from molecules to synapses, neurons, networks, and so forth (Churchland and Sejnowski 1992; fig. 1). Evidence indicates that various structural levels have important functional capacities, and that computation might be carried out not only at the level of the neuron, but also at a finer grain, namely the dendrite, as well as at a larger grain, namely the network. From the perspective of neuroscience, the hardware/software distinction did not fall gracefully onto brains.

What, in neural terms, are representations? Whereas the AI approach equates representations with symbols, a term well defined in the context of conventional computers, connectionists realized that "symbol" is essentially undefined in neurobiological contexts. They therefore aimed to develop a new theory of representation suitable to neurobiology. Thus they hypothesized that occurrent representations (those happening now) are patterns of *activation* across the units in a neural net, characterized as a vector, <x, y, z, . . .>, where each element in the vector specifies the level of activity in a unit. Stored representations, by contrast, are believed to depend on the configuration of *weights* between units. In neural terms, these weights are the strength of synaptic connections between neurons.

Despite considerable progress, exactly how brains represent and compute remains an unsolved problem. This is mainly because many questions about how neurons code and decode information are still unresolved. New techniques in neuroscience have revealed that timing of neuronal spikes is important in coding, but exactly how this works or how temporally structured signals are decoded is not understood.

In exploring the properties of nervous systems, artificial NEURAL NETWORKS (ANNs) have generally been more useful to neuroscience than AI models. A useful strategy for investigating the functional role of an actual neural network is to train an ANN to perform a similar information processing task, then to analyze its properties, and then compare them to the real system. For example, consider certain neurons in the parietal cortex (area 7a) of the brain whose response properties are correlated with the position of the visual stimulus relative to head-centered coordinates. Since the receptor sheets (RETINA, eye muscles) cannot provide that information directly, it has to be computed from various input signals. Two sets of neurons project to these cells: some represent the position of the stimulus on the retina, some represent the position of the eyeball in the head. Modeling these relationships via an artificial neural net shows how the eyeball/retinal position can be used to compute the position of the stimulus relative to the head (see OCULOMOTOR CONTROL). Once trained, the network's structure can be analyzed to determine how the computation was achieved, and this may suggest neural experiments (Andersen 1995; see also COMPUTATIONAL NEUROSCIENCE).

How biologically realistic to make an ANN depends on the purposes at hand, and different models are useful for different purposes. At certain levels and for certain purposes, abstract, simplifying models are precisely what is needed. Such a model will be more useful than a model slavishly realistic with respect to every level, even the biochemical. Excessive realism may mean that the model is too complicated to analyze or understand or run on the available computers. For some projects such as modeling language comprehension, less neural detail is required than for other projects, such as investigating dendritic spine dynamics.

Although the assumption that nervous systems compute and represent seems reasonable, the assumption is not proved and has been challenged. Stressing the interactive and time-dependent nature of nervous systems, some researchers see the brain together with its body and environment as dynamical systems, best characterized by systems of differential equations describing the temporal evolution of states of the brain (*see* DYNAMIC APPROACHES TO COGNITION, and Port and van Gelder 1995). In this view both the brain and the liver can have their conduct adequately described by systems of differential equations. Especially in trying to explain the development of perceptual motor skills in neonates, a dynamical systems approach has shown considerable promise (Thelen and Smith 1994).

The main reason for adhering to a framework with computational resources derives from the observation that neurons represent various nonneural parameters, such as head velocity or muscle tension or visual motion, and that complex neuronal representations have to be constructed from simpler ones. Recall the example of neurons in area 7a. Their response profiles indicate that they represent the position of the visual stimulus in head-centered coordinates. Describing causal interactions between these cells and their input signals without specifying anything about representational role masks their function in the animal's visual capacity. It omits explaining how these cells come to represent what they do. Note that connectionist models can be dynamical when they include back projections, time constants for signal propagation, channel open times, as well as mechanisms for adding units and connections, and so forth.

In principle, dynamical models could be supplemented with representational resources in order to achieve more revealing explanations. For instance, it is possible to treat certain parameter settings as inputs, and the resultant attractor as an output, each carrying some representational content. Furthermore, dynamical systems theory easily handles cases where the "output" is not a single static state (the result of a computation), but is rather a trajectory or limit cycle. Another approach is to specify dynamical subsystems within the larger cognitive system that function as emulators of external domains, such as the task environment (see Grush 1997). This approach embraces both the representational characterization of the inner emulator (it represents the external domain), as well as a dynamical system's characterization of the brain's overall function.

See also AUTOMATA; COGNITIVE MODELING, CONNECTIONIST; COGNITIVE MODELING, SYMBOLIC; COMPUTATIONAL THEORY OF MIND; MENTAL REPRESENTATION

—*Patricia S. Churchland and Rick Grush*

References

Andersen, R. A. (1995). Coordinate transformations and motor planning in posterior parietal cortex. In M. Gazzaniga, Ed., *The Cognitive Neurosciences*. Cambridge, MA: MIT Press.

Churchland, P. S., and T. J. Sejnowski. (1992). *The Computational Brain*. Cambridge, MA: MIT Press.

Grush, R. (1997). The architecture of representation. *Philosophical Psychology* 10 (1): 5–25.

Marr, D. (1982). *Vision*. New York: Freeman.

Port, R., and T. van Gelder. (1995). *Mind as Motion: Explorations in the Dynamics of Cognition*. Cambridge, MA: MIT Press.

Thelen, E., and L. B. Smith. (1994). *A Dynamical Systems Approach to the Development of Cognition and Action*. Cambridge, MA: MIT Press.

Further Readings

Abeles, M. (1991). *Corticonics: Neural Circuits of the Cerebral Cortex*. Cambridge: Cambridge University Press.

Arbib, A. M. (1995). *The Handbook of Brain Theory and Neural Networks*. Cambridge, MA: MIT Press.

Boden, M. (1988). *Computer Models of the Mind*. Cambridge: Cambridge University Press.

Churchland, P. (1995). *The Engine of Reason, the Seat of the Soul*. Cambridge, MA: MIT Press.

Koch, C., and I. Segev. (1997). *Methods in Neuronal Modeling: From Synapses to Networks.* 2nd ed. Cambridge, MA: MIT Press.

Sejnowski, T. (1997). Computational neuroscience. *Encyclopedia of Neuroscience.* Amsterdam: Elsevier Science Publishers.

Computational Complexity

How is it possible for a biological system to perform activities such as language comprehension, LEARNING, ANALOGY, PLANNING, or visual interpretation? The COMPUTATIONAL THEORY OF MIND suggests that it is possible the same way it is possible for an electronic computer to sort a list of numbers, simulate a weather system, or control an elevator: the brain, it is claimed, is an organ capable of certain forms of COMPUTATION, and mental activities such as those listed above are computational ones. But it is not enough to say that a mental activity is computational to account for its physical or biological realizability; it must also be the sort of task that can be performed by the brain in a plausible amount of time.

Computational complexity is the part of computer science that studies the resource requirements in time and memory of various computational tasks (Papadimitriou 1994). Typically, these requirements are formulated as functions of the size of the input to be processed. The central tenet of computability theory (one form of the CHURCH-TURING THESIS) is that any computational task that can be performed by a physical system of whatever form, can be performed by a very simple device called a Turing machine. The central tenet of (sequential) complexity theory, then, is that any computational task that can be performed by any physical system in $F(n)$ steps, where n is the size of the input, can be performed by a Turing machine in $G(n)$ steps, where F and G differ by at most a polynomial. A consequence of this is that any task requiring exponential time on a Turing machine would not be computable in polynomial time by anything physical whatsoever. Because exponentials grow so rapidly, such a task would be physically infeasible except for very small inputs.

How might this argument be relevant to cognitive science? Consider a simple form of visual interpretation, for example. Suppose it is hypothesized that part of how vision works is that the brain determines some property P of the scene, given a visual grid provided by the retina as input. Let us further suppose that the task is indeed computable, but an analysis shows that a Turing machine would require an exponential number of steps to do so. This means that to compute P quickly enough on all but very small grids, the brain would have to perform an unreasonably large number of elementary operations per second. The hypothesis, then, becomes untenable: it fails to explain how the brain could perform the visual task within reasonable time bounds.

Unfortunately, this putative example is highly idealized. For one thing, computational complexity is concerned with how the demand for resources scales as a function of the size of the input. If the required input does not get very large (as with individual sentences of English, say, with a few notable exceptions), complexity theory has little to contribute. For another, to say that the resource demands scale exponentially is to say that there will be inputs that require exponential effort. However, these could turn out to be extremely rare in real life, and the vast majority may very well be unproblematic from a resource standpoint. Thus the actual tractability of a task depends crucially on the range of inputs that need to be processed.

But these considerations do not undermine the importance of complexity. To return to the visual interpretation example, we clearly ought not to be satisfied with a theory that claims that the brain computes P, but that in certain extremely rare cases, it could be busy for hours doing so. Either such cases cannot occur at all for some reason, or the brain is able to deal with them: it gives up, it uses heuristics, it makes do. Either way, what the brain is actually doing is no longer computing P, but some close approximation to P that needs to be shown adequate for vision, and whose complexity in turn ought to be considered.

Another complication that should be noted is that it has turned out to be extremely difficult to establish that a computational task requires an exponential number of steps. Instead, what has emerged is the theory of NP-completeness (Garey and Johnson 1979). This starts with a specific computational task called SAT (Cook 1971), which involves determining whether an input formula of propositional logic can be made true. While SAT is not known to require exponential time, all currently known methods do require an exponential number of steps on some inputs. A computational task is NP-complete when it is as difficult as SAT: an efficient way of performing it would also lead to an efficient method for SAT, and vice versa. Thus, all NP-complete tasks, including SAT itself, and including a very large number seemingly related to assorted mental activities, are strongly believed (but are not known) to require exponential time.

The constraint of computational tractability has ended up being a powerful forcing function in much of the technical work in artificial intelligence. For example, research in KNOWLEDGE REPRESENTATION can be profitably understood as investigating reasoning tasks that are not only semantically motivated and broadly applicable, but are also computationally tractable (Levesque 1986). In many cases, this has involved looking for plausible approximations, restrictions, or deviations from the elegant but thoroughly intractable models of inference based on classical LOGIC (Levesque 1988). Indeed, practical KNOWLEDGE-BASED SYSTEMS have invariably been built around restricted forms of logical or probabilistic inference. Similar considerations have led researchers away from classical decision theory to models of BOUNDED RATIONALITY (Russell and Wefald 1991). In the area of COMPUTATIONAL VISION, it has been suggested that visual attention is the mechanism used by the brain to tame otherwise intractable tasks (Tsotsos 1995). Because the resource demands of a task are so dependent on the range of inputs, recent work has attempted to understand what it is about certain inputs that makes NP-complete tasks problematic (Hogg, Huberman, and Williams 1996). For a less technical discussion of this whole issue, see Cherniak 1986.

See also AUTOMATA; COMPUTATION AND THE BRAIN; RATIONAL AGENCY; TURING, ALAN

—*Hector Levesque*

References

Cherniak, C. (1986). *Minimal Rationality.* Cambridge, MA: MIT Press.

Cook, S. A. (1971). The complexity of theorem-proving procedures. *Proceedings of the 3rd Annual ACM Symposium on the Theory of Computing,* pp. 151–158.

Garey, M., and D. Johnson. (1979). *Computers and Intractability: A Guide to the Theory of NP-Completeness.* New York: Wiley, Freeman and Co.

Hogg, T., B. Huberman, and C. Williams. (1996). Frontiers in problem solving: Phase transitions and complexity. *Artificial Intelligence* 81 (1–2).

Levesque, H. (1986). Knowledge representation and reasoning. *Annual Review of Computer Science* 1: 255–287.

Levesque, H. (1988). Logic and the complexity of reasoning. *Journal of Philosophical Logic* 17: 355–389.

Papadimitriou, C. (1994). *Computational Complexity.* New York: Addison-Wesley.

Russell, S., and E. Wefald. (1991). *Do the Right Thing.* Cambridge, MA: MIT Press.

Tsotsos, J. (1995). Behaviorist intelligence and the scaling problem. *Artificial Intelligence* 75 (2): 135–160.

Computational Learning Theory

Computational learning theory is the study of a collection of mathematical models of machine learning, and has among its goals the development of new algorithms for learning from data, and the elucidation of computational and information-theoretic barriers to learning. As such, it is closely related to disciplines with similar aims, such as statistics and MACHINE LEARNING (see also NEURAL NETWORKS; PATTERN RECOGNITION AND FEEDFORWARD NETWORKS; and BAYESIAN LEARNING). However, it is perhaps coarsely distinguished from these other areas by an explicit and central concern for computational efficiency and the COMPUTATIONAL COMPLEXITY of learning problems.

Most of the problems receiving the greatest scrutiny to date can be traced back to the seminal paper of L. G. Valiant (1984), where a simple and appealing model is proposed that emphasizes three important notions. First, learning is probabilistic: a finite sample of data is generated randomly according to an unknown process, thus necessitating that we tolerate some error, hopefully quantifiable, in the hypothesis output by a learning algorithm. Second, learning algorithms must be computationally efficient, in the standard complexity-theoretic sense: given a sample of m observations from the unknown random process, the execution time of a successful learning algorithm will be bounded by a fixed polynomial in m. Third, learning algorithms should be appropriately general: they should process the finite sample to obtain a hypothesis with good generalization ability under a reasonably large set of circumstances.

In Valiant's original paper, the random process consisted of an unknown distribution or density P over an input space X, and an unknown Boolean (two-valued) target function f over X, chosen from a known class F of such functions. The finite sample given to the learning algorithm consists of pairs $<x, y>$, where x is distributed according to P and $y = f(x)$. The demand that learning algorithms be general is captured by the fact that the distribution P is arbitrary, and the function class F is typically too large to permit an exhaustive search for a good match to the observed data. A typical example sets F to be the class of all linear-threshold functions (perceptrons) over n-dimensional real inputs. In this case, the model would ask whether there is a learning algorithm that, for any input dimension n and any desired error $\varepsilon > 0$, requires a sample size and execution time bounded by fixed polynomials in n and $1/\varepsilon$, and produces (with high probability) a hypothesis function h such that the probability that $h(x) \neq f(x)$ is smaller than ε under P. Note that we demand that the hypothesis function h generalize to unseen data (as represented by the distribution P), and not simply fit the observed training data.

The last decade has yielded a wealth of results and analyses in the model sketched above and related variants. Many of the early papers demonstrated that simple and natural learning problems can be computationally difficult for a variety of interesting reasons. For instance, Pitt and Valiant (1988) showed learning problems for which the "natural" choice for the form of the hypothesis function h leads to an NP-hard problem, but for which a more general hypothesis representation leads to an efficient algorithm. Kearns and Valiant (1994) exhibited close connections between hard learning problems and cryptography by showing that several natural problems, including learning finite automata and boolean formula, are computationally difficult regardless of the method used to represent the hypothesis.

These results demonstrated that powerful learning algorithms were unlikely to be developed within Valiant's original framework without some modifications, and researchers turned to a number of reasonable relaxations. One fruitful variant has been to supplement the random sample given to the learning algorithm with a mechanism to answer *queries* —that is, rather than simply passively receiving $<x, y>$ pairs drawn from some distribution, the algorithm may now actively request the classification of any desired x under the unknown target function f. With this additional mechanism, a number of influential and elegant algorithms have been discovered, including for finite automata by Angluin (1987, 1988; to be contrasted with the intractability without the query mechanism, mentioned above) and for decision trees by Kushelevitz and Mansour (1993).

One drawback to the query mechanism is the difficulty of simulating such a mechanism in real machine learning applications, where typically only passive observations of the kind posited in Valiant's original model are available. An alternative but perhaps more widely applicable relaxation of this model is known as the *weak learning* or *boosting* model. Here it is assumed that we already have possession of an algorithm that is efficient, but meets only very weak (but still nontrivial) generalization guarantees. This is formalized by asserting that the weak learning algorithm always outputs a hypothesis whose error with respect to the unknown target function is slightly better than "random guessing." The goal of a boosting algorithm is then to combine the many mediocre hypotheses' output by several executions of the weak learning algorithm into a single hypothesis that is much better than random guessing. This is made possible by assuming that the weak learning algorithm will perform better than random guessing on many *different* distributions on the inputs. Initially proposed to settle some rather theoretical questions in Valiant's original model, the boosting framework has recently resulted in new learning algorithms enjoying widespread experimental success and influence (Freund and Schapire 1997), as well as new analyses of some classic machine learning heuristics, such as the CART and C4.5 decision tree programs (Kearns and Mansour 1996).

Although computational considerations are the primary distinguishing feature of computational learning theory, and have been the emphasis here, it should be noted that a significant fraction of the work and interest in the field is devoted to questions of a primarily statistical or information-theoretic nature. Thus, characterizations of the number of observations required by any algorithm (computationally efficient or otherwise) for good generalization have been the subject of intense and prolonged scrutiny, building on the foundational work of Vapnik (1982; see STATISTICAL LEARNING THEORY). Recent work has also sought similar characterizations without probabilistic assumptions on the generation of observations (Littlestone 1988), and has led to a series of related and experimentally successful algorithms.

A more extensive bibliography and an introduction to some of the central topics of computational learning theory is contained in Kearns and Vazirani 1994.

See also INDUCTION THEORY; INFORMATION THEORY; LEARNING SYSTEMS; STATISTICAL TECHNIQUES IN NATURAL LANGUAGE PROCESSING

—*Michael Kearns*

References

Angluin, D. (1987). Learning regular sets from queries and counterexamples. *Information and Computation* 75 (2): 87–106.

Angluin, D. (1988). Queries and concept learning. *Machine Learning* 2 (4): 319–342.

Blumer, A., A. Ehrenfeucht, D. Haussler, and M. Warmuth. (1989). Learnability and the Vapnik-Chervonenkis dimension. *Journal of the ACM* 36 (4): 929–965.

Freund, Y., and R. Schapire. (1997). A decision–theoretic generalization of on-line learning and an application to boosting. *Journal of Computer and System Sciences* 55 (1): 119–139.

Kearns, M., and Y. Mansour. (1996). On the boosting ability of top-down decision tree learning algorithms. In *Proceedings of the 28th Annual ACM Symposium on the Theory of Computing.* Forthcoming in *Journal of Computer and Systems Sciences.*

Kearns, M., and L. G. Valiant. (1994). Cryptographic limitations on learning Boolean formulae and finite automata. *Journal of the ACM* 41 (1): 67–95.

Kearns, M., and U. Vazirani. (1994). *An Introduction to Computational Learning Theory.* Cambridge: MIT Press.

Kushelevitz, E., and Y. Mansour. (1993). Learning decision trees using the Fourier Spectrum. *SIAM Journal on Computing* 22 (6): 1331–1348.

Littlestone, N. (1988). Learning when irrelevant attributes abound: A new linear-threshold algorithm. *Machine Learning* 2: 285–318.

Pitt, L., and L. G. Valiant. (1988). Computational limitations on learning from examples. *Journal of the ACM* 35: 965–984.

Schapire, R. (1990). The strength of weak learnability. *Machine Learning* 5 (2): 197–227.

Valiant, L. G. (1984). A theory of the learnable. *Communications of the ACM* 27 (11): 1134–1142.

Vapnik, V. N. (1982). *Estimation of Dependences Based on Empirical Data.* New York: Springer-Verlag.

Computational Lexicons

A computational lexicon has traditionally been viewed as a repository of lexical information for specific tasks, such as parsing, generation, or translation. From this viewpoint, it must contain two types of knowledge: (1) knowledge needed for syntactic analysis and synthesis, and (2) knowledge needed for semantic interpretation. More recently, the definition of a computational lexicon has undergone major revision as the fields of COMPUTATIONAL LINGUISTICS and semantics have matured. In particular, two new trends have driven the design concerns of researchers:

- Attempts at closer integration of compositional semantic operations with the lexical information structures that bear them
- A serious concern with how lexical types reflect the underlying ontological categories of the systems being modeled

Two new approaches to modeling the structure of the LEXICON have recently emerged in computational linguistics: (1) theoretical studies of how computations take place in the mental lexicon; (2) developments of computational models of information as structured in lexical databases. The differences between the computational study of the lexicon and more traditional linguistic approaches can be summarized as follows:

Lexical representations must be explicit. The knowledge contained in them must be sufficiently detailed to support one or more processing applications.

The global structure of the lexicon must be modeled. Real lexicons are complex knowledge bases, and hence the structures relating entire words are as important as those relating components of words. Furthermore, lexical entries consisting of more than one orthographic word (collocations, idioms, and compounds) must also be represented.

The lexicon must provide sufficient coverage of its domain. Real lexicons can typically contain up to 400,000 entries. For example, a typical configuration might be: verbs (5K), nouns (30K), adjectives (5K), adverbs (<1K), logical terms (<1K), rhetorical terms (<1K), compounds (2K), proper names (300K), and various sublanguage terms.

Computational lexicons must be evaluable. Computational lexicons are typically evaluated in terms of: (i) coverage: both breadth of the lexicon and depth of lexical information; (ii) extensibility: how easily can information be added to the lexical entry? How readily is new information made consistent with the other lexical structures? (iii) utility: how useful are the lexical entries for specific tasks and applications?

Viewed independently of any specific application and evaluated in terms of its relevance to cognitive science, the recent work on computational lexicons makes several important points. The first is that the lexical and interlexical structures employed in computational studies have provided some of the most complete descriptions of the lexical bases of natural languages. Besides the broad descriptive coverage of these lexicons, the architectural decisions involved in these systems have important linguistic and psychological consequences. For example, the legitimacy and usefulness of many theoretical constructions and abstract descriptions can be tested and verified by attempting to instantiate them in as complete and robust a lexicon as possible. Of course, completeness doesn't ensure correctness nor does it ensure a particularly interesting lexicon from a theoretical point of view, but explicit representations do reveal the limitations of a given analytical framework.

Content of a Single Lexical Entry

Although there are many competing views on the exact structure of lexical entries, there are some important common assumptions about the content of a lexical entry. It is generally agreed that there are three necessary components to the structure of a lexical item: *orthographic and morphological information*; i.e. how the word is spelled and what forms it appears in; *syntactic information*; for instance, what part of speech the word is; and *semantic information*; i.e., what representation the word translates to.

Syntactic information may be divided into the subtypes of *category* and *subcategory*. Category information includes traditional categories such as noun, verb, adjective, adverb, and preposition. While most systems agree on these "major" categories, there are often great differences in the ways they classify "minor" categories, such as conjunctions, quantifier elements, determiners, etc.

Subcategory information is information that divides syntactic categories into subclasses. This sort of information may be usefully separated into two types, *contextual features* and *inherent features*. The former are features that may be defined in terms of the contexts in which a given lexical entry may occur. *Subcategorization* information marks the local legitimate context for a word to appear in a syntactic structure. For example, the verb *devour* is never intransitive in English and requires a direct object; hence the lexicon tags the verb with a subcategorization requiring an NP object. Another type of context encoding is *collocational information,* where patterns that are not fully productive in the grammar can be tagged. For example, the adjective *heavy* as applied to *drinker* and *smoker* is collocational and not freely productive in nature.

Inherent features are features of lexical entries that cannot, or cannot easily, be reduced to a contextual definition. They include such features as count/mass (e.g., *pebble* vs. *water*), abstract, animate, human, and so on.

Semantic information can also be separated into two subcategories, *base semantic typing* and *selectional typing*. While the former identifies the broad semantic class that a lexical item belongs to (such as event, proposition, predicate), the latter class specifies the semantic features of arguments and adjuncts to the lexical item.

Global Structure of the Lexicon

From the discussion above, the entries in a lexicon would appear to encode only concepts such as category information, selectional restrictions, number, type and case roles of arguments, and so forth. While the utility of this kind of information is beyond doubt, the emphasis on the individual entry misses out on the issue of global lexical organization. This is not to dismiss ongoing work that does focus precisely on this issue; for instance, attempts to relate grammatical alternations with semantic classes (e.g., Levin 1993).

One obvious way to organize lexical knowledge is by means of lexical inheritance mechanisms. In fact, much recent work has focused on how to provide shared data structures for syntactic and morphological knowledge (Flickinger, Pollard, and Wasow 1985). Evans and Gazdar (1990) provide a formal characterization of how to perform inferences in a language for multiple and default inheritance of linguistic knowledge. The language developed for that purpose, DATR, uses value-terminated attribute trees to encode lexical information. Taking a different approach, Briscoe, dePaiva, and Copestake (1993) describe a rich system of types for allowing default mechanisms into lexical type descriptions.

Along a similar line, Pustejovsky and Boguraev (1993) describe a theory of shared semantic information based on orthogonal typed inheritance principles, where there are several distinct levels of semantic description for a lexical item. In particular, a set of semantic roles called *qualia structure* is relevant to just this issue. These roles specify the purpose (telic), origin (agentive), basic form (formal), and constitution (const) of the lexical item. In this view, a lexical item inherits information according to the qualia structure it carries. In this view, multiple inheritance can be largely avoided because the qualia constrain the types of concepts that can be put together. For example, the predicates *cat* and *pet* refer to formal and telic qualia, respectively.

The Computational Lexicon as Knowledge Base

The interplay of the lexical needs of current language processing frameworks and contemporary lexical semantic theories very much influences the direction of computational dictionary analysis research for lexical acquisition. Given the increasingly prominent place the lexicon is assigned—in linguistic theories, in language processing technology, and in domain descriptions—it is no accident, nor is it mere rhetoric, that the term "lexical knowledge base" has become a widely accepted one. Researchers use it to refer to a large-scale repository of lexical information, which incorporates more than just "static" descriptions of words, for example, clusters of properties and associated values. A lexical knowledge base should state constraints on word behavior, dependence of word interpretation on context, and distribution of linguistic generalizations.

A lexicon is essentially a dynamic object, as it incorporates, in addition to its information types, the ability to perform inference over them and thus induce word meaning in context. This is what a computational lexicon is: a theoretically sound and computationally useful resource for real application tasks and for gaining insights into human cognitive abilities.

See also COMPUTATIONAL PSYCHOLINGUISTICS; CONCEPTS; KNOWLEDGE REPRESENTATION; NATURAL LANGUAGE GENERATION; NATURAL LANGUAGE PROCESSING; STATISTICAL TECHNIQUES IN NATURAL LANGUAGE PROCESSING

—*James Pustejovsky*

References

Briscoe, T., V. de Paiva, and A. Copestake, Eds. (1993). *Inheritance, Defaults, and the Lexicon.* Cambridge: Cambridge University Press.

Evans, R., and G. Gazdar. (1990). Inference in DATR. *Proceedings of the Fourth European ACL Conference,* April 10–12, 1989, Manchester, England.

Flickinger, D., C. Pollard, and T. Wasow. (1985). Structure–sharing in lexical representation. *Proceedings of 23rd Annual Meeting of the ACL,* Chicago, IL, pp. 262–267.

Grimshaw, J. (1990). *Argument Structure.* Cambridge, MA: MIT Press.

Guthrie, L., J. Pustejovsky, Y. Wilks, and B. Slator. (1996). The role of lexicons in natural language processing. *Communications of the ACM* 39:1.

Levin, B. (1993). *Towards a Lexical Organization of English Verbs.* Chicago: University of Chicago Press.

Miller, G. WordNet: an on-line lexical database. *International Journal of Lexicography* 3: 235–312.

Pollard, C., and I. Sag. (1987). *Information–Based Syntax and Semantics.* CSLI Lecture Notes Number 13. Stanford, CA: CSLI.

Pustejovsky, J., and P. Boguraev. (1993). Lexical knowledge representation and natural language processing. *Artificial Intelligence* 63: 193–223.

Further Readings

Atkins, B. (1990). Building a lexicon: Reconciling anisomorphic sense differentiations in machine-readable dictionaries. Paper presented at *BBN Symposium: Natural Language in the 90s—Language and Action in the World,* Cambridge, MA.

Boguraev, B., and E. Briscoe. (1989). *Computational Lexicography for Natural Language Processing.* Longman, Harlow and London.

Boguraev, B., and J. Pustejovsky. (1996). *Corpus Processing for Lexical Acquisition.* Cambridge, MA: Bradford Books/MIT Press.

Briscoe, E., A. Copestake, and B. Boguraev. (1990). Enjoy the paper: Lexical semantics via lexicology. *Proceedings of 13th International Conference on Computational Linguistics,* Helsinki, Finland, pp. 42–47.

Calzolari, N. (1992). Acquiring and representing semantic information in a lexical knowledge base. In J. Pustejovsky and S. Bergler, Eds., *Lexical Semantics and Knowledge Representation.* New York: Springer Verlag.

Copestake, A., and E. Briscoe. (1992). Lexical operations in a unification–based framework. In J. Pustejovsky and S. Bergler, Eds., *Lexical Semantics and Knowledge Representation.* New York: Springer Verlag.

Evens, M. (1987). *Relational Models of the Lexicon.* Cambridge: Cambridge University Press.

Grishman, R., and J. Sterling. (1992). Acquisition of selectional patterns. *Proceedings of the 14th International Conf. on Computational Linguistics (COLING 92),* Nantes, France.

Hirst, G. (1987). *Semantic Interpretation and the Resolution of Ambiguity.* Cambridge: Cambridge University Press.

Hobbs, J., W. Croft, T. Davies, D. Edwards, and K. Laws. (1987). Commonsense metaphysics and lexical semantics. *Computational Linguistics* 13: 241–250.

Ingria, R., B. Boguraev, and J. Pustejovsky. (1992). Dictionary/Lexicon. In Stuart Shapiro, Ed., *Encyclopedia of Artificial Intelligence.* 2nd ed. New York: Wiley.

Miller, G. (1991). *The Science of Words.* Scientific American Library.

Pustejovsky, J. (1992). Lexical semantics. In Stuart Shapiro, Ed., *Encyclopedia of Artificial Intelligence.* 2nd ed. New York: Wiley.

Pustejovsky, J. (1995). *The Generative Lexicon.* Cambridge, MA: MIT Press.

Pustejovsky, J., S. Bergler, and P. Anick. (1993). Lexical semantic techniques for corpus analysis. *Computational Linguistics* 19 (2).

Salton, G. (1991). Developments in automatic text retrieval. *Science* 253: 974.

Weinreich, U. (1972). *Explorations in Semantic Theory.* The Hague: Mouton.

Wilks, Y. (1975). An intelligent analyzer and understander for English. *Communications of the ACM* 18: 264–274.

Wilks, Y., D. Fass, C-M. Guo, J. McDonald, T. Plate, and B. Slator. (1989). A tractable machine dictionary as a resource for computational semantics. In B. Boguraev and E. Briscoe, Eds., *Computational Lexicography for Natural Language Processing.* Longman, Harlow and London, pp. 193–228.

Computational Linguistics

Computational linguistics (CL; also called natural language processing, or NLP) is concerned with (1) the study of computational models of the structure and function of language, its use, and its acquisition; and (2) the design, development, and implementation of a wide range of systems such as SPEECH RECOGNITION, language understanding and NATURAL LANGUAGE GENERATION. CL applications include interfaces to databases, text processing, and message understanding, multilingual interfaces as aids for foreign language correspondences, web pages, and speech-to-speech translation in limited domains. On the theoretical side, CL uses computational modeling to investigate syntax, semantics, pragmatics (that is, certain aspects of the relationship of the speaker and the hearer, or of the user and the system in the case of a CL system), and discourse aspects of language. These investigations are interdisciplinary and involve concepts from artificial intelligence (AI), linguistics, logic, and psychology. By connecting the closely interrelated fields of computer science and linguistics, CL plays a key role in cognitive science.

Because it is impossible to cover the whole range of theoretical and practical issues in CL in the limited space available, only a few related topics are discussed here in some detail, to give the reader a sense of important issues. Fortunately, there exists a comprehensive source, documenting all the major aspects of CL (*Survey of the State of Art in Human Language Technology* forthcoming).

Grammars and Parsers

Almost every NLP system has a grammar and an associated parser. A *grammar* is a finite specification of a potentially infinite number of sentences, and a *parser* for the grammar is an ALGORITHM that analyzes a sentence and, if possible, assigns one or more grammar-based structural descriptions to the sentence. The structural descriptions are necessary for further processing—for example, for semantic interpretation.

Many CL systems are based on context-free grammars (CFGs). One such grammar, G, consists of a finite set of nonterminals (for example, S: sentence; NP: noun phrase; VP: verb phrase; V: verb; ADV: adverb), a finite set of terminals, or lexical items, and a finite set of rewrite rules of the form $A \rightarrow W$, where A is a nonterminal and W is a string of nonterminals and terminals. S is a special nonterminal called the "start symbol."

CFGs are inadequate and need to be augmented for a variety of reasons. For one, the information associated with a phrase (a string of terminals) is not just the atomic symbols used as nonterminals, but a complex bundle of information (sets of attribute-value pairs, called "feature structures") that needs to be associated with strings. Moreover, appropriate structures and operations for combining them are needed, together with a CFG skeleton. For another, the string-combining operation in a CFG is concatenation, (for example, if u and v are strings, v concatenated with u gives the string $w = uv$, that is, u followed by v), and more complex string-combining as well as tree-combining operations are needed to describe various linguistic phenomena. Finally, the categories in a grammar need to be augmented by associating them with feature structures, a set of attribute-value pairs that are then combined in an operation called "unification." A variety of grammars such as generalized phrase structure grammar (GPSG), HEAD-DRIVEN PHRASE STRUCTURE GRAMMAR (HPSG), and LEXICAL FUNCTIONAL GRAMMAR (LFG) are essentially CFG-based unification grammars (Bresnan and Kaplan 1983; Gazdar et al. 1985; Pollard and Sag 1994).

Computational grammars need to describe a wide range of dependencies among the different elements in the grammar. Some of these dependencies involve agreement features, such as person, number, and gender. For example, in English, the verb agrees with the subject in person and number. Others involve verb subcategorization, in which each verb specifies one (or more) subcategorization frames for its complements. For instance, *sleep* (as in *Harry sleeps*) does not require any complement, while *like* (as in *Harry likes peanuts*) requires one complement; *give* (as in *Harry gives Susan a flower*) requires two complements; and so forth. Sometimes the dependent elements do not appear in their normal positions. In *Who$_i$ did John invite e$_i$*, where e_i is a stand-in for *who$_i$*, *who$_i$* is the filler for the gap e_i (see WH-MOVEMENT). The filler and the gap need not be at a fixed distance. Thus in *Who$_i$ did Bill ask John to invite e$_i$*, the filler and the gap are more distant than in the previous sentence. Sometimes the dependencies are nested. In German, for example, one could have *Hans$_i$ Peter$_j$ Marie$_k$ schwimmen$_k$ lassen$_j$ sah$_i$* (Hans saw Peter make Marie swim), where the nouns (arguments) and verbs are in nested order, as the subscripts indicate. And sometimes they are crossed. In Dutch, for example, one could have *Jan$_i$ Piet$_j$ Marie$_k$ zag$_i$ laten$_j$ zwemmen$_k$* (Jan saw Piet make Marie swim). There are, of course, situations where the dependencies have

more complex patterns. Precise statements of such dependencies and the domains over which they operate constitute the major activity in the specification of a grammar. Computational modeling of these dependencies is one of the key areas in CL. Many (for example, the crossed dependencies discussed above) cannot be described by context-free grammars and require grammars with larger domains of locality. One such class is constituted by the so-called mildly context-sensitive grammars (Joshi and Schabes 1997). Two grammar formalisms in this class are tree-adjoining grammars (TAGs) and combinatory categorial grammars (CCGs; Joshi and Schabes 1997; Steedman 1997; see also CATEGORIAL GRAMMAR). TAGs are also unification-based grammars.

Parsing sentences according to different grammars is another important research area in CL. Indeed, parsing algorithms are known for almost all context-free grammars used in CL. The time required to parse a sentence of length n is at most Kn^3, where K depends on the size of the grammar and can become very large in the worst case. Most parsers perform much better than the worst case on typical sentences, however, even though there are no computational results, as yet, to characterize their behavior on typical sentences. Grammars that are more powerful than CFGs are, of course, harder to parse, as far as the worst case is concerned. Like CFGs, mildly context-sensitive grammars can all be parsed in polynomial time, although the exponent for n is 6 instead of 3. A crucial problem in parsing is not just to get all possible parses for a sentence but to rank the parses according to some criteria. A grammar can be combined with statistical information to provide this ranking.

Thus far, we have assumed that the parser only handles complete sentences and either succeeds or fails to find the parses. In practice, we want the parser to be flexible. It should be able to handle fragments of sentences, or if it fails, it should fail gracefully, providing as much analysis as possible for as many fragments of the sentence as possible, even if it cannot glue all the pieces together.

Finally, even though the actual grammars in major CL systems are large, their coverage is not adequate. Building a grammar by hand soon reaches its limit in coping with free text (say, text from a newspaper). Increasing attention is being paid both to automatically acquiring grammars from a large corpus and to statistical parsers that produce parses directly based on the training data of the parsed annotated corpora.

Statistical Approaches

Although the idea of somehow combining structural and statistical information was already suggested in the late 1950s, it is only now, when we have formal frameworks suitable for combining structural and statistical information in a principled manner and can use very large corpora to reliably estimate the statistics needed to deduce linguistic structure, that this idea has blossomed in CL.

STATISTICAL TECHNIQUES IN NATURAL LANGUAGE PROCESSING in conjunction with large corpora (raw texts or texts annotated in various ways) have also been used to automatically acquire linguistic information about MORPHOLOGY (prefixes, suffixes, inflected forms), subcategorization, semantic classes (classification of nouns based on what predicates they go with; compound nouns such as *jet engines, stock market prices;* classification of verbs, for example, *to know*, or events, for example, *to look;* and so on), and, of course, grammatical structure itself. Such results have opened up a new direction of research in CL, often described as "corpus-based CL."

It should be clear from the previous discussion that, for the development of corpus-based CL, very large quantities of data are required (the Brown corpus from the 1960s is about 1 million words). Researchers estimate that about 100 million words will be required for some tasks. The technologies that will benefit from corpus-based NLP include speech recognition, SPEECH SYNTHESIS, MACHINE TRANSLATION, full-text information retrieval, and message understanding, among others. The need for establishing very large text and speech databases, annotated in various ways, is now well understood. One such database is the Linguistic Data Consortium (LDC), a national and international resource supported by federal and industrial grants, and useful also for psycholinguistic research (especially in experimental design for controlling lexical and grammatical frequency biases; see http://www.ldc.upenn.edu).

See also COMPUTATIONAL COMPLEXITY; COMPUTATIONAL LEXICONS; COMPUTATIONAL PSYCHOLINGUISTICS; NATURAL LANGUAGE PROCESSING; PSYCHOLINGUISTICS; SENTENCE PROCESSING

—*Aravind K. Joshi*

References

Bresnan, J., and R. M. Kaplan. (1983). *The Mental Representation of Grammatical Relations.* Cambridge, MA: MIT Press.

Gazdar, G., E. Klein, G. K. Pullum, and I. A. Sag. (1985). *Generalized Phrase Structure Grammar.* Cambridge, MA: Harvard University Press.

Joshi, A. K., and Y. Schabes. (1997). Tree-adjoining grammars. In A. Salomma and G. Rozenberg, Eds., *Handbook of Formal Languages and Automata.* Berlin: Springer.

Pollard, C., and I. A. Sag. (1994). *Head-Driven Phrase Structure Grammar.* Chicago: University of Chicago Press.

Steedman, M. (1997). *Surface Structure and Interpretation.* Cambridge, MA: MIT Press.

Survey of the State of Art in Human Language Technology. (Forthcoming). Cambridge: Cambridge University Press. A survey sponsored by the National Science Foundation, the Directorate XIII-E of the Commission of the European Communities, and the Center for Spoken Language Understanding, Oregon Graduate Institute, Corvalis. Currently available at http://www.cse.ogi.edu/CSLU/HLTsurvey.

Computational Neuroanatomy

The term *computational anatomy* was introduced in Schwartz 1980, which suggested that the observables of functional anatomy, such as columnar and topographic structure, be made the basis of the state variables for perceptual computations (rather than, as is universally assumed, some combination of single neuronal response properties). The goal of computational neuroanatomy is to construct a suppraneuronal continuum, or "field theory," approach to neural structure and function, to the "particulate" approach associated with the properties of single neurons. In particular, the details of spatial neuroanatomy of the nervous system are viewed as computational, rather than as mere "packaging" (see Schwartz 1994 for a comprehensive review of the structural and functional correlates of neuroanatomy).

Global Map Structure

It is widely accepted that the cortical magnification factor in primates is approximately inverse linear, at least for the central twenty degrees of field (e.g., Tootell et al. 1985; van Essen, Newsome, and Maunsell 1984; Dow, Vautin, and Bauer 1985), and preliminary results from functional MAGNETIC RESONANCE IMAGING (fMRI) suggest roughly the same for humans. The simple mathematical argument showing there is only one complex analytic two-dimensional map function that has this property, namely, the complex logarithm (Schwartz 1977, 1994), suggested an experiment. Determine the point correspondence data from a 2DG (2-deoxyglucose) experiment, accurately measure the flattened cortical surface, and check the validity of the Reimann mapping theorem prediction of primary visual cortex (V1) topography, or, equivalently, of the hypothesis that global topography in V1 is a generalized conformal map. The results of this experiment (Schwartz, Munsif, and Albright 1989; Schwartz 1994) confirmed that cortical topography is in strong agreement with the conformal mapping hypothesis, up to an error estimated to be roughly 20 percent.

Local Map Structure

A large number of NEURAL NETWORK models have been constructed to address the generation of ocular dominance and orientation columns in cat and monkey VISUAL CORTEX. Surprisingly, the common element in all these models, often not explicitly stated, is the use of a spatial filter applied to spatial white noise (Rojer and Schwartz 1990a). Thus ocular dominance columns are the result of band-pass filtering a scalar white noise variable (ocularity). Orientation columns, as originally pointed out by Rojer and Schwartz (1990a), could be understood as the result of applying a band-pass filter to vector noise, that is, to a vector quantity whose magnitude represented strength of tuning, and whose argument represented orientation. One recent result of this analysis is that the zero-crossings of the cortical orientation map were predicted, on topological grounds, to provide a coordinate system in which left- and right-handed orientation vortices should alternate in handedness (i.e., clockwise or counterclockwise orientation change). This prediction was tested with optical recording data on primate visual cortex orientation maps and found to be in perfect agreement with the data (Tal and Schwartz 1997).

Unified Global and Local Map Structure

A joint map structure to express the global conformal topographic structure, and, at the same time, the local orientation column and ocular dominance column structure of primate V1, was introduced by Landau and Schwartz (1994), making use of a new construct in computational geometry called the "protocolumn."

Global Map Function

One obvious functional advantage of using strongly space-variant (e.g., foveal) architecture in vision is data compression. It has been estimated that a constant-resolution version of visual cortex, were it to retain the full human visual field and maximum human visual resolution, would require roughly 10^4 as many cells as our actual cortex (and would weigh, by inference, roughly 15,000 pounds; Rojer and Schwartz 1990b). The problem of viewing a wide-angle work space at high resolution would seem to be best performed with space-variant visual architectures, an important theme in MACHINE VISION (Schwartz, Greve, and Bonmassar 1995). The complex logarithmic mapping has special properties with respect to size and rotation invariance. For a given fixation point, changing the size or rotating a stimulus causes its cortical representation to shift, but to otherwise remain invariant (Schwartz 1977). This symmetry property provides an excellent example of computational neuroanatomy: simply by virtue of the spatial properties of cortical topography, size and rotation symmetries may be converted into the simpler symmetry of shift. One obvious problem with this idea is that it only works for a given fixation direction. As the eye scans an image, translation invariance is badly broken. Recently, a computational solution to this problem has been found, by generalizing the Fourier transform to complex logarithmic coordinate systems, resulting in a new form of spatial transform, called the "exponential chirp transform" (Bonmassar and Schwartz forthcoming.) The exponential chirp transform, unlike earlier attempts to incorporate Fourier analysis in the context of human vision (e.g., Cavanagh 1978), provides size, rotation, and shift invariance properties, while retaining the fundamental space-variant structure of the visual field.

Local Map Function

The ocular dominance column presents a binocular view of the visual world in the form of thin "stripes," alternating between left- and right-eye representations. One question that immediately arises is how this aspect of cortical anatomy functionally relates to binocular stereopsis. Yeshurun and Schwartz (1989) constructed a computational stereo algorithm based on the assumption that the ocular dominance column structure is a direct representation, as an anatomical pattern, of the stereo percept. It was shown that the power spectrum of the log power spectrum (also known as the "cepstrum") of the interlaced cortical "image" provided a simple and direct measure of stereo disparity of objects in the visual scene. This idea has been subsequently used in a successful machine vision algorithm for stereo vision (Ballard, Becker, and Brown 1988), and provides another excellent illustration of computational neuroanatomy.

The regular local spatial map of orientation response in cat and monkey, originally described by Hubel and Wiesel (1974), suggested the hypothesis that a local analysis of shape, in terms of periodic changes in orientation of a stimulus outline, might provide a basis for shape analysis (Schwartz 1984). A parametric set of shape descriptors, based on shapes whose boundary curvature varied sinusoidally, was used as a probe for the response properties of neurons in infero-temporal cortex, which is one of the final targets for V1, and which is widely believed to be an important site for shape recognition. This work found that a subset of the infero-temporal neurons examined were tuned to stimuli with sinusoidal curvature variation (so-called Fourier descriptors), and that these responses showed a significant amount of size, rotation, and shift invariance (Schwartz et al. 1983).

See also COLUMNS AND MODULES; COMPUTATIONAL NEUROSCIENCE; COMPUTATIONAL VISION; COMPUTING IN SINGLE NEURONS; STEREO AND MOTION PERCEPTION; VISUAL ANATOMY AND PHYSIOLOGY

—*Eric Schwartz*

References

Ballard, D., T. Becker, and C. Brown. (1988). The Rochester robot. *Tech. Report University of Rochester Dept. of Computer Science* 257: 1–65.

Bonmassar, G., and E. Schwartz. (Forthcoming). Space-variant Fourier analysis: The exponential chirp transform. *IEEE Pattern Analysis and Machine Vision*.

Cavanagh, P. (1978). Size and position invariance in the visual system. *Perception* 7: 167–177.

Dow, B., R. G. Vautin, and R. Bauer. (1985). The mapping of visual space onto foveal striate cortex in the macaque monkey. *J. Neuroscience* 5: 890–902.

Hubel, D. H., and T. N. Wiesel. (1974). Sequence regularity and geometry of orientation columns in the monkey striate cortex. *J. Comp. Neurol.* 158: 267–293.

Landau, P., and E. L. Schwartz. (1994). Subset warping: Rubber sheeting with cuts. *Computer Vision, Graphics and Image Processing* 56: 247–266.

Rojer, A., and E. L. Schwartz. (1990a). Cat and monkey cortical columnar patterns modeled by bandpass-filtered 2D white noise. *Biological Cybernetics* 62: 381-391.

Rojer, A., and E. L. Schwartz. (1990b). Design considerations for a space-variant visual sensor with complex-logarithmic geometry. In *10th International Conference on Pattern Recognition*, vol. 2. pp. 278–285.

Schwartz, E. L. (1977). Spatial mapping in primate sensory projection: Analytic structure and relevance to perception. *Biological Cybernetics* 25: 181–194.

Schwartz, E. L. (1980). Computational anatomy and functional architecture of striate cortex: A spatial mapping approach to perceptual coding. *Vision Research* 20: 645–669.

Schwartz, E. L. (1984). Anatomical and physiological correlates of human visual perception. *IEEE Trans. Systems, Man and Cybernetics* 14: 257-271.

Schwartz, E. L. (1994). Computational studies of the spatial architecture of primate visual cortex: Columns, maps, and protomaps. In A. Peters and K. Rocklund, Eds., *Primary Visual Cortex in Primates*, Vol. 10 of *Cerebral Cortex*. New York: Plenum Press.

Schwartz, E. L., R. Desimone, T. Albright, and C. G. Gross. (1983). Shape recognition and inferior temporal neurons. *Proceedings of the National Academy of Sciences* 80: 5776–5778.

Schwartz, E. L., D. Greve, and G. Bonmassar. (1995). Space-variant active vision: Definition, overview and examples. *Neural Networks* 8: 1297–1308.

Schwartz, E. L., A. Munsif, and T. D. Albright. (1989). The topographic map of macaque V1 measured via 3D computer reconstruction of serial sections, numerical flattening of cortex, and conformal image modeling. *Investigative Opthalmol.* Supplement, p. 298.

Tal, D., and E. L. Schwartz. (1997). Topological singularities in cortical orientation maps: The sign theorem correctly predicts orientation column patterns in primate striate cortex. *Network: Computation Neural Sys.* 8: 229–238.

Tootell, R. B., M. S. Silverman, E. Switkes, and R. deValois. (1985). Deoxyglucose, retinotopic mapping and the complex log model in striate cortex. *Science* 227: 1066.

van Essen, D. C., W. T. Newsome, and J. H. R. Maunsell. (1984). The visual representation in striate cortex of the macaque monkey: Asymmetries, anisotropies, and individual variability. *Vision Research* 24: 429–448.

Yeshurun, Y., and E. L. Schwartz. (1989). Cepstral filtering on a columnar image architecture: A fast algorithm for binocular stereo segmentation. *IEEE Trans. Pattern Analysis and Machine Intelligence* 11(7): 759–767.

Computational Neuroscience

The goal of computational neuroscience is to explain in computational terms how brains generate behaviors. Computational models of the brain explore how populations of highly interconnected neurons are formed during development and how they come to represent, process, store, act on, and be altered by information present in the environment (Churchland and Sejnowski 1992). Techniques from computer science and mathematics are used to simulate and analyze these computational models to provide links between the widely ranging levels of investigation, from the molecular to the systems levels. Only a few key aspects of computational neuroscience are covered here (see Arbib 1995 for a comprehensive handbook of brain theory and neural networks).

The term *computational* refers both to the techniques used in computational neuroscience and to the way brains process information. Many different types of physical systems can solve computational problems, including slide rules and optical analog analyzers as well as digital computers, which are analog at the level of transistors and must settle into a stable state on each clock cycle. What these have in common is an underlying correspondence between an abstract computational description of a problem, an algorithm that can solve it, and the states of the physical system that implement it (figure 1). This is a broader approach to COMPUTATION than one based purely on symbol processing.

There is an important distinction between general-purpose computers, which can be programmed to solve many different types of algorithms, and special-purpose computers, which are designed to solve only a limited range of problems. Most neural systems are specialized for particular tasks, such as the RETINA, which is dedicated to visual transduction and image processing. As a consequence of the close coupling between structure and function in a brain area, anatomy and physiology can provide important clues

to the algorithms implemented, and the computational function of that area (figure 1), which might not be apparent in a general-purpose computer whose function depends on software.

Another major difference between the brain and a general-purpose digital computer is that the connectivity between neurons and their properties are shaped by the environment during development and remain plastic even in adulthood. Thus, as the brain processes information, it changes its own structure in response to the information being processed. Adaptation and learning are important mechanisms that allow brains to respond flexibly as the world changes on a wide range of time scales, from seconds to years. The flexibility of the brain has survival advantages when the environment is nonstationary and the evolution of cognitive skills may deeply depend on genetic processes that have extended the time scales for brain plasticity.

Brains are complex, dynamic systems, and brain models provide intuition about the possible behaviors of such systems, especially when they are nonlinear and have feedback loops. The predictions of a model make explicit the consequences of the underlying assumptions, and comparison with experimental results can lead to new insights and discoveries. Emergent properties of neural systems, such as oscillatory behaviors, depend on both the intrinsic properties of the neurons and the pattern of connectivity between them.

Perhaps the most successful model at the level of the NEURON has been the classic Hodgkin-Huxley (1952) model of the action potential in the giant axon of the squid (Koch and Segev 1998). Data were collected under a variety of conditions, and a model later constructed to integrate the data into a unified framework. Because most of the variables in the model are measured experimentally, only a few unknown parameters need to be fit to the experimental data. Detailed models can be used to choose among experiments that could be used to distinguish between different explanations of the data.

The classic model of a neuron, in which information flows from the dendrites, where synaptic signals are integrated, to the soma of the neuron, where action potentials

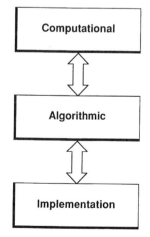

Figure 1. Levels of analysis (Marr 1982). The two-way arrows indicate that constraints between levels can be used to gain insights in both directions.

are initiated and carried to other neurons through long axons, views dendrites as passive cables. Recently, however, voltage-dependent sodium, calcium, and potassium channels have been observed in the dendrites of cortical neurons, which greatly increases the complexity of synaptic integration. Experiments and models have shown that these active currents can carry information in a retrograde direction from the cell body back to the distal synapse tree (see also COMPUTING IN SINGLE NEURONS). Thus it is possible for spikes in the soma to affect synaptic plasticity through mechanisms that were suggested by Donald HEBB in 1949.

Realistic models with several thousand cortical neurons can be explored on the current generation of workstation. The first model for the orientation specificity of neurons in the VISUAL CORTEX was the feedforward model proposed by Hubel and Wiesel (1962), which assumed that the orientation preference of cortical cells was determined primarily by converging inputs from thalamic relay neurons. Although solid experimental evidence supports this model, local cortical circuits have been shown to be important in amplifying weak signals and suppressing noise as well as performing gain control to extend the dynamic range. These models are governed by the type of attractor dynamics analyzed by John Hopfield (1982), who provided a conceptual framework for the dynamics of feedback networks (Churchland and Sejnowski 1992).

Although the spike train of cortical neurons is highly irregular, and is typically treated statistically, information may be contained in the timing of the spikes in addition to the average firing rate. This has already been established for a variety of sensory systems in invertebrates and for peripheral sensory systems in mammals (Rieke et al. 1996). Whether spike timing carries information in cortical neurons remains, however, an open research issue (Ritz and Sejnowski 1997). In addition to representing information, spike timing could also be used to control synaptic plasticity through Hebbian mechanisms for synaptic plasticity.

Other models have been used to analyze experimental data in order to determine whether they are consistent with a particular computational assumption. For example, Apostolos Georgopoulos has used a "vector-averaging" technique to compute the direction of arm motion from the responses of cortical neurons, and William Newsome and his colleagues (Newsome, Britten, and Movshon 1989) have used SIGNAL DETECTION THEORY to analyze the information from cortical neurons responding to visual motion stimuli (Churchland and Sejnowski 1992). In these examples, the computational model was used to explore the information in the data but was not meant to be a model for the actual cortical mechanisms. Nonetheless, these models have been highly influential and have provided new ideas for how the cortex may represent sensory information and motor commands.

A NEURAL NETWORK model that simplifies the intrinsic properties of neurons can help us understand the information contained in populations of neurons and the computational consequences. An example of this approach is a recent model of parietal cortex (Pouget and Sejnowski 1997) based on the response properties of cortical neurons, which are involved in representing spatial location of objects in the environment. Examining which reference frames are used in the cortex for performing sensorimotor transformations, the model makes predictions for experiments performed on patients with lesions of the parietal cortex who display spatial neglect.

Conceptual models can be helpful in organizing experimental facts. Although thalamic neurons that project to the cortex are called "relay cells," they almost surely have additional functions because the visual cortex makes massive feedback projections back to them. Francis Crick (1994) has proposed that the relay cells in the THALAMUS may be involved in ATTENTION, and has provided an explanation for how this could be accomplished based on the anatomy of the thalamus. His searchlight model of attention and other hypotheses for the function of the thalamus are being explored with computational models and new experimental techniques. Detailed models of thalamocortical networks can already reproduce the low-frequency oscillations observed during SLEEP states, when feedback connections to the thalamus affect the spatial organization of the rhythms. These sleep rhythms may be important for memory consolidation (Sejnowski 1995).

Finally, small neural systems have been analyzed with dynamic systems theory. This approach is feasible when the numbers of parameters and variables are small. Most models of neural networks involve a large number of variables, such as membrane potentials, firing rates, and concentrations of ions, with an even greater number of unknown parameters, such as synaptic strengths, rate constants, and ionic conductances. In the limit that the number of neurons and parameters is very large, techniques from statistical physics can be applied to predict the average behavior of large systems. There is a midrange of systems where neither type of limiting analysis is possible, but where simulations can be performed. One danger of relying solely on computer simulations is that they may be as complex and difficult to interpret as the biological systems themselves.

To better understand the higher cognitive functions, we will need to scale up simulations from thousands to millions of neurons. While parallel computers are available that permit massively parallel simulations, the difficulty of programming these computers has limited their usefulness. A new approach to massively parallel models has been introduced by Carver Mead (1989), who builds subthreshold complementary metal-oxide semiconductor Very-Large-Scale Integrated (CMOS VLSI) circuits with components that directly mimic the analog computational operations in neurons. Several large silicon chips have been built that mimic the visual processing found in retinas. Analog VLSI cochleas have also been built that can analyze sound in real time. These chips use analog voltages and currents to represent the signals, and are extremely efficient in their use of power compared to digital VLSI chips. A new branch of engineering called "neuromorphic engineering" has arisen to exploit this technology.

Recently, analog VLSI chips have been designed and built that mimic the detailed biophysical properties of neurons, including dendritic processing and synaptic conductances (Douglas, Mahowald, and Mead 1995), which has opened the possibility of building a "silicon cortex." Protocols are being designed for long-distance communication between analog VLSI chips using the equivalent of all-or-none spikes, to mimic long-distance communication between neurons.

Many of the design issues that govern the evolution of biological systems also arise in neuromorphic systems, such as the trade-off in cost between short-range connections and expensive long-range communication. Computational models that quantify this trade-off and apply a minimization procedure can predict the overall organization of topographical maps and columnar organization of the CEREBRAL CORTEX.

Although brain models are now routinely used as tools for interpreting data and generating hypotheses, we are still a long way from having explanatory theories of brain function. For example, despite the relatively stereotyped anatomical structure of the CEREBELLUM, we still do not understand its computational functions. Recent evidence from functional imaging of the cerebellum suggests that it is involved in higher cognitive functions, and not just a motor controller. Modeling studies may help to sort out competing hypotheses. This has already occurred in the oculomotor system, which has a long tradition of using control theory models to guide experimental studies.

Computational neuroscience is a relatively young, rapidly growing discipline. Although we can now simulate only small parts of neural systems, as digital computers continue to increase in speed, it should become possible to approach more complex problems. Most of the models developed thus far have been aimed at interpreting experimental data and providing a conceptual framework for the dynamic properties of neural systems. A more comprehensive theory of brain function should arise as we gain a broader understanding of the computational resources of nervous systems at all levels of organization.

See also COMPUTATION AND THE BRAIN; COMPUTATIONAL NEUROANATOMY; COMPUTATIONAL THEORY OF MIND

—*Terrence J. Sejnowski*

References

Arbib, A. M. (1995). *The Handbook of Brain Theory and Neural Networks.* Cambridge, MA: MIT Press.

Churchland P. S., and T. J. Sejnowski. (1992). *The Computational Brain.* Cambridge, MA: MIT Press.

Crick, F. H. C. (1994). *The Astonishing Hypothesis: The Scientific Search for the Soul.* New York: Scribner.

Douglas R., M. Mahowald, and C. Mead. (1995). Neuromorphic analogue VLSI. *Annual Review of Neuroscience* 18: 255–281.

Hebb, D. O. (1949). *Organization of Behavior.* New York: Wiley.

Hodgkin, A. L., and A. F. Huxley. (1952). A quantitative description of membrane current and its application to conduction and excitation in nerve. *J. Physiol.* 117: 500–544.

Hopfield, J. J. (1982). Neural networks and physical systems with emergent collective computational abilities. *Proc Natl Acad Sci USA* 79: 2554–2558.

Hubel, D., and T. Wiesel. (1962). Receptive fields, binocular interaction and functional architecture in the cat's visual cortex. *Journal of Physiology* 160: 106–154.

Koch, C., and I. Segev. (1998). *Methods in Neuronal Modeling: From Synapses to Networks.* Second edition. Cambridge, MA: MIT Press.

Marr, D. (1982). *Vision.* San Francisco: Freeman.

Mead, C., and M. Ismail, Eds. (1989). Analog VLSI implementation of neural systems. Boston: Kluwer Academic Publishers.

Newsome, W. T., K. H. Britten, and J. A. Movshon. (1989). Neuronal correlates of a perceptual decision. *Nature* 341: 52–54

Pouget, A., and T. J. Sejnowski. (1997). A new view of hemineglect based on the response properties of parietal neurons. *Philosophical Transactions of the Royal Society* 352: 1449–1459.

Rieke, F., D. Warland, R. de Ruyter van Steveninck, and W. Bialek. (1996). *Spikes: Exploring the Neural Code.* Cambridge, MA: MIT Press.

Ritz, R., and T. J. Sejnowski. (1997). Synchronous oscillatory activity in sensory systems: New vistas on mechanisms. *Current Opinion in Neurobiology* 7: 536–546.

Sejnowski, T. J. (1995). Sleep and memory. *Current Biology* 5: 832–834.

Computational Psycholinguistics

In PSYCHOLINGUISTICS, computational models are becoming increasingly important both for helping us understand and develop our theories and for deriving empirical predictions from those theories. How a theory of language processing behaves usually depends not just on the mechanics of the model itself, but also on the properties of the linguistic input. Even when the theory is conceptually simple, the interaction between theory and language is often too complex to be explored without the benefit of computer simulations. It is no surprise then that computational models have been at the center of some of the most significant recent developments in psycholinguistics.

The main area of contact with empirical data has been made by models operating roughly at the level of the word. Although there are active and productive efforts underway to develop models of higher-level processes such as syntactic parsing (Kempen and Vosse 1989; McRoy and Hirst 1990; Marcus 1980) and discourse (Kintsch and van Dijk 1978; Kintsch 1988; Sharkey 1990), the complexity of these processes makes it harder to derive detailed experimental predictions.

The neighborhood activation model (Luce, Pisoni, and Goldinger 1990) gives a computational account of isolated word recognition, but only TRACE (McClelland and Elman 1986) and Shortlist (Norris 1994a) have been applied to the more difficult problem of how words can be recognized in continuous speech, where the input may contain no reliable cues to indicate where one word ends and another begins. Both of these models are descendants of McClelland and Rumelhart's (1981) connectionist interactive activation model (IAM) of VISUAL WORD RECOGNITION. The central principle of both models is that the input can activate multiple word candidates, represented by nodes in a network, and that these candidates then compete with each other by means of inhibitory links between overlapping candidates. Thus the spoken input "get in" might activate "tin" as well as "get" and "in," but "tin" would be inhibited by the other two overlapping words. TRACE and Shortlist represent opposite positions in the debate over whether SPOKEN WORD RECOGNITION is an interactive process. In TRACE there is continuous interaction between the lexical and phonemic levels of representation, whereas Shortlist has a completely bottom-up, modular architecture. They also differ in their solution to the problem of how to recognize words beginning at different points in time. TRACE uses a permanent set of complete lexical networks beginning at each point where a word might begin. In Shortlist the network performing the lexical competition is created dynamically and contains only those candidates identified by a bottom-up analysis of the input. On a purely practical level, at least, this has the advantage of enabling Shortlist to perform simulations with realistically sized lexicons of twenty or thirty thousand words. Shortlist has also been extended (Norris, McQueen and Cutler 1995) to incorporate the metrical segmentation strategy of Cutler and Norris (1988), which enables the model to make use of metrical cues to word boundaries.

The most significant nonconnectionist model of spoken word recognition has been Oden and Massaro's (1978) fuzzy logical model of perception (FLMP). FLMP differs from TRACE and Shortlist in that it can be seen as a generic account of how decisions are made on the basis of information from different sources. FLMP itself has nothing to say, for example, about the competition process vital for the recognition of words in continuous speech in both TRACE and Shortlist. Comparisons between FLMP and TRACE in terms of their treatment of the relationship between lexical and phonemic information led to a major revision of the IAM framework and the development of the stochastic interactive activation model (Massaro 1989; McClelland 1991).

IAMs and spreading activation models have also been predominant in the area of LANGUAGE PRODUCTION (Dell 1986, 1988; Harley 1993; Roelofs 1992; see also Houghton 1990). Dell's model is designed to account for the nature and distribution of speech errors. It takes as its input an ordered set of word units (lemmas), representing the speaker's intended production, and produces as its output a string of phonemes that may be corrupted or misordered. In Dell (1988) the model consists of a lexical network in which word nodes are connected to their constituent phonemes by reciprocal links and by a word shape network that reads out successive phonemes in the appropriate syllable structure. The main effect of the reciprocal links from phonemes to words is to give the model a tendency for its errors to form real rather than nonsense words. Whether the production system really does contain these feedback links has been the topic of extensive debate between Dell and Levelt. Levelt, Roelofs, and Meyer (forthcoming) describe the latest computational implementation of the WEAVER++ model, which is a noninteractive spreading activation model designed to account for an extensive body of response time (RT) data on production as well as speech error data.

The most controversial connectionist model of language has been the Rumelhart and McClelland (1986) model for acquisition of the past tense of verbs. Conventional linguistic accounts of quasi-regular systems such as the past tense assume that the proper explanation is in terms of rules and a list of exceptions. Rumelhart and McClelland modeled the acquisition of the past tense using a simple pattern associator that mapped the phonology of verb roots (e.g., *kill, run*) onto their past tense forms (*killed, ran*). They claimed that their model not only explained important facts about the acquisition of verbs, but that it did so without using linguistic rules.

The model was fiercely criticized by Pinker and Prince (1988). Later models by MacWhinney and Leinbach (1991) and Plunkett and Marchman (1991, 1993), using backpropagation with hidden units, rectified some of the technical deficiencies of the original model, and claimed to give a more accurate account of the developmental data, but the debate between the connectionist and symbolic camps continues. Recently reported neuropsychological and neuroimaging data suggest a neuroanatomical distinction between mechanisms underlying the rule-based and non-rule-based processes (e.g., Marslen-Wilson and Tyler forthcoming).

A parallel set of arguments has surrounded models of reading aloud. The relationship between spelling and sound is another example of a quasi-regular system where backpropagation networks have been used to give a unitary account of the READING process rather than incorporating spelling-to-sound rules and a list of exception words (e.g., *yacht, choir*) not pronounced according to the rules (Seidenberg and McClelland 1989; Plaut et al. 1996). The more traditional two-process view is represented by Coltheart et al. (1993), while an interactive activation model by Norris (1994b) takes an intermediate stance.

See also COGNITIVE MODELING, CONNECTIONIST; COMPUTATIONAL LINGUISTICS; CONNECTIONIST APPROACHES TO LANGUAGE; PROSODY AND INTONATION, PROCESSING ISSUES; SENTENCE PROCESSING

—Dennis Norris

References

Coltheart, M., B. Curtis, P. Atkins, and M. Haller. (1993). Models of reading aloud: Dual-route and parallel-distributed-processing approaches. *Psychological Review* 100: 589–608.

Cutler, A., and D. Norris. (1988). The role of strong syllables in segmentation for lexical access. *Journal of Experimental Psychology: Human Perception and Performance* 14: 113–121.

Dell, G. S. (1986). A spreading-activation theory of retrieval in sentence production. *Psychological Review* 82: 407–428.

Dell, G. S. (1988). The retrieval of phonological forms in production: Tests of predictions from a connectionist model. *Journal of Memory and Language* 27: 124–142.

Dijkstra, T., and K. de Smedt, Eds. (1996). *Computational Psycholinguistics*. London: Taylor and Francis.

Harley, T. A. (1993). Phonological activation of semantic competitors during lexical access in speech production. *Language and Cognitive Processes* 8: 291–309.

Houghton, G. (1990). The problem of serial order: A neural network model of sequence learning and recall. In R. Dale, C. Mellish, and M. Zock, Eds., *Current Research in Natural Language Generation*. London: Academic Press, pp. 289–319.

Kempen, G., and T. Vosse. (1989). Incremental syntactic tree formation in human sentence processing: A cognitive architecture based on activation decay and simulated annealing. *Connection Science* 1: 273–290.

Kintsch, W. (1988). The role of knowledge in discourse comprehension: A construction-integration model. *Psychological Review* 95: 163–182.

Kintsch, W., and T. A. van Dijk. (1978). Towards a model of text comprehension and production. *Psychological Review* 85: 363–394.

Levelt, W. J. M., A. Roelofs, and A. S. Meyer. (Forthcoming). A theory of lexical access in speech production. *Brain and Behavioural Sciences*.

Luce, P. A., D. B. Pisoni, and S. D. Goldinger. (1990). Similarity neighborhoods of spoken words. In G. T. M. Altmann, Ed., *Cognitive Models of Speech Processing: Psycholinguistic and Computational Perspectives.* Cambridge, MA: MIT Press, pp. 122–147.

MacWhinney, B., and J. Leinbach. (1991). Implementations are not conceptualizations: Revising the verb learning model. *Cognition* 40: 121–157.

Marcus, M. P. (1980). *A Theory of Syntactic Recognition for Natural Language.* Cambridge, MA: MIT Press.

Marslen-Wilson, W. M., and L. K. Tyler. (Forthcoming). Dissociating types of mental computation. *Nature.*

Massaro, D. W. (1989). Testing between the TRACE model and the Fuzzy Logical Model of Perception. *Cognitive Psychology* 21: 398–421.

McClelland, J. L. (1991). Stochastic interactive processes and the effects of context on perception. *Cognitive Psychology* 23: 1–44.

McClelland, J. L., and J. L. Elman. (1986). The TRACE model of speech perception. *Cognitive Psychology* 18: 1–86.

McClelland, J. L., and D. E. Rumelhart. (1981). An interactive activation model of context effects in letter perception: 1. An account of the basic findings. *Psychological Review* 88: 375–407.

McRoy, S. W., and G. Hirst. (1990). Race-based parsing and syntactic disambiguation. *Cognitive Science* 14: 313–353.

Norris, D. (1994a). Shortlist: A connectionist model of continuous speech recognition. *Cognition* 52: 189–234.

Norris, D. (1994b). A quantitative multiple-levels model of reading aloud. *Journal of Experimental Psychology: Human Perception and Performance* 20(6): 1212–1232.

Norris, D., J. M. McQueen, and A. Cutler. (1995). Competition and segmentation in spoken word recognition. *Journal of Experimental Psychology: Learning, Memory, and Cognition* 21: 1209–1228.

Oden, G. C., and D. W. Massaro. (1978). Integration of featural information in speech perception. *Psychological Review* 1985: 172–191.

Pinker, S., and A. Prince. (1988). On language and connectionism: Analysis of a parallel distributed processing model of language acquisition. *Cognition* 28: 73–193.

Plaut, D. C., J. L. McClelland, M. Seidenberg, and K. E. Patterson. (1996). Understanding normal and impaired word reading: Computational principles in quasi-regular domains. *Psychological Review* 103: 56–115.

Plunkett, K., and V. Marchman. (1991). U-shaped learning and frequency effects in a multi-layered perceptron: Implications for child language acquisition. *Cognition* 38: 43–102.

Plunkett, K., and V. Marchman. (1993). From rote learning to system building: Acquiring verb morphology in children and connectionist nets. *Cognition* 48: 21–69.

Roelofs, A. (1992). A spreading-activation theory of lemma retrieval in speaking. *Cognition* 42: 107–142.

Roelofs, A. (1996). Serial order in planning the production of successive morphemes of a word. *Journal of Memory and Language* 35: 854–876.

Rumelhart, D. E., and J. L. McClelland. (1986). On learning the past tense of English verbs. In McClelland and Rumelhart, Eds., *Parallel Distributed Processing: Explorations in the Microstructure of Cognition.* Cambridge, MA: MIT Press.

Seidenberg, M., and J. L. McClelland. (1989). A distributed developmental model of word recognition and naming. *Psychological Review* 96: 523–568.

Sharkey, N. E. (1990). A connectionist model of text comprehension. In D.A. Balota and G. B. Flores d'Arcais, Eds., *Comprehension Processes in Reading.* Hillsdale, NJ: Erlbaum, pp. 487–514.

Computational Theory of Mind

The computational theory of mind (CTM) holds that the mind is a digital computer: a discrete-state device that stores symbolic representations and manipulates them according to syntactic rules; that thoughts are mental representations—more specifically, symbolic representations in a LANGUAGE OF THOUGHT; and that mental processes are causal sequences driven by the syntactic, but not the semantic, properties of the symbols. Putnam (1975) was perhaps the first to articulate CTM, but it has found many proponents, the most influential being Fodor (1975, 1981, 1987, 1990, 1993) and Pylyshyn (1980, 1984).

CTM's proponents view the theory as an extension of the much older idea that thought is MENTAL REPRESENTATION—an extension that shows us how a commitment to mental states can be compatible with a causal account of mental processes and with a commitment to materialism and the generality of physics. Older breeds of representationalism were unable to explain how mental processes could be semantically coherent—how thoughts could follow one another in a fashion appropriate to their meanings, while also being bona fide causal processes that did not depend on an inner homunculus who understood the meanings of the representations. Using formalization and digital computers, however, we can explain how this occurs. Formalization shows us how to link semantics to syntax. For any formalizable symbol system, it is possible to develop a set of formal derivation rules, based wholly on syntactic properties, that license all and only the inferences permissible on semantic grounds. Computers show us how to link syntax to causation. For any finite formal system, it is possible to construct a digital computer that automates the derivations of that system. Thus, together, formalization and computation show us how to link semantics to causation in a material system like a digital computer: design a set of syntactic rules that "track" the semantic properties of the symbols (i.e., formalize the system), and then implement those rules in a computer. Because digital computers are purely physical systems, this shows us it is possible for a purely physical system to carry out symbolic inferences that respect the semantics of the symbols without recourse to a homunculus or to any other nonphysical agency. Syntactic properties are the causal determinants of reasoning, syntax tracks semantics, and syntactic properties can be implemented in a physical system.

CTM has been touted both for its connections to successful empirical research in cognitive science and for its promise in resolving philosophical problems. The main argument in favor of the language of thought hypothesis and CTM has been the "only game in town" argument: cognitive theories of language, learning, and other psychological phenomena are the only viable theories we possess, and these theories presuppose an inner representational system. Therefore we have a prima facie commitment to the existence of such a representational system (Fodor 1975). Some have claimed that CTM also explains the INTENTIONALITY of mental states and that it reconciles mentalism with materialism. The meanings and intentionality of mental states are "inherited from" the meanings and intentionality of the "mentalese" symbols (Fodor 1981). And because symbols, the ultimate bearers of semantic properties and intentionality, can both have meaning and be physical objects, there is not even a prima facie conflict between a commitment to semantics and intentionality and a commitment to materialism. Finally, CTM has been held to explain the generative and creative powers of thought that result from the COMPOSITIONALITY of the language of thought. Chomskian linguistics shows us how an infinite number of possible sentences can be generated out of a finite number of atomic lexical units, syntactic structures, and transformation rules. If the basis of thought is a symbolic language, these same resources can be applied directly to explain the compositionality of thought.

Although CTM gained a great deal of currency in the late 1970s and 1980s, it has since been criticized on a number of fronts. First, with philosophers' rediscovery in the late 1980s of alternative approaches to psychological modeling, represented in NEURAL NETWORKS and dynamic adaptive systems, the empirical premise of the "only game in town" argument has been brought into question. Indeed, the main thrust of philosophical debate about neural networks and connectionism has been over whether their models of psychological phenomena are viable alternatives to rule-and-representation models.

Second, writers such as Dreyfus (1972, 1992) and Winograd and Flores (1986) have claimed that much human thought and behavior cannot be reduced to explicit rules, and hence cannot be formalized or reduced to a computer program. Thus, even if CTM does say something significant about the parts of human cognition that can be formalized, there are large portions of human mental life about which it can say nothing. Dreyfus and others have attempted to argue that this includes all expert knowledge and such simple skills as knowing how to drive a car or order in a restaurant.

A third line of criticism has been directed at CTM's use of symbolic meaning to explain the semantics of thought, on the grounds that symbolic meaning is derivative from the intentionality of thought, either causally (Searle 1980; Haugeland 1978; Sayre 1986) or conceptually (Horst 1996). Thus the attempt to explain intentionality by appeal to symbols is circular and regressive. Searle (1990) and Horst (1996) have taken this line of argument even further, claiming that the "representations" in computers are not even symbolic or syntactic in their own right, but possess these properties by virtue of the intentions and conventions of computer users: a digital machine not connected to our interpretive practices has a "syntax" only in a metaphorical sense of that word. Horst's version of these criticisms also yields an argument against the claim to reconcile mentalism with materialism: what digital computers show us how to do is to link convention-laden symbolic meaning with CAUSATION by way of convention-laden syntax, not to link the sense of "meaning" attributed to mental states with causation.

A fourth line of criticism has come from advocates of externalist theories of meaning. For many years, advocates of CTM tended also to be advocates of a "methodological solipsism" (Fodor 1980) or INDIVIDUALISM who held that the typing of mental states needed to be insensitive to features outside of the cognizer because the computational processes that determined thought have access only to mental representations. At the same time, CTM required that the typing of mental states reflect their semantic properties. These two commitments together seemed to be incompatible with externalist theories of content, which hold that the meanings of many terms are at least partially determined by factors that lie outside of the cognizer, such as its physical (Putnam 1975) and linguistic (Burge 1979, 1986) environment. This was used by some externalists (e.g., Baker 1987) as an argument against computationalism, and was used at least at one time by Fodor (1980) as a reason to reject externalism. Nevertheless, at least some computationalists, including Fodor (1993), have now embraced strategies for reconciling computational theories of mental processes with externalist theories of meaning for mental representations.

See also CHINESE ROOM ARGUMENT; COMPUTATION AND THE BRAIN; CONNECTIONISM, PHILOSOPHICAL ISSUES; FUNCTIONALISM; NARROW CONTENT; RULES AND REPRESENTATIONS

—*Steven Horst*

References

Baker, L. R. (1987). *Saving Belief: A Critique of Physicalism.* Princeton: Princeton University Press.

Burge, T. (1979). Individualism and the mental. In P. French, T. Euhling, and H. Wettstein, Eds., *Studies in Epistemology,* Midwest Studies in Philosophy, vol. 4. Minneapolis: University of Minnesota Press.

Burge, T. (1986). Individualism and psychology. *Philosophical Review* 95(1): 3–45.

Dreyfus, H. (1972). *What Computers Can't Do.* New York: Harper and Row.

Dreyfus, H. (1992). *What Computers Still Can't Do.* Cambridge, MA: MIT Press.

Fodor, J. (1975). *The Language of Thought.* New York: Crowell.

Fodor, J. (1980). Methodological solipsism considered as a research strategy in cognitive science. *Behavioral and Brain Sciences* 3: 63–73.

Fodor, J. (1981). *Representations.* Cambridge, MA: MIT Press.

Fodor, J. (1987). *Psychosemantics.* Cambridge, MA: MIT Press.

Fodor, J. (1990). *A Theory of Content and Other Essays.* Cambridge, MA: MIT Press.

Fodor, J. (1993). *The Elm and the Expert.* Cambridge, MA: MIT Press.

Haugeland, J. (1978). The nature and plausibility of cognitivism. *Behavioral and Brain Sciences* 2: 215–226.

Haugeland, J., Ed. (1981). *Mind Design.* Cambridge, MA: MIT Press.

Horst, S. (1996). *Symbols, Computation and Intentionality: A Critique of the Computational Theory of Mind.* Berkeley and Los Angeles: University of California Press.

Putnam, H. (1975). The Meaning of "Meaning." In K. Gunderson, Ed., *Language, Mind and Knowledge.* Minnesota Studies in the Philosophy of Science, vol. 7. Minneapolis: University of Minnesota Press.

Pylyshyn, Z. (1980). Computation and cognition: Issues in the foundation of cognitive science. *Behavioral and Brain Sciences* 3: 111–132.

Pylyshyn, Z. (1984). *Computation and Cognition: Toward a Foundation for Cognitive Science.* Cambridge, MA: MIT Press.

Sayre, K. (1986). Intentionality and information processing: An alternative model for cognitive science. *Behavioral and Brain Sciences* 9(1): 121–138.

Searle, J. (1980). Minds, brains and programs. *Behavioral and Brain Sciences* 3: 417–424.

Searle, J. (1984). Minds, brains and science. Cambridge, MA: Harvard University Press.

Searle, J. (1990). Presidential address. *Proceedings of the American Philosophical Association.*

Searle, J. (1992). *The Rediscovery of the Mind.* Cambridge, MA: MIT Press.

Winograd, T., and F. Flores. (1986). *Understanding Computers and Cognition.* Norwood, NJ: Ablex.

Further Readings

Cummins, R. (1989). *Meaning and Mental Representation.* Cambridge, MA: MIT Press.

Garfield, J. (1988). *Belief in Psychology: A Study in the Ontology of Mind.* Cambridge, MA: MIT Press.

Newell, A., and H. Simon. (1975). Computer science as empirical inquiry. (1975 Turing Lecture.) Reprinted in J. Haugeland, Ed., *Mind Design.* Cambridge, MA: MIT Press, 1981, pp. 35–66.

Putnam, H. (1960). Minds and machines. In S. Hook, Ed., *Dimensions of Mind.* New York: New York University Press, pp. 138–164.

Putnam, H. (1961). Brains and behavior. Reprinted in Ned Block, Ed., *Readings in Philosophy of Psychology.* Cambridge, MA: Harvard University Press, 1980, pp. 24–36.

Putnam, H. (1967). The nature of mental states. In W. H. Capitan and D. D. Merrill, Eds., *Art, Mind and Religion.* Pittsburgh: University of Pittsburgh Press. Reprinted in Ned Block, Ed., *Readings in Philosophy of Psychology.* Cambridge, MA: Harvard University Press, 1980, pp. 223–231.

Rumelhart, D. E., J. McClelland, and the PDP Research Group. (1986). *Parallel Distributed Processing: Explorations in the Microstructure of Cognition.* Cambridge, MA: MIT Press.

Sayre, K. (1987). Cognitive science and the problem of semantic content. *Synthèse* 70: 247–269.

Smolensky, P. (1988). The proper treatment of Connectionism. *Behavioral and Brain Sciences* 11(1): 1–74.

Computational Vision

The analysis of a visual image yields a rich understanding of what is in the world, where objects are located, and how they are changing with time, allowing a biological or machine system to recognize and manipulate objects and to interact physically with its environment. The computational approach to the study of vision explores the information-processing mechanisms needed to extract this important information. The integration of a computational perspective with experimental studies of biological vision systems from psychology and neuroscience can ultimately yield a more complete functional understanding of the neural mechanisms underlying visual processing.

Vision begins with a large array of measurements of the light reflected from object surfaces onto the eye. Analysis then proceeds in multiple stages, with each producing increasingly more useful representations of information in the scene. Computational studies suggest three primary representational stages. *Early representations* may capture information such as the location, contrast, and sharpness of significant intensity changes or edges in the image. Such changes correspond to physical features such as object boundaries, texture contours, and markings on object surfaces, shadow boundaries, and highlights. In the case of a dynamically changing scene, the early representations may also describe the direction and speed of movement of image intensity changes. *Intermediate representations* describe information about the three-dimensional (3-D) shape of object surfaces from the perspective of the viewer, such as the orientation of small surface regions or the distance to surface points from the eye. Such representations may also describe the motion of surface features in three dimensions. Visual processing may then proceed to higher-level representations of objects that describe their 3-D shape, form, and orientation relative to a coordinate frame based on the objects or on a fixed location in the world. Tasks such as object recognition, object manipulation, and navigation may operate from the intermediate or higher-level representations of the 3-D layout of objects in the world. (See also MACHINE VISION for a discussion of representations for visual processing.)

Models for computing the early representations of intensity edges typically begin by filtering the image with filters that smooth and differentiate the image intensities. Smoothing at multiple spatial scales allows the simultaneous representation of the gross structure of image contours, while preserving the fine detail of surface markings and TEXTURE. The differentiation operation transforms the image into a representation that facilitates the localization of edge contours and computation of properties such as their sharpness and contrast. Significant intensity changes may correspond to maxima, or peaks, in the first derivative, or to zero-crossings in the second derivative, of the image intensities. Subsequent image analysis may operate on a representation of image contours. Alternative models suggest that later processes operate directly on the result of the filtering stage.

Several sources of information are used to compute the 3-D shape of object surfaces. Binocular stereo uses the relative location of corresponding features in the images seen by the left and right eyes to infer the distance to object surfaces. Abrupt changes in motion between adjacent image regions indicate object boundaries, while smooth variations in the direction and speed of motion within image regions can be used to recover surface shape. Other cues include systematic variations in the geometric structure of image textures, such as changes in the orientation, size, or density of texture elements; image shading, which refers to smooth variations of intensity that occur as surfaces bend toward or away from a light source; and perspective, which refers to the distortion of object contours that results from the perspective projection of the 3-D scene onto the two-dimensional (2-D) image. (See STRUCTURE FROM VISUAL INFORMATION SOURCES and STEREO AND MOTION PERCEPTION for further discussion of visual cues to structure and form.)

The computation of 3-D structure cannot proceed unambiguously from the 2-D image alone. Models also incorporate physical constraints that capture the typical behavior of objects in the world. For the early and intermediate stages of processing, these constraints are as general as possible. Existing models use constraints based on the following typical behaviors: object surfaces are coherent and typically vary smoothly and continuously from one image location to the next; objects usually move rigidly, at least within small image regions; illumination usually shines from above the observer; changes in the reflectance properties of a surface (such as its color) usually occur abruptly while illumination may vary slowly across the image. Models also incorporate the known physics of how the image is formed from the perspective projection of light reflected from surfaces onto the eyes. Computational studies of vision identify appropriate physical constraints and show how they can be built into a specific algorithm for computing the image representations.

Among cues for recovering 3-D structure from 2-D images, the two most extensively studied by computational and biological researchers are binocular stereo and motion. For both stereo and motion measurement, the most challenging computational problem is the correspondence problem. Given a representation of features in the left and right images, or two images displaced in time, a matching process must identify pairs of features in the two images that are projections of the same physical structure in space. Many models attempt to match edge features in the two images. Some models, such as an early model of human stereo vision proposed by MARR and Poggio (Marr 1982), simultaneously match image edge representations at multiple spatial scales. The correspondence of features at a coarse scale can provide a rough 3-D layout of a scene that can guide the correspondence of features at finer scales. Information such as the orientation or contrast of edge features can help identify pairs of similar features likely to correspond to one another. Stereo and motion models also typically use physical constraints such as uniqueness (i.e., features in one image have a unique corresponding feature in the other) and continuity or smoothness (i.e., nearby features in the image lie at similar depths or have a similar direction and speed of motion). Many models incorporate some form of optimization: a solution is found that best satisfies a complex set of criteria based on all of the physical constraints taken together. In the case of motion processing, the analysis of the movement of features in the changing 2-D image is followed by a process that infers the 3-D structure of the moving features. Most computational models of this inference use the rigidity constraint: they attempt to find a rigidly moving 3-D structure consistent with the computed 2-D image motion. (For specific models of stereo and motion processing, see Faugeras 1993; Hildreth and Ullman 1989; Kasturi and Jain 1991; Landy and Movshon 1991; Marr 1982; Martin and Aggarwal 1988; and Wandell 1995.)

Much attention has been devoted to the higher-level problem of object recognition, which requires that a representation derived from a viewed object in the image be matched with internal representations of a similar object stored in memory. Most computational models consider the recognition of objects on the basis of their 2-D or 3-D shape. Recognition is difficult because a given 3-D object can have many appearances in the 2-D image. Most recognition models can be classified into three main approaches. The first assumes that objects have certain invariant properties that are common to all of their views. Recognition typically proceeds in this case by first computing a set of simple geometric properties of a viewed object from image information, and then selecting an object model that offers the closest fit to the set of observed property values. The second approach focuses on the decomposition of objects into primitive, salient parts. In this case, models first find primitive parts in an image, and then identify objects on the basis of the detected parts and their spatial arrangement. The best-known model of this type was proposed by Biederman (1985; see Ullman 1996). The third major approach to object recognition uses a process that explicitly compensates for the transformation between a viewed object and its stored model. One example of this approach proposed by Ullman (1996) first computes the geometric transformations that best explain the mapping between a viewed object and each object model in a database. A second stage then recognizes the object by finding which combination of object model and transformation best matches the viewed object. (Some specific models of recognition are described in Faugeras 1993 and Ullman 1996.)

See also OBJECT RECOGNITION, ANIMAL STUDIES; OBJECT RECOGNITION, HUMAN NEUROPSYCHOLOGY; SURFACE PERCEPTION; VISUAL OBJECT RECOGNITION, AI; VISION AND LEARNING

—*Ellen Hildreth*

References

Biederman, I. (1985). Human image understanding: Recent research and a theory. *Computer Vision, Graphics, and Image Processing* 32: 29–73.

Faugeras, O. (1993). *Three-Dimensional Computer Vision: A Geometric Viewpoint.* Cambridge, MA: MIT Press.

Haralick, R. M., and L. G. Shapiro. (1992). *Computer and Robot Vision.* 2 vols. Reading, MA: Addison-Wesley.

Hildreth, E. C., and S. Ullman. (1989). The computational study of vision. In M. Posner, Ed., *Foundations of Cognitive Science.* Cambridge, MA: MIT Press, pp. 581–630.

Horn, B. K. P. (1989). *Shape from Shading.* Cambridge, MA: MIT Press.

Kasturi, R., and R. C. Jain, Eds. (1991). *Computer Vision: Principles.* Los Alamitos, CA: IEEE Computer Society Press.

Landy, M. S., and J. A. Movshon, Eds. (1991). *Computational Models of Visual Processing.* Cambridge, MA: MIT Press.

Marr, D. (1982). *Vision.* San Francisco: Freeman.

Martin, W. N., and J. K. Aggarwal, Eds. (1988). *Motion Understanding: Robot and Human Vision.* Boston: Kluwer.

Ullman, S. (1996). *High-level Vision: Object Recognition and Visual Cognition.* Cambridge, MA: MIT Press.

Wandell, B. A. (1995). *Foundations of Vision.* Sunderland, MA: Sinauer.

Further Readings

Aloimonos, J., and D. Shulman. (1989). *Integration of Visual Modules.* Boston: Academic Press.

Blake, A., and A. Yuille, Eds. (1992). *Active Vision.* Cambridge, MA: MIT Press.

Blake, A., and A. Zisserman. (1987). *Visual Reconstruction.* Cambridge: MIT Press.

Brooks, R. A. (1991). Intelligence without representation. *Artificial Intelligence Journal* 47: 139–160.

Fischler, M. A., and O. Firschein, Eds. (1987). *Readings in Computer Vision: Issues, Problems, Principles, and Paradigms.* Los Altos, CA: Kaufman.

Grimson, W. E. L. (1990). *Object Recognition by Computer: The Role of Geometric Constraints.* Cambridge, MA: MIT Press.

Horn, B. K. P. (1986). *Robot Vision.* Cambridge, MA: MIT Press.

Kanade, T., Ed. (1987). *Three-Dimensional Machine Vision.* Boston: Kluwer.

Koenderink, J. J. (1990). *Solid Shape.* Cambridge, MA: MIT Press.

Levine, M. D. (1985). *Vision in Man and Machine.* New York: McGraw-Hill.

Lowe, D. (1985). *Perceptual Organization and Visual Recognition.* Cambridge, MA: MIT Press.

Malik, J. (1995). Perception. In S. J. Russell and P. Norvig, Eds., *Artificial Intelligence: A Modern Approach.* Englewood Cliffs, NJ: Prentice Hall, pp. 724–756.

Mayhew, J. E. W., and J. P. Frisby. (1991). *3-D Model Recognition from Stereoscopic Cues.* Cambridge, MA: MIT Press.

Mitiche, A. (1994). *Computational Analysis of Visual Motion.* New York: Plenum Press.

Mundy, J. L., and A. Zisserman, Eds. (1992). *Geometric Invariance in Computer Vision.* Cambridge, MA: MIT Press.

Ullman, S. (1984). Visual routines. *Cognition* 18: 97–159.

Computer-Human Interaction

See HUMAN-COMPUTER INTERACTION

Computing in Single Neurons

Over the past few decades, NEURAL NETWORKS have provided the dominant framework for understanding how the brain implements the computations necessary for its survival. At the heart of these networks are very dynamic and complex processing nodes, individual neurons. A typical NEURON in the CEREBRAL CORTEX receives input from a few thousand fellow neurons and, in turn, passes on messages to a few thousand other neurons. One hundred thousand such cells are packed into a cubic millimeter of cortical tissue, which amounts to 4 kilometers of axonal wiring, 500 meters of dendrites, and close to one billion synapses (Braitenberg and Schüz 1991).

Synapses, the specialized connections between two neurons, come in two basic flavors, excitatory and inhibitory. An excitatory synapse will reduce the electrical potential across the membrane of its target cell (that is, it will depolarize the cell), while an inhibitory synapse will hyperpolarize the cell. If the membrane potential at the cell body exceeds a particular threshold value, the neuron generates a short, millisecond-long pulse, called an "action potential" or "spike" (figure 1). Otherwise, it remains silent. The amount of synaptic input determines how fast the cell generates spikes, and these are in turn conveyed to the next target cells through the output axon. Information processing in an average human cortex then relies on the proper interconnection of about 4×10^{10} such neurons in a network of stupendous size.

In 1943, MCCULLOCH and PITTS showed that this view is at least plausible. They described each synapse by a single scalar weight, ranging from positive to negative depending on whether the synapse was excitatory or inhibitory. The contributions from all synapses, multiplied by their synaptic weights, add linearly at the cell body. If this sum exceeds a threshold, a spike is generated. McCulloch and Pitts argued that, with the addition of memory, a sufficiently large number of these logical "neurons," wired together in an appropriate manner, can compute anything that can be computed on any digital computer.

LEARNING entered this picture in the form of HEBB's (1949) rule, postulating that the synapse between neuron A and neuron B increases its "weight" if activity in A occurs at the same time as activity in B. Half a century later, we have solid evidence that such changes do take place in a well-studied phenomenon termed LONG-TERM POTENTIATION (LTP). Here, the synaptic weight increases for days or even weeks. It can be induced by simultaneous activity at the pre- and postsynaptic termini, in agreement with Hebb's rule (Nicoll and Malenka 1995). Of more recent vintage is the discovery of a complementary process, a decrease in synaptic weight called "long-term depression" (Stevens 1996).

Over the last few years, it has become abundantly clear that dendrites do much more than simply convey synaptic inputs to the cell body for linear summation. Dendrites have traditionally been treated as passive cables, surrounded by a membrane that can be modeled by a conductance in parallel with a capacitance (Segev, Rinzel, and Shepherd 1995). When synaptic input is applied, such an arrangement acts as a low-pass filter, removing the high frequencies but performing no other significant information processing. Dendrites with such a passive membrane would not really disturb our view of neurons as linear threshold units.

As long ago as the 1950s, Hodgkin and Huxley (1952) showed how the transient changes in such active voltage-dependent membrane conductances generate and shape the action potential. But it was assumed that they are limited to the axon and the adjacent cell body. We now know that many dendrites of pyramidal cells are endowed with a relatively homogeneous distribution of sodium conductances as

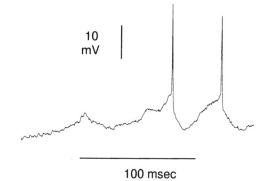

10 mV

100 msec

Figure 1. Action potentials recorded in a single neuron in the visual cortex, shown as a plot of membrane potential against time. (*a*) A visual stimulus causes a sustained barrage of synaptic input, which triggers three cycles of depolarization. The first cycle does not reach the threshold for generating a spike, but the second and third do. Each spike lasts for about 1 msec. (Data provided by B. Ahmed, N. Berman, and K. Martin.)

well as a diversity of calcium membrane conductances (Johnston et al. 1996).

What is the function of these active conductances? One likely explanation (supported by computer models) is that calcium and potassium membrane conductances in the distant dendrites can selectively linearize and amplify this input. Voltage-dependent conductances can also subserve a specific nonlinear operation, multiplication, one of the most common operations carried out in the nervous system (Koch and Poggio 1992). If the dendritic tree contains sodium or calcium conductances, or if the synapses use a particular type of receptor (the so-called NMDA receptor), the inputs can interact synergistically, with the strongest response occurring when inputs from different neurons are located close to each other on a patch of dendritic membrane. Simulations (Mel 1994) show that the firing rate of such a neuron is proportional to the *product*, rather than the *sum*, of its inputs.

Ramòn y CAJAL postulated the law of "dynamic polarization," stipulating that dendrites and cell bodies are the receptive areas for the synaptic input, and that the resulting output pulses are transmitted unidirectionally along the axon to its targets. From work on brain slices, however, it seems that this is by no means the whole story. Single action potentials can propagate not only forward from their initiation site along the axon, but also backward into the dendritic tree, a phenomenon known as antidromic spike invasion (Stuart and Sakmann 1994). It remains unclear whether dendrites themselves can initiate action potentials. If spikes can be generated locally under physiological conditions, they could implement powerful logical operations far away from the cell body (Softky 1994).

What of the role of time in neuronal processing? There are two main aspects to this issue: (1) the relationship between the timing of an event in the external world and the timing of the representation of that event at the single-neuron level; (2) the accuracy and importance of the relative timing of spikes between two or more neurons.

Regarding the first aspect, some animals can discriminate intervals of the order of a microsecond (for instance, to localize sounds), implying that the timing of sensory stimuli must be represented with similar precision in the brain, and is probably based on the average timing of spikes in a population of cells. It is also possible to measure the precision with which individual cells track the timing of external events. For instance, certain cells in the monkey VISUAL CORTEX are preferentially stimulated by moving stimuli, and these cells can modulate their firing rate with a precision of less than 10 msec (Bair and Koch 1996).

The second aspect of the timing issue is the extent to which the exact temporal arrangements of spikes—both within a single neuron and across several neurons—matters for information processing. It is usually assumed that, to cope with the apparent lack of reliability of single cells, the brain makes use of a "firing rate" code. Only the average number of spikes within some suitable time window, say a fraction of a second, matters. The detailed pattern of spikes (figure 2) is thought by many to be largely irrelevant, a hypothesis supported by the existence of a quantitative relationship between the firing rates of single cortical neurons and psychophysical judgments made by monkeys. That is,

the behavior of a monkey in a visual discrimination task can be statistically predicted by counting spikes in a single neuron in the visual cortex (Newsome, Britten, and Movshon 1989). Robustness of this encoding is further ensured by averaging the response over a large number of similar cells (a process known as population coding).

Recent years have witnessed a resurgence in *information-theoretic* approaches to the nervous system (Rieke et al. 1996). We know that individual neurons, such as motion-selective cells in the fly or single auditory inputs in the bullfrog, can encode between 1 and 3 bits of sensory information per output spike, amounting to rates of up to 300 bits per second. This information is encoded using changes in the instantaneous interspike interval between a handful of spikes. Such a temporal encoding mechanism is within 10 to 40 percent of the theoretical maximum allowed by the spike train variability. This implies that individual spikes can carry significant amounts of information, at odds with the idea that neurons are unreliable and can only signal in the aggregate. At these rates, the optic nerve would convey between one and ten million bits per second. (This compares to a ten-speed CD-ROM drive, which transfers information at 1.5 million bits per second.)

Timing precision of spiking across populations of simultaneously firing neurons is believed to be a key element in neuronal strategies for encoding perceptual information in the sensory pathways (Abeles 1990; Singer and Gray 1995). Yet if information is indeed embodied in a temporal code, how, if at all, is it decoded by the target neurons? Do neurons act as *coincidence detectors,* able to detect the arrival time of incoming spikes at a millisecond or better resolution? Or do they integrate more than a hundred or so relatively small inputs over many tens of milliseconds until the threshold for spike initiation is reached (Softky 1995; see figure 1)?

Current thinking about computation has the brain as a hybrid computer. Individual nerve cells convert the incoming streams of binary pulses into analog, spatially distributed variables: the postsynaptic membrane potential and calcium distribution throughout the dendritic tree. This transformation involves highly dynamic synapses that adapt to their input. Information is then processed in the analog domain, using a number of linear and nonlinear operations (multiplication, saturation, amplification, thresholding) implemented

0   1500 msec

Figure 2. Variability in neuronal responses (each line in the trace corresponds to a spike of the type shown in figure 1). If the same stimulus is presented twice in succession, it induces the same average firing rate on both trials (about 50 Hz), although the exact timing of individual spikes shows random variation. (Data provided by W. Newsome and K. Britten.)

in the dendritic cable structure and augmented by voltage-dependent membrane and synaptic conductances. The result is converted into asynchronous binary pulses and conveyed to the following neurons. The functional resolution of these pulses is in the millisecond range, with temporal synchrony across neurons likely to contribute to coding. Reliability could be achieved by pooling the responses of a small number (20–200) of neurons.

And what of MEMORY? It is everywhere (but cannot be randomly accessed). It resides in the concentration of free calcium in dendrites and cell body; in the presynaptic terminal; in the density and exact voltage dependency of the various ionic conductances; in the density and configuration of specific proteins in the postsynaptic terminals; and, ultimately, in the gene in the cell's nucleus for lifetime memories.

See also BINDING BY NEURAL SYNCHRONY; COMPUTATION; COMPUTATION AND THE BRAIN; COMPUTATIONAL NEUROSCIENCE; CORTICAL LOCALIZATION, HISTORY OF; SINGLE-NEURON RECORDING

—*Christof Koch*

References

Abeles, M. (1990). *Corticonics: Neural Circuits of the Cerebral Cortex.* Cambridge University Press.

Bair, W. and C. Koch. (1996). Temporal precision of spike trains in extrastriate cortex of the behaving monkey. *Neural Computation* 8: 1185–1202.

Braitenberg, V., and A. Schüz. (1991). *Anatomy of the Cortex.* Berlin: Springer.

Hebb, D. O. (1949). *The Organization of Behavior: A Neuropsychological Theory.* New York: Wiley.

Hodgkin, A. L., and A. F. Huxley. (1952). A quantitative description of membrane current and its application to conduction and excitation in nerve. *J. Physiol.* 117: 500–544.

Johnston, D., J. Magee, C. Colbert, and B. Christie. (1996). Active properties of neuronal dendrites. *Annu. Rev. Neurosci* 19: 165–186.

Koch, C., and T. Poggio. (1992). Multiplying with synapses and neurons. In T. McKenna, J. Davis, and S. F. Zornetzer, Eds., *Single Neuron Computation.* Boston: Academic Press, pp. 315–345.

McCulloch, W., and W. Pitts. (1943). A logical calculus of the ideas immanent in nervous activity. *Bulletin of Mathematical Biophysics* 5: 115–133.

Mel, B. W. (1994). Information processing in dendritic trees. *Neural Computation* 6: 1031–1085.

Newsome, W. T., K. H. Britten, and J. A. Movshon (1989). *Nature* 341: 52–54.

Nicoll, R. A., and R. C. Malenka. (1995). Contrasting properties of two forms of longterm potentiation in the hippocampus. *Nature* 377: 115–118.

Rieke, F., D. Warland, R. R. D. van Steveninck, and W. Bialek. (1996). *Spikes: Exploring the Neural Code.* Cambridge, MA: MIT Press.

Segev, I., J. Rinzel, and G. Shepherd. (1995). *The Theoretical Foundation of Dendritic Function: Selected Papers of Wilfrid Rall with Commentaries.* Cambridge, MA: MIT Press.

Singer, W., and C. M. Gray. (1995). Visual feature integration and the temporal correlation hypothesis. *Annu. Rev. Neurosci* 18: 555–586.

Softky, W. R. (1994). Sub-millisecond coincidence detection in active dendritic trees. *Neuroscience* 58: 15–41.

Softky, W. R. (1995). Simple codes versus efficient codes. *Curr. Opin. Neurobiol* 5: 239–247.

Stevens, C. F. (1996). Strengths and weaknesses in memory. *Nature* 381: 471–472.

Stuart, G. J., and B. Sakmann. (1994). Active propagation of somatic action potentials into neocortical pyramidal cell dendrites. *Nature* 367: 69–72.

Further Readings

Arbib, M., Ed. (1995). *The Handbook of Brain Theory and Neural Networks.* Cambridge, MA: MIT Press.

Hopfield, J. J. (1995). Pattern-recognition computation using action potential timing for stimulus representation. *Nature* 376: 33–36

Koch, C. (1998) *Biophysics of Computation: Information Processing in Single Neurons.* New York: Oxford University Press.

Koch, C., and I. Segev, Eds. (1998). *Methods in Neuronal Modeling: From Ions to Networks.* Second edition. Cambridge, MA: MIT Press.

Shepherd, G., Ed. (1998). *The Synaptic Organization of the Brain.* Fourth edition. New York: Oxford University Press.

Supplementary information can be found at http://www.klab.caltech.edu

Concepts

The elements from which propositional thought is constructed, thus providing a means of understanding the world, concepts are used to interpret our current experience by classifying it as being of a particular kind, and hence relating it to prior knowledge. The concept of "concept" is central to many of the cognitive sciences. In cognitive psychology, conceptual or semantic encoding effects occur in a wide range of phenomena in perception, ATTENTION, language comprehension, and MEMORY. Concepts are also fundamental to reasoning in both machine systems and people. In AI, concepts are the symbolic elements from which KNOWLEDGE REPRESENTATION systems are built in order to provide machine-based expertise. Concepts are also often assumed to form the basis for the MEANING of nouns, verbs and adjectives (see COGNITIVE LINGUISTICS and SEMANTICS). In behaviorist psychology, a concept is the propensity of an organism to respond differentially to a class of stimuli (for example a pigeon may peck a red key for food, ignoring other colors). In cultural anthropology, concepts play a central role in constituting the individuality of each social group. In comparing philosophy and psychology, it is necessary to distinguish philosophical concepts understood as abstractions, independent of individual minds, and psychological concepts understood as component parts of MENTAL REPRESENTATIONS of the world (see INDIVIDUALISM).

Philosophy distinguishes NARROW CONTENT, which is the meaning of a concept in an individual's mental representation of the world, from *broad content*, in which the meaning of a concept is also partly determined by factors in the external world. There has been much debate on the question of how to *individuate* the contents of different concepts, and whether this is possible purely in terms of narrow content (Fodor 1983; Kripke 1972), and how concepts as purely internal symbols in the mind relate to classes of entities in the external world.

Concepts are considered to play an "intensional" and an "extensional" role (FREGE 1952). There are different technical ways to approach this distinction. One philosophical definition is that the *extension* is the set of all objects in the "actual" world which fall under the concept, whereas the *intension* is the set of objects that fall under the concept in "all possible worlds." In cognitive science a less strict notion of intension has been operationalized as the set of propositional truths associated with a proper understanding of the concept—for example that chairs are for sitting on. It resembles a dictionary definition, in that each concept is defined by its relation to others. Intensions permit inferences to be drawn, as in "This is a chair, therefore it can be sat upon," although, as the example illustrates, these inferences may be fallible. The extension of a concept is the class of objects, actions or situations in the actual external world which the concept represents and to which the concept term therefore refers (Frege's "reference"). Frege argued that intension determines extension; thus the extension is the class of things in the world for which the intension is a true description. This notion of concepts leads to a research program for the analysis of relevant concepts (such as "moral" or "lie") in which proposed intensional analyses of concepts are tested against intuitions of the extension of the concept, either real or hypothetical. Fodor (1994) has advanced arguments against this program. To avoid the circularity found in dictionaries, the intension of a concept must be expressed in terms of more basic concepts (the "symbol grounding problem" in cognitive science). The problems involved in grounding concepts have led Fodor to propose a strongly innatist account of concept acquisition, according to which all simple concepts form unanalyzable units, inherited as part of the structure of the brain. Others have explored ways to ground concepts in more basic perceptual symbolic elements (Barsalou 1993).

In the psychology of concepts, there are three main research traditions. First, the "cognitive developmental" tradition, pioneered by PIAGET (1967), seeks to describe the ages and stages in the growing conceptual understanding of children. Concepts are schemas. Through self-directed action and experience the *assimilation* of novel experiences or situations to a schema leads to corresponding *accommodation* of the schema to the experience, and hence to CONCEPTUAL CHANGE and development. Piaget's theory of adult intelligence has been widely criticized for overestimating the cognitive capacities of most adults. His claims about the lack of conceptual understanding in young children have also been challenged in the literature on conceptual development (Carey 1985; Keil 1989). Research in this tradition has also had a major influence on theories of adult concepts developed within the lexical semantics tradition.

The second research tradition derives from behaviorist psychology, for which concepts involve the ability to classify the world into categories (see also CATEGORIZATION and MACHINE LEARNING). Animal discrimination learning paradigms have been used to explore how people learn and represent new concepts. A typical experiment involves a controlled stimulus set, usually composed of arbitrary and meaningless elements, such as line segments, geometric symbols, or letters, which has to be classified into two or more classes. The stimuli in the set are created by manipulating values on a number of stimulus dimensions (for example, shape or color). A particular value on a particular dimension constitutes a stimulus feature. The distribution of stimuli across the classes to be learned constitutes the structure of the concept. Training in these experiments typically involves using trial-and-error learning with feedback. In a subsequent transfer or generalization phase, novel stimuli are presented for classification without feedback, to test what has been learned. Three types of model have been explored in this paradigm. "Rule-based" learning models propose that participants try to form hypotheses consistent with the feedback in the learning trials (see for example Bruner, Goodnow, and Austin 1956). "Prototype" learning models propose that participants form representations of the average or prototypical stimulus for each class, and classify these by judging how similar the new stimulus is to each prototype. "Exemplar" models propose that participants store individual exemplars and their classification in memory, and base the classification on the relative average similarity of a stimulus to the stored exemplars in each class, with a generally assumed exponential decay of similarity as distance along stimulus dimensions increases (Nosofsky 1988). Exemplar models typically provide the best fits to experimental data, although rules and prototypes may also be used when the experimental conditions are favorable to their formation. NEURAL NETWORK models of category learning capture the properties of both prototype and exemplar models because they abstract away from individual exemplar representations, but at the same time are sensitive to patterns of co-occurrence of particular stimulus features.

The study of categorization learning in the behaviorist tradition has generated powerful models of fundamental learning processes with an increasing range of application, although the connection to other traditions in the psychology of concepts (for example, cognitive development or lexical semantics) is still quite weak. As in much behaviorist-inspired experimental research, the desire to have full control over the stimulus structure has led to the use of stimulus domains with low meaningfulness and hence poor ECOLOGICAL VALIDITY.

The third research tradition derives from the application of psychological methods to lexical semantics, the representation of word meaning, where concepts are studied through their expression in commonly used words. Within the Fregean branch of this tradition, interest has focused on how the intensions of concepts are related to their extensions. Tasks have been devised to examine each of these two aspects of people's everyday concepts. Intensions are typically studied through feature-listing tasks, where people are asked to list relevant aspects or attributes of a concept which might be involved in categorization, and then to judge their importance to the definition of the concept. Extensions are studied by asking people either to generate or to categorize lists of category members. The use of superordinate concepts (for example, birds or tools) allows instances to be named with single words. Extensions may also be studied through the classification of hypothetical or counterfactual examples, or through using pictured objects.

Five broad classes of model have been proposed within the lexical semantics tradition. The "classical" model assumes that concepts are clearly defined by a conjunction of singly necessary and jointly sufficient attributes (Armstrong, Gleitman, and Gleitman 1983; Osherson and Smith 1981). The first problem for this model is that the attributes people list as true or relevant to a concept's definition frequently include nonnecessary information that is not true of all category members (such as that birds can fly), and often fail to provide the basis of a necessary and sufficient classical definition. Second, there are category instances which show varying degrees of disagreement about their classification both between individuals and for the same individuals on different occasions (McCloskey and Glucksberg 1978). Third, clear category members differ in how "typical" they are judged to be of the category (Rosch 1975). The classical view was therefore extended by proposing two kinds of attribute in concept representations—*defining features,* which form the core definition of the class, and *characteristic features,* which are true of typical category members only and which may form the basis of a *recognition procedure* for quick categorization. Keil and Batterman (1984) reported a development with age from the use of characteristic to defining features. Nevertheless, the extended classical model is still incompatible with the lack of clearly expressible definitions for most everyday concept terms.

In the second or "prototype" model, concepts are represented by a prototype with all the most common attributes of the category, which includes all instances sufficiently similar to this prototype (Rosch and Mervis 1975). The typicality of an instance in a category depends on the number of attributes which an instance shares with other category members. Prototype representations lead naturally to non-defining attributes and to the possibility of unstable categorization at the category borderline. Such effects have been demonstrated in a range of conceptual domains. A corollary of the prototype view is that the use of everyday concepts may show nonlogical effects such as intransitivity of categorization hierarchies, and nonintersective conjunctions (Hampton 1982, 1988). Associated with prototype theory is the theory of *basic levels* in concept hierarchies. Rosch, Simpson, and Miller (1976) proposed that the SIMILARITY structure of the world is such that we readily form a basic level of categorization—typically, that level corresponding to high-frequency nouns such as chair, apple, or car—and presented evidence that both adults and children find thinking to be easier at this level of generality (as opposed to superordinate levels such as furniture or fruit, or subordinate levels such as armchair or McIntosh). This intuitive notion has, however, proved hard to formalize in a rigorous way, and the evidence for basic levels outside the well-studied biological and artifact domains remains weak. Attempts to model the combination of prototype concept classes with FUZZY LOGIC (Zadeh 1965) has also proved to be ill founded (Osherson and Smith 1981), although they have led to the development of more general research in conceptual combination (Hampton 1988).

In the third or "exemplar" model, which is only weakly represented in the lexical semantic research tradition, lexical concepts are based not on a prototype but on a number of different exemplar representations. For example, small metal spoons and large wooden spoons are considered more typical than small wooden spoons and large metal spoons (Medin and Shoben 1988). This fact could be evidence for representation through stored exemplars, although it could also be explained by a disjunctive prototype representation. Formally, explicit exemplar models are generally underpowered for representing lexical concepts, having no means to represent intensional information for stimulus domains that do not have a simple dimensional structure. As a result, they have no way to derive logical entailments based on conceptual meaning (for example, that all robins are birds).

The fourth model is the "theory-based" model (Murphy and Medin 1985), which has strong connections with the COGNITIVE DEVELOPMENT tradition. Concepts are embedded in theoretical understanding of the world. While a prototype representation of the concept bird would consist of a list of unconnected attributes, the theory-based representation would also represent theoretical knowledge about the relation of each attribute to others in a complex network of causal and explanatory links, represented in a structured frame or schema. Birds have wings in order to fly, which allows them to nest in trees, which they do to escape predation, and so forth. According to this view, objects are categorized in the class which best explains the pattern of attributes they possess (Rips 1989).

The fifth and final model, psychological ESSENTIALISM (Medin and Ortony 1989), is a development of the classical and theory-based models, and attempts to align psychological models with the philosophical intuitions of Putnam and others. The model argues for a classical "core" definition of concepts, but one which may frequently contain an empty "place holder." People believe that there is a real definition of what constitutes a bird (an *essence* of the category), but they do not know what it is. They are therefore forced to use available information to categorize the world, but remain willing to yield to more expert opinion. Psychological essentialism captures Putnam's intuition (1975) that people defer to experts when it comes to classifying biological or other technical kinds (for example, gold). However, it has not been shown that the model applies well to concepts beyond the range of biological and scientific terms (Kalish 1995) or even to people's use of natural kind terms such as *water* (Malt 1994).

The proliferation of different models for concept representation reflects the diversity of research traditions, the many different kinds of concepts we possess, and the different uses we make of them.

See also BEHAVIORISM; CATEGORIZATION; INTENTIONALITY; NATIVISM; NATURAL KINDS

—*James A. Hampton*

References

Armstrong, S. L., L. R. Gleitman, and H. Gleitman. (1983). What some concepts might not be. *Cognition* 13: 263–308.

Barsalou, L. W. (1993). Structure, flexibility and linguistic vagary in concepts: Manifestations of a compositional system of perceptual symbols. In A. C. Collins, S. E. Gathercole, and M. A. Conway, Eds., *Theories of Memory.* Hillsdale, NJ: Erlbaum.

Bruner, J. S., J. J. Goodnow, and G. A. Austin. (1956). *A Study of Thinking.* New York: Wiley.

Carey, S. (1985). *Conceptual Change in Childhood.* Cambridge, MA: MIT Press.

Fodor, J. A. (1983). *The Modularity of Mind.* Cambridge, MA: MIT Press.

Fodor, J. A. (1994). Concepts—a pot-boiler. *Cognition* 50: 95–113.

Frege, G. (1952). On sense and reference. In P. Geach and M. Black, Eds., *Translations from the Philosophical Writings of Gottlob Frege.* Oxford: Blackwell.

Hampton, J. A. (1982). A demonstration of intransitivity in natural categories. *Cognition* 12: 151–164.

Hampton, J. A. (1988). Overextension of conjunctive concepts: Evidence for a unitary model of concept typicality and class inclusion. *Journal of Experimental Psychology: Learning, Memory and Cognition* 14: 12–32.

Kalish, C. W. (1995). Essentialism and graded membership in animal and artifact categories. *Memory and Cognition* 23: 335–353.

Keil, F. C. (1989). *Concepts, Kinds and Cognitive Development.* Cambridge, MA: MIT Press.

Keil, F. C., and N. Batterman. (1984). A characteristic-to-defining shift in the development of word meaning. *Journal of Verbal Learning and Verbal Behavior* 23: 221–236.

Kripke, S. (1972). Naming and necessity. In D. Davidson and G. Harman, Eds., *Semantics of Natural Language.* Dordrecht: Reidel.

Malt, B. C. (1994). Water is not H$_2$O. *Cognitive Psychology* 27: 41–70.

McCloskey, M., and S. Glucksberg. (1978). Natural categories: Well-defined or fuzzy sets? *Memory and Cognition* 6: 462–472.

Medin, D. L., and A. Ortony. (1989). Psychological essentialism. In S. Vosniadou and A. Ortony, Eds., *Similarity and Analogical Reasoning.* Cambridge: Cambridge University Press, pp. 179–195.

Medin, D. L., and E. J. Shoben. (1988). Context and structure in conceptual combination. *Cognitive Psychology* 20: 158–190.

Murphy, G. L., and D. L. Medin. (1985). The role of theories in conceptual coherence. *Psychological Review* 92: 289–316.

Nosofsky, R. M. (1988). Exemplar-based accounts of relations between classification, recognition and typicality. *Journal of Experimental Psychology: Learning, Memory and Cognition* 14: 700–708.

Osherson, D. N., and E. E. Smith. (1981). On the adequacy of prototype theory as a theory of concepts. *Cognition* 11: 35–58.

Piaget, J. (1967). Piaget's theory. In J. Mussen, Ed., *Carmichael's Manual of Child Psychology,* vol. 1. New York: Basic Books.

Putnam, H. (1975). The meaning of "meaning." In *Mind, Language, and Reality,* vol. 2, *Philosophical Papers.* Cambridge: Cambridge University Press,

Rips, L. J. (1989). Similarity, typicality and categorization. In S. Vosniadou and A. Ortony, Eds., *Similarity and Analogical Reasoning.* Cambridge: Cambridge University Press, pp. 21–59.

Rosch, E. (1975). Cognitive representations of semantic categories. *Journal of Experimental Psychology: General* 104: 192–232.

Rosch, E., and C. B. Mervis. (1975). Family resemblances: Studies in the internal structure of categories. *Cognitive Psychology* 7: 573–605.

Rosch, E., C. Simpson, and R. S. Miller. (1976). Structural bases of typicality effects. *Journal of Experimental Psychology: Human Perception and Performance* 2: 491–502.

Zadeh, L. (1965). Fuzzy sets. *Information and control* 8: 338–353.

Further Readings

Hampton, J. A. (1997). Psychological representation of concepts. In M. A. Conway and S. E. Gathercole, Eds., *Cognitive Models of Memory.* Hove, England: Psychology Press, pp. 81–110.

Lakoff, G. (1987). *Women, Fire and Dangerous Things.* Chicago: University of Chicago Press.

Millikan, R. (1984). *Language, Thought, and Other Biological Categories.* Cambridge, MA: MIT Press.

Neisser, U., Ed. (1993). *Concepts and Conceptual Development: Ecological and Intellectual Bases of Categories.* Cambridge: Cambridge University Press.

Rey, G. (1983). Concepts and stereotypes. *Cognition* 15: 237–262.

Rips, L. J. (1995). The current status of research on concept combination. *Mind and Language* 10: 72–104.

Rosch, E., and B. B. Lloyd, Eds. (1978). *Cognition and Categorization.* Hillsdale, NJ: Erlbaum.

Schwanenflugel, P., Ed. (1991). *The Psychology of Word Meanings.* Hillsdale, NJ: Erlbaum.

Smith, E. E., and D. L. Medin. (1981). *Categories and Concepts.* Cambridge, MA: Harvard University Press.

van Mechelen, I., J. A. Hampton, R. S. Michalski, and P. Theuns, Eds. (1993). *Categories and Concepts: Theoretical Views and Inductive Data Analysis.* London: Academic Press.

Ward, T. B., S. M. Smith, and J. Viad, Eds. (1997). *Conceptual Structures and Processes: Emergence Discovery and Change.* Washington, DC: American Psychological Association.

Conceptual Change

Discussion of conceptual change is commonplace throughout cognitive science and is very much a part of understanding what CONCEPTS themselves are. There are examples in the history and philosophy of science (Kuhn 1970, 1977), in the study of SCIENTIFIC THINKING AND ITS DEVELOPMENT, in discussions of COGNITIVE DEVELOPMENT at least as far back as PIAGET (1930) and VYGOTSKY (1934), in linguistic analysis both of language change over history and of LANGUAGE ACQUISITION, and in computer science and artificial intelligence (AI) (Ram, Nersessian, and Keil 1997). But no one sense of conceptual change prevails, making it difficult to define conceptual change in uncontroversial terms. We can consider four types of conceptual change (see also Keil 1998) as being arrayed along a continuum from the simple accretion of bits of knowledge to complete reorganizations of large conceptual structures, with a fifth type that can involve little or no restructuring of concepts but radical changes in how they are used. Common to all accounts is the idea that either conceptual structure itself or the way that structure is used changes over time. The most discussed account focuses on structural change seen as a dramatic and qualitative restructuring of whole systems of concepts (type 4). All five types are critical to consider, however, because very often the phenomena under discussion have not been studied in sufficient detail to say which type best explains the change.

1. *Feature or property changes and value changes on dimensions.* With increasing knowledge, different clusters of features may come to be weighted more heavily in a

concept, perhaps because they occur more frequently in a set of experiences. A young child might weight shape somewhat more heavily in her concept of a bath towel than texture, while an older child might do the opposite. In its simplest form, such a developmental change may not connect to any other relations or beliefs, such as why texture is now more important. An older child might disagree with a younger one on identifying some marginal feature of bath towels, and while we might thereby attribute this difference to conceptual change, we might not see the concepts as really being very different.

Changes in feature weightings and dimensional value shifts are ubiquitous in cognitive science studies of concepts. They are seen at all ages ranging from studies of infant categorization to adult novice-to-expert shifts (see INFANT COGNITION and EXPERTISE). Any time that some bit of information is incrementally added to a knowledge base and results in a different feature weighting, such a change occurs. When such changes have no other obvious consequences for how knowledge in a domain is represented, they constitute the most minimal sense of conceptual change, and for many who contrast "learning" with true conceptual change, not a real case at all (Carey 1991).

2. *Shifting use of different sorts of properties and relations.* Conceptual change could occur because of changes in the kinds of feature used in representations. Infants and young children have been said to use perceptual and not conceptual features to represent classes of things, or perceptual and not functional ones, or concrete and not abstract ones (e.g., Werner and Kaplan 1963). More recently, young children are said to use one-place predicates and not higher-order relational ones (Gentner and Toupin 1988), or to rely heavily on shape-based features early on in some contexts (Smith, Jones, and Landau 1996). Similar arguments have been made about novice to expert shifts in adults (Chi, Feltovich, and Glaser 1981) and even about the evolution of concepts from those in "primitive" cultures to those in more "advanced" ones (cf. Horton 1967; see also LURIA).

Several forms of conceptual change can be captured by shifts in what feature types are used in concepts. Despite a wide range of proposals in this area, however, it is striking how many have always been controversial, especially in claims of cross-cultural differences (Cole and Means 1981). There is no consensus on changes in the sorts of properties, relations, or both available at different points in development, expertise, or historical change, nor on the very real possibility of no true changes in the availability of property types.

Part of the problem is the need for better theories of property types. It is difficult to make claims about perceptual to conceptual shifts, or perceptual to functional shifts, if the contrast between perceptual and conceptual features is murky. Claims of changes in feature types therefore need to attend closely to philosophical analyses of properties and relations, which in turn need to attend more to the empirical facts.

3. *Changes in computations performed on features.* Conceptual change can also arise from new kinds of computations performed on a constant set of features, such as from tabulations of features based on frequency and correlational information, to more rulelike organizations of the same features (Sloman 1996). In other cases, there have been claims of changes from prelogical to quasi-logical computations over features (Inhelder and Piaget 1958), or changes from integral to separable operations on features and dimensions (Kemler and Smith 1978); or changes from feature frequency tabulations to feature correlation tabulations.

Although most models tend to propose changes in computations that apply across all areas of cognition, such transitions can also occur in circumscribed domains of thought even as there are no global changes in computational ability (Chi 1992). Second, these models do not require that concepts be interrelated in a larger structure. They are neutral in that respect and thus allow each concept to change on its own. In practice, this is highly implausible and may in the end render such models inadequate because they fail to make stronger claims about links among concepts.

There are also cases where there is no absolute change in feature or computational types, but rather a strong change in the ratio of types. Thus a younger child may have true conceptual or functional features but may have ten times as many perceptual ones in her concepts, whereas an older child may have the opposite ratio. Similarly, a younger child may perform logical computations on feature sets, but may do so much more rarely and may more frequently resort to simpler probabilistic tabulations. This variant is important because it offers a very different characterization of the younger child in terms of basic competencies. Younger children are not incapable of representing certain feature types or engaging in certain computations; rather, they do so much less often, perhaps as a function of being much more inexperienced in so many domains (Keil 1989).

4. *Theoretic changes, where theories spawn others and thereby create new sets of concepts.* The most dramatic kinds of conceptual change, and those occupying most discussions in cognitive science at large, are those that view concepts as embedded in larger explanatory structures, usually known as "theories," and whose changes honor DOMAIN SPECIFICITY. Sweeping structural changes are said to occur among whole sets of related concepts in a domain. For example, a change in one concept in biology will naturally lead to simultaneous changes in other biological concepts because they as a cluster tend to complement each other symbiotically. Within this type, three kinds of change are normally described: (a) birth of new theories and concepts through the death of older ones (Gopnik and Wellman 1994); (b) gradual evolution of new theories and concepts out of old ones in a manner that eventually leaves no traces of the earlier ones (Wiser and Carey 1983); and (c) birth of new theories and attendant concepts in a manner that leaves the old ones intact (Carey 1985).

One key issue in choosing among these kinds of theoretic change is the extent to which concepts of one type are incommensurable or contradictory with those of another type (Kuhn 1970, 1982). Kuhn suggested that conceptual changes in domains could lead to "paradigm shifts" in which concepts in a prior system of beliefs might not even be understandable in terms of the new set of beliefs, just as concepts in that newer system might not be understandable in terms of the older one. The ideas of paradigm shifts and ensuing incommensurability have been highly influential in many areas of cognitive science, most notably in the study of conceptual change in childhood (Carey 1985). A related issue asks how contradictions and anomalies in an older theory precipitate change (Chinn and Brewer 1993; Rusnock and Thagard 1995).

Although most discussion of theoretic conceptual change has focused on these three kinds of restructuring, unambiguous empirical evidence for these systemic restructurings as opposed to the other four types of conceptual change (1, 2, 3, 5) is often difficult to come by. For example, when a child undergoes a dramatic developmental shift in how she thinks about the actions of levers, although that change might reflect a restructuring of an interconnected set of concepts in a belief system about physical mechanics, it might also reflect a change in the kinds of features that are most emphasized in mechanical systems, or how the child performs computations on correlations that she notices among elements in mechanical systems.

5. *Shifting relevances.* Children and adults often come to dramatic new insights not because of an underlying conceptual revolution or birth of a new way of thinking, but rather because they realize the relevance or preferred status of an already present explanatory system to a new set of phenomena. Because the realization can be sudden and the extension to new phenomena quite sweeping, it can have all the hallmarks of profound conceptual change. It is, however, markedly different from traditional restructuring notions. Children, for example, can often have several distinct theories available to them throughout an extensive developmental period but might differ dramatically from adults in where they think those theories are most relevant (e.g., Gutheil, Vera, and Keil 1998). Children might not differ across ages in their possession of the theories but rather in their application of them. These kinds of relevance shifts, combined with theory elaboration in each domain, may be far more common than cases of new theories arising de novo out of old ones.

An increasing appreciation of these different types of conceptual change is greatly fostered by a cognitive science perspective on knowledge; for as questions cross the disciplines, they become treated in different ways and different kinds of conceptual change stand out as most prominent. In addition, these types of conceptual change need not be mutually exclusive. For example, changes in the kinds of features that are emphasized and in the kinds of computations performed on those features can occur on a domain-specific basis and might result in a set of concepts having different structural relations among each other.

See also COGNITIVE MODELING, CONNECTIONIST; EDUCATION; EXPLANATION; INDUCTION; MENTAL MODELS; THEORY OF MIND

—*Frank Keil*

References

Carey, S. (1985). *Conceptual Change in Childhood.* Cambridge, MA: MIT Press.

Carey, S. (1991). Knowledge acquisition: Enrichment or conceptual change? In S. Carey and R. Gelman, Eds., *The Epigenesis of Mind: Essays on Biology and Cognition.* Jean Piaget Symposium Series. Hillsdale, NJ: Erlbaum, pp. 257–291.

Chi, M. (1992). Conceptual change within and across ontological categories: Examples from learning and discovery in science. *Minnesota Studies in the Philosophy of Science* 15: 129–186.

Chi, M., P. J. Feltovich, and R. Glaser. (1981). Categorization and representation of physics problems by experts and novices. *Cognitive Science* 5: 121–152.

Chinn, C. A., and W. F. Brewer. (1993). The role of anomalous data in knowledge acquisition: A theoretical framework and implications for science. *Instruction Rev. Educ. Res.* 63(1): 1–49.

Cole, M., and B. Means. (1981). *Comparative Studies of How People Think.* Cambridge, MA: Harvard University Press.

Gentner, D., and C. Toupin. (1988). Systematicity and surface similarity in the development of analogy. *Cognitive Science* 10: 277–300.

Gopnik, A., and H. M. Wellman. (1994). The theory theory. In L. A. Hirschfeld and S. A. Gelman, Eds., *Mapping the Mind: Domain Specificity in Cognition and Culture.* Cambridge: Cambridge University Press, pp. 257–293.

Gutheil, G., A. Vera, and F. C. Keil. (1998). Houseflies don't "think": Patterns of induction and biological beliefs in development. *Cognition,* 66: 33–49.

Horton, R. (1967). African traditional thought and Western science. *Africa* 37: 50–71, 159–187.

Inhelder, B., and J. Piaget. (1958). *The Growth of Logical Thinking from Childhood to Adolescence.* New York: Basic Books.

Keil, F. C. (1989). *Concepts, Kinds and Cognitive Development.* Cambridge, MA: MIT Press.

Keil, F. C. (1998). Cognitive science and the origins of thought and knowledge. In R. M. Lerner, Ed., *Theoretical Models of Human Development.* vol. 1 of *Handbook of Child Psychology,* 5th ed. New York: Wiley.

Kemler, D. G., and L. B. Smith. (1978). Is there a developmental trend from integrality to separability in perception? *Journal of Experimental Child Psychology* 26: 498–507.

Kuhn, T. S. (1970). *The Structure of Scientific Revolutions.* Chicago: University of Chicago Press.

Kuhn, T. S. (1977). A function for thought experiments. In T. Kuhn, Ed., *The Essential Tension: Selected Studies in Scientific Tradition and Change.* Chicago: University of Chicago Press.

Kuhn, T. S. (1982). Commensurability, comparability, and communicability. *PSA* 2: 669–688. East Lansing: Philosophy of Science Association.

Piaget, J. (1930). *The Child's Conception of Physical Causality.* London: Routledge and Keegan Paul.

Ram, A., N. J. Nersessian, and F. C. Keil. (1997). Conceptual change: Guest editors' introduction. *Journal of the Learning Sciences* 6(1): 1–2.

Rusnock, P., and P. Thagard. (1995). Strategies for conceptual change: Ratio and proportion in classical Greek mathematics. *Studies in the History and Philosophy of Science* 26(1): 107–131.

Sloman, S. A. (1996). The empirical case for two systems of reasoning. *Psychological Bulletin* 119(1): 3–22.

Smith, L. B., S. S. Jones, and B. Landau. (1996). Naming in young children: A dumb attentional mechanism? *Cognition* 60: 143–171.

Werner, H., and B. Kaplan. (1963). *Symbol Formation: An Organismic-Developmental Approach to Language and the Expression of Thought.* New York: Wiley.

Wiser, M., and S. Carey. (1983). When heat and temperature were one. In D. Gentner and A. Stevens, Eds., *Mental Models.* Hillsdale, NJ: Erlbaum.

Further Readings

Arntzenius, F. (1995). A heuristic for conceptual change. *Philosophy of Science* 62(3): 357–369.

Bartsch, R. (1996) The relationship between connectionist models and a dynamic data-oriented theory of concept formation. *Synthèse* 108(3): 421–454.

Carey, S., and E. Spelke. (1984). Domain-specific knowledge and conceptual change. In L. A. Hirschfeld and S. A. Gelman, Eds., *Mapping the Mind: Domain Specificity in Cognition and Culture*. New York: Cambridge University Press, pp. 169–200.

Case, R. (1996). Modeling the process of conceptual change in a continuously evolving hierarchical system. *Monographs of the Society for Research in Child Development* 61(1–2): 283–295.

Dunbar, K. (1997). How scientists think: On-line creativity and conceptual change in science. In T. B. Ward, S. M. Smith, and J. Vaid, Eds., *Creative Thought: An Investigation of Conceptual Structures and Processes*. Washington, DC: American Psychological Association, pp. 461–493.

Gentner, D., S. Brem, R. W. Ferguson, et al. (1997). Analogical reasoning and conceptual change: A case study of Johannes Kepler. *Journal of the Learning Sciences* 6(1): 3–40.

Greeno, J. G. (1998). The situativity of knowing, learning, and research. *American Psychologist* 53(1): 5–26.

Hatano, G. (1994). Conceptual Change: Japanese Perspectives: Introduction. *Human Development* 37(4): 189–197.

Kitcher, P. (1988). The child as parent of the scientist. *Mind and Language* 3: 217–227.

Lee, O., and C. W. Anderson. (1993). Task engagement and conceptual change in middle school science classrooms. *American Educational Research Journal* 30(3): 585–610.

Nersessian, N. J. (1989). Conceptual change in science and in science education. *Synthèse* 80(1): 163–183.

Nersessian, N. J. (1992). How do scientists think? Capturing the dynamics of conceptual change in science. *Minnesota Studies in the Philosophy of Science* 15: 3–44.

Nersessian, N. J. (1996). Child's play. *Philosophy of Science* 63: 542–546.

Smith, C., S. Carey, and M. Wiser. (1985). On differentiation: A case study of the development of the concepts of size, weight, and density. *Cognition* 21: 177–237.

Stinner, A., and H. Williams. (1993). Conceptual change, history, and science. *Stories Interchange* 24: 87–103.

Thagard, P. (1990). Concepts and conceptual change. *Synthèse* 82: 255–274.

Vosniadou, S., and W. F. Brewer. (1987). Theories of knowledge restructuring in development. *Review of Educational Research* 57: 51–67.

Vosniadou, S., and W. F. Brewer. (1992). Mental models of the earth: A study of conceptual change in childhood. *Cognitive Psychol.* 24(4): 535–585.

Vygotsky, L. S. (1934/1986). *Thought and Language*. Cambridge, MA: MIT Press.

Wiser, M. (1988). The differentiation of heat and temperature: History of science and novice-expert shift. In S. Strauss, Ed., *Ontogeny, Phylogeny, and Historical Development*. Norwood, NJ: Ablex, pp. 28–48.

Zietsman, A., and J. Clement. (1997). The role of extreme case reasoning in instruction for conceptual change. *Journal of the Learning Sciences* 6(1): 61–89.

Conceptual Role Semantics

See FUNCTIONAL ROLE SEMANTICS

Conditioning

When Ivan Pavlov observed that hungry dogs salivated profusely not only at the taste or sight of food, but also at the sight or sound of the laboratory attendant who regularly fed them, he described this salivation as a "psychical reflex" and later as a "conditional reflex." Salivation was an inborn, reflexive response, unconditionally elicited by food in the mouth, but which could be elicited by other stimuli conditionally on their having signaled the delivery of food. The term *conditional* was translated as "conditioned," whence by back-formation the verb "to condition," which has been used ever since.

In Pavlov's experimental studies of conditioning (1927), the unconditional stimulus (US), food or dilute acid injected into the dog's mouth, was delivered immediately after the presentation of the conditional stimulus (CS), a bell, metronome, or flashing light, regardless of the animal's behavior. The US served to strengthen or reinforce the conditional reflex of salivating to the CS, which would extinguish if the US was no longer presented. Hence the US is often referred to as a "reinforcer." Pavlovian or classical conditioning is contrasted with instrumental or operant conditioning, where the delivery of the reinforcer is dependent on the animal performing a particular response or action. This was first studied in the laboratory by Thorndike (1911), at much the same time as, but quite independently of, Pavlov's experiments. Thorndike talked of "trial-and-error learning," but the "conditioning" terminology was popularized by Skinner (1938), who devised the first successful fully automated apparatus for studying instrumental conditioning.

In Pavlovian conditioning, the delivery of the reinforcer is contingent on the occurrence of a stimulus (the CS), whereas in instrumental conditioning, it is contingent on the occurrence of a designated response. This operational distinction was first clearly articulated by Skinner, but Miller and Konorski (1928) in Poland and Grindley (1932) in England had already argued, on experimental and theoretical grounds, for the importance of this distinction. According to the simplest, and still widely accepted, interpretation of Pavlovian conditioning, the US serves to elicit a response (e.g., salivation), and pairing a CS with this US results in the formation of an association between the two, such that the presentation of the CS can activate a representation of the US, which then elicits the same (or a related) response. This account cannot explain the occurrence of instrumental conditioning. If the delivery of a food reinforcer is contingent on the execution of a particular response, this may well lead to the formation of an association between response and reinforcer. The Pavlovian principle can then predict that the dog performing the required response will salivate when doing so (a prediction that has been confirmed), but what needs to be explained is why the dog learns to perform the response in the first place.

Another way of stating the distinction between Pavlovian and instrumental conditioning is to note that instrumentally conditioned responses are being modified by their consequences, much as Thorndike's law of effect, or Skinner's talk of "controlling contingencies of reinforcement," implied. The hungry rat that presses a lever to obtain food, will desist from pressing the lever if punished for doing so. But Pavlovian conditioned responses are not modified by their consequences; they are simply elicited by a CS associated with a US, as experiments employing omission schedules demonstrate. If, in a Pavlovian experiment, the delivery of food to a hungry pigeon is signaled by the illumination of a small light some distance away from the food hopper, the pigeon will soon learn to approach and peck at this light, even though this pattern of behavior takes it farther away from the food, to the point of reducing the amount of food it obtains. Indeed, it will continue to approach and peck the light on a high proportion of trials even if the experimenter arranges that any such response actually cancels the delivery of food on that trial. The light, as a CS, has been associated with food, as a US, and comes to elicit the same pattern of behavior as food, approach and pecking, regardless of its consequences (Mackintosh 1983).

Most research in COMPARATIVE PSYCHOLOGY accepts that the conditioning process is of wide generality, common at least to most vertebrates, and allows them to learn about the important contingencies in their environment—what events predict danger, what signs reliably indicate the availability of food, how to take effective action to avoid predators or capture prey; in short, to learn about the causal structure of their world. But why should cognitive scientists pay attention to conditioning? One plausible answer is that conditioning experiments provide the best way to study simple associative LEARNING, and associative learning is what NEURAL NETWORKS implement. Conditioning experiments have unique advantages for the study of associative learning: experiments on eyelid conditioning in rabbits, conditioned suppression in rats, or autoshaping in pigeons reveal the operation of simple associative processes untrammeled by other, cognitive operations that people bring to bear when asked to solve problems. And through such preparations researchers can directly study the rules governing the formation of single associations between elementary events. As many commentators have noted, there is a striking similarity between the Rescorla-Wagner (1972) model of Pavlovian conditioning and the Widrow-Hoff or delta rule frequently used to determine changes in connection weights in a parallel distributed processing (PDP) network (Sutton and Barto 1981). The phenomenon of "blocking" in Pavlovian conditioning provides a direct illustration of the operation of this rule: if a given reinforcer is already well predicted by CS1, further conditioning trials on which CS2 is added to CS1 and the two are followed by the reinforcer results in little or no conditioning to CS2. The Rescorla-Wagner model explains this by noting that the strength of an association between a CS and reinforcer will change only when there is a discrepancy between the reinforcer that actually occurs and the one that was expected to occur. According to the delta rule, connections between elements in a network are changed only insofar as is necessary to bring them into line with external inputs to those elements.

But conditioning theorists, not least Rescorla and Wagner themselves, have long known that the Rescorla-Wagner model is incomplete in several important respects. A second determinant of the rate of change in the strength of an association between a CS and a US is the associability of the CS—which can itself change as a consequence of experience. For example, in the phenomenon of latent inhibition, a novel CS will enter into association with a US rapidly, but a familiar one will condition only slowly. Inhibitory conditioning, when a CS signals the absence of an otherwise predicted US, is not the symmetrical opposite of excitatory conditioning, when the CS signals the occurrence of an otherwise unexpected US. Even the rather simple stimuli used in most conditioning experiments are, at least sometimes, represented as configurations of patterns of elements rather than as a simple sum of their elements (Pearce 1994). This last point has indeed been incorporated into many connectionist networks because a simple, elementary representation of stimuli makes the solution of many discriminations impossible. A familiar example is the XOR (exclusive or) problem: if each of two stimuli, A and B, signaled the delivery of a US when presented alone, but their combination, AB, predicted the absence of the US, a simple elementary system would respond more vigorously to the AB compound than to A or B alone, and thus fail to learn the discrimination. The solution must be to represent the compound as something more than, or different from, the sum of its components. But apart from this, not all connectionist models have acknowledged the modifications to error-correcting associative systems that conditioning theorists have been willing to entertain to supplement the simple Rescorla-Wagner model. Conversely, some of the phenomena once thought to contradict, or lie well outside the scope of, standard conditioning theory, such as evidence of so-called constraints on learning (Seligman and Hager 1972), turn out on closer experimental and theoretical analysis to require little more than minor parametric changes to the theory (Mackintosh 1983). Conditioning theory and conditioning experiments may still have some important lessons to teach.

See also BEHAVIORISM; CONDITIONING AND THE BRAIN; PSYCHOLOGICAL LAWS

—*Nicholas J. Mackintosh*

References

Grindley, G. C. (1932). The formation of a simple habit in guinea pigs. *British Journal of Psychology* 23: 127–147.

Mackintosh, N. J. (1983). *Conditioning and Associative Learning.* Oxford: Oxford University Press.

Miller, S., and J. Konorski. (1928). Sur une forme particulière des reflexes conditionnels. *C. R. Sèance. Soc. Biol.* 99: 1155–1157.

Pavlov, I. P. (1927). *Conditioned Reflexes.* Oxford: Oxford University Press.

Pearce, J. M. (1994). Similarity and discrimination: A selective review and a connectionist model. *Psychological Review* 10: 587–607.

Rescorla, R. A., and A. R. Wagner. (1972). A theory of Pavlovian conditioning: Variations in the effectiveness of reinforcement and nonreinforcement. In A. H. Black and W. F. Proskay, Eds., *Classical Conditioning,* vol. 2, *Current Research and Theory.* New York: Appleton-Century-Crofts, pp. 54–99.

Seligman, M. E. P., and J. L. Hager, Eds. (1972). *Biological Boundaries of Learning.* New York: Appleton-Century-Crofts.

Skinner, B. F. (1938). *The Behavior of Organisms.* New York: Appleton-Century-Crofts.

Sutton, R. S., and A. G. Barto. (1981). Toward a modern theory of adaptive networks: Expectation and prediction. *Psychological Review* 88: 135–170.

Thorndike, E. L. (1911). *Animal Intelligence: Experimental Studies.* New York: Macmillan.

Conditioning and the Brain

How the brain codes, stores, and retrieves memories is among the most important and baffling questions in science. The uniqueness of each human being is due largely to the MEMORY store—the biological residue of memory from a lifetime of experience. The cellular basis of this ability to learn can be traced to simpler organisms. In the past generation, it has become clear that various forms and aspects of LEARNING and memory involve particular systems, networks, and circuits in the brain, and it now appears possible we will identify these circuits, localize the sites of memory storage, and ultimately analyze the cellular and molecular mechanism of memory.

All aspects of learning share a common thrust. As Rescorla (1988) has stressed, basic associative learning is the way organisms, including humans, learn about causal relationships in the world. It results from exposure to relations among events in the world. For both modern Pavlovian and cognitive views of learning and memory, the individual learns a representation of the causal structure of the world and adjusts this representation through experience to bring it in tune with the real causal structure of the world, striving to reduce any discrepancies or errors between its internal representation and external reality.

Most has been learned about the simplest forms of learning: nonassociative processes of habituation and sensitization, and basic associative learning and memory. Here we focus on CONDITIONING in the mammalian brain. We emphasize classical or Pavlovian conditioning because far more is known about brain substrates of this form of learning than about more complex instrumental learning. Pavlovian conditioning involves pairing a "neutral" stimulus, for example, a sound- or light-conditioned stimulus (CS) with an unconditioned stimulus (US) that elicits a response, the unconditioned response (UR). As a result of repeated pairings, with the CS onset preceding the US onset by some brief period of time, the CS comes to elicit a conditioned response (CR). Conditioning may be the way organisms, including humans, first learn about the causal structure of the world. Contemporary views of Pavlovian conditioning emphasize the predictive relations between the CS and the US, consistent with cognitive views of learning and memory. The key factor is the contingencies among events in the organism's environment.

When animals, including humans, are faced with an aversive or threatening situation, at least two complementary processes of learning occur. Learned fear or arousal develops very rapidly, often in one trial. Subsequently, the organism learns to make the most adaptive behavioral motor responses to deal with the situation. These observations led to theories of "two-process" learning: an initial learned fear or arousal, followed by slower learning of discrete, adaptive behavioral responses (Rescorla and Solomon 1967). As the latter learning develops, fear subsides. We now think that at least in mammals a third process of "declarative" memory for the events and their relations also typically develops (cf. EPISODIC VS. SEMANTIC MEMORY).

Learned fear develops rapidly, often in one trial, and involves changes in autonomic responses (heart rate, blood pressure, pupillary dilation) and nonspecific skeletal responses (freezing, startle). The afferent limb of the conditioned fear circuit involves projections from sensory relay nuclei via thalamic projections to the AMYGDALA. Although lesions of the appropriate regions of the amygdala can abolish all signs of learned fear, lesions of the efferent targets of the amygdala can have selective effects, for example, lateral hypothalamic lesions abolish cardiovascular signs of learned fear but not behavioral signs (e.g., freezing), whereas lesions of the periqueductal gray abolish learned freezing but not the autonomic signs of learned fear (see, for example, Le Doux et al. 1988). This double disassociation of conditioned responses stresses the key role of the amygdala in learned fear, as do studies involving recording of neuronal activity and electrical stimulation (Davis 1992). The amygdala is critically involved in unlearned fear responses as well. The structures most involved in generating the appropriate responses in basic associative learning and memory seem also to be the most likely sites of memory storage (see below).

Higher brain structures also become critically engaged in learned fear under certain circumstances. Thus when an organism experiences strong shock in a particular environment, reexperiencing that environment elicits learned fear. This context-dependent learned fear involves both the amygdala and the HIPPOCAMPUS for a time-limited period after the experience, a temporal property characteristic of more cognitive aspects of declarative memory (Kim and Fanselow 1992).

A vast amount of research has been done using Pavlovian conditioning of the eye blink response in humans and other mammals (Gormezano, Kehoe, and Marshall-Goodell 1983). The eye blink response exhibits all the basic laws and properties of Pavlovian conditioning equally in humans and other mammals. The basic procedure is to present a neutral CS such as a tone or a light followed a quarter of a second or so later by a puff of air to the eye or a periorbital (around-the-eye) shock (US), the two stimuli terminating together. This is termed the *delay procedure.* If a period of no stimuli intervenes between CS offset and US onset, it is termed the *trace procedure,* which is much more difficult to learn than the delay procedure. Initially, there is no response to the CS and a reflex eye blink to the US. After a number of such trials, the eyelid begins to close in response to the CS before the US occurs, and in a well-trained subject, the eyelid closure CR becomes very precisely timed so that the eyelid is maximally closed about the time that the air puff or shock US onset occurs. This very adaptive timing of the eye blink CR develops over the range of CS-US onset intervals where learning occurs, about 100 milliseconds to 1 second. Thus the conditioned eye blink response is a very precisely timed elementary learned motor skill. The same is true of other discrete behavioral responses learned to deal with aversive stimuli (e.g., the forelimb or hindlimb flexion response, head turn, etc.).

Two brain systems become massively engaged in eye blink conditioning, hippocampus and CEREBELLUM (Thompson and Kim 1996). If the US is sufficiently aversive, learned fear also occurs, involving the amygdala, as noted above. Neuronal unit activity in the hippocampus increases in paired (tone CS–corneal air puff US) training trials very rapidly, shifts forward in time as learning develops, and forms a predictive "temporal model" of the learned behavioral response, both within and over the training trials. The growth of this hippocampal neuronal unit response is, under normal conditions, an invariable and strongly predictive concomitant of subsequent behavioral learning (Berger, Berry, and Thompson 1986).

Interestingly, in the basic delay procedure, hippocampal lesions do not impair the eye blink CR, although if the more difficult trace procedure is used, the hippocampal lesions massively impair learning of the CR and, in trained animals, impair memory in a time-limited manner. These results are strikingly consistent with the literature concerned with declarative memory deficit following damage to the hippocampal system in humans and monkeys, as is the hippocampus-dependent contextual fear discussed above. So even in "simple" learning tasks like eye blink and fear conditioning, hippocampus-dependent "declarative" memory processes develop.

The cerebellum has long been a favored structure for modeling a neuronal learning system, in part because of the extraordinary architecture of the cerebellar cortex, where each Purkinje neuron receives 100,000+ excitatory synapses from mossy-parallel fibers but only one climbing fiber from the inferior olive (see below). The reflex eye blink response pathways activated by the US (corneal air puff or periorbital shock) involve direct and indirect relays through the brain stem from the sensory (trigeminal) nucleus to the relevant motor nuclei (largely the seventh and accessory sixth). The CS (e.g., tone) pathway projects to the forebrain and also, via mossy fibers, to the cerebellum. The US (e.g., corneal air puff) pathway projects from the trigeminal nuclei to the forebrain and also, via the inferior olive, as climbing fibers to the cerebellum. These two projection systems converge on localized regions of the cerebellum, where the memory traces appear to be formed. The CR pathway projects from the cerebellar cortex and nuclei (interpositus nucleus) via the red nucleus to the motor nuclei generating the eye blink response. (The cerebellum does not participate in the reflex eye blink response.) A wide range of evidence, including electrophysiological recording, lesions, electrical stimulation, and reversible inactivation during training, has demonstrated conclusively that the cerebellum is necessary for this form of learning (both delay and trace) and that the cerebellum and its associated circuitry form the essential (necessary and sufficient) circuitry for this learning. Moreover, the evidence strongly suggests that the essential memory traces are formed and stored in the localized regions in the cerebellum (see Thompson and Krupa 1994; Lavond, Kim, and Thompson 1993; Yeo 1991).

These results constitute an extraordinary confirmation of the much earlier theories of the cerebellum as a neuronal learning system, first advanced in the classic papers of MARR (1969) and Albus (1971) and elaborated by Eccles (1977) and Ito (1984). These theories proposed that mossy-parallel fibers conveyed information about stimuli and movement contexts (CSs here) and the climbing fibers conveyed information about specific movement errors and aversive events (USs here) and they converged (e.g., on Purkinje neurons in cerebellar cortex and interpositus nucleus neurons).

The cerebellar system essential for a basic form of learning and memory constitutes the clearest example to date of localizing memory traces to particular sites in the brain (i.e., in the cerebellum).

See also BEHAVIORISM; EMOTION AND THE ANIMAL BRAIN

—*Richard F. Thompson*

References

Albus, J. S. (1971). A theory of cerebellar function. *Mathematical Bioscience* 10: 25–61.

Berger, T. W., S. D. Berry, and R. F. Thompson. (1986). Role of the hippocampus in classical conditioning of aversive and appetitive behaviors. In R. L. Isaacson and K. H. Pribram, Eds., *The Hippocampus.* New York: Plenum Press, pp. 203–239.

Davis, M. (1992). The role of the amygdala in fear and anxiety. *Annual Review of Neuroscience* 15: 353–375.

Eccles, J. C. (1977). An instruction-selection theory of learning in the cerebellar cortex. *Brain Research* 127: 327–352.

Gormezano, I., E. J. Kehoe, and B. S. Marshall-Goodell. (1983). Twenty years of classical conditioning research with the rabbit. In J. M. Sprague and A. N. Epstein, Eds., *Progress in Physiological Psychology.* New York: Academic Press, pp. 197–275.

Ito, M. (1984). *The Cerebellum and Neural Control.* New York: Raven.

Kim, J. J., and M. S. Fanselow. (1992). Modality-specific retrograde amnesia of fear. *Science* 256: 675–677.

Kim, J. J., and R. F. Thompson. (1997). Cerebellar circuits and synaptic mechanisms involved in classical eyeblink conditioning. *Trends in Neurosciences* 20: 177–181.

Krupa, D. J., J. K. Thompson, and R. F. Thompson. (1993). Localization of a memory trace in the mammalian brain. *Science* 260: 989–991.

Lavond, D. G., J. J. Kim, and R. F. Thompson. (1993). Mammalian brain substrates of aversive classical conditioning. *Annual Review of Psychology* 44: 317–342.

LeDoux, J. E., J. Iwata, P. Cicchetti, and D. J. Reis. (1988). Different projections of the central amygdaloid nucleus mediate autonomic and behavioral correlates of conditioned fear. *Journal of Neuroscience* 8: 2517–2529.

Marr, D. (1969). A theory of cerebellar cortex. *Journal of Physiology* (London) 202: 437–470.

McGaugh, J. L. (1989). Involvement of hormonal and neuromodulatory systems in the regulation of memory storage. *Annual Review of Neuroscience* 12: 255–287.

Rescorla, R. A. (1988). Behavioral studies of Pavlovian conditioning. *Annual Review of Neuroscience* 11: 329–352.

Rescorla, R. A., and R. L. Solomon. (1967). Two-process learning theory: Relationships between Pavlovian conditioning and instrumental learning. *Psychological Review* 74: 151–182.

Thompson, R. F., and J. J. Kim. (1996). Memory systems in the brain and localization of a memory. *Proceedings of the National Academy of Sciences* 93: 13438–13444.

Thompson, R. F., and D. J. Krupa. (1994). Organization of memory traces in the mammalian brain. *Annual Review of Neuroscience* 17: 519–549.

Yeo, C. H. (1991). Cerebellum and classical conditioning of motor response. *Annals of the New York Academy of Sciences* 627: 292–304.

Zola-Morgan, S., and L. R. Squire. (1993). Neuroanatomy of memory. *Annual Review of Neuroscience* 16: 547–563.

Connectionism, Philosophical Issues

Since its inception, artificial intelligence (AI) research has had a growing influence on the philosophy of mind. Consequently, the recent development of a radically different style of cognitive modeling—commonly known as "connectionism" (see COGNITIVE MODELING, CONNECTIONIST)—has brought with it a number of important philosophical issues and concerns. Because connectionism is such a dramatic departure from more traditional accounts of cognition, it has forced philosophers to reconsider several assumptions based on earlier theories. Most of these cluster around three central themes: (1) the nature of psychological explanation, (2) forms of mental representation, and (3) nativist and empiricist accounts of learning.

Before the introduction of connectionism in the mid-1980s, the dominant paradigm in cognitive modeling was the COMPUTATIONAL THEORY OF MIND, sometimes referred to by philosophers as "GOFAI" (for "good old-fashioned artificial intelligence"; see also COGNITIVE MODELING, SYMBOLIC). GOFAI accounts treat the mind as a complex organization of interacting subsystems, each performing a specific cognitive function and processing information through the manipulation of discrete, quasi-linguistic symbols whose interactions are governed by explicitly encoded rules. Psychological explanation is treated as a form of FUNCTIONAL DECOMPOSITION, where sophisticated cognitive capacities are broken down and explained through the coordinated activity of individual components. The capacities of the individual components are further explained through a description of their internal symbolic operations (Cummins 1983; see also RULES AND REPRESENTATIONS and ALGORITHM).

Connectionism suggests a very different outlook on the nature of psychological theory. Connectionist networks model cognition through the spreading activation of numerous simple units. The processing is highly distributed throughout the entire system, and there are no task-specific modules, discrete symbols, or explicit rules that govern the operations (Rumelhart, McClelland, and PDP Research Group 1986; McClelland, Rumelhart, and PDP Research Group 1986; Smolensky 1988). This has forced researchers to abandon the functional decomposition approach and search for new ways to understand the structure of psychological explanation. In one popular alternative, DYNAMIC APPROACHES TO COGNITION, cognitive activity is understood as a series of mathematical state transitions plotted along different possible trajectories. Mental operations are described through equations that capture the behavior of the whole system, rather than focusing on the logical or syntactic transformations within specific subsystems. Some writers believe this framework will provide a new paradigm for understanding the nature of COGNITIVE ARCHITECTURE and give rise to psychological explanations that depart dramatically from past accounts (van Gelder 1991; Horgan and Tienson 1996; see also COMPUTATIONAL NEUROSCIENCE).

GOFAI cognitive models rely heavily on explicit, syntactically structured symbols to store and process information. By contrast, connectionist networks employ a very different type of representation, whereby information is encoded throughout the nodes and connections of the entire network. These distributed representations (cf. DISTRIBUTED VS. LOCAL REPRESENTATION) lack the languagelike, syntactic structure of traditional GOFAI symbols. Moreover, their content and representational function is often revealed only through mathematical analysis of the activity patterns of the system's internal units.

The philosophical implications of this new account of representation are far-reaching. Some writers, unhappy with the quasi-linguistic character of GOFAI symbols, have embraced the connectionist picture to support nonsentential theories of representation, including prototype accounts of CONCEPTS (Churchland 1989). Others have suggested parallels between the connectionist representations and the biologically motivated theories of INFORMATIONAL SEMANTICS explored by writers such as Fred Dretske (1988). Many believe the internal units of connectionist networks provide a promising new way to understand MENTAL REPRESENTATION because of their similarity to real neural systems and their sensitivity to environmental stimuli (Bechtel 1989).

On the other hand, some philosophers have argued that the connectionist account of representation is seriously flawed. Jerry Fodor and Zenon Pylyshyn have claimed that the ability to represent some states of affairs (e.g., "John loves Mary") is closely linked to the ability to represent other states of affairs (e.g., "Mary loves John"; Fodor and Pylyshyn 1988). They argue that this feature of cognition, called "systematicity," must be explained by any plausible theory of mind. They insist that because connectionist representations do not have constituent parts, connectionist models cannot explain systematicity. In response to this challenge, several connectionists have argued that it is possible for connectionist representations to produce systematic cognition in subtle ways without merely implementing a symbolic system (Smolensky 1991; Clark 1991).

Connectionist accounts of representations have also influenced philosophical debate concerning the status of PROPOSITIONAL ATTITUDES. ELIMINATIVE MATERIALISM holds that our commonsense conception of the mind is so flawed that there is reason to be skeptical about the existence of states such as beliefs and desires. Some writers have suggested that the style of information encoding in networks is so radically different from what is assumed by common sense that connectionist models actually give credence to eliminativism (Churchland 1986; Ramsey, Stich, and Garon 1990). Others have gone a step further and argued that the internal elements of networks should not be viewed as representations at all (Brooks 1991; Ramsey 1997). In response, several writers have insisted that commonsense psychology and connectionism are quite compatible, once the former is properly construed; moreover, because our commonsense notion of belief is not committed to any specific sort of cognitive architecture, it has nothing to fear from the success of connectionism (Dennett 1991; Bechtel and Abrahamsen 1993; see also FOLK PSYCHOLOGY).

Research in cognitive science has had an important influence on the traditional debate between nativists, who claim that we are born with innate knowledge, and empiricists, who claim that knowledge is derived from experience (see also NATIVISM and RATIONALISM VS. EMPRIRICISM). Nativism has enjoyed popularity in cognitive science because it has proven difficult to explain how cognitive capacities are acquired without assuming some form of preexisting knowledge within the system. Yet one of the most striking features of connectionist networks is their ability to attain capacities with very little help from antecedent knowledge. By relying on environmental stimuli and powerful learning algorithms, networks often appear to program themselves. This has led many to claim that connectionism offers a powerful new approach to learning—one that will resurrect empiricist accounts of the mind.

A mainspring of nativism in cognitive science has been Chomsky's POVERTY OF THE STIMULUS ARGUMENT for the INNATENESS OF LANGUAGE (1975). Chomsky has argued that LANGUAGE ACQUISITION is impossible without a rich store of innate linguistic knowledge. Although several CONNECTIONIST APPROACHES TO LANGUAGE have been developed to demonstrate how areas of linguistic competence—such as knowing regular and irregular past tense forms of verbs—can be obtained without preexisting linguistic rules (Rumelhart, McClelland, and PDP Research Group 1986; Elman et al. 1996), the success of these models in establishing a nonnativist theory of linguistic competence has been heavily debated (Pinker and Prince 1988). One critical issue concerns the degree of DOMAIN SPECIFICITY employed in the learning strategies and initial configuration of the networks (Ramsey and Stich 1990).

A second motivation for nativism stems from the "classical" account of concept acquisition, which assumes that learning occurs when new complex concepts are constructed from more primitive concepts (Fodor 1981), and which suggests there must first exist a prior store of basic concepts that, by hypothesis, are unlearned. However, connectionism appears to offer a different model of concept acquisition. Networks seem to develop new classifications and abstractions that emerge without the recombination of preexisting representations. In other words, there is reason to think connectionist learning gives rise to new primitive concepts that are developed entirely in response to the system's training input (Munakata et al. 1997). To many, this captures the essence of empiricist learning and signals a new direction for understanding CONCEPTUAL CHANGE (Churchland 1989; Elman et al. 1996).

—*William Ramsey*

References

Bechtel, W. (1989). Connectionism and intentionality. In *Proceedings of the Eleventh Annual Meetings of the Cognitive Science Society.* Hillsdale, NJ: Erlbaum, pp. 553–600.

Bechtel, W., and A. Abrahamsen. (1993). Connectionism and the future of folk psychology. In S. Christensen and D. Turner, Eds., *Folk Psychology and the Philosophy of Mind.* Hillsdale, NJ: Erlbaum, pp. 340–367.

Brooks, R. (1991). Intelligence without representation. *Artificial Intelligence* 47: 139–159.

Chomsky, N. (1975). *Reflections on Language.* New York: Pantheon.

Churchland, P. M. (1986). Some reductive strategies in cognitive neurobiology. *Mind* 95(379): 279–309.

Churchland, P. M. (1989). *A Neurocomputational Perspective.* Cambridge, MA: MIT Press.

Clark, A. (1991). Systematicity, structured representations and cognitive architecture: A reply to Fodor and Pylyshyn. In T. Horgan and J. Tienson, Eds., *Connectionism and the Philosophy of Mind.* Dordrecht: Kluwer, pp. 198–218.

Cummins, R. (1983). *The Nature of Psychological Explanation.* Cambridge, MA: MIT Press.

Dennett, D. (1991). Two contrasts: Folk craft versus folk science, and belief vs. opinion. In J. Greenwood, Ed., *The Future of Folk Psychology.* New York: Cambridge University Press, pp. 135–148.

Dretske, F. (1988). *Explaining Behavior.* Cambridge, MA: MIT Press.

Elman, J., E. Bates, M. Johnson, A. Karmiloff-Smith, D. Parisi, and K. Plunkett. (1996). *Rethinking Innateness: A Connectionist Perspective on Development.* Cambridge, MA: MIT Press.

Fodor, J. (1981). The present status of the innateness controversy. In *Representations.* Cambridge, MA: MIT Press, pp. 257–316.

Fodor, J., and Z. Pylyshyn. (1988). Connectionism and cognitive architecture: A critical analysis. *Cognition* 28: 3–71.

Horgan, T., and J. Tienson. (1996). *Connectionism and the Philosophy of Psychology.* Cambridge, MA: MIT Press.

McClelland, J., D. Rumelhart, and PDP Research Group. (1986). *Parallel Distributed Processing: Explorations in the Microstructure of Cognition.* Vol. 2, *Psychological and Biological Models.* Cambridge, MA: MIT Press.

Muntakata, Y., J. L. McClelland, M. H. Johnson, and R. S. Siegler. (1997). Rethinking infant knowledge: Toward an adaptive process account of success and failure in object permanence tasks. *Psychological Review* 104(4): 686–713.

Pinker, S., and A. Prince. (1988). On language and connectionism: Analysis of a parallel distributed processing model of language acquisition. *Cognition* 28: 73–193.

Ramsey, W. (1997). Do connectionist representations earn their explanatory keep? *Mind and Language* 12(1): 34–66.

Ramsey, W., and S. Stich (1990). Connectionism and three levels of nativism. *Synthèse* 82: 177–205.

Ramsey, W., S. Stich, and J. Garon (1990). Connectionism, eliminativism and the future of folk psychology. *Philosophical Perspectives* 4: 499–533.

Rumelhart, D., J. McClelland, and PDP Research Group. (1986). *Parallel Distributed Processing: Explorations in the Microstructure of Cognition.* Vol. 1, *Foundations.* Cambridge, MA: MIT Press.

Smolensky, P. (1988). On the proper treatment of connectionism. *Behavioral and Brain Sciences* 11(1): 1–74.

Smolensky, P. (1991). The constituent structure of mental states: A reply to Fodor and Pylyshyn. In T. Horgan and J. Tienson, Eds., *Connectionism and the Philosophy of Mind.* Dordrecht: Kluwer, pp. 281–308.

van Gelder, T. (1991). Connectionism and dynamical explanation. In *Proceedings of the Thirteenth Annual Conference of the Cognitive Science Society.* Hillsdale, NJ: Erlbaum, pp. 499–503.

Further Readings

Aizawa, K. (1994). Representation without rules, connectionism and the syntactic argument. *Synthèse* 101: 465–492.

Bechtel, W. (1991). Connectionism and the philosophy of mind: An overview. In T. Horgan and J. Tienson, Eds., *Connectionism and the Philosophy of Mind*. Dordrecht: Kluwer, pp. 30–59.

Bechtel, W., and A. Abrahamsen. (1991). *Connectionism and the Mind: An Introduction to Parallel Processing in Networks*. Oxford: Blackwell.

Bechtel, W., and R. Richardson. (1993). *Discovering Complexity*. Princeton, NJ: Princeton University.

Chalmers, D. (1993). Connectionism and compositionality: Why Fodor and Pylyshyn were wrong. *Philosophical Psychology* 6: 305–319.

Churchland, P. S., and T. Sejnowski. (1992). *The Computational Brain*. Cambridge, MA: MIT Press.

Clark, A. (1989). *Microcognition*. Cambridge MA: MIT Press.

Clark, A. (1993). *Associative Engines: Connectionism, Concepts and Representational Change*. Cambridge MA: MIT Press.

Forster, M. R., and E. Saidel. (1994). Connectionism and the fate of folk psychology: A reply to Ramsey, Stich and Garon. *Philosophical Psychology* 7: 437–452.

Garson, J. (1994). Cognition without classical architecture. *Synthèse* 100: 291–306.

Hanson, S., and D. Burr. (1990). What connectionist models learn: Learning and representation in connectionist networks. *Behavioral and Brain Sciences* 13: 471–518.

Haugeland, J. (1978). The nature and plausibility of cognitivism. *Behavioral and Brain Sciences* 2: 215–260.

Horgan, T., and J. Tienson, Eds. (1991). *Connectionism and Philosophy of Mind*. Dordrecht: Kluwer.

Lloyd, D. (1989). *Simple Minds*. Cambridge, MA: MIT Press.

Nadel, L., L. Cooper, P. Culicover, and R. M. Harnish, Eds. (1989). *Neural Connections, Mental Computation*. Cambridge, MA: MIT Press.

Macdonald, C., and G. Macdonald, Eds. (1995). *Connectionism: Debates on Psychological Explanation*. Oxford: Blackwell.

McLaughlin, B. (1993). The connectionism/classicism battle to win souls. *Philosophical Studies* 71: 163–190.

McLaughlin, B., and T. Warfield. (1994). The allure of connectionism re-examined. *Synthèse* 101: 365–400.

Port, F., and T. van Gelder, Eds. (1995). *Mind as Motion: Explorations in the Dynamics of Cognition*. Cambridge, MA: MIT Press.

Ramsey, W., S. Stich, and D. Rumelhart, Eds. (1991). *Philosophy and Connectionist Theory*. Hillsdale, NJ: Erlbaum.

Tomberlin, J., Ed. (1995). *Philosophical Perspectives*. Vol. 9, *AI, Connectionism and the Philosophy of Mind*. Atascadero, CA: Ridgeview.

Connectionist Approaches to Language

In research on theoretical and COMPUTATIONAL LINGUISTICS and NATURAL LANGUAGE PROCESSING, the dominant formal approaches to language have traditionally been theories of RULES AND REPRESENTATIONS. These theories assume an underlying symbolic COGNITIVE ARCHITECTURE based in discrete mathematics, the theory of algorithms for manipulating symbolic data structures such as strings (e.g., of phonemes; see PHONOLOGY), trees (e.g., of nested syntactic phrases; see SYNTAX), graphs (e.g., of conceptual structures deployed in SEMANTICS), and feature structures (e.g., of phonological, syntactic, and semantic properties of nested phrases or their designations). In contrast, connectionist computation is based in the continuous mathematics of NEURAL NETWORKS: the theory of numerical vectors and tensors (e.g., of activation values), matrices (e.g., of connection weights), differential equations (e.g., for the dynamics of spreading activation or learning), probability and statistics (e.g., for analysis of inductive and statistical inference). How can linguistic phenomena traditionally analyzed with discrete symbolic computation be analyzed with continuous connectionist computation? Two quite different strategies have been pursued for facing this challenge.

The dominant, *model-centered* strategy proceeds as follows (see COGNITIVE MODELING, CONNECTIONIST; see also STATISTICAL TECHNIQUES IN NATURAL LANGUAGE PROCESSING): specific data illustrating some interesting linguistic phenomena are identified; certain general connectionist principles are hypothesized to account for these data; a concrete instantiation of these principles in a particular connectionist network—the model—is selected; computer simulation is used to test the adequacy of the model in accounting for the data; and, if the network employs learning, the network configuration resulting from learning is analyzed to discern the nature of the account that has been learned.

For instance, a historically pivotal model (Rumelhart and McClelland 1986) addressed the data on children's overgeneralization of the regular past tense inflection of irregular verbs; connectionist induction from the statistical preponderance of regular inflection was hypothesized to account for these data; a network incorporating a particular representation of phonological strings and a simple learning rule was proposed; simulations of this model documented considerable but not complete success at learning to inflect irregular, regular, and novel stems; and limited post hoc analysis was performed of the structure acquired by the network which was responsible for its performance.

The second, *principle-centered,* strategy approaches language by directly deploying general connectionist principles, without the intervention of a particular network model. Selected connectionist principles are used to directly derive a novel and general linguistic formalism, and this formalism is then used directly for the analysis of particular linguistic phenomena. An example is the "harmonic grammar" formalism (Legendre, Miyata, and Smolensky 1990), in which a grammar is a set of violable or "soft" constraints on the well-formedness of linguistic structures, each with a numerical strength: the grammatical structures are those that simultaneously best satisfy the constraints. As discussed below, this formalism is a consequence of general mathematical principles that can be shown to govern the abstract, high-level properties of the representation and processing of information in certain classes of connectionist systems.

These two connectionist approaches to language are complementary. Although the principle-centered approach is independent from many of the details needed to define a concrete connectionist model, it can exploit only relatively basic connectionist principles. With the exception of the simplest cases, the general emergent cognitive properties of the dynamics of a large number of interacting low-level connectionist variables are not yet characterizable by mathematical analysis—detailed computer simulation of concrete networks is required.

We now consider several connectionist computational principles and their potential linguistic implications. These principles divide into those pertaining to the learning, the processing, and the representational components of connectionist theory.

Connectionist Inductive Learning Principles

These provide one class of solution to the problem of how the large numbers of interactions among independent connectionist units can be orchestrated so that their emergent effect is the computation of an interesting linguistic function. Such functions include those relating a verb stem with its past tense (MORPHOLOGY); orthographic with phonological representations of a word (READING and VISUAL WORD RECOGNITION); and a string of words with a representation of its meaning.

Many learning principles have been used to investigate what types of linguistic structure can be induced from examples. SUPERVISED LEARNING techniques learn to compute a given input or output function by adapting the weights of the network during experience with training examples so as to minimize a measure of the overall output error (e.g., each training example might be a pair consisting of a verb stem and its past tense form). UNSUPERVISED LEARNING methods extract regularities from training data without explicit information about the regularities to be learned, for example, a network trained to predict the next letter in an unsegmented stream of text extracts aspects of the distributional structure arising from the repetition of a fixed set of words, enabling the trained network to segment the stream (Elman 1990).

A trained network capable of computing, to some degree, a linguistically relevant function has acquired a certain degree of internal structure, manifest in the behavior of the learned network (e.g., its pattern of generalization to novel inputs), or more directly discernible under analysis of the learned connection weights. The final network structure is jointly the product of the linguistic structure of the training examples and the a priori structure explicitly and implicitly provided the model via the selection of architectural parameters. Linguistically relevant a priori structure includes what is implicit in the representation of inputs and outputs, the pattern of connectivity of the network, and the performance measure that is optimized during learning.

Trained networks have acquired many types of linguistically relevant structure, including nonmonotonic or "U-shaped" development (Rumelhart and McClelland 1986); categorical perception; developmental spurts (Elman et al. 1996); functional modularity (behavioral dissociations in intact or internally damaged networks; Plaut and Shallice 1994); localization of different functions to different spatial portions of the network (Jacobs, Jordan, and Barto 1991); finite-state, machinelike structure corresponding to a learned grammar (Touretzky 1991). Before a consensus can be reached on the implications of learned structure for POVERTY OF THE STIMULUS ARGUMENTS and the INNATENESS OF LANGUAGE, researchers will have to demonstrate incontrovert-

ibly that models lacking grammatical knowledge in their a priori structure can acquire such knowledge (Elman et al. 1996; Pinker and Mehler 1988; Seidenberg 1997). In addition to this model-based research, recent formal work in COMPUTATIONAL LEARNING THEORY based in mathematical statistics has made considerable progress in the area of inductive learning, including connectionist methods, formally relating the justifiability of induction to general a priori limits on the learner's hypothesis space, and quantitatively relating the number of adjustable parameters in a network architecture to the number of training examples needed for good generalization (with high probability) to novel examples (Smolensky, Mozer, and Rumelhart 1996).

Connectionist Processing Principles

The potential linguistic implications of connectionist principles go well beyond learning and the RATIONALISM VS. EMPIRICISM debate. The processing component of connectionist theory includes several relevant principles. For example, in place of serial stages of processing, a connectionist principle that might be dubbed "parallel modularity" hypothesizes that informationally distinct modules (e.g., phonological, orthographic, syntactic, and semantic knowledge) are separate subnetworks operating in parallel with each other, under continuous exchange of information through interface subnetworks (e.g., Plaut and Shallice 1994).

Another processing principle concerns the transformations of activity patterns from one layer of units to the next: In the processing of an input, the influence exerted by a previously stored item is proportional to both the frequency of presentation of the stored item and its "similarity" to the input, where "similarity" of activity patterns is measured by a training-set–dependent metric (see PATTERN RECOGNITION AND FEEDFORWARD NETWORKS). While such frequency- and similarity-sensitive processing is readily termed associative, it must be recognized that "similarity" is defined relative to the internal activation pattern encoding of the entire set of items. This encoding may itself be sensitive to the contextual or structural role of an item (Smolensky 1990); it may be sensitive to certain complex combinations of features of its content, and insensitive altogether to other content features. For example, a representation may encode the syntactic role and category of a word as well as its phonological and semantic content, and the relevant "similarity" metric may be strongly sensitive to the syntactic information, while being completely insensitive to the phonological and semantic information.

A class of RECURRENT NETWORKS with feedback connections is subject to the following principle: The network's activation state space contains a finite set of attractor states, each surrounded by a "basin of attraction"; any input pattern lying in a given basin will eventually produce the corresponding attractor state as its output (see DYNAMIC APPROACHES TO COGNITION). This principle relates a continuous space of possible input patterns and a continuous processing mechanism to a discrete set of outputs, providing the basis for many connectionist accounts of categorical perception, categorical retrieval of lexical items from memory, and categorization processes generally. For example, the pronunciation model of Plaut et al. (1996) acquires a combinatorially structured set of output attractors encoding phonological strings including monosyllabic English words, and an input encoding a letter string yields an output activation pattern that is an attractor for a corresponding pronunciation.

A related principle governing processing in a class of recurrent networks characterizes the output of the network as an *optimal* activation pattern: among those patterns containing the given input pattern, the output is the pattern that maximizes a numerical well-formedness measure, harmony, or that minimizes "energy" (see also CONSTRAINT SATISFACTION). This principle has been used in combination with the following one to derive a general grammar formalism, harmonic grammar, described above as an illustration of principle-centered research. Harmonic grammar is a precursor to OPTIMALITY THEORY (Prince and Smolensky 1993), which adds further strong restrictions on what constitutes a possible human grammar. These include the universality of grammatical constraints, and the requirement that the strengths of the constraints be such as to entail "strict domination": the cost of violating one constraint can never be exceeded by any amount of violation of weaker constraints.

Connectionist Representational Principles

Research on the representational component of connectionist theory has focused on statistically based analyses of internal representations learned by networks trained on linguistic data, and on techniques for representing, in numerical activation patterns, information structured by linear precedence, attribute/value, and dominance relations (e.g., Smolensky 1990; see BINDING PROBLEM). While this research shows how complex linguistic representations may be realized, processed, and learned in connectionist networks, contributions to the theory of linguistic representation remain largely a future prospect.

See also COGNITIVE MODELING, CONNECTIONIST; DISTRIBUTED VS. LOCAL REPRESENTATION; NATIVISM

—*Paul Smolensky*

References

Elman, J. L. (1990). Finding structure in time. *Cognitive Science* 14: 179–211.

Elman, J., E. Bates, M. H. Johnson, A. Karmiloff-Smith, D. Parisi, and K. Plunkett. (1996). *Rethinking Innateness: A Connectionist Perspective on Development.* Cambridge, MA: MIT Press.

Jacobs, R. A., M. I. Jordan, and A. G. Barto. (1991). Task decomposition through competition in a modular connectionist architecture: The what and where vision tasks. *Cognitive Science* 15: 219–250.

Legendre, G., Y. Miyata, and P. Smolensky. (1990). Harmonic grammar: A formal multi-level connectionist theory of linguistic well-formedness: Theoretical foundations. In *Proceedings of the Twelfth Annual Conference of the Cognitive Science Society.* Cambridge, MA, pp. 388–395.

Pinker, S., and J. Mehler. (1988). *Connections and Symbols.* Cambridge, MA: MIT Press.

Plaut, D., and T. Shallice. (1994). *Connectionist Modelling in Cognitive Neuropsychology: A Case Study.* Hillsdale, NJ: Erlbaum.

Plaut, D. C., J. L. McClelland, M. S. Seidenberg, and K. Patterson. (1996). Understanding normal and impaired word reading: Computational principles in quasi-regular domains. *Psychological Review* 103: 56–115.

Prince, A., and P. Smolensky. (1993). *Optimality Theory: Constraint Interaction in Generative Grammar.* RuCCS Technical Report 2, Rutgers Center for Cognitive Science, Rutgers University, Piscataway, NJ, and Department of Computer Science, University of Colorado at Boulder.

Rumelhart, D., and J. L. McClelland. (1986). On learning the past tenses of English verbs. In J. L. McClelland, D. E. Rumelhart, and the PDP Research Group, *Parallel Distributed Processing: Explorations in the Microstructure of Cognition.* Vol. 2, *Psychological and Biological Models.* Cambridge, MA: MIT Press, pp. 216–271.

Seidenberg, M. (1997). Language acquisition and use: Learning and applying probabilistic constraints. *Science* 275: 1599–1603.

Smolensky, P. (1990). Tensor product variable binding and the representation of symbolic structures in connectionist networks. *Artificial Intelligence* 46: 159–216.

Smolensky, P., M. C. Mozer, and D. E. Rumelhart, Eds. (1996). *Mathematical Perspectives on Neural Networks.* Mahwah, NJ: Erlbaum.

Touretzky, D. S., Ed. (1991). *Machine Learning* 7(2/3). Special issue on connectionist approaches to language learning.

Further Readings

Elman, J. L. (1993). Learning and development in neural networks: The importance of starting small. *Cognition* 48: 71–99.

Goldsmith, J., Ed. (1993). *The Last Phonological Rule: Reflections on Constraints and Derivations.* Chicago: University of Chicago Press.

Hare, M., and J. L. Elman. (1994). Learning and morphological change. *Cognition* 49.

Hinton, G. E. (1991). *Connectionist Symbol Processing.* Cambridge, MA: MIT Press.

Miikkulainen, R. (1993). *Subsymbolic Natural Language Processing: An Integrated Model of Scripts, Lexicon, and Memory.* Cambridge, MA: MIT Press.

Plunkett, K., and V. Marchman. (1993). From rote learning to system building: Acquiring verb morphology in children and connectionist nets. *Cognition* 48: 21–69.

Sharkey, N., Ed. (1992). *Connectionist Natural Language Processing.* Dordrecht: Kluwer.

Wheeler, D. W., and D. S. Touretzky. (1993). A connectionist implementation of cognitive phonology. In J. Goldsmith, Ed., *The Last Phonological Rule: Reflections on Constraints and Derivations.* Chicago: University of Chicago Press, pp. 146–172.

Consciousness

Conscious mental states include sensations, such as the pleasure of relaxing in a hot bath or the discomfort of a hangover, perceptual experiences, such as the visual experience of a computer screen about half a meter in front of me, and occurrent thoughts, such as the sudden thought about how a problem can be solved. Consciousness is thus a pervasive feature of our mental lives, but it is also a perplexing one. This perplexity—the sense that there is something mysterious about consciousness despite our familiarity with sensation, perception, and thought—arises principally from the question of how consciousness can be the product of physical processes in our brains.

Ullin Place (1956) introduced a precursor of central state materialism for conscious states such as sensations. But the idea that types of conscious experience are to be identified with types of brain processes raises an important question, which can be made vivid by using Thomas Nagel's (1974) idea of WHAT-IT'S-LIKE to be in a certain state—and, more generally, the idea of there being something that it is like to be a certain creature or system. The question is, why should there be something that it is like for certain processes to be occurring in our brains? Nagel's famous example of what it is like to be a bat illustrates that our grasp of facts about the subjective character of experiences depends very much on our particular perceptual systems. Our grasp on physical or neurophysiological theories, in contrast, is not so dependent. Thus it may appear that subjective facts are not to be identified with the facts that are spelled out in those scientific theories. This Nagelian argument about the elusiveness of QUALIA is importantly similar to Frank Jackson's (1982, 1986) "knowledge argument" and similar responses have been offered to both (Churchland 1985, 1988; and for a reply, Braddon-Mitchell and Jackson 1996).

Ned Block's (1978) "absent qualia argument" is different from the arguments of Nagel and Jackson because it is specifically directed against FUNCTIONALISM: the idea that mental states are individuated by the causal roles they play in the total mental economy, rather than by the particular neurophysiological ways these roles are realized. The problem for functionalism is that we can imagine a system (e.g., Block's homunculi-headed system) in which there is nothing that it is like to be that system, even though there are, within the system, devices that play the various functional roles associated with sensations, perceptions, and thoughts. This argument is not intended for use against a physicalist who (in the style of Place and subsequent central state materialists) simply identifies conscious mental states with brain processes (pain with C-fibers firing, for example). The examples used in the absent qualia argument may, however, be used to support the claim that it is even logically possible there could be a physical duplicate of a normal human being that nevertheless lacked qualia (a "zombie"; Chalmers 1996).

It is a disputed question whether arguments like Nagel's can establish an ontological conclusion that consciousness involves something nonphysical (see MIND-BODY PROBLEM). But even if they cannot, there still appears to be a problem about consciousness; namely, it is a mystery why there should be something that it is like to undergo certain physical processes. This is what Joseph Levine (1983) has called the EXPLANATORY GAP. Jackson and Block both join Nagel in seeing a puzzle at this point, and Colin McGinn (1989) has argued that understanding how physical processes give rise to consciousness is cognitively beyond us (for a critical appraisal of McGinn's argument, see Flanagan 1992).

One possible strategy for demystifying the notion of consciousness is to claim that consciousness is a matter of thought about mental states. This is the "higher-order thought theory of consciousness" favored by David Rosenthal (1986). In this theory, consciousness, considered as a property of mental states, is analyzed in terms of consciousness *of* mental states, while consciousness *of* something is analyzed in terms of having a thought about that thing. Thus for a mental state to be a conscious mental state is for the subject of that state to have a thought about it. If the higher-order thought theory were to be correct, then the occurrence of consciousness in the physical world would not be any more mysterious than the occurrence of mental states, which are not in themselves conscious states, or the occurrence of thoughts about mental states.

However, there are some quite serious problems for the higher-order thought theory. One is that the theory seems to face a kind of dilemma. If the notion of thought employed is a demanding one, then there could be something that it is like for a creature to be in certain states even though the creature did not have (perhaps, even, could not have) any thoughts about those states. In that case, higher-order thought is not necessary for consciousness. But if the notion of thought that is employed is a thin and undemanding one, then higher-order thought is not sufficient for consciousness. Suppose, for example, that thought is said to require no more than having discriminative capacities. Then it seems clear that a creature, or other system, could be in a certain type of mental state, and could have a capacity to detect whether it was in a state of that type, even though there was nothing that it was like to be that creature or system.

More generally, work toward the demystification of consciousness has a negative and a positive aspect. The negative aspect consists in seeking to reveal unclarities and paradoxes in the notion of the subjective character of experience (e.g., Dennett 1988, 1991). The positive aspect consists in offering putative explanations of one or another property of conscious experience in neural terms. Paul Churchland (1988, 148) clearly illustrates how to explain certain structural features of our experiences of color (for example, that an experience of orange is more like an experience of red than it is like an experience of blue). The explanation appeals to the system of neural coding for colors that involves triples of activation values corresponding to the illumination reaching three families of cones, and to structural properties of the three-dimensional space in which they are plotted (see COLOR VISION). But while this is a satisfying explanation of those structural features of color experiences, it seems to leave us without any account of why it is like *anything at all* to see red. Why there are *any* experiential correlates of the neural codes is left as a brute unexplained fact. The demystifier of consciousness may then reply that this appearance of residual mystery is illusory, and that it is a product either of fallacies and confusions that surround the notion of the subjective character of experience or else of an illegitimately high standard imposed on explanation.

The notion of consciousness associated with the idea of the subjective character of experience, and which generates the "hard problem" of consciousness (Chalmers 1996), is sometimes called "phenomenal consciousness." There are several other notions for which the term *consciousness* is sometimes used (Allport 1988), including being awake, voluntary action, ATTENTION, monitoring of internal states, reportability, INTROSPECTION, and SELF-KNOWLEDGE. The distinctions among these notions are important, especially for the assessment of cognitive psychological and neuroscientific theories of consciousness (see CONSCIOUSNESS, NEUROBIOLOGY OF).

One particularly useful contrast is between phenomenal consciousness and "access consciousness" (Block 1995, 231): "A state is access-conscious if, in virtue of one's having the state, a representation of its content is (1) inferentially promiscuous, that is, poised to be used as a premise in reasoning, (2) poised for rational control of action, and (3) poised for rational control of speech. . . . [Access consciousness is] a cluster concept, in which (3)—roughly, reportability—is the element of the cluster with the smallest weight, though (3) is often the best practical guide to [access consciousness]." The two notions appear to be independent in the sense that it is possible to have phenomenal (P) consciousness without access (A) consciousness, and vice versa. An example of P-consciousness without A-consciousness would be a situation in which there is an audible noise to which we pay no attention because we are engrossed in conversation. As an example of A-consciousness without P-consciousness, Block (1995, 233) suggests an imaginary phenomenon of "superblindsight." In ordinary cases of BLINDSIGHT, patients are able to guess correctly whether there is, for example, an O or an X in the blind region of their visual field, even though they are unable to see either an O or an X there. The state that represents an O or an X is neither a P-conscious nor an A-conscious state. In superblindsight, there is still no P-consciousness, but now the patient is imagined to be able to make free use in reasoning of the information that there is an O, or that there is an X.

While the notion of phenomenal consciousness applies most naturally to sensations and perceptual experiences, the notion of access consciousness applies very clearly to thoughts. It is not obvious whether we should extend the notion of phenomenal consciousness to include thoughts as well as sensory experiences. But the idea of an important connection between consciousness and thought is an engaging one. Sometimes, for example, it seems hard to accept that there could be a fully satisfying reconstruction of thinking in the terms favored by the physical sciences. This intuition is similar to, and perhaps derives from, the intuition that consciousness somehow defies scientific explanation.

The question whether there is an important connection between consciousness and thought divides into two: Does consciousness require thought? Does thought require consciousness? The intuitive answer to the first question is that access consciousness evidently does require thought, but that phenomenal consciousness does not. (The appeal of this intuitive answer is the source of some objections to the higher-order thought theory of consciousness.) The answer to the second question as it concerns access consciousness is that there is scarcely any distance at all between the notion of thought and the notion of access consciousness. But when we focus on phenomenal consciousness, the answer to the second question is less clear.

John Searle (1990, 586) argues for the connection principle: "The ascription of an unconscious intentional phenomenon to a system implies that the phenomenon is in principle accessible to consciousness." This is to say that, while we can allow for unconscious intentional states, such as unconscious thoughts, these have to be seen as secondary, and as standing in a close relation to conscious intentional states. Searle's argument is naturally interpreted as being directed toward the conclusion that central cases of thinking are at least akin to phenomenally conscious states.

Even if one does not accept Searle's argument for the connection principle, there is a plausible argument for a weaker version of his conclusion. The INTENTIONALITY of human thought involves modes of presentation of objects and properties (see SENSE AND REFERENCE); demonstrative modes of presentation afforded by perceptual experience of objects and their properties constitute particularly clear examples. For example, we think of an object as "that [perceptually presented] cat" or of a property as "that color." Suppose now that it could be argued that some theoretical primacy attaches to these "perceptual demonstrative" modes of presentation (Perry 1979). It might be argued, for example, that in order to be able to think about objects at all, a subject needs to be able to think about objects under perceptual demonstrative modes of presentation. Such an argument would establish a deep connection between intentionality and consciousness.

Finally, there is another way phenomenal consciousness might enter the theory of thought. It might be because a thinker's thoughts are phenomenally conscious states, that they also have the more dispositional properties (such as reportability) mentioned in the definition of access consciousness. This phenomenal consciousness property might also figure in the explanation of a thinker's being able to engage in critical reasoning—evaluating and assessing reasons and reasoning as such (Burge 1996). It is far from clear, however, whether this idea can be worked out in a satisfactory way. Would the idea require a sensational phenomenology for thinking? If it does require that, then it might be natural to suggest that phenomenally conscious thoughts are clothed in the phonological or orthographic forms of natural language sentences (Carruthers 1996).

—*Martin Davies*

References

Allport, A. (1988). What concept of consciousness? In A. J. Marcel and E. Bisiach, Eds., *Consciousness in Contemporary Science.* Oxford: Oxford University Press, pp. 159–182.

Block, N. (1978). Troubles with functionalism. In C. Wade Savage, Ed., *Minnesota Studies in the Philosophy of Science,* vol. 9. Minneapolis: University of Minnesota Press, pp. 261–325.

Block, N. (1995). On a confusion about a function of consciousness. *Behavioral and Brain Sciences* 18: 227–287.

Braddon-Mitchell, D., and F. Jackson (1996). *Philosophy of Mind and Cognition.* Oxford: Blackwell.

Burge, T. (1996). Our entitlement to self-knowledge. *Proceedings of the Aristotelian Society* 96: 91–116.

Carruthers, P. (1996). *Language, Thought and Consciousness.* Cambridge: Cambridge University Press.

Chalmers, D. (1996). *The Conscious Mind: In Search of a Fundamental Theory.* New York: Oxford University Press.

Churchland, P. M. (1985). Reduction, qualia and the direct introspection of brain states. *Journal of Philosophy* 82: 8–28.

Churchland, P. M. (1988). *Matter and Consciousness.* Rev. ed. Cambridge, MA: MIT Press.

Dennett, D. C. (1988). Quining qualia. In A. J. Marcel and E. Bisiach, Eds., *Consciousness in Contemporary Science.* Oxford: Oxford University Press, pp. 42–77.

Dennett, D. C. (1991). *Consciousness Explained.* Boston: Little, Brown.

Flanagan, O. (1992). *Consciousness Reconsidered.* Cambridge, MA: MIT Press.

Jackson, F. (1982). Epiphenomenal qualia. *Philosophical Quarterly* 32: 127–136.

Jackson, F. (1986). What Mary didn't know. *Journal of Philosophy* 83: 291–295.

Levine, J. (1983). Materialism and qualia: The explanatory gap. *Pacific Philosophical Quarterly* 64: 354–361.

McGinn, C. (1989). Can we solve the mind-body problem? *Mind* 98: 349–366.

Nagel, T. (1974). What is it like to be a bat? *Philosophical Review* 83: 435–450.

Perry, J. (1979). The problem of the essential indexical. *Noûs* 13: 3–21.

Place, U. T. (1956). Is consciousness a brain process? *British Journal of Psychology* 47: 44–50.

Rosenthal, D. M. (1986). Two concepts of consciousness. *Philosophical Studies* 94: 329–359.

Searle, J. R. (1990). Consciousness, explanatory inversion, and cognitive science. *Behavioral and Brain Sciences* 13: 585–596.

Further Readings

Block, N. (1998). How to find the neural correlate of consciousness. In A. O'Hear, Ed., *Contemporary Issues in the Philosophy of Mind.* Royal Institute of Philosophy Supplement 43. Cambridge: Cambridge University Press, pp. 23–34.

Block, N., O. Flanagan, and G. Güzeldere, Eds. (1997). *The Nature of Consciousness: Philosophical Debates.* Cambridge, MA: MIT Press.

Crick, F., and C. Koch. (1995). Are we aware of neural activity in primary visual cortex? *Nature* 375: 121–123.

Davies, M., and G. W. Humphreys, Eds. (1993). *Consciousness: Psychological and Philosophical Essays.* Oxford: Blackwell.

Dennett, D. C., and M. Kinsbourne. (1992). Time and the observer: The where and when of consciousness in the brain. *Behavioral and Brain Sciences* 15: 183–247.

Metzinger, T., Ed. (1995). *Conscious Experience.* Paderborn: Schöningh.

Nelkin, N. (1996). *Consciousness and the Origins of Thought.* Cambridge: Cambridge University Press.

Peacocke, C. (1998). Conscious attitudes, attention and self-knowledge. In C. Wright, B. C. Smith, and C. Macdonald, Eds., *Knowing Our Own Minds.* Oxford: Oxford University Press, pp. 63–98.

Rolls, E. T. (1997). Consciousness in neural networks? *Neural Networks* 10: 1227–1240.

Schacter, D. L. (1989). On the relation between memory and consciousness: Dissociable interactions and conscious experience. In H. Roediger and F. Craik, Eds., *Varieties of Memory and Consciousness: Essays in Honor of Endel Tulving.* Hillsdale, NJ: Erlbaum.

Shear, J., Ed. (1997). *Explaining Consciousness: The Hard Problem.* Cambridge, MA: MIT Press.

Tye, M. (1995). *Ten Problems of Consciousness: A Representational Theory of the Phenomenal Mind.* Cambridge, MA: MIT Press.

Consciousness, Neurobiology of

After a hiatus of fifty years or more, the physical origins of CONSCIOUSNESS are being once again vigorously debated, in hundreds of books and monographs published in the last decade. What sparse facts can we ascertain about the neurobiological basis of consciousness, and what can we reasonably assume at this point in time?

By and large, neuroscientists have made a number of working assumptions that need to be justified more fully. In particular,

1. There is something to be explained, that is, the subjective content associated with a conscious sensation (what philosophers refer to as QUALIA; see also WHAT-IT'S-LIKE) does exist and has its physical basis in the brain.

2. Consciousness is one of the principal properties of the human brain, a highly evolved system; it must therefore have a useful function to perform. Crick and Koch (1995) assume that the function of visual consciousness is to produce the best current interpretation of the visual scene—in the light of past experiences—and to make it available for a sufficient time to the parts of the brain that contemplate, plan, and execute voluntary motor outputs (including language). This needs to be contrasted with the on-line systems that bypass consciousness but can generate stereotyped behaviors (see below).

3. At least some animal species (i.e., non-human primates such as the macaque monkey) are assumed to possess some aspects of consciousness. Consciousness associated with sensory events is likely to be very similar in humans and monkeys for several reasons. First, trained monkeys behave as humans do under controlled conditions for most sensory tasks (e.g., visual motion discrimination; see MOTION, PERCEPTION OF; Wandell 1995). Second, the gross neuroanatomy of humans and nonhuman primates is the same, once the difference in size has been accounted for. Finally, MAGNETIC RESONANCE IMAGING in humans is confirming the existence of a functional organization very similar to that discovered by single-cell electrophysiology in the monkey (Tootell et al. 1996). As a corollary, it follows that language is not necessary for consciousness to occur (although it greatly enriches human consciousness). In the following, we will mainly concentrate on sensory consciousness, and, in particular, on visual consciousness, because it is experimentally the most accessible and the best understood.

Cognitive and clinical research demonstrates that much complex information processing can occur without involving consciousness, both in normals as well as in patients. Examples of this include BLINDSIGHT (Weiskrantz 1997), priming, and the implicit recognition of complex sequences (Velmans 1991; Berns, Cohen, and Mintun 1997). Milner and Goodale (1995) have made a masterful case for the existence of so-called on-line visual systems that bypass consciousness, and that serve to mediate relative stereotype visual-motor behaviors, such as eye and arm movements as well as posture adjustments, in a very rapid manner. On-line systems work in egocentric coordinate systems and lack both certain types of perceptual ILLUSIONS (e.g. size illusion) and direct access to WORKING MEMORY. Milner and Goodale (1995; see also

Rossetti forthcoming) hypothesize that on-line systems are associated with the dorsal stream of visual information in the CEREBRAL CORTEX, originating in the primary VISUAL CORTEX (V1) and terminating in the posterior parietal cortex (see VISUAL PROCESSING STREAMS). This contrasts well with the function of consciousness alluded to above, namely, to synthesize information from many different sources and use it to plan behavioral patterns over time.

What is the neuronal correlate of consciousness? Most popular has been the belief that consciousness arises as an emergent property of a very large collection of interacting neurons (Popper and Eccles 1981; Libet 1995). An alternative hypothesis is that there are special sets of "consciousness" neurons distributed throughout cortex (and associated systems, such as the THALAMUS and the BASAL GANGLIA) that represent the ultimate neuronal correlate of consciousness (NCC), in the sense that activity of an appropriate subset of them is both necessary and sufficient to give rise to an appropriate conscious experience or percept (Crick and Koch 1995). NCC neurons would, most likely, be characterized by a unique combination of molecular, biophysical, pharmacological, and anatomical traits. It is also possible, of course, that all cortical neurons may be capable of participating in the representation of one percept or another, at one time or another, though not necessarily doing so for all percepts. The secret of consciousness would then consist of all cortical neurons representing that particular percept at that moment (see BINDING BY NEURAL SYNCHRONY).

Where could such NCC neurons be found? Based on clinical evidence that small lesions of the intralaminar nuclei of the thalamus (ILN) cause loss of consciousness and coma and that ILN neurons project widely and reciprocally into the cerebral cortex, ILN neurons have been proposed as the site where consciousness is generated (Bogen 1995; Purpura and Schiff 1997). It is more likely, however, that ILN neurons provide an enabling or arousal signal without which no significant cortical processing can occur. The great specificity associated with the content of our consciousness at any point in time can only be mediated by neurons in the cerebral cortex, its associated specific thalamic nuclei, and the basal ganglia. It is here, among the neurons whose very specific response properties have been extensively characterized by SINGLE-NEURON RECORDING, that we have to look for the NCC.

What, if anything, can we infer about the location of these neurons? In the case of visual consciousness, Crick and Koch (1995) surmised that these neurons must have access to visual information and project to the planning stages of the brain, that is, to premotor and frontal areas (Fuster 1997). Because in the macaque monkey, no neurons in primary visual cortex project to any area anterior to the central sulcus, Crick and Koch (1995) proposed that neurons in V1 do not directly give rise to consciousness (although V1 is necessary for most forms of vision, just as the retina is). Current electrophysiological, psychophysical, and imaging evidence (He, Cavanagh, and Intriligator 1996; Engel, Zhang, and Wandell 1997) supports the hypothesis that the NCC is not to be found among V1 neurons.

A promising experimental approach to locate the NCC has been the use of bistable percepts, that is, pairs of percepts, alternating in time, that arise from a constant visual stimulus as in a Necker cube (Crick and Koch 1992). In one such case, a small image, say of a horizontal grating, is presented to the left eye and another image, say of a vertical grating, is presented to the corresponding location in the right eye. In spite of the constant retinal stimulus, observers "see" the horizontal grating alternate every few seconds with the vertical one, a phenomenon known as "binocular rivalry" (Blake 1989). The brain does not allow for the simultaneous perception of both images.

It is possible, though difficult, to train a macaque monkey to report whether it is currently seeing the left or the right image. The distribution of the switching times and the way in which changing the contrast in one eye affects these times leaves little doubt that monkeys and humans experience the same basic phenomenon (Myerson, Miezin, and Allman 1981). In a series of elegant experiments, Logothetis and colleagues (Logothetis and Schall 1989; Leopold and Logothetis 1996; Sheinberg and Logothetis 1997) recorded from a variety of monkey cortical areas during this task. In early visual cortex, only a small fraction of cells modulated their response as a function of the percept of the monkey, while 20 to 30 percent of neurons in MT and V4 cells did. The majority of cells increased their firing rate in response to one or the other retinal stimulus with no regard to what the animal perceived at the time. In contrast, in a high-level cortical area, such as the inferior temporal cortex (IT), almost all neurons responded only to the perceptual dominant stimulus (in other words, a "face" cell only fired when the animal indicated by its performance that it saw the face and not the sunburst pattern in the other eye). This makes it likely that the NCC is located among—or beyond—IT neurons.

Finding the NCC would only be the first, albeit critical, step in understanding consciousness. We also need to know where these cells project to, their postsynaptic action, and what happens to them in various diseases known to affect consciousness, such as schizophrenia or AUTISM, and so on. And, of course, a final theory of consciousness would have to explain the central mystery—why a physical system with a particular architecture gives rise to feelings and qualia. (Chalmers 1996).

See also ATTENTION; ATTENTION IN THE ANIMAL BRAIN; ATTENTION AND THE HUMAN BRAIN; SENSATIONS

—*Christof Koch and Francis Crick*

References

Berns, G. S., J. D. Cohen, and M. A. Mintun. (1997). Brain regions responsive to novelty in the absence of awareness. *Science* 276: 1272–1275.

Blake, R. (1989). A neural theory of binocular rivalry. *Psychol. Rev.* 96: 145–167.

Bogen, J. E. (1995). On the neurophysiology of consciousness: 1. An overview. *Consciousness and Cognition* 4: 52–62.

Chalmers, D. (1996). *The Conscious Mind: In Search of a Fundamental Theory.* Oxford: Oxford University Press.

Crick, F., and C. Koch. (1992). The problem of consciousness. *Scientific American* 267(3): 153–159.

Crick, F., and C. Koch. (1995). Are we aware of neural activity in primary visual cortex? *Nature* 375: 121–123.

Engel, S., X. Zhang, and B. Wandell (1997). Colour tuning in human visual cortex measured with functional magnetic resonance imaging. *Nature* 388: 68–71.

Fuster, J. M. (1997). *The Prefrontal Cortex: Anatomy, Physiology, and Neuropsychology of the Frontal Lobe.* 3rd ed. Philadelphia: Lippincott-Raven.

He, S., P. Cavanagh, and J. Intriligator. (1996). Attentional resolution and the locus of visual awareness. *Nature* 383: 334–337.

Leopold, D. A., and N. K. Logothetis. (1996). Activity changes in early visual cortex reflect monkeys' percepts during binocular rivalry. *Nature* 379: 549–553.

Libet, B. (1995). *Neurophysiology of Consciousness: Selected Papers and New Essays.* Boston: Birkhäuser.

Logothetis, N., and J. Schall. (1989). Neuronal correlates of subjective visual perception. *Science* 245: 761–763.

Milner, D., and M. Goodale. (1995). *The Visual Brain in Action.* Oxford: Oxford University Press.

Myerson, J., F. Miezin, and J. Allman. (1981). Binocular rivalry in macaque monkeys and humans: A comparative study in perception. *Behav. Anal. Lett.* 1: 149–156.

Popper, K. R., and J. C. Eccles. (1981). *The Self and Its Brain.* Berlin: Springer.

Purpura, K. P., and N. D. Schiff (1997). The thalamic intralaminar nuclei: a role in visual awareness. *Neuroscientist* 3: 8–15.

Rossetti, Y. (Forthcoming). Implicit perception in action: Short-lived motor representations of space evidenced by brain-damaged and healthy subjects. In P. G. Grossenbacher, Ed., *Finding Consciousness in the Brain.* Philadelphia: Benjamins.

Sheinberg, D. L., and N. K. Logothetis. (1997). The role of temporal cortical areas in perceptual organization. *Proc. Natl. Acad. Sci. U.S.A.196* 94: 3408–3413.

Tootell, R. B. H., A. M. Dale, M. I. Sereno, and R. Malach. (1996). New images from human visual cortex. *Trends Neurosci.* 19: 481–489.

Velmans, M. (1991). Is human information processing conscious? *Behavioral Brain Sci.* 14: 651–726.

Wandell, B. A. (1995). *Foundations of Vision.* Sunderland, MA: Sinauer.

Weiskrantz, L. (1997). *Consciousness Lost and Found.* Oxford: Oxford University Press.

Further Readings

Crick, F., and C. Koch. (1998). Consciousness and neuroscience. *Cerebral Cortex* 8: 97–107.

Jackendoff, R. (1987). *Consciousness and the Computational Mind.* Cambridge, MA: MIT Press.

Zeki, S. (1993). *Vision of the Brain.* Oxford: Blackwell.

Consensus Theory

See CULTURAL CONSENSUS THEORY

Constraint Satisfaction

A *constraint satisfaction problem* (CSP) is defined over a *constraint network,* which consists of a finite set of *variables,* each associated with a *domain* of values, and a set of *constraints.* A *solution* is an assignment of a value to each variable from its domain such that all the constraints are satisfied. Typical constraint satisfaction problems are to determine whether a solution exists, to find one or all solutions, and to find an optimal solution relative to a given cost function. A well-known example of a constraint satisfaction problem is *k*-colorability, where the task is to color, if possible, a given graph with *k* colors only, such that any two adjacent nodes have different colors. A constraint satisfaction formulation of this problem associates the nodes of the graph with variables, the possible colors are their domains, and the inequality constraints between adjacent nodes are the constraints of the problem. Each constraint of a CSP may be expressed as a relation, defined on some subset of variables, denoting legal combinations of their values. Constraints can also be described by mathematical expressions or by computable procedures. Another typical constraint satisfaction problem is *SATisfiability,* the task of finding the truth assignment to propositional variables such that a given set of clauses is satisfied. For example, given the two clauses $(A \lor B \lor \neg C)$, $(\neg A \lor D)$, the assignment of *false* to A, *true* to B, *false* to C, and *false* to D, is a satisfying truth value assignment.

The structure of a constraint network is depicted by a constraint graph whose nodes represent the variables and in which any two nodes are connected if the corresponding variables participate in the same constraint. In the *k*-colorability formulation, the graph to be colored is the constraint graph. In our SAT example the constraint graph has A connected to D, and A, B, and C are connected to each other.

Constraint networks have proven successful in modeling mundane cognitive tasks such as vision, language comprehension, default reasoning, and abduction, as well as in applications such as scheduling, design, diagnosis, and temporal and spatial reasoning. In general, constraint satisfaction tasks are computationally intractable ("NP-hard"; see COMPUTATIONAL COMPLEXITY).

ALGORITHMS for processing constraints can be classified into two interacting categories: (1) search and (2) consistency inference. Search algorithms traverse the space of partial instantiations, while consistency inference algorithms reason through equivalent problems. Search algorithms are either systematic and complete or stochastic and incomplete. Likewise, consistency inference algorithms have either complete solutions (e.g., variable-elimination algorithms) or incomplete solutions (i.e., local consistency algorithms).

Local consistency algorithms, also called "consistency-enforcing" or "constraint propagation" algorithms (Montanari 1974; Mackworth 1977; Freuder 1982), are polynomial algorithms that transform a given constraint network into an equivalent, yet more explicit network by deducing new constraints to be added onto the network. Intuitively, a consistency-enforcing algorithm will make any partial solution of a small subnetwork extensible to some surrounding network. For example, the most basic consistency algorithm, called an "arc consistency" algorithm, ensures that any legal value in the domain of a single variable has a legal match in the domain of any other selected variable. A "path consistency" algorithm ensures that any consistent solution to a two-variable subnetwork is extensible to any third variable, and, in general, *i-consistency* algorithms guarantee that any locally consistent instantiation of $i - 1$ variables is extensible to any *i*th variable. Enforcing *i*-consistency is time and space exponential in *i*. Algorithms for *i*-consistency frequently decide *inconsistency*.

A network is *globally consistent* if it is *i*-consistent for *every i*, which means a solution can be assembled by assigning values using any variable ordering without encountering any dead end, namely, in a "backtrack-free" manner. However, it is enough to possess *directional* global consistency relative to a given ordering only. Indeed, an *adaptive consistency* (variable elimination) algorithm enforces global consistency in a given order only, such that every solution can be extracted, with no dead ends along this ordering. Another related algorithm, called a "tree-clustering" algorithm, compiles the given constraint problem into an equivalent tree of subproblems (Dechter and Pearl 1989) whose respective solutions can be efficiently combined into a complete solution. Adaptive consistency and tree-clustering algorithms are time and space exponential in a parameter of the constraint graph called an "induced-width" or "tree-width" (Arnborg and Proskourowski 1989; Dechter and Pearl 1987).

When a problem is computationally hard for the adaptive consistency algorithm, it can be solved by bounding the amount of consistency enforcing (e.g., arc or path consistency), and by augmenting the algorithm with a search component. Generally speaking, search will benefit from network representations that have a high level of consistency. However, because the complexity of enforcing *i*-consistency is exponential in *i*, there is a trade-off between the effort spent on consistency inference and that spent on search. Theoretical and empirical studies of this trade-off, prior to or during search, aim at identifying a problem-dependent cost-effective balance (Haralick and Elliot 1980; Prosser 1993; Sabin and Freuder 1994; Dechter and Rish 1994).

The most common algorithm for performing systematic search is the *backtracking* algorithm, which traverses the space of partial solutions in a depth-first manner. At each step, the algorithm extends a partial solution by assigning a value to one more variable. When a variable is encountered such that none of its values are consistent with the partial solution (a situation referred to as a "dead end"), backtracking takes place. The algorithm is time exponential, but requires only linear space.

Improvements of the backtracking algorithm have focused on the two phases of the algorithm: moving forward (look-ahead schemes) and backtracking (look-back schemes; Dechter 1990). When moving forward, to extend a partial solution, some computation (e.g., arc consistency) is carried out to decide which variable and value to choose next. For variable orderings, variables that maximally constrain the rest of the search space are preferred. For value selection, however, the least constraining value is preferred, in order to maximize future options for instantiations (Haralick and Elliot 1980; Dechter and Pearl 1987; Purdom 1983; Sabin and Freuder 1994).

Look-back schemes are invoked when the algorithm encounters a dead end. These schemes perform two functions: (1) they decide how far to backtrack, by analyzing the reasons for the dead end, a process often referred to as "backjumping" (Gaschnig 1979); (2) they record the reasons for the dead end in the form of new constraints so that the same conflicts will not arise again, a process known as "constraint learning" and "no-good recording" (Stallman and Sussman 1977; Dechter 1990).

Stochastic local search strategies have been recently reintroduced into the satisfiability and constraint satisfaction literature under the umbrella name (GSAT "greedy SAT-isfiability"; see GREEDY LOCAL SEARCH). These methods move in hill-climbing manner in the space of complete instantiations to all the variables (Minton et al. 1990). The algorithm improves its current instantiation by "flipping" a value of a variable that maximizes the number of constraints satisfied. Such search algorithms are incomplete, may get stuck in a local maxima, and cannot prove inconsistency. Nevertheless, when equipped with some heuristics for randomizing the search walksat or for revising the guiding criterion function (constraint reweighting), they prove successful in solving large and hard problems that are frequently hard for backtracking search algorithms (Selman, Levesque, and Mitchell 1992).

Structure-driven algorithms cut across both search and consistency inference algorithms. These techniques emerged from an attempt to topologically characterize constraint problems that are tractable. *Tractable classes* were generally recognized by realizing that enforcing low-level consistency (in polynomial time) guarantees global consistency for some problems. The basic network structure that supports tractability is a tree (Mackworth and Freuder 1985). In particular, enforcing arc consistency on a tree-structured network ensures global consistency along some ordering. Most other graph-based techniques can be viewed as transforming a given network into a metatree. Adaptive consistency, tree clustering, and constraint learning, are all time and space exponentially bounded by the tree width of the constraint graph; the *cycle cutset scheme* combines search and inference and is exponentially bounded by the constraint graph's *cycle-cutset;* the *biconnected component method* is bounded by the size of the constraint graph's largest biconnected component (Freuder 1982); and backjumping is exponentially bounded by the depth of the graph's depth-first search tree. The last three methods require only polynomial space.

Tractable classes were also identified by the properties of the constraints themselves. Such tractable classes exploit notions such as tight domains and tight constraints (van Beek and Dechter 1997), row-convex constraints (van Beek and Dechter 1995), implicational and max-ordered constraints (Kirousis 1993; Jeavons, Cohen, and Gyssens 1997), as well as causal networks. A connection between tractability and algebraic closure was recently discovered (Cohen, Jeavons, and Gyssens 1995).

Finally, special classes of tractable constraints associated with TEMPORAL REASONING have received much attention in the last decade. These include subsets of qualitative interval algebra (Golumbic and Shamir 1993) expressing relationships such as "time interval *A* overlaps or precedes time interval *B*," as well as quantitative binary linear inequalities over the real numbers of the form $X - Y \leq a$ (Dechter, Meiri, and Pearl 1990).

Theoretical evaluation of constraint satisfaction algorithms is accomplished primarily by worst-case analysis (i.e., determining a function of the problem's size that sets the upper bound to the algorithm's performance over all problems of that size), or by dominance relationships (Kondrak and van Beek 1997). However, because worst-case analysis by its nature is too pessimistic and often does not reflect actual performance, empirical evaluation is necessary. Normally, a proposed algorithm is evaluated empirically on a set of randomly generated instances taken from the relatively "hard" "phase transition" region (Selman, Levesque, and Mitchell 1992). Other benchmarks based on real-life applications such as scheduling are also used. Currently, dynamic variable ordering and value selection heuristics that use various forms of constraint inference, backjumping, and constraint learning have been shown to be very effective for various problem classes (Prosser 1993; Frost and Dechter 1994; Sabin and Freuder 1994).

See also HEURISTIC SEARCH

—*Rina Dechter*

References

Arnborg, S., and A. Proskourowski. (1989). Linear time algorithms for NP-hard problems restricted to partial *k*-trees. *Discrete and Applied Mathematics* 23: 11–24.

Dechter, R. (1990). Enhancement schemes for constraint processing: Backjumping, learning, and cutset decomposition. *Artificial Intelligence* 41: 273–312.

Dechter, R., and J. Pearl. (1987). Network-based heuristics for constraint satisfaction problems. *Artificial Intelligence* 34: 1–38.

Dechter, R., and J. Pearl. (1989). Tree clustering for constraint networks. *Artificial Intelligence* 38(3): 353–366.

Dechter, R., I. Meiri, and J. Pearl. (1990). Temporal constraint networks. *Artificial Intelligence* 49: 61–95.

Dechter, R., and I. Rish. (1994). Directional resolution: The Davis-Putnam procedure, revisited. In *Principles of Knowledge Representation and Reasoning*, pp. 134–145.

Freuder, E. C. (1982). A sufficient condition for backtrack-free search. *Journal of the ACM* 29(1): 24–32.

Frost, D., and R. Dechter. (1994). In search of best search: An empirical evaluation. In *AAAI-94: Proceedings of the Twelfth National Conference on Artificial Intelligence*. Seattle, WA, pp. 301–306.

Gaschnig, J. (1979). *Performance Measurement and Analysis of Search Algorithms*. Pittsburgh: Carnegie Mellon University.

Golumbic, M. C., and R. Shamir. (1993). Complexity and algorithms for reasoning about time: A graph-theoretic approach. *Journal of the ACM* 40: 1108–1133.

Haralick, M., and G. L. Elliot. (1980). Increasing tree-search efficiency for constraint satisfaction problems. *Artificial Intelligence* 14: 263–313.

Jeavons, P., D. Cohen, and M. Gyssens. (1997). Closure properties of constraints. *Journal of ACM* 44: 527–548.

Kirousis, L. M. (1993). Fast parallel constraint satisfaction. *Artificial Intelligence* 64: 147–160.

Kondrak, G., and P. van Beek. (1997). A theoretical valuation of selected algorithms. *Artificial Intelligence* 89: 365–387.

Mackworth, A. K. (1977). Consistency in networks of relations. *Artificial Intelligence* 8(1): 99–118.

Mackworth, A. K., and E. C. Freuder. (1985). The complexity of some polynomial network consistency algorithms for constraint satisfaction problems. *Artificial Intelligence* 25.

Minton, S., M. D. Johnson, A. B. Phillips, and P. Laird. (1990). Solving large-scale constraint satisfaction and scheduling problems using heuristic repair methods. In *National Conference on Artificial Intelligence*, Anaheim, CA, pp. 17–24.

Montanari, U. (1974). Networks of constraints: fundamental properties and applications to picture processing. *Information Sciences* 7(66): 95–132.

Prosser, P. (1993). Hybrid algorithms for constraint satisfaction problems. *Computational Intelligence* 9(3): 268–299.

Purdom, P. W. (1983). Search rearrangement backtracking and polynomial average time. *Artificial Intelligence* 21: 117–133.

Sabin, D., and E. C. Freuder. (1994). Contradicting conventional wisdom in constraint satisfaction. In *ECAI-94*, Amsterdam, pp. 125–129.

Selman, B., H. Levesque, and D. Mitchell. (1992). A new method for solving hard satisfiability problems. In *Proceedings of the Tenth National Conference on Artificial Intelligence*, 339–347.

Stallman, M., and G. J. Sussman. (1977). Forward reasoning and dependency-directed backtracking in a system for computer-aided circuit analysis. *Artificial Intelligence* 2: 135–196.

van Beek, P., and R. Dechter. (1995). On the minimality and decomposability of row-convex constraint networks. *Journal of the ACM* 42: 543–561.

van Beek, P., and R. Dechter. (1997). Constraint tightness and looseness versus local and global consistency. *Journal of the ACM* 44(4): 549–566.

Further Readings

Baker, A. B. (1995). *Intelligent Backtracking on Constraint Satisfaction Problems: Experimental and Theoretical Results*. Ph.D. diss., University of Oregon.

Bayardo, R., and D. Mirankar. (1996). A complexity analysis of space-bound learning algorithms for the constraint satisfaction problem. *AAAI-96: Proceedings of the Thirteenth National Conference on Artificial Intelligence*, pp. 298–304.

Bistarelli, S., U. Montanari, and F. Rossi. (Forthcoming). Semiring-based constraint satisfaction and optimization. *Journal of the Association of Computing Machinery*.

Cohen, D. A., M. C. Cooper, and P.G. Jeavons. (1994). Characterizing tractable constraints. *Artificial Intelligence* 65: 347–361.

Dechter, R., and D. Frost. (1997). Backtracking algorithms for constraint satisfaction problems: A survey. *UCI Tech Report*.

Dechter, R. (1992). Constraint networks. In *Encyclopedia of Artificial Intelligence*. 2nd ed. New York: Wiley, pp. 276–285.

Dechter, R., and I. Meiri. (1994). Experimental evaluation of preprocessing algorithms for constraint satisfaction problems. *Artificial Intelligence* 68: 211–241.

Dechter, R., and P. van Beek. (1997). Local and global relational consistency. *Theoretical Computer Science* 173(1): 283–308.

Frost, D. (1997). *Algorithms and Heuristics for Constraint Satisfaction Problems*. Ph.D. diss., University of California, Irvine.

Ginsberg, M. L. (1993). Dynamic backtracking. *Journal of Artificial Intelligence Research* 1: 25–46.

Kumar, V. (1992). Algorithms for constraint satisfaction problems: A survey. *AI magazine* 13(1): 32–44.

Mackworth, A. K. (1992). Constraint Satisfaction. In *Encyclopedia of Artificial Intelligence*. 2nd ed. New York: Wiley, pp. 285–293.

Schwalb, E. and R. Dechter. (1997). Processing disjunctions in temporal constraint networks. *Artificial Intelligence* 93(1–2): 29–61.

Tsang, E. (1993). *Foundation of Constraint Satisfaction*. Academic Press.

Context and Point of View

The content of most linguistic expressions in one way or other depends on the context of utterance; in fact, in logical semantics (literal) meaning is analyzed as a function assigning contents (or intensions) to contexts. The most prominent way for the context to determine content is by way of INDEXICALS, that is, by expressions whose sole function is to contribute a component of the situation in which an utterance is made to the content expressed by that utterance. Indexicals can be either lexical items, such as the English personal pronoun *I*, which always refers to the speaker, or grammatical forms, such as the first person verbal suffix in Latin, which has the same function. Indexicals are special cases of *deictic expressions* whose reference depends on context—a case in point being the possessive pronoun *my*, which describes something as belonging to the speaker as determined by the utterance situation (Zimmermann 1995).

All languages seem to contain deictic expressions and to make ample use of them. Traditionally, deictics are classified according to the aspect or feature of the utterance context that determines their reference. Three major kinds of deixis are usually distinguished: (1) *person deixis,* where the context provides one or more participants of the conversation (speaker, addressee), or a group to which they belong; (2) *spatial deixis,* where the context provides a location or a direction, especially as a reference point for spatial orientation on which other deictics depend (an "origo," in Bühler's 1934 sense); and (3) *temporal deixis,* with the context contributing a specific time, which may be the time of utterance, the time of a reported event, or the like. Among the clear cases of deixis in English are (1) the first and second person pronouns, *I, you, we;* (2) the local adverbs *here* and *there;* and (3) the temporal adverbs *now* and *yesterday*. Other examples of deixis, including demonstratives such as *this* whose referents depend on an accompanying gesture plus the speaker's referential intentions (Kaplan 1989a, 1989b), do not clearly fall under 1–3. DISCOURSE anaphors, such as *aforementioned,* or third person pronouns, such as *he, her,* receive their interpretation by reference to their linguistic context and are thus sometimes also considered as deictic. As has become clear by work in DYNAMIC SEMANTICS, however, such anaphoric elements quite regularly undergo variable binding processes, as in *Every man who owns a donkey beats it,* resulting in a quantified, rather than context-dependent reading. The same has been observed for the context dependence of certain relational nouns (Partee 1989) such as *enemy* whose arguments are usually given by the utterance situation, as in *The enemy is approaching,* but may also be quantified over, as in *Every participant faced an enemy*.

Languages differ considerably in the number and kinds of deictic locutions they have. Some have the place of utterance as their only spatial parameter, where others have complex systems classifying space according to various criteria (Frei 1944), including distance from the speaker's position as measured in varying degrees (up to seven in Malagasy, according to Anderson and Keenan 1985), visibility (also in Malagasy, and in many other languages), and perspective (as

in English *left* and *right*). Person deixis, too, is subject to variation: many languages (e.g., French) distinguish more than one second person, depending on the social relationship between speaker and hearer, a phenomenon known as "social deixis" (Levinson 1979); another common distinction (to be found, for example, in Tagalog) is between an inclusive and an exclusive first person plural, depending on whether the addressee does or does not belong to the group designated. The variation in temporal deixis is harder to estimate, partly because it is not always clear whether tenses are truly deictic, but also because languages tend to be more or less *localistic,* extending their system of spatial deixis to time by analogy and frozen metaphor (cf. TENSE AND ASPECT).

The role of the context in providing the perspective from which the utterance is interpreted becomes particularly vivid in *shifted contexts,* also known as "relativized deixis" (Fillmore 1975), or "Deixis am Phantasma" (Bühler 1934), where at least some of the deictic parameters are not provided by the utterance situation. Among these shifts are various forms of pretense like play-acting, impersonation, *analogous* deixis (Klein 1978)—the speaker of *We took <u>this</u> road* may refer to what is represented by the map in front of her—or even first-person inscriptions on gravestones (Kratzer 1978).

Speakers often take the hearer's perspective in describing the spatial location of objects (Schober 1993), as in *Please press the left button/the button to your left*. This context shift can be made out of politeness or, especially when the hearer does not know the speaker's location, for communicative efficiency. In the latter case, however, deictic orientation may also be replaced by an intrinsic perspective provided by an object with a canonical front (as in *behind the house,* denoting the backyard).

A rather coherent area of regular context shift is known as "free indirect speech" in narrative analysis (Banfield 1982; Ehrlich 1990). In a passage such as *Mary looked out of the window. Her husband was coming soon,* the second sentence is understood to report Mary's thoughts from her own point of view: it is Mary, not the narrator, who believes her husband to be on his way and, whereas the verb *come* normally expresses movement toward the speaker as determined by the context, in this case it is Mary's position toward which her husband is reported to move (Rossdeutscher 1997). Similarly, the adverb *soon* is understood to describe an event as happening shortly after the scene described, rather than the utterance, has taken place. This simultaneous replacement of some (but not all) contextual parameters can be seen as a shift of the *logophoric center* (Kuno 1987), which comprises a large part of the more subjective parameters, including those that determine the interpretation of evaluative adjectives (e.g., *boring*) and free reflexives. Whereas free indirect speech is a rather well understood phenomenon with predictable features (including a restricted choice of tenses), other shifts of the logophoric center are less easily accounted for. Among these are the optional perspectives in overt attitude reports (Mitchell 1987), as in *The CIA agent knows that John thinks that a KGB agent lives <u>across the street</u>,* where the underlined phrase can be evaluated from the speaker's, the CIA agent's, or John's point of view.

See also MEANING; PRAGMATICS; QUANTIFIERS; SITUAT-EDNESS/EMBEDDEDNESS

—*Thomas Ede Zimmermann*

References

Anderson, S. R., and E. L. Keenan. (1985). Deixis. In T. Shopen, Ed., *Language Typology and Syntactic Description.* Vol. 2, *Grammatical Categories and the Lexicon.* Cambridge: Cambridge University Press, pp. 259–308.

Banfield, A. (1982). *Unspeakable Sentences.* London: Routledge.

Bühler, K. (1934). *Sprachtheorie.* Jena, Germany: Fischer.

Ehrlich, S. (1990). *Point of View.* London: Routledge.

Fillmore, C. (1975). *Santa Cruz Lectures on Deixis.* Bloomington: Indiana University Lingustics Club.

Frei, H. (1944). Systèmes de déictiques. *Acta Linguistica* 4: 111–129.

Kaplan, D. (1989a). Demonstratives: An essay on the semantics, logic, metaphysics and epistemology of demonstratives and other indexicals. In J. Almog, J. Perry, and H. Wettstein, Eds., *Themes from Kaplan.* Oxford: Oxford University Press, pp. 481–563.

Kaplan, D. (1989b). Afterthoughts. In J. Almog, J. Perry, and H. Wettstein, Eds., *Themes from Kaplan.* Oxford: Oxford University Press, pp. 565–614.

Klein, W. (1978). Wo ist hier? Präliminarien zu einer Untersuchung der lokalen Deixis. *Linguistische Berichte* 58: 18–40.

Kratzer, A. (1978). *Semantik der Rede: Kontexttheorie—Modalwörter—Konditionalsätze.* Königstein, Germany: Scriptor.

Kuno, S. (1987). *Functional Syntax.* Chicago: University of Chicago Press.

Levinson, S. C. (1979). Pragmatics and social deixis: Reclaiming the notion of conventional implicature. In *Proceedings of the Fifth Annual Meeting of the Berkeley Linguistics Society,* Berkeley, CA: pp. 206–223.

Mitchell, J. (1987). The Formal Semantics of Point of View. Ph.D. diss., University of Massachusetts at Amherst.

Partee, B. (1989). Binding implicit variables in quantified contexts. In C. Wiltshire, R. Graczyk, and B. Music, Eds., *CLS 25. Part One: The General Session,* Chicago, pp. 342–365.

Rossdeutscher, A. (1997). Perspektive und propositionale Einstellung in der Semantik von *kommen.* In C. Umbach, M. Grabski, and R. Hörnig, Eds., *Perspektive in Sprache und Raum.* Wiesbaden: Deutscher Universitätsverlag, pp. 261–288.

Schober, M. F. (1993). Spatial perspective-taking in conversation. *Cognition* 47: 1–24.

Zimmermann, T. E. (1995). Tertiumne datur? Possessivpronomina und die Zweiteilung des Lexikons. *Zeitschrift für Sprachwissenschaft* 14: 54–71. Translated as *Tertiumne datur? Possessive pronouns and the bipartition of the lexicon.* In H. Kamp and B. Partee, Eds., *Context Dependence in the Analysis of Linguistic Meaning.* Vol. 1, *Papers.* Stuttgart, Germany: Institut für maschinelle Sprachverarbeitung, Stuttgart University, 1997, pp. 409–425.

Further Readings

Doron, E. (1990). *Point of View.* CSLI Report 90–143, Stanford University.

Ehrich, V. (1992). *Hier und Jetzt: Studien zur lokalen und temporalen Deixis im Deutschen.* Tübingen, Germany: Niemeyer.

Forbes, G. (1988). Indexicals. In D. Gabbay and F. Guenthner, Eds., *Handbook of Philosophical Logic,* vol. 4. Dordrecht: Kluwer, pp. 463–490.

Jarvella, R. J., and W. Klein, Eds. (1982). *Speech, Place, and Action: Studies of Deixis and Related Topics.* Chichester: Wiley.

Zimmermann, T. E. (1991). Kontextabhängigkeit. In A. v. Stechow and D. Wunderlich, Eds., *Semantik (Semantics).* Berlin/New York: Springer, pp. 156–229.

Control Theory

The modern development of automatic control evolved from the regulation of tracking telescopes, steam engine control using fly-ball governors, the regulation of water turbines, and the stabilization of the steering mechanisms of ships. The literature on the subject is extensive, and because feedback control is so broadly applicable, it is scattered over many journals ranging from engineering and physics to economics and biology. The subject has close links to optimization including both deterministic and stochastic formulations. Indeed, Bellman's influential book on dynamic optimization, *Dynamic Programming* (1957), is couched largely in the language of control.

The successful use of feedback control often depends on having an adequate model of the system to be controlled and suitable mechanisms for influencing the system, although recent work attempts to bypass this requirement by incorporating some form of adaptation, learning, or both. Here we will touch on the issues of modeling, regulation and tracking, optimization, and stochastics.

Modeling

The oldest and still most successful class of models used to design and analyze control systems are input-output models, which capture how certain controllable input variables influence the state of the system and, ultimately, the observable outputs. The models take the form of differential or difference equations and can be linear or nonlinear, finite or infinite dimensional. When possible, the models are derived from first principles, adapted and simplified to be relevant to the situation of interest. In other cases, empirical approaches based on regression or other tools from time series analysis are used to generate a mathematical model from data. The latter is studied under the name of "system identification" (Willems 1986). To fix ideas, consider a linear differential equation model with input vector u, state vector x, and output y

$$\frac{dx}{dt} = Ax + Bu; \quad y = Cx$$

Such models are of fundamental importance because they not only capture the essential behavior of important classes of linear systems but also represent the small signal approximation to a large class of strongly nonlinear systems. Questions of control often center around the design of an auxiliary system, called the "compensator" or "controller," which acts on the measurable variable y to produce a feedback signal that, when added to u, results in better performance. The concepts of controllability, observability, and model reduction play a central role in the theory of linear models (Kalman et al. 1969; Brockett 1970).

There are important classes of systems whose performance can only be explained by nonlinear models. Many of these are prominent in biology. In particular, problems that involve pattern generation, such as walking or breathing, are not well modeled using linear equations. The description of numerically controlled machine tools and robots, both of which convert a formal language input into an analog (continuous) output are also not well modeled by the linear theory, although linear theory may have a role in explaining the behavior of particular subsystems (Brockett 1997, 1993).

Regulation and Tracking

The simplest and most frequently studied problem in automatic control is the regulation problem. Here one has a desired value for a variable, say the level of water in a tank, and wants to regulate the flow of water into the tank to keep the level constant in the face of variable demand. This is a special case of the problem of tracking a desired signal, for example, keeping a camera focused on a moving target (see STEREO AND MOTION PERCEPTION), or orchestrating the motion of a robot so that the end effector follows a certain moving object. The design of stable regulators is one of the oldest problems in control theory. It is often most effective to incorporate additional dynamic effects, such as *integral action,* in the feedback path, thus increasing the complexity of the dynamics and making the issue of stability less intuitive. In the case of systems adequately modeled by linear differential equations, the matter was resolved long ago by the work of Routh, and Hurwitz, which yields, for example, the result that the third-order linear, constant-coefficient differential equation

$$\frac{d^3y}{dt^3} + a\frac{d^2y}{dt^2} + b\frac{dy}{dt} + cy = 0$$

is stable if a, b, and c are all positive and $ab - c \geq 0$. Motivated by feedback stability problems associated with high-gain amplifiers, Nyquist (1932) took a fresh look at the feedback stability problem and formulated a stability criterion directly in terms of the frequency response of the system. This criterion and variations of it form the basis of classical feedback compensation techniques as described in the well-known book of Kuo (1967). In the case of nonlinear systems, the design of stable regulators is more challenging. Liapunov stability theory (Lefschetz 1965) provides a point of departure, but general solutions are not to be expected.

Optimization

A systematic approach to the design of feedback regulators can be based on the minimization of the integral of some positive function of the error and the control effort. For the linear system defined above this might take the form

$$\eta = \int_0^\infty (x^TQx + u^Tu)dt$$

which leads, via the calculus of variations, to a linear feedback control law of the form $u = -B^TKx$, with K being a solution to the quadratic matrix equation $A^TK + KA - KBB^TK + Q = 0$. This methodology provides a reasonably systematic approach to the design of regulators in that only the loss matrix Q is unspecified. Different types of optimization problems associated with trajectory optimization in aerospace applications and batch processing in chemical plants are also quite important. A standard problem formulation in this latter setting would be concerned with problems of the form

$$\frac{dx}{dt} = f(x, u); \quad \eta = \int_0^T L(x, u, t)dt + \phi(x(T))$$

Chapter 7 of Sontag (1990) provides a short introduction including a discussion of the relationships between DYNAMIC PROGRAMMING and the more classical Hamilton-Jacobi theory.

Stochastics

The Kalman-Bucy (1961) filter, one of the most widely appreciated triumphs of mathematical engineering, is used in many fields to reduce the effects of measurement errors and has played a significant role in achieving the first soft landing on the moon, and more recently, achieving closed-loop control of driverless cars on the autobahns of Germany. Developed in the late 1950s as a state space version of the Wiener-Kolomogorov theory of filtering and prediction, it gave rise to a rebirth of this subject. In its basic form, the Kalman-Bucy filter is based on a linear system, white noise (written here as $\dot{w}$ and $\dot{n}$) model

$$\dot{x} = Ax + B\dot{w}; \quad y = Cx + \dot{n}$$

The signal Cx is generated from the white noise $\dot{w}$ by passing it into the linear system, although it is not observed directly, but only after it is corrupted by the additive noise $\dot{n}$. The theory tells us that the best (in several senses including the least squares) way to recover x from y is to generate an estimate $\hat{x}$ using the equation

$$\frac{d\hat{x}}{dt} = A\hat{x} - PC^T(C\hat{x} - y)$$

with P being the solution of the variance equation

$$\dot{P} = AP + PA^T + BB^T - PC^TCP$$

The development of similar theories for counting processes, queuing systems, and the like is more difficult and remains an active area for research (Brémaud 1981).

See also BEHAVIOR-BASED ROBOTICS; DYNAMIC APPROACHES TO COGNITION; MANIPULATION AND GRASPING; MOBILE ROBOTS; WALKING AND RUNNING MACHINES; WIENER

—*Roger W. Brockett*

References

Airy, G. B. (1840). On the regulator of the clock-work for effecting uniform movement of equatoreals. *Memoirs of the Royal Astronomical Society* 11: 249–267.

Bellman, R. (1957). *Dynamic Programming.* Princeton: Princeton University Press.

Brémaud, P. (1981). *Point Processes and Queues.* New York: Springer.

Brockett, R. W. (1970). *Finite Dimensional Linear Systems.* New York: Wiley.

Brockett, R. W. (1993). Hybrid models for motion control systems. In H. Trentelman and J. C. Willems, Eds., *Perspectives in Control.* Boston: Birkhauser, pp. 29–54.

Brockett, R. W. (1997). Cycles that effect change. In *Motion, Control and Geometry.* Washington, DC: National Research Council, Board on Mathematical Sciences.

Hurwitz, A. (1895). Über die Bedingungen, unter welchen eine Gleichung nur Wurzeln mit negativen reellen Theilen besitzt. *Mathematische Annalen* 46: 273–284.

Kalman, R. E., and R. S. Bucy. (1961). New results in linear filtering and prediction theory. *Trans. ASME Journal of Basic Engineering* 83: 95–108.

Kalman, R. E., et al. (1969). *Topics in Mathematical System Theory.* New York: McGraw-Hill.

Kuo, B. C. (1967). *Automatic Control Systems.* Englewood Cliffs, NJ: Prentice-Hall.

Lefschetz, S. (1965). Stability of nonlinear control systems. In *Mathematics in Science and Engineering,* vol. 13. London: Academic Press.

Maxwell, J. C. (1868). On governors. *Proc. of the Royal Soc. London* 16: 270–283.

Minorsky, N. (1942). Self-excited oscillations in dynamical systems possessing retarded action. *J. of Applied Mechanics* 9: 65–71.

Nyquist, H. (1932). Regeneration theory. *Bell Systems Technical Journal* 11: 126–147.

Sontag, E. D. (1990). *Mathematical Control Theory.* New York: Springer.

Willems, J. C. (1986). From time series to linear systems. *Automatica* 22: 561–580.

Cooperation and Competition

Cooperation is a hallmark of all social organisms. Social groups are, in effect, cooperative solutions to the day-to-day problems of survival and reproduction. For some or all members of the group, however, group living invariably incurs costs, which may be reflected in social subordination, restricted access to the best feeding or resting sites, the social suppression of reproduction, or increased ecological costs. Because individuals (or at least, their genes) are by definition in evolutionary competition with each other, this creates a paradox that is not easy to explain in Darwinian terms: Cooperation is a form of ALTRUISM in which one individual gives up something to the benefit of another (see also SOCIOBIOLOGY).

Evolutionary theory identifies three ways cooperation can evolve, which differ in the delay before the "debt" incurred by cooperating is repaid (see Bertram 1982). In *mutualism,* both individuals gain an immediate advantage from cooperating. This may be an appropriate explanation for many cases of group living where individuals gain mutually and simultaneously from living together (e.g., through increased protection from predators, group defense of a territory, etc). In *reciprocal altruism,* the debt is repaid at some future time, providing this is during the lifetime of the altruist. This may be an appropriate explanation for cases where individuals who are unrelated to each other form a coalition for mutual protec-

tion. The ally, even though in no immediate danger, will come to the aid of a beleaguered partner, on the implicit assumption that the partner will come to the ally's aid on some future occasion. And in *kin selection,* the debt is repaid after the death of the altruist because the extra fitness that accrues to the recipient contributes to the altruist's *inclusive fitness,* defined as the number of copies of a given gene contributed to the species' gene pool by an individual as a result of his or her own reproductive output plus the number contributed by his or her relatives as a direct result of that individual helping each relative to breed more successfully. Kin selection can only work when the two individuals are genetically related. It may provide an explanation for assistance freely given to relatives without prior demands for reciprocation.

Although cooperation and the exchange of services or resources occur widely among humans, such exchanges are not wholly altruistic, especially when the actor incurs a significant cost. A number of recent studies of humans have demonstrated that exchange of benefits occurs without preconditions for repayment when it involves relatives, but only with strict reciprocation when it involves nonrelatives, (for example, garden labor exchange among South American K'ekchi' horticulturalists and Nepalese hill farmers (Berté 1988; Panter-Brick 1989); alliance support among historical Vikings (Dunbar, Clark, and Hurst 1995); and exchange of information about good fishing grounds among contemporary Maine lobstermen (Palmer 1991).

Cooperation is an unstable strategy because it is susceptible to cheating by free riders. The ease with which selfish interests can undermine cooperativeness is most conspicuous in the case of common pool resources (e.g., forest resources, communally owned commons or oceanic fishing grounds). Although it may be obvious to everyone that a communal agreement to manage the use of these resources would benefit everyone because the resource would last longer, the advantages to be gained by taking a disproportionate share can be an overwhelming temptation. The result is often the complete destruction of the resource through overuse, the "tragedy of the commons" (see Ortsrom, Gardner, and Walker 1994). Tax avoidance and parking in no parking zones are everyday examples of a similar kind of cheating on socially agreed conventions.

The free rider problem is one of the most serious problems encountered by organisms living in large groups that depend on cooperation for their effectiveness. It acts as a dispersive force that, unless checked, leads inexorably to the disbanding of groups (and thus the loss of the very purpose for which the groups formed). The problem arises because the advantages of free riding are often considerable, especially when the risks of being caught (and thus of being punished or discriminated against) are slight. Perhaps as a result, strategies that help to detect or deter free riders are common in most human societies. These include being suspicious of strangers (whose willingness to cooperate remains in doubt), rapidly changing dialects (which helps identify the group of individuals with whom you grew up, who are likely to be either relatives or to bear obligations of mutual aid; see Nettle and Dunbar 1997), entering into conventions of mutual obligation (e.g., blood brotherhood, exchange of gifts, or formal treaties), and ostracizing or punishing those who cheat on the system (e.g., castigating hunters who eat all their meat rather than sharing it, as among !Kung San bushmen: Lee 1979).

In addition to these purely behavioral mechanisms (perhaps the product of CULTURAL EVOLUTION), there is also evidence to suggest that there may be dedicated "cheat detection" modules hardwired in the human brain. The evidence for this derives from studies that consider abstract and social versions of the *Wason selection task* (a verbal task about logical reasoning: see Table 1). Although most people get the answer wrong when presented with the abstract version of the Wason task, they usually get it right when the task is presented as a logically identical social contract problem that involves detecting who is likely to be cheating the system (see Cosmides and Tooby 1992). This is assumed to happen because we have a cognitive module that is sensitive to social cheats, but that cannot easily recognize the same kind of logical problem in another form.

The mechanisms involved in the evolution of cooperation have been of considerable interest to economists and other social scientists, as well as to evolutionary psychologists (see EVOLUTIONARY PSYCHOLOGY). GAME THEORY, in particular, provides considerable insights into the stability of cooperative behavior. The situation known as "prisoner's dilemma" has been the focus of much of this research. It involves two allies who must independently decide whether to cooperate with each other (to gain a small reward) or defect (to gain a very large reward)—but with the risk of doing very badly if cooperation is met with defection. A computer tournament that pitted alternative algorithms against each other in an evolutionary game revealed that the very simplest rule of behavior is the most successful. This rule is known as "tit-for-tat" (or *TfT*): Cooperate on the first encounter with an opponent and thereafter do exactly what the opponent did on the previous round (cooperate if he cooperated, defect if he defected).

In more conventional face-to-face situations, cues provided by nonverbal behavior may be important in promoting both trust in another individual and the sense of obligation to others required for successful cooperation. Experiments have shown that simply allowing individuals to discuss even briefly which strategy is best greatly increases the frequency of cooperation. Allowing them to exert moral pressure or fines on defectors improves the level of group cooperativeness still further.

Table 1. The Wason Selection Task

Standard version	Logical equivalent	Social contract version
A	P	Drinking a beer
H	Not-P	Drinking a Coke
4	Q	21 years old
7	Not-Q	16 years old

The Wason selection task (table 1) was developed as a test of logical reasoning. When presented with four cards bearing letters and numbers (as shown in column 1) and informed that "an even number always has a vowel on its reverse," the subject has to decide which card or cards to turn over in order to check the validity of the rule. This rule has the standard structure of the logical statement "If P (= even number), then Q (= vowel on reverse)." Because the four cards correspond to the statements P, not-P, Q and not-Q, the correct logical solution is to choose the cards that correspond to P and not-Q. Most subjects incorrectly choose P alone or the P and the Q cards. In the social contract version, the cards correspond to people sitting around a table whose drinks or ages are specified (as in column 3). The rule in this case is "If you want to drink alcoholic beverages, you must be over the age of 21 years." Here it is obvious that only the age of the beer drinker (P) and the drink of the 16-year-old (not-Q) need to be checked. Even though most people get the original abstract Wason task wrong, they get the social contract version right.

See also EVOLUTION

—*R. I. M. Dunbar*

References

Axelrod, R. (1984). *The Evolution of Cooperation.* New York: Basic Books.

Berté, N. A. (1988). K'ekchi' horticultural exchange: Productive and reproductive implications. In L. Betzig, M. Borgerhoff Mulder, and P. Turke, Eds., *Human Reproductive Behavior.* Cambridge: Cambridge University Press, pp. 83–96.

Bertram, B. C. R. (1982). Problems with altruism. In King's College Sociobiology Group, Eds., *Current Problems in Sociobiology.* Cambridge: Cambridge University Press, pp. 251–268.

Boyd, R., and P. Richerson. (1992). Punishment allows the evolution of cooperation (or anything else) in sizeable groups. *Ethology and Sociobiology* 13: 171–195.

Cosmides, L., and J. Tooby. (1992). Cognitive adaptations for social exchange. In J. Barkow, L. Cosmides and J. Tooby, Eds., *The Adapted Mind: Evolutionary Psychology and the Generation of Culture.* Oxford: Oxford University Press, pp. 163–228.

Dunbar, R., A. Clark, and N. L. Hurst. (1995). Conflict and cooperation among the Vikings: Contingent behavioral decisions. *Ethology and Sociobiology* 16: 233–246.

Enquist, M., and O. Leimar. (1993). The evolution of cooperation in mobile organisms. *Animal Behavior* 45: 747–757.

Gigerenzer, G., and K. Hug. (1992). Domain-specific reasoning: Social contracts, cheating and perspective change. *Cognition* 43: 127–171.

Lee, R. B. (1979). *The !Kung San: Men, Women and Work in a Foraging Society.* Cambridge: Cambridge University Press.

Nettle, D., and R. I. M. Dunbar. (1997). Social markers and the evolution of reciprocal exchange. *Current Anthropology* 38: 93–99.

Orstrom, E., R. Gardner, and J. Walker. (1994). *Rules, Games and Common-Pool Resources.* Ann Arbor: University of Michigan Press.

Palmer, C. T. (1991). Kin-selection, reciprocal altruism and information sharing among Maine lobstermen. *Ethology and Sociobiology* 12: 221–235.

Panter-Brick, C. (1989). Motherhood and subsistence work: The Tamang of rural Nepal. *Human Ecology* 17: 205–228.

Trivers, R. L. (1971). The evolution of reciprocal altruism. *Quarterly Review of Biology* 46: 35–57.

Cortex

See CEREBRAL CORTEX; VISUAL CORTEX, CELL TYPES, AND CONNECTIONS IN

Cortical Localization, History of

During the first twenty-five centuries of studies of brain function, almost all investigators ignored or belittled the CEREBRAL CORTEX. One exception was the Alexandrian anatomist Erasistratus (fl. c. 290 B.C.E.), who on the basis of comparative studies attributed the greater intelligence of humans to their more numerous cortical convolutions. This view was ridiculed by Galen (129–199), the most influential of all classical biomedical scientists, whose sarcastic dismissal of any significant role for the cortex continued to be quoted into the eighteenth century. Another major exception was Thomas Willis (1621–1675), a founder of the Royal Society, and author of the first monograph on the brain. On the basis of his dissections, experiments on animals, and clinical studies of humans, he attributed memory and voluntary movement functions to the cortex. However, by far the dominant view on cortical function before the beginning of the nineteenth century was that the cortex was merely a protective rind (*cortex* means "rind" in Latin), a glandular structure (the early microscopists saw globules in cortex, probably artifacts), or a largely vascular structure made up of small blood vessels. The apparent insensitivity of the cortex to direct mechanical and chemical stimulation was used as an argument against the cortex having any important functions in sensation, mentation, or movement.

The systematic localization of different psychological functions in different regions of the cerebral cortex begins with Franz Joseph Gall (1758–1828) and his collaborator J. C. Spurzheim (1776–1832), the founders of phrenology. The central ideas of their phrenological system were that the brain was an elaborately wired machine for producing behavior, thought, and emotion, and that the cerebral cortex consisted of a set of organs with different functions. Postulating about thirty-five affective and intellectual faculties, they assumed that these were localized in specific cortical organs and that the size of each cortical organ was indicated by the prominence of the overlying skull, that is, by cranial bumps. Their primary method was to examine the skulls of a wide variety of people, from lunatics and criminals to the eminent and accomplished. Although the absurdity of their dependence on cranial morphology was quickly recognized in the scientific community, Gall's ideas about the cortex as a set of psychological organs stimulated investigation of the effects of cortical lesions in humans and animals and of structural variations across different cortical regions, and thus had a lasting influence on the development of modern neuroscience.

Examining a variety of animals, Pierre Flourens (1794–1867) found that different major brain regions had different functions; he implicated the cerebral hemispheres in willing, remembering, and perceiving, and the CEREBELLUM in movement. Within the cortex, however, he found no localization of function: only the size and not the site of the lesion mattered. Although these results appeared to refute the punctate localizations of Gall, they actually supported both the general idea of localization of function in the brain and the specific importance Gall had given to the cerebral hemispheres in cognition.

In 1861, Paul BROCA described several patients with longstanding difficulties in speaking, which he attributed to damage to their left frontal lobes. This was the first generally accepted evidence for localization of a specific psychological function in the cerebral cortex (and was viewed at the time as a vindication of Gall's ideas of localization). Soon after, Fritsch and Hitzig demonstrated specific movements from electrical stimulation of the cortex of a dog, and drew the inference that some psychological functions and perhaps all of them need circumscribed centers of the cortex. The next major development was Carl Wernicke's 1876 report of a second type of language difficulty, or APHASIA, namely, one in understanding language; he associated this type of aphasia with damage to the posterior cortex in the region where the occipital, temporal, and parietal areas meet. Furthermore, he extended the idea of specialized cortical areas by stressing the importance of the connections among different areas, particularly for higher mental functions.

The last years of the nineteenth century saw several acrimonious controversies about the location of the various cortical sensory areas, involving such figures as David Ferrier, E. A. Schafer, and Hermann Munk. These issues were resolved first in monkeys and then in humans, so that by the end of World War I (with its rich clinical material), the location and organization of the primary visual, auditory, somesthetic, and motor areas of the cortex had been defined. By this time, the cerebral cortex had been divided up into multiple regions on the basis of regional variations in its cellular or fiber structure. The more lasting of these cortical architectonic parcellations were those by Korbinian Brodmann and Constantin von Economo, who created the numbering and lettering schemes, respectively, that are still in use. Despite their new labels, however, the functions of vast regions of the cortex, other than the primary sensory and motor areas, remained mysterious. These regions were termed *association cortex*, initially because they were thought to be the site of associations among the sensory and motor areas. Under the influence of British association psychology (typified by John Stuart Mill and Alexander Bain), association cortex was believed to be the locus of the association of ideas, and after Pavlov, the locus of the linkage between conditioned stimuli and responses.

Parallel with the success of the localizers around the turn of the century, there was also a strong antilocalization tendency. Adherents of this view, such as C.E. Brown-Sequard, Friedrich Goltz, Camillo GOLGI, and Jacques Loeb, emphasized such phenomena as the variability and recovery of symptoms after brain damage. They stressed that higher cognitive functions, particularly INTELLIGENCE and MEMORY, could not be localized in specific regions of the cortex. Like Flourens, Goltz reported that it was the size and not the location of the lesion that determined the severity of its effects on such higher functions. This holistic view of brain function was reinforced by the rise of GESTALT PSYCHOLOGY.

The best-known investigator of the relative importance of the size and site of a cortical lesion was Karl S. LASHLEY, easily the foremost figure in the study of the brain in the 1940s and 50s. On the basis of a long series of experiments, particularly on rats in a complex maze, he proposed two principles of brain organization, "equipotentiality" and "mass action" (Lashley 1929). *Equipotentiality* was the apparent capacity of any intact part of a functional area to carry out, with or without reduction in efficiency, the functions lost by destruction of the whole. Lashley assumed equipotentiality to vary with different brain areas and with different functions and thought it might only hold for association cortex and for functions more complex than sensory or motor ones such as maze learning. Furthermore, equipotentiality was not absolute but subject to a law of *mass action* whereby the efficiency of a whole complex function might be reduced in proportion to the extent of brain injury within an equipotential area. He stressed that both principles were compatible with cortical localization of functions and himself reported several findings of specific cortical localizations.

Lashley's most famous (or infamous) result was that both principles held for the entire cerebral cortex of rats learning a complex maze. That is, performance in this maze was independent of the site of the cortical lesion and only dependent on its size. We now know that these mass action results were due to increasing encroachment on multiple areas critical for different components of maze learning with increasing size of lesion. In recent years, Lashley's specific ideas on equipotentiality and mass action (and many of his other contributions) are often forgotten, and he is inaccurately described as an extreme "antilocalizer," who thought the brain was like a bowl of jelly.

Starting in the 1930s, systematic evidence for the localization of various cognitive functions in regions of association cortex began to emerge, particularly from students and associates of Lashley. In an experiment still at the core of contemporary research on the frontal lobes, Carlyle Jacobsen showed that frontal cortex lesions impair the performance of delayed response tasks, in which the monkey must remember which of two cups a peanut was placed under, a deficit Jacobsen described as one of short-term memory. (This result, through no fault of Jacobsen's, led directly to the introduction of frontal lobotomy as a psychosurgical procedure in humans.) In another seminal experiment, K.-L. Chow, in 1950, showed that lesions of temporal cortex yield a deficit in pattern recognition, a finding that helped spark the study of extrastriate mechanisms in vision.

Up to the 1950s, the advances in understanding the functions of the cerebral cortex had relied almost entirely on the study of brain damage in humans and other primates. The introduction of evoked response and SINGLE-NEURON RECORDING techniques provided powerful new methods for studying localization of cortical function, methods soon revealing that much of association cortex was made up of areas devoted to processing specific aspects of a single sensory modality. Furthermore, these higher sensory areas were often involved in attentional and mnemonic functions as well as perceptual ones.

Most recently, the introduction of functional MAGNETIC RESONANCE IMAGING (fMRI) and POSITRON-EMISSION TOMOGRAPHY (PET) scanning have begun to radically enhance our understanding of the functional specialization of the cerebral cortex. As we begin to understand the parallel serial and hierarchical ways that the cortex processes, stores, and retrieves information, the phrase "localization of function" sounds increasingly archaic and simplistic.

See also ELECTROPHYSIOLOGY, ELECTRIC AND MAGNETIC EVOKED FIELDS; MEMORY, ANIMAL STUDIES; MEMORY, HUMAN NEUROPSYCHOLOGY

— *Charles Gross*

References

Finger, S. (1994). *Origins of Neuroscience.* Oxford: Oxford University Press.

Gross, C. G. (1987). Early history of neuroscience. In G. Adelman, Ed., *Encyclopedia of Neuroscience,* vol. 2. Boston: Birkhauser, pp. 843–846.

Gross, C. G. (1997). From Imhotep to Hubel and Wiesel: the story of visual cortex. In J. H. Kaas, K. Rockland, and A. Peters, Eds., *Cerebral Cortex.* Vol. 12, *Extrastriate Cortex in Primates.* New York: Plenum Press.

Gross, C. G. (1998). *Brain, Vision, Memory: Tales in the History of Neuroscience.* Cambridge, MA: MIT Press.

Krech, D. (1963). Localization of function. In L. Postman, Ed., *Psychology in the Making.* New York: Knopf.

Lashley, K. S. (1929). *Brain Mechanisms and Intelligence.* Chicago: University of Chicago Press.

Further Readings

Boring, E. (1957). *A History of Experimental Psychology.* 2nd ed. New York: Appleton-Century-Crofts.

Brazier, M. (1988). *A History of Neurophysiology in the 19th Century.* New York: Raven Press.

Clarke, E., and K. Dewhurst. (1972). *An Illustrated History of Brain Function.* 2nd ed. San Francisco: Norman.

Clarke, E., and L. Jacyna. (1987). *Nineteenth-Century Origins of Neuroscientific Concepts.* Berkeley: University of California Press.

Clarke, E., and C. O'Malley. (1996). *The Human Brain and Spinal Cord.: A Historical Study Illustrated by Writings from Antiquity to the Twentieth Century.* San Francisco: Norman.

Corsi, P., Ed. (1991). *The Enchanted Loom. Chapters on the History of Neuroscience.* Oxford: Oxford University Press.

Fearing, F. (1970). *A Study in the History of Physiological Psychology.* Cambridge, MA: MIT Press.

Fulton, J. (1966). *Selected Readings in the History of Physiology.* 2nd ed. Springfield, IL: Thomas.

Harrington, A. (1987). *Medicine, Mind and the Double Brain.* Princeton: Princeton University Press.

Liddell, E. (1960). *The Discovery of Reflexes.* Oxford: Oxford University Press.

Meyer, A. (1971). *Historical Aspects of Cerebral Anatomy.* Oxford: Oxford University Press.

Neuburger, M. (1981). *The Historical Development of Experimental Brain and Spinal Cord Physiology before Flourens.* Baltimore: Johns Hopkins University Press.

Poytner, F. N. (1958). *The History and Philosophy of Knowledge of the Brain and Its Functions.* Oxford: Blackwell.

Polyak, H. (1957). *The Vertebrate Visual System.* Chicago: University of Chicago Press.

Shepherd, G. (1991). *Foundations of the Neuron Doctrine.* Oxford: Oxford University Press.

Singer, C. (1957). *A Short History of Anatomy and Physiology from the Greeks to Harvey.* New York: Dover.

Spillane, J. (1981). *The Doctrine of the Nerves: Chapters in the History of Neurology*. Oxford: Oxford University Press.

Young, R. (1970). *Mind, Brain and Adaptation in the Nineteenth Century*. Oxford: Oxford University Press.

Creativity

In psychology, *creativity* is usually defined as the production of an idea, action, or object that is new and valued, although what is considered creative at any point in time depends on the cultural context.

The early history of research in creativity includes Cesare Lombroso's investigation of the relationship between genius and madness, and Sir Francis Galton's genetic studies of genius. Guilford (1967) developed a theory of cognitive functioning that took creativity into account, and a battery of tests that measured fluency, flexibility, and originality of thought in both verbal and visual domains. His model and the tests he developed, such as the "Brick Uses" and "Unusual Uses" tests, are still the foundation for much of creativity testing and research (e.g., Torrance 1988).

Contemporary approaches to creativity range from mathematical modeling and computer simulations of breakthroughs in science (Langley et al. 1987) to the intensive study of creative individuals (Gruber 1981; Gardner 1993). Other approaches include the historiographic method applied to the content of large numbers of creative works, or to biographies (Martindale 1990; Simonton 1990). Most studies, however, are still done with schoolchildren and students, and assess performance on Guilford-type tests (for reviews, see Sternberg 1988 and Runco and Albert 1990).

Stages of the Creative Process

Contrary to the popular image of creative solutions appearing with the immediacy of a popping flashbulb, most novel achievements are the result of a much longer process, sometimes lasting many years. We can differentiate five stages of this process (Wallas 1926), with the understanding that these stages are recursive, and may be repeated in several full or partial cycles before a creative solution appears.

1. *Preparation* It is almost impossible to have a good new idea without having first been immersed in a particular symbolic system or domain. Creative inventors know the ins and outs of their branch of technology, artists are familiar with the work of previous artists, scientists have learned whatever there is to know about their specialty. One must also feel a certain unease about the state of the art in one's domain. There has to be a sense of curiosity about some unresolved problem—a machine that could be improved, a disease that has to be cured, a theory that could be made simpler and more elegant. Sometimes the problem is presented to the artist, scientist, or inventor by an outside emergency or requirement. The most important creative problems, however, are discovered as the individual is trying to come to terms with the problematic situation (Getzels 1964). In such cases, the problem itself may not be clearly formulated until the very end of the process. As Albert Einstein noted, the solution of an already formulated problem is relatively easy compared to the formulation of a problem no one had previously recognized.

2. *Incubation* Some of the most important mental work in creative problems takes place below the threshold of consciousness, where problematic issues identified during the preceding stage remain active without the person controlling the process. By allowing ideas to be associated with the contents of memory more or less at random, incubation also allows completely unexpected combinations to emerge. As long as one tries to formulate or solve a problem consciously, previous habits of mind will direct thoughts in rational, but predictable directions.

3. *Insight* When a new combination of ideas is strong enough to withstand unconscious censorship, it emerges into awareness in a moment of illumination—the "Eureka!" or "Aha!" experience usually thought to be the essence of creativity. Without preparation evaluation, and elaboration, however, no new idea or product will follow.

4. *Evaluation* The insight that emerges must be assessed consciously according to the rules and conventions of the given domain. Most novel ideas fail to withstand critical examination. One can go wrong by being either too critical or not critical enough.

5. *Elaboration* Thomas Edison made popular the saying "Genius is 1 percent inspiration and 99 percent perspiration." Even the most brilliant insight disappears without a trace unless the person is able and willing to develop its implications, to transform it into a reality. But this stage does not involve a simple transcription of a model perfectly formed in the mind. Most creative achievements involve drastic changes that occur as the creator translates the insight into a concrete product. A painter may approach the canvas with a clear idea of how the finished painting should look, but most original pictures evolve during the process of painting, as the combination of colors and shapes suggests new directions to the artist.

Creativity as a Systemic Phenomenon

No person can be creative without having access to a tradition, a craft, a knowledge base. Nor can we trust the subjective report of a person to the effect that his or her insight was indeed creative. It is one of the peculiarities of human psychology that most people believe their thoughts to be original and valuable. To accept such personal assessment at face value would soon deprive the concept of creativity of any specific meaning.

Creativity can best be understood as a confluence of three factors: a domain, which consists of a set of rules and practices; an individual, who makes a novel variation in the contents of the domain; and a field, which consist of experts who act as gatekeepers to the domain, and decide which novel variation is worth adding to it (Csikszentmihalyi 1996). A burst of creativity is generally caused, not by individuals being more creative, but by domain knowledge becoming more available, or a field being more supportive of change. Conversely, lack of creativity is usually caused, not by individuals lacking original thoughts, but by the domain having exhausted its possibilities, or the field not recognizing the most valuable original thoughts.

The Creative Person

Three aspects of creative persons are particularly important: cognitive processes, personality, and values and motivations. While, in most cases, a certain level of intelligence is a prerequisite—a threshold of 120 IQ is often mentioned (Getzels and Jackson 1962)—the relationship of IQ to creativity varies by domain, and after a relatively low threshold, there seems to be no further contribution of IQ to creativity. The first and longest study of high-IQ children (Terman 1947; see also Sears and Sears 1980) found little evidence of adult creativity in a sample whose mean IQ as children was 152, or even in a subsample with an IQ above 170.

The most obvious characteristic of original thinkers is what Guilford (1967) identified as "divergent thinking" or "thinking outside the box." *Divergent thinking* involves unusual associations of ideas, changing perspectives, and novel approaches to problems, in contrast to *convergent thinking,* which involves linear, logical steps. Correlations between divergent thinking tests and creative achievement tend to be low, however, and some scholars even claim that the cognitive approach of creative individuals does not differ qualitatively from that of normal people except in its speed (Simon 1988) and quantity of ideas produced (Simonton 1990).

Some forms of mental disease such as manic depression, addiction, and suicide are more frequent among individuals involved in artistic and literary pursuits (Andreasen 1987; Jamison 1989), but this might have less to do with creativity than with the lack of recognition that obtains in artistic domains. At the same time, creative individuals appear to be extremely sensitive to all kinds of stimuli, including aversive ones (Piechowski 1991), possibly accounting for their higher rates of emotional instability.

Personality traits often associated with creativity include openness to experience, impulsivity, self-confidence, introversion, aloofness, and rebelliousness (Getzels and Csikszentmihalyi 1976; Feist forthcoming). Such people also seem to have a remarkable ability to be both playful and hard-working, introverted and extroverted, aloof and gregarious, traditional and rebellious, as the occasion requires (Csikszentmihalyi 1996). The creative person might be less distinguished by a set of traits than by the ability to experience the world along modalities that in other people tend to be stereotyped. Throughout their lives, creative persons exhibit a childlike curiosity and interest in their domains, value their work above conventional monetary or status rewards (Getzels and Csikszentmihalyi 1976), and enjoy it primarily for intrinsic reasons (Amabile 1983). Creativity is its own reward.

See also CONCEPTUAL CHANGE; EDUCATION; EXPERTISE; INTELLIGENCE; PICTORIAL ART AND VISION; SCIENTIFIC THINKING AND ITS DEVELOPMENT

—*Mihalyi Csikszentmihalyi*

References

Amabile, T. (1983). *The Social Psychology of Creativity.* New York: Springer.

Andreasen, N. C. (1987). Creativity and mental illness: prevalence rates in writers and first-degree relatives. *American Journal of Psychiatry* 144: 1288–1292.

Csikszentmihalyi, M. (1996). *Creativity: Flow and the Psychology of Discovery and Invention.* New York: HarperCollins.

Feist, G. J. (Forthcoming). Personality in scientific and artistic creativity. In R. J. Sternberg, Ed., *Handbook of Human Creativity.* Cambridge: Cambridge University Press.

Gardner, H. (1993). *Creating Minds.* New York: Basic Books.

Getzels, J. W. (1964). Creative thinking, problem-solving, and instruction. In E. R. Hilgard, Ed., *Theories of Learning and Instruction.* Chicago: University of Chicago Press.

Getzels, J. W., and M. Csikszentmihalyi. (1976). *The Creative Vision: A Longitudinal Study of Problem Finding in Art.* New York: Wiley.

Getzels, J. W., and P. Jackson. (1962). *Creativity and Intelligence.* New York: Wiley.

Gruber, H. (1981). *Darwin on Man.* Chicago: University of Chicago Press.

Guilford, J. P. (1967). *The Nature of Human Intelligence.* New York: McGraw-Hill.

Jamison, K. R. (1989). Mood disorders and patterns of creativity in British writers and artists. *Psychiatry* 52: 125–134.

Kris, E. (1952). *Psychoanalytic Explorations in Art.* New York: International Universities Press.

Langley, P., H. A. Simon, G. L. Bradshaw, and J. M. Zytkow. (1987). *Scientific Discovery: Computational Exploration of the Creative Process.* Cambridge, MA: MIT Press.

Martindale, C. (1990). *The Clockwork Muse: The Predictability of Artistic Change.* New York: Basic Books.

Piechowski, M. J. (1991). Emotional development and emotional giftedness. In N. Colangelo and G. A. Davis, Eds., *Handbook of Gifted Education.* Boston: Allyn and Bacon, pp. 285–306.

Runco, M. A., and S. Albert, Eds. (1990). *Theories of Creativity.* Newbury Park, CA: Sage.

Sears, P., and R. R. Sears. (1980). 1,528 little geniuses and how they grew. *Psychology Today* February: 29–43.

Simon, H. A. (1988). Creativity and motivation: a response to Csikszentmihalyi. *New Ideas in Psychology* 6(2): 177–181.

Simonton, D. K. (1990). *Scientific Genius.* Cambridge: Cambridge University Press.

Sternberg, R. J., Ed. (1988). *The Nature of Creativity.* Cambridge: Cambridge University Press.

Terman, L. M. (1947). Subjects of IQ 170 or above. In *Genetic Studies of Genius,* vol. 4, chap. 21. Stanford: Stanford University Press.

Torrance, E. P. (1988). The nature of creativity as manifest in its testing. In R. J. Sternberg, Ed., *The Nature of Creativity.* Cambridge: Cambridge University Press, pp. 43–75.

Wallas, G. (1926). *The Art of Thought.* New York: Harcourt-Brace.

Further Readings

Sternberg, R. J., Ed. (1998). *Handbook of Human Creativity.* Cambridge: Cambridge University Press.

Creoles

Creoles constitute a unique language group. Other groups consist either of languages derived from a hypothesized protolanguage (as Welsh, English, Greek, and Sanskrit derive from Proto Indo-European) or a single historical ancestor (as Portuguese, Spanish, and Italian derive from Latin). Creoles, however, have no clear affiliation. Although the term *creole* has been used to characterize any language with an appearance of language mixture, languages generally accepted as creoles have all arisen in recent centuries from contacts between speakers of unrelated languages, usually as indirect results of European colonialism. They are found throughout the tropics, especially where large numbers of workers have been imported as slaves (or, occasionally, indentured laborers) to work on European-owned plantations. Because more work has been done on plantation creoles than on other types (those that developed in racially mixed communities on African and Asian coasts, or those derived initially from maritime contacts in the Pacific), most of what follows will apply primarily to plantation creoles.

Until recently, few scholars (e.g., Schuchardt 1882–91; Hesseling 1933) took these languages seriously; most treated them as deformed versions of European languages. Even to scholars who accepted them as true languages, their origins were controversial: some saw them as radical developments of French, English, and other languages, others as non-European languages thinly disguised by European vocabularies, still others as descendants of an Ur-creole perhaps springing from Afro-Portuguese contacts in the fifteenth and sixteenth centuries, perhaps even dating back to the medieval Lingua Franca. Other issues, such as whether creoles were necessarily preceded by, and derived from, some radically impoverished quasi-language (jargon or early-stage pidgin), or whether children or adults played the major role in their creation, were debated with equal heat but equally little agreement.

More than a century ago, Coelho (1880–86) pointed out that creoles showed structural similarities much greater than would be predicted given their wide distribution, their varied histories, and the large number of languages spoken in the contact situation where they arose. However, creoles would have held little interest for cognitive science had it not been proposed that, due to their mode of origin, they reflected universals of language more directly than "normal" languages.

This hypothesis of a species-specific biological program for language, providing default settings where acquisitional input is greatly reduced and/or deformed (often referred to as "bioprogram theory"), assumes a version of GENERATIVE GRAMMAR proposed by Borer (1983), and now widely accepted by generativists, in which parametric variation in SYNTAX arises solely from variability in grammatical MORPHOLOGY. In the (severely depleted) morphology of creoles, many (often most) grammatical morphemes are distinct from those of any language spoken in the contact situation. This indicates that grammatical morphemes, lost in the pidginization process, are replaced by the creation of new morphemes, often from semantically "bleached" referential items (thus the verb for "go" marks irrealis mode, locative verbs mark imperfective aspect, etc.). Some grammatical functions required immediate recreation of new morphemes, whereas morphemes for other functions were recreated centuries later, if at all (Bickerton 1988). The implication of these facts for the study of universal grammar remain, surprisingly, unexplored.

Bioprogram theory has obvious implications for other fields of inquiry. In LANGUAGE ACQUISITION, it suggests that creoles should be acquired more rapidly and with fewer errors than non-creoles, a prediction that has only recently begun to be tested (Adone 1994). In innateness studies (see INNATENESS OF LANGUAGE), it suggests in addition to syntactic principles a default SEMANTICS yielding highly specific analyses of TENSE AND ASPECT, modality, negation, articles, and purposive constructions, among others (an element missing from generative accounts of innateness of language). In the EVOLUTION OF LANGUAGE it suggests that syntactically structured language could have emerged abruptly from a structureless protolanguage (Bickerton 1990a).

Although bioprogram theory has had "an explosive impact . . . upon all aspects of the field" (McWhorter 1996), other approaches to creole genesis continue to flourish. Perhaps the most currently popular alternative is substratism, which claims that languages spoken by non-European ancestors of creole speakers served as sources for characteristically creole structures such as serial verb constructions (e.g., equivalents of "I carry X come give Y" for "I bring X to Y") and focusing of verbs by fronting and copying (e.g., equivalents of "is break he break the glass" for "he *broke* the glass" as opposed to merely cracking it). Alleyne (1980), Boretsky (1983), and Holm (1988–89), among others, exemplify this approach. However, substratists attribute these and other creole features to the Kwa language group in West Africa, heavily represented in some creole-speaking areas (Haiti, Surinam), but more lightly, if at all, in others (the Gulf of Guinea, Mauritius) and not at all in still others (Hawaii, the Seychelles).

Substratism's mirror-image, superstratism—the belief that creoles derive their syntax from colloquial versions of European language—is nowadays largely confined to French creolists (e.g., Chaudenson 1992). More widespread is a "componential" approach (Hancock 1986, Mufwene 1986) claiming that different mixtures of substratal, superstratal, and universal features contributed to different creoles, the mixture being determined in each case by social, historical, and demographic factors. However, because no one has yet proposed a formula for determining the relative contributions of the various components, this approach is at present virtually unfalsifiable, and it constitutes a research program rather than a theory.

Controversies have thus far centered around creole origins. But only recently, after decades of speculation and conjecture, have serious attempts been made to gather historical data (e.g., Arends 1995; Baker 1996). Not all this work is of equal value; claims of a scarcity of children in early colonies are refuted by contemporary statistics (Postma 1990; Bickerton 1990b). Documentation for the earliest stages of creole languages remains sparse, except for Hawaii, where rich data for all phases of the pidgin-creole cycle has been unearthed by Roberts (1995, 1998). These data confirm, at least for Hawaii, the main claims of bioprogram theory: that the creole was created (a) from a primitive, structureless pidgin (b) in a single generation (c) by children rather than adults. Hopefully, ongoing historical research on other creoles will determine the extent to which these conform to Hawaii's pattern.

See also CULTURAL EVOLUTION; LANGUAGE AND CULTURE

—*Derek Bickerton*

References

Adone, D. (1994). *The Acquisition of Mauritian Creole.* Amsterdam: John Benjamins.

Alleyne, M. (1980). *Comparative Afro-American.* Ann Arbor, MI: Karoma.

Arends, J., Ed. (1995). *The Early Stages of Creolization.* Amsterdam: John Benjamins.

Baker, P., Ed. (1996). *From Contact to Creole and Beyond.* London: University of Westminster Press.

Bickerton, D. (1981). *Roots of Language.* Ann Arbor, MI: Karoma.

Bickerton, D. (1984). The language bioprogram hypothesis. *Behavioral and Brain Sciences* 7.

Bickerton, D. (1988). Creole languages and the bioprogram. In F. J. Newmeyer, Ed., *Linguistics: The Cambridge Survey,* vol. 2. Cambridge: Cambridge University Press, pp. 267–284.

Bickerton, D. (1990a). *Language and Species.* Chicago: University of Chicago Press.

Bickerton, D. (1990b). Haitian demographics and creole genesis. *Canadian Journal of Linguistics* 35: 217–219.

Borer, H. (1983). *Parametric Syntax.* Dordrecht: Foris.

Boretsky, N. (1983). *Kreolsprachen, Substrate und Sprachwandel.* Weisbaden: Otto Harrassowitz.

Chaudenson, R. (1992). *Des Iles, des Hommes, des Langues.* Paris: L'Harmattan.

Coelho, F. A. (1880–86). Os dialectos romanicos o neo-latinos na Africa, Asia e America. *Boletin da Sociedade de Geografia de Lisboa* 2: 129–196; 3: 451–478; 6: 705–755.

Hancock, I. (1986). The domestic hypothesis, diffusion and componentiality: an account of Atlantic Anglophone Creole origins. In P. Muysken and N. Smith, Eds., *Substrata Versus Universals in Creole Genesis.* Amsterdam: John Benjamins.

Hesseling, D. C. (1933). Hoe onstond de eigenaardige vorm van het Kreols? *Neophilologus* 18: 209–215.

Holm, J. (1988–89). *Pidgins and Creoles.* 2 vols. Cambridge: Cambridge University Press.

McWhorter, J. (1996). Review of *Pidgins and Creoles, An Introduction,* edited by J. Arends, P. Muysken, and N. Smith. *Journal of Pidgin and Creole Languages* 11: 145–151.

Mufwene, S. (1986). The universalist and substrate hypotheses complement one another. In P. Muysken and N. Smith, Eds., *Substrata Versus Universals in Creole Genesis.* Amsterdam: John Benjamins.

Postma, J. M. (1990). *The Dutch in the Atlantic Slave Trade, 1600–1815.* Cambridge: Cambridge University Press.

Roberts, S. J. (1995). Pidgin Hawaiian: a sociohistorical study. *Journal of Pidgin and Creole Languages* 10: 1–56.

Roberts, S. J. (1998). The role of diffusion in creole genesis. To appear in *Language.*

Schuchardt, H. (1882–91). *Kreolische Studien.* Vienna: G. Gerold's Sohn/K. Tempsky.

Cross-Cultural Variation

See CULTURAL VARIATION; HUMAN UNIVERSALS; LANGUAGE AND CULTURE; LINGUISTIC UNIVERSALS AND UNIVERSAL GRAMMAR

Cultural Consensus Theory

Cultural consensus theory is a collection of formal statistical models designed to measure cultural knowledge shared by a set of respondents. Each respondent is given the same set of items designed to tap the respondents' shared knowledge. The data consist of a respondent-item matrix containing each respondent's answers to each of the items. An appropriate cultural consensus model provides estimates of each respondent's competence (knowledge) as well as an estimate of the culturally correct answer to each item. When the theory was developed in the mid-1980s it was motivated by the observation that when an anthropologist goes to a new culture and asks questions, neither the answers to the questions nor the cultural competence of the respondents is known. It has since been applied to a number of research questions, for example, folk medical beliefs, judgment of personality traits in a college sorority, semiotic characterizations of alphabetic systems, occupational prestige, causes of death, illness beliefs of deaf senior citizens, hot-cold concepts of illness, child abuse, national consciousness in Japan, measuring interobserver reliability, and three-way social network data.

Consensus theory uses much of the accumulated knowledge of traditional psychometric test theory without assuming knowledge of the "correct" answers in advance. Traditional test theory begins with respondent-item "performance" data (i.e., items' scores as "correct" or "incorrect"), whereas consensus theory begins with "response" data (items coded as responses given by the respondent, for example, "true" or "false," without scoring the responses). The different models of the theory depend on the format of the questions, for example, true-false, multiple choice, or ranking. Anthropology is the prototypical social science that can use such a methodology; however, research in other areas of social and behavioral science, such as cognitive psychology, social networks, and sociology, can also benefit from its use.

Cultural consensus theory fits into the category of information-pooling methods in which one has answers from several "experts" to a fixed body of "objective" questions. The goal is to aggregate rationally the experts' responses to select the most likely "correct answer" to each question, and also to assess one's degree of confidence in these selections. Cultural consensus theory provides an information-pooling methodology that does not incorporate a researcher's prior beliefs about the correct answers or any prior calibrations of the experts, and instead, it estimates both the respondents' competencies and the consensus answers from the same set of questionnaire data.

A central concept in the theory is the use of the pattern of agreement or consensus among respondents to make inferences about their differential knowledge of culturally shared information represented in the questions. It is assumed that the sole source of correspondence between the answers of any two respondents is a function of the extent to which the knowledge of each is correlated with (overlaps) this shared information. In other words, when responses are not based on shared information they are assumed to be uncorrelated. More formally, the model is derived from a set of three basic assumptions that are elaborated appropriately for each question format:

Assumption 1: *Common Truth.* There is a fixed answer key applicable to all respondents.

Assumption 2: *Local Independence.* The respondent-item response random variables satisfy conditional independence (conditional on the correct answer key).

Assumption 3: *Homogeneity of Items.* Each respondent has a fixed competence over all questions.

In some contexts Assumption 3 is replaced with a weaker one, *monotonicity*, that allows them to differ in difficulty: Basically, monotonicity says that respondents who have more competence on any subset of questions will have more competence on all subsets.

Formal process models have been derived for the analysis of dichotomous, multiple-choice, matching, and continuous item formats. Informal data models have also been developed for rank order and interval level formats. The theory has also been extended to the analysis of multiple cultures by relaxing the first axiom. In this situation each respondent belongs to exactly one culture, but different cultures may have different answer keys.

For very small sets of respondents (six or fewer), iterative maximum likelihood estimates of the parameters can be obtained by existing methods. For example, in the true-false case, the consensus model is equivalent to the two-class latent structure model with the roles of respondents and items interchanged; thus known estimation methods for that model can be used. For other situations, new estimation methods have been developed and assessed with Monte Carlo data. The theory enables the calculation of the minimal number of respondents needed to reconstruct the correct answers as a function of preselected levels of mean cultural competence of the respondents and levels of confidence in the reconstructed answers. It is also possible to estimate the amount of sampling variability among respondents and thus identify "actual" variance in cultural competence.

The theory performs better than does using a simple majority rule to reconstruct the answer key, especially in cases where there are small numbers of respondents with heterogeneous competence. The success of cultural consensus theory as an information-pooling method can be traced to several factors: (1) it is normally applied to items that tap high concordance cultural codes where mean levels of consensus are high; (2) the theory allows the differential weighting of the respondents' responses in reconstructing the answer key; and (3) the theory uses precise assumptions derived from successful formal models in test theory, latent structure analysis, and signal detection theory. The model has been subjected to extensive testing through simulation and Monte Carlo methods.

See also CONCEPTS; CULTURAL PSYCHOLOGY; RADICAL INTERPRETATION

—A. Kimball Romney and William H. Batchelder

Further Readings

Batchelder, W. H., and A. K. Romney. (1986). The statistical analysis of a general condorcet model for dichotomous choice situations. In B. Grofman and G. Owen, Eds., *Information Pooling and Group Decision Making,* pp. 103–112. Greenwich, Connecticut: JAI Press.

Batchelder, W. H., and A. K. Romney. (1988). Test theory without an answer key. *Psychometrika* 53: 71–92.

Batchelder, W. H., and A. K. Romney. (1989). New results in test theory without an answer key. In E. Roskam, Ed., *Advances in Mathematical Psychology,* vol. 2. Heidelberg and New York: Springer-Verlag, pp. 229–248.

Batchelder, W. H., E. Kumbasar, and J. P. Boyd. (1997). Consensus analysis of three-way social network data. *Journal of Mathematical Sociology* 22: 29–58.

Brewer, D. D., A. K. Romney, and W. H. Batchelder. (1991). Consistency and consensus: a replication. *Journal of Quantitative Anthropology* 3: 195–205.

Klauer, K. C., and W. H. Batchelder. (1996). Structural analysis of subjective categorical data. *Psychometrika* 61: 199–240.

Romney, A. K., W. H. Batchelder, and S. C. Weller. (1987). Recent applications of consensus theory. *American Behavioral Scientist* 31: 163–177.

Romney, A. K., S. C. Weller, and W. H. Batchelder. (1986). Culture as consensus: a theory of culture and accuracy. *American Anthropologist* 88: 313–338.

Weller, S. C. (1987). Shared knowledge, intracultural variation, and knowledge aggregation. *American Behavioral Scientist* 31:178–193.

Weller, S. C., and N. C. Mann. (1997). Assessing rater performance without a "gold standard" using consensus theory. *Medical Decision Making* 17: 71–79.

Weller, S. C., L. M. Pachter, R. T. Trotter, and R. D. Baer. (1993). Empacho in four Latino groups: a study of intra- and intercultural variation in beliefs. *Medical Anthropology* 15: 109–136.

Cultural Evolution

Human cultures include among other things mental representations with some between-group differences and within-group similarities. Ecological constraints, historical conditions, and power relations may influence the transmission of culture. A *cognitive* account assumes that, all these being equal, some trends in culture result from universal properties of human minds. These may account for patterns of change as well as for stability over time and space.

In the past, various forms of evolutionism described cultures as cognitively different and some of them as intrinsically more complex or developed than others (see Ingold 1986). In this view, differences in social and economic complexity between human groups corresponded to cognitive differences between *peoples* or *races.* It is clear to modern cognitive scientists that this is untenable. Different environments make different demands on a cognitive system, but there is no hierarchy of complexity or development between them, and the relevant cognitive structures are typical of the human species as a whole.

A cognitive approach must address three related questions: (1) Is cultural transmission similar to genetic transmission? (2) How did hominization lead to the appearance of culture? and (3) How are cultural representations constrained by the human genotype?

1. Are cultural memes like genes? Many authors have suggested that cultural evolution could be modeled on terms derived from natural selection (Campbell 1970). Mentally represented units of information, usually called *memes* (Dawkins 1976), result in overt behavior, are passed on

through social interaction and modified by memory and inference. Different memes may have different *cultural fitness* values: culture evolves through *differential* transmission of ideas, values and beliefs (Durham 1991: 156).

Coevolution theories describe significant trends in meme transmission using the formal tools of population genetics (Lumsden and Wilson 1981; Boyd and Richerson 1985; Durham 1991). Patterns of transmission and change depend on quantitative factors, such as the frequency of a trait in cultural elders or the number of variants available in a given group, but also on cognitive processes. Durham, for instance, makes a distinction between *primary values*, a set of evolved, universal propensities toward certain representations, and *secondary values*, socially acquired expectations concerning the possible consequences of behavior (1991: 200, 432).

An alternative to replication is an *epidemiological* model, in which cultural evolution is construed as the outcome of mental contagion (Sperber 1985). This approach emphasizes the differences between gene and meme transmission. Cultural representations are not literally *replicated*, because human communication is intrinsically inferential and works by producing publicly available tokens (e.g., utterances, gestures) designed to change other agents' representations (Sperber and Wilson 1986). Cultural epidemics are distinct from a replication process in that acquisition typically produces variants rather than copies of the representations of others; rough replication, then, is an exception that must be explained, rather than the norm (Sperber 1996).

2. What made (and makes) culture possible? There are important differences between various types of animal traditions and complex, flexible human cultures, which often show an accumulation of modifications over generations (i.e., the ratchet effect; Tomasello, Kruger, and Ratner 1993: 508). Humans may have developed very general learning capacities that allow them to acquire whatever information can be found in their environment. Alternatively, EVOLUTION may have given humans a more numerous and complex set of specialized cognitive capacities.

The first type of explanation can be found in Donald's account of the appearance of cognitive plasticity as a crucial evolutionary change. The primate mind became *modern* by developing a powerful learning device without constraining restrictions as to the range of mental contents that could be learned (Donald 1993). An explanation in terms of more specific capacities is Tomasello, Kruger, and Ratner's (1993) account of cultural learning, as distinct from social learning based on IMITATION and found in higher primates. Cultural learning requires *mind-reading* and perspective-taking capacities. Obviously, these capacities would have been boosted by the appearance of verbal communication.

One may push this further and argue that the appearance of culture depended, not on a more powerful general learning capacity, but on a multiplication of specialized capacities (Rozin 1976, Tooby and Cosmides 1989). This would have been less costly in evolutionary terms. It only required gradual addition of small *modules* rather than the sudden appearance of a general and flexible mind. Also, it makes more computational sense. An unbiased all-purpose learning capacity could be overloaded with many adaptively

irrelevant facts and correlations in the environment. These considerations lead to the research program of EVOLUTIONARY PSYCHOLOGY, which specifies a large number of *cognitive adaptations*. These are specialized in particular aspects of experience that would have been of plausible relevance to fitness in the environment of evolutionary adaptation, though not necessarily in a modern environment. To some extent, the archaeological record supports this notion of specialized microcapacities appearing side by side and making up an ever more complex mind. However, late developments (in particular, the cultural differences between Neanderthals and modern humans) may also suggest that communication between modules was as important as development in each of them (Mithen 1996).

3. Is culture constrained by genes? What are the connections between the genotype and recurrent features of culture? Coevolution theories have challenged the assumption of early human SOCIOBIOLOGY that people's concepts and values generally tend to maximize their reproductive potential (Cavalli-Sforza and Feldman 1973). Most cultural variants are adaptively neutral, and many are in fact maladaptive, so coevolution models postulate different evolution tracks for genes and memes. Beyond this, one may argue that evolved properties of human cognition influence cultural evolution in two different ways.

First, human minds comprise a set of ready-made behavioral recipes that are activated by particular cues in the natural and social environment. Whether those cues are present and which capacities are activated may vary from place to place. So different environments set parameters differently for such universal capacities as social exchange, detection of cheaters, or particular strategies in mate-selection and in the allocation of parental investment (see Barkow, Cosmides, and Tooby 1992 for a survey of these domains).

Second, humans develop universal conceptual structures that constrain the transmission of particular representations. This can be observed even in beliefs and values whose overt content seems culturally variable. Children gradually develop a set of quasi-theoretical, domain-specific assumptions about the different types of objects in the world as well as expectations about their observable and underlying properties. The experimental evidence demonstrates the effects of such principles in domains like THEORY OF MIND, the perception of mechanical causation or the specific properties of living things (Hirschfeld and Gelman 1994). This *intuitive ontology* has direct effects on the acquisition of cultural representations.

In some domains, information derived from cultural input is acquired inasmuch as it tends to *enrich* early skeletal principles. This is the case for number systems, for instance, as cultural input provides names for intuitive concepts of *numerosity* (Gallistel and Gelman 1992). In the same way, FOLK PSYCHOLOGY is built by using cultural input, for instance about motivation, emotion, through-processes, and so on, that provide explanations for the intuitions delivered by our theory of mind. In folk biology, too, cultural input that is spontaneously selected tends to enrich intuitive principles about the taxonomic ordering of living species or possession of an *essence* as a feature of each species (Atran 1990). Even such social constructs as kinship terms or notions of *family* and *race* can be construed as enriching an intuitive apprehension of social categories (Hirschfeld 1994).

In other domains, cultural input is selectively attended to inasmuch as it *violates* the expectations of intuitive ontology. Religious ontologies, for instance, postulate agents whose physical or biological properties are counterintuitive, given ordinary expectations about intentional agents. Such combinations are very few in number and account for most cultural variants in religious systems (Boyer 1994). Their presence in individual religious representations can be demonstrated experimentally (Barett and Keil 1996).

In some domains more complex processes are involved. This is the case for scientific theories and other forms of scholarly knowledge that diverge from intuitive ontology. Such systems of representations generally require considerable social support (intensive tuition and specialized institutions like schools). They generally include an explicit description of their divergence from intuitive ontology, and therefore a METAREPRESENTATION of ordinary representations about the natural world. This is why such systems typically require LITERACY, which boosts metarepresentational capacities and provides external memory storage, allowing for incremental additions to cultural representations.

Human cognition comprises a series of specialized capacities. Transmission patterns probably vary as a function of which domain-specific conceptual predispositions are activated. So there may be no overall process of cultural transmission, but a series of domain-specific *cognitive tracks* of transmission. Models of cultural evolution are tautological if they state only that whatever got transmitted must have been better than what did not (Durham 1991: 194). This is where cognitive models are indispensable. Experimental study of cognitive predispositions provides independent evidence for the underlying mechanisms of cultural evolution.

See also ADAPTATION AND ADAPTATIONISM; COGNITIVE ARCHAEOLOGY; COGNITIVE ARTIFACTS; DOMAIN SPECIFICITY; NAIVE BIOLOGY; NAIVE MATHEMATICS

—*Pascal Boyer*

References

Atran, S. (1990). *Cognitive Foundations of Natural History: Towards an Anthropology of Science.* Cambridge: Cambridge University Press.

Barett, J. L., and F. C. Keil. (1996). Conceptualizing a non-natural entity: anthropomorphism in God concepts. *Cognitive Psychology* 31: 219–247.

Barkow, J., L. Cosmides, and J. Tooby, Eds. (1992). *The Adapted Mind: Evolutionary Psychology and the Generation of Culture.* New York: Oxford University Press.

Boyd, R., and P. Richerson. (1985). *Culture and the Evolutionary Process.* Chicago: University of Chicago Press.

Boyer, P. (1994). *The Naturalness of Religious Ideas: A Cognitive Theory of Religion.* Berkeley and Los Angeles: University of California Press.

Campbell, D. T. (1970). Natural selection as an epistemological model. In N. Naroll and R. Cohen, Eds., *A Handbook of Method in Cultural Anthropology.* Garden City, NY: Chapman and Hall.

Cavalli-Sforza, L. L., and M. W. Feldman. (1973). Cultural versus biological inheritance: phenotypic transmission from parents to children. *American Journal of Human Genetics* 25: 618–637.

Dawkins, R. (1976). *The Selfish Gene.* New York: Oxford University Press.

Donald, M. (1993). Precis of origins of the modern mind: three stages in the evolution of culture and cognition. *Behavioral and Brain Sciences* 16: 737–791.

Durham, W. (1991). *Coevolution: Genes, Cultures and Human Diversity.* Stanford, CA: Stanford University Press.

Gallistel, C. R., and R. Gelman. (1992). Preverbal and verbal counting and computation. *Cognition* 44: 79–106.

Hirschfeld, L. A. (1994). The acquisition of social categories. In L. A. Hirschfeld and S. A. Gelman, Eds., *Mapping The Mind: Domain-Specificity in Culture and Cognition.* New York: Cambridge University Press.

Hirschfeld, L. A., and S. A. Gelman, Eds. (1994). *Mapping The Mind: Domain-Specificity in Culture and Cognition.* New York: Cambridge University Press.

Ingold, T. (1986). *Evolution and Social Life.* Cambridge: Cambridge University Press.

Lumsden, C. J., and E. O. Wilson. (1981). *Genes, Minds and Culture.* Cambridge, MA: Harvard University Press.

Mithen, S. (1996). *The Prehistory of the Mind.* London: Thames and Hudson.

Rozin, P. (1976). The evolution of intelligence and access to the cognitive unconscious. In J. M. Sprague and A. N. Epstein, Eds., *Progress in Psychobiology and Physiological Psychology.* New York: Academic Press.

Sperber, D. (1985). Anthropology and psychology: towards an epidemiology of representations. *Man* 20: 73–89.

Sperber, D. (1996). *Explaining Culture: A Naturalistic Approach.* Oxford: Blackwell.

Sperber, D., and D. Wilson. (1986). *Relevance, Communication and Cognition.* New York: Academic Press.

Tomasello, M., A. C. Kruger, and H. H. Ratner. (1993). Cultural learning. *Behavioral and Brain Sciences* 16: 495–510.

Tooby, J., and L. Cosmides. (1989). Evolutionary psychology and the generation of culture (i): theoretical reflections. *Ethology and Sociobiology* 10: 29–49.

Cultural Models

See METAPHOR AND CULTURE; MOTIVATION AND CULTURE

Cultural Psychology

The most basic assumption of cultural psychology can be traced back to the eighteenth-century German romantic philosopher Johann Gottfried von Herder, who proposed that "to be a member of a group is to think and act in a certain way, in the light of particular goals, values, pictures of the world; and to think and act so is to belong to a group" (Berlin 1976: 195). During the past twenty-five years there has been a major renewal of interest in cultural psychology, primarily among anthropologists (D'Andrade 1995; Geertz 1973; Kleinman 1986; Levy 1973; Shore 1996; Shweder 1991; Shweder and LeVine 1984; White and Kirkpatrick 1985), psychologists (Bruner 1990; Cole 1996; Goodnow, Miller, and Kessel 1995; Kitayama and Markus 1994; Markus and Kitayama 1991; Miller 1984; Nisbett and Cohen 1995; Russell 1991; Yang forthcoming) and linguists

(Goddard 1997; Wierzbicka 1992a), although relevant work has been done by philosophers as well (Harre 1986; MacIntyre 1981; Taylor 1989). The contemporary field of cultural psychology is concerned, as was Herder, with both the psychological foundations of cultural communities and the cultural foundations of mind. It is concerned with the way culture and psyche make each other up, over the history of the group and over the life course of the individual.

The word "cultural" in the phrase "cultural psychology" refers to local or community-specific conceptions of what is true, good, beautiful, and efficient ("goals, values and pictures of the world") that are socially inherited, made manifest in the speech, laws, and customary practices of members of some self-monitoring group, and which serve to mark a distinction between different ways of life (the Amish way of life, the way of life of Hindu Brahmans in rural India, the way of life of secular urban middle-class Americans).

A community's cultural conception of things will usually include some vision of the proper ends of life; of proper values; of proper ways to speak; of proper ways to discipline children; of proper educational goals; of proper ways to determine kinship connections and obligations; of proper gender and authority relations within the family; of proper foods to eat; of proper attitudes toward labor and work, sexuality and the body, and members of other groups whose beliefs and practices differ from one's own; of proper ways to think about salvation; and so forth.

A community's cultural conception of things will also usually include some received, favored, or privileged "resolution" to a series of universal, scientifically undecidable, and hence existential questions. These are questions with respect to which "answers" must be given for the sake of social coordination and cooperation, whether or not they are logically or ultimately solvable by human beings, questions such as "What is me and what is not me?", "What is male and what is female?", "How should the burdens and benefits of life be fairly distributed?", "Are there community interests or cultural rights that take precedence over the freedoms (of speech, conscience, association, choice) associated with individual rights?" and "When in the life of a fetus or child does social personhood begin?" Locally favored and socially inherited "answers" to such questions are expressed and made manifest (and are thus discernible) in the speech, laws, and customary practices of members of any self-monitoring group. In sum, local conceptions of the true, the good, the beautiful, the efficient, plus discretionary "answers" to cognitively undecidable existential questions, all made apparent in and through practice, is what the word "cultural" in "cultural psychology" is all about.

The word "psychology" in the phrase "cultural psychology" refers broadly to mental functions, such as perceiving, categorizing, reasoning, remembering, feeling, wanting, choosing, valuing, and communicating. What defines a function as a "mental" function per se (over and above, or in contrast to a "physical" function) has something to do with the capacity of the human mind to grasp ideas, to do things for reasons or with a purpose in mind, to be conscious of alternatives and aware of the content or meaning of its own experience. This is one reason that "mental" states are

sometimes referred to as "intentional" or "symbolic" states. Cultural psychology is the study of those intentional and symbolic states of individuals (a belief in a reincarnating soul, a desire to purify one's soul and protect it from pollutions of various kinds) that are part and parcel of a particular cultural conception of things made manifest in, and acquired by means of involvement with, the speech, laws and customary practices of some group.

It has been noted by Clifford Geertz, and by others interested in lived realities, that "one does not speak language; one speaks a language." Similarly, one does not categorize; one categorizes something. One does not want; one wants something. On the assumption that what you think about can be decisive for how you think, the focus of cultural psychology has been on content-laden variations in human mentalities rather than on the abstract common denominators of the human mind. Cultural psychologists want to know why Tahitians or Chinese react to "loss" with an experience of headaches and back pains rather than with the experience of "sadness" so common in the Euro-American cultural region (Levy 1973; Kleinman 1986). They seek to document population-level variations in the emotions that are salient or basic in the language and feelings of different peoples around the world (Kitayama and Markus 1994; Russell 1991; Shweder 1993; Wierzbicka 1992a). They aim to understand why Southern American males react more violently to insult than Northern American males (Nisbett and Cohen 1996) and why members of sociocentric subcultures perceive, classify, and moralize about the world differently than do members of individualistic subcultures (Markus and Kitayama 1991; Triandis 1989; Shweder 1991).

It is precisely because cultural psychology is the study of the content-laden intentional/symbolic states of human beings that cultural psychology should be thought of as the study of peoples (such as Trobriand Islanders or Chinese Mandarins), not people (in general or in the abstract). The psychological subject matter definitive of cultural psychology thus consists of those aspects of the mental functioning of individuals that have been ontogenetically activated and historically reproduced by means of some particular cultural conception of things, and by virtue of participation in, observation of, and reflection on the activities and practices of a particular group. This definition of research in cultural psychology sets it in contrast (although not necessarily in opposition) to research in general psychology, where the search is for points of uniformity in the psychological functioning of people around the world. Without denying the existence of some empirically manifest psychological uniformities across all human beings, the focus in cultural psychology is on differences in the way members of different cultural communities perceive, categorize, remember, feel, want, choose, evaluate, and communicate. The focus is on psychological differences that can be traced to variations in communally salient "goals, values, and pictures of the world."

Cultural psychology is thus the study of the way the human mind can be transformed, given shape and definition, and made functional in a number of different ways that are not uniformly distributed across cultural communities around the world. "Universalism without the uniformity" is one of the slogans cultural psychologists sometimes use to talk about "psychic unity," and about themselves.

See also CULTURAL EVOLUTION; CULTURAL SYMBOLISM; ETHNOPSYCHOLOGY; HUMAN UNIVERSALS; INTENTIONALITY

—*Richard A. Shweder*

References

Berlin, I. (1976). *Vico and Herder.* London: Hogarth.

Bruner, J. (1990). *Acts of Meaning.* Cambridge, MA: Harvard University Press.

Cole, M. (1996). *Cultural Psychology: A Once and Future Discipline.* Cambridge, MA: Harvard University Press.

D'Andrade, R. (1995). *The Development of Cognitive Anthropology.* Cambridge: Cambridge University Press.

Geertz, C. (1973). *The Interpretation of Cultures.* New York: Basic Books.

Goddard, C. (1997). Contrastive semantics and cultural psychology: "Surprise" in Malay and English. *Culture and Psychology* 2: 153–181.

Goodnow, J., P. Miller, and F. Kessel. (1995). Cultural practices as contexts for development. In *New Directions for Child Development.* Vol. 67. San Francisco: Jossey-Bass.

Harre, R. (1986). *The Social Construction of Emotions.* Oxford: Blackwell.

Kitayama, S., and H. Markus, Eds. (1994). *Emotion and Culture: Empirical Studies of Mutual Influence.* Washington, DC: American Psychological Association.

Kleinman, A. (1986). *Social Origins of Distress and Disease.* New Haven: Yale University Press.

Levy, R. (1973). *Tahitians: Mind and Experience in the Society Islands.* Chicago: University of Chicago Press.

Markus, H., and S. Kitayama. (1991). Culture and the self: implications for cognition, emotion, and motivation. *Psychological Review* 98: 224–253.

Miller, J. (1984). Culture and the development of everyday social explanation. *Journal of Personality and Social Psychology* 46: 961–978.

Nisbett, R., and D. Cohen. (1995). *The Culture of Honor: The Psychology of Violence in the South.* Boulder, CO: Westview Press.

Russell, J. (1991). Culture and the categorization of emotions. *Psychological Bulletin* 110: 426–450.

Shore. B. (1996). *Culture in Mind: Cognition, Culture and the Problem of Meaning.* New York: Oxford University Press.

Shweder, R. (1991). *Thinking Through Cultures: Expeditions in Cultural Psychology.* Cambridge, MA: Harvard University Press.

Shweder, R. (1993). The cultural psychology of the emotions. In M. Lewis and J. Haviland, Eds., *Handbook of Emotions.* New York: Guilford.

Shweder, R., and R. LeVine. (1984). *Culture Theory: Essays on Mind, Self and Emotion.* New York: Cambridge University Press.

Taylor, C. (1989). *Sources of the Self: The Making of Modern Identities.* Cambridge, MA: Harvard University Press.

Triandis, H. (1989). The self and social behavior in differing cultural contexts. *Psychological Review* 93: 506–520.

Wierzbicka, A. (1992*a*). Talking about emotions: semantics, culture and cognition. *Cognition and Emotion* 6: 285–319.

White, G., and J. Kirkpatrick, Eds. (1985). *Person, Self and Experience: Exploring Pacific Ethnopsychologies.* Berkeley: University of California Press.

Yang, K.-S. (1997). Indigenizing westernized Chinese psychology. In M. Bond, Ed., *Working at the Interface of Culture: Twenty Lives in Social Science.* London: Routledge.

Further Readings

Fiske, A. (1992). *The Four Elementary Forms of Sociality: Framework for a Unified Theory of Social Relations.* New York: Free Press.

Jessor, R., A. Colby, and R. Shweder, Eds. (1996). *Ethnography and Human Development: Context and Meaning in Social Inquiry.* Chicago: University of Chicago Press.

Kakar, S. (1978). *The Inner World: A Psychoanalytic Study of Childhood and Society in India.* New York: Oxford University Press.

Kakar, S. (1996). *The Colors of Violence: Cultural Identities, Religion and Conflict.* Chicago: University of Chicago Press.

Lebra, T. (1992). *Culture, Self and Communication.* Ann Arbor: University of Michigan Press.

Lucy, J. (1992). *Grammatical Categories and Cognition: A Case Study of the Linguistic Relativity Hypothesis.* New York: Cambridge University Press.

Lutz, C., and White, G. (1986). The anthropology of emotions. *Annual Review of Anthropology* 15: 405–436.

MacIntyre, A. (1981). *After Virtue: A Study in Moral Theory.* Notre Dame: University of Notre Dame Press.

Markus, H., S. Kitayama, and R. Heiman. (1998). Culture and "basic" psychological principles. In E. T. Higgins and A. W. Kruglanski, Eds., *Social Psychology: Handbook of Basic Principles.* New York: Guilford.

Miller, J. (1994). Cultural psychology: bridging disciplinary boundaries in understanding the cultural grounding of self. In P. Bock, Ed., *Handbook of Psychological Anthropology.* Westport, CT: Greenwood Press.

Much, N. (1995). Cultural psychology. In J. Smith, R. Harre, and L. van Langenhove, Eds., *Rethinking Psychology.* London: Sage.

Shweder, R. (1998). *Welcome to Middle Age! (And Other Cultural Fictions.)* Chicago: University of Chicago Press.

Shweder, R., J. Goodnow, G. Hatano, R. LeVine, H. Markus, and P. Miller. (1997). The cultural psychology of development: one mind, many mentalities. In W. Damon, Ed., *Handbook of Child Psychology,* vol. 1: *Theoretical Models of Human Development.* New York: John Wiley and Sons.

Shweder, R., and M. Sullivan. (1993). Cultural psychology: who needs it? *Annual Review of Psychology* 44: 497–523.

Stigler, J., R. Shweder, and G. Herdt. (1990). *Cultural Psychology: Essays on Comparative Human Development.* Chicago: University of Chicago Press.

Wierzbicka, A. (1992). Defining emotion concepts. *Cognitive Science* 16: 539–581.

Wierzbicka, A. (1993). A conceptual basis for cultural psychology. *Ethos: Journal of the Society for Psychological Anthropology* 21: 205–231

Cultural Relativism

How are we to make sense of the diversity of beliefs and ethical values documented by anthropology's ethnographic record? Cultural relativism infers from this record that significant dimensions of human experience, including morality and ethics, are inherently local and variable rather than universal. Most relativists (with the exception of developmental relativists discussed below) interpret and evaluate such diverse beliefs and practices in relation to local cultural frameworks rather than universal principles.

There are many variations on the theme of cultural relativism. Six important variants are described below:

1. *Epistemological relativism,* the most general phrasing of cultural relativism, proposes that human experience is mediated by local frameworks for knowledge (Geertz 1973). Most epistemological relativism assumes that experienced reality is largely a social and cultural construction and so this position is often called "social constructionism" (Berger and Luckmann 1966).

2. *Logical relativism* claims that there are no transcultural and universal principles of rationality, logic and reasoning. This claim was debated in the 1970s in a series of publications featuring debates among English philosophers, anthropologists, and sociologists about the nature and universality of rationality in logical and moral judgment (B. Wilson 1970).

3. *Historical relativism* views historical eras as a cultural and intellectual history of diverse and changing ideas, paradigms, or worldviews (Burckhardt 1943; Kuhn 1977).

4. *Linguistic relativism* focuses on the effects of particular grammatical and lexical forms on habitual thinking and classification (Whorf 1956; Lucy 1992).

5. *Ethical relativism* claims that behavior can be morally evaluated only in relation to a local framework of values and beliefs rather than universal ethical norms (Ladd 1953). Proponents advocate tolerance in ethical judgments to counter the presumed ethnocentricism of universalistic judgments (Herskovitz 1972; Hatch 1983). Opponents claim that extreme ethical relativism is amoral and potentially immoral since it can justify, by an appeal to local or historical context, any action, including acts like genocide that most people would condemn (Vivas 1950; Norris 1996). This debate engages the highly visible discourse on the doctrine of universal human rights, and the extent to which it reflects natural rights rather than the cultural values of a politically dominant community (R. Wilson 1997). Important and emotionally salient issues engaged in this debate include the status of women, abortion, religious tolerance, the treatment of children, arranged marriages, female circumcision, and capital punishment. A common thread linking many of these issues is the status of "the individual" and by implication social equality versus social hierarchy, and cultural relativism can be used to justify relations of inequality (Dumont 1970).

6. Distinct from evolutionary psychologists mentioned above are *developmental relativists* who ascribe differences in thought or values to different stages of human development, either in terms of evolutionary stages or developmental differences in moral reasoning between individuals. A commonplace assumption of Victorian anthropology, evolutionism still has echoes in the *genetic epistemology* of developmental psychologists like PIAGET, Kohlberg, and Werner (Piaget 1932; Kohlberg 1981, 1983; Werner 1948/1964). Genetic epistemology acknowledges the cultural diversity and relativity of systems of reasoning and symbolism but links these differences to a universalistic developmental (and, by common implication, evolutionary) trajectory.

Both a philosophical and a moral stance, cultural relativism makes two different sorts of claims: (1) an *ontological claim* about the nature of human understanding, a claim subject to empirical testing and verification, and (2) a *moral/political claim* advocating tolerance of divergent cultural styles of thought and action.

Cultural relativism implies a fundamental human psychic diversity. Such diversity need not preclude important universals of thought and feeling. Relativism and universalism are often seen as mutually exclusive. At the relativist end of the spectrum are proponents of CULTURAL PSYCHOLOGY who argue that the very categories and processes by which psychologists understand the person are themselves cultural constructs, and who imply that academic psychology is actually a Western ETHNOPSYCHOLOGY (Shweder 1989). From this perspective comparative or cross-cultural psychology become impossible, inasmuch as the psychology of each community would need to be studied in its own analytical terms. At the universalist end of the spectrum is EVOLUTIONARY PSYCHOLOGY, which looks at human cognitive architecture as having evolved largely during the upper Paleolithic, subject to the general Darwinian forces of natural selection and fitness maximization (Barkow, Cosmides, and Tooby 1992). Local cultural differences are viewed as relatively trivial compared with the shared cognitive abilities that are the products of hominid evolution.

Many cognitive anthropologists see in the relativist/universalist distinction a false dichotomy. An adequate model of mind must encompass both universal and variable properties. Although they acknowledge the importance of a shared basic cognitive architecture and universal process of both information processing and meaning construction, many cognitive anthropologists do not see cultural variation as trivial but stress the crucial mediating roles of diverse social environments and variable cultural models in human cognition (D'Andrade 1987; Holland and Quinn 1987; Hutchins 1996; Shore 1996).

Although cultural relativism has rarely been treated as a problem of cognitive science, COGNITIVE ANTHROPOLOGY is a useful perspective for reframing the issues of cultural relativism. For cognitive anthropologists, a cultural unit comprises a population sharing a large and diverse stock of *cultural models,* which differ from community to community. Once internalized, cultural models become conventional cognitive models in individual minds. Cultural models thus have a double life as both *instituted models* (public institutions) and conventional *mental models* (individuals' mental representations of public forms; Shore 1996). Other kinds of cognitive models include "hardwired" schemas (like those governing facial recognition) and personal/idiosyncratic mental models that differ from person to person. Thus viewed, culture is not a bounded unit but a dynamic social distribution of instituted and mental models.

When culture is conceived as a socially distributed system of models, the sources of cultural relativity become more complex and subtle but are easier to specify. Rather than draw simple oppositions between distinct cultures, we can specify which models (rather than which cultures) are different and how they differ. Thus the similarity or difference between communities is not an all-or-nothing phenomenon, but is a matter of particular differences or similarities.

In addition, significant conflict or contradiction among cultural models within a community becomes easier to account for, as do conflicts between cultural models and personal models or between cultural models and relatively unmodeled (diffuse/inarticulate) feelings and desires. Such internal conflicts do not argue against the intersubjective sharing of cultural models within a community or the important difference between communities. But they suggest a softening of the oppositions between discrete cultures that has been the hallmark of much of the discourse of cultural relativism.

Many within-culture conflicts suggest existential dilemmas that have no final resolution (e.g., autonomy versus dependency needs, equality and hierarchy; Fiske 1990; Nuckolls 1997). There are models and countermodels, as in political discourse. Cultural models sometimes provide temporary resolutions, serving as salient cognitive and emotional resources for clarifying experience. Sometimes, as in religious ritual, cultural models simply crystallize contradictions, representing them as sacred paradox. Such resolutions are never complete, and never exhaust the experience of individuals. In this way, the relativity *between cultures* is complemented by a degree of experiential relativity *within cultures* (variation and conflict) and periodically within individuals (ambivalence).

See also COLOR CATEGORIZATION; CULTURAL SYMBOLISM; CULTURAL VARIATION; LINGUISTIC RELATIVITY HYPOTHESIS; MOTIVATION AND CULTURE; SAPIR, EDWARD

—Bradd Shore

References

Barkow H., L. Cosmides, and J. Tooby, Eds. (1992). *The Adapted Mind: Evolutionary Psychology and the Generation of Culture.* New York: Oxford University Press.

Berger, P., and T. Luckmann. (1966). *The Social Construction of Reality: A Treatise on the Sociology of Knowledge.* Garden City: Doubleday.

Burckhardt, J. (1943). *Reflections on History.* Trans. M. D. Hottinger. London: G. Allen and Unwin.

D'Andrade, R. (1987). Cultural meaning systems. In R. Shweder and R. LeVine, Eds., *Culture Theory: Essays on Mind, Self and Emotion,* pp. 88–119. Cambridge: Cambridge University Press.

Dumont, L. (1970). *Homo Hierarchicus.* Chicago: University of Chicago Press.

Fiske, A. P. (1990). Relativity within Moose ("Mossi") culture: four incommensurable models for social relationships. *Ethos* 18(2): 180–204.

Geertz, C. (1973). *The Interpretation of Cultures.* New York: Basic Books.

Hatch, E. (1983). *Culture and Morality: The Relativity of Values in Anthropology.* New York: Columbia University Press.

Herskovitz, M. J. (1972). *Cultural Relativism: Perspectives in Cultural Pluralism.* New York: Random House.

Holland, D., and N. Quinn, Eds. (1987). *Cultural Models in Language and Thought.* Cambridge: Cambridge University Press.

Hutchins, E. (1996). *Cognition in the Wild.* Cambridge, MA: MIT Press.

Kohlberg, L. (1981). *Essays in Moral Development,* vol. 1: *The Philosophy of Moral Development.* New York: Harper and Row.

Kohlberg, L. (1983). *Essays in Moral Development,* vol. 2: *The Psychology of Moral Development.* New York: Harper and Row.

Kuhn, T. (1977). *The Structure of Scientific Revolutions.* 2nd ed. Chicago: University of Chicago Press.

Ladd, J. (1953). *Ethical Relativism.* Belmont, CA: Wadsworth.

Lakoff, G. (1987). *Women, Fire and Dangerous Things.* Chicago: University of Chicago Press.

Lucy, J. (1992). *Language Diversity and Thought: A Reformulation of the Linguistic Relativity Hypothesis.* New York: Cambridge University Press.

Nuckolls, C. (1997). *Culture and the Dialectics of Desire.* Madison: University of Wisconsin Press.

Piaget, J. (1932). *The Development of Moral Reasoning in Children.* New York: Free Press.

Shore, B. (1996). *Culture in Mind: Cognition, Culture and the Problem of Meaning.* New York: Oxford University Press.

Shweder, R. (1989). Cultural psychology: what is it? In J. Stigler, R. Shweder, and G. Herdt, Eds., *Cultural Psychology: The Chicago Symposia on Culture and Development.* New York: Cambridge University Press, pp. 1–46.

Vivas, E. (1950). *The Moral Life and the Ethical Life.* Chicago: University of Chicago Press.

Werner, H. (1948/1964). *Comparative Psychology of Mental Development.* Rev. ed. New York: International University Press.

Whorf, B. L. (1956). *Language, Thought and Reality.* Cambridge, MA: MIT Press.

Wilson, B., Ed. (1970). *Rationality.* Oxford: Basil Blackwell.

Wilson, R., Ed. (1997). *Human Rights, Cultural Context: Anthropological Perspectives.* London and Chicago: Pluto Press.

Further Readings

Benedict, R. (1934). *Patterns of Culture.* Boston: Houghton Mifflin.

Fernandez, J. (1990). Tolerance in a repugnant world and other dilemmas of cultural relativism in the work of Melville J. Herskovitz. *Ethos* 18(2): 140–164.

Geertz, C. (1984). Distinguished lecture: anti-anti relativism. *American Anthropologist* 86(2): 263–278.

Hartung, F. E. (1954). Cultural relativity and moral judgments. *Philosophy of Science* 21: 118–126.

Horton, R. (1967). African traditional thought and Western science. *Africa* 37: 50–71, 155–187.

Lucy, J. (1985). Whorf's view of the linguistic mediation of thought. In E. Mertz and R. Parmentier, Eds., *Semiotic Mediation: Sociological and Psychological Perspectives.* Orlando, FL: Academic Press, pp. 73–98.

Norris, C. (1996). *Reclaiming Truth: Contribution to a Critique of Cultural Relativism.* Durham: Duke University Press.

Overing, J., Ed. (1985). *Reason and Morality.* London: Tavistock.

Schoeck, H., and J. M. Wiggens. (1961). *Relativism and the Study of Man.* Princeton, NJ: Van Nostrand.

Shweder, R. (1990). Ethical relativism: is there a defensible version? *Ethos* 18(2): 205–218.

Shweder, R., M. Mahapatra, and J. G. Miller. (1987). Culture and moral development. In J. Kagan and S. Lamb, Eds., *The Emergence of Morality in Young Children.* Chicago: University of Illinois Press, pp. 1–90.

Spiro, M. (1986). Cultural relativism and the future of anthropology. *Cultural Anthropology* 1(3): 259–286.

Cultural Symbolism

At about 50,000 B.P., the archaeological record shows a sudden change in the nature and variety of artifacts produced by modern humans, with the massive production of cave paintings, elaborate artifacts of no practical utility, the use of ocher, the introduction of burial practices, and so on. Here we have the first traces of the emergence of cultural symbolism (although the phenomenon itself may have appeared earlier). The term has a wider extension for anthropologists who are not limited to preserved artifacts and can observe such cultural products as public utterances, ritual, clothing, music, etiquette, dance, and prohibitions. All these productions have three main characteristics: (1) their particular features are to a large extent unmotivated by immediate survival needs and are often devoid of any practical purpose; (2) they seemingly involve a capacity to "reify" mental representations, so that certain communicative or memory effects can be achieved by producing material objects and observable events; (3) their features vary from one human group to another.

In the social sciences, the loose term *symbolism* was applied to all such productions for a simple reason: although they often seemed to convey some overt "meaning," this meaning did not seem sufficient to explain their occurrence or transmission. A common strategy, then, was to explain symbolism as a symptom of social relations. Durkheim, for instance, treats religion as a symbol of social order and superhuman agency as a symbol of society itself. For Marx, an ideology symbolizes (and distorts) social relations. Alternatively, hermeneutic approaches to culture emphasize common concerns of mankind that find their expression in cultural symbolism. Religion, for instance, is described as expressing universal metaphysical questions or anxieties. The common thread in these very different frameworks is that cultural productions stand for something else, which may or may not be accessible to people's consciousness and which is encoded in public representations.

From a cognitive perspective, the main question is to account for the capacities that make symbolism possible, and for the causes of acquisition and transmission of particular patterns (see CULTURAL EVOLUTION). An important attempt in this direction can be found in D. Sperber's cognitive account of symbolism (Sperber 1975, 1996). For Sperber, certain cultural phenomena are "symbolic" to particular actors inasmuch as their rational interpretation does not lead to a limited and predictable set of inferences. This triggers a search for conjectural representations that, if true, would make a rational interpretation possible. The production and use of public representations is then described in terms of communicative intentions. What people do with public representations, just as they do with verbal utterances, is to engage in a goal-directed, relevance-optimizing search for possible descriptions of the communicator's intentions (see RELEVANCE).

This conception has two interesting consequences. First, it suggests that there are no such things as "symbols" as a particular class of cultural products. Any conceptual or perceptual item can become symbolic, if there is some index that a rational interpretation is unavailable or insufficient. This conception of cultural symbolism also implies that we cannot assume that material and other public symbols "contain" meanings in the form of a code, in much the same way as the letters of a writing system contain phonological information. Symbolism does not work in that way in our species. Bees or vervet monkeys do produce signals that are reliable indicators of the states of affairs that caused their production. Cultural symbols, much like human communication in general, trigger inferential processes that are not constrained by the features of the public representation itself, but by what these features reveal of the communicator's communicative intentions. In other words, you cannot achieve communication (and this extends to cultural "meanings") unless you activate a rich intuitive psychology (see THEORY OF MIND). This argument finds some support from studies showing that even artifact production among humans requires such perspective-taking and inferences about the other's intentions (see, e.g., Tomasello, Kruger, and Ratner 1993).

Cultural symbolism often combines universal, intuitive concepts (e.g., a theory of physical objects as cohesive, a theory of living things as internally propelled) in counterintuitive ways (e.g., a theory of superhuman agents as nonmaterial and nonbiological; Boyer 1994). This, too, requires an ability to rearrange representations that derive from basic cognitive dispositions. This is why the appearance of cultural symbolism has been linked to the emergence of a "metarepresentational" capacity riding piggyback on more specialized "modular" cognitive systems (Mithen 1996).

All this may explain why, as soon as it appears in the archaeological record and wherever it is found in the anthropological evidence, cultural symbolism is "cultural" in the sense of varying between human groups. Humans tend to talk about the same topics the world over and make use of a similar evolved cognitive architecture (see EVOLUTIONARY PSYCHOLOGY). However, inferences produced on the basis of a public representation depend on cues revealing intentions, which themselves may largely depend on the group's history, in particular on the fact that certain public representations, or elements thereof, have been used in the same group before. Such historical variations may result in different implicit schemata and therefore in differences of cultural "style" between groups (see CULTURAL PSYCHOLOGY).

See also CULTURAL VARIATION; RELIGIOUS IDEAS AND PRACTICES

—*Pascal Boyer*

References

Boyer, P. (1994). Cognitive constraints on cultural representations: Natural ontologies and religious ideas. In L. A. Hirschfeld and S. Gelman, Eds., *Mapping the Mind: Domain-specificity in Culture and Cognition.* New York: Cambridge University Press.

Mithen, S. (1996). *The Prehistory of the Mind.* London: Thames and Hudson.

Sperber, D. (1975). *Rethinking Symbolism.* Cambridge: Cambridge University Press.

Sperber, D. (1996). *Explaining Culture: A Naturalistic Approach.* Oxford: Blackwell.

Tomasello, M., A. C. Kruger, and H. H. Ratner. (1993). Cultural Learning. *Behavioral and Brain Sciences* 16: 495–510.

Cultural Universals

See CULTURAL RELATIVISM; HUMAN UNIVERSALS; LINGUISTIC UNIVERSALS AND UNIVERSAL GRAMMAR

Cultural Variation

Cultural variation refers to differences in knowledge or belief among individuals. This article focuses on intracultural variation, on differences in belief among individual members of the same cultural group. For example, Americans differ in their environmental beliefs and values (Kempton, Boster, and Hartley 1995); Mexicans differ in their beliefs about disease (Weller 1984); Ojibway differ in their knowledge of hypertension (Garro 1988); Aguaruna women differ in their knowledge of the names of manioc varieties (Boster 1985); and Americans differ in their familiarity, vocabulary size, and recognition ability in various semantic domains (Gatewood 1984). Cross-cultural variation, the general differences between cultural groups, is discussed elsewhere (see HUMAN UNIVERSALS, CULTURAL RELATIVISM, and COGNITIVE ANTHROPOLOGY).

Cultural variation (studied by anthropologists) contrasts both with sociolinguistic variation (studied by linguists) and with individual differences (studied by psychologists). "Cultural (or cognitive) variation" refers to relatively stable substantive differences in belief. "Sociolinguistic (or contextual) variation" usually refers to transient stylistic differences in speech. In this case, speakers share a model of what their choices of register say about themselves and make different choices of self-representation in different social contexts. For example, they may choose to show solidarity with other members of their social group in one setting and compete for status in another. "Individual differences" usually refers to differences in task performance attributable to intrinsic differences in the way individuals process information. These differences, though sometimes produced by training, are often interpreted as (biologically based) variation in intelligence, temperament, or cognitive style.

Various patterns of intracultural variation have been proposed. The simplest pattern is one implicit in most classic ethnography and often incorporated into the concept of culture itself: Individual members of a cultural group share knowledge and beliefs with other members of the group. This assumption of within-group uniformity is often coupled with an assumption of between-group divergence. For a classic review of the culture concept, see Kroeber and Kluckhorn (1952).

Wallace (1961), building on Sapir's (e.g., 1938) and Hallowell's (e.g., 1955) emphasis on the uniqueness of individuals, argued against this uniformitarian view of culture and asserted that cognitive *non-sharing* is a "functional prerequisite of society." He identified six possible patterns of the organization of cognitive diversity:

1. Zero diversity (high concordance)
2. Unorganized diversity (random differences or idiosyncrasy)
3. Ad hoc communication (enhanced agreement among individuals engaged in the same task)
4. Inclusion (systematic differences between experts and novices)
5. End linkage (systematic differences between experts engaged in complementary tasks)
6. Administration (systematic differences between managers and subordinates executing sub-plans)

The first two patterns were regarded as logical extremes, the latter four as ways of accepting and organizing cognitive diversity.

Subsequent authors have emphasized one or another of these patterns. Roberts studied high concordance codes (pattern 1) for color, kin, and clothing, among other domains. He argued that "such codes merit the heavy cultural investment made in them, for they aid rapid and accurate communication" (Roberts 1987: 267). D'Andrade (1976) suggested that most cultural beliefs were either generally shared or were idiosyncratic (patterns 1 and 2), using as an example the distribution of disease beliefs in the United States and Mexico. He later (1981) suggested that the division of labor in society would augment the total cultural information pool from two to four orders of magnitude beyond what an individual knows (pattern 5; cf. Gatewood 1983). Gardner (1976) describes Dene bird classification as a case in which cultural norms are absent and most knowledge is unique to the individual (pattern 2). In contrast, Boster describes Aguaruna manioc identification as a case in which there is a single cultural model known to varying degrees by different informants and in which "deviations from the model are patterned according to the sexual division of labor, membership in kin and residential groups, and individual expertise" (1985: 193; patterns 3, 4, and 5).

There appear to be many similar instances in which one can infer the knowledge of individuals from their degree of agreement with others (e.g., Boster 1985, 1991; D'Andrade 1987; Garro 1986; Gatewood 1984; Romney, Weller, and Batchelder 1986; Weller 1984; see CULTURAL CONSENSUS THEORY). In these instances, individuals who give the model responses are more likely to be reliable on retest (Boster 1985), consistent (Weller 1984), and experienced with the domain (Boster 1985; Gatewood 1984; Garro 1986; Weller 1984). This pattern holds even in cases, such as a word association task, in which there are no culturally normative responses (D'Andrade 1987). However, there are some cases in which domain novices agree with each other more than do experts (e.g., similarity judgment of fish; Boster and Johnson 1989). The exceptions are often instances in which domain novices can generate consistent responses with a simple heuristic. It is important to ensure that any task used to assess cultural knowledge be representative of natural uses of domain knowledge and have ECOLOGICAL VALIDITY.

Just as authors have differed in the patterns of intracultural variation they emphasize, they differ in their description of the processes that generate those patterns. For Wallace, cognitive diversity mainly reflects the division of labor: different patterns emerge depending on how tasks are divided among individuals (cf. Durkheim 1933).

Roberts (1964) developed a view of cultures, similar to Wallace's, as "information economies" that create, distribute, and use information. He showed how aspects of social organization affect how cultural groups as a whole store and retrieve information. Elsewhere, he demonstrated how explicit cultural models of error are used to evaluate and correct mistakes, in trapshooting, tavern pool playing, and flying. See Roberts (1987) for a review.

Boster (1991) extended Roberts's model of culture as an information economy. He proposed that patterns of intracultural variation reflect the "quality, quantity, and distribution of individuals' opportunities to learn" (1991: 204). He argues that domains observable by direct inspection (e.g., FOLK BIOLOGY) or introspection (e.g., COLOR CLASSIFICATION) give individuals equal and ample opportunities to learn regardless of their cultural background. These properties give rise to high cross-cultural and intracultural agreement. In contrast, domains that can only be learned from others (e.g., mythologies) are likely to be highly variable both within and between societies, and have a distribution that reflects the social communication network.

Hutchins (1995), like Roberts, sees whole groups as computational engines. But for Hutchins, cognition is distributed not just among humans but also among artifacts such as navigation charts and compasses, for they serve to store, transform, and transmit information, just as do the humans who use them.

See also COGNITIVE ARTIFACTS; CULTURAL SYMBOLISM; FOLK PSYCHOLOGY; LANGUAGE AND CULTURE; LINGUISTIC RELATIVITY HYPOTHESIS

—James Boster

References

Boster, J. S. (1985). Requiem for the omniscient informant: there's life in the old girl yet. In J. Dougherty, Ed., *Directions in Cognitive Anthropology*. Urbana: University of Illinois Press, pp. 177–197.

Boster, J. S. (1991). The information economy model applied to biological similarity judgment. In L. Resnick, J. Levine, and S. Teasley, Eds., *Perspectives on Socially Shared Cognition*. Washington, DC: American Psychological Association, pp. 203–235.

Boster, J. S., and J. C. Johnson. (1989). Form or function: a comparison of expert and novice judgments of similarity among fish. *American Anthropologist* 91(4): 866–889.

D'Andrade, R. G. (1976). A propositional analysis of U.S. American beliefs about illness. In K. H. Basso and H. A. Selby, Eds., *Meaning in Anthropology*. Albuquerque: University of New Mexico Press, pp. 155–180.

D'Andrade, R. G. (1981). The cultural part of cognition. *Cognitive Science* 5: 179–195.

D'Andrade, R. G. (1987). Modal responses and cultural expertise. *American Behavioral Scientist* 31(2): 266–279.

Durkheim, E. (1933). *Division of Labor in Society.* New York: Macmillan.

Gardner, P. (1976). Birds, words, and a requiem for the omniscient informant. *American Ethnologist* 3: 446–468.

Garro, L. (1986). Intracultural variation in folk medical knowledge: a comparison of curers and non-curers. *American Anthropologist* 88(2): 351–370.

Garro, L. (1988). Explaining high blood pressure: variation in knowledge about illness. *American Ethnologist* 15: 98–119.

Gatewood, J. B. (1983). Loose talk: linguistic competence and recognition ability. *American Anthropologist* 85(2): 378–387.

Gatewood, J. B. (1984). Familiarity, vocabulary size, and recognition ability in four semantic domains. *American Ethnologist* 11(3): 507–527.

Hallowell, A. I. (1955). *Culture and Experience.* Philadelphia: University of Pennsylvania Press.

Hutchins, E. (1995). *Cognition in the Wild.* Cambridge, MA: MIT Press.

Kempton, W., J. S. Boster, and J. A. Hartley. (1995). *Environmental Values in American Culture.* Cambridge, MA: MIT Press.

Kroeber, A. L., and C. Kluckhohn. (1952). Culture: a critical review of concepts and definitions. *Papers of the Peabody Museum of American Archaeology and Ethnology,* vol. 47. Cambridge, MA: Harvard University.

Roberts, J. (1964). The self management of cultures. In W. Goodenough, Ed., *Explorations in Cultural Anthropology: Essays in Honor of George Peter Murdock.* New York: McGraw-Hill, pp. 433–454.

Roberts, J. (1987). Within culture variation. *American Behavioral Scientist* 31(2): 266–279.

Romney, A. K., S. C. Weller, and W. H. Batchelder. (1986). Culture as consensus: a theory of culture and informant accuracy. *American Anthropologist* 88: 313–338.

Sapir, E. (1938). Why anthropology needs the psychiatrist. *Psychiatry* 1: 7–12.

Wallace, A. (1961). *Culture and Personality.* New York: Random House.

Weller, S. C. (1984). Consistency and consensus among informants: disease concepts in a rural Mexican town. *American Anthropologist* 86(4): 966–975.

Culture

See INTRODUCTION: CULTURE, COGNITION, AND EVOLUTION

Culture and Language

See CREOLES; LANGUAGE AND CULTURE; LANGUAGE VARIATION AND CHANGE; PARAMETER-SETTING APPROACHES TO ACQUISITION, CREOLIZATION, AND DIACHRONY

Culture and Metaphor

See METAPHOR AND CULTURE

Culture and Representations of Self

See METAPHOR AND CULTURE; MOTIVATION AND CULTURE; SELF

Darwin, Charles

Charles Darwin (1809–1882) formulated the most important biological theory of the last century and a half: his theory of EVOLUTION by natural selection. By explaining that "mystery of mysteries," the origin of species, Darwin overturned long-entrenched biological and religious assumptions. He applied his general theory to the human animal and thereby rendered an account of moral behavior and rational mind that has formed the foundation for many complementary theories today.

Charles Darwin was born on February 12, 1809, the son of Robert Waring Darwin, a Shrewsbury physician, and Susannah Wedgwood Darwin, daughter of Josiah Wedgwood, who founded the famous pottery firm. When he was sixteen, Darwin went to Edinburgh medical school, following in the shadows of his famous grandfather Erasmus Darwin, and of his father and older brother. At Edinburgh, he came into contact with Robert Grant, who helped him cultivate the study of invertebrates and introduced him to the evolutionary works of his own grandfather and of Lamarck. After Darwin left Edinburgh without a degree, his father, greatly disappointed, sent him to Cambridge to become a country parson. He spent most of his time at university in the pursuits of a gentleman, with some added beetle collecting. A teacher and friend, John Henslow, nevertheless detected a spark in the young man and recommended him to serve as naturalist on a vessel that would sail around the world charting the seas for British naval and commercial craft.

Under the command of the twenty-six-year-old Robert FitzRoy, *H.M.S. Beagle* sailed from Falmouth Harbor on December 29, 1831, and reached the coast of South America two months later. While on board, Darwin occupied himself with reading Alexander von Humboldt's *Personal Narrative of Travels* and steering clear of FitzRoy's foul moods. The *Beagle* charted the waters along the east and west coasts of South America, the Pacific islands, and Australia. Darwin traveled into the interior of these lands to record geological information, as well as to collect fossils and animal specimens to be shipped back to London for careful description and cataloguing. The ship docked at Falmouth on October 4, 1836, almost five years after it had departed. During the voyage Darwin seems not to have seriously considered the possibility that species had transmuted, though he may have had some suspicions. Only in March 1837, as he tried to make sense of the morphology of mockingbirds collected on the Galápagos Islands, did his biological orthodoxy begin to crumble.

During the spring and summer of 1837, Darwin became gradually committed to the idea that species had been transformed over time, and he started to develop hypotheses concerning the causes of change. Initially he supposed that the direct impact of the environment and inherited habit had altered species' forms—notions he retained in his later theorizing. He thought that innate behavior, instincts, also underwent transformations through time, being first acquired as habits. On September 28, 1838, Darwin read Malthus's *Essay on the Principle of Population,* which allowed him to formulate, in the words of his *Autobiography,* "a theory by which to work," his theory of natural selection.

Darwin did not wish to exempt human beings from the evolutionary process. During the late 1830s and early 1840s, he devised theories of the evolution of mind and conscience. Influenced by the empiricism of David HUME and his grandfather, Darwin regarded intelligence as a generalizing and loosening of the cerebral structures that underlay instinct.

Human reason, he believed, gradually emerged out of instincts, which themselves derived from inherited habits and selection operating on such habits. From late 1838 to early 1840, in a set of notebooks ("M" and "N") and in loose notes, he worked out a theory of conscience, which would be elaborated thirty years later in the *Descent of Man* (1871).

Darwin continued to work on his basic theory of evolution through the 1840s and into the early 1850s, simultaneously undertaking the time-consuming labor that produced four large volumes on barnacles. In 1856, after prodding by his friend the eminent geologist Charles Lyell, Darwin began to compose a volume that would detail his theory. In mid-June 1858, he received from Alfred Russel Wallace, then in Malaya, a letter describing a theory of species origin that was nearly identical to his own. Darwin thought his originality had now vanished under a veil of honor. It took Lyell and other of Darwin's friends to convince him that he should continue working on his book, which he did, though in abbreviated form. *On the Origin of Species by Means of Natural Selection* was published in November 1859 and sold out within a few weeks. During Darwin's lifetime, the *Origin* went through six editions, each incorporating alterations and responses to critics. With the last edition, the book had changed by some 50 percent.

The *Origin* had barely mentioned humankind. Critics, however, immediately understood the theory's implications, and most of their objections focused on the problem of human evolution. In 1870, when Wallace seemed to have excluded human beings from the natural process of species change, Darwin felt compelled to reveal his full conception. The *Descent of Man and Selection in Relation to Sex,* appearing in 1871, made his theories of the evolution of mind and conscience quite explicit. Mind reached its human form under the aegis of natural selection and language, the latter producing heritable modifications in brain patterns. Darwin argued that human moral instincts would be acquired through community selection, inasmuch as self-sacrificing behavior would do the agent little good but would benefit the clan, which would include many relatives of the agent. In competition among clans, those whose members exercised more altruistic instincts would have the advantage; and so moral conscience would gradually increase in humankind. Because the pricks of such conscience would little directly benefit the moral individual, Darwin thought his theory quite different from those that were based in utilitarian selfishness—the philosophical ground for many comparable theories today in SOCIOBIOLOGY. Darwin had intended to discuss thoroughly the EMOTIONS in the *Descent,* but saved his theories of emotional instinct for his *Expression of the Emotions in Man and Animals* (1872). Though Konrad Lorenz regarded this book as the foundational document for ETHOLOGY, Darwin had explained emotional instincts solely through the inheritance of acquired habit. And so the Darwinian shade that yet hovers over current biology does bear but passing resemblance to the man who lived in the last century.

See also ADAPTATION AND ADAPTATIONISM; ALTRUISM; EVOLUTIONARY PSYCHOLOGY

—*Robert J. Richards*

References

Darwin, C. (1969). *The Autobiography of Charles Darwin.*, N. Barlow, Ed., New York: Norton.

Darwin, C. (1987). *Charles Darwin's Notebooks, 1836–1844.* P. Barrett et al., Eds., Ithaca: Cornell University Press.

Darwin, C. (1985–). *The Correspondence of Charles Darwin.* 9 vols. to date. Cambridge: Cambridge University Press.

Darwin, C. (1871). *The Descent of Man and Selection in Relation to Sex.* 2 vols. London: Murray.

Darwin, C. (1872). *The Expression of the Emotions in Man and Animals.* London: Murray.

Darwin, C. (1839). *Journal of Researches into the Geology and Natural History of the Various Countries Visited by H.M.S. Beagle.* London: Henry Coburn.

Darwin, C. (1854). *A Monograph of the Fossil Balanidae and Verrucidae of Great Britain.* London: Palaeontological Society.

Darwin, C. (1851). *A Monograph of the Fossil Lepadidae or, Pedunculated Cirripedes of Great Britain.* London: Ray Society.

Darwin, C. (1851). *A Monograph of the Sub-Class Cirripedia. The Balanidae (or Sessile Cirripedes), the Verrucidae, &c.* London: Ray Society.

Darwin, C. (1851). *A Monograph of the Sub-Class Cirripedia, with Figures of all the Species. The Lepadidae or, Pedunculated Cirripedes.* London: Ray Society.

Darwin, C. (1859). *On the Origin of Species by Means of Natural Selection.* London: Murray.

Humboldt, A., and A. Bonpland. (1818–1829). *Personal Narrative of Travels to the Equinoctial Regions of the New Continent, during the Years 1799–1804.* 7 vols. London: Longman, Hurst, Rees, Orme, and Brown.

Malthus, T. (1826). *An Essay on the Principle of Population.* 6th ed., 2 vols. London: Murray.

Further Reading

Bowler, P. (1984). *Evolution: The History of an Idea.* Berkeley: University of California Press.

Browne, J. (1995). *Charles Darwin: Voyaging.* New York: Alfred Knopf.

Dennett, D. (1995). *Darwin's Dangerous Idea.* New York: Simon and Schuster.

Desmond, A. (1989). *The Politics of Evolution.* Chicago: University of Chicago Press.

Glass, B., Ed. (1968). *Forerunners of Darwin.* Baltimore: Johns Hopkins University Press.

Hull, D. (1973). *Darwin and His Critics.* Cambridge, MA: Harvard University Press.

Kohn, D., Ed. (1985). *The Darwinian Heritage.* Princeton: Princeton University Press.

Mayr, E. (1991). *One Long Argument: Charles Darwin and the Genesis of Modern Evolutionary Thought.* Cambridge, MA: Harvard University Press.

Ospovat, D. (1981). *The Development of Darwin's Theory.* Cambridge, MA: Harvard University Press.

Richards, R. (1987). *Darwin and the Emergence of Evolutionary Theories of Mind and Behavior.* Chicago: University of Chicago Press.

Ruse, M. (1996). *Monad to Man: The Concept of Progress in Evolutionary Biology.* Cambridge, MA: Harvard University Press.

Data Mining

See KNOWLEDGE ACQUISITION; MACHINE LEARNING

Decision Making

Decision making is the process of choosing a preferred option or course of action from among a set of alternatives. Decision making permeates all aspects of life, including decisions about what to buy, whom to vote for, or what job to take. Decisions often involve uncertainty about the external world (e.g., What will the weather be like?), as well as conflict regarding one's own preferences (e.g., Should I opt for a higher salary or for more leisure?). The decision-making process often begins at the information-gathering stage and proceeds through likelihood estimation and deliberation, until the final act of choosing.

The study of decision making is an interdisciplinary enterprise involving economics, political science, sociology, psychology, statistics, and philosophy. Decisions are made by individuals and by groups. Important results have been obtained both in the theoretical and experimental study of group decision making. With an eye toward the cognitive sciences, this article focuses on the empirical study of decision making at the individual level. (The focus is on choice behavior; for more on judgment, see JUDGMENT HEURISTICS.)

One can distinguish three approaches to the analysis of decision making: normative, descriptive, and prescriptive. The normative approach assumes a rational decision-maker who has well-defined preferences that obey certain axioms of rational behavior. This conception, known as RATIONAL CHOICE THEORY, is based primarily on a priori considerations rather than on empirical observation. The descriptive approach to decision making is based on empirical observation and on experimental studies of choice behavior. It is concerned primarily with the psychological factors that guide behavior in decision-making situations. Experimental evidence indicates that people's choices are often at odds with the normative assumptions of the rational theory. In light of this, the prescriptive enterprise focuses on methods of improving decision making, bringing it more in line with normative desiderata (see, e.g., von Winterfeld and Edwards 1986).

In some decision contexts, the availability of the chosen option is essentially certain (as when choosing among dishes from a menu, or cars at a dealer's lot). Other decisions are made under UNCERTAINTY: they can be "risky," where the probabilities of the outcomes are known (e.g., gambling or insurance), or they can be "ambiguous," as are most real world decisions, in that their precise likelihood is not known and needs to be judged "subjectively" by the decision maker. When making decisions under uncertainty, a person has to consider both the desirability of the potential outcomes and their probability of occurrence (see PROBABILISTIC REASONING). Indeed, part of the study of decision-making concerns the manner in which these factors are combined.

Presented with a choice between a risky prospect that offers a 50 percent chance to win $200 (and a 50 percent chance to win nothing) and an alternative of receiving $100 for sure, most people prefer the sure gain over the gamble, although the two prospects have the same expected value. (The expected value is the sum of possible outcomes weighted by their probability of occurrence. The expected value of the gamble above is .50 × $200 + .50 × 0 = $100.) Preference for a sure outcome over a risky prospect of equal expected value is called *risk aversion*; indeed, people tend to be risk averse when choosing between prospects with positive outcomes. The tendency towards risk aversion can be explained by the notion of *diminishing sensitivity,* first formalized by Daniel Bernoulli (1738), who thought that "the utility resulting from a fixed small increase in wealth will be inversely proportional to the quantity of goods previously possessed." Bernoulli proposed that people have a concave utility function that captures their subjective value for money, and that preferences should be described using expected utility instead of expected value (a function is concave if a line joining two points on the curve lies below it). According to expected utility, the worth of a gamble offering a 50 percent chance to win $200 (and 50 percent chance to win nothing) is .50 × u($200), where u is the person's utility function (u(0) = 0). It follows from a concave function that the subjective value attached to a gain of $100 is more than 50 percent of the value attached to a gain of $200, which entails preference for the sure $100 gain and, hence, risk aversion.

Expected UTILITY THEORY and the assumption of risk aversion play a central role in the standard economic analysis of choice between risky prospects. In fact, a precipitating event for the empirical study of decision making came from economics, with the publication of von Neumann and Morgenstern's (1947) normative treatment of expected utility, in which a few compelling axioms, when satisfied, were then shown to imply that a person's choices can be thought of as favoring the alternative with the highest subjective expected utility. The normative theory was introduced to psychologists in the late 1950s and early 1960s (Edwards 1961; Luce and Raiffa 1957), and has generated extensive research into "behavioral decision theory." Because the normative treatment specifies simple and compelling principles of rational behavior, it has since served as a benchmark against which behavioral studies of decision making are compared. Research over the last four decades has gained important insights into the decision-making process, and has documented systematic ways in which decision-making behavior departs form the normative benchmark (see ECONOMICS AND COGNITIVE SCIENCE).

When asked to choose between a prospect that offers a 50 percent chance to lose $200 (and a 50 percent chance at nothing) and the alternative of losing $100 for sure, most people prefer to take an even chance at losing $200 or nothing over a sure $100 loss. This is because diminishing sensitivity applies to negative as well as to positive outcomes: the impact of an initial $100 loss is greater than that of an additional $100. The worth of a gamble that offers a 50 percent chance to lose $200 is thus greater (i.e., less negative) than that of a sure $100 loss; .50 × u(−$200) > u(−$100). This results in a convex function for losses and a risk-seeking preference for the gamble over a sure loss. Preference for a risky prospect over a sure outcome of equal expected value is called *risk seeking*. With the exception of prospects that involve very small probabilities, risk aversion is generally observed in choices involving gains, whereas risk seeking tends to hold in choices involving losses.

An S-shaped value function, based on these attitudes toward risk, forms part of prospect theory (Kahneman and TVERSKY 1979), an influential descriptive theory of choice. The value function of prospect theory has three important properties: (1) it is defined on gains and losses rather than total wealth, which captures the fact that people normally treat outcomes as departures from a current reference point, rather than in terms of final assets, as posited by the rational theory of choice; (2) it is steeper for losses than for gains: thus, a loss of $X is more aversive than a gain of $X is attractive. The fact that losses loom larger than corresponding gains is known as *loss aversion*; and (3) it is concave for gains and convex for losses, which yields the risk attitudes described above: risk aversion in the domain of gains and risk seeking in the domain of losses.

These attitudes seem compelling and unobjectionable, yet their combination can lead to normatively problematic consequences. In one example (Tversky and Kahneman 1986), respondents are asked to assume themselves to be $300 richer and are then asked to choose between a sure gain of $100 or an equal chance to win $200 or nothing. Alternatively, they are asked to assume themselves to be $500 richer, and made to choose between a sure loss of $100 and an equal chance to lose $200 or nothing. In accord with the properties described above, most subjects choosing between gains are risk averse and prefer the certain $100 gain, whereas most subjects choosing between losses are risk seeking, preferring the risky prospect over the sure $100 loss. The two problems, however, are essentially identical: when the initial $300 or $500 payment is added to the respective outcomes, both problems amount to a choice between $400 for sure as opposed to an even chance at $300 or $500. This is known as a *framing effect*. It occurs when alternative framings of what is essentially the same decision problem give rise to predictably different choices. The way a problem is described—in terms of gains or losses—can trigger conflicting risk attitudes; similarly, different methods of eliciting preference—for example, through choice versus independent evaluation—can lead people to weigh certain aspects of the options differently. This leads to violations of the normative requirements of "description invariance" and "procedure invariance," according to which logically equivalent representations of a decision problem as well as logically equivalent methods of elicitation should yield the same preferences.

Monetary gambles have traditionally served as metaphors for uncertain awards and as frequent stimuli in decision research. However, much attention has also been devoted to choices between nonmonetary awards, which tend to be multidimensional in nature—for example, the need to choose between job options that differ in prestige, salary, and rank, or between apartments that differ in size, price, aesthetic attractiveness, and location. People are typically uncertain about how much weight to assign to the different dimensions of options; such assignments are often contingent on relatively immaterial changes in the task, the description, and the nature of the options under consideration (Hsee 1998; Tversky, Sattath, and Slovic 1988).

The study of decision-making incorporates issues of PLANNING, PROBLEM SOLVING, PSYCHOPHYSICS, MEMORY, and SOCIAL COGNITION, among others. Behavioral studies of decision-making have included process-tracing methods, such as verbal protocols (Ericsson and Simon 1984), information-acquisition sequences (Payne, Bettman, and Johnson 1993), and eye-movement data (Russo and Dosher 1983). Decision patterns involving hypothetical problems have been replicated in real settings and with experts, for example, physicians' decisions regarding patient treatment (McNeil et al. 1982; Redelmeier and Shafir 1995), academics' retirement investment decisions (Benartzi and Thaler 1995), and taxi drivers' allocation of working hours (Camerer et al. 1997). Some replications have provided substantial as opposed to minor payoffs (e.g., the equivalent of a month's salary paid to respondents in the Peoples' Republic of China; Kachelmeier and Shehata 1992).

People's choices are influenced by various aspects of the decision-making situation. Among these are the conflict or difficulty that characterize a decision (March 1978; Tversky and Shafir 1992), the regret anticipated in cases where another option would have been better (Bell 1982), the role that reasons play in justifying one choice over another (Shafir, Simonson, and Tversky 1993), the attachment that is felt for options already in one's possession (Kahneman, Knetsch, and Thaler 1990), the influence exerted by costs already suffered (Arkes and Blumer 1985), the effects of temporal separation on future decisions (Loewenstein and Elster 1992), and the occasional inability to predict future or remember past satisfaction (Kahneman 1994). Research in decision-making has uncovered psychological principles that account for empirical findings that are counterintuitive and incompatible with normative analyses. People do not always have well-ordered preferences: instead, they approach decisions as problems that need to be solved, and construct preferences that are heavily influenced by the nature and the context of decision.

See also BOUNDED RATIONALITY; CAUSAL REASONING; DEDUCTIVE REASONING; RATIONAL DECISION MAKING; TVERSKY

—Eldar Shafir

References

Arkes, H. R., and C. Blumer. (1985). The psychology of sunk cost. *Organizational Behavior and Human Performance* 35: 129–140.

Bell, D. E. (1982). Regret in decision making under uncertainty. *Operations Research* 30: 961–981.

Benartzi, S., and R. Thaler. (1995). Myopic loss aversion and the equity premium puzzle. *Quarterly Journal of Economics* 110 (1): 73–92.

Camerer, C., L. Babcock, G. Loewenstein, and R. Thaler. (1997). A target income theory of labor supply: Evidence from cab drivers. *Quarterly Journal of Economics* 112 (2).

Edwards, W. (1961). Behavioral decision theory. *Annual Review of Psychology* 12: 473–498.

Ericsson, K. A., and H. A. Simon. (1984). *Protocol Analysis: Verbal Reports as Data*. Cambridge, MA: MIT Press.

Hsee, C. K. (1998). The evaluability hypothesis: Explaining joint-separate evaluation preference reversal and beyond. In D. Kahneman and A. Tversky, Eds. *Choices, values and frames*. Cambridge: Cambridge University Press.

Kachelmeier, S. J., and M. Shehata. (1992). Examining risk preferences under high monetary incentives: Experimental evidence from the People's Republic of China. *American Economic Review* 82: 1120–1141.

Kahneman, D. (1994). New challenges to the rationality assumption. *Journal of Institutional and Theoretical Economics* 150 (1): 18–36.

Kahneman, D., J. L. Knetsch, and R. Thaler. (1990). Experimental tests of the endowment effect and the Coase theorem. *Journal of Political Economy* 98 (6): 1325–1348.

Kahneman, D., and A. Tversky. (1979). Prospect theory: An analysis of decision under risk. *Econometrica* 47: 263–291.

Loewenstein, G., and J. Elster, Eds. (1992). *Choice Over Time*. New York: Russell Sage Foundation.

Luce, R. D., and H. Raiffa. (1957). *Games and Decisions*. New York: Wiley.

March, J. (1978). Bounded rationality, ambiguity and the engineering of choice. *Bell Journal of Economics* 9 (2): 587–608.

McNeil, B. J., S. G. Pauker, H. C. Sox, and A. Tversky. (1982). On the elicitation of preferences for alternative therapies. *New England Journal of Medicine* 306: 1259–1262.

Payne, J. W., J. R. Bettman, and E. J. Johnson. (1993). *The Adaptive Decision Maker*. Cambridge: Cambridge University Press.

Redelmeier, D., and E. Shafir. (1995). Medical decision making in situations that offer multiple alternatives. *Journal of the American Medical Association* 273 (4): 302–305.

Russo, J. E., and B. A. Dosher. (1983). Strategies for multiattribute binary choice. *Journal of Experimental Psychology: Learning, Memory, and Cognition* 9 (4): 676–696.

Shafir, E., I. Simonson, and A. Tversky. (1993). Reason-based choice. *Cognition* 49 (2): 11–36.

Tversky, A., and D. Kahneman. (1986). Rational choice and the framing of decisions. *Journal of Business* 59 (4, pt. 2): 251–278.

Tversky, A., S. Sattath, and P. Slovic. (1988). Contingent weighting in judgment and choice. *Psychological Review* 95 (3): 371–384.

Tversky, A., and E. Shafir. (1992). Choice under conflict: The dynamics of deferred decision. *Psychological Science* 3 (6): 358–361.

von Neumann, J., and O. Morgenstern. (1947). *Theory of Games and Economic Behavior*. 2nd ed. Princeton: Princeton University Press.

von Winterfeld, D., and W. Edwards. (1986). *Decision Analysis and Behavioral Research*. Cambridge: Cambridge University Press.

Further Readings

Baron, J. (1994). *Thinking and Deciding*. 2nd ed. Cambridge: Cambridge University Press.

Bell, D. E., H. Raiffa, and A. Tversky, Eds. (1988). *Decision Making: Descriptive, Normative, and Prescriptive Interactions*. New York: Cambridge University Press.

Camerer, C. F. (1995). Individual decision making. In J. H. Kagel and A. E. Roth, Eds., *Handbook of Experimental Economics*. Princeton, NJ: Princeton University Press, pp. 587–703.

Dawes, R. M. (1988). *Rational Choice in an Uncertain World*. New York: Harcourt Brace Jovanovich.

Edwards, W. (1954). The theory of decision making. *Psychological Bulletin* 51: 380–417.

Goldstein, W. M., and R. M. Hogarth. (1997). *Research on Judgment and Decision Making: Currents, Connections, and Controversies*. Cambridge: Cambridge University Press.

Hogarth, R. M. (1987). *Judgment and Choice.* 2nd ed. New York: Wiley.

Raiffa, H. (1968). *Decision Analysis: Introductory Lectures on Choices under Uncertainty.* Reading, MA: Addison-Wesley.

Shafir, E., and A. Tversky. (1995). Decision making. In E. E. Smith and D. N. Osherson, Eds., *An Invitation to Cognitive Science,* 2nd ed. vol. 3: *Thinking).* Cambridge, MA: MIT Press, pp. 77–100.

Tetlock, P. E. (1992). The impact of accountability on judgment and choice: Toward a social contingency model. In M. P. Zanna, Ed., *Advances in Experimental Social Psychology,* vol. 25. New York: Academic Press.

Yates, J. F. (1990). *Judgment and Decision Making.* Englewood Cliffs, NJ: Prentice-Hall.

Decision Theory

See RATIONAL AGENCY; RATIONAL CHOICE THEORY; RATIONAL DECISION MAKING; UTILITY THEORY

Decision Trees

A *decision tree* is a graphical representation of a procedure for classifying or evaluating an item of interest. For example, given a patient's symptoms, a decision tree could be used to determine the patient's likely diagnosis, or outcome, or recommended treatment. Figure 1 shows a decision tree for forecasting whether a patient will die from hepatitis, based on data from the University of California at Irvine repository (Murphy and Aha 1994). A decision tree represents a function that maps each element of its domain to an element of its range, which is typically a class label or numerical value. At each leaf of a decision tree, one finds an element of the range. At each internal node of the tree, one finds a test that has a small number of possible outcomes. By branching according to the outcome of each test, one arrives at a leaf that contains the class label or numerical value that corresponds to the item in hand. In the figure, each leaf shows the number of examples of each class that fall to that leaf. These leaves are usually not of one class, so one typically chooses the most frequently occurring class label.

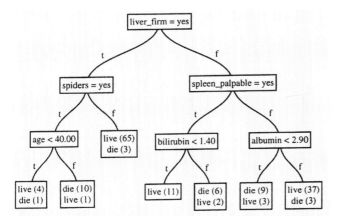

Figure 1.

A decision tree with a range of discrete (symbolic) class labels is called a *classification tree*, whereas a decision tree with a range of continuous (numeric) values is called a *regression tree*. A domain element is called an *instance* or an *example* or a *case*, or sometimes by another name appropriate to the context. An instance is represented as a conjunction of variable values. Each variable has its own domain of possible values, typically discrete or continuous. The space of all possible instances is defined by set of possible instances that one could generate using these variables and their possible values (the cross product).

Decision trees are attractive because they show clearly how to reach a decision, and because they are easy to construct automatically from labeled instances. Two well known programs for constructing decision trees are C4.5 (Quinlan 1993) and CART (Classification and Regression Tree) (Breiman et al. 1984). The tree shown in figure 1 was generated by the ITI (Incremental Tree Inducer) program (Utgoff, Berkman, and Clouse 1997). These programs usually make quick work of training data, constructing a tree in a matter of a few seconds to a few minutes. For those who prefer to see a list of rules, there is a simple conversion, which is available in the C4.5 program. For each leaf of the tree, place its label in the right-hand side of a rule. In the left-hand side, place the conjunction of all the conditions that would need to be true to reach that leaf from the root.

Decision trees are useful for automating decision processes that are part of an application program. For example, for the optical character recognition (OCR) task, one needs to map the optical representation of a symbol to a symbol name. The optical representation might be a grid of pixel values. The tree could attempt to map these pixel values to a symbol name. Alternatively, the designer of the system might include the computation of additional variables, also called *features*, that make the mapping process simpler. Decision trees are used in a large number of applications, and the number continues to grow as practitioners gain experience in using trees to model decision making processes. Present applications include various pixel classification tasks, language understanding tasks such as pronoun resolution, fault diagnosis, control decisions in search, and numerical function approximation.

A decision tree is typically constructed recursively in a top-down manner (Friedman 1977; Quinlan 1986). If a set of labeled instances is sufficiently pure, then the tree is a leaf, with the assigned label being that of the most frequently occurring class in that set. Otherwise, a test is constructed and placed into an internal node that constitutes the tree so far. The test defines a partition of the instances according to the outcome of the test as applied to each instance. A branch is created for each block of the partition, and for each block, a decision tree is constructed recursively.

One needs to define when a set of instances is to be considered sufficiently pure to constitute a leaf. One choice would be to require absolute purity, meaning that all the instances must be of the same class. Another choice would be to require that the class distribution be significantly lopsided, which is a less stringent form of the complete lopsidedness that one gets when the leaf is pure. This is also known as *prepruning* because one restricts the growth of the tree before it occurs.

One also needs a method for constructing and selecting a test to place at an internal node. If the test is to be based on just one variable, called a *univariate test*, then one needs to be able to enumerate possible tests based on that variable. If the variable is discrete, then the possible outcomes could be the possible values of that variable. Alternatively, a test could ask whether the variable has a particular value, making just two possible outcomes, as is the case in figure 1. If the variable is continuous, then some form of discretization needs to be done, so that only a manageable number of outcomes is possible. One can accomplish this by searching for a *cutpoint*, and then forming a test whether the variable value is less than the cutpoint, as shown in figure 1.

If the test is to be based on more than one variable, called a *multivariate test*, then one needs to be able to search quickly for a suitable test. This is often done by mapping the discrete variables to continuous variables, and then finding a good linear combination of those variables. A univariate test is also known as an *axis-parallel split* because in a geometric view of the instance space, the partition formed by a univariate test is parallel to the axes of the other variables. A multivariate test is also known as an *oblique split* because it need not have any particular characteristic relationship to the axes (Murthy, Kasif, and Salzberg 1994).

One must choose the best test from among those that are allowed at an internal node. This is typically done in a *greedy* manner by ranking the tests according to a heuristic function, and picking the test that is ranked best. Many heuristic tests have been suggested, and this problem is still being studied. For classification trees, most are based on entropy minimization. By picking a test that maximizes the purity of the blocks, one will probably obtain a smaller tree than otherwise, and researchers and practitioners alike have a longstanding preference for smaller trees. Popular heuristic functions include *information gain, gain ratio, GINI,* and *Kolmogorov-Smirnoff distance.* For regression trees, most tests are based on variance minimization. A test that minimizes the variance within the resulting blocks will also tend to produce a smaller tree than one would obtain otherwise.

It is quite possible that a tree will overfit the data. The tree may have more structure than is helpful because it is attempting to produce several purer blocks where one less pure block would result in higher accuracy on unlabeled instances (instance not used in training). This can come about due to inaccurate variable measurements or inaccurate label or value assignments. A host of *postpruning* methods are available that reduce the size of the tree after it has been grown. A simple method is to set aside some of the training instances, called the *pruning set*, before building the tree. Then after the tree has been built, do a postorder traversal of the tree, reducing each subtree to a leaf if the proposed leaf would not be significantly less accurate on the pruning set than the subtree it would replace. This issue of balancing the desire for purity with the desire for accuracy is also called the *bias-variance trade-off.* A smaller tree has higher bias because the partition is coarser, but lower variance because the leaves are each based on more training instances.

During the mid-1990s, researchers developed methods for using ensembles of decision trees to improve accuracy (Dietterich and Bakiri 1995; Kong and Dietterich 1995; Breiman 1996). To the extent that different decision trees for the same task make independent errors, a vote of the set of decision trees can correct the errors of the individual trees.

See also DECISION MAKING; GREEDY LOCAL SEARCH; HEURISTIC SEARCH; RATIONAL DECISION MAKING

—*Paul Utgoff*

References

Breiman, L. (1996). Bagging predictors. *Machine Learning* 24: 123–140.

Breiman, L., J. H. Friedman, R. A. Olshen, and C. J. Stone. (1984). *Classification and Regression Trees.* Belmont, CA: Wadsworth International Group.

Dietterich, T. G., and G. Bakiri. (1995). Solving multiclass learning problems via error-correcting output codes. *Journal of Artificial Intelligence* 2: 263–286.

Friedman, J. H. (1977). A recursive partitioning decision rule for nonparametric classification. *IEEE Transactions on Computers,* C-26: 404–408.

Kong, E. B., and T. G. Dietterich. (1995). Error-correcting output coding corrects bias and variance. *Machine Learning: Proceedings of the Twelfth International Conference.* Tahoe City, CA: Morgan Kaufmann, pp. 313–321.

Murphy, P. M., and D. W. Aha. (1994). *UCI Repository of Machine Learning Databases.* Irvine, CA: University of California, Department of Information and Computer Science.

Murthy, S. K., S. Kasif, and S. Salzberg. (1994). A system for induction of oblique decision trees. *Journal of Artificial Intelligence Research* 2: 1–32.

Quinlan, J. R. (1986). Induction of decision trees. *Machine Learning* 1: 81–106.

Quinlan, J. R. (1993). *C4.5: Programs for Machine Learning.* San Mateo, CA: Morgan Kaufmann.

Utgoff, P. E., N. C. Berkman, and J. A. Clouse. (1997). Decision tree induction based on efficient tree restructuring. *Machine Learning* 29: 5–44.

Further Readings

Brodley, C. E., and P. E. Utgoff. (1995). Multivariate decision trees. *Machine Learning* 19: 45–77.

Buntine, W., and T. Niblett. (1992). A further comparison of splitting rules for decision-tree induction. *Machine Learning* 8: 75–85.

Chou, P. A. (1991). Optimal partitioning for classification and regression trees. *IEEE Transactions on Pattern Analysis and Machine Intelligence* 13: 340–354.

Draper, B. A., C. E. Brodley, and P. E. Utgoff. (1994). Goal-directed classification using linear machine decision trees. *IEEE Transactions on Pattern Analysis and Machine Intelligence* 16: 888–893.

Jordan, M. I. (1994). A statistical approach to decision tree modeling. *Machine Learning: Proceedings of the Eleventh International Conference.* New Brunswick, NJ: Morgan Kaufmann, pp. 363–370.

Moret, B. M. E. (1982). Decision trees and diagrams. *Computing Surveys* 14: 593–623.

Murphy, P., and M. Pazzani. (1994). Exploring the decision forest: An empirical investigation of Occam's Razor in decision tree induction. *Journal of Artificial Intelligence Research* 1: 257–275.

Pagallo, G., and D. Haussler. (1990). Boolean feature discovery in empirical learning. *Machine Learning* 5,1: 71–99.

Quinlan, J. R., and R. L. Rivest. (1989). Inferring decision trees using the minimum description length principle. *Information and Computation* 80: 227–248.

Safavian, S. R., and D. Langrebe. (1991). A survey of decision tree classifier methodology. *IEEE Transactions on Systems, Man and Cybernetics* 21: 660–674.

Utgoff, P. E. (1989). Incremental induction of decision trees. *Machine Learning* 4: 161–186.

White, A. P., and W. Z. Liu. (1994). Bias in information-based measures in decision tree induction. *Machine Learning* 15: 321–329.

Decompositional Strategies

See FUNCTIONAL DECOMPOSITION

Deductive Reasoning

Deductive reasoning is a branch of cognitive psychology investigating people's ability to recognize a special relation between statements. *Deductive LOGIC* is a branch of philosophy and mathematics investigating the same relation. We can call this relation *entailment*, and it holds between a set of statements (the *premises*) and a further statement (the *conclusion*) if the conclusion must be true whenever all the premises are true. Consider the premises "Calvin bites his nails while working" and "Calvin is working" and the conclusion "Calvin is biting his nails." Because the latter statement must be true whenever both the former statements are, these premises entail the conclusion. By contrast, the premises "Calvin bites his nails while working" and "Calvin is biting his nails" does not entail "Calvin is working," inasmuch as it is possible that Calvin bites his nails off the job.

Historically, logicians have constructed systems that describe entailments among statements in some domain of discourse. To compare these systems to human intuition, psychologists present to their subjects *arguments* (premise-conclusion combinations), some of which embody the target entailments. The psychologists ask the subjects to identify those arguments in which the conclusion "follows logically" from the premises (or in which the conclusion "must be true whenever the premises are true"). Alternatively, the psychologist can present just the premises and ask the subjects to produce a conclusion that logically follows from them. Whether a subject's answer is correct or incorrect is usually determined by comparing it to the dictates of the logic system.

One purpose of investigating people's ability to recognize entailments is to find out what light (if any) entailment sheds on thinking and to use these findings as a basis for revising theories of logic and theories of mind. Given this goal, certain differences between entailments and psychological decisions about them are uninformative. Subjects' inattention, memory limits, and time limits all restrict their success in distinguishing entailments from nonentailments, but factors such as these affect all human thinking and tell us nothing new about deductive reasoning.

Investigating the role of entailment in thought requires some degree of abstraction from everyday cognitive foibles. But it is not always easy to say how far such abstraction should go. According to GRICE (1989), Lewis (1979), and Sperber and Wilson (1986), among others, ordinary conversational settings impose restrictions on what people say, restrictions that can override entailments or supplement entailments (see PRAGMATICS). If Martha says, "Some of my in-laws are honest," we would probably understand her to imply that some of her in-laws are dishonest. This follows from a conversational principle that enjoins her to make the most informative statement available, all else being equal. If Martha believes that all her in-laws are honest, she should have said so; because she did not say so, we infer that she believes not all are honest. We draw this conversational IMPLICATURE even if we recognize that "Some of my in-laws are honest" does not entail "Some of my in-laws are dishonest."

Experimental results suggest that people do not abandon their conversational principles when they become subjects in reasoning experiments (e.g., Fillenbaum 1977; Sperber, Cara, and Girotto 1995). Moreover, conversational implicatures are just one among many types of nondeductive inferences that people routinely employ. In many situations it is satisfactory to reach conclusions that are plausible on the basis of current evidence, but where the conclusion is not necessarily true when the evidence is. It is reasonable to conclude from "Asteroid gamma-315 contains carbon compounds" that "Asteroid gamma-359 contains carbon compounds," even though the first statement might be true and the second false. Attempts to reduce these plausible inferences to entailments have not been successful (as Osherson, Smith, and Shafir 1986 have argued).

Subjects sometimes misidentify these plausible arguments as deductively correct, and psychologists have labeled this tendency a *content effect* (Evans 1989 contains a review of such effects). These content effects, of course, do not mean that people have no grasp of individual entailments (see, e.g., Braine, Reiser, and Rumain 1984; Johnson-Laird and Byrne 1991; and Rips 1994, for evidence concerning people's mastery of entailments that depend on *logical constants* such as "and," "if," "or," "not," "for all," and "for some"). Subjects may rely on plausible inferences when it becomes difficult for them to judge whether an entailment holds; they may rely on entailments only when the context pushes them to do so; or they may falsely believe that the experiment calls for plausible inferences rather than for entailments.

However, if there is a principled distinction between entailments and other inference relations and if people routinely fail to observe this distinction, then perhaps they have difficulties with the concept of entailment itself. Some psychologists and some philosophers believe that there is no reasoning process that is distinctive to entailments (e.g., Harman 1986). Some may believe that people (at least those without special logic or math training) have no proper concept of entailment that distinguishes it from other inference relations. The evidence is clouded here, however, by methodological issues (see Cohen 1981). For example, psychologists rarely bother to give their subjects a full explanation of entailment, relying instead on phrases like "logically follows." Perhaps subjects interpret these instructions as equivalent to the vaguer sort of relation indicated in natural language by "therefore" or "thus."

The problem of whether people distinguish entailments is complicated on the logic side by the existence of multiple logic systems (see MODAL LOGIC). There is no one logic that captures all purported entailments, but many proposed systems that formalize different domains. Some systems are supersets of others, adding new logical constants to a core logic in order to describe entailments for concepts like time, belief and knowledge, or permission and obligation. Other systems are rival formulations of the same domain. Psychologists sometimes take subjects' rejection of a specific logic principle as evidence of failure in the subjects' reasoning; however, some such rejections may be the result of an incorrect choice of a logic standard. According to many philosophers (e.g., Goodman 1965), justification of a logic system depends in part on how close it comes to human intuition. If so, subjects' performance may sometimes be grounds for revision in logic.

The variety of logic systems also raises the issue of whether human intuitions about entailment are similarly varied. According to one view, the intuitions belong to a unified set that incorporates the many different types of entailment. Within this set, people may recognize entailments that are specialized for broad domains, such as time, obligation, and so on; but intuitions about each domain are internally consistent. Rival analyses of a specific constant (e.g., "it ought to be the case that . . .") compete for which gives the best account of reasoning. According to a second view, however, there are many different intuitions about entailment, even within a single domain. Rival analyses for "it ought to be the case that. . ." may then correspond to different (psychologically real) concepts of obligation, each with its associated inferences (cf. Lemmon 1959).

The first view lends itself to a theory in which people automatically translate natural language arguments into a single LOGICAL FORM on which inference procedures operate. The second view suggests a more complicated process: when subjects decide whether a natural language argument is deductively correct, they may perform a kind of model-fitting, determining if any of their mental inference packages makes the argument come out right (as Miriam Bassok has suggested, personal communication, 1996). Both views have their advantages, and both deserve a closer look.

See also CAUSAL REASONING; EVOLUTIONARY PSYCHOLOGY; INDUCTION; LOGICAL REASONING SYSTEMS; MENTAL MODELS; NONMONOTONIC LOGICS

—*Lance J. Rips*

References

Braine, M. D. S., B. J. Reiser, and B. Rumain. (1984). Some empirical justification for a theory of natural propositional reasoning. In G. H. Bower, Ed., *Psychology of Learning and Motivation,* vol. 18. Orlando: Academic Press.

Cohen, L. J. (1981). Can human irrationality be experimentally demonstrated? *Behavioral and Brain Sciences* 4: 317–370.

Evans, J. St. B. T. (1989). *Bias in Human Reasoning.* Hillsdale, NJ: Erlbaum.

Fillenbaum, S. (1977). Mind your *p*'s and *q*'s: the role of content and context in some uses of *and, or* and *if.* In G. H. Bower, Ed., *Psychology of Learning and Motivation,* vol. 11. Orlando: Academic Press.

Goodman, N. (1965). *Fact, Fiction, and Forecast.* 2nd ed. Indianapolis: Bobbs-Merrill.

Grice, H. P. (1989). *Studies in the Way of Words.* Cambridge, MA: Harvard University Press.

Harman, G. (1986). *Change in View.* Cambridge, MA: MIT Press.

Johnson-Laird, P. N., and R. M. J. Byrne. (1991). *Deduction.* Hillsdale, NJ: Erlbaum.

Lemmon, E. J. (1959). Is there only one correct system of modal logic. *Proceedings of the Aristotelian Society* 23: 23–40.

Lewis, D. (1979). Score keeping in a language game. *Journal of Philosophical Logic* 8: 339–359.

Osherson, D. N., E. E. Smith, and E. B. Shafir. (1986). Some origins of belief. *Cognition* 24: 197–224.

Rips, L. J. (1994). *The Psychology of Proof.* Cambridge, MA: MIT Press.

Sperber, D., F. Cara, and V. Girotto. (1995). Relevance theory explains the selection task. *Cognition* 57: 31–95.

Sperber, D., and D. Wilson. (1986). *Relevance.* Cambridge, MA: Harvard Press.

Further Readings

Braine, M. D. S., and D. P. O'Brien. (1998). *Mental Logic.* Mahwah, NJ: Erlbaum.

Cheng, P. W., K. J. Holyoak, R. E. Nisbett, and L. M. Oliver. (1986). Pragmatic versus syntactic approaches to training deductive reasoning. *Cognitive Psychology* 18: 293–328.

Evans, J. St. B. T., S. E. Newstead, and R. M. J. Byrne. (1993). *Human Reasoning.* Hillsdale, NJ: Erlbaum.

Nisbett, R. E. (1993). *Rules for Reasoning.* Hillsdale, NJ: Erlbaum.

Oaksford, M., and N. Chater. (1994). A rational analysis of the selection task as optimal data selection. *Psychological Review* 101: 608–631.

Polk, T. A., and A. Newell. (1995). Deduction as verbal reasoning. *Psychological Review* 102: 533–566.

Deficits

See MODELING NEUROPSYCHOLOGICAL DEFICITS

Deixis

See INDEXICALS AND DEMONSTRATIVES

Demonstratives

See INDEXICALS AND DEMONSTRATIVES

Dendrite

See COMPUTATIONAL NEUROSCIENCE; NEURON

Density Estimation

See UNSUPERVISED LEARNING

Depth Perception

Depth perception is one of the oldest problems of philosophy and experimental psychology. It has always intrigued people because of the two-dimensionality of the retinal image, although this is not really relevant because, as Descartes (1637) realized, we do not perceive the retinal image. DESCARTES was one of the first to suggest that depth could be computed from changes in the accommodation and convergence of the eyes. Accommodation is the focusing of the lenses and convergence is the inward/outward turning of the eyes stimulated by a change in the distance of the object of regard. Unfortunately, convergence and accommodation vary little beyond a meter or two and we clearly have a sense of depth well beyond that. Cutting and Vishton (1995) note that different cues to depth seem to be operative for near (personal) space, ambient (action) space, and vista (far) space. Convergence and accommodation clearly apply best to the space approximately within arm's reach, but even in that region their effectiveness in giving an impression of absolute distance varies among persons and is imprecise.

Interposition, or the hiding of one object by another, creates an ordinal sense of depth at all distances. But how is interposition specified in visual stimulation? Interposition or occlusion can be indicated monocularly by such contour arrangements as T junctions and alignments (Kanisza 1979) or binocularly by the fact that parts of background objects or regions are hidden from one eye and not the other (Leonardo da Vinci 1505). Current evidence suggests that unlike monocular occlusion cues, binocular occlusion cues can elicit a sense of metric depth (Gillam, Blackburn, and Nakayama 1999).

It is generally found that people are quite accurate in judging ambient distance (up to approximately twenty feet). This is typically demonstrated by having them survey the scene, close their eyes, and walk to a predesignated object (Loomis et al. 1992). Perhaps the most important source of distance information in ambient and far space is spatial layout information of the kind first analyzed by James Jerome GIBSON (1950, 1966), although much of the underlying perspective geometry was known by artists of the Renaissance (Alberti 1435). Gibson pointed out that objects are nearly always located on a ground plane and that if the ground is homogeneously textured, it provides a scale in the "optic array" (the projection of the layout to a station point) which can be used to compare distances between elements in any direction at any distance. If the size of the units of texture are known, for example by their relationship to the observer, the scale may also specify absolute distance. In practice it has been found that random dot textures give a much poorer sense of depth than regular textures, especially regular textures that include lines converging toward a vanishing point. Vanishing points and horizons provide depth information in their own right. (A horizon is the locus of the vanishing

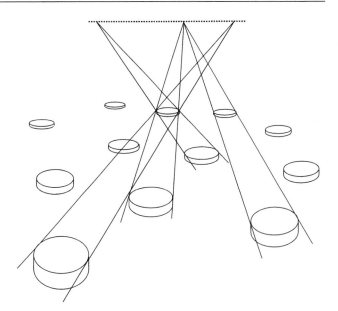

Figure 1.

points of all sets of parallel lines on a planar surface.) For example, the angular extent in the optic array of a location on a surface and the horizon of that surface specifies the absolute distance of that location to a scale factor given by the observer's eye height. Furthermore, the angular distances from two locations on a surface to the horizon can give the relative distances of those locations independently of eye height (Sedgwick 1986). The horizon can be implicitly specified by converging lines even if they do not extend to a vanishing point and also by randomly arranged elements of finite uniform size (see figure 1).

It is generally agreed that the familiar size of isolated objects is not used to derive distance from their angular size although this is possible in principle. However, relative size, especially for objects of a similar shape, is an excellent cue to relative distance. Likewise, an object changing size is normally seen as looming or receding in depth.

Parallax, defined as the difference in the projection of a static scene as viewpoint changes relative to the scene, is a potent source of information about depth. Motion parallax refers to successive viewpoint changes produced by motion of the observer, whereas binocular parallax refers to the simultaneous differences in viewpoint provided by two horizontally separated eyes. The disparate images thus produced result in "stereoscopic vision." Wheatstone (1838), who discovered stereoscopic vision, showed that the projections of a scene to the two eyes differ in a number of ways (see figure 2), and there is some evidence that the visual system responds directly to certain higher order image differences such as contour orientation. Binocular disparity is usually specified, however, as the difference in the horizontal angles subtended at the two eyes by two points separated in depth.

Stereoscopic vision really comes into its own in near vision where it is important in eye-hand coordination, and in ambient vision where it allows discrete elements that do not provide perspective cues, such as the leaves and branches of a forest, to be seen in vivid relief. The disparity produced by a given depth interval declines rapidly as the distance of the

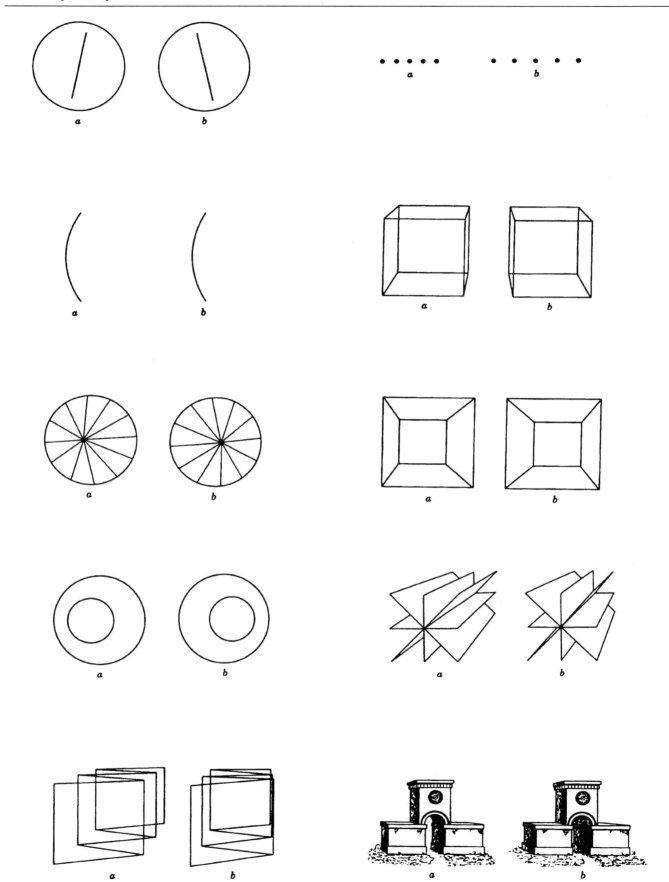

Figure 2.

interval from the observer increases. Nevertheless it is possible with moderate stereoscopic acuity to detect that an object at about five hundred meters is nearer than infinity. Because the binocular disparity produced by a given depth interval declines with its distance, the depth response to disparity must be scaled for distance to reflect depth accurately. Scaling has largely been studied at close distances where it is excellent under full cue conditions although it is not yet clear how the scaling is achieved (Howard and Rogers 1995). The accuracy of scaling in vista space is not known. Stereoscopic depth is best for objects that are laterally close to each other (Gogel 1963). At such separations stereoscopic depth is a "hyperacuity" because disparities of only 10–30 sec of arc can be responded to as a depth separation (Westheimer 1979).

Despite the fact that binocular and motion parallax have identical geometry, stereopsis is the superior sense for depth perception under most conditions, especially when there are only two objects separated in depth. Motion parallax is almost as good as stereopsis, however, in eliciting perception of depth in densely patterned corrugated surfaces (Rogers and Graham 1979). A strong sense of solidity is also obtained monocularly when a skeletal object, such as a tangled wire, is rotated in depth and viewed with a stationary eye (kinetic depth effect). The depth variations in densely textured surfaces can also be perceived on the basis of the monocular transformations they undergo during motion.

Many of the possible sources of information about depth have not yet been adequately investigated, especially the sources used in ambient and vista space. There are also unresolved theoretical issues such as the relationship between the apparent distances of objects to the observer and their apparent distances from each other.

See also HIGH-LEVEL VISION; ILLUSIONS; MID-LEVEL VISION; STRUCTURE FROM VISUAL INFORMATION SOURCES; SURFACE PERCEPTION; VISUAL PROCESSING STREAMS

—*Barbara Gillam*

References

Alberti, L. (1435). *On Painting.* Translated by J. R. Spencer, 1956. New Haven, CT: Yale University Press.

Cutting, J. E., and P. Vishton. (1995). Perceiving layout and knowing distances: The integration, relative potency and contextual use of different information about depth. In W. Epstein and S. Rogers, Eds., *Perception of Space and Motion.* San Diego: Academic Press, pp. 69–117.

Descartes, R. (1637). *Discourse on Method, Optics, Geometry and Meteorology.* Translated by Paul J. Olscamp, 1965. Indianapolis: Bobbs-Merrill.

Gibson, J. J. (1950). *The Perception of the Visual World.* Boston: Houghton Mifflin.

Gibson, J. J. (1966). *The Senses Considered as Perceptual Systems.* Boston: Houghton Mifflin.

Gillam, B. J., S. Blackburn, and K. Nakayama. (1999). Unpaired background stereopsis: Metrical encoding of depth and slant without matching contours. To appear in *Vision Research.*

Gogel, W. C. (1963). The visual perception of size and distance. *Vision Research* 3: 101–120.

Howard, I. P., and B. J. Rogers. (1995). *Binocular Vision and Stereopsis.* New York: Oxford University Press.

Kanisza, G. (1979). *Organization in Vision.* New York: Praeger.

Leonardo da Vinci. (1505). *Codex Manuscript D.* In the Bibliothèque Nationale, Paris. English translation in D. S. Strong (1979), *Leonardo on the Eye.* New York: Garland, pp 41–92.

Loomis, J. M., J. A. Da Silva, N. Fujita, and S. S. Fukusima. (1992). Visual space perception and visually directed action. *Journal of Experimental Psychology: Human Perception and Performance* 18(4): 906–921.

Rogers, B. J., and M. E. Graham. (1979). Motion parallax as an independent cue for depth perception. *Perception* 8: 125–134.

Sedgwick, H. A. (1986). Space perception. In K. Boff, L. Kaufman, and J. Thomas, Eds., *Handbook of Perception and Human Performance,* vol. 1. New York: John Wiley and Sons.

Westheimer, G. (1979) Cooperative neural processes involved in stereoscopic acuity. *Experimental Brain Research* 36: 585–597.

Wheatstone, C. (1838). Contributions to the physiology of vision: 1. On some remarkable and hitherto unobserved phenomena of binocular vision. *Philisophical Transactions of the Royal Society, London* 128: 371–394.

Descartes René

A dominant figure of mid-seventeenth century philosophy and science, René Descartes (1596–1650) developed a sweepingly anti-Aristotelian, mechanist theory of nature, while also advocating a conception of the "rational soul" as a distinct, immaterial entity, endowed by God with certain innate intellectual concepts. Generations of anglophone philosophers have tended (with some notable exceptions) to construe Descartes's importance as deriving mainly from his radical development of problems of scepticism, and his sharp dualistic distinction between mind and body, in his central philosophical work, the *Meditations on First Philosophy* (1641). Today, however, this conception is often criticized as historically naive. On one hand, the *Meditations* themselves were intended by Descartes to provide a "foundation" for his comprehensive mechanistic account of natural phenomena; the doctrines and arguments of the work need to be interpreted in this light. On the other hand, Descartes's vision of a comprehensive, unified theory of nature, grounded in a small number of "distinctly conceivable," quantitatively expressible concepts (especially size, figure and motion) was in itself of incalculable significance in the history of Western thought (cf. UNITY OF SCIENCE).

Prominent among Descartes's aims as a systematic scientist was the incorporation of biological phenomena (such as nutrition and growth), and many psychological phenomena as well (such as reflex behaviors and some kinds of learning), in the universal mechanistic physics that he envisaged. Works in which he develops mechanist approaches to physiology and psychology include the early *Treatise on Man* (published only after his death); the *Dioptrics* (published, together with the *Geometry and Meteors*, with the wideranging, partly autobiographical work, *Discourse on the Method of Rightly Conducting One's Reason and Seeking Truth in the Sciences,* 1637); parts of the compendious *Principles of Philosophy* (1644); and the late *Passions of the Soul* (1649).

Basic to Descartes's approach to the understanding of animal (including human) behavior is the notion that one should push mechanistic-materialist explanations as far as one can. From early in his career he proclaimed that all the behavior of nonhuman animals ("brutes") can be explained in mechanistic terms. In the *Discourse on the Method* (Part V) he defended this position by arguing that the behavior of brutes uniformly fails two tests that he considers to be crucial to establishing the presence of some principle other than the strictly mechanistic. The first is the ability to respond adaptively to a variety of challenging circumstances in appropriate ways. A bird, for instance, might seem to show more "skills" in building a nest that we can summon; but so does a clock show more "skill" than we command in measuring time. Yet neither the bird nor the clock is able to respond to novel circumstances in the inventive way characteristic of humans. Descartes's other, more famous, test for the presence of a nonmechanistic principle is the ability to use language: to "express our thoughts to others," no matter what may be said in our presence. He acknowledges that brutes can utter cries and grunts that have some kind of communicative effect, but he stresses that these fall short, drastically, of the range and versatility of human language. In the case of human beings, however, behavioral adaptability and "true language" demonstrate the presence of a nonmechanistic principle, a conscious rational soul.

Descartes's *Discourse* conception of nonhuman animals as "automata, or self-moving machines" is today sometimes characterized as "mechanomorphism." Widely rejected and even ridiculed in his lifetime, it remains a target, or stalking horse, for contemporary advocates of animal intelligence, consciousness, and (in some species) perhaps language (cf. COGNITIVE ETHOLOGY, PRIMATE LANGUAGE).

In the *Meditations* (as anticipated by Part IV of the *Discourse*) Descartes approaches issues of reason and consciousness from a first-person rather than a behavioral perspective. He argues, first, that all his apparent perceptions of a physical world are initially subject to doubt (in that they could in principle occur even if no physical world existed). In fact, he is able to find reason to doubt even the simplest and most evident propositions. But second, even in the face of such skepticism his own existence as a "thinking thing" at least is indubitable. Later he argues that he is the creature of a perfect God; hence his clearest and most distinct "perceptions" (mainly the deliverances of pure intellect) are beyond doubt. Finally he concludes that as a thinking thing, he is a substance distinct from any body, though (as he goes on to say) one at present closely joined with a body, with which he, as a mind, interacts (cf. SELF and MIND-BODY PROBLEM). He further maintains that, given the goodness of God, his normal conviction that his seeming perceptions of bodies are in fact caused by external physical things must be correct.

Along the way, however, Descartes repeatedly underscores the point that bodies are not in fact as they appear in ordinary sense experience. For instance, their appearances as colored are misleading, in that we tend to suppose that (say) green as we sensibly experience it is a real quality of some bodies; whereas in fact it is just a sensation in our minds, resulting from the effect of external things (constituted of bits of matter in motion) on our nervous systems, and of the latter on us as immaterial mental substances.

In the *Meditations* Descartes characterizes both sensations and our intellectual apprehensions (such as our representation of God) as *ideas*. The Cartesian theory of ideas had great impact on subsequent philosophy. It involves complex notions about representation and misrepresentation that continue to attract the interest of philosophers and scholars today (cf. MENTAL REPRESENTATION).

There is substantial—probably conclusive—evidence in Descartes's post-*Meditations* writings that he intended to limit strictly mental phenomena to those states that are accessible to an individual's conscious awareness. But this austere aspect of his mind-body dualism sits uneasily with some features of his impressive accounts of human visual perception in the first half of the *Dioptrics*; and of human emotions in the *Passions of the Soul*. In both works he not only blends sensational with intellectual states in his explanations of mental phenomena, but also invokes considerations that are hard to apportion between the "conscious-mental" and "purely mechanistic-material" divide. This is particularly true of his account of distance perception in the *Dioptrics*, in which Descartes certainly seems to invoke a kind of COMPUTATION that cannot plausibly be regarded as accessible to consciousness (cf. COMPUTATIONAL VISION).

See also NATIVISM, HISTORY OF; RATIONALISM VS. EMPIRICISM

—*Margaret D. Wilson*

Further Readings

Chomsky, N. (1966). *Cartesian Linguistics*. New York: Harper and Row.

Cottingham, J., Ed. (1992). *The Cambridge Companion to Descartes*. Cambridge: Cambridge University Press.

Descartes, R. (1984–85). *Philosophical Writings*. 3 vols. Trans. J. Cottingham, R. Stoothoff, D. Murdoch. Cambridge, England: Cambridge University Press.

Des Cheyne, D. (1996). *Physiologia: Natural Philosophy in Late Aristotelian and Cartesian Thought*. Ithaca, NY: Cornell University Press.

Garber, D. (1992). *Descartes' Metaphysical Physics*. Chicago: University of Chicago Press.

Gaukroger, S. (1995). *Descartes: An Intellectual Biography*. Oxford: Oxford University Press.

Hoffman, P. (1996). Descartes on misrepresentation. *Journal of the History of Philosophy*. 34: 357–381.

Smith, N. K. (1966). *New Studies in the Philosophy of Descartes: Descartes as Pioneer*. London: Macmillan.

Voss, S., Ed. (1993). *Essays on the Philosophy and Science of René Descartes*. New York: Oxford University Press.

Wilson, M. D. (1995). Animal ideas. *Proceedings of the American Philosophical Association* 69: 7–25.

Wilson, M. D. (1978). *Descartes*. London: Routledge and Kegan Paul.

Wolf-Devine, C. (1993). *Descartes on Seeing*. Carbondale: Southern Illinois University Press.

Detectors

See FEATURE DETECTORS

Development

See COGNITIVE DEVELOPMENT; INFANT COGNITION; NATIVISM; NEURAL DEVELOPMENT

Developmental Language Disorders

See LANGUAGE IMPAIRMENT, DEVELOPMENTAL

Diachrony

See PARAMETER-SETTING APPROACHES TO ACQUISITION, CREOLIZATION, AND DIACHRONY

Discourse

Discourse is the ground of our experience of language and of linguistic meaning. It is in discourse that we learn language as children, and in discourse that we most adequately convey our thought. The individual utterances in a discourse are notoriously vague and full of potential AMBIGUITY. Yet in the context of the discourse in which they occur, vagueness and ambiguity are rarely a problem. That is, the overall discourse profoundly influences the interpretation of individual linguistic constituents within it, as witnessed by our discomfort with the ethics of taking what someone says out of context.

Discourse can be characterized in three principal ways. We may think of discourse as a type of event, in which human agents engage in a *verbal exchange*; in the limit case, the monologue, there is only one agent, but even then there is an intended audience, if only reflexive or imaginary. We may also think of discourse as the *linguistic content* of that exchange, an ordered string of words with their associated syntactic and prosodic structures. Or we may characterize discourse as the more complex *structure of information* that is presupposed and/or conveyed by the interlocutors during the course of the discourse event in view of the explicit linguistic content of the exchange. The information structure of a discourse may be characterized as an ordered set containing several distinguished kinds of information, for example: a set of discourse participants (the *interlocutors*); the linguistic content of the discourse, with each utterance indexed by the speaker; the information presupposed or proffered by speakers during the discourse via the linguistic content of their utterances; an association of the proffered information with various topics or questions under discussion, the topics and subtopics hierarchically organized by virtue of their relations to the (often only inferred) goals and intentions of the various speakers (the *intentional structure* of the discourse); a set of entities discussed (the *domain* of discourse); a changing set of the entities and topics which the interlocutors focus on during their discussion, organized as a function of time (the *attentional structure* of discourse); and other kinds of information and structures on information, as well (Lewis 1979; Grosz and Sidner

1986; Roberts 1996). The information structure of a discourse is far richer than its linguistic content alone. Only the full range of contextual information for a given discourse, including a grasp of the interlocutors' inferred intentions, the intended rhetorical relations among their utterances, and other nonlinguistically given information that they share, can resolve all the potential ambiguities in the linguistic strings uttered, clarify the often inexplicit connections between utterances, and lead us to grasp what the speaker(s) intend to convey.

These three ways of characterizing discourse—as an event revolving around verbal exchange, as the linguistic content of that exchange, and as the structure on the information involved—are not mutually exclusive; there is no verbal exchange without linguistic content, and the latter can be taken as one aspect of the abstract information structure of the exchange. However, most of the work on discourse in artificial intelligence, linguistics, philosophy of language, PSYCHOLINGUISTICS, sociology, and anthropology can be classified according to which of the three aspects it focuses on. For example, sociologists, sociolinguists, and ethnographers interested in *conversational analysis* (Sacks, Schegloff, and Jefferson 1978) focus on the discourse event itself and its social character, including the way that interlocutors organize their participation in such events in an orderly, apparently conventional manner, varying somewhat from culture to culture. Speakers take turns, the opportunity for taking a turn being cued by a number of conventional means (including set phrases, intonation, and pauses), and negotiate the beginning and end of a discourse as well as the shift from topic to topic within it. In sociologically informed anthropological linguistics (Duranti 1997), discourse events are taken to play a crucial role in the creation, reproduction, and legitimation of a community's social alliances and cleavages. Those working in the tradition of *discourse analysis* (see van Dijk 1985; Carlson 1983) focus instead on the linguistic content of the verbal exchange, the text, some arguing that it is generated by the syntactic rules of a text grammar. But probably the majority of theorists who work on discourse today would agree that discourse is not a linguistic structure generated by a grammar, but instead is structured by nonlinguistic, logical, and intentional factors—aspects of what we have called the information structure of discourse.

A number of *prima facie* unrelated pragmatic phenomena depend on the information structure of discourse, suggesting that this aspect of discourse can provide the basis for a unified theory of the role of pragmatic factors in linguistic interpretation. Dynamic theories of semantic interpretation take the meaning of an utterance to be a function from contexts (the context of utterance) to contexts (the context of utterance updated with the information proffered in the utterance). One can view the three basic types of *speech acts*—assertions, questions, and orders—as functions that update the information structure of a discourse in different ways. Assertions update the information proffered in the discourse (see DYNAMIC SEMANTICS; Stalnaker 1979); a question sets up a new (sub)topic for discussion, hence affecting the intentional structure of the discourse (Ginzburg 1996; Roberts 1996); an order, if accepted, commits the person ordered to behave in accordance with the order, and this commitment is part of the information indirectly conveyed by the discourse. Many secondary subtypes of these three basic types of speech acts have been proposed in the literature, including, for example, predictions, confirmations, concessives, and promises; rhetorical questions as well as probes for information; requests, permissions, advisories, and commands; and so forth (see Searle 1969). Work in artificial intelligence on plan inference (see Cohen, Morgan, and Pollack 1990) has argued that the secondary speech act type of an utterance can be derived from its basic speech act type and proffered content, its inferred role in the intentional structure of the discourse, and the inferred *domain goals* of the interlocutor at the time of utterance (i.e., her general goals at that time, not necessarily just those expressed in discourse).

In his important work on meaning in conversation, H. Paul GRICE argued that much of the MEANING conveyed in discourse is not directly proffered via the linguistic content of the utterances in the discourse, but instead follows from what is said in view of the intentions of the interlocutors and a set of guidelines, the conversational maxims, which characterize the rational behavior of agents in a communicative situation (see IMPLICATURE and RELEVANCE). Although the crucial role of interlocutors' intentions is sometimes overlooked in older work on implicature, contemporary work (e.g., McCafferty 1987; Welker 1994) pays considerable attention to the role of that facet of the information structure of discourse that we have called its intentional structure in explaining how implicatures are generated. Similarly, work on ANAPHORA in discourse, especially from a computational point of view (e.g., Grosz and Sidner 1986), emphasizes the role both of intentional structure and of attentional structure in constraining the set of possible antecedents for a given pronoun or other anaphoric element across discourse; see also the related work on *centering* (Walker, Joshi, and Prince 1998). And the intentional structure of discourse may be seen to reflect strategies of inquiry which correspond to classical *rhetorical structures* (Mann and Thompson 1987), connecting work on the role of such structures in interpretation to the general notion of information structure.

Finally, the information structure of discourse is reflected in a number of ways in the structure of linguistic constituents—sentences and sentence fragments. These reflections involve the phenomena variously referred to as *topic* and *comment*, *theme* and *rheme*, *link*, and *focus*, among others. Some have argued that (some subset of) these notions play a role as primitive notions in syntactic structure (e.g., Sgall, Hajicova, and Panevová 1986; Vallduví 1992), while others have argued that they are, instead, only functional characterizations of the accidental role of syntactic constituents in particular discourse contexts. However, it is clear that particular sentential constructions (e.g., topicalization in English) and prosodic features (e.g., prosodic prominence) may be specially associated with these functions via associated conventional presuppositions about the information structure of the discourse in which they occur. Such linguistic structures, along with anaphora and ellipsis, are designed to increase discourse coherence and to help interlocutors keep track of the common ground and other features of the information structure of discourse.

See also FOCUS; PRAGMATICS; PRESUPPOSITION; PROSODY AND INTONATION; STRESS, LINGUISTIC

—*Craige Roberts*

References

Carlson, L. (1983). *Dialogue Games: An Approach to Discourse Analysis*. Dordrecht: Reidel.

Cohen, P., J. Morgan, and M. Pollack. (1990). *Intentions in Communication*. Cambridge, MA: Bradford Books/ MIT Press.

Duranti, A. (1997). *Linguistic Anthropology*. New York: Cambridge University Press.

Ginzburg, J. (1996). The semantics of interrogatives. In S. Lappin, Ed., *The Handbook of Contemporary Semantic Theory*, pp. 385–422. Oxford: Blackwell.

Grosz, B., and C. Sidner. (1986). Attention, intentions, and the structure of discourse. *Computational Linguistics* 12: 175–204.

Lewis, D. (1979). Score-keeping in a language game. In R. Bauerle, U. Egli, and A. von Stechow, Eds., *Semantics from a Different Point of View*. Berlin: Springer.

Mann, W. C., and S. A. Thompson. (1987). *Rhetorical Structure Theory: A Theory of Text Organization*. Information Sciences Institute, University of Southern California.

McCafferty, A. (1987). *Reasoning about Implicature*. Ph.D. diss. University of Pittsburgh.

Roberts, C. (1996). Information structure: Towards an integrated theory of formal pragmatics. In Y.-H. Yoon and A. Kathol, Eds., *OSU Working Papers in Linguistics*, vol. 49: *Papers in Semantics*. Ohio State University Department of Linguistics.

Sacks, H., E. A. Schegloff, and G. Jefferson. (1978). A simplest systematics for the organization of turn-taking in conversation. In J. Schenkein, Ed., *Studies in the Organization of Conversational Interaction*. New York: Academic Press, pp. 7–55.

Searle, J. R. (1969). *Speech Acts*. Cambridge: Cambridge University Press.

Sgall, P., E. Hajicova, and J. Panevova. (1986). *The Meaning of Sentence in its Semantic and Pragmatic Aspect*. Dordrecht: Reidel.

Stalnaker, R. (1979). Assertion. In P. Cole, Ed., *Syntax and Semantics*. New York: Academic Press.

Vallduví, E. (1992). *The Informational Component*. New York: Garland.

van Dijk, T. (1985). *Handbook of Discourse Analysis*, vol. 3: *Discourse and Dialogue*. London: Academic Press.

Walker, M., A. Joshi, and E. Prince, Eds. (1998). *Centering Theory in Discourse*. Oxford: Oxford University Press.

Welker, K. (1994). *Plans in the Common Ground: Toward a Generative Account of Implicature*. Ph.D. diss. Ohio State University.

Further Readings

Brown, G., and G. Yule. (1983). *Discourse Analysis*. Cambridge: Cambridge University Press.

Büring, D. (1994). Topic. In Peter Bosch and Rob van der Sandt, Eds., *Focus and Natural Language Processing*. Heidelberg: IBM, pp. 271–280.

Goffman, E. (1981). *Forms of Talk*. Oxford: Basil Blackwell.

Halliday, M. A. K., and R. Hasan. (1976). *Cohesion in English*. London: Longman.

Kamp, H., and U. Reyle. (1993). *From Discourse to Logic: An Introduction to Model-Theoretic Semantics of Natural Language, Formal Logic and Discourse Representation Theory*. Dordrecht: Kluwer.

Polanyi, L., and R. J. H. Scha. (1983). The syntax of discourse. *Text* 3: 261–270.

Schiffrin, D. (1987). *Discourse Markers.* Cambridge: Cambridge University Press.

Searle, J. R., F. Kiefer, and M. Bierwisch, Eds. (1980). *Speech Act Theory and Pragmatics.* Dordrecht: Reidel.

Dissonance

Festinger's (1957) theory of cognitive dissonance is, by far, the most prominent of several social-psychological theories based on the premise that people are motivated to seek consistency among their beliefs, attitudes, and actions (Abelson et al. 1968). It asserts that people find inconsistency, or "dissonance," among their cognitions to be emotionally aversive and seek to eliminate or reduce any inconsistency.

According to Festinger, cognitive dissonance is a tension state that arises whenever an individual simultaneously holds two or more cognitions that are mutually inconsistent with one another. In this model, any two cognitions, considered by themselves, stand in one of three relations to one another—dissonant (contradictory or inconsistent), consonant (consistent), or irrelevant. The total amount of dissonance for a given person in any particular situation is defined as the ratio of dissonant relations to total relevant relations, with each relation weighted for its importance to that person:

Total Dissonance = (Dissonant Relations) / (Dissonant + Constant Relations)

When cognitive dissonance arises, the individual is motivated to reduce the amount of dissonance. This can be done in many ways—by decreasing the number and/or the importance of dissonant relations, or by increasing the number and/or the importance of consonant relations. Precisely how dissonance is reduced in any particular situation depends on the resistance to change of the various cognitions involved. The resistance-to-change of any cognition in a particular context depends, in turn, on the extent to which a change would produce new dissonant relations, the degree to which the cognition is firmly anchored in reality, and the difficulty of changing those aspects of reality.

Consider a prototypic case: a cigarette smoker, circa 1960, encountering the first medical reports linking smoking to lung cancer, emphysema, and heart disease. His two cognitions, "I smoke," and, "Smoking causes serious diseases," are dissonant because both cognitions are of substantial importance to him and are inconsistent. To reduce this dissonance, he could quit smoking or, if this proved too difficult, could cut back on cigarettes or switch to a brand with lower tar and nicotine. Similarly, he could question the significance of "merely statistical" evidence regarding smoking and disease processes, downplay the relevance or importance of such evidence to his personal situation, avoid subsequent medical reports on the topic, and/or exaggerate the pleasures and positive consequences of smoking (e.g., how it helps him relax or control his weight).

Festinger (1957) used dissonance theory to account for a wide array of psychological phenomena, ranging from the transmission of rumors following disasters to the rationalization of everyday decisions, the consequences of counterattitudinal advocacy, selectivity in information search and interpretation, and responses to the disconfirmation of central beliefs. Of the many new research directions produced by the theory, three paradigms proved most influential.

The first major paradigm involved the attitudinal consequences of making a decision (Brehm 1956). Any choice among mutually exclusive options is postulated to produce dissonance, because any nonoverlapping bad features of the chosen alternative(s) or good features of the rejected alternative(s) are dissonant with the choice itself. To reduce this postdecisional dissonance, the individual is likely to exaggerate the advantages of the option(s) selected and to disparage the advantages of the option(s) rejected. Through this postdecisional reevaluation and "spreading apart" of the alternatives, individuals come to rationalize their decisions. Such effects appear most strongly when the decision is both difficult and irrevocable, and have proved to be highly replicable across a variety of decision contexts (Festinger 1964; Wicklund and Brehm 1976).

A second popular paradigm concerned the selectivity of information-seeking following a decision (Ehrlich et al. 1957). If the decision is difficult to undo (and not all of the attendant dissonance has already been reduced through reevaluation of the alternatives), the individual is motivated both to avoid subsequent information that seems likely to be dissonant with that decision and to seek out subsequent information that seems likely to support that decision. Empirical evidence concerning this aspect of the theory, however, has been much more mixed; and the precise conditions under which such selective exposure effects occur remain unclear (Freedman and Sears 1965; Frey 1986).

Finally, the third, and most influential paradigm examined the effects of "forced compliance," in which an individual is induced to engage in some counterattitudinal action with minimal, "psychologically insufficient," external coercion or incentive (e.g., Aronson and Carlsmith 1963; Festinger and Carlsmith 1959). In this case, dissonance derives from a conflict between the person's action and attitudes. To the extent that an overt action is harder to change than a personal opinion, attitudes are changed to conform more closely to behavior. The less the external pressure used to induce the behavior, the more such subsequent justification of one's actions occurs, because any external pressures provide added consonant relations. Such "insufficient justification" effects have been observed, under free-choice conditions, in a wide variety of situations, particularly when the person's counterattitudinal behavior has aversive consequences for which he/she feels personally responsible (Cooper and Fazio 1984; Harmon-Jones and Mills forthcoming; Lepper 1983).

More recent research on cognitive dissonance has emphasized three additional issues. Some authors have focused on the role of physiological arousal (e.g., Cooper and Fazio 1984) and psychological discomfort (e.g., Elliot and Devine 1994) in the production and reduction of cognitive dissonance, showing the importance of the motivational factors that distinguish dissonance theory from self-perception theory (Bem 1967, 1972) and other nonmotivational alternative explanations. Others have emphasized the importance of the self-concept in cognitive dissonance, arguing that dissonance effects may depend on threats to one's self-concept and may be alleviated by procedures that affirm the SELF (e.g., Steele 1988; Thibodeau and Aronson 1992).

Most recently, computational models of dissonance reduction have sought to quantify dissonance more precisely and have simulated many of the subtleties of psychological findings (e.g., Read and Miller 1994; Shultz and Lepper 1996). These models use artificial NEURAL NETWORKS that treat dissonance reduction as a gradual process of satisfying constraints imposed on the relationships among beliefs by a motive for cognitive consistency. Their success suggests that dissonance, rather than being exotic and unique, may have much in common with other psychological phenomena (e.g., memory retrieval or analogical reasoning) that can also be understood in constraint-satisfaction terms.

The general success of dissonance theory—and the particular power of the "reevaluation of alternatives" and "insufficient justification" paradigms—seems to derive, in large part, from the breadth of the theory and from the ways that apparently "rational" consistency-seeking can, under certain conditions, produce unexpectedly "irrational" changes in actions and attitudes.

See also ATTRIBUTION THEORY; DECISION MAKING; MOTIVATION; MOTIVATION AND CULTURE; SOCIAL COGNITION

—*Mark R. Lepper and Thomas R. Shultz*

References

Abelson, R. P., E. Aronson, W. J. McGuire, T. M. Newcomb, M. J. Rosenberg, and P. H. Tannenbaum, Eds. (1968). *Theories of Cognitive Consistency: A Sourcebook.* Chicago: Rand McNally.

Aronson, E. (1969). The theory of cognitive dissonance: A current perspective. In L. Berkowitz, Ed., *Advances in Experimental Social Psychology,* vol. 4. New York: Academic Press, pp. 1–34.

Aronson, E., and J. M. Carlsmith. (1963). Effect of severity of threat on the devaluation of forbidden behavior. *Journal of Abnormal and Social Psychology* 66: 584–588.

Bem, D. J. (1967). Self-perception: An alternative interpretation of cognitive dissonance phenomena. *Psychological Review* 74: 183–200.

Bem, D. J. (1972). Self-perception theory. In L. Berkowitz, Ed., *Advances in Experimental Social Psychology,* vol. 6. New York: Academic Press, pp. 1–62.

Brehm, J. W. (1956). Post-decision changes in the desirability of choice alternatives. *Journal of Abnormal and Social Psychology* 52: 384–389.

Cooper, J., and R. H. Fazio. (1984). A new look at dissonance theory. In L. Berkowitz, Ed., *Advances in Experimental Social Psychology,* vol. 17. New York: Academic Press, pp. 229–266.

Ehrlich, D., I. Guttman, P. Schoenbach, and J. Mills. (1957). Post-decision exposure to relevant information. *Journal of Abnormal and Social Psychology* 54: 98–102.

Elliot, A. J., and P. G. Devine. (1994). On the motivational nature of cognitive dissonance: Dissonance as psychological discomfort. *Journal of Personality and Social Psychology* 67: 382–394.

Festinger, L. (1957). *A Theory of Cognitive Dissonance.* Evanston, IL: Row, Peterson.

Festinger, L., Ed. (1964). *Conflict, Decision, and Dissonance.* Stanford, CA: Stanford University Press.

Festinger, L., and J. M. Carlsmith. (1959). Cognitive consequences of forced compliance. *Journal of Abnormal and Social Psychology* 58: 203–210.

Freedman, J. L., and D. O. Sears. (1965). Selective exposure. In L. Berkowitz, Ed., *Advances in Experimental Social Psychology,* vol. 2. New York: Academic Press, pp. 57–97.

Frey, D. (1986). Recent research on selective exposure to information. In L. Berkowitz, Ed., *Advances in Experimental Social Psychology,* vol. 19. New York: Academic Press, pp. 41–80.

Harmon-Jones, E. and J. Mills, Eds. (Forthcoming). *Dissonance theory: Twenty-five years later.* Washington, DC: American Psychological Association.

Lepper, M. R. (1983). Social-control processes and the internalization of values: An attributional perspective. In E. T. Higgins, D. N. Ruble, and W. W. Hartup, Eds., *Social Cognition and Social Development.* New York: Cambridge University Press, pp. 294–330.

Read, S. J., and L. C. Miller. (1994). Dissonance and balance in belief systems: The promise of parallel constraint satisfaction processes and connectionist modeling approaches. In R. C. Schank and E. Langer, Eds., *Beliefs, Reasoning, and Decision Making: Psycho-logic in Honor of Bob Abelson.* Hillsdale, NJ: Erlbaum, pp. 209–235.

Shultz, T. R., and M. R. Lepper. (1996). Cognitive dissonance reduction as constraint satisfaction. *Psychological Review* 103: 219–240.

Steele, C. M. (1988). The psychology of self-affirmation: Sustaining the integrity of the self. In L. Berkowitz, Ed., *Advances in Experimental Social Psychology,* vol. 21. New York: Academic Press, pp. 261–302.

Thibodeau, R., and E. Aronson. (1992). Taking a closer look: Reasserting the role of the self-concept in dissonance theory. *Personality and Social Psychology Bulletin* 18: 591–602.

Wicklund, R. A., and J. Brehm. (1976). *Perspectives on Cognitive Dissonance.* Hillsdale, NJ: Erlbaum.

Distinctive Features

Every speech sound shares some articulatory and acoustic properties with other speech sounds. For example, the consonant [*n*] shares nasality with [*m*], complete oral closure with the set [*pbmtdkg*], and an elevated tongue-tip with the set [*tdsz*].

Most contemporary theories of PHONOLOGY posit a universal set of distinctive features to encode these shared properties in the representation of the speech sounds themselves. The hypothesis is that speech sounds are represented mentally by their values for binary distinctive features, and that a single set of about twenty such features suffices for all spoken languages. Thus, the distinctive features, rather than the sounds built from them, are the primitives of phonological description. The sound we write as [*n*] is actually a bundle of distinctive feature values, such as [+nasal], [−continuant] (complete oral closure), and [+coronal] (elevated tongue-tip).

Three principal arguments can be presented in support of this hypothesis:

1. The union of the sound systems of all spoken languages is a smaller set than the physical capabilities of the human vocal and auditory systems would lead one to

expect. The notion "possible speech sound" is defined by higher-level cognitive requirements (the distinctive features) and not lower-level physiological considerations.

2. Distinctive features help to explain the structure of sound systems. For example, many languages have no sounds from the set [*bdg*], but if a language has one of them, it is likely to have all of them. These sounds are all [+voice] (referring to the presence of vocal fold vibration); having the full [*bdg*] set together in a language maximizes the cross-classificatory effect of that distinctive feature.

3. PHONOLOGICAL RULES AND PROCESSES depend on the classes of sounds defined by distinctive feature values, and so the notion "possible phonological process" is, in part, determined by the universal feature theory. The English plural suffix is a typical example. This suffix agrees in the value of [voice] with the sound at the end of the noun: [–voice] in *caps, chiefs, cats, tacks* versus [+voice] in *labs, shelves, pads, bags*. This suffix is pronounced with a vowel if the noun ends in a [+strident] consonant, characterized by turbulent airflow and consequent [s]-like hissing noise: *passes, roses, lashes, garages*. Classes like these—[+voice], [–voice], and [+strident]—are frequently encountered in the phonological processes of the world's languages. In contrast, logically possible but featurally arbitrary classes like [*pbsk*] are rarely or never needed to describe phonological processes.

These considerations not only support the claim that there must be *some* set of universal distinctive features; in their particulars, they also serve as the principal basis for determining what is the *correct* set of distinctive features. Primarily, arguments in support of a feature theory turn on how well it explains the observed structure of sound systems and of well-attested phonological processes. Secondarily, the correct feature theory should support a plausible interface between phonology on one hand and the PHONETICS of ARTICULATION and SPEECH PERCEPTION on the other. This prioritization of phonological evidence over phonetic is appropriate because a theory of distinctive features is, above all, a claim about the mind and not about the mouth or the ear.

The idea that speech sounds can be classified in phonologically relevant ways goes back to antiquity, but the concept of a universal classification is a product of the twentieth century. It emerges from the work of the prewar Prague School theorists, principally N. S. Trubetzkoy and Roman JAKOBSON, who sought to explain the nature of possible phonological contrasts in sound systems. The first fully elaborated theory of distinctive features appeared with the publication in 1952 of Jakobson, Fant, and Halle's *Preliminaries to Speech Analysis*. The *Preliminaries* features are defined in acoustic terms; that is, they are descriptions of the spectral properties of speech sounds. This model was largely superseded in 1968 by the distinctive feature system of Chomsky and Halle's *The Sound Pattern of English* (*SPE*). Nearly all of the *SPE* features are defined in articulatory terms; that is, they are descriptions of vocal tract configurations during the production of speech sounds. Despite these differences of definition, the empirical consequences of the *SPE* model do not differ dramatically from the *Preliminaries* model.

There has been no single broad synthesis of feature theory since *SPE*, but there have been many significant developments in specific areas. The most important is the emergence of autosegmental or nonlinear phonology, with its fundamental thesis that distinctive features are, like TONES, independent objects not necessarily tied to any particular speech sound. In the South American language Terena, the feature [+nasal] is, by itself, the first person prefix; for example, [*owoku*] "house" becomes "my house" by attaching [+nasal] to the initial [*owo*] sequence. This freeing of distinctive features from individual speech sounds has yielded new insights into the nature of the most common phonological process, assimilation (where one sound takes on features from a nearby sound).

A further evolution of the autosegmental view is the theory of feature geometry, which asserts that the distinctive features are hierarchically organized into functionally related classes. The features that characterize states of the larynx, for instance, appear to have a considerable degree of functional cohesion in phonological systems. This leads to the positing of a kind of metafeature [Laryngeal], which has within its scope [voice] and other features.

Along other lines, an improved understanding of feature theory has been achieved through the study of particular types of features (such as those pertaining to the larynx or to degree of oral constriction) and of particular groups of speech sounds (such as the various [*l*]- and [*r*]-like sounds of the world's languages). Much has also been achieved by considering alternatives to binary features, in the direction of both single-valued features (marked only by their presence) and ternary or higher-order features (which are particularly useful for characterizing some natural scales, like degree of oral constriction or tongue height).

Finally, research on SIGN LANGUAGES has showed that they too have representations composed of distinctive features. Thus, while the distinctive features of spoken languages are modality-specific, the existence of a featural level of representation apparently is not.

See also AUDITION; INNATENESS OF LANGUAGE; PHONOLOGY, ACQUISITION OF; PHONOLOGY, NEURAL BASIS OF

—*John McCarthy*

References

Chomsky, N., and M. Halle. (1968). *The Sound Pattern of English*. New York: Harper and Row. (Reprinted MIT Press, 1991.)

Clements, G. N. (1985). The geometry of phonological features. *Phonology Yearbook* 2: 225–252.

Jakobson, R., C. G. M. Fant, and M. Halle. (1952). *Preliminaries to Speech Analysis*. Cambridge, MA: MIT Press.

Keating, P. (1987). A survey of phonological features. *UCLA Working Papers in Phonetics* 66: 124–150.

Ladefoged, P., and I. Maddieson. (1996). *The Sounds of the World's Languages*. Oxford: Blackwell.

McCarthy, J. J. (1988). Feature geometry and dependency: A review. *Phonetica* 45: 84–108.

Further Readings

Browman, C., and L. Goldstein. (1992). Articulatory Phonology: An overview. *Phonetica* 49: 155–180.

Clements, G. N., and E. Hume. (1995). The internal organization of speech sounds. In J. Goldsmith, Ed., *The Handbook of Phonological Theory*. Oxford: Blackwell, pp. 245–306.

Gnanadesikan, A. (1997). *Phonology with Ternary Scales*. Ph.D. diss. University of Massachusetts, Amherst.

Goldsmith, J. A. (1990). *Autosegmental and Metrical Phonology*. Oxford: Blackwell.

Halle, M. (1983). On distinctive features and their articulatory implementation. *Natural Language and Linguistic Theory* 1: 91–105.

Hulst, H. v. d. (1989). Atoms of segmental structure: Components, gestures, and dependency. *Phonology* 6: 253–284.

Lombardi, L. (1994). *Laryngeal Features and Laryngeal Neutralization*. New York: Garland.

Padgett, J. (1995). *Stricture in Feature Geometry*. Stanford: CSLI Publications.

Sandler, W., Ed. (1993). Phonology: special issue on sign language phonology. *Phonology* 10: 165–306.

Schane, S. A. (1984). The fundamentals of particle phonology. *Phonology Yearbook* 1: 129–155.

Walsh, D. L. (1997). *The Phonology of Liquids*. Ph.D. diss. University of Massachusetts, Amherst.

Williamson, K. (1977). Multivalued features for consonants. *Language* 53: 843–871.

Distributed AI

See DISTRIBUTED VS. LOCAL REPRESENTATION; MULTI-AGENT SYSTEMS

Distributed vs. Local Representation

A central problem for cognitive science is to understand how agents represent the information that enables them to behave in sophisticated ways. One long-standing concern is whether representation is localized or distributed (roughly, "spread out"). Two centuries ago Franz Josef Gall claimed that particular kinds of knowledge are stored in specific, discrete brain regions, whereas Pierre Flourens argued that all knowledge is spread across the entire cortex (Flourens 1824; Gall and Spurzheim 1809/1967). This debate has continued in various guises through to the present day (e.g.,

Farah 1994). Meanwhile, the concept of distribution has found mathematical elaboration in fields such as optics and psychology, and the rise of connectionist models has generated interest in a range of related technical and philosophical issues.

In the most basic sense, a distributed representation is one that is somehow "spread out" over some more-than-minimal extent of the resources available for representing. Unfortunately, however, this area is a semantic mess; the terms *local* and *distributed* are used in many different ways, often vaguely or ambiguously. Figure 1 sketches the most common meanings.

Suppose that we have some quantity of resources available for representing items, and that these resources are naturally divisible into minimal chunks or aspects. Connectionist neural processing units are obvious examples, but the discussion here is pitched at a very abstract level, and the term "unit" in what follows might just as well refer to bits in a digital computer memory, single index cards, synaptic interconnections, etc.

- *Strictly Local* The item (in this case, the word "cat") is represented by appropriately configuring a single dedicated unit. The state of the other units is irrelevant.
- *Distributed—basic notion* The word is represented by a distinctive configuration pattern over some subset or "pool" of the available resources (see Hinton, McClelland, and Rumelhart 1986). A different word would be represented by an alternative pattern over that pool or another pool. Each unit in the pool participates in representing the word; the state of units outside the pool are irrelevant. In a *sparse* (*dense*) distributed representation, a small (large) proportion of units in the pool are configured in a non-default or "active" state (Kanerva 1988).
- *Local* The limiting case of a sparse distributed representation is one in which only a single unit in the pool is active. These representations are often also referred to as "local" (e.g., Thorpe 1995). The key difference with strictly local representations is that here it matters what state the other units in the pool are in, viz., they must not be active.

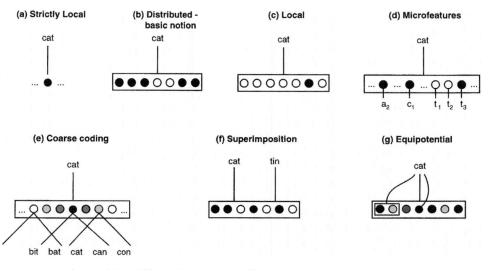

Figure 1. Seven ways to represent the word "cat," illustrating varieties of local and distributed representation.

- *Microfeatures* Sometimes individual units are used to represent "microfeatures" of the domain in strictly local fashion. The pattern representing a given macro-level item is then determined by these microfeatural correspondences. In the example in Figure 1, individual units represent the presence of a letter at a certain spot in the word; the word "cat" is represented just in case the active units are the ones for *c* in the first spot, *a* in the second spot, and *t* in the third spot.
- *Coarse Coding* In these schemes the (micro or macro) features of the domain represented by individual units are relatively broad, and overlapping.

The reader seeking a detailed illustration of these ideas may care to examine the well-known "verb-ending" paper of Rumelhart and McClelland (1986). In that case, verb-base and past-tense forms are represented by sparse distributed patterns over pools of units. Individual units represent microfeatures (ordered triples of phonetic features) in strictly local fashion. Because these triples overlap, the scheme is also coarse.

- *Superimposition* Two or more items are simultaneously represented by one and the same distributed pattern (Murdock 1979). For example, it is standard in feedforward connectionist networks for one and the same set of synaptic weights to represent many associations between input and output.
- *Equipotentiality* In some cases, an item is represented by a pattern over a pool of units, and the pattern over any subpool (up to some resolution limit) also suffices to represent the item. Thus every part or aspect of the item is represented in superimposed fashion over the whole pool. The standard example is the optical hologram (Leith and Uptanieks 1965); see also Plate's "holographic reduced" representations (Plate 1993).

With these various distinctions on board, we can return to the central question: is human knowledge represented in distributed form? This question has been approached at a number of levels, ranging from detailed neurophysiology to pure philosophy of mind. Thus, neuroscientists have debated whether the patterns of neural firing responsible for representing some external event are a matter of single cells (Barlow 1972) or patterns of activity distributed over many cells; if the latter, whether the patterns are sparse, dense, or coarse-coded (e.g., Földiák and Young 1995). At a higher level, they have debated whether knowledge is distributed over large areas of the brain, perhaps in equipotential fashion (LASHLEY 1929/1963), or whether at least some kinds of knowledge are restricted to tightly circumscribed regions (Fodor 1983).

These issues have also been pursued in the context of computer-based cognitive modeling. Connectionists have paid considerable attention to the relative merits of distributed versus local encoding in their networks. Advantages of distribution are generally held to include greater representational capacity, content addressibility, automatic generalization, fault tolerance, and biological plausibility. Disadvantages include slow learning, catastrophic interference (French 1992), and binding problems.

In a famous critique of connectionist cognitive science, Fodor and Pylyshyn (1988) argued that connectionists must either implement "classical" architectures with their traditional symbolic representations or fail to explain the alleged "systematicity" of cognition. The standard connectionist response has been to insist that they can in fact explain systematicity without merely implementing classical architectures by using distributed representations encoding complex structures in a nonconcatenative fashion (e.g., Smolensky 1991).

Implicit in this connectionist response is the idea that distributed representations and standard symbolic representations are somehow deeply different in nature. For millennia, philosophers have attempted to develop a taxonomy of representations. At the highest level, they have usually distinguished just two major kinds—the generically linguistic or symbolic, and the generically imagistic or pictorial. Is distribution just an accidental property of these more basic kinds, or do distributed representations form a third fundamental category?

Answers to questions like these obviously depend on exactly what we mean by "distributed." The standard approach, as exemplified in the preceding discussion, has been to define various notions of distribution in terms of structures of correspondence between the represented items and the representational resources (e.g., van Gelder 1992). This approach may be misguided; the essence of this alternative category of representation might be some other property entirely. For example, Haugeland (1991) has suggested that whether a representation is distributed or not turns on the nature of the knowledge it encodes.

It has been argued that some of the most intransigent problems confronting orthodox artificial intelligence are rooted in its commitment to representing knowledge by means of digital symbol structures (Dreyfus 1992). If this is right, there must be some other form of knowledge representation underlying human capacities. If distributed representation is indeed a fundamentally different form of representation, it may be suited to playing this role (Haugeland 1978).

See also COGNITIVE ARCHITECTURE; COGNITIVE MODELING, CONNECTIONIST; COGNITIVE MODELING, SYMBOLIC; CONNECTIONISM, PHILOSOPHICAL ISSUES; MENTAL REPRESENTATION; NEURAL NETWORKS

—*Tim van Gelder*

References

Barlow, H. B. (1972). Single units and sensation. *Perception* 1: 371–394.

Dreyfus, H. L. (1992). *What Computers Still Can't Do: A Critique of Artificial Reason.* Cambridge MA: The MIT Press.

Farah, M. (1994). Neuropsychological inference with an interactive brain. *Behavioral and Brain Sciences* 17: 43–61.

Flourens, P. (1824). *Recherches Expérimentales sur les Propriétés et les Fonctions du Systeme Nerveux.* Paris: Grevot.

Fodor, J. A. (1983). *The Modularity of Mind.* Cambridge MA: Bradford/MIT Press.

Fodor, J. A., and Z. Pylyshyn. (1988). Connectionism and cognitive architecture: A critical analysis. *Cognition* 28: 3–71.

Földiák, P., and M. P. Young. (1995). Sparse coding in the primate cortex. In M. A. Arbib, Ed., *The Handbook of Brain Theory and Neural Networks*. Cambridge, MA: MIT Press, pp. 895–898.

French, R. (1992). Semi-distributed representations and catastrophic forgetting in connectionist networks. *Connection Science* 4: 365–377.

Gall, F. J., and J. G. Spurzheim. (1809/1967). *Recherches sur le Systeme Nerveux*. Amsterdam: Bonset.

Haugeland, J. (1978). The nature and plausibility of cognitivism. *Behavioral and Brain Sciences* 1: 215–226.

Haugeland, J. (1991). Representational genera. In W. Ramsey, S. P. Stich, and D. E. Rumelhart, Eds., *Philosophy and Connectionist Theory*. Hillsdale, NJ: Lawrence Erlbaum Associates, pp. 61–89.

Hinton, G. E., J. L. McClelland, and D. E. Rumelhart. (1986). Distributed representations. In D. E. Rumelhart and J. L. McClelland, Eds., *Parallel Distributed Processing: Explorations in the Microstructure of Cognition*. Cambridge, MA: MIT Press, pp. 77–109.

Kanerva, P. (1988). *Sparse Distributed Memory*. Cambridge, MA: MIT Press.

Lashley, K. S. (1929/1963). *Brain Mechanisms and Intelligence: A Quantitative Study of Injuries to the Brain*. New York: Dover.

Leith, E. N., and J. Uptanieks. (1965). Photography by laser. *Scientific American* 212(6): 24–35.

Murdock, B. B. (1979). Convolution and correlation in perception and memory. In L. G. Nilsson, Ed., *Perspectives on Memory Research,* pp. 609–626. Hillsdale, NJ: Lawrence Erlbaum Associates.

Plate, T. A. (1993). Holographic recurrent networks. In C. L. Giles, S. J. Hanson, and J. D. Cowan, Eds., *Advances in Neural Processing Systems* 5 (NIPS92). San Mateo, CA: Morgan Kaufmann.

Rumelhart, D. E., and J. L. McClelland. (1986). On learning the past tenses of English verbs. In J. L. McClelland, D. E. Rumelhart, and The PDP Research Group, Eds., *Parallel Distributed Processing: Explorations in the Microstructure of Cognition*. vol. 2: *Psychological and Biological Models*. Cambridge, MA: MIT Press, pp. 216–268.

Smolensky, P. (1991). Connectionism, constituency, and the language of thought. In B. Lower and G. Rey, Eds., *Jerry Fodor and his Critics*. Oxford: Blackwell.

Thorpe, S. (1995). Localized versus distributed representations. In M. A. Arbib, Ed., *Handbook of Brain Theory and Neural Networks*. Cambridge, MA: MIT Press, pp. 549–552.

van Gelder, T. J. (1990). Compositionality: A connectionist variation on a classical theme. *Cognitive Science* 14: 355–384.

van Gelder, T. J. (1991). What is the 'D' in 'PDP'? An overview of the concept of distribution. In S. Stich, D. Rumelhart, and W. Ramsey, Eds., *Philosophy and Connectionist Theory*. Hillsdale, NJ: Lawrence Erlbaum Associates, pp. 33–59.

van Gelder, T. J. (1992). Defining "distributed representation." *Connection Science* 4: 175–191.

Domain Specificity

Cognitive abilities are *domain-specific* to the extent that the mode of reasoning, structure of knowledge, and mechanisms for acquiring knowledge differ in important ways across distinct content areas. For example, many researchers have concluded that the ways in which language is learned and represented are distinct from the ways in which other cognitive skills are learned and represented (Chomsky 1988; but

see Bates, Bretherton, and Snyder 1988). Other candidate domains include (but are not limited to) number processing, face perception, and spatial reasoning. The view that thought is domain-specific contrasts with a long-held position that humans are endowed with a general set of reasoning abilities (e.g., memory, attention, inference) that they apply to any cognitive task, regardless of specific content. For example, Jean PIAGET's (1983) theory of cognitive development is a domain-general theory, according to which a child's thought at a given age can be characterized in terms of a single cognitive level. In contrast, evidence for domain-specificity comes from multiple sources, including variability in cognitive level across domains within a given individual at a given point in time (e.g., Gelman and Baillargeon 1983), neuropsychological dissociations between domains (e.g., Baron-Cohen 1995), innate cognitive capacities in infants (Spelke 1994), evolutionary arguments (Cosmides and Tooby 1994), ethological studies of animal learning (e.g., Marler 1991), coherent folk theories (Gopnik and Wellman 1994), and domain-specific performance in areas of expertise (Chase and Simon 1973).

Domain-specificity is not a single, unified theory of the mind. There are at least three distinct approaches to cognition that assume domain-specificity. These approaches include modules, theories, and expertise (see Hirschfeld and Gelman 1994; Wellman and Gelman 1997).

The most powerful domain-specific approach is modularity theory, according to which the mind consists of "separate systems [i.e., the language faculty, visual system, facial recognition module, etc.] with their own properties" (Chomsky 1988: 161). Proposals regarding modularity have varied in at least two respects: whether modularity is restricted to perceptual processes or affects reasoning processes as well, and whether modularity is innate or constructed. Modularity need not imply evolved innate modules (see Karmiloff-Smith 1992) but for most modular proponents it does. Nonetheless, all modularity views assume domain-specificity. Chomsky's focus was on language, and more specifically SYNTAX or universal grammar. Evidence for the status of syntax as a module was its innate, biologically driven character (evident in all and only humans), its neurological localization and breakdown (the selective impairment of syntactic competence in some forms of brain damage), its rapid acquisition in the face of meager environmental data (abstract syntactic categories are readily acquired by young children), and the presence of critical periods and maturational timetables (see Pinker 1994).

Fodor (1983) extended the logic of modules to cognitive abilities more broadly. He distinguished between central logical processes and perceptual systems, arguing for modularity of the latter. In Fodor's analysis, modules are innately specified systems that take in sensory inputs and yield necessary representations of them. The visual system as characterized by MARR (1982) provides a prototypical example: a system that takes visual inputs and generates 2.5-dimensional representations of objects and space. Like the visual system, by Fodor's analysis, modules are innately specified, their processing is mandatory and encapsulated, and (unlike central knowledge and beliefs) their representational outputs are insensitive to revision via experience. Experience provides specific inputs to modules, which yield mandatory representations of inputs. Certain experiential inputs may be necessary to trigger working of the module in the first place, but the processes by which the module arrives at its representations are mandatory rather than revisable.

Extending Fodor, several writers have argued that certain conceptual processes, not just perceptual ones, are modular (Karmiloff-Smith 1992; Sperber 1994) or supported by systems of cognitive modules (e.g., Baron-Cohen 1995; Leslie 1994). In these claims each module works independently, achieving its own special representations. Thus, for the most part cognitive modules are like Fodor's perceptual ones, except that "perceptual processes have, as input, information provided by sensory receptors, and as output, a conceptual representation categorizing the object perceived . . . conceptual processes have conceptual representations both as input and as output" (Sperber 1994: 40).

The claim that people ordinarily construct or possess folk theories (as distinct from scientific theories) is a controversial one. However, everyday thought may be considered theory-like in its resistance to counterevidence, ontological commitments, attention to domain-specific causal principles, and coherence of beliefs (Carey 1985; Gopnik and Wellman 1994). Like modules, folk theories are also domain-specific. Folk theories make use of domain-specific ontologies (e.g., a folk theory of psychology concerns mental entities such as beliefs and desires, whereas a folk theory of physics concerns physical entities such as objects and substances). Folk theories also entail domain-specific causal explanations (e.g., the law of gravity is not applied to mental states). However, in contrast to modules, which are generally assumed to be innately constrained, biologically determined, and invariant, theories are thought to undergo radical restructuring over time, and to be informed by knowledge and cultural beliefs. On this construal of domain-specificity, candidate domains include psychology (also known as theory of mind; Wellman 1990), physics (McCloskey, Washburn, and Felch 1983), and biology (Keil 1994); see Wellman and Gelman (1997).

Domain-specificity is also apparent in the remarkable pockets of skill that people develop as a result of extensive experience. With enough practice at a task (e.g., playing chess, gathering factual knowledge about dinosaurs), an individual can develop extraordinary abilities within that task domain. For example, experts can achieve unusual feats of MEMORY, reorganize knowledge into complex hierarchical systems, and develop complex networks of causally related information (Chi, Hutchinson, and Robin 1989). These abilities are sufficiently powerful that child experts can even surpass novice adults, in contrast to the usual developmental finding of adults outperforming children (e.g., Chi 1978). Importantly, EXPERTISE skills cannot be explained as individual differences in the general processing talents of experts, because these achievements are limited to the narrow task domain. For example, a chess expert displays advanced memory for arrangements of pieces on a chessboard, but ordinary memory for digit strings.

Modular, theory-theory, and expertise views of domain-specificity differ from one another in several fundamental ways. They make different assumptions concerning what is innate, the role of input, mechanisms of development, interindividual variability in performance, and what constitutes a domain. For example, modular theories propose that mechanisms of developmental change are biological constraints, theory theories propose that the relevant mechanisms are causal-explanatory understandings, and expertise theories propose that such mechanisms are information-processing skills. Nonetheless, they converge on the proposal that cognitive abilities are specialized to handle specific types of information. For critiques of domain-specificity, see Bates, Bretherton, and Snyder (1988) and Elman et al. (1996).

See also FOLK PSYCHOLOGY; INNATENESS OF LANGUAGE; LINGUISTIC UNIVERSALS AND UNIVERSAL GRAMMAR; MODULARITY OF MIND; NAIVE SOCIOLOGY; NATIVISM

—*Susan A. Gelman*

References

Baron-Cohen, S. (1995). *Mindblindness.* Cambridge, MA: MIT Press.

Bates, E., I. Bretherton, and L. Snyder. (1988). *From First Words to Grammar.* New York: Cambridge University Press.

Carey, S. (1985). *Conceptual Change in Childhood.* Cambridge, MA: MIT Press.

Chase, W. G., and H. A. Simon. (1973). The mind's eye in chess. In W. G. Chase, Ed., *Visual Information Processing.* New York: Academic Press.

Chi, M. T. H. (1978). Knowledge structure and memory development. In R. Siegler, Ed., *Children's Thinking: What Develops?* Hillsdale, NJ: Erlbaum, pp. 73–96.

Chi, M. T., J. E. Hutchinson, and A. F. Robin. (1989). How inferences about novel domain-related concepts can be constrained by structured knowledge. *Merrill-Palmer Quarterly* 35: 27–62.

Chomsky, N. (1988). *Language and Problems of Knowledge.* Cambridge, MA: MIT Press.

Cosmides, L., and J. Tooby. (1994). Origins of domain specificity: The evolution of functional organization. In L. A. Hirschfeld and S. A. Gelman, Eds., *Mapping the Mind: Domain Specificity in Cognition and Culture.* New York: Cambridge University Press.

Elman, J. L., E. A. Bates, M. H. Johnson, A. Karmiloff-Smith, D. Parisi, and K. Plunkett. (1996). *Rethinking Innateness: A Connectionist Perspective on Development.* Cambridge, MA: MIT Press.

Fodor, J. A. (1983). *Modularity of Mind.* Cambridge, MA: MIT Press.

Gelman, R., and R. Baillargeon. (1983). A review of some Piagetian concepts. In J. H. Flavell and E. M. Markman, Eds., *Handbook of Child Psychology.* Vol. 3. New York: Wiley, pp. 167–230.

Gopnik, A., and H. M. Wellman. (1994). The theory theory. In L. A. Hirschfeld and S. A. Gelman, Eds., *Mapping the Mind: Domain Specificity in Cognition and Culture.* New York: Cambridge University Press.

Hirschfeld, L. A., and S. A. Gelman. (1994). *Mapping the Mind: Domain Specificity in Cognition and Culture.* New York: Cambridge University Press.

Karmiloff-Smith, A. (1992). *Beyond Modularity.* Cambridge, MA: MIT Press.

Keil, F. C. (1994). The birth and nurturance of concepts by domains: the origins of concepts of living things. In L. A. Hirschfeld and S. A. Gelman, Eds., *Mapping the Mind: Domain Specificity in Cognition and Culture.* New York: Cambridge University Press.

Leslie, A. M. (1994). ToMM, ToBy, and agency: Core architecture and domain specificity in cognition and culture. In L. A. Hirschfeld and S. A. Gelman, Eds., *Mapping the Mind: Domain Specificity in Cognition and Culture.* New York: Cambridge University Press.

Marler, P. (1991). The instinct to learn. In S. Carey and R. Gelman, Eds., *The Epigenesis of Mind: Essays on Biology and Cognition.* Hillsdale, NJ: Erlbaum.

Marr, D. (1982). *Vision.* New York: Freeman.

McCloskey, M., A. Washburn, and L. Felch. (1983). Intuitive physics: The straight-down belief and its origin. *Journal of Experimental Psychology: Learning, Memory, and Cognition* 9: 636–649.

Piaget, J. (1983). Piaget's theory. In W. Kessen, Ed., *Handbook of Child Psychology.* Vol. 1. New York: Wiley.

Pinker, S. (1994). *The Language Instinct.* New York: Penguin Books.

Spelke, E. S. (1994). Initial knowledge: Six suggestions. *Cognition* 50: 431–445.

Sperber, D. (1994). The modularity of thought and the epidemiology of representations. In L. A. Hirschfeld and S. A. Gelman, Eds., *Mapping the Mind: Domain Specificity in Cognition and Culture.* New York: Cambridge University Press.

Wellman, H. M. (1990). *The Child's Theory of Mind.* Cambridge, MA: MIT Press.

Wellman, H. M., and S. A. Gelman. (1997). Knowledge acquisition in foundational domains. In D. Kuhn and R. S. Siegler, Eds., *Handbook of Child Psychology.* Vol. 2. New York: Wiley, pp. 523–573.

Further Readings

Atran, S. (1995). Causal constraints on categores and categorical constraints on biological reasoning across cultures. In D. Sperber, D. Premack, and A. J. Premack, Eds., *Causal Cognition: A Multidisciplinary Debate.* New York: Oxford University Press, pp. 205–233.

Barkow, J. H., L. Cosmides, and J. Tooby, Eds. (1992). *The Adapted Mind: Evolutionary Psychology and the Generation of Culture.* New York: Oxford University Press.

Caramazza, A., A. Hillis, E. C. Leek, and M. Miozzo (1994). The organization of lexical knowledge in the brain: Evidence from category- and modality-specific deficits. In L. A. Hirschfeld and S. A. Gelman, Eds., *Mapping the Mind: Domain Specificity in Cognition and Culture.* New York: Cambridge University Press.

Chase, W. G., and K. A. Ericsson. (1981). Skilled memory. In J. R. Anderson, Ed., *Cognitive Skills and Their Acquisition.* Hillsdale, NJ: Erlbaum.

Cosmides, L. (1989). The logic of social exchange: Has natural selection shaped how humans reason? Studies with the Wason selection task. *Cognition* 31: 187–276.

Ericsson, K. A., Ed. (1996). *The Road to Excellence: The Acquisition of Expert Performance in the Arts and Sciences, Sports, and Games.* Mahwah, NJ: Erlbaum.

Ericsson, K. A., and W. G. Chase. (1982). Exceptional memory. *American Scientist* 70: 607–615.

Gopnik, A., and A. N. Meltzoff. (1997). *Words, Thoughts, and Theories.* Cambridge, MA: MIT Press.

Gottlieb, G. (1991). Experiential canalization of behavioral developments: Results. *Developmental Psychology* 27: 35–39.

Hermer, L., and E. Spelke. (1996). Modularity and development: The case of spatial reorientation. *Cognition* 61: 195–232.

Hirschfeld, L. A. (1996). *Race in the Making.* Cambridge, MA: MIT Press.

Hirschfeld, L. A., and S. A. Gelman. (1994). Toward a topography of mind: An introduction to domain specificity. In L. A. Hirschfeld and S. A. Gelman, Eds., *Mapping the Mind: Domain Specificity in Cognition and Culture.* New York: Cambridge University Press.

Kaiser, M. K., M. McCloskey, and D. R. Proffitt. (1986). Development of intuitive theories of motion: Curvilinear motion in the absence of external forces. *Developmental Psychology* 22: 67–71.

Karmiloff-Smith, A., and B. Inhelder. (1975). If you want to get ahead, get a theory. *Cognition* 3: 195–211.

Marini, Z., and R. Case. (1989). Parallels in the development of preschoolers' knowledge about their physical and social worlds. *Merrill-Palmer Quarterly* 35: 63–86.

Murphy, G. L., and D. L. Medin. (1985). The role of theories in conceptual coherence. *Psychological Review* 92: 289–316.

Sadock, J. M. (1991). *Autolexical Syntax.* Chicago: University of Chicago Press.

Smith, L. B. (1995). Self-organizing processes in learning to learn words: Development is not induction. In C. A. Nelson, Ed., *Basic and Applied Perspectives on Learning, Cognition, and Development.* Vol. 28. Mahwah, NJ: Erlbaum.

Sternberg, R. J. (1989). Domain-generality versus domain-specificity: The life and impending death of a false dichotomy. *Merrill-Palmer Quarterly* 35: 115–130.

Thelen, E., and L. B. Smith. (1994). *A Dynamic Systems Approach to the Development of Cognition and Action.* Cambridge, MA: MIT Press.

Tomasello, M. (1995). Language: Not an instinct. *Cognitive Development* 10: 131–156.

Turiel, E. (1989). Domain-specific social judgments and domain ambiguities. *Merrill-Palmer Quarterly* 35: 89–114.

Dominance in Animal Social Groups

Social dominance refers to situations in which an individual or a group controls or dictates others' behavior primarily in competitive situations. Generally, an individual or group is said to be dominant when "a prediction is being made about the course of future interactions or the outcome of competitive situations" (Rowell 1974: 133). Criteria for assessing and assigning dominance relationships can vary from one situation to another, even for studies of conspecifics (members of the same species), and the burden is on researchers to show that their methods are suitable for the situation at hand (Bekoff 1977; Chase 1980; Lehner 1996). It is difficult to summarize available data succinctly, but generally it has been found that dominant individuals, when compared to subordinate individuals, often have more freedom of movement, have priority of access to food, gain higher-quality resting spots, enjoy favorable grooming relationships, occupy more protected parts of a group, obtain higher-quality mates, command and regulate the attention of other group members, and show greater resistance to stress and disease. Despite assertions that suggest otherwise, it really is not clear how robust the relationship is between an individual's dominance status and its lifetime reproductive success (for comparative data see Dewsbury 1982; McFarland 1982; Clutton-Brock 1988; Alcock 1993; Berger and Cunningham 1994; Altmann et al. 1996; Drickamer, Vessey and Meikle 1996; Byers 1997; Frank 1997; Pusey, Williams, and Goodall 1997). There also can be costs associated with dominance such that dominant individuals suffer because of stresses associated with the possibility of being overthrown by more subordinate individuals or because while they are defending their mates subordinates can sneak in and copulate with them (Wilson 1975; Hogstad 1987).

In practice, the concept of social dominance has proven to be ubiquitous but slippery (Rowell 1974; Bernstein 1981). Some researchers have questioned if dominance relationships are actually recognized by the animals themselves or if they are constructed by the human observers. Some also question if dominance hierarchies widely exist in nature or if they are due to the stresses associated with living in captivity (where much research is performed; see, for example, Rowell 1974). Others also feel that a lack of correlation between dominance in different contexts (for example, the possession of food, the acquisition or retention of a mate or a resting place) or in different locations argues against its conceptual utility (but see Hinde 1978). Nonetheless, many who have casually observed or carefully studied various animals agree that social dominance exists in similar forms and serves many of the same functions in widely diverse taxa, ranging from invertebrates to vertebrates including humans, and that dominance relationships among individuals are powerful organizing principles for animal social systems and population dynamics.

Based on, and expanding from, the classical studies of Schjelderup-Ebbe (1922) on dominance hierarchies in chickens, three basic types of hierarchies are usually recognized: (i) linear hierarchies (pecking-orders), usually in groups of fewer than ten individuals in which all paired relationships among individuals are transitive, such that if individual A dominates ($>$) individual B, and B $>$ C, then A $>$ C (wasps, bumblebees, chaffinches, turkeys, magpies, cows, ponies, coyotes, various nonhuman primates); (ii) nonlinear hierarchies in which there is at least one nontransitive relationship; and (iii) despotisms in which one individual (the alpha) in a group dominates all other individuals among whom dominance relationships are indistinguishable. Many papers concerned with historical aspects of social dominance in animals are reprinted in Schein (1975).

Although there has been little empirical experimental research done on cognitive aspects of, for example, how dominance status is recognized and represented in animals' minds, there are preliminary data that show that some animals have and use knowledge of other individuals' social ranks in their social interactions, and that individuals seem to agree on their ranking of others (Cheney and Seyfarth 1990; de Waal 1996; Tomasello and Call 1997). For example, when adult female vervet monkeys compete for grooming partners in their social group, individuals appear to rank one another and to agree on the rankings of the most preferred grooming partners. The understanding of dominance relationships—having and using the social knowledge needed for making evaluations and decisions—might entail constructing ordinal relationships and transitivity concerning the relationships among individuals with whom one has and has not had personal experience (Cheney and Seyfarth 1990; Tomasello and Call 1997), but the phylogenetic distribution of these skills remains to be determined. Certainly, the formation of alliances and coalitions (who to recruit, how to solicit them,

who to retaliate against, how and when to intervene, with whom to reciprocate; Tomasello and Call 1997) may involve having and using knowledge of others' social ranks, observing the outcomes of encounters between other individuals, and making deductions using this knowledge in the absence of personal experience. Social knowledge of self and others (in the absence of personal experience) may also be important in reconciliation, but detailed comparative data are scant (de Waal 1988, 1989; Harcourt and de Waal 1992; Silk, Cheney, and Seyfarth 1996).

All in all, insight and foresight (planning) seem to be important skills that are shown by a variety of nonhuman primates and nonprimates in their social encounters, but the comparative database is too small to support any general conclusions about whether individuals really do use insight and planning in their social interactions with others. Thus, broadly comparative and detailed research on the cognitive aspects of social dominance is sorely needed. These efforts will also inform other areas in the cognitive arena, including general questions about whether individuals have a theory of mind—whether they make attributions about the mental states of others and use this information in their own social encounters.

See also COGNITIVE ETHOLOGY; COOPERATION AND COMPETITION; ETHOLOGY; PRIMATE COGNITION; SOCIAL COGNITION; SOCIAL COGNITION IN ANIMALS

—Marc Bekoff

References

Alcock, J. (1993). *Animal Behavior: An Evolutionary Approach.* 5th ed. Sunderland, MA: Sinauer Associates, Inc.

Altmann, J., S. C. Alberts, S. A. Haines, J. Dubach, P. Muruthi, T. Cooter, E. Geffen, D. J. Cheeseman, R. S. Mututua, S. N. Saiyalel, R. K. Wayne, R. C. Lacy, and M. W. Bruford. (1996). Behavior predicts genetic structure in a wild primate group. *Proceedings of the National Academy of Sciences* 93: 5797–5801.

Bekoff, M. (1977). Quantitative studies of three areas of classical ethology: Social dominance, behavioral taxonomy, and behavioral variability. In B. A. Hazlett, Ed., *Quantitative Methods in the Study of Animal Behavior.* New York: Academic Press, pp. 1–46.

Berger, J., and C. Cunningham. (1994). *Bison: Mating and Conservation in Small Populations.* New York: Columbia University Press.

Bernstein, I. S. (1981). Dominance: The baby and the bathwater. *Behavioral and Brain Sciences* 4: 419–458.

Byers, J. A. (1997). *American Pronghorn: Social Adaptations and the Ghost of Predators Past.* Chicago: University of Chicago Press.

Chase, I. D. (1980). Social process and hierarchy formation in small groups: A comparative perspective. *American Sociological Review* 45: 905–924.

Cheney, D. L., and R. M. Seyfarth. (1990). *How Monkeys See the World: Inside the Mind of Another Species.* Chicago: University of Chicago Press.

Clutton-Brock, J. H., Ed. (1988). *Reproductive Success: Studies of Individual Variation in Contrasting Breeding Systems.* Chicago: University of Chicago Press.

de Waal, F. (1988). The reconciled hierarchy. In M. R. A. Chance, Ed., *Social Fabrics of the Mind.* Hillsdale, NJ: Erlbaum, pp. 105–136.

de Waal, F. (1989). Dominance 'style' and primate social organization. In V. Standen and R. A. Foley, Eds., *Comparative Socioecology: The Behavioural Ecology of Humans and Other Animals*. Oxford: Blackwell Scientific Publications, pp. 243–263.

de Waal, F. (1996). *Good Natured: The Origins of Right and Wrong in Humans and Other Animals*. Cambridge, MA: Harvard University Press.

Dewsbury, D. A. (1982). Dominance rank, copulatory behavior, and differential reproduction. *Quarterly Review of Biology* 57: 135–159.

Drickamer, L. C., S. H. Vessey, and D. Meikle. (1996). *Animal Behavior: Mechanisms, Ecology, and Evolution*. Dubuque, IA: Wm. C. Brown Publishers.

Frank, L. (1997). Evolution of genital masculinization: Why do female hyaenas have such a large 'penis'? *Trends in Ecology and Evolution* 12: 58–62.

Harcourt, A. H., and F. B. M. de Waal, Eds. (1992). *Coalitions and Alliances in Humans and Other Animals*. New York: Oxford University Press.

Hinde, R. A. (1978). Dominance and role: Two concepts with dual meanings. *Journal of Social and Biological Structure* 1: 27–38.

Hogstad, O. (1987). It is expensive to be dominant. *Auk* 104: 333–336.

Lehner, P. N. (1996). *Handbook of Ethological Methods* 2nd ed. New York: Cambridge University Press.

McFarland, D., Ed. (1982). *The Oxford Companion to Animal Behavior*. New York: Oxford University Press.

Pusey, A., J. Williams, and J. Goodall. (1997). The influence of dominance rank on the reproductive success of female chimpanzees. *Science* 277: 828–831.

Rowell, T. (1974). The concept of social dominance. *Behavioral Biology* 11: 131–154.

Schein, M. W., Ed. (1975). *Social Hierarchy and Dominance*. Stroudsberg, PA: Dowden, Hutchinson and Ross.

Schjelderup-Ebbe, T. (1922). Contributions to the social psychology of the domestic chicken. *Zeitschrift für Psychologie* 88: 225–252. Translated in Schein (1975).

Silk, J. B., D. L. Cheney, and R. M. Seyfarth. (1996). The form and function of post-conflict interactions between female baboons. *Animal Behaviour* 52: 259–268.

Tomasello, M., and T. Call. (1997). *Primate Cognition*. New York: Oxford University Press.

Wilson, E. O. (1975). *Sociobiology: The New Synthesis*. Cambridge, MA: Harvard University Press.

Dreaming

Mental activity does not cease at the onset of sleep. Current scientific evidence suggests instead that it is virtually continuous throughout sleep but that its level of intensity and its formal characteristics change as the brain changes its state with the periodic recurrence of rapid eye movement (REM) and non-REM (NREM) sleep phases.

Until the discovery of REM sleep by Eugene Aserinsky and Nathaniel Kleitman in 1953, interest in the psychology of dreaming was restricted to speculative accounts of its distinctive phenomenology that were linked to schematic efforts to interpret dream content. The best known example of this kind of theorizing is the psychoanalytic model of Sigmund FREUD, which held that dream bizarreness was the result of the mind's effort to disguise and censor unconscious wishes released in sleep that in their unaltered form would over-

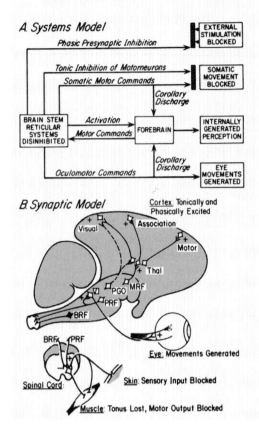

Figure 1. The Activation-Synthesis model. Systems and synaptic model. As a result of disinhibition caused by cessation of aminergic neuronal firing, brainstem reticular systems autoactivate. Their outputs have effects including depolarization of afferent terminals causing phasic presynaptic inhibition and blockade of external stimuli, especially during the bursts of REM, and postsynaptic hyperpolarization causing tonic inhibition of motorneurons that effectively counteract concomitant motor commands so that somatic movement is blocked. Only the oculomotor commands are read out as eye movements because these motorneurons are not inhibited. The forebrain, activated by the reticular formation and also aminergically disinhibited, receives efferent copy or corollary discharge information about somatic motor and oculomotor commands from which it may synthesize such internally generated perceptions as visual imagery and the sensation of movement, both of which typify dream mentation. The forebrain may, in turn, generate its own motor commands that help to perpetuate the process via positive feedback to the reticular formation.

whelm the mind and cause awakening. The discovery of the association of dreaming with REM sleep allowed a quite different approach. Emphasis suddenly shifted from the attempt to analyze the content to an attempt to explain the formal aspects of the distinctive phenomenology in terms of underlying brain activity.

This article gives a summary of how the cellular and molecular changes in the brain which distinguish waking, NREM and REM sleep can be used to account for the concomitant shifts in mental state that result in the shift in consciousness from waking to dreaming. (See also SLEEP for relevant background information.)

Whether subjects are aroused from sleep in a laboratory setting or awaken spontaneously at home, they give reports of preawakening mental experience that are quite different if their brain state is REM than if it is non-REM. REM-sleep dream reports are seven times longer and are far more likely to describe formed sensory perceptions and vivid visual images than are the reports of NREM dreams, which tend to be more thoughtlike and dull. REM sleep reports are also far more likely to be animated, with descriptions of walking, running, playing sports, or even flying. Finally, the REM-sleep dream scenarios are accompanied by strong emotions such as anxiety, elation, and anger, all of which bear a close relationship to details of the plot.

These formal features of dreaming correlate well with changes in the activation level of the brain as measured by the degree of low-voltage, high-frequency power in the sleep electroencephalogram, and they are negatively correlated with high voltage, slow EEG patterns. Because the high-voltage, slow-wave activity of NREM sleep is most intense and prolonged in the first half of the night, reports from awakenings performed then are more likely to show differences from REM reports than are those from the second half of the night. Brain activation is therefore an easily understandable determinant of dream length and visual intensity. Dreamlike mentation may also emerge at sleep onset when the brain activation level is just beginning to fall. Sleep-onset dreaming is likely to be evanescent and fragmentary, with less vivid imagery, less strong emotion, and a less well developed story line than in REM-sleep dreaming.

Collaborating with the still high activation level to produce sleep-onset dreaming is the rapidly rising threshold to external sensory stimulation. This factor allows internal stimuli to dominate the brain. In REM sleep internal stimuli also protect the brain from external sensory influence. If the stimulus level is raised to sufficiently high levels, external information can be incorporated into dream plots, but the critical window for such incorporation is narrow and external stimuli more commonly interrupt dreaming by causing awakening. When dreams are interrupted in this way, recall of dreaming is markedly enhanced to levels as high as 95 percent if the subject is aroused from REM sleep during a cluster of rapid eye movements.

The strong correlation between dreaming and REM sleep has encouraged attempts to model the brain basis of dreaming at the cellular and molecular level. The activation-synthesis hypothesis, first put forward in 1977, ascribed dreaming to activation of the brain in REM sleep by a well-specified pontine brain stem mechanism.

Such distinctive aspects of dream mentation as vivid visual hallucinations, a constant sense of movement, and strong emotion were ascribed to internal stimulation of visual, motor, and limbic regions of the upper brain by signals of brain stem origin. The bizarreness of dream cognition, with its characteristic instability of time, place, and person, was thought to be due to the chaotic nature of the autoactivation process and to the failure of short-term memory caused by the chemical changes in REM described by the reciprocal interaction model of brain state control first advanced in 1975.

Using microelectrode recording techniques to sample individual cell activity during natural sleep and waking in animal models, it has been possible to show that the neuromodulatory systems of the brain stem behave very differently in waking and REM sleep. These differences help to account for the distinctive psychological features of dreaming, especially the bizarreness and recent memory loss. During waking, cells of the noradrenergic locus coeruleus and the serotonergic raphe nuclei are tonically active, but in REM they are shut off. This means that the activated brain of REM is aminergically demodulated so that it cannot process information in the same way as it does in waking. Dream bizarreness and dream amnesia are both the result of this neuromodulatory defect. Compounding this difference, the pontine cholinergic neurones become reciprocally activated in REM, and their intense phasic activity conveys eye movement-related information to the visual sensory and motor areas of the brain (accounting for hallucinated dream vision and movement) and to the amygdala (accounting for the emotion of dreams).

The specification of these neurochemical differences enables a three-dimensional state space model to be constructed that integrates activation level (A), input-output gating (I) with the brain modulatory factor (M). This hybrid psychophysiological construct thus updates both activation synthesis and reciprocal interaction by representing the energy level (A) information source (I) and processing mode (M) of the brain mind as a single point that continuously moves through the state space as a function of the values of A, I, and M.

According to AIM, dreaming is most likely to occur when activation is high, when the information source shifts from external to internal, and when the neuromodulatory balance shifts from aminergic to cholinergic. Because these shifts may occur gradually or suddenly, it is not surprising that the correlation of physiology with psychology is also statistical. REM is the most highly conducive to dreaming, but it can also occur at sleep onset and NREM sleep, both of which fulfill some of the necessary physiological conditions.

Our natural skepticism about the relevance of animal model data for human psychophysiology has been partially dispelled by recent POSITRON EMISSION TOMOGRAPHY (PET) studies of the human brain, which reveal significant regional changes in activation level during REM sleep compared to waking. The subjects of these studies all reported dreams after awakening from REM-sleep in the scanner. First and foremost is activation of the pontine brain stem, the presumed organizer of the REM-sleep brain. Second is the selective activation of the limbic forebrain and paralimbic cortex, the supposed mediator of dream emotion. Third is the selective inactivation of the dorsal prefrontal cortex, a brain region essential to self-reflective awareness and to executively guided thought, judgment, and action. Both of these cognitive functions are markedly deficient in dreaming.

Unfortunately, imaging techniques do not have the spatial or molecular resolution necessary to confirm the neuromodulatory hypothesis of AIM. But an extensive body of

AIM: A THREE DIMENSIONAL STATE SPACE MODEL

2A

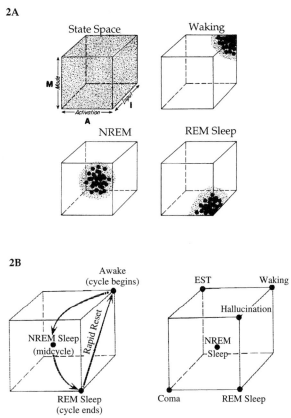

2B

Figure 2a. Three-dimensional state space defined by the values for brain activation (A), input source and strength (I), and mode of processing (M). It is theoretically possible for the system to be at any point in the state space, and an infinite number of state conditions is conceivable. In practice the system is normally constrained to a boomerang-like path from the back upper right in waking (high A, I, and M), through the center in NREM (intermediate A, I, and M) to the front lower right in REM sleep (high A, low I, and M).

Figure 2b. (A) Movement through the state space during the sleep cycle. (B) Segments of the state space associated with some normal, pathological, and artificial conditions of the brain.

human psychopharmacological data is consonant with the basic assumptions of the model. Drugs that act as aminergic agonists (or reuptake blockers) first suppress REM and REM-sleep dreaming. When they are later withdrawn, a marked and unpleasant intensification of dreaming and even psychosis may occur. If those drugs also possess anticholinergic actions, the effects on dreaming are even more pronounced. Finally, and most significantly, human REM-sleep dreaming is potentiated by some of the same cholinergic agonist drugs that experimentally enhance REM sleep in animals.

See also CONSCIOUSNESS; CONSCIOUSNESS, NEUROBIOLOGY OF; LIMBIC SYSTEM; NEUROTRANSMITTERS

—*J. Allan Hobson*

References and Further Readings

Aserinsky, E., and N. Kleitman. (1953). Regularly occurring periods of eye motility and concomitant phenomena during sleep. *Science* 118: 273–274.
Foulkes, D. (1985). *Dreaming: A Cognitive-Psychological Analysis.* Mahwah, NJ: Erlbaum.
Freud, S. (1900). *The Interpretation of Dreams.* Trans. J. Strachey. New York: Basic Books.
Hobson, J. A. (1988). *The Dreaming Brain.* New York: Basic Books.
Hobson, J. A. (1990). Activation, input source, and modulation: A neurocognitive model of the state of the brain-mind. In R. Bootzin, J. Kihlstrom, and D. Schacter, Eds., *Sleep and Cognition.* Washington, DC: American Psychological Association, pp. 25–40.
Hobson, J. A. (1994). *The Chemistry of Conscious States.* Boston: Little Brown.
Hobson, J. A., and R. W. McCarley. (1977). The brain as a dream-state generator: An activation-synthesis hypothesis of the dream process. *Am. J. Psychiat.* 134: 1335–1348.
Hobson, J. A., E. Hoffman, R. Helfand, and D. Kostner. (1987). Dream bizarreness and the activation-synthesis hypothesis. *Human Neurobiology* 6: 157–164.
Llinas, R., and D. Pare. (1991). Commentary on dreaming and wakefulness. *Neuroscience* 44: 521–535.
Solms, M. (1997). *The Neuropsychology of Dreams: A Clinico-Anatomical Study.* Mahwah, NJ: Erlbaum.

Dynamic Approaches to Cognition

The dynamical approach to cognition is a confederation of research efforts bound together by the idea that natural cognition is a dynamical phenomenon and best understood in dynamical terms. This contrasts with the "law of qualitative structure" (Newell and Simon 1976) governing orthodox or "classical" cognitive science, which holds that cognition is a form of digital COMPUTATION.

The idea of mind as dynamical can be traced as far back as David HUME, and it permeates the work of psychologists such as Lewin and Tolman. The contemporary dynamical approach, however, is conveniently dated from the early cybernetics era (e.g., Ashby 1952). In subsequent decades dynamical work was carried out within programs as diverse as ECOLOGICAL PSYCHOLOGY, synergetics, morphodynamics, and neural net research. In the 1980s, three factors—growing dissatisfaction with the classical approach, developments in the pure mathematics of nonlinear dynamics, and increasing availability of computer hardware and software for simulation—contributed to a flowering of dynamical research, particularly in connectionist form (Smolensky 1988). By the 1990s, it was apparent that the dynamical approach has sufficient power, scope, and cohesion to count as a research paradigm in its own right (Port and van Gelder 1995).

In the prototypical case, the dynamicist focuses on some particular aspect of cognition and proposes an abstract dynamical system as a model of the processes involved. The behavior of the model is investigated using dynamical systems theory, often aided by simulation on digital computers. A close match between the behavior of the model and empirical data on the target phenomenon confirms the hypothesis that the target is itself dynamical in nature, and that it can be understood in the same dynamical terms.

Consider, for example, how we make decisions. One possibility is that in our heads there are symbols representing various options and the probabilities and values of their outcomes; our brains then crank through an ALGORITHM for determining a choice (see RATIONAL DECISION-MAKING). But this classical approach has difficulty accounting for the empirical data, partly because it cannot accommodate temporal issues and other relevant factors such as affect and context. Dynamical models treat the process of DECISION-MAKING as one in which numerical variables evolve interactively over time. Such models, it is claimed, can explain a wider range of data and do so more accurately (see, e.g., Busemeyer and Townsend 1993; Leven and Levine 1996).

A better understanding of dynamical work can be gained by highlighting some of its many differences with classical cognitive science. Most obviously, dynamicists take cognitive agents to be dynamical systems as opposed to digital computers. A dynamical system for current purposes is a set of quantitative variables changing continually, concurrently, and interdependently over quantitative time in accordance with dynamical laws described by some set of equations. Hand in hand with this first commitment goes the belief that dynamics provides the right tools for understanding cognitive processes. Dynamics in this sense includes the traditional practice of dynamical modeling, in which scientists attempt to understand natural phenomena via abstract dynamical models; such modeling makes heavy use of calculus and differential or difference equations. It also includes dynamical systems theory, a set of concepts, proofs, and methods for understanding the behavior of systems in general and dynamical systems in particular. A central insight of dynamical systems theory is that behavior can be understood geometrically, that is, as a matter of position and change of position in a space of possible overall states of the system. The behavior can then be described in terms of attractors, transients, stability, coupling, bifurcations, chaos, and so forth—features largely invisible from a classical perspective.

Dynamicists and classicists also diverge over the general nature of cognition and cognitive agents. The pivotal issue here is probably the role of time. Although all cognitive scientists understand cognition as something that happens *over* time, dynamicists see cognition as being *in* time, that is, as an essentially temporal phenomenon. This is manifested in many ways. The time variable in dynamical models is not a mere discrete order, but a quantitative, sometimes continuous approximation to the real time of natural events. Details of timing (durations, rates, synchronies, etc.) are taken to be essential to cognition itself rather than incidental details. Cognition is seen not as having a sequential cyclic (sense-think-act) structure, but rather as a matter of continuous and continual coevolution. The subtlety and complexity of cognition is found not *at* a time in elaborate static structures, but rather *in* time in the flux of change itself.

Dynamicists also emphasize SITUATEDNESS/EMBEDDEDNESS. Natural cognition is always environmentally embedded, corporeally embodied, and neurally "embrained." Classicists typically set such considerations aside (Clark 1997). Dynamicists, by contrast, tend to see cognitive processes as collective achievements of brains in bodies in contexts. Their language—dynamics—can be used to describe change in the environment, bodily movements, and neurobiological processes (e.g., Bingham 1995; Wright and Liley 1996). This enables them to offer integrated accounts of cognition as a dynamical phenomenon in a dynamical world.

In classical cognitive science, symbolic representations and their algorithmic manipulations are the basic building blocks. Dynamical models usually also incorporate representations, but reconceive them as dynamical entities (e.g., system states, or trajectories shaped by attractor landscapes). Representations tend to be seen as transient, context-dependent stabilities in the midst of change, rather than as static, context-free, permanent units. Interestingly, some dynamicists claim to have developed wholly representation-free models, and they conjecture that representation will turn out to play much less of a role in cognition than has traditionally been supposed (e.g., Skarda 1986; Wheeler forthcoming).

The differences between the dynamical and classical approaches should not be exaggerated. The dynamical approach stands opposed to what John Haugeland has called "Good Old Fashioned AI" (Haugeland 1985). However, dynamical systems may well be performing computation in some other sense (e.g., analog computation or "real" computation; Blum, Shub, and Smale 1989; Siegelmann and Sontag 1994). Also, dynamical systems are generally effectively computable. (Note that something can be *computable* without being a digital *computer.*) Thus, there is considerable middle ground between pure GOFAI and an equally extreme dynamicism (van Gelder 1998).

How does the dynamical approach relate to connectionism? In a word, they overlap. Connectionist networks are generally dynamical systems, and much of the best dynamical research is connectionist in form (e.g., Beer 1995). However, the way many connectionists structure and interpret their systems is dominated by broadly computational preconceptions (e.g., Rosenberg and Sejnowski 1987). Conversely, many dynamical models of cognition are not connectionist networks. Connectionism is best seen as straddling a more fundamental opposition between dynamical and classical cognitive science.

Chaotic systems are a special sort of dynamical system, and chaos theory is just one branch of dynamics. So far, only a small proportion of work in dynamical cognitive science has made any serious use of chaos theory. Therefore the dynamical approach should not be identified with the use of chaos theory or related notions such as fractals. Still, chaotic dynamics surely represents a frontier of fascinating possibilities for cognitive science (Garson 1996).

The dynamical approach stands or falls on its ability to deliver the best models of particular aspects of cognition. In any given case its ability to do this is a matter for debate among the relevant specialists. Currently, many aspects of cognition—e.g., story comprehension—are well beyond the reach of dynamical treatment. Nevertheless, a provisional consensus seems to be emerging that some significant range of cognitive phenomena will turn out to be dynamical, and that a dynamical perspective enriches our understanding of cognition more generally.

See also COGNITIVE MODELING, CONNECTIONIST; COMPUTATION AND THE BRAIN; COMPUTATIONAL THEORY OF MIND; CONNECTIONIST APPROACHES TO LANGUAGE; NEURAL NETWORKS; RULES AND REPRESENTATIONS

—*Tim van Gelder*

References

Ashby, R. (1952). *Design for a Brain.* London: Chapman and Hall.

Beer, R. D. (1995). A dynamical systems perspective on agent-environment interaction. *Artificial Intelligence* 72: 173–215.

Bingham, G. (1995). Dynamics and the problem of event recognition. In R. Port and T. van Gelder, Eds., *Mind as Motion: Explorations in the Dynamics of Cognition.* Cambridge, MA: MIT Press.

Blum, L., M. Shub, and S. Smale. (1989). On a theory of computation and complexity over the real numbers: NP completeness, recursive functions and universal machines. *Bulletin of the American Mathematical Society* 21: 1–49.

Busemeyer, J. R., and J. T. Townsend. (1993). Decision field theory: A dynamic-cognitive approach to decision making in an uncertain environment. *Psychological Review* 100: 432–459.

Clark, A. (1997). *Being There: Putting Brain, Body and World Together Again.* Cambridge MA: MIT Press.

Garson, J. (1996). Cognition poised at the edge of chaos: a complex alternative to a symbolic mind. *Philosophical Psychology* 9: 301–321.

Haugeland, J. (1985). *Artificial Intelligence: The Very Idea.* Cambridge MA: MIT Press.

Leven, S. J., and D. S. Levine. (1996). Multiattribute decision making in context: A dynamic neural network methodology. *Cognitive Science* 20: 271–299.

Newell, A., and H. Simon. (1976). Computer science as empirical enquiry: Symbols and search. *Communications of the Association for Computing Machinery* 19: 113–126.

Port, R., and T. J. van Gelder. (1995). *Mind as Motion: Explorations in the Dynamics of Cognition.* Cambridge, MA: MIT Press.

Rosenberg, C. R., and T. J. Sejnowski. (1987). Parallel networks that learn to pronounce English text. *Complex Systems* 1.

Siegelmann, H. T., and E. D. Sontag. (1994). Analog computation via neural networks. *Theoretical Computer Science* 131: 331–360.

Skarda, C. A. (1986). Explaining behavior: Bringing the brain back in. *Inquiry* 29: 187–202.

Smolensky, P. (1988). On the proper treatment of connectionism. *Behavioral and Brain Sciences* 11: 1–74.

van Gelder, T. J. (1998). The dynamical hypothesis in cognitive science. *Behavioral and Brain Sciences* 21: 1–14.

Wheeler, M. (Forthcoming). *The Next Step: Beyond Cartesianism in the Science of Cognition.* Cambridge MA: MIT Press.

Wright, J. J., and D. T. J. Liley. (1996). Dynamics of the brain at global and microscopic scales: Neural networks and the EEG. *Behavioral and Brain Sciences* 19.

Further Readings

Giunti, M. (1997). *Computation, Dynamics, and Cognition.* New York: Oxford University Press.

Gregson, R. A. M. (1988). *Nonlinear Psychophysical Dynamics.* Hillsdale, NJ: Erlbaum.

Haken, H., and M. Stadler, Eds. (1990). *Synergetics of Cognition.* Berlin: Springer.

Horgan, T. E., and J. Tienson. (1996). *Connectionism and the Philosophy of Psychology.* Cambridge, MA: MIT Press.

Jaeger, H. (1996). Dynamische systeme in der kognitionswissenschaft. *Kognitionswissenschaft* 5: 151–174.

Kelso, J. A. S. (1995). *Dynamic Patterns: The Self-Organization of Brain and Behavior.* Cambridge, MA: MIT Press.

Port, R., and T. J. van Gelder. (1995). *Mind as Motion: Explorations in the Dynamics of Cognition.* Cambridge, MA: MIT Press.

Sulis, W., and A. Combs, Eds. (1996). *Nonlinear Dynamics in Human Behavior.* Singapore: World Scientific.

Thelen, E., and L. B. Smith. (1993). *A Dynamics Systems Approach to the Development of Cognition and Action.* Cambridge, MA: MIT Press.

Vallacher, R., and A. Nowak, Eds. (1993). *Dynamical Systems in Social Psychology.* New York: Academic Press.

Wheeler, M. (Forthcoming). *The Next Step: Beyond Cartesianism in the Science of Cognition.* Cambridge MA: MIT Press.

Dynamic Programming

Some problems can be structured into a collection of small problems, each of which can be solved on the basis of the solution of some of the others. The process of working a solution back through the subproblems in order to reach a final answer is called dynamic programming. This general algorithmic technique is applied in a wide variety of areas, from optimizing airline schedules to allocating cell-phone bandwidth to justifying typeset text. Its most common and relevant use, however, is for PLANNING optimal paths through state-space graphs, in order, for example, to find the best routes between cities in a map.

In the simplest case, consider a directed, weighted graph $< S, A, T, L>$, where S is the set of nodes or "states" of the graph, and A is a set of arcs or "actions" that may be taken from each state. The state that is reached by taking action a in state s is described as $T(s,a)$; the positive length of the a arc from state s is written $L(s,a)$. Let $g \in S$ be a desired goal state. Given such a structure, we might want to find the shortest path from a particular state to the goal state, or even to find the shortest paths from each of the states to the goal.

In order to make it easy to follow shortest paths, we will use dynamic programming to compute a distance function, $D(s)$, that gives the distance from each state to the goal state. The ALGORITHM is as follows:

$D(s) := large$
$D(g) := 0$
Loop $|S|$ times
    Loop for s in S
        $D(s) := \min_{a \in A} L(s,a) + D(T(s,a))$
    end loop
end loop

We start by initializing $D(s) = large$ to be an overestimate of the distance between s and g (except in the case of $D(g)$, for which it is exact). Now, we want to improve iteratively the estimates of $D(s)$. The inner loop updates the value for each state s to be the minimum over the outgoing arcs of $L(s,a) + D(T(s,a))$; the first term is the known distance of the first arc and the second term is the estimated distance from the resulting state to the goal. The outer loop is executed as many times as there are states.

The character of this algorithm is as follows: Initially, only $D(g)$ is correct. After the first iteration, $D(s)$ is correct for all states whose shortest path to the goal is one step long. After $|S|$ iterations, it is correct for all states. Note that if L was uniformly 1, then all the states that are i steps from the goal would have correct D values after the ith iteration; however, it may be possible for some state s to be one step from g with a very long arc, but have a much shorter path with more steps, in which case the D value after the iteration would still be an overestimate.

Once D has been computed, then the optimal path can be described by, at any state s, choosing the action a that minimizes $D(a,s)$. Rather than just a single plan, or trajectory of states, we actually have a *policy,* mapping every state to its optimal action.

A generalization of the shortest-paths problem is the problem of finding optimal policies for Markov decision processes (MDPs). An MDP is a tuple $< S, A, T, R >$, where S and A are state and action sets, as before; $T(s,a)$ is a stochastic state-transition function, mapping a state and action into a *probability distribution* over next states (we will write $T(s,a,s')$ as the probability of landing in state s' as a result of taking action a in state s); and $R(s,a)$ is a *reward* function, describing the expected immediate utility resulting from taking action a in state s. In the simplest case, we seek a policy π that will gain the maximum expected total reward over some finite number of steps of execution, k.

In the shortest-paths problem, we computed a distance function D that allowed us to derive an optimal policy cheaply. In MDPs, we seek a value function $V^k(s)$, which is the expected utility (sum of rewards) of being in state s and executing the optimal policy for k steps. This value function can be derived using dynamic programming, first solving the problem for the situation when there are t steps remaining, then using that solution to solve the problem for the situation when there are $t + 1$ steps remaining. If there are no steps remaining, then clearly $V^0(s) = 0$ for all s. If we know V^{t-1}, then we can express $V(t)$ as

$$V^t(s) = \max_{a \in A} R(s, a) + \sum s' \in S\, T(s, a, s') V^{t-1}(s')$$

The t-step value of state s is the maximum over all actions (we get to choose the best one) of the immediate value of the action plus the expected $t - 1$-step value of the next state. Once V has been computed, then the optimal action for state s with t steps to go is the action that was responsible for the maximum value of $V^t(s)$.

Solving MDPs is a kind of planning problem, because it is assumed that a model of the world, in the form of the T and R functions, is known. When the world model is not known, the solution of MDPs becomes the problem of REINFORCEMENT LEARNING, which can be thought of as stochastic dynamic programming.

The theory of dynamic programming, especially as applied to MDPs, was developed by Bellman (1957) and Howard (1960). More recent extensions and developments are described in excellent recent texts by Puterman (1994) and Bertsekas (1995).

See also COMPUTATION; HIDDEN MARKOV MODELS

—*Leslie Pack Kaelbling*

References

Bellman, R. (1957). *Dynamic Programming.* Princeton, NJ: Princeton University Press.

Bertsekas, D. P. (1995). *Dynamic Programming and Optimal Control,* vols. 1–2. Belmont, MA: Athena Scientific.

Howard, R. A. (1960). *Dynamic Programming and Markov Processes.* Cambridge, MA: The MIT Press.

Puterman, M. L. (1994). *Markov Decision Processes.* New York: John Wiley and Sons.

Dynamic Semantics

The term *dynamic interpretation* refers to a number of approaches in formal semantics of natural language that arose in the 1980s and that distinguish themselves from the preceding paradigm by viewing interpretation as an inherently dynamic concept. The phrase *dynamic semantics* is used to denote a specific implementation of this idea, which locates the dynamic aspect in the concept of linguistic meaning proper.

The dominant view on meaning from the origins of logically oriented semantics at the beginning of the twentieth century until well into the 1980s is aptly summarized in the slogan "Meaning equals truth conditions." This formulates a static view on what MEANING is: it characterizes the meaning relation between sentences and the world as a descriptive relation, which is static in the sense that, although the meaning relation itself may change over time, it does not bring about a change itself. The slogan focuses on sentences, but derivatively the same holds for subsentential expressions: their meanings consist in the contribution they make to the truth conditions of sentences, a contribution that is usually formalized in terms of a static relation of reference. Interpretation is the recovery of the meaning of an utterance, and is essentially sentence-based. This static view on meaning and interpretation derives from the development of formal LOGIC, and lies at the basis of the framework of Montague grammar, the first attempt to apply systematically formal semantics to natural language.

Although dominant, the static view did not go unchallenged. The development of speech act theory (Austin, Searle) and work on PRESUPPOSITION (Stalnaker) and IMPLICATURE (GRICE) stressed the dynamic nature of interpretation. However, at first this just led to a division of labor between SEMANTICS and PRAGMATICS, the latter being viewed as something that works on top of the results of the former. This situation began to change in the beginning of the 1980s when people started to realize that certain empirical problems could be solved only by viewing meaning as an integrated notion that accounts for the dynamic aspects of interpretation right from the start and that is essentially concerned with DISCOURSE (or texts), and not with sentences.

A simple but illustrative example is provided by cross-sentential ANAPHORA. In a discourse such as "A man walked into the bar. He was wearing a black velvet hat," the pronoun "he" is naturally interpreted as bound by the indefinite noun phrase "a man." If interpretation proceeds on a sentence-by-sentence basis, this can not be accounted for. And "delayed" interpretation, that is, linking quantified noun phrases and pronouns only when the discourse is finished, makes empirically wrong predictions in other cases, such as: "One man was sitting in the bar. He was wearing a black velvet hat." Such examples rather suggest that interpretation has to be viewed as a dynamic process, which takes place incrementally as a discourse or text proceeds.

Further development of this idea received both an internal and an external stimulus. The main external influence came from natural language research within the context of artificial intelligence, which favored a definitely procedural view and was oriented toward units larger than sentences. The interpretation of utterances is modeled as the execution of procedures that change the state of a system as it proceeds. It took some time before this idea caught on, mainly because it seemed hard to reconcile with the core goal of formal semantics, viz., to account for logical relationships. However, the emergence of formal models within the AI paradigm, in particular the development of NONMONOTONIC LOGICS, provided the necessary link. Also, work on the semantics of programming languages turned out to be concerned with a conceptual machinery that could be applied successfully to natural language.

In the beginning of the 1980s the dynamic view on interpretation was formulated explicitly in discourse representation theory (Kamp 1981; see also Kamp and Reyle 1993) and file change semantics (Heim 1982). The work of Kamp and Heim constitutes an extension and transformation of the framework of Montague grammar. In his original paper Kamp explicitly describes his theory as an attempt to wed the static approach of the logical tradition to the procedural view of the AI paradigm. Within different settings similar ideas developed, for example within the theory of semantic syntax (Seuren 1985), and that of game theoretical semantics (Hintikka 1983).

Discourse representation theory is a dynamic theory of interpretation, not of meaning. The dynamics is located in the process of building up representational structures, so-called discourse representations. These structures are initiated by incoming utterances and added to or modified by subsequent utterances. The structures themselves are interpreted in a static way by evaluating them with respect to a suitable model. For example, anaphoric relations across sentence boundaries are analyzed as follows. A sentence containing a referential expression (such as a proper name, or a quantified term; see QUANTIFIERS) introduces a so-called discourse referent along with restrictions on its interpretation. A subsequent sentence containing an anaphoric expression (such as a pronoun) can "pick up" this referent if certain descriptive and structural conditions are met, and thus be linked to the antecedent referential expression. The semantics of the discourse representation then takes care of the coreference.

Dynamic semantics (Groenendijk and Stokhof 1991; Groenendijk, Stokhof, and Veltman 1996) takes the idea of dynamic interpretation one step further and locates the dynamics in the concept of meaning itself. The basic starting point of dynamic semantics can be formulated in a slogan: "Meaning is context-change potential." In other words, the meaning of a sentence is the change that an utterance of it brings about. And the meanings of subsentential expressions consist in their contribution to the context-change potential of the sentences in which they occur. Unlike discourse representation theory, it tries to do away with semantic representations but assigns various expressions, such as the existential quantifier associated with indefinite noun phrases, a dynamic meaning, which allows it to extend its binding force beyond its ordinary syntactic scope.

The slogan "Meaning is context-change potential" is general in at least two respects: it does not tell us what it is that is changed, and it does not say how the change is brought about. The latter question is answered by giving analyses of concrete linguistic structures. As to the former issue, it is commonly assumed that one of the primary functions of language use is that of information exchange and that, hence, information is what is changed by an utterance. Primary focus is the information state of the hearer, but in dialogical situations that of the speaker also has to be taken into account. Depending on the empirical domain, information concerns different kinds of entities. If the subject is anaphoric relations, information is about entities which are introduced and their properties; for temporal expressions one needs information about events and their location on a time axis; in the case of default reasoning expectation patterns become relevant. In other cases (question-answer dialogues, presuppositions) "higher order" information of the speech participants about each other is also at stake.

A change in the notion of meaning brings along a change in other semantic concepts, such as entailment. In static semantics truth plays a key role in defining meaning and entailment. In dynamic semantics it becomes a limit case. The central notion here is that of support: roughly, an information state s supports a sentence Φ iff an utterance of Φ does not bring about a change in s. Entailment can then be defined as follows (alternative definitions are possible as well): $\Phi_1 \ldots \Phi_n$ entails Ψ iff for every state s it holds that updating s with $\Phi_1 \ldots \Phi_n$ consecutively leads to a state that supports Ψ. (Cf. van Benthem 1996 for discussion of various alternatives.)

Dynamic semantics of natural language can be seen as part of a larger enterprise: the study of how information in general is structured and exchanged. Such a study brings together results from diverse fields such as computer science, cognitive psychology, logic, linguistics, and artificial intelligence. Language is one particular means to structure and exchange information, along with others such as visual representations, databases, and so on. The dynamic viewpoint has considerable merit here, and, conversely, draws on results that have been developed with an eye to other applications.

See also CONTEXT AND POINT OF VIEW; DYNAMIC APPROACHES TO COGNITION; LOGICAL FORM IN LINGUISTICS; POSSIBLE WORLDS SEMANTICS; REFERENCE, THEORIES OF

—*Martin Stokhof and Jeroen Groenendijk*

References

Benthem, J. F. A. K. van. (1996). *Exploring Logical Dynamics.* Stanford: CSLI.

Groenendijk, J. A. G., and M. J. B. Stokhof. (1991). Dynamic Predicate Logic. *Linguistics and Philosophy* 14: 39–100.

Groenendijk, J. A. G., M. J. B. Stokhof, and F. J. M. M. Veltman. (1996). Coreference and modality. In S. Lappin, Ed., *Handbook of Contemporary Semantic Theory.* Oxford: Blackwell, pp. 179–213.

Heim I. (1982). *The Semantics of Definite and Indefinite Noun Phrases.* Ph.D. diss., University of Massachusetts. (Published in 1989 by Garland, New York.)

Hintikka, J. (1983). *The Game of Language.* Dordrecht: Reidel.

Kamp, J. A. W. (1981). A theory of truth and semantic representation. In J. A. G. Groenendijk, T. M. V. Janssen, and M. J. B. Stokhof, Eds., *Formal Methods in the Study of Language.* Amsterdam: Mathematical Centre, pp. 277–322.

Kamp, J. A. W., and U. Reyle. (1993). *From Discourse to Logic.* Dordrecht: Kluwer.

Seuren, P. A. M. (1985). *Discourse Semantics.* Oxford: Blackwell.

Further Readings

Beaver, D. (1997). Presupposition. In J. F. A. K. van Benthem and A. T. M. ter Meulen, Eds., *Handbook of Logic and Linguistics.* Amsterdam: Elsevier, pp. 939–1008.

Benthem, J. F. A. K. van, R. M. Muskens, and A. Visser. (1997). Dynamics. In J. F. A. K. van Benthem and A. T. M. ter Meulen, Eds., *Handbook of Logic and Linguistics.* Amsterdam: Elsevier, pp. 587–648.

Blutner, R. (1993). Dynamic generalized quantifiers and existential sentences in natural languages. *Journal of Semantics* 10: 33–64.

Chierchia, G. (1995). *Dynamics of Meaning.* Chicago: University of Chicago Press.

Dekker, P. (1993). Existential disclosure. *Linguistics and Philosophy* 16: 561–588.

Groeneveld, W. (1994). Dynamic semantics and circular propositions. *Journal of Philosophical Logic* 23: 267–306.

Krifka, M. (1993). Focus and presupposition in dynamic interpretation. *Journal of Semantics* 10: 269–300.

Veltman, F. J. M. M. (1996). Defaults in update Semantics. *Journal of Philosophical Logic* 25: 221–261.

Vermeulen, C. J. M. (1994). Incremental semantics for propositional texts. *Notre Dame Journal of Formal Logic* 35: 243–271.

Zeevat, H. J. (1994). Presupposition and accommodation in update Semantics. *Journal of Semantics* 12: 379–412.

Dynamical Systems

See ARTIFICIAL LIFE; DYNAMIC APPROACHES TO COGNITION; SELF-ORGANIZING SYSTEMS

Dyslexia

Dyslexia is a developmental disorder of READING that is based on abnormal brain development. The brain changes exist from before birth and persist throughout life, although they do not usually manifest themselves clinically until the early school years, and many sufferers of this disorder compensate significantly by the time they reach adult life. The etiology of dyslexia remains unknown, but it is clear that both genetic and environmental factors play a role in its clinical manifestations.

The term *dyslexia* is used in the United States to refer to a developmental disorder of reading, whereas in the United Kingdom acquired disorders of reading may also be called *dyslexias.* Whereas *dyslexia* appears as an entry in *ICD-9-CM for Neurologists* (Neurology 1994) to represent either developmental or acquired disorders of reading, *DSM-IV* (Association 1994) does not have an entry for dyslexia altogether and instead has one for *reading disorder.* In this article only the developmental form is considered.

Some researchers have been unhappy with the term *dyslexia* and prefer to use *developmental reading disorder* instead, even though the term *dyslexia* means reading disorder. In *DSM-IV* the definition for *reading disorder* includes reading achievement (accuracy, speed, and/or comprehension as measured by individually administered standardized tests) that falls substantially below that expected given the individual's chronological age, measured intelligence, and age-appropriate education. Sensory-perceptual, cognitive, psychiatric, or neurological problems may coexist with the reading disorder, but should not be sufficient to explain the reading underachievement.

Other researchers (see Shaywitz et al. 1992) do not consider that intelligence should be a factor in the diagnosis, and prefer to include all individuals with reading difficulties, even those who are frankly mentally retarded. Still others insist that the reading disorder should be the consequence of disturbances of language function (see Vellutino 1987), specifically phonological processing (see PHONOLOGY), and that a reading disorder resulting from other mechanisms not be included.

It is generally accepted that the reading disorder is often accompanied by problems with writing, arithmetic, verbal memory, and subtle motor dysfunction. Sometimes there is also coexistence of anomalous HEMISPHERIC SPECIALIZATION, ATTENTION deficits, and emotional and personality disorders. Subtle problems with oral language are also commonly seen, but the presence of more severe disturbances in oral communication gives rise to the diagnosis of developmental language impairment, albeit with associated disturbances in reading and writing.

Dyslexia is the most commonly recognized form of learning disorder. The prevalence of dyslexia is accepted by most to be in the order of 4–5 percent of the school-age population. Depending on how the condition is defined, the prevalence figures range between 1 percent and 35 percent. Although problems may persist into adulthood, no clear figures about clinical prevalence in adult age groups exist. Most studies have shown a male prevalence in excess of that for females in the range of three to four males to one female. Some of this discrepancy may relate to reporting bias (the argument is that dyslexic girls are better behaved and go unnoticed). However, even when this is taken into consideration, a significant male preponderance still remains. As with other complex behaviors, normal and abnormal, that have their origin in a genetic background with added environmental influences, the prevalence of dyslexia depends in part on its definition, severity, and sociocultural attitudes.

The most common form of dyslexia is associated with deficits in phonological processing (Morais, Luytens, and Alegria 1984; Shankweiler et al. 1995), but other varieties, some based on disturbances affecting the visual system, have also been identified (Lovegrove 1991; Stein 1994). A difficulty with processing rapidly changing stimuli, affecting at least visual and auditory functions has also been implicated, which blurs the distinction between perceptual and cognitive mechanisms in the etiology of dyslexia (Merzenich et al. 1996a, 1996b; Tallal et al. 1995). The temporal processing hypothesis states that sensory-perceptual temporal processing deficits impede the development of normal phonological representations in the brain, which in turn produce the reading disorder. The main idea is that reading requires knowledge of the normal sound structure of the language before appropriate sound-sight associations can be made. Sensory-perceptual temporal processing deficits may lead to difficulties representing some language sounds that require rapid processing, which in turn leads to an incomplete or ambiguous sound repertoire and consequently difficulty with reading. The main objection to this theory is based on observations such as the presence of normal reading in many deaf people, and the counterargument is that the reading disorder rather reflects a deficit in semiconscious parsing (metalinguistic) of the sound stream into phonemes, as a prerequisite for mapping the parsed elements onto visual words.

Neurophysiological and psychophysical studies have shown abnormalities in visual perception and eye movements in dyslexics (Cornelissen et al. 1991). These findings are consistent with dysfunction of the magnocellular pathway of the visual system, which among other functions deals with rapid temporal processing (Greatrex and Drasdo 1995; Livingstone et al. 1991). Psychophysical evidence indicated that language-impaired children exhibit slow processing in the auditory system, too (Tallal and Piercy 1975). More recently studies employing functional MAGNETIC RESONANCE IMAGING showed that the area involved in motion perception, MT, does not activate normally in dyslexics, an area that forms part of the magnocellular system (Eden et al. 1996). In sum, therefore, there is increasing evidence to suggest that rapid processing is impaired in dyslexics, which may help account for the phonological disorder and hence the reading disorder. The ongoing debate has to do with the question of whether the type and degree of temporal processing perceptual difficulty seen in dyslexics is sufficient for explaining their language problems (for instance, see Paulesu et al. 1996).

Dyslexia is associated with anatomic changes in the brain. The normal human brain often shows asymmetry in the planum temporale, a region concerned with language function. Normal brains that are not asymmetric in the planum temporale show two large planums, rather than two small ones or two medium-sized ones. Dyslexic brains fail to show the standard asymmetric or symmetric pattern in the planum temporale (Galaburda 1993), presumably indicating a disturbance in the development of hemispheric specialization for language (see Annett, Eglinton, and Smythe 1996).

There are also subtle changes in the lamination of the CEREBRAL CORTEX, which are focal in nature and affect the left cerebral hemisphere more than the right in most cases (Galaburda 1994). They consist mostly of displaced nests of

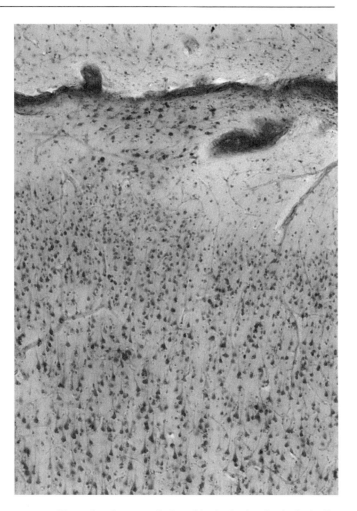

Figure 1. Example of an ectopia found in the brain of a dyslexic. In the upper part of the photomicrograph there is an extrusion of neurons and glia into the molecular layer (uppermost layer of the cortex). This is one example of a neuronal migration anomaly.

neurons and glia in the frontal, parietal, and temporal cortex. These anomalies, called *ectopias* (see figure 1), reflect disturbances in neuronal migration to the cerebral cortex during fetal brain development. The fundamental cause of the migration disturbance, though suspected to be genetic, is not known (for a review of recent work on the genetics of dyslexia, see Pennington 1995).

Associated with the ectopias in the cerebral cortex are changes in the sizes of neurons of some thalamic sensory nuclei, including the visually linked lateral geniculate nucleus (LGN) (Livingstone et al. 1991) and the auditory medial geniculate nucleus (MGN; Galaburda, Menard, and Rosen 1994). These are structures close to the input channels for visual and auditory experience and are not involved in cognitive functions but rather in sensory perceptual functions. In the LGN, the neurons comprising the magnocellular layers are smaller in dyslexic than in control brains, and in the MGN there is a shift toward an excess of small neurons and a paucity of large neurons in the left hemisphere.

Ectopias have been induced in newborn rats, and the displaced neurons exhibit abnormal connections with neurons in the THALAMUS as well as with other cortical areas in the ipsilateral and contralateral cerebral hemispheres (Rosen and Galaburda 1996). This provides a possible conduit for the propagation of changes from the ectopias to the thalamus and/or vice versa. Additional research has shown that induction of cortical malformations related to ectopias lead to secondary changes in the thalamus, namely the appearance of excessive numbers of small neurons and a paucity of large neurons (Herman et al. 1997). The animals with the induced malformations also exhibit slow temporal processing involving rapidly changing sounds. There are sex differences in these findings, such that induction of cortical malformations produce both behavioral changes and changes in thalamic neuronal sizes only in treated males. Females demonstrate the anatomic changes in the cortex, but no changes in the thalamus and no abnormal slowing in auditory processing. Moreover, administration of testosterone to pregnant rat mothers in the perinatal period produces masculinization of the female offspring complete with thalamic neuronal changes (Rosen, Herman, and Galaburda 1997).

In summary, animal models for the brain changes seen in association with developmental dyslexia indicate that abnormal cortical development can lead to abnormal development of the thalamus, and that it is likely that brain areas that deal with cognitive tasks and brain areas that deal with sensory-perceptual tasks are both affected in dyslexia. Moreover, the research indicates that multiple modalities, as well as multiple stages of processing, are involved, which may limit the ability of the developing brain to compensate. On the other hand, because of the relative discreteness of the neural connections even during development, not all cortical and thalamic areas are affected, setting up the possibility for a relatively delimited form of learning disorder.

See also APHASIA; GESCHWIND; LANGUAGE IMPAIRMENT, DEVELOPMENTAL; MODELING NEUROPSYCHOLOGICAL DEFICITS; VISUAL WORD RECOGNITION; WRITING SYSTEMS

—*Albert M. Galaburda*

References

Annett, M., E. Eglinton, and P. Smythe. (1996). Types of dylexia and the shift to dextrality. *J. Child Psychol. Psychiat.* 37: 167–180.

Association, A. P. (1994). *Diagnostic and Statistical Manual of Mental Disorders—DSM-IV.* Washington, DC: 4th ed. American Psychiatric Association.

Cornelissen, P., L. Bradley, S. Fowler, and J. Stein. (1991). What children see affects how they read. *Dev. Med. Child Neurol.* 33: 755–762.

Eden, G. F., J. W. Vanmeter, J. M. Rumsey, J. M. Maisog, R. P. Woods, and T. A. Zeffiro. (1996). Abnormal processing of visual motion in dyslexia revealed by functional brain imaging. *Nature* 382: 66–69.

Galaburda, A. (1993). Neuroanatomic basis of developmental dyslexia. *Behavioral Neurology* 11: 161–173.

Galaburda, A. (1994). Developmental dyslexia and animal studies: At the interface between cognition and neurology. *Cognition* 50: 133–149.

Galaburda, A. M., M. T. Menard, and G. D. Rosen. (1994). Evidence for aberrant auditory anatomy in developmental dyslexia. *Proc. Natl. Acad. Sci. USA* 91: 8010–8013.

Greatrex, J. C., and N. Drasdo. (1995). The magnocellular deficit hypothesis in dyslexia: A review of the reported evidence. *Ophthalmic Physiol. Opt.* 15: 501–506.

Herman, A. E., A. M. Galaburda, H. R. Fitch, A. R. Carter, and G. D. Rosen. (1997). Cerebral thalamic cell size and microgyria auditory temporal processing in male and female rats. *Cerebral Cortex* 7: 453–464.

Livingstone, M., G. Rosen, F. Drislane, and A. Galaburda. (1991). Physiological and anatomical evidence for a magnocellular defect in developmental dyslexia. *Proc. Natl. Acad. Sci.* 88: 7943–7947.

Lovegrove, W. J. (1991). Is the question of the role of visual deficits as a cause of reading disabilities a closed one? Comments on Hulme. *Cognitive Neuropsychology* 8: 435–441.

Merzenich, M. M., W. M. Jenkins, P. Johnston, C. Schreiner, S. L. Miller, and P. Tallal. (1996a). Temporal processing deficits of language-learning impaired children ameliorated by training. *Science* 271: 77–80.

Merzenich, M. M., W. M. Jenkins, P. Johnston, C. Schreiner, S. L. Miller, and P. Tallal. (1996b). Temporal processing deficits of language-learning impaired children ameliorated by training. *Science* 271: 77–81.

Morais, J., M. Luytens, and J. Alegria. (1984). Segmentation abilities of dyslexics and normal readers. *Percep. Motor Skills* 58: 221–222.

Neurology, T. A. A. o. (1994). *ICD-9-CM for Neurologists.* 3rd ed. Minneapolis: The American Academy of Neurology.

Paulesu, E., U. Frith, M. Snowling, A. Gallagher, J. Morton, R. S. J. Frackowiak, and C. D. Frith. (1996). Is developmental dyslexia a disconnection syndrome? Evidence from PET scanning. *Brain* 119: 143–157.

Pennington, B. F. (1995). Genetics of learning disabilities. *J. Chi. Neurol.* 10: S69–S77.

Rosen, G. D., and A. M. Galaburda. (1996). Efferent and afferent connectivity of induced neocortical microgyria. *Soc. Neurosci. Abstr.* 22: 485.

Rosen, G. D., A. E. Herman, and A. M. Galaburda. (1997). MGN neuronal size distribution following induced neocortical malformations: The effect of perinatal gonadal steroids. *Soc. Neurosci. Abstr.* 23: 626.

Shankweiler, D., S. Crain, L. Katz, A. E. Fowler, A. M. Liberman, S. A. Brady, R. Thornton, E. Lundquist, L. Dreyer, J. M. Fletcher, K. K. Stuebing, S. E. Shaywitz, and B. A. Shaywitz. (1995). Cognitive profiles of reading-disabled children: Comparison of language skills in morphology, phonology, and syntax. *Psychological Science* 6: 149–156.

Shaywitz, B., J. Fletcher, J. Holahan, and S. Shaywitz. (1992). Discrepancy compared to low achievement definitions of reading disability: Results from the Connecticut longitudinal study. *Journal of Learning Disabilities* 25: 639–648.

Stein, J. F. (1994). Developmental neural timing and dyslexia hemispheric lateralisation. *Int. J. Psychophysiol.* 18: 241–249.

Tallal, P., S. Miller, R. H. Fitch, J. F. Stein, K. McAnally, A. J. Richardson, A. J. Fawcett, C. Jacobson, and R. I. Nicholson. (1995). Dyslexia update. *The Irish Journal of Psychology* 16: 194–268.

Tallal, P., and M. Piercy. (1975). Developmental aphasia: The perception of brief vowels and extended stop consonants. *Neuropsychologia* 13: 69–74.

Vellutino, F. R. (1987). Dyslexia. *Sci. Amer.* 256: 34–41.

Ebbinghaus, Hermann

Hermann Ebbinghaus (1850–1909) was the first psychologist to apply experimental methods to the study of human MEMORY. His groundbreaking book summarizing his experimental work, *Über das Gedächtnis,* was published in 1885.

The English translation appeared in 1913 as *Memory: A Contribution to Experimental Psychology* and is still in print and well worth reading today.

Ebbinghaus was born in Barmen, Germany, studied at the University of Bonn, and began his pioneering research on memory in Berlin in 1878. His work is notable for its many original features. In addition to performing the first experiments on memory, he provided an authoritative review of probability and statistics, an elegant command of experimental design, a mathematical model of the forgetting function, an enlightened discussion of problems of experimenter bias and demand characteristics in research, and a set of experimental results that has stood the test of time. All the experiments reported by Ebbinghaus have been replicated.

No one knows how he created his ingenious methods, although historians have speculated that his purchase of a copy of Fechner's book (in English) (1860/1966) and his reading about psychophysical methods may have been the source of his own clever methodology (see PSYCHOPHYSICS). Ebbinghaus solved the three problems faced by all cognitive/experimental psychologists in their work: to convert unobservable mental processes into observable behavior; to measure the behavior reliably; and to show how the behavior is systematically affected by relevant factors and conditions.

Ebbinghaus solved these problems by creating long lists of nonsense syllables (ZOK, VAM, etc.) to be memorized. He hoped that using these materials would permit him to study formation of new associations with relatively homogeneous materials. He learned the lists by reciting them in time to a metronome and measuring the amount of time or the number of repetitions taken until he could recite a list perfectly. He discovered quickly that the longer the list, the more repetitions were required to effect a perfect recitation. Although this was hardly a surprising finding, Ebbinghaus plotted the exact relation between the length of the series and the amount of time (or number of repetitions) to recall it once perfectly, a measure known as *trials to criterion*. He then had to determine how to measure retention of the series at some later point in time. Ebbinghaus's clever idea was to have himself relearn the list to the same criterion (of one perfect recitation); he could then obtain the savings (in time or repetitions) in relearning the series and use it as his measure of list retention. The greater the savings (the fewer trials to relearn the series), the greater is retention; conversely, if the same number of trials is needed to relearn the series as was originally required to learn it, then its forgetting was complete.

The beauty of Ebbinghaus's relearning and savings method is that measures of retention could be obtained even when recall of the list items was absent. This is one reason Ebbinghaus preferred his objective savings technique over what he called introspective techniques, such as recall or recognition. In a sense, ten years before FREUD proposed his ideas of unconscious mentation, Ebbinghaus had already devised a method whereby they could be studied. Even if someone failed to bring information to mind consciously, the unconscious residue could be examined through his relearning and savings technique.

Ebbinghaus made many discoveries with his new methods. He obtained a relatively precise relation between number of repetitions and forgetting: For every three repetitions of a list, he saved one repetition in relearning it a week later. He also discovered the logarithmic nature of the forgetting function; great forgetting occurred soon after learning, with the rate of forgetting slowing over time. In addition, he fitted an equation to the forgetting function. He also discovered the advantage of spaced repetitions of lists to massed repetition, when he found that "38 repetitions, distributed in a certain way over the three preceding days, has just as favorable an effect as 68 repetitions made on the day just previous" (page 89).

Ebbinghaus asked the question of whether associations were only formed directly, between adjacent nonsense syllables, or whether in addition remote associations were formed between syllables that were not adjacent. Using the symbols A, B, C, D, E, F, G, and H to represent syllables in a list to be learned, he asked whether there are only associations between A and B, B and C, and so on, or whether there are also associations (albeit presumably weaker ones) between A and C, A and D, and so on. Ebbinghaus developed a clever transfer of training design to answer the question. He derived lists for relearning that had associations of varying remoteness, which can be symbolized as ACEG . . . BDFH (for one degree of remoteness) or ADG . . . BEH . . . CF for two degrees of remoteness, and so on. He discovered that he did show savings in relearning these derived lists relative to control lists (that had no associations), and he concluded that the savings were the result of remote associations. In reviewing Ebbinghaus's work, William JAMES (1890) noted that "Dr. Ebbinghaus's attempt is as successful as it is original, in bringing two views, which seem at first sight inaccessible to proof, to a direct and practical test, and giving the victory to one of them" (page 677). The derived list experiments might be the first case of competitive hypothesis testing between two theories in experimental psychology.

Ebbinghaus was the only subject in all of his experiments, and this fact might give rise to doubt about the results. But he was a meticulous scientist, employing LOGIC, controls, and precise techniques far ahead of this time. All his results have stood the test of time. His particular methods of studying memory were rather quickly supplanted by other techniques—the introspective techniques of recall and recognition that he had wished to avoid—but his great achievements live on. He was the pioneer in showing how complex and unconscious mental processes could be studied through objective means by careful, systematic observation. As such, he helped pave the way for modern cognitive/experimental psychology.

See also BARTLETT; EPISODIC VS. SEMANTIC MEMORY; IMPLICIT VS. EXPLICIT MEMORY; INTROSPECTION

—*Henry L. Roediger*

References

Ebbinghaus, H. (1964). *Memory: A Contribution to Experimental Psychology*. Trans. H. A. Ruber and C. E. Bussenius. New York: Dover. Original work published 1885.

Fechner, G. (1860/1966). *Elements of Psychophysics*. Vol. 1. H. E. Adler, D. H. Howes, and E. G. Boring, Eds. and Trans. New York: Holt, Rinehart, and Winston.

James, W. (1890). *Principles of Psychology.* New York: Holt.

Postman, L. (1968). Hermann Ebbinghaus. *American Psychologist* 23: 149–157.

Roediger, H. L. (1985). Remembering Ebbinghaus. *Contemporary Psychology* 30: 519–523.

Tulving, E. (1992). Ebbinghaus, Hermann. In L. R. Squire, Ed., *Encyclopedia of Learning and Memory.* New York: Macmillan.

Echolocation

Echolocation, a term first coined by Donald Griffin in 1944, refers to the use of sound reflections to localize objects and orient in the environment (Griffin 1958). Echolocating animals transmit acoustic signals and process information contained in the reflected signals, permitting the detection, localization and identification of objects. The use of echolocation has been documented in bats (e.g., Griffin 1958), marine mammals (e.g., Norris et al. 1961; Au 1993), some species of nocturnal birds (e.g., Griffin 1953) and to a limited extent in blind or blindfolded humans (e.g., Rice 1967). Only in bats and dolphins have specialized perceptual and neural processes for echolocation been detailed.

Acoustic signals for echolocation in bats and marine mammals are primarily in the ultrasonic range, above 20 kHz and the upper limit of human hearing. The short wavelengths of these ultrasound signals permit reflections from small objects in the environment. All bat species of the suborder Microchiroptera produce echolocation calls, either through the open mouth or through a nose-leaf, depending on the species. The signal types used by different bat species vary widely, but all contain some frequency modulated (FM) components, which are well suited to carry information about the arrival time of target echoes. Constant frequency (CF) signal components are sometimes combined with FM components, and these signals are well suited to carry information about target movement through Doppler shifts in the returning echoes. There is evidence that species using both FM and CF signals show individual variations in signal structure that could facilitate identification of self-produced echoes (see Suga et al. 1987; Masters, Jacobs, and Simmons 1991). One species of echolocating bat of the suborder Megachiropetera, *Rosettus aegyptiacus,* produces clicklike sounds with the tongue for echolocation (Novick 1958). The most widely studied echolocating marine mammal, the bottlenose dolphin (*Tursiops truncatus*), emits brief clicks, typically less than 50 µs in duration, with spectral energy from 20 kHz to over 100 kHz, depending on the acoustic environment in which the sounds are produced (Au 1993).

In echolocating animals, detection of a sonar target depends on the strength of the returning echo (Griffin 1958). Large sonar targets reflecting strong echoes are detected at greater distances than small sonar targets (Kick 1982; Au 1993). Psychophysical studies of echo detection in bats and dolphins indicate a strong dependence of performance on the acoustic environment. Forward and backward masking, background noise level, and reverberation can all influence sonar target detection (Au 1993; Moss and Schnitzler 1995).

Once an animal detects a sonar target, it must localize the object in three-dimensional space. In bats, the horizontal location of the target influences the features of the echo at the two ears, and these interaural cues permit calculation of a target's azimuthal position in space (Shimozowa et al. 1974). Laboratory studies of target tracking along the horizontal axis in bats suggest an accuracy of approximately 1 deg (Masters et al. 1985). The vertical location of a target results in a distinctive travel path of the echo into the bat's external ear, producing spectral changes in the returning sound that can be used to code target elevation (Grinnell and Grinnell 1965). Accuracy of vertical localization in bats is approximately 3 deg (Lawrence and Simmons 1982). The third dimension, target distance, depends on the time delay between the outgoing sound and returning echo (Hartridge 1945; Simmons 1973). Psychophysical studies of distance discrimination in FM bats report thresholds of about 1 cm, corresponding to a difference in echo arrival time of approximately 60 microseconds. Experiments that require the bat to detect a change in the distance (echo delay) of a jittering target report thresholds of less than 0.1 mm, corresponding to a temporal jitter in echo arrival time of less than 1 microsecond. Successful interception of insect prey by bats requires accuracy of only 1–2 cm (summarized in Moss and Schnitzler 1995). In marine mammals, psychophysical data show that the dolphin can discriminate a target range difference of approximately 1 cm, performance similar to that of the echolocating bat (Murchison 1980).

Many bats that use CF-FM signals are specialized to detect and process frequency and amplitude modulations in the returning echoes that are produced by fluttering insect prey. The CF components of these signals are relatively long in duration (up to 100 ms), sufficient to encode target movement from a fluttering insect over one or more wingbeat cycles. The CF-FM greater horseshoe bat, *Rhinolophus ferrumequinum,* can discriminate frequency modulations in the returning echo of approximately 30 Hz (less than 0.5% of the bat's 83 kHz CF signal component), and can discriminate fluttering insect species with different echo signatures (von der Emde and Schnitzler 1990). Several bat species that use CF-FM signals for echolocation exhibit Doppler shift compensation behavior: the bat adjusts the frequency of its sonar transmission to offset a Doppler shift in the returning echo, the magnitude of which depends on the bat's flight velocity (Schnitzler and Henson 1980). Doppler shift compensation allows the bat to isolate small amplitude and frequency modulations in sonar echoes that are produced by fluttering insects.

High-level perception by sonar has been examined in some bat species. Early work by Griffin et al. (1965) demonstrated that FM-bats can discriminate between mealworms and disks tossed into the air. Both mealworms and disks presented changing surface areas as they tumbled through the air, and this study suggested that FM-bats use complex echo features to discriminate target shape. The acoustic basis for target shape discrimination by FM-bats has been considered in detail by Simmons and Chen (1989); however, researchers have not yet determined whether FM bat species develop three-dimensional representations of objects using sonar (see Moss and Schnitzler 1995). Three-dimensional recognition of fluttering insects has been reported in the greater horseshoe bat, a species that uses a CF-FM signal for echolocation (von der Emde and Schnitzler 1990).

Successful echolocation depends on specializations in the auditory receiver to detect and process echoes of the transmitted sonar signals. Central to the conclusive demonstration of echolocation in bats was data on hearing sensitivity in the ultrasonic range of the biological sonar signals (Griffin 1958), and subsequent research has detailed many interesting specializations for the processing of sonar echoes in the auditory receiver of bats. In dolphins, studies of the central auditory system have been limited, but early work clearly documents high frequency hearing in the ultrasonic range of echolocation calls (e.g., Bullock et al. 1968).

In some CF-FM bat species, there are specializations in the peripheral and central auditory systems for processing echoes in the frequency range of the CF sonar component. The greater horseshoe bat, for example, adjusts the frequency of its sonar emissions to receive echoes at a reference frequency of approximately 83 kHz. The auditory system of this species shows a large proportion of neurons devoted to processing this reference frequency, and this expanded representation of 83 kHz can be traced to mechanical specializations of this bat's cochlea (Kössl and Vater 1995).

There are other specializations in the bat central auditory system for echo processing that may play a role in the perception of target distance. In bat species that utilize CF-FM signals and those that utilize FM sonar components alone, there are neurons in the midbrain, THALAMUS and cortex that respond selectively to pairs of FM sounds separated by a delay (e.g., Yan and Suga 1996). The pairs of FM sounds simulate the bat's sonar transmissions and returning echoes, and the time delay separating the two corresponds to a particular target distance. The pulse-echo delay evoking the largest facilitated response, referred to as the best delay (BD), is in some CF-FM bat species topographically organized (Suga and O'Neill 1979). Neural BD's fall into a biologically relevant range of 2–40 ms, corresponding to target distances of approximately 34 to 690 cm. Such topography has not been demonstrated in FM-bat species (e.g., Dear et al. 1993).

Many specializations in behavior and central auditory processing appear in echolocating animals; however, research findings suggest that echolocation builds on the neural and perceptual systems that evolved for hearing in less specialized animals.

See also ANIMAL COMMUNICATION; AUDITION; AUDITORY PHYSIOLOGY; PSYCHOPHYSICS; SPATIAL PERCEPTION; WHAT-IT'S-LIKE

—*Cynthia F. Moss*

References

Au, W. L. (1993). *The Sonar of Dolphins.* New York: Springer.

Bullock, T. H., A. D. Grinnell, E. Ikenzono, K. Kameda, Y. Katsuki, M. Nomoto, O. Sato, N. Suga, and K. Yanagisawa. (1968). Electrophysiological studies of central auditory mechanisms in cetaceans. *Zeitschrift für Vergleichende Physiologie* 59: 117–316.

Dear, S. P., J. Fritz, T. Haresign, M. Ferragamo, and J. A. Simmons. (1993). Tonotopic and functional organization in the auditory cortex of the big brown bat, *Eptesicus fuscus. Journal of Neurophysiology* 70: 1988–2009.

Emde, G. v. d., and H-V. Schnitzler. (1990). Classification of insects by echolocating greater horseshoe bats. *Journal of Comparative Physiology A* 167: 423–430.

Griffin, D. R. (1944). Echolocation in blind men, bats and radar. *Science* 100: 589–590.

Griffin, D. R. (1953). Acoustic orientation in the oilbird, *Steatornis. Proc. Nat. Acad. Sci. USA* 39: 884–893.

Griffin, D. R. (1958). *Listening in the Dark.* New Haven: Yale University Press.

Griffin, D. R., J. H Friend, and F. A. Webster. (1965). Target discrimination by the echolocation of bats. *Journal of Experimental Zoology* 158: 155–168.

Grinnell, A. D., and V. S. Grinnell. (1965). Neural correlates of vertical localization by echolocating bats. *Journal of Physiology* 181: 830–851.

Hartridge, H. (1945). Acoustic control in the flight of bats. *Nature* 156: 490–494.

Kick, S. A. (1982). Target-detection by the echolocating bat, *Eptesicus fuscus. Journal of Comparative Physiology A* 145: 431–435.

Kössl, M., and M. Vater. (1995). Cochlear structure and function in bats. In R. R. Fay and A. N. Popper, Eds., *Springer Handbook of Auditory Research. Hearing by Bats.* Berlin: Springer-Verlag.

Lawrence, B. D., and J. A. Simmons. (1982). Echolocation in bats: The external ear and perception of the vertical positions of targets. *Science* 218: 481–483.

Masters, W. M., A. J. M. Moffat, and J. R. Simmons. (1985). Sonar tracking of horizontally moving targets by the big brown bat, *Eptesicus fuscus. Science* 228: 1331–1333

Masters, W. M., S. C. Jacobs, and J. A. Simmons. (1991). The structure of echolocation sounds used by the big brown bat *Eptesicus fuscus:* Some consequences for echo processing. *Journal of the Acoustical Society of America* 89: 1402–1413.

Moss, C. F., and H.-U. Schnitzler. (1995). Behavioral studies of auditory information processing. In R. R. Fay and A. N. Popper, Eds., *Springer Handbook of Auditory Research. Hearing by Bats.* Berlin: Springer-Verlag, pp. 87–145.

Murchison, A. E. (1980). Maximum detetion range and range resolution in echolocating bottlenose porpoise *(Tursiops tuncatus).* In R. G. Busnel and J. F. Fish, Eds., *Animal Sonar Systems.* New York: Plenum Press, pp. 43–70.

Norris, K. S., J. W. Prescott, P. V. Asa-Dorian, and P. Perkins. (1961). An experimental demonstration of echolocation behavior in the porpoise, *Tursiops truncatus* (Montagu). *Biological Bulletin* 120: 163–176.

Novick, A. (1958). Orientation in palaeotropical bats. II. Megachiroptera. *Journal of Experimental Zoology* 137: 443–462.

Rice, C. (1967). Human echo perception. *Science* 155: 656–664.

Schnitzler, H.-U., and W. Henson Jr. (1980). Performance of airborne animal sonar systems: 1. Microchiroptera. In R. G. Busnel and J. F. Fish, Eds., *Animal sonar systems* New York: Plenum Press, pp. 109–181.

Shimozawa, T., N. Suga, P. Hendler, and S. Schuetze. (1974). Directional sensitivity of echolocation system in bats producing frequency-modulated signals. *Journal of Experimental Biology* 60: 53–69.

Simmons, J. A. (1973). The resolution of target range by echolocating bats. *Journal of the Acoustical Society of America* 54: 157–173.

Simmons, J. A., and L. Chen. (1989). The acoustic basis for target discrimination by FM echolocating bats. *Journal of the Acoustical Society of America* 86: 1333–1350.

Suga, N., H. Niwa, I. Taniguchi, and D. Margoliash. (1987). The personalized auditory cortex of the mustached bat: Adaptation for echolocation. *Journal of Neurophysiology* 58: 643–654.

Suga, N., and W. E. O'Neill. (1979). Neural axis representing target range in the auditory cortex of the mustache bat. *Science* 206: 351–353.

Yan, J., and N. Suga. (1996). The midbrain creates and the thalamus sharpens echo-delay tuning for the cortical representation of target-distance information in the mustached bat. *Hearing Research* 93: 102–110.

Further Readings

Busnel, R. G., and J. F. Fish. (1980). *Animal Sonar Systems*. New York: Plenum Press.

Dror, I. E., M. Zagaeski, and C. F. Moss. (1995). Three-dimensional target recognition via sonar: A neural network model. *Neural Networks* 8: 143–154.

Fay, R. R., and A. N. Popper. (1995). *Springer Handbook of Auditory Research. Hearing by Bats*. Berlin: Springer.

Nachtigall, P. E., and P. W. B. Moore. (1988). *Animal Sonar: Processes and Performance*. New York: Plenum Press.

Pollak, G. D., and J. H. Casseday. (1989). *The Neural Basis of Echolocation in Bats*. Berlin: Springer.

Rice, C. E., S. H. Feinstein, and R. J. Schusterman. (1965). Echo-detection ability of the blind: Size and distance factors. *Journal of Experimental Psychology* 70: 246–251.

Suga, N. (1988). What does single unit analysis in the auditory cortex tell us about information processing in the auditory system? In P. Rakic and W. Singer, Eds., *Neurobiology of Neocortex*. New York: Wiley.

Supa, M., M. Cotzin, and K. M. Dallenbach. "Facial vision," the perception of obstacles by the blind. *American Journal of Psychology* 57: 133–183.

Ecological Psychology

The term *ecological* has been used to characterize several theoretical positions in psychology, but only one—that of James J. GIBSON (1966, 1979) and his successors—is clearly relevant to cognitive science. (The others are Barker's descriptions of social behavior settings and Bronfenbrenner's analysis of the many contexts that influence the developing child; see ECOLOGICAL VALIDITY.) Gibson's views—and their subsequent development by other theorists—are the focus of the *International Society for Ecological Psychology*. The Society's journal *Ecological Psychology* has been published since 1989; the ecologically oriented *International Conference on Event Perception and Action* has met every two years since 1981.

The ecological approach rejects the cognitivist assumption of the poverty of the stimulus, that is, that perceivers must rely on MENTAL REPRESENTATIONS because they have access only to fragmentary and fallible sense-data. It also rejects many of the conventional variables that are usually regarded as the objects of perception: (absolute) distance, (absolute) size, (two-dimensional) form, etc. What people and animals actually perceive includes the *layout of the environment* (the arrangement of objects and surfaces, relative to one another and to the ground), the *shapes* of objects, the *self* (the perceiver's own situation in and motion through the layout), *events* (various types of movement and change),

and especially AFFORDANCES, possibilities for effective action. These things are perceivable because they are specified by information available to appropriately tuned perceptual systems. The task of ecological psychology is to analyze that information, and to understand how animals regulate their encounters with the environment by taking advantage of it.

The ecological analysis of vision begins not with the retinal image but with the *optic array*. At any point of observation to which an eye might come there is already an optical structure, formed by ambient light reflected to the point from all directions. Even a static array of such points is rich in information, but the transformations generated by observer motion are richer still: they specify the layout of the environment and the perceiver's path of motion uniquely. The *visual system* that evolved to take advantage of this information consists of a hierarchy of active organs: a pair of movable eyes, each with its lens and chamber and retina, stabilized in their orbits by the ocular muscles and set in a mobile head on a moving body (Gibson 1966). Note that the brain does not appear in this definition: the specialized neural mechanisms essential to vision have been of relatively little interest to ecological psychologists. Vision would be impossible without the brain, but it would be equally impossible without the optic array and the mobile organs of vision.

Much of the early research in ecological psychology focused on movement-produced information, which had been largely neglected in other approaches to perception. Kinetic *occlusion*, for example, occurs when nearby objects hide (or reveal) others beyond them as a result of observer or object motion. In occlusion, visible elements of surface texture are systematically deleted at one side of the occluding edge but not at the other. The result is a compelling impression of relative depth as well as a perceptual form of object permanence: one sees that the occluded object is going out of sight without going out of existence (see also DEPTH PERCEPTION). Movement-produced information (including deformations of shading, highlights, etc.) also plays a significant role in the perception of object shape (Norman, Todd, and Phillips 1995).

Another form of kinetic structure is *optic flow*, the characteristic streaming of the array produced by observer motion. Such flows have powerful effects on posture and can create vivid illusions of self-motion. Optic flow also enables perceivers to determine their heading (i.e., the direction in which they are moving), but the details of this process are presently controversial (Cutting 1996; Warren 1995). For more on optic flow, see MID-LEVEL VISION.

Looming is the rapid magnification of a sector of the array that occurs when an object approaches the eye or the eye approaches a surface. Looming specifies impending collision, and animals of many different species—humans, monkeys, chickens, crabs—respond appropriately. The time remaining before collision (assuming unchanged velocity) is optically specified by a variable called *tau* (Lee 1980). (If X is the visual angle subtended by the approaching object or any of its parts, the tau-function is $\tau(X) = X/[dX/dt]$.) A considerable body of evidence suggests that humans and other animals use tau-related information in the control of action (e.g., Lee 1993), although the issue is not closed.

Given their focus on information structures rather than stimuli, ecological psychologists have been especially interested in *amodal invariants* available to more than one perceptual system. It is easy, for example, to match the shapes of seen objects with shapes felt with the hand (Gibson 1962)—easy not just for humans but for chimpanzees (Davenport, Rogers, and Russell 1973). Runeson and Frykholm (1981) have shown that one can judge the weight of a box just as well by watching someone else lift it as by lifting it oneself, even if one's view of the lifter is just a "point-light" display. Even infants can pick up many types of tactile-visual and audiovisual invariants, matching what they see to what they hear or feel. At any age, the perceived unity of environmental events—a person seen and heard as she walks by, the breaking of a glass that falls on the floor—depends on our sensitivity to amodal invariants.

Ecological psychologists have been among the leaders in the study of infant perception and PERCEPTUAL DEVELOPMENT. A case in point is the discovery, cited above, that infants are sensitive to amodal invariants. Another example concerns infant locomotion: reinterpreting her classical studies of the "visual cliff," E. J. Gibson has shown that babies' willingness to venture onto a surface depends on their perception of its affordances. A sharp dropoff affords falling but not crawling; an undulating waterbed affords crawling but not walking (Gibson et al. 1987); sloping surfaces afford various modes of exploration and locomotion (Adolph, Eppler, and Gibson 1993).

J. J. Gibson's (1966) concept of a *perceptual system* (as opposed to a sensory modality) is particularly useful in the study of HAPTIC PERCEPTION and dynamic touch. (The older term *tactile perception* suggests a more passive form of experience.) The haptic system includes a rich complex of afferent and efferent nerves as well as the skin, underlying tissues, muscles, digits, and joints. This system is capable of remarkable feats: one can, for example, determine a great deal about the length, shape, and other properties of an (unseen) rigid rod simply by wielding it with one hand. Michael Turvey (1996) and his associates have shown that the rotational/mechanical invariants on which this form of perception is based can be summarized in the inertia tensor I_{ij}, which represents the moments of inertia specific to a given object rotated around a fixed point. Because we "wield" our own limbs in much the same sense, the inertia tensor may provide a partial basis for self-perception as well. "Simply put, moving one's limbs can be considered a case of dynamic touch" (Pagano and Turvey 1995: 1081).

Ecological psychologists have also made substantial contributions to the study of motor control. Effective action requires the coordination of many simultaneously moving body parts, each with its own inertia and other physical attributes. That coordination must be matched to the specific affordances of the immediate environment, and hence cannot be achieved by any centrally programmed pattern of impulses. This problem has been widely recognized (see MOTOR CONTROL); part of the solution may be the formation of task-specific *coordinative structures*. "A group of muscles spanning several different joints, and capable of contracting independently of each other, can become functionally linked so as to perform as a single task-specific unit" (Turvey 1990: 940). Turvey and his collaborators have developed this concept in a series of studies of coordinated movements.

Other perceptual systems have been studied as well: as a first step toward an ecological analysis of hearing, Gaver (1993) has recently outlined a descriptive framework for the sounds of everyday events. Fowler (1986) has advanced an ecological approach to SPEECH PERCEPTION, which can be regarded as a special case of the perception of events (specifically, the movements of the articulatory organs). Stoffregen and Riccio (1988) have proposed an ecological analysis of the vestibular system and related phenomena such as motion sickness.

Since J. J. Gibson's death in 1979, theory development in ecological psychology has taken two principal forms. On the one hand is the development of increasingly sophisticated formal descriptions of environmental structure and the information that specifies it (e.g., Bingham 1995); more generally, of animal/environment mutuality (Turvey and Shaw 1995). On the other hand are various attempts to broaden the enterprise, using ecological concepts to address a range of classical psychological issues. In this vein are Eleanor Gibson's (1994) elaboration of her theory of development, Walker-Andrews's (1997) account of the perception of emotion, my own analysis of self-perception (Neisser 1993), and the wide-ranging theoretical work of Edward Reed. Reed's book *The Necessity of Experience* (1996b) is a philosophical and political critique of the assumptions underlying standard cognitive science; its companion volume *Encountering the World* (1996a) presents ecological analyses of many topics in psychology. "Cognition," says Reed, "is neither copying nor constructing the world. Cognition is, instead, the process that keeps us active, changing creatures in touch with an eventful, changing world" (1996a: 13).

See also AFFORDANCES; GIBSON, JAMES JEROME; PERCEPTUAL DEVELOPMENT

—*Ulric Neisser*

References

Adolph, K. E., M. A. Eppler, and E. J. Gibson. (1993). Crawling versus walking infants' perception of affordances for locomotion over sloping surfaces. *Child Development* 64: 1158–1174.

Bingham, G. P. (1995). Dynamics and the problem of visual event recognition. In R. Port and T. Van Gelder, Eds., *Mind as Motion: Explorations in the Dynamics of Cognition.* Cambridge, MA: MIT Press.

Cutting, J. E. (1996). Wayfinding from multiple sources of local information in retinal flow. *Journal of Experimental Psychology: Human Perception and Performance* 22: 1299–1313.

Davenport, R. K., C. M. Rogers, and I. S. Russell. (1973). Cross-modal perception in apes. *Neuropsychologia* 11: 21–28.

Fowler, C. A. (1986). An event approach to the study of speech perception from a direct-realist perspective. *Journal of Phonetics* 14: 3–28.

Gaver, W. W. (1993). How do we hear in the world? Explorations in ecological acoustics. *Ecological Psychology* 5: 285–313.

Gibson, E. J. (1994). Has psychology a future? *Psychological Science* 5: 69–76.

Gibson, E. J., G. Riccio, M. A. Schmuckler, T. A. Stoffregen, D. Rosenberg, and J. Taormina. (1987). Detection of the traversability of surfaces by crawling and walking infants. *Journal of Experimental Psychology: Human Perception and Performance* 13: 533–544.

Gibson, J. J. (1966). *The Senses Considered as Perceptual Systems.* Boston: Houghton Mifflin.

Gibson, J. J. (1979). *The Ecological Approach to Visual Perception.* Boston: Houghton Mifflin.

Lee, D. N. (1980). The optic flow field: The foundation of vision. *Philosophical Transactions of the Royal Society of London B* 290: 169–179.

Lee, D. N. (1993). Body-environment coupling. In U. Neisser, Ed., *The Perceived Self.* New York: Cambridge University Press, pp. 43–67.

Neisser, U., Ed. (1993). *The Perceived Self: Ecological and Interpersonal Sources of Self-Knowledge.* New York: Cambridge University Press.

Norman, J. F., J. T. Todd, and F. Phillips. (1995). The perception of surface orientation from multiple sources of information. *Perception and Psychophysics* 57: 629–636.

Pagano, C. C., and M. T. Turvey. (1995). The inertia tensor as a basis for the perception of limb orientation. *Journal of Experimental Psychology: Human Perception and Performance* 21: 1070–1087.

Reed, E. S. (1996a). *Encountering the World: Toward an Ecological Psychology.* New York: Oxford University Press.

Reed, E. S. (1996b). *The Necessity of Experience.* New Haven: Yale University Press.

Runeson, S., and G. Frykholm. (1981). Visual perception of lifted weight. *Journal of Experimental Psychology: Human Perception and Performance* 7: 733–740.

Stoffregen, T. A., and G. E. Riccio. (1988). An ecological theory of orientation and the vestibular system. *Psychological Review* 95: 3–14.

Turvey, M. T. (1990). Coordination. *American Psychologist* 45: 938–953.

Turvey, M. T. (1996). Dynamic touch. *American Psychologist* 51: 1134–1152.

Turvey, M. T., and R. E. Shaw. (1995). Toward an ecological physics and a physical psychology. In R. L. Solso and D. W. Massaro, Eds., *The Science of the Mind: 2001 and Beyond.* New York: Oxford University Press, pp. 144–169.

Walker-Andrews, A. S. (1997). Infants' perception of expressive behaviors: Differentiation of multimodal information. *Psychological Bulletin* 121: 437–456.

Warren, W. H. (1995). Self-motion: Visual perception and visual control. In W. Epstein and S. Rogers, Eds., *Perception of Space and Motion.* New York: Academic Press, pp. 263–325.

Turvey, M. T., R. E. Shaw, E. S. Reed, and W. M. Mace. (1981). Ecological laws of perceiving and acting: In reply to Fodor and Pylyshyn (1981). *Cognition* 9: 237–304.

Warren, W. H. Jr., and R. E. Shaw, Eds. (1985). *Persistence and Change: Proceedings of the First International Conference on Event Perception.* Hillsdale, NJ: Erlbaum.

Further Readings

Gibson, E. J. (1982). The concept of affordances in development: The renascence of functionalism. In W. A. Collins, Ed., *The Concept of Development: Minnesota Symposium on Child Development* vol. 15. Hillsdale, NJ: Erlbaum, pp. 55–81.

Lee, D. N., and C. von Hofsten. (1985). Dialogue on perception and action. In W. Warren and R. Shaw, Eds, *Persistence and Change.* Hillsdale, NJ: Erlbaum.

Reed, E. S. (1988). *James J. Gibson and the Psychology of Perception.* New Haven: Yale University Press.

Reed, E., and R. Jones. (1982). *Reasons for Realism: Selected Essays of James J. Gibson.* Hillsdale, NJ: Erlbaum.

Ecological Validity

The term *ecological validity* refers to the extent to which behavior indicative of cognitive functioning sampled in one environment can be taken as characteristic of an individual's cognitive processes in a range of other environments. Consequently, it is a central concern of cognitive scientists who seek to generalize their findings to questions about "how the mind works" on the basis of behavior exhibited in specially designed experimental or diagnostic settings. This concern was provocatively expressed by Urie Bronfenbrenner (1979), who complained that too much of the study of child development depended on the study of children in strange circumstances for short periods of time, in contrast with the ecologies of their everyday lives.

Discussions of the problem of ecological validity first came to prominence in cognitive research in the United States owing to the work of Egon Brunswik and Kurt Lewin, two German scholars who emigrated to the United States in the 1930s. Other important sources of ideas about ecological validity include Roger Barker (1978), whose work on the influence of social setting on behavior retains its influence to the present day, and J. J. GIBSON (1979), who argued that the crucial questions in the study of perception are to be resolved not so much by an attention to the perceiver as by the description of how the environment in particular everyday life arrangements "affords" a person perceptual information; the issue was given further prominence in Ulric Neisser's influential *Cognition and Reality* in 1976.

Brunswik (1943) proposed an ECOLOGICAL PSYCHOLOGY in which psychological observations would be made by sampling widely the environments within which particular "proximal" tasks are embedded. Brunswik's overall goal was to prevent psychology from being restricted to artificially isolated proximal or peripheral circumstances that are not representative of the "larger patterns of life." In order to avoid this problem, he suggested that situations, or tasks, rather than people, should be considered the basic units of psychological analysis. In addition, these situations or tasks must be "carefully drawn from the universe of the requirements a person happens to face in his commerce with the physical and social environment" (p. 263). To illustrate his approach, Brunswik studied size constancy by accompanying an individual who was interrupted frequently in the course of her normal daily activities and asked to estimate the size of some object she had just been looking at. This person's size estimates correlated highly with physical size of the objects and not with their retinal image size. This result, Brunswik claimed, "possesses a certain generality with regard to normal life conditions" (p. 265).

Lewin proposed a "psychological ecology," as a way of "discovering what part of the physical or social world will determine, during a given period, the 'boundary zone' of the life space" of an individual (1943: 309). By life space, Lewin meant "the person and the psychological environment as it exists for him" (p. 306). He argued that behavior at time *t* is a function of the situation at time *t* only, and hence we must find ways to determine the properties of the lifespace "at a given time." This requirement amounts to what ethnographers refer to as "taking the subject's point of view." It seeks to unite the subjective and the objective.

If one agrees that understanding psychological processes in terms of the life space of the subject is important, following the logic of Lewin's argument, Brunswik's approach was inadequate. His experimental procedures did not allow him to observe someone fulfilling a well-specified task in a real-life environment; rather, it amounted to making experiments happen in a nonlaboratory environment. His procedures, in Lewin's terminology, changed the subject's life space to fit the requirements of his predefined set of observation conditions.

Ulric Neisser (1976) also pointed out marked discontinuities between the "spatial, temporal, and intermodal continuities of real objects and events" and the objects and events characteristic of laboratory-based research as a fundamental shortcoming of cognitive psychology, going so far as to suggest, "It is almost as if ecological *in*validity were a deliberate feature of the experimental design" (1976: 34).

Urie Bronfenbrenner's (1979, 1993) advocacy of ecologically valid research has greatly influenced the study of cognitive social development (Cole and Cole 1996). There are, he writes, three conditions that ecologically valid research must fulfill: (1) maintain the integrity of the real-life situations it is designed to investigate; (2) be faithful to the larger social and cultural contexts from which the subjects come; (3) be consistent with the participants' definition of the situation, by which he meant that the experimental manipulations and outcomes must be shown to be "perceived by the participants in a manner consistent with the conceptual definitions explicit and implicit in the research design" (1979: 35).

Note that there is a crucial difference between Lewin, Neisser, and Bronfenbrenner's interpretations of how to conduct ecologically valid research and the procedures proposed by Brunswik. Neisser, Bronfenbrenner, and others do not propose that we carry around our laboratory task and make it happen in a lot of settings. They propose that we discover and directly observe the ways that tasks occur (or don't occur) in nonlaboratory settings. Moreover, in Bronfenbrenner's version of this enterprise we must also discover the equivalent of Lewin's "life space," for example how the task and all it involves appear to the subject.

Two decades ago, the idea that such discovery procedures are possible was quite widespread among researchers who used experimental procedures and were cognizant of questions of ecological validity. Herbert Simon was echoing common opinion when he asserted that there is

a general experimental paradigm that can be used to test the commonality of cognitive processes over a wide range of task domains. The paradigm is simple. We find two tasks that have the same formal structure (e.g., they are both tasks of multi-dimensional judgment), one of which is drawn from a social situation and the

other is not. If common processes are implicated in both tasks, then we should be able to produce in each task environment phenomena that give evidence of workings of the same basic cognitive mechanisms that appear in the other. (1976: 258)

However, a variety of contemporary research indicates that the requirements for establishing ecological validity place an enormous analytical burden on cognitive scientists (see Cole 1996: ch. 8–9 for an extended treatment of the associated issues). Once we move beyond the laboratory in search of representativeness, the ability to identify tasks is markedly weakened. Failure to define the parameters of the analyst's task or failure to insure that the task-as-discovered is the subject's task can vitiate the enterprise. This point was made clearly by Schwartz and Taylor (1978). Their particular interest was the representativeness of standardized achievement and IQ tests, but their specification of the issues involved has broad applicability in cognitive science. They queried, "Does the test elicit the same behavior as would the same tasks embedded in a real noncontrived situation? . . . Even to speak of the same task across contexts requires a model of the structure of the task. In the absence of such a model, one does not know where the equivalence lies (p. 54)."

As Valsiner and Benigni (1986) point out, standardized cognitive experimental procedures are meant to embody closed analytic systems (the point of the experimental/test procedures being to achieve precisely this closure). Consequently, attempting to establish task equivalence in order to generalize beyond the experimental circumstances amounts to imposing a closed system on a more open behavioral system. To the degree that behavior conforms to the prescribed analytic categories, one achieves ecological validity in Brunswik's sense. Yet a variety of research (reviewed in Cole 1996) has shown that even psychological tests and other presumably "closed system" cognitive tasks are more permeable and negotiable than analysts ordinarily take account of. Insofar as the cognitive scientist's closed system does not capture veridically the elements of the open system it is presumed to model, experimental results systematically misrepresent the life process from which they are derived. The issue of ecological validity then becomes a question of the violence done to the phenomenon of interest owing to the analytic procedures employed (Sbordone and Long 1996).

See also BEHAVIORISM; CULTURAL VARIATION

—*Michael Cole*

References

Barker, R. (1978). *Ecological Psychology.* Stanford, CA: Stanford University Press.

Bronfenbrenner, U. (1979). *The Ecology of Human Development.* Cambridge, MA: Harvard University Press.

Brunswik, E. (1943). Organismic achievement and environmental probability. *The Psychological Review* 50: 255–272.

Cole, M. (1996). *Cultural Psychology: A Once and Future Discipline.* Cambridge, MA: Harvard University Press.

Cole, M., and S. R. Cole. (1996). *The Development of Children.* 3rd ed. New York: Freeman.

Gibson, J. J. (1979). *An Ecological Approach to Visual Perception.* Boston: Houghton-Mifflin.

Lewin, K. (1943). Defining the "field at a given time." *Psychological Review* 50: 292–310.

Sbordone, R. J., and C. J. Long, Eds. (1996). *Ecological Validity of Neuropsychological Testing.* Delray Beach, FL: GR Press/St. Lucie Press, Inc.

Schwartz, J. L., and E. F. Taylor. (1978). Valid assessment of complex behavior. The Torque approach. *Quarterly Newsletter of the Laboratory of Comparative Human Cognition* 2: 54–58.

Simon, H. A. (1976). Discussion: Cognition and social behavior. In J. S. Carroll and J. W. Payne, Eds., *Cognition and Social Behavior.* Hillsdale, NJ: Erlbaum.

Economics and Cognitive Science

Economics is concerned with the equilibria reached by large systems, such as markets and whole economies. The units that contribute to these collective outcomes are the individual participants in the economy. Consequently, assumptions about individual behavior play an important role in economic theorizing, which has relied predominantly on a priori considerations and on normative assumptions about individuals and institutions.

In economics, it is assumed that every option has a subjective "utility" for the individual, a well-established position in his or her preference ordering (von Neumann and Morgenstern 1947; see RATIONAL DECISION MAKING). Because preferences are clear and stable they are expected to be invariant across normatively equivalent assessment methods (procedure invariance), and across logically equivalent ways of describing the options (description invariance). In addition, people are assumed to be good Bayesians (see BAYESIAN LEARNING and BAYESIAN NETWORKS), who hold coherent (and dynamically consistent) preferences through time. Economics also makes a number of secondary assumptions: economic agents are optimal learners, whose selfish focus is on tangible assets (e.g., consumer goods rather than goodwill), who ignore sunk costs, and who do not let good opportunities go unexploited.

Coinciding with the advent of cognitive science, Simon (1957) brought into focus the severe strain that the hypothesis of rationality put on the computing abilities of economic agents, and proposed instead to consider agents whose rationality was bounded (see BOUNDED RATIONALITY). Over the last three decades, psychologists, decision theorists, and, more recently, experimental and behavioral economists have explored people's economic decisions in some detail. These studies have emphasized the role of information processing in people's decisions. The evidence suggests that people often rely on intuitive heuristics that lead to non-Bayesian judgment (see JUDGMENT HEURISTICS), and that probabilities have nonlinear impact on decision (Kahneman and TVERSKY 1979; Wu and Gonzalez 1996). Preferences, moreover, appear to be formed, not merely revealed, in the elicitation process, and their formation depends on the framing of the problem, the method of elicitation, and the valuations and attitudes that these trigger.

Contrary to the assumption of utility maximization, evidence suggests that the psychological carriers of value are gains and losses, rather than final wealth (see DECISION MAKING). Because of diminishing sensitivity to greater amounts, people exhibit risk aversion for gains and risk seeking for losses (except for very low probabilities, where these can reverse). Prospects can often be framed either as gains or as losses relative to some reference point, which can trigger opposing risk attitudes and can lead to discrepant preferences with respect to the same final outcomes (Tversky and Kahneman 1986). People are also loss averse: the loss of utility associated with giving up a good is greater than the utility associated with obtaining it (Tversky and Kahneman 1991). Loss aversion yields "endowment effects," wherein the mere possession of a good can lead to higher valuation of it than if it were not in one's possession (Kahneman, Knetsch, and Thaler 1990), and also creates a general reluctance to trade or to depart from the status quo, because the disadvantages of departing from it loom larger than the advantages of the alternatives (Knetsch 1989; Samuelson and Zeckhauser 1988). In further violation of standard value maximization, decisional conflict can lead to a greater tendency to search for alternatives when better options are available but the decision is hard than when relatively inferior options are present and the decision is easy (Tversky and Shafir 1992).

When a multiattribute option is evaluated, in consumer choice for example, each attribute must be weighted in accord with its contribution to the option's attractiveness. The standard economic assumption is that such evaluation of options is stable and does not depend, for example, on the method of evaluation. Behavioral research, in contrast, has shown that the weight of an attribute is enhanced by its compatibility with a required response. Compatibility effects are well known in domains such as perception and motor performance. In line with compatibility, a gamble's potential payoff is weighted more heavily in a pricing task (where both the price and the payoff are expressed in the same monetary units) than in choice. Consistent with this is the preference reversal phenomenon (Slovic and Lichtenstein 1983), wherein subjects choose a lottery that offers a greater chance to win over another that offers a higher payoff, but then price the latter higher than the former. This pattern has been observed in numerous experiments, including one involving professional gamblers in a Las Vegas casino (Lichtenstein and Slovic 1973), and another offering the equivalent of a month's salary to respondents in the People's Republic of China (Kachelmeier and Shehata 1992).

People's representation of money also systematically departs from what is commonly assumed in economics. According to the fungibility assumption, which plays a central role in theories of consumption and savings such as the life-cycle or the permanent income hypotheses, "money has no labels"; all components of a person's wealth can be collapsed into a single sum. Contrary to this assumption, people appear to compartmentalize wealth and spending into distinct budget categories, such as savings, rent, and entertainment, and into separate mental accounts, such as current income, assets, and future income (Thaler 1985, 1992). These mental accounting schemes lead to differential marginal propensities to consume (MPC) from one's current income (where MPC is high), current assets (where MPC is intermediate), and future income (where MPC is low). Consumption functions thus end up being overly dependent on current income, and people find themselves willing to save and borrow (at a higher interest rate) at the same time (Ausubel 1991). In addition, people often fail to ignore sunk costs (Arkes and Blumer 1985), fail to consider opportunity costs (Camerer et al. 1997), and show money illusion, wherein the nominal worth of money interferes with a representation of its real worth (Shafir, Diamond, and Tversky 1997).

Economic agents are presumed to have a good sense of their tastes and to be consistent through time. People, however, often prove weak at predicting their future tastes or at learning from past experience (Kahneman 1994), and their intertemporal choices exhibit high discount rates for future as opposed to present outcomes, yielding dynamically inconsistent preferences (Loewenstein and Thaler 1992). In further contrast with standard economic assumptions, people show concern for fairness and cooperation, even when dealing with unknown others in limited encounters, where long-term strategy and reputation are irrelevant (see, e.g., Dawes and Thaler 1988; Kahneman, Knetsch and Thaler 1986; Rabin 1993).

The foregoing partial list of empirical observations and psychological principles does not approach a unified theory comparable to that proposed by economics. The empirical evidence suggests that *Homo sapiens* is significantly more difficult to model than *Homo economicus*. Some have argued that the descriptive adequacy of the economic assumptions is unimportant as long as the theory is able to predict observed behaviors. Friedman (1953), for example, has proposed the analogy of an expert billiards player who, without knowing the relevant rules of physics or geometry, is able to play as if he did. Nonetheless, as the preceding list suggests, the tension between economics and the cognitive sciences appears to reside in the actual predictions, not only in the assumptions. Others have argued that individual errors are less important when one is ultimately interested in explaining aggregate behavior. The observed discrepancies, however, are systematic and predictable, and if the majority errs in the same direction there is no reason to expect that the discrepancies should disappear in the aggregate (Akerlof and Yellen 1985). Cognitive scientists and experimental and behavioral economists are trying better to understand and model systematic departures from standard economic theory. The aim is to bring to economics a theory populated with psychologically more realistic agents.

See also COOPERATION AND COMPETITION; RATIONAL AGENCY; RATIONAL CHOICE THEORY

—*Eldar Shafir*

References

Akerlof, G. A., and J. Yellen. (1985). Can small deviations from rationality make significant differences to economic equilibria? *American Economic Review* 75(4): 708–720.

Arkes, H. R., and C. Blumer. (1985). The psychology of sunk cost. *Organizational Behavior and Human Performance* 35: 129–140.

Ausubel, L. M. (1991). The failure of competition in the credit card market. *American Economic Review* 81: 50–81.

Camerer, C., L. Babcock, G. Loewenstein, and R. Thaler. (1997). A target income theory of labor supply: Evidence from cab drivers. *Quarterly Journal of Economics* 112(2).

Dawes, R. M., and R. H. Thaler. (1988). Cooperation. *Journal of Economic Perspectives* 2: 187–197.

Friedman, M. (1953). The methodology of positive economics. In *Essays in Positive Economics*. Chicago: University of Chicago Press.

Kachelmeier, S. J., and M. Shehata. (1992). Examining risk preferences under high monetary incentives: Experimental evidence from the People's Republic of China. *American Economic Review* 82: 1120–1141.

Kahneman, D. (1994). New challenges to the rationality assumption. *Journal of Institutional and Theoretical Economics* 150 (1): 18–36.

Kahneman, D., J. L. Knetsch, and R. H. Thaler. (1986). Fairness as a constraint on profit seeking: Entitlements in the market. *American Economic Review* 76(4): 728–741.

Kahneman, D., J. L. Knetsch, and R. H. Thaler. (1990). Experimental tests of the endowment effect and the Coase theorem. *Journal of Political Economy* 98(6): 1325–1348.

Kahneman, D., and A. Tversky. (1979). Prospect theory: An analysis of decision under risk. *Econometrica* 47: 263–291.

Knetsch, J. L. (1989). The endowment effect and evidence of non-reversible indifference curves. *American Economic Review* 79: 1277–1284.

Lichtenstein, S., and P. Slovic. (1973). Response-induced reversals of preference in gambling: An extended replication in Las Vegas. *Journal of Experimental Psychology* 101: 16–20.

Loewenstein, G., and R. H. Thaler. (1992). Intertemporal choice. In R. H. Thaler, Ed., *The Winner's Curse: Paradoxes and Anomalies of Economic Life*. New York: Free Press.

Rabin, M. (1993). Incorporating fairness into game theory and economics. *American Economic Review* 83: 1281–1302.

Samuelson, W., and R. Zeckhauser. (1988). Status quo bias in decision making. *Journal of Risk and Uncertainty* 1: 7–59.

Shafir, E., P. Diamond, and A. Tversky. (1997). Money illusion. *The Quarterly Journal of Economics* 112 (2): 341–374.

Simon, H. A. (1957). *Models of Man*. New York: Wiley.

Slovic, P., and S. Lichtenstein. (1983). Preference reversals: A broader perspective. *American Economic Review* 73: 596–605.

Thaler, R. H. (1985). Mental accounting and consumer choice. *Marketing Science* 4: 199–214.

Tversky, A., and D. Kahneman. (1986). Rational choice and the framing of decisions. *Journal of Business* 59(4,2): 251–278.

Tversky, A., and D. Kahneman. (1991). Loss aversion in riskless choice: A reference dependent model. *Quarterly Journal of Economics* (November): 1039–1061.

Tversky, A., and E. Shafir. (1992). Choice under conflict: The dynamics of deferred decision. *Psychological Science* 3 (6): 358–361.

von Neumann, J., and O. Morgenstern. (1947). *Theory of Games and Economic Behavior*. 2nd ed. Princeton, NJ: Princeton University Press.

Wu, G., and R. Gonzalez. (1996). Curvature of the probability weighting function. *Management Science* 42(12): 1676–1690.

Further Readings

Benartzi, S., and R. Thaler. (1995). Myopic loss aversion and the equity premium puzzle. *Quarterly Journal of Economics* 110 (1): 73–92.

Camerer, C. F. (1995). Individual decision making. In J. H. Kagel and A. E. Roth, Eds., *Handbook of Experimental Economics*. Princeton, NJ: Princeton University Press.

Heath, C., and A. Tversky. (1990). Preference and belief: Ambiguity and competence in choice under uncertainty. *Journal of Risk and Uncertainty* 4(1): 5–28.

Johnson, E. J., J. Hershey, J. Meszaros, and H. Kunreuther. (1993). Framing, probability distortions, and insurance decisions. *Journal of Risk and Uncertainty* 7: 35–51.

Kagel, J. H., and A. E. Roth, Eds. (1995). *Handbook of Experimental Economics*. Princeton, NJ: Princeton University Press.

Loewenstein, G., and J. Elster, Eds. (1992). *Choice over Time.* New York: Russell Sage Foundation.

March, J. G. (1978). Bounded rationality, ambiguity and the engineering of choice. *Bell Journal of Economics* 9: 587–610.

Plott, C. R. (1987). Psychology and economics. In J. Eatwell, M. Milgate, and P. Newman, Eds., *The New Palgrave: A Dictionary of Economics*. New York: Norton.

Rabin, M. (1998). Psychology and economics. *Journal of Economic Literature.*

Simon, H. A. (1978). Rationality as process and as product of thought. *Journal of the American Economic Association* 68: 1–16.

Thaler, R. H. (1991). *Quasi Rational Economics.* New York: Russell Sage Foundation.

Thaler, R. H. (1992). *The Winner's Curse: Paradoxes and Anomalies of Economic Life.* New York: Free Press.

Tversky, A., and D. Kahneman. (1992). Advances in prospect theory: Cumulative representation of uncertainty. *Journal of Risk and Uncertainty* 5: 297–323.

Tversky, A., S. Sattath, and P. Slovic. (1988). Contingent weighting in judgment and choice. *Psychological Review* 95(3): 371–384.

Tversky, A., P. Slovic, and D. Kahneman. (1990). The causes of preference reversal. *American Economic Review* 80: 204–217.

Tversky, A., and P. Wakker. (1995). Risk attitudes and decision weights. *Econometrica* 63(6): 1255–1280.

Education

In its broadest sense, education spans the ways in which cultures perpetuate and develop themselves, ranging from infant-parent communications to international bureaucracies and sweeping pedagogical or maturational movements (e.g., the constructivist movement attributed to PIAGET). As a discipline of cognitive science, education is a body of theoretical and applied research that draws on most of the other cognitive science disciplines, including psychology, philosophy, computer science, linguistics, neuroscience, and anthropology. Educational research overlaps with the central part of basic cognitive psychology that considers LEARNING. Such research may be idealized as primarily either descriptive or prescriptive in nature, although many research ventures have aspects of both.

Descriptively, educational research focuses on observing *human* learning. Specific areas of study include expert-novice approaches, CONCEPTUAL CHANGE and misconception research, skill learning, and METACOGNITION. Expert-novice research typically explicitly contrasts the extremes of a skill to infer an individual's changes in processes and representations. Misconception research in domain-based education, such as NAIVE PHYSICS, NAIVE MATHEMATICS, writing, and computer programming, implicitly contrasts expert knowledge with that of nonexperts; a person's current understanding may be thought of in terms of SCHEMATA, frames, scripts, MENTAL MODELS, or analogical or metaphorical representations. Child development research often involves studying misconceptions. These constructs

are used for both explanatory and predictive purposes. Research in general skill learning includes psychometric analyses of high-level aptitudes (e.g., spatial cognition), and topics such as INDUCTION, DEDUCTIVE REASONING, abduction (hypothesis generation and evaluation), experimentation, critical or coherent reasoning, CAUSAL REASONING, comprehension, and PROBLEM SOLVING. Some of these skills are analyzed into more specific skills and malskills such as heuristics, organizing principles, bugs, and reasoning fallacies (cf. JUDGMENT HEURISTICS). Increasingly, metacognition research focuses on an individual's learning style, reflections, motivation, and belief systems. Research on learning can often be readily applied predictively (i.e., a priori). For example, Case (1985) predicted specific cognitive performance in balance-beam problem solving within defined stages of development.

Prescriptive elements of education are quite diverse. Some liken such elements to the engineering, as opposed to the science, of learning. Products of prescriptive education include modest reading modules, scientific microworlds, literacy standards, and assessment-driven curricular systems (e.g., Reif and Heller 1982; Resnick and Resnick 1992). The advent of design experiments (Brown 1992; Collins 1992) represents a kind of uneasy compromise between the rigorous control of laboratory research and the potential of greater relevance from classroom interventions.

Educational proponents of situated cognition generally highlight the notion that individuals always learn and perform within rather narrow situations or contexts, but such proponents are often reticent to offer specific pedagogical recommendations. Situated cognition variably borrows pieces of activity theories, ECOLOGICAL VALIDITY, group interaction, hermeneutic philosophies, direct perception, BEHAVIORISM, distributed cognition, cognitive psychology, and social cognition. It generally focuses on naturalistic, apprentice-oriented, artifact-laden, work-based, and even culturally exotic settings. This focus is often represented as a criticism of traditional school-based learning—even though some situated studies are run in schools (which are arguably natural in our society). Situated cognition's critics see it as an unstructured, unfalsifiable melange with near-infinite degrees of explanatory freedom and generally vague prescriptions. Recent disputes between the situated and mainstream camps seem to center on the questions, "What is a symbol?", "How can we separate a learner from a social situation?", and "Is transfer of training common or rare?" (e.g., Vera and Simon 1993, and commentaries). The disputes mirror many core issues from other cognitive science disciplines, as well as questions about the goals of social science.

Several cognitive theories have descriptive, predictive, *and* prescriptive applications to education. For instance, the ACT-based computational models of cognition (Anderson 1993) attempt to account for past data, predict learning outcomes, and serve as the basis for an extended family of intelligent tutoring systems (ITSs). These sorts of models might incorporate proposition-based semantic networks, "adaptive" or "learning" production systems, economic or rational analyses, and representations of individual students' strengths and weaknesses. The contrasts among various computer-based categories of learning-enhancement systems have not been sharp (Wenger 1987). These categories include ITSs, computer-aided instruction, interactive learning environments, computer coaches, and guided discovery environments. Some distinctions among these categories include (a) whether a model of student knowledge or skill is employed, (b) whether a relatively generative knowledge base for a chosen domain is involved, (c) whether feedback comes via hand-coded (or compiled) buggy rules (and lookup tables) or via the interpreted semantics of a knowledge base, and (d) whether a novel, more effective representation is introduced for a traditional one. Superior ITSs demonstrate great effectiveness relative to many forms of standard instruction, but currently have limited interactional sophistication compared to human tutoring (Merrill et al. 1992). Specific ITSs often spawn the following question from both within and without cognitive science: "Where is the intelligence, or the semantics, in this system?"

Distributed cognition systems also face this question, although many proponents are unconcerned about philosophical semantics-from-syntax queries. Constraint-based and connectionist models are not yet commonly employed in educational ventures (cf. Ranney, Schank, and Diehl 1995), which seems surprising, given the efforts focused on learning in parallel distributed processing models of cognition, BAYESIAN NETWORKS, artificial neural or fuzzy networks, and the like.

As with some ITSs, cognitive science approaches to education, in general, often focus on improving students' knowledge representations or on providing more generative or transparent representations. Many such representational systems have evolved with computational technology, particularly as graphical user interfaces supplant text-based, command-line interactions. Clickable, object-oriented interfaces have become the norm, although the complexity of such features sometimes overwhelms and inhibits learners.

Most recently, the Internet and World Wide Web have spawned many research ventures, for instance, involving collaborative learning environments that include the integration of technology and curricula. However, an ongoing danger to education is the proliferation of well-funded research projects developing potentially promising technologies that, relative to the vast majority of classrooms, (a) require intolerable levels of equipment upgrades or technical and systemic support, (b) are unpalatable to classroom teachers, and (c) simply do not "scale up" to populations of nontrivial size (cf. Cuban 1989).

See also COGNITIVE ARTIFACTS; COGNITIVE DEVELOPMENT; HUMAN-COMPUTER INTERACTION

—*Michael Ranney and Todd Shimoda*

References

Anderson, J. R. (1993). *Rules of the Mind.* Hillsdale, NJ: Erlbaum.

Brown, A. L. (1992). Design experiments: Theoretical and methodological challenges in creating complex interventions in classroom settings. *The Journal of the Learning Sciences* 2: 141–178.

Case, R. (1985). *Intellectual Development.* Orlando, FL: Academic Press.

Collins, A. (1992). Toward a design science of education. In E. Scanlon and T. O'Shea, Eds., *Proceedings of the NATO Advanced Research Workshop On New Directions In Advanced Educational Technology.* Berlin: Springer, pp. 15–22.

Cuban, L. (1989). Neoprogressive visions and organizational realities. *Harvard Educational Review* 59: 217–222.

Merrill, D. C., B. J. Reiser, M. Ranney, and J. G. Trafton. (1992). Effective tutoring techniques: A comparison of human tutors and intelligent tutoring systems. *The Journal of the Learning Sciences* 2: 277–305.

Ranney, M., P. Schank, and C. Diehl. (1995). Competence and performance in critical reasoning: Reducing the gap by using *Convince Me. Psychology Teaching Review* 4: 153–166.

Reif, F., and J. Heller. (1982). Knowledge structure and problem solving in physics. *Educational Psychologist* 17: 102–127.

Resnick, L. and D. Resnick. (1992). Assessing the thinking curriculum: New tools for educational reform. In B. Gifford and M. O'Connor, Eds., *Cognitive Approaches to Assessment.* Boston: Kluwer-Nijhoff.

Vera, A. H. and H. A. Simon. (1993). Situated action: A symbolic interpretation. *Cognitive Science* 17: 7–48.

Wenger, E. (1987). *Artificial Intelligence and Tutoring Systems: Computational and Cognitive Approaches to the Communication of Knowledge.* Los Altos, CA: Morgan Kaufman.

Electric Fields

See ELECTROPHYSIOLOGY, ELECTRIC AND MAGNETIC EVOKED FIELDS

Electrophysiology, Electric and Magnetic Evoked Fields

Electric and magnetic evoked fields are generated in the brain as a consequence of the synchronized activation of neuronal networks by external stimuli. These evoked fields may be associated with sensory, motor, or cognitive events, and hence are more generally termed *event-related potentials* ERPs) and *event-related magnetic fields* (ERFs), respectively. Both ERPs and ERFs consist of precisely timed sequences of waves or components that may be recorded noninvasively from the surface of the head to provide information about spatio-temporal patterns of brain activity associated with a wide variety of cognitive processes (Heinze, Münte, and Mangun 1994; Rugg and Coles 1995).

Electric and magnetic field recordings provide complementary information about brain function with respect to other neuroimaging methods that register changes in regional brain metabolism or blood flow, such as POSITRON EMISSION TOMOGRAPHY (PET) and functional MAGNETIC RESONANCE IMAGING (fMRI). Although PET and fMRI provide a detailed anatomical mapping of active brain regions during cognitive performance, these methods cannot track the time course of neural events with the high precision of ERP and ERF recordings. Studies that combine ERP/ERF and PET/fMRI methodologies are needed to resolve both the spatial and temporal aspects of brain activity patterns that underlie cognition.

At the level of SINGLE-NEURON RECORDING, both ERPs and ERFs are generated primarily by the flow of ionic currents

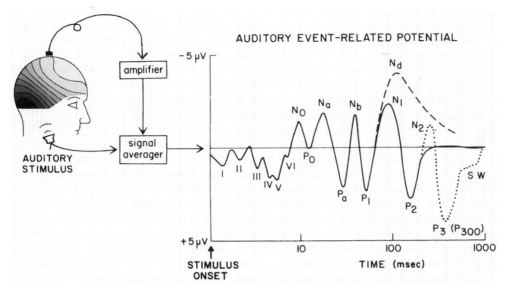

AUDITORY EVENT-RELATED POTENTIAL

Figure 1. The characteristic time-voltage waveform of the auditory ERP in response to a brief stimulus such as a click or a tone. To extract the ERP from the ongoing noise of the electroencephalogram, it is necessary to signal average the time-locked waves over many stimulus presentations. The individual waves or components of the ERP are triggered at specific time delays or latencies after the stimulus (note logarithmic time scale). The earliest waves (I–VI) are generated in the auditory brainstem pathways, while subsequent negative (N) and positive (P) waves are generated in different subregions of primary and secondary auditory cortex. (From Hillyard, S.A. (1993). Electrical and magnetic brain recordings: contributions to cognitive neuroscience. Current Opinion in Neurobiology 3: 217–224.)

across nerve cell membranes during synaptic activity. ERPs arise from summed field potentials produced by synaptic currents passing into the extracellular fluids surrounding active neurons. In contrast, ERFs are produced by the concentrated intracellular flow of synaptic currents through elongated neuronal processes such as dendrites, which gives rise to concentric magnetic fields surrounding the cells. When a sufficiently large number of neurons having a similar anatomical position and orientation are synchronously activated, their summed fields may be strong enough to be detectable as ERPs or ERFs at the surface of the head. The detailed study of scalp-recorded ERPs became possible in the 1960s following the advent of digital signal-averaging computers, whereas analysis of ERFs required the further development in the 1980s of highly sensitive, multichannel magnetic field sensors (Regan 1989).

The anatomical locations of the neuronal populations that generate ERPs and ERFs may be estimated on the basis of their surface field configurations. This requires application of algorithms and models that take into account the geometry of the generator neurons and the physical properties of the biological tissues. Active neural networks may be localized in the brain more readily by means of ERF than by surface ERP recordings, because magnetic fields pass through the brain, skull, and scalp without distortion, whereas ERPs are attenuated by the resistivity of intervening tissues. Both ERP and ERF data have been used successfully to reveal the timing of mental operations with a high degree of precision (of the order of milliseconds) and to localize brain regions that are active during sensory and perceptual processing, selective attention and discrimination, memory storage and retrieval, and language comprehension (Hillyard 1993).

The processing of sensory information in different modalities is associated with characteristic sequences of surface-recorded ERP/ERF components (figure 1). In each modality, components at specific latencies represent evoked activity in subcortical sensory pathways and in primary and secondary receiving areas of the CEREBRAL CORTEX. Cortical components with latencies of 50–250 msec have been associated with perception of specific classes of stimuli (Allison et al. 1994) and with short-term sensory memory processes. Altered sensory experience (e.g., congenital deafness, blindness, or limb amputation) produces marked changes in ERP/ERF configurations that reflect the NEURAL PLASTICITY and functional reorganization of cortical sensory systems (Neville 1995).

Recordings of ERPs and ERFs have revealed both the timing and anatomical substrates of selective ATTENTION operations in the human brain (Näätänen 1992; Hillyard et al. 1995). In dichotic listening tasks, paying attention to sounds in one ear while ignoring sounds in the opposite ear produces a marked enhancement of short-latency ERP/ERF components to attended-ear sounds in auditory cortex. This selective modulation of attended versus unattended inputs during AUDITORY ATTENTION begins as early as 20–50 msec poststimulus, which provides strong support for theories of attention that postulate an "early selection" of stimuli prior to full perceptual analysis. In visual attention tasks, stimuli presented at attended locations in the visual field elicit enlarged ERP/ERF components in secondary (extrastriate) cortical areas as early as 80–100 msec poststimulus. This suggests that visual attention involves a sensory gain control or amplification mechanism that selectively modulates the flow of information through extrastriate cortex. Paying attention to nonspatial features such as color or shape is manifested by longer latency components that index the time course of feature analyses in different visual-cortical areas.

ERPs and ERFs provide a converging source of data about the timing and organization of information processing stages that intervene between a stimulus and a discriminative response. Whereas short-latency components demarcate the timing of early sensory feature analyses, longer latency components ("N200" and "P300" waves) are closely coupled with processes of perceptual discrimination, OBJECT RECOGNITION, and classification. ERP components generated in motor cortex index the timing of response selection and MOTOR CONTROL processes. Studies using these ERP measures have provided strong support for "cascade" theories that posit a continuous flow of partially analyzed information between successive processing stages during sensory-motor tasks (Coles et al. 1995).

Long-latency ERPs have been linked with MEMORY encoding, updating, and retrieval processes (Rugg 1995). ERPs elicited during LEARNING can reliably predict accuracy of recall or recognition on subsequent testing. Some components appear to index conscious recognition of previously learned items, whereas others are sensitive to contextual priming effects. These memory-related components have been recorded both from the scalp surface and from implanted electrodes in hippocampus and adjacent temporal lobe structures in neurosurgical patients.

ERP and ERF recordings are also being used effectively to investigate the NEURAL BASIS OF LANGUAGE, including phonetic, lexical, syntactic, and semantic levels of processing (Kutas and Van Petten 1994). Alterations in specific ERP/ERF components have been linked to syndromes of LANGUAGE IMPAIRMENT. A late negative ERP ("N400") provides a graded, on-line measure of word expectancy and semantic priming during sentence comprehension. Studies of N400 have contributed to understanding the organization of semantic networks in the brain (McCarthy et al. 1995).

See also ATTENTION IN THE HUMAN BRAIN; NEURAL PLASTICITY

—Steven A. Hillyard

References

Allison, T., G. McCarthy, A. C. Nobre, A. Puce, and A. Belger. (1994). Human extrastriate visual cortex and the perception of faces, words, numbers, and colors. *Cerebral Cortex* 5: 544–554.

Coles, M. G. H., G. O. Henderikus, M. Smid, M. K. Scheffers, and L. J. Otten. (1995). Mental chronometry and the study of human information processing. In M. D. Rugg and M. G. H. Coles, Eds., *Electrophysiology of Mind: Event-Related Brain Potentials and Cognition.* Oxford: Oxford University Press, pp. 86–131.

Heinze, H. J., T. F. Münte, and G. R. Mangun, Eds. (1994). *Cognitive Electrophysiology.* Boston: Birkhauser.

Hillyard, S. A. (1993). Electrical and magnetic brain recordings: Contributions to cognitive neuroscience. *Current Opinion in Neurobiology* 3: 217–224.

Hillyard, S. A., G. R. Mangun, M. G. Woldorff, and S. J. Luck. (1995). Neural systems mediating selective attention. In M. S.

Gazzaniga, Ed., *The Cognitive Neurosciences.* Cambridge, MA: MIT Press, pp. 665–681.

Kutas, M., and C. K. Van Petten. (1994). Psycholinguistics electrified: Event-related brain potential investigations. In M. Gernsbacher, Ed., *Handbook of Psycholinguistics.* New York: Academic Press, pp. 83–143.

McCarthy, G., A. C. Nobre, S. Bentin, and D. D. Spence. (1995). Language-related field potentials in the anterior-medial temporal lobe: 1. Intracranial distribution and neural generators. *Journal of Neuroscience* 15: 1080–1089.

Näätänen, R. (1992). *Attention and Brain Function.* Hillsdale, NJ: Erlbaum.

Neville, H. (1995). Developmental specificity in neurocognitive development in humans. In M. S. Gazzaniga, Ed., *The Cognitive Neurosciences.* Cambridge, MA: MIT Press, pp. 219–234.

Regan, D. (1989). *Human Brain Electrophysiology.* New York: Elsevier.

Rugg, M. D. (1995). ERP studies of memory. In M. D. Rugg and M. G. H. Coles, Eds., *Electrophysiology of Mind: Event-Related Brain Potentials and Cognition.* Oxford: Oxford University Press, pp. 132–170.

Rugg, M. D., and M. G. H. Coles, Eds. (1995). *Electrophysiology of Mind: Event-Related Brain Potentials and Cognition.* Oxford: Oxford University Press.

Further Readings

Coles, M. G. H., E. Donchin, and S. W. Porges, Eds. (1986). *Psychophysiology: Systems, Processes, and Applications.* Vol. 1, *Systems.* New York: Guilford Press.

Donchin, E., Ed. (1984). *Cognitive Psychophysiology.* Hillsdale, NJ: Erlbaum.

Gaillard, A. W. K., and W. Ritter, Eds. (1983). *Tutorials in ERP Research: Endogenous Components.* Amsterdam: North-Holland.

Hämäläinen, M., R. Hari, R. J. Ilmoniemi, J. Knuutila, and O. V. Lounasmaa. (1993). Magnetoencephalography: Theory, instrumentation, and applications to noninvasive studies of the working human brain. *Reviews of Modern Physics* 65: 413–497.

Hillyard, S. A., L. Anllo-Vento, V. P. Clark, H. J. Heinze, S. J. Luck, and G. R. Mangun. (1996). Neuroimaging approaches to the study of visual attention: A tutorial. In M. Coles, A. Kramer, and G. Logan, Eds., *Converging Operations in the Study of Visual Selective Attention.* Washington, DC: American Psychological Association, pp. 107–138.

Hillyard, S., and T. W. Picton. (1987). Electrophysiology of cognition. In F. Plum, Ed., *Handbook of Physiology Section 1: The Nervous System.* Vol. 5, *Higher Functions of the Brain.* Bethesda: American Physiological Society, pp. 519–584.

John, E. R., T. Harmony, L. Prichep, M. Valdés, and P. Valdés, Eds. (1990). *Machinery of the Mind.* Boston: Birkhausen.

Näätänen, R. (1992). *Attention and Brain Function.* Hillsdale, NJ: Erlbaum.

Näätänen, R. (1995). The mismatch negativity: A powerful tool for cognitive neuroscience. *Ear and Hearing* 16: 6–18.

Nunez, P. L., Ed. (1981). *Electric Fields of the Brain.* New York: Oxford University Press.

Picton, T. W., O. G. Lins, and M. Scherg. (1994). The recording and analysis of event-related potentials. In F. Boller and J. Grafman, Eds., *Handbook of Neuropsychology.* Vol. 9, *Event-Related Potentials.* Amsterdam: Elsevier, pp.429–499.

Scherg, M. (1990). Fundamentals of dipole source potential analysis. In F. Grandori, M. Hoke, and G. L. Romans, Eds., *Auditory Evoked Magnetic Fields and Electric Potentials, Advances in Audiology.* Basel: Karger, pp. 40–69.

Eliminative Materialism

Eliminative materialism, or "eliminativism" as it is sometimes called, is the claim that one or another kind of mental state invoked in commonsense psychology does not really exist. Eliminativists suggest that the mental states in question are similar to phlogiston or caloric fluid, or perhaps to the gods of ancient religions: they are the nonexistent posits of a seriously mistaken theory. The most widely discussed version of eliminativism takes as its target the intentional states of commonsense psychology, states like beliefs, thoughts and desires (P. M. Churchland 1981; Stich 1983; Christensen and Turner 1993). The existence of conscious mental states such as pains and visual perceptions has also occasionally been challenged (P. S. Churchland 1983; Dennett 1988; Rey 1983).

Though advocates of eliminativism have offered a wide variety of arguments, most of the arguments share a common structure (Stich 1996). The first premise is that beliefs, thoughts, desires, or other mental states whose existence the argument will challenge can be viewed as posits of a widely shared commonsense psychological theory, which is often called "folk psychology." FOLK PSYCHOLOGY, this premise maintains, underlies our everyday discourse about mental states and processes, and terms like "belief," "thought," and "desire" can be viewed as theoretical terms in this commonsense theory. The second premise is that folk psychology is a seriously mistaken theory because some of the central claims that it makes about the states and processes that give rise to behavior, or some of the crucial presuppositions of these claims, are false or incoherent. This second premise has been defended in many ways, some of which will be considered in the following discussion. Both premises of the eliminativist argument are controversial. Indeed, debate about the plausibility of the second premise, and thus about the tenability of commonsense psychology, has been one of the central themes in the philosophy of mind for several decades. From these two premises eliminativists typically draw a pair of conclusions. The weaker conclusion is that the cognitive sciences that ultimately give us a correct account of the workings of the human mind/brain will not refer to commonsense mental states like beliefs and desires; these states will not be part of the ontology of a mature cognitive science. The stronger conclusion is that these commonsense mental states simply do not exist. Most of the discussion of eliminativism has focused on the plausibility of the premises, but several authors have argued that even if the premises are true, they do not give us good reason to accept either conclusion (Lycan 1988; Stich 1996)

Arguments in defense of the second premise typically begin by making some claims about the sorts of states or mechanisms that folk psychology invokes, and then arguing that a mature cognitive science is unlikely to countenance states or mechanisms of that sort. One family of arguments follows Wilfrid Sellars (1956) in maintaining that folk psychology takes thoughts and other intentional states to be modeled on overt linguistic behavior. According to this Sellarsian account, common sense assumes that beliefs are quasi-linguistic states and that thoughts are quasi-linguistic

episodes. But if this is right, one eliminativist argument continues, then either nonhuman animals and prelinguistic children do not have beliefs and thoughts, or they must think in some nonpublic LANGUAGE OF THOUGHT, and both of these options are absurd (P. S. Churchland 1980). Opponents of the argument fall into two camps. Some, following Donald Davidson (1975), argue that children and nonhuman animals *do not* have beliefs or thoughts, whereas others, most notably Jerry Fodor (1975), argue that children and higher animals do indeed think in a nonpublic "language of thought." Another argument that relies on the Sellarsian account of beliefs` and thoughts notes that neuroscience has thus far failed to find syntactically structured, quasi-linguistic representations in the brain and predicts that the future discovery of such quasi-linguistic states is unlikely (Van Gelder 1991).

Many authors have challenged the claim that commonsense psychology is committed to a quasi-linguistic account of intentional states (see, for example, Loar 1983; Stalnaker 1984), and a number of arguments for the eliminativist's second premise rely on less controversial claims about commonsense psychology. One of these arguments (Ramsey, Stich, and Garon 1990) maintains only that, according to commonsense psychology, a belief is a contentful state that can be causally involved in some cognitive episodes while it is causally inert in others. It is not the case that all of our beliefs are causally implicated in all of our inferences. However, there is a family of connectionist models of propositional memory in which information is encoded in a thoroughly holistic way. All of the information encoded in these models is causally implicated in every inference the model makes. Thus, it is claimed, there are *no* contentful states in these models which can be causally involved in some cognitive episodes and causally inert in others. Whether or not connectionist models of this sort will provide the best psychological account of human propositional memory is a hotly disputed question. But if they do, the eliminativist argument maintains, then folk psychology will turn out to be pretty seriously mistaken. A second argument (due to Davies 1991) that relies on connectionist models begins with the claim that commonsense psychology is committed to a kind of "conceptual modularity." It requires that there is "a single inner state which is active whenever a cognitive episode involving a given concept occurs and which can be uniquely associated with the concept concerned" (Clark 1993). In many connectionist models, by contrast, concepts are represented in a context-sensitive way. The representation of coffee in a cup is different from the representation of coffee in a pot (Smolensky 1988). Thus, there is no state of the model that is active whenever a cognitive episode involving a given concept occurs and that can be uniquely associated with the concept concerned. If these models offer the best account of how human concepts are represented, then once again we have the conclusion that folk psychology has made a serious mistake.

Still another widely discussed family of arguments aimed at showing that folk psychology is a seriously mistaken theory focus on the fact that commonsense psychology takes beliefs, desires, and other intentional states to have semantic properties—truth or satisfaction conditions—

and that commonsense psychological explanations seem to attribute causal powers to intentional states that they have in virtue of their semantic content. A number of reasons have been offered for thinking that this reliance on semantic content will prove problematic. Some authors argue that semantic content is "wide"—it depends (in part) on factors outside the head—and that this makes it unsuitable for the scientific explanation of behavior (Stich 1978; Fodor 1987). Others argue that semantic content is "holistic"—it depends on the entire set of beliefs that a person has—and that useful scientific generalizations cannot be couched in terms of such holistic properties (Stich 1983). Still others argue that semantic properties cannot be reduced to physical properties, and that properties that cannot be reduced to physical properties cannot have causal powers. If this is right, then, contrary to what folk psychology claims, semantic properties are causally irrelevant (Van Gulick 1993). Finally, some authors have urged that the deepest problem with commonsense psychology is that semantic properties cannot be "naturalized"—there appears to be no place for them in our evolving, physicalistic view of the world (Fodor 1987; Stich and Laurence 1994).

See also AUTONOMY OF PSYCHOLOGY; CONNECTIONISM; PHILOSOPHICAL ISSUES; INDIVIDUALISM; MIND-BODY PROBLEM; MODULARITY OF MIND; PHYSICALISM

—Stephen Stich

References

Christensen, S., and D. Turner, Eds. (1993). *Folk Psychology and the Philosophy of Mind.* Hillsdale, NJ: Erlbaum.

Churchland, P. M. (1981). Eliminative materialism and the propositional attitudes. *Journal of Philosophy* 78: 67–90.

Churchland, P. S. (1980). Language, thought and information processing. *Nous* 14: 147–170.

Churchland, P. S. (1983). Consciousness: The transmutation of a concept. *Pacific Philosophical Quarterly* 64: 80–95.

Clark, A. (1993). *Associative Engines.* Cambridge, MA: Bradford Books/MIT Press.

Davidson, D. (1975). Thought and talk. In S. Guttenplan, Ed., *Mind and Language.* Oxford: Oxford University Press.

Davies, M. (1991). Concepts, connectionism and the language of thought. In W. Ramsey, S. Stich, and D. Rumelhart, Eds., *Philosophy and Connectionist Theory.* Hillsdale, NJ: Erlbaum, pp. 229–257.

Dennett, D. (1988). Quining qualia. In A. Marcel and E. Bisiach, Eds., *Consciousness in Contemporary Science.* New York: Oxford University Press.

Fodor, J. (1975). *The Language of Thought.* New York: Thomas Y. Crowell.

Fodor, J. (1987). *Psychosemantics.* Cambridge, MA: Bradford Books/MIT Press.

Loar, B. (1983). Must beliefs be sentences? In P. Asquith and T. Nickles, Eds., *PSA 1982. Proceedings of the 1982 Biennial Meeting of the Philosophy of Science Association,* vol. 2. East Lansing, MI: Philosophy of Science Association, pp. 627–643.

Lycan, W. (1988). *Judgement and Justification.* Cambridge: Cambridge University Press.

Ramsey, W., S. Stich, and J. Garon. (1990). Connectionism, eliminativism and the future of folk psychology. *Philosophical Perspectives* 4: 499–533. Reprinted in Stich (1996).

Rey, G. (1983). A reason for doubting the existence of consciousness. In R. Davidson, G. Schwartz, and D. Shapiro, Eds., *Consciousness and Self-Regulation,* vol. 3. New York: Plenum, pp. 1–39.

Sellars, W. (1956). Empiricism and the philosophy of mind. In H. Feigl and M. Scriven, Eds., *The Foundations of Science and the Concepts of Psychology and Psychoanalysis: Minnesota Studies in the Philosophy of Science,* vol. 1. Minneapolis: University of Minnesota Press, pp. 253–329.

Smolensky, P. (1988). On the proper treatment of connectionism. *Behavioral and Brain Sciences* 11: 1–74.

Stalnaker, R. (1984). *Inquiry.* Cambridge, MA: Bradford Books/MIT Press.

Stich, S. (1978). Autonomous psychology and the belief-desire thesis. *The Monist* 61: 573–591.

Stich, S. (1983). *From Folk Psychology to Cognitive Science.* Cambridge, MA: Bradford Books/MIT Press.

Stich, S., and S. Laurence. (1994). Intentionality and naturalism. In Peter A. French and Theodore E. Uehling Jr., Eds., *Midwest Studies in Philosophy.* Vol. 19, *Naturalism.* University of Notre Dame Press. Reprinted in Stich (1996).

Stich, S. (1996). *Deconstructing the Mind.* New York: Oxford University Press.

Van Gelder, T. (1991). What is the 'D' in 'PDP'? A survey of the concept of distribution. In W. Ramsey, S. Stich, and D. Rumelhart, Eds., *Philosophy and Connectionist Theory.* Hillsdale, NJ: Erlbaum, pp. 33–59.

Van Gulick, R. (1993). Who's in charge here? And who's doing all the work? In J. Heil and A. Mele, Eds., *Mental Causation.* Oxford: Clarendon Press, pp. 233–256.

Further Readings

Baker, L. (1987). *Saving Belief.* Princeton: Princeton University Press.

Baker, L. (1995). *Explaining Attitudes.* Cambridge: Cambridge University Press.

Burge, T. (1986). Individualism and psychology. *Philosophical Review* 95: 3–45.

Churchland, P. M. (1970). The logical character of action explanations. *Philosophical Review* 79: 214–236.

Churchland, P. M. (1989). Folk psychology and the explanation of human behavior. In P. M. Churchland, *A Neurocomputational Perspective.* Cambridge, MA: MIT Press, pp. 111–127.

Clark, A. (1989). *Microcognition.* Cambridge, MA: Bradford Books/MIT Press.

Clark, A. (1989/90). Connectionist minds. *Proceedings of the Aristotelian Society* 90: 83–102.

Clark, A. (1991). Radical ascent. *Proceedings of the Aristotelian Society* Supplementary Volume 65: 211–227.

Dretske, F. (1988). *Explaining Behavior.* Cambridge, MA: Bradford Books/MIT Press.

Egan, F. (1995). Folk psychology and cognitive architecture. *Philosophy of Science* 62: 179–196.

Feyerabend, P. (1963). Materialism and the mind-body problem. *Review of Metaphysics* 17: 49–66.

Fodor, J. (1989). Making mind matter more. *Philosophical Topics* 17: 59–80.

Horgan, T. (1982). Supervenience and microphysics. *Pacific Philosophical Quarterly* 63: 29–43.

Horgan, T. (1989). Mental quausation. *Philosophical Perspectives* 3: 47–76.

Horgan, T. (1993). From supervenience to superdupervenience: Meeting the demands of a material world. *Mind* 102: 555–586.

Horgan, T., and G. Graham. (1990). In defense of southern fundamentalism. *Philosophical Studies* 62: 107–134. Reprinted in Christensen and Turner (1993), pp. 288–311.

Horgan, T., and J. Woodward. (1985). Folk psychology is here to stay. *Philosophical Review* 94: 197–226. Reprinted in Christensen and Turner (1993), pp. 144–166.

Jackson, F., and P. Pettit. (1990). In defense of folk psychology. *Philosophical Studies* 59: 31–54.

Kim, J. (1989). Mechanism, purpose and explanatory exclusion. *Philosophical Perspectives* 3: 77–108.

O'Brien, G. (1991). Is connectionism common sense? *Philosophical Psychology* 4: 165–178.

O'Leary-Hawthorne, J. (1994). On the threat of elimination. *Philosophical Studies* 74: 325–346.

Rey, G. (1991). An explanatory budget for connectionism and eliminativism. In T. Horgan and J. Tienson, Eds., *Connectionism and the Philosophy of Mind.* Dordrecht, The Netherlands: Kluwer Academic Publishers, pp. 219–240.

Rorty, R. (1965). Mind-body identity, privacy, and categories. *Review of Metaphysics* 19: 24–54.

Rorty, R. (1970). In defense of eliminative materialism. *Review of Metaphysics* 24: 112–121.

Sterelny, K. (1990). *The Representational Theory of Mind.* Oxford: Blackwell.

Embeddedness

See SITUATED COGNITION AND LEARNING; SITUATEDNESS/ EMBEDDEDNESS

Embodiment

See MIND-BODY PROBLEM; SITUATEDNESS/EMBEDDEDNESS

Emergent Structuring

See EMERGENTISM; SELF-ORGANIZING SYSTEMS

Emergentism

George Henry Lewes coined the term *emergence* (Lewes 1875). He drew a distinction between emergents and resultants, a distinction he learned from John Stuart Mill. In his *System of Logic* (1843), Mill drew a distinction between "two modes of the conjoint action of causes, the mechanical and the chemical" (p. xviii). According to Mill, when two or more causes combine in the mechanical mode to produce a certain effect, the effect is the sum of what would have been the effects of each of the causes had it acted alone. Mill's principal example of this is the effect of two or more forces acting jointly to produce a certain movement: the movement is the vector sum of what would have been the effect of each force had it acted alone. According to Mill, two or more causes combine in the chemical mode to produce a certain effect if and only if they produce the effect, but not in the mechanical mode. Mill used the term *chemical mode* because chemical agents produce effects in a nonmechanical way. Consider a chemical process such as $CH_4 + 2O_2 \rightarrow CO_2 + 2H_2O$ (methane → oxygen produces carbon dioxide + water). The product of these reactants acting jointly is not in any sense the sum of what would have been the effects of each acting alone. Mill labeled the

effects of two or more causes acting in the mechanical mode "homopathic effects," and effects of two or more causes acting in the chemical mode "heteropathic effects." Lewes called heteropathic effects emergents and homopathic ones resultants (McLaughlin 1992).

Mill's work launched a tradition, British Emergentism, that flourished through the first third of the twentieth century (McLaughlin 1992). The main works in this tradition are Alexander Bain's *Logic* (1843), George Henry Lewes's *Problems of Life and Mind* (1875), Samuel Alexander's *Space, Time, and Deity* (1920), Lloyd Morgan's *Emergent Evolution* (1923), and C. D. Broad's *The Mind and Its Place in Nature* (1925). There were also prominent American emergentists: William JAMES, Arthur Lovejoy, and Roy Wood Sellars; and in France, Henri Bergson developed a brand of emergent evolution (Blitz 1992; Stephan 1992). In the 1920s in the former Soviet Union, the members of the Debron School, headed by A. M. Debron, spoke of the emergence of new forms in nature and maintained that the mechanists "neglected the specific character of the definite levels or stages of the development of matter" (Kamenka 1972: 164).

Alexander (1920) spoke of levels of qualities or properties, maintaining that "the higher-level quality emerges from the lower level of existence and has its roots therein, but it emerges therefrom, and it does not belong to that lower level, but constitutes its possessor a new order of existent with its special laws of behavior. The existence of emergent qualities thus described is something to be noted, as some would say, under the compulsion of brute empirical fact, or, as I should prefer to say in less harsh terms, to be accepted with the 'natural piety' of the investigator. It admits no explanation" (1920: 46). Morgan (1923) connected the notions of emergence and evolution and argued for an evolutionary cosmology. Morgan maintained that through a process of evolution genuinely new qualities emerge that generate new fundamental forces that effect "the go" of events in ways unanticipated by force-laws governing matter at lower levels of complexity.

Broad (1925) contrasted "the ideal of Pure Mechanism" with emergentism. Of the ideal of pure mechanism, he said: "On a purely mechanical theory all the apparently different kinds of matter would be made of the same stuff. They would differ only in the number arrangement and movements of their constituent particles. And their apparently different kinds of behaviour would not be ultimately different. For they would all be deducible from a single simple principle of composition from the mutual influences of the particles taken by pairs [he cites the Parallelogram Law]; and these mutual influences would all obey a single law which is quite independent of the configuration and surroundings in which the particles happen to find themselves" (1925: 45–46). He noted that "a set of gravitating particles, on the classical theory of gravitation, is an almost perfect example of the ideal of Pure Mechanism" (1925: 45). He pointed out that according to pure mechanism, "the external world has the greatest amount of unity which is conceivable. There is really only one science and the various 'special sciences' are just particular cases of it" (1925: 76). In contrast, on the emergentist view "we have to reconcile ourselves to much less unity in the external world and a much less intimate connexion between the various sciences. At best the external world and the various sciences that deal with it will form a hierarchy" (1925: 77). He noted that emergentism can "keep the view that there is only one fundamental kind of stuff" (1925: 77). However, if emergentism is true, then "we should have to recognize aggregates of various orders. And there would be two fundamentally different types of laws, which might be called 'intra-ordinal' and 'trans-ordinal' respectively. A trans-ordinal law would be one which connects the properties of adjacent orders. . . . An intra-ordinal law would be one which connects the properties of aggregates of the same order. A trans-ordinal law would be a statement of the irreducible fact that an aggregate composed of aggregates of the next lower order in such and such proportions and arrangements has such and such characteristic and non-deducible properties" (1925: 77–78). Broad maintained that transordinal laws are irreducible, emergent laws because they cannot be deduced from laws governing aggregates at lower levels and any compositional principle governing lower levels.

The British emergentists intended their notion of emergence to imply irreducibility. However, they presupposed a Newtonian conception of mechanistic reduction. Quantum mechanics broadened our conception of mechanistic reduction by providing holistic reductive explanations of chemical bonding that make no appeal to additive or even linear compositional principles. The quantum mechanical explanation of chemical bonding is a paradigm of a reductive explanation. Chemical phenomena are indeed emergent in the sense that the product of chemical reactants is a heteropathic effect of chemical agents; moreover, the chemical properties of atoms are not additive resultants of properties of electrons, and so chemical properties of atoms are emergent. However, the quantum mechanical explanation of chemical bonding teaches us that reductive explanations need not render the reduced property of a whole as an additive resultant of properties of its parts. Reductions need not invoke additive or even linear compositional principles. The quantum mechanical explanation of chemical bonding, and the ensuing successes of molecular biology (such as the discovery of the structure of DNA) led to the almost complete demise of the antireductionist, emergentist view of chemistry and biology (McLaughlin 1992).

Nonetheless, the British emergentists' notion of an emergent property as a property of a whole that is not an additive resultant of, or even linear function of, properties of the parts of the whole continues to be fairly widely used (Kauffman 1993a, 1993b). The term *emergent computation* is used to refer to the computation of nonlinear functions (see the essays in Forrest 1991).

In philosophical circles, there have been some attempts to develop a notion of emergence, loosely based on the British emergentist notion, but that actually implies ontological irreducibility (Klee 1984; Van Cleve 1990; Beckermann, Flohr, and Kim 1992; Kim 1992; McLaughlin 1992, 1997). These attempts invoke the notion of SUPERVENIENCE and make no appeal to nonadditivity or nonlinearity. On one view, bridge laws linking micro and macro properties are emergent laws if they are not semantically implied by initial microconditions and microlaws (McLaughlin 1992). One issue that remains a topic of intense debate is whether, in something like this sense of emergence, bridge laws linking conscious properties with physical properties are irreducible, emergent psychophysical laws, and conscious properties thereby irreducible, emergent properties (Popper and Eccles 1977; Sperry 1980; Van Cleve 1990; Chalmers 1996).

See also ANOMALOUS MONISM; CONSCIOUSNESS; PHYSICALISM; PSYCHOLOGICAL LAWS; REDUCTIONISM

—*Brian P. McLaughlin*

References

Alexander, S. (1920). *Space, Time, and Deity.* 2 vols. London: Macmillan.

Bain, A. (1870). *Logic, Books II and III.* London.

Beckermann, A., H. Flohr, and J. Kim, Eds. (1992). *Emergence or Reduction?* Berlin: Walter de Gruyter.

Blitz, D. (1992). *Emergent Evolution: Qualitative Novelty and the Levels of Reality.* Dordrecht: Kluwer Academic Publishers.

Chalmers, D. (1996). *The Conscious Mind: In Search of a Theory of Conscious Experience.* New York: Oxford University Press.

Forrest, S., Ed. (1991). *Emergent Computation.* Cambridge, MA: MIT Press/Bradford Books.

Kamenka, E. (1972). Communism, philosophy under. In P. Edwards, Ed., *Encyclopedia of Philosophy,* vol. 2. 2nd ed. New York: Macmillan.

Kauffman, S. (1993a). *The Origins of Order: Self-Organization and Selection in Evolution.* New York: Oxford University Press.

Kauffman, S. (1993b). *At Home in the Universe: The Search for the Laws of Self-Organization and Complexity.* New York: Oxford University Press.

Lewes, G. H. (1875). *Problems of Life and Mind,* vol. 2. London: Kegan Paul, Trench, Turbner, and Co.

Lovejoy, A. O. (1926). The meanings of "emergence" and its modes. In E. S. Brightman, Ed., *Proceedings of the Sixth International Congress of Philosophy.* New York, pp. 20–33.

McLaughlin, B. P. (1992). The rise and fall of British emergentism. In A. Beckermann, H. Flohr, J. Kim, Eds., *Emergence or Reduction?* Berlin: Walter de Gruyter.

McLaughlin, B. P. (1997). Emergence and supervenience. *Intellectia* 25: 25–43.

Mill, J. S. (1843). *System of Logic.* London: Longmans, Green, Reader, and Dyer. 8th ed., 1872.

Morgan, C. L. (1923). *Emergent Evolution.* London: Williams and Norgate.

Popper, K. R., and J. C. Eccles. (1977). *The Self and Its Brain.* New York: Springer.

Smart, J. J. C. (1981). Physicalism and emergence. *Neuroscience* 6: 1090–1113.

Sperry, R. W. (1980). Mind-brain interaction: Mentalism, yes; dualism, no. *Neuroscience* 5: 195–206.

Stephan, A. (1992). Emergence—A systematic view of its historical facets. In A. Beckermann, H. Flohr, J. Kim, Eds., *Emergence or Reduction?* Berlin: Walter de Gruyter.

Van Cleve, J. (1990). Emergence vs. panpsychism: Magic or mind dust? In J. E. Tomberlin, Ed., *Philosophical Perspectives,* vol. 4. Atascadero, CA: Ridgeview, pp. 215–226.

Further Readings

Caston, V. (1997). Epiphenomenals, ancient and modern. *Philosophical Review* 106.

Hempel, C. G., and P. Oppenheim. (1948). Studies in the logic of explanation. *Philosophy of Science* 15: 135–175.

Henle, P. (1942). The status of emergence. *Journal of Philosophy* 39: 486–493.

Horgan, T. (1993). From supervenience to superdupervenience: Meeting the demands of a material world. *Mind* 102: 555–586.

Jones, D. (1972). Emergent properties, persons, and the mind-body problem. *The Southern Journal of Philosophy* 10: 423–433.

Kim, J. (1992). "Downward causation" in emergentism and non-reductive materialism. In A. Beckermann, H. Flohr, and J. Kim, Eds., *Emergence or Reduction?* Berlin: Walter de Gruyter.

Klee, R. (1984). Micro-determinism and the concepts of emergence. *Philosophy of Science* 51: 44–63.

Meehl, P. E., and W. Sellars. (1956). The concept of emergence. In H. Feigl and M. Scriven, Eds., *The Foundations of Science and the Concepts of Psychology and Psychoanalysis. Minnesota Studies in the Philosophy of Science,* vol. 1. Minneapolis: University of Minnesota Press, pp. 239–252.

Morris, C. R. (1926). The notion of emergence. *Proceedings of the Aristotelian Society Suppl.* 6: 49–55.

Nagel, E. (1961). *The Structure of Science.* New York: Harcourt, Brace and World.

Pap, A. (1951). The concept of absolute emergence. *British Journal for the Philosophy of Science* 2: 302–311.

Pepper, S. (1926). Emergence. *Journal of Philosophy* 23: 241–245.

Popper, K. (1979). Natural selection and the emergence of mind. *Dialectica* 32: 279–355.

Stace, W. T. (1939). Novelty, indeterminism, and emergence. *Philosophical Review* 48: 296–310.

Stephan, A. (1997). Armchair arguments against emergentism. *Erkenntnis* 46: 305–314.

Emotion and the Animal Brain

Emotion, long ignored within the field of neuroscience, has at the end of the twentieth century been experiencing a renaissance. Starting around mid-century, brain researchers began to rely on the LIMBIC SYSTEM concept as an explanation of where emotions come from (MacLean 1949), and subsequently paid scant attention to the adequacy of that account. Riding the wave of the cognitive revolution (Gardner 1987), brain researchers have instead concentrated on the neural basis of perception, MEMORY, ATTENTION, and other cognitive processes. However, starting in the 1980s, studies of a particular model of emotion, classical fear conditioning, began to suggest that the limbic system concept could not provide a meaningful explanation of the emotional brain (LeDoux 1996). The success of these studies in identifying the brain pathways involved in a particular kind of emotion has largely been responsible for the renewed interest in exploring more broadly the brain mechanisms of emotion, including a new wave of studies of EMOTION AND THE HUMAN BRAIN. This article briefly reviews the neural pathways involved in fear conditioning, and then considers how the organization of the fear pathways provides a neuroanatomical framework for understanding emotional processing, including emotional stimulus evaluation (appraisal), emotional response control, and emotional experience (feelings).

The brain circuits involved in fear CONDITIONING have been most thoroughly investigated for situations involving an auditory conditioned stimulus (CS) paired with footshock (see LeDoux 1996; Davis 1992; Kapp et al. 1992; McCabe et al. 1992; Fanselow 1994). In order for conditioning to take place and for learned responses to be evoked by the CS after conditioning, the CS has to be relayed through the auditory system to the amygdala. If the CS is relatively simple (a single tone), it can reach the amygdala either from the auditory thalamus or the auditory cortex. In more complex stimulus conditions that require discrimination or CATEGORIZATION, the auditory cortex becomes involved, though the exact nature of this involvement is poorly understood (see Jarrell et al. 1987; Armony et al. 1997).

CS information coming from either the auditory THALAMUS or the cortex arrives in the lateral nucleus of the amygdala and is then distributed to the central nucleus by way of internal amygdala connections that have been elucidated in some detail (Pitkanen et al. 1997). The central nucleus, in turn, is involved in the control of the expression of conditioned responses through its projections to a variety of areas in the brainstem. These behavioral (e.g., freezing, escape, fighting back), autonomic (e.g. blood pressure, heart rate, sweating), and hormonal (adrenaline and cortisol released from the adrenal gland) responses mediated by the central nucleus are involuntary and occur more or less automatically in the presence of danger (though they are modulated somewhat by the situation).

Other brain areas implicated in fear conditioning are the HIPPOCAMPUS and prefrontal cortex. The hippocampus is important in conditioning to contextual stimuli, such as the situation in which an emotional event occurs. Its role is more of that of a high-level sensory/cognitive structure that integrates the situation into a spatial or conceptual "context" rather than that of an emotional processor per se (Kim and Fanselow 1992; Phillips and LeDoux 1992; LeDoux 1996). The medial area of the prefrontal cortex is important for extinction, the process by which the CS stops eliciting emotional reactions when its association with the shock is weakened (Morgan and LeDoux 1995). Fear/anxiety disorders, where fear persists abnormally, may involve alterations in the function of this region (LeDoux 1996).

The fear pathways can be summarized very succinctly. They involve the transmission of information about external stimuli to the amygdala and the control of emotional responses by way of outputs of the amygdala. The simplicity of this scheme suggests a clear mapping of certain psychological processes (stimulus evaluation and response control) onto brain circuits, and leads to hypotheses about how other aspects of emotion (feeling or experience) come about. However, it is important to point out that the ideas in the discussion that follows mainly pertain to the fear system of the brain, inasmuch as other emotions have not been studied in sufficient detail to allow these kinds of relations to be discussed.

Stimulus evaluation or *appraisal* is a key concept in the psychology of emotion (Lazarus 1991; Scherer 1988; Frijda 1986). Although most psychological work treats appraisal as a high-level cognitive process, often involving conscious access to underlying evaluations, it is clear from studies of animals and people that stimuli are first evaluated at a lower (unconscious) level prior to, and perhaps independent of, higher-level appraisal processes (see LeDoux 1996). In particular, the amygdala, which sits between sensory processes (including low-level sensory processes originating precortically and higher-level cortical processes) and motor control systems, is likely to be the neural substrate of early (unconscious) appraisal in the fear system. Not only do cells in the amygdala respond to conditioned fear stimuli, but they also learn the predictive value of new stimuli associated with danger (Quirk, Repa, and LeDoux 1995; Rogan, Staubli, and LeDoux 1997).

The amygdala receives inputs from a variety of cortical areas involved in higher cognitive functions. These areas project to the basal and accessory basal nuclei of the amygdala (Pitkanen et al. 1997). Thus, the emotional responses controlled by the amygdala can be triggered by low-level physical features of stimuli (intensity, color, form), higher-level semantic properties (objects), situations involving configurations of stimuli, and thoughts or memories about stimuli, and imaginary stimuli or situations. In this way higher-level appraisal processes can be critically involved in the functioning of this system. It is important to note that these hypotheses about the neural substrate of higher-level processes have emerged from a detailed elucidation of the physiology of lower-level processes. A bottom-up approach can be very useful when it comes to figuring out how psychological processes are represented in the brain.

Involuntary emotional responses are EVOLUTION's immediate solution to the presence of danger. Once these responses occur, however, higher-level appraisal mechanisms are often activated. We begin planning what to do, given the circumstances. We then have two kinds of response possibilities. Habits are well-practiced responses that we have learned to use in routine situations. Emotional habits can enable us to avoid danger and escape from it once we are in it. These kinds of responses may involve the amygdala, cortex, and BASAL GANGLIA (see LeDoux 1996; Everitt and Robbins 1992; McDonald and White 1993). Finally, there are emotional actions, such as choosing to run away rather than to stay put in the presence of danger, given our assessment of the possible outcomes of each course of action. These voluntary actions are controlled by cortical decision processes, most likely in the frontal lobe (Damasio 1994; Goldman-Rakic 1992; Georgopolous et al. 1989). Voluntary processes allow us to override the amygdala and become emotional actors rather than simply reactors (LeDoux 1996). The ability to shift from emotional reaction to action is an important feature of primate and especially human evolution.

The problem of feelings is really the problem of CONSCIOUSNESS (LeDoux 1996). Emotion researchers have been particularly plagued by this problem. Although we are nowhere near solving the problem of consciousness (feelings), there have been some interesting ideas in the area of consciousness that may be useful in understanding feelings. In particular, it seems that consciousness is closely tied up with the process we call WORKING MEMORY (Baddeley 1992), a mental workspace where we think, reason, solve problems, and integrate disparate pieces of information from immediate situations and long-term memory (Kosslyn and Koenig 1992; Johnson-Laird 1988; Kihlstrom 1987). In light of this, we might postulate that feelings result when working memory is occupied with the fact that one's brain

and body are in a state of emotional arousal. By integrating immediate stimuli with long-term memories about the occurrence of such stimuli in the past, together with the arousal state of the brain and feedback from the bodily expression of emotion, working memory might just be the stuff that feelings are made of.

Ever since William JAMES raised the question of whether we run from the bear because we are afraid or whether we are afraid because we run, the psychology of emotion has been preoccupied with questions about where fear and other conscious feelings come from. Studies of fear conditioning have gone a long way by addressing James's other question —what causes bodily emotional responses (as opposed to feelings)? Although James was correct in concluding that rapid-fire emotional responses are not caused by feelings of fear, he did not say much about how these come about. However, as we now see, by focusing on the responses we have been able to get a handle on how the system works, and even have gotten some ideas about where the feelings come from.

See also CEREBRAL CORTEX; CONDITIONING AND THE BRAIN; CONSCIOUSNESS, NEUROBIOLOGY OF; EMOTIONS; MEMORY, ANIMAL STUDIES; SENSATIONS

—*Joseph LeDoux and Michael Rogan*

References

Armony, J. L., D. Servan-Schreiber, L. M. Romanski, J. D. Cohen, and J. E. LeDoux. (1997). Stimulus generalization of fear responses: Effects of auditory cortex lesions in a computational model and in rats. *Cerebral Cortex* 7: 157–165.

Baddeley, A. (1992). Working memory. *Science* 255: 556–559.

Damasio, A. (1994). *Descarte's error: Emotion, reason, and the human brain.* New York: Gosset/Putnam.

Davis, M. (1992). The role of the amygdala in conditioned fear. In J. P. Aggleton, Ed., *The Amygdala: Neurobiological Aspects of Emotion, Memory and Mental Dysfunction.* New York: Wiley-Liss, pp. 255–306.

Everitt, B. J., and T. W. Robbins. (1992). Amygdala-ventral striatal interactions and reward-related processes. In J. P. Aggleton, Ed., *The Amygdala: Neurobiological Aspects of Emotion, Memory and Mental Dysfunction.* New York: Wiley-Liss, pp. 401–429.

Fanselow, M. S. (1994). Neural organization of the defensive behavior system responsible for fear. *Psychonomic Bulletin and Review* 1: 429–438.

Frijda, N. (1986). *The Emotions.* Cambridge: Cambridge University Press.

Gardner, H. (1987). *The Mind's New Science: A History of the Cognitive Revolution.* New York: Basic Books.

Georgopoulos, A., J. T. Lurito, M. Petrides, A. B. Schwartz, and J. T. Massey. (1989). Mental rotation of the neuronal population vector. *Science* 243: 234–236.

Goldman-Rakic, P. S. (1992). Circuitry of primate prefrontal cortex and regulation of behavior by representational memory. In J. M. Brookhart and V. B. Mountcastle, Eds., *Handbook of Physiology—The Nervous System V.* Baltimore, MD: American Physiological Society, pp. 373–417.

Jarrell, T. W., C. G. Gentile, L. M. Romanski, P. M. McCabe, and N. Schneiderman. (1987). Involvement of cortical and thalamic auditory regions in retention of differential bradycardia conditioning to acoustic conditioned stimuli in rabbits. *Brain Research* 412: 285–294.

Johnson-Laird, P. N. (1988). *The computer and the mind: An introduction to cognitive science.* Cambridge, MA: Harvard University Press.

Kapp, B. S., P. J. Whalen, W. F. Supple, and J. P. Pascoe. (1992). Amygdaloid contributions to conditioned arousal and sensory information processing. In J. P. Aggleton, Ed., *The Amygdala: Neurobiological Aspects of Emotion, Memory and Mental Dysfunction.* New York: Wiley-Liss.

Kihlstrom, J. F. (1987). The cognitive unconscious. *Science* 237: 1445–1452.

Kim, J. J., and M. S. Fanselow. (1992). Modality-specific retrograde amnesia of fear. *Science* 256: 675–677.

Kosslyn, S. M., and O. Koenig. (1992). *Wet Mind: The New Cognitive Neuroscience.* New York: Macmillan.

Lazarus, R. S. (1991). Cognition and motivation in emotion. *American Psychologist* 46: 352–367.

LeDoux, J. E. (1996). *The Emotional Brain.* New York: Simon and Schuster.

MacLean, P. D. (1949). Psychosomatic disease and the "visceral brain": Recent developments bearing on the Papez theory of emotion. *Psychosomatic Medicine* 11: 338–353.

McCabe, P. M., N. Schneiderman, T. W. Jarrell, C. G. Gentile, A. H. Teich, R. W. Winters, and D. R. Liskowsky. (1992). Central pathways involved in differential classical conditioning of heart rate responses. In I. Gormezano, Ed., *Learning and Memory: The Behavioral and Biological Substrates.* Hillsdale, NJ: Erlbaum, pp. 321–346.

McDonald, R. J., and N. M. White. (1993). A triple dissociation of memory systems: Hippocampus, amygdala, and dorsal striatum. *Behavioral Neuroscience* 107(1): 3–22.

Morgan, M., and J. E. LeDoux. (1995). Differential contribution of dorsal and ventral medial prefrontal cortex to the acquisition and extinction of conditioned fear. *Behavioral Neuroscience* 109: 681–688.

Phillips, R. G., and J. E. LeDoux. (1992). Differential contribution of amygdala and hippocampus to cued and contextual fear conditioning. *Behavioral Neuroscience* 106: 274–285.

Pitkanen, A., V. Savander, and J. E. LeDoux. (1997). Organization of intra-amygdaloid circuitries: An emerging framework for understanding functions of the amygdala. *Trends in Neurosciences* 20: 517–523.

Quirk, G. J., J. C. Repa, and J. E. LeDoux. (1995). Fear conditioning enhances short-latency auditory responses of lateral amygdala neurons: Parallel recordings in the freely behaving rat. *Neuron* 15: 1029–1039.

Rogan, M. T., U. V. Staubli, and J. E. LeDoux. (1997). Fear conditioning induces associative long-term potentiation in the amygdala. *Nature* 390: 604–607.

Scherer, K. R. (1988). Criteria for emotion-antecedent appraisal: A review. In V. Hamilton, G. H. Bower, and N. H. Frijda, *Cognitive Perspectives on Emotion and Motivation.* Norwell, MA: Kluwer, pp. 89–126.

Further Readings

Davis, M., W. A. Falls, S. Campeau, and M. Kim. (1994). Fear potentiated startle: A neural and pharmacological analysis. *Behavioral Brain Research* 53: 175–198.

Gray, J. A. (1987). *The Psychology of Fear and Stress*, vol. 2. New York: Cambridge University Press.

LeDoux, J. E. (1994). Emotion, memory and the brain. *Scientific American* 270: 32–39.

Maren, S., and M. S. Fanselow. (1996). The amygdala and fear conditioning: Has the nut been cracked? *Neuron* 16: 237–240.

Ono, T., and H. Nishijo. (1992). Neurophysiological basis of the Kulver-Bucy Syndrome: Responses of monkey amygdaloid neurons to biologically significant objects. In J. P. Aggleton, Ed., *The Amygdala: Neurobiological Aspects of Emotion, Memory, and Mental Dysfunction.* New York: Wiley-Liss, pp. 167–191.

Rolls, E. T. (1992). Neurophysiology and functions of primate amygdala. In J. P. Aggleton, Ed., *The Amygdala: Neurobiological Aspects of Emotion, Memory, and Mental Dysfunction.* New York: Wiley-Liss, pp. 143–166.

Emotion and the Human Brain

Popular ideas about the mind evolve over time: emotion came to have its contemporary meaning only in the late nineteenth century (Candland 1977). In current usage, the concept of emotion has two aspects. One pertains to a certain kind of subjective experience, "feeling." The other relates to expression, the public manifestation of feeling. These dual aspects of emotion—the subjective and the expressive—were represented a century ago in the writings of William JAMES (1884), who speculated on the neural and somatic basis of feeling, and Charles DARWIN (1872), who examined the evolution of emotional expression in various species. Most workers in this area have also pointed out that feelings and the actions that go with them are an essential part of an organism's relation to its environment. Thus, together with more elaborated cognition, emotions can be said to be the means by which an animal or person appraises the significance of stimuli so as to prepare the body for an appropriate response.

Emotion is traditionally distinguished from cognition, and for most of this century received little research attention in its own right—excepting possibly studies of the brain mechanisms of aggression. Emotion per se has come to be embraced as a legitimate topic only in the last several decades. Its acceptance was probably due in part to Ekman's influential cross-cultural studies of human facial expression (Ekman, Sorenson, and Friesen 1969), which implied an innate, biological basis for emotional experience. Social factors have undoubtedly also facilitated the entry of emotion into the arena of neuroscience research, for current popular culture upholds emotion as a significant feature of human life (McCarthy 1989).

An additional factor in the acceptance of emotion as a neurobiological entity was MacLean's (1952) persuasive account of a brain system specialized for emotion. Building on earlier anatomical theories, MacLean grouped together certain evolutionarily ancient brain structures, primarily regions of medial cortex and interconnected subcortical regions such as the hypothalamus, and called them the "visceral brain." He suggested that activity in this region was responsible for the subjective aspect of emotional experience. Later, following terminology introduced by the anatomist BROCA, he called these structures the LIMBIC SYSTEM.

In the years following MacLean's account, researchers have debated exactly which structures can be said to be "limbic." Most often included are the AMYGDALA, septum, hippocampal formation, orbitofrontal cortex, and cingulate gyrus. However, it is now appreciated that no criteria—be they anatomic, association with visceral function, or association with the behavioral manifestations of emotional experience—bind the regions traditionally called "limbic" unequivocally and uniquely together, leaving the status of this proposal in doubt (LeDoux 1991). Indeed, James had asserted a century ago that there is no special brain system mediating emotional experience. Instead, he held, the bodily changes brought about by a stimulus are themselves experienced in turn through interoceptive pathways that project to sensory cortex; the latter somatic sensations "are" emotional experience. The role of afferent activity from the body in producing states of feeling continues to be emphasized: indeed, the idea that somatic sensations form the critical core of ongoing subjective experience has been repeatedly proposed by philosophers and psychologists. Most neuroscientists accept the idea that the body plays a role, but they also believe that there are particular structures in the human brain that are specialized for emotional experience and behavior.

There are several distinct themes in studies of the neural basis of human emotion. One pertains to the role of neural structures in producing states of feeling. In the 1950s, neurosurgeons demonstrated that subjective emotional experiences, especially fear, could be produced by electrical stimulation in the temporal lobes, particularly in the amygdala and hippocampal formation. The amygdala has come to the fore again in modern imaging studies that suggest that individuals with familial depression have increased metabolic activity in the left amygdala. Depression has been associated with both decreased and increased activity in orbitofrontal cortex. Several decades ago, before the rise of activity-dependent imaging techniques, there was an interest in the relation between mood and hemispheric side of brain lesions, with several researchers concluding that strokes involving the left hemisphere, particularly the frontal regions, produce depression, whereas strokes in the right produce euphoria. Although this interpretation of lesion data has been debated subsequently, stable differences in individual temperament have been attributed to differing patterns of activation of anterior frontal and temporal regions in the two hemispheres.

Links between emotion, memory, and learning have also attracted interest. Normal subjects seem to show a right hemisphere superiority for recall of affective material, and subjects with greater activation of the right amygdala appear to have a greater ability to recall emotional movies. Damasio (1994) has emphasized the role of central representations of relevant somatic states for acquiring appropriate responses to positive and negative situations. In support of his thesis, he has demonstrated that certain patients with orbitofrontal lesions, who seem unable to make appropriate decisions in real life situations, are also deficient in their autonomic responses to arousing stimuli.

A second major theme in emotion research relates to the production and understanding of expressive behavior. The right hemisphere appears to predominate for the production and the perception of expressions, both facial and vocal. Indeed, the temporal cortex of the right hemisphere may have a region specialized for decoding facial expression. Furthermore, some patients with bilateral damage to the amygdala are deficient in understanding facial expressions, especially expressions of fear. One such patient was also

found to have difficulty interpreting emotional and non-emotional intonations of voice. These findings are consistent with a number of lesion studies carried out from the 1930s to the 1960s in nonhuman primates, involving structures such as the amygdala, orbital frontal cortex, and cortex of the temporal pole. Researchers had concluded, based on the animals' impaired ability to interpret social signals, that these structures are part of a brain system specialized for social responsiveness in primates (Kling and Steklis 1976). Indeed, case reports have repeatedly shown that humans with lesions in structures such as the hypothalamus, amygdala, cingulate gyrus, and orbitofrontal cortex exhibit altered social behavior and expressiveness. It is at present uncertain whether one should conceptualize the defective performance of patients with amygdala lesions in terms of a primary deficiency of emotional state (e.g., fear) or a primary deficiency of social communication (e.g., ability to interpret expression).

A third theme in emotion research is the neurochemistry of mood. The discovery that the antihypertensive drug reserpine induced depression gave rise to models of depression that invoked catecholamine transmission. Subsequently, the discovery of abnormally low levels of serotonin in the cerebrospinal fluid of suicide victims gave rise to hypotheses invoking serotonin. Both theories are supported by the efficacy of medications that enhance catecholaminergic and serotonergic transmission for the treatment of depression, but empirical confirmation of hypotheses regarding the specific sites and mechanisms of action remains lacking. Other workers have proposed a role for dopamine in disorders of mood. At present, the clear efficacy of antidepressant medications is not matched by an equally clear understanding of their mechanisms. Likewise, roles for GABAergic and serotonergic systems in anxiety have been postulated, based on the clinical effects of agents that interact with these neurotransmitters. Imaging studies show some promise of illuminating the relation between neurotransmitters and mood in the future.

There are some persisting uncertainties in emotion research. For one, workers have long debated the relative contributions of somatic states and cognition to emotional experience. A principled distinction between somatic states that are emotional and those that are not is impossible: as a result, emotion cannot be defined in terms of somatic states alone. Furthermore, there is general agreement that somatic changes cannot be specific enough by themselves to yield the various discriminable emotional experiences. But because somatic elements seem indispensable to emotion, researchers such as Schachter and Singer (1962) have argued that cognitive appraisal of the stimulus must be combined with physiological arousal in order for an emotion to be produced. However, the notion of appraisal itself is complex. Another area of uncertainty concerns which emotions deserve to be called "basic" (Ortony and Turner 1990). Finally, one of the pillars of the emotion concept is the idea of subjective experience—feeling. This raises the thorny problem of QUALIA, a philosophical term for the felt nature of experience (cf. MIND-BODY PROBLEM). Nevertheless, despite—or even because of—these uncertainties, emotion will continue to attract interest as a topic in cognitive science.

See also EMOTIONS; EMOTION AND THE ANIMAL BRAIN; FREUD; INTERSUBJECTIVITY

—*Leslie Brothers*

References

Candland, D. (1977). The persistent problems of emotion. In D. Candland, J. Fell, E. Keen, A. Leshner, R. Tarpy, and R. Plutchik, Eds., *Emotion.* Monterey, CA: Brooks-Cole, pp. 2–84.

Damasio, A. (1994). *Descartes' Error: Emotion, Reason, and the Human Brain.* New York: G. P. Putnam's Sons.

Darwin, C. (1872). *The Expression of the Emotions in Man and Animals.*

Ekman, P., E. Sorenson, and W. Friesen. (1969). Pan-cultural elements in facial displays of emotion. *Science* 186: 86–88.

James, W. (1884). What is an emotion? *Mind* 9: 188–205.

Kling, A., and H. D. Steklis. (1976). A neural substrate for affiliative behavior in nonhuman primates. *Brain, Behavior and Evolution* 13: 216–238.

LeDoux, J. (1991). Emotion and the limbic system concept. *Concepts Neurosci.* 2: 169–199.

MacLean, P. (1952). Some psychiatric implications of physiological studies on frontotemporal portion of limbic system (visceral brain). *Electroencephalog. Clin. Neurophysiol.* 4: 407–418.

McCarthy, E. D. (1989). Emotions are social things: An essay in the sociology of emotions. In D. Franks and E. D. McCarthy, Eds., *The Sociology of Emotions: Original Essays and Research Papers.* Greenwich, CT: JAI Press, pp. 51–72.

Ortony, A., and T. Turner. (1990). What's basic about basic emotions? *Psychological Review* 97: 315–331.

Schachter, S., and J. Singer. (1962). Cognitive, social, and physiological determinants of emotional state. *Psychological Review* 69: 379–399.

Further Readings

Adolphs, R., H. Damasio, D. Tranel, and A. Damasio. (1996). Cortical systems for the recognition of emotion in facial expressions. *J. Neurosci.* 16: 7678–7687.

Asberg, M., P. Thoren, L. Traskman, L. Bertilsson, and V. Ringberger. (1976). "Serotonin Depression"—a biochemical subgroup within the affective disorders? *Science* 191: 478–480.

Cahill, L., R. Haier, J. Fallon, M. Alkire, C. Tang, D. Keator, J. Wu, and J. McGaugh. (1996). Amygdala activity at encoding correlated with long-term, free recall of emotional information. *Proc. Natl. Acad. Sci. USA* 93: 8016–8021.

Calder, A., A. Young, D. Rowland, D. Perrett, J. Hodges, and N. Etcoff. (1996). Facial emotion recognition after bilateral amygdala damage: Differentially severe impairment of fear. *Cognitive Neuropsychology* 13: 699–745.

Davidson, R. (1992). Anterior cerebral asymmetry and the nature of emotion. *Brain and Cognition* 20: 125–151.

Drevets, W., and M. Raichle. (1995). Positron emission tomographic imaging studies of human emotional disorders. In M. Gazzaniga, Ed., *The Cognitive Neurosciences.* Cambridge, MA: MIT Press, pp. 1153–1164.

Drevets, W., J. Price, J. Simpson, R. Todd, T. Reich, M. Vannier, and M. Raichle. (1997). Subgenual prefrontal cortex abnormalities in mood disorders. *Nature* 386: 824–827.

Duffy, E. (1941). An explanation of "emotional" phenomena without the use of the concept "emotion." *J. Gen. Psychology* 25: 283–293.

Fried, I., C. Mateer, G. Ojemann, R. Wohns, and P. Fedio. (1982). Organization of visuospatial functions in human cortex: Evidence from electrical stimulation. *Brain* 105: 349–371.

Gainotti, G. (1972). Emotional behavior and hemispheric side of the lesion. *Cortex* 8: 41–55.

Gold, P., F. Goodwin, and G. Chrousos. (1988). Clinical and biochemical manifestations of depression. *NEJM* 319: 348–420.

House, A., M. Dennis, C. Warlow, K. Hawton, and A. Molyneux. (1990). Mood disorders after stroke and their relation to lesion location: A CT scan study. *Brain* 113: 1113–1128.

Mayberg, H., S. Starkstein, C. Peyser, J. Brandt, R. Dannals, and S. Folstein. (1992). Paralimbic frontal lobe hypometabolism in depression associated with Huntington's disease. *Neurology* 42: 1791–1797.

Morris, J., D. Frith, D. Perrett, D. Rowland, A. Young, A. Calder, and R. Dolan. (1996). A differential neural response in the human amygdala to fearful and happy facial expressions. *Nature* 383: 812–815.

Papez, J. (1937). A proposed mechanism of emotion. *Arch. Neurol. Psychiat.* 38: 725–743.

Scott, S., A. Young, A. Calder, D. Hellawell, J. Aggleton, and M. Johnson. (1997). Impaired auditory recognition of fear and anger following bilateral amygdala lesions. *Nature* 385: 254–257.

Suberi, M., and W. McKeever. (1977). Differential right hemispheric memory storage of emotional and non-emotional faces. *Neuropsychologia* 15: 757–768.

Swerdlow, N., and G. Koob. (1987). Dopamine, schizophrenia, mania, and depression: Toward a unified hypothesis of cortico-striato-pallido-thalamic function. *Behav. Brain Sciences* 10: 197–245.

Weintraub, S., and M-M. Mesulam. (1983). Developmental learning disabilities of the right hemisphere. *Arch. Neurol.* 40: 463–468.

Weintraub, S., M-M. Mesulam, and L. Kramer. (1981). Disturbances in prosody: A right-hemisphere contribution to language. *Arch. Neurol.* 38: 742–744.

Emotions

An emotion is a psychological state or process that functions in the management of goals. It is typically elicited by evaluating an event as relevant to a goal; it is positive when the goal is advanced, negative when the goal is impeded. The core of an emotion is readiness to act in a certain way (Frijda 1986); it is an urgency, or prioritization, of some goals and plans rather than others. Emotions can interrupt ongoing action; also they prioritize certain kinds of social interaction, prompting, for instance, COOPERATION or conflict.

The term *emotional* is often used synonymously with the term *affective*. Emotions proper usually have a clear relation to whatever elicited them. They are often associated with brief (lasting a few seconds) expressions of face and voice, and with perturbation of the autonomic nervous system. Such manifestations often go unnoticed by the person who has the emotion. A consciously recognized emotion lasts minutes or hours. A *mood* has similar bases to an emotion but lasts longer; whereas an emotion tends to change the course of action, a mood tends to resist disruption. At the longer end of the time spectrum, an emotional disorder, usually defined as a protracted mood plus specific symptoms, lasts from weeks to years. Personality traits, most with an emotional basis, last for years or a lifetime. (Definitions, distinctions, and the philosophical and psychological background of emotions discussed in the next paragraphs, are described in more detail by Oatley and Jenkins 1996.)

Emotions have been analyzed by some of the world's leading philosophers, including Aristotle, DESCARTES, and Spinoza. Following Aristotle, in whose functionalist account emotions were species of cognitive evaluations of events, most philosophical work on emotions has been cognitive. The stoics developed subtle analyses of emotions, arguing that most were deleterious, because people had wrong beliefs and inappropriate goals. Stoic influence has continued. Its modern descendent is cognitive therapy for emotional disorders.

Charles DARWIN (1872) argued that emotional expressions are behavioral equivalents of vestigial anatomical organs like the appendix; they derive from earlier phases of EVOLUTION or of individual development, and in adulthood they occur whether or not they are of any use. According to William JAMES (1884), FOLK PSYCHOLOGY wrongly assumes that an event causes an emotion, which in turn causes a reaction. Instead, he argued that an emotion is a perception of the physiological reactions by the body to the event; emotions give color to experience but, as perceptions of physiological changes, they occur after the real business of producing behavior is over. Following James, there has been a long tradition of regarding emotions as bodily states, and although cognitive approaches now dominate the field, body-based research on emotions continues to be influential (see the third and fourth approaches following). FREUD developed theories of emotional disorder, proposing that severe emotional experiences, whether of trauma or conflict, undermine RATIONAL AGENCY subsequently, and interfere with life.

Cultural distrust of emotions was exacerbated by the work of Darwin, James, and Freud. There seemed to be something wrong with emotions; they were either without useful function in adult life or actively dysfunctional. Starting in the 1950s, however, several influential movements began with cognitive emphases, all stressing function, and all making it clear that emotions typically contribute to rationality instead of being primarily irrational. One result of these movements has been to expand concepts of cognition to include emotion. Among the first cognitive approaches to emotions, in the 1950s, was Bowlby's (see e.g., 1971). Bowlby proposed the idea of emotional attachment of infant to a mother or other caregiver. He was influenced by theories of evolution and of PSYCHOANALYSIS. His compelling analogy was with the ethological idea of imprinting. With attachment—love—in infancy, a child's emotional development is based on the child's building a MENTAL MODEL of its relationship with the caregiver (Bowlby called it a "working model") to organize the child's relational goals and plans.

Mental models are also known as *schemas*. Developmentalists have done much to demonstrate the importance of emotional schemas for structuring close relationships (see SOCIAL COGNITION). Such demonstrations include those of children's models of interaction with violent parents, probably functional in the family where they first occur, but often maladaptive in the outside world where they play a large role in later aggressive delinquency (Dodge, Bates, and Pettit 1990). A parallel, second approach was that of Arnold (e.g.,

Arnold and Gasson 1954). She proposed that emotions are relational: they relate selves, including physiological substrates, to events in the world. Events are appraised, consciously or unconsciously, for their suitability to the subject's goals, for whether desired objects are available or not, and according to several other features of the event and its context. Appraisal researchers have shown that which emotion is produced by any event depends on which appraisals are made (e.g., Frijda 1986). Work on appraisal was extended by Lazarus (1991) to research on coping and its effects on health. A third approach was also begun in the 1950s, by Tomkins (see, e.g., 1995). He proposed that, based on feedback from bodily processes, particularly from expressions of the face, emotions act as amplifiers to specific motivational systems. Personality is structured by schemas, each with a theme of some emotional issue. Tomkins inspired a surge of research (e.g., Scherer and Ekman 1984) that did much to place the study of emotions on an accepted empirical base. Notable has been the study of facial expressions and their relation to emotions, both developmentally and cross-culturally. Some aspects of such expressions are agreed to be HUMAN UNIVERSALS, although how they are best analyzed remains controversial. A fourth approach occurred with attempts to reconcile the work of James with cognitive ideas: notable were Schachter and Singer (1962), who proposed that emotion was a physiological perturbation, as had also been proposed by James, although not with the distinctive patterning that James had suggested; instead an undifferentiated arousal was made recognizable by cognitive labeling (a kind of appraisal). This work has been extended by Mandler (1984) who, like Simon (see next paragraph) stressed that emotions occur when an ongoing activity is interrupted, and an expectancy is violated.

Prompted by difficulties of COGNITIVE MODELING in capturing what is essential about the organization of human action, Simon (1967) argued that because resources are always finite, any computational system operating in any complex environment needs some system to manage PLANNING, capable of interrupting ongoing processes. The system for handling interruptions can be identified with the emotional system of human beings. An extended idea of Simon's proposal can be put like this: In the ordinary world there are three large problems for orchestrating cognitively based action.

1. Mental models are always incomplete and sometimes incorrect; resources of time and power are always limited.
2. Human beings typically have multiple goals, not all of which can be reconciled.
3. Human beings are those agents who accomplish together what they cannot do alone; hence individual goals and plans are typically parts of distributed cognitive systems.

Although cooperation helps overcome limitations of resources, it exacerbates problems of multiple goals and requires coordination of mental models among distributed agents. These three problems ensure that fully rational solutions to most problems in life are rare. Humans' biologically based solution is the system of emotions. These provide genetically based heuristics for situations that affect ongoing action and that have recurred during evolution (e.g., threats, losses, frustrations), they outline scripts for coordination with others during cooperation, social threat, interpersonal conflict, etc.; and they serve as bases for constructing new parts of the cognitive system when older parts are found wrong or inadequate.

Much recent research is concerned with effects of emotions and moods. Emotions bias cognitive processing during judgment and inference, giving preferential availability to some heuristics rather than others. For instance, happiness allows unusual associations and improves creative PROBLEM SOLVING (Isen, Daubman, and Nowicki 1987); anxiety constrains ATTENTION to features of the environment concerned with safety or danger; sadness prompts recall from MEMORY of incidents from the past that elicited comparable sadness. Such biases provide bases for both normal functions, and for disordered emotional processing (Mathews and MacLeod 1994).

As compared with research on learning or perception, research on emotions has been delayed. With newer cognitive emphases, however, emotions are seen to serve important intracognitive and interpersonal functions. A remarkable convergence is occurring: as well as support from evidence of social and developmental psychology, the largely functionalist account given here is supported by evidence from animal neuroscience (EMOTION AND THE ANIMAL BRAIN) and human neuropsychology (EMOTION AND THE HUMAN BRAIN). There is growing consensus: emotions are managers of mental life, prompting heuristics that relate the flow of daily events to goals and social concerns.

—Keith Oatley

References

Arnold, M. B., and J. Gasson. (1954). Feelings and emotions as dynamic factors in personality integration. In M. B. Arnold and J. Gasson, Eds., *The Human Person.* New York: Ronald, pp. 294–313.

Bowlby, J. (1971). *Attachment and Loss, vol. 1: Attachment.* London: Hogarth.

Darwin, C. (1872). *The Expression of the Emotions in Man and Animals.* London: Murray.

Dodge, K. A., J. Bates, and G. Pettit. (1990). Mechanisms in the cycle of violence. *Science* 250: 1678–1683.

Frijda, N. H. (1986). *The Emotions.* Cambridge: Cambridge University Press.

Isen, A. M., K. Daubman, and G. Nowicki. (1987). Positive affect facilitates creative problem solving. *Journal of Personality and Social Psychology* 52: 1122–1131.

James, W. (1884). What is an emotion? *Mind* 9: 188–205.

Lazarus, R. S. (1991). *Emotion and Adaptation.* New York: Oxford University Press.

Mandler, G. (1984). *Mind and Body: Psychology of Emotions and Stress.* New York: Norton.

Mathews, A., and C. MacLeod. (1994). Cognitive approaches to emotion and emotional disorders. *Annual Review of Psychology* 45: 25–50.

Oatley, K., and J. M. Jenkins. (1996). *Understanding Emotions.* Cambridge, MA: Blackwell.

Schachter, S., and J. Singer. (1962). Cognitive, social and physiological determinants of emotional state. *Psychological Review* 69: 379–399.

Scherer, K., and P. Ekman. (1984). *Approaches to Emotion.* Hillsdale, NJ: Erlbaum.

Simon, H. A. (1967). Motivational and emotional controls of cognition. *Psychological Review* 74: 29–39.

Tomkins, S. S. (1995). *Exploring Affect: Selected Writings of Sylvan S. Tomkins.* E. V. Demos., Ed. New York: Cambridge University Press.

Empiricism

See INTRODUCTION: PHILOSOPHY; BEHAVIORISM; RATIONALISM VS. EMPIRICISM

Epiphenomenalism

The traditional doctrine of epiphenomenalism is that mental phenomena are caused by physical phenomena but do not themselves cause anything. Thus, according to this doctrine, mental states and events are causally inert, causally impotent; they figure in the web of causal relations only as effects, never as causes. James Ward (1903) coined the term *epiphenomenalism* for this doctrine. However, William JAMES (1890) was the first to use the term *epiphenomena* to mean phenomena that lack causal efficacy. (It is possible that his use of the term was inspired by the medical use of *epiphenomena* to mean symptoms of an underlying condition.) Huxley (1874) and Hodgson (1870) earlier discussed the doctrine of epiphenomenalism under the heading of "Conscious Automatism." They both held that conscious states are caused by physiological states but have no causal effect on physiological states (see Caston 1997).

According to proponents of epiphenomenalism, mental phenomena seem to be causes only because they figure in regularities. For example, instances of a certain type of mental occurrence M (e.g., trying to raise one's arm) might tend to be followed by instances of a type of physical occurrence P (e.g., one's arm's rising). But it would be fallacious to infer from that regularity that instances of M tend to cause instances of P: it would be to commit the fallacy of *post hoc, ergo propter hoc.* According to the epiphenomenalist, when an M-type occurrence is followed by a P-type occurrence, the occurrences are dual effects of some common physical cause.

Epiphenomenalism is a shocking doctrine. If it is true, then a PAIN could never cause us to wince or flinch, something's looking red to us could never cause us to think it is red, and a nagging headache could never cause us to be in a bad mood. Indeed, if epiphenomenalism is true, then although one thought may follow another, one thought never results in another. If thinking is a causal process, it follows that we never engage in the activity of thinking.

A central premise in the argument for epiphenomenalism is that for every (caused) event, e, there is a causal chain of physical events leading to e such that each link in the chain determines (or, if strict determinism is false, determines the objective probability of) its successor. Such physical causal chains are said to leave "no gap" to be filled by mental occurrences, and it is thus claimed that mental occurrences are epiphenomena (McLaughlin 1994).

One critical response to this no-gap line of argument for epiphenomenalism is that physical events underlie mental events in such a way that mental events are causally efficacious by means of the causal efficacy of their underlying physical events. The task for proponents of this response is to say what it is, exactly, for a physical event to underlie a mental event, and to explain how mental events can count as causes in virtue of the causal efficacy of their underlying physical events. The underlying relationship is typically spelled out in terms of some relationship between mental and physical event types. An explication of the relationship should yield an account of how causal efficacy can transmit from underlying physical events to mental events. (See the discussion of realization that follows.)

Perhaps the leading response to the no-gap line of argument, however, is that every token mental event is identical with some token physical event or other. According to this token physicalism, an event can be both an instance of a mental type (e.g., belief) and an instance of a distinct physical type (e.g., a neurophysiological type). CAUSATION is an extensional relation between states and events: if two states or events are causally related, they are so related however we may type or describe them. Given that the causal relation is extensional, because particular mental states and events are physical states and events with causal effects, mental states and events are causes, and thus epiphenomenalism is false (Davidson 1970, 1993).

The token-identity response to epiphenomenalism does not, however, escape the issue of how mental and physical types (or properties) are related (McLaughlin 1989; 1993). For it prompts a concern about the relevance of mental properties or types to causal relations. C. D. Broad (1925) characterized the view that mental events are epiphenomena as the view "that mental events either (a) do not function at all as causal-factors; or that (b) if they do, they do so in virtue of their physiological characteristics and not in virtue of their mental characteristics" (1925: 473).

Following Broad, we can distinguish two kinds of epiphenomenalism (McLaughlin 1989):

Token Epiphenomenalism Physical events cause mental events, but mental events have no causal effects.
Type Epiphenomenalism Events are causes in virtue of falling under physical types, but no event causes anything in virtue of falling under a mental type.

(*Property epiphenomenalism* is the thesis that no event can cause anything in virtue of having or being an exemplification of a mental property.) Token epiphenomenalism implies type epiphenomenalism; for if an event can cause something in virtue of falling under a mental type, then an event could be both a mental event and a cause, and thus token epiphenomenalism would be false. However, type epiphenomenalism is compatible with the denial of token epiphenomenalism: mental events may be causes, but only in virtue of falling under physical types, and not in virtue of falling under mental types. Whether type epiphenomenalism is true, and whether certain doctrines about the mind (such as Davidson's (1970) doctrine of ANOMALOUS MONISM, which implies token physicalism) imply type epiphenomenalism, have been subjects of intense debate in recent years (see the essays in Heil and Mele 1993). But one can find the concern about type or property epiphenomenalism even in ancient philosophical texts. Aristotle appears to have criticized the *harmonia* theory of the soul—the theory according to which the soul is like the harmonia of a musical instrument, its tuning or mode—on the grounds that it implies property epiphenomenalism (see Caston 1997).

Type epiphenomenalism is itself a stunning doctrine. If type epiphenomenalism is true, then nothing has any causal powers in virtue of (because of) being an instance of a mental type (or having a mental property). Thus, it could never be the case that it is in virtue of being an urge to scratch that a state results in scratching behavior; and it could never be the case that it is in virtue of a state's being a belief that danger is near that it results in fleeing behavior. If type epiphenomenalism is true, the mental *qua* mental, so to speak, is causally inert: mental types and properties make no difference to causal transactions between states and events (Sosa 1984; Horgan 1989).

How can mental types be related to physical types so that type epiphenomenalism fails? How can mental types be related to physical types so that an event can be a cause in virtue of falling under a mental type? How must mental types relate to physical types so as not to compete for causal relevance?

The notion of multiple realization is often invoked in response to such questions. It is claimed that mental types are multiply realized by physical types and that sometimes a mental type is causally relevant to a certain effect type, whereas the relevant underlying, realizing physical type is merely a matter of implementational detail (Putnam 1975a; Yablo 1992a, 1992b). This happens whenever instances of the mental type would produce an effect of the sort in question however the mental type is in fact physically realized.

This, of course, raises the issue of what realization is. On one notion of realization, the realization relation is that of determinable to determinate (Yablo 1992a, 1992b). But it is highly controversial whether mental types are determinables of physical types. On a related notion of realization, realization is spelled out in terms of the notion of a causal role and the notion of a role-player. Mental state types are types of functional states: they are second-order states, states of being in a state that plays a certain causal role (Loar 1981). The first-order states that realize them are physical states that play the causal roles in question. The second-order state may be multiply realizable in that there are many different first-order states that play the causal role. It is controversial whether appeal to this notion of realization can warrant the rejection of type epiphenomenalism. For it is arguable that second-order state types are themselves epiphenomena. It is arguably not in virtue of falling under such a second-order state type that a state has causal effects, but rather in virtue of falling under some (relevant) first-order state type (Block 1990).

Another notion of realization treats mental concepts (i.e., concepts of mental states) as equivalent to functional concepts, but treats mental states themselves as first-order states that play the relevant causal role (Armstrong 1968; Lewis 1980). On this view, the concept of mental state *M* of an organism (or system) is equivalent to the concept of being a state of the organism (or system) that plays a certain causal role *R*. It is claimed that the states that answer to the functional concepts in question are invariably physical states, but which physical states they are may vary from species to species, or even within a species, perhaps even within a given individual at different times.

Concerns about type epiphenomenalism remain, however. We type intentional mental states not only by their intentional mode (e.g., belief, desire, intention), but also by their content (by what is believed, what is desired, or what is intended). According to externalist theories of content, the content of a mental state can fail to supervene on intrinsic physical states of its occupant (Putnam 1975b; Burge 1979). Two intrinsic physical duplicates could have mental states (e.g., beliefs) with different contents. Thus intentional state types seem to involve contextual, environmental factors. The concern is that the contextual, environmental component of content is causally irrelevant to behavior. This is a problem in that the contents of beliefs and desires figure essentially in belief-desire explanations of behavior. The problem is exacerbated by the fact that on some externalist theories, content depends on historical context (Dretske 1988), and that on some it can depend on social context (Burge 1979).

A concern also remains about whether qualitative mental states (states that have a subjective experiential aspect) are epiphenomena. Our concepts of sensory states—e.g., aches, pains, itches, and the like—are arguably not functional concepts in either sense of functional concepts (Hill 1991). This has led some philosophers to embrace token dualism for such states and to maintain both type and token epiphenomenalism for them (Jackson 1982; Chalmers 1996). In rejection of epiphenomenalism for qualitative states, some philosophers argue that sensory concepts are equivalent to functional concepts (White 1991). And some argue that although sensory concepts are not equivalent to functional concepts or physical concepts, nonetheless, sensory properties are identical with neural properties (Hill 1991). Whether PHYSICALISM is true for sensory states raises the mind-body problem in perhaps its toughest form. That a nagging headache can cause one to be in a bad mood and that an itch can cause one to scratch seem to be as intuitive cases of mental causation as one can find. But how, and indeed even whether, a qualitative aspect of a mental state (e.g., the achiness of the headache) can be causally relevant remains an issue of intense debate.

See also INDIVIDUALISM; MENTAL CAUSATION; MENTAL REPRESENTATION; NARROW CONTENT

—*Brian P. McLaughlin*

References

Armstrong, D. M. (1968). *A Materialist Theory of Mind.* London: Routledge and Kegan Paul.

Block, N. (1990). Can the mind change the world? In G. Boolos, Ed., *Meaning and Method: Essays in Honor of Hilary Putnam.* Cambridge: Cambridge University Press.

Broad, C. D. (1925). *The Mind and Its Place in Nature.* London: Routledge and Kegan Paul.

Burge, T. (1979). Individualism and the mental. *Midwest Studies in Philosophy* 4: 73–121.

Caston, V. (1997). Epiphenomenalisms, ancient and modern. *Philosophical Review* 106.

Chalmers, D. (1996). *The Conscious Mind: In Search of a Theory of Conscious Experience.* New York: Oxford University Press.

Davidson, D. (1970). Mental events. In L. Foster and J. W. Swanson, Eds., *Experience and Theory.* Amherst: University of Massachusetts Press.

Davidson, D. (1993). Thinking causes. In J. Heil and A. Mele, Eds., *Mental Causation.* Oxford: Oxford University Press.

Dretske, F. (1988). *Explaining Behavior: Reasons in a World of Causes.* Cambridge, MA: MIT Press/Bradford Books.

Heil, J., and A. Mele, Eds. (1993). *Mental Causation.* Oxford: Oxford University Press.

Hill, C. (1991). *Sensations: A Defense of Type Materialism.* Cambridge: Cambridge University Press.

Hodgson, S. H. (1870). *The Theory of Practice: An Ethical Enquiry.* 2 vols. London: Longmans, Green, Reader, and Dyer.

Horgan, T. (1989). Mental quasation. *Philosophical Perspectives* 3: 47–76.

Huxley, T. H. (1874/1901). On the hypothesis that animals are automata, and its history. Reprinted in T. H. Huxley, *Method and Results. Collected Essays,* vol. 1. New York: D. Appleton and Company.

Jackson, F. (1982). Epiphenomenal qualia. *Philosophical Quarterly* 32: 127–136.

Lepore, E., and B. Loewer. (1987). Mind matters. *Journal of Philosophy* 84: 630–642.

Lewis, D. (1980). Mad pain and martian pain. In N. Block, Ed., *Readings in the Philosophy of Psychology,* vol. 1. Cambridge, MA: Harvard University Press.

Loar, B. (1981). *Mind and Meaning.* Cambridge: Cambridge University Press.

McLaughlin, B. P. (1989). Type dualism, type epiphenomenalism, and the causal priority of the physical. *Philosophical Perspectives* 3: 109–135.

McLaughlin, B. P. (1993). On Davidson's response to the charge of epiphenomenalism. In Heil, J., and A. Mele, Eds., *Mental Causation.* Oxford: Oxford University Press, 27–40.

McLaughlin, B. P. (1994). Epiphenomenalism. In S. Guttenplan, Ed., *A Companion to the Philosophy of Mind.* Oxford: Blackwell, pp. 277–288

McLaughlin, B. P. (1995). Mental causation. In *Encyclopedia of Philosophy, Supplementary Volume.* London: Routledge and Kegan Paul.

Putnam, H. (1975a). Philosophy and our mental life. In H. Putnam, Ed., *Philosophical Papers,* vol. 2. Cambridge: Cambridge University Press.

Putnam, H. (1975b). The meaning of "meaning." In H. Putnam, Ed., *Philosophical Papers,* vol. 2. Cambridge: Cambridge University Press.

Sosa, E. (1984). Mind-body interaction and supervenient causation. *Midwest Studies in Philosophy* 9: 271–281.

Ward, J. (1896–98/1903). The Conscious Automaton Theory. Lecture XII of *Naturalism or Agnosticism,* vol. 2. London: Adam and Charles Black, pp. 34–64.

White, S. L. (1991). *The Unity of the Self.* Cambridge, MA: MIT/Bradford Books.

Yablo, S. (1992a). Mental causation. *Philosophical Review* 101: 245–280.

Yablo, S. (1992b). Cause and essence. *Synthese* 93: 403–499.

Further Readings

Fodor, J. A. (1987). *Psychosemantics.* Cambridge, MA: MIT Press.

Jackson, F., and P. Pettit. (1988). Broad contents and functionalism. *Mind* 47: 381–400.

Kim, J. (1984). Epiphenomenal and supervenient causation. *Midwest Studies in Philosophy* 9: 257–270.

Kim, J. (1993). *Supervenience and Mind.* Cambridge: Cambridge University Press.

Episodic vs. Semantic Memory

Episodic memory is a recently evolved, late developing, past-oriented memory system, probably unique to humans, that allows remembering of previous experiences as experienced. William JAMES (1890) discussed it as simply "memory." The advent of many different forms of memory since James's time has made adjectival modifications of the term necessary. Semantic memory is the closest relative of episodic memory in the family of memory systems. It allows humans and nonhuman animals to acquire and use knowledge about their world. Although humans habitually express and exchange their knowledge through language, language is not necessary for either remembering past experiences or knowing facts about the world.

Episodic and semantic memory are alike in many ways, and for a long time were thought of and classified together as an undifferentiated "declarative" memory that was distinguished from "procedural" memory. Nevertheless, rapidly accumulating evidence suggests that episodic and semantic memory are fundamentally different in a number of ways, and therefore need to be treated separately. In what follows, the similarities and differences are briefly summarized.

Episodic and semantic systems share a number of features that collectively define "declarative" (or "cognitive") memory in humans.

1. Both are large and complex, and have unmeasurable capacity to hold information, unlike WORKING MEMORY, which has limited capacity.
2. Cognitive operations involved in encoding of information are similar for both episodic and semantic memory. Frequently a single short-lived event is sufficient for a permanent "addition" to the memory store, unlike in many other forms of learning that require repeated experiences of a given kind.
3. Both are open to multimodal influences and can receive information for storage through different sensory modalities, as well as from internally generated sources.
4. The operations of both systems are governed by principles such as encoding specificity and transfer-appropriate processing.
5. Stored information in both systems represents aspects of the world, and it has truth value, unlike many other forms of learned behavior that do not.
6. Both are "cognitive" systems: their informational "contents" can be thought about independently of any overt action, although such action can be and frequently is taken. As cognitive systems, episodic and semantic memory differ from all forms of procedural memory in which overt behavior at input and output is obligatory.
7. Information in both systems is flexibly accessible through a variety of retrieval queries and routes.
8. Information retrieved from either system can be expressed and communicated to others symbolically.
9. Information in both systems is accessible to INTROSPECTION: we can consciously "think" about things and events in the world, as we can "think" about what we did yesterday afternoon, or in the summer camp at age ten.
10. The processes of both forms of memory depend critically on the integrity of the medial temporal lobe and diencephalic structures of the brain.

Consider now the differences.

1. The simplest way of contrasting episodic and semantic memory is in terms of their functions: episodic memory is concerned with *remembering,* whereas semantic memory is concerned with *knowing.* Episodic remembering takes the form of "mental travel through subjective time," accompanied by a special kind of awareness ("autonoetic," or self-knowing, awareness). Semantic knowing takes the form of thinking about what there is, or was, or could be in the world; it is accompanied by another kind of awareness ("noetic," or knowing awareness). Language is frequently involved in both episodic and semantic memory, but it need not be.
2. The relation between remembering and knowing is one of embeddedness: remembering always implies knowing, whereas knowing does not imply remembering.
3. Episodic memory is arguably a more recent arrival on the evolutionary scene than semantic memory. Many animals other than humans, especially mammals and birds, possess well-developed knowledge-of-the-world (semantic memory) systems. But there is no evidence that they have the ability to autonoetically remember past events in the way that humans do.
4. Episodic lags behind semantic memory in human development. Young children acquire a great deal of knowledge about their world before they become capable of adult-like episodic remembering.
5. Episodic memory is the only form of memory that is oriented toward the past: retrieval in episodic memory necessarily involves thinking "back" to an earlier time. All other forms of memory, including semantic memory, are present-oriented: utilization (retrieval) of information usually occurs for the purpose of whatever one is doing now without any thinking "back" to the experiences of the past.
6. Episodic remembering is characterized by a state of awareness (autonoetic) that is different from that in semantic memory (noetic). When one recollects an event autonoetically, one reexperiences aspects of a past experience; when one recalls a fact learned in the past, reexperiencing of the learning episode is not necessary.
7. Episodic remembering has an affectively laden "tone" that is absent in semantic knowing. William James (1890) referred to is as a "feeling of warmth and intimacy."

Given the many similarities and some fundamental differences between episodic and semantic memory, it is difficult to provide a simple description of the relation between the two. According to one proposal, however, the relation is process-specific: The two systems operate serially at the time of encoding: information "enters" episodic memory "through" semantic memory. They operate in parallel in holding the stored information: a given datum may be stored in one or both systems. And the two systems can act independently at the time of retrieval: recovery of episodic information can occur separately of retrieval of semantic information (Tulving 1995).

The term "episodic memory" is sometimes used in senses that differ from the memory-systems orientation presented here. Some writers use "episodic memory" in its original sense of task orientation: Episodic memory refers to tasks in which information is encoded for storage on a particular occasion. This kind of usage is popular in work with animals. Other writers use "episodic memory" as a particular kind of memory information or "material," namely past "events," in contrast with the "facts" of semantic memory. The systems-based definition of episodic memory as described here is more comprehensive than either the task-specific and material-specific definitions. Finally, some writers still prefer the traditional view that there is only one kind of declarative memory, and they use the terms "episodic" and "semantic" for descriptive purposes only.

The evidential basis for the distinction between episodic and semantic memory has been growing steadily over the past ten or fifteen years. General reviews have been provided by Nyberg and Tulving (1996), Nyberg, McIntosh, and Tulving (1997), and Wheeler, Stuss, and Tulving (1997). Functional dissociations between autonoetic and noetic awareness in memory retrieval have been reviewed by Gardiner and Java (1993). Developmental evidence for the distinction has been presented by Mitchell (1989), Nelson (1993), Nilsson et al. (1997), and Perner and Ruffman (1995). Pertinent psychopharmacological data have been reported by Curran et al. (1993). Dissociations between episodic and semantic memory produced by known or suspected brain damage have been reported, among others, by Hayman, Macdonald, and Tulving (1993); Markowitsch (1995); Shimamura and Squire (1987); and Vargha-Khadem et al. (1997). Electrophysiological correlates of "remembering" versus "knowing" have been described by Düzel et al. (1997), and differences in EEG power spectra in episodic versus semantic retrieval by Klimesch, Schimke, and Schwaiger (1994). Finally, evidence in support of the distinction between episodic and semantic memory has been provided by a number of recent studies of functional neuroimaging, especially POSITRON EMISSION TOMOGRAPHY (Buckner and Tulving 1995). One of the most persistent findings is that episodic retrieval is accompanied by changes in neuronal activity in brain regions such as the right prefrontal cortex, medial parietal cortical regions, and the left CEREBELLUM, whereas comparable semantic retrieval processes are accompanied by changes in the left frontal and temporal regions (Buckner 1996; Cabeza and Nyberg 1997; Fletcher, Frith, and Rugg 1997; Haxby et al. 1996; Nyberg, Cabeza, and Tulving 1996, Nyberg, McIntosh, and Tulving 1997; Shallice et al. 1994; Tulving et al. 1994). Future studies will undoubtedly further clarify the emerging picture of the functional neuroanatomy of episodic and semantic memory.

It is a moot question whether episodic and semantic memory are basically similar or basically different. The question is not unlike one about basic similarities and differences between, say, vertebrates and invertebrates. As frequently happens in science, it all depends on one's interest and purpose.

See also AGING, MEMORY, AND THE BRAIN; IMPLICIT VS. EXPLICIT MEMORY; MEMORY, HUMAN NEUROPSYCHOLOGY; WORKING MEMORY, NEURAL BASIS OF

—*Endel Tulving*

References

Buckner, R. (1996). Beyond HERA: Contributions of specific prefrontal brain areas to long-term memory. *Psychonomic Bulletin and Review* 3: 149–158.

Buckner, R., and E. Tulving. (1995). Neuroimaging studies of memory: Theory and recent PET results. In F. Boller and J. Grafman, Eds., *Handbook of Neuropsychology*, vol. 10. Amsterdam: Elsevier. pp. 439–466.

Cabeza, R., and L. Nyberg. (1997). Imaging cognition: An empirical review of PET studies with normal subjects. *Journal of Cognitive Neuroscience.*

Curran, H. V., J. M. Gardiner, R. Java, and D. Allen. (1993). Effects of lorazepam upon recollective experience in recognition memory. *Psychopharmacology* 110: 374–378.

Düzel, E., A. P. Yonelinas, H-J. Heinze, G. R. Mangun, and E. Tulving. (1997). Event-related brain potential correlates of two states of conscious awareness in memory. *Proceedings of National Academy of Sciences USA* 94: 5973–5978.

Fletcher, P. C., C. D. Frith, and M. D. Rugg. (1997). The functional neuroanatomy of episodic memory. *Trends in Neurosciences* 20: 213–218.

Gardiner, J. M., and R. Java. (1993). Recognizing and remembering. In A. F. Collins, S. E. Gathercole, M. A. Conway, and P. E. Morris, Eds., *Theories of Memory*. Hove, England: Erlbaum.

Haxby, J. V., L. G. Ungerleider, B. Horwitz, J. M. Maisog, S. L. Rapoport, and C. L. Grady. (1996). Face encoding and recognition in the human brain. *Proceedings of the National Academy of Sciences USA* 93: 922–927.

Hayman, C. A. G., C. A. Macdonald, and E. Tulving. (1993). The role of repetition and associative interference in new semantic learning in amnesia. *Journal of Cognitive Neuroscience* 5: 375–389.

James, W. (1890). *Principles of Psychology.* New York: Dover.

Klimesch, W., H. Schimke, and J. Schwaiger. (1994). Episodic and semantic memory: An analysis in the EEG theta and alpha band. *Electroencephalography and Clinical Neurophysiology* 91: 428–441.

Markowitsch, H. J. (1995). Which brain regions are critically involved in the retrieval of old episodic memory. *Brain Research Reviews* 21: 117–127.

Mitchell, D. B. (1989). How many memory systems? Evidence from aging. *Journal of Experimental Psychology: Learning, Memory and Cognition* 15: 31–49.

Nelson, K. (1993). The psychological and social origins of autobiographical memory. *Psychological Science* 4: 7–14.

Nilsson, L. G., L. Bäckman, K. Erngrund, L. Nyberg, R. Adolfsson, G. Bucht, S. Karlsson, M. Widing, and B. Winblad. (1997). The Betula prospective cohort study: Memory, health, and aging. *Aging and Cognition* 1: 1–36.

Nyberg, L., and E. Tulving. (1996). Classifying human long-term memory: Evidence from converging dissociations. *European Journal of Cognitive Psychology* 8: 163–183.

Nyberg, L., R. Cabeza, and E. Tulving. (1996). PET studies of encoding and retrieval: The HERA model. *Psychonomic Bulletin and Review* 3: 135–148.

Nyberg, L., A. R. McIntosh, and E. Tulving. (1997). Functional brain imaging of episodic and semantic memory. *Journal of Molecular Medicine* 76: 48–53.

Perner, J., and T. Ruffman. (1995). Episodic memory and autono-etic consciousness: Developmental evidence and a theory of childhood amnesia. *Journal of Experimental Child Psychology* 59: 516–548.

Shallice, T., P. Fletcher, C. D. Frith, P. Grasby, R. S. J. Fracowiak, and R. J. Dolan. (1994). Brain regions associated with acquisition and retrieval of verbal episodic memory. *Nature* 368: 633–635.

Shimamura, A. P., and L. R. Squire. (1987). A neuropsychological study of fact memory and source amnesia. *Journal of Experimental Psychology: Learning, Memory, and Cognition* 13: 464–473.

Tulving, E., S. Kapur, F. I. M. Craik, M. Moscovitch, and S. Houle. (1994). Hemispheric encoding/retrieval asymmetry in episodic memory: Positron emission tomography findings. *Proceedings of the National Academy of Sciences USA* 91: 2016–2020.

Tulving, E. (1995). Organization of memory: Quo vadis? In M. S. Gazzaniga, Ed., *The Cognitive Neurosciences.* Cambridge, MA: MIT Press, pp. 839–847.

Vargha-Khadem, F., D. G. Gadian, K. E. Watkins, A. Connelly, W. Van Paesschen, and M. Mishkin. (1997). Differential effects of early hippocampal pathology on episodic and semantic memory. *Science* 277: 376–380.

Wheeler, M. A., D. T. Stuss, and E. Tulving. (1997). Toward a theory of episodic memory: The frontal lobes and autonoetic consciousness. *Psychological Bulletin* 121: 331–354.

Further Readings

Dalla Barba, G., M. C. Mantovan, E. Ferruzza, and G. Denes. (1997). Remembering and knowing the past: A case study of isolated retrograde amnesia. *Cortex* 33: 143–154.

Horner, M. D. (1990). Psychobiological evidence for the distinction between episodic and semantic memory. *Neuropsychology Review* 1: 281–321.

Humphreys, M. S., J. D. Bain, and R. Pike. (1989). Different ways to cue a coherent memory system: A theory for episodic, semantic, and procedural tasks. *Psychological Review* 96: 208–233.

Humphreys, M. S., J. Wiles, and S. Dennis. (1994). Toward a theory of human memory: Data structures and access processes. *Behavioral and Brain Sciences* 17: 655–692.

Huron, C., J. M. Danion, F. Giacomoni, D. Grange, P. Robert, and L. Rizzo. (1995). Impairment of recognition memory with, but not without, conscious recollection in schizophrenia. *American Journal of Psychiatry* 152: 1737–1742.

Kihlstrom, J. F. (1984). A fact is a fact is a fact. *Behavioral and Brain Sciences* 7: 243–244.

Kitchner, E. G., J. R. Hodges, and R. McCarthy. (1998). Acquisition of post-morbid vocabulary and semantic facts in the absence of episodic memory. *Brain* 121: 1313–1327.

Mandler, G. (1987). Memory: Conscious and unconscious. In P. R. Solomon, G. R. Goethals, C. M. Kelley, and B. R. Stephens, Eds., *Memory—An Interdisciplinary Approach.* New York: Springer, p. 42.

McKoon, G., R. Ratcliff, and G. S. Dell. (1985). A critical evaluation of the semantic-episodic distinction. *Journal of Experimental Psychology: Learning, Memory and Cognition* 12: 295–306.

Roediger, H. L., M. S. Weldon, and B. H. Challis. (1989). Explaining dissociations between implicit and explicit measures of retention: A processing account. In H. L. Roediger and F. I. M. Craik, Eds., *Varieties of Memory and Consciousness: Essays in Honour of Endel Tulving.* Hillsdale, N.J: Erlbaum, pp. 3–41.

Roediger, H. L., S. Rajaram, and K. Srinivas. (1990). Specifying criteria for postulating memory systems. Conference of the National Institute of Mental Health et al: The development and neural bases of higher cognitive functions. (1989, Philadelphia, Pennsylvania). *Annals of the New York Academy of Sciences* 608: 572–595.

Schacter, D. L., and E. Tulving. (1994). What are the memory systems of 1994? In D. L. Schacter and E. Tulving, Eds., *Memory Systems 1994.* Cambridge, MA: MIT Press, pp. 1–38.

Squire, L. R. (1993). Memory and the hippocampus: A synthesis from findings with rats, monkeys, and humans. *Psychological Review* 99: 195–231.

Tulving, E. (1983). *Elements of Episodic Memory.* Oxford: Clarendon Press.

Tulving, E. (1985). How many memory systems are there? *American Psychologist* 40: 385–398.

Tulving, E. (1985). Memory and consciousness. *Canadian Psychology* 26: 1–12.

Tulving, E. (1991). Concepts of human memory. In L. Squire, G. Lynch, N. M. Weinberger, and J. L. McGaugh, Eds., *Memory: Organization and Locus of Change.* New York: Oxford University Press, pp. 3–32.

Tulving, E. (1993). What is episodic memory? *Current Perspectives in Psychological Science* 2: 67–70.

Tulving, E. (1998). Brain/mind correlates of memory. In M. Sabourin, M. Robert, and F. I. M. Craik, Eds., *Advances in Psychological Science,* vol. 2: *Biological and cognitive aspects.* Hove, England: Psychology Press.

Epistemology and Cognition

Epistemology and cognition is the confluence of the philosophy of knowledge and the science of cognition. Epistemology is concerned with the prospects for human knowledge, and because these prospects depend on the powers and frailties of our cognitive equipment, epistemology must work hand in hand with cognitive science. Epistemology centers on normative or evaluative questions about cognition: what are the good or right ways to think, reason, and form beliefs? But normative assessments of cognitive systems and activities must rest on their descriptive properties, and characterizing those descriptive properties is a task for cognitive science. Historically rationalism and empiricism exemplified this approach by assigning different values to reason and the senses based on different descriptions of their capacities.

Epistemic evaluation can take many forms. First, it can evaluate entire cognitive systems, selected cognitive subsystems, or particular cognitive performances. Second, there are several possible criteria of epistemic assessment. (1) A system or process might be judged by its *accuracy* or veridicality, including its *reliability*—the proportion of true judgments it generates—and its *power*—the breadth of tasks or situations in which it issues accurate judgments (Goldman 1986). (2) It can be judged by its conformity or nonconformity with normatively approved *formal standards*, such as deductive validity or probabilistic coherence. (3) It might be evaluated by its *adaptiveness*, or conduciveness for achieving desire-satisfaction or goal-attainment (Stich 1990). Normative assessments of these kinds are not only of theoretical interest, but also admit of several types of application. You might judge another person's belief to be untrustworthy if the process productive of that belief is unreliable, or you might deploy a powerful intellectual strategy to improve your own cognitive attainments.

To illustrate the reliability and power criteria, as well as the two types of application just mentioned, consider MEMORY and its associated processes (Schacter 1996). Studies partly prompted by "recovered" memory claims show that memory is strongly susceptible to postevent distortions, both in adults and especially in children. Suggestive questioning of preschool children can have devastating effects on the reliability of their memories (Ceci 1995). Knowing that someone underwent suggestive questioning should give third parties grounds for distrusting related memories. Another application is the use of encoding strategies to boost memory power. A runner hit on the technique of coding a series of digits in terms of running times. After months of practice with this coding strategy, he could recall over eighty digits in correct order after being exposed to them only once (Chase and Ericsson 1981). Analogous encoding strategies can help anyone increase his memory power. A third memory example illustrates tradeoffs between different epistemic standards. Reliable recollection often depends on "source memory," the recall of how you encountered an object or event. Witnesses have erroneously identified alleged criminals because they had seen them outside the context of the crime, for example, on television. A sense of familiarity was retained, but the source of this familiarity was forgotten (Thomson 1988). People often fail to keep track of the origins of their experience or beliefs. Is this epistemically culpable? The adaptiveness criterion suggests otherwise: forgetting sources is an economical response to the enormous demands on memory (Harman 1986).

The formal-standards criterion of epistemic normativity is applied to both DEDUCTIVE REASONING and PROBABILISTIC REASONING. It is unclear exactly which formal standards are suitable criteria for epistemic rationality. Must a cognitive system possess *all* sound rules of a natural deduction system to qualify as deductively rational? Or would *many* such rules suffice? Must these rules be natively endowed, or would it suffice that the system acquires them under appropriate experience? Whether human deductive capacities qualify as rational depends on which normative criterion is chosen, as well as on the descriptive facts concerning these capacities, about which there is ongoing controversy.

One psychological approach says that people's deductive competence does come in the form of abstract rules akin to natural deduction rules (Rips 1994). On this view, people's native endowments might well qualify as rational, at least under the weaker criterion ("many rules") mentioned above. Other approaches deny that people begin with purely abstract deductive principles, a conclusion supported by content effects discovered in connection with Wason's selection task. Cheng and Holyoak (1985) suggest that generalized rules are induced from experience because of their usefulness. They explain (modest) deductive competence by reference to inductive capacities for acquiring rules, thereby allowing for rationality under one of the foregoing proposals. Cosmides (1989) contends that evolution provided us with specific contentful rules, ones useful in the context of social exchange. Reasoning capacities might qualify as rational under the social exchange approach if the criterion of adaptiveness is applied.

The dominant approach to probabilistic reasoning is the judgments and heuristics (or "heuristics and biases") approach (Tversky and Kahneman 1974; see JUDGMENT HEURISTICS). Its proponents deny that people reason by means of normatively appropriate rules. Instead, people allegedly use shortcuts such as the "representativeness heuristic," which can yield violations of normative rules such as nonutilization of base rates and commission of the conjunction fallacy (Tversky and Kahneman 1983). If someone resembles the prototype of a feminist bank teller more than the prototype of a bank teller, subjects tend to rate the probability of her being both a feminist and a bank teller higher than the probability of her being a bank teller. According to the probability calculus, however, a conjunction cannot have a higher probability than one of its conjuncts.

Recent literature challenges the descriptive claims of the heuristics approach as well as its normative conclusions. Gigerenzer (1991) finds that many so-called cognitive biases or illusions "disappear" when tasks are presented in frequentist terms. People do understand probabilities, but only in connection with relative frequencies, not single cases. Koehler (1996) surveys the literature on the base-rate fallacy and disputes on empirical grounds the conventional wisdom that base rates are routinely ignored. He adds that because base rates are not generally equivalent to prior probabilities, a Bayesian normative standard does not mandate such heavy emphasis on base rates. It is not easy to decide, then, whether people have a general competence at probabilistic reasoning, or the circumstances in which such a competence will be manifested. A related subject is the forms of teaching that can successfully train people in normatively proper reasoning (Nisbett 1993).

Epistemologists are traditionally interested in deciding which beliefs or classes of belief meet the standard for knowledge, where knowledge includes at least true justified belief. The crucial normative notion here is JUSTIFICATION (rather than rationality). Can cognitive science help address this question? One affirmative answer is supported by a reliable process theory of justification (Goldman 1986). If a justified belief is (roughly) a belief produced by reliable cognitive processes, that is, processes that usually output truths, then cognitive science can assist epistemology by determining which mental processes are reliable. Reliabilism is not the only theory of justification, however, that promotes a tight link between epistemology and cognitive science. Any theory can do so that emphasizes the cognitive sources or context of belief.

Assuming that humans do have extensive knowledge, both epistemologists and cognitive scientists ask how such knowledge is possible. During much of the twentieth century, philosophers and psychologists assumed that general-purpose, domain-neutral learning mechanisms, such as deductive and inductive reasoning, were responsible. The most influential approach in current cognitive science, however, is DOMAIN SPECIFICITY (Hirschfeld and Gelman 1994). On this view, the mind is less an all-purpose problem solver than a collection of independent subsystems designed to perform circumscribed tasks. Whether in language, vision,

FOLK PSYCHOLOGY, or other domains, special-purpose modules have been postulated. As the philosopher Goodman (1955) emphasized, wholly unconstrained INDUCTION leads to indeterminacy or antinomy. To resolve this indeterminacy, cognitive scientists have sought to identify constraints on learning or representation in each of multiple domains (Keil 1981; Gelman 1990).

See also NATIVISM; NATIVISM, HISTORY OF; PROPOSITIONAL ATTITUDES; RATIONALISM VS. EMPIRICISM; TVERSKY, AMOS

—Alvin Goldman

References

Ceci, S. (1995). False beliefs: Some developmental and clinical considerations. In D. Schacter, J. Coyle, G. Fischbach, M. Mesulam, and L. Sullivan, Eds., *Memory Distortion.* Cambridge, MA: Harvard University Press, pp. 91–128

Chase, W., and K. Ericsson. (1981). Skilled memory. In J. Anderson, Ed., *Cognitive Skills and Their Acquisition.* Hillsdale, NJ: Erlbaum.

Cheng, P., and K. Holyoak. (1985). Pragmatic reasoning schemas. *Cognitive Psychology* 17: 391–416.

Cosmides, L. (1989). The logic of social exchange: Has natural selection shaped how humans reason? *Cognition* 31: 187–276.

Gelman, R. (1990). First principles organize attention to and learning about relevant data: Number and the animate-inanimate distinction as examples. *Cognitive Science* 14: 79–106.

Gigerenzer, G. (1991). How to make cognitive illusions disappear: Beyond "heuristics and biases." *European Review of Social Psychology* 2: 83–115.

Goldman, A. (1986). *Epistemology and Cognition.* Cambridge, MA: Harvard University Press.

Goodman, N. (1955). *Fact, Fiction, and Forecast.* Cambridge, MA: Harvard University Press.

Harman, G. (1986). *Change in View.* Cambridge, MA: MIT Press.

Hirschfeld, L., and S. Gelman, Eds. (1994). *Mapping the Mind: Domain Specificity in Cognition and Culture.* Cambridge: Cambridge University Press.

Keil, F. (1981). Constraints on knowledge and cognitive development. *Psychological Review* 88: 197–227.

Koehler, J. (1996). The base rate fallacy reconsidered: Descriptive, normative, and methodological challenges. *Behavioral and Brain Sciences* 19: 1–17.

Nisbett, R., Ed. (1993). *Rules for Reasoning.* Hillsdale, NJ: Erlbaum.

Rips, L. (1994). *The Psychology of Proof.* Cambridge, MA: MIT Press.

Schacter, D. (1996). *Searching for Memory.* New York: Basic Books.

Stich, S. (1990). *The Fragmentation of Reason.* Cambridge, MA: MIT Press.

Thomson, D. (1988). Context and false recognition. In G. Davies and D. Thomson, Eds., *Memory in Context: Context in Memory,* Chichester, England: Wiley, pp. 285–304.

Tversky, A., and D. Kahneman. (1974). Judgment under uncertainty: Heuristics and biases. *Science* 185: 1124–1131.

Tversky, A., and D. Kahneman. (1983). Extensional vs. intuitive reasoning: The conjunction fallacy in probability judgment. *Psychological Review* 91: 293–315.

Further Readings

Carey, S. (1985). *Conceptual Change in Childhood.* Cambridge, MA: MIT Press.

Cherniak, C. (1986). *Minimal Rationality.* Cambridge, MA: MIT Press.

Churchland, P. (1989). *A Neurocomputational Perspective.* Cambridge, MA: MIT Press.

Dretske, F. (1981). *Knowledge and the Flow of Information.* Cambridge, MA: MIT Press.

Fodor, J. (1983). *Modularity of Mind.* Cambridge, MA: MIT Press.

Gilovich, T. (1991). *How We Know What Isn't So.* New York: Free Press.

Goldman, A. (1993). *Philosophical Applications of Cognitive Science.* Boulder, CO: Westview Press.

Gopnik, A., and A. Meltzoff. (1997). *Words, Thoughts, and Theories.* Cambridge, MA: MIT Press.

Johnson-Laird, P., and R. Byrne. (1991). *Deduction.* Hillsdale, NJ: Erlbaum.

Karmiloff-Smith, A. (1992). *Beyond Modularity.* Cambridge, MA: MIT Press.

Kornblith, H., Ed. (1993). *Naturalizing Epistemology.* 2nd ed. Cambridge, MA: MIT Press.

Nisbett, R., and L. Ross. (1980). *Human Inference.* Englewood Cliffs, NJ: Prentice-Hall.

Pollock, J. (1995). *Cognitive Carpentry.* Cambridge, MA: MIT Press.

Spelke, E., K. Breinlinger, J. Macomber, and K. Jacobson. (1992). Origins of knowledge. *Psychological Review* 99: 605–632.

Sperber, D., D. Premack, and A. Premack, Eds. (1995). *Causal Cognition.* New York: Oxford University Press.

Stein, E. (1996). *Without Good Reason.* Oxford: Oxford University Press.

Thagard, P. (1992). *Conceptual Revolutions.* Princeton, NJ: Princeton University Press.

Essentialism

Psychological essentialism is any folk theory of concepts positing that members of a category have a property or attribute (*essence*) that determines their identity. Psychological essentialism is similar to varieties of philosophical essentialism, with roots extending back to ancient Greek philosophers such as Plato and Aristotle. One important difference, however, is that psychological essentialism is a claim about human reasoning, and not a metaphysical claim about the structure of the real world. Psychological essentialism may be divided into three types: sortal, causal, and ideal (see Gelman and Hirschfeld in press).

The *sortal* essence is the set of defining characteristics that all and only members of a category share. This notion of essence is captured in Aristotle's (1924) distinction between essential and accidental properties (see also Keil's 1989 defining versus characteristic properties): the essential properties constitute the essence. For example, on this view the essence of a grandmother would be the property of being the mother of a person's parent (rather than the accidental or characteristic properties of wearing glasses and having gray hair). In effect, this characterization is a restatement of the classical view of concepts: meaning (or identity) is supplied by a set of necessary and sufficient features that determine whether an entity does or does not belong in a category (Smith and Medin 1981). Specific essentialist accounts then provide arguments concerning which sorts of features are essential. The viability of this account has been called into question by more recent models of concepts that stress the importance of probabilistic features, exemplars, and theories in concepts.

In contrast, the *causal* essence is the substance, power, quality, process, relationship, or entity that causes other category-typical properties to emerge and be sustained, and that confers identity. Locke (1894/1959: Book III, p. 26) describes it as "the very being of anything, whereby it is what it is. And thus the real internal, but generally . . . unknown constitution of things, whereon their discoverable qualities depend, may be called their essence." The causal essence is used to explain the observable properties of category members. Whereas the sortal essence could apply to any entity, the causal essence applies only to entities for which inherent, hidden properties determine observable qualities. For example, the causal essence of water may be something like H_2O, which is responsible for various observable properties that water has. Thus, the cluster of properties "odorless, tasteless, and colorless" is not a causal essence of water, despite being true of all members of the category Water, because the properties have no direct causal force on other phenomenal properties of that kind.

Causal essentialism requires no specialized knowledge, and, in contrast to sortal essentialism, people may possess an "essence placeholder" without knowing what the essence is (Medin 1989; Medin and Ortony 1989). For example, a child might believe that girls have some inner, nonobvious quality that distinguishes them from boys and that is responsible for the many observable differences in appearance and behavior between boys and girls, before ever learning about chromosomes or human physiology.

The *ideal* essence is assumed to have no actual instantiation in the world. For example, on this view the essence of "goodness" is some pure, abstract quality that is imperfectly realized in real-world instances of people performing good deeds. None of these good deeds perfectly embodies "the good," but each reflects some aspect of it. Plato's cave allegory (*The Republic*), in which what we see of the world are mere shadows of what is real and true, exemplifies this view. The ideal essence thus contrasts with both the sortal and the causal essences. There are relatively little empirical data available on ideal essences in human reasoning (but see Barsalou 1985).

Most accounts of psychological essentialism focus on causal essences. Causal essentialism has important implications for category-based inductive inferences, judgments of constancy over time, and stereotyping. By two to three years of age, children expect category members to share nonobvious similarities, even in the face of salient perceptual dissimilarities. For example, on learning that an atypical exemplar is a member of a category (e.g., that a penguin is a bird), children and adults draw novel inferences from typical instances to the atypical member (Gelman and Markman 1986). By four years of age children judge nonvisible internal parts to be especially crucial to the identity and functioning of an item. Children also treat category membership as stable and unchanging over transformations such as costumes, growth, metamorphosis, or changing environmental conditions (Keil 1989; Gelman, Coley, and Gottfried 1994). The finding that young children hold essentialist beliefs thus suggests that human concepts are not constructed atomistically from perceptual features.

Causal essentialism is closely related to the notion of "kinds" or NATURAL KINDS (Schwartz 1977). Whereas a category is any grouping together of two or more discriminably different things, a kind is a category that is believed to be based in nature, discovered rather than invented, and capturing indefinitely many similarities. "Tigers" is a kind; the set of "striped things" (including tigers, striped shirts, and barbershop poles) is not, because it captures only a single, superficial property (stripedness); it does not capture nonobvious similarities, nor does it serve as a basis of induction (e.g., Mill 1843; Markman 1989). Similarly, the ad hoc category of "things to take on a camping trip" does not form a kind (Barsalou 1991). Whereas kinds are treated as having essences, other categories are not. It is not yet known which categories are construed as "kinds" over development. The majority of evidence for causal essentialism obtains from animal categories. However, similar beliefs seem to characterize how people construe social categories such as race, gender, and personality. These racial, gender, or personality "essences" may be analogical extensions from a folk biological notion, or an outgrowth of a more general "essentialist construal" (see Atran 1990; Carey 1995; Keil 1994; Pinker 1994 for discussion).

Essentialism is pervasive across history, and initial evidence suggests that it may be pervasive across cultures (Atran 1990). Whether biological taxa truly possess essences is a matter of much debate (Sober 1994; Mayr 1982; Kornblith 1993; Dupré 1993), although essentialism is largely believed to be incompatible with current biological knowledge. Some scholars have proposed that essentialist views of the species as fixed and unchanging may present obstacles for accurately learning scientific theories of EVOLUTION (Mayr 1982).

See also COGNITIVE DEVELOPMENT; CONCEPTS; CONCEPTUAL CHANGE; FOLK BIOLOGY; NAIVE SOCIOLOGY; STEREOTYPING

—*Susan A. Gelman*

References

Aristotle. (1924). *Metaphysics.* Oxford: Clarendon Press.

Atran, S. (1990). *Cognitive Foundations of Natural History.* New York: Cambridge University Press.

Barsalou, L. W. (1985). Ideals, central tendency, and frequency of instantiation as determinants of graded structure in categories. *Journal of Experimental Psychology: Learning, Memory, and Cognition* 11: 629–654.

Barsalou, L. W. (1991). Deriving categories to achieve goals. In G. H. Bower, Ed., *The Psychology of Learning and Motivation.* New York: Academic Press, pp. 1–64.

Carey, S. (1995). On the origins of causal understanding. In D. Sperber, D. Premack, and A. J. Premack, Eds., *Causal Cognition: A Multi-Disciplinary Approach.* Oxford: Clarendon Press, pp. 268–308.

Dupré, J. (1993). *The Disorder of Things: Metaphysical Foundations of the Disunity of Science.* Cambridge, MA: Harvard University Press.

Gelman, S. A., J. D. Coley, and G. M. Gottfried. (1994). Essentialist beliefs in children: The acquisition of concepts and theories. In L. A. Hirschfeld and S. A. Gelman, Eds., *Mapping the Mind:*

Domain Specificity in Cognition and Culture., pp. 341–366. New York: Cambridge University Press.

Gelman, S. A., and L. A. Hirschfeld. How biological is essentialism? Forthcoming in D. Medin and S. Atran, Eds., *Folkbiology.* Cambridge, MA: MIT Press.

Gelman, S. A., and E. M. Markman. (1986). Categories and induction in young children. *Cognition* 23: 183–209.

Keil, F. (1989). *Concepts, Kinds, and Cognitive Development.* Cambridge, MA: Bradford Books/MIT Press.

Keil, F. (1994). The birth and nurturance of concepts by domains: The origins of concepts of living things. In L. A. Hirschfeld and S. A. Gelman, Eds., *Mapping the Mind: Domain Specificity in Cognition and Culture.* New York: Cambridge University Press.

Kornblith, H. (1993). *Inductive Inference and its Natural Ground.* Cambridge, MA: MIT Press.

Locke, J. (1894/1959). *An Essay Concerning Human Understanding,* vol. 2. New York: Dover.

Markman, E. M. (1989). *Categorization and Naming in Children: Problems in Induction.* Cambridge, MA: Bradford Books/MIT Press.

Mayr, E. (1982). *The Growth of Biological Thought.* Cambridge, MA: Harvard University Press.

Medin, D. (1989). Concepts and conceptual structure. *American Psychologist* 44: 1469–1481.

Medin, D. L., and A. Ortony. (1989). Psychological essentialism. In S. Vosniadou and A. Ortony, Eds., *Similarity and Analogical Reasoning.* Cambridge: Cambridge University Press, pp. 179–195.

Mill, J. S. (1843). *A System of Logic, Ratiocinative and Inductive.* London: Longmans.

Pinker, S. (1994). *The Language Instinct.* New York: W. Morrow.

Schwartz, S. P., Ed. (1977). *Naming, Necessity, and Natural Kinds.* Ithaca, NY: Cornell University Press.

Smith, E. E., and D. L. Medin. (1981). *Categories and Concepts.* Cambridge, MA: Harvard University Press.

Sober, E. (1994). *From a Biological Point of View.* New York: Cambridge University Press.

Further Readings

Atran, S. (1996). Modes of thinking about living kinds: science, symbolism, and common sense. In D. Olson and N. Torrance, Eds., *Modes of Thought: Explorations in Culture and Cognition.* New York: Cambridge University Press.

Braisby, N., B. Franks, and J. Hampton. (1996). Essentialism, word use, and concepts. *Cognition* 59: 247–274.

Fuss, D. (1989). *Essentially Speaking: Feminism, Nature, and Difference.* New York: Routledge.

Gelman, S. A., and J. D. Coley. (1991). Language and categorization: The acquisition of natural kind terms. In S. A. Gelman and J. P. Byrnes, Eds., *Perspectives on Language and Thought: Interrelations in Development.* Cambridge: Cambridge University Press, pp. 146–196.

Gelman, S. A., and D. L. Medin. (1993). What's so essential about essentialism? A different perspective on the interaction of perception, language, and conceptual knowledge. *Cognitive Development* 8: 157–167.

Gelman, S. A., and H. M. Wellman. (1991). Insides and essences: Early understandings of the nonobvious. *Cognition* 38: 213–244.

Gopnik, A., and H. M. Wellman. (1994). The theory theory. In L. A. Hirschfeld and S. A. Gelman, Eds., *Mapping the Mind: Domain Specificity in Cognition and Culture.* New York: Cambridge University Press.

Hirschfeld, L. (1995). Do children have a theory of race? *Cognition* 54: 209–252.

Hirschfeld, L. (1996). *Race in the Making: Cognition, Culture, and the Child's Construction of Human Kinds.* Cambridge, MA: MIT Press.

Jones, S., and L. B. Smith. (1993). The place of perception in children's concepts. *Cognitive Development* 8: 113–139.

Kalish, C. (1995). Essentialism and graded membership in animal and artifact categories. *Memory and Cognition* 23: 335–353.

Keil, F. (1995). The growth of causal understandings of natural kinds. In D. Sperber, D. Premack, and A. Premack, Eds., *Causal Cognition: A Multidisciplinary Debate.* Oxford: Oxford University Press.

Kripke, S. (1972). Naming and necessity. In D. Davidson and G. Harman, Eds., *Semantics of Natural Language.* Dordrecht: D. Reidel.

McNamara, T. P., and R. J. Sternberg. (1983). Mental models of word meaning. *Journal of Verbal Learning and Verbal Behavior* 22: 449–474.

Malt, B. (1994). Water is not H_2O. *Cognitive Psychology* 27: 41–70.

Putnam, H. (1975). The meaning of "meaning." In H. Putnam, Ed., *Mind, Language and Reality: Philosophical Papers,* vol. 2. New York: Cambridge University Press.

Rips, L. J., and A. Collins. (1993). Categories and resemblance. *Journal of Experimental Psychology: General* 122: 468–486.

Rorty, R. (1979). *Philosophy and the Mirror of Nature.* Princeton: Princeton University Press.

Rothbart, M., and M. Taylor. (1990). Category labels and social reality: Do we view social categories as natural kinds? In G. Semin and K. Fiedler, Eds., *Language and Social Cognition.* London: Sage.

Solomon, G. E. A., S. C. Johnson, D. Zaitchik, and S. Carey. (1996). Like father, like son: Young children's understanding of how and why offspring resemble their parents. *Child Development* 67: 151–171.

Springer, K. (1996). Young children's understanding of a biological basis for parent-offspring relations. *Child Development* 67: 2841–2856.

Taylor, M. (1996). The development of children's beliefs about social and biological aspects of gender differences. *Child Development* 67: 1555–1571.

Wierzbicka, A. (1994). The universality of taxonomic categorization and the indispensability of the concept "kind." *Rivista di Linguistica* 6: 347–364.

Ethics

See CULTURAL RELATIVISM; ETHICS AND EVOLUTION; MORAL PSYCHOLOGY

Ethics and Evolution

When Charles DARWIN wrote *The Origin of Species,* he withheld discussion of the origins of human morality and cognition. Despite Darwin's restraint, some of the strongest reactions to the theory of natural selection had to do with its connection to ethical matters. The intersection between evolution and ethics continues to be a site of controversy. Some claim that human ethical judgments are to be explained by their adaptive value. Others claim that human ethical systems are the result of cultural evolution, not biological evolution. In the context of cognitive science, the central issue is whether humans have ethics-specific beliefs or cognitive mechanisms that are the result of biological evolution.

There is increasing evidence that the human brain comes prewired for a wide range of specialized capacities (see NATIVISM and DOMAIN SPECIFICITY). With regard to ethics, the central questions are to what extent the human brain is prewired for ethical thinking and, insofar as it is, what the implications of this are.

There is one sense in which humans are prewired for ethics: humans have the capacity for ethical reasoning and reflection while amoebas do not. This human capacity is biologically based and results from EVOLUTION. *Ethical nativism* is the view that there are specific, prewired mechanisms for ethical thought. Adherents of SOCIOBIOLOGY, the view that evolutionary theory can explain all human social behavior, are among those who embrace ethical nativism. E. O. Wilson, in *Sociobiology: The New Synthesis* (1975), goes so far as to say that ethics can be "biologized." Sociobiologists claim that humans have specific ethical beliefs and an associated ethical framework that are innate and are the result of natural selection. They support this view with evidence that humans in all cultures share certain ethical beliefs and certain underlying ethical principles (see HUMAN UNIVERSALS), evidence of ethical or "pre-ethical" behavior among other mammals, especially primates (see de Waal 1996), and with evolutionary accounts of the selective advantage of having innate ethical mental mechanisms. Most notably, they talk about the selective advantage (to the individual or to the species) of ALTRUISM.

Consider a particular moral belief or feeling for which an evolutionary explanation has been offered, namely the belief that it is wrong to have (consensual) sex with one's sibling. Some sociobiologists have argued that this belief (more precisely, the feeling that there is something wrong about having sex with a person one was raised with) is innate and that we have this belief because of its selective advantage. When close blood relatives reproduce, there is a relatively high chance that traits carried on recessive genes (most notably, serious diseases like sickle-cell anemia and hemophilia) will be exhibited in the resulting offspring. Such offspring are thus more likely to fail to reproduce. Engaging in incest is thus an evolutionarily nonadaptive strategy. If a mutation occurred that caused an organism to feel or believe that it is wrong to engage in incest, then, all else being equal, this gene would spread through the population over subsequent generations. Sociobiologists think they can give similar accounts of our other ethical beliefs and the mechanisms that underlie them.

What are the implications for ethics if ethical nativism and some version of the sociobiological story behind it are true? Some philosophers have denied there are any interesting implications. Ethics, they note, is *normative* (it says what we ought to do), whereas biology—in particular, the details of the evolutionary origins of humans and our various capacities—is *descriptive*. One cannot derive normative conclusions from empirical premises. To do so is to commit the naturalistic fallacy. It would be a mistake, for example, to infer from the empirical premise that our teeth evolved for tearing flesh to the normative conclusions that we ought to eat meat. This empirical premise is compatible with ethical arguments that it is morally wrong to eat meat. By the same reasoning, the fact that evolution produced in us the tendency to have some moral feeling or belief does not necessarily entail that we ought to act on that feeling or accept that belief on reflection. In fact, some commentators have suggested, following Thomas Huxley (1894), that "the ethical progress of society depends, not on imitating [biological evolution], . . . but in combating it."

Ethical nativists have various responses to the charge that they commit the naturalistic fallacy. Some allow that the fact that humans have some innate moral belief does not entail that we ought to act on it, while insisting that nativism has something to tell us about ethics. Perhaps biology can tell us that we are not able to do certain things and thus that it cannot be the case that we ought to do this. For example, concerning feminism, some sociobiologists have claimed that many of the differences between men and women are biologically based and unchangeable; a feminist political agenda that strives for equality is therefore destined to failure. This argument has been criticized on both empirical and normative grounds (see Kitcher 1985 and Fausto-Sterling 1992).

Some sociobiologists (Wilson 1975 and Ruse 1986) have argued that the facts of human evolution have implications for moral realism, the metaethical position that there are moral facts like, for example, the moral fact that it is wrong to torture babies for fun. A standard argument for moral realism says that the existence of moral facts explains the fact that we have moral beliefs (on moral realism, see Harman 1977; Mackie 1977; Brink 1989). If, however, ethical nativism is true and an evolutionary account can be given for why people have the moral beliefs they do, then an empirical explanation can be given for why we have the ethical capacities that we do. The standard argument for moral realism is thus undercut.

One promising reply to this line of thought is to note that moral facts might be involved in giving a biological account of why we humans have the moral beliefs that we do. In the case of incest, the moral status of incest might be related to the selective advantageousness of incest. Consider an analogy to mathematics. Although we might give an evolutionary explanation of the spread of mathematical abilities in humans (say, because the ability to perform addition was useful for hunting), mathematical facts, like $2 + 2 = 4$, would still be required to explain *why* mathematical ability is selectively advantageous. Many of our mathematical beliefs are adaptive because they are true. The idea is to give the same sort of account for moral beliefs: they are selectively advantageous because they are true. Selective advantage and moral status can, however, come apart in some instances. One can imagine a context in which it would be selectively advantageous for men to rape women. In such a context, it might be selectively advantageous to have the belief that rape is morally permissible. Rape would, however, remain morally reprehensible and repugnant even if it were selectively advantageous to believe otherwise.

Even if there is a tension between ethical nativism and moral realism, the tension might not be so serious if only a few of our ethical beliefs are in fact innate. Many of our ethical beliefs come from and are justified by a reflective process that involves feedback among our various ethical beliefs; this suggests that many of them are not innate. The nativist argument against moral realism depends on the strength of its empirical premises.

See also ADAPTATION AND ADAPTATIONISM; CULTURAL EVOLUTION; CULTURAL VARIATION; EVOLUTIONARY PSYCHOLOGY; MORAL PSYCHOLOGY

—*Edward Stein*

References

Brink, D. O. (1989). *Moral Realism and the Foundations of Ethics.* Cambridge: Cambridge University Press.

de Waal, F. (1996). *Good Natured: The Origins of Right and Wrong in Humans and Other Animals.* Cambridge: Harvard University Press.

Fausto-Sterling, A. (1992). *Myths of Gender: Biological Theories about Women and Men.* Rev. ed. New York: Basic Books.

Harman, G. (1977). *The Nature of Morality.* Oxford: Oxford University Press.

Huxley, T. H. (1894). *Evolution and Ethics and Other Essays.* New York: D. Appleton.

Kitcher, P. (1985). *Vaulting Ambition.* Cambridge, MA: MIT Press.

Mackie, J. L. (1977). *Ethics: Inventing Right and Wrong.* New York: Penguin.

Ruse, M. (1986). *Taking Darwin Seriously.* Oxford: Blackwell.

Wilson, E. O. (1975). *Sociobiology: The New Synthesis.* Cambridge, MA: Harvard University Press.

Further Readings

Bradie, M. (1994). *The Secret Chain: Evolution and Ethics.* Albany: SUNY Press.

Goldman, A. (1993). Ethics and cognitive science. *Ethics* 103: 337–360.

Lumsden, C., and E. O. Wilson. (1981). *Genes, Minds and Culture.* Cambridge, MA: Harvard University Press.

Nitecki, M., and D. Nitecki, Eds. (1993). *Evolutionary Ethics.* Albany: SUNY Press.

Nozick, R. (1981). *Philosophical Explanations.* Cambridge, MA: Harvard University Press.

Thompson, P., Ed. (1995). *Issues in Evolutionary Ethics.* Albany: SUNY Press.

Ethnopsychology

Ethnopsychology refers to cultural or "folk" models of subjectivity, particularly as applied to the interpretation of social action. It also refers to the comparative, anthropological study of such models as used in particular languages and cultures. Whereas the fields of psychology and philosophy have both given concerted attention to folk theories of the mind (see FOLK PSYCHOLOGY and THEORY OF MIND), the hallmark of anthropological studies has been the empirical study of commonsense psychologies in comparative perspective (Heelas and Lock 1981; White and Kirkpatrick 1985; see also CULTURAL PSYCHOLOGY).

A growing body of ethnographic work has established that (1) people everywhere think and talk in ordinary language about subjective states and personal qualities (D'Andrade 1987), that (2) cultures vary in the conceptual elaboration and sociocultural importance of such concepts, and that (3) determining conceptual universals in this

domain is made difficult by problems of translation, interpretation and representation. So, for example, studies of complex emotion concepts such as Ilongot *liget* (roughly, "anger") or Japanese *amae* ("dependent love") have produced extended debates about issues of meaning and representation (see Rosaldo 1980 and Doi 1973, respectively, for extended analyses of these terms).

Beginning in the early 1950s, at about the same time that social psychologists were examining English-language folk psychology (Heider 1958), A. I. Hallowell called for the comparative study of "ethnopsychology," by which he meant "concepts of self, of human nature, of motivation, of personality" (1967: 79). With the advent of COGNITIVE ANTHROPOLOGY and the development of lexical techniques for the semantic analysis of terminological domains such as color, kinship, or botany, anthropologists initially approached ethnopsychology in much the same way as other areas of ethno- or "folk" knowledge, as an essentially cognitive system that could be studied as a set of interrelated categories and propositions. The semantic theories that informed this work derived largely from the study of referential meaning, analyzed in terms of category structures and distinctive features or dimensions (see D'Andrade 1995; Quinn and Holland 1987 for historical overviews).

The two types of psychological vocabulary most frequently studied with lexical methods are personality and emotion. In both cases, comparative research has sought linguistic evidence for cognitive and psychological universals. Studies of personality terms in both English (Schneider 1973) and non-Western languages (e.g., Shweder and Bourne 1982) indicate that two or three dimensions of interpersonal meaning, particularly "solidarity" and "power," structure person concepts across cultures (White 1980). Similarly, studies of emotion vocabularies have found complex patterns of convergence interpreted as evidence for a small number of basic or universal affects (Gerber 1985; Romney, Moore, and Rusch 1997). Claims for universal emotion categories, however, are often complicated by detailed accounts of the relevance of culture-specific models for emotional understanding (Lutz 1988; Heider 1991).

The search for linguistic correlates of basic emotions is motivated by robust findings of biological invariance in facial expressions associated with five or six discrete emotions, often labeled with the English language terms "anger," "disgust," "fear," "happiness," "surprise," and "shame" (Ekman 1992). Inspired by research on COLOR CATEGORIZATION that shows color lexicons everywhere to be structured according to a small set of prototypic categories, numerous authors have speculated that prototype models may be an effective means of representing emotion concepts as internally structured categories (Gerber 1985; Russell 1991) or scenarios (Lakoff and Kövecses 1987).

Lexical studies of an entire corpus of terms extracted from linguistic and social context generally produce highly abstract results. Analyses focusing on the conceptualization of emotion in ordinary language have identified more complex cultural or propositional networks of meaning associated with key emotion terms (e.g., Rosaldo 1980). In particular, analyses of METAPHOR show that metaphorical associations play a central role in the elaboration of cultural models of emotion. Emotion metaphors often acquire their significance by linking together other metaphors pertaining to the conceptualization of bodies, persons, and minds. So, for example, the English language expression "He is about to explode" obtains its meaning in relation to such metaphorical propositions as *anger is heat* and *the body is a container for emotions* (Lakoff and Kövecses 1987).

Both comparative and developmental studies show that implicit models of emotion frequently take the form of event schemas in which feelings and other psychological states mediate antecedent events and behavioral responses (Harris 1989; Lutz 1988). The most systematic framework developed for the analysis of emotion language is that of linguist Anna Wierzbicka (1992), who has proposed a metalanguage capable of representing the meanings of emotion words in terms of a limited number of semantic primitives. In this approach, scriptlike understandings of emotion are represented as a string of propositions forming prototypic event schemas. Application of this framework has clarified a number of debates about the nature of emotional meaning in specific languages and cultures (White 1992).

The relevance of prototype schemas for emotional understanding follows from the wider salience of narrative as an organizing principle in ethnopsychological thought generally (Bruner 1990; Johnson 1993). Among the many types of narrative used to represent and communicate social experience, "life stories" appear to be an especially salient genre across cultures (Linde 1993; Ochs and Capps 1996; Peacock and Holland 1993). There is, however, some evidence that Euro-American cultures tend to "package" experience in the form of individualized life stories more than many non-Western cultures that do not value or elaborate individual self-narrative.

Research on talk about personal experience in ordinary social contexts indicates that self-reports are often interactively produced by narrators and audiences intent on rendering experience in moral terms and on actively directing the course of social interaction (Miller et al. 1990). This line of sociolinguistic research has identified the importance of sociocultural institutions for analyzing the pragmatic force of psychological talk in context. Ethnographic research in small-scale societies finds that verbal representations of the thoughts and feelings of others are likely to carry considerable moral weight and may be limited to specific, culturally defined occasions.

By raising interpretive questions, the comparative perspective has drawn attention to the constructed nature of commonsense psychologies, noting that concepts of emotion, person, and so forth generally derive their significance from wider systems of cultural meaning and value. The comparative approach of ethnopsychological research focuses attention back on psychological theory itself, noting ways in which English language constructs and paradigms are constrained by implicit cultural concepts of person. The major theme in this line of criticism is that the values and ideology of Euro-American individualism systematically influence a range of psychological concepts, including personality (White 1992), emotion (Markus and Kitayama 1991), and moral reasoning (Shweder 1990).

As is often the case for comparative research, ethnopsychological studies raise questions about the validity of the domain under study, of "psychology" as a basis for cross-cultural interpretation. As working concepts of psychology are adjusted for purposes of comparison, the boundaries between ethnopsychology, NAIVE SOCIOLOGY, and FOLK BIOLOGY, among other areas, are likely to be remapped as psychology's metalanguage comes to terms with the diversity of psychological forms and practices worldwide.

See also CULTURAL EVOLUTION; CULTURAL VARIATION; HUMAN UNIVERSALS; MOTIVATION AND CULTURE

—*Geoffrey White*

References

Bruner, J. (1990). *Acts of Meaning.* Cambridge, MA: Harvard University Press.

D'Andrade, R. G. (1987). A folk model of the mind. In D. Holland and N. Quinn, Eds., *Cultural Models in Language and Thought.* Cambridge: Cambridge University Press.

D'Andrade, R. G. (1995). *The Development of Cognitive Anthropology.* Cambridge: Cambridge University Press.

Doi, T. (1973). *The Anatomy of Dependence.* Tokyo: Kodansha International Ltd.

Ekman, P. (1992). An argument for basic emotions. *Cognition and Emotion* 6: 169–200.

Gerber, E. (1985). Rage and obligation: Samoan emotions in conflict. In G. White and J. Kirkpatrick, Eds., *Person, Self and Experience: Exploring Pacific Ethnopsychologies.* Berkeley: University of California Press.

Hallowell, A. I. (1967). The self and its behavioral environment. In *Culture and Experience.* New York: Schocken Books (originally published in 1954).

Harris, P. (1989). *Children and Emotion: The Development of Psychological Understanding.* Oxford: Blackwell.

Heelas, P., and A. Lock, Eds. (1981). *Indigenous Psychologies: The Anthropology of the Self.* London and New York: Academic Press.

Heider, F. (1958). *The Psychology of Interpersonal Relations.* New York: Wiley.

Heider, K. (1991). *Landscapes of Emotion: Mapping Three Cultures in Indonesia.* Cambridge: Cambridge University Press.

Johnson, M. (1993). The narrative context of self and action. In *Moral Imagination: Implications of Cognitive Science for Ethics.* Chicago: University of Chicago Press.

Lakoff, G., and Z. Kövecses. (1987). The cognitive model of anger inherent in American English. In D. Holland and N. Quinn, Eds., *Cultural Models in Language and Thought.* Cambridge: Cambridge University Press.

Linde, C. (1993). *Life Stories: The Creation of Coherence.* Oxford: Oxford University Press.

Lutz, C. A. (1988). *Unnatural Emotions: Everyday Sentiments on a Micronesian Atoll and Their Challenge to Western Theory.* Chicago: University of Chicago Press.

Markus, H., and S. Kitayama. (1991). Culture and the Self: Implications for Cognition, Emotion and Motivation. *Psychological Review* 98: 224–253.

Miller, P. J., R. Potts, H. Fung, L. Hoogstra, and J. Mintz. (1990). Narrative practices and the social construction of self in childhood. *American Ethnologist* 17: 292–311.

Ochs, E., and L. Capps. (1996). Narrating the self. *Annual Review of Anthropology* 25:19–43.

Peacock, J., and D. Holland. (1993). The narrated self: life stories in process. *Ethos* 21(4): 367–383.

Quinn, N., and D. Holland. (1987). Culture and cognition. In D. Holland and N. Quinn, Eds., *Cultural Models in Language and Thought*. Cambridge: Cambridge University Press.

Romney, A. K., C. Moore, and C. Rusch (1997). Cultural universals: measuring the semantic structure of emotion terms in English and Japanese. *Proceedings of the National Academy of Science* 94: 5489–5494.

Rosaldo, M. Z. (1980). *Knowledge and Passion: Ilongot Notions of Self and Social Life*. Cambridge: Cambridge University Press.

Russell, J. (1991). Culture and the categorization of emotion. *Psychological Bulletin* 110: 426–450.

Schneider, D. J. (1973). Implicit personality theory: a review. *Psychological Bulletin* 79: 294–309.

Shweder, R. (1990). Cultural psychology: what is it? In J. Stigler, R. Shweder, and G. Herdt, Eds., *Cultural Psychology: Essays on Comparative Human Development*. Cambridge: Cambridge University Press.

Shweder, R., and E. Bourne. (1982). Does the concept of the person vary cross-culturally? In A. J. Marsella and G. M. White, Eds., *Cultural Conceptions of Mental Health and Therapy*. Boston: D. Reidel.

White, G. M. (1980). Conceptual universals in interpersonal language. *American Anthropologist* 82: 759–781.

White, G. M. (1992). Ethnopsychology. In T. Schwartz, G. White, and C. Lutz, Eds., *New Directions in Psychological Anthropology*. Cambridge: Cambridge University Press.

White, G. M., and J. Kirkpatrick, Eds. (1985). *Person, Self and Experience: Exploring Pacific Ethnopsychologies*. Berkeley: University of California Press.

Wierzbicka, A. (1992). *Semantics, Culture, and Cognition: Universal Human Concepts in Culture-Specific Combinations*. Chicago: University of Chicago Press.

Ethology

Ethology had the most impact from about 1940 to 1970, when it took the discipline of animal behavior by storm, earning Konrad Lorenz and Niko Tinbergen, with Karl von Frisch, a Nobel Prize in 1973. The underlying concepts were biological rather than psychological, derived from a Darwinian approach to naturally occurring animal behavior. Historically, the naturalistic aspect was crucial, with an emphasis lacking in psychology at the time. Although anticipated by American behaviorists, ethology came of age as a mature discipline in Europe. The proceedings of a 1949 conference in Cambridge, England, on physiological mechanisms in animal behavior presented a full exposition of the ideas of Lorenz, Tinbergen, and other participants in the emerging discipline (Lorenz 1950; see 1970, 1971 for collected works). Tinbergen's classical treatise on "The Study of Instinct" followed a year later (Tinbergen 1951). Ethology provided a comprehensive framework for studying the functions, evolution, and development of behavior and its physiological basis. Some insights were conceptual and others methodological. Four historically important aspects were the basic endogeneity of behavior, the concept of sign stimuli, the reinstatement of instincts, and the importance of cross-species comparisons.

Lorenz's medical training in Vienna exposed him to concepts of phylogeny emerging from comparative anatomy, but behavior was viewed as too amorphous to be amenable to the same kind of study. Encouraged by Berlin zoo direc-

tor Oscar Heinroth, who was intimate with the behavior of scores of animals, Lorenz became convinced that comparative ethological studies could be as objective as anatomical investigations. Young animals of diverse species, raised under similar conditions, consistently develop distinctive behaviors, stable enough to yield insights into taxonomy and phylogeny. Many of the species-specific displays of captive ducks match those in the wild. The emphasis on comparative study, rendered more quantitative by Tinbergen and his students, was an important innovation, embodied in Lorenz's term "fixed action patterns." Although action patterns are not completely "fixed," any more than is morphology, careful scrutiny reveals consistent species and individual differences in modal action patterns. Descriptive studies of behavior took on new momentum, shifting focus somewhat from species comparisons to intraspecific variation, culminating more than a generation later in the quantitative sophistication of mating choice theory, and cladistic and other approaches to problems in phylogeny (Harvey and Pagel 1991).

A second innovation emphasized endogenous sources of motivation. The BEHAVIORISM of Watson (1924), given a more biological flavor by Schneirla and his colleagues, stressed the role of external forces in the control of behavior, perhaps initially as a healthy antidote to the indulgences of introspectionist psychology. Ethologists provided a refreshing reminder that without a genome you have no organism, and no instructions on how to respond to external stimuli or how to learn as a consequence of experience, countering such excesses as "psychology without heredity" (Kuo 1924). The notion of "instinct," eloquently championed by Darwin, had fallen into disrepute. Lorenz redressed this balance by stressing the importance of endogeneity, both in the motivational sense, manifest in the inherent rhythmicity of many behaviors, and in the ontogenetic sense, with certain patterns of behavior developing endogenously, only minimally perturbed or adjusted according to the vagaries of individual experience. The notion of strong internal forces driving behavior was then highly controversial. We now accept that the underlying neural circuitry of many behaviors includes neuronal pacemakers as key components. The theme of endogenous forces came to pervade research at the Institute for Behavioral Physiology established for Lorenz and codirector Eric von Holst by the Max Planck Gesellschaft in Bavaria in 1956, including pioneering studies of swimming rhythms, and later circadian and circannual behavioral cycles. Across the Atlantic, ethologically inspired insect physiologists Kenneth Roeder and Donald Wilson convincingly demonstrated the delicate interplay of exogenous and endogenous forces underlying locomotion and other behaviors (Roeder 1963; reviewed in detail in Gallistel 1980).

The interpretation of responses to external situations not as driven from without but as interactions between changing environments and purposively changing organismal states was not unique to ethology. A generation previously, in an essay on "appetites and aversions as constituents of instincts," the American ethologist Wallace Craig (1918) clarified the issues of uniformity and plasticity with a distinction made previously by Sherrington, and later by

Lorenz, between appetitive (i.e., proceptive) behavior, endogenously motivated and variable, and consummatory behavior, externally triggered and more stereotyped. Craig was a student of Charles Otis Whitman, whose 1898 Woods Hole lectures on animal behavior anticipated other aspects of ethological thinking. But Craig's message fell on deaf ears, appreciated by few psychologists, and apparently known to Lorenz only after his career was well launched. He may also have been unaware of Craig's assertion that aggression is less endogenously driven than most behaviors (Craig 1928). Lorenz's controversial 1966 book "On Aggression," presented the contrary case, that there are strong endogenous wellsprings for agonistic behavior. Few of the many critics of Lorenz's position acknowledged Craig's thoughtful counterargument (see also Heiligenberg and Kramer 1972).

Until the postwar years, American biologists and psychologists alike were curiously unresponsive to efforts within their ranks to instate ethologically styled concepts. A prophetic paper by one of its most respected pioneers, titled "Experimental analysis of instinctive behavior" (LASHLEY 1938; see Beach et al. 1960), anticipated some developments in ethology but had much less impact than his work on cortical memory mechanisms. Lashley's preoccupation with endogenous motivational forces was evident in his arguments with Pavlovian theorists who reduced all behavioral and psychological activity to chains of conditioned reflexes. There had also been limited appreciation of the case made a generation previously by Lashley's teacher, Jennings (1906), for the existence, even in single-celled organisms, of complex, sometimes purposive, endogenously driven behaviors. His suggestion that equivalent observations in higher organisms would suffice to encourage cognitive theorizing may have helped to spur his later colleague Watson (1924) to put an end to subjective, introspective psychologizing. Instead, Watson shifted the emphasis to observable behaviors and Pavlovian reflexes, thus launching behaviorism. But what began as a worthy effort to reintroduce objectivity into comparative psychology hardened into dogma, and the importance of endogenous factors was again forgotten until reinstated by Beach and other students of Lashley, increasingly preoccupied with physiological psychology as an emerging discipline (Beach et al. 1960). The notion of instinct met a similar fate, swept aside by the appeals of pragmatism. In developmental studies, American comparative psychologists grappling with the nature/nurture problem lost sight of the need to balance environmental influences with contributions of the genome, a primary emphasis in ethology.

Environmental factors were not neglected by ethologists. Tinbergen and his students, more experimentally oriented than Lorenz, focused on key components of complex situations to which animals actually respond (collected in Tinbergen 1971, 1973). Many of these "sign stimuli," or "social releasers," often a small fraction of the total that the animal can perceive, were communicative signals (see ANIMAL COMMUNICATION). Physiological mechanisms were inferred for filtering incoming stimuli, apparently operating at birth in many young organisms, such as the nestling birds that Tinbergen studied. Lorenz posited central "innate release

mechanisms" with properties varying according to genetically encoded instructions. The determination of ethologists to reinstate concepts of innateness led to the sometimes legitimate criticism that they caricatured young animals as completely preprogrammed automata (Lehrman 1953). It became clear later that even young organisms with well-defined innate responsiveness, such as herring gulls, display great developmental plasticity, quickly acquiring new information about their parents and other aspects of life around them. But they do so by learning processes that are canalized by innate predispositions, insuring a certain range of trajectories for development, whether behavioral or neurological (Hailman 1967; Waddington 1966; Rauschecker and Marler 1987).

The importance of innately guided learning, well illustrated by song learning in birds, was the special province of British ethologist William Homan Thorpe (1956). More than Lorenz or Tinbergen, Thorpe prepared the way for the emergence of COGNITIVE ETHOLOGY (Griffin 1976). He was the first to formalize criteria for different types of learning, some very basic, others with clear cognitive implications. His thoughtful scholarship emphasized the importance of internalized processing in perception and the purposiveness of behavior. The interplay of nature and nurture is most evident in "imprinting," the developmental process for which Lorenz is best known. During imprinting, young of some organisms learn to recognize and bond with their parents, or parent surrogates, and others like them, by processes destined to become favored paradigms for investigating the neural basis of memory formation (Horn 1985). Imprinting occurs most rapidly during sensitive periods, as experience interacts with innate preferences for visual and auditory stimuli that capture attention and initiate the imprinting process. That these early experiences sometimes influence later social and sexual preferences, with varying degrees of reversibility, attracted special attention in psychiatry and the social sciences (Bowlby 1969, 1973; Hinde 1982). There are parallels with song learning in birds and with human speech acquisition, where the choice of what to learn is guided by generalized innate preferences, resulting ultimately in specific learned vocal traditions (Marler 1991; Pinker 1994). The interplay of inheritance and experience that canalizes the development of many behaviors is epitomized by the apparently paradoxical term "instincts to learn" (Gould and Marler 1987). More than any other, the concept of instinctively guided learning captures the essence of what was uniquely distinctive about classical ethology, still providing a valued heuristic framework for contemporary research on behavioral ontogeny (see EVOLUTIONARY PSYCHOLOGY).

See also SOCIAL COGNITION IN ANIMALS; SOCIAL PLAY BEHAVIOR

—*Peter Marler*

References

Beach, F. A., D. O. Hebb, C. T. Morgan, and H. W. Nissen. (1960). *The Neuropsychology of Lashley: Selected Papers of K. S. Lashley.* New York: McGraw-Hill.

Bowlby, J. (1969, 1973). *Attachment and Loss.* Vols. 1 and 2. London: Hogarth Press.

Craig, W. (1918). Appetites and aversions as constituents of instincts. *Biological Bulletin* 34: 91–107.

Craig, W. (1928). Why do animals fight? *International Journal of Ethics* 31: 264–278.

Gallistel, C. R. (1980). *The Organization of Action: A New Synthesis.* Hillsdale, NJ: Erlbaum.

Gould, J. L., and P. Marler. (1987). Learning by instinct. *Scientific American* 256(1):62–73.

Griffin, D. R. (1976). *The Question of Animal Awareness: Evolutionary Continuity of Mental Experience.* New York: Rockefeller University Press.

Hailman, J. P. (1967). The ontogeny of an instinct. *Behavior* 15: 1–142.

Harvey, P. H., and M. D. Pagel. (1991). *The Comparative Method in Evolutionary Biology.* Oxford: Oxford University Press.

Heiligenberg, W., and U. Kramer. (1972). Aggressiveness as a function of external stimulation. *Journal of Comparative Physiology* 77: 332–340.

Hinde, R. A. (1982). *Ethology: Its Nature and Relations with Other Sciences.* New York: Oxford University Press.

Horn, B. (1985). *Memory, Imprinting and the Brain.* Oxford: Clarendon Press.

Jennings, H. S. (1906). *Behavior of the Lower Organisms.* Bloomington: Indiana University Press. (reprint, 1962.)

Kuo, Z. Y. (1924). A psychology without heredity. *Psychology Review* 31:427–448.

Lashley, K. S. (1938). Experimental analysis of instinctive behavior. *Psychological Review* 45: 445–471.

Lehrman, D. S. (1953). A critique of Konrad Lorenz's theory of instinctive behavior. *Quarterly Review of Biology* 28: 337–363.

Lorenz, K. Z. (1950). The comparative method in studying innate behaviour patterns. *Symposia of the Society for Experimental Biology No. IV.* Cambridge: Cambridge University Press, 221–268

Lorenz, K. Z. (1966). *On Aggression.* New York: Harcourt, Brace and World.

Lorenz, K. Z. (1970, 1971). *Studies in Animal and Human Behavior,* vols. 1 and 2. Cambridge, MA: Harvard University Press.

Marler, P. (1991). The instinct to learn. In S. Carey and R. Gelman, Eds., *The Epigenesis of Mind: Essays on Biology and Cognition.* Hillsdale, NJ: Erlbaum, pp. 37–66.

Pinker S. (1994). *The Language Instinct.* New York: William Morrow.

Rauschecker, J, and P. Marler, Eds. (1987). *Imprinting and Cortical Plasticity.* New York: Wiley.

Roeder, K. D. (1963). *Nerve Cells and Insect Behavior.* Cambridge, MA: Harvard University Press.

Thorpe, W. H. (1956). *Learning and Instinct in Animals.* Cambridge, MA: Harvard University Press.

Tinbergen, N. (1951). *The Study of Instinct.* Oxford: Clarendon Press.

Tinbergen, N. (1971, 1973). *The Animal in its World: Explorations of an Ethologist,* vols. 1 and 2. Cambridge, MA: Harvard University Press.

Waddington, C. H. (1966). *Principles of Development and Differentiation.* New York: Macmillan.

Watson, J. B. (1924). *Behaviorism.* Chicago: University of Chicago Press.

Further Readings

Alcock, J. (1997). *Animal Behavior: An Evolutionary Approach.* Sunderland, MA: Sinauer Associates Inc.

Baerends, G. P. (1988). Ethology. In R. C. Atkinson, R. J. Herrnstein, G. Lindzey, and R. D. Luce, Eds., *Stevens' Handbook of Experimental Psychology,* vol. 1: Perception and Motivation. New York: Wiley, pp. 765–830.

Barlow, G. W. (1977). Modal action patterns. In T. A. Sebeok, Ed., *How Animals Communicate.* Bloomington: University of Indiana Press.

Bateson, P. P. G. (1966). The characteristics and context of imprinting. *Biological Reviews* 41: 177–220.

Bateson, P. P. G. (1978). Early experience and sexual preferences. In J. B. Hutchison, Ed., *Biological Determinants of Sexual Behavior.* New York: Wiley, pp. 29–53.

von Cranach, M., K. Foppa, W. Lepenies, and D. Ploog, Eds. (1979). *Human Ethology.* Cambridge: Cambridge University Press.

Eibl-Eibesfeldt, I. (1975). *Ethology: The Biology of Behavior.* New York: Holt, Rinehart and Winston.

Gottlieb, G. (1979). Comparative psychology and ethology. In E. Hearst, Ed., *The First Century of Experimental Psychology.* Hillsdale, NJ: Erlbaum.

Gould, J. L., and P. Marler. (1987). Learning by instinct. *Scientific American* 256(1): 62–73.

Grillner, S., and P. Wallen. (1985). Central pattern generators for locomotion with special reference to vertebrates. *Annual Review of Neuroscience* 8: 233–261.

Hess, E. H. (1973). *Imprinting: Early Experience and the Developmental Psychobiology of Attachment.* New York: Van Nostrand.

Hinde, R. A. (1960). Energy models of motivation. *Sym. Soc. Exp. Biol.* 14: 199–213.

Hinde, R. A. (1970). *Animal Behavior: A Synthesis of Ethology and Comparative Psychology.* 2nd ed. New York: McGraw-Hill.

von Holst, E. (1973). *The Behavioral Physiology of Animals and Man. Selected Papers of Eric von Holst.* Coral Gables, FL: University of Miami Press.

Maier, N. R. F., and T. C. Schneirla. (1935). *Principles of Animal Psychology.* New York: McGraw-Hill.

Marler, P. (1985). Ethology of communicative behavior. In H. I. Kaplan and B. J. Sadock, Eds., *Comprehensive Textbook of Psychiatry,* vol. 1. Baltimore/London: Williams and Wilkins, pp. 237–246.

Marler, P. R., and W. J. Hamilton III. (1966). *Mechanisms of Animal Behavior.* New York: Wiley.

Schleidt, W. M. (1962). Die historische Entwicklung der Begriffe "Angeborenes auslösendes Schema": und "Angeborener Auslösemechanismus". *Z. Tierpsychol.* 19: 697–722.

Seligman, M. E. P., and J. L. Hager, Eds. (1972). *Biological Boundaries of Learning.* New York: Appleton-Century Crofts.

Thorpe, W. H. (1961). *Bird Song.* Cambridge: Cambridge University Press.

Evoked Fields

See ELECTROPHYSIOLOGY, ELECTRIC AND MAGNETIC EVOKED FIELDS

Evolution

In its simplest form, the theory of evolution is just the idea that life has changed over time, with younger forms descending from older ones. This idea existed well before the age of Charles DARWIN, but he and his successors developed it to explain both the diversity of life, and the adaptation of living things to their circumstances. Ernest Mayr (1991) argues that this developed conception of evolution combines five main ideas:

1. The living world is not constant; evolutionary change occurs.
2. Evolutionary change has a branching pattern. The species that we see are descended from one (or a few) remote ancestors.
3. New species form when a population splits into isolated fragments which then diverge.
4. Evolutionary change is gradual. Very few organisms that differ dramatically from their parents are able to survive. Of those few that survive, only a small proportion found populations that preserve these differences.
5. The mechanism of adaptive change is natural selection.

Darwin, Wallace, and others rapidly convinced their scientific contemporaries of the fact of evolution (Darwin 1859/1964; Wallace 1870). They persuaded that community of the existence of the tree of life. Darwin himself was a gradualist, thinking that tiny increments across great periods of time accumulate as evolutionary change, and he thought that the main agent of that change was natural selection. But his views on gradual change and on the importance of selection were not part of the biological consensus until the synthesis of population genetics with evolutionary theory by Fisher, Wright, Haldane, and others in the 1930s (Depew and Weber 1995). The importance of isolation in the generation of new species remained controversial even longer. It became part of the consensus view on evolution only after Mayr's postwar work on speciation and evolution (Mayr 1942, 1976, 1988).

The biological world confronted Darwin, Wallace, and their successors with two central problems. The world of life as we know it is fabulously diverse, even though today's life is only a tiny fraction of its total historical diversity. We tend to underestimate that diversity, because most large animals—animals that we notice—are vertebrates like us. But many organisms are weirdly different from us and from one another, and weird not just in finished adult form, but also in their developmental history. Humans do not undergo major physical reorganizations during their growth from children, whereas (for example) many parasites' life cycles take them through a number of hosts, and in their travels they experience complete physical transformation. Yet though life is diverse, that diversity is clumped in important ways. Arthropods have jointed, segmented bodies with various limbs and feelers attached, the whole covered with an exoskeleton. They are very different from anything else, from vertebrates, worms, and other invertebrates. Before Darwin, the differences between arthropods, vertebrates, worms, and other great branches of life seemed so vast as to rule out evolutionary transitions between them. They are so distinctive that even after the universal acceptance of the evolutionary descent of life, arthropod affinities remain controversial. Thus one task of evolutionary biology is in the explanation of diversity and its clumping, both on the large scale of different kinds of organism, and on the smaller scale of the difference between species of the same general kind.

If diversity is important, so too is ADAPTATION. The structured complexity of organisms, and their adaptation to their environment, is every bit as striking as the diversity of organisms through their environment. Perceptual systems are classic examples of complex, fine-tuned adaptation. Bat ECHOLOCATION requires mechanisms that enable bats to produce highly energetic sound waves. So they also have mechanisms that protect their ears while they are making such loud sounds. They have elaborately structured facial architectures to maximize their chances of detecting return echoes, together with specialized neural machinery to use the information in those echoes to guide their flight to their target. But there are many other examples of complex adaptation. Many parasites, for example, manufacture chemicals that they use to manipulate the morphology and behavior of their host.

Darwin's greatest achievement was to give a naturalistic explanation of adaptation. His key idea, natural selection, can explain both adaptation and diversity. Imagine the population ancestral to the Australasian bittern. Let us suppose that this population, like current bitterns, lived in reeds adjacent to wetlands and sought to escape predation by crouching still when a threatening creature was near. It is quite likely that the color and pattern of the plumage of this ancestral population varied. If so, some birds were favored. Their plumage made them somewhat harder to see when they froze among the reeds. They were more likely to survive to breed. If the plumage patterns of their offspring were like those of their parents, the plumage patterns of the descendant generation would be somewhat different from that of the ancestral generation. Over time, the colors and patterns characteristic of the population would change. Thus we could reach today's superbly well-concealed bitterns. Natural selection selects fitter organisms, and the heritability of their traits ensures a changed descendant population. Evolutionary change depends on variation in a population, fitness differences in the population consequent on that variation and heritability. Adaptive change takes place despite the fact that the mechanisms that generate variation in the population are decoupled from the adaptive needs of the population. But it depends on more than those principles. The adaptive shift to good camouflage took place gradually, over many generations. It depended on cumulative selection. If selection is to explain major adaptation it must be cumulative. Innovation is the result of a long sequence of selective episodes rather than one, for the chances of a single mutation producing a new adaptation are very low.

Thus evolution under natural selection can produce adaptation. At the same time, it can produce diversity, as populations become adapted to different local environments, and thus diverge from one another.

Evolutionary biology has developed a consensus on the broad outline of life's history. There is agreement on important aspects of the mechanism of evolution. Everyone agrees that selection is important, but that chance and other factors play an important role too. No one doubts the importance of isolation in generating diversity. But important disagreements remain. The nature of species and speciation remains problematic. Although everyone agrees that selection, chance, history, and development combine to generate life's history, the nature of that combination remains controversial. Though all agree that selection matters, the mode of its action remains contested. Dawkins and others think of selection as primarily selecting lineages of genes in virtue of their differing capacities to get themselves replicated (Dawkins 1982). Others—for example, Gould (1989) and Sober (1984)—conceive of selection as acting on many different kinds of entities: genes, organisms, colonies and groups, and even species. Finally, some—David Hull (1988) being one—think of evolution in biology as just a special case of a general mechanism of change involving undirected variation and selective retention. These controversial ideas lead to attempts to give evolutionary accounts of scientific and cultural change.

See also COGNITIVE ETHOLOGY; CULTURAL EVOLUTION; ETHOLOGY; EVOLUTION OF LANGUAGE; EVOLUTIONARY COMPUTATION; EVOLUTIONARY PSYCHOLOGY

—Kim Sterelny

References

Darwin, C. (1859/1964). *On the Origin of Species: A Facsimile of the First Edition.* Cambridge, MA: Harvard University Press.

Dawkins, R. (1982). *The Extended Phenotype.* Oxford: Oxford University Press.

Depew, D., and B. H. Weber. (1995). *Darwinism Evolving: Systems Dynamics and the Genealogy of Natural Selection.* Cambridge, MA: MIT Press.

Gould, S. J. (1989). *Wonderful Life: The Burgess Shale and the Nature of History.* New York: W. W. Norton.

Hull, D. (1988). *Science as a Process.* Chicago: University of Chicago Press.

Mayr, E. (1942). *Systematics and the Origin of Species.* New York: Columbia University Press.

Mayr, E. (1976). *Evolution and the Diversity of Life.* Cambridge, MA: Harvard University Press.

Mayr, E. (1988). *Towards a New Philosophy of Biology.* Cambridge, MA: Harvard University Press.

Mayr, E. (1991). *One Long Argument: Charles Darwin and the Genesis of Modern Evolutionary Thought.* London: Penguin.

Sober, E. (1984). *The Nature of Selection: Evolutionary Theory in Philosophical Focus.* Cambridge, MA: MIT Press.

Wallace, A. R. (1870). *Contributions to the Theory of Natural Selection.* London: Macmillan.

Further Readings

Bowler, P. (1989). *Evolution: The History of an Idea.* Berkeley: University of California Press.

Williams, G. C. (1966). *Adaptation and Natural Selection: A Critique of Some Current Evolutionary Thought.* Princeton, NJ: Princeton University Press.

Williams, G. C. (1992). *Natural Selection: Domains, Levels and Challenges.* Oxford: Oxford University Press.

Evolution and Ethics

See ETHICS AND EVOLUTION

Evolution of Language

The question of how language evolved has never been a respectable one. In the nineteenth century it motivated so much wild speculation that the Société de Linguistique de Paris banned all discussion on the topic—and many academics today wish this ban were still in place. Over the last thirty or so years, however, findings from psychology, evolutionary biology, and linguistics have radically changed the way that scholars approach this issue, leading to some surprising insights and opening up areas of fruitful empirical investigation.

For one thing, proposals that language is entirely a cultural innovation, akin to agriculture or bowling, can be safely dismissed. Historical linguistics gives no support to the speculation that language was invented once and then spread throughout the world; instead, the capacity to create language is to some extent within every human, and it is invented anew each generation (Pinker 1994). This is most apparent from studies of creolization; children who are exposed to a rudimentary communication system will embellish and expand it, transforming it into a full-fledged language within a single generation—a CREOLE (Bickerton 1981). A similar process might occur in all normal instances of LANGUAGE ACQUISITION: Children are remarkably proficient at obeying subtle syntactic and morphological constraints for which there is little evidence in the sentences they hear (e.g., Crain 1991), suggesting that some capacity for language has emerged through biological evolution.

Could this capacity have emerged as an accidental result of the large brains that humans have evolved, or as a by-product of some enhanced general intelligence? Probably not; there are people of otherwise normal intelligence and brain size who have severe problems learning language (e.g., Gopnik 1990), as well as people with reduced intelligence or small brains who have no problems with language (e.g., Lenneberg 1967). Furthermore, the human language capacity cannot be entirely explained in terms of the evolution of mechanisms for the production and comprehension of speech. Although the human vocal tract shows substantial signs of design for the purpose of articulation—something observed by both DARWIN and the theologian William Paley, though they drew quite different morals from it—humans are equally proficient at learning and using SIGN LANGUAGES (Newport and Meier 1985).

How else could language have evolved? Modern biologists have elaborated Darwin's insight that although natural selection is the most important of all evolutionary mechanisms, it is not the only one. Many traits that animals possess are not adaptations, but emerge either as by-products of adaptations ("spandrels") or through entirely nonselectionist processes, such as random genetic drift (Gould and Lewontin 1979). Natural selection is necessary only in order to explain the evolution of what Darwin (1859) called "organs of extreme perfection and complexity," such as the heart, the hand, and the eye. This is because only a selectionist process can evolve biological traits capable of accomplishing impressive engineering tasks of adaptive benefit to organisms (Dawkins 1986; Williams 1966). Although there is controversy about the proper scope of selectionist theories, this much at least is agreed on, even by those who are most cautious about applying adaptive explanations (e.g., Gould 1977).

Does language show signs of complex adaptive design to the same extent as organs such as the hand and the eye? Many linguists would claim that it does, arguing that language is composed of different parts, including PHONOLOGY,

MORPHOLOGY, and SYNTAX, that interact with one another, as well as with perceptual, motoric, and conceptual systems, so as to make possible an extraordinarily complicated engineering task—the transduction of thoughts into speech or sign. The conclusion that language decomposes into distinct neural and computational components is supported by independent data from studies of acquisition, processing, and pathology (Pinker 1994).

Based on these conclusions, some scholars have argued that language has evolved as a biological adaptation for the function of communication (Newmeyer 1991; Pinker and Bloom 1990). Others have proposed instead that the ability to learn and use language is a by-product of brain mechanisms evolved for other purposes, such as motor control (Lieberman 1984), social cognition (Tomasello 1995) and internal computation and representation (Bickerton, 1995)—and that such mechanisms have been exploited, with limited subsequent modification, for speech and sign.

To put the issue in a different context, nobody doubts that the acquisition and use of human language involves capacities we share with other animals; the interesting debate is over whether the uniquely human ability to learn language can be explained entirely in terms of enhancements of such capacities, or whether much of language has been specifically evolved in the millions of years that separate us from other primates. The study of the communication systems of nonhuman primates is plainly relevant here (e.g., Cheney and Seyfarth 1990) as is the study of their conceptual and social capacities (e.g., Povinelli and Eddy 1996).

The more we learn about the cognitive and neural mechanisms underlying language, the more we will know about how it evolved—which aspects are adaptations for different purposes, which are by-products of adaptations, and which are accidents (Bloom 1998). Perhaps more importantly, we can gain insights in the opposite direction. As Mayr (1983) points out, asking about the function of a given structure or organ "has been the basis for every advance in physiology." And although one can ask about function without considering evolutionary biology, an appreciation of how natural selection works is necessary in order to discipline and guide functional inquiry; this is especially so for the quite nonintuitive functional considerations that arise in the evolution of communication systems (Dawkins and Krebs 1978; Hauser 1996). To the extent that language is part of human physiology, exploring how it evolved will inevitably lead to insights about its current nature.

See also ADAPTATION AND ADAPTATIONISM; CULTURAL EVOLUTION; EVOLUTION; INNATENESS OF LANGUAGE; LANGUAGE AND CULTURE; PRIMATE COGNITION; PRIMATE LANGUAGE

—*Paul Bloom*

References

Bickerton, D. (1981). *Roots of Language.* Ann Arbor, MI: Karoma.

Bickerton, D. (1995). *Language and Human Behavior.* Seattle: University of Washington Press.

Bloom, P. (1998). Some issues in the evolution of language and thought. In D. Cummins and C. Allen, Eds., *Evolution of the Mind.* Oxford: Oxford University Press.

Cheney, D. L., and R. M. Seyfarth. (1990). *How Monkeys See the World.* Chicago: University of Chicago Press.

Chomsky, N. (1980). *Rules and Representations.* New York: Columbia University Press.

Crain, S. (1991). Language acquisition in the absence of experience. *Behavioral and Brain Sciences* 14: 597–650.

Darwin, C. (1859). *On the Origin of Species.* London: John Murray.

Dawkins, R. (1986). *The Blind Watchmaker.* New York: W. W. Norton.

Dawkins, R., and Krebs, J. R. (1978). Animal signals: information or manipulation. In J. R. Krebs and N. B. Davies, Eds., *Behavioral Ecology.* Oxford: Blackwell.

Gopnik, M. (1990). Feature blindness: a case study. *Language Acquisition* 1: 139–164.

Gould, S. J. (1977). Darwin's untimely burial. In *Ever Since Darwin: Reflections on Natural History.* New York: W. W. Norton.

Gould, S. J., and R. Lewontin. (1979). The spandrels of San Marco and the Panglossian Paradigm: a critique of the Adaptationist Programme. *Proceedings of the Royal Society* 205: 581–598.

Hauser, M. D. (1996). *The Evolution of Communication.* Cambridge, MA: MIT Press.

Lenneberg, E. H. (1967). *Biological Foundations of Language.* New York: Wiley.

Lieberman, P. (1984). *The Biology and Evolution of Language.* Cambridge, MA: Harvard University Press.

Mayr, E. (1983). How to carry out the adaptationist program? *The American Naturalist* 121: 324–334.

Newmeyer, F. J. (1991). Functional explanations in linguistics and the origin of language. *Language and Communication* 11: 1–28.

Newport, E. L., and R. P. Meier. (1985). The acquisition of American Sign Language. In D. I. Slobin, Ed., *The Crosslinguistic Study of Language Acquisition.* Vol. 1, *The Data.* Hillsdale, NJ: Erlbaum.

Pinker, S. (1994). *The Language Instinct.* New York: Morrow.

Pinker, S., and P. Bloom. (1990). Natural language and natural selection. *Behavioral and Brain Sciences* 13: 585–642.

Povinelli, D. J., and T. J. Eddy. (1996). What young chimpanzees know about seeing. *Monographs of the Society for Research in Child Development* 61(3): 1–152.

Tomasello, M. (1995). Language is not an instinct. *Cognitive Development* 10: 131–156.

Williams, G. C. (1966). *Adaptation and Natural Selection: A Critique of Some Current Evolutionary Thought.* Princeton: Princeton University Press.

Evolutionary Computation

Evolutionary computation is a collection of computational search, learning, optimization, and modeling methods loosely inspired by biological EVOLUTION. The methods most often used are called *genetic algorithms* (GAs), *evolution strategies* (ESs), and *evolutionary programming* (EP). These three methods were developed independently in the 1960s: GAs by Holland (1975), ESs by Rechenberg (1973) and Schwefel (1977), and EP by Fogel, Owens, and Walsh (1966). (Genetic programming, a variant of genetic algorithms, was developed in the 1980s by Koza 1992, 1994.) Such methods are part of a general movement for using biological ideas in computer science that started with pioneers such as VON NEUMANN, TURING, and WIENER, and continues today with evolutionary computation, NEURAL NETWORKS, and methods inspired by the immune system, insect colonies, and other biological systems.

Imitating the mechanisms of evolution has appealed to computer scientists from nearly the beginning of the computer age. Very roughly speaking, evolution can be viewed as searching in parallel among an enormous number of possibilities for "solutions" to the problem of survival in an environment, where the solutions are particular designs for organisms. Viewed from a high level, the "rules" of evolution are remarkably simple: species evolve by means of heritable variation (via mutation, recombination, and other operators), followed by natural selection in which the fittest tend to survive and reproduce, thus propagating their genetic material to future generations. Yet these simple rules are thought to be responsible, in large part, for the extraordinary variety and complexity we see in the biosphere. Seen in this light, the mechanisms of evolution can inspire computational search methods for finding solutions to hard problems in large search spaces or for automatically designing complex systems.

In most evolutionary computation applications, the user has a particular problem to be solved and a way to encode candidate solutions so that the solution space can be searched. For example, in the field of computational protein design, the problem is to design a one-dimensional sequence of amino acids that will fold up into a three-dimensional protein with desired characteristics. Assuming that the sequence is of length l, candidate solutions can be expressed as strings of l amino-acid codes. There are twenty different amino acids, so the number of possible strings is 20^l. The user also provides a "fitness function" or "objective function" that assigns a value to each candidate solution measuring its quality.

Evolutionary computation (EC) methods all begin with a population of randomly generated candidate solutions ("individuals"), and perform fitness-based selection and random variation to create a new population. Typically, some number of the highest-fitness individuals are chosen under selection to create offspring for the next generation. Often, an offspring will be produced via a crossover between two or more parents, in which the offspring receives "genetic material"—different parts of candidate solutions—from different parents. Typically the offspring is also mutated randomly—parts of the candidate solution are changed at random. (Mutation and crossover in evolutionary computation are meant to mimic roughly biological mutation and sexual recombination, two main sources of genetic variation.) Offspring are created in this way until a new generation is complete. This process typically iterates for many generations, often ending up with one or more optimal or high-quality individuals in the population.

GA, EP, and ES methods differ in the details of this process. In general, ESs and EP each define fairly specific versions of this process, whereas the term "genetic algorithm," originally referring to a specific algorithm, has come to refer to many considerably different variations of the basic scheme.

ESs were originally formulated to work on real-valued parameter optimization problems, such as airplane wing-shape optimization. They are still most commonly applied to numerical optimization problems. In the original formulation of EP, candidate solutions to given tasks were represented as finite-state machines, which were evolved by randomly mutating their state-transition diagrams and selecting the fittest. Since that time a somewhat broader formulation has emerged. In contrast with ESs and EP, GAs were originally formulated not to solve specific problems, but rather as a means to study formally the phenomenon of adaptation as it occurs in nature and to develop ways in which the mechanisms of natural adaptation might be imported into computer systems. Only after Holland's original theoretical work were GAs adapted to solving optimization problems. Since the early 1990s there has been much cross-fertilization among the three areas, and the original distinctions among GAs, ESs, and EP have blurred considerably in the current use of these labels.

Setting the parameters for the evolutionary process (population size, selection strength, mutation rate, crossover rate, and so on) is often a matter of guesswork and trial and error, though some theoretical and heuristic guidelines have been discovered. An alternative is to have the parameters "self-adapt"—to change their values automatically over the course of evolution in response to selective pressures. Self-adapting parameters are an intrinsic part of ESs and EP, and are the subject of much research in GAs.

EC methods have been applied widely. Examples of applications include numerical parameter optimization and combinatorial optimization, the automatic design of computer programs, bioengineering, financial prediction, robot learning, evolving production systems for artificial intelligence applications, and designing and training neural networks. In addition to these "problem-solving" applications, EC methods have been used in models of natural systems in which evolutionary processes take place, including economic systems, immune systems, ecologies, biological evolution, evolving systems with adaptive individuals, insect societies, and more complex social systems. (See Mitchell 1996 for an overview of applications in some of these areas.)

Much current research in the EC field is on making the basic EC framework more biologically realistic, both for modeling purposes and in the hope that more realism will improve the search performance of these methods. One approach is incorporating more complex genetic information in individuals in the population, such as sexual differentiation, diploidy, and introns. Another is incorporating additional genetic operators, such as inversion, translocation, and gene doubling and deletion. A third is embedding more complex ecological interactions into the population, such as host-parasite coevolution, symbiosis, sexual selection, and spatial migration. Finally, there has been considerable success in combining EC methods with other types of search methods, such as simple gradient ascent and simulated annealing. Such hybrid algorithms are thought by many to be the best approach to optimization in complex and ill-understood problem spaces (Davis 1991).

EC is relevant for the cognitive sciences both because of its applications in the fields of artificial intelligence and MACHINE LEARNING and because of its use in models of the interaction of evolution and cognitive processes. For example, researchers in EVOLUTIONARY PSYCHOLOGY and other areas have used EC methods in their models of interactions between evolution and LEARNING (e.g., Ackley and Littman 1992; Belew and Mitchell 1996; Miller and Todd 1990; Parisi, Nolfi and Elman 1994; Todd 1996). Likewise, EC methods have been used in models of the relationship between evolution and development (e.g., Belew 1993; Dellaert and Beer 1994). Social scientists and linguists have used EC methods to study, for example, the evolution of cooperation and communication in multiagent systems (e.g., Ackley and Littman 1994; Axelrod 1987; Batali 1994; Batali and Kitcher 1995; Stanley, Ashlock, and Tesfatsion 1994). Many of these models are considered to fall in the purview of the field of ARTIFICIAL LIFE. These examples by no means exhaust the uses of EC in cognitive science, and the literature is growing as interest increases in the role of evolution in shaping cognition and behavior.

—*Melanie Mitchell*

References

Ackley, D., and M. Littman. (1992). Interactions between learning and evolution. In C. G. Langton, C. Taylor, J. D. Farmer, and S. Rasmussen, Eds., *Artificial Life II*. Reading, MA: Addison-Wesley, pp. 487–509.

Ackley, D., and M. Littman. (1994). Altruism in the evolution of communication. In R. A. Brooks and P. Maes, Eds., *Artificial Life IV*. Cambridge, MA: MIT Press, pp. 40–48.

Axelrod, R. (1987). The evolution of strategies in the iterated Prisoner's Dilemma. In L. D. Davis, Ed., *Genetic Algorithms and Simulated Annealing*, New York: Morgan Kaufmann, pp. 32–41.

Back, T. (1996). *Evolutionary Algorithms in Theory and Practice: Evolution Strategies, Evolutionary Programming, Genetic Algorithms*. New York: Oxford University Press.

Batali, J. (1994). Innate biases and critical periods: combining evolution and learning in the acquisition of syntax. In R. A. Brooks and P. Maes, Eds., *Artificial Life IV*. Cambridge, MA: MIT Press, pp. 160–177.

Batali, J., and P. Kitcher. (1995). Evolution of altruism in optional and compulsory games. *Journal of Theoretical Biology* 175(2): 161.

Belew, R. K. (1993). Interposing an ontogenic model between genetic algorithms and neural networks. In S. J. Hanson, J. D. Cowan, and C. L. Giles, Eds., *Advances in Neural Information Processing* (NIPS 5). New York: Morgan Kaufmann.

Belew, R. K., and M. Mitchell, Eds. (1996). *Adaptive Individuals in Evolving Populations: Models and Algorithms*. Reading, MA: Addison-Wesley.

Davis, L. D., Ed. (1991). *Handbook of Genetic Algorithms*. New York: Van Nostrand Reinhold.

Dellaert, F., and R. D. Beer. (1994). Toward an evolvable model of development for autonomous agent synthesis. In R. A. Brooks and P. Maes, Eds., *Artificial Life IV*. Cambridge, MA: MIT Press, pp. 246–257.

Fogel, D. B. (1995). *Evolutionary Computation: Toward a New Philosophy of Machine Intelligence*. Los Angeles: IEEE Press.

Fogel, L. J., A. J. Owens, and M. J. Walsh. (1966). *Artificial Intelligence through Simulated Evolution*. New York: Wiley.

Goldberg, D. E. (1989). *Genetic Algorithms in Search, Optimization, and Machine Learning*. Reading, MA: Addison-Wesley.

Holland, J. H. (1975). *Adaptation in Natural and Artificial Systems*. Ann Arbor, MI: University of Michigan Press. 2nd ed: MIT Press, 1992.

Koza, J. R. (1992). *Genetic Programming: On the Programming of Computers by Means of Natural Selection*. Cambridge, MA: MIT Press.

Koza, J. R. (1994). *Genetic Programming II: Automatic Discovery of Reusable Programs*. Cambridge, MA: MIT Press.

Michalewicz, Z. (1992). *Genetic Algorithms + Data Structures = Evolution Programs*. New York: Springer.

Miller, G. F., and P. M. Todd. (1990). Exploring adaptive agency I: Theory and methods for simulating the evolution of learning. In D. S. Touretzky, J. L. Elman, T. J. Sejnowski, and G. E. Hinton, Eds., *Proceedings of the (1990) Connectionists Models Summer School*. New York: Morgan Kaufmann, pp. 65–80.

Mitchell, M. (1996). *An Introduction to Genetic Algorithms*. Cambridge, MA: MIT Press.

Mitchell, M., and S. Forrest. (1994). Genetic algorithms and artificial life. *Artificial Life* 1(3): 267–289.

Parisi, D., S. Nolfi, and J. L. Elman. (1994). Learning and evolution in neural networks. *Adaptive Behavior* 3(1): 5–28.

Rechenberg, I. (1973). *Evolutionsstrategie: Optimierung Technischer Systeme nach Prinzipien der Biologischen Evolution*. Stuttgart: Frommann-Holzboog.

Schwefel, H.-P. (1977). *Numerische Optimierung von Computer-Modellen mittels der Evolutionsstrategie*. Basel: Birkhauser.

Stanley, E. A., D. Ashlock, and L. Tesfatsion. (1994). Iterated Prisoner's Dilemma with choice and refusal of partners. In C. G. Langton, Ed., *Artificial Life III*. Reading, MA: Addison-Wesley, pp. 131–175.

Todd, P. M. (1996). Sexual selection and the evolution of learning. In R. K. Belew and M. Mitchell, Eds., *Adaptive Individuals in Evolving Populations: Models and Algorithms*. Reading, MA: Addison-Wesley, pp. 365–393.

von Neumann, J. (1966). *Theory of Self-Reproducing Automata*. Ed. A. W. Burks. Urbana: University of Illinois Press.

Further Readings

Holland, J. H., K. J. Holyoak, R. Nisbett, and P. R. Thagard. (1986). *Induction: Processes of Inference, Learning and Discovery*. Cambridge, MA: MIT Press.

Langton, C. G., Ed. (1995). *Artificial Life: An Overview*. Cambridge, MA: MIT Press.

Schwefel, H.-P. (1995). *Evolution and Optimum Seeking*. New York: Wiley.

Evolutionary Psychology

Evolutionary psychology is an approach to the cognitive sciences in which evolutionary biology is integrated with the cognitive, neural, and behavioral sciences to guide the systematic mapping of the species-typical computational and neural architectures of animal species, including humans.

Although the field draws on many disciplines, of particular importance was the integration of (1) the cognitive study of functional specializations pioneered in perception and Chomskyan psycholinguistics (MARR 1982); (2) hunter-gatherer and primate studies (Lee and DeVore 1968); and (3) the revolution that placed evolutionary biology on a more rigorous, formal foundation of replicator dynamics (Williams 1966; Dawkins 1982). Beginning in the 1960s, this revolution catalyzed the derivation of a set of theories about how evolution shapes organic design with respect to kinship, foraging, parental care, mate selection, COOPERATION AND COMPETITION, aggression, communication, life history, and so forth—theories that were refined and tested on an empirical base that now includes thousands of species. This body of theory has allowed evolutionary psychologists to apply the concepts and methods of the cognitive sciences to nontraditional topics, such as reciprocation, foraging memory, parental motivation, coalitional dynamics, incest avoidance, sexual jealousy, and so on. Evolutionary psychology is unusual in that a primary goal is the construction of a comprehensive map of the entire species-typical computational architecture of humans, including motivational and emotional mechanisms, and that its scope includes all human behavior, rather than simply "cold cognition."

George Williams's (1966) volume *Adaptation and Natural Selection* was of particular formative significance to evolutionary psychology. Williams identified the defects in the imprecise, panglossian functionalist thinking that had pervaded evolutionary biology and that continues, implicitly, to permeate other fields. The book outlined the principles of modern adaptationism (see ADAPTATION AND ADAPTATIONISM), showed how tightly constrained any adaptationist (i.e., functionalist) or by-product claim had to be to be consistent with neo-Darwinism, and identified the empirical tests such claims had to pass. Until Williams, many biologists explained the existence of a trait (or attributed functionality to traits) by identifying some beneficial consequence (to the individual, the social group, the ecosystem, the species, etc.). They did so without regard to whether the functionality or benefit was narrowly coupled, as neo-Darwinism requires, to a design that led to systematic genic propagation of replicas of itself within the context of the species' ancestral environment. Evolutionary psychologists apply these precise adaptationist constraints on functionalism to the cognitive, neural, and social sciences, and maintain that cognitive scientists should at least be aware that many cognitive theories routinely posit complex functional organization of kinds that evolutionary processes are unlikely to produce.

Evolutionary psychologists consider their field methodologically analogous to reverse engineering in computer science. In such an enterprise, evolutionary psychologists argue, knowledge of the evolutionary dynamics and ancestral task environments responsible for the construction of each species' architecture can provide valuable, although incomplete, models of the computational problems (sensu Marr 1982) that each species regularly encountered. These, in turn, can be used to pinpoint many candidate design features of the computational devices that could have evolved to solve these problems, which can then be used to guide empirical investigations. For example, if eye direction reliably provided useful information ancestrally about the intentions of conspecifics or predators, then specialized eye direction detectors may have evolved as a component of SOCIAL COGNITION, and it may prove worthwhile testing for their existence and design (Baron-Cohen 1995).

Evolutionary psychologists consider it likely that cognitive architectures contain a large number of evolved computational devices that are specialized in function (Gallistel 1995), such as FACE RECOGNITION systems, a language acquisition device, navigation specializations, and animate motion recognition. They are skeptical that an architecture consisting predominantly of content-independent cognitive processes, such as general-purpose pattern associators, could solve the diverse array of adaptive problems efficiently enough to reproduce themselves reliably in complex, unforgiving natural environments that include, for example, antagonistically coevolving biotic adversaries, such as parasites, prey, predators, competitors, and incompletely harmonious social partners.

Selection drives design features to become incorporated into architectures in proportion to the actual distribution of adaptive problems encountered by a species over evolutionary time. There is no selection to generalize the scope of problem solving to include never or rarely encountered problems at the cost of efficiency in solving frequently encountered problems. To the extent that problems cluster into types (domains) with statistically recurrent properties and structures (e.g., facial expression statistically cues emotional state), it will often be more efficient to include computational specializations tailored to inferentially exploit the recurrent features of the domain (objects always have locations, are bounded by surfaces, cannot pass through each other without deformation, can be used to move each other, etc.). Because the effects of selection depend on iteration over evolutionary time, evolutionary psychologists expect the detailed design features of domain-specific inference engines to intricately reflect the enduring features of domains. Consequently, evolutionary psychologists are very interested in careful studies of enduring environmental and task regularities, because these predict details of functional design (Shepard 1987). Adaptationist predictions of DOMAIN SPECIFICITY have gained support from many sources, for example, from cognitive neuroscience, demonstrating that many dissociable cognitive deficits show surprising content-specificity, and from developmental research indicating that infants come equipped with evolved domain-specific inference engines (e.g., a NAIVE PHYSICS, a THEORY OF MIND module; Hirschfeld and Gelman 1994).

A distinguishing feature of evolutionary psychology is that evolutionary psychologists have principled theoretical reasons for their hypotheses derived from biology, paleoanthropology, GAME THEORY, and hunter-gatherer studies. Such theoretically derived prior hypotheses allow researchers to devise experiments that make possible the detection and mapping of computational devices that no one would otherwise have thought to test for in the absence of such theories. To the extent that the evolutionary theory used is accurate, evolutionary psychologists argue that this practice allows a far more efficient research strategy than experiments designed and conducted in ignorance of the principles of evolved design or the likely functions of the brain. Using this new research program, many theoretically motivated discoveries have been made about, for instance, internal representations of trajectories; computational specializations for reasoning about danger, social exchanges, and threats; female advantage in the incidental learning of the spatial locations of objects; the frequency format of probabilistic reasoning representations; the decision rules governing risk aversion and its absence; universal mate selection criteria and standards of beauty; eye direction detection and its relationship to theory of mind; principles of generalization; life history shifts in aggression and parenting decisions; social memory; reasoning about groups and coalitions; the organization of jealousy, and scores of other topics (see Barkow, Cosmides, and Tooby 1992 for review).

Although some critics (Gould 1997) have argued that the field consists of post hoc storytelling, it is difficult to reconcile such claims with the actual practice of evolutionary psychologists, inasmuch as in evolutionary psychology the evolutionary model or "explanation" precedes the empirical discovery and guides researchers to it, rather than being constructed post hoc to explain some known fact. Although critics have also plausibly maintained that reconstructions of the past are inherently speculative, evolutionary psychologists have responded that researchers know with certainty or high confidence thousands of important things about our ancestors, many of which can be deployed in designing cognitive experiments: our ancestors had two sexes; lived in an environment where self-propelled motion reliably predicted that the entity was an animal; inhabited a world where the motions of objects conformed to the principles of kinematic geometry; chose mates; had color vision; were predated upon; had faces; lived in a biotic environment with a hierarchical taxonomic structure; and so on. Moreover, evolutionary psychologists point out that, to the extent that reconstructions are uncertain, they will simply lead to experiments that are no more or less likely to be productive than evolutionarily agnostic empiricism, the alternative research strategy.

Similarly, critics have argued that adaptationist analysis is misconceived, because adaptations are of poor quality, rendering functional predictions irrelevant (Gould 1997). Evolutionary psychologists respond that although selection does not optimize, it demonstrably produces well-engineered adaptations to long-enduring adaptive problems. Indeed, whenever engineers have attempted to duplicate any natural competence (color vision, object recognition, grammar acquisition, texture perception, object manipulation, locomotion over natural terrains, language comprehension, etc.), even when using huge budgets, large research teams, and decades of effort, they are unable to engineer artificial systems that can come close to competing with naturally engineered systems.

The processes of evolutionary change divide into two families: chance and selection. Chance processes (drift, mutation pressure, environmental change, etc.) produce random evolutionary change, and so cannot build organic structure more functionally organized than chance could account for. Natural selection, in contrast, is the only component of the evolutionary process that sorts features into or out of the architecture on the basis of how well they function. Consequently, all cognitive organization that is too improbably well-ordered with respect to function to have arisen by chance must be attributed to the operation of selection, a constrained set of processes that restrict the kinds of functional organization that can appear in organisms. As a result,

features of a species' cognitive or neural architecture can be partitioned into adaptations, which are present because they were selected for (e.g., the enhanced recognition system for snakes coupled with a decision-rule to acquire a motivation to avoid them); by-products, which are present because they are causally coupled to traits that were selected for (e.g., the avoidance of harmless snakes); and noise, which was injected by the stochastic components of evolution (e.g., the fact that a small percentage of humans sneeze when exposed to sunlight). One payoff of integrating adaptationist analysis with cognitive science was the realization that complex functional structures (computational or anatomical), in species with life histories like humans, will be overwhelmingly species-typical (Tooby and Cosmides 1990a). That is, the complex adaptations that compose the human COGNITIVE ARCHITECTURE must be human universals, while variation caused by genetic differences are predominantly noise: minor random perturbations around the species-typical design. This principle allows cross-cultural triangulation of the species-typical design, which is why many evolutionary psychologists include cross-cultural components in their research.

Evolutionary psychologists emphasize the study of adaptations and their by-products not because they think all or most traits are adaptations (or their side effects), but because (1) at present, adaptationist theories of function provide clear and useful prior predictions about cognitive organization; (2) the functional elements are far more likely to be species-typical and hence experimentally extractable; (3) analysis of the random or contingent components of evolution provides very few constrained or falsifiable predictions about cognitive architecture; and (4) theories of phylogenetic constraint are not yet very useful or well developed, although that may change. Evolutionary psychologists do not maintain that all traits are adaptive, that the realized architecture of the human mind is immune to modification, that genes or biology are deterministic, that culture is unimportant, or that existing human social arrangements are fair or inevitable. Indeed, they provide testable theories about the developmental processes that build (and can change) the mechanisms that generate human behavior.

See also ALTRUISM; EVOLUTION; MODULARITY OF MIND; SEXUAL ATTRACTION, EVOLUTIONARY PSYCHOLOGY OF; SOCIAL COGNITION IN ANIMALS; SOCIOBIOLOGY

—*Leda Cosmides and John Tooby*

References

Barkow, J., L. Cosmides, and J. Tooby, Eds. (1992). *The Adapted Mind: Evolutionary Psychology and the Generation of Culture.* New York: Oxford University Press.

Baron-Cohen, S. (1995). *Mindblindness: An Essay on Autism and Theory of Mind.* Cambridge, MA: MIT Press.

Dawkins, R. (1982) *The Extended Phenotype.* San Francisco: W. H. Freeman.

Gallistel, C. R. (1995) The replacement of general-purpose theories with adaptive specializations. In M. S. Gazzaniga, Ed., *The Cognitive Neurosciences.* Cambridge, MA: MIT Press.

Gould, S. J. (1997). Evolution: the pleasures of pluralism. *New York Review of Books* 44(11): 47–52.

Hirschfeld, L., and S. Gelman, Eds. (1994). *Mapping the Mind: Domain Specificity in Cognition and Culture.* New York: Cambridge University Press.

Lee, R. B., and I. DeVore, Eds. (1968) *Man the Hunter.* Aldine: Chicago.

Marr, D. (1982). *Vision.* Cambridge, MA: MIT Press.

Shepard, R. N. (1987). Evolution of a mesh between principles of the mind and regularities of the world. In J. Dupre, Ed., *The Latest on the Best: Essays on Evolution and Optimality.* Cambridge, MA: The MIT Press.

Tooby, J., and L. Cosmides. (1990a). On the universality of human nature and the uniqueness of the individual: the role of genetics and adaptation. *Journal of Personality* 58: 17–67.

Tooby, J., and L. Cosmides. (1992). The psychological foundations of culture. In J. Barkow, L. Cosmides, and J. Tooby, Eds., *The Adapted Mind: Evolutionary Psychology and the Generation of Culture.* New York: Oxford University Press.

Williams, G. C. (1966). *Adaptation and Natural Selection.* Princeton: Princeton University Press.

Further Readings

Atran, S. (1990). *The Cognitive Foundations of Natural History.* New York: Cambridge University Press.

Brown, D. E. (1991). *Human Universals.* New York: McGraw-Hill.

Buss, D. M. (1994). *The Evolution of Desire.* New York: Basic Books.

Carey, S., and R. Gelman, Eds. (1991). *Epigenesis of the Mind: Essays in Biology and Knowledge.* Hillsdale, NJ: Erlbaum.

Cosmides, L., and J. Tooby. (1992). Cognitive adaptations for social exchange. In J. Barkow, L. Cosmides, and J. Tooby, Eds., *The Adapted Mind: Evolutionary Psychology and the Generation of Culture.* New York: Oxford University Press.

Daly, M., and M. Wilson. (1995). Discriminative parental solicitude and the relevance of evolutionary models to the analysis of motivational systems. In M. S. Gazzaniga (Ed.), *The Cognitive Neurosciences.* Cambridge, MA: MIT Press.

Daly, M., and M. Wilson. (1988) *Homicide.* New York: Aldine.

Ekman, P. (1993). Facial expression and emotion. *American Psychologist* 48: 384–392.

Gigerenzer, G., and K. Hug. (1992). Domain specific reasoning: social contracts, cheating, and perspective change. *Cognition* 43: 127–171.

Krebs, J. R., and N. B. Davies. (1997). *Behavioural Ecology: An Evolutionary Approach.* 4th ed. Sunderland, Mass.: Sinauer Associates.

Maynard Smith, J. (1982) *Evolution and the Theory of Games.* Cambridge: Cambridge University Press.

Pinker, S. (1997). *How the Mind Works.* New York: W. W. Norton.

Rozin, P. (1976) The evolution of intelligence and access to the cognitive unconscious. In J. M. Sprague and A. N. Epstein, Eds., *Progress in Psychobiology and Physiological Psychology.* New York: Academic Press.

Shepard, R. N. (1987). Toward a universal law of generalization for psychological science. *Science* 237: 1317–1323.

Sherry, D., and D. Schacter. (1987). The evolution of multiple memory systems. *Psychological Review* 94: 439–454.

Spelke, E. (1990). Principles of object perception. *Cognitive Science* 14: 29–56.

Sperber, D. (1994). The modularity of thought and the epidemeology of representations. In L. Hirschfeld and S. Gelman, Eds., *Mapping the Mind: Domain-Specificity in Cognition and Culture.* Cambridge: Cambridge University Press.

Sperber, D. (1996). *Explaining Culture: A Naturalistic Approach.* Cambridge: Blackwell.

Staddon, J. E. R. (1988). Learning as inference. In R. C. Bolles and M. D. Beecher, Eds., *Evolution and Learning.* Hillsdale, NJ: Erlbaum.

Stephens, D., and J. Krebs. (1986). *Foraging Theory.* Princeton, NJ: Princeton University Press.

Symons, D. (1979). *The Evolution of Human Sexuality.* New York: Oxford University Press.

Tooby, J., and L. Cosmides. (1990b). The past explains the present: emotional adaptations and the structure of ancestral environments. *Ethology and Sociobiology* 11: 375–424.

Expert Systems

See EXPERTISE; KNOWLEDGE-BASED SYSTEMS

Expertise

Expertise refers to the mechanisms underlying the superior achievement of an expert, that is, "one who has acquired special skill in or knowledge of a particular subject through professional training and practical experience" (Webster's, 1976: 800). The term *expert* is used to describe highly experienced professionals such as medical doctors, accountants, teachers, and scientists, but has been expanded to include individuals who attained their superior performance by instruction and extended practice: highly skilled performers in the arts, such as music, painting, and writing; sports, such as swimming, running, and golf; and games, such as bridge, chess, and billiards.

When experts exhibit their superior performance in public their behavior looks so effortless and natural that we are tempted to attribute it to special talents. Although a certain amount of knowledge and training seems necessary, the role of acquired skill for the highest levels of achievement has traditionally been minimized. However, when scientists began measuring the experts' supposedly superior powers of speed, memory and intelligence with psychometric tests, no general superiority was found—the demonstrated superiority was domain-specific. For example, the superiority of the CHESS experts' memory was constrained to regular chess positions and did not generalize to other types of materials (Djakow, Petrowski and Rudik 1927). Not even IQ could distinguish the best among chess-players (Doll and Mayr 1987) nor the most successful and creative among artists and scientists (Taylor 1975). Ericsson and Lehmann (1996) found that

1. Measures of general basic capacities do not predict success in a domain.
2. The superior performance of experts is often very domain-specific, and transfer outside their narrow area of expertise is surprisingly limited.
3. Systematic differences between experts and less proficient individuals nearly always reflect attributes acquired by the experts during their lengthy training.

In a pioneering empirical study of the thought processes mediating the highest levels of performance, de Groot (1978) instructed expert and world-class chess players to think aloud while they selected their next move for an unfamiliar chess position. The world-class players did not differ in the speed of their thoughts or the size of their basic memory capacity, and their ability to recognize promising potential moves was based on their extensive experience and knowledge of patterns in chess. In their influential theory of expertise, Chase and Simon (1973; Simon and Chase 1973) proposed that experts with extended experience acquire a larger number of more complex patterns and use these new patterns to store knowledge about which actions should be taken in similar situations. According to this influential theory, expert performance is viewed as an extreme case of skill acquisition (Proctor and Dutta 1995; Richman et al. 1996; VanLehn 1996) and as the final result of the gradual improvement of performance during extended experience in a domain. Furthermore, the postulated central role of acquired knowledge has encouraged efforts to extract experts' knowledge so that computer scientists can build expert systems that would allow a computer to act as an expert (Hoffman 1992).

Among investigators of expertise, it has generally been assumed that the performance of experts improves as a direct function of increases in their knowledge through training and extended experience. However, recent studies show that there are, at least, some domains where "experts" perform no better then less trained individuals (cf. outcomes of therapy by clinical psychologists; Dawes 1994) and that sometimes experts' decisions are no more accurate than beginners' decisions and simple decision aids (Camerer and Johnson 1991; Bolger and Wright 1992). Most individuals who start as active professionals or as beginners in a domain change their behavior and increase their performance for a limited time until they reach an acceptable level. Beyond this point, however, further improvements appear to be unpredictable, and the number of years of work and leisure experience in a domain is a poor predictor of attained performance (Ericsson and Lehmann 1996). Hence, continued improvements (changes) in achievement are not automatic consequences of more experience, and in those domains where performance consistently increases, aspiring experts seek out particular kinds of experience, that is, deliberate practice (Ericsson, Krampe, and Tesch-Römer 1993)— activities designed, typically by a teacher, for the sole purpose of effectively improving specific aspects of an individual's performance. For example, the critical difference between expert musicians differing in the level of attained solo performance concerned the amounts of time they had spent in solitary practice during their music development, which totaled around ten thousand hours by age twenty for the best experts, around five thousand hours for the least-accomplished expert musicians, and only two thousand hours for serious amateur pianists. More generally, the accumulated amount of deliberate practice is closely related to the attained level of performance of many types of experts, such as musicians (Ericsson, Krampe, and Tesch-Römer 1993; Sloboda et al. 1996), chess players (Charness, Krampe, and Mayr 1996) and athletes (Starkes et al. 1996).

The recent advances in our understanding of the complex representations, knowledge and skills that mediate the superior performance of experts derive primarily from studies where experts are instructed to think aloud while completing representative tasks in their domains, such as chess, music,

physics, sports, and medicine (Chi, Glaser, and Farr 1988; Ericsson and Smith 1991; Starkes and Allard 1993). For appropriate challenging problems experts do not just automatically extract patterns and retrieve their response directly from memory. Instead, they select the relevant information and encode it in special representations in WORKING MEMORY that allow PLANNING, evaluation and reasoning about alternative courses of action (Ericsson and Lehmann 1996). Hence, the difference between experts and less skilled subjects is not merely a matter of the amount and complexity of the accumulated knowledge; it also reflects qualitative differences in the organization of knowledge and its representation (Chi, Glaser, and Rees 1982). Experts' knowledge is encoded around key domain-related concepts and solution procedures that allow rapid and reliable retrieval whenever stored information is relevant. Less skilled subjects' knowledge, in contrast, is encoded using everyday concepts that make the retrieval of even their limited relevant knowledge difficult and unreliable. Furthermore, experts have acquired domain-specific memory skills that allow them to rely on long-term memory (Ericsson and Kintsch 1995) to dramatically expand the amount of information that can be kept accessible during planning and during reasoning about alternative courses of action. The superior quality of the experts' mental representations allow them to adapt rapidly to changing circumstances and anticipate future events in advance. The same acquired representations appear to be essential for experts' ability to monitor and evaluate their own performance (Ericsson 1996; Glaser 1996) so that they can keep improving their own performance by designing their own training and assimilating new knowledge.

See also DOMAIN SPECIFICITY; EXPERT SYSTEMS; KNOWLEDGE-BASED SYSTEMS; KNOWLEDGE REPRESENTATION; PROBLEM SOLVING

—*Anders Ericsson*

References

Bolger, F., and G. Wright. (1992). Reliability and validity in expert judgment. In G. Wright and F. Bolger, Eds., *Expertise and Decision Support.* New York: Plenum, pp. 47–76.

Camerer, C. F., and E. J. Johnson. (1991). The process-performance paradox in expert judgment: how can the experts know so much and predict so badly? In K. A. Ericsson and J. Smith (Eds.), *Towards a General Theory of Expertise: Prospects and Limits.* Cambridge: Cambridge University Press, pp. 195–217.

Charness, N., R. T. Krampe, and U. Mayr. (1996). The role of practice and coaching in entrepreneurial skill domains: an international comparison of life-span chess skill acquisition. In K. A. Ericsson, Ed., *The Road to Excellence: The Acquisition of Expert Performance in the Arts and Sciences, Sports, and Games.* Mahwah, NJ: Erlbaum, pp. 51–80.

Chase, W. G., and H. A. Simon. (1973). The mind's eye in chess. In W. G. Chase, Ed., *Visual Information Processing.* New York: Academic Press, pp. 215–281.

Chi, M. T. H., R. Glaser, and M. J. Farr, Eds. (1988). *The Nature of Expertise.* Hillsdale, NJ: Erlbaum.

Chi, M. T. H., R. Glaser, and E. Rees. (1982). Expertise in problem solving. In R. S. Sternberg, Ed., *Advances in the Psychology of Human Intelligence,* vol. 1. Hillsdale, NJ: Erlbaum, pp. 1–75.

Dawes, R. M. (1994). *House of Cards: Psychology and Psychotherapy Built on Myth.* New York: Free Press.

Djakow, I. N., N. W. Petrowski, and P. Rudik. (1927). *Psychologie des Schachspiels [Psychology of Chess].* Berlin: Walter de Gruyter.

Doll, J. and U. Mayr. (1987). Intelligenz und Schachleistung—eine Untersuchung an Schachexperten. [Intelligence and achievement in chess—a study of chess masters]. *Psychologische Beitrge* 29: 270–289.

de Groot, A. (1978). *Thought and Choice in Chess.* The Hague: Mouton. (Original work published 1946.)

Ericsson, K. A. (1996). The acquisition of expert performance: an introduction to some of the issues. In K. A. Ericsson, Ed., *The Road to Excellence: The Acquisition of Expert Performance in the Arts and Sciences, Sports, and Games.* Mahwah, NJ: Erlbaum, pp. 1–50.

Ericsson, K. A., and W. Kintsch. (1995). Long-term working memory. *Psychological Review* 102: 211–245.

Ericsson, K. A., R. T. Krampe, and C. Tesch-Römer. (1993). The role of deliberate practice in the acquisition of expert performance. *Psychological Review* 100: 363–406.

Ericsson, K. A., and A. C. Lehmann. (1996). Expert and exceptional performance: evidence on maximal adaptations on task constraints. *Annual Review of Psychology* 47: 273–305.

Ericsson, K. A., and J. Smith, Eds. (1991). *Toward a General Theory of Expertise: Prospects and Limits.* Cambridge, England: Cambridge University Press.

Glaser, R. (1996). Changing the agency for learning: acquiring expert performance. In K. A. Ericsson, Ed., *The Road to Excellence: The Acquisition of Expert Performance in the Arts and Sciences, Sports, and Games.* Mahwah, NJ: Erlbaum, pp. 303–311.

Hoffman, R. R., Ed. (1992). *The Psychology of Expertise: Cognitive Research and Empirical AI.* New York: Springer.

Proctor, R. W., and A. Dutta. (1995). *Skill Acquisition and Human Performance.* Thousand Oaks, CA: Sage.

Richman, H. B., F. Gobet, J. J. Staszewski, and H. A. Simon. (1996). Perceptual and memory processes in the acquisition of expert performance: the EPAM model. In K. A. Ericsson, Ed., *The Road to Excellence: The Acquisition of Expert Performance in the Arts and Sciences, Sports, and Games.* Mahwah, NJ: Erlbaum, pp. 167–187.

Simon, H. A., and W. G. Chase. (1973). Skill in chess. *American Scientist* 61: 394–403.

Sloboda, J. A., J. W. Davidson, M. J. A. Howe, and D. G. Moore. (1996). The role of practice in the development of performing musicians. *British Journal of Psychology* 87: 287–309.

Starkes, J. L., and F. Allard, Eds. (1993). *Cognitive Issues in Motor Expertise.* Amsterdam: North Holland.

Starkes, J. L., J. Deakin, F. Allard, N. J. Hodges, and A. Hayes. (1996). Deliberate practice in sports: what is it anyway? In K. A. Ericsson, Ed., *The Road to Excellence: The Acquisition of Expert Performance in the Arts and Sciences, Sports, and Games.* Mahwah, NJ: Erlbaum, pp. 81–106.

Taylor, I. A. (1975). A retrospective view of creativity investigation. In I. A. Taylor and J. W. Getzels, Eds., *Perspectives in Creativity.* Chicago: Aldine. pp. 1–36.

VanLehn, K. (1996). Cognitive skill acquisition. *Annual Review of Psychology* 47: 513–539.

Webster's Third New International Dictionary. (1976). Springfield, MA: Merriam.

Explanation

An explanation is a structure or process that provides understanding. Furnishing explanations is one of the most important activities in high-level cognition, and the nature of explanation and its role in thinking has been addressed by philosophers, psychologists, and artificial intelligence researchers.

The main philosophical concern has been to characterize the nature of explanations in science. In 1948, Hempel and Oppenheim proposed the deductive-nomological (D-N) model of explanation, according to which an explanation is an argument that deduces a description of a fact to be explained from general laws and descriptions of observed facts (Hempel 1965). For example, to explain an eclipse of the sun, scientists use laws of planetary motion to deduce that at a particular time the moon will pass between the earth and the sun, producing an eclipse. Many artificial intelligence researchers also assume that explanations consist of deductive proofs (e.g., Mitchell, Keller, and Kedar-Cabelli 1986).

Although the D-N model gives a good approximate account of explanation in some areas of science, particularly mathematical physics, it does not provide an adequate general account of explanation. Some explanations are inductive and statistical rather than deductive, showing only that an event to be explained is likely or falls under some probabilistic law rather than that it follows deductively from laws (see DEDUCTIVE REASONING and INDUCTION). For example, we explain why people get influenza in terms of their exposure to the influenza virus, but many people exposed to the virus do not get sick. In areas of science such as evolutionary biology, scientists cannot predict how different species will evolve, but they can use the theory of evolution by natural selection and the fossil record to explain how a given species has evolved. Often, the main concern of explanation is not so much to deduce what is to be explained from general laws as it is to display causes (Salmon 1984). Understanding an event or class of events then consists of describing the relevant causes and causal mechanisms that produce such events. Salmon (1989) and Kitcher (1989) provide good reviews of philosophical discussions of the nature of scientific explanation. According to Friedman (1974) and Kitcher, explanations yield understanding by unifying facts using common patterns.

Deduction from laws is just one of the ways that facts can be explained by fitting them into a more general, unifying framework. More generally, explanation is a process of applying a schema that fits what is to be explained into a system of information. An explanation schema consists of an explanation target, which is a question to be answered, and an explanatory pattern, which provides a general way of answering the question. For example, when you want to explain why a person is doing an action such as working long hours, you may employ a rough explanation schema like:

Explanation target:
Why does a *person* with a set of *beliefs* and *desires* perform a particular *action*?

Explanatory pattern:
The *person* has the *belief* that the *action* will help fulfil the *desires.* This *belief* causes the *person* to pursue the *action.*

To apply this schema to a particular case, we replace the italicized terms with specific examples, as in explaining

Mary's action of working long hours in terms of her belief that this will help her to fulfill her desire to finish her Ph.D. dissertation. Many writers in philosophy of science and cognitive science have described explanations and theories in terms of schemas, patterns, or similar abstractions (Kitcher 1989, 1993; Kelley 1972; Leake 1992; Schank 1986; Thagard 1992).

One kind of explanation pattern that is common in biology, psychology, and sociology explains the presence of a structure or behavior in a system by reference to how the structure or behavior contributes to the goals of the system. For example, people have hearts because this organ functions to pump blood through the body, and democracies conduct elections in order to allow people to choose their leaders. These functional (teleological) explanations are not incompatible with causal/mechanical ones: in a biological organism, for example, the explanation of an organ in terms of its function goes hand in hand with a causal explanation that the organ developed as the result of natural selection. Craik (1943) originated the important idea that an explanation of events can be accomplished by mental models that parallel the events in the same way that a calculating machine can parallel physical changes.

Analogies can contribute to explanation at a more specific level, without requiring explicit use of laws or schemas. For example, DARWIN's use of his theory of natural selection to explain evolution frequently invoked the familiar effects of artificial selection by breeders of domesticated animals. Pasteur formed the germ theory of disease by analogy with his earlier explanation that fermentation is caused by bacteria. In analogical explanations, something puzzling is compared to a familiar phenomenon whose causes are known (see ANALOGY).

In both scientific and everyday understanding, there is often more than one possible explanation. Perhaps Mary is working long hours merely because she is a workaholic and prefers working to other activities. One explanation of why the dinosaurs became extinct is that they were killed when an asteroid hit the earth, but acceptance of this hypothesis must compare it with alternative explanations. The term *inference to the best explanation* refers to acceptance of a hypothesis on the grounds that it provides a better explanation of the evidence than alternative hypotheses (Harman 1986; Lipton 1991; Thagard 1992). Examples of inference to the best explanation include theory choice in science and inferences we make about the mental states of other people. What social psychologists call *attribution* is inference to the best explanation of a person's behavior (Read and Marcus-Newhall 1993).

Explanations are often useful for improving the performance of human and machine systems. Automated expert systems are sometimes enhanced by giving them the ability to produce computer-generated descriptions of their own operation so that people will be able to understand the inferences underlying their conclusions (Swartout 1983). Chi et al. (1989) found that students learn better when they use "self-explanations" that monitor progress or lack of progress in understanding problems.

See also CONCEPTUAL CHANGE; EXPLANATION-BASED LEARNING; REALISM AND ANTIREALISM; UNITY OF SCIENCE

—*Paul Thagard*

References

Chi, M. T. H., M. Bassok, M. W. Lewis, P. Reimann, and R. Glaser. (1989). Self-explanations: how students study and use examples in learning to solve problems. *Cognitive Science* 13: 145–182.

Craik, K. (1943). *The Nature of Explanation.* Cambridge: Cambridge University Press.

Friedman, M. (1974). Explanation and scientific understanding. *Journal of Philosophy* 71: 5–19.

Harman, G. (1986). *Change in View: Principles of Reasoning.* Cambridge, MA: MIT Press/Bradford Books.

Hempel, C. G. (1965). *Aspects of Scientific Explanation.* New York: Free Press.

Kelley, H. H. (1972). Causal schemata and the attribution process. In E. E. Jones, D. E. Kanouse, H. H. Kelley, R. E. Nisbett, S. Valins, and B. Weiner, Eds., *Attribution: Perceiving the Causes of Behavior.* Morristown, NJ: General Learning Press.

Kitcher, P. (1989). Explanatory unification and the causal structure of the world. In P. Kitcher and W. C. Salmon (Eds.), *Scientific Explanation.* Minneapolis: University of Minnesota Press, pp. 410–505.

Kitcher, P. (1993). *The Advancement of Science.* Oxford: Oxford University Press.

Kitcher, P. and W. Salmon. (1989). *Scientific Explanation.* Minneapolis: University of Minnesota Press.

Leake, D. B. (1992). *Evaluating Explanations: A Content Theory.* Hillsdale, NJ: Erlbaum.

Lipton, P. (1991). *Inference to the Best Explanation.* London: Routledge.

Mitchell, T., R. Keller, and S. Kedar-Cabelli. (1986). Explanation-based generalization: a unifying view. *Machine Learning* 1: 47–80.

Read, S. J., and A. Marcus-Newhall. (1993). Explanatory coherence in social explanations: a parallel distributed processing account. *Journal of Personality and Social Psychology* 65: 429–447.

Salmon, W. (1984). *Scientific Explanation and the Causal Structure of the World.* Princeton: Princeton University Press.

Salmon, W. C. (1989). Four decades of scientific explanation. In P. Kitcher and W. C. Salmon, Eds., *Scientific Explanation (Minnesota Studies in the History of Science,* vol. 13. Minneapolis: University of Minnesota Press.

Schank, R. C. (1986). *Explanation Patterns: Understanding Mechanically and Creatively.* Hillsdale, NJ: Erlbaum.

Swartout, W. (1983). XPLAIN: a system for creating and explaining expert consulting systems. *Artificial Intelligence* 21: 285–325.

Thagard, P. (1992). *Conceptual Revolutions.* Princeton: Princeton University Press.

Further Readings

Keil, F., and R. Wilson, Eds. (1997). *Minds and Machines* 8: 1–159.

Explanation-Based Learning

Explanation-based learning (EBL) systems attempt to improve the performance of a problem solver (PS) by first examining how the PS solved previous problems, then modifying the PS to enable it to solve similar problems *better* (typically, *more efficiently*) in the future.

Many problem-solving tasks—which here include diagnosis, classification, PLANNING, scheduling and parsing (see also KNOWLEDGE-BASED SYSTEMS; NATURAL LANGUAGE

PROCESSING; CONSTRAINT SATISFACTION)—are combinatorially difficult, inasmuch as they require finding a (possibly very long) sequence of rules to reduce a given goal to a set of operational actions, or to a set of facts, and so forth. Unfortunately, this can force a problem solving system (PS) to take a long time to solve a problem. Fortunately, many problems are similar, which means that information obtained from solving one problem may be useful for solving subsequent, related problems. Some PSs therefore include an "explanation-based learning" module that learns from each solution: after the basic problem-solving module has solved a specific problem, the EBL module then modifies the solver (perhaps by changing its underlying rule base, or by adding new control information), to produce a new solver that is able to solve this problem, and related problems, more efficiently.

As a simple example, given the information in the Prolog-style logic program

$$
\begin{aligned}
&\text{lender}(X,Y) \; \text{:-} \; \text{relative}(X,Y), \text{rich}(Y). \\
&\text{relative}(X,Y) \; \text{:-} \; \text{aunt}(X,Y) \\
&\text{relative}(X,Y) \; \text{:-} \; \text{uncle}(X,Y) \\
\\
&\text{rich}(X,Y) \quad \text{:-} \; \text{ceo}(Y,B), \text{bank}(B). \\
&\text{rich}(Y) \qquad \text{:-} \; \text{own}(Y,H), \text{house}(H). \\
\\
&\text{uncle}(me,u_1) \quad \text{own}(u_1,h_2). \; \text{house}(h_2)
\end{aligned}
$$

(where the first rule states that a person Y may lend money to X if Y is a relative of X and Y is rich, etc., as well as information about a house-owning uncle u_1), the PS would correctly classify u_1 as a lender—that is, return yes to the query lender(me, u_1).

Most PSs would have had to backtrack here; first asking if u_1 was an aunt, and only when this subquery failed, then asking whether u_1 was an uncle; similarly, to establish rich(u_1), it would first see whether u_1 was the CEO of a bank before backtracking to see if he owns a house. In general, PSs may have to backtrack many times as they search through a combinatorial space of rules until finding a sequence of rules that successfully reduces the given query to a set of known facts.

Although there may be no way to avoid such searches the first time a query is posed (note that many of these tasks are NP-hard; see COMPUTATIONAL COMPLEXITY), an EBL module will try to modify the PS to help it avoid this search the second time it encounters the same query, or one similar to it. As simply "caching" or "memorizing" (Michie 1967) the particular conclusion—here, lender(me, u_1)—would only help the solver if it happens to encounter this exact query a second time, most EBL modules instead incorporate more general information, perhaps by adding in a new rule that directly encodes the fact that any uncle who owns a house is a lender; that is,

lender(X, Y) :– uncle(X, Y), owns(Y, H), house(H).

Many EBL systems would then store this rule—call it r_{new}—in the *front* of the PS's rule set, which means it will be the first rule considered the next time a lender was sought. This would allow the modified solver—call it PS′—to handle houseowning uncles in a single backward-chaining step, without any backtracking.

Such EBL modules first "explain" why u_1 was a lender by examining the derivation structure obtained for this query; hence the name "explanation-based learning." Many such systems then "collapse" the derivation structure of the motivating problem: directly connecting a variablized form of the conclusion to the atomic facts used in its derivation. In general, the antecedents of the new rule are the weakest set of conditions required to establish the conclusion (here lender(X, Y)) in the context of the given instance. The example itself was used to specify what information—in particular, which of the facts about me and u_1—were required.

Although the new r_{new} rule is useful for queries that deal with houseowning uncles, it will not help when dealing with house-owning *aunts* or with *CEO* uncles. In fact, r_{new} will be counterproductive for such queries, as the associated solver PS′ will have to first consider r_{new} before going on to find the appropriate derivation. If only a trivial percentage of the queries deal with houseowning uncles, then the performance of PS′ will be *worse* than the original problem solver, as PS′ will take longer, on average, to reach an answer. This degradation is called the "utility problem" (Minton 1988; Tambe, Newell, and Rosenbloom 1990).

One way to address this problem is first to estimate the distribution of queries that will be posed, then evaluate the efficiency of a PS against that distribution (Greiner and Orponen 1996; Segre, Gordon, and Elkan 1996; Cohen 1990; Zweben et al. 1992). (Note that this estimation process may require the EBL module to examine more than a single example before modifying the solver.) The EBL module can then decide whether to include a new rule, and if so, where it should insert that rule. (Storing the rule in front of the rule set may not be optimal, especially after other EBL-generated rules have already been added.) Because the latter task is unfortunately intractable (Greiner 1991), many EBL systems involve hill-climbing to a local optimum (Greiner 1996; Gratch and DeJong 1996; see GREEDY LOCAL SEARCH).

There are, however, some implemented systems that have successfully addressed these challenges. As examples, the Samuelsson and Rayner EBL module improved the performance of a natural language parsing system by a factor of three (Samuelsson and Rayner 1991); Zweben et al. (1992) improved the performance of their constraint-based scheduling system by about 34 percent on realistic data, and Gratch and Chien (1996), by about 50 percent.

Explanation-based learning differs from typical MACHINE LEARNING tasks in several respects. First, standard learners try to acquire new domain-level information, which the solver can then use to solve problems that it could not solve previously; for example, many INDUCTION learners learn a previously unknown classification function, which can then be used to classify currently unclassified instances. By contrast, a typical EBL module does not extend the set of problems that the underlying solver could solve (Dietterich 1986); instead, its goal is to help the solver to solve problems more efficiently. Stated another way, explanation-based learning does not extend the deductive closure of the information already known by the solver. Such knowledge-preserving transformations can be critical, as they can turn correct, but inefficient-to-use information (e.g., first-principles knowledge) into useful, efficient, special-purpose expertise.

Of course, the solver must know a great deal initially. There are other learning systems that similarly exploit a body of known information, including work in INDUCTIVE LOGIC PROGRAMMING (attempting to build an accurate deductive knowledge base from examples; Muggleton 1992) and theory revision (modifying a given initial knowledge base, to be more accurate over a set of examples; Ourston and Mooney 1994; Wogulis and Pazzani 1993; Greiner 1999; Craw and Sleeman 1990). However, these other learning systems differ from EBL (and resemble standard learning algorithms) by changing the deductive closure of the initial theory (see DEDUCTIVE REASONING).

Finally, most learners require a great number of training examples to be guaranteed to learn effectively; by contrast, many EBL modules attempt to learn from a single solved problem. As we saw above, this single "solved problem" is in general very structured, and moreover, most recent EBL modules use *many* samples to avoid the utility problem.

This article has focused on EBL modules that add new (entailed) base-level rules to a rule base. Other EBL modules instead try to speed up a performance task by adding new control information, for example, which help the solver to select the appropriate operator when performing a state space search (Minton 1988). In general, EBL modules first detect characteristics that make the search inefficient, and then modify the solver to avoid poor performance in future problems. Also, although our description assumes the background theory to be "perfect," there have been extensions to deal with theories that are incomplete, intractable, or inconsistent (Cohen 1992; Ourston and Mooney 1994; DeJong 1997).

The rules produced by an EBL module resemble the "macro-operators" built by the Abstrips planning system (Fikes, Hart, and Nilsson 1972), as well as the "chunks" built by the Soar system (Laird and Rosenbloom 1986). (Note that Rosenbloom showed that this "chunking" can model the practice effects in humans.)

See also EXPLANATION; KNOWLEDGE REPRESENTATION; PROBLEM SOLVING

—*Russell Greiner*

References

Cohen, W. W. (1990). Using distribution-free learning theory to analyze chunking. *Proceeding of* CSCSI–90 177–83.

Cohen, W. W. (1992). Abductive explanation-based learning: a solution to the multiple inconsistent explanation problems. *Machine Learning* 8(2): 167–219.

Craw, S., and D. Sleeman. (1990). Automating the refinement of knowledge-based systems. In L. C. Aiello, Ed., *Proceedings of ECAI 90*. Pitman.

DeJong, G. (1997). Explanation-base learning. In A. Tucker, Ed., *The Computer Science and Engineering Handbook*. Boca Raton, FL: CRC Press, pp. 499–520.

DeJong, G., and R. Mooney. (1986). Explanation-based learning: an alternative view. *Machine Learning* 1(2): 145–76.

Dietterich, T. G. (1986). Learning at the knowledge level. *Machine Learning* 1(3): 287–315. (Reprinted in *Readings in Machine Learning*.)

Ellman, T. (1989). Explanation-based learning: a survey of programs and perspectives. *Computing Surveys* 21(2): 163–221.

Fikes, R., P. E. Hart, and N. J. Nilsson. (1972). Learning and executing generalized robot plans. *Artificial Intelligence* 3: 251–288.

Gratch, J., and S. Chien. (1996). Adaptive problem-solving for large-scale scheduling problems: a case study. *Journal of Artificial Intelligence Research* 4: 365–396.

Gratch, J., and G. DeJong. (1996). A decision-theoretic approach to adaptive problem solving. *Artificial Intelligence* 88(1–2): 365–396.

Greiner, R. (1991). Finding the optimal derivation strategy in a redundant knowledge base. *Artificial Intelligence* 50(1): 95–116.

Greiner, R. (1996). PALO: A probabilistic hill-climbing algorithm. *Artificial Intelligence* 83(1–2).

Greiner, R. (1999). The complexity of theory revision. *Artificial Intelligence*.

Greiner, R., and P. Orponen. (1996). Probably approximately optimal satisficing strategies. *Artificial Intelligence* 82(1–2): 21–44.

Laird, J. E., P. S. Rosenbloom, and A. Newell. (1986). *Universal Subgoaling and Chunking: The Automatic Generation and Learning of Goal Hierarchies*. Hingham, MA: Kluwer Academic Press.

Michie, D. (1967). Memo functions: a language facility with "rote learning" properties. Research Memorandum MIP–r–29, Edinburgh: Department of Machine Intelligence and Perception.

Minton, S. (1988). *Learning Search Control Knowledge: An Explanation-Based Approach*. Hingham, MA: Kluwer Academic Publishers.

Minton, S., J. Carbonell, C. A. Knoblock, D. R. Kuokka, O. Etzioni, and Y. Gil. (1989). Explanation-based learning: a problem solving perspective. *Artificial Intelligence* 40(1–3): 63–119.

Mitchell, T. M., R. M. Keller, and S. T. Kedar-Cabelli. (1986). Example-based generalization: a unifying view. *Machine Learning* 1(1): 47–80.

Muggleton, S. H. (1992). *Inductive Logic Programming*. Orlando, FL: Academic Press.

Ourston, D. and R. J. Mooney. (1994). Theory refinement combining analytical and empirical methods. *Artificial Intelligence* 66(2): 273–310.

Samuelsson, C., and M. Rayner. (1991). Quantitative evaluation of explanation-based learning as an optimization tool for a large-scale natural language system. In *Proceedings of the 12th International Joint Conference on Artificial Intelligence*. Los Angeles, CA: Morgan Kaufmann, pp. 609–615.

Segre, A. M., G. J. Gordon, and C. P. Elkan. (1996). Exploratory analysis of speedup learning data using expectation maximization. *Artificial Intelligence* 85(1–2): 301–319.

Tambe, M., A. Newell, and P. Rosenbloom. (1990). The problem of expensive chunks and its solution by restricting expressiveness. *Machine Learning* 5(3): 299–348.

Wogulis, J., and M. J. Pazzani. (1993). A methodology for evaluating theory revision systems: results with Audrey II. *Proceedings of IJCAI–93:* 1128–1134.

Zweben, M., E. Davis, B. Daun, E. Drascher, M. Deale, and M. Eskey. (1992). Learning to improve constraint-based scheduling. *Artificial Intelligence* 58: 271–296.

Explanatory Gap

The MIND-BODY PROBLEM—the problem of understanding the relation between physical and mental phenomena—has both a metaphysical side and an epistemological side. On the metaphysical side, there are arguments that purport to show that mental states could not be (or be realized in) physical states, and therefore some version of dualism must be true. On the epistemological side, there are arguments to the effect that even if in fact mental states are (or are realized in) physical states, there is still a deep problem about how we can explain the distinctive features of mental states in terms of their physical properties. In other words, there seems to be an "explanatory gap" between the physical and the mental (see Levine 1983 and 1993).

The distinctive features that seem to give rise to the explanatory gap are the qualitative characters of conscious experiences (or QUALIA), such as the smell of a rose or the way the blue sky looks on a clear day. With conscious creatures it seems sensible to ask, with regard to their conscious mental states, WHAT-IT'S-LIKE to have them. The answers to these questions refer to properties that seem quite unlike the sorts of properties described by neurophysiologists or computational psychologists. It is very hard to see how the qualitative character of seeing blue can be explained by reference to neural firings, or even to the information flow that encodes the spectral reflectance properties of distal objects. It always seems reasonable to ask, but why should a surface with this specific spectral reflectance look like *that* (as one internally points at one's experience of blue)? For that matter, it seems reasonable to ask why there should be anything it is like at all to see blue, inasmuch as detecting and encoding information about the external world does not automatically entail having a genuine experience. After all, thermometers and desktop computers detect and encode information, but few people are tempted to ascribe experience to them.

Traditionally, dualists have employed conceivability arguments to demonstrate a metaphysical distinction between the mental and the physical. Whether or not these arguments work to establish the metaphysical thesis of dualism (for arguments pro and con see Chalmers 1996; Jackson 1993; Block and Stalnaker forthcoming), they can be employed to support the existence of the explanatory gap. We start with the assumption that adequate explanations reveal a necessary relation between the factors cited in the explanation (the *explanans*) and the phenomenon to be explained (the *explanandum*). For example, suppose we want to know why water boils at 212° F. at sea level. Given the molecular analysis of water, boiling, and temperature, together with the relevant physical and chemical laws, it becomes apparent that under these conditions water just has to boil. The point is, we can see why we should not expect anything else.

Contrast this example with what it is like to see blue. After an exhaustive specification of both the neurological and the computational details, we really do not know why blue should look the way it does, as opposed, say, to the way red or yellow looks. That is, we can still conceive of a situation in which the very same neurological and computational facts obtain, but we have an experience that is like what seeing red or yellow is like. Because we can imagine a device that processed the same information as our visual systems but was not conscious at all, it is also clear that we do not really know why our systems give rise to conscious experience of any sort, much less of this specific sort. Again, the contrast with the boiling point of water is instructive. Once we fill in the appropriate microphysical details, it does not seem conceivable that water should not boil at 212° F. at sea level.

One final example is quite helpful to make the point. Frank Jackson (1982) imagines a neuroscientist, Mary, who knows all there is to know about the physical mechanisms underlying color vision. However, she has been confined all her life to a black and white environment. One day she is allowed to emerge into the world of color and sees a ripe tomato for the first time. Does she learn anything new? Jackson claims that obviously she does; she learns what red looks like. But if all the information she had before really explained what red looked like, it seems as if she should have been able to predict what it would look like. Thus her revelation on emerging from the colorless world supports the existence of the explanatory gap.

There are various responses to the explanatory gap. One view (see McGinn 1991) is that it reflects a limitation on our cognitive capacities. We just do not have, and are constitutionally incapable of forming, the requisite concepts to bridge the gap. Others argue that the gap is real but that it is to be expected given certain peculiarities associated with our first-person access to experience (see Lycan 1996; Rey 1996; Tye 1995). Just as one cannot derive statements involving indexicals from those that do not—e.g., "I am here now" from "Joe Levine is at home on Saturday, June 27, 1997"—so one cannot derive statements containing terms like "the way blue looks" from those that contain only neurological or computational terms. Still others (see Churchland 1985) argue that advocates of the explanatory gap just do not appreciate how much one could explain given a sufficient amount of neurological detail. Finally, some see in the explanatory gap evidence that the very notion of qualitative character at issue is confused and probably inapplicable to any real phenomenon (see Dennett 1991 and Rey 1996). On this view qualia literally do not exist. Although we have experiences, they do not actually possess the features we naively take to be definitive of them.

There are complex and subtle issues involved with each of these responses. For instance, the precise role of identity statements in explanations, and the degree to which identities themselves are susceptible of explanation, must be explored more fully. (For a lengthy discussion of the conceivability argument that deals with these issues, see Levine forthcoming.) Suffice it to say that no consensus yet exists on the best way to respond to the explanatory gap.

See also CONSCIOUSNESS; EXPLANATION; INTENTIONALITY; PHYSICALISM

—*Joseph Levine*

References

Block, N. J., and R. Stalnaker. (Forthcoming). *Conceptual Analysis and the Explanatory Gap.*

Chalmers, D. (1996). *The Conscious Mind.* Oxford: Oxford University Press.

Churchland, P. (1985). Reduction, qualia, and the direct introspection of brain states. *Journal of Philosophy* 82: 8–28.

Dennett, D. C. (1991). *Consciousness Explained.* Boston: Little, Brown.

Jackson, F. (1982). Epiphenomenal qualia. *Philosophical Quarterly* 32: 127–136.

Jackson, F. (1993). Armchair metaphysics. In J. O'Leary-Hawthorne and M. Michael, Eds., *Philosophy in Mind.* Dordrecht: Kluwer.

Levine, J. (1983). Materialism and qualia: the explanatory gap. *Pacific Philosophical Quarterly* 64: 354–361.

Levine, J. (1993). On leaving out what it's like. In M. Davies and G. Humphreys, Eds., *Consciousness: Psychological and Philosophical Essays.* Oxford: Blackwell, pp. 121–136.

Levine, J. (Forthcoming). Conceivability and the metaphysics of mind.

Lycan, W. G. (1996). *Consciousness and Experience.* Cambridge, MA: Bradford Books/MIT Press.

McGinn, C. (1991). *The Problem of Consciousness.* Oxford: Blackwell.

Rey, G. (1996). *Contemporary Philosophy of Mind: A Contentiously Classical Approach.* Oxford: Blackwell.

Tye, M. (1995). *Ten Problems of Consciousness: A Representational Theory of the Phenomenal Mind.* Cambridge, MA: Bradford Books/MIT Press.

Further Readings

Clark, A. (1993). *Sensory Qualities.* Oxford: Oxford University Press.

Dretske, F. (1995). *Naturalizing the Mind.* Cambridge, MA: Bradford Books/MIT Press.

Flanagan, O. (1992). *Consciousness Reconsidered.* Cambridge, MA: Bradford Books/MIT Press.

Hardcastle, V. G. (1995). *Locating Consciousness.* Amsterdam/Philadelphia: John Benjamins.

Hardin, C. L. (1987). Qualia and materialism: closing the explanatory gap. *Philosophy and Phenomenological Research* 47(2).

Levin, J. (1983). Functionalism and the argument from conceivability. *Canadian Journal of Philosophy*, sup. vol. 11.

Loar, B. (1990). Phenomenal states. In J. Tomberlin, Ed., *Action Theory and Philosophy of Mind; Philosophical Perspectives 4.* Atascadero, CA: Ridgeview Publishing Co., pp. 81–108.

Metzinger, T., Ed. (1995). *Conscious Experience.* Paderborn: Ferdinand Schöningh/ Imprint Academic.

Yablo, S. (1993). Is conceivability a guide to possibility? *Philosophy and Phenomenological Research* 53 (1): 1–42.

Explicit Memory

See IMPLICIT VS. EXPLICIT MEMORY

Extensionality, Thesis of

The thesis of extensionality says that every meaningful declarative sentence is *equivalent* to some *extensional sentence.* Understanding this thesis requires understanding the terms in italics.

Two sentences are *equivalent* if and only if they have the same truth-value in all possible circumstances. The following are equivalent because no matter how far Jody actually ran, the sentences are either both true or both false:

Jody just jogged 3.1 miles.
Jody just jogged 5 kilometers.

When the replacement of a component of a sentence with another component always results in a sentence that has the same truth-value as the original (true if the original is true and false if the original if false) this is a *replacement that preserves truth-value.*

Terms of different kinds have extensions of different kinds. The extension of a name or description is the individual or individuals to which the name or description applies. The extension of a one-place predicate such as "is a synapse" applies to the class of all the individuals, in this case, all the synapses, to which the predicate applies. The extension of an *n*-place predicate is a set of ordered *n*-tuples to which the predicate applies. The extension of a declarative sentence, which one can regard as a zero-place predicate, is its truth value.

Two terms are *coextensive* only when they have the same extension, two sentences that have the same truth value, two names that refer to exactly the same thing (or things), and so on.

A sentence is *extensional* only when each and every replacement of a component of a sentence with a coextensive term preserves truth value.

If "Stan's car" and "the oldest Volvo in North Carolina" are coextensive, then replacing the first with the second in (a) "Stan's car is in the driveway" preserves truth-value. So far as this replacement shows, then, (a) is extensional. A similar replacement in (b) "Hillis thinks that Stan's car is a new Jaguar" does not preserve truth value. Hillis does not think that the oldest Volvo in North Carolina is a new Jaguar. Statements about PROPOSITIONAL ATTITUDES such as thinking, believing, fearing, and hoping are typically not extensional.

If "The Mercury Track Team" and "The Vanguard Video Club" are coextensive because each expression names a group with exactly the same members, then replacing the first with the second in (c) "Nobody in the Mercury Track Team smokes cigars" preserves truth-value. A similar replacement in (d) "The Captain of the Mercury Track Team is Lou Silver" will not preserve truth-value if (d) is true and the Vanguard Video Club does not have a captain. Examples of this sort show at least that clubs are not sets.

"Vicki will discover the greatest prime number" and "Vicki will win the New Jersey Lottery" are coextensive because they are both false. Replacing the first with the second in (e) "It isn't so that Vicki will discover the greatest prime number" preserves truth-value. A similar replacement in (f), "It is absolutely impossible that Vicki will discover the greatest prime number," does not preserve truth value. However unlikely, it is still possible that Vicki will hit the jackpot. The existence of a largest prime number, in contrast, is not merely unlikely; it is impossible. Modal statements about what is possible or necessary, treated by MODAL LOGIC, are often not extensional. The connectives of standard propositional LOGIC such as *not, and, or, if,* and *if and only if* are *truth-functional.* Replacement in a truth-functional sentence of any component with another with the same truth-value preserves the truth-value of the original.

The thesis of extensionality, a version of REDUCTIONISM, says that every meaningful, declarative sentence is equivalent to some extensional sentence. This does not require that every sentence be extensional but rather that every nonextensional sentence about psychological attitudes, modality, laws, counterfactual conditionals, and so forth, have an extensional equivalent.

An historically important statement of the thesis of extensionality appears in Wittgenstein (1922): "A proposition is a truth-function of elementary propositions (Proposition 5)."

Wittgenstein's later philosophy abandons both elementary propositions and the thesis of extensionality. Russell expresses sympathy for the thesis in several places including "Truth-Functions and Others," Appendix C of Whitehead and Russell (1927).

Rudolf Carnap formulates the thesis of extensionality (hereafter abbreviated TOE) as a relation between extensional and nonextensional languages (see especially Carnap 1937, sect. 67). The truth of TOE promises a greater intelligibility of the world. Extensional languages have "radically simpler structures and hence simpler constitutive rules" than nonextensional languages (Carnap 1958: 42). If "the universal language of science" (Carnap 1937: 245) is extensional, therefore, we can discuss exhaustively every scientific phenomenon in a language that has a radically simple structure.

Carnap defends TOE by finding an extensional sentence about language that he thinks is equivalent to a given nonextensional sentence. The modal, nonextensional sentence "Necessary, if you steal this book, then you steal this book" is equivalent to the extensional sentence "'If you steal this book, then you steal this book' is true in a certain formal metalanguage L" (cf. Carnap 1958: 42). The psychological, nonextensional sentence "John believes that raccoons have knocked over the garbage cans" is equivalent, perhaps, to the extensional sentence "John is disposed to an affirmative response to some sentence in some language which expresses the proposition that raccoons have knocked over the garbage cans" (cf. Carnap 1947: 55).

Although he devotes much time and effort to defend TOE, Carnap does not claim to establish it. He regards it as a likely conjecture. The project, however, now appears to be more difficult than Carnap predicted. A successful translation of a nonextensional sentence must satisfy two requirements: (1) the new sentence must really be equivalent to the original, and (2) the new sentence must really be extensional. In the example above, if someone can have such a belief about raccoons without being disposed to respond to any sentences, (1) is violated. If one cannot understand affirmative response except as a nonextensional notion, then (2) is violated.

In terms of INTENTIONALITY, Chisholm (1955–56) formulates a thesis resembling that of Brentano (1874) about the distinctiveness of the psychological: (A) TOE is true for all nonpsychological sentences, and (B) TOE is false for all psychological sentences. In the 1950s, Chisholm defended (B) by attacking translations of sentences about believing

that Carnap and others proposed. (See Hahn 1998 for a Chisholm bibliography.)

Clause (A), however, cannot be taken for granted. The project of finding extensional equivalents of nonextensional modal sentences also faces difficulties. Quine (1953), like Carnap, attempts syntactic translations that are about language. (See chapter 10, section 3, "The Problems of Intensionality," in Kneale and Kneale 1962.) Montague (1963) derives significant negative results that are beyond the scope of this article.

See also UNITY OF SCIENCE; INDEXICALS AND DEMONSTRATIVES; FREGE, GOTTLOB

—*David H. Sanford*

References

Brentano, F. (1874). *Psychologie vom empirischen Standpunkt.* Vienna.

Carnap, R. (1937). *The Logical Syntax of Language.* London: Routledge and Kegan Paul. First published in German in 1934.

Carnap, R. (1947). *Meaning and Necessity.* Chicago: University of Chicago Press.

Carnap, R. (1958). *Introduction to Symbolic Logic and Its Applications.* New York: Dover. First published in German in 1954.

Chisholm, R. M. (195556). Sentences about believing. *Proceedings of the Aristotelian Society* 56: 125–148.

Hahn, L. E., Ed. (1998). *The Philosophy of Roderick M. Chisholm: The Library of Living Philosophers.* Peru, IL: Open Court.

Kneale, W., and M. Kneale. (1962). *The Development of Logic.* Oxford: Oxford University Press.

Montague, R. (1963). Syntactical treatments of modality, with corollaries on reflexion principles and finite axiomatizability. Reprinted in R. H. Thomason, Ed., 1974, *Formal Philosophy; Selected Papers of Richard Montague.* New Haven: Yale University Press.

Quine, W. (1953). Three grades of modal involvement. Reprinted in Quine (1966), *The Ways of Paradox.* New York: Random House.

Whitehead, A. N., and B. Russell. (1927). *Principia Mathematica.* 2nd ed. Cambridge: Cambridge University Press.

Wittgenstein, L. (1922). *Tractatus Logico-Philosophicus.* First published in German in 1921. Recent English translation by D. F. Pears and B. F. McGuinness (1961), London: Routledge and Kegan Paul.

Externalism

See INDIVIDUALISM; MENTAL CAUSATION; NARROW CONTENT

Eye Movements and Visual Attention

Visual scenes typically contain more objects than can ever be recognized or remembered in a single glance. Some kind of sequential selection of objects for detailed processing is essential if we are to cope with this wealth of information. Built into the earliest levels of vision is a powerful means of accomplishing the selection, namely, the heterogeneous RETINA. Fine grain visual resolution is possible only within

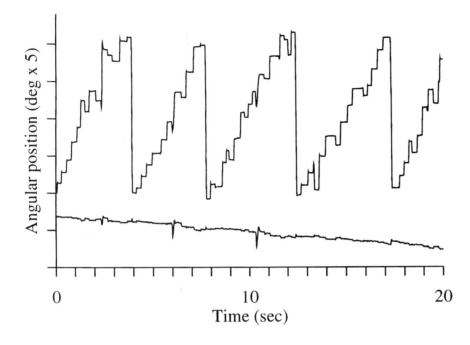

Figure 1. Sequence of saccadic eye movements during reading. The graph on top shows horizontal (top trace) and vertical (bottom trace) eye movements over time. The abrupt changes in eye position are the saccades. The figure shows the sequences of rightward saccades (upward deflections in the trace) made to read a line of text, followed by large leftward resetting saccades made to the beginning of each successive line of text. The locations of the saccadic endpoints are shown in numbered sequence, superimposed on the text, at the bottom of the figure. The figure was made by J. Epelboim from recordings made with R. Steinman's Revolving Magnetic Field Sensor Coil monitor at the University of Maryland (see Epelboim et al. 1995, for a description of the instrument).

the central retinal region known as the fovea, whose diameter is approximately 2 degrees of visual angle (about the size of eight letters on a typical page of text). Eye movements are important because they bring selected images to the fovea, and also keep them there for as long as needed to recognize the object.

Eye movements fall into two broad classes. *Saccadic eye movements* (saccades) are rapid jumps of the eye used to shift gaze to any chosen object. In READING, for example, saccades typically occur about three times each second and are generally made to look from one word to the next (see figure 1). *Smooth eye movements* keep the line of sight on the selected object during the intervals between saccades, compensating for motion on the retina that might be caused either by motion of the object or by motion of the head or body. Intervals between saccades can be as long as several seconds during steady fixation of stationary or moving objects. Saccades can be made in any chosen direction, even in total darkness, whereas directed smooth eye movements cannot be initiated or maintained without some kind of motion signal.

There are two natural links between eye movements and visual attention. One is the role played by ATTENTION in OCULOMOTOR CONTROL. The other is the way in which eye

movements provide overt indicators of the locus of attention during performance of complex cognitive tasks, such as reading or visual search.

Consider first the role of attention in programming smooth eye movements. When we walk forward in an otherwise stationary scene, trying to keep our gaze fixed on our goal ahead, the flow of image motion generated on the retina by our own forward motion creates a large array of motion signals that could potentially drag the line of sight away from its intended goal (a problem described originally by Ernst Mach in 1906). Laboratory simulations of this common situation show that smooth eye movements can maintain a stable line of sight on a small, attended, stationary target superimposed on a large, vivid moving background. Similarly, smooth eye movements can accurately track a target moving across a stationary background. With more complex stimuli (letters, for example), perceptual identification of tracked targets is better than identification of untracked backgrounds (a result that holds after any differences in identification due to different retinal velocities of target and background are taken into account). The greater perceptibility of the target compared to the background implies that the same attentional mechanism serves both perception and eye movements (Khurana and Kowler 1987).

Attention contributes to the control of saccades in an analogous way, namely, attention is allocated to the chosen target shortly before the saccade is made to look at it (Hoffman and Subramaniam 1995; Kowler et al. 1995). Some attention can be transferred to nontargets, with no harmful effect on the latency or accuracy of the eye movements, showing that the attentional demands of eye movements are modest (Kowler et al. 1995; Khurana and Kowler 1987).

On the whole, the arrangement is very efficient. By allowing oculomotor and perceptual systems to share a common attentional filter, the eye will be directed to the object we are most interested in without the need for a separate selective attentional decision. At the same time, the modest attentional requirements of effective oculomotor control mean that it is very likely that we can look wherever we choose with little danger of the eye's being drawn to background objects, regardless of how large, bright, or vivid they may be. Modest attentional requirements also imply that there will be ample cognitive resources left over for identification and recognition; all our efforts need not be devoted to targeting eye movements.

The close link between attention and eye movements is supported by neurophysiology. Cortical centers containing neurons that are active before eye movements also contain neurons (sometimes the same ones) that are active before shifts of attention while the eye is stationary (Colby and Duhamel 1996; Andersen and Gnadt 1989). Some have gone so far as to consider whether shifting attention to an eccentric location while the eye remains stationary is equivalent to planning a saccadic eye movement (Kustov and Robinson 1997; Rizzolatti et al. 1987; Klein 1980).

Attention is involved in the programming of eye movements, and at the same time observations of eye movements provide a record of where someone chooses to attend during performance of complex cognitive tasks. Yarbus's (1967) well-known recordings of eye movements made while inspecting various paintings show systematic preferences to repeatedly look at those elements that would seem to be most relevant to evaluating the content of the picture. Despite the detailed record of preferences that eye movements provide, it has nevertheless proven to be surprisingly difficult to develop valid models of underlying cognitive processing based on eye movements alone (Viviani 1990). More recent work has taken a different tack by using highly constrained and novel tasks. Sequences of fixations have been used to study the modularity of syntactic processing during reading (Tanenhaus et al. 1995), the role of WORKING MEMORY during visual problem-solving tasks (Ballard, Hayhoe, and Pelz 1995; Epelboim and Suppes 1996), the coordination of eye and arm movements (Epelboim et al. 1995), and the size of the effective processing region during reading or search (McConkie and Rayner 1975; Motter and Belky 1998; O'Regan 1990).

This article has emphasized the importance of eye movements for selecting a subset of the available information for detailed processing. The price paid for having this valuable tool is that the visual system must cope with the continual shifts of the retinal image that eye movements will produce. Remarkably, despite the retinal perturbations, the visual scene appears stable and unimpaired. Evidence from studies in which subjects look at or point to targets presented briefly during saccades suggests that stored representations of oculomotor commands ("efferent copies") are used to take the effect of eye movements into account and create a representation of target location with respect to the head or body (Hansen and Skavenski 1977). Other evidence suggests that shifts of the retinal image are effectively ignored. According to these views, visual analysis begins anew each time the line of sight arrives at a target, with attended visual information converted rapidly to a high-level semantic code that can be remembered across sequences of saccades (e.g., O'Regan 1992).

The advantages to visual and cognitive systems of having a fovea are evidently so profound that it has been worth the cost of developing both the capacity for accurate control of eye movements and a tolerance for the retinal perturbations that eye movements produce. Visual attention is crucial for accomplishing both.

See also OBJECT RECOGNITION, ANIMAL STUDIES; OBJECT RECOGNITION, HUMAN NEUROPSYCHOLOGY; ATTENTION IN THE HUMAN BRAIN; VISUAL WORD RECOGNITION; TOP-DOWN PROCESSING IN VISION

—Eileen Kowler

References

Andersen, R. A., and J. W. Gnadt. (1989). Posterior parietal cortex. In R. H. Wurtz and M. E. Goldberg, Eds., *Reviews of Oculomotor Research*, vol. 3: *The neurobiology of saccadic eye movements*. Amsterdam: Elsevier, pp. 315–336.

Ballard, D. H., M. M. Hayhoe, and J. B. Pelz. (1995). Memory representation in natural tasks. *Journal of Cognitive Neuroscience* 7: 66–80.

Colby, C. L., and J.-R. Duhamel. (1996). Spatial representations for action in parietal cortex. *Cognitive Brain Research* 5: 105–115.

Epelboim, J., R. M. Steinman, E. Kowler, M. Edwards, Z. Pizlo, C. J. Erkelens, and H. Collewijn. (1995). The function of visual search and memory in sequential looking tasks. *Vision Research* 35: 3401–3422.

Epelboim, J., and P. Suppes. (1996). Window on the mind? What eye movements reveal about geometrical reasoning. *Proceedings of the Cognitive Science Society* 18: 59.

Hansen, R. H., and A. A. Skavenski. (1977). Accuracy of eye position information for motor control. *Vision Research* 17: 919–926.

Hoffman, J., and B. Subramaniam. (1995). Saccadic eye movements and visual selective attention. *Perception and Psychophysics* 57: 7787–7795.

Khurana, B., and E. Kowler. (1987). Shared attentional control of smooth eye movements and perception. *Vision Research* 27: 1603–1618.

Klein, R. (1980). Does oculomotor readiness mediate cognitive control of visual attention? In R. Nickerson, Ed., *Attention and Performance III*. Hillsdale, NJ: Erlbaum, pp. 259–276.

Kowler, E. (1990). The role of visual and cognitive processes in the control of eye movement. In E. Kowler, Ed., *Reviews of Oculomotor Research*, vol. 4: *Eye Movements and Their Role in Visual and Cognitive Processes*. Amsterdam: Elsevier, pp. 1–70.

Kowler, E., E. Anderson, B. Dosher and E. Blaser. (1995). The role of attention in the programming of saccades. *Vision Research* 1897–1916.

Kustov, A. A., and D. L. Robinson. (1997). Shared neural control of attentional shifts and eye movements. *Nature* 384: 74–77.

Mach, E. (1906/1959). *Analysis of Sensation.* New York: Dover.

McConkie, G. W., and K. Rayner. (1975). The span of the effective stimulus during a fixation in reading. *Perception and Psychophysics* 17: 578–586.

Motter, B. C., and E. J. Belky. (1998). The zone of focal attention during active visual search. *Vision Research* 38: 1007–1022.

O'Regan, J. K. (1990). Eye movements and reading. In E. Kowler, Ed., *Reviews of Oculomotor Research,* vol. 4: *Eye Movements and Their Role in Visual and Cognitive Processes.* Amsterdam: Elsevier, pp. 395–453.

O'Regan, J. K. (1992). Solving the "real" mysteries of visual perception: the world as an outside memory. *Canadian Journal of Psychology* 46: 461–488.

Rizzolatti, G., L. Riggio, I. Dascola, and C. Umita. (1987). Reorienting attention across the horizontal and vertical meridians: evidence in favor of a premotor theory of attention. *Neuropsychologia* 25: 31–40.

Tanenhaus, M. K., M. J. Spivey-Knowlton, K. M. Eberhard, and J. C. Sedivy. (1995). Integration of visual and linguistic information in spoken language comprehension. *Science* 268: 1632–1634.

Viviani, P. (1990). Eye movements in visual search: cognitive, perceptual and motor control aspects. In E. Kowler, Ed., *Reviews of Oculomotor Research,* vol. 4: *Eye Movements and Their Role in Visual and Cognitive Processes.* Amsterdam: Elsevier, pp. 353–393.

Yarbus, A. L. (1967). *Eye Movements and Vision.* New York: Plenum Press.

Further Readings

Hoffman, J. E. (1997). Visual attention and eye movements. In H. Pashler, Ed., *Attention.* London: University College London Press.

Kowler, E. (1995). Eye movement. In S. Kosslyn, Ed., *Invitation to Cognitive Science,* vol. 2. Cambridge, MA: MIT Press, pp. 215–265.

Rayner, K, Ed. (1992). *Eye Movements and Visual Cognition: Scene Perception and Reading.* New York: Springer.

Steinman, R. M., and J. Z. Levinson. (1990). The role of eye movement in the detection of contrast and spatial detail. In E. Kowler, Ed., *Reviews of Oculomotor Research,* vol. 4: *Eye Movements and Their Role in Visual and Cognitive Processes.* Amsterdam: Elsevier, pp. 115–212

Suppes, P. (1990). Eye movement models for arithmetic and reading performance. In E. Kowler, Ed., *Reviews of Oculomotor Research,* vol. 4: *Eye Movements and Their Role in Visual and Cognitive Processes.* Amsterdam: Elsevier, pp. 455–477.

Face Recognition

Analysis and retention of facial images is a crucial skill for primates. The survival value of this skill is reflected in our extraordinary MEMORY for faces, in the visual preferences for face stimuli shown by infants, and in our remarkable sensitivity to subtle differences among faces. Striking parallels have emerged between the results of perceptual, developmental, neuropsychological, neurophysiological, and functional neuroimaging studies of face recognition. These indicate that face recognition in primates is a specialized capacity consisting of a discrete set of component processes with neural substrates in ventral portions of occipito-temporal and frontal cortices and in the medial temporal lobes.

Appreciation of the specialness of the face for social organisms can be traced back at least to Darwin's *The Expression of Emotion in Man and Animals* (1872). Moreover, face agnosia—a selective deficit in recognizing faces—has been inferred from the clinical literature since the turn of the century. Intensive research on face perception of normal individuals has a more recent history, linked to a growing interest in INFANT COGNITION and perception. One early milestone was Yin's (1969) demonstration of the *inversion effect,* the tendency for recognition of faces to be differentially impaired (relative to that of other "mono-oriented" stimuli such as houses) by turning the stimulus upside down. This finding has been widely interpreted to mean that face recognition depends on specialized mechanisms for configural processing (i.e., analysis of small differences in details and spatial relations of features within a prototypical organization). Face "specialness" is also supported by data showing that infants preferentially look at or track facelike arrangements of features relative to jumbles of features or control stimuli. Nonetheless, the protracted development of adult levels of performance indicates that face recognition additionally involves either a long period of NEURAL DEVELOPMENT and/or cognitive processing capacity, specific experience with faces, or both. Exactly what improves with maturation or experience remains unclear (Chung and Thomson 1995).

The fascinating syndrome of face agnosia (prosopagnosia) has spurred considerable controversy regarding the "specialness" of faces. The degree of DOMAIN SPECIFICITY present in prosopagnosia is relevant to whether face recognition is best viewed as a unique capacity, or merely as an example of general mechanisms of OBJECT RECOGNITION (Farah 1996). Although prosopagnosics are aware that faces are faces—that is, they know the basic level category—they fail to identify reliably or achieve a sense of familiarity from faces of family members, famous persons, and other individuals they previously knew well. Typically, they also have trouble forming memories of new faces, even if other new objects are learned. However, prosopagnosics may identify individuals by salient details such as clothing and hairstyle, or by nonvisual features such as voice.

Varying patterns of deficits in processing faces occur in brain-damaged individuals, and these differing patterns provide evidence for dissociable component operations in face recognition. Some patients show sparing of ability to judge the age, gender, and even emotional expression of faces whose identity they cannot grasp. Others have difficulty with all aspects of face processing; such patients are unable even to analyze facial features normally, a necessary precondition to identification. Finally, some brain-damaged patients can perceive structural attributes of faces adequately for judgments about emotion and gender, and even judge if a face is familiar, but show a specific inability to recall the associated name.

In both humans and monkeys, faces are analyzed in subregions of the visual-cortical object recognition pathway. In particular, the temporal neocortex in nonhuman primates (notably inferior temporal cortex or "area TE") contains neurons that fire selectively to face stimuli (Gross and Sergent 1992). The question arises as to whether such cells truly respond to visual information unique to faces, or whether their selectivity is more parsimoniously explained as responsiveness to features shared by faces and other object classes; the bulk of the evidence supports the former description. For example, although face-selective neurons vary in the degree of their preference for face stimuli, many respond to both real faces and pictures of faces, but give nearly no response to any other stimuli tested, including other complex objects and pictures in which features making up the face are rearranged or "scrambled." Moreover, for many such neurons, specificity of response is maintained over transformations in size, stimulus position, angle of lighting of the face, blurring, and so forth. Thus, at least some face-selective neurons are sensitive to the global aspects of a face, such as prototypical configuration of stimulus features. Finally, face-selective neurons are present very early in life (Rodman, Gross, and Ó Scalaidhe 1993), consistent with the idea that they represent inborn "prototypes" for faces.

Subsets of face-selective neurons appear to participate in specific aspects of face coding. For example, some respond selectively to distinctive features, such as eyes per se, distance between the eyes, or extent of the forehead. Others do not respond to isolated features but instead are selective for orientation of a face (e.g., profile or frontal view). Still others have responses specific for particular expressions; a final subset are particularly sensitive to eye gaze direction (looking back or looking to the side), an important social signal in both monkeys and humans. Cells selectively responsive to faces have a localized distribution in several senses. First, although face cells make up only a tiny fraction of neurons (1–5%) within TE and adjacent areas as a whole, their concentration is much higher in irregular localized clumps. Second, different types of face-selective cells are found in different regions, such that cells sensitive to facial expression and gaze direction tend to be found within the superior temporal sulcus, whereas cells more generally selective for faces and, purportedly, for individuals tend to be located in TE on the inferior temporal gyrus.

Electrophysiological correlates of face recognition have also been obtained from humans (Allison et al. 1994). A large evoked potential (called the N200) is generated by faces (but not other stimulus types) at small sites in the ventral occipitotemporal cortex. These sites or "modules" may be comparable to the clumps of face neurons found in monkeys. Longer-latency face-specific potentials were also recorded from the anterior portions of ventral temporal cortex activated by face recognition in POSITRON EMISSION TOMOGRAPHY (PET) studies. Moreover, N200s to inverted faces recorded from the right hemisphere were smaller and longer than for normally oriented faces; the left hemisphere generated comparable N200s under both conditions. These studies thus provide correlates of both the "inversion effect" and of HEMISPHERIC SPECIALIZATION for some aspects of face processing noted in the clinical literature and in tachistoscopic studies of face recognition in normal humans.

Brain imaging studies in normal humans provide converging evidence for the involvement of the ventral occipitotemporal cortices in face recognition and for the existence of dissociable component operations. Sergent et al. (1992), for example, used PET to compare brain activation while sub-

jects either made discriminations of the gender of faces (perceptual task) or judged their identity. In the perceptual task, selective activation was found in the right ventral occipitotemporal cortex, to a lesser extent in the same area on the left, and in a more lateral left focus as well. These areas overlap, but are generally anterior to, domains activated by other categories of objects. Judgments of face identity, requiring reactivation of stored information about individuals, also activated the right parahippocampal gyrus, anterior temporal cortex, and temporal pole on both sides. These studies and those of Haxby and colleagues have additionally implicated lateralized portions of frontal cortex in face encoding, perceptual judgments of faces, and subsequent recognition of faces. In particular, a right frontal focus appears to be involved in recognizing facial emotion. Finally, the HIPPOCAMPUS appears to participate, along with parahippocampal cortices, primarily at the time of encoding new faces.

Neuropathological data are generally consistent with results of imaging and evoked potential studies regarding anatomical substrates for face recognition. Initially, prosopagnosia was associated clinically with right posterior cortical damage. In the 1980s, a number of cases came to autopsy. The damage in these lay very ventrally and medially at the occipitotemporal junction, in roughly the same region activated in recent PET studies. However, in all such cases this area (or underlying white matter) was damaged bilaterally, and consequently bilateral damage became thought of as a necessary precondition to prosopagnosia. Recently, cases with proposagnosia and right cortical damage alone, along with the results of imaging and evoked potential studies reviewed above, have reaffirmed the critical role of the right hemisphere in face recognition in humans.

Many explanations have been given for the apparent "specialness" of faces. Face perception and recognition may indeed be unique behavioral capacities and reflect dedicated neural circuits that can be selectively damaged. Such uniqueness of faces might result both from their behavioral significance and from the fact that they differ structurally from most other object classes, necessitating different perceptual strategies (such as encoding on the basis of prototypical configuration), strategies selectively lost in prosopagnosia. An alternative explanation is that faces are processed and stored in a manner similar to that for other objects, but faces are simply harder to tell apart than other kinds of objects; this view is consistent with observations that prosopagnosia is often accompanied by some degree of general object agnosia. A related account holds that face processing requires subtle discriminations between *highly similar exemplars within a category,* and that it is this capacity, not processing of the facial configuration, that is disrupted in prosopagnosia. Interestingly, recent studies show that face processing is still disproportionately impaired when discriminations of face and nonface stimuli are equated for difficulty, so this view has lost some force. A final suggestion is that face processing represents acquisition of EXPERTISE associated with very protracted experience with a category of complex visual stimuli (Carey 1992). Prosopagnosics with deficits in other object recognition domains in which they had previously acquired expertise over long periods (e.g., a show dog expert who lost the ability to differentiate breeds) support this idea.

Growing acceptance of faces as a distinct stimulus type has led, along with growing evidence for component processes, to emergence of theoretical accounts of face recognition tied to central ideas in COMPUTATIONAL NEUROSCIENCE. For example, drawing on the notion of a computational model advanced by David MARR, Bruce and Young (1986) analyzed face processing as a set of seven types of information code (or representation). In their scheme, which fits well with neuropsychological dissociations, everyday face recognition involves the use of "structural" codes to access identity-specific semantic information, and then finally the attachment of a name to the percept. Other recent theoretical accounts have modeled face recognition using artificial neural network architectures derived from parallel-distributed processing accounts of complex systems. Future advances in understanding face recognition will likely require further incorporation of data on self-organizing (developmental and environmental) and modulatory (emotional and motivational) aspects of face processing into existing models.

See also AMYGDALA, PRIMATE; COGNITIVE ARCHITECTURE; EMOTION AND THE HUMAN BRAIN; HIGH-LEVEL VISION; MID-LEVEL VISION

—*Hillary R. Rodman*

References

Allison, T., C. McCarthy, A. Nobre, A. Puce, and A. Belger. (1994). Human extrastriate visual cortex and the perception of faces, words, numbers and colors. *Cereb. Cortex* 5: 544–554.

Bruce, V., and A. Young. (1986). Understanding face recognition. *Br. J. Psych.* 77: 305–327.

Carey, S. (1992). Becoming a face expert. *Phil. Trans. R. Soc. Lond. B* 335: 95–103.

Chung, M-S., and D. M. Thomson. (1995). Development of face recognition. *Br. J. Psych.* 86: 55–87.

Farah, M. J. (1996). Is face recognition "special"? Evidence from neuropsychology. *Beh. Brain Res.* 76: 181–189.

Gross, C. G., and J. Sergent. (1992). Face recognition. *Curr. Opin. Neurobiol.* 2: 156–161.

Haxby, J. V., L. G. Ungerleider, B. Horwitz, J. M. Maisog, S. I. Rapoport, and C. L. Grady. (1996). Face encoding and recognition in the human brain. *Proc. Nat. Acad. Sci.* 93: 922–927.

Rodman, H. R., C. G. Gross, and S. P. Ó Scalaidhe. (1993). Development of brain substrates for pattern recognition in primates: physiological and connectional studies of inferior temporal cortex in infant monkeys. In B. de Boysson-Bardies, S. de Schonen, P. Jusczyk, P. MacNeilage, and J. Morton, Eds., *Developmental Neurocognition: Speech and Face Processing in The First Year of Life*. Dordrecht: Kluwer Academic, pp. 63–75.

Sergent, J., S. Ohta, and B. MacDonald. (1992). Functional neuroanatomy of face and object processing: a positron emission tomography study. *Brain* 115: 15–36.

Yin, R. K. (1969). Looking at upside-down faces. *J. Exp. Psychol.* 81: 141–145.

Further Readings

Benton, A. L. (1980). The neuropsychology of facial recognition. *American Psychologist* 35: 176–186.

Damasio, A. R., D. Tranel, and H. Damasio. (1990). Face agnosia and the neural substrates of memory. *Ann. Rev. Neurosci.* 13: 89–109.

Desimone, R., T. D. Albright, C. G. Gross, and C. Bruce. (1984). Stimulus selective properties of inferior temporal neurons in the macaque. *J. Neurosci.* 4: 2051–2062.

Dror, I., F. L. Florer, D. Rios, and M. Zagaeski. (1996). Using artificial bat sonar neural networks for complex pattern recognition: recognizing faces and the speed of a moving target. *Biol. Cybern.* 74: 331–338.

Farah, M. J. (1991). Patterns of co-occurrence among the associative agnosias: implications for visual object representations. *Cog. Neuropsychol.* 8:1–19.

Farah, M. J., K. L. Levinson, and K. L. Klein. (1994). Face perception and within-category discrimination in prosopagnosia. *Neuropsychologia* 33: 661–674.

Field, T. M., R. Woodson, R. Greenberg, and D. Cohen. (1982). Discrimination and imitation of facial expressions by neonates. *Science* 218: 179–181.

Flude, B. M., A. W. Ellis, and J. Kay. (1989). Face processing and name retrieval in an anomic aphasic: names are stored separately from semantic information about familiar people. *Brain and Cog.* 11: 60–72.

George, M. S., T. A. Ketter, D. S. Gill, J. V. Haxby, L. G. Ungerleider, P. Herscovitch, and R. I. Post. (1993). Brain regions involved in recognizing emotion or identity: an oxygen-15 PET study. *J. Neuropsychiat. Clin. Neurosci.* 5: 384–394.

Gross, C. G., H. R. Rodman, P. M. Gochin, and M. W. Colombo. (1993). Inferior temporal cortex as a pattern recognition device. In E. Baum, Ed., *Computational Learning and Cognition*. Philadelphia: SIAM Press.

Haxby, J. V., C. L. Grady, B. Horwitz, L. G. Ungerleider, M. Mishkin, R. E. Carson, P. Herscovitch, M. B. Schapiro, and S. I. Rapoport. (1991). Dissociation of object and spatial vision processing pathways in human extrastriate cortex. *Proc. Natl. Acad. Sci.* 88: 1621–1625.

Heywood, C. A., and A. Cowey. (1992). The role of the "face cell" area in the discrimination and recognition of faces by monkeys. *Phil. Trans. Roy. Soc. Lond. B* 335: 31–38.

Perrett, D. I., P. A. J. Smith, D. D. Potter, A. J. Mistlin, A. S. Head, A. D. Milner, and M. A. Jeeves. (1985). Visual cells in the temporal cortex sensitive to face view and gaze direction. *Proc. Roy. Soc. Lond* B 223: 293–317.

Rodman, H. R. (1994). Development of inferior temporal cortex in the monkey. *Cereb. Cortex* 5: 484–498.

Rolls, E. T., and G. C. Baylis. (1986). Size and contrast have only small effects on the responses to faces of neurons in the cortex of the superior temporal sulcus of the monkey. *Exp. Brain Res.* 65: 38–48.

Yamane, S., S. Kaji, and K. Kawano. (1988). What facial features activate face neurons in inferotemporal cortex of the monkey. *Exp. Brain Res.* 73: 209–214.

Feature Detectors

The existence of feature detectors is based on evidence obtained by recording from single neurons in the visual pathways (Barlow 1953; Lettvin et al. 1959; Hubel and Wiesel 1962; Waterman and Wiersma 1963; see also SINGLE-NEURON RECORDING). It was found that responses from many types of NEURON do not correlate well with the straightforward physical parameters of the stimulus, but instead require some specific *pattern* of excitation, often a spatio-temporal pattern that involves movement. The rabbit retina provides some well-documented examples, though they were not the first to be described. *Direction-*

ally selective ganglion cells respond to movements of the image in one direction, but respond poorly to the reverse motion, however bright or contrasty the stimulus; there are two classes of these ganglion cells, distinguished by the fast or slow speed of movement that each prefers, and within each class there are groups responding to different directions of motion (Barlow, Hill, and Levick 1964). Another class, found mainly in the central zone of the RETINA, are *local edge detectors* that respond only to an edge moving very slowly over precisely the right position in the visual field (Levick 1967). These units are often highly specific in their stimulus requirements, and it can be a difficult task to find out what causes such a unit to fire reliably; yet once the appropriate *trigger feature* has been properly defined it will work every time. Another class, the *fast movement detectors,* respond only to very rapid image movements, and yet another, the *uniformity detectors,* fire continuously at a high rate *except* when patterned stimulation is delivered to the part of the retina they are connected to.

All classes have a restricted retinal region where the appropriate feature has to be positioned, and this is described as the unit's *receptive field,* even though the operations being performed on the input are very different from simple linear summation of excitatory and inhibitory influences, which the term *receptive field* is sometimes thought to imply. Units often show considerable *invariance of response* for changes of the luminance, contrast, and even polarity of the light stimulus, while maintaining selectivity for their particular patterned spatio-temporal feature. There is also evidence for feature detectors in auditory (Evans 1974; Suga 1994; see also DISTINCTIVE FEATURES) and tactile pathways.

Feature detection in the retina makes it clear that complicated logical operations can be achieved in simple neural circuits, and that these processes need to be described in computational, rather than linear, terms. For a time there was some rivalry between *feature creatures,* who espoused this logical, computational view of the operation of visual neurons, and *frequency freaks,* who were devoted to the use of sine wave spatial stimuli and Fourier interpretations. The latter had genuine successes that yielded valid new insights (Braddick, Campbell, and Atkinson 1978), but their approach works best for systems that operate nearly linearly. Object recognition is certainly not a linear process, and the importance of feature detectors lies in the insight they give into how the brain achieves this very difficult task. But first, glance back at the history of feature detection before single-neuron feature-detectors were discovered.

Sherrington found that to elicit the *scratch reflex*—the rhythmical scratching movements made by a dog's hind leg—a tactile stimulus had to be applied to a particular region of the flank, and it was most effective if it was applied to several neighboring cutaneous regions in succession. This must require a tactile feature detector not unlike some of those discovered in visual pathways.

Some years later the ethologists Lorenz (1961) and Tinbergen (1953) popularized the notion of *innate releasers:* these are special sensory stimuli that trigger specific behavioral responses when delivered under the appropriate cir-

cumstances. One example is the red dot on a herring gull's beak, which has been shown to cause the chick to open its bill to receive regurgitated food from its mother. Another example is the stimulus for eliciting the rather stereotyped feeding behavior shown by many vertebrates: a small moving object first alerts the animal, then causes it to orient itself toward the stimulus, next to approach it, and finally to snap at it. It was early suggested that the retinal ganglion cells in the frog that respond to small moving objects might act as such *bug detectors* (Barlow 1953; Lettvin et al. 1959).

Such feature detectors must be related to the specific requirements of particular species in particular ecological niches, but feature detection may have a more general role in perception and classification. A clue to their significance in object recognition may be found in the early attempts by computer scientists to recognize alphanumeric characters (Grimsdale et al. 1959; Selfridge and Neisser 1960; Kamentsky and Liu 1963). It was found that fixed templates, one for each letter, perform very badly because the representation of the same character varies in different fonts. Performance could be much improved by detecting the features (bars, loops, intersections etc.) that make up the characters, for latitude could then be allowed in the positioning of these relative to each other. This is the germ of an idea that seems to provide a good qualitative explanation for the feature detectors found at successive levels in the visual system: operations that restrict response or increase selectivity for one aspect of the stimulus are combined with operations that generalize or relax selectivity for another aspect. In the preceding example the components of letters vary less from font to font than the overall pattern of the letters, so the initial feature detectors can be rather selective. But having found that certain features are present, the system can be less demanding about how they are positioned relative to each other, and this achieves some degree of font-invariant character recognition.

In the primate visual system some retinal ganglion cells are excited by a single foveal cone, so they are very selective for position. Several of these connect, through the lateral geniculate nucleus, to a single neuron in primary visual cortex, but the groups that so connect are arranged along lines: the cortical neuron thus maintains selectivity for position orthogonal to the line, but relaxes selectivity and summates along the line (Hubel and Wiesel 1962). This makes each unit selectively responsive to lines of a particular orientation, and they may be combined together at later stages to generalize in various ways.

The best-described examples of units that generalize for position are provided by the cortical neurons of area MT or V5 that specialize in the analysis of image motion: these collect together information from neurons in cortical area V1 that come from a patch several degrees in diameter in the visual field (Newsome et al. 1990; Raiguel et al. 1995), but all the neurons converging on one MT neuron signal movements of similar direction and velocity. Thus all the information about motion with a particular direction and velocity occurring in a patch of the visual field is pooled onto a single MT neuron, and such neurons have been shown to be as sensitive to weak motion cues as the intact, behaving animal (Newsome, Britten, and Movshon 1989).

Possibly the whole sensory cortex should be viewed as an immense bank of tuned filters, each collecting the information that enables it to detect with high sensitivity the occurrence of a patterned feature having characteristics lying within a specific range (Barlow and Tripathy 1997). The existence of this enormous array of near-optimal detectors, all matched to stimuli of different characteristics, would explain why the mammalian visual system can perform detection and discrimination tasks with a sensitivity and speed that computer vision finds hard to emulate.

Another aspect of the problem is currently arousing interest: Why do we have detectors for some features, but not others? What property of a spatio-temporal pattern makes it desirable as a feature? A suggestion (Barlow 1972; Field 1994) currently receiving some support (Bell and Sejnowski 1995; Ohlshausen and Field 1996) is that the feature detectors we possess are able to create a rather complete representation of the current sensory scene using the principle of *sparse coding*; this means that at any one time only a small selection of all the units is active, yet this small number firing in combination suffices to represent the scene effectively. The types of feature that will achieve this double criterion, sparsity with completeness, can be described as *suspicious coincidences*: they are local patterns in the image that would be expected, from the probabilities of their constituent elements, to occur rarely, but in fact occur more commonly.

Sparse coding goes some way toward preventing accidental conjunctions of attributes, which is the basis for the so-called BINDING PROBLEM. Although sparsely coded features are not mutually exclusive, they nonetheless occur infrequently: hence accidental conjunctions of them will only occur very infrequently, possibly no more often than they do in fact occur.

Like the basis functions that are used for *image compression,* those suitable for sparse coding achieve their result through being adapted to the statistical properties of natural images. This adaptation must be done primarily through evolutionary selection molding their pattern selective mechanisms, though it is known that they are also modified by experience during the *critical period* of development of the visual system (Hubel and Wiesel 1970; Movshon and Van Sluyters 1981), and perhaps also through short term processes of contingent adaptation (Barlow 1990). Feature detectors that exploit statistical properties of natural images in this way could provide a representation that is optimally up-to-date, minimizes the effects of delays in afferent and efferent pathways, and perhaps also achieves some degree of prediction (see also CEREBRAL CORTEX).

Although we are far from being able to give a complete account of the physiological mechanisms that underlie even the simplest examples of object recognition, the existence of feature detecting neurons, and these theories about their functional role, provide grounds for optimism.

See also OBJECT RECOGNITION, ANIMAL STUDIES; OBJECT RECOGNITION, HUMAN NEUROPSYCHOLOGY; VISUAL ANATOMY AND PHYSIOLOGY; VISUAL PROCESSING STREAMS

—*Horace Barlow*

References

Barlow, H. B. (1953). Summation and inhibition in the frog's retina. *Journal of Physiology, London* 119: 69–88.

Barlow, H. B. (1972). Single units and sensation: a neuron doctrine for perceptual psychology? *Perception* 1: 371–394.

Barlow, H. B. (1990). A theory about the functional role and synaptic mechanism of visual after-effects. In C. B. Blakemore, Ed., *Vision: Coding and Efficiency.* Cambridge: Cambridge University Press.

Barlow, H. B., R. M. Hill, and W. R. Levick. (1964). Retinal ganglion cells responding selectively to direction and speed of motion in the rabbit. *Journal of Physiology, London* 173: 377–407.

Barlow, H. B., and S. P. Tripathy. (1997). Correspondence noise and signal pooling as factors determining the detectability of coherent visual motion. *Journal of Neuroscience* 17 7954–7966.

Bell, A. J., and T. J. Sejnowski. (1995). An information maximisation approach to blind separation and blind deconvolution. *Neural Computation* 7: 1129–1159.

Braddick, O. J., F. W. Campbell, and J. Atkinson. (1978). Channels in vision: basic aspects. In R. Held, H. W. Leibowicz, and H. L. Teuber, Eds., *Handbook of Sensory Physiology,* New York: Springer, pp. 1–38.

Evans, E. F. (1974). Feature- and call-specific neurons in auditory pathways. In F. C. S. and F. G. Worden, Eds., *The Neurosciences: Third Study Program.* Cambridge, MA: MIT Press.

Field, D. J. (1994). What is the goal of sensory coding? *Neural Computation* 6: 559–601.

Grimsdale, R. L., F. H. Sumner, C. J. Tunis, and T. Kilburn. (1959). A system for the automatic recognition of patterns. *Proceedings of the Institute of Electrical Engineers, B* 106: 210–221.

Hubel, D. H., and T. N. Wiesel. (1962). Receptive fields, binocular interaction, and functional architecture in the cat's visual cortex. *Journal of Physiology, London* 195: 215–243.

Hubel, D. H., and T. N. Wiesel. (1970). The period of susceptibility to the physiological effects of unilateral eye closure in kittens. *Journal of Physiology, London* 206: 419–436.

Kamentsky, L. A., and C. N. Liu. (1963). Computer-automated design of multifont print recognition logic. *IBM Journal of Research and Development* 7: 2–13.

Lettvin, J. Y., H. R. Maturana, W. S. McCulloch, and W. H. Pitts. (1959). What the frog's eye tells the frog's brain. *Proceedings of the Institute of Radio Engineers* 47: 1940–1951.

Levick, W. R. (1967). Receptive fields and trigger features of ganglion cells in the visual streak of the rabbit's retina. *Journal of Physiology, London* 188: 285–307.

Lorenz, K. (1961). *King Solomon's Ring.* Trans. M. K. Wilson. Cambridge: Cambridge University Press.

Movshon, J. A., and R. C. Van Sluyters. (1981). Visual neural development. *Annual Review of Psychology* 32: 477–522.

Newsome, W. T., K. H. Britten, and J. A. Movshon. (1989). Neuronal correlates of a perceptual decision. *Nature* 341: 52–54.

Newsome, W. T., K. H. Britten, C. D. Salzman, and J. A. Movshon. (1990). Neuronal mechanisms of motion perception. *Cold Spring Harbor Symposia on Quantitative Biology* 55: 697–705.

Olshausen, B. A., and D. J. Field. (1996). Emergence of simple-cell receptive-field properties by learning a sparse code for natural images. *Nature* 381: 607–609.

Raiguel, S., M. M. Van Hulle, D.-K. Xiao, V. L. Marcar, and G. A. Orban. (1995). Shape and spatial distribution of receptive fields and antagonistic motion surrounds in the middle temporal area (V5) of the macaque. *European Journal of Neuroscience* 7: 2064–2082.

Selfridge, O., and U. Neisser. (1960). Pattern recognition by machine. *Scientific American* 203(2): 60–68.

Suga, N. (1994). Multi-function theory for cortical processing of auditory information: implications of single-unit and lesion data for future research. *Journal of Comparative Physiology A* 175: 135–144.

Tinbergen, N. (1953). *The Herring Gull's World.* London: Collins.

Waterman, T. H., and C. A. G. Wiersma. (1963). Electrical responses in decapod crustacean visual systems. *Journal of Cellular and Comparative Physiology* 61: 1–16.

Further Readings

Ballard, D. H. (1997). *An Introduction to Natural Computation.* Cambridge, MA: MIT Press.

Barlow, H. B. (1995). The neuron doctrine in perception. In M. Gazzaniga, Ed., *The Cognitive Neurosciences.* Cambridge, MA: MIT Press, pp. 415–435.

Features

See DISTINCTIVE FEATURES; FEATURE DETECTORS

Feedforward Networks

See PATTERN RECOGNITION AND FEEDFORWARD NETWORKS; SUPERVISED LEARNING IN MULTILAYER NEURAL NETWORKS

Figurative Language

Figurative language allows speakers/writers to communicate meanings that differ in various ways from what they literally say. People speak figuratively for reasons of politeness, to avoid responsibility for the import of what is communicated, to express ideas that are difficult to communicate using literal language, and to express thoughts in a compact and vivid manner. Among the most common forms of figurative language, often referred to as "tropes" or "figures of speech," are *metaphor,* where ideas from dissimilar knowledge domains are either explicitly, in the case of *simile* (e.g., "My love is like a red, red rose"), or implicitly (e.g., "Our marriage is a roller-coaster ride") compared; *metonymy,* where a salient part of a single knowledge domain is used to represent or stand for the entire domain (e.g., "The White House issued a statement"); *idioms,* where a speaker's meaning cannot be derived from an analysis of the words' typical meanings (e.g., "John let the cat out of the bag about Mary's divorce"); *proverbs,* where speakers express widely held moral beliefs or social norms (e.g.,"The early bird captures the worm"); *irony,* where a speaker's meaning is usually, but not always, the opposite of what is said (e.g., "What lovely weather we're having" stated in the midst of a rainstorm); *hyperbole,* where a speaker exaggerates the reality of some situation (e.g., "I have ten thousand papers to grade by the morning"); *understatement,* where a speaker says less than is actually the case (e.g., "John seems a bit tipsy" when John is clearly very drunk); *oxymora,* where two contradictory ideas/concepts are fused together (e.g., "When parting is such sweet sorrow"); and *indirect requests,* where speakers make requests of others in indirect ways by asking questions (e.g., "Can you pass the salt?"), or stating a simple fact (e.g., "It seems cold in here" meaning "Go close the window").

One traditional assumption, still held in some areas of cognitive science, is that figurative language is deviant and requires special cognitive processes to be understood. Whereas literal language can be understood via normal cognitive mechanisms, listeners must recognize the deviant nature of a figurative utterance before determining its nonliteral meaning (Grice 1989; Searle 1979). For instance, understanding a metaphorical comment, such as "Criticism is a branding iron," requires that listeners must first analyze what is stated literally, then recognize that the literal meaning (i.e., that criticism is literally a tool to mark livestock) is contextually inappropriate, and then infer some meaning consistent with the context and the idea that the speaker must be acting cooperatively and rationally (i.e., criticism can psychologically hurt the person who receives it, often with long-lasting consequences). This traditional view suggests, then, that figurative language should always be more difficult to process than roughly equivalent literal speech.

But the results of many psycholinguistic experiments have shown this idea to be false (see Gibbs 1994 for a review). Listeners/readers can often understand the figurative interpretations of metaphors, irony/sarcasm, idioms, proverbs, and indirect speech acts without having to first analyze and reject their literal meanings when these expressions are seen in realistic social contexts. People can read figurative utterances as quickly as, sometimes even more quickly than, they read literal uses of the same expressions in different contexts, or equivalent nonfigurative expressions. These experimental findings demonstrate that the traditional view of figurative language as deviant and ornamental, requiring additional cognitive effort to be understood, has little psychological validity. Although people may not always process the complete literal meanings of different figurative expressions before inferring their nonliteral interpretations, people may analyze aspects of word meaning as part of their understanding of what different phrases and expressions figuratively mean as wholes (Blasko and Connine 1993; Cacciari and Tabossi 1988). At the same time, listeners/readers certainly may slowly ponder the potential meanings of a figurative expression, such as the literary metaphor from Shakespeare, "The world is an unweeded garden." It is this conscious experience that provides much of the basis for the mistaken assumption that figurative language always requires "extra work" to be properly understood.

A great deal of empirical research from all areas of cognitive science has accumulated on how people learn, produce, and understand different kinds of figurative language (see ANALOGY and METAPHOR). Several notable findings have emerged from this work. To give just a few examples, many idioms are analyzable with their individual parts contributing something to what these phrases figuratively mean, contrary to the traditional view (Gibbs 1994). People also learn and make sense of many conventional and idiomatic phrases, not as "frozen" lexical items, but because they tacitly recognize the metaphorical mapping of information between two conceptual domains (e.g., "John spilled the beans" maps our knowledge of someone tipping over a container of beans to a person revealing some previously hidden secret; Gibbs 1994). Ironic and sarcastic expressions are understood when listeners recognize the pretense underlying a speaker's remark. For instance, a speaker who says "What lovely weather we're having" in the midst of a rainstorm pretends to be an unseeing person, perhaps a weather forecaster, exclaiming about the beautiful weather to an unknown audience (Clark and Gerrig 1984). In many cases, ironic utterances accomplish their communicative intent by reminding listeners of some antecedent event or statement (Sperber and Wilson 1986), or by reminding listeners of a belief or social norm jointly held by a speaker and listener (Kreuz and Glucksberg 1989).

Some cognitive scientists now argue that metaphor, metonymy, irony, and other tropes are not linguistic distortions of literal, mental thought, but constitute basic schemes by which people conceptualize their experience and the external world (Gibbs 1994; Johnson 1987; Lakoff and Johnson 1980; Lakoff 1987; Lakoff and Turner 1989; Sweetser 1990; Turner 1991). Speakers cannot help but employ figurative language in conversation and writing because they conceptualize much of their experience through the figurative schemes of metaphor, metonymy, irony, and so on. Listeners often find figurative discourse easy to understand precisely because much of their thinking is constrained by figurative processes. For instance, people often talk about the concept of time in terms of the widely shared conceptual metaphor *time is money* (e.g., "I saved some time," I wasted my time," "I invested time in the relationship," "We can't spare you any time"). These conventional expressions are not "dead metaphors," but reflect metaphorical conceptualizations of experience that are very much alive and part of ordinary cognition, one reason why these same metaphors are frequently seen in novel expressions and poetic language (Lakoff and Turner 1989). There is much debate over whether people's understanding of various conventional expressions, idioms, proverbs, and metaphors necessarily requires activation of underlying conceptual metaphors that may motivate the existence of these statements in the language (Gibbs 1994; Gibbs et al. 1997; Glucksberg, Brown, and McGlone 1993; McGlone 1996). Nevertheless, there is a growing appreciation from scholars in many fields that metaphors and other tropes not only serve as the foundation for much everyday thinking and reasoning, but also contribute to scholarly theory and practice in a variety of disciplines, as well as providing much of the foundation for our understanding of culture (see Fernandez 1991; Gibbs 1994).

See also CONCEPTS; MEANING; METAPHOR AND CULTURE; SEMANTICS

—Raymond W. Gibbs

References

Blasko, D., and C. Connine. (1993). Effects of familiarity and aptness of metaphor processing. *Journal of Experimental Psychology: Learning, Memory and Cognition* 19: 295–308.

Cacciari, C., and P. Tabossi. (1988). The comprehension of idioms. *Journal of Memory and Language* 27: 668–683.

Clark, H., and R. Gerrig. (1984). On the pretense theory of irony. *Journal of Experimental Psychology: General* 113: 121–126.

Fernandez, J., Ed. (1991). *Beyond Metaphor: The Theory of Tropes in Anthropology.* Stanford, CA: Stanford University Press.

Gibbs, R. (1994). *The Poetics of Mind: Figurative Thought, Language and Understanding.* New York: Cambridge University Press.

Gibbs, R., J. Bogdonovich, J. Sykes, and D. Barr. (1997). Metaphor in idiom comprehension. *Journal of Memory and Language* 36.

Glucksberg, S., and B. Keysar. (1990). Understanding metaphorical comparisons: beyond literal similarity. *Psychological Review* 97: 3–18.

Glucksberg, S., M. Brown, and M. McGlone. (1993). Conceptual metaphors are not automatically accessed during idiom comprehension. *Memory and Cognition* 21: 711–719.

Grice, H. P. (1989). *Studies in the Ways of Words.* Cambridge, MA: Harvard University Press.

Happe, F. (1994). Understanding minds and metaphors: insights from the study of figurative language in autism. *Metaphor and Symbolic Activity* 10: 275–295.

Johnson, M. (1987). *The Body in the Mind.* Chicago: University of Chicago Press.

Kreuz, R., and S. Glucksberg. (1989). How to be sarcastic: the echoic reminder theory of verbal irony. *Journal of Experimental Psychology: General* 120: 374–386.

Lakoff, G., (1987). *Woman, Fire and Dangerous Things.* Chicago: University of Chicago Press.

Lakoff, G., and M. Johnson. (1980). *Metaphors We Live By.* Chicago: University of Chicago Press.

Lakoff, G., and M. Turner. (1989). *No Cool Reason: The Power of Poetic Metaphor.* Chicago: University of Chicago Press.

McGlone, M. (1996). Conceptual metaphors and figurative language interpretation: food for thought. *Journal of Memory and Language* 35: 544–565.

Searle, J. (1979). Metaphor. In A. Ortony, Ed., *Metaphor and Thought.* New York: Cambridge University Press, pp. 92–123.

Sperber, D. (1994). Understanding verbal understanding. In J. Khalfa, Ed., *What is Intelligence?* New York: Cambridge University Press, pp. 179–198.

Sperber, D., and D. Wilson. (1986). *Relevance: Communication and Cognition.* Oxford: Blackwell.

Sweetser, E. (1990). *From Etymology to Pragmatics: The Mind-Body Metaphor in Semantic Structure and Semantic Change.* Cambridge: Cambridge University Press.

Turner, M. (1991). *Reading Minds: The Study of English in the Age of Cognitive Science.* Princeton: Princeton University Press.

fMRI

See MAGNETIC RESONANCE IMAGING

Focus

The term *focus* is used to refer to the highlighting of parts of utterances for communicative purposes, typically by accent. For example, a question like *Who did Mary invite for dinner* is answered by *Mary invited BILL for dinner,* not by *Mary invited Bill for DINner* (capitals mark the syllable with main accent, cf. STRESS, LINGUISTIC and PROSODY AND INTONATION). A contrastive statement like *Mary didn't invite BILL for dinner, but JOHN* is also fine, whereas *Mary didn't invite Bill for DINner, but JOHN* is odd. Finally, notice that *Mary only invited BILL for dinner* means something different from *Mary only invited Bill for DINner.* Expressions like *only* that depend on the choice of focus are said to *associate with focus* (Jackendoff 1972).

Focus is typically expressed in spoken language by pitch movement, duration, or intensity on a syllable (cf. Ladd 1996). In addition, we often find certain syntactic constructions, like cleft sentences (*It was BILL that she invited for dinner*). There are languages that make use of specific syntactic positions (e.g., the preverbal focus position in Hungarian), dedicated particles (e.g., Quechua), or syntactic movement of nonfocused expressions from their regular position (e.g., Catalan; cf. É Kiss 1995). In American Sign Language (see SIGN LANGUAGES), focus is marked by a non-manual gesture, the brow raise (cf. Wilbur 1991).

Focus marking is often ambiguous, which gives rise to misunderstandings and jokes. When the notorious bank robber Willie Sutton was asked by a reporter, *Why do you rob banks?* he replied: *Because that's where the money is.* The answer makes sense with focus on *banks,* but the intended focus clearly was on *rob banks;* Sutton was asked why he robs banks in contrast to doing other things. The focus is marked by accent on *banks* in both cases. In general, accent on a syntactic *argument* often helps to mark broad focus on predicate + argument (cf. Schmerling 1976; Gussenhoven 1984; Selkirk 1984). Take the difference between (a) *John has PLANS to leave* and (b) *John has plans to LEAVE.* (a) is understood as *John has to leave plans,* with *plans* as object argument, whereas (b) is understood as *John plans to leave,* with VP argument *to leave.* In both cases, *plans to leave* is in focus.

On the semantic side, one influential line of research has been to analyze focus as expressing what is *new* in an utterance (DISCOURSE; cf. Halliday 1967; Sgall, Hajicová, and Panenová 1986; Rochemont 1986). The question *Who did Mary invite for dinner?* can be answered by *Mary invited BILL for dinner,* inasmuch as it presupposes that Mary invited someone for dinner, and the new information is that this person was Bill. Consequently, *Bill* is accented, and the other constituents, which are *given* information, are deaccented. What should count as "given" often requires inferencing, as in the following example: *Many tourists visit (a) Israel / (b) Jerusalem. When BILL arrived in the Holy City, all hotels were booked.* In the (a) case, *Holy City* is accented, while in the (b) case, it is deaccented because it is mentioned before, though not literally.

Another influential research program sees focus as indicating the presence of *alternatives* to the item in focus (cf. Rooth 1992, 1995). For example, a question like *Who did Mary invite for dinner?* asks for answers of the form *Mary invited X for dinner,* where X varies over persons. The focus in the answer, *Mary invited BILL for dinner,* identifies a particular answer of this form. In general, focus on an expression marks the fact that alternatives to this expression are under consideration. This idea naturally also applies to the contrastive use of focus and to association with focus. A sentence like *Mary invited BILL for dinner* can be used in contrast to sentences of the type

Mary invited X for dinner, where X applies to some alternative to *Bill.* And a sentence like *Mary only invited BILL for dinner* says that Mary did not invite any alternative to Bill to dinner. Other focus-sensitive operators can be explained similarly. For example, *Mary also invited BILL for dinner* presupposes that there is an alternative X to *Bill* such that *Mary invited X for dinner* is true. And *Mary unfortunately invited BILL for dinner* presupposes that there is an alternative X to *Bill* such that it would have been more fortunate for Mary to invite X for dinner. Sedivy et al. (1994) have used eyetracking techniques to observe the construction of such alternative sets during sentence processing.

The two lines of research sometimes lead to different analyses. Consider the following exchange: A: *My car broke down.* B: *What did you do?* A can answer with (a) *I called a meCHAnic* or with (b) *I FIXed the car.* If focus expresses newness, (a) should have focus on *called a mechanic,* and (b) should have focus just on *fixed,* as *the car* is given. But if focus indicates the presence of alternatives, (b) should have focus on *fixed the car,* as the question asks for an activity. The lack of accent on *the car* in (b) shows that even focus theories based on alternatives must allow for givenness as a factor in accentuation. Notice that there are expressions that are never accentuated, for example, the indefinite pronoun *something,* as in A: *What did you do?* B: *I FIXed something.*

Focus is of interest for the study of the SYNTAX-SEMANTICS INTERFACE, as focus-sensitive operators require a liberal understanding of the principle of COMPOSITIONAL-ITY. Take the view that focus indicates the presence of alternatives. As the VPs *only invited BILL for dinner* and *only invited Bill for DINner* differ in meaning, the placement of focus must lead to differences in the interpretation of the embedded VP *invited Bill for dinner.* One proposal assumes that the item in focus is somehow made "visible," for example by movement on the syntactic level of LOGI-CAL FORM (cf. MINIMALISM). In this theory, a sentence like *Mary only invited BILL for dinner* means something like "The only X such that *invited X for dinner* is true of Mary is Bill" (cf., e.g., von Stechow 1990; Jacobs 1991). A problem is that association with focus seems to disregard syntactic islands (cf. WH-MOVEMENT), as in *Mary only invited [BILL's mother] for dinner.* Another proposal assumes that expressions in focus introduce alternatives, which leads to alternatives for the expressions with embedded focus constituents ("Alternative Semantics," cf. Rooth 1992). Our example is analyzed as "The only predicate of the form *invite X for dinner* that applies to Mary is *invite Bill for dinner.*" In general, alternative semantics is more restrictive, but it may not be sufficient for more complex cases in which multiple foci are involved, as in, A: *Mary only invited BILL for dinner. She also$_1$ only$_2$ invited BILL$_2$ for LUNCH$_1$,* where the second sentence presupposes that there is another person X besides *Bill* such that Mary invited only *Bill* to x.

There is another use of the term *focus,* unrelated to the one discussed here, in which it refers to discourse referents that are salient at the current point of discourse and are potential antecedents for pronouns (cf. Grosz and Sidner 1986).

See also DYNAMIC SEMANTICS; SEMANTICS; SYNTAX

—Manfred Krifka

References

Grosz, B., and C. Sidner. (1986). Attention, intention and the structure of discourse. *Journal of Computational Linguistics* 12: 175–204.

Gussenhoven, C. (1984). *On the Grammar and Semantics of Sentence Accent.* Dordrecht: Foris.

Halliday, M. A. K. (1967). Notes on transitivity and theme in English, part 2. *Journal of Linguistics* 3: 199–244.

Jacobs, J. (1991). Focus ambiguities. *Journal of Semantics* 8: 1–36.

Jackendoff, R. (1972). *Semantic Interpretation in Generative Grammar.* Cambridge, MA: MIT Press.

É Kiss, K., Ed. (1995). *Discourse Configurational Languages.* Oxford: Oxford University Press.

Ladd, R. (1996). *Intonational Phonology.* Cambridge: Cambridge University Press.

Rochemont, M. (1986). *Focus in Generative Grammar.* Amsterdam: John Benjamins.

Rooth, M. (1992). A theory of focus interpretation. *Natural Language Semantics* 1: 75–116.

Rooth, M. (1995). Focus. In S. Lappin, Ed., *Handbook of Contemporary Semantic Theory.* London: Blackwell, pp. 271–298.

Schmerling, S. (1976). *Aspects of English Sentence Stress.* Austin: University of Texas Press.

Sedivy, J., G. Carlson, M. Tanenhaus, M. Spivey-Knowlton, and K. Eberhard. (1994). The cognitive function of contrast sets in processing focus constructions. In P. Bosch and R. van der Sandt, Eds., *Focus and Natural Language Processing.* IBM Deutschland Informationssysteme GmbH, Institute for Logic and Linguistics, pp. 611–620.

Selkirk, E. (1984). *Phonology and Syntax: The Relation Between Sound and Structure.* Cambridge, MA: MIT Press.

Sgall, P., E. Hajicová, and J. Panenová. (1986). *The Meaning of the Sentence in Its Semantic and Pragmatic Aspects.* Dordrecht: Reidel.

Von Stechow, A. (1990). Focusing and backgrounding operators. In W. Abraham, Ed., *Discourse Particles.* Amsterdam: John Benjamins, pp. 37–84.

Wilbur, R. (1991). Intonation and focus in American Sign Language. In Y. No and M. Libucha, Eds., *ESCOL '90: Proceedings of the Seventh Eastern States Conference on Linguistics.* Columbus: Ohio State University Press, pp. 320–331.

Further Readings

Bayer, J. (1995). *Directionality and Logical Form. On the Scope of Focussing Particles and Wh-in-Situ.* Dordrecht: Kluwer.

König, E. (1991). *The Meaning of Focus Particles: A Comparative Perspective.* London: Routledge.

Lambrecht, K. (1994). *Information Structure and Sentence Form. Topic, Focus and the Mental Representation of Discourse Referents.* Cambridge: Cambridge University Press.

Selkirk, E. (1995). Sentence prosody. In J. A. Goldsmith, Ed., *Handbook of Phonological Theory.* London: Blackwell, pp. 550–569.

Taglicht, J. (1984). *Message and Emphasis: On Focus and Scope in English.* London: Longman.

Von Stechow, A. (1991). Current issues in the theory of focus. In A. v. Stechow and D. Wunderlich, Eds., *Semantik: Ein internationales Handbuch der zeitgenössischen Forschung.* Berlin: de Gruyter, pp. 804–825.

Winkler, S. (1997). *Focus and Secondary Predication.* Berlin: Mouton de Gruyter.

Folk Biology

Folk biology is the cognitive study of how people classify and reason about the organic world. Humans everywhere classify animals and plants into species-like groups as obvious to a modern scientist as to a Maya Indian. Such groups are primary loci for thinking about biological causes and relations (Mayr 1969). Historically, they provided a transtheoretical base for scientific biology in that different theories—including evolutionary theory—have sought to account for the apparent constancy of "common species" and the organic processes centering on them. In addition, these preferred groups have "from the most remote period . . . been classed in groups under groups" (Darwin 1859: 431). This taxonomic array provides a natural framework for inference, and an inductive compendium of information, about organic categories and properties. It is not as conventional or arbitrary in structure and content, nor as variable across cultures, as the assembly of entities into cosmologies, materials, or social groups. From the vantage of EVOLUTIONARY PSYCHOLOGY, such natural systems are arguably routine "habits of mind," in part a natural selection for grasping relevant and recurrent "habits of the world."

The relative contributions of mind and world to folk biology are current research topics in COGNITIVE ANTHROPOLOGY and COGNITIVE DEVELOPMENT (Medin and Atran 1998). *Ethnobiology* is the anthropological study of folk biology; a research focus is *folk taxonomy,* which describes the hierarchical structure, organic content, and cultural function of folk biological classifications the world over. *Naive biology* is the psychological study of folk biology in industrialized societies; a research focus is *category-based induction,* which concerns how children and adults learn about, and reason from, biological categories.

Ethnobiology roughly divides into adherents of cultural universals versus CULTURAL RELATIVISM (debated also as "intellectualism" versus "utilitarianism," Brown 1995). Universalists highlight folk taxonomic principles that are only marginally influenced by people's needs and uses to which taxonomies are put (Berlin 1992). Relativists emphasize those structures and contents of folk biological categories that are fashioned by cultural interest, experience, and use (Ellen 1993). Universalists grant that even within a culture there may be different special-purpose classifications (beneficial/noxious, domestic/wild, edible/inedible, etc.). However, there is only one cross-culturally universal kind of general-purpose taxonomy, which supports the widest possible range of inductions about living kinds. This distinction between special- and general-purpose folk biological classifications parallels the distinction in philosophy of science between artificial versus natural classification (Gilmour and Walters 1964).

A culture's general-purpose folk taxonomy is composed of a stable hierarchy of inclusive groups of organisms, or taxa, which are mutually exclusive at each level of the hierarchy. These absolutely distinct levels, or ranks, are: folk kingdom (e.g., animal, plant), life form (e.g., bug, fish, bird, mammal/animal, tree, herb/grass, bush), generic species (gnat, shark, robin, dog, oak, clover, holly), folk specific (poodle, white oak), and folk varietal (toy poodle; swamp white oak). Ranking is a cognitive mapping that projects living kind categories onto fundamentally different levels of reality. Ranks, not taxa, are universal. Taxa of the same rank tend to display similar linguistic, psychological, and biological characteristics. For example, most generic species are labeled by short, simple words (i.e., unanalyzable lexical stems: "oak," "dog"). In contrast, subordinate specifics are usually labelled binomially (i.e., attributive + lexical stem: "white oak") unless culturally very salient (in which case they may also merit simple words: "poodle," "collie"). Relativists agree there is a preferred taxonomic level roughly corresponding to that of the scientific species (e.g., dog) or genus (e.g., oak). Phenomenally salient species for humans, including most species of large vertebrates and trees, belong to monospecific genera in any given locale, hence the term "generic species" for this preferred taxonomic level (also called "folk generic" or "specieme"). Nevertheless, relativists note that even in seemingly general-purpose taxonomies, categories superordinate or subordinate to generic species can reflect "special-purpose" distinctions of cultural practice and expertise. For example, the Kalam of New Guinea deny that cassowaries fall under the bird life form, not only because flightless cassowaries are physically unlike other birds, but also because they are ritually prized objects of the hunt (Bulmer 1967).

Universalism in folk biology may be further subdivided into tendencies that parallel philosophical and psychological distinctions between RATIONALISM VS. EMPIRICISM (Malt 1995). Empiricists claim that universal structures of folk taxonomy owe primarily to perceived structures of "objective discontinuities" in nature rather than to the mind's conceptual structure. On this view, the mind/brain merely provides domain-general mechanisms for assessing perceptual similarities, which are recursively applied to produce the embedded similarity-structures represented in folk taxonomy (Hunn 1976). Rationalists contend that higher-order cognitive principles are needed to produce regularities in folk biological structures (Atran 1990). For example, one pair of principles is that every object is either an animal or plant or neither, and that no animal or plant can fail to belong uniquely to a generic species. Thus, the rank of folk kingdom—the level of plant and animal—is a category of people's intuitive ontology, and conceiving an object as plant or animal entails notions about generic species that are not applied to objects thought to belong to other ontological categories, such as person, substance, or artifact. Although such principles may be culturally universal, cognitively compelling, and adaptive for everyday life, they no longer neatly accord with the known scientific structure of the organic world.

In the study of naive biology, disagreement arises over whether higher-order principles evince strong or weak NATIVISM; that is, whether they reflect the innate modularity and DOMAIN SPECIFICITY of folk biology (Inagaki and Hatano 1996), or are learned on the basis of cognitive principles inherent to other domains, such as NAIVE PHYSICS or FOLK PSYCHOLOGY (Carey 1995). One candidate for a domain-specific principle involves a particular sort of ESSENTIALISM, which carries an invariable presumption that the various members of each generic species share a unique underlying nature, or biological essence. Such an essence may be considered domain-specific insofar as it is an intrinsic (i.e., nonartifactual) teleological agent, which physically (i.e., nonintentionally) causes the biologically relevant parts and properties of a generic species to function and cohere "for the sake of" the generic species itself. Thus, American preschoolers consistently judge that thorns on a rose bush exist for the sake of there being more roses, whereas physically similar depictions of barbs on barbed wire or the protuberances of a jagged rock do not elicit indications of inherent purpose and design (Keil 1994). People everywhere expect the disparate properties of a generic species to be integrated without having to know the precise causal chains linking universally recognized relationships of morpho-behavioral functioning, inheritance and reproduction, disease and death.

This essentialist concept shares features with the broader philosophical notion NATURAL KIND in regard to category-based induction. Thus, on learning that one cow is susceptible to "mad cow" disease, one might reasonably infer that all cows, but not all mammals or animals, are susceptible to the disease. This is presumably because disease is related to "deep" biological properties, and because *cow* is a generic species with a fairly uniform distribution of such properties. The taxonomic arrangement of generic species systematically extends this inductive power: it is more "natural" to infer a greater probability that all mammals share the disease than that all animals do. Taxonomic stability allows formulation of a general principle of biological induction: a property found in two organisms is most likely found in all organisms belonging to the lowest-ranked taxon containing the two. This powerful inferential principle also underlies systematics, the scientific classification of organic life (Warburton 1967). Still, relativists can point to cultural and historical influences on superordinate and subordinate taxa as suggesting that biologically relevant properties can be weighted differently for induction in different traditions.

See also CONCEPT; COLOR CLASSIFICATION; NAIVE SOCIOLOGY

—*Scott Atran*

References

Atran, S. (1990). *Cognitive Foundations of Natural History*. Cambridge: Cambridge University Press.

Berlin, B. (1992). *Ethnobiological Classification*. Princeton: Princeton University Press.

Brown, C. (1995). Lexical acculturation and ethnobiology: utilitarianism and intellectualism. *Journal of Linguistic Anthropology* 5: 51–64.

Bulmer, R. (1967). Why is the cassowary not a bird? *Man* 2: 5–25.

Carey, S. (1995). On the origins of causal understanding. In S. Sperber, D. Premack, and A. Premack, Eds., *Causal Cognition*. Oxford: Clarendon Press.

Darwin, C. (1859). *On the Origins of Species by Natural Selection*. London: Murray.

Ellen, R. (1993). *The Cultural Relations of Classification*. Cambridge: Cambridge University Press.

Gilmour, J., and S. Walters. (1964). Philosophy and classification. In W. Turrill, Ed., *Vistas in Botany*, vol. 4: *Recent Researches in Plant Taxonomy*. Oxford: Pergamon Press.

Hunn, E. (1976). Toward a perceptual model of folkbiological classification. *American Ethnologist* 3: 508–524.

Inakagi, K., and G. Hatano. (1996). Young children's recognition of commonalities between plants and animals. *Child Development* 67: 2823–2840.

Keil, F. (1994). The birth and nurturance of concepts by domains. In L. Hirschfeld and S. Gelman, Eds., *Mapping the Mind: Domain Specificity in Cognition and Culture*. New York: Cambridge University Press.

Malt, B. (1995). Category coherence in crosscultural perspective. *Cognitive Psychology* 29: 85–148.

Mayr, E. (1969). *Principles of Systematic Zoology*. New York: McGraw-Hill.

Medin, D., and S. Atran, Eds. (1998). *Folk Biology*. Cambridge, MA: MIT Press.

Warburton, F. (1967). The purposes of classification. *Systematic Zoology* 16: 241–245.

Folk Psychology

In recent years, folk psychology has become a topic of debate not just among philosophers, but among developmental psychologists and primatologists as well. Yet there are two different things that "folk psychology" has come to mean, and they are not always distinguished: (1) commonsense psychology that explains human behavior in terms of beliefs, desires, intentions, expectations, preferences, hopes, fears, and so on; (2) an interpretation of such everyday explanations as part of a folk theory, comprising a network of generalizations employing concepts like *belief, desire,* and so on. The second definition—suggested by Sellars (1963) and dubbed "theory-theory" by Morton (1980)— is a philosophical account of the first.

Folk psychology(1) concerns the conceptual framework of explanations of human behavior: If the explanatory framework of folk psychology(1) is correct, then "because Nan wants the baby to sleep," which employs the concept of wanting, may be a good (partial) explanation of Nan's turning the TV off. Folk psychology(2) concerns how folk-psychological(1) explanations are to be interpreted: If folk psychology(2) is correct, then "because Nan wants the baby to sleep" is an hypothesis that Nan had an internal (brain) state of wanting the baby to sleep and that state caused Nan to turn the TV off.

Although the expression *folk psychology* came to prominence as a term for theory-theory, that is, folk psychology(2), it is now used more generally to refer to commonsense psychology, that is, folk psychology(1). This largely unnoticed broadening of the term has made for confusion in the literature. Folk psychology (in one or the other sense, or sometimes equivocally) has been the focus of two debates.

The first is the so-called use issue: What are people doing when they explain behavior in terms of beliefs, desires, and so on? Some philosophers (Goldman 1993; Gordon 1986) argue that folk psychology, in sense (1) is a matter of simulation. Putting it less precisely than either Goldman or Gordon would, to use commonsense psychology is to exercise a skill; to attribute a belief is to project oneself into the situation of the believer. The dominant view, however, is that users of concepts like believing, desiring, intending—folk psychology(1)—are deploying a theory—

folk psychology(2). To attribute a belief is to make an hypothesis about the internal state of the putative believer. Some psychologists (e.g., Astington, Harris, and Olson 1988) as well as philosophers simply assume the theory-theory interpretation, and some, though not all, fail to distinguish between folk psychology(1) and folk psychology(2).

The second is the so-called status issue. To what extent is the commonsense belief/desire framework correct? The "status" issue has turned on this question: To what extent will science vindicate (in some relevant sense) commonsense psychology? The question of scientific vindication arises when commonsense psychology is understood as folk psychology(2). On one side are intentional realists like Fodor (1987) and Dretske (1987), who argue that science will vindicate the conceptual framework of commonsense psychology. On the other side are proponents of ELIMINATIVE MATERIALISM like Churchland (1981) and Stich (1983), who argue that as an empirical theory, commonsense psychology is susceptible to replacement by a better theory with radically different conceptual resources (but see Stich 1996 for a revised view). Just as other folk theories (e.g., FOLK BIOLOGY) have been overthrown by scientific theories, we should be prepared for the overthrow of folk psychology by a scientific theory—scientific psychology or neuroscience. Eliminative materialists make the empirical prediction that science very probably will not vindicate the framework of commonsense psychology.

The question of scientific vindication, however, does not by itself decide the "status" issue. To see this, consider an argument for eliminative materialism (EM):

a. Folk psychology will not be vindicated by a physicalistic theory (scientific psychology or neuroscience).

b. Folk psychology is correct if and only if it is vindicated (in some relevant sense) by a physicalistic theory.

So,

c. Folk psychology is incorrect.

Premise (b), which plays an essential role in the argument, has largely been neglected (but see Baker 1995; Horgan and Graham 1991). If premise (b) refers to folk psychology(2), then premise (b) is plausible; but then the conclusion would establish only that commonsense psychology *interpreted as a theory* is incorrect. However, if premise (b) refers to folk psychology(1), then premise (b) is very probably false. If folk psychology is not a putative scientific theory in the first place, then there is no reason to think that a physicalistic theory will reveal it to be incorrect. (Similarly, if cooking, say, is not a scientific theory in the first place, then we need not fear that chemistry will reveal that you cannot really bake a cake.) So, the most that (EM) could show would be that if the theory-theory is the correct philosophical account of folk psychology(1), then folk psychology is a false theory. (EM) would not establish the incorrectness of commonsense psychology on other philosophical accounts (as, say, understood in terms of Aristotle's account of the practical syllogism).

Other positions on the "status" issue include these: commonsense psychology—folk psychology(1)—will be partly confirmed and partly disconfirmed by scientific psychology (von Eckardt 1994, 1997); commonsense psychology is so robust that we should affirm its physical basis regardless of the course of scientific psychology (Heil 1992); commonsense psychology is causal, and hence, though attributions of attitudes are interpretive and normative, explanations of behavior in terms of attitudes are backed by strict laws (Davidson 1980); commonsense psychology is useless as science, but remains useful in everyday life (Dennett 1987; Wilkes 1991). Still others (Baker 1995; Horgan and Graham 1991) take the legitimacy of commonsense psychology to be borne out in everyday cognitive practice—regardless of the outcome of scientific psychology or neuroscience.

See also AUTISM; FUNCTIONALISM; INTENTIONALITY; LANGUAGE OF THOUGHT; PHYSICALISM; PROPOSITIONAL ATTITUDES; SIMULATION VS. THEORY-THEORY; THEORY OF MIND

—*Lynne Rudder Baker*

References

Astington, J. W., P. L. Harris, and D. R. Olson, Eds. (1988). *Developing Theories of Mind*. Cambridge, MA: Cambridge University Press.

Baker, L. R. (1995). *Explaining Attitudes: A Practical Approach to the Mind*. Cambridge, MA: Cambridge University Press.

Churchland, P. M. (1981). Eliminative Materialism and the Propositional Attitudes. *Journal of Philosophy* 78: 67–90.

Churchland, P. M. (1989). Eliminative materialism and the propositional attitudes. In *A Neurocomputational Perspective: The Nature of Mind and the Structure of Science*. Cambridge, MA: MIT Press.

Davidson, D. (1980). *Essays on Actions and Events*. Oxford: Clarendon Press.

Dennett, D. C. (1987). *The Intentional Stance*. Cambridge, MA: MIT Press.

Dretske, F. (1987). *Explaining Behavior: Reasons in a World of Causes*. Cambridge, MA: MIT Press.

Fodor, J. A. (1987). *Psychosemantics: The Problem of Meaning in the Philosophy of Mind*. Cambridge, MA: MIT Press.

Goldman, A. I. (1993). The Psychology of Folk Psychology. *Behavioral and Brain Sciences* 16: 15–28.

Gordon, R. M. (1986). Folk Psychology as Simulation. *Mind and Language* 1: 158–171.

Heil, J. (1992). *The Nature of True Minds*. Cambridge, MA: Cambridge University Press.

Horgan, T., and G. Graham. (1991). In defense of southern fundamentalism. *Philosophical Studies* 62: 107–134.

Morton, A. (1980). *Frames of Mind: Constraints on the Commonsense Conception of the Mental*. Oxford: Clarendon Press.

Sellars, W. (1963). Empiricism and the philosophy of mind. In *Science, Perception and Reality*. London: Routledge and Kegan Paul.

Stich, S. P. (1983). *From Folk Psychology to Cognitive Science: The Case Against Belief*. Cambridge, MA: MIT Press.

Stich, S. P. (1996). *Deconstructing the Mind*. Oxford: Oxford University Press.

von Eckardt, B. (1994). Folk psychology and scientific psychology. In S. Guttenplan, Ed., *A Companion to the Philosophy of Mind*. Oxford: Blackwell, pp. 300–307.

von Eckardt, B. (1997). The empirical naivete of the current philosophical conception of folk psychology. In M. Carrier and P. K. Machamer, Eds., *Mindscapes: Philosophy, Science, and the Mind*. Pittsburgh, PA: University of Pittsburgh Press, pp. 23–51.

Wilkes, K. V. (1991). The relationship between scientific psychology and common-sense psychology. *Synthese* 89: 15–39.

Further Readings

Baker, L. R. (1988). *Saving Belief: A Critique of Physicalism*. Princeton: Princeton University Press.

Burge, T. (1979). Individualism and the mental. *Studies in Metaphysics: Midwest Studies in Philosophy*, vol. 4. Minneapolis: University of Minnesota Press.

Churchland, P. S. (1988). *Neurophilosophy: Toward a Unified Science of the Mind/Brain*. Cambridge, MA: MIT Press.

Dennett, D. C. (1978). *Brainstorms: Philosophical Essays on Mind and Psychology*. Montgomery, VT: Bradford Books.

Fodor, J. A. (1990). *A Theory of Content and Other Essays*. Cambridge, MA: MIT Press.

Goldman, A. (1989). Interpretation psychologized. *Mind and Language* 4: 161–185.

Graham, G. L., and T. Horgan. (1988). How to be realistic about folk psychology. *Philosophical Psychology* 1: 69–81.

Greenwood, J. D. (1991). *The Future of Folk Psychology: Intentionality and Cognitive Science*. Cambridge: Cambridge University Press.

Horgan, T., and J. Woodward. (1985). Folk psychology is here to stay. *Philosophical Review* 94: 197–225.

Kitcher, P. (1984). In defense of intentional psychology. *Journal of Philosophy* 71: 89–106.

Lewis, D. (1972). Psychophysical and theoretical identifications. *Australasian Journal of Philosophy* 50: 249–258.

Premack, D., and G. Woodruff. (1978). Does the chimpanzee have a theory of mind? *Behavioral and Brain Sciences* 1: 515–526.

Putnam, H. (1988). *Representation and Reality*. Cambridge, MA: MIT Press.

Ramsey, W., S. Stich, and J. Garon. (1990). Connectionism, eliminativism, and the future of folk psychology. In J. E. Tomberliin, Ed., *Action Theory and Philosophy of Mind—Philosophical Perspectives 4*. Atascadero, CA: Ridgeview.

Ryle, G. (1949). *The Concept of Mind*. London: Hutchinson.

Searle, J. (1980). Minds, brains and programs. *Behavioral and Brain Sciences* 3: 417–424.

Wellman, H. (1990). *The Child's Theory of Mind*. Cambridge, MA: MIT Press.

Form/Content

See COMPUTATIONAL THEORY OF MIND; INTENTIONALITY; LOGICAL FORM, ORIGINS OF

Formal Grammars

A grammar is a definition of a set of linguistic structures, where the linguistic structures could be sequences of words (sentences), or "sound-meaning" pairs (that is, pairs $<s,m>$ where s is a representation of phonetic properties and m is a representation of semantic properties), or pairs $<t,p>$ where t is a tree and p is a probability of occurrence in a discourse. A *formal grammar*, then, is a grammar that is completely clear and unambiguous. Obviously, this account of what qualifies as "formal" is neither formal nor rigorous, but in practice there is little dispute.

It might seem that formalization would always be desirable in linguistic theory, but there is little point in spelling out the details of informal hypotheses when their weaknesses can readily be ascertained and addressed without working out the details. In fact, there is considerable variation in the degree to which empirical proposals about human grammars are formalized, and there are disputes in the literature about how much formalization is appropriate at this stage of linguistic theory (Pullum 1989; Chomsky 1990).

Given this controversy, and given the preliminary and changing nature of linguistic theories, formal studies of grammar have been most significant when they have focused not on the details of any particular grammar, but rather on the fundamental properties of various *kinds* of grammars. Taking this abstract, metagrammatical approach, formal studies have identified a number of basic properties of grammars that raise new questions about human languages.

One basic division among the various ways of defining sets of linguistic structures classifies them as *generative* or *constraint-based*. A GENERATIVE GRAMMAR defines a set of structures by providing some basic elements and applying rules to derive new elements. Again, there are two basic ways of doing this. The first approach, common in "formal language theory" involves beginning with a "category" like "sentence," applying rules that define what parts the sentence has, what parts those parts have, and so on until the sentence has been specified all the way down to the level of words. This style of language definition has proven to be very useful, and many fundamental results have been established (Harrison 1978; Rozenberg and Salomaa 1997).

A second "bottom-up" approach, more common in CATE-GORIAL GRAMMAR and some related traditions, involves starting with some lexical items ("generators") and then applying rules to assemble them into more complex structures. This style of language definition comes from LOGIC and algebra, where certain sets are similarly defined by "closing" a set of basic elements with respect to some generating relations. In these formal grammars, the structures of the defined language are analogous to the theorems of formal logic in that they are derived from some specified basic elements by rigorously specified rules. A natural step from this idea is to treat a grammar explicitly as a logic (Lambek 1958; Moortgat 1997).

Unlike the generative methods, which define a language by applying rules to a set of initial elements of some kind, a *constraint grammar* specifies a set by saying what properties the elements of that set must have. In this sort of definition, the structures in the language are not like the (generated, enumerable) theorems of a logic, but more like the sentences that could possibly be true (the "satisfiable" sentences of a logic). This approach to grammar is particularly prominent in linguistic traditions like HEAD-DRIVEN PHRASE STRUCTURE GRAMMAR (Pollard and Sag 1994). However, most linguistic theories use both generative and constraint-based specifications of structure.

Recently, linguists have also shown interest in a special variety of constraint grammar that is sometimes called "over-constrained." These grammars impose constraints that cannot all be met, and the interest then is in the linguistic structures that meet the constraints of the grammar to the greatest degree, the structures that are "most economical" or "most optimal" in some sense. Systems of this kind have been studied in a variety of contexts, but have recently become prominent in OPTIMALITY THEORY. Parts of the transformational grammar tradition called MINIMALISM have a fundamentally similar character, with constraints that can be violated when there is no better option.

The various different kinds of formal grammars have all been studied formally, particularly with regard to the complexities of sets they can define, and with regard to the succinctness of the definitions of those sets.

The study of various kinds of formal grammars has led linguists to consider whether we can determine, in advance of knowing in full detail what the grammars for human languages are like, whether human languages have one or another of the fundamental properties that are well understood in the context of artificial languages. Regardless of how a set of linguistic structures is defined, whether by a generative grammar or constraint grammar or over-constrained grammar, we can consider questions like the following about the complexity of the defined sets of "grammatical" structures. (Of course, such questions apply only to formal grammars for which some significant criterion of "grammaticality" can be formulated, which is a controversial empirical question.)

Is the set of linguistic structures finite? Although there are obvious practical limitations on the lengths of sentences that any human will ever pronounce, these bounds do not seem to be linguistic in nature, but rather derive from limitations in our life span, requirements for sleep, and so on. As far as the grammars of natural languages go, there seems to be no longest sentence, and consequently no maximally complex linguistic structure, and we can conclude that human languages are infinite. This assumption makes all of the following questions more difficult, because it means that the languages that people speak contain structures that no human will ever produce or understand. This basic point is also one of the basic motivations for the competence/performance distinction.

Is the set of linguistic structures "recursive"? That is, is there an algorithm that can effectively decide whether a given structure is in the set or not? This question is more interesting than it looks, because the mere fact that humans use languages does not show they are recursive (Matthews 1979). However, there seems to be no good reason to assume that languages are not recursive.

Is the set of linguistic structures one that is recognized by a finite computing device? As Chomsky (1956) pointed out, as far as the principles of language are concerned, not only are there sentences that are too long for a human to pronounce, but there are sentences that require more memory to recognize than humans have. To recognize an arbitrary sentence of a human language requires infinite memory, just as computing arbitrary multiplication problems does. (In a range of important cases, the complexity of grammatical descriptions of formal languages corresponds to the complexity of the machines needed to recognize those languages, as we see here. The study of formal languages overlaps extensively with the theory of AUTOMATA.)

Is the set of linguistic structures generated by a "context free grammar"? Because "context free grammars" can define languages that cannot be accepted by a finite machine, this more technical question has received a lot of attention, particularly in studies of the syntax of human languages. The received view is that the sentences of natural languages are not generally definable by context free grammars (Chomsky 1956; Savitch et al. 1987). So the human languages seem to be more complex than context free languages, but still recursive. There have been a number of attempts to pin the matter down more precisely (Joshi 1985; Vijay-Shanker and Weir 1994).

Is the set of linguistic structures "efficiently parsable"? That is, roughly, can the structures be computed efficiently from their spoken or written forms? For human languages, the answer appears to be negative, as argued for example in Barton, Berwick, and Ristad (1987) and in Ristad (1993), but the matter remains controversial. Questions like this one are at the foundations of work in NATURAL LANGUAGE PROCESSING.

Is a set of formal languages "learnable"? Results in formal studies of learning often depend on the particular sets that are learned (in some precise sense of "learned"), and so formal grammars play a fundamental role in LEARNING SYSTEMS; COMPUTATIONAL LEARNING THEORY; SUPERVISED LEARNING; UNSUPERVISED LEARNING; MACHINE LEARNING; STATISTICAL LEARNING THEORY.

—*Edward Stabler*

References

Barton, E., R. C. Berwick, and E. S. Ristad (1987). *Computational Complexity and Natural Language.* Cambridge, MA: MIT Press.

Chomsky, N. (1956). Three models for the description of language. *IRE Transactions on Information Theory* IT-2: 113–124.

Chomsky, N. (1990). On formalization and formal linguistics. *Natural Language and Linguistic Theory* 8: 143–147.

Harrison, M. A. (1978). *Introduction to Formal Language Theory.* Reading, MA: Addison-Wesley.

Joshi, A. (1985). How much context-sensitivity is necessary for characterizing structural descriptions? In D. Dowty, L. Karttunen, and A. Zwicky, Eds., *Natural Language Processing: Theoretical, Computational and Psychological Perspectives.* New York: Cambridge University Press.

Lambek, J. (1958). The mathematics of sentence structure. *American Mathematical Monthly* 65: 154–170.

Matthews, R. (1979). Do the grammatical sentences of language form a recursive set? *Synthese* 40: 209–224.

Moortgat, M. (1997). Categorial type logics. In J. van Benthem and A. ter Meulen, Eds., *Handbook of Logic and Language.* New York: Elsevier.

Pollard, C., and I. Sag. (1994). *Head-driven Phrase Structure Grammar.* Chicago: University of Chicago Press.

Pullum, G. K. (1989). Formal linguistics meets the boojum. *Natural Language and Linguistic Theory* 7: 137–143.

Ristad, E. S. (1993). *The Language Complexity Game.* Cambridge, MA: MIT Press.

Rozenberg, G., and A. Salomaa, Eds. (1997). *Handbook of Formal Languages.* New York: Springer.

Savitch, W. J., E. Bach, W. Marsh, and G. Safran-Naveh, Eds. (1987). *The Formal Complexity of Natural Language.* Boston: Reidel.

Vijay-Shanker, K., and D. Weir (1994). The equivalence of four extensions of context free grammar formalisms. *Mathematical Systems Theory* 27: 511–545.

Further Readings

Basic Mathematical Properties of Generative Grammars

Harrison, M. A. (1978). *Introduction to Formal Language Theory.* Reading, MA: Addison-Wesley.

Hopcroft, J. E., and J. D. Ullman. (1979). *Introduction to Automata Theory, Languages and Computation.* Reading, MA: Addison-Wesley.

Moll, R. N., M. A. Arbib, and A. J. Kfoury (1988). *An Introduction to Formal Language Theory.* New York: Springer.

On Formal Properties of Human Languages

Barton, E., R. C. Berwick, and E. S. Ristad (1987). *Computational Complexity and Natural Language.* Cambridge, MA: MIT Press.

Savitch, W. J., E. Bach, W. Marsh, and G. Safran-Naveh, Eds. (1987). *The Formal Complexity of Natural Language.* Boston: Reidel.

Basic Mathematical Properties of Some Linguistic Theories

Perrault, R. C. (1983). On the mathematical properties of linguistic theories. *Proceedings of the Association for Computational Linguistics* 21: 98–105.

Recent Work on Grammars-as-Logic

Moortgat, M. (1997). Categorial type logics. In J. van Benthem and A. ter Meulen, Eds., *Handbook of Logic and Language.* New York: Elsevier.

Recent Work on Over-Constrained Systems

Jampel, M., E. Freunder, and M. Maher, Eds. (1996). *Over-Constrained Systems.* New York: Springer.

Prince, A., and P. Smolensky. (1993). *Optimality Theory: Constraint Interaction in Generative Grammar. Technical Report 2.* Center for Cognitive Science, Rutgers University.

Formal Systems, Properties of

Formal systems or theories must satisfy requirements that are sharper than those imposed on the structure of theories by the axiomatic-deductive method, which can be traced back to Euclid's *Elements.* The crucial additional requirement is the regimentation of inferential steps in proofs: not only axioms have to be given in advance, but also the logical rules representing argumentative steps. To avoid a regress in the definition of proof and to achieve intersubjectivity on a minimal basis, the rules are to be "mechanical" and must take into account only the syntactic form of statements. Thus, to exclude any ambiguity, a precise symbolic language is needed and a logical calculus. Both the concept of a "formula" (i.e., statement in the symbolic language) and that of a "rule" (i.e., inference step in the logical calculus) have to be effective; by the Church-Turing Thesis, this means they have to be recursive.

FREGE (1879) presented a symbolic language (with relations and quantifiers) together with an adequate logical calculus, thus providing the means for the completely formal representation of mathematical proofs. The Fregean framework was basic for the later development of mathematical logic; it influenced the work of Whitehead and Russell that culminated in *Principia Mathematica*. The next crucial step was taken most vigorously by Hilbert; he built on Whitehead and Russell's work and used an appropriate framework for the development of parts of mathematics, but took it also as an object of mathematical investigation. The latter metamathematical perspective proved to be extremely important. Clearly, in a less rigorous way it goes back to the investigations concerning non-Euclidean geometry and Hilbert's own early work (1899) on independence questions in geometry.

Hilbert's emphasis on the mathematical investigation of formal systems really marked the beginning of *mathematical* logic. In the lectures (1918), prepared in collaboration with Paul Bernays, he isolated the language of first order logic as the central language (together with an informal semantics) and developed a suitable logical calculus. Central questions were raised and partially answered; they concerned the completeness, consistency, and decidability of such systems and are still central in mathematical logic and other fields, where formal systems are being explored. Some important results will be presented paradigmatically; for a real impression of the richness and depth of the subject readers have to turn to (classical) textbooks or to up-to-date handbooks (see Further Readings.)

Completeness has been used in a number of different senses, from the *quasi-empirical* completeness of Zermelo Fraenkel set theory (being sufficient for the formal development of mathematics) to the *syntactic completeness* of formal theories (shown to be impossible by Gödel's First Theorem for theories containing a modicum of number theory). For logic the central concept is, however, *Semantic completeness*: a calculus is (semantically) complete, if it allows to prove all statements that are true in all interpretations (models) of the system. In sentential logic these statements are the tautologies; for that logic Hilbert and Bernays (1918) and Post (1921) proved the completeness of appropriate calculi; for first order logic completeness was established by Gödel (1930). Completeness expresses obviously the adequacy of a calculus to capture all logical consequences and entails almost immediately the logic's compactness: if every finite subset of a system has a model, so does the system. Ironically, this immediate consequence of its adequacy is at the root of real inadequacies of first order logic: the existence of nonstandard models for arithmetic and the inexpressibility of important concepts (like "finite," "well-order"). The relativity of "being countable" (leading to the so-called Skolem paradox) is a direct consequence of the proof of the completeness theorem.

Relative *consistency* proofs were obtained in geometry by semantic arguments: given a model of Euclidean geometry one can define a Euclidean model of, say, hyperbolic geometry; thus, if an inconsistency could be found in hyperbolic geometry it could also be found in Euclidean geometry. Hilbert formulated as the central goal of his program to establish by elementary, so-called finitist means the consistency of formal systems. This involved a direct examination of formal proofs; the strongest results before 1931 were obtained by Ackermann, VON NEUMANN, and Herbrand: they established the consistency of number theory with a very restricted induction principle. A basic limitation had indeed been reached, as was made clear by Gödel's Second Theorem; see

GÖDEL'S THEOREMS. Modern proof theory—by using stronger than finitist, but still "constructive" means—has been able to prove the consistency of significant parts of analysis. In pursuing this generalized consistency program, important insights have been gained into structural properties of proofs in special calculi ("normal form" of proofs in sequent and natural deduction calculi; cf. Gentzen 1934–35, 1936; Prawitz 1966). These structural properties are fundamental not only for modern LOGICAL REASONING SYSTEMS, but also for interesting psychological theories of human reasoning (see DEDUCTIVE REASONING and Rips 1994).

Hilbert's *Entscheidungsproblem*, the decision problem for first order logic, was one issue that required a precise characterization of "effective methods"; see CHURCH-TURING THESIS. Though partial positive answers were found during the 1920s, Church and TURING proved in 1936 that the general problem is undecidable. The result and the techniques involved in its proof (not to mention the very mathematical notions) inspired the investigation of the recursion theoretic complexity of sets that led at first to the classification of the arithmetical, hyperarithmetical, and analytical hierarchies, and later to that of the computational complexity classes.

Some general questions and results were described for particular systems; as a matter of fact, questions and results that led to three branches of modern logic: model theory, proof theory, and computability theory. However, to reemphasize the point, from an abstract recursion theoretic point of view any system of "syntactic configurations" whose "formulas" and "proofs" are effectively decidable (by a Turing machine) is a formal system. In a footnote to his 1931 paper added in 1963, Gödel made this point most strongly: "In my opinion the term 'formal system' or 'formalism' should never be used for anything but this notion. In a lecture at Princeton . . . I suggested certain transfinite generalizations of formalisms; but these are something radically different from formal systems in the proper sense of the term, whose characteristic property is that reasoning in them, in principle, can be completely replaced by mechanical devices." Thus, formal systems in this sense can in principle be implemented on computers and provide (at least partial) models for a wide variety of mental processes.

See also COMPUTATION; COMPUTATIONAL THEORY OF MIND; LANGUAGE AND THOUGHT; MENTAL MODELS; RULES AND REPRESENTATIONS

—*Wilfried Sieg*

References

Frege, G. (1879). *Begriffsschrift, eine der arithmetischen nachgebildete Formelsprache des reinen denkens*. Halle: Nebert.

Frege, G. (1893). *Grundgesetze der Arithmetik, begriffsschriftlich abgeleitet*, vol. 1. Jena: Pohle.

Gentzen, G. (1934–35). Untersuchungen über das logische Schliessen 1, 2. *Math. Zeitschrift* 39: 176–210, 405–431. Translated in Gentzen (1969).

Gentzen, G. (1936). Die Widerspruchsfreiheit der reinen Zahlentheorie. *Mathematische Annalen* 112: 493–565. Translated in Gentzen (1969).

Gentzen, G. (1969). *The Collected Papers of Gerhard Gentzen*. M. E. Szabo, Ed. Amsterdam: North-Holland.

Gödel, K. (1930). Die Vollständigkeit der Axiome des logischen Funktionenkalküls. *Monatshefte für Mathematik und Physik* 37: 349–360. Translated in *Collected Works 1.*

Gödel, K. (1931). Über formal unentscheidbare Sätze der *Principia Mathematica* und verwandter Systeme 1. *Monatshefte für Mathematik und Physik* 38: 173–198. Translated in *Collected Works 1.*

Gödel, K. (1986). *Collected Works 1.* Oxford: Oxford University Press.

Hilbert, D. (1899). *Grundlagen der Geometrie.* Leipzig: Teubner.

Hilbert, D. (1918). *Die Prinzipien der Mathematik.* Lectures given during the winter term 1917–18. Written by Paul Bernays. Mathematical Institute, University of Göttingen.

Hilbert, D., and W. Ackermann. (1928). *Grundzüge der theoretichen Logik.* Berlin: Springer.

Post, E. (1921). Introduction to a general theory of elementary propositions. *Amer. J. Math.* 43: 163–185.

Prawitz, D. (1966). *Natural Deduction: A Proof-Theoretical Study.* Stockholm: Almqvist and Wiskell.

Rips, L. (1994). *The Psychology of Proof-Deductive Reasoning in Human Thinking.* Cambridge, MA: MIT Press.

Further Readings

Barwise, J., Ed. (1977). *Handbook of Mathematical Logic.* Amsterdam: North-Holland.

Börger, E., E. Graedel, and Y. Gurevich. (1997). *The Classical Decision Problem.* New York: Springer.

Kleene, S. C. (1952). *Introduction to Metamathematics.* Groningen: Wolters-Noordhoff Publishing.

Rogers, H. Jr. (1967). *Theory of Recursive Functions and Effective Computability.* New York: McGraw Hill.

Shoenfield, J. R. (1967). *Mathematical Logic.* Reading, MA: Addison-Wesley.

van Dalen, D. (1989). *Logic and Structure.* New York: Springer.

Formal Theories

See ACQUISITION, FORMAL THEORIES OF; FORMAL GRAMMARS; FORMAL SYSTEMS, PROPERTIES OF; LEARNING SYSTEMS

Frame-Based Systems

Frame-based systems are knowledge representation systems that use *frames,* a notion originally introduced by Marvin Minsky, as their primary means to represent domain knowledge. A frame is a structure for representing a CONCEPT or situation such as "living room" or "being in a living room." Attached to a frame are several kinds of information, for instance, definitional and descriptive information and how to use the frame. Based on the original proposal, several knowledge representation systems have been built and the theory of frames has evolved. Important descendants of frame-based representation formalisms are *description logics* that capture the declarative part of frames using a logic-based semantics. Most of these logics are decidable fragments of *first order logic* and are very closely related to other formalisms such as modal logics and *feature logics.*

In the seminal paper "A framework for representing knowledge," Minsky (1975) proposed a KNOWLEDGE REPRESENTATION scheme that was completely different from formalisms used in those days, namely, rule-based and logic-based formalisms. Minsky proposed organizing knowledge into chunks called *frames.* These frames are supposed to capture the essence of concepts or stereotypical situations, for example being in a living room or going out for dinner, by clustering all relevant information for these situations together. This includes information about how to use the frame, information about expectations (which may turn out to be wrong), information about what to do if expectations are not confirmed, and so on. This means, in particular, that a great deal of procedurally expressed knowledge should be part of the frames. Collections of such frames are to be organized in *frame systems* in which the frames are interconnected. The processes working on such frame systems are supposed to match a frame to a specific situation, to use default values to fill unspecified aspects, and so on. If this brief summary sounds vague, it correctly reproduces the paper's general tone. Despite the fact that this paper was a first approach to the idea of what frames could be, Minsky explicitly argued in favor of staying flexible and nonformal.

Details that had been left out in Minsky's 1975 paper were later filled in by knowledge representation systems that were inspired by Minsky's ideas—the most prominent being FRL and KRL (Bobrow and Winograd 1977). KRL was one of the most ambitious projects in this direction. It addressed almost every representational problem discussed in the literature. The net result is a very complex language with a very rich repertoire of representational primitives and almost unlimited flexibility.

Features that are common to FRL, KRL, and later frame-based systems (Fikes and Kehler 1985) are: (1) frames are organized in (tangled) *hierarchies*; (2) frames are composed out of *slots* (attributes) for which *fillers* (scalar values, references to other frames or procedures) have to be specified or computed; and (3) properties (fillers, restriction on fillers, etc.) are inherited from superframes to subframes in the hierarchy according to some *inheritance strategy.* These organizational principles turned out to be very useful, and, indeed, the now popular object-oriented languages have adopted these organizational principles.

From a formal point of view, it was unsatisfying that the *semantics* of frames and of inheritance was specified only operationally. So, subsequent research in the area of knowledge representation addressed these problems. In the area of *defeasible inheritance,* principles based on nonmonotonic logics together with preferences derived from the topology of the inheritance network were applied in order to derive a formal semantics (Touretzky 1986; Selman and Levesque 1993). The task of assigning *declarative semantics* to frames was addressed by applying methods based on first order LOGIC.

Hayes (1980) argued that "most of frames is just a new syntax for parts of first order logic." Although this means that frames do not offer anything new in expressiveness, there are two important points in which frame-based systems may have an advantage over systems using first-order logic. Firstly, they offer a concise way to express knowledge in an *object-oriented* way (Fikes and Kehler 1985). Secondly, by using only a fragment of first order logic, frame-based systems may offer more efficient means for reasoning.

These two points are addressed by the so-called *description logics* (also called terminological logics, concept languages, and attributive description languages; Nebel and Smolka 1991), which formalize the declarative part of frame-based systems and grew out of the development of the frame-based system KL-ONE (Brachman and Schmolze 1985). In description logics, it is possible to build up a concept hierarchy out of *atomic concepts* (interpreted as unary predicates and denoted by capitalized words) and attributes, usually called *roles* (interpreted as binary predicates and denoted by lowercase words). The intended meaning of atomic concepts can be specified by providing *concept descriptions* made up of other concepts and *role restrictions,* as in the following informal example:

Woman = Person and Female
Parent = Person with some child
Grandmother = Woman with some child who is a Parent

One of the most important reasoning tasks in this context is the determination of *subsumption* between two concepts, that is, determining whether all instances of one concept are necessarily instances of the other concept taking into account the definitions. For example, "Grandmother" is subsumed by "Parent" because everything that is a "Grandmother" is—by definition—also a "Parent." Similar to the subsumption task is the *instance-checking* task, where one wants to know if a given object is an *instance* of the specified concept.

Starting with a paper by Brachman and Levesque (1984), the COMPUTATIONAL COMPLEXITY of subsumption determination for different variants of description logics has extensively been analyzed and a family of algorithms for solving the subsumption problem has been developed (Schmidt-Schauss and Smolka 1991).

Although in most cases subsumption is decidable, that is, easier than inference in full first order logic, there are cases when subsumption becomes undecidable (Schmidt-Schauss 1989). Aiming for polynomial-time decidability, however, leads to very restricted description logics, as shown by Donini et al. (1991). Further, if definitions of concepts as in the example above are part of the language, even the weakest possible description logic has an NP-hard subsumption problem (Nebel 1990). Although these results seem to suggest that description logics are not usable because the computational complexity of reasoning is too high, experience with implemented systems shows that moderately expressive description logics are computationally feasible (Heinsohn et al. 1994). In fact, current frame-based systems are efficient enough to support large configuration systems that are in everyday use at AT&T (Brachman 1992).

In the course of analyzing the logical and computational properties of frame-based systems, it turned out that description logics are very similar to other formalisms used in computer science and COMPUTATIONAL LINGUISTICS (Nebel and Smolka 1991). First of all, the declarative part of *object-oriented database languages* bears a strong resemblance to description logics, and it is possible to apply techniques and methods developed for description logics in this area (Buch-

heit et al. 1994). Second, there is a very strong connection to modal logics and to dynamic logics (Schild 1991). In fact, the "standard" description logic ALC (Schmidt-Schauss and Smolka 1991) is simply a notational variant of the MODAL LOGIC K with multiple agents. Third, *feature logics,* which are the constraint logic part of so-called unification grammars such as HPSG, are very similar to description logics. The only difference is that attributes in feature logics are single-valued, whereas they are multivalued in description logics. Although this seems to be a minor difference, it can make the difference between decidable and undecidable reasoning problems (Nebel and Smolka 1991).

See also KNOWLEDGE-BASED SYSTEMS; KNOWLEDGE ACQUISITION; NONMONOTONIC LOGICS; SCHEMATA

—Bernhard Nebel

References

Bobrow, D. G., and T. Winograd. (1977). An overview of KRL-0, a knowledge representation language. *Cognitive Science* 1(1): 3–46.

Brachman, R. J. (1992). Reducing CLASSIC to practice: knowledge representation theory meets reality. In B. Nebel, W. Swartout, and C. Rich, Eds., *Principles of Knowledge Representation and Reasoning: Proceedings of the 3rd International Conference (KR-92).* Cambridge, MA, pp. 247–258.

Brachman, R. J., and H. J. Levesque. (1984). The tractability of subsumption in framebased description languages. In *Proceedings of the 4th National Conference of the American Association for Artificial Intelligence* (AAAI-84). Austin, TX, pp. 34–37.

Brachman, R. J., and J. G. Schmolze. (1985). An overview of the KL-ONE knowledge representation system. *Cognitive Science* 9(2): 171–216.

Buchheit, M., M. A. Jeusfeld, W. Nutt, and M. Staudt. (1994). Subsumption between queries to object-oriented databases. In K. Jeffery, M. Jarke, and J. Bubenko, Eds., *Advances in Database Technology—EDBT-94. 4th International Conference on Extending Database Technology.* Cambridge, pp. 15–22.

Donini, F. M., M. Lenzerini, D. Nardi, and W. Nutt. (1991). Tractable concept languages. In *Proceedings of the 12th International Joint Conference on Artificial Intelligence (IJCAI-91).* Sydney, pp. 458–465.

Fikes, R. E., and T. Kehler. (1985). The role of frame-based representation in knowledge representation and reasoning. *Communications of the ACM* 28(9): 904–920.

Hayes, P. J. (1980). The logic of frames. In D. Metzing, Ed., *Frame Conceptions and Text Understanding.* Berlin: deGruyter, pp. 46–61.

Heinsohn, J., D. Kudenko, B. Nebel, and H.-J. Profitlich. (1994). An empirical analysis of terminological representation systems. *Artificial Intelligence* 68(2): 367–397.

Minsky, M. (1975). A framework for representing knowledge. In P. Winston, Ed., *The Psychology of Computer Vision.* New York: McGraw-Hill, pp. 211–277.

Nebel, B. (1990). Terminological reasoning is inherently intractable. *Artificial Intelligence* 43: 235–249.

Nebel, B., and G. Smolka. (1991). Attributive description formalisms . . . and the rest of the world. In O. Herzog and C.-R. Rollinger, Eds., *Text Understanding in* LILOG. Berlin: Springer, pp. 439–452.

Schild, K. (1991). A correspondence theory for terminological logics: preliminary report. In *Proceedings of the 12th International Joint Conference on Artificial Intelligence (IJCAI-91).* Sydney, pp. 466–471.

Schmidt-Schauss, M. (1989). Subsumption in KL-ONE is undecidable. In R. Brachman, H. J. Levesque, and R. Reiter, Eds., *Principles of Knowledge Representation and Reasoning: Proceedings of the 1st International Conference (KR-89)*. Toronto, pp. 421–431.

Schmidt-Schauss, M., and G. Smolka. (1991). Attributive concept descriptions with complements. *Artificial Intelligence* 48: 1–26.

Selman, B., and H. J. Levesque. (1993). The complexity of path-based defeasible inheritance. *Artificial Intelligence* 62: 303–339.

Touretzky, D. S. (1986). *The Mathematics of Inheritance Systems*. Los Altos, CA: Morgan Kaufmann.

Frame Problem

From its humble origins labeling a technical annoyance for a particular AI formalism, the term *frame problem* has grown to cover issues confronting broader research programs in AI. In philosophy, the term has come to encompass allegedly fundamental, but merely superficially related, objections to computational models of mind in AI and beyond.

The original frame problem appears within the SITUATION CALCULUS for representing a changing world. In such systems there are "axioms" about changes conditional on prior occurrences—that pressing a switch changes the illumination of a lamp, that selling the lamp changes who owns it, and so on. Unfortunately, because inferences are to be made solely by deduction, axioms are needed for purported *non*changes—that pressing the switch does not change the owner, that selling the lamp does not change its illumination, and so on. Without such "frame axioms," a system is unable strictly to deduce that any states *persist*. The resulting problem is to do without huge numbers of frame axioms potentially relating *each* representable occurrence to *each* representable nonchange.

A common response is to handle nonchanges *implicitly* by allowing the system to assume *by default* that a state persists, unless there is an axiom specifying that it is changed by an occurrence, given surrounding conditions. Because such assumptions are not *deducible* from the axioms of change (even given surrounding conditions), and because the licensed conclusions are not *cumulative* as evidence is added, the frame problem helps motivate the development of special NONMONOTONIC LOGICS intended to minimize the assumptions that must be *retracted* given further evidence. This is related to discussions of defeasibility and *ceteris paribus* reasoning in epistemology and philosophy of science (e.g., Harman 1986).

A related challenge is to determine *which* assumptions to retract when necessary, as in the "Yale Shooting Problem" (Hanks and McDermott 1986). Let a system assume by default (1) that live creatures remain alive, and (2) that loaded guns remain loaded. Confront it with this information: Fred is alive, then a gun is loaded, then, after a delay, the gun is fired at Fred. If assumption (2) is in force through the delay, Fred probably violates (1). But equally, if assumption (1) is in force after the shooting, the gun probably violates (2). Why is (2) the more natural assumption to enforce? Some favor (2) because the delay occurs *before* the shooting (e.g., Shoham 1988). Others favor (2) because there is no represented *reason* to believe it violated, although the shooting provides some reason for believing (1) violated (e.g., Morgenstern 1996; cf. philosophical discussions of inference to the best EXPLANATION, e.g., Thagard 1988). Work continues in this vein, seeking to formalize the relevant temporal and rational notions, and to insure that the strategies apply more broadly than the situation calculus.

Another approach to the frame problem seeks to remain within the strictures of classical (monotonic) logic (Reiter 1991). In most circumstances, it avoids the use of huge *numbers* of axioms about nonchanges, but at the cost of using hugely and implausibly *bold* axioms about nonchanges. For example, it is assumed that all the possible causes of a certain kind of effect are known, or that all the actual events or actions operating on a given situation are known.

Some philosophers of mind maintain that the original frame problem portends deeper problems for traditional AI, or at least for cognitive science more broadly. (Unless otherwise mentioned, the relevant papers of the authors cited may be found in Pylyshyn 1987.) Daniel Dennett wonders how to ignore information *obviously irrelevant to one's goals*, as one ignores many obvious nonchanges. John Haugeland wonders how to keep track of *salient side effects* without constantly checking for them. This includes the "ramification" and "qualification" problems of AI; see Morgenstern (1996) for a survey. Jerry Fodor wonders how to avoid the use of *"kooky" concepts* that render intuitive nonchanges as changes —for instance, "fridgeon" which applies to physical particles if and only if Fodor's fridge is on, so that Fodor can "change" the entire universe simply by unplugging his fridge. AI researchers, including Drew McDermott and Pat Hayes, protest that these further issues are unconnected to the original frame problem.

Nevertheless, the philosophers' challenges must be met somehow if human cognition is to be understood in computational terms (see CAUSAL REASONING). Exotic suggestions involve mental IMAGERY as opposed to a LANGUAGE OF THOUGHT (Haugeland, cf. Janlert in AI), nonrepresentational practical skills (Dreyfus and Dreyfus), and emotion-induced temporary modularity (de Sousa 1987, chap. 7). The authors of the Yale Shooting Problem argue, as well, against the hegemony of logical deduction — whether classical or nonmonotonic— in AI simulations of commonsense reasoning. More conservative proposed solutions appeal to HEURISTIC SEARCH techniques and ideas about MEMORY long familiar in AI and cognitive psychology (Lormand, in Ford and Pylyshyn 1996; Morgenstern 1996 provides an especially keen survey of AI proposals).

See also EMOTIONS; FRAME-BASED SYSTEMS; KNOWLEDGE REPRESENTATION; PROPOSITIONAL ATTITUDES; SCHEMATA; SITUATEDNESS/EMBEDDEDNESS

—*Eric Lormand*

References

de Sousa, R. (1987). *The Rationality of Emotion*. Cambridge, MA: MIT Press.

Ford, K., and Z. Pylyshyn, Eds. (1996). *The Robot's Dilemma Revisited.* Norwood, NJ: Ablex.

Hanks, S., and D. McDermott. (1986). Default reasoning, non-monotonic logic, and the frame problem. *Proceedings of the American Association for Artificial Intelligence* 328-333.

Harman, G. (1986). *Change in View.* Cambridge, MA: MIT Press.

Morgenstern, L. (1996). The problem with solutions to the frame problem. In K. Ford and Z. Pylyshyn, Eds., (1996), pp. 99–133.

Pylyshyn, Z., Ed. (1987). *The Robot's Dilemma.* Norwood, NJ: Ablex.

Reiter, R. (1991). The frame problem in the situation calculus: a simple solution (sometimes) and a completeness result for goal regression. In V. Lifschitz, Ed., *Artificial Intelligence and Mathematical Theory of Computation: Papers in Honor of John McCarthy.* Boston: Academic Press, pp. 359–380.

Shoham, Y. (1988). *Reasoning about Change.* Cambridge, MA: MIT Press.

Thagard, P. (1988). *Computational Philosophy of Science.* Cambridge, MA: MIT Press.

Frege, Gottlob

Gottlob Frege (1848–1925) was a professional mathematician who, together with Bertrand Russell, is considered to be one of the two grandfathers of modern analytic philosophy. However, the importance of his work extends far beyond the field of philosophy. Frege first introduced the concepts of modern quantificational LOGIC (1879). Indeed, with apologies to C. S. Pierce, it is no exaggeration to call modern quantificational logic Frege's discovery. Frege was also the first to present a formal system in the modern sense in which it was possible to carry out complex mathematical investigations (cf. FORMAL SYSTEMS, PROPERTIES OF).

In addition to contemporary, second-order quantificational logic, a host of logical and semantical techniques occur explicitly for the first time in his work. In Part III of his 1879 work, he introduced the notion of the ancestral of a relation, which yields a logical characterization of one important notion of mathematical sequence; for example, the ancestral can be used to define the notion of natural number. Indeed, the ancestral provides a general technique for transforming an inductive definition of a concept into an explicit one (Dedekind was the codiscoverer of this notion). Frege's later work was also of logico-semantical significance. The "smooth-breathing" operator of his *Grund-gesetze der Arithmetik*, a variable binding device for the formation of complex names for extensions of functional expressions, is the inspiration for lambda abstraction. The brilliant semantic discussion in Part I, though hindered by the lack of an analysis of the consequence relation, nonetheless anticipated many future developments in logic and semantics. For instance, Frege's hierarchy of functions (see Dummett 1973: chap. 3) could be taken as the catalyst for CATEGORIAL GRAMMAR. Even the influential technique of treating two-place functional expressions as denoting functions from objects to one-place functions described in Schoenfinkel (1924) is anticipated by Frege in his discussion of the extensions of two-place functional expressions (1893: §36).

Other ideas of Frege have also had a tremendous impact on research in the cognitive sciences. Perhaps the most important of these is the distinction between sense and reference, which occurs in his 1892 paper, "On Sense and Reference," the defining article of the analytic tradition in philosophy (see SENSE AND REFERENCE for an extended discussion). In that paper, he also gave the first modern informal semantical analysis of PROPOSITIONAL ATTITUDES and introduced the notion of presupposition into the literature (though he introduced the negation test for presupposition, it is clear that he was unaware of the Projection Problem; see PRESUPPOSITION). His 1918 essay "Thoughts" contains a sophisticated discussion of indexicality (cf. INDEXICALS AND DEMONSTRATIVES). Though some of the students of BRENTANO also made distinctions like the one between sense and reference, and even had interesting discussions of indexicals and demonstratives (e.g., Husserl 1903: Book VI), none of them achieved the conceptual clarity of Frege on these topics. Furthermore, Frege's conception of thoughts as structured in a way similar to sentences is a precursor to one aspect of Fodor's (1975) LANGUAGE OF THOUGHT, though Frege's conception of the ontology of thoughts as abstract, mind independent entities, much like numbers and sets, is incompatible with a Fodorian construal of them, and indeed with much of what is said on the matter in the philosophy of mind today.

Though Frege's ideas and discoveries have clearly had a profound effect on subsequent research in philosophy, computer science, and linguistics, his life's project, logicism, is usually considered to be a failure (for an influential defense of part of Frege's version of logicism, see Wright 1983). Logicism is the doctrine that arithmetic is reducible to logic. Frege announced this project in his *Foundations of Arithmetic,* which contained the most sophisticated discussion of the concept of number in the history of philosophy, together with an informal description of how the logicist program could be carried out. In his Magnum Opus, *Grundgesetze der Arithmetik (Basic Laws of Arithmetic)* (1893, 1903), Frege tried to carry out the logicist program in full detail, attempting to derive the basic laws of arithmetic, and indeed analysis, within a formal system whose axioms he believed expressed laws of logic. Unfortunately, the theory was inconsistent. This discovery, by Bertrand Russell, devastated Frege, and essentially ended his career as a mathematician. Recent research has shown, however, that there is a great deal of interest that is salvageable from his mathematical work (Wright 1983; and the essays in Demopoulos 1995).

Frege is not merely of historical interest for the student of cognitive science. Rather than being interested in how we in fact reason, he is interested in how we ought to reason, and rather than being interested in the biological component of mentality, he is interested in the abstract structure of thought. Studying his works provides a useful curative for those who need to be reminded about the public and normative aspects of the notions that concern cognitive science.

—*Jason C. Stanley*

References

Demopoulos, W., Ed. (1995). *Frege's Philosophy of Mathematics.* Cambridge, MA: Harvard University Press.

Dummett, M. (1973). *Frege: Philosophy of Language.* London: Duckworth.

Fodor, J. (1975). *The Language of Thought.* New York: Thomas Crowell.

Frege, G. (1879). Begriffsschrift: a formula language, modeled upon that of arithmetic, for pure thought. In Jean Van Heihenoort, Ed., 1967, *From Frege to Goedel: A Source Book in Mathematical Logic, 1879–1931.* Cambridge: Harvard University Press, pp. 5–82.

Frege, G. (1884/1980). *The Foundations of Arithmetic.* Evanston, IL: Northwestern University Press.

Frege, G. (1891). On Sense and Reference. In Peter, Geach, and Max Black, Eds., (1993). *Translations from the Philosophical Writings of G Frege.* Oxford: Blackwell, pp. 56–78 (there translated as "On Sense and Meaning").

Frege, G. (1893, 1903/1966). *Grundgesetze der Arithmetik.* Hildesheim: Georg Olms Verlag.

Frege, G. (1918). Thoughts. In Brian McGuiness, Ed., 1984, *Collected Papers.* Oxford: Blackwell, pp. 351–372.

Frege, G. (1984). *Collected Papers.* Brian McGuiness, Ed. Oxford: Blackwell.

Husserl, E. (1903/1980). *Logische Untersuchungen.* Tuebingen: Max Niemeyer.

Schoenfinkel, M. (1924). On the building blocks of mathematical logic. In J. Van Heihenoort, Ed., 1967, *From Frege to Goedel: A Source Book in Mathematical Logic, 1879–1931.* Cambridge, MA: Harvard University Press, pp. 357–366.

Wright, C. (1983). *Frege's Conception of Numbers as Objects.* Aberdeen: Aberdeen University Press.

Freud, Sigmund

A prolific and gifted writer, whose broad learning extended from neurophysiology and EVOLUTION to the literature of six languages, Sigmund Freud (1826–1939) was one of the most influential scientists of the late nineteenth and early twentieth centuries. He was also one of the most controversial scientists of any time, so much so that both his critics and admirers have occasionally succumbed to the temptation to deny that he was a scientist at all.

Freud's positive and negative reputations flow from the same source—the extraordinary scope of his theories. Although the notions of unconscious ideas and processes did not originate with Freud, having philosophical antecedents in Gottfried Leibniz's (1646–1716) theory of *petites perceptions* and psychiatric antecedents in the work of, *inter alia,* Pierre Janet (1859–1947), Freud made them the centerpiece of his complex theory of the mind. Unlike other psychiatrists, Freud took unconscious ideas and processes to be critical in explaining the behavior of all people in all circumstances and not merely the outré actions of psychotics. Unlike Leibniz and his followers, Freud presented unconscious ideas not merely as a theoretical necessity, but as the key to human action. Through his spirited defense of the necessity and importance of unconscious ideas and processes, he gave these concepts theoretical respectability, almost in spite of their associations with him.

The explanatory scope of unconscious ideas and processes was enormous for Freud, because he saw psychoanalysis (see PSYCHOANALYSIS, CONTEMPORARY VIEWS OF and PSYCHOANALYSIS, HISTORY OF) as bridging the gap between the biological and the "human" sciences. Freud's early training in neurophysiology led him to try to ground psychological theorizing in the known structures of the brain. His incomplete manuscript, "Project for a Scientific Psychology" attempted to relate specific psychological functions, such as learning and memory, to recently discovered properties of the neurons. In this respect, his methodological principles exactly paralleled the current view in cognitive science that psychological theorizing must be consistent with and informed by the most recent knowledge in neuroscience. Freud was also an avid supporter of DARWIN and was explicit in stating that his theory of sexual and self-preservative instincts was firmly rooted in (evolutionary) biology. Prototypical of his synthetic approach to knowledge, he made a bold conjecture about an important relation between the findings of neurophysiology and evolutionary biology. If, as nearly all psychologists agreed, the mind functioned as a reflex, then it required constant stimulation, and if, as Darwin argued, the sexual instinct is one of the two most important forces governing animal life, then these findings could be brought together under a more comprehensive theory that sexual instincts (libido) drove the nervous system. Although Freud, his disciples, and his critics often present libido theory as an extrapolation from the sexual difficulties of his patients, its real strength and appeal came from its plausible biological premises.

Thanks to Darwin's influence, sexuality also played an important role in the social sciences of the late nineteenth century. A methodological imperative of evolutionary anthropology and sociology was to connect sophisticated human achievements to "primitive" conditions shared with animals, and sexual behavior was the most obvious point of connection. Given these trends in social science, Freud was able to make "upward" connections between psychoanalysis and the social sciences, as well as "downward" connections to neurophysiology and biology. In his efforts to find links among all the "mental" sciences, Freud's methodological approach again bears a striking resemblance to the interdisciplinary emphasis of current cognitive science. This approach was also the basis of the tremendous appeal of psychoanalysis: he believed that he had a theory that could provide biologically grounded explanations, in terms of sexual and self-preservative instincts and the various mental processes that operated on them, for everything from psychotic symptoms, dreams, and jokes to cultural practices such as art and religion.

Freud's theories of CONSCIOUSNESS and the EMOTIONS were also the product of an interdisciplinary synthesis between psychiatry and philosophy. Individuals whose behavior was driven by natural, but unconscious, emotional forces needed treatment in order to gain control of their lives by bringing the forces that govern them to consciousness. This was possible, Freud believed, because affective states were also cognitive and so could be made conscious through their ideational components. Although the *Project* offered some speculations about the qualitative character of consciousness, Freud's later approach was functionalist. Conscious ideas differed from the unconscious, because they could be expressed verbally, because they were subject to rational constraints such as consistency, and because they could interact with sensory evidence.

Although Freud regarded the consilience of psychoanalysis with the biological and social sciences as the strongest argument in its favor, important changes in both the biological and social sciences undermined the plausibility of his basic assumptions about how mental processes worked. Rather than alter the scientific foundations of psychoanalysis, he continued to try to increase its scope and influence, leading to charges of disingenuousness and even pseudoscience. Despite Freud's tarnished reputation, many of his central substantive and methodological assumptions about studying the mind have reemerged with the rise of cognitive science, in particular, the assumption (from his teacher BRENTANO) that mental states are intentional (see INTENTIONALITY) and must be understood in terms of their contents, but that they are likewise physical and must be related to neuroscience, the assumption (which he described as an extension of KANT) that most mental processes are unconscious, the view that cognition and emotion are not separate faculties, but deeply intertwined aspects of mentality, and the basic methodological assumption that the biological and "human" sciences must learn from each other, because the ultimate goal is to develop a comprehensive theory of the social, psychological, and physical aspects of mentality. Further, although its emphasis on input-output computation has given cognitive science a synchronic time scale for much of its history, recent work on ARTIFICIAL LIFE and EVOLUTIONARY COMPUTATION reintroduces the sort of diachronic or genetic approach that Freud thought was essential in understanding the complexities of a mentality that was produced via individual development and the evolution of the species.

See also FOLK PSYCHOLOGY; FUNCTIONALISM; UNITY OF SCIENCE

—*Patricia Kitcher*

References

Ellenberger, H. (1970). *The Discovery of Consciousness.* New York: Basic Books.

Erdelyi, M. H. (1985). *Psychoanalysis: Freud's Cognitive Psychology.* New York: W. H. Freeman.

Freud, S. (1966). Project for a Scientific Psychology. Preliminary Communication (to *Studies in Hysteria,* with (Josef Brauer)). Three Essays on Sexuality. The Unconscious. Instincts and their Vicissitudes. The Ego and the Id. All can be found in *The Complete Psychological Works of Sigmund Freud.* James Strachey., Ed. 24, vol. London: The Hogarth Press.

Kitcher, P. (1992). *Freud's Dream: A Complete Interdisciplinary Science of Mind.* Cambridge, MA: Bradford/MIT Press.

Sulloway, F. (1994). *Freud: Biologist of the Mind.* New York: Basic Books.

Functional Decomposition

Functional decomposition is the analysis of the activity of a system as the product of a set of subordinate functions performed by independent subsystems, each with its own characteristic domain of application. It assumes that there are a variety of functionally independent units, with intrinsically determined functions, that are minimally interactive. Functional decomposition plays important roles in engineering, physiology, biology, and in artificial intelligence. Functional morphologists, for example, distinguish the causal or functional roles of structures within organisms, the extent to which one structure may be altered without changing overall function, and the effects of these structures for evolutionary change. Within cognitive science, the assumption is that there are a variety of mechanisms underlying our mental life, which are domain specific and functionally independent. The classical distinction in DESCARTES between understanding, imagination and will is a functional decomposition, which postulates at least three independent faculties responsible for specific mental functions; likewise, the distinction drawn by KANT between sensation, judgment, understanding, and reason offers a partitioning of our mental faculties based on their cognitive functions, and is equally one that postulates a variety of independent faculties responsible for specific mental operations. In more recent psychological work, the distinction between sensory stores, short-term MEMORY, and long-term memory elaborated by Richard Atkinson and Richard Shiffrin (1968) is a functional decomposition of memory, based on their domains of application (for a classic source, see Neisser 1967).

Functional decomposition typically assumes a hierarchical organization, though a hierarchical organization is consistent with different modes of organization. Thus, the mind is conceived as having a modular organization (cf. MODULARITY OF MIND), with a variety of faculties, each with independent, intrinsically determined functions. Each of those modules in turn may have a modular organization, with a variety of independent, intrinsically determined functions. Sensory systems are relatively independent of one another, and independent of memory, language, and cognition. Language in turn may be taken to consist of a variety of relatively independent subsystems (cf. MODULARITY AND LANGUAGE), including modules responsible for PHONOLOGY, PHONETICS, SEMANTICS, and SYNTAX. The extent to which a hierarchical organization, or functional independence, is realistic can be decided only empirically, by seeing the extent to which we can approximate or explain system behavior by assuming it.

Functional decomposition is easily illustrated by appealing to the understanding of language. In the early nineteenth century, Franz Joseph Gall (1758–1828) defended the view that the mind consists of a variety of "organs" or "centers," each subserving specific intellectual or moral (that is, practical) functions, with dedicated locations in the cerebral hemispheres. These intellectual and moral functions were sharply distinguished at a higher level from the "vital" functions and affections that Gall located in the "lower" portions of the brain, and the specific functions in turn were distinguished from one another. There were differences between Gall and his fellow phrenologists concerning the number and characterization of the specific faculties, but within the intellectual faculties, phrenologists typically distinguished broadly between the external senses, various "perceptive" faculties (including faculties for perceiving weight, color, tune, and language, among others), and the "reflective" faculties constitutive of reason. The primary faculties were the species of intellection, and they were assumed to belong to specific organs in the brain. Gall held an extreme view, assuming that the basic functions were strictly limited in application, invariable in their operation, and wholly independent of the activities of other faculties. That is, he assumed that the mind was simply an aggregate of its independent functions and that there was no overlap or interaction between these organs. Because he recognized no interaction between the faculties, complex abilities became simply the aggregates of simple abilities. Gall assumed, in other words, that the mind was both hierarchical and aggregative, or simply decomposable.

Paul Pierre BROCA (1824–1880) was also a defender of "organology," retaining both the discrete localizations of the phrenologists and the view that the size of organs was responsible for differing mental abilities. Following Jean Baptiste Bouillard (1796–1881), Broca emphasized the importance of dysfunction in determining functional organization. By August 1861, Broca had described in some detail the anatomical changes accompanying a disorder of speech that he called "aphemia," and that we would describe as an APHASIA. The patient, known as "Tan," lost the ability to speak by the time he was thirty, and over the years his case degenerated. Broca relied on interviews with the hospital staff to discover that Tan's initial "loss of articulate language" was due to a focal lesion in the frontal lobe. Broca's conclusion was that there were a variety of "organs" corresponding to discrete mental functions. Karl Wernicke (1848–1905) subsequently elaborated the basic model, reframing it in terms of an associationistic psychology rather than a faculty psychology and distinguishing sensory and motor aphasias. Wernicke concluded that there was a series of discrete loci mediating the comprehension and production of speech. On the basis of clinical observations, Wernicke concluded there were three distinctive "centers" associated with language use: a center for the acoustic representations of speech, a center for motor representations of speech, and a center for concepts typically mediating between the two. Disruptions of the various associations between these centers resulted in the various aphasias. The resulting functional decomposition for language use thus had at least three components, and a linear organization: the output of one "organ" serves as the input for the next, though the function performed or realized by each module is intrinsically determined. This basic model has since been elaborated by a number of clinical neurologists, including Norman GESCHWIND. The organization is no longer aggregative, but sequential, with relatively independent functional units. This is near decomposability.

A commitment to functional decomposition has continued in a variety of forms in more recent work in cognitive science, including the new "organology" of Noam Chomsky (1980), the "modularity" defended by Jerry Fodor (1983), and the FUNCTIONALISM of William Lycan (1987). Steven Pinker (1994), for example, argues that language is an ability that is relatively independent of cognitive abilities in general. The clear implication of such independence is that

it should be possible to disrupt linguistic abilities without impairing cognition, and vice versa. The studies of aphasia exhibit such patterns. A commitment to some form of functional decomposition or modularity might seem inevitable when dealing with a phenomenon as complex as mental life. Herbert Simon (1969) has emphasized the importance of simple decomposability and near decomposability, as well as of hierarchical organization in complex systems. In explaining the behavior of a complex system, it is often possible to establish independent functional characterizations for components, ignoring both the contributions of other components at the same level as well as the influences operative at higher or lower levels. This is, however, not always true, and the cases are often more complex than they might initially appear.

Numerous examples of functional decomposition are available from recent work in cognitive science. It is common, as noted, to analyze memory into distinctive subsystems. Commonly, it is assumed that there are at least two stages, presumably with discrete physiological mechanisms: the first process is short-lived, lasting from minutes to hours, and the second is of indefinite duration. Conventionally, this distinction between short-term and long-term memory is assayed by recall tests. This is by no means the only decomposition of memory, and is anything but unproblematic; more specifically, the experimental evidence leaves it unclear whether the distinction between short- and long-term memory is a distinction between modules, or modes of processing, and whether short-term memory is a unitary entity. Experimentation in memory typically involves some measure of retention based on recall or recognition of some predetermined material, and more recently using dual tasks in parallel. This research has led to a variety of ways of understanding the organization of memory, including distinctions between working memory, semantic memory, and declarative memory. There is currently no clear consensus concerning the most appropriate theory, and no model that naturally accommodates the entire range of the phenomena. In a similar way, linguistic competence is generally understood as the product of a set of distinct subsystems. Wernicke's distinction between comprehension and production has been replaced with distinct processes involved in language use, typically distinguishing between semantic and syntactic functions. Again, this decomposition is not unproblematic, and there is some evidence suggesting that such decompositions do not yield functionally independent subsystems.

See also COGNITIVE ARCHITECTURE; DOMAIN SPECIFICITY; HEMISPHERIC SPECIALIZATION; IMPLICIT VS. EXPLICIT MEMORY; LANGUAGE, NEURAL BASIS OF; MEMORY, HUMAN NEUROPSYCHOLOGY

—*Robert C. Richardson*

References

Atkinson, R., and R. Shiffrin. (1968). Human memory: A proposed system and its control processes. In K. W. Spence and J. T. Spence, Eds., *The Psychology of Learning and Motivation,* vol. 2. New York: Academic Press.

Broca, P. (1861*a*). Perte de la parole. *Bulletins de la Société Anthropologie* 2: 235–238.

Broca, P. (1861*b*). Remarques sur le siège de la faculté suivies d'une observation d'aphémie. *Bulletin de la Société Anatomique de Paris* 6: 343–357.

Chomsky, N. (1980). *Rules and Representations.* New York: Columbia University Press.

Fodor, J. A. (1983). *Modularity of Mind.* Cambridge, MA: MIT Press/Bradford Books.

Lycan, W. (1987). *Consciousness.* Cambridge, MA: MIT Press/Bradford Books.

Neisser, U. (1967). *Cognitive Psychology.* New York: Appleton-Century-Crofts.

Pinker, S. (1974). *The Language Instinct.* New York: William Morrow.

Simon, H. A. (1969). *The Sciences of the Artificial.* Cambridge, MA: MIT Press.

Wernicke, C. (1874). *Der Aphasische Symptomcomplex: Eine Psychologische Studie auf Anatomischer Basis.* Breslau: Cohen and Weigert.

Further Readings

Amundson, R., and G. V. Lauder. (1994). Function without purpose: the uses of causal role function in evolutionary biology. *Biology and Philosophy* 9: 443–470.

Bechtel, W., and R. C. Richardson. (1993). *Discovering Complexity.* Princeton: Princeton University Press.

Bradley, D. C., M. F. Garrett, and E. Zurif. (1980). Syntactic deficits in Broca's aphasia. In D. Caplan, Ed., *Biological Studies of Mental Processes.* Cambridge, MA: MIT Press, pp. 269–286.

Cummins, R. (1983). *The Nature of Psychological Explanation.* Cambridge, MA: MIT Press.

Gregory, R. L. (1961). The brain as an engineering problem. In W. H. Thorpe and O. L. Zangwill, Eds., *Current Problems in Animal Behaviour.* Cambridge: Cambridge University Press, pp. 307–330.

Gregory, R. L. (1968). Models and the localization of function in the central nervous system. In C. R. Evans and A. D. J. Robertson, Eds., *Key Papers: Cybernetics.* London: Butterworths.

Gregory, R. L. (1981). *Mind in Science.* Cambridge: Cambridge University Press.

Johnson-Laird, P. N. (1983). *Mental Models.* Cambridge: Harvard University Press.

Schacter, D. L. (1993). Memory. In M. I. Posner, Ed., *Foundations of Cognitive Science.* Cambridge, MA: MIT Press, pp. 683–725.

Functional Explanation

See EXPLANATION; FUNCTIONAL DECOMPOSITION

Functional Grammar

See LEXICAL FUNCTIONAL GRAMMAR

Functional Role Semantics

According to functional role semantics (FRS), the meaning of a MENTAL REPRESENTATION is its role in the cognitive life of the agent, for example in perception, thought and DECISION MAKING. It is an extension of the well-known "use" theory of meaning, according to which the meaning of a word is its use in communication and more generally, in social interaction. FRS supplements external use by including the role of a symbol inside a computer or a brain. The uses appealed to are not just actual, but also counterfactual: not only what effects a thought does have, but also what effects it would have had if stimuli or other states had differed. The view has arisen separately in philosophy (where it is sometimes called "inferential," or "functional" role semantics) and in cognitive science (where it is sometimes called "procedural semantics"). The view originated with Wittgenstein and Sellars, but the source in contemporary philosophy is a series of papers by Harman (see his 1987) and Field (1977). Other proponents in philosophy have included Block, Horwich, Loar, McGinn, and Peacocke; in cognitive science, they include Woods, Miller, and Johnson-Laird.

FRS is motivated in part by the fact that many terms seem definable only in conjunction with one another, and not in terms outside of the circle they form. For example, in learning the theoretical terms of Newtonian mechanics—force, mass, kinetic energy, momentum, and so on—we do not learn definitions outside the circle. There are no such definitions. We learn the terms by learning how to use them in our thought processes, especially in solving problems. Indeed, FRS explains the fact that modern scientists cannot understand the phlogiston theory without learning elements of an old language that expresses the old concepts. The functional role of, for example, "principle" as used by phlogiston theorists is very different from the functional role of any term or complex of terms of modern physics, and hence we must acquire some approximation of the eighteenth century functional roles if we want to understand their ideas.

FRS seems to give a plausible account of the meanings of the logical connectives. For example, we could specify the meaning of "and" by noting that certain inferences—for example, the inferences from sentences *p* and *q* to *p and q*, and the inference from *p and q* to *p*—have a special status (they are "primitively compelling" in Peacocke's 1992 terminology). But it may be said that the logical connectives are a poor model for language and for concepts more generally. One of the most important features of our CONCEPTS is that they refer—that is, that they pick out objects in the world.

In part for this reason, many theorists prefer a two-factor version of FRS. On this view, meaning consists of an internal, "narrow" aspect of meaning—which is handled by functional roles that are within the body—and an external referential/truth-theoretic aspect of meaning. According to the external factor, "Superman flies" and "Clark Kent flies" are semantically the same because Superman = Clark Kent; the internal factor is what distinguishes them. But the internal factor counts "Water is more greenish than bluish" as semantically the same in my mouth as in the mouth of my twin on TWIN EARTH. In this case, it is the external factor that distinguishes them.

Two-factor theories gain some independent plausibility from the need of them to account for indexical thought and assertions, assertions whose truth depends on facts about when and where they were made and by whom. For example, suppose that you and I say "I am ill." One aspect of the meaning of "I" is common to us, another aspect is different. What is the same is that our terms are both used according to the rule that they refer to the speaker; what is different is that the speakers are different. White (1982) generalized this distinction to apply to the internal and external factors for all referring expressions, not just INDEXICALS.

In a two-factor account, the functional roles stop at the skin in sense and effector organs; they are "short-arm" roles. But FRS can also be held in a one-factor version in which the functional roles reach out into the world—these roles are "long-arm." Harman (1987) has advocated a one-factor account that includes in the long-arm roles much of the machinery that a two-factor theorist includes in the referential factor, but without any commitment to a separable narrow aspect of meaning. Harman's approach and the two-factor theory show that the general approach of FRS is actually compatible with metaphysical accounts of reference such as the causal theory or teleological theories, for they can be taken to be partial specifications of roles.

Actual functional roles involve errors, even dispositions to err. For example, in applying the word *dog* to candidate dogs, one will make errors, for example in mistaking coyotes for dogs (see Fodor 1987). This problem arises in one form or another for all naturalistic theories of truth and reference, but in the case of FRS it applies to erroneous inferences as well as to erroneous applications of words to things. Among all the conceptual connections of a symbol with other symbols, or (in the case of long-arm roles) with the world, which ones are correct and which ones are errors? One line of reply is to attempt to specify some sort of naturalistic idealization that specifies roles that abstract away from error, in the way that laws of free fall abstract away from friction.

FRS is often viewed as essentially holistic, but the FRS theorist does have the option of regarding some proper subset of the functional roles in which an expression participates as the ones that constitute its meaning. One natural and common view of what distinguishes the meaning-constitutive roles is that they are "analytic." Proponents of FRS are thus viewed as having to choose between accepting holism and accepting that this distinction between the analytic and synthetic is scientifically respectable, a claim that has been challenged by Quine. Indeed, Fodor and Lepore (1992) argue that, lacking an analytic/synthetic distinction, FRS is committed to semantic holism, regarding the meaning of any expression as depending on its inferential relations to every other expression in the language. This, they argue, amounts to the denial of a psychologically viable account of meaning.

Proponents of FRS can reply that the view is not committed to regarding what is meaning constitutive as analytic. In terms of our earlier two-factor account, they can, for example, regard the meaning-constitutive roles as those that are primitively compelling, or perhaps as ones that are explanatorily basic: they are the roles that explain other roles (see Horwich 1994). Another approach to accommodating holism with a psychologically viable account of meaning is to substitute close enough similarity of meaning for strict

identity of meaning. That may be all we need for making sense of psychological generalizations, interpersonal comparisons, and the processes of reasoning and changing one's mind.

See also INDIVIDUALISM; NARROW CONTENT; REFERENCE, THEORIES OF; SEMANTICS; SENSE AND REFERENCE

—*Ned Block*

References

Block, N. (1987). Functional role and truth conditions. *Proceedings of the Aristotelian Society* LXI: 157–181.

Field, H. (1977). Logic, meaning and conceptual role. *Journal of Philosophy* 69: 379–408.

Fodor, J., and E. LePore. (1992). *Holism: A Shoppers' Guide*. Oxford: Blackwell.

Harman, G. (1987). (Non-solipsistic) Conceptual Role Semantics. In E. Lepore, Ed., *New Directions in Semantics*. London: Academic Press.

Horwich, P. (1994). What it is like to be a deflationary theory of meaning. In E. Villanueva, Ed., *Philosophical Issues 5: Truth and Rationality*. Ridgeview, pp. 133–154.

White, S. (1982). Partial character and the language of thought. *Pacific Philosophical Quarterly* 63: 347–365.

Further Readings

Block, N. (1986). Advertisement for a semantics for psychology. *Midwest Studies in Philosophy* 10.

Devitt, M. (1996). *Coming to Our Senses*. New York: Cambridge University Press.

Fodor, J. (1978). Tom Swift and his procedural grandmother. In *Representations*. Sussex: Harvester.

Fodor, J. (1987). *Psychosemantics*. Cambridge, MA: MIT Press.

Kripke, S. (1982). *Wittgenstein: On Rules and Private Language*. Oxford: Blackwell.

Johnson-Laird, P. (1977). Procedural Semantics. *Cognition* 5: 189–214.

Loar, B. (1981). *Mind and Meaning*. Cambridge: Cambridge University Press.

McGinn, C. (1982). The structure of content. In A. Woodfield, Ed., *Thought and Object*. Oxford: Clarendon Press.

Miller, G., and P. Johnson-Laird. (1976). *Language and Perception*. Cambridge, MA: MIT Press.

Peacocke, C. (1992). *A Theory of Concepts*. Cambridge, MA: MIT Press.

Wittgenstein, L. (1953). *The Philosophical Investigations*. New York: Macmillan.

Woods, W. (1981). Procedural Semantics as a theory of meaning. In A. Joshi, B. Webber, and I. Sag, Eds., *Elements of Discourse Understanding*. Cambridge, MA: MIT Press.

Functionalism

Compare neurons and neutrons to planets and pendula. They all cluster into kinds or categories conforming to nomic generalizations and comporting with scientific investigation. However, whereas all neurons and neutrons must be composed of distinctive types of matter structured in ruthlessly precise ways, individual planets and pendula can be made of wildly disparate sorts of differently structured stuff. Neurons and neutrons are examples of physical kinds; planets and pendula exemplify functional kinds. Physical kinds are identified by their material composition, which in turn determines their conformity to the laws of nature. Functional kinds are not identified by their material composition but rather by their activities or tendencies. All planets, no matter the differences in their composition, orbit or tend to. All pendula, no matter the differences in their composition, oscillate or tend to.

What, then, of minds or mental states, kinds that process information and control intelligent activity or behavior? Do they define physical or functional kinds? Naturally occurring minds, at least those most familiar to us, are brains. The human mind is most certainly the human brain; the mammal mind, the mammal brain (Kak 1996). Hence, under the assumption that brains are physical kinds, we might conjecture that all minds must be brains and, therefore, physical kinds. If so, we should study the brain if curious about the mind.

However, perhaps we are misled by our familiar, local and possibly parochial sample of minds. If all the pendula at hand happened to be aluminum, we might, failing to imagine copper ones, mistakenly suppose that pendula must—of *necessity*—be aluminum. Maybe, then, we should ask whether it is *possible* that minds occur in structures other than brains. Might there be silicon Martians capable of reading *Finnegan's Wake* and solving differential equations? Such fabled creatures would have minds although, being silicon instead of carbon, they could not have brains. Moving away from fiction and closer toward fact, what should we make of artificially intelligent devices? They can be liberated from human biochemistry while exhibiting talents that appear to demand the kind of cognition that fuels much of what is psychologically distinctive in human activity.

Possibly, then, some minds are not brains. These minds might be made of virtually any sort of material as long as it should be so organized as to process information, control behavior and generally support the sort of performances indicative of minds. Minds would then be functional, not physical, kinds. Respectively like planets and pendula, minds might arise naturally or artificially. Their coalescing into a single unified kind would be determined by their proclivity to process information and to control behavior independently of the stuff in which individual minds might happen to reside. Terrestrial evolution may here have settled on brains as the local natural solution to the problem of evolving minds. Still, because differing local pressures and opportunities may induce evolution to offer up alternative solutions to the same problem (say, mammals versus marsupials), evolution could develop minds from radically divergent kinds of matter. Should craft follow suit, art might fabricate intelligence in any computational medium. Functionalism, then, is the thesis that minds are functional kinds (Putnam 1960; Armstrong 1968; Lewis 1972; Cummins 1983).

The significance of functionalism for the study of the mind is profound, for it liberates cognitive science from concern with how the mind is embodied or composed. Given functionalism, it may be true that every individual mind is itself a physical structure. Nevertheless, by the lights of functionalism, physical structure is utterly irrelevant to the deep nature of the mind. Consequently, function-alism is foundational to those cognitive sciences that would abstract from details of physical implementation in order to discern principles common to all possible cognizers, thinkers who need not share any physical features immediately relevant to thought. Such a research strategy befriends Artificial Intelligence inasmuch as it attends to algorithms, programs, and computation rather than cortex, ganglia, and neurotransmitters. True, the study of *human or mammalian* cognition might focus on the physical properties of the brain. But if functionalism is true, the most general features of cognition must be independent of neurology.

According to functionalism, a mind is a physical system or device—with a host of possible internal states—normally situated in an environment itself consisting of an array of possible external states. External states can induce changes in such a device's internal states, and fluctuations in these internal states can cause subsequent internal changes determining the device's overt behavior. Standard formulations of functionalism accommodate the mind's management of information by treating the internal, that is, cognitive, states of the device as its representations, symbols, or signs of its world (Dennett 1978; Fodor 1980; Dretske 1981). Hence, disciplined change in internal state amounts to change in representation or manipulation of information.

Some (Pylyshyn 1985), but not all (Lycan 1981), formulations of functionalism model the mind in terms of a TURING machine (Turing 1950), perhaps in the form of a classical digital computer. A Turing machine possesses a segmented tape with segments corresponding to a cognitive device's internal states or representations. The machine is designed to read from and write to segments of the tape according to rules that themselves are sensitive to how the tape may be antecedently marked. If the device is an information processor, the marks on the tape can be viewed as semantically disciplined symbols that resonate to the environment and induce the machine appropriately to respond (Haugeland 1981). For functionalism, then, the mind, like a computer, may process information and control behavior simply by implementing a Turing machine.

In allowing that minds are functional kinds, one supposes that mental state types (for example, believing, desiring, willing, hoping, feeling, and sensing) are themselves functionally characterized. Thus belief, as a type of mental state, would be a kind of mental state with characteristic causes and effects (Fodor 1975; Block and Fodor 1972). The idea can be extended to identify or individuate specific beliefs (Harman 1973; Field 1977). The belief, say, that snow is white might be identified by its unique causal position in the mental economy (see FUNCTIONAL ROLE SEMANTICS). On this model, specific mental states are aligned with the unobservable or theoretical states of science generally and identified by their peculiar potential causal relations.

Although functionalism has been, and remains, the dominant position in the philosophy of mind since at least 1970, it remains an unhappy hostage to several important objections. First, the argument above in favor of functionalism begins with a premise about how it is *possible* for the mind to be realized or implemented outside of the brain. This premise is dramatized by supposing, for example, that it is possible that carbon-free Martians have minds but lack brains. However, what justifies the crucial assumption of the real possibility of brainless, silicon Martian minds?

It is no answer to reply that anything imaginable is possible. For in that case, one can evidently imagine that it is *necessary* that minds are brains. If the imaginable is possible, it would follow that it is *possible* that it is *necessary* that minds are brains. However, on at least one version of modal logic it is axiomatic that whatever is *possibly necessary* is simply *necessary*. Hence, if it is *possible* that it is *necessary* that minds are brains, it is simply *necessary* that minds are brains. This, however, is in flat contradiction to the premise that launches functionalism, namely the premise that it is *possible* that minds are not brains! Evidently, what is desperately wanting here is a reasonable way of justifying premises about what is genuinely possible or what can be known to be possible. Until the functionalist can certify the possibility of a mind without a brain, the argument from such a possibility to the plausibility of functionalism appears disturbingly inconclusive (Maloney 1987).

Beyond this objection to the functionalist program is the worry that functionalism, if unwittingly in the service of a false psychology, could fly in the face of good scientific practice. To see this, suppose that minds are *defined* in terms of current (perhaps popular or folk) psychology and that this psychology turns out, unsurprisingly, to be false. In this case, minds—as defined by a false theory—would not be real, and that would be the deep and true reason why minds are not identical with real physical types such as brains. Nevertheless, a misguided functionalism, because it construes the mind as "whatever satisfies the principles of (false current) psychology," would wrongly bless the discontinuity of mind and brain and insist on the reality of mind disenfranchised from any physical kind. Put differently, our failure to identify phlogiston with any physical kind properly leads us to repudiate phlogiston rather than to elevate it to a functional kind. So too, the objection goes, perhaps our failure to identify the mind with a physical type should lead us to repudiate the mind rather than elevate it to a functional kind (Churchland 1981).

Others object to functionalism charging that it ignores the (presumed) centrality of CONSCIOUSNESS in cognition (Shoemaker 1975; Block 1978; Lewis 1980). They argue that functionally identical persons could differ in how they feel, that is, in their conscious, qualitative, or affective states. For example, you and I might be functionally isomorphic in the presence of a stimulus while we differ in our consciousness of it. You and I might both see the same apple and treat it much the same. Yet, this functional congruence might mask dramatic differences in our color QUALIA, differences that might have no behavioral or functional manifestation. If these conscious, qualitative differences differentiate our mental states, functionalism would seem unable to recognize them.

Finally, mental states are semantically significant representational states. As you play chess, you are thinking *about* the game. You realize that your knight is threatened but that its loss shall ensure the success of the trap you have set. But consider a computer programmed perfectly to emulate you at chess. It is your functional equivalent. Hence, according to functionalism it has the same mental states as do you. But does it think the same as you; does it

realize, genuinely realize in exactly the manner that you do, that its knight is threatened but that the knight's loss ensures ultimate success? Or is the computer a semantically impoverished device designed merely to mimic you and your internal mental states without ever representing its world in anything like the manner in which you represent and recognize your world through your mental states (Searle 1980; Dennett and Searle 1982)? If you and the computer differ in how you represent the world, if you represent the world but the computer does not, then functionalism may have obscured a fundamentally important aspect of our cognition.

See also COMPUTATION AND THE BRAIN; FOLK PSYCHOLOGY; FUNCTIONAL DECOMPOSITION; MENTAL REPRESENTATION; MIND-BODY PROBLEM; PHYSICALISM

—*J. Christopher Maloney*

References

Armstrong, D. (1968). *A Materialist Theory of the Mind.* London: Routledge and Kegan Paul.

Block, N. (1978). Troubles with functionalism. In C. W. Savage, Ed., *Perception and Cognition: Issues in the Philosophy of Science.* Minneapolis: University of Minnesota Press, 9: 261–325.

Block, N., and J. Fodor. (1972). What psychological states are not. *Philosophical Review* 81: 159–181.

Churchland, P. (1981). Eliminative materialism and the propositional attitudes. *Journal of Philosophy* LXXVIII: 67–90.

Cummins, R. (1983). *The Nature of Psychological Explanation.* Cambridge, MA: MIT Press/Bradford Books.

Dennett, D. (1978). *Brainstorms.* Montgomery, VT: Bradford Books.

Dennett, D., and J. Searle. (1982). The myth of the computer: an exchange. *New York Review of Books* June 24: 56–57.

Dretske, F. I. (1981). *Knowledge and the Flow of Information.* Cambridge, MA: Bradford Books/MIT Press.

Field, H. (1977). Mental representations. *Erkenntnis* 13: 9–16.

Fodor, J. (1975). *The Language of Thought.* New York: Thomas Crowell.

Fodor, J. (1980). Methodological solipsism considered as a research strategy in cognitive psychology. *The Behavioral and Brain Sciences* 3: 63–109.

Harman, G. (1973). *Thought.* Princeton: Princeton University Press.

Haugeland, J. (1981). On the nature and plausibility of cognitivism. In J. Haugeland, Ed., *Mind Design.* Cambridge, MA: MIT Press/Bradford Books, pp. 243–281.

Kak, S. C. (1996). Can we define levels of artificial intelligence? *Journal of Intelligent Systems* 6: 133–144.

Lewis, D. (1972). Psychophysical and theoretical identifications. *Australasian Journal of Philosophy* 50: 249–258.

Lewis, D. (1980). Mad pain and martian pain. In N. Block, Ed., *Readings in the Philosophy of Psychology, I.* Cambridge, MA: MIT Press, pp. 216–222.

Lycan, W. (1981). Form, function and feel. *Journal of Philosophy* 78: 24–50.

Maloney, J. C. (1987). *The Mundane Matter of the Mental Language.* Cambridge: Cambridge University Press.

Putnam, H. (1960). Minds and machines. In S. Hook, Ed., *Dimensions of Mind.* New York: N.Y.U. Press. Reprinted along with other relevant papers in Putnam's *Mind, Language and Reality, Philosophical Papers 2.* Cambridge: Cambridge University Press, 1975.

Pylyshyn, Z. (1985). *Computation and Cognition: Toward a Foundation for Cognitive Science.* Cambridge, MA: MIT Press/ Bradford Books.

Searle, J. (1980). Minds, brains and computers. *The Behavioral and Brain Sciences* 3: 417–457 (including peer review).

Shoemaker, S. (1975). Functionalism and qualia. *Philosophical Studies* 27: 291–315.

Turing, A. (1950). Computing machinery and intelligence. *Mind* 59: 433–460.

Fuzzy Logic

What is fuzzy logic? This question does not have a simple answer because fuzzy logic, or FL for short, has many distinct facets—facets that overlap and have unsharp boundaries (Zadeh 1996a; Dubois, Prade, and Yager 1993).

To a first approximation, fuzzy logic is a body of concepts, constructs, and techniques that relate to modes of reasoning that are approximate rather than exact. Much of—perhaps most—human reasoning is approximate in nature. In this perspective, the role model for fuzzy logic is the human mind. By contrast, classical LOGIC is normative in spirit in the sense that it is aimed at serving as a role model for human reasoning rather than having the human mind as its role model. Fundamentally, fuzzy logic is a generalization of classical logic and rests on the same mathematical foundations. However, as a generalization that reflects the pervasive imprecision of human reasoning, fuzzy logic is much better suited than classical logic to serve as the logic of human cognition.

Among the many facets of fuzzy logic there are four that stand out in importance. They are the following:

1. the logical facet, FL/L;
2. the set-theoretic facet, FL/S;
3. the relational facet, FL/R;
4. the epistemic facet, FL/E (see figure 1).

The logical facet of FL, FL/L, is a logical system or, more accurately, a collection of logical systems that include as a special case both two-valued and multiple-valued systems. As in any logical system, at the core of the logical facet of FL lies a system of rules of inference. In FL/L, however, the rules of inference play the role of rules that govern propagation of various types of fuzzy constraints. Concomitantly, a proposition, p, is viewed as a fuzzy constraint on an explicitly or implicitly defined variable. For example, the proposition "Mary is young" may be viewed as a fuzzy constraint on the variable Age (Mary), with "young" playing the role of a constraining fuzzy relation. Similarly, the proposition "Most students are young" may be viewed as a fuzzy

constraint on the proportion of young students among students, with the fuzzy quantifier "most" playing the role of a fuzzy constraint on the proportion. The logical facet of FL plays a pivotal role in the applications of FL to knowledge representation and to inference from information that is imprecise, incomplete, uncertain, or partially true.

The set-theoretic facet of FL, FL/S, is concerned with fuzzy sets, that is, classes or sets whose boundaries are not sharply defined. The initial development of FL was focused on this facet. Most of the applications of FL in mathematics have been and continue to be related to the set-theoretic facet. Among the examples of such applications are: fuzzy topology, fuzzy groups, fuzzy differential equations, and fuzzy arithmetic. Actually, any concept, method or theory can be generalized by fuzzification, that is, by replacing the concept of a set with that of a fuzzy set. Fuzzification serves an important purpose: it provides a way of constructing theories that are more general and more reflective of the imprecision of the real world than theories in which the sets are assumed to be crisp.

The relational facet of FL, FL/R, is concerned in the main with representation and manipulation of imprecisely defined functions and relations. It is this facet of FL that plays a pivotal role in its applications to systems analysis and control. The three basic concepts that lie at the core of this facet of FL are those of a linguistic variable, fuzzy if-then rule, and fuzzy graph. The relational facet of FL provides a foundation for the fuzzy-logic-based methodology of computing with words (CW).

Basically, a linguistic variable is a variable whose values are words drawn from a natural or synthetic language, with words playing the role of labels of fuzzy sets. For example, Height is a linguistic variable if its values are assumed to be: tall, very tall, quite tall, short, not very short, and so on. The concept of a linguistic variable plays a fundamentally important role in fuzzy logic and in particular, in computing with words. The use of words instead of—or in addition to—numbers serves two major purposes: (1) exploitation of the tolerance for imprecision; and (2) reflection of the finite ability of the human mind to resolve detail and store precise information.

The epistemic facet of FL, FL/E, is linked to its logical facet and is focused on the applications of FL to knowledge representation, information systems, fuzzy databases, and the theories of possibility and probability. A particularly important application area for the epistemic facet of FL relates to the conception and design of information/intelligent systems.

At the core of FL lie two basic concepts: (1) fuzziness/ fuzzification; and (2) granularity/granulation. As was alluded to already, fuzziness is a condition that relates to classes whose boundaries are not sharply defined, whereas fuzzification refers to replacing a crisp set, that is, a set with sharply defined boundaries, with a set whose boundaries are fuzzy. For example, the number 5 is fuzzified when it is transformed into approximately 5.

In a similar spirit, granularity relates to clumpiness of structure, whereas granulation refers to partitioning an object into a collection of granules, with a granule being a clump of objects (points) drawn together by indistinguishability,

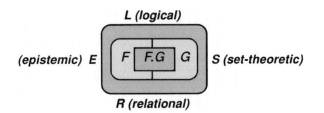

Figure 1. Conceptual structure of fuzzy logic.

similarity, proximity, or functionality. For example, the granules of an article might be the introduction, section 1, section 2, and so forth. Similarly, the granules of a human body might be the head, neck, chest, stomach, legs, and so on. Granulation may be crisp or fuzzy, dense or sparse, physical or mental.

A concept that plays a pivotal role in fuzzy logic is that of *fuzzy information granulation,* or fuzzy IG, for short. In crisp IG, the granules are crisp, whereas in fuzzy IG the granules are fuzzy. For example, when the variable Age is granulated into the time intervals {0,1}, {1,2}, {2,3}, . . . , the granules {0,1}, {1,2}, {2,3}, . . . are crisp; when Age is treated as a linguistic variable, the fuzzy sets labeled young, middle-aged, old, are fuzzy granules that play the role of linguistic values of Age. The importance of fuzzy logic— especially in the realm of applications—derives in large measure from the fact that FL is the only methodology that provides a machinery for fuzzy information granulation. In the figure, the core concept of fuzzy granulation is represented as the conjunction F. G.

The point of departure in fuzzy logic is the concept of a fuzzy set. A fuzzy set A in a universe U is characterized by its grade of membership μ_A, which associates with every point u in U its grade of membership $\mu_A(u)$, with $\mu_A(u)$ taking values in the unit interval [0,1]. More generally, μ_A may take values in a partially ordered set. For crisp sets, the concept of a membership function reduces to the familiar concept of a characteristic function, with $\mu_A(u)$ being 1 or 0 depending, respectively, on whether u belongs or does not belong to A.

Two interpretations of A play basic roles in fuzzy logic: *possibilistic* and *veristic*. More specifically, assume that X is a variable taking values in U, and A is a fuzzy set in U. In the possibilistic interpretation, in the proposition X is A, A plays the role of the possibility distribution of X, and $\mu_A(u)$ is the possibility that X can take the value u. In the veristic interpretation, $\mu_A(u)$ is the truth value (verity) of the proposition $X = u$. As an illustration, in the proposition *Mary is young* if $\mu_{young}(25) = 0.8$, then the possibility that Mary is twenty-five given that *Mary is young* is 0.8. Reciprocally, given that *Mary is 25,* the truth value (verity) of the proposition *Mary is young* is 0.8.

In addition to the concept of a fuzzy set, the basic concepts in fuzzy logic are those of a linguistic variable, fuzzy if-then rule, and fuzzy graph. In combination, these concepts provide a foundation for the theory of fuzzy information granulation (Zadeh 1997), the calculus of fuzzy if-then rules (Zadeh 1996a), and, ultimately, the methodology of computing with words (Zadeh 1996b). Most of the practical applications of fuzzy logic, especially in the realm of control and information/intelligent systems, involve the use of the machinery of computing with words.

Fuzzy if-then rules can assume a variety of forms. The simplest rule can be expressed as: if X is A then Y is B, where X and Y are variables taking values in universes of discourse U and V, respectively; and A and B are fuzzy sets in U and V. Generally, A and B play the role of linguistic values of X and Y; for example, if Pressure is high then Volume is low. In practice, the membership functions of A and B are usually triangular or trapezoidal.

A fuzzy graph is a union of fuzzy points (granules) each of which represents a fuzzy if-then rule. A fuzzy graph of a function f may be interpreted as a granular approximation to f. In most of the practical applications of fuzzy logic, fuzzy graphs are employed in this role as granular approximations to functions and relations.

In computing with words, the initial data set (IDS) and the terminal data set (TDS) are assumed to consist of collections of propositions expressed in a natural language. An input interface transforms IDS into a system of fuzzy constraints that are propagated from premises to conclusions through the use of the inference rules in fuzzy logic. The output interface transforms the conclusions into TDS.

The machinery for computing with words instead of or in addition to numbers may be viewed as one of the principal contributions of fuzzy logic. In a way, computing with words may be regarded as a step toward a better understanding of the remarkable human ability to perform complex tasks without any measurements and any numerical computations.

See also AMBIGUITY; COMPUTATION; DEDUCTIVE REASONING; UNCERTAINTY

—*Lotfi A. Zadeh*

References

Dubois, D., H. Prade, and R. Yager. (1993). *Readings in Fuzzy Sets for Intelligent Systems.* San Mateo: Morgan Kaufmann.

Zadeh, L. A. (1996a). *Fuzzy Sets, Fuzzy Logic and Fuzzy Systems.* Singapore: World Scientific.

Zadeh, L. A. (1996b). Fuzzy logic and the calculi of fuzzy rules and fuzzy graphs: a precis. *Multiple Valued Logic* 1: 1–38.

Zadeh, L. A. (1996c). Fuzzy logic = computing with words. *IEEE Transactions on Fuzzy Systems* 4(2): 103–111.

Zadeh, L. A. (1997). Toward a theory of fuzzy information granulation and its centrality in human reasoning and fuzzy logic. *Fuzzy Sets and Systems* 90: 111–127.

Further Readings

Bandemer, H., and S. Gottwald. (1995). *Fuzzy Sets, Fuzzy Logic and Fuzzy Methods with Applications.* Chichester: Wiley.

Bouchon-Meunier, B., R. Yager, and L. A. Zadeh, Eds. (1995). *Fuzzy Logic and Soft Computing.* Singapore: World Scientific Publishing.

Dubois, D., H. Prade, and R. R. Yager, Eds. (1997). *Fuzzy Information Engineering: A Guided Tour of Applications.* New York: Wiley.

Kruse, R., J. Gebhardt, and F. Klawonn. (1994). *Foundations of Fuzzy Systems.* Chichester: Wiley.

Game-Playing Systems

Games have long been popular in Artificial Intelligence as idealized domains suitable for research into various aspects of search, KNOWLEDGE REPRESENTATION, and the interaction between the two. CHESS, in particular, has been dubbed the "Drosophila of Artificial Intelligence" (McCarthy 1990), suggesting that the role of games in Artificial Intelligence is akin to that of the fruit fly in genetic research. In each case, certain practical advantages compensate for the lack of intrinsic importance of the given problem. In genetic research. In each case, certain practical advantages compensate for the lack of intrinsic importance of the given problem. In genetic research, fruit flies make it easy to maintain large populations with a short breeding cycle at low cost. In Artificial Intelligence research, games generally have rules that are well defined and can be stated in a few sentences, thus allowing for a relatively straightforward computer implementation. Yet the combinatorial complexity of interesting games can create immensely difficult problems. It has taken many decades of research combined with sufficiently powerful computers in order to approximate the level of leading human experts in many popular games. And in some games, human players still reign supreme.

Games can be classified according to a number of criteria, among them number of players, perfect versus hidden information, presence of a stochastic element, zero-sum versus non-zero-sum, average branching factor, and the size of the state space. Different combinations of characteristics emphasize different research issues. Much of the early research in game-playing systems concentrated on two-person zero-sum games of perfect information with low or moderate branching factors, in particular chess and checkers. Claude Shannon's 1950 paper on programming a computer to play chess mapped out much territory for later researchers. Alan TURING wrote a chess program (Turing et al. 1953), which he hand-simulated in the early 1950s. The earliest fully functioning chess program was described in Bernstein et al. (1958). The first chess program demonstrably superior to casual human chess players appeared in the mid-sixties (Greenblatt et al. 1967), and progress continued as faster machines became available and algorithms were refined (Slate and Atkin 1977; Condon and Thompson 1982; Hyatt, Gower, and Nelson 1990; Berliner and Ebeling 1990; Hsu et al. 1990). But it took until 1997 for a computer, the IBM Deep Blue chess machine, to defeat the human world chess champion, Gary Kasparov, in a regulation match.

Much of the success in game-playing systems has come from approaches based on depth-first minimax search with alpha-beta pruning in two-person zero-sum games of perfect information. This is essentially a brute-force search technique, searching forward as many moves as possible in an allotted time, assessing positions according to an evaluation function, and choosing the best move based on the minimax principle. The evaluation function captures essential domain knowledge. In fact, there is often a trade-off between the quality of the evaluation function and the depth of search required to achieve a given level of play. Minimax search is made more efficient through the use of alpha-beta pruning (Knuth and Moore 1975), which allows searching roughly twice as deep as would be possible in a pure minimax search. Notable examples of this approach include Deep Blue; Chinook (Schaeffer et al. 1992), which has defeated the world's best checkers players; and Logistello (Buro 1995), which has easily beaten the top human Othello players. The methods used in these programs and others of this type have been constantly improved and refined, and include such techniques as iterative deepening, transposition tables, null-move pruning, endgame databases, and singular extensions, as well as increasingly sophisticated evaluation functions.

In spite of the success of high-performance alpha-beta-based game-playing systems, there has been limited transference of ideas generated in this work to other areas of Artificial Intelligence (although see, for example, Newborn's work on theorem proving; Newborn 1992). There are, however, many alternatives to minimax alpha-beta that have been examined. Conspiracy numbers search (McAllester 1988) counts the number of positions whose evaluations must change in order for a different move choice to be made. This idea has led to methods that are capable of solving some interesting nontrivial games (Allis 1994). Decision-theoretic approaches to game playing, particularly under constraints of limited resources (BOUNDED RATIONALITY), are promising and have broad applicability outside the game-playing area. For example, Russell and Wefald (1991) reasoned specifically about when to terminate a search, based on the expected utility of further search and the cost of the time required for the additional work. Statistical methods for search and evaluation (Baum and Smith 1997) also have shown promise, adding uncertainty to a standard evaluation function and then using the inexact statistical information to approximate the exploration of the most important positions.

MACHINE LEARNING has a long history of using games as domains for experimentation. Samuel's checkers program (Samuel 1959), originally developed in the 1950s, employed both a rote-learning scheme and a method for tuning the coefficients of his evaluation function. Many current chess and Othello programs use forms of rote learning to avoid losing the same game twice. The Logistello program has also used an automatically tuned evaluation function with excellent results. However, the most noteworthy example of learning in game-playing systems is TD-Gammon (Tesauro 1995), a neural network program for playing backgammon. For games with stochastic elements, for instance the dice in backgammon, forward searching approaches are less efficient, which places a premium on the quality of the evaluation function. TD-Gammon used a reinforcement learning algorithm to train its neural network solely by playing against itself and learning from the results. This network, with or without some limited search, produces world-class play in backgammon (Tesauro and Galperin 1997). Reinforcement learning also has applications in other decision making and scheduling problems.

Some games are very difficult for computers at the present time. Go programs are actively being developed (Chen et al. 1990), but are far from the level of the best human players. The alpha-beta search paradigm, which is so successful in chess, checkers, and the like, is not directly applicable to Go because of the large branching factor. More subtle approaches involving decomposition of a game state into subproblems appear to be necessary. Hidden information games, such as bridge, are also not appropriate for direct application of the alpha-beta ALGORITHM, and have begun to receive more attention (Ginsberg 1996). Some other games are too difficult for even initial attempts. For example, in the game of Nomic (Suber 1990) a player's turn involves an amendment or addition to an existing set of rules. Initially players vote on proposed changes, but the game can evolve into something completely different. There is no clear way at present to design a game-playing system to play a game such as Nomic due to the tremendous amount of world knowledge required.

Game-playing systems have helped illustrate the role of search and knowledge working together in systems for solving complex problems, but games have also been useful as domains for experimentation with various types of machine learning and HEURISTIC SEARCH. The absence of significant learning capabilities in most game-playing systems, as well as the difficulty in creating high-performance programs for games such as Go, suggest that games are still fertile domains for Artificial Intelligence research.

See also EXPERTISE; GREEDY LOCAL SEARCH; NEURAL NETWORKS; PROBLEM SOLVING

—*Murray Campbell*

References

Allis, V. (1994). *Searching for Solutions in Games and Artificial Intelligence.* Maastricht: University of Limburg.

Baum, E. B., and W. D. Smith. (1997). A bayesian approach to game playing. Artificial Intelligence 97: 195–242.

Berliner, H., and C. Ebeling. (1990). Hitech. In T. A. Marsland and J. Schaeffer, Eds., *Computers, Chess, and Cognition.* New York: Springer, pp. 79–110.

Bernstein, A., M. deV. Roberts, T. Arbuckle, and M. A. Belsky. (1958). A chess-playing program for the IBM 704. *Proceedings of the Western Joint Computer Conference.* New York: The American Institute of Electrical Engineers.

Buro, M. (1995). Statistical feature combination for the evaluation of game positions. *Journal of Artificial Intelligence Research* 3: 373–382.

Chen, K., A. Kierult, M. Muller, and J. Nievergelt. (1990). The design and evolution of Go explorer. In T. A. Marsland and J. Schaeffer, Eds., *Computers, Chess, and Cognition.* New York: Springer, pp. 271–286.

Condon, J., and K. Thompson. (1982). Belle chess hardware. In M. Clarke, Ed., *Advances in Computer Chess 3.* New York: Pergamon, pp. 45–54.

Ginsberg, M. (1996). Partition search. *Proceedings of AAAI-96.*

Greenblatt, R. D., D. E. Eastlake, and S. D. Crocker. (1967). The Greenblatt Chess Program. *Proceedings of the Fall Joint Computer Conference.* The American Federation of Information Processing Societies.

Hsu, F., T. Anantharman, M. Campbell, and A. Nowatzyk. (1990). Deep Thought. In T. A. Marsland and J. Schaeffer, Eds., *Computers, Chess, and Cognition.* New York: Springer, pp. 55–78.

Hyatt, R., A. Gower, and H. Nelson. (1990). Cray Blitz. In T. A. Marsland and J. Schaeffer, Eds., *Computers, Chess, and Cognition.* New York: Springer, pp. 111–130.

Knuth, D., and R. Moore. (1975). An analysis of alpha-beta pruning. *Artificial Intelligence* 6: 293–326.

McAllester, D. (1988). Conspiracy numbers for min-max search. *Artificial Intelligence* 35: 287-310

McCarthy, J. (1990). Chess as the Drosophila of AI. In T. A. Marsland and J. Schaeffer, Eds., *Computers, Chess, and Cognition.* New York: Springer, pp. 227–238.

Newborn, M. (1992). A theorem-proving program for the IBM PC. In D. Kopec and R. B. Thompson, Eds., *Artificial Intelligence and Intelligent Tutoring Systems.* Upper Saddle River, NJ: Prentice Hall, pp. 65–92.

Russell, S., and E. Wefald. (1991). Principles of metareasoning. *Artificial Intelligence* 49: 361–395.

Samuel, A. L. (1959). Some studies in machine learning using the game of checkers. *IBM Journal of Research and Development* 3: 210–229.

Schaeffer, J., J. Culberson, N. Treloar, B. Knight, P. Lu, and D. Szafron. (1992). A world championship caliber checkers program. *Artificial Intelligence* 53: 273–290.

Shannon, C. (1950). Programming a computer for playing chess. *Philosophical Magazine* 41: 256–275.

Slate, D., and L. Atkin. (1977). Chess 4.5—The Northwestern Chess Program. In P. Frey, Ed., *Chess Skill in Man and Machine.* Berlin: Springer, pp. 82–118.

Suber, P. (1990). *The Paradox of Self-Amendment: A Study of Law, Logic, Omnipotence and Change.* New York: Peter Lang.

Tesauro, G. (1995). Temporal difference learning and TD-Gammon. *Communications of the ACM* 38: 58–68.

Tesauro, G., and R. Galperin. (1997). On-line policy improvement using Monte-Carlo search. In M. I. Jordan and M. C. Mozer, Eds., *Advances in Neural Information Processing Systems 9: Proceedings of the 1996 Conference.* Cambridge, MA: MIT Press.

Turing, A., C. Strachey, M. Bates, and B. Bowden. (1953). Digital computers applied to games. In B. Bowden, Ed., *Faster Than Thought.* New York: Pitman, pp. 286–310.

Game Theory

Game theory is a mathematical framework designed for analyzing the interaction between several agents whose decisions affect each other. In a game-theoretic analysis, an interactive situation is described as a *game*: an abstract description of the players (agents), the courses of actions available to them, and their preferences over the possible outcomes. The game-theoretic framework assumes that the players employ RATIONAL DECISION MAKING, that is, they act so as to achieve outcomes that they prefer (VON NEUMANN and Morgenstern 1944). Typically, preferences are modeled using numeric utilities, and players are assumed to be expected utility maximizers.

Unlike decision making for a single agent, in the multi-agent case this assumption is not enough to define an "optimal decision," because the agent cannot unilaterally control the outcome. One of the roles of game theory is to define notions of "optimal solution" for different classes of games. These solutions assume that players reason strategically, basing their decisions on their expectations regarding the behavior of other players. Typically, players are assumed to have *common knowledge* that they are all rational (see MODAL LOGIC).

A large part of game theory deals with noncooperative situations, where each player acts independently. In such a game, a *strategy* s_i for player i specifies the action player i should take in any state of the game. A *solution* to the game is a strategy combination $s_1, \ldots, s_n$ satisfying certain optimality conditions.

Most abstractly, a situation is represented as a *strategic form* game, where the possible strategies for the players are simply enumerated. Each strategy combination $s_1, \ldots, s_n$ leads to some outcome, whose value to player i is a payoff $u_i(s_1, \ldots, s_n)$. A two-player strategic form game is often represented by a matrix where the rows are player 1 strategies, the columns are player 2 strategies, and the matrix entries are the associated payoff pairs.

	heads	tails
heads	1, -1	-1, 1
tails	-1, 1	1, -1

(a)

	silent	confess
silent	-1,-1	0,-10
confess	-10,0	-8,-8

(b)

Figure 1. (a) Flipping Pennies. (b) Prisoner's Dilemma: Two conspirators, in prison, are each given the opportunity to confess in return for a reduced prison sentence; the payoffs correspond to numbers of years in prison.

The simplest game is a two-player *zero-sum* game, where the players' interests are completely opposed (see figure 1). Because any gain for one player corresponds to a loss for the other, each player should make a worst-case assumption about the behavior of the other. Thus, it appears that player 1 should choose the *maximin* strategy s_1^* that achieves $\max_{s_1^i} \min_{s_1^j} u_1(s_1^i, s_1^j)$; player 2 has an analogous rational strategy s_2^*. Common knowledge of rationality implies that the "rational" strategy of one player will be known to the other. However, s_1^* may not be optimal against s_2^*, making it irrational for player 1 to play as anticipated. This circularity can be avoided if we allow the players to use randomness. In game (a), player 2 can play the *mixed* strategy μ_2^* where he chooses heads and tails each with probability *1/2*. If each player plays the maximin mixed strategy μ_i^*, we avoid the problem: μ_1^* and μ_2^* are in equilibrium, that is, each is optimal against the other (von Neumann and Morgenstern 1944).

The equilibrium concept can be extended to general *n*-player games. A strategy combination $\mu_1^* \ldots \mu_n^*$ is said to be in *Nash equilibrium* (Nash 1950) if no player i can benefit by deviating from it (playing a strategy $\mu_i \neq \mu_i^*$). In game (b), the (unique) equilibrium is the nonrandomized strategy combination (confess, confess). An equilibrium in mixed strategies is always guaranteed to exist.

The Nash equilibrium is arguably the most fundamental concept in noncooperative games. However, several problems reduce its intuitive appeal. Many games have several very different equilibria. In such games, it is not clear which equilibrium should be the "recommended solution," nor how the players can pick a single equilibrium without communication. One important mechanism that addresses these concerns is based on the assumption that the game is played repeatedly, allowing players to adapt their strategies gradually over time (Luce and Raiffa 1957; Battigalli, Gilli, and Milinari 1992). This process is a variant of multiagent REINFORCEMENT LEARNING. Some variants are related to BAYESIAN LEARNING (Milgrom and Roberts 1989). Others are related to the evolution of biological populations, and have led to a branch of game theory called *evolutionary games* (Maynard Smith 1982).

Furthermore, many equilibria are unintuitive. In game (b), the Nash equilibrium has a utility of –8,–8, which is worse for both players than the "desired" outcome –1,–1. There have been many attempts to find alternative models where the desired outcome is the solution. Some success has been achieved in the case of infinitely repeated play where the players have BOUNDED RATIONALITY (e.g., when their strategies are restricted to be finite-state AUTOMATA; Abreu and Rubenstein 1992).

A more refined representation of a game takes into consideration the evolution of the game. A game in *extensive form* (Kuhn 1953) is a tree whose edges represent possible actions and whose leaves represent outcomes. Most simply, the players have *perfect information*—any action taken is revealed to all players.

The notion of equilibrium often leads to unintuitive results when applied to extensive-form games. For example, in game (a), the strategy combination (*R, a*) is one equilibrium: given that player 2 will play *a*, player 1 prefers *R*, and given that player 1 plays *R*, player 2's choice is irrelevant. This equilibrium is sustained only by a noncredible "threat" by player 2 to play the suboptimal move *a*. The extensive-form equilibrium concept has been refined to deal with this issue, by adding the requirement that, at each point in the game, the player's chosen action be optimal (Selten 1965). In our example, the optimal move for player 2 is *b*, and therefore player 1's optimal action is *L*. This process, whereby optimal moves are selected at the bottom of the tree, and these determine optimal moves higher up, is called *backward induction*. In the context of zero-sum games, the algorithm is called the *minimax algorithm,* and is the fundamental technique used in GAME-PLAYING SYSTEMS.

The extensive form also includes imperfect information games (Kuhn 1953): the tree is augmented with *information sets,* representing sets of nodes among which the player cannot distinguish. For example, a simultaneous-move game such as Flipping Pennies can be represented as in figure (2). Clearly, imperfect information games require the use of randomization in order to guarantee the existence of a Nash

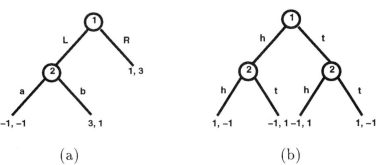

(a)   (b)

Figure 2. (a) Unintuitive equilibrium. (b) Flipping Pennies.

equilibrium. Refinements of the Nash equilibrium concept addressing the temporal sequencing of decisions have also been proposed for imperfect information games (Kreps and Wilson 1982; Selten 1975; Fudenberg and Tirole 1991), largely based on the intuition that the player's actions must be optimal relative to his or her *beliefs* about the current state.

Game theory also deals with *cooperative* games, where players can form coalitions and make binding agreements about their choice of actions (von Neumann and Morgenstern 1944; Luce and Raiffa 1957; Shapley and Shubik 1953). In this case, the outcome of the game is determined by the coalition that forms and the joint action it takes. The game-theoretic models for such situations typically focus on how the payoff resulting from the optimal group action is divided between group members. Various solution concepts have been proposed for coalition games, essentially requiring that the payoff division be such that no subgroup is better off by leaving the coalition and forming another (see Aumann 1989 for a survey).

Game theory is a unified theory for rational decision making in multiagent settings. It encompasses bargaining, negotiation, auctions, voting, deterrence, competition, and more. It lies at the heart of much of economic theory, but it has also been used in political science, government policy, law, military analysis, and biology (Aumann and Hart 1992, 1994, 1997). One of the most exciting prospects for the future is the wide-scale application of game theory in the domain of autonomous computer agents (Rosenschein and Zlotkin 1994; Koller and Pfeffer 1997).

See also ECONOMICS AND COGNITIVE SCIENCE; MULTI-AGENT SYSTEMS; RATIONAL CHOICE THEORY

—*Daphne Koller*

References

Abreu, D., and A. Rubinstein. (1992). The structure of Nash equilibria in repeated games with finite automata. *Econometrica* 56: 1259–1281.

Aumann, R. J., and S. Hart, Eds. (1992; 1994; 1997). *Handbook of Game Theory with Economic Applications,* vols. 1–3. Amsterdam: Elsevier.

Aumann, R. J. (1976). Agreeing to disagree. *Annals of Statistics* 4(6): 1236–1239.

Aumann, R. J. (1989). *Lectures on Game Theory.* Boulder, CO: Westview Press.

Battigalli, P., M. Gilli, and M. C. Milinari. (1992). Learning and convergence to equilibrium in repeated strategic interactions: An introductory survey. *Ricerche Economiche* 46: 335–377.

Fudenberg, D., and J. Tirole. (1991). Perfect Bayesian equilibrium and sequential equilibrium. *Journal of Economic Theory* 53: 236–260.

Koller, D., and A. Pfeffer. (1997). Representations and solutions for game-theoretic problems. *Artificial Intelligence.*

Kreps, D. M., and R. B. Wilson. (1982). Sequential equilibria. *Econometrica* 50: 863–894.

Kuhn, H. W. (1953). Extensive games and the problem of information. In H. W. Kuhn and A. W. Tucker, Eds., *Contributions to the Theory of Games II.* Princeton: Princeton University Press, pp. 193–216.

Luce, R. D., and H. Raiffa. (1957). *Games and Decisions—Introduction and Critical Survey.* New York: Wiley.

Maynard Smith, J. (1982). *Evolution and the Theory of Games.* Cambridge: Cambridge University Press.

Milgrom, P., and J. Roberts. (1989). *Adaptive and Sophisticated Learning in Repeated Normal Forms.* Mimeo, Stanford University.

Nash, J. F. (1950). Equilibrium points in n-person games. *Proceedings of the National Academy of Sciences* 36: 48–49.

Nash, J. F. (1951). Non-cooperative games. *Annals of Mathematics* 54: 286–295.

Rosenschein, J. S., and G. Zlotkin. (1994). Consenting agents: designing conventions for automated negotiation. *AI Magazine* 15(3): 29–46.

Selten, R. (1965). Spieltheoretische behandlung eines oligopolmodells mit nachfragetragheit. *Zeitschrift für die gesamte Staatswissenschaft* 121: 301–324.

Selten, R. (1975). Reexamination of the perfectness concept for equilibrium points in extensive games. *International Journal of Game Theory* 4: 25–55.

Shapley, L. S., and M. Shubik. (1953). Solutions of n-person games with ordinal utilities. *Econometrica* 21: 348–349.

von Neumann, J., and O. Morgenstern. (1944). *Theory of Games and Economic Behavior.* Princeton: Princeton University Press.

Further Readings

Aumann, R. J. (1985). What is game theory trying to accomplish? In K. J. Arrow and S. Honkapohja, Eds., *Frontiers of Economics.* Oxford: Blackwell, pp. 28–76.

Aumann, R. J. (1987). Game theory. In J. Eatwell, M. Milgate, and P. Newman, Eds., *The New Palgrave,* vol. 2. New York: Macmillan, pp. 460–482.

Fudenberg, D., and J. Tirole. (1991). *Game Theory.* Cambridge, MA: MIT Press.

Fudenberg, D. (1992). Explaining cooperation and commitment in repeated games. In J.-J. Laffont, Ed., *Advances in Economic Theory,* vol. 1. Cambridge: Cambridge University Press.

Kreps, D. M. (1990). *Game Theory and Economic Modelling.* Oxford: Clarendon Press.

McKelvey, R. D., and A. McLennan. (1996). Computation of equilibria in finite games. In H. Amman, D. Kendrick, and J. Rust, Eds., *Handbook of Computational Economics,* vol. 1. Amsterdam: Elsevier.

Megiddo, N., Ed. (1994). *Essays in Game Theory.* New York: Springer.

Myerson, R. B., Ed. (1991). *Game Theory.* Cambridge, MA: Harvard University Press.

Osborne, M. J., and A. Rubinstein. (1994). *A Course in Game Theory.* Cambridge, MA: MIT Press.

Van Damme, E. (1991). *Stability and Perfection of Nash Equilibria.* Berlin: Springer.

Gender

See LANGUAGE AND GENDER; METAPHOR AND CULTURE; NAIVE SOCIOLOGY; STEREOTYPING

Generative Grammar

The motivating idea of generative grammar is that we can gain insight into human language through the construction of explicit grammars. A language is taken to be a collection of structured symbolic expressions, and a generative grammar is simply an explicit theoretical account of one such collection.

Simple finite sets of rules can describe infinite languages with interesting structure. For example, the following instruction describes all palindromes over the alphabet {A, B}:

Start with S and recursively replace S by ASA, BSB, or nothing.

We prove that ABBA is a palindrome by constructing the sequence S—ASA—ABSBA—ABBA, which represents a *derivation* of the string. The instruction, or rule, constitutes a generative grammar for the language comprising such palindromes; for every palindrome over the alphabet {A,B} the grammar provides a derivation. S can be regarded as a grammatical category analogous to a sentence, and A and B are analogous to words in a language.

The following condition on nodes in trees turns out to be equivalent to the above grammar:

Nodes labeled S have left and right daughters either both labeled A or both labeled B; optionally these are separated by a node labeled S; nodes labeled A or B have no daughters.

If a set of trees T satisfies this condition, then its frontier (the sequence of daughterless nodes) is a palindrome of A's and B's; and any such palindrome is the frontier of some such tree. This is a declarative definition of a set of trees, not a procedure for deriving strings. But it provides an alternative way of defining the same language of strings, a different type of generative grammar.

Studying English in generative terms involves trying to determine whether some finite set of rules could generate the entire set of strings of words that a native speaker of (say) English would find acceptable. It presumably is possible, because speakers, despite their finite mental capacities, seem to have a full grasp of what is in their language.

A fundamental early insight was that limitations on the format of rules or constraints set limits on definable languages, and some limits are too tight to allow for description of languages like English. String-rewriting rules having the form "rewrite X as wY," where w is a string of words and X and Y are grammatical categories, are too weak. (This limitation would make grammars exactly equivalent to finite automata, so strictly speaking English cannot be recognized by any finite computer.) However, if limits are too slack, the opposite problem emerges: the theory may be Turing-equivalent, meaning that it provides a grammar for any recursively enumerable set of strings. That means it does not make a formal distinction between natural languages and any other recursively enumerable sets. Building on work by Zellig Harris, Chomsky (1957) argued that a grammar for English needed to go beyond the sort of rules seen so far, and must employ transformational rules that convert one structural representation into another. For example, using transformations, passive sentences might be described in terms of a rearrangement of structural constituents of corresponding active sentences:

Take a subjectless active sentence structure with root label S and move the postverbal noun phrase leftward to become the subject (left branch) of that S.

Several researchers (beginning with Putnam 1961) have noted that transformational grammars introduce the undesirable property of Turing-equivalence. Others, including Chomsky, have argued that this is not a vitiating result.

Generative grammatical study and the investigation of human mental capacities have been related via widely discussed claims, including the following:

1. People tacitly know (and learn in infancy) which sentences are grammatical and meaningful in their language.
2. They possess (and acquire) such knowledge even about novel sentences.
3. Therefore they must be relying not on memorization but on mentally represented rules.
4. Generative grammars can be interpreted as models of mentally represented rule sets.
5. The ability to have (and acquire) such rules must be a significant (probably species-defining) feature of human minds.

Critics have challenged all these claims. (It has been a key contribution of generative grammar to cognitive science to have stimulated enormous amounts of interesting critical discussion on issues of this sort.) Psycholinguistic studies of speakers' reactions to novel strings have been held to undercut (1). One response to (2) is that speakers might simply generalize or analogize from familiar cases. Regarding (3), some philosophers object that one cannot draw conclusions about brain inscriptions (which are concrete objects) from properties of sentences (arguably abstract objects). In response to (4), it has been noted that the most compact and nonredundant set of rules for a language will not necessarily be identical with the sets people actually use, and that the Turing-equivalence results mean that (4) does not imply any distinction between being able to learn a natural language and being able to learn any arbitrary finitely representable subject matter. And primatologists have tried to demonstrate language learning in apes to challenge (5).

Two major rifts appeared in the history of generative grammar, one in the years following 1968 and the other about ten years later. The first rift developed when a group of syntacticians who became known as the generative semanticists suggested that syntactic investigations revealed that transformations must act directly on semantic structures that looked nothing like superficial ones (in particular, they did not respect basic constituent order or even integrity of words), and might represent *They persuaded Mike to fell the tree* thus (a predicate-initial representation of clauses is adopted here, though this is not essential):

[$_S$PAST [$_S$CAUSE they [$_S$AGREE Mike [$_S$CAUSE Mike [$_S$FALL the tree]]]]].

The late 1960s and early 1970s saw much dispute about the generative semantics program (Harris 1993), which ultimately dissolved, though many of its insights have been revived in recent work. Some adherents became interested in the semantic program of logician Richard Montague (1973), bringing the apparatus of model-theoretic semantics into the core of theoretical linguistics; others participated in the development of RELATIONAL GRAMMAR (Perlmutter and Postal 1983).

The second split in generative grammar, which developed in the late 1970s and persists to the present, is between those who continue to employ transformational analyses (especially movement transformations) and hence derivations, and those who by 1980 had completely abandoned them to formulate grammars in constraint-based terms. The transformationalists currently predominate. The constraint-based minority is a heterogenous group exemplified by the proponents of, inter alia, relational grammar (especially the formalized version in Johnson and Postal 1980), HEAD-DRIVEN PHRASE STRUCTURE GRAMMAR (Pollard and Sag 1994), LEXICAL FUNCTIONAL GRAMMAR (Bresnan and Kaplan 1982), and earlier frameworks including tree adjoining grammar (Joshi, Levy, and Takahashi 1975) and generalized phrase structure grammar (Gazdar et al. 1985).

In general, transformationalist grammarians have been less interested, and constraint-based grammarians more interested, in such topics as COMPUTATIONAL LINGUISTICS and the mathematical analysis of properties of languages (sets of expressions) and classes of formalized grammars.

Transformationalists formulate grammars procedurally, defining processes for deriving a sentence in a series of steps. The constraint-based minority states them declaratively, as sets of constraints satisfied by the correct structures. The derivational account of passives alluded to above involves a movement transformation: a representation like

$$[[_{\text{NP}}\_\_] \text{ } PAST \text{ } made \text{ } [_{\text{NP}} mistakes] \text{ } ([_{\text{PP}} by \text{ people}])]$$

is changed by transformation into something more like

$$[[_{\text{NP}} mistakes] \text{ } were \text{ } made \text{ } [_{\text{NP}}\_\_]] \text{ } ([_{\text{PP}} by \text{ people}])]$$

The same facts might be described declaratively by means of constraints ensuring that for every transitive verb *V* there is a corresponding intransitive verb *V** used in such a way that *for B to be V*ed by A means the same as for A to V B.* This is vague and informal, but may serve to indicate how passive sentences can be described without giving instructions for deriving them from active structures, yet without missing the systematic synonymy of actives and their related passives.

There is little explicit debate between transformationalists and constraint-based theorists, though there have been a few interchanges on such topics as (1) whether a concern with formal exactitude in constructing grammars (much stressed in the constraint-based literature) is premature at the present stage of knowledge; (2) whether claims about grammars can sensibly be claimed to have neurophysiological relevance (as transformationalists have claimed); and (3) whether progress in computational implementation of nontransformational grammars is relevant to providing a theoretical argument in their favor.

At least two topics can be identified that have been of interest to both factions within generative grammar. First, broadening the range of languages from which data are drawn is regarded as most important. The influence of relational grammar during the 1980s helped expand considerably the number of languages studied by generative grammarians, and so did the growth of the community of generative grammarians in European countries after 1975. Second, the theoretical study of how natural languages might be learned by infants—particularly how SYNTAX is learned—has been growing in prominence and deserves some further discussion here.

Transformationalists argue that what makes languages learnable is that grammars differ only in a finite number of parameter settings triggered by crucial pieces of evidence. For example, identifying a clause with verb following object might trigger the "head-final" value for the head-position parameter, as in Japanese (where verbs come at the ends of clauses), rather than the "head-initial" value that characterizes English. (In some recent transformationalist work having the head-final parameter actually corresponds to having a required leftward movement of postverbal constituents into preverbal positions, but the point is that it is conjectured that only finitely many distinct alternatives are made available by universal grammar.) Theories of learning based on this idea face significant computational problems, because even quite simple parameter systems can define local blind alleys from which a learning algorithm cannot escape regardless of further input data (see Gibson and Wexler 1995).

The general goal is seen as that of overcoming the problem of the POVERTY OF THE STIMULUS: the putative lack of an adequate evidential basis to support induction of a grammar via general knowledge acquisition procedures (see LEARNING SYSTEMS and ACQUISITION, FORMAL THEORIES OF).

Nontransformationalists are somewhat more receptive than transformationalists to the view that the infant's experience might not be all that poverty-stricken: once one takes account of the vast amount of statistical information contained in the corpus of observed utterances (see STATISTICAL TECHNIQUES IN NATURAL LANGUAGE PROCESSING), it can be seen that the child's input might be rich enough to account for language acquisition through processes of gradual generalization and statistical approximation. This idea, familiar from pre-1957 structuralism, is reemerging in a form that is cognizant of the past four decades of generative grammatical research without being wholly antagonistic in spirit to such trends as CONNECTIONIST APPROACHES TO LANGUAGE. The research on OPTIMALITY THEORY that has emerged under the influence of connectionism meshes well both with constraint-based approaches to grammar and with work on how exposure to data can facilitate identification of constraint systems.

There is no reason to see such developments as being at odds with the original motivating idea of generative grammar, inasmuch as rigorous and exact description of human languages and what they have in common—that is, a thorough understanding of what is acquired—is surely a prerequisite to any kind of language acquisition research, whatever its conclusions.

See also COGNITIVE LINGUISTICS; LANGUAGE ACQUISITION; LINGUISTIC UNIVERSALS AND UNIVERSAL GRAMMAR; MINIMALISM; PARAMETER-SETTING APPROACHES TO ACQUISITION, CREOLIZATION, AND DIACHRONY

—Geoffrey K. Pullum

References

Bresnan, J., and R. Kaplan. (1982). *The Mental Representation of Grammatical Relations.* Cambridge, MA: MIT Press.

Chomsky, N. (1957). *Syntactic Structures.* The Hague: Mouton.

Chomsky, N. (1965). *Aspects of the Theory of Syntax.* Cambridge, MA: MIT Press.

Chomsky, N. (1994). *The Minimalist Program.* Cambridge, MA: MIT Press.

Gazdar, G., E. Klein, G. K. Pullum, and I. A. Sag. (1985). *Generalized Phrase Structure Grammar.* Cambridge, MA: Harvard University Press.

Gibson, T., and K. Wexler. (1995). Triggers. *Linguistic Inquiry* 25: 407–454.

Harris, R. A. (1993). *The Linguistic Wars.* New York: Oxford University Press.

Johnson, D. E., and P. M. Postal. (1980). *Arc Pair Grammar.* Princeton: Princeton University Press.

Joshi, A., L. S. Levy, and M. Takahashi. (1975). Tree adjunct grammars. *Journal of Computing and System Sciences* 19: 136–163.

Montague, R. (1993). *Formal Philosophy.* New Haven: Yale University Press.

Perlmutter, D. M., and P. M. Postal. (1983). *Studies in Relational Grammar 1.* Chicago: University of Chicago Press.

Pollard, C., and I. A. Sag. (1994). *Head-driven Phrase Structure Grammar.* Chicago: University of Chicago Press.

Putnam, H. (1961). Some issues in the theory of grammar. *Proceedings of the Twelfth Symposium in Applied Mathematics.* Providence: American Mathematical Society. Reprinted in *Philosophical Papers,* vol. 2: *Mind, Language and Reality.* New York: Cambridge University Press, 1975, pp. 85–106; and in G. Harman, Ed., *On Noam Chomsky.* New York: Anchor, 1974, pp. 80–103.

Genetic Algorithms

See EVOLUTIONARY COMPUTATION

Geschwind, Norman

Norman Geschwind (1926–1984) was an eminent American neurologist whose major contribution was to help revive the CORTICAL LOCALIZATION-based anatomophysiological analysis of human behavior and behavioral disorders typical of the approach of the last decades of the nineteenth century. In this way, in the early 1960s and almost single-handedly, he brought the study of behavior back into the framework of neurology and away from purely behavioral explanations characteristic of most of the first half of the twentieth century. Thus, he helped to pave the way to what is now the domain of cognitive neuroscience. His research interests included the study of brain connections as a way of explaining the neural basis and disorders of language, knowledge, and action (Geschwind 1965a, 1965b), the study of HEMISPHERIC SPECIALIZATION and its biological underpinnings (Geschwind and Levitsky 1968; Geschwind and Galaburda 1984), and the study of developmental learning disorders such as DYSLEXIA (Geschwind and Galaburda 1987).

Geschwind was born in New York City on January 8, 1926 (for a more extensive biographical sketch, see Gala-

burda 1985 and Damasio and Galaburda 1985). His parents had emigrated from Poland at the turn of the century. Geschwind graduated from Boys' High School in Brooklyn, New York, in 1942, and attended Harvard College on a Pulitzer Scholarship from 1942 until 1944, when his studies were interrupted by service in the United States Army in the last years of World War II. After the war, Geschwind finished his undergraduate studies and then attended Harvard Medical School. After graduation in 1951 he carried out an internship at Boston's Beth Israel Hospital (to which he would return at the end of his life as chair of neurology). Afterward Geschwind traveled to England to study muscle physiology with neurologist Ian Simpson at the National Hospital in Queen Square. He returned from London to continue his neurological training under Derek Denny-Brown at the Boston City Hospital. In 1958, Geschwind joined Fred Quadfasel at the Boston's Veterans Administration Hospital, where his education and work on the neurology of behavior began. When Quadfasel retired in 1963, Geschwind replaced him as chief of service and remained at that post until 1969. That year Geschwind returned to Harvard as the James Jackson Putnam Professor of Neurology and chief of the neurological unit of Boston City Hospital. He continued to be involved in the APHASIA Research Center, which he had founded while at the Veterans Hospital.

Initially Geschwind was influenced in his thinking about behavior by the holistic views of Hughlings Jackson, Kurt Goldstein, Henry Head, and Carl LASHLEY (Geschwind 1964). In the early 1960s, however, he was seduced by the style of explanation of neurologists BROCA, Wernicke, Bastian, Dejerine, and Charcot, and others, which relied heavily on anatomical relationships among areas of the brain by way of neural connections. From that time on Geschwind became the clearest and most forceful and incisive champion of this localizationist approach to the understanding of behavior and behavioral disorders. Geschwind's analysis of the case of a patient with a brain tumor who could write correct language with his right hand but not with his left showed the power of this approach and launched Geschwind's career as a behavioral neurologist (Geschwind and Kaplan 1962). The explanation was damage to the large bundle of neural connections linking the two hemispheres of the brain, the corpus callosum, whose importance was also being recognized by the neurobiologist Roger SPERRY through his work with monkeys. Additional reports and impressive review of the world's literature led to Geschwind's famous two-part paper in the journal *Brain,* 'Disconnexion syndromes in animals and man' (1965a and b). The clarity of exposition and conviction about the power of the anatomical method produced a strong following and established Geschwind as the leading figure in American behavioral neurology, which he remained until his death.

Irked by a statement by the anatomist Gerhard von Bonin that there were no anatomical asymmetries in the human brain to account for the striking hemispheric specialization the brain exhibits, Geschwind undertook his own literature review and laboratory studies and published an important paper, together with Walter Levitsky, which disclosed striking asymmetries in a region of the temporal lobe, in an area important to language, called the planum temporale

(Geschwind and Levitsky 1968). Several others confirmed these findings, and the paper stimulated a great deal of additional research on brain asymmetries, some of which are still actively studied using anatomical brain imaging techniques such as computed assisted tomography (CAT scans) and MAGNETIC RESONANCE IMAGING (MRI scans) in living subjects, as well as functional MRI and POSITRON EMISSION TOMOGRAPHY (PET).

During the last few years of his life Geschwind became interested in developmental learning disabilities. In Geschwind's mind, strict localization theory began to give way to localization with NEURAL PLASTICITY resulting from early extrinsic influences on brain development occurring in utero or soon after birth. These effects were capable of changing standard patterns of brain asymmetry and could lead to developmental learning disorders. His keen clinical acumen led to his noticing that mothers of dyslexic children often reported left-handedness, atopic illnesses such as asthma, and autoimmune diseases such as hypothyroidism. In an epidemiological study carried out with Peter Behan in London, they showed an association between stuttering, dyslexia, colitis, thyroid disease, and myasthenia gravis in left-handers (Geschwind and Behan 1983). This work engendered massive additional research and debate and may constitute Geschwind's most creative contribution to new knowledge. Since his death a slightly larger number of reports have found support for this last of Geschwind's insight than the number finding no support.

Norman Geschwind wrote more than 160 journal articles and books, and his name became a household word among not only neurologists but also psychologists, philosophers of mind, educators, and neurobiologists. He was recognized by many prizes, honorary degrees, and visiting professorships, which led him to travel widely. He spoke several languages and possessed a strong memory, a sharp logical mind, and a broad culture, which turned him into a powerful adversary in debate and discussion. He left a legacy of knowledge and ideas, as well as a long list of students and followers, many of whom became leaders in behavioral neurology in the United States and abroad.

See also HEBB, DONALD O.; LANGUAGE IMPAIRMENT, DEVELOPMENTAL; LANGUAGE, NEURAL BASIS OF; LURIA, ALEXANDER ROMANOVICH

—*Albert M. Galaburda*

References

Damasio, A. R., and A. M. Galaburda. (1985). Norman Geschwind. *Archives of Neurology* 42: 500–504.

Galaburda, A. M. (1985). Norman Geschwind. *Neuropsychologia* 23: 297–304.

Geschwind, N. (1964). The paradoxical position of Kurt Goldstein in the history of aphasia. *Cortex* 1: 214–224.

Geschwind, N. (1965a). Disconnexion syndromes in animals and man. *Brain* 88: 237–294.

Geschwind, N. (1965b). Disconnexion syndromes in animals and man. *Brain* 88: 585–644.

Geschwind, N., and P. Behan (1983). Left-handedness: association with immune disease, migraine, and developmental learning disorder. *Proceedings of the National Academy of Sciences (U.S.A.)* 79: 5097–5100.

Geschwind, N., and A. M. Galaburda, Eds. (1984). *Cerebral Dominance: The Biological Foundations.* Cambridge, MA: Harvard University Press.

Geschwind, N. and A. M. Galaburda. (1987). *Cerebral Lateralization: Biological Mechanisms, Associations, and Pathology.* Cambridge, MA: MIT Press.

Geschwind, N., and E. Kaplan. (1962). A human reconnection syndrome: a preliminary report. *Neurology* 12: 675–685.

Geschwind, N., and W. Levitsky. (1968). Human brain: left-right asymmetries in temporal speech region. *Science* 161: 186–187.

Gestalt Perception

Gestalt perception is the name given to various perceptual phenomena and theoretical principles associated with the school of GESTALT PSYCHOLOGY (Koffka 1935). Its most important contributions concerned *perceptual organization*: the nature of relations among parts and wholes and how they are determined. Previously, perceptual theory was dominated by the *structuralist* proposal that complex perceptions were constructed from *atoms* of elementary color sensations and unified by *associations* due to spatial and temporal contiguity. Gestalt theorists rejected both assumptions, arguing that perception was *holistic* and *organized* due to interactions between stimulus structure and underlying brain processes.

Wertheimer (1923) posed the problem of perceptual organization in terms of how people manage to perceive organized scenes consisting of surfaces, parts, and whole objects coherently arranged in space rather than the chaotic, dynamic juxtaposition of millions of different colors registered by retinal receptors. He attempted to answer this question by identifying stimulus factors that caused simple arrays of elements to be perceived as organized in distinct groups. The factors he identified are usually called the *laws* (or *principles*) of grouping, several of which are illustrated in figures A–F: *proximity* (A), *similarity of color* (B), *similarity of size* (C), *common fate* (D), *good continuation* (E), and *closure* (F). More recently other principles have been identified (Palmer and Rock 1994), including *common region* (G) and *element connectedness* (H). In each case, elements that have a stronger relation in terms of the specified property (i.e., those that are closer, more similarly colored, etc.) tend to be grouped together. These "laws" are actually *ceteris paribus rules*: all else being equal, the elements most closely related by the specified factor will be grouped together. They cannot predict the result when two or more factors vary in opposition because the rules fail to specify how multiple factors are integrated. No general theory has yet been formulated that overcomes this problem.

A second important phenomenon of Gestalt perception is *figure-ground organization* (Rubin 1921). In figure I, for instance, one can perceive either a white object on a black background or a black object on a white background. The crucial feature of figure-ground organization is that the boundary is perceived as belonging to the figural region. As a result, it seems "thing-like," has definite shape, and appears closer, whereas the ground appears farther and to extend behind the figure. Gestalt psychologists identified several factors that govern figure-ground organization,

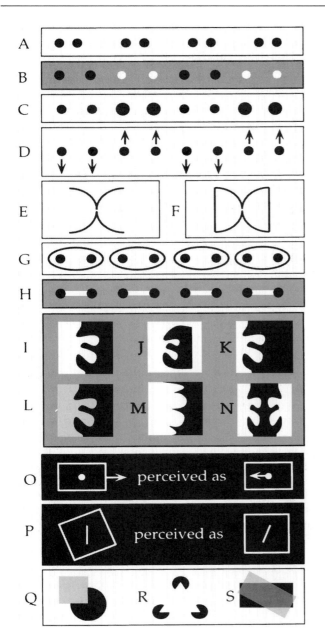

Figure 1.

the *rod-and-frame effect* (P), observers perceive an upright rod as tilted when it is presented inside a large tilted rectangle in an otherwise darkened environment (Asch and Witkin 1948), much as one perceives a vertical chandelier as hanging askew inside a tilted room in a fun house. Larger, surrounding objects or surfaces thus tend to be taken as the frame of reference for the smaller objects they enclose.

Several other organizational phenomena are strongly identified with the Gestalt approach to perception. *Amodal completion* refers to the perception of partly visible figures as completed behind an occluding object. Figure Q, for example, is invariably perceived as a complete circle behind a square even though only three-fourths of it is actually showing. *Illusory contours* refer to the perception of a figure defined by edges that are not physically present in the image. As figure R illustrates, an illusory figure is perceived when aligned contours in the inducing elements cause them to be seen as partly occluded by a figure that has the same color as the background (Kanisza 1979). *Color scission* (figure S) refers to the splitting of perceived color into one component due to an opaque figure and another component due to a translucent figure through which the farther figure is seen (Metelli 1974).

Although these examples do not exhaust the perceptual contributions of Gestalt psychologists and their followers, they are representative of the phenomena they studied in the visual domain. They also investigated the perceptual organization of sounds, a topic that has been extended significantly by modern researchers (Bregman 1990). Recent studies of PERCEPTUAL DEVELOPMENT demonstrate that, contrary to the nativistic beliefs of Gestalt theorists, most principles of organization are not present at birth, but develop at different times during the first year of life (Kellman and Spelke 1983).

Theoretically, Gestalt psychologists maintained that these phenomena of perceptual organization support *holism*, the doctrine that the whole is different from the sum of its parts. They attempted to explain such holistic effects in terms of their *principle of Prägnanz* (or *minimum principle*), the claim that the percept will be as "good" as the stimulus conditions allow. This means that the preferred organization should be the simplest, most regular possibility compatible with the constraints imposed by the retinal image. Unfortunately, they did not provide an adequate definition of goodness, simplicity, or regularity, so their central claim was untestable in any rigorous way. Later theorists have attempted to ground these concepts in objective analyses, suggesting that simple perceptions correspond to low information content, economy of symbolic representation, and/or minimal transformational distance. Non-Gestalt theorists typically appeal instead to HELMHOLTZ's *likelihood principle* that the perceptual system is biased toward the most likely (rather than the simplest) interpretation. The difficulty in discriminating between these two alternatives arises in part from the fact that the most likely interpretation is usually the simplest in some plausible sense. (See Pomerantz and Kubovy 1986 for a review of this issue.)

Most phenomena of Gestalt perception have resisted explanation at computational, algorithmic, and physiological levels. Köhler (1940) suggested that the best organization

including *surroundedness* (J), *size* (K), *contrast* (L), *convexity* (M), and *symmetry* (N). These principles are also *ceteris paribus* rules: all else being equal, the surrounded, smaller, higher contrast, more convex, or symmetrical region tends to be seen as the figure. They therefore suffer from the same problem as the laws of grouping: they cannot predict the result when two or more factors conflict.

A third important phenomenon of Gestalt perception is that certain properties of objects are perceived relative to a *frame of reference*. MOTION and orientation provide two compelling examples. In *induced motion* (O), a slowly moving larger object surrounds a smaller stationary object in an otherwise dark environment. Surprisingly, observers perceive the frame as still and the dot as moving in the opposite direction (Duncker 1929)—for example, when the moon appears to move through a cloud that appears stationary. In was achieved by *electromagnetic fields* in the CEREBRAL CORTEX that settled into states of *minimum energy*, much as soap bubbles stabilize into perfect spheres, which are minimal in both energy and complexity. Although subsequent physiological findings have discredited the brain-field conjecture, the more abstract idea of a *physical Gestalt* is compatible with modern investigations of RECURRENT NETWORKS (e.g., Grossberg and Mingolla 1985) that converge on a solution by reaching a minimum in an energy-like function. This suggests new theoretical approaches to the many important organizational phenomena Gestalt psychologists discovered more than a half century ago.

See also HIGH-LEVEL VISION; ILLUSIONS; MID-LEVEL VISION; NATIVISM; OBJECT RECOGNITION, ANIMAL STUDIES; OBJECT RECOGNITION, HUMAN; PICTORIAL ART AND VISION; VISION AND LEARNING

—*Stephen Palmer*

References

Asch, S. E., and H. A. Witkin. (1948). Studies in space orientation: I and II. *Journal of Experimental Psychology* 38: 325–337, 455–477.

Bregman, A. S. (1990). *Auditory Scene Analysis: The Perceptual Organization of Sound.* Cambridge, MA: MIT Press.

Duncker, K. (1929). Über induzierte Bewegung. *Psychologishe Forschung* 12: 180–259. Condensed translation published as Induced motion, in W. D. Ellis (1938), *A Sourcebook of Gestalt Psychology.* New York: Harcourt, Brace, pp. 161–172.

Grossberg, S., and E. Mingolla. (1985). Neural dynamics of form perception: boundary completion, illusory contours, and neon color spreading. *Psychological Review* 92: 173–211.

Kanisza, G. (1979). *Organization in Vision.* New York: Praeger.

Kellman, P. J., and E. S. Spelke. (1983). Perception of partly occluded objects in infancy. *Cognitive Psychology* 15: 483–524.

Koffka, K. (1935). *Principles of Gestalt Psychology.* New York: Harcourt Brace.

Köhler, W. (1940). *Dynamics in Psychology.* New York: Liveright Publishing Corp.

Metelli, F. (1974). The perception of transparency. *Scientific American* 230(4): 90–98.

Pomerantz, J. R., and M. Kubovy. (1986). Theoretical approaches to perceptual organization. In K. R. Boff, L. Kaufman, and J. P. Thomas, Eds., *Handbook of Perception and Human Performance.* Vol. 2, *Cognitive Processes and Performance.* New York: Wiley, pp. 36–1 to 36–46.

Palmer, S. E., and I. Rock. (1994). Rethinking perceptual organization: the role of uniform connectedness. *Psychonomic Bulletin and Review* 1: 29–55.

Rubin, E. (1921). *Visuell Wahrgenommene Figuren.* Copenhagen: Glydendalske.

Wertheimer, M. (1923). Untersuchungen zur Lehre von der Gestalt, II. *Psychologische Forschung* 4: 301–350. Condensed translation published as Laws of organization in perceptual forms, in W. D. Ellis (1938), *A Sourcebook of Gestalt Psychology.* New York: Harcourt, Brace, pp. 71–88.

Gestalt Psychology

The scope of Gestalt psychology goes beyond its origins in research on perception. The founder of the Gestalt school, Max Wertheimer, invested much of his energies in other topics, such as epistemology (Wertheimer 1934), ethics (1935), problem solving (1920), and creativity (1959/1978; see also Duncker 1945/1972; Luchins 1942). Koffka, one of Wertheimer's foremost collaborators, devoted more than half of his *Principles of Gestalt Psychology* (1935) to attitudes, emotion, the will, memory (see also Wulf 1921; Restorff 1933), learning, and the relations between society and personality (see also Lewin 1935; Dembo 1931/1976). Köhler, the third member of the leadership of the Gestalt school, did research on the insightful problem-solving of apes (1921/1976) and wrote about ethics (claiming that value is an emergent property of situations) and *requiredness* (1938), which anticipates Gibson's notion of AFFORDANCES.

After the dismantling of German psychology—beginning with the coming to power of Hitler in 1933—American psychology, dominated by doctrinaire BEHAVIORISM, was disdainful of cognitive ideas and saw Gestalt psychology as outmoded and suspiciously vitalistic. These suspicions were reinforced by the views of some Gestalt psychologists about the way the brain creates Gestalts, views that seemed to have been spectacularly refuted (for a summary, see Pomerantz and Kubovy 1981). It was perhaps for this reason that during this period, the influence of Gestalt psychologists—many of whom were refugees from Nazi Germany—on American psychology was felt mostly in social psychology (e.g., Lewin 1951; Heider 1958/1982; Krech and Crutchfield 1948) and psychology of art (e.g., Arnheim 1974, 1969), which were not under the control of behaviorists and were not concerned with brain theory (Zajonc 1980).

During the eclipse of Gestalt psychology as cognitive psychology, some of the questions posed by the Gestalt psychologists were kept alive by Attneave (1959), Garner (1974), Goldmeier (1973), and Rock (1973). A more general revival of these questions took place in the early 1980s with the publication of three edited books: Kubovy and Pomerantz (1981), Beck (1982), and Dodwell and Caelli (1984).

Gestalt psychology can be characterized by four main features: (1) its method: phenomenology; (2) its attitude towards REDUCTIONISM: brain-experience isomorphism; (3) its focus of investigation: part-whole relationships; (4) its theoretical principle: Prägnanz (Pomerantz and Kubovy 1981; Epstein and Hatfield 1994). Let us consider these features one by one.

Phenomenology. The application of phenomenology to perception involves a descriptive text laced with pictures (exemplified by GESTALT PERCEPTION, and Ihde 1977). According to Bozzi (1989: chap. 7), a conventional psychological experiment (in any field of psychology) differs from a phenomenological experiment in the way summarized in Table 1. This comparison shows how close phenomenological research is to protocol analysis, the use of verbal reports as data, often used in research on problem-solving (Simon and Kaplan 1989: 21–29). In recent years some psychologists have confirmed and elaborated results obtained with the phenomenological method by using more conventional experimental methodology (Kubovy, Holcombe, and Wagermans forthcoming). Phenomenology as practiced by the Gestalt psychologists should not be confused with introspec-

Table 1. Comparison of conventional and phenomenological experiments (after Bozzi 1989: chap. 7)

	Conventional	Phenomenological
environment	isolated (such as a laboratory)	any (preferably not a laboratory)
participants	kept naive about the topic or purpose of the research (to minimize *demand characteristics*)	are told everything
task	well-defined	jointly defined by participant and researcher
participants' response	• often the first that comes to mind	• may transcend their first impression, and thus provide information about their solution space
	• may not be modified	• may be reconsidered
	• are either correct or incorrect	• all answers are valid
	• unambiguous, or are filtered into a set of mutually exclusive and collectively exhaustive a priori categories	• responses are classified only after all the data have been examined

tionism as practiced by early psychologists such as Titchener (cf. INTROSPECTION). In fact, in its methodological assumptions, introspectionism is closer to contemporary experimental psychology than to phenomenology. Any account of the introspectionists' methods (Lyons 1986) will confirm that they are well described by Bozzi's six features of conventional psychological experiments (Table 1).

Brain Theory. Despite the refutation of the specifics of the Gestalt psychologists' brain theory, their search for specific correspondences between experiences and brain events and their idea of brain fields anticipated important current foci of research (e.g., NEURAL NETWORKS and massively parallel processing). Köhler (1947: 132–133) predicted that future psychological research would study "dynamic self-distribution. . . which Gestalt Psychology believes to be essential in neurological and psychological theory," whose "final result always constitutes an orderly distribution," that is, a "balance of forces" (p. 130; this is a statement of the principle of Prägnanz, discussed below). It is impossible to read this prophecy without thinking of Hopfield networks and Boltzman machines, that can be thought of as minimizing a system energy function (Anderson 1995; Kelso 1995).

It should be noted that for all their emphasis on brain theory, the Gestalt psychologists did not think of themselves as nativists (Köhler 1947: 113, 117, 215). They were nevertheless vigorously opposed to the behaviorists' empirism (a psychological metatheory that gives primacy to learning theories; to be carefully distinguished from the epistemological theory of empiricism).

Part-whole relationships. The problem of part-whole relationships, which is currently under vigorous investigation in perception, was first discussed by Christian von Ehrenfels, in

a seminal essay "On 'Gestalt Qualities'" (1988) written twenty-two years before Wertheimer's (1912a) first discussion of the subject. He is the one who first asked, "Is a melody (i) a mere *Zusammenfassung* of elements, or (ii) something novel in relation to this *Zusammenfassung,* something that. . . is distinguishable from the *Zusammenfassung* of the elements?" (p. 82). Although *Zusammenfassung* has usually been translated as "sum," this translation may have led to confusion because the notion of *Zusammenfassung* is more vague than the word "sum" suggests. The word means "combination," "summing-up," "summary," "synopsis," that is to say, "sum" as in the expression "in sum," rather than as an arithmetic operation (Grelling and Oppenheim 1939/1988: 198, propose the translation "totality").

Consider the tune *Row Your Boat.* The melody is different from the following *Zusammenfassung:* "10 Cs, 3 Ds, 7 Es, 2 Fs, and 5 Gs," because the duration of the notes is important. The melody is also different from a more detailed *Zusammenfassung* (if the time signature is $\frac{6}{8}$): "1 × < C,6>, 2 × <C,3S>, 1 × <C,2> , 6 × <C,1>, 3 × <D,1>, . . ." where 2 × <C,3>, means two tokens of C whose duration is equivalent to three eighth notes, because the order of the notes is important. But even the score—which specifies the notes, their duration, and their order—does not capture the melody. The tune could be transposed from the key of C to the key of F#, and played at a faster tempo so that it would share no pitches and no absolute durations with the original version. It would still be the same tune. What is preserved are the ratios of frequencies (musical intervals) and the ratios of durations (rhythm). Melody is a property of the whole that depends on *relationships* among the elements, not on the elements themselves. According to von Ehrenfels, the Gestalt is a quality one perceives *in addition to* perceiving the individual elements. It was Wertheimer who reformulated this idea of the Gestalt as a whole embracing perceived elements as parts.

Prägnanz. The notion of Prägnanz (introduced by Wertheimer 1912b) is of great importance to the understanding of cognition. Textbooks define Prägnanz as the tendency of a process to realize the most regular, ordered, stable, balanced state possible in a given situation. This notion is illustrated by the behavior of soap films, which are laminae of minimal potential energy. Unconstrained, a soap film becomes a spherical bubble, but when constrained by a wire, the film takes on a graceful and seemingly complex shape (Hildebrandt and Tromba 1985: chap. 5). But the standard definition of Prägnanz ignores an important difference between physical and cognitive systems. Physical systems are exquisitely sensitive to the exact form of the constraints: small changes in the constraints can make a big difference to the shape of the soap film. In contrast, cognitive systems are relatively insensitive to the details of the input, because they decompose it into a *schema* that has Prägnanz, to which a *correction* is added to characterize the input (Woodworth 1938: chap. 4). Cognitive systems have several ways to extract Prägnanz from inputs (Rausch 1966—summarized by Smith 1988—proposed seven of them). Here are five of them (the first three are exemplified in figure 1): (1) *Lawfulness:* extract the part of an event or an object that conforms to a law or a rule. (2) *Originality:* extract the part of

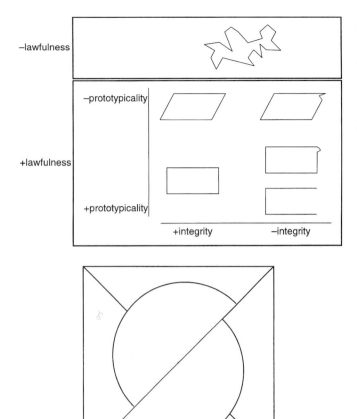

Attneave, F. (1959). *Applications of Information Theory to Psychology.* New York: Holt, Rinehart and Winston.

Beck, J., Ed. (1982). *Organization and Representation in Perception.* Hillsdale, NJ: Erlbaum.

Birenbaum, G. (1930). Das Vergessen einer Vornahmen. Isolierte seelische Systeme und dynamische Gesamtbereiche. [Forgetting a person's name. Isolated mental systems and dynamical global fields.] *Psychologische Forschung* 13: 218–284.

Bozzi, P. (1989). *Fenomenologia Sperimentale.* [Experimental Phenomenology]. Bologna, Italy: Il Mulino.

Dembo, T. (1976). The dynamics of anger. In J. De Rivera, Ed., *Field Theory as Human-Science: Contributions of Lewin's Berlin Group.* New York: Gardner Press. pp. 324–422. Original work published 1931.

Dodwell, P. C., and T. Caelli, Eds. (1984). *Figural Synthesis.* Hillsdale, NJ: Erlbaum.

Duncker, K. (1972). *On Problem-Solving.* Trans. L. S. Lees. Westport, CT: Greenwood Press. Original work published 1945.

Ehrenfels, C. von. (1988). On "Gestalt qualities". In B. Smith, Ed., *Foundations of Gestalt Theory.* Munich: Philosophia Verlag, pp. 82–117. Original work published 1890.

Ellis, W. D., Ed. (1938). *A Source Book of Gestalt Psychology.* London: Kegan, Paul, Trench, Trubner.

Epstein, W., and G. Hatfield. (1994). Gestalt psychology and the philosophy of mind. *Philosophical Psychology* 7: 163–181.

Garner, W. R. (1974). *The Processing of Information and Structure.* Potomac, MD: Erlbaum.

Goldmeier, E. (1973). Similarity in visually perceived form. *Psychological Issues* 8: Whole No.1.

Grelling, K., and P. Oppenheim. (1988). Logical analysis of "Gestalt" as "Functional whole". In B. Smith, Ed., *Foundations of Gestalt Theory.* Munich: Philosophia Verlag, pp. 210–226. Original work published 1939.

Heider, F. (1982). *The Psychology of Interpersonal Relations.* Hillsdale, NJ: Erlbaum. Original work published 1958.

Hildebrandt, S., and S. Tromba. (1985). *Mathematics and Optimal Form.* New York: Scientific American Books.

Ihde, D. (1977). *Experimental Phenomenology: An Introduction.* New York: Putnam.

Kanizsa, G. (1979). *Organization in Vision.* New York: Praeger.

Kelso, J. A. S. (1995). *Dynamic Patterns: The Self-Organization of Brain and Behavior.* Cambridge, MA: MIT Press.

Köhler, W. (1938). *The Place of Value in a World of Facts.* New York: Liveright.

Köhler, W. (1947). *Gestalt Psychology: An Introduction to New Concepts in Modern Psychology.* Rev. ed. New York: Liveright.

Köhler, W. (1976). *The Mentality of Apes.* 2nd ed. Trans. by E. Winter. New York: Liveright. Original work published 1921.

Figure 2. A puzzle that is hard to solve because of Prägnanz.

an event or an object that is a prototype (in the sense currently used in theories of the structure of CONCEPTS) with respect to other events or objects. (3) *Integrity:* extract the part of an event or an object that is whole, complete or intact, rather than partial, incomplete or flawed. (4) *Simplicity:* extract that part of an event or an object that is simple or "good." (5) *Diversity:* extract that part of an event or an object that is "pregnant," that is, rich, fruitful, significant, weighty.

Much of the work of Gestalt psychologists on obstacles to PROBLEM SOLVING has implicated Prägnanz. For example, if the six pieces shown in figure 2 are scattered in front of you, and you are asked to make a square out of them, you are likely to start by forming a disk—a good form that delays the solution (Kanizsa 1979: chap. 14).

See also EMERGENCE; GIBSON, JAMES JEROME; ILLUSIONS; RECURRENT NETWORKS

—*Michael Kubovy*

References

Anderson, J. A. (1995). *An Introduction to Neural Networks.* Cambridge, MA: MIT Press.

Arnheim, R. (1969). *Visual Thinking.* Berkeley: University of California Press.

Arnheim, R. (1974). *Art and Visual Perception: A Psychology of the Creative Eye.* Berkeley: University of California Press.

Figure 1. Three ways to apply Prägnanz to the perception of shape. For each of these ways, the smaller the "correction" to the "schema," the greater the Prägnanz of the shape. *Originality:* A shape can be seen as a transformed prototype: a parallelogram can be seen as a skewed rectangle. *Integrity:* A shape can be seen as an intact shape ("rectangle") modified by a feature or a flaw: "rectangle with a bump," "rectangle with one side missing." *Lawfulness:* A hard-to-name irregular shape can be said to be roughly rectangular in form.

Koffka, K. (1963). *Principles of Gestalt psychology*. New York: Harcourt, Brace and World. Original work published 1935.

Krech, D., and R Crutchfield. (1948). *Theory and Problems in Social Psychology*. New York: McGraw-Hill.

Kubovy, M., and J. R. Pomerantz, Eds. (1981). *Perceptual Organization*. Hillsdale, NJ: Erlbaum.

Kubovy, M., A. O. Holcombe, and J. Wagemans. (1998). On the lawfulness of grouping by proximity. *Cognitive Psychology* 35: 71–98.

Lewin, K. (1935). *A Dynamic Theory of Personality*. New York: McGraw-Hill.

Lewin, K. (1951). *Field Theory in Social Science*. New York: Harper.

Luchins, A. S. (1942). Mechanization in problem solving: the effect of "Einstellung." *Psychological Monographs* 54(6): whole no. 248.

Lyons, W. (1986). *The Disappearance of Introspection*. Cambridge, MA: MIT Press.

Metzger, W. (1962). *Schöpferische Freiheit*. [Creative Freedom]. Frankfurt-am-Main: Kramer.

Pomerantz, J. R., and M. Kubovy. (1981). Perceptual organization: an overview. In M. Kubovy and J. R. Pomerantz, Eds., *Perceptual Organization*. Hillsdale, NJ: Erlbaum, pp. 423–456.

Pomerantz, J. R., and M. Kubovy. (1986). Theoretical approaches to perceptual organization: Simplicity and likelihood principles. In K. R. Boff, L. Kaufman, and J. P. Thomas, Eds., *Handbook of Perception and Human Performance*. Vol. 2: *Cognitive Processes and Performance*. New York: Wiley, pp. 36-1–36-46.

Rausch, E. (1966). Das Eigenschaftsproblem in der Gestalttheorie der Wahrnehmung. [The problem of properties in the Gestalt theory of perception]. In W. Metzger and H. Erke, Eds., *Handbuch der Psychologie [Handbook of Psychology]*, vol. 1: *Wahrnehmung und Bewusstsein [Perception and Consciousness]*. Göttingen: Hogrefe, pp. 866–953.

von Restorff, H. (1933). Analyse von Vorgängen in Spurenfeld. I. Über die Wirkung von Bereichtsbildungen im Spurenfeld. [Analysis of processes in the memory trace. I. On the effect of region-formation on the memory trace]. *Psychologische Forschung* 18: 299–342.

Rock, I. (1973). *Orientation and Form*. New York: Academic Press.

Rosch, E., and C. B. Mervis. (1975). Family resemblances: studies in the internal structure of categories. *Cognitive Psychology* 7: 573–605.

Shipley, T., Ed. (1961). *Classics in Psychology*. New York: Philosophical Library.

Simon, H. A., and C. A Kaplan. (1989). Foundations of cognitive science. In M. I. Posner, Ed., *Foundations of Cognitive Science*. Cambridge, MA: MIT Press, pp. 1–47.

Smith, B. (1988). Gestalt theory: an essay in philosophy. In B. Smith, Ed., *Foundations of Gestalt Theory*. Munich: Philosophia Verlag, pp. 11–81.

Wertheimer, M. (1912a). Über das Denken der Naturvölker. I. Zahlen und Zahlgebilde. [On the thought-processes in preliterate groups. I. Numbers and numerical concepts]. *Zeitschrift für Psychologie* 60: 321–378. (Excerpts in Ellis 1938: 265–273.)

Wertheimer, M. (1912b). Experimentelle Studien über das Sehen von Bewegung. [Experiments on the perception of motion]. *Zeitschrift für Psychologie* 61: 161–265. (Excerpts in Shipley 1961: 1032–1089.)

Wertheimer, M. (1920). *Über Schlussprozesse im produktiven Denken*. Berlin: de Gruyter.

Wertheimer, M. (1934). On truth. *Social Research* 1: 135–146.

Wertheimer, M. (1935). Some problems in the theory of ethics. *Social Research* 2: 353–367.

Wertheimer, M. (1978). *Productive Thinking*. Enlarged ed. Westport, CT: Greenwood Press. Original work published 1959.

Woodworth, R. S. (1938). *Experimental Psychology*. New York: Henry Holt.

Wulf, F. (1921). Über die Veränderung von Vorstellungen (Gedächtnis und Gestalt). [On the modification of representations (memory and Gestalt)]. *Psychologische Forschung* 1: 333–373. (Excerpts in Ellis 1938: 136–148).

Zajonc, R. B. (1980). Cognition and social cognition: a historical perspective. In L. Festinger, Ed., *Retrospections on Social Psychology*. New York: Oxford University Press, pp. 180–204.

Gibson, James Jerome

In his last book, *The Ecological Approach to Visual Perception*, James Gibson (1904–1979) concluded with a plea that the terms and concepts of his theory "...never shackle thought as the old terms and concepts have!" He was referring to the framework of traditional perception, as was reflected, for example, in the classical problem of space perception Bishop Berkeley posed more than three hundred years ago (Berkeley 1963). How is it possible to perceive three-dimensional space when the input to our senses is a two-dimensional retinal surface in the case of vision, or a skin surface in the case of touch? Logically, it seemed this inadequate stimulation had to be supplemented somehow to account for our ordinary perception of a three-dimensional world. There have been two general proposals for the nature of this supplementation. An empiricist proposal, advocated by Berkeley himself, based the supplementation in the prior experience of the individual. The alternative nativist proposal based the supplementation in the innate functioning of the mental apparatus which intrinsically imposes a three-dimensional structure on two-dimensional stimulation. These two alternatives in only slightly modified forms persist to this day.

Gibson challenged Berkeley's initial assumption, asserting that there is indeed sufficient information available to observers for perceiving a three-dimensional world. It does not have to be supplemented from our past experience or from our innate mental operations. Gibson's refutation of the traditional formulation depended on confirming the hypothesis that information is sufficient to account for what we perceive. He argued that the traditional physical analysis of energy available to our senses (rays of light and sound waves) is the wrong level of analysis for perceiving organisms with mobile eyes in mobile heads who look and walk around. Rather, light in ambient arrays (as opposed to radiant light) is structured by, and fully specifies, its sources in the objects and events of the world we perceive. He showed that if the entire structure of the optic array at any point in space were examined, rather than punctate stimuli impinging on the retina, the information available is exceedingly rich. Moreover it specifies important features of the environment. Thus textured optic arrays specify surfaces, gradients of texture specify slanted or receding surfaces, changing patterns in the structure are specific to particular types of object and observer movement, and so on.

Two implications of Gibson's reformulation need to be emphasized. First, patterns of stimulation change when an observing organism is active. The very act of moving makes information available. Gibson showed that the transformations in the optic array sampled by a moving observer simultaneously specify the path of locomotion (perspective structure) and the stable environment (invariant structure). The traditional formulation of perception involves a passive observer with stimulation imposed by the natural physical world or by a psychological experimenter; either observer or object movement is a complication. Gibson emphasized the active nature of perceiving, and the idea that movement is essential. Second, in Gibson's formulation perception is of properties that are relevant to an organism's being in contact with its environment: things like surfaces and changes in surface layout, places that enclose, paths that are open for mobility, objects approaching or receding, and so on. In the traditional Berkeley perspective perception is of abstract three-dimensional space. For Gibson abstract three-dimensional space is a conceptual achievement. Perception is concerned with guiding behavior in a populated and cluttered environment.

Gibson's emphasis on the functional aspects of perception had roots in his work on pilot selection and training in the Army Air Force during World War II (Gibson 1947). This functional emphasis was developed most thoroughly in his last book, where he presented his ecological approach (Gibson 1979). The first section of the book included an analysis of the physical world at a level ecologically relevant to the activity of a perceiving organism. This provided a taxonomy of the features that are perceived and an analysis of how the physical world structures light so as to provide the information for the meaningful properties to be perceived.

Gibson's ecological perspective emphasizes both the environment/organism mutuality of perception and its intrinsic meaningfulness. This emphasis has the radical implication of breaking down the subject/object distinction pervasive in Western philosophy and psychology as well as solving the psychological riddle of how perception is meaningful. The meaningfulness of perception is reflected in his concept of *affordance* which is currently the source of some controversy. AFFORDANCES are the properties of the environment, taken with reference to creatures living in it, that make possible or inhibit various kinds of activity: surfaces of a certain height, size, and inclination afford sitting on by humans, those of a different height and size afford stepping up on, objects moving at a certain speed afford catching, and so forth. For Gibson, perception of these possibilities for action are primary, and they are specified by information in the optic array.

The concept of affordance is implicated in another controversial concept of Gibson's formulation, that of direct perception. Gibson argued that perception is direct in the sense that perceiving a property, for instance an affordance, is based on detection of the information specifying that property. (For affordances the meaning is appreciated in the very detection of the information.) Critics of his theory interpret direct perception as implying that perception is automatic and argue that it is easy to find examples where it is not. This is a misunderstanding. Direct perception does not imply automaticity, rather the processes involved are

different from the traditional ones; they are not association or computation but exploration, detection of invariant relations, and perceptual learning.

Many of Gibson's empirical discoveries were incorporated into mainstream theories of perception during his lifetime. From early in his career adaptation to prolonged inspection of curved and tilted lines (e.g., Gibson 1937) became a prototype of subsequent research concerned with perceptual and perceptual-motor adaptation to visual-motor rearrangements. TEXTURE gradients have long been accepted as one of the "cues" of DEPTH PERCEPTION. The investigation of the use of motion transformations for guiding locomotion and the analysis of active perception in general, particularly in computer science, are very active research areas. Gibson's theoretical influence has been extended by many of his former colleagues and students whose research is motivated by his ecological framework. Many groups and research problems illustrate this influence: Lee (1980), Warren, Morris, and Kalish (1988), and others have investigated the geometric nature of motion-generated information available for the guidance of locomotion. Turvey, Shaw, and others (e.g., Turvey et al. 1981) have integrated Gibson's ideas with those of Nicolai Bernshtein, the Russian action physiologist, in investigations and analyses of both visual and haptic perception. Edward Reed has extended his views to what he terms ecological philosophy, described in three recent books (Reed 1996a, 1996b, 1997). Gibson's closest and most influential colleague was his wife, Eleanor Jack Gibson, who has elaborated a theory of perceptual learning and development, complementary to his theory of perception (E. J. Gibson 1969). Most recently she and her colleagues (e.g., Adolph, Eppler, and Gibson 1993; A. D. Pick 1997; Walker-Andrews 1988; and others) have been applying the concept of affordance in the study of PERCEPTUAL DEVELOPMENT in a way that simultaneously refines the concept itself. Such investigations have shown the promise and utility of Gibson's radical formulation. Such success will really be complete when it permits and encourages further development of his theoretical concepts without the shackling which he feared.

This article was to have been written by Gibson's close friend and younger colleague, Edward Reed. His untimely death in February, 1997, has deprived the field of a brilliant and humane scholar.

See also ECOLOGICAL PSYCHOLOGY; MARR, DAVID; MOTION, PERCEPTION OF; RATIONALISM VS. EMPIRICISM; STRUCTURE FROM VISUAL INFORMATION SOURCES; VISION AND LEARNING

—Herb Pick, Jr., and Anne Pick

References

Adolph, K. E., M. A. Eppler, and E. J. Gibson. (1993). Development of perception of affordances. In C. Rovee-Collier and L. P. Lipsitt, Eds., *Advances in Infancy Research,* vol. 8. Norwood, NJ: Ablex, pp. 51–98.

Berkeley, G. (1709/1963). An essay towards a new theory of vision. In C. Turbayne, Ed., *Berkeley: Works on Vision.* Indianapolis: Bobbs-Merrill.

Gibson, E. J. (1969). *Principles of Perceptual Learning and Development.* New York: Appleton-Century-Crofts.

Gibson, J. J. (1937). Adaptation with negative after-effect. *Psychological Review* 44: 222–244.

Gibson, J. J. (1947). Motion picture testing and research. *Aviation Psychology Research Reports* No. 7. Washington, DC: U.S. Government Printing Office.

Gibson, J. J. (1979). *The Ecological Approach to Visual Perception.* Boston: Houghton Mifflin.

Lee, D. N. (1980). The optic flow field: the foundation of vision. *Philosophical Transactions of the Royal Society, London* Series B, 290: 169–179.

Pick, A. D. (1997). Perceptual learning, categorizing, and cognitive development. In C. Dent-Read and P. Zukow-Goldring, Eds., *Evolving Explanations of Development.* Washington, DC: American Psychological Association, pp. 335–370.

Reed, E. S. (1996a). *Encountering the World.* New York: Oxford University Press.

Reed, E. S. (1996b). *The Necessity of Experience.* New Haven: Yale University Press.

Reed, E. S. (1997). *From Soul to Mind. The Emergence of Psychology, from Erasmus Darwin to William James.* New Haven: Yale University Press.

Turvey, M. T., R. E. Shaw, E. S. Reed, and W. M. Mace. (1981). Ecological laws of perceiving and acting: in reply to Fodor and Pylyshyn (1981). *Cognition* 9: 237–304.

Walker-Andrews, A. S. (1988). Infant perception of the affordances of expressive behaviors. In L. P. Lipsitt and C. Rovee-Collier, Eds., *Advances in Infancy,* vol. 5. Norwood, NJ: Ablex, pp. 173–221.

Warren, W. H., M. W. Morris, and M. Kalish. (1988). Perception of translation heading from optical flow. *Journal of Experimental Psychology: Human Perception and Performance* 14: 646–660.

Further Readings

Gibson, J. J. (1950). *The Perception of the Visual World.* Boston: Houghton Mifflin.

Gibson, J. J. (1968). *The Senses Considered as Perceptual Systems.* London: Allen and Unwin.

Michaels, C., and C. Carello. (1981). *Direct Perception.* New York: Prentice-Hall.

Reed, E. S. (1988). *James J. Gibson and the Psychology of Perception.* New Haven: Yale University Press.

Reed, E. S., and R. K. Jones, Eds. (1982). *Reasons for Realism:*

Selected Essays of James J. Gibson. Hillsdale, NJ: Erlbaum.

Gödel's Theorems

Kurt Gödel was one of the most influential logicians of the twentieth century. He established a number of absolutely central facts, among them the semantic completeness of first order logic and the relative consistency of the axiom of choice and of the generalized continuum hypothesis. However, the theorems that have been most significant—for the general discussion concerning the foundations of mathematics—are his two *incompleteness theorems* published in 1931; they are also referred to simply as Gödel's theorems or *the Gödel theorems.*

The early part of the twentieth century saw a dramatic development of logic in the context of deep problems in the foundations of mathematics. This development provided for the first time the basic means to reflect mathematical practice in formal theories; see FORMAL SYSTEMS. One fundamental question was: Is there a formal theory such that mathematical truth is co-extensive with provability in that theory? Russell's type theory *P* of *Principia Mathematica* and axiomatic set theory as formulated by Zermelo seemed to make a positive answer plausible. A second question emerged from the research program that had been initiated by Hilbert around 1920 (with roots going back to the turn of the century): Is the consistency of mathematics in its formalized presentation provable by restricted mathematical, so-called finitist means? The incompleteness theorems gave negative answers to both questions for the particular theories mentioned. To be more precise, a negative answer to the second question is provided only if finitist mathematics itself can be formalized in these theories; that was not claimed by Gödel in 1931, only in his (1933) did he assert it with great force.

The first incompleteness theorem states (making use of an improvement due to Rosser):

If P is consistent, then there is a sentence σ in the language of *P*, such that neither σ nor its negation ¬ σ is provable in *P*.

σ is thus *independent* of *P*. As σ is a number theoretic statement it is either true or false for the natural numbers; in either case, we have a statement that is true and not provable in *P*. This incompleteness of *P* cannot be remedied by adding the true statement to *P* as an axiom: for the theory so expanded, the same incompleteness phenomenon arises.

Gödel's second theorem claims the unprovability of a (meta-) mathematically meaningful statement:

If P is consistent, then *cons,* the statement in the language of *P* that expresses the consistency of *P*, is not provable in *P*.

Some, for example Church, raised the question whether the proofs in some way depended on special features of *P*. In his Princeton lectures of 1934, Gödel tried to present matters in a more general way; he succeeded in addressing Church's concerns, but continued to strive for even greater generality in the formulation of the theorems. To understand in what direction, we first review the very basic ideas underlying the proofs and then discuss why Turing's work is essential for a general formulation.

Crucial are the *effective presentation* of *P*'s syntax and its *(internal) representation.* Gödel uses a presentation by primitive recursive functions, that is, the basic syntactic objects (strings of letters of *P*'s alphabet and strings of such strings) are "coded" as natural numbers, and the subsets corresponding to formulas and proofs are given by primitive recursive characteristic functions. Representability conditions are established for all syntactic notions R, that is, really for all primitive recursive sets (and relations): if $R(m)$ holds then *P* proves $r(\overline{m})$, and if not $R(m)$ holds then *P* proves $\neg r(\overline{m})$, where r is a formula in the language of *P* and $\overline{m}$ the numeral for the natural number m. Thus, the metamathematical talk about the theory can be represented within it. Then the self-referential statement σ (in the language of *P*) is constructed in conscious analogy to the liar sentence; σ expresses that it is not provable in *P*. An argument similar to that showing the liar sentence not to be true establishes that σ is not provable in *P*, thus we have part of the first theorem. The second theorem is obtained, very roughly speaking, by formalizing the proof of the first theorem concerning σ, but additional derivability conditions are needed: this yields a proof in *P* of (cons → σ). Now, clearly, cons cannot be provable in *P*, otherwise σ were provable, contradicting the part of the first theorem we just established. The proof of the second theorem was given in detail only by Hilbert and Bernays (1939). A gem of an informal presentation of this material is (Gödel 1931b); for a good introduction to the mathematical details see Smorynski (1977).

Gödel viewed in (1934) the primitive recursiveness of the syntactic notions as "a precise condition which in practice suffices as a substitute for the unprecise requirement . . . that the class of axioms and relation of immediate consequence be constructive," that is, have an effectively calculable characteristic function. What was needed, in principle, was a precise concept capturing the informal notion of an effectively calculable function, and that would allow a perfectly general characterization of formal theories. Such a notion emerged from the investigations of Church and TURING; see CHURCH-TURING THESIS. Only then was it possible to state and prove the Incompleteness Theorems for all formal theories satisfying representability (for all recursive relations) and derivability conditions. In the above statement of the theorems, the premise "*P* is consistent" can now be replaced by "*P* is any consistent formal theory satisfying the representability conditions," respectively "*P* is any consistent formal theory satisfying the representability and derivability conditions." It is this generality of his results that Gödel emphasized again and again; for example, in his (1964) work: "In consequence of later advances, in particular of the fact that, due to A. M. Turing's work, a precise and unquestionably adequate definition of the general concept of formal system can now be given, the existence of undecidable arithmetical propositions and the non-demonstrability of the consistency of a system in the same system can now be proved rigorously for *every* consistent formal system containing a certain amount of finitary number theory."

Gödel exploited this general formulation of his theorems (based on Turing's work) and analyzed their broader significance for the philosophy of mathematics and mind most carefully in (1951). The first section is devoted to a discussion of the Incompleteness Theorems, in particular of the second theorem, and argues for a "mathematically established fact" which is of "great philosophical interest" to Gödel: either the humanly evident axioms of mathematics cannot be comprised by a finite rule given by a Turing machine, or they can be and thus allow the successive development of all of demonstrable mathematics. In the latter case human mathematical abilities are in principle captured by a Turing machine, and thus there will be absolutely undecidable problems. That is what can be strictly inferred from Gödel's theorems, counter to Lucas, Penrose, and others. Gödel thought that the first disjunct held, as he believed that the second disjunct had to be false; he emphasized repeatedly, for example in (1964), that his

results do not establish "any bounds for the powers of human reason, but rather for the potentialities of pure formalism in mathematics." Indeed, in the Gibbs lecture Gödel reformulated the first disjunct as this dramatic and vague statement: "the human mind (even within the realm of pure mathematics) infinitely surpasses the powers of any finite machine."

See also COMPUTATION AND THE BRAIN; COMPUTATIONAL THEORY OF MIND; LOGIC

—*Wilfried Sieg*

References

Gödel, K. (1931a). Über formal unentscheidbare Sätze der *Principia Mathematica* und verwandter Systeme I. Translated in *Collected Works I*, pp. 144–195.

Gödel, K. (1931b). Über unentscheidbare Sätze. Translated in *Collected Works III*, pp. 30–35.

Gödel, K. (1933). The present situation in the foundations of mathematics. In *Collected Works III*, pp. 45–53.

Gödel, K. (1934). On undecidable propositions of formal mathematical systems (Princeton Lectures). In *Collected Works I*, pp. 346–369.

Gödel, K. (1951). Some basic theorems on the foundations of mathematics and their implications (Gibbs Lecture). In *Collected Works III*, pp. 304–323.

Gödel, K. (1964). Postscriptum to Gödel (1934). In *Collected Works I*, pp. 369–371.

Gödel, K. (1986). *Collected Works I*. Oxford: Oxford University Press.

Gödel, K. (1990). *Collected Works II*. Oxford: Oxford University Press.

Gödel, K. (1995). *Collected Works III*. Oxford: Oxford University Press.

Hilbert, D. and P. Bernays. (1939). *Grundlagen der Mathematik II*. Berlin: Springer.

Lucas, J. R. (1961). Minds, machines and Gödel. *Philosophy* 36: 112–127.

Penrose, R. (1989). *The Emperor's New Mind*. New York: Oxford University Press.

Rosser, B. (1936). Extensions of some theorems of Gödel and Church. *J. Symbolic Logic* 2: 129–137.

Smorynski, C. (1977). The incompleteness theorem. In J. Barwise, Ed., *Handbook of Mathematical Logic*. Amsterdam. North-Holland, pp. 821–865.

Further Readings

Dawson, J. W. (1997). *Logical Dilemmas—The Life and Work of Kurt Gödel*. New York: A. K. Peters.

Golgi, Camillo

Camillo Golgi (1843–1926) was one of a generation of great neurohistologists that included Kölliker, Gerlach, Nissl, and CAJAL. For these scientists, the cellular nature of nervous tissue was still enigmatic and controversial, decades after Schleiden and Schwann had promulgated the theory that cells are the basic architectonic units of living tissues. What we now somewhat nonchalantly identify as nerve cells had been visualized as early as 1836 (by Valentin); but, with the techniques then available, the relationship between cell bodies and their protoplasmic extensions could not be clear. A natural interpretation, bizarre as it may now seem, was that nerve cells were nodes, perhaps nutritive in function, embedded within a continuous reticulum of nerve fibers.

Golgi's unique and enduring contribution is generally cited as the discovery of the silver dichromate stain for nerve tissue, which for the first time allowed visualization of nerve cells in their entirety. The actual discovery is surrounded with a certain romanticism, an admixture of luck and perseverance. Golgi, the son of a medical practitioner, had taken his degree in medicine (1865), and spent six years (1865–71) tending patients at the Ospedale di San Matteo in Pavia while also doing research in brain histology in the laboratory of his younger friend and mentor, Giulio Cesare Bizzozero. The actual discovery, however, came while he was first resident physician in the home for incurables at Abbiategrasso. Working in the evenings by candlelight in the kitchen of his hospital apartment (da Fano 1926), he continued the research that led to the new technique. The resulting article, published in 1873 ("On the structure of the gray matter of the brain"), has a refreshing simplicity: "Using the method I have developed for staining brain elements . . . I was able to discover several facts about the structure of the grey brain matter which I believe worth making known" (in Corsi 1988).

The silver stain, although used to advantage by Golgi himself (who subsequently moved to the faculty at Pavia, as professor of general pathology and histology, where he remained until his retirement in 1918), was at first dismissed by the mainstream school of German histologists. In 1887 the Golgi stain was itself discovered by Ramon y Cajal, who used it to impressive advantage in the first great investigations of functional neuroanatomy. Throughout the twentieth century, the Golgi stain remained important in investigations of normative structure and of changes associated with development, pathology, or plasticity. It has to some extent been superseded by intracellular injection of tracers (such as biocytin or horseradish peroxidase), but remains a valuable method for visualizing larger populations of cells and when experimental injection is not feasible (i.e., in most human material). In tribute to the elegance of the original silver methods, high-quality cellular images, immunocytochemical or intracellular, are still evaluated as "pseudo-Golgi" or "Golgi-like."

Golgi further deserves acknowledgment for his role in the early polemics surrounding the NEURON doctrine. This debate was articulated dramatically, almost scandalously from the modern perspective, in the Nobel addresses for 1906, when Golgi and Cajal were jointly awarded the prize in physiology and medicine. Golgi defended the reticularist position, while Cajal championed the neuron doctrine (respectively representing the "continualists" and the "contiguists"; Van der Loos 1967). Golgi's position, in light of the facts, has come to be viewed as archaic, and an unfortunate example of dogma winning out over observation. In his defense, it is worth remembering that synaptic morphology —and in particular the discontinuity of the pre- and postsynaptic elements—was not definitively demonstrated until electron microscopic studies in the 1950s (see Peters, Palay, and de Webster 1991). Moreover, at least some of Golgi's

reservations can be seen as an arguably legitimate concern about the neuron doctrine in its most stringent formulation. Thus, he makes the interesting distinction between a "nerve cell," which corresponds to a distinct histological entity, and a "neuron," the definition of which, he suggests, should include its functional operation. In the functional domain, the concept of the "neuron" is indeed elusive and continues to evolve even at the present moment.

Golgi's reticularist stance may have derived from a strong conviction in the unified or holistic nature of brain function, or at least a preoccupation with how unity (of perception, of consciousness) can result from individualized elements. So stated, this is not necessarily dissimilar from modern discussions of the BINDING PROBLEM. It is interesting to read Golgi's prose against the backdrop of current work on functional ensembles linked by temporal response properties ("l'action d'ensemble des cellules nerveuses, que j'ai ainsi définée par opposition à la prétendue action individuelle," Golgi 1908; "the group action of nerve cells which I have defined as being opposite to their alleged individual action," Golgi 1967: 202).

Golgi is also known for his discovery of the "internal reticular apparatus" (smooth endoplasmic reticulum or "Golgi apparatus;" see Peters, Palay, and de Webster 1991), and for his distinction between neurons with long or local axons (respectively, Golgi Type I and Type II, also observed early on by Cajal).

In summary, Golgi's silver stain has become, rightly or not, a favorite illustration of the role of serendipity in scientific discovery. It is an early example of the importance of new techniques for advancing the investigation of brain and cognitive processes. The story is also a lesson in the potential deceptiveness of "concrete" images—whether we read it as a case of missed opportunity and intransigence, or of being right for the wrong reasons.

See also BINDING BY NEURAL SYNCHRONY; CORTICAL LOCALIZATION, HISTORY OF

—*Kathleen S. Rockland*

References

Clark, E., and C. D. O'Malley. (1968). *The Human Brain and Spinal Cord.* Berkeley: University of California Press.

Corsi, P. (1988). Camillo Golgi's morphological approach to neuroanatomy. In R. L. Masland, A. Portera Sanchez, and G. Toffano, Eds., *Neuroplasticity: A New Therapeutic Tool in the CNS Pathology.* Padova: Liviana Press—Springer (Fidia Research Series 12), pp. 1–7.

Da Fano, C. (1926). Camillo Golgi. *Journal of Pathology and Bacteriology* 29: 500–514.

Mazzarello, P. (1996). *La Struttura Segreta.* Pavia: Edizioni Cisalpino.

Peters, A., S. L. Palay, and H. de Webster. (1991). *The Fine Structure of the Neuron's System.* 3rd ed. New York: Oxford University Press.

Santini, M., Ed. (1975). *Golgi Centennial Symposium: Perspectives in Neurobiology.* New York: Raven Press.

Shepherd, G. M. (1991). *Foundations of the Neuron Doctrine.* Oxford: Oxford University Press.

Van der Loos, H. (1967). The history of the neuron. In H. Hyden, Ed., *The Neuron.* Amsterdam: Elsevier, pp. 1–47.

Selected Works by Golgi

Golgi, C. (1903–1923). *Opera Omnia*. R. Fusati, G. Marenghi, and S. Sala, Eds., 4 vols. Milan: Hoepli.

Golgi, C. (1908). La doctrine du neurone. In *Les Prix Nobel en 1906* Stockholm: P.A. Norstedt and Söner.

Golgi, C. (1967). The neuron doctrine—theory and facts. In *Nobel Lectures: Physiology or Medicine 1901–1921*. Amsterdam: Elsevier, pp. 189–217.

Good Old Fashioned AI (GOFAI)

See INTRODUCTION: COMPUTATIONAL INTELLIGENCE; CONNECTIONISM, PHILOSOPHICAL ISSUES

GPSG

See GENERATIVE GRAMMAR; HEAD-DRIVEN PHRASE STRUCTURE GRAMMAR

Grammar, Neural Basis of

Grammar refers to the syntactic structure of sentences that allows the meanings of words to be related to each other to form propositions. Linguistics has been concerned with the way humans' unconscious knowledge of this structure is represented. PSYCHOLINGUISTICS has been concerned with how this knowledge is used in speaking and comprehension. There is no way at present to investigate how the nervous system represents syntactic knowledge, but there are two approaches to the neural basis for syntactic processing. One has been the traditional deficit-lesion correlational approach in patients with brain lesions. The second is the observation of neurophysiological and metabolic activity associated with syntactic processing in normal subjects. Both approaches have made some progress, but there are many gaps in our scientific investigation of the question.

Deficit-lesion correlations are available for patients with disorders of both production and receptive processing of syntactic structures. With respect to the production of syntactic form, the speech of patients with a symptom known as agrammatism is characterized by short phrases with simple syntactic structures and omission of grammatical markers and function words. These patients tend to have lesions that include Broca's area (pars triangularis and opercularis of the left third frontal convolution), which has led some researchers to suggest that this region is responsible for syntactic planning in LANGUAGE PRODUCTION (Zurif 1982). Several studies have shown, however, that lesions in other brain areas can produce agrammatism, suggesting that other left hemisphere areas can be responsible for this function in some individuals (Vanier and Caplan 1990; Dronkers et al. 1994).

Syntactic processing can also be impaired in comprehension, as shown by patients' failure to understand sentences with more complex syntactic structures whose meaning cannot be simply inferred (e.g., *The boy was pushed by the girl*). More detailed studies of disorders of the time-course of syntactic processing in sentence comprehension have also been carried out (Tyler 1985; Swinney and Zurif 1995). The original studies of patients with syntactic comprehension disorders also focused on agrammatic Broca's aphasics (Caramazza and Zurif 1976). However, patients whose lesions lie outside Broca's area also often show impairments of syntactically-based sentence comprehension (Berndt, Mitchum, and Haendiges 1996; Caplan 1987; Caplan and Hildebrandt 1988; Caplan, Baker, and Dehaut 1985; Caplan, Hildebrandt, and Makris 1996; Tramo, Baynes, and Volpe 1988), and patients with agrammatism often show good syntactic comprehension (Berndt, Mitchum, and Haendiges 1996). This has led some researchers to suggest that a more distributed neural system in the left perisylvian cortex, of which Broca's area may be a specialized part, is responsible for this function (Mesulam 1990; Damasio and Damasio 1992). One study (Caplan, Hildebrandt, and Makris 1996) reported a small but clear impairment in syntactic processing in comprehension after right hemisphere strokes, suggesting some role of the nondominant hemisphere in this function.

Physiological and metabolic studies in normal subjects have also provided information about the brain regions involved in syntactic processing in comprehension. Event related potentials (ERPs) have shown components, such as the P600 or "syntactic positive shift" in the central parietal region and the "left anterior negativity," that may be associated with syntactic processing (Hagoort, Brown, and Groothusen 1993; Munte, Heinze, and Mangun 1993; Neville et al. 1991; Rosler et al. 1993). Recently, functional neuroimaging with POSITRON EMISSION TOMOGRAPHY (PET) and functional MAGNETIC RESONANCE IMAGING (fMRI) has been used to investigate the regional cerebral blood flow (rCBF) associated with sentence-level language processing. Using PET, Mazoyer et al. (1993) reported inconsistent rCBF increases associated with syntactic processing, but it may be that their experimental conditions did not differ in the minimal ways necessary to isolate the neural correlates of the various components of linguistic processing above the single-word level. Stromswold et al. (1996) reported an isolated increase in rCBF in part of Broca's area associated with syntactic processing. Using a slightly different experimental paradigm with fMRI, Just et al. (1996) reported an increase in rCBF in both Broca's area and a second language area—Wernicke's area in the left first temporal gyrus —as well as smaller increases in rCBF in the right hemisphere homologues of these structures. The Just et al. results are consistent with those of Caplan, Hildebrandt, and Makris (1996), but more research is needed to understand the differences across various studies.

In summary, the dominant perisylvian cortex is the region of the brain most involved in syntactic processing and production. Whether there is any further specialization within this region for these functions remains to be established.

See also APHASIA; LANGUAGE, NEURAL BASIS OF; PHONOLOGY, NEURAL BASIS OF; SENTENCE PROCESSING; SYNTAX; SYNTAX, ACQUISITION OF

—*David N. Caplan*

References

Berndt, R., C. Mitchum, and A. Haendiges. (1996). Comprehension of reversible sentences in "agrammatism": a meta-analysis. *Cognition* 58: 289–308.

Caplan, D. (1987). Discrimination of normal and aphasic subjects on a test of syntactic comprehension. *Neuropsychologia* 25: 173–184.

Caplan, D., and N. Hildebrandt. (1988). *Disorders of Syntactic Comprehension.* Cambridge, MA: MIT Press/Bradford Books.

Caplan, D., C. Baker, and F. Dehaut. (1985). Syntactic determinants of sentence comprehension in aphasia. *Cognition* 21: 117–175.

Caplan, D., N. Hildebrandt, and G. S. Waters. (1994). Interaction of verb selectional restrictions, noun animacy and syntactic form in sentence processing. *Language and Cognitive Processes* 9: 549–585.

Caplan, D., N. Hildebrandt, and N. Makris. (1996). Location of lesions in stroke patients with deficits in syntactic processing in sentence comprehension. *Brain* 119: 933–949

Caramazza, A., and E. B. Zurif. (1976). Dissociation of algorithmic and heuristic processes in language comprehension: evidence from aphasia. *Brain and Language* 3: 572–582.

Damasio, A. R., and H. Damasio. (1992). Brain and language. *Scientific American* (September): 89–95.

Dronkers, N. F., D. P. Wilkins, R. D. van Valin, B. B. Redfern, and J. J. Jaeger. (1994). A reconsideration of the brain areas involved in the disruption of morphosyntactic comprehension. *Brain and Language* 47: 461–463.

Hagoort, P., C. Brown, and J. Groothusen. (1993). The syntactic positive shift (SPS) as an ERP measure of syntactic processing. *Language and Cognitive Processes* 8(4): 485–532.

Just, M. A., P. A. Carpenter, T. A. Keller, W. F. Eddy, and K. R. Thulborn. (1996). Brain activation modulated by sentence comprehension. *Science* 274: 114–116.

Mazoyer, B., N. Tzourio, V. Frak, A. Syrota, N. Murayama, O. Levrier, and G. Salamon. (1993). The cortical representation of speech. *Journal of Cognitive Neuroscience* 5: 467–479.

Mesulam, M.-M. (1990). Large-scale neurocognitive networks and distributed processing for attention, language and memory. *Annals of Neurology* 28(5): 597–613.

Munte, T. F., H. J. Heinze, and G. R. Mangun. (1993). Dissociation of brain activity related to syntactic and semantic aspects of language. *Journal of Cognitive Neuroscience* 5: 335–344.

Neville, H., J. L. Nicol, A. Barss, K. I. Forster, and M. F. Garrett. (1991). Syntactically based sentence processing classes: evidence from event-related brain potentials. *Journal of Cognitive Neuroscience* 3: 151–165.

Rosler, F., P. Putz, A. Friederici, and A. Hahne. (1993). Event-related potentials while encountering semantic and syntactic constraint violations. *Journal of Cognitive Neuroscience* 5: 345–362.

Stromswold, K., D. Caplan, N. Alpert, and S. Rauch. (1996). Localization of syntactic comprehension by positron emission tomography. *Brain and Language* 52: 452–473

Swinney, D., and E. Zurif. (1995). Syntactic processing in aphasia. *Brain and Language* 50: 225–239.

Tramo, M. J., K. Baynes, and B. T. Volpe. (1988). Impaired syntactic comprehension and production in Broca's aphasia: CT lesion localization and recovery patterns. *Neurology* 38: 95–98.

Tyler, L. (1985). Real-time comprehension processes in agrammatism: a case study. *Brain and Language* 26: 259–275.

Vanier, M., and D. Caplan. (1990). CT-scan correlates of agrammatism. In L. Menn and L. K. Obler, Eds., *Agrammatic Aphasia.* Amsterdam: Benjamins, pp. 97–114.

Zurif, E. B. (1982). The use of data from aphasia in constructing a performance model of language. In M. A. Arbib, D. Caplan, and J. C. Marshall, Eds., *Neural Models of Language Processes.* New York: Academic Press, pp. 203–207.

Grammatical Relations

In its broadest sense, the term *grammatical relation* (or *grammatical role* or *grammatical function*) can be used to refer to almost any relationship within grammar, or at least within SYNTAX and MORPHOLOGY. In its narrowest sense, grammatical relation is a cover term for grammatical subject, object, indirect object, and the like. To understand what grammatical relations are, in this more specific sense, it will help to contrast them with intuitively similar but distinct syntactic concepts such as thematic roles, Cases, and syntactic positions.

We can see the difference between surface grammatical relations and semantic relations or THEMATIC ROLES (e.g., agent, goal, theme, etc.) by examining examples (1) and (2). In these examples, the noun phrase "that story" has the same thematic role (theme or patient) in both the active and the passive versions of the sentence; however, the grammatical relation of "that story" differs in the two sentences. In the active sentence, "that story" has the grammatical relation of object, whereas in the passive sentence, it has the grammatical relation of subject.

(1) active: This girl wrote that story.

(2) passive: That story was written by this girl.

It is not necessary, however, to appeal to derived contexts in order to distinguish surface grammatical relations and thematic roles. Although the subject of an active sentence is very often an agent, there are sentences without an agent role and in such sentences, some other thematic role such as theme, goal, or experiencer is associated with the grammatical relation of subject:

(3) The ball rolled down the hill.

(4) The woman received the letter.

(5) The boy enjoyed the ice cream.

Grammatical relations are also distinct from Cases (e.g. nominative, accusative, dative, etc.). Although the grammatical relation of subject is often associated with nominative Case, whereas the grammatical relation of object is often associated with accusative Case, there are many examples of other pairings of these grammatical relations and Cases. For example, in Icelandic some verbs take a dative subject and a nominative object:

(6) Barninu   batnaði   veikin.
    the.child-DAT recovered.from the.disease-NOM(*ACC)
    'The child recovered from the disease.' (Yip, Maling, and Jackendoff 1987: 223)

Hindi also has verbs that take dative subjects, but most transitive verbs in Hindi take an ergative subject and a nominative object (in the perfective aspect):

(7) Raam-ne   roTii   khaayii   thii.
    Ram(masc.)-ERG bread(fem)-NOM eat(perf, fem)
    be(past, fem) "Ram had eaten bread." (Mahajan 1990:
    73)

Thus we see that grammatical relations are distinct from
Cases.

Finally, grammatical relations can also be distinguished
from syntactic positions. If an object is fronted in a topicalization construction, for example, it remains an object
despite the fact that it is located above the subject in the syntactic structure.

(8) a. I read *that book.*
    b. *That book,* I read.

Similarly, grammatical relations remain constant across
many word orders in languages that allow scrambling. For
example, in all of the word order variants of the Hindi sentence below, *Ram* has the grammatical relation of subject
and *banana* has the grammatical relation of object:

(9) a. Raam-ne   kelaa   khaayaa.
       Ram-ERG   banana-NOM   ate
       'Ram ate a banana.'
    b. Raam-ne khaayaa kelaa.
    c. Kelaa raam-ne khaayaa.
    d. Kelaa khaayaa raam-ne.
    e. Khaayaa raam-ne kelaa.
    f. Khaayaa kelaa raam-ne. (Mahajan 1990: 19)

So far, we have been discussing only surface grammatical relations; that is, the grammatical relations that hold at
surface structure after all movements or other grammatical
relation-changing processes have occurred. However, one
may also speak of deep or initial grammatical relations. In
both the active sentence in (10) and the passive sentence in
(11), one may say that *that banana* has the initial grammatical relation of object.

(10) Ram ate that banana.

(11) That banana was eaten by Ram.

Thus there is a closer association between initial grammatical relations and thematic roles than there is between surface grammatical relations and thematic roles.

Almost all linguists use the terms *grammatical relation,*
subject, object, and the like in a descriptive sense. However,
theories of grammar differ widely with respect to the question of the theoretical status of grammatical relations. The
controversy centers around the question of how many formal devices of what kind the correct theory of grammar
includes. Proponents of RELATIONAL GRAMMAR (Perlmutter
and Postal 1977; Perlmutter 1983) maintain that grammatical relations are primitive notions in the theory of grammar
and that universal generalizations about language are formulated in terms of those primitives. Others maintain that
no grammatical rules make crucial reference to grammatical
relations, as distinct from thematic roles, Cases, or syntactic
positions and that adding grammatical relations to the the-

ory of grammar is unnecessary and therefore undesirable
(e.g., Chomsky 1981; Hoekstra 1984; Williams 1984; Bhat
1991). Between these poles, there are several middle and
variant positions. Some take the position that although
grammatical relations are not primitive notions of grammar,
they do play an important role in grammar as derived
notions (Anderson 1978). Some argue for the need for finer-
grained grammatical relations, such as adding "restricted
object" (Bresnan and Kanerva 1989), within the theory of
LEXICAL FUNCTIONAL GRAMMAR.

Many works whose titles contain the phrase "grammatical relations" are not so much concerned with this theoretical controversy, but rather with a somewhat broader sense
of grammatical relations, pertaining to how Case, agreement, and/or word order identify or distinguish subjects
and objects. In this broader sense, a "theory of grammatical relations" is assumed to include a theory of Case and
agreement systems that can account for all of the cross-linguistic differences that occur (see TYPOLOGY). Such work
often focuses on languages or particular constructions in
which the familiar associations between subjects and nominative Case or objects and accusative Case do not hold.
For example, they address the question of how or why
dative or ergative Case is assigned to subjects in constructions such as (6) or (7), instead of nominative Case; and
why nominative Case is instead assigned to the objects in
those constructions. One approach to this problem of non-
prototypic associations between Cases and grammatical
relations has been to propose that at some level, the prototypic association (e.g., between nominative Case and subjects) actually does hold, but that grammatical relations (or
structural positions) are inverted at some level in the derivation (e.g., Harris 1976; Marantz 1984). Others maintain
that assuming such a close association between Case and
grammatical relations (or syntactic positions) is not correct
and that there are conditions under which subjects can take
other Cases, especially lexical (inherent, quirky) Cases,
freeing up the nominative Case which can then be assigned
to an object (e.g., Yip, Maling, and Jackendoff 1987).

Other works with "grammatical relations" in the title
focus on the question of how to describe and analyze a
range of constructions that appear to involve changes in
grammatical relations, such as passive, causative, or appli-
cative constructions, or on restrictions on various grammatical processes such as relativization that may be stated in
terms of grammatical relations (e.g., Gary and Keenan
1977; Marantz 1984; Baker 1988).

See also HEAD-DRIVEN PHRASE STRUCTURE GRAMMAR;
SYNTAX, ACQUISITION OF

—*Ellen Woolford*

References

Anderson, J. (1978). On the derivative status of grammatical rela-
    tions. In W. Abraham, Ed., *Valence, Semantic Case, and Gram-
    matical Relations.* Amsterdam: John Benjamins.
Baker, M. (1988). *Incorporation: A Theory of Grammatical Func-
    tion Changing.* Chicago: University of Chicago Press.
Bhat, D. N. S. (1991). *Grammatical Relations: The Evidence
    Against Their Necessity and Universality.* London: Routledge.

Bresnan, J., and J. Kanerva. (1989). Locative inversion in Chichewa: a case study of factorization in grammar. *Linguistic Inquiry* 20: 1–50.

Chomsky, N. (1981). *Lectures on Government and Binding.* Dordrecht: Foris.

Gary, J. O., and E. Keenan. (1977). Grammatical relations in Kinyarwanda and universal grammar. In Paul F. Kotey and H. Der-Houssikian, Eds., *Language and Linguistic Problems in Africa.* Columbia, SC: Hornbeam Press, pp. 315–329.

Harris, A. C. (1976). *Grammatical Relations in Modern Georgian.* Ph.D. diss., Harvard University.

Hoekstra, T. (1984). *Transitivity: Grammatical Relations in Government-Binding Theory.* Dordrecht: Foris.

Mahajan, A. (1990). *The A/A-Bar Distinction and Movement Theory.* Ph.D. diss., MIT. Distributed by MIT Working Papers in Linguistics.

Marantz, A. (1984). *On the Nature of Grammatical Relations.* Cambridge, MA: MIT Press.

Perlmutter, D., Ed. (1983). *Studies in Relational Grammar I.* Chicago: University of Chicago Press.

Perlmutter, D., and P. Postal. (1977). Toward a universal characterization of passive. *Proceedings of the Berkeley Linguistics Society* 3: 394–417.

Williams, E. (1984). Grammatical relations. *Linguistic Inquiry* 15: 639–673.

Yip, M., J. Maling, and R. Jackendoff. (1987). Case in tiers. *Language* 63: 217–250.

Further Readings

Abraham, W., Ed. (1978) *Valence, Semantic Case, and Grammatical Relations.* Amsterdam: John Benjamins.

Anderson, J. M. (1977). *On Case Grammar: Prolegomena to a Theory of Grammatical Relations.* London: Croom Helm.

Bowers, J. (1981). *The Theory of Grammatical Relations.* Ithaca: Cornell University Press.

Bresnan, J., Ed. (1982). *The Mental Representation of Grammatical Relations.* Cambridge, MA: MIT Press.

Burgess, C., K. Dziwirek, and D. Gerdts. (1995). *Grammatical Relations: Theoretical Approaches to Empirical Questions.* Stanford: CSLI Publications.

Campe, P. (1994). *Case, Semantic Roles, and Grammatical Relations: A Comprehensive Bibliography.* Amsterdam: John Benjamins.

Cole, P., and J. Sadock, Eds. (1977). *Grammatical Relations (Syntax and Semantics 8).* New York: Academic Press.

Croft, W. (1991). *Syntactic Categories and Grammatical Relations: The Cognitive Organization of Information.* Chicago: University of Chicago Press.

Dziwirek, P. F., and E. Mejías-Bikandi. (1990). *Grammatical Relations: A Cross-Theoretical Perspective.* Stanford: CSLI Publications.

Faarlund, J. T. (1987). On the history of grammatical relations. *Proceedings of the Chicago Linguistic Society* 23: 64–78.

Gary, J. O., and E. Keenan. (1977). On collapsing grammatical relations in universal grammar. *Syntax and Semantics* 8: 83–120.

Gerdts, D. (1993). Mapping Halkomelem grammatical relations. *Linguistics* 31: 591–621.

Hudson, R. A. (1988). Extraction and grammatical relations. *Lingua* 76: 177–208.

Jake, J. (1983). *Grammatical Relations in Imabaura Quechua.* Ph.D. diss., University of Illinois.

Keenan, E., and B. Comrie. (1977). Noun phrase accessibility and universal grammar. *Linguistic Inquiry* 8: 63–99.

Maxwell, E. M. (1981). Question strategics and hierarchies of grammatical relations in Kinyarwanda. *Proceedings of the Berkeley Linguistics Society* 7: 166–177.

Palmer, F. R. (1994). *Grammatical Roles and Relations.* Cambridge: Cambridge University Press.

Perlmutter, D. (1978). Impersonal passives and the unaccusative hypothesis. *Proceedings of the Berkeley Linguistics Society* 4: 157–189.

Perlmutter, D., and C. G. Rosen, Eds. (1984). *Studies in Relational Grammar 2.* Chicago: University of Chicago Press.

Plank, F., Ed. (1979). *Ergativity: Toward a Theory of Grammatical Relations.* London: Academic Press.

Plank, F., Ed. (1984). *Objects: Towards A Theory of Grammatical Relations.* London: Academic Press.

Postal, P., and B. D. Joseph. (1990). *Studies in Relational Grammar 3.* Chicago: University of Chicago Press.

Scancarelli, J. (1987). *Grammatical Relations and Verb Agreement in Cherokee.* Ph.D. diss., UCLA.

Woolford, E. (1993). Symmetric and asymmetric passives. *Natural Language and Linguistic Theory* 11: 679–728.

Woolford, E. (1997). Four-way case systems: nominative, ergative, objective, and accusative. *Natural Language and Linguistic Theory* 15: 181–227.

Grammatical Theory

See INTRODUCTION: LINGUISTICS AND LANGUAGE; GENERATIVE GRAMMAR

Grasping

See MANIPULATION AND GRASPING

Greedy Local Search

Greedy local search search methods are widely used to solve challenging computational problems. One of the earliest applications of local search was to find good solutions for the traveling salesman problem (TSP). In this problem, the goal is to find the shortest path for visiting a given set of cities. The TSP is prototypical of a large class of computational problems for which it is widely believed that no efficient (i.e., polynomial time) ALGORITHM exists. Technically speaking, it is an NP-hard optimization problem (Cook 1971; Garey and Johnson 1979; Papadimitriou and Steiglitz 1982). A local search method for the TSP proceeds as follows: start with an arbitrary path that visits all cities, such a path will define an order in which the cities are to be visited. Subsequently, one makes small ("local") changes to the path to try to find a shorter one. An example of such a local change is to swap the position of two cities on the tour. One continues making such changes until no swap leads to a shorter path. Lin (1965) and Lin and Kernighan (1973) show that such a simple procedure, with only a slightly more complex local change, leads to solutions that are surprisingly close to the shortest possible path.

The basic local search framework allows for several variations. For example, there is the choice of the initial solution, the nature of the local changes considered, and the manner in which the actual improvement of the current solution is selected. Lin and Kernighan found that multiple runs with different random initial paths lead to the best solutions. Somewhat surprisingly, starting with good initial paths did not necessarily lead to better final solutions. The reason for this appears to be that the local search mechanism itself is powerful enough to improve on the initial solutions—often quickly giving better solutions than those generated using other methods. Choosing the best set of local changes to be considered generally requires an empirical comparison of various kinds of local modifications that are feasible. Another issue is that of how to select the actual improvement to be made to the current solution. The two extremes are *first-improvement* (also called "hill-climbing"), in which any favorable change is accepted, and *steepest-descent,* in which the *best* possible local improvement is selected at each step. Steepest-descent is sometimes referred to as *greedy* local search, but this term is also used to refer to local search in general.

A local search method does not necessarily reach a global optimum because the algorithm terminates when it reaches a state where no further improvement can be found. Such states are referred to as *local optima.* In 1983, Kirkpatrick, Gelatt, and Vecchi introduced a technique for escaping from such local optima. The idea is to allow the algorithm to make occasional changes that do not improve the current solution, that is, changes that lead to equally good or possibly inferior solutions. Intuitively speaking, these nonimproving moves can be viewed as injecting *noise* into the local search process. Kirkpatrick, Gelatt, and Vecchi referred to their method as *simulated annealing,* because it was inspired by the annealing technique used to reach low energy states in glasses and metals. The amount of "noise" introduced is controlled with a parameter, called the temperature T. Higher values of T correspond to more noise. The search starts off at a high temperature, which is slowly lowered during the search in order to reach increasingly better solutions.

Another effective way of escaping from local minima is the *tabu search* method (Glover 1989). During the search, the algorithm maintains a "tabu" list containing the last L changes, where L is a constant. The local search method is prevented from making a change that is currently on the tabu list. With the appropriate choice of L, this methods often forces the search to make upward (nonimproving) changes, again introducing noise into the search.

Genetic algorithms can also be viewed as performing a form of local search (Holland 1975). In this case, the search process proceeds in parallel. Solutions are selected based on their "fitness" (i.e., solution quality) from an evolving population of candidates. Noise is introduced in the search process via random mutations (see EVOLUTIONARY COMPUTATION).

A recent new area of application for local search methods is in solving NP-complete *decision problems,* such as the Boolean satisfiability (SAT) problem. An instance of SAT is a logical expression over a set of Boolean variables. An example expression is "(a or (not b)) and ((not a) or (not c))." The formula has a, b, and c as Boolean variables. The satisfiability problem is to find an assignment to the Boolean variables such that the various parts of the logical expression are simultaneously satisfied. That is, the overall expression should evaluate to "true." In our example, setting a to "true," b to "true," and c to "false" satisfies the formula. Finding a satisfying assignment for arbitrary formulas is a computationally difficult task (Cook 1971). Note that the obvious algorithm would enumerate all 2^N Boolean truth assignments, where N is the number of Boolean variables. The SAT problem is of particular interest to computer scientists because many other problems can be efficiently represented as Boolean satisfiability problems. The best traditional methods for solving the SAT problem are based on a systematic backtrack-style search procedure, called the Davis, Putnam, and Loveland procedure (Davis and Putnam 1960; Davis, Logemann, and Loveland 1962). These procedures can currently solve hard, randomly generated instances with up to four hundred variables (Mitchell, Selman, and Levesque 1992; Crawford and Auton 1993; Kirkpatrick and Selman 1994). In 1992, Selman, Livesque, and Mitchell showed that a greedy local search method, called GSAT, could solve instances with up to seven hundred variables. Recent improvements on the local search strategy enable us to solve instances with up to three thousand variables (Selman, Kautz, and Cohen 1994). The GSAT procedure starts with a randomly generated truth assignment. It then considers changing the truth value of one of the Boolean variables in order to satisfy more of the given logical expression. It keeps making those changes until a satisfying truth assignment is found or until the procedure reaches some preset maximum number of changes. When it reaches this maximum, GSAT restarts with a new initial random assignment. (For closely related work in the area of scheduling, see Minton et al. 1992.) One inherent limitation of local search procedures applied to decision problems is that they cannot be used to determine whether a logical expression is inconsistent, that is, no satisfying truth assignment exists. In practice, this means that one has to use model-based formulations, where solutions correspond to models or satisfying assignments.

An important difference in applying local search to decision problems, as opposed to optimization problems, is that *near*-solutions are of no particular interest. For decision problems, the goal is to find a solution that satisfies all constraints of the problem under consideration (see also CONSTRAINT SATISFACTION and HEURISTIC SEARCH). In practice, this means that, for example, GSAT and related local search procedures spend most of their time satisfying the last few remaining constraints. Recent work has shown that incorporating random walk-style methods in the search process greatly enhances the effectiveness of these procedures.

Since Lin and Kernighan's successful application of local search to the TSP, and the many subsequent enhancements to the local search method, local search techniques have proved so powerful and general that such procedures have become the method of choice for solving hard computational problems.

See also COMPUTATIONAL COMPLEXITY; GAME–PLAYING SYSTEMS; INTELLIGENT AGENT ARCHITECTURE; PROBLEM SOLVING; RATIONAL DECISION MAKING

—*Bart Selman*

References

Cook, S. A. (1971). The complexity of theorem–proving procedures. *Proc.* STOC–71, pp. 151–158.

Crawford, J. M., and L. D. Auton. (1993). Experimental results on the cross–over point in satisfiability problems. *Proc.* AAAI–93, pp. 21–27.

Davis, M., G. Logemann, and D. Loveland. (1962). A machine program for theorem-proving. *Comm. Assoc. for Comput. Mach.* 5: 394–397.

Davis, M., and H. Putnam. (1960). A computing procedure for quantification theory. *J. of the ACM* 7: 201–215.

Garey, M. R., and D. S. Johnson. (1979). *Computers and Intractability, A Guide to the Theory of NP-Completeness.* New York: W. H. Freeman.

Glover, F. (1989) Tabu search—part I. ORSA Journal on Computing 1(3): 190–206.

Holland, J. H. (1975). *Adaptation in Natural and Artificial Systems.* Ann Arbor: University of Michigan Press.

Kirkpatrick, S., C. D. Gelatt, and M. P. Vecchi. (1983). Optimization by simulated annealing. *Science* 220: 671–680.

Kirkpatrick, S., and B. Selman. (1994). Critical behavior in the satisfiability of random Boolean expressions. *Science* 264: 1297–1301.

Lin, S. (1965). Computer solutions of the traveling salesman problem. BSTJ 44 (10): 2245–2269.

Lin, S., and B. W. Kernighan. (1973). An effective heuristic for the traveling–salesman problem. *Oper. Res.* 21: 498–516.

Minton, S., M. Johnston, A. B. Philips, and P. Laird. (1992). Minimizing conflicts: a heuristic repair method for constraint satisfaction and scheduling problems. *Artificial Intelligence* 58: 161–205.

Mitchell, D., B. Selman, and H. J. Levesque. (1992). Hard and easy distributions of SAT problems. *Proc.* AAAI–92, pp. 459–465.

Papadimitriou, C. H., and K. Steiglitz. (1982). *Combinatorial Optimization.* Englewood Cliffs, NJ: Prentice–Hall.

Selman, B., H. A. Kautz, and B. Cohen. (1994). Noise strategies for improving local search. *Proc.* AAAI–94, pp. 337–343.

Selman, B., H. J. Levesque, and D. Mitchell. (1992). A new method for solving hard satisfiability problems. *Proc.* AAAI–92, pp. 440–446.

Grice, H. Paul

H. Paul Grice (1913–1988), the English philosopher, is best known for his contributions to the theory of meaning and communication. This work (collected in Grice 1989) has had lasting importance for philosophy and linguistics, with implications for cognitive science generally. His three most influential contributions concern the nature of communication, the distinction between speaker's meaning and linguistic meaning, and the phenomenon of conversational IMPLICATURE.

Grice's concept of speaker's meaning was an ingenious refinement of the crude idea that communication is a matter of intentionally affecting another person's psychological states. He discovered that there is a distinctive, rational means by which the effect is achieved: by way of getting one's audience to recognize one's intention to achieve it. The intention includes, as part of its content, that the audience recognize this very intention by taking into account the fact that they are intended to recognize it. A communi-

cative intention is thus a self-referential, or reflexive, intention. It does not involve a series of nested intentions—the speaker does not have an intention to convey something and a further intention that the first be recognized, for then this further intention would require a still further intention that it be recognized, and so on ad infinitum. Confusing reflexive with iterated intentions, to which even Grice himself was prone, led to an extensive literature replete with counterexamples to ever more elaborate characterizations of the intentions required for genuine communication (see, e.g., Strawson 1964 and Schiffer 1972), and to the spurious objection that it involves an infinite regress (see Sperber and Wilson 1986, whose own RELEVANCE theory neglects the reflexivity of communicative intentions). Although the idea of reflexive intentions raises subtle issues (see the exchange between Recanati 1987 and Bach 1987), it clearly accounts for the essentially overt character of communicative intentions, namely, that their fulfillment consists of their recognition (by the intended audience). This idea forms the core of a Gricean approach to the theory of speech acts, including nonliteral and indirect speech acts (Bach and Harnish 1979). Different types of speech acts (statements, requests, apologies, etc.) may be distinguished by the type of propositional attitude (belief, desire, regret, etc.) being expressed by the speaker.

Grice's distinction between speaker's and linguistic MEANING reflects the fact that what a speaker means in uttering a sentence often diverges from what the sentence itself means. A speaker can mean something other than what the sentence means, as in "Nature abhors a vacuum," or something more, as in "Is there a doctor in the house?" Grice invoked this distinction for two reasons. First, he thought linguistic meaning could be reduced to (standardized) speaker's meaning. This reductive view has not gained wide acceptance, because of its extreme complexity (see Grice 1989: chaps. 6 and 14, and Schiffer 1972) and because it requires the controversial assumption that language is essentially a vehicle for communicating thoughts rather than a medium of thought itself. Even so, many philosophers would at least concede that mental content is a more fundamental notion than linguistic meaning, and perhaps even that SEMANTICS reduces to the psychology of PROPOSITIONAL ATTITUDES.

Grice's other reason for invoking the distinction between speaker's and linguistic meaning was to combat extravagant claims, made by so-called ordinary language philosophers, about various important philosophical terms, such as *believes* or *looks*. For example, it was sometimes suggested that believing implies not knowing, because to say, for example, "I believe that alcohol is dangerous" is to imply that one does not know this, or to say "The sky looks blue" is to imply that the sky might not actually be blue. However, as Grice pointed out, what carries such implications is not what one is saying but that one is saying it (as opposed to the stronger "I know that alcohol is dangerous" or "The sky is blue"). Grice also objected to certain ambiguity claims, for instance that *or* has an exclusive as well as inclusive sense, as in "I would like an apple or an orange," by pointing out that it is the use of *or*, not the word itself, that carries the implication of exclusivity. Grice's Modified Occam's Razor ("Senses are not to be multiplied beyond necessity") cut back on a growing conflation of (linguistic) meaning with use, and has since helped linguists appreciate the importance of separating, so far as possible, the domain of PRAGMATICS from semantics.

Conversational implicature is a case in point. What a speaker implicates is distinct from what the speaker says and from what his words imply. Saying of an expensive dinner, "It was edible," implicates that it was mediocre at best. This simple example illustrates a general phenomenon: a speaker can say one thing and manage to mean something else or something more by exploiting the fact that he may be presumed to be cooperative, in particular, to be speaking truthfully, informatively, relevantly, and otherwise appropriately. The listener relies on this presumption to make a contextually driven inference from what the speaker says to what the speaker means. If taking the utterance at face value is incompatible with this presumption, one may suppose that the speaker intends one to figure out what the speaker does mean by searching for an explanation of why the speaker said what he said.

Although Grice's distinction between what is said and what is implicated is not exhaustive (for what it omits, see Bach 1994), the theoretical strategy derived from it aims to reduce the burden on semantics and to explain a wide range of nonsemantic phenomena at an appropriate level of generality. This strategy has had lasting application to a wide range of problems in philosophy of language as well as other areas of philosophy, such as epistemology and ethics, and to various areas of research in linguistics and computer science, such as the LEXICON, ANAPHORA, DISCOURSE, and PLANNING. Economy and plausibility of theory require heeding Grice's distinction between speaker's and linguistic meaning, and the correlative distinction between speaker's and linguistic reference. Rather than overly attribute features to specific linguistic items, one can proceed on the default assumption that uses of language can be explained in terms of a core of linguistic meaning together with general facts about rational communication.

See also FOLK PSYCHOLOGY; FREGE, GOTTLOB; LANGUAGE AND COMMUNICATION; SENSE AND REFERENCE

—*Kent Bach*

References

Bach, K. (1987). On communicative intentions: a reply to Recanati. *Mind and Language* 2: 141–154.

Bach, K. (1994). Conversational implicature. *Mind and Language* 9: 124–162.

Bach, K., and R. M. Harnish. (1979). *Linguistic Communication and Speech Acts.* Cambridge, MA: MIT Press.

Grice, P. (1989). *Studies in the Way of Words.* Cambridge, MA: Harvard University Press.

Recanati, F. (1986). On defining communicative intentions. *Mind and Language* 1: 213–242.

Schiffer, S. (1972). *Meaning.* Oxford: Oxford University Press.

Sperber, D., and D. Wilson. (1986). *Relevance.* Cambridge, MA: Harvard University Press.

Strawson, P. F. (1964). Intention and convention in speech acts. *Philosophical Review* 73: 439–460.

Further Readings

Carston, R. (1988). Implicature, explicature, and truth-theoretic semantics. In R. Kempson, Ed., *Mental Representations: The Interface between Language and Reality.* Cambridge: Cambridge University Press. Reprinted in Davis (1991), pp. 33–51.

Davis, S., Ed. (1991). *Pragmatics: A Reader.* Oxford: Oxford University Press.

Grandy, R., and R. Warner, Eds. (1986). *Philosophical Grounds of Rationality: Intentions, Categories, Ends.* Oxford: Oxford University Press.

Harnish, R. M. (1976). Logical form and implicature. In T. Bever, J. Katz, and T. Langendoen, Eds., *An Integrated Theory of Linguistic Ability.* New York: Crowell. Reprinted in Davis (1991), pp. 316–364.

Horn, L. (1984). Toward a new taxonomy for pragmatic inference: Q-based and R-based implicature. In D. Schiffrin, Ed., *Meaning, Form, and Use in Context.* Washington, DC: Georgetown University Press, pp. 11–42.

Levinson, S. (Forthcoming). *Default Meanings: The Theory of Generalized Conversational Implicature.*

Lewis, D. (1979). Scorekeeping in a language game. *Journal of Philosophical Logic* 8: 339–359.

Neale, S. (1992). Paul Grice and the philosophy of language. *Linguistics and Philosophy* 15: 509–559.

Recanati, F. (1989). The pragmatics of what is said. *Mind and Language* 4: 295–328. Reprinted in Davis (1991), pp. 97–120.

Gustation

See TASTE

Haptic Perception

The haptic sensory modality is based on cutaneous receptors lying beneath the skin surface and kinesthetic receptors found in muscles, tendons, and joints (Loomis and Lederman 1986). The haptic modality primarily provides information about objects and surfaces in contact with the perceiver, although heat and vibration from remote sources can be sensed (see also PAIN). Haptic perception provides a rich representation of the perceiver's proximal surroundings and is critical in guiding manipulation of objects.

Beneath the surface of the skin lie a variety of structures that mediate cutaneous (or tactile) perception (see, e.g., Bolanowski et al. 1988; Cholewiak and Collins 1991). These include four specialized end organs: Meissner corpuscles, Merkel disks, Pacinian corpuscles, and Ruffini endings. There is substantial evidence that these organs play the role of mechanoreceptors, which transduce forces applied to the skin into neural signals. The mechanoreceptors can be functionally categorized by the size of their receptive fields (large or small) and their temporal properties (fast adapting, FA, or slowly adapting, SA). The resulting 2×2 classification comprises (1) FAI receptors, which are rapidly adapting, have small receptive fields, and are believed to correspond to the Meissner corpuscles; (2) FAII receptors, which are rapidly adapting, have large receptive fields, and likely correspond to the Pacinian corpuscles (hence also called PCs); (3) SAI receptors, which are slowly adapting, have small receptive fields, and likely correspond to the Merkel disks; and (4) SAII receptors, which are slowly adapting, have large receptive fields, and likely correspond to the Ruffini endings. Among other cutaneous neural populations are thermal receptors that respond to cold or warmth.

By virtue of differences in their temporal and spatial responses, the various mechanoreceptors mediate different types of sensations. The Pacinian corpuscles have a maximum response for trains of impulses on the order of 250 Hz and hence serve to detect vibratory signals, like those that arise when very fine surfaces are stroked or when an object is initially contacted. The SAI receptors, by virtue of their sustained response and relatively fine spatial resolution, are implicated in the perception of patterns pressed into the skin, such as braille symbols (Phillips, Johansson, and Johnson 1990). The SAIs also appear to mediate the perception of roughness, when surfaces have raised elements separated by about 1 mm or more (Connor and Johnson 1992; see TEXTURE).

The responses of haptic receptors are affected by movements of the limbs, which produce concomitant changes in the nature of contact between the skin and touched surfaces. This dependence of perception on movement makes haptic perception active and purposive. Characteristic, stereotyped patterns of movement arise when information is sought about a particular object property. For example, when determining the roughness of a surface, people typically produce motion laterally between the skin and the surface, by stroking or rubbing. Such a specialized movement pattern is called an exploratory procedure (Lederman and Klatzky 1987).

An exploratory procedure is said to be associated with an object property if it is typically used when information about that property is called for. A number of exploratory procedures have been documented. In addition to the lateral motion procedure associated with surface texture, there is unsupported holding, used to sense weight; pressure, used to sense compliance; enclosure, used to sense global shape and volume; static contact, used to determine apparent temperature; and contour following, used to determine precise shape. The exploratory procedure associated with a property during free exploration also turns out to be optimal, in terms of speed and/or accuracy, or even necessary (in the case of contour following), for extracting information about that property; an exploratory procedure that is optimal for one property may also deliver relatively coarse information about others (Lederman and Klatzky 1987).

The exploratory procedures appear to optimize perception of an object property by facilitating a computational process that derives that property from sensory signals. For example, the exploratory procedure called static contact promotes perception of surface temperature, because it characteristically involves a large skin surface and therefore produces a summated signal from spatially distributed thermal receptors (Kenshalo 1984). Texture perception is enhanced by lateral motion of the skin across a surface, because the scanning motion increases the response of the SA units (Johnson and Lamb 1981). It has been proposed

that weight can be judged by wielding an object (as occurs during unsupported holding), because the motion provides information about the object's resistance to rotation, which is related to its mass and volume (Amazeen and Turvey 1996).

With free exploration, familiar common objects can usually be identified haptically (i.e., without vision) with virtually no error, within a period of 1–2 s (Klatzky, Lederman, and Metzger 1985; see also OBJECT RECOGNITION). The sequence of exploratory procedures during identification appears to be driven both by the goal of maximizing bottom-up information and by top-down hypothesis testing. Object exploration tends to begin with general-purpose procedures, which provide coarse information about multiple object properties, and proceed to specialized procedures, which test for idiosyncratic features of the hypothesized object (Lederman and Klatzky 1990).

Although haptic object identification usually has a time-course of seconds, considerable information about objects can be acquired from briefer contact. Intensive properties of objects—those that can be coded unidimensionally (i.e., not with respect to layout in 2-D or 3-D space)—can be extracted with minimal movement of the fingers and in parallel across multiple fingers (Lederman and Klatzky 1997). When an array of surface elements is simultaneously presented across multiple fingers, the time to determine whether an intensively coded target feature (e.g., a rough surface) is present can average on the order of 400 ms, including response selection and motor output. Properties extracted during such early touch can form the basis for object identification: a 200-ms period of contact, without finger movement, is sufficient for identification at levels above chance (Klatzky and Lederman 1995).

A critical role for haptic perception is to support manipulatory actions on objects (see also MOTOR CONTROL). When an object is lifted, signals from cutaneous afferents allow a grip force to be set to just above the threshold needed to prevent slip (Westling and Johannson 1987). During lifting, incipient slip is sensed by the FA receptors, leading to corrective adjustments in grip force (Johannson and Westling 1987). Adjustments also occur during initial contact in response to perceived object properties such as coefficient of friction (Johannson and Westling 1987). Age-related elevations in cutaneous sensory thresholds lead older adults to use grip force that is substantially greater than the level needed to prevent slip (Cole 1991).

See also ECOLOGICAL PSYCHOLOGY; MANIPULATION AND GRASPING; SMELL; TASTE

—*Roberta Klatzky*

References

Amazeen, E. L., and M. T. Turvey. (1996). Weight perception and the haptic size-weight illusion are functions of the inertia tensor. *Journal of Experimental Psychology: Human Perception and Performance* 22: 213–232.

Bolanowski, S. J., Jr., G. A. Gescheider, R. T. Verrillo, and C. M. Checkosky. (1988). Four channels mediate the mechanical aspects of touch. *Journal of the Acoustical Society of America* 84(5): 1680–1694.

Cholewiak, R., and A. Collins. (1991). Sensory and physiological bases of touch. In M. A. Heller and W. Schiff, Eds., *The Psychology of Touch*. Mahwah, NJ: Erlbaum, pp. 23–60.

Cole, K. J. (1991). Grasp force control in older adults. *Journal of Motor Behavior* 23: 251–258.

Connor, C. E., and K. O. Johnson. (1992). Neural coding of tactile texture: Comparison of spatial and temporal mechanisms for roughness perception. *The Journal of Neuroscience* 12: 3414–3426.

Johannson, R. S., and G. Westling. (1987). Signals in tactile afferents from the fingers eliciting adaptive motor responses during precision grip. *Experimental Brain Research* 66: 141–154.

Johnson, K. O., and G. D. Lamb. (1981). Neural mechanisms of spatial tactile discrimination: Neural patterns evoked by Braille-like dot patterns in the monkey. *Journal of Physiology* 310: 117–144.

Kenshalo, D. R. (1984). Cutaneous temperature sensitivity. In W. W. Dawson and J. M. Enoch, Eds., *Foundations of Sensory Science*. Berlin: Springer, pp. 419–464.

Klatzky, R., S. Lederman, and V. Metzger. (1985). Identifying objects by touch: an "expert system." *Perception and Psychophysics* 37: 299–302.

Klatzky, R. L., and S. J. Lederman. (1995). Identifying objects from a haptic glance. *Perception and Psychophysics* 57(8): 1111–1123.

Lederman, S. J., and R. L. Klatzky. (1987). Hand movements: a window into haptic object recognition. *Cognitive Psychology* 19: 342–368.

Lederman, S. J., and R. L. Klatzky. (1990). Haptic object classification: knowledge driven exploration. *Cognitive Psychology* 22: 421–459.

Lederman, S. J., and R. L. Klatzky. (1997). Relative availability of surface and object properties during early haptic processing. *Journal of Experimental Psychology: Human Perception and Performance* 23: 1680–1707.

Loomis, J., and S. Lederman. (1986). Tactual perception. In K. Boff, L. Kaufman, and J. Thomas, Eds., *Handbook of Human Perception and Performance*. New York: Wiley, pp. 1–41.

Phillips, J. R., R. S. Johansson, and K. D. Johnson. (1990). Representation of braille characters in human nerve fibres. *Experimental Brain Research* 81: 589–592.

Westling, G., and R. S. Johannson. (1987). Responses in glabrous skin mechanoreceptors during precision grip in humans. *Experimental Brain Research* 66: 128–140.

Further Readings

Heller, M. A., and W. Schiff. (1991). *The Psychology of Touch*. Mahwah, NJ: Erlbaum.

Jeannerod, M., and J. Grafman., Eds. (1997). *Handbook of Neuropsychology*, vol. 11. *(Section 16: Action and Cognition)*. Amsterdam: Elsevier.

Katz, D. (1989). *The World of Touch*. L. E. Krueger, Ed., Mahwah, NJ: Erlbaum.

Nicholls, H. R., Ed. (1992). *Advanced Tactile Sensing for Robotics*. River Edge, NJ: World Scientific.

Schiff, W., and E. Foulke. (1982.) *Tactual Perception: A Sourcebook*. New York: Cambridge University Press.

Wing, A. M., P. Haggard, and J. R. Flanagan, Eds. (1996). *Hand and Brain: The Neurophysiology and Psychology of Hand Movements*. San Diego: Academic Press.

Head-Driven Phrase Structure Grammar

Head-driven phrase structure grammar (HPSG) is a lexicalist, constraint-based family of theories of GENERATIVE GRAMMAR to which Sag and Wasow (1998) offers an elementary introduction. Two assumptions underlie the theory of head-driven phrase structure grammars. The first is that languages are systems of types of linguistic objects like *word, phrase, clause, person, index, form-type, content,* rather than collections of sentences. The other is that grammars are best represented as process-neutral systems of declarative constraints (as opposed to constraints defined in terms of operations on objects as in transformational grammar). Representations are structurally uniform: all objects of a particular type have all and only the attributes defined for that type. What attributes are defined for an object type is restricted empirically, not by a priori conditions; they cover phonological, semantic, structural, contextual, formal and selectional (subcategorizational) properties.

A grammar (and for that matter, a theory of universal grammar) is thus seen as consisting of an inheritance hierarchy of such types (an "is-a" hierarchy similar to familiar semantic networks of the sort that have "creature" as a root and progressively more specific nodes on a branch leading to a particular canary "Tweety"). The types are interrelated in two ways. First, some types are defined in terms of other types. Second, the hierarchy allows for multiple inheritance, in that linguistic objects can belong to multiple categories at the same time, just as other conceptual objects do. The constraints in the linguistic hierarchy are all local, so that well-formedness is determined exclusively with reference to a given structure, and not by comparison to any other candidate structures. The LEXICON is a rich subhierarchy within the larger hierarchy constituting the grammar. Having declarative constraints on a hierarchy of interrelated types of linguistic objects is seen as enabling an account of language processing which is incremental and pervasively integrative. Thus, as long as information about grammatical number is consistent, it does not matter whether it comes from a verb or its subject, as shown by the fact that (1–3) are acceptable, whereas (4) is not.

1. The dogs slept in the barn.
2. The sheep which was mine stayed in the pen.
3. The sheep which stayed in the pen were mine.
4. *The sheep which was mine are in the pen.

Linguistic objects are modeled as feature structures. Feature structures are complete specifications of values for all the attributes that are appropriate for the particular sort of object that they model, and they are the entities constrained by the grammar. Feature structure descriptions describe classes of feature structures, by means of familiar attribute-and-value matrices (AVMs) that (partially) describe them. A partial description constrains all the members of whatever class of feature structures it describes, while a total description is a constraint that limits the class to a single member. For the most part, grammar specification deals with generalizations over classes of objects like words and phrase-types, and therefore with (partial) feature structure descriptions. Feature-based unification grammar formalisms like HPSG are thus conceptually lean and computationally tractable, and are being used in increasing numbers of NATURAL LANGUAGE PROCESSING systems.

A feature's value is of one of four possible types: atom, feature structure, set of feature structures, or list of feature structures. (Set values are represented as sequences within curly brackets: SLASH {①②}. The empty set is denoted: { } while { [ ] } denotes a singleton set. List values are represented as sequences within angled brackets: COMPS < NP, VP[*inf*] >. The empty list is denoted: < >, and < [ ] > denotes a singleton list.) Values that are not specified in a feature-structure description are still constrained to be among the legitimate values for the features that the constraints on the types to which it belongs require.

Like other linguistic objects, categories that figure in the SYNTAX have rich internal structure and constituency descriptions. But HPSG is a "WYSIWYG" theory; empty categories are avoided rather than exploited.

The general outlines of the HPSG approach to constituent order derive from the theory of linear precedence rules sketched in GPSG (Gazdar and Pullum 1981; Gazdar et al. 1985), and discussed at some length in Pollard and Sag (1987). As in GPSG, so-called free word order (i.e., free phrase order) is a consequence of not constraining the order of constituents at all. (Genuinely free word order, where (any) words of one phrase can precede (any) words of any other phrase requires a word-order function that allows constituents of one phrase to be recursively interleaved with constituents of another; see Gazdar and Pullum 1981; Pollard and Sag 1987; Dowty 1996; Reape 1994).

As grammar-writing research on a number of languages (especially notably, German and French) has made abundantly clear, word order constraints are not always compatible with the semantic and syntactic evidence for constituency, and the exact form of the resolution to this dilemma constitutes a lively topic in current research.

Constraints on phrase types project meanings, subcategorization requirements, and head properties from subconstituents. The HEAD-feature principle, for example, represented in figure 1, constrains HEAD properties of a phrase (i.e., category information like person, number, case, inflection) to be the same as that of its head daughter.

Constraints on phrase types also provide COMPOSITIONALITY in the semantics by specifying how the semantics of a phrase type is a function of the semantics of its daughter constituents.

Equi and raising structures (like *Kim tried to run* and *Kim seemed to run,* respectively) are both projections of heads that subcategorize for an unsaturated predicative complement, and have the same sorts of constituent structure. Equi verbs like *try,* however, systematically assign one more semantic role than raising verbs like *seem* do. Pollard and Sag (1994) represent this difference by saying that an equi verb subcategorizes for an NP with a referential index (i.e., one that is not an expletive), which is the same as the index

of the subject element that its complement subcategorizes for, and assigns a semantic role to that index, whereas a raising verb just subcategorizes for whatever its infinitive VP complement subcategorizes for, and assigns no semantic role to the index of that element.

The general outlines of the HPSG treatment of unbounded extractions (WH-MOVEMENT) follow the three-part strategy developed in GPSG (Gazdar 1981; Gazdar et al. 1985). An extra constituent is licensed just in case it matches a missing constituent. Something must ensure that the missing constituent is missing. The correspondence between the gap and the extra constituent (the *filler*) is recorded via constraints on local (i.e., depth one) constituency relations over an indefinitely large array of structure.

In HPSG, the extra constituent is licensed in strong (topicalization-type) extractions by the schema or sort declaration that defines head-filler clauses (topicalization structures), and for weak extraction phenomena such as *tough*-constructions, by subcategorization and sort specifications that require a complement daughter to not be lexically realized. Gaps (or traces) are licensed in phrases by constraints or rules that allow dependents to be unrealized when the lexical head that selects them inherits information that a matching element should be missing. As in GPSG, "a linked series of local mother-daughter feature correspondences" (Gazdar et al. 1985: 138), embodied as constraints on phrase-types, entail that the extra constituent and the missing constituent match.

The HPSG account of the binding of indexical elements like *her* and *themselves* is stated in terms of the relative obliqueness of the GRAMMATICAL RELATIONS of the indexical and its antecedent relative to a predicate. Considering its nonconfigurational approach, the HPSG binding theory nonetheless resembles familiar configurational accounts:

- A locally commanded anaphor must be locally o-bound.
- A personal pronoun must be locally o-free.
- A non-pronoun must be o-free.

However, it differs crucially from typical configurational accounts in that it has an inherently narrower scope. Principle A does not constrain all anaphors to be locally o-bound (coindexed to something before them on a predicate's argument-structure list); it constrains only those that are locally o-commanded (i.e., the ones that are noninitial on the list). This makes strong, vulnerable, and apparently correct claims. First, pronouns that are initial elements on argument-structure lists are unconstrained—free to be anaphors, coindexed to anything, and vacuously satisfying principle A, or to be pronouns, substantively satisfying principle B. Thus, the theory predicts that phrases in these "exempt" conditions, which are coindexed to anything anywhere in a higher clause, or even outside the sentence altogether, can be either anaphors or pronouns. This is correct; the reflexive pronouns that contradict the naive versions of principle A are generally replaceable with personal pronouns with the same reference.

Unification-based, declarative models of grammar like HPSG are attractive for natural language processing applications (e.g., as interfaces to expert systems) precisely

$$\begin{bmatrix} \text{SYNSEM | LOCAL | CATEGORY | HEAD } ① \\ \text{HEAD-DTR } <[\text{SYNSEM | LOCAL | CATEGORY | HEAD } ①]> \end{bmatrix}$$

headed-phrase

Figure 1.

because they are nondirectional and suited to the construction of application-neutral systems serving NATURAL LANGUAGE GENERATION as well as parsing and interpretation.

See also ANAPHORA; BINDING THEORY; COMPUTATIONAL LEXICONS; COMPUTATIONAL LINGUISTICS; FORMAL GRAMMARS

—Georgia M. Green

References

Dowty, D. (1996). Towards a minimalist theory of syntactic structure. In H. Bunt and A. van Horck, Eds., *Discontinuous Constituency*. Berlin: Mouton de Gruyter.

Gazdar, G. (1981). Unbounded dependencies and coordinate structure. *Linguistic Inquiry* 12: 155–184.

Gazdar, G., and G. K. Pullum. (1981). Subcategorization, constituent order, and the notion "head." In M. Moortgat, H. v. D. Hulst, and T. Hoekstra, Eds., *The Scope of Lexical Rules*. Dordrecht: Foris, pp. 107–123.

Gazdar, G., E. Klein, G. K. Pullum, and I. A. Sag. (1985). *Generalized Phrase Structure Grammar*. Cambridge, MA: Harvard University Press.

Pollard, C., and I. Sag. (1987). *Information-based Syntax and Semantics,* vol. 1. Stanford: CSLI.

Pollard, C., and I. Sag. (1994). *Head-driven Phrase Structure Grammar*. Chicago: University of Chicago Press.

Reape, M. (1994). Domain union and word order variation in German. In J. Nerbonne, K. Netter, and C. Pollard, Eds., *German in Head-driven Phrase Structure Grammar*. CSLI Lecture Notes No. 46. Stanford: CSLI.

Sag, I. A., and T. Wasow. (1998). *Syntactic Theory: A Formal Introduction*. Stanford: CSLI.

Further Readings

Carpenter, B. (1992). The logic of typed feature structures. *Cambridge Tracts in Theoretical Computer Science 32*. New York: Cambridge University Press.

Copestake, A., D. Flickinger, R. Malouf, S. Riehemann, and I. A. Sag. (1995). Translation using Minimal Recursion Semantics. *Proceedings of the Sixth International Conference on Theoretical and Methodological Issues in Machine Translation (TMI-95)* Leuven, Belgium.

Kay, M., J. M. Gawron, and P. Norvig. (1994). *Verbmobil: A Translation System for Face-to-Face Dialog*. CSLI Lecture Notes No. 33. Stanford: CSLI.

Lappin, S., and H. Gregory. (1997). A computational model of ellipsis resolution. Master's thesis, School of Oriental and African Studies, University of London. Available from website http://semantics.soas.ac.uk/ellip/.

Meurers, W. D., and G. Minnen. (1995). A computational treatment of HPSG lexical rules as covariation in lexical entries. *Proceedings of the Fifth International Workshop on Natural Language Understanding and Logic Programming*. Lisbon, Portugal.

Pollard, C. (1996). The nature of constraint-based grammar. Talk presented at Pacific Asia Conference on Language, Information, and Computation. Seoul, Korea: Kyung Hee University.

Pollard, C., and D. Moshier. (1990). Unifying partial descriptions of sets. Information, Language and Cognition. *Vancouver Studies in Cognitive Science,* vol. 1. Vancouver: University of British Columbia Press, pp. 285–322.

Shieber, Stuart. (1986). *An Introduction to Unification-based Approaches to Grammar*. CSLI Lecture Notes Series. Stanford:

Center for the Study of Language and Information. (Distributed by University of Chicago Press.)

Head Movement

Within the syntactic framework that grew out of Chomsky (1965), elements that appear in unexpected positions are often said to have undergone movement. One case of this is wh-movement where a maximal projection (see X-BAR THEORY) moves to Spec, CP. Heads of maximal projections may also be displaced as seen by the following triple. "The children will not *have* done their homework." "The children *have* not done their homework." "*Have* the children done their homework?" The verb *have* appears in three different positions with respect to negation *not* and the subject *the children*. A head movement account assumes that *have* originates in V (head of VP), moves to T(ense) (head of TP), and then to C (head of CP).

(1) [$_{CP}$C [$_{TP}$ the children T [$_{VP}$ V [$_{VP}$ do their homework]]]].

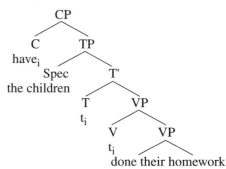

By positing a process by which heads may be moved, languages that appear to have quite different surface realizations may be seen as having similar abstract underlying representations that are then disrupted by language-specific rules of head movement. For instance, if one assumes that VPs containing the V and the object are universal (see LINGUISTIC UNIVERSALS), one can account for VSO languages (see TYPOLOGY) by positing obligatory movement of the V to a head higher in the syntactic tree in these languages.

(2)

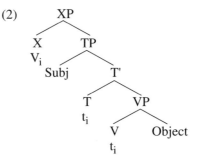

The word order in verb second languages such as German is characterized by obligatory movement of a topic to Spec, CP and head movement of the verb to C (see PARAMETER-SETTING APPROACHES TO ACQUISITION, CREOLIZATION, AND DIACHRONY).

Another use of head movement has been to explain the tight correlation between morpheme orders and phrase structure (the mirror principle of Baker 1985) through local iterative head movement. Although the movement in English discussed earlier transposes words by moving a word into an empty head position, head movement may also move a stem into a head which contains an affix (or force movement of a word which contains this affix in MINIMALISM). For example, in Japanese where the morpheme order is V-Tense-C as in *tabe-ta-to,* "eat-pst-Comp(that)," the verb has undergone the same movement that we saw for English from V to T to C, picking up the head-related MORPHOLOGY.

This use of head movement to create morphologically complex words can be further extended to account for processes such as noun incorporation where the noun head of the object NP incorporates into the verb through head movement to form complex verbs like the Mohawk form in (3) (see POLYSYNTHETIC LANGUAGES as well as Baker 1988 and 1996).

(3) wa-hake-'sereht-uny-λ-'
    fact-agr(3sS)+agr(1sO)-car-make-ben-punc
    'He made a car for me'

Head movement as a mechanism to build complex words interacts in obvious ways with questions concerning morphology and the LEXICON (see, e.g., diSciullo and Williams 1988 for arguments against this account of incorporation).

As well as creating morphologically complex words, head movement has been used to represent words that are morphologically simple but semantically complex. Hale and Keyser (1993) have suggested that denominal and deadjectival verbs such as *shelve* and *thin* are formed through head movement. "The children shelved the books" would be derived from a structure similar to "The children put the books on the shelf." The verb and the preposition would be null, however, allowing the movement of *shelve* as the head of the prepositional object NP to move iteratively through the empty P to the empty V. (The structure below contains an extra VP; see Hale and Keyser 1993 for details.)

(4) the children [VP shelved [the books] [PP P [NP N]].

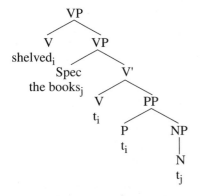

Like other movements, head movement in not unconstrained but must obey a locality condition. Descriptively this locality condition requires movement to the most local possible landing site (the Head Movement Constraint of Travis 1984). Baker (1988) and Rizzi (1990) have subsequently reformulated this locality condition, collapsing it with the locality condition on rules that move maximal projections. The existence of this locality condition on head movement and the similarity of this condition to the condition for movement of maximal projections strengthens the claim that head movement is one instance of a more general movement rule. Further, the fact that this locality condition shows up in noun incorporation and denominal verb formation as well as the English verb movement facts strengthens the claim that they are all part of the same phenomenon. For instance, the following strings are ungrammatical for the same reason:

(5) a. *Have the children will ___ done their homework
    b. *wa-hake-'sereht-uny-λ-' wa'-ke-nohare-'
       fact-agr(3sS)+agr(1sO)-car-make-ben-punc fact-
       agr(1sS)-wash-punc)
       'He made me wash the car' (lit: he me-car-made wash)
    c. *The children shelved the books on ___.

In all three cases an intervening head position has been skipped (the T *will,* the V *ohare,* "wash," and the P *on*), violating the Head Movement Constraint.

If heads must always move to head positions, then head movement may be used as a probe to determine phrase structure. For instance, Pollock (1989) has argued that there must be (at least) two head positions between C and V due to the fact that, in French, there are two possible landing sites for the verb—one between the subject and negation (as in the English example above) and one between negation and an adverb. This may be extended as in Cinque (forthcoming) to posit head positions between different classes of adverbs in order to account for the possible placement of the participle *rimesso* (marked with an X) in the following Italian sentence.

(6) Da allora, non hanno X di solito X mica X più X sempre
    X completamente *rimesso* tutto bene in ordine
    "Since then, they haven't usually not any longer always put everything well in order"

It has also been proposed that head movement cannot proceed from a lexical category (N, V, A, P) through a functional category (T, C, D(et)) back to a lexical category to explain why functional (grammatical) morphemes are not found in, say, causative structures (*make-fut-work; see Li 1990). A typology of head movement has also been proposed (Koopman 1983) that includes one type of head movement with the characteristics of NP-Movement (like passive and raising), and another with the characteristics of WH-MOVEMENT.

Head movement is different from maximal projection movement in that it can be seen to create both morphologically complex as well as (the meaning of) morphologically simple words, arguably putting it into direct competition with lexical and semantic rules. Yet because it shows parallel restrictions and typology to rules that permute maximal projections, it can be said to be part of the computational component of SYNTAX.

See also BINDING THEORY; GENERATIVE GRAMMAR; SYNTAX, ACQUISITION OF

—Lisa Travis

References

Baker, M. (1985). The Mirror Principle and morphosyntactic explanation. *Linguistic Inquiry* 16: 373–415.

Baker, M. (1988). *Incorporation: A Theory of Grammatical Function Changing.* Chicago: University of Chicago Press.

Baker, M. (1996). *The Polysynthesis Parameter.* Oxford: Oxford University Press.

Chomsky, N. (1965). *Aspects of the Theory of Syntax.* Cambridge, MA: MIT Press.

Cinque, G. (Forthcoming). *Adverbs and Functional Heads: A Cross-Linguistic Perspective.* Oxford: Oxford University Press.

diSciullo, A.-M., and E. Williams. (1988). *On the Definition of Word.* Cambridge, MA: MIT Press.

Hale, K., and S. J. Keyser. (1993). On argument structure and the lexical expression of syntactic relations. In K. Hale and S. J. Keyser, Eds., *The View from Building 20.* Cambridge, MA: MIT Press, pp. 53–110.

Koopman, H. (1983). *The Syntax of Verbs.* Dordrecht: Foris.

Li, Y. (1990). X°-binding and verb incorporation. *Linguistic Inquiry* 21: 399–426.

Pollock, J.-Y. (1989). Verb movement, UG, and the structure of IP. *Linguistic Inquiry* 20: 365–424.

Rizzi, L. (1990). *Relativized Minimality.* Cambridge, MA: MIT Press.

Travis, L. (1984). *Parameters and Effects of Word Order Variation.* Ph.D. diss., Massachusetts Institute of Technology.

Further Readings

Belletti, A. (1990). *Generalized Verb Movement: Aspects of Verb Syntax.* Torino: Rosenberg and Sellier.

Borsley, R. D., M.-L. Rivero, and J. Stephens. (1996). Long head movement in Breton. In R. D. Borsley and I. Roberts, Eds., *The Syntax of Celtic Languages.* Cambridge: Cambridge University Press, pp. 53–74.

Lema, J., and M.-L. Rivero. (1989). Long head movement: ECP vs. HMC. In J. Carter, R.-M. Dechaine, B. Philip, and T. Sherer, Eds., *NELS.* Carnegie Mellon University: GLSA, pp. 333–347.

Lema, J., and M.-L. Rivero. (1991). Types of verbal movement in Old Spanish: modals, futures, and perfects. *Probus* 3: 237–278.

Lema, J., and M.-L. Rivero. (1989). Inverted conjugations and V-second effects in Romance. In C. Laeufer and T. Morgan, Eds., *Theoretical Analyses in Contemporary Romance Linguistics: Selected Papers from the Nineteenth Symposium on Romance Linguistics.* London: John Benjamins, pp. 311–328.

Rivero, M.-L. (1991). Long head movement and negation: Serbo-Croation vs Slovak and Czech. *The Linguistic Review* 8: 319–351.

Rivero, M.-L. (1994). Clause structure and V-movement in the languages of the Balkans. *Natural Language and Linguistic Theory* 12: 63–120.

Rizzi, L., and I. Roberts. (1989). Complex inversion in French. *Probus* 1: 1–30.

Roberts, I. (1994). Two types of head movement in Romance. In D. Lightfoot and N. Hornstein, Eds., *Verb Movement.* Cambridge: Cambridge University Press, pp. 207–242.

Roberts, I. (1991). Excorporation and Minimality. *Linguistic Inquiry* 22: 209–218.

Hearing

See AUDITION; AUDITORY PHYSIOLOGY; SPEECH PERCEPTION

Hebb, Donald O.

Donald Olding Hebb (1904–1985) was, during his lifetime, an extraordinarily influential figure in the discipline of psychology. His principled opposition to radical BEHAVIORISM and emphasis on understanding what goes on between stimulus and response (perception, LEARNING, thinking) helped clear the way for the cognitive revolution. His view of psychology as a biological science and his neuropsychological cell-assembly proposal rejuvenated interest in physiological psychology. Since his death, Hebb's seminal ideas exert an ever-growing influence on those interested in mind (cognitive science), brain (neuroscience), and how brains implement mind (cognitive neuroscience).

On graduating from Dalhousie University in 1925, Hebb aspired to write novels, but chose instead the more practical field of education and quickly became a school principal. The writings of JAMES, FREUD, and Watson stimulated his interest in psychology, and as a part-time graduate student at McGill University, Hebb was exposed to Pavlov's program. Unimpressed, Hebb was "softened up for [his] encounter with Kohler's GESTALT PSYCHOLOGY and LASHLEY's critique of reflexology." Hebb went to work with Lashley, and in 1936 completed his doctorate at Harvard on the effects of early visual deprivation on size and brightness perception in the rat. He accepted Wilder PENFIELD's offer of a fellowship at the Montreal Neurological Institute, where he explored the impact of brain injury and surgery, particularly lesions of the frontal lobes, on human intelligence and behavior. From his observations that removal of large amounts of tissue might have little impact on MEMORY and INTELLIGENCE, Hebb inferred a widely distributed neural substrate. At Queens University, Hebb developed human and animal intelligence tests (including the "Hebb-Williams" maze) and concluded that experience played a much greater role in determining intelligence than was typically assumed (Hebb 1942).

In 1942 Hebb rejoined Lashley, who had become director of the Yerkes Laboratory of Primate Biology. There Hebb explored fear, anger, and other emotional processes in the chimpanzee (cf. EMOTION AND THE ANIMAL BRAIN). Stimulated by the intellectual climate at Yerkes, Hebb began writing a book synthesizing different lines of research into a "general theory of behavior that attempts to bridge the gap between neurophysiology and psychology" (Hebb 1949: vii). Hebb returned to McGill as professor of psychology and in 1948 was appointed chair. His book *The Organization of Behavior: A Neuropsychological Theory* wielded a kind of magic in the years after its appearance (Hebb 1949). It attracted many brilliant scientists into psychology, made McGill University a North American mecca for scientists interested in the brain mechanisms of behavior, led to many important discoveries, and steered contemporary psychology onto a more fruitful path.

For Hebb "the problem of understanding behavior is the problem of understanding the total action of the nervous system, and vice versa" (1949: xiv), and his advocacy of an interdisciplinary effort to solve this "neuropsychological" problem was his most general theme. When Hebb's book was published physiological psychology was in decline, and there was a growing movement in psychology to reject physiological concepts (Skinner 1938). *The Organization of Behavior* marked a turning point away from this trend. Metaphors, using nonbiological devices with well-understood properties, figure prominently in the history of attempts to explain behavior and thought. The mental chemistry of the British Associationists, hydraulics of psychotherapy, magnetic fields of Gestalt psychology, and the computer metaphor of information processing psychology were all fruitful to a point, but then limited and misleading. Hebb's appealingly simple alternative was to explain human and animal behavior and thought in terms of the actual device that produces them—the brain. In *The Organization of Behavior,* Hebb presented just such a *neuropsychological* theory.

There were three pivotal postulates: (1) Connections between neurons increase in efficacy in proportion to the degree of correlation between pre- and postsynaptic activity. In neuroscience this corresponds to the "Hebb synapse," the first instances of which were later discovered in LONG-TERM POTENTIATION and kindling, whereas in cognitive science this postulate provides the most basic learning algorithm for adjusting connection weights in artificial NEURAL NETWORK models. (2) Groups of neurons that tend to fire together form a cell-assembly whose activity can persist after the triggering event and serves to represent it. (3) Thinking is the sequential activation of a set of cell-assemblies.

Hebb knew that his theory was speculative, vague, and incomplete. Missing from the model, for example, was neural inhibition (Milner 1957), a concept Hebb later incorporated (1959). But Hebb believed that a class of theory was needed, of which his was merely one specific form—subject to modification or rejection in the face of new evidence. Hebb's ideas were certainly fruitful in generating new evidence, as whole literatures on the role of early experience in PERCEPTUAL DEVELOPMENT (Hunt 1979), sensory deprivation (Zubek 1969), self stimulation (Olds and Milner 1954), the stopped retinal image (Pritchard, Heron, and Hebb 1960), synaptic modifiability (Goddard 1980), and learning without awareness (McKelvie 1987), were provoked or fostered by them.

When philosophy and physiology converged in the nineteenth century, psychology emerged with the promise of a science of mental life (Boring 1950). By providing a neural implementation of the Associationists' mental chemistry Hebb fulfilled this promise and laid the foundation for neoconnectionism, which seeks to explain cognitive processes in terms of connections between assemblies of real or artificial neurons.

See also COGNITIVE MODELING, CONNECTIONIST; CONDITIONING; CONDITIONING AND THE BRAIN

—*Raymond M. Klein*

References

Boring, E. G. (1950). *A History of Experimental Psychology.* 2nd ed. New York: Appleton-Century-Crofts.

Goddard, G. V. (1980). Component properties of the memory machine: Hebb revisited. In P. W. Jusczyk and R. M. Klein, Eds., *The Nature of Thought: Essays in Honor of D. O. Hebb.* Hillsdale, NJ: Erlbaum, pp. 231–247.

Hebb, D. O. (1942). The effects of early and late brain injury upon test scores, and the nature of normal adult intelligence. *Proceedings of the American Philosophical Society* 85: 275–292.

Hebb, D. O. (1949). *The Organization of Behavior: A Neuropsychological Theory.* New York: Wiley.

Hebb, D. O. (1959). A neuropsychological theory. In S. Koch, Ed., *Psychology: A Study of a Science,* vol. 1. New York: McGraw-Hill.

Hunt, J. M. (1979). Psychological development: early experience. *Annual Review of Psychology* 30: 103–143.

McKelvie, S. (1987). Learning and awareness in the Hebb digits task. *Journal of General Psychology* 114: 75–88.

Milner, P. M. (1957). The cell assembly: Mark II. *Psychological Review* 64: 242–252.

Olds, J., and P. M. Milner. (1954). Positive reinforcement produced by electrical stimulation of the septal area and other regions of the rat brain. *Journal of Comparative and Physiological Psychology* 47: 419–427.

Pritchard, R. M., W. Heron, and D. O. Hebb. (1960). Visual perception approached by the method of stabilized images. *Canadian Journal of Psychology* 14: 67–77.

Skinner, B. F. (1938). *The Behavior of Organisms: An Experimental Analysis.* New York: Appleton-Century.

Zubek, P. (1969). *Sensory Deprivation: 15 Years of Research.* New York: Meredith.

Further Readings

Glickman, S. (1996). Donald Olding Hebb: Returning the nervous system to psychology. In G. Kimble, C. Boneau, and M. Wertheimer, Eds., *Portraits of Pioneers in Psychology,* vol. 2. Hillsdale, NJ: Erlbaum.

Hebb, D. O. (1980). D. O. Hebb. In G. Lindzey, Ed., *A History of Psychology in Autobiography,* vol. 8. San Francisco: W. H. Freeman.

Hebb, D. O. (1953). Heredity and environment in mammalian behavior. *British Journal of Animal Behavior* 1: 43–47.

Hebb, D. O. (1958). *A Textbook of Psychology.* Philadelphia: Saunders.

Hebb, D. O. (1955). Drives and the CNS (conceptual nervous system). *Psychological Review* 62: 243–254.

Hebb, D. O. (1980). *Essay on Mind.* Hillsdale, NJ: Erlbaum Associates.

Klein, R. M. (1980). D. O. Hebb: An appreciation. In P. W. Jusczyk and R. M. Klein, Eds., *The nature of Thought: Essays in Honour of D. O. Hebb.* Hillsdale, New Jersey: Erlbaum, pp. 1–18.

Milner, P. M. (1986). The mind and Donald O. Hebb. *Scientific American* 268(1): 124–129.

Hebbian Learning

See COMPUTATIONAL NEUROSCIENCE; HEBB, DONALD O.; NEURON

Helmholtz, Hermann Ludwig Ferdinand von

Hermann Ludwig Ferdinand von Helmholtz (1821–1894) was born on August 31, 1821, in Potsdam. His father, Ferdinand Helmholtz, was a respected teacher of philology and philosophy at the gymnasium. His mother was the daughter of a Hanoverian artillery officer with the surname Penne, descended from the Quaker William Penn, founder of Pennsylvania.

After serving as an army surgeon, Helmholtz held a succession of academic positions—lecturer at the Berlin Anatomy Museum, professor of physiology at Konigsberg, professor of physiology at Bonn, professor of physiology at Heidelberg, professor of physics at the Military Institute for Medicine and Surgery in Berlin, first president of the Imperial Physico-Technical Institute in Berlin. He married and had two children, his son Richard becoming a physical chemist. During his extremely distinguished life he was ennobled by the emperor: hence the "von" in his name.

Helmholtz was no less than a hero of nineteenth-century science, making major contributions to physics and the foundations of geometry, and founding the modern science of visual and auditory perception. He formulated the principle of conservation of energy in 1847, and made significant contributions to the philosophy of non-Euclidean geometry. This fueled his rejection of the prevailing Kantian philosophy in favor of a thoroughly empirical approach to the natural and biological sciences. He was the last scholar to combine both in depth.

Helmholtz was the first to see a living human RETINA. The wonderful memory of doing so remained with him for the rest of his life. His discovery was made with the extraordinarily useful instrument, the ophthalmoscope, which he invented in 1851. He explained why the pupil is black—the observing eye and head gets in the way of light reaching the observed retina—so he introduced light onto the retina with a part-reflecting 45° mirror, using thin microscope slides for part-reflecting mirrors, and also a concave lens. Although Helmholtz immediately saw its general medical significance, doctors were slow to adopt it. It became his most famous invention, which set him up as a scientist commanding support for any future work he chose to undertake.

A guiding principle for Helmholtz's physiological psychology was his teacher Johannes Muller's law of specific energies (perhaps better called law of specific qualities): "In whatever way a terminal organ of sense may be stimulated, the result in CONSCIOUSNESS is always of the same kind." Various SENSATIONS are given not by different nerve signals but according to which part of the "sensory" brain is stimulated. The eyes, ears, and the other organs of sense convert patterns of various kinds of physical energies into the same neural coding, now known to be trains of minute electrical impulses called action potentials, varying in frequency according to strength of stimulation. It was Helmholtz who first measured the rate of conduction of nerve, and recorded reaction times to unexpected events. His teacher Johannes Muller thought the speed must be too great to measure, probably greater than the speed of light; but Helmholtz showed him to be wrong with a very simple technique. For noninvasive measures on humans, he touched the shoulder or the wrist and noted the difference in reaction times. Knowing the difference in length of nerve between shoulder and wrist, it was easy to calculate the conduction rate, and also to find the brain's processing delay time. For a long time Muller could not believe that nerve conduction rate is slower than sound!

Helmholtz followed the English philosopher John Locke (1632–1704) in holding that sensations are symbols for external objects, no more like external objects than words used to describe them. Thus the physical world is separated from experience, and perception is only indirectly related to external events or objects. This, and Muller's law of specific energies, are basic to his theory that visual perceptions are unconscious inferences. This was a generation before Freud's unconscious mind, which also evoked much criticism as it challenged the right to blame, or indeed praise, actions that are unconscious. Yet studying unconscious processes has proved vital for investigating brain and mind, perhaps ultimately to understanding consciousness. For Helmholtz phenomena of ILLUSIONS are important evidence for understanding perceptions as inferences, depending on assumptions that may be wrong. His basic principle was: "We always think we see such objects before us as would have to be present in order to bring about the same retinal images under normal conditions of observation." So afterimages and even crude pictures are seen as objects.

Apart from the mathematical and experimental sciences as well as philosophy, he was talented in languages and in music, playing the piano. He conveyed science and something of the arts to the public with notable popular lectures that remain interesting to read. Remarkably active throughout his life, he suffered occasional migraines, which interrupted his work, and hay fever, which spoiled his holidays. He traveled widely, often to the British Isles, and was a particular friend of the physicist Lord Kelvin, meeting in Glasgow, Scotland. He attributed his success to the unusual range of his knowledge, which indeed was exceptional.

Helmholtz's death on September 8, 1894, a few days after his seventy-third birthday, resulted from an accidental fall while on a ship bound for America, which, sadly, he never visited. Neither of his biographies mentions his account of perception as unconscious inference, which after a long delay is now seen as centrally important in current cognitive psychology. There should be a fuller and more readable life of this major scientist and philosopher, who gave psychology a scientific basis that is still not fully appreciated, and championed thoroughgoing empiricism for understanding physics and biology, and even the misleading yet highly suggestive phenomena of illusions.

See also AUDITION; FREUD, SIGMUND; LIGHTNESS PERCEPTION; RATIONALISM VS. EMPIRICISM; WUNDT, WILHELM

—*Richard L. Gregory*

References

Helmholtz, H. von. (1866). *Treatise on Physiological Optics.* vol. 3. 3rd ed. Trans. by J. P. C. Southall. New York: Opt. Soc. Amer., 1924. Dover reprint, 1962.

Helmholtz, H. von. (1881). *Popular Lectures.* London: Longmans Green. Dover reprint, 1962.

Koenigsberger, Leo. (1906). *Hermann von Helmholtz.* Oxford: Oxford University Press. Dover reprint, 1965.

M'Kendrick, John. (1899). *Hermann von Helmholtz.* London: Fisher Unwin.

Hemispheric Specialization

The modern era of neuroscientific investigation into the asymmetry of the cerebral hemispheres began in the 1860s when localization of function within the cerebral cortex was thrust into the forefront of scientific thought by Paul BROCA. Broca etched out his place in history by announcing that language resided in the frontal lobes and that the left hemisphere played the predominant role. Although neither of these ideas originated with Broca, the recognition that the brain may be functionally asymmetric opened up new avenues of cognitive and neurobiological investigation that have persisted for well over a century. This summary paper will briefly describe a number of lateralized cognitive functions, including language, FACE RECOGNITION, fine MOTOR CONTROL, visuospatial skills, and EMOTIONS, and will examine whether structural asymmetries in the organization of cerebral cortex are related to these functional specializations. The interested reader is referred to several thorough reviews on the topic of lateralization (see further readings).

Language Lateralization

Language is perhaps the most notable and strongly lateralized function in the human brain. Much of our knowledge of the organization of language in the brain is based on the correlation of behavioral deficits with the location of lesions in the neocortex of patient populations. Several language areas are found to be located within the left hemisphere and the behavioral outcome of injury to these particular cerebral locations is generally predictable (e.g., Broca's APHASIA, Wernicke's aphasia, conduction aphasia). In other cases uniquely specific linguistic deficits can result. For example, one case has been reported in which the subject showed an unusual disability at naming fruits and vegetables despite normal performance on a variety of other lexical/semantic tasks following injury to the frontal lobe and BASAL GANGLIA (Hart, Berndt, and Caramazza 1985). Recent reports describe two more patients who are able to produce a normal complement of verbs, but are extremely deficient in noun production, while a third case shows exactly the reverse deficit. Despite the variety of deficits and lesion locations, all are associated with the left hemisphere (Damasio and Tranel 1993).

Modern research techniques including regional cerebral blood flow, POSITRON EMISSION TOMOGRAPHY (PET), functional MAGNETIC RESONANCE IMAGING (fMRI), and intraoperative cortical stimulation, have continued to localize cortical regions that are activated during language tasks and further support the left hemisphere's special role in language functions.

Although it is true that individuals can be right hemisphere, or bilaterally, dominant for language, 90 percent of the adult population (both left- and right-handed) have language functions that are predominantly located within the left hemisphere. Even in seemingly anomalous situations the left hemisphere maintains its "specialized" role in language functions. Studies of bilingual subjects indicate that both languages are located in the same hemisphere, but may be differentially distributed (Mendelsohn 1988). In addition, language lateralization is not dependent on the vocal-auditory modality. Disturbances of SIGN LANGUAGE in deaf subjects are also consistently associated with left hemisphere damage, and signing deficits are typically analogous to the language deficits one observes in hearing subjects with the same lesion location (Bellugi, Poizner, and Klima 1989).

In early decorticate patients with one hemisphere missing, language development proceeds relatively normally in either hemisphere (Carlson et al. 1968). Language development in the right hemisphere, while retaining its phonemic and semantic abilities, has deficient syntactic competence that is revealed when meaning is conveyed by syntactic diversity, such as repeating stylistically permuted sentences and determining sentence implication (Dennis and Whitaker 1976). These results suggest that although the right hemisphere is capable of supporting language, language usage does not reach a fully normal state.

In adults who have had language develop in the dominant hemisphere, but later became available for the testing of language in their right hemisphere due to commissurotomy or hemispherectomy, the right hemisphere appears capable of understanding a limited amount of vocabulary, but is usually unable to produce speech. In recent years speech production by the right hemisphere of commissurotomy patients has also been reported, albeit in an extremely limited context (Baynes, Tramo, and Gazzaniga 1992).

Motor Control and the Left Hemisphere

Nine out of ten individuals demonstrate a clear preference for using the right hand. Broca inferred that the hemisphere dominant for language would also control the dominant hand; however, it soon became clear that this was not universally true. Most studies suggest that over 95 percent of right-handers are left-hemisphere dominant for language; however, only 15 percent of left-handers show the expected right-hemisphere dominance. Of left-handers, a full 70 percent are left-hemisphere dominant, while the remaining 15 percent have bilateral language abilities.

Disorders of skilled movement are referred to as *apraxia*. These disorders are characterized by a loss of the ability to carry out familiar purposeful movements in the absence of sensory or motor impairment. The preponderance of apraxia following left hemisphere damage has led many researchers to suggest that this hemisphere may be specialized for complex motor programming. Although lesion studies argue for the left hemisphere's dominance of complex motor control, the lateralization of this function is not nearly as strong as that seen for language. In addition, studies of commissurotomy patients suggest that the right hemisphere is capable of independently directing motor function in response to visual nonverbal stimuli without the help of the left hemisphere (Geschwind 1976).

Right Hemisphere Specializations

The right hemisphere also plays a predominant role in several specialized tasks. Right hemisphere lesion patients have greater difficulties localizing points, judging figure from ground, and performing tasks that require stereoscopic depth discriminations than do patients suffering damage to the left hemisphere. Additionally, commissurotomy patients show a right hemisphere advantage for a number of visuoperceptual tasks (Gazzaniga 1995). Many investigators have also reported a right hemisphere advantage for visuoperceptual tasks in normal subjects, but these results are controversial. On the whole visuoperceptual abilities do not appear to be strongly lateralized as both hemispheres are capable of performing these types of low level perceptual tasks. Several suggestions have been made to account for the asymmetries that are present. One suggestion is that there is no right hemisphere advantage for visuoperception, but a left hemisphere disadvantage due to that hemisphere's preoccupation with language functions (Corballis 1991; Gazzaniga 1985). Other authors have reported a difference in the ability of each hemisphere to process global versus local patterns or in terms of a hemispheric specialization for different spatial frequencies. The right hemisphere is typically much better at representing the whole object while the left hemisphere shows a slight advantage for recognizing the parts of an object (Hellige 1995).

One specific task that does show convincing evidence for a right hemisphere advantage is face perception. Prosopagnosia, the inability to recognize familiar faces, occurs more often following damage to the right hemisphere than the left (although most cases result from bilateral damage). In addition, commissurotomy patients have a right hemisphere advantage in their ability to recognize upright faces (Gazzaniga and Smylie 1983; Puce et al. 1996).

In support of a facial processing asymmetry, a number of cognitive studies have indicated that normal subjects attend more to the left side of a face than the right and that the information carried by the left side of the face is more likely to influence a subject's response. Finally, numerous imaging studies have demonstrated right hemispheric activation using a variety of facial stimuli.

The right hemisphere may also be superior at tasks requiring spatial attention (Mangun et al. 1994). Hemineglect patients typically do not attend to one side of space and do not recognize the presence of individuals in the other hemifield. Additionally, they ignore one side of their body and copy drawings in a manner that entirely ignores half of the picture. This attentional deficit is more often observed following right hemisphere damage.

Studies of normal subjects, psychiatric patients, and lesion patients indicate that the right hemisphere is dominant in the recognition and expression of emotion and is preferentially activated during the experience of emotion. Lesions of the right hemisphere are also often associated with affective disorders. Many of the lesion results remain controversial, but experimental studies do demonstrate a left visual field/right hemisphere superiority for the recognition of emotions.

Structural Asymmetry

If the hemispheres are not symmetrical in their functioning then the physical structure of the brain may also be asymmetrical. Although many contradictory reports regarding the weight and volume of the two cerebral hemispheres were published following the discovery of the left hemisphere's role in language, it was not long before the differences between the length of the left and right sylvian (lateral) fissures were described. Related to this difference in sylvian fissure length are the casual reports by von Economo and Horn in 1930 and later Pfeifer (1936) that the planum temporale, the dorsal surface of the temporal lobe, is typically larger in the left hemisphere than the right. This very specific size difference between the two hemispheres became a focus of research in the late 1960s after it was described that the left planum temporale (the dorsal surface of the temporal lobe) is significantly larger than the right in 65 percent of the population (GESCHWIND and Levitsky 1968). Based on these studies, it was commonly accepted that a difference in the size of cortical regions could account for the left hemisphere's specialization for language.

A recent reanalysis of this question using computer-generated three-dimensional reconstruction techniques has revealed a different story. The right lateral fissure rises dramatically at its caudal extent which results in an apparent foreshortening of the planum in the right hemisphere when it is studied using the previously applied methods (i.e., photographic tracings and slice reconstruction). Three-dimensional measurements that accurately map the highly convoluted cortical surface reveal no size difference between the left and right planum temporale (Loftus et al. 1993). Thus these anatomical differences may not reflect size differences between the hemispheres, but rather differences in gross cortical folding.

Many modern authors have also continued to report the difference in the length of the sylvian fissure that borders the lateral aspect of the planum on the dorsal surface of the temporal lobes (Rubens et al. 1976). Subsequently these findings have been corroborated in certain primate species, human fossils, infants, and, interestingly enough, in the male cat (Tan 1992).

Lateralized Cortical Circuitry

Although many studies have examined gross size differences between the two hemispheres, relatively few have directly examined whether connectional or organizational specializations underlie lateralized functions. Not surprisingly, both neurochemical and structural differences have been found between the hemispheres.

Columnar organization also varies between the left and right posterior temporal areas. The left hemisphere has been reported to be organized into clear columnar units, while columns in the right hemisphere appear to be much less distinct (Ong and Garey 1990; cf. COLUMNS AND MODULES). This difference may be related to previous reports that the left temporal lobe has greater columnar widths and intercolumnar distances. Sex differences in the density of neurons within cortical lamina have also been documented in posterior temporal regions (Witelson, Glezer, and Kigar 1995), and these results are beginning to support cognitive data suggesting that language functions in women are less lateralized than those in men (Strauss, Wada, and Goldwater 1992).

Differences in the fine dendritic structure of pyramidal cells in each hemisphere have also been reported within the frontal lobes (Scheibel 1984), and it has been suggested that the total dendritic length of left hemisphere pyramidal cells is greater than that of right hemisphere pyramidal cells and that this asymmetry may decrease with age (Jacobs and Scheibel 1993).

Cell size asymmetries have also been documented in these same areas. The cell size differences appear to be restricted to the largest of the large pyramidal cells within layer III of Broca's area and are not apparent in adjacent cortical regions (Hayes and Lewis 1995). This same size difference also exists in posterior language regions, but is spread throughout auditory areas, including the primary auditory cortex (Hutsler and Gazzaniga 1995). What is the functional meaning of larger cell sizes? The answer is unclear, but differences in cell body size may indicate differences in the length of a cell's axon or degree of bifurcation. Thus, pyramidal cell size may be related to connectivity differences between the two hemispheres. Recent studies of temporal lobe connectivity using newly-developed tract-tracing methods may support this notion. These studies demonstrate patchy connectivity within the posterior segment of Brodmann's area 22 (Wernicke's area) of both the left and right hemisphere. Additionally, the size of individual patches is quite symmetric, but the distance between individual patches of the left hemisphere is consistently greater than that found in the right (Schmidt et al. 1997). These connectional differences may play a role in the anatomical underpinnings of temporal processing differences between the two hemispheres that could be critical in asymmetric cognitive functions such as language analysis.

Although one might expect that symmetrical structure should be the norm in the human brain, symmetrical organization of the body may largely be due to the requirements of locomotion (Corballis 1991). In addition to the symmetrical placement of the limbs, sense organs may be placed symmetrically so that an organism can attend and respond equally to both sides of the world. Brain organization for these functions might mirror the body organization, but the hemispheric distribution of many cognitive functions may not be constrained in this way. Although there could be some advantage to having dual representations of functions not involved with locomotion (for instance, in the case of damage to one side of the brain), these benefits are likely outweighed by the disadvantages of delayed transmission across long fibers of the corpus callosum. When viewed in this context, it makes sense that certain functions would become largely the domain of one cerebral hemisphere and that damage to the normal brain, either through unilateral lesions or commissurotomy, would reveal a remarkable array of behavioral results.

See also BILINGUALISM AND THE BRAIN; MODULARITY AND LANGUAGE; SIGN LANGUAGE AND THE BRAIN

—*Michael S. Gazzaniga and Jeffrey J. Hutsler*

References

Baynes, K., M. J. Tramo, and M. S. Gazzaniga. (1992). Reading with a limited lexicon in the right hemisphere of a callosotomy patient. *Neuropsychologia* 30: 187–200.

Bellugi, U., H. Poizner, and E. S. Klima. (1989). Language, modality and the brain. *Trends in Neuroscience* 12: 380–388.

Carlson, J., C. Netley, E. B. Hendrick, and J. S. Prichard. (1968). A reexamination of intellectual disabilities in hemispherectomized patients. *Transactions of the American Neurological Association* 93: 198–201.

Corballis, M. C. (1991). *The Lopsided Ape.* New York: Oxford University Press.

Damasio, A. R., and D. Tranel. (1993). Nouns and verbs are retrieved with differently distributed neural systems. *Proceedings of the National Academy of Sciences, USA* 90: 4957–4960.

Davidson, R. J., Ed. (1995). *Cerebral Asymmetry.* Cambridge, MA: MIT Press.

Dennis, M., and H. A. Whitaker. (1976). Language acquisition following hemidecortication: linguistic superiority of the left over the right hemisphere. *Brain and Language* 3: 404–433.

Gazzaniga, M. S., and C. Smylie. (1983). Facial recognition and brain asymmetries: clues to underlying mechanisms. *Annals of Neurology* 13: 536–540.

Gazzaniga, M. S. (1985). *The Social Brain: Discovering the Networks of the Mind.* New York: Basic Books.

Gazzaniga, M. S. (1995). Principles of human brain organization derived from split-brain studies. *Neuron* 14: 217–228.

Geschwind, N. (1976). The apraxias. *American Scientist* 63: 188–195.

Geschwind, N., and W. Levitsky. (1968). Human brain: left-right asymmetries in temporal speech region. *Science* 162: 186–187.

Hart, J., R. S. Berndt, and A. Caramazza. (1985). Category-specific naming deficit following cerebral infarction. *Nature* 316: 439–440.

Hayes, T. L., and D. A. Lewis. (1995). Anatomical specilization of the anterior motor speech area: Hemispheric differences in magnopyramidal neurons. *Brain and Language* 49: 289–308.

Hellige, J. B. (1993). *Hemispheric Asymmetry.* Cambridge, MA: Harvard University Press.

Hellige, J. B. (1995). Hemispheric asymmetry for components of visual information processing. In R. J. Davidson and K. Hugdahl, Eds., *Brain Asymmetry.* Cambridge, MA: MIT Press, pp. 99–121.

Hutsler, J. J., and M. S. Gazzaniga. (1995). Hemispheric differences in layer III pyramidal cell sizes—a critical evaluation of asymmetries within auditory and language cortices. *Society for Neuroscience Abstracts* 21: 180.1.

Jacobs, B., and A. B. Scheibel. (1993). A quantitative dendritic analysis of Wernicke's area in humans. I. Lifespan changes. *Journal of Comparative Neurology* 327: 83–96.

Loftus, W. C., M. J. Tramo, C. E. Thomas, R. L. Green, R. A. Nordgren, and M. S. Gazzaniga. (1993). Three-dimensional analysis of hemispheric asymmetry in the human superior temporal region. *Cerebral Cortex* 3: 348–355.

Mangun, G. R., R. Plager, W. Loftus, S. A. Hillyard, S. J. Luck, V. Clark, T. Handy, and M. S. Gazzaniga. (1994). Monitoring the visual world: hemispheric asymmetries and subcortical processes in attention. *Journal of Cognitive Neuroscience* 6: 265–273.

Mendelsohn, S. (1988). Language lateralization in bilinguals: facts and fantasy. *Journal of Neurolinguistics* 3: 261–292.

Nass, R. D., and M. S. Gazzaniga. (1985). Cerebral lateralization and specialization in human central nervous system. In F. Plum, Ed., *Handbook of Physiology.* Bethesda, MD: The American Physiological Society, pp. 701–761.

Ong, Y., and L. J. Garey. (1990). Neuronal architecture of the human temporal cortex. *Anatomy and Embryology* 181: 351–364.

Pfeifer, R. A. (1936). Pathologie der Horstrahlung und der Corticalen Horsphare. In O. Bumke, Ed., *Foerster, O,* vol. 6. Berlin: Springer.

Puce, A., T. Allison, M. Asgari, J. C. Gore, and G. McCarthy. (1996). Differential sensitivity of human visual cortex to faces, letterstrings and textures: a functional magnetic resonance imaging study. *Journal of Neuroscience* 16: 5205–5215.

Rubens, A. B., M. W. Mahowald, and T. Hutton. (1976). Asymmetry of the lateral (Sylvian) fissures in man. *Neurology* 26: 620–624.

Scheibel, A. B. (1984). A dendritic correlate of human speech. In N. Geschwind and A. M. Galaburda, Eds., *Cerebral Dominance: The Biological Foundations.* Cambridge, MA: Harvard University Press, pp. 43–52.

Schmidt, K. E., W. Schlote, H. Bgratzke, T. Rauen, W. Singer, and R. A. W. Galuske. (1997). Patterns of long range intrinsic connectivity in auditory and language areas of the human temporal cortex. *Society for Neuroscience Abstracts* 23: 415.13.

Strauss, E., J. Wada, and B. Goldwater. (1992). Sex differences in interhemispheric reorganization of speech. *Neuropsychologia* 30: 353–359.

Tan, Ü. (1992). Similarities between sylvian fissure asymmetries in cat brain and planum temporale asymmetries in human brain. *International Journal of Neuroscience* 66: 163–175.

von Economo, C., and L. Horn. (1930). Uber windungsrelief, masse, und rindenarchtektonik der supratemporalfalche. *Z Gest Neurol. Psychiat.* 130: 678–755.

Witelson, S. F., I. I. Glezer, and D. L. Kigar. (1995). Women have greater density of neurons in posterior temporal cortex. *Journal of Neuroscience* 15: 3418–3428.

Heuristic Search

Heuristic search is the study of computer algorithms designed for PROBLEM SOLVING, based on trial-and-error exploration of possible solutions. Problem solving tasks include "pathfinding problems," game playing, and CONSTRAINT SATISFACTION.

The task of navigating in a network of roads from an initial location to a desired goal location, with the aid of a roadmap, is an example of a pathfinding problem. The "states" of the problem are decision points, or intersections of two or more roads. The "operators" are segments of road between two adjacent intersections. The navigation problem can be viewed as finding a sequence of operators (road segments) that go from the initial state (location) to the goal state (location). In a game such as CHESS, the states are the legal board configurations, and the operators are the legal moves.

A search algorithm may be systematic or nonsystematic. A systematic algorithm is guaranteed to find a solution if one exists, and may in fact guarantee a lowest-cost solution. Nonsystematic algorithms, such as GREEDY LOCAL SEARCH, EVOLUTIONARY COMPUTATION, and other stochastic approaches, are not guaranteed to find a solution. We focus on systematic algorithms here.

The simplest systematic algorithms, called "brute-force search" algorithms, do not use any knowledge about the problem other than the states, operators, and initial and goal states. For example, "breadth-first search" starts with the initial state, then considers all states one operator away from the initial state, then all states two operators away, and so on until the goal is reached. Uniform-cost search, or Dijkstra's algorithm (Dijkstra 1959), considers the different costs of operators, or lengths of road segments in our example, and

visits the states in increasing order of their distance from the start. A drawback of both these algorithms is that they require enough memory to hold all the states considered so far, which is prohibitive in very large problems (see the following).

"Depth-first search" more closely approximates how one would search if actually driving in the road network, rather than planning with a map. From the current location, depth-first search extends the current path by following one of the roads until a dead end is reached. It then backtracks to the last decision point that has not been completely explored, and chooses a new path from there. The advantage of depth-first search is that it only requires enough memory to hold the current path from the initial state.

"Bi-directional search" (Pohl 1971) searches forward from the initial state and backward from the goal state simultaneously, until the two searches meet. At that point, a complete path from the initial state to the goal state has been found.

A drawback of all brute-force searches is the amount of time they take to execute. For example, a breadth-first search of a road network will explore a roughly circular region whose center is the initial location, and whose radius is the distance to the goal. It has no sense of where the goal is until it stumbles upon it.

Heuristic search, however, is directed toward the goal. A heuristic search, such as the "A* algorithm" (Hart, Nilsson, and Raphael 1968), makes use of a "heuristic evaluation function," which estimates the distance from any location to the goal. For example, the straight-line distance from a given location to the goal is often a good estimate of the actual road distance. For every location visited by A*, it estimates the total distance of a path to the goal that passes through that location. This is the sum of the distance from the start to the location, plus the straight-line distance from the location to the goal. A* starts with the initial location, and generates all the locations immediately adjacent to it. It then evaluates these locations in the above way. At each step, it generates and evaluates the neighbors of the unexplored location with the lowest total estimate. It stops when it chooses a goal location.

A* is guaranteed to find a solution if one exists. Furthermore, if the heuristic function never overestimates actual cost, A* is guaranteed to find a shortest solution. For example, because the shortest path between two points is a straight line, A* using the straight-line distance heuristic function is guaranteed to find a shortest solution to the road navigation problem.

The bane of all search algorithms is called "combinatorial explosion." In road navigation, the total number of intersections is quite manageable for a computer. Consider, however, the traveling salesman problem (TSP). Given a set of N cities, the TSP is to find a shortest tour that visits all the cities and returns to the starting city. Given N cities, there are $(N-1)!$ different orders in which the cities could be visited. Clever algorithms can reduce the number of possibilities to 2^N, but even if N is as small as 50, 2^N is approximately 10^{15}. Even if a computer could examine a million possibilities per second, examining 10^{15} possibilities would take 31.7 years.

An algorithm that is well suited to problems such as the TSP is called depth-first branch-and-bound. A TSP solution is a sequence of cities. Depth-first branch-and-bound systematically searches the possible tours depth-first, adding one city at a time to a partial tour, and backtracks when a tour is completed. In addition, it keeps track of the length of the shortest complete tour found so far, in a variable α. Whenever a partial tour is found in which the sum of the trip segments already included exceeds α, we need not consider any extensions of that partial tour, inasmuch as the total cost can only be greater. In addition, a heuristic evaluation function can be used to estimate the cost of completing a partial tour. If the heuristic function never overestimates the lowest completion cost, whenever the cost of the segments so far, plus the heuristic estimate of the completion cost, exceeds α, we can backtrack. All known algorithms that are guaranteed to find an optimal solution to such "combinatorial problems" are variants of branch-and-bound.

See also ALGORITHM; COMPUTATIONAL COMPLEXITY

—Richard Korf

References

Dijkstra, E. W. (1959). A note on two problems in connexion with graphs. *Numerische Mathematik* 1: 269–271.

Hart, P. E., N. J. Nilsson, and B. Raphael. (1968). A formal basis for the heuristic determination of minimum cost paths. *IEEE Transactions on Systems Science and Cybernetics* 4(2): 100–107.

Pohl, I. (1971). Bi-directional search. In B. Meltzer and D. Michie, Eds., *Machine Intelligence 6*. New York: American Elsevier, pp. 127–140.

Further Readings

Bolc, L., and J. Cytowski. (1992). *Search Methods for Artificial Intelligence*. London: Academic Press.

Kanal, L., and V. Kumar, Eds. (1988). *Search in Artificial Intelligence*. New York: Springer.

Korf, R. E. (1985). Depth-first iterative-deepening: an optimal admissible tree search. *Artificial Intelligence* 27(1): 97–109.

Korf, R. E. (1998). Artificial intelligence search algorithms. To appear in M. J. Atallah, Ed., *CRC Handbook of Algorithms and Theory of Computation*. Boca Raton, FL: CRC Press.

Newell, A., and H. A. Simon. (1972). *Human Problem Solving*. Englewood Cliffs, NJ: Prentice-Hall.

Pearl, J. (1984). *Heuristics*. Reading, MA: Addison-Wesley.

Heuristics

See GREEDY LOCAL SEARCH; HEURISTIC SEARCH; JUDGMENT HEURISTICS

Hidden Markov Models

A *hidden Markov model* (HMM) is a widely used probabilistic model for data that are observed in a sequential fashion (e.g., over time). A HMM makes two primary assumptions. The first assumption is that the observed data arise from a mixture of K probability distributions. The second assumption is that there is a discrete-time Markov chain with K states, which is generating the observed data by visiting the K distributions in Markov fashion. The "hidden" aspect of the model arises from the fact that the state-sequence is not directly observed. Instead, one must infer the state-sequence from a sequence of observed data using the probability model. Although the model is quite simple, it has been found to be very useful in a variety of sequential modeling problems, most notably in SPEECH RECOGNITION (Rabiner 1989) and more recently in other disciplines such as computational biology (Krogh et al. 1994). A key practical feature of the model is the fact that inference of the hidden state sequence given observed data can be performed in time linear in the length of the sequence. Furthermore, this lays the foundation for efficient estimation algorithms that can determine the parameters of the HMM from training data.

A HMM imposes a simple set of dependence relations between a sequence of discrete-valued state variables S and observed variables Y. The state sequence is usually assumed to be first-order Markov, governed by a $K \times K$ matrix of transition probabilities of the form $p(S_{t+1} = i \mid S_{t+1} = j)$, that is, the conditional probability that the system will transit to state i at time $t + 1$ given that the system is in state j at time t (Markov 1913). The K probability distributions associated with each state, $p(Y_t \mid S_t = i)$, describe how the observed data Y are distributed given that the system is in state i. The transition probability matrix and the parameters of the K probability distributions are usually assumed not to vary over time. The independence relations in this model can be summarized by the simple graph in figure 1. Each state depends only on its predecessor, and each observable depends only on the current state. A large number of variations of this basic model exist, for example, constraints on the transition matrix to contain "null" transitions, generalizations of the first-order Markov dependence assumption, generalizations to allow the observations Y_t to depend on past observations Y_{t-2}, Y_{t-3}, . . . , and different flexible parametrizations of the K probability distributions for the observable Ys (Poritz 1988; Rabiner 1989).

The application of HMMs to practical problems involves the solution of two related but distinct problems. The first is the *inference* problem, where one assumes that the parameters of the model are known and one is given an observed data sequence $\{Y_1, . . . , Y_T\}$. How can one calculate $p(Y_1, . . . , Y_T \mid \text{model})$, as in speech recognition (for example) when finding which word model, from a set of word models, explains the observed data best? Or how can one calculate the most likely sequence of hidden states to have generated $\{Y_1, . . . , Y_T\}$, as in applications such as decoding error-correcting codes, where the goal is to determine which specific sequence of hidden states is most likely to have generated the data. Both questions can be answered in an exact and computationally efficiently manner by taking advantage of the independence structure of the HMM. Finding $p(Y_1, . . ., Y_T \mid \text{model})$ can be solved by the forward-backward procedure, which, as the name implies, amounts to a forward pass through the possible hidden state sequences followed by a backward pass (Rabiner 1989). This procedure takes on the order of TK^2

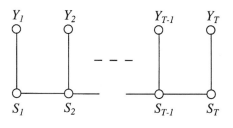

Figure 1. A graphical representation of the dependencies in a Hidden Markov Model.

operations (linear in the length of the observed sequence). Similarly, the most likely sequence of hidden states for a given observation sequence can be found by the well-known Viterbi algorithm, which is a general application of DYNAMIC PROGRAMMING to this problem (Forney 1973). It also involves a forward and backward pass through the data and also takes order of TK^2 operations.

The second general problem to be solved in practice is that of *estimation,* that is, finding values for the HMM parameters; the $K \times K$ transition matrix, the parameters of the K observable probability distributions, and an initial probability distribution over the states. Implicit is the assumption that K is known (usually assumed to be the case in practice). Given K, the most widely used technique for estimation of HMM parameters is the Baum-Welch algorithm (Baum et al. 1970). The general idea behind the algorithm is as follows. Assume that the parameters are fixed at some tentative estimate. Use the forward-backward algorithm described earlier to infer the probabilities of all the possible transitions $p(S_{t+1} = j \mid S_t = i)$ between hidden states and all probabilities of observed data $p(Y_t \mid S_t = i)$, keeping the tentative parameters fixed. Now that one has estimates of the transitions and observation probabilities, it is possible to reestimate a new set of parameters in closed form. Remarkably, it can be shown that $p(Y_1, \ldots, Y_T \mid \theta_{new}) \geq p(Y_1, \ldots, Y_T \mid \theta_{old})$, that is, the likelihood of the new parameters is at least as great as that of the old, where θ denotes the particular HMM parameter set. Thus, iterative application of this two-step procedure of forward-backward calculations and parameter estimation yields an algorithm that climbs to a maximum of the likelihood function in parameter space. It turns out that this procedure is a special case of a general technique (known as the expectation-maximization or EM procedure; McLachlan and Krishnan 1997) for generating maximum-likelihood parameter estimates in the presence of hidden variables. Variations of the EM algorithm are widely used in machine learning and statistics for solving UNSUPERVISED LEARNING problems. The HMM parameter space can have many local maxima, making estimation nontrivial in practice. The Baum-Welch and EM procedures can also be generalized to maximum a posteriori and Bayesian estimation, where prior information and posterior uncertainty are explicitly modeled (e.g., Gauvain and Lee 1994).

It can be also be useful to look at HMMs from other viewpoints. For example, figure 1 can be interpreted as a simple Bayesian network and, thus, a HMM can be treated in complete generality as a particular member of the Baye-

sian network family (Smyth, Heckerman, and Jordan 1997). An advantage of this viewpoint is that it allows one to leverage the flexible inference and estimation techniques of BAYESIAN NETWORKS when investigating more flexible and general models in the HMM class, such as more complex sequential dependencies and multiple hidden chains.

See also BAYESIAN LEARNING; FOUNDATIONS OF PROBABILITY; PROBABILISTIC REASONING

—*Padhraic Smyth*

References

Baum, L. E., T. Petrie, G. Soules, and N. Weiss. (1970). A maximization technique occurring in the statistical analysis of probabilistic functions of Markov chains. *Ann. Math. Stat.* 41: 164–171.

Forney, G. D. (1973). The Viterbi algorithm. *Proceedings of the IEEE* 61: 268–278.

Gauvain, J., and C. Lee. (1994). Maximum a posteriori estimation for multivariate Gaussian mixture observations of Markov chains. *IEEE Trans. Sig. Audio Proc.* 2: 291–298.

Krogh, A., M. Brown, I. S. Mian, K. Sjolander, and D. Haussler. (1994). Hidden Markov models in computational biology: applications to protein modeling. *J. Mol. Bio.* 235: 1501–1531.

Markov, A. A. (1913). An example of statistical investigation in the text of "Eugene Onyegin" illustrating coupling of "tests" in chains. *Proc. Acad. Sci. St. Petersburg VI Ser.* 7: 153–162.

McLachlan, G. J., and T. Krishnan. (1997). *The EM Algorithm and Extensions.* New York: Wiley.

Poritz, A. M. (1988). Hidden Markov models: a guided tour. *Proceedings of the IEEE International Conference on Acoustics, Speech and Signal Processing* 1: 7–13.

Rabiner, L. R. (1989). A tutorial on hidden Markov models and selected applications in speech recognition. *Proceedings of the IEEE* 77: 257–285.

Smyth, P., D. Heckerman, and M. I. Jordan. (1997). Probabilistic independence networks for hidden Markov probability models. *Neural Computation* 9: 227–269.

Further Readings

Elliott, R. J., L. Aggoun, and J. B. Moore. (1995). *Hidden Markov Models: Estimation and Control.* New York: Springer.

Huang, X. D., Y. Ariki, and M. A. Jack. (1990). *Hidden Markov Models for Speech Recognition.* Edinburgh: Edinburgh University Press.

MacDonald, I. L., and W. Zucchini. (1997). *Hidden Markov and Other Models for Discrete-Valued Time Series.* New York: Chapman and Hall.

High-Level Vision

Aspects of vision that reflect influences from memory, context, or intention are considered "high-level vision," a term originating in a hierarchical approach to vision. In currently popular interactive hierarchical models, however, it is almost impossible to distinguish where one level of processing ends and another begins. This is because partial outputs from lower-level processes initiate higher-level processes, and the outputs of higher-level processes feed back to influence processing at the lower levels (McClelland and Rumelhart 1986). Thus, the distinctions between processes residing at high, intermediate, and low levels are difficult to draw. Indeed, substantial empirical evidence indicates that some high-level processes influence behaviors that are traditionally considered low-level or MID-LEVEL VISION. With this caveat in mind, the following topics will be considered under the heading "high-level vision": object and face recognition, scene perception and context effects, effects of intention and object knowledge on perception, and the mental structures used to integrate across successive glances at an object or a scene.

One major focus of theory and research in high-level vision is an attempt to understand how humans manage to recognize and categorize familiar objects quickly and reliably. An adequate theory of OBJECT RECOGNITION must account for (1) the accuracy of object recognition over changes in object size, location, and orientation (preferably, this account would not posit a different memory record for each view of every object ever seen); (2) the means by which the spatial relationships between the parts or features of an object are represented (given that objects and spaces seem to be coded in different VISUAL PROCESSING STREAMS, with object processing occurring in ventral pathways and space processing occurring in dorsal pathways); and (3) the attributes of both basic-level and subordinate-level recognition (e.g., recognition of a finch as both a bird and as a specific kind of bird). Current competing object recognition theories differ in their approach to each of these factors (see Biederman 1987; Tarr 1995). According to Biederman (1987), objects are parsed into parts at concave portions of their bounding contours, and the parts are represented in memory by a set of abstract components (generalized cylinders); the claim is that these components can be extracted from an image independent of changes in orientation (up to an accidental view rendering certain component features invisible). On Biederman's view, (1) object recognition should be robust to orientation changes as long as the same components can be extracted from the image; and (2) very few views of each object need be represented in memory. Tarr (1995) adopts a different theoretical approach, proposing that specific views of objects are represented by salient features, and that object recognition is orientation-dependent. On Tarr's approach, multiple views of each object are stored in memory, and objects seen in new views must undergo some time-consuming process before they are recognized. The empirical evidence suggesting that object recognition is orientation-dependent is accumulating, favoring the multiple-views approach. However, evidence indicates that the concave portions of bounding contours are more important for recognition than other contour segments, supporting the idea that part structure is critically important for object recognition, consistent with an approach like Biederman's.

A related, but independent, research focus is FACE RECOGNITION. Behavioral evidence obtained from both normal and brain damaged populations suggests that different mechanisms are used to represent faces and objects, and in particular, that holistic, configural processing seems to be more critical for face than for object recognition (e.g., Farah, Tanaka, and Drain 1995; Moscovitch, Winocur, and Behrmann 1997).

A second major problem in high-level vision is the question of how scenes are perceived and, in particular, how the semantic and spatial context provided by a scene influences the identification of the individual objects within the scene. Any effects of scene context require the interaction of spatially local and spatially global processing mechanisms; the means by which this is accomplished have yet to be identified. Research indicates that scene-consistent objects are identified faster and more accurately when placed in a contextually appropriate spatial location rather than one that is contextually inappropriate (Biederman, Mezzanotte, and Rabinowitz 1982). In addition, recent evidence (Diwadkar and McNamara 1997) suggests that scene memory is viewpoint dependent, just as object memory is orientation-dependent. Such dependencies and similarities in the processing of scenes and objects raise questions about the extent to which the mechanisms for processing scenes and objects overlap, despite the apparent specialization of the two different visual processing streams. Nevertheless, much research continues to argue for fundamental differences in the representation of spaces and objects. An example is evidence that when no semantic context is present, memory for spatial configuration is excellent under conditions in which memory for object identity is impaired (Simons 1996). It is worth pointing out that whereas context effects are prevalent in visual perception, their influence may not extend to motor responses generated on the basis of visual input (Milner and Goodale 1995). Experiments measuring motor responses raise the possibility that the different visual processing streams associated with ventral and dorsal anatomical pathways are specialized for vision and action, respectively, rather than for the visual perception of objects and spaces, as originally hypothesized.

A third question central to investigations of high-level vision concerns the mechanisms by which successive glances at an object or a scene are integrated. Phenomenologically, perception of objects and scenes seems to be holistic and fully elaborated rather than piecemeal, abstract, and schematic. Contrary to the phenomenological impressions, evidence indicates that perception is not "everywhere dense" (Hochberg 1968); instead, visual percepts are largely determined by the stimulation obtained at the locus of fixation or attention, even when inconsistent information lies nearby (Hochberg and Peterson 1987; Peterson and Gibson 1991; Rensink O'Regan, and Clark 1997). It has been shown that the structures used to integrate the information obtained in successive glances are abstract and schematic in nature (Irwin 1996); hence, they can tolerate the integration of inconsistent information. Similarly, visual memories, assessed via mental IMAGERY research, are known to be schematic compared to visual percepts (Kosslyn 1990; Peterson 1993). One of the abiding questions in high-level vision is, given such circumstances, how can one account for the phenomenological impressions that percepts are detailed and fully elaborated? A recent appealing proposal is that the apparent richness of visual percepts is an illusion, made possible because eye movements (see EYE MOVEMENTS AND VISUAL ATTENTION) can be made rapidly to real world locations containing the perceptual details required to answer perceptual inquiries (O'Regan 1992). On this view, the world serves as an external memory, filling in and supplementing abstract percepts on demand.

Other research in high-level vision investigates various forms of TOP-DOWN PROCESSING IN VISION. Included in this domain are experiments concerning the effects of observers' intentions on perception (where intentions are manipulated via instructions; Hochberg and Peterson 1987) and investigations of how object knowledge affects the perception of moving or stationary displays. For example, detection thresholds are lower for known objects than for their scrambled counterparts (Purcell and Stewart 1991). In addition, object recognition cues contribute to DEPTH PERCEPTION, along with the classic depth cues and the configural cues of GESTALT PERCEPTION (Peterson 1994). For moving displays, influences from object memories affect the direction in which ambiguous displays appear to move (McBeath, Morikowa, and Kaiser 1992). Moreover, although apparent motion typically seems to take the shortest path between two locations, Shiffrar and Freyd (1993) found that, under certain timing conditions, object-appropriate pathways are preferred over the shortest pathways. Much early research investigating the contributions to perception from knowledge, motivation, and intention was discredited by later research showing that the original results were due to response bias (Pastore 1949). Hence, it is important to ascertain whether effects of knowledge and intentions lie in perception *per se* rather than in memory or response bias. One way to do this is to measure perceptual processes online; another way is to measure perception indirectly by asking observers to report about variables that are perceptually coupled to the variable to which intention or knowledge refers (Hochberg and Peterson 1987). Many of these recent experiments have succeeded in localizing the effects of intention and knowledge in perception *per se* by using one or more of these methods; hence, representing an advance over previous attempts to study top-down effects on perception.

It is important to point out that not all forms of knowledge or memory can influence perception and not all aspects of perception can be influenced by knowledge and memory. Consider the moon illusion, for example. When the moon is viewed near the horizon, it appears much larger than it does when it is viewed in the zenith; yet the moon itself does not change size, nor does it cover areas of different size on the viewer's retina in the two viewing conditions. The difference in apparent size is an illusion, most likely caused by the presence of many depth cues in the horizon condition and by the absence of depth cues in the zenith condition. However, knowledge that the apparent size difference is an illusion does not eliminate or even reduce the illusion; the same is true for many illusions. The boundaries of the effects of knowledge and intentions on perception have yet to be firmly established. One possibility is that perception can be altered only by knowledge residing in the structures normally accessed in the course of perceptual organization (Peterson et al. 1996).

In summary, research in high-level vision focuses on questions regarding how context, memory, knowledge, and intention can influence visual perception. In the course of investigations into the interaction between perception and these higher-order processes, we will undoubtedly learn more about both. The result will be a deeper understanding of high-level vision and its component processes.

See also PICTORIAL ART AND VISION; SHAPE PERCEPTION; SPATIAL PERCEPTION; STRUCTURE FROM VISUAL INFORMATION SOURCES; VISUAL OBJECT RECOGNITION, AI

—*Mary A. Peterson*

References

Biederman, I. (1987). Recognition by components: a theory of human image understanding. *Psychological Review* 94: 115–147.

Biederman, I., R. J. Mezzanotte, and J. C. Rabinowitz. (1982). Scene perception: detecting and judging objects undergoing relational violations. *Cognitive Psychology* 14: 143–177.

Diwadkar, V. A., and T. P. McNamara. (1997). Viewpoint dependence in scene recognition. *Psychological Science* 8: 302–307.

Farah, M. J., J. W. Tanaka, and H. M. Drain. (1995). What causes the face inversion effect? *Journal of Experimental Psychology: Human Perception and Performance* 21: 628–634.

Hochberg, J. (1968). In the mind's eye. In R. N. Haber, Ed., *Contemporary Theory and Research in Visual Perception.* New York: Holt, Rinehart, and Winston, pp. 309–331.

Hochberg, J., and M. A. Peterson. (1987). Piecemeal organization and cognitive components in object perception: perceptually coupled responses to moving objects. *Journal of Experimental Psychology: General* 116: 370–380.

Irwin, D. E. (1996). Integrating information across saccadic eye movements. *Current Directions in Psychological Science* 5: 94–100.

Kosslyn, S. M. (1990). Mental imagery. In D. N. Osherson, S. M. Kosslyn, and J. M. Hollerbach, Eds., *Visual Cognition and Action: An Invitation to Cognitive Science,* vol. 2. Cambridge, MA: MIT Press.

McBeath, M. C., K. Morikowa, and M. Kaiser. (1992). Perceptual bias for forward-facing motion. *Psychological Science* 3: 362–367.

McClelland, J. L., and D. E. Rumelhart. (1986). *Parallel Distributed Processing: Explorations in the Microstructure of Cognition,* vol. 2. Cambridge, MA: MIT Press.

Milner, A. D., and M. Goodale. (1995). *The Visual Brain in Action.* Oxford: Oxford University Press.

Moscovitch, M., G. Winocur, and M. Behrmann. (1997). What is special about face recognition? Nineteen experiments on a person with visual object agnosia and dyslexia but normal face recognition. *Journal of Cognitive Neuroscience* 9: 555–604.

O'Regan, D. (1992). Solving the "real" mysteries of visual perception: the world as an outside memory. *Canadian Journal of Psychology* 46: 461–488.

Pastore, N. (1949). Need as a determinant of perception. *The Journal of Psychology* 28: 457–475.

Peterson, M. A. (1993). The ambiguity of mental images: Insights regarding the structure of shape memory and its function in creativity. In B. Roskos-Ewoldsen, M. J. Intons-Peterson, and R. Anderson, Eds., *Imagery, Creativity, and Discovery: A Cognitive Perspective.* Amsterdam: North Holland, pp. 151–185.

Peterson, M. A. (1994). Shape recognition can and does occur before figure-ground organization. *Current Directions in Psychological Science* 3: 105–111.

Peterson, M. A., and B. S. Gibson. (1991). Directing spatial attention within an object: Altering the functional equivalence of shape descriptions. *Journal of Experimental Psychology: Human Perception and Performance* 17: 170–182.

Peterson, M. A., L. Nadel, P. Bloom, and M. F. Garrett. (1996). Space and Language. In P. Bloom, M. A. Peterson, L. Nadel, and M. F. Garrett, Eds., *Language and Space*. Cambridge, MA: MIT Press, pp. 553–577.

Purcell, D. G., and A. L. Stewart. (1991). The object-detection effect: configuration enhances perception. *Perception and Psychophysics* 50: 215–224.

Rensink, R. A., J. K. O'Regan, and J. J. Clark. (1997). To see or not to see: the need for attention to perceive changes. *Psychological Science* 8: 368–373.

Shiffrar, M., and J. J. Freyd. (1993). Timing and apparent motion path choice with human body photographs. *Psychological Science* 4: 379–384.

Simons, D. (1996). In sight, out of mind: when object representations fail. *Psychological Science* 5: 301–305.

Tarr, M. J. (1995). Rotating objects to recognize them: a case study on the role of viewpoint dependency in the recognition of three-dimensional objects. *Psychonomic Bulletin and Review* 2: 55–82.

Hippocampus

The hippocampus is a brain structure located deep within the temporal lobe, surrounded by the lateral ventricle, and connected to subcortical nuclei via the fornix and to the neocortex via the parahippocampal region. Considerations of the information-processing functions of the hippocampus highlight its position as the final convergence site for outputs from many areas of the CEREBRAL CORTEX, and its divergent outputs that return to influence or organize cortical memory representations (figure 1).

The neocortex provides information to the hippocampus only from the highest sensory processing areas, plus multimodal and LIMBIC SYSTEM cortical areas and the olfactory cortex. These inputs follow a coarse rostral-to-caudal topography arriving in the parahippocampal region, composed of the perirhinal, parahippocampal, and entorhinal cortices (Burwell, Witter, and Amaral 1995). The latter areas project onto the hippocampus itself at each of its main subdivisions, the dentate gyrus, the CA3 and CA1 components of Ammon's horn, and the subiculum (figure 1). The main flow of information through the hippocampus involves serial connections from the dentate gyrus to CA3, CA3 to CA1, and then CA1 to the subiculum (Amaral and Witter 1989). The intrinsic hippocampal pathway partially preserves the topographical gradients of neocortical input, but there is also considerable divergence and associational connections particularly at the CA3 stage. Outputs of the subiculum, and to a lesser extent CA1, are directed back to the parahippocampal region, which in turn projects back onto the neocortical and olfactory areas that were the source of cortical inputs. These aspects of hippocampal organization maximize the potential for association of information from many cortical streams, and the potential for such associations to influence cortical processing broadly. Furthermore, the capacity for associative plasticity in the form of LONG-TERM POTENTIATION at dentate and CA1 synapses is well established, and has been related to normal rhythmic (theta) bursting activity in the hippocampus and to hippocampal memory function.

In 1957 Scoville and Milner described a patient known as H. M. who suffered profound amnesia following bilateral

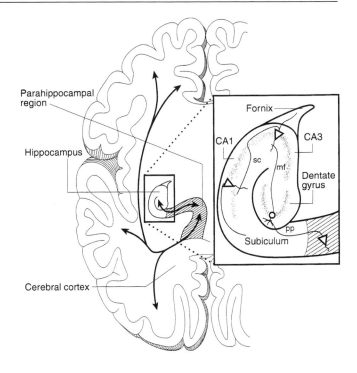

Figure 1.

removal of substantial portions of both the hippocampus and parahippocampal region. H. M. demonstrated an almost complete failure to learn new material, whereas his remote autobiographical memories and short term memory were completely intact, leading to the view that the hippocampal region plays a specific role in the consolidation of short term memories into a permanent store. In addition, the amnesic impairment is also selective to declarative or explicit memory (cf. IMPLICIT VS. EXPLICIT MEMORY), the capacity for conscious and direct expression of both episodic and semantic memory (Corkin 1984; Squire et al. 1993; see also EPISODIC VS. SEMANTIC MEMORY). Conversely, amnesiacs demonstrate normal MOTOR LEARNING and CONDITIONING, and normal sensory adaptations and "priming" of perceptual stimuli; such forms of implicit memory occur despite their inability to recall or recognize the learning materials or the events surrounding the learning experience (see MEMORY, HUMAN NEUROPSYCHOLOGY). The development of a nonhuman primate model has demonstrated a parallel dissociation between severely impaired recognition memory and preserved acquisition of motor skills and perceptual discriminations following damage to the same hippocampal areas removed in H. M. (see MEMORY, ANIMAL STUDIES).

A central open question is precisely what role the hippocampus plays in declarative memory processing. Studies of the consequences of hippocampal damage in animals have generated several proposals about hippocampal function, each suggesting a specific form of hippocampal-dependent and hippocampal-independent memory. Perhaps the most prominent of these is the hypothesis that the hippocampus constitutes a COGNITIVE MAP, a representation of allocentric space (O'Keefe and Nadel 1978). This notion captures the multimodal nature of hippocampal inputs and accounts for deficits in place learning observed following hippocampal damage. However, this view does not account for the global amnesia observed in humans or for impairments observed on some nonspatial learning tasks in animals with hippocampal damage. A reconciliation of its declarative and spatial functions may be possible by considering a fundamental role for the hippocampus in representing relations among items in a memory network and in "flexibility" of memory expression by which all items can be accessed through any point in the network (Dusek and Eichenbaum 1997). Recent findings using both monkeys and rats have shown that animals with hippocampal damage are severely impaired when challenged to express learned relations between items in a flexible way, and the lack of such flexibility is characteristic of human amnesia (see Eichenbaum 1997; Squire 1992).

Complementary evidence about the memory processing accomplished by the hippocampus has been derived from studies of the firing patterns of cortical and hippocampal neurons in behaving animals. Recordings at successive cortical stages leading to the hippocampus reflect increasing sensory convergence, from the encoding of specific perceptual features or movement parameters in early cortical areas to that of increasingly complicated and multimodal objects and behaviors at higher cortical stages. Consistent with the view that the hippocampus is the ultimate stage of hierarchical processing, the functional correlates of hippocampal cells are "supramodal" in that they appear to encode the abstract stimulus configurations that are independent of any particular sensory input. Most prominent among the functional types of hippocampal principal neurons are cells that fire selectively when a rat is in a particular location in its environment as defined by the spatial relations among multiple and multimodal stimuli (O'Keefe 1976). The firing of such "place cells" is characteristically not dependent upon any particular stimulus element and is not affected even if all the stimuli are removed, so long as the animal behaves as if it is in the same environment. However, hippocampal neuronal activity is not limited to the encoding of spatial cues, but has also been related to meaningful movement trajectories and actions in rats as well as conditioned motor responses in restrained rabbits and monkeys. In addition, across a variety of learning tasks hippocampal neurons are activated by relevant olfactory, visual, tactile, or auditory cues, and these encodings prominently reflect nonallocentric spatial, temporal, and other relations among the cues that guide performance (Wood, Dudchencko, and Eichenbaum, 1999; Deadwyler and Hampson 1997). These findings extend the range of hippocampal coding to reflect its global involvement in memory and serve to reinforce the conclusion that the hippocampus supports relational representations.

Efforts to understand how hippocampal circuitry mediates memory processing have focused on special aspects of hippocampal architecture: a high convergence of sensory information onto the hippocampus, sparse connectivity within the broad serial divergence and associative connections across the cell population, recurrent connections that characterize dentate gyrus and CA3 pyramidal cells, the small fraction of excited afferent fibers required to drive CA1 cells, and rapid adjustments of synaptic weights at each stage via long term potentiation. These anatomical and physiological features have been simulated in artificial associative networks employed to accomplish distributed recodings of inputs and to perform basic computations that are reflected in hippocampal neural activity (see Gluck 1996). Some models have focused on the central features of cognitive maps, such as the ability to solve problems from partial information, take shortcuts, and navigate via novel routes. Other models have focused on sequence prediction that employs the recall of temporal patterns to accomplish spatial and nonspatial pattern completion and disambiguation, and more generally show how such network memory representations can provide the flexibility of memory expression conferred by the hippocampus.

See also MEMORY; MEMORY STORAGE, MODULATION OF; WORKING MEMORY, NEURAL BASIS OF

—*Howard Eichenbaum*

References

Amaral, D. G., and M. P. Witter. (1989). The three-dimensional organization of the hippocampal formation: a review of anatomical data. *Neuroscience* 31: 571–591.

Burwell R. D., M. P. Witter, and D. G. Amaral. (1995). Perirhinal and postrhinal cortices in the rat: a review of the neuroanatomical literature and comparison with findings from the monkey brain. *Hippocampus* 5: 390–408.

Deadwyler, S. A., and R. E. Hampson. (1997). The significance of neural ensemble codes during behavior and cognition. *Annual Review of Neuroscience* 20: 217–244.

Dusek, J. A., and H. Eichenbaum. (1997). The hippocampus and memory for orderly stimulus relations. *Proceedings of the National Acadamy of Sciences USA* 94: 7109–7114.

Eichenbaum, H. (1997). Declarative memory: insights from cognitive neurobiology. *Annual Review of Psychology* 48: 547–572.

Gluck, M. A., Ed. (1996). Computational models of hippocampal function in memory. Special Issue of *Hippocampus*, vol. 6, no. 6.

O'Keefe, J. A. (1976). Place units in the hippocampus of the freely moving rat. *Experimental Neurology* 51: 78–109.

O'Keefe, J., and L. Nadel. (1978). *The Hippocampus as a Cognitive Map.* New York: Oxford University Press.

Scoville, W. B., and B. Milner. (1957). Loss of recent memory after bilateral hippocampal lesions. *Journal of Neurology, Neurosurgery and Psychiatry* 20: 11–12.

Squire, L. R. (1992). Memory and the hippocampus: a synthesis of findings with rats, monkeys, and humans. *Psychological Reviews* 99: 195–231.

Squire, L. R., B. Knowlton, and G. Musen. (1993). The structure and organization of memory. *Annual Review of Psychology* 44: 453–495.

Wood, E. R., P. A. Dudchencko, and H. Eichenbaum. (1999). The global record of memory in hippocampal neuronal activity. *Nature* (in press).

Further Readings

Cohen, N. J., and H. Eichenbaum. (1993). *Memory, Amnesia, and the Hippocampal System.* Cambridge, MA: MIT Press.

Historical Linguistics

See CREOLES; LANGUAGE VARIATION AND CHANGE; TYPOLOGY

HMMs

See HIDDEN MARKOV MODELS

Hopfield Networks

See RECURRENT NETWORKS

HPSG

See HEAD-DRIVEN PHRASE STRUCTURE GRAMMAR

Human-Computer Interaction

Human-computer interaction (HCI) studies how people design, implement, and use computer interfaces. With computer-based systems playing increasingly significant roles in our lives and in the basic infrastructure of science, business, and society, HCI is an area of singular importance. A key to understanding human-computer interaction is to appreciate that interactive interfaces mediate redistribution of cognitive tasks between people and machines.

Designed to aid cognition and simplify tasks, interfaces function as COGNITIVE ARTIFACTS. Two features distinguish interfaces from other cognitive artifacts: they provide the most plastic representational medium we have ever known, and they enable novel forms of communication. Interfaces are plastic in the sense that they can readily mimic representational characteristics of other media. This plasticity in combination with the dynamic character of computation makes possible new interactive representations and forms of communication that are impossible in other media.

The historical roots of human-computer interaction can be traced to a human information-processing approach to cognitive psychology. Human information processing (Card, Moran, and Newell 1983; Lindsay and Norman 1977) explicitly took the digital computer as the primary metaphorical resource for thinking about cognition. HCI as a field grew out of early human information-processing research and still reflects that lineage. Just as cognitive psychology focused on identifying the characteristics of individual cognition, human-computer interaction has, until very recently, focused almost exclusively on single individuals interacting with applications derived from decompositions of work activities into individual tasks. This theoretical approach has dominated human-computer interaction for over twenty years, leading to a computing infrastructure built around the personal computer and based on the desktop interface metaphor.

The desktop metaphor and associated graphical user interface evolved from Sutherland's Sketchpad (Sutherland 1963), a seminal system that introduced the interactive graphical interface in the early 1960s. The desktop metaphor and underlying technologies on which it is based were cast in modern form in a number of university and industrial research centers, most notably Xerox Parc. We now see the legacy of that work in the ubiquitous graphical interface of current commercial systems. Their interfaces bear startling resemblances to those of the early Xerox Alto (Lampson 1988). What has changed since the days of the Alto, in addition to the continual doubling of computing power every eighteen months and all that this doubling makes possible, is that we now have more principled understandings of how to create effective interfaces. This is primarily a result of the development and acceptance of user-centered approaches (Norman and Draper 1986; Nielsen 1993; Nickerson and Landauer 1997) to system design.

Research in human-computer interaction (Helenader, Landauer, and Prabhu 1997), as in most of the cognitive sciences, draws on many disciplines in that it involves both people and computer technologies. The goal of creating effective and enjoyable systems for people to use makes HCI a design activity (Winograd 1996). As designed artifacts, interface development involves what Schon (1983) terms *a reflective conversation with materials*. To be effective, though, interfaces must be well suited to and situated in the environments of users. Designers must ensure that they remain centered on human concerns. Thus, although HCI can be viewed simply as an important area of software design, inasmuch as interfaces account for more than 50 percent of code and significant portions of design effort, it is much more than that. Interfaces are the locus for new interactive representations and make possible new classes of computationally based work materials.

There are many spheres of research activity in HCI. Three areas are of special interest. The first draws on what we know about human perception and cognition, coupling it with task analysis methods, to develop an engineering discipline for HCI. For examples, see the early work of Card, Moran, and Newell (1983) on the psychology of human-computer interaction, analysis techniques based on models of human performance (John and Kieras 1997), the evolving subdiscipline of usability engineering (Nielsen 1993), work on human error (Woods 1988; Reason 1990), and the development of toolkits for interface design (Myers, Hollan, and Cruz 1996).

A second research activity explores interfaces that expand representational possibilities beyond the menus and icons of the desktop metaphor. The new field of information visualization (Hollan, Bederson, and Helfman 1997) provides many examples. The Information Visualizer (Card, Robertson, and Mackinlay 1991), a cognitive coprocessor architecture and collection of 3-D visualization techniques, supports navigation and browsing of large information spaces. Numerous techniques are being developed to help visualize large complex systems (Eick and Joseph 1993; Church and Helfman 1993), gather histories of interactions with digital objects (Hill and Hollan 1994; Eick and Joseph 1993), and provide interactive multiscale views of information spaces (Perlin and Fox 1993; Bederson et al. 1996).

A third active research area is computer-supported cooperative work (CSCW). (See Olson and Olson [1997] for a recent survey.) The roots of CSCW can be traced to Engelbart's NLS system (Engelbart and English 1994). Among other things, it provided the first demonstration of computer-mediated interactions between people at remote sites. CSCW takes seriously what Hutchins (1995) has termed *distributed cognition* to highlight the fact that most thinking tasks involve multiple individuals and shared artifacts.

Overall, as Grudin (1993) has pointed out, we can view the development of HCI as a movement from early concerns with low-level computer issues, to a focus on people's individual tasks and how better to support them, to current concerns with supporting collaboration and sharing of information within organizations. The phenomenal growth of the World Wide Web and the associated changes in the way we work and play are important demonstrations of the impact of interface changes on sharing information. Not to minimize the importance of the underlying technologies required for the Web (networks, file transfer protocols, etc.), it is instructive to realize that they have all been available since the early days of the Arpanet, the precursor to the modern Internet. Changes at the level of the interface, making access to information on systems almost anywhere only a matter of clicking on a link, opened the Web to users and resulted in its massive impact not only on scientific activities but also on commercial and social interaction.

Myriad important issues, ranging from complex issues of privacy and ownership of information to the challenges of creating new representations and understanding how to effectively accomplish what one might term *urban planning for electronic communities,* face the HCI discipline. As long as the evaluative metric continues to be whether interfaces help us accomplish our tasks more effectively and enjoyably and we continue to explore the potential of new interactive representations to allow us to know the world better and improve our relationships with others, the future of HCI will remain bright and exciting.

See also MULTIAGENT SYSTEMS; SITUATEDNESS/EMBEDDEDNESS

—*James D. Hollan*

References

Bederson, B. B., J. D. Hollan, K. Perlin, J. Meyer, D. Bacon, and G. Furnas. (1996). Pad++: a zoomable graphical sketchpad for exploring alternate interface physic. *Journal of Visual Languages and Computing* 7: 3–31.

Card, S., T. Moran, and A. Newell. (1983). *The Psychology of Human-Computer Interaction.* Hillsdale, NJ: Erlbaum.

Card, S., G. Robertson, and J. Mackinlay. (1991). The information visualizer. *Proceedings of ACM CHI '91 Conference on Human Factors in Computing Systems,* pp. 181–188.

Church, K. W., and J. I. Helfman. (1993). Dotplot: a program for exploring self-similarity in millions of lines of text and code. *Journal of Computational and Graphical Statistics* 2(2): 153–174.

Eick, S. G., and L. S. Joseph. (1993). Seesoft: a tool for visualizing line-oriented software statistics. *IEEE Transactions on Software Engineering* 18(11): 957–968.

Engelbart, D., and W. A. English. (1994). Research center for augmenting human intellect. *ACM Siggraph Video Review,* p. 106.

Grudin, J. (1993). Interface: an evolving concept. *Communications of the ACM* 236(4): 110–119.

Helenander, M. G., T. K. Landauer, and P. Prabhu, Eds. (1997). *The Handbook of Human Computer Interaction.* Amsterdam: Elsevier Science.

Hill, W. C., and J. D. Hollan. (1994). History-enriched digital objects: prototypes and policy issues. *The Information Society* 10: 139–145.

Hollan, J. D., B. B. Bederson, and J. Helfman. (1997). Information visualization. In M. G. Helenander, T. K. Landauer, and P. Prabhu, Eds., *The Handbook of Human Computer Interaction.* Amsterdam: Elsevier Science, pp. 33–48.

Hutchins, E. (1995). *Cognition in the Wild.* Cambridge, MA: MIT Press.

John, B. E. and D. E. Kieras. (1997). Using GOMS for user interface design and evaluation: which technique? *ACM Transactions on Computer-Human Interaction.*

Lampson, B. W. (1988). Personal distributed computing: the Alto and Ethernet software. In A. Goldberg, Ed., *A History of Personal Workstations.* New York: ACM Press, pp. 293–335.

Lindsay, P. H., and D. A. Norman. (1977). *Human Information Processing: An Introduction to Psychology.* 2nd ed. New York: Academic Press.

Myers, B. A., J. D. Hollan, and I. F. Cruz. (1996). Strategic directions in human-computer interaction. *ACM Computing Surveys* 28(4): 794–809.

Nickerson, R. S., and T. K. Landauer. (1997). Human-computer interaction: background and issues. In G. Helenander, T. K. Landauer, and P. Prabhu, Eds., *The Handbook of Human Computer Interaction.* Amsterdam: Elsevier Science, pp. 3–31.

Nielsen, J. (1993). *Usability Engineering.* New York: Academic Press.

Norman, D. A., and S. Draper. (1986). *User Centered System Design.* Hillsdale, NJ: Erlbaum.

Olson, G. M., and J. S. Olson. (1997). Research on computer supported cooperative work. In M. G. Helenander, T. K. Landauer, and P. Prabhu, Eds., *The Handbook of Human Computer Interaction.* Amsterdam: Elsevier Science, pp. 1433–1456.

Perlin, K., and D. Fox. (1993). D. Pad: an alternative approach to the computer interface. In J. T. Kajiya, Ed., *Computer Graphics (SIGGRAPH '93 Proceedings).* Vol. 27, pp. 57–64.

Reason, J. (1990). *Human Error.* New York: Cambridge University Press.

Schon, D. A. (1983). *The Reflective Practitioner: How Professionals Think in Action.* New York: Basic Books.

Sutherland, I. E. (1963). Sketchpad: a man-machine graphical communication system. *Proceedings AFIPS Spring Joint Computer Conference 1* 23: 329–346.

Winograd, T., Ed. (1996). *Bringing Design to Software.* Reading, MA: Addison-Wesley.

Woods, D. D. (1988). Coping with complexity: the psychology of human behaviour in complex systems. In L. P. Goodstein, H. B. Anderson, and S. E. Olsen, Eds., *Task, Errors and Mental Models.* London: Taylor and Francis, pp. 128–148.

Human Nature

See CULTURAL RELATIVISM; CULTURAL VARIATION; HUMAN UNIVERSALS

Human Navigation

Although the term *navigation* originates from the Latin word for ship, the term has come to be used in a very general way. It refers to the practice and skill of animals as well as humans in finding their way and moving from one place to another by any means. Generally moving from place to place requires knowledge of where one is starting, where the goal is, what the possible paths are, and how one is progressing during the movement.

Knowledge of where one is starting in one sense is obvious; one can see the immediate surrounds. However, this is of little help if the relation of that place to the rest of the spatial layout is not known. This becomes of practical interest in the so-called drop-off situation, where one is dropped off at an unknown position and has to determine the location. Practically, this could happen in a plane crash when flying over unknown territory, or more generally if one is lost for any reason.

In such cases having a map is useful but requires matching the perception of the surrounding environment with a particular position on the map. That problem can be cognitively quite difficult. An observer has a particular viewpoint of the environment that in general is rather limited. The map typically covers a much larger area and, of course, has an infinite number of possible viewpoints. In addition, in many locales the individual features are ambiguous; limited views of any one hill, valley, or stream often look like others. Very experienced map readers have strategies that help them overcome these difficulties (Pick et al. 1995). For example, in trying to figure out where on a topographical map they are, successful readers focus initially on the terrain rather than the map. This makes sense inasmuch as knowing the details of the terrain would constrain the possibilities more than knowledge of the big picture provided by the map. Successful readers look for configurations of features. As noted, any individual feature is ambiguous; configurations provide powerful constraints as to where one might be.

Identifying possible paths from one place to another can be based on prior spatial layout knowledge (see COGNITIVE MAPS), but it can also be accomplished on the basis of maps. Depending on the type of map, constraints on possible paths will also be indicated, for example, roads on urban and highway maps; mountains, streams, and the like on topographic maps; and reefs, islands, water depths, and so forth on nautical charts. Many maps provide a very general and powerful reference system. The geographic coordinate system, as Hutchins (1995) points out, not only enables specification of the location of starting point and destination, but also permits easy determination of paths by graphic or numerical computation.

In many cases such as piloting a ship along a coast line, navigation often involves specifying position in relation to landmarks rather than the coordinate systems of maps or charts. Keeping track of one's progress during travel is particularly problematic when information about position in relation to landmarks is impoverished. One of the most impressive and cognitively interesting examples of sea navigation is that of Micronesian islanders who traditionally traveled from island to island across wide-open stretches of the South Pacific without navigational instruments. Their skill has been carefully studied by anthropologists (e.g., Gladwin 1970; Lewis 1978; Hutchins 1995). The islanders' knowledge of the paths from one island to another is in the form of sailing directions as to courses to steer and features that are observable along the way. By our standards, information in relation to such features is clearly impoverished. However, there are observable features to which Micronesian sailors attend that others might miss, such as slight changes of water color indicating underwater landmarks, changes in the wave patterns indicating disturbance by nearby islands, the sighting of birds flying toward or away from islands at different times of the day, and so on.

Across the open sea there are few constraints on what paths to take, so maintaining a steady course becomes quite important. Micronesian navigators have developed a form of celestial navigation in which direction at night is determined in relation to the position on the horizon at which particular stars rise and set. In fact, stars rising at the same point on the horizon all follow the same track across the sky and set at the same place in what is called a linear constellation (Hutchins 1995). During the day the direction of the sun at different times and the direction of wave patterns can be used to maintain course.

Most intriguing about the Micronesian system is how the islanders keep track of where along the journey they are. The Micronesian navigators conceptualize the trip in terms of a stationary canoe with an out-of-sight reference island moving past it. Thus the bearing from the canoe to such an island changes as the journey progresses. Because the reference islands are generally out of sight, it makes no difference if the island really exists and, in fact, if there is not an actual convenient reference island an imaginary one is used.

Because motion is relative, it makes no logical difference whether one conceptualizes travel as involving a stationary world and a moving canoe or a stationary canoe and a moving world. Hutchins and Hinton (1984) hypothesize a very interesting explanation for why this conceptualization makes sense on the basis of the sensory information available at sea to the Micronesians.

The changing bearing of a reference island is a convenient way to keep track of where one is on a journey, as is plotting one's position on a map or chart. But how does one know how fast the bearing is changing or how far to move one's chart position? If the environment is too impoverished to keep track of position with respect to features, it must be done by somehow keeping track of one's velocity and integrating over time to obtain distance moved, a procedure known as dead reckoning (Gallistel 1990). Crossing undifferentiated expanses of sea or land, dead reckoning must be relied on for registering progress between celestial fixes unless modern navigational instruments are used.

Another relevant case of impoverished environmental information is the very mundane activity of walking without vision. This is, of course, the common situation of blind people. They, like the Micronesian sailors, are able to keep track of their progress by attending to information often ignored by others, for example odors marking particular locations, and changes of air currents and acoustic resonance properties that signify open passageways and the like (Welsh and Blasch 1980). However, internal information also specifies movement, for example by proprioception and/or motor commands. There is some evidence that blind people do not use this source of information to update their position as well as do blindfolded sighted persons (Rieser, Guth, and Hill 1987; but see Loomis et al. 1993). This advantage of sighted people may be due to optical flow information when walking with vision serving to calibrate nonvisual locomotion (Rieser et al. 1995). Thus movement in nonvisual locomotion presents on a small scale some of the same problems involved in much grander global navigation.

See also ANIMAL NAVIGATION; ANIMAL NAVIGATION, NEURAL NETWORKS; BEHAVIOR-BASED ROBOTICS; COGNITIVE ARTIFACTS; MOBILE ROBOTS; SPATIAL PERCEPTION

—*Herbert Pick*

References

Gallistel, C. R. (1990). *The Organization of Learning.* Cambridge, MA: MIT Press.

Gladwin, T. (1970). *East is a Big Bird.* Cambridge, MA: Harvard University Press.

Hutchins, E. (1995). *Cognition in the Wild.* Cambridge, MA: MIT Press.

Hutchins, E., and G. E. Hinton. (1984). Why the islands move. *Perception* 13: 629–632.

Lewis, D. (1978). *The Voyaging Stars: Secrets of Pacific Island Navigators.* New York: W. W. Norton.

Loomis, J. M., R. L. Klatzky, R. G. Golledge, J. G. Cicinelli, J. W. Pellegrino, and P. A. Fry. (1993). Nonvisual navigation by blind and sighted: assessment of path integration ability. *Journal of Experimental Psychology: General* 122: 73–91.

Pick, H. L., M. R. Heinrichs, D. R. Montello, K. Smith, C. N. Sullivan, and W. B. Thompson. (1995). Topographic map reading. In J. Flach, P. A. Hancock, J. K. Caird, and K. Vincente, Eds., *The Ecology of Human-Machine Systems,* vol. 2. Hillsdale, NJ: Erlbaum.

Rieser, J. J., D. A. Guth, and E. W. Hill. (1986). Sensitivity to perceptive structure while walking without vision. *Perception* 15: 173–188.

Rieser, J. J., H. L. Pick, Jr., D. H. Ashmead, and A. E. Garing. (1995). Calibration of human locomotion and models of perceptual-motor organization. *Journal of Experimental Psychology: Human Perception and Performance* 21: 480–497.

Welsh, R. L., and B. B. Blasch. (1980). *Foundations of Orientation and Mobility.* New York: American Foundation for the Blind.

Further Readings

Cornell, E. H., C. D. Heth, and D. M. Alberts. (1994). Place recognition and way finding by children and adults. *Memory and Cognition* 22: 633–643.

Eley, M. G. (1988). Determining the shapes of land surfaces from topographical maps. *Ergonomics* 31: 355–376.

Maguire, E. A., N. Burgess, J. G. Donnett, R. S. J. Frackowiak, C. D. Frith, and J. O'Keefe. (1998). Knowing where and getting there: a human navigational network. *Science* 280: 921–924.

Thorndyke, P. W., and B. Hayes-Roth. (1982). Differences in spatial knowledge acquired from maps and navigation. *Cognitive Psychology* 14: 560–589.

Human Universals

Human universals comprise those features of culture, society, language, behavior, and psyche for which there are no known exceptions to their existence in all ethnographically or historically recorded human societies. Among the many examples are such disparate phenomena as tools, myths and legends, sex roles, social groups, aggression, gestures, grammar, phonemes, EMOTIONS, and psychological defense mechanisms. Broadly defined universals often contain more specific universals, as in the case of kinship statuses, which are universally included among social statuses. In some cases, the content of a universal is highly specific, as in the smile, frown, or other facial expressions of basic emotions (Ekman, Sorenson, and Friesen 1969) and in the more complex "coyness display" (Eibl-Eibesfeldt 1989).

Some universals have a collective referent-being found in all societies, languages, or cultures, but having a contingent relation to individuals. Thus, dance is found in all societies or cultures, but not all individuals dance. Other universals, such as a grasp of elementary logical concepts (not, and, or, kind of, greater/lesser, etc.) or the use of gestures, characterize the psyche or behavior of all (normal) individuals. Some universals—such as the predominance of women in infant socialization (Levy 1989) or the ease with which youngsters acquire language—characterize all (normal) individuals of one sex or age range.

Human universals commanded attention from the founding of academic anthropology, but for much of this century a variety of factors promoted an emphasis of cultural particulars and a deemphasis of universals and the psychobiological features that might underlie them (Brown 1991; Degler 1991; see also CULTURAL RELATIVISM). Seminal mid-century essays on human universals (Murdock 1945; Kluckhohn 1953) were followed by the emergence of COGNITIVE ANTHROPOLOGY, a fruitful field for the discovery and persuasive demonstration of universals (D'Andrade 1995). Cognitive anthropology and the study of universals in general have drawn heavily on developments in linguistics (see LINGUISTIC UNIVERSALS).

Anthropologists and linguists generally assume that claims of universality should be validated by cross-cultural or cross-language research. However, a considerable amount of research in economics, political science, psychology, and sociology implicitly assumes universality without demonstrating it (but see COMPARATIVE PSYCHOLOGY). Thus, many research findings from these fields may or may not have universal validity.

Because of the practical difficulties that are involved, the existence of particular universals is normally demonstrated not by exhaustive examination of the historical and ethnographic records but rather by some form of sampling. In spite of these difficulties, existing lists of universals show substantial overlap (e.g., Brown 1991; Murdock 1945; Hockett 1973; Tiger and Fox 1971).

Among the variations on the basic concept of human universals are conditional (or implicational) universals, statistical universals, near universals, and universal pools. A conditional universal refers to a cross-culturally invariant rule or linkage whereby if condition *x* obtains, then *y* will obtain. The evolution of "basic color terms" provides a well-documented example: if a language possesses only three basic color terms, they will be black, white, and red (Berlin and Kay 1969; see also COLOR CATEGORIZATION). The real universality in such cases consists not in the manifest occurrence of specific phenomena but in a pattern of co-occurrences and its underlying causation (see the discussion of universal mechanisms beneath variable behavior in Tooby and Cosmides 1992).

Similarly, although the manifest cross-cultural frequency of occurrence of a statistical universal need only be greater than chance, it implies a universal explanation rather than a series of culturally specific explanations. For example, given all the possible terms that might be used to refer to the pupil of the eye, in a very disproportionate number of languages the term refers to a little person, presumably because people everywhere see their own reflections in the pupils of other people's eyes (Brown and Witkowski 1981; see also FIGURATIVE LANGUAGE).

Keeping domestic dogs is only a near universal, as there were peoples who, until recently, lacked them. In many cases the explanations for near universals and (absolute) universals are essentially the same. The designation of near universality sometimes merely indicates uncertainty about the (absolute) universality of the item in question.

A universal pool is a fixed set of possibilities from which particular manifestations are everywhere drawn. For example, a classic study found that in a sample of diverse kinship terminologies only a small pool of semantic features (e.g., sex of speaker, sex of relative, lineal versus collateral relative, etc.) were drawn upon to distinguish one kin term from another (Kroeber 1909).

There are only a few general explanations for universals. Some cultural universals, for example, appear to be inventions that, due to their great antiquity and usefulness, have diffused to all societies. The use of fire and the more specific use of fire to cook food are examples. The dog achieved near universality for the same reasons. Other universals appear to be reflections in culture of noncultural features that are ubiquitous and important for one reason or another. Kinship terminologies (which are simultaneously social, cultural, and linguistic) are found among all peoples, and in all cases they reflect (at least in part) the relationships necessarily generated by the facts of biological reproduction. Systems of classification—of plants and animals as well as kin—were among the most important arenas for the development of cognitive studies in anthropology (Berlin 1992; D'Andrade 1995; see NATURAL KINDS).

Yet other universals spring more or less directly from human nature and, thus, are causally formative of societies, cultures, and languages—and even the course of history. The syndrome of cognitive and emotional traits comprising romantic love, for instance, is known everywhere, inspiring poetry as well as reproduction, while giving rise to families and much human conflict (Harris 1995; Jankowiak 1995).

In recent decades, an inclusive framework for explaining those universals embodied in or springing from human nature has emerged from a combination of fields. From ETHOLOGY and animal behavior have come the identification of species-typical behaviors and the developmental processes (combining innateness and learning) that produce them (see, e.g., Eibl-Eibesfeldt 1989; Seligman and Hager 1972; Tiger and Fox 1971); from SOCIOBIOLOGY have come ultimate explanations for such universals as kin altruism and the norm of reciprocity (Hamilton 1964; Trivers 1971); from Chomsky (1959) has come the notion of mental organs or

modules that underpin complex, innate features of the human psyche (Hirschfeld and Gelman 1994; see also DOMAIN SPECIFICITY). Elucidating the evolved architecture of the (universal) human mind and its causal role in the construction of society and culture is the domain of EVOLUTIONARY PSYCHOLOGY (Barkow, Cosmides, and Tooby 1992).

Studies within this framework seek to specify the universals of mind that underlie manifest universals and to explain them in both ultimate (evolutionary) and proximate terms. Thus Symons (1979) explains several species-typical sex differences in human sexuality in terms of a theory derived from a wide comparison of animal species. For example, men compete more intensely or violently for mates, desire more variety of sexual partners, and attend more to the physical features (especially signs of youth) of their mates. Both sexes assume that sex is a service or favor that women provide to men. The theory (Trivers 1972) predicts these differences as consequences of the typically larger female investment in each offspring (e.g., the minimum investments are the female's nine months of gestation and the male's insemination). Studies of this sort offer a more comprehensive illumination of human universals than had hitherto been the case.

See also ADAPTATION AND ADAPTATIONISM; COGNITIVE ARCHITECTURE; CULTURAL VARIATION; SEXUAL ATTRACTION, EVOLUTIONARY PSYCHOLOGY OF

—Donald Brown

References

Barkow, J. H., L. Cosmides, and J. Tooby, Eds. (1992). *The Adapted Mind: Evolutionary Psychology and the Generation of Culture.* New York: Oxford University Press.

Berlin, B. (1992). *Ethnobiological Classification: Principles of Categorization of Plants and Animals in Traditional Societies.* Princeton: Princeton University Press.

Berlin, B., and P. Kay. (1969). *Basic Color Terms: Their Universality and Evolution.* Berkeley: University of California Press.

Brown, C. H., and S. R. Witkowski. (1981). Figurative language in a universalist perspective. *American Ethnologist* 9: 596–615.

Brown, D. E. (1991). *Human Universals.* New York: McGraw-Hill.

Chomsky, N. (1959). Review of B. F. Skinner's verbal behavior. *Language* 35: 26–58.

D'Andrade, R. G. (1995). *The Development of Cognitive Anthropology.* Cambridge: Cambridge University Press.

Degler, C. (1991). *In Search of Human Nature: The Decline and Revival of Darwinism in American Social Thought.* New York: Oxford University Press.

Eibl-Eibesfeldt, I. (1989). *Human Ethology.* New York: Aldine de Gruyter.

Ekman, P., E. R. Sorenson, and W. V. Friesen. (1969). Pan-cultural elements in facial displays of emotion. *Science* 164: 86–88.

Hamilton, W. D. (1964). The genetical evolution of social behavior, parts 1 and 2. *Journal of Theoretical Biology* 7: 1–52.

Harris, H. (1995). *Human Nature and the Nature of Romantic Love.* Ph.D. diss., University of California at Santa Barbara.

Hirschfeld, L. A., and S. A. Gelman, Eds. (1994). *Mapping the Mind: Domain Specificity in Cognition and Culture.* Cambridge: Cambridge University Press.

Hockett, C. F. (1973). *Man's Place in Nature.* New York: McGraw-Hill.

Jankowiak, W. (1995). *Romantic Passion: A Universal Experience?* New York: Columbia University Press.

Kluckhohn, C. (1953). Universal categories of culture. In *Anthropology Today: An Encyclopedic Inventory.* Chicago: University of Chicago Press, pp. 507–523.

Kroeber, A. L. (1909). Classificatory systems of relationship. *Journal of the Royal Anthropological Institute* 39: 77–84.

Levy, M. J. Jr. (1989). *Maternal Influence: The Search For Social Universals.* Berkeley: University of California Press.

Murdock, P. (1945). The common denominator of cultures. In R. Linton, Ed., *The Science of Man in the World Crisis.* New York: Columbia University Press, pp. 123–142.

Seligman, M. and J. Hager. (1972). *Biological Boundaries of Learning.* New York: Appleton-Century-Crofts.

Symons, D. (1979). *The Evolution of Human Sexuality.* New York: Oxford University Press.

Tiger, L., and R. Fox. (1971). *The Imperial Animal.* New York: Holt, Rinehart and Winston.

Tooby, J., and L. Cosmides. (1992). The evolutionary and psychological foundations of culture. In J. H. Barkow, L. Cosmides, and J. Tooby, Eds., *The Adapted Mind: Evolutionary Psychology and the Generation of Culture.* New York: Oxford University Press, pp. 3–136.

Trivers, R. L. (1971). The evolution of reciprocal altruism. *Quarterly Review of Biology* 46: 35–57.

Trivers, R. L. (1972). Parental investment and sexual selection. In B. Campbell, Ed., *Sexual Selection and the Descent of Man.* Chicago: Aldine, pp. 136–179.

Hume, David

Impressed by Isaac Newton's success at explaining the apparently diverse and chaotic physical world with a few universal principles, David Hume (1711–1776), while still in his teens, proposed that the same might be done for the realm of the mind. Through observation and experimentation, Hume hoped to uncover the mind's "secret springs and principles." Hume's proposal for a science of the mind was published as *A Treatise of Human Nature* in 1740, and subtitled "An Attempt to introduce the experimental Method of Reasoning into moral subjects." Though it is now one of the most widely read works in Western philosophy, the reception of the *Treatise* in Hume's lifetime was disappointing. In *My Own Life* Hume says that the *Treatise* "fell dead-born from the press." Considered an atheist by the clergy, which controlled university appointments, Hume sought but never received a professorship.

Hume is widely regarded as belonging with Locke and Berkeley to the philosophical movement called British Empiricism (see RATIONALISM VS. EMPIRICISM). The mind contains two kinds of perceptions: impressions and ideas. Impressions are the original lively SENSATIONS and EMOTIONS. Ideas are fainter copies of impressions. Like Locke, Hume rejected the NATIVISM of the rationalists. There are no ideas without prior impressions, so no ideas are innate. Impressions and ideas may be simple or complex. The imagination freely concatenates perceptions; the understanding and the passions organize perceptions by more regular rules of association. MEMORY ideas, for example, preserve the order and position of the impressions from which they derive. Hume's theory of ideas is an empiricist account of concept formation (see CONCEPTS).

Hume held that the ability to form beliefs, in contrast to having sensations and emotions, was a matter of inference. The belief that bread nourishes is an inference from the constant conjunction of the ingestion of bread with nourishment. In what is now called the problem of INDUCTION, Hume argued that this inference is not a deductive inference, because the proof of the conclusion is not guaranteed by the truth of the premises, and any proof based on experience is itself an inductive inference, making it thus a circular proof. Hume's conclusion is a skeptical one. There is no rational justification for CAUSAL REASONING.

Causal inference leading to belief is a matter of custom and habit. The constant conjunction of perceptions experienced lead cognitive agents to have certain lively ideas or beliefs. One cannot help but believe that fire is hot. Hume emphasized that both humans and other animals make such inductive or causal inferences to predict and explain the world, in spite of the fact that such inferences cannot be rationally justified. In the section of the *Treatise* entitled "Of the reason of animals," Hume anticipated COGNITIVE ETHOLOGY by appealing to evidence about nonhuman animals in support of the claim that inferences from past instances are made by members of many species. The possession of language by humans, Hume held, makes it possible for humans to make more precise inferences than other animals, but this is a matter of degree, not of kind.

If beliefs are habitual responses to environmental regularities, how is it that beliefs that deny such regularities are held? Hume's critical examination of religious belief and the belief in the existence of miracles inspired him to offer a fuller account of the nature of belief formation and credulity. Hume noted several belief-enlivening associative mechanisms in addition to constant conjunction. Belief is influenced by such factors as proximity, resemblance, and repetition. A pilgrimage to the Red Sea, for example, will serve to make one more receptive to the claim that the sea parted. Hume's treatment of the factors influencing belief anticipates the studies of Kahneman and TVERSKY (Tversky and Kahneman 1974) on the selective availability of evidence in PROBABILISTIC REASONING.

Hume rejected DESCARTES's claim that the mind is a mental substance on the grounds that there is no impression from which such an idea of mental substance could be derived. Introspection provides access to the mind's perceptions, but not to anything in which those perceptions inhere. "When I enter most intimately into what I call myself, I always stumble on some particular perception or other, of heat or cold, light or shade, love or hatred, pain or pleasure. I never can catch myself at any time without a perception, and never can observe any thing but the perception" (*Treatise,* p. 252). The mind, Hume concludes, "is nothing but a heap or collection of different perceptions."

The bundle theory of the mind has been criticized by recent philosophers of mind. Hume attempted to account for mental representation by the dynamic interaction of mental items—impressions and ideas. It is not clear that Hume was able to characterize such interaction as mental without appealing to the fact that impressions and ideas are the perceptions *of a mind.* According to Hume's critics, Hume helps himself to the concept of mind rather than account for it in nonmentalistic terms. Dennett (1978) refers to this as Hume's Problem. Haugeland (1984) argues that such mechanistic accounts of the mind, which predate the notion of automatic symbol manipulation, cannot avoid Hume's problem.

The perceptions of the mind include emotions and passions as well as beliefs, and Hume attempted to offer a unified account of all mental operations. Beliefs are lively or vivacious ideas that result from a certain kind of mental preparation, a constant conjunction of pairs of impressions such as impressions of flame joined with impressions of heat. The lively idea of heat gets its vivacity from the habit or custom formed by the experience of the constantly conjoined impression pair. Beliefs, then, are themselves feelings. Both emotions and beliefs are strongly held perceptions, and the mechanisms that actuate one can influence the other. Fear of falling from a precipice may, for example, displace a belief that one is secure. Like recent theorists, Hume held that both probability and the degree of the severity of anticipated pain or pleasure play a role in the resolution of conflicts of emotion and judgment.

See also CAUSATION; KANT, IMMANUEL; NATIVISM, HISTORY OF; RELIGIOUS IDEAS AND PRACTICES; SELF

—*Saul Traiger*

References

Dennett, D. C. (1978). A cure for the common code? In *Brainstorms*. Montgomery, VT: Bradford Books.

Haugeland, J. (1984). *Artificial Intelligence: The Very Idea.* Cambridge, MA: MIT Press.

Hume, D. (1973). *A Treatise of Human Nature.* 2nd ed. L. A. Selby-Bigge and P. H. Nidditch, Eds. Oxford: Oxford University Press.

Hume, D. (1975). *Enquiries concerning Human Understanding and concerning the Principles of Morals.* 3rd ed. L. A. Selby-Bigge and P. H. Nidditch, Eds. Oxford: Oxford University Press.

Hume, D. (1874). My own life. In T. H. Green and T. H. Grose, Eds., *The Philosophical Works of David Hume.* London.

Tversky, A., and D. Kahneman. (1974). Judgments under uncertainty: heuristics and biases. *Science* 185: 1124–1131.

Further Readings

Baier, A. C. (1991). *A Progress of Sentiments: Reflections on Hume's Treatise.* Cambridge, MA: Harvard University Press.

Biro, J. (1985). Hume and cognitive science. *History of Philosophy Quarterly* 2(3) July.

Flanagan, O. (1992). *Consciousness Reconsidered.* Cambridge, MA: MIT Press.

Kemp Smith, N. (1941). *The Philosophy of David Hume.* London: Macmillan.

Smith, J.-C. (1990). *Historical Foundations of Cognitive Science.* Dordrecht: Kluwer Academic.

Traiger, S. (1994). The secret operations of the mind. *Minds and Machines* 4(3): 303–316.

Wright, J. P. (1983). *The Sceptical Realism of David Hume.* Minneapolis: University of Minnesota Press.

Identity Theory

See MIND-BODY PROBLEM; PHYSICALISM

Illusions

A hallucination is a false perception seen by one person, often drugged or mentally ill, in the absence of stimulation, whereas an illusion is a misinterpretation of a stimulus consistently experienced by most normal people. Illusions are characteristic errors of the visual system that may give us clues to underlying mechanisms. There are several types of visual illusion:

Geometrical: Illusions of Angle and Size

Angles: In the Zollner and Hering (1861) illusions, the long parallel lines appear to be tilted away from the orientation of the background fins (figure 1). Blakemore (1973) attributes this to "tilt contrast," caused by lateral inhibition between neural signals of orientation, which will expand the appearance of acute angles. This theory has problems with the Poggendorff (1860) illusion, which still persists when only the obtuse angles are present, but vanishes when only the acute angles are present (see Burmester 1986). In Fraser's (1908) twisted-rope spiral illusion, the circles look like spirals because of the twisted local ropes, abetted by the diamonds in the background. The visual system seems to take "local votes" of orientation and fails to integrate them correctly.

Size: Gregory points out that size constancy scaling allows the correct perception of the size of objects even when their distance, and hence retinal size, changes. He attributes the geometrical illusions of size to an inappropriate application of size constancy. Thus the nearby man in figure 1 looks tiny compared to the distant man, even though the retinal sizes are identical: depth cues from the ground plane allow size constancy perceptually to expand distant objects. More subtly, in the Muller Lyer illusion, the arrow fins provide cues similar to those from receding and advancing corners, and in Roger Shepard's table illusion (figure 2, top), the two table tops are geometrically identical on the page but look like completely different 3-D shapes, because size and shape constancy subjectively expand the near-far dimension along the line of sight to compensate for geometrical foreshortening.

Illusions of Lightness and Color

A gray cross looks darker on a white than on a black surround. On a red surround it looks greenish, probably owing to lateral inhibition from neurons that sense the white or

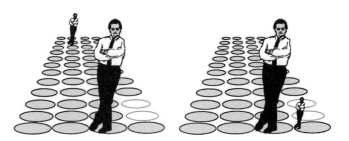

Figure 1. Illusion of size

Tables (Shepard)

Sara Nader (Shepard)   Elephant (Shepard)

Figure 2. Top: Illusion of size; Bottom: Illusions of interpretation.

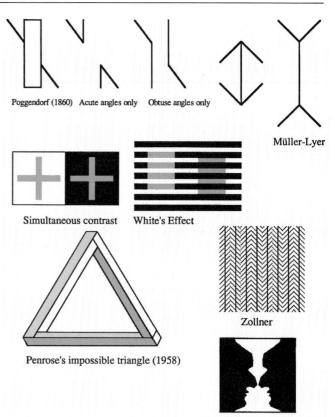

Poggendorf (1860)   Acute angles only   Obtuse angles only

Müller-Lyer

Simultaneous contrast   White's Effect

Zollner

Penrose's impossible triangle (1958)

Ambiguous face/vase (Rubin)

Figure 3. Top: Illusions of angle and size; Middle: Illusions of lightness and color; Bottom: Illusions of interpretation.

colored surround. In White's illusion, the grey segments that replace black bars are bordered by much white above and below, so they "ought" to look darker than the gray segments that replace white bars. But in fact they look lighter. This might show that lateral inhibition operates more strongly along the bars than across them, but more likely it is a top-down "belongingness" effect based on colinearity.

Illusions of Interpretation: Ambiguous, Impossible, and Puzzle Pictures

In *ambiguous* pictures, the brain switches between two possible figure-ground interpretations—in figure 3, faces and a vase—even though the stimulus does not change. The shape of the region selected as figure is perceived and remembered; that of the ground is not.

Impossible figures embody conflicting 3-D cues. Penrose's "impossible triangle" (figure 3) is not the projection of any possible physical object. It holds together by means of incorrect connections between its corners, which are correct locally but incorrect globally. Shepard's elephant (figure 2) confuses its legs with the spaces in between. Local votes about depth are not properly integrated. Impossible objects cannot be consistently painted with colors.

In *puzzle* pictures there is one possible interpretation, but reduced cues make it hard to find. (Shepard's Sara Nader, figure 2, is unusual in having two different possibilities). Once found, immediate perceptual learning makes the picture easier to remember, and immediately recognizable the next time it is seen.

The Belgian surrealist painter René Magritte (1898–1967) and the Dutch engraver Maurits Escher (1898–1972) filled their works with splendid visual illusions (http://www.bright-ideas.com/magrittegallery/aF.html and http://lonestar.texas.net/~escher/gallery/). Collections of illusions can be seen on CD-ROM (Scientific American) and on Al Seckel's Web page at http://www.lainet.com/illusions/.

See also COLOR VISION; LIGHTNESS PERCEPTION; PICTORIAL ART AND VISION; SPATIAL PERCEPTION; TOP-DOWN PROCESSING IN VISION

—*Stuart Anstis*

References

Blakemore, C. B. (1973). The baffled brain. In R. L. Gregory and E. H. Gombrich, Eds., *Illusion in Nature and Art.* London: Duckworth.

Block, J. R., and H. Yuker. (1992) *Can You Believe Your Eyes?* Brunner/Mazel.

Burmester, E. (1986). Beitrag zur experimentellen Bestimmung geometricsh–optischen. *Z. Psychol.* 12: 355

Ernst, B. (1985). *The Magic Mirror of M. C. Escher.* Stradbroke, England: Tarquin.

Fraser, J. (1908). A new illusion of directing. *British Journal of Psychology* 2, 307–320.

Gregory, R. L. (1974). *Concepts and Mechanisms of Perception.* London: Duckworth.

Robinson, J. (1971). *The Psychology of Visual Illusions.* London: Hutchinson.

Rock, I., and D. H. Hubel. (1997). *Illusion* (CD-ROM). Scientific American Library. Simon and Schuster/Byron Preiss Multimedia.

Shepard, R. N. (1990). *Mindsights.* New York: Freeman.

Wade, N. (1982) *The Art and Science of Visual Illusions.* London: Routledge and Kegan Paul.

Imagery

The term *imagery* is inherently ambiguous—it can refer to iconography, visual effects in cinematography, mental events, or even to some types of prose. This article focuses on mental imagery. For example, when asked to recall the number of windows in one's living room, most people report that they visualize the room, and mentally scan over this image, counting the windows. In this article we consider not the introspections themselves, but rather the nature of the underlying representations that give rise to them. Because most research on imagery has addressed visual mental imagery, we will focus on that modality.

Unlike most other cognitive activities (such as language and memory), we only know that visual mental image representations are present because we have the experience of seeing, but in the absence of the appropriate sensory input. And here lies a central problem in the study of imagery (the "introspective dilemma"): there is no way that another person can verify what we "see" with our inner eye, and hence the phenomenon smacks of unscientific, fanciful confabulation.

Nevertheless, imagery played a central role in theories of the mind for centuries. For example, the British Associationists conceptualized thought itself as sequences of images. And, WILHELM WUNDT, the founder of scientific psychology, emphasized the analysis of images. However, the central role of imagery in theories of mental activity was undermined when Kulpe, in 1904, pointed out that some thoughts are not accompanied by imagery (e.g., one is not aware of the processes that allow one to decide which of two objects is heavier).

The observation that images are not the hallmark of all thought processes was soon followed by the notion that images as ordinarily conceived (and, indeed, thoughts themselves) may not even exist! John Watson (1913)—the founder of BEHAVIORISM—argued that images actually correspond to subtle movements of the larynx. Watson emphasized the precept that scientific phenomena must be publicly observable, and imagery clearly is not. This line of argument led to diminished interest in imagery until the early 1960s.

Behaviorism ultimately had a salutary effect on the study of imagery; it made it rigorous. Whereas researchers in Wundt's lab were trained in INTROSPECTION, modern researchers are trained in measuring subtle aspects of behavior. In such cases, the behavior is like the track left by a cosmic ray passing through a cloud chamber: It is a kind of signature, a hallmark, that allows us to draw inferences about the phenomena that produced it.

Imagery has effects on the accuracy of LEARNING and MEMORY. In the early 1960s the behaviorist approach to language led to the study of "verbal learning": words were treated as stimuli that could be learned like any other. Paivio and his colleagues (e.g., Paivio 1971) showed that imagery is a major factor that affects the ease of learning words. Not only is a picture worth a thousand words, it is also easier to remember. The same is true for "mental pictures." Words are better learned and remembered if they name an object that can be visualized, such as "boat" or "cat," than they are if they name an abstract idea, such as "justice" or "kindness." The way objects are visualized can, however, affect how easily the words they correspond to are remembered; Bower (1972) found that forming an image of the interaction between a pair of objects made it easier to remember the names of those objects than was the case by simply forming an image of the objects existing separately.

Imagery also affects the detection of perceptual stimuli. Studies of imagery benefited from new techniques developed to investigate perception. For example, SIGNAL DETECTION THEORY (e.g., Green and Swets 1966) has been used to show that forming a visual mental image interrupts vision more than it does hearing, but forming an auditory image interrupts hearing more than vision. Such results reveal that imagery draws on mechanisms used in like-modality perception. However, Craver-Lemley and Reeves (1992) report, this interference occurs only if the image overlaps the target. It is also worth noting that images can be mistaken for percepts, both at the time and in memory (e.g., Johnson and Raye 1981; see Kosslyn 1994 for a review).

One reason that behaviorism failed to hold sway was that a viable alternative was introduced: cognitive psychology. Cognitive psychology likened the mind to software running on a computer, and imagery—along with all other mental processes—was conceptualized in terms of such "information processing." This approach stressed that different sets of processes are used to accomplish different ends. For example, to plan how to arrange furniture in an empty room, one could *generate* an image of the furniture and then mentally *transform* it (rotate it, perhaps imagine stacking a shelf on a crate or desk); one must *maintain* the image as it is being *inspected*. Sometimes imagery involves only some of these processes; for instance, image transformation is irrelevant in remembering the way to get to the train station. Information processing is often studied by measuring response times.

Consider tasks that require image inspection. Do you know the shape of a Saint Bernard's ears? Subjects will require more time to perform this task if they are first told to visualize the dog far off in the distance; before they can answer the question, they will "zoom in" on the part of their image containing the dog's head. Similarly, subjects will require more time to answer this question if they are first told to visualize a Saint Bernard's tail; they will now mentally "scan" across the image of the dog in order to "look" at its ears. Indeed, the time to respond increases linearly with the amount of distance scanned—even though the subject's eyes are closed. Such results suggest that the image representations embody spatial extent (see Kosslyn 1994).

Now consider image generation. Images are generated by activating stored information. Images are created "piece by piece," and thus an image with more parts takes longer to form. Indeed, the time to form an image often increases linearly with the number of parts that are assembled.

Finally, consider image transformation. When objects in images are transformed, they often mimic the movements of real objects. For example, rotating objects appear to shift through a trajectory; the farther one rotates an imaged object, the longer it takes to do so (see MENTAL ROTATION).

Shepard (1984) suggests that this occurs because, due to natural selection, certain laws of physics have been internalized in the brain and act as constraints on the imagery process. Alternatively, it is possible that motor programs guide imagery and, consequently, objects are mentally manipulated in the same manner that real objects would be physically manipulated. In fact, motor parts of the brain have been shown to be activated during some image transformation tasks (e.g., Georgopoulos et al. 1989).

The computer metaphor encouraged a kind of "disembodied mind" approach, which ignored certain classes of data and constraints on theories. Recent years have seen a sharp increase in research on the neural bases of imagery. Such research has addressed each of the processes noted earlier, as well as the issue of how images are internally represented.

It has long been known that some parts of the brain are spatially organized (see Felleman and Van Essen 1991); the pattern of activity on the retina is projected onto these areas (albeit distorted in several ways). Studies reported by five laboratories have now shown that some of these areas, such as primary VISUAL CORTEX, are activated when people visualize. Moreover, the pattern of activation is systematically altered by spatial properties of the image, in a way similar to what occurs in perception. Such results suggest that imagery relies on "depictive" representations, which use space to represent space. This result bears directly on the "imagery debate" of the 1970s and 1980s, which focused on the question of whether a depictive representation is used during imagery. However, this result is not always obtained, and the crucial differences between the tasks that do and do not engender such representations have not yet been identified (Mellet et al. 1998).

Image *generation* is most often disrupted by damage to the posterior left hemisphere (Farah 1984). However, recent studies have shown that images can be generated in at least two ways, one of which uses stored descriptions to arrange parts and relies primarily on left-hemisphere processes, and the other of which uses stored metric spatial information to arrange parts and relies primarily on the right hemisphere (for a review of the literature on this topic, see Behrmann, Kosslyn and Jeannerod 1996).

Patients with brain damage that impairs visual perception sometimes also have corresponding deficits when they *inspect* imaged objects. For example, some patients who have suffered damage to the posterior right parietal lobe display a phenomenon known as "unilateral VISUAL NEGLECT"; they ignore objects to the left side of space. These patients may display the same behavior when visualizing—they ignore objects on the left half of their images (e.g., Bisiach and Luzzatti 1978).

Image *transformations* are accomplished by a complex set of brain areas. However, studies with brain-damaged patients suggest that the right hemisphere plays a crucial role in the transformation process itself (e.g., Corballis and Sergent 1989; Ratcliff 1979).

In conclusion, the recent research on visual mental imagery reveals that imagery is not a unitary phenomenon, but rather is accomplished by a collection of distinct processes. These processes are implemented by neural systems, not discrete "centers." These processes can be combined in different ways (with each combination corresponding to a distinct method or strategy) to allow one to accomplish any given imagery task.

See also WORD MEANING, ACQUISITION OF; DREAMING; HAPTIC PERCEPTION; PICTORIAL ART AND VISION

—*Stephen M. Kosslyn and Carolyn S. Rabin*

References

Behrmann, M., S. M. Kosslyn, and M. Jeannerod, Eds. (1996). *The Neuropsychology of Mental Imagery.* New York: Pergamon.

Bisiach, E., and C. Luzzatti. (1978). Unilateral neglect of representational space. *Cortex* 14: 129–133.

Boring, E. G. (1950). *A History of Experimental Psychology.* 2nd ed. New York: Appleton-Century-Crofts.

Bower, G. H. (1972). Mental imagery and associative learning. In L. Gregg, Ed., *Cognition in Learning and Memory.* New York: Wiley.

Corballis, M. C., and J. Sergent. (1989). Hemispheric specialization for mental rotation. *Cortex* 25: 15–25.

Craver-Lemley, C., and A. Reeves. (1992). How visual imagery interferes with vision. *Psychological Review* 99: 633–649.

Farah, M. J., (1984). The neurological basis of mental imagery: a componential analysis. *Cognition* 18: 245–272.

Felleman, D. J., and D. C. Van Essen. (1991). Distributed hierarchical processing in the primate cerebral cortex. *Cerebral Cortex* 1: 1–47.

Georgopolous, A. P., J. T. Lurito, M. Petrides, A. B. Schwartz, and J. T. Massey. (1989). Mental rotation of the neuronal population vector. *Science* 243: 234–236.

Green, D. M., and J. A. Swets. (1966). *Signal Detection Theory and Psychophysics.* New York: Wiley.

Johnson, M. K., and C. L. Raye. (1981). Reality monitoring. *Psychological Review* 88: 67–85.

Kosslyn, S. M. (1994). *Image and Brain: The Resolution of the Imagery Debate.* Cambridge, MA: MIT Press.

Logie, R. H., and M. Denis. (1991). *Mental Images in Human Cognition.* Amsterdam: North Holland.

Mellet, E., L. Petit, B. Mazoyer, M. Denis, and N. Tzourio. (1998). Reopening the mental imagery debate: Lessons from functional neuroanatomy. *NeuroImage* 8: 129–139.

Paivio, A. (1971). *Imagery and Verbal Processes.* New York: Holt, Rinehart and Winston.

Ratcliff, G. (1979). Spatial thought, mental rotation and the right cerebral hemisphere. *Neuropsychologia* 17: 49–54.

Shepard, R. N. (1984). Ecological constraints on internal representation: resonant kinematics of perceiving, imagining, thinking, and dreaming. *Psychological Review* 91: 417–447.

Watson, J. B. (1913). Psychology as the behaviorist views it. *Psychological Review* 20: 158–177.

Further Readings

Anderson, J. R. (1978). Arguments concerning representations for mental imagery. *Psychological Review* 85: 249–277.

Arditi, A., J. D. Holtzman, and S. M. Kosslyn. (1988). Mental imagery and sensory experience in congenital blindness. *Neuropsychologia* 26: 1–12.

Behrmann, M., G. Winocur, and M. Moscovitch. (1992). Dissociation between mental imagery and object recognition in a brain-damaged patient. *Nature* 359: 636–637.

Block, N. (1981). *Imagery.* Cambridge, MA: MIT Press.

Brandimonte, M., and W. Gerbino. (1993). Mental image reversal and verbal recoding: when ducks become rabbits. *Memory and Cogniton* 21: 23–33.

Chambers, D., and D. Reisberg. (1985). Can mental images be ambiguous? *Journal of Experimental Psychology: Human Perception and Performance* 11: 317–328.

Charlot, V., M. Tzourio, M. Zilbovicius, B. Mazoyer, and M. Denis. (1992). Different mental imagery abilities result in different regional cerebral blood flow activation patterns during cognitive tasks. *Neuropsychologia* 30: 565–580.

Corballis, M. C., and R. McLaren. (1982). Interactions between perceived and imagined rotation. *Journal of Experimental Psychology: Human Perception and Performance* 8: 215–224.

Denis, M., and M. Carfantan. (1985). People's knowledge about images. *Cognition* 20: 49–60.

Eddy, J. K., and A. L. Glass. (1981). Reading and listening to high and low imagery sentences. *Journal of Verbal Learning and Verbal Behavior* 20: 333–345.

Farah, M. J. (1988). Is visual imagery really visual? Overlooked evidence from neuropsychology. *Psychological Review* 95: 301–317.

Farah, M. J., and G. Ratcliff, Eds. (1994). *The Neural Bases of Mental Imagery*. Hillsdale, NJ: Erlbaum.

Farah, M. J., M. J. Soso, and R. M. Dasheiff. (1992). Visual angle of the mind's eye before and after unilateral occipital lobectomy. *Journal of Experimental Psychology: Human Perception and Performance* 18: 241–246.

Finke, R. A. (1989). *Principles of Mental Imagery*. Cambridge, MA: MIT Press.

Finke, R. A., and S. Pinker. (1982). Spontaneous imagery scanning in mental extrapolation. *Journal of Experimental Psychology: Learning, Memory, and Cognition* 8: 142–147.

Finke, R. A., and R. N. Shepard. (1986). Visual functions of mental imagery. In K. R. Boff, L. Kaufman, and J. P. Thomas, Eds., *Handbook of Perception and Human Performance*. New York: Wiley-Interscience, pp. 37–1 to 37–55.

Hampson, P. J., D. F. Marks, and J. T. E. Richardson. (1990). *Imagery: Current Developments*. London: Routledge.

Hinton, G. (1979). Some demonstrations of the effects of structural descriptions in mental imagery. *Cognitive Science* 3: 231–250.

Jolicoeur, P., and S. M. Kosslyn. (1985). Is time to scan visual images due to demand characteristics? *Memory and Cognition* 13: 320–332.

Kosslyn, S. M., and O. Koenig. (1992). *Wet Mind: The New Cognitive Neuroscience*. New York: Free Press.

Paivio, A. (1986). *Mental Representations*. New York: Oxford University Press.

Pylyshyn, Z. W. (1973). What the mind's eye tells the mind's brain: a critique of mental imagery. *Psychological Bulletin* 80: 1–24.

Sergent, J. (1990). The neuropsychology of visual image generation: data, method, and theory. *Brain and Cognition* 13: 98–129.

Shepard, R. N., and L. A. Cooper. (1982). *Mental Images and Their Transformations*. Cambridge, MA: MIT Press.

Tye, M. (1991). *The Imagery Debate*. Cambridge, MA: MIT Press.

Imitation

There has been an explosion of research in the development, evolution, and brain basis of imitation. Human beings are highly imitative. Recent discoveries reveal that newborn infants have an innate ability to imitate facial expressions. This has important implications for theories of FOLK PSYCHOLOGY, MEMORY, CULTURE, and LANGUAGE.

Classical theories of COGNITIVE DEVELOPMENT postulated that newborns did not understand the similarity between themselves and others. Newborns were said to be "solipsistic," experiencing their own internal sensations and seeing the movements of others without linking the two (Piaget 1962). According to Jean PIAGET, the imitation of facial gestures was first possible at one year of age, a landmark development that was a prerequisite for representational abilities. In sharp contrast, modern empirical work has shown that infants as young as forty-two minutes old successfully imitate adult facial gestures (Meltzoff and Moore 1983). Imitation is innate in humans (figure 1).

Facial imitation presents a puzzle. Infants can see an adult's face but cannot see their own faces. They can feel their own faces move but have no access to the feelings of movement in another person. How is facial imitation possible? One candidate is "active intermodal mapping." The crux of the view is that an infant represents the adult facial expression and actively tries to make his or her own face match that target. Of course, infants do not see their own facial movements, but they can use proprioception to monitor their own unseen actions and to correct their behavior. According to this view, the perception and production of human acts are represented in a common "supramodal" framework and can be directly compared to one another. Meltzoff and Moore (1997) provide a detailed account of the metric used for establishing cross-modal equivalence of human acts and its possible brain basis.

The findings on imitation suggest a common coding for perception and production. Work with adults analyzing brain sites and cognitive mechanisms involved in the imitation, perception, and imagination of human acts suggests they tap common processes (Jeannerod and Decety 1995; Prinz 1990). Neurophysiological studies show that in some cases the same neurons become activated when monkeys perform an action as when they observe a similar action

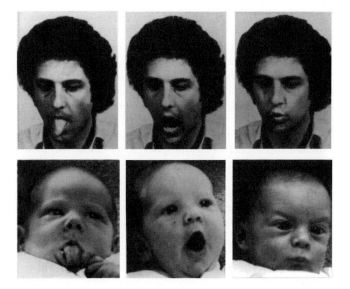

Figure 1. Photographs of two- to three-week-old infants imitating facial acts demonstrated by an adult. From A. N. Meltzoff and M. K. Moore (1977). *Science* 198 : 75–78.

made by another (Rizzolatti et al. 1996). Such "mirror neurons" may provide a neurophysiological substrate for imitation.

Early imitation has implications for the philosophical problem of other minds. Imitation shows that young infants are sensitive to the movements of themselves and other people and can map self-other isomorphisms at the level of actions (see INTERSUBJECTIVITY). Through experience they may learn that when they act in particular ways, they themselves have certain concomitant internal states (proprioception, emotions, intentions, etc.). Having detected this regularity, infants have grounds for making the inference that when they see another person act in the same way that they do, the person has internal states similar to their own. Thus, one need not accept Fodor's (1987) thesis that the adult THEORY OF MIND must be innate in humans (because it could not be learned via classical reinforcement procedures. Imitation of body movements, vocalizations, and other goal-directed behavior provides a vehicle for infants discovering that other people are "like me," with internal states just like the SELF. Infant imitation may be a developmental precursor to developing a theory of mind (Meltzoff and Moore 1995, 1997; Gopnik and Meltzoff 1997; see also SIMULATION VS. THEORY-THEORY).

What motivates infants to imitate others? Imitation serves many cognitive and social functions, but one possibility is that very young infants use behavioral imitation to sort out the identity of people. Young infants are concerned with determining the identity of objects as they move in space, disappear, and reappear (see INFANT COGNITION). Research shows that young infants use imitation of a person's acts to help them distinguish one individual from another and reidentify people on subsequent encounters (Meltzoff and Moore 1998). Infants use the distinctive actions of people as if they were functional properties that can be elicited through interaction. Thus, infants identify a person not only by featural characteristics (lips, eyes, hair), but by how that individual acts and reacts.

As adults, we ascribe mental states to others. One technique for investigating the origins of theory of mind capitalizes on the proclivity for imitation (Meltzoff 1995a). Using this technique, the adult tries but fails to perform certain target acts. The results show that eighteen-month-olds imitate what the adult "is trying to do," not what that adult literally does do. This establishes that young children are not strict behaviorists, attuned only to the surface behavior of people. By eighteen months of age children have already adopted a fundamental aspect of a folk psychology—actions of persons are understood within a framework involving goals and intentions.

Imitation illuminates the nature of preverbal memory (Meltzoff 1995b). In these tests infants are shown a series of acts on novel objects but are not allowed to touch the objects. A delay of hours or weeks is then imposed. Infants from six to fifteen months of age have been shown to perform deferred imitation after the delay, which establishes preverbal recall memory, not simply recognition of the objects. The findings suggest that infants operate with what cognitive neuroscientists call declarative memory as opposed to procedural or habit memory (Sherry and Schacter 1987; Squire,

Knowlton, and Musen 1993), inasmuch as learning and recall of novel material occurs after one brief observation with no motor training. Research is being directed to determining the brain structures that mediate deferred imitation. Amnesic adults (see MEMORY, HUMAN NEUROPSYCHOLOGY) are incapable of the same deferred imitation tasks accomplished by infants, suggesting that it is mediated by the HIPPOCAMPUS and related anatomical structures (McDonough et al. 1995). Compatible evidence comes from a study showing that children with AUTISM have a deficit in imitation, particularly deferred imitation, compared to mental-age matched controls (Dawson et al. 1998).

Comparative psychologists hotly debate the nature and scope of imitation in nonhuman animals (Heyes and Galef 1996). Imitation among nonhuman animals is more limited than human imitation (Tomasello, Kruger, and Ratner 1993; Tomasello and Call 1997). Animals modify their behavior when observing others, but even higher primates are most often limited to duplicating the goal rather than the detailed means used to achieve it. Moreover, social learning in animals is typically motivated by obtaining food and other extrinsic rewards, whereas imitation is its own reward for the human young. In humans, aspects of language development depend on imitation. Vocal imitation is a principal vehicle for infants' learning of the phonetic inventory and prosodic structure of their native language (Kuhl and Meltzoff 1996; see PHONOLOGY, ACQUISITION OF and SPEECH PERCEPTION).

Human beings are the most imitative species on earth. Imitation plays a crucial role in the development of culture and the distinctively human ability to pass on learned abilities from one generation to another. A current challenge in artificial intelligence is to create a robot that can learn through imitation (Demiris and Hayes 1996). Creating more "humanlike" devices may hinge on embodying one of the cornerstones of the human mind, the ability to imitate.

See also COMPARATIVE PSYCHOLOGY; CULTURAL EVOLUTION; LANGUAGE ACQUISITION; LEARNING; NATIVISM; PRIMATE COGNITION

—*Andrew N. Meltzoff*

References

Dawson, G., A. N. Meltzoff, J. Osterling, and J. Rinaldi. (1998). Neurophysiological correlates of early symptoms of autism. *Child Development* 69: 1276–1285.

Demiris, J., and G. Hayes. (1996). Imitative learning mechanisms in robots and humans. In V. Klingspor, Ed., *Proceedings of the 5th European Workshop on Learning Robots.* Bari, Italy.

Fodor, J. A., (1987). *Psychosemantics: The Problem of Meaning in the Philosophy of Mind.* Cambridge, MA: MIT Press.

Gopnik, A., and A. N. Meltzoff. (1997). *Words, Thoughts, and Theories.* Cambridge, MA: MIT Press.

Heyes, C. M., and B. G. Galef. (1996). *Social Learning in Animals: The Roots of Culture.* New York: Academic Press.

Jeannerod, M., and J. Decety. (1995). Mental motor imagery: a window into the representational stages of action. *Current Opinion in Neurobiology* 5: 727–732.

Kuhl, P. K., and A. N. Meltzoff. (1996). Infant vocalizations in response to speech: vocal imitation and developmental change. *Journal of the Acoustical Society of America* 100: 2425–2438.

McDonough, L., J. M. Mandler, R. D. McKee, and L. R. Squire. (1995). The deferred imitation task as a nonverbal measure of declarative memory. *Proceedings of the National Academy of Science* 92: 7580–7584.

Meltzoff, A. N. (1995a). Understanding the intentions of others: re-enactment of intended acts by 18-month-old children. *Developmental Psychology* 31: 838–850.

Meltzoff, A. N. (1995b). What infant memory tells us about infantile amnesia: Long-term recall and deferred imitation. *Journal of Experimental Child Psychology* 59: 497–515.

Meltzoff, A. N., and M. K. Moore. (1977). Imitation of facial and manual gestures by human neonates. *Science* 198: 75–78.

Meltzoff, A. N., and M. K. Moore. (1983). Newborn infants imitate adult facial gestures. *Child Development* 54: 702–709.

Meltzoff, A. N., and M. K. Moore. (1995). Infants' understanding of people and things: from body imitation to folk psychology. In J. Bermudez, A. J. Marcel, and N. Eilan, Eds., *The Body and the Self*. Cambridge, MA: MIT Press, pp. 43–69.

Meltzoff, A. N., and M. K. Moore. (1997). Explaining facial imitation: a theoretical model. *Early Development and Parenting* 6: 179–192.

Meltzoff, A. N., and M. K. Moore. (1998). Object representation, identity, and the paradox of early permanence: steps toward a new framework. *Infant Behavior and Development* 21: 201–235.

Piaget, J. (1962). *Play, Dreams and Imitation in Childhood*. New York: Norton.

Prinz, W. (1990). A common coding approach to perception and action. In O. Neumann and W. Prinz, Eds., *Relationships Between Perception and Action*. Berlin: Springer, pp. 167–201.

Rizzolatti, G., L. Fadiga, V. Gallese, and L. Fogassi. (1996). Premotor cortex and the recognition of motor actions. *Cognitive Brain Research* 3: 131–141.

Sherry, D. F., and D. L. Schacter. (1987). The evolution of multiple memory systems. *Psychological Review* 94: 439–454.

Squire, L. R., B. Knowlton, and G. Musen. (1993). The structure and organization of memory. *Annual Review of Psychology* 44: 453–495.

Tomasello, M., and J. Call. (1997). *Primate Cognition*. New York: Oxford University Press.

Tomasello, M., A. C. Kruger, and H. H. Ratner. (1993). Cultural learning. *Behavioral and Brain Sciences* 16: 495–552.

Further Readings

Barr, R., A. Dowden, and H. Hayne. (1996). Developmental changes in deferred imitation by 6- to 24-month-old infants. *Infant Behavior and Development* 19: 159–170.

Bauer, P. J., and J. M. Mandler. (1992). Putting the horse before the cart: The use of temporal order in recall of events by one-year-old children. *Developmental Psychology* 28: 441–452.

Braten, S. (1998). *Intersubjective Communication and Emotion in Early Ontogeny*. New York: Cambridge University Press.

Campbell, J. (1994). *Past, Space, and Self*. Cambridge, MA: MIT Press.

Cole, J. (1998). *About Face*. Cambridge, MA: MIT Press.

Decety, J., J. Grezes, N. Costes, D. Perani, M. Jeannerod, E. Procyk, F. Grassi, and F. Fazio. (1997). Brain activity during observation of actions: influence of action content and subject's strategy. *Brain* 120: 1763–1777.

Gallagher, S. (1996). The moral significance of primitive self-consciousness. *Ethics* 107: 129–140.

Gallagher, S., and A. N. Meltzoff. (1996). The earliest sense of self and others: Merleau-Ponty and recent developmental studies. *Philosophical Psychology* 9: 211–233.

Meltzoff, A. N. (1990). Towards a developmental cognitive science: the implications of cross-modal matching and imitation for the development of representation and memory in infancy. In A. Diamond, Ed., *The Development and Neural Bases of Higher Cognitive Functions*. New York: Annals of the New York Academy of Sciences, vol. 608, 1–31.

Meltzoff, A. N., and A. Gopnik. (1993). The role of imitation in understanding persons and developing a theory of mind. In S. Baron-Cohen, H. Tager-Flusberg, and D. J. Cohen, Eds., *Understanding Other Minds: Perspectives from Autism*. New York: Oxford University Press, pp. 335–366.

Nadel, J., and G. E. Butterworth. (1998). *Imitation in Infancy: Progress and Prospects of Current Research*. Cambridge: Cambridge University Press.

Rochat, P. (1995). *The Self in Early Infancy: Theory and Research*. Amsterdam: North-Holland—Elsevier Science.

Visalberghi, E., and D. M. Fragaszy. (1990). Do monkeys ape? In S. Parker and K. Gibson, Eds., *Language and Intelligence in Monkeys and Apes: Comparative Developmental Perspectives*. New York: Cambridge University Press, pp. 247–273.

Whiten, A., and R. Ham. (1992). On the nature and evolution of imitation in the animal kingdom: reappraisal of a century of research. In P. Slater, J. Rosenblatt, C. Beer, and M. Milinski, Eds., *Advances in the Study of Behavior*, vol. 21. New York: Academic Press, pp. 239–283.

Implicature

Implicature is a nonlogical inference constituting part of what is conveyed by S[peaker] in uttering U within context C, without being part of what is said in U. As stressed by H. PAUL GRICE (1989), what is conveyed is generally far richer than what is directly expressed; linguistic MEANING radically underdetermines utterance interpretation. Pragmatic principles must be invoked to bridge this gap, for example, (1) (Harnish 1976: 340):

1. Make the strongest relevant claim justifiable by your evidence.

Precursors of (1) were proposed by Augustus De Morgan and John Stuart Mill in the mid-nineteenth century, and by P. F. Strawson and Robert Fogelin in the mid-twentieth (see Horn 1990), but the central contribution is Grice's, along with the recognition that such principles are not simply observed but rather systematically exploited to generate nonlogically valid inferences. From S's assertion that *Some of the apples are ripe,* H[earer] will tend to infer that (for all S knows) not all the apples are ripe, because if S had known all were ripe, she would have said so, given (1).

The first explicit and general account of such inferences is given by Grice (1961: §3), who distinguishes the nonentailment relations operative in (2):

2. a. She is poor but honest.
   a´. There is some contrast between her poverty and her honesty.
   b. Jones has beautiful handwriting and his English is grammatical.
      [Context: recommendation letter for philosophy job candidate]
   b´. Jones is no good at philosophy.
   c. My wife is either in the kitchen or in the bathroom.
   c´. I don't know for a fact that my wife is in the kitchen.

Grice observes that although the inference in (2a,a´) cannot be cancelled (#*She is poor but honest, but there's no contrast between the two*), it is detachable, because the same truth-conditional content is expressible in a way that detaches (removes) the inference: *She is poor and honest.* It is also irrelevant to truth conditions: (2a) is true if "she" is poor and honest, false otherwise. Such detachable but noncancelable inferences that are neither constitutive of what is said nor calculable in any general way from what is said are conventional implicata, related to pragmatic presuppositions (see PRAGMATICS). Indeed, classic instances of conventional implicature involve the standard pragmatic presupposition inducers: focus particles like *even* and *too*, truth-conditionally transparent verbs like *manage to* and *bother to,* and syntactic constructions like clefts. Because conventional implicata are non-truth-conditional aspects of the conventional meaning of linguistic expressions, which side of the semantics/pragmatics border they inhabit depends on whether pragmatics is identified with the non-truth-conditional (as on Gazdar's intentionally oversimplified equation: pragmatics = semantics – truth conditions) or with the nonconventional. (Karttunen and Peters 1979 provide a formal compositional treatment of conventional implicature.)

The inferences associated with (2b,c) are nonconventional, being calculable from the utterance of such sentences in a particular context. In each case, the inference of the corresponding primed proposition is cancelable (either explicitly by appending material inconsistent with it—"*but I don't mean to suggest that . . .*"—or by altering the context of utterance) but nondetachable, given that truth-conditionally equivalent expressions license the same inference. An utterance of (2b) "does not standardly involve the implication . . . attributed to it; it requires a special context to attach the implication to its utterance" (Grice 1961: 130), whereas the default inference from (2c), that S did not know in which of the two rooms his wife was located, is induced in the absence of a marked context (e.g., that of a game of hide-and-seek). (2b) exemplifies particularized conversational implicature, (2c) the more linguistically significant category of generalized conversational implicature. In each case, it is not the proposition or sentence, but the speaker or utterance, that induces the relevant implicatum in the appropriate context.

Participants in a conversational exchange compute what was meant (by S's uttering U in context C) from what was said by assuming the application of the cooperative principle (Grice 1989: 26)—"Make your conversational contribution such as is required, at the stage at which it occurs"—and the four general and presumably universal maxims of conversation on which all rational interchange is grounded:

3. Maxims of Conversation (Grice [1967]1989: 26–27):
Quality: Try to make your contribution one that is true.

1. Do not say what you believe to be false.
2. Do not say that for which you lack evidence.

Quantity:

1. Make your contribution as informative as is required (for the current purposes of the exchange).
2. Do not make your contribution more informative than is required.

Relation: Be relevant.
Manner: Be perspicuous.

1. Avoid obscurity of expression.
2. Avoid ambiguity.
3. Be brief. (Avoid unnecessary prolixity.)
4. Be orderly.

Although implicata generated by the first three categories of maxims are computed from propositional content (what is said), Manner applies to the way what is said is said; thus the criterion of nondetachability applies only to implicata induced by the "content" maxims.

Since this schema was first proposed, it has been challenged, as well as defended and extended, on conceptual and empirical grounds (Keenan 1976; Brown and Levinson 1987), while neo- and post-Gricean pragmaticists have directed a variety of reductionist efforts at the inventory of maxims. The first revisionist was Grice himself, maintaining that all maxims are not created equal, with a privileged status accorded to Quality (though see Sperber and Wilson 1986 for a dissenting view): "False information is not an inferior kind of information; it just is not information . . . . The importance of at least the first maxim of Quality is such that it should not be included in a scheme of the kind I am constructing; other maxims come into operation only on the assumption that this maxim of Quality is satisfied" (Grice 1989: 371).

Of those "other maxims," the most productive is Quantity-1, which is systematically exploited to yield upper-bounding generalized conversational implicatures associated with scalar operators (Horn 1972, 1989; Gazdar 1979; Hirschberg 1985). Grice seeks to defend a conservative bivalent semantics; the shortfall between what standard logical semantics yields and what an intuitively adequate account of utterance meaning requires is addressed by a pragmatic framework grounded on the assumption that S and H are observing CP and the attendant maxims. Quantity-based scalar implicature in particular—my inviting you to infer from my use of *some . . .* that for all I know *not all . . .*—is driven by your knowing (and my knowing your knowing) that I expressed a weaker proposition, bypassing an equally unmarked utterance that would have expressed a stronger proposition, one unilaterally entailing it. What is said in the use of a weak scalar value is the lower bound (*at least some, at least possible*), with the upper bound (*at most some, at most necessary*) implicated as a cancelable inference (*some and possibly all, possible if not necessary*). Negating such predications denies the lower bound: to say that something is not possible is to say that it is impossible (less than possible). When the upper bound is denied (*It's not possible, it's necessary*), grammatical and phonological diagnostics reveal a metalinguistic or echoic use of negation, in which the negative particle is used to object to any aspect of a quoted utterance, including its conventional and conversational implicata, register, morphosyntactic form or pronunciation (Horn 1989; Carston 1996).

One focus of pragmatic research has been on the interaction of implicature with grammar and the LEXICON, in particular on the conventionalization or grammaticalization of conversational implicatures (see Bach and Harnish 1979 on standardized nonliterality). Another issue is whether Grice's inventory of maxims is necessary and sufficient. One response is a proposal (Horn 1984, 1989; see also Levinson 1987) to collapse the non-Quality maxims into two basic principles regulating the economy of linguistic information. The Q Principle, a hearer-based guarantee of the sufficiency of informative content ("Say as much as you can, modulo Quality and R"), collects Quantity-1 and Manner-1,2. It is systematically exploited (as in the scalar cases) to generate upper-bounding implicata, based on H's inference from S's failure to use a more informative and/or briefer form that S was not in a position to do so. The R Principle, a correlate of the law of least effort dictating minimization of form ('Say no more than you must, modulo Q'), encompasses Relation, Quantity-2, and Manner-3,4. It is exploited to induce strengthening (lower-bounding) implicata typically motivated on social rather than purely linguistic grounds, as exemplified by indirect speech acts (e.g., euphemism) and so-called neg-raising, as in the tendency to pragmatically strengthen *I don't think that f* to *I think that not-f.*

A more radically reductionist model is offered in relevance theory (Sperber and Wilson 1986), in which one suitably elaborated principle of RELEVANCE suffices for the entire gamut of inferential work performed by the Gricean maxims. (The monistic approach of RT is closer to the dualistic Q/R model than it appears, both frameworks being predicated on a minimax or cost/benefit tradeoff that sees the goal of communication as maximizing contextual effects while minimizing processing effort.) RT stresses the radical underspecification of propositional content by linguistic meaning; pragmatically derived aspects of meaning include not only implicatures but "explicatures," that is, components of enriched truth-conditional content.

Although the issues surrounding the division of labor between Gricean implicature and RT-explicature await resolution (see Horn 1992; Récanati 1993), relevance theory has proved a powerful construct for rethinking the role of pragmatic inferencing in utterance interpretation and other aspects of cognitive structure; see Blakemore (1992) for an overview.

See also DISCOURSE; LANGUAGE AND COMMUNICATION; LANGUAGE AND THOUGHT; METAREPRESENTATION; SEMANTICS

—*Laurence Horn*

References

Bach, K., and R. M. Harnish. (1979). *Linguistic Communication and Speech Acts.* Cambridge, MA: MIT Press.

Blakemore, D. (1992). *Understanding Utterances.* Oxford: Blackwell.

Brown, P., and S. C. Levinson. (1987). *Politeness: Some Universals in Language Usage.* Cambridge: Cambridge University Press.

Carston, R. (1996). Metalinguistic Negation and Echoic Use. *Journal of Pragmatics* 25: 309–330.

Gazdar, G. (1979). *Pragmatics.* New York: Academic Press.

Grice, H. P. (1961). The causal theory of perception. *Proceedings of the Aristotelian Society,* sup. vol. 35: 121–152.

Grice, H. P. (1989). *Studies in the Way of Words.* Cambridge: Harvard University Press.

Harnish, R. M. (1976). Logical form and implicature. In S. Davis, Ed., *Pragmatics: A Reader.* New York: Oxford University Press, pp. 316–364.

Hirschberg, J. (1985). *A Theory of Scalar Implicature.* Ph. D. diss., University of Pennsylvania.

Horn, L. (1972). *On the Semantic Properties of Logical Operators in English.* Ph.D. diss., UCLA. Distributed by Indiana University Linguistics Club, 1976.

Horn. L. (1984). Toward a new taxonomy for pragmatic inference: Q-based and R-based implicature. In D. Schiffrin, Ed., *Meaning, Form, and Use in Context* (GURT '84). Washington: Georgetown University Press, pp. 11–42.

Horn, L. (1989). *A Natural History of Negation.* Chicago: University of Chicago Press.

Horn, L. (1990). Hamburgers and truth: Why Gricean inference is Gricean. *Berkeley Linguistics Society* 16: 454–471.

Horn, L. (1992). The said and the unsaid. *Proceedings of the Second Conference on Semantics and Linguistic Theory*: 163–192.

Karttunen, L., and S. Peters. (1979). Conventional implicature. In C.-K. Oh and D. Dinneen, Eds., *Presupposition. Syntax and Semantics*, vol. 11. New York: Academic Press, pp. 1–56.

Keenan, E. O. (1976). The universality of conversational postulates. *Language in Society* 5: 67–80.

Levinson, S. C. (1987). Minimization and conversational inference. In J. Verschueren and M. Bertucelli-Papi, Eds., *The Pragmatic Perspective.* Amsterdam: John Benjamins, pp. 61–130.

Récanati, F. (1993). *Direct Reference.* Oxford: Blackwell.

Sperber, D., and D. Wilson. (1986). *Relevance.* Cambridge, MA: Harvard University Press.

Further Readings

Atlas, J. D., and S. C. Levinson. (1981). It-clefts, informativeness, and logical form. In P. Cole, Ed., *Radical Pragmatics.* New York: Academic Press, pp. 1–61.

Bach, K. (1994). Conversational implicature. *Mind and Language* 9: 125–162.

Carston, R. (1988). Implicature, explicature, and truth-theoretic semantics. In S. Davis, Ed., *Pragmatics: A Reader.* New York: Oxford University Press, pp. 33–51.

Cole, P., Ed. (1978). *Syntax and Semantics 9: Pragmatics.* New York: Academic Press.

Davis, S., Ed. (1991). *Pragmatics: A Reader.* New York: Oxford University Press.

Green, G. (1989). *Pragmatics and Natural Language Understanding.* Hillsdale, NJ: Erlbaum.

Green, G. (1990). The universality of Gricean explanation. *Berkeley Linguistics Society* 16: 411–428.

Levinson, S. C. (1983). *Pragmatics.* Cambridge: Cambridge University Press.

Levinson, S. C. (1987). Pragmatics and the grammar of anaphora: a partial pragmatic reduction of binding and control phenomena. *Journal of Linguistics* 23: 379–434.

McCawley, J. D. (1978). Conversational implicature and the lexicon. In P. Cole, Ed., *Syntax and Semantics 9: Pragmatics.* New York: Academic Press, pp. 245–258.

Morgan, J. (1978). Two types of convention in indirect speech acts. In P. Cole, Ed., *Syntax and Semantics 9: Pragmatics.* New York: Academic Press, pp. 261–280.

Neale, S. (1992). Paul Grice and the philosophy of language. *Linguistics and Philosophy* 15: 509–559.

Récanati, F. (1989). The pragmatics of what is said. In S. Davis, Ed., *Pragmatics: A Reader.* New York: Oxford University Press, pp. 97–120.

Sadock, J. M. (1978). On testing for conversational implicature. In P. Cole, Ed., *Syntax and Semantics 9: Pragmatics.* New York: Academic Press, pp. 281–298.

Walker, R. (1975). Conversational implicatures. In S. Blackburn, Ed., *Meaning, Reference, and Necessity.* Cambridge: Cambridge University Press, pp. 133–181.

Wilson, D., and D. Sperber. (1986). Inference and implicature. In S. Davis, Ed., *Pragmatics: A Reader.* New York: Oxford University Press, pp. 377–392.

Implicit vs. Explicit Memory

Psychological studies of human MEMORY have traditionally been concerned with conscious recollection or explicit memory for specific facts and episodes. During recent years, there has been growing interest in a nonconscious form of memory, referred to as *implicit memory* (Graf and Schacter 1985; Schacter 1987), that does not require explicit recollection for specific episodes. Numerous experimental investigations have revealed dramatic differences between implicit and explicit memory, which have had a major impact on psychological theories of the processes and systems involved in human memory (cf. Roediger 1990; Schacter and Tulving 1994; Ratcliff and McKoon 1997).

The hallmark of implicit memory is a change in performance—attributable to information acquired during a specific prior episode—on a test that does not require conscious recollection of the episode. This change is often referred to as direct or repetition priming. One example of a test used to assess priming is known as stem completion, where people are asked to complete word stems (e.g., TAB) with the first word that comes to mind (e.g., TABLE); priming is inferred from an enhanced tendency to complete the stems with previously studied words relative to nonstudied words (for reviews, see Roediger and McDermott 1993; Schacter and Buckner 1998; Schacter, Chiu, and Ochsner 1993). Priming is not the only type of implicit memory. For instance, tasks in which people learn to perform motor or cognitive skills may involve implicit memory, because skill acquisition does not require explicit recollection of a specific previous episode (for review, see Salmon and Butters 1995).

Implicit memory can be separated or dissociated from explicit memory through experimental manipulations that affect implicit and explicit memory differently (for methodological considerations, see Jacoby 1991; Schacter, Bowers, and Booker 1989), and neurological conditions in which explicit memory is impaired while implicit memory is spared. For example, it has been well established that performance on explicit recall and recognition tests is higher following semantic than following nonsemantic study of an item—the well-known levels of processing effect. In contrast, however, the magnitude of priming on tasks that involve completing word stems or identifying briefly flashed words is often less affected, and sometimes unaffected, by semantic versus nonsemantic study (see reviews by Roediger and McDermott 1993; Schacter, Chin, and Ochsner 1993).

Perhaps the most dramatic dissociation between implicit and explicit memory has been provided by studies of brain-damaged patients with organic amnesia. Amnesic patients are characterized by a severe impairment in explicit memory for recent events, despite relatively normal intelligence, perception, and language. This memory deficit is typically produced by lesions to either medial temporal or diencephalic brain regions. In contrast, a number of studies have demonstrated that amnesic patients show intact implicit memory on tests of priming and skill learning. These observations suggest that implicit memory is supported by different brain systems than is explicit memory (Squire 1992).

The evidence also shows that various forms of implicit memory can be dissociated from one another. A number of studies point toward a distinction between perceptual priming and conceptual priming. Perceptual priming is little affected by semantic versus nonsemantic study processing. It is also modality specific (i.e., priming is enhanced when the sensory modality of study and test are the same), and in some instances may be specific to the precise physical format of stimuli at study and test (cf. Church and Schacter 1994; Curran, Schacter, and Bessenoff 1996; Graf and Ryan 1990; Tenpenny 1995). Conceptual priming, in contrast, is not tied to a particular sensory modality and is increased by semantic study processing; it is observed most clearly on tests that require semantic analysis, such as producing category exemplars in response to a category cue (Hamman 1990). Other evidence indicates that priming and skill learning are dissociable forms of implicit memory. For instance, studies of patients suffering from different forms of dementia indicate that patients with Alzheimer's dementia often show impaired priming on stem completion tasks, yet show normal learning of motor skills; in contrast, patients with Huntington's disease (which affects the motor system) show normal stem completion priming together with impaired learning of motor skills (Salmon and Butters 1995).

Recent studies using newly developed brain imaging techniques, such as POSITRON EMISSION TOMOGRAPHY (PET) and functional MAGNETIC RESONANCE IMAGING (fMRI) have demonstrated that visual priming on such tests as stem completion is accompanied by decreased blood flow in regions of visual cortex (Squire et al. 1992). Various other neuroimaging studies have produced similar priming-related blood flow decreases (see Schacter and Buckner 1998). These observations are consistent with the idea that visual priming effects depend on a perceptual representation system that includes posterior cortical regions that are involved in perceptual analysis (Tulving and Schacter 1990); priming may produce more efficient processing of test cues, perhaps resulting in decreased neural activity. Other studies have shown that conceptual priming is associated with blood flow reductions in regions of left inferior frontal cortex that are known to be involved in semantic processing (for review, see Schacter and Buckner 1998). In contrast, neuroimaging studies of motor skill learning have shown that the development of skill across many sessions of practice is accompanied by increased activity in regions involved in motor processing, such as motor cortex (Karni et al. 1995). Neuroimaging studies are also beginning to illuminate the networks of structures involved in explicit remembering of recent episodes, including the regions within the prefrontal cortex and medial temporal lobes (e.g., Buckner et al. 1995; Schacter et al. 1996; Tulving et al. 1994; for review, see Cabeza and Nyberg 1997).

The exploration of implicit memory has opened up new vistas for memory research, providing a vivid reminder that many aspects of memory are expressed through means other than conscious, explicit recollection of past experiences. Nonetheless, a great deal remains to be learned about the cognitive and neural mechanisms of implicit memory, and it seems likely that further empirical study and theoretical analysis will continue to pay handsome dividends in the future.

See also AGING, MEMORY, AND THE BRAIN; EBBINGHAUS, HERMANN; EPISODIC VS. SEMANTIC MEMORY; MEMORY, HUMAN NEUROPSYCHOLOGY; MEMORY STORAGE, MODULATION OF; MOTOR LEARNING

—*Daniel L. Schacter*

References

Buckner, R. L., S. E. Petersen, J. G. Ojemann, F. M. Miezin, L. R. Squire, and M. E. Raichle. (1995). Functional anatomical studies of explicit and implicit memory retrieval tasks. *Journal of Neuroscience* 15: 12–29.

Cabeza, R., and L. Nyberg. (1997). Imaging cognition: an empirical review of PET studies with normal subjects. *Journal of Cognitive Neuroscience* 9: 1–26.

Church, B. A., and D. L. Schacter. (1994). Perceptual specificity of auditory priming: implicit memory for voice intonation and fundamental frequency. *Journal of Experimental Psychology: Learning, Memory, and Cognition* 20: 521–533.

Curran, T., D. L. Schacter, and G. Bessenoff. (1996). Visual specificity effects on word stem completion: beyond transfer appropriate processing? *Canadian Journal of Experimental Psychology* 50: 22–33.

Gabrieli, J. D. E., D. A. Fleischman, M. M. Keane, S. L. Reminger, and F. Morrell. (1995). Double dissociation between memory systems underlying explicit and implicit memory in the human brain. *Psychological Science* 6: 76–82.

Graf, P., and L. Ryan. (1990). Transfer-appropriate processing for implicit and explicit memory. *Journal of Experimental Psychology: Learning, Memory, and Cognition* 16: 978–992.

Graf, P., and D. L. Schacter. (1985). Implicit and explicit memory for new associations in normal subjects and amnesic patients. *Journal of Experimental Psychology: Learning, Memory, and Cognition* 11: 501–518.

Hamman, S. B. (1990). Level-of-processing effects in conceptually driven implicit tasks. *Journal of Experimental Psychology: Learning, Memory, and Cognition* 16: 970–977.

Jacoby, L. L. (1991). A process dissociation framework: separating automatic from intentional uses of memory. *Journal of Memory and Language* 30: 513–541.

Karni, A., G. Meyer, P. Jezzard, M. M. Adams, R. Turner, and L. G. Ungerleider. (1995). Functional MRI evidence for adult motor cortex plasticity during motor skill learning. *Nature* 377: 155–158.

Nyberg, L., A. R. McIntosh, S. Houle, L -G. Nilsson, and E. Tulving. (1996). Activation of medial temporal structures during episodic memory retrieval. *Nature* 380: 715–717.

Ratcliff, R., and G. McKoon. (1997). A counter model for implicit priming in perceptual word identification. *Psychological Review* 104: 319–343.

Roediger, H. L. (1990). Implicit memory: retention without remembering. *American Psychologist* 45: 1043–1056.

Roediger, H. L., and K. B. McDermott. (1993). Implicit memory in normal human subjects. In H. Spinnler and F. Boller, Eds., *Handbook of Neuropsychology*, vol. 8. Amsterdam: Elsevier, pp. 63–131.

Salmon, D. P., and N. Butters. (1995). Neurobiology of skill and habit learning. *Current Opinion in Neurobiology* 5: 184–190.

Schacter, D. L. (1987). Implicit memory: history and current status. *Journal of Experimental Psychology: Memory Learning and Cognition* 13: 501–518.

Schacter, D. L., N. M. Alpert, C. R. Savage, S. L. Rauch, and M. S. Albert. (1996). Conscious recollection and the human hippocampal formation: evidence from positron emission tomography. *Proceedings of the National Academy of Sciences* 93: 321–325.

Schacter, D. L., J. Bowers, and J. Booker. (1989). Awareness, intention and implicit memory: the retrieval intentionality criterion. In S. J. C. Lewandowsky Dunn and K. Kirsner, Eds., *Implicit Memory: Theoretical Issues*. Hillsdale, NJ: Erlbaum, pp. 47–69.

Schacter, D. L., and R. L. Buckner. (1998). Priming and the brain. *Neuron* 20: 185–195.

Schacter, D. L., C. Y. P. Chiu, and K. N. Ochsner. (1993). Implicit memory: a selective review. *Annual Review of Neuroscience* 16: 159–182.

Schacter, D. L., and E. Tulving. (1994). What are the memory systems of 1994? In D. L. Schacter and E. Tulving, Eds., *Memory Systems*. Cambridge, MA: MIT Press, pp. 1–38.

Squire, L. R. (1992). Memory and the hippocampus: a synthesis from findings with rats, monkeys and humans. *Psychological Review* 99: 195–231.

Squire, L. R., J. G. Ojemann, F. M. Miezin, S. E. Petersen, T. O. Videen, and M. E. Raichle. (1992). Activation of the hippocampus in normal humans: a functional anatomical study of memory. *Proceedings of the National Academy of Sciences* 89: 1837–1841.

Tenpenny, P. L. (1995). Abstractionist versus episodic theories of repetition priming and word identification. *Psychonomic Bulletin and Review* 2: 339–363.

Tulving, E., S. Kapur, H. J. Markowitsch, F. I. M. Craik, R. Habib, and S. Houle (1994). Neuroanatomical correlates of retrieval in episodic memory: auditory sentence recognition. *Proceedings of the National Academy of Sciences* 91: 2012–2015.

Tulving, E., and D. L. Schacter. (1990). Priming and human memory systems. *Science* 247: 301–306.

Incompleteness

See FORMAL SYSTEMS, PROPERTIES OF; GÖDEL'S THEOREMS

Indexicals and Demonstratives

When you use "I," you refer to yourself. When I use it, I refer to myself. We use the same linguistic expression with the same conventional meaning. It is a matter of who uses it that determines who is the referent. Moreover, when Jon, pointing to Sue, says "she" or "you," he refers to Sue, whereas Sue can neither use "she" nor "you" to refer to herself, unless she is addressing an image of herself. If we change the context—the speaker, time, place, addressee, or audience—in which these expressions occur, we may end up with a different referent. Among the expressions that may switch reference with a change in context are personal pronouns (*my, you, she, his, we, . . .*), demonstrative pronouns (*this, that*), compound demonstratives (*this table, that woman near the window, . . .*), adverbs (*today, yesterday, now, here, . . .*), adjectives (*actual* and *present*), possessive adjectives (*my pen, their house,* . . .). The reference of other words (e.g., *local, Monday,* . . .) seems also to depend on the context in which they occur. These words capture the interest of those working within the boundaries of cognitive science for several reasons: they play crucial roles when dealing with such puzzling notions as the nature of the SELF, the nature of perception, the nature of time, and so forth.

Reichenbach (1947) characterized this class of expressions *token reflexive* and argued that they can be defined in terms of the locution "this token," where the latter (reflexively) self-refers to the very token used. So, "I" can be defined in terms of "the person who utters this token," "now" in terms of "the time at which this token is uttered," "this table" in terms of "the table pointed to by a gesture accompanying this token," and so on.

One of the major features of token reflexive expressions—also called indexical expressions—that differentiates them from other referential expressions (e.g., proper names: "Socrates," "Paris"; mass terms: "gold," "water"; terms for species: "tiger," "rose"; and so on) is that they are usually used to make reference *in praesentia*. That is, a use of a token reflexive expression exploits the presence of the referent. In a usual communicative interaction the referent is in the perceptual field of the speaker and some contextual clues are used to make the referent salient.

When token reflexive expressions are not used to make reference *in praesentia* they exploit a previously fixed reference. "That man" in *That man we saw last night is handsome* does not refer to a present man. The use of token reflexive expressions to make reference *in absentia* forces the distinction between the context of utterance and the context of reference fixing. In our example, to fix the reference the speaker and the hearer appeal to a past context. The gap between the two contexts is bridged by memory.

The general moral seems to be that the paradigmatic use of a token reflexive expression cannot be deferential. Although one often relies on the so-called division of linguistic labor when using nontoken reflexive expressions, one cannot appeal to the same phenomenon when using a token reflexive expression: for example, one can competently use "Spiro Agnew" or "roadrunner" even if one does not know who Spiro Agnew is or is unable to tell a roadrunner from a rabbit. This parallels the fact that when using proper names, mass terms, and the like, context is in play before the name is used: we first fix the context and then use the name, whereas with token reflexive expressions context is at work the very moment we use them. As Perry (1997) suggests, we often use context to disambiguate a mark or noise (e.g., "bank;" "Aristotle" used either as a tag for the philosopher or for Onassis). These are presemantic uses of context. With token reflexive expressions, though, context is used semantically. It remains relevant after the language, words, and meaning are all known; the meaning directs us to certain aspects of context. This distinction reflects on the fact that proper names, mass terms, and so on, unlike token reflexive expressions, contribute to building context-free (eternal) sentences, that is, sentences that are true or false independently of the context in which they are used.

These general features of token reflexive expressions depend on their particular linguistic meaning: "the utterer of this token" is the linguistic meaning (the character, Kaplan 1977, or role, Perry 1977) of "I," whereas "the day in which this token is uttered" is the linguistic meaning of "today," and so on. As such, their linguistic meaning can be viewed as a function taking as argument the context and giving as value the referent (Kaplan 1977).

It is often the case, though, that the linguistic MEANING of expressions like "this," "that," "she," and so on, together with context, is not enough to select a referent. These expressions are often accompanied by a pointing gesture or demonstration and the referent will be what the demonstration demonstrates. Kaplan (1977) distinguishes between *pure indexicals* ("I," "now," "today,". . .) and *demonstratives* ("this," "she," . . .). The former, unlike the latter, do not need a demonstration to secure the refererence.

Another way to understand the distinction between pure indexicals and demonstratives is to argue that the latter, unlike pure indexicals, are perception based. When one says "I" or "today," one does not have to perceive oneself or the relevant day to be able to use and understand these expressions competently. To use and understand "this," "she," and the like competently, one ought to perceive the referent or demonstratum. For this very reason, when a pure indexical is involved, the context of reference fixing and the context of utterance cannot diverge: the reference of a pure indexical, unlike the reference of a demonstrative, cannot be fixed by a past perception.

Moreover, a demonstrative, unlike a pure indexical, can be a vacuous term. "Today," "I," and so on never miss the referent. Even if I do not know whether today is Monday or Tuesday and I am amnesiac, if I say "Today I am tired," I refer to the relevant day and myself. By contrast, if hallucinating one says "She is funny," or pointing to a man, "This car is green," "she" and "this car" are vacuous.

Besides, pure indexicals cannot be coupled with sortal predicates, whereas "this" and "that" are often accompanied by sortal predicates to form compound demonstratives like "this *book*" and "that *water*." Sortal predicates can be considered to be *universe narrowers* which, coupled with other contextual clues, help us fix the reference. If when pointing to a bottle one says "This liquid is green," the sortal "liquid" helps us to fix the liquid and not the bottle as referent. Moreover, personal pronouns that work like demonstratives (e.g., "she," "he," "we," . . .) have a built-in or hidden sortal. "She," unlike "he," refers to a female, whereas "we" refers to a plurality of people among whom is the speaker.

See also CONTEXT AND POINT OF VIEW; PRAGMATICS; REFERENCE, THEORIES OF; SENSE AND REFERENCE

—*Eros Corazza*

References

Biro, J. (1982). Intention, demonstration, and reference. *Philosophy and Phenomenological Research* XLIII(1): 35–41.

Castañeda, H. (1966). "He": a study in the logic of self-consciousness. *Ratio* 8(2): 130–157.

Castañeda, H. (1967). Indicators and quasi-indicators. *American Philosophical Quarterly* 4(2): 85–100.

Evans, G. (1981). Understanding demonstratives. In G. Evans (1985), *Collected Papers*. Oxford: Oxford University Press, pp. 291–321.

Frege, G. (1918/1988). Thoughts. In N. Salmon and S. Soaemes, Eds., *Propositions and Attitudes*. Original work published 1918. Oxford: Oxford University Press, pp. 33–55.

Kaplan, D. (1977/1989). Demonstratives. In J. Almog et al., Eds., *Themes from Kaplan*. Original work published 1977. Oxford: Oxford University Press, pp. 481–563.

Kaplan, D. (1989). Afterthoughts. In J. Almog et al., Eds., *Themes from Kaplan*. Oxford: Oxford University Press, pp. 565–614.

Lewis, D. (1979). Attitudes de dicto and de se. *The Philosophical Review* 88: 513–543. Reprinted in D. Lewis (1983), *Philosophical Papers:* vol. 1. Oxford: Oxford University Press.

Perry, J. (1977). Frege on demonstratives. *The Philosophical Review* 86(4): 476–497. Reprinted in J. Perry (1993), *The Problem of the Essential Indexical and Other Essays*. Oxford: Oxford University Press.

Perry, J. (1979). The problem of the essential indexical. *Nous* 13(1): 3–21. Reprinted in J. Perry (1993), *The Problem of the Essential Indexical and Other Essays*. Oxford: Oxford University Press.

Perry, J. (1997). Indexicals and demonstratives. In R. Hale and C. Wright, Eds., *Companion to the Philosophy of Language*. Oxford: Blackwell, pp. 586–612.

Reichenbach, H. (1947). *Elements of Symbolic Logics*. New York: Free Press, pp. 284–286.

Yourgrau, P., Ed. (1990). *Demonstratives*. Oxford: Oxford University Press.

Further Readings

Austin, D. (1990). *What's the Meaning of This?* Ithaca: Cornell University Press.

Bach, K. (1987). *Thought and Reference*. Oxford: Clarendon Press.

Boër, S. E., and W. G. Lycan. (1980). Who, me? *The Philosophical Review* 89 (3): 427–466.

Burks, A. W. (1949). Icon, index, and symbol. *Philosophy and Phenomenological Research* 10: 673–689.

Castañeda, H-N. (1989). *Thinking, Language, and Experience*. Minneapolis: University of Minnesota Press.

Chisholm, R. (1981). *The First Person*. Minneapolis: University of Minnesota Press.

Corazza, E. (1995). *Référence, Contexte et Attitudes*. Montréal and Paris: Bellarmin/Vrin.

Evans, G. (1982). *The Varieties of Reference*. Oxford: Oxford University Press.

Mellor, D. H. (1989). I and now. *Proceedings of the Aristotelian Society* 89: 79–84. Reprinted in D. H. Mellor (1991), *Matters of Metaphysics*. Cambridge: Cambridge University Press.

Numberg, G. (1993). Indexicality and deixis. *Linguistics and Philosophy* 16: 1–43.

Perry, J. (1986). Thoughts without representation. *Proceedings of the Aristotelian Society* 60: 137–152. Reprinted in J. Perry, (1993), *The problem of the Essential Indexical and Other Essays*. Oxford: Oxford University Press.

Récanati, F. (1993). *Direct Reference*. London: Blackwell.

Vallée, R. (1996). Who are we? *Canadian Journal of Philosophy*. Vol. 26, no. 2: 211–230.

Wettstein, H. (1981). Demonstrative reference and definite descriptions. *Philosophical Studies* 40: 241–257. Reprinted in H. Wettstein (1991), *Has Semantics Rested on a Mistake? and Other Essays*. Stanford: Stanford University Press.

Individualism

Individualism is a view about how psychological states are taxonomized that has been claimed to constrain the cognitive sciences, a claim that remains controversial. Individualists view the distinction between the psychological states *of individuals* and the physical and social environments of those individuals as providing a natural basis for demarcating properly scientific, psychological kinds. Psychology in particular and the cognitive sciences more generally are to be concerned with natural kinds whose instances end at the boundary of the individual. Thus, although individualism is sometimes glossed as the view that psychological states are "in the head," it is a more specific and stronger view than suggested by such a characterization. Individualism is sometimes (e.g., van Gulick 1989) called "internalism," and its denial "externalism." Its acceptance or rejection has implications for accounts of MENTAL REPRESENTATION, MENTAL CAUSATION, and SELF-KNOWLEDGE.

The dominant research traditions in cognitive science have been at least implicitly individualistic. Relatively explicit statements of a commitment to an individualistic view of aspects of cognitive science include Chomsky's (1986, 1995) deployment of the distinction between two conceptions of language (the "I"-language and the "E"-language, for "internal" and "external," respectively), Jackendoff's (1991) related, general distinction between "psychological" and "philosophical" conceptions of the mind, and Cosmides and Tooby's (1994) emphasis on the constructive nature of our internal, evolutionary-specialized cognitive modules.

Individualism is controversial for at least three reasons. First, individualism appears incompatible with FOLK PSYCHOLOGY and, more controversially, with a commitment to INTENTIONALITY more generally. Much contemporary cognitive science incorporates and builds on the basic concepts of the folk (e.g., belief, memory, perception) and at least appears to rely on the notion of mental content. Second, despite the considerable intuitive appeal of individualism, arguments for it have been less than decisive. Third, the relationship between individualism and cognitive science has been seen to be more complicated than initially thought, in part because of varying views of how to understand explanatory practice in the cognitive sciences.

One formulation of individualism, expressed in Putnam (1975), but also found in the work of Carnap and early twentieth century German thinkers, is *methodological solipsism*. Following Putnam, Fodor views methodological solipsism as the doctrine that psychology ought to concern itself only with *narrow* psychological states, where these are states that do not presuppose "the existence of any individual other than the subject to whom that state is ascribed" (Fodor 1980: 244). An alternative formulation of individualism offered by Stich (1978), the *principle of autonomy*, says that "the states and processes that ought to be of concern to the psychologist are those that supervene on the current, internal, physical state of the organism" (Stich 1983: 164–165; see SUPERVENIENCE). Common to both expressions is the idea that an individual's psychological states should be *bracketed off* from the mere, beyond-the-head environments that individuals find themselves in.

Fodor and Stich used their respective principles to argue for substantive conclusions about the scope and methodology of psychology and the cognitive sciences. Fodor contrasted a solipsistic psychology with what he called a naturalistic psychology, arguing that the latter (among which he included JAMES JEROME GIBSON's approach to perception, learning theory, and the naturalism of WILLIAM JAMES) was unlikely to prove a reliable research strategy in psychology. Stich argued for a syntactic or computational theory of mind that made no essential use of the notion of intentionality or mental content. Although these arguments themselves have not won widespread acceptance, many philosophers interested in the cognitive sciences are attracted to individualism because of a perceived connection to FUNCTIONALISM in the philosophy of mind, the idea being that the functional or causal roles of psychological states are individualistic.

A point initially made in different ways by both Putnam and Stich—that our folk psychology violates individualism—was developed by Tyler Burge (1979) as part of a wide-ranging attack on individualism. Putnam had argued that "'meanings' just ain't in the head" by developing a causal theory of reference for natural kind terms, introducing TWIN EARTH thought experiments into the philosophy of mind. Stich identified intuitive cases (including two of Putnam's) in which our folk psychological ascriptions conflicted with the principle of autonomy. Burge introduced *individualism* as a term for an overall conception of the mind, extended the Twin Earth argument from language to thought, and showed that the conflict between individualism and folk psychology did not turn on a perhaps controversial claim about the semantics of natural kind terms. Together with Burge's (1986) argument that DAVID MARR's celebrated computational theory of vision was *not* individualistic, Burge's early arguments have posed the deepest and most troubling challenges to individualism (cf. Fodor 1987: chap. 2; 1994).

Individualism is motivated by several clusters of powerful intuitions. A "Cartesian" cluster that goes most naturally with the methodological solipsism formulation of individualism revolves around the idea that an organism's mental states could be just as they are even were its environment radically different. Perhaps the most extreme case is that of a brain-in-a-vat: were you a brain-in-a-vat, not an embodied person actively interacting with the world, you could have just the same psychological states that you have now, provided that you were supplied with just the right stimulation and feedback from the "vat" that replaces the world you are actually in. A second, "physicalist" cluster that complements the principle of autonomy formulation appeals to the idea that physically identical individuals *must have* the same psychological states—again, no matter how different their environments.

So much for the intuitions; what about the *arguments*? Empirical and methodological (rather than *a priori*) arguments for or against individualism are perhaps of most interest to cognitive scientists (Wilson 1995: chaps. 2–5). Because of the centrality of computation to cognitive sci-

ence, the most powerful empirical arguments appeal to the computational nature of cognition. At times, such arguments have involved detailed examination of particular theories or research programs, most notably Marr's theory of vision (Egan 1992; Segal 1989; Shapiro 1997), the discussion of which forms somewhat of an industry within philosophical psychology. A different sort of challenge to the inference from computationalism to individualism is posed by Wilson's (1994) *wide computationalism*, a view according to which some of our cognitive, computational systems literally extend into the world (and so cannot be individualistic).

Those rejecting individualism on empirical or methodological grounds have appealed to the situated or embedded nature of cognition, seeking more generally to articulate the crucial role that an organism's environment plays in its cognitive processing. For example, McClamrock (1995: chap. 6) points to the role of improvisation in planning, and Wilson (1999) points to the ways in which informational load is shifted from organism to environment in metarepresentation. But despite the suggestiveness of such appeals, the arguments here remain relatively undeveloped; further attention to the relationships between culture, external symbols, and cognition (Donald 1991; Hutchins 1995) is needed.

Further issues: First, faced with the prima facie conflict between individualism and representational theories of the mind, including folk psychology, individualists have often invoked a distinction between wide content and NARROW CONTENT and argued that cognitive science should use only the latter. The adequacy of competing accounts of narrow content, and even whether there *is* a notion of content that meets the constraint of individualism, are matters of continuing debate.

Second, little of the debate over individualism in cognitive science has reflected the increasing prominence of neuroscientific perspectives on cognition. Although one might assume that the various neurosciences must be individualistic, this issue remains largely unexplored.

Finally, largely unasked questions about the relationship between individualism in psychology and other "individualistic" views—for example, in evolutionary biology (Williams 1966; cf. Wilson and Sober 1994) and in the social sciences (e.g., Elster 1986)—beckon discussion as the boundaries and focus of traditional cognitive science are challenged. Answering such questions will require discussion of the place of the cognitive sciences among the sciences more generally, and of general issues in the philosophy of science.

See also COMPUTATIONAL THEORY OF MIND; PHYSICALISM; SITUATEDNESS/EMBEDDEDNESS

—*Robert A. Wilson*

References

Burge, T. (1979). Individualism and the mental. In P. French, T. Uehling Jr., and H. Wettstein, Eds., *Midwest Studies in Philosophy,* vol. 4 *(Metaphysics).* Minneapolis: University of Minnesota Press.

Burge, T. (1986). Individualism and Psychology. *Philosophical Review* 95: 3–45.

Chomsky, N. (1986). *Knowledge of Language.* New York: Praeger.

Chomsky, N. (1995). Language and nature. *Mind* 104: 1–61.

Cosmides, L., and J. Tooby. (1994). Foreword to S. Baron-Cohen, *Mindblindness.* Cambridge, MA: MIT Press.

Donald, M. (1991). *Origins of the Modern Mind.* Cambridge, MA: Harvard University Press.

Egan, F. (1992). Individualism, computation, and perceptual content. *Mind* 101: 443–459.

Elster, J. (1986). *An Introduction to Karl Marx.* New York: Cambridge University Press.

Fodor, J. A. (1980). Methodological solipsism considered as a research strategy in cognitive psychology. Reprinted in his *Representations.* Sussex: Harvester Press, 1981.

Fodor, J. A. (1987). *Psychosemantics.* Cambridge, MA: MIT Press.

Fodor, J. A. (1994). *The Elm and the Expert.* Cambridge, MA: MIT Press.

Hutchins, E. (1995). *Cognition in the Wild.* Cambridge, MA: MIT Press.

Jackendoff, R. (1991). The problem of reality. Reprinted in his *Languages of the Mind.* Cambridge, MA: MIT Press, 1992.

McClamrock, R. (1995). *Existential Cognition: Computational Minds in the World.* Chicago: University of Chicago Press.

Putnam, H. (1975). The meaning of "meaning." Reprinted in his *Mind, Language, and Reality.* New York: Cambridge University Press.

Segal, G. (1989). Seeing what is not there. *Philosophical Review* 98: 189–214.

Shapiro, L. (1997). A clearer vision. *Philosophy of Science* 64: 131–153.

Stich, S. (1978). Autonomous psychology and the belief-desire thesis. *Monist* 61: 573–591.

Stich, S. (1983). *From Folk Psychology to Cognitive Science.* Cambridge, MA: MIT Press.

van Gulick, R. (1989). Metaphysical arguments for internalism and why they don't work. In S. Silvers, Ed., *Rerepresentation.* Dordrecht: Kluwer.

Williams, G. (1966). *Adaptation and Natural Selection.* Princeton, NJ: Princeton University Press.

Wilson, D. S., and E. Sober. (1994). Re-introducing group selection to the human behavioral sciences. *Behavioral and Brain Sciences* 17: 585–608.

Wilson, R. A. (1994). Wide computationalism. *Mind* 103: 351–372.

Wilson, R. A. (1995). *Cartesian psychology and physical minds: individualism and the sciences of the mind.* New York: Cambridge University Press.

Wilson, R. A. (1999). The mind beyond itself. In D. Sperber, Ed., *Metarepresentation.* New York: Oxford University Press.

Further Readings

Adams, F., D. Drebushenko, G. Fuller, and R. Stecker. (1990). Narrow content: Fodor's folly. *Mind and Language* 5: 213–229

Block, N. (1986). Advertisement for a semantics for psychology. In P. French, T. Uehling, Jr., and H. Wettsten, Eds., *Midwest Studies in Philosophy,* vol. 10: *Philosophy of Mind.* Minneapolis: University of Minnesota Press.

Burge, T. (1988). Individualism and self-knowledge. *Journal of Philosophy* 85: 649–663.

Burge, T. (1989). Individuation and causation in psychology. *Pacific Philosophical Quarterly* 70: 303–322.

Crane, T. (1991). All the difference in the world. *Philosophical Quarterly* 41: 1–25.

Davies, M. (1991). Individualism and perceptual content. *Mind* 100: 461–484.

Devitt, M. (1990). A narrow representational theory of mind. In W. Lycan, Ed., *Mind and Cognition: A Reader.* New York: Blackwell.

Fodor, J. A. (1982). Cognitive science and the Twin Earth problem. *Notre Dame Journal of Formal Logic* 23: 98–118.

Houghton, D. (1997). Mental content and external representation. *Philosophical Quarterly* 47: 159–177

Jacob, P. (1997). *What Minds Can Do: Intentionality in a Non-Intentional World.* New York: Cambridge University Press.

Kitcher, Pat. (1985). Narrow taxonomy and wide functionalism. *Philosophy of Science* 52: 78–97.

Lewis, D. L. (1994). Reduction of mind. In S. Guttenplan, Ed., *Companion to the Philosophy of Mind.* New York: Blackwell.

Marr, D. (1982). *Vision: A Computational Approach.* San Francisco: Freeman.

McGinn, C. (1989). *Mental Content.* New York: Blackwell.

Millikan, R. G. (1993). *White Queen Psychology and Other Essays for Alice.* Cambridge, MA: MIT Press.

Patterson, S. (1991). Individualism and semantic development. *Philosophy of Science* 58: 15–35.

Pylyshyn, Z. (1984). *Computation and Cognition.* Cambridge, MA: MIT Press.

Segal, G. (1991). Defense of a reasonable individualism. *Mind* 100: 485–494.

Stalnaker, R. C. (1989). On what's in the head. In J. Tomberlin, Ed., *Philosophical Perspectives 3.* Atascadero, CA: Ridgeview.

Walsh, D. (1998). Wide content individualism. *Mind* 107: 625–651

White, S. (1991). *The Unity of the Self.* Cambridge, MA: MIT Press.

Woodfield, A., Ed. (1982). *Thought and Object: Essays on Intentionality.* Oxford: Oxford University Press.

Induction

Induction is a kind of inference that introduces uncertainty, in contrast to DEDUCTIVE REASONING in which the truth of a conclusion follows necessarily from the truth of the premises. The term *induction* sometimes has a narrower meaning to describe a particular kind of inference to a generalization, for example from "All the cognitive scientists I've met are intelligent" to "All cognitive scientists are intelligent." In the broader sense, induction includes all kinds of nondeductive LEARNING, including concept formation, ANALOGY, and the generation and acceptance of hypotheses (abduction).

The traditional philosophical problem of induction is whether inductive inference is legitimate. Because induction involves uncertainty, it may introduce error: no matter how many intelligent cognitive scientists I have encountered, one still might turn up who is not intelligent. In the eighteenth century, DAVID HUME asked how people could be justified in believing that the future will be like the past and concluded that they cannot: we use induction out of habit but with no legitimate basis. Because no deductive justification of induction is available, and any inductive justification would be circular, it seems that induction is a dubious source of knowledge. Rescher (1980) offers a pragmatic justification of induction, arguing that it is the best available means for accomplishing our cognitive ends. Induction usually works, and even when it leads us into error, there is no method of thinking that would work better.

In the 1950s, Nelson Goodman (1983) dissolved the traditional problem of induction by pointing out that the validity of deduction consists in conformity to valid deductive principles at the same time that deductive principles are evaluated according to deductive practice. Justification is then just a matter of finding a coherent fit between inferential practice and inferential rules. Similarly, inductive inference does not need any general justification but is a matter of finding a set of inductive principles that fit well with inductive practice after a process of improving principles to fit with practice and improving practice to fit with principles. Instead of the old problem of coming up with an absolute justification of induction, we have a new problem of compiling a set of good inductive principles.

The task that philosophers of induction face is therefore very similar to the projects of researchers in psychology and artificial intelligence who are concerned with learning in humans and machines. Psychologists have investigated a wide array of inductive behavior, including rule learning in rats, category formation, formation of models of the social and physical worlds, generalization, learning inferential rules, and analogy (Holland et al. 1986). AI researchers have developed computational models of many kinds of MACHINE LEARNING, including learning from examples and EXPLANATION-BASED LEARNING, which relies heavily on background knowledge (Langley 1996; Mitchell 1997).

Most philosophical work on induction, however, has tended to ignore psychological and computational issues. Following Carnap (1950), much research has been concerned with applying and developing probability theory. For example, Howson and Urbach (1989) use Bayesian probability theory to describe and explain inductive inference in science. Similarly, AI research has investigated inference in BAYESIAN NETWORKS (Pearl 1988). In contrast, Thagard (1992) offers a more psychologically oriented view of scientific induction, viewing theory choice as a process of parallel constraint satisfaction that can be modeled using connectionist networks. There is room for both psychological and nonpsychological investigations of induction in philosophy and artificial intelligence: the former are concerned with how people do induction, and the latter pursue the question of how probability theory and other mathematical methods can be used to perform differently and perhaps better than people typically do. It is possible, however, that psychologically motivated connectionist approaches to learning may approximate to optimal reasoning.

Here are some of the inductive tasks that need to be understood from a combination of philosophical, psychological, and computational perspectives:

1. *Concept learning.* Given a set of examples and a set of prior concepts, formulate new CONCEPTS that effectively describe the examples. A student entering the university, for example, needs to form new concepts that describe kinds of courses, professors, and students.
2. *Rule learning.* Given a set of examples and a set of prior rules, formulate new rules that improve problem solving. For example, a student might generalize that early morning classes are hard to get to. According to some linguists, LANGUAGE ACQUISITION is essentially a matter of learning rules.
3. *Hypothesis formation.* Given a puzzling occurrence such as a friend's not showing up for a date, generate hypoth-

eses about why this happened. Pick the best hypothesis, which might be done probabilistically or qualitatively by considering which hypothesis is the best explanation. Forming and evaluating explanatory hypotheses is a kind of CAUSAL REASONING. Medical diagnosis is one kind of hypothesis formation.
4. *Analogical inference.* To solve a given target problem, look for a similar problem that can be adapted to infer a possible solution to the target problem. ANALOGY and hypothesis formation are often particularly risky kinds of induction, inasmuch as they both tend to involve substantial leaps beyond the information given and introduce much uncertainty; alternative analogies and hypotheses will always be possible. Nevertheless, these risky kinds of induction are immensely valuable to everyday and scientific thought, because they can bring new creative insights that induction of rules and concepts from examples could never provide.

How much of human thinking is deductive and how much is inductive? No data are available to answer this question, but if Harman (1986) is right that inference is always a matter of coherence, then all inference is inductive. He points out that the deductive rule of modus ponens, from *P* and *if P then Q* to infer *Q*, does not tell us that we should infer *Q* from *P* and *if P then Q*; sometimes we should give up *P* or *if P then Q* instead, depending on how these beliefs and *Q* cohere with our other beliefs. Many kinds of inductive inference can be interpreted as maximizing coherence using parallel constraint satisfaction (Thagard and Verbeurgt 1998).

See also CATEGORIZATION; EPISTEMOLOGY AND COGNITION; JUSTIFICATION; LOGIC; PRODUCTION SYSTEMS

—Paul Thagard

References

Carnap, R. (1950). *Logical Foundations of Probability.* Chicago: University of Chicago Press.

Goodman, N. (1983). *Fact, Fiction and Forecast.* 4th ed. Indianapolis: Bobbs-Merrill.

Harman, G. (1986). *Change in View: Principles of Reasoning.* Cambridge, MA: MIT Press/Bradford Books.

Holland, J. H., K. J. Holyoak, R. E. Nisbett, and P. R. Thagard. (1986). *Induction: Processes of Inference, Learning, and Discovery.* Cambridge, MA: MIT Press/Bradford Books.

Howson, C., and P. Urbach. (1989). *Scientific Reasoning: The Bayesian Tradition.* Lasalle, IL: Open Court.

Langley, P. (1996). *Elements of Machine Learning.* San Francisco: Morgan Kaufmann.

Mitchell, T. (1997). *Machine Learning.* New York: McGraw-Hill.

Pearl, J. (1988). *Probabilistic Reasoning in Intelligent Systems.* San Mateo: Morgan Kaufman.

Rescher, N. (1980). *Induction.* Oxford: Blackwell.

Thagard, P. (1992). *Conceptual Revolutions.* Princeton: Princeton University Press.

Thagard, P., and K. Verbeurgt. (1998). Coherence as constraint satisfaction. *Cognitive Science* 22: 1–24.

Inductive Logic Programming

Inductive logic programming (ILP) is the area of computer science involved with the automatic synthesis and revision of logic programs from partial specifications. The word "inductive" is used in the sense of philosophical rather than mathematical induction. In his *Posterior Analytics* Aristotle introduced philosophical induction (in Greek *epagogue*) as the study of the derivation of general statements from specific instances (see INDUCTION). This can be contrasted with deduction, which involves the derivation of specific statements from more general ones. For instance, induction might involve the conjecture that (a) "all swans are white" from the observation (b) "all the swans in that pond are white," where (b) can be derived deductively from (a). In the *Principles of Science* the nineteenth-century philosopher and economist William Stanley Jevons gave some simple demonstrations that inductive inference could be carried out by reversal of deductive rules of inference. The idea of reversing deduction has turned out to be one of the strong lines of investigation within ILP.

In ILP the general and specific statements are in both cases logic programs. A logic program is a set of Horn clauses (see LOGIC PROGRAMMING). Each Horn clause has the form *Head ← Body*. Thus the definite clause active(X) ← *charged(X), polar(X)* states that any X that is charged and polar is also active. In this case, active, charged, and polar are called "predicates," and they are properties that are either true or false of X. Within deductive logic programming the inference rule of *resolution* is used to derive consequences from logic programs. According to resolution, given atom a and clauses $C, D,$ from the clauses $a \lor C$ and $D \lor \bar{a}$ the clause $C \lor D$ can be concluded. A connected set of resolutions is called a proof or deductive derivation.

The inductive derivations in ILP are sometimes thought of as inversions of resolution-based proofs (see "inverse resolution" in Muggleton and de Raedt 1994). Following Plotkin's work in the 1970s, the logical specification of an ILP problem is thought of as consisting of three primary components: $B,$ the background knowledge (e.g., things cannot be completely black and completely white), E the examples (e.g., the first swan on the pond is white) and $H,$ the hypothesis (e.g., all swans are white). The primary relation between these three components is that the background together with the hypothesis should allow the derivation of the examples. This can be written in logical notation as follows:

$$B, H \vdash E$$

Given only such logical specifications, it has long been known that induction is not sound. That is to say, H is not a necessary conclusion from knowing B and E.

A sound treatment is possible by viewing inductive inference as the derivation of statements with associated probabilities. This approach was advocated by the philosopher Carnap in the 1950s and has been taken up more recently in a revised form within ILP. The framework typically chosen is that of Bayesian inference (see BAYESIAN LEARNING). This is a probabilistic framework that allows calculations of the probability of certain events' happening given that other events have happened. Thus suppose we imagine that nature, or a teacher, randomly and independently chooses a series of concepts to be learned, where each concept has an associated probability of coming up. Suppose also that for each concept a series of instances are randomly and inde-

pendently chosen and associated with the label true or false depending on whether they are or are not examples of the chosen concept. From an inductive agent's point of view, prior to receipt of any examples the probability that any particular hypothesis H will fit the data is $p(H),$ the probability of H being chosen by the teacher. Likewise, $p(E)$ denotes the probability that the teacher will provide the example sequence $E,$ $p(H \mid E)$ is the probability the hypothesis chosen was H given that the example sequence was E and $p(E \mid H)$ is the probability that the example sequence was E given that the hypothesis chosen was $H.$ According to Bayes's theorem

$$p(H|E) = \frac{p(H)p(E|H)}{p(E)}.$$

The most likely hypothesis H given the example E is the one that maximizes $p(H \mid E).$ In fact it is sufficient to maximize $p(H)$ $p(E \mid H)$ because $p(E)$ is common to all candidate hypotheses. As with all Bayesian approaches the main issue is how to choose the inductive agent's prior probabilities over hypotheses. In common with other forms of machine learning, this is usually done within ILP systems using a MINIMUM DESCRIPTION LENGTH (MDL) approach, that is, a probability distribution that assigns higher probabilities to textually simple hypotheses.

Within any computational framework such as ILP, a key question involves the efficiency with which the inductive agent converges on the "correct" solution. Here a number of ILP researchers have taken the approach of COMPUTATIONAL LEARNING THEORY, which studies the numbers of examples required for an inductive algorithm to return with high probability an hypothesis which has a given degree of accuracy (this is Valiant's Probably Approximately Correct [PAC] model). One interesting result of these investigations has been that though it has been shown that logic programs cannot be PAC-learned as a class, time-bound logic programs (those in which the derivation of instances are of bounded length) are efficiently learnable within certain Bayesian settings in which the probability of hypotheses decays rapidly (e.g., exponentially or with the inverse square) relative to their size.

One of the hard and still largely unsolved problems within ILP is that of *predicate invention*. This is the process by which predicates are added to the background knowledge in order to provide compact representations for foreground concepts. Thus suppose you were trying to induce a phrase structured grammar for English, and you already have background descriptions for noun, verb, and verb phrase, but no definition for a noun phrase. "Inventing" a definition for noun phrase would considerably simplify the overall hypothesized descriptions. However, the space of possible new predicates that could be invented is clearly large, and its topology not clearly understood.

ILP has found powerful applications in areas of scientific discovery in which the expressive power of logic programs is necessary for representing the concepts involved. Most notably, ILP techniques have been used to discover constraints on the molecular structures of certain biological molecules. These semiautomated scientific "discoveries" include a new structural alert for mutagenesis and the suggestion of a new binding site for an HIV protease inhibitor. ILP techniques have also been demonstrated capable of building large grammars automatically from example sentences.

The philosopher of science Gillies (1996) has made a careful comparison of techniques used in ILP with Bacon and Popper's conception of scientific induction. Gillies concludes that ILP techniques combine elements from Bacon's "pure" knowledge-free notion of induction and Popper's falsificationist approach. ILP has helped clarify a number of issues in the theory, implementation, and application of inductive inference within a computational logic framework.

See also DEDUCTIVE REASONING; PROBABILITY, FOUNDATIONS OF

—*Stephen Muggleton*

References and Further Readings

Bratko, I., and S. Muggleton. (1995). Applications of Inductive Logic Programming. *Communications of the ACM* 38(11): 65–70.

Carnap, R. (1952). *The Continuum of Inductive Methods.* Chicago: University of Chicago Press.

Gillies, D. A. (1996). *Artificial Intelligence and Scientific Method.* Oxford: Oxford University Press.

Jevons, W. S. (1874). *The Principles of Science: a Treatise on Logic and Scientific Method.* London: Macmillan. Republished in 1986 by IBIS publishing.

King R., S. Muggleton, A. Srinivasan, and M. Sternberg. (1996). Structure-activity relationships derived by machine learning: the use of atoms and their bond connectives to predict mutagenicity by inductive logic programming. *Proceedings of the National Academy of Sciences* 93: 438–442.

Lavrac, N., and S. Dzeroski. (1994). *Inductive Logic Programming.* Ellis Horwood.

Muggleton, S. (1995). Inverse entailment and Progol. *New Generation Computing Journal* 13: 245–286.

Muggleton, S., and L. de Raedt. (1994). Inductive Logic Programming: theory and methods. *Journal of Logic Programming* 19(20): 629–679.

Plotkin, G. (1971). A further note on inductive generalisation. In *Machine Intelligence 6.* Edinburgh: Edinburgh University Press.

Sternberg, M., R. King, R. Lewis, and S. Muggleton. (1994). Application of machine learning to structural molecular biology. *Philosophical Transactions of the Royal Society B* 344: 365–371.

Zelle, J. M., and R. J. Mooney. (1996). Comparative results on using inductive logic programming for corpus-based parser construction. In *Connectionist, Statistical and Symbolic Approaches to Learning for Natural Language Processing.* Berlin: Springer, pp. 355–369.

Infant Cognition

Questions about the origins and development of human knowledge have been posed for millennia. What do newborn infants know about their new surroundings, and what do they learn as they observe events, play with objects, or interact with people? Behind these questions are deeper ones: By what processes does knowledge grow, how does it change, and how variable are its developmental paths and endpoints?

Studies of cognition in infancy have long been viewed as a potential source of answers to these questions, but they face a problem: How does one find out what infants know? Before the twentieth century, most studies of human knowledge depended either on the ability to reflect on one's knowledge or on the ability to follow instructions and perform simple tasks with focused attention. Infants obviously are unfit subjects for these studies, and so questions about their knowledge were deemed unanswerable by scientists as different as HERMAN VON HELMHOLTZ and Edward Bradford Titchener.

The study of cognition in infancy nevertheless began in earnest in the 1920s, with the research of JEAN PIAGET. Piaget observed his own infants' spontaneous, naturally occurring actions under systematically varying conditions. Some of his most famous observations centered on infants' reaching for objects under different conditions of visibility and accessibility. Infants under nine months of age, who showed intense interest in visible objects, either failed to reach for objects or reached to inappropriate locations when the objects were occluded. Search failures and errors declined with age, a change that Piaget attributed to the emergence of abilities to represent objects as enduring, mechanical bodies. He proposed a domain-general, constructivist theory of cognitive development, according to which the development of object representations was just one manifestation of a more general change in cognitive functioning over the period from birth to eighteen months.

Later investigators have confirmed Piaget's central observations but questioned his conclusions. Studies of motor development suggest that developmental changes in infants' search for hidden objects stem in part from developing abilities to reach around obstacles, manipulate two objects in relation to one another, and inhibit prepotent actions. When these abilities are not required (for example, when infants are presented with an object that is obscured by darkness rather than by occlusion), successful search occurs at younger ages. The causes of developmental changes in search are still disputed, however, with different accounts emphasizing changes in action, ATTENTION, MEMORY, object representations, and physical knowledge.

Recent studies of cognition in infancy have tended to focus on early-developing actions such as kicking, sucking, and looking. Experiments have shown that even newborn infants learn to modify their actions so as to produce or change a perceived event: for example, babies will suck on a pacifier with increased frequency or pressure if the action is followed by a sound, and they will suck harder or longer for some sounds than for others. Studies using this method provide evidence that newborn infants recognize their parents' voices (they suck harder to hear the voice of their mother than the voice of a different woman) and their native language (they suck harder to produce speech in their own community's language). Both abilities likely depend on auditory perception and learning before birth.

A variant of this method is based on the finding that infants' sucking declines over time when followed by the same sound and then increases if the sound changes. This pattern is the basis of studies of infants' auditory discrimination, CATEGORIZATION, and memory, and it reveals remarkably acute capacities for SPEECH PERCEPTION in the first days of life. Indeed, young infants are more sensitive than adults to speech contrasts outside their native language. Studies of older infants, using similar procedures and a headturn response, reveal abilities to recognize the sounds of individual words and predictable sequences of syllables well before speech begins. The relation between these early-developing abilities and later LANGUAGE ACQUISITION is an open question guiding much current research.

Since the middle of the twentieth century, many studies of cognition in infancy have used some aspect of visual attention as a window on the development of knowledge. Even newborn infants show systematic differences in looking time to different displays, preferring patterned to homogeneous pictures, moving to stationary objects, and familiar people to strangers. Like sucking, looking time declines when a single display is repeated and increases when a new display appears. Both intrinsic preferences and preferences for novelty provide investigators with measures of detection and discrimination not unlike those used by traditional psychophysicists. They have produced quite a rich body of knowledge about early PERCEPTUAL DEVELOPMENT. Investigators now know, for example, that one-week-old infants perceive depth and the constant sizes of objects over varying distances, that two-month-old infants have begun to perceive the stability of objects over self motion and consequent image displacements in the visual field, and that three-month-old infants perceive both similarities among animals within a single species and differences across different species.

Perhaps the most intriguing, and controversial, studies using preferential looking methods have focused on more central aspects of cognitive development in infancy. Returning to knowledge of objects, experiments have shown that infants as young as three months look systematically longer at certain events that adults find unnatural or unexpected, relative to superficially similar events that adults find natural. In one series of studies, for example, three-month-old infants viewed an object that was initially fully visible on a horizontal surface, an opaque screen in front of the object rotated upward and occluded the object, and then the screen either stopped at the location of the object (expected for adults) or rotated a full half turn, passing through the space that the object had occupied (unexpected). Infants looked longer at the latter event, despite the absence of any intrinsic preference for the longer rotation. Infants' looking patterns suggested that they represented the object's continuous existence, stable location, and solidity, and that they reacted with interest or surprise when these properties were violated.

In further investigations of these abilities, the limits of early-developing object knowledge have been explored. Thus, four-month-old infants have been found to be more sensitive to the contact relations among object motions (they represent objects as initiating motion on contact with other objects) than to the inertial properties of object motions (they fail to represent objects as moving at constant or smoothly changing velocities in the absence of obstacles). Very young infants also have been shown to detect and discriminate different numbers of objects in visible and partly occluded displays when numbers are small or numerical differences are large. With large set sizes and small differences, in contrast, infants fail to respond reliably to number. Studies of cognition in infancy are most revealing where they show contrasting patterns of success and failure, as in these examples, because the patterns provide insight into the nature of the cognitive systems underlying their performance.

Where infants have shown visual preferences for events that adults judge to be unnatural, controversy has arisen concerning the interpretation of infants' looking patterns. For example, Baillargeon (1993) has proposed that the patterns provide evidence for early-developing, explicit knowledge of objects; Karmiloff-Smith (1992) has proposed that the patterns provide evidence for an initial system of object representation not unlike early-developing perceptual systems; and Haith (Haith and Bensen 1998) has proposed that preferential looking to unnatural events depends on sensory or motor systems attuned to subtle, superficial properties of the events. These contrasting possibilities animate current research.

Alongside these studies is a rich tradition of research on infants' social development, providing further insight into their cognitive capacities. Newborn infants attend to human faces, recognize familiar people, and even imitate some facial gestures and expressions in a rudimentary way. By six months, infants follow people's gaze and attend to objects on which people have acted. By nine months, infants reproduce other people's actions on objects, and they communicate about objects with gestures such as pointing. These patterns suggest that infants have considerable abilities to learn from other people, and they testify to early-developing knowledge about human action. Studies probing the nature of this knowledge, using methods parallel to the preferential looking methods just described, reveal interesting differences. Whereas infants represent inanimate object motions as initiated on contact, they represent human actions as directed to goals; whereas continuity of motion provides the strongest information for object identity, constancy of properties such as facial features provides stronger information for personal identity. Evidence for these differences has been obtained only recently and much remains to be learned, but research already suggests that distinct systems of knowledge underlie infants' reasoning about persons and inanimate objects.

In sum, the descriptive enterprise of characterizing infants' developing knowledge is well under way, both in the preceding domains and in others not mentioned. In contrast, the deeper and more important enterprise of explaining early cognitive development has hardly begun. Most investigators agree that knowledge is organized into domain-specific systems at a very early age, but they differ in their characterizations of those systems and their explanations for each system's emergence and growth. Elman et al. (1996) suggest that infants are endowed with a collection of connectionist learning systems whose differing architectures and processing characteristics predispose them to treat information from different domains. Spelke and others suggest that infants are endowed with systems of core knowledge that remain central to humans as adults. Carey (1991) proposes that infants are endowed with modular systems for processing perceptual information, but CONCEPTUAL CHANGE occurs as these systems are partly superceded over development by more central systems of representation. As research on infants' learning, knowledge, and perception progresses, these views and others will become more amenable to empirical test.

References to the experiments discussed earlier can be found in Bertenthal (1996), Haith and Bensen (1998), Mandler (1998), and Spelke and Newport (1998). Discussions of infant cognition from diverse theoretical perspectives are listed in the references.

See also COGNITIVE DEVELOPMENT; INTERSUBJECTIVITY; NAIVE PHYSICS; NATIVISM; PHONOLOGY, ACQUISITION OF

—Elizabeth S. Spelke

References

Baillargeon, R. (1993). The object concept revisited: New directions in the study of infants' physical knowledge. In C. Granrud, Ed., *Perception and Cognition in Infancy*. Hillsdale, NJ: Erlbaum.

Bertenthal, B. I. (1996). Origins and early development of perception, action, and representation. *Annual Review of Psychology* 47: 431–459.

Carey, S. (1991). Knowledge acquisition: enrichment or conceptual change? In S. Carey and R. Gelman, Eds., *Epigenesis of Mind: Essays on Biology and Cognition*. Hillsdale, NJ: Erlbaum, pp. 1257–1291.

Elman, J., E. Bates, M. H. Johnson, A. Karmiloff-Smith, D. Parisi, and K. Plunkett. (1996). *Rethinking Innateness: A Connectionist Perspective on Cognitive Development*. Cambridge, MA: MIT Press.

Haith, M. M., and J. B. Bensen. (1998). Infant cognition. In D. Kuhn and R. Siegler, Eds., *Handbook of Child Psychology*, vol. 3: *Cognition, Perception, and Language*. 5th ed. New York: Wiley.

Jusczyk, P. (1997). *The Discovery of Spoken Language*. Cambridge, MA: MIT Press.

Karmiloff-Smith, A. (1992). *Beyond Modularity: A Developmental Perspective on Cognitive Science*. Cambridge, MA: MIT Press.

Kellman, P. J., and M. Arterberry. (Forthcoming). *The Cradle of Knowledge: Development of Perception in Infancy*. Cambridge, MA: MIT Press.

Leslie, A. M. (1988). The necessity of illusion: perception and thought in infancy. In L. Weiskrantz, Ed., *Thought Without Language*. Oxford: Clarendon Press.

Mandler, J. M. (1998). Representation. In D. Kuhn and R. Siegler, Eds., *Handbook of Child Psychology*, vol. 3: *Cognition, Perception, and Language*. 5th ed. New York: Wiley.

Munakata, Y., J. L. McClelland, M. H. Johnson, and R. S. Siegler. (1997). Rethinking infant knowledge: toward an adaptive process account of successes and failures in object permanence tasks. *Psychological Review* 104: 686–713.

Piaget, J. (1954). *The Construction of Reality in the Child*. New York: Basic Books.

Spelke, E. S., K. Breinlinger, J. Macomber, and K. Jacobson. (1992). Origins of knowledge. *Psychological Review* 99: 605–632.

Spelke, E. S., and E. L. Newport. (Forthcoming). Nativism, empiricism, and the development of knowledge. In R. Lerner and W. Damon, Eds., *Handbook of Child Psychology*, vol. 1: *Theoretical Models of Human Development*. 5th ed. New York: Wiley.

Thelen, E., and L. B. Smith. (1994). *A Dynamical Systems Approach to the Development of Cognition and Action*. Cambridge, MA: Bradford Books/MIT Press.

Wynn, K. (1995). Infants possess a system of numerical knowledge. *Current Directions in Psychological Science* 4: 172–176.

Inference

See DEDUCTIVE REASONING; INDUCTION; LOGIC; LOGICAL REASONING SYSTEMS

Influence Diagrams

See BAYESIAN NETWORKS

Information Processing

See INTRODUCTION: COMPUTATIONAL INTELLIGENCE; INTRODUCTION: PSYCHOLOGY

Information Theory

Information theory is a branch of mathematics that deals with measures of information and their application to the study of communication, statistics, and complexity. It originally arose out of communication theory and is sometimes used to mean the mathematical theory that underlies communication systems. Based on the pioneering work of Claude Shannon (1948), information theory establishes the limits to the shortest description of an information source and the limits to the rate at which information can be sent over a communication channel. The results of information theory are in terms of fundamental quantities like entropy, relative entropy, and mutual information, which are defined using a probabilistic model for a communication system. These quantities have also found application to a number of other areas, including statistics, computer science, complexity and economics. In this article, we will describe these basic quantities and some of their applications. Terms like *information* and *entropy* are richly evocative with multiple meanings in everyday usage; information theory captures only some of the many facets of the notion of information. Strictly speaking, information theory is a branch of mathematics, and care should be taken in applying its concepts and tools to other areas.

Information theory relies on the theory of PROBABILITY to model information sources and communication channels. A source of information produces a message out of a set of possible messages. The difficulty of communication or storage of the message depends only on length of the representation of the message and can be isolated from the meaning of the message. If there is only one possible message, then no information is transmitted by sending that message. The amount of information obtained from a message is related to its UNCERTAINTY—if something is very likely, not much information is obtained when it occurs. The simplest case occurs when there are two equally likely messages—the messages can then be represented by the symbols 0 and 1 and the amount of information transmitted by such a message is one bit. If there are four equally likely messages, the messages can be represented by 00, 01,10 and 11, and thus require two bits for its representation. For equally likely messages, the number of bits required grows logarithmically with the number of possibilities. When the messages are not equally likely, we can model the message source by a random variable X, which takes on values 1, 2, . . . with probabilities $p1, p2, . . .$, with associated entropy defined as

$$H(X) = -\sum_i p_i \log_2 p_i \text{ bits.}$$

The entropy is a measure of the average uncertainty of the random variable. It can be shown (Cover and Thomas 1991) that the entropy of a random variable is a lower bound to the average length of any uniquely decodable representation of the random variable. For a uniformly distributed random variable taking on 2^k possible values, the entropy of the random variable is k bits, and it is easy to see how an outcome could be represented by a k bit number. When the random variable is not uniformly distributed, it is possible to get a lower average length description by using fewer bits to describe the most frequently occurring outcomes, and more bits to describe the less frequent outcomes. For example, if a random variable takes on the values A, B, C, and D with probabilities 0.5, 0.25, 0.125, and 0.125 respectively, then we can use a code 0, 10, 110, 111 to represent these four outcomes with an average length of 1.75 bits, which is less than the two bits required for the equal length code. Note that in this example, the average codeword length is equal to the entropy. In general, the entropy is a lower bound on the average length of any uniquely decodable code, and there exists a code that achieves an average length that is within one bit of the entropy.

Traditional information theory was developed using probabilistic models, but it was extended to arbitrary strings using notions of program length by the work of Kolmogorov (1965), Chaitin (1966), and Solomonoff (1964). Suppose one has to send a billion bits of π to a person on the moon. Instead of sending the raw bits, one could instead send a program to calculate π and let the receiver reconstruct the bits. Because the length of the program would be much shorter than the raw bits, we compress the string using this approach. This motivates the following definition for *Kolmogorov complexity* or *algorithmic complexity:* The Kolmogorov complexity $K_u(x)$ is the length of the shortest program for a universal TURING machine U (see AUTOMATA) that prints out the string x and halts. Using the fact that any universal Turing machine can simulate any other universal Turing machine using a fixed length simulation program, it is easy to see that the Kolmogorov complexity with respect to two different Turing machines differs by at most a constant (the length of the simulation program). Thus the notion of Kolmogorov complexity is

universal up to a constant. For random strings, it can be shown that with high probability, the Kolmogorov complexity is equivalent to the entropy rate of the random process. However, due to the halting problem, it is not always possible to discover the shortest program for a string, and thus it is not always possible to determine the Kolmogorov complexity of a string. But Kolmogorov or algorithmic complexity provides a natural way to think about complexity and data compression and has been developed into a rich and deep theory (Li and Vitanyi 1992) with many applications (see MINIMUM DESCRIPTION LENGTH and COMPUTATIONAL COMPLEXITY).

Transmission of information over a communication channel is subject to noise and interference from other senders. A fundamental concept of information theory is the notion of channel capacity, which plays a role very similar to the capacity of a pipe carrying water—information is like an incompressible fluid that can be sent reliably at any rate below capacity. It is not possible to send information reliably at a rate above capacity. A communication channel is described by a probability transition function $p(y|x)$, which models the probability of a particular output message y when input signal x is sent. The capacity C of the channel can then be calculated as

$$C = \max_{p(x)} \sum_x \sum_y p(x)p(y|x)\log\frac{p(x)p(y|x)}{p(x)\Sigma_x p(y|x)} \qquad (4)$$

A key result of information theory is that if the entropy rate of a source is less than the capacity of a channel, then the source can be reproduced at the output of the channel with negligible error, whereas if the entropy rate is greater than the capacity, the error cannot be made arbitrarily small. This result, due to Shannon (1948), created a sensation when it first appeared. Before Shannon, communication engineers believed that the only way to increase reliability in the presence of noise was to reduce the rate by repeating messages, and that to get arbitrarily high reliability one would need to send at a vanishingly small rate. Shannon proved that this was not necessary; at any rate below the capacity of the channel, it is possible to send information with arbitrary reliability by appropriate coding and decoding. The methods used by Shannon were not explicit, but subsequent research has developed practical codes that allow communication at rates close to capacity. These codes are used in combating errors and noise in most current digital systems, for example, in CD players and modems.

Another fundamental quantity used in information theory and in statistics is the relative entropy or Kullback-Leibler distance $D(p \| q)$ between probability mass functions p and q, which is defined as

$$D(p \| q) = \sum_i p_i \log\frac{p_i}{q_i} \qquad (5)$$

The relative entropy is a measure of the difference between two distributions. It is always nonnegative, and is zero if and only if the two distributions are the same. However, it is not a true distance measure, because it is not symmetric. The relative entropy plays a key role in large deviation theory, where it is the exponent in the probability that data drawn according to one distribution looks like data from the other distribution. Thus if a experimenter observes n samples of data and wants to decide if the data that he has observed is drawn from the distribution p or the distribution q, then the probability that he will think that the distribution is p when the data is actually drawn from q is approximately $2^{-nD(p\|q)}$.

We have defined entropy and relative entropy for single discrete random variables. The definitions can be extended to continuous random variables and random processes as well. Because a real number cannot be represented fully with a finite number of bits, a branch of information theory called rate distortion theory characterizes the tradeoff between the accuracy of the representation (the distortion) and the length of the description (the rate). The theory of communication has also been extended to networks with multiple senders and receivers and to information recording (which can be considered as information transmission over time as opposed to information transmission over space).

Information theory has had a profound impact on the technology of the information age. The fact that most information now is stored and transmitted in digital form can be considered a result of one of the fundamental insights of the theory, that the problem of data compression can be separated from the problem of optimal transmission over a communication channel without any loss in achievable performance. Over the half century since Shannon's original work, complex source coding and channel coding schemes have been developed that have come close to fulfilling the bounds that are derived in the theory. These fundamental bounds on description length and communication rates apply to all communication systems, including complex ones like the nervous system or the brain (Arbib 1995). The quantities defined by information theory have also found application in many other fields, including statistics, computer science, and economics.

See also ALGORITHM; COMPUTATION; ECONOMICS AND COGNITIVE SCIENCE; INFORMATIONAL SEMANTICS; LANGUAGE AND COMMUNICATION; WIENER, NORBERT

—*Thomas M. Cover and Joy A. Thomas*

References

Arbib, M. A. (1995). *The Handbook of Brain Theory and Neural Networks.* Cambridge, MA: Bradford Books/MIT Press.

Chaitin, G. J. (1966). On the length of programs for computing binary sequences. *J. Assoc. Comp. Mach.* 13: 547–569.

Cover, T. M., and J. A. Thomas. (1991). *Elements of Information Theory.* New York: Wiley.

Kolmogorov, A. N. (1965). Three approaches to the quantitative definition of information. *Problems of Information Transmission* 1: 4–7.

Li, M., and P. Vitanyi. (1992). *Introduction to Kolmogorov Complexity and its Applications.* New York: Springer.

Shannon, C. E. (1948). A mathematical theory of communication. *Bell Sys. Tech. Journal* 27: 379–423, 623–656.

Solomonoff, R. J. (1964). A formal theory of inductive inference. *Information and Control* 7: 1–22, 224–254.

Informational Semantics

Informational semantics is an attempt to ground meaning—as this is understood in the study of both language and mind—in an objective, mind (and language) independent, notion of information. This effort is often part of a larger effort to naturalize INTENTIONALITY and thereby exhibit semantic—and, more generally, mental—phenomena as an aspect of our more familiar (at least better understood) material world.

Informational semantics locates the primary source of meaning in symbol-world relations (the symbols in question can occur either in the language of thought or in a public language). The symbol-world relations are sometimes described in information-theoretic terms (source, receiver, signal, etc.) and sometimes in more general causal terms. In either case, the resulting semantics is to be contrasted with *conceptual role* (also called *procedural*) semantics, which locates meaning in the relations symbols have to one another (or, more broadly, the way they are related to one another, sensory input, and motor output). Because on some interpretations of information, the information a signal carries is what it indicates about a source, informational semantics is sometimes referred to as *indicator semantics*. The concept of information involved is inspired by, but is only distantly related to, the statistical construct in INFORMATION THEORY (Dretske 1981).

The word "meaning" is multiply ambiguous. Two of its possible meanings (Grice 1989) are: (1) *nonnatural* meaning—the sense in which the word "fire" stands for or means fire; and (2) *natural* meaning—the way in which smoke means (is a sign of, indicates) fire. Nonnatural meaning has no necessary connection with truth: "Jim has the measles" means that Jim has the measles whether or not he has the measles. Natural meaning, on the other hand, requires the existence of the condition meant: if Jim doesn't have the measles, the red spots on his face do not mean (indicate) that he has the measles. Perhaps all they mean is that he has been eating too much candy. Natural meaning, what one event indicates about another, is taken to be a relation between sign and signified that does not depend on anyone recognizing or identifying what is meant. Tracks in the snow can mean there are deer in the woods even if no one identifies them that way—even if they do not mean that *to* anyone.

Information, as this is used in informational semantics, is akin to natural meaning. It is an objective (mind-independent) relation between a sign or signal—tracks in the snow, for instance—and what that sign or signal indicates—deer in the woods. The information a signal carries about a source is what that signal indicates (*means* in a natural way) about that source. Informational semantics, then, is an effort to understand non-natural meaning—the kind of meaning characteristic of thought and language—as arising out of and having its source in natural meaning. The word "meaning" will hereafter be used to refer to nonnatural meaning; "information" and "indication" will be reserved for natural meaning.

Informational semantics takes the primary home of meaning to be in the mind—as the meaning or content of a thought or intention. Sounds and marks of natural language derive their meaning from the communicative intentions of the agents who use them. As a result, the information of primary importance to informational semantics is that occurring in the brains of conscious agents. Thus, for informational semantics, the very existence of thought and, thus, the possibility of language depends on the capacity of systems to transform information (normally supplied by perception) into meaning.

Not all information-processing systems have this capacity. Artifacts (measuring instruments and computers) do not. To achieve this conversion, two things are required. First, because meaning is fine grained (even though 3 *is* $^3\sqrt{27}$, thinking or saying that x = 3 is not the same as thinking or saying that x = $^3\sqrt{27}$) and information is coarse grained (a signal that carries the information that x = 3 necessarily carries the information that x = $^3\sqrt{27}$), a theory of meaning must specify how coarse grained information is converted into fine grained meaning. Which of the many pieces of information an event (normally) carries is to be identified as its meaning? Second, in order to account for the fact that something (e.g., a thought) can mean (have the content) that x = 3 when x ≠ 3, a way must be found to "detach" information from the events that normally carry it so that something can mean that x = 3 when it does not carry this information (because x ≠ 3).

One of the strategies used by some (e.g., Dretske 1981, 1986; Stampe 1977, 1986) to achieve these results is to identify meaning with the environmental condition with which a state is, or is supposed to be, correlated. For instance, the meaning of a state might be the condition about which it is *supposed* to carry information where the "supposed to" is understood in terms of the state's teleofunction. Others—for example, Fodor (1990)—reject teleology altogether and identify meaning with the sort of causal antecedents of an event on which other causes of that event depend. Still others—for example, Millikan (1984)—embrace the teleology but reject the idea that the relevant functions are informational. For Millikan a state can mean *M* without having the function of carrying this information. By combining teleology with information, informational semantics holds out the promise of satisfying the desiderata described in the last paragraph. Just as the pointer reading on a measuring instrument—a speedometer, for example—can misrepresent the speed of the car because there is something (viz., the speed of the car) it is supposed to indicate that it can fail to indicate, so various events in the brain can misrepresent the state of the world by failing to carry information it is their function to carry. In the case of the nervous system, of course, the information-carrying functions are not (as with artifacts) assigned by designers or users. They come, in the first instance, from a specific evolutionary (selectional) history—the same place the heart and kidneys get their function—and, in the second, from certain forms of learning. Not only do information-carrying functions give perceptual organs and the central nervous system the capacity to misrepresent the world (thus solving the second of the above two problems), they also help solve the grain problem. Of the many things the heart does, only one, pumping blood, is its (biological) function. So too, perhaps, an internal state has the function of indicating only one of the many things it carries information about. Only one piece of information is it supposed to carry. According to informational semantics, this would be its meaning.

Informational semantics—as well as any other theory of meaning—has the problem of saying of what relevance the meaning of internal states is to the behavior of the systems in which it occurs. Of what relevance is meaning to a science of intentional systems? Is not the behavior of systems completely explained by the nonsemantic (e.g., neurobiological or, in the case of computers, electrical and mechanical) properties of internal events? This question is sometimes put by asking whether, in addition to syntactic engines, there are (or could be) *semantic* engines. The difficulty of trying to find an explanatory role for meaning in the behavior of intentional (i.e., semantic) systems has led some to abandon meaning (and with it the mind) as a legitimate scientific construct (ELIMINATIVE MATERIALISM), others to regard meaning as legitimate in only an instrumental sense (Dennett 1987), and still others (e.g., Burge 1989; Davidson 1980; Dretske 1988; Fodor 1987; Kim 1996) to propose indirect—but nonetheless quite real—ways meaning figures in the explanation of behavior.

See also MEANING; MENTAL REPRESENTATION

—*Fred Dretske*

References

Burge, T. (1989). Individuation and causation in psychology. *Pacific Philosophical Quarterly* 70: 303–322.

Davidson, D. (1980). *Essays on Actions and Events.* Oxford: Oxford University Press.

Dennett, D. (1987). *The Intentional Stance.* Cambridge, MA: MIT Press.

Dretske, F. (1981). *Knowledge and the Flow of Information.* Cambridge, MA: MIT Press.

Dretske, F. (1986). Misrepresentation. In R. Bogdan, Ed., *Belief.* Oxford: Oxford University Press, pp. 17–36.

Dretske, F. (1988). *Explaining Behavior.* Cambridge, MA: MIT Press.

Fodor, J. (1987). *Psychosemantics: The Problem of Meaning in the Philosophy of Mind.* Cambridge, MA: MIT Press.

Fodor, J. (1990). *A Theory of Content and Other Essays.* Cambridge, MA: MIT Press.

Grice, P. (1989). *Studies in the Way of Words.* Cambridge, MA: Harvard University Press.

Kim, J. (1996). *Philosophy of Mind.* Boulder, CO: Westview Press.

Millikan, R. (1984). *Language, Thought, and Other Biological Categories.* Cambridge, MA: MIT Press.

Stampe, D. (1977). Towards a causal theory of linguistic representation. In P. French, T. Uehling, and H. Wettstein, Eds., *Midwest Studies in Philosophy 2.* Minneapolis: University of Minnesota Press, pp. 42–63.

Stampe, D. (1986). Verificationism and a causal account of meaning. *Synthèse* 69: 107–137.

Further Readings

Barwise, J., and J. Perry. (1983). *Situations and Attitudes.* Cambridge, MA: MIT Press.

Block, N. (1986). Advertisement for a semantics for psychology. In *Midwest Studies in Philosophy,* vol. 10. Minneapolis: University of Minnesota Press, pp. 615–678.

Fodor, J. (1984). Semantics, Wisconsin style. *Synthèse* 59: 231–250.

Israel, D., and J. Perry. (1990). What is information? In P. Hanson, Ed., *Information, Language, and Cognition.* Vancouver: University of British Columbia Press, pp. 1–19.

Lepore, E., and B. Loewer. (1987). Dual aspect semantics. In E. Lepore, Ed., *New Directions in Semantics.* London: Academic Press.

Papineau, D. (1987). *Reality and Representation.* Oxford: Blackwell.

Inheritance

See FRAME-BASED SYSTEMS; LOGICAL REASONING SYSTEMS

Innateness of Language

Although the idea has a large philosophical tradition (especially in the work of the Continental rationalists; see RATIONALISM VS. EMPIRICISM), modern ideas concerning the innateness of language originated in the work of Chomsky (1965 etc.) and the concomitant development of GENERATIVE GRAMMAR. Chomsky's hypothesis is that many aspects of the formal structure of language are encoded in the genome. The hypothesis then becomes an empirical hypothesis, to be accepted or validated according to standard empirical methods.

As with any other hypothesis in the natural sciences, the innateness hypothesis (that there exist genetically specified aspects of language) has to be evaluated alongside competing hypotheses. Clearly, the competing hypothesis is that there are no genetically specified aspects of language. If one accepts that any genetically specified aspects of language exist, then there is no more debate about a general innateness hypothesis, but only a debate about exactly which aspects of language are innate. This debate, in fact, is central to current research in linguistics and PSYCHOLINGUISTICS.

There are many arguments for the innateness hypothesis. But the most significant one in Chomsky's writings, and the one that has most affected the field, is the argument from the POVERTY OF THE STIMULUS (APS; see also Wexler 1991). As Chomsky points out, this argument in the study of language is a modern version of DESCARTES's argument concerning human knowledge of CONCEPTS. The basic thrust of the argument goes as follows:

(1) Human language has the following complex form: G (for Grammar)

(2) The nature of the information about G available to the learner is the following: I (for Input/Information, called Primary Linguistic Data in Chomsky 1965).

(3) No learner could take the information in I and transform it into G.

In other words, the argument from the poverty of the stimulus is that the information in the environment is not rich enough to allow a human learner to attain adult competence.

The arguments to support APS in linguistic theory usually involve linguistic structures that do not seem to be encoded in environmental events. Thus (4a,b) seem to have identical surface structures, yet in (4a) *Mary* is the subject of *please* (she will do the pleasing) and in (4b) *Mary* is the object of *please* (she will be pleased). How will a learner learn this, inasmuch as it seems that the information is not directly provided to the learner in the surface form of the sentence?

(4) a. Mary is eager to please.
    b. Mary is easy to please.

The field of learnability theory (Wexler and Hamburger 1973; Wexler and Culicover 1980) developed as an attempt to provide mathematical preciseness to the APS, and to derive exact consequences. Learnability theory provides an exact characterization of the class of possible grammars, the nature of the input information, and the learning mechanisms, and asks whether the learning mechanism can in fact learn any possible grammar. The basic results of the field include the formal, mathematical demonstration that without serious constraints on the nature of human grammar, no possible learning mechanism can in fact learn the class of human grammars. In some cases it is possible to derive from learnability considerations the existence of specific constraints on the nature of human grammar. These predictions can then be tested empirically.

The strongest, most central arguments for innateness thus continue to be the arguments from APS and learnability theory. This is recognized by critics of the Innateness Hypothesis (e.g., Elman et al. 1996; Quartz and Senjowski 1997). The latter write (section 4.1):

> The best known characterization of a developing system's learning properties comes from language acquisition—what syntactic properties a child could learn, what in the environment could serve as evidence for that learning, and ultimately, what must be prespecified by the child's genetic endowment. From these questions, 30 years of research have provided mainly negative results. . . . In the end, theorists concluded that the child must bring most if its syntactic knowledge, in the form of a universal grammar, to the problem in advance. . . . The perception that this striking view of syntax acquisition is based primarily on rigorous results in formal learning theory makes it especially compelling. Indeed, above all, it is this formal feature that has prompted its generalization from syntax to the view of the entire mind as a collection of innately specified, specialized modules. . . . It is probably no overstatement to suggest that much of cognitive science is still dominated by Chomsky's nativist view of the mind.

In addition to the APS, there are a number of other arguments for the innateness hypothesis. These include (1) the similarity of languages around the world on a wide array of abstract features, even when the languages are not in contact, and the features do not have an obvious functional motivation; (2) the rapid and uniform acquisition of language by most children, without instruction (see PHONOLOGY, ACQUISITION OF; SEMANTICS, ACQUISITION OF; SYNTAX, ACQUISITION OF) whereas many other tasks (e.g., problem solving of various kinds) need instruction and are not uniformly attained by the entire population.

Over the years there have been many attempts (currently fashionable ones include Elman et al. 1996; Quartz and Senjowski 1996) to suggest that perhaps learning could explain

LANGUAGE ACQUISITION after all. However, no arguments have been given that overcome the central learnability argumentation for the innateness hypothesis. For example, neither Elman et al. nor Quartz and Senjowski explain via "learning" any of the properties of universal grammar or how they are attained. Quartz and Sejnowski attempt to critique learnability theory, but their critique does not apply to actual studies in learnability theory. For example, they characterize learnability theory as assuming that learners must enumerate every possible language in the class as part of the learning procedure. This is false of Gold (1967) and explicitly argued against in Wexler and Culicover (1980). Wexler and Culicover, who are greatly concerned with the psychological plausibility of the learning procedure, derive their results under some quite severe restrictions, making their learning procedure much more empirically adequate on psychological grounds than the procedures that are considered in so-called learning accounts. (See Gibson and Wexler 1994 for an analysis of psychologically plausible learning mechanisms in the principles and parameters framework in which there is much innate knowledge.) One simply has to say that CONNECTIONIST APPROACHES TO LANGUAGE and its acquisition are simply programmatic statements without any kind of theoretical or empirical support. To be taken seriously as a competitor to the innateness hypothesis, these approaches will have to attain real results.

See also COGNITIVE DEVELOPMENT; CONNECTIONISM, PHILOSOPHICAL ISSUES; LANGUAGE AND CULTURE; MODULARITY AND LANGUAGE; NATIVISM; NATIVISM, HISTORY OF

—*Kenneth Wexler*

References

Chomsky, N. (1965). *Aspects of the Theory of Syntax*. Cambridge, MA: MIT Press.

Elman, J. L., E. A. Bates, M. H. Johnson, A. Karmiloff-Smith, D. Parisi, and K. Plunkett. (1996). *Rethinking Innateness: A Connectionist Perspective on Development*. Cambridge, MA: MIT Press.

Gibson, E., and K. Wexler. (1994). Triggers. *Linguistic Inquiry* 25(3): 407–454.

Gold, E. M. (1967). Language identification in the limit. *Information and Control* 10: 447–474.

Quartz, S. R., and T. J. Sejnowski. (1997). The neural basis of cognitive development: a constructivist manifesto. *Behavioral and Brain Sciences* 20(4): 537–596.

Wexler, K. (1991). On the argument from the poverty of the stimulus. In A. Kasher, Ed., *The Chomskyan Turn*. Cambridge: Blackwell, pp. 253–270.

Wexler, K., and P. Culicover. (1980). *Formal Principles of Language Acquisition*. Cambridge, MA: MIT Press.

Wexler, K., and H. Hamburger. (1973). On the insufficiency of surface data for the learning of transformational languages. In K. J. J. Hintikka, J. M. E. Moravcsik, and P. Suppes, Eds., *Approaches to Natural Language. Proceedings of the 1970 Standard Workshop on Grammar and Semantics*. Dordrecht: Reidel, pp. 167–179.

Inner Sense

See INTROSPECTION; SELF

Integration

See MULTISENSORY INTEGRATION

Intelligence

Intelligence may be defined as the ability to adapt to, shape, and select environments, although over the years many definitions of intelligence have been offered (e.g., see symposia in *Journal of Educational Psychology* 1921; Sternberg and Detterman 1986). Various approaches have been proposed in attempts to understand it (see Sternberg 1990). The emphasis here will be on cognitive-scientific approaches.

Historically, two major competing approaches to understanding intelligence were offered, respectively, by Sir Francis Galton in England and Alfred Binet in France. Galton (1883) sought to understand (and measure) intelligence in terms of psychophysical skills, such as an individual's just noticeable difference (JND) for discriminating weights or the distance on the skin two points needed to be separated in order for them to be felt as having occurred in distinct locations. Binet and Simon (1916), in contrast, conceptualized intelligence in terms of complex judgmental abilities. Binet believed that three cognitive abilities are key to intelligence: (1) direction (knowing what has to be done and how it should be done), (2) adaptation (selection and monitoring of one's strategies for task performance), and (3) control (the ability to criticize one's own thoughts and judgments). The "metacognitive" emphasis in this conception is apparent. Binet's views have had more impact, both because his theory seemed better to capture intuitive notions of intelligence and because Binet devised a test of intelligence that successfully predicted children's performance in school.

Charles Spearman (1923) was a forerunner of contemporary cognitive approaches to intelligence in suggesting three information processes underlying intelligence: (1) apprehension of experience, (2) eduction of relations, and (3) eduction of correlates. Spearman used the four-term ANALOGY problem (A : B :: C : D) as a basis for illustrating these processes, whereby the first process involved encoding the terms; the second, inferring the relation between A and B; and the third, applying that relation from C to D.

The early part of the twentieth century was dominated by psychometric approaches to intelligence, which emphasized the measurement of individual differences but had relatively less to say about the cognitive processing underlying intelligence (see Sternberg 1990 for a review). These approaches for the most part used factor analysis, a statistical technique for discovering possible structures underlying correlational data. For example, Spearman (1927) believed that a single factor, *g* (general ability), captured most of what is important about intelligence, whereas Thurstone (1938) believed in a need for seven primary factors. More recently, Carroll (1993) has proposed a three-tier hierarchical model that is psychometrically derived, but is expressed in information-processing terms, with *g* at the top and successively more narrow cognitive skills at each lower level of the hierarchy.

A change in the field occurred when Estes (1970) and Hunt, Frost, and Lunneborg (1973) proposed what has come to be called the cognitive-correlates approach to intelligence, whereby relatively simple information-processing tasks used in the laboratories of cognitive psychologists were related to scores on conventional psychometric tests of intelligence. Hunt and his colleagues found correlations of roughly −.3 between parameters of rate of information processing in tasks such as a letter-identification task (Posner and Mitchell 1967)—where participants had to say whether letter pairs like A A, A a, or A b were the same either physically or in name—and scores on psychometric tests of verbal abilities. This approach continues actively today, with investigators proposing new tasks that they believe to be key to intelligence, such as the inspection time task, whereby individuals are assessed psychophysically for the time it takes them accurately to discern which of two lines is longer than the other (e.g., Deary and Stough 1996).

An alternative, cognitive-components approach was proposed by Sternberg (1977), who suggested that intelligence could be understood in terms of the information-processing components underlying complex reasoning and problem-solving tasks such as analogies and syllogisms. Sternberg used information-processing and mathematical modeling to decompose cognitive task performance into its elementary components and strategies. Some theorists, such as Hunt (1974) and Carpenter, Just, and Shell (1990), have used computer-simulation methodology in order to identify such components and strategies in complex tasks, such as the Raven progressive matrices.

Building on his earlier work, Sternberg (1985) proposed a triarchic theory of intelligence, according to which these information-processing components are applied to experience to adapt to, shape, and select environments. Intelligence is best understood in terms of performance on either relatively novel cognitive tasks or in terms of automatization of performance on familiar tasks. Sternberg argued that intelligence comprises three major aspects: analytical, creative, and practical thinking.

Howard Gardner (1983, 1995), in contrast, has suggested that intelligence is not unitary, but rather comprises eight distinct multiple intelligences: linguistic, logical-mathematical, spatial, musical, bodily-kinesthetic, interpersonal, intrapersonal, and naturalist. Each of these intelligences is a distinct module in the brain and operates more or less independently of the others. Gardner has offered a variety of kinds of evidence to support his theory—including cognitive-scientific research—although he has not conducted research directly to test his model.

Other theorists have tried directly to link information processing to physiological processes in the brain. For example, Haier and his colleagues (Haier et al. 1988; Haier et al. 1992) have shown via POSITRON EMISSION TOMOGRAPHY (PET) scans that brains of intelligent individuals generally consume less glucose in doing complex tasks such as Raven matrices or the game of TETRIS, suggesting that the greater expertise of intelligent people enables them to expend less effort on the tasks. Vernon and Mori (1992), among others, have attempted directly to link measured speed of neural conduction to intelligence, although there is

some question as to the replicability of the findings (Wickett and Vernon 1994).

The field of intelligence has many applied offshoots. For example, a number of cognitive tests have been proposed to measure intelligence (see Sternberg 1993), and a number of different programs have been developed, based on cognitive theory, to modify intelligence (see Nickerson 1994). Some investigators have also argued that there are various kinds of intelligence, such as practical intelligence (Sternberg et al. 1995) and emotional intelligence (Goleman 1995; Salovey and Mayer 1990). The field is an active one today, and it promises to change rapidly as new theories are proposed and new data collected. The goal is not to choose among alternative paradigms, but rather for them to work together ultimately to help us produce a unified understanding of intellectual phenomena.

See also CREATIVITY; MACHIAVELLIAN INTELLIGENCE HYPOTHESIS; PROBLEM SOLVING; PSYCHOPHYSICS

—*Robert J. Sternberg*

References

Binet, A., and T. Simon. (1916). *The Development of Intelligence in Children.* Baltimore: Williams and Wilkins. (Originally published in 1905.)

Carpenter, P. A., M. A. Just, and P. Shell. (1990). What one intelligence test measures: a theoretical account of the processing in the Raven Progressive Matrices Test. *Psychological Review* 97: 404–431.

Carroll, J. B. (1993). *Human Cognitive Abilities: A Survey of Factor-Analytic Studies.* New York: Cambridge University Press.

Deary, I. J., and C. Stough. (1996). Intelligence and inspection time: achievements, prospects, and problems. *American Psychologist* 51(6): 599–608.

Estes, W. F. (1970). *Learning Theory and Mental Development.* New York: Academic Press.

Galton, F. (1883). *Inquiry into Human Faculty and its Development.* London: Macmillan.

Gardner, H. (1983). *Frames of Mind: The Theory of Multiple Intelligences.* New York: Basic.

Gardner, H. (1995). Reflections on multiple intelligences: myths and messages. *Phi Delta Kappan* 77: 200–203, 206–209.

Goleman, D. (1995). *Emotional Intelligence.* New York: Bantam.

Haier, R. J., K. H. Nuechterlein, E. Hazlett, J. C. Wu, J. Pack, H. L. Browning, and M. S. Buchsbaum. (1988). Cortical glucose metabolic rate correlates of abstract reasoning and attention studied with positron emission tomography. *Intelligence* 12: 199–217.

Haier, R. J., B. Siegel, C. Tang, L. Abel, and M. S. Buchsbaum. (1992). Intelligence and changes in regional cerebral glucose metabolic rate following learning. *Intelligence* 16: 415–426.

Hunt, E. (1974). Quote the raven? Nevermore! In L. W. Gregg, Ed., *Knowledge and Cognition.* Hillsdale, NJ: Erlbaum, pp. 129–157.

Hunt, E., N. Frost, and C. Lunneborg. (1973). Individual differences in cognition: a new approach to intelligence. In G. Bower, Ed., *The Psychology of Learning and Motivation,* vol. 7. New York: Academic Press, pp. 87–122.

"Intelligence and its measurement": A symposium. (1921). *Journal of Educational Psychology* 12: 123–147, 195–216, 271–275.

Nickerson, R. S. (1994). The teaching of thinking and problem solving. In R. J. Sternberg, Ed., *Thinking and Problem Solving.* San Diego: Academic Press, pp. 409–449.

Posner, M. I., and R. F. Mitchell. (1967). Chronometric analysis of classification. *Psychological Review* 74: 392–409.

Salovey, P., and J. D. Mayer. (1990). Emotional intelligence. *Imagination, Cognition, and Personality* 9: 185–211.

Spearman, C. (1923). *The Nature of "Intelligence" and the Principles of Cognition.* 2nd ed. London: Macmillan. (1923 edition reprinted in 1973 by Arno Press, New York.)

Spearman, C. (1927). *The Abilities of Man.* London: Macmillan.

Sternberg, R. J. (1977). *Intelligence, Information Processing, and Analogical Reasoning: The Componential Analysis of Human Abilities.* Hillsdale, NJ: Erlbaum.

Sternberg, R. J. (1985). *Beyond IQ: A Triarchic Theory of Human Intelligence.* New York: Cambridge University Press.

Sternberg, R. J. (1990). *Metaphors of Mind: Conceptions of the Nature of Intelligence.* New York: Cambridge University Press.

Sternberg, R. J. (1993). *Sternberg Triarchic Abilities Test.* Unpublished test.

Sternberg, R. J., and D. K. Detterman, Eds. (1986). *What is Intelligence? Contemporary Viewpoints on its Nature and Definition.* Norwood, NJ: Ablex.

Sternberg, R. J., R. K. Wagner, W. M. Williams, and J. A. Horvath. (1995). Testing common sense. *American Psychologist* 50(11): 912–927.

Thurstone, L. L. (1938). Primary mental abilities. *Psychometric Monographs* 1.

Vernon, P. A., and M. Mori. (1992). Intelligence, reaction times, and peripheral nerve conduction velocity. *Intelligence* 8: 273–288.

Wickett, J. C., and P. A. Vernon. (1994). Peripheral nerve conduction velocity, reaction time, and intelligence: an attempt to replicate Vernon and Mori. *Intelligence* 18: 127–132.

Intelligent Agent Architecture

Intelligent agent architecture is a model of an intelligent information-processing system defining its major subsystems, their functional roles, and the flow of information and control among them.

Many complex systems are made up of specialized subsystems that interact in circumscribed ways. In the biological world, for example, organisms have modular subsystems, such as the circulatory and digestive systems, presumably because nature can improve subsystems more easily when interactions among them are limited (see, for example, Simon 1969). These considerations apply as well to artificial systems: vehicles have fuel, electrical, and suspension subsystems; computers have central-processing, mass-storage, and input-output subsystems; and so on. When variants of a system share a common organization into subsystems, it is often useful to characterize abstractly the elements shared by all variants. For example, a family of integrated circuits might vary in clock speed or specialized data operations, while sharing a basic instruction set and memory model. In the engineering disciplines, the term *architecture* has come to refer to generic models of shared structure. Architectures serve as templates, allowing designers to develop, refine, test, and maintain complex systems in a disciplined way.

The benefits of architectures apply to the design of intelligent agents as well. An intelligent agent is a device that interacts with its environment in flexible, goal-directed ways, recognizing important states of the environment and acting to achieve desired results. Clearly, when designing a particular agent, many domain-specific features of the environment must be reflected in the detailed design of the agent. Still, the general form of the subsystems underlying intelligent interaction with the environment may carry over from domain to domain. Intelligent agent architectures attempt to capture these general forms and to enforce basic system properties such as soundness of reasoning, efficiency of response, or interruptibility. Many architectures have been proposed that emphasize one or another of these properties, and these architectures can be usefully grouped into three broad categories: the deliberative, the reactive, or the distributed.

The deliberative approach, inspired in part by FOLK PSYCHOLOGY, models agents as symbolic reasoning systems. In this approach, an agent is decomposed into data subsystems that store symbolic, propositional representations, often corresponding to commonsense beliefs, desires, and intentions, and processing subsystems responsible for perception, reasoning, planning, and execution. Some variants of this approach (Genesereth 1983; Russell 1991) emphasize formal methods and resemble approaches from formal philosophy of mind and action, especially with regard to soundness of logical reasoning, KNOWLEDGE REPRESENTATION, and RATIONAL DECISION MAKING. Others (Newell 1990) emphasize memory mechanisms, general PROBLEM SOLVING, and search. Deliberative architectures go beyond folk psychology and formal philosophy by giving concrete computational interpretations to abstract processes of representation and reasoning. Ironically, the literal-minded interpretation of mental objects has also been a source of difficulty in building practical agents: symbolic reasoning typically involves substantial search and is of high COMPUTATIONAL COMPLEXITY, and capturing extensive commonsense knowledge in machine-usable form has proved difficult as well. These problems represent significant challenges to the deliberative approach and have stimulated researchers to investigate other paradigms that might address or sidestep them.

The reactive approach to intelligent-agent design, for example, begins with the intuition that although symbolic reasoning may be a good model for certain cognitive processes, it does not characterize well the information processing involved in routine behavior such as driving, cooking, taking a walk, or manipulating everyday objects. These abilities, simple for humans, remain distant goals for robotics and seem to impose hard real-time requirements on an agent. Although these requirements are not in principle inconsistent with deliberative architectures (Georgeff and Lansky 1987), neither are they guaranteed, and in practice they have not been easily satisfied. Proponents of the reactive approach, therefore, have argued for architectures that insure real-time behavior as part of their fundamental design. Drawing on the mathematical and engineering tradition of feedback control, advocates of reactive architectures model agent and environment as coupled dynamic systems, the inputs of each being the outputs of the other. The agent contains behavioral modules that are self-contained feedback-control systems, each responsible for detecting states of the environment based on sensory data and generating appropriate output. The key is for state-estimation and output calculations to be performed fast enough to keep up with the sampling rates of the system. There is an extensive literature on how to build such behaviors (control systems) when a mathematical description of the environment is available and is of the proper form; reactive architectures advance these traditional control methods by describing how complex behaviors might be built out of simpler ones (Brooks 1986), either by switching among a fixed set of qualitatively different behaviors based on sensed conditions (see Miller, Galanter, and Pribram 1960 for precursors), by the hierarchical arrangement of behaviors (Albus 1992), or by some more intricate principle of composition. Techniques have also been proposed (Kaelbling 1988) that use off-line symbolic reasoning to derive reactive behavior modules with guaranteed real-time on-line performance.

A third architectural paradigm, explored by researchers in distributed artificial intelligence, is motivated by the following observation. A local subsystem integrating sensory data or generating potential actions may have incomplete, uncertain, or erroneous information about what is happening in the environment or what should be done. But if there are many such local nodes, the information may in fact be present, in the aggregate, to assess a situation correctly or select an appropriate global action policy. The distributed approach attempts to exploit this observation by decomposing an intelligent agent into a network of cooperating, communicating subagents, each with the ability to process inputs, produce appropriate outputs, and store intermediate states. The intelligence of the system as a whole arises from the interactions of all the system's subagents. This approach gains plausibility from the success of groups of natural intelligent agents, for example, communities of humans, who decompose problems and then reassemble the solutions, and from the parallel, distributed nature of neural computation in biological organisms. Although it may be stretching the agent metaphor to view an individual neuron as an intelligent agent, the idea that a collection of units might solve one subproblem while other collections solve others has been an attractive and persistent theme in agent design.

Intelligent-agent research is a dynamic activity and is much influenced by new trends in cognitive science and computing; developments can be anticipated across a broad front. Theoretical work continues on the formal semantics of MENTAL REPRESENTATION, models of behavior composition, and distributed problem solving. Practical advances can be expected in programming tools for building agents, as well as in applications (spurred largely by developments in computer and communications technology) involving intelligent agents in robotics and software.

See also BEHAVIOR-BASED ROBOTICS; COGNITIVE ARCHITECTURE; FUNCTIONAL DECOMPOSITION; MODULARITY OF MIND; MULTIAGENT SYSTEMS

—*Stanley J. Rosenschein*

References

Albus, J. S. (1992). RCS: A reference model architecture for intelligent control. *IEEE Comput.* 25(5): 56–59.

Brooks, R. A. (1986). A robust layered control system for a mobile robot. *IEEE Trans. Rob. Autom.* 2: 14–23.

Genesereth, M. R. (1983). An overview of metalevel architecture. *Proceedings AAAI* 83: 119–123.

Georgeff, M., and A. Lansky. (1987). Reactive reasoning and planning. *Proceedings AAAI* 87.

Kaelbling, L. (1988). Goals as parallel program specification. *Proceedings AAAI* 88.

Miller, G., E. Galanter, and K. H. Pribram. (1960). *Plans and the Structure of Behavior.* New York: Henry Holt and Company.

Newell, A. (1990). *Unified Theories of Cognition.* Cambridge, MA: Harvard University Press.

Russell, S., and E. Wefald. (1991). *Do the Right Thing.* Cambridge, MA: MIT Press.

Simon, H. A. (1969). *The Sciences of the Artificial.* Cambridge, MA: MIT Press.

Intentional Stance

The *intentional stance* is the strategy of interpreting the behavior of an entity (person, animal, artifact, or the like) by treating it as if it were a rational agent that governed its "choice" of "action" by a "consideration" of its "beliefs" and "desires." The distinctive features of the intentional stance can best be seen by contrasting it with two more basic stances or strategies of prediction, the physical stance and the design stance. The physical stance is simply the standard laborious method of the physical sciences, in which we use whatever we know about the laws of physics and the physical constitution of the things in question to devise our prediction. When I predict that a stone released from my hand will fall to the ground, I am using the physical stance. For things that are neither alive nor artifacts, the physical stance is the only available strategy. Every physical thing, whether designed or alive or not, is subject to the laws of physics and hence behaves in ways that can be explained and predicted from the physical stance. If the thing I release from my hand is an alarm clock or a goldfish, I make the same prediction about its downward trajectory, on the same basis.

Alarm clocks, being designed objects (unlike the rock), are also amenable to a fancier style of prediction—prediction from the design stance. Suppose I categorize a novel object as an alarm clock: I can quickly reason that if I depress a few buttons just so, then some hours later the alarm clock will make a loud noise. I do not need to work out the specific physical laws that explain this marvelous regularity; I simply assume that it has a particular design—the design we call an alarm clock—and that it will function properly, as designed. Design-stance predictions are riskier than physical-stance predictions, because of the extra assumptions I have to take on board: that an entity is designed as I suppose it to be, and that it will operate according to that design—that is, it will not malfunction. Designed things are occasionally misdesigned, and sometimes they break. But this moderate price I pay in riskiness is more than compensated for by the tremendous ease of prediction.

An even riskier and swifter stance is the intentional stance, a subspecies of the design stance, in which the designed thing is an agent of sorts. An alarm clock is so simple that this fanciful anthropomorphism is, strictly speaking, unnecessary for our understanding of why it does what it does, but adoption of the intentional stance is more useful—indeed, well-nigh obligatory—when the artifact in question is much more complicated than an alarm clock. Consider chess-playing computers, which all succumb neatly to the same simple strategy of interpretation: just think of them as rational agents that want to win, and that know the rules and principles of chess and the positions of the pieces on the board. Instantly your problem of predicting and interpreting their behavior is made vastly easier than it would be if you tried to use the physical or the design stance. At any moment in the chess game, simply look at the chessboard and draw up a list of all the legal moves available to the computer when it is its turn to play (there will usually be several dozen candidates). Now rank the legal moves from best (wisest, most rational) to worst (stupidest, most self-defeating), and make your prediction: the computer will make the best move. You may well not be sure what the best move is (the computer may "appreciate" the situation better than you do!), but you can almost always eliminate all but four or five candidate moves, which still gives you tremendous predictive leverage.

The intentional stance works (when it does) whether or not the attributed goals are genuine or natural or "really appreciated" by the so-called agent, and this tolerance is crucial to understanding how genuine goal-seeking could be established in the first place. Does the macromolecule really want to replicate itself? The intentional stance explains what is going on, regardless of how we answer that question. Consider a simple organism—say a planarian or an amoeba—moving nonrandomly across the bottom of a laboratory dish, always heading to the nutrient-rich end of the dish, or away from the toxic end. This organism is seeking the good, or shunning the bad—its own good and bad, not those of some human artifact-user. Seeking one's own good is a fundamental feature of any rational agent, but are these simple organisms seeking or just "seeking"? We do not need to answer that question. The organism is a predictable intentional system in either case.

By exploiting this deep similarity between the simplest—one might as well say mindless—intentional systems and the most complex (ourselves), the intentional stance also provides a relatively neutral perspective from which to investigate the differences between our minds and simpler minds. For instance, it has permitted the design of a host of experiments shedding light on whether other species, or young children, are capable of adopting the intentional stance—and hence are higher-order intentional systems. Although imaginative hypotheses about "theory of mind modules" (Leslie 1991) and other internal mechanisms (e.g., Baron-Cohen 1995) to account for these competences have been advanced, the evidence for the higher-order competences themselves must be adduced and analyzed independently of these proposals, and this has been done by cognitive ethologists (Dennett 1983; Byrne and Whiten 1991) and developmental psychologists, among others, using the intentional stance to generate the attributions that in turn generate testable predictions of behavior.

Although the earliest definition of the intentional stance (Dennett 1971) suggested to many that it was merely an instrumentalist strategy, not a theory of real or genuine belief, this common misapprehension has been extensively discussed and rebutted in subsequent accounts (Dennett 1987, 1991, 1996).

See also COGNITIVE DEVELOPMENT; COGNITIVE ETHOLOGY; FOLK PSYCHOLOGY; INTENTIONALITY; PROPOSITIONAL ATTITUDES; RATIONAL AGENCY; REALISM AND ANTIREALISM

—*Daniel Dennett*

References

Baron-Cohen, S. (1995). *Mindblindness: An Essay on Autism and Theory of Mind.* Cambridge, MA: MIT Press.

Byrne, R., and A. Whiten. (1991). *Machiavellian Intelligence: Social Expertise and the Evolution of Intellect in Monkeys, Apes and Humans.* New York: Oxford University Press.

Dennett, D. (1971). Intentional systems. *Journal of Philosophy* 68: 87–106.

Dennett, D. (1983). Intentional systems in cognitive ethology: the "panglossian paradigm" defended. *Behavioral and Brain Sciences* 6: 343–390.

Dennett, D. (1987). *The Intentional Stance.* Cambridge, MA: Bradford Books/MIT Press.

Dennett, D. (1991). Real patterns. *Journal of Philosophy* 87: 27–51.

Dennett, D. (1996). *Kinds of Minds.* New York: Basic Books.

Leslie, A. (1991). The theory of mind impairment in autism: evidence for a modular mechanism of development? In A. Whiten, Ed., *Natural Theories of Mind.* Oxford: Blackwell.

Intentionality

The term *intentional* is used by philosophers, not as applying primarily to actions, but to mean "directed upon an object." More colloquially, for a thing to be intentional is for it to be *about something.* Paradigmatically, mental states and events are intentional in this technical sense (which originated with the scholastics and was reintroduced in modern times by FRANZ BRENTANO). For instance, beliefs and desires and regrets are about things, or have "intentional objects": I have beliefs about Boris Yeltsin, I want a beer and world peace, and I regret agreeing to write so many encyclopedia articles.

A mental state can have as intentional object an individual (John loves *Marsha*), a state of affairs (Marsha thinks that *it's going to be a long day*) or both at once (John wishes *Marsha were happier*). Perception is intentional: I see John, and that John is writing Marsha's name in his copy of *Verbal Behavior.* The computational states and representations posited by cognitive psychology and other cognitive sciences are intentional also, inasmuch as in the course of computation something gets computed and something gets represented. (An exception here may be states of NEURAL NETWORKS, which have computational values but arguably not representata.)

What is at once most distinctive and most philosophically troublesome about intentionality is its indifference to reality. An intentional object need not actually exist or obtain: the Greeks worshiped Zeus; a friend of mine believes that corks grow on trees; and even if I get the beer, my desire for world peace is probably going to go unfulfilled.

Brentano argued both (A) that this reality-neutral feature of intentionality makes it the distinguishing mark of the mental, in that all and only mental things are intentional in that sense, and (B) that purely physical or material objects cannot have intentional properties—for how could any purely physical entity or state have the property of being "directed upon" or *about* a nonexistent state of affairs? (A) and (B) together imply the Cartesian dualist thesis that no mental thing is also physical. And each is controversial in its own right.

Thesis (A) is controversial because it is hardly obvious that every mental state has a possibly nonexistent intentional object; bodily sensations such as itches and tickles do not seem to, and free-floating anxiety is notorious in this regard. Also, there seem to be things other than mental states and events that "aim at" possibly nonexistent objects. Linguistic items such as the name "Santa Claus" are an obvious example; paintings and statues portray fictional characters; and one might ignorantly build a unicorn trap. More significantly, *behavior* as usually described is intentional also: I reach for the beer; John sends a letter to Marsha; Marsha throws the letter at the cat; Macbeth tries to clutch the dagger he sees. (Though some philosophers, such as Chisholm 1958 and Searle 1983, argue that the aboutness of such nonmental things as linguistic entities and behavior is second-rate because it invariably derives from the more fundamental intentionality of someone's mental state.)

Dualism and immaterialism about the mind are unpopular both in philosophy and in psychology—certainly cognitive psychologists do not suppose that the computational and representational states they posit are states of anything but the brain—so we have strong motives for rejecting thesis (B) and finding a way of explaining how a purely physical organism can have intentional states. (Though some behaviorists in psychology and eliminative materialists in philosophy have taken the bolder step of simply denying that people do in fact ever have intentional states; see BEHAVIORISM and ELIMINATIVE MATERIALISM.) The taxonomy of such explanations is now fairly rich. It divides first between theories that ascribe intentionality to presumed particular states of the brain and those that attribute intentional states only to the whole subject.

Many theorists, especially those influenced by cognitive science, do believe that not only the intentionality of cognitive computational states but also that of everyday intentional attitudes such as beliefs and desires (also called PROPOSITIONAL ATTITUDES) inhere in states of the brain. On this view, all intentionality is at bottom MENTAL REPRESENTATION, and propositional attitudes have Brentano's feature because the internal physical states and events that realize them represent actual or possible states of affairs. Some evidence for this is that intentional features are semantical features: Like undisputed cases of representation, beliefs are true or false; they entail or imply other beliefs; they are (it seems) composed of concepts and depend for their truth on a match between their internal structures and the way the world is; and so it is natural to regard their aboutness as a matter of mental referring or designation. Sellars (1963) and

Fodor (1975, 1981) have argued that intentional states are just physical states that have semantical properties, and the existent-or-nonexistent states of affairs that are their objects are just representational contents.

The main difficulty for this representationalist account is that of saying exactly *how* a physical item's representational content is determined; in virtue of what does a neurophysiological state represent precisely *that the Republican candidate will win*? An answer to that general question is what Fodor has called a "psychosemantics"; the question itself has also been called the "symbol grounding problem." Several attempts have been made on it (Devitt 1981; Millikan 1984; Block 1986; Dretske 1988; Fodor 1987, 1990).

One serious complication is that, surprisingly, ordinary propositional attitude contents do not seem to be determined by the states of their subjects' nervous systems, not even by the total state of their subjects' entire bodies. Putnam's (1975) TWIN EARTH and indexical examples are widely taken to show that, surprising as it may seem, two human beings could be molecule-for-molecule alike and still differ in their beliefs and desires, depending on various factors in their spatial and historical environments. (For dissent, however, see Searle 1983.) Thus we can distinguish between "narrow" properties, those that are determined by a subject's intrinsic physical composition, and "wide" properties, those that are not so determined, and representational contents are wide. So it seems an adequate psychosemantics cannot limit its resources to narrow properties such as internal functional or computational roles; it must specify some scientifically accessible relations between brain and environment. (Though some theorists continue to maintain that a narrow notion of content—see NARROW CONTENT—and accordingly a narrow psychosemantics are needed and will suffice for cognitive science; see Winograd 1972; Johnson-Laird 1977; and Fodor 1987. A few maintain the same for the everyday propositional attitudes; see Loar 1988; Devitt 1990.)

A second and perhaps more serious obstacle to the representational view of thinking is that the objects of thought need not be in the environment at all. They may be abstract; one can think about a number, or about an abstruse theological property, and as always they may be entirely unreal. (The same things are true of representations posited by cognitive psychology.) An adequate psychosemantics must deal just as thoroughly with Arthur's illiterate belief that the number of the Fates was six, and with a visual system's hallucinatory detection of an edge that isn't really there, as much as with a real person's seeing and wanting to eat a muffin that is right in front of her.

In view of the foregoing troubles and for other reasons as well, other philosophers have declined to ascribe intentionality to particular states of subjects, and they insist that ascriptions of commonsense intentional attitudes, at least, are not about inner states at all, much less about internal causes of behavior. Some such theories maintain just that the attitudes are states, presumably physical states, of a whole person (Strawson 1959; McDowell 1994; Baker 1995; Lewis 1995). Others are overtly instrumentalist: Philosophers influenced by W.V. Quine (1960) or by continental hermeneuticists maintain that what a subject believes or desires is entirely a matter of how that person is interpreted or translated into someone else's preferred idiom for one purpose or another, there being no antecedent or inner fact of the matter. A distinctive version of this view is that of Donald Davidson (1970) and D. C. Dennett (1978, 1987), who hold that intentional ascriptions express nonfactual, normative calculations that help to predict behavior but not in the same way as the positing of inner mechanisms does— in particular, not causally (see INTENTIONAL STANCE). Such views are usually defended epistemologically, by reference to the sorts of evidence we use in ascribing propositional attitudes.

Perhaps suspiciously, the instrumentalist views are not usually extrapolated to the aboutness of perceptual states or of representations posited by cognitive scientists; they are restricted to commonsense beliefs and desires. They do shed the burden of psychosemantics, that is, of explaining how a particular brain state can have a particular content, but they do no better than did the representationalist views in explaining how thoughts can be about abstracta or about nonexistents.

See also INFORMATIONAL SEMANTICS; MENTAL CAUSATION; MIND-BODY PROBLEM; PHYSICALISM

—*William Lycan*

References

Baker, L. R. (1995). *Explaining Attitudes*. Cambridge: Cambridge University Press.

Block, N. J. (1986). Advertisement for a semantics for psychology. In P. French, T. E. Uehling, and H. Wettstein, Eds., *Midwest Studies,* vol. 10: *Studies in the Philosophy of Mind.* Minneapolis: University of Minnesota Press, pp. 615–678.

Chisholm, R. M. (1958). Sentences about believing. In H. Feigl, M. Scriven, and G. Maxell, Eds., *Minnesota Studies in the Philosophy of Science,* vol. 2. Minneapolis: University of Minnesota Press, pp. 510–520.

Davidson, D. (1970). Mental events. In L. Foster and J. W. Swanson, Eds., *Experience and Theory.* Amherst: University of Massachusetts Press, pp. 79–101.

Dennett, D. C. (1978). *Brainstorms.* Montgomery, VT: Bradford Books.

Dennett, D. C. (1987). *The Intentional Stance.* Cambridge, MA: Bradford Books/MIT Press.

Devitt, M. (1981). *Designation.* New York: Columbia University Press.

Devitt, M. (1990). A narrow representational theory of the mind. In W. G. Lycan, Ed., *Mind and Cognition.* Oxford: Blackwell, pp. 371–398.

Dretske, F. (1988). *Explaining Behavior.* Cambridge, MA: Bradford Books/MIT Press.

Fodor, J. A. (1975). *The Language of Thought.* Hassocks, England: Harvester Press.

Fodor, J. A. (1981). *RePresentations.* Cambridge, MA: Bradford Books/MIT Press.

Fodor, J. A. (1987). *Psychosemantics.* Cambridge, MA: Bradford Books/MIT Press.

Fodor, J. A. (1990). *A Theory of Content and Other Essays.* Cambridge, MA: Bradford Books/MIT Press.

Johnson-Laird, P. (1977). Procedural semantics. *Cognition* 5: 189–214.

Lewis, D. (1995). Lewis, David: reduction of mind. In S. Guttenplan, Ed., *A Companion to the Philosophy of Mind.* Oxford: Blackwell, pp. 412–431.

Loar, B. (1988). Social content and psychological content. In R. Grimm and D. Merrill, Eds., *Contents of Thought.* Tucson: University of Arizona Press, pp. 99–110.

McDowell, J. (1994). *Mind and World.* Cambridge, MA: Harvard University Press.

Millikan, R. G. (1984). *Language, Thought, and Other Biological Categories.* Cambridge, MA: MIT Press/Bradford Books.

Putnam, H. (1975). The meaning of "meaning." In K. Gunderson, Ed., *Minnesota Studies in the Philosophy of Science,* vol. 7: *Language, Mind and Knowledge.* Minneapolis: University of Minnesota Press.

Quine, W. V. (1960). *Word and Object.* Cambridge, MA: MIT Press.

Searle, J. R. (1983). *Intentionality.* Cambridge: Cambridge University Press.

Sellars, W. (1963). *Science, Perception, and Reality.* London: Routledge and Kegan Paul.

Strawson, P. F. (1959). *Individuals.* London: Methuen and Co.

Winograd, T. (1972). *Understanding Natural Language.* New York: Academic Press.

Further Readings

Chisholm, R. M. (1967). Intentionality. In P. Edwards, Ed., *Encyclopedia of Philosophy.* London: Macmillan.

Lycan, W. G. (1988). *Judgement and Justification, Part 1.* Cambridge: Cambridge University Press.

Perry, J. (1995). Intentionality (2). In S. Guttenplan, Ed., *A Companion to the Philosophy of Mind.* Oxford: Blackwell, pp. 386–395.

Searle, J. (1995). Intentionality (1). In S. Guttenplan, Ed., *A Companion to the Philosophy of Mind.* Oxford: Blackwell, pp. 379–386.

Sterelny, K. (1990). *The Representational Theory of Mind: An Introduction.* Oxford: Blackwell.

Internalism

See INDIVIDUALISM

Interpretation

See DISCOURSE; PRAGMATICS; RADICAL INTERPRETATION; SENTENCE PROCESSING

Intersubjectivity

Intersubjectivity is the process in which mental activity— including conscious awareness, motives and intentions, cognitions, and emotions—is transferred between minds. ANIMAL COMMUNICATION and cooperative social life require intersubjective signaling (Marler, Evans, and Hauser 1992). Individuals must perceive and selectively respond to the motives, interests, and emotions behind perceived movement in bodies of other animals, especially in conspecifics. Such communication has attained a new level of complexity in human communities, with their consciousness of collectively discovered cultural meanings.

Human intersubjectivity manifests itself as an immediate sympathetic awareness of feelings and conscious, purposeful intelligence in others. It is transmitted by body movements (especially of face, vocal tract, and hands) that are adapted to give instantaneous visual, auditory, or tactile information about purposes, interests, and emotions and symbolic ideas active in subjects' minds. On it depends cultural learning, and the creation of a "social reality," of conventional beliefs, languages, rituals, and technologies. Education of children is rooted in preverbal, mimetic intersubjectivity. Human linguistic dialogue also rests on intersubjective awareness, as do the phenomena of "self-awareness" in society. A psychology of intersubjectivity concerns itself with analysis of this innate capacity for intimate and efficient intermental coupling, and attempts to assess what must be learned, through imitation or instruction, to advance intelligent cooperation.

Research on communication with infants and young children proves the existence in the developing human brain of emotional and cognitive regulators for companionship in thought and purposeful action (Aitken and Trevarthen 1997). The theory of innate intersubjectivity (Trevarthen 1998), like the theory of the virtual other (Braten 1988), invites new concepts of language and thinking, as well as of music and all temporal arts, and it requires deep examination of cognitive processing models of CONSCIOUSNESS.

Infants demonstrate that they perceive persons as essentially different "objects" from anything nonliving and nonhuman (Legerstee 1992; Trevarthen 1998). They are acutely sensitive to time patterns in human movement (manifestations of TIME IN THE MIND), and can react in synchrony, or with complementary "attunement" of motives and feelings (Stern 1985, 1993; Trevarthen, Kokkinaki, and Fiamenghi 1998). Dynamic forms of vocal, facial, and gestural emotional expression are recognized and employed in interactions with other persons from birth, before intentional use of objects is effective. Scientific research into the earliest orientations, preferences, and intentional actions of newborns when they encounter evidence of a person, and their capacities for IMITATION, prove that the newborn human is ready for, and needs, mutually regulated intersubjective transactions (Kugiumutzakis 1998). Infants do not acquire intersubjective powers in "pseudo dialogues" by being treated "as if" they wish to express intentions, thoughts, and feelings (Kaye 1982), but they do find satisfying communication only with partners who accept that they have such powers, because such acceptance releases intuitive patterns of "parenting" behavior that infants can be aware of, and with which they can enter into dialogue (Papoušek and Papoušek 1987). Infants' emotional well-being depends on a mutual regulation of consciousness with affectionate companions (Tronick and Weinberg 1997). Events in the infant-adult "dynamic system" (Fogel and Thelen 1987) are constrained by intrinsic human psychological motives on both sides (Aitken and Trevarthen 1997). These intrinsic constraints are psychogenic adaptations for cultural learning.

Human knowledge begins in exchange and combination of purposes between the young child and more experienced companions—in "joint attention" (Tomasello 1988). A "primary intersubjectivity" is active, in "protoconversational" play, soon after birth (Bateson 1975; Trevarthen 1979), and this develops by the end of the first year into "secondary intersubjectivity"—sympathetic intention toward shared

environmental AFFORDANCES and objects of purposeful action (Trevarthen and Hubley 1978). Before they possess any verbalizable THEORY OF MIND, children share purposes and their consequences through direct other-awareness of persons' interests and moods (Reddy et al. 1997). Acquired beliefs and concepts of a young child are redescriptions of narrativelike patterns of intention and consciousness that can be shared, without verbal or rational analysis, in a familiar "common sense" world. Narrative expression by rhythmic posturing and gesturing with prosodic or melodic vocalisation, or "mimesis," may have been a step in the prelinguistic evolution of hominid communication and cognition (Donald 1991). Pretense and socially demonstrated METACOGNITION is natural in infant play, and imitation of pretend actions and attitudes is essential in the development of imaginative representational play in toddlers of modern *Homo sapiens*.

Language and other symbolic conventions enrich intersubjectivity, generating and storing limitless common meaning and strategies of thought, but they do not constitute the basis for interpersonal awareness. Rather, as Wittgenstein perceived, the reverse is the case—all language develops from experience negotiated, with emotion, in intersubjectivity, whatever innate predispositions there may be to acquire language qua language (see PRAGMATICS). The acquisition of syntax is derived from expressive sequences that are perceived as emotional narratives in game rituals (Bruner 1983). Word meaning is acquired by imitation in narrative exchanges modulated by dynamic affects and expressions of interest, intention, and feeling deployed by the child and companions in a familiar, common world (Locke 1993; see WORD MEANING, ACQUISITION OF).

Intersubjective sympathy is shown when persons synchronize or alternate their motor impulses, demonstrating "resonance" of motives that have matching temporospatial dimensions (rhythms and morphology or "embodiment") in all individuals, and that, consequently, can be perceived by one to forecast the other's acts and their perceptual consequences (Trevarthen 1998). Psychophysical and physiological research proves that cognitive processes of perceptual information uptake, thoughts, and memories are organized by intrinsically generated "motor images" or "dynamic forms" (Jeannerod 1994). The same motor forms are demonstrated in communication. The discovery of "mirror neurons" in the ventral premotor cortex of monkeys, which discharge both when the monkey grasps or manipulates something and when the human experimenter makes similar manipulations, indicates how "self" and "other," or observer and actor, can be matched, and it helps explain how the essential intersubjective neural mechanisms of communication by language may have evolved (Rizzolatti and Arbib 1998). Conscious monitoring of intersubjective motives is asymmetric; in normal circumstances we are more aware of others' feelings and intentions than of our own inner states. However, we do not have to be in the presence of others to have them in mind. As Adam Smith explained, the moral sense, built around representations of an innate sympathy, takes the form of an "other-awareness" or "conscience." In his words, "When I endeavour to examine my own conduct, I divide myself, as it were, into two persons. The first is the spectator . . . the second is the agent, the person whom I properly call myself, and of whose conduct, under the character of the spectator, I was endeavouring to form an opinion." (Smith 1759: 113, 6).

The aptitude of human minds for imitation does not mean, as social learning theory asserts, that a SELF-KNOWLEDGE is possible only as a result of learning how others see us, and how to talk about oneself. Impulses of purpose and interest, with the emotions that evaluate their prospects and urgency, have, as motives, similar status for the self as for others, and independently of culture. This consequence of immediate, innate intersubjective sympathy is overlooked by empiricists, including theorists of ECOLOGICAL PSYCHOLOGY, in their accounts of how perceptual information is taken up by behaving subjects, individually. There is a historical reason for the idea of the separate self.

The Western philosophical tradition (exemplified by RENÉ DESCARTES and IMMANUEL KANT) generally assumes that human minds are inherently separate in their purposes and experiences, seeking rational clarity, autonomous skills, and self-betterment. Subjects take in information for consciousness of reality or truth, become aware of other people as objects that have particular properties and affordances. They construct an awareness of the SELF in society, but remain single subjectivities. Interpersonal life and collective understanding result from individuals communicating thoughts in language, the grammar of which is derived from innate rational processes. The rational individual has both self-serving emotions and instinctive "biological" reactions to others, which must be regulated by conventional rules of socially acceptable behavior. With good management of education and social government, individuals learn how to negotiate with social partners and converge in awareness of transcendental universals in their individual consciousness and purposes, to their mutual benefit. We will call this view of intelligent and civilized cooperation as an artificial acquisition the "extrinsic intersubjectivity" or "subjective first" position. Psychology and cognitive science analyze awareness, thinking, learning, and skill in action from this position, which must find immediate intersubjectivity difficult to explain.

A different conception of human consciousness, exhibiting affinity with some philosophies of religious experience, perceives interpersonal awareness, cooperative action in society, and cultural learning as manifestations of innate motives for sympathy in purposes, interests, and feelings—that is, that a human mind is equipped with needs for dialogic, intermental engagement with other similar minds (Jopling 1993). Notions of moral obligation are conceived as fundamental to the growth of consciousness of meaning in every human being. Language is neither just a learned skill, nor the product of an instinct for generating grammatical structures to model subjective agency and to categorize awareness of objects. It emerges as an extension of the natural growth of a sympathy in purposes and experiences that is already clearly demonstrated in the mimetic narratives of an infant's play in reciprocal attention with an affectionate companion. We will call this view of how human cooperative awareness arises the "intrinsic intersubjectivity" or "intersubjective first" position.

Psychoanalysis, though interested in rational representations of self and others by introjection and projection, or transference and countertransference, seeks intersubjective explanations for psychopathology, and for the relation of disorders in child development to the acquisition of an emotionally communicated self-awareness (Stern 1985). Theories of childhood AUTISM, a challenging but highly instructive pathology, necessarily confront hypotheses concerning how engagement with mind states is normally possible between individuals from infancy (Hobson 1993).

As the political offspring of the subjective first position, individualism sees a society as animated by stressful encounters between competitors who survive and prosper by Machiavellian deceit. Positive relationships or attachments merely serve to build alliances that increase chances of success for their members in competition with the rest of the group. Like the misnamed "social Darwinism," SOCIOBIOLOGY is founded on the tacit belief that there is no natural ALTRUISM, no capacity to link purposes for collective goals that are valued because they are products of intuitive sympathy and cooperative awareness. Closer study of animal behaviors shows contrary evidence (De Waal 1996). The evidence that infants learn by emotional referencing to evaluate experiences through attunement with motives of familiar companions, for whom they have, and from whom they receive, affectionate regard, proves that it is the sense of individuality in society that is the derived state of mind, developed in contrast to more fundamental intersubjective needs and obligations.

—*Colwyn Trevarthen*

References

Aitken, K. J., and C. Trevarthen. (1997). Self-other organization in human psychological development. *Development and Psychopathology* 9: 651–675.

Bateson, M. C. (1975). Mother-infant exchanges: the epigenesis of conversational interaction. In D. Aaronson and R. W. Rieber, Eds., *Developmental Psycholinguistics and Communication Disorders (Annals of the New York Academy of Sciences,* vol. 263. New York: New York Academy of Sciences, pp. 101–113.

Bråten, S. (1988). Dialogic mind: the infant and adult in protoconversation. In M. Cavallo, Ed., *Nature, Cognition and System.* Dordrecht: Kluwer Academic, pp. 187–205.

Bruner, J. S. (1983). *Child's Talk: Learning to Use Language.* New York: Norton.

De Waal, F. (1996). *Good Natured: The Origins of Right and Wrong in Human and Other Animals.* Cambridge, MA: Harvard University Press.

Donald, M. (1991). *Origins of the Modern Mind.* Cambridge and London: Harvard University Press.

Fogel, A., and E. Thelen. (1987). Development of early expressive action from a dynamic systems approach. *Developmental Psychology* 23: 747–761.

Hobson, P. (1993). *Autism and the Development of Mind.* Hillsdale, NJ: Erlbaum.

Jeannerod, M. (1994). The representing brain: Neural correlates of motor intention and imagery. *Behavioral and Brain Sciences* 17: 187–245.

Jopling, D. (1993). Cognitive science, other minds, and the philosophy of dialogue. In U. Neisser, Ed., *The Perceived Self:*

Ecological and Interpersonal Sources of Self-Knowledge. New York: Cambridge University Press, pp. 290–309.

Kaye, K. (1982). *The Mental and Social Life of Babies.* Chicago: University of Chicago Press.

Kugiumutzakis, G. (1998). Neonatal imitation in the intersubjective companion space. In S. Bråten, Ed., *Intersubjective Communication and Emotion in Early Ontogeny.* Cambridge: Cambridge University Press.

Legerstee, M. (1992). A review of the animate-inanimate distinction in infancy: Implications for models of social and cognitive knowing. *Early Development and Parenting* 1: 59–67.

Locke, J. L. (1993). *The Child's Path to Spoken Language.* Cambridge, MA: Harvard University Press.

Marler, P., C. S. Evans, and M. C. Hauser. (1992). Animal signals: motivational, referential or both? In H. Papoušek, U. Jurgens, and M. Papoušek, Eds., *Nonverbal Vocal Communication: Comparative and Developmental Aspects.* Cambridge: Cambridge University Press, pp. 66–86.

Papoušek, H., and M. Papoušek. (1987). Intuitive parenting: a dialectic counterpart to the infant's integrative competence. In J. D. Osofsky, Ed., *Handbook of Infant Development.* 2nd ed. New York: Wiley, pp. 669–720.

Reddy, V., D. Hay, L. Murray, and C. Trevarthen. (1997) Communication in infancy: mutual regulation of affect and attention. In G. Bremner, A. Slater, and G. Butterworth, Eds., *Infant Development: Recent Advances.* Hillsdale, NJ: Erlbaum, pp. 247–273.

Rizzolatti, A., and M. A. Arbib. (1998). Language within our grasp. *Trends in the Neurosciences* 21: 188–194.

Smith, A. (1759). *Theory of Moral Sentiments.* Edinburgh. Modern edition: D. D. Raphael and A. L. Macfie, Gen. Eds., Glasgow Edition. Oxford: Clarendon, 1976. Reprint, Indianapolis: Liberty Fund, 1984.

Stern, D. N. (1985). *The Interpersonal World of the Infant: A View from Psychoanalysis and Developmental Psychology.* New York: Basic Books.

Stern, D. N. (1993). The role of feelings for an interpersonal self. In U. Neisser, Ed., *The Perceived Self: Ecological and Interpersonal Sources of Self-Knowledge.* New York: Cambridge University Press, pp. 205–215.

Tomasello, M. (1988). The role of joint attentional processes in early language development. *Language Sciences* 10: 69–88.

Trevarthen, C. (1979). Communication and cooperation in early infancy. A description of primary intersubjectivity. In M. Bullowa, Ed., *Before Speech: The Beginning of Human Communication.* London: Cambridge University Press, pp. 321–347.

Trevarthen, C. (1998). The concept and foundations of infant intersubjectivity. In S. Bråten, Ed., *Intersubjective Communication and Emotion in Early Ontogeny.* Cambridge: Cambridge University Press, pp. 15–46.

Trevarthen, C., and P. Hubley. (1978). Secondary intersubjectivity: confidence, confiding and acts of meaning in the first year. In A. Lock, Ed., *Action, Gesture and Symbol.* London: Academic Press, pp. 183–229.

Trevarthen, C., T. Kokkinaki, and G. A. Fiamenghi Jr. (1998). What infants' imitations communicate: With mothers, with fathers and with peers. In J. Nadel and G. Butterworth, Eds., *Imitation in Infancy.* Cambridge: Cambridge University Press.

Tronick, E. Z., and M. K. Weinberg. (1997). Depressed mothers and infants: failure to form dyadic states of consciousness. In L. Murray and P. J. Cooper, Eds., *Postpartum Depression and Child Development.* New York: Guilford Press, pp. 54–81.

Further Readings

Bakhtine, M. M. (1981). *The Dialogic Imagination.* Austin: University of Texas Press.

Barnes, B. (1995). *The Elements of Social Theory.* London: UCL Press.

Beebe, B., J. Jaffe, S. Feldstein, K. Mays, and D. Alson. (1985). Inter-personal timing: the application of an adult dialogue model to mother-infant vocal and kinesic interactions. In F. M. Field and N. A. Fox, Eds., *Social Perception in Infants.* Norwood, NJ: Ablex, 217–248.

Bretherton, I., S. McNew, and M. Beeghley-Smith. (1981). Early person knowledge as expressed in gestural and verbal communication: when do infants acquire "theory of mind"? In M. E. Lamb and L. R. Sherrod, Eds., *Infant Social Cognition.* Hillsdale, NJ: Erlbaum.

Bruner, J. S. (1996). *The Culture of Education.* Cambridge, MA: Harvard University Press.

Donaldson, M. (1978). *Children's Minds.* Glasgow: Fontana/Collins.

Halliday, M. A. K. (1975). *Learning How to Mean: Explorations in the Development of Language.* London: Edward Arnold.

Hondereich, T., Ed. (1995). *The Oxford Companion to Philosophy.* Oxford and New York: Oxford University Press.

Leslie, A. (1987). Pretense and representation: the origins of "theory of mind." *Psychological Review* 94: 412–426.

Meltzoff, A. N. (1985). The roots of social and cognitive development: models of man's original nature. In T. M. Field and N. A. Fox, Eds., *Social Perception in Infants.* Norwood, NJ: Ablex, pp. 1–30.

Nadel, J., and A. Pezé. (1993). Immediate imitation as a basis for primary communication in toddlers and autistic children. In J. Nadel and L. Camioni, Eds., *New Perspectives in Early Communicative Development.* London: Routledge, 139–156.

Neisser, U. (1993). The self perceived. In U. Neisser, Ed., *The Perceived Self: Ecological and Interpersonal Sources of Self-Knowledge.* New York: Cambridge University Press, pp. 3–21.

Rogoff, B. (1990). *Apprenticeship in Thinking: Cognitive Development in Social Context.* New York: Oxford University Press.

Ryan, J. (1974). Early language development: towards a communicational analysis. In M. P. M. Richards, Ed., *The Integration of a Child into a Social World.* London: Cambridge University Press, pp. 185–213.

Schore, A. (1994). *Affect Regulation and the Origin of the Self: The Neurobiology of Emotional Development.* Hillsdale, NJ: Erlbaum.

Searle, J. R. (1995). *The Construction of Social Reality.* New York: Simon and Schuster.

Sluga, H. (1996). Ludwig Wittgenstein: life and work. An introduction. In H. Sluga and D. G. Stern, Eds., *The Cambridge Companion to Wittgenstein.* Cambridge: Cambridge University Press.

Tomasello, M., A. C. Kruger, and H. H. Ratner. (1993). Cultural learning. *Behavioral and Brain Sciences* 16(3): 495–552.

Trehub, S. E., L. J. Trainor, and A. M. Unyk. (1993). Music and speech processing in the first year of life. *Advances in Child Development and Behaviour* 24: 1–35.

Trevarthen, C. (1980). The foundations of intersubjectivity: development of interpersonal and cooperative understanding of infants. In D. Olson, Ed., *The Social Foundations of Language and Thought: Essays in Honor of J. S. Bruner.* New York: W. W. Norton, pp. 316–342.

Trevarthen, C. (1986). Development of intersubjective motor control in infants. In M. G. Wade and H. T. A. Whiting, Eds., *Motor Development in Children: Aspects of Coordination and Control.* Dordrecht: Martinus Nijhof, pp. 209–261.

Trevarthen, C. (1993). The self born in intersubjectivity: the psychology of an infant communicating. In U. Neisser, Ed., *The Perceived Self: Ecological and Interpersonal Sources of Self-Knowledge.* New York: Cambridge University Press, pp. 121–173.

Trevarthen, C. (1994). Infant semiosis. In W. Noth, Ed., *Origins of Semiosis*. Berlin: Mouton de Gruyter, pp. 219–252.

Trevarthen, C. (1995). Contracts of mutual understanding: negotiating meaning and moral sentiments with infants. In P. Wohlmuth, Ed., *The Crisis of Text: Issues in the Constitution of Authority*. San Diego: University of San Diego School of Law, Journal of Contemporary Legal Issues, Spring 1995, vol. 6: 373–407.

Intonation

See PROSODY AND INTONATION; PROSODY AND INTONATION, PROCESSING ISSUES

Introspection

Introspection is a process by which people come to be attentively conscious of mental states they are currently in. This focused CONSCIOUSNESS of one's concurrent mental states is distinct from the relatively casual, fleeting, diffuse way we are ordinarily conscious of many of our mental states. "Introspection" is occasionally applied to both ways of being conscious of one's mental states (e.g., Armstrong 1968/1993), but is most often used, as in what follows, for the attentive way only.

Introspection involves both the mental states introspected and some mental representation of those very states (as suggested by the etymology, from the Latin *spicere* "look" and *intra* "within"; looking involves mental representations of what is seen). Because it involves higher-order mental representations of introspected states, introspection is a kind of conscious METAREPRESENTATION or METACOGNITION.

WILHELM WUNDT (1911/1912) held that introspection provides an experimental method for psychology, and relied on it in setting up, in 1879 in Leipzig, the first experimental psychology laboratory. Some challenged this introspectionist method, following Auguste Comte's (1830–42) denial that a single mind can be both the agent and object of introspection. This, Comte had held, would divide attention between the act and object of introspecting, which he thought impossible. These concerns led WILLIAM JAMES (1890) and others to propound instead a method of immediate retrospection.

Introspectionist psychology foundered mainly not for these reasons, but because results from different introspectionist laboratories frequently conflicted. Still, experimental procedures in psychology continue to rely on subjects' access to their current mental states, though the theoretical warrant for this reliance is seldom discussed.

The phenomenological movement in philosophy, pioneered by Wundt's contemporary Edmund Husserl (1913/1980), held that introspection, by "bracketing" consciousness from its object, enables us to describe and analyze consciousness, and thereby solve many traditional philosophical problems. This methodology encountered difficulties similar to those that faced introspectionist psychology.

Some have questioned whether higher-order mental representations of concurrent mental states ever actually occur

and hence whether introspection, properly so-called, exists. According to Gilbert Ryle (1949) and William Lyons (1986), what we loosely describe as attending to current perceptions is really just perceiving in an attentive manner. But perceiving attentively itself sometimes involves attending to the perceiving, as when one is explicitly aware of visually concentrating on something. Moreover, when we report what mental states we are in, those reports express higher-order mental representations of the states we report; Ryle's denial that remarks such as "I am in pain" are literally about one's mental states is groundless.

It is often held that introspection involves some "inner sense" by which we perceive our own mental states. The seemingly spontaneous and unmediated character of perceiving generally would then explain why introspection itself seems spontaneous and immediate. This model could, in addition, appeal to mechanisms of perceptual attention to explain how we come to focus attentively on our concurrent mental states.

But introspection cannot be a form of perceiving. Perception invariably involves sensory qualities, and no qualities ever occur in introspection other than those of the sensations and perceptions we introspect; the introspecting itself produces no additional qualities. Moreover, speech acts generally express not perceptions, but thoughts and other intentional states (see INTENTIONALITY). So introspective reports express intentional states about the mental states we introspect, and introspective representations of concurrent mental states involve assertive intentional states, or thoughts. Introspection is deliberate and attentive because these higher-order intentional states are themselves attentive and deliberate. And our introspecting seems spontaneous and unmediated presumably because we remain unaware of any mental processes that might lead to these higher-order intentional states. Introspection consists in conscious, attentively focused, higher-order thoughts about our concurrent mental states.

Despite Comte's claim that attention cannot be divided, people can with a little effort attend to more than one thing. And attentive consciousness of concurrent mental states could in any case occur whenever the target mental state was not itself an attentive state.

A related concern is that attending to concurrent mental states may distort their character. But it is unclear why that should happen, inasmuch as attention does not generally alter the properties of its object. Introspection itself cannot show that distortion occurs, because even if it seems to, that appearance might be due not to the distorting effect of introspection, but to introspection's making us aware of more of a state's properties or of a different range of properties. Similarly for the idea that introspective attention might actually bring the introspected state into existence (Hill 1991: chap. 5). That may well happen, but it may instead be that, when that seems to happen, introspection simply makes one newly aware of a state that already existed.

Work by John H. Flavell (1993) has raised doubt about whether children five and younger have introspective access to their mental states. Four- and five-year-olds describe themselves and others as thinking, feeling, and experiencing. But they also describe people while awake as going for significant periods without thinking or feeling anything whatever. Doubtless these children themselves have, when awake, normal streams of consciousness. But they seem not to think of themselves in that way and, hence, not to introspect their streams of consciousness. Flavell also reports that these children determine what people attend to and think about solely on the basis of behavioral cues and environmental stimulation. So perhaps their inability to introspect results from their simply not conceiving of thoughts and experiences as states that are sometimes conscious (see THEORY OF MIND).

Some have held that introspective access to one's mental states cannot be erroneous or, at least, that it overrides all other evidence (see SELF-KNOWLEDGE). RENÉ DESCARTES (1641/1984) famously noted that one cannot, when thinking, doubt that one is thinking. But this hardly shows that when one is thinking one always knows one is, much less that one is invariably right about which thoughts one has. In a similar spirit, Sydney Shoemaker (1996) has urged that when one has a belief one always knows one does, because a rational person's believing something itself involves cognitive dispositions that constitute that person's knowing about the belief. But the relevant rationality often fails to accompany our beliefs and other first-order mental states.

Indeed, psychological research reveals many such lapses of rationality. In addition to the misrepresentations of one's own mental states discovered by SIGMUND FREUD, other work (e.g., Nisbett and Wilson 1977) shows that introspective judgments frequently result from confabulation. People literally invent mental states to explain their own behavior in ways that are expected or acceptable. Daniel Dennett (1991) in effect seeks to generalize this finding by arguing that all introspective reports can be treated as reports of useful fictions.

Introspection not only misrepresents our mental states, but it also fails to reveal many concurrent states, both in ordinary and exotic situations (see BLINDSIGHT and IMPLICIT VS. EXPLICIT MEMORY). And it is likely that introspection seldom if ever reveals all the mental properties of target states. Many, moreover, would endorse KARL LASHLEY's (1958) dictum that introspection never makes mental processes accessible, only their results. At best, introspection is one tool among many for learning about the mind.

See also ATTENTION; INTERSUBJECTIVITY; SELF

—*David M. Rosenthal*

References

Armstrong, D. M. (1968/1993). *A Materialist Theory of the Mind.* New York: Humanities Press. Rev. ed., London: Routledge and Kegan Paul.

Comte, A. (1830–42). *Cours de Philosophie Positive.* 6 vols. Paris: Bachelier.

Dennett, D. (1991). *Consciousness Explained.* Boston: Little, Brown.

Descartes, R. (1641/1984). Meditations on first philosophy. In *The Philosophical Writings of Descartes,* vol. 2. Trans. J. Cottingham, R. Stoothoff, and D. Murdoch. Cambridge: Cambridge University Press.

Flavell, J. H. (1993). Young children's understanding of thinking and consciousness. *Current Directions in Psychological Science* 2(2): 40–43.

Hill, C. S. (1991). *Sensations: A Defense of Type Materialism.* Cambridge: Cambridge University Press.

Husserl, E. (1913/1980). *Ideas Pertaining to a Pure Phenomenology and to a Phenomenological Philosophy,* vol. 1. Trans. T. E. Klein and W. E. Pohl. The Hague and Boston: M. Nijhoff.

James, W. (1890). *The Principles of Psychology.* 2 vols. New York: Henry Holt.

Lashley, K. S. (1958). Cerebral organization and behavior. In H. C. Solomon, S. Cobb, and W. Penfield, Eds., *The Brain and Human Behavior,* vol. 36. Association for Research in Nervous and Mental Diseases, Research Publications. Baltimore: Williams and Wilkins, pp. 1–18.

Lyons, W. (1986). *The Disappearance of Introspection.* Cambridge, MA: MIT Press/Bradford Books.

Nisbett, R. E., and T. DeCamp Wilson. (1977). Telling more than we can know: verbal reports on mental processes. *Psychological Review* 84 (3): 231–259.

Ryle, G. (1949). *The Concept of Mind.* London: Hutchinson.

Shoemaker, S. (1996). *The First-Person Perspective and Other Essays.* Cambridge: Cambridge University Press.

Wundt, W. (1911/1912). *An Introduction to Psychology.* Trans. Rudolf Pintner. London: George Allen and Unwin.

Further Readings

Brentano, F. (1874/1973). *Psychology from an Empirical Standpoint.* O. Kraus, Ed., L. L. McAlister, Eng. ed. Trans. A. C. Rancurello, D. B. Terrell, and L. L. McAlister. London: Routledge and Kegan Paul.

Broad, C. D. (1925). *The Mind and Its Place in Nature.* London: Routledge and Kegan Paul.

Burge, T. (1988). Individualism and self-knowledge. *The Journal of Philosophy* 85 (11): 649–663.

Cassam, Q. (1995). Introspection and bodily self-ascription. In J. Luis Bermudez, A. Marcel, and N. Eilan, Eds., *The Body and the Self.* Cambridge, MA: MIT Press/Bradford Books.

Churchland, P. M. (1985). Reduction, qualia, and the direct introspection of brain states. *The Journal of Philosophy* 82 (1): 8–28.

Dretske, F. (1994/95). Introspection. *Proceedings of the Aristotelian Society* CXV: 263–278.

Goldman, A. I. (1993). The psychology of folk psychology. *The Behavioral and Brain Sciences* 16(1): 15–28. Open peer commentary, 29–90; author's response: Functionalism, the theory-theory and phenomenology, 101–113.

Gopnik, A. (1993). How do we know our minds: the illusion of first-person knowledge of intentionality. *The Behavioral and Brain Sciences* 16(1): 1–14. Open peer commentary, 29–90; author's response: Theories and illusion, 90–100.

Locke, J. (1700/1975). *Essay Concerning Human Understanding.* Nidditch, P. H., Ed. Oxford: Oxford University Press.

Lycan, W. (1996). *Consciousness and Experience.* Cambridge, MA: MIT Press/Bradford Books.

Metcalfe, J., and A. P. Shimamura, Eds. (1994). *Metacognition: Knowing About Knowing.* Cambridge, MA: MIT Press/Bradford Books.

Nelson, T. O., Ed. (1992). *Metacognition: Core Readings.* Boston: Allyn and Bacon.

Nelson, T. O. (1996). Consciousness and metacognition. *American Psychologist* 51(2): 102–116.

Rosenthal, D. M. (1997). A theory of consciousness. In N. Block, O. Flanagan, and G. Güzeldere, Eds., *The Nature of Consciousness: Philosophical Debates.* Cambridge, MA: MIT Press, pp. 729–753.

Rosenthal, D. M. (Forthcoming). Consciousness and metacognition. In D. Sperber, Ed., *Metarepresentation: Proceedings of the Tenth Vancouver Cognitive Science Conference*. New York: Oxford University Press.

Titchener, E. B. (1909). *A Text-Book of Psychology*. New York: Macmillan.

Uleman, J. S., and J. A. Bargh, Eds. (1989). *Unintended Thought*. New York: Guilford Press.

Weinert, F. E., and R. H. Kluwe, Eds. (1987). *Metacognition, Motivation, and Understanding*. Hillsdale, NJ: Erlbaum.

Weiskrantz, L. (1997). *Consciousness Lost and Found: A Neuropsychological Exploration*. Oxford: Oxford University Press.

White, P. A. (1988). Knowing more than we can tell: "introspective access" and causal report accuracy 10 years later. *British Journal of Psychology* 79(1): 13–45.

Wilson, T. D., S. D. Hodges, and S. J. LaFleur. (1995). Effects of introspecting about reasons: inferring attitudes from accessible thoughts. *Journal of Personality and Social Psychology* 69: 16–28.

Intuitive Biology

See FOLK BIOLOGY

Intuitive Mathematics

See NAIVE MATHEMATICS

Intuitive Physics

See NAIVE PHYSICS

Intuitive Psychology

See FOLK PSYCHOLOGY

Intuitive Sociology

See NAIVE SOCIOLOGY

ILP

See INDUCTIVE LOGIC PROGRAMMING

Jakobson, Roman

Roman Jakobson (1896–1982), one of the foremost students of linguistics, literature, and culture of the twentieth century, was born and educated in Moscow. In 1920 he moved to Czechoslovakia, where he remained until the Nazi occupation in 1939. During 1939–1941 Jakobson was in Scandinavia, and in 1941 he emigrated to the United States, where he served on the faculties of Columbia University (1946–1949), Harvard (1949–1966), and MIT (1958–1982).

The eight published volumes of Jakobson's *Selected Writings* reflect the impressive breadth and variety of his contributions. These include, in addition to linguistics proper, discussions of the foundations of literary theory; research into formal devices of literature, including pioneering inquiries into the principles governing meter in poetry; analyses of poetic texts in many languages; philological investigations into literary monuments; studies of Slavic folklore and comparative mythology; inquiries into the cultural history of the Slavs; and some of the finest literary criticism of modern Russian poetry. A bibliography of Jakobson's writing is Jakobson (1990).

Jakobson's chief contribution to linguistics concerns the nature of the speech sounds (phonemes). It has been accepted for well over a century that the phonemes that make up the words in all languages differ fundamentally from other, acoustically similar sounds that humans produce with the lips, tongue and larynx, for example yawns, burps, or coughs. (See, e.g., chap. 5 of Sievers 1901, the standard phonetics text of the time.) It was also understood that the sounds of a given language are not a random collection, but are made up of various intersecting groups of sounds; for example, [p t k] or [p b f v m] or [m n]. What was not understood was the basis on which speech and nonspeech sounds are differentiated, and how, short of listing, phonemes can be assigned to groups. It was Jakobson who proposed an answer to these fundamental questions.

In a 1928 paper written by Jakobson and co-signed by the Russian linguists N. S. Trubetzkoy (1890–1938) and S. Karcevskij (1884–1955), Jakobson proposed that the phonemes of all languages are complexes of a small number of DISTINCTIVE FEATURES such as nasal, labial, voicing, fricative, and so on. Although many features were used by phoneticians, they were viewed as somewhat accidental attributes of sounds. By contrast, for Jakobson the features are the raw material of which the phonemes—and only phonemes—are made. The fact that only phonemes, but no other sounds, are feature complexes differentiates phonemes from the rest, and this fact also explains the grouping of phonemes into intersecting sets, each defined by one or more shared features; for example, [m n] are nasal, [p b f v m] are labial, and [p t k] are voiceless. This conception of phonemes as feature bundles is fundamental to subsequent developments in PHONOLOGY.

In exploring the consequences of this proposal, Jakobson was joined by Trubetzkoy, whose important *Grundzüge der Phonologie* (1939) summarizes many results of these early investigations. Jakobson's own contributions to feature theory are reflected in such papers as Jakobson (1929), where the evolution of the phoneme system of modern Russian is reviewed in light of the feature concept; Jakobson (1939), where it is shown—contra Trubetzkoy (1939)—that such apparently multivalued features as "place of articulation" can be reanalyzed in terms of binary features, and that this makes it possible to analyze both vowels and consonants with the same set of features; Jakobson (1941), where facts of phoneme acquisition by children, phoneme loss in aphasia, phoneme distribution in different languages, and other phonological phenomena are reviewed in feature terms; and Jakobson, Fant, and Halle (1952), where the acoustic correlates of individual features were first described and many consequences of these new facts discussed. Jakobson also made enduring contributions to the phonological study of individual languages, for instance Russian (Jakobson 1948), Slovak (Jakobson 1931), Arabic (Jakobson 1957a), and Gilyak (Jakobson 1957b).

In addition to phonology, Jakobson's major contributions to linguistics were in the area of MORPHOLOGY, the study of the form of words and their minimal syntactic constituents, the morphemes. Among the new ideas in these studies (collected in Jakobson 1984) is Jakobson's attempt to extend the feature analysis to morphemes, which, like its phonological counterpart, has been adopted in subsequent work.

See also BLOOMFIELD, LEONARD; PHONOLOGY, ACQUISITION OF

—*Morris Halle*

References

Jakobson, R. (1929). Remarques sur l'évolution phonologique du russe comparée à celle des autres langues slaves. *SW* 1: 7–116.

Jakobson, R. (1931). Phonemic notes on standard Slovak. *SW* 1: 221–230.

Jakobson, R. (1939). Observations sur le classement phonologique des consonnes. *SW* 1: 272–279.

Jakobson, R. (1941). Kindersprache, Aphasie, und allgemeine Lautgesetze. *SW* 1: 328–401.

Jakobson, R. (1948). Russian conjugation. *SW* 2: 119–129.

Jakobson, R. (1957a). Mufaxxama—the "emphatic" phonemes in Arabic. *SW* 1: 510–522.

Jakobson, R. (1957b). Notes on Gilyak. *SW* 2: 72–97.

Jakobson, R. (1962–88). *Selected Writings.* (SW) 8 vols. Berlin: Mouton de Gruyter.

Jakobson, R. (1984). *Russian and Slavic Grammar.* L. R. Waugh and M. Halle, Eds. Berlin: Mouton de Gruyter.

Jakobson, R. (1990). *A Complete Bibliography of His Writings.* Ed. S. Rudy. Berlin: Mouton de Gruyter.

Jakobson, R., C. G. M. Fant, and M. Halle. (1952). Preliminaries to speech analysis. *SW* 8: 583–660.

Jakobson, R., S. Karcevskij, and N. S. Trubetzkoy. (1928). Quelles sont les méthodes les mieux appropiées à un exposé complet et pratique de la phonologie d'une langue quelconque? *SW* 1: 3–6.

Sievers, E. (1901). *Grundzüge der Phonetik.* 5th ed. Leipzig: Breitkopf und Härtel.

Trubetzkoy, N. S. (1939). Grundzüge der Phonologie. *Travaux du Cercle linguistique de Prague* 7.

James, William

William James (1842–1910) was born in New York City into a cultivated, liberal, financially comfortable and deeply religious middle-class family. It was also a very literary family. His father wrote theological works, his brother Henry became famous as a novelist, and his sister Alice acquired a literary reputation on the posthumous publication of her diaries. As his parents took to traveling extensively in Europe, William James was educated at home and in various parts of Europe by a succession of private tutors and through brief attendance at whatever school was at hand. After an unsuccessful attempt to become a painter in Newport, Rhode Island, James began to study comparative anatomy at the Lawrence Scientific School of Harvard University. After a few years, James moved to the Harvard Medical School, graduating in medicine in 1869.

After teaching anatomy and physiology at Harvard for two years, James began teaching physiological psychology in 1875. In 1879 James gave his first lectures in philosophy at Harvard. As he himself put it, these lectures of his own were the first lectures in philosophy that he had ever heard. In 1884 James helped found the American Society for Psychical Research and, in the following year, was appointed professor of philosophy at Harvard. In 1890, after some twelve years of labor on the project, James published his magnum opus, the two volumes of *The Principles of Psychology.* In that same year, James established the psychological laboratory at Dane Hall in Harvard, one of the first such laboratories to be set up in America. In 1892 James wrote a textbook of psychology for students derived from *The Principles,* entitled *Textbook of Psychology: Briefer Course.*

The next twenty years saw a rapid succession of books: *The Will to Believe, and Other Essays in Popular Philosophy* (1897), *Human Immortality: Two Supposed Objections to the Doctrine* (1898), *Talks to Teachers on Psychology: and to Students on Some of Life's Ideals* (1899), *The Varieties of Religious Experience* (1902—his Gifford lectures at Edinburgh), *Pragmatism* (1907—lectures delivered at the Lowell Institute in Boston and at Columbia University), *A Pluralistic Universe* (1909—his Hibbert lectures at Oxford) and *The Meaning of Truth: A Sequel to Pragmatism* (1909). These unusually accessible books of philosophy and psychology achieved a wide readership and acclaim. After a long period of illness, James died at his summer home in Chocorua, New Hampshire, in 1910.

At his death James left behind an uncompleted work that was published as *Some Problems of Philosophy: A Beginning of an Introduction to Philosophy* (1911). This work was followed by a number of other posthumous volumes, mainly collections of his essays and reviews: *Memories and Studies* (1911), *Essays in Radical Empiricism* (1912), *Selected Papers in Philosophy* (1917) and *Collected Essays and Reviews* (1920). A collection of his letters was published in 1920, and a reconstruction of his 1896 Lowell lectures on "exceptional mental states" was issued in 1982.

James's best known contributions can most readily be understood when seen against the background of the temperament of his thought. One central strand of this temperament was his desire always to emphasize the practical, particular, and concrete over the theoretical, abstract and metaphysical. Thus his doctrine of *pragmatism,* which he shared with Charles Sanders Peirce and John Dewey, was a plea that an abstract concept of modern philosophy, MEANING, was best understood in terms of the practical effects of the words or the concepts embodying it. The *meaning* of a word or concept was only discernible in the practical effects of its employment, and its *meaningfulness* was a function of its success (or failure) in practice.

Most famously, or in some quarters, notoriously, this account of meaning was clearly illustrated by James's account of *truth.* For James there was no "final, complete fact of the matter," no truth with a capital T. Truth was simply a word that we applied to a "work-in-progress belief," that is, a belief which we held and have continued to hold because it enables us to make our way in the world in the long run. A true belief, then, is one that is useful and one that has survived, in Darwinian fashion, the pressures of its environment. Such "truths" are always revisable. As James himself put it, "The true is the name of whatever proves itself to be good in the way of belief, and good, too, for definite, assignable reasons" (*Pragmatism*).

James has sometimes been referred to as the first American phenomenologist, though he himself preferred to call this aspect of his thinking *radical empiricism*. Both these labels have some cash value, because another strand of James's temperament was his evangelical holism in regard to all experiences. By experience, James meant any subject's current stream of consciousness. Such a stream was always experienced as a seamless flux. It alone was what was real for any subject. Any concepts, categories, or distinctions that we might refer to in regard to CONSCIOUSNESS, indeed even to speak of consciousness in the traditional way as inner, subjective, and mental, were, strictly speaking, artificial conceptual matrices that we have placed over the flow of experience for particular pragmatic purposes. Although James's fascination with consciousness has led many to refer to him as a Cartesian or as an introspectionist like WILHELM WUNDT, it is more fruitful to see him in relation to Heraclitus and Henri Bergson.

James's evangelical holism regarding the nature of experience should be coupled with what might be called an evangelical pluralism about its scope. For James believed that all experiences, whether mystical, psychical, or "normal," were of equal value. They were properly to be differentiated only in terms of the purposes for which these experiences had been deployed. So James's lectures on *The Varieties of Religious Experience,* his championing of psychical research, and his interest in "exceptional mental states" associated with cases of multiple personality and other mental illnesses, were in harmony with his radical empiricism.

James connected his radical empiricism with mainstream psychology and physiology by taking as the central task of *The Principles of Psychology* "the empirical correlation of the various sorts of thought or feeling [as known in consciousness] with definite conditions of the brain." In the *Principles* James also connected his radical empiricism with his unyielding advocacy of the freedom of the will by analyzing this freedom as involving the momentary endorsement of a particular thought in our stream of consciousness such that this thought would thereby become the cause of some appropriate behavior.

In the *Principles,* as well as in some other texts, James also made important contributions to the psychology of MEMORY, self-identity, habit, instinct, the subliminal and religious experiences. For example, his distinction between *primary* and *secondary* memory was the precursor of the modern distinction between short-term and long-term memory, and his work on ATTENTION has influenced recent work on the human capacity for dividing attention between two or more tasks. However, the most influential part of the *Principles* has been the theory of emotion that James developed in parallel with the Danish physiologist Carl Lange. As James himself put it, *"bodily changes follow directly the perception of the exciting fact, . . . [so that] our feeling of the same changes as they occur IS the emotion."* That is, an emotional state *is* the feeling in our stream of consciousness of the

behavior and physiological effects that we usually associate with a particular emotion. "Common sense says, we lose our fortune, are sorry and weep. . . . The hypothesis here to be defended says. . . that we feel sorry because we cry."

See also DESCARTES, RENÉ; EMOTIONS; INTROSPECTION; SELF

—William Lyons

References

Bird, G. (1986). *William James.* London: Routledge.

James, W. *The Works of William James.* Cambridge, MA: Harvard University Press.

Myers, G. E. (1986). *William James: His Life and Thought.* New Haven, CT: Yale University Press.

Perry, R. B. (1935). *The Thought and Character of William James,* vols. 1 and 2. Boston: Little, Brown.

Taylor, E. (1982). *William James on Exceptional Mental States.* New York: Charles Scribners Sons.

Judgment Heuristics

People sometimes need to know quantities that they can neither look up nor calculate. Those quantities might include the probability of rain, the size of a crowd, the future price of a stock, or the time needed to complete an assignment. One coping strategy is to use a *heuristic*, or rule of thumb, to produce an approximate answer. That answer might be used directly, as the best estimate of the desired quantity, or adjusted for suspected biases. Insofar as heuristics are, by definition, imperfect rules, it is essential to know how much confidence to place in them.

Heuristics are common practice in many domains. For example, skilled tradespeople have rules for bidding contracts, arbitrageurs have ones for making deals, and operations researchers have ones for predicting the behavior of complex processes. These rules may be more or less explicit; they may be computed on paper or in the head. The errors that they produce are the associated "bias."

Heuristics attained prominence in cognitive psychology through a series of seminal articles by Amos TVERSKY and Daniel Kahneman (1974), then at the Hebrew University of Jerusalem. They observed that judgments under conditions of uncertainty often call for heuristic solutions. The precise answers are unknown or inaccessible. People lack the training needed to compute appropriate estimates. Even those with training may not have the intuitions needed to apply their textbook learning outside of textbook situations.

The first of these articles (Tversky and Kahneman 1971) proposed that people expect future observations of uncertain processes to be much like past ones, even when they have few past observations to rely on. Such people might be said to apply a "law of small numbers," which captures some properties of the statistical "law of large numbers" but is insufficiently sensitive to sample size. The heuristic of expecting past observations to predict future ones is useful but leads to predictable problems, unless one happens to have a large sample. Tversky and Kahneman demonstrated these problems, with quantitative psychologists as subjects. For example, their scientist subjects overestimated the probability that small samples would affirm research hypotheses, leading them to propose study designs with surprisingly low statistical power. Of course, well-trained scientists can calculate the correct value for power analyses. However, to do so, they must realize that their heuristic judgment is faulty. Systematic reviews have found a high rate of published studies with low statistical power, suggesting that practicing scientists often lack this intuition (Cohen 1962).

Kahneman and Tversky (1972) subsequently subsumed this tendency under the more general *representativeness* heuristic. Users of this rule assess the likelihood of an event by how well it captures the salient properties of the process producing it. Although sometimes useful, this heuristic will produce biases whenever features that determine likelihood are insufficiently salient (or when irrelevant features capture people's attention). As a result, predicting the behavior of people relying on representativeness requires both a substantive understanding of how they judge salience and a normative understanding of what features really matter. Bias arises when the two are misaligned, or when people apply appropriate rules ineffectively.

Sample size is one normatively relevant feature that tends to be neglected. A second is the population frequency of a behavior, when making predictions for a specific individual. People feel that the observed properties of the individual (sometimes called "individuating" or "case-specific" information) need to be represented in future events, even when those observations are not that robust (e.g., small sample, unreliable source).

Bias can also arise when normatively relevant features are recognized but misunderstood. Thus, people know that random processes should show variability, but expect too much of it. One familiar expression is the "gambler's fallacy," leading people to expect, say, a "head" coin flip after four tails, but not after four alternations of head-tail. An engaging example is the unwarranted perception that basketball players have a "hot hand," caused by not realizing how often such (unrandom-looking) streaks arise by chance (Gilovich, Vallone, and Tversky 1985). In a sense, representativeness is a metaheuristic, a very general rule from which more specific ones are derived for particular situations. As a result, researchers need to predict how a heuristic will be used in order to generate testable predictions for people's judgments. Where those predictions fail, it may be that the heuristic was not used at all or that it was not used in that particular way.

Two other (meta)heuristics are *availability* and *anchoring and adjustment*. Reliance on availability means judging an event as likely to the extent that one can remember examples or imagine it happening. It can lead one astray when instances of an event are disproportionately (un)available in MEMORY. Reliance on anchoring and adjustment means estimating a quantity by thinking of why it might be larger or smaller than some initial value. Typically, people adjust too little, leaving them unduly "anchored" in that initial value, however arbitrarily it has been selected. Obviously, there are many ways in which examples can be produced, anchors selected, and adjustments made. The better these processes are understood, the sharper the predictions that can be made for heuristic-based judgments.

These seminal papers have produced a large research literature (Kahneman, Slovic, and Tversky 1982). Their influence can be traced to several converging factors (Dawes 1997; Jungermann 1983), including: (1) The initial demonstrations have proven quite robust, facilitating replications in new domains and the exploration of boundary conditions (e.g., Plous 1993). (2) The effects can be described in piquant ways, which present readers and investigators in a flattering light (able to catch others making mistakes). (3) The perspective fits the cognitive revolution's subtext of tracing human failures to unintended side effects of generally adaptive processes. (4) The heuristics operationalize Simon's (1957) notions of BOUNDED RATIONALITY in ways subject to experimental manipulation.

The heuristics-and-biases metaphor also provides an organizing theme for the broader literature on failures of human DECISION MAKING. For example, many studies have found people to be insensitive to the extent of their own knowledge (Keren 1991; Yates 1990). When this trend emerges as overconfidence, one contributor is the tendency to look for reasons supporting favored beliefs (Koriat, Lichtenstein, and Fischhoff 1980). Although that search is a sensible part of hypothesis testing, it can produce bias when done without a complementary sensitivity to disconfirming evidence (Fischhoff and Beyth-Marom 1983). Other studies have examined hindsight bias, the tendency to exaggerate the predictability of past events (or reported facts; Fischhoff 1975). One apparent source of that bias is automatically making sense of new information as it arrives. Such rapid updating should facilitate learning—at the price of obscuring how much has been learned. Underestimating what one had to learn may mean underestimating what one still has to learn, thereby promoting overconfidence.

Scientists working within this tradition have, naturally, worried about the generality of these behavioral patterns. One central concern has been whether laboratory results extend to high-stakes decisions, especially ones with experts working on familiar tasks. Unfortunately, it is not that easy to provide significant positive stakes (or threaten significant losses) or to create appropriate tasks for experts. Those studies that have been conducted suggest that stakes alone do not eliminate bias nor lead people, even experts, to abandon faulty judgments (Camerer 1995).

In addition to experimental evidence, there are anecdotal reports and systematic observations of real-world expert performance showing biases that can be attributed to using heuristics (Gilovich 1991; Mowen 1993). For example, overconfidence has been observed in the confidence assessments of particle physicists, demographers, and economists (Henrion and Fischhoff 1986). A noteworthy exception is weather forecasters, whose assessments of the probability of precipitation are remarkably accurate (e.g., it rains 70 percent of the times that they forecast a 70 percent chance of rain; Murphy and Winkler 1992). These experts make many judgments under conditions conducive to LEARNING: prompt, unambiguous feedback that rewards them for accuracy (rather than, say, for bravado or hedging). Thus, these judgments may be a learnable cognitive skill. That process may involve using conventional heuristics more effectively or acquiring better ones.

Given the applied interests of decision-making researchers, other explorations of the boundary conditions on suboptimal performance have focused on practical procedures for reducing bias. Given the variety of biases and potential interventions, no simple summary can be comprehensive (Kahneman, Slovic, and Tversky 1982; von Winterfeldt and Edwards 1986). One general trend is that merely warning about bias is not very useful. Nor is teaching statistics, unless direct contact can be made with people's intuitions. Making such contact requires an understanding of natural thought processes and plausible alternative ones. As a result, the practical goal of debiasing has fostered interest in basic cognitive processes, in areas such as reasoning, memory, METACOGNITION, and PSYCHOPHYSICS (Nisbett 1993; Svenson 1996; Tversky and Koehler 1994). For example, reliance on availability depends on how people encode and retrieve experiences; any quantitative judgment may draw on general strategies for extracting hints at the right answer from the details of experimental (or real-world) settings (Poulton 1995).

See also DEDUCTIVE REASONING; METAREASONING; RATIONAL DECISION MAKING

—*Baruch Fischhoff*

References

Camerer, C. (1995). Individual decision making. In J. Kagel and A. Roth, Eds., *The Handbook of Experimental Economics.* Princeton, NJ: Princeton University Press.

Cohen, J. (1962). The statistical power of abnormal social psychological research. *Journal of Abnormal and Social Psychology* 65: 145–153.

Dawes, R. M. (1997). Behavioral decision making, judgment, and inference. In D. Gilbert, S. Fiske, and G. Lindzey, Eds., *The Handbook of Social Psychology.* Boston, MA: McGraw-Hill, pp. 497–548.

Fischhoff, B. (1975). Hindsight | foresight: The effect of outcome knowledge on judgment under uncertainty. *Journal of Experimental Psychology: Human Perception and Performance* 104: 288–299.

Fischhoff, B., and R. Beyth-Marom. (1983). Hypothesis evaluation from a Bayesian perspective. *Psychological Review* 90: 239–260.

Gilovich, T. (1991). *How We Know What Isn't So.* New York: Free Press.

Gilovich, T., R. Vallone, and A. Tversky. (1985). The hot hand in basketball: On the misperception of random sequences. *Journal of Personality and Social Psychology* 17: 295–314.

Henrion, M., and B. Fischhoff. (1986). Assessing uncertainty in physical constants. *American Journal of Physics* 54: 791–798.

Jungermann, H. (1983). The two camps on rationality. In R. W. Scholz, Ed., *Decision Making Under Uncertainty.* Amsterdam: Elsevier, pp. 63–86.

Kahneman, D., and A. Tversky. (1972). Subjective probability: A judgment of representativeness. *Cognitive Psychology* 3: 430–454.

Kahneman, D., P. Slovic, and A. Tversky, Eds. (1982). *Judgments Under Uncertainty: Heuristics and Biases.* New York: Cambridge University Press.

Keren, G. (1991). Calibration and probability judgment. *Acta Psychologica* 77: 217–273.

Koriat, A., S. Lichtenstein, and B. Fischhoff. (1980). Reasons for confidence. *Journal of Experimental Psychology: Human Learning and Memory* 6: 107–118.

Mowen, J. C. (1993). *Judgment Calls.* New York: Simon and Schuster.

Murphy, A. H., and R. L. Winkler. (1992). Approach verification of probability forecasts. *International Journal of Forecasting* 7: 435–455.

Nisbett, R., Ed. (1993). *Rules for Reasoning.* Hillsdale, NJ: Erlbaum.

Plous, S. (1993). *The Psychology of Judgment and Decision Making.* New York: McGraw Hill.

Poulton, E. C. (1995). *Behavioral Decision Making.* Hillsdale, NJ: Erlbaum.

Simon, H. (1957). *Models of Man: Social and Rational.* New York: Wiley.

Svenson, O. (1996). Decision making and the search for fundamental psychological regularities. *Organizational Behavior and Human Performance* 65: 252–267.

Tversky, A., and D. Kahneman. (1974). Judgment under uncertainty: Heuristics and biases. *Science* 185: 1124–1131.

Tversky, A., and D. Kahneman. (1971). Belief in the "law of small numbers." *Psychological Bulletin* 76: 105–110.

Tversky, A., and D. J. Koehler. (1994). Support theory. *Psychological Review* 101: 547–567.

Yates, J. F. (1990). *Judgement and Decision Making.* New York: Wiley.

von Winterfeldt, D., and W. Edwards. (1986). *Decision Making and Behavioral Research.* New York: Cambridge University Press.

Further Readings

Baron, J. (1994). *Thinking and Deciding.* 2nd ed. New York: Cambridge University Press.

Bazerman, M., and M. Neale. (1992). *Negotiating Rationally.* New York: The Free Press.

Berkeley, D., and P. C. Humphreys. (1982). Structuring decision problems and the "bias heuristic." *Acta Psychologica* 50: 201–252.

Dawes, R. (1988). *Rational Choice in an Uncertain World.* San Diego, CA: Harcourt Brace Jovanovich.

Hammond, K. R. (1996). *Human Judgment and Social Policy.* New York: Oxford University Press.

Morgan, M. G., and M. Henrion. (1990). *Uncertainty.* New York: Cambridge University Press.

Nisbett, R., and L. Ross. (1980). *Human Inference: Strategies and Shortcomings of Social Judgment.* Englewood Cliffs, NJ: Prentice-Hall.

Thaler, R. H. (1992). *The Winner's Curse: Paradoxes and Anomalies of Economic Life.* New York: Free Press.

Justification

Philosophers distinguish between *justified* and *unjustified* beliefs. The former are beliefs a cognizer is entitled to hold by virtue of his or her evidence or cognitive operations. The latter are beliefs he or she is unwarranted in holding, for example, beliefs based on sheer fantasy, popular superstition, or sloppy thinking. Some justified beliefs are based on scientific findings, but scientific beliefs do not exhaust the class of justified beliefs. Ordinary perceptual and memorial beliefs, such as "There is a telephone before me" and "Nixon resigned from the Presidency," are also normally justified.

A belief's justification is usually assumed to be something that makes it probable that the belief is true. But justified beliefs are not guaranteed to be true. Even sound scientific evidence can support a hypothesis that is actually false. Almost all contemporary epistemologists accept this form of fallibilism.

There are three principal approaches to the theory of justification: *foundationalism, coherentism,* and *reliabilism.* The historical inspiration for foundationalism was RENÉ DESCARTES (1637), who launched the project of erecting his system of beliefs on solid, indeed indubitable, foundations. Most contemporary foundationalists reject Descartes's insistence on indubitable or infallible foundations, because they doubt that there are enough infallible propositions (if any) to support the rest of our beliefs. On their view, the core of foundationalism is the notion that justification has a vertical structure. Some beliefs are directly or immediately justified independently of inference from other beliefs, for example, by virtue of current perceptual experience. These beliefs are called *basic* beliefs, and they comprise the foundations of a person's justificational structure. Nonbasic justified beliefs derive their justification via reasoning from basic beliefs. It has been widely rumored that foundationalism is dead, perhaps because few people still believe in infallible foundations. But most epistemologists regard weak versions of foundationalism—those that acknowledge fallibility—as still viable.

Coherentism rejects the entire idea of basic beliefs, and the image of vertical support that begins at the foundational level. Instead, beliefs coexist on the same level and provide mutual support for one another. Each member of a belief system can be justified by meshing, or cohering, with the remaining members of that system. Beliefs get to be justified not by their relationship with a small number of basic beliefs, but by their fit with the cognizer's total corpus of beliefs.

Reliabilism, a theory of more recent vintage, holds (in its simplest form) that a belief is justified if it is produced by a sequence of reliable psychological processes (Goldman 1979). Reliable processes are ones that usually output true beliefs, or at least output true beliefs when taking true beliefs as inputs. Perceptual processes are reliable if they typically output accurate beliefs about the environment, and reasoning processes are (conditionally) reliable if they output beliefs in true conclusions when applied to beliefs in true premises. Some types of belief-forming processes are unreliable, and they are responsible for unjustified beliefs. This might include beliefs formed by certain kinds of biases or illegitimate inferential methods.

Because reliabilism's account of justification explicitly invokes psychological processes, its connection to cognitive science is fairly straightforward. To determine exactly which of our beliefs are justified or unjustified, we should determine which of the belief-forming practices that generate them are reliable or unreliable, and that is a task for cognitive science (Goldman 1986). There is no special branch of cognitive science that addresses this topic, but it is sprinkled across a range of cognitive scientific projects.

Although most perceptual beliefs are presumably justified, some applications of our visual object-recognition system are fairly unreliable. Biederman's (1987) account of visual object recognition posits a process of matching

visually detected components of a stimulus with the component types associated with object categories, such as "cup," "elephant," or "airplane." Object recognition is sometimes produced by partial matching, however, as when an occluded or degraded stimulus reveals only a few of its contours. When partial matching is unreliable, beliefs so formed are unjustified. An example of unreliable reasoning is the overuse of confirming information and the neglect of disconfirming information in drawing covariational conclusions: "I am convinced you can cure cancer with positive thinking because I know somebody who whipped the Big C after practicing mental imagery." People focus on instances that confirm their hypothesis without attending to evidence that might disconfirm it (Crocker 1982; Gilovich 1991). The search for evidence can also be biased by desire or preference. If we prefer to believe that a political assassination was a conspiracy, this may slant our evidence collection. In one study, subjects were led to believe that either introversion or extroversion was related to academic success. Those who were led to believe that introversion was predictive of success (a preferred outcome) came to think of themselves as more introverted than those who were led to believe that extroversion was associated with success (Kunda and Sanitioso 1989).

Proponents of foundationalism and coherentism often reject the relevance of experimental science to the theory of justification (e.g., Chisholm 1989). But even these types of theories might benefit from psychological research. What makes a memory belief about a past event justified or unjustified, according to foundationalism? It is the conscious memory traces present at the time of belief. Exactly what kinds of memory traces are available, however, and what kinds of clues do they contain about the veridicality of an apparent memory? This question can be illuminated by psychology. Johnson and Raye (1981) suggest that memory traces can be rich or poor along a number of dimensions, such as their sensory attributes, the number of spatial and temporal contextual attributes, and so forth. Johnson and Raye suggest that certain of these dimensions are evidence that the trace originated from external sources (obtained through perception) and other of these dimensions are evidence of an internal origin (imagination or thought). A characterization of these dimensions could help epistemologists specify when a memory belief about an allegedly external past event is justified and when it is unjustified (Goldman forthcoming).

Epistemological theories of justification sometimes ignore computational considerations, which are essential from a cognitivist perspective. Coherentism, for example, usually requires of a justified belief that it be logically consistent with the totality of one's current beliefs. But is this logical relationship computationally feasible? Cherniak (1986) argues that even the apparently simple task of checking for truth-functional consistency would overwhelm the computational resources available to human beings. One way to check for truth-functional consistency is to use the familiar truth-table method. But even a supermachine that could check a line in a truth-table in the time it takes a light ray to traverse the diameter of a proton would require 20 billion years to check a belief system containing only 138 logically independent propositions. Thus, the coherence theory implicitly requires a humanly impossible feat, thereby rendering justification humanly unattainable (Kornblith 1989). Attention to computational feasibility, obviously, should be an important constraint on theories of justification.

See also EPISTEMOLOGY AND COGNITION; INDUCTION; JUDGMENT HEURISTICS; RATIONAL AGENCY

—*Alvin I. Goldman*

References

Biederman, I. (1987). Recognition-by-components: A theory of human image understanding. *Psychological Review* 94: 115–147.

Cherniak, C. (1986). *Minimal Rationality*. Cambridge, MA: MIT Press.

Chisholm, R. (1989). *Theory of Knowledge*. 3rd ed. Englewood Cliffs, NJ: Prentice Hall.

Crocker, J. (1982). Biased questions in judgment of covariation studies. *Personality and Social Psychology Bulletin* 8: 214–220.

Descartes, R. (1637). *Discourse on Method*.

Gilovich, T. (1991). *How We Know What Isn't So*. New York: Free Press.

Goldman, A. (1979). What is justified belief? In G. Pappas, Ed., *Justification and Knowledge*. Dordrecht: Reidel. Reprinted in Goldman (1992).

Goldman, A. (1986). *Epistemology and Cognition*. Cambridge, MA: Harvard University Press.

Goldman, A. (Forthcoming). Internalism exposed. In M. Steup, Ed., *Knowledge, Truth, and Obligation: Essays on Epistemic Responsibility and the Ethics of Belief*. New York: Oxford University Press.

Johnson, M., and C. Raye (1981). Reality monitoring. *Psychological Review* 88: 67–85.

Kornblith, H. (1989). The unattainability of coherence. In J. Bender, Ed., *The Current State of the Coherence Theory*. Dordrecht: Kluwer.

Kunda, Z., and R. Sanitioso. (1989). Motivated changes in the self- concept. *Journal of Experimental Social Psychology* 25: 272–285.

Further Readings

Alston, W. (1989). *Epistemic Justification*. Ithaca, NY: Cornell University Press.

BonJour, L. (1985). *The Structure of Empirical Knowledge*. Cambridge, MA: Harvard University Press.

Goldman, A. (1992). *Liaisons: Philosophy Meets the Cognitive and Social Sciences*. Cambridge, MA: MIT Press.

Harman, G. (1986). *Change in View*. Cambridge, MA: MIT Press.

Lehrer, K. (1990). *Theory of Knowledge*. Boulder, CO: Westview Press.

Pollock, J. (1986). *Contemporary Theories of Knowledge*. Totowa, NJ: Rowman and Littlefield.

Steup, M. (1996). *An Introduction to Contemporary Epistemology*. Upper Saddle River, NJ: Prentice Hall.

Kant, Immanuel

Immanuel Kant (1724–1804) is perhaps the single most influential figure in the pre-twentieth-century history of cognitive research. He was a devoutly religious man from a very humble background: his father was a saddlemaker. Though one-quarter Scottish (it is said that Kant is a Germanization of Candt), he lived his whole life in Königsberg (now Kaliningrad), just below Lithuania. By his death he was virtually the official philosopher of the German-speaking world.

Until middle age, he was a prominent rationalist in the tradition of Leibniz and Wolff. Then DAVID HUME, as he put it, "awoke me from my dogmatic slumbers." The critical philosophy ensued. One of its fundamental questions was, what must we be like to have the experiences we have? The view of the mind that Kant developed to answer this question framed virtually all cognitive research until very recently.

Philosophy of mind and knowledge were by no means the only areas in which Kant made seminal contributions. He founded physical geometry. (Fieldwork must not have been too important—he is said never to have traveled more than thirty-five miles from Königsberg in his whole life!) His work on political philosophy grounds modern liberal democratic theory. And his deontology put ethics on a new footing, one that remains influential to this day.

It is his view of the mind, however, that influenced cognitive research. Four things in particular shaped subsequent thought:

1. MENTAL REPRESENTATION requires both CONCEPTS and SENSATIONS (percepts). As Kant put it, "concepts without intuitions are empty, intuitions without concepts are blind." To represent something, we require both acts of judgment and material from the senses to judge. Put another way, to discriminate, we need information; but we also need the ability to discriminate. This doctrine is now orthodoxy in cognitive science.

2. The method of transcendental argument. Kant's central methodological innovation, transcendental arguments are inferences from phenomena of a certain kind to what must be the case for those phenomena to exist. Applied to mental representations, such arguments are about what must be true of the thing that has those representations. Because this move allows us to infer the unobservable psychological antecedents of observed behavior, it is now central to most experimental cognitive science.

3. The mind as a system of functions. Kant was the first theorist to think of the mind as a system of functions, conceptual functions transforming ("taking") percepts into representations, at any rate of the modern era (Sellars 1968). (Aristotle may have had the same idea much earlier.) FUNCTIONALISM is by far the most influential philosophy of mind of cognitive science. Even the recent antisententialism of ELIMINATIVE MATERIALISM and CONNECTIONISM still see the mind as a system of functions.

Indeed, Kant's notorious "noumenalism" about the mind might be simply an early expression of FUNCTIONALISM. Noumenalism is the idea that we cannot know what the mind is like, not even something as basic as whether it is simple or complex. Part of Kant's argument is that we cannot infer how the mind is built from how it functions: function does not determine form. (The other part is an equally contemporary-sounding rejection of INTROSPECTION. Both arguments occur in his most important treatment of the mind, the chapter attacking rationalism's paralogisms of pure reason in the *Critique of Pure Reason*.)

4. Faculties: Kant developed a theory of mental faculties that strongly anticipates Fodor's (1983) well-known modularity ac-count (see MODULARITY OF MIND).

Kant also developed important ideas about the mind that have not played much of a role in subsequent cognitive research, though perhaps they should have. Two of them concern mental unity.

5. Synthesis: Kant urged that to represent the world, we must perform two kinds of synthesis. First we must synthesize colors, edges, textures, and the like into representations of single objects. Then we must tie the various represented objects together into a single representation of a world. The first kind of synthesis is now studied under the name "binding" (e.g., Treisman and Gelade 1980). The second receives little attention, though it would appear to be equally central to cognition.

6. Unity of CONSCIOUSNESS: The unity of consciousness is our ability to be aware of a great many things at the same time, or better, as parts of a single global representation.

Finally, Kant articulated some striking ideas about:

7. Consciousness and the SELF. The awareness that we have of ourselves is one form of unified consciousness; we are aware of ourselves as the "single common subject" of our representations. But Kant had insights into it that go well beyond that. Ideas he articulated about the peculiar barrenness of one form of consciousness of self and about the referential apparatus that we use to attain it did not reappear until Castañeda (1966) and Shoemaker (1968).

In sum, Kant articulated the view of the mind behind most of cognitive science (see Brook 1994 for further discussion).

See also BINDING PROBLEM; FREUD, SIGMUND

—*Andrew Brook*

References

Brook, A. (1994). *Kant and the Mind.* New York: Cambridge University Press.
Castañeda, H.-N. (1966). "He": A study in the logic of self-consciousness. *Ratio* 8: 130–157.
Fodor, J. (1983). *Modularity of Mind.* Cambridge: MIT Press.
Kant, I. (1781/1787). *Critique of Pure Reason.* London: Macmillan, 1963.
Sellars, W. (1968). *Science and Metaphysics.* New York: Humanities Press.
Shoemaker, S. (1968). Self-reference and self-awareness. *Journal of Philosophy* 65(2): 555–567.
Treisman, A., and G. Gelade. (1980). A feature-integration theory of attention. *Cognitive Psychology* 12: 97–136.

Further Readings

Ameriks, K. (1983). *Kant's Theory of the Mind.* Oxford: Oxford University Press.
Brook, A. (1994). *Kant and the Mind.* New York: Cambridge University Press.
Falkenstein, L. (1996). *Kant's Intuitionism: A Commentary on the Transcendental Aesthetic.* Toronto: University of Toronto Press.

Kant, I. (1798). *Anthropology from a Pragmatic Point of View.* Trans. Mary Gregor. The Hague: Martinus Nijhoff, 1974.
Kitcher, P. (1990). *Kant's Transcendental Psychology.* New York: Oxford University Press.

Kinds

See NATURAL KINDS

Knowledge Acquisition

Knowledge acquisition is a phase in the building of knowledge-based or expert systems. Knowledge-based systems are a kind of computer program that apply technical knowledge, or expertise, to PROBLEM SOLVING. Knowledge acquisition involves identifying the relevant technical knowledge, recording it, and getting it into computable form so it can be applied by the problem-solving engine of the expert system. Knowledge acquisition is the most expensive part of building and maintaining expert systems.

The area of expertise represented in the expert system is called the "domain." For example, a system that diagnoses malfunctioning VCRs and suggests remedies has VCR repair as its domain. An expert VCR repairman would be a "domain expert" for the system. The domain knowledge a developer, or "knowledge engineer," might acquire includes the types of problems VCRs exhibit, the symptoms a domain expert would look for to figure out the underlying cause of the problem, and the types of repairs that could cure the problem.

One of the big challenges of knowledge acquisition is finding a source of EXPERTISE that can be harvested. Written manuals are typically incomplete and sometimes even misleading. Manuals may contain technical details not actually applied in solving the problem. At the same time, manuals often leave out crucial "tricks" that experts have discovered in the field. The best, most experienced domain experts are generally in high demand and do not have much time for system building. Furthermore, experts may perform very well but have difficulty describing what cues they are responding to and what factors contribute to decisions they make. Very often multiple experts equally skilled in the same field disagree on how to do their job.

Another challenge addressed by approaches to knowledge acquisition is the maintenance of the knowledge. Especially in technical fields dealing with fast-changing product lines, domain knowledge may be extensive and dynamic. A VCR repair system may need to know technical details of the construction of every brand and make of VCR as well as likely failures. New knowledge will need to be added as new VCRs come on the market and technical innovations are incorporated into the products.

Most approaches to knowledge acquisition make the task manageable by identifying the problem-solving method that will be applied by the knowledge-based system. The problem-solving method then identifies what kinds of knowledge the developer should go after and organizes the knowledge so that it is easy to access for maintenance. (For more detail on using structure in knowledge acquisition and building expert systems, see Clancey 1983, 1985; Swartout 1983; Chandrasekaran 1983; Gruber and Cohen 1987; McDermott 1988; Steels 1990; Wielinga, Schreiber, and Breuker 1992.)

For example, in our VCR repair domain, we may decide that, based on symptoms the user describes, the system will classify VCR problems into categories that represent the most probable cause of the problem. The system will then choose a repair based on that suspected problem. What is "probable" will just be based on our domain experts' experience of what's worked in the past. If we use this problem-solving method, then the knowledge we need to acquire includes symptom-to-probable-cause associations and probable-cause-to-repair recommendations.

Alternatively, we may decide the system will diagnose the VCR by simulating failures of components on a schematic model until the simulated system shows readings that match the readings on the sick VCR. The system will then suggest replacing the failed components. If we use this problem-solving method, then the knowledge we need to acquire includes an internal model of a VCR identifying components, their dynamic behavior both when healthy and when sick, and their effect on the simulation readings.

A method-based approach to knowledge acquisition extends traditional software engineering for building expert systems (see, for example, Scott, Clayton, and Gibson 1991). During requirements analysis, while developers are figuring out what the system needs to do, they are also figuring out how it is going to do it. Developers interview domain experts and check additional knowledge sources and manuals to see how the expert goes about problem-solving and what types of knowledge are available for application in a method. This information helps them select a method for the system. Establishing a method focuses further specifications and knowledge gathering; the method serves to organize the acquired knowledge into the roles the knowledge plays in the method. (See also Schreiber et al. 1994 for extensive organizational schemes.)

To assist in the knowledge acquisition process, researchers have developed automated tools (Davis 1982; Boose 1984; Musen et al. 1987; Gaines 1987; Marcus 1988). The earliest tools assumed a single problem-solving method and had a user interface dedicated to extracting the knowledge needed by that method. For example, a knowledge-acquisition tool for diagnostic tasks might query a user for symptoms, causes, and the strengths of association between symptoms and causes. Queries would be phrased in a general way so that they could be answered as easily with symptoms of malfunctioning VCRs as with symptoms of sick humans. Such tools might employ specialized interviewing techniques to help get at distinctions experts find difficult to verbalize. They might also analyze the knowledge for completeness and consistency, looking, for example, for symptoms that have no causes, causes without symptoms, or circular reasoning.

Once the domain knowledge is built up, such an interviewing tool is typically used with a "shell" for this kind of diagnosis. A shell is an empty problem-solving engine that knows, for example, what to do with symptoms, causes, and symptom-cause association weights to select a probable cause. Domain knowledge gathered by the interviewing tool is added to the problem-solving shell to produce a functioning expert system.

A further development has been the creation of layered tools that handle multiple problem-solving methods (Musen 1989; Eriksson et al. 1995; Klinker et al. 1990; Runkel and Birmingham 1993). These layered tools help the system-builder select a problem-solving method and then, based on that method, query for domain terms and knowledge, conduct completeness and consistency analyses, and integrate with an appropriate problem-solving shell.

The techniques described so far have mainly focused on interviewing a domain expert in order to encode their knowledge into the system. Knowledge acquisition for expert systems has also benefited from the related field of MACHINE LEARNING (Michalski and Chilausky 1980; Quinlan 1986; Bareiss, Porter, and Murray 1989; Preston, Edwards, and Compton 1994). Machine learning focuses on getting computer programs to learn autonomously from examples or from feedback to their own behavior. Machine learning techniques have been used most effectively to train expert systems that need to make distinctions such as the distinction between symptoms caused by immune-deficiency diseases versus cancers. The knowledge of the domain is acquired through the machine's experience with training cases rather than by directly encoding instructions from an interview. In domains where the cases and training are available, the knowledge acquisition effort can be quite efficient and effective.

Finally, knowledge acquisition challenges have inspired efforts to get the most mileage out of the knowledge that is so expensive to acquire (Lenat and Guha 1990; Gruber 1991). Many of the method-based acquisition tools represent knowledge in a way that is specific to how it is used by the method. A use-specific representation simplifies the job of getting the knowledge into computable form to match the problem-solving shell. However, knowledge that was acquired to design car electrical systems might also be useful in diagnosing their failures. A use-neutral representation makes it easier to reuse the same knowledge with multiple problem-solving methods provided a mechanism to transform or integrate the knowledge with particular problem-solvers. Large knowledge-base efforts focus on storing knowledge in a use-neutral way and making it available to many knowledge-based systems.

See also DOMAIN SPECIFICITY; KNOWLEDGE-BASED SYSTEMS; SCHEMATA

—*Sandra L. Marcus*

References

Bareiss, R., B. W. Porter, and K. S. Murray. (1989). Supporting start-to-finish development of knowledge bases. *Machine Learning* 4: 259–283.

Boose, J. (1984). Personal construct theory and the transfer of human expertise. In *Proceedings of the Fourth National Conference on Artificial Intelligence.* Austin, Texas.

Chandrasekaran, B. (1983). Towards a taxonomy of problem solving types. *AI Magazine* 4: 9–17.

Clancey, W. (1983). The advantages of abstract control knowledge in expert system design. In *Proceedings of the Third National Conference on Artificial Intelligence.* Washington, D.C.

Clancey, W. (1985). Heuristic classification. *Artificial Intelligence* 27: 289–350.

Davis, R. (1982). TEIRESIAS: Applications of meta-level knowledge. In R. Davis and D. Lenat, Eds., *Knowledge-Based Systems in Artificial Intelligence*. New York: McGraw-Hill.

Eriksson, H., Y. Shahar, S. W. Tu, A. R. Puerta, and M. A. Musen. Task modeling with reusable problem-solving methods. In *International Journal of Expert Systems: Research and Applications* 9.

Gaines, B. R. (1987). An overview of knowledge acquisition and transfer. *International Journal of Man-Machine Studies.* 26: 453–472.

Gruber, T. R. (1991). *The Role of Common Ontology in Achieving Sharable, Reusable Knowledge Bases.* San Mateo, CA: Morgan Kaufmann.

Gruber, T. R., and P. Cohen. (1987). Design for acquisition: Principles of knowledge-system design to facilitate knowledge acquisition. *International Journal of Man-Machine Studies* 26: 143–159.

Klinker, G., C. Bhola, G. Dallemagne, D. Marques, and J. McDermott. (1990). *Usable and Reusable Programming Constructs. Fifth Banff Knowledge Acquisition for Knowledge-Based Systems Workshop.* Banff, Alberta, Canada.

Lenat, D. B., and R. V. Guha. (1990). *Building Large Knowledge-Based Systems.* Reading, MA: Addison-Wesley.

Marcus, S., Ed. (1988). *Automating Knowledge Acquisition for Expert Systems.* Boston: Kluwer Academic.

McDermott, J. (1988). Preliminary steps toward a taxonomy of problem-solving methods. In S. Marcus, Ed., *Automating Knowledge Acquisition for Expert Systems.* Boston: Kluwer Academic.

Michalski, R. S., and R. L. Chilausky. (1980). Learning by being told and learning from examples: An experimental comparison of the two methods of knowledge acquisition in the context of developing an expert system for soybean disease diagnosis. *Policy Analysis and Information Systems* 4: 125–160.

Musen, M. A. (1989). Knowledge acquisition at the metalevel: Creation of custom-tailored knowledge acquisition tools. In C. R. McGraw and K. L. McGraw, Eds., *Special Issue of ACM SIGART Newsletter on Knowledge Acquisition,* no. 108. April: 45–55.

Musen, M. A., L. M. Fagan, D. M. Combs, and E. H. Shortliffe. (1987). Using a domain model to drive an interactive knowledge editing tool. *International Journal of Man-Machine Studies* 26: 105–121.

Preston, P., G. Edwards, and P. Compton. (1994). A 2000 rule expert system without knowledge engineers. In *Proceedings of the 8th Banff Knowledge Acquisition for Knowledge-Based Systems Workshop.* Banff, Alberta, Canada.

Quinlan, J. R. (1986). Induction of decision trees. *Machine Learning,* 1: 81–106.

Runkel, J. T., and W. P. Birmingham. (1993). Knowledge acquisition in the small: Building knowledge-acquisition tools from pieces. In *Knowledge Acquisition* 5(2), 221–243.

Schreiber, A. T., B. J. Wielinga, R. de Hoog, H. Akkermans, and W. van de Velde. (1994). CommonKADS: A comprehensive methodology for KBS development. *IEEE Expert,* December: 28–37.

Scott, A. C., J. E. Clayton, and E. L. Gibson. (1991). *A Practical Guide to Knowledge Acquisition.* Reading, MA: Addison-Wesley.

Steels, L. (1990). Components of expertise. *AI Magazine* 11: 28–49.

Swartout, W. (1983). XPLAIN: A system for creating and explaining expert consulting systems. *Artificial Intelligence* 21: 285–325.

Wielinga, B. J., A. T. Schreiber, and A. J. Breuker. (1992). KADS: A modeling approach to knowledge engineering. *Knowledge Acquisition* 4: 1–162.

Further Readings

Chandrasekaran, B. (1986). Generic tasks in knowledge-based reasoning: High-level building blocks for expert system design. *IEEE Expert* 1: 23–29.

Quinlan, J. R., Ed. (1989). *Applications of Expert Systems.* London: Addison Wesley.

Knowledge-Based Systems

Knowledge-based systems (KBS) is a subfield of artificial intelligence concerned with creating programs that embody the reasoning expertise of human experts. In simplest terms, the overall intent is a form of intellectual cloning: find persons with a reasoning skill that is important and rare (e.g., an expert medical diagnostician, chess player, chemist), talk to them to determine what specialized knowledge they have and how they reason, then embody that knowledge and reasoning in a program.

The undertaking is distinguished from AI in general in several ways. First, there is no claim of breadth or generality; these systems are narrowly focused on specific domains of knowledge and cannot venture beyond them. Second, the systems are often motivated by a combination of science and application on real-world tasks; success is defined at least in part by accomplishing a useful level of performance on that task.

Third, and most significant, the systems are knowledge based in a technical sense: they base their performance on the accumulation of a substantial body of task-specific knowledge. AI has examined other notions of how intelligence might arise. GPS (Ernst 1969), for example, was inspired by the observation that people can make some progress on almost any problem we give them, and it depended for its power on a small set of very general problem-solving methods. It was in that sense methods based.

Knowledge-based systems, by contrast, work because of what they know and in this respect are similar to human experts. If we ask why experts are good at what they know, the answer will contain a variety of factors, but to some significant degree it is that they simply know more. They do not think faster, nor in fundamentally different ways (though practice effects may produce shortcuts); their expertise arises because they have substantially more knowledge about the task.

Human EXPERTISE is also apparently sharply domain-specific. Becoming a chess grandmaster does not also make one an expert physician; the skill of the master chemist does not extend to automobile repair. So it is with these programs.

The systems are at times referred to as *expert systems* and the terms are informally used interchangeably. "Expert system" is however better thought of as referring to the level of aspiration for the system. If it can perform as well as an expert, then it can play that role; this has been done, but is relatively rare. More commonly the systems perform as intelligent assistants, making recommendations for a human to review. Speaking of them as expert systems thus sets too narrow a perspective and restricts the utility of the technology.

Although knowledge-based systems have been built with a variety of representation technologies, two common architectural characteristics are the distinction between inference engine and knowledge base, and the use of declarative style representations. The knowledge base is the system's repository of task-specific information; the inference engine is a (typically simple) interpreter whose job is to retrieve relevant knowledge from the knowledge base and apply it to the problem at hand. A declarative representation is one that aims to express knowledge in a form relatively independent of the way in which it is going to be used; predicate calculus is perhaps the premier example.

The separation of inference engine and knowledge base, along with the declarative character of the knowledge, facilitates the construction and maintenance of the knowledge base. Developing a knowledge-based system becomes a task of debugging knowledge rather than code; the question is, what should the program know, rather than what should it do.

Three systems are frequently cited as foundational in this area: SIN (Moses 1967) and its descendant MACSYMA (Moses 1971), DENDRAL (Feigenbaum et al. 1971), and MYCIN (Davis 1977). SIN's task domain was symbolic integration. Although its representation was more procedural than would later become the norm, the program was one of the first embodiments of the hypothesis that problem solving power could be based on knowledge. It stands in stark contrast to SAINT (Slagle 1963), the first of the symbolic integration programs, which was intended by its author to work by tree search, that is, methodically exploring the space of possible problem transformations. SIN, on the other hand, claimed that its goal was the *avoidance* of search, and that search was to be avoided by knowing what to do. It sought to bring to bear all of the cleverness that good integrators used, and attempted to do so using its most powerful techniques first. Only if these failed would it eventually fall back on search.

DENDRAL's task was analytic chemistry: determining the structure of a chemical compound from a variety of physical data about the compound, particularly its mass spectrum (the way in which the compound fragments when subjected to ionic bombardment). DENDRAL worked by generate and test, generating possible structures and testing them (in simulation) to see whether they would produce the mass spectrum observed. The combinatorics of the problem quickly become unmanageable: even relatively modest sized compounds have tens of millions of isomers (different ways in which the same set of atoms can be assembled). Hence in order to work at all, DENDRAL's generator had to be informed. By working with the expert chemists, DENDRAL's authors were able to determine what clues chemists found in the spectra that permitted them to focus their search on particular subclasses of molecules. Hence DENDRAL's key knowledge was about the "fingerprints" that different classes of molecules would leave in a mass spectrum; without this it would have floundered among the millions of possible structures.

MYCIN's task was diagnosis and therapy selection for a variety of infectious diseases. It was the first system to have all of the hallmarks that came to be associated with knowledge-based systems and as such came to be regarded as a prototypical example. Its knowledge was expressed as a set of some 450 relatively independent if/then rules; its inference engine used a simple backward-chaining control structure; and it was capable of explaining its recommendations (by showing the user a recap of the rules that had been used).

The late 1970s and early 1980s saw the construction of a wide variety of knowledge-based systems for tasks as diverse as diagnosis, configuration, design, and tutoring. The decade of the 1980s also saw an enormous growth in industrial interest in the technology. One of the most successful and widely known industrial systems was XCON (for expert configurer), a program used by Digital Equipment Corporation (DEC) to handle the wide variation in the ways a DEC VAX computer could be configured. The system's task was to ensure that an order had all the required components and no superfluous ones. This was a knowledge-intensive task: factors to be considered included the physical layout of components in the computer cabinet, the electrical requirements of each component, the need to establish interrupt priorities on the bus, and others. Tests of XCON demonstrated that its error rate on the task was below 3 percent, which compared quite favorably to human error rates in the range of 15 percent (Barker and O'Connor 1989). Digital has claimed that over the decade of the 1980s XCON and a variety of other knowledge-based systems saved it over one billion dollars. Other commercial knowledge-based systems of pragmatic consequence were constructed by American Express, Manufacturer's Hanover, duPont, Schlumberger, and others.

The mid-1980s also saw the development of BAYESIAN NETWORKS (Pearl 1986), a form of KNOWLEDGE REPRESENTATION grounded in probability theory, that has recently seen wide use in developing a number of successful expert systems (see, e.g., Heckerman, Wellman, and Mamdani 1995).

Work in knowledge-based systems is rooted in observations about the nature of human intelligence, viz., the observation that human expertise of the sort involved in explicit reasoning is typically domain specific and dependent on a large store of task specific knowledge. Use of simple if/then rules—production rules—is drawn directly from the early work of Newell and Simon (1972) that used production rules to model human PROBLEM SOLVING.

The conception of knowledge-based systems as attempts to clone human reasoning also means that these systems often produce detailed models of someone's mental conception of a problem and the knowledge needed to solve it. Where other AI technologies (e.g., predicate calculus) are more focused on finding a way to achieve intelligence without necessarily modeling human reasoning patterns, knowledge-based systems seek explicitly to capture what people know and how they use it. One consequence is that the effort of constructing a system often produces as a side effect a more complete and explicit model of the expert's conception of the task than had previously been available. The system's knowledge base thus has independent value, apart from the program, as an expression of one expert's mental model of the task and the relevant knowledge.

MYCIN and other programs also provided one of the early and clear illustrations of Newell's concept of the knowledge level (Newell 1982), that is, the level of abstraction of a system (whether human or machine) at which one can talk coherently about what it knows, quite apart from the details of how the knowledge is represented and used.

These systems also offered some of the earliest evidence that knowledge could obviate the need for search, with DENDRAL in particular offering a compelling case study of the power of domain specific knowledge to avoid search in a space that can quickly grow to hundreds of millions of choices.

See also AI AND EDUCATION; DOMAIN SPECIFICITY; FRAME-BASED SYSTEMS; KNOWLEDGE ACQUISITION

—*Randall Davis*

References

Barker, V., and D. O'Connor. (1989). Expert systems for configuration at Digital: XCON and beyond. *Communications of the ACM* March: 298–318.

Davis, R. (1977). Production rules as a representation for a knowledge–based consultation program. *Artificial Intelligence* 8:15–45.

Ernst, G. W. (1969). *GPS: A Case Study in Generality and Problem Solving.* New York: Academic Press.

Feigenbaum, E. A., B. G. Buchanan, and J. Lederberg. (1971). On generality and problem solving: A case study using the DENDRAL program. In B. Meltzer and D. Michie, Eds., *Machine Intelligence 6*, pp. 165–189.

Heckerman, D., M. Wellman, and A. Mamdani, Eds. (1995). Real world applications of Bayesian networks. *Communications of the ACM,* vol. 38, no. 3.

Moses, J. (1967). *Symbolic Integration.* Ph.D. diss., Massachusetts Institute of Technology.

Moses, J. (1971). Symbolic integration: The stormy decade. *Communications of the ACM* 14: 548–560.

Newell, A. (1982). The knowledge level. *Artificial Intelligence* 18(1): 87–127.

Newell, A., and H. A. Simon. (1972). *Human Problem Solving.* Englewood Cliffs, NJ: Prentice-Hall.

Pearl, J. (1986). Fusion, propagation, and structuring in belief networks. *Artificial Intelligence* (29)3: 241–288.

Slagle, J. (1963). A heuristic program that solves symbolic integration problems in freshman calculus. In E. A. Feigenbaum and J. Feldman, Eds., *Computers and Thought*, pp. 191–206.

Further Readings

Bachant, J., and J. McDermott. (1984). R1 revisited: Four years in the trenches. *Artificial Intelligence Magazine* 21–32.

Buchanan, B. G., and E. H. Shortliffe. (1984). *Rule-Based Expert Systems.* Reading, MA: Addison-Wesley.

Clancey, W., and E. Shortliffe. (1984). *Readings in Medical Artificial Intelligence.* Reading, MA: Addison-Wesley.

Davis, E. (1990). *Representations of Commonsense Knowledge.* San Mateo, CA: Morgan Kaufmann.

Davis, R., and D. Lenat. (1982). *Knowledge-Based Expert Systems.* New York: McGraw-Hill.

Lenat, D. B., and R. V. Guha. (1990). *Building Large Knowledge-Based Systems.* Reading, MA: Addison-Wesley.

Lockwood, S., and Z. Chen. (1995). Knowledge validation of engineering expert systems. *Advances in Engineering Software* 23(2): 97–104.

O'Leary, D. E. (1994). Verification and validation of intelligent systems: Five years of AAAI workshops. *International Journal of Intelligent Systems* 9(8): 953–957.

Schreiber, G., B. Wielinga, and J. Breuker, Eds. (1993). *KADS: A Principled Approach to Knowledge–Based System Development.* New York: Academic Press.

Shrobe, H. E., Ed. (1988). *Exploring Artificial Intelligence.* San Mateo, CA: Morgan Kaufmann.

Knowledge Compilation

See EXPLANATION-BASED LEARNING; METAREASONING

Knowledge Representation

Knowledge representation (KR) refers to the general topic of how information can be appropriately encoded and utilized in computational models of cognition. It is a broad, rather catholic field with links to logic, computer science, cognitive and perceptual psychology, linguistics, and other parts of cognitive science. Some KR work aims for psychological or linguistic plausibility, but much is motivated more by engineering concerns, a tension that runs through the entire field of AI. KR work typically ignores purely philosophical issues, but related areas in philosophy include analyses of mental representation, deductive reasoning and the "language of thought," philosophy of language, and philosophical logic.

Typically, work in knowledge representation focuses either on the representational formalism or on the information to be encoded in it, sometimes called *knowledge engineering.* Although many AI systems use ad-hoc representations tailored to a particular application, such as digital maps for robot navigation or graphlike story scripts for language comprehension, much KR work is motivated by the perceived need for a uniform representation, and the intuition that because human intelligence can rapidly draw appropriate conclusions, KR should seek conceptual frameworks in which these conclusions have short derivations. The philosophical integrity or elegance of this assumed framework is less important than its practical effectiveness; for example, Jerry Hobbs (1985) urges a principle of *ontological promiscuity* in KR.

The central topic in knowledge engineering is to identify an appropriate conceptual vocabulary; a related collection of formalized concepts is often called an *ontology.* For example, temporal or dynamic knowledge is often represented by describing actions as functions on states of the world, using axioms to give sufficient conditions for the success of the action, and then using logical reasoning to prove constructively that a state exists that satisfies a goal. The name of the final state then provides a "plan" of the actions necessary to achieve the goal, such as: *drink(move(mouth,pickup(cup,start-state))).* Though useful, this ontology has several stubborn difficulties, notably the FRAME PROBLEM, that is, how compactly to state what remains *unchanged* by an action. (For example, picking up something from a table obviously leaves the table in the same place and doesn't change the color of anything, but because the state has changed this needs to be made explicit; and some actions do have such side effects, so the possibility cannot be ruled out on logical grounds.) Many solutions to the frame problem have been proposed, but none are fully satisfactory. Other approaches divide the world into objects with spatial and temporal boundaries (Hayes 1985), or use transformations on state descriptions to model actions more directly. Several areas of knowledge engineering have received detailed attention, notably intuitive physical knowledge, often called *qualitative physics* (Davis 1990; Weld and de Kleer 1990).

KR formalisms need a precisely defined SYNTAX, a useful SEMANTICS, and a computationally tractable inference procedure. A wide variety have been studied. Typical features include a notation for describing concept hierarchies and mechanisms to maintain property inheritance; an ability to check for, and correct, propositional inconsistency in the light of new information ("truth-maintenance"; see Forbus and de Kleer 1993); and ways of expressing a "closed world" assumption, that is, that a representation contains all facts of a certain kind (so if one is omitted it can be assumed to be false).

Many notations are inspired by sentential logics, some by semantic networks, others, often called "frame-based," resemble object-oriented programming languages. Most of these can be regarded as syntactic variations on subsets of first-order relational logic, sometimes extended to allow Bayesian probabilistic inference, fuzzy reasoning, and other ways to express partial or uncertain information or degrees of confidence. Many also use some form of default or *non-monotonic* reasoning, allowing temporary assumptions to be cancelled by later or more detailed information. For example, if told that something is an elephant one can infer that it is a mammal, but this inference would be withdrawn given the further information that it is a toy elephant. More recently there has been considerable interest in diagrammatic representations that are supposed to represent by being directly similar to the subject being represented (Glasgow, Narayan, and Chandrasekharan 1995). These are sometimes claimed to be plausible models of mental IMAGERY, but Levesque and Brachman (1985) point out that a set of ground propositions together with a closed-world assumption has many of the functional properties of a mental image.

A central issue for KR formalisms is the tradeoff between expressive power and deductive complexity. At one extreme, propositional logic restricted to Horn clauses (disjunctions of atomic propositions with at most one negation) admits a very efficient decision procedure but cannot express any generalizations; at another, full second-order logic is capable of expressing most of mathematics but has no complete inference procedure. Most KR formalisms adopt various compromises. Network and frame-based formalisms often gain deductive efficiency by sacrificing the ability to express arbitrary disjunctions. Description logics (Borgida et al. 1989) guarantee polynomial-time decision algorithms by using operators on concept descriptions instead of quantifiers.

Commercial applications use knowledge representation as an extension of database technology, where the "knowledge" is seen as a reservoir of useful information rather than as supporting a model of cognitive activity. Here action planning is often unnecessary, and the ontology fixed by the particular application—for example, medical diagnosis or case law—but issues of scale become important. The contents of such systems can often be thought of either as sentential knowledge or as program code; one school of thought in KR regards this distinction as essentially meaningless in any case. More recently, increased available memory size has made it feasible to use "compute-intensive" representations that simply list all the particular facts rather than stating general rules. These allow the use of statistical techniques such as Markov simulation, but seem to abandon any claim to psychological plausibility.

Commercial use of knowledge bases and a proliferation of Krep systems with various ad-hoc syntactic restrictions has created a need for "standard" or "interchange" formalisms to allow intertranslation. These include the Knowledge Interchange Format, a blend of first-order set theory and LISP (Genesereth et al. 1992) and conceptual graphs, a graphical notation inspired by C. S. Peirce (Sowa 1997). There is also considerable interest in compiling standard ontologies for commonly used concepts such as temporal relations or industrial process control (see the "ontology page" http://mnemosyne.itc.it:1024/ontology.html for the current state of research in this area).

Although there has been a great deal of work on KR, much intuitive human knowledge still resists useful formalization. Even such apparently straightforward areas as temporal and spatial knowledge are still subjects of active research, and the knowledge involved in comprehending simple stories or understanding simple physical situations is still yet to be adequately formalized. Many ideas have been developed in NL research, such as "scripts" or idealized story-frameworks and the use of a limited number of conceptual primitive categories, but none have achieved unqualified success.

Early work in AI and cognitive science assumed that suitably represented information must be central in a proper account of cognition, but more recently this assumption has been questioned, notably by "connectionist" and "situated" theories. Connectionism seeks to connect cognitive behavior directly to neurally inspired mechanisms, whereas situated theories focus on how behavior emerges from interaction with the environment (Brooks 1991). Both were initially seen as in direct opposition to knowledge-representation ideas, but reconciliations are emerging. In particular, phase-encoding seems to enable connectionist networks to perform quite sophisticated logical reasoning. The single most important lesson to emerge from these controversies is probably that the representation of knowledge cannot be completely isolated from its hypothesized functions in cognition.

See also COGNITIVE MODELING, CONNECTIONIST; COGNITIVE MODELING, SYMBOLIC; COMPUTATIONAL THEORY OF MIND; CONNECTIONISM, PHILOSOPHICAL ISSUES; KNOWLEDGE ACQUISITION; LOGICAL REASONING SYSTEMS; NEURAL NETWORKS; PROBLEM SOLVING

—Patrick Hayes

References

Borgida, A., R. J. Brachman, D. L. McGuinness, and A. L. Resnick. (1989). CLASSIC: A structural data model for objects. *SIGMOD Record* 18(2): 58–67.

Brooks, R. A. (1991). Intelligence without representation. *Artificial Intelligence* 47(1–3): 139–160.

Davis, E. (1990). *Representations of Common-Sense Knowledge.* Stanford: Morgan Kaufmann.

Forbus, K., and J. de Kleer. (1993). *Building Problem Solvers.* Cambridge, MA: MIT Press.

Genesereth, M., and R. E. Fikes. (1992). *Knowledge Interchange Format Reference Manual.* Stanford University Logic Group, report 92-1, Stanford University.

Glasgow, J., N. H. Narayan, and B. Chandrasekharan, Eds. (1995). *Diagrammatic Reasoning: Cognitive and Computational Perspectives.* Cambridge, MA: AAAI/MIT Press.

Hayes, P. (1985). Naive Physics I: Ontology for liquids. In Hobbs and Moore (1985), pp. 71–107.

Hobbs, J. R. (1985). Ontological promiscuity. *Proc. 23rd Annual Meeting of the Association for Computational Linguistics* 61–69.

Levesque, H., and R. Brachman. (1985). A fundamental tradeoff in knowledge representation and reasoning. In Brachman and Levesque (1985).

Sowa, J. F. (1997). *Knowledge Representation: Logical, Philosophical and Computational Foundations.* Boston: PWS.

Weld, D., and J. de Kleer, Eds. (1990). *Readings in Qualitative Reasoning about Physical Systems.* San Francisco: Morgan Kaufmann.

Further Readings

Brachman, R., and H. Levesque. (1985). *Readings in Knowledge Representation.* Stanford: Morgan Kaufmann.

Hobbs, J., and R. Moore, Eds. (1985). *Formal Theories of the Common-Sense World.* Norwood, NJ: Ablex.

McCarthy, J., and V. Lifschitz, Eds. (1990). *Formalizing Common Sense.* Norwood, NJ: Ablex.

Russell, S., and P. Norvig. (1995). *Artificial Intelligence; A Modern Approach.* Englewood Cliffs, NJ: Prentice-Hall.

Language Acquisition

Language acquisition refers to the process of attaining a specific variant of human language, such as English, Navajo, American Sign Language, or Korean. The fundamental puzzle in understanding this process has to do with the open-ended nature of what is learned: children appropriately use words acquired in one context to make reference in the next, and they construct novel sentences to make known their changing thoughts and desires. In light of the creative nature of this achievement, it is striking that close-to-adult proficiency is attained by the age of 4–5 years despite large differences in children's mentalities and motivations, the circumstances of their rearing, and the particular language to which they are exposed. Indeed, some linguists have argued that the theoretical goal of their discipline is to explain how children come to have knowledge of language through only limited and impoverished experience of it in the speech of adults (i.e., "Plato's problem"; Chomsky 1986). For closely related reasons, philosophers, evolutionary biologists, and psychologists have long used language acquisition as a testbed for exploring and contrasting theories of learning, development, and representation. Neither the natural communication systems of infrahumans nor the outcomes for apes specially tutored in aspects of spoken or signed systems approach in content or formal complexity the achievements of the most ordinary 3-year-old human (see also PRIMATE LANGUAGE). Because children are the only things (living or nonliving) that are capable of this learning, computer scientists concerned with simulating the process study language acquisition for much the same reason that Leonardo Da Vinci, who was interested in building a flying machine, chose to study birds.

Language acquisition begins at birth, if not earlier. Children only a few days old can discriminate their own language from another, presumably through sensitivity to language-specific properties of prosody and phonetic patterning. In the first several months of life, they discriminate among all known phonetic contrasts used in natural languages, but this ability diminishes over time such that by about 12 months, children distinguish only among the contrasts made in the language they are exposed to. Between about the seventh and tenth month, infants begin reduplicative babbling, producing sounds such as "baba" and "gaga" (see also PHONOLOGY, ACQUISITION OF). At this age, deaf children too begin to babble—with their hands—producing repetitive sequences of sign-language formatives that resemble the syllabic units of vocal babbling. In general, the acquisition sequence does not seem to differ for spoken and signed languages, suggesting that the language-learning capacity is geared to abstract linguistic structure, not simply to speech (see SIGN LANGUAGES).

Comprehension of a few words has been demonstrated as early as 9 months, and first spoken words typically appear between 12 and 14 months. The most common early words are names for individuals (*Mama*), objects (*car*), and substances (*water*); these nominal terms appear early in language development for children in all known cultures. Other common components of the earliest vocabulary are animal names, social terms such as *bye-bye* and—of course—*no*. Verbs and adjectives as well as members of the functional categories (such as *the, -ed, is,* and *with*) are rare in the early vocabulary compared to their frequency in the input corpus. At this initial stage, new words appear in speech at the rate of about two or three a week and are produced in isolation (that is, in "one word sentences"). The rate of vocabulary growth increases and so does the character of the vocabulary, with verbs and adjectives being added and functional morphemes beginning to appear. This change in growth rate and lexical class typology coincides with the onset of syntax (for further discussion and references, see WORD MEANING, ACQUISITION OF and SYNTAX, ACQUISITION OF).

The most obvious sign of early syntactic knowledge is canonical phrasal order: Children's speech mirrors the canonical sequence of phrases (be it Subject-Verb-Object, Verb-Subject-Object, etc.) of the exposure language as soon as they begin to combine words at all (Pinker 1984). English-speaking children's first word combinations were originally called "telegraphic" by investigators (Brown and Bellugi 1964) because they are short and because they lack most function words and morphemes, giving the speech the minimalist flavor of telegrams and classified ads. But more recent investigation shows this characterization to be inadequate, in part because this pattern of early speech is not universal. In languages where closed-class morphemes are stressed and syllabic, they appear before age 2 (Slobin 1985).

Another problem with calling children's language "telegraphic" is that this characterization underestimates the extent of child knowledge. There is significant evidence that infants' knowledge of syntax, including the forms and semantic roles played by functional elements, is radically in advance of their productive speech. One source of evidence is preferential looking behavior in tasks where a heard sentence matches only one of two visually displayed scenes. Such methods have shown, for example, that appreciation of word order and its semantic implications are in place well before the appearance of two-word speech. For example, infants will look primarily to the appropriate action video in response to hearing *Big Bird tickles Cookie Monster* versus *Cookie Monster tickles Big Bird* (Hirsh-Pasek and Golinkoff 1996) and show a rudimentary understanding of the semantic implications of functional elements (Snedeker 1996). Another compelling source of evidence for underlying syntactic knowledge is that analyses of the relative positioning of subjects, negative words, and verbs, and their interaction with verb morphology, makes clear that children have significant implicit knowledge of functional projections; for example, they properly place negative words with respect to finite versus infinitive forms of the verb. That is, the French toddler regularly says "mange pas" but "pas manger" (Deprez and Pierce 1993).

By the age of 3 years or before, the "telegraphic" stage of speech ends and children's utterances increase in length and complexity. For instance, at age 3 and 4 we hear such constructions as inverted yes/no questions (*Is there some food over there?*), relative clauses (*the cookie that I ate*), and control structures (*I asked him to go*). Production errors at this stage are largely confined to morphological regularizations (e.g., *goed* for *went*) and syntactic overextensions (*She giggled the baby* for *She made the baby giggle*; see Bowerman 1982), though even these errors are rare (Marcus et al. 1992).

One important commitment that all acquisition theories make is to the sort of input that is posited to be required by the learner. After all, the richer and more informative the information received, the less preprogrammed capacity and inductive machinery the child must supply "from within." Adults tend to communicate with their offspring using slow, high-pitched speech with exaggerated intonation contours, a relatively simple and restricted vocabulary, and short sentences. Although whimsically dubbed "Motherese" (Newport, Gleitman, and Gleitman 1977), this style of speech is characteristic of both males and females, and even of older children when talking to younger ones. DARWIN, who was interested in language learning and kept diaries of his children's progress, called this style of speech "the sweet music of the species." Infants resonate to it, strongly preferring Motherese to the adult-to-adult style of speech (Fernald and Kuhl 1987). Although it is possible that these apparent adult simplifications might facilitate aspects of learning, there is plenty of evidence that the abused and neglected children of the world, regardless of their other difficulties, adequately acquire the language of their communities.

Because speech to children is almost perfectly grammatical and meaningful, it seems to offer a pretty straightforward model for acquisition. Yet in principle such a "good sample" of, say, English, is a limited source of information for of necessity it doesn't explicitly expose the full range of structure and content of the language. Notice, as an example, that although an adjective can appear in two structural positions in certain otherwise identical English sentences (e.g., *Paint the red barn* and *Paint the barn red*), this is not always so: Woe to the learner who generalizes from *See the red barn* to *See the barn red*. It has been proposed, therefore, that "negative evidence"—information about which sentences are ill-formed in some way—might be crucial for deducing the true nature of the input language. Such information might be available in parents' characteristic reactions to the child's ill-formed early speech, thus providing statistical evidence as to right and wrong ways to speak the language. However, a series of studies beginning with Brown and Hanlon (1970) have demonstrated that there is little reliable correlation between the grammaticality of children's utterances and the sorts of responses to these that their parents give, even for children raised in middle-class American environments. Moreover, children learn language in cultures in which nobody speaks to infants until the infants themselves begin to talk (Lieven 1994).

As mentioned above, neonates can detect and store at least some linguistic elements and their patterning from minimal distributional information (Saffran, Aslin, and Newport 1997). Recent computational simulations suggest that certain lexical category, selectional, and syntactic properties of the language can be gleaned from such patterns in text (e.g., Cartwright and Brent 1997). Most theories of language development, following Chomsky (1965) and Macnamara (1972), assume that children also have access to some nonlinguistic encoding of the context. That is, they are more likely to hear *hippopotamus* in the presence of hippos than of aardvarks, and *The cat is on the mat* is, other things being equal, a more likely sentence in the presence of cats and mats than in their absence. The effects of such contextual support are obvious for learning the meanings of words, but they are likely to be critical as well for the acquisition of syntax (Bloom 1994; Pinker 1984).

Whatever the detailed cause-and-effect relations between input properties and learning functions, it seems a truism that the variant of human language attained by young children is that modeled by the adult community of language users. Yet even in this regard, there are significant exceptions. For example, isolated deaf children not exposed to signed languages spontaneously generate gestural systems that share many formal and substantive features with the received languages (e.g., Feldman, Golden-Meadow, and Gleitman 1978; see also SIGN LANGUAGES). Similarly, children whose linguistic exposure is to "pidgin" languages (simple contact systems with little grammatical structure) elaborate and regularize these in the course of learning them (Bickerton 1981; Newport 1990; see CREOLES). Much of language change can be explained as part of this process of regularization and elaboration of received systems by children. In a very real sense, then, children do not merely learn language; they create it.

The acquisition properties just described sketch the known facts about this process as it unfolds in young children, under all the myriad personal, cultural, and linguistic circumstances into which they are born. Acquisition is astonishingly "robust" to environmental circumstance. This finding is at the heart of theorizing that assigns the child's acquisition in large part to internal, biological, predispositions that can correct for adventitious properties of the environment. One more stunning indication of the merit of such a view is that young children simultaneously exposed to two—or even three—languages in infancy and early childhood acquire them all as rapidly and systematically as the child in monolingual circumstances acquires one language. That is, if the child in a bilingual home sleeps as much as her monolingual cousin, she necessarily hears a smaller sample of each of the languages; yet attainment of each is at age-level under conditions where both languages are in regular use in the child's immediate environment.

If it is true that biologically "prepared" factors in young children significantly support and constrain the learning process, then learning might look different when those biological factors vary. And indeed it does. The most obvious first case to inspect is that of learners who come into a language-learning situation at a later brain-maturational state. In contrast to the almost universal attainment of a high level of language knowledge by humans exposed to a model in infancy or early childhood stand the sharply different results for such late learners. In the usual case, these are second-language learners, and the level of their final attainment is inferior to infant learners as a direct negative function of maturational status at first exposure. However, the same generalizations apply to acquisition of a primary language late in life (Newport 1990). Apparently, these increasing decrements in language-acquisition skills over maturational time apply both to learning idiosyncratic details of the exposure language and to language universals, properties common across the languages of the world. Such "critical period" or "sensitive period" effects, though undeniable on the obtained evidence, cannot by themselves reveal just what is being lost or diminished in the late learner: This could be some aspects of learning specific to language itself, general capacities for structured cognitive learning, or some combination of the two (for discussion of the complex interweave of nature and nurture in accounting for critical period effects, see Marler 1991).

A large and informative literature considers tragedies of nature, populations of learners with conceptually or linguistically relevant deficits. The effect of these studies, taken as a whole, is to demonstrate, first, that linguistic and general-cognitive capacities are often dissociated in pathology. For example, in Williams syndrome (Bellugi et al. 1988), language-learning abilities are virtually unscathed but these children's IQs are severely below normal; in SLI (Specific Language Impairment; van der Lely 1997), children with normal and even superior IQs exhibit defects in the timing and content of language acquisition. The second overall finding from these unusual populations is that language deficiencies are not across-the-board but may affect only a single aspect. For example, both in SLI (Rice and Wexler 1996) and in Down's syndrome (Fowler 1990), word learning and some aspects of syntax (e.g., word order) are adequate, but there is a specific deficit for functional projections (i.e., knowledge of the interaction of verb morphology and syntactic structure).

To many theorists the bottom-line message from joint investigation of normal and unusual learning is this: Language acquisition is little affected by the ambiance in which learners find themselves, so long as they have intact young human brains; whereas any change in mentality (even: growing up!) massively, and negatively, impacts the learning process.

Beyond questions of nature-nurture in the acquisition process are more specific questions about acquisition functions for language at various levels in the linguistic hierarchy, including PHONOLOGY, SYNTAX, SEMANTICS, and word learning. At this moment in the progress of the field, interpretation of such results is limited to the extent that a number of viable theories of language design—that is, of the targets of acquisition—contend in the linguistic literature. Moreover, theoretical pressure to account for the emerging facts about language learning often motivates revision of the linguistic theory. One way to think about how language and its learning are jointly explored, then, is to contrast two different questions that investigators ask, depending on their orientations: "What is a child, such that it can learn language?" versus "What is language, such that every child can learn it?"

Particularly informative in adjudicating these issues are studies that contrast learning and language effects crosslinguistically (a classic collection of such articles appears in Slobin 1985). Another useful direction has been to consider acquisition across various levels of the linguistic hierarchy, to examine the extent of their interaction. For example, phonological and semantic knowledge underlie aspects of how children understand the syntax of a sentence; syntactic and morphological cues support the acquisition of word meaning; and so on. Recent technological developments are beginning to enable acquisition work in directions unforeseen and infeasible up until the last few years. One important example concerns child on-line language processing, an area that has remained largely closed to investigation (for an exception, see McKee 1996) until the advent of eyetracking equipment that can monitor the child's linguistic representations as these are constructed, in milliseconds, dependent on the reference world (Trueswell, Sekerina, and Hill 1998). Another is neuropsychological investigation employing techniques such as POSITRON EMISSION TOMOGRAPHY and functional MAGNETIC RESONANCE IMAGING (fMRI) recording of neural activity during linguistic processing. Finally, the increasing use of computer models and simulations allows explicit and detailed theories to be tested on large bodies of computerized linguistic data.

In light of the growing armamentarium of investigative technique and increasingly sophisticated linguistic analysis, understanding of language acquisition can be expected to increase rapidly in the coming decade. All current theoretical positions, no matter how different in other ways, acknowledge that language acquisition is the result of an interaction between aspects of the human mind and aspects of the environment: children learn language but rocks and dogs do not; children in France learn French and children in Mawu learn Mawukakan. Substantive debates in the present literature largely center on the nature of the learning mechanism. One issue is whether language is learned through a specialized organ or module or is the product of more general learning capacities. A further issue, logically distinct from the question of specialization, is whether the mechanisms of language acquisition and representation exploit symbolic rules, associations, or some combination of the two.

In conclusion, we should stress that language acquisition is a diverse process. It is extremely likely, for instance, that the right explanation for how children learn to form *wh*-questions will involve different cognitive mechanisms from those required for learning proper names or learning to take turns in conversation. We suspect, in fact, that there is no single story to be told about how children acquire language. Rather, the formatives, the learning machinery, and the combinatorial schemata at each level of the final system can be expected to vary. At the same time, knowledge of one aspect of the system can be expected to piggyback on the next in a complex incremental learning scheme, some of whose dimensions and procedures cannot now even be guessed at.

See also INDUCTION; INNATENESS OF LANGUAGE; NATIVISM, HISTORY OF; POVERTY OF THE STIMULUS ARGUMENTS; THEMATIC ROLES

—*Lila Gleitman and Paul Bloom*

References

Bellugi, U., S. Marks, A. Bihrle, and H. Sabo. (1988). Dissociation between language and social functions in Williams syndrome. In K. Mogford and D. Bishop, Eds., *Language Development in Exceptional Circumstances*. New York: Churchill-Livingstone Inc., pp. 177–189.

Bickerton, D. (1981). *Roots of Language*. Ann Arbor, MI: Karoma.

Bloom, P. (1994). Semantic competence as an explanation for some transitions in language development. In Y. Levy and I. Schlesinger, Eds., *Other Children, Other Languages: Theoretical Issues in Language Development*. Hillsdale, NJ: Erlbaum.

Bowerman, M. (1982). Starting to talk worse: Clues to language acquisition from children's late speech errors. In S. Strauss, Ed., *U-Shaped Behavioral Growth*. New York: Academic Press.

Brown, R., and U. Bellugi. (1964). Three processes in the child's acquisition of syntax. In E. H. Lenneberg, Ed., *New Directions in the Study of Language*. Cambridge, MA: MIT Press.

Brown, R., and C. Hanlon. (1970). Derivational complexity and order of acquisition in child speech. In J. R. Hayes, Ed., *Cognition and the Development of Language*. New York: Wiley.

Cartwright, T. A., and M. R. Brent. (1997). Syntactic categorization in early language acquisition: Formalizing the role of distributional analysis. *Cognition* 63(2): 121–170.

Chomsky, N. (1965). *Aspects of the Theory of Syntax*. Cambridge, MA: MIT Press.

Chomsky, N. (1986). *Knowledge of Language: Its Nature, Origin, and Use*. New York: Praeger.

Deprez, V., and A. Pierce. (1993). Negation and functional projections in early grammar. *Linguistic Inquiry* 24(1): 25–67.

Feldman, H., S. Goldin-Meadow, and L. R. Gleitman. (1978). Beyond Herodotus: The creation of language by linguistically deprived deaf children. In A. Lock, Ed., *Action, Gesture, and Symbol*. New York: Academic Press.

Fernald, A., and P. Kuhl. (1987). Acoustic determinants of infant preference for motherese speech. *Infant Behavior and Development* 10: 279–293.

Fowler, A. (1990). Language abilities in children with Down's syndrome: Evidence for a specific syntactic delay. In D. Cicchetti and M. Beeghly, Eds., *Children with Down's Syndrome: A Developmental Perspective*. Cambridge: Cambridge University Press, pp. 302–328.

Hirsh-Pasek, K., and R. Golinkoff (1996). *The Origins of Grammar: Evidence from Early Language Comprehension*. Cambridge, MA: MIT Press.

Lieven, E. V. M. (1994). Crosslinguistic and crosscultural aspects of language addressed to children. In C. Gallaway and B. J. Richards, Eds., *Input and Interaction in Language Acquisition*. Cambridge: Cambridge University Press.

Macnamara, J. (1972). Cognitive basis of language learning in infants. *Psychological Review* 79: 1–13.

Marcus, G. F., S. Pinker, M. Ullman, M. Hollander, T. Rosen, and F. Xu. (1992). Overgeneralization in language acquisition. *Monographs of the Society for Research in Child Development*.

Marler, P. (1991). The instinct to learn. In S. Carey and R. Gelman, Eds., *The Epigenesis of Mind: Essays on Biology and Cognition*. Hillsdale, NJ: Erlbaum.

McKee, C. (1996). On-line methods. In D. McDaniel, C. McKee, and H. Smith-Cairns, Eds., *Methods for Assessing Children's Syntax*. Cambridge, MA: MIT Press, pp. 190–208.

Newport, E. L. (1990). Maturational constraints on language learning. *Cognitive Science* 14: 11–28.

Newport, E. L., L. Gleitman, and H. Gleitman. (1977). Mother, I'd rather do it myself: Some effects and non-effects of maternal speech style. In C. E. Snow and C. A. Ferguson, Eds., *Talking to Children: Language Input and Acquisition*. Cambridge: Cambridge University Press.

Pinker, S. (1984). *Language Learnability and Language Development*. Cambridge, MA: Harvard University Press.

Rice, M., and K. Wexler. (1996). Toward tense as a clinical marker of Specific Language Impairment in English-speaking children. *Journal of Speech and Hearing Research* 39: 1239–1257.

Saffran, J. R., R. N. Aslin, and E. L. Newport. (1996). Statistical learning by 8-month old infants. *Science* 274: 1926–1928.

Slobin, D. I., Ed. (1985). *The Crosslinguistic Study of Language Acquisition*. Vol. 1, *The Data*. Hillsdale, NJ: Erlbaum.

Snedeker, J. (1996). "With" or without: children's use of a functional preposition in sentence comprehension. Unpublished manuscript, University of Pennsylvania.

Trueswell, J., I. Sekerina, and N. Hill. (1998). On-line sentence processing in children: Evidence from experiments during listening. Paper presented at the CUNY Sentence Processing Conference, Rutgers, NJ, March 19, 1998.

van der Lely, H. K. J. (1997). Language and cognitive development in a Grammatical SLI boy: Modularity and innateness. *Journal of Neurolinguistics* 10: 75–107.

Further Readings

Aksu-Koc, A. A., and Slobin D. I. (1985). The acquisition of Turkish. In D. I. Slobin, Ed., *The Crosslinguistic Study of Language Acquisition*. Vol. 1, *The Data*. Hillsdale, NJ: Erlbaum.

Bickerton, D. (1984). The language bioprogram hypothesis. *Behavioral and Brain Sciences* 7: 173–187.

Bloom, L. (1970). *Language Development: Form and Function in Emerging Grammars*. Cambridge, MA: MIT Press.

Bloom, P. (1990). Syntactic distinctions in child language. *Journal of Child Language* 17: 343-355.

Bloom, P. (1994). Recent controversies in the study of language acquisition. In M. A. Gernsbacher, Ed., *Handbook of Psycholinguistics*. San Diego, CA: Academic Press.

Braine, M. D. S. (1976). Children's first word combinations. *Monographs of the Society for Research in Child Development* 41.

Brown, R. (1973). *A First Language: The Early Stages.* Cambridge, MA: Harvard University Press.

Chomsky, N. (1965). *Aspects of the Theory of Syntax.* Cambridge, MA: MIT Press.

Darwin, C. H. (1877). A biographical sketch of a young child. *Kosmos* 1: 367–376.

Gleitman, L. R., and Gleitman, H. (1992). A picture is worth a thousand words but that's the problem: The role of syntax in vocabulary acquisition. *Current Directions in Psychological Science* 1(1): 31–35.

Gleitman, L., H. Gleitman, B. Landau, and E. Wanner. (1988). Where learning begins: Initial representations for language learning. In F. Newmeyer, Ed., *Language: Psychological and Biological Aspects.* Vol. 3, *Linguistics. The Cambridge Survey.* New York: Cambridge University Press.

Gleitman, L., and E. L. Newport. (1995). The invention of language by children: Environmental and biological influences on the acquisition of language. In L. Gleitman and M. Liberman, Eds., *An Invitation to Cognitive Science,* 2nd ed. Vol. 1, *Language.* Cambridge MA: MIT Press, pp. 1–24.

Johnson, J. S., and E. L. Newport. (1989). Critical period effects in second language learning: The influence of maturational state on the acquisition of English as a second language. *Cognitive Psychology* 21: 60–99.

Jusczyk, P. W. (1997). *The Discovery of Spoken Language.* Cambridge, MA: MIT Press/Bradford Books.

Kelly, M. H., and S. Martin. (1994). Domain general abilities applied to domain specific tasks: Sensitivity to probabilities in perception, cognition, and language. *Lingua* 92: 105–140.

Lenneberg, E. (1967). *Biological Foundations of Language.* New York: Wiley.

Marcus, G. F. (1993). Negative evidence in language acquisition. *Cognition* 46: 53–85.

Mintz, T. H., E. L. Newport, and T. G. Bever. (1995). Distributional regularities of grammatical categories in speech to infants. In J. Beckman, Ed., *Proceedings of the North East Linguistic Society 25,* vol. 2. Amherst, MA: GLSA.

Mehler, J., P. W. Jusczyk, N. Lambertz, J. Halsted, J. Bertoncini, and C. Amiel-Tison. (1988). A precursor of language acquisition in young infants. *Cognition* 29: 143–178.

Newport, E. L., and R. P. Meier. (1985). The acquisition of American Sign Language. In D.I. Slobin, Ed., *The Cross-Linguistic Study of Language Acquisition.* Hillsdale, NJ: Erlbaum.

Petitto, L. A., and P. F. Marentette. (1991). Babbling in the manual mode: Evidence for the ontogeny of language. *Science* 251: 1493–1496.

Piaget, J. (1926). *The Language and Thought of the Child.* New York: Routledge and Kegan Paul.

Pinker, S. (1994). *The Language Instinct.* New York: Morrow.

Pinker, S., and A. Prince. (1988). On language and connectionism: Analysis of a Parallel Distributed Processing model of language acquisition. *Cognition* 28: 73–193.

Plunkett, K., and V. Marchman. (1991). U-shaped learning and frequency effects in a multi-layered perceptron: Implications for child language acquisition. *Cognition* 38: 43–102.

Shatz, M., and R. Gelman. (1973). The development of communication skills: Modifications in the speech of young children as a function of listener. *Monographs of the Society for Research in Child Development* 38 (5, Serial No. 152).

Singleton, J. L., and E. L. Newport. (1994). When learners surpass their models: The acquisition of American Sign Language from impoverished input. Unpublished manuscript, University of Illinois.

Slobin, D. I., and T. G. Bever. (1982). Children's use of canonical sentence schemas: A crosslinguistic study of word order and inflections. *Cognition* 12: 229–265.

Werker, J. F., and R. C. Tees. (1984). Cross-linguistic speech perception: Evidence for perceptual reorganiztion in the first year of life. *Infant Behavior and Development* 7: 49–63.

Wexler, K. (1982). A principle theory for language acquisition. In E. Wanner and L. Gleitman, Eds., *Language Acquisition: The State of the Art.* Cambridge: Cambridge University Press, pp. 288–318.

Language and Cognition

See INTRODUCTION: LINGUISTICS AND LANGUAGE; LANGUAGE AND THOUGHT; LANGUAGE OF THOUGHT

Language and Communication

Language and communication are often defined as the human ability to refer abstractly and with intent to influence the thinking and actions of other individuals. Language is thought of as the uniquely human part of a broader system of communication that shares features with other ANIMAL COMMUNICATION systems. In the twentieth century, language research has focused largely on those aspects of vocal communication (or their homologs in SIGN LANGUAGES) that are organized as categorial oppositions (de Saussure (1916/1959); for example, categories of sound, grammar, and meaning. The domain of language research has been largely speech. In 1960, the linguist Charles Hockett advocated restricting the term "[human] language" to just those dimensions of communication that are vocal, syntactic, arbitrary in relation to their referents, abstractly referential (that is, meaning is determinable independently of the immediate context of utterance), and learned. The host of other patterned dimensions of communicative acts—social, kinesic and affective-volitional: vocal and nonvocal—has often been labeled "paralanguage" and regarded as outside the proper domain of linguistic inquiry.

The dominant paradigm in linguistics since the 1950s (Piatelli-Palmarini 1980) has as its foundation some notion of language as a disembodied symbol manipulation device. This Cartesian rationalist approach (Dreyfus 1992) has informed much research in experimental PSYCHOLINGUISTICS. The approach meshes with a general theory of mind in cognitive science whose influence has spread with the increasing use of computer technology. Based on the metaphor of the mind as a computer, higher human mental functions (language among them) are modeled on analogy with the operating principles of formal information processing (IP) systems, including, "decomposition of complexity into simpler units; routines and subroutines that automatically and recursively operate on atomic units" (Gigerenzer and Goldstein 1996). In modular IP models, subroutines are "unintelligent" and encapsulated; that is, each functions in relative isolation from other modules in the system. Gigerenzer and Goldstein cite Levelt's (1989) influential model of LANGUAGE PRODUCTION as representative of this general approach. As well, a great deal of basic research on SPEECH PERCEPTION, SENTENCE PROCESSING, and LANGUAGE ACQUISITION has been concerned with the nature of psycholinguistic functions when variables of meaning and context enter the experimental format only in a controlled manner, via symbol and syntax. One goal has been to understand how arbitrary symbol and syntax, thought of as the "purely linguistic" dimensions of human communicative acts, function as pointers to extralinguistic meaning and context. Olson (1994) implicates the technology of writing as another source for this way of thinking about language, saying, "we introspect our language in terms of the categories laid down by our script." In this view, spoken linguistic units are containers to carry abstract reference and these units have an existence independent from the context that gives rise to them. (That linguistic units can be made to function in this way *in vitro* is an issue crucially distinct from what their nature and functions may be in the organic whole of face-to-face communication.)

Research cued by formal linguistics links to the combined senses of what language is (speech and syntax) and what its "main function" is (abstract reference). Lieberman's (1991) research on the evolution of the human vocal tract, for instance, pinpoints when in evolutionary time humans became capable of producing the modern range of spoken phonetic categorial distinctions, identifying this with the onset of human language as a whole. Research on PRIMATE LANGUAGE often imports frameworks and units of analysis from linguistic analyses of human language. For example, reports of chimpanzee and gorilla attempts to use artificial and signed languages give totals of the words in the animals' vocabularies and comment on the extent to which the animals are able to negotiate task demands absent information from context on the basis of symbol manipulation alone. Cheney and Seyfarth's (1990) finding that vervet monkeys have distinct calls to alert conspecifics to the presence of different types of predators gives rise to discussions about the role of something like "words" in these animals' natural communication system.

The dominant paradigm puts a chasm between animal communication and human language, one that has been notably difficult for theories of the EVOLUTION OF LANGUAGE to bridge. Saltationist evolutionary accounts assume a significant structure-producing genetic mutation that makes human-language syntax possible. Some researchers hypothesize that humans are uniquely capable of developing a THEORY OF MIND necessary for intentional communication; some that a particular mimetic ability is the key. Other accounts emphasize the continuity between human cognitive, social, and communicative abilities and those of our primate relatives (see the collected papers in Hurford, Studdert-Kennedy, and Knight 1998). The crucial evolutionary join, however, remains underspecified.

Alternative research strategies in linguistics, sociolinguistics, anthropology, and psychology have assembled evidence of much interpenetration and interdependence of the many dimensions of human communicative acts that have been theorized to be functionally independent. Sociolinguistics (for example, Labov 1980) has shown that individuals' attempts to position themselves relative to different groups or social strata can have effects even to the level of language phonology. The psycholinguist Locke (1994) has noted that, "linguists have neglected the role of language as a medium for social interaction and emotional expression." He distinguishes "talk" (loosely: social speech) in human communication from a more restricted sense of speech and claims that the language acquisition process targets talk first, assembling an essential social-interactional framework within which speech is then acquired. The anthropologist Kendon (1994) assigns equal status to gesture and speech as communicative resources. Cognitive and functional linguistic theory (Lakoff 1987) attempts to ground language in embodied experience and rejects the analytic separation of grammar from meaning. In later years, Hockett himself (1987), in writing about "how language means," acknowledged the difficulty of drawing a sharp boundary in situated language use between language and "paralanguage"; between the arbitrary and the iconic. He exhorted linguists to learn about language by studying the communicative package as a whole, "*in vivo*," and to avoid focusing too exclusively on, thereby making too much of, the abstract referring and symbol manipulation properties of language.

The linguist Dwight Bolinger (Bolinger and Sears 1975) pursued linguistic research with a very different focus, stating, "language is speech embedded in gesture." This statement puts paralanguage ("gesture," both vocal and kinesic) before abstract, syntactic speech in studies of human language. The "gesture" with which Bolinger was primarily concerned is prosody, the patterns of stress and intonation in speech. He also reported, however, observations of the facial and bodily gestures that occur together with speech and noted their relation to prosody. He was interested, for example, in how a prosodic contour determines the meaning of an utterance as much as do the combined meanings of the words in the sentence; also in how gesture expresses affect or can reveal a speaker's perspective on her own utterance at the moment of speaking.

McNeill and Duncan (1999) largely reject the language/paralanguage distinction. These authors theorize that gesture, broadly construed to include prosodic and rhythmic phenomena (cf. Tuite 1993), iconic gestures, nonrepresentational movements of the hands and body, semiotic valuation of gesture space, as well as analog (as opposed to discrete) patterning on other communicative dimensions, is intrinsic to language. On this view, language is an organized form of on-line, interactive, embodied, and contextualized human cognition. By hypothesis, the initial organizing impulse of a communicative production is a unit of thinking patterned simultaneously according to two distinct representational systems: one categorial, compositional, and analytic; the other imagistic, synthetic, and holistic. Patterning in either system may emerge in speech or gesture production, though it has often been convenient to think of speech as the embodiment of the categorial, and gesture as the embodiment of the noncategorial. According to McNeill and Duncan, reductionist accounts that isolate categorial speech from image, prosody, and gesture in separate processing modules (Levelt 1989; Krauss, Chen, and Gottesman 1999) will fail to account for the way language production and comprehension evolve on-line in real-time communication. Speech and gesture together provide an enhanced window on cognition during communication. Much is externalized, a fact that minimizes the burden on interlocutors' theories of mind.

Gigerenzer and Goldstein (1996) identify the information encapsulation feature of modularist IP models such as Levelt's as the Achilles' heel of these models. Pushed by cross-disciplinary study of language *in vivo*, there is growing consensus that models must deal with the massive interpenetration of what have traditionally been analyzed as functionally distinct levels of linguistic analysis. Such consensus points to a paradigm shift underway, one that encompasses Saussure's paradigm-shifting formulation but moves beyond it. It locates human language in the human body and postulates as its theoretic atom the conversational dyad, rather than a monad with a message to transmit or receive (Goodwin 1986; Schegloff 1984). The shift was foreshadowed by Lev Semenovich VYGOTSKY (1934/1986), who analyzed communicative events as developing simultaneously on an "inter-" as well as an "intra-psychic plane." At the vangard are socio- and psycholinguistic gesture research, research on sign languages liberated from earlier constraints to minimize iconic dimensions of patterning (Armstrong, Stokoe, and Wilcox 1995), cognitive and functional linguistic research, as well as philosophical (Heidegger: see Dreyfus 1991) and anthropological (Levinson, forthcoming) re-search that highlights the situated, culturally embedded character of language use.

See also MODULARITY AND LANGUAGE; MODULARITY OF MIND; PROSODY AND INTONATION; PROSODY AND INTONATION, PROCESSING ISSUES; SITUATEDNESS/EMBEDDEDNESS

—*Susan Duncan*

References

Armstrong, D. F., W. C. Stokoe, and S. E. Wilcox. (1995). *Gesture and the Nature of Language.* Cambridge: Cambridge University Press.

Bolinger, D. L., and D. A. Sears. (1975). *Aspects of Language.* 2nd ed. New York: Harcourt, Brace, Jovanovich.

Cheney, D. L., and S. M. Seyfarth. (1990). *How Monkeys See the World.* Chicago: University of Chicago Press.

Dreyfus, H. L. (1991). *Being-in-the-World: A Commentary on Heidegger's Being and Time, Division I.* Cambridge, MA: The MIT Press.

Dreyfus, H. L. (1992). *What Computers Still Can't Do: A Critique of Artificial Reason.* Cambridge, MA: MIT Press.

Gigerenzer, G., and D. Goldstein. (1996). Mind as computer: The birth of a metaphor. *Creativity Research Journal* 9: 131–144.

Goodwin, C. (1986). Gesture as a resource for the organization of mutual orientation. *Semiotica* 62(1–2): 29–49.

Hockett, C. F. (1987). *Refurbishing our Foundations.* Amsterdam: John Benjamins.

Hockett, C. F. (1960). Logical considerations in the study of animal communication. In W. E. Lanyon and W. N. Tavolga, Eds., *Animal Sounds and Communication.* Washington: American Institute of Biological Science, pp. 392–430.

Hurford, J. R., M. Studdert-Kennedy, and C. Knight, Eds. (1998). *Approaches to the Evolution of Language: Social and Cognitive Bases.* Edinburgh: Edinburgh University Press.

Kendon, A. (1994). Do gestures communicate? *Research on Language and Social Interaction* 27(3): 3–28.

Krauss, R. M., Y. Chen, and R. F. Gottesman. (1999). Lexical gestures and lexical access: A process model. In D. McNeill, Ed., *Language and Gesture: Window into Thought and Action.* Cambridge: Cambridge University Press.

Labov, W. (1980). The social origins of sound change. In W. Labov, Ed., *Locating Language in Time and Space.* New York: Academic Press, pp. 251–266.

Lakoff, G. (1987). *Women, Fire, and Dangerous Things: What Categories Reveal about the Mind.* Chicago: University of Chicago Press.

Levelt, W. J. M. (1989). *Speaking: From Intention to Articulation.* Cambridge, MA: MIT Press.

Levinson S. C. (Forthcoming). The body in space: Cultural differences in the use of body-schema for spatial thinking and gesture. In G. Lewis and F. Sigaud, Eds., *Culture and Uses of the Body.* Cambridge: Oxford University Press.

Lieberman, P. (1991). *Uniquely Human: The Evolution of Speech, Thought, and Selfless Behavior.* Cambridge, MA: Harvard University Press.

Locke, J. (1994). Phases in a child's development of language. *American Scientist* 82: 436–445.

McNeill, D., and S. Duncan. (1999). Growth points in thinking for speaking. In D. McNeill, Ed., *Language and Gesture: Window into Thought and Action.* Cambridge: Cambridge University Press.

Olson, D. R. (1994). *The World on Paper: Conceptual and Cognitive Implications of Writing and Reading.* Cambridge: Cambridge University Press.

Piatelli-Palmarini, M., Ed. (1980). *Language and Learning: The Debate Between Jean Piaget and Noam Chomsky.* Cambridge, MA: Harvard University Press.

Saussure, F. de. [1916] (1959). *Course in General Linguistics.* Translated by W. Baskin. Reprint. New York: Philosophical Library.

Schegloff, E. A. (1984). On some gestures' relation to talk. In J. M. Atkinson and J. Heritage, Eds., *Structures of Social Action.* Cambridge: Cambridge University Press, pp. 266–295.

Tuite, K. (1993). The production of gesture. *Semiotica* 93(1–2): 83–105.

Vygotsky, L. S. [1934] (1986). *Thought and Language,* A. Kozulin, ed. and trans. Cambridge, MA: MIT Press.

Further Readings

Armstrong, D. (1983). Iconicity, arbitrariness, and duality of pattering in signed and spoken language: Perspectives on language evolution. *Sign Language Studies* 38(Spring): 51–69.

Bavelas, J. B. (1994). Gestures as part of speech: Methodological implications. *Research on Language and Social Interaction* 27(3): 201–221.

Bernieri, F. J., and R. Rosenthal. (1991). Interpersonal coordination: Behavior matching and interactional synchrony. In R. Feldman and B. Rime, Eds., *Fundmentals of Nonverbal Behavior.* Cambridge: Cambridge University Press, pp. 401–432.

Bickerton, D. (1990). *Language and Species.* Chicago: University of Chicago Press.

Bolinger, D. L. (1946). Thoughts on "yep" and "nope." *American Speech* 21: 90–95.

Crystal, D. (1976). Paralinguistic behavior as continuity between animal and human communication. In W. C. McCormack and S. A. Wurm, Eds., *Language and Man: Anthropological Issues.* The Hague: Mouton, pp. 13–27.

Givon, T. (1985). Iconicity, isomorphism, and non-arbitrary coding in syntax. In J. Haiman, Ed., *Iconicity in Syntax.* Amsterdam: John Benjamins, pp. 187–219.

Hockett, C. F. (1978). In search of Jove's brow. *American Speech* 53: 243–313.

Kendon, A. (1980). Gesticulation and speech: Two aspects of the process of utterance. In M. R. Key, Ed., *The Relationship Between Verbal and Nonverbal Communication*. The Hague: Mouton, pp. 207–228.

Kendon, A. (1972). Some relationships between body motion and speech: An analysis of an example. In A. Siegman and B. Pope, Eds., *Studies in Dyadic Communication*. New York: Pergamon Press, pp. 177–210.

McNeill, D. (1985). So you think gestures are nonverbal? *Psychological Review* 92(3): 350–371.

McNeill, D. (1992). *Hand and Mind: What Gestures Reveal About Thought*. Chicago: Chicago University Press.

Streeck, J. (1994). Gesture as communication II: the audience as co-author. *Research on Language and Social Interaction* 27(3): 239–267.

Language and Culture

Languages differ in fundamental ways: their phoneme inventories vary from 11 to 141 (Maddieson 1984), they may have elaborate or no morphology, may or may not use word order or constituent structure or case to signify syntactic relations, may or may not have word roots of fixed grammatical word class, may make use of quite different semantic parameters, and so on (see TYPOLOGY). There are an estimated 7000 or more distinct languages in the world, each a cultural tradition of (generally) thousands of years in the making, and there are at least 20 (how many is controversial) language families across which relationships cannot be demonstrated. Each is adapted to a unique cultural and social environment, with striking differences in usage patterns (Bauman and Sherzer 1974). This cultural adaptation constitutes the cultural capital of language, and language differences are perhaps the most perduring of all aspects of culture. On the other hand, language is a biological capacity, instantiated in the anatomy of our vocal tract and the corresponding acuity of our hearing and in dedicated areas of the brain (see LANGUAGE, NEURAL BASIS OF). In fact, language provides the best evidence for the thesis of coevolution, whereby cultural replication and genetic replication became intertwined, each providing the context for the evolution of the other (see EVOLUTION OF LANGUAGE; also Durham 1991). CULTURAL VARIATION also requires that the biological capacity for language be malleable (see NEURAL PLASTICITY)—for example, able to learn and parse speech of quite different sound and structural type (see PSYCHOLINGUISTICS)—although this malleability is progressively lost during maturation of the individual.

Most models of human cognition abstract away from variation, whether cultural or individual. But in the case of language, the capacity to handle the cultural variation is a central property of cognitive ability. Consider for example that language ability is modality independent; according to cultural tradition it can be not only spoken or signed (see SIGN LANGUAGES) but also represented visually by reference to sounds, meanings, or both (according to the writing system) or signed with the hands as in auxiliary hand-sign systems. In this modality independence it is very unlike any other sensory input or motor output system.

Current linguistic theory proceeds by positing universal hypotheses across all languages, and workers in other branches of cognitive science may therefore be led to think that large numbers of universals of language have been established. In actual fact these have proved very hard to formulate, and nearly all successful generalizations are either very abstract (and correspondingly difficult to test) or of the form "if a language is of a certain type T, then it tends to have property P" (see Greenberg 1978), usually with exceptions rapidly discovered. Most databases for extrapolation cover less than 10% of the world's languages; the great majority of languages have never been described, let alone carefully analyzed.

Through language, and to a lesser extent other semiotic systems, individuals have access to the large accumulation of cultural ideas, practices, and technology that instantiate a distinct cultural tradition. The question then arises as to what extent these ideas and practices are actually embodied in the language in lexical and grammatical distinctions. Humboldt, and later SAPIR and Whorf, are associated with the theory that a language encapsulates a cultural perspective and actually creates conceptual categories (see CONCEPTS; LINGUISTIC RELATIVITY HYPOTHESIS; Gumperz and Levinson 1996). In some respects this seems clearly true (consider notions like "tort" or "manslaughter" that reflect and constitute part of the English legal tradition, not an aspect of culture-independent reality); in other respects it seems to be false ("black" appears to be a universal concept, reflecting aspects of PSYCHOPHYSICS). Yet many cognitive scientists assume that basic semantic parameters are universal, culture-specific notions like "tort" being constructed from such universal semantic primitives (an influential exception is Fodor, who claims that all such notions are universal unanalyzed wholes in the LANGUAGE OF THOUGHT). Current work on semantics, however, makes it clear than even apparently fundamental notions may vary crosslinguistically, and children learning language do not invariably appear to make the same initial assumptions about meaning (Slobin 1985). Take for example spatial notions: readers are likely to think of the things on the desk before them in terms of things "in front" of themselves, "to the left," or "to the right." But some languages do not lexicalize these notions at all. Instead one must refer to things as, for example, "to the north," "to the east" or "to the west," and so forth, as appropriate. Consequently, speakers of these languages must keep their bearings, and they can be shown to conceive of spatial arrangements differently in nonverbal memory and inference (Levinson 1996).

There are many aspects of the cultural patterning of language that may be fundamental to its role in cognition. One is special elaborations of linguistic ability—for instance, highly skilled performance as in simultaneous translation or rapid sports commentary that can be delivered at twice the speed of the fastest conversation. Perhaps the majority of the world's population are multingual, and multilingualism is a capacity largely beyond current psycholinguistic understanding. Another is the elaboration of technologies of language, of which writing is the most fundamental (Goody 1977) and NATURAL LANGUAGE PROCESSING the most advanced. Natural languages are learned in and through social interaction and constitute probably the most complex cognitive task that humans routinely undertake (and quite plausibly the major pressure for brain evolution in our species; see Byrne and Whiten 1988; COOPERATION AND COMPETITION). Many aspects of natural language can only be understood in relation to this interactional context, including INDEXICALS AND DEMONSTRATIVES, speech acts, and conveyed politeness (Brown and Levinson 1987).

Cognitive scientists are not interested in all aspects of language (most aspects of their history for example, but see LANGUAGE VARIATION AND CHANGE). Four aspects though are of particular importance. One is how language is learned (see LEARNING). A second is how language is processed (viewing the mind or the brain as an information-processing device), both in comprehension (Tyler 1992) and production (Levelt 1989). A third is how language interfaces with other cognitive abilities and how semantic representations are related to other conceptual representations (Nuyts and Pederson 1997). A fourth concerns how linguistic ability is instantiated in neurophysiology.

In all four aspects, the complex interplay between culture and biology in language is crucial to our understanding of the phenomena. In LANGUAGE ACQUISITION, the cultural variability makes learning a fundamental puzzle; even if there are significant universals, the child must still pair sounds and meanings, where the analysis of neither is given by first principles. For language processing, again language variation is highly problematic: it is hard to see how the same mechanisms can be involved in radically different languages. For example, languages with verbs in medial or final position in the sentence allow one to start speech production before the sentence is fully worked out; but languages with verbs in initial position, fully marked for agreement with subject and object, would seem to require a different production strategy. Similarly, parsing strategies for comprehension would seem necessarily divergent in languages with fixed word order or no fixed word order, with rich morphology or none. Thirdly, fundamental variation in semantic parameters makes the interface between language and general cognition look much more problematic than is commonly assumed. Not all concepts are directly expressible in a language. Further, the semantic distinctions obligatorily required by the grammar are not necessarily of the kind that would universally be noted and memorized for future possible linguistic expression (e.g., was the referent visible at event time, was the participant to be described of greater or lesser rank than the speaker and the addressee, was the referent a singleton or not, etc.). This points to the likelihood that to speak a particular language, experience must be coded in the appropriate categories, and it also raises questions about the universality of the language of thought. Finally, with regards to brain and language, there is evidence from selective brain damage (see APHASIA) that linguistic abilities are localized partly in accordance with the structure of a particular language (Bates and Wulfreck 1989).

See also HUMAN UNIVERSALS; INNATENESS OF LANGUAGE; LANGUAGE AND THOUGHT; LANGUAGE PRODUCTION; LINGUISTIC UNIVERSALS AND UNIVERSAL GRAMMAR

—*Stephen C. Levinson*

References

Bates, E., and B. Wulfek. (1989). Crosslinguistic studies of aphasia. In B. Macwhinney and E. Bates, Eds., *The Crosslinguistic Study of Sentence Processing.* New York: Cambridge University Press, pp. 328–374.

Bauman, R., and J. Sherzer, Eds. (1974). *Explorations in the Ethnography of Speaking.* Cambridge: Cambridge University Press.

Brown, P., and S. Levinson. (1987) *Politeness.* Cambridge, UK: Cambridge University Press.

Byrne, R. W., and A. Whiten. (1988). *Machiavellian Intelligence.* Oxford: Clarendon Press.

Durham, W. (1991). *Coevolution: Genes, Cultures, and Human Diversity.* Palo Alto, CA: Stanford.

Goody, J. (1977). *The Domestication of the Savage Mind.* Cambridge: Cambridge University Press.

Greenberg, J. (1978). *Universals of Language,* vols. 1–4. Stanford, CA: Stanford University Press.

Gumperz, J., and S. Levinson. (1996). *Rethinking Linguistic Relativity.* Cambridge: Cambridge University Press.

Levelt, W. (1989). *Speech Production.* Cambridge, MA: MIT Press.

Levinson, S. C. (1996). Frames of reference and Molyneux's question: Crosslinguistic evidence. In I. P. Bloom, M. Peterson, L. Nadel, and M. Garnett, Eds., *Language and Space.* Cambridge, MA: MIT Press.

Maddieson, I. (1984). *Patterns of Sounds.* Cambridge: Cambridge University Press.

Nuyts, J., and E. Pederson, Eds. (1997). *Linguistic and Conceptual Representation.* Cambridge: Cambridge University Press.

Slobin, D. (1985). *The Crosslinguistic Study of Language Acquisition.* Vols. 1 and 2. Hillsdale, NJ: Erlbaum.

Tyler, L. (1992). *Spoken Language Comprehension.* Cambridge, MA: MIT Press.

Language and Gender

Exploring the interaction of language and gender raises many fundamental questions of cognitive science. What are the connections of LANGUAGE AND THOUGHT, of LANGUAGE AND CULTURE, of language and action? What role do LANGUAGE ACQUISITION and language processing play in forging these connections? Even research on language and gender that does not address such questions explicitly can usually be seen as implicitly relevant to them. Relatively few language and gender researchers have cast their work in primarily cognitive terms, more often emphasizing social or economic or political phenomena, but of course such phenomena can themselves be fruitfully approached from the perspective of cognitive science—for example, in work on SOCIAL COGNITION.

Two basic families of questions have dominated language and gender research. First, does gender influence language and, if so, how? That is, how might gender identities and relations of interlocutors be connected to the form and content of what they say? There is considerable sociolinguistic research on how women and men use language in different situations (see, e.g., Coates 1992; Coates and Cameron 1988; Eckert 1990); there is some developmental research that looks at gender issues and a very little neurolinguistic work on sex differences in brain activity during language processing (along with sociolinguistic work, Philips, Steele, and Tanz 1987 include contributions addressing both language development and neurolinguistics). There is also a very little work on phonetic issues (e.g., Hanson 1996; Henton 1992). With the exception of some of the best sociolinguistic work (e.g., Brown 1990; Goodwin 1991; and a number of the articles in Coates 1998), most research on how gender affects language conflates gender with sex, focusing on overall sex differences while ignoring the intertwining of gender with other aspects of social identity and social relations (see Eckert and McConnell-Ginet 1992, 1996; Ochs 1992) and also ignoring other aspects of intrasex variation as well as complexities in sexual classification. Some work has addressed ways in which gender arrangements may affect the development of linguistic conventions (e.g., McConnell-Ginet 1989 discusses how changes in lexical meaning might be driven by certain features of gender arrangements, including, for example, practices that give greater voice in public contexts to men than to women). And much sociolinguistic work has addressed the question of how gender affects changes in patterns of pronunciation and other aspects of language use that ultimately can change language structure (e.g., Milroy et al. 1995).

Second, does language influence gender and, if so, how? That is, how might linguistic resources and conventions affect the shape of a culture's gender arrangements? There have been a number of psycholinguistic studies on such topics as masculine generics (see, e.g., Sniezek and Jazwinski 1986) and studies in PRAGMATICS and related fields on topics like METAPHOR and linguistic discrimination (see, e.g., papers in Vetterling-Braggin 1981). There is also considerable work on these topics from anthropologists and cultural theorists, who look at a culture's favored figures of speech (e.g., using the terminology of delectable edibles to talk about women) and other linguistic clues to cultural assumptions in order to map the gender terrain. There is some evidence that gender (and other) stereotypes help drive inferencing even in those who don't accept them, suggesting that linguistically triggered stereotyping may be consequential both in acculturating children and in helping to maintain the gender status quo. What should be seen as the direction of influence is certainly not clear, however, and many studies of gender biases evident in linguistic resources are positing the influence of gender arrangements on language as much as the other way around (McConnell-Ginet 1989 and others suggest that influences typically go in both directions). Some of the same sociolinguistic studies that explore how women and men speak also look at the social and political effects of different speech styles and interactional dynamics. Lakoff (1975) made popular the idea that women's language use is part of what contributes to men's dominance over them. Although Lakoff herself and others would frame matters somewhat differently now, looking also at men's language use and at attitudes toward different speech styles, there continues to be considerable research suggesting that ways of speaking often play a role in maintaining male dominance (see, e.g., Henley and Kramarae 1991). Much of this research, however, also emphasizes the advantages that can accrue to women who have developed certain kinds of interactionally useful speech skills that many men lack (Tannen 1994 makes this kind of point, as does Holmes 1995).

As the discussion of these questions suggests, the distinction between these two families of questions is not as clearcut as it might at first seem. To talk in this way is to suppose that gender and language are somehow quite separate phenomena and that our goal is to articulate their connections. While useful for certain purposes, this supposition can mislead us. In particular, it does not come to grips with the rooting of both language use and gender in situated social practices, which involve the jointly orchestrated actions of groups of cognitive agents. Gal (1991) and Eckert and McConnell-Ginet (1992) have argued that the real interaction of gender and language, their coevolution, can be best illumined by examining both language and gender as they are manifest in social practice.

Both language and gender are of course also partly biological phenomena. In the view of most linguists and many other cognitive scientists, the possibilities for human language systems are very much constrained by the biologically given language capacity. There are, however, not only parameters along which language systems can vary; there are also many different ways that communities can (and do) use language in their activities. And gender is linked to sexual difference. Biological sex itself, however, is far less dichotomous than many assume (English speakers show little tolerance for gradations between "female" and "male," insisting on classifying intersexed people in one or the other category; see Bing and Bergvall 1996), and there is considerable intrasex variation on many dimensions (including cognitive functioning as well as physical and behavioral attributes), even among those whose classification seems biologically quite unproblematic. There is an extraordinary amount of sociocultural work done to elaborate femaleness and maleness, to construct gender identities (not limited to two in all cultures) and also gender relations. Most of this work is at the same time also shaping other aspects of social identities and relations (e.g., ethnicity, race, class). Because language use is an integral component of most social practices, language is necessarily a major instrument of the sociocultural construction of gender. Thus an emerging research goal is exploration of the linguistic practices through which sex and gender are elaborated in a wide range of different communities (see, e.g., Hall and Bucholtz 1996). Although rather little of this research has a cognitive orientation and some interesting work is not really empirical or scientific, it raises many important questions for cognitive scientists to address.

See also CULTURAL EVOLUTION; LANGUAGE AND COMMUNICATION; LANGUAGE AND CULTURE; METAPHOR AND CULTURE

—*Sally McConnell-Ginet*

References

Bing, J. M., and V. L. Bergvall. (1996). The question of questions: Beyond binary thinking. In V. L. Bergvall, J. M. Bing, and A. F. Freed, Eds., *Rethinking Language and Gender Research: Theory and Practice.* London: Longman.

Brown, P. (1990). Gender, politeness, and confrontation in Tenejapa. *Discourse Processes* 13: 123–141.

Coates, J. (1992). *Women, Men, and Language.* 2nd ed. London: Longman.

Coates, J. (1993). *Language and Gender: A Reader.* Oxford: Blackwell.

Coates, J., and D. Cameron, Eds. (1988). *Women in their Speech Communities: New Perspectives on Language and Sex.* London: Longman.

Eckert, P. (1990). The whole woman: Sex and gender differences in variation. *Language Variation and Change* 1: 245–267.

Eckert, P., and S. McConnell-Ginet. (1992). Think practically and look locally: Language and gender as community-based practice. *Annual Review of Anthropology* 21: 461–490.

Eckert, P., and S. McConnell-Ginet. (1996). Constructing meaning, constructing selves: Snapshots of language, gender, and class from Belten High. In K. Hall and M. Bucholtz, Eds., *Gender Articulated: Language and the Socially Constructed Self.* London: Routledge, pp. 459–507.

Gal, S. (1991). Between speech and silence: The problematics of research on language and gender. In M. DiLeonardo, Ed., *Gender at the Crossroads of Knowledge: Feminist Anthropology in the Postmodern Era.* Berkeley and Los Angeles: University of California Press, pp. 175–203.

Goodwin, M. H. (1991). *He-Said-She-Said.* Bloomington: Indiana University Press.

Hall, K., and M. Bucholtz, Eds. (1996). *Gender Articulated: Language and the Socially Constructed Self.* London: Routledge.

Hanson, H. (1996). Synthesis of female speech using the Klatt synthesizer. *Speech Communication Group Working Papers,* vol. 10. MIT Research Laboratory of Electronics, pp. 84–103.

Henley, N. M., and C. Kramarae. (1991). Gender, power, and miscommunication. In N. Coupland, H. Giles, and J. M. Wiemann, Eds., *Miscommunication and Problematic Talk.* Newbury Park, CA: Sage Publications.

Henton, C. (1992). The abnormality of male speech. In G. Wolf, Ed., *New Departures in Linguistics.* New York: Garland, pp. 27–59.

Holmes, J. (1995). *Women, Men, and Politeness.* London: Longman.

Lakoff, R. (1975). *Language and Woman's Place.* New York: Harper and Row.

McConnell-Ginet, S. (1989). The sexual (re-)production of meaning: A discourse-based theory. In F. W. Frank and P. A. Treichler, Eds., *Language, Gender, and Professional Writing: Theoretical Approaches and Guidelines for Nonsexist Usage.* New York: Modern Language Association.

Milroy, J., L. Milroy, S. Hartley, and D. Walshaw. (1995). Glottal stops and Tyneside glottalization: Competing patterns of variation and change in British English. *Language Variation and Change* 6: 327–357.

Ochs, E. (1992). Indexing gender. In A. Duranti and C. Goodwin, Eds., *Rethinking Context: Language as an Interactive Phenomenon.* Cambridge: Cambridge University Press, pp. 335–358.

Philips, S. U., S. Steele, and C. Tanz, Eds. (1987). *Language, Gender, and Sex in Comparative Perspective.* Cambridge: Cambridge University Press.

Sniezek, J. A., and C. H. Jazwinski. (1986). Gender bias in English: In search of fair language. *Journal of Applied Social Psychology* 16: 642–662.

Tannen, D. (1994). *Talking from 9 to 5: How Women's and Men's Conversational Styles Affect Who Gets Heard, Who Gets Credit, and What Gets Done at Work.* New York: William Morrow.

Vetterling-Braggin, M., Ed. (1981). *Sexist Language: A Modern Philosophical Analysis.* Totawa, NJ: Littlefield.

Language and Modularity

See MODULARITY AND LANGUAGE

Language and Thought

Perhaps because we typically think in words, language and thought seem completely intertwined. Indeed, scholars in various fields—psychology, linguistics, anthropology—as well as laypeople have entertained these questions: Is thought possible without language? Does the structure of our language shape our thinking? Does our perception/cognition shape the structure of language? Are our abilities to learn and use language part of our general intelligence?

Is thought possible without language? Research on babies and children who have not yet acquired any language suggests that little babies muse over rather important things. For instance, 3- to 4-month-old babies seem to think that each object occupies its own space and so one solid object cannot go through another solid object. Five-month-old babies can do simple arithmetic. If they see a hand carrying two objects to the back of a screen and reappearing empty-handed, they seem to expect two more objects behind the screen than before this addition event. When developmental psychologists such as Renee Baillargeon and Karen Wynn concocted "magic shows" that violated fundamental principles of physics or numbers by clever subterfuge, preverbal babies showed surprise by staring at the scenes longer than they would at physically plausible scenes. Other evidence for thought without language came from profoundly deaf children who had not been exposed to any sign language. Susan Goldin-Meadow, a psychologist, found several such children growing up in loving families. They invented their own signs and gestures to communicate their thoughts and needs (e.g., talking about shoveling snow, requesting someone to open a jar).

Still other evidence for thinking without language has to do with mental images. Scientists and writers as well as visual artists have claimed that some of their most creative work was inspired by their mental images. One of the best known examples, perhaps, is James Watson and Francis Crick's discovery of the double helix structure of DNA. Albert Einstein was another self-described visual thinker. It seems, then, brilliant as well as mundane thought is eminently possible without language.

Does language shape or even dictate thought? The linguistic anthropologist Edward SAPIR argued, "No two languages are ever sufficiently similar to be considered as representing the same social reality." His student, Benjamin Lee Whorf, asserted, "The world is presented in a kaleidoscopic flux of impressions which has to be organized . . . largely by the linguistic systems in our minds." The Sapir-Whorf hypothesis has two tenets: LINGUISTIC RELATIVITY HYPOTHESIS (i.e., structural differences between languages will generally be paralleled by nonlinguistic cognitive differences) and linguistic determinism (i.e., the structure of a language strongly influences or fully determines the way its native speakers perceive and reason about the world).

John Lucy, an anthropologist, has written about language differences associated with perceptual differences. For example, speakers of languages with different basic color vocabularies might sort nonprimary colors (e.g., turquoise, chartreuse) in slightly different ways. But such subtle effects were hardly what Sapir and Whorf had in mind when they wrote about how language might be related to, or might even shape, its speakers' worldview (e.g., time, causality, ontological categories).

One notable exception is the psychologist Alfred Bloom's intriguing claim that the lack of a distinct counterfactual marker in the Chinese language might make it difficult for Chinese speakers to think counterfactually—that is, to think hypothetically about what is not true (e.g., If Plato had been able to read Chinese, he could have . . .). Upon close scrutiny, however, Chinese speakers' purported difficulty in understanding Bloom's counterfactual stories disappeared when researchers such as Terry Au and Lisa Liu rewrote those stories in idiomatic Chinese with proper counterfactual markers. With 20/20 hindsight, perhaps we should have realized that Bloom's initial finding had to be too fascinating to be true. Note that when we feel lucky and realize that things could have turned out badly but didn't, or when we regret having done something and wish that we had acted differently, we have to think counterfactually. How can something so fundamental and pervasive in human thinking be difficult in any human language?

Despite early disappointing efforts to uncover evidence for language shaping thought, a "Whorfian Renaissance" seems to be in the making. For instance, the anthropologist Stephen Levinson has reported interesting variations in spatial language across cultures (see LANGUAGE AND CULTURE). However, how each language carves up space seems to be principled—influenced by the direction of gravity (e.g., up, down), human perception (e.g., near, far, front, back) and so forth—rather than random or arbitrary. Moreover, there is as yet no evidence for fundamental differences in spatial cognition associated with linguistic variations. For example, unlike some Papuan languages, English has no simple word meaning "that far away up there." Are English speakers less capable than Papuan speakers to construe such a location? Probably not. While the jury is still out for the Sapir-Whorf hypothesis, it is probably safe to say that important aspects of our worldview are unlikely to be at the mercy of arbitrary aspects of our language.

How about the other way around? By virtue of being human, we tend to perceive, organize, and reason about the world in certain ways. Do languages build upon our perceptual categories and conceptual organization? Consider color perception. Four-month-old babies prefer looking at primary colors (red, blue, green, yellow) to colors near the boundaries of primary colors; toddlers can identify primary colors better than nonprimary ones. Interestingly, anthropologists Brent Berlin and Paul Kay found that, if a language has fewer than five basic color words, it would include red, blue, green, and yellow (in addition to black and white). Nonprimary colors such as brown, pink, orange, and purple are encoded only in languages that have encoded the four primary colors (see COLOR CATEGORIZATION). Perceptual salience, then, seems to shape the encoding of color words rather than the other way around.

Our cognition also seems to shape our language. For instance, when asked in their native language "Paul amazes Mary. Why?" and "Paul admires Mary. Why?", the psychologist Roger Brown found that both Chinese and English speakers tended to talk about something amazing about Paul and something admirable about Mary. Note that in English, "amazing" and "admirable"—rather than "amazable" and "admiring"—are entrenched adjectives for describing people's disposition. These cognitive causal schemas, then, might be a universal and may have influenced the derivation of dispositional adjectives in English, rather than the other way around.

One more central issue in the study of language and thought: Are our abilities to learn and use language part of our general intelligence? Or, are they subserved by a special "language faculty"? Recent findings on language-specific impairments (i.e., language delay or disorder experienced by children who are not hearing or cognitively impaired) and Williams syndrome (i.e., extreme mental retardation with almost intact language abilities) suggest that cognition and language can be decoupled (see LANGUAGE IMPAIRMENT, DEVELOPMENTAL). In short, although language and thought might be quite modular (see also MODULARITY OF MIND), there is some evidence for our cognition and perception shaping the evolution of our language. Evidence for influence in the opposite direction, however, seems more elusive.

See also CATEGORIZATION; IMAGERY; MODULARITY AND LANGUAGE; NATIVISM; VYGOTSKY

—*Terry Au*

References

Au, T. K. (1983). Chinese and English counterfactuals: The Sapir-Whorf hypothesis revisited. *Cognition* 15: 155–187.

Au, T. K. (1986). A verb is worth a thousand words: The causes and consequences of interpersonal events implicit in language. *Journal of Memory and Language* 25: 104–122.

Baillargeon, R. (1993). The object concept revisited: New directions in the investigation of infants' physical knowledge. In C. Granrud, Ed., *Visual Perception and Cognition in Infancy.* Hillsdale, NJ: Erlbaum, pp. 265–315.

Bellugi, U., A. Bihrle, H. Neville, and S. Doherty. (1992). Language, cognition, and brain organization in a neurodevelopmental disorder. In M. Gunnar and C. Nelson, Eds., *Developmental Behavioral Neuroscience.* Hillsdale, NJ: Erlbaum, pp. 201–232.

Berlin, B., and P. Kay. (1969). *Basic Color Terms: Their Universality and Evolution.* Berkeley and Los Angeles: University of California Press.

Bloom, A. H. (1981). *The Linguistic Shaping of Thought: A Study in the Impact of Language on Thinking in China and the West.* Hillsdale, NJ: Erlbaum.

Bornstein, M. H. (1975). Qualities of color vision in infancy. *Journal of Experimental Child Psychology* 19: 410–419.

Brown, R., and D. Fisher. (1983). The psychological causality implicit in language. *Cognition* 14: 237–273.

Chomsky, N. (1959). A review of B. F. Skinner's monograph "Verbal Behavior." *Language* 35: 26–58.

Goldin-Meadow, S., and C. Mylander. (1990). Beyond the input given: The child's role in the acquisition of language. *Language* 66: 323–355.

Leonard, L. (1987). Is specific language impairment a useful construct? In S. Rosenberg, Ed., *Advances in Applied Psycholinguistics*. Vol. 1., *Disorders of First-language Development*. Cambridge: Cambridge University Press.

Levinson, S. C. (1996). Language and space. *Annual Review of Anthropology* 25: 353–382.

Lucy, J. A. (1992). *Language Diversity and Thought: A Reformulation of the Linguistic Relativity Hypothesis*. Cambridge: Cambridge University Press.

Pinker, S. (1994). *The Language Instinct*. New York: William Morrow.

Shepard, R. N. (1978). The mental image. *American Psychologist* 33: 125–137.

Wynn, K. (1992). Addition and subtraction in human infants. *Nature* 358: 749–750.

Further Readings

Au, T. K. (1988). Language and cognition. In L. Lloyd and R. Schiefelbusch, Eds., *Language Perspectives II*. Austin, TX: Pro-Ed, pp. 125–146.

Au, T. K. (1992). Counterfactual reasoning. In G. R. Semin and K. Fiedler, Eds., *Language, Interaction, and Social Cognition*. London: Sage, pp. 194–213.

Language Change

See CREOLES; LANGUAGE VARIATION AND CHANGE; PARAMETER-SETTING APPROACHES TO ACQUISITION, CREOLIZATION, AND DIACHRONY; TYPOLOGY

Language Development

See INNATENESS OF LANGUAGE; LANGUAGE ACQUISITION; PHONOLOGY, ACQUISITION OF; SEMANTICS, ACQUISITION OF

Language Evolution

See EVOLUTION OF LANGUAGE; LANGUAGE VARIATION AND CHANGE

Language Impairment, Developmental

It has been estimated that approximately thirteen percent of all children have some form of language impairment (Beitchman et al. 1986a). The most common known causes of developmental language impairments are hearing loss (including intermittent hearing loss resulting from chronic otitis media), general MENTAL RETARDATION, neurological disorders such as lesions or epilepsy affecting the auditory processing or language areas of the brain, and motor defects affecting the oral musculature. Many other developmental disorders, such as pervasive developmental disability (including AUTISM), attention deficit disorder, central auditory processing disorder, and Down's syndrome, may include delay in language development. In addition to these known causes of developmental language impairment, a recent epidemiological study of monolingual English-speaking kindergarten children in the United States found that approximately 8 percent of boys and 6 percent of girls have a significant developmental language impairment of unknown origin, referred to as specific language impairment (SLI; Tomblin et al. 1997). This epidemiological study also showed that the clinical identification of language impairments remains low. Only 29 percent of the parents of children identified as having SLI had previously been informed that their child had a speech or language problem.

The differential diagnosis of developmental language impairments is based on behavioral evaluations that include audiological, neurological, psychological, and speech and language testing. Developmental language disorders are divided into two basic categories, expressive language disorder and mixed receptive-expressive language disorder, a disorder encompassing both language comprehension and production deficits (DSM-IV. 1994). Comprehension or production problems may occur within one or more of the components of language, including PHONOLOGY, MORPHOLOGY, SEMANTICS, or SYNTAX. Problems with PRAGMATICS, that is, conversational skills, also occur frequently. A high proportion of children with developmental language disorders also have concomitant speech articulation defects, that is, they have difficulty clearly and correctly producing one or more of the speech sounds of their language. However, speech articulation defects and developmental language impairments can occur independently of each other.

Developmental language impairment has been shown to be a risk factor for other childhood disorders. For example, epidemiological studies showed that children referred to child guidance clinics for a variety of social and emotional conditions were found to have a higher-than-expected incidence of developmental language disorders (Beitchman et al. 1986b). Conversely, children diagnosed with developmental language disorders also have been found, upon examination, to have a preponderance of behavioral and emotional disorders (Cantwell, Baker, and Mattison 1979). Longitudinal research studies that have followed children with early developmental language impairments prospectively from the preschool though elementary school years have demonstrated a striking link between early developmental language impairments and subsequent learning disabilities, especially DYSLEXIA, a developmental reading disability (Aram et al. 1984; Bishop and Adams 1990; Rissman, Curtiss, and Tallal 1990; Catts 1993). Research that has compared children classified as SLI with those classified as dyslexic has shown that both groups are characterized by a variety of oral language deficits, specifically phonological analysis deficits (Liberman et al. 1974; Wagner and Torgeson 1987; Shankweiler et al. 1995). Whether the phonological deficit derives from speech-specific mechanisms, or from more basic acoustic processing deficits, has been the focus of considerable research and theoretical debate.

Phonological processing deficits are generally accompanied by central auditory processing disorders, particularly in the areas of AUDITORY ATTENTION and serial memory. These processing problems may result from a more basic impairment in the rate of neural information processing, specifically a severe backward masking deficit (Tallal, Miller, and Fitch 1993a; Tallal et al. 1993b; Wright et al.

1997). Tallal and colleagues have shown that children with phonologically based speech, language, and READING disorders need significantly more neural processing time (hundreds of milliseconds instead of tens of milliseconds) between brief, rapidly successive acoustic cues in order to process them correctly. This slowed processing rate has a particularly detrimental effect on phonological processing. Many acoustic changes occurring within syllables and words, necessary to distinguish the individual phonological elements (speech sounds), occur within the tens-of-milliseconds time window. Research has demonstrated that perception of those speech syllables that incorporate rapidly successive acoustic cues is most problematic for these children (see Tallal et al. 1993a for review).

These findings linking slow auditory processing rate and phonological processing deficits to developmental language and reading disorders have recently led to the development of novel remediation strategies for the treatment of developmental language-learning impairments. In a treatment-controlled study, using speech that was acoustically computer modified to extend and amplify the rapidly successive components, it was shown that intensive, individually adaptive daily training with computer-based exercises resulted in highly significant gains in auditory processing rate, speech discrimination, and language comprehension of syntax and grammar (Merzenich et al. 1996; Tallal et al. 1996).

There also have been considerable advances made in understanding the specific linguistic deficits of these children. Research has demonstrated particular difficulty with components of syntax and morphology (see Leonard 1998 for review). The results of longitudinal studies have shown, however, that children with developmental language impairments develop the linguistic structures of language along a similar linguistic trajectory to that observed in normal younger children. There is little evidence that these children make linguistic errors that are deviant or substantially different from younger children at the same stage of language development. Rather, children with language impairments take much longer to progress through the stages of normal language development (Curtiss, Katz, and Tallal 1992). A similar pattern of delay, rather than deviance, occurs across most populations of children with developmental language impairment. Looking cross-linguistically at children with developmental language impairments learning different languages in different countries, it also has been shown that whatever linguistic structures are unstressed or of weak phonetic substance in a particular language are the most difficult for children to learn and also the most delayed in children with language impairments (Leonard 1992). That the same order of development occurs across populations and language environments gives strong support that there is a potent metric of sheer difficulty (whether representational or perceptual) that is imposed on the learning of linguistic structures and contents.

There is growing evidence from family and twin studies that developmental language impairments may aggregate in families and may be genetically transmitted. Twin studies have shown a high concordance rate (heritability) for measures of phonological analysis (Bishop, North, and Donlan 1995). As a group, infants born into families with a positive history of developmental language impairment demonstrate longer processing times than matched infants born into families with a negative family history for SLI. When followed prospectively, the processing rate established at six months of age has been shown to predict the rate of language development, with the infants showing impaired processing rate subsequently being most likely to be delayed in language development (Benasich and Tallal 1996). It also has been found that adults with dyslexia, or who have a family history of language-learning impairments, show significant psychoacoustic deficits, particularly a slower auditory processing rate. These adults also show poorer phonological analysis abilities when compared with matched adults who are family history–negative for developmental language learning disorders (Tomblin, Freese, and Records 1992).

Recently, brain imaging technologies also have been used to examine the neurobiological basis of developmental language impairment. Electrophysiological studies support the results of behavioral studies showing specific deficits in acoustic analysis and phonological processing (Kraus et al. 1995). Results from MAGNETIC RESONANCE IMAGING (MRI) show that the pars triangularis (Broca's area) is significantly smaller in the left hemisphere of children with SLI and that these children are more likely to have rightward asymmetry of language structures. The opposite pattern is seen in children developing language normally (Jernigan et al. 1991; Gauger, Lombardino, and Leonard 1997).

See also APHASIA; GRAMMAR, NEURAL BASIS OF; LANGUAGE, NEURAL BASIS OF; PHONOLOGY, NEURAL BASIS OF

—*Paula Tallal*

References

Aram, D. M., B. L. Ekelman, and J. E. Nation. (1984). Preschoolers with language disorders: 10 years later. *Journal of Speech and Hearing Research* 27: 232–244.

Beitchman, J. H., R. Nair, M. Clegg, and P. G. Patel. (1986a). Prevalence of speech and language disorders in 5-year-old kindergarten children in the Ottawa-Careton region. *Journal of Speech and Hearing Disorders* 51: 98–110.

Beitchman, J. H., R. Nair, M. Ferguson, and P. G. Patel. (1986b). Prevalence of psychiatric disorders in children with speech and language disorders. *Journal of American Academy of Child Psychiatry* 24: 528–535.

Benasich, A. A., and P. Tallal. (1996). Auditory temporal processing thresholds, habituation, and recognition memory over the first year. *Infant Behavior and Development* 19: 339–357.

Bishop, D. V., and C. Adams. (1990). A prospective study of the relationship between specific language impairment, phonological disorders and reading retardation. *Journal of Child Psychology and Psychiatry Allied Disciplines* 31: 1027–1050.

Bishop, D. V. M., T. North, and C. Donlan. (1995). Genetic basis of specific language impairment: Evidence from a twin study. *Developmental Medicine and Child Neurology* 37: 56–71.

Cantwell, D. P., L. Baker, and R. E. Mattison. (1979). The prevalence of psychiatric disorder in children with speech and language disorder: An epidemiological study. *Journal of the American Academy of Child Psychiatry* 18(3): 450–461.

Catts, H. W. (1993). The relationship between speech-language impairments and reading disabilities. *Journal of Speech and Hearing Research* 36: 948–958.

Curtiss, S., W. Katz, and P. Tallal. (1992). Deviance versus delay in language acquisition of language impaired children. *Journal of Speech and Hearing Research* 35: 373–383.

Diagnostic and Statistical Manual of Mental Disorders, 4th ed. (DSM-IV). (1994). Washington, DC: American Psychiatric Association.

Gauger, L. M., L. J. Lombardino, and C. M. Leonard. (1997). Brain morphology in children with specific language impairment. *Journal of Speech, Language, and Hearing Research* 40: 1272–1284.

Jernigan, T. L., J. R. Aesselink, E. Sowell, and P. Tallal. (1991). Cerebral structure on magnetic resonance imaging in language and learning impaired children. *Archives of Neurology* 48: 539–545.

Kraus, N., T. McGee, T. Carrell, C. King, K. Tremblay, and T. Nicol. (1995). Central auditory system plasticity with speech discrimination. *Journal of Cognitive Neuroscience* 7: 25–32.

Leonard, L. (1992). Specific language impairments in three languages: Some cross-linguistic evidence. In P. Fletcher and D. Hall, Eds., *Specific Speech and Language Disorder in Children.* London: Whurr, pp. 119–126.

Leonard, L. B. (1998). *Children with Specific Language Impairment.* Cambridge, MA: MIT Press.

Liberman I., D. Shankweiler, F. W. Fischer, and B. Carter. (1974). Explicit syllable and phoneme segmentation in the young child. *Journal of Experimental Child Psychology* 18: 201–212.

Merzenich, M., W. Jenkins, P. S. Johnston, C. Schreiner, S. L. Miller, and P. Tallal. (1996). Temporal processing deficits of language-learning impaired children ameliorated by training. *Science* 271: 77–80.

Rissman, M., S. Curtiss, and P. Tallal. (1990). School placement outcomes of young language impaired children. *Journal of Speech and Language Pathology and Audiology* 14: 49–58.

Shankweiler, D., S. Crain, L. Katz, A. Fowler, A. Liberman, S. Brady, R. Thorton, E. Lundquist, L. Dreyer, J. Fletcher, K. Stuebing, S. Shaywitz, and B. Shaywitz. (1995). Cognitive profiles of reading disabled children: Comparisons of language skills in phonology, morphology, and syntax. *Psychological Science* 6(3): 149–155.

Tallal, P., S. Miller, and R. H. Fitch. (1993a). Neurobiological basis of speech: A case for the preeminence of temporal processing. *Annals of the New York Academy of Sciences* 682: 27–47.

Tallal, P., A. M. Galaburda, R. R. Llinas, and C. von Euler, Eds. (1993b). Temporal information processing in the nervous system: Special reference to dyslexia and dysphasia. *Annals of the New York Academy of Sciences* 682.

Tallal, P., S. L. Miller, G. Bedi, G. Byma, X. Wang, S. S. Nagarajan, C. Schreiner, W. M. Jenkins, and M. M. Merzenich. (1996). Language comprehension in language-learning impaired children improved with acoustically modified speech. *Science* 271: 81–84.

Tomblin, J. B., P. R. Freese, and N. L. Records. (1992). Diagnosing specific language impairment in adults for the purpose of pedigree analysis. *Journal of Speech and Hearing Research* 35: 332–343.

Tomblin, J. B., N. L. Records, P. Buckwalter, X. Zhang, E. Smith, and M. O'Brien. (1997). The prevalence of specific language impairment in kindergarten children. *Journal of Speech, Language, and Hearing Research* 40: 1245–1260.

Wagner, R. K., and J. K. Torgeson. (1987). The nature of phonological processing and its causal role in the acquisition of reading skills. *Psychological Bulletin* 102: 192–212.

Wright, B. A., L. J. Lombardino, W. M. King, C. S. Puranik, C. M. Leonard, and M. M. Merzenich. (1997a). Deficits in auditory temporal and spectral processing in language-impaired children. *Nature* 387: 176–178.

Further Readings

Blachman, B., Ed. (1997). *Foundations of Reading Acquisition and Dyslexia.* Hillsdale, NJ: Erlbaum.

Farmer, M. E., and R. Klein. (1995). The evidence for a temporal processing deficit linked to dyslexia: A review. *Psychonomic Bulletin Reviews* 2: 460–493.

Gowasmi, U., and P. Bryant. (1990). *Phonological Skills and Learning to Read.* Hillsdale, NJ: Erlbaum.

Mauer, D. M., and A. G. Kamhi. (1996). Factors that influence phoneme-grapheme correspondence learning. *Journal of Learning Disabilities* 29: 359–370.

Merzenich, M. M., and W. M. Jenkins. (1995). Cortical plasticity, learning and learning dysfunction. In B. Julesz and I. Kovacs, Eds., *Maturational Widows and Adult Cortical Plasticity.* Santa Fe, NM: Addison-Wesley, pp. 247–272.

Protopapas, A., M. Ahissar, and M. M. Merzenich. (1997). Auditory processing deficits in adults with a history of reading difficulty. *Society for Neuroscience Abstracts* 23: 491.

Reed, M. A. (1989). Speech perception and the discrimination of brief auditory cues in reading disabled children. *Journal of Experimental Child Psychology* 48: 270–292.

Tallal, P. (1980). Auditory temporal perception, phonics, and reading disabilities in children. *Brain and Language* 9: 182–198.

Tallal, P., D. Dukette, and S. Curtiss. (1989). Behavioral/emotional profiles of preschool language-impaired children. *Development and Psychopathology* 1: 51–67.

Tallal, P., J. Townsend, S. Curtiss, and B. Wulfeck. (1991). Phenotypic profiles of language-impaired children based on genetic/family history. *Brain and Language* 41: 81–95.

The following Web site contains information on developmental language disorders, as well as links to related sites: http://www.scientificlearning.com.

Language, Innateness of

See INNATENESS OF LANGUAGE; LANGUAGE ACQUISITION; PARAMETER SETTING APPROACHES TO ACQUISITION, CREOLIZATION, AND DIACHRONY

Language, Neural Basis of

Investigations into the neural basis of language center around how the brain processes language. To do this, we must understand that language is a most complex function, one that encompasses numerous subprocesses, including the recognition and articulation of speech sounds, the comprehension and production of words and sentences, and the use of language in pragmatically appropriate ways. Underlying and interacting with these are also the functions of ATTENTION and MEMORY. All contribute in special ways to our ability to process language, and each may, in fact, be handled differently by the human brain. Classic neurolinguistic theories, developed over a hundred years ago, have suggested that certain brain areas play specific roles in the process of language. Since then, modern techniques are offering us new data on what these areas might actually do and how they might contribute to a network of brain areas that collectively participate in language processing.

Most of our information about how the brain processes language has been gleaned from studies of brain-injured patients who have suffered strokes due to blockage of blood flow to the brain or from gunshot wounds to the head during wartime. In these cases, the language deficits resulting from these injuries have been compared to the areas of the brain which became lesioned.

In the past, such investigations had to rely on autopsy data obtained long after the behavioral data had been collected. These days, structural neuroimaging using computed tomography (CT) and MAGNETIC RESONANCE IMAGING (MRI) can help us view the location and extent of the brain lesion while behavioral data can be collected concurrently. Modern electrophysiology studies as well as functional neuroimaging with POSITRON EMISSION TOMOGRAPHY (PET) and functional magnetic resonance imaging (fMRI) are now being conducted with normal non–brain-injured subjects and are also beginning to assist in our understanding of the brain mechanisms involved in language.

Classic descriptions of the brain areas involved in language have largely implicated those in the left cerebral hemisphere known as Broca's area, Wernicke's area, and the connecting bundle of fibers between them, the arcuate fasciculus. These descriptions began in 1861 when Pierre Paul BROCA described his examination of a chronically ill patient with an unusual speech deficit that restricted his ability to communicate (Broca 1861). Whenever the patient attempted to speak, his utterance was reduced to the single recurring syllable "tan," though he could intone it in different ways to change its meaning. When the patient died a few days after the examination, Broca discovered a lesion involving the posterior inferior frontal gyrus (i.e., the back part of the lowest section within the frontal lobe). Though Broca never cut the brain to examine the extent of this lesion, he suggested that this specific region was responsible for the articulation of speech. The area later became known as Broca's area and the behavioral deficit as Broca's APHASIA.

In 1874, Carl Wernicke reported on two patients with a language disturbance that was very different from the one Broca described (Wernicke 1874). These patients had difficulty with what Wernicke described as the "auditory memory for words." In short, they had trouble understanding spoken language, even though their own speech was fluent and unencumbered. Wernicke examined the brain of one of these patients at autopsy and thought that the most significant area of damage in this patient was in the superior temporal gyrus (i.e., the top part of the temporal lobe). He concluded that this region was crucial to the purpose of language comprehension, and subsequently the disorder in language comprehension was referred to as Wernicke's aphasia. Wernicke also developed an elaborate model of language processing that was revived by the neurologist Norman GESCHWIND in the 1960s, and which has formed the basis of our current investigations (Geschwind 1965, 1972).

The Wernicke-Geschwind model holds that the comprehension and formulation of language is dependent on Wernicke's area, after which the information is transmitted over the arcuate fasciculus to Broca's area where it can be prepared for articulation. In general, data from patients with lesions in these areas support this model. Those patients with injuries that involve temporal lobe structures have easily articulated speech but do not always understand spoken or written language. Those with frontal lobe lesions generally have speech or articulation difficulty but tend to understand simple sentences fairly well.

Like most theories, this one has its problems. First, the correlation between lesions to Broca's area and language deficits is far from perfect. Lesions to Broca's area alone never result in a persisting Broca's aphasia. The language deficits that are seen in these patients during the first few weeks after the injury always resolve into a mild or nonexistent problem (Mohr 1976). Several patients have also been reported that suffer from a persisting Broca's aphasia with no involvement of Broca's area whatsoever (Dronkers et al. 1992). Furthermore, Broca's original patient, on whom a significant part of the model is based, had multiple events that led to his aphasia. Since Broca never cut the brain, he could not have seen that other brain areas were also affected by these injuries.

Similar discrepancies can be seen with regard to Wernicke's area. Lesions to this area alone do not result in a persisting language comprehension problem, nor do all chronic Wernicke's aphasia patients have lesions in Wernicke's area (Dronkers, Redfern, and Ludy 1995). In fact, the data that originally predicted the participation of Wernicke's area in language comprehension were based on Wernicke's two problematic cases. One of these was noted to have resolved the comprehension problem after seven weeks and was never even brought to autopsy, while the second was a demented patient with numerous other pathological changes besides just those in the superior temporal gyrus. Current findings are showing that lesions must encompass far more than just the inferior frontal gyrus or superior temporal gyrus to produce the respective chronic Broca's or Wernicke's aphasia.

Still, those who study language and the brain have clung to traditional theory for several good reasons. First, there have been no good substitute theories that can explain as much of the data as the classic theories have been able to do. Most aphasic patients do show the pattern of behaviors described by Broca, Wernicke, and Geschwind. Furthermore, physicians and speech pathologists have found it easy to diagnose and treat their aphasic patients within this framework. While the original cases may have been faulty, the theories that resulted have served to answer most of the questions that surround these patients.

Modern techniques and technologies may gradually be changing the classic model. Most of these contributions concern the roles of traditional language areas, the possibility that other brain areas might also be important, and the likelihood that language processing involves a network of brain areas that contribute in individual but interactive ways. Being so new, these conclusions have not yet made it into neuroscience or linguistics textbooks. Still, it is clear that the classic model, despite its important contributions to understanding language mechanisms in the brain, will see some revision in the next decade.

Take the elusive role of Broca's area as an example. Though Broca thought it was concerned only with the articulation of speech, it has since been associated with many functions. Work in the 1970s included the manipulation of grammatical rules as a function of Broca's area, since those patients with a "Broca's aphasia" and lesions encompassing

Broca's area had difficulty in using and comprehending grammatical information (Zurif, Caramazza, and Meyerson 1972). Recent functional imaging work with PET has suggested that it may play a role in short-term memory for linguistic information (Stromswold et al. 1996). Still other PET studies conclude that it is part of an articulatory loop (Paulesu, Frith, and Frackowiak 1993), while those that involve electrically stimulating the exposed brain during neurosurgery specify it as an end stage for motor speech (Ojemann 1994).

Lesion studies, coupled with high-resolution structural neuroimaging, continue to give us new information regarding other brain regions that might participate in speech and language. One new area that may participate in the articulation of speech is deep in the insula, the island of cortex that lies beneath the frontal, temporal, and parietal lobes. A recent study used computerized lesion reconstructions to find that a very specific area of the insula (high on its precentral gyrus) was lesioned in twenty-five stroke patients who all had a disorder in coordinating the movements for speech articulation (Dronkers 1996). Nineteen stroke patients without this particular disorder had lesions that spared the same area.

The insula is also lesioned in the majority of cases of Broca's aphasia (Vanier and Caplan 1990). This is not surprising, since Broca's aphasia patients have trouble in coordinating articulatory movements in addition to their other language deficits. Even Broca's original case had a large lesion that included the insula, as confirmed by a CT scan of the preserved brain done a hundred years later (Signoret et al. 1984). The fact that Broca's aphasia requires a large lesion that involves multiple brain areas supports the idea that many different regions must participate in the normal processing of language.

The functional imaging literature has given us new insight into areas of the brain that are actively engaged during a language task. Some of these areas would not have been detected from traditional lesions studies because the vascular supply to the brain is more susceptible to stroke in certain areas than others. For example, the supplementary motor area is consistently activated in functional imaging studies involving speech, but strokes to this area are relatively uncommon or do not come to the attention of those who study or treat language disorders. The same holds for posterior temporal areas that appear to be active in word form recognition. Also, functional imaging studies can signal the involvement of the right hemisphere in a given speech or language task, in addition to activation of traditional areas within the left hemisphere.

One area of the frontal lobe that has received a fair amount of attention in the functional imaging literature is the left inferior prefrontal cortex, the area of the brain in front of and below Broca's area. Peterson and colleagues found it to be activated in semantic retrieval tasks where subjects generated verbs associated with nouns presented to them (Peterson et al. 1988). Others have also found it involved in tasks requiring word retrieval or semantic encoding (e.g., Demb et al. 1995; Warburton et al. 1996). Still, it is not clear whether the role played by this area is one that is truly related to language or whether it is related to attention or executive functioning and merely plays an assistive role in language processing. Patients with lesions to this area do show deficits on constrained verbal fluency tasks in which they must generate words that begin only with certain letters or belong only to certain semantic categories, yet these patients are not obviously aphasic. Thus, the true contribution of this area to language must still be determined.

The basal temporal area is another region that was not implicated in classic models. This region lies at the base of the temporal lobe and is not usually affected by stroke, though it can be the source of epileptic seizure activity. Some epileptic patients have had electrodes temporarily placed under the skull directly on the cortex to monitor seizure activity. These electrodes can also deliver small electrical charges to the cortex that interfere with normal functioning. When placed over the basal temporal area, stimulation disrupts patients' ability to name objects, implying that this area is somehow involved in word retrieval (Luders et al. 1986). In a different kind of study, an epileptic patient with a seizure focus in the basal temporal area had an aphasia associated with the duration of the seizures that resolved once the seizures were stopped (Kirshner et al. 1995). All these data are derived from a different source than are most of the data from stroke patients, but still provide strong evidence that this area may also be important for normal language processing.

There are several other areas that may also contribute to language in their own way. The cingulate gyrus has been implicated in word retrieval, possibly because of its role in maintaining attention to the task. The anterior superior temporal gyrus, just in front of primary auditory cortex, may also play a role in sentence comprehension because of its rich connections to hippocampal structures important in memory. The fact that there are so many new brain regions emerging in modern lesion and functional imaging studies of language suggests that the classic Wernicke-Geschwind model, though useful for so many years, is now seen as oversimplified. Areas all over the brain are recruited for language processing; some are involved in lexical retrieval, some in grammatical processing, some in the production of speech, some in attention and memory. These new findings are still too fresh for any overarching theories to have developed that might explain how these areas interact. Future imaging and electrophysiological studies will undoubtedly show us not only the areas involved in language but also the recruitment of these areas at any stage of the process, the manner in which they interact, the time course of these activities, and the change in activation and allocation of resources relative to task complexity. The study of the neural mechanisms of language is evolving rapidly in conjunction with advances in the technologies that allow us to study it.

Other avenues of interest that are being pursued include the intriguing possibility that the brain may choose where to store lexical information depending on the semantic category to which the word belongs (Damasio et al. 1996; Martin et al. 1996). Another is that the brain might store and process language in different ways depending on the modality of acquisition (auditory vs. visual) (Neville, Mills, and Lawson 1992). Others question whether the brain mechanisms involved in language may differ for men and women, left-handers and right-handers, or monolinguals and bilinguals. These are all challenges for continued exploration whose findings are shaping contemporary models of language processing.

See also BILINGUALISM AND THE BRAIN; CORTICAL LOCALIZATION, HISTORY OF; GRAMMAR, NEURAL BASIS OF; HEMISPHERIC SPECIALIZATION; LEXICON, NEURAL BASIS; SIGN LANGUAGE AND THE BRAIN

—*Nina F. Dronkers*

References

Broca, P. (1861). Remarques sur le siège de la faculté du langage articulé, suivies d'une observation d'aphémie (perte de la parole). *Bulletin de la Société Anatomique de Paris* 6: 330–357.

Damasio, H., T. J. Grabowski, D. Tranel, R. D. Hichwa, and A. Damasio. (1996). A neural basis for lexical retrieval. *Nature* 499–505.

Demb, J., J. Desmond, A. Wagner, C. Valdya, G. Glover, and J. Gabrieli. (1995). Semantic encoding and retrieval in the left inferior prefrontal cortex: A functional MRI study of task difficulty and process specificity. *Journal of Neuroscience* 15(9): 5870–5878.

Dronkers, N. F. (1996). A new brain region for coordinating speech articulation. *Nature* 384: 159–161.

Dronkers, N. F., B. B. Redfern, and C. A. Ludy. (1995). Lesion localization in chronic Wernicke's aphasia. *Brain and Language* 51(1): 62–65.

Dronkers, N. F., J. K. Shapiro, B. Redfern, and R. T. Knight. (1992). The role of Broca's area in Broca's aphasia. *Journal of Clinical and Experimental Neuropsychology* 14: 52–53.

Geschwind, N. (1965). Disconnexion syndromes in animals and man. *Brain* 88: 237–294.

Geschwind, N. (1972). Language and the brain. *Scientific American* 226: 76–83.

Kirshner, H., T. Hughes, T. Fakhoury, and B. Abou-Khalil. (1995). Aphasia secondary to partial status epilepticus of the basal temporal language area. *Neurology* 45(8): 1616–1618.

Luders, H., R. P. Lesser, J. Hahn, D. S. Dinner, H. Morris, S. Resor, and M. Harrison. (1986). Basal temporal language area demonstrated by electrical stimulation. *Neurology* 36: 505–510.

Martin, A., C. L. Wiggs, L. G. Ungerleider, and J. V. Haxby. (1996). Neural correlates of category-specific knowledge. *Nature* 379: 649–652.

Mohr, J. P. (1976). Broca's area and Broca's aphasia. In H. Whitaker and H. Whitaker, Eds., *Studies in Neurolinguistics,* vol. 1. New York: Academic Press, pp. 201–233.

Neville, H., D. Mills, and D. Lawson. (1992). Fractionating language: Different neural subsystems with different sensitive periods. *Cerebral Cortex* 2(3): 244–258.

Ojemann, G. (1994). Cortical stimulation and recording in language. In A. Kertesz, Ed., *Localization and Neuroimaging in Neuropsychology.* San Diego: Academic Press, pp. 35–55.

Paulesu, E., C. D. Frith, and R. S. J. Frackowiak. (1993). The neural correlates of the verbal component of working memory. *Nature* 362: 342–345.

Peterson, S. E., P. T. Fox, M. I. Posner, M. Mintun, and M. E. Raichle. (1988). Positron emission tomographic studies of the cortical anatomy of single-word processing. *Nature* 331: 585–589.

Signoret, J., P. Castaigne, F. Lehrmitte, R. Abelanet, and P. Lavorel. (1984). Rediscovery of Leborgne's brain: Anatomical description with CT scan. *Brain and Language* 22: 303–319.

Stromswold, K., D. Caplan, N. Alpert, and S. Rauch. (1996). Localization of syntactic comprehension by positron emission tomography. *Brain and Language* 52: 452–473.

Vanier, M., and D. Caplan. (1990). CT-scan correlates of agrammatism. In L. Menn and L. Obler, Eds., *Agrammatic Aphasia: A Cross-Linguistic Narrative Sourcebook.* Amsterdam: John Benjamins, pp. 37–114.

Warburton, E., R. Wise, C. Price, C. Weiller, U. Hadar, S. Ramsey, and R. Frackowiak. (1996). Noun and verb retrieval by normal subjects. Studies with PET. *Brain* 119: 159–179.

Wernicke, C. (1874). *Der aphasische Symptomencomplex.* Breslau: Kohn und Weigert.

Zurif, E. B., A. Caramazza, and R. Meyerson. (1972). Grammatical judgements of agrammatic aphasics. *Neuropsychologia* 10: 405–417.

Further Readings

Benson, D. F., and A. Ardila. (1996). *Aphasia: A Clinical Perspective.* New York: Oxford University Press.

Caplan, D. (1987). *Neurolinguistics and Linguistic Aphasiology.* New York: Cambridge University Press.

Dronkers, N., and R. T. Knight. (Forthcoming). The neural architecture of language disorders. In M. Gazzaniga, Ed., *The Cognitive Neurosciences.*

Goodglass, H. (1993). *Understanding Aphasia.* San Diego: Academic Press.

Stemmer, B., and H. Whitaker, Eds. (1998). *Handbook of Neurolinguistics.* New York: Academic Press.

Language of Thought

The language of thought hypothesis is an idea, or family of ideas, about the way we represent our world, and hence an idea about how our behavior is to be explained. Humans are marvelously flexible organisms. The commuter surviving her daily trip to New York, the subsistence agriculturalist, the inhabitant of a chaotic African state all thread their different ways through the maze of their day. This ability to adapt to a complex and changing world is grounded in our mental capacities. We navigate our way through our social and physical world by constructing an inner representation, an inner map of that world, and we plot our course from that inner map and from our representation of where we want to get to. Our capacity for negotiating our complex and variable environment is based on a representation of the world as we take it to be, and a representation of the world as we would like it to be. In the language of FOLK PSYCHOLOGY— our everyday set of concepts for thinking about ourselves and others—these are an agent's beliefs and desires. Their interaction explains action. Thus Truman ordered the bombing of Japan because he wanted to end World War II as quickly as possible, and he believed that bombing offered his best chance of attaining that end.

We represent—think about—many features of our world. We have opinions on politics, football, food, the best way to bring up children, and much more. Our potential range of opinion is richer still. You may not have had views on the pleasures of eating opossum roadkills, but now that you are prompted, you quickly will. This richness of our cognitive range is important to the language of thought hypothesis. Its defenders take our powers of MENTAL REPRESENTATION to be strikingly similar to our powers of *linguistic representation*. Neither language nor thought are stimulus bound: we can both speak and think of the elsewhere and the elsewhen. Both language and thought are counterfactual: we can both speak and think of how the world might be, not just how it is. We can misrepresent the world; we can both say and think that it is infested by gods, ghosts, and dragons. Moreover, thoughts and sentences can be indefinitely complex. Of course, if sentences are too long and complex, we cease to understand them. But this limit does not seem intrinsic to our system of linguistic representation but is instead a feature of our capacities to use it. Under favorable circumstances, our capacity to handle linguistic complexity extends upwards; in unfavorable circumstances, downwards. Moreover, the boundary between the intelligible and the unintelligible is fuzzy and not the result of hitting the system's walls. The same seems true of mental representation. These similarities are no surprise. Although there may be thoughts we cannot express, surely there are no utterances we cannot think.

The power of linguistic representation comes from the organization of language. Sentences are structures built out of basic units, words or morphemes. The meaning of the sentence—what it represents—depends on the meaning of those words together with its structure. So when we learn a language, we learn the words together with recipes for building sentences out of them. We thus acquire a representational system of great power and flexibility, for indefinitely many complex representations can be constructed out of its basic elements. Since mental representation exhibits these same properties, we might infer that it is organized in the same way. Thoughts consist of CONCEPTS assembled into more complex structures. A *minimal* language of thought hypothesis is the idea that our capacities to think depend on a representational system, in which complex representations are built from a stock of basic elements; the meaning of complex representations depend on their structure and the representational properties of those basic elements; and the basic elements reappear with the same meaning in many structures. This representational system is "Mentalese."

This minimal version of the language of thought hypothesis leaves many important questions open. (1) Just how "languagelike" is the language of thought? Linguists emphasize the complexity and abstractness of natural-language sentence structure. Our thoughts might be complex structures built out of simple elements without thought structures being as complex as those of natural language. Mentalese may have no equivalent of the elaborate MORPHOLOGY and PHONOLOGY of natural languages. Natural languages probably have features that reflect their history as spoken systems. If so, these are unlikely to be part of Mentalese. (2) The minimal hypothesis leaves open the nature of the basic units. Perhaps the stock of concepts is similar to the stock of simple words of a natural language. Just as there are words for tigers and trucks, there are concepts of them amongst the basic stock out of which thoughts are built. But the minimal version is also compatible with the idea that the basic units out of which complexes are built are

nothing like the semantic equivalent of words. Thus the concept "tiger" might itself be a complex semantic structure. (3) The minimal version leaves open the relationship between Mentalese and natural languages. Perhaps only learning a natural language powers the development of Mentalese. Perhaps learning a natural language enhances and transforms the more rudimentary language of thought with which one begins. Perhaps learning a natural language is just learning to produce linguistic representations that are equivalent to those that can already be formulated in Mentalese.

Jerry Fodor goes beyond the minimal language of thought hypothesis. Fodor argues for Mentalese not just from intentional psychology but from cognitive psychology. He argues that our best accounts, and often our only accounts, of cognitive abilities presuppose the existence of a rich, language-like internal code. So, for example, any account of rational action presupposes that rational agents have a rich enough representational system to represent a range of possible actions and possible outcomes. They must have the capacity not just to represent actual states of the world but possible ones as well. Most importantly, learning in general, and concept acquisition in particular, depends on hypothesis formation in the inner code. You cannot learn the concept "leopard" or the word *leopard* unless you already have an inner code in which you can formulate an appropriate hypothesis about leopards. So Fodor thinks of Mentalese as semantically rich, with a large, word-like stock of basic units. For example, he expects the concepts "truck," "elephant," and even "reactor" to be semantically simple. Moreover, this large stock of basic units is innate. Experience is causally relevant to an agent's conceptual repertoire. But we do not learn our basic concepts from experience. Concept acquisition is more like the development of secondary sexual characteristics than like learning the dress code at the local pub. So Mentalese is independent of any natural language we speak. The expressive power of natural language depends on the expressive power of Mentalese, not vice versa.

The language of thought hypothesis has been enormously controversial. One response focuses on the inference from intentional psychology to the language of thought. For example, Daniel Dennett has long argued that the relationship between an agent's intentional profile—the beliefs and desires she has—and her internal states is likely to be very indirect. In a favorite illustration, he asks us to consider a chess-playing computer. These play good chess, so we treat them as knowing a lot about the game, as knowing, for example, that the passed-rook pawn is dangerous. We are right to do so, even though there is no single causally salient inner state that corresponds to that belief. Dennett thinks that the relationship between our beliefs and our causally efficacious inner states is likely to be equally indirect. I think this argument is best seen as a response to Fodor's strong version of the language of thought hypothesis. The same is true of many other critical responses, for these often focus on Fodor's denial that learning increases the expressive capacity of our thoughts. The Churchlands, for example, have taken this to be a reduction of the language of thought hypothesis itself, but if anything, it is a reduction only of Fodor's strong version of it. Connectionist models of cognition, on the other hand, do seem to be a threat to any version of a language of thought hypothesis, for in connectionist mental representation, meaning is not a function of the structure plus the meaning of the atomic units (see CONNECTIONISM, PHILOSOPHICAL ISSUES).

See also IMAGERY; INTENTIONALITY; LANGUAGE AND THOUGHT; MENTAL CAUSATION; PROPOSITIONAL ATTITUDES

—*Kim Sterelny*

References

Churchland, P. S. (1986). *Neurophilosophy*. Cambridge, MA: MIT Press.

Dennett, D. C. (1987). True believers. In D. C. Dennett, *The Intentional Stance*. Cambridge, MA: MIT Press.

Fodor, J. A. (1975). *The Language of Thought*. Sussex: Harvester Press.

Fodor, J. A. (1981). The present status of the innateness controversy. In J. A. Fodor, *Representations*. Cambridge, MA: MIT Press.

Fodor, J. A., and Z. Pylyshyn. (1988). Connectionism and cognitive architecture: a critical analysis. *Cognition* 28: 3–71.

Further Readings

Clark, A. (1989). *Microcognition: Philosophy, Cognitive Science, and Parallel Distributed Processing*. Cambridge, MA: MIT Press.

Clark, A. (1993). *Associative Engines: Connectionism, Concepts, and Representational Change*. Cambridge, MA: MIT Press.

Fodor, J. A. (1987). *Psychosemantics: The Problem of Meaning in the Philosophy of Mind*. Cambridge, MA: MIT Press.

Fodor, J. A. (1990). *A Theory of Content and Other Essays*. Cambridge, MA: MIT Press.

Harman, G. (1975). Language, thought, and communication. In K. Gunderson, Ed., *Minnesota Studies in the Philosophy of Science*. Vol. 7, *Language, Mind, and Knowledge*. Minneapolis: University of Minnesota Press.

Lower, B., and G. Rey, Eds. (1991). *Jerry Fodor and His Critics*. Oxford: Blackwell, ch.11–13.

Smolensky, P. (1988). On the proper treatment of connectionism. *Behavioral and Brain Sciences* 11: 1–84.

Language Processing

See LANGUAGE PRODUCTION; PSYCHOLINGUISTICS; SENTENCE PROCESSING; SPEECH PERCEPTION

Language Production

Language production means talking, but not merely that. When people talk, it is usually because they have something to say. Psycholinguistic research on language production concerns itself with the cognitive processes that convert nonverbal communicative intentions into verbal actions. These processes must translate perceptions or thoughts into sounds, using the patterns and elements of a code that constitutes the grammar of a language. For theories of language production, the goal is to explain how the mind uses this code when converting messages into spontaneous speech in ongoing time. This requires an explanation of the action system that puts language knowledge to use.

The action system for language production has a COGNITIVE ARCHITECTURE along the lines shown in figure 1. Imagine a speaker who wishes to draw a listener's attention to a rabbit browsing in the garden. The process begins with a communicative intention, a *message,* that stands at the interface between thought and language. Little is known about the content or structure of messages, but they are assumed to include at least conceptual categorizations (in figure 1, tacit rabbit-knowledge) and the information needed for making distinctions such as tense, number, aspect, and speaker's perspective. Less certain is whether messages habitually include different kinds of information as a function of the language being spoken, along the lines proposed in the Sapir-Whorf hypothesis (see LINGUISTIC RELATIVITY HYPOTHESIS; Slobin 1996).

Of primary interest to contemporary theories of production are the processing components dubbed *grammatical* and *phonological* in figure 1 (following Levelt 1989). These are the processes immediately responsible for recruiting the linguistic information to create the utterances that convey messages. Grammatical encoding refers to the cognitive mechanisms for retrieving, ordering, and adjusting words for their grammatical environments, and phonological encoding refers to the mechanisms for retrieving, ordering, and adjusting sounds for their phonological environments.

The motivation for separating these components comes from several lines of evidence for a division between word-combining and sound-combining processes. Speech errors suggest that there are two basic sorts of elements that are manipulated by the processes of production, roughly corresponding to words and sounds (Dell 1995). So-called tip-of-the-tongue states (the familiar frustration of being unable to retrieve a word that one is certain one knows) can carry word-specific grammatical information, in the absence of sound information (Miozzo and Caramazza 1997; Vigliocco, Antonini, and Garrett 1997). Electrophysiological evidence also suggests that grammatical information about words is accessible about 40 ms before information about sounds (van Turennout, Hagoort, and Brown 1998). Finally, the arbitrariness of the linguistic mapping from meaning to sound creates a computational problem that can only be solved by a mediating mechanism (Dell et al. 1997). These and other observations argue that there are distinct grammatical and phonological encoding mechanisms.

Grammatical encoding Adult speakers of English know between 30,000 and 80,000 words. The average for high-school graduates has been estimated at 45,000 words. These words can be arranged in any of an infinite number of ways that conform to the grammar of English. The ramifications of this can begin to be appreciated in the number of English sentences with 20 or fewer words, which is about 10^{30}. Using these resources, speakers must construct utterances to convey specific messages. They normally do so in under two seconds, although disruptions are common enough that average speakers spend about half of their speaking time in *not* speaking—hemming, hawing, and pausing between three and twelve times per minute (Goldman-Eisler 1968). These

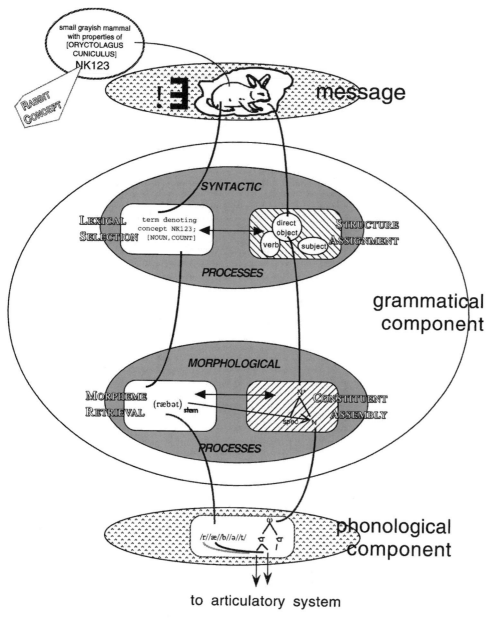

Figure 1. A cognitive architecture for language production.

disfluencies reflect problems in retrieving a suitable set of words and arranging them into a suitable syntactic structure. What is suitable, of course, is not merely a matter of grammaticality (though it is also that) but of adequacy for conveying a particular message to particular listeners in particular places and times.

Lexical selection and retrieval are integral to grammatical processing because of the kinds of information that words carry about their structural and positional requirements. In everyday language use, words are rarely produced in isolation. Instead, they occupy places within strings of words, with their places determined in part by their grammatical categories (e.g., in most English declarative sentences, at least one noun will precede a verb) and their MORPHOLOGY determined in part by their positions with respect to other words (e.g., a present-tense English verb accompanying a

singular subject will be inflected differently than the same verb accompanying a plural subject: *A razor cuts,* whereas *Scissors cut*). Thus, speakers must recover information about grammatical class and morphology.

Lexical selection involves locating a lexical entry (technically, a *lemma*) that adequately conveys some portion of a message, ensuring that there exists a word in one's mental lexicon that will do the job. A rough analogy is looking for a word in a reverse dictionary, which is organized semantically rather than alphabetically. If the desired meaning is listed in the dictionary with a single word that expresses the sense, there is an appropriate word to be had in the language; if not, the search fails. The mental lexicon is presumably accessible in a comparable fashion, permitting speakers to determine whether they know a word that conveys the meaning they intend. Most English speakers, for example, will find at least one lemma for their concept of a member of the family *Oryctolagus cuniculus.*

Locating a lemma yields basic information about how a word combines with other words. This corresponds to information about grammatical class (noun, verb, adjective, etc.) and other grammatical features that control a word's combinatorial privileges and requirements (e.g., nouns must be specified as mass or count, and if count, as singular or plural; verbs must be specified as intransitive or transitive, and if transitive, as simple or ditransitive, etc.; cf. LEXICON). The lemma for an instance of *Oryctolagus cuniculus,* for example, is a noun, count, and singular. These features in turn affect the determination of syntactic functions such as subject phrases, predicate phrases, and their arrangement (cf. SYNTAX).

Once a lemma is found, the word's morphology (technically, its *lexeme*) may have to be adjusted to its syntactic environment. In connected speech, this will encompass inflectional processes (e.g., making a verb singular or plural). Lexical retrieval processes yield an abstract specification of the morphological structure of the selected word. So, retrieving the lexeme for the count noun that denotes a member of the family *Oryctolagus cuniculus* should yield a word stem for *rabbit.*

The role of active morphological processes in language use is currently disputed in some quarters. The issue is whether regularly inflected words are stored and retrieved from memory in the same way as uninflected words (Seidenberg 1997) or require a separable set of specifically inflectional operations (Marslen-Wilson and Tyler 1997). Although this debate has been confined primarily to research on word recognition, logically comparable issues arise regarding language production. In production, however, it may be harder to account for the available data with passive retrieval mechanisms (see Bock, Nicol, and Cutting, forthcoming).

Phonological encoding Words can be comfortably articulated at a rate of four per second, calling on more muscle fibers than may be required for any other mechanical performance of the human body (Fink 1986). Yet errors in the production of speech sounds are rare, only occurring once in every 5,000 words or so (Deese 1984). Controlling the activity requires some specification of phonological segments (/r/, /æ/, /b/, etc.), syllabification, and metrical structure. The broad outlines of phonological encoding are sketched similarly in current theories (Dell et al. 1997; Levelt, Roelofs, and Meyer, forthcoming). Counter to the intuition that words are stored as wholes, sound segments are actually assembled into word forms during the encoding process. Consonantal and vocalic segments must be selected and assigned to positions within syllabic frames. Additionally, the syllables and sounds must be integrated into the stream of speech: In a sequence of words such as *rabbit in,* the /t/ in rabbit will be produced differently than it is in *rabbit by.* One implication is that a description of the sound segments in an isolated word is insufficient to explain the word's form in connected speech.

Where theories of word production diverge is in their view of the relationship between phonological encoding and the higher level processes of lexical selection and retrieval.

The *discrete-stage* view (Levelt, Roelofs, and Meyer, forthcoming) argues that each step of the retrieval process is completed before the next is begun (*discrete* processing), and without feedback to higher level processes from lower levels (strict *feedforward* processing). In contrast, *interactive* views (Dell et al. 1997) embrace the possibilities of partial information from one stage affecting the next (*cascaded* processing) and of information from lower levels affecting higher levels of processing (*feedback*).

What is at stake in this theoretical battle, in part, is the role that an explanation for speech errors should play in the account of normal speech. Speech errors are a traditional foundation for the study of language production (Dell 1986; Fromkin 1973; Garrett 1988), and the properties of errors have long been viewed as informative about the production of error-free speech. Consider the word exchange by a speaker who intended to say *minds of the speakers* and instead uttered "speakers of the minds." Or the sound exchange that yielded "accipital octivity" instead of *occipital activity.* Such errors point to the embodiment of rule-like constraints in the arrangement process. When words exchange, they exchange almost exclusively with other words from the same syntactic class (noun, verb, adjective, and so on). When sounds exchange, they exchange almost exclusively with other sounds from the same phonological class (consonant or vowel). The net effect is that erroneous utterances are almost always grammatical, albeit often nonsensical. In the spirit of exceptions proving the rule, this has been taken to mean that speech errors represent small, local, and most importantly, principled departures from normal retrieval or assembly operations.

Models of word production that incorporate discrete stages have been less successful in accounting for the distribution and the features of speech errors than interactive views, in part because of a difference in explanatory emphasis. Levelt, Roelofs, and Meyer, forthcoming) elaborate a discrete-stage approach that is designed primarily to account for experimental data about the time course of word production, and not for errors, for the simple reason that errors are departures from the norm. What the production system does best, and remarkably well under the circumstances, is retrieve words and sounds appropriate for speakers' communicative intentions. Within the approach endorsed by Levelt, Roelofs, and Meyer, errors are a product of aberrations from the basic operating principles of the production system and are correspondingly rare events. By this argument, errors demand a separate theory.

Despite these differences, the leading theories of language production are in agreement that knowledge about words comes in pieces and that the pieces are not recovered all at once. In normal speaking, the semantic, syntactic, and phonological properties of words are called upon in quick succession, not simultaneously. Thus, what normally feels like a simple, unitary act of finding-and-saying-a-word is actually a complicated but fast assembly of separate, interlocking features. More broadly, speaking cannot be likened to the recitation of lines, as E. B. Titchener once did in describing it as "reading from a memory manuscript" (1909). It involves active, ongoing construction of utterances from rudimentary linguistic parts.

Communicative processes All the processes of language production serve communication, but certain activities tailor messages and utterances to the needs of particular listeners at particular places and times. The tailoring requirements are legion. They range from such patent demands as choosing language (English? Spanish?) and gauging loudness (whisper? shout?) to the need to infer what the listener is likely to be thinking or capable of readily recollecting. These are aspects of PRAGMATICS (cf. PSYCHOLINGUISTICS). A common shortcoming of speakers is presuming too much, failing to anticipate the myriad misconstruals to which any given utterance or expression is vulnerable. The source of this presumptuousness is transparent: Speakers know what they intend. For them, there is no ambiguity in the message.

The direct apprehension of the message sets speakers apart from their listeners, for whom ambiguity is rife. In this crucial respect, language production has little in common with language comprehension. In other respects, however, successful communication demands that production and comprehension share certain competencies. They must somehow draw on the same linguistic knowledge, because we speak as well as understand our native languages.

The cognitive processing systems responsible for comprehension and production may nonetheless be distinct. Research on language disorders suggests a degree of independence between them, because people with disorders of production can display near-normal comprehension abilities, and vice versa (Caramazza 1997). At a minimum, the flow of information must differ, leading from meaning to sound in production and from sound to meaning in comprehension.

This simple truth about information flow camouflages the deep questions that are at stake in current debates about the isolability and independence of the several cognitive and linguistic components of production. The questions are a piece of the overarching debate about modularity, to do with whether language and its parts are in essence the same as other forms of cognition and more broadly, whether all types of knowledge are in essence the same in acquisition and use. Accordingly, answers to the important questions about language production bear on our understanding of fundamental relationships between LANGUAGE AND THOUGHT, between free will and free speech, and between natural and artificial intelligence.

See also CONCEPTS; CONNECTIONIST APPROACHES TO LANGUAGE; MEANING; NATURAL LANGUAGE GENERATION; SENTENCE PROCESSING

—*Kathryn Bock*

References

Bock, K. (1995). Sentence production: From mind to mouth. In J. L. Miller and P. D. Eimas, Eds., *Handbook of Perception and Cognition*. Vol. 11, *Speech, Language, and Communication*. Orlando, FL: Academic Press, pp. 181–216.

Bock, J. K., J. Nicol, and J. C. Cutting. (Forthcoming). The ties that bind: Creating number agreement in speech. *Journal of Memory and Language*.

Caramazza, A. (1997). How many levels of processing are there in lexical access? *Cognitive Neuropsychology* 14: 177–208.

Deese, J. (1984). *Thought into Speech: The Psychology of a Language*. Englewood Cliffs, NJ: Prentice-Hall.

Dell, G. S. (1986). A spreading-activation theory of retrieval in sentence production. *Psychological Review* 93: 283–321.

Dell, G. S. (1995). Speaking and misspeaking. In L. R. Gleitman and M. Liberman, Eds., *An Invitation to Cognitive Science*. Vol. 1, *Language*. Cambridge, MA: MIT Press, pp. 183–208.

Dell, G. S., M. F. Schwartz, N. Martin, E. M. Saffran, and D. A. Gagnon. (1997). Lexical access in aphasic and nonaphasic speakers. *Psychological Review* 104: 801–838.

Fink, B. R. (1986). Complexity. *Science* 231: 319.

Fromkin, V. A., Ed. (1973). *Speech Errors as Linguistic Evidence*. The Hague: Mouton.

Garrett, M. F. (1982). Production of speech: Observations from normal and pathological language use. In A. Ellis, Ed., *Normality and Pathology in Cognitive Functions*. London: Academic Press, pp. 19–76.

Garrett, M. F. (1988). Processes in language production. In F. J. Newmeyer, Ed., *Linguistics: The Cambridge Survey*. Vol. 3, *Language: Psychological and Biological Aspects*. Cambridge: Cambridge University Press, pp. 69–96.

Goldman-Eisler, F. (1968). *Psycholinguistics: Experiments in Spontaneous Speech*. London: Academic Press.

Levelt, W. J. M. (1989). *Speaking: From Intention to Articulation*. Cambridge, MA: MIT Press.

Levelt, W. J. M., A. Roelofs, and A. S. Meyer. (Forthcoming). A theory of lexical access in speech production. *Behavioral and Brain Sciences*.

Marslen-Wilson, W. D., and L. K. Tyler. (1997). Dissociating types of mental computation. *Nature* 387: 592–594.

Miozzo, M., and A. Caramazza. (1997). Retrieval of lexical-syntactic features in tip-of-the-tongue states. *Journal of Experimental Psychology: Learning, Memory and Cognition* 23: 1410–1423.

Seidenberg, M. S. (1997). Language acquisition and use: Learning and applying probabilistic constraints. *Science* 275: 1599–1603.

Slobin, D. I. (1996). From "thought and language" to "thinking for speaking." In J. Gumperz and S. C. Levinson, Eds., *Rethinking Linguistic Relativity*. Cambridge: Cambridge University Press.

Titchener, E. B. (1909). *Lectures on the Experimental Psychology of the Thought-Processes*. New York: Macmillan.

van Turennout, M., P. Hagoort, and C. M. Brown. (1998). Brain activity during speaking: From syntax to phonology in 40 milliseconds. *Science* 280: 572–574.

Vigliocco, G., T. Antonini, and M. F. Garrett. (1997). Grammatical gender is on the tip of Italian tongues. *Psychological Science* 8: 314–317.

Language Universals

See LANGUAGE AND CULTURE; LINGUISTIC UNIVERSALS AND UNIVERSAL GRAMMAR; TYPOLOGY

Language Use

See INTRODUCTION: LINGUISTICS AND LANGUAGE; DISCOURSE; MEANING; PRAGMATICS

Language Variation and Change

The speech of no two people is identical, so it follows that if one takes manuscripts from two eras, one will be able to identify differences and so point to language "change." In this sense, languages are constantly changing in piecemeal, gradual, chaotic, and relatively minor fashion. However, historians also know that languages sometimes change abruptly, several things changing at the same time, and then settle into relative stasis, in a kind of "punctuated equilibrium."

So, all of the long vowels in English were raised (and the highest vowels diphthongized) in the famous Great Vowel Shift, which took place in late Middle English. Similarly, the language lost several uses of the verb *be* simultaneously in the nineteenth century (*I wish our opinions were the same, but in time they will; you will be to visit me in prison; their being going to be married*) and developed the first progressive passives: *everything is being done* (Warner 1995).

We may adopt a cognitive view of grammars, that they are mental entities that arise in the mind/brain of individual children. Hermann Paul (1880) was the first person to study change with roughly this view of grammars. Then it is natural to try to interpret cascades of changes in terms of changes in grammars, a new setting for some parameter, sometimes having a wide variety of surface effects and perhaps setting off a chain reaction. Such "catastrophic" changes are recognizable by the distinctive features discussed in Lightfoot 1991 (chap. 7). So grammatical approaches to language change have focussed on these large-scale changes, assuming that the clusters of properties tell us about the harmonies that follow from particular parameters. By examining the clusters of simultaneous changes and by taking them to be related by properties of Universal Grammar, we discover something about the scope and nature of parameters and about how they are set. Work on language change from this perspective is fused with work on language variation and acquisition. Change illuminates the principles and parameters of Universal Grammar in the same way that, when we view a forest at some distance, we may not see the deer until it moves.

This grammatical approach to diachrony explains changes at two levels. First, the set of parameters postulated as part of UG explains the unity of the changes, why superficially unrelated properties cluster in the way that they do.

Second, historical records, where they are rich, show not only when catastrophic change takes place but also what kinds of changes were taking place in the language prior to the parametric shift. This enables us to identify in what ways the trigger experiences of children who underwent the parametric shift differed from those of people with the older grammar. This, in turn, enables us to hypothesize what the crucial trigger experience is for setting a given parameter.

Recent work has treated this topic in terms of cue-based learning (Dresher and Kaye 1990; Dresher 1997; Lightfoot 1997): under this view, parameters have a designated cue; children scan their linguistic environment for the relevant cues and set parameters accordingly. The distribution of those cues may change in such a way that a parameter was set differently.

This model has nothing to say about why the distribution of the cues should change. That may be explained by claims about language contact or socially defined speech fashions, and it is a function of the use of grammars and not a func-tion of theories of grammar, acquisition, or change—except under one set of circumstances, where the new distribution of cues results from an earlier parametric shift; in that circumstance, one has a "chain" of grammatical changes.

This approach to change is not tied to any particular grammatical model. Warner (1995) offers a persuasive analysis of parametric shift using a lexicalist HEAD-DRIVEN PHRASE STRUCTURE GRAMMAR model. Interesting diachronic analyses have been offered for a wide range of phenomena, invoking different grammatical claims; see the Further Readings for examples.

This approach to abrupt change, where children acquire different systems from those of their parents, is echoed in work on creolization (see CREOLES) under the view of Bickerton (1984), and the acquisition of signing systems by children exposed largely to unnatural input (Goldin-Meadow and Mylander 1990; Newport 1999; Supalla 1990; see SIGN LANGUAGES). Bickerton argues that situations in which "the normal transmission of well-formed language data from one generation to the next is most drastically disrupted" will tell us something about the innate component and how it determines acquisition (Bickerton 1999).

The vast majority of deaf children are exposed initially to fragmentary signed systems that have not been internalized well by their primary models. Goldin-Meadow and Mylander (1990) take these to be artificial systems, and they show how deaf children go beyond their models in such circumstances and "naturalize" the system, altering the code and inventing new forms that are more consistent with what one finds in natural languages. The acquisition of signed languages under these circumstances casts light on abrupt language change, creolization, and on cue-based learning (Lightfoot 1998).

There has been interesting work on the replacement of one grammar by another—that is, the spread of change through a community. So, Kroch and his associates (Kroch 1989; Kroch and Taylor 1997; Pintzuk 1990; Santorini 1992, 1993; Taylor 1990) have argued for coexisting grammars. That work postulates that speakers may operate with more than one grammar in a kind of "internalized diglossia" and it enriches grammatical analyses by seeking to describe the variability of individual texts and the spread of a grammatical change through a population.

Niyogi and Berwick (1995) have offered a population genetics computer model for describing the spread of new grammars. Certain changes progress in an S-curve and now Niyogi and Berwick provide a model of the emergent, global population behavior, which derives the S-curve. They postulate a learning theory and a population of child learners, a small number of whom fail to converge on preexisting grammars, and they produce a plausible model of population changes for the loss of null subjects in French.

Taking grammars to be elements of cognition has been productive for work on language change, but it is not as common an approach as one that takes grammars to be social entities. The distinction and its implications for historical linguistics are discussed by Lightfoot (1995). The approach described here is analogous to the study of evolutionary change in order to learn about general biological principles and about particular species.

See also LANGUAGE ACQUISITION; LANGUAGE AND CUL-
TURE; LINGUISTIC UNIVERSALS AND UNIVERSAL GRAMMAR;
PARAMETER-SETTING APPROACHES TO ACQUISITION, CRE-
OLIZATION, AND DIACHRONY

—*David Lightfoot*

References

Bickerton, D. (1984). The language bioprogram hypothesis. *Behavioral and Brain Sciences* 7(2): 173–222.

Bickerton, D. (1999). How to acquire language without positive evidence: What acquisitionists can learn from creoles. In DeGraff, Ed. (1999).

DeGraff, M., Ed. (1999). *Language Creation and Language Change.* Cambridge, MA: MIT Press.

Dresher, B. E. (1997). Charting the learning path: Cues to parameter setting. To appear in *Linguistic Inquiry.*

Dresher, B. E., and J. Kaye. (1990). A computational learning model for metrical phonology. *Cognition* 137–195.

Goldin-Meadow, S., and C. Mylander. (1990). Beyond the input given: The child's role in the acquisition of language. *Language* 66: 323–355.

Kemenade, A. van, and N. Vincent, Eds. (1997). *Parameters of Morphosyntactic Change.* Cambridge: Cambridge University Press.

Kroch, A. (1989). Reflexes of grammar in patterns of language change. *Journal of Language Variation and Change* 1: 199–244.

Kroch, A., and A. Taylor. (1997). Verb movement in Old and Middle English: Dialect variation and language contact. In van Kemenade and Vincent (1997).

Lightfoot, D. W. (1991). *How to Set Parameters: Arguments from Language Change.* Cambridge, MA: MIT Press.

Lightfoot, D. W. (1995). Grammars for people. *Journal of Linguistics* 31: 393–399.

Lightfoot, D. W. (1997). Catastrophic change and learning theory. *Lingua* 100: 171–192.

Lightfoot, D. W. (1998). *The Development of Language: Acquisition, Change, and Evolution.* Oxford: Blackwell.

Newport, E. L. (1999). Reduced input in the acquisition of signed languages: Contributions to the study of creolization. In DeGraff, Ed. (1999).

Niyogi, P., and R. C. Berwick. (1995). The logical problem of language change. *MIT A. I. Memo No. 1516.*

Paul, H. (1880). *Prinzipien der Spachgeschichte.* Tübingen: Niemeyer.

Pintzuk, S. (1990). *Phrase Structures in Competition: Variation and Change in Old English Word Order.* Ph.D. diss., University of Pennsylvania.

Santorini, B. (1992). Variation and change in Yiddish subordinate clause word order. *Natural Language and Linguistic Theory* 10: 595–640.

Santorini, B. (1993). The rate of phrase structure change in the history of Yiddish. *Journal of Language Variation and Change* 5: 257–283.

Supalla, S. (1990). *Segmentation of Manually Coded English: Problems in the Mapping of English in the Visual/Gestural Mode.* Ph.D. diss., University of Illinois.

Taylor, A. (1990). *Clitics and Configurationality in Ancient Greek.* Ph.D. diss., University of Pennsylvania.

Warner, A. R. (1995). Predicting the progressive passive: Parametric change within a lexicalist framework. *Language* 71(3): 533–557.

Further Readings

Battye, A., and I. Roberts, Eds. (1995). *Clause Structure and Language Change.* Oxford: Oxford University Press.

Clark, R., and I. Roberts. (1993). A computational approach to language learnability and language change. *Linguistic Inquiry* 24: 299–345.

Fontana, J. M. (1993). *Phrase Structure and the Syntax of Clitics in the History of Spanish.* Ph.D. diss., University of Pennsylvania.

Jespersen, O. (1922). *Language, Its Nature, Development, and Origin.* London: Allen and Unwin.

Kemenade, A. van. (1987). *Syntactic Case and Morphological Case in the History of English.* Dordrecht: Foris.

Kiparsky, P. (1995). Indo-European origins of Germanic syntax. In Battye and Roberts (1995).

Kiparsky, P. (1997). The rise of positional licensing in Germanic. In van Kemenade and Vincent (1997).

Lass, R. (1997). *Historical Linguistics and Language Change.* Cambridge: Cambridge University Press.

Lightfoot, D. W. (1979). *Principles of Diachronic Syntax.* Cambridge: Cambridge University Press.

Lightfoot, D. W. (1993). Why UG needs a learning theory: Triggering verb movement. In C. Jones, Ed., *Historical Linguistics: Problems and Perspectives.* London: Longman, pp. 190–214. Reprinted in Battye and Roberts (1995).

Lightfoot, D. W. (1997). Shifting triggers and diachronic reanalyses. In van Kemenade and Vincent (1997).

Lightfoot, D. W. (1999). Creoles and cues. In DeGraff, Ed. (1999).

Pearce, E. (1990). *Parameters in Old French Syntax.* Dordrecht: Kluwer.

Roberts, I. G. (1985). Agreement patterns and the development of the English modal auxiliaries. *Natural Language and Linguistic Theory* 3: 21–58.

Roberts, I. G. (1993a). *Verbs and Diachronic Syntax.* Dordrecht: Kluwer.

Roberts, I. G. (1993b). A formal account of grammaticalization in the history of Romance futures. *Folia Linguistica Historica* 13: 219–258.

Roberts, I. G. (1998). Verb movement and markedness. In DeGraff, Ed.(1999).

Sprouse, R., and B.Vance. (1999). An explanation for the loss of null subjects in certain Romance and Germanic languages. In DeGraff, Ed. (1999).

Vance, B. (1995). On the decline of verb movement to Comp in Old and Middle French. In A. Battye and I. Roberts, Eds., *Clause Structure and Language Change.* Oxford: Oxford University Press.

Warner, A. R. (1983). Review article on Lightfoot 1979. *Journal of Linguistics* 19: 187–209.

Warner, A. R. (1993). *English Auxiliaries: Structure and History.* Cambridge: Cambridge University Press.

Warner, A. R. (1997). The structure of parametric change, and V movement in the history of English. In van Kemenade and Vincent (1997).

Lashley, Karl Spencer (1890–1958)

Donald HEBB described Karl Lashley's career as "perhaps the most brilliant in the psychology of this century" (Hebb 1959: 142). Lashley's intellectual odyssey about brain and behavior extended from the earliest days of Watsonian BEHAVIORISM to astonishingly modern cognitive views.

Lashley attended the University of West Virginia, where he studied with John Black Johnston, a neurologist. When taking his first class from Johnston in zoology, Lashley "knew that I had found my life's work." Lashley plunged into the study of zoology, neuroanatomy, embryology, and animal behavior, graduating in 1910. He received an M.S. in bacteriology at the University of Pittsburgh in 1911, where he studied experimental psychology with K. M. Dallenbach. Following this he enrolled for the Ph.D. in zoology at Johns Hopkins with H. S. Jennings, with a minor in psychology with Adolf Meyer and John B. Watson. Watson's developing theory of behaviorism, and Watson himself, had a profound influence on Lashley.

In a letter written much later to Ernest Hilgard at Stanford, Lashley described taking a seminar with Watson in 1914. Watson called attention in the seminar to the writings of Bechterev and Pavlov on conditioned reflexes, which they translated.

In the spring I served as an unpaid assistant and we constructed apparatus and did experiments, repeating a number of their experiments. Our whole program was then disrupted by the move to the lab in Meyer's Clinic. There were no adequate animal quarters there. Watson started work with infants as the next best material available. I tagged along for awhile but disliked the babies and found me a rat lab in another building.

We accumulated a considerable amount of experimental material on the conditioned reflex that was never published. Watson sought the basis of a systemic psychology and was not greatly concerned with the reaction itself.

The conditioned reflex thus came to form the basis of Watson's behaviorism. Lashley, on the other hand, had become interested in the physiology of the reaction and the attempt to trace conditioned reflex paths through the central nervous system.

During the period at Hopkins, Lashley worked with Shepherd Irvory Franz at St. Elizabeth's Hospital in Washington. Together, they developed a new approach to the study of brain mechanisms of learning and memory and published landmark papers on the effect of cortical lesions on learning in rats. From this time (1916) until 1929, Lashley systematically used the lesion method in an attempt to localize memory traces in the brain. Following Watson (and Pavlov), Lashley conceived of the brain as a massive reflex switchboard, with sequential chaining of input-output circuitries via the cerebral cortex as the basis of memory. This work culminated in his classic 1929 monograph *Brain Mechanisms of Intelligence*. He was also president of the American Psychological Association that year. His presidential address, and his 1929 monograph, destroyed the switchboard reflexology theory of brain function and learning as it existed at that time. In complex mazes, rats were impaired in LEARNING and MEMORY in proportion to the degree of cerebral cortex destroyed, independent of locus. He employed the terms "mass action" and "equipotentiality" more to describe his results than as a major theory. Lashley did not deny localization of function in the neocortex. Rather, he argued that the neural substrate for higher-order memorial functions—he often used the term "intelligence"—as in complex maze learning in rats, was widely distributed in the CEREBRAL CORTEX.

Lashley was perhaps the most formidable critical thinker of his time, successfully demolishing all major theories of brain behavior, from Pavlov to the Gestalt psychologists to his own views. "He remarked that he had destroyed all theories of behavior, including his own" (Hebb 1959: 149). Near the end of his career, looking over his lifetime of research on memory, Lashley (1950) concluded that

This series of experiments has yielded a good bit of information about what and where the memory trace is not. It has discovered nothing directly of the real nature of the memory trace. I sometimes feel, in reviewing the evidence of the localization of the memory trace, that the necessary conclusion is that learning is just not possible. It is difficult to conceive of a mechanism that can satisfy the conditions set for it. Nevertheless, in spite of such evidence against it, learning sometimes does occur. (477–478).

Lashley's positive contributions were extraordinary. Perhaps most striking was his brilliant analysis of the "problem of serial order in behavior" (Lashley 1951). Ranging from the properties of language to the performance of complex motor sequences, he showed that "associative chaining" cannot account for serial behavior. Rather, higher-order representations must exist in the brain in the form of patterns of action "where spatial and temporal order are. . .interchangeable." (Lashley 1951: 128).

Lashley made a number of other major contributions, including an insightful analysis of "instinctive" behaviors, analysis of sexual behaviors, characterization of the patterns of thalamocortical projections, functions of the visual cortex, a rethinking of cortical cytoarchitectonics (Beach et al. 1960).

In 1936 James B. Conant, then the new president of Harvard, appointed an ad hoc committee to find "the best psychologist in the world" (Beach 1961). Lashley, then at the University of Chicago, was chosen and hired in 1937. He became director of the Yerkes Laboratory of Primate Biology in Florida but maintained his chair at Harvard, traveling to Cambridge once each year to give his two-week graduate seminar. The roster of eminent psychologists and neuroscientists who worked with Lashley is without parallel.

According to his student Roger SPERRY (personal communication), Lashley was interested in the problem of CONSCIOUSNESS but refused to write about it, considering it something of an epiphenomenon. He did, however, speculate about the mind, in itself heretical for a behaviorist:

"Mind is a complex organization, held together by interaction processes and by time scales of memory, centered about the body image. It has no distinguishing features other than its organization . . . there is no logical or empirical reason for denying the possibility that the correlation (between mental and neural activities) may eventually show a complete identity of the two organizations" (Lashley 1958: 542).

In his biographical memoir of Lashley, Frank Beach (1961) offered the following tribute (163):

Eminent psychologist with no earned degree in psychology
Famous theorist who specialized in disproving theories, including his own
Inspiring teacher who described all teaching as useless.

See also CORTICAL LOCALIZATION, HISTORY OF; GESTALT PSYCHOLOGY

—Richard F. Thompson

References

Beach, F. A. (1961). A biographical memoir [of Karl Lashley]. *Biographical Memoirs of the National Academy of Sciences* 35: 162–204.

Beach, F. A., D. D. Hebb, C. T. Morgan, and H. W. Nissen, Eds. (1960). *The Neuropsychology of Lashley*. New York: McGraw-Hill.

Hebb, D. D. (1959). Karl Spencer Lashley, 1890-1958. *The American Journal of Psychology* 72: 142–150.

Lashley, K. S. (1929). *Brain Mechanisms and Intelligence*. Chicago: University of Chicago Press.

Lashley, K. S. (1950). In search of the engram. *Society of Experimental Biology, Symposium 4*, pp. 454–482.

Lashley, K. S. (1951). The problem of serial order in behavior. In *Cerebral Mechanisms in Behavior*. New York: Wiley, pp. 112–136.

Lashley, K. S. (1958). Cerebral organization and behavior. *Proceedings of the Association for Research in Nervous and Mental Diseases* 36: 1–18.

Laws

See CAUSATION; PSYCHOLOGICAL LAWS

Learning

Although learning can be understood as a change in an organism's capacities or behavior brought about by experience, this rough definition encompasses many cases usually not considered examples of learning (e.g., an increase in muscular strength brought about through exercise). More important, it fails to reflect the many forms of learning, which may be distinguished, for example, according to what is learned, may be governed by different principles, and may involve different processes.

One form of learning is *associative learning,* in which the learner is exposed to pairs of events or stimuli and has the opportunity to learn these pairings—which event or stimulus goes with which (see CONDITIONING). The study of associative learning has led to the discovery of numerous learning principles applicable to species as diverse as flatworms and humans, and behaviors as different as salivation and the onset of fear. Investigators have also learned a great deal about the biological bases for this form of learning (see CONDITIONING AND THE BRAIN).

Another crucial form of learning involves the acquisition of knowledge about the spatial layout of the organism's surrounding—these COGNITIVE MAPS can include the locations of food sources or of dangers, the boundaries of one's territory, and so on. The acquisition of this spatial knowledge often involves *latent learning*: The organism derives some knowledge from its experiences, but with no immediately visible change in the organism's behavior. (The latent learning does become visible later on, however, when the organism finds occasion to use what it has earlier learned.) In many species, this learning about spatial layout can be extraordinarily sophisticated, allowing the organism to navigate across great distances, or to remember the locations of hundreds of food caches, or to navigate by dead reckoning, with little or no reliance on sensory landmarks (see ANIMAL NAVIGATION and ANIMAL NAVIGATION, NEURAL NETWORKS).

Spatial learning may be considered a special case within a broader category of learning, in which an organism gains ("memorizes") information about its environment (see MEMORY). In humans, this information may be derived directly from firsthand experience, or indirectly, from what one reads or hears from others. This information may then be used later on for some memory-based report (e.g., a response to the question, "What happened yesterday?"), or as a basis for modifying future action. In any of these cases, one *encodes* the information into memory during the initial exposure, and then *retrieves* this stored information later on. The initial encoding may be *intentional* (if one is seeking to memorize the target information) or *incidental* (if the learning is a by-product of one's ordinary commerce with the world, with no intention of learning). Similarly, the subsequent use of the information may involve *explicit* memory (if one wittingly and deliberately seeks to use the stored information later on) or *implicit* memory (if the stored information has an unwitting and automatic influence on one's subsequent behavior; see IMPLICIT VS. EXPLICIT MEMORY).

Still another form of learning is *skill learning,* in which one learns how to perform some action or procedure, often without any ability to describe the acquired skill (also see MOTOR LEARNING). In this case, one is said to have acquired "procedural knowledge" (knowing how to carry out some procedure), as opposed to "declarative knowledge" (knowing that some proposition is correct). It should be emphasized, however, that skill learning is not limited to the acquisition of motor skills (such as learning how to serve a tennis ball or how to ride a bicycle). In addition, much of our mental activity can be understood in terms of skill acquisition—we acquire skills for reading, solving problems within a particular domain, recognizing particular patterns, and so on. Thus, for example, chess masters have acquired the skill of recognizing specific configurations of chess pieces, a skill that helps them both in remembering the arrangement of the game pieces and (probably more important) allows them to think about the game in terms of strategy-defined, goal-oriented patterns of pieces, rather than needing to focus on individual pieces (see EXPERTISE and PROBLEM SOLVING).

Skill learning can also lead to AUTOMATICITY for the particular skill or procedure. Once automatized, a skill can be run off as a single, integrated action, even though the skill was initially composed of numerous constituent actions. The skilled tennis player, for example, need not focus on wrist position, the arch of the back, and the position of the shoulders, but instead launches the single (complex) behavior, "backhand swing." This automatization promotes fluency among the constituents of a complex behavior, dramatically decreases the extent to which one must attend to the various elements of the behavior, and thus frees ATTENTION for other tasks. On the other hand, automatic behaviors are often inflexible and difficult to control, leading some to speak of them as "mental reflexes."

A further form of learning is INDUCTION, in which the learner is exposed to a series of stimuli or events and has the opportunity to discover a general rule or pattern that summarizes these experiences. In some cases, induction is produced by the simple forgetting of an episode's details and the consequent blurring together in memory of that episode with other similar episodes. This blurring together is, for example, the source of our knowledge of, say, what a kitchen is likely to contain. Investigators refer to knowledge acquired in this fashion as "generic" or "schematic knowledge" (see EPISODIC VS. SEMANTIC MEMORY and SCHEMATA).

In other cases, induction results from a more deliberate judgment process in which one actively seeks to generalize from one's previous experiences, a process that seems to rely on a relatively small number of strategies or JUDGMENT HEURISTICS. For example, subjects in many studies seem to rely on the assumption that the categories they encounter are relatively homogeneous, and this encourages them to extrapolate freely from the sample of observations made so far, even if that sample is relatively small, and even (in some cases) if warnings are in place that the sample is not representative of the larger category (see CATEGORIZATION).

Some aspects of induction seem to be governed by highly specialized domain-specific skills. One clear example is provided by LANGUAGE ACQUISITION in the small child. The human infant appears to be well prepared to induce the regularities of language, so that language acquisition is relatively swift and successfully achieved by virtually all children, independent (within certain boundary conditions) of the child's individual abilities or circumstances. The same learning skills, however, seem irrelevant to the acquisition of information in other domains (also see COGNITIVE DEVELOPMENT and DOMAIN SPECIFICITY).

Finally, let us note still other forms of learning: Many species are capable of learning through IMITATION, in which an action is first observed and then copied. A number of species display *imprinting,* in which a young organism learns to recognize its parents or its conspecifics. Human learning often also involves DEDUCTIVE REASONING, in which one is able to discover (or generate) new knowledge, based on beliefs one already holds. In some cases of deduction, one's reasoning is guided by relatively abstract rules or principles. In others, one's reasoning is guided by a specific remembered experience; one then draws an analogy, based on that experience, and the analogy indicates how one should act, or what one should conclude, for the current problem (see CASE-BASED REASONING AND ANALOGY).

Thus the term *learning* plainly covers a diversity of phenomena. But having now emphasized this diversity, we should ask what these many forms of learning have in common. At a general level, some principles may apply across domains—for example, the importance of acknowledging task-specific learning skills, or the possibility of latent learning, not immediately manifest in behavioral change. At a much finer-grained level, it is likely that similar processes in the nervous system provide the substrate for diverse forms of learning, including, for example, the process of LONG-TERM POTENTIATION, in which the pattern of interaction among neurons is modified through experience. Similarly, it is plausible that connectionist models may provide powerful accounts of many of these forms of learning (see COGNITIVE MODELING, CONNECTIONIST). In between these extremes, however, we may be unable to formulate general "laws of learning," applicable to all learning types.

See also BAYESIAN LEARNING; BEHAVIORISM; COMPUTATIONAL LEARNING THEORY; EXPLANATION-BASED LEARNING; STATISTICAL LEARNING THEORY; VISION AND LEARNING

—*Daniel Reisberg*

Further Readings

Reisberg, D. (1997). *Cognition: Exploring the Science of the Mind.* New York: Norton.

Schwartz, B., and S. Robbins. (1995). *Psychology of Learning and Behavior.* New York: Norton.

Tarpy, R. M. (1997). *Contemporary Learning Theory and Research.* New York: McGraw-Hill.

Learning and Vision

See VISION AND LEARNING

Learning Systems

The ability to formulate coherent and predictive theories of the environment is a salient characteristic of our species. We perform this feat at diverse stages of development and with respect to sundry features of our experience. For example, almost all infants construct grammatical theories of their caretakers' language; most children master the moral and aesthetic codes of their household and community; and selected adults discover scientific principles that govern fundamental aspects of the physical world. In each case, our theories are underdetermined by the data that trigger them in the sense that there exist alternative hypotheses (with different predictive consequences) that are equally compatible with the evidence in hand. In some cases, the underdetermination reaches dramatic proportions, revealed by comparing the fragmentary nature of available data to the scope and apparent accuracy of the theories they engender. Such appears to be the case in the physical sciences. For example, Dodelson, Gates, and Turner (1996) describe a theory of the origin of astrophysical structure, from stars to great walls of galaxies, presenting evidence that such structure arose from quantum mechanical fluctuations during the first 10^{-34} seconds in the life of the universe. If the theory is true, surely one of its most curious features is that it could be known by a human being. Similarly, radical underdetermination has also been suggested for the grammatical theories constructed by infants learning their first language (for elaboration of this view, see Chomsky 1988 and POVERTY OF THE STIMULUS ARGUMENTS; a critical rejoinder is provided by Pullum 1996; see also INDUCTION and LANGUAGE ACQUISITION).

The psychological processes mediating discovery no doubt vary with the specific problem to which they must apply. There may be little in common, for example, between the neural substrate of grammatical hypotheses and that underlying the conjectures of professional geologists. Such matters are controversial, so it will be prudent to limit the remainder of our discussion to discovery of a patently scientific kind.

The psychological study of discovery has focused on how people choose tests of specific hypotheses, and how they modify hypotheses in the face of confirming or disconfirming data. Many of the experiments are inspired by "Mill's methods" of causal inquiry, referring to the nineteenth-century logician John Stuart Mill. The results suggest that both children and adults are apt to test hypotheses by seeking data that cannot be disconfirmatory, and to retain hypotheses whose predictions are observed to be falsified (see, for example, Kuhn 1996). In contrast to this bleak picture of intuitive science, other researchers believe that Mill's methods are too crude for the framing of pertinent questions about the psychology of empirical inquiry. A different assessment of lay intuition is thought to arise from a subtler account of normative science (see, for example, Koslowski 1996 and SCIENTIFIC THINKING AND ITS DEVELOPMENT).

More generally, investigation of the psychology of theory discovery can benefit from a convincing model of rational inquiry, if only to help define the task facing the reasoner. Two formal perspectives on discovery have been developed in recent years, both quite primitive but in different ways. One view focuses on the credibility that scientists attach to alternative theories, and on the evolution of these credibilities under the impact of data. Interpreting credibility as probability leads to the *Bayesian analysis* of inquiry, which has greatly illuminated diverse aspects of scientific practice (see BAYESIAN LEARNING). For example, it is widely acknowledged that a theory T is better confirmed by data D_s, which verify a surprising prediction, than by data D_o, which verify an obvious one. The Bayesian analysis of this fact starts by interpreting surprise probabilistically: $0 < P(D_s) < P(D_o) \leq 1$. Because both predictions are assumed to follow deductively from T, the probability calculus implies $P(D_s \mid T) = P(D_o \mid T) = 1$, and Bayes's theorem yields

$$P(T \mid D_s) = \frac{P(D_s \mid T) \times P(T)}{P(D_s)} = \frac{P(T)}{P(D_s)} > \frac{P(T)}{P(D_o)}$$
$$= \frac{P(D_o \mid T) \times P(T)}{P(D_o)} = P(T \mid D_o).$$

The greater support of T offered by D_s compared to D_o is thus explained in terms of the posterior probabilities $P(T \mid D_s)$ and $P(T \mid D_o)$. This example and many others are discussed in Earman (1992), Horwich (1982), Howson and Urbach (1993), and Rosenkrantz (1977).

A second perspective on inquiry is embodied in the "theory of scientific discovery" (see, for example, Kelly 1996; Martin and Osherson 1998; for a computational perspective, see Langley et al. 1987; COMPUTATIONAL LEARNING THEORY; and MACHINE LEARNING). Scientific success here consists not in gradually increasing one's confidence in the true theory, but rather in ultimately accepting it and holding on to it in the face of new data. This way of viewing inquiry is consonant with the philosophy of Karl Popper (1959), and was first studied from an algorithmic point of view in Put-

nam (1975), Solomonoff (1964), and Gold (1967). Analysis proceeds by distinguishing five components of empirical inquiry, namely: (1) potential realities or "worlds"; (2) a scientific problem; (3) a set of potential data streams or "environments" for each world, which provide information about the world; (4) scientists; and (5) a criterion of success that stipulates the conditions under which a scientist is credited with solving a given problem. Any precise formalization of the preceding items is called a "model" or "paradigm" of inquiry, and may be analyzed mathematically using the techniques developed within the general theory (the five components are adapted from Wexler and Culicover 1980). Particular attention is devoted to characterizing the kinds of problems that can be solved, distinguishing them from problems that resist solution by any scientist.

One of the simplest paradigms to be studied in depth has a numerical character, and may be described as follows (for fuller treatment see Jain et al. forthcoming). Let N be the set $\{0,1,2,\ldots\}$ of natural numbers.

1. A world is any infinite subset of N, for example: $N - \{0\}$ or $N - \{1\}$. The numbers making up a world are conceived as codes for individual facts that call for prediction and explanation.

2. A scientific problem is any collection of worlds, for example, the collection $\mathbf{P} = \{ N - \{x\} \mid x \in N \}$ of all subsets of N with just one number missing. A problem thus specifies a range of theoretically possible worlds, the "real" member of which must be recognized by the scientist.

3. An environment for a world is any listing of all of its members. For example, one environment for $N - \{3\}$ starts off: $0,1,2,4,5,6\ldots$. We emphasize that an environment for a world S may list S in *any* order.

4. A scientist is any mapping from initial segments of environments into worlds. To illustrate, consider the scientist S that responds to each initial segment of its environment with the set $N - \{x\}$, where x is the least number not yet encountered. Then faced with the environment $0,1,2,4,5,6\ldots$ shown above, S would first conjecture $N - \{1\}$, then $N - \{2\}$, then $N - \{3\}$, then again $N - \{3\}$, and so on.

5. A scientist is said to "solve" a given problem just in case the following is true. No matter what world W is drawn from the problem, and no matter how the members of W are listed to form an environment e, the scientist's conjectures on e are wrong only finitely often. That is, starting at some point in e, the scientist begins to (correctly) hypothesize W, and never deviates thereafter.

It is not difficult to see that the scientist S solves the problem $\mathbf{P}$ described above. In contrast, it can be demonstrated that no scientist whatsoever solves the problem that results from adding the additional world N to $\mathbf{P}$. This new problem is *unsolvable*.

The foregoing model of inquiry can be progressively enriched to provide more faithful portraits of science. In one version, worlds are relational structures for a first-order language, scientists implement belief revision operators in the sense of Gärdenfors (1988), and success consists in fixing upon an adequate theory of the structure giving rise to the atomic facts of the environment (see Martin and Osherson 1998).

See also INNATENESS OF LANGUAGE; LEARNING; PROBLEM SOLVING

—Daniel Osherson

References

Chomsky, N. (1988). *Language and Problems of Knowledge: The Managua Lectures.* Cambridge, MA: MIT Press.

Dodelson, S., E. Gates, and M. Turner. (1996). Cold dark matter. *Science* 274: 69–75.

Earman, J. (1992). *Bayes or Bust?* Cambridge, MA: MIT Press.

Gärdenfors, P. (1988). *Knowledge in Flux: Modeling the Dynamics of Epistemic States.* Cambridge, MA: MIT Press.

Gold, E. M. (1967). Language identification in the limit. *Information and Control* 10: 447–474.

Horwich, P. (1982). *Probability and Evidence.* Cambridge: Cambridge University Press.

Howson, C., and P. Urbach. (1993). *Scientific Reasoning: The Bayesian Approach.* 2nd ed. La Salle, IL: Open Court.

Jain, S., E. Martin, D. Osherson, J. Royer, and A. Sharma. (Forthcoming). *Systems That Learn.* 2nd ed. Cambridge, MA: MIT Press.

Kelly, K. T. (1996). *The Logic of Reliable Inquiry.* New York: Oxford University Press.

Koslowski, B. (1996). *Theory and Evidence: The Development of Scientific Reasoning.* Cambridge, MA: MIT Press.

Kuhn, D. (1996). Children and adults as intuitive scientists. *Psychological Review* 96(4).

Langley, P., H. A. Simon, G. L. Bradshaw, and Z. M. Zytkow. (1987). *Scientific Discovery.* Cambridge, MA: MIT Press.

Martin, E., and D. Osherson. (1998). *Elements of Scientific Inquiry.* Cambridge, MA: MIT Press.

Popper, K. (1959). *The Logic of Scientific Discovery.* London: Hutchinson.

Pullum, G. (1996). Learnability, hyperlearning, and the poverty of the stimulus. In J. Johnson, M. L. Juge, and J. L. Moxley, Eds., *Proceedings of the Twenty-second Annual Meeting: General Session and Parasession on the Role of Learnability in Grammatical Theory.* Berkeley, CA: Berkeley Linguistics Society, pp. 498–513.

Putnam, H. (1975). Probability and confirmation. In *Mathematics, Matter and Method.* Cambridge: Cambridge University Press.

Rosenkrantz, R. (1977). *Inference, Method and Decision.* Dordrect: Reidel.

Solomonoff, R. J. (1964). A formal theory of inductive inference. *Information and Control* 7: 1–22, 224–254.

Wexler, K., and P. Culicover. (1980). *Formal Principles of Language Acquisition.* Cambridge, MA: MIT Press.

Lévi-Strauss, Claude

The most remarkable aspect of the French anthropologist Lévi-Strauss's (1908–) undertaking is his ambition to take seriously the very idea of anthropology. His aim has been to develop anthropology not just as an inventory of human cultures or of types of institutions (kinship, myths, rituals, arts, technologies, knowledge systems), but also as an investigation of the mental equipment common to all humans. This has not always been understood. It has been seen as an overambitious philosophical project when in fact it is better understood as a cognitivist project.

Lévi-Strauss develops this approach by taking up the concept of *structure* and by proposing a new use of this concept in anthropology. He abandons the notion of social structure (promoted by A. R. Radcliffe-Brown and G. P. Murdock) as the totality of directly observable relations in a society (a notion that still refers to the traditional understanding of "structure" as architectural frame or organic system). Lévi-Strauss's conception of structure as a *model* stems directly from linguistics (particularly from Troubetskoi and JAKOBSON) where structure refers to a recurring relation between terms (such as phonemes) considered as minimal units. The second source is mathematics where it refers to constant relations between elements regardless of what the set in question is. Lévi-Strauss admits that this kind of stable relations only appears in certain objects and under certain conditions. In other words, in the field of social sciences, a structural analysis is productive and legitimate only in such cases as phonology, kinship, taxonomies, "totemic" phenomena, rituals, mythical narratives, and certain artifacts. It is better avoided in domains where probabilistic factors prevail over the mechanical order.

From a cognitivist point of view, Lévi-Strauss's most interesting contribution is linked to his conviction that there is a continuity between forms of organization of external reality (matter, living organisms, social groups, artifacts) and the human mind. To understand a specific field of objects is to show how that field produces its own rationality, that is, how it is regulated by a spontaneous intelligible order. This is the epistemological presupposition behind Lévi-Strauss's analyses of kinship systems. This aim dominates the following inquiries he has conducted on the traditional forms of classification of objects in the natural world. He began his research by going back to an old controversial and seemingly insoluble problem, that of so-called totemism, and by showing that it was a nonissue, first because it was badly stated. In fact, totemism is not a one-to-one correspondence between the human and the natural world but a way of establishing and expressing a system of differences between humans (individuals and groups), with the help of a system of differences between things (animals, plants, or artifacts). What resembles each other are not humans and things but their differential relations.

Of course, this presupposes that the human mind has the capacity and a disposition to recognize differences and to classify things themselves. In fact, traditional forms of knowledge show that this spontaneous work of classification is very sophisticated. This means that it is not primarily guided by vital need (such as food or survival) but indeed by the desire to understand and interpret the world; in short, as Lévi-Strauss reminds us, things are not just "good for eating," but also "good for thinking." From this perspective it is therefore important not to underestimate the power of "untamed thinking" (literally: *la pensée sauvage*). There, the flourishing symbolic systems are based on the differential values themselves that have come out of the operations of classification of the observed world.

What is finally the difference between "untamed thinking" and "domesticated thinking," between traditional forms of knowledge and modern reason? According to Lévi-Strauss, it stems from the progressive branching out of two types of society at the end of the neolithic period: some evolved toward the pursuit and preservation of a stable equilibrium between the human and the natural world, while others turned toward change by developing technologies for mastery over nature, which involved the explicit recognition and formalization of abstract representations, as was the case of the civilizations of writing, particularly those where alphabetical writing developed.

This exercise of traditional knowledge appears particularly in the production of mythical narratives. According to Lévi-Strauss, myths are a complex expression of forms of thought inherent in a culture or a group of cultures (which refers back to an empirical corpus); at the same time they reveal mental processes that are verifiable everywhere (this concerns operations that are part of the basic equipment of every human mind). In the interpretation of myths it is therefore impossible to maintain a purely functionalist approach (which seeks an explanation of narrative based on need alone), or a symbolist approach (which seeks for keys of universal interpretation), or a psychological approach (which seeks archetypes). To be sure, myths do refer back to an empirical environment (geographical, technical, social) and express it directly or not, but above all they construct representations where through the categorial use of sensory elements (such as diversity of species, places, forms, colors, materials, directions, sounds, temperatures) emerges a symbolic order of things and humans (cosmogony, sociogony) and where, above all, the logical faculties of the mind are at work—for example, opposition, symmetry, contradiction, disjunction, negation, inclusion, exclusion, complementarity. Hence the surprising character of certain myths that do not correspond to any etiology, that is, to any specific referential situation, but seem to arise and develop just for the sake of pure speculative play. Therefore a narrative cannot be interesting in itself. Some elements reappear from one myth to another (mythemes or segments); there are clusters of narratives related in various ways (symmetrical, oppositional, etc.); and finally there are whole cycles with groups of myths that are linked in networks and constitute complete systems of representation. Lévi-Strauss's most original and ambitious theoretical contribution has been to demonstrate that those networks consist of transformation groups (in the mathematical sense of the term).

The recourse to the structural model stemming from linguistics and mathematics allowed Lévi-Strauss to bring to the fore invariants hitherto only seen as simple empirical recurrences, if not residues of lost history—invariants that he attributes to the propensitites of the human mind. This is unquestionably pioneering work for a cognitivist approach to traditional societies and for the elaboration of a global theory of the human mind.

See also CATEGORIZATION; CULTURAL SYMBOLISM; HUMAN UNIVERSALS; MAGIC AND SUPERSTITION

—*Marcel Hénaff*

Works by Lévi-Strauss

Lévi-Strauss, C. (1969). *The Elementary Structures of Kinship.* Translated by J. Bell, J. von Sturmer, and R. Needham. Boston: Beacon Press.

Lévi-Strauss, C. (1974). *Tristes Tropiques.* Translated by John and Doreen Weightman. New York: Athenaeum.

Lévi-Strauss, C. (1963). *Structural Anthropology,* vol. 1. Translated by C. Jacobson and B. Graundfest Schoepf. New York: Basic Books.

Lévi-Strauss, C. (1963). *Totemism.* Translated by Rodney Needham. Boston: Beacon.

Lévi-Strauss, C. (1966). *The Savage Mind.* Chicago: University of Chicago Press.

Lévi-Strauss, C. (1969). *Mythologiques I: The Raw and the Cooked.* Translated by John and Doreen Weightman. New York: Harper and Row.

Lévi-Strauss, C. (1973). *Mythologiques II: From Honey to Ashes.* Translated by John and Doreen Weightman. London: Cape.

Lévi-Strauss, C. (1978). *Mythologiques III: The Origin of Table Manners.* Translated by John and Doreen Weightman. London: Cape.

Lévi-Strauss, C. (1981). *Mythologiques IV: The Naked Man.* Translated by John and Doreen Weightman. New York: Harper and Row.

Lévi-Strauss, C. (1976). *Structural Anthropology,* vol. 2. Translated by M. Layton. New York: Basic Books.

Lévi-Strauss, C. (1985). *The View from Afar.* Translated by J. Neugroschel and P. Hoss. New York: Basic Books.

Lévi-Strauss, C. (1988). *The Jealous Potter.* Translated by Benedicte Chorier. Chicago: University of Chicago Press.

Lévi-Strauss, C. (1995). *The Story of Lynx.* Chicago: University of Chicago Press.

Further Readings

Badcock, C. R. (1975). *Lévi-Stauss, Structuralism and Sociological Theory.* London: Hutchinson.

Hénaff, M. (1998). *Lévi-Strauss and the Making of Structural Anthropology.* University of Minnesota Press.

Leach, E. (1970). *Claude Lévi-Strauss.* New York: Viking Press.

Sperber, D. (1973). *Le Structuralisme en Anthropologie.* Paris: Seuil.

Sperber, D. (1985). *On Anthropological Knowledge.* Cambridge: Cambridge University Press.

Lexical Access

See COMPUTATIONAL LEXICONS; LEXICON; SPOKEN WORD RECOGNITION; VISUAL WORD RECOGNITION

Lexical Functional Grammar

Lexical Functional Grammar (LFG) is a theory of the structure of natural language and how different aspects of linguistic structure are related. The name of the theory expresses two ways in which it differs from other theories of linguistic structure and organization. LFG is a lexical theory: relations between linguistic forms, such as the relation between an active and passive form of a verb, are generalizations about the structure of the lexicon, not transformational operations that derive one form on the basis of another one. And LFG is a functional theory: GRAMMATICAL RELATIONS such as subject and object are basic, primitive constructs, not defined in terms of phrase-structure configurations or of semantic notions such as agent or patient.

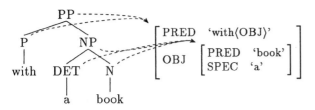

Figure 1. Simplified constituent structure and functional structure for the prepositional phrase *with a book*.

Two aspects of syntactic structure are copresent in the LFG analysis of a sentence or phrase. The concrete, perceptible relations of dominance, precedence, and phrasal grouping are represented by a phrase structure tree, the constituent structure or *c-structure*. More abstract functional syntactic information such as the relation of subjecthood or objecthood is represented by an attribute-value matrix, the functional structure or *f-structure*. Each node of the constituent structure is related to its corresponding functional structure by a functional correspondence Φ, illustrated in Figure 1 by dotted lines. This functional correspondence induces equivalence classes of structural positions that can be related to a particular grammatical function. There may be functional structures that are not related to any constituent structure node (that is, the Φ correspondence function is not onto); for example, in so-called pro-drop languages, a verb may appear with no overtly expressed arguments. In such a case, the verb's arguments are represented at functional structure but not at constituent structure.

Information about the constituent structure category of each word as well as its functional structure is contained in the LEXICON, and the constituent structure is annotated with information specifying how the functional structures of the daughter nodes are related to the functional structure of the mother node. The functional structure must also obey the well-formedness conditions of *completeness* and *coherence*: all grammatical functions required by a predicate must be present, and no other grammatical functions may be present. For example, a transitive verb requires the presence of a subject and an object (completeness) and no other grammatical functions (coherence). Thus, the universally applicable principles of completeness and coherence together with a language-specific lexicon and principles for phrase-structure annotation provide the criteria for determining the constituent-structure tree and the functional structure that corresponds to it for a sentence or phrase of a language.

LFG adheres to the lexical integrity principle, which states that morphological composition does not interact with syntactic composition: the minimal unit analyzed by the constituent structure is the word, and the internal morphological structure of the word is not accessible to syntactic processes (Bresnan and Mchombo 1995). However, it is possible for words and phrases to have similarly articulated functional structure: a verb with a morphologically incorporated pronominal object may have the same functional structure as a verb phrase with a verb and an independent pronoun. A number of apparent paradoxes are explained by distinguishing between syntactic phenomena at the two different syntactic levels.

Distinguishing the outer, crosslinguistically variable constituent structure from the functional structure, which encodes relations that hold at a more abstract level in every language, allows for the incorporation of a comparative assessment of grammatical structures as proposed in OPTIMALITY THEORY (Bresnan 1997; Choi 1996).

The formal generative properties of LFG grammars are fairly well described. Like context-free languages, LFG languages are closed under union, concatenation, and Kleene closure (Kelly Roach, unpublished work). The recognition problem (whether a given string is in the language generated by a given LFG grammar) was shown to be decidable by Kaplan and Bresnan (1982). The emptiness problem (whether a given LFG grammar generates a nonempty set of strings) was shown to be undecidable in further unpublished work by Roach. A synopsis of Roach's results is given by Dalrymple et al. (1995).

The efficient processing of LFG grammars, both from a psycholinguistic and a computational standpoint, is a central concern of the theory. It has been shown that LFG recognition is *NP*-complete (Berwick 1982): for some string (not necessarily a string in any natural language) and some LFG grammar, no known algorithm exists to determine in polynomial time whether that string is in the language generated by that grammar. Kaplan (1982) proposes that the *NP*-complete class is actually a psycholinguistically plausible one for a linguistic model: the exponentially many candidate analyses of a string can be heuristially winnowed, and subsequent verification of the correct analysis can be accomplished very quickly. Strategies can also be devised to optimize the distribution of processing work between the two syntactic structures (Maxwell and Kaplan 1993). In recent unpublished work, Ronald M. Kaplan and Rens Bod explore the Data-Oriented Parsing approach within the LFG framework; this approach assumes that LANGUAGE ACQUISITION proceeds by forming generalizations over fragments of constituent structures and functional structures of previously encountered utterances and by inducing the most likely structure of newly encountered utterances based on these generalizations.

Besides constituent structure and functional structure, LFG assumes other structures for other aspects of linguistic form. These structures are generally assumed to be related by functional correspondence to the constituent structure, the functional structure, and/or one another (Kaplan 1987). Argument structure encodes the THEMATIC ROLES of the arguments of predicates and plays an important role in LFG's linking theory, principles for how the thematic role of an argument affects its grammatical function and realization in the functional structure (Bresnan and Kanerva 1989; Alsina 1994). The meaning of a phrase or sentence is represented at semantic structure (Halvorsen 1983), related directly to functional structure and indirectly to other linguistic structures. The relation between semantic structures and their corresponding functional structures is exploited in recent deductive accounts of the SYNTAX-SEMANTICS INTERFACE; syntactic relations established at functional structure interact with lexically specified information about the meaning of individual words in a logical deduction of the meaning of larger phrases and sentences (Dalrymple, Lamping, and Saraswat 1993).

Further information about LFG, including a continually updated bibliography, is available at http://clwww.essex.ac.uk/LFG/.

See also GENERATIVE GRAMMAR; HEAD-DRIVEN PHRASE STRUCTURE GRAMMAR; MINIMALISM; RELATIONAL GRAMMAR

—*Mary Dalrymple*

References

Alsina, A. (1994). *Predicate Composition: A Theory of Syntactic Function Alternations.* Ph.D. diss., Stanford University.

Berwick, R. (1982). Computational complexity and Lexical Functional Grammar. *American Journal of Computational Linguistics* 8: 97–109.

Bresnan, J. (1997). The emergence of the unmarked pronoun: Chichewa pronominals in Optimality Theory. Paper presented at the BLS 23 Special Session on Syntax and Semantics in Africa. http://www-csli.stanford.edu/bresnan/jb-bls-roa.ps.

Bresnan, J., and J. Kanerva. (1989). Locative inversion in Chichewa: A case study of factorization in grammar. *Linguistic Inquiry* 20(1): 1–50. Reprinted in T. Stowell and E. Wehrli, Eds., *Syntax and Semantics No. 26: Syntax and the Lexicon.* New York: Academic Press, pp. 53–101.

Bresnan, J., and S. A. Mchombo. (1995). The lexical integrity principle: Evidence from Bantu. *Natural Language and Linguistic Theory* 13(2): 181–254.

Choi, H.-W. (1996). *Optimizing Structure in Context: Scrambling and Information Structure.* Ph.D. diss., Stanford University.

Dalrymple, M., R. M. Kaplan, J. T. Maxwell, and A. Zaenen. (1995). Mathematical and computational issues. In M. Dalrymple, R. M. Kaplan, J. T. Maxwell, and A. Zaenen, Eds., *Formal Issues in Lexical Functional Grammar.* Stanford, CA: CSLI Publications, pp. 331–338.

Dalrymple, M., J. Lamping, and V. Saraswat. (1993). LFG semantics via constraints. *Proceedings of the 6th Meeting of the European Association for Computational Linguistics,* University of Utrecht, April. ftp://ftp.parc.xerox.com/pub/nl/eacl93-lfg-sem.ps.

Halvorsen, P.-K. (1983). Semantics for Lexical Functional Grammar. *Linguistic Inquiry* 14(4): 567–615.

Kaplan, R. M. (1982). Determinism and nondeterminism in modelling psycholinguistic processes. Paper presented to the Conference on Linguistic Theory and Psychological Reality Revisited, Princeton University.

Kaplan, R. M. (1987). Three seductions of computational psycholinguistics. In P. Whitelock, M. McGee Wood, H. L. Somers, R. Johnson, and P. Bennett, Eds., *Linguistic Theory and Computer Applications.* London: Academic Press, pp. 149–181. Reprinted in M. Dalrymple, R. M. Kaplan, J. Maxwell, and A. Zaenen, Eds., *Formal Issues in Lexical Functional Grammar.* Stanford, CA: CSLI Publications, pp. 337–367.

Kaplan, R. M., and J. Bresnan. (1982). Lexical Functional Grammar: A formal system for grammatical representation. In J. Bresnan, Ed., *The Mental Representation of Grammatical Relations.* Cambridge, MA: MIT Press, pp. 173–281. Reprinted in M. Dalrymple, R. M. Kaplan, J. Maxwell, and A. Zaenen, Eds., *Formal Issues in Lexical Functional Grammar.* Stanford, CA: CSLI Publications, pp. 29–130.

Maxwell, J. T., III, and R. M. Kaplan. (1993). The interface between phrasal and functional constraints. *Computational Linguistics* 19(4): 571–590. Reprinted in M. Dalrymple, R. M. Kaplan, J. Maxwell, and A. Zaenen, Eds., *Formal Issues in Lexical Functional Grammar.* Stanford, CA: CSLI Publications, pp. 403–429.

Further Readings

Alsina, A. (1992). On the argument structure of causatives. *Linguistic Inquiry* 23(4): 517–555.

Alsina, A. (1996). *The Role of Argument Structure in Grammar: Evidence from Romance.* Stanford, CA: CSLI Publications.

Andrews, A. D. (1990). Unification and morphological blocking. *Natural Language and Linguistic Theory* 8(4): 507–557.

Andrews, A., and C. Manning. (1993). Information spreading and levels of representation in LFG. *Technical Report CSLI–93–176* Stanford, CA: CSLI Publications.

Bresnan, J., Ed. (1982). *The Mental Representation of Grammatical Relations.* Cambridge, MA: MIT Press.

Bresnan, J. (1994). Locative inversion and the architecture of universal grammar. *Language* 70(1): 2–31.

Bresnan, J., and L. Moshi. (1990). Object asymmetries in comparative Bantu syntax. *Linguistic Inquiry* 21(2): 147–185. Reprinted in S. A. Mchombo, Ed., *Theoretical Aspects of Bantu Grammar 1.* Stanford: CSLI Publications, pp. 47–91.

Bresnan, J., and S. A. Mchombo. (1987). Topic, pronoun, and agreement in Chichewa. *Language* 63(4): 741–782. Reprinted in M. Iida, S. Wechsler, and D. Zec, Eds., *Working Papers in Grammatical Theory and Discourse Structure: Interactions of Morphology, Syntax, and Discourse.* Stanford, CA: CSLI Publications, pp. 1–59.

Bresnan, J., and A. Zaenen. (1990). Deep unaccusativity in LFG. In K. Dziwirek, P. Farrell, and E. M. Bikandi, Eds., *Grammatical Relations: A Cross-Theoretical Perspective.* Stanford CA: CSLI Publications/Stanford Linguistics Association, pp. 45–57.

Butt, M. (1995). *The Structure of Complex Predicates in Urdu.* Stanford, CA: CSLI Publications.

Dalrymple, M. (1993). *The Syntax of Anaphoric Binding.* Stanford, CA: CSLI Publications. *CSLI Lecture Notes,* no. 36.

Dalrymple, M., R. M. Kaplan, J. T. Maxwell, and A. Zaenen, Eds. (1995). *Formal Issues in Lexical Functional Grammar.* Stanford, CA: CSLI Publications.

Fenstad, J.-E., P.-K. Halvorsen, T. Langholm, and J. van Benthem. (1987). *Situations, Language, and Logic.* Dordrecht: Reidel.

Johnson, M. (1988). *Attribute-Value Logic and the Theory of Grammar.* Stanford, CA: CSLI Publications. *CSLI Lecture Notes,* no. 16.

King, T. H. (1995). *Configuring Topic and Focus in Russian.* Stanford, CA: CSLI Publications.

Kroeger, P. (1993). *Phrase Structure and Grammatical Relations in Tagalog.* Stanford, CA: CSLI Publications.

Laczko, T. (1995). *The Syntax of Hungarian Noun Phrases: A Lexical Functional Approach.* Frankfurt am Main: Peter Lang GmbH.

Levin, L. (1986). *Operations on Lexical Forms: Unaccusative Rules in Germanic Languages.* Ph.D. diss., Massachusetts Institute of Technology.

Levin, L. S., M. Rappaport, and A. Zaenen, Eds. (1983). *Papers in Lexical Functional Grammar.* Bloomington, IN: Indiana University Linguistics Club.

Matsumoto, Y. (1996). *Complex Predicates in Japanese: A Syntactic and Semantic Study of the Notion "Word".* Stanford and Tokyo: CSLI Publications and Kuroiso Publishers.

Mohanan, K. P. (1983). Functional and anaphoric control. *Linguistic Inquiry* 14(4): 641–674.

Neidle, C. (1988). *The Role of Case in Russian Syntax.* Dordrecht: Kluwer.

Pinker, S. (1984). *Language Learnability and Language Development.* Cambridge, MA: Harvard University Press.

Simpson, J. (1991). *Warlpiri Morphology and Syntax: A Lexicalist Approach.* Dordrecht: Reidel.

Zaenen, A. (1994). Unaccusativity in Dutch: Integrating syntax and lexical semantics. In J. Pustejovsky, Ed., *Semantics and the Lexicon*. Dordrecht: Kluwer, pp. 129–161.

Lexicon

The lexicon is a list of the morphemes in a language, containing information that characterizes the SYNTAX (hence distribution), MORPHOLOGY (hence PHONOLOGY), and meaning for every morpheme. Thus, for a word such as *forget*, the lexical entry states its meaning, that it is a verb and takes a nominal or clause complement (*I forgot the picnic, I forgot that the picnic was at 3:00*), and that its phonological representation is /fərgɛt/.

However, the study of the lexicon in linguistics and in cognitive science saw a major shift in perspective in the 1980s and early 1990s stemming from the realization that lexicons are much more than this: they are studded with principled phenomena, which any lexical theory must explicate (Wasow 1977 is a classic study). In particular, the lexicon is the domain of a set of linguistic operations or regularities that govern the formation of complex words from lexical components. A much-studied example is passivization (e.g., *arrest > arrested* as in *The thief was arrested by the police*). Why does the passive form of *arrest*, unlike the active, require that its "logical subject" (see GRAMMATICAL RELATIONS) *the police* appear in a prepositional phrase beginning with *by*, instead of in object position, or indeed subject position? Why does a verb like *suffocate* have both a causative and a change-of-state meaning (*The pillow suffocated Mary, Mary suffocated*), and why is the object of one verb the subject of the other? Work on the lexicon has aimed to uncover the principles underlying regular lexical phenomena and to examine their implications for learning and processing.

Most lexical research has centered on the words of obvious semantic importance in a sentence, primarily substantives such as nouns and verbs, treating words like determiners and complementizers (e.g., *that* in *I think that it is raining*) as peripheral to linguistic structure. Recent work argues, however, that these words determine properties of entire phrases, hence their lexical properties are now of considerable interest.

In sum, the theory of the lexicon must encompass two subtheories: one (the primary focus of this article) governing words that are "meaningful" in the obvious if pretheoretic sense, and the other governing words that are functional, or grammatical in character.

The Lexicon for Substantives

The lexicon determines the ability of nouns, verbs and adjectives to combine with arguments. For example *give* takes three arguments (*She gave the box to Peter*), *eat* takes two (*She ate the sandwich*) and *rise* takes one (*The balloon rose rapidly*). The representation that includes this information is often called an "argument structure" (Williams 1981; Grimshaw 1990; Levin and Rappaport Hovav 1995).

The most important source of evidence concerning the representation of argument structure is alternations in argument organization, such as active/passive and causative/change-of-state mentioned above. Others include the "dative alternation": *They gave a present to the teachers/They gave the teachers a present*; morphological causativization: *large > enlarge*; and nominalization: *legislate > legislator, legislation*.

Certain properties of arguments are important in explaining their behavior. Arguments can be usefully classified according to their semantic role as agent, theme, or goal (Jackendoff 1972; see THEMATIC ROLES). Williams (1981) argued that the "external argument" is singled out for special grammatical and lexical treatment. Thus the argument structure of *give* might be (1), where the first argument is marked as external, the others as internal.

(1) *give* (ext, int, int)

Further work on morphology and syntax suggests that some verbs have no external argument, including unaccusatives and perhaps some psychological predicates, and that this has important morphological and syntactic consequences (Burzio 1986; Belletti and Rizzi 1988; see also RELATIONAL GRAMMAR).

The existence of strong semantic regularities within the alternation system sheds light on the semantic representation of substantives, most prominently verbs. For example, the alternation of argument realization seen in the *suffocate* examples above, where the object of the transitive verb corresponds to the subject of the intransitive, is a completely regular phenomenon but is found only with causative verbs. *The pillow suffocated Mary* can be paraphrased roughly as "The pillow caused Mary to suffocate". Verbs that lack this interpretation do not show the alternation, thus *The thief robbed the bank* does not have a counterpart **The bank robbed*.

This constellation of facts, which is crosslinguistically remarkably stable, can be explained by lexical theory, if the verb meanings can be broken down or decomposed into smaller meaning components, one of which (represented here by CAUSE) is part of the meaning of causative verbs. A verb like *suffocate* has two semantic representations, often called "lexical conceptual structures," one with the CAUSE component and one without.

(2) *suffocate*
   a. (x CAUSE (y suffocate));
   b. (y suffocate)

Because the CAUSE component has its own argument, the causative version has one more argument than the noncausative: this holds mutatis mutandis for all causative verbs in all languages. Because the argument of CAUSE is higher in the argument structure than the other, it occupies the syntactic subject position when it is present; when it is absent, the other argument occupies this position in English, which requires that the subject position be filled in all sentences. Hence we find the alternation in argument realization with these verbs. Verbs like *rob* do not have an intransitive counterpart because their semantic analysis does not have the required properties.

A related line of reasoning allows us to explain why verbs like *apologize* occur only intransitively (**He apologized the impolite clerk*). Argument structures are subject to a very general constraint: only one argument of a given semantic type is allowed in each one. Analysis shows that *apologize* and CAUSE have arguments of the same type, with the thematic role agent. Hence the two cannot be combined into a single argument structure, hence the causative cannot exist. Thus generalizations and gaps in the system can be explained, not merely described within this system of representation. Further quite remarkable evidence comes from the discovery by Talmy (1985) that there are crosslinguistic differences in what meaning components can be combined. He showed that French systematically lacks verbs like English *float*, which encode motion and manner in a single morpheme.

Despite the progress that has been made in understanding lexical alternations, they still pose some powerful challenges. On the one hand, many verbs participate in them and many languages show similar patterns. On the other hand, not *all* verbs participate in them, and some fail to show the alternation, apparently for no very good reason. For example, *donate* appears in only the first of the two configurations that *give* occurs in above, and similarly, *rise* does not occur in the causative (*The balloon rose into the sky,* **They rose the balloon into the sky*). Yet *rise* does not have an argument that is plausibly an agent, unlike *apologize*. Gaps such as these pose an important problem for learning: we can explain the existence of lexical generalizations only if learners generalize heavily, but then how can we explain the existence of exceptions? (See WORD MEANING, ACQUISITION OF; Pinker 1989, Gleitman and Landau 1994.)

A very appealing answer holds that there are no entirely arbitrary exceptions once the generalizations themselves are properly understood. This is probably a fair way to characterize the general direction of the field, but it is not an easy commitment to make good on. One idea is that the meaning of the verb in one configuration is systematically different from the meaning of the verb in others, as the result of a lexical rule changing the verb's semantic representation (see Levin and Rappaport Hovav 1995). Each such lexical rule carries out a specified meaning change on any verb with the appropriate semantics, with syntactic changes emerging as a consequence.

However, consider a marginal but interpretable example like *He sang his mother out of the house,* where *sang,* under this line of analysis, would mean "to cause Y to move by singing." Why couldn't there be a verb which meant *only* this and did not also mean what *sang* usually does? The best answer is that this is not a possible word meaning, but then it cannot be the meaning of *sang* as used here. Some current work suggests that effects such as this extended use of *sang* are due to an interaction between the verb meaning and the syntactic and semantic context the verb appears in, which makes it possible to construe the verb in a certain way. From this perspective, related to that developed by Pustejovsky (1995) and in Construction Grammar (Goldberg 1994), verbs that do not alternate have some special property prohibiting alternation; massive alternation is the norm rather than the exception.

The Functional Lexicon

Although the argument structure of the predicate of a clause determines the number and kind of arguments that can appear in it, the grammatical structure of the entire clause is determined by properties of the function words, previously labeled misleadingly as "minor categories." A noun along with its satellite expressions forms a noun phrase of which it is the "head," the element that determines the properties of the phrase as a whole. Remarkably, it turns out that the same is true for the "minor" syntactic categories, like complementizer and determiner: they also head phrases. Thus the head of the entire complement clause in *I think that it is raining* is *that,* and not, as previously thought, *raining* or a phrase of some kind. It follows then that the primary item determining the grammatical properties of the clause is the complementizer itself (see HEAD MOVEMENT and X-BAR THEORY). Since this discovery, the field has faced a completely new question: what properties does the lexicon of functional morphemes have? Clearly, notions like thematic role are entirely irrelevant for words like *that* and *the*. These morphemes code properties like "type" (e.g., interrogative versus propositional) or definiteness. How much crosslinguistic variation can be shown to follow from differences in the functional lexicon? Related work on learning attempts to establish whether these morphemes and associated phrases are present in early child language (Déprez and Pierce 1993; Clahsen 1990/91; Radford 1990; see also PARAMETER-SETTING APPROACHES TO ACQUISITION, CREOLIZATION, AND DIACHRONY; and MINIMALISM).

The content-function word distinction has a long history in cognitive science (see Halle, Bresnan, and Miller 1978). The lexical representation of both types of morpheme is now an issue of central importance within linguistic theory.

See also COMPUTATIONAL LEXICONS; LANGUAGE ACQUISITION; PSYCHOLINGUISTICS; SEMANTICS; SENTENCE PROCESSING

—*Jane Grimshaw*

References

Belletti, A., and L. Rizzi. (1988). Psych verbs and theta theory. *Natural Language and Linguistic Theory* 6: 291–352.

Burzio, L. (1986). *Italian Syntax: A Government-Binding Approach.* Dordrecht: Reidel.

Clahsen, H. (1990/91). Constraints on parameter setting: a grammatical analysis of some acquisition stages in German child language. *Language Acquisition* 1: 361–391.

Déprez, V., and A. Pierce. (1993). Negation and functional projections in early grammar. *Linguistic Inquiry* 24: 25–67.

Gleitman, L., and B. Landau, Eds. (1994). Lexical acquisition. *Lingua* 92: 1.

Goldberg, A. E. (1994). *Constructions: A Construction Grammar Approach to Argument Structure.* Chicago: University of Chicago Press.

Grimshaw, J. (1990). *Argument Structure.* Linguistic Inquiry Monograph 18. Cambridge, MA: MIT Press.

Halle, M., J. Bresnan, and G. Miller, Eds. (1978). *Linguistic Theory and Psychological Reality.* Cambridge, MA: MIT Press.

Jackendoff, R. (1972). *Semantic Interpretation in Generative Grammar.* Cambridge, MA: MIT Press.

Levin, B., and M. Rappaport Hovav (1995). *Unaccusativity: at the Syntax-Semantics Interface.* Cambridge, MA: MIT Press.

Pinker, S. (1989). *Learnability and Cognition: The Acquisition of Argument Structure.* Cambridge, MA: MIT Press.

Pustejovsky, J. (1995). *The Generative Lexicon.* Cambridge, MA: MIT Press.

Radford, A. (1990). *Syntactic Theory and the Acquisition of English Syntax.* Oxford: Blackwell.

Talmy, L. (1985). Lexicalization patterns: semantic structure in lexical forms. In T. Shopen, Ed., *Language Typology and Syntactic Description 3: Grammatical Categories and the Lexicon.* Cambridge: Cambridge University Press, pp. 57–149.

Wasow, T. (1977). *Transformations and the Lexicon, in Formal Syntax.* In P. Culicover, T. Wasow, and A. Akmajian, Eds. New York: Academic Press, pp. 327–360.

Williams, E. (1981). Argument structure and morphology. *Linguistic Review* 1: 81–114.

Further Readings

Baker, M. (1988). *Incorporation: A Theory of Grammatical Function Changing.* Chicago: University of Chicago Press.

Dowty, D. (1991). Thematic proto-roles and argument selection. *Language* 67: 547–619.

Hale, K., and J. Keyser. (1993). On argument structure and the lexical expression of syntactic relations. In K. Hale and J. Keyser, Eds., *The View from Building 20.* Cambridge, MA: MIT Press.

Grimshaw, J. (1979). Complement selection and the lexicon. *Linguistic Inquiry* 10: 279–326.

Jackendoff, R. (1990). *Semantic Structures.* Cambridge, MA: MIT Press.

Lexicon, Neural Basis of

The lexical processing system is the collection of mechanisms that are used to store and retrieve our knowledge of the words of the language. Knowing a word means knowing its meaning, its phonological and orthographic forms, and its grammatical properties. How is this knowledge organized and represented in the brain? Two types of evidence have been used to answer this question. The major source of evidence has been the patterns of lexical deficits associated with brain damage in aphasic patients. More recently, functional neuroimaging methods—POSITRON EMISSION TOMOGRAPHY (PET) and functional MAGNETIC RESONANCE IMAGING (fMRI)—have played an increasingly important role. Evidence from neuropsychological and neuroimaging studies has converged on one widely shared conclusion: the mental LEXICON is organized into relatively autonomous neural subsystems in the left hemisphere, each dedicated to processing a different aspect of lexical knowledge.

One of the classic syndromes of APHASIA, anomia—a deficit in retrieving words for production—provides prima facie evidence for distinct representation of meaning and of lexical forms in the brain. Studies of anomic patients have shown that they are unable to produce the names of objects despite normal ability to recognize and define them, indicating a selective deficit in processing lexical forms. These patients tend to have more narrowly circumscribed damage, involving most often the left temporal lobe, but sometimes the parietal or frontal lobe or both. There is also evidence that the semantic system can be damaged independently of knowledge of lexical forms. The latter evidence has been obtained both with patients who have sustained focal brain damage due to strokes and patients with degenerative disorders such as Alzheimer's disease. Both types of patients make semantic errors (e.g., they might produce "table" in naming a chair or "tastes good, a fruit" in naming a pear) in all lexical processing tasks. Patients with selective damage to the semantic component of the lexicon typically have extensive left hemisphere damage involving the temporal, parietal, and frontal lobes. Converging evidence in support of the view that semantic information is distributed widely in the left hemisphere has been obtained in functional neuroimaging studies with PET.

Some brain-damaged patients are selectively impaired in retrieving only the orthographic form (e.g., the spelling of the word *chair*) or only the phonological form of words (e.g., the sound of the word *chair*). Patients of this type can be entirely normal in their ability to understand and define words, but fail to retrieve the correct word form in one, but not the other, modality of output. These patterns of performance attest to the autonomy of phonological and orthographic lexical forms from each other and from meaning. Converging evidence for this conclusion comes from functional neuroimaging studies which have shown that distinct brain regions are activated when neurologically intact participants are engaged in processing the phonological (frontal-temporal) versus the orthographic (parietal-occipital) forms of words.

Damage to the semantic system can lead to disproportionate difficulties with specific semantic categories. The most frequently observed category-specific deficits have concerned the contrast between living and nonliving things. However, the deficits can be quite selective, affecting (or sparing) only animals or only plant life. The lesion sites typically associated with these deficits include the left temporal lobe, the posterior frontal lobe, and the inferior junction of the parietal and occipital lobes. The existence of semantic category-specific deficits was originally interpreted as reflecting a modality-based organization of conceptual knowledge in the brain. It was proposed that visual and functional/associative properties are represented in distinct areas of the brain and that these two sets of properties are differentially important in distinguishing between living and nonliving things, respectively. On this view, selective damage to one of the modality-specific knowledge subsystems would result in a semantic category-specific deficit. However, recent results have shown that category-specific deficits are not the result of damage to modality-specific but rather to modality-independent knowledge systems. These results, and the fact that the reliable categories of category-specific deficits are those of animals, plant life, artifacts, and conspecifics, have led to the proposal that conceptual knowledge is organized into broad, evolutionarily determined domains of knowledge. Functional neuroimaging results with neurologically intact participants have confirmed that the inferior temporal lobe and parts of the occipital lobe are activated in response to animal pictures and words, whereas more dorsal areas of the temporal lobe and parts of the frontal lobe are activated in response to artifacts.

One of the classic features of the speech of some aphasic patients is agrammatic production—a form of speech characterized by a relative paucity of function or closed-class words (articles, prepositions, auxiliaries, etc.). The disproportionate difficulty in producing closed-class words in some patients is in contrast to patients who show the reverse pattern of dissociation—selective difficulty with open-class words (nouns, verbs, and adjectives). But, the dissociations of lexical processing deficits can be even more fine-grained than that: some patients are disproportionately impaired in producing verbs while others are disproportionately impaired in producing nouns, and some patients can be disproportionately impaired in comprehending one or the other class of words. Grammatical class effects can even be restricted to one modality of output or input. For example, there are patients who are impaired in producing verbs only in speaking (they can write verbs and can produce nouns both in speaking and in writing) and patients who are impaired in producing nouns only in speaking; and there are patients who fail to understand written but not spoken verbs. The fact that grammatical class effects can also be modality-specific implies a close link between word form and grammatical information. These results challenge the view that there exists a modality-neutral lexical node mediating between modality-specific lexical representations and word meaning. Damage to the left frontal lobe is typically associated with disproportionate difficulty in processing verbs and closed-class words, while damage to the left temporal lobe is associated with disproportionate difficulty in producing and comprehending nouns. Recent investigations with PET and event-related potentials (ERPs) have confirmed this general characterization of the roles of the frontal and temporal lobes in processing words of different grammatical classes.

Brain damage can also selectively affect different parts of words, revealing their internal structure. It is now well established that some aphasic patients have no difficulty in processing the stem of words (e.g., *walk* in *walked*) but fail to retrieve their correct inflectional suffixes (e.g. the *-ed* in *walked*), and that some patients can process normally the morphological affixes of words but not their stems. This double dissociation in processing different types of morphemes implies that the units of lexical representation in the brain are stems and inflectional affixes, and not whole words. Detailed single-case studies of aphasic patients have confirmed this conclusion, and have shown that difficulties in processing inflectional morphology tend to be associated with damage to more frontal areas of the left hemisphere, while difficulties in processing the stems of words are more likely to be associated with temporal lobe damage.

Although we still do not have a detailed understanding of the neural substrates of the lexicon, its general outlines are beginning to emerge, and it looks to be as follows: (1) the lexical processing system is distributed over a large area of the left hemisphere, involving the temporal, frontal, and parietal lobes; (2) different parts of the left hemisphere are dedicated to the storage and computation of different aspects of lexical knowledge—meaning, form, and grammatical information are represented autonomously; and (3) within each of the major components of the lexicon, the semantic and lexical form components, there are further fine-grained functional and neural distinctions.

See also BILINGUALISM AND THE BRAIN; GRAMMAR, NEURAL BASIS OF; LANGUAGE, NEURAL BASIS OF; SEMANTICS

—*Alfonso Caramazza*

Further Readings

Badecker, W., and A. Caramazza. (1991). Morphological composition in the lexical output system. *Cognitive Neuropsychology* 8(5): 335–367.

Buckingham, H. W., and A. Kertesz. (1976). *Neologistic Jargon Aphasia.* Amsterdam: Swets and Zeitlinger.

Butterworth, B., and D. Howard. (1987). Paragrammatism. *Cognition* 26: 1–37.

Caplan, D., L. Keller, and S. Locke. (1972). Inflection of neologisms in aphasia. *Brain* 95: 169–172.

Caramazza, A. (1997). How many levels of processing are there in lexical access? *Cognitive Neuropsychology* 14: 177–208.

Caramazza, A., and A. Hillis. (1990). Where do semantic errors come from? *Cortex* 16: 95–122.

Caramazza, A., and A. E. Hillis. (1991). Lexical organization of nouns and verbs in the brain. *Nature* 249: 788–790.

Caramazza, A., and J. Shelton. (1998). Domain-specific knowledge systems in the brain: The animate/inanimate distinction. *Journal of Cognitive Neuroscience* 10: 1–34.

Chertkow, H., D. Bub, and D. Caplan. (1992). Constraining theories of semantic memory processing: Evidence from dementia. *Cognitive Neuropsychology* 9: 327–365.

Damasio, A. R., and D. Tranel. (1993). Verbs and nouns are retrieved from separate neural systems. *Proceedings of the National Academy of Sciences* 90: 4957–4960.

Gainotti, G., and M. C. Silveri. (1996). Cognitive and anatomical locus of lesion in a patient with a category-specific semantic impairment for living beings. *Cognitive Neuropsychology* 13: 357–389.

Garrett, M. F. (1992). Disorders of lexical selection. *Cognition* 42: 143–180.

Goodglass, H. (1976). Agrammatism. In N. H. Whitaker and H. A. Whitaker, Eds., *Studies in Neurolinguistics.* New York: Academic Press.

Hart, J., R. S. Brendt, and A. Caramazza. (1985). Category-specific naming deficit following cerebral infarction. *Nature* 316: 439–440.

Hillis, A. E., and A. Caramazza. (1991). Category specific naming and comprehension impairment: A double dissociation. *Brain* 110: 613–629.

Kay, J., and A. W. Ellis. (1987). A cognitive neuropsychological case study of anomia: Implications for psychological models of word retrieval. *Brain* 110: 613–629.

McCarthy, R., and E. W. Warrington. (1985). Category specificity in an agrammatic patient: The relative impairment of verb retrieval and comprehension. *Neuropsychologia* 23: 709–727.

Martin, A., J. V. Haxby, F. M. Lalonde, C. L. Wiggs, and L. G. Ungerleider. (1995). Discrete cortical regions associated with knowledge of color and knowledge of action. *Science* 270: 868–889.

Martin, A., C. L. Wiggs, L. G. Ungerleider, and J. V. Haxby. (1996). Neural correlates of category-specific knowledge. *Nature* 379: 649–652.

Petersen, S. E., P. T. Fox, M. I. Posner, M. Mintem, and M. E. Raichle. (1989). Positron emission tomographic studies of the processing of single words. *Journal of Cognitive Neuroscience* 1: 153–170.

Rapp, B., and A. Caramazza. (1997). The modality-specific organization of grammatical categories: Evidence from impaired spoken and written sentence production. *Brain and Language* 56: 248–286.

Rumsey, J. M., B. Horwitz, B. C. Donohue, K. Nace, J. M. Maisog, and P. Andreason. (1970). Phonologic and orthographic components of word recognition: A PET-rCFB study. *Brain* 120: 729–760.

Shallice, T. (1988). *From Neuropsychology to Mental Structure*. Oxford: Oxford University Press.

Vanderberghe, R., C. Price, R. Wise, D. Josephs, and R. S. J. Frackowiak. (1996). Functional anatomy of a common semantic system for words and pictures. *Nature* 282: 254–256.

Warrington, E. K., and R. A. McCarthy. (1987). Categories of knowledge: Further fractionations and an attempted integration. *Brain* 110: 1269–1273.

Warrington, E. K., and T. Shallice. (1984) Category specific semantic impairments. *Brain* 107: 829–853.

Zingeser, L., and R. S. Berndt. (1990). Retrieval of nouns and verbs in agrammatism and anomia. *Brain and Language* 39: 14–32.

LFG

See LEXICAL FUNCTIONAL GRAMMAR

Life

See ARTIFICIAL LIFE; EVOLUTION; SELF-ORGANIZING SYSTEMS

Lightness Perception

The term *lightness* refers to the perceived whiteness or blackness of an opaque surface. The physical counterpart of lightness is *reflectance,* or the percentage of light a surface reflects. A good white surface reflects about ninety percent of the light that illuminates it, absorbing the rest; black reflects only about three percent. The eye, having no reflectance detectors, must compute lightness based only on the light reflected from the scene. But the intensity of light reflected from any given surface, called *luminance,* is a product of both its reflectance and the level of illumination. And although luminance thus varies with every change of illumination, lightness remains remarkably stable, an achievement referred to as *lightness constancy*.

There is a perceptual quality that corresponds to luminance called *brightness*. Brightness is to lightness as perception of visual angle is to perception of object size (see SPATIAL PERCEPTION). While brightness might be said to refer to our sensation of light intensity, lightness refers to a perceived property of the object itself and is essential to object recognition (see SURFACE PERCEPTION).

Despite the remarkable correlation between lightness and physical reflectance, neither the stimulus variable on which it is based nor the computation that finally produces lightness has been agreed upon. HELMHOLTZ (1866), recognizing that lightness cannot be based simply on luminance, argued that the level of illumination is unconsciously taken into account, but this approach has remained vague and unconvincing. Wallach (1948) avoided the whole issue of computing the illumination with the dramatically simple proposal that lightness depends on the ratio between the luminance of a surface and the luminance of its background. He demonstrated that such a local edge ratio predicts perceived lightness in very simple displays such as a disk surrounded by an annulus. And he observed that, even for complex images, luminance ratios, unlike absolute luminance values, tend to remain invariant when the illumination changes. Others (Hurvich and Jameson 1966; Cornsweet 1970), lured by the prospect of a physiological account of lightness, have sought to reduce Wallach's ratio findings to the neural mechanism of lateral inhibition.

Subsequent research has suggested that what gets encoded are luminance ratios at edges, not the absolute luminances of points, and that lateral inhibition plays a key role in the neural encoding of these ratios. But both Wallach's ratio principle and its physiological reduction are now viewed as much too simplistic an account of lightness. Recent work has dealt with three important limitations: (1) the computation is too local; (2) it produces large errors when applied to illuminance edges; and (3) only relative lightness values can be determined, unless an anchoring rule is also given.

1. The first of these can be illustrated in simultaneous lightness contrast, the familiar textbook illusion, shown in figure 1. On its face this contrast illusion appears to provide further evidence of the relational determination of lightness. But if lightness depended simply on local luminance ratios, the two targets should look as different as black and white. So, in fact, the very weakness of the illusion shows that lightness is not tied to background luminance as strongly as Wallach's ratio rule implies. Quantitative work (Gilchrist 1988) has shown that lightness is just as independent of background luminance as it is of illumination level and this appears to require the ability to compute luminance ratios between remote regions of the image. In the early 1970s several writers (Land and McCann 1971; Arend, Buehler, and Lockhead 1971; Whittle and Challands 1969) proposed a process of edge integration by which all edge ratios along a path between two remote regions are mathematically combined.

2. Gilchrist (1979), noting that many edges in the retinal image represent changes in the illumination (such as shadow boundaries), not changes in reflectance, argued that edge integration cannot work without some prior process of edge classification (see figure 2). Recent computational models (Bergström 1977; Adelson 1993; Gilchrist 1979) have relied on concepts like edge integration and edge classification to decompose the retinal image into component images—called intrinsic images—that represent the physical values of surface reflectance and illumination. This approach has the advantage of providing an

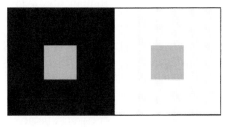

Figure 1. Simultaneous lightness contrast. Although this illusion shows an influence of the target/background luminance ratio, the weakness of the illusion shows that lightness is no simple product of that ratio.

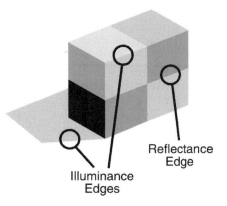

Reflectance Edge

Illuminance Edges

Figure 2. Lightness could not be based on local edge ratios unless the edges were first classified. (After Adelson 1993.)

account of our perception of the illumination, not just of surface lightness.

3. Computing absolute or specific shades of gray requires an anchoring rule, a rule that ties some locus on the scale of perceived grays to some feature of the retinal image. One candidate rule, endorsed by Wallach (1948) and by Land and McCann (1971), says that the highest luminance is white, with lower luminances scaled relative to this standard. An alternative rule, implicit in concepts like the *gray world assumption* and Helson's adaptation-level theory (1964), says that the average luminance is middle gray, with higher and lower values scaled relative to the average. When these rules are tested by presenting a display consisting of a very restricted range of grays, it is found that the highest luminance appears white, but the average does not appear middle gray (Cataliotti and Gilchrist 1995; Li and Gilchrist in press). But relative area also plays an important role. An increase in the area of the darker regions at the expense of the lighter causes the darker regions to lighten in gray value and the lightest region to appear self-luminous.

These rules of anchoring by highest luminance and relative area apply to both simple visual displays and to frameworks or groups embedded within complex images. In complex images, however, perceived lightness can be predicted by a compromise between lightness values computed within these relatively local frameworks and lightness values computed across the entire visual field. The weighting in this compromise increasingly shifts to the local framework as that becomes larger and more highly articulated. If the study of anchoring has undermined the portrait of a highly ratiomorphic lightness computation recovering veridical values of reflectance and illumination, it has nevertheless provided a remarkable account of perceptual errors. Emerging anchoring models portray a more rough-and-ready system (see MID-LEVEL VISION) that, while subject to apparently unnecessary errors, is nevertheless quite robust in the face of a wide variety of challenges to perceptual veridicality.

See also COLOR VISION; DEPTH PERCEPTION; GESTALT PERCEPTION; STEREO AND MOTION PERCEPTION; TEXTURE; TRANSPARENCY

—*Alan Gilchrist*

References

Adelson, E. (1993). Perceptual organization and the judgment of brightness. *Science* 262: 2042–2044.

Arend, L. E., J. N. Buehler, and G. R. Lockhead. (1971). Difference information in brightness perception. *Perception and Psychophysics* 9: 367–370.

Bergström, S. S. (1977). Common and relative components of reflected light as information about the illumination, colour, and three-dimensional form of objects. *Scandinavian Journal of Psychology* 18: 180–186.

Cataliotti, J., and A. L. Gilchrist. (1995). Local and global processes in lightness perception. *Perception and Psychophysics* 57(2): 125–135.

Cornsweet, T. N. (1970). *Visual Perception.* New York: Academic Press.

Gilchrist, A. (1979). The perception of surface blacks and whites. *Scientific American* 240: 112–123.

Gilchrist, A. (1988). Lightness contrast and failures of constancy: a common explanation. *Perception and Psychophysics* 43(5): 415–424.

Helmholtz, H. von. (1866/1924). *Helmholtz's Treatise on Physiological Optics.* New York: Optical Society of America.

Helson, H. (1964). *Adaptation-Level Theory.* New York: Harper and Row.

Hurvich, L., and D. Jameson. (1966). *The Perception of Brightness and Darkness.* Boston: Allyn and Bacon.

Land, E. H., and J. J. McCann. (1971). Lightness and retinex theory. *Journal of the Optical Society of America* 61: 1–11.

Li, X., and A. Gilchrist. (Forthcoming). Relative area and relative luminance combine to anchor surface lightness values. *Perception and Psychophysics.*

Wallach, H. (1948). Brightness constancy and the nature of achromatic colors. *Journal of Experimental Psychology* 38: 310–324.

Whittle, P., and P. D. C. Challands. (1969). The effect of background luminance on the brightness of flashes. *Vision Research* 9: 1095–1110.

Further Readings

Gilchrist, A., Ed. (1994). *Lightness, Brightness, and Transparency.* Hillsdale, NJ: Erlbaum.

Gilchrist, A., C. Kossyfidis, F. Bonato, T. Agostini, J. Cataliotti, X. Li, B. Spehar, V. Annan, and E. Economou. (Forthcoming). An anchoring theory of lightness perception. *Psychological Review.*

Hurlbert, A. (1986). Formal connections between lightness algorithms. *Journal of the Optical Society of America A. Optics and Image Science* 3: 1684–1693.

Koffka, K. (1935). *Principles of Gestalt Psychology.* New York: Harcourt, Brace, and World, pp. 240–264.

MacLeod, R. B. (1932). An experimental investigation of brightness constancy. *Archives of Psychology* 135: 5–102.

Wallach, H. (1976). *On Perception.* New York: Quadrangle/The New York Times Book Co.

Limbic System

Much as other systems with a historic origin (e.g., the reticular system), the limbic system (LS) is difficult to define as it has gone through numerous modifications, adaptations, refinements, and expansions during the more than 100 years of its existence. Furthermore, problems with its description arise from the facts that it is frequently composed of only portions of larger units (e.g., only a minority of the thalamic nuclei are included), and that it varies considerably among species (e.g., the olfactory system, a portion of the LS, first expands considerably in mammals as opposed to nonmammals such as birds, but then shrinks again in whales and primates). Basically the LS constitutes an agglomerate of brain structures with a cortical core around the corpus callosum and within the medial temporal lobe and with a number of subcortical structures extending from the hindbrain to the forebrain (figure 1). Many of these structures are central to the processing of EMOTIONS and MEMORY, including the evaluation of sensory functions such as PAIN.

The term *le grand lobe limbique* was coined by BROCA (1878) as an anatomical structure. Broca and his contemporaries nevertheless thought that the limbic structures were largely olfactory and might therefore be subsumed under the term *rhinencephalon* (cf. Laurent 1997 for olfactory processing). Later research shifted the dominant functional implications of the LS to the processing of emotions and memory and modified the regions to be subsumed under this term. This discussion has continued until today (Papez 1937; MacLean 1952, 1970; Nauta 1979; LeDoux 1996; Nieuwenhuys 1996). While the LS (the term was introduced by MacLean 1952) is frequently regarded as an ancient brain system which regresses during phylogeny, numerous more recent studies have shown that, on the contrary—with the exception of the olfactory regions—most

structures of this system expand and increase in differentiation (e.g., Stephan 1975; Armstrong 1986). (This expansion is, however, less prominent than that of neocortical areas.)

Based on comparative anatomy and evolutionary theory, MacLean (1970) divided the brain into three general compartments: (1) a protoreptilian portion (spinal cord, parts of the midbrain and diencephalon, BASAL GANGLIA); (2) a paleomammalian one—in principle the LS—, and (3), a neomammalian one, largely the neocortical mantle. The LS therefore constitutes a link between the oldest and the newest attributes of the mammalian, in particular the human, brain. It includes (1) the limbic cortex, a circumscribed cortical region along the medial rim of the cerebrum; (2) the limbic nuclei of the tel-, di-, and mesencephalon; and (3) the fiber tracts interconnecting these structures. The limbic cortex is further subdividable into an inner ("allocortical," i.e., constituted of the phylogenetically oldest, three-layered cortex) and an outer ring ("juxtallocortical," i.e., constituted of transitional, four- or five-layered cortex; Isaacson 1982).

The core of the LS is included in the so-called Papez circuit (Papez 1937) or medial limbic circuit (see figure 1). This circuit is primarily engaged in the transfer of information from short-term to long-term memory. Another circuit that is more closely related to emotional processing but still relevant to mnemonic information processing as well is the

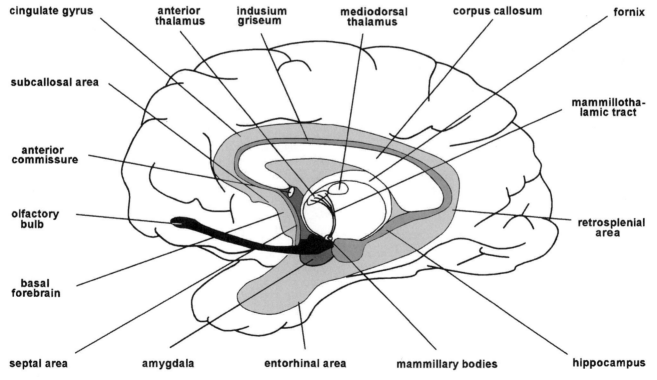

Figure 1. Schematic section through the forebrain (i.e., without the brain stem) showing the ringlike arrangement of the limbic structures around the corpus callosum and below it. The Papez circuit is formed principally by the HIPPOCAMPUS, mammillary bodies, anterior thalamus, cingulate gyrus, and is interconnected via the fornix, mammillothalamic tract, fibers from the anterior

thalamus to the cingulate gyrus and to portions of the hippocampal region, and the cingulum fibers that run near the indusium griseum, an extension of the hippocampal formation (Irle and Markowitsch 1982). All other structures mentioned are usually regarded as belonging to the limbic system as well. Some brain stem nuclei might be added.

basolateral limbic circuit, or lateral limbic circuit (Sarter and Markowitsch 1985). It is constituted by the triangle formed by the amygdala, the mediodorsal thalamic nucleus, and the basal forebrain regions. Interconnecting fibers are the ventral amygdalofugal pathway, the anterior thalamic peduncle, and the bandeletta diagonalis (the circuit is depicted in figure 48.4 of Markowitsch 1995).

As mentioned above, there have been various attempts to expand the LS (Isaacson 1982; Nauta 1979; Nieuwenhuys 1996). All of these nevertheless agree in principle with MacLean's (1970) proposal to see this system as the mediator between the neocortical mantle (dealing with sensory processing, memory storage, and the initiation and supervision of behavior) and the "lower," largely motoric regions of the brain stem and the basal ganglia.

Though the structures of the LS are predominantly involved in emotional, motivational, and memory-related aspects of behavior, some subclustering should be noted: the septal region, the amygdala, and the cingulate cortex are largely engaged in the control of emotions ranging from heightened ATTENTION and arousal to rage and aggression. In evaluating emotions the septum may partly act in opposition to amygdala and cingulate cortex. The amygdala is furthermore involved in motivational regulations and in evaluating information of biological or social significance (and therefore indirectly in memory processing). Damage to the amygdala may result in conditions of tameness, hypersexuality, amnesia, agnosia, aphagia, and hyperorality (Klüver-Bucy syndrome). The hippocampal formation and surrounding structures are principally engaged in transferring memories from short-term to long-term storage, but do have additional functions (e.g., in the spatial and possibly also in the time domains). Anterior and medial nuclei of the thalamus and the mammillary body of the hypothalamus control memory transfer as well ("bottleneck structures"; Markowitsch 1995). Also, these nuclear configurations (to which nonspecific thalamic nuclei belong as well) control further forms of behavior ranging from sleep to possibly consciousness. Between different species, functional shifts of limbic structures have been noted.

There is consequently both functional unity and diversity within the LS. As an example, it is still largely unknown whether the medial temporal lobe structures (with the hippocampus as core) and the medial diencephalic structures (medial and anterior thalamus, mammillary bodies) constitute one or two memory systems. One reason for this uncertainty can be sought in the multitude of fiber bundles interconnecting LS structures in an extensive network. High-resolution dynamic imaging research (e.g., POSITRON EMISSION TOMOGRAPHY) may provide answers in the near future.

See also EMOTION AND THE ANIMAL BRAIN; EMOTION AND THE HUMAN BRAIN; THALAMUS

—*Hans J. Markowitsch*

References

Armstrong, E. (1986). Enlarged limbic structures in the human brain: the anterior thalamus and medial mamillary body. *Brain Research* 362: 394–397.

Broca, P. (1878). Anatomie comparée des circonvolutions cérébrales. Le grand lobe limbique et la scissure limbique dans le série des mammifères. *Revue Anthropologique* 2: 385–498.

Irle, E., and H. J. Markowitsch. (1982). Connections of the hippocampal formation, mamillary bodies, anterior thalamus and cingulate cortex. A retrograde study using horseradish peroxidase in the cat. *Experimental Brain Research* 47: 79–94.

Isaacson, R. L. (1982). *The Limbic System.* 2nd ed. New York: Plenum Press.

Laurent, G. (1997). Olfactory processing: maps, time and codes. *Current Opinion in Neurobiology* 7: 547–553.

LeDoux, J. E. (1996). *The Emotional Brain.* New York: Simon and Schuster.

MacLean, P. D. (1952). Some psychiatric implications of physiological studies of frontotemporal portion of limbic system (visceral brain). *Electroencephalography and Clinical Neurophysiology* 4: 407–418.

MacLean, P. D. (1970). The triune brain, emotion and scientific bias. In F. O. Schmitt, Ed., *The Neurosciences: Second Study Program.* New York: Rockefeller University Press, pp. 336–348.

Markowitsch, H. J. (1995). Anatomical basis of memory disorders. In M. S. Gazzaniga, Ed., *The Cognitive Neurosciences.* Cambridge, MA: MIT Press, pp. 665–679.

Nauta, W. J. H. (1979). Expanding borders of the limbic system concept. In T. Rasmussen and R. Marino, Eds., *Functional Neurosurgery.* New York: Raven Press, pp. 7–23.

Nieuwenhuys, R. (1996). The greater limbic system, the emotional motor system and the brain. *Progress in Brain Research* 107: 551–580.

Papez, J. W. (1937). A proposed mechanism of emotion. *Archives of Neurology and Psychiatry* 38: 725–743.

Sarter, M., and H. J. Markowitsch. (1985). The amygdala's role in human mnemonic processing. *Cortex* 21: 7–24.

Stephan, H. (1975). *Allocortex. Handbuch der mikroskopischen Anatomie des Menschen*, vol. 4, part 9. Berlin: Springer-Verlag.

Further Readings

Cahill, L., R. Babinsky, H. J. Markowitsch, and J. L. McGaugh. (1995). Involvement of the amygdaloid complex in emotional memory. *Nature* 377: 295–296.

Cramon, D.Y. von, H. J. Markowitsch, and U. Schuri. (1993). The possible contribution of the septal region to memory. *Neuropsychologia* 31: 1159–1180.

Groenewegen, H. J., C. I. Wright, and A. V. J. Beijer. (1996). The nucleus accumbens: gateway for limbic structures to reach the motor system? *Progress in Brain Research* 107: 485–511.

Lilly, R., J. L. Cummings, D. F. Benson, and M. Frankel. (1983). The human Klüver-Bucy syndrome. *Neurology* 33: 1141–1145.

Macchi, G. (1989). Anatomical substrate of emotional reactions. In L. R. Squire and G. Gainotti, Eds., *Handbook of Neuropsychology,* vol. 3. Amsterdam: Elsevier, pp. 283–304.

Markowitsch, H. J., P. Calabrese, M. Würker, H. F. Durwen, J. Kessler, R. Babinsky, D. Brechtelsbauer, L. Heuser, and W. Gehlen. (1994). The amygdala's contribution to memory—a PET-study on two patients with Urbach-Wiethe disease. *Neuroreport* 5: 1349–1352.

Mesulam, M.-M. (1985). Patterns in behavioral neuroanatomy: association areas, the limbic system, and behavioral specialization. In M.-M. Mesulam, Ed., *Principles of Behavioral Neurology.* Philadelphia: F. A. Davis, pp. 1–70.

Reep, R. (1984). Relationship between prefrontal and limbic cortex: a comparative anatomical review. *Brain, Behavior and Evolution* 25: 5–80.

Schneider, F., R. E. Gur, L. H. Mozley, R. J. Smith, P. D. Mozley, D. M. Censits, A. Alavi, and R. C. Gur. (1995). Mood effects on limbic blood flow correlate with emotional self-rating: a PET study with oxygen-15 labeled water. *Psychiatry Research: Neuroimaging* 61: 265–283.

Scoville, W. B., and B. Milner. (1957). Loss of recent memory after bilateral hippocampal lesions. *Journal of Neurology, Neurosurgery and Psychiatry* 20: 11–21.

Tulving, E., and H. J. Markowitsch. (1997). Memory beyond the hippocampus. *Current Opinion in Neurobiology* 7: 209–216.

Linguistic Relativity Hypothesis

The linguistic relativity hypothesis is the proposal that the particular language one speaks influences the way one thinks about reality. The hypothesis joins two claims. First, languages differ significantly in their interpretations of experience—both what they select for representation and how they arrange it. Second, these interpretations of experience influence thought when they are used to guide or support it. Because the first claim is so central to the hypothesis, demonstrations of linguistic differences in the interpretation of experience are sometimes mistakenly regarded as demonstrations of linguistic relativity and demonstrations of some commonalities are taken as disproof, but the assessment of the hypothesis necessarily requires evaluating the cognitive influence of whatever language differences do exist. Accounts vary in the proposed mechanisms of influence and in the power attributed to them—the strongest version being a strict linguistic determinism (based, ultimately, on the identity of language and thought). Linguistic relativity proposals should be distinguished from more general concerns about how speaking any natural language whatsoever influences thinking (e.g., the general role of language in human intellectual functioning) and discourse-level concerns with how using language in a particular way influences thinking (e.g., schooled versus unschooled). Ultimately, however, all these levels interrelate in determining how language influences thought.

Interest in the intellectual significance of the diversity of language categories has deep roots in the European tradition (Aarsleff 1982). Formulations related to contemporary ones appeared in England (Locke), France (Condillac, Diderot), and Germany (Hamman, Herder) near the beginning of the eighteenth century. They were stimulated by opposition to the universal grammarians, by concerns about the reliability of language-based knowledge, and by practical efforts to consolidate national identities and cope with colonial expansion. Work in the nineteenth century, notably that of Humboldt in Germany and SAUSSURE in Switzerland and France, drew heavily on this earlier tradition and set the stage for contemporary approaches. The linguistic relativity proposal received new impetus and reformulation in America during the early twentieth century in the work of anthropological linguists SAPIR (1949) and Whorf (1956) (hence the common designation as "the Sapir-Whorf hypothesis"). They emphasized direct study of diverse languages and rejected the hierarchical rankings of languages and cultures characteristic of many European approaches.

Despite enduring philosophical interest in the question (e.g., Quine 1960), there has been little empirical research that both compares linguistic meaning structures and then independently assesses thought (Lucy 1992a). This stems partly from the interdisciplinary nature of the problem and partly from concern about the implications of relativism and determinism. Empirical efforts fall into three broad types.

Structure-centered approaches begin with an observed difference between languages, elaborate the interpretations of reality implicit in them, and then seek evidence for their influence on thought. The approach remains open to unexpected interpretations of reality but often has difficulty establishing a neutral basis for comparison. The classic example of a language-centered approach is Whorf's pioneering comparison of Hopi and English (1956) in which he argues for different conceptions of 'time' in the two languages as a function of whether cyclic experiences are classed as like ordinary objects (English) or as recurrent events (Hopi). The most extensive recent effort to extend and improve the comparative fundamentals in a structure-centered approach has sought to establish a relation between variations in grammatical number marking and attentiveness to number and form (Lucy 1992b).

Domain-centered approaches begin with a domain of experienced reality, typically characterized independently of language(s), and ask how various languages select from and organize it. The approach facilitates controlled comparison but often at the expense of regimenting the linguistic data rather narrowly. The classic example of this approach shows that some colors are more lexically encodable than others and that more codable colors are remembered better (Brown and Lenneberg 1954). This approach was later extended to argue that there are cross linguistic universals in the encoding of the color domain such that a small number of "basic" color terms emerge in languages as a function of biological constraints (Berlin and Kay 1969). This research has been widely accepted as evidence against the linguistic relativity hypothesis, although it actually deals with constraints on linguistic diversity. Subsequent research has challenged the universal claim and shown that different color term systems do influence COLOR CATEGORIZATION and memory. The most successful effort to improve the quality of the linguistic comparison in a domain-centered approach has sought to show cognitive differences in the spatial domain between languages favoring the use of body coordinates to describe arrangements of objects (e.g., the man is left of the tree) and those favoring systems anchored in cardinal direction terms or topographic features (e.g., the man is east/uphill of the tree; Levinson 1996).

Behavior-centered approaches begin with a marked difference in behavior that the researcher comes to believe has its roots in a pattern of thinking arising from language practices. The behavior at issue typically has clear practical consequences (either for theory or for native speakers), but because the research does not begin intending to address the linguistic relativity question, the theoretical and empirical analyses of language and reality are often weak. An example of a behavior-centered approach is the effort to account for differences in Chinese and English speakers' facility with counterfactual or hypothetical reasoning by reference to the marking of counterfactuals in the two languages (Bloom 1981).

The continued relevance of the linguistic relativity issue seems assured by the same impulses found historically: the patent relevance of language to human sociality and intellect, the reflexive concern with the role of language in intellectual method, and the practical encounter with diversity.

See also CONCEPTS; CULTURAL VARIATION; LANGUAGE AND CULTURE; LANGUAGE AND THOUGHT; LINGUISTIC UNIVERSALS AND UNIVERSAL GRAMMAR; LINGUISTICS, PHILOSOPHICAL ISSUES

—*John A. Lucy*

References

Aarsleff, H. (1982). *From Locke to Saussure.* Minneapolis, MN: University of Minnesota Press.

Berlin, B., and P. Kay. (1969). *Basic Color Terms.* Berkeley and Los Angeles: University of California Press.

Bloom, A. H. (1981). *The Linguistic Shaping of Thought.* Hillsdale, NJ: Erlbaum.

Brown, R. W., and E. H. Lenneberg. (1954). A study in language and cognition. *Journal of Abnormal and Social Psychology* 49: 454–462.

Levinson, S. C. (1996). Relativity in spatial conception and description. In J. J. Gumperz and S .C. Levinson, Eds., *Rethinking Linguistic Relativity.* Cambridge: Cambridge University Press.

Lucy, J. A. (1992a). *Language Diversity and Thought.* Cambridge: Cambridge University Press.

Lucy, J. A. (1992b). *Grammatical Categories and Cognition.* Cambridge: Cambridge University Press.

Quine, W. (1960). *Word and Object.* Cambridge, MA: MIT Press.

Sapir, E. (1949). The selected writings of Edward Sapir. In D.G. Mandelbaum, Ed., *Language, Culture, and Personality.* Berkeley and Los Angeles: University of California Press.

Whorf, B. L. (1956). *Language, Thought, and Reality: Selected Writings of Benjamin Lee Whorf,* J. B. Carroll, Ed. Cambridge, MA: MIT Press.

Further Readings

Aarsleff, H. (1988). Introduction. In W. von Humboldt, Ed., *On Language: The Diversity of Human Language-Structure and its Influence on the Mental Development of Mankind,* trans. by P. Heath. Cambridge: Cambridge University Press.

Grace, G. W. (1987). *The Linguistic Construction of Reality.* London: Croom Helm.

Gumperz, J. J., and S. C. Levinson, Eds. (1996). *Rethinking Linguistic Relativity.* Cambridge: Cambridge University Press.

Hardin, C. L., and L. Maffi, Eds. (1997). *Color Categories in Thought and Language.* Cambridge: Cambridge University Press.

Hill, J. H., and B. Mannheim. (1992). Language and world view. *Annual Review of Anthropology* 21: 381–406.

Hunt, E., and F. Agnoli. (1991). The Whorfian Hypothesis: a cognitive psychology perspective. *Psychological Review* 98: 377–389.

Kay, P., and C. K. McDaniel. (1978). The linguistic significance of the meanings of basic color terms. *Language* 54: 610–646.

Koerner, E. F. K. (1992). The Sapir-Whorf Hypothesis: a preliminary history and a bibliographic essay. *Journal of Linguistic Anthropology* 2: 173–178.

Lakoff, G. (1987). *Women, Fire, and Dangerous Things: What Categories Reveal about the Mind.* Chicago: University of Chicago Press.

Lee, P. (1997). *The Whorf Theory Complex: A Critical Reconstruction.* Amsterdam: John Benjamins.

Levinson, S. C. (1997). From outer to inner space: linguistic categories and nonlinguistic thinking. In J. Nuyts and E. Pederson, Eds., *The Relationship between Linguistic and Conceptual Representation.* Cambridge: Cambridge University Press.

Lucy, J. A. (1996). The scope of linguistic relativity: an analysis and review of empirical research. In J. J. Gumperz and S. C. Levinson, Eds., *Rethinking Linguistic Relativity.* Cambridge: Cambridge University Press.

Lucy, J. A. (1997). Linguistic relativity. *Annual Review of Anthropology* 26:291-312.

Lucy, J. A., and R. A. Shweder. (1979). Whorf and his critics: linguistic and nonlinguistic influences on color memory. *American Anthropologist* 81: 581–615.

Putnam, H. (1981). *Philosophical Papers.* Cambridge: Cambridge University Press.

Schultz, E. A. (1990). *Dialogue at the Margins: Whorf, Bakhtin, and Linguistic Relativity.* Madison: University of Wisconsin Press.

Silverstein, M. (1979). Language structure and linguistic ideology. In P. Clyne, W. Hanks, and C. Hofbauer, Eds., *The Elements: A Parasession on Linguistic Units and Levels.* Chicago: Chicago Linguistic Society.

Wierzbicka, A. (1992). *Semantics, Culture, and Cognition: Universal Human Concepts in Culture-Specific Configurations.* Oxford: Oxford University Press.

Linguistic Stress

See STRESS, LINGUISTIC

Linguistic Theory

See INTRODUCTION: LINGUISTICS AND LANGUAGE

Linguistic Universals and Universal Grammar

A child's linguistic system is shaped to a significant degree by the utterances to which that child has been exposed. That is why a child speaks the language and dialect of his family and community. Nonetheless, there are aspects of the linguistic system acquired by the child that do *not* depend on input data in this way. Some cases of this type, it has been argued, reflect the influence of a genetically prespecified body of knowledge about human language. In the literature on GENERATIVE GRAMMAR, the term *Universal Grammar*—commonly abbreviated UG—refers to this body of "hardwired" knowledge.

Questions concerning the existence and nature of UG arise in all areas of linguistics (see discussion in SYNTAX, PHONOLOGY, and SEMANTICS). Research on these questions constitutes a principal point of contact between linguistics and the other cognitive sciences.

Three streams of evidence teach us about the existence and nature of UG. One stream of evidence comes from crosslinguistic investigation of linguistic universals, discussed in the article on TYPOLOGY. Crosslinguistic investigations help us learn whether a property found in one language is also found in other unrelated languages, and, if so, why. Another stream of evidence concerning UG comes from investigation of LANGUAGE ACQUISITION and learnability, especially as these investigations touch on issues of POVERTY OF THE STIMULUS ARGUMENTS. Work on acquisition and learnability helps us understand whether a property found in the grammar of an individual speaker is acquired by imitation of input data or whether some other reason for the existence of this property must be sought. Finally, evidence bearing on the specially *linguistic* nature of UG comes from research on MODULARITY AND LANGUAGE. Features of language whose typological and acquisitional footprint suggests an origin in UG may be confirmed as reflections of UG if they reflect aspects of cognition that are to some degree language-specific and "informationally encapsulated." If a fact about an individual speaker's grammar turns out to be a fact about grammars of all the world's languages, if it is demonstrably not a fact acquired in imitation of input data, and if it appears to be specific to language, then we are warranted to suspect that the fact arose from a specific feature of UG.

The questions one asks in the process of building the theory of UG are varied and complex. Suppose the linguist discovers that a property P of one language is present in a variety of other languages. It is often possible that P arises from some more general property of cognition. For example, the repertoire of linguistically relevant THEMATIC ROLES such as "experiencer" or "agent" may reflect language-independent facts about the categorization of events —and therefore fall outside of UG. On the other hand, while the repertoire of thematic roles may be language-independent, the opposite is true of the apparently universal mapping of specific thematic roles onto specific designated syntactic positions—for example, the fact that agents are mapped universally onto a structurally more prominent position than patients (e.g., subject position). This specifically linguistic mapping thus constitutes one of the properties attributed to UG.

It is also important to try to distinguish UG-based universals from apparent universals that merely reflect usability conditions on languages that must serve a communicative function (*functional* universals). For example, there is probably a lower bound to the size of a language's phonemic inventory. Does this restriction form part of UG? Not necessarily. It is equally possible that the limitation merely reflects a consequence of usability conditions for linguistic systems. The words of a language whose only phonemes are /m/ and /a/ would be extraordinarily long and hard to distinguish. Such a language might fall within the range permitted by UG, yet never occur in nature because of its dysfunctionality.

Because of the ever-present possibility that a universal may have a functional explanation, researchers interested in discovering properties of language that derive from UG often focus on those universals for which functional explanations are the *least* likely. For example, syntactic research has paid particular attention to a number of limitations on form-meaning pairs that have just this property of "dysfunc-

tionality." One example is a set of restrictions specific to *how* and *why* questions. *How did you think Mary solved the problem?* can be a question about Mary's problem-solving methods, but the sentence *How did you ask if Mary solved the problem?* cannot. (It can only be a question about methods of asking.) The restriction concerns the domains from which WH-MOVEMENT may apply, which in turn correlates with sentence meaning. The restriction appears to be a genuine universal, already detected in a wide variety of languages whose grammars otherwise diverge in a number of ways. Crucially, the restriction makes no evident contribution to usability. Just the opposite: it prevents speakers from posing perfectly sensible questions, except through circumlocution—for example, *I know that you asked if Mary had solved the problem in some particular way. What was that way?* The study of such seemingly dysfunctional aspects of language has provided an especially clear path to a preliminary understanding of UG. This fact also explains why the data of generative grammar stray so often from "everyday" linguistic facts—a central difference between the concerns of generative grammarians and those researchers more concerned with "everyday" language use (a group that includes some sociolinguists as well as computational linguists interested in practical language technologies).

The existence of "Universal Grammar" (uppercase) does not necessarily entail the existence of a "universal grammar" (lowercase)—in the sense of a usable linguistic system wholly determined by genetic factors. UG must allow for language variation, though by its very nature it restricts the range of variation. This is why certain nonuniversal properties of language nonetheless recur in widely scattered, unrelated languages, while other equally imaginable properties are never found. For example, the placement of the finite verb in "second" position characteristic of the Germanic languages (see HEAD MOVEMENT) is also found in Vata (Ivory Coast; Koopman 1983), Kashmiri (Bhatt 1995), and Karitiana (Brazil; Storto 1996). By contrast, in no known language are verbs obligatorily placed in third position. In other words, UG allows languages to vary—but only up to a point.

There are several theories of how variation is built into UG. One proposal holds that the principles of UG define the parameters of possible variation. Language acquisition involves "setting" these parameters (see PARAMETER-SETTING APPROACHES TO ACQUISITION, CREOLIZATION, AND DIACHRONY). Another suggestion, advanced by Borer (1981) and Borer and Wexler (1987), holds that true variation is limited to the LEXICON (one aspect of language that we know must vary from language to language). Apparent syntactic variation on this view arises from the differing syntactic requirements of lexical items (see also SYNTAX, ACQUISITION OF). Another proposal, developed within OPTIMALITY THEORY, attributes variation to differences in the ability of particular grammatical principles to nullify the action of other principles with which they conflict (i.e., differences in "constraint ranking").

It is not entirely clear what aspects of UG are subject to variation. In particular, though no one doubts that syntactic and phonological systems vary across languages, the question of variation in semantics is more contested. The details of semantic interpretation are probably less obvious to young children acquiring language than are the details of word positioning and word pronunciation that provide evidence about syntax and phonology. Consequently, it is conceivable (though not inevitable) that the laws governing compositional semantic interpretation of syntactic structures are wholly determined by UG—hence invariant across languages. In fact, the notion and the term was borrowed by Chomsky (1965, 1966) from an earlier grammatical tradition that explicitly sought universal semantic roots of syntax (for example, the 1660 Port-Royal *Grammaire générale et raisonée*). Semantic universals do exist, of course. Not only basic laws of semantic composition (Heim and Kratzer 1998), but also many details recur in language after language. For example, the classification of predicates into something like "states" versus "events," and the interaction of this classification with such properties as quantifier interpretation, seems to be invariant (or nearly so) across the languages that have been studied. On the other hand, other facts might cause one to doubt whether all languages command exactly the same semantic resources. For example, although "multiple questions" such as *Who bought what?* receive similar interpretations in many languages (as questions whose answer provides a list of pairs; e.g., *John bought the wine and Mary bought the dessert*), this semantic possibility is entirely absent in some languages, including Italian and Irish. To native speakers of these languages, the counterparts to *Who bought what?* (e.g., Italian **Chi a comprato che cosa?*) seem quite uninterpretable. Whether such facts indicate the existence of semantic variation, or merely reveal lexical or syntactic differences with a predictable impact on semantics, remains an open question.

The fact that variation is "built into" some aspects of UG does not preclude the possibility that UG might characterize a usable "default" grammar on its own. This is also a matter of considerable controversy. Bickerton (1981), for example, has suggested that CREOLES represent the spontaneous flowering of a purely UG-based grammar, but this view is controversial (Mufwene 1996, 1999). Furthermore, a precedent for "usable UG" is provided elsewhere in the animal kingdom by songbird species whose song is partly learned rather than totally innate. Researchers have identified a "UG" for the song of several such species. When birds of these species are reared in isolation, they spontaneously develop a song that falls recognizably within the parameters of their UG, though rudimentary in many ways (Marler 1991, 1996; see also ANIMAL COMMUNICATION). The UG of songbirds is of importance for another reason. Among those who have not made a study of the relevant evidence, theories of UG are often thought to require special pleading, as if the hypothesis of species-specific innate knowledge constituted a violation of Occam's razor. The evidence from songbirds makes it clear that a priori objections to UG are nothing more than a prejudice. The nature of human UG remains, however, a topic of lively debate and continued research.

See also CONNECTIONIST APPROACHES TO LANGUAGE; HUMAN UNIVERSALS; INNATENESS OF LANGUAGE; LANGUAGE AND CULTURE; LANGUAGE VARIATION AND CHANGE; NATIVISM

—*David Pesetsky*

References

Bhatt, R. (1995). Verb movement in Kashmiri. In R. Izvorski and V. Tredinnick, Eds., *U. Penn Working Papers in Linguistics,* vol. 2. Philadelphia: University of Pennsylvania Department of Linguistics.

Bickerton, D. (1981). *Roots of Language.* Ann Arbor, MI: Karoma.

Borer, H. (1983). *Parametric Syntax.* Dordrecht: Foris.

Borer, H., and K. Wexler. (1987). The maturation of syntax. In T. Roeper and E. Williams, Eds., *Parameter Setting.* Dordrecht: Reidel.

Chomsky, N. (1965). *Aspects of the Theory of Syntax.* Cambridge, MA: MIT Press.

Chomsky, N. (1966). *Cartesian Linguistics.* New York: Harper and Row.

Heim, I., and A. Kratzer. (1997). *Semantics in Generative Grammar.* Oxford: Blackwell.

Koopman, H. (1983). *The Syntax of Verbs: from Verb Movement Rules in the Kru Language to Universal Grammar.* Dordrecht: Foris.

Marler, P. (1991). Differences in behavioural development in closely related species: birdsong. In P. Bateson, Ed., *The Development and Integration of Behaviour.* Cambridge: Cambridge University Press, pp. 41–70.

Marler, P. (1996). Song Learning. http://www.hip.atr.co.jp/~bateson/hawaii/abstracts/marler_ms.html.

Mufwene, S. S. (1996). The Founder Principle in creole genesis. *Diachronica* 13: 83–134.

Mufwene, S. (1999). On the language bioprogram hypothesis: Hints from Tazie. In M. DeGraff, Ed., *Language Creation and Language Change: Creolization, Diachrony, and Development.* Cambridge, MA: MIT Press.

Storto, L. (1996). Verb Raising and Word Order Variation in Karitiana. Unpublished manuscript, Massachusetts Institute of Technology.

Linguistics, Philosophical Issues

As with any rapidly developing science, GENERATIVE GRAMMAR has given rise to a number of interesting philosophical puzzles and controversies. These controversies range from disputes about the object of study in linguistics, to issues about the relation between the language faculty and the external world, to questions about the legitimacy of appeal to rules and representations, to questions about proper empirical methodology.

One of the prominent philosophical debates in generative grammar has centered around the question of what sort of objects languages and grammars are. Katz (1985) distinguishes three general approaches to the question, roughly paralleling three traditional approaches to the nature of abstract objects: platonism, conceptualism, and nominalism. The platonist view would take the object of study in linguistics to be an abstract mathematical object outside of space and time, the conceptualist position would be a position like Chomsky's in which the object of study is a mental object of some form, and the nominalist view would hold that the object of study is a corpus of inscriptions or utterances.

The platonist view has been advanced most visibly by Katz (1981), although it may be that the position rests on a confusion. For example, Higginbotham (1983) has observed that even if grammars are abstract objects, there is still the empirical question of which grammar a particular agent is employing. George (1989) has further clarified the issue, holding that we need to distinguish between a grammar, which is the abstract object that we know, a psycho-grammar, which is the cognitive state that constitutes our knowledge of the grammar, and a physio-grammar, which is the physical manifestation of the psycho-grammar in the brain. If this picture is right, then the platonist/conceptualist dispute in linguistics may be trading on a failure to distinguish between grammars and psycho-grammars.

Perhaps more pressing is the dispute between the nominalist and conceptualist positions, a dispute that Chomsky (1986) has characterized as being between E-language and I-language conceptions of language. From the E-language perspective, a natural language is a kind of social object, the structure of which is purported to be established by convention (see Lewis 1975), and persons may acquire varying degrees of competence in their knowledge and use of that social object. On Chomsky's views, such objects would be of little scientific interest if they did exist (since they would not be "natural" objects), but in any case such objects don't exist. Alternatively, an I-language is not an external object but is rather a state of an internal system that is part of our biological endowment. An agent might have I-language representations of English sentences, but those internal representations are not to be confused with spoken or written English sentences. They are rather data structures in a kind of internal computational system.

Chomsky understands the I-language computational system to be individualistic (see INDIVIDUALISM). That means that the properties of the system can be specified independently of the environment that the agent is embedded in. Thus, it involves properties like the agent's rest mass and genetic make-up (and unlike relational properties like the agent's weight and IQ).

By itself, the dispute between I-language and E-language approaches has little philosophical traction; the actual direction of the field presumably settles the issue as to which is the object of study. Nevertheless, some normative claims have been offered. For example, Soames (1984) has suggested that if we attend to the leading questions of linguistics in the past, then linguistics has been (and ought to be) concerned with E-language. Of course, one might wonder why past investigations should restrict the direction (and leading questions) of current research. Chomsky (1993, 1995) not only disputes this historical story but has argued that E-languages are not suitable for naturalistic inquiry, because they constitute artifacts rather than natural objects. In other words, it is fine to talk about E-languages as long as one doesn't think one is doing science.

As we will see, the choice between these two general approaches to language is very rich in consequences. Both the claim that I-language is individualistic and the claim that it is computational have led to a number of philosophical skirmishes.

One of the immediate questions raised by the idea that I-language is individualistic has to do with the nature of SEMANTICS, and in particular *referential* semantics—construed as theories of the relation between linguistic forms and aspects of the external world (see REFERENCE, THEORIES OF). In short, the worry is this: Putnam (1975) and many other philosophers have held that we need referential semantics to characterize linguistic MEANING—that meanings "ain't in the head." But if this is right, then it is hard to see how semantics can be part of the language faculty, which is supposed to be individualistic (and hence "in the head").

This tension between I-language and referential semantics has led commentators such as Hornstein (1984) and Chomsky (1993, 1995) to be skeptical of the possibility of a referential semantics. However, Ludlow (forthcoming) has argued that the tension in these views is apparent only, because the connection between I-languages and referential semantics would parallel the connection between individualistic and relational sciences in other domains (for example, it would be similar to the connection that holds between the studies of primate physiology and primate ecology—facts about physiology can shed light on the primate's relation to its environment, and vice versa). Inferences between individualistic and relational sciences are imperfect, but data from one domain can nevertheless be relevant to the other.

The idea that linguistic theory involves the investigation of RULES AND REPRESENTATIONS (or principles and parameters) of an internal computational system has also led to philosophical questions about the nature of these rules and representations. For example, Quine (1970) has argued that because many possible grammars may successfully describe an agent's linguistic behavior, there is no way in principle for us to determine which grammar an agent is using. For his part, Chomsky (1980) has argued that if we consider the *explanatory adequacy* of a grammar in addition to its *descriptive adequacy,* then the question of which grammar is correct is answerable in principle. That is, if we consider that a grammar must be consistent with the theory of LANGUAGE ACQUISITION, acquired language deficits, and more generally with cognitive psychology, then there are many constraints available to rule out competing grammatical theories.

Another set of worries about rule following have stemmed from Kripke's (1982) reconstruction of arguments in Wittgenstein (1953, 1956). The idea is that there can be no brute fact about what rules and representations a system is running apart from the intentions of the designer of the system. Because, when studying humans, we have no access to the intentions of the designer, there can be no fact of the matter about what rules and representations underlie our linguistic abilities. The conclusion drawn by Kripke is that "it would seem that the use of the idea of rules and of competence in linguistics needs serious reconsideration, even if these notions are not rendered meaningless." (1982: 31 fn 22)

Chomsky (1986) appears to argue that one can know certain facts about computers in isolation, but Chomsky's current position (1995) is that computers, unlike the human language faculty, are artifacts and hence the product of human intentions. The language faculty is a natural object and embedded within human biology, so the facts about its structure are no more grounded in human intentions than are facts about the structure of human biology.

If the language faculty is an internal computational/representational system, a number of questions arise about how to best go about investigating and describing it. For example, there has been considerable attention paid to the role of formal rigor in linguistic theory. On this score, a number of theorists (e.g., Gazdar, Klein, Pullum, and Sag 1985; Bresnan and Kaplan 1982; Pullum, 1989) have argued that the formal rigor of their approaches—in particular, their use of well-defined recursive procedures—counts in their favor. However, Ludlow (1992) has argued that this sort of approach to rigorization would be out of synch with the development of other sciences (and indeed, branches of mathematics) where formalization follows in the wake of the advancing theory.

A second methodological issue relates to the use of PARSIMONY AND SIMPLICITY in the choice between linguistic theories. Although tight definitions of simplicity within a linguistic theory seem to be possible (see Halle 1961; Chomsky and Halle 1968; Chomsky 1975), finding a notion of simplicity that allows us to chose between two competing theoretical frameworks is another matter. Some writers (e.g., Postal 1972; Hornstein 1995) have argued that generative semantics and the minimalist program (see MINIMALISM), respectively, are simpler than their immediate competitors because they admit fewer levels of representation. In response, Ludlow (1998) has maintained that there is no objective criterion for evaluating the relative amount of theoretical machinery across linguistic theories. Ludlow offers that the only plausible definition of simplicity would be one that appealed to "simplicity of use," suggesting that simplicity in linguistics may not be a feature of the object of study itself but rather our ability to easily grasp and utilize certain kinds of theories.

Finally, there is the matter of the nature of evidence available for investigating the language faculty. Evidence from a written or spoken corpus is at best twice removed from the actual object of investigation, and given the possibility of performance errors, is notoriously unreliable at that. Much of the evidence adduced in linguistic theory has therefore been from speakers' intuitions of acceptability, as well as intuitions about possible interpretations. This raises a number of interesting questions about the reliability of introspective data (see INTROSPECTION) and the kind of training required to have reliable judgements. There is also the question of why we should have introspective access to the language faculty at all. It is fair to say that these questions have not been adequately explored to date (except in a critical vein; see Devitt 1995; Devitt and Sterelny 1987).

Katz (1985: Introduction) offers that the philosophy of linguistics could soon emerge as a domain of inquiry in its own right, on the model of the philosophy of physics and the philosophy of biology. Given the number of interesting questions and disputes that have arisen in the interim, it is fair to say that Katz's prediction is coming true. The issues canvassed above provide a mere sketch of the current topics under discussion and point to a rich field of investigation in the years to come.

See also FREGE; INNATENESS OF LANGUAGE; LOGICAL FORM, ORIGINS OF; SENSE AND REFERENCE

—Peter Ludlow

References

Bresnan, J., and R. Kaplan. (1982). Introduction: Grammars as mental representations of language. In J. Bresnan, Ed., *The Mental Representation of Grammatical Relations.* Cambridge, MA: MIT Press, pp. xvii–lii.

Chomsky, N. (1975). *The Logical Structure of Linguistic Theory.* New York: Plenum.

Chomsky, N. (1980). *Rules and Representations.* New York: Columbia University Press.

Chomsky, N. (1986). *Knowledge of Language.* New York: Praeger.

Chomsky, N. (1993). Explaining language use. In J. Tomberlin, Ed., *Philosophical Topics 20.* pp. 205–231.

Chomsky, N. (1995). Language and nature. *Mind* 104: 1–61.

Chomsky, N., and M. Halle. (1968). *The Sound Pattern of English.* New York: Harper and Row.

Devitt, M. (1995). *Coming to Our Senses: A Naturalistic Program for Semantic Localism.* Cambridge: Cambridge University Press.

Devitt, M., and K. Sterelny. (1987). *Language and Reality: An Introduction to the Philosophy of Language.* Cambridge, MA: MIT Press.

Gazdar, G., E. Klein, G. Pullum, and I. Sag. (1985). *Generalized Phrase Structure Grammar.* Cambridge, MA: Harvard University Press.

George, A. (1989). How not to become confused about linguistics. In A. George, Ed., *Reflections on Chomsky.* Oxford: Blackwell, pp. 90–110.

Halle, M. (1961). On the role of simplicity in linguistic description. *Proceedings of Symposia in Applied Mathematics 12 (Structure of Language and its Mathematical Aspects),* pp. 89–94. Providence: American Mathematical Society.

Higginbotham, J. (1983). Is grammar psychological? In L. Cauman, I. Levi, C. Parsons, and R. Schwartz, Eds., *How Many Questions: Essays In Honor of Sydney Morgenbesser.* Indianapolis, IN: Hackett.

Hornstein, N. (1984). *Logic as Grammar.* Cambridge, MA: MIT Press.

Hornstein, N. (1995). *Logical Form: From GB to Minimalism.* Oxford: Blackwell.

Katz, J. (1981). *Language and Other Abstract Objects.* Totowa, NJ: Rowman and Littlefield.

Katz, J., Ed. (1985). *The Philosophy of Linguistics.* Oxford: Oxford University Press.

Kripke, S. (1982). *Wittgenstein on Rules and Private Language.* Cambridge: Harvard University Press.

Lewis, D. (1975). Language and languages. In K. Gunderson, Ed., *Language, Mind, and Knowledge.* Minneapolis: University of Minnesota Press, pp. 3–35.

Ludlow, P. (1992). Formal Rigor and Linguistic Theory. *Natural Language and Linguistic Theory* 10: 335–344.

Ludlow, P. (1998). Simplicity and generative grammar. In R. Stainton and K. Murasugi, Eds., *Philosophy and Linguistics.* Boulder, CO: Westview Press.

Ludlow, P. (Forthcoming). Referential semantics for I-languages? In N. Hornstein and L. Antony, Eds., *Chomsky and His Critics.* Oxford: Blackwell.

Postal, P. (1972). The best theory. In S. Peters, Ed., *Goals of Linguistic Theory.* Englewood Cliffs, NJ: Prentice-Hall, pp. 131–179.

Pullum, G. (1989). Formal linguistics meets the boojum. *Natural Language and Linguistic Theory* 7: 137–143.

Putnam, H. (1975). The meaning of meaning. In K. Gunderson, Ed., *Language, Mind, and Knowledge.* Minneapolis: University of Minnesota Press, pp. 131–193.

Quine, W. V. O. (1970). Methodological reflections on current linguistic theory. *Synthese* 21: 368–398.

Soames, S. (1984). Linguistics and psychology. *Linguistics and Philosophy* 81: 155–179.

Wittgenstein, L. (1953). *Philosophical Investigations.* Translated by G. E. M. Anscombe. New York: MacMillan.

Wittgenstein, L. (1956). *Remarks on the Foundations of Mathematics.* Translated by G. E. M. Anscombe. Cambridge, MA: MIT Press.

Literacy

Literacy is competence with a written language, a script. This competence includes not only an individual's ability to read and write a script but also one's access to and competence with the documentary resources of a literate society. Literacy holds a prominent place in the political goals of both developed and developing nations as manifest in universal, compulsory education where literacy is seen as a means to personal, social, and economic fulfillment. Literacy is a more general concept than READING and writing, including not only competence with and uses of reading and writing but also the roles that reading and writing play in the formation and accumulation of the procedures, laws, and texts that serve as the primary embodiment of historical culture. Literate, bureaucratic, or "document" societies are those in which such archival texts and documents play a central and authoritative role. Such societies depend on highly literate specialists.

Writing and communication Writing has obvious advantages over speech for communication across space and through time, factors which various media, including the book, the printing press, the telegraph, and computer technologies, exploit and extend in various ways. Writing played an essential role in the formation and operation of the first large-scale societies, whether as cities, nations, or empires in ancient China, Sumer, Egypt, and Mesoamerica, where it played a critical role in record keeping (Nissen, Damerow, and Englund 1993), codification and publication of law (Harris 1989), the development of literature (Havelock 1963), and the accumulation of knowledge whether as history or science (Eisenstein 1969).

Writing and representation Not only does writing alter patterns of communication, written texts and commentaries on texts build up a tradition of scholarship. Such accumulations tend to lose their connections with personal authorship and may come to be treated as objects in their own rights, as Scripture, as Law, or as Science. Consequently, writing comes to serve as a mode of representation of what is taken as "known." Three aspects of this problem have been taken up in the cognitive sciences: the relation between speech and writing, the acquisition of literacy, and the effects of literate representations on the formation of mind.

Speech and writing Although scripts are not designed according to fixed principles, WRITING SYSTEMS may be classified according to type, each type bearing a particular relation to the structure of speech. Each type of script, consequently, requires a reader to carve up the stream of speech in a distinctive, graphically determined way. The problem for the learner is to analyze, that is, conceive of, oral speech in terms of the categories offered by the script (Shankweiler and Liberman 1972; Faber 1992; Harris 1986; Olson 1994).

On this view, the properties of speech available for INTROSPECTION, such as words, sentences, syllables, and phonemic segments, are the consequence of literacy, of applying written models to speech. A major problem in learning to read is learning to "hear" speech in a new way, that is, in a way compatible with the items—words and letters—composing the script. Studies of nonliterate adults' (Morais, Alegria, and Content 1987) and of prereading children's beliefs about writing (Ferreiro and Teberosky 1982) as well as the vast literature on metalinguistic awareness (Goswami and Bryant 1990) tend to support this view.

Writing and the mind Although the mind as a biological organ is common to all humans, mind as a conscious, conceptual system is in part the product of culture. In a modern bureaucratic culture, mind is closely linked to literacy but just how remains the subject of research and theory. Although the theory linking forms of writing with levels of culture and thought is to be found in such eighteenth-century writers as Vico and Condorcet, modern theory is more clearly traced to Levy-Bruhl's theory of "primitive thought," now widely criticized, and the theories that first appeared in the 1960s by Goody (1968), McLuhan (1962), Havelock (1963), and later Ong (1982), which contrasted "orality" and "literacy" both as modes of communication and modes of thought. Writing allowed, it was argued, a particular form of study and contemplation, the formation of logics and dictionaries, a focus on "verbatim" interpretation and memorization with an interpretive bias to literalism. Although the increasing and pervasive reliance on written records and other written documents in many societies is undeniable (Clanchy 1992; Thomas 1992), the relations between "orality" and "literacy" continue to be debated. CULTURAL PSYCHOLOGY attempts to understand the cognitive implications of such developments. Although writing never replaces speaking but rather preserves aspects of speech and other forms of information as permanent visible artifacts, these literate artifacts may in turn alter the very linguistic and conceptual practices of a social group, activities that blur, almost to the point of obliterating, the distinction between orality and literacy.

Literate thought Although mind reflects as well as invents culture and although human competence must be analyzed in terms of the available technologies (Clark 1996: 61), the technology of greatest importance for understanding conceptual and intellectual advance in the arts and sciences is the invention of writing and other notational systems (Donald 1991; Olson 1994).

Conceptual development in children is, in part, the consequence of the acquisition of these systems for representing thought (VYGOTSKY 1986). Furthermore, writing is instrumental to thinking in general as a form of metalinguistic knowledge—that is, knowledge *about* the lexical, grammatical, and logical properties of the language. Vocabulary knowledge, for example, is greatly extended by reading (Anglin 1993; Anderson 1985), and reflective knowledge about words serves as a major aspect of measured intelligence in a literate society (Stanovich 1986).

Literacy and social development Because literacy plays such a prominent role in modern societies, it is often assumed that the route to social development is through teaching people to read and write (UNESCO 1985). Current research and practice has shown that in order to bring about cultural and social transformation, literacy must be seen as an activity embedded in social and cultural practice. Literacy, bureaucratic institutional structures with explicit procedures and accountability, and democratic participation are mutually reinforcing. Rather than being seen simply as a goal, literacy has come to be seen as a means to fuller participation in the institutions of the society, whether in law, science, or literature (Street 1985) as well as a means for their transformation.

See also LANGUAGE AND COMMUNICATION; LANGUAGE AND CULTURE; LEXICON; NUMERACY AND CULTURE

—*David Olson*

References

Anderson, R. C. (1985). *Becoming a Nation of Readers: The Report of the Commission on Reading.* Pittsburgh, PA: National Academy of Education.

Anglin, J. M. (1993). Vocabulary development: a morphological analysis. *Monographs of the Society for Research in Child Development* 58, no. 10: 1–66.

Clanchy, M. (1992). *From Memory to Written Record.* Oxford: Blackwell.

Clark, A. (1996). *Being There: Putting Brain, Body, and World Together Again.* Cambridge, MA: Bradford/MIT Press.

Donald, M. (1991). *Origins of the Modern Mind.* Cambridge, MA: Harvard University Press.

Eisenstein, E. (1979). *The Printing Press as an Agent of Change.* Cambridge: Cambridge University Press.

Faber, A. (1992). Phonemic segmentation as epiphenomenon: evidence from the history of alphabetic writing. In P. Dowling, S. D. Lima, and M. Noonan, Eds., *The Linguistics of Literacy.* Amsterdam: John Benjamins.

Ferreiro, E., and A. Teberosky. (1982). *Literacy before Schooling.* Exeter, NH: Heinemann.

Goody, J. (1968). *Literacy in Traditional Societies.* Cambridge: Cambridge University Press.

Goswami, U., and P. Bryant. (1990). *Phonological Skills and Learning to Read.* Hillsdale, NJ: Erlbaum.

Harris, R. (1986). *The Origin of Writing.* London: Duckworth.

Harris, W. V. (1989). *Ancient Literacy.* Cambridge, MA: Harvard University Press.

Havelock, E. (1963). *Preface to Plato.* Cambridge: Cambridge University Press.

McLuhan, M. (1962). *The Gutenberg Galaxy.* Toronto: University of Toronto Press.

Morais, J., J. Alegria, and A. Content. (1987). The relationships between segmental analysis and alphabetic literacy: an interactive view. *Cahiers de Psychologie Cognitive* 7: 415–538.

Nissen, H. J., P. Damerow, and R. K. Englund. (1993). *Archaic Bookkeeping: Early Writing and Techniques of Economic Administration in the Ancient Near East.* Chicago: University of Chicago Press.

Olson, D. R. (1994). *The World on Paper.* Cambridge: Cambridge University Press.

Ong, W. (1982). *Orality and Literacy: The Technologizing of the Word.* London: Methuen.

Shankweiler, D., and I. Liberman. (1972). Misreading: a search for causes. In J. Kavanaugh and I. Mattingly, Eds., *Language by Ear and Language by Eye: The Relationships between Speech and Reading.* Cambridge, MA: MIT Press, pp. 293–317.

Stanovich, K. E. (1986). Matthew effects in reading: some consequences of individual differences in the acquisition of literacy. *Reading Research Quarterly* 21: 360–407.

Street, B. (1985). *Literacy in Theory and Practice.* Cambridge: Cambridge University Press.

Thomas, R. (1992). *Literacy and Orality in Ancient Greece.* Cambridge: Cambridge University Press.

UNESCO. (1985). *The Current Literacy Situation in the World.* Paris: UNESCO.

Vygotsky, L. (1986). *Thought and Language,* A. Kozulin, Ed. Cambridge, MA: MIT Press.

Further Readings

Bruner, J. S. (1996). *The Culture of Education.* Cambridge, MA: Harvard University Press.

Cole, M. (1996). *Cultural Psychology.* Cambridge, MA: Harvard University Press.

Condorcet, M. de. (1802). *Outlines of an Historical View of the Progress of the Human Mind, Being a Posthumous Work of the Late M. De Condorcet.* Baltimore, MD: G. Fryer.

Karmiloff-Smith, A. (1992). *Beyond Modularity: A Developmental Perspective on Cognitive Science.* Cambridge, MA: MIT Press.

Levy-Bruhl, L. (1923). *Primitive Mentality.* London: George Allen and Unwin.

Nelson, K. (1996). *Language in Cognitive Development: The Emergence of the Mediated Mind.* Cambridge: Cambridge University Press.

Vico, G. (1744/1984). *The New Science of Giambattista Vico,* T. Bergin and M. Fish, Eds. Ithaca, NY: Cornell University Press.

Local Representation

See CONNECTIONISM, PHILOSOPHICAL ISSUES; DISTRIBUTED VS LOCAL REPRESENTATION; KNOWLEDGE REPRESENTATION

Logic

> All the children in Lake Woebegone are above average.
> Most people in Lake Woebegone are children.
> Therefore, most people in Lake Woebegone are above average.

No matter what "Lake Woebegone" refers to, what time is being talked about, exactly what kind of majority "most" refers to, or what sense of "above average" is meant, this little proof is valid—as long as the meaning of these terms is held constant. If we replace "most" by the determiner "all," "some," or "at least three," the proof remains valid, but if we replace it by "no" or "few," the proof becomes invalid. As the science of reasoning, logic attempts to understand such phenomena.

It is instructive to compare logic with linguistics, the science of language. Reasoning and using language have a number of properties in common. Both characterize human cognitive abilities. Both exhibit INTENTIONALITY—they refer to objects, events, and other situations typically outside the skin of the agent. And both involve an interaction of SYNTAX, SEMANTICS, and PRAGMATICS. Given these similarities, one might expect logic and linguistics to occupy similar positions vis-à-vis cognitive science, but while linguistics is usually considered a branch of cognitive science, logic is not. To understand why, we must recognize that, apart from the properties noted above, logic and linguistics are strikingly dissimilar. What constitutes a proper sentence varies from language to language. Linguistics looks for what is common to the world's many languages as a way to say something about the nature of the human capacity for language. By contrast, what constitutes a proper (i.e., valid) piece of reasoning is thought to be universal. Twentieth-century logic holds that no matter what language our sample argument is couched in, it will remain valid, not because of some cognitive property of human beings, but because valid reasoning is independent of how it was discovered, produced, or expressed in natural language.

Since antiquity Euclidean geometry, with its system of postulates and proofs, was taken as the shining example of a logical edifice, having its foundations in what we would now call "cognitive science." Under the influence of KANT, nineteenth-century mathematicians and philosophers had assumed that the truth of Euclid's postulates was built into human perceptual abilities, and that methods of proof embodied laws of thought. For example, the great mathematical logician David Hilbert (1928 p. 475) wrote, "The fundamental idea of my proof theory is none other than to describe the activity of our understanding, to make a protocol of the rules according to which our thinking actually proceeds."

Given this historical relationship between logic, geometry, and cognition, it is not surprising that logic was profoundly influenced by the discovery of non-Euclidean geometries, which challenged the Kantian view, and which brought with them both a deep distrust of psychology and an urgent need to understand the differences between valid and invalid reasoning. What were the valid principles of reasoning? What made a principle of reasoning valid or invalid? Refocusing on such normative questions led logicians, following Gödel and Tarski in the mid-twentieth century, to the semantic aspects of logic—truth, reference, and meaning—whose relationships must be honored in valid reasoning. In particular, a valid proof clearly demonstrates that whenever the premises of an argument are true, its conclusion is also true. That is why our sample argument is valid, not because of cognitive abilities of humans, but because, if its premises are true, so is its conclusion.

Cognitive science, on the other hand, is concerned with mechanism, with *how* humans reason. Why do they make the reasoning errors they do? Systematic reasoning errors are at least as interesting as valid reasoning if one is looking for clues as to how people reason. Why are some inferences harder than others? For example, people seem to take longer on average to process the inference in our original sample argument than they do the one in the variant where "most" is replaced by "some" or "at least three," even though all three versions are valid. (This claim is based on informal surveys; I know of no careful work on this question.)

The logician's distrust of psychological aspects of reasoning has led to a de facto division of labor. The relationship between mind and representation is considered the subject matter of psychology, that between representation and the world the subject matter of logic. (There is no such division of labor involving linguistics since it has long been interested in mechanism.) This division has resulted in a distance between the fields of logic and cognitive science. Still, ideas and results from logic have had a profound influence on cognitive science.

Late-nineteenth- and early-twentieth-century logicians (e.g., Hilbert, FREGE, Russell, and Gentzen, before the shift to semantics noted above), developed FORMAL SYSTEMS, mathematical models of reasoning based on the syntactic manipulation of sentencelike representations. The import of "formal" in this context is that the acceptability of an inference step should be a function solely of the shape or "form" of the representations, independent of what they mean. Within linguistics, this has led to the view that a sentence has an underlying LOGICAL FORM that represents its meaning, and that reasoning involves computations over logical forms.

One might postulate that the logical forms involved in our sample argument are something like

> All C are A
> Most P are C
> Most P are A

(Early work did not treat determiners such as "most" and "few" at all—only "every," "some," and others that could be defined in terms of them.) In this view, recognizing the validity of the argument would be a matter of computing the logical forms of the natural language sentences and then recognizing the validity of the inference in terms of these forms (see, for example, Rips 1994).

As models of valid reasoning, formal systems have important uses within mathematical logic and computer science, but as models of human performance, they have been frequently criticized for their poor predictions of successes, errors, and difficulties in human reasoning. Johnson-Laird and Byrne (1991) have argued that postulating more imagelike MENTAL MODELS make better predictions about the way people actually reason. Their proposal, applied to our sample argument, might well help to explain the difference in difficulty in the various inferences mentioned earlier, because it is easier to visualize "some people" and "at least three people" than it is to visualize "most people." Cognitive scientists have recently been exploring computational models of reasoning with diagrams. Logicians, with the notable exceptions of Euler, Venn, and Peirce, have until the past decade paid scant attention to spatial forms of representation, but this is beginning to change (Hammer 1995).

In the 1930s, Alan TURING, a pioneer in computability theory, developed his famous machine model of the way people carry out routine computations using symbols, a model exploited in the design of modern-day digital computers (Turing 1936). Combining Turing's machines and the formal system model of reasoning, cognitive scientists (e.g., Fodor 1975) have proposed formal symbol processing as a metaphor for all cognitive activity: the so-called COMPUTATIONAL THEORY OF MIND. Indeed, some cognitive scientists go so far as to define cognitive science in terms of this metaphor. This suggestion has played a very large role in cognitive science, some would say a defining role, and it is implicit in Turing's original work. Still the idea is highly controversial; connectionists, for example, reject it.

A third contribution of logic to cognitive science arose from research in logic on semantics. Most famously, the logician Montague (1974), borrowing ideas from modern logic, developed the first serious account of the semantics of natural languages; known as "Montague grammar", it has proven quite fruitful. One successful development in this area has been use of generalized QUANTIFIERS to interpret natural language determiners and their associated noun phrases (Barwise and Cooper 1981). The meaning of each determiner is modeled by a binary relation between sets; the relations themselves have very different properties, properties that can be used in accounting for associated logical and processing differences.

Our final application has to do with cognitive interpretations of the first of GÖDEL'S THEOREMS. This theorem, one of the most striking achievements of logic, demonstrates strict limitations on what can be done using formal systems and hence digital computers. Various writers, most famously Penrose (1991), have attempted to use Gödel's first theorem to argue that because there are things people can do that computers in principle cannot do, the formal systems of logic are irrelevant to understanding human cognition, although this argument is very controversial (see, for example, Feferman 1996).

If it is to be the science of full-fledged reasoning, logic still has much to accomplish. What features might this more complete logic have? The logician C. S. Peirce suggested that the relationship between mind, language, and the world was irreducibly ternary, that one could not give an adequate account of the binary relation between mind and language, or between language and the world, without giving an account of the relationship among all three. According to this view, the division of labor depicted above, and with it the divorce of logic from cognition, is misguided. Peirce's thinking has been reincarnated in the situated cognition movement, which argues that any adequate cognitive theory must take account of the agent's physical embeddedness in its environment and its exploitation of regularities in that environment (see SITUATEDNESS/EMBEDDEDNESS).

Situatedness infects reasoning and logic (Barwise 1987). The ease or difficulty of an inference, for example, depends on the agent's context in many ways. Even the validity of an inference is in a limited sense a situated matter because validity depends not just on the sentences used, but on how they are used by the agent. This arises in our sample argument in the requirement that the meaning of the terms be held constant. The way the agent is situated in the world in part determines whether this caveat is satisfied. For example, if the agent uttered the two premises in different years, the conclusion would not follow.

Logic has had a profound impact on cognitive science, as the above examples show. The impact in the other direction has been less than one might have expected, due to the distrust of cognitive aspects of reasoning by the logic community. One hopes that the synergy between the two fields will be greater in years to come.

See also CAUSAL REASONING; DEDUCTIVE REASONING; INDEXICALS AND DEMONSTRATIVES; LANGUAGE OF THOUGHT; LOGIC PROGRAMMING; LOGICAL OMNISCIENCE, PROBLEM OF; POSSIBLE WORLDS SEMANTICS

—K. Jon Barwise

References

Barwise, J. (1987). *The Situation in Logic.* Stanford, CA: CSLI Publications.

Barwise, J., and R. Cooper. (1981). Generalized quantifiers and natural language. *Linguistics and Philosophy* 4: 137–154.

Fodor, J. A. (1975). *The Language of Thought.* New York: Crowell.

Feferman, S. (1996). Penrose's Goedelian argument. *Psyche* 2: 21–32.

Glasgow, J. I., N. H. Narayan, and B. Chandrasekaran, Eds. (1991). *Diagrammatic Reasoning: Cognitive and Computational Perspectives.* Cambridge, MA: AAAI/MIT Press.

Hammer, E. (1995). *Logic and Visual Information. Studies in Logic, Language, and Computation.* Stanford, CA: CSLI Publications.

Hilbert, D. (1928/1967). Die Grundlagen der Mathematik. Eng. title (The foundations of mathematics). *Abhandlugen aus dem mathematischen Seminar der Hamburgischen Universität* 6: 65–85. In J. van Heijenoort, Ed., *From Frege to Gödel.* Cambridge, MA: Harvard University Press, pp. 464–479.

Johnson-Laird, P. N., and R. Byrne. (1991). *Deduction. Essays in Cognitive Psychology.* Mahwah, NJ: Erlbaum.

Montague, R. (1974). *Formal Philosophy: Selected Papers of Richard Montague.* Edited with an introduction by Richmond Thomason. New Haven: Yale University Press.

Penrose, R. (1991). *The Emperor's New Mind: Concerning Computers, Minds, and the Laws of Physics.* New York: Penguin.

Rips, L. (1994). *The Psychology of Proof.* Cambridge, MA: MIT Press.

Turing, A. (1936). On computable numbers, with an application to the Entscheidungsproblem. *Proc. London Math. Soc.* Series 2, 42: 230–265.

Further Readings

Barwise, J., Ed. (1977). *Handbook of Mathematical Logic.* Amsterdam: Elsevier.

Barwise, J., and J. Etchemendy. (1993). *The Language of First-Order Logic.* 3rd ed. Stanford, CA: CSLI Publications.

Barwise, J., and J. Perry. (1983). *Situations and Attitudes.* Cambridge, MA: MIT Press.

Devlin, L. (1991). *Logic and Information.* Cambridge: Cambridge University Press.

Gabbay, D., and F. Guenther, Eds. (1983). *Handbook of Philosophical Logic*, 4 vols. Dordrecht: Kluwer.

Gabbay, D., Ed. (1994). *What is a Logical System? Studies in Logic and Computation.* Oxford: Oxford University Press.

Haugland, J. (1985). *Artificial Intelligence: The Very Idea.* Cambridge, MA: MIT Press.

Stenning, K., and P. Yule. (1997). Image and language in human reasoning: A syllogistic illustration. *Cognitive Psychology* 34: 109–159.

Van Benthem, J. and A. ter Meulen, Eds. (1997). *Handbook of Logic and Language.* Amsterdam: Elsevier.

Logic Programming

Logic programming is the use of LOGIC to represent programs and of deduction to execute programs in LOGICAL

FORM. To this end, many different forms of logic and many varieties of deduction have been investigated. The simplest form of logic, which is the basis of most logic programming, is the Horn clause subset of logic, where programs consist of sets of implications: A_0 if A_1 and A_2 and ... and A_n. Here each A_i is a simple (i.e., atomic) sentence.

Because deduction by backward reasoning interprets such implications as procedures, it is usual to write them backward: to solve the goal A_0, solve the subgoals A_1 and A_2 and . . . and A_n. The number of conditions, n, can be 0, in which case the implication is simply a fact, which behaves as a procedure which solves goals directly without introducing subgoals.

The procedural interpretation of implications can be used for declarative programming, where the programmer describes information in logical form and the deduction mechanism uses backward reasoning to achieve problem solving behavior. Consider, for example, the implication

X is a citizen of the United States
    if X was born in the United States.

Backward reasoning treats the sentence as a procedure:

To show X is a citizen of the United States,
    show that X was born in the United States.

In fact, backward reasoning can be used, not only to show a particular person is a citizen, but also to find people who are citizens by virtue of having been born in the United States.

Logic programs are nondeterministic in the sense that many different procedures might apply to the same goal. For example, naturalization and being the child of a citizen provide alternative procedures for obtaining citizenship. The nondeterministic exploration of alternative procedures, to find one or more which solve a given goal, can be performed by many different search strategies. In the logic programming language Prolog, search is performed depth-first, trying procedures one at a time, in the order in which they are written, backtracking in case of failure.

Declarative programming is an ideal. The programmer specifies what the problem is and what knowledge should be used in solving problems, and the computer determines how the knowledge should be used. The declarative programming ideal works in some cases where the knowledge has a particularly simple form. But it fails in many others, where nondeterminism leads to an excessively inefficient search. This failure has led many programmers to reject logic programming in favor of conventional, imperative programming languages.

The following example shows the kind of problem that can arise with declarative programming:

There is a path from X to Y if there is a step from X to Y.

There is a path from X to Y if there is a path from X to Z and there is a path from Z to Y.

Given no other information and the goal of showing whether there is a path from a node a to a node b, Prolog fails to find a step from a to b using the first procedure. It therefore tries to find a path from a to some Z using the second procedure. There is no step from a to any Z using the first procedure. So Prolog tries to find a path from a to some Z using the second procedure. Continuing in this way, it goes into an infinite loop, looking for paths from a to Z, to Z' to Z'', ...

The alternative to rejecting logic programming because of such problems or of restricting it to niche applications, is for the programmer to take responsibility for both the declarative correctness and the procedural efficiency of programs. The following is such a correct and efficient logic program for the path-finding problem. It incrementally constructs a path of nodes already visited and ensures that no step is taken that revisits a node already in the path. The goal of showing there is a path from X to Y is reformulated as the goal of extending the path consisting of the single node X to a path ending at Y. For simplicity, a path is regarded as a trivial extension of itself.

The path P can be extended to a path ending at Y
    if P ends at Y.
The path P can be extended to a path ending at Y
    if P ends at X
and there is a step from X to Z
and Z is not in P
and P' extends P by adding Z to the end of P
and the path P' can be extended to a path ending at Y.

It is usual to interpret the negation in a condition, such as "Z is not in P" above, as negation by failure. A subgoal of the form "not A" is deemed to hold if and only if the positive subgoal "A" cannot be shown to hold. Programs containing such negative conditions, extending the Horn clause subset of logic programming, are called "normal logic programs."

The use of negation as failure renders logic programming a NONMONOTONIC LOGIC, where addition of new information may cause a previously justified conclusion to be withdrawn. A simple example is the sentence

X is innocent if not X is guilty.

The condition "not X is guilty" is interpreted as "it cannot be shown that X is guilty."

Many extensions of normal logic programming have been investigated. Among the most important of these is the extension that includes METAREASONING. For example, the following implication is a fragment of a metalevel logic program that can be used to reason about the interval of time for which a conclusion holds:

"R" holds for interval I
    if "R if S" holds for interval I_1
and "S" holds for interval I_2
and I is the intersection of I_1 and I_2.

Similar metalevel programs are used to construct explanations and to implement resource-bounded reasoning and reasoning with UNCERTAINTY.

Among the other extensions of logic programming being investigated are extensions to incorporate constraint processing, a second "strong" form of negation, disjunctive conclusions, and abductive reasoning. Methods are being developed both to execute programs efficiently and to transform inefficient programs into more efficient ones.

Applications range from natural language processing and legal reasoning to commercial knowledge management systems and parts of the Windows NT operating system.

See also BOUNDED RATIONALITY; CONSTRAINT SATISFACTION; DEDUCTIVE REASONING; INDUCTIVE LOGIC PROGRAMMING; LOGICAL REASONING SYSTEMS; SITUATION CALCULUS

—*Robert Kowalski*

Further Readings

Apt, K., and F. Turini, Eds. (1995). *Meta-Logics and Logic Programming*. Cambridge, MA: MIT Press.

Bratko, I. (1988). *Prolog Programming for Artificial Intelligence*. Reading, MA: Addison-Wesley.

Clark, K. L. (1978). Negation by failure. In H. Gallaire and J. Minker, Eds., *Logic and Databases*. New York: Plenum Press, pp. 293–322.

Colmerauer, A., H. Kanoui, R. Pasero, and P. Roussel. (1973). Un système de communication homme-machine en français. Research report, Groupe d'Intelligence Artificielle. Université d'Aix-Marseilles II, Luminy, France.

Flach, P. (1994). *Simply Logical: Intelligent Reasoning by Example*. New York: Wiley.

Gabbay, D., C. Hogger, and J. A. Robinson. (1993). *Handbook of Logic in Artificial Intelligence and Logic Programming*. Vol. 1, *Logic Foundations*. Oxford: Clarendon Press.

Gabbay, D., C. Hogger, and J. A. Robinson. (1997). *Handbook of Logic in Artificial Intelligence and Logic Programming*. Vol. 5, *Logic Programming*. Oxford: Clarendon Press.

Gillies, D. (1996). *Artificial Intelligence and Scientific Method*. New York: Oxford University Press.

Kowalski, R. (1974). Predicate logic as programming language. In *Proceedings IFIP Congress,* Stockholm. Amsterdam: Elsevier, pp. 569–574.

Kowalski, R. (1979). *Logic for Problem Solving*. Amsterdam: Elsevier.

Kowalski, R. (1992). Legislation as logic programs. In G. Comyn, N. E. Fuchs, and M. J. Ratcliffe, Eds., *Logic Programming in Action*. New York: Springer, pp. 203–230.

Lloyd J. W. (1987). *Foundations of Logic Programming*. 2nd ed. New York: Springer.

Logical Form in Linguistics

The logical form of a sentence (or utterance) is a formal representation of its logical structure—that is, of the structure that is relevant to specifying its logical role and properties. There are a number of (interrelated) reasons for giving a rendering of a sentence's logical form. Among them is to obtain proper inferences (which otherwise would not follow; cf. Russell's theory of descriptions), to give the proper form for the determination of truth-conditions (e.g., Tarski's method of truth and satisfaction as applied to quantification), to show those aspects of a sentence's meaning that follow from the logical role of certain terms (and not from the lexical meaning of words; cf. the truth-functional account of conjunction), and to formalize or regiment the language in order to show that it is has certain metalogical properties (e.g., that it is free of paradox or that there is a sound proof procedure).

Logical analysis—that is, the specification of logical forms for sentences of a language—presumes that some distinction is to be made between the grammatical form of sentences and their logical form. In LOGIC, of course, there is no such distinction to be drawn. By design, the grammatical form of a sentence specified by the syntax of, for instance, first-order predicate logic simply is its logical form. In the case of natural language, however, the received wisdom of the tradition of FREGE, Russell, Wittgenstein, Tarski, Carnap, Quine, and others has been that on the whole, grammatical form and logical form cannot be identified; indeed, their nonidentity has often been given as the *raison d'être* for logical analysis. Natural languages have been held to be insufficiently specified in their grammatical form to reveal directly their logical form, and that no mere paraphrase within the language would be sufficient to do so. This led to the view that, as far as natural languages were concerned, logical analysis was a matter of rendering sentences of the language in some antecedently defined logical (or formal) language, where the relation between the sentences in the languages is to be specified by some sort of contextual definition or rules of translation.

In contemporary linguistic theory, there has been a continuation of this view in work inspired largely by Montague (especially, Montague 1974). In large part because of technical developments in both logic (primarily in the areas of type theories and POSSIBLE WORLDS SEMANTICS) and linguistics (with respect to categorial rule systems), this approach has substantially extended the range of phenomena that could be treated by translation into an interpreted logical language, shedding the pessimism of prior views as to how systematically techniques of logical analysis can be formally applied to natural language (see Partee 1975; Dowty, Wall, and Peters 1981; Cooper 1983). Within linguistic theory, however, the term "logical form" has been much more closely identified with a different view that takes natural language to be in an important sense logical, in that grammatical form can be identified with logical form. The hallmark of this view is that the derivation of logical forms is continuous with the derivation of other syntactic representations of a sentence. As this idea was developed initially by Chomsky and May (with precursors in generative semantics), the levels of syntactic representation included Deep Structure, Surface Structure, and Logical Form (LF), with LF—the set of syntactic structures constituting the "logical forms" of the language—derived from Surface Structure by the same sorts of transformational rules that derived Surface Structure from Deep Structure.

As with other approaches to logical form, quantification provides a central illustration. This is because, since Frege, it has been generally accepted that the treatment of quantification requires a "transformation" of a sentence's surface form. On the LF approach, it was hypothesized (originally in May 1977) that the syntax of natural languages contains a rule—QR, for Quantifier Raising—that derives representations at LF for sentences containing quantifier phrases, functioning syntactically essentially as does WH-MOVEMENT (the rule that derives the structure of "What did Max read?"). By QR, (1) is derived as the representation of

"Every linguist has read *Syntactic Structures*" at LF, and because QR may iterate, the representations in (2) for "Every linguist has read some book by Chomsky".

(1) [every linguist$_1$ [t$_1$ has read *Syntactic Structures*]]

(2) a. [every linguist$_1$ [some book by Chomsky$_2$ [t$_1$ has read t$_1$]]]
    b. [some book by Chomsky$_2$ [every linguist$_1$ [t$_1$ has read t$_2$]]]

With the aid of the syntactic notions of "trace of movement" (t$_1$, t$_2$) and "c-command" (both of which are independently necessary within syntactic theory), the logically significant distinctions of open and closed sentence, and of relative scope of quantifiers, can be easily defined with respect to the sort of representations in (1) and (2). Interpreting the trace in (1) as a variable, "t$_1$ has read *Syntactic Structures*" stands as an open sentence, falling within the scope of the c-commanding quantifier phrase "every linguist$_1$;" similar remarks hold for (2), except that (2a) and (2b) can be recognized as representing distinct scope orderings of the quantifiers (see Heim 1982; May 1985, 1989; Hornstein and Weinberg 1990; Fox 1995; Beghelli and Stowell 1997; and Reinhart 1997 for further discussion of the treatment of quantification within the LF approach). A wide range of arguments have been made for the LF approach to logical form. Illustrative of the sort of argument presented is the argument from antecedent-contained deletion (May 1985). A sentence such as "Dulles suspected everyone that Angleton did" has a verb phrase elided (its position is marked by the pro-form "did"). If, however, the ellipsis is to be "reconstructed" on the basis of the surface form, the result will be a structural regress, as the "antecedent" verb phrase, "suspected everyone that Angleton did" itself contains the ellipsis site. However, if the reconstruction is defined with respect to a structure derived by QR:

(3) everyone that Angleton did [Dulles suspected t],

the antecedent is now the VP "suspected t," obtaining, properly, an LF-representation comparable in form to that which would result if there had been no deletion:

(4) everyone that Angleton suspected t [Dulles suspected t].

Among other well-known arguments for LF are weak crossover (Chomsky 1976), the interaction of quantifier scope and bound variable anaphora (Higginbotham 1980; Higginbotham and May 1981), superiority effects with multiple *wh*-constructions (Aoun, Hornstein, and Sportiche 1981) and *wh*-complementation in languages without overt *wh*-movement (Huang 1982). Over the past two decades, there has been active discussion in linguistic theory of the precise nature of representations at LF, in particular with respect to the representation of binding (see BINDING THEORY) as this pertains to quantification and ANAPHORA, and of the semantic interpretation of such representations (cf. Larson and Segal 1995). This has taken place within a milieu of evolving conceptions of SYNTAX and SEMANTICS and has led to considerable refinement in our conceptions of the structure of logical forms and the range of phenomena

that can be analyzed. Constant in these discussions has been the assumption that logical form is integrated into syntactic description generally, and hence that the thesis that natural languages are logical is ultimately an empirical issue within the general theory of syntactic rules and principles.

See also COMPOSITIONALITY; LOGICAL FORM, ORIGINS OF; MORPHOLOGY; QUANTIFIERS; SYNTAX-SEMANTICS INTERFACE

—Robert C. May

References

Aoun, J., N. Hornstein, and D. Sportiche (1981). Some aspects of wide scope quantification. *Journal of Linguistic Research* 1: 69–95.

Beghelli, F., and T. Stowell (1997). Distributivity and negation: The syntax of *each* and *every*. In A. Szabolcsi, Ed., *Ways of Taking Scope*. Dordrecht: Kluwer.

Chomsky, N. (1976). Conditions on rules of grammar. *Linguistic Analysis* 2: 303–351.

Cooper, R. (1983). *Quantification and Syntactic Theory*. Dordrecht: Reidel.

Dowty, D., R. E. Wall, and S. Peters. (1981). *Introduction to Montague Semantics*. Dordrecht: Reidel.

Fox, D. (1995). Economy and scope. *Natural Language Semantics* 3: 283–341.

Higginbotham, J. (1980). Pronouns and bound variables. *Linguistic Inquiry* 11: 679–708.

Higginbotham, J., and R. May (1981). Questions, quantifiers, and crossing. *The Linguistic Review* 1: 41–79.

Heim, I. (1982). *The Semantics of Definite and Indefinite Noun Phrases*. Ph.D. diss., University of Massachusetts, Amherst.

Hornstein, N., and A. Weinberg. (1990). The necessity of LF. *The Linguistic Review* 7: 129–168.

Huang, C.-T. J. (1982). *Logical Relations in Chinese and the Theory of Grammar*. Ph.D. diss., Massachusetts Institute of Technology.

Larson, R., and G. Segal. (1995). *Knowledge of Meaning*. Cambridge, MA: MIT Press.

May, R. (1977). *The Grammar of Quantification*. Ph.D. diss., Massachusetts Institute of Technology. (Facsimile edition published by Garland Publishing, New York, 1991.)

May, R. (1985). *Logical Form: Its Structure and Derivation*. Cambridge, MA: MIT Press.

May, R. (1989). Interpreting logical form. *Linguistics and Philosophy* 12: 387–435.

Montague, R. (1974). The proper treatment of quantification in ordinary English. In R. Thomason, Ed., *Formal Philosophy: Selected Papers of Richard Montague*. New Haven, CT: Yale University Press.

Partee, B. (1975). Montague grammar and transformational grammar. *Linguistic Inquiry* 6: 203–300.

Reinhart, T. (1997). Quantifier scope: How labor is divided between QR and choice functions. *Linguistics and Philosophy* 20: 399–467.

Further Readings

Chomsky, N. (1995). *The Minimalist Program*. Cambridge, MA: MIT Press.

Fiengo, R., and R. May (1994). *Indices and Identity*. Cambridge, MA: MIT Press.

Frege, G. (1892). On Sense and Reference, trans. by M. Black. In P. Geach and M. Black, Eds., *Translations from the Philosophical Writings of Gottlob Frege*. Oxford: Blackwell.

Hornstein, N. (1984). *Logic as Grammar.* Cambridge, MA: MIT Press.

Hornstein, N. (1995). *Logical Form.* Oxford: Blackwell.

Jaeggli, O. (1980). *On Some Phonologically Null Elements of Syntax.* Ph.D. diss., Massachusetts Institute of Technology.

Koopman, H., and D. Sportiche. (1982). Variables and the bijection principle. *The Linguistic Review* 2: 139–161.

Lakoff, G. (1972). On Generative Semantics. In D. Steinberg and L. Jakobovits, Eds., *Semantics.* Cambridge: Cambridge University Press, pp. 232–296.

May, R. (1991a). Syntax, semantics, and logical form. In A. Kasher, Ed., *The Chomskyan Turn.* Oxford: Blackwell.

May, R. (1991b). Linguistic theory and the naturalist approach to semantics. In D. J. Napoli and J. Kegl, Eds., *Bridges Between Psychology and Linguistics: A Swarthmore Festschrift for Lila Gleitman.* Hillsdale, NJ: Erlbaum.

Pesetsky, D. (1987). Wh-in-situ: movement and selective binding. In E. Reuland and A. ter Meulen, Eds., *The Representation of (In)definiteness.* Cambridge, MA: MIT Press.

Quine, W. V. O. (1960). *Word and Object.* Cambridge, MA: MIT Press.

Russell, B. (1905). On denoting. *Mind* 14: 479–493.

Wittgenstein, L. (1922). *Tractatus Logico-Philosophicus,* trans. by D. F. Pears and B. F. McGuiness. London: Routledge and Kegan Paul.

Logical Form, Origins of

When philosophers use the expression "the Logical Form of a sentence," they refer to a linguistic representation whose desirable properties the surface grammatical form of the sentence either masks or lacks completely. Because philosophers have found ever so many desirable properties hidden or absent in grammatical form, there are ever so many different notions of Logical Form.

According to one tradition, which one might call the "descriptive conception" of Logical Form, the Logical Form of a sentence is something like the "deep structure" of that sentence (e.g., Harman 1972), and we may discover that the "real" structure of a natural language sentence is in fact quite distinct from its surface grammatical form. Talk of Logical Form in this sense involves attributing hidden complexity to natural language, complexity that may be revealed by philosophical, and indeed empirical, inquiry (see LOGICAL FORM IN LINGUISTICS). However, perhaps more common in the recent history of philosophy is what one might call the "revisionary conception" of Logical Form. According to it, natural language is defective in some fundamental way. Appeals to Logical Form are appeals to a kind of linguistic representation which is intended to replace natural language for the purposes of scientific or mathematical investigation (e.g., Frege 1879, preface; Whitehead and Russell 1910, introduction; Russell 1918, 58).

Nineteeth-century debates concerning the foundations of the calculus are one source of the revisionary flavor of some contemporary conceptions of Logical Form (e.g., Quine 1960, 248ff.). Perhaps the most vivid example is the overthrow of the infinitesimal calculus, which began with the work of Cauchy in the 1820s. Cauchy took the notation of the infinitesimal calculus, which contained explicit reference to infinitesimals, and reanalyzed it in terms of a notation that exploited the limit concept, and made no reference to infinitesimals. It subsequently emerged that the limit concept was analyzable in terms of logical notions, such as quantification, together with unproblematic numerical concepts. Thus progress in nineteenth-century mathematics involved replacing a notation that made explicit reference to undesirable entities (viz., infinitesimals) with a notation in which reference to such entities was replaced by logical and numerical operations on more acceptable ones (noninfinitesimal real numbers).

Bertrand Russell (e.g., 1903) was clearly affected by the developments in nineteenth-century mathematics, though his proposals (1905) have both revisionary and descriptive aspects. In them Russell treated the problem of negative existential sentences, such as "Pegasus does not exist." The difficulty with this sentence is that its grammatical form suggests that endorsing its truth commits one to the existence of a denotation for the proper name "Pegasus," which could be none other than that winged horse. Yet what the sentence seems to assert is precisely the nonexistence of such a being.

According to Russell, the problem lies in taking the grammatical form to be a true guide to the structure of the proposition it expresses, that is, in taking the surface grammatical form to exhibit the commitments of its endorsement. In Russell's view, the structure of the proposition expressed by "Pegasus does not exist" differs markedly from the grammatical form. Rather than being "about" Pegasus, its structure is more adequately reflected by a sentence such as "It is not the case that there exists a unique thing having properties F, G, and H," where F, G, and H are the properties we typically associate with the fictional winged horse. Once this is accepted, we may endorse the truth of "Pegasus does not exist" without fear of admitting Pegasus into the realm of being.

Russell took himself not as proposing a special level of linguistic representation, but rather as proposing what the true structure of the (nonlinguistic) proposition expressed by the sentence was. Russell's early writings are therefore no doubt the origin of the occasional usage of "Logical Form" as referring to the structure of a nonlinguistic entity such as a proposition or a fact (e.g., Wittgenstein 1922, 1929; Sainsbury 1991, 35). However, Russell's proposal could just as easily be adopted as a claim about a special sort of linguistic representation, one that allows us to say what we think is true, while freeing us from the absurd consequences endorsement of the original grammatical form would entail (Russell, after his rejection of propositions, himself construed it in this way). Thus arises a conception of Logical Form as a level of linguistic representation at which the metaphysical commitments of the sentences are completely explicit. This conception of Logical Form was later to achieve full articulation in the works of Quine (e.g., 1960, chaps. 5, 7).

Nineteenth-century mathematics not only provided successful examples of notational revision; it also provided many examples of notational confusion (Wilson 1994 argues that this was not necessarily a tragic situation). One of Frege's central purposes (1879, Preface) was to provide a notation free of such confusion, devoid of vagueness, ambiguity, and context dependence, whose purpose was "to provide us with the most reliable test of the validity of a chain of inferences and to point out every presupposition that tries to sneak in unnoticed . . . ." Frege's remarks here suggest a test of the validity of arguments in terms of the syntax of his idealized language. According to this criterion, a chain of reasoning is logically valid if and only if its translation into his idealized "Begriffsschrift" proceeds by transitions, each of which is of the right syntactic form. Thus arises a conception of Logical Form as a linguistic representation for which it is possible to designate certain syntactic forms such that all and only basic logical transitions are translatable into instances of those forms (see LOGIC).

The purpose of formalization into Logical Form is to replace one notation by another, which has desirable properties which the original notation lacked. In the case of the Quinean conception of Logical Form, the purpose of formalization is to replace a notation (in the usual case, natural language) by one which more accurately reveals ontological commitments. In the case of the Fregean conception, the purpose of formalization is to replace notations which obscure the logical structure of sentences by one which makes this structure explicit (these are not necessarily conflicting goals). Many other conceptions of Logical Form have been proposed. For example, Richard Montague's favored way of giving an interpretation to a fragment of natural language involved translating that fragment into an artificial language, for example, the language of "tensed intensional logic" (Montague 1973), and then giving a formal semantic interpretation to the artificial language. This produces a conception of Logical Form as a level of linguistic representation at which a compositional semantics is best given (see COMPOSITIONALITY and SEMANTICS).

Strictly revisionary conceptions of Logical Form involve abstracting from features of the original notation that are problematic in various ways. Because notations may be problematic in some ways and not in others, in such a use of "Logical Form," there is no issue about what the "correct" notion of Logical Form is. Descriptive conceptions, on the other hand, involve claims about the "true" structure of the original notation, structure that is masked by the surface grammatical form. Someone who makes a proposal, in the purely descriptive mode, about the "true" Logical Form of a natural language sentence thus runs the risk that her claims will be vitiated by linguistic theory. To avoid this danger, most philosophers vascillate between a revisionary and descriptive use of the expression "Logical Form."

The tension between descriptive and revisionary conceptions of Logical Form mirrors a tension in the cognitive sciences generally. According to some, cognitive science should be interested in explaining the possession of abstract cognitive abilities such as thinking and language use in humans, and we should be interested, not in the most ideal representations of thought and language, but rather in how humans think and speak. If so, we should be interested in Logical Form only insofar as it is plausibly associated with natural language on some level of empirical analysis. According to others, cognitive sciences should be interested in the abstract properties of thinking and speaking, and we

should be interested in arriving at an ideal representational system, one that may abstract from the defects of human natural language. Among such thinkers, the revisionary project of replacing natural language by a representation more suitable for scientific purposes is fundamental to the aims of cognitive science.

See also EXTENSIONALITY, THESIS OF; FREGE; LANGUAGE AND THOUGHT; REFERENCE, THEORIES OF; SYNTAX-SEMANTICS INTERFACE

—*Jason Stanley*

References

Frege, G. (1879). Begriffsschrift: A formula language, modeled upon that of arithmetic, for pure thought. In Van Heijenoort, Ed., *From Frege to Godel: A Sourcebook in Mathematical Logic, 1879–1931*. Cambridge: Harvard University Press, 1967, pp. 5–82.

Harman, G. (1972). Deep structure as logical form. In D. Davidson and G. Harman, Eds., *Semantics of Natural Language*. Dordrecht: Reidel.

Montague, R. (1973). The proper treatment of quantification in ordinary English. In J. Hintikka, H. Moravcsik, and P. Suppes, Eds., *Approaches to Natural Language: Proceedings of the 1970 Stanford Workshop on Grammar and Semantics*. Dordrecht: Reidel, pp. 221–242.

Quine, W. V. O. (1960). *Word and Object*. Cambridge, MA: MIT Press.

Russell, B. (1903). *Principles of Mathematics*. Cambridge: Cambridge University Press.

Russell, B. (1905). On denoting. *Mind* 14: 479–493.

Russell, B. (1918/1985). *The Philosophy of Logical Atomism*. LaSalle: Open Court.

Sainsbury, M. (1991). *Logical Forms: An Introduction to Philosophical Logic*. London: Routledge and Kegan Paul.

Whitehead, A., and B. Russell. (1910). *Principia Mathematica*. Cambridge: Cambridge University Press.

Wilson, M. (1994). Can we trust Logical Form? *Journal of Philosophy* October 91: 519–544.

Wittgenstein, L. (1922). *Tractatus Logico-Philosophicus*. Translated by C. K. Ogden. London: Routledge and Kegan Paul.

Wittgenstein, L. (1929). Some remarks on Logical Form. Vol 9, *Proceedings of the Aristotelean Society*.

Logical Omniscience, Problem of

Knowers or believers are *logically omniscient* if they know or believe all of the consequences of their knowledge or beliefs. That is, x is a logically omniscient believer (knower) if and only if the set of all of the propositions believed (known) by x is closed under logical consequence. It is obvious that if belief and knowledge are understood in their ordinary sense, then no nonsupernatural agent, real or artificial, will be logically omniscient. Despite this obvious fact, many formal representations of states of knowledge and belief, and some explanations of what it is to know or believe, have the consequence that agents are logically omniscient. This is why there is a problem of logical omniscience.

There are a number of different formal representations of knowledge and belief that face a problem of logical omniscience. POSSIBLE WORLDS SEMANTICS for knowledge and belief, first developed by Jaakko Hintikka, represent a state of knowledge by a set of possible worlds—the worlds that are epistemically possible for the knower. According to this analysis, x knows that P if and only if P is true in all epistemically possible worlds. Epistemic models using this kind of analysis have been widely applied by theoretical computer scientists studying distributed systems (see MULTIAGENT SYSTEMS), and by economists studying GAME THEORY. As Hintikka noted from the beginning of the development of semantic models for epistemic logic, this analysis implies that knowers are logically omniscient.

Because all logical truths in any probability function must receive probability one, and because any logical consequences of a proposition P must receive at least as great a probability as P (at least if one holds fixed the context in which probability assessments are made; see RATIONAL DECISION MAKING), any use of probability theory to represent the beliefs and partial beliefs of an agent will face a version of the problem of logical omniscience.

It is not only abstract formal representations, but also some philosophical explanations of the nature of belief and knowledge that seem to imply that knowers and believers are logically omniscient. First, pragmatic or INTENTIONAL STANCE accounts of belief assume that belief and desire are correlative dispositions displayed in rational action. Roughly, according to such accounts, to believe that P is to act in ways that would be apt in situations in which P (together with one's other beliefs) is true. This kind of analysis of belief will imply that believers are logically omniscient. Second, because the logical consequences of any information carried by some state of a system are also information implicit in the state (see also INFORMATIONAL SEMANTICS and PROPOSITIONAL ATTITUDES), any account of knowledge based on INFORMATION THEORY will face a prima facie problem of logical omniscience.

There are two contrasting ways to reconcile a theory implying that agents are logically omniscient with the obvious fact that they are not. First, one may take the theory to represent a special sense of knowledge or belief that diverges from the ordinary one. For example, one may take the theory to be modeling *implicit knowledge,* understood to include, by definition, all of the consequences of one's knowledge; ordinary knowers are logically omniscient with respect to their implicit knowledge, but have no extraordinary computational powers. Alternatively, one may take the theory to be modeling the knowledge (in the ordinary sense) of an idealized agent, a fictional ideal agent with infinite computational capacities that enable her to make all her implicit knowledge explicit.

Either of these approaches may succeed in reconciling the counterintuitive consequences of theories of belief and knowledge with the phenomena, but there remains a problem, for the first approach, of explaining what explicit knowledge is, and how it is distinguished from merely implicit knowledge. And the second approach must explain the relevance an idealized agent, all of whose implicit beliefs are available, to the behavior of real agents. If the knowledge and beliefs of nonideal agents—agents who have only BOUNDED RATIONALITY—are to contribute to an explanation of their behavior, we need to be able to distinguish the beliefs that are accessible or available to the agent, and to do this, we need an account of what it means for a belief to be available. Because a belief might be available to influence the rational behavior of an agent even if the agent is unable to produce or recognize a linguistic expression of the belief, it will not suffice to distinguish *articulate* beliefs—those beliefs that an agent can express or to which he is disposed to assent. And because one's beliefs about one's beliefs may themselves be merely implicit, and unavailable, one cannot explain the difference between available and merely implicit belief in terms of higher-order belief.

It may appear to be an advantage of a LANGUAGE OF THOUGHT account of belief that it avoids the problem of logical omniscience. If it is assumed that an agent's explicit beliefs are beliefs encoded in a mental language and stored in the "belief box," then one's theory will not imply that the consequences of the agent's explicit beliefs are also explicit beliefs. But explicit belief in this sense is neither necessary nor sufficient for a plausible notion of accessible or available belief. Although the immediate and obvious consequences of one's explicit beliefs may count intuitively as beliefs in the ordinary sense, thus also as available beliefs even if they are not explicitly represented, beliefs that are explicitly represented may nevertheless remain inaccessible. If the set of explicit beliefs is large, the search required to access an explicit belief could be a nontrivial computational task.

A general problem for the analysis of available belief is that one can distinguish between beliefs that are available or accessible and those that are not only in relation to the particular uses of the belief. Consider the talented but inarticulate chess player whose implicit knowledge of the strategic situation is available to guide her play, but not to explain or justify her choices.

While it is obvious that real agents are never logically omniscient, it is not at all clear how to give a plausible account of knowledge and belief that does not have the consequence that they are.

See also COMPUTATIONAL COMPLEXITY; IMPLICIT VS. EXPLICIT MEMORY; RATIONAL AGENCY

—*Robert Stalnaker*

Further Readings

Dretske, F. (1981). *Knowledge and the Flow of Information.* Cambridge, MA: MIT Press.

Fagin, R., J. Y. Halpern, Y. Moses, and M. Y. Vardi. (1995). *Reasoning about Knowledge.* Cambridge, MA: MIT Press.

Hintikka, J. J. K. (1962). *Knowledge and Belief.* Ithaca, NY: Cornell University Press.

Levesque, H. J. (1984). A logic of implicit and explicit belief. In *Proceedings of the Conference on Artificial Intelligence.* Menlo Park, CA: AAAI Press, pp. 188–202.

Lipman, B. L. (1994). An axiomatic approach to the logical omniscience problem. In R. Fagin, Ed., *Theoretical Aspects of Reasoning about Knowledge: Proceedings of the Fifth Conference.* San Francisco: Morgan Kaufman, pp. 182–196.

Parikh, R. (1987). Knowledge and the problem of logical omniscience. In Z. W. Ras and M. Zemankova, Eds., *Methodologies of Intelligent Systems.* The Hague: Elsevier, pp. 432–439.

Stalnaker, R. (1991). The problem of logical omniscience, I. *Synthese* 89: 425–440.

Logical Reasoning Systems

Logical reasoning systems derive sound conclusions from formal declarative knowledge. Such systems are usually defined by abstract *rules of inference*. For example, the rule of modus ponens states that given P, and "P implies Q" (usually written $P \rightarrow Q$), we can infer Q. Logical systems have a rich history, starting with Greek syllogisms and continuing through the work of many prominent mathematicians such as DESCARTES, Leibniz, Boole, FREGE, Hilbert, Gödel, and Cohen. (For a good discussion of the history of logical reasoning systems, see Davis 1983.)

Logical reasoning provides a well-understood general method of symbolic COMPUTATION. Symbolic computation manipulates expressions involving variables. For example, a computer algebra system can simplify the expression $x(x + 1)$ to $x^2 + x$. The equation $x(x + 1) = x^2 + x$ is true under any interpretation of x as a real number. Unlike numerical computation, symbolic computation derives truths that hold under a wide variety of interpretations and can be used when only partial information is given, for example, that x is some (unknown) real number. Logical inference systems can be used to perform symbolic computation with variables that range over conceptual domains such as sets, sequences, graphs, and computer data structures. Symbolic computation underlies essentially all modern efforts to formally verify computer hardware and software.

There are at least two ways in which symbolic inference is relevant to cognitive science. First, symbolic inference rules have traditionally been used as models of human mathematical reasoning. Second, symbolic computation also provides a model of certain commonsense inferences. For example, suppose one is given a bag of marbles and continues removing marbles from the bag for as long as it remains nonempty. People easily reach the conclusion that, barring unusual or magical circumstances, the bag will eventually become empty. They reach this conclusion without being told any particular number of marbles—they reach a conclusion about an arbitrary set s. Computer systems for drawing such conclusions based on "visualization" do not currently work as well as approaches based on symbolic computation (McAllester 1991).

Here I will divide symbolic computation research into five general approaches. First are the so-called symbolic algebra systems such as Maple or Mathematica (Wolfram 1996), designed to manipulate expressions satisfying certain algebraic properties such as those satisfied by the real numbers. Although they have important applications in the physical sciences, these systems are not widely used for hardware or software verification and seem too specialized to provide plausible models of commonsense reasoning. Second are the symbolic model-checking systems (Burch et al. 1990), which perform symbolic inference where the variables range over finite sets such as the finite set of possible states of a certain piece of computer hardware. Although very effective for the finitary problems where they apply, these systems are too restricted for software verification and also seem too restricted to provide plausi-

ble models of commonsense reasoning. The remaining three approaches to symbolic computation all claim to be general purpose or domain independent. I will call these the "first-order approach," the "higher-order approach," and the "induction approach," respectively, and discuss each in turn.

The first-order approach is based on making inferences from axioms written in first-order LOGIC, which includes a wide variety of resolution and term-rewriting systems (Fitting 1996). For problems that can be naturally axiomatized in first-order logic, the first-order approach seems superior to other approaches. Unfortunately, most mathematical theorems and verification problems have no natural first-order formulation. Although detailed discussion of first-order logic and inference methods is beyond the scope of this entry, it is possible to give a somewhat superficial description of its limitations. First-order logic allows us to state properties of concepts, but not generally to *define* concepts. For example, suppose we want to describe the concept of a finite set. We can write a formal expression stating, "A set is finite if it is either empty or can be derived by adding a single element to some other finite set." Unfortunately, this statement does not uniquely determine the concept—it is also true that "a set is countable if it is either empty or can be derived by adding a single element to some other countable set." Statements true of a concept often fail to uniquely specify them. Finiteness is not definable in first-order logic. The bag of marbles inference mentioned above implicitly relies on finiteness. Almost all program verfication problems involve concepts not definable in first-order logic. Methods of simulating more expressive logics in first-order logic are generally inferior in practice to systems specifically designed to go beyond first-order logic.

Higher-order systems allow quantification over predicates (i.e., concepts; Gordon 1987). Finiteness is definable in higher-order logics—by quantifying over predicates, we can say that "finite" is the *least* predicate satisfying the condition given in the paragraph above. Unfortunately, because higher-order logic makes automation difficult, computer systems based on higher-order logic typically verify human-written derivations rather than attempt to find derivations automatically.

Induction systems represent a middle ground between the expressively weak first-order resolution and term-rewriting systems and the expressively strong systems based on higher-order logic (Boyer and Moore 1979). Induction systems are "first-order" in the sense that they do not typically allow quantification over predicates. But, unlike true first-order systems, all objects are assumed to be finite. A variable in a symbolic expression ranges over infinitely many different possible values, each of which is a finite object. This is different from symbolic model checking, where each variable ranges over only a finite number of possible values. Also, induction systems allow well-founded recursive definitions of the kind used in functional programming languages. The underlying logic of an induction system is best viewed as a programming language, such as cons-car-cdr Lisp. But unlike traditional implementations of a programming language, an induction system can derive symbolic equations that are true under any allowed interpretation of the variables appearing in the expressions, such as the following:

$$append(x,append(y,z)) = append(append(x,y),z).$$

Induction systems seem most appropriate for program verification and for modeling commonsense reasoning about an arbitrary (or unknown) finite set.

See also CAUSAL REASONING; DEDUCTIVE REASONING; FORMAL SYSTEMS, PROPERTIES OF; MENTAL MODELS; PROBABILISTIC REASONING; RULES AND REPRESENTATIONS

—David McAllester

References

Boyer, R. S., and J. S. Moore. (1979). *A Computational Logic.* ACM Monograph Series. Academic Press.

Burch, J. R., E. M. Clarke, K. L. McMillan, D. L. Dill, and J. Hwang. (1990). Symbolic model checking: 10^{20} states and beyond. In *Proceedings of the Fifth Annual* IEEE *Symposium on Logic in Computer Science.* IEEE Computer Society Press.

Davis, M. (1983). The prehistory and early history of automated deduction. In J. Seikmann and G. Wrightson, Eds., *Automation of Reasoning*, vol. 1. Springer.

Fitting, M. (1996). *First-Order Logic and Automated Theorem Proving.* 2nd ed. Springer.

Gordon, M. (1987). Hol: A proof generating system for higher-order logic. In G. Birtwistle and P. A. Subrahmanyam, Eds., *VLSI Specification, Verification, and Synthesis.* Kluwer.

McAllester, D. (1991). Some observations on cognitive judgments. In *AAAI-91* Kaufmann, pp. 910–915.

Wolfram, S. (1996). *Mathematica.* 3rd ed. Wolfram Media and Cambridge University Press.

Long-Term Potentiation

Long-term potentiation (LTP) is operationally defined as a long-lasting increase in synaptic efficacy in response to high-frequency stimulation of afferent fibers. The increase in synaptic efficacy persists from minutes to days and is thus a robust example of a long-term increase in synaptic strength. LTP was first observed in the rabbit hippocampus (Bliss and Lomo 1973), but has since been observed in numerous brain structures, including the cortex, brain stem, and amygdala. LTP is not limited to the mammalian brain, but occurs in other vertebrates such as fish, frogs, birds, and reptiles, as well as in some invertebrates (Murphy and Glanzman 1997).

LTP occurs at all three major synaptic connections in the HIPPOCAMPUS: the perforant path synapse to dentate gyrus granule cells, mossy fibers to CA3 pyramidal cells, and the Schaffer collaterals of CA3 cells to CA1 pyramidal cells. Based on its prevalence and initial discovery there, LTP is most often studied in the hippocampus. Within the hippocampus, the cellular and molecular mechanisms that underlie the induction and expression of LTP are varied. In the dentate gyrus and area CA1, the induction of LTP occurs through activation of the postsynaptic *N*-methyl-*D*-aspartate (NMDA) type of glutamate receptor and consequent calcium influx (Collingridge, Kehl, and McLennan 1983), while its expression is accompanied by an increase in postsynaptic current mediated by the AMPA (α-amino-3-hydroxy-5-methyl-4-isoxazole propionic acid) type of glutamate receptor. In contrast, the induction of mossy fiber LTP in area CA3 is not dependent on NMDA receptor activation, but is dependent on an increase in presynaptic glutamate release (Castillo et al. 1997).

A primary focus of those involved in LTP research is to elucidate the cellular and molecular mechanisms necessary for sustaining the increase in synaptic efficacy over long periods of time. Most of these studies are conducted in neural tissue that is excised and maintained in an in vitro slice environment for physiological recording. Using this technique, it has been determined that the late phases of LTP maintenance are dependent on protein synthesis and there is some evidence that gene transcription is required. Although controversial, it has been proposed that LTP in the dentate gyrus and CA1 is expressed as an increase in affinity or number of postsynaptic AMPA receptors (Lynch and Baudry 1991). Others postulate that the expression is mediated by a persistent increase in the release of presynaptic glutamate, which is induced by a release of retrograde messengers from the postsynaptic neuron during LTP induction. In area CA1 and the dentate gyrus, the long-term expression of LTP is likely to be mediated by a combination of postsynaptic and presynaptic events, and a consequence of activation of various enzyme systems (Roberson, English, and Sweatt 1996; Abel et al. 1997). There is some evidence that LTP induces structural changes at the synapse (Buchs and Muller 1996), as well as induction of new sites of synaptic transmission (Bolshakov et al. 1997). Based on this cursory review, it should be clear that LTP is a complex phenomenon that involves the interaction of multiple cellular and molecular systems; the exact contribution of each has yet to be determined.

In addition to being a robust example of persistent changes in synaptic plasticity, LTP has been promoted as a putative neural mechanism of associative MEMORY formation or storage in the mammalian brain. It is generally believed that memory formation occurs through a strengthening of connections between neurons. In 1949, Donald HEBB wrote that, "When an axon of cell A ... excite(s) cell B and repeatedly or persistently takes part in firing it, some growth process or metabolic change takes place in one or both cells so that A's efficiency as one of the cells firing B is increased" (p. 62). This supposition, known as Hebb's rule, is similar to the operational definition of LTP and is often cited as theoretical support for the putative role of LTP in learning and memory. In addition to theoretical support, the biological characteristics of LTP are in some respects similar to those of memory. First, LTP is prominent in the hippocampus, a structure considered necessary for aspects of declarative and spatial memory (Squire 1992). Second, LTP is long lasting, as is memory. Most forms of electrophysiological plasticity last milliseconds to seconds, while LTP persists from minutes to hours, even days (Staubli and Lynch 1987). In addition, LTP possesses physiological correlates of associativity and cooperativity, both properties of learning associated with classical CONDITIONING (Brown, Kairiss, and Keenan 1990). Finally, hippocampal LTP is optimally induced with a pattern of stimulation that mimics "theta," a naturally occurring brain rhythm (Larson and Lynch 1989). Theta rhythms are most often associated with motor activity and dreaming (Vanderwolf and Cain 1994), although they have been reported to occur in the hippocampus during learning (Otto et al. 1991) and stressful experience (Vanderwolf and Cain 1994; Shors and Matzel 1997).

Many behavioral studies addressing the role of LTP in memory take advantage of the fact that most types of LTP are dependent on NMDA receptor activation (Collingridge, Kehl, and McLennan 1983). When these receptors are blocked with competitive antagonists, rats are impaired in their ability to perform the Morris water maze, a spatial memory task that requires the hippocampus for acquisition. Recent evidence suggests that even during NMDA receptor blockade, rats can learn the location of new spatial cues if they were previously trained on a similar spatial task (Saucier and Cain 1995; Bannerman et al. 1995). Thus, NMDA receptor activation may not be necessary for learning about spatial cues per se, but may be involved in other aspects of performance necessary for successful completion of the task (Morris and Frey 1997; Shors and Matzel 1997). In addition to maze performance, NMDA receptor antagonists prevent fear conditioning (Kim et al. 1991), fear-potentiated startle (Campeau, Miserendino, and Davis 1992) and classic eyeblink conditioning (Servatius and Shors 1996). These tasks are not dependent on the hippocampus but rather are dependent on the AMYGDALA and CEREBELLUM, respectively. Thus, if LTP does play a role in memory, it may not be limited to hippocampal-dependent memories.

The relationship between LTP and learning has also been addressed using genetic techniques. Using a transgenic mouse in which a mutated and calcium-independent form of calmodulin (CaM) kinase II was expressed, researchers reported that LTP in response to theta-burst stimulation was reduced, as was the acquisition of spatial memories. In addition, the mutant mice possessed unstable and imprecise place cells in the hippocampus (Rotenberg et al. 1996). In another study, researchers expressed an inhibitory form of a protein kinase A regulatory subunit in mice and observed deficits in the late phase of LTP as well as deficits in hippocampal-dependent conditioning (Abel et al. 1997). Because the genes are altered throughout the life span, some deficits in plasticity and learning could be due to the abnormal developmental responses. Recently, transient knockouts have become available, providing more temporally and anatomically discrete lesions. Removal of a specific subunit of the NMDA receptor in the hippocampus after development disrupted LTP and spatial learning in the Morris water maze (Tsien, Huerta, and Tonegawa 1996).

A long-term increase in synaptic strength and efficacy is considered by many to be the best candidate to date for mediating the storage and retrieval of memories in the mammalian brain. This application of synaptic potentiation would constitute a memory system with massive storage capacity and fine resolution. Although appealing in principle, it remains to be determined whether increases in synaptic efficacy, such as LTP, are necessary for memory storage, whether they modify the rate and efficiency of memory formation (Shors and Matzel 1997), or do neither.

See also MEMORY, ANIMAL STUDIES; MEMORY STORAGE, MODULATION OF; NEUROTRANSMITTERS

—*Tracey J. Shors*

References

Abel, T., P. V. Nguyen, M. Barad, T. Deuel, E. R. Kandel, and R. Bourtchouladze. (1997). Genetic demonstration of a role for PKA in the late phase of LTP and in hippocampus-based long-term memory. *Cell* 88: 615–626.

Bannerman, D. M., M. A. Good, S. P. Butcher, M. Ramsay, and R. G. M. Morris. (1995). Distinct components of spatial learning revealed by prior train and NMDA receptor blockade. *Nature* 378: 182–186.

Bliss, T. V. P., and T. Lomo. (1973). Long-lasting potentiation of synaptic transmission in the dentate gyrus of the anesthetized rabbit following stimulation of the perforant path. *Journal of Physiology* 232: 331–356.

Bolshakov, V. Y., H. Golan, E. R. Kandel, and S. A. Siegelbaum. (1997). Recruitment of new sites of synaptic transmission during the cAMP-dependent late phase of LTP at CA3-CA1 synapses in the hippocampus. *Neuron* 19: 635–651.

Brown, T. H., E. W. Kairiss, and C. L. Keenan. (1990). Hebbian synapses: Biophysical mechanisms and algorithms. *Annual Review of Neuroscience* 13: 475–511.

Buchs, P. A., and D. Muller. (1996). Induction of long-term potentiation is associated with major ultrastructural changes of activated synapses. *Proceedings of the National Academy of Sciences* 93: 8040–8045.

Campeau, S., M. J. Miserendino, and M. Davis. (1992). Intra-amygdaloid infusion of the *N*-methyl-*d*-aspartate receptor antagonist AP5 blocks acquisition but not expression of fear-potentiated startle to a conditioned stimulus. *Behavioral Neuroscience* 106: 569–574.

Castillo, P. E., R. Janz, T. C. Sudhof, T. Tzounopoulos, R. C. Malenka, and R. A. Nicoll. (1997). Rab3A is essential for mossy fiber long-term potentiation in the hippocampus. *Nature* 388: 590–593.

Collingridge, C. L., S. J. Kehl, and H. McLennan. (1983). Excitatory amino acids in synaptic transmission in the Schaffer-commissural pathway of the rat hippocampus. *Journal of Physiology* 334: 33–46.

Hebb, D. O. (1949). *The Organization of Behavior.* New York: Wiley.

Kim, J. J., J. P. DeCola, J. Landeira-Fernandex, and M. S. Fanselow. (1991). *N*-methyl-*D*-aspartate receptor antagonist APV blocks acquisition but not expression of fear conditioning. *Behavioral Neuroscience* 1005: 160–167.

Larson, J., and G. Lynch. (1989). Theta pattern stimulation and the induction of LTP: The sequence in which synapses are stimulated determines the degree to which they potentiate. *Brain Research* 489: 49–58.

Lynch, G., and M. Baudry. (1991). Reevaluating the constraints on hypotheses regarding LTP expression. *Hippocampus* 1: 9–14.

Morris, R. G., and U. Frey. (1997). Hippocampal synaptic plasticity: Role in spatial learning or the automatic recording of attended experience? *Philosophical Transactions of the Royal Society of London. Series B: Biological Sciences* 352: 1489–1503.

Murphy, G. G., and D. L. Glanzman. (1997). Mediation of classical conditioning in *Aplysia californica* by long-term potentiation of sensorimotor synapses. *Science* 278: 467–471.

Otto, T., H. Eichenbaum, S. I. Wiener, and C. G. Wible. (1991). Learning-related patterns of CA1 spike trains parallel stimulation parameters optimal for inducing hippocampal long-term potentiation. *Hippocampus* 1: 181–192.

Roberson, E. D., J. D. English, and J. D. Sweatt. (1996). A biochemist's view of long-term potentiation. *Learning and Memory* 3: 1–24.

Rotenberg, A., M. Mayford, R. D. Hawkins, E. R. Kandel, and R. U. Muller. (1996). Mice expressing activated CaMKII lack low-frequency LTP and do not form stable place cells in the CA1 region of the hippocampus. *Cell* 87: 1351–1361.

Saucier, D., and D. P. Cain. (1995). Spatial learning without NMDA receptor-dependent long-term potentiation. *Nature* 378: 186–189.

Servatius, R. J., and T. J. Shors. (1996). Early acquisition but not retention of the classically conditioned eyeblink response is *N*-methyl-*d*-aspartate (NMDA) receptor dependent. *Behavioral Neuroscience* 110: 1040–1048.

Shors, T. J., and L. D. Matzel. (1997). Long-term potentiation (LTP): What's learning got to do with it? *Behavioral and Brain Sciences* 20: 597–655.

Squire, L. (1992). Memory and the hippocampus: A synthesis from findings in rats, monkeys, and humans. *Psychological Review* 99: 195–231.

Staubli, U., and G. Lynch. (1987). Stable hippocampal long-term potentiation elicited by "theta" pattern stimulation. *Brain Research* 435: 227–234.

Tsien, J. Z., P. T. Huerta, and S. Tonegawa. (1996). The essential role of hippocampal CA1 NMDA receptor-dependent synaptic plasticity in spatial memory. *Cell* 87: 264–297.

Vanderwolf, C. H., and D. P. Cain. (1994). The behavioral neurobiology of learning and memory: A conceptual reorientation. *Brain Research Reviews* 19: 264–297.

LOT

See LANGUAGE OF THOUGHT

LTP

See LONG-TERM POTENTIATION

Luria, Alexander Romanovich

Alexander Romanovich Luria (1902–1977) was born in Kazan, an old Russian university city east of Moscow. He entered Kazan University at the age of 16 and obtained his degree in 1921 at the age of 19. While still a student, he established the Kazan Psychoanalytic Association and planned on a career in psychology. His earliest research sought to establish objective methods of assessing Freudian ideas about abnormalities of thought and the effects of fatigue on mental processes.

In 1923 Luria's use of reaction time measures to study thought processes in the context of work settings won him a position at the Institute of Psychology in Moscow where he developed a psychodiagnostic procedure, the "combined motor method," for diagnosing individual subjects' thought processes. In this method (described in detail in Luria 1932), subjects are asked to carry out three tasks simulta-

neously. One hand is to be held steady while the other is used to press a key or squeeze a rubber bulb in response to verbal stimuli presented by the experimenter, to which the subject is asked to respond verbally with the first word to come to mind. Preliminary trials are presented until a steady baseline of coordination is established. At this point, "critical" stimuli which the experimenter believes to be related to specific thoughts in the subject are presented. Evidence for the ability to "read the subject's mind" is the selective disruption of the previously established coordinated system by the critical test stimuli. This method was applied to a variety of naturally occurring and experimentally induced cases, providing a model system for psychodiagnosis that won widespread attention in the West when it was published. The book describing these studies has to date never been published in Russian, owing to its association with psychoanalytic theorizing which was disapproved of by Soviet authorities.

In 1924 Luria met Lev Semionovich VYGOTSKY, whose influence was decisive in shaping his future career. Together with Vygotsky and Alexei Nikolaivitch Leontiev, Luria sought to establish an approach to psychology that would enable them to "discover the way natural processes such as physical maturation and sensory mechanisms become intertwined with culturally determined processes to produce the psychological functions of adults" (Luria 1979: 43). Vygotsky and his colleagues referred to this new approach variably as "cultural," "historical," and "instrumental" psychology. These three labels all index the centrality of cultural mediation in the constitution of specifically human psychological processes, and the role of the social environment in structuring the processes by which children appropriate the cultural tools of their society in the process of ontogeny. An especially heavy emphasis was placed on the role of language, the "tool of tools" in this process; the acquisition of language was seen as the pivotal moment when phylogeny and cultural history are merged to form specifically human forms of thought, feeling, and action.

From the late 1920s until his death, Luria sought to elaborate this synthetic, cultural-historical psychology in different content areas of psychology. In the early 1930s he led two expeditions to central Asia where he investigated changes in perception, problem solving, and memory associated with historical changes in economic activity and schooling. During this same period he carried out studies of identical and fraternal twins raised in a large residential school to reveal the dynamic relations between phylogenetic and cultural-historical factors in the development of LANGUAGE AND THOUGHT.

In the late 1930s, largely to remove himself from public view during the period of purges initiated by Stalin, Luria entered medical school where he specialized in the study of aphasia, retaining his focus on the relation between language and thought in a politically neutral arena. The onset of World War II made his specialized knowledge of crucial importance to the Soviet war effort, and the widespread availability of people with various forms of traumatic brain injury provided him with voluminous materials for developing his theories of brain function and methods for the remediation of focal brain lesions. It was during this period that he developed the systematic approach to brain and cognition which has come to be known as the discipline of neuropsychology. Central to his approach was the belief that "to understand the brain foundations for psychological activity, one must be prepared to study both the brain and the system of activity" (1979: 173). This insistence on linking brain structure and function to the proximal, culturally organized environment provides the thread of continuity between the early and later parts of Luria's career.

Following the war Luria sought to continue his work in neuropsychology. His plans were interrupted for several years when he was removed from the Institute of Neurosurgery during a period of particularly virulent antisemitic repression. During this time he pursued his scientific interests through a series of studies of the development of language and thought in mentally retarded children.

In the late 1950s Luria was permitted to return to the study of neuropsychology, which he pursued until his death of heart failure in 1977. In the years just prior to his death, he returned to his earliest dreams of constructing a unified psychology. He published two case studies, one of a man with an exceptional and idiosyncratic memory (Luria 1968), the other of a man who suffered a traumatic brain injury (Luria 1972). These two case studies illustrate his blend of classic, experimental approaches with clinical and remediational approaches, a synthesis that stands as a model for late twentieth-century cognitive science.

See also COGNITIVE DEVELOPMENT; CULTURAL PSYCHOLOGY; PIAGET, JEAN; PSYCHOANALYSIS, HISTORY OF

—*Michael Cole*

Works By A. R. Luria

Luria, A. R. (1932). *The Nature of Human Conflicts.* New York: Liveright.

Luria, A. R. and F. A. Yudovich. (1959). *Speech and the Development of Mental Processes.* London: Staples Press.

Luria, A. R. (1960). *The Role of Speech in the Regulation of Normal and Abnormal Behavior.* New York: Irvington.

Luria, A. R. (1966). *Higher Cortical Functions in Man.* New York: Basic Books.

Luria, A. R. (1970). *Traumatic Aphasia: Its Syndromes, Psychology, and Treatment.* The Hague: Mouton.

Luria, A. R. (1968). *The Mind of Mnemonist.* New York: Basic Books.

Luria, A. R. (1972). *The Man with a Shattered World.* New York: Basic Books.

Luria, A. R. (1973). *The Working Brain.* New York: Basic Books.

Luria, A. R. (1979). *The Making of Mind.* Cambridge, MA: Harvard University Press.

Machiavellian Intelligence Hypothesis

The Machiavellian intelligence hypothesis takes several forms, but all stem from the proposition that the advanced cognitive processes of primates are primarily adaptations to *the special complexities of their social lives,* rather than to nonsocial environmental problems such as finding food, which were traditionally thought to be the province of intelligence. The new "social" explanation for the evolution of INTELLIGENCE arose in the context of proliferating field studies of primate societies in the 1960s and 1970s. The paper generally recognized as pivotal in launching this wave of studies was Nicholas Humphrey's "The Social Function of Intellect" (1976), the first to spell out the idea explicitly, although important insights were offered by earlier writers, notably Alison Jolly (see Whiten and Byrne 1988a for a review). By 1988 the idea had inspired sufficient interesting empirical work to produce the volume *Machiavellian Intelligence* (Byrne and Whiten 1988; now see also Whiten and Byrne 1997), which christened the area.

The Machiavellian intelligence hypothesis has been recognized as significant beyond the confines of primatology, however. On the one hand, it is relevant to all the various disciplines that study human cognitive processes. Because the basic architecture of these processes is derived from the legacy of our primate past, a more particular Machiavellian subhypothesis is that developments in specifically human intelligence were also most importantly shaped by social complexities. On the other hand, looking beyond primates, the hypothesis has been recognized as of relevance to any species of animal with sufficient social complexity.

Why "Machiavellian" intelligence? Humphrey talked of "the social function of intellect" and some authors refer to the "social intelligence hypothesis" (Kummer et al. 1997). But "social" is not really adequate as a label for the hypothesis. Many species are social (some living in much larger groups than primates) without being particularly intelligent; what is held to be special about primate societies is their *complexity,* which includes the formation of sometimes fluid and shifting alliances and coalitions. Within this context, primate social relationships have been characterized as manipulative and sometimes deceptive at sophisticated levels (Whiten and Byrne 1988b). Primates often act as if they were following the advice that Niccolo Machiavelli offered to sixteenth-century Italian prince-politicians to enable them to socially manipulate their competitors and subjects (Machiavelli 1532; de Waal 1982). "Machiavellian intelligence" therefore seemed an appropriate label, and it has since passed into common usage.

An important prediction of the hypothesis is that greater social intellect in some members of a community will exert selection pressures on others to show greater social expertise, so that over evolutionary time there will be an "arms race" of Machiavellian intelligence. Indeed, one of the questions the success of the hypothesis now begins to raise is why such escalation has not gone further than it has in many species.

But the way in which the hypothesis highlights competitive interactions must not be interpreted too narrowly. "Machiavellianism" in human affairs is often taken to include only a subset of social dealings characterized by their proximally selfish and exploitative nature (Wilson, Near, and Miller 1996). Although animal behavior is expected to be ultimately selfish in the face of natural selection (by definition a competition), COOPERATION with some individuals against others can be one means to that end. Primate coalitions provide good examples. Indeed, because an important component of exploiting one's social environment includes learning socially from others, primate "culture" also comes within the scope of Machiavellian intelligence.

As noted at the outset, the Machiavellian hypothesis is not so much a single hypothesis as a cluster of related hypotheses about the power of social phenomena to shape cognitive processes. Two main variants may be distinguished here. In one version of the hypothesis, intelligence is seen as a relatively domain-general capacity, with degrees of intelligence in principle distinguishable among different taxa of animals. In this case, the hypothesis proposes that different grades of intelligence will be correlated significantly and most closely with variations in the social complexity of the taxa concerned. This should apply to any taxon with the right kind of social complexity. Although primate research was the arena from which the ideas sprang, related kinds of complexity are now being described in other taxa, like the alliances of dolphins and hyenas (Harcourt and de Waal 1992).

Another version of the hypothesis proposes that the very nature of the cognitive system will be shaped to handle social phenomena: a domain-specific social intelligence (see DOMAIN SPECIFICITY). This possibility has been examined in both human and nonhuman primates, with the bulk of work done on humans. Influential research includes the work of Cosmides (1989) on the power of cheater detection mechanisms to handle logical problems humans find difficult in equivalent nonsocial contexts (see EVOLUTIONARY PSYCHOLOGY). Another well-documented case is our everyday THEORY OF MIND, whose social domain specificity is highlighted by autistic individuals' difficulty in reading other minds, despite high levels of nonsocial intelligence (Baron-Cohen 1995; see AUTISM). For nonhuman primates, Cheney and Seyfarth (1990) report the results of both observational and experimental studies in which vervet monkeys demonstrate social expertise in excess of that operating in equivalent nonsocial contexts. For example, the monkeys may discriminate as targets of aggression those individuals whose kin have fought their own kin, yet fail to read the signs of a recent python track entering a bush (see SOCIAL COGNITION IN ANIMALS).

A different kind of test of the Machiavellian hypothesis is based on examining the correlates of relative brain size across primate and other animal taxa. Contrary to some earlier findings, the strongest predictors of encephalization that have emerged consistently in recent studies are not measures of physical ecological complexity such as home range size, but the size of the social group or clique, an indicator (even if a crude one) of social complexity (Dunbar 1995; Barton and Dunbar 1997). Although this approach conflates the two alternative versions of the hypothesis discriminated above (because we do not know how modular the mechanisms are that contribute to greater encephalization) the results obviously support the Machiavellian intelligence hypothesis in the general form stated at the start of this entry.

See also COGNITIVE ETHOLOGY; MODULARITY OF MIND; PRIMATE COGNITION; SOCIAL COGNITION

—*Andrew Whiten*

References

Baron-Cohen, S. (1995). *Mindblindness: An Essay on Autism and Theory of Mind.* Cambridge, MA: The MIT Press.

Barton, R. A., and R. I. M. Dunbar. (1997). Evolution of the social brain. In A. Whiten and R. W. Byrne, Eds., *Machiavellian Intelligence.* Vol. 2, *Evaluations and Extensions.* Cambridge: Cambridge University Press, pp. 240–263.

Byrne, R. W., and A. Whiten. (1988). *Machiavellian Intelligence: Social Expertise and the Evolution of Intellect in Monkeys, Apes and Humans.* Oxford: Oxford University Press.

Cheney, D. L., and R. M. Seyfarth. (1990). *How Monkeys See the World: Inside the Mind of Another Species.* Chicago: University of Chicago Press.

Cosmides, L. (1989). The logic of social exchange: Has natural selection shaped how humans reason? Studies with the Wason selection task. *Cognition* 31: 187–276.

de Waal, F. (1982). *Chimpanzee Politics.* London: Cape.

Dunbar, R. I. M. (1995). Neocortex size and group size in primates: A test of the hypothesis. *Journal of Human Evolution* 28: 287–296.

Harcourt, A. H., and F. B. deWaal. (1992). *Coalitions and Alliances in Humans and Other Animals.* Oxford: Oxford University Press.

Humphrey, N. K. (1976). The social function of intellect. In P. P. G. Bateson and R. A. Hinde, Eds., *Growing Points in Ethology.* Cambridge: Cambridge University Press, 1976, pp. 303–321.

Kummer, H., L. Daston, G. Gigerenzer, and J. Silk. (1997). The social intelligence hypothesis. In P. Weingart, P. Richerson, S. D. Mitchell, and S. Maasen, Eds., *Human by Nature: Between Biology and the Social Sciences.* Hillsdale, NJ: Erlbaum, pp. 157–179.

Machiavelli, N. (1532). *The Prince.* Harmondsworth, England: Penguin, 1961.

Whiten, A., and R. W. Byrne. (1988a). The Machiavellian intellect hypotheses. In R. W. Byrne and A. Whiten, Eds., *Machiavellian Intelligence.* Oxford: Oxford University Press, pp. 1–9.

Whiten, A., and R. W. Byrne. (1988b). Tactical deception in primates. *Behavioral and Brain Sciences* 11: 233–273.

Whiten, A., and R. W. Byrne. (1997). *Machiavellian Intelligence.* Vol. 2, *Evaluations and Extensions.* Cambridge: Cambridge University Press.

Wilson, D. S., D. Near, and R. R. Miller. (1996). Machiavellianism: A synthesis of the evolutionary and psychological literatures. *Psychological Bulletin* 119: 285–299.

Further Readings

Brothers, L. (1990). The social brain: A project for integrating primate behavior and neurophysiology in a new domain. *Concepts in Neuroscience* 1: 27–51.

Byrne, R. W. (1995). *The Thinking Ape: Evolutionary Origins of Intelligence.* Oxford: Oxford University Press.

Byrne, R. W., and A. Whiten. (1990). Tactical deception in primates: The 1990 database. *Primate Report* 27: 1–101.

Crow, T. J. (1993). Sexual selection, Machiavellian intelligence, and the origins of psychosis. *Lancet* 342: 594–598.

Dunbar, R. I. M. (1992). Neocortex size as a constraint on group size in primates. *Journal of Human Evolution* 20: 469–493.

Erdal, D., and A. Whiten. (1996). Egalitarianism and Machiavellian intelligence in human evolution. In P. Mellars and K. Gibson, Eds., *Modelling the Early Human Mind.* Cambridge, England: McDonnell Institute, pp. 139–150.

Sambrook, T., and A. Whiten. (1997). On the nature of complexity in cognitive and behavioural science. *Theory and Psychology* 7: 191–213.

Venables, J. (1993). *What is News?* Huntingdon, England: ELM.

Whiten, A. (1991). *Natural Theories of Mind: Evolution, Development and Simulation of Everyday Mindreading.* Oxford: Blackwell.

Whiten, A. (1993). Deception in animal communication. In R. E. Asher, Ed., *The Pergamon Encyclopedia of Language and Linguistics,* vol. 2. Pergamon Press, pp. 829–832.

Whiten, A. (1996). Imitation, pretence and mindreading: Secondary representation in comparative primatology and developmental psychology. In A. Russon, K. A. Bard, and S. T. Parker, Eds., *Reaching into Thought: The Minds of the Great Apes.* Cambridge University Press, pp. 300–324.

Whiten, A. (Forthcoming). Primate culture and social learning. *Cognitive Science.*

Machine Learning

The goal of machine learning is to build computer systems that can adapt and learn from their experience. Different learning techniques have been developed for different performance tasks. The primary tasks that have been investigated are SUPERVISED LEARNING for discrete decision-making, supervised learning for continuous prediction, REINFORCEMENT LEARNING for sequential decision making, and UNSUPERVISED LEARNING.

The best-understood task is one-shot decision making: the computer is given a description of an object (event, situation, etc.) and it must output a classification of that object. For example, an optical character recognizer must input a digitized image of a character and output the name of that character ("A" through "Z"). A machine learning approach to constructing such a system would begin by collecting training examples, each consisting of a digitized image of a character and the correct name of that character. These would be analyzed by a learning ALGORITHM to produce an optical character recognizer for classifying new images.

Machine learning algorithms search a space of candidate classifiers for one that performs well on the training examples and is expected to generalize well to new cases. Learning methods for classification problems include DECISION TREES, NEURAL NETWORKS, rule-learning algorithms (Cohen 1995), nearest-neighbor methods (Dasarathy 1991), and certain kinds of BAYESIAN NETWORKS.

There are four questions to answer when developing a machine learning system:

1. How is the classifier represented?
2. How are the examples represented?
3. What objective function should be employed to evaluate candidate classifiers?
4. What search algorithm should be used?

Let us illustrate these four questions using two of the most popular learning algorithms, C4.5 and backpropagation.

The C4.5 algorithm (Quinlan 1993) represents a classifier as a decision tree. Each example is represented as a vector of features. For example, one feature describing a printed character might be whether it has a long vertical line segment (such as the letters B, D, E, etc.).

Each node in the decision tree tests the value of one of the features and branches to one of its children, depending on the result of the test. A new example is classified by starting at the root of the tree and applying the test at that node. If the test is true, it branches to the left child; otherwise, it branches to the right child. The test at the child node is then applied, recursively, until one of the leaf nodes of the tree is reached. The leaf node gives the predicted classification of the example.

C4.5 searches the space of decision trees through a constructive search. It first considers all trees consisting of only a single root node and chooses one of those. Then it considers all trees having that root node and various left children, and chooses one of those, and so on. This process constructs the tree incrementally with the goal of finding the decision tree that minimizes the so-called pessimistic error, which is an estimate of classification error of the tree on new training examples. It is based on taking the upper endpoint of a confidence interval for the error of the tree (computed separately for each leaf).

Although C4.5 *constructs* its classifier, other learning algorithms begin with a *complete* classifier and modify it. For example, the backpropagation algorithm for learning neural networks begins with an initial neural network and computes the classification error of that network on the training data. It then makes small adjustments in the weights of the network to reduce this error. This process is repeated until the error is minimized.

There are two fundamentally different theories of machine learning. The classical theory takes the view that, before analyzing the training examples, the learning algorithm makes a "guess" about an appropriate space of classifiers to consider (e.g., it guesses that decision trees will be better than neural networks). The algorithm then searches the chosen space of classifiers hoping to find a good fit to the data. The Bayesian theory takes the view that the designer of a learning algorithm encodes all of his or her prior knowledge in the form of a prior probability distribution over the space of candidate classifiers. The learning algorithm then analyzes the training examples and computes the posterior probability distribution over the space of classifiers. In this view, the training data serve to reduce our remaining uncertainty about the unknown classifier.

These two theories lead to two different practical approaches. The first theory encourages the development of large, flexible hypothesis spaces (such as decision trees and neural networks) that can represent many different classifiers. The second theory encourages the development of representational systems that can readily express prior knowledge (such as Bayesian networks and other stochastic models).

The discussion thus far has focused on discrete classification, but the same issues arise for the second learning task: supervised learning for continuous prediction (also called "regression"). In this task, the computer is given a description of an object and it must output a real-valued quantity. For example, given a description of a prospective student (high school grade-point average, SAT scores, etc.), the system must predict the student's college grade-point average (GPA). The machine learning approach is the same: a collection of training examples describing students and their college GPAs is provided to the learning algorithm, which outputs a predictor to predict college GPA. Learning methods for continuous prediction include neural networks, regression trees (Breiman et al. 1984), linear and additive models (Hastie and Tibshirani 1990), and kernel regression methods (Cleveland and Devlin 1988). Classification and prediction are often called "supervised learning" tasks, because the training data include not only the input objects but also the corresponding output values (provided by a "supervisor").

We now turn from supervised learning to reinforcement learning tasks, most of which involve sequential decision making. In these tasks, each decision made by the computer affects subsequent decisions. For example, consider a computer-controlled robot attempting to navigate from a hospital kitchen to a patient's room. At each point in time, the computer must decide whether to move the robot forward, left, right, or backward. Each decision changes the location of the robot, so that the next decision will depend on previous decisions. After each decision, the environment provides a real-value reward. For example, the robot may receive a positive reward for delivering a meal to the correct patient and a negative reward for bumping into walls. The goal of the robot is to choose *sequences* of actions to maximize its long-term reward. This is very different from the standard supervised learning task, where each classification decision is completely independent of other decisions.

The final learning task we will discuss is unsupervised learning, where the computer is given a collection of objects and is asked to construct a model to explain the observed properties of these objects. No teacher provides desired outputs or rewards. For example, given a collection of astronomical objects, the learning system should group the objects into stars, planets, and galaxies and describe each group by its electromagnetic spectrum, distance from earth, and so on.

Although often called "cluster analysis" (Everitt 1993), unsupervised learning arises in a much wider range of tasks. Indeed, there is no single agreed-upon definition of unsupervised learning, but one useful formulation views unsupervised learning as density estimation. Define a probability distribution P(X) to be the probability that an object X will be observed. The goal of unsupervised learning is to find this probability distribution, given a sample of the Xs. This is typically accomplished by defining a family of possible stochastic models and choosing the model that best accounts for the data.

For example, one might model each group of astronomical objects as having a spectrum that is a multivariate normal distribution (centered at a "typical" spectrum). The probability distribution P(X) describing the whole collection of astronomical objects could then be modeled as a mixture of normal distributions—one distribution for each group of objects. The learning process determines the number of groups and the mean and covariance matrix of each multivariate distribution. The Autoclass program discovered a new class of astronomical objects in just this way (Cheeseman et al. 1988).

Another widely used unsupervised learning model is the HIDDEN MARKOV MODEL (HMM). An HMM is a stochastic finite-state machine that generates strings. In speech recognition applications, the strings are speech signals, and one HMM is trained for each word in the vocabulary (Rabiner 1989).

Once a stochastic model has been fitted to a collection of objects, that model can be applied to classify new objects. Given a new astronomical object, we can determine which multivariate Gaussian is most likely to have generated it, and we can assign it to the corresponding group. Similarly, given a new speech signal, we can determine which HMM is most likely to have generated it, and thereby guess which word was spoken. A general algorithm schema for training both HMMs and mixture models is the expectation maximization (EM) algorithm (Dempster, Laird, and Rubin 1976).

See also COMPUTATIONAL LEARNING THEORY; DECISION MAKING; EXPLANATION-BASED LEARNING; INDUCTIVE LOGIC PROGRAMMING; LEARNING; PATTERN RECOGNITION AND LAYERED NETWORKS; RATIONAL DECISION MAKING; SPEECH RECOGNITION IN MACHINES; STATISTICAL LEARNING THEORY

—*Tom Dieterich*

References

Breiman, L., J. H. Friedman, R. A. Olshen, and C. J. Stone. (1984). *Classification and Regression Trees.* Monterey, CA: Wadsworth.

Cheeseman, P., J. Kelly, M. Self, J. Stutz, W. Taylor, and D. Freeman. (1988). Autoclass: A Bayesian classification system. *Proceedings of the Fifth International Conference on Machine Learning.* San Francisco: Kaufmann, pp. 54–64.

Cleveland, W. S., and S. J. Devlin. (1988). Locally-weighted regression: An approach to regression analysis by local fitting. *Journal of the American Statistical Association* 83: 596–610.

Cohen, W. W. (1995). Fast effective rule induction. In *Proceedings of the Twelfth International Conference on Machine Learning.* San Francisco: Kaufmann, pp. 115–123.

Dasarathy, B. V., Ed. (1991). *Nearest Neighbor (NN) Norms: NN Pattern Classification Techniques.* Los Alamitos, CA: IEEE Computer Society Press.

Dempster, A. P., N. M. Laird, and D. B. Rubin. (1976). Maximum likelihood from incomplete data via the EM algorithm. *Proceedings of the Royal Statistical Society* B39: 1–38.

Everitt, B. (1993). *Cluster Analysis.* London: Halsted Press.

Hastie, T. J., and R. J. Tibshirani. (1990). *Generalized Additive Models.* London: Chapman and Hall.

Quinlan, J. R. (1993). *C4.5: Programs for Empirical Learning.* San Francisco: Kaufmann.

Rabiner, L. R. (1989). A tutorial on hidden Markov models and selected applications in speech recognition. *Proceedings of the IEEE* 77(2): 257–286.

Further Readings

Bishop, C. M. (1996). *Neural Networks for Pattern Recognition.* Oxford: Oxford University Press.

Mitchell, T. M. (1997). *Machine Learning.* New York: McGraw-Hill.

Machine Translation

Machine translation (MT), which celebrated its fiftieth anniversary in 1997, uses computers to translate texts written in one human language, such as Spanish, into another human language, such as Ukrainian. In the ideal situation, sometimes abbreviated as FAHQMT (for Fully Automated

High Quality Machine Translation) the computer program produces fully automatic, high-quality translations of text. Programs that assist human translators are called "machine-aided translators" (MATs).

MT is the intellectual precursor to the field of COMPUTATIONAL LINGUISTICS (also called NATURAL LANGUAGE PROCESSING), and shares interests with computer science (artificial intelligence), linguistics, and occasionally anthropology. Machine translation dates back to the work of Warren Weaver (1955), who suggested applying ideas from cryptography, as employed during World War II, and information theory, as outlined in 1947 by Claude Shannon, to language processing. Not surprisingly, the first large-scale MT project was funded by the U.S. government to translate Russian Air Force manuals into English. After an initial decade of naive optimism, the ALPAC (for Automatic Language Processing Advisory Committee) report (Pierce et al. 1966), issued by a government-sponsored study panel, put a damper on research in the United States for many years. Research and commercial development continued largely in Europe and after 1970 also in Japan. Today, over fifty companies worldwide produce and sell translation by computer, whether as translation services to outsiders, as in-house translation bureaus, or as providers of on-line multilingual chat rooms. Some 250 of the world's most widely spoken languages have been translated, at least in pilot systems. By some estimates, expenditures for MT in 1989 exceeded $20 million worldwide, involving 200–300 million pages per year (Wilks 1992).

Translation is not easy—even humans find it hard to translate complex texts such as novels. Current technology produces output whose quality level varies from perfect (for very circumscribed domains with just a few hundred words) to hardly readable (for unrestricted domains requiring lexicons of a quarter million words or more). Research groups continue to investigate unsolved issues. Recent large government-sponsored research collaborations include CICC in Japan (Tsujii 1990), Eurotra in Europe (Johnson, King, and des Tombes 1985), and the DARPA MT effort in the United States (White et al. 1992–1994). (For reviews of the history, theory, and applications of MT, see Hutchins and Somers 1992; Nirenburg et al. 1992; and Hovy 1993; useful collections of papers can be found in AMTA 1996, 1994; CL 1985.)

Before producing their output, all MT systems perform some analysis of the input text. The degree of analysis largely determines what type of translation is being performed, and what the average output quality is. Generally, the more refined or "deeper" the analysis, the better the output quality. Three major levels of analysis are traditionally recognized:

1. *Direct replacement.* The simplest systems perform very little analysis of the input, essentially replacing source language (input) words with equivalent target language (output) words, inflected as necessary for tense, number, and so on. When the source and target languages are fairly similar in structure and word use, as between Italian, Spanish, and French, this approach can produce surprisingly understandable results. However, as soon as the word order starts to differ (say, if the verb appears at the end of the sentence, as in Japanese), then some syntactic analysis is required.

Modern research using this approach has focused on the semiautomated construction of large word and phrase correspondence "tables," extracting this information from human translations as examples (Nirenburg, Beale, and Domashnev 1994) or using statistics (Brown et al. 1990, 1993).

2. *Transfer.* In order to produce grammatically appropriate translations, syntactic transfer systems include so-called parsers, transfer modules, and realizers or generators (see NATURAL LANGUAGE GENERATION). A *parser* is a computer program that accepts a natural language sentence as input and produces a parse tree of that sentence as output. A *transfer module* applies transfer rules to convert the source parse tree into a tree conforming to the requirements of the target language grammar—for example, by shifting the verb from the end of the sentence (Japanese) to the second position (English). A *realizer* then converts the target tree back into a linear string of words in the target language, inflecting them as required. (For more details, see Kinoshita, Phillips, and Tsujii 1992; Somers et al. 1988; and Nagao 1987.)

Unfortunately, syntactic analysis is often not enough. Effective translation may require the system to "understand" the actual meaning of the sentence. For example, "I am small" is expressed in many languages using the verb "to be," but "I am hungry" is often expressed using the verb "to have," as in "I have hunger." For the translation system to handle such cases (and their more complex variants), it needs to have information about the meaning of size, hunger, and so on (see SEMANTICS). Often such information is represented in *case frames*, small collections of attributes and their values. The translation system then requires an additional analysis module, usually called the "semantic analyzer," additional (semantic) transfer rules, and additional rules for the realizer. The *semantic analyzer* produces a case frame from the syntax tree, and the transfer module converts the case frame derived from the source language sentence into the case frame required for the target language.

3. *Interlinguas.* Although transfer systems are common, because a distinct set of transfer rules must be created for each language pair in each direction—for N languages, one needs about N^2 pairs of rule sets—they require a great deal of effort to build. The solution is to create a single intermediate representation scheme to capture the language-neutral meaning of any sentence in any language. Then only 2N sets of mappings are required—from each language into the interlingua and back out again.

This idea appeals to many. Despite numerous attempts, however, it has never yet been achieved on a large scale; all interlingual MT systems to date have been at the level of demonstrations (a few hundred lexical items) or prototypes (a few thousand). A great deal has been written about interlinguas, but no clear methodology exists for determining exactly how one should build a true language-neutral meaning representation, if such a thing is possible at all (Nirenburg et al. 1992; Dorr 1994; Hovy and Nirenburg 1992).

Machine translation applications are classified into two traditional and one more recent types:

1. *Assimilation.* People interested in tracking the multilingual world use MT systems for assimilation—to produce (rough) translations of many externally created

documents, from which they then select the ones of interest (and then possibly submit them for more refined, human translation). Typical users are commercial and government staff who monitor developments in areas of interest. The desired output quality need not be very high, but the MT system should cover a large domain, and it should be fast.

2. *Dissemination.* People wishing to disseminate their own documents to the world in various languages use MT systems to produce the translations. Typical users are manufacturers such as Caterpillar, Honda, and Fujitsu. In this case, the desired output quality should be as high as possible, but the system need cover only the application domain, and speed is not generally a consideration.

3. *Interaction.* People wanting to converse with others in foreign countries via E-mail or chat rooms use MT systems on-line to translate their messages. Typical users are chat room participants and business travelers setting up meetings and reserving hotel rooms. CompuServe currently supports MT for some of its highly popular chat rooms at the cost of one cent per word. The desired output quality should be as high as possible, given the requirements of system speed and relatively broad coverage.

A great deal of effort has been devoted to the evaluation of MT systems (see White et al. 1992–1994: AMTA 1992: Nomura 1992; Church and Hovy 1993; King and Falkedal 1990; Kay 1980; and Van Slype 1979). No single measure can capture all the aspects of a translation system. While, from the ultimate user's point of view, the major dimensions will probably be cost, output quality, range of coverage, and degree of automation, numerous more specific evaluation metrics have been developed. These range from system-internal aspects such as number of grammar rules and treatment of multisentence phenomena to user-related aspects such as the ability to extend the lexicon and the quality of the system's interface.

See also SPEECH RECOGNITION IN MACHINES; STATISTICAL TECHNIQUES IN NATURAL LANGUAGE PROCESSING; SYNTAX

—*Eduard Hovy*

References

AMTA (Association for Machine Translation in the Americas). (1992). *MT Evaluation: Basis for Future Directions.* San Diego, CA.

AMTA. (1994). *Proceedings of the Conference of the AMTA.* Columbia, MD.

AMTA. (1996). *Proceedings of the Conference of the AMTA.* Montreal, CAN.

Brown, P. F., J. Cocke, S. A. Della Pietra, V. J. Della Pietra, F. Jelinek, J. D. Lafferty, R. L. Mercer, and P. S. Roossin. (1990). A statistical approach to machine translation. *Computational Linguistics* 16(2): 79–85.

Brown, P. F., S. Della Pietra, V. Della Pietra, and R. Mercer. (1993). The mathematics of statistical machine translation: Parameter estimation. *Computational Linguistics* 19(2): 263–311.

Church, K. W., and E. H. Hovy. (1993). Good applications for crummy machine translation. *Machine Translation* 8: 239–258.

CL (Computational Linguistics). (1985). Special issues on machine translation. Vol. 11, nos. 2–3.

Dorr, B. J. (1994). Machine translation divergences: A formal description and proposed solution. *Computational Linguistics* 20(4): 597–634.

Hovy, E. H. (1993). How MT works. *Byte.* January: 167–176. Special feature on machine translation.

Hovy, E. H., and S. Nirenburg. (1992). Approximating an interlingua in a principled way. In *Proceedings of the DARPA Speech and Natural Language Workshop,* New York: Arden House.

Hutchins, W. J., and H. Somers. (1992). *An Introduction to Machine Translation.* San Diego: Academic Press.

Johnson, R., M. King, and L. des Tombes. (1985). Eurotra: A multilingual system under development. *Computational Linguistics* 11(2–3): 155–169.

Kay, M. (1980). The proper place of men and machines in language translation. XEROX PARC Research Report CSL-80-11. Palo Alto, CA: Xerox Parc.

King, M., and K. Falkedal. (1990). Using test suites in evaluation of machine translation systems. In *Proceedings of the Eighteenth COLING Conference,* vol. 2, pp. 435–447.

Kinoshita, S., J. Phillips, and J. Tsujii. (1992). Interactions between structural changes in machine translation. In *Proceedings of the Twentieth COLING Conference,* pp. 679–685.

Nagao, M. (1987). Role of structural transformation in a machine translation system. In S. Nirenburg, Ed., *Machine Translation: Theoretical and Methodological Issues.* Cambridge: Cambridge University Press, pp. 262–277.

Nirenburg, S., S. Beale, and C. Domashnev. (1994). A full-text experiment in example-based machine translation. In *Proceedings of the International Conference on New Methods in Language Processing,* pp. 95–103.

Nirenburg, S., J. C. Carbonell, M. Tomita, and K. Goodman. (1992). *Machine Translation: A Knowledge-Based Approach.* San Mateo, CA: Kaufmann.

Nomura, H. (1992). *JEIDA Methodology and Criteria on Machine Translation Evaluation* (JEIDA Report). Tokyo: Japan Electronic Industry Development Association.

Pierce, J. R., J. B. Carroll, E. P. Hamp, D. G. Hays, C. F. Hockett, A. G. Dettinger, and A. Perlis (1966). *Computers in Translation and Linguistics* (ALPAC Report). National Academy of Sciences/National Research Council Publication 1416. Washington, DC: NAS Press.

Somers, H., H. Hirakawa, S. Miike, and S. Amano. (1988). The treatment of complex English nominalizations in machine translation. *Computers and Translation* (now *Machine Translation*) 3(1): 3–22.

Tsujii, Y. (1990). Multi-language translation system using interlingua for Asian languages. In *Proceedings of International Conference Organized by IPSJ for its Thirtieth Anniversary.*

Van Slype, G. (1979). *Critical Study of Methods for Evaluating the Quality of Machine Translation.* Prepared for the European Commission Directorate on General Scientific and Technical Information and Information Management. Report BR 19142. Brussells: Bureau Marcel van Dijk.

White, J., and T. O'Connell (1992–1994). *ARPA Workshops on Machine Translation.* Series of four workshops on comparative evaluation. McLean, VA: Litton PRC Inc.

Wilks, Y. (1992). MT contrasts between the U.S. and Europe. In J. Carbonell, E. Rich, D. Johnson, M. Tomita, M. Vasconcellos, and Y. Wilks, Eds., *JTEC Panel Report.* Commissioned by DARPA and Japanese Technology Evaluation Center.

Weaver, W. (1955). Translation. In W. N. Locke and A. D. Booth, Eds., *Machine Translation of Languages.* Cambridge, MA: MIT Press.

Further Readings

TMI. (1995). *Proceedings of the Conference on Theoretical and Methodological Issues in Machine Translation.* Leuven, Belgium.

TMI. (1997). *Proceedings of the Conference on Theoretical and Methodological Issues in Machine Translation.* Santa Fe, NM.

Whorf, B. L. (1956). *Language, Thought, and Reality: Selected Writings of Benjamin Lee Whorf.* J. B. Carroll, Ed. Cambridge, MA: MIT Press.

Machine Vision

Machine vision is an applied science whose objective is to take two-dimensional (2-D) images as input and extract information about the three-dimensional (3-D) environment adequate for tasks typically performed by humans using vision. These tasks fall into four broad categories:

1. *Reconstruction.* Examples are building 3-D geometric models of an environment, determining spatial layout by finding the locations and poses of objects, and estimating surface color, reflectance, and texture properties.
2. *Visually guided control of locomotion and manipulation.* Locomotion tasks include navigating a robot around obstacles or controlling the speed and direction of a car driving down a freeway. Manipulation tasks include reaching, grasping, and insertion operations (see MANIPULATION AND GRASPING).
3. *Spatiotemporal grouping and tracking. Grouping* is the association of image pixels into regions corresponding to single objects or parts of objects. *Tracking* is matching these groups from one time frame to the next. Grouping is used in the segmentation of different kinds of tissues in an ultrasound image or in traffic monitoring to distinguish and track individual vehicles.
4. *Recognition of objects and activities.* Object recognition tasks include determining the class of particular objects that have been imaged ("This is a face") and recognizing specific instances such as faces of particular individuals ("This is Nixon's face"). Activity recognition includes identifying gaits, expressions, and gestures. (See VISUAL OBJECT RECOGNITION, AI Ullman 1996 provides a book-length account.)

Reconstruction Tasks

The most basic fact about vision, whether machine or human, is that images are produced by perspective projection. Consider a coordinate system with origin at the optical center of a camera whose optical axis is aligned along the Z axis. A point P with coordinates (X,Y,Z) in the scene gets imaged at the point P', with image plane coordinates (x,y) where

$$x = \frac{-fX}{Z}, y = \frac{-fY}{Z},$$

and f is the distance from the optical center of the camera to the image plane. All points in the 3-D world that lie on a ray passing through the optical center are mapped to the same point in the image. During reconstruction, we seek to recover the 3-D information lost during perspective projection.

Many cues are available in the visual stimulus to make this possible, including structure from motion, binocular stereopsis, texture, shading, and contour. Each of these relies on background assumptions about the physical scene (Marr 1982).

The cues of stereopsis and structure from motion rely on the presence of multiple views, either acquired simultaneously from multiple cameras or over time from a single camera during the relative motion of objects. When the projections of a sufficient number of points in the world are observed in multiple images, it is theoretically possible to deduce the 3-D locations of the points as well as of the cameras (Faugeras 1993; for further discussion of the mathematics, see STEREO AND MOTION PERCEPTION).

Shape can be recovered from visual TEXTURE—a spatially repeating pattern on a surface such as windows on a building, spots on a leopard, or pebbles on a beach. If the arrangement is periodic, or at least statistically regular, it is possible to recover surface orientation and shape from a single image (Malik and Rosenholtz 1997). While the sizes, shapes, and spacings of the texture elements (*texels*) are roughly uniform in the scene, the projected size, shape, and spacing in the image vary, principally because

1. Distances of the different texels from the camera vary. Recall that under perspective projection, distant objects appear smaller. The scaling factor is $1/Z$.
2. Foreshortening of the different texels varies. This is related to the orientation of the texel relative to the line of sight of the camera. If the texel is perpendicular to the line of sight, there is no foreshortening. The magnitude of the foreshortening effect is proportional to $\cos \sigma$, where σ is the angle between the surface normal and the ray from the viewer.

Expressions can be derived for the rate of change of various image texel features, for example, area, foreshortening, and density (GIBSON's texture gradients), as functions of surface shape and orientation. One can then estimate the surface shape, slant, and tilt that would give rise to the measured texture gradients.

Shading—spatial variation in the image brightness—is determined by the spatial layout of the scene surfaces, their reflectance properties, and the arrangement of light sources. If one neglects interreflections—the fact that objects are illuminated not just by light sources but also by light reflected from other surfaces in the scene—then the shading pattern is determined by the orientation of each surface patch with respect to the light sources. For a diffusely reflecting surface, the brightness of the patch varies as the cosine of the angle between the surface normal and the light source direction. A number of techniques have been developed that seek to invert the process—to recover the surface orientation and shape giving rise to the observed brightness pattern (Horn and Brooks 1989).

Humans can perceive 3-D shape from line drawings, which suggests that useful information can be extracted from the projected image of the contour of an object (Koenderink 1990). It is easiest to do this for objects that belong to parametrized classes of shapes, such as polyhedra or surfaces of revolution, for which the ambiguity resulting from perspective projection can be resolved by considering only those scene configurations that satisfy the constraints appropriate to the particular class of shapes.

Finally, it should be noted that shape and spatial layout are only some of the scene characteristics that humans can infer from images. Surface color, reflectance, and texture are also perceived simultaneously. In machine vision, there has been some work in this direction. For example, attempts have been made to solve the color constancy problem—to estimate true surface color, given that the apparent color in the image is determined both by the surface color and the spectral distribution of the illuminant.

Visually Guided Control

One of the principal uses of vision is to provide information for manipulating objects and guiding locomotion. Consider the use of vision in driving on a freeway. A driver needs to

1. Keep moving at a reasonable speed.
2. Control the lateral position of the vehicle in its lane—make sure it stays in the center and is oriented properly.
3. Control the longitudinal position of the vehicle—keep a safe distance from the vehicle in front of it.

The lateral and longitudinal control tasks do not require a complete reconstruction of the environment. For instance, lateral control of the car only requires the following information: the position of the car relative to the left and right lane markers, its orientation relative to the lanes, and the curvature of the upcoming road. A feedback control law can be designed using these measurements and taking into account the dynamics of the car. Several research groups (e.g., Dickmanns and Mysliwetz 1992) have demonstrated vision-based automated driving.

For dynamic tasks, it is important that measurements can be integrated over time to yield better estimates—Kalman filtering provides one formalism. Often the motion of the sensing device is known (perhaps because it has been commanded by the agent) and estimation of relevant scene properties can be made even more robust by exploiting this knowledge.

It is worth noting that even a partial reconstruction of scene information, as suggested above, may not be necessary. Lateral control could be achieved by feedback directly on image (as opposed to scene) measurements. Just steer so that the left and right lane markers are seen by the forward pointing camera in a symmetric position with respect to the center of the image. For the more general task of navigation around obstacles, other variables computable from the optical flow field have been proposed.

Grouping and Tracking

Humans have a remarkable ability to organize their perceptual input—instead of a collection of values associated with individual photoreceptors, we perceive a number of visual groups, usually associated with objects or well-defined parts of objects. This ability is equally important for machine vision. To recognize objects, we must first separate them from their backgrounds. Monitoring and surveillance applications require the ability to detect individual objects, and track them over time. Tracking can be viewed as grouping in the temporal dimension.

Most machine vision techniques for grouping and tracking can be viewed as attempts to construct algorithmic implementations of various grouping factors studied in the context of humans under the rubric of GESTALT PERCEPTION. For instance, the Gestaltists listed similarity as a major grouping factor—humans readily form groups from parts of an image that are uniform in color, such as a connected red patch, or uniform in texture, such as a plaid region. Computationally, this has motivated edge detection, a technique based on marking boundaries where neighboring pixels have significant differences in brightness or color. If we look for differences in texture descriptors of image patches, suitably defined, we can find texture edges.

Similarity is only one of the factors that can promote grouping. Good continuation suggests linking edge segments that have directions consistent with being part of a smoothly curving extended contour. Relaxation methods and dynamic programming approaches have been proposed to exploit this factor.

Earlier work in machine vision was based primarily on local methods, which make decisions about the presence of boundaries purely on the information in a small neighborhood of an image pixel. Contemporary efforts aim to make use of global information. A number of competing formalisms, such as Markov random fields (Geman and Geman 1984), layer approaches (Wang and Adelson 1994) based on the expectation maximization technique from statistics, and cut techniques drawn from spectral graph theory (Shi and Malik 1997) are being explored. Some of these allow for the combined use of multiple grouping factors such as similarity in brightness as well as common motion.

The temporal grouping problem, visual tracking, lends itself well to the Kalman filtering formalism for dynamic estimation. At each frame, the position of a moving object is estimated by combining measurements from the current time frame with the predicted position from previous data. Generalizations of this idea have also been developed (see Isard and Blake 1996).

See also COLOR VISION; COMPUTATIONAL VISION; STRUCTURE FROM VISUAL INFORMATION SOURCES; SURFACE PERCEPTION; OBJECT RECOGNITION; HUMAN NEUROPSYCHOLOGY; VISION AND LEARNING

—*Jitendra Malik*

References

Dickmanns, E. D., and B. D. Mysliwetz. (1992). Recursive 3-D road and relative ego-state recognition. *IEEE Transactions on Pattern Analysis and Machine Intelligence* 14: 199–213.

Faugeras, O. (1993). *Three-Dimensional Computer Vision: A Geometric Viewpoint.* Cambridge, MA: MIT Press.

Geman, S., and D. Geman. (1984). Stochastic relaxation, Gibbs distributions, and the Bayesian restoration of images. *IEEE Transactions on Pattern Analysis and Machine Intelligence* 6: 721–741.

Horn, B. K. P., and M. J. Brooks. (1989). *Shape from Shading.* Cambridge, MA: MIT Press.

Isard, M., and A. Blake. (1996). Contour tracking by stochastic propagation of conditional density. In B. Buxton and R. Cipolla, Eds., *Proceedings of the Fourth European Conference on Computer Vision.* (ECCV 1996), Cambridge. Berlin: Springer, vol. 1, p. 343–356.

Koenderink, J. J. (1990). *Solid Shape.* Cambridge, MA: MIT Press.

Malik, J., and R. Rosenholtz. (1997). Computing local surface orientation and shape from texture for curved surfaces. *International Journal of Computer Vision* 23(2): 149–168.

Shi, J., and J. Malik. (1997). Normalized cuts and image segmentation. In *Proceedings of the 1997 IEEE Computer Society Conference on Computer Vision and Pattern Recognition,* San Juan, Puerto Rico, pp. 731–737.

Ullman, S. (1996). *High-Level Vision: Object Recognition and Visual Cognition.* Cambridge, MA: MIT Press.

Wang, J. Y. A., and E. H. Adelson. (1994). Representing moving images with layers. *IEEE Transactions on Image Processing* 3(5): 625–638.

Further Readings

Haralick, R. M., and L. G. Shapiro. (1992). *Computer and Robot Vision.* 2 vols. Reading, MA: Addison-Wesley.

Horn, B. K. P. (1986). *Robot Vision.* Cambridge, MA: MIT Press.

Marr, D. (1982). *Vision.* San Francisco: Freeman.

Nalwa, V. S. (1993). *A Guided Tour of Computer Vision.* Reading, MA: Addison Wesley.

Trucco, E., and A. Verri. (1998). *Introductory Techniques for 3-D Computer Vision.* Englewood Cliffs, NJ: Prentice-Hall.

Machines and Cognition

See INTRODUCTION: COMPUTATIONAL INTELLIGENCE; INTRODUCTION: PHILOSOPHY

Magic and Superstition

We generally call something magical or superstitious if it involves human agency (as distinct from religion), and invokes causes inconsistent with *current* understandings, by relevant "experts," (e.g., Western scientists) of how the world operates.

Magical beliefs and activities have been understood by historians (Thomas 1971), psychologists (Freud 1950; Piaget 1929), and anthropologists (Frazer 1890; Mauss 1902) as primitive attempts to understand and control the world. Some of these authors posit an "evolutionary" or developmental course, with magic replaced over historical time, first by religion and ultimately by science. This hypothesized progression cannot account for the high incidence of magical beliefs in educated late twentieth century adults in the developed world, in the face of the great advances of science in the twentieth century.

Why do these beliefs (and actions) persist? The adaptive human tendency to understand, control, and make meaning out of occurrences in the world probably lies at the heart of magic and religion. Reliance by scientific explanations on impersonal forces and random events fails to satisfy the human mind, which is inclined to personalize and humanize accounts of events in the world. The pervasiveness of magical beliefs can probably be attributed to three causes: (1) this type of thinking is natural and intuitive for the human mind (though some, e.g., Sperber 1985, propose that ideas such as this may survive because they strikingly depart from intuition and expectations); (2) magical thinking often makes moderately accurate predictions; and (3) a major function of magical acts and rituals is performative (Tambiah 1990).

Why do magical beliefs take the particular form they do? They seem heavily guided by natural intuitions about the nature of the world, and are selected for their ability to give satisfying (including anxiety-reducing) as much as accurate accounts. These intuitions may derive from primary process thought (FREUD), failure to distinguish the self from the world (PIAGET), preprogrammed or readily acquired cognitive heuristics, or the very nature of symbolic thinking.

Since some "magical" beliefs have proven true over time (e.g., the folk belief in mid-19th-century America that cholera was contagious), and since scientific knowledge is by definition open to continuous revision, we focus on the form rather than the accuracy of magical beliefs. We examine two principles that are widespread, specific, and relatively well studied. These are two of the three "laws of sympathetic magic," originally described as aspects of the "primitive" mind by Tylor (1879), Frazer (1890), and Mauss (1902). The laws were conceived as basic features of human thought, projected onto the world, leading to beliefs that things associated or symbolically related in the mind actually go together, and may be causally linked, in the world (see Rozin and Nemeroff 1990; Nemeroff and Rozin 1998; Tambiah 1990 for reviews).

The law of similarity has been summarized as "like produces like," "like goes with like," or "the image equals the object." Likeness is elevated to a basic, often causal principle; the simplest example confounds likeness with identity, hence "appearance equals reality." The adaptive value of this law is clear: generally speaking, if it looks like a tiger, it *is* a tiger. For humans, this law becomes problematic because humans make artifacts that are imitations of entities in the world, as in drawings or photographs, or more abstractly, the words that represent them. A picture of a tiger does not justify fear. Similarity functions in nonhumans and in young children (presumably from birth); one feature of development is learning about situations in which appearance does not correspond to reality.

Examples of similarity include burning effigies of persons in order to cause harm to them, or reliance on appearance in judging objects when the appearance is known to be deceiving (e.g., avoidance by educated adults of chocolate shaped to look like feces; or difficulty experienced in throwing darts at a picture of a respected person). In the domain of words, Piaget (1929) described as "nominal realism" the child's difficulty in understanding the arbitrary relation of word and referent. Similarly, educated people have difficulty disregarding a label on a bottle (e.g., "poison") that they know does not apply.

The law of contagion holds that when two objects come into even brief physical contact, properties are permanently transmitted between them ("once in contact, always in contact"). Contagion typically flows from a valenced source (e.g., a detested or favorite person), often through a vehicle (e.g., clothing or food) to a target, usually a person. Traditional examples include the idea that food or objects that have been in contact with death, disease, or enemies will cause harm if eaten or contacted, or that damage done to a separated part of a person (e.g., a piece of hair) will damage that person (sorcery).

Contagion has clear adaptive value by reducing the risk of transmitting microbes. It is closely associated with the emotion of disgust (disgusting entities are contaminating, i.e., negative contagion), and may have originated in the food context. On the positive side, contagion provides a concrete representation of kinship as shared blood, and may serve as the proximal means to induce kin preferences.

Contagion, in opposition to similarity, holds that things are often not what they appear to be, since they bear invisible "traces" of their histories. Consistent with this sophistication, contagion seems to be absent in young children and all nonhumans. However, contagion is probably present in all normal adult humans.

Magical contagion is shown by educated adults, who, for example, reject a preferred beverage after brief contact with a dead cockroach (Rozin and Nemeroff 1990). Western subjects in situations such as these generally attribute their aversion to health risks; however, they quickly realize that this account is insufficient when their aversion remains after the contaminant has been rendered harmless (e.g., sterilized). Magical thinking often exposes such "head vs. heart" conflicts.

Other examples of contagion in everyday life include celebrity token hunting, valuing of family heirlooms, and the reluctance of many individuals to share or buy used clothing. Sources capable of producing positive contagion ("transvaluation") include loved ones and celebrities. Those capable of producing substantial aversions include virtually any disgusting substance, and a wide variety of people; even unknown healthy others contaminate for most persons, and contamination is enhanced if the person is described as ill or morally tainted.

Some properties of contagion (Rozin and Nemeroff 1990) across situations and cultures are: (1) Physical contact is either definitionally necessary or almost always present; (2) Effects are relatively permanent; (3) Even very brief contact with any part of the source produces almost the full effect (dose and route insensitivity); (4) Negative contagion is more widespread and powerful than positive (negativity dominance); (5) Properties passed may be physical or mental, including intentions and "luck"; (6) Contagion can operate in a "backward" direction, with effects flowing from recipient or vehicle back on to the source (as when one attempts to harm someone by burning a lock of their hair).

The contagious entity or "essence" may be mentally represented in at least three ways (depending on culture, nature of the source, and individual within-culture differences). One is pure association (which does not entail contact, and can be thought of as an artifactual account of contagion), a second is the passage of a material-like essence, and a third is the passage of a spiritual, nonmaterial essence (Nemeroff and Rozin 1994).

Magical thinking varies substantially in quality and quantity across cultures, lifetimes, and history, as well as among adults within a culture. Contagion, particularly via contact with those perceived as undesirable, is omnipresent, and is potentially crippling. While this type of interpersonal contagion is universal, in Hindu India and many of the cultures in Papua, New Guinea (Meigs 1984), it is especially salient in daily life, and has an overt moral significance.

See also CULTURAL SYMBOLISM; CULTURAL VARIATION; ESSENTIALISM; LÉVI-STRAUSS, CLAUDE; RELIGIOUS IDEAS AND PRACTICES; SCIENTIFIC THINKING AND ITS DEVELOPMENT

—*Paul Rozin and Carol Nemeroff*

References

Frazer, J. G. (1890/1959). *The Golden Bough: A Study in Magic and Religion.* New York: Macmillan. (Reprint of 1922 abr. ed. T. H. Gaster; original work published 1890.)

Freud, S. (1950). *Totem and Taboo: Some Points of Agreement between the Mental Lives of Savages and Neurotics.* Translated by J. Strachey. New York: W. W. Norton. (Original work published 1913.)

Mauss, M. (1902/1972). *A General Theory of Magic.* Translated by R. Brain. New York: W. W. Norton. (Original work published 1902: Esquisse d'une theorie generale de la magie. *L'Annee Sociologique* 1902–1903.)

Meigs, A. (1994). *Food, Sex, and Pollution: A New Guinea Religion.* New Brunswick, NJ: Rutgers University Press.

Nemeroff, C., and P. Rozin. (Forthcoming). The makings of the magical mind. In K. Rosengren, C. Johnson, and P. Harris, Eds., *Imagining the Impossible: The Development of Magical, Scientific, and Religious Thinking in Contemporary Society.* Oxford: Oxford University Press.

Nemeroff, C. and P. Rozin. (1994). The contagion concept in adult thinking in the United States: Transmission of germs and interpersonal influence. *Ethos. The Journal of Psychological Anthropology* 22: 158–186.

Piaget, J. (1929/1967). *The Child's Conception of the World.* Totawa, NJ: Littlefield and Adams. (Original work published 1929.)

Rozin, P., and C. J. Nemeroff. (1990). The laws of sympathetic magic: A psychological analysis of similarity and contagion. In J. Stigler, G. Herdt, and R. A. Shweder, Eds., *Cultural Psychology: Essays on Comparative Human Development.* Cambridge, UK: Cambridge University Press, pp. 205–232.

Sperber, D. (1985). Anthropology and psychology. Towards an epidemiology of representations. *Man* 20: 73–89.

Tambiah, S. J. (1990). *Magic, Science, Religion, and the Scope of Rationality.* Cambridge, UK: Cambridge University Press.

Thomas, K. (1971). *Religion and the Decline of Magic.* London: Weidenfeld and Nicolson.

Tylor, E. B. (1871/1974). *Primitive Culture: Researches into the Development of Mythology, Philosophy, Religion, Art and Custom.* New York: Gordon Press. (Original work published 1871.)

Further Readings

Boyer, P. (1995). Causal understandings in cultural representations: Cognitive constraints on inferences from cultural input. In D. Sperber, D. Premack, and A. J. Premack, Eds., *Causal Cognition: A Multidisciplinary Debate.* Oxford: Clarendon Press, pp. 615–644.

Evans-Pritchard, E. E. (1976). *Witchcraft, Oracles and Magic among the Azande.* Oxford: Oxford University Press. (Original work published 1937.)

Horton, R. (1967). African traditional thought and Western science. *Africa* 37(1–2): 50–71, 155–187.

Humphrey, N. (1996). *Leaps of Faith.* New York: Basic Books.

Nemeroff, C., A. Brinkman, and C. Woodward. (1994). Magical cognitions about AIDS in a college population. *AIDS Education and Prevention* 6: 249–265.

Rosengren, K., C. Johnson, and P. Harris, Eds. (Forthcoming). *Imagining the Impossible: The Development of Magical, Scien-*

tific, and Religious Thinking in Contemporary Society. Oxford: Oxford University Press.

Rozin, P., M. Markwith, and C. R. McCauley. (1994). The nature of aversion to indirect contact with other persons: AIDS aversion as a composite of aversion to strangers, infection, moral taint and misfortune. *Journal of Abnormal Psychology* 103: 495–504.

Shweder, R. A. (1977). Likeness and likelihood in everyday thought: magical thinking in judgments about personality. *Current Anthropology* 18: 637–658.

Siegel, M., and D. L. Share. (1990). Contamination sensitivity in young children. *Developmental Psychology* 26: 455–458.

Magnetic Fields

See ELECTROPHYSIOLOGY, ELECTRIC AND MAGNETIC EVOKED FIELDS

Magnetic Resonance Imaging

Magnetic resonance imaging (MRI) is based on the phenomenon of nuclear magnetic resonance (NMR), first described in landmark papers over fifty years ago (Rabi et al. 1938; Rabi, Millman, and Kusch 1939; Purcell et al. 1945; Bloch, Hansen, and Packard 1946). In the presence of an external magnetic field, atomic nuclei with magnetic moments, such as ^{1}H, ^{13}C, and ^{31}P nuclei, encounter a separation in the energy levels of their quantum mechanically allowed orientations relative to the external field. Transitions between these orientations can be induced with electromagnetic radiation typically in the radiofrequency range. The discrete frequency associated with such a transition is proportional to the external magnetic field strength and to two parameters that are determined by the intrinsic properties of the nucleus and its chemical environments, the nuclear gyromagnetic ratio, and the chemical shift, respectively. Based on the ability to obtain discrete resonances sensitive to the chemical environment, NMR has evolved rapidly to become an indispensable tool in chemical and biological research focused on molecular composition, structure, and dynamics.

In 1973, a novel concept of using NMR of the hydrogen atoms in the human body as an imaging modality was introduced (Lauterbur 1973). While all NMR applications of the time were singularly concerned with eliminating inhomogeneities in magnetic field magnitude over the sample, this new concept embraced them and proposed to utilize them to extract spatial information. Consequently, today magnetic resonance is solidly established as a noninvasive imaging technique suitable for use with humans.

MRI is essentially based on two fundamental ideas, "spatial encoding" and "contrast." The former is the means by which the NMR data contain information on the spatial origin of the NMR signal. The latter must provide the ability to distinguish and visualize different structures or processes occurring within the imaged object and is ultimately translated into gray scale or color coding for presentation. Spatial encoding is accomplished by external magnetic fields whose magnitude depend linearly on spatial coordinates in any one of three orthogonal directions. Contrast is achieved either based on the regional density of the nuclear species imaged or by the impact of the chemical and biological environment on parameters that determine the behavior or relaxation of a population of spins from a nonequilibrium state toward thermal equilibrium. Improving contrast and spatial encoding strategies are central to developments in MRI as the field strives to image faster, with higher resolution and structural detail, and image not only anatomy but also physiological processes such as blood flow, perfusion, organ function, and intracellular chemistry.

An avidly pursued new dimension in the acquisition of physiological and biochemical information with MRI is mapping human brain function, referred to as fMRI. The first fMRI image of the human brain was based on measurements of task-induced blood volume change assessed with intravenous bolus injection of an MRI contrast agent, a highly paramagnetic substance, into the human subject and tracking the bolus passage through the brain with consecutive, rapidly acquired images (Belliveau et al. 1991). However, this method was quickly rendered obsolete with the introduction of totally noninvasive methods of fMRI. Of the two current ways of mapping alterations in neuronal activation noninvasively, the most commonly used method relies on the weak magnetic interactions between the nuclear spins of water protons in tissue and blood, and the paramagnetic deoxyhemoglobin molecule, termed BOLD (blood oxygen level–dependent) contrast, first described for the brain by Ogawa (Ogawa et al. 1990a, 1990b; Ogawa and Lee 1990) and is similar to the effect described for blood alone by Thulborn et al. (1982). The presence of paramagnetic deoxyhemoglobin, compartmentalized in red blood cells and in blood vessels, generates local magnetic field inhomogeneities surrounding these compartments which are dynamically (due to rapid diffusion) or statically averaged over the smallest volume element in the image and lead to signal loss when a delay is introduced between signal excitation and subsequent sampling.

In the original papers describing the BOLD effect, functional mapping in the human brain using BOLD was anticipated (Ogawa et al. 1990a) based on data documenting regional elevation in blood flow and glucose metabolism without a commensurate increase in oxygen consumption rate during increased neuronal activity (Fox and Raichle 1985; Fox et al. 1988); these data would predict a task-induced decrease in deoxyhemoglobin content in the human brain and a consequent alteration in MRI signal intensity when the signal intensity difference between two states, for example, in the absence and presence of a mental task or sensory stimulation, is examined. This was demonstrated and the first BOLD-based fMRI images of the human brain were published in 1992 by three groups in papers submitted within five days of each other (Bandettini et al. 1992; Kwong et al. 1992; Ogawa et al. 1992). Initial functional brain mapping studies were focused on simple sensory stimulation and regions of the brain that are relatively well understood. These studies were aimed at demonstrating and evaluating the validity of the technique rather than addressing the plethora of as yet unanswered questions concerned with aspects of brain function. In the short period of time since its introduction, however, BOLD fMRI has been used to map functions in the whole brain, including subcortical nuclei, with a few millimeters resolution and has been shown to display specificity at the level of ocular dominance columns in humans at the high magnetic field of 4 tesla (Menon, Ogawa, and Ugurbil 1996; Menon et al. 1997). At present field strengths, the sensitivity and hence the spatial resolution attainable, however, is at the margin of what is required for visualizing human ocular dominance columns which are approximately 1×1 mm in cross-sectional dimensions.

A second approach to generating functional maps of the brain with fMRI relies on the task-induced increase in regional blood flow alone. This method is analogous to the POSITRON EMISSION TOMOGRAPHY (PET)–based functional brain mapping using water labeled with a positron emitter ($H_2^{15}O$). In the noninvasive MRI approach, however, the label is simply the collective spins of the water molecules whose net bulk magnetization is inverted or nulled (saturated) either within a slice to be imaged or outside of the slice to be imaged. For example, if the slice to be imaged is inverted, the inverted magnetization must relax back to its thermal equilibrium value and does so in a few seconds; in the absence of flow, this occurs with what is termed spin-lattice relaxation mechanisms. However, when flow is present, apparent relaxation occurs because of replacement of inverted spins by unperturbed spins coming from outside the inversion slice. Such flow-based fMRI methods were first demonstrated in 1992 (Kwong et al. 1992), and significantly refined subsequently (Edelman et al. 1992; Kim 1995). While flow-based techniques have some advantages over BOLD methods, such as simplicity of interpretation and ability to poise the sensitivity to perfusion as opposed to macrovascular flow, rapid imaging of large sections of the brain or whole brain is not yet possible.

fMRI techniques rely on secondary and tertiary responses, metabolic and hemodynamic, to increased neuronal activity. Hence, they are subject to limitations imposed by the temporal characteristics and spatial specificity of these responses. Current data suggest that BOLD images, when designed with appropriate paradigms, may have spatial specificity down to the millimeter to submillimiter scale (e.g., ocular dominance columns) presumably because the spatial extent of altered oxygen consumption, hence deoxyhemoglobin alterations, coupled to neuronal activity, is confined accurately to the region of elevated neuronal activity; this scale may be coarser, possibly in the range of several millimeters, for perfusion images if blood flow response extends beyond the region of increased activity (Malonek and Grinvald 1996). With respect to temporal resolution, the sluggish metabolic response and even more sluggish hemodynamic response to changes in neuronal activity suggest that better than approximately 0.5-sec time resolution may not be achievable with current fMRI techniques even though image acquisition can be accomplished in as little as 20 to 30 msec. While this excludes a very large temporal domain of interest, the plethora of mental processes accomplished in the seconds domain by the human brain remains accessible to fMRI.

See also ELECTROPHYSIOLOGY, ELECTRIC AND MAGNETIC EVOKED FIELDS; MOTION, PERCEPTION OF; PHONOL-OGY, NEURAL BASIS OF; POSITRON EMISSION TOMOGRAPHY; SINGLE-NEURON RECORDING

—Kamil Ugurbil

References

Bandettini, A., E. C. Wang, R. S. Hinks, R. S. Rikofsky, and J. S. Hyde. (1992). Time course EPI of human brain function during task activation. *Magn. Reson. Med.* 25: 390.

Belliveau, J. W., D. N. Kennedy, R. C. McKinstry, B. R. Buchbinder, R. M. Weisskoff, M. S. Cohen, J. M. Vevea, T. J. Brady, and B. R. Rosen. (1991). Functional mapping of the human visual cortex by magnetic resonance imaging. *Science* 254: 716–719.

Bloch, F., W. W. Hansen, and M. Packard. (1946). The nuclear induction experiment. *Physical Review* 70: 474–485.

Edelman, R. E., B. Siewer, D. G. Darby, V. Thangaraj, A. C. Nobre, M. M. Mesulam, and S. Warach. (1992). Qualitative mapping of cerebral blood flow and functional localization with echo-planar MR imaging and signal targeting with alternating radio frequency. *Radiology* 192: 513–520.

Fox, P. T., and M. E. Raichle. (1985). Stimulus rate determines regional brain blood flow in striate cortex. *Ann. Neurol.* 17: 303–305.

Fox, P. T., M. E. Raichle, M. A. Mintun, and C. Dence. (1988). Nonoxidative glucose consumption during focal physiologic neural activity. *Science* 241: 462–464.

Kim, S.-G. (1995). Quantification of relative cerebral blood flow change by flow-sensitive alternating inversion recovery (FAIR) technique: Application to functional mapping. *Magn. Reson. Med.* 34: 293–301.

Kwong, K. K., J. W. Belliveau, D. A. Chesler, I. E. Goldberg, R. M. Weisskoff, B. Poncelet, D. N. Kennedy, B. E. Hoppel, M. S. Cohen, R. Turner, H. -M. Cheng, T. J. Brady, and B. R. Rosen. (1992). Dynamic magnetic resonance imaging of human brain activity during primary sensory stimulation. *Proc. Natl. Acad. Sci. U. S. A.* 89: 5675–5679.

Lauterbur, P. C. (1973). Image formation by induced local interaction: Examples employing nuclear magnetic resonance. *Nature* 242: 190–191.

Malonek, D., and A. Grinvald. (1996). Interactions between electrical activity and cortical microcirculation revealed by imaging spectroscopy: Implication for functional brain mapping. *Science* 272: 551–554.

Menon, R. S., S. Ogawa, and K. Ugurbil. (1996). Mapping ocular dominance columns in human V1 using fMRI. *Neuroimage* 3: S357.

Menon, R. S., S. Ogawa, J. P. Strupp, and K. Ugurbil. (1997). Ocular dominance in human V1 demonstrated by functional magnetic resonance imaging. *J. Neurophysiol.* 77(5): 2780–2787.

Ogawa, S., and T.-M. Lee. (1990). Magnetic resonance imaging of blood vessels at high fields: In vivo and in vitro measurements and image simulation. *Magn. Reson. Med.* 16: 9–18.

Ogawa, S., T. -M. Lee, A. R. Kay, and D. W. Tank. (1990a). Brain magnetic resonance imaging with contrast dependent on blood oxygenation. *Proc. Natl. Acad. Sci. U. S. A.* 87: 9868–9872.

Ogawa, S., T. -M. Lee, A. S. Nayak, and P. Glynn. (1990b). Oxygenation-sensitive contrast in magnetic resonance image of rodent brain at high magnetic fields. *Magn. Reson. Med.* 14: 68–78.

Ogawa, S., D. W. Tank, R. Menon, J. M. Ellermann, S. -G. Kim, H. Merkle, and K. Ugurbil. (1992). Intrinsic signal changes accompanying sensory stimulation: Functional brain mapping with magnetic resonance imaging. *Proc. Natl. Acad. Sci. U. S. A.* 89: 5951–5955.

Purcell, E. M., H. C. Torrey, and R. V. Pound. (1945). Resonance absorption by nuclear magnetic moments in a solid. *Physical Review* 69: 37.

Rabi, I. I., S. Millman, and P. Kusch. (1939). The molecular beam resonance method for measuring nuclear magnetic moments. *Physical Review* 55: 526–535.

Rabi, I. I., J. R. Zacharias, S. Millman, and P. Kusch. (1938). A new method of measuring nuclear magnetic moment. *Physical Review* 53: 318.

Thulborn, K. R., J. C. Waterton, P. M. Mathews, and G. K. Radda. (1982). Oxygenation dependence of the transverse relaxation time of water protons in whole blood at high field. *Biochem. Biophys. Acta* 714: 265–270.

Malinowski, Bronislaw

Bronislaw Malinowski (1884–1942), founder of British social anthropology and first thorough-going practitioner (if not the inventor) of the fieldwork method known as "participant observation," continues to be read with fascination and admiration. His reputation rests on six classic monographs he wrote between 1922 and 1935 about the lives and ideas of the world of the people of the Trobriands, a group of islands off the northeast coast of Papua New Guinea.

Malinowski was born in Cracow in 1884 to aristocratic parents. His father—a linguist and professor of Slavic philology at the University of Cracow—died when he was 12. His evidently clever mother taught herself Latin and mathematics in order to tutor him during a long illness in his midteens. In 1902 he entered the University of Cracow to study physics and philosophy and graduated with a Ph.D. in 1908—his thesis influenced by the empiricist epistemology of Ernst Mach. Afterward, at Leipzig, he studied economic history with Bucher and psychology with WUNDT, whose "folk psychology" concerned people's day-to-day ideas and their interconnections—their language, customs, art, myths, religion—in short, their "culture." Frazer's *The Golden Bough* was another definitive influence (see Kuper 1996: 1–34; Stocking 1995: 244–297).

In 1910 Malinowski left Leipzig for the London School of Economics where, under Westermarck, he worked on *The Family among the Australian Aborigines,* published in 1913. In 1914, aged 30, he made his first field trip to Papua New Guinea, where, following the wishes of his mentor, W. H. R. Rivers, he worked for some months among the Mailu; but this was "no more than an apprentice's trial run, conventional enough in method and results" (Kuper 1966: 12). The ground-breaking fieldwork came in 1915–1916 and 1917–1918 in Kiriwina, the largest of the Trobriand Islands.

Malinowski's first Trobriand ethnography was written in Australia in 1916. *Baloma: The Spirits of the Dead in the Trobriand Islands* (1916) is an engaging study of magic, witchcraft, and religious beliefs that also reveals Malinowski's tenacity in investigation. *Argonauts of the Western Pacific* (1922) describes the ceremonial exchange known as the Kula; a key text for anthropologists, it influenced, for example, Marcel Mauss and Claude LÉVI-STRAUSS. *Crime and Custom in Savage Society* (1926) examines reciprocity as an underlying principle of social control. *Sex and Repression in Savage Society* (1927) looks at the implications for

Freudian theory of relations within the Trobriand family. *The Sexual Life of Savages* (1929) focuses on sexuality, marriage, and kinship and includes vivid descriptions of children's daily lives. *Coral Gardens and their Magic* (1935, two volumes) deals with horticulture, land tenure, and the language of magic and gardening. Here Malinowski draws out his idea of "the context of situation," first put forward in an essay published twelve years earlier: "The conception of meaning as contained in an utterance is false and futile. A statement, spoken in real life, is never detached from the situation in which it has been uttered" (1952: 307). This perspective on language—radical in its time—is consistent with Malinowski's empiricism, which was always tempered by an awareness that "any belief or any item of folklore is not a simple piece of information . . . [it] must be examined in the light of diverse types of minds and of the diverse institutions in which it can be traced. To ignore this social dimension [of belief] . . . is unscientific" (1974: 239–240).

Malinowski's evolutionist view took for granted the cultural superiority of Europeans over other peoples; this idea is evident in his various works, especially in his private Trobriand diaries, which, being somewhat at odds with the ethnographies, caused controversy when they were published posthumously in 1967. Even so, and despite his sometimes patronizing and even spiteful asides on "the natives," Malinowski was clearly genuine both in his pursuit of his fieldwork aims and in the often admiring respect for Trobriand people he expressed in his works and in person to his students (Firth 1957, 1989; Young 1979).

A charismatic teacher, revered by his students at the London School of Economics, where he held the first chair in social anthropology, Malinowski spent a good deal of his intellectual force engaged in the battle to make his functionalist theory of human behavior dominant in social anthropology. He argued that "culture is essentially an instrumental apparatus by which man is put in a position the better to cope with the concrete specific problems that face him in his environment in the course of the satisfaction of his needs" (1944: 150). This perspective had stood Malinowski in good stead in gathering field data, but it assumed "culture" to be an integrated whole, left no place for change as a condition of human existence, and lacked any analytical power to explain cross-cultural similarities and differences.

In 1938 Malinowski went to the United States, where he was caught by the outbreak of World War II and remained, as a visiting professor at Yale, until he died suddenly in 1942. His work was developed and sometimes amended by later ethnographers of the Trobriands, but "the legacy of his Trobriand ethnography continues to play an unprecedented role in the history of anthropology" (Weiner 1988: 4).

See also BOAS, FRANZ; CULTURAL EVOLUTION; CULTURAL PSYCHOLOGY; RELIGIOUS IDEAS AND PRACTICES; SAPIR, EDWARD

—*Christina Toren*

References

Firth, R., Ed. (1957). *Man and Culture: An Evaluation of the Work of Bronislaw Malinowski.* London: Routledge and Kegan Paul.

Firth, R. (1989). Introduction. In B. Malinowski, *A Diary in the Strict Sense of the Term*. Stanford University Press.

Kuper, A. (1996). *Anthropologists and Anthropology: The Modern British School*. 3rd ed. London: Routledge.

Malinowski, B. (1916). Baloma: Spirits of the dead in the Trobriand Islands. *Journal of the Royal Anthropological Institute* 46: 354–430.

Malinowski, B. (1922). *Argonauts of the Western Pacific*. London: Routledge.

Malinowski, B. (1926). *Crime and Custom in Savage Society*. London: Kegan Paul.

Malinowski, B. (1927). *Sex and Repression in Savage Society*. London: Kegan Paul.

Malinowski, B. (1929). *The Sexual Life of Savages*. London: Routledge.

Malinowski, B. (1935). *Coral Gardens and their Magic: A Study of the Methods of Tilling the Soil and of Agricultural Rites in the Trobriand Islands*. Two vols. London: George Allen and Unwin.

Malinowski, B. (1944). *A Scientific Theory of Culture and Other Essays*. Chapel Hill: University of North Carolina Press.

Malinowski, B. (1952). The problem of meaning in primitive languages. In C. K. Ogden and I. A. Richards, Eds., *The Meaning of Meaning: A Study of the Influence of Language upon Thought and of the Science of Symbolism*. London: Routledge and Kegan Paul.

Malinowski, B. (1974). *Magic, Science and Religion*. London: Souvenir Press.

Malinowski, B. (1967). *A Diary in the Strict Sense of the Term*. London: Routledge and Kegan Paul.

Stocking, G. W. (1995). *After Tylor: British Social Anthropology 1888–1951*. Madison: University of Wisconsin Press.

Weiner, A. (1988). *The Trobrianders of Papua New Guinea*. New York: Holt, Rinehart and Winston.

Young, M. W., Ed. (1979). *The Ethnography of Malinowski: The Trobriand Islands 1915–18*. London: Routledge and Kegan Paul.

Further Readings

Wayne Malinowska, H. (1985). Bronislaw Malinowski: The influence of various women on his life and works. *American Ethnologist* 12:529–40.

Manipulation and Grasping

Manipulation and grasping are branches of robotics and involve notions from kinematics, mechanics, and CONTROL THEORY. Grasping is concerned with characterizing and achieving the conditions that will ensure that a robot gripper holds an object securely, preventing, for example, any motion due to external forces. Manipulation, on the other hand, is concerned with characterizing and achieving the conditions under which a robot or a part held by a robot will perform a certain motion. Research in both areas has led to practical systems for picking up parts from a conveyor belt or a pallet, reorienting them, and inserting them into an assembly (e.g., Tournassoud, Lozano-Perez, and Mazer 1987; Peshkin and Sanderson 1988; Goldberg 1993), with promising applications in flexible manufacturing.

This entry focuses on a quasi-static model of mechanics that neglects inertial forces and dynamic effects. This is valid in typical grasping and manipulation tasks when all velocities are small enough, and allows for a geometric analysis of object motion under kinematic constraints. Our discussion of manipulation is restricted to the problem of characterizing the motion of an object pushed by one or several fingers, and it excludes some fundamental problems such as general robot motion planning in the presence of obstacles.

Grasping emerged as a field of its own in the early eighties with the introduction of dextrous multifinger grippers such as the Salisbury Hand (Salisbury 1982) and the Utah-MIT Dextrous Hand (Jacobsen et al. 1984). Much of the early work was conducted in Roth's research group at Stanford (e.g., Salisbury 1982; Kerr and Roth 1986) drawing on notions of form and force closure from *screw theory* (Ball 1900), which provides a unified representation for displacements and velocities as well as forces and torques using a line-based geometry. Namely, when a hand holds an object at rest, the forces and moments exerted by the fingers should balance each other so as not to disturb the position of this object. Such a grasp is said to achieve *equilibrium*. An equilibrium grasp achieves *force closure* when it is capable of balancing any external force and torque, thus holding the object securely. A *form closure* grasp achieves the same result by preventing any small object motion through the geometric constraints imposed by the finger contacts. Intuition suggests that the two conditions are equivalent, and it can indeed be shown that force closure implies form closure and vice versa (Mishra and Silver 1989). A secure grasp should also be *stable;* in particular, a compliant grasp submitted to a small external disturbance should return to its equilibrium state. Nguyen (1989) has shown that force or form closure grasps are indeed stable.

Screw theory can be used to show that, in the frictionless case, four or seven fingers are both necessary and, under very general conditions, sufficient (Lakshminarayana 1978; Markenscoff, Ni, and Papadimitriou 1990) to construct frictionless form or force closure grasps of two- or three-dimensional objects, respectively. As could be expected, friction "helps" and it can also be shown that only three or four fingers are sufficient in the presence of Coulomb friction (Markenscoff, Ni, and Papadimitriou 1990). In fact, it can also be shown that any grasp achieving equilibrium for some friction coefficient μ will also achieve form or force closure for any friction coefficient $\mu' > \mu$ (Nguyen 1988; Ponce et al. 1997).

Screw theory can also be used to characterize the geometric arrangement of contact forces that achieve equilibrium (and thus form or force closure under friction). In particular, two forces are in equilibrium when they oppose each other and share the same line of action, and three forces are in equilibrium when they add to zero and their lines of action intersect at a point. The four-finger case is more involved, but a classical result from line geometry is that the lines of action of four noncoplanar forces achieving equilibrium lie on the surface of a (possibly degenerated) hyperboloid (Ball 1990). In turn, these geometric conditions have been used in algorithms for computing optimal grasp forces given fixed finger positions (e.g., Kerr and Roth 1986), constructing at least one (maybe optimal) configuration of the fingers that will achieve force closure (e.g.,

Mishra, Schwartz, and Sharir 1987; Markenscoff and Papadimitriou 1989), and computing entire ranges of finger positions that yield force closure (e.g., Nguyen 1988; Ponce et al. 1997). The latter techniques provide some degree of robustness in the presence of the unavoidable positioning uncertainties of real robotic systems.

As shown in Rimon and Burdick (1993), for example, certain grasps that are not form closure nevertheless immobilize the grasped object. For example, three frictionless fingers positioned at the centers of the edges of an equilateral triangle cannot prevent an infinitesimal rotation of the triangle about its center of mass, although they can prevent any finite motion. Rimon and Burdick (1993) have shown how to characterize these grasps by mapping the constraints imposed by the fingers on the motion of an object onto its *configuration space,* that is, the set of object positions and orientations. In this setting, screw theory becomes a *first-order* theory of mobility, where the curved obstacle surfaces are approximated by their tangent planes, and where immobilized object configurations correspond to isolated points of the free configuration space. Rimon and Burdick have shown that second-order (curvature) effects can effectively prevent any finite object motion, and they have given operational conditions for immobilization and proven the dynamic stability of immobilizing grasps under various deformation models (Rimon and Burdick 1994). An additional advantage of this theory is that second-order immobility can be achieved with fewer fingers than form closure (e.g., four fingers instead of seven are in general sufficient to guarantee immobility in the frictionless case). Techniques for computing second-order immobilizing grasps have been proposed in Sudsang, Ponce, and Srinivasa (1997) for example.

Once an object has been grasped, it can of course be manipulated by moving the gripper while keeping its fingers locked, but the range of achievable motions is limited by physical constraints. For example, the rotational freedom of a gripper about its axis is usually bounded by the mechanics of the attached robot wrist. A simple approach to fine manipulation in the plane is to construct *finger gaits* (Hong et al. 1990). Assume that a disk is held by a four-finger hand in a three-finger force closure grasp. A certain amount of, say, counterclockwise rotation can be achieved by rotating the wrist. To achieve a larger rotation, first position the fourth finger so that the disk will be held in force closure by the second, third, and fourth fingers, then release the first finger and reposition it. By repositioning the four fingers in turn so that their overall displacement is clockwise, we can then apply a new counterclockwise rotation of the wrist, and repeat the process as many times as necessary. (See Li, Canny, and Sastry 1989 for a related approach to dextrous manipulation, which includes coordinated manipulation, as well as rolling and sliding motions.)

Thus far, our discussion has assumed implicitly that a workpiece starts *and remains* at rest while it is grasped. This will be true when the part is very heavy or bolted to a table, but in a realistic situation, it is likely to move when the first contact is established and contact may be immediately broken. Moreover, the actual position and orientation of the object with respect to the hand are usually (at best) close to the nominal ones. Mason (1986) proposed that an appropri-ate characterization of the mechanics of pushing would at the same time provide the means of (1) predicting (at least partially) the motion of the manipulated object once contact is established, and (2) reducing the uncertainty in object position without sensory feedback. Assuming Coulomb friction, he constructed a program that predicts the motion of an object with a known distribution of support forces being pushed at a single contact point. He also devised a simple rule for determining the rotation sense of the pushed object when the distribution is unknown.

Extensions of this approach have been applied to a number of other manipulation problems. Fearing (1986) has shown how to exploit local tactile information to determine how a polygonal object rotates while it is grasped, and demonstrated the capture of an object by the three-finger Salisbury hand as well as the execution of other complex manipulation tasks such as part "twirling." In the manufacturing domain, Peshkin and Sanderson (1988) have shown how to use static fences to reorient parts carried by a conveyor belt, and Goldberg (1993) has used a modified two-jaw gripper to plan a sequence of grasping operations that will reorient a part with unknown original orientation. A variant of this approach has also been used to plan a set of tray-tilting operations that will reorient a part lying in a tray (Erdmann and Mason 1988). More recently, Lynch and Mason (1995) have derived sufficient conditions for *stable pushing,* namely, for finding a set of pushing directions that will guarantee that the pushed object remains rigidly attached to the pusher during the manipulation task. They have also proven conditions for local and global controllability, and given an algorithm for planning pushing tasks in the presence of obstacles.

The kinematics of pushing are important as well, because they determine the relative positions and orientations of the gripper-object pair during the execution of a manipulation task. Brost (1991) has shown how to construct plans for pushing and compliant motion tasks through a detailed geometric analysis of the obstacle formed by a rigid polygon in the configuration space of a second polygon. More recently, Sudsang, Ponce, and Srinivasa (1997) have introduced the notion of *inescapable configuration space* (ICS) region for a grasp. As noted earlier, an object is immobilized when it rests at an isolated point of its free configuration space. A small motion of a finger away from the object will transform this isolated point into a compact region of free space (the ICS) that cannot be escaped by the object. For simple pushing mechanisms, it is possible to compute the maximum ICS regions and the corresponding range of finger motions, and to show that moving the finger from the far end of this range to its immobilizing position will cause the ICS to continuously shrink, ensuring that the object ends up in the planned immobilizing configuration. Thus a grasp can be executed in a robust manner, without requiring a model of the part motion at contact. More complex manipulation tasks can also be planned by constructing a graph of overlapping maximum ICS regions. This approach has been applied to grasping and in-hand manipulation with a multifingered reconfigurable gripper (Sudsang, Ponce, and Srinivasa 1997), and more recently, to manipulation tasks using disk-shaped mobile platforms in the plane.

See also BEHAVIOR-BASED ROBOTICS; HAPTIC PERCEPTION; MOBILE ROBOTS; ROBOTICS AND LEARNING; WALKING AND RUNNING MACHINES

—Jean Ponce

References

Ball, R. S. (1900). *A Treatise on the Theory of Screws.* New York: Cambridge University Press.

Brost, R. C. (1991). *Analysis and planning of planar manipulation tasks.* Ph.D. diss., Carnegie-Mellon University.

Erdmann, M. A., and M. T. Mason. (1988). An exploration of sensorless manipulation. *IEEE Journal of Robotics and Automation* 4: 369–379.

Fearing, R. S. (1986). Simplified grasping and manipulation with dextrous robot hands. *IEEE Transactions on Robotics and Automation* 4(2): 188–195.

Goldberg, K. Y. (1993) Orienting polygonal parts without sensors. *Algorithmica* 10(2): 201–225.

Hong, J., G. Lafferriere, B. Mishra, and X. Tan. (1990). Fine manipulation with multifinger hands. In *Proc. IEEE Int. Conf. on Robotics and Automation.* IEEE Press, 1568–1573.

Jacobsen, S. C., J. E. Wood, D. F. Knutti, and K. B. Biggers. (1984). The Utah-MIT Dextrous Hand: Work in progress. *International Journal of Robotics Research* 3(4): 21–50.

Kerr, J. R., and B. Roth. (1986). Analysis of multi-fingered hands. *International Journal of Robotics Research* 4(4).

Lakshminarayana, K. (1978). Mechanics of form closure. *Technical Report* 78-DET-32.: American Society of Mechanical Engineers.

Li, Z., J. F. Canny, and S. S. Sastry. (1989). On motion planning for dextrous manipulation: 1. The problem formulation. In *Proc. IEEE Int. Conf. on Robotics and Automation,* Scottsdale, AZ, pp. 775–780.

Lynch, K. M., and M. T. Mason. (1995). Stable pushing: Mechanics, controllability, and planning. In K. Y. Goldberg, D. Halperin, J-C. Latombe, and R. Wilson, Eds., *Algorithmic Foundations of Robotics.* A. K. Peters, pp. 239–262.

Markenscoff, X., L. Ni, and C. H. Papadimitriou. (1990). The geometry of grasping. *International Journal of Robotics Research* 9(1): 61–74.

Markenscoff, X., and C. H. Papadimitriou. (1989). Optimum grip of a polygon. *International Journal of Robotics Research* 8(2): 17–29.

Mason, M. T. (1986). Mechanics and planning of manipulator pushing operations. *International Journal of Robotics Research* 5(3): 53–71.

Mishra, B., J. T. Schwartz, and M. Sharir. (1987). On the existence and synthesis of multifinger positive grips. *Algorithmica, Special issue on robotics* 2(4): 541–558.

Mishra, B., and N. Silver. (1989). Some discussion of static gripping and its stability. *IEEE Systems, Man, and Cybernetics* 19(4): 783–796.

Nguyen, V-D. (1988). Constructing force-closure grasps. *International Journal of Robotics Research* 7(3): 3–16.

Nguyen, V-D. (1989). Constructing stable grasps. *International Journal of Robotics Research* 8(1): 27–37.

Peshkin, M. A., and A. C. Sanderson. (1988). Planning robotic manipulation strategies for workpieces that slide. *IEEE Journal of Robotics and Automation* 4(5).

Ponce, J., S. Sullivan, A. Sudsang, J-D. Boissonnat, and J-P. Merlet. (1997). On computing four-finger equilibrium and force-closure grasps of polyhedral objects. *International Journal of Robotics Research* 16(1): 11–35.

Rimon, E., and J. W. Burdick. (1993). Towards planning with force constraints: On the mobility of bodies in contact. In *Proc. IEEE Int. Conf. on Robotics and Automation*: Atlanta, GA, pp. 994–1000.

Rimon, E. and J. W. Burdick. (1994). Mobility of bodies in contact: 2. How forces are generated by curvature effects. In *Proc. IEEE Int. Conf. on Robotics and Automation,* San Diego, CA.

Salisbury, J. K. (1982). *Kinematic and force analysis of articulated hands.* Ph.D. diss., Stanford University.

Sudsang, A., J. Ponce, and N. Srinivasa. (1997). Algorithms for constructing immobilizing fixtures and grasps of three-dimensional objects. In J-P. Laumont and M. Overmars, Eds., *Algorithmic Foundations of Robotics,* vol. 2. Peters, pp. 363–380.

Tournassoud, P., T. Lozano-Perez, and E. Mazer. (1987). Regrasping. In *Proc. IEEE Int. Conf. on Robotics and Automation,* Raleigh, NC, pp. 1924–1928.

Further Readings

Akella, S., and M. T. Mason. (1995). Parts orienting by push-aligning. In *Proc. IEEE Int. Conf. on Robotics and Automation.* Nagoya, Japan, pp. 414–420.

Baker, B. S., S. J. Fortune, and E. H. Grosse. (1985). Stable prehension with a multi-fingered hand. In *Proc. IEEE Int. Conf. on Robotics and Automation,* St. Louis, MO. pp. 570–575.

Brost, R. C., and K. Goldberg. (1996). A complete algorithm for designing planar fixtures using modular components. *IEEE Transactions on Robotics and Automation* 12(1): 31–46.

Cutkosky, M. R. (1984). Mechanical properties for the grasp of a robotic hand. *Technical Report* CMU-RI-TR-84-24, Carnegie-Mellon University Robotics Institute.

Ferrari, C., and J. F. Canny. (1992). Planning optimal grasps. In *Proc. IEEE Int. Conf. on Robotics and Automation,* Nice, France, pp. 2290–2295.

Goldberg, K., and M. T. Mason. (1990). Bayesian grasping. In *Proc. IEEE Int. Conf. on Robotics and Automation,* IEEE Press, pp. 1264–1269.

Howard, W. S., and V. Kumar. (1994). Stability of planar grasps. In *Proc. IEEE Int. Conf. on Robotics and Automation,* San Diego, CA, pp. 2822–2827.

Ji, Z., and B. Roth. (1988). Direct computation of grasping force for three-finger tip-prehension grasps. *Journal of Mechanics, Transmissions, and Automation in Design* 110: 405–413.

Kirkpatrick, D. G., B. Mishra, and C. K. Yap. (1990). Quantitative Steinitz's theorems with applications to multifingered grasping. In *Twentieth ACM Symp. on Theory of Computing,* Baltimore, MD, pp. 341–351.

Latombe, J-C. (1991). *Robot Motion Planning.* Dordrecht: Kluwer.

Laugier, C. (1981). A program for automatic grasping of objects with a robot arm. In *Eleventh International Symposium on Industrial Robots.*

Li, Z., and S. Sastry. (1987). Task-oriented optimal grasping by multifingered robot hands. *In Proc. IEEE Int. Conf. on Robotics and Automation,* IEEE Press, pp. 389–394.

Lozano-Perez, T. (1976). The design of a mechanical assembly system. MIT AI Memo 397. Cambridge, MA: MIT Artificial Intelligence Lab.

Mason, M., and J. K. Salisbury. (1985). *Robot Hands and the Mechanics of Manipulation.* Cambridge, MA: MIT Press.

Murray, R. M., Z. Li, and S. S. Sastry. (1994). *A Mathematical Introduction to Robotic Manipulation.* CRC Press.

Pertin-Troccaz, J. (1987). On-line automatic programming: A case study in grasping. In *Proc. IEEE Int. Conf. on Robotics and Automation,* Raleigh, NC, pp. 1292–1297.

Pollard, N. S., and T. Lozano-Perez. (1990). Grasp stability and feasibility for an arm with an articulated hand. In *Proc. IEEE*

Int. Conf. on Robotics and Automation, IEEE Press, pp. 1581–1585.

Ponce, J., and B. Faverjon. (1995). On computing three-finger force-closure grasps of polygonal objects. *IEEE Transactions on Robotics and Automation* 11(6): 868–881.

Ponce, J., D. Stam, and B. Faverjon. (1993). On computing force-closure grasps of curved two-dimensional objects. *International Journal of Robotics Research* 12(3): 263–273.

Reulaux, F. (1876/1963). *The Kinematics of Machinery.* New York: Macmillan. Reprint, New York: Dover.

Rimon, E., and A. Blake. (1996). Caging 2D bodies by one-parameter two-fingered gripping systems. In *Proc. IEEE Int. Conf. on Robotics and Automation*, Minneapolis, MN, pp. 1458–1464.

Roth, B. (1984). Screws, motors, and wrenches that cannot be bought in a hardware store. In *Int. Symp. on Robotics Research* Cambridge, MA: MIT Press, pp. 679–693.

Trinkle, J. C. (1992). On the stability and instantaneous velocity of grasped frictionless objects. *IEEE Transactions on Robotics and Automation* 8(5): 560–572.

Wallack, A., and J. F. Canny. (1994). Planning for modular and hybrid fixtures. In *Proc. IEEE Int. Conf. on Robotics and Automation,* San Diego, CA, pp. 520–527.

Markov Decision Problems

See DYNAMIC PROGRAMMING; RATIONAL DECISION MAKING; REINFORCEMENT LEARNING

Marr, David

David Marr (1945–1980), theoretical neurophysiologist and cognitive scientist, integrated neurophysiological and psychophysical studies with the computational methods of artificial intelligence (AI) to found a new, more powerful approach to understanding biological information-processing systems. The approach has come to redefine the standard for achieving a suitable comprehension of brain structure and function.

Marr was born in Essex, England on 19 January 1945 to Douglas and Madge Marr, and died at age thirty-five of leukemia. After attending Rugby, he entered Trinity College, Cambridge in 1963, obtaining the B.S. degree in mathematics in 1966 with first-class honors. Shortly thereafter, under the guidance of Giles Brindley, he began an intensive year of study on all aspects of brain function, with the intent of focusing on the neural implementation of efficient associative memories. By the end of 1968 he had submitted a dissertation for a title, a fellowship at Trinity College, and was elected. He received two advanced degrees from Trinity in 1971: an M.S. in mathematics and a Ph.D. in theoretical neurophysiology. The first part of his thesis was a theoretical analysis of the cerebellar cortex, published in the *Journal of Physiology* in 1969. This work was the first detailed theory on any really complex piece of neural machinery, with very specific predictions concerning the input-output relations and details of synaptic modifiabilities during the learning of new motor movements. The essence of this theory is still viable today, and continues to be the benchmark for further advances in understanding cerebellar cortex. Two other papers also appeared before 1971: one on the archicortex, the other on the neocortex, both of which remain landmarks in theoretical neurophysiology.

After obtaining his Ph.D., Marr accepted an appointment at the MRC Laboratory of Molecular Biology under Sydney Brenner and Francis Crick, and he retained an affiliation with MRC until 1976. The thrust of Marr's work changed rather dramatically in 1972, however, following an interdisciplinary workshop on the brain where he met Marvin Minsky and Seymour Papert, who extended an invitation to visit the MIT Artificial Intelligence Laboratory. This visit reinforced Marr's growing conviction that a complete theory of any brain structure must go beyond interpreting anatomical and physiological facts to include an analysis of the task being performed, or more specifically, an understanding of the problem that the information-processing device was "solving." Equally important, he recognized the weakness of theories that appeared explanatory but were not demonstrative. However, demonstrative theories of brain function required large and flexible computing resources such as those available at MIT. Consequently, Marr's initial three-month visit to the AI lab oratory in 1973 became extended, extended again, and then by 1976 became permanent. In 1977 he was appointed to the faculty of the (current) Department of Brain and Cognitive Sciences, becoming full professor at MIT in 1980, while continuing to hold his AI Lab appointment.

Marr's years at the AI laboratory were incredibly productive. The goal was to understand both the competence as well as the performance of a biological information-processing system. Although some studies of movement continued, the primary thrust was understanding the mammalian visual system. Although small, Marr's remarkably talented group included Tomaso Poggio and Shimon Ullman. They shared Marr's conviction that explanations of a complex system are found at several levels. A complete study should address at least three levels: an analysis of the competence, the design of an algorithm and choice of representation, and an implementation. In order to provide a coherent framework for organizing and attacking visual problems—more properly, problems of "seeing"—Marr proposed separating perceptual processing tasks into three main stages: a primal sketch, where properties of the image are made explicit; a 2½-D sketch, which is a viewer-centered representation of the surface geometry and surface properties; and lastly a 3-D model representation, which is object centered rather than viewer based. His 1982 book, *Vision: A Computational Investigation into the Human Representation and Processing of Visual Information,* published posthumously, summarizes these ideas, as well as the contributions to image processing, grouping, color, stereopsis, motion, surface geometry, TEXTURE, SHAPE PERCEPTION, and OBJECT RECOGNITION. Many of these contributions had appeared by the late 1970s, and in recognition of this work, Marr received in 1979 the Computers and Thought Award from the International Joint Conference on Artificial Intelligence. More recently, "best paper" awards in the name of David Marr have been created by the International Conference on Computer Vision and by the Cognitive Science Society.

As a person, David Marr was charismatic and inspiring. He was both fun and brilliant, enjoying the adventures of understanding brain structure and function, as well as life itself. He communicated his pleasure in clear and compelling ways, not only in personal exchanges and in his writing but also in music. He was an accomplished clarinetist. His early death was a great loss but even in his short life, he was able to bring together two previously diverse disciplines, set a higher standard for explanatory understanding, and open new doors to unraveling the mysteries of mind and brain.

See also CEREBELLUM; COMPUTATIONAL VISION; MACHINE VISION; MID-LEVEL VISION; STEREO AND MOTION PERCEPTION

—*Whitman A. Richards*

References and Further Readings

Marr, D. (1982). *Vision: A Computational Investigation into the Human Representation and Processing of Visual Information.* San Francisco: W. H. Freeman.

Vaina, L. (1991). *From Retina to Cortex: Selected Papers of David Marr.* Boston: Birkhäuser.

Materialism

See MIND-BODY PROBLEM; PHYSICALISM

Maximum Likelihood Density Estimation

See MINIMUM DESCRIPTION LENGTH; UNSUPERVISED LEARNING

McCulloch, Warren S.

Warren McCulloch (1898–1968) was a physician turned physiologist. After medical school, he trained in neurology from 1928–1931, studied mathematical physics in 1931–1932, worked as a clinician from 1932–34, then joined the Yale Laboratory of Neurophysiology and by 1941 became an assistant professor in the department. His main work at Yale was on the functional connections in the CEREBRAL CORTEX of primates. Dusser de Barenne, his mentor and collaborator, had developed the method of strychnine neuronography, a way of determining the direct projection of one architectonically specified region in the cortex of the forebrain to other regions. It is a clever and reliable technique that served well to show in a single day of experiment what would take years to work out by the standard anatomical procedures at the time. Little of what the technique revealed has been faulted, but it never caught on for a variety of reasons, the main one being a general misunderstanding of the underlying physiology.

In 1941 McCulloch came to the Illinois Neuropsychiatric Institute as Associate Professor of Psychiatry at the College of Medicine, University of Illinois. Percival Bailey, Professor of Neurosurgery, had worked with McCulloch at Yale, as had Gerhardt van Bonin, Professor of Anatomy. The neuronography of primate cortex work continued and attracted many visiting collaborators, and McCulloch developed an enduring interest in the bulbo-reticular system, due mainly to the innovative studies of Magvin and Snyder at Northwestern University.

In 1942 he took a medical student, Jerry Lettvin, together with his friend Walter PITTS, into his laboratory, and by mid-year, into his home. Pitts, taking an interest in the nervous system, told McCulloch of Gottfried Wilhelm Leibniz's dictum that any task that can be completely and unambiguously set forth in logical terms can be performed by a logical engine. In the previous year, David Lloyd had demonstrated monosyllabic excitation, facilitation, and inhibition. And in 1936–37 Alan TURING had published his brilliant essay on the universal logical engine. It seemed to McCulloch and Pitts that neurons could be conceived as logical elements, pulsatile rather than two-state devices, and capable of realizing logical process. The ensuing paper, "A Logical Calculus of the Ideas Immanent in Nervous Activity" (McCulloch and Pitts 1943) became the inspiration for a new view of the nervous system, and a justification for the project of artificial intelligence.

In a later second paper, "On how we know universals: The perception of auditory and visual forms," Pitts and McCulloch implemented their notions by showing how the anatomy of the cerebral cortex might accommodate the identification of form independent of its angular size in the image, and other such operations in perception.

McCulloch at the same time carried on a full load of his studies in the physiology of the cortex and other parts of the nervous system. That was his daytime work. But, having become enamored of LOGIC, his evenings were devoted to problems in logical representation of mental operations. After all, he had developed a profound interest in philosophy while at Yale.

By the end of the 1940s, with John VON NEUMANN's first digital computers, Norbert Wiener's linear prediction theory, and the massive and singularly intellectual thrust of the military and industrial complex, it was evident that a new era was opening. In 1951, Jerome Wiesner, on Norbert Wiener's advice, offered a place at the Research Laboratory of Electronics at MIT to McCulloch, Pat Wall, and Lettvin. There McCulloch and Wall worked on spinal cord physiology. Pitts was already at MIT. At the time McCulloch was full professor at the University of Illinois, and Wall was assistant professor at the University of Chicago. Although the move brought loss of academic status and a serious cut in pay, the three of them accepted the invitation.

Beginning in 1951, McCulloch became a magnet for a most diverse company of those concerned with the new communications revolution. Benoit Mandelbrot, Manuel Blum, Marvin Minsky, Seymour Papert, and a host of others, then young and eager and hungry for discovery, visited frequently and stayed for long discussions.

Several major works were issued before 1960. One that charmed McCulloch particularly was the arduous source-sink analysis of currents in the spinal cord. Pitts had laid out the general method behind the effort; published in 1954–1955, it was the first demonstration of presynaptic inhibition between the collaterals of dorsal root fibers. A year and a half had been spent on computations that would occupy about an hour on today's machines. Then there was the demonstration of the action of strychnine, which provided the ground needed to justify strychnine neuronography. Wall turned his interest to the mechanism involved in pain. H. R. Maturana joined the group from Harvard and, thanks to his patience and skill, "What the Frog's Eye Tells the Frog's Brain" was published (Lettvin et al. 1959).

Bob Gesteland joined the group as McCulloch's graduate student, addressing himself, under the urging of Pitts and McCulloch, to the problem of olfaction. His were the first recordings of the activity of single olfactory cells in the nasal mucosa of frogs. And his results—namely, that every cell responds to almost every odorant but with different coding patterns of activity, for different odorants, and that cells differ among themselves in their coding patterns for the odorants—are just bearing fruit today. In short, McCulloch was the center of a new thrust in nervous physiology, even more fascinating than what he envisioned before coming to MIT.

McCulloch had great generosity of spirit. He treated everyone as an equal and made an effort to encourage the best in everyone he met. He never showed the faintest hint of malice or envy or deviousness, but spoke, wrote, and carried himself as a nineteenth-century cavalier. A complete list of his publications is given in his *Collected Works,* and a small indication of his influence is evidenced by the Further Readings below.

See also AUTOMATA; COMPUTATION AND THE BRAIN; NEURAL NETWORKS; NEWELL; VON NEUMANN; WIENER

—*Jerome Lettvin*

References

Lettvin, J., H. Maturana, W. McCulloch, and W. Pitts. (1959). What the frog's eye tells the frog's brain. *Proceedings of the IRE* 47: 1940–1959. Reprinted in *Embodiments of Mind.*

McCulloch, R., Ed. (1989). *Collected Works of Warren S. McCulloch.* 4 volumes. Salinas, CA: Intersystems Publications.

McCulloch, W. S. (1988). *Embodiments of Mind.* Cambridge, MA: MIT Press. Originally published 1965.

McCulloch, W., and W. Pitts. (1943). A logical calculus of the ideas immanent in nervous activity. *Bulletin of Mathematical Biophysics* 5: 115–133. Reprinted in *Embodiments of Mind.*

Pitts, W., and W. McCulloch. (1947). On how we know universals: The perception of auditory and visual forms. *Bulletin of Mathematical Biophysics* 9:127–147. Reprinted in *Embodiments of Mind.*

Further Readings

Anderson, J. A. (1996). From discrete to continuous and back again. In Moreno-Diaz and Mira-Mira (1996).

Arbib, M. A. (1996). Schema theory: From Kant to McCulloch and beyond. In Moreno-Diaz and Mira-Mira (1996).

Cull, P. (1996). Neural nets: Classical results and current problems. In Moreno-Diaz and Mira-Mira (1996).

Lettvin, J. (1988). Foreword to the 1988 reprint of *Embodiments of Mind.*

Lettvin, J. (1989). Introduction to vol. 1. R. McCulloch, Ed., *Collected Works of Warren S. McCulloch.*

Lindgren, N. (1969). The birth of cybernetics—an end to the old world: The heritage of Warren S. McCulloch. *Innovation* 6: 12–15.

Moreno-Diaz, R., and J. Mira-Mira, Eds. (1996). *Brain Processes, Theories and Models: An International Conference in Honor of W. S. McCulloch 25 Years after His Death.* Cambridge, MA: MIT Press.

Papert, S. (1965). Introduction to *Embodiments of Mind.*

Perkel, D. H. Logical neurons: The enigmatic legacy of Warren McCulloch. *Trends in Neuroscience* 11: 9–12.

Weir, M. K. (1996). Putting the mind inside the head. In Moreno-Diaz and Mira-Mira (1996).

McCulloch-Pitts Neurons

See AUTOMATA; MCCULLOCH, WARREN S.; PITTS, WALTER; VON NEUMANN, JOHN

Meaning

The meaning of an expression, as opposed to its form, is that feature of it which determines its contribution to what a speaker says in using it. Meaning conveyed by a speaker is the speaker's communicative intent in using an expression, even if that use departs from the expression's meaning. Accordingly, any discussion of meaning should distinguish speaker's meaning from linguistic meaning.

We think of meanings as what synonyms (or translations) have in common, what ambiguous expressions have more than one of, what meaningful expressions have and gibberish lacks, and what competent speakers grasp. Yet linguistic meaning is a puzzling notion. The traditional view is that the meaning of a word is the concept associated with it and, as FREGE suggested, what determines its reference, but this plausible view is problematic in various ways. First, it is not clear what CONCEPTS are. Nor is it clear what the relevant sort of association with words is, or, indeed, that every word has a concept, much less a unique concept, associated with it. Wittgenstein (1953) even challenged the Platonic assumption that all the items to which a word applies must have something in common. Unfortunately, there is no widely accepted alternative to the traditional view. Skepticism about meaning, at least as traditionally conceived, has also been registered in various ways by such prominent philosophers as Quine (1960), Davidson (1984), Putnam (1975), and Kripke (1982); for review of the debates these philosophers have generated see Hale and Wright 1997 (chaps. 8 and 14–17). Psychological approaches based on prototypes or on semantic networks, as well as COGNITIVE LINGUISTICS, seem to sever the connection between meaning and reference. The most popular philosophical approaches to sentence meaning, such as truth-conditional, model-theoretic, and POSSIBLE WORLDS SEMANTICS, also have their limitations. They seem ill equipped to distinguish meanings of expressions that necessarily apply in the same circumstances or to handle non-truth-conditional aspects of meaning.

Here are six foundational questions about meaning, as difficult as they are basic:

1. What are meanings?
2. What is it for an expression to have meaning?
3. What is it to know the meaning(s) of an expression? (More generally, what is it to understand a language?)

4. What is the relationship between the meaning of an expression and what, if anything, the expression refers to?

5. What is the relationship between the meaning of a complex expression and the meanings of its constituents?

An answer to question 1 would say whether meanings are psychological, social, or abstract, although many philosophers would balk at the question, insisting that meanings are not entities in their own right and that answering question 2 would take care of question 1. An answer to question 3 would help answer question 2, for what expressions mean cannot be separated from (and is perhaps reducible to) what people take them to mean. And question 4 bears on question 3. It was formerly assumed that the speaker's internal state underlying his knowledge of the meaning of a term determines the term's reference, but Putnam's (1975) influential TWIN EARTH thought experiments have challenged this "internalist" or "individualist" assumption. In reaction, Chomsky (1986, 1995) and Katz (1990) have defended versions of internalism about knowledge of language and meaning.

Question 5 points to the goal of linguistic theory: to provide a systematic account of the relation between form and meaning. SYNTAX is concerned with linguistic form, including LOGICAL FORM, needed to represent scope relationships induced by quantificational phrases and modal and other operators; SEMANTICS, with how form maps onto linguistic meaning. The aim is to characterize the semantic contributions made by different types of expression to sentences in which they occur. The usual strategy is to seek a systematic, recursive way of specifying the meanings of a complex expression (a phrase or sentence) in terms of the meanings of its constituents and its syntactic structure (see Larson and Segal 1995 for a detailed implementation). Underlying this strategy is the principle of semantic COMPOSITIONALITY, which seems needed to explain how a natural language is learnable (but see Schiffer 1987). Compositionality poses certain difficulties, however, regarding conditional sentences, PROPOSITIONAL ATTITUDE ascriptions, and various constructions of concern to linguists, such as genitives and adjectival modification. For example, although *Rick's team* is a so-called possessive phrase, Rick's team need not be the team Rick owns—it might be the team he plays for, coaches, or just roots for. Or consider how the force of the adjective *fast* varies in the phrases *fast car, fast driver, fast track,* and *fast race* (see Pustejovsky 1995 for a computational approach to such problems).

The study of speaker's meaning belongs to PRAGMATICS. What a speaker means in uttering a sentence is not just a matter of what his words mean, for he might mean something other than or more than what he says. For example, one might use "You're another Shakespeare" to mean that someone has little literary ability and "The door is over there" to mean also that someone should leave. The listener has to figure out such things, and also resolve any AMBIGUITY or VAGUENESS in the utterance and identify the references of any INDEXICALS AND DEMONSTRATIVES. GRICE (1989) ingeniously proposed that communicating involves a distinctive sort of audience-directed intention: that one's audience is to recognize one's intention partly on the suppo-

sition that they are intended to recognize it. This idea, which has important applications to GAME THEORY (communication is a kind of cooperative game), is essential to explaining how a speaker can make himself understood even if he does not make fully explicit what he means, as in IMPLICATURE. Understanding a speaker is not just a matter of understanding his words but of identifying his communicative intention. One must rely not just on knowledge of linguistic meaning but also on collateral information that one can reasonably take the speaker to be intending one to rely on (see Bach and Harnish 1979 for a detailed account). Communication is essentially an intentional-inferential affair, and linguistic meaning is just the input to the inference.

See also INDIVIDUALISM; NARROW CONTENT; RADICAL INTERPRETATION; SENSE AND REFERENCE; REFERENCE, THEORIES OF

—*Kent Bach*

References

Bach, K., and R. M. Harnish. (1979). *Linguistic Communication and Speech Acts.* Cambridge, MA: MIT Press.

Chomsky, N. (1986). *Knowledge of Language.* New York: Praeger.

Chomsky, N. (1995). Language and nature. *Mind* 104: 1–61.

Davidson, D. (1984). *Essays on Truth and Interpretation.* Oxford: Oxford University Press.

Grice, P. (1989). *Studies in the Way of Words.* Cambridge, MA: Harvard University Press.

Hale, B., and C. Wright, Eds. (1997). *The Blackwell Companion to the Philosophy of Language.* Oxford: Blackwell.

Katz, J. J. (1990). *The Metaphysics of Meaning.* Cambridge, MA: MIT Press.

Kripke, S. (1982). *Wittgenstein on Rules and Private Language.* Cambridge, MA: Harvard University Press.

Larson, R., and G. Segal. (1995). *Knowledge of Meaning.* Cambridge, MA: MIT Press.

Lyons, J. (1995). *Linguistic Semantics: An Introduction.* Cambridge: Cambridge University Press.

Pustejovsky, J. (1995). *The Generative Lexicon.* Cambridge, MA: MIT Press.

Putnam, H. (1975). The meaning of "meaning." In K. Gunderson, Ed., *Language, Mind, and Knowledge.* Minneapolis: University of Minnesota Press, pp. 131–193.

Quine, W. V. (1960) *Word and Object.* Cambridge, MA: MIT Press.

Schiffer, S. (1972). *Meaning.* Oxford: Oxford University Press.

Schiffer, S. (1987). *The Remnants of Meaning.* Cambridge, MA: MIT Press.

Wittgenstein, L. (1953). *Philosophical Investigations.* New York: Macmillan.

Memory

The term *memory* implies the capacity to encode, store, and retrieve information. The possibility that memory might not be a unitary system was proposed by William JAMES (1898) who suggested two systems which he named *primary* and *secondary memory.* Donald HEBB (1949) also proposed a dichotomy, suggesting that the brain might use two separate neural mechanisms with primary or short-term storage being based on electrical activation, while long-term memory reflected the growth of relatively permanent neuronal links between assemblies of cells.

Empirical support for a two-component view began to emerge in the late 1950s, when Brown (1958) and Peterson and Peterson (1959) observed that even small amounts of information would show rapid forgetting, provided the subject was prevented from maintaining it by active rehearsal. The characteristic forgetting pattern appeared to differ from that observed in standard long-term memory experiments, leading to the suggestion that performance depended on a separate short-term store. Such a view was vigorously opposed by Melton (1963), leading to a period of intense activity during the early 1960s that was concerned with the question of whether memory should be regarded as a unitary or dichotomous system.

By the late 1960s, the evidence seemed to strongly favor the dichotomous view. A particularly influential source of evidence was provided by a small number of neuropsychological patients who appeared to have a specific deficit of either the short-term or the long-term system. The clearest evidence of preserved short-term (STM) and impaired long-term memory (LTM) comes in the classic amnesiac syndrome. Particularly influential was case H.M. who underwent bilateral excision of the HIPPOCAMPUS in an attempt to treat intractable epilepsy. H.M. was left with a profound amnesia, unable to commit new material to memory, whether visual or verbal, and showing no capacity to learn his way around a new environment, to recognize people who worked with him regularly, or to remember the content of anything he read or saw. His STM, on the other hand, as evidenced by the capacity to hear and repeat back a string of digits such as a telephone number, was quite normal (Milner 1966).

The opposite pattern of memory deficit was demonstrated by Shallice and Warrington (1970) in a patient, K.F., who was unable to repeat back more than two digits, but whose long-term learning capacity and everyday memory were well within the normal range. His lesion was in the left hemisphere in an area known to be associated with language. Subsequent studies have shown that language and short-term phonological memory are often impaired in the same patient, but that the two areas are separable and the symptoms dissociable. When tested on the Petersons' short-term forgetting task, patients like K.F. proved to show very rapid forgetting, whereas densely amnesiac patients show normal performance, provided their amnesia is pure and unaffected by more general intellectual deficits (Baddeley and Warrington 1970).

Evidence from normal subjects paralleled the neuropsychological research in suggesting the need for at least two separate memory systems. Many memory tests appeared to show two separate components, one that was durable and long-term while the other showed rapid dissipation. For example, if a subject hears a list of twenty unrelated words and is asked to recall as many as possible in any order, there will be a tendency for the last few words to be well recalled, the so-called recency effect. However a delay of only a few seconds is sufficient for the effect to disappear, while recall of earlier items remains stable. When this paradigm was applied to neuropsychological patients, those with STM deficits showed preservation of the long-term component, but little or no recency, while amnesiac patients showed the opposite pattern.

Finally the learning characteristics of the two systems appeared to differ. The short-term system has a limited capacity, but appears to be relatively insensitive to speed of presentation, and in the case of verbal material to be sensitive to the sound or phonological characteristics of the material presented. The long-term system, on the other hand, has a huge capacity but a relatively slow rate of acquisition of new material, and a tendency to encode verbal material in terms of its meaning rather than sound (Baddeley 1966a, 1966b; Waugh and Norman 1965).

The 1960s saw a growing interest in developing mathematical models of learning and memory, with the most influential of these being that of Atkinson and Shiffrin (1968) which became known as the modal model. However, problems with a simple dichotomy rapidly emerged, leading to the wide-scale abandonment of the field by many of its investigators.

One problem stemmed from Atkinson and Shiffrin's assumption that the probability of an item being stored in LTM was a simple function of how long it was maintained in the short-term system. A number of studies demonstrated that active and vigorous verbal rehearsal might link to very little durable LTM (Craik and Watkins 1973; Bjork and Whitten 1974). This prompted Craik and Lockhart (1972) to propose their *levels of processing* theory of memory. This proposed that an item to be remembered, such as a word, could be processed at a series of encoding levels, beginning with the visual appearance of the word on the page, moving on to the sound of the word when pronounced, and, given further and deeper processing, to the meaning of that word and its relationship to other experiences of the subject. Craik and Lockhart suggested that the deeper the level of encoding, the more durable the memory trace. There is no doubt that this simple formulation does capture an important characteristic of long-term learning, namely, that encoding material richly and elaborately in terms of prior experience will lead to a comparatively durable and readily retrievable memory trace.

Note however that levels of processing is not an alternative to a dichotomous view; indeed Craik and Lockhart themselves postulate a primary memory system as part of their model, although this aspect of their work receives very much less attention than the concept of encoding levels.

A second difficulty for the modal model lay in the neuropsychological evidence. It may be recalled that patients with an STM deficit performed poorly on tasks such as immediate memory span and recency, but were normal in their LTM performance. The modal model suggested, however, that the short-term system acts as a crucial antechamber to long-term learning, hence predicting that such patients should have impaired learning capacity, and indeed should show poor performance on a wide range of tasks that were assumed to be dependent on the limited-capacity short-term system. They showed no evidence of this, with one such patient being an efficient secretary, while another ran a shop and raised a family.

This problem formed the focus of work by Baddeley and Hitch (1974), who attempted to simulate the neuropsychological STM deficit by means of a dual task technique. Subjects were required to hold and rehearse sequences of digits varying in length while at the same time performing a range of other tasks that were assumed to depend upon the limited-capacity store. It was assumed that longer sequences of digits would absorb more of the store, until eventually capacity was reached, leaving the main tasks to be performed without the help of the short-term system. A range of tasks were studied including long-term learning, reasoning, and comprehension. A clear pattern emerged suggesting that concurrent digits did impair performance systematically, but by no means obliterated it. This led to a reformulation of the STM hypothesis and the postulation of a multicomponent system which was termed *working memory*. It was suggested that this comprised a limited capacity attentional control system, the *central executive,* together with at least two slave systems, one concerned with maintaining visual-spatial information, the *sketchpad,* while the other was responsible for holding and manipulating speech-based information, the *phonological loop.*

The concept of working memory has proved extremely fruitful, not only in accounting for the initial neuropsychological evidence but also in being applicable to a wide range of tasks and subject groups, and more recently, providing a very fruitful basis for a range of neuroradiological studies concerned with the neuroanatomical basis of working memory (see Smith and Jonides 1995).

As in the case of STM, the concept of LTM has also undergone a detailed analysis in the last twenty years, again resulting in a degree of fractionation. One of the strongest cases for a basic distinction is that between implicit and explicit memory (see IMPLICIT VS. EXPLICIT MEMORY). Once again this distinction was heavily influenced by neuropsychological evidence, when it was observed that even densely amnesiac patients could nevertheless show comparatively normal learning on certain tasks, including the acquisition of motor skills, classical conditioning, and a whole range of procedures that come under the general term of *priming.* The classic demonstration within this area was that of Warrington and Weiskrantz (1968), who showed that amnesiac patients who were shown a list of words were totally unable to recall or recognize the words, but were able to demonstrate learning by perceiving the words more rapidly when they were presented in fragmented form. Subsequent work showed that learning was also preserved when tested by cueing with the first few letters of the word (e.g., present CROCODILE, test with CRO____), or with a fragment of the word, (C__O__O__I__E). Equivalent phenomena have been demonstrated in other modalities, and have shown to be widely demonstrable in normal subjects (see Roediger 1990 for a review).

Over the last decade there has been substantial controversy as to how best to explain this pattern of results. There is still some support for attempts to account for the data within a unitary system, but my own view (Baddeley 1998) is that this is no longer a tenable position. In particular, the neuropsychological evidence seems to argue for a distinction between an episodic LTM system (depending on a circuit linking the temporal lobes, the frontal lobes, and parahippocampal regions), and a whole range of implicit learning systems, each tending to reflect a different brain region.

While these systems are of considerable interest in their own right, and as ways of analyzing perceptual and motor processing, it can be questioned as to whether they should be referred to as *memory* systems, as they typically involve relatively automatic retrieval processes that are often not under the direct control of the subject. In contrast, episodic memory is the system that typifies our experience of recollecting the past. Indeed, Tulving (1985) suggests that its crucial and defining feature is the recollective process, accompanied by the feeling of familiarity, a process he refers to as *ecphory.* There have in recent years been a growing number of studies concerned with the phenomenological aspect of memory, often with considerable success (see Gardiner 1988).

A second proposed distinction within LTM is that between *semantic* and *episodic* memory (see EPISODIC VS. SEMANTIC MEMORY). Semantic memory refers to the stored knowledge of the world that underlies not only our capacity to understand language but also our ability to take advantage of prior knowledge in perceiving and organizing both the physical and social world around us. The need for such a store of information was initially made obvious by attempts to develop computer-based systems for comprehending text, such as that of Quillian (1969). These stimulated attempts to understand semantic memory in human subjects, and prompted Tulving (1972) to propose that semantic and episodic memory are distinct systems. At first sight, the evidence appeared persuasive. Densely amnesiac patients may perform normally on semantic memory tests while showing no evidence of new episodic learning (Wilson and Baddeley 1988). However, semantic memory tests typically involve accessing old memories, whereas episodic tests are principally concerned with the laying down of new memory traces. When amnesiac patients are required to extend their existing semantic memory systems, for example, by learning about the developing political system within their country, or learning new routes within their town, learning appears to be catastrophically bad. An alternative way of conceptualizing semantic memory is to suggest that it represents the residue of many episodic memories, with access being based on generic commonalities, rather than the retrieval of a specific episode. The nature of semantic memory and its neuroanatomical basis continues to be a very active research area, with neuropsychological evidence again being particularly cogent (see Patterson and Hodges 1996).

No survey of memory would be complete without comment on one aspect of memory that has been both active and controversial in recent years, namely, the attempt to apply the lessons learned in the laboratory to everyday functioning. Although the link between the laboratory and the field has occasionally appeared to be excessively confrontational (e.g., see Neisser 1978; Banaji and Crowder 1989), the interaction has on the whole been a fruitful one. This is particularly true of clinical applications of the psychology of memory, where, as we have seen, the study of memory deficits in patients has been enormously influential in changing our views of the normal functioning of human memory.

See also ECOLOGICAL PSYCHOLOGY; MEMORY, ANIMAL STUDIES; MEMORY, HUMAN NEUROPSYCHOLOGY

—*Alan Baddeley*

References

Atkinson, R. C., and R. M. Shiffrin. (1968). Human memory: A proposed system and its control processes. In K. W. Spence, Ed., *The Psychology of Learning and Motivation: Advances in Research and Theory.* New York: Academic Press, pp. 89–195.

Baddeley, A. D. (1966a). Short-term memory for word sequences as a function of acoustic, semantic and formal similarity. *Quarterly Journal of Experimental Psychology* 18: 362–365.

Baddeley, A. D. (1966b). The influence of acoustic and semantic similarity on long-term memory for word sequences. *Quarterly Journal of Experimental Psychology* 18: 302–309.

Baddeley, A. D. (1998). *Human Memory: Theory and Practice,* Revised ed. Needham Heights, MA: Allyn and Bacon.

Baddeley, A. D., and G. Hitch. (1974). Working memory. In G. A. Bower, Ed., *The Psychology of Learning and Motivation.* New York: Academic Press, pp. 47–89.

Baddeley, A. D., and E. K. Warrington. (1970). Amnesia and the distinction between long- and short-term memory. *Journal of Verbal Learning and Verbal Behavior* 9: 176–189.

Banaji, M. R., and R. G. Crowder. (1989). The bankruptcy of everyday memory. *American Psychologist* 44: 1185–1193.

Bjork, R. A., and W. B. Whitten. (1974). Recency-sensitive retrieval processes. *Cognitive Psychology* 6: 173–189.

Brown, J. (1958). Some tests of the decay theory of immediate memory. *Quarterly Journal of Experimental Psychology* 10: 12–21.

Craik, F. I. M., and R. S. Lockhart. (1972). Levels of processing: A framework for memory research. *Journal of Verbal Learning and Verbal Behavior* 11: 671–684.

Craik, F. I. M., and M. J. Watkins. (1973). The role of rehearsal in short-term memory. *Journal of Verbal Learning and Verbal Behavior* 12: 599–607.

Gardiner, J. M. (1988). Functional aspects of recollective experience. *Memory and Cognition* 16: 309–313.

Hebb, D. O. (1949). *Organization of Behavior.* New York: Wiley.

James, W. (1890). *The Principles of Psychology.* New York: Holt, Rinehart and Winston.

Melton, A. W. (1963). Implications of short-term memory for a general theory of memory. *Journal of Verbal Learning and Verbal Behavior* 2: 1–21.

Milner, B. (1966). Amnesia following operation on the temporal lobes. In C. W. M. Whitty and O. L. Zangwill, Eds., *Amnesia.* London: Butterworths, pp. 109–133.

Neisser, U. (1978). Memory: What are the important questions? In M. M. Gruneberg, P. E. Morris, and R. N. Sykes, Eds., *Practical Aspects of Memory.* London: Academic Press.

Patterson, K. E., and J. R. Hodges. (1996). Disorders of semantic memory. In A. D. Baddeley, B. A. Wilson, and F. N. Watts, Eds., *Handbook of Memory Disorders.* Chichester, England: Wiley, pp. 167–186.

Peterson, L. R., and M. J. Peterson. (1959). Short-term retention of individual verbal items. *Journal of Experimental Psychology* 58: 193–198.

Quillian, M. R. (1969). The teachable language comprehender: A simulation program and theory of language. *Communication of the ACM* 12: 459–476.

Roediger, H. L. (1990). Implicit memory: Retention without remembering. *American Psychologist* 45: 1043–1056.

Shallice, T., and E. K. Warrington. (1970). Independent functioning of verbal memory stores: A neuropsychological study. *Quarterly Journal of Experimental Psychology* 22: 261–273.

Smith, E. E., and J. Jonides. (1995). Working memory in humans: Neuropsychological evidence. In M. Gazzaniga, Ed., *The Cognitive Neurosciences.* Cambridge, MA: MIT Press, pp. 1009–1020.

Tulving, E. (1972). Episodic and semantic memory. In E. Tulving and W. Donaldson, Eds., *Organization of Memory.* New York: Academic Press, pp. 381–403.

Tulving, E. (1985). How many memory systems are there? *American Psychologist* 40: 385–398.

Warrington, E. K., and L. Weiskrantz. (1968). New methods of testing long-term retention with special reference to amnesic patients. *Nature* 217: 972–974.

Waugh, N. C., and D. A. Norman. (1965). Primary memory. *Psychological Review* 72: 89–104.

Wilson, B. A., and A. D. Baddeley. (1988). Semantic, episodic and autobiographical memory in a post-meningitic amnesic patient. *Brain and Cognition* 8: 31–46.

Further Readings

Baddeley, A. D. (1999). *Essentials of Human Memory.* Hove: Psychology Press.

Parkin, A. (1987). *Memory and Amnesia: An Introduction.* Oxford: Blackwell.

Memory, Animal Studies

Information about which structures and connections in the brain are important for MEMORY has come from studies of amnesiac patients and from systematic experimental work with animals. Work in animals includes studies which assess the effects of selective brain lesions on memory, as well as studies using neurophysiological recording and stimulating techniques to investigate neural activity within particular brain regions (for discussions of the latter two approaches, see OBJECT RECOGNITION, ANIMAL STUDIES; FACE RECOGNITION; SINGLE-NEURON RECORDING). An important development that has occurred in the area of memory during the past two decades was the establishment of an animal model of human amnesia in the monkey (Mahut and Moss 1984; Mishkin 1982; Squire and Zola-Morgan 1983). In the 1950s, Scoville and Milner (1957) described the severe amnesia that followed bilateral surgical removal of the medial temporal lobe (patient H.M.). This important case demonstrated that memory is a distinct cerebral function, dissociable from other perceptual and cognitive abilities.

In monkeys, surgical lesions of the medial temporal lobe, which were intended to approximate the damage sustained by patient H.M., reproduced many features of human memory impairment. In particular, both monkeys and humans were impaired on tasks of declarative memory, but fully intact at skills and habit learning and other tasks of nondeclarative memory. This achievement set the stage for additional work in monkeys and for work in rodents that has identified structures in the medial temporal lobe that are important for declarative memory. These structures include the hippocampal region (i.e., the cell fields of the HIPPO-CAMPUS, the dentate gyrus, and the subiculum), and adjacent cortical areas that are anatomically related to the hippocampal region, namely, the entorhinal, perirhinal, and parahippocampal cortices (Zola-Morgan and Squire 1993).

The midline diencephalon is another brain area important for memory, although less is known about which specific structures in this region contribute to memory function. Findings from work in animals, including the development of an animal model of alcoholic Korsakoff's syndrome in the rat (Mair et al., 1992), have been consistent with the anatomical findings from human amnesia in showing the importance of damage within the medial THALAMUS, especially damage in the internal medullary lamina, for producing memory loss. Lesions in the internal medullary lamina would be expected to disconnect or damage several thalamic nuclei, including intralaminar nuclei, the mediodorsal nucleus, and the anterior nucleus (Aggleton and Mishkin 1983; Mair et al. 1991; Zola-Morgan and Squire 1985). However, the separate contributions to memory of the mediodorsal nucleus, the anterior nucleus, and the intralaminar nuclei remain to be explored systematically with well-circumscribed lesions in animals.

A major criterion for demonstrating that an animal has a memory deficit is to show that performance is impaired at long-delay intervals, but is intact at short-delay intervals, that is, no impairment in perception, attention, or general intellectual function. A successful strategy for demonstrating intact short-term memory and impaired long-term memory has involved training normal monkeys and monkeys with medial temporal lobe lesions on the delayed nonmatching-to-sample task, a recognition memory task sensitive to amnesia in humans. In this task, the monkey first sees an object, and then after a prescribed delay the animal is given a choice between the previously seen object and a novel one. The key feature of this experimental approach is the use of very short delay intervals (e.g., 0.5 sec). The absence of an impairment at a delay of 0.5 sec would indicate that the medial temporal lobe lesions do not affect short-term memory. Using this strategy, Alvarez-Royo, Zola-Morgan, and Squire (1992) and Overman, Ormsby, and Mishkin (1990) showed that medial temporal lobe lesions impair memory at long delays, but not at very short delays. Studies in rats using delayed nonmatching-to-sample as well as a variety of other memory tasks have also demonstrated that long-term memory is impaired while short-term memory is spared following lesions that involve the hippocampal region (Kesner and Novak 1982; for recent reviews of work in rats, see Further Readings). These findings underscore the idea that medial temporal lobe lesions reproduce a key feature of human amnesia, that is, the distinction between intact short-term memory and impaired long-term memory.

It was originally supposed that damage to the AMYGDALA directly contributed to the memory impairment associated with large medial temporal lobe lesions (Murray and Mishkin 1984). Subsequent work showed that monkeys with virtually complete lesions of the amygdala performed as well as normal monkeys on four different memory tasks, including delayed nonmatching-to-sample task (Zola-Morgan et al. 1989). Other experiments with rats and monkeys suggest that the amygdala is important for other kinds of memory, including the development of conditioned fear and other forms of affective memory (see EMOTION AND THE ANIMAL BRAIN). These and other findings (Murray 1992) focused attention away from the amygdala toward the cortical structures of the medial temporal lobe, that is, the perirhinal, entorhinal, and parahippocampal cortices, in addition to the hippocampal region itself.

Direct evidence for the importance of the cortical regions has come from studies in which circumscribed damage has been done to the perirhinal, entorhinal, or parahippocampal cortices, either separately or in combination (Moss, Mahut, and Zola-Morgan 1981; Zola-Morgan et al. 1989; Gaffan and Murray 1992; Meunier et al. 1993; Suzuki et al. 1993; Leonard et al. 1995). For example, monkeys with combined lesions of the perirhinal and parahippocampal cortices exhibited severe, multimodal, and long-lasting memory impairment (Zola-Morgan et al. 1989; Suzuki et al. 1993). More limited lesions of the cortical regions also produce memory impairment. For example, several studies found that monkeys with bilateral lesions limited to the perirhinal cortex exhibit long-lasting memory impairment (Meunier et al. 1993; Ramus, Zola-Morgan, and Squire 1994). Additionally, a large number of individual studies in monkeys and in rats with varying extents of damage to the medial temporal lobe, together with work in humans, has led to the idea that the severity of memory impairment increases as more components of the medial temporal lobe memory system are damaged.

A long-standing and controversial issue in work on memory has been whether the hippocampal region is disproportionately involved in spatial memory, or whether spatial memory is simply a good example of a broader category of memory that requires the hippocampal region. One view of the matter comes from earlier work with monkeys (Parkinson, Murray, and Mishkin 1988). Monkeys with lesions that involved the hippocampal formation (hippocampus plus underlying posterior entorhinal cortex and parahippocampal cortex) were severely impaired in acquiring an object-place association task, whereas lesions that involved the amygdala plus underlying anterior entorhinal cortex and perirhinal cortex were only mildly impaired. The authors suggested that the hippocampus has an especially important role in spatial memory, an idea developed originally by O'Keefe and Nadel (1978), based mostly on rat work. It was unclear from this monkey study, however, whether the observed spatial deficit was due to hippocampal damage, the adjacent cortical damage, or both. Additional work from both humans and animals suggests another view. In one formal study (Cave and Squire 1991), spatial memory was found to be proportionately impaired in amnesiac patients relative to object recognition memory and object recall memory. The same (nonspatial) view of hippocampal function has also been proposed for the rat, based, for example, on demonstrated deficits in odor memory tasks after ibotenate hippocampal lesions (Bunsey and Eichenbaum 1996). The role of the hippocampus in spatial memory remains unclear. Recent commentaries on the issue of the hippocampus and spatial memory can be found under Further Reading.

Uncertainty about the function of the hippocampus has been due, in part, to the inability until recently to make circumscribed lesions limited to the hippocampal region in experimental animals. Studies in which selective lesions of the hippocampal region could be accomplished became possible only with the development of (a) a technique for producing restricted ibotenate lesions of the hippocampus in the rat and (b) a technique that uses MAGNETIC RESONANCE IMAGING to guide the placement of radiofrequency or ibotenic acid stereotaxic lesions of the hippocampal region in the monkey. Monkeys with bilateral, radiofrequency lesions of the hippocampal region, which spared almost entirely the perirhinal, entorhinal, and parahippocampal cortices, exhibited impaired performance at long delays (ten minutes and forty minutes) on the delayed nonmatching-to-sample task (Alvarez, Zola-Morgan, and Squire 1995).

Ibotenic acid lesions cause cell death but, unlike radio-frequency lesions, spare afferent and efferent white matter fibers within the region of the lesion. If it should turn out, after systematic study, that ibotenic acid lesions of the hippocampal region do not impair performance on the delayed nonmatching task, the interpretation of such studies should not be overstated. The results concern recognition memory, not memory in general, and only the kind of recognition memory measured by the nonmatching-to-sample task itself. The delayed nonmatching task has been extraordinarily useful for evaluating the effects on visual recognition memory of damage to the medial temporal lobe memory system and for measuring the severity of recognition memory impairment. However, in the case of human memory, recognition memory tests are known to be rather easy and not as sensitive to memory impairment as other tests, for instance, tests of recall or cued recall. The issue of task sensitivity is crucially important. Other kinds of recognition memory tasks, for example, the paired comparisons task (a task of spontaneous novelty preference; Bachevalier, Brickson, and Hagger 1993) and tasks that are thought to be more sensitive than tasks of simple recognition memory, for example the transverse patterning, the transitive inference, and naturalistic association tasks, have recently been developed to assess memory in animals.

An important question with respect to the components of the medial temporal lobe memory system is whether these structures all share similar functions as part of a common memory system, or do they have distinct and dissociable functions? In this regard, one must consider the neuroanatomy of the medial temporal lobe system and its pattern of connectivity with association cortex. An extensive anatomical investigation by Suzuki and Amaral (1994) showed that different areas of neocortex gain access to the medial temporal lobe memory system at different points. Visual information arrives preferentially to perirhinal cortex. Approximately 65 percent of the input reaching the perirhinal cortex is unimodal visual information, mostly from TE and TEO. By contrast, about 40 percent of the input reaching parahippocampal cortex is visual, mostly from area V4. Cortical areas that are believed to be important for processing spatial information project preferentially to parahippocampal cortex. Approximately 8 percent of the input to parahippocampal cortex originates in the parietal cortex, whereas virtually none of the input to perirhinal cortex originates in the parietal cortex. These anatomical considerations lead to the expectation that perirhinal cortical lesions might impair visual memory more than spatial memory and that the reverse might be true for parahippocampal cortex. Furthermore, because both the perirhinal and the parahippocampal cortices project to the hippocampus, one might expect that hippocampal damage will similarly impair visual memory and spatial memory. The establishment of new, more sensitive behavioral tests and the development of new techniques for producing selective brain lesions have now made it possible to address these possibilities and to systematically clarify the separate contributions to memory of structures in the medial temporal lobe and the diencephalon.

See also ATTENTION IN THE ANIMAL BRAIN; EPISODIC VS. SEMANTIC MEMORY; IMPLICIT VS. EXPLICIT MEMORY; MEMORY, HUMAN NEUROPSYCHOLOGY; WORKING MEMORY; WORKING MEMORY, NEURAL BASIS OF

—*Stuart Zola*

References

Aggleton, J. P., and M. Mishkin. (1983). Memory impairments following restricted medial thalamic lesions. *Exp. Brain Res.* 52: 199–209.

Alvarez-Royo, P., S. Zola-Morgan, and L. R. Squire. (1992). Impairment of long-term memory and sparing of short-term memory in monkeys with medial temporal lobe lesions: A response to Ringo. *Behav. Brain Res.* 52: 1–5.

Alvarez, P., S. Zola-Morgan, and L. R. Squire. (1995). Damage limited to the hippocampal region produces long-lasting memory impairment. *J. Neurosci.* 15: 3796–3807.

Bachevalier, J., M. Brickson, and C. Hagger. (1993). Limbic-dependent recognition memory in monkeys develops early in infancy. *Neuroreport* 4: 77–80.

Bunsey, M., and H. Eichenbaum. (1996). Conservation of hippocampal memory function in rats and humans. *Nature* 379: 255–257.

Cave, C. B., and L. R. Squire. (1991). Equivalent impairment of spatial and nonspatial memory following damage to the human hippocampus. *Hippocampus* 1: 329–340.

Gaffan, D., and E. A. Murray. (1992). Monkeys (*Macaca fascicularis*) with rhinal cortex ablations succeed in object discrimination learning despite 24-hr intertrial intervals and fail at matching to sample despite double sample presentations. *Behav. Neurosci.* 106: 30–38.

Kesner, R. P., and J. M. Novak. (1982). Serial position curve in rats: Role of the dorsal hippocampus. *Science* 218: 173–175.

Leonard, B. W., D. G. Amaral, L. R. Squire, and S. Zola-Morgan. (1995). Transient memory impairment in monkeys with bilateral lesions of the entorhinal cortex. *J. Neurosci.* 15: 5637–5659.

Mahut, H., and M. Moss. (1984). Consolidation of memory: The hippocampus revisited. In L. R. Squire and N. Butters, Eds., *Neuropsychology of Memory*, vol 1. New York: Guilford Press, pp. 297–315.

Mair, R. G., R. L. Knoth, S. A. Rabehenuk, and P. J. Lanlais. (1991). Impairment of olfactory, auditory, and spatial serial reversal learning in rats recovered from pyrithiamine induced thiamine deficiency. *Behav. Neurosci.* 105: 360–374.

Mair, R. G., J. K. Robinson, S. M. Koger, G. D. Fox, and Y. P. Zhang. (1992). Delayed non-matching to sample is impaired by extensive, but not by limited lesions of thalamus in rats. *Behav. Neurosci.* 106: 646–656.

Meunier, M., J. Bachevalier, M. Mishkin, and E. A. Murray. (1993). Effects on visual recognition of combined and separate ablations of the entorhinal and perirhinal cortex in rhesus monkeys. *J. Neurosci.* 13: 5418–5432.

Mishkin, M. (1982). A memory system in the monkey. *Philos. Trans. R. Soc. Lond. B. Biol. Sci.* 98: 85–95.

Moss, M., H. Mahut, and S. Zola-Morgan. (1981). Concurrent discrimination learning of monkeys after hippocampal, entorhinal, or fornix lesions. *J. Neurosci.* 1: 227–240.

Murray, E. A. (1992). Medial temporal lobe structures contributing to recognition memory: The amygdaloid complex versus the rhinal complex. In J. P. Aggleton, Ed., *The Amygdala: Neurobiological Aspects of Emotion, Memory, and Mental Dysfunction.* New York: Wiley-Liss, pp. 453–470.

Murray, E. A., and M. Mishkin. (1984). Severe tactual as well as visual memory deficits following combined removal of the amygdala and hippocampus in monkeys. *J. Neurosci.* 4: 2565–2580.

O'Keefe, J., and L. Nadel. (1978). *The Hippocampus as a Cognitive Map.* Oxford: Clarendon Press.

Overman, W. H., G. Ormsby, and M. Mishkin. (1990). Picture recognition vs. picture discrimination learning in monkeys with medial temporal removals. *Exp. Brain Res.* 79: 18–24.

Parkinson, J. K., E. A. Murray, and M. Mishkin. (1988). A selective mnemonic role for the hippocampus in monkeys: Memory for the location of objects. *J. Neurosci.* 8: 4159–4167.

Ramus, S. J., S. Zola-Morgan, and L. R. Squire. (1994). Effects of lesions of perirhinal cortex or parahippocampal cortex on memory in monkeys. *Soc. Neurosci. Abst.* 20: 10–74.

Scoville, W. B., and B. Milner. (1957). Loss of recent memory after bilateral hippocampal lesions. *J. Neurol. Neurosurg. Psychiatry* 20: 11–21.

Squire, L. R., and S. Zola-Morgan. (1983). The neurology of memory: The case for correspondence between the findings for human and nonhuman primates. In J. A. Deutsch, Ed., *The Physiological Basis of Memory.* New York: Academic Press, pp. 199–268.

Suzuki, W. A., and D. G. Amaral. (1994). Perirhinal and parahippocampal cortices of the macaque monkey: Cortical afferents. *J. Comp. Neurol.* 350: 497–533.

Suzuki, W. A., S. Zola-Morgan, L. R. Squire, and D. G. Amaral. (1993). Lesions of the perirhinal and parahippocampal cortices in the monkey produce long-lasting memory impairment in the visual and tactual modalities. *J. Neurosci.* 13: 2430–2451.

Zola-Morgan, S. M., and L. R. Squire. (1985). Amnesia in monkeys following lesions of the mediodorsal nucleus of the thalamus. *Ann. Neurol.* 17: 558–564.

Zola-Morgan, S. M., and L. R. Squire. (1993). Neuroanatomy of memory. *Ann. Rev. Neurosci.* 16: 547–563.

Zola-Morgan, S., L. R. Squire, D. G. Amaral, and W. A. Suzuki. (1989). Lesions of perirhinal and parahippocampal cortex that spare the amygdala and hippocampal formation produce severe memory impairment. *J. Neurosci.* 9: 4355–4370.

Further Readings

Alvarado, M. C., and J. W. Rudy. (1995). Rats with damage to the hippocampal-formation are impaired on the transverse-patterning problem but not on elemental discriminations. *Behav. Neurosci.* 109: 204–211.

Alvarez-Royo, P., R. P. Clower, S. Zola-Morgan, and L. R. Squire. (1991). Stereotaxic lesions of the hippocampus in monkeys: Determination of surgical coordinates and analysis of lesions using magnetic resonance imaging. *J. Neurosci. Methods* 38: 223–232.

Amaral, D. G., Ed. (1991). Is the hippocampal formation preferentially involved in spatial behavior? *Hippocampus* (special issue) 1: 221–292.

Bunsey, M., and H. Eichenbaum. (1995). Selective damage to the hippocampal region blocks long-term retention of a natural and nonspatial stimulus-stimulus association. *Hippocampus* 5: 546–556.

Eichenbaum, H. (1997). Declarative memory: Insights from cognitive neurobiology. *Annu. Rev. Psychol.* 48: 547–572.

Eichenbaum, H., T. Otto, and N. J. Cohen. (1994). Two functional components of the hippocampal memory system. *Behav. and Brain Sci.* 17: 449–517.

Horel, J. A., D. E. Pytko-Joiner, M. Voytko, and K. Salsbury. (1987). The performance of visual tasks while segments of the inferotemporal cortex are suppressed by cold. *Behav. Brain Res.* 23: 29–42.

Jaffard, R., and M. Meunier. (1993). Role of the hippocampal formation in learning and memory. *Hippocampus* 3: 203–218.

Jarrard, L. E. (1993). On the role of the hippocampus in learning and memory in the rat. *Behav. Neural Biol.* 60: 9–26.

Jarrard, L. E., and B. S. Meldrum. (1993). Selective excitotoxic pathology in the rat hippocampus. *Neuropathol. Appl. Neurobiol.* 19: 381–389.

Mair, R. G., C. D. Anderson, P. J. Langlais, and W. J. McEntree. (1988). Behavioral impairments, brain lesions and monoaminergic activity in the rat following a bout of thiamine deficiency. *Behav. Brain Res.* 27: 223–239.

Mishkin, M. (1978). Memory in monkeys severely impaired by combined but not separate removal of the amygdala and hippocampus. *Nature* 273: 297–298.

Nadel, L. (1995). The role of the hippocampus in declarative memory: A comment on Zola-Morgan, Squire, and Ramus (1994). *Hippocampus* 5: 232–234.

Vnek, N., T. C. Gleason, and L. F. Kromer. (1995). Entorhinal-hippocampal connections and object memory in the rat: Acquisition versus retention. *J. Neurosci.* 15: 3193–3199.

Zola-Morgan, S., L. R. Squire, and S. J. Ramus. (1995). The role of the hippocampus in declarative memory: A reply to Nadel. *Hippocampus* 5: 235–239.

Memory, Human Neuropsychology

LEARNING is the process by which new knowledge is acquired about the world. MEMORY is the process by which what is learned can be retained in storage with the possibility of drawing on it later. Most of what humans know about the world is not built into the brain at the time of birth but is acquired through experience. It is learned, stored in the brain as memory, and is available later to be retrieved.

Memory is localized in the brain as physical changes produced by experience. Memory is thought to be stored as changes in synaptic connectivity within large ensembles of neurons. New synaptic connections may be formed, and there are changes as well in the strength of existing synapses. What makes a memory is not the manufacture of some chemical code, but rather increases and decreases in the strength of already existing neural connections and formation of new connections. What makes the memory specific (memory of a trip to England instead of memory of a drive to the hardware store) is not the kind of cellular and molecular event that occurs in the brain, but where in the nervous system the changes occur and along which pathways.

The brain is highly specialized and differentiated, organized so that different regions of neocortex simultaneously carry out computations on separate features of the external world (e.g., the analysis of form, color, and movement). Memory of a specific event, or even memory of something so apparently simple as a single object, is thought to be stored in a distributed fashion, essentially in component parts. These components are stored in the same neural systems in neocortex that ordinarily participate in the processing and analysis of what is to be remembered. In one sense, memory is the persistence of perception. It is stored as outcomes of perceptual operations and in the same cortical regions that are ordinarily involved in the processing of the items and events that are to be remembered.

It has long been appreciated that severe memory impairment can occur against a background of otherwise normal intellectual function. This dissociation shows that the brain has to some extent separated its intellectual and perceptual functions from its capacity for laying down in memory the records that ordinarily result from intellectual and perceptual work. Specifically, the medial temporal lobe and the midline diencephalon of the brain have specific memory functions, and bilateral damage to these regions causes an amnesic syndrome. The amnesic syndrome is characterized by profound forgetfulness for new material (anterograde amnesia), regardless of the sensory modality through which the material is presented and regardless of the kind of material that is presented (faces, names, stories, musical passages, or shapes). Immediate memory, as measured by digit span, is intact. However, a memory deficit is easily detected with conventional memory tests that ask subjects to learn and remember an amount of information that exceeds what can be held in immediate memory or with memory tests that ask subjects to learn even a small amount of information and then hold onto it for several minutes in the face of distraction. The impairment appears whether memory is tested by unaided (free) recall, by recognition, or by cued recall. As assessed by these various instruments, the deficit in amnesic patients is proportional to the sensitivity with which these tests measure memory in intact subjects. Recognition is easier than recall for all subjects, amnesic patients and normal subjects alike.

The same brain lesions that cause difficulties in new learning also cause retrograde amnesia, difficulty in recollecting events that occurred prior to the onset of amnesia. Typically, retrograde amnesia is temporally graded such that very old (remote) memory is affected less than recent memory. Retrograde amnesia can cover as much as a decade or two prior to the onset of amnesia. These observations show that the structures damaged in amnesia are not the repositories of long-term memory. Rather, these structures are essential, beginning at the time of learning, and they are thought to drive a gradual process of memory consolidation in neocortex. As the result of this process, memory storage in neocortex comes to be independent of the medial temporal lobe and diencephalic structures that are damaged in amnesia.

Information about what specific structures are important for human memory comes from carefully studied cases of amnesia, which provide both neuropsychological and neurohistological information, and from the study of an animal model of human amnesia in the monkey. The available human cases make several points. First, damage limited bilaterally to the CA1 region of the HIPPOCAMPUS is sufficient to cause a moderately severe anterograde amnesia. Second, when more damage occurs in the hippocampal formation, (e.g., damage to the CA fields, dentate gyrus, subicular complex, and some cell loss in entorhinal cortex), the anterograde amnesia becomes more severe. Third, damage limited bilaterally to the hippocampal formation is sufficient to produce temporally limited retrograde amnesia covering more than 10 years.

Systematic and cumulative work in monkeys has further demonstrated that the full medial temporal lobe memory system consists of the hippocampus and adjacent, anatomically related structures: entorhinal cortex, perirhinal cortex, and parahippocampal cortex. The critical regions of the medial diencephalon important for memory appear to be the mediodorsal thalamic nucleus, the anterior nucleus, the mammillary nuclei, and the structures within and interconnected by the internal medullary lamina.

One fundamental distinction in the neuropsychology of memory separates immediate memory from long-term memory. Indeed, this is the distinction that is revealed by the facts of human amnesia. In addition, a number of distinctions can be made within long-term memory. Memory is not a unitary mental faculty but depends on the operation of several separate systems that operate in parallel to record the effects of experience. The major distinction is between the capacity for conscious recollection about facts and events (so-called declarative or explicit memory) and a collection of nonconscious memory abilities (so-called nondeclarative or implicit memory), whereby memory is expressed through performance without any necessary conscious memory content or even the experience that memory is being used.

Declarative memory is the kind of memory that is impaired in amnesia. Declarative memory is a brain-systems construct. It is the kind of memory that depends on the integrity of the medial temporal lobe–diencephalic brain structures damaged in amnesia. Declarative memory is involved in modeling the external world, in storing representations of objects, episodes, and facts. It is fast, specialized for one-trial learning, and for making arbitrary associations or conjunctions between stimuli. The acquired representations are flexible and available to multiple response systems. Nondeclarative memory is not itself a brain-systems construct, but rather an umbrella term for several kinds of memory, each of which has its own brain organization. Nondeclarative memory underlies changes in skilled behavior, the development through repetition of appropriate ways to respond to stimuli, and it underlies the phenomenon of priming—a temporary change in the ability to identify or detect perceptual objects. In these cases, performance changes as the result of experience and therefore deserves the name memory, but like drug tolerance or immunological memory, performance changes without providing a record of the particular episodes that led to the change in performance. What is learned tends to be encapsulated and inflexible, available most readily to the same response systems that were involved in the original learning.

Among the prominent kinds of nondeclarative memory are procedural memory (memory for skills and habits), simple classical CONDITIONING, and the phenomenon of priming. Skill and habit memory depends importantly on the dorsal striatum, even when motor activity is not an important part of the task. Thus, nondemented patients with Parkinson's disease, who have dorsal striatal damage, are impaired at learning a two-choice discrimination task where the correct answer on each trial is determined probabilistically. In this task, normal subjects learn gradually, not by memorizing the cues and their outcomes, but by gradually developing a disposition to respond differentially to the cues that are presented. Classical conditioning of skeletal musculature (e.g., eyeblink conditioning) depends on cerebellar and brain stem pathways. Emotional learning, including fear conditioning, depends on the amygdaloid complex. In the case of fear conditioning, subjects will often remember the unpleasant, aversive event. This component of memory is declarative and depends on the medial temporal lobe and diencephalon. But subjects may also develop a negative feeling about the stimulus object, perhaps even a phobia, and this component of remembering depends on the amygdala. The AMYGDALA also appears to be an important modulator of both declarative and nondeclarative forms of memory. For example, activity originating in the amygdala appears to underlie the observation that emotional events are typically remembered better than neutral events. Finally, the phenomenon of priming appears to depend on the neocortical pathways that are involved in processing the material that is primed. Neuroimaging studies have described reductions in activity in posterior neocortex in correspondence with perceptual priming.

Information is still accumulating about how memory is organized, what structures and connections are involved, and what jobs they do. The disciplines of both psychology and neuroscience contribute to this enterprise.

See also AGING, MEMORY, AND THE BRAIN; EPISODIC VS. SEMANTIC MEMORY; IMPLICIT VS. EXPLICIT MEMORY; MEMORY, ANIMAL STUDIES; MEMORY STORAGE, MODULATION OF; WORKING MEMORY; WORKING MEMORY, NEURAL BASIS OF

—Larry Squire

Further Readings

Knowlton, B. J., J. Mangels, and L. R. Squire. (1996). A neostriatal habit learning system in humans. *Science* 273: 1399–1402.

Rempel-Clower, N., S. M. Zola, L. R. Squire, and D. G. Amaral. (1996). Three cases of enduring memory impairment following bilateral damage limited to the hippocampal formation. *Journal of Neuroscience* 16: 5233–5255.

Squire, L. R., B. J. Knowlton, and G. Musen. (1993). The structure and organization of memory. *Annual Review of Psychology* 44: 453–495.

Squire, L. R., and S. Zola-Morgan. (1991). The medial temporal lobe memory system. *Science* 253: 1380–1386.

Memory Storage, Modulation of

The formation of lasting, long-term memory occurs gradually, over time, following learning. A century ago Mueller and Pilzecker (1900) proposed that the neural processes underlying new memories persist in a short-lasting modifiable state and then, with time, become consolidated into a relatively long-lasting state. Later, HEBB (1949) proposed that the first stage of the "dual-trace" memory system is based on reverberating neural circuits and that such neural activity induces lasting changes in synaptic connections that provide the basis for long-term memory.

Clinical and experimental evidence strongly supports the hypothesis that memory storage is time-dependent. Disruption of brain activity shortly after learning impairs long-term memory. In humans, acute brain trauma produces retrograde amnesia, a selective loss of memory for recent experiences (Burnham 1903; Russell and Nathan 1946) and in animals retrograde amnesia is induced by many treatments that impair brain functioning, including electrical brain stimulation and drugs (McGaugh and Herz 1972). Additionally, and more importantly, in humans as well as animals (Soetens et al. 1995), stimulant drugs administered shortly after learning enhance memory. Drugs affecting many neurotransmitter and hormonal systems improve long-term memory when they are administered within a few minutes or hours after training (McGaugh 1973, 1983). Extensive evidence indicates that the drugs enhance the consolidation of long-term memory.

Our memories of experiences vary greatly in strength. Some memories fade quickly and completely, whereas others last a lifetime. Generally, remembrance of experiences varies with their significance; emotionally arousing events are better remembered (Christianson 1992). William JAMES observed that, "An experience may be so exciting emotionally as almost to leave a scar on the cerebral tissue" (James 1890). Studies of retrograde amnesia and memory enhancement provide important clues to the physiological systems underlying variations in memory strength. In particular, the finding that drugs enhance memory consolidation suggests that hormonal systems activated by emotional arousal may influence consolidation (Cahill and McGaugh 1996).

Emotionally exciting experiences induce the release of adrenal hormones, including the adrenal medullary hormone epinephrine (Adrenaline) and the adrenal cortex hormone corticosterone (in humans, cortisol). Experiments with animal and human subjects indicate that these hormones, as well as other hormones released by learning experiences, play an important role in regulating memory storage (Izquierdo and Diaz 1983; McGaugh and Gold 1989). Administration of epinephrine to rats or mice shortly after training enhances their long-term memory of the training (Gold, McCarty, and Sternberg 1982). β-adrenergic antagonists such as propranolol block the memory enhancement induced by epinephrine. Comparable findings have been obtained in studies with human subjects. The finding that β-adrenergic antagonists block the enhancing effects of emotional arousal on long-term memory formation in humans supports the hypothesis that β-adrenergic agonists, including epinephrine, modulate memory storage (Cahill et al. 1994). Additionally, studies of the effects of corticosterone, as well as synthetic glucocorticoid receptor agonists and antagonists, indicate that memory storage is enhanced by glucocorticoid agonists and impaired by antagonists. Furthermore, hormones of the adrenal medulla and adrenal cortex interact in modulating memory storage: metyrapone, a drug that impairs the synthesis and release of corticosterone, blocks the effects of epinephrine on memory consolidation (Sandi and Rose 1994; De Kloet 1991; Roozendaal, Cahill, and McGaugh 1996).

Recent research has revealed brain regions mediating drug and hormone influences on memory storage. Considerable evidence indicates that many drugs and hormones modulate memory through influences involving the amygdaloid complex. It is well established that electrical stimulation of the AMYGDALA modulates memory storage and that the effect is influenced by adrenal hormones (Liang, Bennett, and McGaugh 1985). Lesions of the stria terminalis (a major amygdala pathway that connects the amygdala with many brain regions) block the memory-modulating effects of many drugs and hormones, including those of adrenal hormones. Furthermore, lesions of the amygdala and, more specifically, lesions of the basolateral amygdala nucleus, also block the effects of adrenal hormones on memory storage (McGaugh, Cahill, and Roozendaal 1996).

In humans, amygdala lesions block the effects of emotional arousal on long-term memory (Cahill et al. 1995). In animals, infusions of β-adrenergic and glucocorticoid antagonists into the amygdala impair memory, whereas infusions of β-adrenergic agonists (e.g., norepinephrine) and glucocorticoid receptor agonists into the amygdala after training enhance memory. As was found with lesions, the critical site for infusions is the basolateral amygdala nucleus (Gallagher et al. 1981; Liang, Juler, and McGaugh 1986; McGaugh et al. 1996). Findings such as these indicate that the basolateral amygdala nucleus is an important and perhaps critical brain region mediating arousal-induced neuromodulatory influences on memory storage.

Thus, there is extensive evidence from human and animal studies that the amygdala is critically involved in modulating memory consolidation. However, it is also clear from the findings of many studies that the amygdala is not the neural locus of long-term memory. Lesions of the amygdala induced after training do not block retention of the memory of the training (Parent, West, and McGaugh 1994). Additionally, the amygdala is not the locus of neural changes underlying the enhanced memory induced by infusing drugs into the amygdala immediately after training. Drug infusions administered into the amygdala post training enhance long-term memory for training in many types of tasks, including tasks known to involve the HIPPOCAMPUS or caudate nucleus. Furthermore, inactivation of the amygdala with lidocaine infusions prior to retention testing does not block the enhanced memory (Packard, Cahill, and McGaugh 1994).

Research with humans has provided additional evidence that amygdala activation is involved in modulating the consolidation of long-term memory. In subjects tested several weeks after viewing emotionally arousing film clips, memory of the content of the film clips correlated very highly with activation of the amygdala when viewing the film clips, as indicated by POSITRON EMISSION TOMOGRAPHY (PET) brain scans (Cahill et al. 1996).

The formation of new long-term memory must, of course, involve the formation of lasting neural changes. Additionally, the strength of the induced neural changes, as subsequently reflected in long-term memory, is modulated by the actions of specific hormonal and brain systems activated by learning experiences. Such modulation serves to ensure that the significance of experiences will influence their remembrance. Investigations of the processes and systems underlying the modulation of memory storage are providing new insights into how memories are created and sustained.

See also EPISODIC VS. SEMANTIC MEMORY; IMPLICIT VS. EXPLICIT MEMORY; MEMORY; NEUROTRANSMITTERS

—*James L. McGaugh*

References

Burnham, W. H. (1903). Retrograde amnesia: Illustrative cases and a tentative explanation. *Am. J. Psychol.* 14: 382–396.

Cahill, L., and J. L. McGaugh. (1996). Modulation of memory storage. *Current Opinion in Neurobiology* 6: 237–242.

Cahill, L., B. Prins, M. Weber, and J. L. McGaugh. (1994). β-Adrenergic activation and memory for emotional events. *Nature* 371: 702–704.

Cahill, L., R. Babinsky, H. J. Markowitsch, and J. L. McGaugh. (1995). The amygdala and emotional memory. *Nature* 377: 295–296.

Cahill, L., R. J. Haier, J. Fallon, M. Alkire, C. Tang, D. Keator, J. Wu, and J. L. McGaugh. (1996). *Proc. Natl. Acad. Sci. U.S.A.* 93: 8016–8021.

Christianson, S. -A., Ed. (1992). *Handbook of Emotion and Memory: Current Research and Theory.* Hillsdale, NJ: Erlbaum.

De Kloet, E. R. (1991). Brain corticosteriod receptor balance and homeostatic control. *Neuroendocrinology* 12: 95–164.

Gallagher, M., B. S. Kapp, J. P. Pascoe, and P. R. Rapp. (1981). A neuropharmacology of amygdaloid systems which contribute to learning and memory. In Y. Ben-Ari, Ed., *The Amygdaloid Complex.* Amsterdam: Elsevier.

Gold, P. E., R. McCarty, and D. B. Sternberg. (1982). Peripheral catecholamines and memory modulation. In C. Ajmone Marson and H. Matthies, Eds., *Neuronal Plasticity and Memory Formation.* New York: Raven Press, pp. 327–338.

Hebb, D. O. (1949). *The Organization of Behavior.* New York: Wiley.

Izquierdo, I., and R. D. Diaz. (1983). Effect of ACTH, epinephrine, β-endorphin, naloxone and of the combination of naloxone or β-endorphin with ACTH or epinephrine on memory consolidation. *Psychoneuroendocrinology* 8: 81–87.

James, W. (1890). *The Principles of Psychology.* New York: Henry Holt.

Liang, K. C., C. Bennett, and J. L. McGaugh. (1985). Peripheral epinephrine modulates the effects of posttraining amygdala stimulation on memory. *Behav. Brain Res.* 15: 83–91.

Liang, K. C., R. G. Juler, and J. L. McGaugh. (1986). Modulating effects of posttraining epinephrine on memory: Involvement of the amygdala noradrenergic system. *Brain Research* 368: 125–133.

McGaugh, J. L. (1973). Drug facilitation of learning and memory. *Ann. Rev. Pharmacol.* 13: 229–241.

McGaugh, J. L. (1983). Hormonal influences on memory. *Ann. Rev. Psychol.* 34: 297–323.

McGaugh, J. L., and P. E. Gold. (1989). Hormonal modulation of memory. In R. B. Rush and S. Levine, Eds., *Psychoendocrinology*. New York: Academic Press.

McGaugh, J. L., and M. J. Herz. (1972). *Memory Consolidation*. San Francisco: Albion.

McGaugh, J. L., L. Cahill, and B. Roozendaal. (1996). Involvement of the amygdala in memory storage: Interaction with other brain systems. *Proc. Natl. Acad. Sci. U.S.A.* 93: 13508–13514.

Mueller, G. E., and A. Pilzecker. (1900). Experimentelle Beiträge zur Lehre vom Gedächtnis. *Z. Psychol.* 1: 1–288.

Packard, M. G., L. Cahill, and J. L. McGaugh. (1994). Amygdala modulation of hippocampal-dependent and caudate nucleus-dependent memory processes. *Proc. Natl. Acad. Sci. U.S.A.* 91: 8477–8481.

Parent, M. B., M. West, and J. L. McGaugh. (1994). Memory of rats with amygdala lesions induced 30 days after footshock-motivated escape training reflects degree of original training. *Behavioral Neuroscience* 6: 1959–1064.

Roozendaal, B., L. Cahill, and J. L. McGaugh. (1996). Interaction of emotionally activated neuromodulatory systems in regulating memory storage. In K. Ishikawa, J. L. McGaugh, and H. Sakata, Eds., *Brain Processes and Memory, Excerpta Medica International Congress Series 1108*. Amsterdam: Elsevier, pp. 39–54.

Russell, W. R., and P. W. Nathan. (1946). Traumatic amnesia. *Brain* 69: 280–300.

Sandi, C., and S. P. R. Rose. (1994). Corticosterone enhances long-term retention in one-day old chicks trained in a weak passive avoidance paradigm. *Brain Research* 647: 106–112.

Soetens, E., S. Casear, R. D'Hooge, and J. E. Hueting. (1995). Effect of amphetamine on long-term retention of verbal material. *Psychopharmacology* 119: 155–162.

Mental Causation

The problem of mental causation is the most recent incarnation of the venerable MIND-BODY PROBLEM, Schopenhauer's "world knot". DESCARTES held that mind and body were distinct kinds of entity that interact causally, but waffled over the question how this was possible. Mind-body dualism of the Cartesian sort is no longer popular, but variants of the Cartesian problem remain, and waffling is still in fashion. Current worries about mental causation stem from two sources: (1) "nonreductive" conceptions of the mental; and (2) externalism (or anti-INDIVIDUALISM) about mental "content."

Although most theorists have left dualism behind, many remain wedded to the Cartesian idea that the mental and the physical are fundamentally distinct. Mental properties, though properties of physical systems, are "higher-level" properties not reducible to or identifiable with "lower-level" properties of those systems. Most functionalist accounts of the mind embrace this picture, endorsing the slogan that mental properties are "multiply realizable." Take the property of being in pain. This property, like the property of being an eye, is said to be a functional, "second-order" property, one that a creature possesses by virtue of possessing some first-order "realizer"—a particular physical configuration or process, for instance. Pains are capable of endless "realizations" in the human nervous system, in the very different nervous system of a cephalopod, and perhaps

in silicon-based systems of Alpha Centaurians—or appropriately programmed computing machines. There is, then, no prospect of locating a unique physical property to identify with pain.

When, however, we try to reconcile "multiple realizability" with the idea that the physical realm is causally self-contained, trouble arises. Consider your body, a complex physical system composed of microparticles interacting in accord with fundamental physical laws. The behavior of those particles, hence the behavior of your body, is completely determined (albeit probabilistically) by those laws. Now suppose you step on a tack, experience a pain, and quickly withdraw your foot. Common sense tells us that your pain played a causal role in your foot's moving. But can this be right? Your experiencing a pain is a matter of your possessing a "higher-level" property, a property thought to be distinct from any of the properties possessed by your "lower-level" physical constituents. It appears, however, that your behavior is entirely determined by "lower-level" nonmental goings-on. In what sense, then, is your experience of pain "causally relevant" to the movement of your foot?

Some philosophers have responded to this difficulty by adopting a deflationary view of CAUSATION. As they see it, causation is just counterfactual dependence: roughly, if E would not have occurred unless C had, then C causes E (LePore and Loewer 1987). Others, appealing to scientific practice, have suggested that we replace metaphysically loaded references to causes with talk of causal explanation (Wilson 1995). Still others argue that the causal relevance of "higher-level" properties requires reduction: "Higher-level" mental properties must be identified with "lower-level" properties (Kim 1989). This strategy resolves one problem of mental causation, but at a cost few philosophers seem willing to pay.

Lack of enthusiasm for reduction is due in part to the widespread belief that mental properties are "multiply realizable," hence distinct from their physical realizers, and in part to a no less widespread commitment to externalism. Externalists hold that the "contents" of states of mind depend on agents' contexts. Wayne, for example, believes that water is wet. Wayne's belief concerns water, and the "content" of his belief is that water is wet. Imagine an exact duplicate of Wayne, Dwayne, who inhabits a distant planet, TWIN EARTH, an exact duplicate of Earth with one important difference: the colorless, tasteless, transparent liquid that fills rivers and bathtubs on Twin Earth differs in its molecular constitution from water. Water is H_2O. The substance on Twin Earth that Dwayne and his fellows call "water" is XYZ. Now, so the story goes, although Wayne and Dwayne are alike intrinsically, their thoughts differ. Wayne believes that water is wet; whereas Dwayne's beliefs concern, not water, but what we might call "twin water" (see Putnam 1975).

Thought experiments of this sort have convinced many philosophers that the contents of thoughts depend, at least in part, on thinkers' surroundings and causal histories (see Burge 1986; Davidson 1987; Baker 1987). A contextualism of this sort introduces a new twist on the problem of mental causation, and simultaneously renders REDUCTIONISM even less attractive. Surely the contents of your thoughts are relevant to what those thoughts lead you to do. You flee because you believe the creature on the path in front of you is a skunk. Had you believed instead that the creature was a cat, you would have behaved differently. If the content of your belief—its being a belief about a skunk—depends on your causal history, however, how could it make a here-and-now physical difference to the way you move your body?

A molecule, a billiard ball, a planet, or a brain behaves as it does and reacts to incoming stimuli because of its intrinsic physical makeup. But if everything you do is a function of your intrinsic physical properties, and if the contents of your thoughts depend on relations you bear to other things, then it is hard to see how the contents of your thoughts could make any difference at all to what you do.

Again, some philosophers have sought to accommodate externalism and mental causation via deflationary accounts of causation or appeals to explanatory norms. Others have defended a notion of "narrow content," mental content that depends only on agents' intrinsic composition (Fodor 1987). Wayne and Dwayne, for instance, are said to entertain thoughts that have the same "narrow content" but differ in their "broad content." Externalists have been unenthusiastic about "narrow content." And, in any case, even if we embrace "narrow content," so long as we assume that mental properties are irreducible "higher-level" properties of physical systems, we are left with our initial worry about the causal irrelevance of "higher-level" properties.

Externalism aside, perhaps we could make progress by distinguishing predicates and properties. Predicates apply to objects by virtue of properties those objects possess, but not every predicate designates a property. The predicate "is a tree" applies to objects by virtue of their properties, but there is no property of being a tree common to all trees. Perhaps mental predicates are like this. The predicate "pain," for instance, might apply to many different kinds of object, not because these objects share some single property, but because they are similar in important ways: they possess distinct, though similar, first-order physical properties (which have uncontroversial causal roles). A view of this sort allows that "pain" applies truly to creatures in distress, although it obliges us to abandon the philosopher's conceit that the predicate "pain" thereby designates a property shared by every creature to whom "pain" is truly predicable.

Whether these remarks are on the right track, they suggest that the philosophy of mind would benefit from an infusion of good old-fashioned metaphysics. Until we are clear on the nature of properties, for instance, or the character of "multiple realizability," we shall not be in a position to make headway on the problem of mental causation.

See also EPIPHENOMENALISM; INTENTIONALITY; PHYSICALISM; PROPOSITIONAL ATTITUDES; SUPERVENIENCE

—*John Heil*

References

Baker, L. R. (1987). *Saving Belief.* Princeton: Princeton University Press.
Burge, T. (1986). Individualism and psychology. *Philosophical Review* 45: 3–45.
Davidson, D. (1987). Knowing one's own mind. *Proceedings and Addresses of the American Philosophical Association* 60: 441–458.
Fodor, J. (1987). *Psychosemantics.* Cambridge: MIT Press.
Heil, J., and A. Mele, Eds. (1993). *Mental Causation.* Oxford: Clarendon Press.
Jackson, F. (1996). Mental causation. *Mind* 105: 377–413.
Kim, J. (1989). The myth of nonreductive materialism. *Proceedings and Addresses of the American Philosophical Association* 63: 31–47. Reprinted in *Supervenience and Mind.* Cambridge: Cambridge University Press, 1993, pp. 265–284.
LePore, E., and B. Loewer. (1987). Mind matters. *Journal of Philosophy* 84: 630–642.
Putnam, H. (1975). The meaning of "meaning." In *Mind, Language and Reality.* Cambridge: Cambridge University Press, pp. 215–271.
Wilson, R. (1995). *Cartesian Psychology and Physical Minds.* Cambridge: Cambridge University Press.

Mental Models

As psychological representations of real, hypothetical, or imaginary situations, mental models were first postulated by the Scottish psychologist Kenneth Craik (1943), who wrote that the mind constructs "small-scale models" of reality to anticipate events, to reason, and to underlie EXPLANATION. The models are constructed in working memory as a result of perception, the comprehension of discourse, or imagination (see MARR 1982; Johnson-Laird 1983). A crucial feature is that their structure corresponds to the structure of what they represent. Mental models are accordingly akin to architects' models of buildings and to chemists' models of complex molecules.

The structure of a mental model contrasts with another sort of MENTAL REPRESENTATION. Consider the assertion

The triangle is on the right of the circle.

Its meaning can be encoded in the mind in a *propositional representation,* for example:

(right-of triangle circle)

The structure of this representation is syntactic, depending on the conventions governing the LANGUAGE OF THOUGHT: The predicate "right-of" precedes its subject "triangle" and its object "circle." In contrast, the situation described by the assertion can be represented in a mental model:

The structure of this representation is spatial: it is isomorphic to the actual spatial relation between the two objects. The model captures what is common to any situation where a triangle is on the right of a circle. Although it represents nothing about their distance apart or other such matters, the shape and size of the tokens can be revised to take into account subsequent information. Mental models appear to underlie visual IMAGERY. Unlike images, however, they can represent three dimensions (see MENTAL ROTATION), negation, and other abstract notions. The construction of models from propositional representations of discourse is part of the process of comprehension and of establishing that different expressions refer to the same entity. How this process occurs has been investigated in detail (e.g., Garnham and Oakhill 1996).

If mental models are the end result of perception and comprehension, they can underlie reasoning. Individuals use them to formulate conclusions, and test the strength of these conclusions by checking whether other models of the premises refute them (Johnson-Laird and Byrne 1991). This theory is an alternative to the view that DEDUCTIVE REASONING depends on formal rules of inference akin to those of a logical calculus. The distinction between the two theories parallels the one in LOGIC between proof-theoretic methods based on formal rules and model-theoretic methods based, say, on truth tables. Which psychological theory provides a better account of human reasoning is controversial, but mental models have a number of advantages. They provide a unified account of deductive, probabilistic, and modal reasoning. People infer that a conclusion is necessary —it *must* be true—if it holds in all of their models of the premises; that it is probable—it is *likely* to be true—if it holds in most of their models of the premises; and that it is possible—it *may* be true—if it holds in at least one of their models of the premises. Thus an assertion such as

There is a circle or there is a triangle, or both

yields three models, each of which corresponds to a *true* possibility, shown here on separate lines:

O

Δ

O   Δ

The modal conclusion

It is possible that there is both a circle and a triangle

follows from the assertion, because it is supported by the third model. Experiments show that the more models needed for an inference, the longer the inference takes and the more likely an error is to occur (Johnson-Laird and Byrne 1991). Models also have the advantage that they can serve as counterexamples to putative conclusions—an advantage over formal rules of inference that researchers in artificial intelligence exploit in LOGICAL REASONING SYSTEMS (e.g., Halpern and Vardi 1991).

Mental models represent explicitly what is true, but not what is false (see the models of the disjunction above). An unexpected consequence of this principle is the existence of "illusory inferences" to which nearly everyone succumbs (Johnson-Laird and Savary 1996). Consider the following problem:

Only one assertion is true about a particular hand of cards:

There is a king in the hand or there is an ace, or both.
There is a queen in the hand or there is an ace, or both.
There is a jack in the hand or there is a ten, or both.

Is it possible that there is an ace in the hand?

Nearly everyone responds "yes" (Johnson-Laird and Goldvarg 1997). Yet the response is a fallacy. If there were an ace in the hand, then two of the assertions would be true, contrary to the rubric that only one of them is true. The illusion arises because individuals' mental models represent what is true for each premise, but not what is false concomitantly for the other two premises. A variety of such illusions occur in all the main domains of reasoning. They can be reduced by making what is false more salient.

The term *mental model* is sometimes used to refer to the representation of a body of knowledge in long-term memory, which may have the same sort of structure as the models used in reasoning. Psychologists have investigated mental models of such physical systems as handheld calculators, the solar system, and the flow of electricity (Gentner and Stevens 1983). They have studied how children develop such models (Halford 1993), how to design artifacts and computer systems for which it is easy to acquire models (Ehrlich 1996), and how models of one domain may serve as an ANALOGY for another domain. Researchers in artificial intelligence have similarly developed qualitative models of physical systems that make possible "commonsense" inferences (e.g., Kuipers 1994). To understand phenomena as a result either of short-term processes such as vision and inference or of long-term experience appears to depend on the construction of mental models. The embedding of one model within another may play a critical role in METAREPRESENTATION and CONSCIOUSNESS.

See also CAUSAL REASONING; SCHEMATA

—*Philip N. Johnson-Laird*

References

Craik, K. (1943). *The Nature of Explanation.* Cambridge: Cambridge University Press.

Ehrlich, K. (1996). Applied mental models in human-computer interaction. In J. Oakhill and A. Garnham, Eds., *Mental Models in Cognitive Science.* Mahwah, NJ: Erlbaum.

Garnham, A., and J. V. Oakhill. (1996). The mental models theory of language comprehension. In B. K. Britton and A. C. Graesser, Eds., *Models of Understanding Text.* Hillsdale, NJ: Erlbaum, pp. 313–339.

Gentner, D., and A. L. Stevens, Eds. (1983). *Mental Models.* Hillsdale, NJ: Erlbaum.

Halford, G. S. (1993). *Children's Understanding: The Development of Mental Models.* Hillsdale, NJ: Erlbaum.

Halpern, J. Y., and M. Y. Vardi. (1991). Model checking vs. theorem proving: A manifesto. In J. A. Allen, R. Fikes, and E. Sandewall, Eds., *Principles of Knowledge Representation and Reasoning: Proceedings of the Second International Conference.* San Mateo, CA: Kaufmann, pp. 325–334.

Johnson-Laird, P. N. (1983). *Mental Models: Towards a Cognitive Science of Language, Inference, and Consciousness.* Cambridge: Cambridge University Press; Cambridge, MA: Harvard University Press.

Johnson-Laird, P. N., and R. M. J. Byrne. (1991). *Deduction.* Hillsdale, NJ: Erlbaum.

Johnson-Laird, P. N., and Y. Goldvarg. (1997). How to make the impossible seem possible. In *Proceedings of the Nineteenth Annual Conference of the Cognitive Science Society,* Stanford, CA. Hillsdale, NJ: Erlbaum, pp. 354–357.

Johnson-Laird, P. N., and F. Savary. (1996). Illusory inferences about probabilities. *Acta Psychologica* 93: 69–90.

Kuipers, B. (1994). *Qualitative Reasoning: Modeling and Simulation with Incomplete Knowledge.* Cambridge, MA: MIT Press.

Marr, D. (1982). *Vision: A Computational Investigation into the Human Representation and Processing of Visual Information.* San Francisco: Freeman.

Further Readings

Byrne, R. M. J. (1996). A model theory of imaginary thinking. In J. Oakhill and A. Garnham, Eds., *Mental Models in Cognitive Science.* Hove, England: Taylor and Francis. pp. 155–174.

Garnham, A. (1987). *Mental Models as Representations of Discourse and Text.* Chichester: Ellis Horwood.

Glasgow, J. I. (1993). Representation of spatial models for geographic information systems. In N. Pissinou, Ed., *Proceedings of the ACM Workshop on Advances in Geographic Information Systems.* Arlington, VA: Association for Computing Machinery, pp. 112–117.

Glenberg, A. M., M. Meyer, and K. Lindem. (1987). Mental models contribute to foregrounding during text comprehension. *Journal of Memory and Language* 26: 69–83.

Hegarty, M. (1992). Mental animation: Inferring motion from static diagrams of mechanical systems. *Journal of Experimental Psychology: Learning, Memory, and Cognition* 18: 1084–1102.

Johnson-Laird, P. N. (1993). *Human and Machine Thinking.* Hillsdale, NJ: Erlbaum.

Legrenzi, P., V. Girotto, and P. N. Johnson-Laird. (1993). Focussing in reasoning and decision making. *Cognition* 49: 37–66.

Moray, N. (1990). A lattice theory approach to the structure of mental models. *Philosophical Transactions of the Royal Society of London* B 327: 577–583.

Polk, T. A., and A. Newell. (1995). Deduction as verbal reasoning. *Psychological Review* 102: 533–566.

Rogers, Y., A. Rutherford, and P. A. Bibby, Eds. (1992). *Models in the Mind: Theory, Perspective and Application.* London: Academic Press.

Schaeken, W., P. N. Johnson-Laird, and G. d'Ydewalle. (1996). Mental models and temporal reasoning. *Cognition* 60: 205–234.

Schwartz, D. (1996). Analog imagery in mental model reasoning: Depictive models. *Cognitive Psychology* 30: 154–219.

Stevenson, R. J. (1993). *Language, Thought and Representation.* New York: Wiley.

Mental Representation

To understand the nature of mental representation posited by cognitive scientists to account for various aspects of human and animal cognition (see Von Eckardt 1993 for a more detailed account), it is useful to first consider representation in general. Following Peirce (Hartshorne, Weiss, and Burks 1931–1958), we can say that any representation has four essential aspects: (1) it is realized by a representation bearer; (2) it has content or represents one or more objects; (3) its representation relations are somehow "grounded"; and (4) it can be interpreted by (will function as a representation for) some interpreter.

If we take one of the foundational assumptions of cognitive science to be that the mind/brain is a computational device (see COMPUTATIONAL THEORY OF MIND), the mental representation bearers will be computational structures or states. The specific nature of these structures or states depends on what kind of computer the mind/brain is hypothesized to be. To date, cognitive science research has focused on two kinds: conventional (von Neumann, symbolic, or rule-based) computers and connectionist (parallel distributed processing) computers (see COGNITIVE MODELING, SYMBOLIC and COGNITIVE MODELING, CONNECTIONIST). If the mind/brain is a conventional computer, then the mental representation bearers will be data structures. Kosslyn's (1980) work on mental IMAGERY provides a nice illustration. If the mind/brain is a connectionist computer, then the representation bearers of occurrent mental states will be activation states of connectionist nodes or sets of nodes. In the first case, representation is considered to be "local"; in the second, "distributed" (see DISTRIBUTED VS. LOCAL REPRESENTATION and McClelland, Rumelhart, and Hinton 1986). There may also be implicit representation (storage of information) in the connections themselves, a form of representation appropriate for dispositional mental states.

While individual claims about what our representations are about are frequently made in the cognitive science literature, we do not know enough to theorize about the semantics of our mental representation system in the sense that linguistics provides us with the formal SEMANTICS of natural language (see also POSSIBLE WORLDS SEMANTICS and DYNAMIC SEMANTICS). However, if we reflect on what our mental representations are hypothesized to explain—namely, certain features of our cognitive capacities—we can plausibly infer that the semantics of our mental representation system must have certain characteristics. Pretheoretically, human cognitive capacities have the following three properties: (1) each capacity is intentional, that is, it involves states that have content or are "about" something; (2) virtually all of the capacities can be pragmatically evaluated, that is, they can be exercised with varying degrees of success; and (3) most of the capacities are productive, that is, once a person has the capacity in question, he or she is typically in a position to manifest it in a practically unlimited number of novel ways. To account for these features, we must posit mental representations that can represent specific objects; that can represent many different kinds of objects—concrete objects, sets, properties, events, and states of affairs in this world, in possible worlds, and in fictional worlds as well as abstract objects such as universals and numbers; that can represent both an object (in and of itself) and an aspect of that object (or both extension and intension); and that can represent both correctly and incorrectly. In addition, if we take the productivity of our cognitive capacities seriously, we must posit representations with constituent structure and a compositional semantics. (Fodor and Pylyshyn 1988 use this fact to argue that our mental representation system cannot be connectionist; see CONNECTIONISM, PHILOSOPHICAL ISSUES.)

Cognitive scientists are interested not only in the content of mental representations, but also in where this content comes from, that is, in what makes a mental representation of a tree have the content of being about a tree. Theories of what determines content are often referred to as this-or-that kind of "semantics." Note, however, that it is important to distinguish such "theories of content determination" (Von Eckardt 1993) from the kind of semantics that systematically describes the content being determined (i.e., the kind referred to in the previous paragraph).

There are currently five principal accounts of how mental representational content is grounded. Two are discussed elsewhere (see FUNCTIONAL ROLE SEMANTICS and INFORMATIONAL SEMANTICS). The remaining three are characterized below.

1. *Structural isomorphism.* A representation is understood to be "some sort of model of the thing (or things) it represents" (Palmer 1978). The representation (or more precisely, the representation bearer) represents aspects of the represented object by means of aspects of itself. Palmer (1978) treats both the representation bearer and the represented object as relational systems, that is, as sets of constituent objects and sets of relations defined over these objects. A representation bearer then represents a represented object under some aspect if there exists a set G of relations constituting the representation bearer and a set D of relations constituting the object such that G is isomorphic to D.

2. *Causal historical.* (Devitt 1981; Sterelny 1990) Intended to apply only to the mental analogues of designational expressions, this account holds that a token designational "expression" in the LANGUAGE OF THOUGHT designates an object if there is a certain sort of causal chain connecting the representation bearer with the object. Such causal chains include perceiving the object, designating the object in natural language, and borrowing a designating expression from another person (see REFERENCE, THEORIES OF).

3. *Biological function.* In this account (Millikan 1984), mental representations, like animal communication signals, are "intentional icons," a form of representation that is "articulate" (has constituent structure and a compositional semantics) and mediates between producer mechanisms and interpreter mechanisms. The content of any given representation bearer will be determined by two things—the systematic natural associations that exist between the family of intentional icons to which the representation bearer belongs and some set of representational objects, and the biological functions of the interpreter device. More specifically, a representation bearer will represent an object if the existence of a mapping from the representation bearer family to the object family is a condition of the interpreter device successfully performing its biological functions. Take the association between bee dances and the location of nectar relative to the hive. The interpreter device for bee dances consists of the gatherer bees, among whose biological functions are those adapted to specific bee dances, for example, finding nectar 120 feet to the north of the hive in response to, say, bee dance 23. The interpreter function can successfully perform its function, however, only if bee dance 23 is in fact associated with the nectar's being at that location.

It can be argued that for a mental entity or state to be a representation, it must not only have content, it must also be significant for the subject who has it. According to Peirce, a representation having such significance can produce an "interpretant" state or process in the subject, and this state or process is related to both the representation and the subject in such a way that, by means of the interpretant, what the representation represents can make a difference to the internal states and behavior of the subject. This aspect of mental representation has received little explicit attention; indeed, its importance and even its existence have been disputed by some. Nevertheless, many cognitive scientists hold that the interpretant of a mental representation, for a given subject, consists of all the possible (token) computational consequences, including both the processes and the results of these processes, contingent on the subject's actively "entertaining" that representation.

Cognitive scientists engaged in the process of modeling or devising empirical theories of specific cognitive capacities (or specific features of those capacities) often posit particular kinds of mental representations. For pedagogical purposes, Thagard (1995) categorizes representations into six main kinds, each of which is typically associated with certain types of computational processes: sentences or well-formed formulas of a logical system (see LOGICAL REASONING SYSTEMS); rules (see PRODUCTION SYSTEMS and NEWELL); representations of concepts such as frames; SCHEMATA; scripts (see CATEGORIZATION), analogies (see ANALOGY), images; and connectionist representations. Another popular distinction is between symbolic representation (found in "conventional" computational devices) and subsymbolic representation (found in connectionist devices). There is unfortunately no conceptually tidy taxonomy of representational kinds. Sometimes such kinds are distinguished by their computational or formal characteristics—for example, local versus distributed representation in connectionist systems. Sometimes they are distinguished in terms of what they represent—for example, phonological, lexical, syntactic, and semantic representation in linguistics and psycholinguistics. And sometimes both form and content play a role. Paivio's (1986) dual-coding theory claims that there are two basic modes of representation—imagistic and propositional. According to Eysenck and Keane (1995), imagistic representations are modality-specific, nondiscrete, implicit, and involve loose combination rules, whereas propositional representations are amodal, discrete, explicit, and involve strong combination rules. The first contrast, modality-specific versus amodal, refers to the aspect under which the object is represented, hence to content; the other three contrasts all concern form.

Not all philosophers interested in cognitive science regard the positing of mental representations as being necessary or even unproblematic. Stich (1983) argues that if one compares a "syntactic theory of mind" (STM), which treats mental states as relations to purely syntactic mental sentence tokens and which frames generalizations in purely formal or computational terms, with representational approaches, STM will win. Representational approaches, in his view, necessarily encounter difficulties explaining the cognition of young children, "primitive" folk, and the mentally and neurally impaired. STM does not. Nor is it clear that cognitive science ought to aim at explaining the sorts of intentional phenomena (capacities or behavior) that mental representations are typically posited to explain.

Even more damning critiques of mental representation can be found in Judge (1985) and Horst (1996). Judge accepts the Peircean tripartite conception of representation according to which a representation involves a representation bearer R, an object represented O, and an interpretant I, but takes the interpretant to require an agent performing an intentional act such as understanding R to represent O, which causes problems for mental representation, in her view. Understanding R to represent O itself necessitates that the agent have nonmediated access to O. But, if we assume that all cognition is mediated by mental representation, this is impossible. (Another problem with this view of the interpretant, not discussed by Judge, is that it leads to an infinite regress of mental representations.)

Horst (1996) also believes that cognitive science's attempt to explain INTENTIONALITY by positing mental representations is fundamentally confused. Mental representations are usually taken to be symbols. But a symbol, in the standard semantic sense, involves conventions, both with respect to its meaning and with respect to its syntactic type. And because conventions themselves involve intentionality, intentionality cannot be explained by positing mental representations. An alternative is to treat "mental symbol" as a technical term. But Horst argues that, viewed in this technical way, the positing of mental representations also fails to be explanatory. Furthermore, even if such an alternative approach were to work, cognitive science would still be saddled with the conventionality of mental syntax.

See also CONCEPTS; KNOWLEDGE REPRESENTATION; MENTAL MODELS

—*Barbara Von Eckardt*

References

Devitt, M. (1981). *Designation.* New York: Columbia University Press.

Eysenck, M. W., and M. T. Keane. (1995). *Cognitive Psychology: A Student's Handbook.* Hillsdale, NJ: Erlbaum.

Fodor, J. A., and Z. W. Pylyshyn. (1988). Connectionism and cognitive architecture: A critical analysis. In S. Pinker and J. Mehler, Eds., *Connections and Symbols.* Cambridge, MA: MIT Press, pp. 3–71.

Hartshorne, C., P. Weiss, and A. Burks, Eds. (1931–1958). *Collected Papers of Charles Sanders Peirce.* Cambridge, MA: Harvard University Press.

Horst, S. W. (1996). *Symbols, Computation, and Intentionality: A Critique of the Computational Theory of Mind.* Berkeley: University of California Press.

Judge, B. (1985). *Thinking About Things: A Philosophical Study of Representation.* Edinburgh: Scottish Academic Press.

Kosslyn, S. M. (1980). *Image and Mind.* Cambridge, MA: Harvard University Press.

McClelland, J. L., D. E. Rumelhart, and G. E. Hinton, Eds. (1986). *Parallel Distributed Processing: Explorations in the Microstructures of Cognition.* 2 vols. Cambridge, MA: MIT Press.

Millikan, R. (1984). *Language, Thought, and Other Biological Categories.* Cambridge, MA: MIT Press.

Paivio, A. (1986). *Mental Representations: A Dual Coding Approach.* Oxford: Oxford University Press.

Palmer, S. E. (1978). Fundamental aspects of cognitive representation. In E. Rosch and B. Lloyd, Eds., *Cognition and Categorization.* Mahwah, NJ: Erlbaum.

Sterelny, K. (1990). *The Representational Theory of Mind: An Introduction.* Oxford: Blackwell.

Stich, S. P. (1983). *From Folk Psychology to Cognitive Science.* Cambridge, MA: MIT Press.

Thagard, P. (1995). *Mind: Introduction to Cognitive Science.* Cambridge, MA: MIT Press.

Von Eckardt, B. (1993). *What is Cognitive Science?* Cambridge, MA: MIT Press.

Further Readings

Anderson, J. R. (1983). *The Architecture of Cognition.* Cambridge, MA: Harvard University Press.

Anderson, J. R. (1993). *Rules of the Mind.* Hillsdale, NJ: Erlbaum.

Bechtel, W., and A. Abrahamson. (1991). *Connectionism and the Mind: An Introduction to Parallel Processing in Networks.* Oxford: Blackwell.

Block, N. (1986). Advertisement for a semantics for psychology. In P. A. French, T. E. Uehling, Jr., and H. K. Wettstein, Eds., *Studies in the Philosophy of Mind,* vol. 10. Minneapolis: University of Minnesota Press, pp. 615–678.

Cummins, R. (1989). *Meaning and Mental Representation.* Cambridge, MA: MIT Press.

Devitt, M., and K. Sterelny. (1987). *Language and Reality.* Cambridge, MA: MIT Press.

Dretske, F. (1981). *Knowledge and the Flow of Information.* Cambridge, MA: MIT Press.

Fodor, J. (1975). *The Language of Thought.* New York: Crowell.

Fodor, J. (1981). *Representations.* Cambridge, MA: MIT Press.

Fodor, J. (1987). *Psychosemantics.* Cambridge, MA: MIT Press.

Fodor, J. (1990). *A Theory of Content and Other Essays.* Cambridge, MA: MIT Press.

Genesereth, M. R., and N. J. Nilsson. (1987). *Logical Foundations of Artificial Intelligence.* Los Altos, Ca.: Kaufmann.

Hall, R. (1989). Computational approaches to analogical reasoning: A comparative analysis. *Artificial Intelligence* 39: 39–120.

Holyoak, K. J., and P. Thagard. (1995). *Mental Leaps: Analogy in Creative Thought.* Cambridge, MA: MIT Press.

Johnson-Laird, P. N. (1983). *Mental Models.* Cambridge, MA: Harvard University Press.

Kosslyn, S. M. (1994). *Image and Brain: The Resolution of the Imagery Debate.* Cambridge, MA: MIT Press.

Lloyd, D. (1987). Mental representation from the bottom up. *Synthèse* 70: 23–78.

Loar, B. (1981). *Mind and Meaning.* Cambridge: Cambridge University Press.

Millikan, R. (1989). Biosemantics. *Journal of Philosophy* 86: 281–297.

Minsky, M. (1975). A framework for representing knowledge. In P. H. Winston, Ed., *The Psychology of Computer Vision.* New York: McGraw-Hill, pp. 211–277.

Newell, A. (1990). *Unified Theories of Cognition.* Cambridge, MA: Harvard University Press.

Rumelhart, D. E. (1980). Schemata: The building blocks of cognition. In R Spiro, B. Bruce, and W. Brewer, Eds., *Theoretical Issues in Reading Comprehension.* Hillsdale, NJ: Erlbaum, pp. 33–58.

Schank, R. C., and R. P. Abelson. (1977). *Scripts, Plans, Goals, and Understanding: An Inquiry into Human Knowledge Structures.* Hillsdale, NJ: Erlbaum.

Searle, J. R. (1983). *Intentionality.* Cambridge: Cambridge University Press.

Smith, E. E., and D. L. Medin. (1981). *Categories and Concepts.* Cambridge, MA: Harvard University Press.

Mental Retardation

Definitions of mental retardation characteristically include three criteria: (1) significantly subaverage INTELLIGENCE accompanied by (2) significant limitations in adaptive skills with (3) an onset during the developmental period. Thus, according to the DSM-IV (American Psychiatric Association 1994), individuals are considered to have mental retardation if (1) they have a current IQ, based on an individually administered test, of approximately two or more standard deviations below the mean (e.g., ~70); (2) they have significant limitations (relative to those expected for chronological age and sociocultural background) in two or more of the following domains: communication, social/interpersonal skills, self-care, home living, self-direction, leisure, functional academic skills, use of community resources, work, health, and safety; and (3) these difficulties were first evidenced prior to age 18 years. Each of the other major organizations involved in the treatment of individuals with mental retardation—the American Association on Mental Retardation (AAMR), the American Psychological Association (APA), and the World Health Organization (WHO)—accepts the same three criteria, but implements them in slightly different ways (see Luckasson et al. 1992; American Psychological Association 1996; World Health Organization 1996). The DSM-IV, APA, and WHO ICD-10 definitions further divide mental retardation into four levels: mild (IQ between 50–55 and approximately 70); moderate (IQ between 35–40 and 50–55); severe (IQ between 20–25 and 35–40); and profound (IQ below 20). The AAMR definition also recognizes four levels of mental retardation, based on the intensity of support needed to enhance independence, productivity, and community integration: intermittent, limited, extensive, and pervasive.

Epidemiological research indicates a prevalence of mental retardation at between 0.8 and 1.2 percent. Per 1,000 individuals, approximately 3–6 have mild mental retardation, 2 have moderate mental retardation, 1.3 have severe mental retardation, and 0.4 have profound mental retardation. The cause of mental retardation is known for approximately 33–52 percent of individuals with IQs between 50 and 69: chromosomal: 4–8 percent; prenatal (multifactorial or environmental): 11–23 percent; perinatal or postnatal: 21 percent. For individuals with IQs below 50, the cause of mental retardation is known for 60–75 percent: chromosomal: 20–40 percent; prenatal: 20–30 percent; perinatal or postnatal: less than 20 percent (Pulsifer 1996). The most common known causes of mental retardation are fetal alcohol syndrome, Down's syndrome, and fragile X syndrome. Individuals with mental retardation often have additional disabilities (Batshaw and Shapiro 1997). Seizure disorders and cerebral palsy are present in about 10 percent of individuals with mild mental retardation and more than 20 percent of individuals with severe mental retardation. Individuals with mental retardation are three or four times more likely than the general population to have a psychiatric disorder (Kymissis and Leven 1994), with the likelihood of comorbid psychiatric disorder increasing as a function of severity of mental retardation (mild mental retardation: 25 percent, severe: 50 percent). Sensory impairments are also frequent (mild mental retardation: 24 percent, severe: 55 percent).

Historically, psychologists and educators have focused on level of mental retardation rather than cause (etiology), both for research purposes and for educational intervention (Goodman 1990; Hodapp 1997). Extensive characterizations are provided in the *Manual of Diagnosis and Professional Practice in Mental Retardation* (American Psychological Association 1996). Individuals with mild mental retardation are expected to attain a mental age of between 8 and 12 years. Many individuals acquire fluent language by adolescence; READING and arithmetic skills are usually between the first and sixth grade levels. Independence in both employment and daily living is typically attained. Individuals with moderate mental retardation are expected to attain a mental age of between 6 and 8 years, to acquire functional language abilities, but not functional reading or arithmetic skills, and to require supervision during adulthood. Individuals with severe mental retardation are expected to attain a mental age of between 4 and 6 years, although language abilities will be at a lower level. During adulthood, assistance is required for self-care skills. Individuals with profound mental retardation attain a mental age of between birth and 4 years. Many of these individuals are medically fragile, with a very high early mortality rate. During adulthood, some individuals will be able to walk and to produce single words. Pervasive supervision is required throughout the life span.

More recently, some researchers have begun to emphasize the importance of etiology. There are more than 500 known genetic causes of mental retardation (Flint and Wilkie 1996), in addition to a wide range of teratogenic causes (e.g., prenatal alcohol exposure). Each of these may be expected to affect brain structure and function. The particular areas and functions impacted will vary due to differences in which genes are affected and the roles the particular genes play in development, or which aspects of the brain were developing most rapidly at the time of exposure to a particular teratogen. It is likely that some aspects of cognition will be more severely impacted than others, and that areas of severe impact will vary from syndrome to syndrome. If so, the overall mental age attributed to a given individual (which is used to indicate level of mental retardation) may not accurately reflect his or her abilities in specific domains. For example, consider Williams syndrome, which is caused by a hemizygous microdeletion of chromosome 7q11.23, encompassing at least fifteen genes. Full-scale IQs range from less than 40 to about 90, with a mean of 55–60. Despite the fact that this mean IQ is in the range of mild mental retardation, individuals with Williams syndrome evidence a wide range of ability levels, as a function of domain. Their auditory rote memory ability is typically within the normal range (greater than second percentile), and about half have vocabulary or grammatical abilities, or both, within the normal range. In contrast, levels of visual-spatial constructive ability typically fall within the moderate to severe range of mental retardation (Mervis et al. forthcoming; see also Bellugi, Wang, and Jernigan 1994). In addition, unlike the typical characterization of individuals with mild mental retardation, most individuals with Williams syndrome evidence additional psychopathology: attention deficit hyperactivity disorder, anxiety disorder, or both (e.g., Dykens and Hodapp 1997). Perhaps because of these problems, individuals with Williams syndrome also differ from the typical characterization of individuals with mild mental retardation, by seldom being able to live independently.

As evidenced by the example of Williams syndrome, summary test scores often do not represent well the level of ability within individual domains. Thus it is crucial to take into account etiology when planning either basic research or intervention. At the same time, it is important to remember that there is within-syndrome variability, both in overall IQ and fit to the behavioral phenotype associated with the syndrome. Explication of both within- and between-syndrome variability depends on coordination of research efforts among researchers studying cognition, personality, brain structure and development, and genetics. Such interdisciplinary efforts should lead to a deeper understanding of basic processes and their relation to intelligence and adaptive functioning, whether the goal is to explain more fully a specific etiology or to elucidate processes relevant to mental retardation as a whole.

See also AUTISM: LANGUAGE AND THOUGHT; LANGUAGE IMPAIRMENT, DEVELOPMENTAL; LURIA

—*Carolyn B. Mervis and Byron F. Robinson*

References

American Psychiatric Association. (1994). *Diagnostic and Statistical Manual of Mental Disorders.* 4th ed. Washington, DC.

American Psychological Association. (1996). Definition of mental retardation. In J. W. Jacobson and J. D. Mulick, Eds., *Manual of Diagnosis and Professional Practice in Mental Retardation.* Washington, DC: American Psychological Association, Editorial Board of Division 33, pp. 13–38.

Batshaw, M. L., and B. K. Shapiro (1997). Mental retardation. In M. L. Batshaw, Ed., *Children with Disabilities.* 4th ed. Baltimore: Brookes.

Bellugi, U., P. P. Wang, and T. L. Jernigan. (1994). Williams syndrome: An unusual neuropsychological profile. In S. H. Broman and J. Grafman, Eds., *Atypical Cognitive Deficits in Developmental Disorders: Implications for Brain Function.* Hillsdale, NJ: Erlbaum, pp. 23–56.

Burack, J. A., R. M. Hodapp, and E. Zigler. (1988). Issues in the classification of mental retardation: Differentiating among organic etiologies. *Journal of Child Psychology and Psychiatry* 29: 765–779.

Dykens, E. M., and R. M. Hodapp. (1997). Treatment issues in genetic mental retardation syndromes. *Professional Psychology: Research and Practice* 28: 263–270.

Flint, J., and A. O. M. Wilkie. (1996). The genetics of mental retardation. *British Medical Bulletin* 52: 453-464.

Goodman, J. F. (1990). Technical note: Problems in etiological classifications of mental retardation. *Journal of Child Psychology and Psychiatry* 31: 465–469.

Hodapp, R. M. (1997). Direct and indirect behavioral effects of different genetic disorders of mental retardation. *American Journal on Mental Retardation* 102: 67–79.

Kymissis, P., and L. Leven. (1994). Adolescents with mental retardation and psychiatric disorders. In N. Bouras, Ed., *Mental Health in Mental Retardation: Recent Advances and Practices.* Cambridge: Cambridge University Press, pp. 102–107.

Luckasson, R., D. L. Coulter, E. A. Polloway, S. Reiss, R. L. Schalock, M. E. Snell, D. M. Spitalnik, and J. A. Stark. (1992). *Mental Retardation: Definition, Classification, and System of Supports.* 9th ed. Washington, DC: American Association on Mental Retardation.

Mervis, C. B., C. A. Morris, J. Bertrand, and B. F. Robinson. (Forthcoming). Williams syndrome: Findings from an integrated program of research. In H. Tager-Flusberg, Ed., *Neurodevelopmental Disorders.* Cambridge, MA: MIT Press.

Pulsifer, M. B. (1996). The neuropsychology of mental retardation. *Journal of the International Neuropsychological Society* 2: 159–176.

World Health Organization (1996). *Multiaxial Classification of Child and Adolescent Psychiatric Disorders: The ICD-10 Classification of Mental and Behavioral Disorders in Children and Adolescents.* Cambridge: Cambridge University Press.

Further Readings

Adams, J. (1996). Similarities in genetic mental retardation and neuroteratogenic syndromes. *Pharmacology Biochemistry and Behavior* 55: 683–690.

Batshaw, M. L., Ed. (1997). *Children with Disabilities.* 4th ed. Baltimore: Brookes.

Bouras, N., Ed. (1994). *Mental Health in Mental Retardation: Recent Advances and Practices.* Cambridge: Cambridge University Press.

Detterman, D. K. (1987). Theoretical notions of intelligence and mental retardation. *American Journal of Mental Deficiency* 92: 2–11.

Hodapp, R. M., and E. Zigler. (1995). Past, present, and future issues in the developmental approach to mental retardation and developmental disabilities. In D. Cicchetti and D. J. Cohen, Eds., *Developmental Psychopathology,* vol. 2, *Risk, Disorder, and Adaptation.* New York: Wiley.

O'Brien, G., and W. Yule. (1995). *Behavioral Phenotypes.* Clinics in Developmental Medicine 138. London: MacKeith Press.

Simonoff, E., P. Bolton, and M. Rutter. (1996). Mental retardation: Genetic findings, clinical implications, and research agenda. *Journal of Child Psychology and Psychiatry* 37: 259-280.

Tager-Flusberg, H., Ed. (Forthcoming). *Neurodevelopmental Disorders.* Cambridge, MA: MIT Press.

Mental Rotation

In Douglas Adams's (1988) novel *Dirk Gently's Holistic Detective Agency,* a sofa gets stuck on a stairway landing. Throughout the remainder of the novel, Dirk Gently ponders how to get it unstuck by imagining the sofa rotating into various positions (he eventually solves the problem using a time machine). The well-known psychologist Roger Shepard once had a somewhat similar experience, awakening one morning to "a spontaneous kinetic image of three-dimensional structures majestically turning in space" (Shepard and Cooper 1982, 7). That experience inspired Shepard and his student Jacqueline Metzler to run what has become a seminal experiment in cognitive science—one that both defines and operationalizes mental rotation.

Shepard and Metzler (1971) presented subjects with images of novel three-dimensional (3-D) objects at various orientations—on each trial a pair of images appeared side-by-side and subjects decided whether the two images depicted the same (figures 1a and 1b) or different objects (figure 1c) regardless of any difference in orientation. A given 3-D object had two "handedness" versions: its "standard" version and a mirror-reflected version (equivalent to the relationship between left- and right-handed gloves).

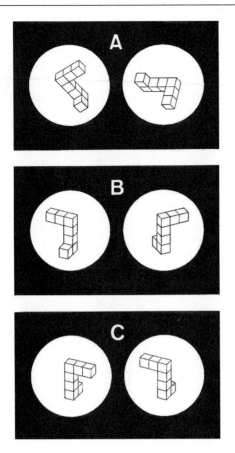

Figure 1. Illustrative pairs of perspective views, including a pair differing by an 80-degree rotation in the picture plane (a), a pair differing by an 80-degree rotation in depth (b), and a pair differing by a reflection as well as a rotation (c).

Different objects were always mirror reflections of one another, so objects could never be discriminated using distinctive local features. Shepard and Metzler measured the time it took subjects to make same/different discriminations as a function of the angular difference between them. What they found was a remarkably consistent pattern across both picture plane and depth rotations—mean response times increased linearly with increasing angular separation. This outcome provides evidence that subjects mentally rotate one or both objects until they are (mentally) aligned with one another. Shepard and Metzler suggest that the mental rotation process is an internal analogue of physical rotation, that is, a continuous shortest path 3-D rotation that would bring the objects into alignment.

A variation on Shepard and Metzler's experiment demonstrated that mental rotation is also used when subjects judge the handedness of familiar objects. Another student of Shepard's, Lynn Cooper, presented subjects with single English letters or digits (Cooper and Shepard 1973). On each trial a standard (e.g., "R") or a mirror-reflected version (e.g., "Я") of a letter or digit was shown at some misorientation in the picture plane. Because subjects had to judge whether the misoriented character was of standard or mirror handedness they could not use local distinguishing features

to make the discrimination. Moreover, because handedness is only defined relative to the viewer, subjects presumably needed to align each test character with their egocentric reference frame in which left and right are defined. The results, quite similar to those obtained with 3-D objects, confirmed this assumption—mean response times for judging handedness increased monotonically as the test characters were misoriented farther and farther from their canonical upright orientations. Response times turned out to be symmetric around 180 degrees—the point at which the characters were exactly upside down. Thus subjects were apparently mentally rotating the characters in the shortest direction to the upright regardless of whether this rotation was clockwise or counterclockwise.

Why are these findings so important? Much of the theorizing about COGNITIVE ARCHITECTURE during the 1960s assumed a symbolic substrate (e.g., PRODUCTION SYSTEMS) in which all mental representations were thought to have a common amodal format. Shepard's results demonstrated that at least some cognitive processes were modal, and, in particular, tied to visual perception. The hypothesis that mental rotation is a continuous process akin to a real-world rotation also has implications for the nature of IMAGERY, namely, that humans have the capacity to make judgments using inherently spatial representations and that such representations are sophisticated enough to support PROBLEM SOLVING, spatial reasoning, and SHAPE PERCEPTION. Not surprisingly, this claim evoked a great deal of skepticism.

In response, Shepard and Cooper went on to meticulously demonstrate that mental rotation indeed involved a continuous mental transformation. Three critical results provide converging evidence for this conclusion. First, Cooper and Shepard (1973) ran a variant of their familiar characters experiment in which they preceded each letter or digit with a cue to the test character's orientation, identity, or both. They found that neither orientation nor identity alone was sufficient to diminish the effect of stimulus orientation on response times. In contrast, providing both, along with sufficient time for the subject to prepare, removed almost all effects of orientation. Thus it appears that mental rotation operates on a representation that depicts a particular shape at a particular position in space—properties associated with an image.

Second, Cooper and Shepard (1973; see also Cooper 1976) ran an experiment in which they controlled an individual subject's putative rate of rotation across a series of trials. Given this information, for a misoriented test letter or digit, they could predict the instantaneous orientation of the rotating mental image of that character. On each trial, a test character was presented, followed at some point by a probe character. The task was to begin rotating the test character, but then to judge the handedness of the probe. Under these conditions, response times were essentially unrelated to the absolute orientation of the probe, but increased monotonically with increasing angular distance from the presumed orientation of the rotating mental image of the test character. For example, when the predicted orientation of the test character image and the visible probe corresponded, response times were independent of the actual orientation of the probe. Thus the changing image actually passes through all of the intermediate orientations—a property expected for a truly analog transformation mechanism.

Third, Cooper and Shepard ran an experiment in which subjects were given extensive practice judging the handedness of characters mentally rotated in only one direction, for example, 0 degrees to 180 degrees counterclockwise. When these subjects were tested with characters misoriented slightly past 180 degrees, say 190 degrees, the distribution of response times had two peaks—one corresponding to mentally rotating the short way around (clockwise) and one corresponding to mentally rotating the long way around (counterclockwise and consistent with the practice subjects had received). Thus it was the actual angular distance traversed by a rotation that determined the time consumed—again consistent with an analog mechanism.

In summary, there is compelling evidence for the use of a continuous mental rotation process that brings images of two objects into correspondence or the image of a single object into alignment with an internal representation. The existence of such a mechanism suggests that models of cognitive architecture should include modality-specific mechanisms that can support mental imagery. Mental rotation may also play a role in HIGH-LEVEL VISION, for example, in shape perception (Rock and Di Vita 1987), FACE RECOGNITION (Hill, Schyns, and Akamatsu 1997; Troje and Bülthoff 1996), and OBJECT RECOGNITION (Jolicoeur 1985; Tarr 1995; Tarr and Pinker 1989).

See also MENTAL MODELS; MENTAL REPRESENTATION; MODULARITY OF MIND

—*Michael Tarr*

References

Adams, D. (1988). *Dirk Gently's Holistic Detective Agency.* New York: Pocket Books.

Cooper, L. A. (1976). Demonstration of a mental analog of an external rotation. *Perception and Psychophysics* 19: 296–302.

Cooper, L. A., and R. N. Shepard. (1973). Chronometric studies of the rotation of mental images. In W. G. Chase, Ed., *Visual Information Processing.* New York: Academic Press, pp. 75–176.

Hill, H., P. G. Schyns, and S. Akamatsu. (1997). Information and viewpoint dependence in face recognition. *Cognition* 62: 201–222.

Jolicoeur, P. (1985). The time to name disoriented natural objects. *Memory and Cognition* 13: 289–303.

Rock, I., and J. Di Vita. (1987). A case of viewer-centered object perception. *Cognitive Psychology* 19: 280–293.

Shepard, R. N., and L. A. Cooper. (1982). *Mental Images and Their Transformations.* Cambridge, MA: MIT Press.

Shepard, R. N., and J. Metzler. (1971). Mental rotation of three-dimensional objects. *Science* 171: 701–703.

Tarr, M. J. (1995). Rotating objects to recognize them: A case study of the role of viewpoint dependency in the recognition of three-dimensional objects. *Psychonomic Bulletin and Review* 2: 55–82.

Tarr, M. J., and S. Pinker. (1989). Mental rotation and orientation-dependence in shape recognition. *Cognitive Psychology* 21, 233–282.

Troje, N., and H. H. Bülthoff. (1996). Face recognition under varying pose: The role of texture and shape. *Vision Research* 36: 1761–1771.

Further Readings

Carpenter, P. A., and M. A. Just. (1978). Eye fixations during mental rotation. In J. W. Senders, D. F. Fisher, and R. A. Monty, Eds., *Eye Movements and the Higher Psychological Functions.* Hillsdale, NJ: Erlbaum, pp. 115–133.

Cohen, M. S., S. M. Kosslyn, H. C. Breiter, G. J. Digirolamo, W. L. Thompson, A. K. Anderson, S. Y. Bookheimer, B. R. Rosen, and J. W. Belliveau. (1996). Changes in cortical activity during mental rotation: A mapping study using functional MRI. *Brain* 119: 89–100.

Cohen, D., and M. Kubovy. (1993). Mental rotation, mental representation and flat slopes. *Cognitive Psychology* 25: 351–382.

Cooper, L. A., and R. N. Shepard. (1984). Turning something over in the mind. *Scientific American* 251(6): 106–114.

Georgopoulos, A. P., J. T. Lurito, M. Petrides, A. B. Schwartz, and J. T. Massey. (1989). Mental rotation of the neuronal population vector. *Science* 243: 234–236.

Jolicoeur, P., S. Regehr, L. B. J. P. Smith, and G. N. Smith. (1985). Mental rotation of representations of two-dimensional and three-dimensional objects. *Canadian Journal of Psychology* 39: 100–129.

Pinker, S. (1984). Visual cognition: An introduction. *Cognition* 18: 1–63.

Rock, I. (1973). *Orientation and Form.* New York: Academic Press.

Rock, I., D. Wheeler, and L. Tudor. (1989). Can we imagine how objects look from other viewpoints? *Cognitive Psychology* 21: 185–210.

Tarr, M. J., and S. Pinker. (1990). When does human object recognition use a viewer-centered reference frame? *Psychological Science* 1: 253–256.

Metacognition

Broadly defined, *metacognition* is any knowledge or cognitive process that refers to, monitors, or controls any aspect of cognition. Although its historical roots are deep (e.g., James 1890), the study of metacognition first achieved widespread prominence in the 1970s through the work of Flavell (1979) and others on developmental changes in children's cognition about MEMORY ("metamemory"), understanding ("metacomprehension"), and communication ("metacommunication"). Metacognition is now seen as a central contributor to many aspects of cognition, including memory, ATTENTION, communication, PROBLEM SOLVING, and INTELLIGENCE, with important applications to areas like EDUCATION, aging, neuropsychology, and eyewitness testimony (Flavell, Miller, and Miller 1993; Metcalfe and Shimamura 1994). In this sense at least, metacognition is a domain-general facet of cognition.

Although theorists differ in how to characterize some aspects of metacognition (see Schneider and Pressley 1989), most make a rough distinction between metacognitive knowledge and metacognitive regulation. *Metacognitive knowledge* refers to information that individuals possess about their own cognition or cognition in general. Flavell (1979) further divides metacognitive knowledge into knowledge about persons (e.g., knowing that one has a very good memory), tasks (e.g., knowing that categorizable items are typically easier to recall than noncategorizable items), strategies (e.g., knowledge of mnemonic strategies such as rehearsal or organization), and their interactions (e.g., knowing that organization is usually superior to rehearsal if the task involves categorizable items). Although even preschool children have some metacognitive knowledge, marked developmental progress occurs in all these areas and, indeed, continues to be made in adolescence and beyond (e.g., Brown et al. 1983; Schneider and Pressley 1989).

Metacognitive regulation includes a variety of executive functions such as planning, resource allocation, monitoring, checking, and error detection and correction (Brown et al. 1983). Nelson and Narens (1990) divide metacognitive regulation into monitoring and control processes, defined in terms of whether information is flowing to or from the "meta-level." In monitoring (e.g., tracking one's comprehension of material while READING), the meta-level receives information from ongoing, "object-level" cognition, whereas in control (e.g., allocating effort and attention to important rather than trivial material), the meta-level modifies cognition. Again, important developmental advances occur in both these metacognitive processes (e.g., Garner 1987).

Although monitoring may occur without explicit awareness, it often produces, and is in turn affected by, conscious metacognitive experiences (Flavell 1979): for example, the feeling of knowing something but being unable to recall it. Even two-year-olds may have some metacognitive experiences, although older children and adults appear to be much better at interpreting and taking advantage of them (Flavell 1987). An important question concerns whether metacognitive experiences such as feelings of knowing are actually veridical indicators of underlying cognition. This issue has received close attention in recent years in the field of adult cognition (e.g., Metcalfe and Shimamura 1994; Nelson 1992). The findings suggest that the presence or absence of feelings of knowing does predict later recognition memory (see Hart 1965 for the seminal finding). However, although the accuracy of such feelings is typically above chance, it is far from perfect and appears to be somewhat task-dependent. Moreover, the mechanisms underlying feelings of knowing are not yet fully clear: Individuals may have partial access to the unrecalled item, or alternatively, they may simply infer the likelihood of knowing from other related information that is accessible (Nelson 1992).

Metacognitive knowledge and regulation are often closely intertwined. For example, knowing that a task is difficult can lead an individual to monitor cognitive progress very carefully. Conversely, successful cognitive monitoring can lead to knowledge of which tasks are easy and which difficult.

Precisely how metacognitive abilities are acquired is not known, but the process is almost certainly multifaceted. Likely contributors include general advances in self-regulation and reflective thinking, the demands of formal schooling, and the modeling of metacognitive activity by parents, teachers, and peers (see Flavell 1987). A critical precursor to the development of metacognition is the acquisition of initial knowledge about the existence of the mind and mental states (i.e., the development of a THEORY OF MIND). Well established by the end of the preschool years, such knowledge continues to develop in tandem with metacognition throughout middle childhood and adolescence (Moses and Chandler 1992). Somewhat curiously, theory of mind and metacognition are often thought of as separate research domains. Certainly, the two areas of inquiry tend to have different foci: Prototypical theory of mind studies assess younger children's appreciation of the role of mental states in the prediction and explanation of other people's behavior, whereas classical metacognitive studies examine older children's knowledge of mental processes in the self, often in an academic context. Still, no absolute distinction between the two areas should be drawn: Both are centrally concerned with the study of cognition about cognition.

Metacognitive impairments are not limited to very young children. Poor metacognitive skills can also be found in learning disabled and mentally retarded individuals. Conversely, gifted individuals often have excellent metacognitive abilities (Jarman, Vavrik, and Walton 1995) which may be especially evident in domains where they have special expertise (Alexander, Carr, and Schwanenflugel 1995). Some aspects of metacognition may also be deficient in the aged, although whether the impairments are a function of aging or some other factor (e.g., lack of college experience) is not always clear (Nelson 1992). Finally, individuals with frontal lobe damage frequently show metacognitive deficits, whereas those with damage to other parts of the cortex typically do not (Shimamura 1996). For example, frontal lobe patients are often unaware of their cognitive deficits, they lack knowledge of and are impaired in their use of metacognitive strategies, and the accuracy of their feelings of knowing is poor. That the locus of metacognition in the brain might be the frontal lobes should come as no surprise, given the extensive overlap between metacognitive regulation and executive functioning, an aspect of cognition long associated with the prefrontal cortex.

Much of the interest in metacognition derives from the belief that metacognitive skills significantly influence cognitive performance. Of course, many factors are likely to affect behavior in a specific cognitive situation (Flavell, Miller, and Miller 1993), including implicit processes of which the individual is unaware (Reder 1996). Nevertheless, in the case of memory (where the issue has been examined most thoroughly), a moderately high correlation is often found between metamemory and task performance (Schneider and Pressley 1989). The association tends to be stronger for older children, for more difficult tasks, and for certain types of metamemory (e.g., memory monitoring). Not surprisingly, the correlation between metamemory (e.g., strategy knowledge) and strategy use is typically higher than that between metamemory and performance, confirming that the links between metacognition and task success are indeed complex.

Given that metacognitive abilities actually do enhance cognitive performance, their acquisition should have far-reaching educational implications. In this respect, it is encouraging that metacognitive strategies can sometimes be successfully taught (e.g., Brown and Campione 1990). The teaching is most effective if individuals are explicitly taught how a strategy works and the conditions under which to use it, and if they attribute performance gains to the strategy (e.g., Schneider and Pressley 1989). Importantly, it is under these teaching conditions that individuals are most likely to maintain and generalize their newly acquired metacognitive skills.

See also COGNITIVE DEVELOPMENT; FOLK PSYCHOLOGY; INTROSPECTION; LITERACY; METAREASONING; METAREPRESENTATION

—*Louis J. Moses and Jodie A. Baird*

References

Alexander, J. M., M. Carr, and P. J. Schwanenflugel. (1995). Development of metacognition in gifted children: Directions for future research. *Developmental Review* 15: 1–37.

Brown, A. L., J. D. Bransford, R. A. Ferrara, and J. C. Campione. (1983). Learning, remembering, and understanding. In J. H. Flavell and E. M. Markman, Eds., *Handbook of Child Psychology*. Vol. 3, *Cognitive Development*. 4th ed. New York: Wiley, pp. 77–166.

Brown, A. L., and J. C. Campione. (1990). Communities of learning and thinking, or a context by any other name. In D. Kuhn, Ed., *Developmental Perspectives on Teaching and Learning Thinking Skills*. Basel: Karger, pp. 108–126.

Flavell, J. H. (1979). Metacognition and cognitive monitoring: A new area of cognitive-developmental inquiry. *American Psychologist* 34: 906–911.

Flavell, J. H. (1987). Speculations about the nature and development of metacognition. In F. E. Weinert and R. H. Kluwe, Eds., *Metacognition, Motivation, and Understanding*. Hillsdale, NJ: Erlbaum, pp. 21–29.

Flavell, J. H., P. H. Miller, and S. A. Miller. (1993). *Cognitive Development*. 3rd ed. Englewood Cliffs, NJ: Prentice Hall.

Garner, R. (1987). *Metacognition and Reading Comprehension*. Norwood, NJ: Ablex.

Hart, J. T. (1965). Memory and the feeling-of-knowing experience. *Journal of Educational Psychology* 56: 208–216.

James, W. (1890). *Principles of Psychology,* vol. 1. New York: Holt.

Jarman, R. F., J. Vavrik, and P. D. Walton. (1995). Metacognitive and frontal lobe processes: At the interface of cognitive psychology and neuropsychology. *Genetic, Social, and General Psychology Monographs* 121: 153–210.

Metcalfe, J., and A. P. Shimamura, Eds. (1994). *Metacognition: Knowing about Knowing*. Cambridge, MA: MIT Press.

Moses, L. J., and M. J. Chandler. (1992). Traveler's guide to children's theories of mind. *Psychological Inquiry* 3: 286–301.

Nelson, T. O., Ed. (1992). *Metacognition: Core Readings*. Boston: Allyn and Bacon.

Nelson, T. O., and L. Narens. (1990). Metamemory: A theoretical framework and new findings. In G. Bower, Ed., *The Psychology of Learning and Motivation*, vol. 26. New York: Academic Press, pp. 125–141.

Reder, L. M., Ed. (1996). *Implicit Memory and Metacognition*. Mahwah, NJ: Erlbaum.

Schneider, W., and M. Pressley. (1989). *Memory Development between 2 and 20*. New York: Springer.

Shimamura, A. P., (1996). The role of the prefrontal cortex in controlling and monitoring memory processes. In L. M. Reder, Ed., *Implicit Memory and Metacognition*. Mahwah, NJ: Erlbaum, pp. 259–274.

Further Readings

Borkowski, J. G., M. Carr, E. Rellinger, and M. Pressley. (1990). Self-regulated cognition: Interdependence of metacognition, attributions, and self-esteem. In B. F. Jones and L. Idol, Eds., *Dimensions of Thinking and Cognitive Instruction*. Hillsdale, NJ: Erlbaum, pp. 53–92.

Brown, A. L., and A. S. Palincsar. (1989). Guided cooperative learning and individual knowledge acquisition. In L. B. Resnick, Ed., *Knowing, Learning, and Instruction: Essays in Honor of Robert Glaser*. Hillsdale, NJ: Erlbaum, pp. 393–451.

Duell, O. K. (1986). Metacognitive skills. In G. D. Phye and T. Andre, Eds., *Cognitive Classroom Learning: Understanding, Thinking, and Problem Solving*. Orlando, FL: Academic Press, pp. 205–242.

Flavell, J. H., and H. M. Wellman. (1977). Metamemory. In R. V. Kail, Jr., and J. W. Hagen, Eds., *Perspectives on the Development of Memory and Cognition*. Hillsdale, NJ: Erlbaum, pp. 3–33.

Forrest-Pressley, D. L., G. E. MacKinnon, and T. G. Waller, Eds. (1985). *Metacognition, Cognition, and Human Performance*, 2 vols. Orlando, FL: Academic Press.

Garner, R., and P. A. Alexander. (1989). Metacognition: Answered and unanswered questions. *Educational Psychology* 24: 143–158.

Kluwe, R. H. (1982). Cognitive knowledge and executive control: Metacognition. In D. R. Griffin, Ed., *Animal Mind-Human Mind*. New York: Springer, pp. 201–224.

Markman, E. M. (1981). Comprehension monitoring. In W. P. Dickson, Ed., *Children's Oral Communication Skills*. New York: Academic Press, pp. 61–84.

McGlynn, S. M., and D. L. Schacter. (1989). Unawareness of deficits in neuropsychological syndromes. *Journal of Clinical and Experimental Neuropsychology* 11: 143–205.

Paris, S. G., and P. Winograd. (1990). How metacognition can promote academic learning and instruction. In B. F. Jones and L. Idol, Eds., *Dimensions of Thinking and Cognitive Instruction*. Hillsdale, NJ: Erlbaum, pp. 15–51.

Pressley, M., J. J. Borkowski, and W. Schneider. (1987). Cognitive strategies: Good strategy users coordinate metacognition and knowledge. In R. Vasta and G. Whitehurst, Eds., *Annals of Child Development*, vol. 5. Greenwich, CT: JAI Press, pp. 89–129.

Schneider, W., and F. E. Weinert, Eds. (1990). *Interactions among Aptitudes, Strategies, and Knowledge in Cognitive Performance*. New York: Springer-Verlag.

Schraw, G., and D. Moshman. (1995). Metacognitive theories. *Educational Psychology Review* 7: 351–371.

Schwanenflugel, P. J., W. V. Fabricius, and C. R. Noyes. (1996). Developing organization of mental verbs: Evidence for the development of a constructivist theory of mind in middle childhood. *Cognitive Development* 11: 265–294.

Weinert, F. E., and R. H. Kluwe, Eds. (1987). *Metacognition, Motivation, and Understanding*. Hillsdale, NJ: Erlbaum.

Wellman, H. M. (1983). Metamemory revisited. In M. T. H. Chi, Ed., *Trends in Memory Development Research*. Basel: Karger, pp. 31–51.

Yussen, S. R., Ed. (1985). *The Growth of Reflection in Children*. Orlando, FL: Academic Press.

Metaphor

Metaphor, from the Greek for "transference," is the use of language that designates one thing to designate another in order to characterize the latter in terms of the former. *Nominal metaphors* use nouns in this way, as in "My daughter is an *angel.*" *Predicative metaphors* use verbs, as in "The dog *flew* across the back yard." In addition to single words being used metaphorically, phrases, sentences, and more extended texts can also function as metaphors, as in the assertion "Bravely the troops carried on" to refer to telephone operators who continued to work during a natural disaster. Sometimes a metaphor can be recognized because it is literally false. When a proud father says, "My daughter is an angel," no one believes that she has wings. But a metaphor need not be literally false. The opposite assertion—that one's daughter is no angel—is literally true; she does not have wings. Yet this is not likely to be the speaker's intended meaning, nor is it likely to be a hearer's interpretation. In each of these two cases, hearers must go beyond the literal meaning to arrive at the speaker's intention—what the hearer is intended to understand (see PSYCHOLINGUISTICS and PRAGMATICS).

Does the need to go beyond literal meanings imply that literal meanings have unconditional priority? The standard pragmatic theory of metaphor assumes that literal meanings are always computed first, and only when a literal meaning makes no sense in context are alternative, metaphorical meanings derived (Searle 1979). If this is so, then metaphorical meaning should be ignored whenever a literal meaning makes sense. However, people cannot ignore metaphors. Whenever metaphorical meanings are available, they are automatically processed, even when there is no apparent need to do so (Glucksberg, Gildea, and Bookin 1982). Furthermore, metaphors are no more difficult to understand than comparable literal expressions (Ortony et al. 1978), suggesting that literal meanings do not have priority.

Metaphors have traditionally been viewed as implicit comparisons. According to this view, metaphors of the form *X is a Y* are understood by converting them into simile form, X is *like* a Y. The simile is then understood by comparing the properties of X and Y. This view has been challenged on both theoretical and empirical grounds. One finding is particularly telling. Metaphors in class inclusion form, such as "My lawyer is a shark" take less time to understand than when in simile form, such as "My lawyer is *like* a shark" (Johnson 1996).

That metaphors can be understood more easily than similes argues that metaphors are exactly what they seem to be, namely, class inclusion assertions (Glucksberg and Keysar 1990). In such assertions, the metaphor vehicle (e.g., *shark*) is used to refer to the category of predatory creatures in general, not to the marine creature that is also named "shark." This dual reference function of metaphor vehicles is clear in metaphors such as "Cambodia was Vietnam's Vietnam." Here, the first mention of *Vietnam* refers to the nation of Vietnam. In contrast, the second mention of *Vietnam* does not refer to that nation, but instead to the American involvement in Vietnam, which has come to epitomize the category of disastrous military interventions. That intervention has become a metaphor for such disasters, and so the word *Vietnam* can be used as a metaphor vehicle to characterize other ill-fated military actions, such as Vietnam's invasion of Cambodia. More generally, metaphor vehicles such as *Vietnam* can be used as names for categories that have no names of their own (Brown 1958). With continued use, once-novel metaphors become frozen, their original metaphorical meanings become literal, and their senses become dictionary entries. The word "butcher" is a case in point: It can be taken to mean a meat purveyor, a bungler, or a vicious murderer, depending on the context.

Thus, while metaphors can suggest a comparison, they are primarily attributive assertions, not merely comparisons. To say that someone's job is a jail is to attribute (i.e., *transfer,* in the original Greek sense) salient properties of the category *jail* to a particular job (Ortony 1979). That particular job is now included in the general, abstract category of *jail*, and as a consequence of that categorization is now similar in relevant respects to literal jails (Glucksberg, McGlone, and Manfredi 1997). Predicative metaphors, in which verbs are used figuratively, function similarly. The verb *to fly* literally entails movement in air. Because flying through the air epitomizes speed, expressions such as "He hopped on his bike and flew home" are readily understood, just as nominal metaphors, such as "His bike was an arrow," are readily understood. Arrows are prototypical members of the category of speeding things; flying is a prototypical member of the category of fast travel. For both nominal and predicative metaphors, prototypical members of categories can be used as metaphors to attribute properties to topics of interest.

Why are metaphors used instead of comparable literal expressions? Often there are no comparable literal expressions (Black 1962), particularly when metaphor is used systematically to describe one domain in terms of another. Perceptual metaphors enable us to describe experiences in one sense modality in terms of another, as in *bright sound*. Theories can be described in terms of structures, with correspondences between the blueprints and foundations of a structure on the one hand, and those of a theory on the other. Once a target domain (e.g., theories) has been described in terms of a source domain (e.g., buildings), then new correspondences can be introduced, as in "The theory's superstructure is collapsing of its own weight." Whether such systematic correspondences constitute conceptual knowledge per se or are primarily a means of describing and transmitting such knowledge remains an unresolved issue (see COGNITIVE LINGUISTICS and METAPHOR AND CULTURE; Lakoff and Johnson 1980; McGlone 1996; Murphy 1996; Quinn 1991).

Domains for which metaphors seem particularly apt include science, emotions, personality characteristics, and politics (Cacciari forthcoming). Indeed, any domain can be effectively framed by choice of metaphor. Immigration, for example, can be viewed either as an invigorating process ("New blood has been pumped into the city's economy") or as a threat ("The tide of refugees will soon drown us"). Similarly, different interpretations of feelings and interpersonal relations can be effectively revealed and communicated via metaphor in clinical settings (Rothenberg 1984).

Given the importance and ubiquity of metaphor, it is not surprising that the beginnings of metaphorical thought and language appear early in children's cognitive and linguistic development. Infants as young as two months can detect intermodal correspondences (Starkey, Spelke, and Gelman 1983). Such correspondences represent a rudimentary form of metaphorical conceptualization (Marks 1982). Children as young as two years use and understand more abstract metaphorical correspondences, such as between the shoulders of a person and those of a mountain, although sophisticated use of metaphors comes only with complex knowledge of relations among CONCEPTS and facility in analogical reasoning (Gentner and Markman 1977). As children learn to distinguish between figurative and literal language, they use the same "psychological mechanisms" to understand the one as they do the other (Miller 1979; 248). Literal and nonliteral understanding develop hand in hand.

See also ANALOGY; DISCOURSE; FIGURATIVE LANGUAGE; MEANING

—Sam Glucksberg

References

Black, M. (1962). *Models and Metaphors.* New York: Cornell University Press.

Black, M. (1979). More about metaphor. In A. Ortony, Ed., *Metaphor and Thought.* Cambridge: Cambridge University Press, pp. 19–43.

Brown, R. (1958). *Words and Things.* New York: Free Press.

Cacciari, C. (Forthcoming). Why do we speak metaphorically? Reflections on the functions of metaphor in discourse and reasoning. In A. Katz, Ed., *Figurative Language and Thought.* New York: Oxford University Press.

Gentner, D., and A. B. Markman. (1977). Structure-mapping in analogy and similarity. *American Psychologist* 52: 45–56.

Glucksberg, S., P. Gildea, and H. A. Bookin. (1982). On understanding nonliteral speech: Can people ignore metaphors? *Journal of Verbal Learning and Verbal Behavior* 21: 85–98.

Glucksberg, S., and B. Keysar. (1990). Understanding metaphoric comparisons: Beyond similarity. *Psychological Review* 97: 3–18.

Glucksberg, S., M. S. McGlone, and D. A. Manfredi. (1997). Property attribution in metaphor comprehension. *Journal of Memory and Language* 36: 50–67.

Johnson, A. T. (1996). Comprehension of metaphor and similes: A reaction time study. *Journal of Psycholinguistic Research* 11: 145–160.

Lakoff, G., and M. Johnson. (1980). *Metaphors We Live By.* Chicago: University of Chicago Press.

Marks, L. E. (1982). Bright sneezes and dark coughs, loud sunlight and soft moonlight. *Journal of Experimental Psychology: Human Perception and Performance* 8: 77–193.

McGlone, M. S. (1966). Conceptual metaphors and figurative language interpretation: Food for thought? *Journal of Memory and Language* 35: 544–565.

Miller, G. A. (1979). Images and models: Similes and metaphors. In A. Ortony, Ed., *Metaphor and Thought.* Cambridge: Cambridge University Press, pp. 202–250.

Murphy, G. L. (1996). On metaphoric representation. *Cognition* 60: 173–204.

Ortony, A. (1979). Beyond literal similarity. *Psychological Review* 86: 161–180.

Ortony, A., D. Schallert, R. Reynolds, and S. Antos. (1978). Interpreting metaphors and idioms: Some effects of context on comprehension. *Journal of Verbal Learning and Verbal Behavior* 17: 465–478.

Quinn, N. (1991). The cultural basis of metaphor. In J. W. Fernandez, Ed., *Beyond Metaphor: The Theory of Tropes in Anthropology.* Stanford, CA: Stanford University Press, pp. 56–93.

Rothenberg, A. (1984). Creativity and psychotherapy. *Psychoanalysis and Contemporary Thought* 7: 233–268.

Searle, J. (1979). Metaphor. In A. Ortony, Ed., *Metaphor and Thought.* Cambridge: Cambridge University Press, pp. 92–123.

Starkey, P., E. Spelke, and R. Gelman. (1988). Detection of intermodal correspondences by human infants. *Science* 222: 179–181.

Vosniadou, S., and A. Ortony. (1983). The emergence of the literal-metaphorical-anomalous distinction in young children. *Child Development* 54: 154–161.

Further Readings

Black, M. (1962). *Models and Metaphors.* Ithaca, NY: Cornell University Press.

Cacciari, C., and S. Glucksberg. (1994). Understanding figurative language. In M. A. Gernsbacher, Ed., *Handbook of Psycholinguistics.* New York: Academic Press, pp. 447–477.

Fernandez, J. W., Ed. (1991). *Beyond Metaphor: The Theory of Tropes in Anthropology.* Stanford, CA: Stanford University Press.

Gentner, D. (1983). Structure-mapping: A theoretical framework for analogy. *Cognitive Science* 7: 155–170.

Gibbs, R. W., Jr. (1994). *The Poetics of Mind: Figurative Thought, Language and Understanding.* Cambridge: Cambridge University Press.

Keysar, B. (1989). On the functional equivalence of literal and metaphorical interpretations in discourse. *Journal of Memory and Language* 28: 375–385.

Kittay, E. (1987). *Metaphor: Its Cognitive Force and Linguistic Structure.* Oxford: Clarendon Press.

Ortony, A. (1979). Beyond literal similarity. *Psychological Review* 86: 151–180

Ortony, A. (1993). *Metaphor and Thought.* 2nd ed. Cambridge: Cambridge University Press.

Way, E. C. (1991). *Knowledge Representation and Metaphor.* Dordrecht: Kluwer.

Winner, E. (1988). *The Point of Words: Children's Understanding of Metaphor and Irony.* Cambridge, MA: Harvard University Press.

Metaphor and Culture

How culture might figure in the conceptual domain-to-domain mappings that characterize METAPHOR has gone largely unaddressed. On the one hand, this is because anthropologists who study metaphor, and who belong to the interpretivist school and its offshoots, take the position that culture resides in metaphors, as it does in other symbols—and not in the use and sense people make of these. These scholars draw on literary criticism, semiotics, structuralism, and the like to interpret metaphors and other tropes (Linger 1994).

On the other hand, the role of culture in the production and comprehension of metaphor tends to be crowded out of systematic consideration by linguists, many of whom, perhaps understandably, have treated the metaphors occurring in language as direct reflections of deeper conceptual structures. On grounds of the ubiquity and automaticity of metaphor in speech, Lakoff and his colleagues (e.g., Lakoff and Johnson 1980) have made broad claims for the indispensable role of what they call "conceptual metaphors" in comprehension. In a characteristic assertion of this position, Lakoff and Turner (1989, xi) propose that "metaphor allows us to understand our selves and our world in ways that no other modes of thought can." One challenge to this view, from COGNITIVE ANTHROPOLOGY (Quinn 1991; 1997), holds that the metaphors expressed in language are underlain by cultural understandings, which cannot be read directly from linguistic metaphors but must be investigated independently.

Cultural understandings govern metaphor use in two ways. Sometimes a given domain of experience is understood by analogy to another domain. Such an analogy and the extensive metaphorical language it provides may be culturally and historically quite distinctive. Yet the analogy may be so well established that it is naturalized in thinking, and the metaphors it provides have become standard parts of language, making it, not impossible, but difficult, for those who have learned to conceptualize the world in this way to think and talk in any other terms (Reddy 1979). Perhaps the most famous case is that of the "conduit" metaphor (Reddy 1979) for talking in English about meanings as transmitted in words—as in "Did I get my point across?" Various authors have pointed to the force of the conduit model and its metaphorical language, arguing that it has seriously constrained mathematical information theory (Reddy 1979); led the aforementioned interpretive anthropologists to mistakenly locate culture in symbols (Linger 1994); and bedeviled linguists themselves (Langacker 1991), possibly including those who study metaphor.

Cultural understandings enter the use of metaphors in a second way, one that depends on their intentional selection. Metaphors are commonly employed in ordinary speech to clarify to their audiences points that speakers are trying to convey. This communication task depends on knowledge that the audience can be counted on to share intersubjectively with the speaker. Cultural knowledge is reliably so shared. A common misconception has been that metaphoric target domains are less well understood, perhaps because they are abstract or intangible or unseen or unfamiliar, and that metaphoric source domains are better understood (e.g., Lakoff and Turner 1989), perhaps because they are physical in nature or otherwise concretely experienced. Rather, metaphors intended for clarification are typically selected from among cultural exemplars of that feature of the target domain under discussion (Glucksberg 1991; Quinn 1997). Indeed, this is how metaphors do their work of clarifying, by introducing an outstanding and unambiguous instance of the point being made.

Thus marriage, in the following example, is no more concrete, tangible, knowable, familiar, or well understood to the speaker than baseball. In a newspaper story on his retirement, Kansas City Royals third baseman George Brett was quoted as saying, "I compare it to a marriage. We've had our problems, but overall, we have had a good relationship. I never, ever want to put on another uniform" (*USA Today*, Wednesday, May 5, 1993). What is the case is that marriage is exemplary, for Brett and his American audience, of a relationship that is meant to endure and that does so (when it does so) because it is rewarding despite its difficulties. This is why his metaphor gives readers a surer sense of the complex idea Brett wants to convey about his relationship with the Royals.

When metaphors serve in this way to clarify what we mean to say, the cultural understandings that underlie what we mean may lend considerable regularity to the metaphors chosen. Thus, for example, in Americans' DISCOURSE, metaphors for marriage all fall into eight classes that reflect an underlying cultural model of marriage. For instance, marriage is seen as an ongoing journey ("Once the marriage was formalized it was an unalterable course"), a durable material ("You really have to start out with something strong if it's going to last"), and a firmly held possession ("I think we got

it!"). Each metaphor exemplifies a different kind of lasting thing, and all convey the expectation that marriage is lasting—a key piece of Americans' model of it. That different metaphors are used to capture the same shared understanding is strong evidence that a speaker must have had this point already in mind and selected the metaphor to match it. Indeed, speakers will occasionally concatenate two or three different metaphors to emphasize a point and also readily convey the same understanding nonmetaphorically. Far from following the entailments of a chosen metaphor, reasoning in discourse on marriage commonly follows the idealized cultural model of marriage, and employs different metaphors or no metaphor at all, or at times switches from one metaphor to another in midstream to reach the conclusion being reasoned to (Quinn 1991).

Cultural exemplars such as being married in the Brett quote, or ongoing journeys, durable materials, and firmly held possessions in the examples from discourse about marriage, can usefully be viewed as COGNITIVE ARTIFACTS, though wholly internalized ones. That is to say, they mediate performance of a commonplace cognitive task—in this case, the task of communicating accurately and efficiently. The psychological processing required for this task lends itself to a straightforward connectionist interpretation. Connections built up from experience between properties of the world and their known exemplars permit rapid, automatic identification of apposite metaphors. Of course, for metaphors to do their work of clarification, members of a speech community must, and do, share a large stock of such cultural exemplars. Knowledge of these is accumulated from a variety of experience, both first- and secondhand. Crucial is the ongoing experience of hearing and using metaphors in speech, not only because it presents individuals with many more exemplars than could possibly be encountered otherwise, but also because it weeds out more idiosyncratic choices that would be ill understood by audiences, in favor of more widely agreed upon cultural exemplars that communicate well. Through their repeated use as metaphors, these more readily understood examplars gain even wider acceptance, sometimes becoming wholly conventional.

See also ANALOGY; COGNITIVE LINGUISTICS; CULTURAL SYMBOLISM; CULTURAL PSYCHOLOGY; FIGURATIVE LANGUAGE; LANGUAGE AND CULTURE; LANGUAGE AND GENDER

—*Naomi Quinn*

References

Glucksberg, S. (1991). Beyond literal meanings: The psychology of allusion. *Psychological Science* 2: 146–152.

Lakoff, G., and M. Johnson (1980). *Metaphors We Live By*. Chicago: University of Chicago Press.

Lakoff, G., and M. Turner. (1989). *More Than Cool Reason: A Field Guide to Poetic Metaphor*. Chicago: University of Chicago Press.

Langacker, R. W. (1991). *Foundations of Cognitive Grammar*. Vol. 2, *Descriptive Application*. Stanford: Stanford University Press.

Linger, D. T. (1994). Has culture theory lost its minds? *Ethos* 22: 284–315.

Quinn, N. (1991). The cultural basis of metaphor. In J. W. Fernandez, Ed., *Beyond Metaphor: The Theory of Tropes in Anthropology*. Stanford: Stanford University Press.

Quinn, N. (1997). Research on shared task solutions. In C. Strauss and N. Quinn, Eds., *A Cognitive Theory of Cultural Meaning*. Cambridge: Cambridge University Press.

Reddy, M. J. (1979). The conduit metaphor: A case of frame conflict in our language about language. In A. Ortony, Ed., *Metaphor and Thought*. Cambridge: Cambridge University Press.

Metareasoning

Metareasoning is reasoning about reasoning—in its broadest sense, any computational process concerned with the operation of some other computational process within the same entity. The term relies on a conceptual distinction between *object-level* deliberation about *external* entities, for example, considering the merits of various opening moves one might make in a game of chess, and *metalevel* deliberation about internal entities (computations, beliefs, and so on), for example, deciding that it is not worth spending much time deliberating about which opening move to make. Genesereth and Nilsson (1987) provide formal definitions along these lines. Smith (1986) makes a further distinction between INTROSPECTION about purely internal entities and *reflection* relating internal and external entities. In this view, a proposition such as "If I open the window I will know if the birds are singing" is reflective, because it relates a physical action to a future state of knowledge.

The capacity for metareasoning serves several purposes in an intelligent agent. First, it allows the agent to *control* its object-level deliberations—to decide which ones to undertake and when to stop deliberating and act. This is essential, given the pervasive problem of COMPUTATIONAL COMPLEXITY in decision making, and the consequent need for BOUNDED RATIONALITY. In GAME-PLAYING SYSTEMS, for example, the *alpha-beta* ALGORITHM makes a simple metalevel decision to avoid certain lines of deliberation about future moves, taking advantage of a metalevel theorem to the effect that these lines cannot affect the ultimate object-level decision. Second, metareasoning allows the agent to *generate* computational and physical behaviors, such as planning to obtain information, that require introspective or reflective reasoning. Third, it allows the agent to recover from errors or impasses in its object-level deliberations.

Most early work on metareasoning focused on designing an INTELLIGENT AGENT ARCHITECTURE (see also COGNITIVE ARCHITECTURE) that could support introspection and reflection. The use of metareasoning to control deduction seems to have been proposed first by Hayes (1973), although the first implementation was in the TEIRESIAS system (Davis 1980), which used metarules to control deliberation within a rule-based expert system. The Metalevel Representation System, or MRS, (Genesereth and Smith 1981) used LOGIC PROGRAMMING for both object and metalevel inference and provided a very flexible interface between the two. Because MRS allowed reasoning about which procedure to use for each object-level inference, and about which representation to use for each object-level fact, it enabled many different representations and reasoning methods to operate together seamlessly. By far the most ambitious metalevel architecture is Soar (Laird, Newell, and Rosenbloom 1987), whose fundamental mode of computation is based on PROBLEM SOLVING. Whenever Soar does not have an unambiguous rule telling it which problem-solving step to take next, it invokes *universal subgoaling* to set up a metalevel problem space that will resolve the issue. As might be imagined from these examples, designers of such systems must take care to avoid an *infinite regress* of metameta . . . reasoning.

Does metareasoning differ from "ordinary" reasoning? In all metalevel architectures, the metalevel is given direct access to object-level data structures. Thus metareasoning (at least in computers) can assume a completely and perfectly observable object-level state—which is seldom the case with ordinary reasoning about the external world. Furthermore, it is possible to represent fully and exactly the nature of the available object-level computations. Thus it is possible for the metalevel to simulate completely the object-level computations under consideration (as is done in Soar). This would seem counterproductive, however, as a way of selecting among object-level computations because simulating a computation (and hence knowing its outcome) is just a very slow way of doing the computation itself—knowledge of the outcome of a computation *is* the outcome. For this reason, Soar always compiles the results of subgoaling into a new rule, thereby avoiding deliberation in similar cases in future. Compilation of metareasoning into more efficient forms is perhaps the principal way an agent's computational performance can improve over time.

In the research outlined thus far, the metareasoning consisted mostly of applying simple "IF-THEN" rules encoding the system designer's computational EXPERTISE; no standard of rationality for metareasoning was provided. The concept of *rational metareasoning* (Horvitz 1989; Russell and Wefald 1989) had its roots in early work by I. J. Good (1971) on "Type II rationality" and in *information value theory* (Howard 1966), which places a value on acquiring a piece of information based on the expected improvement in decision quality that results from its acquisition. A COMPUTATION can be viewed as the process of making explicit some information that was previously implicit, and therefore value can be placed on computations in the same way. That is, a computation can be viewed as an action whose benefit is that it may result in better external decisions, and whose cost is the delay it incurs. Thus, given a model of the effects of computations and information about object-level utility, the metalevel can infer the value of computations. It can decide which computations to do and when computation should give way to action.

The simplest applications of rational metareasoning arise in the context of *anytime algorithms* (Horvitz 1987; Dean and Boddy 1988), that is, algorithms that can be interrupted at any time and whose output quality improves continuously with time. Each such algorithm has an associated *performance profile* describing its output quality as a function of time. The availability of the profile makes the metalevel decision problem—which algorithm to run and when to terminate—fairly trivial. The use of anytime algorithms devised for a wide variety of computational tasks has resulted in a widely applicable methodology for building complex, real-time decision-making systems (Zilberstein and Russell 1996).

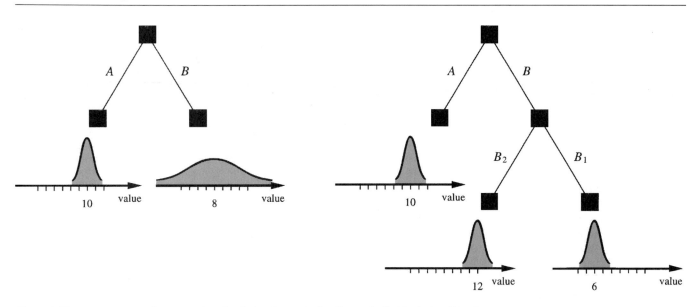

Figure 1. The consequence of computation: Lookahead reveals that *B* may in fact be better than *A*.

A finer-grained approach to metareasoning can be obtained by evaluating individual computation steps within an algorithm. Consider the decision-making situation shown in figure 1a. An agent has two possible actions, *A* and *B*. Based on a quick assessment, the outcome of *A* appears to be worth 10 with a standard deviation of 1, whereas the outcome of *B* seems to be worth 8 with a standard deviation of 4. The agent can choose *A* immediately, or it can refine its estimates by looking further into the future. For example (figure 1b), it can consider the actions B_1 and B_2, with the outcomes shown. At this point, action *B* (followed by B_1) seems to lead to a state with value 12; thus the lookahead computation has changed the agent's decision, with an apparent benefit of 2. Obviously, this is a post hoc analysis, but, as shown by Russell and Wefald (1991), an expected value of computation can be computed efficiently—*prior* to performing the lookahead. In figure 1a, this value is 0.3 for lookahead from *A* and 0.82 for lookahead from *B*. If the initial estimated outcome of *A* were 12, however, these values would drop to 0.002 and 0.06, respectively. Hence, as one would expect, the value of computation depends strongly on whether a clear choice of action has already emerged. If, however, the initial estimates for *A* and *B* were both 10, with standard deviations of 0.1, then the value of computation becomes 0.03. Computation is worthless when it does not matter which action one eventually chooses.

Rational metareasoning can be applied to control deliberations in a wide variety of object-level algorithms including HEURISTIC SEARCH and game playing (Russell and Wefald 1991), LOGICAL REASONING SYSTEMS (Smith 1989), and MACHINE LEARNING (Rivest and Sloan 1988). An important insight to emerge from this work is that a metareasoning capability can, in principle, be *domain independent* (Russell and Wefald 1991; Ginsberg and Geddis 1991) because the necessary domain-specific information (such as the utility function) can be extracted from the object level. One can therefore view successful computational behavior as emerging not from carefully crafted, domain-specific algorithms

but from the interaction of a general capacity for rational metareasoning with object-level domain knowledge. More efficient, domain-specific computational behaviors might then result from processes of compilation and metalevel REINFORCEMENT LEARNING.

See also LOGIC; METACOGNITION; METAREPRESENTATION; MODAL LOGIC; RATIONAL AGENCY

—*Stuart J. Russell*

References

Davis, R. (1980). Meta-rules: Reasoning about control. *Artificial Intelligence* 15(3): 179–222.

Dean, T., and M. Boddy. (1988). An analysis of time-dependent planning. In *Proceedings of the Seventh National Conference on Artificial Intelligence* (AAAI-88). St. Paul, MN: Kaufmann, pp. 49–54.

Genesereth, M. R., and D. Smith. (1981). Meta-level architecture. *Memo HPP-81-6*. Computer Science Department, Stanford University.

Genesereth, M. R., and N. J. Nilsson. (1987). *Logical Foundations of Artificial Intelligence.* San Mateo, CA: Kaufmann.

Ginsberg, M. L., and D. F. Geddis. (1991). Is there any need for domain-dependent control information? In *Proceedings of the Ninth National Conference on Artificial Intelligence,* vol. 1. (AAAI-91). Anaheim, California: AAAI Press, pp. 452–457.

Good, I. J. (1971). Twenty-seven principles of rationality. In V. P. Godambe and D. A. Sprott, Eds., *Foundations of Statistical Inference.* Toronto: Holt, Rinehart and Winston, pp. 108–141.

Hayes, P. J. (1973). Computation and deduction. In *Proceedings of the Second Symposium on Mathematical Foundations of Computer Science Czechoslovakia.* Czechoslovakian Academy of Science.

Horvitz, E. J. (1987). Problem-solving design: Reasoning about computational value, trade-offs, and resources. In *Proceedings of the Second Annual NASA Research Forum.* Moffett Field, CA: NASA Ames Research Center, pp. 26–43.

Horvitz, E. J. (1989). Reasoning about beliefs and actions under computational resource constraints. In L. N. Kanal, T. S. Levitt, and J. F. Lemmer, Eds., *Uncertainty in Artificial Intelligence*, vol. 3. Amsterdam: Elsevier, pp. 301–324.

Howard, R. A. (1966). Information value theory. *IEEE Transactions on Systems Science and Cybernetics* SSC-2: 22–26.

Laird, J. E., A. Newell, and P. S. Rosenbloom. (1987). SOAR: An architecture for general intelligence. *Artificial Intelligence* 33(1): 1–64.

Rivest, R. L., and R. Sloan. (1988). A new model for inductive inference. In M. Vardi, Ed., *Proceedings of the Second Conference on Theoretical Aspects of Reasoning about Knowledge*. San Mateo, CA: Kaufmann, pp. 13–27.

Russell, S. J., and E. H. Wefald. (1989). On optimal game-tree search using rational metareasoning. *Proceedings of the Eleventh International Joint Conference on Artificial Intelligence* (IJCAI-89). Detroit: Kaufmann, pp. 334–340.

Russell, S. J., and E. H. Wefald. (1991). *Do the Right Thing: Studies in Limited Rationality*. Cambridge, MA: MIT Press.

Smith, B. C. (1986). Varieties of self-reference. In J. Halpern, Ed., *Theoretical Aspects of Reasoning about Knowledge*. San Mateo, CA: Kaufmann.

Smith, D. E. (1989). Controlling backward inference. *Artificial Intelligence* 39(2): 145–208.

Zilberstein, S., and S. Russell. (1996). Optimal composition of real-time systems. *Artificial Intelligence* 83.

Metarepresentation

Cognitive systems are characterized by their ability to construct and process representations of objects and states of affairs. MENTAL REPRESENTATIONS and public representations such as linguistic utterances are themselves objects in the world, and therefore potential objects of second-order representations, or "metarepresentations." Under this or another name, (e.g., "higher-order representations"), metarepresentations are evoked in evolutionary approaches to INTELLIGENCE, in philosophical and developmental approaches to commonsense psychology, in pragmatic approaches to communication, in theories of consciousness, and in the study of reasoning.

It is assumed that the members of most animal species are incapable of recognizing in themselves or attributing to conspecifics mental representations such as beliefs or desires: they utterly lack metarepresentational abilities. Highly intelligent social animals such as primates, on the other hand, are believed to have evolved an ability to interpret and predict the behavior of others by recognizing their mental states. Indeed, Dennett (1987) has described some primates as "second-order intentional systems," capable of having "beliefs and desires about beliefs and desires." Second-order intentional systems are, for instance, capable of deliberate deception. In a population of second-order intentional systems, a third-order intentional system would be at a real advantage, if only because it would be able to see through deception. Similarly, in a population of third-order intentional systems, a fourth-order intentional system would be a greater advantage still, with greater abilities to deceive others and avoid being deceived itself, and so on. Hence the hypothesis, supported by some ethological evidence, that primates have developed a kind of strategic MACHIAVELLIAN INTELLIGENCE (Byrne and Whiten 1988) involving higher-order metarepresentational abilities. These evolutionary and ethological arguments have in part converged, in part conflicted with experimental studies of primates' metarepresentational abilities that have started with Premack and Woodruff's pioneering article "Does the Chimpanzee Have a Theory of Mind?" (1978). Though the level of metarepresentational sophistication of other primates is still disputed, that of human beings is not. The human lineage may be the only one in which a true escalation of metarepresentational abilities has taken place.

Humans are all spontaneous psychologists. They have some understanding of cognitive functions such as perception and MEMORY (see METACOGNITION). They also attribute to one another PROPOSITIONAL ATTITUDES such as beliefs and desires, and do so as a matter of course. While philosophers have described the basic tenets of this commonsense or FOLK PSYCHOLOGY and discussed its empirical adequacy, psychologists have focused on the development of this cognitive ability, often described as a THEORY OF MIND. Philosophers and psychologists have been jointly involved in discussing the mechanism through which humans succeed in metarepresenting other people's thoughts and their own. This investigation has taken the form of a debate between those who believe attribution of mental states to others is done by simulation (e.g., Goldman 1993; Gordon 1986; Harris 1989), and those who believe it is done by inference from principles and evidence (e.g., Gopnik 1993; Leslie 1987; Perner 1991; Wellman 1990). In this debate (see SIMULATION VS. THEORY-THEORY), much attention has been paid to different degrees of metarepresentational competence that may be involved in attributing mental states to others. In particular, the ability to attribute *false* beliefs is seen as a sufficient, if not necessary, proof of basic metarepresentational competence. This metarepresentational competence can be impaired—the basis of a new, cognitive approach to AUTISM. Conversely, the study of autism has contributed to the development of a finer-grained understanding of metarepresentations (see Baron-Cohen 1995; Frith 1989).

Cognitive approaches have stressed the metarepresentational complexity of human communication. The very act of communicating involves, on the part of the communicator and addressee, mutual metarepresentations of each other's mental states. In ordinary circumstances, the addressee of a speech act is interested in the linguistic MEANING of the utterance only as a means of discovering the speaker's meaning. Speaker's meaning has been analyzed by the philosopher Paul GRICE (1989) in terms of several layers of metarepresentational intentions, in particular the basic metarepresentational intention to cause in the addressee a certain mental state (e.g., a belief), and the higher-order metarepresentational intention to have that basic intention recognized by the addressee. Grice's analysis of metarepresentational intentions involved in communication has been discussed and developed by numerous philosophers and linguists (e.g., Bach and Harnish 1979; Bennett 1976; Recanati 1986; Schiffer 1972; Searle 1969; Sperber and Wilson 1986).

It has long been observed that human languages have the semantic and syntactic resources to serve as metalanguages. In direct and indirect quotations, utterances and meanings are metarepresented. The study of such metalinguistic devices has been developed in semiotics (see SEMIOTICS AND COGNITION), in philosophy of language, and in PRAGMATICS. In particular, in the study of FIGURATIVE LANGUAGE, irony has been described as a means of distancing oneself from some propositional attitude by metarepresenting it (see Gibbs 1994; Sperber and Wilson 1986).

The ability to metarepresent one's own mental states plays an important role in CONSCIOUSNESS, and may even be seen as defining it. For David Rosenthal (1986; 1997) in particular, a mental state is conscious if it is represented in a higher-order thought. When a thought itself is conscious, then the higher-order thought that represents it is a straight-forward metarepresentation. These higher-order thoughts may themselves be the object of yet higher-order thoughts: The reflexive character of consciousness (i.e., that one can be conscious of being conscious) is then explained in terms of a hierarchy of metarepresentations. While many philosophers do not accept this "higher-order thought" theory of consciousness, the role of metarepresentations at least in aspects of consciousness and in related phenomena such as INTROSPECTION is hardly controversial.

Much of spontaneous human reasoning is about states of affairs and how they relate to one another. But some reasoning, especially deliberate reasoning as occurs in science or philosophy, is about hypotheses, theories, or claims—representations—and only indirectly about the state of affairs represented in these representations. In the psychology of DEDUCTIVE REASONING, growing attention has been paid to such metarepresentational reasoning, in particular by experimenting with liar and truth teller problems, either from the point of view of "mental logic" (Rips 1994) or from that of MENTAL MODELS (Johnson-Laird and Byrne 1991). In artificial intelligence, too, there is a growing interest in modeling such METAREASONING.

This rapid overview does not exhaust the areas of cognitive science where metarepresentation (whether so named or not) plays an important role. In a great variety of cognitive activities, humans exhibit unique metarepresentational virtuosity. This, together with the possession of language, may be their most distinctive cognitive trait.

See also INTENTIONAL STANCE; PRIMATE COGNITION; RELEVANCE AND RELEVANCE THEORY

—*Dan Sperber*

References

Bach, K. and R. Harnish. (1979). *Linguistic Communication and Speech Acts.* Cambridge, MA: MIT Press.

Baron-Cohen, S. (1995). *Mindblindness: An Essay on Autism and Theory of Mind.* Cambridge, MA: MIT Press.

Bennett, J. (1976). *Linguistic Behaviour.* Cambridge: Cambridge University Press.

Byrne, R. W., and A. Whiten. (1988). *Machiavellian Intelligence: Social Expertise and the Evolution of Intellect in Monkeys, Apes and Humans.* Oxford: Oxford University Press.

Dennett, D. (1987). *The Intentional Stance.* Cambridge, MA: MIT Press.

Frith, U. (1989). *Autism: Explaining the Enigma.* Oxford: Blackwell.

Gibbs, R. (1994). *The Poetics of Mind: Figurative Thought, Language and Understanding.* Cambridge: Cambridge University Press.

Goldman, A. (1993). The psychology of folk psychology. *Behavioral and Brain Sciences* 16: 15–28.

Gopnik, A. (1993). How we know our minds: The illusion of first-person knowledge of intentionality. *Behavioral and Brain Sciences* 16: 1–14.

Gordon, R. M. (1986). Folk psychology as simulation. *Mind and Language* 1: 158–171.

Grice, H. P. (1989). *Studies in the Way of Words.* Cambridge, MA: Harvard University Press.

Harris, P. L. (1989). *Children and Emotion: The Development of Psychological Understanding.* Oxford: Blackwell.

Johnson-Laird, P. N., and R. M. J. Byrne. (1991). *Deduction.* Hove: Erlbaum.

Leslie, A. M. (1987). Pretence and representation: The origins of "theory of mind." *Psychological Review* 94: 412–426.

Perner, J. (1991). *Understanding the Representational Mind.* Cambridge, MA: MIT Press.

Premack, D., and G. Woodruff. (1978). Does the chimpanzee have a theory of mind? *Behavioral and Brain Sciences* 1: 515–526.

Recanati, F. (1986). On defining communicative intentions. *Mind and Language* 1(3): 213–242.

Rips, L. (1994). *The Psychology of Proof.* Cambridge, MA: MIT Press.

Rosenthal, D. M. (1986). Two concepts of consciousness. *Philosophical Studies* 49(3): 329–359.

Rosenthal, D. M. (1997). A theory of consciousness. In N. Block, O. Flanagan, and G. Güzeldere, Eds., *The Nature of Consciousness: Philosophical Debates.* Cambridge, MA: MIT Press, pp. 729–753.

Schiffer, S. (1972). *Meaning.* Oxford: Clarendon Press.

Searle, J. (1969). *Speech Acts.* Cambridge: Cambridge University Press.

Sperber, D., and D. Wilson. (1986). *Relevance: Communication and Cognition.* Oxford: Blackwell.

Wellman, H. M. (1990). *The Child's Theory of Mind.* Cambridge, MA: MIT Press.

Whiten, A. (1991). *Natural Theories of Mind: Evolution, Development and Simulation of Everyday Mindreading.* Oxford: Blackwell.

Further Readings

Baron-Cohen, S., A. Leslie, and U. Frith. (1985). Does the autistic child have a "theory of mind"? *Cognition* 21: 37–46

Baron-Cohen, S., H. Tager-Flusberg, and D. J. Cohen, Eds. (1993). *Understanding Other Minds: Perspectives from Autism.* Oxford: Oxford University Press.

Bogdan, R. J. (1997). *Interpreting Minds: The Evolution of a Practice.* Cambridge, MA: MIT Press.

Carruthers, P. (1996). *Language, Thought and Consciousness.* Cambridge: Cambridge University Press.

Carruthers, P., and P. Smith, Eds. (1996). *Theories of Theories of Mind.* Cambridge: Cambridge University Press.

Clark, H., and Gerrig, R. (1990). Quotations as demonstrations. *Language* 66: 764–805.

Davies, M., and T. Stone, Eds. (1995). *Folk Psychology: The Theory of Mind Debate.* Oxford: Blackwell.

Davies, M., and Humphreys, G., Eds. (1993). *Consciousness.* Oxford: Blackwell.

Davies, M., and T. Stone, Eds. (1995). *Mental Simulation: Evaluations and Applications.* Oxford: Blackwell.

Frith, U., and F. Happé. (1994b). Autism: Beyond "theory of mind." *Cognition* 50: 115–132.

Happé, F. (1994). *Autism: An Introduction to Psychological Theory.* London: UCL Press.

Lehrer, K. (1990). *Metamind.* Oxford: Oxford University Press.

Mithen, S. (1996). *The Prehistory of the Mind.* London: Thames and Hudson.

Sperber, D. (1994). Understanding verbal understanding. In J. Khalfa, Ed., *What is Intelligence?* Cambridge: Cambridge University Press.

Sperber, D., Ed. (Forthcoming). *Metarepresentations.* Oxford: Oxford University Press.

Sperber, D., and D. Wilson. (1981). Irony and the use-mention distinction. In P. Cole, Ed., *Radical Pragmatics.* New York: Academic Press, pp. 295–318.

Whiten, A., and R. W. Byrne. (1997). *Machiavellian Intelligence.* Vol. 2, *Evaluations and Extensions.* Cambridge: Cambridge University Press.

Meter and Poetry

The fundamental formal distinction between poetry and all other forms of literary art is this: poems are made up of lines. But how long is a line? Lines of metrical verse are subject to measurement just as surely as if they were made of cloth and both poet and reader has a yardstick. In the case of cloth, you measure physical distance by counting in yards. What do you use to measure the length of a line of poetry? The simplest kinds of meters are measured in syllables. There are only so many in a line.

Such meters occur in the poetry of languages all over the world. Much of the poetry in the Romance languages counts syllables (Halle and Keyser 1980). Hebrew poetry of the Old Testament does as well (Halle 1997). So, too, do the Japanese verse forms known as *tanka* and *haiku* (Halle 1970). In the five-line *tanka,* lines are 5-7-5-7-7 syllables long. In the three-line *haiku,* the lines are 5-7-5 syllables long. As shown by the poems in (1) and (2), syllables with double vowels (i.e., long syllables) are counted as two units; all other syllables count as one.

(1) Haru tateba   5   When spring comes
    Kiyuru koori no   7   the ice melts away
    Nokori naku   5   without trace
    Kimi ga kokoro mo   7   your heart
    Ware ni tokenamu   7   melts into me
    (Kokinshuu)

(2) Kaki kueba   5   Eating persimmons
    Kanega narunari   7   the bell rings
    Hooryuu-ji   5   Hooryuuji
    (Masaoka)

Japanese poets and their readers both know what a syllable is. They also know the difference between a long syllable and a short one. This shared knowledge is what Japanese meter depends upon. Segmenting a word into syllables requires a great deal of sophisticated knowledge about such things as the difference between a vowel, a consonant, a liquid, and a glide. No modern computer can reliably segment a stretch of speech into syllables. Yet speakers of all languages do this constantly and unconsciously.

Much more complex linguistic machinery is involved in verse where line length is measured by counting feet rather than syllables. Foot-counting verse is encountered in a wide range of poetic traditions, among them Homer and much of the poetry of classical Greek and Latin antiquity, the Old Norse bards, English poetry from Chaucer to Frost, German poetry from Hans Sachs to Rilke, and Russian poetry from the eighteenth century to the present.

To illustrate the more complex machinery of foot-counting meters, we look at the so-called syllabo-tonic meters of English and, in particular, iambic pentameter. This meter is made up, as its name suggests, of five feet. An iambic foot is made up of two syllables followed by a boundary. There is a specific procedure that divides the line into iambic feet. Consider the opening line of Gray's "Elegy Written in a Country Churchyard":

(3) The curfew tolls the knell of parting day.
      *   *   *   *   *   *   * *   *   *

We represent each syllable in the verse by an asterisk beneath the line. The procedure is: insert right parenthesis from left to right, starting at the left edge so as to group asterisks into pairs:

(4) The curfew tolls the knell of parting day.
) *   *) *   *)   *   *) * *) * *)

Although there are six parentheses in this line, there are only five feet because an iambic foot is defined as a sequence of two syllables followed by a parenthesis. The rule that inserts parentheses is:

(5) Insert a right parenthesis ")" at the beginning of the line and, proceeding rightward, after every other syllable (thus generating binary feet).

Readers familiar with iambic verse know that many lines of iambic pentameter verse are often longer than 10 syllables. These exhibit what the textbooks call "feminine rhymes." The following couplet from Byron's "Don Juan" (Canto 65) is illustrative:

(6) Yet he was jealous, though he did not show it,
     For jealousy dislikes the world to know it.

The line-final rhyming pair is *show it: know it.* Each member of the pair has a so-called extrametrical syllable—namely, *it.* Rule (5) automatically accounts for the possibility of such syllables in iambic verse:

(7) Yet he was jealous, though he did not show it.
) * *) * *) *   *) * *) * *) *
     For jealousy dislikes the world to know it.
) * *) * *) * *) *   *) * *) *

As before, right parentheses are inserted, beginning at the left. Notice, however, that a right parenthesis cannot be inserted to the right of the final * in (7) because (5) requires that two syllables are skipped before a right parenthesis can be inserted. Here only a single * follows the last parenthesis. Therefore, no parenthesis is inserted line finally and the line is correctly scanned as containing only five iambic feet.

Just as readers familiar with poetry written in iambic pentameter recognize that some lines are longer than 10 syllables, they also know certain lines are not possible iambic pentameter lines, even though they may be composed of 10 syllables. For example, a line like (8) is not a possible iambic pentameter line.

(8) On cutting Lucretia Borgia's bright hair

This causes a problem for the account given so far because (5) scans the line without difficulty:

(9) On cutting Lucretia Borgia's bright hair
) * *) * *) * *) * *)   *   *)

(5) must be modified in such a way that it will continue to scan lines like those in (4) and (7) while ruling out lines like (9).

It is well known that in foot-based meters not only does line length play a role but so does the placement of certain marked syllables. In the English iambic meters, these are the syllables that bear the main stress of the word. We mark such metrically important syllables by inserting a bracket before or after them. The marked syllables in stress-based verse are called stress maxima. A stress maximum is the main stressed syllable in a polysyllabic word. In the history of English, poets made use of slightly different definitions, extending the definition in some cases and restricting it in others. For present purposes, the stress maximum is defined as:

(10) The stressed syllable of a polysyllabic word that is preceded by a lesser stressed syllable is a stress maximum.

The stressed syllables in the following words are instances of stress maxima:

(11) Lucrétia   meándering
      autobiográphic   pellúcid

Rule (12) accounts for the placement of such syllables in an iambic pentameter line.

(12) In an iambic line, insert a right bracket after (to the right of) a stress maximum.

Let us see how rules (5) and (12) construct feet within a line like (13).

(13) The curfew tolls the knell of parting day.

The square brackets called for by stress maxima are inserted first. They are no different from parentheses, but we use them to help the reader keep track of which rule is responsible for a given boundary:

(14) The cúrfew tolls the knell of párting day.
      *   *] *   *   *   * * *] *   *

Next come the parentheses inserted by (5):

(15) The curfew tolls the knell of parting day.
      * *]) * *) *   *) * *]) * *)

The line is correctly divided into five feet and, significantly, where right parentheses and right brackets occur in the line, they coincide. Now consider how (5) and (12) assign boundaries to the unmetrical (8):

(16) On cutting Lucretia Borgia's bright hair
      *   *]) *   *) *]) * *]) *   *)   *

Unlike the metrical lines discussed thus far, this line contains two feet that end on consecutive syllables, namely:

(17) -ing Lucrétia
      *   *) *] *

This is not a well-formed configuration. We exclude it by means of prohibition (18):

(18) Feet may not end on consecutive syllables.

Rule (18) applies after the insertion of parentheses by (5) and (12). All scansions that conform to it are well-formed. Scansions that fail to do so are not.

The theory of meter proposed contains two rules, one output constraint, and a definition of stress maximum. The rules insert right foot boundaries, either to the right of stress maxima or else iteratively from left to right. The constraint rules out scansions with unary feet. The grammar is summarized in (19):

(19) Rule: a. Insert a right bracket "]" to the right of a stress maximum.
            b. Insert a right parenthesis ")" from left to right, skipping two consecutive syllables.
      Constraint: In iambic verse feet may not end on consecutive syllables.
      Stress Maximum: The stressed syllable of a polysyllabic word preceded by a lesser stressed syllable.

Just as two speakers of a language share a body of linguistic knowledge called a grammar, which enables them to speak to one another, so, too, do poets and their readers share a body of knowledge that enables the one to write metrically and the other to scan what has been put into meter. The rules in (19) are an attempt at illustrating what this body of shared metrical knowledge looks like.

Up to now, nothing has been said about the machinery used to scan iambic pentameter lines. That machinery is identical to that needed to account for the way ordinary speakers assign stress to the words of English (see STRESS, LINGUISTIC), and is part of the natural endowment of human beings that enables them to speak a language—what linguists have come to call Universal Grammar (UG). In other words, poets who write metrically do so using the same theoretical apparatus provided by UG that speakers use to assign stress to the words of their language. This convergence of the machinery of meter with the machinery of stress assignment is the essence of PROSODY.

See also LINGUISTIC UNIVERSALS AND UNIVERSAL GRAMMAR; FIGURATIVE LANGUAGE; PHONOLOGICAL RULES AND PROCESSES; PHONOLOGY; PROSODY AND INTONATION, PROCESSING ISSUES

—*Samuel Jay Keyser*

References

Halle, M. (1970). What is meter in poetry? In R. Jakobson and S. Hattori, Eds., *Sciences of Language: The Journal of the Tokyo Institute for Advanced Studies in Languages,* vol. 2. Japan: Tokyo Institute for Advanced Studies of Language, pp. 124–138.

Halle, M. (1997). Metrical verse in the Psalms. In V. van der Meij, Ed., *India and Beyond: Aspects of Literature, Meaning, Ritual and Thought. Essays in Honour of Frits Staal.* London: Kegan Paul International, in association with the International Institute for Asian Studies, Leiden, pp. 207–225.

Halle, M., and S. J. Keyser. (1980). Metrica. *Enciclopedia IX.* Torino, Italy: Einaudi.

Further Readings

Halle, M., and S. J. Keyser. (1998). Robert Frost's loose and strict iambics. In E. Iwamoto, M. Muraki, M. Tokunaga, and N. Hasegawa, Eds., *Festschrift in Honor of Kazuko Inoue.* Tokyo, Japan: Kanda University of International Studies.

Mid-Level Vision

Mid-level vision refers to a putative level of visual processing, situated between the analysis of the image (lower-level vision) and the recognition of specific objects and events (HIGH-LEVEL VISION). It is largely a viewer-centered process, seemingly concerned explicitly with real-world scenes, not simply images (see Nakayama, He, and Shimojo 1995). Yet, in distinction to high-level vision, mid-level vision represents the world only in a most general way, dealing primarily with surfaces and objects and the fact that they can appear at different orientations, can be variously illuminated, and can be partially occluded.

Vision as we understand it today is far more complicated than had been recognized even thirty to forty years ago. Despite the seeming unity of our visual experience, there is mounting evidence that vision is not a single function but is likely to be a conglomerate of functions, each acting with considerable autonomy (Goodale 1995; Ungerleider and Mishkin 1982). Along with this new appreciation of vision's complexity comes the striking fact that from a purely anatomical point of view, the portion of the brain devoted to vision is also much greater than previously supposed (Allman and Kaas 1975; Felleman and van Essen 1991). For example, about 50 percent of the CEREBRAL CORTEX of primates is devoted exclusively to visual processing, and the estimated territory for humans is nearly comparable. So vision by itself looms very large even when stacked up against all other conceivable functions of the brain. As such, subdivisions in vision, particularly principled ones that delineate qualitatively different processes, are sorely needed, and Marr's (1982) seminal argument for three levels provides the broad base for what we outline here.

Let us consider what processes might constitute mid-level vision, and then contrast them with low-level and high-level vision. Good examples of mid-level visual processing can be seen in the work of Kanizsa (1979). Compare figure 1a where we see many isolated fragments with figure 1b where the same fragments are accompanied by additional diagonal line segments. In figure 1b there is a dramatic shift in what is perceived. The isolated pieces seen in figure 1a now form a single larger figure, the familiar Necker cube.

The phenomenon just described is characterized by several things, which all appear to be related to objects and surfaces and their boundaries. Furthermore, they are examples of occlusion, the partial covering of one surface by another. There is also the indication of inferences being made, enabling us to represent something that has been made invisible. We are thus aware of something continuing behind, which in turn enables us to see a single figure, not isolated fragments.

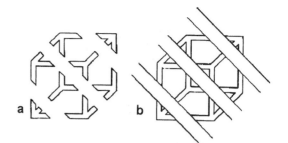

Figure 1.

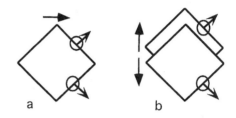

Figure 2.

These characteristics, while not delineating mid-level vision in its entirety, provide sufficient basis for characterizing it as qualitatively different from low- and high-level vision. Consider the "aperture" problem for motion and its solution, something that until recently has been considered as within the province of low-level vision. Since Wallach's work (1935/1997), it has been recognized that there is an inherent ambiguity of perception if motion is analyzed locally, as would be the case for directionally selective receptive fields (see circles in figure 2). Thus in the case of a rightward-moving diamond (figure 2a), the local motions of the edges are very different from the motion of the whole figure. Yet, we are unaware of these local motions and see unified motion to the right. Computational models based on local motion measurements alone can recover the horizontal motion of the single figure on the left, but they cannot account for the perceived motion of one figure moving differently from another on the right (figure 2b). Although the local motions here are essentially identical, our visual system sees the motion in each case to be very different. It sees rightward motion of a single object versus opposing vertical motion of two objects. Only by the explicit parsing of the moving scene into separate surfaces can the correct motion be recovered. Thus, directionally selective neurons by themselves cannot supply reliable information regarding the motion of objects. Mid-level vision, with its explicit encoding of distinct surfaces, is required.

How might we distinguish mid-level from high-level vision? Consider figure 3. Most obvious is the reversal of the duck and the rabbit. From the above discussion, it should be clear that this reversal cannot be happening at the level of mid-level vision, which concerns itself more generally with surfaces and objects, but at higher levels where specific objects, like rabbits and ducks, are represented. For mid-level vision there is *no* reversal. Here mid-level vision's

Figure 3.

Figure 4.

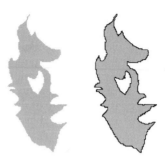

Figure 5.

job is to make sure we see a single thing or surface, despite its division into four separate image fragments by the overlying occluder and despite the change in its identity (the rabbit vs. the duck).

Another job of mid-level vision is to cope effectively with the characteristics of reflected light as it plays across surfaces in natural scenes. Surfaces can appear in various guises in the image, the result of being illuminated from various angles, being shaded by themselves or other surfaces, and by being viewed through transparent media. It would thus seem natural that various visual mechanisms would have developed or evolved to deal with these issues of illumination just as they have for cases of occlusion. This view is strengthened by the existence of perceptual phenomena that provide at least some hint as to how such processes may be occurring, also demonstrating the existence of processing that cannot be explained by low-level vision, say by lateral interactions of neurons with various types of receptive fields. Consider White's illusion shown in figure 4 where the apparent difference in brightness of the gray squares (top vs. bottom row) is very large despite being of equal luminance. Each identical gray patch is bounded by identical amounts of black and white areas, thus ruling out any explanation based on simultaneous contrast or lateral inhibition. The major difference is the nature of the junction structure bounding the areas, properties very important in mid-level vision processing. Figure 5 suggests that mid-level vision's role is the processing of shadows, showing how specific are the requirements for a dark region to be categorized as shadow and how consequential this categorization is for higher-level recognition. On the left we see a 3-D figure, a face. On the right, it looks more 2-D, where the outline around the dark region diminishes the impression that the figure contains shadows.

Although phenomena related to mid-level vision have been well-known, starting with GESTALT PSYCHOLOGY and more recently with work by Kanizsa (1979), the scope and positioning of mid-level vision in the larger scheme of visual processing has been unclear. Recently, Nakayama et al. (1995) have suggested that mid-level vision, in the form

of surface representation, is required for a range of processes more traditionally associated with early vision, including motion perception (see MOTION, PERCEPTION OF), forms of stereopsis, TEXTURE segregation and saliency coding. More speculatively, there has been a proposal that mid-level vision is the first level of processing, the results of which are available to conscious awareness (Jackendoff 1987; Nakayama, He, and Shimojo 1995), thus implying that mid-level vision is the earliest level to which ATTENTION can be deployed.

See also CONSCIOUSNESS; GESTALT PERCEPTION; ILLUSIONS; SHAPE PERCEPTION; SURFACE PERCEPTION; VISUAL PROCESSING STREAMS

—*Ken Nakayama*

References

Allman, J. M., and J. H. Kaas. (1975). The dorsomedial cortical visual area: a third tier area in the occipital lobe of the owl monkey (*Aotus trivirgatus*). *Brain Research* 100: 473–487.

Felleman, D. J., and D. C. van Essen. (1991). Distributed hierarchical processing in the primate cerebral cortex. *Cerebral Cortex* 1: 1–47.

Goodale, M. A. (1995). The cortical organization of visual perception and visuomotor control. In S. M. Kosslyn and D. N. Osherson, Eds., *Visual Cognition.* Cambridge, MA: MIT Press.

Jackendoff, R. (1987). *Consciousness and the Computational Mind.* Cambridge, MA: MIT Press.

Kanizsa, G. (1979). *Organization in Vision: Essays on Gestalt Perception.* New York: Praeger.

Marr, D. (1982). *Vision.* San Francisco, CA: Freeman.

Nakayama, K., Z. J. He, and S. Shimojo. (1995). Visual surface representation: a critical link between lower-level and higher-level vision. In S. M. Kosslyn and D. N. Osherson, Eds., *Visual Cognition.* Cambridge, MA: MIT Press, pp. 1–70.

Ungerleider, L. G., and M. Mishkin. (1982). Two cortical visual systems. In D. J. Ingle, M. A. Goodale, and R. J. W. Mansfield, Eds., *Analysis of Visual Behavior.* Cambridge, MA: MIT Press.

Wallach, H. (1935). Über visuell wahrgenommene Bewegungsrichtung. *Psychol. forschung* 20: 325–380. Translated (1997) by S. Wuenger, R. Shapley, and N. Rubin. On the visually perceived direction of motion. *Perception* 25: 1317–1368.

Mind-Body Problem

The *mind-body problem* is the problem of explaining how our mental states, events, and processes are related to the physical states, events, and processes in our bodies. A question of the form "How is A related to B?" does not by itself pose a philosophical problem. To pose such a problem, there has to be something about A and B that makes the relation between them seem problematic. Many features of mind and body have been cited as responsible for our sense of the problem. Here I will concentrate on two: the apparent causal interaction of mind and body, and the distinctive features of CONSCIOUSNESS.

A long tradition in philosophy has held, with René DESCARTES, that the mind must be a nonbodily entity: a soul or mental substance. This thesis is called "substance dualism" or "Cartesian dualism" because it says that there are two kinds of substance in the world, mental and physical or material. Belief in such dualism is based on belief that the soul is immortal, and that we have free will, which seems to require that the mind be a nonphysical thing because all physical things are subject to the laws of nature.

To say that the mind (or soul) is a mental substance is not to say that the mind is made up of nonphysical "stuff" or material. Rather, the term *substance* is used in the traditional philosophical sense: a *substance* is an entity that has properties and that persists through change in its properties. A tiger, for instance, is a substance, whereas a hurricane is not. To say there are mental substances—individual minds or souls—is to say there are objects that are nonmaterial or nonphysical, and these objects can exist independently of physical objects, such as a person's body. These objects, if they exist, are not made of nonphysical "stuff"—they are not made of "stuff" at all.

But if there are such objects, then how do they interact with physical objects? Our thoughts and other mental states often seem to be caused by events in the world external to our minds, and our thoughts and intentions seem to make our bodies move. A perception of a glass of wine can be caused by the presence of a glass of wine in front of me, and my desire for some wine plus the belief that there is a glass of wine in front of me can cause me to reach toward the glass. But many think that all physical effects are brought about by purely physical causes: The physical states of my brain are enough to cause the physical event of my reaching toward the glass. So how can my mental states play any causal role in bringing about my actions?

Some dualists react to this by denying that such psychophysical causation really exists (this view is called EPIPHENOMENALISM). Some philosophers have thought that mental states are causally related only to other mental states, and physical states are causally related only to other physical states: The mental and physical realms operate independently. This "parallelist" view has been unpopular in the twentieth century, as have most dualist views. For if we find dualism unsatisfactory, there is another way to answer the question of psychophysical causation. We can say that mental states have effects in the physical world precisely because they are, contrary to appearances, physical states (see Lewis 1966). This is a *monist* view because it holds that there is only one kind of substance, physical or material substance. Therefore it is also known as PHYSICALISM or "materialism."

Physicalism comes in many forms. The strongest form is the form just mentioned, which holds that mental *states* or *properties* are identical with physical states or properties. Sometimes called the "type-identity theory," this view is considered an empirical hypothesis, awaiting confirmation by science. The model for such an identity theory is the identification of properties such as the heat of a gas with the mean kinetic energy of its constituent molecules. Because such an identification is often described as part of the *reduction* of thermodynamics to statistical mechanics, the parallel claim about the mental is often called a "reductive" theory of mind, or "reductive physicalism" (see Lewis 1994).

Because it seems committed to the implausible claim that all creatures who believe that grass is green have one physical property in common—the property identical to the belief that grass is green—many philosophers find reductive physicalism an excessively bold empirical speculation. For this reason (and others), some physicalists adopt a weaker version of physicalism, which holds that all particular objects and events are physical, but that there are mental properties not identical to physical properties. (Davidson 1970 is one inspiration for such views; see ANOMALOUS MONISM.) Such "non-reductive physicalism" is a kind of dualism because it holds there are two kinds of properties, mental and physical, but it is not *substance* dualism because it holds that all substances are physical substances.

Nonreductive physicalism is also sometimes called a "token identity theory" because it identifies mental and physical particulars or tokens, and it is invariably supplemented by the claim that mental properties *supervene* on physical properties. Though the notion can be refined in many ways, SUPERVENIENCE is essentially a claim about the dependence of the mental on the physical: There can be no difference in mental facts without a difference in some physical facts (see Kim 1993; Horgan 1993).

If the problem of psychophysical causation was the whole of the mind-body problem, then it might seem that physicalism is a straightforward solution to that problem. If the only question is, How do mental states have effects in the physical world?, then it seems that the physicalist can answer this by saying that mental states are identical with physical states.

But there is a complication here. For it seems that physicalists can only propose this solution to the problem of psychophysical causation if mental causes are identical with physical causes. Yet if properties or states are causes, as many reductive physicalists assume, then nonreductive physicalists are not entitled to this solution because they do not identify mental and physical properties. This is the problem of MENTAL CAUSATION for nonreductive physicalists (see Davidson 1993; Crane 1995; Jackson 1996).

On the other hand, even if the physicalist can solve this problem of mental causation, there is a deeper reason why there is more to the mind-body problem than the problem of psychophysical interaction. The reason is that, according to many philosophers, physicalism is not the "solution" to the mind-body problem, but something that gives rise to a particular version of that problem. They reason as follows: Because we know that the world is completely physical, if the mind exists, it too must be physical. However, it seems hard to understand how certain aspects of mind—notably, consciousness—could just be physical features of the brain.

How can the complex subjectivity of a conscious experience be produced by the gray matter of the brain? As McGinn (1989) puts it, neurons and synapses seem "the wrong kind" of material to produce consciousness. The problem here is one of intelligibility: Because we know that the mental is physical, consciousness must have its origins in the brain. But how can we make sense of this mysterious fact?

Thomas Nagel (1974) dramatized this in a famous paper, saying that when a creature is conscious, there is something it is *like* to be that creature: There is something it is like to be a bat, but there is nothing it is like to be a stone. The heart of the mind-body problem for Nagel was the apparent fact that we cannot understand *how* consciousness can just be a physical property of the brain, even though we know that in some sense physicalism is true (see also Chalmers 1996).

Some physicalists respond by saying that this problem is illusory: if physicalism *is* true, then consciousness is just a physical property, and it simply begs the question against physicalism to wonder whether this *can* be true (see Lewis 1983). But Nagel's criticism can be sharpened, as it has been by what Frank Jackson calls the "knowledge argument" (Jackson 1982; see also Robinson 1982). Jackson argues that even if we knew all the physical facts about, say, pain, we would not ipso facto know what it is like to be in pain. Someone omniscient about the physical facts about pain would learn something new when they learn what it is like to be in pain. Therefore there is some knowledge— knowledge of WHAT-IT'S-LIKE—that is not knowledge of any physical fact. Hence not all facts are physical facts. (For physicalist responses to Jackson's argument, see Lewis 1990; Dennett 1991; Churchland 1985.)

In late-twentieth-century philosophy of mind, discussions of the mind-body problem revolve around the twin poles of the problem of psychophysical causation and the problem of consciousness. And while it is possible to see these as independent problems, there is nonetheless a link between them, which can be expressed as a dilemma: if the mental is not physical, then how can we make sense of its causal interaction with the physical? But if it is physical, how can we make sense of the phenomena of consciousness? These two questions, in effect, define the contemporary debate on the mind-body problem.

See also CAUSATION; CONSCIOUSNESS, NEUROBIOLOGY OF; EXPLANATORY GAP; QUALIA

—Tim Crane

References

Chalmers, D. (1996). *The Conscious Mind: In Search of a Fundamental Theory.* Oxford: Oxford University Press.

Churchland, P. M. (1985). Reduction, qualia and the direct introspection of brain states. *Journal of Philosophy* 82: 8–28.

Crane, T. (1995). The mental causation debate. *Proceedings of the Aristotelian Society* (supp. vol.) 69: 211–236.

Davidson, D. (1970). Mental events. In L. Foster and J. Swanson, Eds., *Experience and Theory.* London: Duckworth, pp. 79–101.

Davidson, D. (1993). Thinking causes. In J. Heil and A. Mele, Eds., *Mental Causation.* Oxford: Oxford University Press, pp. 1–17.

Dennett, D. C. (1991). *Consciousness Explained.* Harmondsworth: Allen Lane.

Horgan, T. (1993). From supervenience to superdupervenience: Meeting the demands of a material world. *Mind* 102: 555–586.

Jackson, F. (1982). Epiphenomenal qualia. *Philosophical Quarterly* 32: 127–136.

Jackson, F. (1996). Mental causation. *Mind* 105: 377–413.

Kim, J. (1993). *Supervenience and Mind.* Cambridge: Cambridge University Press.

Lewis, D. (1966). An argument for the identity theory. *Journal of Philosophy* 63: 17–25.

Lewis, D. (1983). Mad pain and Martian pain. In D. Lewis, *Philosophical Papers,* vol. 1. Oxford: Oxford University Press, pp. 122–132.

Lewis, D. (1990). What experience teaches. In W. Lycan, Ed., *Mind and Cognition.* Oxford: Blackwell, pp. 499–519.

Lewis, D. (1994). Reduction of mind. In S. Guttenplan, Ed., *A Companion to the Philosophy of Mind.* Oxford: Blackwell, pp. 412–431.

McGinn, C. (1989). Can we solve the mind-body problem? *Mind* 98: 349–366.

Nagel, T. (1974). What is it like to be a bat? *Philosophical Review* 4: 435–450.

Robinson, H. (1982). *Matter and Sense.* Cambridge: Cambridge University Press.

Further Readings

Armstrong, D. M. (1968). *A Materialist Theory of the Mind.* London: Routledge and Kegan Paul.

Campbell, K. (1970). *Body and Mind.* New York: Doubleday.

Churchland, P. M. (1986). *Matter and Consciousness.* Cambridge, MA: MIT Press.

Flanagan, O. (1992). *Consciousness Reconsidered.* Cambridge, MA: MIT Press.

Foster, J. (1991). *The Immaterial Self: A Defence of the Cartesian Dualist Conception of the Mind.* London: Routledge.

Levine, J. (1983). Materialism and qualia: The explanatory gap. *Pacific Philosophical Quarterly* 64: 354–361.

Szubka, T., and R. Warner, Eds. (1994). *The Mind-Body Problem: A Guide to the Current Debate.* Oxford: Blackwell.

Mind Design

See INTRODUCTION: COMPUTATIONAL INTELLIGENCE; INTRODUCTION: PHILOSOPHY; COGNITIVE ARCHITECTURE

Minimalism

Minimalism is the latest (though still programmatic) development of an approach to SYNTAX—transformational GENERATIVE GRAMMAR—first developed by Noam Chomsky in the 1950s and successively modified in the four decades since. The fundamental idea was and continues to be that a sentence is the result of some sort of computation producing a derivation, beginning with an abstract structural representation, sequentially altered by structure-dependent transformations. The Minimalist Program maintains that these derivations and representations conform to an "economy" criterion demanding that they be minimal in a sense determined by the language faculty: no extra steps in derivations, no extra symbols in representations, and no representations beyond those that are conceptually necessary.

As articulated by Chomsky (1995), minimalism can best be understood in juxtaposition to its predecessor, the "Government-Binding" (GB) model of Chomsky (1981, 1982). (It should be pointed out that Chomsky prefers the name "principles and parameters" for the model, reasoning that government and binding are just two among many technical devices in the theory, and not necessarily the most important ones. For some discussion, see Chomsky and Lasnik 1993, a work that can be regarded as the culmination of the GB framework or the beginnings of minimalism.) In that model, there are four significant levels of representation, related by derivation as in following diagram:

(1)   D(eep)-Structure
                    |
           S(urface)-Structure
              /   \
         PF   LF
   (Phonetic Form)   (Logical Form)

Items are taken from the LEXICON and inserted into the D-Structure in accord with their thematic (θ) relations (roughly, *subject of . . . object of . . .* etc.). Transformations alter this D-Structure representation, the movement transformations leaving traces that mark the positions from which movement took place, eventually producing an S-Structure. Transformations of the same character (and arguably the same transformations) continue the derivation to LF, the SYNTAX-SEMANTICS INTERFACE with the conceptual-intentional system of the mind (cf. LOGICAL FORM). Rules of the phonological component continue the derivation from S-Structure to PF, the interface with the articulatory-perceptual system. The portion of the derivation between D-Structure and S-Structure is often called "overt syntax"; that between S-Structure and LF is called "covert syntax" because operations in that portion of the derivation have no phonetic effects, given the organization in (1). Under the traditional view that a human language is a way of relating sound (more generally, gesture, as in SIGN LANGUAGES) and meaning, the interface levels PF and LF are assumed to be ineliminable. Minimalism seeks to establish that these necessary levels of representation are the only levels.

Introduced into syntactic theory by Chomsky (1965), D-Structure was stipulated to be the locus of all lexical insertion, the input to the transformational component, and, most importantly, the representation determining thematic relations, as indicated above. Given traces, already a central part of the GB theory, the role of D-Structure in determining thematic relations becomes insignificant. Being theory internal, the other arguments for its existence disappear under more recent developments of the theory. S-Structure, the terminus of overt syntax within the GB framework, has a number of central properties, particularly concerning abstract case (dubbed "Case" by Chomsky 1980) and binding (structural constraints on anaphoric relations; cf. BINDING THEORY and ANAPHORA).

In a partial return to the technical apparatus of pre-1965 transformational theory (as in Chomsky 1955), minimalism has lexical items inserted "on-line" in the course of the syntactic derivation, roughly in accord with the fundamental notions of X-BAR THEORY and θ-theory. The derivation proceeds bottom-up: the most deeply embedded structural unit is created first, then combined with the head of which it is the complement to create a larger unit, and so on. Consider first the following simplified example (assuming the widely accepted "VP-internal subject hypothesis," under which the subject is initially introduced into the structure inside VP, then moves to an external position):

(2) [$_{IP}$ The woman [$_{I'}$ will [$_{VP}$ t [$_{V'}$ see [$_{DP}$ the man]]]]]

In the derivation of (2), first the noun (N) *man* is combined with the determiner (D) *the* to form the determiner phrase (DP) *the man*. This DP then combines with the verb *see* to produce an intermediate projection V'. (Phrase labels of the X' type, while convenient for exposition, are largely holdovers from earlier models, with no particular significance within the minimalist approach.) The DP *the woman* is created in the same fashion as *the man,* and is combined with the V' to produce the VP. Next, this VP merges with the tense/inflectional element *will* producing I'. The DP *the woman* finally moves to the specifier position of I', yielding the full clausal projection IP. In a more complicated derivation, such as that yielding (3), the derivation of the embedded clause proceeds exactly as in the case of (2):

(3) I think the woman will see the man

(2) has combined with the verb *think* to produce a V', and so on. Notice that the movement of *the woman* to the embedded subject position precedes the merger of the embedded sentence into the larger V', so that there is no one representation following all lexical insertion and preceding all transformations. That is, there is no D-Structure.

On the other hand, S-Structure, persists in one trivial sense: it is the point where the derivation divides, branching toward LF on one path and toward PF on the other. The more significant question is whether it has any of the further properties it has in the GB framework. One of the primary technical goals of the minimalist research program is to establish that these further properties (involving Case and binding, for instance) are actually properties of LF, contrary to previous arguments (as suggested in Chomsky 1986, contra Chomsky 1981). The attempts to attain this goal generally involve more operations attributed to covert syntax than in previous models.

Another technical goal is to reduce all constraints on representation to *bare output conditions,* determined by the properties of the external systems that PF and LF must interface with. Internal to the computational system, the desideratum is that constraints on transformational derivations will be reduced to general principles of economy. Derivations beginning from the same lexical choices (the *numeration,* in Chomsky's term) are compared in terms of number of steps, length of movements, and so on, with the less economical ones being rejected. An example is the minimalist deduction of the Chomsky (1973) *Superiority Condition,* which demands that when multiple items are available for WH-MOVEMENT in a language, such as English, allowing only one item to move, it is the "highest" item that will be chosen:

(4) Who t will read what

(5) *What will who read t.

Economy, in the form of "Shortest Move," selects (4) over (5) because the sentence-initial interrogative position "needs" a *Wh*-expression, and is closer to the subject than it is to the object. Many of the movement constraints falling under the *Relativized Minimality Constraint* of Rizzi (1990) are susceptible to a parallel analysis. This constraint, which had an important impact on the developing Minimalist Program, forbids movement to a position of a certain type: head position, A(rgument type)-position, A' (non-A)-position across an intervening position of the same type. Within the minimalist approach, the effects of this constraint are taken to fall under general economy constraints on derivation.

Theoretical developments in the minimalist direction, many well before minimalism was formulated as a program, have generally led to greater breadth and depth of understanding. Thus there is reason to expect that the Minimalist Program may eventually give rise to an articulated theory of linguistic structure, one that can resolve the traditional tension in linguistic theory between *descriptive adequacy* (the need to account for the phenomena of particular languages) and *explanatory adequacy* (the goal of explaining how linguistic knowledge arises in the mind so quickly and on the basis of such limited evidence).

See also HEAD MOVEMENT; LINGUISTIC UNIVERSALS AND UNIVERSAL GRAMMAR; PARAMETER-SETTING APPROACHES TO ACQUISITION, CREOLIZATION, AND DIACHRONY

—*Howard Lasnik*

References

Chomsky, N. (1955). *The logical structure of linguistic theory.* Harvard University and Massachusetts Institute of Technology. Revised 1956 version published in part by Plenum Press, New York (1975) and by University of Chicago Press, Chicago, (1985).

Chomsky, N. (1965) *Aspects of the Theory of Syntax.* Cambridge, MA: MIT Press.

Chomsky, N. (1973). Conditions on transformations. In S. Anderson and P. Kiparsky, Eds., *A Festschrift for Morris Halle.* New York: Holt, Rinehart and Winston, pp. 232–286.

Chomsky, N. (1980). On binding. *Linguistic Inquiry* 11: 1–46.

Chomsky, N. (1981). *Lectures on Government and Binding.* Dordrecht: Foris.

Chomsky, N. (1982). *Some Concepts and Consequences of the Theory of Government and Binding.* Cambridge, MA: MIT Press.

Chomsky, N. (1986). *Knowledge of Language.* New York: Praeger.

Chomsky, N. (1995). *The Minimalist Program.* Cambridge, MA: MIT Press.

Chomsky, N., and H. Lasnik. (1993). The theory of principles and parameters. In J. Jacobs, A. von Stechow, W. Sternefeld, and T. Vennemann, Eds., *Syntax: An International Handbook of Contemporary Research,* vol. 1. Berlin: Walter de Gruyter, pp. 506–569. Reprinted in Chomsky (1995).

Rizzi, L. (1990). *Relativized Minimality.* Cambridge, MA: MIT Press.

Further Readings

Abraham, W., S. D. Epstein, H. Thráinsson, and C. Jan-Wouter Zwart, Eds. (1996). *Minimal Ideas: Syntactic Studies in the Minimalist Framework.* Amsterdam: Benjamins.

Bošković, Ž. (1997). *The Syntax of Nonfinite Complementation: An Economy Approach.* Cambridge, MA: MIT Press.

Collins, C. (1997). *Local Economy.* Cambridge, MA: MIT Press.

Freidin, R. (1997). Review of Noam Chomsky. *The Minimalist Program, Language* 73:571–582.

Kayne, R. S. (1994). *The Antisymmetry of Syntax.* Cambridge, MA: MIT Press.

Kitahara, H. (1997). *Elementary Operations and Optimal Derivations.* Cambridge, MA: MIT Press.

Lasnik, H. (1993). Lectures on minimalist syntax. University of Connecticut Occasional Papers in Linguistics, 1. Storrs: University of Connecticut.

Lasnik, H., and M. Saito. (1991). On the subject of infinitives. In L. M. Dobrin, L. Nichols, and R. M. Rodriguez, Eds., *Papers from the Twenty-seventh Regional Meeting of the Chicago Linguistic Society.* Pt. 1, *The General Session.* Chicago: Chicago Linguistic Society, University of Chicago, pp. 324–343.

Lasnik, H., and J. Uriagereka. (1988). *A Course in GB Syntax: Lectures on Binding and Empty Categories.* Cambridge, MA: MIT Press.

Uriagereka, J. (1998). *Rhyme and Reason: An Introduction to Minimalist Syntax.* Cambridge, MA: MIT Press.

Watanabe, A. (1996). *Case Absorption and WH-Agreement.* Dordrecht: Kluwer.

Zwart, C. J.-W. (1997). *Morphosyntax of Verb Movement. A Minimalist Approach to the Syntax of Dutch.* Dordrecht: Kluwer.

Minimum Description Length

Minimum message length (MML) is a criterion for comparing competing theories about, or inductive inferences from, a given body of data. A very similar criterion, also to be described, is *minimum description length* (MDL). The basic concept behind both criteria is an operational form of Occam's razor (see PARSIMONY AND SIMPLICITY). A "good" theory induced from some data should enable the data to be encoded briefly. In human terms, a good theory introduces concepts, assumptions, and inference rules or "laws" that, if taken as true, allow much of the data to be deduced.

For example, suppose the data to be measurements of the forces applied to several physical bodies, and their resulting accelerations, where each body is subjected to a number of experiments using different forces. If we propose the concept that each body has a "mass," and the law that acceleration is given by force divided by mass, then the given data may be restated more briefly. If for each body, we state an assumed value for its mass, then for each experiment on that body we need only state the applied force because its acceleration can then be deduced. In practice, matters are a little more complicated: we cannot expect the measured acceleration in each case to equal the deduced value exactly because of inaccuracies of measurement (and because our proposed "law" is not quite right). Thus, for each experiment, the restatement of the data must include a statement of the small amount by which the measured acceleration differs from the deduced value, but if these corrections are sufficiently small, writing them out will need much less space than writing out the original data values.

Note that the restated data are unintelligible to a reader who does not know the "law" we have induced and the body masses we have estimated from the original data. Thus we insist that the restated data be preceded by a statement of whatever theory, laws, and quantities we have inferred and assumed in the restating.

This leads to the idea of a special form of message for encoding data, termed an EXPLANATION. An *explanation* is a message that first states a theory (or hypothesis) about the data, and perhaps also some values estimated for unobserved concepts in the theory (e.g., the masses of the bodies in our example), and that then states the data in a short encoding that assumes the theory and values are correct. Equivalently, the second part of the message states all those details of the data which cannot be deduced from the first part of the message.

The MML principle is to prefer that theory which leads to the shortest explanation of the data. As the explanation contains a statement of the theory as well as the data encoded by assuming the theory, overly complex theories will not give the shortest explanations. A complex theory, by implying much about the data, gives a short second part, but a long first part. An overly simple theory needs only a short first part for its assertion, but has few or imprecise implications for the data, needing a long second part.

Message length can be quantified using INFORMATION THEORY: An event of probability P can be encoded in −log P binary digits, or bits, using base 2 logs. Hence the length of the second part of an explanation is just −log (probability of data given the theory). Also, if a Bayesian "prior probability" over theories is assumed, the length of the first part is −log (prior probability of theory). The shortest explanation then yields the theory of highest posterior probability, as do some other Bayesian methods. However, MML actually achieves a shorter message by choosing a code for theories that, in general, does not provide for all possible theories. Theories so similar that the available data cannot be expected to reliably distinguish between them are amalgamated and represented in the code by a single theory, credited with the sum of their prior probabilities. In particular, when a theory includes a real-valued parameter, only a subset of the possible values for the parameter is allowed for in the code. Although the prior over the parameter must be a density, this amalgamation gives a nonzero prior probability to each of the subset of parameter values. This makes MML invariant under transformations of the parameter space, unlike Bayesian maximum A-posterior density (MAP) methods.

MDL differs from MML in replacing Bayesian coding of theories with coding deemed to be efficient and "natural." In practice, there is usually little difference in the two approaches, but in some cases MML gives better parameter estimates than MDL, which usually relies on *maximum likelihood* estimates.

General theoretical results show MML optimally separates information about general patterns in the data, which appears in the first part, from patternless "noise," which appears in the second part. The method is statistically consistent: if the "true" model of the data is in the set of theories considered, enough data will reveal it. It also is not misleading: If there is no pattern in the data, no theory-based explanation will be shorter than the original statement of the data, thus no theory will be inferred. Successful applications of MML in MACHINE LEARNING include clustering, DECISION TREES, factor analysis, ARMA processes, function estimation, and BAYESIAN NETWORKS.

Message length can also be quantified via Kolmogorov complexity: The information in a given binary string is the length of the shortest input to a TURING machine causing output of the given string. This approach is equivalent to MML, with the set of possible "theories" including all computable functions. Practical applications, while very general, are limited by the undecidability of the "halting problem," although such quantification may provide a basis for a descriptive account of scientific process, which seems to evolve and retain those theories best able to give short explanations.

See also COMPUTATIONAL COMPLEXITY; FORMAL SYSTEMS, PROPERTIES OF; FOUNDATIONS OF PROBABILITY

—Chris Wallace

Further Readings

Barron, A. R., and T. M. Cover. (1991). Minimum complexity density estimation. *IEEE Transactions on Information Theory* 37: 1034–1054.

Dowe, D. L., K. B. Korb, and J. J. Oliver, Eds. (1996). *ISIS: Information, Statistics and Induction in Science.* Singapore: World Scientific.

Kolmogorov, A. N. (1965). Three approaches to the quantitative definition of information. *Problems of Information Transmission* 1: 4–7.

Li, M., and P. M. B. Vitanyi. (1997). *An Introduction to Kolmagorov Complexity and its Applications.* 2nd ed. New York: Springer.

Rissanen, J. (1978). Modeling by shortest data description. *Automatica* 14: 465–471.

Rissanen, J., C. S. Wallace, and P. R. Freeman. (1987). Stochastic complexity: Estimation and inference by compact coding. *J. Statist. Soc.* B49(3): 223–265.

Rissanen, J. (1989). *Stochastic Complexity in Statistical Inquiry.* Singapore: World Scientific.

Solomonoff, R. J. (1964). A formal theory of inductive inference, parts 1 and 2. *Information and Control* 7: 1–22, 224–254.

Wallace, C. S., and D. M. Boulton. (1968). An information measure for classification. *Computer Journal* 11: 185–194.

Mobile Robots

Mobile robots have long held a fascination, from science fiction (*Star Wars'* R2D2 and C3PO, *Forbidden Planet*'s Robby) to science fact. For artificial intelligence researchers, the lure has been to enable a machine to emulate the behavioral, perceptual, and cognitive skills of humans, and to investigate how an artifact can successfully interact, in real time, with an uncertain, dynamic environment. While most research has focused on autonomous navigation and on software architectures for autonomous robots, mobile robots have also been used for investigating planning, MANIPULATION AND GRASPING, learning, perception, human-robot interaction (such as gesture recognition), and robot-robot (multiagent) interaction. Representative applications for mobile robots include service robots (mail delivery, hospital delivery, cleaning), security, agriculture, mining, waste remediation and disposal, underwater exploration, and planetary exploration, such as NASA's *Sojourner* Rover on Mars.

At the most basic level, mobile robots must perceive the world, decide what to do based on their goals and perceptions, and then act. The first two issues are the most challenging: how to reliably perceive the world with uncertain, unreliable sensors, and how to make rational decisions about what to do in the face of UNCERTAINTY about the perceived world and the effects of actions (both the robot's and those of other agents). For example, a mobile robot for the home must perceive furniture, stairs, children, pets, toys, and so on, and decide how to act correctly in a myriad of different situations.

Early work in indoor mobile robots demonstrated some basic capabilities of robots to perceive their environment (e.g., Stanford's CART; Moravec 1983), plan how to accomplish relatively simple tasks (e.g., SRI's Shakey; Fikes, Hart, and Nilsson 1972), and successfully move about in (relatively) unstructured environments. Early outdoor mobile robots, such as Carnegie Mellon's Navlab (Thorpe 1990), demonstrated similar capabilities for on-road vehicles. For these robot systems, speed was not much of an issue, nor was reacting to a dynamically changing environment—it was enough just to operate successfully using a sequential perceive/decide/act cycle in a previously unknown, albeit static, world. These and similar efforts resulted in new planning and plan execution algorithms (e.g., STRIPS; Fikes, Hart, and Nilsson 1972; see also PLANNING), new techniques to perceive the environment (Moravec 1983, 1988), and new software architectures for integrating and controlling complex robot systems (Thorpe 1990).

Starting in the mid-1980s, research focused more heavily on improving capabilities for navigating in more unstructured, dynamic environments, which typically involved handling greater levels of uncertainty. Notable advances were made in perceiving obstacles, avoiding obstacles, and in *map-based navigation* (following a map to get from location to location, without getting lost).

A key component to successful navigation is reliable perception of objects (obstacles) that may impede motion. For indoor mobile robots, a ring of ultrasonic sensors is often used for obstacle detection. These sensors give reasonably good range estimates, and the data can be improved by integrating measurements over time to reduce sensor noise (e.g., the *occupancy grids* of Moravec 1988). Outdoor robots often use stereo vision (see also MACHINE VISION and STEREO AND MOTION PERCEPTION). While computationally expensive, stereo has the advantages of being able to detect objects at greater distances and with good resolution. It also gives three-dimensional data, which is important for outdoor, rough-terrain navigation. Color vision has also been successfully employed, especially to detect boundaries, such as between walls and floors. Other researchers have investigated using lasers (e.g., *Sojourner*), radar, and infrared sensors to detect objects in the environment.

Deciding how to move is often divided into local navigation (obstacle avoidance), for reacting quickly, and global, map-based navigation, for planning good routes. Many techniques have been developed for avoiding obstacles

while continuing to move toward some desired goal. The *potential field* approach (Khatib 1985; Arkin 1989) treats obstacles as repulsive forces and goals as attractors. The vector sum of all forces is used to determine the desired robot heading. This calculation can be done very quickly, enabling robots to avoid moving obstacles, as well. The *vector field histogram* approach (Borenstein 1991) essentially looks for wide openings through which to head. It overcomes some of the problems the *potential field* approach has in dealing with crowded environments. More recently, real-time obstacle avoidance algorithms have been developed that take the robot's dynamics into account, enabling much higher travel speeds (Fox, Burgard, and Thrun 1997). Also, approaches using machine learning techniques to learn how to avoid obstacles have proven effective, especially for high-speed highway travel (Thorpe 1990; see also ROBOTICS AND LEARNING and REINFORCEMENT LEARNING)

Early approaches to global, map-based navigation were based on metric maps—geometrically accurate, usually grid-based, representations. To estimate position with respect to the map, robots would typically use *dead reckoning,* (also called "internal odometry"—measuring position and orientation by counting wheel rotations). Such approaches were not very reliable: Position, and especially orientation, error would gradually increase until the robot was hopelessly lost. (On the other hand, widespread use of the Global Positioning System or GPS and inertial navigation units or INUs have made position estimation a non-issue for many outdoor robots.)

To avoid this problem of "dead reckoning error," and to avoid the need for geometrically accurate maps, researchers developed *landmark-based* navigation schemes (Kuipers and Byun 1993; Kortenkamp and Weymouth 1994). In these approaches, the map is represented as a topological graph, with nodes representing *landmarks* ("important places," such as corridor junctions or doorways) and with arcs representing methods for traveling from landmark to landmark (e.g., "Turn right and travel forward, using local obstacle avoidance"). Each landmark is associated with a set of features that can be used by the robot to determine when it has arrived at that place. Researchers have used both sonar (e.g., to detect corridor junctions) and vision as the basis for defining landmarks (Kortenkamp and Weymouth 1994). Landmark-based navigation can be fairly reliable and is readily amenable to learning a map of the environment. It has difficulties, however, in situations where landmarks can be easily confused (e.g., two junctions very near one another) or where the robot misses seeing particular landmarks.

To combine the best of the metric and landmark-based schemes, some researchers have investigated *probabilistic* approaches that explicitly represent map, actuator, and sensor uncertainty. One approach uses partially observable Markov decision process (POMDP) models to model the robot's state—its position and orientation (Nourbakhsh, Powers, and Birchfield 1995; Simmons and Koenig 1995). The robot maintains a probability distribution over what state it is in, and updates the probability distribution based on Bayes's rule as it moves and observes features (see also HIDDEN MARKOV MODELS). The robot associates actions with either states or probability distributions, and uses its

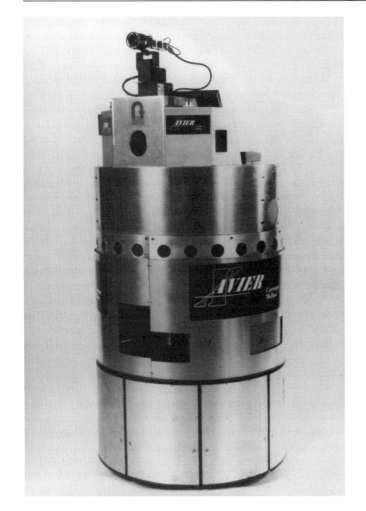

Figure 1.

belief state to decide how to best move. Such probabilistic navigation approaches tend to be very reliable: While the robot may never know exactly where it is, neither does it ever (or rarely) get lost. The approach has been used in an office delivery robot, Carnegie Mellon's Xavier (Simmons et al. 1997; see figure 1), which has traveled over 150 kilometers with a 95 percent success rate, and in a museum tour guide robot, Bonn University's Rhino, which has a greater than 98 percent success rate in achieving its intended tasks.

A sequential perceive/decide/act cycle is often inadequate to ensure real-time response. Mobile robots must be able to do all this concurrently. To this end, much research in mobile robots has focused on *execution architectures* that support concurrent perception, action, and planning (see also INTELLIGENT AGENT ARCHITECTURE). *Behavior-based* architectures consist of concurrently operating sets of behaviors that process sensor information and locally determine the best action to take (Brooks 1986; see also BEHAVIOR-BASED ROBOTICS). The decisions of all applicable behaviors are *arbitrated* using different types of voting mechanisms. Behavior-based systems tend to be very reactive to change in the environment and can be very robust, but it is often difficult to ensure that unintended interactions

among behaviors do not occur. An *executive* (or *sequencer*) is often used to manage the flow of control in robot systems. The executive is typically responsible for decomposing tasks into subtasks, sequencing tasks and dispatching them at the right times, and providing constructs for monitoring execution and handling exceptions (Firby 1987; Gat 1996; Simmons 1994). *Tiered* (or *layered*) architectures integrate planners, an executive, and behaviors in a hierarchical fashion, to enable very complex and reliable behavior (Bonasso et al. 1997). While such layered architectures are relatively new, they have proven to be quite flexible and are rapidly gaining popularity. Other architectural approaches include layers of more and more abstract feedback loops (Albus 1991) and architectures where the role of the planner is to provide schedules that can be guaranteed to run on a real-time system (Musliner, Durfee, and Shin 1993).

See also ANIMAL NAVIGATION; FOUNDATIONS OF PROBABILITY; WALKING AND RUNNING MACHINES

—*Reid G. Simmons*

References

Albus, J. (1991). Outline for a theory of intelligence. *IEEE Transactions on Systems, Man and Cybernetics* 21(3): 473–509.

Arkin, R. (1989). Motor schema-based mobile robot navigation. *International Journal of Robotics Research* 8(4): 92–112.

Bonasso, R. P., R. J. Firby, E. Gat, D. Kortenkamp, D. Miller, and M. Slack. (1997). Experiences with an architecture for intelligent, reactive agents. *Journal of Experimental and Theoretical Artificial Intelligence* 9(2).

Borenstein, J., and Y. Koren. (1991). The vector field histogram: Fast obstacle avoidance for mobile robots. *IEEE Transactions on Robotics and Automation* 7(3): 278–288.

Brooks, R. (1986). A robust layered control system for a mobile robot. *IEEE Journal of Robotics and Automation* RA-2(1).

Fikes, R., P. Hart, and N. Nilsson. (1972). Learning and executing generalized robot plans. *Artificial Intelligence* 3: 1–4.

Firby, R. J. (1987). An investigation into reactive planning in complex domains. In *Proceedings of the Sixth National Conference on Artificial Intelligence,* San Francisco: Morgan Kaufman, pp. 202–206.

Fox, D., W. Burgard, and S. Thrun. (1997). The dynamic window approach to collision avoidance. *IEEE Robotics and Automation* 4(1): 23–33.

Gat, E. (1996). ESL: A language for supporting robust plan execution in embedded autonomous agents. In *Proceedings AAAI Fall Symposium on Plan Execution: Problems and Issues.* Boston, MA: AAAI Press, Technical Report FS-96-01.

Khatib, O. (1985). Real-time obstacle avoidance for manipulators and mobile robots. In *Proceedings IEEE International Conference on Robotics and Automation*, St. Louis, pp. 500–505.

Kortenkamp, D., and T. Weymouth. (1994). Topological mapping for mobile robots using a combination of sonar and vision sensing. In *Proceedings of the Twelfth National Conference on Artificial Intelligence,* Seattle.

Kuipers, B., and Y. Byun. (1993). A robot exploration and mapping strategy based on a semantic hierarchy of spatial representations. *Journal of Robotics and Autonomous Systems* 8: 47–63.

Moravec, H. (1983). The Stanford Cart and the CMU Rover. *Proceedings of the IEEE* 71: 872–884.

Moravec, H. (1988). Sensor fusion in certainty grids for mobile robots. *AI* magazine 9(2): 61–74.

Musliner D., E. Durfee, and K. Shin. (1993). CIRCA: A cooperative intelligent real-time control architecture. *IEEE Transactions on Systems, Man, and Cybernetics* 23(6).

Nourbakhsh, I., R. Powers, and R. Birchfield. (1995). DERVISH: An office-navigating robot. *AI* magazine 16: 53–60.

Simmons, R. (1994). Structured control for autonomous robots. *IEEE Transactions on Robotics and Automation* 10(1): 34–43.

Simmons, R., and S. Koenig. (1995). Probabilistic navigation in partially observable environments. In *Fourteenth International Joint Conference on Artificial Intelligence,* San Francisco: Morgan Kaufman, pp. 1080–1087.

Simmons. R, R. Goodwin, K. Z. Haigh, S. Koenig, and J. O'Sullivan. (1997). A layered architecture for office delivery robots. In *First International Conference on Autonomous Agents.* Marina del Rey, CA.

Thorpe, C., Ed. (1990). *Vision and Navigation: The Carnegie Mellon Navlab.* Norwell: Kluwer.

Further Readings

Arkin, R. (1998). *Behavior-Based Robotics.* Cambridge, MA: MIT Press.

Balabanovic, M., et al. (1994). The winning robots from the 1993 Robot Competition. *AI* magazine.

Brooks, R. (1991). Intelligence without representation. *Artificial Intelligence* 47(1–3): 139–160.

Hinkle, D., D. Kortenkamp, and D. Miller. (1995). The 1995 Robot Competition and Exhibition (plus related articles in same issue). *AI* magazine 17(1).

Jones, J., and A. Flynn. (1993). *Mobile Robots: Inspiration to Implementation.* Wellesley: Peters.

Kortenkamp, D., I. Nourbakhsh, and D. Hinkle. (1996). The 1996 AAAI Mobile Robot Competition and Exhibition (plus related articles in same issue). *AI* magazine 18(1).

Kortenkamp, D., P. Bonasso, and R. Murphy, Eds. (1998). *Artificial Intelligence and Mobile Robots.* Cambridge, MA: MIT Press.

Raibert, M. (1986). *Legged Robots That Balance.* Cambridge, MA: MIT Press.

Simmons, R. (1994). The 1994 AAAI Robot Competition and Exhibition (plus related articles in same issue). *AI* magazine 16(2).

Song, S., and K. Waldron. (1989). *Machines That Walk: The Adaptive Suspension Vehicle.* Cambridge, MA: MIT Press.

Modal Logic

In classical propositional LOGIC all the operators are *truth-functional.* That is to say, the truth or falsity of a complex formula depends only on the truth or falsity of its simpler propositional constituents. Modal logic is concerned to understand propositions about what *must* or *might* be the case. We might, for example, have two propositions alike in truth value, both true say, where one is true and could not possibly be false, while the other is true but might easily have been false. Thus it *must* be that $2 + 2 = 4$, but while it is true that I am writing this entry, it might easily not have been. Modal logic extends the well-formed formulas (wff) of classical logic by the addition of a one-place sentential operator L (or $\Box$), interpreted as meaning "It is necessary that." Using this operator, a one-place operator M (or $\Diamond$) meaning "It is possible that" may be defined as $\sim L\sim$, where $\sim$ is a (classical) negation operator, and a two-place operator

$\dashv$ meaning "entails" may be defined as $\alpha \dashv \beta =_{df} L(\alpha \supset \beta)$, where $\supset$ is classical material implication. In fact, any one of L, M, or $\dashv$ can be taken as primitive, and the others defined in terms of it.

Although Lp is usually read as "Necessarily p," it need not be restricted to a single narrowly conceived sense of "necessarily." Very often, for example, when we say that something *must* be so, we can be taken to be claiming that it *is* so; and if we take L to express "must be" in this sense, we shall want to have it as a principle that whenever Lp is true, so is p itself. A system of logic that expresses this idea will have $Lp \supset p$ as one of its valid formulas. On the other hand, there are uses of words such as "must" and "necessary" that express not what necessarily *is so* but rather what *ought to be so,* and if we interpret L in accordance with these uses, we shall want to allow the possibility that Lp may be true but p itself false because people do not always do what they ought to do. And fruitful systems of logic have been inspired by the idea of taking the necessity operator to mean, for example, "It will always be the case that," "It is known that," or "It is provable that." In fact, one of the important features of modal logic is that out of the same basic material can be constructed a variety of systems that reflect a variety of interpretations of L, within a range that can be indicated, somewhat loosely, by calling L a "necessity operator."

In the early days of modal logic, disputes centered round the question of whether a given principle of modal logic was correct. Typically, these disputes involved formulas in which one modal operator occurs within the scope of another—formulas such as $Lp \supset LLp$. Is a necessary proposition necessarily necessary? A number of different modal systems were produced that reflected different views about which principles were correct. Until the early sixties, however, modal logics were discussed almost exclusively as axiomatic systems without access to a notion of validity of the kind used, for example, in the truth table method for determining the validity of wff of the classical propositional calculus. The semantical breakthrough came by using the idea that a necessary proposition is one true in all possible worlds. But whether another world counts as possible may be held to be relative to the world of origin. Thus an interpretation or *model* for a modal system would consist of a set W of possible worlds and a relation R of *accessibility* between them. For any wff α and world w, $L\alpha$ will be true at w iff α itself is true at every w' such that wRw'. It can then happen that whether a principle of modal logic holds can depend on properties of the accessibility relation. Suppose that R is required to be transitive, that is, suppose that, for any worlds w_1, w_2, and w_3, if w_1Rw_2 and w_2Rw_3, then w_1Rw_3. If so, then $Lp \supset LLp$ will be valid, but if nontransitive models are permitted, it need not be. If R is reflexive, that is, if wRw for every world w, then $Lp \supset p$ is valid. Thus different systems of modal logic can represent different ways of restricting necessity.

It is possible to extend modal logic by having logics that involve more than one modal operator. One particularly important class of multimodal systems is the class of *tense logics.* A tense logic has two operators, L_1 and L_2, where L_1 means "it always will be the case that" and L_2 means "it always has been the case that". (In a tense logic L_1 and L_2

are often written G and H, with their possibility versions as P for ~H~, and F for ~G~.) More elaborate families of modal operators are suggested by possible interpretations of modal logic in computer science. In these interpretations the "worlds" are states in the running of a program. If π is a computer program, then $[\pi]\alpha$ means that after program π has been run, α will be true. If w is any "world," then $wR_{\pi}w'$ means that state w' results from the running of program π. This extension of modal logic is called "dynamic logic."

First-order predicate logic can also be extended by the addition of modal operators. The most interesting consequences of such extensions are those which affect "mixed" principles, principles that relate quantifiers and modal operators and that cannot be stated at the level of modal propositional logic or nonmodal predicate logic. Thus where α is any wff, $\exists xL\alpha \supset L\exists x\alpha$ is valid, but for some wff $L\exists x\alpha \supset \exists xL\ \alpha$ need not be. (Even if a game must have a winner, there need be no one who must win.) In some cases the principles of the extended system will depend on the propositional logic on which it is based. An example is the schema $\forall xL\alpha \supset L\forall x\alpha$ (often known as the "Barcan formula"), which is provable in some modal systems but not in others. If both directions are assumed, so that we have $\forall xL\alpha \equiv L\forall x\alpha$, then this formula expresses the principle that the domain of individuals is held constant as we move from one world to another accessible world.

When identity is added, even more questions arise. The usual axioms for identity easily allow the derivation of $(x = y) \supset L(x = y)$, but should we really say that all identities are necessary? Questions like this bring us to the boundary between modal logic and metaphysics and remind us of the rich potential that the theory of possible worlds has for illuminating such issues. POSSIBLE WORLDS SEMANTICS can be generalized to deal with any operators whose meanings are operations on propositions as sets of possible worlds, and form a congenial tool for those who think that the meaning of a sentence is its truth conditions, and that these should be taken literally as a set of possible worlds—the worlds in which the sentence is true. Such generalizations give rise to fruitful tools in providing a framework for semantical theories for natural languages.

See also LOGICAL FORM; NONMONOTONIC LOGICS; QUANTIFIERS

—*Max Cresswell*

Further Readings

Chellas, B. F. (1980). *Modal Logic: An Introduction.* Cambridge: Cambridge University Press.
Hughes, G. E., and M. J. Cresswell. (1996). *A New Introduction to Modal Logic.* London: Routledge.

Modeling Neuropsychological Deficits

Patterns of cognitive breakdown after brain damage in humans can often be interpreted in terms of damage to particular components of theories of normal cognition developed within cognitive science. Along with the new methods of functional neuroimaging, neurological impairments of cognition provide us with prime evidence about the organization of cognitive systems in the human brain. Yet neuropsychologists have long been aware that the relation between a behaviorally manifest cognitive deficit and an underlying cognitive lesion may be complex. As early as the nineteenth century, authors such as John Hughlings-Jackson (1873) cautioned that the brain is a distributed and highly interactive system, such that local damage to one part can unleash new modes of functioning in the remaining parts of the system. As a result, one cannot assume that a patient's behavior following brain damage is the direct result of a simple subtraction of one or more components of the mind, with those that remain functioning normally. More likely, it results from a combination of the subtraction of some components, and changes in the functioning of other components that had previously been influenced by the missing components. At stake in deciding between these two types of account is not only our understanding of cognition in neurological patients but also the inferences we draw from such patients about the organization of the normal cognitive system.

Computational modeling provides a conceptual framework, and concrete tools, for reasoning about the effects of local lesions in distributed, interactive systems such as the brain (Farah 1994). It has proved helpful in understanding a number of different neuropsychological disorders. In the second part of this article, three examples will be presented of computational models that provide alternative interpretations of a neuropsychological disorder, with correspondingly different implications for theories of normal cognition.

Many of the computational models used in neuropsychology are parallel distributed processing (PDP) models (see COGNITIVE MODELING, CONNECTIONIST and NEURAL NETWORKS), which share certain features with what is known of brain function. These brain-like features include the use of distributed representations, the large number of inputs to and outputs from each unit, the modifiable connections between units, the existence of both inhibitory and excitatory connections, summation rules, bounded activations, and thresholds. Of course, there are many important differences between the computation of PDP models and real brains; for example, even the biggest PDP networks are tiny compared to the brain, PDP models have just one kind of "unit," compared to a variety of types of neurons, and just one kind of activation (which can act excitatorily or inhibitorily) rather than a multitude of different neurotransmitters, and so on. Computational architectures other than PDP, which have fewer patent correspondences to real neural computation, have also been used to mediate inferences between the behavioral impairments of brain-damaged patients and theories of normal cognition. The final example to be summarized here is a production system model (see also PRODUCTION SYSTEMS), which sacrifices some explicit resemblances to brain function in the service of making explicit other key aspects of the theory used to explain patient behavior.

Computational models in neuropsychology, like all models in science, are simplifications of reality, with some theory-relevant features and some theory-irrelevant ones.

Our models allow us to find out what aspects of behavior, normal and pathological, can be explained by the theory-relevant attributes, that is, those that are shared with real brain function. Of course, some behavior may be explainable only with the incorporation of other features of neuroanatomy and neurophysiology not used in current computational models. But this is not a problem for models that already account well for patient data. In such cases, the only worry is that the model's success might depend on some theory-irrelevant simplification. We must be on the lookout for such cases, but also recognize that it is unlikely that the success of most models will happen to depend critically on their unrealistic features.

In closing, I provide pointers to three concrete examples of computational modeling in neuropsychology. Only the barest outlines can be given here of the questions to which the models are addressed, and the mechanisms by which the models provide answers.

Deep Dyslexia: Interpreting Error Types

Patients with a READING disorder known as "deep DYSLEXIA" make two very different types of reading errors, which have been interpreted as indicating that two functionally distinct lesions are needed to account for the reading errors of these patients. Deep dyslexic patients make semantic errors, that is, errors that bear a semantic similarity to the correct word, such as reading *cat* as "dog." They also make visual errors, that is, errors that bear a visual (graphemic) similarity to the correct word, such as reading *cat* as "cot." The fact that both semantic and visual errors are common in deep dyslexia has been taken to imply that deep dyslexic patients have multiple lesions, with one affecting the visual system and another affecting semantic knowledge. However, Hinton and Shallice (1991) showed that a single lesion (removal of units) in an attractor network that has been trained to associate visual patterns with semantic patterns is sufficient to account for these patients' errors. Indeed, they showed that mixtures of error types will be the rule, rather than the exception, when a system normally functions to transform the stimulus representation from one form that has one set of similarity relations (e.g., visual, in which *cot* and *cat* are similar) to another form with different similarity relations (e.g., semantic, in which *cot* and *bed* are similar).

Covert Face Recognition: Dissociation Without Separate Systems

Prosopagnosia is an impairment of FACE RECOGNITION that can occur relatively independently of impairments in object recognition (Farah, Klein, and Levinson 1995; see OBJECT RECOGNITION, HUMAN NEUROPSYCHOLOGY). Recently it has been observed that some prosopagnosic patients retain a high degree of face recognition ability when tested in certain ways ("covert recognition"), while performing poorly on more conventional tasks ("overt recognition") and professing no conscious awareness of face recognition. This has been taken to imply that recognition and awareness depend on dissociable and distinct brain systems (De Haan, Bauer, and Greve 1992). My colleagues and I were able to account for covert recognition with a network consisting of units representing facial appearance, general information

about people, and names, but without any part of the network dedicated to awareness (Farah, O'Reilly, and Vecera 1993). The dissociations between overt and covert recognition observed in three different tasks were simulated by lesioning the visual face representations of the network. Our conclusion was that it is unnecessary to hypothesize separate cognitive components for recognition and awareness of recognition; covert recognition tasks are simply those that can tap the residual knowledge of a damaged visual system.

Frontal Lobe Impairments: Loss of an Executive System, or Working Memory?

Studies of frontal lobe function in nonhuman primates have overwhelmingly focused on WORKING MEMORY, the capacity to hold information "on-line" for an interval of seconds or minutes. By contrast, studies of frontal lobe function in humans have documented a broad array of abilities, including PLANNING, PROBLEM SOLVING, sequencing, and inhibiting impulsive responses (Kimberg, D'Esposito, and Farah 1997). The diversity of abilities affected, and their "high-level" nature, has led many to infer that the cognitive system contains a supervisory "executive," residing in the frontal lobes.

With the animal literature in mind, Dan Kimberg and I wondered whether damage to working memory might produce the varied and apparently high-level behavioral impairments associated with frontal lobe damage (Kimberg and Farah 1993). We used a production system architecture because it makes very explicit the process of weighing different sources of information to select an action. We found that damaging working memory resulted in the system failing a variety of frontal-sensitive tasks, and indeed committing the same types of errors as frontal-damaged patients. This could be understood in terms of the decreased influence of working memory on action selection, and the consequently greater contribution of other influences, including priming of recently executed actions and habit. We concluded that the behavior of frontal-damaged patients does not imply the existence of an executive.

See also COGNITIVE ARCHITECTURE; COGNITIVE MODELING, SYMBOLIC; LEXICON, NEURAL BASIS OF; VISUAL NEGLECT; WORKING MEMORY, NEURAL BASIS OF

—*Martha J. Farah*

References

De Haan, E. H., R. M. Bauer, and K. W. Greve. (1992). Behavioral and physiological evidence for covert face recognition in a prosopagnosic patient. *Cortex* 28: 77–95.

Farah, M. J. (1994). Neuropsychological inference with an interactive brain: A critique of the "locality assumption." *Behavioral and Brain Sciences* 17: 43–61.

Farah, M. J., K. L. Klein, and K. L. Levinson. (1995). Face perception and within-category discrimination in prosopagnosia. *Neuropsychologia* 33: 661–674.

Farah, M. J., R. C. O'Reilly, and S. P. Vecera. (1993). Dissociated overt and covert recognition as an emergent property of a lesioned neural network. *Pychological Review* 100: 571–588.

Hinton, G. E., and T. Shallice, (1991). Lesioning an attractor network: Investigations of acquired dyslexia. *Psychological Review* 98: 74–95.

Hughlings-Jackson, J. (1873). On the anatomical and physiological localization of movements in the brain. *Lancet* 1: 84–85, 162–164, 232–234.

Kimberg, D.Y., M. D'Esposito, and M. J. Farah. (1997). Frontal lobes: Cognitive neuropsychological aspects. In T. E. Feinberg and M. J. Farah, Eds., *Behavioral Neurology and Neuropsychology*. New York: McGraw-Hill.

Kimberg, D. Y., and M. J. Farah. (1993). A unified account of cognitive impairments following frontal lobe damage: The role of working memory in complex, organized behavior. *Journal of Experimental Psychology: General* 112: 411–428.

Modularity and Language

Is language a separate mental faculty? Or is it just part of a monolithic general-purpose cognitive system? The idea that the human mind is composed of distinct faculties was hotly debated in the nineteenth century, and the debate continues today. Genetic disorders such as Williams syndrome show that individuals who cannot count to three or solve simple spatial tasks nevertheless develop remarkable language skills that resemble those of a fully fluent and proficient second-language learner (Bellugi et al. 1993; Karmiloff-Smith et al. 1997). The striking disparity in the levels of attainment of Williams syndrome individuals in different cognitive domains clearly argues for differentiated mental capacities.

Studies of the brain lead to the same conclusion. The left hemisphere of the brain is the language-dominant hemisphere for right-handed individuals. In 1861, Paul BROCA identified the third frontal gyrus of the language-dominant hemisphere as an important language area. Performing autopsies on brain-damaged individuals with expressive difficulties characterized by slow, effortful "telegraphic" speech, he found that their lesions involved the third frontal gyrus, now known as "Broca's area." Using modern neuroimaging techniques, Smith and Jonides (1997) have implicated Broca's area specifically in the rehearsal of material in verbal WORKING MEMORY in normal adults, showing an increase in activation with increasing memory load. Spatial tasks requiring active maintenance of spatial information in working memory do not activate Broca's area in the left hemisphere but rather the premotor cortex of the right hemisphere. Though the overall picture of language representation in the brain is far from clear, the debates today mostly concern, not whether areas specialized for language (or object recognition or spatial relations) exist, but how these areas are distributed in the brain and organized.

In studies of normal adult language processing, modularity is discussed in broad terms where the questions concern the separability of grammatical processing from general cognitive processing and in narrow terms where the questions concern the isolability of distinct components of the grammar. One central question is whether a syntactic parser exists that is concerned only with the construction of syntactic structure in production or the identification of syntactic structure in comprehension. In studies of sentence production, Bock (1989) presents evidence for purely syntactic priming not dependent on semantic content or the particular words in a sentence. In other words, having just produced a sentence with a particular syntactic structure, speakers tend to use that same structure again even under circumstances where there is no semantic relation between the two sentences. This result is expected if syntax is a specialized component of a modular language processor in the narrow sense. Similarly in comprehension, Clifton (1993) has shown that a phrase following an optionally transitive verb is first analyzed as an object of that verb even if semantic properties of the clause dictate that ultimately it must be the subject of a following clause. Both studies provide evidence for the existence of autonomous syntactic structures that participate in language processing.

Laying out a very specific modularity thesis, Fodor (1983) hypothesizes that perceptual, or "input," systems share several important characteristics. They apply only to a limited domain, visual inputs, for example. Only domain-specific information (e.g., visual information) is applied in the input system. The operation of the input system is fast and reflexive (automatic and mandatory). There is limited access to the intermediate representations computed—essentially only the final output of the system is available to other systems. Each input system is biologically determined in the sense that its development exhibits a characteristic pace and sequence, it has an associated neural basis, and when that neural basis is damaged, characteristic deficits result. Fodor claims that language is an input system—it exhibits all of the properties of a perceptual system.

To argue that the language system, or more accurately the grammatical system, is domain-specific, Fodor notes that perceivers integrate auditory and visual information about a speech input, perceiving an "average" when the two conflict. Presented with a videotaped speaker forming a consonant in the back of the mouth ("ga") and a synchronized auditory input "ba," perceivers will integrate the forward (labial) articulation of the "ba" with the evidence about the place of articulation of "ga" from the video and perceive "da"—a sound produced farther back in the mouth than labials such as "ba" but farther forward than sounds such as "ga." This is known as the "McGurk effect" (McGurk and MacDonald 1976). The point about the McGurk effect is that it is not simply a guess on the part of confused perceivers about how they can resolve conflicting perceptual inputs. It is an actual perceptual illusion, as expected if SPEECH PERCEPTION is part of an input system specialized for speech inputs.

The most controversial aspect of Fodor's thesis is the claim that language processing is "informationally encapsulated," that only domain-specific information is consulted within a module. The question is whether the massive effects of nonlinguistic world knowledge actually occur after an initial hypothesis has already been identified within the language module on the basis of purely linguistic knowledge or whether world knowledge can direct the grammatical processing of the input. Word recognition is one area where this debate has been played out.

Word recognition studies demonstrate that both meanings of an ambiguous word are activated (Swinney 1979), at least when the word occurs in a semantically neutral sentence. In a semantically biased sentence favoring the more frequent meaning of the ambiguous word, only the dominant (frequent) meaning of the word is activated, suggesting that perhaps word recognition is not informationally encapsulated. On the other hand, in a sentence biased toward the less frequent meaning of the ambiguous word, *both* the contextually appropriate and the contextually inappropriate meaning of the ambiguous words are activated, as we would expect if word recognition were informationally encapsulated. Proponents of modularity take heart in this latter finding and explain the former finding in terms of the frequent meaning being activated and accepted so quickly that it can inhibit the activation of the less frequent meaning (Rayner and Frazier 1989). Opponents of modularity focus on the former finding and note that it indicates that context can influence word recognition under at least some circumstances (Duffy, Morris, and Rayner 1988, for example).

Ultimately, the survival of Fodor's modularity thesis may depend on its explanatory value. Precisely because a module operates mandatorily and consults only restricted information (identifiable in advance of any particular input), the identification, access, or computation of information can be fast. The grammatical processor's job is a structured and limited one.

If the grammar or grammatical subsystems act as modules, it also becomes less surprising that grammars have the eccentric properties that they do, relying on strict module-internal notions of prominence such as "c-command" (Reinhart 1983), rather than on generally available notions based on, say, precedence, loudness, or the importance of the information conveyed. For many linguists, it is the reappearance within and across languages of the same peculiar notion of prominence or locality that most convincingly argues that grammars form, not loose associations of "biases" or co-occurrence probabilities, but specialized systems or modules.

See also DOMAIN SPECIFICITY; INNATENESS OF LANGUAGE; MODULARITY OF MIND; SPOKEN WORD RECOGNITION; VISUAL WORD RECOGNITION

—*Lyn Frazier*

References

Bellugi, U., S. Marks, A. Bihrle, and H. Sabo. (1993). Dissociation between language and cognitive function in Williams syndrome. In D. Bishop and K. Mogford, Eds., *Language Development in Exceptional Circumstances.* Mawah, NJ: Erlbaum.

Bock, K. (1989). Closed class immanence in sentence production. *Cognition* 31: 163–186.

Clifton, C. (1993). Thematic roles in sentence parsing. *Canadian Journal of Psychology* 47: 222–246.

Duffy, S. A., R. K. Morris, and K. Rayner. (1988). Lexical ambiguity and fixation times in reading. *Journal of Memory and Language* 27: 429–446.

Fodor, J. A. (1983). *Modularity of Mind.* Cambridge, MA: MIT Press.

Karmiloff-Smith, A., J. Grant, I. Berthoud, M. Davies, P. Howlin, and O. Udwin. (1997). Language and Williams syndrome: How intact is "intact"? *Child Development* 68(2): 246–262.

McGurk, H., and J. MacDonald. (1976). Hearing lips and seeing voices. *Nature* 264: 746–748.

Rayner, K., and L. Frazier. (1989). Selection mechanisms in reading lexically ambiguous words. *Journal of Experimental Psychology: Learning, Memory and Cognition* 15: 779–790.

Reinhart, T. (1983). *Anaphora and Semantic Interpretation.* London: Croom Helm.

Smith, E. E., and J. Jonides. (1997). Working memory: A view from neuroimaging. *Cognitive Psychology* 33: 5–42.

Swinney, D. (1979). Lexical access during sentence comprehension: (Re-)consideration of context effects. *Journal of Verbal Learning and Verbal Behavior* 18: 645–659.

Modularity of Mind

Two influential theoretical positions have permeated cognitive science: (1) that the mind/brain is a general-purpose problem solver (NEWELL and Simon 1972; PIAGET 1971); and (2) that it is made up of special-purpose modules (Chomsky 1980; Fodor 1983; Gardner 1985). The concept of modular organization dates back to KANT (1781/1953) and to Gall's faculty theory (see Hollander 1920). But it was the publication of Fodor's *Modularity of Mind* (1983) that set the stage for recent modularity theorizing and which provided a precise set of criteria about what constitutes a module.

Fodor holds that the mind is made up of genetically specified, independently functioning modules. Information from the external environment passes first through a system of sensory transducers that transform the data into formats each special-purpose module can process. Each module, in turn, outputs data in a common format suitable for central, domain-general processing. The modules are deemed to be hardwired (not assembled from more primitive processes), of fixed neural architecture (specified genetically), domain-specific (a module computes a constrained class of specific inputs bottom-up, focusing on entities relevant only to its particular processing capacities), fast, autonomous, mandatory (a module's processing is set in motion whenever relevant data present themselves), automatic, stimulus-driven, and insensitive to central cognitive goals. A further characteristic of modules is that they are informationally encapsulated. In other words, other parts of the mind can neither influence nor have access to the internal workings of a module, only to its outputs. Modules only have access to information from stages of processing at lower levels, not from top-down processes. Take, for example, the Muller-Lyer illusion, where, even if a subject explicitly knows that two lines are of equal length, the perceptual system cannot see them as equal. Explicit knowledge about equal line length, available in what Fodor calls the "central system," cannot infiltrate the perceptual system's automatic, mandatory computation of relative lengths.

For Fodor, it is the co-occurrence of all the properties discussed above that defines a module. Alone, particular properties do not necessarily entail modularity. For instance, automatic, rapid processing can also take place outside input systems such as in skill learning (Anderson 1980). Task-specific EXPERTISE should not be confounded with the Fodorian concept of a module. Rather, each module is like a special-purpose computer with a proprietary database. A Fodorian module can only process certain types of data; it automatically ignores other, potentially competing input. This enhances automaticity and speed of computation by ensuring that the organism is insensitive to many potential classes of information from other input systems and to top-down expectations from central processing. In other words, Fodor divides the mind/brain into two very different parts: innately specified modules and the nonmodular central processes responsible for deductive reasoning and the like.

Fodor's modularity theory had a strong impact on researchers in cognitive development. Until the 1980s BEHAVIORISM and Piaget's constructivism had been dominant forces in development. Both these theories maintain that the infant and child learn about all domains—SYNTAX, SEMANTICS, number, space, THEORY OF MIND, physics, and so forth—via a single set of domain-general mechanisms (the actual types of mechanism invoked are very different in the two theories). By contrast, with Chomskyan linguistics and Fodorian modularity, a sizable number of developmentalists opted for an innately specified, modular view of the infant mind. Not only did Chomskyan psycholinguists argue for the innately specified modularity of syntax (e.g., Smith and Tsimpli 1995; see Garfield 1987; but see also Marslen-Wilson and Tyler 1987 for a different view), but developmentalists also supported a modular view of semantics (Pinker 1994), of theory of mind (Anderson 1992; Baron-Cohen 1995; Leslie 1988), of certain aspects of the infant's knowledge of physics (Spelke et al. 1992; but see Baillargéon 1994 for a different view), and of number in the form of a set of special-purpose, number-relevant principles (Gelman and Gallistel 1978).

Data from normal adults whose brains become damaged from stroke or accident seem to support the modular view (Butterworth, Cipolotti, and Warrington 1996; Caramazza, Berndt, and Basili 1983). Indeed, brain-damaged adults often display dissociations where, say, face processing is impaired, while other aspects of visual-spatial processing are spared, or where semantics is spared in the face of impaired syntax, and so forth. On the other hand, several authors have now challenged these seemingly clear-cut dissociations, demonstrating, for instance, that supposedly damaged syntax can turn out to be intact if one uses on-line tasks tapping automatic processes rather than off-line, meta-linguistic tasks (e.g., Tyler 1992), and that a single underlying deficit can give rise to behavioral dissociations (Farah and McClelland 1991; Plaut 1995).

Evidence from idiots savants (Smith and Tsimpli 1995) and from persons having certain developmental disorders (e.g., Baron-Cohen 1995; Leslie 1988; Pinker 1994) has also been used to lend support to the modularity view. There are, for instance, developmental disorders where theory of mind is impaired in otherwise high functioning people with AUTISM (Frith 1989), or where face processing scores are in the normal range but visuo-spatial cognition is seriously impaired, as in the case of people with Williams syndrome (Bellugi, Wang and Jernigan 1994). These data have led some theorists to claim that such modules must be innately specified because they are left intact or impaired in genetic disorders of development. Yet this claim has also been recently challenged. In almost every case of islets of so-called intact modular functioning, serious impairments within the "intact" domain have subsequently been identified (e.g., Karmiloff-Smith 1998; Karmiloff-Smith et al. 1997), and in cases of purported singular modular deficits, more general impairments have frequently been brought to light (e.g., Bishop 1997; Frith 1989; Pennington and Welsh 1995). In other words, abnormal development does not point to isolated, prespecified modules divorced from the rest of the cognitive, motor, and emotional systems. Genetic impairments affect various aspects of the developmental process, in some domains very subtly and in others more seriously.

In normal development, too, new research is also pointing to gradual specialization rather than prespecification. Take the case of syntax, a particularly popular domain for claimants of modularity. Brain imaging studies of infants and toddlers have shown a changing pattern of HEMISPHERIC SPECIALIZATION (Mills, Coffey-Corina, and Neville 1993, 1994). Initially, the infant processes syntax in various parts of the brain across both hemispheres. It is only with time that parts of the left hemisphere become increasingly specialized. This also obtains for other aspects of language and for face processing in which infant imaging studies using high-density ERPs show progressive localization and specialization (Johnson 1997). The human cortex takes time to structure itself as a function of complex interactions at multiple levels: differential timing of the development of parts of cortex, the predispositions each part has for different types of computation, and the structure of the inputs it receives (for detailed discussion, see for example Elman et al. 1996; Johnson 1997; Quartz and Sejnowsky forthcoming). While there may be prespecification at the cellular level, this does not seem to hold for synaptogenesis at the cortical level. Specialized circuitry and the rich network of connections between cells appear to develop as a function of experience, which challenges the notion of prespecified modules.

Although the fully developed adult brain may include a number of module-like structures, it does not follow that these must be innately specified. Given the lengthy period of human postnatal brain development and what we know about the necessary and complex interaction of the genome with environmental influences (e.g., Elman et al. 1996; Johnson, 1997; Quartz and Sejnowsky 1997; Rose 1997), modules could be the product in adulthood of a gradual developmental process (Karmiloff-Smith 1992), rather than being fully prespecified, as Fodorians maintain. This is not a return to a general-purpose, equipotential view of the infant brain. On the contrary, an alternative to representational nativism (the innate knowledge position on which modularity theory is based) has been proposed by several theorists who have formulated hypotheses about what might be innately specified in terms of computational and timing constraints, while leaving ample room for epigenetic processes (Elman et al. 1996; Quartz and Sejnowsky 1997).

While the concept of prespecified modules has been challenged on a number of fronts, it has also become increasingly clear that the general-purpose view of the brain is inadequate. The human mind/brain is not a single, domain-general processing system, either in infancy or in adulthood. Nor is the alternative a return to simple behaviorism. The genome and sociophysical environment both place constraints on development. A different way to conceive of modularity might therefore be to adopt a truly developmental perspective and acknowledge that the structure of minds could emerge from dynamically developing brains, whether normal or abnormal, in interaction with the environment. The long period of human postnatal cortical development and the considerable plasticity it displays suggest that progressive modularization may arise simply as a consequence of the developmental process. Variations in developmental timing and the brain's capacity to carry out subtly different kinds of computation, together with differential structures in the environmental input, could suffice to structure the brain (Elman et al. 1996; Karmiloff-Smith 1992, 1995; Quartz and Sejnowsky 1997; Rose 1997). Nativists of course recognize that environmental input is essential to trigger developmental processes, but the environment only plays a very secondary role to the genome in such theories. In the alternative framework suggested above, there is no need to invoke innate knowledge or representations to account for resulting specialization, because of variations in developmental timing, different learning algorithms together with information inherent in different environmental inputs would together play a central role in the dynamics of development and in the gradual formation of module-like structures.

See also LANGUAGE, NEURAL BASIS OF; MODULARITY AND LANGUAGE; NAIVE PHYSICS; NEURAL PLASTICITY

—*Annette Karmiloff-Smith*

References

Anderson, J. R. (1980). *Cognitive Psychology and its Implications.* San Francisco: Freeman.

Anderson, M. (1992). *Intelligence and Development: A Cognitive Theory.* Oxford: Blackwell.

Baillargéon, R. (1994). How do infants reason about the physical world? *Current Directions in Psychological Science* 3: 133–140.

Baron-Cohen, S. (1995). *Mindblindness: An Essay on Autism and Theory of Mind.* Cambridge, MA: MIT Press.

Bellugi, U., P. P. Wang, and T. L. Jernigan. (1994). Williams syndrome: An unusual neuropsychological profile. In S. H. Broman and J. Grafman, Eds., *Atypical Cognitive Deficits in Developmental Disorders: Implications for Brain Function.* Hillsdale, NJ: Erlbaum, pp. 23–56.

Bishop, D. V. M. (1997). *Uncommon Understanding: Development and Disorders of Language Comprehension in Children.* Hove, England: Psychology Press.

Butterworth, B., L. Cipolotti, and E. K. Warrington. (1996). Short-term memory impairment and arithmetical ability. *Quarterly Journal of Experimental Psychology: Human Experimental Psychology* 49A(1): 251–262.

Caramazza, A., R. S. Berndt, and A. G. Basili. (1983). The selective impairment of phonological processing: A case study. *Brain and Language* 18: 128–174.

Chomsky, N. (1980). *Rules and Representations.* New York: Columbia University Press.

Elman, J. L., E. Bates, M. H. Johnson, A. Karmiloff-Smith, D. Parisi, and K. Plunkett. (1996). *Rethinking Innateness: A Connectionist Perspective on Development.* Cambridge, MA: MIT Press.

Farah, M. J., and J. L. McClelland. (1991). A computational model of semantic memory impairment: Modality-specificity and emergent category-specificity. *Journal of Experimental Psychology: General* 120: 339–357.

Fodor, J. A. (1983). *The Modularity of Mind.* Cambridge, MA: MIT Press.

Frith, U. (1989). *Autism: Explaining the Enigma.* Oxford: Blackwell.

Gardner, H. (1985). *Frames of Mind: The Theory of Multiple Intelligences.* London: Heinemann.

Garfield, J. L., Ed. (1987). *Modularity in Knowledge Representation and Natural-Language Understanding.* Cambridge, MA: MIT Press.

Gelman, R., and C. R. Gallistel. (1978). *The Child's Understanding of Number.* Cambridge, MA: Harvard University Press.

Hollander, B. (1920). *In Search of the Soul.* New York: Dutton.

Johnson, M. H. (1997). *Developmental Cognitive Neuroscience.* Oxford: Blackwell.

Kant, E. (1781/1953). *Critique of Pure Reason.* Translated N. K. Smith. New York: Macmillan.

Karmiloff-Smith, A. (1992). *Beyond Modularity: A Developmental Perspective on Cognitive Science.* Cambridge, MA: MIT Press.

Karmiloff-Smith, A. (1995). Annotation: The extraordinary cognitive journey from foetus through infancy. *Journal of Child Psychology and Child Psychiatry* 36(8): 1293–1313.

Karmiloff-Smith, A. (1998). Development itself is the key to understanding developmental disorders. *Trends in Cognitive Sciences* 2(10): 389–398.

Karmiloff-Smith, A., J. Grant, I. Berthoud, M. Davies, P. Howlin, and O. Udwin. (1997). Language and Williams syndrome: How intact is "intact"? *Child Development* 68: 246–262.

Leslie, A. M. (1988). The necessity of illusion: perception and thought in infancy. In L. Weiskrantz, Ed., *Thought without language.* Oxford: Oxford University Press.

Marslen-Wilson, W. D., and L. K. Tyler. (1987). Against modularity. In J. L. Garfield, Ed., *Modularity in Knowledge Representations and Natural-Language Understanding.* Cambridge, MA: MIT Press.

Mills, D. L., S. A. Coffey-Corina, and H. J. Neville. (1993). Language acquisition and cerebral specialization in 20-month-old infants. *Journal of Cognitive Neuroscience* 5(3): 317–334.

Mills, D. L., S. A. Coffey-Corina, and H. J. Neville. (1994). Variability in cerebral organization during primary language acquisition. In G. Dawson and K. Fischer, Eds., *Human Behavior and the Developing Brain.* New York: Guilford Press.

Newell, A., and H. Simon. (1972). *Human Problem Solving.* Englewood Cliffs, NJ: Prentice Hall.

Pennington, B. F., and M. C. Welsh. (1995). Neuropsychology and developmental psychopathology. In D. Cicchetti and D. J. Cohen, Eds., *Manual of Developmental Psychopathology,* vol. 1. New York: Wiley, pp. 254–290.

Piaget, J. (1971). *Biology and Knowledge.* Chicago: University of Chicago Press. Originally published 1967.

Pinker, S. (1994). *The Language Instinct.* London: Lane.

Plaut, D. (1995). Double dissociation without modularity: Evidence from connectionist neuropsychology. *Journal of Clinical and Experimental Neuropsychology* 17: 291–231.

Quartz, S. R., and T. J. Sejnowsky. (1997). A neural basis of cognitive development: A constructivist manifesto. *Behavioral and Brain Sciences* 20:537–556.

Rose, S. (1997). *Lifelines: Biology, Freedom, Determinism.* London: Lane.

Smith, N. V., and I. M. Tsimpli. (1995). *The Mind of a Savant: Language Learning and Modularity.* Oxford: Blackwell.

Spelke, E. S., K. Breinlinger, J. Macomber, and K. Jacobson. (1992). Origins of knowledge. *Psychological Review* 99: 605–632.

Tyler, L. K. (1992). *Spoken Language Comprehension: An Experimental Approach to Disordered and Normal Processing.* Cambridge, MA: MIT Press.

Modulation of Memory

Monism

Monte Carlo Simulation

Morality

Moral Psychology

Moral psychology is a branch of ethics. It concerns the features of human psychology whose study is necessary to the examination of the main questions of ethics, questions about what is inherently valuable, what constitutes human well-being, and what justice and decency toward others demand. Adequate examination of these questions requires an understanding of the primary motives of human behavior, the sources of pleasure and pain in human life, the capacity humans have for voluntary action, and the nature of such psychological states and processes as desire, emotion, conscience, deliberation, choice, character or personality, and volition. The study of these phenomena in relation to the main questions of ethics defines the field of moral psychology.

At the heart of this study are questions about the intellectual and emotional capacities in virtue of which human beings qualify as moral agents. Humans, in being capable of moral agency, differ from all other animals. This difference explains why human action, unlike the actions of other animals, is subject to moral assessment and why humans, unlike other animals, are morally responsible for their actions. At the same time, not every human being is morally responsible for his or her actions. Some like the very young and the utterly demented are not. They lack the capacities that a person must have to be morally responsible, capacities that equip people for understanding the moral quality of their actions and for being motivated to act accordingly. Full possession of these capacities is what qualifies a person as a moral agent, and it is the business of moral psychology to specify what they are and to determine what full possession of them consists in.

In modern ethics the study of these questions has largely concentrated on the role and importance of reason in moral thought and moral motivation. The overarching issue is whether reason alone, if fully developed and unimpaired, is sufficient for moral agency, and the field divides into affirmative and negative positions on this issue. Rationalist philosophers, among whom KANT is foremost in the modern period, defend the former. On their view, reason works not only to instruct one about the moral quality of one's actions but also to produce motivation to act morally. Human beings, on this view, are moved by two fundamental kinds of desire, rational and nonrational. Rational desires have their source in the operations of reason, nonrational in animal appetite and passion. Accordingly, moral motivation, on this position, is a species of rational desire, and reason not only produces such desire but is also capable of investing it with enough strength to suppress the conflicting impulses of appetite and passion. Moral agency in human beings thus consists in the governance of appetite and passion by reason, and the possession of reason is therefore alone ordinarily sufficient to make one responsible for one's actions.

The chief opposition to this view comes from philosophers such as HUME and Mill. They deny that reason is ever the source of moral motivation and restrict its role in moral agency to instructing one about the moral quality of one's actions. On this view, all desires originate in animal appetite and passion, and reason works in the service of these desires to produce intelligent action, action that is well aimed for attaining the objects of the desires it serves. Consequently, the primary forms of moral motivation, on this position, the desire to act rightly, the aversion to acting wrongly, are not products of reason but are instead acquired through some mechanical process of socialization by which their objects become associated with the objects of natural desires and aversions. Moral agency in human beings thus consists in cooperation among several forces, including reason, but also including a desire to act rightly and an aversion to acting wrongly that originate in natural desires and aversions. Hence, because the acquisition of these desires and aversions is not guaranteed by the maturation of reason, the possession of reason is never alone sufficient to make one responsible for one's actions.

This anti-rationalist view is typically inspired by, when not grounded in, the methods and theories of natural science as applied to human psychology. In this regard, the most influential elaboration of the view in twentieth century thought is Freud's. Applying the general principles of personality development central to his mature theory, FREUD gave an account of the child's development of a conscience and a sense of guilt that explained the independence and seeming authority of these phenomena consistently with their originating in emotions and drives that humans like other animals possess innately. His account in this way speaks directly to the challenge that the rationalist view represents, for rationalists, such as Kant, make the independence and seeming authority of conscience the basis for attributing the phenomena of conscience, including their motivational force, to the operations of reason.

A second dispute between rationalists and their opponents concerns the nature of moral thought. Rationalists hold that moral thought at its foundations is intelligible independently of all sensory and affective experiences. It is, in this respect, like arithmetic thought at its foundations. Kant's view again sets the standard. In brief, it is that the concepts and principles constitutive of moral thought are formal and universal, that their application defines an attitude of impartiality toward oneself and others, and that through their realization in action, that is, by following the judgments one makes in applying them, one achieves a certain kind of freedom, which Kant called autonomy. This view, unlike Kant's view about moral motivation, which has little currency outside of philosophy, deeply informs various programs in contemporary developmental psychology, notably those of PIAGET and his followers, whose work on moral judgment and its development draws heavily on the formalist and universalist elements in Kant's ethics.

Opponents of this view maintain that some moral thought is embodied by or founded on certain affective experiences. In this respect they follow common opinion. Sympathy, compassion, love, humanity, and attitudes of caring and friendship are commonly regarded as moral responses, and in the views of leading anti-rationalist thinkers one or another of these responses is treated as fundamental to ethics. Accordingly, the cognitions that each embodies or the beliefs about human needs and well-being (or the needs and well-being of other animals) that each presupposes and to which each gives force count on these views as forms of foundational moral thought. Such thought, in contrast to the rationalist conception, is not resolvable into formal concepts and principles, does not necessarily reflect an attitude of impartiality toward oneself and others, and brings through its realization, not autonomy, but connection with others. In contemporary developmental psychology, this view finds support in work on gender differences in moral thinking and on the origins of such thinking in the child's capacity for empathy.

—*John Deigh*

References

Eisenberg, N., and J. Strayer, Eds. (1987). *Empathy and Its Development.* Cambridge: Cambridge University Press.

Freud, S. (1923). *The Ego and the Id.* New York: Norton.

Freud, S. (1931). *Civilization and Its Discontents.* New York: Norton.

Gilligan, C. (1982). *In a Different Voice: Psychological Theory and Women's Development.* Cambridge, MA: Harvard University Press.

Hume, D. (1751). *Enquiry Concerning the Principles of Morals.* Indianapolis: Hackett.

Kant, I. (1788). *Critique of Practical Reason.* Indianapolis: Bobbs-Merrill.

Kohlberg, L. (1981). *Essays on Moral Development,* vol. 1. San Francisco: Harper and Row.

Mill, J. S. (1861). *Utilitarianism.* Indianapolis: Hackett.

Nagel, T. (1970). *The Possibility of Altruism.* Oxford: Oxford University Press.

Piaget, J. (1932). *The Moral Judgment of the Child.* New York: Free Press.

Further Readings

Blum, L. A. (1995). *Moral Perception and Particularity.* Cambridge: Cambridge University Press.

Deigh, J. (1992). *Ethics and Personality: Essays in Moral Psychology.* Chicago: University of Chicago Press.

Deigh, J. (1996). *The Sources of Moral Agency: Essays in Moral Psychology and Freudian Theory.* Cambridge: Cambridge University Press.

Dillon, R. S., Ed. (1995). *Dignity, Character, and Self-Respect.* New York: Routledge.

Flanagan, O. (1991). *Varieties of Moral Personality: Ethics and Psychological Realism.* Cambridge, MA: Harvard University Press.

Flanagan, O., and A. Rorty, Eds. (1990). *Identity Character and Morality: Essays in Moral Psychology.* Cambridge, MA: MIT Press.

Hoffman, M. L. (1982). Development of prosocial motivation: Empathy and guilt. In N. Eisenberg, Ed., *The Development of Prosocial Behavior.* New York: Academic Press, pp. 281–313.

Johnson, M. (1993). *Moral Imagination: Implications of Cognitive Science for Ethics.* Chicago: University of Chicago Press.

May, L., M. Friedman, and A. Clark, Eds. (1996). *Mind and Morals: Essays on Ethics and Cognitive Science.* Cambridge, MA: MIT Press.

Morris, H. (1976). *On Guilt and Innocence: Essays in Legal Theory and Moral Psychology.* Berkeley and Los Angeles: University of California Press.

Rawls, J. (1971). *A Theory of Justice.* Cambridge, MA: Harvard University Press.

Rorty, A. (1988). *Mind in Action: Essays in the Philosophy of Mind.* Boston: Beacon Press.

Rousseau, J.-J. (1763). *Émile.* New York: Basic Books.

Schoeman, F., Ed. (1988). *Responsibility, Character, and the Emotions: New Essays in Moral Psychology.* Cambridge: Cambridge University Press.

Stocker, M. (1990). *Plural and Conflicting Values.* Oxford: Oxford University Press.

Stocker, M. (1996). *Valuing Emotions.* Cambridge: Cambridge University Press.

Strawson, P. F. (1962). Freedom and resentment. *Proceedings of the British Academy* 48: 1–25.

Taylor, G. (1985). *Pride, Shame and Guilt: Emotions of Self-Assessment.* Oxford: Oxford University Press.

Thomas, L. (1989). *Living Morally: A Psychology of Moral Character.* Philadelphia: Temple University Press.

Williams, B. (1981). *Moral Luck.* Cambridge: Cambridge University Press.

Williams, B. (1993). *Shame and Necessity.* Berkeley and Los Angeles: University of California Press.

Wollheim, R. (1984). *The Thread of Life.* Cambridge, MA: Harvard University Press.

Wollheim, R. (1993). *The Mind and its Depths.* Cambridge, MA: Harvard University Press.

Morphology

Morphology is the branch of linguistics that deals with the internal structure of those words that can be broken down further into meaningful parts. Morphology is concerned centrally with how speakers of language understand complex words and how they create new ones. Compare the two English words *marry* and *remarry*. There is no way to break the word *marry* down further into parts whose meanings contribute to the meaning of the whole word, but *remarry* consists of two meaningful parts and therefore lies within the domain of morphology. It is important to stress that we are dealing with meaningful parts. If we look only at sound, then *marry* consists of two syllables and four or five phonemes, but this analysis is purely a matter of PHONOLOGY and has nothing to do with meaningful structure and hence is outside morphology.

The first part of *remarry* is a prefix (*re-*), which means approximately 'again'; it is joined together with the second component, the verb *marry*, to form another verb with the predictable meaning 'marry again'. The same prefix *re-* occurs in many other words (e.g., *reacquaint, redesign, refasten,* and *recalibrate*) and can also be used to form novel words like *redamage* or *retarget* whose meaning is understood automatically by speakers of English. The additional fact that verbs like *reweep or *relike are impossible tells us that there are restrictions on this prefix. It is the morphologist's job to discover the general principles that underlie our ability to form and understand certain complex words but not others.

Languages differ quite greatly in both the complexity and the type of their morphology. Some languages (e.g., Mandarin Chinese and Vietnamese) have very little in the way of morphology. Others (e.g., Turkish, Sanskrit, Swahili, and Navajo) are famous for their complex morphology. English falls somewhere in the middle. It is quite normal for an English sentence to contain no complex words. Even Shakespeare, who is commonly thought of as using complex language, tended to use morphologically simple words. That most famous of Shakespeare's sentences, "To be or not to be, that is the question," is morphologically very simple.

The atomic meaningful units of language are traditionally called *morphemes*. Morphemes are classified into two very basic types: *free morphemes* and *bound morphemes,* the difference between them being that a bound morpheme is defined in terms of how it attaches to (or is bound to) another form (called its *stem*). The most common types of bound morphemes are *prefixes* and *suffixes*. The other major device for forming complex words in English is *compounding,* whereby free morphemes are put together to form a word like *doghouse* or *ready-made*. Although these devices are quite simple, repeated application allows for the formation of fairly complex words by piling one prefix or suffix on another or by successive compounding. The word *unmanageableness* contains three bound morphemes and has been built up in stages from *manage* by first adding the suffix *-able* to produce *manageable*, then the prefix *un-* to form *unmanageable*, and finally the suffix *-ness*, resulting in $[[un[[manage]_V able]_A]_A ness]_N$.

Among the world's languages, suffixation is the most common morphological device and there are quite a few languages (including Japanese, Turkish, and the very large Dravidian family of South India) that have no prefixes but permit long sequences of suffixes. Languages with many prefixes and few or no suffixes are quite rare (Navajo is one example). Some languages use *infixes,* which are placed at a specific place inside their stems. In Tagalog, the national language of the Philippines, for example, the infix *-um-* may be added in front of the first vowel of a stem, after any consonants that may precede it, to mark a completed event. Alongside *takbuh* 'run' and *lakad* 'walk,' we find *tumakbuh* 'ran' and *lumakad* 'walked'. Another internal morphological device is to change a sound in the stem. A fairly small number of English verbs form their past tenses by changing the vowel: *write/wrote, sing/sang, hold/held*. These are irregular in English, because the vast majority of English

verbs form their past tense by suffixation, but in some languages, most prominently the Semitic languages, this type of vowel substitution is normal. Consonants as well as vowels may be altered in a meaningful way. One example of this in English is the relation between nouns like *cloth* that end in voiceless fricatives (in which there is no vibration of the vocal folds) and corresponding verbs like *clothe*, which end in the corresponding voiced fricative sound. Bound morphemes thus modify the sound shape of the words to which they attach, either by adding something to the stem or by changing it. In the limiting case, known as *conversion,* there is no change at all in the shape of the word. This device is very common in English, where basic nouns like *ship* and *sand* are routinely turned into verbs, and verbs like *run* can similarly be turned into nouns.

Linguists distinguish *derivational morphology* from *inflectional morphology*. Derivational morphology, as just discussed, deals with how distinct words (*lexemes*) are related to one another; inflectional morphology is concerned with the different forms that a word may take, depending on its role in a sentence. English is quite poor inflectionally. Nouns have at most a singular and a plural form, and only pronouns have special *case* forms that depend on the role of the word in a sentence; regular verbs have only four distinctive forms, and the different tenses, aspects, and moods are formed by means of auxiliary verbs. But in many other languages, all nouns have distinct case forms, adjectives must often agree with the nouns that they modify, and verbs may have not only distinct forms for each TENSE AND ASPECT, *voice* and *mood,* but may also agree with their subject or object. In Classical Greek, each noun will have 11 different forms, each adjective 30, and every regular verb over 300. Other languages are even more complex in their inflection.

An important difference between morphology and SYNTAX is that morphological patterns vary greatly in their *productivity,* the ease with which new words can be created and understood. If we compare the three English noun-forming suffixes *-ness*, *-ity*, and *-th*, we find that there are many existing nouns ending in *-ness*, a somewhat smaller number ending in *-ity*, and only a dozen or so nouns ending in *-th*. The numbers correlate roughly with the productivity of new words: experiments show that a new noun ending in *-ness* will be more readily accepted as English than a new noun ending in *-ity*, and no new noun in *-th* has been added to the language since about 1600.

The study of productivity shows that the distinct lexemes and their forms comprise a complex network. A major research focus for the experimental study of morphology has been the nature of this network. The prevailing model is that speakers each have a mental LEXICON in which is stored every word of their language, inflected or derived, that has any unpredictable feature. Completely regular words are produced on the fly by productive patterns as they are needed and then discarded. Less productive patterns may also be used, but the words formed in these patterns are less predictable in their meaning and are more likely to be stored once they have been used.

Morphology lies at the heart of language. It interacts with syntax, phonology, SEMANTICS, PRAGMATICS, and the lexicon. Through this interaction, it also relates to numerous aspects of NATURAL LANGUAGE PROCESSING and cognition. Morphology can thus provide a window onto detailed aspects of language and cognition. The more we discover about the rest of language and cognition, the more important the study of morphology will become.

See also BINDING THEORY; LINGUISTIC UNIVERSALS AND UNIVERSAL GRAMMAR; POLYSYNTHETIC LANGUAGES; STRESS, LINGUISTIC; WORD MEANING, ACQUISITION OF

—*Mark Aronoff*

Further Readings

Aronoff, M. (1976). *Word Formation in Generative Grammar.* Cambridge, MA: MIT Press.

Bauer, L. (1983). *English Word-Formation.* Cambridge: Cambridge University Press.

Carstairs-McCarthy, A. (1992). *Current Morphology.* London: Routledge.

Feldman, L. B., Ed. (1995). *Morphological Aspects of Language Processing.* Hillsdale, NJ: Erlbaum.

Matthews, P. H. (1991). *Morphology.* 2nd ed. Cambridge: Cambridge University Press.

Mel'cuk, I. A. (1992). *Cours de Morphologie Générale,* vol. 1. Montreal: Presses de l'Université de Montréal.

Nida, E. A. (1949). *Morphology: The Descriptive Analysis of Words.* 2nd ed. Ann Arbor: University of Michigan Press.

Scalise, S. (1986). *Generative Morphology.* Dordrecht: Foris.

Spencer, A. (1991). *Morphological Theory.* Oxford: Blackwell.

Zwicky, A., and A. Spencer, Eds. (1998). *Handbook of Morphology.* Oxford: Blackwell.

Motion, Perception of

The visual environment of most animals consists of objects that move with respect to one another and to the observer. Detection and interpretation of these motions are not only crucial for predicting the future state of one's dynamic world—as would be necessary to escape an approaching predator, for example—but also provide a wealth of information about the 3-D structure of the environment. Not surprisingly, motion perception is one of the most phylogenetically well conserved of visual functions. In primates, who rely heavily on vision, motion processing has reached a peak of computational sophistication and neuronal complexity.

The neuronal processes underlying perceived motion first gained widespread attention in the nineteenth century. Our present understanding of this topic is a triumph of cognitive science, fueled by coordinated application of a variety of techniques drawn from the fields of COMPUTATIONAL NEUROSCIENCE, ELECTROPHYSIOLOGY, ELECTRIC AND MAGNETIC EVOKED FIELDS, PSYCHOPHYSICS, and neuroanatomy. Most commonly the visual stimulus selectivities of individual neurons are assessed via the technique of SINGLE-NEURON RECORDING, and attempts are made to link selectivities to well-defined computational steps, to behavioral measures of perceptual state, or to specific patterns of neuronal circuitry. The product of this integrative approach has been a broad perspective on the neural structures and events responsible for visual motion perception.

Motion processing serves a number of behavioral goals, from which it is possible to infer a hierarchy of computational steps. An initial step common to all aspects of motion processing is detection of the displacement of retinal image features, a process termed "motion detection." In the primate visual system, neurons involved in motion detection are first seen at the level of primary VISUAL CORTEX (area V1; Hubel and Wiesel 1968). Many V1 neurons exhibit selectivity for the direction in which an image feature moves across the retina and hence are termed "directionally selective." These V1 neurons give rise to a larger subsystem for motion processing that involves several interconnected regions of the dorsal (or "parietal") VISUAL PROCESSING STREAMS (Felleman and Van Essen 1991). Most notable among these cortical regions is the middle temporal visual area, commonly known as area MT (or V5)—a small visual-otopically organized area with a striking abundance of directionally selective neurons (Albright 1993).

Several detailed models have been proposed to account for neuronal motion detection (Borst and Egelhaaf 1993). The earliest was developed over forty years ago to explain motion sensitivity in flying insects. According to this model and its many derivatives, motion is computed through spatiotemporal correlation. This COMPUTATION is thought to be achieved neuronally via convergence of temporally staggered outputs from receptors with luminance sensitivity profiles that are spatially displaced. The results of electrophysiological experiments indicate that a mechanism of this type can account for directional selectivity seen in area V1 (Ganz and Felder 1984).

While motion detection is thus implemented at the earliest stage of cortical visual processing in primates, a number of studies (Shadlen and Newsome 1996) have demonstrated a close link between the discriminative capacity of motion-sensitive neurons at subsequent stages—particularly area MT—and perceptual sensitivity to direction of motion. Using a stimulus in which the "strength" of a motion signal can be varied continuously, Newsome and colleagues have shown that the ability of individual MT neurons to discriminate different directions of motion is, on average, comparable to that of the nonhuman primate observer in whose CEREBRAL CORTEX the neurons reside. In a related experiment, these investigators found that they could predictably bias the observer's perceptual report of motion direction by electrically stimulating a cortical column of MT neurons that represent a known direction. Finally, direction discrimination performance was severely impaired by ablation of area MT. In concert, the results of these experiments indicate that MT neurons provide representations of image motion upon which perceptual decisions can be made.

Once retinal image motion is detected and discriminated, the resultant signals are used for a variety of purposes. These include (1) establishing the 3-D structure of a visual scene, (2) guiding balance and postural control, (3) estimating the observer's own path of locomotion and time to collision with environmental objects, (4) parsing retinal image features into objects, and—perhaps most obviously—(5) identifying the trajectories of moving objects and predicting their future positions in order to elicit an appropriate behavioral response (e.g., ducking). Computational steps and corresponding neural substrates have been identified for many of these perceptual and motor functions.

Establishing 3-D scene structure from motion and estimating the path of locomotion, for example, both involve detection of complex velocity gradients in the image (e.g., rotation, expansion, tilt; see STRUCTURE FROM VISUAL INFORMATION SOURCES). Psychophysical studies demonstrate that primates possess fine sensitivity to such gradients (Van Doorn and Koenderink 1983) and electrophysiological evidence indicates that neurons selective for specific velocity gradients exist in the medial superior temporal (MST) area, and other higher areas of the parietal stream (Duffy and Wurtz 1991).

Establishing the trajectory of a moving object—another essential motion-processing function—is also an area of considerable interest. This task is fundamentally one of transforming signals representing retinal image motions, such as those carried by V1 neurons, into signals representing visual scene motions. Computationally, this transformation is complex (indeed, the solution is formally underconstrained), owing, in part, to spurious retinal image motions that are generated by the incidental overlap of moving objects. Contextual cues for visual scene segmentation play an essential role in achieving this transformation. This process has been explored extensively using visual stimuli that simulate retinal images rendered by one object moving past another (Stoner and Albright 1993). A variety of real-world contextual cues, including brightness differences (indicative of shading, transparency, or differential surface reflectance) and binocular positional disparity ("stereoscopic" cues), have been used in psychophysical studies to manipulate perceptual interpretation of the spatial relationships between the objects in the scene. This interpretation has, in turn, a profound influence upon the motion that is perceived. Electrophysiological experiments have been conducted using stimuli containing similar contextual cues for scene segmentation. Neuronal activity in area MT is altered by context, such that the direction of motion represented neuronally matches the direction of object motion perceived (Stoner and Albright 1992). These results suggest that the transformation from a representation of retinal image motion to one of scene motion occurs in, or prior to, area MT and is modulated by signals encoding the spatial relationships between moving objects.

The final utility of visual motion processing is, of course, MOTOR CONTROL—for example, reaching a hand to catch a ball, adjusting posture to maintain balance during figure skating, or using smooth eye movements to follow a moving target. The OCULOMOTOR CONTROL system is particularly well understood and has served as a model for investigation of the link between vision and action. The motion-processing areas of the parietal cortical stream (e.g., areas MT and MST) have anatomical projections to brain regions known to be involved in control of smooth pursuit EYE MOVEMENTS (e.g., dorsolateral pons). Electrophysiological data linking the activity of MT and MST neurons to smooth pursuit are plentiful. For one, the temporal characteristics of neuronal responses in area MT are correlated with the dynamics of pursuit initiation, suggesting a causal role. MST neurons respond well during visual pursuit; many even do so through the momentary absence of a pursuit target. The latter finding suggests that such neurons receive a "copy" of the efferent motor command, which may be used to interpret retinal motion signals during eye movements, as well as to perpetuate pursuit when the target briefly passes behind an occluding surface. Finally, neuropsychological studies have shown that smooth pursuit is severely impaired following damage to areas MT and MST. In concert, these studies demonstrate that cortical motion-processing areas—particularly MT and MST—forward precise measurements of object direction and speed to the oculomotor system to be used for pursuit generation. Similar visual-motor links are likely to be responsible for head, limb, and body movements.

As evident from the foregoing discussion, basic knowledge of the neural substrates of motion perception has come largely from investigation of nonhuman primates and other mammalian species. The general mechanistic and organizational principles gleaned from this work are believed to hold for the human visual system as well. Neuropsychological studies, in conjunction with recent advances in functional brain imaging tools such as MAGNETIC RESONANCE IMAGING (MRI) and POSITRON EMISSION TOMOGRAPHY (PET), have yielded initial support to this hypothesis. In particular, clinical cases of selective impairment of visual motion perception following discrete cortical lesions have been hailed as evidence for a human homologue of areas MT and MST (Zihl, von Cramon, and Mai 1983). Neuronal activity-related signals (PET and functional MRI) recorded from human subjects viewing moving stimuli have identified a motion-sensitive cortical zone in approximately the same location as that implicated from the effects of lesions (Tootell et al. 1995).

These observations from the human visual system, in combination with fine-scale electrophysiological, anatomical, and behavioral studies in nonhuman species, paint an increasingly rich portrait of cortical motion-processing substrates. Indeed, motion processing is now arguably the most well-understood sensory subsystem in the primate brain. As briefly revealed herein, one can readily identify the computational goals of the system, link them to specific loci in a distributed and hierarchically organized neural system, and document their functional significance in a real-world sensory-behavioral context. The technical and conceptual roots of this success provide a valuable model for the investigation of other sensory, perceptual, and cognitive systems.

See also ATTENTION IN THE HUMAN BRAIN; MACHINE VISION; MID-LEVEL VISION; OBJECT RECOGNITION, HUMAN NEUROPSYCHOLOGY; SPATIAL PERCEPTION; VISUAL ANATOMY AND PHYSIOLOGY

—*Thomas D. Albright*

References

Albright, T. D. (1993). Cortical processing of visual motion. In J. Wallman and F. A. Miles, Eds., *Visual Motion and Its Use in the Stabilization of Gaze.* Amsterdam: Elsevier, pp. 177–201.

Borst, A., and M. Egelhaaf. (1993). Detecting visual motion: Theory and models. In J. Wallman and F. A. Miles, Eds., *Visual*

Motion and Its Use in the Stabilization of Gaze. Amsterdam: Elsevier, pp. 3–26.

Duffy, C. J., and R. H. Wurtz. (1991). Sensitivity of MST neurons to optic flow stimuli, I. A continuum of response selectivity to large-field stimuli. *J. Neurophysiol.* 65(6): 1329–1345.

Felleman, D. J., and D. C. Van Essen. (1991). Distributed hierarchical processing in the primate cerebral cortex. *Cerebral Cortex* 1: 1–47.

Ganz, L., and R. Felder. (1984). Mechanism of directional selectivity in simple neurons of the cat's visual cortex analyzed with stationary flash sequences. *J. Neurophysiol.* 51(2): 294–324.

Hubel, D. H., and T. N. Wiesel. (1968). Receptive fields and functional architecture of monkey striate cortex. *J. Physiol.* 195: 215–243.

Shadlen, M. N., and W. T. Newsome. (1996). Motion perception: Seeing and deciding. *Proc. Natl. Acad. Sci. U.S.A.* 93(2): 628–633.

Stoner, G. R., and T. D. Albright. (1992). Neural correlates of perceptual motion coherence. *Nature* 358: 412–414.

Stoner, G. R., and T. D. Albright. (1993). Image segmentation cues in motion processing: Implications for modularity in vision. *J. Cogn. Neurosci.* 5(2): 129–149.

Tootell, R. B., J. B. Reppas, K. K. Kwong, R. Malach, R. T. Born, T. J. Brady, B. R. Rosen, and J. W. Belliveau. (1995). Functional analysis of human MT and related visual cortical areas using magnetic resonance imaging. *J. Neurosci.* 15(4): 3215–3230.

Van Doorn, A. J., and J. J. Koenderink. (1983). Detectability of velocity gradients in moving random-dot patterns. *Vision Res.* 23: 799–804.

Zihl, J., D. von Cramon, and N. Mai. (1983). Selective disturbance of movement vision after bilateral brain damage. *Brain* 106(2): 313–340.

Motivation

Motivation is a modulating and coordinating influence on the direction, vigor, and composition of behavior. This influence arises from a wide variety of internal, environmental, and social sources and is manifested at many levels of behavioral and neural organization.

As an illustration of motivational influence, consider the cyclical changes in sexual interest and receptivity shown by a female rat (McClintock 1984). Two days following the onset of her last period of sexual receptivity, she encounters one of the male rats with which she shares a communal burrow. The rats sniff each other indifferently and continue on their separate ways. Two days later, their paths cross again. Levels of gonadal hormones in the female's blood (see NEUROENDOCRINOLOGY) have increased markedly since her last encounter with the male, and she now responds in a strikingly different fashion, approaching, nuzzling, and crawling over him. Turning away, she runs a short distance and stops. The male follows hesitantly, but then spies a puddle and stops to drink, appearing to lose interest in the female. Undeterred, the female returns and repeats the pattern of approach and contact followed by turning, running away, and stopping. She soon succeeds in attracting and holding the attention of the male, and he follows her on a tortuous high-speed chase. The female then halts abruptly, and coitus ensues.

During the first encounter, the female treats the male as a neutral stimulus, whereas during the second, she treats him as a valuable goal object. Had he grasped her flanks with his forepaws during the first encounter, the female would have kicked him away, but when he delivers similar sensory stimulation during the second encounter, she responds by adopting a posture that allows him to mount her and mate. During the first encounter, the female's gait is similar to that of the male, whereas during the second encounter, her gait includes a distinctive combination of darts and hops followed by pauses that may be accompanied by vigorous ear wiggling. Finally, her prodding of the male, distinctive motor patterns, and postural response vary in intensity as a function of her hormonal status and recent experience. Such coordinated changes in the evaluation of goal objects (Shizgal forthcoming), the impact of external stimuli, the prepotency of sensorimotor units of action (Gallistel 1980), and the vigor of performance can be said to reflect a common motivational influence; the set of internal conditions responsible for this common influence can be said to constitute a motivational state.

The response of the male to the solicitation of the female illustrates the contribution of external as well as internal inputs to the genesis and maintenance of a motivational state (Bindra 1969). Such external inputs, called "incentive stimuli," are important both to behavioral continuity and change. Positive feedback between incentive stimuli and motivational states tends to lock in commitment to a particular course of action. The more the male interacts with the female, the more he exposes himself to olfactory, tactile, and visual stimuli that increase the likelihood of further interaction. Thus his initial hesitancy gives way to vigorous pursuit. Moreover, sufficiently powerful incentive stimuli incompatible with a current objective can trigger an abrupt, self-reinforcing switch in the direction of the solicited behavior, as when the male rat is sidetracked from slaking his thirst by the intervention of the female.

Motivational states not only modulate the stimulus control of behavior, they also act as intermediaries in its temporal control by transducing internal and external signals indicating the season and time of day into changes in the likelihood of initiating different goal-directed activities. Timing signals make it possible for behavior to anticipate physiological need states, thus lessening the risk that supplies will be depleted and that the physiological imbalance will compromise the capacity of the animal to procure additional resources. For example, migrating birds eat voraciously and greatly increase their body weight prior to their departure. Nonetheless, anticipatory intake may prove insufficient to meet later needs or may exceed subsequent expenditures. Thus the contribution of motivation to the regulation of the internal environment depends both on signals that predict future physiological states and on signals that reflect current ones (Fitzsimons 1979).

To illustrate the regulatory challenges addressed by the motivational modulation of behavior, let us revisit the female rat as she begins to wean her litter, about six weeks after she has mated successfully. The total weight of her pups now exceeds her own. First via her bloodstream and then via her milk, she has succeeded in providing the necessary resources without seriously compromising her own viability. Accomplishing this feat has required dramatic

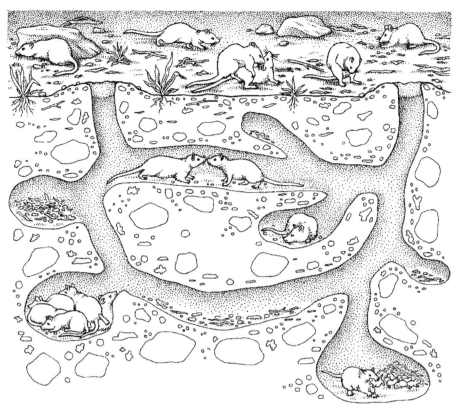

Figure 1. The reproductive behavior of rats illustrates multiple facets of motivational influence (from McClintock 1987). Changes in hormonal status and experience alter the evaluation and selection of goal objects, the impact of external stimuli, the vigor of goal-directed behavior, and the prepotency of sensorimotor units of action.

alteration in her intake patterns. For example, her caloric intake and calcium consumption during lactation will have reached 2–3 times postweaning levels, reflecting both hormonally driven anticipatory changes and feedback from the physiological consequences of increased expenditures (Millelire and Woodside 1989).

The motivational modulation of preferences can extend beyond the point of neutrality, rendering previously repulsive stimuli attractive and vice versa (Cabanac 1971). Prior to her first pregnancy, a female rat will treat a rat pup as an aversive stimulus, positioning herself as far away from it as possible when placed together with the pup in an enclosure. In contrast, when she is in the maternal state, the female will actively retrieve pups, even if they are not her own (Fleming 1986).

Changes in motivational state are expressed at many levels of behavioral and neural organization. For example, the posture adopted by a receptive female rat during copulation reflects the highly stereotyped operation of a spinal reflex (Pfaff 1982). Provided the female is sexually receptive, the reflex can be triggered in response to pressure on the flanks regardless of whether the stimulus is applied by the forepaws of the male rat or the hand of a human. Although facilitation from brain stem neurons is necessary for execution of the reflex (Pfaff 1982), the integrity of the cerebral cortex is not (Beach 1944). In contrast, the organization of the individual components of solicitation into the pattern of approach, contact, withdrawal, and pausing is context-sensitive, flexible (McClintock 1984), and dependent on cortical integrity (Beach 1944). The solicitation behavior of the intact female is directed preferentially at an appropriate

sexual partner, and each of the constituent acts may be varied in intensity and duration or omitted entirely, depending on the response of the male. Following removal of the CEREBRAL CORTEX, components of the behavior survive, but their patterning is disrupted and is no longer well coordinated with the behavior of the male.

At higher levels of behavioral and neural organization, motivational states interact with cognitive processes in influencing behavior. For example, the information directing ongoing behavior may be drawn from COGNITIVE MAPS of the environment rather than from current sensory input (Gallistel 1990; Marlow and Tollestrup 1982; see ANIMAL NAVIGATION). Another point of contact between motivation and cognition is the control of ATTENTION (Simon 1993). Changes in motivational state alter the likelihood that a stimulus will attract attentional resources, and directing these resources at a stimulus can boost its incentive effects (Shizgal 1996). By gating input to WORKING MEMORY, attention can restrict the set from which goals are selected and control the access of goal-related information to the processes involved in PLANNING.

In the examples provided above, the objects of evaluation and goal selection are physical resources and activities. In humans, and perhaps in other animals as well, abstractions can serve as goals and as the objects of evaluation (see MOTIVATION AND CULTURE). For example, our evaluations of ourselves have profound motivational consequences (Higgins, Strauman, and Klein 1986), and our objectives may be defined with respect to current and projected self-concepts (Cantor and Fleeson 1993). Nonetheless, the psychological and neural foundations for such abstract expressions of motivational influence may have much in common with mechanisms, perhaps highly conserved across animal species, that modulate pursuit of concrete biological goals.

Motivational influences are incorporated in some artificial intelligence models. For example, such signals provide contextual information in an important model of REINFORCEMENT LEARNING (Barto 1995), although the manner in which motivational signals are processed to modulate the impact of rewards and to guide action tends to be left unspecified in such models. A hierarchical account of motor control (Gallistel 1980) and recent modeling (Shizgal 1997, forthcoming) of the neural and computational processes underlying goal evaluation and selection (see DECISION MAKING and UTILITY THEORY) represent early steps toward formal description of the motivational influence on behavior.

See also COMPARATIVE PSYCHOLOGY; RATIONAL AGENCY

—*Peter Shizgal*

References

Barto, A. G. (1995). Adaptive critics and the basal ganglia. In J. C. Houk, J. L. Davis, and D. G. Beiser, Eds., *Models of Information Processing in the Basal Ganglia.* Cambridge, MA: MIT Press, pp. 215–232.

Beach, F. A. (1944). Effects of injury to the cerebral cortex upon sexually receptive behavior in the female rat. *Psychosomatic Medicine* 6: 40–55.

Bindra, D. (1969). A unified interpretation of emotion and motivation. *Annals of the New York Academy of Sciences* 159: 1071–1083.

Cabanac, M. (1971). Physiological role of pleasure. *Science* 173: 1103–1107.

Cantor, N., and W. Fleeson. (1993). Social intelligence and intelligent goal pursuit: A cognitive slice of motivation. In W. D. Spaulding, Ed., *Integrative Views of Motivation, Cognition and Emotion.* Lincoln: University of Nebraska Press, pp. 125–179.

Fitzsimons, J. T. (1979). *The Physiology of Thirst and Sodium Appetite,* vol. 35. Cambridge: Cambridge University Press.

Fleming, A. (1986). Psychobiology of rat maternal behavior: How and where hormones act to promote maternal behavior at parturition. *Annals of the New York Academy of Sciences* 474: 234–251.

Gallistel, C. R. (1980). *The Organization of Action: A New Synthesis.* Hillsdale, NJ: Erlbaum.

Gallistel, C. R. (1990). *The Organization of Learning.* Cambridge, MA: MIT Press.

Higgins, E. T., T. Strauman, and R. Klein. (1986). Standards and the process of self-evaluation: Multiple affects from multiple stages. In R. M. Sorrentino and E. T. Higgins, Eds., *Handbook of Motivation and Cognition.* New York: Guilford Press, pp. 23–63.

Marlow, R. W., and K. Tollestrup. (1982). Mining and exploitation of natural deposits by the desert tortoise, *Gopherus agassizii. Animal Behaviour* 30: 475–478.

McClintock, M. K. (1984). Group mating in the domestic rat as a context for sexual selection: Consequences for the analysis of sexual behavior and neuroendocrine responses. In J. Rosenblatt, C. Beer, and R. Hinde, Eds., *Advances in the Study of Behavior.* New York: Academic Press, pp. 1–50.

McClintock, M. K. (1987). A functional approach to the behavioral endocrinology of rodents. In D. Crews, Ed., *Psychobiology of Reproductive Behavior: An Evolutionary Perspective.* Englewood Cliffs, NJ: Prentice Hall.

Millelire, L., and B. Woodside. (1989). Factors influencing the self-selection of calcium in lactating rats. *Physiology and Behavior* 46: 429–439.

Pfaff, D. W. (1982). Neurobiological mechanisms of sexual motivation. In D. W. Pfaff, Ed., *The Physiological Mechanisms of Motivation.* New York: Springer, pp. 287–317.

Shizgal, P. (1996). The Janus faces of addiction. *Behavioral and Brain Sciences* 19(4): 595–596.

Shizgal, P. (1997). Neural basis of utility estimation. *Current Opinion in Neurobiology* 7(2): 198–208.

Shizgal, P. (Forthcoming). On the neural computation of utility: Implications from studies of brain stimulation reward. In D. Kahneman, E. Diener, and N. Schwarz, Eds., *Foundations of Hedonic Psychology: Scientific Perspectives on Enjoyment and Suffering.* New York: Russell Sage Foundation.

Simon, H. A. (1993). The bottleneck of attention: Connecting thought with motivation. In W. D. Spaulding, Ed., *Integrative Views of Motivation, Cognition and Emotion.* Lincoln: University of Nebraska Press, pp. 1–21.

Further Readings

Bindra, D. (1976). *A Theory of Intelligent Behaviour.* New York: Wiley.

Bolles, R. C. (1975). *Theory of Motivation.* New York: Harper and Row.

Dienstbier, R., and W. D. Spaulding, Eds. (1993). *Nebraska Symposium on Motivation.* Vol. 41, *Integrative Views of Motivation, Cognition and Emotion.* Lincoln: University of Nebraska Press.

Mook, D. G. (1996). *Motivation.* 2nd ed. New York: Norton.

Pfaff, D. W., Ed. (1982). *The Physiological Mechanisms of Motivation.* New York: Springer.

Satinoff, E., and P. Teitelbaum, Eds. (1983). *Handbook of Behavioral Neurobiology,* vol. 6, *Motivation.* New York: Plenum Press.

Sorrentino, R. M., and E. T. Higgins, Eds. (1986). *Handbook of Motivation and Cognition.* 3 vols. New York: Guilford Press.

Toates, F. (1986). *Motivational Systems.* Cambridge: Cambridge University Press.

Motivation and Culture

Studies of motivation try to explain the initiation, persistence, and intensity of behavior (Geen 1995; see also MOTIVATION). Culture, learned schemas shared by some people due to common, humanly mediated experiences, as well as the practices and objects creating and created by these schemas, plays a large role in nearly all human behavior. Even such biologically adaptive motivations as hunger and sex instigate somewhat different behaviors in different societies, depending on learned schemas for desirable objects, appropriate and effective ways to obtain these, and skills for doing so (Mook 1987).

The motivational effects of culturally variable beliefs can be illustrated by considering causal attribution processes. Weiner (1991) argues that we are unlikely to persist at a voluntary behavior if we have failed in the past and we attribute that failure to an unchanging and uncontrollable aspect of ourselves or the situation. Some studies show that people in Japan tend to attribute poor academic performance to insufficient effort, while people in the United States give greater weight than do their Japanese counterparts to lack of ability (Markus and Kitayama 1991; Weiner 1991). Given these assumptions, U.S. schoolchildren who receive poor grades should thereafter put less effort into their schoolwork, while Japanese schoolchildren who receive poor grades should increase their effort.

Is there a fixed, limited number of universal basic motives, which vary cross-culturally only in their strength? Or is cross-cultural variation qualitative as well as quantitative, making it impossible to delimit universally applicable basic motives? McClelland (1985; Weinberger and McClelland 1990) has argued for the first position. He has found cross-societal as well as intrasocietal differences in the average levels of such basic motives as achievement and affiliation, and he posits that human as well as other animal behavior is motivated by a limited set of stable, "implicit motives" such as these, which draw on the "natural incentive" of neurohormone release. Cantor and her colleagues (1986), by contrast, focus on idiosyncratically variable self-concepts. These are conscious, change over time, and include a variety of understandings and images, positive and negative roles and behaviors in the past and present as well as various future "possible selves," namely, "those selves that individuals *could* become, would *like* to become, or are *afraid* of becoming" (p. 99). They illustrate the possible variability among such self-conceptions with the example of students preparing for a final examination. One, fearing exposure as a fraud, parties the night before the exam so that no one will attribute her failure to lack of ability. Another, having a feared "careless failure" possible self, studies very hard. The enormous variability among such self-conceptions, even within a single society, suggests the potential for limitless cross-cultural variation. Markus and Kitayama (1991), on the other hand, while continuing to link motivation to self-conceptions, posit a general distinction between societies with conceptions of self as independent of others and societies with conceptions of self as interdependent with others (see also Miller 1997). D'Andrade (1992) likewise advocates the infinite variability position. Discussing the potential for a wide variety of schemas (not just self or conscious schemas) to function as goals, he offers as a classic example from the ethnographic literature the intensity of most Nuers's interest in cattle (Evans-Pritchard 1947).

McClelland proposes (Weinberger and McClelland 1990) that the differences between his approach and that of Cantor et al. (1986) can be resolved by treating them as describing two sorts of motivation. He provides evidence that the implicit motives he discusses are derived largely from preverbal "affective experiences" (such as early parent-child interaction in feeding, elimination control, and so on) and explain behavior over the long term and in less structured situations. In contrast, the explicit self-conceptions discussed by Cantor et al. are acquired with the mediation of language and explain choices in structured tasks, especially ones that make self-conceptions salient.

This categorization of kinds of motivation could be expanded. Neither McClelland's nor Cantor et al.'s model accounts for the sort of behavior that is enacted because it is typical in one's social group, making other behaviors less available for consideration, likely to provoke disapproval, or inconvenient. Examples are body language, table manners and food choices, house design, mode of dress, occupations, and forms of worship. When action follows the patterns learned from repeated observation of the typical behavior of other people like oneself, as well as social facilitation of certain ways of acting over others, it could be said to draw on routine motivation (Strauss and Quinn 1997). In many cases, routine motivation is acquired nonverbally, is internalized as implicit schemas, and is not strongly affectively charged or linked to self-conceptions. Particularly important routine motivations (e.g., schemas for being a good parent or reliable breadwinner), however, may be internalized with an explicit verbal component and linked to emotions (e.g., fear or pride) and self-conceptions, depending on how they were learned.

The different forms of motivation, and various ways in which these are learned, highlight the fact that a culture is not a single thing. In particular, cultures cannot be thought of as master programmers loading up instructions that determine people's behavior. In every society various, not always consistent, values are proclaimed explicitly. Some of these values are the basis for motivations that socializers try to teach children, others are ignored, remaining "cultural clichés" (Spiro 1987; see also Strauss 1992; and Strauss and Quinn 1997). Finally, in addition to motivations that are deliberately instilled, there are needs and expectations derived from preverbal parent-child interactions (McClelland 1985, Weinberger and McClelland 1990, see also Paul 1990), as well as ongoing observations of the normal way of acting in one's social group.

See also DECISION MAKING; RATIONAL CHOICE THEORY; SELF

—*Claudia Strauss*

References

Cantor, N., H. Markus, P. Niedenthal, and P. Nurius. (1986). On motivation and the self-concept. In R. M. Sorrentino and E. T. Higgins, Eds., *Handbook of Motivation and Cognition: Foundations of Social Behavior.* New York: Guilford Press, pp. 96–121.

D'Andrade, R. G. (1992). Schemas and motivation. In R. G. D'Andrade and C. Strauss, Eds., *Human Motives and Cultural Models.* Cambridge: Cambridge University Press, pp. 23–44.

Evans-Pritchard, E. E. (1947). *The Nuer: A Description of the Modes of Livelihood and Political Institutions of a Nilotic People.* Oxford: Clarendon Press.

Geen, R. G. (1995). *Human Motivation: A Social Psychological Approach.* Pacific Grove, CA: Brooks/Cole.

Markus, H. R., and S. Kitayama. (1991). Culture and the self: Implications for cognition, emotion, and motivation. *Psychological Review* 98: 224–253.

McClelland, D. C. (1985). *Human Motivation.* Glenview, IL: Scott, Foresman.

Miller, J. (1997). Cultural conceptions of duty: Implications for motivation and morality. In D. Munro, J. E. Schumaker, and S. C. Carr, Eds., *Motivation and Culture.* New York: Routledge, pp. 178–192.

Mook, D. G. (1987). *Motivation: The Organization of Action.* New York: Norton.

Paul, R. (1990). What does anybody want? Desire, purpose, and the acting subject in the study of culture. *Cultural Anthropology* 5: 431–451.

Spiro, M. E. (1987). Collective representations and mental representations in religious symbol systems. In B. Kilborne and L. L. Langness, Eds., *Culture and Human Nature: Theoretical Papers of Melford E. Spiro.* Chicago: University of Chicago Press, pp. 161–184.

Strauss, C. (1992). What makes Tony run? Schemas as motives reconsidered. In R. G. D'Andrade and C. Strauss, Eds., *Human Motives and Cultural Models.* Cambridge: Cambridge University Press, pp. 197–224.

Strauss, C., and N. Quinn. (1997). *A Cognitive Theory of Cultural Meaning.* Cambridge: Cambridge University Press.

Weinberger, J., and D. C. McClelland. (1990). Cognitive versus traditional motivational models: Irreconcilable or complementary? In E. T. Higgins and R. M. Sorrentino, Eds., *Handbook of Motivation and Cognition.* Vol. 2, *Foundations of Social Behavior.* New York: Guilford Press, pp. 562–597.

Weiner, B. (1991). On perceiving the other as responsible. In R. A. Dienstbier, Ed., *Nebraska Symposium on Motivation, 1990.* Lincoln: University of Nebraska Press, pp. 165–198.

Further Readings

Holland, D., and N. Quinn. (1987). *Cultural Models in Language and Thought.* Cambridge: Cambridge University Press.

Motor Control

To specify a plan of action, the central nervous system (CNS) must first transfer sensory inputs into motor goals such as the direction, amplitude, and velocity of the intended movement. Then, to execute movements, the CNS must convert these desired goals into signals controlling the muscles that are active during the execution of even the simplest kind of limb trajectory. Thus, the CNS must transform information about a small number of variables (direction, amplitude, and velocity) into a large number of signals to many muscles. Any transformation of this type is "ill-posed" in the sense that an exact solution may be either not available or not unique. How the nervous system computes these transformations has been the focus of recent studies.

Specifically, to plan an arm trajectory toward an object, the CNS first must locate the position of the object with respect to the body and represent the initial position of the arm. Recordings from single neurons in the parietal cortex and superior colliculus in awake monkeys have significantly contributed to our understanding of how space is represented. There is some evidence that in the parietal cortical areas there are retinotopic neurons whose activity is tuned by signals derived from somatosensory sources. Their visual receptive field is modified by signals representing both eye and head position. This result suggests that parietal area 7a contains a representation of space in body-centered space. Neurons representing object location in body-independent (allocentric) coordinates have also been found in the parietal cortex and in the HIPPOCAMPUS (Andersen et al. 1993).

To specify the limb's trajectory toward a target, the CNS must locate not only the position of an object with respect to the body but also the initial position of the arm. The conventional wisdom is that proprioception provides information about arm configuration to be used in the programming of the arm's trajectory. However there is experimental evidence indicating that information about the initial position of the limb derives from a number of sources, including the visual afferences (Ghez, Gordon, and Ghilardi 1993).

The current view on the formation of arm trajectories is that the CNS formulates the appropriate command for the desired trajectory on the basis of knowledge about the initial arm position and the target's location. Recent psychophysical evidence supports the hypothesis that the planning of limbs' movements constitutes an early and separate stage of information processing. According to this view, during planning the brain is mainly concerned with establishing movement kinematics, a sequence of positions that the hand is expected to occupy at different times within the extrapersonal space. Later, during execution, the dynamics of the musculoskeletal system are controlled in such a way as to enforce the plan of movement within different environmental conditions.

There is evidence indicating that the planning of arm trajectories is specified by the CNS in extrinsic coordinates. The analysis of arm movements has revealed kinematic invariances (Abend, Bizzi, and Morasso, 1982; Morasso 1981). Remarkably, these simple and invariant features were detected only when the hand motion was described with respect to a fixed Cartesian reference frame, a fact suggesting that CNS planning takes place in terms of the hand's motion in space (Flash and Hogan 1985). Even complex curved movements performed by human subjects in an obstacle-avoidance task displayed invariances in the hand's motion and not in joint motion (Abend et al. 1982). The data derived from straight and curved movements indicate that the kinematic invariances could be derived from a single organizing principle based on optimizing endpoint smoothness (Flash and Hogan 1985). It follows that if actions are planned in spatial or extrinsic coordinates, then for the execution of movement, the CNS must convert the desired direction and velocity of the limb into signals that control muscles.

Investigators of motor control have been well aware of the computational complexities involved in the production of muscle forces. A variety of proposals have been made to explain these complexities. In theory, in a multijoint limb, the problem of generation forces may be addressed only after the trajectory of the joint angles has been derived from the trajectory of the endpoint—that is, after an inverse kinematics problem has been solved. Investigations in robot control in the late 1970s and early 1980s have shown that both the inverse kinematic and inverse dynamic problems may be efficiently implemented in a digital computer for many robot geometries. On the basis of these studies, investigators have argued that the brain may be carrying out inverse kinematic and dynamic computations when moving the arm in a purposeful way.

One way to compute inverse dynamics is based on carrying out explicitly the algebraic operations after representing variables such as positions, velocity acceleration, torque, and inertia. This hypothesis, however, is unsatisfactory because there is no allowance for the inevitable mechanical vagaries associated with any interaction with the environment.

Alternative proposals have been made that do not depend on the solution of the complicated inverse-dynamic problem. Specifically, it has been proposed that the CNS may transform the desired hand motion into a series of equilibrium positions (Bizzi et al. 1984). The forces needed to track the equilibrium trajectory result from the intrinsic elastic properties of the muscles (Feldman 1974).

According to the equilibrium-point hypothesis, as first proposed by Feldman, limb movements result from a shift in the neurally specified equilibrium point. Studies of single and multijoint movements have provided experimental evidence that supports the equilibrium-point hypothesis (Bizzi et al. 1984). The equilibrium-point hypothesis has implications both for the control and for the computation of movements. With respect to control, the elastic properties of the muscles provide instantaneous correcting forces when a limb is moved away from the intended trajectory by some external perturbation. With respect to computation, the same elastic properties offer the brain an opportunity to deal with the inverse-dynamics problem. Once the brain has achieved the ability to represent and control equilibrium postures, it can master movements as temporal sequences of such postures. In this context, a representation in the CNS of the inertial, viscous, and gravitational parameters contained in the equations of motion is no longer necessary.

Recently, a set of experiments performed in frogs with spinal cords that were surgically disconnected from the brain stem has provided neurophysiological support for the equilibrium-point hypothesis. Microstimulation of the spinal cord demonstrated that this region is organized to produce the neural synergies necessary for the expression of equilibrium points. These experiments have indicated that the spinal cord contains circuitry that, when activated, produces precisely balanced contractions in groups of muscles. These synergistic contractions generate forces that direct the limb toward an equilibrium point in space (Bizzi, Mussa-Ivaldi, and Giszter 1991).

Experimental evidence also indicates that microstimulation of the lumbar gray results in a limited number of force patterns. More importantly, the simultaneous stimulation of two sites, each generating a force field, results in a force field proportional to the vector sum of the two fields (Mussa-Ivaldi, Giszter, and Bizzi 1994). Vector summation of force fields implies that the complex nonlinearities that characterize the interactions both among neurons and between neurons and muscles are in some way eliminated. This result has led to a novel hypothesis for explaining movement and posture based on combinations of a few basic elements. The limited-force pattern may be viewed as representing an elementary alphabet from which, through superimposition, a vast number of movements could be fashioned by impulses conveyed by supraspinal pathways. With mathematical modeling, experimenters have verified that this novel view of the generation of movement and posture has the competence required for controlling a wide repertoire of motor behaviors.

The hypothesis that the premotor zones in the spinal gray may be the structures underlying the transformation from extrinsic to intrinsic coordinates is consistent with the results obtained by other groups of investigators, who have demonstrated the existence of a few separate circuits for controlling horizontal and vertical head movements in the owl. These structures, which are located in the brain stem, receive inputs from the tectum and transform the tectal movement vectors into the neck motor-neural activation.

See also MANIPULATION AND GRASPING; MOTION, PERCEPTION OF; MOTOR LEARNING; ROBOTICS AND LEARNING; SINGLE-NEURON RECORDING; WALKING AND RUNNING MACHINES

—*Emilio Bizzi*

References

Abend, W., E. Bizzi, and P. Morasso. (1982). Human arm trajectory formation. *Brain* 105: 331–348.

Andersen, R. A., L. H. Snyder, C.-S. Li, and B. Stricanne. (1993). Coordinate transformations in the representation of spatial information. *Current Opinion in Neurobiology* 3: 171–176.

Bizzi, E., N. Accornero, W. Chapple, and N. Hogan. (1984). Posture control and trajectory formation during arm movement. *Journal of Neuroscience* 4: 2738–2744.

Bizzi, E., F. A. Mussa-Ivaldi, and S. Giszter. (1991). Computations underlying the execution of movement: A biological perspective. *Science* 253: 287–291.

Feldman, A. G. (1974). Change of muscle length due to shift of the equilibrium point of the muscle-load system. *Biofizika* 19: 534–538.

Flash, T., and N. Hogan. (1985). The coordination of arm movements: An experimentally confirmed mathematical model. *Journal of Neuroscience* 5: 1688–1703.

Ghez, C., J. Gordon, and M. F. Ghilardi. (1993). Programming of extent and direction in human reaching movements. *Biomedical Research* 14 (Suppl 1): 1–5.

Masino, T., and E. I. Knudsen. (1990). Horizontal and vertical components of head movement are controlled by distinct neural circuits in the barn owl. *Nature* 345: 434–437.

Morasso, P. (1981). Spatial control of arm movements. *Experimental Brain Research* 42: 223–227.

Mussa-Ivaldi, F. A., S. F. Giszter, and E. Bizzi. (1994). Linear combinations of primitives in vertebrate motor control. *Proceedings of the National Academy of Sciences* 91: 7534–7538.

Motor Learning

Humans are capable of an impressive repertoire of motor skills that range from simple movements, such as looking at an object of interest by turning the head and eyes, to complex and intricate series of movements, such as playing a violin or executing a triple somersault from a balance beam. Most movements are not performed perfectly the first time around, but instead require extensive periods of practice. During practice, we detect errors in motor performance and then modify subsequent movements to reduce or eliminate those errors. The iterative process of improving motor performance by executing movements, identifying errors, and correcting those errors in subsequent movements is called motor learning.

Motor learning occurs in behaviors that range in complexity from simple reflexive movements to highly developed skills. The simplest form of motor learning is adaptation, in which muscular force generation changes to compensate for altered mechanical loads or sensory inputs. Adaptation can involve movements across either a single joint or multiple joints, and can occur in both reflexive and voluntary movements. The best understood example of this type of motor learning is in the vestibulo-ocular reflex, in which EYE MOVEMENTS normally compensate for motion of the head such that images remain stable on the RETINA during head movements. If subjects experience persistent image motion during head movements (e.g., after vestibular trauma or when wearing new corrective lenses), motor learning produces adaptive increases or decreases in compensatory eye movements that restore image stability during head movements.

Motor learning is not a unitary phenomenon, but can affect many different components of sensory and motor processing. MOTOR CONTROL involves both simple movement trajectories and complex series of movements in which multiple muscles and joints must be controlled in precise temporal sequence. Motor learning refines simple movements by altering the magnitude and timing of muscular force generation. For complex movements, motor learning is required to select and coordinate the appropriate muscular contractions, to link together motor subroutines, and to create new motor synergies by combining forces generated across multiple joints in novel spatial and temporal patterns.

Sensory processing is intimately linked with motor learning. Sensory information about the outcome of a movement is used to detect and evaluate errors in motor performance. The nature of the sensory information used can vary and depends on the movement being learned. For example, when one is learning to hit a tennis ball, vision provides the most salient information about the accuracy of the shot, but somatosensory information about the angles of the elbow and wrist and the feel of the ball against the racket also provide important cues. A violin player evaluates his or her performance with the auditory system, by listening for mistakes, and also by monitoring the pressure of strings against fingers. As subjects attempt new movements and refine existing skills, they develop expectations of the sensory consequences of their movements. During motor learning, the expected sensory outcomes of a movement are compared with the actual outcomes, and the difference between what was expected and what actually occurred is used to drive changes in subsequent movements.

The sensory inputs used to detect and correct errors in motor performance can change with practice. At the initial stages of motor learning, a subject may attend to a variety of sensory stimuli, but as learning proceeds, attention becomes restricted to salient sensory stimuli until eventually, as the movement becomes perfected, the reliance on sensory cues can disappear altogether.

The memories formed during motor learning are not accessible to conscious recall, but instead are expressed in the context of motor performance. This type of subconscious recollection of gradually learned skills is called "procedural" (or "implicit") memory and is also a feature of the expression and formation of mental habits. In contrast, the memory of facts and events, which can be learned in a single trial and are subject to conscious recall, is termed "declarative" (or "explicit") memory (see IMPLICIT VS.

EXPLICIT MEMORY and MEMORY). The distinction between procedural and declarative memory was prompted by studies of patients with amnesia caused by dysfunction of the part of the cerebral cortex called the medial temporal lobe. Despite a profound inability to remember the training sessions and other events and facts, amnesiac patients could be trained to learn new motor skills or to improve existing skills with practice. This finding indicates that procedural and declarative memory involve distinct brain areas and mechanisms.

Our knowledge of the brain regions involved in motor learning and memory derives from clinical studies of patients who have neurological diseases, stroke, or other localized brain dysfunction, from brain imaging studies in humans, and from neurophysiological recordings in animal models. A number of distinct brain regions are involved in motor learning. The CEREBELLUM is required for adaptation, for conditioning, and for the learning and coordination of movements that involve multiple joints and muscles. The BASAL GANGLIA are involved in learning sequences of movements, and are also critical for habit formation. Although the studies of amnesiac patients indicate that the medial temporal lobes are not required for motor learning, other cortical regions are clearly involved in the learning of motor skills and the associations of sensory cues with appropriate motor programs. These include primary motor cortex, somatosensory cortex, prefrontal cortex, and the supplementary motor areas. As learning proceeds and motor memories become consolidated, the relative contributions of neuronal activity in the various brain regions involved in motor learning can vary. The precise roles of distinct brain areas in motor learning and the neural mechanisms that underlie the acquisition and retention of motor skills are areas of active investigation in neuroscience.

See also AGING, MEMORY, AND THE BRAIN; LEARNING

—*Sascha du Lac*

References and Further Readings

du Lac, S., J. L. Raymond, T. J. Sejnowski, and S. G. Lisberger. (1995). Learning and memory in the vestibulo-ocular reflex. *Annual Review of Neuroscience* 18: 409–441.

Halsband, U., and H. J. Freund. (1993). Motor learning. *Current Opinion in Neurobiology* 3(6): 940–949.

Hikosaka, O. (1996). MRI in sequence learning. *J. Neurophysiol.* 76(1): 617–621.

Knowlton, B. J., J. Mangels, and L. R. Squire. (1996). A neostriatal habit learning system in humans. *Science* 273(5280): 1399–1402.

Pascual-Leone, A., J. Grafman, and M. Hallett. (1995). Procedural learning and prefrontal cortex. *Annals of the New York Academy of Sciences* 769: 61–70.

Salmon, D. P., and N. Butters. (1995). Neurobiology of skill and habit learning. *Current Opinion in Neurobiology* 5 (2): 184–190.

Shadmehr, R., and H. H. Holcomb. (1997). Neural correlates of motor memory consolidation. *Science* 277(5327): 821–825.

Thach, W. T., H. P. Goodkin, and J. G. Keating. (1992). The cerebellum and the adaptive coordination of movement. *Annual Review of Neuroscience* 15: 403–442.

Ungerleider, L. G. (1995). Functional brain imaging studies of cortical mechanisms for memory. *Science* 270(5237): 769–775.

MRI

See MAGNETIC RESONANCE IMAGING

Multiagent Systems

Multiagent systems are distributed computer systems in which the designers ascribe to component modules autonomy, mental state, and other characteristics of agency. Software developers have applied multiagent systems to solve problems in power management, transportation scheduling, and a variety of other tasks. With the growth of the Internet and networked information systems generally, separately designed and constructed programs increasingly need to interact substantively; such complexes also constitute multiagent systems.

In the study of multiagent systems, including the field of "distributed AI" (Bond and Gasser 1988) and much of the current activity in "software agents" (Huhns and Singh 1997), researchers aim to relate aggregate behavior of the composite system with individual behaviors of the component agents and properties of the interaction protocol and environment. Frameworks for constructing and analyzing multiagent systems often draw on metaphors—as well as models and theories—from the social and ecological sciences (Huberman 1988). Such social conceptions are sometimes applied within an agent to describe its behaviors in terms of interacting subagents, as in Minsky's *society of mind* theory (Minsky 1986).

Design of a distributed system typically focuses on the *interaction mechanism*—specification of agent communication languages and interaction protocols. The interaction mechanism generally includes means to implement decisions or agreements reached as a function of the agents' interactions. Depending on the context, developers of a distributed system may also control the configuration of participating agents, the INTELLIGENT AGENT ARCHITECTURE, or even the implementation of agents themselves. In any case, principled design of the interaction mechanism requires some model of how agents behave within the mechanism, and design of agents requires a model of the mechanism rules, and (sometimes) models of the other agents.

One fundamental characteristic that bears on design of interaction mechanisms is whether the agents are presumed to be *cooperative,* which in the technical sense used here means that they have the same objectives (they may have heterogeneous capabilities, and may also differ on beliefs and other agent attitudes). In a cooperative setting, the role of the mechanism is to coordinate local decisions and disseminate local information in order to promote these global objectives. At one extreme, the mechanism could attempt to *centralize* the system by directing each agent to transmit its local state to a central source, which then treats its problem as a single-agent decision. This approach may be infeasible or expensive, due to the difficulty of aggregating belief states, increased complexity of scale, and the costs and delays of communication. Solving the problem in a *decentralized* manner, in contrast, forces the designer to deal directly with issues of reconciling inconsistent beliefs and accommodating local decisions made on the basis of partial, conflicting information (Durfee, Lesser, and Corkill 1992).

Even among cooperative agents, *negotiation* is often necessary to reach joint decisions. Through a negotiation process, for example, agents can convey the relevant information about their local knowledge and capabilities necessary to determine a principled allocation of resources or tasks among them. In the *contract net protocol* and its variants, agents submit "bids" describing their abilities to perform particular tasks, and a designated contract manager assigns tasks to agents based on these bids. When tasks are not easily decomposable, protocols for managing shared information in global memory are required. Systems based on a *blackboard architecture* use this global memory both to direct coordinated actions of the agents and to share intermediate results relevant to multiple tasks.

In a noncooperative setting, objectives as well as beliefs and capabilities vary across agents. Noncooperative systems are the norm when agents represent the interests of disparate humans or human organizations. Note that having distinct objectives does not necessarily mean that the agents are adversarial or even averse to cooperation. It merely means that agents cooperate exactly when they determine that it is in their individual interests to do so.

The standard assumption for noncooperative multiagent systems is that agents behave according to principles of RATIONAL DECISION MAKING. That is, each agent acts to further its individual objectives (typically characterized in terms of UTILITY THEORY), subject to its beliefs and capabilities. In this case, the problem of designing an interaction mechanism corresponds to the standard economic concept of *mechanism design,* and the mathematical tools of GAME THEORY apply. Much current work in multiagent systems is devoted to game-theoretic analyses of interaction mechanisms, and especially negotiation protocols applied within such mechanisms (Rosenschein and Zlotkin 1994). Economic concepts expressly drive the design of multiagent interaction mechanisms based on market price systems (Clearwater 1996).

Both cooperative and noncooperative agents may derive some benefit by reasoning expressly about the other agents. Cooperative agents may be able to propose more effective joint plans if they know the capabilities and intentions of the other agents. Noncooperative agents can improve their bargaining positions through awareness of the options and preferences of others (agents that exploit such bargaining power are called "strategic"; those that neglect to do so are "competitive"). Because direct knowledge of other agents may be difficult to come by, agents typically induce their models of others from observations (e.g., "plan recognition"), within an interaction or across repeated interactions.

See also AI AND EDUCATION; COGNITIVE ARTIFACTS; HUMAN-COMPUTER INTERACTION; RATIONAL AGENCY

—*Michael P. Wellman*

References

Bond, A. H., and L. Gasser, Eds. (1988). *Readings in Distributed Artificial Intelligence*. San Francisco: Kaufmann.

Clearwater, S. H., Ed. (1996). *Market-Based Control: A Paradigm for Distributed Resource Allocation.* Singapore: World Scientific.

Durfee, E. H., V. R. Lesser, and D. D. Corkill. (1992). Distributed problem solving. In *Encyclopedia of Artificial Intelligence.* 2nd ed. New York: Wiley.

Huberman, B. A., Ed. (1988). *The Ecology of Computation.* Amsterdam: Elsevier.

Huhns, M., and M. Singh, Eds. (1997). *Readings in Agents.* San Francisco: Kaufmann.

Minsky, M. (1986). *The Society of Mind.* New York: Simon and Schuster.

Rosenschein, J. S., and G. Zlotkin. (1994). *Rules of Encounter: Designing Conventions for Automated Negotiation among Computers.* Cambridge, MA: MIT Press.

Multisensory Integration

Because of its importance in forming an appropriate picture of the external world, the representation of sensory information has been a powerful driving force in EVOLUTION. Extant organisms possess an impressive array of specialized sensory systems that allow them to monitor simultaneously a host of environmental cues. This "parallel" processing of multiple cues not only increases the probability of detecting a given stimulus but, because the information carried along each sensory channel reflects a different feature of that stimulus, it also increases the likelihood of its accurate identification. For example, stimuli that are similar along one physical dimension (how they sound) might be identified on the basis of a second dimension (how they look). But if a coherent representation of the external world is to be constructed, and if the appropriate responses are to be generated, the brain must synthesize the information originating from these different sensory channels. One way in which such a multimodal representation is generated is by having information from different sensory systems converge on a common group of neurons.

During the evolution of sensory systems, mechanisms were preserved or elaborated so that the combined action of sensory systems would provide information not available within any single sensory channel. Indeed, in many circumstances, events are more readily perceived, have less ambiguity, and elicit a response far more rapidly when signaled by the coordinated action of multiple sensory modalities. Sensory systems have evolved to work in concert, and normally, different sensory cues that originate from the same event are concordant in both space and time. The products of this spatial and temporal coherence are synergistic intersensory interactions within the central nervous system (CNS), interactions that are presumed to enhance the salience of the initiating event. For example, seeing a speaker's face makes the spoken message far easier to understand, especially in a noisy room (Sumby and Pollack 1954).

Similarly, discordant cues from different modalities can have powerful effects on perception, as illustrated by a host of interesting cross-modal illusions. One of the most compelling of these is the so-called McGurk effect, wherein a speaker lip-synchs the syllable "ga" in time with the sound "ba" (McGurk and MacDonald 1976). The perception is of neither "ga" nor "ba," but a synthesis of the two, "da." Similarly, in the "ventriloquism effect," the sight of movement (i.e., the dummy's head and lips) compels one to believe it is also the source of the sound.

Multisensory neurons, which receive input from more than a single sensory modality, are found in many areas of the CNS (see Stein and Meredith 1993 for a review). These neurons are involved in a number of circuits, and presumably in a variety of cognitive and behavioral functions. Thus, for example, multisensory neurons in neocortex are likely participants in the perceptual, mnemonic, and associative processes that serve to bind together the modality-specific components of a multisensory experience. Still other multisensory neurons, positioned at the sensorimotor interface, are known to mediate goal-directed orientation behavior. Such neurons, a high incidence of which are found in the superior colliculus (SC), have been the most extensively studied, and serve as the model for deciphering how multiple sensory cues are integrated at the level of the single neuron (see Stein and Meredith 1993 for review). Visual, auditory, and somatosensory inputs converge on individual neurons in the SC, where each of these modalities is represented in a common coordinate frame. As a result, the modality-specific receptive fields of an individual multisensory neuron represent similar regions of space.

An example of an SC neuron's ability to integrate two different sensory inputs is illustrated in figure 1. When presented simultaneously and paired within their receptive fields, a visual and auditory stimulus result in a substantial response enhancement, well above the sum of the two individual responses (see A_1V). Conversely, when the auditory stimulus is presented outside its receptive field, the neuron's ability to generate a vigorous response to the visual stimulus is suppressed (see A_2V). The timing of these stimuli is critical, and the magnitude of their interaction changes when the interval between the two stimuli is manipulated (Meredith and Stein 1986). However, this interval or "temporal window" generally is quite broad (e.g., several hundred milliseconds).

The multisensory interactions that are observable at the level of the single neuron are reflected in the animal's behavior (Stein et al. 1989). Thus, its ability to detect and orient toward a visual stimulus is markedly enhanced when it is paired with a neutral auditory cue at the same position in space. However, if the auditory cue is spatially disparate from the visual, the response is strongly degraded.

Although SC neurons can respond to different sensory stimuli via inputs from a variety of structures, their ability to integrate multisensory information depends on projections from a specific region of neocortex (Wallace and Stein 1994). If these inputs from cortex are removed, SC neurons continue to respond to stimuli from different sensory modalities but fail to exhibit the synergistic interactions that characterize multisensory integration. At the behavioral level, animals can still orient normally to unimodal cues, but the benefit derived from combined cues is markedly diminished (Wilkinson, Meredith, and Stein 1996). This intimate relationship between cortex and SC suggests that the higher-level cognitive functions of the neocortex play a substantial role in controlling the information-processing capability of multisensory neurons in the SC, as well as the overt behaviors they mediate.

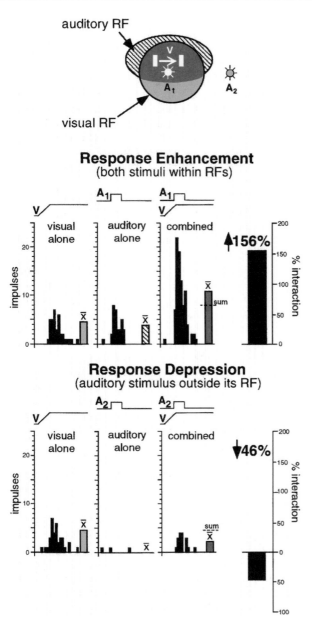

Figure 1. Multisensory integration in a visual-auditory SC neuron. The two receptive fields (RFs) of this neuron (dark gray shading shows the region of their overlap) are shown at the top. Icons depict stimuli: visual (V) is a moving bar of light, auditory is a broad-band noise burst from a speaker either within (A1), or outside (A2) the RF. Below, peristimulus time histograms and bar graphs (means) show responses to the visual stimulus alone (movement is represented by a ramp), the within-field auditory stimulus alone (square wave), and the stimulus combination. The summary bar graph shows that the large response enhancement is greater than the sum of A+V. The bottom panel illustrates the inhibition of the visual response when the auditory stimulus is outside its RF.

At present, comparatively little is known about the multisensory integrative properties of the cortical multisensory neurons presumed to be involved in various aspects of perception. However, they have been shown to share some of the features of SC neurons (Wallace, Meredith, and Stein 1992). Future studies detailing their response properties and associated circuitry should greatly aid in our understanding of how multisensory information is used in higher cognitive functions and, in doing so, reveal the neural basis of a fully integrated multisensory experience.

See also BINDING PROBLEM; CONSCIOUSNESS, NEUROBIOLOGY OF; MODULARITY OF MIND

—*Barry E. Stein, Terrence R. Stanford, J. William Vaughan, and Mark T. Wallace*

References

McGurk, H., and J. MacDonald. (1976). Hearing lips and seeing voices. *Nature* 264: 746–748.

Meredith, M. A., and B. E. Stein. (1986). Visual, auditory and somatosensory convergence on cells in superior colliculus results in multisensory integration. *J. Neurophysiol.* 56: 640–662.

Stein, B. E., and M. A. Meredith. (1993). *The Merging of the Senses.* Cambridge, MA: MIT Press.

Stein, B. E., M. A. Meredith, W. S. Huneycutt, and L. McDade. (1989). Behavioral indices of multisensory integration: orientation to visual cues is affected by auditory stimuli. *J. Cogn. Neurosci.* 1: 12–24.

Sumby, W. H., and I. Pollack. (1954). Visual contribution to speech intelligibility in noise. *J. Acoust. Soc. Am.* 26: 212–215.

Wallace, M. T., M. A. Meredith, and B. E. Stein. (1992). Integration of multiple sensory modalities in cat cortex. *Exp. Brain Res.* 91: 484–488.

Wallace, M. T., and B. E. Stein. (1994). Cross-modal synthesis in the midbrain depends on input from cortex. *J. Neurophysiol.* 71: 429–432.

Wilkinson, L. K., M. A. Meredith, and B. E. Stein. (1996). The role of anterior ectosylvian cortex in cross-modality orientation and approach behavior. *Exp. Brain Res.* 112:1–10.

Further Readings

Cytowic, R. E. (1989). *Synesthesia: A Union of the Senses.* New York: Springer-Verlag.

Lewkowicz, D. J., and R. Lickliter. (1994). *The Development of Intersensory Perception: Comparative Perspectives.* Hillsdale, NJ: Erlbaum.

Stein, B. E., M. A. Meredith, and M. T. Wallace. (1994). Neural mechanisms mediating attention and orientation to multisensory cues. In M. Gazzaniga, Ed., *The Cognitive Neurosciences.* Cambridge, MA: MIT Press, pp. 683–702.

Walk, R. D., and L. H. Pick. (1981). *Intersensory Perception and Sensory Integration.* New York: Plenum Press.

Welch, R. B., and D. H. Warren. (1986). Intersensory interactions. In K. R. Boff, L. Kaufman, and J. P. Thomas, Eds., *Handbook of Perception and Human Performance,* vol. 1: *Sensory Processes and Perception.* New York: Wiley, pp. 25-1–25-36.

Naive Biology

See FOLK BIOLOGY

Naive Mathematics

Whether or not schooling is offered, children and adults all over the world develop an intuitive, naive mathematics. As long as number-relevant examples are part of their culture, people will learn to reason about and solve addition and subtraction problems with positive natural numbers. They also will rank order and compare continuous amounts, if they do not have to measure with equal units. The notion of equal units is hard, save for the cases of money and time. Universally, and without formal instruction, everyone can use money. Examples abound of child candy sellers, taxicab drivers, fishermen, carpenters, and so on developing fluent quantitative scripts, including one for proportional reasoning. Of note is that almost always these strategies use the natural numbers and nonformal notions of mathematical operations. For example, the favored proportions strategy for Brazilian fishermen can be dubbed the "integer proportional reasoning": the rule for reasoning is that one whole number goes into another X number of times and there is no remainder.

Intuitive mathematics serves a wide range of everyday math tasks. For example, Liberian tailors who have no schooling can solve arithmetic problems by laying out and counting familiar objects, such as buttons. Taxicab drivers and child fruit vendors in Brazil invent solutions that serve them well (Nunes, Schliemann, and Carraher 1993).

Two kinds of theories vie for an account of the origins and acquisition of intuitive arithmetic. One idea is that knowledge of the counting numbers and their use in arithmetic tasks builds from a set of reinforced bits of learning about situated counting number routines. Given enough learning opportunities, principles of counting and arithmetic are induced (Fuson 1988). Despite the clear evidence that there are pockets of early mathematical competence, young children are far from perfect on tasks they can negotiate. Additionally, the range of set sizes and tasks they can deal with is limited. These facts constitute the empirical foundation for the "bit-bit" theory and would seem to constitute a problem for the "principle-first" account of intuitive mathematics, which proposes an innate, domain-specific, learning-enabling structure. Although skeleton-like to start, such a structure serves to draw the beginning learner's attention to seek out, attend to, and assimilate number-relevant data—be these in the physical, social, cultural and mental environments—that are available for the epigenesis of number-specific knowledge.

True, there are many arithmetic reasoning tasks that young children cannot do, and early performances are shaky. But this would be expected for any learning account. Those who favor the principle-first account (Geary 1996; Gelman and Williams 1997) point to an ever-increasing number of converging lines of evidence: animals and infants respond to the numerical value of displays (Gallistel and Gelman 1992; Wynn 1995); retarded children have considerable difficulty with simple arithmetic facts, money, time, and novel counting or arithmetic tasks—despite extensive in-school practice (e.g., Gelman and Cohen 1988); preschool children distinguish between novel count sequences that are wrong and those which are unusual but correct; they also invent counting solutions to solve arithmetic problems (Siegler and Shrager 1984; Starkey and Gelman 1982); and elementary school children invent counting solutions to solve school arithmetic tasks in ways that differ from those they are taught in school (Resnick 1989). Moreover, there is

cross-language variability in the transparency of the base rules for number word generation. For example, in Chinese, the words for 10, 11, 12, 13 . . . 20, 21 . . . 30, 31 . . . and so forth, translate as 10, 10–1, 10–2, 10–3, . . . 2–10s-1 . . . 3–10s-1 . . . 3–10s, and so forth. English has no comparable pattern for the teens. This difference influences the rate at which children in different countries master the code for generating large numbers although it does not affect rate of learning of the count words for 1–9. American and Chinese children learn these at comparable rates and use them equally well to solve simple arithmetic problems (Miller et al. 1995).

Almost all of the mathematics or arithmetic revealed in the above examples from divergent settings, ages, and cultural conditions map onto a common structure. Different count lists all honor the same counting principles, and different numbers are made by adding, subtracting, composing, and decomposing natural numbers that are thought of in terms of counted sets. The favored mathematical entities are the natural numbers; the favored operations addition and subtraction, even if the task is stated as multiplication or division. The general rule seems to be, find a way to use whole numbers, either by counting, decomposing N, subtracting, or doing repeated counting and subtraction with whole numbers. Notions about continuous quantity usually are not integrated with those about discrete quantities, where people prefer to use repeated addition or subtraction if they can. This commonality of the underlying arithmetic structure and reliance on natural numbers is an important line of evidence for the idea that counting principles and simple arithmetic are universal. The reliance on whole number strategies, even when proportional reasoning is used, is consistent with this conclusion.

Understanding the mathematician's zero, negative numbers, rational and irrational numbers, and all other higher mathematics does not contribute to the knowledge base of intuitive mathematics. The formal side of mathematical understanding is outside the realm of intuitive mathematics (Hartnett and Gelman 1998). Even the mathematical concept of a fraction develops with considerable difficulty, a fact that is surely related to the problems people have learning to measure and understand the concept of equal units. Reliance on intuitive mathematics is ubiquitous, sometimes even to the point where it becomes a barrier to learning new mathematical concepts that are related to different structures (Gelman and Williams 1997). A salient case in point is the concept of rational numbers and the related symbol systems for representing them. Rational numbers are not generated by the counting principles. They are the result of dividing one cardinal number by another. Nevertheless, there is a potent tendency for elementary school children to interpret lessons about rational numbers as if these were opportunities to generalize their knowledge of natural numbers. For example, they rank order fractions on the basis of the denominator and therefore say 1/75 is larger than 1/56, and so on. There is a growing body of evidence that the mastery of mathematical concepts outside the range of those encompassed by intuitive mathematics constitutes a difficult conceptual challenge.

See also DOMAIN SPECIFICITY; HUMAN UNIVERSALS; INFANT COGNITION; NATIVISM; NUMERACY AND CULTURE; SCIENTIFIC THINKING AND ITS DEVELOPMENT

—Rochel Gelman

References

Fuson, K. C. (1988). *Children's Counting and Concepts of Number.* New York: Springer.

Gallistel, C. R., and R. Gelman. (1992). Preverbal and verbal counting and computation: *Cognition* 44(1–2), 43–74. Special issue on numerical cognition.

Geary, D. C. (1996). Biology, culture, and cross-national differences in mathematical ability. In R. J. Sternberg and T. Ben-Zeev, Eds., *The Nature of Mathematical Thinking.* The Studies in Mathematical Thinking and Learning Series. Mahwah, NJ: Erlbaum, pp. 145–171.

Gelman, R. (1993). A rational-constructivist account of early learning about numbers and objects. In D. Medin, Ed., *Learning and Motivation,* vol. 30. New York: Academic Press.

Gelman, R., and M. Cohen. (1988). Qualitative differences in the way Down's syndrome and normal children solve a novel counting problem. In L. Nadel, Ed., *The Psychobiology of Down's Syndrome.* Cambridge, MA: MIT Press, pp. 51–99.

Gelman, R., and B. Meck. (1992). Early principles aid initial but not later conceptions of number. In J. Bideaud, C. Meljac, and J. Fischer, Eds., *Pathways to Number.* Hillsdale, NJ: Erlbaum, pp. 171–189.

Gelman, R., and E. Williams. (1997). Enabling constraints for cognitive development and learning: Domain-specificity and epigenesis. In D. Kuhn and R. Siegler, Eds., *Cognition, Perception, and Language,* 5th ed., vol. 2 of W. Damon, Ed., *Handbook of Child Psychology.* New York: Wiley.

Hartnett, P. M., and R. Gelman. (1998). Early understandings of number: Paths or barriers to the construction of new understandings? *Learning and Instruction* 8, 341–374.

Miller, K. F., C. M. Smith, J. Zhu, and H. Zhang. (1995). Preschool origins of cross-national differences in mathematical competence: The role of number-naming systems. *Psychological Science* 6: 56–60.

Nunes, T., A. D. Schliemann, and D. W. Carraher. (1993). *Street Mathematics and School Mathematics.* Cambridge: Cambridge University Press.

Resnick, L. (1989). Developing mathematical knowledge. *American Psychologist* 44: 162–169.

Siegler, R. S., and J. Shrager. (1984). Strategy choices in addition: How do children know what to do? In C. Sophian, Ed., *Origins of Cognitive Skills.* Hillsdale, NJ: Erlbaum.

Starkey, P., and R. Gelman. (1982). The development of addition and subtraction abilities prior to formal schooling. In T. P. Carpenter, J. M. Moser, and T. A. Romberg, Eds., *Addition and Subtraction: A Developmental Perspective.* Hillsdale, NJ: Erlbaum.

Further Readings

Behr, M. J., G. Harrell, T. Post, and R. Lesh. (1992). Rational number, ratio, and proportion. In D. A. Grouws, Ed., *Handbook of Research on Mathematics Teaching and Learning: A Project of The National Council of Teachers of Mathematics.* New York: Macmillan.

Fischbein, E., M. Deri, M. Nello, and M. Marino. (1985). The role of implicit models in solving problems in multiplication and division. *Journal of Research in Mathematics Education* 16: 3–17.

Gelman, R., and C. R. Gallistel. (1978). *The Child's Understanding of Number.* Cambridge, MA: Harvard University Press.

Greer, B. (1992). Multiplication and division as models of situations. In D. A. Grouws, Ed., *Handbook of Research on Mathematics Teaching and Learning: A Project of The National Council of Teachers of Mathematics.* New York: Macmillan.

Groen, G., and L. B. Resnick. (1977). Can preschool children invent addition algorithms? *Journal of Educational Psychology* 69: 645–652.

Lave, J., and E. Wenger. (1991). *Situated Learning: Legitimate Peripheral Participation.* Cambridge: Cambridge University Press.

Saxe, G. B., S. R. Guberman, and M. Gearhart. (1987). Social processes in early development. *Monographs of the Society for the Research in Child Development* 52.

Sophian, C. (1994). *Children's Numbers.* Madison, WI: W. C. B. Brown and Benchmark.

Starkey, P., E. S. Spelke, and R. Gelman. (1990). Numerical abstraction by human infants. *Cognition* 36(2): 97–127.

Stevenson, H., and J. Stigler. (1992). *The Learning Gap.* New York: Summit Books.

Wynn, K. (1995). Infants possess a system of numerical knowledge. *Current Directions in Psychological Science* 4: 172–177.

Naive Physics

Naive physics refers to the commonsense beliefs that people hold about the way the world works, particularly with respect to classical mechanics. Being the oldest branch of physics, classical mechanics has priority because mechanical systems can be seen, whereas the motions relevant to other branches of physics are invisible. Because the motions of mechanical systems are both lawful and obvious, it is always intriguing to find instances in which people hold beliefs about mechanics that are not just underdeveloped but systematically wrong.

Jean PIAGET (1952, 1954) studied how young children acquire an understanding of the basic physical dimensions of the world and demonstrated that at young ages, children are systematically disposed to construe the world in biased ways. Interestingly, it was also found that adults often do not exhibit simple physical concepts that Piaget assumed they must have. A notable example of this is the water level problem introduced by Piaget and Inhelder (1956). When asked to indicate the surface orientation of water in a tilted container, about 40 percent of the adult population produce estimates that systematically deviate from the horizontal by more than 5 degrees (cf. McAfee and Proffitt 1991).

A large number of studies have found that adults express systematic errors in their reasoning about how objects naturally move in the world (Champagne, Klopher, and Anderson 1980; Clement 1982; Kaiser, Jonides, and Alexander 1986; McCloskey 1983; McCloskey, Caramazza, and Green 1980; McCloskey and Kohl 1983; Shanon 1976). An excellent introduction to this research can be found in McCloskey (1983), who dubbed this field of study "Intuitive Physics." The best-known example of these problems is the C-shaped tube problem, in which a participant is asked to predict the trajectory taken by a ball after it exits a C-shaped tube lying flat on a table (McCloskey, Caramazza, and Green 1980). The correct answer is that the ball will follow a straight trajectory tangent to the tube's curvature at the point of exit. About 40 percent of college students get this problem wrong and predict instead that the ball will continue to curve after exiting the tube.

There are two classes of explanations for these findings. The first supposes that people possess a general mental model that dictates the form of their errors (*see* MENTAL MODELS). One such proposal is that naive physics reflects an Aristotelian model of mechanics. Shanon (1976) found that many people reasoned, like Aristotle, that objects will fall at a constant velocity proportional to their mass. In his early writings, diSessa (1982) also argued that people display Aristotelian tendencies. McCloskey (1983) suggested that people's intuitive model resembled medieval impetus theory. By this account, an object is made to move by an impetus that dissipates over time. However, there are at least two problems with these mental model approaches to naive physics. The first is that people are not internally consistent (Cooke and Breedin 1994; diSessa 1983; Kaiser et al. 1992; Ranney and Thagard 1988; Shanon 1976). The same person will respond to different problems in a manner that suggests the application of different models. The second problem is that people are strongly influenced by the surface structure of the problem. Kaiser, Jonides, and Alexander (1986) found that people do not err on the C-shaped tube problem when the situation is put in a more familiar context. For example, no one predicts that water exiting a curved hose will continue to curve upon exit. Although people's dynamical judgments seem not to adhere to either implicit Aristotelian or impetus theories, this does not imply that they have no mental models applicable to natural dynamics. People may possess general models having some as yet undetermined structure, or their models may be domain specific.

The second type of EXPLANATION for people's systematic errors appeals to issues of problem complexity. Proffitt and Gilden (1989) proposed an account of dynamical event complexity that parsed mechanical systems into two classes. Particle motions are those that can be described mathematically by treating the moving object as if it were a point located at its center of mass. Extended-body motions are those contexts in which the object's mass distribution, size, and orientation influence its motion. As an example, consider a wheel. If the wheel is dropped in a vacuum, then its velocity is simply a function of the distance that its center of mass has fallen. Ignoring air resistance, freefall is a particle motion. On the other hand, if the wheel is placed on an inclined plane and released, then the wheel's shape—its moment of inertia—is dynamically relevant. This is an extended-body motion context. People reason fairly well about particle motion problems but not extended-body motion ones. In addition, people also err when they misrepresent a particle motion as being an extended-body motion as, for example, in the C-shaped tube problem. In doing so, they attribute more dimensionality to the problem than is actually there.

Given that people often predict that events will follow unnatural courses—for example, that a ball exiting a C-shaped tube will persist to follow a curved path—it is interesting to ask what would happen if they actually saw such an event occur. Would it look odd or natural? Kaiser and Proffitt (Kaiser, Proffitt, and Anderson 1985; Kaiser et al.

1992; Proffitt, Kaiser, and Whelan 1990) found that when presented with animations of particle motion problems, people judged their own predictions to be unnatural and selected natural motions as appearing correct. For example, when contrived animations were presented to people who drew curved paths on the paper-and-pencil version of the problem, these people reported that balls rolling through a C-shaped tube and continuing to curve upon exit looked very odd, whereas straight paths appeared natural. Animations, however, did not evoke more accurate judgments for extended-body motions (Proffitt, Kaiser, and Whelan 1990). For example, Howard (1978) and McAfee and Proffitt (1991) found that viewing animations of liquids moving to nonhorizontal orientations in tilting containers did not evoke more accurate judgments from people prone to err on this problem.

Adults' naive conceptions about how the world works appear to be simplistic, inconsistent, and situation-specific. However, recent research with infants suggests that a few core beliefs may underlie all dynamical reasoning (*see* INFANT COGNITION). Baillargeon (1993) and Spelke et al. (1992) have shown that, by around 2 1/2 months of age, infants can reason about the continuity and solidity of objects involved in simple events. Other physical concepts, such as gravity and inertia, do not seem to enter infants' reasoning until much later, around 6 months of age (Spelke et al. 1992). Spelke et al. proposed the intriguing notion that continuity and solidity are core principles that persist throughout the development of people's naive physics.

See also COGNITIVE DEVELOPMENT; FOLK BIOLOGY; NAIVE MATHEMATICS; SCIENTIFIC THINKING AND ITS DEVELOPMENT; THEORY OF MIND

—*Dennis Proffitt*

References

Baillargeon, R. (1993). The object concept revisited: New directions in the investigation of infants' physical knowledge. In C. E. Granrud, Ed., *Carnegie Symposium on Cognition: Visual Perception and Cognition in Infancy*. Hillsdale, NJ: Erlbaum, pp. 265–315.

Champagne, A. B., L. E. Klopher, and J. H. Anderson. (1980). Factors influencing the learning of classical mechanics. *American Journal of Physics* 48: 1074–1079.

Clement, J. (1982). Students' preconceptions in introductory mechanics. *American Journal of Physics* 50: 66–71.

Cooke, N. J., and S. D. Breedin. (1994). Constructing naive theories of motion on the fly. *Memory and Cognition* 22: 474–493.

diSessa, A. (1982). Unlearning Aristotelian physics: A study of knowledge-based learning. *Cognitive Science* 6: 37–75.

diSessa. A. (1983). Phenomenology and the evolution of intuition. In D. Gentner and A. L. Stevens, Eds., *Mental Models*. Hillsdale, NJ: Erlbaum, pp. 15–33.

Howard, I. (1978). Recognition and knowledge of the water-level problem. *Perception* 7: 151–160.

Kaiser, M. K., J. Jonides, and J. Alexander. (1986). Intuitive reasoning about abstract and familiar physics problems. *Memory and Cognition* 14: 308–312.

Kaiser, M. K., D. E. Proffitt, and K. A. Anderson. (1985). Judgments of natural and anomalous trajectories in the presence and absence of motion. *Journal of Experimental Psychology: Human Perception and Performance* 11: 795–803.

Kaiser, M. K., D. R. Proffitt, S. M. Whelan, and H. Hecht. (1992). Influence of animation on dynamical judgments. *Journal of Experimental Psychology: Human Perception and Performance* 18: 384–393.

McAfee, E. A., and D. R. Proffitt. (1991). Understanding the surface orientation of liquids. *Cognitive Psychology* 23: 669–690.

McCloskey, M. (1983). Intuitive physics. *Scientific American* 248: 122–130.

McCloskey, M., A. Caramazza, and B. Green. (1980). Curvilinear motion in the absence of external forces: Naive beliefs about the motion of objects. *Science* 210: 1139–1141.

McCloskey, M., and D. Kohl. (1983). Naive physics: The curvilinear impetus principle and its role in interactions with moving objects. *Journal of Experimental Psychology: Learning, Memory, and Cognition* 9: 146–156.

Piaget, J. (1952). *The Origins of Intelligence in Childhood.* New York: International Universities Press.

Piaget, J. (1954). *The Construction of Reality in the Child.* New York: Basic Books.

Piaget, J., and B. Inhelder. (1956). *The Child's Conception of Space.* London: Routledge and Kegan Paul.

Proffitt, D. R., and D. L. Gilden. (1989). Understanding natural dynamics. *Journal of Experimental Psychology: Human Perception and Performance* 15: 384–393.

Proffitt, D. R., M. K. Kaiser, and S. M. Whelan. (1990). Understanding wheel dynamics. *Cognitive Psychology* 22: 342–373.

Ranney, M., and P. Thagard. (1988). Explanatory coherence and belief revision in naive physics. In *Proceedings of the Tenth Annual Conference of the Cognitive Science Society.* Hillsdale, NJ: Erlbaum, pp. 426–432.

Shanon, B. (1976). Aristotelianism, Newtonianism, and the physics of the layman. *Perception* 5: 241–243.

Spelke, E. S., K. Breinlinger, J. Macomber, and K. Jacobson. (1992). Origins of knowledge. *Psychological Review* 99: 605–632.

Further Readings

Caramazza, A., M. McCloskey, and B. Green. (1981). Naive beliefs in "sophisticated" subjects: Misconceptions about trajectories of objects. *Cognition* 9: 117–123.

Chi., M. T. H., and J. D. Slotta. (1993). The ontological coherence of intuitive physics. *Cognition and Instruction* 10: 249–260.

Clement, J. (1983). A conceptual model discussed by Galileo and used intuitively by physics students. In D. Gentner and A. L. Stevens, Eds., *Mental Models.* Hillsdale, NJ: Erlbaum, pp. 325–339.

diSessa, A. (1993). Toward an epistemology of physics. *Cognition and Instruction* 10: 105–225.

Gilden, D. L. (1991). On the origins of dynamical awareness. *Psychological Review* 98: 554–568.

Hubbard, T. L. (1996). Representational momentum: Centripetal force, and curvilinear impetus. *Journal of Experimental Psychology: Learning, Memory, and Cognition* 22: 1049–1060.

Kaiser, M. K., D. R. Proffitt, and M. McCloskey. (1985). The development of beliefs about falling objects. *Perception and Psychophysics* 38: 533–539.

Larkin, J. H. (1983). The role of problem representation in physics. In D. Gentner and A. L. Stevens, Eds., *Mental Models.* Hillsdale, NJ: Erlbaum, pp. 75–98.

McCloskey, M. (1983). Naive theories of motion. In D. Gentner and A. L. Stevens, Eds., *Mental Models.* Hillsdale, NJ: Erlbaum, pp. 299–324.

McCloskey, M., A. Washburn, and L. Felch. (1983). Intuitive physics: The straight-down belief and its origin. *Journal of Experimental Psychology: Learning, Memory, and Cognition* 9: 636–649.

Smith, B., and R. Casati. (1994). Naive physics. *Philosophical Psychology* 7: 227–247.

Spelke, L. S. (1991). Physical knowledge in infancy: Reflections on Piaget's theory. In S. Carey and R. Gelman, Eds., *The Epigenesis of Mind: Essays on Biology and Cognition.* Hillsdale, NJ: Erlbaum.

Naive Psychology

See FOLK PSYCHOLOGY

Naive Sociology

Humans everywhere possess elaborate and often articulate knowledge of the social world. Central to this knowledge is the recognition of and reasoning about those groupings of individuals that constitute the social world. Naive sociology is the study of the cognitive processes underlying these everyday beliefs about human groups and human group affiliation.

That humans develop complex representations of society is not surprising. Humans almost certainly know more about other humans than they do about any other aspect of the world, and group living is a hallmark of human existence. Group living likely includes adaptation to the fact that humans may be the only species in which conspecifics are the principal predator (Alexander 1989). Since much of this predation is regulated by and implemented through social groups, cognitive skills, like the capacity to rapidly and accurately interpret the behavior and motivations of others, are critical for survival.

Human social groupings are more complex and more fluid than those of other social species. Consequently, the rapid and accurate appraisal of the social environment is both difficult to achieve and demanding of cognitive resources. Major tasks include the capacity to represent and to compute information about (1) large numbers of groups, (2) varied group affiliations, and (3) shifting coalitions between groups. A number of mechanisms underlie these capacities, and their precise nature remains a matter of some controversy.

Considerable research in social psychology, particularly group dynamics, has revealed and interpreted many processes pertinent to these capacities. Like the bulk of psychology, work in SOCIAL COGNITION tends to approach sociality from a domain-general perspective. Thus, representations of group-level phenomena, like social identity, are typically interpreted as instances of general cognitive strategies for processing categories. Patterns of inferencing associated with social categories (e.g., STEREOTYPING and prejudice), on this view, involve general category effects that simply happen to target person categories (Fiske and Taylor 1991; Hamilton 1981).

Other research in social psychology has identified mechanisms that specifically act on mental representations of human groupings. Research on stereotyping has contributed important insights into cognitions of group-level phenomena, particularly insights into the relationship between ascribed group affiliation and explanations for the beliefs and behaviors of members of other groups (Hogg and Abrams 1988; Pettigrew 1979; Taylor and Fiske 1991; Miller and Prentice forthcoming).

Influential studies by Tajfel (1981) demonstrate that biases of this sort may be extremely general in the sense that they are not tethered to any actual group affiliation. Tajfel and his colleagues have shown that individuals, in virtually any situation, privilege members of their own group (ingroup) vis-à-vis members of other groups (outgroups). Thus, even when subjects know that the ingroup has no real-world group status (e.g., when the ingroup is composed of all persons whose social security numbers end in the same digit), they distribute pretend money more readily to members of their own group than to members of an outgroup. Biases of this sort are extremely resistant to change and attempts to inhibit spontaneous group-related favoritism have been largely ineffective (Miller and Brewer 1984; Gaertner et al. 1993).

These studies typically approach group-relevant cognitions from the perspective of the individual, both with respect to the individual who perceives group affiliation from the vantage point of him or herself and with respect to the individual as target of bias.

Evolutionary and comparative studies have been especially important in making clear that mental representations of group-level phenomena also include beliefs about groups themselves. EVOLUTIONARY PSYCHOLOGY, COGNITIVE ANTHROPOLOGY, AND ETHNOPSYCHOLOGY all speak directly or indirectly to the role representations of groups play in sociality (Alexander 1989; Dunbar 1988; Brereton 1996; Warnecke, Masters, and Kempter 1992; Fishbein 1996; Shaw and Wong 1989; Reynolds, Falger, and Vine 1987; Cosmides 1989; LeVine and Campbell 1972), as does comparative research on DOMINANCE IN ANIMAL SOCIAL GROUPS and SOCIAL COGNITION IN ANIMALS.

Much of this work reveals the importance of domain-specific and modular mechanisms to naive sociology. Evolution prepares all living things to resolve (or attempt to resolve) recurrent problems facing the organism. It is extremely likely that evolved adaptations emerged in response to recurring social problems that our ancestral populations faced (Baron-Cohen 1995). Relevant evolved adaptations include specialized mechanisms in both humans and nonhuman animals (particularly primates) such as a THEORY OF MIND; domain-specific devices for the recognition of faces, voices, and affective states; cheater detectors; and capacities for representing social dominance.

Other capacities that evolved to coordinate information relevant to nonsocial phenomena may have also been recruited to treat social group-level phenomena. Scholars in the domain-specific tradition, using beliefs about NATURAL KINDS as a point of departure, have proposed that concepts of human groupings are organized around principles that initially emerge in naive understanding of nonhuman groupings (particularly the folk notion of species). Strategies for classifying and reasoning about human groups are strikingly similar to strategies for classifying and reasoning about nonhuman species. It has been argued that notions that capture

human diversity (e.g., race, ethnicity, nationality, and gender) may derive via analogy from the notion of species in FOLK BIOLOGY (Atran 1990; Boyer 1990; Rothbart and Taylor 1990). In much the same vein, other aspects of social reasoning (e.g., the willingness to interpret behavior in terms of traits and dispositions) have been attributed to theory of mind (Wellman 1990).

Hirschfeld (1995) and Jackendoff (1992) argue that mental representations of human groups are also governed by a distinct cognitive faculty of social cognition or naive sociology. Noam Chomsky (1988), in a discussion of bilingualism, implies something of the same when he observes that young children have theories of both language and society that they must coordinate in determining, among other things, the particular language to speak in a given context. The basic task of a faculty of social cognition is to develop an integrated picture of the self in society. Whereas the fundamental units of spatial cognition are physical objects in space, those of social cognition are persons in social interaction (Jackendoff 1992: 72). On this view, the notion of *persons in social interaction* involves at least two elements that set the domain of social cognition apart from other domains. First, the causal principles of social relations (e.g., consanguinity, group membership, and dominance) appear to be unrelated to those underlying other domains of knowledge. Second, the fundamental unit of social cognition, the person, is a singular conceptual entity. As already noted, humans have a number of highly specialized input devices that allow the identification of specific persons and the interpretation of their actions.

The concept of the person itself may be contingent on group-relevant cognitions. The image of a social person, for instance, may be a conceptual prerequisite for other individually oriented domain-specific competencies. Recent work with young children, for example, suggests that the notion *group* may developmentally preceed the notion of self (Hirschfeld 1996). Similarly, in theory of mind the person is the entity to which beliefs and desires are attributable (except in rare and pathological circumstances, like multiple personality disorder; see Hacking 1995). Yet belief/desire psychology, taken by some to be the backbone of social reasoning (e.g., Baron-Cohen 1995), may well be insufficient to account for social reasoning in that it is insufficient to account for representations of groups. For instance, it is a commonplace in anthropological analysis to proceed without reference to individuals at all on the belief that social groups and social affiliation are distinct from (and perhaps antecedent to) knowledge of individuals (Mauss 1985). Indeed, social analysis would be impoverished without invoking the notion of corporate groups (groups that are conceptualized as corporate individuals rather than collections of individuals; Brown 1976).

A major cognitive issue in this regard is the nature and scope of cognitive resources that human sociality demands. The social units with which any individual can affiliate are many and varied. A critical task for both children and adults is to develop skills at high-speed scanning of social contexts and high-speed identification of the appropriate (or strategic) affiliations and allegiances invoked in a given context. For example, choosing something as "simple" as the correct register of speech for a particular situation depends on adequately parsing the social affiliations of the individuals in that context (Hirschfeld and Gelman 1997).

The complexity of the social environment led Hirschfeld (1996) to propose the existence of specialized knowledge structures dedicated to social group understanding. He argues that identifying and reasoning about "natural" groupings (i.e., groups such as race and gender that are considered immutable and derived from a unique group essence) rest on mechanisms unique to social reasoning. Thus, despite the predominant view that preschoolers are conceptually unable to reason beyond external properties (Aboud 1988), Hirschfeld found that even quite young children represent the social environment in terms of abstract principles and nonvisible qualities. For instance, even 3-year-olds distinguish "natural" human kinds from other ways of sorting people and attribute group membership to underlying and unique essences that are transmitted from parent to child.

In sum, cognitive science has provided important insights into the nature and scope of group living. Many questions remain open. What is the relationship between knowledge of group-level and individual-level phenomena? Given the marked variation in sociality, what role does the cultural environment play in shaping social understanding? To what extent does this marked variation preclude evolutionary accounts? If it does not, what kinds of adaptations evolved to treat social phenomena? What was the evolutionary environment like in which these adaptations emerged?

See also DOMAIN SPECIFICITY; ESSENTIALISM; NAIVE PHYSICS

—*Lawrence A. Hirschfeld*

References and Further Readings

Aboud, F. E. (1988). *Children and Prejudice.* New York: Blackwell.

Alexander, R. (1989). Evolution of the human psyche. In P. Mellars and C. Stringer, Eds., *The Human Revolution: Behavioural and Biological Perspectives on the Origins of Modern Humans.* Princeton: Princeton University Press.

Atran, S. (1990). *Cognitive Foundations of Natural History.* New York: Cambridge University Press.

Baron-Cohen, S. (1995). *Mindblindness: An Essay on Autism and Theory of Mind.* Cambridge, MA: MIT Press.

Boyer, P. (1990). *Tradition as Truth and Communication.* New York: Cambridge University Press.

Brereton, A. (1996). Coercion-defense hypothesis: The evolution of primate sociality. *Folia Primatol.* 64: 207–214.

Brown, D. (1976). *Principles of Social Structure: Southeast Asia.* London: Duckworth.

Chomsky, N. (1988). *Language and Problems of Knowledge: The Managua Lectures.* Cambridge, MA: MIT Press.

Cosmides, L. (1989). The logic of social exchange: Has natural selection shaped how humans reason? Studies with the Wason selection task. *Cognition* 31: 187–276.

Dunbar, R. (1988). *Primate Social Systems.* Ithaca: Cornell University Press.

Fishbein, H. (1996). *Peer Prejudice and Discrimination: Evolutionary, Cultural, and Developmental Dynamics.* Boulder, CO: Westview Press.

Fiske, S., and S. Taylor. (1991). *Social Cognition.* New York: McGraw Hill.

Gaertner, S., J. Dovidio, A. Anastasio, B. Bachman, and M. Rust. (1993). The common in-group identity: Recategorization and the reduction of intergroup bias. *European Review of Social Psychology* 4: 1–26.

Hacking, I. (1995). *Rewriting the Soul: Multiple Personality and the Sciences of Memory.* Princeton: Princeton University Press.

Hamilton, D. (1981). Illusory correlation as a basis for stereotyping. In D. Hamilton, Ed., *Cognitive Processes in Stereotyping and Intergroup Behavior.* Hillsdale, NJ: Erlbaum.

Hirschfeld, L. (1995). Do children have a theory of race? *Cognition* 54: 209–252.

Hirschfeld, L. (1996). *Race in the Making: Cognition, Culture, and the Child's Construction of Human Kinds.* Cambridge: MIT Press.

Hirschfeld, L., and S. Gelman. (1997). Discovering social difference: the role of appearance in the development of racial awareness. *Cognitive Development* 25: 317–350.

Hogg, M., and D. Abrams. (1988). *Social Identifications: A Social Psychology of Intergroup Relations and Group Processes.* London: Routledge.

Jackendoff, R. (1992). *Language of the Mind: Essays on Mental Representation.* Cambridge, MA: MIT Press.

LeVine, R., and D. Campbell. (1972). *Ethnocentrism: Theories of Conflict, Ethnic Attitudes, and Group Behavior.* New York: Wiley.

Mauss, M. (1985). A category of the human mind: The notion of person. In M. Carrithers, S. Collins, and S. Lukes, Eds., *The Category of Person.* New York: Cambridge University Press.

Miller, D., and D. Prentice. (Forthcoming). Social consequences of a belief in group essence: the category divide hypothesis. In D. Prentice and D. Miller, Eds., *Cultural Divides: Understanding and Resolving Group Conflict.* New York: Russell Sage Foundation.

Miller, N., and M. Brewer. (1984). *Groups in Contact: The Psychology of Desegregation.* New York: Academic Press.

Pettigrew, T. (1979). The ultimate attribution error: Extending Allports' cognitive analysis. *Personality and Social Psychology Bulletin* 5: 461–476.

Reynolds, V., V. Falger, and I. Vine. (1987). *The Sociobiology of Ethnocentrism: Evolutionary Dimensions of Xenophobia, Discrimination, Racism, and Nationalism.* London: Croom Helm.

Rothbart, M., and M. Taylor. (1990). Category labels and social reality: Do we view social categories as natural kinds? In G. Semin and K. Fiedler, Eds., *Language and Social Cognition.* London: Sage.

Shaw, R., and Y. Wong. (1989). *Genetic Seeds of Warfare: Evolution, Nationalism, and Patriotism.* Boston: Unwin Hyman.

Tajfel, H. (1981). *Human Groups and Social Categories.* Cambridge: Cambridge University Press.

Taylor, S., S. Fiske, N. Etcoff, and A. Ruderman. (1978). The categorical and contextual bases of person memory and stereotyping. *Journal of Personality and Social Psychology* 36: 778–793.

Warnecke, A., R. Masters, and G. Kempter. (1992). The roots of nationalism: Nonverbal behavior and xenophobia. *Ethology and Sociobiology* 13: 267–282.

Wellman, H. (1990). *The Child's Theory of Mind.* Cambridge: MIT Press.

Narrow Content

According to some causal theories, the referent of a term like "water" is whatever substance bears the appropriate causal relation to the use of that term (Putnam 1975; Kripke

1980; see also Fodor 1987; Dretske 1981; Stampe 1977). This view is supported by Putnam's TWIN EARTH example, according to which the referents of our terms, and hence the truth conditions and meanings of utterances and the contents of our thoughts, depend on conditions in our environment and so are not determined by (do not supervene on) our individual, internal psychology alone. Content that does not supervene on an individual subject's internal psychology is called broad content.

Several considerations, however, suggest the need for a concept of content that *would* supervene on internal psychology, that is, a concept of narrow content. We normally assume that our behavior is causally explained by our intentional states such as beliefs and desires (see INTENTIONALITY). We also assume that our behavior has its causal explanation in our individual, internal psychological makeup (see INDIVIDUALISM). But if the explanation of behavior supervenes on individual, internal psychology, and the broad contents of our intentional states do not, then it seems that either those states will not figure in the causal explanations of a genuine psychological science or that a notion of narrow content is required. Some theorists have challenged this argument, however, by denying the first assumption (Stich 1978; 1983), some have denied the second (Wilson 1995), and some have denied that the conclusion follows (Fodor 1994). Even the legitimacy of a distinction between broad and narrow content along these lines has been challenged (Bilgrami 1992; Chomsky 1995). Thus the implication that the scientific explanation of behavior requires narrow content remains controversial.

For this reason, other arguments for narrow content have been advanced that involve not just the causal explanation of behavior but explanations that capture the subject's own perspective on the world and thus rationalize and justify that behavior. For example, if all content is the broad content postulated by causal theories, a brain in a vat being fed artificial sensory inputs by a computer will either have no beliefs or its beliefs will be about the computer's internal states, regardless of the nature of the stimulus inputs. Thus although the question how the world presents itself seems just as legitimate for the brain in the vat as for a normal subject, a theory of belief that restricts itself to broad content apparently cannot provide an adequate account.

A third consideration favoring narrow content derives from a problem raised by Gottlob FREGE (1952). Though the expressions "Hesperus" and "Phosphorus" both refer to the same object—Venus—a person who was sufficiently uninformed could be perfectly rational in believing and assenting to what he would express by saying both "Hesperus is inhabited" and "Phosphorus is not inhabited." The problem is that according to the causal theory these two beliefs are about the same object and say contradictory things about it. And we cannot counter the implication of the causal theory that the subject is irrational by appeal to the different descriptions that the subject associates with the two terms; to do so would undermine the claim of the causal theory that reference is independent of the descriptions available to the subject. Nor can we appeal to the differences in the causal chains connecting Venus with "Hesperus" and "Phospho-

rus," because these are unavailable to the subject and so cannot explain how it could be rational to hold these beliefs simultaneously. This last point reveals a problem for conceptual or FUNCTIONAL ROLE SEMANTICS and for procedural semantics as accounts of narrow content (Block 1986; Loar 1982; Field 1977; Schiffer 1981; Miller and Johnson-Laird 1976; Johnson-Laird 1977; see also Harman 1982). Functional role semantics answers the question what the subjects and their Twin Earth doppelgängers have in common by reference to the equivalence of the functional states underlying their beliefs (see FUNCTIONALISM). But, because these functional properties, like the causal chains, are not available to the subject in question, this approach cannot characterize the world as it presents itself to the brain in the vat or rationalize and justify the behavior of the uninformed subject.

Another approach to narrow content exploits an analogy between broad contents and the contents of token-reflexive utterances involving INDEXICALS AND DEMONSTRATIVES (White 1982; Fodor 1987). Suppose Jones and Jones' doppelgänger on Twin Earth both say "It's warm here." Because they have different locations, they say different things and express different belief contents. What is common to the two expressions, however, is a function from their *contexts of utterance* to the contents expressed. If Jones had uttered what he did at his doppelgänger's location, he would have expressed what his doppelgänger did and vice versa. Suppose now that Jones and his duplicate both say "Water is wet." What Jones says is true just in case H_2O is wet, and the same goes for his duplicate and the twin Earth analogue of water, XYZ. Again they express different propositions, and their utterances have different broad contents. But suppose Jones had acquired his word "water" not on Earth but on Twin Earth. Then the broad content of his utterance would have been the same as that of his duplicate. In this case too, what the broad contents of their utterances have in common can be expressed as a function—this time from *contexts of acquisition* to broad contents.

We can also appeal to such functions to show what the brain in the vat has in common with normal subjects. Had the brain acquired its beliefs in the same context as normal subjects, it would have had the same broad-content beliefs that they have, and vice versa. Thus in this example as well, the narrow contents that the beliefs have in common can be expressed as functions from contexts of acquisition to broad contents. Furthermore, we can appeal to the same functions to distinguish the content the uninformed subject would express in saying "Hesperus is inhabited" from what that subject would express in saying "Phosphorus is inhabited." Though there is no possible world at which Hesperus is not identical with Phosphorus, there are worlds epistemically identical with the actual one such that had the subject acquired the terms at those worlds they would have referred to different planets. Thus the terms "Hesperus" and "Phosphorus," though they have the same referent, are associated with different functions from contexts of acquisition to referents. Hence the two beliefs whose broad contents are contradictory have narrow contents that do not support the charge of irrationality.

The appeal to narrow content in this sense answers the three objections to broad content that we have been considering. This approach, however, is not fully satisfactory. First, it underestimates the theoretical significance of narrow content by making its ascription parasitic on the ascription of broad content. Second, it provides only an indirect answer to the question *what* the subject believes, where the question concerns narrow belief. Third, narrow contents, so defined, do not lend themselves easily to a characterization of the logical or epistemic relations among a subject's beliefs, nor to an analysis of the relations in virtue of which they figure in practical reasoning or decision-making.

An alternative approach to narrow content takes its cue from the fact that the truth conditions of a belief or utterance are often represented as the set of possible worlds at which that belief or utterance is true. As we have seen, the causal theorist's notion of truth and truth conditions leads directly to broad content. However, we can represent the narrow contents of the subject's beliefs as the set of worlds where those beliefs are accurate or veridical and then define these in a way that is independent of truth. One suggestion is that there is a conceptual connection between possible worlds at which one's beliefs are accurate and worlds at which one's actions are optimal (and nonaccidentally so), given one's desires and one's available alternatives. The intuition is that if one performs an action that from one's own point of view is the best action under the circumstances (it is not weak willed, etc.), then it could only fail to be optimal if some of one's beliefs were inaccurate (White 1991).

See also POSSIBLE WORLDS SEMANTICS; PROPOSITIONAL ATTITUDES; SENSE AND REFERENCE

—*Stephen L. White*

References

Bilgrami, A. (1992). *Belief and Meaning.* Oxford: Blackwell.

Block, N. (1986). Advertisement for a semantics for psychology. In P. French, T. Uehling, and H. Wettstein, Eds., *Midwest Studies in Philosophy,* vol 10. Minneapolis: University of Minnesota Press.

Chomsky, N. (1995). Language and nature. *Mind* 104: 1–61.

Dretske, F. (1981). *Knowledge and the Flow of Information.* Cambridge, MA: Bradford/MIT Press.

Field, H. (1977). Logic, meaning, and conceptual role. *Journal of Philosophy* 74: 379–409.

Fodor, J. A. (1987). *Psychosemantics: The Problem of Meaning in the Philosophy of Mind.* Cambridge, MA: Bradford/MIT Press.

Fodor, J. A. (1994). *The Elm and the Expert: Mentalese and Its Semantics.* Cambridge, MA: Bradford/MIT Press.

Frege, G. (1952). On sense and reference. In P. Geach and M. Black, Eds., *Translations from the Philosophical Writings of Gottlob Frege.* Oxford: Blackwell.

Harman, G. (1982). Conceptual role semantics. *Notre Dame Journal of Formal Logic* 23: 242–256.

Johnson-Laird, P. N. (1977). Procedural semantics. *Cognition* 5: 189–214.

Kripke, S. A. (1980). *Naming and Necessity.* Cambridge, MA: Harvard University Press.

Loar, B. (1982). Conceptual role and truth conditions. *Notre Dame Journal of Formal Logic* 23: 272–283.

Miller, G. A., and P. N. Johnson-Laird. (1976). *Language and Perception.* Cambridge, MA: Harvard University Press.

Putnam, H. (1975). The meaning of "meaning." In H. Putnam, Ed., *Mind, Language and Reality.* New York: Cambridge University Press.

Schiffer, S. (1981). Truth and the theory of content. In H. Parret and J. Bouveresse, Eds., *Meaning and Understanding.* New York: Walter de Gruyter.

Stampe, D. W. (1977). Toward a causal theory of linguistic representation. In P. French, T. Uehling, and H. Wettstein, Eds., *Midwest Studies in Philosophy,* vol. 2. Minneapolis: University of Minnesota Press.

Stich, S. (1978). Autonomous psychology and the belief-desire thesis. *Monist* 61: 573–591.

Stich, S. (1983). *From Folk Psychology to Cognitive Science.* Cambridge, MA: MIT Press.

White, S. L. (1982). Partial character and the language of thought. *Pacific Philosophical Quarterly* 63: 347–365. Reprinted in S. L. White, *The Unity of the Self.* Cambridge, MA: Bradford/MIT Press.

White, S. L. (1991). Narrow content and narrow interpretation. In S. L. White, Ed., *The Unity of the Self.* Cambridge, MA: Bradford/MIT Press.

Wilson, R. A. (1995). *Cartesian Psychology and Physical Minds: Individualism and the Sciences of the Mind.* New York: Cambridge University Press.

Further Readings

Burge, T. (1979). Individualism and the mental. In P. French, T. Uehling, and H. Wettstein, Eds., *Midwest Studies in Philosophy,* vol. 4. Minneapolis: University of Minnesota Press.

Field, H. (1978). Mental representation. *Erkenntnis* 13: 9–61.

Fodor, J. A. (1978). Tom Swift and his procedural grandmother. *Cognition* 6: 229–247.

Fodor, J. A. (1980). Methodological solipsism considered as a research strategy in cognitive psychology. *Behavioral and Brain Sciences* 3: 63–73. Reprinted in J. A. Fodor, *Representations.* Cambridge, MA: MIT Press.

Johnson-Laird, P. (1978). What's wrong with grandma's guide to procedural semantics: A reply to Jerry Fodor. *Cognition* 6: 241–261.

Kaplan, D. (1989). Demonstratives. In J. Almog, J. Perry, and H. Wettstein, Eds., *Themes from Kaplan.* New York: Oxford University Press.

Stalnaker, R. (1989). On what's in the head. In J. Tomberlin, Ed., *Philosophical Perspectives,* vol. 3, *Philosophy of Mind and Action Theory.* Atascadero, CA: Ridgeview.

Woodfield, A., Ed. (1982). *Thought and Content.* New York: Oxford University Press.

Nativism

Nativism is often understood as the view that a significant body of knowledge is "built in" to an organism, or at least innately predetermined. This characterization, however, fails to capture contemporary nativism as well as being inadequate for many older views (see NATIVISM, HISTORY OF). Few nativists argue today for the full predetermination of specific concepts, ideas, or cognitive structures such as a language's grammar; and few empiricists fail to argue for certain kinds of information processing, such as back propagation (see SUPERVISED LEARNING), as being built in. Every party to current debates about nativism in fact shares the view that there is something special and intrinsic, that is innate, to particular types of organisms that enables them to more easily come to engage in some behaviors as opposed to others. It is the nature of those intrinsic structures and processes that is the true focus of debates about whether some aspect of cognition or perception is compatible with a nativist perspective. In particular, nativist views endorse the presence of multiple learning systems each of which is especially effective at acquiring a particular kind of information and where that effectiveness arises from specializations for information that occurs at all levels in that learning system, not just in the initial stages of processing. The rise of connectionism (see CONNECTIONISM, PHILOSOPHICAL ISSUES and COGNITIVE MODELING, CONNECTIONIST) has been said to pose a fatal challenge to nativism; but as seen later in this article, it in itself in no way renders nativism obsolete.

Confusions about nativism often arise in cases where one organism can acquire a body of knowledge or an ability that another cannot. Thus, attempts to teach human language to primates are often seen as bearing directly on nativist views of an innate language even as the researchers on such topics are usually much more cautious (e.g., Savage-Rumbaugh et. al. 1993). But differential success at learning is in itself not relevant. This irrelevance is clear when more extreme comparisons are made. When a child acquires language and a pet gerbil in the same environment does not, no one argues that language is therefore innate in humans. Failure to learn can arise for many reasons, only some of which support a nativist perspective. There may be general cognitive capacity requirements necessary for learning complex knowledge that exceed the capacities of some organisms. When a gerbil fails to learn language, we might well assume that it simply could not acquire any knowledge system with the structural complexity and memory loads imposed by language. When a primate fails to learn a language, it too may fail to pass some general capacity threshold. Alternatively, a primate that is highly adept in some sorts of complex cognitions might fail at language acquisition because it does not have capacities that are specifically tailored for the pickup and learning of linguistic structure. It may fail because it does not "know" enough in advance about some specific properties in the domain of natural language, a pattern of failure that is compatible with a nativist view of knowledge and its origins. But that prior "knowledge" does not have to be in the form of an innately represented set of grammatical rules; it can be a set of powerful biases for interpreting linguistic information in highly constrained ways. Specifying those biases and constraints is where the real distinctions between contemporary nativists and empiricists reside (Keil 1981, 1998). Indeed, it has recently been argued that, even in traditional biology, constraints thought of as "canalization" are the best way of understanding innateness (Ariew 1996).

Although it is more common in philosophy to distinguish RATIONALISM VS. EMPIRICISM, in cognitive science today it is nativism that is usually pitted against empiricism, where, for a nativist, knowledge of such things as grammar or folk psychology does not arise from simply having rational thought and its logical consequences, but rather from having information-specific learning biases that go beyond the more content-neutral mechanisms of learning favored by empiricists, such as unconstrained associationism. Nativists

and empiricists disagree on whether one organism achieves greater learning success than another because it is more cognitively capable in general or because it has specialized structures tuned to learn a particular kind of knowledge. This is the question of DOMAIN SPECIFICITY that has become such a pivotal issue in cognitive science today, especially in EVOLUTIONARY PSYCHOLOGY (Fodor 1983; Hirschfeld and Gelman 1994; Keil 1981; Cosmides and Tooby 1994).

Domain specificity alone, however, is not enough to characterize nativism. The specialization for information must involve a certain kind and "level" of processing. The eye is tailored for different kinds of information than the ear (VISUAL ANATOMY AND PHYSIOLOGY, AUDITORY PHYSIOLOGY), a fact well known to both nativists and empiricists for centuries. But empiricists see those specializations as soon disappearing when that information flows beyond the sensory transducers. If all of thought and all patterns of learning can be explained by general laws, such as those of association, once one goes beyond the specializations of the sense organs, then nativism founders. If, however, there are specialized systems for building up representations and processes in specific domains, whether they be language, biology, or number (LANGUAGE ACQUISITION, FOLK BIOLOGY, NAIVE MATHEMATICS), and general learning principles seem inadequate, nativism is supported.

Consider the difference between having a system that is tuned to expect certain patterns in a specific modality, such as the eye's "expectations" concerning reflected light patterns, and a system that has expectations that transcend modalities, such as that two physical bodies cannot interpenetrate (Spelke 1994). The second expectation can be borne out tactilely, visually, and possibly even auditorily. This expectation is still domain specific in that it applies only to bounded physical objects and not fluids, gases, or aggregates. Systems that are tuned to patterns that transcend modalities would therefore be more likely to fit with a nativist stance.

Connectionist architectures can favor either empiricist or nativist orientations depending on their implementation. A system with preset weights and compression algorithms that seem to be optimized for learning only certain kinds of information, such as that of spatial layout, might well support a nativist account. If such weights, however, only bias the learner toward low-level perceptual features, an empiricist approach is supported (Seidenberg 1992). In some models, a low-level bias, such as selective attention in human infants for moving triangular dot patterns, has been argued to result in a "face processing area of the brain," even though there were no initial biases in that region for faces initially (Johnson and Morton 1991). Thus, an end state of domain-specific processing of a particular kind of information that is localized in a specific region of the brain is not by itself nativist. The way in which that specialized processing was set up is critical. Similarly, a recent interest in "emergentism" in connectionist systems, namely ways in which general learning systems can yield unpredictable emergent higher-order properties (MacWhinney forthcoming), does not displace nativism as much as it makes apparent the subtlety needed for arguments about the origins of various types of knowledge.

In short, nativists and empiricists primarily disagree on the extent to which pre-existing biases for specific domains of information go beyond those in effect at the levels of sensory transducers. The sense of domain also shifts, with domains at the sensory levels being patterns of information such as "light" or "sound waves" and domains at higher levels being patterns corresponding to such things as bounded physical objects, intentional agents, number, or spatial layout. All of these domains of the second sort clearly are amodal and more cognitive than perceptual.

Biases on high-level cognition that work in domain-general ways do not need to support nativism. For example, the base rate fallacy (Kahneman, Slovic, and Tversky 1982) would seem to apply to any kind of experienced information, regardless of its domain. As such, it would seem to be a further modification of general laws of learning, such as those on association, all of which fits with empiricism. If, however, this bias were to be much more prominent in cases of social attribution, and seemed to help learning about social situations, it would be considered domain specific.

Some have argued that the nativism/empiricism controversy is seriously misguided because of the intrinsically interactional nature of development (Lehrman 1953). This notion has been raised again more recently (Elman et al. 1996) in attempts to argue that it makes no sense to ask what is innate in dynamic learning systems. These objections, however, attack a caricature of "innate structures" and not the current debate between nativists and empiricists. Part of the confusion is between specifying particular behaviors or pieces of knowledge as innate, as opposed to being products of the learning function itself and the cognitive biases it engenders. When learning is considered as a function from sets of environments to sets of mental representations (Chomsky 1980), the intrinsically interactional nature of learning is part of the formulation.

See also CONNECTIONIST APPROACHES TO LANGUAGE; EVOLUTION OF LANGUAGE; INNATENESS OF LANGUAGE; LEARNING; LINGUISTIC UNIVERSALS AND UNIVERSAL GRAMMAR; MODULARITY OF MIND

—*Frank Keil*

References

Ariew, A. (1996). Innateness and canalization. *Philosophy of Science* 63: 19–27.

Chomsky, N. (1980). *Rules and Representations.* New York: Columbia University Press.

Cosmides, L., and J. Tooby. (1994). The evolution of domain specificity: The evolution of functional organization. In L. A. Hirschfeld and S. A. Gelman, Eds., *Mapping the Mind: Domain Specificity in Cognition and Culture.* Cambridge: Cambridge University Press.

Elman, J. L., E. A. Bates, M. H. Johnson, A. Karmiloff-Smith, D. Parisi, and K. Plunkett. (1996). *Rethinking Innateness.* Cambridge, MA: MIT Press.

Fodor, J. A. (1983). *Modularity of Mind.* Cambridge, MA: MIT Press.

Hirschfeld, L. A., and S. A. Gelman, Eds. (1994). *Mapping the Mind: Domain Specificity in Cognition and Culture.* Cambridge: Cambridge University Press.

Johnson, M. H., and J. Morton. (1991). *Biology and Cognitive Development: The Case of Face Recognition.* Cambridge, MA: Blackwell.

Kahneman, D., P. Slovic, and A. Tversky. (1982). *Judgement under Uncertainty: Heuristics and Biases.* New York: Cambridge University Press.

Keil, F. C. (1981). Constraints on knowledge and cognitive development. *Psychological Review* 88: 197–227.

Keil, F. C. (1998). Cognitive science and the origins of thought and knowledge. In R. M. Lerner, Ed., *Theoretical Models of Human Development.* Vol. 1, *Handbook of Child Psychology.* New York: Wiley.

Lehrman, D. (1953). A critique of Konrad Lorenz's theory of instinctive behavior. *Quarterly Review of Biology* 28: 337–363.

MacWhinney, B. J., Ed. (Forthcoming). *Emergentist Approaches to Language.* Hillsdale, NJ: Erlbaum.

Savage-Rumbaugh, E. S., J. Murphy, R. A. Sevick, K. E. Brakke, S. L. Williams, and D. Rumbaugh. (1993). *Language Comprehension in Ape and Child.* Monographs of the Society for Research in Child Development, 233. Chicago: University of Chicago Press.

Seidenberg, M. S. (1992). Connectionism without tears. In S. Davis, Ed., *Connectionism: Theory and Practice.* Oxford: Oxford University Press.

Spelke, E. (1994). Initial knowledge: Six suggestions. *Cognition* 50: 431–445.

Further Readings

Chomsky, N. (1988). *Language and Problems of Knowledge: The Managua Lectures.* Cambridge, MA: Bradford Books/MIT Press.

Fischer, K. W., and T. Bidell. (1991). Constraining nativist inferences about cognitive capacities. In S. C. A. R. Gelman, Ed., *The Epigenesis of Mind: Essays on Biology and Knowledge.* Hillsdale, NJ: Erlbaum, pp. 199–235.

Fodor, J. (1981). *Representations: Philosophical Essays on the Foundations of Cognitive Science.* Cambridge, MA: MIT Press.

Keil, F. C. (1990). Constraints on constraints: Surveying the epigenetic landscape. *Cognitive Science* 14: 135–168.

Keil, F., C. Smith, D. Simons, and D. Levin. (1998). Two dogmas of conceptual empiricism. *Cognition* 65(2).

Lerner, R. M. (1984). *On the Nature of Human Plasticity.* New York: Cambridge University Press.

Leslie, A. (1995). A theory of agency. In A. L. Premack, D. Premack, and D. Sperber, Eds., *Causal Cognition: A Multi-Disciplinary Debate.* New York: Oxford, pp. 121–141.

Lightfoot, D. (1982). *The Language Lottery: Toward a Biology of Grammars.* Cambridge, MA: MIT Press.

Mandler, J. M. (1992). How to build a baby: II. Conceptual primitives. *Psychological Review* 99: 587–604.

McClelland, J. L., M. Bruce, L. O'Reilly, and C. Randall. (1995). Why there are complementary learning systems in the hippocampus and neocortex: Insights from the successes and failures of connectionist models of learning and memory. *Psychological Review* 102 (3): 419–437.

Meltzoff, A. N., and M. K. Moore. (1989). Imitation in newborn infants: Exploring the range of gestures imitated and the underlying mechanisms. *Developmental Psychology* 25: 954–962.

Piatelli-Palmarini, M. (1994). Ever since language and learning: Afterthoughts on the Piaget-Chomsky debate. *Cognition* 50: 315–346.

Pinker, S. (1994). *The Language Instinct.* New York: Morrow.

Pinker, S. (1997). *How the Mind Works.* New York: W. W. Norton.

Prince, A., and P. Smolensky. (1997). Optimality: From neural networks to universal grammar. *Science* 275: 1604–1610.

Spelke, E., and E. Newport. (1998). Nativism. In R. M. Lerner, Ed., *Theoretical Models of Human Development.* Vol. 1, *Handbook of Child Psychology.* New York: Wiley.

Wynn, K. (1995). Origins of numerical knowledge. *Mathematical Cognition* 1.

Nativism, History of

Our understanding of ourselves and of our world rests on two factors: the innate nature of our minds and the specific character of our experience. For 2,500 years there has been an on-again off-again debate over which of these factors is paramount. NATIVISM champions our innate endowment; *empiricism,* the role of experience (cf. RATIONALISM VS. EMPIRICISM). There have been three significant moments in the historical development of nativism: Plato's doctrine of anamnesis, the rationalist defense of innateness in the seventeenth and eighteenth centuries, and the contemporary revival of nativism in the cognitive sciences.

Platonic Nativism

Plato presents the first explicit defense of nativism in the *Meno,* where Socrates draws out a geometrical theorem from an uneducated slave, and argues that this is possible only because the slave implicitly had the theorem in him all along. He had merely forgotten it, and questioning helped him to recollect. For Plato, all genuine learning is a matter of recollecting (*anamnesis*) what is innate but forgotten. Socrates goes on to argue that because the slave had not been taught geometry, he must have acquired the knowledge in an earlier existence. In the *Phaedo,* Plato connects innateness to the theory of forms and argues that our grasp of the form of equality could not come from perceived equals, and must therefore also be innate. For Plato, nativism is more than a solution to the epistemological problem of knowledge acquisition; it also provides evidence for the preexistence and immortality of the soul.

Plato's claims have served as the touchstone for defenders of nativism (so much so that the doctrine is sometimes referred to as "Platonism"), but it is difficult to pin down a specific Platonic innateness "doctrine." The problem is that Plato's nativism is embedded in an epistemological framework that takes transcendent forms to be the only objects of genuine knowledge, and there are unresolved questions about the exact nature of that framework. Plato never definitively says what forms there are, or what role our grasp of the forms plays in ordinary cognition. It is therefore difficult to say confidently what Plato took to be innate, or how he conceived the influence of the innate in thinking. Apart from these uncertainties, his argument seems threatened by a potentially devastating regress: if knowledge acquisition is recollection, how is it that we acquire knowledge in an earlier existence?

Nativism and Continental Rationalism

In the *Meditations,* René DESCARTES argues that concepts such as God and infinity can not be derived from experience and must therefore be innate. At some points he even suggests that no ideas can come to us via experience; all must be innate. Gottfried Wilhelm Leibniz, the main rationalist spokesman for nativism, argues that our certain knowledge of necessary truths (of mathematics, logic, metaphysics, and so on) is wholly inexplicable on the empiricist position. Our experience is always particular and contingent; how could our knowledge be universal and necessary? Such knowledge must instead rest on innate principles. Leibniz also argues that even our ordinary empirical concepts contain an innate element. Our concept of a man, for instance, draws upon our innate general concept of substance as well as on the specific features of men that we discover in experience. A priori knowledge about substance is possible because we can mine this innate source, and such knowledge is therefore immune from the contingencies of the specific substances we experience.

Leibniz's position illustrates the fit between seventeenth-century rationalism and nativism. Rationalism holds that the mind can go beyond appearances and provide us with insight into the intelligible nature of things; this insight yields a priori knowledge. But how do we get such insight? Here nativism is invoked: our innate ideas and principles are the source of our a priori understanding. The problem with this package is that even if something is innate, that does not in itself establish its truth; it certainly cannot establish its necessity. René Descartes implicitly recognizes this when he introduces a benevolent God into his epistemology as the ultimate guarantor of our knowledge. The idea is that if something is innate, a benevolent God must have put it there for our edification, and a benevolent God would not mislead us.

The historical result was that nativism became entangled with an excess of philosophical baggage. Plato, as we saw, joined it to a transcendent world of forms and a mystical doctrine of the preexistence of the soul. From rationalism it inherited an exalted conception of the power of pure reason and an epistemology that seemed to ultimately require a theological basis. Whatever the original merits of the basic nativist claim about the initial state of the mind, the position began to seem out of step with the more naturalistic world view of the Newtonian revolution.

Empiricism

John Locke's *Essay,* the first systematic defense of empiricism, is a philosophical expression of this more naturalistic perspective. Locke begins with an extended polemic against nativism, in which he charges that it is either blatantly false, because there are no principles that can claim the "universal consent" that an innate principle would produce, or that it reduces to the trivial claim that we have an inborn capacity to come to know everything we know. Leibniz responds to these preemptive strikes in his *New Essays,* where a number of innovative ideas are introduced—for example, the notion of unconscious knowledge, the procedural-declarative distinction, the suggestion of innate biases that may or may not be expressed. But although this part of the debate has had greater visibility, the more important empiricist attack—and this is the main point of Locke's *Essay* and of subsequent empiricist theorizing—is that nativism is an unnecessary extravagance, because our knowledge can be explained with the simpler empiricist hypothesis. The empiricist project exerted a dominant influence in both philosophy and psychology well into the twentieth century. It was widely assumed that the program had to eventually succeed, because nativism was stigmatized as a backward superstition and not a serious "scientific" alternative. Empiricist-oriented psychologists carried over the early associationist thinking of David HUME, John Stuart Mill, and others into the behaviorist analyses of learning, while their counterparts in philosophy pursued technical analyses of INDUCTION and CONCEPT formation.

Chomsky and the INNATENESS OF LANGUAGE

The reign of this presumptive empiricism ended at mid-century with Noam Chomsky's groundbreaking work in linguistics. Chomsky has revived nativism by arguing that a child's mastery of language cannot be accounted for in terms of empiricist learning mechanisms. His case rests on the POVERTY OF THE STIMULUS ARGUMENTS. Speakers adhere to a complex system of grammatical rules that must somehow be reflected in the speaker's psychological processors; otherwise we cannot explain the adherence. But these rules involve categories and classifications that are abstract and far removed from the linguistic evidence available to the learner, and their specific content is underdetermined by the evidence available. The empiricist's inductive manipulation of the data available to the child cannot produce the rule-information that the child must have. But despite this shortfall, normal children acquire the right set of rules with little or no rule-instruction, and at an age at which they cannot master much else. Chomsky's hypothesis is that language learners have innately specified information that is specifically about the nature of human language ("universal grammar"). The child is not simply dropped into the wholly alien terrain of language; instead she comes to the language-learning task with a "head start"—a rough map giving her some idea of what to look for. Chomsky's claims have attracted criticism both from within and outside linguistics, but the preponderant view is that as far as language goes, empiricism is wrong and nativism is right.

This nativist revival in linguistics led to the reassessment of established empiricist approaches to development in other areas like mathematics, physical causality, visual perception, and so on. In many of these areas, nativists have developed new evidence to support their positions, and in some cases have argued that older findings were misinterpreted. A case in point is Jerry Fodor's contention that the whole empiricist "concept-learning" paradigm—the sort of "learning by example" that has been championed from Locke to the present—has at its core a surprising and unavoidable nativist commitment. Empiricists have of course not given up; new connectionist models of learning have been touted as using only empiricist-sanctioned principles, but as nevertheless being able to learn what nativists have claimed was unlearnable without domain-specific innate structure.

Regardless of how the empirical issues are resolved in any particular domain, nativism has been at least reestab-

lished in contemporary cognitive science as a viable alternative to empiricism. The core question-schema it addresses remains cogent: are our ideas, beliefs, knowledge, and so forth in any particular domain derived solely from experience, or are they to some extent traceable to domain-specific features of the mind's initial endowment? There is nothing obscure or unscientific about nativist answers. They are on the contrary very much in line with our understanding of the way brain adaptations equip organisms to function in their environmental niches. Cognitive ethologists (*see* COGNITIVE ETHOLOGY) have shown that rats are born with a grasp of their nutritional needs, and that ants do not need to be taught the system of dead reckoning they use in foraging expeditions. Nativists extend this pattern of findings to the higher cognitive functions found in humans. The new field of EVOLUTIONARY PSYCHOLOGY, which adopts a thoroughgoing nativist perspective, focuses especially on the sorts of cognitive and motivational structures that might have developed as adaptations in the original ancestral settings in which humans evolved.

This newly secured scientific respectability has come at a philosophical price. The "transcendental" nativism of Plato and Descartes had significant epistemological and metaphysical ramifications that the new nativism cannot secure with the same ease.

See also COGNITIVE ARCHITECTURE; CONNECTIONIST APPROACHES TO LANGUAGE; DOMAIN SPECIFICITY; KANT; LINGUISTIC UNIVERSALS AND UNIVERSAL GRAMMAR; PARAMETER-SETTING APPROACHES TO ACQUISITION, CREOLIZATION, AND DIACHRONY

—*Jerry Samet*

References

Chomsky, N. (1965). *Aspects of a Theory of Syntax.* Cambridge, MA: MIT Press.

Descartes, R. (1641). Meditations on first philosophy. In E. Haldane and G. R. T. Ross, Eds., (1967). *The Philosophical Works of Descartes.* Cambridge: Cambridge University Press.

Fodor, J. (1981). *Representations: Philosophical Essays on the Foundation of Cognitive Science.* Cambridge, MA: MIT Press.

Leibniz, G. W. (1704). *New Essays on Human Understanding.* Translated and edited by P. Remnant and J. Bennett. Cambridge: Cambridge University Press, 1981.

Locke, J. (1690). *An Essay Concerning Human Understanding.* P. H. Nidditch, Ed. Oxford: Oxford University Press, 1975.

Plato. (c. 380 B.C.). *Meno* (key passages: 80a–86c) and *Phaedo* (key passages: 73c–78b).

Further Readings

Chomsky, N. (1988). *Language and Problems of Knowledge.* Cambridge, MA: MIT Press.

Edgley, R. (1970). *Knowledge and Necessity, Royal Institute of Philosophy Lectures,* vol. 3. London: Macmillan.

Hook, S., Ed. (1969). *Language and Philosophy: A Symposium.* New York: NYU Press.

Jolley, N. (1984). *Leibniz and Locke.* Oxford: Clarendon Press.

Piattelli-Palmerini, M., Ed. (1980). *Language and Learning.* Cambridge, MA: Harvard University Press.

Samet, J. (Forthcoming). *Nativism.* Cambridge, MA: MIT Press.

Scott, D. (1996). *Recollection and Experience: Plato's Theory of Learning and its Successors.* Cambridge: Cambridge University Press.

Stich, S., Ed. (1975). *Innate Ideas.* Berkeley: University of California Press.

Natural Kinds

Some systems of classification are *merely conventional:* they divide a population of objects into kinds, and the principles by which objects are categorized are designed to answer to some specific purpose. There is no antecedently correct or incorrect way to categorize various objects apart from the purposes to which the system of classification will be put. Thus, for example, we divide the world into different time zones, and our purpose in so doing is to allow for coordination of activities in different locales, but there is no right or wrong way to draw the boundaries of time zones; there are merely more or less convenient ways that answer better or worse the concerns that led us to devise these categories in the first place. The view that all systems of categorization are merely conventional is called *conventionalism* about kinds.

Some systems of CATEGORIZATION, however, do not seem to be merely conventional. Rather, they attempt to draw conceptual boundaries that correspond to real distinctions in nature, boundaries which, in Plato's phrase, "cut nature at its joints." Thus, for example, the periodic table of elements seems not merely an arbitrary or convenient system of classification, a system that makes certain calculations or predictions easier; rather, it seems to describe real kinds in nature, kinds whose existence is not just a product of our classificatory activity. Kinds of this sort, which are not merely conventional, are called *natural kinds.* Those who believe that there are natural kinds, called *realists* about kinds, believe that it is part of the business of the various sciences to discover what the natural kinds are; scientific taxonomies, in this view, attempt to provide a proper account of these kinds.

The notion of a natural kind figures in to important questions in the methodology of the cognitive sciences, as well as work in COGNITIVE DEVELOPMENT, the psychology of reasoning, and COGNITIVE ANTHROPOLOGY.

According to conventionalism, many disputes about proper taxonomy in the sciences are misguided. Taxonomic systems, in this view, cannot themselves "get things right" or "get things wrong," although some will, of course, be more convenient than others. Disputes about taxonomy, in this view, do not involve genuine disagreement about substantive scientific questions. Realists, however, regard disputes about proper taxonomy in the various sciences as substantive. Consider, for example, the categorization of psychopathologies in the *Diagnostic and Statistical Manual* (1994). Those who think of psychodiagnostic categories as merely conventional will regard questions about categorization here as ones of convenience; a proper system of categorization is merely one that well serves the purposes for which it was designed. If, however, the various psychodiagnostic categories constitute a system of natural kinds, then there are substantive theoretical questions about the boundaries of those kinds. In this view, certain ways of drawing the boundaries among psychopathologies are simply mistaken, and not merely inconvenient or ill-suited to the purposes for which we have devised our classificatory scheme. More important, some systems of classification might be extremely useful for certain purposes without giving a proper account of the nature and boundaries of the items classified.

Those who believe that all classification is merely conventional thus see taxonomic disputes as shallow and the search for substantive theory to guide taxonomy as misguided; substantive scientific questions arise only *after* the choice of a taxonomic system. Realists about natural kinds, on the other hand, see taxonomic disputes as potentially important; a proper taxonomy must be guided by theoretical insight into the underlying causal structure of the phenomena under study. The dispute between conventionalists and realists is thus significant not only in issues concerning psychodiagnosis, but also in addressing taxonomic questions throughout the cognitive sciences.

The way in which questions about natural kinds influence taxonomic issues demonstrates the importance of this concept for methodological concerns in the cognitive sciences. Questions about natural kinds arise more directly, however, as well. First, natural kind CONCEPTS play a crucial role in inductive inference. Second, and relatedly, the acquisition of natural kind concepts plays an important role in cognitive development.

Natural kind concepts play an important role in successful inductive inference because members of a given natural kind tend to have many of their most fundamental properties in common. Thus, finding that one member of a kind has a certain property gives one reason for believing that others will share that property as well. This uniformity of natural kinds is part of what distinguishes them from arbitrarily specified classes of individuals, for in the case of arbitrary classes, noting that one member of the class has a certain property (other than the ones that are used to define the class) provides one with no reason at all to believe that other members of the class will share that property. Our ability to make successful inductive inferences thus depends on our ability to recognize natural kinds. Not surprisingly, many suggest an evolutionary basis for such a preestablished harmony between folk and scientific taxonomies. While no one believes that our native categories simply mirror those of the sciences, the suggestion here is that natural selection provides us with a starting point that approximately captures some of the real distinctions in nature, thereby allowing for the possibility of more elaborate and more accurate scientific taxonomies. Without some native help in identifying the real categories in nature, some have argued, we would be unable to develop accurate taxonomies at all.

It is for this reason that the acquisition of natural kind concepts is such an important intellectual achievement. Two developmental questions need to be separated here: (1) At what point are various natural kind concepts acquired? For example, when do children acquire the concept of a living thing, of an animal, of a being with mental states, and so on?

(2) At what point do children acquire the concept of a natural kind itself? A good deal of work has been done on each of these questions. Although an explicitly articulated concept of a natural kind is certainly found in no children, and indeed, in few adults, the ways in which children classify objects and the ways in which they respond to the information that two objects are members of a single taxonomic category suggest that there is a strong tendency to view the world as having a structure that presupposes the existence of natural kinds. In particular, children do not tend to classify objects merely on the basis of their most obvious observable features, features that may be unrevealing of natural kind membership; and when children are told that two individuals are members of a single category, they tend to assume that these individuals will share many fundamental properties, even when the most obvious observable features of the objects differ. Some authors have suggested that these tendencies may be innate; this would help to explain the possibility of successful inductive inference by explaining the source of the human ability to identify kinds that support inductive generalizations. A tendency to view the world in terms of the structure required by natural kinds seems, at a minimum, to be an ability already in place early in cognitive development.

Relevant here too is work in cognitive anthropology. Atran's work (1990) on folk taxonomies reveals deep similarities in the ways in which different cultures divide up the biological world. More than this, these taxonomies have much more than just a passing resemblance to the more refined taxonomic categories of the biological sciences.

Not everyone is entirely optimistic about the possibility of filling in the details of the picture presented here. Some deny that the taxonomies of the different sciences have enough in common with one another to speak of them all as displaying a single structure, the structure of natural kinds. This skepticism has been fueled by a number of factors, including the recognition that the physical world is not deterministic, as well as the fact that the kinds of the biological world crosscut one another. That scientific taxonomies are simply more messy than was once assumed has thus not only complicated the picture of natural kinds, but also made some doubt the very usefulness of the notion. Moreover, the similarity between folk taxonomies and the taxonomies of the various sciences differ substantially. The connection between our conceptual capacities and the causal structure of the world thus leaves a good deal to be discovered on all accounts.

See also CAUSAL REASONING; FOLK BIOLOGY; INDUCTION; NATIVISM; REALISM AND ANTIREALISM; REFERENCE, THEORIES OF

—*Hilary Kornblith*

References

American Psychiatric Association. (1994). *Diagnostic and Statistical Manual of Mental Disorders*. 4th ed. Washington, D.C.

Atran, S. (1990). *Cognitive Foundations of Natural History*. Cambridge: Cambridge University Press.

Boyd, R. (1991). Realism, anti-foundationalism and the enthusiasm for natural kinds. *Philosophical Studies* 61: 127–148.

Carey, S. (1985). *Conceptual Change in Childhood*. Cambridge, MA: MIT Press.

Dupre, J. (1993). *The Disorder of Things*. Cambridge, MA: Harvard University Press.

Gelman, S. A., and H. M. Wellman. (1991). Insides and essences: Early understanding of the non-obvious. *Cognition* 38: 213–244.

Gopnik, A., and A. Meltzoff. (1997). *Words, Thoughts, and Theories*. Cambridge, MA: MIT Press.

Hacking, I. (1995). *Rewriting the Soul*. Princeton, NJ: Princeton University Press.

Keil, F. (1989). *Concepts, Kinds, and Cognitive Development*. Cambridge, MA: MIT Press.

Kornblith, H. (1993). *Inductive Inference and Its Natural Ground*. Cambridge, MA: MIT Press.

Locke, J. (1690). *An Essay Concerning Human Understanding*. London: Thomas Bassett.

Markman, E. (1989). *Categorization and Naming in Children*. Cambridge, MA: MIT Press.

Medin, D., and A. Ortony. (1989). Psychological essentialism. In S. Vosniadou and A. Ortony, Eds., *Similarity and Analogical Reasoning*. Cambridge: Cambridge University Press, pp. 179–195.

Putnam, H. (1975). *Mind, Language and Reality*. Cambridge: Cambridge University Press.

Quine, W. V. O. (1969). *Ontological Relativity and Other Essays*. New York: Columbia University Press.

Schwartz, S. P. (1977). *Naming, Necessity and Natural Kinds*. Ithaca, NY: Cornell University Press.

Wellman, H. M., and S. A. Gelman. (1988). Children's understanding of the non-obvious. In R. Sternberg, Ed., *Advances in the Psychology of Intelligence*, vol. 4. Hillsdale, NJ: Erlbaum.

Natural Language Generation

Automated natural language generation (NLG), currently about 25 years old, investigates how to build computer programs to produce high-quality text from computer-internal representations of information. Generally, NLG does not include research on the automatic production of speech, whether from text or from a more abstract input (see SPEECH SYNTHESIS). Also, with few exceptions, research has steadily moved away from modeling how people produce language to developing methods by which computers can be made to do so robustly.

The information provided to a language generator is produced by some other system (the "host" program), which may be an expert system, database access system, MACHINE TRANSLATION engine, and so on. The outputs of various host systems can differ quite significantly, a fact that makes creating a standardized input notation for generators a perennial problem.

Traditionally, workers on NLG have divided the problem into two major areas: content selection ("what shall I say?") and content expression ("how shall I say it?"). Processing in these stages is generally performed by so-called text planners and sentence realizers, respectively. More recently, two further developments have occurred: first, as generators became more expressive, the control of stylistic variation ("why should I say it this way?") has become important; second, an intermediate stage of sentence planning has been introduced to fill the "generation gap" between text planners and sentence realizers. The canonical generator architecture

Input: communicative goals

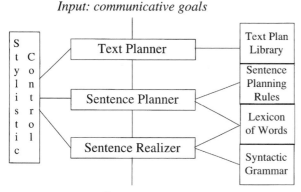

Output: text

Figure 1.

appears in figure 1. No generator created to date fully embodies all these modules. Pilot attempts at comprehensive architectures are ERMA (Clippinger 1974) and PAULINE (Hovy 1988). Most generators contain just some of these stages, in various arrangements; see Reiter (1994) and De Smedt, Horacek, and Zock (1995).

Stage 1: Text Planning

Accepting one or more communicative goals from the host system, the text planner's two tasks are to select the appropriate content material to express, and to order that material into a coherently flowing sequence. A typical input goal might be [DESCRIBE HOUSE-15] or [MOTIVATE GOING-ON-VACATION-12], where the terms with numbers denote specific packages of information. After planning, the output is generally a tree structure or an ordered list of more detailed content propositions, linked together by discourse connectives signaled by "therefore," "and," "however," and so on. Usually, each proposition represents approximately the information contained in a single-clause sentence. Thus, the initial goal [DESCRIBE HOUSE-15] may be expanded into a text plan containing (in simplified notation) [GENERATE HOUSE-IDENTIFIER] [GENERATE ADDRESS] [INTRODUCE FLOORPLAN] [ELABORATE [GENERATE GROUND-FLOOR] "and" [GENERATE TOP-FLOOR] "and" [GENERATE BASEMENT]] and so on. Generally, text planning is considered to be language-independent.

The two principal methods for performing the text planning tasks involve schemas and so-called rhetorical relations. Schemas (McKeown 1985; Paris 1993; see SCHEMATA) are the simplest and most popular, useful when the texts follow a fairly stereotypical structure, such as short encyclopedia articles or business reports. Each schema specifies the typical sequence of units of content material (or of other schemata; they may be nested); for example, the order of floors. Rhetorical relations (e.g., Elaboration, Justification, Background) organize material by specifying which units of material (or blocks of units) should be selected and linked in sequence. Several collections of relations have been proposed; Rhetorical Structure Theory (Mann and Thompson

1988) and the associated method of planning (Hovy 1993; Moore 1989) are typical.

Stage 2: Sentence Planning

Until the early 1990s, sentence-planning tasks were performed during text planning or sentence realization. Increasingly, however, sentence planning is seen as a distinct stage; this clarifies the generation process and makes focused investigation of subtasks easier.

Accepting from the text planner a text structure, some of the sentence planner's tasks include: specifying sentence boundaries; organizing (ordering, relativizing, etc.) the material internal to each sentence; planning cross-sentence reference and other anaphora; selecting appropriate words and phrases to express content; and specifying tense, mode (active or passive), as well as other syntactic parameters. The ideal output of a sentence planner is a list of clause-sized units containing a fairly complete syntactic specification for each clause; see Meteer (1990) for a thoughtful study.

In the example, the sentence planner must decide whether to generate each floor plan as a separate sentence or to conjoin them (and if so, to choose an appropriate conjunction). It must decide whether to say, for example, "the ground floor contains . . ." or "the ground floor has the following rooms . . . ," or any of numerous other formulations. It must decide whether to say "living room" or "sitting room"; "den" or "family room." The interrelatedness and wide range of variation of such individual aspects makes sentence planning a difficult task, as anyone who has ever written an essay knows. A considerable amount of research on individual sentence-planning tasks exists (see the readings below), but there is relatively little on their integration (see Appelt 1985; Nirenburg et al. 1988).

Stage 3: Sentence Realization

Accepting from the sentence planner a list of sentence specifications, the sentence realizer's tasks are to determine the grammatically correct order of words; to inflect words for tense, number, and so on, as required by the language; and to add punctuation, capitalization, and the like. These tasks are language-dependent.

Realization is the most extensively studied stage of generation. The principal knowledge required is a grammar of syntactic rules and a lexicon of words. Different theories of SYNTAX have led to very different approaches to realization. Realization algorithms include unification (Elhadad 1992), Systemic network traversal (Mann and Matthiessen 1985), phrase expansion (Meteer et al. 1987), head-driven and reversible methods (Van Noord 1990; St. Dizier 1992), simulated annealing (De Smedt 1990), connectionist architectures (Ward 1990), and statistically based management of underspecification (Knight and Hatzivassiloglou 1995). The systems Penman (Mann and Matthiessen 1985; later extended as KPML; Bateman 1994), FUF/SURGE (Elhadad 1992), and MUMBLE (Meteer et al. 1987) have been distributed and used by several external users.

In the example, the specification (in simplified form):

(1) [GENERATE (TYPE: DECLARATIVE-SENTENCE)
      (HEAD: POSSESS)
      (SUBJECT:((HEAD: FLOOR) (LEVEL-MODI-
      FIER: GROUND) (DETERMINED: YES)))
      (OBJECT:((HEAD: ROOM) (NUMBER: 4)
      (DETERMINED: NO)))
      (TENSE: PRESENT)]

as produced by the sentence planner will be interpreted by the grammar rules to form a sentence such as "the ground floor has four rooms."

Stylistic Control

Throughout the generation process, some agency has to ensure the consistency of choices, whose net effect is the style of the text. Since different styles have different communicative effects, the stylistic control module must use high-level pragmatic parameters initially specified for the system (such as degree of formality, the addressee's language level, amount of time available, communication genre) to govern its overall decision policies. These policies determine the selection of the most appropriate option from the options facing any generator module at each point during the planning and realization process.

Few studies have been performed on this aspect of generation; lexicons, grammars, and sets of planning rules are still too small to necessitate much stylistic guidance. Furthermore, the complexity of interaction of choices across the stages of generation requires deep attention: how does the choice of word "freedom fighter"/"terrorist"/"guerrilla" interact with the length of the sentences near it, or with the choice of active or passive mode? See Jameson (1987), Hovy (1988), and DiMarco and Hirst (1990) for studies.

Generation Techniques

Two core operations are performed throughout the generation process: content selection and ordering. For text planning, the items are units of meaning representation; for realization, the items are grammatical constituents and/or words. To do this, almost all generators use one of the following four basic techniques.

Canned items: Predefined sentences or paragraphs are selected and printed without modification. This approach is used for simple applications.

Templates: Predefined structures that allow some variation are selected, and their blank spaces filled with items specified by the content. The blanks usually have associated requirements that specify what kinds of information may fill them.

Cascaded patterns: An initial abstract pattern is selected, and each of its pieces are replaced by successively more detailed patterns, forming a tree structure with, at its leaves, the target elements. An example is traditional phrase-structure grammars, with words as target elements. The selection of suitable patterns for further expansion is guided by the content to be generated. Example realizer: MUMBLE (Meteer et al. 1987), using grammar rules as patterns; exam-

ple text planner: TEXT (McKeown 1985), using schemas as patterns.

Features: In the most sophisticated approach to realization, grammar rules, lexical items, and the input notation are all encoded as collections of features, using the same type of notation. A process called unification is employed to compare the input's features against all possible grammar rules and lexical items to determine which combination of rules and items matches. For example, the specification for the sentence "the ground floor has four rooms" given above will unify with the feature-based grammar rule:

(2) [SENTENCE (TYPE: DECLARATIVE-SENTENCE)
      (HEAD: X0)
      (SUBJECT: X1)
      (OBJECT: X2)
      (TENSE: X3)]

where each variable X is then associated with the appropriate portion of the input and subsequently unified against other rules. And the word "rooms" is obtained from the lexicon by successfully unifying the input's subject with the lexical item.

(3) [LEXITEM (HEAD: ROOM) (NUMBER: >1) (LEX-
      EME: "rooms")]

Example realizer: FUF/SURGE (Elhadad 1992).

Using features a different way, the influential Penman system (Mann and Matthiessen 1985) contains a network of decision points that guide the system to identify appropriate features, whose ultimate combination specifies the desired sentence structure and lexical items.

See also KNOWLEDGE-BASED SYSTEMS; LANGUAGE PRODUCTION; NATURAL LANGUAGE PROCESSING

—*Eduard Hovy*

References

Appelt, D. E. (1985). *Planning English Sentences.* Cambridge: Cambridge University Press.

Bateman, J. A. (1994). KPML: The KOMET-Penman (Multilingual) Development Environment. Darmstadt, Germany: Technical Report, IPSI Institute.

Clippinger, J. H. (1974). *A Discourse Speaking Program as a Preliminary Theory of Discourse Behavior and a Limited Theory of Psychoanalytic Discourse.* Ph.D. diss., University of Pennsylvania.

De Smedt, K. J. M. J. (1990). *Incremental Sentence Generation.* Ph.D. diss., University of Nijmegen.

De Smedt, K. J. M. J., H. Horacek, and M. Zock. (1995). Architectures for natural language generation: problems and perspectives. In G. Adorni and M. Zock, Eds., *Trends in Natural Language Generation: An Artificial Intelligence Perspective.* Heidelberg, Germany: Springer-Verlag Lecture Notes in AI, No. 1036, pp. 17–46.

DiMarco, C., and G. Hirst. (1990). A computational theory of goal-directed style in syntax. *Computational Linguistics* 19(3): 451–500.

Elhadad, M. (1992). *Using Argumentation to Control Lexical Choice: A Functional Unification-Based Approach.* Ph.D. diss., Columbia University.

Hovy, E. H. (1988). *Generating Natural Language under Pragmatic Constraints.* Hillsdale: Erlbaum.

Hovy, E. H. (1993). Automated discourse generation using discourse structure relations. *Artificial Intelligence* 63(1–2): 341–386 Special Issue on Natural Language Processing.

Jameson, A. (1987). How to appear to be conforming to the "maxims" even if you prefer to violate them. In G. Kempen, Ed., *Natural Language Generation: Recent Advances in Artificial Intelligence, Psychology, and Linguistics.* Dordrecht: Kluwer, pp. 19–42.

Knight, K., and V. Hatzivassiloglou. (1995). Two-level, many-paths generation. In *Proceedings of the 33rd Conference of the Association for Computational Linguistics,* pp. 252–260.

Mann, W. C., and C. M. I. M. Matthiessen. (1985). Nigel: A systemic grammar for text generation. In R. Benson and J. Greaves, Eds., *Systemic Perspectives on Discourse: Selected Papers from the Ninth International Systemics Workshop.* London: Ablex, pp. 95–135.

Mann, W. C., and S. A. Thompson. (1988). Rhetorical structure theory: Toward a functional theory of text organization. *Text* 8: 243–281. Also available as USC/Information Sciences Institute Research Report RR-87-190.

McKeown, K. R. (1985). *Text Generation: Using Discourse Strategies and Focus Constraints to Generate Natural Language Text.* Cambridge: Cambridge University Press.

Meteer, M. W. (1990). *The Generation Gap: The Problem of Expressibility in Text Planning.* Ph.D. diss., University of Massachusetts. Available as BBN Technical Report 7347.

Meteer, M., D. D. McDonald, S. Anderson, D. Foster, L. Gay, A. Huettner, and P. Sibun. (1987). *Mumble-86: Design and Implementation.* Amherst: University of Massachusetts Technical Report COINS-87-87.

Moore, J. D. (1989). *A Reactive Approach to Explanation in Expert and Advice-Giving Systems.* Ph.D. diss., University of California at Los Angeles.

Nirenburg, S., R. McCardell, E. Nyberg, S. Huffman, E. Kenschaft, and I. Nirenburg. (1988). Lexical realization in natural language generation. In *Proceedings of the 2nd Conference on Theoretical and Methodological Issues in Machine Translation.* Pittsburgh, pp. 18–26.

Paris, C. L. (1993). *The Use of Explicit Models in Text Generation.* London: Francis Pinter.

Reiter, E. B. (1994). Has a consensus NL generation architecture appeared, and is it psychologically plausible? In *Proceedings of the 7th International Workshop on Natural Language Generation.* Kennebunkport, pp. 163–170.

St. Dizier, P. (1992). A constraint logic programming treatment of syntactic choice in natural language generation. In R. Dale, E. H. Hovy, D. Roesner, and O. Stock, Eds., *Aspects of Automated Natural Language Generation.* Heidelberg, Germany: Springer-Verlag Lecture Notes in AI, No. 587, pp. 119–134.

Van Noord, G. J. M. (1990). An overview of head-driven bottom-up generation. In R. Dale, C. S. Mellish, and M. Zock, Eds., *Current Research in Natural Language Generation.* London: Academic Press, pp. 141–165.

Ward, N. (1990). A connectionist treatment of grammar for generation. In *Proceedings of the 5th International Workshop on Language Generation.* University of Pittsburgh, pp. 95–102.

Further Readings

Adorni, G., and M. Zock, Eds. (1996). *Trends in Natural Language Generation: An Artificial Intelligence Perspective.* Heidelberg, Germany: Springer-Verlag Lecture Notes in AI, No. 1036.

Bateman, J. A., and E. H. Hovy. (1992). An overview of computational text generation. In C. Butler, Ed., *Computers and Texts: An Applied Perspective.* Oxford: Blackwell, pp. 53–74.

Cole, R., J. Mariani, H. Uszkoreit, A. Zaenen, and V. Zue. (1996). *Survey of the State of the Art of Human Language Technology.* Report commissioned by NSF and LRE; http://www.cse.ogi.edu/CSLU/HLTsurvey/.

Dale, R. (1990). Generating recipes: An overview of EPICURE. In R. Dale, C. Mellish, and M. Zock, Eds., *Current Research in Natural Language Generation.* New York: Academic Press, pp. 229–255.

Dale, R., E. H. Hovy, D. Röesner, and O. Stock, Eds. (1992). *Aspects of Automated Natural Language Generation.* Heidelberg, Germany: Springer-Verlag Lecture Notes in AI, No. 587.

Goldman, N. M. (1974). *Computer Generation of Natural Language from a Deep Conceptual Base.* Ph.D. diss., Stanford University. Also in R. C. Schank, Ed., (1975) *Conceptual Information Processing.* Amsterdam: Elsevier, pp. 54–79.

Horacek, H. (1992). An integrated view of text planning. In R. Dale, E. H. Hovy, D. Röesner, and O. Stock, Eds., *Aspects of Automated Natural Language Generation.* Heidelberg, Germany: Springer-Verlag Lecture Notes in AI, No. 587, pp. 57–72.

Kempen, G., Ed. (1987). *Natural Language Generation: Recent Advances in Artificial Intelligence, Psychology, and Linguistics.* Dordrecht: Kluwer.

Lavoie, B., and O. Rambow. (1997). A fast and portable realizer for text generation systems. In *Proceedings of the 5th Conference on Applied Natural Language Processing.* Washington, pp. 73–79.

Paris, C. L., W. R.Swartout, and W. C. Mann, Eds. (1990). *Natural Language Generation in Artificial Intelligence and Computational Linguistics.* Dordrecht: Kluwer.

Reiter, E. B. (1990). *Generating Appropriate Natural Language Object Descriptions.* Ph.D. diss., Harvard University.

Reiter, E. B., C. Mellish, and J. Levine. (1992). Automatic generation of on-line documentation in the IDAS project. In *Proceedings of the 3rd Conference on Applied Natural Language Processing.* Association for Computational Linguistics, pp. 64–71.

Robin, J. (1990). *Lexical Choice in Language Generation.* Ph.D. diss., Columbia University, Technical Report CUCS-040-90.

Natural Language Processing

Natural language processing is a subfield of artificial intelligence involving the development and use of computational models to process language. Within this, there are two general areas of research: *comprehension,* which deals with processes that extract information from language (e.g., natural language understanding, information retrieval), and *generation,* which deals with processes of conveying information using language. Traditionally, work dealing with speech has been considered separate fields of SPEECH RECOGNITION and SPEECH SYNTHESIS. We will continue with this separation here, and the issues of mapping sound to words and words to sound will not be considered further.

There are two main motivations underlying work in this area. The first is the technological goal of producing automated systems that perform various language-related tasks, such as building automated interactive systems (e.g., automated telephone-operator services) or systems to scan databases of documents to articles on a certain topic (e.g., finding relevant pages on the world wide web). The second, the one most relevant to cognitive science, seeks to better understand how language comprehension and generation occurs in humans. Rather than performing experiments on humans as done in psycholinguistics, or developing theories that account for the data with a focus on handling possible counterexamples as in linguistics and philosophy, researchers in natural language processing test theories by building explicit computational models to see how well they behave. Most research in the field is still more in the exploratory stage of this endeavor and trying to construct "existence proofs" (i.e., find any mechanism that can understand language within limited scenarios), rather than building computational models and comparing them to human performance. But once such existence-proof systems are completed, the stage will be set for more detailed comparative study between human and computational models. Whatever the motivation behind the work in this area, however, computational models have provided the inspiration and starting point for much work in psycholinguistics and linguistics in the last twenty years.

Although there is a diverse set of methods used in natural language processing, the techniques can generally be broadly classified in three general approaches: statistical methods, structural/pattern-based methods and reasoning-based methods. It is important to note that these approaches are not mutually exclusive. In fact, the most comprehensive models combine all three techniques. The approaches differ in the kind of processing tasks they can perform and in the degree to which systems require handcrafted rules as opposed to automatic training/learning from language data. A good source that gives an overview of the field involving all three approaches is Allen 1995.

Statistical methods involve using large corpora of language data to compute statistical properties such as word co-occurrence and sequence information (see also STATISTICAL TECHNIQUES IN NATURAL LANGUAGE PROCESSING). For instance, a *bigram* statistic captures the probability of a word with certain properties following a word with other properties. This information can be estimated from a corpus that is labeled with the properties needed, and used to predict what properties a word might have based on its preceding context. Although limited, bigram models can be surprisingly effective in many tasks. For instance, bigram models involving part of speech labels (e.g., noun, verb) can typically accurately predict the right part of speech for over 95 percent of words in general text. Statistical models are not restricted to part of speech tagging, however, and they have been used for semantic disambiguation, structural disambiguation (e.g., prepositional phrase attachment), and many other properties. Much of the initial work in statistical language modeling was performed for automatic speech-recognition systems, where good word prediction can double the word-recognition accuracy rate. The techniques have also proved effective in tasks such as information retrieval and producing rough "first-cut" drafts in machine translation. A big advantage to statistical techniques is that they can be automatically trained from language corpora. The challenge for statistical models concerns how to capture higher level structure, such as semantic information, and

structural properties, such as sentence structure. In general, the most successful approaches to these problems involve combining statistical approaches with other approaches. A good introduction to statistical approaches is Charniak 1993.

Structural and pattern-based approaches have the closest connection to traditional linguistic models. These approaches involve defining structural properties of language, such as defining FORMAL GRAMMARS for natural languages. Active research issues include the design of grammatical formalisms to capture natural language structure yet retain good computational properties, and the design of efficient parsing algorithms to interpret sentences with respect to a grammar. Structural approaches are not limited solely to syntax, however. Many more practical systems use semantically based grammars, where the primitive units in the grammar are semantic classes rather than syntactic. And other approaches dispense with fully analyzing sentence structure altogether, using simpler patterns of lexical, syntactic and semantic information that match sentence fragments. Such techniques are especially useful in limited-domain speech-driven applications where errors in the input can be expected. Because the domain is limited, certain phrases (e.g., a prepositional phrase) may have only one interpretation possible in the application. Structural models also appear at the DISCOURSE level, where models are developed that capture the interrelationships between sentences and build models of topic flow. Structural models provide a capability for detailed analysis of linguistic phenomena, but the more detailed the analysis, the more one must rely on hand-constructed rules rather than automatic training from data. An excellent collection of papers on structural approaches, though missing recent work, is Grosz, Sparck Jones, and Webber 1986.

Reasoning-based approaches involve encoding knowledge and reasoning processes and use these to interpret language. This work has much in common with work in KNOWLEDGE REPRESENTATION as well as work in the philosophy of language. The idea here is that the interpretation of language is highly dependent on the context in which the language appears. By trying to capture the knowledge a human may have in a situation, and model common-sense reasoning, problems such as word sense and sentence-structure disambiguation, analysis of referring expressions, and the recognition of the intentions behind language can be addressed. These techniques become crucial in discourse, whether it be extended text that needs to be understood or a dialogue that needs to be engaged in. Most dialogue-based systems use a speech-act–based approach to language and computational models of PLANNING and plan recognition to define a conversational agent. Specifically, such systems first attempt to recognize the intentions underlying the utterances they hear, and then plan their own utterances based on their goals and knowledge (including what was just recognized about the other agent). The advantage of this approach is that is provides a mechanism for contextual interpretation of language. The disadvantage is the complexity of the models required to define the conversational agent. Two good sources for work in this area are Cohen, Morgan, and Pollack 1990 and Carberry 1991.

There are many applications for natural language processing research, which can be roughly categorized into three main areas:

Information Extraction and Retrieval

Given that much of human knowledge is encoded in textual form, work in this area attempts to analyze such information automatically and develop methods for retrieving information as needed. The most obvious application area today is in developing internet web browsers, where one wants to find web pages that contain specific information. While most web-based techniques today involve little more than sophisticated keyword matching, there is considerable research in using more sophisticated techniques, such as classifying the information in documents based on their statistical properties (e.g., how often certain word patterns appear) as well as techniques that use robust parsing techniques to extract information. A good survey of applications for information retrieval can be found in Lewis and Sparck Jones (1996). Many of the researchers in this area have participated in annual evaluations and present their work at the MUC conferences (Chincor, Hirschman, and Lewis 1993).

Machine Translation

Given the great demand for translation services, automatic translation of text and speech (in simultaneous translation) is a critical application area. This is one area where there is an active market for commercial products, although the most useful products to date have aimed to enhance human translators rather than to replace them. They provide automated dictionary/translation aids and provide rough initial translations that can be post-edited. In applications where the content is stylized, such as technical and user manuals for products, it is becoming feasible to produce reasonable-quality translations automatically. A good reference for the machine-translation area is Hutchins and Somers 1992.

Human-Machine Interfaces

Given the increased availability of computers in all aspects of everyday life, there are immense opportunities for defining language-based interfaces. A prime area for commercial application is in telephone applications for customer service, replacing the touch-tone menu-driven interfaces with speech-driven language-based interfaces. Even the simplest applications, such as a ten-word automated operator service for long-distance calls, can save companies millions of dollars a year. Another important but longer-term application concerns the computer interface itself, replacing current interfaces with multimedia language-based interfaces that enhance the usability and accessibility of personal computers for the general public. Although general systems are a long way off, it will soon be feasible to define such interfaces for limited applications.

Although natural language processing is an area of great practical importance and commercial application, it is important to remember that its main contribution to cognitive science will remain the powerful metaphor that the computer provides for understanding human language processing. It allows us to specify models at a level of detail that would otherwise be unimaginable. We are now at the stage where end-to-end models of conversational agents can be constructed in simple domains. Work in this area will continue to further our knowledge of language processing and suggest novel ideas for experimentation.

See also COMPUTATIONAL LEXICONS; COMPUTATION LINGUISTICS; COMPUTATIONAL PSYCHOLINGUISTICS; CONNECTIONIST APPROACHES TO LANGUAGE; HIDDEN MARKOV MODELS; NATURAL LANGUAGE GENERATION

—*James Allen*

References

Allen, J. F. (1995). *Natural Language Understanding.* 2nd ed. Menlo Park, CA: Benjamin-Cummings.

Carberry, S. (1991). *Plan Recognition in Natural Language Dialogue.* Cambridge, MA: MIT Press.

Charniak, E. (1993). *Statistical Language Learning.* Cambridge, MA: MIT Press.

Cohen, P., J. Morgan, and M. Pollack. (1990). *Communication and Intention.* Cambridge, MA: MIT Press.

Chincor, N., L. Hirschman, and D. Lewis. (1993). Evaluation of message understanding systems. *Computational Linguistics* 19(3): 409–450.

Grosz, B., K. Sparck Jones, and B. Webber (1986). *Readings in Natural Language Processing.* San Francisco: Kaufmann.

Hutchins, W. J., and H. Somers. (1992). *An Introduction to Machine Translation.* New York: Academic Press.

Lewis, D. D., and K. Sparck Jones. (1996). Natural language processing for information retrieval. *Communications of the ACM* 39(1): 92–101.

Navigation

See ANIMAL NAVIGATION; ANIMAL NAVIGATION, NEURAL NETWORKS; COGNITIVE ARTIFACTS; HUMAN NAVIGATION

Neural Development

Neural development is the mechanistic link between the shaping forces of EVOLUTION and the physical and computational architecture of the mature brain. A growing knowledge of how the genome is expressed in development in the progressive specification of cell fates and neural structures is being combined with a better understanding of the functional organization of the adult brain to define the questions of neural development in a way never before possible. Until recently, questions in neural development were problem-centered—for example, how do axons locate a target?, how is a neuron's neurotransmitter specified?, how are topographic maps made? While most current research remains directed at such empirical problems, advances in our understanding of genetics and evolution have begun to give the questions of neural development a more principled structure.

The most surprising insight of molecular genetics and evolution regarding the brain is the extreme conservation of fundamental genetic and physical structures across vertebrate orders, and even across phyla. Specification of gene expression at the level of the individual neuron is too expensive of the genome; a better solution is to divide areas of the developing nervous system into domains specified by overlapping patterns of gene expression that, in combination, confer unique information to each zone. Such a solution was originally found to be operating in the control of head development in the fruit fly *Drosophila*. Through a mosaic pattern of expression, the HOM-C class of homeotic genes specify segmentation during *Drosophila* development (Lewis 1978), regulating expression of other genes that direct differentiation of structures along the anterior-posterior neuraxis. Since this discovery, these genes or their homologues have been found throughout the animal world; vertebrate homologues of the HOM-C genes, known as Hox genes, were found to delineate various aspects of segmentation of the vertebrate hindbrain and midbrain (Keynes and Krumlauf 1994). An immediate benefit from this descriptive work is a better understanding of the segmental architecture of the forebrain, which had been enigmatic and controversial. The overlapping pattern of Hox and other regulator gene expression allowed the first characterization of a continuous pattern of segmental architecture from spinal cord to olfactory bulb in the vertebrate brain, even in the elaborate forebrain (Puelles and Rubenstein 1993).

This type of conservation of developmental patterning has been apparent not only in fundamental segmental divisions but in many other features of development. In morphogenesis, for example, the same regulator gene (reviewed in Zuker 1994) is implicated in the proper development of eyes both in *Drosophila* and mammals, even though their common ancestor could not have had an image-forming eye. Formation of initial axonal scaffolding and the mechanisms of axon extension are strikingly similar in both vertebrate and complex invertebrate brains (Easter, Ross, and Frankfurter 1993; Goodman 1994; Reichert and Boyan 1997). Within mammals, and possibly most vertebrates, the sequence and relative timing of events in both early neurogenesis and process extension produce extremely predictable alterations in morphology as brains enlarge in various radiations (Finlay and Darlington 1995). That the structures that underlie cognitive processes in complex animals can be found, albeit in reduced form, in animals without such capacities is an important consideration for future theory building in COMPUTATIONAL NEUROSCIENCE.

The actual solutions found in neural development to clearly stated, logical problems seem bound to defy standard hypothesis testing. For example, a central and conspicuous feature of brain organization is the topographic representation of sensory surfaces and the preservation of topographic order as one brain structure maps to the next, though the information-bearing dimensions being mapped are sometimes unclear. How are such maps formed? A number of mechanisms could independently produce an acceptable solution: (1) the spatial relationship of elements in connecting maps could be passively apposed; (2) temporal gradients could map one element to another in an organized sequence; (3) neighboring elements in a map could actively recognize one another so that the map might travel in a coherent pattern of axons to its target; (4) different parts of the map might have different "road maps" to find the target; (5) the elements in the first map might recognize locations in the target map at varying degrees of specificity; (6) the map might develop from trial and error, based on experience; or (7) statistical regularities in the activity pattern of the input array could be used to confer order in the target array. In the highly studied, paradigmatic case of map formation in the retinotectal system begun with the work of Roger SPERRY over fifty years ago, every one of the logical possibilities described above has been shown to contribute to the formation of the adult map (Udin and Fawcett 1988), and unsurprisingly (given the multiplicity of mechanisms), multiple genes are required for its successful development (Karlstrom et al. 1996). The cause of such (at least conceptually) uneconomical solutions is unclear; because this is an evolved system, it could be an accretion of solutions and exaptations, spandrels on spandrels (Gould 1997). Different features of the solution come in at different developmental times, and as a whole this apparent redundancy of mechanism may be responsible for the robust nature of much of neural development.

Conversely, single mechanisms often appear in the solution to multiple developmental problems. Such a mechanism is the Hebbian, activity-dependent stabilization of the synapse. This single mechanism serves in diverse areas such as stabilization of the neuromuscular junction, refinement of topographic maps due to the correlation of firing of neighboring units in a topographic map, sorting of unlike from like inputs in such notable cases as the formation of ocular dominance columns in the VISUAL CORTEX, and basic associative learning both in development and in adulthood (Katz and Shatz 1996). A particularly interesting developmental use of this mechanism is the "retinal waves" described in the ferret where, prior to actual visual experience, the RETINA appears to generate its own highly self-correlated waves of activation that propagate through the nervous system and can initiate the various axonal sorting processes described above (Wong, Meister, and Shatz 1993). A challenge for future work is to describe how this mechanism might function in the creation of neural networks capable of detecting more complex aspects of information structure than temporal association.

The CEREBRAL CORTEX or isocortex has always commanded special attention as the structure of largest volume in the human brain, and the one most closely associated with complex cognitive skills. In this case, the principal developmental questions have been motivated by the adult functional architecture of the isocortex, a structure with a rather uniform architecture which nevertheless carries out a number of distinct and diverse functions. Is the isocortex a structure that performs some sort of standard transformation of its input, with differences in cortical areas (e.g., visual, motor, secondary sensory) arising epigenetically from interaction with the input, or are early regions in some way optimized for their future roles in adult isocortex?

Both positions capture aspects of the true state of affairs, as the following list of features of cortical development will illustrate. The neurons of the isocortex arise from a sheet of cells in the ventricular zone that is not fully uniform in its neurochemical identity or rate of neurogenesis (reviewed in Levitt, Barbe, and Eagleson 1997). Neuroblasts migrate out on radial glial cells to the cortical plate in a well-described "inside-out" settling pattern, thus potentially retaining positional information of the ventricular zone, though considerable dispersion also occurs (Rakic 1995). The cortical plate shows some neurochemical nonuniformity before it is innervated by any outside structure (Cohen-Tannoudji, Babinet, and Wassef 1994). The innervation of cortex by the THALA-MUS is extremely specific and mosaic, while by contrast, the large majority of intracortical connectivity can be accounted for by the generic rule, "connect to your two nearest neighbors" (Scannell, Blakemore, and Young 1995). The specific outputs of discrete cortical areas emerge from a generic set of intracortical and subcortical connections in mid- to late development, dependent on activity. There are several notable examples of plasticity: the isocortex can represent and transform visual input artificially induced to project to the auditory thalamus (Roe et al. 1990), and also, early transplants of one cortical area to another can accept innervation and make connections characteristic of the new area (O'Leary, Schlaggar, and Stanfield 1992). However, neither the new innervation nor the new connectivity is identical to the unaltered state.

Thus, the isocortex does not fall clearly into either the equipotential or modular description, but rather shows evidence of some early channeling of the epigenetic landscape in the context of a great deal of equipotentiality. When the isocortex first encounters the information of the external world, the separation of modalities and the topographic mapping of surfaces available already in the thalamus is preserved and available. Overall, the evolutionarily conservative primary sensory cortices show the most evidence of early morphological and connectional specialization, while those areas of frontal and parietal cortex that proliferate in the largest brains show the least. The specification of intracortical connectivity, both short- and long-range, occurs concurrent with early experience, and it seems likely that it is in this circuitry that the isocortex will represent the predictability and variability of the outside world.

See also AUDITORY PLASTICITY; COGNITIVE DEVELOPMENT; NATIVISM; NEURAL PLASTICITY

—Barbara Finlay and John K. Niederer

References

Cohen-Tannoudji, M., C. Babinet, and M. Wassef. (1994). Early determination of a mouse somatosensory cortex marker. *Nature* 368: 460–463.

Easter, S. S., L. S. Ross, and A. Frankfurter. (1993). Initial tract formation in the mouse brain. *Journal of Neuroscience* 13: 285–299.

Finlay, B. L., and R. B. Darlington. (1995). Linked regularities in the development and evolution of mammalian brains. *Science* 268: 1578–1584.

Goodman, C. (1994). The likeness of being: Phylogenetically conserved molecular mechanisms of growth cone guidance. *Cell* 78: 353–373.

Gould, S. J. (1997). The exaptive excellence of spandrels as a term and prototype. *Proc. Natl. Acad. Sci. U.S.A.* 94: 10750–10755.

Karlstrom, R. O., T. Trowe, S. Klostermann, H. Baier, M. Brand, A. D. Crawford, B. Grunewald, P. Haffter, H. Hoffmann, S. U. Meyer, B. K. Muller, S. Richter, F. J. M. van Eeden, C. Nusslei-Volhard, and F. Bonhoeffer. (1996). Zebrafish mutations affecting retinotectal axon pathfinding. *Development* 123: 427–438.

Katz, L. C., and C. J. Shatz. (1996). Synaptic activity and the construction of cortical circuits. *Science* 274: 1133–1138.

Keynes, R., and R. Krumlauf. (1994). Hox genes and the regionalization of the nervous system. *Annual Review of Neuroscience* 17: 109–132.

Levitt, P., M. F. Barbe, and K. L. Eagleson. (1997). Patterning and specification of the cerebral cortex. *Annual Review of Neuroscience* 20: 1–24.

Lewis, E. B. (1978). A gene complex controlling segmentation in *Drosophila. Nature* 276: 565–570.

O'Leary, D. D. M., B. L. Schlaggar, and B. B. Stanfield. (1992). The specification of sensory cortex: Lessons from cortical transplantation. *Experimental Neurology* 115: 121–126.

Puelles, L., and J. L. R. Rubenstein. (1993). Expression patterns of homeobox and other regulatory genes in the embryonic mouse forebrain suggest a neuromeric organization. *Trends in Neurosciences* 16: 472–479.

Rakic, P. (1995). Radial versus tangential migration of neuronal clones in the developing cerebral cortex. *Proc. Nat. Acad. Sci. U. S. A.* 92: 11323–11327.

Reichert, H., and G. Boyan. (1997). Building a brain: Developmental insights in insects. *Trends in Neuroscience* 20: 258–264.

Roe, A. W., S. L. Pallas, J.-O. Hahm, and M. Sur. (1990). A map of visual space induced in primary auditory cortex. *Science* 250: 818–820.

Scannell, J. W., C. Blakemore, and M. P. Young. (1995). Analysis of connectivity in the cat cerebral cortex. *Journal of Neuroscience* 15: 1463–1483.

Udin, S. B., and J. W. Fawcett. (1988). The formation of topographic maps. *Annual Review of Neuroscience* 11: 289–328.

Wong, R. O. L., M. Meister, and C. J. Shatz. (1993). Transient period of correlated bursting activity during development of the mammalian retina. *Neuron* 11: 923–938.

Zuker, C. S. (1994). On the evolution of eyes: Would you like it simple or compound? *Science* 265: 742–743.

Further Readings

Fraser, S. E., and D. H. Perkel. (1990). Competitive and positional cues in the patterning of nerve connections. *Journal of Neurobiology* 21: 51–72.

Gould, S. J., and R. C. Lewontin. (1979). Spandrels of San Marco and the Panglossian paradigm: A critique of the adaptationist programme. *Proceedings of the Royal Society of London. Series B: Biological Sciences* 205: 581–598.

Miller, K. D., and M. P. Stryker. (1990). The development of ocular dominance columns: Mechanisms and models. In S. J. Hanson and C. R. Olson, Eds., *Connectionist Modeling and Brain Functions, The Developing Interface.* Cambridge, MA: MIT Press, pp. 255–350.

O'Leary, D. D. M. (1989). Do cortical areas emerge from a protocortex? *Trends in Neurosciences* 12: 400–406.

Oppenheim, R. W. (1991). Cell death during development of the nervous system. *Annual Review of Neuroscience* 14: 453–502.

Rakic, P. (1990). Critical cellular events in cortical evolution: Radial unit hypothesis. In B. L. Finlay, G. Innocenti, and H. Scheich, Eds., *The Neocortex: Ontogeny and Phylogeny.* New York: Plenum Press, pp. 21–32.

Neural Networks

The study of neural networks is the study of information processing in networks of elementary numerical processors. In some cases these networks are endowed with a certain degree of biological realism and the goal is to build models that account for neurobiological data. In other cases abstract networks are studied and the goal is to develop a computational theory of highly parallel, distributed information-processing systems. In both cases the emphasis is on accounting for intelligence via the statistical and dynamic regularities of highly interconnected, large-scale networks.

Historically, neural networks arose as a number of loosely connected strands, many of which were subsequently absorbed into mainstream engineering disciplines. Some of the earliest research on neural networks (in the 1940s and 1950s) involved the study of interconnected systems of binary switches, or MCCULLOCH-PITTS neurons. This research also contributed to the development of AUTOMATA theory and dynamic systems theory. Links between these fields and neural networks continue to the present day.

Other early research efforts emphasized adaptive systems. In the 1950s and 1960s, Widrow and others studied adaptive linear systems and in particular the *LMS algorithm* (cf. SUPERVISED LEARNING IN MULTILAYER NEURAL NETWORKS). This work led to the field of adaptive signal processing and provided the basis for later extensions to nonlinear neural networks. Adaptive classifiers (systems with a discrete output variable) were also studied during the same period in the form of the "perceptron" algorithm and related schemes; these developments contributed to the development of the engineering field of PATTERN RECOGNITION, which continues to house much neural network research. Finally, efforts in the area of REINFORCEMENT LEARNING formed a strand of neural network research with strong ties to CONTROL THEORY. In the 1980s, these ties were further solidified by research establishing a link between reinforcement learning and optimal control theory, in particular the optimization technique of DYNAMIC PROGRAMMING.

Neural networks received much attention during the 1970s and 1980s, partly as a reaction against the prevailing symbolic approach to the study of intelligence in artificial intelligence (AI). Emphasizing architectures that largely dispense with centralized sequential processing and strict separation between process and data, researchers studied distributed processing in highly parallel architectures (cf. COGNITIVE MODELING, CONNECTIONIST). Intelligence was viewed in terms of mechanisms of CONSTRAINT SATISFACTION and pattern recognition rather than explicit symbol manipulation. A number of technical developments sustained research during this period, two of which stand out.

First, the dynamics of symmetrical networks (networks in which a connection from node A to node B of a given strength implies a connection from B to A of the same strength) was elucidated by the discovery of *energy functions* (see RECURRENT NETWORKS). This allowed network dynamics to be understood in terms of a (generally finite) set of *attractors,* points in the state space toward which trajectories tend as the nodes in the network are updated. This gave a satisfying formal interpretation of constraint satisfaction in neural networks—as the minimization of an energy function—and provided an interesting implementation of an associative memory: the attractors are the memories.

The second important technical development was the discovery of a class of learning algorithms for general networks. The focus on learning algorithms can either be viewed as a natural outgrowth of the earlier research on adaptive algorithms for simple one-layer networks (e.g., the LMS algorithm and the perceptron), or as a necessity born of the fact that general networks are difficult to analyze and accordingly difficult to program. In any case, the algorithms have greatly extended the range of the networks that can be utilized in models and in practical applications, so much so that in AI and engineering the topic of neural networks has become essentially synonymous with the study of numerical learning algorithms.

The earliest successes were obtained with SUPERVISED LEARNING algorithms. These algorithms require an error signal at each of the output nodes of the network. The paradigm case is that of the layered *feedforward network,* a network with no feedback connections between layers and no lateral connections within a layer. Input patterns are presented at the first layer, and each subsequent layer is updated in turn, resulting in an output at the final layer. This output is compared to a desired output pattern, yielding an error signal. Algorithms differ in how they utilize this error signal, but in one way or another the error signal is propagated backward into the network to compute updates to the weights and thereby decrease the error.

A wide variety of theoretical results are available concerning neural network computation. Layered neural networks have been shown to be *universal,* in the sense of being able to represent essentially any function. *Best approximation* results are available for large classes of feedforward networks. Recurrent neural networks have been shown to be TURING-equivalent and have also been shown to be able to represent a wide class of nonlinear dynamic systems. A variety of results are also available for supervised learning in neural networks. In particular, the Vapnik-Chervonenkis (VC) dimension (a measure of the sample complexity of a learning system; see COMPUTATIONAL LEARNING THEORY and STATISTICAL LEARNING THEORY) has been computed for simple networks, and bounds on the VC dimension are available for more complex networks. In classification problems, network learning algorithms have been shown to converge to the posterior probabilities of the classes. Methods from statistical physics have been utilized to characterize learning curves. Finally, Bayesian statistical methods (see BAYESIAN LEARNING) have been exploited both for the analysis of supervised learning and for the design of new algorithms.

Recent years have seen an increase in interest in UNSUPERVISED LEARNING and a concomitant growth in interest in fully probabilistic approaches to neural network design. The unsupervised learning framework is in many ways more powerful and more general than supervised learning, requiring no error signal and no explicit designation of nodes as input nodes or output nodes. One general way to approach the problem involves specifying a *generative model*—an explicit model of the way in which the environment is assumed to generate data. In the neural network setting, such models are generally realized in the form of a network. The learner's uncertainty about the environment is formalized by annotating the network with probabilities. The learning problem in this setting becomes the classic statistical problem of finding the best model to fit the data. The learner may either explicitly manipulate an instantiation of the generative model, or may utilize a network that is obtained by inverting the generative model (e.g., via an application of Bayes's rule). The latter network is often referred to as a *discriminative* network.

Probabilistic network models are studied in other areas of AI. In particular, BAYESIAN NETWORKS provide a general formalism for designing probabilistic networks. It is interesting to note that essentially all of the unsupervised learning architectures that have been studied in the neural network literature can be obtained by specifying a generative model in the form of a Bayesian network.

This rapprochement between neural networks and Bayesian networks has a number of important consequences that are of current research interest. First, the Bayesian network formalism makes it natural to specify and manipulate prior knowledge, an ability that eluded earlier, nonprobabilistic neural networks. By associating a generative model with a neural network, prior knowledge can be more readily incorporated and posterior knowledge more readily extracted from the network. Second, the relationship between generative models and discriminative models can be exploited, yielding architectures that utilize feedback connections and lateral connectivity. Third, the strengths of the neural network focus on LEARNING—particularly discriminative learning—and the Bayesian network focus on inference can be combined. Indeed, learning and inference can be fruitfully viewed as two sides of the same coin. Finally, the emphasis on approximation techniques and laws of large numbers that is present in the neural network literature can be transferred to the Bayesian network setting, yielding a variety of methods for approximate inference in complex Bayesian networks.

See also COGNITIVE ARCHITECTURE; COMPUTATION AND THE BRAIN; COMPUTATIONAL NEUROSCIENCE; CONNECTIONISM, PHILOSOPHICAL ISSUES; DISTRIBUTED VS. LOCAL REPRESENTATION; MODELING NEUROPSYCHOLOGICAL DEFICITS

—*Michael I. Jordan*

Further Readings

Bishop, C. M. (1995). *Neural Networks for Pattern Recognition.* New York: Oxford University Press.

Duda, R. O., and P. E. Hart. (1973). *Pattern Classification and Scene Analysis.* New York: Wiley.

Haykin, S. (1994). *Neural Networks: A Comprehensive Foundation.* New York: Macmillan College Publishing.

Hertz, J., A. Krogh, and R. G. Palmer. (1991). *Introduction to the Theory of Neural Computation.* Redwood City, CA: Addison-Wesley.

Jensen, F. (1996). *An Introduction to Bayesian Networks.* London: UCL Press.

Jordan, M. I., Ed. (1998). *Learning in Graphical Models.* Cambridge, MA: MIT Press.

Ripley, B. D. (1996). *Pattern Recognition and Neural Networks.* Cambridge: Cambridge University Press.

Vapnik, V. (1995). *The Nature of Statistical Learning Theory.* New York: Springer.

Whittaker, J. (1990). *Graphical Models in Applied Multivariate Statistics.* New York: Wiley.

Neural Plasticity

The functional properties of neurons and the functional architecture of the CEREBRAL CORTEX are dynamic, constantly under modification by experience, expectation, and behavioral context. Associated with functional plasticity is a process of modification of circuits, either by altering the strength of a given synaptic input or by axonal sprouting and synaptogenesis. Plasticity has been seen under a number of conditions, including functional recovery following lesions of the sensory periphery of central structures, perceptual learning and learning of object associations, spatial learning, visual-motor adaptation, and context-dependent changes in receptive field properties. This discussion will compare plasticity observed early in development with that seen in adulthood, and then discuss the role of plasticity in recovery of function after lesions, in learning in sensory systems, and in visual-spatial integration.

Much of the original work on neural plasticity in the central nervous system was done in the context of experience-dependent plasticity in the period of postnatal development during which cortical connections, functional architecture, and receptive field properties continue to be refined. Hubel and Wiesel (1977) showed that in the visual system, the balance of input from the two eyes, known as ocular dominance, can be influenced by keeping one eye closed, which shifts the balance toward the open eye, or by induced strabismus (where the two eyes are aimed at different points in the visual field), which blocks the development of binocular cells. The substrate of these changes is an alteration in the extent of thalamocortical axonal arbors, which, immediately after birth, are undergoing a process of collateral sprouting and pruning. The plasticity of these arbors, of ocular dominance columns, and of the ocular dominance of receptive fields, is under experience-dependent regulation for a limited period early in the life of animals that is known as the *critical period.* The length of the critical period is species-dependent, and can extend for the first few months (cats) or years (humans and nonhuman primates) of life. After the end of the critical period the properties involved become fixed for the rest of the life of the animal.

The model of ocular dominance plasticity has been a prime example of the role of activity and of experience in the formation of the functional properties of neurons and of the refinement of connectivity between neurons. Models of cortical development have shown how spontaneous activity in utero can lead to the formation of cortical functional architecture and receptive field properties in the absence of visual experience, and prenatal patterned activity in the RETINA and cortex has been discovered. It has been shown that the effects of monocular deprivation can be prevented by blockade of retinal activity. Some of the molecular intermediaries implicated in the competition between different populations of cortical afferents and of activity-dependent plasticity include neurotrophins and their receptors and glutamate and *N*-methyl-*d*-aspartate (NMDA) receptors. The fundamental rule underlying this plasticity, originating from work in the HIPPOCAMPUS and the ideas of HEBB, is that *neurons that fire together wire together,* and that LONG-TERM POTENTIATION is involved in the consolidation of connections.

Given this background it had been widely assumed that all cortical areas, at least those involved in early sensory processing, would have fixed properties and connections. Of course, some measure of plasticity would have to accompany the ability to acquire and store new percepts throughout life, but this had been thought to be a special property of higher-order cortical areas, particularly those in the temporal lobe, associated with object memory. A radical change has occurred in this view with the growing body of evidence that experience-dependent plasticity is a universal property of cortex, even primary sensory areas.

Each area of sensory cortex, particularly those at early stages in the sensory pathway, has a representation of the sensory surface on the cortical surface. Somatosensory cortex contains a representation of the body map (somatotopy), auditory cortex of the cochlea (tonotopy), and visual cortex of the retina (visuotopy). The integrity of these maps depends on ongoing stimulation of the periphery. Removal of input from any part of the sensory surface, such as by digit amputation or retinal lesion, leads to a reorganization of the cortical maps. Some of the initial evidence for cortical plasticity in the adult came from changes in somatotopic maps following digit amputation (see Merzenich and Sameshima 1993). Amputation of a body part or transection of a sensory nerve causes the area of cortex initially representing that part to be remapped toward a representation of the adjacent body parts. Retinal lesions lead to a shrinkage of the cortical representation of the lesioned part of retina and an expansion in the representation of the part of retina surrounding the lesion.

The mechanism of the reorganization varies with the sensory pathways involved. Generally, the site of reorganization depends on the existence of exuberant connections linking cells representing widely separated parts of the map. Thus, in the somatosensory system, a measure of lesion-induced plasticity can be observed in the spinal cord, although it is likely that a considerable degree of plasticity is based in the somatosensory cortex. In the plasticity observed in the visual system, most of the changes are intrinsic to the visual cortex, and are likely to involve the long-range horizontal connections formed by cortical pyramidal cells. The unmasking of these connections seen with long-term topographic reorganization involves a sprouting of axonal collaterals and synaptogenesis.

There is a wide range of time scales over which the plasticity of topography takes place. The changes occurring over the largest spatial scales in cortex (topographic shifts of up to a centimeter) require several months or years. Smaller but significant changes can be seen within minutes following a lesion, and this is likely to involve changes in the strength of existing connections. Exuberant connections can be unmasked by a potentiation of excitatory connections or by a suppression of inhibitory connections.

The perceptual consequences of lesion-induced plasticity can include, depending on the site of the lesion, a recovery of function or perceptual distortions. PHANTOM LIMB sensation following limb amputation has been linked by Ramachandran (1993) to experimentally induced somatosensory cortical plasticity. For arm amputations, there is often a sensation of stimulation of the absent hand when stroking the limb stump or the cheek. Human patients suffering a loss of central retinal input (by, e.g., age-related macular degeneration) often adopt a preferred retinal locus in the intact retina for targeting visually guided eye movements. Lesions in area MT, an area that plays a role in the perception of movement and the tracking of moving objects by the eyes, initially leads to a loss of smooth pursuit eye movements, but within a few days this function recovers. It is well known that following stroke there are varying degrees of functional recovery. Though this recovery had been thought to involve a return to health of metabolically compromised but not destroyed tissue, it may well be that intact areas of cortex are taking over the function of adjacent cortical regions that have been destroyed.

The mechanisms available to the cortex for functional recovery following lesions are likely to be used for normal sensory processing. It is likely that perceptual learning involves analogous changes in cortical topography. LEARNING in general has been divided into categories including declarative or explicit learning (including the learning of events, facts, and objects) and nondeclarative or implicit learning (including procedural, classical CONDITIONING, priming, and perceptual learning). These different forms of learning may be distinguished less on the basis of the underlying synaptic mechanisms than on the brain region in which the memory is stored. While one ordinarily associates sensory learning with the acquisition and storage of complex percepts and with the temporal lobe, it has been known for well over a hundred years that it is possible to improve one's ability to discriminate simple sensory attributes. Some characteristics of perceptual learning are suggestive of the involvement of early stages in sensory processing.

Perceptual learning has been shown to apply to a wide range of sensory tasks, including visual acuity, hue discrimination, velocity estimation, acoustic pitch discrimination, and two-point somatosensory acuity. This is a form of implicit learning, generally not reaching conscious awareness or requiring error feedback, but is associated with repetitively performing discrimination tasks.

The evidence supporting the idea that the neural substrate for perceptual learning is found in primary sensory cortex comes from the specificity of the learning and from physiological studies demonstrating cortical changes in animals trained on simple discrimination tasks. Improvement in a visual discrimination task at one position in the visual field, for example, does not transfer to other locations. Since the highest spatial resolution is seen in primary visual cortex, where the receptive fields are the smallest and the topography most highly ordered, one might expect to find the basis for specificity there. The learning also shows no transfer to orthogonal orientations, again indicative of early cortical stages where selectivity for stimulus orientation is sharpest. On the other hand, the learning is also specific for stimulus configuration or the context within which a feature is embedded during the training period, which may point toward a feedback influence from higher-order cortical areas providing information about more complex features.

The physiological studies show changes in cortical magnification factor, or cortical recruitment, associated with training. Training a monkey to do a texture discrimination task with a particular digit will increase the area of primary somatosensory cortex representing that digit. Similarly, it has been suggested that training on an auditory frequency discrimination task increases the representation of that frequency in primary auditory cortex. Not only these forms of implicit learning but associative learning as well causes changes in the receptive fields of cells in primary sensory cortex. When a tone is associated with an aversive stimulus, cells in auditory cortex tend to shift their critical frequency toward that of the tone. The reward component of the training may come from basal forebrain structures, involving the diffuse ascending cholinergic input to cortex.

The storage of more complex information has been identified in the inferior temporal cortex. There, animals trained to recognize complex forms, particularly in association with other forms, have cells that showed elevated activity when a given form is presented. The acquisition of the trained information may depend on input from more medial structures, such as the perirhinal cortex.

A central focus for studies of neural plasticity is the hippocampus. As a consequence of neuropsychological findings showing that persons with medial temporal lesions suffer an inability to acquire and store recent memories, the hippocampus has been an active area of study for neural mechanisms of MEMORY. At the systems level, the hippocampus was shown by O'Keefe (1976) to play a role in spatial learning, with cells being tuned for an animal's position in its external environment, known as a *place field*. At the synaptic level, the hippocampus has become the prime model for changes in synaptic weight, through the phenomenon of long-term potentiation originally described by Bliss and Lomo (1973), and long-term depression. While it has been presumed that these forms of synaptic plasticity account for the storage of complex information in the hippocampus, the linkage has not yet been established. It is clear, however, that cells in the hippocampus are capable of rapidly changing their place fields as the external environment is altered, and this alteration is associated with changes in effective connectivity between hippocampal neurons.

The functional properties of cells in cerebral cortex and in brain stem have been shown to be modifiable over much shorter time scales, potentially involving neural plasticity in the ongoing processing of sensory information and in sensorimotor integration.

One of the earliest and most active areas of investigation of adult plasticity is the vestibulo-ocular reflex, the compensatory movement of the eyes associated with rotation of the head or body to keep the visual field stabilized on the retina. Melville-Jones and Gonshor (1975) found that if prisms are put on the eyes to reduce the amount of retinal slip associated with a given amount of head rotation, the *gain* of the reflex is reduced, and eventually settles to a level where once again the world is stabilized on the eyes. Various brain structures have been suggested to be involved in this phenomenon, including the CEREBELLUM and pontine nuclei. Another revealing model of sensorimotor adaptation has been studied in the owl by Knudsen and Brainard (1995). In the tectum of the owl (analogous to the mammalian superior colliculus), there are superimposed maps of visual and auditory space. When prisms are placed over the owl's eyes, shifting the visual map, there is a compensatory shift of the auditory map, so that once again there is a registration between the two maps for a given elevation and azimuth in the external world. This enables the owl to make accurate targeting movements for catching prey, as detected by both visual and sound cues.

Within sensory cortex, rapid changes in receptive field properties have been associated with perceptual fill-in. When an occluder, or *artificial scotoma,* is placed within a background of a uniform color or a textured pattern, and when this stimulus is stabilized on the retina, the occluder disappears over a few seconds, becoming filled with the surrounding pattern. It is supposed that this phenomenon may be a manifestation of the process of linkage and segmentation of the visual scene into contours and surfaces belonging to particular objects. At the cellular level, at several stages in the visual pathway, cells tend to change their response properties when their receptive fields are placed within the artificial scotoma. Assuming that each cell represents a line label signaling, when active, the presence of a feature centered within its receptive field, the response of a cell whose receptive field is centered within the artificial scotoma is interpreted by the visual system as a shift of stimulus features toward its center.

A growing body of evidence reveals a remarkable degree of mutability of function in primary sensory cortex that is not limited to the first months of life but extends throughout adulthood. It is becoming increasingly clear that rather than performing a fixed and stereotyped calculation on their input, cells in all cortical areas represent active filters. Various components of cortical circuitry have been implicated as the likely source of the changes, including intrinsic horizontal connections and feedback connections from higher-order cortical areas. Neural plasticity serves a wide variety of functional roles, and the extent to which it plays a role in the ongoing processing of sensory information depends on the rapidity with which cells can alter their response properties. To date, it has been shown that substantial changes can be induced within seconds of exposure to novel stimuli. It remains to be seen whether even shorter-term modifications of cortical circuits and receptive field properties may underlie the recognition of objects as the eyes move from saccade to saccade.

See also NEURAL DEVELOPMENT; PERCEPTUAL DEVELOPMENT; VISION AND LEARNING; VISUAL ANATOMY AND PHYSIOLOGY

—*Charles Gilbert*

References

Bliss, T. V. P., and T. Lomo. (1973). Long-lasting potentiation of synaptic transmission in the dentate area of the anesthetized rabbit following stimulation of the perforant path. *Journal of Physiology* 232: 331–356.

Gibson, E. J. (1953). *Psychol. Bull.* 50: 401–431.

Gilbert, C. D. (1994). Early perceptual learning. *Proc. Natl. Acad. Sci. U.S.A.* 91: 1195–1197.

Gilbert, C. D., A. Das, M. Ito, M. Kapadia, and G. Westheimer. (1996). Spatial integration and cortical dynamics. *Proc. Natl. Acad. Sci U.S.A.* 93: 615–622.

Hubel, D. H., and T. N. Wiesel. (1977). Functional architecture of macaque monkey visual cortex. *Proc. R. Soc. Lond B. Biol. Sci.* 198: 1–59.

Knudsen, E. I., and M. S. Brainard. (1995). Creating a unified representation of visual and auditory space in the brain. *Annu. Rev. Neurosci.* 18: 19–43.

Linsker, R. (1986). From basic network principles to neural architecture, III: Emergence of orientation columns. *Proc. Natl. Acad. Sci. U.S.A.* 83: 8779–8783.

Melville-Jones, G., and A. Gonshor. (1975). Goal-directed flexibility in the vestibulo-ocular reflex arc. In G. Lennerstrand and P. Bach-y-Rita, Eds., *Basic Mechanisms of Ocular Motility and Their Clinical Implications.* New York: Pergamon Press.

Merzenich, M. M., and K. Sameshima. (1993). Cortical plasticity and memory. *Current Opinion in Neurobiology* 3: 187–196.

O'Keefe, J. (1976). Place units in the hippocampus of the freely moving rat. *Expt. Neurol.* 51: 78–109.

Ramachandran, V. S. (1993). Filling in gaps in perception: Part 2. Scotomas and phantom limbs. *Curr. Dir. Psychol. Sci.* 2: 56–65.

Squire, L. (1994). Declarative and nondeclarative memory: Multiple brain systems supporting learning and memory. In D. L. Schachter and E. Tulving, Eds., *Memory Systems.* Cambridge, MA: MIT Press, pp. 203–231.

Weinberger, N. M. (1995). Dynamic regulation of receptive fields and maps in the adult sensory cortex. *Annu. Rev. Neurosci.* 18: 129–158.

Neural Synchrony

See BINDING BY NEURAL SYNCHRONY

Neuroendocrinology

Neuroendocrinology studies the relationships between the endocrine system and the brain. The endocrine system produces a variety of hormones, which are chemical messengers that signal changes that the body needs to make to adapt to new situations. The brain controls the endocrine system through the hypothalamus and pituitary gland, and the secretions of the gonads, adrenals, and thyroid act on tissues throughout the body, and on the brain and pituitary, to produce a wide variety of effects. Some hormone effects occur during development and are generally long lasting and even permanent for the life of the individual. Other hormone actions take place in the mature nervous system and are usually reversible. Still other hormone actions in adult life are related to permanent changes in brain function associated with disease processes or with aging.

Nerve cells in the hypothalamus produce hormones, called releasing factors, which are released into a portal blood supply and travel to the anterior pituitary gland where they trigger the release of trophic hormones such as adrenocorticotropic hormone (ACTH), thyroid-stimulating hormone (TSH), luteinizing hormone (LH), follicle-stimulating hormone (FSH), prolactin, and growth hormone. These hormones, in turn, regulate endocrine responses—for example, ACTH stimulates glucocorticoid secretion by the adrenal cortex; TSH, thyroid hormone secretion; and LH, sex hormone production. Other hypothalamic neurons produce the hormones vasopressin and oxytocin and release these hormones at nerve terminals located in the posterior lobe of the pituitary gland. Brain activity stimulates the secretion of these hormones; for example, oxytocin and prolactin release are stimulated by suckling, and the sight and sound of an infant can stimulate "milk letdown" in the mother; ACTH is driven by stressful experiences and by an internal clock in the brain that is entrained by the light-dark cycle; and LH and FSH secretion are influenced by season of the year in some animals.

Thyroid hormone and sex hormones act early in life to regulate development and differentiation of the brain, whereas the activity of the stress hormone axis is programmed by early experiences via mechanisms which may depend to some degree on the actions of glucocorticoid hormones.

For thyroid hormone, both excesses and deficiencies of thyroid hormone secretion are associated with altered brain development; extremes in thyroid hormone secretion lead to major deficiencies in cognitive function (e.g., cretinism), whereas smaller deviations in thyroid hormone secretion are linked to more subtle individual variations in brain function and cognitive activity.

For sex hormones, the story is more complicated in that testosterone secretion during midgestation in the human male and then again during the first two years of postnatal life alters brain development and affects cognitive function as well as reproductive function. There are comparable periods of testosterone production in early development in other mammals. Absence of testosterone in females leads to the female behavioral and body phenotype; and absence of androgen receptors or the lack of normal androgen secretion in genetic males leads to a feminine phenotype, whereas exposure of genetic females to androgens early in development produces a masculine phenotype. Sexual differentiation of the brain has been investigated in animals, and there are subtle sex differences in a variety of brain structures, ranging from the hypothalamus (which governs reproduction) to the HIPPOCAMPUS and CEREBRAL CORTEX (which subserve cognitive function). There are also indications for structural and functional sex differences in the human brain that are similar to those found in lower animals. For example, in both animals and humans, sex differences are found in the strategies used for spatial learning and memory, with males using the more global spatial cues and females relying upon local contextual cues.

For stress hormones, early experience has a profound role in shaping the reactivity of the stress hormone axis and the secretion not only of ACTH and glucocorticoids but also the activity of the autonomic nervous system. Prenatal stress and certain types of aversive experience in infant rodents (e.g., several hours of separation from the mother) increase reactivity of the stress hormone axis for the lifetime of the individual. In contrast, handling of newborn rat pups (a much briefer form of separation of the pup from the mother) produces a lifelong reduction in activity of the stress hormone axis. Actions of glucocorticoid and thyroid hormones play a role in these effects. There is growing evidence that for rodents elevated stress hormone activity over a lifetime increases the rate of brain aging, whereas a lifetime of reduced stress hormone activity reduces the rate of brain aging (see below).

Whereas the developmental actions of hormones on the brain are confined to windows of early development during fetal and neonatal life and the peripubertal period, these same hormones produce reversible effects on brain structure and function throughout the life of the mature nervous system. Sex hormones activate reproductive behaviors, including defense of territory, courtship, and mating, and they regulate neuroendocrine function to ensure successful reproduction; however, reflecting sexual differentiation of the brain and secondary sex characteristics of the body, the activational effects of sex hormones in adult life are often gender-specific.

Thyroid hormone actions maintain normal neuronal excitability and promote a normal range of nerve cell structure and function; excesses or insufficiencies of thyroid hormone have adverse effects on brain function and cognition, which are largely reversible. Among these effects are exacerbation of depressive illness.

There are two types of adrenal steroids—mineralocorticoids and glucocorticoids—which regulate salt intake and food intake, respectively, and also modulate metabolic and cognitive function during the diurnal cycle of activity and rest. Adrenal steroids act to maintain homeostasis and glucocorticoids do so in part by opposing, or containing, the actions of other neural systems that are activated by stress and also by promoting adaptation of the brain to repeatedly stressful experiences. Containment effects of glucocorticoids oppose stress-induced activity of the noradrenergic arousal system and the hypothalamic system that releases ACTH from the pituitary. Adaptational effects of stress hormones during prolonged or repeated stress increase or decrease neurochemicals related to brain excitability and neurotransmission and produce changes in neuronal structure. Adrenal steroids biphasically modulate LONG-TERM POTENTIATION (LTP) in the hippocampus, with high levels of stress hormones also promoting long-term depression (LTD). LTP and LTD may be involved in learning and memory mechanisms.

Primary targets of stress hormones are the hippocampal formation and also the AMYGDALA. Repeated stress causes atrophy of hippocampal pyramidal neurons and inhibits the replacement of neurons of the dentate gyrus by cognitive function, enhancing episodic and declarative memory at low to moderate levels but inhibiting these same functions at high levels or after acute stress. Along with adrenal steroids, the sympathetic nervous system participates in creating the powerful memories associated with traumatic events, in which the amygdala plays an important role. Glucocorticoid hormones act in both the amygdala and hippocampus to promote consolidation.

Steroid hormones and thyroid hormone act on cells throughout the body via intracellular receptors that regulate gene expression. Such intracellular receptors are found heterogeneously distributed in the brain, with each hormone having a unique regional pattern of localization across brain regions. The hypothalamus and amygdala have receptors for sex hormones, with both sexes expressing receptors for androgens, estrogens, and progestins, although, because of sexual differentiation, there are somewhat different amounts of these receptors expressed in male and female brains. The hippocampus and amygdala have receptors for adrenal steroids, whereas thyroid hormone receptors are widely distributed throughout the nervous system, particularly in the forebrain and CEREBELLUM.

Effects mediated by intracellular receptors are generally slow in onset over minutes to hours and long-lasting because alterations in gene expression produce effects on cells that can last for hours and days, or longer. Steroid hormones also produce rapid effects on the membranes of many brain cells via cell surface receptors that are like the receptors for neurotransmitters. These actions are rapid in onset and short in duration. However, the precise nature of the receptors for these rapid effects is in most cases largely unknown.

Hormones participate in many disease processes, in some cases as protectors and in other cases as promoters of abnormal function. Adrenal steroids exacerbate neural damage from strokes and seizures and mediate damaging effects of severe and prolonged stress. Estrogens enhance normal declarative and episodic memory in estrogen-deficient women, and estrogen replacement therapy appears to reduce the risk of Alzheimer's disease in postmenopausal women. Estrogens also have antidepressant effects; they modulate pain mechanisms; and they regulate the neural pathways involved in movement, with the result that estrogens enhance performance of fine motor skills and enhance reaction times in a driving simulation test in women. Androgen effects are less well studied in these regards.

Age-related decline of gonadal function reduces the beneficial and protective actions of these hormones on brain function. At the same time, age-related increases in adrenal steroid activity promote age-related changes in brain cells that can culminate in neuronal damage or cell death. Lifelong patterns of adrenocortical function, determined by early experience (see above), contribute to rates of brain aging, at least in experimental animals.

Hormones are mediators of change, acting in large part by modulating expression of the genetic code, and they provide an interface between experiences of the individual and the structure and function of the brain, as well as other organs of the body. Hormone action during development and in adult life participates in the processes that determine individual differences in physiology, behavior, and cognitive function.

See also AGING AND COGNITION; AGING, MEMORY, AND THE BRAIN; MOTOR CONTROL; NEUROTRANSMITTERS; STRESS

—*Bruce S. McEwen*

Further Readings

Adkins-Regan, E. (1981). Early organizational effects of hormones. In N. T. Adler, Ed., *Neuroendocrinology of Reproduction.* New York: Plenum Press, pp. 159–228.

Cahill, L., B. Prins, M. Weber, and J. L. McGaugh. (1994). Beta-adrenergic activation and memory for emotional events. *Nature* 347: 702–704.

Conn, P. M., and S. Melmud. (1997). *Endocrinology: Basic and Clinical Principles.* Totowa, NJ: Humana Press.

Kimura, D. (1992). Sex differences in the brain. *Sci. Amer.* 267: 119–125.

Kimura, D. (1995). Estrogen replacement therapy may protect against intellectual decline in postmenopausal women. *Horm. Behav.* 29: 312–321.

Lupien, S., A. R. Lecours, I. Lussier, G. Schwartz, N. P. V. Nair, and M. J. Meaney. (1994). Basal cortisol levels and cognitive deficits in human aging. *J. Neurosci.* 14: 2893–2903.

McEwen, B. S. (1991). Non-genomic and genomic effects of steroids on neural activity. *Trends in Pharmacological Sciences* 12: 141–147.

McEwen, B. S. (1992). Re-examination of the glucocorticoid hypothesis of stress and aging. In D. Swaab, M. Hofman, M. Mirmiran, R. Ravid, and F. van Leeuwen, Eds., *Prog. Brain Res.* 93: 365–383.

McEwen, B. S. (1995). Neuroendocrine interactions. In *Psychopharmacology: The Fourth Generation of Progress.* New York: Raven Press, pp. 705–718.

McEwen, B. S. (1995). Stressful experience, brain, and emotions: Development, genetic and hormonal influences. In M. S. Gazzaniga, Ed., *The Cognitive Neurosciences.* Cambridge, MA: MIT Press, pp. 1117–1135.

McEwen, B. S. (1998). Protective and damaging effects of stress mediators. *N. Eng. J. Med.* to appear.

McEwen, B. S., R. Sakai, and R. Spencer. (1993). Adrenal steroid effects on the brain: Versatile hormones with good and bad effects. In J. Schulkin, Ed., *Hormonally Induced Changes in Mind and Brain.* San Diego: Academic Press, pp. 157–189.

McEwen, B. S., and R. M. Sapolsky. (1995). Stress and cognitive function. *Current Opinion in Neurobiology* 5: 205–216.

McEwen, B. S., and E. Stellar. (1993). Stress and the individual: Mechanisms leading to disease. *Arch. Intern. Med.* 153: 2093–2101.

McEwen, B. S., E. Gould, M. Orchinik, N. G.Weiland, and C. S. Woolley. (1995). Oestrogens and the structural and functional plasticity of neurons: Implications for memory, ageing and neurodegenerative processes. *Ciba Foundation Symposium* 191: 52–73.

McEwen, B. S., D. Albeck, H. Cameron, H. Chao, E. Gould, N. Hastings, Y. Kuroda, V. Luine, A. M. Magarinos, C. R. McKittrick, M. Orchinik, C. Pavlides, P. Vaher, Y. Watanabe, and N. Weiland. (1995). Stress and the brain: A paradoxical role for adrenal steroids. *Vitamins and Hormones* 51: 371–402.

McGaugh, J. L., L. Cahill, and B. Roozendaal. (1996). Involvement of the amygdala in memory storage: Interaction with other brain systems. *Proc. Natl. Acad. Sci. U.S.A.* 93: 13508–13514.

Meaney, M. J., B. Tannenbaum, D. Francis, S. Bhatnagar, N. Shanks, V. Viau, D. O'Donnell, and P. M. Plotsky. (1994). Early environmental programming hypothalamic-pituitary-adrenal responses to stress. *Seminars in the Neurosciences* 6: 247–259.

Pfaff, D. W. (1980). *Estrogens and Brain Function.* Heidelberg: Springer-Verlag.

Pugh, C. R., D. Tremblay, M. Fleshner, and J. W. Rudy. (1997). A selective role for corticosterone in contextual-fear conditioning. *Behav. Neurosci.* 111: 503–511.

Purifoy, F. (1981). Endocrine-environment interaction in human variability. *Annu. Rev. Anthropol.* 10: 141–162.

Roozendaal, B., and J. L. McGaugh. (1997). Glucocorticoid receptor agonist and antagonist administration into the basolateral but not central amygdala modulates memory storage. *Neurobiology of Learning and Memory* 67:176–179.

Sapolsky, R. (1992). *Stress, the Aging Brain and the Mechanisms of Neuron Death.* Cambridge, MA: MIT Press.

Sapolsky, R. M., L. C. Krey, and B. S. McEwen. (1986). The neuroendocrinology of stress and aging: The glucocorticoid cascade hypothesis. *Endocr. Rev.* 7: 284–301.

Tallal, P., and B. S. McEwen., Eds. (1991). Special Issue: Neuroendocrine Effects on Brain Development and Cognition. *Psychoneuroendocrinology* 16: 1–3.

Neuroimaging

See INTRODUCTION: NEUROSCIENCES; MAGNETIC RESONANCE IMAGING; POSITRON EMISSION TOMOGRAPHY

Neuron

The neuron is the main type of cell in the nervous system that, in association with neuroglial cells, mediates the information processing that underlies nervous function. As the main building block of the brain, the nerve cell is fundamental to the neural basis of cognitive abilities. Much of the research in contemporary neuroscience focuses on neuronal structure, function, and pharmacology, using modern techniques of molecular and cell biology. Based on these results, computational models of neurons and neuronal circuits are being constructed to provide increasingly powerful insights into how the brain mediates cognitive functions.

In their speculations on the mind, the ancients knew nothing of cells or neurons, nor did DESCARTES, Locke, or KANT, or any other scientist or natural philosopher until the nineteenth century. The first step toward this understanding was the cell theory of Schwann, in 1839, which stated that all body organs and tissues are composed of individual cells. A nerve cell was recognized to consist of three main parts: the cell body (soma), containing the nucleus; short processes (dendrites); and a single long process (axon) that connects to the dendrites or somata of other nerve cells within the region or of cells in other regions. However, the branches of dendrites and axons could not be clearly visualized, leading to the belief among some workers that nerve cells are different from other cells in that their finest branches form a continuous functional network (called the reticular theory). It was also recognized that numerous non-neuronal cells, called neuroglia, surround the neurons and contribute to their functions.

Led by Ramón y CAJAL, neuroanatomists in the 1880s and 1890s, using the GOLGI stain, showed that most regions of the brain contain several distinctive types of nerve cell with specific axonal and dendritic branching patterns. Dendrites and axons were found not to be continuous, so that the nerve cell belongs under the cell theory, as summarized in the neuron doctrine. How then are signals transferred between neurons? Sherrington in 1897 suggested that this occurs by means of specialized junctions which he termed *synapses*. Electron microscopists in the 1950s showed that such contacts between neurons exist. Since that time, neuroanatomists have elucidated the ultrastructure of the synapse as well as the patterns of synaptic connections between the different types of neurons. The patterns of connections within a region are called canonical circuits, mediating the main types of information processing within each region. Neurons and their canonical circuits are organized at the next higher level into neural modules, such as the columns found in the CEREBRAL CORTEX (see also VISUAL CORTEX). At a still higher organization level, the patterns of neuronal connections between regions are called distributed circuits, which constitute the pathways and systems underlying behavior (e.g., see VISUAL ANATOMY AND PHYSIOLOGY).

Physiological studies of neuron properties have paralleled these anatomical developments. The axon generates a nerve impulse (action potential), a wave of depolarization of the surface membrane, which propagates rapidly along the membrane from its site of initiation (the axon hillock) to the axon terminals. Already in 1850 a finite rate of propagation (approximately 100 m per second in the largest axons) was established; this overturned the historical assumption of a mysterious instantaneous "nervous force" underlying the mind.

In the 1950s a slower potential (synaptic potential) was discovered by Katz at the synapse. It was found that an action potential invading a synapse causes it to secrete small vesicles containing a chemical neurotransmitter, which diffuses across the cleft from the presynaptic to the postsynaptic cell. There it acts on a membrane receptor to bring about an opening of membrane channels; this lets electrically charged ions flow across the membrane to change the membrane potential of the postsynaptic site. Membrane proteins that contain both receptor sites and ionic channels are called ionotropic receptors. Depending on which ions flow, the membrane may be depolarized (excitatory postsynaptic potential, EPSP) or hyperpolarized (inhibitory postsynaptic potential, IPSP). Among the cells of the body, chemical synapses are unique to neurons. Thus the study of synapses lies at the heart of the study of brain function at the neuronal level. In addition to these chemical synapses, neurons, like other cells, may be interconnected by gap junctions (electrical synapses), which permit electric currents and small molecules to pass directly between cells. These also connect neuroglial cells, and are especially prevalent during development.

Knowledge of NEUROTRANSMITTERS and how they generate EPSPs and IPSPs began with the study of the autonomic nervous system around 1900. The first neurotransmitter to be identified was acetylcholine, shown by Loewi in the 1920s to mediate the slow action of the vagus nerve in slowing the heart rate, and by Katz in the 1950s to mediate the rapid action of motor nerves in exciting skeletal muscles. Cannon in the 1920s established epinephrine (Adrenaline) as the neurohormone mediating "flight-or-fight" responses, and other biogenic amines acting on autonomic organs were revealed in the 1930s. The introduction of the neuroleptics chlorpromazine and reserpine for the treatment of schizophrenia in the 1950s shifted interest in the pharmacology of neurotransmitters to the central nervous system. The resultant growth of the field of psychopharmacology has generated mechanistic hypotheses for all the major mental disorders. For example, a common action of neuroleptic (antipsychotic) drugs is a blockade of D2 receptors at dopaminergic synapses. And current research on antidepressant drugs is focused on their ability to act as selective serotonin reuptake inhibitors (SSRIs).

Many of the neurotransmitters can activate not only ionotropic receptors but also metabotropic receptors coupled to second messenger systems, which then phosphorylate target proteins or bring about other slower metabolic changes in the postsynaptic neuron (and also can act back on the presynaptic terminal as well). Acetylcholine acting on the heart and epinephrine acting as a hormone are examples, as are a wide range of neuropeptides. These include such molecules as hypothalamic factors (e.g., luteinizing hormone–releasing hormone, corticotropin), opioids (e.g., enkephalins and endorphins), and numerous types found also in the gut and other organs (vasoactive intestinal polypeptide, cholecystokinin, substance P, etc.; see NEUROENDOCRINOLOGY). These molecules, acting as neuromodulators, set behavioral states (e.g., the role of acetylcholine, norepinephrine, and serotonin in waking, sleeping, and levels of consciousness, or the role of neuropeptide Y in feeding behavior and anxiety and stress responses). Another role is in learning and memory; LONG-TERM POTENTIATION (LTP) and long-term depression (LTD) of synaptic responses involve second messengers, calcium, and cyclic nucleotides, and actions on the genome that may implement associative (Hebbian) learning. These latter actions overlap with the activation of receptors controlling growth and differentiation during development.

In summary, a better understanding of the effects of neurotransmitters and neuromodulators on different types of neurons and neuronal circuits is the necessary foundation for an understanding of normal cognition and changes underlying psychotic states.

Analysis of neuronal function has been aided enormously by the development of modern techniques. With the advent of DNA engineering in the 1970s, the molecular basis of neuronal structure and function is being increasingly elucidated. Modern physiological research employs a variety of methods in analyzing neuronal function. These include single- and multiple-neuron recordings in awake behaving animals (SINGLE-NEURON RECORDING); patch pipette recordings from neurons in slices taken from different brain regions (this includes slices of human cerebral cortex in tissue obtained in operations for relief of chronic epilepsy); patch recordings of single membrane channels in isolated cells grown in tissue culture; and different types of functional imaging (including movement of calcium ions, glucose uptake, and voltage-sensitive dyes). A long-term goal is to relate these changes at the neuronal level to changes in blood flow revealed by brain imaging methods (POSITRON EMISSION TOMOGRAPHY, functional MAGNETIC RESONANCE IMAGING, fMRI) at the systems level. This will enable an integrated view of neuronal function and the neural basis of cognition and cognitive disorders to begin to emerge. Databases to support this effort are becoming available on the World Wide Web. Examples are membrane receptors and channels (www.le.ac.uk/csn), canonical neurons and their compartmental models (http://senselab.med.yale.edu/neuron), and brain scans (human brain project).

Experimental approaches to the study of the neuron are being greatly aided by the development of computer models and the emergence of the new field of COMPUTATIONAL NEUROSCIENCE. This began in the 1950s with the pioneering model of the axonal action potential by Hodgkin and Huxley. In the 1960s Rall showed that complex dendritic trees could be modeled as chains of compartments incorporating properties representing action potentials and synaptic potentials. With the rise of powerful modern desktop computers it is now possible for neuroscientists to construct increasingly accurate models of different types of neurons to aid them in analyzing the neural basis of function of a given neuron in a given region. This work is reported in mainstream neuroscience journals as well as in new journals such as *Neural Computation* and the *Journal of Computational Neuroscience*. In contrast to this approach, connectionist networks reduce the soma and dendrite of a neuron to a single node, thereby excluding most of the interesting properties of neurons as summarized above. A merging of neuron-based compartmental models with NEURAL NETWORKS will therefore be welcome, because it will provide insights into how real brains actually carry out their system functions in mediating cognitive behavior. It is not unreasonable to expect that this will also provide the philosophical foundation for a more profound functional explanation of the relation between the brain and the mind.

See also CORTICAL LOCALIZATION, HISTORY OF; ELECTROPHYSIOLOGY, ELECTRIC AND MAGNETIC EVOKED FIELDS

—*Gordon Shepherd*

Further Readings

Shepherd, G. M. (1991). *Foundations of the Neuron Doctrine.* New York: Oxford University Press.
Snyder, S. H. (1996). *Drugs and the Brain.* New York: Scientific American Books.

Neuropsychological Deficits

See MENTAL RETARDATION; MODELING NEUROPSYCHOLOGICAL DEFICITS

Neurotransmitters

Neurotransmitters are chemicals made by neurons and used by them to transmit signals to other neurons or non-neuronal cells (e.g., skeletal muscle, myocardium, pineal glandular cells) that they innervate. The neurotransmitters produce their effects by being released into synapses when their neuron of origin fires (i.e., becomes depolarized) and then attaching to receptors in the membrane of the postsynaptic cells. This causes changes in the fluxes of particular ions across that membrane, making cells more likely to become depolarized if the neurotransmitter happens to be excitatory, or less likely if it is inhibitory. Neurotransmitters can also produce their effects by modulating the production of other signal-transducing molecules (second messengers) in the postsynaptic cells (Cooper, Bloom, and Roth 1996). Nine compounds—belonging to three chemical families—are generally believed to function as neurotransmitters some-

where in the central nervous system (CNS) or periphery. In addition, certain other body chemicals, for example, adenosine, histamine, enkephalins, endorphins, and epinephrine, have neurotransmitter-like properties, and many additional true neurotransmitters may await discovery.

The first of these families, and the group about which most is known, are the amine neurotransmitters, a group of compounds containing a nitrogen molecule that is not part of a ring structure. Among the amine neurotransmitters are acetylcholine, norepinephrine, dopamine, and serotonin. *Acetylcholine* is possibly the most widely used neurotransmitter in the body, and all axons that leave the CNS (e.g., those running to skeletal muscle, or to sympathetic or parasympathetic ganglia) use acetylcholine as their neurotransmitter. Within the brain, acetylcholine is the transmitter of, among other neurons, those generating the tracts that run from the septum to the HIPPOCAMPUS, and from the nucleus basalis to the CEREBRAL CORTEX—both of which seem to be needed to sustain memory and learning. It is also the neurotransmitter released by short-axon interneurons of the BASAL GANGLIA. *Norepinephrine* is the neurotransmitter released by sympathetic nerves (e.g., those innervating the heart and blood vessels) and, within the brain, those of the locus ceruleus, a nucleus activated in the process of focusing attention. *Dopamine* and *serotonin* apparently are neurotransmitters only within the CNS. Some dopaminergic (i.e., dopamine-releasing) neurons run from the substantia nigra to the corpus striatum; their loss gives rise to the clinical manifestations of Parkinson's disease (Korczyn 1994); others, involved in the rewarding effects of drugs and natural stimuli, run from the mesencephalon to the nucleus accumbens. Dopaminergic neurons involved in the actions of most antipsychotic drugs (which antagonize the effects of dopamine on its receptors) run from the brain stem to limbic cortical structures in the frontal region, while the dopamine released from hypothalamic cells travels via a private blood supply, the pituitary portal vascular system, to the anterior pituitary gland, where it tonically suppresses release of the hormone prolactin. (Drugs that interfere with the release or actions of this dopamine can cause lactation as a side effect, even in men.)

The cell bodies, or perikarya, of serotoninergic (serotonin-releasing) neurons reside in the brain stem; their axons can descend in the spinal cord (where they "gate" incoming sensory inputs and also decrease sympathetic nervous outflow, thus lowering blood pressure) or ascend to other parts of the brain. Within the brain such serotoninergic nerve terminals are found in virtually all regions, enabling this transmitter to modulate a wide variety of behavioral and nonbehavioral functions, including, among others, mood, sleep, total food intake and macronutrient (carbohydrate vs. protein) selection (Wurtman and Wurtman 1989), aggressive behaviors, and PAIN sensitivity (Frazer, Molinoff, and Winokur 1994). Brains of women produce only about two thirds as much serotonin as those of men (Nishizawa et al. 1997); this may explain their greater vulnerability to serotonin-related diseases like depression and obesity. Within the pineal gland serotonin is also the precursor of the sleep-inducing hormone melatonin (Dollins et al. 1994).

The second neurotransmitter family includes amino acids, compounds that contain both an amino group (NH$_2$) and a carboxylic acid group (COOH) and which are also the building blocks of peptides and proteins. The amino acids known to serve as neurotransmitters are glycine, and glutamic and aspartic acids, present in all proteins, and γ-aminobutyric acid (GABA), produced only in brain neurons. Glutamic acid and GABA are the most abundant neurotransmitters within the CNS, particularly in the cerebral cortex; glutamic acid tends to be excitatory and GABA inhibitory. Aspartic acid and glycine subserve these functions in the spinal cord (Cooper et al. 1996).

The third neurotransmitter family is composed of peptides, compounds that contain at least two and sometimes as many as 100 amino acids. Peptide neurotransmitters are poorly understood: evidence that they are, in fact, transmitters tends to be incomplete and restricted to their location within nerve terminals and to the physiological effects produced when they are applied to neurons. Probably the best understood peptide neurotransmitter is substance P, a compound that transmits signals generated by pain.

In general each neuron uses only a single compound as its neurotransmitter. However some neurons contain both an amine and a peptide and may release both into synapses. Moreover, many neurons release adenosine, an inhibitory compound, along with their "true" transmitter, for instance, norepinephrine or acetylcholine. The stimulant effect of caffeine results from its ability to block receptors for this adenosine.

Neurotransmitters are manufactured from circulating precursor compounds like amino acids, glucose, and the dietary amine choline. Neurons modify the structure of these precursor compounds through a series of enzymatic reactions that often are limited not by the amount of enzyme present but by the concentration of the precursor, which can change, for example, as a consequence of eating (Wurtman 1988). Neurotransmitters that come from amino acids include serotonin, which is derived from tryptophan; dopamine and norepinephrine, which are derived from tyrosine; and glycine, which is derived from threonine. Among the neurotransmitters made from glucose are glutamate, aspartate, and GABA. Choline serves as the precursor of acetylcholine.

Once released into the synapse, each neurotransmitter combines chemically with one or more highly specific receptors; these are protein molecules which are embedded in the postsynaptic membrane. As noted above, this interaction can affect the electrical properties of the postsynaptic cell, its chemical properties, or both. When a NEURON is in its resting state, it sustains a voltage of about -70 mV as the consequence of differences between the concentrations of certain ions at the internal and external sides of its bounding membrane. Excitatory neurotransmitters either open protein-lined channels in this membrane, allowing extracellular ions, like sodium, to move into the cell, or close channels for potassium. This raises the neuron's voltage toward zero, and makes it more likely that—if enough such receptors are occupied—the cell will become depolarized. If the postsynaptic cell happens also to be a neuron (i.e., as opposed to a muscle cell), this depolarization will cause it to release its own neurotransmitter from its terminals. Inhibitory neurotransmitters

like GABA activate receptors that cause other ions—usually chloride—to pass through the membrane; this usually hyperpolarizes the postsynaptic cell, and decreases the likelihood that it will become depolarized. (The neurotransmitter glutamic acid, acting via its N-methyl-d-aspartate (NMDA) receptor, can also open channels for calcium ions. Some investigators believe that excessive activation of these receptors in neurological diseases can cause toxic quantities of calcium to enter the cells and kill them.)

If the postsynaptic cell is a muscle cell rather than a neuron, an excitatory neurotransmitter will cause the muscle to contract. If the postsynaptic cell is a glandular cell, an excitatory neurotransmitter will cause the cell to secrete its contents.

While most neurotransmitters interact with their receptors to change the voltage of postsynaptic cells, some neurotransmitter interactions, involving a different type of receptor, modify the chemical composition of the postsynaptic cell by either causing or blocking the formation of second messenger molecules. These second messengers regulate many of the postsynaptic cell's biochemical processes, including gene expression; they generally produce their effects by activating enzymes that add high-energy phosphate groups to specific cellular proteins. Examples of second messengers formed within the postsynaptic cell include cyclic adenosine monophosphate, diacylglycerol, and inositol phosphates. Once neurotransmitters have been secreted into synapses and have acted on their receptors, they are cleared from the synapse either by enzymatic breakdown—for example, acetylcholine, which is converted by the enzyme acetylcholinesterase to choline and acetate, neither of which has neurotransmitter activity—or, for neurotransmitters like dopamine, serotonin, and GABA, by a physical process called *reuptake*. In reuptake, a protein in the presynaptic membrane acts as a sort of sponge, causing the neurotransmitter molecules to reenter their neuron of origin, where they can be broken down by other enzymes (e.g., monoamine oxidase, in dopaminergic, serotoninergic, or noradrenergic neurons) or repackaged for reuse.

As indicated above, particular neurotransmitters are now known to be involved in many neurological and behavioral disorders. For example, in Alzheimer's disease, whose victims exhibit loss of intellectual capacity (particularly short-term memory), disintegration of personality, mental confusion, hallucinations, and aggressive—even violent—behaviors, many families of neurons, utilizing many neurotransmitters, die (Wurtman et al. 1996). However, the most heavily damaged family seems to be the long-axon acetylcholine-releasing neurons, originating in the septum and the nucleus basalis, which innervate the hippocampal and cerebral cortices. Acetylcholinesterase inhibitors, which increase brain levels of acetylcholine, can improve short-term memory, albeit transiently, in some Alzheimer's disease patients.

Most drugs—therapeutic or recreational—that affect brain and behavior do so by acting at synapses to affect the production, release, effects on receptors, or inactivation of neurotransmitter molecules (Bernstein 1988). Such drugs can also constitute important and specific probes for understanding cognition and other brain functions.

References

Bernstein, J. G. (1988). *Drug Therapy in Psychiatry,* 2nd ed. Littleton, MA: PSG Publishing.

Cooper, J. R., F. E. Bloom, and R. H. Roth. (1996). *The Biochemical Basis of Neuropharmacology.* 7th ed. New York: Oxford University Press.

Dollins, A. B., I. V. Zhdanova, R. J. Wurtman, H. J. Lynch, and M. H. Deng. (1994). Effect of inducing nocturnal serum melatonin concentrations in daytime on sleep, mood, body temperature, and performance. *Proc. Natl. Acad. Sci. U.S.A.* 91:1824–1828.

Frazer, A., P. Molinoff, and A. Winokur. (1994). *Biological Bases of Brain Function and Disease.* New York: Raven Press.

Korczyn, A. D. (1994). Parkinson's disease. In F. E. Bloom and D. J. Kupfer, Eds., *Psychopharmacology: The Fourth Generation of Progress.* New York: Raven Press, pp. 1479–1484.

Nishizawa, S., C. Benkelfat, S. N. Young, M. Leyton, S. Mzengeza, C. de Montigny, P. Blier, and M. Diksic. (1997). Differences between males and females in rates of serotonin synthesis in human brain. *Proc. Natl. Acad. Sci U.S.A.* 94: 5308–5313.

Wurtman, R. J. (1988). Effects of their nutrient precursors on the synthesis and release of serotonin, the catecholamines, and acetylcholine: Implications for behavioral disorders. *Clin. Neuropharmacol.* 11 (Suppl. 1): S187–193.

Wurtman, R. J., and J. J. Wurtman. (January, 1989). Carbohydrates and depression. *Scientific American* 260: 50–57.

Wurtman, R. J., S. Corkin, J. H. Growdon, and R. M. Nitsch. (1996). The neurobiology of Alzheimer's disease. *Annals of the New York Academy of Sciences* 777.9.

Newell, Allen

Allen Newell (1927–1992), cognitive psychologist and computer scientist, made profound contributions to fields ranging from computer architecture and programming software to artificial intelligence, cognitive science, and psychology. One of the founding fathers of the new domains of artificial intelligence and cognitive science, his work continues to exercise a major influence on these developing fields.

Newell was born on March 19, 1927, in San Francisco, the son of Dr. Robert R. Newell, a distinguished radiologist on the faculty of the Stanford Medical School, and Jeanette LeValley Newell. He attended San Francisco public schools, and served in the Navy after World War II, assisting in mapping radiation intensities at the Eniwetok A-bomb tests, an experience that awoke his interest in science. In 1949, he received a B.S. degree in Physics at Stanford, then spent a postgraduate year studying mathematics at Princeton University. A desire to learn more about applications domains led him to a position studying logistics and air defense organization at Rand in Santa Monica, a "think tank" supported by the U.S. Air Force, and gave him early contact with the then emerging electronic digital computers.

At almost the beginning of the computer era, Newell, collaborating with J. C. Shaw and H. A. Simon, conceived that computers might solve problems, non-numerical or numerical, by selective HEURISTIC SEARCH, as people do. Needing programming languages that would provide flexible memory structures, they invented list processing languages (or Information Processing Languages, IPLs) in 1956. Today, list processing is an indispensable tool for artificial intelligence and computer science, central to such widely used languages as LISP and OPS5, and providing a basis for structured programming.

The research continued at Carnegie Institute of Technology (after 1965, Carnegie Mellon University), where Newell enrolled in 1955 to pursue a Ph.D. in Industrial Administration, with a thesis—probably the first—in artificial intelligence. Over the next few years, Newell and his associates at Rand and Carnegie used the IPLs to create the first artificial intelligence programs, including the Logic Theorist (1956), the General Problem Solver (1959), and the NSS chess program (1958), introducing fundamental ideas that are still at the core of PROBLEM SOLVING theory, including means-ends analysis and PLANNING. To test how well these simulations accounted for human problem solving, the group used thinking-aloud protocols. Newell received his doctorate in 1958, joined the faculty of Carnegie Tech in 1961 as a full professor, and retained this position for the remaining three decades of his life.

In 1972, Newell and Simon summarized their psychological research, which employed verbal protocols and computer simulation, in their book *Human Problem Solving.* Recognizing the potential of PRODUCTION SYSTEMS (programs consisting of condition-action statements, employed in most AI programs and expert systems), in 1981, Newell designed the language OPS5.

To generalize psychological simulations and endow them with a more realistic control structure, Newell's research focused increasingly on devising a powerful and veridical cognitive architecture that would provide a framework for general cognitive theories. A major product of this work was the Soar system, developed with Paul Rosenbloom and John Laird, a substantial extension of GPS that operates in multiple problem spaces and has powerful learning capabilities. Dozens of investigators are now using Soar as the architecture for intelligent systems, both simulations of human thinking and expert systems for AI. Soar and the future of unified theories were the subject of Newell's last book, *Unified Theories of Cognition* (1990), based on his William James Lectures at Harvard.

Apart from the Soar research, much of Newell's productive effort went into what he called his "diversions," which almost all produced important contributions to cognitive science. These included investigations with Gordon Bell of computer architectures, reported in *Computer Structures* (1971), and participation in a team at CMU designing parallel computer architectures. He also served as chair of the committee that monitored the research in computer SPEECH RECOGNITION sponsored by the Defense Department's Advanced Research Projects Agency (ARPA). Yet another "diversion" was research with Card and Moran (*The Psychology of Human-Computer Interaction,* 1983) that reinvigorated human factors studies, extending them to complex cognitive processes.

See also MEMORY STORAGE, MODULATION OF; NEUROENDOCRINOLOGY; WORKING MEMORY, NEURAL BASIS OF

—Richard J. Wurtman

In addition to his scientific work, Newell provided leadership in such organizations as the American Association for Artificial Intelligence, and the Cognitive Science Society (serving as president of both), and he provided advice to agencies of the national government. He played a leading role in creating and developing the School of Computer Science at Carnegie Mellon University and the innovations in computing and electronic networking of its campus.

For his scientific and professional contributions, Newell received numerous honors and awards, including the U.S. National Medal of Science, the Lifetime Contributions Award of the International Joint Conference on Artificial Intelligence, the Distinguished Scientific Contributions Award of the American Psychological Association, and the A. M. Turing Award of the Association for Computing Machinery, and honorary degrees from the Universities of Groningen (Netherlands) and Pennsylvania. He was elected to both the National Academy of Engineering and the National Academy of Sciences.

See also COGNITIVE MODELING, SYMBOLIC; HUMAN-COMPUTER INTERACTION; INTELLIGENT AGENT ARCHITECTURE

—*Herbert A. Simon*

References

Bell, C. G., and A. Newell. (1971). *Computer Structures: Readings and Examples.* New York: McGraw-Hill.

Brownston, L., Farrell, R., and E. Kent. (1985). *Programming Expert Systems in OPS5: An Introduction to Rule-Based Programming.* Reading, MA: Addison-Wesley.

Card, S., T. P. Moran, and A. Newell. (1983). *The Psychology of Human-Computer Interaction.* Hillsdale, NJ: Erlbaum.

Forgy, C. L. (1979). *On the Efficient Implementation of Production Systems.* Ph.D. diss., Department of Computer Science, Carnegie Mellon University.

Newell, A. (1990). *Unified Theories of Cognition.* Cambridge, MA: Harvard University Press.

Newell, A., and J. C. Shaw. (1957). Programming the logic theory machine. *Proceedings of the 1957 Western Joint Computer Conference.* New York: Institute of Radio Engineers. pp. 230–240.

Newell, A., J. C. Shaw, and H. A. Simon. (1959). *Report on a general problem-solving program. Proceedings of the International Conference on Information Processing.* Paris, pp. 256–264.

Newell, A., J. C. Shaw, and H. A. Simon. (1958b). Chess-playing programs and the problem of complexity. *IBM Journal of Research and Development* 2: 320–335.

Newell, A., J. C. Shaw, and H. A. Simon. (1960). Report on a general problem-solving program for a computer. *Proceedings of the International Conference on Information Processing.* Paris: UNESCO, pp. 256–264.

Newell, A., and H. A. Simon. (1956). The logic theory machine: a complex information processing system. *IRE Transactions on Information Theory* IT-2, no. 3: 61–79.

Newell, A., and H. A. Simon. (1972). *Human Problem Solving.* Englewood Cliffs, NJ: Prentice-Hall.

Nonmonotonic Logics

Nonmonotonic logics are used to formalize plausible reasoning. They allow more general reasoning than standard logics, which deal with universal statements. For example,

standard logics can easily represent the argument:

All men are mortal
Socrates is a man

Therefore, Socrates is mortal

$(\forall x)(Man(x) \Rightarrow Mortal(x)); Man(Socrates)$

Mortal(Socrates)

but cannot represent reasoning such as:

Birds typically fly
Tweety is a bird

Therefore, Tweety (presumably) flies

Such arguments are characteristic of commonsense reasoning, where *default* rules and the absence of complete information are prevalent.

The most salient feature of nonmonotonic reasoning is that the conclusion of a nonmonotonic argument may not be correct. For example, if Tweety is a penguin, it is incorrect to conclude that Tweety flies. Nonmonotonic reasoning often requires jumping to a conclusion and subsequently retracting that conclusion as further information becomes available. Thus, as the set of assumptions grows, the set of conclusions (theorems) may shrink. This reasoning is called *nonmonotonic* in contrast to standard logic, which is *monotonic:* as one's set of assumptions grows, one's set of theorems grows as well. (Formally, a system is monotonic if for any two theories A and B, whenever A is a subset of B, the theorems of A are a subset of the theorems of B.)

All systems of nonmonotonic reasoning are fundamentally concerned with the issue of consistency: ensuring that conclusions drawn are consistent with one another and with the assumptions.

Major Systems of Nonmonotonic Reasoning

Default Logic (Reiter 1980) introduces a *default rule,* an inference rule consisting of an assumption, an appeal to the consistency of some formula, and a conclusion. For example, the rule *Birds typically fly* could be written as

Bird(x):Fly(x)

Fly(x)

which reads: if x is a bird, and it is consistent that x flies, then conclude that x flies.

Default rules must be applied with care, since conflicting default rules could cause inconsistency if used together. For example, the default *Quakers are usually pacifists* conflicts with the default *Republicans are usually nonpacifists* in the case of Richard Nixon, who was both a Quaker and a Republican. Applying the first default yields the conclusion that Nixon was a pacifist; applying the second default yields the conclusion that Nixon was a nonpacifist; applying both yields inconsistency. One generates *extensions* of a default theory by applying as many default rules as possible. Multiple extensions, or their equivalent, arise in all nonmonotonic logics. The existence of multiple extensions may be seen as a feature or a problem. On the one hand, they allow the expression of reasonable but conflicting arguments within one system, and thus model well commonsense reasoning and discourse. However, conflicting defaults may give rise to unexpected extensions, corresponding to arguments that seem odd or unreasonable. An example of problematic multiple extensions is the Yale shooting problem, discussed below.

Autoepistemic Logic (Moore 1985) formalizes nonmonotonicity using sentences of a MODAL LOGIC of belief with belief operator L. Autoepistemic Logic focuses on *stable sets* of sentences (Stalnaker 1980)—sets of sentences that can be viewed as the beliefs of a rational agent—and the *stable expansions* of a premise set. Properties of stable sets include consistency and a version of negative introspection: if a sentence P does not belong to a belief set, then the sentence $\neg L P$ belongs to the belief set. This corresponds to the principle that if an agent does not believe a particular fact, he believes that he does not believe it. To formalize the Tweety example, one represents the rule that birds typically fly as an appeal to an agent's beliefs: $L(Bird\,(x)) \wedge \neg L\,(\neg Fly\,(x)) \Rightarrow Fly\,(x)$. If I believe that x is a bird and I don't believe that x cannot fly, then (I will conclude that) x flies. Any stable expansion of the premise set consisting of this premise and the premise that Tweety is a bird will contain the conclusion that Tweety flies.

Circumscription (McCarthy 1980, 1986) seeks to formalize nonmonotonic reasoning within classical logic by circumscribing, or limiting the extension of, certain predicates. The logic limits the objects in a particular class to those that *must be* in the class. For example, consider the theory containing assumptions that typical birds fly, atypical (usually called *abnormal*) birds do not fly, penguins are atypical, Opus is a penguin, and Tweety is a bird. Opus *must* be in the class of atypical, nonflying birds, but there is no reason for Tweety to be in that class; thus we conclude that Tweety can fly. The circumscription of a theory is achieved by adding a second-order axiom (or, in a first-order theory, an axiom schema), limiting the extension of certain predicates, to a set of axioms.

The systems above describe different ways of determining the nonmonotonic consequences of a set of assumptions. *Entailment Relations* (Kraus, Lehmann, and Magidor 1990) generalize these approaches by considering a nonmonotonic entailment operator $\mid\sim$, where $P \mid\sim Q$ means that Q is a nonmonotonic consequence of P, and by formulating general principles characterizing the behavior of $\mid\sim$. These principles specify how $\mid\sim$ relates to the standard entailment operator $\vdash$ of classical logic, and how meta-statements referring to the entailment operator can be combined.

Belief Revision (Alchourron, Gardenfors, and Makinson 1985) studies nonmonotonic reasoning from the dynamic point of view, focusing on how old beliefs are retracted as new beliefs are added to a knowledge base. There are four interconnected operators of interest: contraction, withdrawal, expansion, and revision. In general, revising a knowledge base follows the principle of minimal change: one conserves as much information as possible.

Integrating Nonmonotonic Reasoning with Other Theories

Nonmonotonic reasoning systems are useful only if they can be successfully *integrated* with other theories of commonsense reasoning. Attempts at integration are often surprisingly difficult. For example, the Yale shooting problem (Hanks and McDermott 1987) showed that integrating nonmonotonic reasoning with TEMPORAL REASONING was complicated by the multiple extension problem. The Yale shooting problem consists of determining what happens to a turkey when we know that

1. a gun is loaded at 1:00 and fired at 3:00
2. firing a loaded gun at a turkey results in the turkey's immediate death
3. guns typically stay loaded (default rule D1)
4. turkeys typically stay alive (default rule D2)

Two extensions arise, only one of which is expected. In the expected extension, D1 is applied, the gun remains loaded at 3:00, and the turkey dies. In the unexpected extension, D2 is applied and the turkey is therefore alive after 3:00. This entails that the gun mysteriously becomes unloaded between 1:00 and 3:00. The problem of formalizing a system of temporal reasoning so that these unexpected extensions do not arise has become a central topic in nonmonotonic research. In nonmonotonic temporal reasoning, it has resulted in the development of theories of CAUSATION and EXPLANATION (Morgenstern 1996 and Shanahan 1997 give summaries and analyses).

Integrating nonmonotonic logics with MULTIAGENT SYSTEMS is also difficult. The major problem is modeling nested nonmonotonic reasoning: agents must reason about other agents' nonmonotonic reasoning processes. Most nonmonotonic formalisms are not expressive enough to model such reasoning. Moreover, nested nonmonotonic reasoning requires that agents know what other agents do *not* believe, a difficult requirement to satisfy (Morgenstern and Guerreiro 1993).

In general, integration may require extending both the nonmonotonic formalism and the particular theory of commonsense reasoning.

Implementations and Applications

Applications of nonmonotonic systems are scarce. Implementors run into several difficulties. First, most nonmonotonic logics explicitly refer to the notion of consistency of a set of sentences. Determining consistency is in general undecidable for first-order theories; thus predicate nonmonotonic logic is undecidable. Determining inconsistency is decidable but *intractable* for propositional logic; thus performing propositional nonmonotonic reasoning takes exponential time. This precludes the development of general efficient nonmonotonic reasoning systems (Selman and Levesque 1993).

However, efficient systems have been developed for limited cases. LOGIC PROGRAMMING, the technique of programming using a set of logical sentences in clausal form, uses a nonmonotonic technique known as "negation as failure": a literal, consisting of an atomic formula preceded by a nonclassical negation operator, is considered true if the atomic formula cannot be proven. Although logic programs cannot express all types of nonmonotonic reasoning, they can be very efficient (Gottlob 1992). Likewise, inheritance with exceptions is an efficient, although limited, form of nonmonotonic reasoning (Horty, Thomason, and Touretzky 1990; Stein 1992). These limited cases handle many common types of nonmonotonic reasoning.

Due to its efficiency, logic programming has been used for many applications, ranging from railway control to medical diagnosis (*Proceedings of the Conference on Practical Applications of Prolog* 1996, 1997), although few applications exploit logic programming's nonmonotonic reasoning abilities. Aside from logic programming, nonmonotonic logic is still rarely used in the commercial world. This may be because the nonmonotonic reasoning community and the commercial world focus on different problems, and because there are few industrial-strength nonmonotonic tools (Morgenstern 1998).

There are similarities between nonmonotonic logics and other areas of research that seek to formalize reasoning under UNCERTAINTY, such as FUZZY LOGIC and PROBABILISTIC REASONING (especially BAYESIAN NETWORKS). These fields are united in their attempt to represent and reason with incomplete knowledge. The character of nonmonotonic reasoning is different in that it uses a qualitative rather than a quantitative approach to uncertainty. Attempts to investigate the connections between these areas include the work of Goldszmidt and Pearl (1992, 1996).

See also COMPUTATIONAL COMPLEXITY; FRAME PROBLEM; KNOWLEDGE REPRESENTATION; MULTIAGENT SYSTEMS; PROBABILITY, FOUNDATIONS OF

—*Leora Morgenstern*

References

Alchourron, C. E., P. Gardenfors, and D. Makinson. (1985). On the logic of theory change: Partial meet functions for contraction and revision. *Journal of Symbolic Logic* 50: 510–530.

Goldszmidt, M., and J. Pearl. (1992). Rank-based systems: A simple approach to belief revision, belief update, and reasoning about evidence and actions. *Third International Conference on Principles of Knowledge Representation and Reasoning:* (KR-92). San Mateo, CA: Morgan Kaufmann, pp. 661–672.

Goldszmidt, M., and J. Pearl. (1996). Qualitative probabilities for default reasoning, belief revision, and causal modeling. *Artificial Intelligence,* 84: 57–112.

Gottlob, G. (1992). Complexity results for nonmonotonic logics. *Journal of Logic and Computation* 2 (3): 397–425.

Hanks, S., and D. McDermott. (1987). Nonmonotonic logic and temporal projection. *Artificial Intelligence* 33 (3): 379–412.

Horty, J., R. Thomason, and D. Touretzky. (1990). A skeptical theory of inheritance in nonmonotonic semantic networks. *Artificial Intelligence* 42: 311–349.

Kraus, S., D. Lehmann, and M. Magidor. (1990). Nonmonotonic reasoning, preferential models, and cumulative logics. *Artificial Intelligence* 44: 167–207.

McCarthy, J. (1980). Circumscription—a form of nonmonotonic reasoning. *Artificial Intelligence* 13: 27–39.

McCarthy, J. (1986). Applications of circumscription to formalizing common-sense knowledge. *Artificial Intelligence* 28: 86–116.

Moore, R. (1985). Semantical considerations on nonmonotonic logic. *Artificial Intelligence* 25 (1): 75–94.

Morgenstern, L. (1996). The problem with solutions to the frame problem. In K. Ford and Z. Pylyshyn, Eds., *The Robot's Dilemma Revisited.* Norwood: Ablex, pp. 99–133.

Morgenstern, L. (1998). Inheritance comes of age: Applying nonmonotonic techniques to problems in industry. *Artificial Intelligence* (103): 237–271. Shorter version in *Proceedings of the Fifteenth International Joint Conference on Artificial Intelligence (IJCAI-97).* Los Altos: Morgan Kaufmann, pp. 1613–1621.

Morgenstern, L., and R. Guerreiro. (1993). Epistemic logics for multiple agent nonmonotonic reasoning I. *Proceedings of the Second Symposium on Logical Formalizations of Commonsense Reasoning* (CS-93). Austin, TX, pp. 147–156.

Reiter, R. (1980). A logic for default reasoning. *Artificial Intelligence* 13: 81–132.

Selman, B., and H. Levesque. (1993). The complexity of path-based defeasible inheritance. *Artificial Intelligence* 62 (2): 303–340.

Shanahan, M. (1997). *Solving the Frame Problem.* Cambridge, MA: MIT Press.

Stalnaker, R. (1980). A note on nonmonotonic modal logic. Ithaca, NY: Department of Philosophy, Cornell University.

Stein, L. (1992). Resolving ambiguity in nonmonotonic inheritance hierarchies. *Artificial Intelligence* 55: 259–310.

Further Readings

Antoniou, G. (1997). *Nonmonotonic Reasoning.* Cambridge, MA: MIT Press.

Besnard, P. (1989). *An Introduction to Default Logics.* Berlin: Springer.

Brewka, G. (1991). *Nonmonotonic Reasoning: Logical Foundations of Commonsense.* Cambridge: Cambridge University Press.

Dix, J., U. Furbach, and A. Nerode, Eds. (1997). *Logic Programming and Nonmonotonic Reasoning.* Berlin: Springer.

Etherington, D. (1988). *Reasoning with Incomplete Information.* London: Pitman.

Gabbay, D., C. J. Hogger, and J. A. Robinson, Eds. (1994). *Handbook of Logic in Artificial Intelligence and Logic Programming,* vol. 3: *Nonmonotonic Reasoning and Uncertain Reasoning.* Oxford: Clarendon Press.

Gardenfors, P. (1988). *Knowledge in Flux: Modeling the Dynamics of Epistemic States.* Cambridge, MA: MIT Press.

Gardenfors, P., Ed. (1992). *Belief Revision.* Cambridge: Cambridge University Press.

Geffner, H. (1992). *Default Reasoning: Causal and Conditional Theories.* Cambridge: MIT Press.

Genesereth, M., and N. Nilsson. (1987). *Foundations of Artificial Intelligence.* San Mateo: Morgan Kaufmann.

Ginsberg, M., Ed. (1987). *Readings in Nonmonotonic Reasoning.* San Mateo: Morgan Kaufmann.

Konolige, K. (1988). On the relation between default and autoepistemic logic. *Artificial Intelligence* 35: 343–382.

Lloyd, J. (1987). *Foundations of Logic Programming.* 2nd ed. Springer.

Marek, W., and M. Truszcyznski. (1993). *Nonmonotonic Logic.* Springer.

McDermott, D. (1982). Non-monotonic logic II: Non-monotonic modal theories. *Journal of the Association for Computing Machinery* 29: 33–57.

McDermott, D., and J. Doyle (1980). Non-monotonic logic I. *Artificial Intelligence* 25: 41–72.

Pearl, J. (1990). Probabilistic semantics for nonmonotonic reasoning: A survey. In G. Shafer and J. Pearl, Eds., *Readings in Uncertain Reasoning.* San Mateo: Morgan Kaufmann, pp. 699–710.

Poole, D. (1988). A logical framework for default reasoning. *Artificial Intelligence* 36: 27–47.

Shoham, Y. (1988). *Reasoning about Change: Time and Causation from the Standpoint of Artificial Intelligence.* Cambridge, MA: MIT Press.

Williams, M. (1995). Iterated theory base change: A computational model. *Proceedings of the Fourteenth International Joint Conference on Artificial Intelligence (IJCAI-95).* Los Altos: Morgan Kaufmann, pp. 1541–1547.

Numeracy and Culture

Numeracy is a term that has been used in a variety of ways. It encompasses formal and informal mathematics, cultural practices with mathematical content, and behavior mediated by mathematical properties even when these properties are not verbally accessible. The study of numeracy explores a broad range of mathematical competencies across species, cultures, and the human lifespan. Human numeracy has universal characteristics based on biological mechanisms and developmental trajectories as well as culturally variable representation systems, practices, and values.

Studies with diverse species show that animals are sensitive to number (see Gallistel 1990 for a review). This literature suggests that there are innate capabilities that have evolved to support numeracy in humans (Gallistel and Gelman 1992). A variety of sources of evidence point to early numerical abilities in human infants (see INFANT COGNITION). For example, infants as early as the first week of life have been shown to discriminate between different small numbers (Antell and Keating 1983). The possibility that this discrimination is carried out by a cognitive mechanism encompassing several modalities has been debated (Starkey, Spelke, and Gelman 1990). In addition, studies have shown that infants have some knowledge of the effects of numerical transformations such as addition and subtraction (Wynn 1992).

Numerical competencies evident in the human infant are strong candidates for universal aspects of human numeracy. However, this does not necessarily discount the role of culture in developing human numeracy. Within the framework of EVOLUTIONARY PSYCHOLOGY, it is argued that universal characteristics of numeracy provide innate starting points for numeracy development, which, in turn, is influenced by culturally specific systems of knowledge (Cosmides and Tooby 1994). Similarly, within the neo-Piagetian framework, children are seen not simply as passing through a universal set of stages, but also as setting out on a unique cognitive journey that is guided by cultural practices (Case and Okamoto 1996). In this sense, numeracy is viewed as a cultural practice that builds on innate mechanisms for understanding quantities. The result is a conceptual structure for numeracy that reflects both universal and culture-sensitive characteristics. These conceptual structures are relatively similar across cultures that provide similar problem-solving experiences in terms of schooling and everyday life. On the other hand, mastery levels of particular tasks or skills may differ from one culture to another depending on the degree to which they are valued in each culture (Okamoto et al. 1996). In addition, cultures influence mathematical practices through the belief systems associated with numeracy, as well as through tools and artifacts (e.g., symbol systems) that support numeracy. A broad array of human activities to which mathematical thinking is applied are interwoven with cultural artifacts, social conventions, and social interactions (Nunes, Schliemann, and Carraher 1993; Saxe 1991).

Cultures have developed systems of signs that provide ways of thinking about quantitative information (see LANGUAGE AND CULTURE). Different systems shed light on different aspects of knowing. That is, they provide a means to extend the ability to deal with numbers; at the same time, they constrain numerical activities. For example, the Oksapmin of Papua New Guinea have a counting system using body parts, with no base structure, that only goes up to 27 (Saxe 1982). This way of quantifying is fully adequate for the numerical tasks of traditional life. It does not, however, facilitate easy computation or the counting of objects beyond 27. In contrast, the perfectly regular base-10 system of many Asian languages appears to make the mastery of base-10 concepts easier for children beginning school than the less regular base-10 systems of many European languages, including English (Miura et al. 1993). These various representational systems are culture-specific tools to deal with counting and computing, and all cultures seem to have them. Other culture-specific representation systems have been identified for locating (geometry, navigation), measuring, designing (form, shape, pattern), playing (rules, strategies), and explaining (Bishop 1991).

Further cultural variations in mathematical behavior are manifest in the ways that people use mathematical representations in the context of everyday activities (see SITUATED COGNITION AND LEARNING). Although they use the same counting numbers for different activities, child street vendors in Brazil were observed to use different computational strategies when selling than when doing school-like problems (Nunes, Schliemann, and Carraher 1993). While selling, they chose to use oral computation and strategies such as decomposition and repeated groupings. On school-like problems, they chose to use paper and pencil with standard algorithms and showed a markedly higher rate of error. Research in other domains, for example measurement (Gay and Cole 1967) and proportional reasoning (Nunes, Schliemann, and Carraher 1993), further confirms that informal mathematics can be effective and does not depend upon schooling for its development.

One characteristic of ethnomathematics, as informal mathematics or NAIVE MATHEMATICS is commonly called, is that the mathematics is used in pursuit of other goals rather than solely for the sake of the mathematics as in school or among professional mathematicians. As new goals arise, representational systems and practices develop to address the emergent goals. For instance, as the Oksapmin became more involved with the money economy, their "body" counting system began to change toward a base system (Saxe 1982). Although the differences between informal and school mathematics are often stressed (Bishop 1991), skills developed in the informal domain can be used to address new goals and practices in the school setting. In Liberian schools it was found that the most successful elementary students were those who combined the strategies from their indigenous mathematics with the algorithms taught in school (Brenner 1985). Similarly, Oksapmin and Brazilian children benefit from using their informal mathematics to learn school mathematics (Saxe 1985, 1991). Because conflicts between informal and school mathematics frequently arise, a number of authors have argued for building bridges between these different cultures of mathematics (Bishop 1991; Gay and Cole 1967; Gerdes 1988).

In addition to the overt mathematical practices already described, Gerdes (1988) has described *frozen* mathematics as the mathematics embodied in the products of a culture such as baskets, toys, and houses. Although the history of these objects has typically been lost, the original designers of these cultural artifacts employed mathematical principles in their design, according to Gerdes. Mathematical traditions embodied in these artifacts can provide interesting mathematical investigations that help children understand their own cultural heritage as well as contemporary school mathematics.

The study of numeracy and culture draws from diverse disciplines within the cognitive sciences including psychology, linguistics, biology, and anthropology. The strengths of each discipline should be utilized to provide a more coherent view of what numeracy is and how it interacts with culture. Much future work remains to be done to better understand the universal and culture-specific aspects of numeracy.

See also COGNITIVE ARTIFACTS; COGNITIVE DEVELOPMENT; CULTURAL VARIATION; NATIVISM

—*Yukari Okamoto, Mary E. Brenner, and Reagan Curtis*

References

Antell, S., and D. Keating. (1983). Perception of numerical invariance in neonates. *Child Development* 54: 695–701.

Bishop, A. (1991). *Mathematical Enculturation: A Cultural Perspective on Mathematics Education*. Dordrecht: Kluwer.

Brenner, M. E. (1985). The practice of arithmetic in Liberian schools. *Anthropology and Education Quarterly* 16: 177–186.

Case, R., and Y. Okamoto. (1996). The role of central conceptual structures in the development of children's thought. *Monographs of the Society for Research in Child Development* 61 (1–2, serial no. 246).

Cosmides, L., and J. Tooby. (1994). Origins of domain specificity: The evolution of functional organization. In L. A. Hirschfeld and S. A. Gelman, Eds., *Mapping the Mind: Domain Specificity in Cognition and Culture*. Cambridge: Cambridge University Press, pp. 85–116.

Gallistel, C. R. (1990). *The Organization of Learning*. Cambridge, MA: MIT Press.

Gallistel, C. R., and R. Gelman. (1992). Preverbal and verbal counting and computation. *Cognition* 44: 43–74.

Gay, J., and M. Cole. (1967). *The New Mathematics and an Old Culture*. New York: Holt, Rinehart and Winston.

Gerdes, P. (1988). On culture, geometrical thinking and mathematics education. *Educational Studies in Mathematics* 19: 137–162.

Miura, I. T., Y. Okamoto, C. C. Kim, M. Steere, and M. Fayol. (1993). First graders' cognitive representation of number and understanding of place value: Cross-national comparisons—France, Japan, Korea, Sweden, and the United States. *Journal of Educational Psychology* 85: 24–30.

Nunes, T., A. D. Schliemann, and D. W. Carraher. (1993). *Street Mathematics and School Mathematics*. New York: Cambridge University Press.

Okamoto, Y., R. Case, C. Bleiker, and B. Henderson. (1996). Cross cultural investigations. In R. Case and Y. Okamoto, Eds., *The Role of Central Conceptual Structures in the Development of Children's Thought*. Monographs of the Society for Research in Child Development 61 (1–2, serial no. 246), pp. 131–155.

Saxe, G. B. (1982). Developing forms of arithmetic operations among the Oksapmin of Papua New Guinea. *Developmental Psychology* 18: 583–594.

Saxe, G. B. (1985). The effects of schooling on arithmetical understandings: Studies with Oksapmin children in Papua New Guinea. *Journal of Educational Psychology* 77: 503–513.

Saxe, G. B. (1991). *Culture and cognitive development: Studies in mathematical understanding*. Hillsdale, NJ: Erlbaum.

Starkey, P., E. S. Spelke, and R. Gelman. (1990). Numerical abstraction by human infants. *Cognition* 36: 97–128.

Wynn, K. (1992). Addition and subtraction by human infants. *Nature* 358: 749–750.

Further Readings

Barkow, J. H., L. Cosmides, and J. Toob, Eds. (1992). *The Adapted Mind: Evolutionary Psychology and the Generation of Culture*. New York: Oxford University Press.

Crump, T. (1990). *The Anthropology of Numbers*. New York: Cambridge University Press.

Ginsburg, H. P., J. K. Posner, and R. L. Russell. (1981). The development of mental addition as a function of schooling and culture. *Journal of Cross-cultural Psychology* 12: 163–178.

Hatano, G., S. Amaiwa, and K. Shimizu. (1987). Formation of a mental abacus for computation and its use as a memory device for digits: A developmental study. *Developmental Psychology* 23: 832–838.

Lancy, D. F. (1983). *Cross-Cultural Studies in Cognition and Mathematics*. New York: Academic Press.

Miller, K. F., and J. W. Stigler. (1987). Counting in Chinese: Cultural variation in a basic cognitive skill. *Cognitive Development* 2: 279–305.

Moore, D., J. Beneson, J. S. Reznick, P. Peterson, and J. Kagan. (1987). Effect of auditory numerical information on infants' looking behavior: Contradictory evidence. *Developmental Psychology* 23: 665–670.

Nunes, T. (1992). Ethnomathematics and everyday cognition. In D. Grouws, Ed., *Handbook of Research on Mathematics Teaching and Learning*. New York: Macmillan, pp. 557–574.

Reed, H. J., and J. Lave. (1981). Arithmetic as a tool for investigating relations between culture and cognition. In R. W. Casson, Ed., *Language, Culture and Cognition: Anthropological Perspectives*. New York: Macmillan, pp. 437–455.

Saxe, G. B., and J. K. Posner. (1983). The development of numerical cognition: Cross-cultural perspectives. In H. P. Ginsburg, Ed., *The Development of Mathematical Thinking*. Rochester, NY: Academic Press, pp. 291–317.

Song, M. J., and H. P. Ginsburg. (1987). The development of informal and formal mathematics thinking in Korean and U. S. children. *Child Development* 58: 1286–1296.

Sophian, C., and N. Adams. (1987). Infants' understanding of numerical transformations. *British Journal of Developmental Psychology* 5: 257–264.

Starkey, P., and R. G. Cooper, Jr. (1980). Perception of numbers by human infants. *Science* 210: 1033–1035.

Stevenson, H. W., T. Parker, A. Wilkinson, B. Bonnevaux, and M. Gonzalez. (1978). Schooling, environment and cognitive development: A cross-cultural study. *Monographs of the Society for Research in Child Development* 43 (3, serial no. 175).

Strauss, M. S., and L. E. Curtis. (1981). Infant perception of numerosity. *Child Development* 52: 1146–1152.

Object Recognition, Animal Studies

One of the major problems which must be solved by a visual system used for object recognition is the building of a representation of visual information which allows recognition to occur relatively independently of size, contrast, spatial frequency, position on the RETINA, and angle of view, etc. It is important that invariance in the visual system is made explicit in the neuronal responses, for this simplifies greatly the output of the visual system to memory systems such as the HIPPOCAMPUS and AMYGDALA, which can then remember or form associations about *objects* (Rolls 1999). The function of these memory systems would be almost impossible if there were no consistent output from the visual system about objects (including faces), for then the memory systems would need to learn about all possible sizes, positions, etc. of each object, and there would be no easy generalization from one size or position of an object to that object when seen with another retinal size, position, or view (see Rolls and Treves 1998).

The primate inferior temporal visual cortex is implicated by lesion evidence in providing invariance. For example, Weiskrantz and Saunders (1984; see also Weiskrantz 1990) showed that macaques with inferior temporal cortex lesions performed especially poorly in visual discrimination tasks when one of the objects was shown in a different size or in different lighting.

Using the population of neurons in the cortex in the superior temporal sulcus and inferior temporal cortex with responses selective for faces, it has been found that the responses are relatively invariant with respect to size and contrast (Rolls and Baylis 1986); spatial frequency (Rolls, Baylis, and Leonard, 1985; Rolls, Baylis, and Hasselmo, 1987) and retinal translation, that is, position in the visual field (Tovee, Rolls, and Azzopardi 1994; cf. earlier work by Gross 1973; Gross et al. 1985). Some of these neurons even have relatively view-invariant responses, responding to different views of the same face but not of other faces (Hasselmo et al. 1989; see FACE RECOGNITION).

To investigate whether view-invariant representations of objects are also encoded by some neurons in the inferior temporal cortex (area TE) of the rhesus macaque, the activity of single neurons was recorded while monkeys were shown very different views of ten objects (Booth and Rolls 1998). The stimuli were presented for 0.5 sec on a color video monitor while the monkey performed a visual fixation task. The stimuli were images of ten real plastic objects which had been in the monkey's cage for several weeks to enable him to build view-invariant representations of the objects. Control stimuli were views of objects which had never been seen as real objects. The neurons analyzed were in the TE cortex in and close to the ventral lip of the anterior part of the superior temporal sulcus. Many neurons were found that responded to some views of some objects. However, for a smaller number of neurons, the responses occurred only to a subset of the objects, irrespective of the viewing angle. These latter neurons thus conveyed information about which object had been seen, independently of

view, as confirmed by information-theoretic analysis of the neuronal responses.

The representation of objects or faces provided by these neurons is distributed, in that each NEURON does not, in general, respond to only one object or face, but instead responds to a subset of the faces or objects. They thus showed ensemble, sparsely distributed, encoding (Rolls and Tovee 1995; Rolls et al. 1997). One advantage of this encoding is that it allows receiving neurons to generalize to somewhat similar exemplars of the stimuli, because effectively it is the activity of the population vector of neuronal firing which can be read out by receiving neurons (Rolls and Treves 1998). A second advantage is that the information available from such a population about which face or object was seen increases approximately linearly with the number of neurons in the sample (Abbott, Rolls, and Tovee 1996; Rolls et al. 1997). This means that the number of stimuli that can be represented increases exponentially with the number of cells in the sample (because information is a logarithmic measure). This has major implications for brain operation, for it means that a receiving neuron or neurons can receive a great deal of information from a sending population if each receiving neuron receives only a limited number of afferents (100–1000) from a sending population.

A way in which artificial vision systems might encode information about objects is to store the relative coordinates in 3-D object-based space of parts of objects in a database, and to use general-purpose algorithms on the inputs to perform transforms such as translation, rotation, and scale change in 3-D space to see if there is any match to a stored 3-D representation (e.g., Marr 1982). One problem (see also Rolls and Treves 1998) with implementing such a scheme in the brain is that a detailed syntactical description of the relations between the parts of the 3-D object is required, for example, body > thigh > shin > foot > toes. Such syntactical networks are difficult to implement in neuronal networks, because if the representations of all the features just mentioned were active simultaneously, how would the spatial relations between the features also be encoded? (How would it be apparent just from the firing of neurons that the toes were linked to the rest of foot but not to the body?) Another more recent suggestion for a syntactically linked set of descriptors is that of Biederman (1987; see also Hummel and Biederman 1992).

An alternative, more biologically plausible scheme is that the brain might store a few associated 2-D views of objects, with generalization within each 2-D view, in order to perform invariant object and face recognition (Koenderink and Van Doorn 1979; Poggio and Edelman 1990; Rolls 1992, 1994; Logothetis et al. 1994; Wallis and Rolls 1997). The way in which the brain could learn and access such representations is described next.

Cortical visual processing for object recognition is considered to be organized as a set of hierarchically connected cortical regions consisting at least of V1, V2, V4, posterior inferior temporal cortex (TEO), inferior temporal cortex (e.g., TE3, TEa, and TEm), and anterior temporal cortical areas (e.g., TE2 and TE1). There is convergence from each small part of a region to the succeeding region (or layer in the hierarchy) in such a way that the receptive field sizes of neurons (e.g., one degree near the fovea in V1) become larger by a factor of approximately 2.5 with each succeeding stage (and the typical parafoveal receptive field sizes found would not be inconsistent with the calculated approximations of, for example, eight degrees in V4, twenty degrees in TEO, and fifty degrees in inferior temporal cortex; Boussaoud, Desimone, and Ungerleider 1991; see figure 1). Such zones of convergence would overlap continuously with each other. This connectivity would be part of the architecture by which translation-invariant representations are computed. Each layer is considered to act partly as a set of local self-organizing competitive neuronal networks with overlapping inputs. These competitive nets (described, e.g, by Rolls and Treves 1998) operate to detect correlations between the activity of the input neurons, and to allocate output neurons to respond to each cluster of such correlated inputs. These networks thus act as categorizers, and help to build feature analyzers. In relation to visual information processing, they would remove redundancy from the input representation.

Translation invariance would be computed in such a system by utilizing competitive learning to detect statistical regularities in inputs when real objects are translated in the physical world. The hypothesis is that because objects have continuous properties in space and time in the world, an object at one place on the retina might activate feature analyzers at the next stage of cortical processing, and when the object was translated to a nearby position, because this would occur in a short period (e.g., 0.5 sec), the membrane of the postsynaptic neuron would still be in its "Hebb-modifiable" state (caused for example by calcium entry as a result of the voltage-dependent activation of N-methyl-d-aspartate receptors), and the presynaptic afferents activated with the object in its new position would thus become strengthened on the still-activated postsynaptic neuron. It is proposed that the short temporal window (e.g., 0.5 sec) of Hebb modifiability helps neurons to learn the statistics of objects moving in the physical world, and at the same time to form different representations of different feature combinations or objects, as these are physically discontinuous and present less regular statistical correlations to the visual system. Foldiak (1991) has proposed computing an average activation of the postsynaptic neuron to assist with the same problem. The idea here is that the temporal properties of the biologically implemented learning mechanism are such that it is well suited to detecting the relevant continuities in the world of real objects. Rolls (1992, 1994) has also suggested that other invariances, for example, size, spatial frequency, and rotation invariance, could be learned by a comparable process. (Early processing in V1, which enables different neurons to represent inputs at different spatial scales, would allow combinations of the outputs of such neurons to be formed at later stages. Scale invariance would then result from detecting at a later stage which neurons are almost conjunctively active as the size of an object alters.) It is proposed that this process takes place at each stage of the multiple-layer cortical-processing hierarchy, so that invariances are learned first over small regions of space, and then over successively larger regions. This limits the size of the connection space within which correlations must be sought.

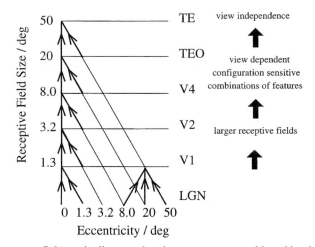

Figure 1. Schematic diagram showing convergence achieved by the forward projections in the visual system, and the types of representation that may be built by competitive networks operating at each stage of the system, from the primary visual cortex (V1) to the inferior temporal visual cortex (area TE; see text). LGN—lateral geniculate nucleus. Area TEO forms the posterior inferior temporal cortex. The receptive fields in the inferior temporal visual cortex (e.g., in the TE areas) cross the vertical midline (not shown).

View-independent representations could be formed by the same type of computation, operating to combine a limited set of views of objects. Consistent with the suggestion that the view-independent representations are formed by combining view-dependent representations in the primate visual system is the fact that in the temporal cortical areas, neurons with view-independent representations of faces are present in the same cortical areas as neurons with view-dependent representations (from which the view-independent neurons could receive inputs; Hasselmo et al. 1989; Perrett, Mistlin, and Chitty 1987).

This hypothesis about the computation of invariant representations has been implemented in a computational model by Wallis and Rolls (1997), and a related model with a trace version of the Hebb rule implemented in recurrent collateral connections has been analyzed using the methods of statistical physics (Parga and Rolls 1998).

Another suggestion for the computation of translation invariance is that the image of an object is translated to standard coordinates using a circuit in V1 that has connections for every possible translation, and switching on in a multiplication operation just the correct set of connections (Olshausen, Anderson, and Van Essen 1993). This scheme does not appear to be fully plausible biologically, in that all possible sets of connections do not appear to be present (in the brain), the required multiplier inputs and multiplication synapses do not appear to be present; and such a scheme could perform translation-invariant mapping in one stage, whereas in the brain it takes place gradually over the whole series of visual cortical areas V1, V2, V4, posterior inferior temporal, and anterior inferior temporal, with an expansion of the receptive field size (and thus of translation invariance) of approximately 2.5 at each stage (see figure 1 and Rolls 1992, 1994; Wallis and Rolls 1997; Rolls and Treves 1998).

See also HIGH-LEVEL VISION; MEMORY, ANIMAL STUDIES; MID-LEVEL VISION; OBJECT RECOGNITION, HUMAN NEUROPSYCHOLOGY; VISUAL OBJECT RECOGNITION, AI; VISUAL PROCESSING STREAMS

—*Edmund T. Rolls*

References

Abbott, L. A., E. T. Rolls, and M. J. Tovee. (1996). Representational capacity of face coding in monkeys. *Cerebral Cortex* 6: 498–505.

Biederman, I. (1987). Recognition-by-components: A theory of human image understanding. *Psychological Review* 94: 115–147.

Booth, M. C. A., and E. T. Rolls. (1998). View-invariant representations of familiar objects by neurons in the inferior temporal visual cortex. *Cerebral Cortex* 8: 510–523.

Boussaoud, D., R. Desimone, and L. G. Ungerleider. (1991). Visual topography of area TEO in the macaque. *Journal of Comparative Neurology* 306: 554–575.

Foldiak, P. (1991). Learning invariance from transformation sequences. *Neural Computation* 3: 193–199.

Gross, C. G. (1973). Inferotemporal cortex and vision. *Progress in Psychobiology and Physiological Psychology.* 5: 77–123.

Gross, C. G., R. Desimone, T. D. Albright, and E. L. Schwartz. (1985). Inferior temporal cortex and pattern recognition. *Experimental Brain Research* 11 (Suppl.) 179–201.

Hasselmo, M. E., E. T. Rolls, G. C. Baylis, and V. Nalwa. (1989). Object-centered encoding by face-selective neurons in the cortex in the superior temporal sulcus of the monkey. *Experimental Brain Research* 75: 417–429.

Hummel, J. E., and I. Biederman. (1992). Dynamic binding in a neural network for shape recognition. *Psychological Review* 99: 480–517.

Koenderink, J. J., and A. J. Van Doorn. (1979). The internal representation of solid shape with respect to vision. *Biological Cybernetics* 32: 211–216.

Logothetis, N. K., J. Pauls, H. H. Bülthoff, and T. Poggio. (1994). View-dependent object recognition by monkeys. *Current Biology* 4: 401–414.

Marr, D. (1982). *Vision.* San Francisco: W. H. Freeman.

Olshausen, B. A., C. H. Anderson, and D. C. Van Essen. (1993). A neurobiological model of visual attention and invariant pattern recognition based on dynamic routing of information. *Journal of Neuroscience* 13: 4700–4719.

Parga, N., and E. T. Rolls. (1998). Transform invariant recognition by association in a recurrent network. *Neural Computation* 10: 1507–1525.

Perrett, D. I., A. J. Mistlin, and A. J. Chitty. (1987). Visual neurons responsive to faces. *Trends in Neuroscience* 10: 358–364.

Poggio, T., and S. Edelman. (1990). A network that learns to recognize three-dimensional objects. *Nature* 343: 263–266.

Rolls, E. T. (1992). Neurophysiological mechanisms underlying face processing within and beyond the temporal cortical visual areas. *Philosophical Transactions of the Royal Society of London, Series B: Biological Sciences* 335: 11–21.

Rolls, E. T. (1994). Brain mechanisms for invariant visual recognition and learning. *Behavioural Processes* 33: 113–138.

Rolls, E. T. (1995). Learning mechanisms in the temporal lobe visual cortex. *Behavioural Brain Research* 66: 177–185.

Rolls, E. T. (1999). *The Brain and Emotion.* Oxford: Oxford University Press.

Rolls, E. T., and G. C. Baylis. (1986). Size and contrast have only small effects on the responses to faces of neurons in the cortex of the superior temporal sulcus of the monkey. *Experimental Brain Research* 65: 38–48.

Rolls, E. T., G. C. Baylis, and M. E. Hasselmo. (1987). The responses of neurons in the cortex in the superior temporal sulcus of the monkey to band-pass spatial frequency filtered faces. *Vision Research* 27: 311–326.

Rolls, E. T., G. C. Baylis, and C. M. Leonard. (1985). Role of low and high spatial frequencies in the face-selective responses of neurons in the cortex in the superior temporal sulcus. *Vision Research* 25: 1021–1035.

Rolls, E. T., and M. J. Tovee. (1995). Sparseness of the neuronal representation of stimuli in the primate temporal visual cortex. *Journal of Neurophysiology* 73: 713–726.

Rolls, E. T., and A. Treves. (1998). *Neural Networks and Brain Function.* Oxford: Oxford University Press.

Rolls, E. T., A. Treves, M. Tovee, and S. Panzeri. (1997). Information in the neuronal representation of individual stimuli in the primate temporal visual cortex. *Journal of Computational Neuroscience* 4: 309–333.

Tovee, M. J., E. T. Rolls, and P. Azzopardi. (1994). Translation invariance and the responses of neurons in the temporal visual cortical areas of primates. *Journal of Neurophysiology* 72: 1049–1060.

Wallis, G., and E. T. Rolls. (1997). Invariant face and object recognition in the visual system. *Progress in Neurobiology* 51: 167–194.

Weiskrantz, L. (1990). Visual prototypes, memory and the inferotemporal cortex. In E. Iwai and M. Mishkin, Eds., *Vision, Memory and the Temporal Lobe.* New York: Elsevier, pp. 13–28.

Weiskrantz, L., and R. C. Saunders. (1984). Impairments of visual object transforms in monkeys. *Brain* 107: 1033–1072.

Further Readings

Ullman, S. (1996). *High-Level Vision: Object Recognition and Visual Cognition.* Cambridge, MA: MIT Press/Bradford Books.

Object Recognition, Human Neuropsychology

Most of what we know about the neural mechanisms of object recognition in humans has come from the study of *agnosia*, or impaired object recognition following brain damage. In addition, in recent years, functional neuroimaging in normal humans has begun to offer insights into object recognition. This article reviews both literatures, with greater emphasis accorded to agnosia because of its currently greater contribution to our understanding of human object recognition.

To be considered agnosia, an object recognition impairment must be selective in the sense of not being attributable to impaired elementary perceptual function or general intellectual decline. It must also be a true impairment of recognition, as opposed to an impairment of naming. Agnosias are generally confined to a single perceptual modality, such as auditory (Vignolo 1969), tactile (Reed, Caselli, and Farah 1996), or visual (Farah 1990), suggesting that for each perceptual modality there is a stage of processing beyond elementary perceptual processes that is nevertheless modality-specific, and that represents learned information about objects' sounds, tactile qualities, and visual appearances. In the case of visual agnosia, which is the focus of this article, this stage presumably corresponds to the inferior temporal regions that have been studied using physiological techniques in the monkey (see also OBJECT RECOGNITION, ANIMAL STUDIES). The different types of visual agnosia provide insights into the organization of high-level visual object representations in humans, by showing us the "fracture lines" of the system.

Lissauer (1890) introduced a fundamental distinction between two broad classes of agnosia: those in which perception seemed clearly at fault, which he termed *apperceptive*, and those in which perception seemed at least roughly intact, which he termed *associative*. Lissauer hypothesized that the latter type of patient suffered from an inability to associate percepts with meaning. Although the theory behind this classification system is now widely questioned, the classification itself—that is, the separation of patients with obvious perceptual disorders from patients without obvious perceptual disorders—has proved useful.

The apperceptive agnosias have received less attention than the associative agnosias, perhaps because they are less surprising or counterintuitive. Although such elementary visual functions as acuity and color perception are roughly intact, higher levels of perception such as visual grouping appear to be disrupted, and the object recognition impairment is secondary to these perceptual impairments. In this article I focus on the associative agnosias because they are the most directly relevant to object recognition per se. Readers may consult chapters 2 and 3 of Farah (1990) for further information on the apperceptive agnosias.

In contrast to the apperceptive agnosias, perception seems roughly normal in associative agnosia, and yet patients cannot recognize much of what they see. Most often, associative agnosia follows bilateral inferior occipitotemporal lesions, although unilateral lesions of either the left or right hemisphere are sometimes sufficient (see the final section). The classic case of Rubens and Benson (1971) shows all of the cardinal signs of associative agnosia, including preserved recognition of objects through modalities other than vision, failure to indicate visual recognition verbally and nonverbally, and apparently good visual perception.

The patient could not identify common objects presented visually, and did not know what was on his plate until he tasted it. He identified objects immediately on touching them. When shown a stethoscope, he described it as "a long cord with a round thing at the end," and asked if it could be a watch. He identified a can opener as "could be a key. . . ." He was never able to describe or demonstrate the use of an object if he could not name it. . . . He could match identical objects but not group objects by categories (clothing, food). He could draw the outlines of objects which he could not identify. . . . Remarkably, he could make excellent copies of line drawings and still fail to name the subject.

The modality-specific failure of object recognition, in the context of normal intellect, is what one would expect following destruction of the kinds of object representations found at higher levels of the primate visual system, and indeed the most common lesion locations are roughly consistent with this hypothesis (the human lesions are perhaps a bit more posterior). Although the good copies and successful matching performance of associative agnosic patients might seem inconsistent with the hypothesis of a visual perceptual impairment, these perceptual tasks do not require the use of object representations per se. Indeed, the manner

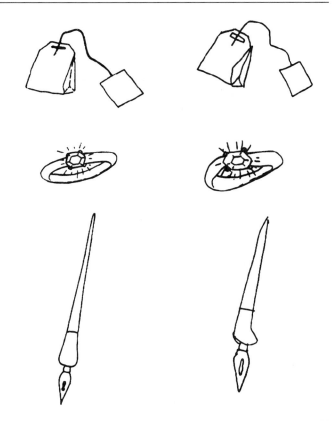

Figure 1. Three drawings that an associative agnosic patient could not recognize (left) and the good-quality copies that he was nevertheless able to produce (right).

in which associative agnosic patients copy and match is consistent with the use of lower-level visual representations in which objects per se are not explicitly represented: they copy line by line, and match feature by feature, unlike normal subjects who organize their copying and matching of these local elements into more global, object-based units (see Farah 1990, chaps. 4 and 5 for a review). The left side of figure 1 shows three drawings that an associative agnosic patient was unable to recognize. When I asked him to copy the drawings, he produced the very adequate copies shown on the right, but only after a laborious, line-by-line process.

Studies using POSITRON EMISSION TOMOGRAPHY (PET) and functional MAGNETIC RESONANCE IMAGING (fMRI) have confirmed the most basic conclusion to be drawn from the agnosia literature, namely, that there are visual modality-specific brain regions in inferior temporo-occipital cortex whose function is object perception. Relative to baselines involving the viewing of gratings, random lines, or disconnected object pieces, the viewing of objects is generally associated with temporal or occipital activation, or both, in both hemispheres (e.g., see Menard et al. 1996; Kanwisher et al. 1996, 1997; Sergent, Ohta, and MacDonald 1992; see Aguirre and Farah 1998 for a review). Furthermore, this localization held both for studies that required subjects to perform active information retrieval (e.g., is the depicted object living or nonliving?) and for others that required only passive viewing, suggesting that the critical determinant of the region's activation is object perception, rather than the association of stored memory knowledge with a percept. Indeed, Kanwisher et al. (1997) found no greater activation for unfamiliar objects than for familiar objects, which have a preexisting memory representation.

Agnosia does not always affect all types of stimuli equally. The scope of the deficit varies from case to case, with recognition of faces, objects, and printed words all pairwise dissociable. These dissociations provide us with insights into the internal organization of high-level visual object representation. Similarly, neuroimaging studies have sometimes found differing patterns of activation for different stimulus types (Aguirre and Farah 1998).

When agnosia is confined to faces or is disproportionately severe for faces, it is prosopagnosia. There are many cases of profound FACE RECOGNITION impairment, with little or no evident object agnosia, in the literature. Pallis (1955) provides a detailed case study of a patient whose impairment of face recognition was so severe, he mistook his own reflection in a mirror for a rude stranger staring at him.

Are faces really disproportionately impaired in prosopagnosia, consistent with a distinct subsystem for face recognition, or does the appearance of a selective deficit result from the need for exceedingly fine discrimination among visually similar members of a single category? Recent evidence suggests that there is specialization within the visual system for faces. McNeill and Warrington (1993) showed that a prosopagnosic patient was better able to recognize individual sheep faces than individual human faces, even though normal subjects find the human faces easier to recognize. Farah, Klein, and Levinson (1995) showed that a prosopagnosic patient was disproportionately impaired at face recognition relative to common object recognition, taking into account the difficulty of the stimulus sets for normal subjects. This was true even when the common objects were all eyeglass frames, a large and visually homogeneous category. Farah et al. (1995) showed that the same subject was impaired at upright face perception relative to inverted face perception, even though normal subjects find the latter harder. The existence of patients who are more impaired with objects than with faces also supports the independence of prosopagnosia and object agnosia. Feinberg et al. (1994) documented impaired object recognition in a series of patients with preserved face recognition.

Attempts to dissociate face and object perception using neuroimaging have produced variable results, although in at least some studies the patterns of activation were different (Sergent et al. 1992; Kanwisher et al. 1996).

Orthography-specific processing systems? So-called pure alexics typically read words letter by letter, in a slow and generally error-prone manner. Their impairment is called "pure" because they are able to comprehend spoken words, they have no problem writing words, and their recognition of objects and faces seems normal. Although pure alexia is generally discussed in the context of language and reading disorders, it is clearly also an impairment of visual recognition affecting printed words. Furthermore, in all the cases so far examined, the visual recognition impairment is not confined to words, but also affects the processing of nonorthographic stimuli whenever rapid processing of multiple shapes is required, be they letters in words or sets of

abstract shapes (Farah and Wallace 1991; Kinsbourne and Warrington 1962; Levine and Calvanio 1978; Sekuler and Behrmann 1996; see Farah and Wallace 1991 for a discussion of some apparently conflicting data). Although clinical descriptions suggest that in some cases orthographic stimuli may be disproportionately affected, for example, relative to numerical stimuli, this can be understood in terms of segregation of representations for orthographic stimuli within a visual area dedicated to rapid encoding of multiple shapes in general (Farah in press). Polk and Farah (1995) describe and test a mechanism by which such segregation could occur in a self-organizing network, based on the statistics of co-occurrence among letter and nonletter stimuli in the environment.

Just as pure alexia is an impairment of printed word recognition in the absence of obvious impairments of single-object recognition, there are cases of object recognition impairment with preserved reading. For example, the case of Gomori and Hawryluk (1984) was impaired at recognizing a variety of objects and the faces of his friends and family. He nevertheless continued to read with ease, even when interfering lines were drawn across the words. Thus, like prosopagnosia and object agnosia, pure alexia and object agnosia are doubly dissociable.

Only one neuroimaging study has directly compared the patterns of activation evoked by printed words and objects, and did find a degree of separation (Menard et al. 1996).

Localization of high-level object representation in the human visual system: Ironically, although the primary goal of neuroimaging is localization, and agnosia research is subject to the vagaries of naturally occurring lesions, the clearest evidence concerning the anatomy of object recognition comes from patient research. In general, the intrahemispheric location of damage is generally occipitotemporal, involving both gray and white matter. In order to understand the laterality of visual recognition processes, it is crucial to distinguish between subtypes of agnosia. Cases of associative agnosia have been reported following unilateral right hemisphere lesions, unilateral left hemisphere lesions, and bilateral lesions. The dual systems hypothesis presented above helps reduce the variability in lesion site. Agnosic patients presumed to have an impairment of just the first ability (in mild form affecting just faces, in more severe form affecting faces and objects but not words) usually have bilateral inferior lesions, although occasionally unilateral right hemisphere lesions are reported (Farah 1991). Agnosic patients presumed to have an impairment of just the second ability (in mild form affecting just words, in more severe form affecting words and objects but not faces) generally have unilateral left inferior lesions (Farah 1991; Feinberg et al. 1994). Agnosic patients presumed to have an impairment in both abilities (affecting faces, objects, and words) generally have bilateral lesions.

Aside from confirming the generalization that face, object, and VISUAL WORD RECOGNITION tasks involve posterior cortices, the neuroimaging literature tells us little about the localization of different subtypes of object recognition (Aguirre and Farah 1998). The precise locations of areas responsive to faces, nonface objects, and words differ widely, from study to study, within posterior association cortex.

Whether this reflects individual variability in brain organization, problems with normalization and statistical procedures for analyzing images of brain activity, or the difference between localizing areas that are activated (as revealed by neuroimaging) vs. areas that are necessary (as revealed by lesions) for visual recognition remains to be discovered.

See also AMYGDALA, PRIMATE; HIGH-LEVEL VISION; MODELING NEUROPSYCHOLOGICAL DEFICITS; SELF-ORGANIZING SYSTEMS; SHAPE PERCEPTION; VISUAL OBJECT RECOGNITION, AI

—*Martha J. Farah*

References

Aguirre, G. K., and M. J. Farah. (1998). Imaging visual recognition. *Trends in Cognitive Sciences* to appear.

Farah, M. J. (1990). *Visual Agnosia: Disorders of Object Recognition and What They Tell Us About Normal Vision.* Cambridge, MA: MIT Press/Bradford Books.

Farah, M. J. (1991). Patterns of co-occurrence among the associative agnosias: Implications for visual object representation. *Cognitive Neuropsychology* 8: 1–19.

Farah, M. J. (Forthcoming). Are there orthography-specific brain regions? Neuropsychological and computational investigations. In R. M. Klein and P. A. McMullen, Eds., *Converging Methods for Understanding Reading and Dyslexia.* Cambridge, MA: MIT Press.

Farah, M. J., K. L. Klein, and K. L. Levinson. (1995). Face perception and within-category discrimination in prosopagnosia. *Neuropsychologia* 33: 661–674.

Farah, M. J., and M. A. Wallace. (1991). Pure alexia as a visual impairment: A reconsideration. *Cognitive Neuropsychology* 8: 313–334.

Farah, M. J., K. D. Wilson, H. M. Drain, and J. R. Tanaka. (1995). The inverted inversion effect in prosopagnosia: Evidence for mandatory, face-specific perceptual mechanisms. *Vision Research* 35: 2089–2093.

Feinberg, T. E., R. J. Schindler, E. Ochoa, P. C. Kwan, and M. J. Farah. (1994). Associative visual agnosia and alexia without prosopagnosia. *Cortex* 30: 395–411.

Gomori, A. J., and G. A. Hawryluk. (1984). Visual agnosia without alexia. *Neurology* 34: 947–950.

Kanwisher, N., M. M. Chun, J. McDermott, and P. J. Ledden. (1996). Functional imaging of human visual recognition. *Cognitive Brain Research* 5: 55–67.

Kanwisher, N., R. Woods, M. Ioacoboni, and J. Mazziotta. (1997). A locus in human extrastriate cortex for visual shape analysis. *Journal of Cognitive Neuroscience* 9: 133–142.

Kinsbourne, M., and E. K. Warrington. (1962). A disorder of simultaneous form perception. *Brain* 85: 461–486.

Levine, D. N., and R. Calvanio. (1978). A study of the visual defect in verbal alexia-simultanagnosia. *Brain* 101: 65–81.

Lissauer, H. (1890). Ein Fall von Seelenblindheit nebst einem Beitrag zur Theorie derselben. *Archiv für Psychiatrie und Nervenkrankheiten* 21: 222–270.

McNeil, J. E., and E. K. Warrington. (1993). Prosopagnosia: A face-specific disorder. *Quarterly Journal of Experimental Psychology A. Human Experimental Psychology* 46: 1–10.

Menard M. T., S. M. Kosslyn, W. L. Thompson, N. M. Alpert, and S. L. Rauch. (1996). Encoding words and pictures: A positron emission tomography study. *Neuropsychologia* 34: 185–194.

Pallis, C. A. (1955). Impaired identification of faces and places with agnosia for colors. *Journal of Neurology, Neurosurgery and Psychiatry* 18: 218–224.

Polk, T. A., and M. J. Farah. (1995). Brain localization for arbitrary stimulus categories: A simple account based on Hebbian learning. *Proceedings of the National Academy of Sciences* 92: 12370–12373.

Reed, C. L., R. Caselli, and M. J. Farah. (1996). Tactile agnosia: Underlying impairment and implications for normal tactile object recognition. *Brain* 119: 875–888.

Rubens, A. B., and D. F. Benson. (1971). Associative visual agnosia. *Archives of Neurology* 24: 305–316.

Sekuler, E., and M. Behrmann. (1996). Perceptual cues in pure alexia. *Cognitive Neuropsychology* 13: 941–974.

Sergent, I., S. Ohta, and B. MacDonald. (1992). Functional neuroanatomy of face and object processing. *Brain* 115: 15–36.

Vignolo, L. A. (1969). Auditory agnosia. In A. L. Benton, Ed., *Contributions to Clinical Neuropsychology.* Chicago: Aldine.

Oculomotor Control

Eye movements fall into two broad classes. *Gaze-stabilization* movements shift the lines of sight of the two eyes to precisely compensate for an animal's self-motion, stabilizing the visual world on the RETINA. *Gaze-aligning* movements point a portion of the retina specialized for high resolution (the *fovea* in primates) at objects of interest in the visual world.

In mammals, gaze-stabilization movements are accomplished by two partially independent brain systems. The *vestibulo-ocular system* employs the inertial velocity sensors attached to the skull (the *semicircular canals*) to determine how quickly and in what direction the head is moving and then rotates the eyes an equal and opposite amount to keep the visual world stable on the retina. The *optokinetic system* extracts information from the visual signals of the retina to determine how quickly and in what direction to rotate the eyes to stabilize the visual world.

Gaze-aligning movements also fall into two broad classes: *saccades* and *smooth pursuit* movements. Saccadic eye movements rapidly shift the lines of sight of the two eyes, with regard to the head, from one place in the visual world to another at rotational velocities up to 1000°/sec. Smooth pursuit eye movements rotate the eyes at a velocity and in a direction identical to those of a moving visual target, stabilizing that moving image on the retina. In humans and other binocular animals, a third class of gaze-shifting movements, *vergence* movements, operates to shift the lines of sight of the two eyes with regard to each other so that both eyes can remain fixated on a visual stimulus at different distances from the head.

In humans, all eye movements are rotations accomplished by just six muscles operating in three antagonistic pairs. One pair of muscles located on either side of each eyeball controls the horizontal orientation of each eye. A second pair controls vertical orientation and a third pair controls rotations of the eye around the line of sight (*torsional movements*). These torsional movements are actually quite common, though usually less than 10° in amplitude.

These six muscles are controlled by three brain stem nuclei. These nuclei contain the cell bodies for all of the motor neurons that innervate the oculomotor muscles and thus serve as a final common path through which all eye movement control must be accomplished. Engineering models of the eye and its muscles indicate that motor neurons must generate two classes of muscle forces to accomplish any eye rotation: a pulsatile burst of force that regulates the *velocity* of an eye movement and a long-lasting increment or decrement in maintained force that, after the movement is complete, holds the eye stationary by resisting the elasticity of the muscles which would slowly draw the eye back to a straight-ahead position (Robinson 1964). Physiological experiments have demonstrated that all motor neurons participate in the generation of both of these two types of forces.

These two forces, in turn, appear to be generated by separable neural circuits. In the 1960s it was suggested that changes to the long-lasting force required after each eye rotation could be computed from the pulse, or velocity, signal by the mathematical operation of integration. In the 1980s the lesion of a discrete brain area, the nucleus prepositus hypoglossi, was shown to eliminate from the motor neurons the long-lasting force change required for leftward and rightward movements without affecting eye velocity during these movements (Cannon and Robinson 1987). This, in turn, suggested that most or all eye movements are specified as velocity commands and that brain stem circuits involving the nucleus prepositus hypoglossi compute, by integration, the long-lasting force required by a particular velocity command. More recently, a similar circuit has been identified that appears to generate the holding force required for upward, downward, and torsional movements.

The saccadic system, in order to achieve a precise gaze shift, must supply these brain stem circuits with a command that controls the *amplitude and direction* of a movement. Considerable research now focuses on how this signal is generated. Current evidence indicates that this command can originate in either of two brain structures: the *superior colliculus* of the midbrain or the *frontal eye fields* of the neocortex. Both of these structures contain laminar sheets of neurons that code all possible saccadic amplitudes and directions in a topographic maplike organization (Robinson 1972; Wurtz and Goldberg 1972; Bruce and Goldberg 1985). Activation of neurons at a particular location in these maps is associated with a particular saccade, and activation of neurons adjacent to that location is associated with saccades having adjacent coordinates. Lesion experiments indicate that either of these structures can be removed without permanently preventing the generation of saccades. How these signals that topographically encode the amplitude and direction of a saccade are translated into a form appropriate for the control of the oculomotor brain stem is not known. One group of theories proposes that these signals govern a brain stem feedback loop which accelerates the eye to a high velocity and keeps the eye in motion until the desired eye movement is complete (cf. Robinson 1975). Other theories place this feedback loop outside the brain stem or generate saccadic commands without the explicit use of a feedback loop. In any case, it seems clear that the superior colliculus and frontal eye fields are important sources of these signals because if both of these structures are removed, no further

saccades are possible (Shiller, True, and Conway 1980). The superior colliculus and frontal eye fields, in turn, receive input from many areas within the VISUAL PROCESSING STREAMS, including the VISUAL CORTEX, as well as the BASAL GANGLIA and brain structures involved in audition and somatosensation. These areas are presumed to participate in the processes that must precede the decision to make a saccade, processes like ATTENTION.

In the smooth pursuit system, signals carrying information about target MOTION are extracted by motion-processing areas in visual cortex and then passed to the dorsolateral pontine nucleus of the brain stem. There, neurons have been identified which code either the direction and velocity of pursuit eye movements, the direction and velocity of visual target motion, or both. These signals proceed to the cerebellum where neurons have been shown to specifically encode the velocity of pursuit eye movements (Suzuki and Keller 1984). These neurons, in turn, make connections with cells known to be upstream of the nucleus prepositus hypoglossi (the integrator of the oculomotor system described above). As in the saccadic system, the brain stem integrator appears to compute the long-term holding force from this signal and then to pass the sum of these signals to the motor neurons.

All eye movement control signals must pass through the ocular motor neurons which serve as a final common path. In all cases these neurons carry signals associated both with the instantaneous velocity of the eye and the holding force required at the end of the movement. Eye movement systems must provide control signals of this type, presumably by first specifying a velocity command from which changes in holding force can be computed. In the case of saccades, this command is produced by brain structures that topographically map all permissible saccades in amplitude and direction coordinates. In the case of pursuit, the brain appears to extract target motion and to use this signal as the oculomotor control input. Together these systems allow humans to redirect the lines of sight to stimuli of interest and to stabilize moving objects on the retina for maximum acuity.

See also ATTENTION IN THE HUMAN BRAIN; EYE MOVEMENTS AND VISUAL ATTENTION

—*Paul W. Glimcher*

References

Bruce, C. J., and M. E. Goldberg. (1985). Primate frontal eye fields I. Single neurons discharging before saccades. *Journal of Neurophysiology* 53: 603–635.

Cannon, S. C., and D. A. Robinson. (1987). Loss of the neural integrator of the oculomotor system from brainstem lesions in the monkey. *Journal of Neurophysiology* 57: 1383–1409.

Robinson, D. A. (1964). The mechanics of human saccadic eye movements. *Journal of Physiology* 174: 245–264.

Robinson, D. A. (1972). Eye movements evoked by collicular stimulation in the alert monkey. *Vision Research* 12: 1795–1808.

Robinson, D. A. (1975). Oculomotor control signals. In G. Iennerstrand and P. Bach-y-Rita, Eds., *Basic Mechanisms of Ocular Motility and Their Clinical Implications.* Oxford: Pergamon Press, pp. 337–374.

Schiller, P. H., S. D. True, and J. L. Conway. (1980). Deficits in eye movements following frontal eye field and superior colliculus ablations. *Journal of Neurophysiology* 44: 1175–1189.

Suzuki, D A., and E. L. Keller. (1984). Visual signals in the dorsolateral pontine nucleus of the monkey: Their relationship to smooth pursuit eye movements. *Experimental Brain Research* 53: 473–478.

Wurtz, R. H., and M. E. Goldberg. (1972). Activity of superior colliculus in the behaving monkey. 3. Cells discharging before eye movements. *Journal of Neurophysiology* 35: 575–586.

Further Readings

Berthoz, A., and G. M. Jones, Eds. (1985). *Mechanisms in Gaze Control: Facts and Theories. Reviews of Oculomotor Research,* vol. 1. New York: Elsevier.

Buttner-Ennever, J. A., Ed. (1988). *Neuroanatomy of the Oculomotor System. Reviews of Oculomotor Research,* vol. 2. New York: Elsevier.

Carpenter, R. H. S. (1988). *Movements of the Eyes.* 2nd ed. London: Pion.

Carpenter, R. H. S., Ed. (1991). *Eye Movements. Vision and Visual Dysfunction,* vol. 8. Boston: CRC Press.

Collewijn, H. (1981). *The Oculomotor System of the Rabbit and Its Plasticity.* New York: Springer.

Fuchs, A. F., C. R. S. Kaneko, and C. A. Scudder. (1985). Brainstem control of saccadic eye movements. *Annual Review of Neuroscience* 8: 307–337.

Fuchs, A. F., and E. S. Lushei. (1970). Firing patterns of abducens neurons of alert monkeys in relationship to horizontal eye movements. *Journal of Neurophysiology* 33: 382–392.

Jones, G. M. (1991). The vestibular contribution. In R. H. S. Carpenter, Ed., *Eye Movements.* Boston: CRC Press, pp.13–44.

Keller, E. L. (1974). Participation of the medial pontine reticular formation in eye movement generation in the monkey. *Journal of Neurophysiology* 37: 316–332.

Kowler, E., Ed. (1990). *Eye Movements and Their Role in Visual and Cognitive Processes. Reviews of Oculomotor Research,* vol. 4. New York: Elsevier.

Leigh, R. J., and D. S. Zee. (1991). *The Neurology of Eye Movements,* 2nd ed. Philadelphia: F. A. Davis.

Lisberger, S. G., E. J. Morris, and L. Tychsen. (1987). Visual motion processing and sensory-motor integration for smooth pursuit eye movements. *Annual Reviews of Neuroscience* 10: 97–129.

Lushei, E. S., and A. F. Fuchs. (1972). Activity of brainstem neurons during eye movements of alert monkeys. *Journal of Neurophysiology* 35: 445–461.

Miles, F. A., and J. Wallman, Eds. (1993). *Visual Motion and Its Role in the Stabilization of Gaze. Reviews of Oculomotor Research,* vol. 5. New York: Elsevier.

Raphan, T., and B. Cohen. (1978). Brainstem mechanisms for rapid and slow eye movements. *Annual Review of Physiology* 40: 527–552.

Robinson, D. A. (1981). Control of eye movements. In V. B. Brooks, Ed., *The Nervous System. Handbook of Physiology,* part 2, vol. 2. Baltimore: Williams and Wilkins, pp. 1275–1320.

Sparks, D. L. (1986). Translation of sensory signals into commands for saccadic eye movements: Role of primate superior colliculus. *Physiological Reviews* 66: 118–171.

Sparks, D. L., R. Holland, and B. L. Guthrie. (1976). Size and distribution of movement fields in the monkey superior colliculus. *Brain Research* 113: 21–34.

Wurtz, R. H., and M. E. Goldberg, Eds. (1989). *The Neurobiology of Saccadic Eye Movements. Reviews of Oculomotor Research,* vol. 3. New York: Elsevier.

Olfaction

See SMELL

Ontology

See CONCEPTS; KNOWLEDGE REPRESENTATION; MIND-BODY PROBLEM; NATURAL KINDS

Optimality Theory

Optimality Theory ("OT," Prince and Smolensky 1991, 1993) is a theory of LINGUISTIC UNIVERSALS AND UNIVERSAL GRAMMAR. According to OT, the grammars of all human languages share a set of constraints, denoted *Con.* These constraints are sufficiently simple and general that they conflict in many contexts: they cannot all be satisfied simultaneously. The grammar of an individual language resolves these conflicts: it ranks the universal constraints of *Con* into a *constraint hierarchy,* conflicts being resolved in favor of higher-ranked constraints, with each constraint having absolute priority over all lower-ranked constraints. Grammars may differ *only* in how they rank the universal constraints; the TYPOLOGY of all possible human languages may be computed as the result of all possible rankings of these constraints. An OT analysis explains why some grammatical patterns are possible while others are not. (That a particular language happens to have a particular constraint ranking is not considered a fact to be explained within grammatical theory proper.)

Consider, for example, the difference between the simple English sentence *it rains* and its Italian counterpart *piove*—literally, "rains." What do these sentences reveal about the commonalities and differences between the two grammars? According to the OT analysis of Grimshaw and Samek-Lodovici (1995, 1998), at issue here is a conflict between two constraints—SUBJECT: "Every sentence has a subject," and FULL-INT(ERPRETATION): "Every element of a linguistic expression contributes to its interpretation." In English, the conflict is resolved in favor of SUBJECT: to provide a subject, *it* must appear, even though it has no referent and contributes nothing to the interpretation of the sentence, violating FULL-INT. In Italian, the conflict is resolved the other way: no meaningless subject may appear, and FULL-INT prevails over SUBJECT.

In many other contexts, SUBJECT and FULL-INT do not conflict, and both constraints must be satisfied in both languages. Both constraints are parts of the grammars of both languages, but they do not have equal status: in English, SUBJECT has priority, or *dominates*; we write: SUBJECT >> FULL-INT. In Italian, the reverse *constraint ranking* holds. The lower-ranked constraint in each language must be obeyed, except in contexts in which doing so would violate the higher-ranked constraint; in this sense, constraints in OT are *minimally violable.* OT thus differs from earlier grammatical theories employing *inviolable* constraints, where any violation of a constraint renders a structure ungrammatical (e.g., RELATIONAL GRAMMAR, LEXICAL FUNCTIONAL GRAMMAR, HEAD-DRIVEN PHRASE STRUCTURE GRAMMAR).

To sketch the broad outline of the OT picture of cross-linguistic variation, we fix attention on a universal constraint C (e.g., FULL-INT). In some languages, C is very highly ranked (e.g., Italian); the effect is that those linguistic structures (e.g., meaningless *it*) that violate the constraint—those that are *marked* by it—are altogether banned from the language. In other languages, C is somewhat lower ranked, so that the structures it marks (e.g., *it*) now appear—but only in those highly restricted contexts in which the marked element is needed to satisfy one of the few constraints more highly ranked than C (e.g., SUBJECT in English). Looking across still other languages, C is ranked lower and lower, so that the structures it marks appear in more and more contexts, as more and more other constraints force violations of because they outrank it. The OT literature documents many specific cases of this general cross-linguistic pattern, which can be captured entirely by the simple statement: C ∈ *Con.* Once this has been stated, the rest of the pattern follows from the formal structure of OT: languages differ in how they rank C, and depending on this ranking, those structures marked by C will be either banned altogether (highest ranking), allowed but only in a highly restricted set of contexts, or allowed in a wide range of contexts (lowest ranking).

Each universal constraint C defines a class of dispreferred or *marked* structures: those that violate it. Through the single mechanism of constraint ranking, such marked elements are banned in some languages, and restricted in their distribution in all languages. OT thus builds on the notion of *markedness* developed in the 1930s by N. S. Trubetzkoy, Roman JAKOBSON, and others of the Prague Linguistics Circle; OT provides a formal, general markedness-based calculus within the tradition of GENERATIVE GRAMMAR. OT's formalization of markedness computation brings into sharp focus a number of issues otherwise obscure.

Competition

To say that a linguistic structure *S* is grammatical in a language *L* because it optimally satisfies *L*'s constraint hierarchy is to exploit a *comparative* property: even though *S* might not satisfy all the universal constraints, *every alternative* incurs more serious violations of *L*'s hierarchy than does *S*. Specifying an OT grammar includes specifying the *candidate sets* of linguistic structures that compete for optimality. This must be universal, for in OT, only constraint ranking varies across grammars.

Aggregation of Multiple Dimensions of Markedness

What defines optimality when the constraints defining different dimensions of markedness disagree on which candidate is preferred? OT's answer is constraint ranking. *S* is optimal if and only if it is *more harmonic* than all other members *S'* of its candidate set, written S ≻ S': this means that, of the constraints differentiating the markedness of *S* and *S'*, *S* is favored by the highest ranked. It is perhaps surprising that within such a simple mechanism, reranking can succeed in accounting for such a diversity of observed grammatical patterns.

Faithfulness to Targets

Why is *it rains* optimal, when its violation of FULL-INT could be avoided by selecting another candidate with an interpreted subject, say, *John smiles*? Implicit thus far in the competition for optimality is the *target* proposition, <rain(), tense = present>, to which *it rains,* but not *John smiles,* is *faithful.* In OT, each candidate is evaluated relative to a target, faithfulness to which is demanded by constraints in *Con* collectively called FAITHFULNESS. *John smiles* is indeed optimal, but for a different target, <smile(x), x = John, tense = present>. The multiplicity of grammatical—optimal—structures in a single language arises from the multiplicity of possible targets. In PHONOLOGY, the target is a sequence of phones, an *underlying form* such as /bat + d/ for the past tense of *to bat.* Optimal for this target is [batɪd] "batted"; this includes a vowel ([ɪ]) not present in the target, so it violates a FAITHFULNESS constraint, F. This minimally unfaithful candidate is optimal because of a universal constraint against certain word-final consonant clusters, including *td;* this constraint is higher ranked than F in the phonological component of the English grammar. That a morpheme (like past-tense /d/) receives different (but closely related) pronunciations, depending on its context, follows in OT from a fixed underlying form for the morpheme, FAITHFULNESS to which is (minimally) violated in many optimal forms, forced by higher-ranked well-formedness constraints governing phones in various contexts. Violability of FAITHFULNESS plays a less obvious role in SYNTAX; Legendre, Smolensky, and Wilson (1998) use it to explain why some syntactic targets have *no* grammatical expression in a particular language: for such an ineffable target, every faithful candidate violates sufficiently high-ranking constraints that an unfaithful candidate, with a different interpretation, is optimal.

The candidates competing for a target *I* form a set written *Gen(I); I* is often called the *input,* and sometimes the *index,* of this candidate set. The set of targets and the candidate-generating function *Gen* are universal.

Implications

A framework employing a novel type of grammatical computation, optimization, OT has cognitive implications for the classic questions of generative grammar that concern the nature of knowledge of language, its use, its acquisition, and its neural realization.

Violable constraints profoundly alter the analytic options in syntactic theory. When a grammatical sentence *S appears* to violate a putative simple, general, universal constraint C, it becomes possible to simply say that it *actually does*; with inviolable constraints, it is typically necessary to posit invisible structures that allow *S* to covertly satisfy C, or to complicate C, often via language-particular parameters, so that it is no longer violated by *S.* Topics of OT syntactic analyses include grammatical voice alternations (GRAMMATICAL

RELATIONS and THEMATIC ROLES), case, ANAPHORA, HEAD MOVEMENT, subject distribution, *wh*-questions (WH-MOVEMENT), scrambling, and clitic inventories and placement.

In phonological theory, the shift from serial, process-oriented frameworks (PHONOLOGICAL RULES AND PROCESSES) to OT's parallel, violable constraint optimization has enabled explanation of typological variation in a number of areas: segmental inventories, syllable structure, STRESS, TONE, vowel harmony, reduplicative and templatic MORPHOLOGY, phonology-morphology relations, the phonology-PHONETICS interface, and many others. (For an extensive bibliography and on-line database of OT papers and software, see the Rutgers Optimality Archive ROA at http://ruccs.rutgers.edu/roa.html.)

A unified grammatical framework for syntax and phonology, OT also provides results that span both these modules, including the relation of general to more specific constraints, the compatibility among related grammatical processes, and the computation and learnability of grammars. Formal results on the latter topics address algorithms for learning constraint rankings from positive examples, algorithms for computing optimal forms, and the complexity of formal languages specified by OT grammars. Empirical findings on the course of acquisition of PHONOLOGY in children, and on real-time SENTENCE PROCESSING, have been analyzed within OT. While detailed OT proposals for the neural basis of language and the neural basis of phonology do not currently exist, theoretical connections between optimization in OT and in NEURAL NETWORK models have proved fruitful for the continuing development of both OT and the theory of complex symbol processing in neural networks (Prince and Smolensky 1997).

See also CONNECTIONIST APPROACHES TO LANGUAGE; LANGUAGE, NEURAL BASIS OF; PHONOLOGY, NEURAL BASIS OF

—*Paul Smolensky*

References

Grimshaw, J., and V. Samek-Lodovici. (1995). Optimal subjects. In J. Beckman, L. Walsh-Dickey, and S. Urbanczyk, Eds., *University of Massachusetts Occasional Papers in Linguistics* 18: *Papers in Optimality Theory.* Amherst, MA: GLSA, University of Massachusetts, pp. 589–605.

Grimshaw, J., and V. Samek-Lodovici. (1998). Optimal subjects and subject universals. In P. Barbosa, D. Fox, P. Hagstrom, M. McGinnis, and D. Pesetsky, Eds., *Is the Best Good Enough? Papers from the Workshop on Optimality in Syntax.* Cambridge, MA: MIT Press and MIT Working Papers in Linguistics.

Legendre, G., P. Smolensky, and C. Wilson. (1998). When is less more? Faithfulness and minimal links in *wh*-chains. In P. Barbosa, D. Fox, P. Hagstrom, M. McGinnis, and D. Pesetsky, Eds., *Is the Best Good Enough? Papers from the Workshop on Optimality in Syntax.* Cambridge, MA: MIT Press and MIT Working Papers in Linguistics.

Prince, A., and P. Smolensky. (1991). *Notes on Connectionism and Harmony Theory in Linguistics.* Technical Report CU-CS-533-91. Boulder, CO: Department of Computer Science, University of Colorado.

Prince, A., and P. Smolensky. (1993). *Optimality Theory: Constraint Interaction in Generative Grammar.* RuCCS Technical Report 2. Piscataway, NJ: Rutgers Center for Cognitive Science, Rutgers University, and Boulder, CO: Department of Computer Science, University of Colorado.

Prince, A., and Smolensky, P. (1997). Optimality: From neural networks to universal grammar. *Science* 275: 1604–1610.

Further Readings

Barbosa, P., D. Fox, P. Hagstrom, M. McGinnis, and D. Pesetsky, Eds. (1998). *Is the Best Good Enough? Papers from the Workshop on Optimality in Syntax.* Cambridge, MA: MIT Press and MIT Working Papers in Linguistics.

Beckman, J., L. Walsh-Dickey, and S. Urbanczyk, Eds. (1995). *University of Massachusetts Occasional Papers in Linguistics 18: Papers in Optimality Theory.* Amherst, MA: GLSA, University of Massachusetts.

Grimshaw, J. (1997). Projection, heads, and optimality. *Linguistic Inquiry* 28: 373–422.

Legendre, G., W. Raymond, and P. Smolensky. (1993). An Optimality-Theoretic typology of case and grammatical voice systems. In *Proceedings of the Nineteenth Annual Meeting of the Berkeley Linguistics Society.* Berkeley, CA, pp. 464–478.

Legendre, G., and P. Smolensky. (Forthcoming). *Towards a Calculus of the Mind/Brain: Neural Network Theory, Optimality, and Universal Grammar.*

Legendre, G., S. Vikner, and J. Grimshaw, Eds. (Forthcoming). *Optimal Syntax.*

McCarthy, J., and A. Prince. (1993). *Prosodic Morphology* I: *Constraint Interaction and Satisfaction.* RuCCS Technical Report 3. Piscataway, NJ: Rutgers Center for Cognitive Science, Rutgers University.

McCarthy, J., and A. Prince. (1993). Generalized Alignment. In G. Booij and J. van Marle, Eds., *Yearbook of Morphology* 1993. Dordrecht: Kluwer, pp. 79–153.

McCarthy, J., and A. Prince. (1995). Faithfulness and reduplicative identity. In J. Beckman, L. Walsh Dickey, and S. Urbanczyk, Eds., *University of Massachusetts Occasional Papers in Linguistics* 18: *Papers in Optimality Theory.* Amherst, MA: GLSA, University of Massachusetts, pp. 249–384.

Smolensky, P. (1996). On the comprehension/production dilemma in child language. *Linguistic Inquiry* 27: 720–731.

Tesar, B., and P. Smolensky. (1998). Learnability in Optimality Theory. *Linguistic Inquiry* 29: 229–268.

Origins of Intelligence

See COGNITIVE ARCHAEOLOGY; EVOLUTIONARY PSYCHOLOGY; INTELLIGENCE; MACHIAVELLIAN INTELLIGENCE HYPOTHESIS

PAC Learning

See COMPUTATIONAL LEARNING THEORY; MACHINE LEARNING

Pain

To a degree matched by no other component of somatic sensation and by no other sensory system, pain carries with it an emotional quality. From one person to the next, differences in personal traits and past experience play major roles in the perception of pain. For any individual, changes in mood or expectation are similarly important for judging and reacting to pain. Moreover, thresholds for a stimulus perceived as painful vary across the body surface, as every person can attest to by comparing how he or she reacts to one grain of sand under the eyelid vs. thousands of grains under the feet. These variations in the perception of pain and its strong affective component make it difficult to study clinically and experimentally.

The anatomy and physiology of pain (nociception) begin with two types of specialized receptors in the skin, muscles, and viscera. One responds only to very forceful mechanical energy and the other to noxious stimuli of many kinds. The first of these is the mechanical nociceptor, a type of afferent that responds only to physical force intense enough to produce tissue damage. Far more general is the response of polymodal nociceptors, as seen by comparing the response of the two receptor types to heat: mechanical nociceptors have a very high threshold for the initial application of heat, whereas polymodal nociceptors begin responding to stimuli of 40° C and show a linear increase in response to stimuli up to 60° C. Both receptor types are notable for the fact that, unlike all other somatosensory receptors, they are left uncovered by specialized cells or connective tissue sheaths and are thus unprotected from the diffusion of chemical agents released by surrounding cells. These agents include a variety of small molecules such as amines and peptides that can produce or change activity in nociceptors over a distance of several millimeters.

Whereas other somatosensory receptors adapt to repeated stimulation by becoming less sensitive and less responsive to each subsequent stimulus, nociceptors participate in a heightened response to repeated noxious stimulation, referred to as hyperalgesia. Both neural and non-neuronal mechanisms appear to participate in this phenomenon by which application of noxious thermal or mechanical stimuli produces a lower threshold for and a greater response to other noxious stimuli. Primary hyperalgesia occurs at the site of injury through the local release of chemical agents, such as bradykinin, which directly stimulate nociceptors to become active. Other chemical agents, including prostaglandin E_2, also play a role in primary hyperalgesia, not by directly driving nociceptors, but by making them much more responsive to subsequent non-noxious mechanical stimuli. It is through inhibition of these chemical agents that aspirin and ibuprofen work as analgesics. A second type of hyperalgesia is of strictly neural origin and probably includes a component that originates in the spinal cord rather than in the periphery.

The two nociceptor types send their responses into the central nervous system (CNS) by way of different kinds of peripheral axons. Larger, lightly myelinated (Aδ) axons end as mechanical nociceptors, whereas the smallest, unmyelinated (C) axons end as polymodal nociceptors. These differences in axon diameter and level of myelination necessarily translate into differences of conduction velocity and thus in the time over which signals from the two nociceptor types reach the CNS. Pricking pain, carried by Aδ fibers, is the more rapidly transmitted, better localized, and more easily tolerated component of pain. The perception of pricking pain is followed after a substantial delay by second or burning pain, a poorly localized, agonizing pain carried by C fibers.

Pain afferents are segregated from other somatosensory afferents that carry discriminative information of touch and body position. They enter the spinal cord in the dorsal root as a more lateral bundle and synapse directly upon neurons of the cord's dorsal and intermediate horns. Convergence of inputs from many pain afferents at this level produces a situation amplified at higher levels in which painful stimuli are localized very poorly when unaccompanied by information from other cutaneous afferents. Further synaptic convergence at higher levels between cutaneous nociceptors and visceral nociceptors leads to the misplacement of pain occurring in viscera to sites that are more peripheral. This referred pain is a common part of abnormal situations, such as those that occur during heart attacks.

Many spinal neurons driven by nociceptive afferents send their axons across the spinal cord, where they ascend to various locations in the brain stem and THALAMUS. That immediate crossing in the cord of pain information contrasts with the delayed crossing of fine touch and proprioceptive axons, which occurs in the medulla. Such a wide difference in the site of crossing produces a situation in which hemisection of the cord leads to a loss of pain sensation on the contralateral side of the body but loss of discriminative sensation on the ipsilateral side. Other neurons directly driven by nociceptive afferents have intraspinal axons that end on spinal motor neurons. These synapses are part of a rapid reflex that produces withdrawal of a limb from the location of a painful stimulus.

Much of the ascending pain information reaches a region of the midbrain around the cerebral aqueduct of the ventricular system. This periaqueductal gray (PAG) region is a principal component of a descending system, stimulation of which relieves pain. Axons from the PAG innervate a collection of serotonin-synthesizing and -secreting neurons of the medulla, the nucleus raphe magnus. These neurons, in turn, send long, descending axons into the dorsal horn of the spinal cord, where they form synapses with interneurons that use opiate-like peptides, the enkephalins, as NEUROTRANSMITTERS. By modulating the activity of nociceptor afferents and of spinal pain neurons, the enkephalinergic interneurons control the perception of the intensity of a noxious stimulus. Opiates and other pharmacological agents that mimic the effects of enkephalins are effective as analgesics in part because of their action at these spinal synapses.

A fraction of spinal neurons that respond to nociceptive inputs send their axons to the contralateral thalamus. Part of that spinothalamic system reaches nuclei of the intralaminar group, which provides the great mass of the cerebral cortex with a diffuse innervation. That system and the projection of spinal nociceptive neurons to the brain stem reticular formation are the anatomical substrates for the generally arousing and motivating qualities of pain. Most spinothalamic axons, however, synapse on clusters of small cells in the ventral posterior lateral (VPL) nucleus, which together make up a complete body representation of pain. A comparable group of cells in the ventral posterior medial (VPM) nucleus is innervated by neurons in the pars caudalis of the spinal trigeminal system and includes a nociceptive representation of the face. Both VPL and VPM send axons to the first somatosensory area of the cerebral cortex, found in the postcentral gyrus of monkeys, apes, and humans. By this route and by a separate innervation of the second somatosensory area, nociceptive information reaches the CEREBRAL CORTEX in a way that it can be compared with other somatosensory information and localized with some precision to particular sites along the body. Neurological studies of soldiers suffering head wounds in the two world wars clearly demonstrate that injuries confined to the postcentral gyrus produce permanent analgesia along the contralateral body surface.

Where the affective quality to pain arises is poorly understood. Those few studies to have addressed the question have focused on areas of temporal and orbitofrontal cortex in humans and nonhuman primates. Perhaps the best current guess is that more than one area of cerebral cortex is involved in the agony that accompanies extreme pain such as that produced by solid tumors or burns. These extreme cases of pain and the need to control them and other lesser or more acute nociceptive events often raise questions of the advantage conferred by painful affect. Rare clinical cases of patients who perceive a painful event as differing from an innocuous stimulus but who experience no affect accompanying that event are test cases for such a question. Most of these patients die at an early age, victims of numerous destructive wounds and crippling conditions of joints. Apparently the failure of these patients to avoid or discontinue actions that are painful significantly shortens their lives despite intensive training in detecting and responding to painful stimuli. From these cases, then, it can be concluded that both precise localization and emotional reaction to pain are parts of successful strategies for survival.

See also EMOTION AND THE ANIMAL BRAIN; EPIPHENOMENALISM; PHANTOM LIMB; WHAT-IT'S-LIKE

— *Stewart Hendry*

Further Readings

Basbaum, A. I., and H. L. Fields. (1984). Endogenous pain control systems: Brainstem spinal pathways and endorphin circuitry. *Annual Review of Neuroscience* 7: 309–338.

Dubner, R., and C. J. Bennett. (1983). Spinal and trigeminal mechanisms of nociception. *Annual Review of Neuroscience* 6: 381–418.

Light, A. R. (1992). *The Initial Processing of Pain and Its Descending Control: Spinal and Trigeminal Systems*. Basel: Karger.

Perl, E. R. (1984). Pain and nociception. In *The Handbook Of Physiology*, sec. 1: *The Nervous System*, vol. 3. *Sensory Processes*, part 2. Bethesda, MD: American Physiological Society.

Price, D. D. (1988). *Psychological and Neural Mechanisms of Pain*. New York: Raven Press.

Willis, W. D. (1985). *The Pain System: The Neural Basis of Nociceptive Transmission in the Mammalian Nervous System*. Basel: Karger.

Parallelism in AI

See COGNITIVE MODELING, CONNECTIONIST; NEURAL NETWORKS

Parameter-Setting Approaches to Acquisition, Creolization, and Diachrony

How is knowledge of one's idiolect—*I(nternal)-language,* in Noam Chomsky's (1986) terminology—represented in the mind/brain? How is such knowledge acquired by children? Answers to these questions are intricately and constructively related. In the principles and parameters/minimalist approach (Chomsky 1981, 1986, 1995; see SYNTAX, ACQUISITION OF and MINIMALISM), linguistic knowledge, in addition to a (language-specific) LEXICON (see WORD MEANING, ACQUISITION OF and COMPUTATIONAL LEXICONS), consists of a computational system that is subject to an innate set of formal constraints, partitioned into *principles* and *parameters*. The *principles* are argued to be universal; they formalize constraints obeyed by *all* languages (see LINGUISTIC UNIVERSALS). Alongside these principles—and perhaps *within* some of these principles (e.g., Rizzi 1982)—what allows for diversity in TYPOLOGY (possibly, in addition to the lexicon proper) are the *parameters*. These parameters constitute an innate and finite set of "switches," each with a fixed range of settings. These switches give the learner a restricted number of options in determining the complete shape of the attained I-language. In such a framework, syntax acquisition reduces to fixing the values of parameters on the basis of primary linguistic data (PLD) (cf. LANGUAGE ACQUISITION). Taken together, principles and parameters bring a solution to the "logical problem of language acquisition":

(1) UG / S_0
    (universal principles cum *UNSET* parameters)

+

PLD / "triggers"

=

Idiolect-Specific Grammar / S_f
(universal principles cum SET parameters)

Per (1), language acquisition is the process in which exposure to PLD transforms our innately specified *faculté de langage* (from an initial state S_0) into a language-specific grammar (at the final state S_f) by assigning values (settings) to an array of (initially unset) parameters (see Chomsky 1981, HISTORICAL LINGUISTICS, and INNATENESS OF LANGUAGE).

The schema just sketched delineates a fascinating and productive research program. Yet our understanding is still very incomplete as to how (which aspects of) the PLD "lead" the learner to adopt (what) settings for (what) parameters. What are the major questions raised by this program? In order to flesh out the structure in (1), generativists are advancing on three complementary theoretical fronts toward:

1. A characterization of parameters. For example, are parameters distributed across various grammatical principles (cf. Rizzi 1982; Chomsky 1986) or are parameters restricted to "inflectional systems" (Borer 1983; Chomsky 1995: ch 2), to the inventory and properties of functional heads (Ouhalla 1991; cf. SYNTAX and HEAD

MOVEMENT), or to ("weak" vs. "strong") morphological features of functional heads (see Chomsky 1995: ch. 3)?

2. A theory that would delineate what (kinds and amounts of) forms from the PLD are used by the learner in what contexts and at what stages as *triggers* or *cues* for assigning particular settings to particular parameters (cf. Gibson and Wexler 1994; Lightfoot 1999; Roberts 1999; also see further readings below).

3. A proposal as to how (i.e., by what chains of deductions) the triggering in (2) takes place.

Current approaches to 1–3 still remain controversial and in need of refinements. Here I discuss one proposal with *some* promise regarding certain (diachronic and ontogenetic) developmental data. Rohrbacher (1994), following insights from works by, among others, Borer, Pollock, Platzack and Holmberg, Roberts, and Chomsky, proposes that "rich" verbal inflections constitute a trigger for verb displacement (V-raising) because such MORPHOLOGY is listed in the lexicon and inserted in the syntax outside of the verbal phrase (VP): as affixal heads, such verbal inflection induces the verb to raise outside VP via head movement in order for the verb stem to become bound with its affixes. Such verb raising is diagnosed by, for example, placement of the finite verb to the left of certain adverbs, as in French. In languages with "poor" verbal inflection, affixes (if any) generally do not behave as independent *syntactic* elements that induce V-raising; they are introduced post-syntactically in the morpho-phonological component. Such proposals for the morphology-syntax interface in parameter-setting are not unproblematic. Yet they make interesting predictions that can (in principle, if not always in practice) be tested against phenomena in language acquisition, creolization, and language change. In turn, research in these three areas has brought forward data and insights that may prove useful in elucidating parameter setting.

Starting with CREOLES, there has been much recent work by young creolists proceeding from the hunch that paths of creolization may provide much needed hints toward understanding: the mechanics of parameter-setting in acquisition and through language change; and whether parameter settings are hierarchically organized along a cline of (un)markedness (with unmarked settings being those that are attained with few or no triggers of the appropriate type). The hunch that creolization phenomena should shed light on parameter setting essentially goes back to Derek Bickerton's language bioprogram hypothesis. In Bickerton's hypothesis, creoles by and large manifest the sort of properties a language learner would attain in the absence of reliable PLD, for example, in the presence of the overly impoverished and unstable patterns that are typical of speakers in (early) pidgin/interlanguage stages. Thus creole settings tend to indicate values accessible with few or no triggers in the PLD. Why should this state of affairs hold?

For Bickerton, structural similarities across creoles arise as creole grammars tend to instantiate genetically specified *default* values of parameter settings due to: (1) the restricted nature of the PLD: the source of the PLD that gave rise to the creole is a pidgin that is itself the outcome of adult language acquisition under duress, that is, with restricted input in contact situations that are unfriendly toward the learner;

thus, pidgin grammatical morphologies tend to be impoverished; (2) the privileged role of children in creole genesis: in acquiring their native language with pidgin PLD, such children appear to stabilize and expand inconsistent, unstable, and restricted patterns in their PLD.

Regarding the morphologies of contact languages, it was noted long ago (e.g., by Meillet 1919) that inflectional paradigms are singularly susceptible to the vagaries of language learning in contact situations. Thus, in a theory where parameter settings are derived from the properties of inflectional morphemes (cf. Borer 1983; see e.g., Rohrbacher 1994), the question arises as to what settings are attainable in an environment that causes attrition to the PLD's inflectional morphemes. Bickerton's proposal is that, in the absence of the relevant (morphological) triggers, certain parameters are assigned default settings by UG. Although various creole structures are inherited from the parent languages, contra Bickerton (see e.g., Chaudenson 1992; Lumsden 1999), Bickerton's intuition seems partly confirmed in certain domains of creole syntax, for example, for Haitian Creole, in the domains of nonverbal predication (*sans* verbal copulas; DeGraff 1992), and of verb and object-pronoun syntax (with adverb-verb-pronoun order; DeGraff 1994, 1997). These are among patterns that distinguish Haitian Creole both from its European ancestor (French) and from its West-African ancestors (e.g., Kwa). Much recent work in this vein (see further readings below) is preliminary and exploratory, but appears to hold promise toward understanding the mechanics of parameter-setting and of creole genesis.

Beyond creolization, Bickerton's proposal, once embedded in a parameter-setting framework, also has ramifications for the relationship between acquisition and language change. Given (1) and some implementation thereof, the language acquisition device with the appropriate parameter-setting algorithm is one locus of confluence for creolization and language-change data (cf. DeGraff 1999b; Lightfoot 1999). As language learners and field and historical linguists often experience (the learners more successfully than the linguists), "language data do not wear their grammars on their sleeves," and parameter values must be fixed anew each time an I-language is attained, that is, at each instantiation of (1). This is in keeping with Meillet's (1929: 74) and others' classic idea that the transmission of language is inherently discontinuous: the grammar of each speaker is an individual re-creation, based on limited evidence. Furthermore, parameter-setting takes the learner through parametric configurations distinct from the target grammar(s) (see e.g., the papers in Roeper and Williams 1987). One must also remark that PLD sets—as uttered by the learner's various model speakers (caretakers, older peers, etc.)—are themselves determined by parameter-setting arrays that, although overlapping, are in most cases (subtly) distinct from one another idiolect-wise. Thus, even in unexceptional instances of acquisition, target grammars, and the final grammars attained by the learners ineluctably diverge, if only along relatively few parameters. Yet such localized parametric shifts are noticeable via the innovative structural patterns they give rise to. In any case, it has been claimed (e.g., in DeGraff 1999b) that such innovation is of the same character as that found in creolization and in the early stages of language acquisition (modulo the degree of divergence); they all are rooted in (1), which is a modern rendering of Meillet's observation about the discontinuity of language transmission. As for the more radical nature of the changes observed in creolization, this stems from the unusual nature of the PLD.

Thus, it should not come as surprise that creolization patterns (e.g., in Haitian Creole's verbal syntax and morphology; see DeGraff 1997) present uncanny parallels with: (1) patterns in language acquisition, as with children who, in the initial stages of acquiring V-raising languages like French, (optionally) use noninflected unraised verbs in contexts where the target language requires inflected raised verbs (Pierce 1992); and (2) patterns in language change, as for example in the history of English where V-raising in Middle English gave way to V-in-situ in Modern English with a prior decrease in verbal inflections (Rohrbacher 1994; Vikner 1997; Roberts 1999; Lightfoot 1999).

Results of this sort would then confirm the view that morphology is one major source of syntactic variations and that functional categories and their associated morphemes are the locus for parameter-setting. In this view, the learner, unlike the linguist, need not consult actual "constructions" in order to set parameters. Instead, inflectional paradigms (once their "richness" and frequencies exceed certain thresholds) serve as triggers for syntax-related settings such as V-raising vs V-in-situ, possibly alongside *syntactic* triggers qua robust and localized distributional patterns (e.g., verb-negation/adverb orders; see, e.g., Roberts 1999; Lightfoot 1999). (As noted by Rohrbacher 1994: 274, the inflectional paradigms may be key because they must be learned anyway.) In absence of relatively copious morphological (and syntactic) triggers, the learner initially falls back on default options (e.g., V-in-situ) as in the earliest stages of acquisition and in the linguistic environments that produced Haitian Creole and Modern English—and other languages that lost V-raising through language contact.

The hypothesis sketched above regarding parameter-setting (in verbal syntax) has been much debated; see, inter alios, Vikner 1997 for counterexamples, and Thráinsson 1996 and Lightfoot 1999 for alternative proposals. Yet, to advance our understanding of parameter-setting within current (provisional) assumptions in syntax (particularly minimalism), one may ask whether morphological triggering (or any other triggering that relies on narrowly defined, easily accessible paradigms) *must* be the null hypothesis in any theory that both assumes "constructions" to be epiphenomenal (see Chomsky 1995) and potentially ambiguous parameter-wise (e.g., Gibson and Wexler 1994), and seeks to solve the logical problem of language acquisition by keeping learning and induction from PLD to a strict minimum (see POVERTY OF THE STIMULUS ARGUMENTS).

—*Michel DeGraff*

References

Borer, H. (1983). *Parametric Syntax*. Dordrecht: Foris.

Chaudenson, R. (1992). *Des Iles, des Hommes, des Langues*. Paris: L'Harmattan.

Chomsky, N. (1981). Principles and parameters in syntactic theory. In N. Hornstein and D. Lightfoot, Eds., *Explanation in Linguistics*. London: Longman, pp. 123–146.

Chomsky, N. (1986). *Knowledge of Language*. New York: Praeger.

Chomsky, N. (1995). *The Minimalist Program*. Cambridge, MA: MIT Press.

DeGraff, M. (1992). The syntax of predication in Haitian. In *Proceedings of the 22nd Annual Meeting of the North Eastern Linguistics Society*. University of Massachusetts at Amherst: Graduate Linguistics Students Association.

DeGraff, M. (1994). To move or not to move? Placement of verbs and object pronouns in Haitian Creole and in French. In K. Beals, J. Denton, R. Knippen, L. Melnar, H. Suzuki, and E. Zeinfeld, Eds., *Papers from the 30th Meeting of the Chicago Linguistic Society*. Chicago: Chicago Linguistics Society.

DeGraff, M. (1997). Verb syntax in creolization (and beyond). In L. Haegeman, Ed., *The New Comparative Syntax*. London: Longman, pp. 64–94.

DeGraff, M., Ed. (1999a). *Language Creation and Language Change: Creolization, Diachrony and Development*. Cambridge, MA: MIT Press.

DeGraff, M., Ed. (1999b). Creolization, language change and language creolization: An epilogue. In M. DeGraff, Ed., *Language Creation and Language Change: Creolization, Diachrony and Development*. Cambridge, MA: MIT Press.

Gibson, E., and K. Wexler. (1994). Triggers. *Linguistic Inquiry* 25 (3): 407–454.

Lightfoot, D. (1999). Creoles and cues. In M. DeGraff, Ed., *Language Creation and Language Change: Creolization, Diachrony and Development*. Cambridge, MA: MIT Press.

Lumsden, J. (1999). Language acquisition and creolization. In M. DeGraff, Ed., *Language Creation and Language Change: Creolization, Diachrony and Development*. Cambridge, MA: MIT Press.

Meillet, A. (1919). Le genre grammaticale et l'élimination de la flexion. *Scientia. (Rivista di Scienza)* 25, 86, 6. Reprinted in Meillet (1958), *Linguistique Historique et Linguistique Générale*, tome 1, pp. 199–211.

Meillet, A. (1929). Le développement des langues. In *Continu et Discontinu*. Reprinted in Meillet (1951), *Linguistique Historique et Linguistique Générale*, tome 2, pp. 70–81.

Ouhalla, J. (1991). *Functional Categories and Parametric Variation*. London: Routledge.

Pierce, A. (1992). *Language Acquisition and Syntactic Theory: A Comparative Analysis of French and English Child Grammars*. Dordrecht: Kluwer.

Platzack, C., and A. Holmberg. (1989). The role of Agr and finiteness. *Working Papers in Scandinavian Syntax* 43: 51–76.

Pollock, J.-Y. (1989). Verb movement, Universal Grammar and the structure of IP. *Linguistic Inquiry* 20: 365–424.

Rizzi, L. (1982). *Issues in Italian Syntax*. Dordrecht: Foris.

Roberts, I. (1999). Verb movement and markedness. In M. DeGraff, Ed., *Language Creation and Language Change: Creolization, Diachrony and Development*. Cambridge, MA: MIT Press.

Roeper, T., and E. Williams, Eds. (1987). *Parameter Setting*. Dordrecht: Reidel.

Rohrbacher, B. (1994). *The Germanic VO Languages and the Full Paradigm: A Theory of V to I raising*. PhD. diss., University of Massachusetts.

Thráinsson, H. (1996). On the (non-)universality of functional categories. In W. Abraham, S. Epstein, and H. Thráinson, Eds., *Minimal Ideas*. Amsterdam: Benjamins, pp. 253–281.

Vikner, S. (1997). V^0-to-I^0 movement and inflection for person in all tenses. In L. Haegeman, Ed., *The New Comparative Syntax*. London: Longman, pp. 189–213.

Further Readings

Adone, D. (1994). *The Acquisition of Mauritian Creole.* Amsterdam: Benjamins.

Adone, D., and A. Vainikka. (1999). Acquisition of WH-Questions in Mauritian Creole. In M. DeGraff, Ed., *Language Creation and Language Change: Creolization, Diachrony and Development.* Cambridge, MA: MIT Press.

Arends, J., P. Muysken, and N. Smith. (1994). *Pidgins and Creoles: An Introduction.* Amsterdam: Benjamins.

Baptista, M. (1997). *The Morpho-Syntax of Nominal and Verbal Categories in Capeverdean Creole.* Ph.D. diss., Harvard University.

Bobaljik, J. (1995). *Morphosyntax: The Syntax of Verbal Inflection.* Ph.D. diss., MIT. Distributed by MIT Working Papers in Linguistics.

Bruyn, A., P. Muysken, and M. Verrips. (1999). Double object constructions in the creole languages: Development and acquisition. In M. DeGraff, Ed., *Language Creation and Language Change: Creolization, Diachrony and Development.* Cambridge, MA: MIT Press.

Clark, R., and I. Roberts. (1993). A computational model of language learnability and language change. *Linguistic Inquiry* 24: 299–345.

DeGraff, M. (1993). A riddle on negation in Haitian. *Probus* 5: 63–93.

DeGraff, M. (1995). On certain differences between Haitian and French predicative constructions. In J. Amastae, G. Goodall, M. Montalbetti, and M. Phinney, Eds., *Contemporary Research in Romance Linguistics.* Amsterdam: Benjamins, pp. 237–256.

DeGraff, M. (1996a). Creole languages and parameter setting: A case study using Haitian Creole and the pro-drop parameter. In H. Wekker, Ed., *Creole Languages and Language Acquisition.* Berlin: Mouton de Gruyter, pp. 65–105.

DeGraff, M. (1996b). UG and acquisition in pidginization and creolization. Open peer commentary on Epstein et al. (1996). *Behavioral and Brain Sciences* 19 (4): 723–724.

DeGraff, M., Ed. (1999). *Language Creation and Language Change: Creolization, Diachrony and Development.* Cambridge, MA: MIT Press.

Déprez, V. (1999). The roots of negative concord in French and French-based creoles. In M. DeGraff, Ed., *Language Creation and Language Change: Creolization, Diachrony and Development.* Cambridge, MA: MIT Press.

Dresher, E. (Forthcoming). Charting the learning path: Cues to parameter setting. *Linguistic Inquiry* (to appear).

Fodor, J. (1995). Fewer but better triggers. *CUNY Forum* 19: 39–64.

Hymes, D., Ed. (1971). *Pidginization and Creolization of Languages.* Cambridge: Cambridge University Press.

Lightfoot, D. (1991). *How to Set Parameters: Arguments from Language Change.* Cambridge, MA: MIT Press.

Lightfoot, D. (1995). Why UG needs a learning theory: Triggering verb movement. In A. Battye and I. Roberts, Eds., *Clause Structure and Language Change.* New York: Oxford University Press, pp. 31–52.

Mufwene, S. (1996). The Founder Principle in creole genesis. *Diachronica* 13 (1): 83–134.

Roberts, I. (1993). *Verbs and Diachronic Syntax: A Comparative History of English and French.* Dordrecht: Kluwer.

Veenstra, T. (1996). *Serial Verbs in Saramaccan: Predication and Creole Genesis.* Ph.D. diss., University of Amsterdam. Distributed by Holland Academic Graphics, The Hague.

Vrzić, Z. (1997). A minimalist approach to word order in Chinook Jargon and the theory of creole genesis. In B. Bruening, Ed., *Proceedings of the Eighth Student Conference in Linguistics.* Cambridge, MA: MIT Working Papers in Linguistics, 31.

Weinreich, U. (1953). *Languages in Contact.* Publications of the Linguistic Circle of New York, no. 1. Reprint: The Hague: Mouton (1968).

Wekker, H., Ed. (1996). *Creole Languages and Language Acquisition.* Berlin: Mouton.

Wexler, K. (1994). Finiteness and head movement in early child grammars. In D. Lightfoot and N. Hornstein, Eds., *Verb Movement.* Cambridge: Cambridge University Press.

Parsimony and Simplicity

The law of parsimony, or Ockham's razor (also spelled "Occam"), is named after William of Ockham (1285–1347/49). His statement that "entities are not to be multiplied beyond necessity" is notoriously vague. What counts as an entity? For what purpose are they necessary? Most agree that the aim of postulated entities is to represent reality, or to "get at the truth" in some sense. But when are entities postulated *beyond* necessity?

The role of parsimony and simplicity is important in all forms of INDUCTION, LEARNING, STATISTICAL LEARNING THEORY, and in the debate about RATIONALISM VS. EMPIRICISM. However, Ockham's razor is better known in scientific theorizing, where it has two aspects. First, there is the idea that one should not postulate entities that make *no* observable difference. For example, Gottfried Wilhelm Leibniz objected to Isaac Newton's absolute space because one absolute velocity of the solar system would produce the same observable behavior as any other absolute velocity.

The second aspect of Ockham's razor is that the *number* of postulated entities should be minimized. One of the earliest known examples was when Copernicus (1473–1543) argued in favor of his stationary-sun theory of planetary motion by arguing that it endowed one cause (the motion of the earth around the sun) with many effects (the apparent motions of the planets). In contrast, his predecessor (Ptolemy) unwittingly duplicated the Earth's motion many times in order to "explain" the same effects. Newton's version of Ockham's razor appeared in his first and second rules of philosophizing: "We are to admit no more causes of natural things than such as are both true and sufficient to explain their appearances. Therefore, to the same natural effects we must, as far as possible, assign the same causes."

Both aspects arise in modern empirical science, including psychology. When data are modeled by an equation or set of equations, they are usually designed so that all theoretical parameters can be *uniquely* estimated for the data using standard statistical estimation techniques (like the method of least squares, or maximum likelihood estimation). When this condition is satisfied, the parameters are said to be *identifiable*. This practice ensures the satisfaction of Ockham's razor in its first aspect. For example, suppose we have a set of data consisting in n pairs of (x, y) values: $\{(x_1, y_1), (x_2, y_2), \ldots (x_n, y_n)\}$. The model $y_i = a + b\, x_i$, for $i = 1, 2, \ldots n$, is identifiable because the parameters a and b can be uniquely estimated by sufficiently varied data. But a model like $y_i = a + (b + c)\, x_i$ is not identifiable, because many pairs of values of b and c fit the data equally well. Different parameter values make no empirical difference.

Normally, this desideratum is so natural and common-sensical that nonidentifiable models are not used. B. F. Skinner resisted the introduction of intervening variables in BEHAVIORISM for this reason. However, they do arise in NEURAL NETWORKS (see also COGNITIVE MODELING, CONNECTIONIST). In the simplest possible two-layered network, one would have one input neuron, or node, with an activation x, one hidden node, with activation y, and an output node, with activation z, where the output is a function of the hidden node activation, which is in turn a function of the input activation. In a simple linear network, this would mean that $z = a.y$, and $y = b.x$, where a and b are the connection weights between the layers. The connection weights are the parameters of the model. But the hidden activations are not observed, and so the only testable consequence of the model is the input-output function, $z = (ab)x$. Different pairs of values of the parameters a and b lead to the same input-output function. Therefore, the model is not identifiable.

Perhaps the more difficult problem is to understand how to draw the line in cases in which extra parameters make a difference, but a very little difference. This is the second aspect of Ockham's razor. For example, how do we select between competing models like $y = a + b\,x_1$ and $y = a + b\,x_1 + c\,x_2$, where the parameters a, b, and c are *adjustable* parameters that range over a set of possible values? Each equation represents a different model, which may be thought of as a *family* of curves. Under one common notion of simplicity, the first *model* is simpler than the second model because it has fewer adjustable parameters. Simplicity is measured by the size, or dimension, of the *family* of curves. (Note that, in this definition, models are of greater or lesser simplicity, but all curves are equally simple because their equations have zero adjustable parameters.)

How does one decide when an additional parameter makes "enough" of an empirical difference to justify its inclusion, or when an additional parameter is "beyond necessity"? If the choice is among models that fit the data *equally well* (where the fit of a model is given by the fit of its best case), then the answer is that simplicity should break the tie. But in practice, competing models do not fit equally well. For instance, when one model is a special case of, or nested in, another (as in the previous example), the more complex model will always fit better (if only because it is able to better fit the noise in the data).

So, the real question is: How much better must the complex model fit before we say that the extra parameter is necessary? Or, when should the better fit of the complex model be "explained away" as arising from the greater tendency of complex models to fit noise? How do we trade off fit with simplicity? That is the motivation for standard significance testing in statistics. Notice that significance testing does not always favor the simpler model. Nor is the practice motivated by any belief in the simplicity of nature. In fact, when enough data accumulates, the choice will favor the complex model eventually even if the added parameters have very small (but nonzero) values.

In recent years, there have been many new model selection criteria developed in statistics, all of which define simplicity in terms of the paucity of parameters, or the dimension of a model (see Forster and Sober 1994 for a nontechnical introduction). These include Akaike's Information Criterion (AIC; Akaike 1974, 1985), the Bayesian Information Criterion (BIC; Schwarz 1978), and MINIMUM DESCRIPTION LENGTH (MDL; Rissanen 1989). They trade off simplicity and fit a little differently, but all of them address the same problem as significance testing: Which of the estimated "curves" from competing models best represents reality? This work has led to a clear understanding of why this form of simplicity is relevant to that question.

However, the paucity of parameters is a limited notion. It does not mark a difference in simplicity between a wiggly curve and a straight curve. Nor does it capture the idea of simpler theories having fewer numbers of fundamental principles or laws. Nor does it reward the repeated use of equations of the same *form*. A natural response is to insist that there must be other kinds of simplicity or unification that are relevant to theory choice. But there are well-known problems in defining these alternative notions of simplicity (e.g., Priest 1976; Kitcher 1976). Moreover, there are no precise proposals about how these notions of simplicity are traded off with fit. Nor are there any compelling ideas about why such properties *should* count in favor of one theory being closer to the truth than another.

See also EXPLANATION; JUSTIFICATION; SCIENTIFIC THINKING AND ITS DEVELOPMENT; SIMILARITY; UNITY OF SCIENCE

—Malcolm R. Forster

References

Akaike, H. (1974). A new look at the statistical model identification. *IEEE Transactions on Automatic Control,* vol. AC-19: 716–723.

Akaike, H. (1985). Prediction and entropy. In A. C. Atkinson and S. E. Fienberg, Eds., *A Celebration of Statistics.* New York: Springer, pp. 1–24.

Forster, M. R., and E. Sober. (1994). How to tell when simpler, more unified, or less ad hoc theories will provide more accurate predictions. *British Journal for the Philosophy of Science* 45: 1–35.

Kitcher, P. (1976). Explanation, conjunction and unification. *Journal of Philosophy* 73: 207–212.

Priest, G. (1976). Gruesome simplicity. *Philosophy of Science* 43: 432–437.

Rissanen, J. (1989). *Stochastic Complexity in Statistical Inquiry.* Singapore: World Books.

Schwarz, G. (1978). Estimating the dimension of a model. *Annals of Statistics* 6: 461–465.

Further Readings

Forster, M. R. (1995). The curve-fitting problem. In R. Audi, Ed., *The Cambridge Dictionary of Philosophy.* Cambridge University Press.

Forster, M. R. (1999). The new science of simplicity. In H. A. Keuzenkamp, M. McAleer, and A. Zellner, Eds., *Simplicity, Inference and Economertric Modelling.* Cambridge: Cambridge University Press.

Gauch, H. G., Jr. (1993). Prediction, parsimony and noise. *American Scientist* 81: 468–478.

Geman, S., E. Bienenstock, and R. Doursat. (1992). Neural networks and the bias/variance dilemma. *Neural Computation* 4: 1–58.

Jefferys, W., and J. Berger. (1992). Ockham's razor and Bayesian analysis. *American Scientist* 80: 64–72.

Popper, K. (1959). In *The Logic of Scientific Discovery.* London: Hutchinson.

Sakamoto, Y., M. Ishiguro, and G. Kitagawa. (1986). *Akaike Information Criterion Statistics.* Dordrecht: Kluwer.

Sober, E. (1990). Let's razor Ockham's razor. In D. Knowles, Ed., *Explanation and Its Limits.* Royal Institute of Philosophy supp. vol. 27. Cambridge: Cambridge University Press, pp. 73–94.

Parsing

See PSYCHOLINGUISTICS; SENTENCE PROCESSING

Pattern Recognition and Feedforward Networks

A feedforward network can be viewed as a graphical representation of a parametric function which takes a set of input values and maps them to a corresponding set of output values (Bishop 1995). Figure 1 shows an example of a feedforward network of a kind that is widely used in practical applications.

Vertices in the graph represent either inputs, outputs, or "hidden" variables, while the edges of the graph correspond to the adaptive parameters. We can write down the analytic function corresponding to this network as follows. The output of the jth hidden node is obtained by first forming a weighted linear combination of the d input values x_i to give

$$a_j = \sum_{i=1}^{d} u_{ji}x_i + b_j. \tag{1}$$

The value of hidden variable j is then obtained by transforming the linear sum in (1) using an activation function $g(\cdot)$ to give

$$z_j = g(a_j). \tag{2}$$

Finally, the outputs of the network are obtained by forming linear combinations of the hidden variables to give

$$a_k = \sum_{j=1}^{M} v_{kj}z_j + c_k. \tag{3}$$

The parameters $\{u_{ji}, v_{kj}\}$ are called *weights* while $\{b_j, c_k\}$ are called *biases,* and together they constitute the adaptive parameters in the network. There is a one-to-one correspondence between the variables and parameters in the analytic function and the nodes and edges respectively in the graph.

Historically, feedforward networks were introduced as models of biological neural networks (McCulloch and Pitts 1943), in which nodes corresponded to neurons and edges corresponded to synapses, and with an activation function $g(a)$ given by a simple threshold. The recent development of feedforward networks for pattern recognition applications has, however, proceeded largely independently of any biological modeling considerations.

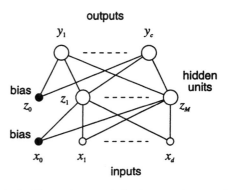

Figure 1. A feedforward network having two layers of adaptive parameters.

The goal in pattern recognition is to use a set of example solutions to some problem to infer an underlying regularity which can subsequently be used to solve new instances of the problem. Examples include handwritten digit recognition, medical image screening, and fingerprint identification. In the case of feedforward networks, the set of example solutions (called a training set) comprises instances of input values together with corresponding desired output values. The training set is used to define an error function in terms of the discrepancy between the predictions of the network for given inputs and the desired values of the outputs given by the training set. A common example of an error function would be the squared difference between desired and actual output, summed over all outputs and summed over all patterns in the training set. The learning process then involves adjusting the values of the parameters to minimize the value of the error function. Once the network has been trained, that is, once suitable values for the parameters have been determined, new inputs can be applied and the corresponding predictions (i.e., network outputs) calculated.

The use of layered feedforward networks for pattern recognition was widely studied in the 1960s. However, effective learning algorithms were only known for the case of networks in which, at most, one of the layers comprised adaptive interconnections. Such networks were known variously as perceptrons (Rosenblatt 1962) and adalines (Widrow and Lehr 1990), and were seriously limited in their capabilities (Minsky and Papert 1969/1990). Research into artificial NEURAL NETWORKS was stimulated during the 1980s by the development of new algorithms capable of training networks with more than one layer of adaptive parameters (Rumelhart, Hinton, and Williams 1986). A key development involved the replacement of the nondifferentiable threshold activation function by a differentiable nonlinearity, which allows gradient-based optimization algorithms to be applied to the minimization of the error function. The second key step was to note that the derivatives could be calculated in a computationally efficient manner using a technique called backpropagation, so called because it has a graphical interpretation in terms of a propagation of error signals from the output nodes backward through the network. Originally these gradients were used in simple steepest-descent algorithms to minimize the error function. More recently, however, this has given way to the use of more sophisticated algorithms, such as conjugate gradients, borrowed from the field of nonlinear optimization (Gill, Murray, and Wright 1981).

During the late 1980s and early 1990s, research into feedforward networks emphasized their role as function approximators. For example, it was shown that a network consisting of two layers of adaptive parameters could approximate any continuous function from the inputs to the outputs with arbitrary accuracy provided the number of hidden units is sufficiently large and provided the network parameters are set appropriately (Hornik, Stinchcombe, and White 1989). More recently, however, feedforward networks have been studied from the much richer probabilistic perspective (see PROBABILITY, FOUNDATIONS OF), which sets neural networks firmly within the field of *statistical pattern recognition* (Fukunaga 1990). For instance, the outputs of the network can be given a probabilistic interpretation, and the role of network training is then to model the probability distribution of the target data, conditioned on the input variables. Similarly, the minimization of an error function can be motivated from the well-established principle of maximum likelihood that is widely used in statistics. An important advantage of this probabilistic viewpoint is that it provides a theoretical foundation for the study and application of feedforward networks (see STATISTICAL LEARNING THEORY), as well as motivating the development of new models and new learning algorithms.

A central issue in any pattern recognition application is that of generalization, in other words the performance of the trained model when applied to previously unseen data. It should be emphasized that a small value of the error function for the training data set does not guarantee that future predictions will be similarly accurate. For example, a large network with many parameters may be capable of achieving a small error on the training set, and yet fail to model the underlying distribution of the data and hence achieve poor performance on new data (a phenomenon sometimes called "overfitting"). This problem can be approached by limiting the complexity of the model, thereby forcing it to extract regularities in the data rather than simply memorizing the training set. From a fully probabilistic viewpoint, learning in feedforward networks involves using the network to define a *prior* distribution over functions, which is converted to a *posterior* distribution once the training data have been observed. It can be formalized through the framework of BAYESIAN LEARNING, or equivalently through the MINIMUM DESCRIPTION LENGTH approach (MacKay 1992; Neal 1996).

In practical applications of feedforward networks, attention must be paid to the representation used for the data. For example, it is common to perform some kind of preprocessing on the raw input data (perhaps in the form of "feature extraction") before they are used as inputs to the network. Often this preprocessing takes into consideration any prior knowledge we might have about the desired properties of the solution. For instance, in the case of digit recognition we know that the identity of the digit should be invariant to the position of the digit within the input image.

Feedforward neural networks are now well established as an important technique for solving pattern recognition prob-

lems, and indeed there are already many commercial applications of feedforward neural networks in routine use.

See also COGNITIVE MODELING, CONNECTIONIST; CONNECTIONIST APPROACHES TO LANGUAGE; MCCULLOCH; NEURAL NETWORKS; PITTS; RECURRENT NETWORKS

—*Christopher M. Bishop*

References

Anderson, J. A., and E. Rosenfeld, Eds. (1988). *Neurocomputing: Foundations of Research.* Cambridge, MA: MIT Press.

Bishop, C. M. (1995). *Neural Networks for Pattern Recognition.* Oxford: Oxford University Press.

Fukunaga, K. (1990). *Introduction to Statistical Pattern Recognition.* 2nd ed. San Diego: Academic Press.

Gill, P. E., W. Murray, and M. H. Wright. (1981). *Practical Optimization.* London: Academic Press.

Hornik, K., M. Stinchcombe, and H. White. (1989). Multilayer feedforward networks are universal approximators. *Neural Networks* 2(5): 359–366.

MacKay, D. J. C. (1992). A practical Bayesian framework for back-propagation networks. *Neural Computation* 4(3): 448–472.

McCulloch, W. S., and W. Pitts. (1943). A logical calculus of the ideas immanent in nervous activity. *Bulletin of Mathematical Biophysics* 5: 115–133. Reprinted in Anderson and Rosenfeld (1988).

Minsky, M. L., and S. A. Papert. (1969/1990). *Perceptrons.* Cambridge, MA: MIT Press.

Neal, R. M. (1996). *Bayesian Learning for Neural Networks.* Lecture Notes in Statistics 118. Springer.

Rosenblatt, F. (1962). *Principles of Neurodynamics: Perceptrons and the Theory of Brain Mechanisms.* Washington, DC: Spartan.

Rumelhart, D. E., G. E. Hinton, and R. J. Williams. (1986). Learning internal representations by error propagation. In D. E. Rumelhart, J. L. McClelland, and the PDP Research Group, Eds., *Parallel Distributed Processing: Explorations in the Microstructure of Cognition,* vol. 1: *Foundations.* Cambridge, MA: MIT Press, pp. 318–362. Reprinted in Anderson and Rosenfeld (1988).

Widrow, B., and M. A. Lehr. (1990). 30 years of adaptive neural networks: Perceptron, madeline, and backpropagation. *Proceedings of the IEEE* 78(9): 1415–1442.

Further Readings

Anderson, J. A., A. Pellionisz, and E. Rosenfeld, Eds. (1990). *Neurocomputing 2: Directions for Research.* Cambridge, MA: MIT Press.

Arbib, M. A. (1987). *Brains, Machines, and Mathematics.* 2nd ed. New York: Springer-Verlag.

Bishop, C. M. (1994). Neural networks and their applications. *Review of Scientific Instruments* 65(b): 1803–1832.

Bishop, C. M., P. S. Haynes, M. E. U. Smith, T. N. Todd, and D. L. Trotman. (1995). Real-time control of a tokamak plasma using neural networks. *Neural Computation* 7: 206–217.

Block, H. D. (1962). The perceptron: A model for brain functioning. *Reviews of Modern Physics* 34(1): 123–135. Reprinted in Anderson and Rosenfeld (1988).

Broomhead, D. S., and D. Lowe. (1988). Multivariable functional interpolation and adaptive networks. *Complex Systems* 2: 321–355.

Duda, R. O., and P. E. Hart. (1973). *Pattern Classification and Scene Analysis.* New York: Wiley.

Geman, S., E. Bienenstock, and R. Doursat. (1992). Neural networks and the bias/variance dilemma. *Neural Computation* 4(1): 1–58.

Hertz, J., A. Krogh, and R. G. Palmer. (1991). *Introduction to the Theory of Neural Computation*. Redwood City, CA: Addison-Wesley.

Jacobs, R. A., M. I. Jordan, S. J. Nowlan, and G. E. Hinton. (1991). Adaptive mixtures of local experts. *Neural Computation* 3(1): 79–87.

Jordan, M. I., and C. M. Bishop. (1997). Neural networks. In A. B. Tucker, Ed., *The Computer Science and Engineering Handbook*. Boca Raton, FL: CRC Press, pp. 536–556.

Le Cun, Y., B. Boser, J. S. Denker, D. Henderson, R. E. Howard, W. Hubbard, and L. D. Jackel. (1989). Backpropagation applied to handwritten zip code recognition. *Neural Computation* 1(4): 541–551.

Lowe, D., and A. R. Webb. (1990). Exploiting prior knowledge in network optimization: An illustration from medical prognosis. *Network: Computation in Neural Systems* 1(3): 299–323.

MacKay, D. J. C. (1995). Bayesian non-linear modelling for the 1993 energy prediction competition. In G. Heidbreder, Ed., *Maximum Entropy and Bayesian Methods, Santa Barbara 1993*. Dordrecht: Kluwer.

MacKay, D. J. C. (1995). Probable networks and plausible predictions—a review of practical Bayesian methods for supervised neural networks. *Network: Computation in Neural Systems* 6(3): 469–505.

Penfield, Wilder

Our knowledge about the organization of the CEREBRAL CORTEX is derived, in part, from the search for a therapeutic intervention for a particular disease—*epilepsy*. Wilder Penfield (1891–1976), stimulated by his postgraduate work with Otfrid Foerster, a pioneer in the development of modern neurosurgical procedures to relieve seizures in epileptic patients, began a prolonged scientific study of the surgical treatment of epilepsy at McGill University in 1928. By 1934, Penfield had founded Montreal Neurological Institute (MNI), which he served as director until his retirement in 1960. Penfield was soon joined by others, including Herbert Jasper, who introduced the EEG to the operating room, and by D. O. HEBB and Brenda Milner, who introduced the idea of systematic neuropsychological assessment of surgical patients. The foundation and the establishment of the endowment for the MNI, or "Neuro," which has become an international center for training, research, and treatment related to the brain and diseases of the nervous system, may be Penfield's most lasting legacy. The idea of a neurological hospital, integrated with a multidisciplinary brain research complex, providing a center where a mutidisciplinary team of both scientists and physicians might study the brain, has served as a model for the establishment of similar units throughout the world.

By the mid-1930s, Penfield and his colleagues were employing electrical stimulation and systematic mapping techniques adapted from physiological work with animals. These procedures were employed to aid in excising those regions of brain tissue that served as the focus of epileptic activity in patients whose seizures were not adequately controlled by available drugs. Electrical brain stimulation provided the "gold standard" by which the functional properties of brain regions might be determined. This *Montreal Procedure* was used both to localize the epileptogenic tissue itself and to minimize surgical damage by first mapping critical motor, somatosensory, language-related brain tissue by applying brief, low-voltage electrical current through thin wire electrodes to sites on the cortical surface of the brains of fully conscious human patients. It was then noted which parts of the body moved, or what bodily sensations were reported in response to each stimulus. By the late 1930s, Penfield and his coworkers had created the first systematic maps of both the human primary motor and somatosensory cortex. Their data indicated there was a point-to-point relation between parts of the body and these neocortical regions (i.e., that motor and somatosensory cortex were both somatotopically organized) and that these distributions of the body surface were distorted, leading to the construction of his famous sensory and motor homunculistylized cartoons of the body surface with the relative prominence of different body parts reflecting the extent of their representation in the cortex. A *sensorimotor* integrative conception of brain organization was also promoted by his finding that 25 percent of the stimulation points yielding sensory experiences were located in precentral *motor* cortical regions. Subsequent investigation of nonhuman subjects led to identification of analogous maps or representations of visual and auditory external worlds and, together with Penfield's own mapping work, helped shape our view of cortical organization for decades. While his original work suggested that there were several somatosensory cortical representations of the external environment, it was not until the late 1970s that more refined anatomical and physiological techniques revealed dozens of maps in each modality, rather than just one or two.

Careful study of hundreds of patients by Penfield and his coworkers (and more recently by George Ojemann and his colleagues at the University of Washington) also provided clear evidence of cerebral asymmetry or HEMISPHERIC SPECIALIZATION. For example, the pooled data from many patients yielded the first direct confirmation of conclusions inferred from previous postmortem correlations, by establishing a map of language-related zones of the left hemisphere that included not only the traditional areas of Paul BROCA and Carl Wernicke, but also the supplementary speech zone. Stimulation in these regions of the left hemisphere usually arrested (or initiated) speech during the stimulation period or produced other forms of language interference such as misnaming and impaired word repetition, whereas stimulation of the right hemisphere seldom did. Penfield's research also furnished other evidence that did not support traditional localizationist models of language. For example, stimulation of anterior and posterior speech zones had remarkably similar effects on speech function, and the extent of these cortical language zones varied considerably among patients.

Accounts of apparent awaking of long-lost childhood and other memories by temporal lobe epileptics during electrical stimulation of the region were recorded by Penfield in the 1930s. This data, together with evidence provided in the neuropsychological studies of such patients after surgery by Brenda Milner and others, made it clear to Penfield that the medial temporal region, including the HIPPOCAMPUS, was of special importance in respect to human MEMORY (and emotion).

Penfield's early observations on seizures arising from deep midline portions of the brain also had an important impact on the development of ideas about the neural substrate of CONSCIOUSNESS. In 1938 he proposed a *"centrencephalic"* system that stressed the role of the upper brain stem in the integration of higher functions. In arguing that consciousness is more closely related to the brainstem than the cortex, he foreshadowed Moruzzi and Magouns's (1949) conception about the role of the midbrain reticular formation. "Consciousness," he later wrote, "exists only in association with the passage of impulses through ever-changing circuits between the brainstem and cortex. One can not say that consciousness is here or there. But certainly without centrencephalic integration, it is nonexistent." Penfield's lifelong search for a better understanding of the functional organization of the brain and its disorders during epileptic seizures is symbolized by this hypothesis of the central integrating mechanism. Never localized in any specific area of gray matter, but "in wider-ranging mechanisms," it represented a conceptual bridge he envisaged between brain and mind (cf. MIND-BODY PROBLEM).

See also CONSCIOUSNESS, NEUROBIOLOGY OF; CORTICAL LOCALIZATION, HISTORY OF

—*Richard C. Tees*

References

Moruzzi, G., and H. W. Magoun. (1949). Brain stem reticular formation and activation of EEG. *EEG and Clinical Neurophysiology* 1: 455–473.
Penfield, W. (1938). The cerebral cortex in man: 1. The cerebral cortex and consciousness. *Archives of Neurology and Psychiatry* 40: 417–442.

Further Readings

Finger, S. (1994). *The Origins of Neuroscience.* New York: Oxford University Press.
Hebb, D. O. (1949). *The Organization of Behavior: A Neuropsychological Theory.* New York: Wiley.
Hebb, D. O., and W. Penfield. (1940). Human behavior after extensive bilateral removals from the frontal lobe. *Archives of Neurology and Psychiatry* 44: 421–438.
Penfield, W. (1958). *The Excitable Cortex in Conscious Man.* Springfield, IL: Charles C. Thomas.
Penfield, W., and E. Boldrey. (1937). Somatic motor and sensory representation in the cerebral cortex of man as studied by electrical stimulation. *Brain* 60: 389–443.
Penfield, W., and H. Jasper. (1954). *Epilepsy and the Functional Anatomy of the Human Brain.* Boston: Little Brown.
Penfield, W., and B. Milner. (1958). Memory deficit produced by bilateral lesions in the hippocampal zone. *Archives of Neurology and Psychiatry* 79: 475–498.
Penfield, W., and T. Rasmussen. (1950). *The Cerebral Cortex of Man.* New York: MacMillan.
Penfield, W., and L. Roberts. (1959). *Speech and Brain Mechanisms.* Princeton, NJ: Princeton University Press.

Perception

See HAPTIC PERCEPTION; HIGH-LEVEL VISION; MID-LEVEL VISION; PERCEPTUAL DEVELOPMENT

Perception of Motion

See MOTION, PERCEPTION OF

Perceptrons

See COMPUTING IN SINGLE NEURONS; NEURAL NETWORKS; PATTERN RECOGNITION AND FEEDFORWARD NETWORKS; RECURRENT NETWORKS

Perceptual Development

Just a century ago it was widely believed that the world perceived by newborn infants was, in the words of WILLIAM JAMES, a "blooming, buzzing confusion." In the decades since then, developmental research has demonstrated dramatically that James's view was erroneous. The shift in view was prompted by research from various domains. In the 1930s, Piaget's detailed descriptions of his infant children and Gesell's charting of infants' motor milestones created a climate of interest in infants as research subjects and in developmental questions. The work of ethologists studying the behavior of animals in their natural habitats (COMPARATIVE PSYCHOLOGY) paved the way for careful observations of spontaneous activity in even the youngest animals. Observation of spontaneous activity ran counter to theories of stimulus-response (S-R) chaining and the radical BEHAVIORISM fashionable in the 1930s; at the same time, it inspired the design of new methods for studying infants, including methods for asking what infants perceive.

By the 1960s, methods for studying infant perception had multiplied as psychologists exploited infants' natural exploratory behaviors, especially looking. Preferential looking at one of two displays, habituation to one display followed by a new display, and a paired comparison test of old and new displays were highly effective methods for studying visual discrimination of simple contrasting properties and even more complex patterns. Spontaneous exploratory behavior was also the basis for research methods, particularly operant conditioning of responses such as sucking, head turning, or moving a limb. Methods which provide infants with opportunities to control their environment (e.g., operant conditioning, infant-controlled habituation) were shown to be more effective than methods without consequences for changing behavior (Horowitz et al. 1972). Psychologists found that they could also investigate what is perceived utilizing natural actions in controlled experimental situations, such as reaching for objects varying in bulk or attainability, and locomotion across surfaces varying in rigidity, pitfalls, obstacles, and slope. Methods borrowed from physiological research, including heart rate and electrophysiological responses, have been used effectively in studying sensitivity to change in stimulus dimensions. These measures, along with psychophysical procedures, have revealed impressive discriminatory abilities in very young infants. (See VISION AND LEARNING; AUDITION; TASTE; and SMELL.) Researchers are now discovering the precursors of some of these competencies during the fetal period of prenatal development.

Major research topics include development of perception of events, the persistent properties of objects, and the larger layout of surfaces. Five key points that emerge are the following:

1. The perception of events is prospective or forward-looking. One example is infants' differential response to approaching obstacles and apertures, the so-called looming studies (Yonas, Petterson, and Lockman 1979). Infants respond with defensive blinking and head retraction to approaching objects, but not to approaching apertures or to withdrawing objects. Studies of neonates reaching out to catch moving objects provide another compelling demonstration of anticipatory perception as skilled reaching develops (Hofsten 1983). Infants also anticipate occurrence of environmental happenings, for example, by looking toward the locus of a predictable event (Haith 1993).

2. Motion is important for revealing the persistent properties of events, objects, and layout of the world. A striking example is the perception of biological motion when visual information is minimized. When spots of light are placed on key joints (e.g., elbows, ankles, hips), and all other illumination is eliminated, observers immediately perceive a person engaging in a uniquely specified activity, such as walking, dancing, or lifting a heavy box, but only when the actor is moving. Infants differentiate these biological motion displays from inverted displays and from spots of light moving in a random fashion (Bertenthal 1993). Motion makes possible pickup of information about social (communicative) events, such as smiling and talking, at an early age. The role of motion is also critical in visual detection of constant properties of objects, such as unity, size, shape (SHAPE PERCEPTION), and substance. At four months of age, infants perceive the unity of an object despite partial occlusion by another object, provided that the occluded object is in motion (Kellman and Spelke 1983). Constant size of an object is given in changes in distance relative to self and background, and neonates appear to detect size as invariant (Slater, Mattock, and Brown 1990). Shape constancy, invariant over changes in orientation of an object, is perceived by five months (Gibson et al. 1979). Rigidity or elasticity of substance is differentiated via mouthing in neonates (Rochat 1983), and visually by five months (Gibson and Walker 1984). Methods of visual habituation and observation of grasping skills converge on evidence for perceiving these properties. Such convergence is not surprising, since exploration of object properties is naturally multimodal. Surface properties of objects, such as color (see COLOR VISION), are not necessarily dependent on motion, but texture of an object's surface is accessed by haptic as well as visual information and is differentiated early in the first year (SURFACE PERCEPTION; see also HAPTIC PERCEPTION).

3. Perception is multimodally unified (MULTISENSORY INTEGRATION). From the earliest moments of life, infants orient to sounds, particularly human voices, and they engage in active visual exploration of faces and sounding objects (Gibson 1988). In fact, infants as young as five months can match the sounds and visible motions of faces and voices in a bimodal matching task (Kuhl and Meltzoff 1982; Walker 1982). Infants can also match the sounds and visible motions of object events (Spelke 1976), evidently perceiving a unified event. At one month, infants appear to detect and unify haptic and visual information for object substance (Gibson and Walker 1984).

4. Properties of the larger layout are made available multimodally as motor skills and new action patterns develop. Experience and practice play an important role in this development. How far away things are must be perceived in units of body scale by infants. Observation of the hands, in relation to surrounding objects, occurs spontaneously within the first month (van der Meer, van der Weel, and Lee 1995). When reaching for objects emerges as a skill, judging not only the distance of an object but its size improves rapidly. Information for the major properties of the layout is best accessed when babies begin locomotion. While recognition of obstacles, approaching objects, and surface properties is not unprepared, experience in traversing the ground surface brings new lessons. Crawling infants tend to avoid a steep drop in the surface of support (Gibson and Walk 1960). The affordance of falling is perceived early in locomotor history, but becomes more dependable with experience in locomotion. Properties of the surface of support that afford locomotion (its rigidity, smoothness, slope, etc.) are detected by experienced crawling infants. They learn to cope effectively with steep slopes by avoiding them or adopting safe methods of travel, but the same infants as novice upright walkers attempt dangerous slopes and must learn new strategies (Adolph 1997). Bipedal locomotion requires extensive adjustments of perceptual and locomotor skills, as infants learn a new balancing act, using multimodal information from ankles, joints, and visual cues provided by flow patterns created by their own movements. Novice walkers fall down in a "moving room," despite a firm and stable unmoving ground surface (Lee and Aronson 1974). Flow patterns created by the room's motion give false information that they are falling forward or backward. Perceiving the world entails coperception of the self; in this case, via visual information from perspective changes in the room's walls in relation to vestibular information about one's own upright posture.

5. Infants perceive the SELF as a unit distinct from the world (see SELF-KNOWLEDGE). By four to five months, infants watch their own legs moving currently on a television screen, contrasted with views of similarly clad legs of another infant or their own at an earlier moment

(Bahrick and Watson 1985). They reliably prefer to gaze at the novel display rather than their own ongoing movements. However, introduction of a target that can be kicked changes the preference to monitoring the ongoing self kicking at the target (Morgan and Rochat 1995). An opportunity for making contact with an object provides motivation for controlling the encounter. Considerable other research in a contingent reinforcement situation (e.g., kicking to rotate a mobile) confirms infants' perception of a self in control. Disruption of control results in frustration and emotional disturbance (Lewis, Sullivan, and Brooks-Gunn 1985).

Early reaction to the explosion of knowledge about the perceptual abilities of young infants was a burst of astonished admiration ("Aren't babies wonderful?"), and little concern was given to how development progresses, although previously popular Piagetian views were questioned. Three current views vary in their assumptions about processes involved in perceptual development. Two are construction theories: (1) The information processing view assumes that bare sensory input is subject to cognitive processing that constructs meaningful perception. (2) The nativist view assumes that rules about order governing events in the world are inherently given and used to interpret observed events. (3) The third view combines an ecological approach to perception and a systems view. Infants actively seek information that comes to specify identities, places, and affordances in the world. Processes that influence development are the progressive growth and use of action systems, and learning through experience. Perceptual learning is viewed as a selective process, beginning with exploratory activity, leading to observation of consequences, and to selection based on two criteria, an affordance fit and reduction of uncertainty, exemplified by detection of order and unity in what is perceived.

We know much less about perceptual development after the first two years. After infancy, perceptual development takes place mainly in complex tasks such as athletic skills, tool use, way-finding, steering vehicles, using language, and READING—all tasks in which experience and learning become more and more specialized (cf. COGNITIVE DEVELOPMENT). Theoretical applications to specialized tasks involving perceptual learning can be profitable (Abernathy 1993).

See also AFFORDANCES; ECOLOGICAL PSYCHOLOGY; IMITATION; INFANT COGNITION; NATIVISM; PIAGET

—*Eleanor J. Gibson, Marion Eppler, and Karen Adolph*

References

Abernathy, B. (1993). Searching for the minimal information for skilled perception and action. *Psychological Research* 55: 131–138.

Adolph, K. E. (1997). *Learning in the Development of Infant Locomotion.* Monographs of the Society for Research in Child Development. Serial No. 251, vol. 62, no. 3.

Bahrick, L. E., and J. S. Watson. (1985). Detection of intermodal proprioceptive-visual contingency as a potential basis of self-perception in infancy. *Developmental Psychology* 21: 963–973.

Bertenthal, B. (1993). Infants' perception of biological motions. In C. Granrud, Ed., *Visual Perception and Cognition in Infancy.* Hillsdale, NJ: Erlbaum, pp. 175–214.

Gibson, E. J. (1988). Exploratory behavior in the development of perceiving, acting and the acquiring of knowledge. *Annual Review of Psychology* 39: 1–41.

Gibson, E. J., and R. D. Walk. (1960). The "visual cliff." *Scientific American* 202: 64–71.

Gibson, E. J., and A. S. Walker. (1984). Development of knowledge of visual-tactual affordances of substance. *Child Development* 55: 453–460.

Gibson, E. J., C. J. Owsley, A. S. Walker, and J. S. Megaw-Nyce. (1979). Development of the perception of invariants: Substance and shape. *Perception* 5: 609–619.

Haith, M. M. (1993). Future-oriented processes in infancy: The case of visual expectations. In C. Granrud, Ed., *Visual Perception and Cognition in Infancy.* Hillsdale, NJ: Erlbaum, pp. 235–264.

Hofsten, C. von (1983). Catching skills in infancy. *Journal of Experimental Psychology: Human Perception and Performance* 2: 75–85.

Horowitz, F., L. Paden, W. Bhana, and P. Self. (1972). An "infant control" procedure for studying infant visual fixations. *Developmental Psychology* 7: 90.

Kellman, P. J., and E. Spelke. (1983). Perception of partly occluded objects in infancy. *Cognitive Psychology* 15: 483–524.

Kuhl, P. K., and A. N. Meltzoff. (1982). The bimodal perception of speech in infancy. *Science* 218: 1138–1141.

Lee, D. N., and E. Aronson. (1974). Visual proprioceptive control of standing in human infants. *Perception and Psychophysics* 15: 529–532.

Lewis, M., M. W. Sullivan, and J. Brooks-Gunn. (1985). Emotional behavior during the teaming of a contingency in early infancy. *British Journal of Developmental Psychology* 3: 307–316.

Morgan, R., and P. Rochat. (1995). The perception of self-produced leg movements in self- vs. object-oriented contexts by 3- to 5-month-old infants. In B. C. Bardy, R. J. Bootsma, and Y. Guiard, Eds., *Studies in Perception and Action* 3. Hillsdale, NJ: Erlbaum.

Rochat, P. (1983). Oral touch in young infants: Response to variations of nipple characteristics in the first month of life. *International Journal of Behavioral Development* 6: 123–133.

Slater, A., A. Mattock, and E. Brown. (1990). Size constancy at birth: Newborn infants' responses to retinal and real size. *Journal of Experimental Child Psychology* 49: 314–322.

Spelke, E. S. (1976). Infants' intermodal perception of events. *Cognitive Psychology* 8: 533–560.

van der Meer, A. L. H., F. R. van der Weel, and D. N. Lee. (1995). The functional significance of arm movements in neonates. *Science* 267: 693–695.

Walker, A. S. (1982). Intermodal perception of expressive behavior by human infants. *Journal of Experimental Child Psychology* 23: 514–535.

Yonas, A., L. Petterson, and J. Lockman. (1979). Young infants' sensitivity to optical information for collision. *Canadian Journal of Psychology* 33: 1285–1290.

Further Readings

Bertenthal, B., and R. K. Clifton. (1997). Perception and action. In D. Kuhn and R. Siegler, Eds., *Handbook of Child Psychology,* vol. 2: *Cognition, Perception and Language.* New York: Wiley, pp. 51–102.

Bertenthal, B. (1996). Origins and early development of perception, action, and representation. *Annual Reviews of Psychology* 47: 431–459.

Fantz, R. L. (1961). The origins of form perception. *Scientific American* 204: 66–72.

Gesell, A. (1928). *Infancy and Human Growth.* New York: Macmillan.

Gibson, E. J. (1969). *Principles of Perceptual Learning and Development.* New York: Appleton-Century-Crofts.

Gibson, E. J., and E. S. Spelke. (1983). The development of perception. In P. H. Mussen, Ed., *Handbook of Child Psychology,* 4th ed., vol. 3: *Cognitive Development.* New York: Wiley, pp. 1–76.

Johansson, G. (1973). Visual perception of biological motion and a model for its analysis. *Perception and Psychophysics* 14: 201–211.

Piaget, J. (1952). *The Origins of Intelligence in Children.* New York: International Universities Press.

Teller, D. Y. (1979). The forced-choice preferential looking procedure: A psychophysical technique for use with human infants. *Infant Behavior and Development* 2: 135–153.

Phantom Limb

Phantom limbs occur in 95 to 100 percent of amputees who lose an arm or leg. The phantom is usually described as having a tingling feeling and a definite shape that resembles the somatosensory experience of the physical limb before amputation. It is reported to move through space in much the same way as the normal limb would move when the person walks, sits down, or stretches out on a bed. At first, the phantom limb feels perfectly normal in size and shape —so much so that the amputee may reach out for objects with the phantom hand, or try to step onto the floor with the phantom leg. As time passes, however, the phantom limb begins to change shape. The arm or leg becomes less distinct and may fade away altogether, so that the phantom hand or foot seems to be hanging in midair. Sometimes, the limb is slowly "telescoped" into the stump until only the hand or foot remains at the stump tip.

Amputation is not essential to the occurrence of a phantom. After avulsion of the brachial plexus of the arm, without injury to the arm itself, most patients report a phantom arm that is usually extremely painful. Even nerve destruction is not necessary. About 95 percent of patients who receive an anesthetic block of the brachial plexus for surgery of the arm report a vivid phantom, usually at the side or over the chest, which is unrelated to the position of the real arm when the eyes are closed but "jumps" into it when the patient looks at the arm. Similarly, a spinal anesthetic block of the lower body produces reports of phantom legs in most patients, and total section of the spinal cord at thoracic levels leads to reports of a phantom body, including genitalia and many other body parts, in virtually all patients.

The most astonishing feature of the phantom limb is its "reality" to the amputee, which is enhanced by wearing an artificial arm or leg; the prosthesis feels real, "fleshed out." Amputees in whom the phantom leg has begun to "telescope" into the stump, so that the foot is felt to be above floor level, report that the phantom fills the artificial leg when it is strapped on and the phantom foot now occupies the space of the artificial foot in its shoe. The reality of the phantom is reinforced by the experience of details of the limb before amputation. For example, the person may feel a painful bunion that had been on the foot or even a tight ring on a phantom finger.

Phantoms of other body parts feel just as real as limbs do. Heusner describes two men who underwent amputation of the penis. One of them, during a four-year period, was intermittently aware of a painless but always erect phantom penis. The other man had severe PAIN of the phantom penis. Phantom bladders and rectums have the same quality of reality. The bladder may feel so real that patients, after a bladder removal, sometimes complain of a full bladder and even report that they are urinating. Patients with a phantom rectum may actually feel that they are passing gas or feces. Menstrual cramps may continue to be felt after a hysterectomy. A painless phantom breast, in which the nipple is the most vivid part, is reported by about 25 percent of women after a mastectomy and 13 percent feel pain in the phantom.

The reality of the phantom body is evident in paraplegic patients who suffer a complete break of the spinal cord. Even though they have no somatic sensation or voluntary movement below the level of the break, they often report that they still feel their legs and lower body. The phantom appears to inhabit the body when the person's eyes are open and usually moves coordinately with visually perceived movements of the body. Initially, patients may realize the dissociation between the two when they see their legs stretched out on the road after an accident yet feel them to be over the chest or head. Later, the phantom becomes coordinate with the body, and dissociation is rare.

Descriptions given by amputees and paraplegic patients indicate the range of qualities of experience of phantom body parts. Touch, pressure, warmth, cold, and many kinds of pain are common. There are also feelings of itch, tickle, wetness, sweatiness, and tactile texture. Even the experience of fatigue due to movement of the phantom limb is reported. Furthermore, male paraplegics with total spinal sections report feeling erections, and paraplegic women describe sexual sensations in the perineal area. Both describe feelings of pleasure, including orgasms.

A further striking feature of the phantom limb or any other body part, including half of the body in many paraplegics, is that it is perceived as an integral part of one's SELF. Even when a phantom foot dangles "in midair" (without a connecting leg) a few inches below the stump, it still moves appropriately with the other limbs and is unmistakably felt to be part of one's body-self. The fact that the experience of "self" is subserved by specific brain mechanisms is demonstrated by the converse of a phantom limb —the denial that a part of one's body belongs to one's self. Typically, the person, after a lesion of the right parietal lobe or any of several other brain areas, denies that a side of the body is part of himself.

There is convincing evidence that a substantial number of children who are born without all or part of a limb feel a vivid phantom of the missing part. The long-held belief that phantoms are experienced only when an amputation has occurred after the age of six or seven years is not true. Phantoms are experienced by about 20 percent of children who are born without all or part of a limb (congenital limb deficiency), and 20 percent of these children report pain in their phantom. Persons with congenital limb deficiency sometimes perceive a phantom for the first time after minor surgery or an injury of the stump when they are adults.

The innate neural substrate implied by these data does not mean that sensory experience is irrelevant. Learning obviously plays a role because persons' phantoms often assume the shape of the prosthesis, and persons with a deformed leg or a painful corn may report, after amputation, that the phantom is deformed or has a corn. That is, sensory inputs play an important role in the experience of the phantom limb. Heredity and environment clearly act together to produce the phenomena of phantom limbs.

See also ILLUSIONS; SENSATIONS; WHAT-IT'S-LIKE

—*Ronald Melzack*

Further Readings

Bors, E. (1951). Phantom limbs of patients with spinal cord injury. *Archives of Neurology and Psychiatry* 66: 610–631.

Heusner, A. P. (1950) Phantom genitalia. *Transactions of the American Neurological Association* 75: 128–131.

Katz, J. (1993). The reality of phantom limbs. *Motivation and Emotion* 17: 147–179.

Katz, J., and R. Melzack. (1990). Pain "memories" in phantom limbs: Review and clinical observations. *Pain* 43: 319–336.

Lacroix, R., R. Melzack, D. Smith, and N. Mitchell. (1992). Multiple phantom limbs in a child. *Cortex* 28: 503–507.

Melzack, R. (1989). Phantom limbs, the self and the brain. The D. O. Hebb Memorial Lecture *Canadian Psychology* 30: 1–16.

Melzack, R., and P. R. Bromage. (1973). Experimental phantom limbs. *Experimental Neurology* 39: 261–269.

Melzack, R., R. Israel, R. Lacroix, and G. Schultz. (1997). Phantom limbs in people with congenital limb deficiency or amputation in early childhood. *Brain* to appear.

Melzack, R., and J. D. Loeser. (1978). Phantom body pain in paraplegics: Evidence for a central "pattern generating mechanism for pain." *Pain* 4: 195–210.

Mesulam, M.-M. (1981). A cortical network for directed attention and unilateral neglect. *Annals of Neurology* 10: 309–325.

Riddoch, G. (1941). Phantom limbs and body shape. *Brain* 64: 197–222.

Saadah, E. S. M., and R. Melzack. (1994). Phantom limb experiences in congenital limb-deficient adults. *Cortex* 30: 479–485.

Sherman, R. A. (1997). *Phantom Pain*. New York: Plenum Press.

Philosophical Issues in Linguistics

See LINGUISTICS, PHILOSOPHICAL ISSUES

Philosophy of Mind

See INTRODUCTION: PHILOSOPHY

Phonetics

Speech is the most common medium by which language is transmitted. Phonetics is the science or study of the physical aspects of speech events. It has a long history. For centuries, phonetic descriptions of particular languages have been undertaken to preserve or reconstruct their pronunciation. Phonetics developed rapidly in the nineteenth century in connection with spelling reform, language (pronunciation) teaching, speech training for the deaf, stenographic shorthands, and the study of historical sound changes. Today phonetics is an interdisciplinary field combining aspects of linguistics, psychology (including perception and motor control), computer science, and engineering. However, in the United States especially, "phonetics" is commonly considered a subfield of linguistics, and "speech science" or "speech" is the more general term.

A common question among linguists and nonlinguists alike is, "What is the difference between phonetics and phonology?" One answer is that phonetics is concerned with actual physical properties that are measured or described with some precision, whereas phonology is concerned with (symbolic) categories. For example, the phonology of a language might describe and explain the allowed sequences of consonants in the language, and the phonetics of the language would describe and explain the physical properties of a given consonant in these different allowed sequences. Nonetheless, even though phonetics deals with physical properties, it is just as much concerned with linguistic knowledge as with behavior. It is not the case that phonology can be identified with "competence" and phonetics with "performance," for example.

Phonetics is usually divided into three areas: speech production, acoustics, and perception. Phoneticians want to understand not only how speech is produced, perceived, and acoustically structured, but how these mechanisms shape the sound systems of human languages. What is the range of speech sounds found in human languages? Why do languages prefer certain sounds and combinations of sounds? How does speech convey linguistic structure to listeners? These are some of the key questions in phonetics. Phoneticians stress that only if the array of sounds used across languages is studied can complete models of speech be developed.

Speech production is the basis of traditional phonetic transcription systems such as the International Phonetic Alphabet (IPA), as well as some phonological feature systems (Catford 1977; Ladefoged 1993; Laver 1994; see PHONOLOGY and DISTINCTIVE FEATURES). The components of speech production are the airstream mechanism (the process by which air flow for speech is initiated), phonation or voicing (production of a sound source by the vibrating vocal cords inside the larynx—this is the most important sound source in speech), ARTICULATION (modification of the phonation sound source, and introduction of additional sound sources, by the movements of articulators), and the oronasal process (modification of the sound source by the flow of air through the nose). Speech sounds are traditionally described as combinations of these components. On the other hand, PROSODY (the suprasegmental variation of loudness, length, and pitch that makes some segments, or larger groupings of segments, more prominent or otherwise set off from others) is traditionally described not in speech-production terms but more in terms of the dimensions of amplitude, duration, and frequency (Lehiste 1970; see STRESS, LINGUISTICS; TONE).

Speech acoustics concerns the properties of speech transmitted from speaker to hearer. Speech sounds are usually described in terms of their prominent frequency components and the durations of intervals within each sound. The source-filter theory of speech production and acoustics (Fant 1960; Stevens, forthcoming) describes speech as the result of modifying acoustic sources by vocal-tract filter functions. The acoustic sources in speech include phonation (described above), noise produced in the larynx (such as for aspiration and breathiness), and noise produced by air flowing through a constriction anywhere in the vocal tract (such as for a fricative sound or after the release of a stop). Every speech sound must involve one or more such sources. The source(s) is then modified by the filter function of the vocal tract. The most important aspect of this filtering is that the airways of the vocal tract have particular resonances, called formants, which serve to enhance any corresponding frequencies in a source. The resonance frequencies depend on the size and shape of the airway, which in turn depend on the positions of all the articulators; thus, as the articulators move during speech, the formant frequencies are varied.

At the same time, phonetics can be divided into practical, experimental, and theoretical approaches. Practical phonetics concerns skills of aural transcription and oral production of speech sounds, usually in conjunction with a descriptive system like the IPA. Different levels of phonetic transcription are traditionally recognized. In a phonemic transcription, the only phonetic symbols used are those representing the phonemes, or basic sounds, of the language being transcribed. In an allophonic transcription, additional symbols are used, to represent more detailed variants (or allophones) of the phonemes. The more such detail included, the narrower the allophonic transcription.

Experimental phonetics is based on the use of laboratory equipment. Laboratory techniques (see Hardcastle and Laver 1997) are generally needed to understand exactly how some sound is produced and to detail its acoustic and/or perceptually relevant properties. When experimental phonetic methods are used to answer questions of interest to phonologists, it is sometimes called "laboratory phonology".

Certain acoustic measurements of speech sounds have become common, especially since the advent of the sound spectrograph, which produces visual displays (spectrograms) of frequency and intensity over time. The most common frequency measurements are the frequencies of vowel formants, of the formant transitions between consonants and vowels, and of the fundamental frequency of phonation. Changes in the source, and the durations of intervals with different sources, are also important in speech; for example the duration between the release of a stop and the onset of voicing (an interval filled with aspiration) is called voice onset time (VOT). There is now a wide range of the world's languages receiving detailed experimental descriptions in terms of these and other measures (e.g., Ladefoged and Maddieson 1996), although of course there remain many languages with unusual sounds whose production, acoustics, and/or perception are not well understood. Furthermore, manipulation of such measures to provide a range of artificial speech stimuli is an important tool of SPEECH PERCEPTION, in determining which acoustic properties matter most to listeners. Experimental phonetics

also contributes to the development of speech technology (see SPEECH SYNTHESIS and SPEECH RECOGNITION IN MACHINES).

Theoretical phonetics is concerned not only with theories of speech production, acoustics, and perception but also with theories to explain why languages have the sounds, grammatical structures, and historical sound changes that they do, and theories to describe the interrelationship of the more abstract patterns of phonology and the physical forms of speech sounds. Phoneticians look for recurring patterns of variation in sounds (see PHONOLOGICAL RULES AND PROCESSES), and then try to understand why they should occur. Phonetic constraints on phonology may be proposed as part of either a reductionist program (see REDUCTIONISM), in which phonology is reduced to phonetics, or an interface program, in which phonetics and phonology are usually recognized as separate components of a grammar.

—*Patricia A. Keating*

References

Catford, J. C. (1977). *Fundamental Problems in Phonetics.* Bloomington: Indiana University Press.

Fant, G. (1960). *Acoustic Theory of Speech Production.* The Hague: Mouton.

Hardcastle, W. J., and J. Laver. (1997). *The Handbook of Phonetic Sciences.* Oxford: Blackwell.

Ladefoged, P. (1993). *A Course in Phonetics.* 3rd ed. Fort Worth, TX and Orlando, FL: Harcourt Brace Jovanovich.

Ladefoged, P., and I. Maddieson. (1996). *The Sounds of the World's Languages.* Oxford: Blackwell.

Laver, J. (1994). *Principles of Phonetics.* Cambridge: Cambridge University Press.

Lehiste, I. (1970). *Suprasegmentals.* Cambridge, MA: MIT Press.

Stevens, K. N. (Forthcoming). *Acoustic Phonetics.* Cambridge, MA: MIT Press.

Further Readings

Asher, R. E., and E. J. A. Henderson, Eds. (1981). *Towards a History of Phonetics.* Edinburgh: Edinburgh University Press.

Connell, B., and A. Arvaniti, Eds. (1995). *Phonology and Phonetic Evidence: Papers in Laboratory Phonology* 4. Cambridge: Cambridge University Press.

Denes, P. B., and E. N. Pinson. (1993). *The Speech Chain: The Physics and Biology of Spoken Language.* 2nd ed. New York: W. H. Freeman and Company.

Docherty, G. J., and D. R. Ladd, Eds. (1992). *Gesture, Segment, Prosody: Papers in Laboratory Phonology* 2. Cambridge: Cambridge University Press.

Keating, P. A., Ed. (1994). *Phonological Structure and Phonetic Form: Papers in Laboratory Phonology* 3. Cambridge: Cambridge University Press.

Kingston, J., and M. E. Beckman, Eds. (1990). *Papers in Laboratory Phonology* 1: *Between the Grammar and Physics of Speech.* Cambridge: Cambridge University Press.

Ladefoged, P. (1996). *Elements of Acoustic Phonetics.* 2nd ed. Chicago: University of Chicago Press.

Phonological Rules and Processes

Phonological processes were first systematically studied in the nineteenth century under the rubric of sound laws relating the various Indo-European languages. In the twentieth century, attention shifted to a synchronic perspective, prompted by observations such as Edward SAPIR's that as part of their grammatical competence mature speakers unconsciously and effortlessly assign (sometimes radically) different pronunciations to a lexical item drawn from memory and inserted in different grammatical or prosodic contexts. For example, in the pronunciation of the word *átom* American English speakers "flap" the intervocalic consonant to [ɾ] and reduce the unstressed vowel to schwa [ə] so that it merges with *Adam*: ['ærəm]. The underlying phonemes emerge when the stress is shifted under affixation: *atóm-ic* [ətʰam-ɪk]. Processes also figure in the neutralizations found in child language such as the loss of the tongue-tip articulation of *r* so that *room* merges with *womb*.

Phonological processes fall into two broad categories: sound change and prosodic grouping. We briefly illustrate each type. In *in-articulate* versus *im-possible* the prefixal nasal *assimilates* the labial feature of the [p] thereby changing from [n] to [m]. *Dissimilation* alters neighboring sounds that share the same feature so that they become more distinct from one another (see DISTINCTIVE FEATURES). For example, the vocalic nucleus and offglide comprising the [au] diphthong of *how* share a retracted tongue position in most English dialects. In broad Australian English the nucleus is fronted to the [æ] vowel of *cat*: *h[æu]*. Assimilation and dissimilation are subject to a strict locality condition requiring that they apply in the context of the closest sound with the appropriate feature. The phonological features that define a sound are also subject to *deletion* and *insertion*: the former typically operates in prosodically weak contexts (reduction of unstressed vowels to schwa in *át[ə]m* but *[ə]tóm-ic*) and the latter in strong contexts (aspiration of [t] before stress in *a[tʰ]ómic*).

Processes of prosodic grouping include the organization of phonemes into syllables. In English a consonant cluster such as [rt] easily combines with the preceding vowel into a single syllable: monosyllabic *mart*. But in order to syllabify the inverse cluster [tr], a helping schwa is required: disyllabic *me.t[ə]r* (cf. *metr-ic*). Languages such as Japanese have simpler syllabic structures that bar syllable-internal consonant clusters and place rigid restrictions on syllable-final consonants. Accordingly, the [rt] cluster in a loanword such as French *courte* [kurt] 'short' receives two extra syllables when it is adapted into Japanese: *kuruto* (Shinohara 1997). At the next level of prosodic organization, syllables are grouped into strong-weak (trochaic) or weak-strong (iambic) rhythmic units known as metrical feet. Native Australian languages impose trochaic rhythm so that words have a canonical SsSsSs . . . syllabic structure in comparison to the iambic grouping sSsSsS . . . found in many Native American languages. English has trochaic grouping as shown by the strong-weak template imposed on nickname formation: *Elízabeth* shortens to Ss *Lísa*; sS *Elí* is impossible.

Some linguists (e.g., Stampe 1979) distinguish between "processes" that reflect phonetically motivated limitations on which sounds can appear where in pronunciation and more arbitrary and conventional "rules" that are typically restricted to particular morphological or lexical contexts

such as the voicing of [f] in the plural of *leaf*: *leaves* but *reefs* (*reeves*) and verbal *he leafs* (*leaves*) *through the paper*). A plausible but unsubstantiated hypothesis is that rules relate different lexical items stored in memory while processes operate online.

Phonological processes are often phonetically motivated, seeming either to enhance the perceptibility of a sound, especially in "strong" contexts or more formal speaking styles (aspiration of prestressed [t] in *a[tʰ]ómic*), or to minimize articulatory gestures, especially in "weak" contexts or fast tempos (flapping of the stop and reduction of the unstressed vowel of *átom* ['ærəm]). Besides a typology based on their formal properties, phonological processes are also usefully viewed as different solutions to a common phonetic difficulty. For example, the transition from the nasal to the fricative in the consonant cluster of *dense* is relatively complex because it requires synchronization of two independent gestures: raising the velum to shut off nasal airflow and shifting the tongue tip from a closure to a constriction. Common responses include insertion of a transitional stop *den[t]se* (to rhyme with *dents*) or deletion of the tongue-tip closure d[ɛ̃]s. An example from prosody is provided by the widespread tendency to avoid syllables beginning with a vowel. When morphological or syntactic rules juxtapose vowels, a variety of processes come into play to avoid a syllable break between the vowels. These include deletion of one of the vowels (Slavic), contraction of the vowels into a diphthong (Polynesian) or long vowel (Sanskrit), or insertion of a consonantal onset (British English intrusive [r] as in *the idea [r] is*).

Processes are characteristically myopic in the sense that in solving one phonetic problem they often create another. Popular London (Cockney) deletion of initial [h] creates a vowel cluster with the indefinite article ("a hedge" [ə ɛdʒ]— a situation that is otherwise avoided by substitution of the *an* allomorph (cf. "an edge" [ən ɛdʒ]; Wells 1982). To take another example (data from Bethin 1992), in Polish [n] assimilates the place of articulation of a following velar: *ba[ŋ]k* 'bank'. In the Southwestern dialect, the process is extended to clusters arising from the deletion of a weak vowel, whereas in the Northeastern dialect, such derived *nk* clusters remain unassimilated: *ganek* 'porch', *ga[ŋ]ka* SW versus *ga[n]ka* NE genitive singular. Many phonologists (e.g., Halle 1962) conclude from examples like this that processes apply in a linear sequence: in the Southwestern dialect, vowel deletion precedes nasal assimilation, whereas in the Northeastern dialect, nasal assimilation precedes vowel deletion (and so sees /ganek+a/ at its point of application). An alternative interpretation (Donegan and Stampe 1979) sees all processes as applying simultaneously to the input with each given the option to iterate (Southwestern) or not (Northeastern).

Although myopic, phonological processes are typically not self-defeating in the sense of recreating the same problem they are called upon to solve. An example is provided by the liquid [l,r] dissimilation inherited from Latin (Steriade 1995), in which the suffixal [l] of *nav-al, fat-al, mor-al* is turned into [r] when the stem contains an [l]: *stell-ar, lun-ar, column-ar, nucle-ar*. The process systematically blocks when an [r] intervenes between the suffixal and stem [l]'s:

flor-al, plur-al, later-al. If the point of the change is to avoid successive identical liquids, an output such as **flor-ar* is no better than the input *flor-al* and hence the process is suspended.

Providing empirical substantiation to the notion "phonetic motivation" as well as determining the principles that underlie the interaction of rules and constraints remain outstanding research objectives.

See also ARTICULATION; LANGUAGE PRODUCTION; PHONETICS; PHONOLOGY; PROSODY AND INTONATION; PROSODY AND INTONATION, PROCESSING ISSUES; STRESS, LINGUISTIC

—Michael Kenstowicz

References

Bethin, C. (1992). *Polish Syllables.* Columbus, OH: Slavica Publishers.

Donegan, P., and D. Stampe. (1979). The study of natural phonology. In D. Dinnsen, Ed., *Current Approaches to Phonological Theory.* Bloomington, IN: Indiana University Press, pp. 126–173.

Halle, M. (1962). Phonology in generative grammar. *Word* 18: 54–72.

Makkai, V. B. (1972). *Phonological Theory: Evolution and Current Practice.* New York: Holt.

Sapir, E. (1925). Sound patterns in language. *Language* 1: 37–51. Reprinted in Makkai 1972, pp. 13–21.

Sapir, E. (1933). The psychological reality of phonemes. Reprinted in Makkai 1972, pp. 22–31.

Shinohara, S. (1997). *Analyse phonologique de l'adaptation japonaise de mots étrangers.* Paris: Université de la Sorbonne Nouvelle, Paris 3.

Stampe, D. (1979). *A Dissertation on Natural Phonology.* New York: Garland.

Steriade, D. (1995). Underspecification and markedness. In J. Goldsmith, Ed., *Handbook of Phonological Theory.* Oxford: Blackwell, pp. 114–174.

Wells, J. (1982). *Accents of English.* Cambridge: Cambridge University Press.

Further Readings

Archangeli, D. and D. Pulleyblank. (1993). *Grounded Phonology.* Cambridge, MA: MIT Press.

Greenberg, J. (1978). *Universals of Human Language.* Stanford, CA: Stanford University Press.

Kenstowicz, M. (1994). *Phonology in Generative Grammar.* Oxford: Blackwell.

Phonology

Phonology addresses the question of how the words, phrases, and sentences of a language are transmitted from speaker to hearer through the medium of speech. It is easy to observe that languages differ considerably from one another in their choice of speech sounds and in the rhythmic and melodic patterns that bind them together into units of structure and sense. Less evident to casual observation, but equally important, is the fact that languages differ greatly in the way their basic sounds can be combined to form sound patterns. The phonological system of a given language is the part of its grammar that determines what its basic phonic units are and how they are put together to create intelligible and natural-sounding spoken utterances.

Let us consider what goes into making up the sound system of a language. One ingredient, obviously enough, is its choice of speech sounds. All languages deploy a small set of consonants and vowels, called *phonemes*, as the basic sequential units from which the minimal units of word structure are constructed. The phonemes of a language typically average around 30, although many have considerably more or less. The Rotokas language of Papua New Guinea has just 11 phonemes, for example, whereas the !Xũ language of Namibia has 141. English has about 43, depending on how we count and what variety of English we are describing. Although this number may seem relatively small, it is sufficient to distinguish the 50,000 or so items that make up the normal adult LEXICON. This is due to the distinctive role of order: thus, for example, the word s*tep* is linked to a sequence of phonemes that we can represent as /stɛp/, whereas *pest* is composed of the same phonemes in a different order, /pɛst/.

Phonemes are not freely combinable as a maximally efficient system would require but are sequenced according to strict patterns that are largely specific to each language. One important organizing principle is *syllabification*. In most languages, all words can be exhaustively analyzable into syllables. Furthermore, many languages require all their syllables to have vowels. The reason why a fictional patronymic like *Btfsplk* is hard for most English speakers to pronounce is that it violates these principles—it has no vowels, and so cannot be syllabified. In contrast, in one variety of the Berber language spoken in Morocco, syllables need not have vowels, and utterances like *tsqssft stt* ("you shrank it") are quite unexceptional. Here is a typical, if extreme, example of how sound patterns can differ among languages.

Speech sounds themselves are made up of smaller components called DISTINCTIVE FEATURES, which recur in one sound after another. For example, a feature of tongue-front ARTICULATION (or *coronality,* to use the technical term) characterizes the initial phoneme in words like *tie, do, see, zoo, though, lie, new, shoe, chow,* and *jay,* all of which are made by raising the tip or front of the tongue. This feature minimally distinguishes the initial phoneme of *tie* from that of *pie,* which has the feature of labiality (lip articulation). Features play an important role in defining the permissible sound sequences of a language. In English, for instance, only coronal sounds like those just mentioned may occur after the diphthong spelled *ou* or *ow:* We consequently find words like *out, loud, house, owl, gown,* and *ouch,* all words ending in coronal sounds, but no words ending in sound sequences like *owb, owf, owp, owk,* or *owg.* All speech sounds and their regular patterns can be described in terms of a small set of such features.

A further essential component of a sound system is its choice of "suprasegmental" or prosodic features such as LINGUISTIC STRESS, by which certain syllables are highlighted with extra force or prominence; TONE, by which vowels or syllables bear contrastive pitches; and intonation, the overall "tune" aligned with phrases and sentences. Stress and tone may be used to distinguish different words. In some varieties of Cantonese, for example, only tone distinguishes *si* "poem" (with high pitch), *si* "cause" (with rising pitch), and *si* "silk" (with falling pitch). Prosodic features may also play an important role in distinguishing different sentence types, as in conversational French where only intonation distinguishes the statement *tu viens* "you come" (with falling intonation) from the corresponding question *tu viens?* (with rising intonation). In many languages, stress is used to highlight the part of the sentence that answers a question or provides new information (cf. FOCUS). Thus in English, an appropriate reply to the question "Where did Calvin go?" is *He went to the STORE*, with main stress on the part of the sentence providing the answer, whereas an appropriate reply to the question "Did you see Calvin with Laura?" might be *No, I saw FRED with her*, where the new information is emphasized. Though this use of stress seems natural enough to the English speaker, it is by no means universal, and Korean and Yoruba, to take two examples, make the same distinctions with differences in word order.

Although phonological systems make speech communication possible, there is often no straightforward correspondence between underlying phoneme sequences and their phonetic realization. This is due to the cumulative effects of sound changes on a language, many of them ongoing, that show up not only in systematic gaps such as the restriction on vowel + consonant sequences in English noted above but also in regular alternations between different forms of the same word or morpheme. For example, many English speakers commonly pronounce *fields* the same way as *feels*, while keeping *field* distinct from *feel*. This is not a matter of sloppy pronunciation but of a regular principle of English phonology that disallows the sound [d] between [l] and [z]. Many speakers of American English pronounce *sense* in the same way as *cents*, following another principle requiring the sound [t] to appear between [n] and [s]. These principles are fully productive in the sense that they apply to any word that contains the underlying phonological sequence in question. Hosts of PHONOLOGICAL RULES AND PROCESSES such as these, some easily detected by the untrained ear and others much more subtle, make up the phonological component of English grammar, and taken together may create a significant "mismatch" between mentally represented phoneme sequences and their actual pronunciation. As a result, the speech signal often provides an imperfect or misleading cue to the lexical identity of spoken words. One of the major goals of speech analysis—one that has driven much research over the past few decades—is to work out the complex patterns of interacting rules and constraints that define the full set of mappings between the underlying phonemic forms of a language and the way these forms are realized in actual speech.

Why should phonological systems include principles that are so obviously dysfunctional from the point of view of the hearer (not to mention the language learner)? The answer appears to lie in the constraints imposed "from above" by the brain and "from below" by the size, shape, and muscular structure of the speech-producing apparatus (the lungs, the larynx, the lips, and the tongue). The fact that languages so commonly group their phonemes into syllables and their syllables into higher-level prosodic groupings (metrical feet,

phrases, etc.) may reflect a higher-order disposition to group serially ordered units into hierarchically organized structures, reflected in many other complex activities such as memorization, versification (see METER AND POETRY), and jazz improvisation. On the other hand, human biology imposes quite different demands, often requiring that complex phonemes and phoneme sequences be simplified to forms that are more readily articulated or that can be more easily distinguished by the ear.

Research on phonology dates back to the ancient Sanskrit, Greek, and Roman grammarians, but it received its modern foundations in the work of Henry Sweet, Jan Baudouin de Courtenay, Ferdinand de SAUSSURE, and others in the late nineteenth century. Principles of phonemic analysis were subsequently worked out in detail by linguists such as BLOOMFIELD, SAPIR, Harris, Pike, and Hockett in the United States and Trubetzkoy, Hjelmslev, and Martinet in Europe. Feature theory was elaborated principally by Roman JAKOBSON and his associates in the United States, and the study of suprasegmental and prosodic features by Kenneth Pike as well as by J. R. Firth and his associates in London. Since mid-century, linguists have increasingly attempted to develop explicit formal models of phonological structure, including patterns of phonologically conditioned morpheme alternation. In their watershed work *The Sound Pattern of English* (1968), Noam Chomsky and Morris Halle proposed to characterize the phonological competence of English speakers in terms of an ordered set of rewrite rules, applying in strict order to transform underlying representations into surface realizations. More recent trends taking such an approach as their point of departure have included the development of so-called nonlinear (autosegmental, metrical, prosodic) models for the representation of tone, stress, syllables, feature structure, and prosodic organization, and the study of the interfaces between phonology and other areas of language, including SYNTAX; MORPHOLOGY; AND PHONETICS. At the present time, newer phonological models emphasizing the role of constraints over rewrite rules have become especially prominent, and include principles-and-parameters models, constraint-and-repair phonology, declarative phonology, connectionist-inspired approaches, and most recently OPTIMALITY THEORY.

Viewed from a cognitive perspective, the task of phonology is to find the mental representations that underlie the production and perception of speech and the principles that relate these representations to the physical events of speech. This task is addressed hand-in-hand with research in related areas such as LANGUAGE ACQUISITION and language pathology, acoustic and articulatory phonetics, PSYCHOLINGUISTICS, neurology, and computational modeling. The next decades are likely to witness increased cross-disciplinary collaboration in these areas.

As one of the basic areas of grammar, phonology lies at the heart of all linguistic description. Practical applications of phonology include the development of orthographies for unwritten languages, literacy projects, foreign language teaching, speech therapy, and man-machine communication (see SPEECH SYNTHESIS and SPEECH RECOGNITION IN MACHINES).

See also PHONOLOGY, ACQUISITION OF; PHONOLOGY, NEURAL BASIS OF; PROSODY AND INTONATION; PROSODY AND INTONATION, PROCESSING ISSUES

— *G. N. Clements*

References

Anderson, S. R. (1985). *Phonology in the Twentieth Century.* Chicago: University of Chicago Press.

Chomsky, N., and M. Halle. (1968). *The Sound Pattern of English.* New York: Harper and Row.

Durand, J. (1990). *Generative and Non-linear Phonology.* London: Longman.

Goldsmith, J. A., Ed. (1995). *The Handbook of Phonological Theory.* Oxford: Blackwell.

Hockett, C. F. (1974/1955). *A Manual of Phonology.* Chicago: University of Chicago Press.

Jakobson, R. (1971). *Selected Writings,* vol. 1: *Phonological Studies.* The Hague: Mouton.

Kenstowicz, M. (1994). *Phonology in Generative Grammar.* Oxford: Blackwell.

Spencer, A. (1995). *Phonology: Theory and Description.* Oxford: Blackwell.

Trubetzkoy, N. S. (1969/1939). *Principles of Phonology.* Berkeley and Los Angeles: University of California.

Further Readings

Archangeli, D., and D. Pulleyblank. (1994). *Grounded Phonology.* Cambridge, MA: MIT Press.

Bloomfield, L. (1933). *Language.* New York: Holt.

Clark, J., and C. Yallop. (1995). *Introduction to Phonetics and Phonology.* 2nd ed. Oxford: Blackwell.

Clements, G. N., and S. J. Keyser. (1983). *CV Phonology: A Generative Theory of the Syllable.* Cambridge, MA: MIT Press.

Dell, F. (1980). *Generative Phonology and French Phonology.* Cambridge: Cambridge University Press.

Dressler, W. (1985). *Morphophonology.* Ann Arbor, MI: Karoma.

Ferguson, C., L. Menn, and C. Stoel-Gammon, Eds. (1992). *Phonological Development.* Timonium, MD: York Press.

Fischer-Jörgensen, E. (1975). *Trends in Phonological Theory: A Historical Introduction.* Copenhagen: Akademisk Forlag.

Goldsmith, J. A. (1990). *Autosegmental and Metrical Phonology.* Oxford: Blackwell.

Greenberg, J. H. (1978). *Universals of Human Language,* vol. 2: *Phonology.* Stanford, CA: Stanford University Press.

Hyman, L. (1975). *Phonology: Theory and Analysis.* New York: Holt, Rinehart, and Winston.

Inkelas, S., and D. Zec. (1990). *The Phonology-Syntax Connection.* Chicago: University of Chicago Press.

Jakobson, R. (1941). *Child Language, Aphasia, and Phonological Universals.* The Hague: Mouton.

Kenstowicz, M., and C. W. Kisseberth. (1979). *Generative Phonology: Description and Theory.* New York: Academic Press.

Kiparsky, P. (1995). Phonological basis of sound change. In J. Goldsmith, Ed., *The Handbook of Phonological Theory.* Oxford: Blackwell, pp. 640–670.

Labov, W. (1994). *Principles of Linguistic Change: Internal Factors.* Oxford: Blackwell.

Maddieson, I. (1984). *Patterns of Sounds.* Cambridge: Cambridge University Press.

Makkai, V. B., Ed. (1972). *Phonological Theory: Evolution and Current Practice.* New York: Holt, Rinehart, and Winston.

Martinet, A. (1955). *Economie des Changements Phonétiques: Traité de Phonologie Diachronique.* Bern: Francke.

Ohala, J. (1983). The origin of sound patterns in vocal tract constraints. In P. F. MacNeilage, Ed., *The Production Of Speech.* New York: Springer, pp. 189–216.

Palmer, F. R., Ed. (1970). *Prosodic Analysis.* London: Oxford University Press.

Phonology, Published three times a year by Cambridge University Press: Cambridge.

Sapir, E. (1925). Sound patterns in language. *Language* 1: 37–51.

Vihman, M. (1995). *Phonological Development: The Origins of Language in the Child.* Oxford: Blackwell.

Phonology, Acquisition of

The acquisition of PHONOLOGY—or rather its development—may be divided into two fields: SPEECH PERCEPTION and speech production. There are two reasons why the development of perception is prior to the development of production. One is that although the human ear is almost completely formed when the fetus is 7 months, the oral cavity of a human at birth is very different from the adult's oral cavity. The second reason is that in order to produce the sounds of a given language, a child must be exposed to the relevant linguistic experience. Babbling infants, in fact, produce all sorts of linguistic sounds, even ones they have never heard in their linguistic environment. Although the first reason why perception is prior to production holds exclusively for the acquisition of the mother tongue (L1), the second holds both for the acquisition of L1 and of whichever language comes after L1 (L2).

A child comes into life well equipped to hear subtle differences in sounds (Eisenberg 1976). Though it is conceivable that some speech perception development starts before birth, because newborns discriminate the mother language from a foreign one (Mehler et al. 1988), it is generally assumed that the development of language perception starts at birth.

The most widely accepted theory of speech perception is the innatist theory, first proposed by JAKOBSON and much influenced by the work of Chomsky and other generative linguists. A mechanism, called the LANGUAGE ACQUISITION device (LAD), is assumed to be responsible for the ability humans have to analyze linguistic inputs and to construct grammars that generate them (see GENERATIVE GRAMMAR). Given that some properties of language are common to all languages of the world, it may be assumed that these are the consequences of the innate human endowment. The development of a specific language is achieved through the setting of the values of a set of parameters on the basis of the linguistic data one is exposed to.

According to the innatist hypothesis, a newborn can discriminate between pairs of segments (consonant and vowels) attested in at least one language of the world, even if they are not distinctive in the language they are exposed to (Jakobson 1941). Testing what infants hear has become possible only in the last twenty years. The methodology to test young infants' perception is the nonnutritive (or high amplitude) sucking method (Eimas et al. 1971). When infants are 6 months or older, the preferential headturn procedure is commonly used to test sound discrimination (Moore, Wilson, and Thomson 1977). It has been shown that, indeed, for the newborn, the ability to discriminate does not appear to be related to the language he or she is exposed to (Streeter 1976). At a later stage of development, around 10 months, infants start losing the ability to discriminate sounds that are not distinctive in the language(s) they are exposed to (Werker and Tees 1984; Kuhl et al. 1992). This is in line with the learning by selection theory of neurological development (Changeux, Heidmann, and Patte 1984). It has also been shown that already from 1 month, infants represent linguistic sounds categorically, that is, different acoustic variants of a sound are identified with one category (Eimas, Miller, and Jusczyk 1987; Kuhl 1993).

Perceiving phonological distinctions is not only relevant to the acquisition of a phonological system but is also essential to the development of both LEXICON and SYNTAX. Newborns are in a position similar to that of adults when they hear a language unrelated to any other language of which they have some experience. One of the problems in constructing a lexicon is segmenting a continuous stream of sounds. In order to build a lexicon, a child must come to understand where each word ends and the next one begins. Because newborns are sensitive to edges of phonological or prosodic constituents (Christophe et al. 1994) and to LINGUISTIC STRESS (Sansavini et al. 1995), it is conceivable that they use these prosodic cues to segment the continuous input (cf. PROSODY AND INTONATION).

According to the theory of language initialization known as prosodic bootstrapping, the prosody of a language also provides a cue to its syntactic structure (Gerken, Jusczyk, and Mandel 1994). Given its sensitivity to prosody, an infant should thus be capable of setting certain syntactic parameters long before the period in which he or she shows some knowledge of the lexicon (Mazuka 1996; Nespor, Guasti, and Christophe 1996). The early setting of parameters responsible for word order accounts for the fact that the monolingual child hardly makes any mistakes in the relative order of words when he or she starts combining them into small sentences.

Speech production starts with babbling, the first approximation to language. The vocal apparatus approaches an adult state at about 6 months of age, so it is only from this period that it is safe to talk about babbling. Though the segmental categories in babbling do not resemble those of the adult language (de Boysson-Bardies 1993), even at this first stage, speech production is influenced by speech perception: babbling does not develop normally without an auditory input (Oller and Eilers 1988). In auditorily unimpaired infants, suprasegmentals (i.e., rhythm and intonation) are acquired before segments are, as early as at 6 months (Whalen, Levitt, and Wang 1991). Around the first year of age, both the vowel quality and the syllabic structure of auditorily unimpaired babbling infants is much influenced by that of the adult language (de Boysson-Bardies et al. 1989; Vihman 1992). The first syllable type produced throughout the languages of the world is one formed by a consonant (C) followed by a vowel (V). This is also the only syllable type universally present. The segmental content of the first syllables is such that C and V are as far apart as possible in sonority—that is, C is pronounced with high air pressure in the oral cavity compared to the external air pressure, as in [p], whereas in the pronunciation of V, the internal pressure is similar to the external one, as in [a]. Subsequently different CV combinations develop and different parameters are set to give the full range of adult syllables such as whether a prevocalic consonant is obligatory or not or whether a postvocalic consonant is allowed or not. PHONOLOGICAL RULES AND PROCESSES also develop with time. For example, the centralization to schwa of unstressed vowels in English is not part of early productions.

The acquisition of the phonology (and of grammar in general) of L1 appears to be impaired after the fifth year of life. This claim is based on the experience of humans who have not been in contact with a speaking community and have been found at age 5 or more. The acquisition of the phonology of L2 appears to be impaired after puberty, as witnessed by the foreign-accent phenomenon, responsible for the fact that we can distinguish a native speaker from a nonnative one. Interestingly, the acquisition of syntax (i.e., the computational system) is not so impaired.

See also PHONOLOGY, NEURAL BASIS OF; SYNTAX, ACQUISITION OF

—*Marina Nespor*

References

Boysson-Bardies, B. de. (1993). Ontogeny of language-specific syllabic productions. In B. de Boysson-Bardies, S. de Schonen, P. Jusczyk, P. McNeilage, and J. Morton, Eds., *Developmental Neurocognition: Speech and Face Processing in the First Year of Life.* Dordrecht: Kluwer, pp. 353–363.

Boysson-Bardies, B. de, P. Halle, L. Sagart, and C. Durand. (1989). A cross-linguistic investigation of vowel formants in babbling. *Journal of Child Language* 11:1–17.

Changeux, J. P., T. Heidmann, and P. Patte. (1984). Learning by selection. In P. Marler and H. S. Terrace, Eds., *The Biology of Learning.* Berlin: Springer, pp.115–133.

Christophe, A., E. Dupoux, J. Bertoncini, and J. Mehler. (1994). Do infants perceive word boundaries? An empirical approach to the bootstrapping problem for lexical acquisition. *Journal of the Acoustical Society of America* 95: 1570–1580.

Eimas, P. D., E. R. Siqueland, P. W. Jusczyk, and J. Vigorito. (1971). Speech perception in infants. *Science* 171: 303–306.

Eimas, P. D., J. L. Miller, and P. W. Jusczyk. (1987). On infant speech perception and the acquisition of language. In S. Harnad, Ed., *Categorical Perception: The Ground Work of Cognition.* Cambridge: Cambridge University Press, pp. 161–195.

Eisenberg, R. B. (1976). *Auditory Competence in Early Life.* Unpublished MS. Baltimore, MD:

Gerken, L.-A., P. W. Jusczyk, and D. R. Mandel. (1994). When prosody fails to cue syntactic structure: Nine-months olds' sensitivity to phonological versus syntactic phrases. *Cognition* 51: 237–265.

Jakobson, R. (1941). *Kindersprache, Aphasie, und Allegemeine Lautgesetze.* (Child Language, Aphasia, and Phonological Universals, 1968.) Uppsala. The Hague: Mouton.

Kuhl, P. K. (1993). Innate predispositions and the effects of experience in speech perception: The native language magnet theory. In B. de Boysson-Bardies, S. de Schonen, P. Jusczyk, P. McNeilage, and J. Morton, Eds., *Developmental Neurocognition: Speech and Face Processing in the First Year of Life.* Dordrecht: Kluwer, pp. 259–274.

Kuhl, P. K., K. A. Williams, F. Lacerda, K. N. Stevens, and B. Lindblom. (1992). Linguistic experiences alter phonetic perception in infants by 6 months of age. *Science* 255: 606–608.

Mazuka, R. (1996). How can a grammatical parameter be set before the first word? In J. L. Morgan and K. Demuth, Eds., *Signal to Syntax.* Hillsdale, NJ: Erlbaum, pp. 313–330.

Mehler, J., P. W. Jusczyk, G. Lambertz, N. Halsted, J. Bertoncini, and C. Amiel-Tison. (1988). A precursor of language acquisition in young infants. *Cognition* 29: 143–178.

Moore, J. M., W. R Wilson, and G. Thomson. (1977). Visual reinforcement of head-turn responses in infants under 12 months of age. *Journal of Speech and Hearing Disorders* 42: 328–334.

Nespor, M., M.-T. Guasti, and A. Christophe. (1996). Selecting word order: The Rhythmic Activation Principle. In U. Kleinhenz, Ed., *Interfaces in Phonology.* Berlin: Akademie Verlag, pp. 1–26.

Oller, D. K., and R. E. Eilers. (1988). The role of audition in infant babbling. *Child Development* 59: 441–449.

Sansavini, A., J. Bertoncini, and G. Giovanelli. (1997). Newborns discriminate the rhythm of multisyllabic stressed words. *Developmental Psychology* 33: 3–11.

Streeter, L. A. (1976). Language perception of 2-month-old infants shows effects of both innate mechanisms and experience. *Nature* 259: 39–41.

Vihman, M. M. (1992). Early syllables and the construction of phonology. In C. A. Ferguson, L. Menn, and C. Stoel-Gammon, Eds., *Phonological Development: Models, Research, Implications.* Timonium, MD: York Press, pp. 393–422.

Werker, J. F., and R. C. Tees. (1984). Cross-linguistic speech perception: Evidence for perceptual reorganization in the first year of life. *Infant Behavior and Development* 7: 49–63.

Whalen, D. H., A. Levitt, and Q. Wang. (1991). Intonational differences between the reduplicative babbling of French and English-learning infants. *Journal of Child Language* 18: 501–506.

Further Readings

Dehaene-Lambertz, G. (1995). *Capacités Linguistiques Précoces et leurs Bases Cérébrales.* Ph.D. diss., Université de Paris VI.

Fikkert, P. (1994). *On the Acquisition of Prosodic Structure.* The Hague: Holland Academic Graphics.

Ingram, D. (1989). *First Language Acquisition.* Cambridge: Cambridge University Press.

Jusczyk, P. W. (1997). *The Discovery of Spoken Language.* Cambridge, MA: MIT Press.

Mehler, J., and A. Christophe. (1995). Maturation and learning of language in the first year of life. In M. S. Gazzaniga, Ed., *The Cognitive Neurosciences.* Cambridge, MA: MIT Press, pp. 943–954.

Mehler, J., and E. Dupoux. (1990). *Naître Humain.* (What Infants Know, 1994.) Paris: Editions Odile Jacob. Oxford: Blackwell.

Morgan, J. L., and K. Demuth, Eds. (1995). *Signal to Syntax.* Mahwah, NJ: Erlbaum.

Repp, R. (1983). Categorical perception: Issues, methods, findings. In N. J. Lass, Ed., *Speech and Language: Advances in Basic Research and Practice,* vol. 10. New York: Academic Press, pp. 243–335.

Smith, N. V. (1973). *The Acquisition of Phonology: A Case Study.* Cambridge: Cambridge University Press.

Strozer, J. R. (1994). *Language Acquisition After Puberty.* Washington, DC: Georgetown University Press.

Werker, J. F. (1995). Exploring developmental changes in cross-language speech perception. In L. R. Gleitman and M. Liberman, Eds., *An Invitation to Cognitive Science.* Vol. 1, *Language.* Cambridge, MA: MIT Press, pp. 87–106.

Phonology, Neural Basis of

PHONOLOGY refers to the sound structure of language. As such, the study of phonology includes investigation of the representations and organizational principles underlying the sound systems of language, as well as the exploration of the mechanisms and processes used by the listener in speech perception or by the speaker in speech production. The study of the neural basis of phonology is guided by an attempt to understand the neural mechanisms contributing to the perception and production of speech. This domain of inquiry has largely focused on investigations of adult aphasics who have language deficits subsequent to brain damage, exploring their language impairments and accompanying lesion localization. These "experiments in nature" provide the traditional approach to the study of the neural bases of phonology. More recently, neuroimaging techniques, such as POSITRON EMISSION TOMOGRAPHY (PET) and functional MAGNETIC RESONANCE IMAGING (fMRI), have provided a new window into the neural mechanisms contributing to phonology, allowing for investigation of neural activity in normal subjects as well as brain-damaged patients.

It has been long known that the left hemisphere is dominant for language for most speakers, and that the peri-sylvian regions of the left hemisphere are most directly involved in LANGUAGE PRODUCTION and SPEECH PERCEPTION. The classical view has characterized speech/language deficits in APHASIA in terms of broad anatomical (left anterior and left posterior) and functional (expressive and receptive) dichotomies (Geschwind 1965). In this view, expressive language deficits occur as a result of damage to the motor (anterior) areas, and receptive language deficits occur as a result of damage to the auditory association (posterior) areas. Nonetheless, the processing components involved in both speech production and perception are complex and appear to involve more extensive neural structures than originally proposed.

In order to produce a word or group of words, a speaker must select the word(s) from the set of words in long-term memory, encode its phonological form in a short-term buffer in order to plan the phonetic shape, which will vary as a function of the context (*articulatory phonological planning*), and convert this phonetic string into a set of motor commands or motor programs to the vocal tract (*articulatory implementation*). Results from studies with aphasic patients show that all patients, regardless of clinical syndrome and accompanying lesion localization, display deficits in the processes of selection and planning (Blumstein 1994). That is, they may produce the wrong sound segment, a selection error, such as "keams" for "teams", or they may produce the wrong sound segment because of the influence of a neighboring sound, a planning error, such as "rof beef" for "roast beef." The patterns of errors that occur show that the sounds of speech are organized in terms of smaller units called phonetic features (cf. DISTINCTIVE FEATURES), and that patients tend to make errors involving a change in the value of a phonetic feature. For example, the production of "keams" for "teams" reflects a change in the place of articulation of the initial stop consonant. Of importance, phonetic features are not "lost," but the patterns of errors reflect statistical tendencies. Sometimes the patients produce a word correctly, sometimes not; and sometimes they may make one type of error on a word, and other times a different type of error on the same word. These phonological deficits arise in nearly all aphasic patients including Broca's aphasics who may have brain damage in Broca's area and other anterior brain structures such as the precentral gyrus and the BASAL GANGLIA, and Wernicke's aphasics who may have brain damage in the third temporal gyrus and other posterior structures such as the second temporal gyrus and the supramarginal gyrus.

Although speech-production deficits that relate to selection and planning may not have a distinct neural locus, speech-production impairments that relate to articulatory implementation processes do. Such deficits seem to stem from impaired timing and coordination of articulatory movements (Ryalls 1987). The correct sound may be selected, but the articulatory system cannot implement it normally. For example, for "teams" the patient may produce an overly aspirated initial /t/. Lesion data from aphasic patients and evoked potential and PET data from normal subjects implicate the left inferior frontal gyrus (including Broca's area), the precentral gyrus, the basal ganglia, the precentral gyrus of the insula, and the supplementary motor areas, in the articulatory implementation of speech (Baum et al. 1990; Dronkers 1996; Petersen et al. 1989). Interestingly, although the speech musculature is bilaterally innervated, speech-production deficits emerge only as a consequence of left-brain damage and not right-brain damage to these structures.

Speech perception processes are also complex. They require a transformation of the auditory input from the peripheral auditory system to a spectral representation based on more generalized auditory patterns or properties, followed by the conversion of this spectral representation to a more abstract feature (phonological) representation, and ultimately the mapping of this sound structure onto its lexical representation. Presumably, the word is selected from a set of potential word candidates that are phonologically similar. Speech perception studies support the view that the neural basis of speech perception is dominant in the left hemisphere. However, they challenge the classical view that these deficits underlie the auditory comprehension impairments of Wernicke's aphasics and that speech perception impairments are restricted to patients with temporal lobe pathology. Nearly all aphasic patients, regardless of their lesion localization, display some deficits in perceiving the sounds of speech, as demonstrated by discrimination experiments with words, "pear" versus "bear," or nonwords, "pa" versus "ba." These patients do not seem to have impairments in transforming the auditory input into a phonological form nor do they show impairments in phonological structure. Differences among aphasic patients relate to the quantity of errors, not the patterns of errors. The basis for the different quantity of errors might reflect a greater involvement of posterior structures in such speech processing tasks. Nonetheless, differential patterns of performance do emerge in studies exploring the mapping of sound structure onto lexical representations, implicating lexical processing deficits for Broca's and Wernicke's aphasics rather than speech

processing impairments (Milberg, Blumstein, and Dworetzky 1988).

PET and fMRI studies provide converging evidence consistent with the results from studies with aphasic patients. These studies have shown activation in a number of posterior and anterior structures when passively listening to words or in making phonetic judgments. These structures include the first and second temporal gyri, the supramarginal gyrus, the inferior frontal gyrus, as well as premotor areas. Nonetheless, direct comparisons between the behavioral/lesion studies and the neuroimaging studies are difficult because the experimental tasks used have not been comparable. For example, patients may be required to listen to pairs of words and make same/different judgments, whereas normal subjects may be required to listen to pairs of words and determine whether the final consonant of the stimuli is the same. Even so, it seems clear that the processes involved in the perception of speech are complex and invoke a neural system that encompasses both anterior and posterior brain structures.

See also LANGUAGE, NEURAL BASIS OF

—Sheila E. Blumstein

References

Blumstein, S. E. (1994). The neurobiology of the sound structure of language. In M. Gazzaniga, Ed., *Handbook of the Cognitive Neurosciences.* Cambridge: MIT Press.

Baum, S. R., S. E. Blumstein, M. A. Naeser, and C. L. Palumbo. (1990). Temporal dimensions of consonant and vowel production: An acoustic and CT scan analysis of aphasic speech. *Brain and Language* 39: 33–56.

Dronkers, N. F. (1996). A new brain region for coordinating speech articulation. *Nature* 384: 159–161.

Geschwind, N. (1965). Disconnexion syndromes in animals and man. *Brain* 88: 237–294, 585–644.

Milberg, W., S. E. Blumstein, and B. Dworetzky. (1988). Phonological processing and lexical access in aphasia. *Brain and Language* 34: 279–293.

Petersen, S. E., P. T. Fox, M. I. Posner, M. Mintun, and M. E. Raichle. (1989). Positron emission tomographic studies of the processing of single words. *Journal of Cognitive Neuroscience* 1: 153–170.

Ryalls, J., Ed. (1987). *Phonetic Approaches to Speech Production in Aphasia and Related Disorders.* Boston: College-Hill Press.

Further Readings

Binder, J. R., J. A. Frost, T. A. Hammeke, R. W. Cox, S. M. Rao, and T. Prieto. (1997). Human brain language areas identified by functional magnetic resonance imaging. *Journal of Neuroscience* 171: 353–362.

Binder, J. R., S. M. Rao, T. A. Hammeke, Y. Z. Yetkin, A. Jesmanowicz, P. A. Bandettini, E. C. Wong, L. D. Estkowski, M. D. Goldstein, V. M. Haughton, and J. S. Hyde. (1994). Functional magnetic resonance imaging of human auditory cortex. *Annals of Neurology* 35: 662–672.

Binder, J. R., J. A. Frost, T. A. Hammeke, S. M. Rao, and R. W. Cox. (1996). Function of the left planum temporale in auditory and linguistic processing. *Brain* 119: 1239–1247.

Damasio, H. (1991). Neuroanatomical correlates of the aphasias. In M. T. Sarno, Ed., *Acquired Aphasia.* 2nd ed. New York: Academic Press.

Demonet, J. F., J. A. Fiez, E. Paulesu, S. E. Petersen, and R. J. Zatorre. (1996). PET studies of phonological processing: A critical reply to Poeppel. *Brain and Language* 55: 352–379.

Gandour, J., and Dardarananda, R. (1982). Voice onset time in aphasia: Thai, I. Perception. *Brain and Language* 1: 24–33.

Gandour, J., and R. Dardarananda. (1984). Voice-onset time in aphasia: Thai, II: Production. *Brain and Language* 18: 389–410.

McAdam, D. W., and H. A. Whitaker. (1971). Language production: Electroencephalographic localization in the normal human brain. *Science* 172: 499–502.

Petersen, S. E., P. T. Fox, M. I. Posner, M. Mintun, and M. E. Raichle. (1988). Positron emission tomographic studies of the cortical anatomy of single-word processing. *Nature* 331: 585–589.

Poeppel, D. (1996). A critical review of PET studies of phonological processing. *Brain and Language* 55: 317–351.

Posner, M. I. and M. E. Raichle. (1994). *Images of Mind.* New York: W. H. Freeman and Co.

Price, C. J., R. J. S. Wise, E. A. Warburton, C. J. Moore, D. Howard, K. Patterson, R. S. J. Frackowiak, and K. J. Friston. (1996). Hearing and saying: The functional neuro-anatomy of auditory word processing. *Brain* 119: 919–931.

Rosenbek, J., M. McNeil, and A. Aronson, Eds. (1984). *Apraxia of Speech.* San Diego, CA: College-Hill Press.

Zatorre, R. J., A. C. Evans, E. Meyer, and A. Gjedde. (1992). Lateralization of phonetic and pitch discrimination in speech processing. *Science* 256: 846–849.

Zatorre, R. J., E. Meyer, A. Gjedde, and A. C. Evans. (1996). PET studies of phonetic processes in speech perception: Review, replication, and re-analysis. *Cerebral Cortex* 6: 21–30.

Physicalism

Physicalism is the doctrine that everything that exists in the spacetime world is a physical thing, and that every property of a physical thing is either a physical property or a property that is related in some intimate way to its physical nature. Stated this way, the doctrine is an ontological claim, but it has important epistemological and methodological corollaries.

Physicalists in general will accept the following thesis of "ontological physicalism" (Hellman and Thompson 1975): Every object in spacetime is wholly material—that is, it is either a basic particle of matter (proton, electron, quark, or whatever) or an aggregate structure composed exclusively of such particles. Ontological physicalism, therefore, denies the existence of things like Cartesian souls, supernatural divinities, "entelechies," "vital forces," and the like. Physicalists, however, differ widely when it comes to the question of *properties* of physical objects—whether complex physical systems can have properties that are in some sense non-physical. But what is a *physical property*?

It is difficult to give a clear-cut answer to this question. In a narrow sense, physical properties are those properties, relations, quantities, and magnitudes that figure in physics, such as mass, energy, shape, volume, entropy, temperature, spatiotemporal position and distance, and the like. Most will also include chemical properties like valence, inflammability, and acidity, although these are not among the basic physical properties—properties that figure in basic physical laws (in this sense entropy and temperature are not basic

either). In discussions of the status of cognitive/psychological properties, physical properties are usually also taken to include such *higher-level* properties as biological properties and computational properties. This broad sense of physical property seems appropriate to the discussion of the question how psychological properties are related to physical properties—that is, the MIND-BODY PROBLEM. In its broad sense, therefore, "physical" essentially amounts to *"nonpsychological."* This leaves our previous question unanswered: what is a physical property? Mass, charge, energy, and the like are of course important properties in current physics, but the physics of the future may invoke properties quite different from those in today's physics. How would we recognize them as physical properties rather than properties of another sort? That is, how would we know that future physics is *physics*?

As noted, physicalists differ on the status of higher-level properties in relation to lower-level, basic physical properties. *Reductive physicalism* claims that higher-level properties, including psychological properties, are reducible to, and hence turn out to be, physical properties. Opposed to reductive physicalism is *nonreductive physicalism,* also called *property dualism,* which takes at least some higher-level properties, in particular cognitive/psychological properties, to form an irreducible autonomous domain. This would mean that psychology is a special science whose object is to investigate the causal/nomological connections involving these irreducible psychological properties and generate distinctively psychological explanations in terms of them. In this view, these laws and explanations cannot be formulated in purely physical terms—not even in an ideally complete physical theory—and a purely physical description of the world, however physically complete it may be, would leave out something important about the world. Nonreductive physicalism, therefore, leads to the doctrine of the AUTONOMY OF PSYCHOLOGY and, more generally, the autonomy of all special sciences in relation to basic physics (Davidson 1970; Fodor 1974).

The mind-brain identity theory (Feigl 1958; Smart 1959; Armstrong 1968) is a form of reductive physicalism. This approach proposes to identify psychological properties with their neural correlates; for example, pain is to be identified with its neural substrate ("C-fiber stimulation," according to armchair philosophical neurophysiology). These mental-neural identities are claimed to be just like the familiar identities discovered by science, for example, "Water = H_2O," "Light = electromagnetic radiation," and "Genes = DNA molecules." Just as the "true nature" of water is being composed of H_2O molecules, advances in neurophysiology will reveal to us the true nature of each type of mental state by identifying it with a specific kind of brain state.

EMERGENTISM, a doctrine popular in the first half of the twentieth century, is a form of nonreductive physicalism (Morgan 1923; Sperry 1969; McLaughlin 1992). Its central tenet is the claim that certain higher-level properties, in particular consciousness and intentionality, are *emergent* in the sense that, although they appear only when a propitious set of physical conditions are present, they are genuinely novel properties that are neither explainable nor predictable in terms of their underlying physical conditions. Moreover, these emergent properties bring into the world their own distinctive causal powers, thereby enriching the causal structure of the world. FUNCTIONALISM is also often thought to be a form of nonreductive physicalism. According to this position, psychological properties are not physical or neural properties, but rather *functional kinds,* where a functional kind is a property defined in terms of causal inputs and outputs. To give a familiar example, pain is said to be a functional kind in that being in pain is to be in some physical/ biological state that is typically caused by certain types of physical inputs (e.g., tissue damage) and that causes certain behavioral outputs (e.g., groaning, wincing, escape behavior). It is then noted that a psychological kind when given a functional interpretation of this kind has *multiple physical realizers* (Putnam 1967; Block and Fodor 1972; Fodor 1974); that is, the neural mechanism that realizes or implements pain in humans is probably vastly different from the pain mechanisms in reptiles, mollusks, and perhaps certain complex electromechanical systems. This is "the multiple realization argument" against reductionism: because pain is multiply realized in diverse physical/biological mechanisms, it cannot be identified with any single physical or biological property. This has led to the view that cognitive/ psychological properties are at a higher level of abstraction and formality than the physical/biological properties that implement them (Kim 1992).

However, nonreductive physicalists, insofar as they are physicalists, will acknowledge that psychological properties, although physically irreducible, are in some sense dependent on, or determined by, physical properties— unless, that is, one is prepared to take their physical irreducibility as proof of their unreality and adopt eliminativism/ irrealism (or ELIMINATIVE MATERIALISM) about the mental (Churchland 1981). That is, physicalists who accept the reality of the mental will accept the mind-body SUPERVENIENCE thesis (Hellman and Thompson 1975; Horgan 1982; Kim 1984): the psychological character of an organism or system is entirely fixed by its total physical nature. From this it follows that any two systems with a relevantly similar physical structure will exhibit an identical or similar psychological character. Even emergentists will grant that when identical physical conditions are replicated, the same mental phenomenon will emerge, or fail to emerge. Supervenience is also a commitment of functionalism: systems in identical physical conditions presumably have the same causal powers and so will instantiate the same functional properties. It is a basic commitment of all forms of physicalism that the world is the way it is because the physical facts of the world are the way they are. That is, physical facts fix all the facts.

Among the facts of this world are causal facts, including those involving mental and other higher properties. The supervenience thesis implies then that these higher-level causal facts are fixed by lower-level physical facts, presumably facts about physical causal relations. The same goes for higher-level laws: under supervenience, these laws are fixed once basic physical facts, in particular basic laws of physics, are fixed. According to the supervenience thesis, therefore, physical laws and causal relations are fundamental; they, and they alone, are ultimately responsible for the causal/nomic structure of the world. But this conclusion does not comport

comfortably with the claim that the special sciences are autonomous vis-à-vis basic physics. For if the laws and causal relations obtaining at the basic physical level determine all higher-level causal relations and laws, it should be possible in principle, or at least so it seems, to formulate explanations of higher-level laws and phenomena within the physical domain. If the world works the way it does because the physical world works the way it does, why is it not possible to explain everything in terms of how the physical world works?

Some will challenge this reasoning. They will argue that for *X* to *determine Y* is one thing, but that for *X* to *explain* or *make intelligible* why *Y* occurs is quite another. Pain emerges whenever C-fibers are firing, and this may well be a lawlike correlation. But the correlation is "brute": it is not possible to explain why pain, rather than tickle or itch, emerges when C-fibers fire, or why pain emerges from C- fiber excitation but not from other kinds of neural activity. Nor do we seem able to explain why any conscious states should emerge from neural processes. For the emergentists, then, although all higher-level facts are determined by lower-level physical facts, the latter are powerless to explain the former. The world may be a fundamentally physical world, but it may well include physically inexplicable facts.

Whether and how the functionalist can resist the reductionist pressure is less clear. Suppose, as functionalism has it, that being in mental state *M* is to be in some physical state or other meeting a certain causal specification *D.* It would seem then that we could easily explain why something is in *M* by pointing out that it is in *P* and that *P* meets causal specification *D*—namely that *P* is a realizer of *M.* And given the functional characterization of *M,* it seems to follow that the causal powers of a given instance of *M* are just the causal powers of its realizer *P* on this occasion. Thus, if it is a special-science law that *M*-events cause *M**-events, that must be so because each of *M*'s physical realizers causes a physical realizer of *M**. In this way, special-science laws would seem reductively explainable in terms of laws governing the realizers of the special-science properties involved.

"Materialism" is often used interchangeably with "physicalism." However, there are some subtle differences between these terms, the most salient of which is that physicalism indicates acknowledgment that something like current physics is the ultimate explanatory theory of all the facts, whereas materialism is not necessarily allied with the success of physics as a basic explanatory theory of the world.

See also ANOMALOUS MONISM; CONSCIOUSNESS; EXPLANATORY GAP; INDIVIDUALISM; INTENTIONALITY

—*Jaegwon Kim*

References

Armstrong, D. M. (1968). *A Materialist Theory of Mind.* New York: Humanities Press.

Block, N., and J. A. Fodor. (1972). What psychological states are not. *Philosophical Review* 81: 159–181.

Churchland, P. M. (1981). Eliminative materialism and the propositional attitudes. *Journal of Philosophy* 78: 68–90.

Davidson, D. (1970). Mental events. In L. Foster and J. W. Swanson, Eds., *Experience and Theory.* Amherst, MA: University of Massachusetts Press, pp. 79–101.

Feigl, H. (1958). The "mental" and the "physical." *Minnesota Studies in the Philosophy of Science* 2: 370–497.

Fodor, J. A. (1974). Special sciences, or the disunity of science as a working hypothesis. *Synthese* 28: 97–115.

Hellman, G., and F. Thompson. (1975). Physicalism: Ontology, determination, and reduction. *Journal of Philosophy* 72: 551–564.

Horgan, T. (1982). Supervenience and microphysics. *Pacific Philosophical Quarterly* 63: 29–43.

Kim, J. (1984). Concepts of supervenience. *Philosophy and Phenomenological Research* 45: 153–176.

Kim, J. (1992). Multiple realization and the metaphysics of reduction. *Philosophy and Phenomenological Research* 52: 1–26.

Lewis, D. (1972). Psychophysical and theoretical identifications. *Australasian Journal of Philosophy* 50: 249–258.

McLaughlin, B. (1992). The rise and fall of British emergentism. In A. Beckermann, H. Flohr, and J. Kim, Eds., *Emergence or Reduction*. Berlin: De Gruyter, pp. 49–93.

Morgan, C. L. (1923). *Emergent Evolution*. London: William and Norgate.

Putnam, H. (1967). Psychological predicates. In W. H. Capitan and D. D. Merrill, Eds., *Art, Mind, and Religion*. Pittsburgh, PA: University of Pittsburgh Press, pp. 37–48.

Smart, J. J. C. (1959). Sensations and brain processes. *Philosophical Review* 68: 141–156.

Sperry, R. W. (1969). A modified concept of consciousness. *Psychological Review* 76: 532–536.

Further Readings

Broad, C. D. (1925). *The Mind and Its Place in Nature*. London: Routledge and Kegan Paul.

Kim, J. (1989). The myth of nonreductive materialism. *Proceedings and Addresses of the American Philosophical Association* 63: 31–47.

Levine, J. (1983). Materialism and qualia: The explanatory gap. *Pacific Philosophical Quarterly* 64: 354–361.

McLaughlin, B. (1989). Type epiphenomenalism, type dualism, and the causal priority of the physical. *Philosophical Perspectives* 3: 109–136.

Moser, P. K., and J. D. Trout, Eds. (1995). *Contemporary Materialism*. London: Routledge.

Poland, J. (1994). *Physicalism*. Oxford: Clarendon Press.

Rosenthal, D. M., Ed. (1991). *The Nature of Mind*. New York: Oxford University Press.

Physiology

See AUDITORY PHYSIOLOGY; ELECTROPHYSIOLOGY, ELECTRIC AND MAGNETIC EVOKED FIELDS; VISUAL ANATOMY AND PHYSIOLOGY; VISUAL CORTEX, CELL TYPES AND CONNECTIONS IN

Piaget, Jean

Jean Piaget's (1896–1930) research program about human knowledge counts as one of the major contributions to psychology and epistemology because it has translated philosophical questions into empirical ones, setting a standard against which any new paradigm about the nature and growth of knowledge is still measured today. Hence its pertinence for cognitive sciences because, like them, Piaget departed from the limited aims of psychology to discover the most general principles of cognition.

Piaget's basic idea is that knowledge continues biological ADAPTATION by different means. This means that intelligence is considered as a sort of organ and, as such, has both a functional side and a structural one. But, whereas other organs have fixed structures and fixed functions, cognitive organs present a functional continuity within structural discontinuities. The functional continuity is the emergence and growth of knowledge during evolution. Structural discontinuities are the different forms knowledge takes during the course of the growth of a species, a culture, or an individual. These discontinuities are marked by a stage like construction of successive invariants ensuring a certain stability to the world in which the organism lives (homeostasis).

Such a position is called constructivism in epistemology, because it is a sort of midway between two opposites: realism and nominalism. REALISM pretends that things exist independently of their instances in the actual world by necessity. Such a view secures the objectivity and universality of knowledge. Nominalism considers that what we call things are mere conveniences that vary according to one's needs and conventions. This relativistic approach accounts for the variability of things according to cultural changes. As one can see, constructivism being both fixed in its functional dimension and ever changing in its structural one solves the opposition gracefully without reducing one perspective to the other or excluding one in favor of the other.

The rest of Piaget's program characterizes the sequences and mechanisms by which rational knowledge develops.

Sequences of development are marked by a constant abstraction of conservation from the mere permanence of objects to the laws of conservation in physics and chemistry. In order for the world to acquire the minimum stability requested to retrieve an object once it has disappeared from perception, space must be conceived as a container within which all the moves of an observer form a mathematical group of displacements. Then time, matter, weight, and volume need to be conserved first in action, symbols, and concepts, as well as logical classes, relations, and numbers, on the logico-mathematical side.

Conservation accounts for the preservation of knowledge at each level of development but not for the acquisition of new knowledge. This is made possible by *novelty* or the attainment of better knowledge and by *necessity* or the interconnection of all available knowledge into logically necessary systems.

Novelty plays an important role in Piaget's theorizing. First, the emergence of novelty in knowledge is considered by him as evidence in favor of his constructivistic view and against the two extreme positions in the nature-nurture dilemma. NATIVISM and environmentalism both exclude novelty because it is mere unfolding in nativism and a matter of learning in environmentalism. Second, the sudden emergence of novelty proves the stage like nature of the growth of knowledge. But, third and above all, novelty changes the face of knowledge both in the child and in science. Once a child has discovered that, when one gets the concept of number, all the numerical operations will yield a number and nothing else but a number ad infinitum, this novel knowledge changes the child's outlook of the world in the very same way that the discovery of object permanence makes the baby search for objects that have disappeared and abandon the "out of sight out of mind" attitude so typical of newborns. In science, the double movement of geometrization of physics and physicalization of space accomplished by Albert Einstein when he applied Georg Riemann's geometry to gravity modified completely the way physicists looked at the world. Thus progress in cognition both generates and is generated by novelty.

But novelty is not enough. Knowledge needs to be true knowledge (novelty) and knowledge of the truth (necessity). This could not be explained only in terms of an interaction between nature and nurture because how could mere contingencies generate necessity? Piaget offers a more general factor: *equilibration,* subsuming nature and nurture, under one explanatory system transcending them in levels of generality, necessity, and abstraction. To understand the abstract nature of equilibration, let us suppose that living organisms are governed by the second law of thermodynamics. If this is so, then the resulting increase in entropy of the system cannot be considered as either innate or acquired but as depending on a law of probability. In the very same way, equilibration is the law of development, an abstract necessary principle independent of any contingencies and resulting in an endless optimization of living systems (homeorhesis) in a stage like sequence considered as the ideal course of evolution or chreode.

A number of criticisms have been raised against Piaget's psychological points: age of attainment, neuropsychological mechanisms of concept acquisition, etc. These criticisms have unfortunately confused Piaget's epistemological points that are essential to his theory with psychological ones that are contingent and thus open to change for him too, because they were just algorithms.

See also ANIMISM; COGNITIVE DEVELOPMENT; INFANT COGNITION; NAIVE MATHEMATICS; NAIVE PHYSICS; NATIVISM; THEORY OF MIND

—*Jacques Vonèche*

References

Inhelder, B., and J. Piaget. (1953). *The Growth of Logical Thinking from Childhood to Adolescence: An essay on the construction of formal operational structures.* Translated by A. Parsons and S. Milgam (1972). London: Routledge and Kegan Paul.

Piaget, J. (1926). *The Child's Conception of the World.* Translated by J. A. Thomlinson (1929). London: Kegan Paul, Trench, Trubner.

Piaget, J. (1932). *The Moral Judgment of the Child.* Translated (1932). London: Kegan Paul, Trench, Trubner.

Piaget, J. (1936). *The Origin of Intelligence in Children.* Translated (1952). New York: International University Press.

Piaget, J. (1937). *The Construction of Reality in the Child.* Translated (1954). New York: Basic Books.

Piaget, J., and B. Inhelder. (1948). *The Child's Conception of Space.* Translated (1956). London: Routledge and Kegan Paul.

Piaget, J., and B. Inhelder. (1966). *The Psychology of the Child.* Translated (1969). New York: Basic Books.

Piaget, J. (1945). *Play, Dreams and Imitation in Childhood.* Translated (1962). New York: W. W. Norton.

Piaget, J. (1947). *The Psychology of Intelligence.* Translated (1950). New York: Harcourt Brace.

Piaget, J. (1953). *Logic and Psychology.* Manchester: Manchester University Press.

Piaget, J. (1967). *Biology and Knowledge: An Essay on the Relations Between Organic Regulations and Cognitive Processes.* Translated (1971). Chicago: University of Chicago Press.

Piaget, J. (1968). *Structuralism.* Translated (1971). New York: Harper and Row.

Piaget, J. (1970). *The Principles of Genetic Epistemology.* Translated (1972). New York: Basic Books.

Piaget, J. (1975). *The Development of Thought: Equilibration of Cognitive Structures.* Translated (1977). New York: Viking Press.

Piaget, J., and J.-C. Bringuier. (1977). *Conversations with J. Piaget.* Translated (1980). Chicago: University of Chicago Press.

Piaget, J., and R. Garcia. (1987). *Towards a Logic of Meanings.* Translated (1991). Hillsdale, NJ: Erlbaum.

Piaget, J., and B. Inhelder. (1941). *The Child's Construction of Quantities: Conservation and Atomism.* Translated by Arnold J. Pomerans (1974). New York: Basic Books.

Piaget, J., and A. Szeminska. (1941). *The Child's Conception of Number.* Translated (1965). London: Routledge and Kegan Paul.

Further Readings

Gruber, H. and J. Vonèche. (1966). *The Essential Piaget: An Interpretative Reference and Guide.* North Vale, NJ: J. Aronson.

Chapman, M. (1988). *Constructive Evolution: Origins and Development of Piaget's Thought.* Cambridge: Cambridge University Press.

Pictorial Art and Vision

Pictorial art attempts to capture the three-dimensional structure of a scene—some chosen view of particular objects, people, or a landscape. The artist's goal is to convey a message about the world around us, but we can also find in art a message about the workings of the brain. Many look to art for examples of pictorial depth cues—perspective, occlusion, TEXTURE gradients, and so on—as these are the only cues available for depth in pictures. DEPTH PERCEPTION based on binocular disparity, vergence, and accommodation is inappropriate for the depths depicted, and head movements no longer provide new views of the scene. However, pictorial cues are abundant in real scenes—that is why they work in pictures—and there is no obvious benefit in studying their effectiveness in art as opposed to their effectiveness in natural scenes.

And yet pictorial art can tell us a great deal about vision and the brain if we pay attention to the ways in which paintings differ from the scenes they depict. First of all, we learn that artists get away with a great deal—impossible colors, inconsistent shading and shadows, inaccurate perspective, the use of lines to stand for sharp discontinuities in depth or brightness. These representational "errors" do not prevent human observers from perceiving robust three-dimensional forms. Art that captures the three-dimensional structure of the world without merely recreating or copying it offers a

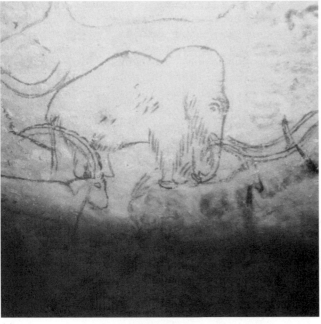

(a)

(b)

11083 - MILANO - La Flagellazione di N. S. - Signorelli - Brera   Anderson - Rom

(c)

Figure 1. (a) An early example of outline drawing from France. (b) As you view this image from different angles, the changes in the distance from face to hand and in the shape of the head are subtle. A 3-D computer model of this scene would require large-scale relative motions and 3-D shape changes to maintain the 2-D view seen with changing viewpoints. (c) Impossible lighting, highlights, or shadows (note the overlapping cast shadows at the bottom) are difficult to spot in paintings, implying that human observers use a simplistic local model of light and shade.

revealing glimpse of the short cuts and economies of the inner codes of vision. The nonveridicality of representation in art is so commonplace that we seldom question the reason why it works.

A line drawing of a building or an elephant can convey its 3-D structure very convincingly, but remember that there are no lines in the real world corresponding to the lines used in the drawings. The surface occlusions, folds, or creases that are represented by lines in drawings are revealed by changes in, say, brightness or texture in the real world, and these changes have one value extending on one side and a different value on the other. This is not a line. It is not obvious why lines should work at all. The effectiveness of line drawings is not based simply on learned convention, passed on through our culture. This point has been controversial (Kennedy 1975; see Deregowski 1989, and its following comments), but most recent evidence suggests that line drawings are universally interpreted in the same way—infants (Yonas and Arterberry 1994), stone-age tribesmen (Kennedy and Ross 1975), and even monkeys (Itakura 1994) appear to be capable of interpreting line drawings as we do. Nor is it the case that the lines in line drawings just trace the brightness discontinuities in the image, because this type of representation is rendered meaningless by the inclusion of cast shadow and pigment contours. By a quirk of design or an economy of encoding, lines may be directly activating the internal code for object structure, but only object contours can be present in the drawing for this shortcut to work. The shortcut, discovered and exploited by artists, hints at the simplicity of the internal code that underlies the vision of 3-D structures. This code is both simpler than the 2 ½-D sketch of David MARR and sparser than the compact, reversible codes (Olshausen and Field 1996) that may reflect the workings of early areas of VISUAL CORTEX. Both artists and brains have found out which are the key contours necessary to represent the essential structure of an object. By studying the nature of lines used in line drawings, scientists too may eventually join this group.

Another aspect as commonplace and as informative as the effectiveness of lines is that pictures are flat and yet they provide consistent, apparently 3-D interpretations from a wide range of viewpoints. This is not only convenient for the artist, but also prime evidence that our impressions of a 3-D world are not supported by true, 3-D internal representations. If we had real 3-D vision, the scene depicted in a flat picture would have to distort grotesquely in 3-D space as we moved about the picture. To the contrary, however, objects in pictures seem reassuringly the same as we change our vantage point (with some interesting exceptions; see Gregory 1994). We don't experience the distortions probably because the visual system does not generate a true 3-D representation of the object. It has some qualities of three dimensions but it is far from Euclidean. It may follow some other geometry, affine or nonmetric in nature (Todd and Reichel 1989; Busey, Brady, and Cutting 1990). The effectiveness of flat images is of course a boon to artists who do not have to worry about special vantage points and to film makers who can have theaters with more than one seat in them. It is also of great importance for understanding the internal representations of objects and space.

Finally, consider the enormous range of discrepancies between light and shade in the world and their renditions in art. When light and shade were introduced into art about 2,200 years ago, it was through the use of local techniques such as lightening a surface fold to make it come forward (a Greek technique described by Pliny the Elder; see Gombrich 1976 for a beautiful reinterpretation of this ancient presentation of painting techniques). These local techniques of shading, shadows, and highlights were applied with little thought to making them all consistent with a given light source—and yet they all work very well. Even 500 years ago, when the geometry of perspective was well understood, the geometry of light was still ignored. The resulting errors in light and shadow would be caught immediately by any analysis based on physical optics, but pass unnoticed to human observers. Modern artists with a full understanding of the physics of light and shade available to them often still choose inconsistencies in lighting either because it never matters much, or perhaps because it looks better.

Evidently, we as observers do not reconstruct a light source in order to recover the depth from shading and shadow, we do not act as optical geometers in the way that computer graphics programs can. We do not notice inconsistencies across different portions of a painting but recover depth cues locally. The message here is that in the real world, the information is rich and redundant, so we do not have to analyze the image much beyond a local region to resolve any ambiguities. When faced with the sparser cues of pictorial art, we do not adopt a larger region of analysis—the local cues are meaningful, albeit inconsistent with cues in other areas of the painting. To the advantage of the artist, the inconsistencies go unnoticed. And again, like many aspects of art, this discrepancy between the art and the scene it depicts informs us about the brain within us as much as about the world around us.

See also GESTALT PERCEPTION; ILLUSIONS; LIGHTNESS PERCEPTION; SHAPE PERCEPTION; STRUCTURE FROM VISUAL INFORMATION SOURCES; SURFACE PERCEPTION

—*Patrick Cavanagh*

References

Busey, T. A., N. P. Brady, and J. E. Cutting. (1990). Compensation is unnecessary for the perception of faces in slanted pictures. *Perception and Psychophysics* 48: 1–11.

Deregowski, J. B. (1989). Real space and represented space: Cross-cultural perspectives. *Behavioral and Brain Sciences* 12: 51–119.

Gombrich, E. H. (1976). *The Heritage of Apelles.* Oxford: Phaidon Press.

Gregory, R. (1994). Experiments for a desert island. *Perception* 23: 1389–1394.

Itakura, S. (1994). Recognition of line-drawing representations by a chimpanzee (*Pan troglodytes*). *Journal of General Psychology* 121: 189–197.

Kennedy, J. M. (1975). Drawings were discovered, not invented. *New Scientist* 67: 523–527.

Kennedy, J. M., and A. S. Ross. (1975). Outline picture perception by the Songe of Papua. *Perception* 4: 391–406.

Olshausen, B. A., and D. J. Field. (1996). Emergence of simple-cell receptive field properties by learning a sparse code for natural images. *Nature* 381: 606–607.

Todd, J. T., and F. D. Reichel. (1989). Ordinal structure in the visual perception and cognition of smoothly curved surfaces. *Psychological Review* 96: 643–657.

Yonas, A., and M. E. Arterberry. (1994). Infants perceive spatial structure specified by line junctions. *Perception* 23: 1427–1435.

Further Readings

Gombrich, E. H. (1960). *Art and Illusion.* Princeton: Princeton University Press.

Gregory, R., J. Harris, P. Heard, and D. Rose. (1995). *The Artful Eye.* Oxford: Oxford University Press.

Kennedy, J. M. (1974). *The Psychology of Picture Perception.* San Francisco: Jossey-Bass Inc.

Maffei, L., and A. Fiorentini. (1995). *Arte e Cervello.* Bologna: Zanichelli Editore.

Willats, J. (1997). *Art and Representation.* Princeton: Princeton University Press.

Pitts, Walter

Walter Pitts was born in 1923, vanished from the scene in the late 1950s, and died at the end of the 1960s, having destroyed, as much as he could, any traces of his past existence. He is a peculiarly difficult subject for a biography because, although he remains a vividly haunting memory to those who knew him, he seems only a group delusion to others. At least that was the opinion of the neurologist Norman GESCHWIND.

Pitts appeared as a penniless 14-year-old at the University of Chicago in 1937, attended various classes, though unregistered, and was accepted by Rashevsky's coterie as a very talented but mysterious junior. All that was known of him was that he came from Detroit, and that would be all that was known thereafter.

An autodidact, he read Latin, Greek, Sanskrit, and German (though did not speak them) and apparently was advanced well beyond his years in LOGIC. The last can be illustrated by a confirmable anecdote. In 1938 he appeared at the office of Rudolf Carnap, whose most recent book on logic had appeared the previous year. Without introducing himself, Pitts laid out his copy opened to a section annotated marginally, and proceeded to make critical comments on the material. Carnap, after initial shock, defended his work and engaged with Pitts in an hour or so of talk. Pitts then left with his copy. For several weeks, Carnap hunted through the university for "that newsboy who understood logic," finally located him, and found a job for him, for Pitts had no funds and lived only on what he could earn from ghosting papers for other students.

In 1938, Pitts, Jerry Lettvin, and Hy Minsky (the future economist) formed a friendship that would endure over the years. When Lettvin went to medical school in 1939 at the University of Chicago, they would still meet often. In 1941, Warren MCCULLOCH came to the University of Illinois from Yale and Gerhardt von Bonin introduced Pitts and Lettvin to him. Thereafter Pitts joined the laboratory unofficially.

Pitts was homeless, Lettvin wanted to escape his family, and so McCulloch, together with his remarkable wife Rook, in spite of having four children already, brought the pair into their household. In late 1942, after weeks of reviewing the material in neurophysiology, Pitts told McCulloch of Leibniz's dictum that any task which can be described completely and unambiguously by a finite set of terms can be performed by a logical machine. Six years earlier TURING had published his marvelous essay on the universal computing engine. The analogy of neurons (as pulsatile rather than two-state devices) to the elements of a logical machine was inescapable. By 1943 McCulloch and Pitts published their famous paper, "A Logical Calculus of the Ideas Immanent in Nervous Activity." In 1947 they added the work "How We Know Universals." It was an attempt to interpret the structure of cortex as providing the sort of net that could abstract form independent of scale.

In 1943 Pitts, visiting Lettvin (who was interning in Boston), met Norbert WIENER and was invited to come to MIT as a research assistant. By the beginning of 1944, Pitts had been taken by the Kellex Corporation (a branch of the atomic bomb project). In the late 1940s he returned to MIT and began a project extending the work of Caianiello (on two-dimensionally connected nets) to three-dimensionally connected arrays—an extremely difficult problem.

In 1951, Jerry Wiesner, at the behest of Wiener, invited McCulloch, Patrick Wall, and Lettvin to join the Research Laboratory of Electronics (RLE) as research associates. Despite the loss of status and income, the three accepted with the full enthusiasm of their wives. They and Pitts formed a new laboratory at RLE.

But in late 1952, Wiesner received a letter from Mexico City where Wiener and his wife were visiting Arthur Rosenblueth. Viciously phrased, it severed all relations with McCulloch's group, which included Pitts. Only after a decade did Rosenblueth reveal what had set off this explosion. It had nothing to do with any substantive cause but was the result of a deliberate and cynical manipulation designed to sever Wiener's connection with McCulloch and his group. The details are not edifying; Wiener was victimized as much as the group.

The effect on Pitts was devastating; he was the most vulnerable. Wiener had become the father he had never had. From that point on, Pitts went into a steep decline. He abandoned interest in the work, and though willing enough to help, lost all initiative. Nothing could be done to arrest his decline. Pitts would have nothing to do with any psychiatrist, even those whom he met at the Macy symposia and other such roundtables. He destroyed all of his past work that he could find and became a ghost long before he died.

On a personal level, Pitts was a wonderful friend, and an inexhaustible fount of knowledge about everything, the arts as much as the sciences. One asked him a serious question only if there was enough time to hear the full answer, which was sometimes several hours long, but never didactic, rather, extremely witty and tailored to the understanding of the inquirer.

All that vanished before the end of the 1950s. He died alone in a boarding house in Cambridge after doing his best for close to a decade to avoid being found by his friends. Nothing of his work was left. But beyond question his influence shaped much of the thought of the laboratory and the approach to physiology from a philosophical view.

See also AUTOMATA; CHURCH-TURING THESIS; NEURAL NETWORKS; VON NEUMANN

—*Jerome Lettvin*

References

McCulloch, W., and W. Pitts. (1943). A logical calculus of the ideas immanent in nervous activity. *Bulletin of Mathematical Biophysics* 5: 115–133. Reprinted in W. S. McCulloch (1965/1988), *Embodiments of Mind.* Cambridge, MA: MIT Press.

Pitts, W., and W. McCulloch. (1947). On how we know universals: The perception of auditory and visual forms. *Bulletin of Mathematical Biophysics* 9: 127–147. Reprinted in W. S. McCulloch (1965/1988), *Embodiments of Mind.* Cambridge, MA: MIT Press.

Further Readings

Anderson, J. A. (1996). From discrete to continuous and back again. In R. Moreno-Diaz and J. Mira-Mira, Eds., *Brain Processes, Theories and Models: An International Conference in Honor of W. S. McCulloch 25 Years After His Death.* Cambridge, MA: MIT Press.

Cull, P. (1996). Neural nets: classical results and current problems. In R. Moreno-Diaz and J. Mira-Mira, Eds., *Brain Processes, Theories and Models: An International Conference in Honor of W. S. McCulloch 25 Years After his Death.* Cambridge, MA: MIT Press.

Howland, R., J. Y. Lettvin, W. S. McCulloch, W. Pitts, and P. D. Wall (1955). Reflex inhibition by dorsal root interaction. *Journal of Neurophysiology* 18: 1–17. Reprinted in W. S. McCulloch (1965/1988), *Embodiments of Mind.* Cambridge, MA: MIT Press.

Lettvin, J. (1989). Introduction. In R. McCulloch, Ed., *Collected Works of Warren S. McCulloch,* vol. 1. Salinas, CA: Intersystems Publications.

Lettvin, J., H. Maturana, W. McCulloch, and W. Pitts. (1959). What the frog's eye tells the frog's brain. *Proceedings of the IRE* 47: 1940–1959. Reprinted in W. S. McCulloch (1965/1988), *Embodiments of Mind.* Cambridge, MA: MIT Press.

Wall, P. D., W. S. McCulloch, J. Y. Lettvin, and W. H. Pitts. (1955). Effects of strychnine with special reference to spinal afferent fibres. *Epilepsia* Series 3, 4: 29–40. Reprinted in W. S. McCulloch (1965/1988), *Embodiments of Mind.* Cambridge, MA: MIT Press.

Planning

Planning is the process of generating (possibly partial) representations of future behavior prior to the use of such plans to constrain or control that behavior. The outcome is usually a set of actions, with temporal and other constraints on them, for execution by some agent or agents. As a core aspect of human intelligence, planning has been studied since the earliest days of AI and cognitive science. Planning research has led to many useful tools for real-world applications, and has yielded significant insights into the organization of behavior and the nature of reasoning about actions.

Early work in cognitive science sought to create general domain-independent problem solvers that exhibited some of the characteristics observed in human problem solving. The most influential early example was the General Problem Solver (GPS) proposed in 1959 (Newell and Simon 1963). It introduced techniques still in regular use today: means-ends analysis or goal directed problem solving, and finding "differences" between goal and current states.

This work was combined with search methods being studied in operations research (e.g., branch-and-bound methods), and with research on representation and reasoning from predicate logic in various theorem proving methods (e.g., Green 1969), so that by the end of the 1960s some long-lasting methods were emerging (*see* HEURISTIC SEARCH and SITUATION CALCULUS).

In 1969, the Stanford Research Institute Problem Solver, or STRIPS, (Fikes, Hart, and Nilsson 1971) represented application domain states in first-order logic, introduced a way to represent the actions of the domain in terms of changes to the world state, used means-end analysis to identify goals and subgoals that needed to be solved as stepping stones to a solution, searched through a space of possible solutions, and employed a simple but effective representation of the actions possible in the domain—as STRIPS operators. Many of these techniques form the basis for later work in planning.

Many planning techniques are formulated as search problems. Early planning approaches, including STRIPS, used a search technique in which the nodes of the search represented application domain states directly and the search arcs were the domain actions that could transform those states. This is termed "application state space" or "situation space." For example, the node state might represent the position of a robot waiter and the items on various tables:

At(Robot,Counter) and On(Cup-a,Table-1) and On(Plate-a,Table-1),

and the action arcs might represent the movement of a robot waiter, or a pickup action of the robot:

Operator Pickup(x)
Preconditions: On(x,y) and At(Robot,y)
Delete list: On(x,y)
Add list: Held(x)

STRIPS operators represent an action as having preconditions that have to be satisfied in the state in which the action is performed, and a delete list and add list of effects that represent changes made to the state following the performance of the action.

Later approaches have concentrated on searching through a different space—that of partially defined plans. A search space node is a partial plan and an arc is a partial plan modification operator (PMO). For example, a PMO might ensure the satisfaction of a condition on some activity in the partial plan. Each node of the search space defines an entire set of possible plan elaborations that fit within the constraints in the partial-plan. This method therefore can support "constraint posting" or "least commitment planning" in which decisions are postponed rather than a selection being made arbitrarily.

The integration of powerful constraint management techniques alongside planning methods is possible within this framework (e.g., as in MOLGEN (Stefik 1981) for plan object constraints, Deviser (Vere 1981) and FORBIN (Dean, Firby, and Miller 1990) for temporal constraints, and SIPE (Wilkins 1988) for resource constraints). This means that planning and scheduling techniques can be intermixed (*see* TEMPORAL REASONING).

Partial-plan search spaces lend themselves very well to "refinement planning" approaches (Kambhampati, Knoblock, and Yang 1996), where an outline plan is refined to address outstanding flaws or issues. However, it also lends itself to refining existing partial descriptions of a solution to a problem, to instantiating previously created generic plans, or to adapting plans drawn from case libraries (*see* CASE-BASED REASONING AND ANALOGY).

In the mid-1970s, NOAH (for Net of Action Hierarchies) (Sacerdoti 1977), and then "Nonlin" (the nonlinear planner built by Austin Tate) (Tate 1977), began to allow plans to be represented as partial orders on the actions contained within them, rather than insisting on the activities within plans being fully ordered. (Unfortunately, the terminology of the time led to partially ordered plans also being called "nonlinear" plans, which caused confusion with the "linear" and "nonlinear" planning approaches to the order in which goals and sub goals were solved in planners.) Some problems that had caused difficulty for earlier planners such as STRIPS were more easily addressed when a partially ordered plan representation was used, but it became more difficult to ensure that conditions on actions in the plan were satisfied from the effects of earlier actions. Potential interactions with parallel actions had to be resolved in a valid plan. Means to "protect" the condition establishment had to be added to planners (as introduced in HACKER; Sussman 1975). The "Nonlin" planner's question answering procedure (Tate 1977) included means to decide whether a specified condition was already satisfied at a given point in a partially ordered network of actions and, if necessary, could propose orderings to be added to the plan to satisfy such a condition. This provides information that can support the protection of the plan's causal structure (also called "goal structure" or "teleology"). This work was later used as the basis for the formalization of the "modal truth criterion" (Chapman 1991) used at the heart of later planners for condition establishment and protection.

Partially ordered planning (POP) algorithms are the basis for a number of modern planners such as SIPE (Wilkins 1988), O-Plan (Currie and Tate 1991), and UCPOP (Penberthy and Weld 1992).

The hierarchical organization of action descriptions is an important technique that may reduce complexity and significantly increase the scale of plans that can be generated in some domains. Most practical planners employ "hierarchical planning" methods. A library of action descriptions is maintained, some of which have a decomposition into a number of subactions at a more detailed level, and some of which are considered "primitive." For example, in the robot waiter domain, a high-level "Cleartable" action may be decomposed into primitive subactions to move to a table, pick up an item on the table, move to the counter, and put down the item held in the robot hand. A higher-level action in the plan can then be replaced with some suitable decomposition into more detailed actions. This is sometimes referred to as "hierarchical task network" (HTN) planning.

HTN planning lends itself to the refinement planning model. An initial plan can incorporate the task specification, assumptions about the situation in which the plan is to be executed, and perhaps a partial solution. This can then be refined through the hierarchy into greater levels of detail while also addressing outstanding issues and flaws in the plan.

Researchers and technologists in the planning field have added many extra features to the basic STRIPS action representation over the years. These have included:

1. Abstraction of the levels of conditions and effects (as in ABSTRIPS (for ABstract STRIPS); Sacerdoti 1974) where a skeleton plan is first developed that addresses important preconditions before refining that to deal with other detailed preconditions; for example, in the robot waiter domain, we may first develop a plan that ignores details of the robot's movements between tables.
2. The addition of resource, time, and spatial constraints to reflect the scheduling requirements on actions.
3. The use of universally quantified preconditions or effects; for example, a "Clearall" action to move all items on a given table to the counter.

The expressiveness of a planner's action representation is a major contributor to the effectiveness of a planning system, but can also lead to very large search spaces if used in uncontrolled ways (see COMPUTATIONAL COMPLEXITY).

Techniques from knowledge engineering and knowledge acquisition are beginning to be used to improve the modeling and capture of information about planning domains. In common with experience in KNOWLEDGE-BASED SYSTEMS, the use of richer models of the application domain have been found to be beneficial, such as in search space pruning and guidance.

Planning as a field has branched out in recent years to include a wide range of research topics related to reasoning about activities. One important area of investigation involves planning for activities that take place in environments where the outcome of actions is uncertain. For example, the robot waiter "Pickup" action may fail if an object is too heavy. Some of the techniques used in "classical" AI planning assume "perfect" information about the outcomes of actions. However, there is also a great deal of work on coping with uncertainty during the planning process or during the execution of plans.

Conditional or "contingency" branches may be included in a plan to allow for the most likely scenarios. "Reactive planning" techniques can be used to select activities at execution time on the basis of the situation that a system finds itself in. Uncertainty has also been addressed by general-purpose algorithms for solving planning problems cast as Markov decision processes (Dean et. al. 1995; see also MULTIAGENT SYSTEMS).

The volume *Readings in Planning* (Allen, Hendler, and Tate 1990) collects together many seminal papers that have documented the main advances in the field of planning. It presents a historical perspective to the work undertaken in this field. Several overviews in the *Readings* volume from different perspectives serve as an introduction to research on planning.

See also KNOWLEDGE REPRESENTATION; ROBOTICS; PROBLEM SOLVING; INTELLIGENT AGENT ARCHITECTURE

—*Austin Tate*

References

Allen, J. F., J. Hendler, and A. Tate. (1990). *Readings in Planning.* San Francisco: Kaufmann.

Chapman, D. (1991). Planning for conjunctive goals. *Artificial Intelligence* 32: 333–377.

Currie, K. W., and A. Tate. (1991). O-Plan: The Open Planning Architecture. *Artificial Intelligence* 52 (1): 49–86.

Dean, T., J. Firby, and D. Miller. (1990). Hierarchical planning involving deadlines, travel time and resources. *Computational Intelligence* 4 (4): 381–398.

Dean, T., L. Kaebling, J. Kirman, and A. Nicholson. (1995). Planning under time constraints in stochastic domains. *Artificial Intelligence* 76 (1–2): 35–74.

Fikes, R. E., P. E. Hart, and N. J. Nilsson. (1971). STRIPS: A new approach to the application of theorem proving to problem solving. *Artificial Intelligence* 3 (4): 251–288.

Green, C. (1969). Application of theorem proving to problem solving. *Proceedings of the First International Joint Conference on Artificial Intelligence (IJCAI-69).* Washington, DC: IJCAII, pp. 219–239.

Kambhampati, S., C. Knoblock, and Q. Yang. (1995). Planning as refinement search: A unified framework for evaluating design tradeoffs in partial order planning. *Artificial Intelligence* 76: 167–238.

Newell, A., and H. A. Simon. (1963). GPS, a program that simulates human thought. In E. A. Fiegenbaum and J. Feldman, Eds., *Computers and Thought.* New York: McGraw Hill, pp. 279–293.

Penberthy, J. S., and D. S. Weld. (1992). UCPOP: A sound, complete, partial order planner for ADL. *Proceedings of Knowledge Representation 1992 (KR-92)* pp. 103–114.

Sacerdoti, E. D. (1974). Planning in a hierarchy of abstraction spaces. *Artificial Intelligence* 5(2): 115–135.

Sacerdoti, E. D. (1977). *A Structure for Plans and Behavior.* Amsterdam: Elsevier.

Stefik, M. J. (1981). Planning with constraints. *Artificial Intelligence* 16: 111–140.

Sussman, G. J. (1975). *A Computer Model of Skill Acquisition.* Elsevier/North-Holland.

Tate, A. (1977). Generating project networks. In *Proceedings of the International Joint Conference on Artificial Intelligence (IJCAI-77)* San Francisco: Kaufmann.

Vere, S. (1981). Planning in time: Windows and durations for activities and goals. In *IEEE Transactions on Pattern Analysis and Machine Intelligence,* vol. 5. Los Alamitos, CA: IEEE Press.

Wilkins, D. (1988). *Practical Planning.* San Francisco: Morgan Kaufmann.

Further Readings

Drabble, B. (1996). *Proceedings of the Third International Conference on Artificial Intelligence Planning Systems.* Menlo Park, CA: AAAI Press.

Georgeff, M. P., and A. L. Lansky. (1986). Reasoning about actions and plans. In *Proceedings of the 1986 Workshop, Timberline, Oregon.* San Francisco: Morgan Kaufmann.

Kambhampati, S., and D. S. Nau. (1996). On the nature and role of modal truth criteria in planning. *AIJ* 82: 129–155.

McAllister, D., and D. Rosenblitt. (1991). Systematic non-linear planning. In *Proceedings of the Ninth National Conference on Artificial Intelligence* (AAAI-91), vol. 2. Anahiem, CA: AAAI Press, pp. 634–639.

Russell, S. J., and P. Norvig. (1995). *Artificial Intelligence: A Modern Approach.* Englewood, NJ: Prentice-Hall.

Simmons, R., and M. Veloso. (1998). *Proceedings of the Fourth International Conference on Artificial Intelligence Planning Systems.* Menlo Park, CA: AAAI Press.

Tate, A., Ed. (1996). *Advanced Planning Technology—The Technological Achievements of the* ARPA/*Rome Laboratory Planning Initiative.* Menlo Park, CA: AAAI Press.

Weld, D. (1994). An introduction to least-commitment planning. *Artificial Intelligence* 15: 27–61.

Zweben, M., and M. E. Fox, Eds. (1995). *Intelligent Scheduling.* San Francisco: Kaufmann.

Plasticity

See AUDITORY PLASTICITY; NEURAL DEVELOPMENT; NEURAL PLASTICITY

Play

See SOCIAL PLAY BEHAVIOR

Poetry

See METER AND POETRY

Polysynthetic Languages

Polysynthetic languages are languages that allow the formation of extremely long and complex words that are built up spontaneously out of many smaller parts. One such word can typically be the functional equivalent of an entire sentence in a language like English. For example, a speaker of the Mohawk language might make up the word *wahonwatia'tawitsherahetkenhten',* and this would immediately be understood by other Mohawk speakers as meaning "She made the thing that one puts on one's body ugly for him." The term *polysynthesis* was coined in the late 1800s, when linguists began to develop typologies of natural languages based on knowledge of languages from outside Europe and the Middle East. For these early typologists, a *synthetic* language was one like Latin and Greek, which use affixes to express the structural and meaning relationships among the words in a sentence. A polysynthetic language, then, is one that carries this method of expression to an extreme (Boas 1911; Sapir 1921; the first important discussion of the concept is Humboldt 1836, although he doesn't use this term). Polysynthesis is particularly associated with the languages of North America, Inuit and Aztec being two paradigm-defining cases. Nevertheless, it refers to a structural type of language, not a linguistic area: there are polysynthetic languages spoken in Australia, New Guinea, Siberia, and India, whereas many native American languages are not polysynthetic. The polysynthetic languages probably do not constitute a discrete type; rather there seems to be a continuum of languages determined by how much they rely on complex words to express various linguistic relationships.

The study of polysynthetic languages has been important for several reasons. First, they present an excellent way of exploring the relationships between the different branches of linguistics. In particular, ideas about the connections between SYNTAX and MORPHOLOGY are well studied by looking at these languages, because they seem to use a different division of labor from languages like English, with more burden on morphology and less on syntax. Thus, the study of such languages has led to new proposals about the relationship between these components (e.g., Sadock 1980, 1985; Baker 1988). These languages also raise interesting questions about the LEXICON and its relationship to both syntax and morphology, because it is clear that speakers of a polysynthetic language cannot possibly learn more than a tiny fraction of the expressions that count as words in their language.

However, the first and most important reason for studying polysynthetic languages is that they constitute one of the most extreme and "exotic" classes of language in a linguistic TYPOLOGY. As such, they provide one of the strongest testing grounds for the validity of proposed LINGUISTIC UNIVERSALS. In this way, they become indirectly relevant to questions about the INNATENESS OF LANGUAGE, because that idea implies that there must be many substantive features of natural language that are attested across the whole human species (see also RATIONALISM VS. EMPIRICISM). Finally, polysynthetic languages raise questions about the EVOLUTION OF LANGUAGE: their existence forces one to ask how it is that human linguistic capacities are articulated enough to account for the ease of language acquisition and yet flexible enough to generate languages that are superficially so different.

What linguists think they have learned about such matters from studying polysynthetic languages has varied over time. These languages contributed greatly to the impression of Boas and Sapir that "language is a human activity that varies without assignable limit" (Sapir 1921), leading away from linguistic universals, innateness, and rationalism. However, more recent research has uncovered facts that point toward the opposite conclusion. For example, one common aspect of polysynthesis is noun incorporation, whereby the noun referring to the thing affected by an action is expressed inside the verb, rather than as a separate direct object (see THEMATIC ROLES and GRAMMATICAL RELATIONS). Thus, in Mohawk one can say *wa'kana'tara-kwetare'* 'It cut the bread,' a single word that contains both *na'tar* 'bread' and *kwetar* 'cut'. This is unlike English, where one cannot naturally say *It bread-cut*. However, there is a point of similarity as well. English does allow affected objects and verbs to be compounded in other environments: one can refer to a long, serrated knife as a *bread-cutter,* for example. Significantly, neither language allows a noun that refers to the cause of the event to be inside the verb. Thus, in Mohawk one cannot say *wawasharakwetare'* (containing *ashar* 'knife') for 'The knife cut it'; neither in English could one call a sliced-up loaf a *knife-cuttee*. Moreover, there is evidence that the verb and the affected object form a relatively tight unit in the syntax of English (the verb phrase) to the exclusion of the causer of the event (see X-BAR THEORY). Collating facts like these, one finds a true universal: affected objects form tighter constructions with verbs than causers do. This universal property then manifests itself in

different ways in English syntax, English morphology, and Mohawk syntax, because of differences in whether HEAD MOVEMENT takes place (Baker 1988).

Another property of polysynthetic languages is that their verbs contain elements that indicate the person, number, and gender of both the subject and object. As a result, the verb, subject, and object can appear in any imaginable word order, in addition to the subject-verb-object order that is required in English. The subject and the object can also be left out entirely. (Languages with these properties are called *nonconfigurational*; Hale 1983.) All this contributes to the impression that these languages have no syntactic structure to speak of—in contrast to English. The view changes, however, once one realizes that the elements in the verb are really the equivalent of English pronouns (Jelinek 1984; Van Valin 1985; Bresnan and Mchombo 1987; Mithun 1987). Thus, the Mohawk sentence *Sak wahahninu' atyatawi* is not best compared to English "Sak bought a dress," but rather to a colloquial dislocated structure "Sak, he finally bought it, the dress." Such structures allow some freedom of word order ("That dress, he finally bought it, Sak") and the omission of noun phrases ("He bought it") even in English. Baker (1996) argues that there are in fact many such abstract similarities between polysynthetic languages and more familiar ones. If this is correct, then polysynthetic languages could actually give some of the most striking evidence in favor of linguistic universals, the innateness of language, and a rationalist view.

—*Mark Baker*

References

Baker, M. (1988). *Incorporation: A Theory of Grammatical Function Changing.* Chicago: University of Chicago Press.

Baker, M. (1996). *The Polysynthesis Parameter.* New York: Oxford University Press.

Boas, F. (1911). Introduction. In F. Boas, Ed., *Handbook of American Indian Languages* pp. 1–83.

Bresnan, J., and S. Mchombo. (1987). Topic, pronoun, and agreement in Chichewa. *Language* 63: 741–782.

Hale, K. (1983). Warlpiri and the grammar of nonconfigurational languages. *Natural Language and Linguistic Theory* 1: 5–49.

Humboldt, W. von (1836). *Über die Verschiedenheit des menschlichen Sprachbaues und ihren Einfluss auf die geistige Entwicklung des Menschengeschlechts.* Berlin: Königliche Akademie der Wissenschaften.

Jelinek, E. (1984). Empty categories, case, and configurationality. *Natural Language and Linguistic Theory* 2: 39–76.

Mithun, M. (1987). Is basic word order universal? In R. Tomlin, Ed., *Coherence and Grounding in Discourse.* Amsterdam: Benjamins, pp. 281–328.

Sadock, J. (1980). Noun incorporation in Greenlandic. *Language* 56: 300–319.

Sadock, J. (1985). Autolexical syntax: A proposal for the treatment of noun incorporation and similar phenomena. *Natural Language and Linguistic Theory* 3: 379–440.

Sapir, E. (1921). *Language.* New York: Harcourt Brace Jovanovich.

Van Valin, R. (1985). Case marking and the structure of the Lakhota clause. In J. Nichols and A. Woodbury, Eds., *Grammar Inside and Outside the Clause.* Cambridge: Cambridge University Press, pp. 363–413.

Further Readings

Bach, E. (1993). On the semantics of polysynthesis. *Berkeley Linguistics Society* 19: 361–368.

Baker, M. (1997). Complex predicates and agreement in polysynthetic languages. In A. Alsina, J. Bresnan, and P. Sells, Eds., *Complex Predicates*. Stanford, CA: CSLI Publications, pp. 247–288.

Foley, W. (1991). *The Yimas language of New Guinea*. Stanford, CA: Stanford University Press.

Mithun, M. (1984). The evolution of noun incorporation. *Language* 60: 847–893.

Reinholtz, C., and K. Russell. (1994). Quantified NPs in pronominal argument langauges: Evidence from Swampy Cree. *North Eastern Linguistics Society* 25: 389–403.

Sadock, J. (1991). *Autolexical Syntax*. Chicago: University of Chicago Press.

Population-Level Cognitive Phenomena

See INTRODUCTION: CULTURE, COGNITION, AND EVOLUTION

Positron Emission Tomography

Emission tomography is a visualization technique in nuclear medicine that yields an image of the distribution of a previously administered radionuclide in any desired transverse section of the body. Positron emission tomography (PET) utilizes the unique properties of the annihilation radiation generated when positrons are absorbed in matter. It is characterized by the fact that an image reconstructed from the radioactive counting data is an accurate and quantitative representation of the spatial distribution of a radionuclide in the chosen section. This approach is analogous to quantitative antoradiography performed in laboratory animals but has the added advantage of allowing in vivo studies and, hence, studies to be performed safely in human subjects.

PET, now along with MAGNETIC RESONANCE IMAGING (MRI), is at the forefront of cognitive neuroscience research in normal humans. The signal used by PET and MRI in this research is based on the fact that changes in the cellular activity of the brain of normal, awake humans and unanesthetized laboratory animals are invariably accompanied by changes in local blood flow (for reviews, see Raichle 1987, 1998). While PET measures blood flow directly, functional MRI or fMRI as it is now called, relies on the local changes in magnetic field properties occurring in the brain that result from changes in the blood flow that exceed changes in oxygen consumption (Raichle 1998). This is known as the blood oxygen level–dependent or BOLD signal.

This robust, empirical relationship between blood flow and brain function has fascinated scientists for well over a hundred years. One has only to consult William JAMES's monumental two-volume text *Principles of Psychology* (James 1890) on page 97 of the first volume to find reference to changes in brain blood flow during mental activities. He references primarily the work of the Italian physiologist Angelo Mosso (1881) who recorded the pulsation of the human cortex in patients with skull defects following neurosurgical procedures. Mosso showed that these pulsations

increased regionally during mental activity and concluded, correctly we now know, that brain circulation changes selectively with neuronal activity.

At the close of World War II, Seymour Kety and his colleagues opened the modern era of studies of brain circulation and metabolism, introducing the first quantitative methods for measuring whole-brain blood flow and metabolism in humans. The introduction by Kety's group of an in vivo tissue autoradiographic measurement of regional blood flow applicable only in laboratory animals (Kety 1960; Landau et al. 1955) provided the first glimpse of quantitative changes in blood flow in the brain related directly to brain function. This work clearly foretold what was to come in the modern era of functional brain imaging with PET and MRI.

Soon after Kety and his colleagues introduced their quantitative methods for measuring whole-brain blood flow and metabolism in humans, David Ingvar, Neils Lassen, and their Scandinavian colleagues introduced methods applicable to humans that permitted regional blood flow measurements to be made using scintillation detectors arrayed like a helmet over the head (Lassen et al. 1963). They demonstrated directly in normal human subjects that blood flow changed regionally during changes in brain functional activity.

In 1973 Godfrey Hounsfield (Hounsfield 1973) introduced x-ray computed tomography (CT), a technique based upon principles presented in 1963 by Alan Cormack (Cormack 1963, 1973). Overnight the way in which we looked at the human brain changed. Immediately, researchers envisioned another type of tomography, positron emission tomography, or PET (Hoffman et al. 1976; Ter-Pogossian et al. 1975).

With the introduction of PET (Hoffman et al. 1976; Ter-Pogossian et al. 1975) a new era of functional brain mapping began. The autoradiographic techniques for the measurement of blood flow (Kety 1960; Landau et al. 1955) and glucose metabolism (Sokoloff et al. 1977) in laboratory animals could now be performed safely in humans (Raichle et al. 1983; Reivich et al. 1979).

Soon it was realized that highly accurate measurements of brain functional anatomy in humans could be performed with PET (Posner and Raichle 1994). While such functional brain imaging could be accomplished with either measurements of blood flow or metabolism (Raichle 1987), blood flow became the favored technique with PET because it could be measured quickly (in less than one minute) using an easily produced radiopharmaceutical ($H_2{}^{15}O$) with a short half-life (123 sec) which allowed many repeat measurements in the same subject (Raichle 1998).

The study of human cognition with PET was aided greatly by the involvement of cognitive psychologists in the 1980s whose experimental designs for dissecting human behaviors using information processing theory fit extremely well with the emerging functional brain imaging strategies (Posner and Raichle 1994). As a result of collaboration among neuroscientists, imaging scientists, and cognitive psychologists, a distinct behavioral strategy for the functional mapping of neuronal activity emerged. This strategy was based on a concept introduced by the Dutch physiologist Franciscus C. Donders in 1868 (reprinted in Donders 1969).

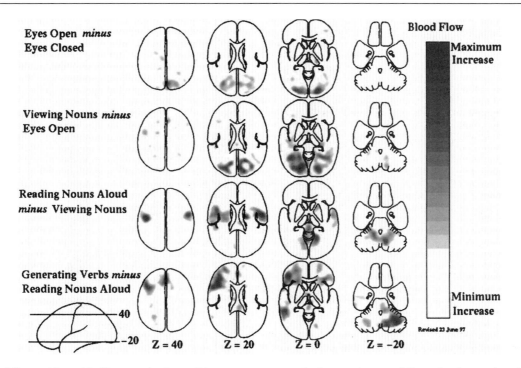

Figure 1. Four different hierarchically organized conditions are represented in these mean blood flow difference images obtained with PET. All of the changes shown in these images represent increases over the control state for each task. A group of normal subjects performed these tasks involving common English nouns (Petersen et al. 1988; Petersen et al. 1989) to demonstrate the spatially distributed nature of the processing by task elements going on in the normal human brain during a simple language task. Task complexity was increased from simply opening the eyes (row 1) through passive viewing of nouns on the television monitor (row 2); reading aloud the nouns as they appear on the screen (row 3); and saying aloud an appropriate verb for each noun as it appeared on the screen (row 4). These horizontal images are oriented with the front of the brain on top and the left side to the reader's left. The marking "Z = 40" indicates milimeters above and below a horizontal plane through the brain marked "Z = 40".

Donders proposed a general method of measuring thought processes based on a simple logic. He subtracted the time needed to respond to a light (say, by pressing a key) from the time needed to respond to a particular color of light. He found that discriminating color required about 50 msec. In this way, Donders isolated and measured a mental process for the first time by subtracting a control state (i.e., responding to a light) from a task state (i.e., discriminating the color of the light). This strategy (figure 1) was first introduced to functional brain imaging with PET in the study of single-word processing (Petersen et al. 1988, 1989, 1990) but quickly became the dominant approach to the study of all aspects of human cognition with functional brain imaging.

One criticism of this subtractive approach has been that the time necessary to press a key after a decision to do so has been made, for instance, is affected by the nature of the decision process itself. By implication, the nature of the processes underlying key press, in this example, may have been altered. Although this issue (known in cognitive science jargon as the assumption of pure insertion) has been the subject of continuing discussion in cognitive psychology, it finds its resolution in functional brain imaging, where changes in any process are directly signaled by changes in observable brain states. Events occurring in the brain are not hidden from the investigator as in the purely cognitive experiments. Careful analysis of the changes in the functional images reveals whether processes (e.g., spe-

cific cognitive decisions) can be added or removed without affecting ongoing processes (e.g., motor processes). Processing areas of the brain whose activity is differentially altered at various stages of a hierarchically organized cognitive paradigm can be readily seen with imaging (figure 2). Clearly, extant data now provide many examples of areas of the brain active at one stage in a hierarchically designed paradigm which become inactive as task complexity is increased (for a recent review, see Raichle 1998). While changes of this sort are hidden from the view of the cognitive scientist they become obvious when brain imaging is employed.

A final caveat with regard to imaging certain cognitive paradigms is that the brain systems involved do not necessarily remain constant through many repetitions of the task (e.g., see Raichle et al. 1994; Raichle 1998). While simple habituation might be suspected when a task is tedious, this is not the issue referred to here. Rather, when a task is novel and, more importantly, conflicts with a more habitual response to the presented stimulus, major changes can occur in the systems allocated to the task. Such changes have both practical and theoretical implications when it comes to the design and interpretation of cognitive activation experiments.

Functional brain imaging provides a unique perspective on the relationship between brain function and behavior in humans that is unavailable in the purely cognitive experiments and, in many instances, unattainable in experiments

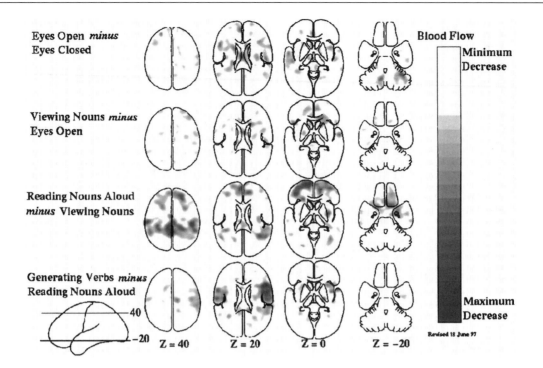

Figure 2. Hierarchically organized subtraction involving the same task conditions as shown in Figure 1 with the difference being that these images represent areas of decreased activity in the condition as compared with the control condition. Combining the information available in Figures 1 and 2 provides a fairly complete picture of the interactions between tasks and brain systems in hierarchically organized cognitive tasks when studied with functional brain imaging.

restricted to laboratory animals. fMRI has greatly expanded the work initiated with PET owing to its better spatial and temporal resolution. Using fMRI it is now possible, for example, to image the brain changes associated with single cognitive events in individual subjects (Buckner et al. 1996).

One of the great challenges remaining in the use of functional imaging with either PET or MRI is to understand more fully the relationship between brain blood flow and brain function (Raichle 1998).

See also CEREBRAL CORTEX; CORTICAL LOCALIZATION, HISTORY OF; ELECTROPHYSIOLOGY, ELECTRIC AND MAGNETIC EVOKED FIELDS; PSYCHOPHYSICS; UNITY OF SCIENCE; SINGLE-NEURON RECORDING

—Marcus Raichle

References

Buckner, R. L., P. A. Bandettini, K. M. O'Craven, R. L. Savoy, S. E. Petersen, M. E. Raichle, and B. R. Rosen. (1996). Detection of cortical activation during averaged single trials of a cognitive task using functional magnetic resonance imaging. *Proceedings of the National Academy of Sciences* 93: 14878–14883.

Cormack, A. M. (1963). Representation of a function by its line integrals, with some radiological physics. *Journal of Applied Physics* 34: 2722–2727.

Cormack, A. M. (1973). Reconstruction of densities from their projections, with applications in radiological applications. *Phys. Med. Biol.* 18: 195–207.

Donders, F. C. (1869/1969). On the speed of mental processes. *Acta Psychologia* 30: 412–431.

Hoffman, E. J., M. E. Phelps, N. A. Mullani, C. S. Higgins, and M. M. Ter-Pogossian. (1976). Design and performance characteristics of a whole-body positron tranxial tomograph. *Journal of Nuclear Medicine* 17: 493–502.

Hounsfield, G. N. (1973). Computerized transverse axial scanning (tomography): Part I. Description of system. *British Journal of Radiology* 46: 1016–1022.

James, W. (1890). *Principles of Psychology.* New York: Henry Holt, pp. 97–99.

Kety, S. (1960). Measurement of local blood flow by the exchange on an inert diffusible substance. *Methods in Medical Research* 8: 228–236.

Landau, W. M., W. H. Freygang Jr., L. P. Roland, L. Sokoloff, and S. Kety. (1955). The local circulation of the living brain: Values in the unanesthetized and anesthetized cat. *Transactions of the American Neurological Association* 80: 125–129.

Lassen, N. A., K. Hoedt-Rasmussen, S. C. Sorensen, E. Skinhoj, B. Cronquist, E. Bodforss, and D. H. Ingvar. (1963). Regional cerebral blood flow in man determined by Krypton-85. *Neurology* 13: 719–727.

Mosso, A. (1881). *Über den Kreislauf des Blutes im menschlichen Gehirn.* Leipzig: Verlag von Veit.

Petersen, S. E., R. T. Fox, M. I. Posner, M. Mintum, and M. E. Raichle. (1988). Positron emission tomographic studies of the cortical anatomy of single-word processing. *Nature* 331: 585–589.

Petersen, S. E., P. T. Fox, M. I. Posner, M. A. Mintun, and M. E. Raichle. (1989). Positron emission tomographic studies of the processing of single words. *Journal of Cognitive Neuroscience* 1: 153–170.

Petersen, S. E., P. T. Fox, A. Z. Snyder, and M. E. Raichle. (1990). Activation of extrastriate and frontal cortical areas by visual words and word-like stimuli. *Science* 249: 1041–1044.

Posner, M. I., and M. E. Raichle. (1994). *Images of Mind*. New York: W. H. Freeman.

Raichle, M. E. (1987). Circulatory and metabolic correlates of brain function in normal humans. In F. Plum, Ed., *Handbook of Physiology: The Nervous System V. Higher Functions of the Brain*. Bethesda, MD: American Physiological Society, pp. 643–674.

Raichle, M. E. (1998). Behind the scenes of function brain imaging: A historical and physiological perspective. *Proceedings of the National Academy of Sciences* 95: 765–772.

Raichle, M. E., W. R. W. Martin, P. Herscovitch, M. A. Mintun, and J. Markham. (1983). Brain blood flow measured with intravenous $H_2^{15}O$. 2. Implementation and validation. *Journal of Nuclear Medicine* 24: 790–798.

Raichle, M. E., J. A. Fiez, T. O. Videen, A. K. MacLeod, J. V. Pardo, P. T. Fox, and S. E. Petersen. (1994). Practice-related changes in human brain functional anatomy during nonmotor learning. *Cerebral Cortex* 4: 8–26.

Reivich, M., D. Kuhl, A. Wolf, J. Greenberg, M. Phelps, T. Ido, V. Casella, E. Hoffman, A. Alavi, and L. Sokoloff. (1979). The [18F] flourodeoxyglucose method for the measurement of local cerebral glucose utilization in man. *Circulation Research* 44: 127–137.

Sokoloff, L., M. Reivich, C. Kennedy, M. H. Des Rosiers, C. S. Patlak, K. D. Pettigrew, O. Sakurada, and M. Shinohara. (1977). The [14C]deoxyglucose method for the measurement of local glucose utilization: Theory, procedure and normal values in the conscious and anesthetized albino rat. *Journal of Neurochemistry* 28: 897–916.

Ter-Pogossian, M. M., M. E. Phelps, E. J. Hoffman, and N. A. Mullani. (1975). A positron-emission tomograph for nuclear imaging (PET). *Radiology* 114: 89–98.

Possible Worlds Semantics

The use of possible worlds as a part of a semantic theory of natural language is based on the truth-conditional theory of meaning, that is, that the meaning of a sentence in a language is constituted by the conditions under which that sentence is true. On this view, to know the meaning of a sentence is to know what the world would have to be like if that sentence were true. If the way the world is construed as the actual world, then other ways the world could be may be thought of as alternative possible but nonactual worlds. Knowing how the world would be if a particular sentence were true does not require knowledge of whether it *is* true, because in a given world *w*, a person need not know in *w* that *w* is the actual world. Thus, if I know the meaning of "Wellington is the capital of New Zealand," I do not have to know whether in fact it is the capital, but I do have to know what it would be like for it to be the capital. In possible worlds terms I have to know of any given world *w*, whether *w* is a world in which the sentence is true or whether *w* is a world in which it is false, but I do not have to know whether *w* is the actual world. To know which world is actual would be to be omniscient.

Our language has to be able to talk about things that may not exist. In a sentence that has become rather famous in the semantical literature, "Someone seeks a unicorn," there need be no particular unicorn that is being sought, and so in some way the idea of a unicorn, a creature that does not actually exist, has to be involved in the content of that sentence—a sentence, moreover, that all of us understand.

Possible worlds semantics is used in compositional theories of meaning, where the meaning of a complex sentence is to be obtained from the meaning of its parts (*see* COMPOSITIONALITY). It developed from the languages of MODAL LOGIC where the meaning of "*p* is true by necessity" (written Lp or $\Box p$) is obtained from the meaning of *p* by specifying the worlds in which Lp is true given the worlds in which *p* is. To be specific, Lp is true in *w* provided *p* is true in every *w'* possible relative to *w*. Dual to necessity is possibility. "It is possible that *p*" (written Mp or $\Diamond p$) is true at a world *w* if *p* itself is true in at least one *w'* possible relative to *w*. A more elaborate example is found in the semantics of counterfactual sentences. Where $p \Box\!\!\rightarrow q$ means that if *p* were the case, then *q* would be too, then (on one account) $p \Box\!\!\rightarrow q$ is true in a world *w* iff there is a world *w'* in which *p* and *q* are both true that is more similar to *w* than any world in which *p* is true but *q* is not. In studying these as logics it is customary (depending on which logic is being studied) to set up first a structure in which relations are given to specify that one world is or is not possible relative to another, or that a world w_1 is further from a world w_2 than a world w_3 is. But for studying natural language we cannot assume that any particular words like "possibly" are in any way special.

Typically, an implementation of possible worlds semantics for a language will require the language to be specified by a system of rules that give the LOGICAL FORM of every sentence. Then values are assigned to the simple symbols of a sentence in logical form in such a way that a set of indices (worlds, times, speaker, and whatever else is involved in the meaning of the sentence) emerges as the meaning of the final sentence. Thus in the sentence "Possibly Felix lives," the name "Felix" will have a person Felix as value, the verb "lives" will have as its value an operation that associates with an individual (in this case Felix) the set of worlds (and times) at which that individual lives; the adverb "possibly" will have as its value an operation that associates with a set of worlds (in this case the set of worlds in which it is the case that Felix lives) another set of worlds, in fact all the worlds from which the worlds in the first set are possible. The final sentence will then be true in a world *w* if there is a world *w'* possible relative to *w*, such that *w'* is in the set assigned to "Felix lives," that is, in the set of worlds in which Felix lives.

To deal with tensed languages worlds can be thought of as worlds at times. More neutrally these are called "semantical indices." Possible worlds semantics requires supplementation by generalizing such indices in various ways. Thus, to interpret "I" in a sentence like "I'd like an apple," one needs an index to supply a speaker (or someone regarded as the speaker). To interpret a sentence like "Everyone is present" one requires an index to supply a domain of people, because the sentence is presumably not intended to claim that everyone in the world is present, but only everyone in some contextually provided universe.

Possible worlds semantics abstracts from many features of linguistic behavior that have sometimes been thought important, though the extent to which this should be done can be controversial. Thus, for some possible worlds theorists the ascription of truth conditions to a sentence is intended to be completely neutral on the question of what an utterance of that sentence is being used to do. It might be being used to report a fact or issue an order or ask a question. Other theorists may be more hesitant to speak of nondeclaratives as having truth conditions. But perhaps more importantly for cognitive science, the ascription of truth conditions to a sentence is neutral on the question of just how those truth conditions are represented in the mind of a speaker. It is concerned with the question of how to categorize what constitutes a representation's having a certain content, not on the nature of the representation itself.

Possible worlds semantics as such can be neutral on the metaphysical status of possible worlds. At one extreme is the view that other possible worlds are just as real as the actual world. At another extreme is the view that possible worlds are no more than linguistic descriptions of how the world might be. For certain limited purposes, as for example in describing the language of a computer where the possibilities that can be represented are fixed and limited, it may be plausible to consider worlds to be descriptions. But it is plausible to claim that a general theory of MEANING should not presuppose any particular way of representing worlds.

See also INTENTIONALITY; LOGIC; PRAGMATICS; PROPOSITIONAL ATTITUDES; SEMANTICS; TENSE AND ASPECT.

—*Max Cresswell*

Further Readings

Cresswell, M. J. (1973). *Logics and Languages.* London: Methuen.

Cresswell, M. J. (1978). Semantic competence. In F. Guenthner and M. Guenthner-Reutter, Eds., *Meaning and Translation.* London: Duckworth, pp. 9–43. Reprinted in M. J. Gresswell, *Semantical Essays* 1988. Dordrecht: Kluwer, pp. 12–33.

Cresswell, M. J. (1985). *Structured Meanings.* Cambridge, MA: MIT Press/Bradford Books.

Cresswell, M. J. (1994). *Language in the World.* Cambridge: Cambridge University Press.

Lewis, D. K. (1972). General semantics. In D. Davidson and G. Harman, Eds., *Semantics of Natural Language.* Dordrecht: Reidel, pp. 169–218.

Lewis, D. K. (1973). *Counterfactuals.* Oxford: Blackwell.

Lewis, D. K. (1975). Languages and language. In K. Gunderson, Ed., *Language, Mind and Knowledge.* Minneapolis: University of Minnesota Press, pp. 3–35.

Lewis, D. K. (1986). *On the Plurality of Worlds.* Oxford: Blackwell.

Loux, M. J., Ed. (1979). *The Possible and the Actual.* Ithaca: Cornell University Press.

Putnam, H. (1975). The meaning of "meaning." In K. Gunderson, Ed., *Language, Mind and Knowledge.* Minneapolis: University of Minnesota Press, pp. 131–193. Reprinted in H. Putnam, *Mind, Language and Reality* (1975). Cambridge: Cambridge University Press, pp. 215–271.

Schiffer, S. (1987). *Remnants of Meaning.* Cambridge, MA: MIT Press.

Stalnaker, R. C. (1968). A theory of conditionals. In N. Rescher, Ed., *Studies in Logical Theory.* Oxford: Blackwell, pp. 98–112.

Stalnaker, R. C. (1978). Assertion. In P. Cole, Ed., *Syntax and Semantics,* vol. 9: *Pragmatics.* New York: Academic Press, pp. 315–332.

Stalnaker, R. C. (1984). *Inquiry.* Cambridge, MA: MIT Press.

Stalnaker, R. C. (1989). On what's in the head. In J. E. Tomberlin, Ed., *Philosophical Perspectives* 3: *Philosophy of Mind and Action Theory.* Atascadero, CA: Ridgeview Publishing Co., pp. 287–316.

Poverty of the Stimulus Arguments

The "poverty of the stimulus argument" is a form of the problem of the under-determination of theory by data, applied to the problem of language learning. Two other well-known problems of under-determination include Willard Van Orman Quine's (1960) Gavagai example (a visitor to a foreign country sees a rabbit pass just as his informant utters the word "gavagai;" given only this evidence, "gavagai" might mean anything from *rabbit, furry* or *nice day, isn't it?* to *undetached part of rabbit*) and Nelson Goodman's Grue paradox (why is it that we take our experience in which all emeralds that we have thus far observed have been green to suggest that emeralds are green rather than the (equally confirmed so far) possibility that emeralds are grue, namely "green when examined before the year 2000, and blue when examined thereafter"?).

Learning a language involves going beyond the data: a child hears only a finite number of sentences, yet learns to speak and comprehend sentences drawn from a grammar that can represent an infinite number of sentences. The trouble that the child faces is thus a problem of under-determination: any finite set of example sentences is compatible with an infinite number of grammars. The child's task is to pick among those grammars.

The term "poverty of the stimulus" itself is relatively recent, perhaps first used by Noam Chomsky (1980: 34); but the argument as applied to language learning goes at least as far back as Chomsky's (1959) review of B. F. Skinner's *Verbal Behavior.* The exact formulation of the argument varies (Chomsky 1980; Crain 1991; Garfield 1994; Wexler 1991), but a typical version states that (1) children rapidly and, to first approximation, uniformly acquire language; (2) children are only exposed to a finite amount of data; yet (3) children appear to converge on a grammar capable of interpreting unfamiliar sentences; the conclusion is often argued to be that some aspect of grammar is innate.

Although the poverty of the stimulus argument is sometimes described in conjunction with the claim that children do not receive correction for their grammatical errors (for a recent review of the role of parental correction in the acquisition of grammar, see Marcus 1993), it is important to reject the notion that nativist explanations of language acquisition depend on the lack of parental correction. Even if parents did provide reliable correction to their children, innate constraints on the generalizations that children make would be necessary, because many plausible errors simply never occur. For instance, children never go through a period where they erroneously form yes-no questions by moving the first *is* to the front of the sentence. Although one can turn *The man is hungry* into *Is the man hungry?,* children never, by a false analogy, turn *The man who is hungry is ordering dinner* into *Is the man who hungry is ordering dinner?* (e.g., Chomsky 1965; Crain and Nakayama 1987). More generally, at every stage of LANGUAGE ACQUISITION—inferring the meaning of a new word or morpheme, creating a morphological or syntactic rule, or determining the subcategorization frame of a new verb—the child can make an infinity of logically possible generalizations, regardless of whether negative evidence exists. But children do not simply cycle through all logical possibilities and check to see what their parents say about each one; their choice of hypotheses instead must, in part, be dictated by innately given learning mechanisms. The open question is not whether there are innately given constraints, but rather whether those constraints are specific to language.

An excellent example of the poverty of the stimulus argument comes from Peter Gordon's (1985) work on the relation between plural formation and compounding. Paul Kiparsky (1983) had noted that while irregular plurals can appear in compounds (*mice-infested*), regular plurals sound awkward inside of compounds (*rats-infested*), perhaps because the design of the grammar is such that the process of compounding can only use stored (irregular) plurals as input, whereas the process of compounding serves as input to the process of regular plural formation. If irregular plurals inside compounds were common, it would be easy to see how a general purpose learning device might learn the contrast between regulars and irregulars, but in fact, as Gordon noted, plurals inside compounds are rare. Given this, one might expect that children would not be able to systematically distinguish between regulars and irregulars appearing in compounds. But Gordon found that although children allow irregular plurals inside of compounds, they systematically exclude regulars from compounds; children say things like *mice-eater*, but not *rats-eater*. As Gordon put it, "it would seem that of all the hypotheses available, there would be little to persuade an open-minded learner to choose this, rather than some other path." Instead, Gordon suggests, the child's mind is structured such that it is predisposed to learn one kind of grammar rather than another.

Recently, some scholars have tried to use CONNECTIONIST APPROACHES TO LANGUAGE learning to challenge the poverty of the stimulus argument, but connectionist models cannot obviate the need for innate constraints; instead they would simply provide a different theory of what those constraints are. Different connectionist models differ from one another in their architecture, representational schemes, learning algorithms, and so forth; each model thus differs from every other model in its innate design (Marcus 1998a, 1998b). Advocates of radical connectionism often overlook the importance of these innate design features, but such models cannot refute the poverty of stimulus argument; instead they can only show that (at most) the innate constraints are different in character than those suggested by other researchers. Moreover, such researchers have yet to provide any concrete example of a putatively unlearnable aspect of language that has been later shown to be learnable; hence their critique of the poverty of the stimulus argument is for now without much force.

See also INDUCTION; INNATENESS OF LANGUAGE; NATIVISM; RADICAL TRANSLATION; WORD MEANING, ACQUISITION OF

—*Gary Marcus*

References

Chomsky, N. A. (1959). Review of *Verbal Behavior. Language* 35: 26–58.

Chomsky, N. A. (1965). *Aspects of a Theory of Syntax.* Cambridge, MA: MIT Press.

Chomsky, N. A. (1980). *Rules and Representations.* New York: Columbia University Press.

Crain, S. (1991). Language acquisition in the absence of experience. *Behavioral and Brain Sciences* 14.

Crain, S., and M. Nakayama. (1987). Structure dependence in grammar formation. *Language* 63: 522–543.

Garfield, J. L. (1994). Innateness. In S. Guttenplan, Ed., *A Companion to the Philosophy of Mind.* Oxford: Blackwell.

Gordon, P. (1985). Level-ordering in lexical development. *Cognition* 21: 73–93.

Kiparsky, P. (1983). Word-formation and the lexicon. In F. Ingemann, Ed., *Proceedings of the 1982 Mid-American Linguistics Conference.* Lawrence, KS: University of Kansas.

Marcus, G. F. (1993). Negative evidence in language acquisition. *Cognition* 46: 53–85.

Marcus, G. F. (1998a). Can connectionism save constructivism? *Cognition* 66: 153–182.

Marcus, G. F. (1998b). Rethinking eliminative connectionism. *Cognitive Psychology* 37(3).

Quine, W. V. O. (1960). *Word and Object.* Cambridge, MA: MIT Press.

Wexler, K. (1991). On the arguments from the poverty of the stimulus. In A. Kasher, Ed., *The Chomskyan Turn.* Oxford: Blackwell.

Pragmatics

Pragmatics is the study of the context-dependent aspects of MEANING that are systematically abstracted away from in the construction of LOGICAL FORM. In the semiotic trichotomy developed by Charles Morris, Rudolf Carnap, and C. S. Peirce in the 1930s, SYNTAX addresses the formal relations of signs to one another, SEMANTICS the relation of signs to what they denote, and pragmatics the relation of signs to their users and interpreters. Although some have argued for a pragmatics module within the general theory of speaker/hearer competence (or even a pragmatic component in the grammar), Sperber and Wilson (1986) argue that, like scientific reasoning—the paradigm case of a nonmodular, horizontal system—pragmatics cannot be a module, given the indeterminacy of the predictions it offers and the global knowledge it invokes (see MODULARITY AND LANGUAGE). In any case, a regimented account of language use facilitates a simpler, more elegant description of language structure. Those areas of context-dependent yet rule-governed aspects of meaning reviewed here include deixis, speech acts, presupposition, reference, and information structure; see also IMPLICATURE.

Pragmatics seeks to "characterize the features of the speech context which help determine which proposition is expressed by a given sentence" (Stalnaker 1972: 383). The meaning of a sentence can be regarded as a function from a context (including time, place, and possible world) into a proposition, where a proposition is a function from a possible world into a truth value. Pragmatic aspects of meaning involve the interaction between an expression's context of utterance and the interpretation of elements within that expression. The pragmatic subdomain of deixis or indexicality seeks to characterize the properties of shifters, indexicals, or token-reflexives (expressions like *I, you, here, there, now, then, hereby,* tense/aspect markers, etc.) whose meanings are constant but whose referents vary with the speaker, hearer, time and place of utterance, style or register, or purpose of speech act (see Levinson 1983, chap. 2).

If pragmatics is "the study of linguistic acts and the contexts in which they are performed" (Stalnaker 1972: 383), speech-act theory constitutes a central subdomain. It has long been recognized that the propositional content of utterance U can be distinguished from its illocutionary force, the speaker's intention in uttering U. The identification and classification of speech acts was initiated by Wittgenstein, Austin, and Searle. In an explicit performative utterance (e.g., *I hereby promise to marry you*), the speaker does something—that is—performs an act whose character is determined by her intention, rather than merely saying something. Austin (1962) regards performatives as problematic for truth-conditional theories of meaning, because they appear to be devoid of ordinary truth value; an alternate view is that a performative is automatically self-verifying when felicitous, constituting a contingent a priori truth like *I am here now*. Of particular linguistic significance are indirect speech acts, where the form of a given sentence (e.g., the yes/no question in *Can you pass the salt?*) belies the actual force (here, a request for action) characteristically conveyed by the use of that sentence. (See Levinson 1983; chap. 4, and Searle and Vanderveken 1985 for more on speech-act theory and its formalization.)

Although a semantic or logical presupposition is a necessary condition on the truth or falsity of statements (Frege 1892, Strawson 1950), a pragmatic presupposition is a restriction on the common ground, the set of propositions constituting the current context. Its failure or nonsatisfaction results not in truth-value gaps or nonbivalence but in the inappropriateness of a given utterance in a given context (Stalnaker 1974; Karttunen 1974). In presupposing Φ, I treat Φ as an uncontroversial element in the context of utterance; in asserting Ψ, I propose adding the propositional content of Ψ to the common ground or, equivalently, discarding $\sim\Psi$ from the set of live options, winnowing down the context set (possible worlds consistent with the shared beliefs of S[peaker] and H[earer]) by jettisoning worlds in which Ψ does not hold.

In stating *Even Kim left* I assert that Kim left while presupposing that others left and that Kim was unlikely to have left. Such presuppositions can be communicated as new information by a speaker who "tells his auditor something . . . by pretending that his auditor already knows it" (Stalnaker 1974: 202). S's disposition to treat a proposition as part of the common ground, thereby getting H to adjust his model of the common ground to encompass it, is codified in Lewis's rule of accommodation for presupposition (1979: 340): "If at time t something is said that requires presupposition P to be acceptable, and if P is not presupposed just before t, then—*ceteris paribus* and within certain limits—presupposition P comes into existence at t'." Accommodation, a special case of Gricean exploitation, is generalized by Lewis to descriptions, modalities, vagueness, and performatives.

How are the presuppositions of a larger expression determined compositionally as a function from those of its subexpressions? Karttunen's (1974) solution to this "projection problem" partitions operators into plugs, holes, and filters, according to their effect on presupposition inheritance, whereas Karttunen and Peters (1979) propose a formalization of inheritance of pragmatic presuppositions qua "conventional implicatures." Gazdar (1979) offers an alternative mechanism in which the potential presuppositions induced by subexpressions are inherited as a default but are canceled if they clash with propositions already entailed or implicated by the utterance or prior discourse context.

Subsequent work identifies empirical and conceptual problems for these models. Heim (1983) identifies an operator's projection properties with its context-change potential. Presuppositions are invariant pragmatic inferences: A sentence Σ presupposes ϕ if every context admitting entails ϕ. If a context c (a conjunction of propositions) is true and c admits Σ, then Σ is true with respect to c if the context incremented by Σ is true. But if Σ is uttered in a context c not admitting it, the addressee will adjust c to c', a context close to c but consistent with Σ. Heim's projection theory thus incorporates Stalnaker-Lewis accommodation, which appeals in turn to the Gricean model of a cooperative conversational strategy dynamically exploited to generate pragmatic inferences (see DYNAMIC SEMANTICS).

Soames (1989) provides a conspectus of formal approaches to presupposition, and see also van der Sandt (1992) for an anaphoric account of PRESUPPOSITION, projection, and accommodation formulated within discourse representation theory. On van der Sandt's theory, the very presupposition that presuppositions are determined compositionally is challenged, leading to a reassessment of the entire projection-problem enterprise.

Although speech acts and presuppositions operate primarily on the propositional level, reference operates on the phrasal level. Reference is the use of a linguistic expression (typically a noun phrase) to induce a hearer to access or create some entity in his mental model of the discourse. A discourse entity represents the referent of a linguistic expression—that is, the actual individual (or event, property, relation, situation, etc.) that the speaker has in mind and is saying something about.

Within philosophy, the traditional view has been that reference is a direct *semantic* relationship between linguistic expressions and the real world objects they denote (see SENSE AND REFERENCE and REFERENCE, THEORIES OF). Researchers in computer science and linguistics, however, have taken a different approach, viewing this relation as mediated through the (assumed) mutual beliefs of speakers and hearers, and therefore as quintessentially pragmatic. Under this view, the form of a referring expression depends on the assumed information status of the referent, which in turn depends on the assumptions that a speaker makes regarding the hearer's knowledge store as well as what the hearer is attending to in a given discourse context.

Given that every natural language provides its speakers with various ways of referring to discourse entities, there are two related issues in the pragmatic study of reference: (1) What are the referential options available to a speaker of a given language? (2) What are the factors that guide a speaker on a given occasion to use one of these forms over another? The speaker's choice among referring expressions (e.g., zero forms, pronominals, indefinites, demonstratives, definite descriptions, proper names) is constrained by the information status of discourse entities. Unidimensional accounts (e.g,. Gundel, Hedberg, and Zacharski 1993) provide a single, exhaustively ordered dimension ("assumed familiarity," "accessibility," "givenness") along which the various types of referring expressions are arranged. More recently, Prince (1992) offers a two-dimensional account in which entities are classified as, on the one hand, either discourse-old or discourse-new (based on whether or not they have been evoked in the prior discourse) and, on the other hand, either hearer-old or hearer-new (based on whether they are assumed to be present within the hearer's knowledge-store).

Related to information status is the notion of definiteness, which has been defined both as a formal marking of NPs and as an information status. Research into the meaning of the English definite article has generally been approached from one of two perspectives (Birner and Ward 1994); its felicitous use has been argued to require that the referent of the NP be either familiar within the discourse or uniquely identifiable to the hearer. In the absence of prior linguistic evocation, the referent must be accommodated (Lewis 1979) into the discourse model by the hearer.

Research into the discourse functions of syntax is based on the observation that every language provides its speakers with various ways to structure the same proposition. That is, a given proposition may be variously realized by a number of different sentence-types, or constructions, each of which is associated with a particular function in discourse. Consider the sentences in (1).

(1) a. John did most of the work on that project.
    b. Most of the work on that project was done by John.
    c. Most of the work on that project John did.
    d. It's John who did most of the work on that project.

The same proposition expressed by the canonical word-order sentence in (1a) can also be expressed by the (truth-conditionally equivalent) passive sentence in (1b), by the topicalization in (1c), and by the cleft sentence in (1d), among others, each of which reflects the speaker's view on how it is to be integrated by the hearer into the current discourse. For example, the topicalization (1c) allows the speaker to situate familiar, or discourse-old (Prince 1992) information in preposed position, thus marking the preposed constituent as related—or "linked"—to the prior discourse, whereas use of the cleft in (1d) reflects the speaker's belief that her hearer has in mind the fact that somebody did most of the work in question. Finally, with the passive in (1b), in which the canonical order of arguments is reversed, the speaker may present information that is relatively familiar within the discourse before information that is relatively unfamiliar within the discourse.

Such constructions serve an information-packaging function in that they allow speakers to structure their discourse in a maximally accessible way, thereby facilitating the incorporation of new information into the hearer's knowledge-store.

Like referring expressions, propositions contain information that can be either discourse-new/old and hearer-new/old.

Vallduví (1992) proposes a hierarchical articulation of information within his theory of informatics. Sentences are divided into the focus, which represents that portion of information that is hearer-new, and the ground, which specifies how that information is situated within the hearer's knowledge-store. The ground is further divided into the link, which denotes an address in the hearer's knowledge-store under which he is instructed to enter the information, and the tail, which provides further directions on how the information must be entered under a given address (see also Rooth 1992). Lambrecht (1994) identifies three categories of information structure: presupposition and assertion (the structure of propositional information into given and new); identifiability and activation (the information status of discourse referents); and topic and focus (the relative predictability of relations among propositions). (See also the Functional Sentence Perspective frameworks of Firbas 1966 and Kuno 1972 and the overview in Birner and Ward, 1998.)

See also DISCOURSE; FIGURATIVE LANGUAGE; GRICE, H. PAUL; INDEXICALS AND DEMONSTRATIVES; PROPOSITIONAL ATTITUDES

—*Laurence Horn and Gregory Ward*

References

Austin, J. L. (1962). *How To Do Things With Words.* Oxford: Clarendon Press.

Birner, B. J., and G. Ward. (1994). Uniqueness, familiarity, and the definite article in English. *Berkeley Linguistics Society* 20: 93–102.

Birner, B. J., and G. Ward. (1998). *Information Status and Noncanonical Word Order in English.* Amsterdam: Benjamins.

Firbas, J. (1966). Non-thematic subjects in contemporary English. *Travaux Linguistiques de Prague* 2: 239–56.

Frege, G. (1952/1892). On sense and reference. In P. Geach and M. Black, Eds., *Translations from the Philosophical Writings of Gottlob Frege.* Oxford: Blackwell, pp. 56–78.

Gazdar, G. (1979). *Pragmatics.* New York: Academic Press.

Gundel, J., N. Hedberg, and R. Zacharski. (1993). Givenness, implicature, and the form of referring expressions in discourse. *Language* 69: 274–307.

Heim, I. (1983). On the projection problem for presuppositions. *WCCFL* 2 pp. 114–25.

Karttunen, L. (1974). Presupposition and linguistic context. *Theoretical Linguistics* 1: 181–193.

Karttunen, L., and S. Peters. (1979). Conventional implicature. In C.-K. Oh and D. A. Dinneen, Eds., *Syntax and Semantics* 11: *Presupposition.* New York: Academic Press, pp. 1–56.

Kuno, S. (1972). Functional sentence perspective: A case study from Japanese and English. *Linguistic Inquiry* 3: 269–320.

Lambrecht, K. (1994). *Information Structure and Sentence Form.* Cambridge: Cambridge University Press.

Levinson, S. (1983). *Pragmatics.* Cambridge: Cambridge University Press.

Lewis, D. (1979). Scorekeeping in a language game. *Journal of Philosophical Logic* 8: 339–359.

Prince, E. F. (1981). Toward a taxonomy of given/new information. In P. Cole, Ed., *Radical Pragmatics.* New York: Academic Press, pp. 223–254.

Prince, E. F. (1992). The ZPG letter: Subjects, definiteness, and information-status. In S. Thompson and W. Mann, Eds.,

Discourse Description: Diverse Analyses of a Fundraising Text. Amsterdam: John Benjamins, pp. 295–325.

Rooth, M. (1992). A theory of focus interpretation. *Natural Language Semantics* 1: 75–116.

Searle, J., and D. Vanderveken. (1985). *Foundations of Illocutionary Logic.* Cambridge: Cambridge University Press.

Soames, S. (1989). Presupposition. In D. Gabbay and F. Guenthner, Eds., *Handbook of Philosophical Logic, 4.* Dordrecht: Reidel, pp. 553–616.

Sperber, D., and D. Wilson. (1986). *Relevance.* Cambridge, MA: Harvard University Press.

Stalnaker, R. (1972). Pragmatics. In D. Davidson and G. Harman, Eds., *Semantics of Natural Language.* Dordrecht: Reidel, pp. 380–397.

Stalnaker, R. (1974). Pragmatic presuppositions. In M. Munitz and P. Unger, Eds., *Semantics and Philosophy.* New York: New York University Press, pp. 197–214.

Strawson, P. F. (1950). On referring. *Mind* 59: 320–344.

Vallduví, E. (1992). *The Informational Component.* New York: Garland.

van der Sandt, R. A. (1992). Presupposition projection as anaphora resolution. *Journal of Semantics* 9: 333–378.

Further Readings

Ariel, M. (1990). *Accessing Noun-Phrase Antecedents.* London: Routledge.

Atlas, J. D. (1989). *Philosophy Without Ambiguity.* Oxford: Clarendon Press.

Birner, B. J. (1996). Form and function in English *by*-phrase passives. *Chicago Linguistic Society* 32.

Christophersen, P. (1939). *The Articles: A Study of their Theory and Use in English.* Copenhagen: Munksgaard.

Clark, H., and C. Marshall. (1981). Definite reference and mutual knowledge. In A. Joshi, B. Webber, and I. Sag, Eds., *Elements of Discourse Understanding.* Cambridge: Cambridge University Press, pp. 10–63.

Cole, P., Ed. (1981). *Radical Pragmatics.* New York: Academic Press.

Givón, T. (1979). *On Understanding Grammar.* New York: Academic Press.

Green, G. (1989). *Pragmatics and Natural Language Understanding.* Hillsdale, NJ: Erlbaum.

Grosz, B., and C. Sidner. (1986). Attention, intentions, and the structure of discourse. *Computational Linguistics* 12: 175–204.

Halliday, M. A. K. (1967). Notes on transitivity and theme in English, part 2. *Journal of Linguistics* 3: 199–244.

Hawkins, J. A. (1991). On (in)definite articles: Implicatures and (un)grammaticality prediction. *Journal of Linguistics* 27: 405–442.

Horn, L. R. (1986). Presupposition, theme and variations. *Papers from the Parasession on Pragmatics and Grammatical Theory, Chicago Linguistic Society* 22: pp. 168–92.

Horn, L. R. (1988). Pragmatic theory. In F. Newmeyer, Ed., *Linguistics: The Cambridge Survey.* Vol. 1, *Linguistic Theory: Foundations.* Cambridge: Cambridge University Press, pp. 113–145.

Kadmon, N. (1990). Uniqueness. *Linguistics and Philosophy* 13: 273–324.

Kuno, S. (1986). *Functional Syntax: Anaphora, Discourse, and Empathy.* Chicago: University of Chicago Press.

Morgan, J. (1978). Towards a rational model of discourse comprehension. *Proceedings of Tinlap-2: Theoretical Issues in Natural Language Processing.* New York: ACM and ACL, pp. 109–114.

Prince, E. F. (1978). A comparison of *wh*-clefts and *it*-clefts in discourse. *Language* 54: 883–906.

Prince, E. F. (1988). Discourse analysis: A part of the study of linguistic competence. In F. Newmeyer, Ed., *Linguistics: The Cambridge Survey.* Vol. 2, *Linguistic Theory: Extensions and Implications.* Cambridge: Cambridge University Press, pp. 164–182.

Rochemont, M., and P. Culicover. (1990). *English Focus Constructions and the Theory of Grammar.* Cambridge: Cambridge University Press.

Searle, J. (1969). *Speech Acts.* Cambridge: Cambridge University Press.

Searle, J. (1975). Indirect speech acts. In P. Cole and J. Morgan, Eds., *Syntax and Semantics 3: Speech Acts.* New York: Academic Press, pp. 59–82.

Sidner, C. (1979). *Towards a Computational Theory of Definite Anaphora Comprehension in English Discourse.* Ph.D. diss., MIT.

Ward, G. (1988). *The Semantics and Pragmatics of Preposing.* New York: Garland.

Webber, B. L. (1979). *A Formal Approach to Discourse Anaphora.* New York: Garland.

Webber, B. L. (1991). Structure and ostension in the interpretation of discourse deixis. *Language and Cognitive Processes* 6: 107–135.

Presupposition

There are two principal aspects of the MEANING conventionally conveyed by a linguistic expression, its *presupposed content* and its *proffered content* (Stalnaker 1979; Karttunen and Peters 1979; Heim 1982; Roberts 1996b). The proffered content is what we usually think of as the literal content of the expression: what is asserted by using a declarative sentence, the question raised by an interrogative, the command (or wish, or suggestion, etc.) posed by an imperative. It is the information that is treated as new by the speaker (or writer, etc.). The presupposed content is ostensibly old information: it is information that the speaker (behaves as if she) assumes is already known in the context of the discourse in progress. Hence, a presupposition imposes a requirement on the context of use, the requirement that it already contain the presupposed information. An older view of presuppositions treats them as *semantic*—that is, as entailments of both a sentence and its negation (Van Fraassen 1971). By contrast, the present notion is called *pragmatic presupposition,* because a presupposition so analyzed is an entailment not of the utterance itself, but of any context which satisfies the imposed requirement.

Consider (1), where the capital letters indicate emphasis on the subject.

(1) MARCIA has a bicycle, too.

(1) cannot be used without presuming that someone other than Marcia has a bicycle, demonstrating that this proposition is in some way conventionally associated with the utterance. This contrasts with conversational implicatures, which in general only arise when context interacts with the conventional content of an utterance in a certain way. That the presupposed proposition in (1) isn't part of what's directly asserted is suggested by the fact that if the addressee directly denies the speaker's assertion of (1), for example replying *No,* he is not taken thereby to deny that someone

other than Marcia has a bicycle but rather to deny that Marcia has a bicycle. In fact, such a reply implicitly acknowledges the truth of the presupposition, as reflected in the dilemma of the man under oath who must reply to the question *Have you stopped stealing bicycles?* The indirectness of presuppositions and their conventional (i.e., noncancellable) nature is also reflected in the behavior of examples like (1) under negation, interrogation, and conditional assumption, as in the following:

(2) It's not as if MARCIA has a bicycle, too.

(3) Does MARCIA have a bicycle, too?

(4) If MARCIA has a bicycle, too, we can go for a ride by the river.

The retention in such variants of the presupposition that someone other than Marcia has a bicycle demonstrates that presuppositions are logically stronger than mere entailments, which are lost under negation, interrogation, or conditional assumption: Here, what is directly entailed by (1), that Marcia has a bicycle, is not entailed by (2), (3), or (4).

There are many kinds of expressions that conventionally trigger presuppositions, including inflectional affixes, lexical items, and syntactic constructions. Among others in English, besides *too,* we find presuppositions conventionally associated with the possessive case, as in *Marcia's bicycle* (which presupposes that Marcia has a bicycle), with the adverbials *only* and *even,* with factive predicates like *regret,* and with constructions like the pseudo-cleft construction, as illustrated by the following. (The reader may use the negated, interrogative, and conditional forms of these examples to test that the presuppositions noted are implicated.)

(5) Marcia even sold her BICYCLE.
Presupposed: Her bicycle was one of the least likely things for Marcia to have sold, and there are other things that she sold.
Asserted: Marcia sold her bicycle.

(6) Marcia regrets that she sold her bicycle.
Presupposed: Marcia sold her bicycle.
Asserted: Marcia regrets having done so.

(7) What Marcia sold is her bicycle.
Presupposed: Marcia sold something.
Asserted: Marcia sold her bicycle.

If the interlocutors in a conversation do not already agree on the truth of a presupposition associated with an utterance, then we say that the presupposition has failed to be *satisfied* in the context of utterance. Presupposition failure often leads to infelicity. Following the seminal work of Karttunen (1973) and Stalnaker (1974), an utterance with presupposition *p* is *felicitous* in context *c* iff *c* entails *p*. If one utters (1) in a conversation whose interlocutors don't have in their common ground the information that someone besides Marcia has a bicycle, then it will sound distinctly odd. If the interlocutors haven't been discussing what Marcia (perhaps among others) sold, then (7) will seem infelicitous. That the presupposition *p* itself needn't have been directly asserted is demonstrated by the following type of example:

(8) a. All Dutch people own bicycles.
b. Marcia is Dutch.
c. She rides her bicycle to work.

(8c) contains the noun phrase *her bicycle,* with *her* anaphoric to *Marcia,* and hence presupposes that Marcia has a bicycle. This presupposition is satisfied in the context suggested, where (8a) and (8b) together (though neither alone) entail that Marcia owns a bicycle.

But presupposition failure doesn't always lead to infelicity. Sometimes a cooperative addressee will be willing to accommodate the speaker by assuming the truth of the presupposed proposition after the fact, as if it had been true all along (Lewis 1979; Heim 1983; Thomason 1990). In such a case, we say that the addressee has *accommodated* the failed presupposition, saving the conversation from infelicity. This is not uncommon with factive verbs, such as *regret* in (6), and in fact gossips often use factives as a way of reporting juicy news while pretending it was already common knowledge.

The linguistic and philosophical literature on presupposition since the early 1970s has largely focused on the so-called *projection problem:* how to predict the presuppositions that a possibly complex sentence will inherit from the words and phrases that constitute it. Uttered out of the blue, (9) seems to presuppose that Marcia has a bicycle. However, this is only apparent, as we can see when we put (9) in the appropriate sort of context, illustrated by (9').

(9) Marcia believes that she sold her bicycle.

(9') Marcia is quite mad. Last week, she imagined that she had acquired a bicycle and a motorscooter. Now, she believes that she sold her bicycle.

Hence, the effect of the main verb *believe* in (9) is quite different from that of *regret* in the otherwise identical (6): *regret* always passes along the presuppositions of its sentential complement *she sold her bicycle,* (that is, the proposition that Marcia had a bicycle), to the matrix sentence; we say that the complement sentence's presuppositions are *projected.* But *believe* doesn't necessarily do so—whether it does depends on the context of utterance.

Karttunen (1973) classifies so-called *factive* predicates like *regret* as *holes to presupposition,* because they pass along the presuppositions of their complements to become presuppositions of the clause of which they are the main verb. Other holes include negation (in (2)), the interrogative construction (in (3)), and the antecedent of a conditional (in (4)). Predicates like *say* are said to be presupposition *plugs,* not passing along any of the presuppositions of a complement; replacing *regrets* with *says* in (6) gets rid of the presupposition that Marcia sold her bicycle. Predicates like *believe* are said to be presupposition *filters,* since they only pass along their complement's presuppositions under certain conditions. Filters include a number of syntactic constructions, as well as embedding predicates and other operators. The filtering behavior of the conditional construction is illustrated in (10):

(10) If Marcia sold her bicycle, then by now she regrets selling it.

The consequent of (10) carries the presupposition that Marcia regrets selling her bicycle; but (10) as a whole does not presuppose this. Although one can utter (10) in a context in which it's known that Marcia sold the bicycle, it would also be felicitous in a context in which we only know that she was contemplating doing so.

The merits of three principal types of theories of presupposition and of presupposition projection are currently being debated: satisfaction theories (Karttunen 1973; Stalnaker 1974, 1979; Heim 1983, 1992), cancellation theories (Gazdar 1979; Soames 1989), and anaphoric theories (Van der Sandt 1989, 1992). See Beaver 1998 for an excellent technical overview of current theory with extensive comparison. For historical overviews of the linguistic and philosophical literature on presupposition (including the important debate on the purported presuppositions of definite Noun Phrases in Frege 1892; Russell 1905, and Strawson 1950), the reader is referred to Levinson (1983) and Soames (1989). Evans (1977), Heim (1982), Kadmon (1990), and Neale (1990), among others, continue the Russell/Strawson debate. And Roberts (1996a) discusses a phenomenon dubbed *modal subordination,* which poses *prima facie* problems for most theories of presupposition

See also ANAPHORA; GRICE, H. PAUL; IMPLICATURE; PRAGMATICS

—*Craige Roberts*

References

Beaver, D. (1997). Presupposition. In J. van Benthem and A. ter Meulen, Eds., *Handbook of Logic and Language.* Amsterdam: Elsevier/Cambridge: MIT Press, pp. 939–1008.

Chierchia, G. (1995). *Dynamics of Meaning: Anaphora, Presupposition, and the Theory of Grammar.* Chicago: University of Chicago Press.

Evans, G. (1977). Pronouns, quantifiers and relative clauses (1). *Canadian Journal of Philosophy* 7: 467–536. Reprinted in M. Platts, Ed., *Reference, Truth, and Reality: Essays on the Philosophy of Language.* London; Routledge and Kegan Paul, pp. 255–317.

Frege, G. (1892). Über Sinn und Bedeutung. *Zeitschrift für Philosophie und philosophische Kritik* 22–50.

Gazdar, G. (1979). *Pragmatics: Implicature, Presupposition, and Logical Form.* New York: Academic Press.

Heim, I. (1982). *The Semantics of Definite and Indefinite Noun Phrases.* Ph.D. diss., University of Massachusetts, Amherst.

Heim, I. (1983). On the projection problem for presuppositions. In M. Barlow, D. Flickinger, and M. Wescoat, Eds., *Proceedings of the Second Annual West Coast Conference on Formal Linguistics.* Stanford University, pp. 114–125.

Heim, I. (1992). Presupposition projection and the semantics of attitude verbs. *Journal of Semantics* 9: 183–221.

Kadmon, N. (1990). Uniqueness. *Linguistics and Philosophy* 13: 273–324.

Karttunen, L. (1973). Presuppositions of compound sentences. *Linguistic Inquiry* 4: 169–193.

Karttunen, L., and S. Peters. (1979). Conventional implicature. In C. K. Oh and D. A. Dinneen, Eds., *Syntax and Semantics 11: Presupposition.* New York: Academic Press, pp. 1–56.

Levinson, S. C. (1983). *Pragmatics.* Cambridge: Cambridge University Press.

Lewis, D. (1979). Score-keeping in a language game. In B. Egli and A. von Stechow, Eds., *Semantics from a Different Point of View.* Berlin: Springer.

Neale, S. (1990). *Descriptions.* Cambridge, MA: MIT Press.

Roberts, C. (1996a). Anaphora in intensional contexts. In S. Lappin, Ed., *Handbook of Semantics.* Oxford: Blackwell, pp. 215–246.

Roberts, C. (1996b). Information structure in discourse: Towards an integrated formal theory of pragmatics. In J.-H. Yoon and A. Kathol, Eds., *OSU Working Papers in Linguistics* 49: *Papers in Semantics.* Ohio State University, pp. 91–136.

Russell, B. (1905). On denoting. *Mind* 66: 479–493.

Soames, S. (1989). Presupposition. In D. Gabbay and F. Guenthner, Eds., *Handbook of Philosophical Logic.* Vol. 4. Dordrecht: Reidel, pp. 553–616.

Stalnaker, R. C. (1974). Pragmatic presuppositions. In M. Munitz and D. Unger, Eds., *Semantics and Philosophy.* New York: New York University Press, pp. 197–219.

Stalnaker, R. C. (1979). Assertion. In P. Cole, Ed., *Syntax and Semantics 9: Pragmatics.* New York: Academic Press, pp. 315–332.

Strawson, P. F. (1950). On referring. *Mind* 59: 320–344.

Thomason, R. H. (1990). Accommodation, meaning, and implicature: Interdisciplinary foundations for pragmatics. In P. R. Cohen, J. Morgan, and M. E. Pollack, Eds., *Intentions in Communication.* Cambridge, MA: MIT Press, pp. 325–363.

Van der Sandt, R. A. (1989). Presupposition and discourse structure. In R. Bartsch, J. van Benthem, and P. van Emde Boas, Eds., *Semantics and Contextual Expression.* Dordrecht: Foris.

Van der Sandt, R. A. (1992). Presupposition projection as anaphora resolution. *Journal of Semantics* 9(4): 333–377.

Van Fraassen, B.C. (1971). *Formal Semantics and Logic.* New York: Macmillan.

Primate Amygdala

See AMYGDALA, PRIMATE

Primate Cognition

Ludwig Wittgenstein remarked that if lions could speak we would not understand them. David Premack (1986), following this conceptual thread, commented that if chickens had syntax they would have nothing much to say. The first comment raises a methodological challenge, the second a conceptual one. Studies of primate cognition have faced both.

For some, monkeys and apes appear much smarter than nonprimates. If so, why might this be the case? One dominant perspective suggests that social life has exerted extraordinary pressure on brain structure and function, and has led to a mind that is capable of tracking dynamically changing social relationships and political struggles (Byrne and Whiten 1988; Cheney and Seyfarth 1990; Humphrey 1976; Povinelli 1993). In primates—but few other species—individuals form coalitions to outcompete others, and following aggressive attack, subordinates often reconcile their differences with a dominant, engaging in exceptional acts of kindness and trust such as kissing and testicle holding (de Waal 1996; Harcourt and de Waal 1992). Such behavior, along with apparent acts of deception (Hauser 1996), has provided the foundation for experimental investigations of underlying cognitive mechanisms. Here, I tackle three problems so as to shed light on the architecture of the primate mind: (1) IMITATION, (2) abstract CONCEPTS, and (3) mental state attribution.

Imitation

In some monkey species, all chimpanzee populations, and one orangutan population—but in no gorilla populations—individuals use tools to gain access to food (Matsuzawa and Yamakoshi 1996; McGrew 1992; Visalberghi and Fragaszy 1991). The observation that individuals within a population ultimately acquire the same tool-using technique has been taken as evidence that primates are capable of imitation. There are, however, several paradoxical findings and controversies over the interpretation of these observations (Heyes and Galef 1996; Tomasello and Call 1997; Byrne and Russon forthcoming). First, in some study populations, young require 5–10 years before they master tool technology. Although some of this can be accounted for by maturational issues associated with motor control, one would expect faster acquisition if imitation, or a more effective teaching system, was in place (Caro and Hauser 1992). Second, most experiments conducted in the lab have failed to provide evidence that naturally reared monkeys and apes can imitate (Whiten and Ham 1992), although a recent set of studies on chimpanzees and marmosets suggest that some of the previous failures may be due to methodological problems rather than conceptual ones (Heyes and Galef 1996). Third, and perhaps most paradoxical of all, apes reared by humans can imitate human actions (reviewed in Tomasello and Call 1997). This suggests that the ape mind has been designed for imitation, but requires a special environment for its emancipation—a conceptual puzzle that has yet to be resolved (see SOCIAL COGNITION IN ANIMALS).

Abstract Concept

In several primates, the number of food calls produced is positively correlated with the amount of food discovered (reviewed in Hauser 1996). In chimpanzees, a group from one community will kill a lone individual from another community, but will avoid others if there are two or more individuals. Are such assessments based on an abstract conceptual system, akin to our number system? Recent experiments, using different experimental procedures, reveal that both apes and monkeys have quite exceptional numerical skills (reviewed in Gallistel 1990; Hauser and Carey forthcoming). Thus, chimpanzees who have learned arabic numbers understand the primary principles of a count system (e.g., one-one mapping, item indifference, cardinality) and can count up to and label nine items (Boysen 1996; Matsuzawa 1996). Using the violation of expectancy procedure designed for human infants, studies of rhesus monkeys and cotton-top tamarins have revealed that they can spontaneously carry out simple arithmetical calculations, such as addition and subtraction (Hauser and Carey forthcoming; Hauser, MacNeilage, and Ware 1996). Although nonhuman primates will never join the intellectual ranks of our mathematical elite, they clearly have access to an abstract number concept, in addition to other abstract concepts (e.g., transitivity, color names, sameness,

cause-effect, identity, kinship) that contribute to the intricacies of their social life. And primates are probably not even unique within the animal kingdom in terms of such conceptual capacities, as other species have demonstrated comparable cognitive prowess (see review in Thompson 1995).

Mental State Attribution

Are primates intuitive psychologists in that they can reflect upon their own beliefs and desires and understand that others may or may not share such mental states? Consider the following observation: a low-ranking male chimpanzee who is about to mate sees a more dominant male approaching. The low-ranking male covers his erect penis as the dominant walks by. This kind of interaction—and there are thousands of observations like this in the literature—suggests a capacity for intentional deception (see MACHIAVELLIAN INTELLIGENCE HYPOTHESIS). If true, the following capacities must be in place: the ability to represent one's own beliefs and desires, the ability to understand perspective, and the ability to attribute intentions to others. The evidence for each of these capacities is weak, at best, but the experimental research program is only in its infancy. Studies using mirrors suggest that all of the apes, and at least one monkey (cotton-top tamarins), respond to their reflection as if they see themselves, rather than a conspecific (Gallup 1970; Hauser et al. 1995; Povinelli et al. 1993). Self-recognition can be computed by perceptual mechanisms alone, whereas self-awareness implies some access to one's own beliefs and desires, how they can change, and how they might differ from those of another individual. The mirror test is blind to issues of awareness.

Many animals, primates included, follow the direction of eye gaze. However, current evidence suggests that neither monkeys nor apes understand that seeing provides a window into knowledge. A suite of experiments now show that monkeys and apes do not use eye gaze to infer what other individuals know, and thus do not alter their behavior as a function of differences in knowledge (Cheney and Seyfarth 1990; Povinelli and Eddy 1996). Given that this capacity emerges in the developing child well before the capacity to attribute intentional states to others and that perspective taking plays such a critical role in mental state attribution, it seems unlikely that primates have access to a theory of mind. But we should withhold final judgment until additional experiments have been conducted.

The human primate once held hands with a nonhuman primate ancestor. But this phylogenetic coupling happened 5–6 million years ago, ample time for fundamental differences to have emerged in the human branch of the tree. Nonetheless, many features of the primate mind have been left unchanged, including some capacity for imitation and some capacity to represent abstract concepts. The future lies in uncovering the kinds of selective pressures that led to changes in and conservation of the general architecture of the primate mind.

See also LANGUAGE AND THOUGHT; METAREPRESENTATION; PRIMATE LANGUAGE; THEORY OF MIND

—Marc D. Hauser

References

Boysen, S. T. (1996). "More is less": The distribution of rule-governed resource distribution in chimpanzees. In A. E. Russon, K. A. Bard, and S. T. Parker, Eds., *Reaching into Thought: The Minds of the Great Apes.* Cambridge: Cambridge University Press, pp. 177–189.

Byrne, R. W., and A. Russon. (Forthcoming). Learning by imitation: A hierarchical approach. *Behavioral and Brain Sciences.*

Byrne, R. W., and A. Whiten. (1988). *Machiavellian Intelligence: Social Expertise and the Evolution of Intellect in Monkeys, Apes and Humans.* Oxford: Oxford University Press.

Caro, T. M., and M. D. Hauser. (1992). Is there teaching in nonhuman animals? *Quarterly Review of Biology* 67: 151–174.

Cheney, D. L., and R. M. Seyfarth. (1990). *How Monkeys See the World: Inside the Mind of Another Species.* Chicago: University of Chicago Press.

de Waal, F. B. M. (1996). *Good Natured.* Cambridge, MA: Harvard University Press.

Gallistel, C. R. (1990). *The Organization of Learning.* Cambridge, MA: MIT Press.

Gallup, G. G., Jr. (1970). Chimpanzees: Self-recognition. *Science* 167: 86–87.

Harcourt, A. H., and F. B. M. de Waal. (1992). *Coalitions and Alliances in Humans and Other Animals.* Oxford: Oxford University Press.

Hauser, M. D. (1996). *The Evolution of Communication.* Cambridge, MA: MIT Press.

Hauser, M. D., and S. Carey. (1998). Building a cognitive creature from a set of primitives: Evolutionary and developmental insights. In D. Cummins and C. Allen, Eds., *The Evolution of Mind.* Oxford: Oxford University Press, pp. 51–106.

Hauser, M. D., J. Kralik, C. Botto, M. Garrett, and J. Oser. (1995). Self-recognition in primates: Phylogeny and the salience of species-typical traits. *Proceedings of the National Academy of Sciences* 92: 10811–10814.

Hauser, M. D., P. MacNeilage, and M. Ware. (1996). Numerical representations in primates. *Proceedings of the National Academy of Sciences* 93: 1514–1517.

Heyes, C. M., and B. G. Galef. (1996). *Social Learning and Imitation in Animals.* Cambridge: Cambridge University Press.

Humphrey, N. K. (1976). The social function of intellect. In P. P. G. Bateson and R. A. Hinde, Eds., *Growing Points in Ethology.* Cambridge: Cambridge University Press, pp. 303–321.

Matsuzawa, T. (1996). Chimpanzee intelligence in nature and in captivity: Isomorphism of symbol use and tool use. In W. C. McGrew, L. F. Nishida, and T. Nishida, Eds., *Great Ape Societies.* Cambridge: Cambridge University Press, pp. 196–209.

Matsuzawa. T., and G. Yamakoshi. (1996). Comparision of chimpanzee material culture between Bossou and Nimba, West Africa. In A. E. Russon, K. A. Bard, and S. T. Parker, Eds., *Reaching into Thought: The Mind of the Great Apes.* Cambridge: Cambridge University Press.

McGrew, W. C. (1992). *Chimpanzee Material Culture.* Cambridge: Cambridge University Press.

Povinelli, D. J. (1993). Reconstructing the evolution of mind. *American Psychologist* 48: 493–509.

Povinelli, D. J., and T. J. Eddy. (1996). What young chimpanzees know about seeing. *Monographs of the Society for Research in Child Development* 247.

Povinelli, D. J., A. B. Rulf, K. R. Landau, and D. T. Bierschwale. (1993). Self-recognition in chimpanzees (*Pan troglodytes*): Distribution, ontogeny and patterns of emergence. *Journal of Comparative Psychology* 107: 347–372.

Premack, D. (1986). *Gavagai! or the Future History of the Animal Language Controversy.* Cambridge, MA: MIT Press.

Thompson, R. K. R. (1995). Natural and relational concepts in animals. In H. L. Roitblat and J. A. Meyer, Eds., *Comparative Approaches to Cognitive Science.* Cambridge, MA: MIT Press, pp. 175–224.

Tomasello, M., and J. Call. (1997). *Primate Cognition.* Oxford: Oxford University Press.

Visalberghi, E., and D. Fragaszy. (1991). Do monkeys ape? In S. T. Parker and K. R. Gibson, Eds., *"Language" and Intelligence in Monkeys and Apes.* Cambridge: Cambridge University Press, pp. 247–273.

Visalberghi, E., and L. Limongelli. (1996). Acting and understanding: Tool use revisited through the minds of capuchin monkeys. In A. E. Russon, K. A. Bard, and S. T. Parker, Eds., *Reaching into Thought: The Minds of the Great Apes.* Cambridge: Cambridge University Press, pp. 57–79.

Whiten, A., and R. Ham. (1992). On the nature and evolution of imitation in the animal kingdom: Reappraisal of a century of research. In P. J. B. Slater, J. S. Rosenblatt, C. Beer, and M. Milinski, Eds., *Advances in the Study of Behavior.* New York: Academic Press, pp. 239–283.

Further Readings

Boesch, C., and H. Boesch. (1992). Transmission aspects of tool use in wild chimpanzees. In T. Ingold and K. R. Gibson, Eds., *Tools, Language and Intelligence: Evolutionary Implications.* Oxford: Oxford University Press.

Boysen, S. T., and G. G. Bernston. (1989). Numerical competence in a chimpanzee. *Journal of Comparative Psychology* 103: 23–31.

Bugnyar, T., and L. Huber. (1997). Push or pull: An experimental study on imitation in marmosets. *Animal Behaviour* 54: 817–831.

Byrne, R. (1996). *The Thinking Ape.* Oxford: Oxford University Press.

Byrne, R., and A. Whiten. (1990). Tactical deception in primates: The 1990 database. *Primate Report* 27: 1–101.

Cheney, D. L., and R. M. Seyfarth. (1988). Assessment of meaning and the detection of unreliable signals by vervet monkeys. *Animal Behaviour* 36: 477–486.

Cheney, D. L., and R. M. Seyfarth. (1990). Attending to behaviour versus attending to knowledge: Examining monkeys' attribution of mental states. *Animal Behaviour* 40: 742–753.

Dasser, V. (1987). Slides of group members as representations of real animals (*Macaca fascicularis*). *Ethology* 76: 65–73.

Galef, B. G., Jr. (1992). The question of animal culture. *Human Nature* 3: 157–178.

Gallup, G. G., Jr. (1987). Self-awareness. In J. R. Erwin and G. Mitchell, Eds., *Comparative Primate Biology,* vol. 2B. *Behavior, Cognition and Motivation.* New York: Alan Liss, Inc.

Hauser, M. D. (1997). Tinkering with minds from the past. In M. Daly, Ed., *Characterizing Human Psychological Adaptations.* New York: Wiley, pp. 95–131.

Hauser, M. D., and J. Kralik. (Forthcoming). Life beyond the mirror: A reply to Anderson and Gallup. *Animal Behaviour.*

Hauser, M. D., and P. Marler. (1993). Food-associated calls in rhesus macaques (*Macaca mulatta*). 1. Socioecological factors influencing call production. *Behavioral Ecology* 4: 194–205.

Hauser, M. D., P. Teixidor, L. Field, and R. Flaherty. (1993). Food-elicited calls in chimpanzees: Effects of food quantity and divisibility? *Animal Behaviour* 45: 817–819.

Hauser, M. D., and R. W. Wrangham. (1987). Manipulation of food calls in captive chimpanzees: A preliminary report. *Folia Primatologica* 48: 24–35.

Matsuzawa, T. (1985). Use of numbers by a chimpanzee. *Nature* 315: 57–59.

Povinelli, D. J., K. E. Nelson, and S. T. Boysen. (1990). Inferences about guessing and knowing by chimpanzees (*Pan troglodytes*). *Journal of Comparative Psychology* 104: 203–210.

Povinelli, D. J., K. A. Parks, and M. A. Novak. (1991). Do rhesus monkeys (*Macaca mulatta*) attribute knowledge and ignorance to others? *Journal of Comparative Psychology* 105: 318–325.

Premack, D. (1978). On the abstractness of human concepts: Why it would be difficult to talk to a pigeon. In S. H. Hulse, H. Fowler, and W. K. Konig, Eds., *Cognitive Processes in Animal Behavior.* Hillsdale, NJ: Erlbaum, pp. 423–451.

Tomasello, M., E. S. Savage-Rumbaugh, and A. Kruger. (1993). Imitative learning of actions on objects by children, chimpanzees and enculturated chimpanzees. *Child Development* 64: 1688–1706.

Whiten, A. (1993). Evolving a theory of mind: The nature of non-verbal mentalism in other primates. In S. Baron-Cohen, H. T. Flusberg, and D. J. Cohen, Eds., *Understanding other minds.* Oxford: Oxford University Press, pp. 367–396.

Wrangham, R. W., and D. Peterson. (1996). *Demonic Males.* New York: Houghton Mifflin.

Primate Language

Curiosity regarding apes' capacity for language has a long history. From DARWIN's nineteenth century postulations of both biological and psychological continuities between animals and humans, to the more recent discovery (Sibley and Ahlquist 1987) that chimpanzee *(Pan)* DNA is more similar to human than to gorilla *(Gorilla)* DNA, scientific findings have encouraged research into the language potential of apes. A recent report (Gannon et al. 1998) that the chimpanzee planum temporale is enlarged in the left hemisphere, with a humanlike pattern of Wernicke's brain language-area homolog, will provide additional impetus. That area is held basic to human language. Does, in fact, elaboration in the chimpanzee's planum temporale provide for language-relevant processes or potential? Is its elaboration an instance of homoplasy (convergent evolution)? Or is its function not necessarily related to language?

Language research with apes was revitalized in the 1960s as Beatrix and Allen Gardner (Gardner, Gardner, and Cantfort 1989) used a variation of American Sign Language to establish two-way communication with their chimpanzee, Washoe, and as David Premack (Premack and Premack 1983) used an artificial language system of plastic tokens with his chimpanzee, Sarah. In the 1970s, Sue Savage-Rumbaugh's group (1977) developed a computer-monitored keyboard of distinctive geometric patterns, called *lexigrams,* to foster studies of language capacity with Lana, a chimpanzee. Herbert Terrace's (1979) chimpanzee Project Nim, Lynn Miles's (1990) orangutan Project Chantek, and Roger and Deborah Fouts's (1989) project with Washoe and other chimpanzees obtained from the Gardners also started during the '70s.

These projects initially emphasized language production. It was assumed that if an ape appropriately produced a sign then it must also understand its meaning. That assumption proved unwarranted. Apes were proved capable of selecting seemingly appropriate symbols without understanding their meanings, even at a level grasped by 2- and 3-year-old children as they use words. Studies of comprehension ensued.

But how can one assess whether symbol meaningfulness and comprehension are present, given that apes can't speak? There are several ways. First, the meaningfulness of symbols with Sherman and Austin chimpanzees (Savage-Rumbaugh 1986) was documented by their symbol-based, cross-modal matching. Without specific training, they could look at a lexigram and select the appropriate object, by touch, from others in a box into which they could not see. They also could label, by use of word-lexigrams, single objects that they could feel but not see. Second, and more importantly, they learned word-lexigrams for the *categories* of "food" and "tool" to which they appropriately sorted 17 individual lexigrams, each representing a specific food and implement. (Each lexigram represented either a food or a tool, such as a banana, magnet, cheese, lever, etc.) Thus, their lexigrams represented things not necessarily present— the essence of SEMANTICS or *word meaning.*

Comprehension became of special interest with the discovery that Kanzi, a bonobo (a rare species of chimpanzee, *Pan paniscus*), *spontaneously* learned the meanings of word-lexigrams and later came to understand human speech—both single words and novel sentences of request (Savage-Rumbaugh et al. 1993). The discovery was made in the course of research with Matata, his adoptive mother. Matata's essential failure in learning lexigrams was likely a reflection of her feral birth and development.

Though always present during Matata's language training, Kanzi was not taught; but later, when separated from her, it became clear that he had learned a great deal! Spontaneously, he began to request and go get specific foods and drinks, to label objects, and to announce what he was about to do with the appropriate lexigrams.

From that time forward, Kanzi was reared in an even richer language-structured milieu. Caregivers commented on events (present, future, and past) and particularly on things of special interest to him. Where possible, caregivers used word-lexigrams as they spoke specific words. Kanzi was not required to use a keyboard to receive objects or to participate in activities and was given no formal lessons.

Kanzi quickly learned by observation how to ask to travel to specific sites in the forest, to play a number of games, to visit other chimps, to get and even cook specific foods, and to watch television. He also commented on things and events and continued to announce eminent actions. In sharp contrast with our other apes, Kanzi also began to comprehend human speech—not just single words but also sentences.

Consequently, Kanzi's (8 yrs.) speech comprehension was compared with that of a human child, Alia (2½ yrs.). In controlled tests, they were given 415 novel requests—to take a specific object to a stated location or person ("Take the gorilla (doll) to the bedroom"), to do something to an object ("Hammer the snake!"), to do something with a specific object relative to another object ("Put a rubber band on your ball"), to go somewhere and retrieve a specific object ("Get the telephone that's outdoors"), and so on. An ever-changing variety of objects was present on each trial, and the ape and child were asked to fulfil various requests with them. Each request was novel and had not been modeled by others.

Both Kanzi and Alia were about 70 percent correct in carrying out the requests on their first presentation. As with the human child, Kanzi's comprehension skills outpaced those of production. Kanzi understood much more than he "could say." Though his comprehension skills compared favorably with those of a 2½-year-old child, his productive skills were more limited and approximate those of the average 1 to 1½-year-old child (Greenfield and Savage-Rumbaugh 1993). These major findings were replicated in subsequent research with two other apes (Savage-Rumbaugh and Lewin 1994).

Thus, speech comprehension can be acquired spontaneously (e.g., without formal training) by apes if from birth they are reared much as one would rear human children—with language used by caregivers throughout the day to describe, to announce, and to coordinate social activities (i.e., feeding, traveling, and playing).

These findings indicate that language acquisition (1) is based in the social-communicative experiences of early infancy; (2) is based, first, in comprehension, not production or speech; and (3) is based in the evolutionary processes that have selected for primate taxa that have large and complex brains (Rumbaugh, Savage-Rumbaugh, and Washburn 1996).

Thus, the question should not be, "Do apes have language?" Given a brain only about one third the size of ours, it would be unreasonable to expect the ape to have full competence for language and its several dimensions. Rather, the question should be, "Which aspects of language can they acquire, and under what conditions do they do so?"

Just as the discovery of even elementary forms of life on another planet will not be trivialized, the documentation of elementary language competence in species other than humans has significant implications for the understanding of evolution and brain. Although the capacity for acquiring even elementary language skills is surely limited among animal species, at least some ape, marine mammal, and avian species have capacities that include the abilities to name, to request, to comprehend, and both to use and to comprehend symbols as representations of things and events not necessarily present in space and time. These capacities are inherently in the domain of language.

See also DOMAIN SPECIFICITY; INNATENESS OF LANGUAGE; LANGUAGE ACQUISITION; PRIMATE COGNITION; SYNTAX

—*Duane Rumbaugh and Sue Savage-Rumbaugh*

References

Fouts, R. S., and D. H. Fouts. (1989). Loulis in conversation with cross-fostered chimpanzees. In R. A. Gardner, B. T. Gardner, and T. E. Van Cantfort, Eds., *Teaching Sign Language in Chimpanzees*. Albany: SUNY Press.

Gannon, P. J., R. L. Holloway, D. C. Broadfield, and A. R. Braun. (1998). Asymmetry of chimpanzee planum temporale: Human-like pattern of Wernicke's brain language area homolog. *Science* 279: 220–222.

Gardner, R. A., B. T. Gardner, and T. E. Van Cantfort. (1989). *Teaching Sign Language to Chimpanzee*. New York: SUNY Press.

Greenfield, P. M., and E. S. Savage-Rumbaugh. (1993). Comparing communicative competence in child and chimp: The pragmatics. *Journal of Child Language* 20: 1–26.

Miles, L. (1990). The cognitive foundations for reference in a signing orangutan. In *"Language" and Intelligence in Monkeys and Apes: Comparative Developmental Perspectives*. Cambridge: Cambridge University Press, pp. 511–539.

Premack, D., and A. J. Premack. (1983). *The Mind of an Ape*. New York: Norton Company.

Rumbaugh, D. M. (1977). *Language Learning by a Chimpanzee: The LANA Project*. New York: Academic Press.

Rumbaugh, D. M., E. S. Savage-Rumbaugh, and D. A. Washburn. (1996). Toward a new outlook on primate learning and behavior: Complex learning and emergent processes in comparative psychology. *Japanese Psychological Research* 38: 113–125.

Savage-Rumbaugh, E. S. (1986). *Ape Language: From Conditioned Response to Symbol*. New York: Columbia University Press.

Savage-Rumbaugh, E. S., and R. Lewin. (1994). *Kanzi: The Ape at the Brink of the Human Mind*. New York: Wiley.

Savage-Rumbaugh, E. S., J. Murphy, R. A. Sevcik, K. E. Brakke, S. Williams, and D. M. Rumbaugh. (1993). Language comprehension in ape and child. *Monographs of the Society for Research in Child Development* no. 233, 58: 3–4.

Sibley, C. C., and J. E. Ahlquist. (1987). DNA hybridization evidence of hominoid phylogeny: Results from an expanded data set. *Journal of Molecular Evolution* 26: 99–121.

Terrace, H. S. (1979). *Nim*. New York: Alfred A. Knopf.

Further Readings

Bates, E., D. Thal, and V. Marchman. (1991). Symbols and syntax: A Darwinian approach to language development. In N. A. Krasnegor, D. M. Rumbaugh, R. L. Schiefelbush, and M. Studdert-Kennedy, Eds., *Biological and Behavioral Determinants of Language Development*. Hillsdale, NJ: Erlbaum, pp. 29–65.

Jerison, H. J. (1985). The evolution of mind. In D. A. Lakley, Ed., *Brain and Mind*. London: Methuen, pp. 1–33.

Lieberman, P. (1984). *The Biology and Evolution of Language*. Cambridge, MA: Harvard University Press.

Matsuzawa, T. (1990). *The Perceptual World of a Chimpanzee*. Project no. 63510057, Kyoto University, Kyoto, Japan.

Pepperberg, I. M. (1993). Cognition and communication in an African grey parrot (*Psittacus erithacus*): Studies on a nonhuman, nonprimate, nonmammalian subject. In H. Roitblat, L. M. Herman, and P. E. Nachtigall, Eds., *Language and Communication: Comparative Perspectives*. Hillsdale, NJ: Erlbaum, pp. 221–248.

Roitblat, H. L., L. M. Herman, and P. E. Nachtigall. (1993). *Language and Communication: Comparative Perspectives*. Hillsdale, NJ: Erlbaum.

Rumbaugh, D. M. (1997). Competence, cortex and primate models—a comparative primate perspective. In N. A. Krasnegor, G. R. Lyon, P. S. Goldman-Rakic, Eds., *Development of the Prefrontal Cortex: Evolution, Neurobiology and Behavior*. Baltimore, MD: Paul H. Brookes Publisher, pp. 117–139.

Rumbaugh, D. M., and E. S. Savage-Rumbaugh. (1994). Language in comparative perspective. In N. J. Mackintosh, Ed., *Animal Learning and Cognition*. New York: Academic Press.

Savage-Rumbaugh, E. S., K. E. Brakke, and S. S. Hutchins. (1992). Linguistic development: Contrasts between co-reared *Pan troglodytes* and *Pan paniscus*. In T. Nishida, W. C. McGrew, P. Marler, M. Pickford, and F. B. M. deWaal, Eds., *Topics in Primatology*. Vol. 1, *Human Origins*. Tokyo: University of Tokyo Press, pp. 51–66.

Schusterman, R. L., R. Gisiner, B. K. Grimm, and E. B. Hanggi. (1993). Behavior control by exclusion and attempts at establishing semanticity in marine mammals using match-to-sample. In H. Roiblat, L. M. Herman, and P. E. Nachtigall, Eds., *Language and Communication: Comparative Perspectives.* Hillsdale, NJ: Erlbaum, pp. 249–274.

Tuttle, R. H. (1986). *Apes of the World: Their Social Behavior, Communication and Ecology.* Park Ridge, NJ: Noyes Publications.

Probabilistic Reasoning

Probabilistic reasoning is the formation of probability judgments and of subjective beliefs about the likelihoods of outcomes and the frequencies of events. The judgments that people make are often about things that are only indirectly observable and only partly predictable. Whether it is the weather, a game of sports, a project at work, or a new marriage, our willingness to engage in an endeavor and the actions that we take depend on our estimated likelihood of the relevant outcomes. How likely is our team to win? How frequently have projects like this failed before? And what is likely to ameliorate those chances?

Like other areas of reasoning and decision making, the study of probabilistic reasoning lends itself to normative, descriptive, and prescriptive approaches. The normative approach to probabilistic reasoning is constrained by the same mathematical rules that govern the classical, set-theoretic conception of probability. In particular, probability judgments are said to be "coherent" if and only if they satisfy conditions commonly known as Kolmogorov's axioms: (1) No probabilities are negative. (2) The probability of a tautology is 1. (3) The probability of a disjunction of two logically exclusive statements equals the sum of their respective probabilities. And (4), the probability of a conjunction of two statements equals the probability of the first, assuming that the second is satisfied, times the probability of the second. Whereas the first three axioms involve unconditional probabilities, the fourth introduces conditional probabilities. When applied to hypotheses and data in inferential contexts, simple arithmatic manipulation of rule (4) leads to the result that the (posterior) probability of a hypothesis conditional on the data is equal to the probability of the data conditional on the hypothesis times the (prior) probability of the hypothesis, all divided by the probability of the data. Although mathematically trivial, this is of central importance in the context of so-called Bayesian inference, which underlies theories of belief updating and is considered by many to be a normative requirement of probabilistic reasoning (see BAYESIAN NETWORKS and INDUCTION).

There are at least two distinct philosophical conceptions of probability. According to one, probabilities refer to the relative frequencies of objective physical events in repeated trials; according to the other, probabilities are epistemic in nature, expressing degrees of belief in specific hypotheses. While these distinctions are beyond the scope of the current entry, they are related to ongoing debate concerning the status and interpretation of some experimental findings (see, e.g., Cosmides and Tooby 1996; Gigerenzer 1994, 1996; Kahneman and Tversky 1996). What is notable, however, is the fact that these different conceptions are arguably constrained by the same mathematical axioms above. Adherence to these axioms suffices to insure that probability judgment is coherent. Conversely, incoherent judgment entails the holding of contradictory beliefs and leaves the person open to possible "Dutch books." These consist of a set of probability judgments that, when translated into bets that the person deems fair, create a set of gambles that the person is bound to lose no matter how things turn out (Osherson 1995; Resnik 1987; see also DECISION MAKING).

Note that coherent judgment satisfies a number of logical, set-theoretic requirements. It does not insure that judgment is correct or even "well calibrated." Thus, a person whose judgment is coherent may nonetheless be quite foolish, believing, for example, that there is a great likelihood that he or she will soon be the king of France. Normative probabilistic judgment needs to be not only coherent but also well calibrated. Consider a set of propositions each of which a person judges to be true with a probability of .90. If she is right about 90 percent of these, then she is said to be well calibrated. If she is right about less or more than 90 percent, then she is said to be overconfident or underconfident, respectively.

A great deal of empirical work has documented systematic discrepancies between the normative requirements of probabilistic reasoning and the ways in which people reason about chance. In settings where the relevance of simple probabilistic rules is made transparent, subjects often reveal appropriate statistical intuitions. Thus, for example, when a sealed description is pulled at random out of an urn that is known to contain the descriptions of thirty lawyers and seventy engineers, people estimate the probability that the description belongs to a lawyer at .30. In richer contexts, however, people often rely on less formal considerations emanating from intuitive JUDGMENT HEURISTICS, and these can generate judgments that conflict with normative requirements. For example, when a randomly sampled description from the urn sounds like that of a lawyer, subjects' probability estimates typically rely too heavily on how representative the description is of a lawyer and too little on the (low) prior probability that it in fact belongs to a lawyer.

According to the representativeness heuristic, the likelihood that observation A belongs to class B is evaluated by the degree to which A resembles B. Sample sizes and prior odds, both of which are highly relevant to likelihood, do not impinge on how representative an observation appears and thus tend to be relatively neglected. In general, the notion that people focus on the strength of the evidence (e.g., the warmth of a letter of reference) with insufficient regard for its weight (e.g., how well the writer knows the candidate) can explain various systematic biases in probabilistic judgment (Griffin and Tversky 1992), including the failure to appreciate regression phenomena, and the fact that people are generally overconfident (when evidence is remarkable but its weight is low), and occasionally underconfident (when the evidence is unremarkable but its reliability high). Probability judgments based on the support, or strength of evidence, of focal relative to alternative hypotheses form part of a theory of subjective probability, called support theory. According to support theory, which has received substantial empirical validation, unpacking a description of an event into disjoint components generally increases its support and, hence, its perceived likelihood.

As a result, different descriptions of the same event can give rise to different judgments (Rottenstreich and Tversky 1997; Tversky and Koehler 1994).

Probability judgments often rely on sets of attributes— for example, a prospective applicant's exams scores, relevant experience, and letters of recommendation—which need to be combined into a single rating, say, likelihood of success at a job. Because people have poor insight into how much weight to assign to each attribute, they are typically quite poor at combining attributes to yield a final judgment. Much research has been devoted to the tension between intuitive ("clinical") judgment and the greater predictive success obtained by linear models of the human judge (Meehl 1954; Dawes 1979; Dawes and Corrigan 1974; Hammond 1955). In fact, it has been repeatedly shown that a linear combination of attributes, based, for example, on a judge's past probability ratings, does better in predicting future (as well as previous) instances than the judge on whom these ratings are based. This bootstrapping method takes advantage of the person's insights captured across numerous ratings, and improves on any single rating where less than ideal weightings of attributes may intrude. Moreover, because attributes are often highly correlated and systematically misperceived, a unit assignment of weights, not properly devised for the person, can often still outperform the human judge (Dawes 1988).

While human intuition can be a useful guide to the likelihoods of events, it often exhibits instances of incoherence, in the sense defined above. Methods have been explored that extract from a person's judgments a coherent core that is maximally consistent with those judgments, and at the same time come closer to the observed likelihoods than do the original (incoherent) judgments (Osherson, Shafir, and Smith 1994; Pearl 1988). Probabilistic reasoning occurs in complex situations, with numerous variables and interactions influencing the likelihood of events. In these situations, people's judgments often violate basic normative rules. At the same time, people can exhibit sensitivity to and appreciation for the normative principles. The coexistence of fallible intuitions along with an underlying appreciation for normative judgment yield a subtle picture of probabilistic reasoning, and interesting possibilities for a prescriptive approach. In this vein, a large literature on expert systems has provided analyses and applications.

See also CAUSAL REASONING; DEDUCTIVE REASONING; EVOLUTIONARY PSYCHOLOGY; PROBABILITY, FOUNDATIONS OF; TVERSKY

—*Eldar Shafir*

References

Cosmides, L., and J. Tooby. (1996). Are humans good intuitive statisticians after all? Rethinking some conclusions from the literature on judgment under uncertainty. *Cognition* 58: 1–73.

Dawes, R. M. (1979). The robust beauty of improper linear models in decision making. *American Psychologist* 34: 571–582.

Dawes, R. M., (1988). *Rational Choice in an Uncertain World*. New York: Harcourt Brace Jovanovich.

Dawes, R. M., and B. Corrigan. (1974). Linear models in decision making. *Psychological Bulletin* 81: 97–106.

Gigerenzer, G. (1994). Why the distinction between single-event probabilities and frequencies is important for psychology (and vice versa). In G. Wright and P. Ayton, Eds., *Subjective Probability*. New York: Wiley.

Gigerenzer, G. (1996). On narrow norms and vague heuristics: A rebuttal to Kahneman and Tversky (1996). *Psychological Review* 103: 592–596.

Griffin, D., and A. Tversky. (1992). The weighing of evidence and the determinants of confidence. *Cognitive Psychology* 24: 411–435.

Hammond, K. R. (1955). Probabilistic functioning and the clinical method. *Psychological Review* 62: 255–262.

Kahneman, D., and A. Tversky. (1996). On the reality of cognitive illusions. *Psychological Review* 103: 582–591.

Meehl, P. E. (1954). *Clinical Versus Statistical Prediction: A Theoretical Analysis and a Review of the Evidence*. Minneapolis: University of Minnesota Press.

Osherson, D. N. (1995). Probability judgment. In E .E. Smith and D. N. Osherson, Eds., *An Invitation to Cognitive Science*. 2nd ed. Cambridge, MA: MIT Press.

Osherson, D. N., E. Shafir, and E. E. Smith. (1994). Extracting the coherent core of human probability judgment. *Cognition* 50: 299–313.

Pearl, J. (1988). *Probabilistic Reasoning in Intelligent Systems: Networks of Plausible Inference*. San Mateo, CA: Kaufmann.

Resnik, M. D. (1987). *Choices: An Introduction to Decision Theory*. Minneapolis: University of Minnesota Press.

Rottenstreich, Y., and A. Tversky. (1997). Unpacking, repacking, and anchoring: Advances in support theory. *Psychological Review* 104: 406–415.

Tversky, A., and D. Kahneman. (1983). Extensional versus intuitive reasoning: The conjunction fallacy in probability judgment. *Psychological Review* 90: 293–315.

Tversky, A., and D. J. Koehler. (1994). Support theory: A nonextensional representation of subjective probability. *Psychological Review* 101: 547–567.

Yates, J. F. (1990). *Judgment and Decision Making*. Englewood Cliffs, NJ: Prentice-Hall.

Further Readings

Arkes, H. R., and K. R. Hammond. (1986). *Judgment and Decision Making: An Interdisciplinary Reader*. Cambridge: Cambridge University Press.

Goldstein, W. M., and R. M. Hogarth. (1997). *Research on Judgment and Decision Making: Currents, Connections and Controversies*. Cambridge: Cambridge University Press.

Hacking, I. (1975). *The Emergence of Probability*. Cambridge: Cambridge University Press.

Heath, C., and A. Tversky. (1990). Preference and belief: Ambiguity and competence in choice under uncertainty. *Journal of Risk and Uncertainty* 4 (1): 5–28.

Howson, C., and P. Urbach. (1989). *Scientific Reasoning: The Bayesian Approach*. La Salle, IL: Open Court Publishers.

Kahneman, D., P. Slovic, and A. Tversky, Eds. (1982). *Judgment under Uncertainty: Heuristics and Biases*. New York: Cambridge University Press.

Shafer, G., and J. Pearl, Eds. (1990). *Readings in Uncertain Reasoning*. San Mateo, CA: Kaufmann.

Skyrms, B. (1975). *Choice and Chance* 2nd ed. Belmont, CA: Dickensen.

von Winterfeld, D., and W. Edwards. (1986). *Decision Analysis and Behavioral Research*. Cambridge: Cambridge University Press.

Wu, G., and R. Gonzalez. (1996). Curvature of the probability weighting function. *Management Science* 42 (12): 1676–1690.

Probability, Foundations of

According to one widely held interpretation of probability, the numerical probability assigned to a proposition given particular evidence is a measure of belief in that proposition given the evidence. For example, the statement "The probability that the next nerve impulse will occur within .1 seconds of the previous impulse is .7, given that 70 of the last 100 impulses occured within .1 seconds" is an assertion of degree of belief about a future event given evidence of previous similar events. In symbols this would be written:

P(impulse-within-.1-seconds | 70 out of 100 previous within .1 sec.) = .7,

where the "|" symbol (called the "givens") separates the target proposition (on the left) from the evidence used to support it (on the right), the *conditioning evidence*. It is now widely accepted that unconditioned probability statements are either meaningless or a shorthand for cases where the conditioning information is understood.

Probability can be viewed as a generalization of classical propositional LOGIC that is useful when the truth of particular propositions is uncertain. This generalization has two important components: one is the association of a numerical degree of belief with the proposition; the other is the explicit dependence of that degree of belief on the evidence used to assess it. Writers such as E. T. Cox (1989) and E. T. Jaynes (1998) have derived standard probability theory from this generalization and the requirement that probability should agree with standard propositional logic when the degree of belief is 1 (true beyond doubt) or 0 (false beyond doubt). This means that any entity that assigns degrees of belief to uncertain propositions, given evidence, must use probability to do so, or be subject to inconsistencies, such as assigning different degrees of belief to the same proposition given the same evidence depending on the order that the evidence is evaluated. The resulting laws of probability are:

1. $0 \leq P(A|I) \leq 1$
2. $P(A|I) + P(\text{not } A|I) = 1$ (Probabilistic Law of excluded middle)
3. $P(A \text{ or } B|I) = P(A|I) + P(B|I) - P(A \& B|I)$
4. $P(A \& B|I) = P(A|I)*P(B|A \& I)$ (Product Law)

All other probability laws, such as Bayes's theorem, can be constructed from the above laws.

This derivation of probability provides a neat resolution to the old philosophical problem of justifying INDUCTION. In the eighteenth century, the philosopher David HUME disproved the assumption that all "truth" could be established deductively, as in mathematics, by showing that propositions such as "The sun will rise tomorrow" can never be known with certainty, no matter how may times the sun has risen in the past. That is, generalizations induced from particular evidence are always subject to possible refutation by further evidence. However, an entity using probability will assign such a high probability to the sun rising tomorrow, given the evidence, that it is rational for it to make decisions based on this belief, even in the absence of complete certainty.

Several important consequences follow from this "conditioned degree of belief" interpretation of probability. One consequence is that two different probability assertions, such as the one above, and

P(impulse-within-.1-seconds | 70 out of 100 previous within .1 sec. & dead(cell)) = 0

are not contradictory because the probabilities involve different conditioning evidence, although the latter assertion is a better predictor if its conditioning evidence is correct. Different entities can condition on different evidence, and so can assign different probability values to the same proposition. This means that there is a degree of subjectivity in evaluating probabilities, because different subjects generally have different experience. However, when different subjects agree on the evidence, they typically give the same probabilities. That is, a degree of objectivity with probabilities can be achieved through intersubjective agreement. Another consequence of the degree of belief interpretation of probability is that the conditioning propositions do not have to be true—a probability assertion gives the numeric probability *assuming* the conditioning information is true. This means that probability theory can be used for hypothetical reasoning, such as "If I drop this glass, it will probably break."

Another consequence of the degree of belief interpretation of probability is that there is no such thing as *the* probability of a proposition; the numerical degree is always dependent on the conditioning evidence. This means that a statement such as "the probability of a coin landing tails is 1/2," is meaningless—some experts are able to flip coins on request so that they land heads or tails. The existence of such experts refutes the view that the probability of 1/2 for tails is a physical property of the coin, just like its mass, as has been asserted by some writers. The reason many users of probability talk about "the" probability of tails for a coin or any other event is that the event occurence is assumed to be under "typical" or "normal" conditions. In a "normal" coin toss, we expect tails with a probability of 1/2, but this probability is conditioned on the normality of the toss and the coin, and has no absolute status relative to any other conditional probability about coins. Probabilities that are implicitly conditioned by "normal" operation are called by some "propensities," and assumed to be an intrinsic property of a proposition. For example, an angry patient has a propensity to throw things, even if that patient is physically restrained. However, this statement is just a shorthand for the probability of the patient to behave in a particular way, conditioned on being angry and unconstrained—"normal" behavior for an angry person.

Although there is universal agreement on the fundamental laws of probability, there is much disagreement on interpretation. The two main interpretations are the "degree of belief" (subjective) interpretation and the "long run frequency" (frequentist or objective) interpretation. In the frequentist interpretation, it is meaningless to assign a probability to a particular proposition, such as "This new type of rocket will launch successfully on the first try," because there are no previous examples on which to base a relative frequency. The degree of belief interpretation can assign a probability in this case by using evidence such as the previous history of other rocket launches, the complexity of the new rocket, the failure rate of machinery of comparable complexity, knowing who built it, and so on. When sufficient frequency evidence is available, and this is the best evidence, then the frequentist and the subjectivist will give essentially the same probability. In other words, when the observed frequency of similar events is used as the conditioning information, both interpretations agree, but the degree of belief interpretation gives reasonable answers even when there is insufficient frequency information.

The main form of probabilistic inference in the degree of belief interpretation is to use Bayes's theorem to go from a prior probability (or just "prior") on a proposition to a posterior probability conditioned on the new evidence. For this reason, the degree of belief interpretation is referred to as *Bayesian inference.* It dates back to its publication in 1763 in a posthumous paper by the Rev. Thomas Bayes. However, before any specific evidence has been incorporated in Bayesian inference, a prior probability distribution must be given over the propositions of interest. In 1812, Pierre Simon Laplace proposed using the "principle of indifference" to assign these initial (prior) probabilities. This principle gives equal probability to each possibility. When there are constraints on this set of possibilities, the "principle of maximum entropy" (Jaynes 1989) must be used as the appropriate generalization of the principle of indifference. Even here, subjectivity is apparent, as different observers may perceive different sets of possibilities, and so assign different prior probabilities using the principle of indifference. For example, a colorblind observer may see only small and large flowers in a field, and so assign a prior probability of 1/2 to the small size possibility; but another observer sees that the large flowers have two distinct colors, and so assigns a prior probability of 1/3 to the small size possibility because this is now one of three possibilities. There is no inconsistency here, as the different observers have different information. As specific flower data is collected, a better estimate of the small flower probability can be obtained by calculating the posterior probability conditioned on the flower data. If there is a large flower sample, the posterior probabilities for both observers converges to the same value. In other words, data will quickly "swamp" weak prior probabilities such as those based on the principle of indifference, which is why different priors are typically not important in practice.

The main reason for the vehement disagreement between the frequentist (or classical statistics) interpretation and the degree of belief (or Bayesian) interpretation is the perjorative label "subjective" associated with the Bayesian approach, particularly in the assignment of prior probabilities. This dispute is largely academic, as in practice, domain knowledge usually suggests appropriate priors. Because priors are inherently subjective does not mean that they are arbitrary, as they are based on the subject's experience. Recently, writers such as J. O. Berger (1985) have shown that the "objective" frequentist interpretation is just as subjective as the Bayesian. In other words, the attempt to circumscribe the definition of probability to "objective" long-run frequencies not only greatly reduced its applicability but did not succeed in eliminating the inherent subjectivity in reasoning under UNCERTAINTY.

See also BAYESIAN LEARNING; BAYESIAN NETWORKS; PROBABILISTIC REASONING; RATIONAL CHOICE THEORY; RATIONAL DECISION MAKING; STATISTICAL LEARNING THEORY

—*Peter Cheeseman*

References

Bayes, T. (1763). An essay towards solving a problem in the doctrine of chances. *Philosophical Transactions of the Royal Society of London* 53: pp. 370–418.

Berger, J. O. (1985). *Statistical Decision Theory and Bayesian Analysis.* 2nd ed. Springer.

Cox, E. T. (1989). *Bayesian Statistics: Principles, Models, and Applications.* S. James Press, Wiley.

Jaynes, E. T. (1989). Where do we stand on maximum entropy. In R. Rosenkrantz, Ed., *E. T. Jaynes: Papers on Probability, Statistics and Statistical Physics.* Dordrecht: Kluwer.

Jaynes, E. T. (1998). "Probability Theory: The Logic of Science." Not yet published book available at http://omega.albany.edu:8008/JaynesBook.html.

Laplace, P. S. (1812). *Théorie Analytique des Porbabiletés.* Paris: Courcier.

Problem Solving

Solving a problem is transforming a given situation into a desired situation or goal (Hayes 1989). Problem solving may occur inside a mind, inside a computer, in some combination of both, or in interaction with an external environment. An example of the first would be generating an English sentence; of the last, driving to the airport. If a detailed strategy is already known for reaching the goal, no problem solving is required. A strategy may be generated in advance of any action (planning) or while seeking the goal.

Studying how humans solve problems belongs to *cognitive psychology.* How computers solve problems belongs to *artificial intelligence.* ROBOTICS studies how computers solve problems requiring interaction with the environment. As similar processes are often used, there is frequent exchange of ideas among these three subdisciplines.

To solve a problem, a *representation* must be generated, or a preexisting representation accessed. A representation includes (1) a *description* of the given situation, (2) *operators* or actions for changing the situation, and (3) *tests* to determine whether the goal has been achieved. Applying operators creates new situations, and potential applications of all permissible operators define a branching tree of achievable situations, the *problem space.* Problem solving amounts to searching through the problem space for a situation that satisfies the tests for a solution (VanLehn 1989).

In computer programs and (as cumulating evidence indicates) in people, operators usually take the form of condition-action rules (*productions*). When the system notices that the conditions of a production are satisfied, it takes the corresponding action of accessing information in memory, modifying information, or acting on the environment (Newell and Simon 1972).

In most problems of interest, the problem space is very large (in CHESS, it contains perhaps 10^{20} states; in real life, many more). Even the fastest computers cannot search such spaces exhaustively, and humans require several seconds to examine each new state. Hence, search must be highly selective, using *heuristic rules* to select a few promising states for consideration. Chess grandmasters seldom search more than 100 states before making a move; the most powerful chessplaying computer programs search tens of billions, still a minuscule fraction of the total. In such tasks, expert computer programs trade off computer speed for some human selectivity (De Groot 1965).

The *heuristics* that guide search derive from properties of the task (e.g., in chess, "Ignore moves that lose pieces without compensation"). If a domain has strong mathematical structure (e.g., is describable as a linear programming problem), strategies may exist that always find an optimal solution in acceptable computation time. In less well structured domains (including most real-life situations) the heuristics follow plausible paths that often find satisfactory (not necessarily optimal) solutions with modest computation but without guarantees of success. In puzzles, the problem space may be small, but misleadingly constructed so that plausible heuristics avoid the solution path. For example, essential intermediate moves may increase the distance from the goal, whereas heuristics usually favor moves that decrease the distance.

An important heuristic is *means-ends* analysis (Newell and Simon 1972). Differences between the current situation and the goal situation are detected, and an operator selected that usually removes one of these differences. After application of the operator eliminates or decreases the difference, the process is repeated. If the selected operator is not applicable to the current situation, a subgoal is established of applying the operator. Means-ends analysis is powerful and general, but is not useful in all problems: for example, it cannot solve the Rubik's Cube puzzle in any obvious way.

Problems are called *well structured* if the situations, operators, and goal tests are all sharply defined; *ill structured*, to the extent that they are vaguely defined. Blending petroleum in a refinery, using linear programming, is a well-structured problem. Playing chess is less well structured, as it requires fallible heuristics to seek and evaluate moves.

Designing buildings and writing novels are highly ill-structured tasks. The tests of success are complex and ill defined, and are often elaborated during the solution process (Akin 1986). The alternative operations for synthesizing a design are innumerable, and may be discovered only by inspecting a partially completed product. As optimization is impossible and several satisfactory solutions may be encountered, the order in which alternatives are synthesized strongly affects the final product. Starting with the floor plan produces a different house than starting with the facade.

The study of problem solving has led to considerable understanding of the nature of EXPERTISE (human and automated). The expert depends on two main processes: HEURISTIC SEARCH of problem spaces, and *recognition* of cues in the situation that access relevant knowledge and suggest heuristics for the next step. In domains that have been studied, experts store tens of thousands or hundreds of thousands of "chunks" of information in memory, accessible when relevant cues are recognized (Chi, Glaser, and Farr 1988). Medical diagnosis (by physicians or computers) pro-

ceeds largely by recognition of symptoms, reinforced by inference processes. Most of what is usually called "intuition," and even "inspiration," can be accounted for by recognition processes.

Testing theories of problem solving, usually expressed as computer programs that simulate the processes, requires observing both outcomes and the steps along the way. At present, the most fine-grained techniques for observation of the processes are verbal (*thinking aloud*) or video protocols, and eye movement records (Ericsson and Simon 1993). Studies of brain damage and MAGNETIC RESONANCE IMAGING (MRI) of the brain are beginning to provide some sequential information, but most current understanding of problem solving is at the level of symbolic processes, not neural events.

Research has progressed from well-structured problems calling for little specific domain knowledge to ill-structured problems requiring extensive knowledge. As basic understanding of problem solving in one domain is achieved, research moves to domains of more complex structure. There has also been considerable movement "downward" from theories, mainly serial, of symbolic structures that model processes over intervals of a fraction of a second or longer, to theories, mainly parallel, that use *connectionist networks* to represent events at the level of neural circuits. Finally, there has been movement toward linking problem solving with other cognitive activities through *unified models of cognition* (Newell 1990).

Recent explorations extend to such ill-structured domains as *scientific discovery* (e.g., Langley et al. 1987) and architectural design (Akin 1986). In modeling scientific discovery and similarly complex phenomena, multiple problem spaces are required (spaces of alternative hypotheses, alternative empirical findings, etc.). We are learning how experimental findings induce changes in representation, and how such changes suggest new experiments. Allen Newell's (1990) Soar system operates in such multiple problem spaces. Kim, Lerch, and Simon (1995) have explored the generation of problem representations, and there is increasing attention to nonpropositional inference (e.g., using mental IMAGERY in search; Glasgow, Narayanan, and Chandrasekaran 1995). Several models now can represent information in both propositional (verbal or mathematical) and diagrammatic forms, and can use words and mental images conjointly to reason about problems.

Another important area of recent research activity explains intuition and insight in terms of the recognition processes of the large memory structures found in knowledge-rich domains (Kaplan and Simon 1990; Simon 1995). Yet another area, robotics, shows, by studying problem solving in real-world environments (Shen 1994), how the problem-solver's incomplete and inaccurate models of changing situations are revised and updated by sensory feedback from the environment.

Finally, interest in knowledge-rich domains has called attention to the essential ties between problem solving and LEARNING (Kieras and Bovair 1986). Both connectionist learning systems and serial symbolic systems have shown considerable success in accounting for concept learning (CATEGORIZATION), a key to the recognition capabilities of knowledge-rich systems. Self-modifying systems of condition-action rules (*adaptive production systems*) have been shown capable, under classroom conditions, of accounting for students' success in learning such subjects as algebra and physics from *worked-out examples* (Zhu et al. 1996).

See also DECISION MAKING; KNOWLEDGE REPRESENTATION; PRODUCTION SYSTEMS; NEWELL, ALLEN

—*Herbert A. Simon*

References

Akin, O. (1986). *Psychology of Architectural Design.* London: Pion.

Chi, M. T. H., R. Glaser, and M. Farr. (1988). *The Nature of Expertise.* Hillsdale, NJ: Erlbaum.

De Groot, A. (1965). *Thought and Choice in Chess.* The Hague: Mouton.

Ericsson, K. A., and H. A. Simon. (1993). *Protocol Analysis.* Rev. ed. Cambridge, MA: MIT Press.

Glasgow, J., N. H. Narayanan, and B. Chandrasekaran, Eds. (1995). *Diagrammatic Reasoning: Computational and Cognitive Perspectives.* Menlo Park, CA: AAAI/MIT Press, pp. 403–434.

Hayes, J. R. (1989). *The Complete Problem Solver.* 2nd ed. Hillsdale, NJ: Erlbaum.

Kaplan, C., and H. A. Simon. (1990). In search of insight. *Cognitive Psychology* 22: 374–419.

Kieras, D. E., and S. Boviar. (1986). The acquisition of procedures from text. *Journal of Memory and Language* 25: 507–524.

Kim, J., J. Lerch, and H. A. Simon. (1995). Internal representation and rule development in object-oriented design. *ACM Transactions on Computer-Human Interaction* 2 (4): 357–390.

Langley, P., H. A. Simon, G. L. Bradshaw, and J. M. Zytkow. (1987). *Scientific Discovery: Computational Explorations of the Creative Processes.* Cambridge, MA: MIT Press.

Newell, A. (1990). *Unified Theories of Cognition.* Cambridge, MA: Harvard University Press.

Newell, A., and H. A. Simon. (1972). *Human Problem Solving.* Englewood Cliffs, NJ: Prentice-Hall.

Shen, W. (1994). *Autonomous Learning from the Environment.* New York: W. H. Freeman.

Simon, H. A. (1995). Explaining the ineffable: AI on the topics of intuition, insight and inspiration. *Proceedings of the Fourteenth International Joint Conference on Artificial Intelligence* 1: 939–948.

VanLehn, K. (1989). Problem solving and cognitive skill acquisition. In M. L. Posner, Ed., *Foundations of Cognitive Science.* Cambridge, MA: MIT Press.

Zhu, X., Y. Lee, H. A. Simon, and D. Zhu. (1996). Cue recognition and cue elaboration in learning from examples. *Proceedings of the National Academy of Sciences* 93: 1346–1351.

Further Readings

Larkin, J. H. (1983). The role of problem representation in physics. In D. Gentner, and A. Collins, Eds., *Mental Models.* Hillsdale, NJ: Erlbaum.

McCorduck, P. (1979). *Machines Who Think.* San Francisco: Freeman.

Polya, G. (1957). *How to Solve It.* Garden City, NY: Doubleday-Anchor.

Simon, H. A. (1996). *The Sciences of the Artificial.* 3rd ed. Cambridge, MA: MIT Press.

Wertheimer, M. (1945). *Productive Thinking.* New York: Harper and Row.

Procedural Semantics

See FUNCTIONAL ROLE SEMANTICS

Production Systems

Production systems are computer languages that are widely employed for representing the processes that operate in models of cognitive systems (NEWELL and Simon 1972).

In a production system, all of the instructions (called productions) take the form:

IF<<conditions>, THEN<<actions>,

That is to say, "if certain conditions are satisfied, then take the specified actions" (abbreviated C → A). Production system languages have great generality: they can possess the full power and generality of a Turing machine (see TURING). They have an obvious affinity to the classical stimulus-response (S → R) connections in psychology, but greater complexity and flexibility, for, in production systems, both the conditions and the actions may, and generally do, contain variables that are instantiated to the appropriate values in each separate application.

The conditions of a production are propositions that state properties of, or relations among, the components of the system being modeled, in its current state. In implementing production systems the conditions are usually stored in a WORKING MEMORY, which may represent short-term memory or current sensory information, or an activated portion of semantic memory (Anderson 1993). To activate a production, all of the conditions specified in its "IF" clause must be satisfied by one or more elements in working memory. The actions that are then initiated may include actions on the system's environment (e.g., motor actions) or actions that alter its memories, including erasing and creating working memory elements.

The operation of a production system can be illustrated by a simple algebraic example that solves linear equations in one unknown:

1. IF the expression has the form $X = N$, where N is a number, THEN halt and check by substituting N in the original equation.
2. IF there is a term in X on the right-hand side, THEN subtract it from both sides, and collect terms.
3. IF there is a numerical term on the left-hand side, THEN subtract it from both sides, and collect terms.
4. IF the equation has the form $NX = M$, $N \neq 1$, THEN divide both sides by N.

If, for instance, the equation were $7X + 6 = 4X + 12$, the condition of the second production would be satisfied, and $4X$ would be subtracted from both sides, yielding $3X + 6 = 12$. Now the condition of the third production is satisfied, and 6 is subtracted from both sides, yielding $3X = 6$. Next, the condition of the fourth production is satisfied and both sides are divided by 3, yielding $X = 2$. Finally, the condition of the first production is satisfied, and substituting 2 for X in the original equation and simplifying gives $14 + 6 = 8 + 12$, or $20 = 20$.

Notice that at the outset, the conditions of both productions 2 and 3 were satisfied. A production system must contain precedence rules that select which production will be executed when the conditions of more than one are satisfied (Brownston et al. 1985). One way in which the set of productions that are executable at any time can be limited is by including goals among their conditions. A goal is simply a symbol that must be present in working memory in order for a production containing that goal among its conditions to execute. Goals are set (i.e., goal symbols are placed in working memory) as part of the actions of other productions. Goals establish contexts so that only productions relevant to the current context will be executed. For example, we could add to the condition side of each production in the system for algebra described above "IF the goal is to solve an equation &." Then, even if the other conditions of these productions were satisfied, if that goal symbol were not in working memory, the productions would not execute.

Production systems were first invented by the logician Emil Post (1943) to provide a simple, clean language for the investigation of questions in the foundations of LOGIC and mathematics. They were borrowed, sometimes under the label of "Markov productions," for use in computer systems programming (languages for compiling compilers). In about the mid-1960s, they were introduced into cognitive science at Carnegie Mellon University, some of their early uses being in the General Problem Solver (GPS; Newell, Shaw, and Simon 1960), and in Tom Williams' thesis (Williams 1972) on a general game-playing program (*see* GAME-PLAYING SYSTEMS). They also found early use as languages for FORMAL GRAMMARS of natural language. Among production systems widely used in cognitive simulation are OPS5 (Brownston et al. 1985; Cooper and Wogrin 1988), Prolog (Clocksin and Mellish 1994), and Act-R (Anderson et al. 1993).

Adaptive production systems are production systems that contain a learning component that is capable of modifying productions already in the system and of creating new productions that can be added to the system (Neves 1978; see LEARNING SYSTEMS). Neves showed how this could be done for algebra by the method of learning from worked-out examples. Consider our earlier example:

$$7X + 6 = 4X + 12$$
$$3X + 6 = 12$$
$$3X = 6$$
$$X = 2$$

Assume that the adaptive production system had learned previously that the allowable actions include adding or subtracting the same numbers from both sides of an equation, or multiplying or dividing both sides by the same number, and simplifying by combining similar terms, but did not know when these actions should be applied to solve a problem. It would now examine the first two lines above, discovering that the unwanted $4X$ ("unwanted" because there is no such term in the last line) had been removed from the right-hand side, and that the action was to subtract this term. In the same way it would find that the condition "unwanted numerical term on left-hand side" characterized the second change, and "unwanted numerical coefficient of X," the third. It would create three new productions (the ones we

have already seen above) and add them to its production system. Thenceforth, it would be capable of solving equations of this general kind.

This method, widely applied in adaptive production systems, of noting and eliminating from an equation expressions that are absent from the final result, is essentially the method of means-ends analysis incorporated in the General Problem Solver (Newell and Simon 1972; see also HEURISTIC SEARCH and PROBLEM SOLVING). The key steps in means-ends analysis are (1) to detect differences between the current and goal situations and (2) to find actions capable of removing these differences. The set of productions shown earlier is simply the "Table of Connections" between differences and operations in the GPS system.

Adaptive production systems, using the method of worked-out examples, today provide the theoretical foundation for a number of computer tutoring systems and mathematics textbooks and workbooks employed successfully in the United States and China (Anderson et al. 1995; Zhu et al. 1996)

See also COGNITIVE ARCHITECTURE; COGNITIVE MODELING, SYMBOLIC; CHURCH-TURING THESIS

—Herbert A. Simon

References

Anderson, J. R. (1993). *Rules of the Mind.* Hillsdale, NJ: Erlbaum.

Anderson, J. R., A. T. Corbett, K. R. Koedinger, and R. Pelletier. (1995). Cognitive tutors: Lessons learned 94. *Journal of Learning Science* 4: 167–207.

Brownston, L., R. Ferrell, E. Kant, and N. Martin. (1985). *Programming Expert Systems in OPS5: An Introduction to Rule-based Programming.* Reading, MA: Addison-Wesley.

Clocksin, W. F., and C. S. Mellish. (1994). *Programming in Prolog.* 4th ed. New York: Springer.

Cooper, T., and N. Wogrin. (1988). *Rule-Based Programming with OPS5.* San Mateo, CA: Kaufmann.

Neves, D. M. (1978). A computer program that learns algebraic procedures by examining examples and working problems in a textbook. *Proceedings of the Second Conference of Computational Studies of Intelligence.* Toronto: Canadian Society for Computational Studies of Intelligence, pp. 191–195.

Newell, A., and H. A. Simon. (1972). *Human Problem Solving.* Englewood Cliffs, NJ: Prentice-Hall.

Newell, A., J. C. Shaw, and H. A. Simon. (1960). Report on a general problem solving program for a computer. *Proceedings of the International Conference on Information Processing.* Paris: UNESCO, pp. 256–264.

Post, E. L. (1943). Formal reductions of the general combinatorial decision problem. *American Journal of Mathematics* 65: 197–215.

Williams, T. (1972). Some studies in game playing with a digital computer. In H. A. Simon and L. Siklossy, Eds., *Representation and Meaning: Experiments with Information Processing Systems.* Englewood Cliffs, NJ: Prentice-Hall.

Zhu, X., Y. Lee, H. A. Simon, and D. Zhu. (1996). Cue recognition and cue elaboration in learning from examples. *Proceedings of the National Academy of Sciences* 93: 1346–1351.

Further Readings

Langley, P., H. A. Simon, G. L. Bradshaw, and J. M. Zytkow. (1987). *Scientific Discovery: Computational Explorations of the Creative Process.* Cambridge, MA: MIT Press.

Newell, A. (1973). Production systems: Models of control structures. In W. G. Chase, Ed., *Visual Information Processing.* New York: Academic Press.

Newell, A. (1990). *Unified Theories of Cognition.* Cambridge, MA: Harvard University Press.

Quinlan, J. R. (1993). *C4.5: Programs for Machine Learning.* San Francisco: Kaufmann.

Shen, W. M. (1994). *Autonomous Learning from the Environment.* New York: W. H. Freeman and Co.

Simon, H. A. (1996). *The Sciences of the Artificial.* 3rd ed. Cambridge, MA: MIT Press.

Tabachneck-Schijf, H. J. M., A. M. Leonardo, and H. A. Simon. (1997). CaMeRa: a computational model of multiple representations. *Cognitive Science* 21: 305–330.

Waterman, D. A., and F. Hayes-Roth, Eds. (1978). *Pattern-Directed Inference Systems.* New York: Academic Press.

Propositional Attitudes

Propositional attitudes are mental states with representational content. Belief is the most prominent example of a propositional attitude. Others include intention, wishing and wanting, hope and fear, seeming and appearing, and tacit presupposition. Verbs of propositional attitude express a relation between an agent and some kind of abstract object—the content of the attitude, the object that is denoted by a nominalized sentence. So a statement such as "Fred believes that fleas have wings" says that Fred stands in the *believes* relation to *that fleas have wings.* The predicate *"believes that fleas have wings"* expresses a property that is ascribed to Fred. A philosophical account of propositional attitudes must answer two interrelated kinds of questions: first, what kind of thing is the content of an attitude (what is the object denoted by the *that*-clause)? Second, how can the states of mind of agents relate them to such objects? The problem of explaining how mental states can have representational content is the problem of INTENTIONALITY.

A propositional attitude—more generally, any state or act that can be said to be representational—represents the world as being a certain way, and the content of the attitude is what determines the way the world is represented (see MENTAL REPRESENTATION). So propositions must be objects that have truth conditions that must be satisfied for a representational state with that content to correctly represent the world.

Many different accounts of the contents of propositional attitudes have been proposed. Often, propositions are assumed to be complex objects, ordered sequences with ordered sequences as parts that reflect the recursive semantic structure of the sentences that express the proposition. In one kind of account of structured propositions, the primitive constituents are taken to be Fregean senses, modes of presentation (see SENSE AND REFERENCE), or CONCEPTS. In an alternative account of structured propositions, the constituents are individuals, properties, and relations. So, for example, the proposition that Booth killed Lincoln might contain, as constituents, the senses of the names "Booth" and "Lincoln" and of the verb "kill," or alternatively, the men Booth and Lincoln and the killing relation.

Both of these kinds of account treat the content of propositional attitudes as a recipe for determining the truth condi-

tions of the representation. A third alternative is to take propositional contents—the referents of that-clauses—to be the truth conditions themselves. In this account, the proposition that Booth killed Lincoln can be identified with the set of possible circumstances in which Booth killed Lincoln. This conception of a proposition—call it an *informational content*—is the most coarse-grained conception of representational content. Any structured proposition will determine a unique informational content, but different structured propositions may have the same informational content.

The choice between different accounts of content depends on the role of content in determining the propositional attitudes—the way in which the properties such as *believing that Booth killed Lincoln* are determined as a function of the content *that Booth killed Lincoln.* The more fine-grained conceptions of content will be justifiable only if the distinctions between different fine-grained contents with the same informational content play a role in distinguishing different states. We also need a conception of content that can account for intuitive judgments about attitudes. If it is intuitively obvious that believing that P is different from believing that Q, then we need a notion of content according to which "that P" and "that Q" denote different propositions. The defender of the coarse-grained conception of content needs to reconcile this account with apparently conflicting intuitions (see LOGICAL OMNISCIENCE).

The problem of propositional attitudes is often discussed in the context of a problem of semantics: the problem of giving the compositional semantics for propositional attitude *reports.* The focus of attention in such discussions has been on the role of pronouns and other context dependent expressions, and of quantification in belief contexts. The problems are closely connected: obviously, the question, "what kind of object is the content of a belief?" cannot be answered independently of the question, "what kind of object is the referent of a that-clause?" But the question about the semantics of attitude reports needs to be distinguished from the philosophical problem of explaining what propositional attitude properties are, and what it is that gives them their content. There are a number of alternative strategies that have been developed for giving such explanations.

First, in one familiar kind of account of propositional attitudes, belief and desire are correlative dispositions that are displayed in rational action (see RATIONAL AGENCY and INTENTIONAL STANCE). Roughly, to believe that P is to be disposed to act in ways that would satisfy one's desires if P (along with one's other beliefs) were true, and to desire that P is to be disposed to act in ways that would tend to bring it about in situations in which one's beliefs were true. This is only a very rough sketch of a strategy of locating belief and desire in a general theory of action. Because belief and desire are explained in terms of each other, the strategy does not offer the promise of a reductive analysis of propositional attitudes, and must be supplemented with additional constraints if the contents of attitudes are not to be wholly indeterminate.

A second strategy that may supplement the first—the informational theoretic strategy—is to explain representational states in terms of causal and counterfactual dependencies between the agent and the world (see INFORMATIONAL SE-MANTICS). One may explain the content of the representational states of an agent in terms of the way those states tend to vary systematically in response to states of the environment. A state of a person or thing *carries the information that P* if the person or thing is in the state because of the fact that P, and would not be in the state if it were not the case that P. The strategy is to explain the content of representational states in terms of the information that the states tend to carry, or the information that the states would carry if they were functioning properly, or if conditions were normal. The information theoretic strategy will give determinate content to representational states only relative to some specification of the relevant normal conditions. A central task of the development and defense of the information-theoretic strategy is to give an account of these conditions.

A third strategy—the *linguistic strategy*—is to begin with linguistic representation, and to explain the content of mental states in terms of the content of sentences that realize the mental states, or of sentences to which the agent is disposed to assent. One version of this strategy, defended by Jerry Fodor (1987) among others, assumes that propositional attitudes are realized by the storage (in the "belief box," to use the popular metaphor) of sentences of a LAN-GUAGE OF THOUGHT. Another version takes a social practice of speech as primary, accounting for the contents of beliefs in terms of the contents of the sentences of the public language that the agent "holds true," or to which the agent is disposed to assent. Donald Davidson (1984) has defended this kind of strategy (see RADICAL INTERPRETATION). The first version of the linguistic strategy needs a distinction between explicit or "core" beliefs and implicit beliefs, because it would not be plausible to say that everything believed is explicitly stored. The second version has a problem explaining attitudes with content that is not easily expressed in linguistic form (for example, perceptual states), and it seems to conflict with the intuition that thought without the capacity for speech is at least a possibility. Both accounts need to be supplemented with some account of what it is in virtue of which the relevant kind of linguistic representations have content.

See also COMPOSITIONALITY; FOLK PSYCHOLOGY; GRICE; INTENTIONAL STANCE; MEANING

—*Robert Stalnaker*

References and Further Readings

Barwise, J., and J. Perry. (1983). *Situations and Attitudes.* Cambridge, MA: MIT Press.

Burge, T. (1978). Individualism and the mental. *Midwest Studies in Philosophy, 4, Studies in Metaphysics.* Minneapolis: University of Minnesota Press.

Crimmins, M. (1992). *Talk about Belief.* Cambridge, MA: MIT Press.

Davidson, D. (1984). *Inquiries into Truth and Interpretation.* Oxford: Oxford University Press.

Dennett, D. (1987). *The Intentional Stance.* Cambridge, MA: MIT Press.

Dretske, F. (1988). *Explaining Behavior.* Cambridge, MA: MIT Press.

Field, H. (1978). Mental representation. *Erkenntnis* 13: 9–61.

Fodor, J. A. (1987). *Psychosemantics: The Problem of Meaning in Psychology of Mind.* Cambridge, MA: MIT Press.

Quine, W. V. (1956). Quantifiers and propositional attitudes. *Journal of Philosophy* 53: 177–187.

Richard, M. (1990). *Propositional Attitudes.* Cambridge: Cambridge University Press.

Salmon, N., and S. Soames, Eds. (1982). *Propositional Attitudes.* Oxford: Oxford University Press.

Stalnaker, R. (1984). *Inquiry.* Cambridge, MA: MIT Press.

Stich, S. (1983). *From Folk Psychology to Cognitive Science: The Case Against Belief.* Cambridge, MA: MIT Press.

Proprioception

See AFFORDANCES; IMITATION; SELF; SENSATIONS

Prosody and Intonation

The term *prosody* refers to the grouping and relative prominence of the elements making up the speech signal. One reflex of prosody is the perceived rhythm of the speech. Prosodic structure may be described formally by a hierarchical structure in which the smallest units are the internal components of the syllable and the largest is the intonation phrase. Units of intermediate scale include the syllable, the metrical foot, and the prosodic word (Selkirk 1984; Hayes 1995).

Intonation refers to phrase-level characteristics of the melody of the voice. Intonation is used by speakers to mark the pragmatic force of the information in an utterance. The alignment of the intonation contour with the words is constrained by the prosody, with intonational events falling on the most prominent elements of the prosodic structure and at the edges. As a result, intonational events can often provide information to the listener about the prosodic structure, in addition to carrying a pragmatic message. The term intonation is often used, by extension, to refer to systematic characteristics of the voice melody at larger scales, such as the discourse segment or the paragraph (Beckman and Pierrehumbert 1986; Pierrehumbert and Hirschberg 1990; Ladd 1996).

The primary phonetic correlate of intonation is the fundamental frequency of the voice (F0), which is perceived as pitch and which arises from the rate of vibration of the vocal folds. The F0 is determined by the configuration of the larynx, the subglottal pressure, and the degree of oral closure (Clark and Yallop 1990; Titze 1994). Articulatory maneuvers that change the rate of vibration of the vocal folds also affect the exact shape of the glottal waveform and hence the voice timbre (or voice quality). Perceived voice quality is probably used in perception to assist in the identification of intonation patterns (Pierrehumbert 1997). Intonation is not the only source of F0 variation. Speech segments also have systematic effects on F0. However, the largest segmental effects are on the time-frequency scale of the smaller intonational effects. Thus, F0 contours can be roughly viewed as a superposition of segmental factors on the intonationally determined contour.

Many experimental studies show that prosody affects all aspects of the speech signal (see *Papers in Laboratory*

Phonology and references cited there). In general, elements found in prosodically prominent positions are more forcefully and fully articulated than elements in prosodically weak positions. The space of acoustic contrasts is therefore expanded in strong positions compared to that in weak positions. Edges of prosodic units also affect phonetic outcomes. Consonantal articulations tend to be strengthened at initial edges of prosodic words and intonation phrases. Final syllables of words and intonation phrases are regularly lengthened. An extensive literature on isochrony addresses the possibility that speech has a steady beat with a constant interval between the stresses. This literature has established that interstress intervals in fact vary widely as a function of the material comprising the interval. However, when the principle determinants of duration are controlled for, evidence of a tendency towards isochrony is reported in some studies.

Contextual effects related to prosody are substantial and rank with speech style and speaker characteristics as sources of variation in the realization of phonemes and DISTINCTIVE FEATURES. The variation is great enough that a token of one phoneme in one prosodic position can be identical to a token of a different phoneme in some other prosodic position. For example, in American English, a phrase-final /z/ is virtually identical to a medial /s/. Similarly, a 20-story building in Evanston, Illinois, provides an example of a "tall building," but it would be an example of a "short building" if it were in downtown Chicago. That is, the context-dependence of the phonetic realizations of phonemes is similar in character to context-dependence found in other domains, and it provides an example of the abstractness and adaptability of human cognition.

Because of intense research activity over the last two decades, the phonological theory of prosody and intonation is now well developed. It characterizes the cognitive structures that must be viewed as implicitly present in the minds of speakers in order to explain their use of prosody and intonation in both speech production and SPEECH PERCEPTION.

The central concepts of prosodic theory are the prosodic units (the syllable, the foot, the intonation phrase, etc.) and the relations defined among these units. The units are temporally ordered. Bigger units dominate smaller ones. Within each unit, a relationship of strength is available that singles out one element as more prominent than the other elements of the same type in the group. Strength is inherited through the hierarchy; the head syllable of an intonation phrase can be defined as the strongest syllable in the strongest foot in the strongest word in that phrase. Although it is generally agreed that prosodic structures are hierarchical, they contrast with syntactic structures in making much less use of recursion. In SYNTAX, we find clauses embedded within other clauses, but in PHONOLOGY, we do not find syllables embedded within other syllables. The only serious candidate for a recursive node in prosody is the prosodic word, and scholars do not agree about whether this node is recursive or not. As a consequence of the relative flatness of the prosodic structure, syntactic structures are flattened when the prosodic phrasing is computed. For example, in sentence (1), a recursive syntactic structure corresponds to a prosodic structure in which three intonation phrases are on a par with each other.

(1) This is the cat % that ate the rat % that stole the cheese.

The intonation system of English has been extensively studied. Points of agreement among many researchers in the English-speaking countries have recently been codified in the ToBI transcription standard, for which on-line training materials are available (Pitrelli, Beckman, and Hirschberg 1994; Beckman and Ayers Elam 1994/97). According to this standard, intonation contours may be "spelled" using three basic tonal elements: low tone (L), high tone (H), and downstepped high tone (!H). !H represents the combination of high tone with a compression and lowering of the pitch range; a sequence of !Hs generates an F0 contour with a descending staircase. Pitch accents, which mark prominently stressed syllables in the phrase, are made up of these elements. The nuclear accent is defined as the accent on the main stress of the entire phrase. The prenuclear accents fall on prominent syllables earlier in the phrase. Every complete utterance must have (at least one) nuclear accent, but some utterances lack prenuclear accents. In addition to the pitch accents, each contour has boundary tones which mark the edges of the intonation phrase.

All languages have prosody and intonation, but there are many important differences among the systems found in various languages. They differ in the total inventory of intonational patterns and in the pragmatic meanings assigned to particular patterns. Languages with lexical tone (whether tone languages such as Mandarin or classic pitch accent languages such as Japanese) tend to have somewhat simpler intonational systems than English, presumably because much of the F0 contour is taken up with providing phonetic expression of the tones in the words (see Pierrehumbert and Beckman 1988; Hayes and Lahiri 1991; Hayes 1995; Myers 1996).

In the prosodic domain, languages differ in the constraints they impose on the composition of the various units. At the phrasal level, they differ in how they set up the correspondance between intonational phrases and syntactic and semantic structures. Some languages tend to locate prosodic breaks after a syntactic head, whereas others tend to locate breaks before. Some languages (such as English) permit the main prominence to be located anywhere in the phrase (for the purpose of highlighting or foregrounding particular words). Other languages make little or no use of variable placement of prominence within the phrase, instead moving new information to fixed prosodically prominent positions. Turning to smaller prosodic units, some languages permit syllables with complicated consonant clusters and others do not (Goldsmith 1990). Languages also differ in foot structure (Hayes 1995) and in the salience or importance of the different prosodic units (Beckman 1995). For example, in English the foot structure conspicuously shapes the lexical inventory and greatly affects how phonemes are pronounced. Foot structure exists in Japanese but smaller units (the syllable and the mora) vary much less with position in the foot and, as a result, exhibit a robustness that they lack in English.

In considering the contribution of prosody to interpretation, it is useful to separate prosodic structure within the word from prosodic structure above the word level. Prosodic structure within the word (i.e., syllable and foot structure) is an important factor in lexical access, shaping the segmentation strategy in each language and the set of active competitors for any given word at any given time (Cutler 1995). Prosodic structure above the word level (phrasing and phrasal prominence) reflects syntax, SEMANTICS, and DISCOURSE structure. As a result, it has repercussions for syntactic parsing, for the scope of operators such as "only," "even," and "not," for the understood reference of pronouns, and for the topic/comment structure of the discourse (Jackendoff 1972; Terken and Nooteboom 1987; Hirschberg and Ward 1991).

Intonation contours function as independent pragmatic morphemes. According to Pierrehumbert and Hirschberg (1990), the contour indicates the relationship of each utterance to the mutual beliefs that are developed and modified in the course of a conversation. For example, an H accent marks an intended addition to the mutual beliefs, whereas L accents mark information that is marked as salient but not to be added. The tremendous variety of understood meanings of patterns in context arises from the interplay of these factors with the goals and assumptions of the interlocutors. (For other treatments of the pragmatic meaning of intonational morphemes, see Gussenhoven 1983, Ward and Hirschberg 1985, and Morel 1995.)

Intonation and prosody are obligatory. Every single utterance has a prosodic analysis and represents some choice of intonation pattern, just as it represents some choice of phonemes and syllables. In experimental studies with aural stimuli, it is not possible to avoid or omit the contribution of intonation by using a monotone F0 contour. Similarly, experiments on words "in isolation" are in fact using words which are phrase-initial, phrase-final, and under main stress in the phrase (if the stimuli are well formed), because linguistic structure requires that every utterance no matter how short be a full intonation phrase. As a result, words produced "in isolation" also carry a complete phrasal melody. Results of experiments on words in isolation often show artifacts of this prosodic positioning and fail to generalize to words in running speech, which most often constitute only a part of a full intonation phrase.

The outcomes of experiments on syntactic processing, scope, and reference resolution in running speech are likely to be affected by the phrasal prosody of the stimuli. It is therefore desirable to control for this factor and to use an established transcriptional standard to report the prosody of the stimuli actually used. Orthogonal variation of the word string and the prosodic pattern may be used to factor out the prosodic and nonprosodic factors in the domain under investigation.

Experimental work on intonational meaning is challenging because the meanings by their very nature are highly variable with context. Judgments of intonational meaning obtained for materials out of context are variable and difficult to interpret because they are affected by the subjects' uncontrolled imaginings of what the context might be. However, very good results have been achieved with experimental studies in which subjects evaluate the felicity of particular patterns for specified discourse contexts or the understood force of patterns as they are presented in context. With a careful eye to the discourse context, experimental work on intonational meaning is one of the more feasible and promising areas for experimental work in PRAGMATICS.

See also PHONETICS; PRESUPPOSITION; PROSODY AND INTONATION, PROCESSING ISSUES; SPOKEN WORD RECOGNITION; STRESS, LINGUISTIC; TONE

—*Janet Pierrehumbert*

References

Beckman, M. E. (1995). On blending and the mora. *Papers in Laboratory Phonology* 4: 157–167.

Beckman, M. E., and G. Ayers Elam. (1994/1997). Guide to ToBI Labelling. Electronic text and accompanying audio example files available at http://ling.ohio-state.edu/Phonetics/E_ToBI/etobi_homepage.html.

Beckman, M. E., and J. Pierrehumbert. (1986). Intonational structure in Japanese and English. *Phonology Yearbook* 3: 15–70.

Clark, J. E., and C. Yallop. (1990). *An Introduction to Phonetics and Phonology.* Oxford: Blackwell.

Cutler, A. (1995). Spoken word recognition and production. In J. Miller and P. Eimas, Eds., *Speech, Language, and Communication.* New York: Academic Press, pp. 97–136.

Goldsmith, J. (1990). *Autosegmental and Metrical Phonology.* Oxford: Blackwell.

Gussenhoven, G. (1983). *On the Grammar and Semantics of Sentence Accents.* Publications in the Linguistics Sciences 16. Dordrecht: Foris.

Hayes, B. (1995). *Metrical Stress Theory: Principles and Case Studies.* Chicago: University of Chicago Press.

Hayes, B., and A. Lahiri. (1991). Bengali intonational phonology. *Natural Language and Linguistic Theory* 9: 47–96.

Hirschberg, J., and G. Ward. (1991). Accent and bound anaphora. *Cognitive Linguistics* 2: 101–121.

Jackendoff, R. (1972). *Semantic Interpretation in Generative Grammar.* Cambridge, MA: MIT Press.

Ladd, D. R. (1996). *Intonational Phonology.* Cambridge: Cambridge University Press.

Morel, M.-A. (1995). Valeur énonciative des variations de hauteur mélodique en français. *French Language Studies* 5: 189–202. Cambridge: Cambridge University Press.

Myers, S. (1996). Boundary tones and the phonetic implementation of tone in Chichewa. *Studies in African Linguistics* 25: 29–60.

Papers in Laboratory Phonology. Cambridge: Cambridge University Press. Vol. 1, (1990). J. Kingston and M. E. Beckman, Eds.; Vol. 2, (1992). G. Docherty and D. R. Ladd, Eds.; Vol. 3, (1994). P. Keating, Ed.; Vol. 4, (1995). B. Connell and A. Arvaniti, Eds.; Vol. 5, Forthcoming, Broe and J. Pierrehumbert, Eds.; Vol 6, Forthcoming, Ogden and Local, Eds.

Pierrehumbert, J., (1997). Consequences of intonation for the voice Source. In S. Kiritani, H. Hirose, and H. Fujisaki, Eds., *Speech Production and Language, Speech Research* 13. Berlin: Mouton, pp. 111–131.

Pierrehumbert, J., and M. E. Beckman. (1988). *Japanese Tone Structure.* Cambridge, MA: MIT Press.

Pierrehumbert, J., and J. Hirschberg. (1990). The meaning of intonation contours in the interpretation of discourse. In P. Cohen, J. Morgan, and M. Pollack, Eds., *Plans and Intentions in Communication.* Cambridge, MA: MIT Press, pp. 271–312.

Pitrelli, J. F., M. E. Beckman, and J. Hirschberg. (1994). Evaluation of prosodic transcription labeling reliability in the ToBI framework. *Proceedings of the International Conference on Spoken Language Processing,* Yokohama, Japan.

Selkirk E. O. (1984). *Phonology and Syntax.* Cambridge, MA: MIT Press.

Terken, J. M. B., and S. G. Nooteboom. (1987). Opposite effects of accentuation and deaccentuation on verification latencies for given and new information. *Language and Cognitive Processes* 2: 145–163.

Titze, I. (1994). *Principles of Voice Production.* Englewood Cliffs, NJ: Prentice-Hall.

Ward, G., and J. Hirschberg. (1985). Implicating uncertainty: The pragmatics of fall-rise. *Language* 61: 747–776.

Further Readings

Bird, S. (1995). *Computational Phonology: A Constraint-Based Approach.* Cambridge: Cambridge University Press.

Grice, M., and R. Benzmueller. (1997). Transcribing German intonation with GToBI. http://www.coli.uni-sb.de/phonetik/projects/Tobi/gtobi.html.

Horne, M., Ed. (1998). *Prosody: Theory and Experiment. Studies Presented to Gosta Bruce.* Dordrecht: Kluwer.

Ladd, D. R. (1980). *The Structure of Intonational Meaning.* Bloomington, IN: University of Indiana Press.

Levelt, W. J. M. (1989). *Speaking: From Intention to Articulation.* Cambridge, MA: MIT Press.

Pierrehumbert, J., and S. Steele. (1990). Categories of tonal alignment in English. *Phonetica* 46: 181–196.

Venditti, J. (1995). Japanese ToBI Labelling Guidelines. http://ling.ohio-state.edu/Phonetics/J_ToBI/jtobi_homepage.html. Also in K. Ainsworth-Darnell and M. D'Imperio, Eds., *Ohio State Working Papers in Linguistics.* 50: 127–162.

Prosody and Intonation, Processing Issues

PROSODY AND INTONATION determine much of the form of spoken language. An account of the processing of language—the production and comprehension of words and sentences—must therefore pay attention to prosodic (rhythmic, grouping) and intonational (melodic) structure. The fact that more research in PSYCHOLINGUISTICS has involved written language than spoken language, however, means that the role of prosody and intonation in processing is not yet fully described.

In studies of language comprehension, prosody and intonation have figured in research on SPOKEN WORD RECOGNITION, on SENTENCE PROCESSING (the computation of syntactic structure) and on DISCOURSE processing. One role of prosody and intonation in word recognition is to aid in the operation of segmenting a continuous input into its component words. Studies in many languages (see, for example, the summaries in Otake and Cutler 1996) have shown that listeners can use the rhythmic structure of utterances to determine where word boundaries are most likely to fall. Because rhythmic structure differs across languages, this means that the processes involved in segmenting utterances into words can also be language-specific—stress-based in English (Cutler and Norris 1988), syllable-based in French (Mehler et al. 1981), and mora-based in Japanese (Otake et al. 1993). This language specificity can result in inappropriate application of native-language segmentation procedures to foreign languages with a different rhythmic structure (Otake and Cutler 1996). Young infants can discriminate between rhythmically dissimilar but not rhythmically similar languages (Nazzi, Bertoncini, and Mehler 1998).

Whether prosodic and intonational information play a role in the processing of word forms per se—for instance, in the activation of lexical entries—is as yet unresolved. The structure of spoken words again differs across languages in ways that affect this issue. Explicit suprasegmental distinctions between words—for example, TONE in languages such as Thai, pitch accent in languages such as Japanese—constrain word activation and thus show that suprasegmental information can play a role at this level. Suprasegmental cues to LINGUISTIC STRESS in English nevertheless appear to play no part in word activation (Cutler 1986): two words that differ solely in suprasegmental structure, such as *foregoing* (primary stress on the first syllable) and *forgoing* (primary stress on the second syllable), are both activated when listeners hear either one, just as is the case with two words pronounced in every respect identically (such as *sale* and *sail*). However, stress in English is, except in rare pairs such as *foregoing/forgoing*, expressed segmentally (in vowel quality) as well as suprasegmentally, so that segmental information alone may in practice suffice for lexical activation in this language. This is not necessarily the case in other stress languages (Cutler, Dahan, and van Donselaar 1997).

In syntactic processing, the relevant questions have been: do prosody and intonation serve to divide the input into major syntactically motivated chunks? Does such information help to resolve ambiguity, such that sentences which allow more than one interpretation when they are written—for example, *I read about the repayment with interest*—are effectively unambiguous when spoken? And does prosodic and intonational information determine selection between alternative syntactic analyses that present themselves, albeit temporarily, during the processing even of an unambiguous sentence—for example, between possible continuations of *The horse raced by the—(—gate;—Queen won)*? The evidence is mixed (see special issues of *Language and Cognitive Processes* and *Journal of Psycholinguistic Research* in 1996 for overviews) but in general offers little support for direct availability of syntactic information in prosodic and intonational structure. Prosodic hierarchies, after all, encode specifically prosodic, not syntactic relationships (Shattuck-Hufnagel and Turk 1996; Beckman 1996). Prosody may signal syntactic cohesion (Tyler and Warren 1987), and the presence of a sentence accent or of prosodic correlates of a syntactic boundary can have an effect on syntactic analysis in that it can, for example, lead the listener to prefer analyses that are consistent with the prosody (Nespor and Vogel 1983). But no evidence suggests that syntactic analysis is directly derived from prosodic or intonational cues.

In the comprehension of discourse structure, prosodic salience appears most important; speakers highlight via accent the words that are semantically more central to a message (Bolinger 1978; Ladd 1996), and listeners actively search for accented words because of their central semantic role (Cutler 1982; Sedivy et al. 1995). Furthermore, processing is facilitated by the placement of accent on new information, and the deaccenting of old information (Bock and Mazzella 1983). Experimental evidence suggests that the processing of deaccented words involves integration with an existing discourse model (Fowler and Housum 1987), but it is unclear whether the facilitation observed with deaccentuation reflects direct exploitation of accent information in discourse-structure decisions or arises indirectly via reference to an existing discourse model in the course of decoding the poorer acoustic information available from deaccented speech. Finally, listeners can interpret prosodic information to derive cues to topic and turn-taking structure in discourse (Hirschberg and Pierrehumbert 1986). Intonational structure is also important for the interpretation of discourse (Pierrehumbert and Hirschberg 1990); the derivation of meaning from intonation involves simultaneous consideration of contours and of the sentential and discourse context in which they appear (Grabe et al. 1997).

The computation of both prosodic and intonational form must of course likewise play a role in speakers' utterance production (Levelt 1989), with prosodic generation referring both to the lexical items and the syntactic structure selected (Ferreira 1993; Meyer 1994), and intonational generation referring to both the sentence to be spoken and its context (Ladd 1996). Production of phonologically alternative forms of words (e.g., via deletion or addition of sounds, as when the middle vowel of *family* is deleted, or a vowel is inserted between the last two sounds of *film*) can be prompted by the prosodic pattern in which the word is uttered (Kuijpers and van Donselaar 1998).

Because, as noted above, there has been less psycholinguistic research on issues specific to spoken language than on the processing of written language, and because it is in addition true that LANGUAGE PRODUCTION has so far attracted far less experimental research than language comprehension, it will be obvious that the production of prosody and intonation is a research area very much in need of wider empirical attention.

See also COMPUTATIONAL PSYCHOLINGUISTICS; INNATENESS OF LANGUAGE; PHONOLOGY; SPEECH PERCEPTION; SYNTAX

—*Anne Cutler*

References

Beckman, M. E. (1996). The parsing of prosody. *Language and Cognitive Processes* 11: 17–67.

Bock, J. K., and J. R. Mazzella. (1983). Intonational marking of given and new information: Some consequences for comprehension. *Memory and Cognition* 11: 64–76.

Bolinger, D. L. (1978). Intonation across languages. In J. Greenberg, Ed., *Universals of Human Language,* vol. 2, *Phonology.* Palo Alto, CA: Stanford University Press, pp. 471–524.

Cutler, A. (1982). Prosody and sentence perception in English. In J. Mehler, E. C. T. Walker, and M. F. Garrett, Eds., *Perspectives on Mental Representation: Experimental and Theoretical Studies of Cognitive Processes and Capacities.* Hillsdale, NJ: Erlbaum, pp. 201–216.

Cutler, A. (1986). Forbear is a homophone: Lexical prosody does not constrain lexical access. *Language and Speech* 29: 201–220.

Cutler, A., D. Dahan, and W. van Donselaar. (1997). Prosody in the comprehension of spoken language: A literature review. *Language and Speech* 40: 141–201.

Cutler, A., and D. G. Norris. (1988). The role of strong syllables in segmentation for lexical access. *Journal of Experimental Psychology: Human Perception and Performance* 14: 113–121.

Ferreira, F. (1993). Creation of prosody during sentence production. *Psychological Review* 100: 233–253.

Fowler, C. A., and J. Housum. (1987). Talkers' signaling of "new" and "old" words in speech and listeners' perception and use of the distinction. *Journal of Memory and Language* 26: 489–504.

Grabe, E., C. Gussenhoven, J. Haan, E. Marsi, and B. Post. (1998). Preaccentual pitch and speaker attitude in Dutch. *Language and Speech* 41, 63–85.

Hirschberg, J., and J. Pierrehumbert. (1986). The intonational structuring of discourse. *Proceedings of Twentyfourth Association Computational Linguistics* 134–144.

Kuijpers, C., and W. van Donselaar. (1998). The influence of rhythmic context on schwa epenthesis and schwa deletion. *Language and Speech* 41: 87–108.

Ladd, D. R. (1996). *Intonational Phonology.* Cambridge: Cambridge University Press.

Levelt, W. J. M. (1989). *Speaking: From Intention to Articulation.* Cambridge, MA: MIT Press.

Mehler, J., J.-Y. Dommergues, U. Frauenfelder, and J. Segui. (1981). The syllable's role in speech segmentation. *Journal of Verbal Learning and Verbal Behavior* 20: 298–305.

Meyer, A. S. (1994). Timing in sentence production. *Journal of Memory and Language* 33: 471–492.

Nazzi, T., J. Bertoncini, and J. Mehler. (1998). Language discrimination by newborns: Towards an understanding of the role of rhythm. *Journal of Experimental Psychology: Human Perception and Performance* 24: 756–766.

Nespor, M., and I. Vogel. (1983). Prosodic structure above the word. In A. Cutler and D. R. Ladd, Eds., *Prosody: Models and Measurements.* Heidelberg: Springer, pp. 123–140.

Otake, T., and A. Cutler, Eds. (1996). *Phonological Structure and Language Processing: Cross-Linguistic Studies.* Berlin: Mouton.

Otake, T., G. Hatano, A. Cutler, and J. Mehler. (1993). Mora or syllable? Speech segmentation in Japanese. *Journal of Memory and Language* 32: 358–378.

Pierrehumbert, J., and J. Hirschberg. (1990). The meaning of intonational contours in the interpretation of discourse. In P. R. Cohen, J. Morgan, and M. E. Pollack, Eds., *Intentions in Communication.* Cambridge, MA: MIT Press, pp. 271–323.

Sedivy, J., M. Tanenhaus, M. Spivey-Knowlton, K. Eberhard, and G. Carlson. (1995). Using intonationally marked presuppositional information in on-line language processing: Evidence from eye movements to a visual model. *Proceedings of the Seventeenth Annual Conference of the Cognitive Science Society.* Hillsdale, NJ: Erlbaum, pp. 375–380.

Shattuck-Hufnagel, S., and A. E. Turk. (1996). A prosody tutorial for investigators of auditory sentence processing. *Journal of Psycholinguistic Research* 25: 193–247.

Tyler, L. K., and P. Warren. (1987). Local and global structure in spoken language comprehension. *Journal of Memory and Language* 26: 638–657.

Further Readings

Friederici, A., Ed. (1998). *Language Comprehension: A Biological Perspective.* Heidelberg: Springer.

Journal of Psycholinguistic Research. (1996). *Special Issue on Prosodic Effects on Parsing* 25(2).

Language and Cognitive Processes. (1996). *Special Issue on Prosody and Parsing* 11(½).

Psychoanalysis, Contemporary Views

Though a number of key issues have been clarified, there is no more agreement now than there was half a century ago concerning the status and objectivity of psychoanalysis.

Controversy in the understanding and evaluation of psychoanalysis has its origin in the multifaceted character of Sigmund FREUD's theorizing—the plurality of other disciplines with which Freud allied it, and the mix of methodologies that he employed—but it is also a function of several other variables, including the diversity of schools (Kleinian, Jungian, ego-psychological, etc.) within the psychoanalytic movement itself, the uncertainty as to whether psychoanalysis is fundamentally a theory or a practice, and the variety of philosophical outlooks that have had an interest in either assimilating or repudiating psychoanalytic ideas.

It is helpful to distinguish in the diversity of schools two modes of approach to psychoanalysis: those that locate discussion of psychoanalysis firmly in the context of scientific methodology, and those that give priority to issues in the philosophy of mind. There is a tendency for this distinction to be correlated with contrasting estimates—respectively negative and positive—of the objectivity of psychoanalysis.

In the first group, the two landmark writings are Karl Popper 1963 (ch. 1) and Adolf Grünbaum 1984. Popper's enormously influential attack on psychoanalysis, in the context of a general rejection of inductivism in the philosophy of science, consists of the claim that psychoanalysis fails to open itself to refutation and so does not satisfy the condition of falsifiability that (in his account) supplies the only alternative to inductive support. On account of its alleged immunity to counter-evidence, psychoanalysis is classified as a "pseudoscience." Popper's criticisms (which in part stand independently of his own philosophy of science) had the effect of making untenable the naive view of psychoanalysis as a set of hypotheses unproblematically grounded in experience, and of provoking attempts—the results of which have been markedly inconclusive—to test psychoanalytic hypotheses experimentally in controlled, extra-clinical contexts (see Eysenck and Wilson 1973).

In direct opposition to Popper, Grünbaum maintains that psychoanalysis can be evaluated scientifically, and has elaborated a highly detailed critique of psychoanalysis centered on Freud's avowed aspiration to provide a theory of the mind that is successful by the canons of natural science, these being inductive, in Grünbaum's view. Grünbaum argues that Freudian theory reposes on claims that only psychoanalysis can give correct insight into the cause of neurosis, and that such insight is causally necessary for a durable cure. Grünbaum then proceeds to underline the empirical weakness of psychoanalysis' claim to causal efficacy, and presses the familiar objection that the therapeutic effects of psychoanalysis may be due to suggestion. Furthermore, Grünbaum argues that even if the clinical data is taken at face value, the inferences that Freud draws are unwarranted. (For further discussion of psychoanalysis' scientificity, see Hook 1964 and Sachs 1991.)

Discussion of psychoanalysis was initiated by philosophers sensitized by Wittgenstein's work in the philosophy of psychology to a set of issues independent from scientific methodology. They addressed the more basic conceptual question of whether psychoanalytic explanations are causal or rationalizing in form—the common assumption being that these are exclusive modes of explanation—and on this basis formulated different views of psychoanalysis' cogency, some

of them positive (see MacDonald 1954: pt. VI). In response to the perceived problem of mechanism in Freudian metapsychology, Schafer (1976) undertook to translate its terms into those of "action language," an approach found attractive by many psychoanalytic theorists.

Contemporary developments in this vein bear witness to the subsequent explosion of work in the philosophy of mind, particularly to the influence of Donald Davidson's compatibilism of reasons and causes, and his ANOMALOUS MONISM. The significance of Davidson's work is to allow a reading of psychoanalysis that is consistent with physicalism and does justice simultaneously to psychoanalysis' commitment to search for meaningful connections among mental phenomena and its claim to provide causal explanation, while freeing it from the obligation to come up with strict causal laws. Against this background it becomes possible to argue that psychoanalysis is an extension of commonsense FOLK PSYCHOLOGY, arrived at by modifying the familiar "belief-desire" schema of practical reason explanation, for which it substitutes the concepts of wish and fantasy. (Melanie Klein's development of Freud's theories assumes, in this approach, special importance.) In such a view, psychoanalysis does not, contra Grünbaum, repose logically on therapeutic claims, and the specific inductive canons of the natural sciences are inappropriate to its evaluation; the grounds for psychoanalysis lie instead in its offering a unified explanation for phenomena (DREAMING, psychopathology, mental conflict, sexuality, and so on) that commonsense psychology is unable, or poorly equipped, to explain. (Defending this broadly circumscribed approach, see above all Wollheim 1984, 1991, and 1993, Hopkins 1988, 1991, and 1992; and also Davidson 1982; Lear 1990; Cavell 1993; and Gardner 1993.) This approach can be vindicated only if there is a determinate interpretative path from the attributions of commonsense psychology to those of psychoanalysis, a matter that can be decided only by examining clinical material. The central philosophical difficulty facing this approach is to show that psychoanalysis can extend commonsense psychology at the same time as revising it, that is, that the modifications psychoanalysis makes to commonsense psychology are not so radical as to effectively cut it loose from the latter. Thus two important questions for this approach, which continue to generate controversy, concern the intelligibility of postulating mental states that are unconscious (see Searle 1992: ch. 7) and mental content that is prelinguistic, unconceptualized, or nonpropositional (see Cavell 1993).

The ascent of cognitive science has encouraged the formulation of a further set of positions on psychoanalysis, which stand midway between the two groups just described. Freud's very early "Project for a scientific psychology" (1950/1895), an attempt at a general neurological theory of mental functioning, allows itself to be recast in more contemporary, computational terms (see Gill and Pribram 1976), and subpersonal reconstructions of Freud's properly psychoanalytic theories, implying their fundamental continuity with the "Project," have been offered (see Erdelyi 1985). Kitcher (1992) has made a detailed case for the stronger thesis that Freud should be interpreted as seeking to establish an interdisciplinary science of the mind of the sort that cognitive science now aims at. Cummins (1983: ch. 4) offers an understanding of psychoanalysis as striving to coordinate an interpretive level of description of the mind with an underlying functional story. Assuming psychoanalysis and cognitive science to be both empirically well grounded, some degree of fit between their functional delineations of the mind is almost certain. Whether any substantial theoretical integration of psychoanalysis with cognitive science can reasonably be expected is moot, however, and arguably stands or falls with the success of cognitive science in analyzing higher-level, propositional attitude-involving cognitive capacities.

The positions indicated above are far from exhaustive, and a comprehensive survey would include also Continental developments. One particularly influential early contribution is Jürgen Habermas's (1971/1968) hermeneutic reading, which seeks to separate psychoanalysis wholly from the natural sciences—this association being attributed to a naturalistic and scientific misconception of psychoanalysis on Freud's part—and integrate it with communication theory. Later Continental writers, having Lacanian psychoanalysis as a model, have tended to develop theories of psychoanalysis strongly oriented toward purely philosophical themes of representation and subjectivity.

Collections discussing psychoanalysis from various philosophical angles include Wollheim and Hopkins 1982, Clark and Wright 1988, and Neu 1991.

See also PSYCHOANALYSIS, HISTORY OF

—Sebastian Gardner

References

Cavell, M. (1993). *The Psychoanalytic Mind: From Freud to Philosophy.* Cambridge, MA: Harvard University Press.

Clark, P., and C. Wright, Eds. (1988). *Mind, Psychoanalysis and Science.* Oxford: Blackwell.

Cummins, R. (1983). *The Nature of Psychological Explanation.* Cambridge, MA: MIT Press.

Davidson, D. (1982). Paradoxes of irrationality. In R. Wollheim and J. Hopkins, Eds., *Philosophical Essays on Freud.* Cambridge: Cambridge University Press, pp. 289–305.

Erdelyi, M. (1985). *Psychoanalysis: Freud's Cognitive Psychology.* New York: Freeman.

Eysenck, H., and G. Wilson, Eds. (1973). *The Experimental Study of Freudian Theories.* London: Methuen.

Freud, S. (1950/1895). Project for a scientific psychology. In *The Standard Edition of the Complete Psychological Works of Sigmund Freud.* 24 vols. Translated by J. Strachey, Ed., in collaboration with A. Freud, assisted by A. Strachey and A. Tyson. London: Hogarth (1953–74), vol. 1, pp. 281–397.

Gardner, S. (1993). *Irrationality and the Philosophy of Psychoanalysis.* Cambridge: Cambridge University Press.

Gill, M., and K. Pribram. (1976). *Freud's "Project" Re-Assessed.* London: Hutchinson.

Grünbaum, A. (1984). *The Foundations of Psychoanalysis.* Berkeley: University of California Press.

Habermas, J. (1968/1971). *Knowledge and Human Interests.* Translated by J. Shapiro. Boston: Beacon.

Hook, S., Ed. (1964). *Psychoanalysis, Scientific Method and Philosophy.* New York: New York University Press.

Hopkins, J. (1988). Epistemology and depth psychology: Critical notes on "The Foundations of Psychoanalysis." In P. Clark and

C. Wright, Eds., *Mind, Psychoanalysis and Science.* Oxford: Blackwell, pp. 33–60.

Hopkins, J. (1991). The interpretation of dreams. In J. Neu, Ed., *The Cambridge Companion to Freud.* Cambridge: Cambridge University Press, pp. 86–135.

Hopkins, J. (1992). Psychoanalysis, interpretation, and science. In J. Hopkins and A. Savile, Eds., *Psychoanalysis, Mind and Art: Perspectives on Richard Wollheim.* Oxford: Blackwell, pp. 3–34.

Kitcher, P. (1992). *Freud's Dream: A Complete Interdisciplinary Science of Mind.* Cambridge, MA: MIT Press.

Lear, J. (1990). *Love and its Place in Nature: A Philosophical Reconstruction of Psychoanalysis.* London: Faber.

MacDonald, M., Ed. (1954). *Philosophy and Analysis.* Oxford: Blackwell.

Neu, J., Ed. (1991). *The Cambridge Companion to Freud.* Cambridge: Cambridge University Press.

Popper, K. (1963). *Conjectures and Refutations: The Growth of Scientific Knowledge.* London: Routledge and Kegan Paul.

Sachs, D. (1991). In fairness to Freud: A critical notice of "The Foundations of Psychoanalysis," by Adolf Grünbaum. In J. Neu, Ed., *The Cambridge Companion to Freud.* Cambridge: Cambridge University Press, pp. 309–338.

Schafer, R. (1976). *A New Language for Psychoanalysis.* New Haven: Yale University Press.

Searle, J. (1992). *The Rediscovery of the Mind.* Cambridge, MA: MIT Press.

Wollheim, R. (1984). *The Thread of Life.* Cambridge: Cambridge University Press.

Wollheim, R. (1991). *Freud.* 2nd ed. London: Fontana Collins.

Wollheim, R. (1993). Desire, belief and Professor Grünbaum's Freud. In *The Mind and Its Depths.* Cambridge, MA: Harvard University Press, pp. 91–111.

Wollheim, R., and J. Hopkins, Eds. (1982). *Philosophical Essays on Freud.* Cambridge: Cambridge University Press.

Psychoanalysis, History of

One of Sigmund Freud's basic psychoanalytic claims was that dreams and symptoms were *wish fulfillments* (Freud 1900; for italicized terms see Laplanche and Pointalis 1973). A particularly simple example is that in which a thirsty person dreams of drinking, and thereby temporarily pacifies the underlying desire. Schematically, in the case of real satisfaction, a desire that P (that I get a drink) brings about a real situation that P (I get a drink), and this in turn brings about an experience or belief that P which pacifies the desire, that is, causes it to cease to operate. In Freudian wish fulfillment, by contrast, a desire operates to bring about an experience- or belief-like representation of satisfaction (I dream of drinking) and so pacifies the desire in the absence of the real thing. Freud hypothesized that this process was effected by the activation of neural prototypes of past desire-satisfaction sequences, and he took this to be the mind/brain's earliest and most basic way of coping with *desire* (1895).

FREUD found this pattern of representational pacification in more complex instances, and was thus able to see dreams, symptoms, and many other depictive phenomena as representing the satisfaction of unfulfilled wishes or desires, which could be traced back to childhood and bodily experience. Analysis indicated that little children attached great and formative emotional significance to very early interactions with their parents in such basic proto-social activities as feeding and the expulsion and management of waste. These involved the first use of the mouth, genitals, and anus, and the early stimulus of these organs apparently roused feelings continuous with their later uses in normal and abnormal *sexuality* (1905). Little children's motives thus included desires to harm or displace each parent, envied and hated as a rival for the love of the other, as well as to preserve and protect that same parent, loved both sensually and as a caretaker, helper, and model. Because these desires were subject to particularly radical conflict they were characteristically *repressed,* and thus rendered *unconscious,* and kept from everyday planning and thought.

Repression entailed that such desires could enter consciousness only in a symbolic form, and so could be expressed in intentional action only via symbol-forming processes such as *sublimation* (1908). Symbolizing incestuous desires in terms of ploughing and planting mother earth, for example, could render such activities meaningful as expressions of wish fulfilling *phantasy.* Thus, according to Freud, the activities of everyday life acquired the kind of unconscious representational significance he had found in dreams and symptoms, and were accordingly subject to unconscious reinforcement, inhibition, etc. Infantile desires (or the contents of infantile neural prototypes) were not lost, but were continually rearticulated through symbolism so as to direct action toward their pacification throughout life. This was thus the *primary process* through which desire was regulated.

Particular phantasies also realize many of the mechanisms described in psychoanalytic theory. Thus phantasies of *projection* assign (usually undesirable) traits from the self to another, whereas those of *introjection* assign (usually desired) traits of the other to the self. The "good in/bad out" operation of these mechanisms, and the processes of *identification* that they effect, are significant for both individual development and social organization.

The young child achieves self-control partly by forming phantasy images derived from the parents as regulators of its early bodily activities. Because these "earliest parental *imagoes*" (1940) embody the child's infantile aggression in a projected form, they are introjected as a *super-ego* far more threatening and punitive than the actual parents. Later the child identifies with its parents in their role as agents, that is, as satisfiers and pacifiers of their own desires, and these identifications form the *ego*. The members of many groups identify with one another by introjecting a common idealized leader or cause (1921: 67ff), or by projecting their destructive motives into a common locus that thereby becomes a legitimated focus of collective hate. Those who find such a common good or bad object feel united, purified, and able to validate destructive motives by common ideals. The processes that establish the individual conscience thus also create a pattern of "good us/bad them" that enlists its ferocity in the service of group aggression.

After the Nazi occupation many analysts left Europe, and post-Freudian psychoanalysis evolved in distinct ways in different countries, often in response to analysts who settled there. In England, Anna Freud and Melanie Klein developed techniques for analyzing the play of children. This made it possible for child analysts to confirm and revise Freud's descriptions of childhood, and to propose further hypotheses about infancy.

Klein (1975) noted that the uninhibited play of children in analysis showed that their conflicts were rooted in unconscious images that represented versions of their parents as both unrealistically good and extremely bad and malevolent. She explained these as resulting from a process of projection that represented the other as containing disowned aspects of the self, which in turn was fragmented and depleted by the projective loss. Klein called this *projective identification,* and hypothesized that it operated most forcefully before the child gained a working grasp of the concept of identity, and hence before it recognized that the parental figures it felt as bad were the same as those it felt as good. Klein called this preobjectual phase of development the *paranoid-schizoid position,* the term "paranoid" marking the extremity of the baby's potential for anxiety, and "schizoid" the fragmentary way it represents both itself and its objects. As the infant starts unifying its images, this phase yields to the *depressive position,* so named because unification entails liability to depression about harming or losing the object (principally the feeding, caring mother), now seen as complex (frustrating as well as gratifying) and liable to be misconceived, but also as unique and irreplaceable.

Klein's discussions of the child's relation to phantasied objects, characteristically different from those in the actual environment, inaugurated the *object-relations* approach to psychoanalysis, continued by Ronald Fairbairn (1954), Donald Winnicott (1958), and a number of others of the so-called British School. Accounts in these terms have now been elaborated by all schools (see Kernberg 1995). Klein's ideas were applied to groups by Wilfred Bion (1961), and by Bion (1989) and Hanna Segal (1990) to the infantile origins of symbolism and thought. They also influenced John Bowlby (1980), whose work fostered extensive study of child-parent attachment (Ainsworth 1985; Karen 1994).

Freud introduced the ego and super-ego both as functional systems mediating between the individual's innate *drives* and the external world, and as modeled on persons. In this he attempted to combine functional explanation with the empirical claim that the way persons function depends upon their internal representations of themselves and others. This mode of explanation, called *ego-psychology,* was elaborated by Anna Freud (1936), and by Heinz Hartmann (1958) and his colleagues in the United States. Hartmann focused particularly upon the attainment of autonomy in object-relations, which he took to be dependent upon object constancy, the ability to represent self and other consistently, despite absence and changes in emotion. This was carried into empirical research on children by Renee Spitz (1965), and developed further by Edith Jackobsen (1964) and Margaret Mahler (1968) and her associates, who sought to describe the process of individuation that issued in object constancy.

More recently, Heinz Kohut (1977) has argued that the pathology of the "fragmented" or "depleted" SELF requires a new "self-psychology" for its conceptualization. He introduces the notion of "self-object," that is, another who is experienced as performing essential psychological functions for the self, and so felt part of it. When the parents fail in essential self-object functions the child—or the analytic patient in whom such needs have been re-activated—responds with narcissistic rage, and may become convinced that the environment is fundamentally hostile. Kohut compares this situation to Klein's paranoid-schizoid position, and the fragmentation and depletion with which he is concerned is evidently linked to that which Klein describes as consequent on infantile projective identification (for a recent synthesis see Kumin 1996).

Psychoanalysis in France has been particularly influenced by Jacques Lacan, whose resonant formulations (1977) link analytic ideas with themes in French philosophy, linguistics, and anthropology. A baby who joyfully identifies itself in a mirror, according to Lacan, thereby represents itself as having a wholeness, permanence, and unity that anticipates and facilitates its ability to move and relate to others. But this identification is also an alienation, for the infant now regards itself as something it does not actually feel itself to be, and which it may yet fail to become. Identifications with others are simultaneously enabling and alienating in the same way, so that the external images by which the self is constituted always threaten to confront it as reminders of its own lack of being.

Lacan assigns these images to an order of representations that he describes as the *imaginary,* and contrasts with the *symbolic order* of personal and social sign-systems whose elements are constrained by rules of combination and substitution comparable to those of natural language. The combinations/substitutions of (representations of) objects in dreams and symptoms, or again in the course of development, can be seen as constrained by such rules, and so as instances of metaphor, metonymy, and other linguistic forms. So, Lacan argues, the unconscious is structured like a language. Comparable structuring holds for social phenomena. Thus the resolution of the *Oedipus Complex* is a development in which the boy forgoes an imaginary relation with the mother to occupy a place in the social order that is symbolic, social, and constitutive of human culture. As in the prior instance of the mirror, the child secures a potentially fulfilling identity via the enabling but alienating assumption of an image, this time of the symbolic father, who embodies the social laws regulating sexual desire and providing for its procreative satisfaction.

See also DREAMING; EMOTIONS; PSYCHOANALYSIS, CONTEMPORARY VIEWS; SELF-KNOWLEDGE

—*James Hopkins*

References

Ainsworth, M. D. S. (1985). 1: Patterns of infant-mother attachment: Antecedents and effects on development. 2. Attachment across the life span. *Bull. N.Y. Acad. Med.* 6: 771–812.

Bion, W. R. (1961). *Experiences in Groups.* New York: Basic Books.

Bion, W. R. (1989). *Second Thoughts: Selected Papers on Psychoanalysis.* London: Heinemann.

Bowlby, J. (1980). *Attachment and Loss.* Vols. 1–3. New York: Basic Books.

Fairbairn, W. R. D. (1954). *An Object-Relations Theory of the Personality.* New York: Basic Books.

Freud, A. (1936). *The Ego and the Mechanisms of Defense.* London: Hogarth Press.

Freud, S. (1895). *Project for a Scientific Psychology.* In Freud (1974) vol. 1.

Freud, S. (1900). *The Interpretation of Dreams.* In Freud (1974) vols. 4, 5.

Freud, S. (1905). *Three Essays on the Theory of Sexuality.* In Freud (1974) vol. 6.

Freud, S. (1908). *Civilized Sexual Morality and Modern Nervous Illness.* In Freud (1974) vol. 9.

Freud, S. (1921). *Group Psychology and the Analysis of the Ego.* In Freud (1974) vol. 18.

Freud, S. (1940). *A Short Outline of Psycho-Analysis.* In Freud (1974) vol. 22.

Freud, S. (1974). *The Standard Edition of the Collected Psychological Works of Sigmund Freud.* Translated by J. Strachey, Ed. London: Hogarth Press.

Hartmann, H. (1958). *Ego Psychology and the Problem of Adaptation.* New York: International Universities Press.

Jackobson, E. (1964). *The Self and the Object World.* New York: International Universities Press.

Karen, R. (1994). *Becoming Attached: Unfolding the Mystery of the Mother-Infant Bond and its Impact on Later Life.* New York: Warner Books.

Kernberg, O. (1995). Psychoanalytic object relations theories. In B. Moore and B. Fine, Eds., *Psychoanalysis: The Major Concepts.* New Haven: Yale University Press.

Kohut, H. (1977). *The Restoration of the Self.* New York: International Universities Press.

Klein, M. (1975). *The Writings of Melanie Klein.* London: Karnac Books and the Institute of Psychoanalysis.

Kumin, I. (1996). *Pre-Object Relatedness: Early Attachment and the Psychoanalytic Situation.* New York: Guilford Press.

Lacan, J. (1977). *Écrits.* New York: Norton.

Laplanche, J., and J. B. Pontalis. (1973). *The Language of Psycho-Analysis.* London: Hogarth Press.

Mahler, M. S. (1968). *On Human Symbiosis and the Vicissitudes of Individuation.* New York: International Universities Press.

Moore, B., and B. Fine. (1995). *Psychoanalysis: The Major Concepts.* New Haven: Yale University Press.

Segal, H. (1990). *Dream, Phantasy, and Art.* London: Tavistock/Routledge.

Spitz, R. (1965). *The First Year of Life: A Psychoanalytic Study of Normal and Deviant Development of Object Relations.* New York: International Universities Press.

Winnicott, D. (1958). *Collected Papers: Through Pediatrics to Psychoanalysis.* New York: Basic Books.

Further Readings

Cavell, M. (1993). *The Psychoanalytic Mind.* Cambridge, MA: Harvard University Press.

Clark, P., and C. Wright, Eds. (1988). *Mind, Psychoanalysis, and Science.* Oxford: Blackwell.

Erwin, E. (1996). *A Final Accounting: Philosophical and Empirical Issues in Freudian Psychology.* Cambridge, MA: MIT Press.

Fink, B. (1997). *A Clinical Introduction to Lacanian Psychoanalysis.* Cambridge, MA: Harvard University Press.

Gardner, S. (1993). *Irrationality and the Philosophy of Psychoanalysis.* Cambridge: Cambridge University Press.

Gay, P. (1988). *Freud, A Life for Our Time.* London: J. M. Dent.

Gill, M., and K. Pribram. (1976). *Freud's Project Re-assessed.* London: Hutchinson.

Glymour, C. (1992). Freud's androids. In J. Neu, Ed., *The Cambridge Companion to Freud.* Cambridge: Cambridge University Press.

Grunbaum, A. (1984). *The Foundations of Psychoanalysis: A Philosophical Critique.* Berkeley: University of California Press.

Grunbaum, A. (1993). *Validation in the Clinical Theory of Psychoanalysis.* Madison, CT: International Universities Press.

Hinshelwood, R. D. (1990). *A Dictionary of Kleinian Thought.* London: Free Associations Books.

Hopkins, J. (1997). Psychoanalysis, post-Freudian. In E. Craig, Ed., *The Routledge Encyclopaedia of Philosophy.* London: Routledge.

Hopkins, J. (1998). Freud and the science of mind. In S. Glendinning, Ed., *The Edinburgh Encyclopaedia of Continental Philosophy.* Edinburgh: Edinburgh University Press.

Kitcher, P. (1992). *Freud's Dream: A Complete Interdisciplinary Science of Mind.* Cambridge, MA: MIT Press.

Kline, P. (1984). *Psychology and Freudian Theory: An Introduction.* London: Methuen.

Lear, J. (1990). *Love and Its Place in Nature.* New York: Farrar, Strauss, and Giroux.

MacDonald, C., and D. MacDonald, Eds. (1995). *Philosophy of Psychology: Debates on Psychological Explanation.* Oxford: Blackwell.

Masson, J., Ed. (1985). *The Complete Letters of Sigmund Freud to Wilhelm Fliess* 1887–1904. Cambridge, MA: Harvard University Press.

Moore, B., and B. Fine. (1990). *Psychoanalytic Terms and Concepts.* New Haven: Yale University Press.

Neu, J. (1992). *The Cambridge Companion to Freud.* Cambridge: Cambridge University Press.

Wollheim, R. (1991). *Freud.* 2nd ed. London: Fontana.

Wollheim, R. (1994). *The Mind and its Depths.* Cambridge, MA: Harvard University Press.

Psycholinguistics

Psycholinguistics is the study of people's actions and mental processes as they use language. At its core are speaking and listening, which have been studied in domains as different as LANGUAGE ACQUISITION and language disorders. Yet the primary domain of psycholinguistics is everyday language use.

Speaking and listening have several levels. At the bottom are the perceptible sounds and gestures of language: how speakers produce them, and how listeners hear, see, and identify them (see PHONETICS, PHONOLOGY, SIGN LANGUAGES). One level up are the words, gestural signals, and syntactic arrangement of what is uttered: how speakers formulate utterances, and how listeners identify them (see SENTENCE PROCESSING). At the next level up are communicative acts: what speakers do with their utterances, and how listeners understand what they mean (see PRAGMATICS). At the highest level is DISCOURSE, the joint activities people engage in as they use language. At each level, speakers and listeners have to coordinate their actions.

Speakers plan what they say more than one word at a time. In conversation and spontaneous narratives, they tend to plan in *intonation units,* generally a single major clause or phrase delivered under a unifying intonation contour (Chafe 1980). Intonation units take time to plan, so they often begin with pauses and disfluencies (*uh* or *um,* elongated words, repeated words). For example, one speaker recounting a film said: "[1.0 sec pause] A--nd u--m [2.6 sec pause] you see him taking . . . picking the pears off the leaves."

Planning such units generally proceeds from the top level of language down—from intention to ARTICULATION (Levelt 1989). Speakers decide on a message, then choose constructions for expressing it, and finally program the phonetic segments for articulating it. They do this in overlapping stages.

Formulation starts at a *functional level.* Consider a woman planning "Take the steaks out of the freezer." First she chooses the subject, verb, direct object, and source she wants to express, roughly "the addressee is to get meat from a freezer." Then she chooses an appropriate syntactic frame, an imperative construction with a verb, object, and source location. She then finds the noun and verbs she needs, *take, steak,* and *freeze.* Finally, she fills in the necessary syntactic elements—the article *the,* the preposition *out of,* and the suffixes *-s* and *-er.* Formulation then proceeds to a *positional level.* She creates a phonetic plan for what she has formulated so far. She uses the plan to program her articulatory organs (tongue, lips, glottis) to produce the actual sounds, "Take the steaks out of the freezer." Processing at these levels overlaps as she plans later phrases while articulating earlier ones.

Much of the evidence for these stages comes from slips of the tongue collected over the past century (Fromkin 1973; Garrett 1980). Suppose that the speaker of the last example had, by mistake, transposed *steak* and *freeze* as she introduced them. She would then have added *-s* to *freeze* and *-er* to *steak* and produced "Take the freezes out of the steaker." Other slips occur at the positional level, as when the initial sounds in *left hemisphere* are switched to form *heft lemisphere.*

Listeners are often thought to work from the bottom up. They are assumed to start with the sounds they hear, infer the words and syntax of an utterance, and, finally, infer what the speakers meant. The actual picture is more complicated. In everyday conversation, listeners have a good idea of what speakers are trying to do, and working top down, they use this information to help them identify and understand what they hear (Tanenhaus and Trueswell 1995).

Spoken utterances are identified from left to right by an incremental process of elimination (Marslen-Wilson 1987). As listeners take in the sounds of "elephant," for example, they narrow down the words it might be. They start with an *initial cohort* of all words beginning with "e" (roughly 1000 words), narrow that to the cohort of all words beginning with "el" (roughly 100 words), and so on. By the sound "f" the cohort contains only one word, allowing them to identify the word as "elephant." This way listeners often identify a word before it is complete. Evidence also suggests that listeners access all of the meanings of the words in these cohorts (Swinney 1979). For example, the moment they identify "bugs" in "He found several bugs in the corner of his room" they activate the two meanings "insects" and "hidden microphones." Remarkably, they activate the same two meanings in "He found several spiders, roaches, and other bugs in the corner of his room," even though the context rules out microphones. But after only .2 to .4 seconds "hidden microphones" gets suppressed in favor of "insects."

Still, listeners do use top-down information in identifying words and constructions (Tanenhaus et al. 1995). When people are placed at a table with many objects on it and are asked, "Pick up the candle," they move their gaze to the candle before they reach for it. Indeed, they start to move their eyes toward the candle about 50 msec *before* the end of "candle." But if there is candy on the table along with the candle, they do not start to move their eyes until 30 msec *after* the end of "candle." As a sentence, "Put the apple on the towel in the box" may mean either (1) an apple is to go on a towel that is in a box, or (2) an apple on a towel is to go into a box. Without context, listeners strongly prefer interpretation 1. But when people are placed at a table with two apples, one on a towel and another on a napkin, their eye movements show that they infer interpretation 2 from the beginning. In identifying utterances, then, listeners are flexible in the information they exploit—auditory information, knowledge of syntax, and the context.

Speaking and listening aren't autonomous processes. People talk in order to do things together, and to accomplish that they have to coordinate speaking with listening at many levels (Clark 1996).

One way people coordinate in conversation is with *adjacency pairs*. An adjacency pair consists of two turns, the first of which projects the second, as in questions and answers:

Sam: And what are you then?
Duncan: I'm on the academic council.

In his first turn Sam *proposes* a simple joint project, that he and Duncan exchange information about what Duncan is. In the next turn Duncan *takes up* his proposal, completing the joint project, by giving the information Sam wanted. People use adjacency pairs for establishing joint commitments throughout conversations. They use them for openings (as in the exchange "Hey, Barbara" "Yes?") and closings ("Bye" "Bye"). They use them for setting up narratives ("Tell you who I met yesterday—" "Who?"), elaborate questions ("Oh there's one thing I wanted to ask you" "Mhm"), and other extended joint projects.

Speakers use their utterances to perform *illocutionary acts*—assertions, questions, requests, offers, promises, apologies, and the like—acts that differ in the uptake they project. Most constructions (e.g., "Sit down") can be used for more than one illocutionary act (e.g., a command, a request, an advisory), so speakers and listeners have to coordinate on what is intended. One way they coordinate is by treating each utterance as a contribution to a larger joint project. For example, when restaurant managers were asked on the telephone, "Do you accept American Express cards?" they inferred that the caller had an American Express card and wanted a "yes" or "no" answer. But when they were asked "Do you accept any kinds of credit cards?" they inferred the caller had more than one credit card and wanted a list of the cards they accepted ("Visa and Mastercard"). Listeners draw such inferences more quickly when the construction is conventionally used for the intended action.

"Can you tell me the time?" is a conventional way to ask for the time, making it harder to construe as a question about ability (Gibbs 1994).

People work hard in conversation to establish that each utterance has been understood as intended (Clark 1996). To do that, speakers *monitor* their speech for problems and repair them as quickly as reasonable (Levelt 1983; Schegloff, Jefferson, and Sacks 1977). In "if she'd been—he'd been alive," the speaker discovers that "she" is wrong, replaces it with "he," and continues. Listeners also monitor and, on finding problems, often ask for repairs, as Barbara does here:

Alan: Now,—um do you and your husband have a j- car?
Barbara: Have a car?
Alan: Yeah.
Barbara: No.

People monitor at all levels of speaking and listening. Speakers, for example, monitor their addressees for lapses of attention, mishearings, and misunderstandings. They also monitor for positive evidence of attention, hearing, and understanding, evidence that addressees provide. Addressees, for example, systematically signal their attention with eye gaze and acknowledge hearing and understanding with "yeah" and "uh huh."

Speaking and listening are not the same in all circumstances. They vary with the language (English, Japanese, etc.), with the medium (print, telephones, video, etc.), with age (infants, adults, etc.), with the genre (fiction, parody, etc.), with the trope (irony, metaphor, etc.), and with the joint activity (gossip, court trials, etc.). Accounting for these variations remains a major challenge for psycholinguistics.

See also FIGURATIVE LANGUAGE; LANGUAGE AND COMMUNICATION; LANGUAGE PRODUCTION; LEXICON; METAPHOR; SPOKEN WORD RECOGNITION; VISUAL WORD RECOGNITION

—*Herbert H. Clark*

References

Chafe, W. (1980). The deployment of consciousness in the production of a narrative. In W. Chafe, Ed., *The Pear Stories*. Norwood, NJ: Ablex, pp. 9–50.

Clark, H. H. (1996). *Using Language.* Cambridge: Cambridge University Press.

Fromkin, V. A., Ed. (1973). *Speech Errors as Linguistic Evidence.* The Hague: Mouton.

Garrett, M. F. (1980). Syntactic processes in sentence production. In B. Butterworth, Ed., *Speech Production.* New York: Academic Press, pp. 170–220.

Gibbs, R. W., Jr. (1994). *The Poetics of Mind: Figurative Thought, Language, and Understanding.* Cambridge: Cambridge University Press.

Levelt, W. J. M. (1983). Monitoring and self-repair in speech. *Cognition*, 14: 41–104.

Levelt, W. J. M. (1989). *Speaking.* Cambridge, MA: MIT Press.

Marslen-Wilson, W. (1987). Functional parallelism in spoken word recognition. *Cognition* 25: 71–102.

Schegloff, E. A., G. Jefferson, and H. Sacks. (1977). The preference for self-correction in the organization of repair in conversation. *Language* 53: 361–382.

Swinney, D. A. (1979). Lexical access during sentence comprehension: (Re)consideration of context effects. *Journal of Verbal Learning and Verbal Behavior* 18: 645–660.

Tanenhaus, M. K., M. J. Spivey-Knowlton, K. M. Eberhard, and J. C. Sedivy. (1995). Integration of visual and linguistic information in spoken language comprehension. *Science* 268: 1632–1634.

Tanenhaus, M. K., and J. C. Trueswell. (1995). Sentence comprehension. In J. L. Miller and P. D. Eimas, Eds., *Handbook of Perception and Cognition: Speech, Language, and Communication.* 2nd ed. San Diego: Academic Press, pp. 217–262.

Psychological Laws

Psychology is a science. Sciences are supposed to feature laws, that is, laws of nature, generalizations that are strongly projectible past the actual data that confirm them. Yet in general, psychologists are reluctant to dub their generalizations "laws," even when they have great confidence in those generalizations; some are even uncomfortable in talking of psychological laws at all.

Over the decades, a few generalizations or regularities have explicitly been called laws, in GESTALT PSYCHOLOGY (the laws of organization), in the theory of conditioning (the law of effect, the law of exercise, Jost's law, the law of generalization), in neuropsychology (Bowditch's laws, Hebb's law), and of course in psychophysics (Weber, Fechner, Thurstone, Steven, Bloch, Ricco, Bunsen-Roscoe, Ferry-Porter, Grassmann, Yerkes-Dodson, Schachter). For the most part—the law of effect being arguably an exception—these are empirical generalizations.

Most such laws are equations relating one measurable magnitude to one or more other, independently measurable, magnitudes. Laws of this particular type are of course found throughout the natural and social sciences. But there are psychological generalizations of other kinds that are laws or lawlike as well, even if they are not commonly called by that name. For example, some of the empirical laws are thought to be explained by higher-level theoretical principles or hypotheses, which would themselves have to be considered lawlike in order to play that explanatory role. And surely there are qualitative rather than quantitative generalizations, truths of the form "Whenever organism S is in state A and X occurs, S goes into state B," that are lawlike.

Such qualitative laws would be derived from a standard explanatory pattern in psychology: the *function-analytical* explanation in the sense of Cummins (1983), as found in much of current cognitive theory, perceptual psychology, and PSYCHOLINGUISTICS. (The pattern is ubiquitous in biology, in computer science, and in electronics as well.) Some psychological questions take the form, "How does S Φ?," where "Φ" designates some accomplishment carried out by the organism S (e.g., "How do speakers of English understand novel sentences?" or "How does an experimental subject estimate the distance in miles from her present location to the place she was born?" or "How do dogs recognize individual human smells?"). In answer to such a question, the theorist appeals to a functional or componential analysis of S. S's performance is explained as being the joint product of several constituent operations, individually less demanding, by components or subagencies of the subject acting in concert. The components' individual functions are specified first, and then the explanation details the ways in which they cooperate in producing the more sophisticated corporate explanandum activity.

For example, to explain language understanding, a psycholinguist posits a phonological segmenter, a parser, a SYNTAX, a LEXICON, and (notoriously) a store of real-world knowledge, and starts to tell a story of how those components interact. Of any functionary figuring in that story, we might want to ask in turn how it performs its own particular job. This is another psychological question of just the same form as the first, only this time about the functional organization of one of the subagencies. It is important to see that we can go on asking our function-analytical questions at considerable length. (What neural structures ultimately realize the lexicon?)

Thus we can see human beings and other psychological subjects as *being* simply functionally organized systems, corporate entities that have myriad behavioral capacities by virtue of their internal bureaucratic organizations. An organism's complete psychological description would consist of a flow chart depicting the organism's immediate subagencies and their routes of cooperative access to each other, followed by a set of lower-level flow charts—"detail" maps or "blowups"—for each of the main components, and so on down. At any given level, the flow charts show how the components depicted at that level cooperate to realize the capacities of the single agency whose functional analysis they corporately constitute.

Function-analytical *laws* of two kinds could be read off such diagrams. First there would be qualitative laws of the sort mentioned above; a given flow chart would show what a creature would do, given that it is in such-and-such a state and that (say) it received a stimulus of a certain sort. These "horizontal" laws would be of direct use in the prediction and control of behavior. Second, there would be "vertical" laws, relating lower-level states to the higher-level states that they constitute at a time. Of course, all such laws would be qualified by normalcy or "ceteris paribus" clauses because exceptions to them can be created by hardware breakdown or by perturbation of the system by some external agent.

Philosophers have raised several deeper, skeptical questions about putative laws that are more distinctive to psychology than to the natural sciences, though none of these questions is directed at the acknowledged empirical laws with which we began. The questions stem from the widely shared assumption that many psychological states are representational (see MENTAL REPRESENTATION). One might suggest that what distinguishes psychological laws from those of other natural sciences is that they concern representational states of organisms, but that would seem to rule out laws of conditioning.

Contemporary cognitive and perceptual psychology do traffic in representations, information-carrying states produced and computationally manipulated by psychological mechanisms. By its nature, a representation represents *something*. That is, it has a content or, as the medieval philosophers called it, an "intentional object." And, remarkably, that content or object need not exist in reality; for instance, through deceptive environment or malfunction, a visual edge detector may signal an edge that is not really there (see INTENTIONALITY).

A first skeptical question is this: *Representation of a possibly inexistent object* is a property not found in physics or chemistry—and it is a relational property, ostensibly a relation that its subject bears to an external thing, determined in part by factors external to the organism. Yet natural laws are causal, and some philosophers (notably Fodor 1987 and Searle 1983) have argued that because an entity's causal powers are intrinsic to the entity itself, either representational properties cannot properly figure in psychological laws or there must be a kind of "narrow" representational content that is intrinsic to the subject and independent of environmental factors. (See INDIVIDUALISM. Against that view, see Burge 1986; McClamrock 1995; and Wilson 1995.)

A second set of questions concerns commonsense mental notions, such as those of believing, desiring, seeing, feeling pain, and the like (see PROPOSITIONAL ATTITUDES). Jerry Fodor (1975, 1981) argues that only slightly cleaned-up versions of those concepts have a home in scientific psychology and indeed will figure explicitly in laws; certainly some current psychological experiments make unabashed reference to subjects' beliefs, desires, memories, etc.

However, Donald Davidson (1970, 1974) and Daniel Dennett (1978, 1987) contend that such commonsense concepts correspond to no NATURAL KINDS, not even within psychology. This is in part because they are ascribed to subjects on grounds that are in large part normative rather than empirical, and in part because (Davidson alleges) the "ceteris paribus" clauses needed as qualifying such commonsense generalizations as "If a man wants to eat an acorn omelette, then he generally will if the opportunity exists and no other desire overrides" (1974: 45) are open-ended and unverifiable in a way that such clauses are not when they occur in biology or chemistry. For somewhat different reasons, Paul Churchland (1989) agrees that commonsense concepts correspond to nothing real in psychology or biology and that they will very probably be dropped from science altogether (see ELIMINATIVE MATERIALISM).

See also ANOMALOUS MONISM; FOLK PSYCHOLOGY; PSYCHOPHYSICS

—*William Lycan*

References

Burge, T. (1986). Individualism and psychology. *Philosophical Review* 95: 3–45.

Churchland, P. M. (1989). *A Neurocomputational Perspective.* Cambridge, MA: Bradford Books/MIT Press.

Cummins, R. (1983). *The Nature of Psychological Explanation.* Cambridge, MA: MIT Press/Bradford Books.

Davidson, D. (1970). Mental events. In L. Foster and J. W. Swanson, Eds., *Experience and Theory.* Amherst, MA: University of Massachusetts Press, pp. 79–101.

Davidson, D. (1974). Psychology as philosophy. In S. C. Brown, Ed., *Philosophy of Psychology.* London: Macmillan, pp. 41–52.

Dennett, D. C. (1978). *Brainstorms.* Montgomery, VT: Bradford Books.

Dennett, D. C. (1987). *The Intentional Stance.* Cambridge, MA: MIT Press.

Fodor, J. A. (1975). *The Language of Thought.* Hassocks, England: Harvester Press.

Fodor, J. A. (1981). *RePresentations.* Cambridge, MA: MIT Press.

Fodor, J. A. (1987). *Psychosemantics.* Cambridge, MA: MIT Press.

McClamrock, R. (1995). *Existential Cognition.* Chicago: University of Chicago Press.

Searle, J. (1983). *Intentionality.* Cambridge: Cambridge University Press.

Wilson, R. A. (1995). *Cartesian Psychology and Physical Minds.* Cambridge: Cambridge University Press.

Further Readings

Fodor, J. A. (1974). Special sciences. *Synthese* 28: 77–115. (Reprinted in Fodor 1981.)

Kim, J. (1996). *Philosophy of Mind.* Boulder, CO: Westview Press.

Lycan, W. (1981). Psychological laws. *Philosophical Topics* 12: 9–38.

Psychology, History of

See INTRODUCTION: PSYCHOLOGY; EBBINGHAUS, HERMANN; HELMHOLTZ, HERMANN LUDWIG FERDINAND VON; WUNDT, WILHELM

Psychophysics

Psychophysics is the scientific study of relationships between physical stimuli and perceptual phenomena. For example, in the case of vision, one can quantify the influence of the physical intensity of a spot of light on its detectability, or the influence of its wavelength on its perceived hue. Examples could as well be selected from the study of AUDITION or other sensory systems.

In a typical psychophysical experiment, subjects are tested in an experimental environment intended to maximize the control of stimulus variations over variations in the subject's responses. Stimuli are carefully controlled, often varying along only a single physical dimension (e.g., intensity). The subject's responses are highly constrained (e.g., "Yes, I see the stimulus," or "No, I don't see it"). Small numbers of subjects are tested with extensive within-subject designs. Individual differences are small in the normal population. Experiments are routinely replicated and replicable across laboratories.

Theoretical treatments of the data consist of computational or physiological models, which attempt to provide an account of the transformation between stimulus and perception within the sensory neural system. The classic modeling approach is SIGNAL DETECTION THEORY. Many other experimental uses and theoretical treatments are illustrated in the related entries listed below.

A *detection threshold* is the smallest amount of physical energy required for the subject to detect a stimulus. The example of the intensity required to detect a spot of light will be used throughout the following paragraphs.

There are a variety of formalized methods for measuring detection thresholds (Gescheider 1997). In the *method of adjustment,* the subject is given control of the intensity of the stimulus and asked to vary it until her perception reaches some criterion value (e.g., the light is just barely visible). In the *method of constant stimuli,* a set of intensities of the light is preselected and presented many times in a random series. The result is a *psychometric function,* describing the percent of a particular response (e.g., "Yes") as a function of light intensity. In *staircase* or *iterative* methods, the stimulus in each trial is chosen based on the accumulated data from previous trials, using a rule designed to optimize the efficiency of threshold estimation.

When a series of trials is used, there are two major options concerning the subject's task and responses. In *Yes/No techniques,* the subject reports whether she did or did not see the stimulus in each trial. In *forced-choice techniques,* the stimulus is presented in one of two spatial locations or temporal intervals, and the subject's task is to judge in which location or interval the stimulus occurred.

Briefly, the method of adjustment has the advantage of maximal efficiency if the effects of stimulus history and subject bias are small. The method of constant stimuli reduces the influence of stimulus history. Forced-choice techniques have the advantage of minimizing the influence of subject bias, and forced-choice iterative techniques often provide an optimal balance of efficiency and bias minimization.

A *discrimination threshold* is the smallest physical difference between two stimuli required for the subject to discriminate between them. Measurement techniques are analogous to those used for detection thresholds.

In *supra-threshold* experiments, the subject views readily visible stimuli and is asked to report the quantity or quality of her own SENSATIONS. For example, in a *scaling* experiment, a subject could be shown lights of different intensities. The task would be to describe the perceived brightness of each stimulus by assigning a number to it. The result is a description of how brightness grows with intensity. In a *color-naming* experiment, a subject could be shown lights of different wavelengths. The task would be to describe the perceived hues using a constrained set of color names (e.g., red, yellow, green, and blue), and partitioning the perceived hue among them (e.g., "10% Green, 90% Blue"). The result is a description of the variations in hue across the spectrum.

Psychophysics is also marked by a variety of experimental paradigms with established theoretical interpretations (Graham 1989; Wandell 1995). For example, in the *summation-at-threshold* paradigm, thresholds are measured for two component stimuli and for a compound made by superimposing the two. The goal is to quantify the energy required for detection of the compound stimulus with respect to the energy required for detection of each of the components. Outcomes vary widely, from facilitation to linear summation to independent detection to interference, and lead to different theoretical conclusions concerning the degree and form of interaction of the mechanisms detecting the two components.

Similarly, *selective adaptation* paradigms examine the extent to which adaptation to one stimulus affects the threshold for another, and are used to argue for independent or nonindependent processing of the two stimuli. *Identification/detection* paradigms examine whether or not two different stimuli can be identified (discriminated) at detection threshold, and are used to determine the extent to which the mechanisms that detect the stimuli also code the properties required for identification.

Much psychophysical research is guided and united by sophisticated mathematical modeling. For example, spatiotemporal aspects of vision have been treated in extensive theories centered around the concept of multiple, more or less independent processing mechanisms (e.g., Graham 1989; see also SPATIAL PERCEPTION), and COLOR VISION has been similarly unified by models of the encoding and recoding of wavelength and intensity information (e.g., Wandell 1995).

Models of psychophysical data are often heavily influenced by the known anatomy and physiology of sensory systems, and advances in each field importantly influence the experiments done in the other. For example, the psychophysical trichromacy of color vision provided the first evidence for the presence of three and only three channels underlying color vision, and provided the impetus for a century of anatomical, physical, physiological, and genetic as well as psychophysical attempts to identify the three cone types. As a converse example, anatomically and physiologically based models of parallel processing of color and motion have importantly influenced the psychophysical investigation of losses of motion perception for purely chromatic (isoluminant) stimuli (see MOTION, PERCEPTION OF). Treatments are also available of the need for special bridge laws, or *linking propositions,* in arguments that attempt to explain perceptual events on the basis of physiological events (Teller 1984).

In sum, psychophysics underlies the accumulation of knowledge in many parts of perception. It has many tools to offer to cognitive scientists. Its empirical successes illustrate the value of tight experimental control of stimuli and responses. It provides experimental paradigms that can be generalized successfully to higher level perceptual and cognitive problems (e.g., Palmer 1995). The extensive modeling in the field provides successes that might be worth emulating, and perhaps blind alleys that might be worth avoiding. Finally, and most importantly, in combination with direct studies of the neural substrates of sensory processing, psychophysics provides an important example of interdisciplinary research efforts that illuminate the relationship between mind and brain.

See also DEPTH PERCEPTION; HIGH-LEVEL VISION; LIGHTNESS PERCEPTION; MID-LEVEL VISION; SURFACE PERCEPTION; TOP-DOWN PROCESSING IN VISION

—*Davida Teller and John Palmer*

References

Gescheider, G. A. (1997). *Psychophysics: The Fundamentals.* 3rd ed. Hillsdale, NJ: Erlbaum.

Graham, N. V. S. (1989). *Visual Pattern Analysers.* New York: Oxford.

Palmer, J. (1995). Attention in visual search: Distinguishing four causes of a set-size effect. *Current Directions in Psychological Science* 4: 118–123.

Teller, D. Y. (1984). Linking propositions. *Vision Research* 24: 1233–1246.

Wandell, B. A. (1995). *Foundations of Vision Science.* Sunderland, MA: Sinauer.

Qualia

The terms *quale* and *qualia* (pl.) are most commonly used to characterize the qualitative, experiential, or felt properties of mental states. Some philosophers take qualia to be essential features of all conscious mental states; others only of SEN-SATIONS and perceptions. In either case, qualia provide a particularly vexing example of the MIND-BODY PROBLEM, because it has been argued that their existence is incompatible with a physicalistic theory of the mind (see PHYSICAL-ISM).

Three recent antiphysicalist arguments have been especially influential. The first claims that one can conceive of the qualitative features of one's pains or perceptions in the absence of any specific physical or functional properties (and vice versa), and that properties that can be so conceived must be distinct (Kripke 1980). The second argument claims that one cannot know, even in principle, WHAT-IT'S-LIKE to be in pain or see a color before actually having these (or similar) experiences, and that no physical or functional properties can afford this perspectival or subjective knowledge (Nagel 1974; Jackson 1982). The third states that no physical or functional characterization of mental states can explain what it's like to have them, and that such an EXPLANATORY GAP raises doubts about whether qualia can be identified with such properties (Levine 1983). They conclude that qualia cannot be (or, at least, cannot be easily believed to be) identical with physical or functional properties.

These arguments are linked in that each first premise assumes (a) that there is no conceptual connection between qualitative and physicalistic terms or concepts. Otherwise, it would be impossible to conceive (for example) of pain qualia existing apart from the relevant physical or functional properties, and it would be possible to know all there is to know about pain without ever having experienced pain oneself; it would also be easy to explain why it feels painful to have the associated physical or functional property. The second premise also depends upon a common thesis, (b) that given this lack of connection, the use of qualitative terms or concepts requires (or at least suggests) the existence of irreducibly qualitative properties. This thesis is supported, at least implicitly, by a theory of reference, deriving from Gottlob FREGE, that permits nonequivalent concepts to denote the same item only by picking out different properties (modes of presentation) of it; in this view, if pain is not equivalent to any physical or functional concept, then even if pain denotes the same property as some physicalistic concept, this can only be by introducing a mode of presentation that is distinct from anything physical or functional. In addition, anti-physicalists have cited inductive evidence for this premise, namely, that in all other cases of intertheoretic reduction, there have been successful analyses, using terms constructed from those of the reducing theory, of the concepts of the theory to be reduced (Jackson 1993; Chalmers 1996).

Physicalists, in turn, have attempted to deny both theses. Those denying (a) have argued that there is in fact a conceptual connection between qualitative and physicalistic concepts, the best candidates being causal or functional concepts that have claim to being part of our commonsense understanding of mental states (see FUNCTIONALISM). Many have doubted, however, that commonsense characterizations could be necessary or sufficient to capture qualitative concepts (Block 1978). In response, some physicalists argue that there are ways to broaden the scope of commonsense characterization (Levin 1991), others that any knowledge we gain uniquely from experience is merely a kind of *practical* knowledge—the acquisition of new imaginative or recognitional abilities, rather than concepts that one previously lacked (Nemirow 1990; Lewis 1990). Yet others suggest that, despite appearances to the contrary, there is no determinate, coherent content to our qualitative concepts over and above that which can be explicated by functional or causal characterizations (Dennett 1991).

Another physicalist strategy is to reject thesis (b) and argue that the irreducibility of qualitative to physicalistic *concepts* does not entail the irreducibility of qualitative to physicalistic *properties*. Some have argued that there can be plausible non-Fregean, direct accounts of how qualitative concepts denote physical states—on the model of INDEXICALS AND DEMONSTRATIVES—that do not require the introduction of further irreducible properties (Loar 1990; Tye 1995). Others have argued that the lack of conceptual connection between qualitative and physicalistic concepts is not unique, but occurs in many cases of successful intertheoretic reduction (Block and Stalnaker forthcoming).

It is also commonly thought that (sincere) beliefs about our own qualia have special authority (that is, necessarily are for the most part true), and are also self-intimating (that is, will necessarily produce, in individuals with adequate conceptual sophistication, accurate beliefs about their nature). Insofar as they have these special epistemic features, qualia are importantly different from physical properties such as shape, temperature, and length, about which beliefs may be both fallible and uncompelled. Can they nonetheless be physical or functional properties?

Functionalists can claim that qualia have these features as a matter of conceptual necessity, because according to (at least some versions of) this doctrine, states with qualitative properties and the beliefs they produce are interdefined (Shoemaker 1990). Physicalists who deny such definitional connections have argued instead that sufficient introspective accuracy is insured by the proper operation of our cognitive faculties; thus, as a matter of law, we cannot be mistaken about (or fail to notice certain properties of) our mental states (Hill 1991). In such a view, these epistemic features of our mental states will be nomologically necessary, but not necessary in any stronger sense (*see* INTROSPECTION and SELF-KNOWLEDGE).

There are many other interesting issues regarding qualia, among them whether qualia, if physical, are to be identified with neural or narrow functional properties of the individual who has them (Block 1990), or whether, to have qualia, one must also be related to properties of objects in the external world (Lycan 1996; Dretske 1995; cf. INTENTIONALITY). Yet another question is whether (and if so, how) the myriad qualia we seem to experience at any given time are bound together at a given moment, and are continuous with our experiences at previous and subsequent times, or whether the commonsense view that we enjoy a unity of consciousness, and a stream of consciousness, is rather an illusion to be dispelled (Dennett 1991).

See also CONSCIOUSNESS; SELF

—*Janet Levin*

References

Block, N. (1978). Troubles with Functionalism. In C. W. Savage, Ed., *Perception and Cognition: Issues in the Foundations of Psychology.* Minneapolis: University of Minnesota Press. Reprinted in N. Block, Ed., *Readings in Philosophy and Psychology,* vol. 1. Cambridge, MA: Harvard University Press, 1980.

Block, N. (1990). Inverted Earth. In J. Tomberlin, Ed., *Philosophical Perspectives,* no. 4. Atascadero, CA: Ridgeview Publishing.

Block, N., and R. Stalnaker. (Forthcoming). Conceptual analysis and the explanatory gap. *Philosophical Review.*

Chalmers, D. (1996). *The Conscious Mind: In Search of a Fundamental Theory.* Oxford: Oxford University Press.

Dennett, D. (1991). *Consciousness Explained.* Boston: Little, Brown.

Dretske, F. (1995). *Naturalizing the Mind.* Cambridge, MA: MIT Press.

Hill, C. (1991). *Sensations: A Defense of Type Materialism.* New York: Cambridge University Press.

Jackson, F. (1982). Epiphenomenal qualia. *Philosophical Quarterly* 32: 127–136.

Jackson, F. (1993). Armchair metaphysics. In J. O'Leary-Hawthorne and M. Michael, Eds., *Philosophy in Mind.* Dordrecht: Kluwer.

Kripke, S. (1980). *Naming and Necessity.* Cambridge, MA: Harvard University Press.

Levin, J. (1991). Analytic functionalism and the reduction of phenomenal state. *Philosophical Studies* 61.

Levine, J. (1983). Materialism and qualia: The explanatory gap. *Pacific Philosophical Quarterly* 64 (4).

Lewis, D. (1990). What experience teaches. In W. G. Lycan, Ed., *Mind and Cognition.* Cambridge, MA: Blackwell.

Loar, B. (1990). Phenomenal states. In J. Tomberlin, Ed., *Philosophical Perspectives 4.* Atascadero, CA: Ridgeview.

Lycan, W. G. (1996). *Consciousness and Experience.* Cambridge, MA: MIT Press.

Nagel, T. (1974). What is it like to be a bat? *Philosophical Review* 82: 435–456.

Nemirow, L. (1990). Physicalism and the cognitive role of acquaintance. In W. G. Lycan, Ed., *Mind and Cognition.* Cambridge, MA: Blackwell.

Shoemaker, S. (1990). First-person access. In J. Tomberlin, Ed., *Philosophical Perspectives 4.* Atascadero, CA: Ridgeview.

Tye, M. (1995). *Ten Problems of Consciousness: A Representational Theory of the Phenomenal Mind.* Cambridge, MA: MIT Press.

Quantifiers

Sentences (Ss) such as *All cats are grey* consist of a predicate *are grey* and a noun phrase (NP) *all cats,* itself consisting of a noun *cats* and a determiner (Det), of which the quantifiers *all, some,* and *no* are special cases. Semantically we treat both the noun and the predicate as denoting *proper-*ties of individuals, and we interpret the S as True in a situation *s* if the individuals with those properties (in *s*) stand in the relation expressed by the quantifier. Different quantifiers typically denote different relations. ALL (we write denotations in upper case) says that the individuals that have the noun property (CAT) are included in those with the predicate property (GREY). SOME says that the individuals with the CAT property overlap with those that are GREY; NO says there is no overlap. EXACTLY TEN says the overlap has exactly ten members. MOST, in the sense of MORE THAN HALF, expresses a *proportion:* The overlap between CAT and GREY is larger than that between CAT and NON-GREY; that is, the number of grey cats is larger than the number of non-grey ones. LESS THAN HALF makes the opposite claim.

The role of the noun is crucial. Syntactically it forms an NP constituent (*all cats*) with the quantifier. We interpret this NP as a function, called a *generalized quantifier,* that maps the predicate property to True or False (in a situation). So we interpret *All cats are grey* by (ALL CAT)(GREY), where ALL CAT is a function mapping a property P to True in a situation s if the cats in s are a subset of the objects with P in s. More generally, Ss of the form [[Det+N]+Predicate] denote the truth value given by $(D(N))(P)$, where P is the property denoted by the predicate, N that denoted by the noun, D the denotation of the Det, and $D(N)$ the denotation of Det+noun NP.

Semantically the noun property N serves to *restrict* the class of things we are quantifying over. The literature captures this intuition with two very general constraints on possible Det denotations. These constraints limit both the logical expressive power of natural languages and the hypotheses children need consider in learning the meanings of the Dets in their language (Clark 1996; see SEMANTICS, ACQUISITION OF).

One condition is *extensions* (Van Benthem 1984), which says in effect that the truth of *Det Ns are Ps* cannot depend on which individuals are non-Ns. For example, scouring Old English texts, you will never stumble upon a Det *blik* that guarantees that *Blik cats are grey* is true if and only if the number of non-cats that are grey is ten.

The second condition is *conservativity* (Keenan 1981; Barwise and Cooper 1981; Higginbotham and May 1981; Keenan and Stavi 1986), which says that the truth of *Det Ns are Ps* cannot depend on Ps that lack N. So *Det Ns are Ps* must have the same truth value as *Det Ns are Ns that are Ps.* For instance, *Most cats are grey* is equivalent to *Most cats are cats that are grey.* And *most* can be replaced by any Det, including syntactically complex ones: *most but not all, every child's,* or *more male than female.* Despite appearances this semantic equivalence is not trivial. Keenan and Stavi show that in a situation with only two individuals there are 65,536 logically possible Det denotations (functions from pairs of properties to truth values). Only 512 of them are conservative!

The restricting role of the noun property distinguishes natural languages from first-order LOGIC (FOL). FOL essentially limits its quantifiers to $(\forall x)$ *every object* and $(\exists x)$ *some object* and forces logical forms to vary considerably and nonuniformly from the English Ss they represent. *All cats are grey* becomes "For all objects *x*, if *x* is a cat *then x* is grey"; *Some cats are grey* becomes "For some object *x*, *x* is a cat *and x* is grey." Now proportionality quantifiers (*most, less than half, a third of the, ten percent of the*) are *inherently* restricted (Keenan 1993): there is no Boolean compound S of *cat(x)* and *grey(x)* such that *(for most x)S* is True if and only if the grey cats outnumber the non-grey ones. Indeed the proper proportionality Dets are not even definable in FOL (see Barwise and Cooper (1981) for *most*), whence the logical expressive power of natural languages properly extends that of FOL.

English presents subclasses of Dets of both semantic and syntactic interest. We note two such: First, *simplex* (= single word) Dets satisfy stronger conditions than conservativity and extension. We say that an NP X is *increasing* (↑) if and only if *X is a P* (or *X are Ps*) and *all Ps are Qs* entails that X is a Q. Proper names are ↑: If all cats are grey and Felix is a cat, then Felix is grey. An NP of the form [Det+N] is ↑ when Det is *every, some, both, most, more than half, at least ten, infinitely many,* or a possessive Det like *some boy's* whose possessor NP *(some boy)* is itself increasing. X is *decreasing* (↓) if *all Ps are Qs and X is a Q* entails *X is a P*. [Det+N] is ↓ when Det is *no, neither, fewer than ten, less than half, not more than five, at most five* or *NP's,* for NP ↓. X is *monotonic* if it is either increasing or decreasing. [Det+N] is non-monotonic if Det equals *exactly five, between five and ten, all but ten, more male than female, at least two and not more than ten.* Simplex Dets build monotonic NPs (usually increasing), a very proper subset of the NPs of English.

Syntactically note that ↓ NPs license negative polarity items in the predicate, ↑ ones do not (Ladusaw 1983). Thus *ever* is natural in *No/Fewer than five students here have ever been to Pinsk* but not in *Some/More than five students here have ever been to Pinsk.* Often, as here, grammatical properties of NPs are determined by their Dets.

Second, many English Dets are *intersective,* in that we determine the truth of *Det Ns are Ps* just by checking which Ns are Ps, ignoring Ns that aren't Ps. Most intersective Dets are *cardinal,* in that they just depend on *how many* Ns are Ps. *Some* is cardinal: whether *Some Ns are Ps* is decided just by checking that the number of Ns that are Ps is greater than 0. Some other cardinal Dets are *no, (not) more than ten, fewer than/exactly/at most ten, between five and ten, about twenty, infinitely many* and *just finitely many. No . . . but John* (as in *no student but John*) is intersective but not cardinal. *All* and *most* are not intersective: if we are just given the set of Ns that are Ps we cannot decide if all or most Ns are Ps.

Intersectivity applies to two-place Dets like *more . . . than . . .* that combine with two Ns to form an NP, as in *More boys than girls were drafted.* It is intersective in that the truth of the S is determined once we are given the intersection of the predicate property with each of the noun properties. Other such Dets are *fewer . . . than . . . , exactly as many . . . as . . . , more than twice as many . . . as . . . , the same number of . . . as . . . .* In general these Dets are also not first-order definable (even on finite domains). Moreover, of syntactic interest, it is the intersective Dets that build NPs that occur naturally in existential *There* contexts: *There*

weren't exactly ten cats/more cats than dogs in the yard is natural but becomes ungrammatical when *exactly ten* is replaced by *most* or *all.*

Finally, we can isolate the purely "quantitative" or "logical" Dets as those whose denotations are invariant under permutations p of the domain of objects under discussion. So they satisfy $D(N)(P)) = D(pN)(pP)$, where *p* is a permutation and *p(A)* is $\{p(x)|x \in A\}$. *All, most but not all, just finitely many* always denote permutation invariant functions, but *no student's, every . . . but John, more male than female* don't.

Cognitive and logical complexity increases with Ss built from transitive verbs (P2s) and two NPs. For example *Some editor reads every manuscript* has two interpretations: One, there is at least one editor who has the property that he reads every manuscript; and two, for each manuscript there is at least one editor who reads it (possibly different editors read different manuscripts). Cognitively, language acquisition studies (Lee 1986; Philip 1992) support that children acquire adult-level competence with such Ss years after they are competent on Ss built from one-place predicates (P1s). And mathematically, whether a sentence is logically true is mechanically decidable in first-order languages with just P1s but loses this property once a single P2 is added (Boolos and Jeffrey 1989).

But some Ss built from P2s and two NPs cannot be adequately represented by iterated application of generalized quantifiers (Keenan 1987, 1992; van Benthem 1989): *Different people like different things; No two students answered exactly the same questions; John criticized Bill but no one else criticized anyone else.* Adequate intrepretations treat the pair of NPs in each S as a function mapping the binary relation denoted by the P2 to a truth value.

Lastly, quantification can also be expressed outside of Dets and NPs: *Students rarely/never/always/often/usually take naps after lunch* (Lewis 1975; Heim 1982; de Swart 1996). Bach et al. 1995 contains several articles discussing languages in which non-Det quantification is prominent: Eskimo (Bittner), Mayali (Evans), or possibly even absent: Straits Salish (Jelinek) and Asurini do Trocará (Vieira). Recent overviews of Det type quantification are Keenan (1996) and the more technical Keenan and Westerståhl (1997).

See also AMBIGUITY; LOGICAL FORM IN LINGUISTICS; LOGICAL FORM, ORIGINS OF; POSSIBLE WORLDS SEMANTICS

—*Edward L. Keenan*

References

Bach, E., E. Jelinek, A. Kratzer, and B. Partee, Eds. (1995). *Quantification in Natural Languages.* Dordrecht: Kluwer.

Barwise, J., and R. Cooper. (1981). Generalized quantifiers and natural language. *Linguistics and Philosophy* 4: 159–219.

Boolos, G., and R. Jeffrey. (1989). *Computability and Logic.* 3rd ed. New York: Cambridge University Press.

Clark, R. (1996). Learning first order quantifier denotations, an essay in semantic learnability. *Technical Reports I.R.C.S.–96–19,* University of Pennsylvania.

de Swart, H. (1996). Quantification over time. In J. van der Does and J. van Eijck 1996, pp. 311–336.

Gärdenfors, P., Ed. (1987). *Generalized Quantifier: Linguistic and Logical Approaches.* Dordrecht: Reidel.

Heim, I. R. (1982). *The Semantics of Definite and Indefinite Noun Phrases.* Ph.D. diss., University of Massachusetts, Amherst.

Higginbotham, J., and R. May. (1981). Questions, quantifiers and crossing. *The Linguistic Review* 1: 41–79.

Keenan, E. L. (1981). A boolean approach to semantics. In J. Groenendijk et al., Eds., *Formal Methods in the Study of Language.* Amsterdam: Math Centre, pp. 343–379.

Keenan, E. L. (1987). Unreducible *n*-ary quantifiers in natural language. In P. Gärdenfors (1987).

Keenan, E. L. (1992). Beyond the Frege boundary. *Linguistics and Philosophy* 15: 199–221. (Augmented and reprinted in van der Does and van Eijck 1996).

Keenan, E. L. (1993). Natural language, sortal reducibility, and generalized quantifiers. *J. Symbolic Logic* 58: 314–325.

Keenan, E. L. (1996). The semantics of determiners. In S. Lappin, Ed., *The Handbook of Contemporary Semantic Theory.* Oxford: Blackwell, pp. 41–63.

Keenan, E. L., and J. Stavi. (1986). A semantic characterization of natural language determiners. *Linguistics and Philosophy* 9: 253–326.

Keenan, E. L., and D. Westerståhl. (1997). Generalized quantifiers in linguistics and logic. In J. van Benthem and A. ter Meulen (1997), pp. 837–893.

Ladusaw, W. (1983). Logical form and conditions on grammaticality. *Linguistics and Philosophy* 6: 389–422.

Lee, T. (1986). Acquisition of quantificational scope in Mandarin Chinese. *Papers and Reports on Child Language Development* No. 25. Stanford University.

Lewis, D. (1975). Adverbs of quantification. In E. L. Keenan, Ed., *Formal Semantics of Natural Language.* Cambridge: Cambridge University Press, pp. 3–15.

Philip, W. (1992). Distributivity and logical form in the emergence of universal quantification. In *Proceedings of the Second Conference on Semantics and Linguistic Theory.* Ohio State University Dept. of Linguistics, pp. 327–345.

Szabolcsi, A., Ed. (1997). *Ways of Scope Taking.* Dordrecht: Kluwer.

Van Benthem, J. (1984). Questions about quantifiers. *J. Symbolic Logic* 49: 443–466.

Van Benthem, J. (1989). Polyadic quantifiers. *Linguistics and Philosophy* 12: 437–465.

Van Benthem, J., and A. ter Meulen, Eds. (1997). *The Handbook of Logic and Language.* Amsterdam: Elsevier.

Van der Does, J., and J. van Eijck. (1996). Quantifiers, logic, and language. *CSLI Lecture Notes.* Stanford.

Further Readings

Beghelli, F. (1992). Comparative quantifiers. In P. Dekker and M. Stokhof, Eds., *Proceedings of the Eighth Amsterdam Colloquium.* ILLC, University of Amsterdam.

Cooper, R. (1983). *Quantification and Syntactic Theory.* Dordrecht: Reidel.

Gil, D. (1995). Universal quantifiers and distributivity. In E. Bach et al. 1995, pp. 321–362.

Kanazawa, M., and C. Pion, Eds. (1994). *Dynamics, Polarity and Quantification.* Stanford, CA: CSLI Publications, pp. 119–145.

Kanazawa, M., C. Pion, and H. de Swart, Eds. (1996). *Quantifiers, Deduction and Context.* Stanford, CA: CSLI Publications.

Keenan, E. L., and L. Faltz. (1985). *Boolean Semantics for Natural Language.* Dordrecht: Reidel.

Keenan, E. L., and L. Moss. (1985). Generalized quantifiers and the expressive power of natural language. In van Benthem and

ter Meulen, Eds., *Generalized Quantifiers.* Dordrecht: Foris, pp. 73–124.

Lindström, P. (1966). First order predicate logic with generalized quantifiers. *Theoria* 35: 186–195.

Montague, R. (1969/1974). English as a formal language. In R. Thomason, Ed., *Formal Philosophy.* New Haven, CT: Yale University Press.

Partee, B. H. (1995). Quantificational structures and compositionality. In Bach et al. 1995, pp. 541–560.

Reuland, E., and A. ter Meulen. (1987). *The Representation of (In)definiteness.* Cambridge, MA: MIT Press.

van Benthem, J. (1986). *Essays in Logical Semantics.* Dordrecht: Reidel.

Westerståhl, D. (1989). Quantifiers in formal and natural languages. In D. Gabbay and F. Guenthner, Eds., *Handbook of Philosophical Logic,* vol. 4. Dordrecht: Reidel, pp. 1–131.

Radical Interpretation

Radical interpretation is interpretation from scratch—as would be necessary if we found ourselves in a community whose language and way of life were completely alien to us, without bilingual guides, dictionaries, grammars, or previous knowledge of the culture. Recent interest in radical interpretation focuses on two related but significantly different sets of investigations, the first initiated by Quine (1960), the second by Davidson ("Truth and Meaning," 1967, collected with other relevant papers in his 1984). It will be convenient to start with Davidson's work which, though later, is the more immediately intelligible (as will be seen when Quine's views are presented).

If we knew what the foreigners meant by their sentences, we could discover their beliefs and desires; if we knew their beliefs and desires, we could discover what they meant. Knowing neither, "we must somehow deliver simultaneously a theory of belief and a theory of meaning" (Davidson 1984: 144). Davidson offers suggestions about both the form of a theory of meaning and how to make sure we have the correct one for a given language.

It seems reasonable to require a theory of meaning for English to tell us things like "'Snow is white' means (in English) that snow is white." To do so, it must presumably explain how the meanings of whole sentences depend on the meanings of their parts. Davidson's suggestion is that this can be done by a theory of *truth* for the given language, of broadly the type proposed by Tarski (1936). Tarski aimed to explain what it was for the sentences of a language to be true without introducing into the explanation either the notion of truth itself or other problematic notions such as reference (see SENSE AND REFERENCE; REFERENCE, THEORIES OF). To get some idea of his approach, which in detail is technical, notice that if we knew all the basic predicates of a given language, we could explain what it was for them to be *true of* things by listing "axioms," one for each basic predicate, on the lines of "'Snow' is true of *x* (in English) if and only if *x* is snow." To ensure that such a theory genuinely explained what it is for the sentences of the given language to be true, Tarski required it to entail all sentences such as:

(1) "Snow is white" is true-in-English if, and only if, snow is white.

These are the famous T-sentences. In contrast to Tarski, Davidson assumes we start with an adequate understanding of truth: "Our outlook inverts Tarski's: we want to achieve an understanding of meaning or translation by assuming a prior grasp of the concept of truth" (1984: 150).

He points out that the T-sentences may be regarded as giving the meanings of the sentences named on the left-hand side—provided the theory of truth satisfies sufficiently strong constraints. One powerful constraint is the circumstances in which the foreigners *hold true* the sentences of their language. He invokes a "principle of charity": optimize agreement with the foreigners unless disagreements are explicable on the basis of known error.

One acknowledged difficulty is that Tarski's theory as it stands applies only to formalized languages, which lack many important features such as INDEXICALS AND DEMONSTRATIVES, proper names, and indirect speech (see Davidson 1984 and essays in LePore 1986).

Davidson believes that although there will be some *indeterminacy* of interpretation, it will be superficial: just a matter of stating the facts in alternative ways, as with Fahrenheit and Celsius scales. In this and other respects, his position contrasts strongly with Quine's, which has also proved more liable to be misunderstood.

Suppose the radical interpreter has worked out a translation manual that, given a foreign sentence, enables a translation to be constructed. Quine maintains we could devise a rival manual so different that it would reject "countless" translations offered by the first. Both manuals would fit all the objective facts, yet competing versions of the same foreign sentence would not even be loosely equivalent (Quine 1960, 1969, 1990).

Here is a famous line of supporting argument. Imagine the foreigners use the one-word sentence "Gavagai" in situations where English speakers would use "Rabbit." Quine suggests that this does not establish that the native *term* "gavagai" refers to rabbits. It might refer instead to such radically different items as undetached rabbit-parts, or rabbit-phases, or rabbithood. Nor could we rule out any of these alternatives by pointing, or by staging experiments, since those operations would depend on untestable assumptions. Such "inscrutability of reference" appears to involve indeterminacy of sentence translation (Quine 1960, 1969).

All this is part of Quine's wider campaign against our tendency to think of MEANING and synonymy as matters of fact. He argues that the notion of meaning is not genuinely explanatory. It makes us think we can explain behavior, but it is a sham. It fails to mesh in with matters of fact in an explanatorily useful way. The indeterminacy thesis, if true, would powerfully support that contention.

Quine's thesis is easily confused with others. It is not, for example, an instance of the truism that there is no limit to the number of different ways to extrapolate beyond finite data. He claims that two schemes of translation could disagree with one another even when both fitted not just actual verbal and other behavior, but the totality of relevant facts. The indeterminacy "withstands even . . . the whole truth about nature" (Davidson and Hintikka 1969: 303). Nor is it any ordinary sort of scepticism. The idea is not that we cannot know we have hit on the right interpretation, but that there is nothing to be right or wrong about (Quine 1960: 73, 221; 1969: 30, 47). Nor will bilinguals help, since he thinks their translations are as much subject to the indeterminacy as others. Nor, finally, is he laboring the familiar point that in translation between relatively remote languages and cultures, nonequivalent sentences of one language will often do equally well as rough translations of a sentence of the other. This is made clear by his application of the indeterminacy thesis to the "translation" of sentences within one and the same language. We assume that for each sentence of our shared language, what you mean by it is also what I mean by it. Quine thinks that if I were perverse and ingenious I could "scorn" that scheme and devise an alternative that would attribute to you "unimagined views" while still fitting all the relevant objective facts.

Quine's indeterminacy thesis is highly contentious (see Kirk 1986 for discussions). But if correct it has profound implications for psychology and philosophy of mind. If beliefs and desires were matters of objective fact, those facts would settle significant differences over translation. So if it is a mistake to think translation is determinate, it is also a mistake to think our beliefs and desires are matters of fact. Quine and others (e.g., Stich 1983) regard his arguments as undermining intentional psychology and supporting ELIMINATIVE MATERIALISM.

See also INTENTIONALITY; MEANING; SEMANTICS

—*Robert Kirk*

References

Davidson, D. (1984). *Inquiries into Truth and Interpretation.* New York: Oxford University Press.

Davidson, D., and J. Hintikka, Eds. (1969). *Words and Objections.* Dordrecht: Reidel.

Kirk, R. (1986). *Translation Determined.* Oxford: Clarendon Press.

LePore, E., Ed. (1986). *Truth and Interpretation: Perspectives on the Philosophy of Donald Davidson.* Oxford: Blackwell.

Quine, W. V. (1960). *Word and Object.* Cambridge, MA and New York: MIT Press/Wiley.

Quine, W. V. (1969). *Ontological Relativity and Other Essays.* New York: Columbia University Press.

Quine, W. V. (1990). *Pursuit of Truth.* Cambridge, MA: Harvard University Press.

Stich, S. (1983). *From Folk Psychology to Cognitive Science: The Case Against Belief.* Cambridge, MA: MIT Press.

Tarski, A. (1936). The concept of truth in formalized languages. In A. Tarski (1956), *Logic, Semantics, Metamathematics.* Oxford: Clarendon Press, pp. 152–278 (translated from the German of 1936).

Further Readings

Dummett, M. (1978). The significance of Quine's indeterminacy thesis. In M. Dummett, *Truth and Other Enigmas.* London: Duckworth, pp. 375–419 (reprinted from 1973).

Fodor, J., and E. LePore (1992). *Holism: A Shopper's Guide.* Oxford: Blackwell.

Hahn, L. E., and P. A. Schilpp, Eds. (1986). *The Philosophy of W. V. Quine.* La Salle, IL: Open Court.

Hookway, C. (1988). *Quine: Language, Experience and Reality.* Stanford, CA: Stanford University Press.

Kripke, S. (1982). *Wittgenstein on Rules and Private Language.* Oxford: Blackwell.

Lewis, D. (1974). Radical interpretation. *Synthese* 27: 331–344.

Massey, G. (1992). The indeterminacy of translation: A study in philosophical exegesis. *Philosophical Topics* 20: 317–345.

Putnam, H. (1981). *Reason, Truth and History.* Cambridge: Cambridge University Press.

Quine, W. V. (1981). *Theories and Things.* Cambridge, MA: Harvard University Press.

Tarski, A. (1949). The semantic conception of truth. In H. Feigl and W. Sellars, Eds., *Readings in Philosophical Analysis.* New York: Appleton Century Crofts, pp. 52–84.

Rational Agency

In philosophy of mind, rationality is conceived of as a coherence requirement on personal identity: roughly, "No rationality, no agent." The agent must have a means-ends competence to fit its actions or decisions, according to its beliefs or knowledge-representation, to its desires or goal-structure. That agents possess such rationality is more than an empirical hypothesis; for instance, as a putative set of beliefs, desires, and decisions accumulated inconsistencies, the set would cease even to qualify as containing beliefs, etc., and disintegrate into a mere set of sentences. This agent-constitutive rationality is distinguished from more stringent normative rationality standards, for agents can and often do possess cognitive systems that fall short of epistemic uncriticizability (e.g., with respect to perfect consistency) without thereby ceasing to constitute agents.

Standard philosophical conceptions of rationality derive from models of the rational agent in microeconomic, game, and decision theory earlier this century (e.g., Von Neumann and Morgenstern 1944; Hempel 1965). The underlying idealization is that the agent, given its belief-desire system, *optimizes* its choices. While this optimization model was proposed as either a normative standard or an empirically predictive account (or both), the philosophical model concerns the idea that we cannot even make sense of agents that depart from such optimality. Related ideal-agent concepts can be discerned in principles of charity for RADICAL INTERPRETATION of human behavior of W. V. Quine (1960) and of Donald Davidson (1980), and in standard epistemic logic (Hintikka 1962). To accomplish this perfection of appropriate decisions in turn would require vast inferential insight: for example, the ideal agent must possess a deductive competence that includes a capacity to identify and eliminate any and all inconsistencies arising in its cognitive system.

While such LOGICAL OMNISCIENCE might appropriately characterize a deity, prima facie it seems at odds with the most basic law of human psychology, that we are finite entities. A wide range of experimental studies since the 1970s indicate interesting and persistent patterns of our departures from ideal logician (Tversky and Kahneman 1974), for instance in harboring inconsistent preferences. A more extreme departure from reality is that for such ideal agents, major portions of the deductive sciences would be trivial (e.g., the role of the discovery of the semantic and set-theoretic paradoxes in the development of logic in this century would then cease even to be intelligible). For a COMPUTATIONAL THEORY OF MIND, where the agent's deductive competence must be represented as a finite algorithm, the ideal agent would in fact have to violate Church's undecidability theorem for first-order logic (Cherniak 1986).

The agent-idealizations—within the limits of their applicability—of course have served very successfully as simplified approximations in economic, game, and decision theory. Nonetheless, a sense of their psychological unreality has motivated two types of subsequent theorizing. One type reinforces an eliminativist impulse, that the whole framework of intentional psychology—with rationality at its core—ought to be cleared away as prescientific pseudotheory (see ELIMINATIVE MATERIALISM); a related response is a quasi-eliminativist instrumentalism (e.g., Dennett 1978), where the agent's cognitive system and its rationality diminish to no more than convenient (but impossible) fictions of the theoretician that may help in predicting agent behavior, but cannot be psychologically real. Ultimately, a sense of the unreality of ideal agent models can spur doubts about the very possibility of a cognitive science.

The other type of response to troubles with the idealizations is a *via media* strategy. After recognizing that nothing could count as an agent or person that satisfied *no* rationality constraints, one stops to wonder whether one must jump to a conclusion that the agent has to be ideally rational. Is rationality all or nothing, or is there some golden mean between unattainable, perfect unity of mind and utter, chaotic disintegration of personhood? The normative and empirical rationality models of Simon (1982) are among the earliest of this less stringent sort: the central principle is that, rather than optimizing or maximizing, the agent only "satisfices" its expected utility, choosing decisions that are good enough according to its belief-desire set, rather than perfect. Such modest coherence realistically is all that an agent ought to attempt, and all that can in general be expected. What amounts to a corresponding account for agent-constitutive rationality appears in Cherniak (1981), with a requirement of minimal, rather than ideal, charity on making sense of an agent's actions. An even more latitudinarian conception can be found in Stich (1990). Related limited-resource models are now also employed in artificial intelligence (see BOUNDED RATIONALITY).

Moderate rationality conceptions leave room for the above-mentioned widely observed phenomena of suboptimal human reasoning, rather than excluding them as unintelligible behavior. We are, after all, only human. Indeed, these more psychologically realistic models can explain the departures from correctness as symptoms of our having to use more efficient but formally imperfect "quick but dirty" heuristic procedures. Formally correct and complete inference procedures are typically computationally complex, with surprisingly small-sized problem instances sometimes requiring vastly unfeasible time and memory resources. (To an extent, this practical intractability parallels, and extends, classical absolute unsolvability; see GÖDEL'S THEOREMS.) Antinomies like Russell's paradox lurking at the core of our conceptual scheme can then be interpreted similarly as signs of our having to use heuristic procedures to avoid computational paralysis.

To conclude, some vigilance about unwarranted reification of cognitive architecture remains advisable. Just as attention has turned to evaluation of uncritical idealizing, scope continues for scrutiny of tacit assumptions in rationality models about psychologically realistic representational format (if any)—for example, the discussions reviewed above tend to presuppose agents as sentence-processors, rather than as, say, quasi-picture processors. Finally, the familiar uneasy coexistence of the intentional framework—having rationality at its core—with the scientific worldview is worth recalling. Yet probably much of the groundplan of our species' model of an agent is innate (see AUTISM and THEORY OF MIND); the framework therefore may be a ladder we cannot kick away. It is as if the scientific worldview can comfortably proceed neither with, nor without, an intentional-cognitive paradigm.

See also ANOMALOUS MONISM; COMPUTATIONAL COMPLEXITY; FOLK PSYCHOLOGY; INTENTIONAL STANCE

—*Christopher Cherniak*

References

Cherniak, C. (1981). Minimal rationality. *Mind* 90: 161–183.

Cherniak, C. (1986). *Minimal Rationality.* Cambridge, MA: MIT Press.

Davidson, D. (1980). Psychology as philosophy. In D. Davidson, *Essays on Actions and Events.* New York: Oxford University Press.

Dennett, D. (1978). Intentional systems. In *Brainstorms.* Cambridge, MA: MIT Press.

Hempel, C. (1965). Aspects of scientific explanation. In *Aspects of Scientific Explanation.* New York: Free Press.

Hintikka, J. (1962). *Knowledge and Belief.* Ithaca, NY: Cornell University Press.

Quine, W. (1960). *Word and Object.* Cambridge, MA: MIT Press.

Simon, H. (1982). *Models of Bounded Rationality,* vol. 2. Cambridge, MA: MIT Press.

Stich, S. (1990). *The Fragmentation of Reason.* Cambridge, MA: MIT Press.

Tversky, A., and D. Kahneman. (1974). Judgment under uncertainty: Heuristics and biases. *Science* 185: 1124–1131.

Von Neumann, J., and O. Morgenstern. (1944). *Theory of Games and Economic Behavior.* New York: Wiley

Rational Choice Theory

The theory of rational choice was developed within the discipline of economics by JOHN VON NEUMANN and Oskar Morgenstern (1947) and Leonard Savage (1954). Although its roots date back as far as Thomas Hobbes's denial that reason can fix our ends or desires (instrumental rationality), and David HUME's relegation of reason to the role of "slave of the passions," having no motivating force, via the utilitarians' definition of rationality as the maximization of "utility" and the neoclassical school of economics' theory of revealed preferences, rational choice theory (RCT) purports to be neutral relative to all forms of psychological assumptions or philosophies of mind. In this respect, its relevance for the cognitive sciences is problematic. However, its most recent developments have been marked by the discovery of paradoxes (Binmore 1987a, b; Campbell and Sowdon 1985;

Eells 1982; Gauthier 1988/89; Gibbard and Harper 1985; Kavka 1983; Lewis 1985; McClennen 1989; Nozick 1969; Rosenthal 1982) whose interpretation and resolution call for the return of the repressed: an explicit psychology of DECISION MAKING and a full-blown theory of mind. No wonder more and more cognitive scientists today (philosophers, artificial intelligence specialists, psychologists) participate, along with economists and game theorists, in the debates about RCT.

It is ironic that Savage's expected utility theory, in which most economists see the perfect embodiment of instrumental rationality, is a set of axioms, admittedly purely syntactic in nature, that constrain the rational agent's ends for the sake of consistency (see RATIONAL DECISION MAKING). For instance, her preferences must be transitive: if she prefers x to y and y to z, she *must* prefer x to z. If, no matter the state of the world, she prefers x to y, she *must* prefer x to y even in the ignorance of the state of the world (*sure-thing principle*). Savage proves that an agent whose preferences satisfy all the axioms of the theory chooses *as if* she were maximizing her expected utility while assigning subjective probabilities to the states of the world. It is not at all that her choices can be *explained* by her setting out to maximize her utility, because it is tautological, by construction, that the utility of x is larger to her than that of y if she chooses x over y. The claim is that agents whose preferences were not consistent (i.e., violated the axioms) could not achieve the maximal satisfaction of their ends.

This removal of all psychological content and motivational assumptions from the theory of utility is untenable. Consider the obvious possibility that preferences may change over time. Which of one's preferences should be subjected to the coherence constraints set by the theory? Only the occurrent ones, because future preferences are not motivationally efficacious now? Should we rather postulate second-order preferences that weigh future versus occurrent first-order preferences? Or are there (noninstrumental) *external* reasons that will do the weighing? Dispensing with a theory of mind proves impossible (Hampton 1998; Hollis and Sugden 1993).

According to RCT, an act is an assignment of consequences to states of the world, and the description of a consequence must include no reference to how that consequence was brought about. The only legitimate motivations are forward-looking reasons: only the future matters. Using an equipment just because one has invested a lot in it is taken to be irrational ("sunk cost fallacy"; see Nozick 1993). Experiments in cognitive psychology reveal that most of us commit that alleged fallacy most of the time, proving that we care about the consistency between past and present, maybe for the sake of personal identity (we violate as well Savage's axioms, especially the sure-thing principle; see Shafir and Tversky 1993; cf. also JUDGMENT HEURISTICS). Does that mean that we are irrational, or just that our mind works differently from what RCT, in spite of its proclaimed neutrality, presupposes?

When RCT is applied to a strategic setting, leading to GAME THEORY, some of its implications are plainly paradoxical. In an ideal world where all agents are rational, this fact being common knowledge (everyone knows it, knows that everyone knows it, etc.), rational behavior may be quite unreasonable: the agents are unable to cooperate in a *finitely repeated prisoner's dilemma* setting (Kreps and Wilson 1982); they don't make good on their promises when it goes against their current interest (*assurance game*; see Bratman 1992); their threats are not credible (*chain-store paradox*; Selten 1978); trust proves impossible (*centipede game* and *backward induction paradox*; Reny 1992; Pettit and Sugden 1989), etc. A remarkable feature is that a small departure from complete transparency is enough to bring back the rational close to the reasonable. Imperfect or BOUNDED RATIONALITY would be that which keeps the social world moving.

Philosophers have recently taken up these paradoxes. Although diverging, their conclusions make it clear that there is no way out without completing or amending RCT with theories of, among others, rational planning and intention-formation, belief revision, counterfactual and probabilistic reasoning in strategic settings, and even temporality and self-deception (Dupuy 1998). Some authors think it possible to ground a form of Kantian rationalism in such an expanded or revised RCT, so that to choose rationally entails that one chooses morally (Gauthier 1986).

Take as an example the assurance game. A mutually beneficial exchange is possible between you and me, but you have to take the first step and I will then decide whether I reciprocate or not. Is my proclaimed intention that I will reciprocate a good enough assurance for you to engage in the deal, and can I rationally form this intention? Forming it has positive autonomous effects for me, independent of my carrying it out (it will provide an incentive for you to cooperate), and no cost. If it were an act of the will, it would be rational for me to form it, and we might be tempted to conclude that it would also be rational to execute it. However, some authors contend, *one cannot will oneself to form an intention* any more than a belief, and it is impossible to form the intention to do X if one knows that when the time comes it will be irrational to do (Kavka 1983). Others maintain that it is possible to be "resolute" in this case, and rational not only to form the intention but to make good on it (McClennen 1989). Only a full-blown theory of the mind can adjudicate between these two positions.

See also ECONOMICS AND COGNITIVE SCIENCE

—*Jean-Pierre Dupuy*

References

Binmore, K. (1987a). Modeling rational players: part 1. *Economics and Philosophy* 3: 9–55.

Binmore, K. (1987b). Modeling rational players: part 2. *Economics and Philosophy* 4: 179–214.

Bratman, M. (1992). Planning and the stability of intention. *Minds and Machines* 2: 1–16.

Campbell, R., and L. Sowden, Eds. (1985). *Paradoxes of Rationality and Cooperation: Prisoner's Dilemma and Newcomb's Problem.* Vancouver: University of British Columbia Press.

Dupuy, J.-P. (1998). Rationality and self-deception. In J.-P. Dupuy, Ed., *Self-Deception and Paradoxes of Rationality.* Stanford: CSLI Publications, 113–150.

Eells, E. (1982). *Rational Decision and Causality.* Cambridge: Cambridge University Press.

Gauthier, D. (1986). *Morals by Agreement.* Oxford: Oxford University Press.

Gauthier, D. (1988/89). In the neighbourhood of the Newcomb-Predictor (Reflections on Rationality). *Proceedings of the Aristotelian Society* 89, part 3.

Gibbard, A., and W. Harper. (1985). Counterfactuals and two kinds of expected utility. In R. Campbell and L. Sowden, Eds., *Paradoxes of Rationality and Cooperation: Prisoner's Dilemma and Newcomb's Problem.* Vancouver: University of British Columbia Press. pp. 133–158. Originally published in Hooker, Leach, and McClennen, Eds. *Foundations and Applications of Decision Theory* vol. 1. Dordrecht: Reidel, 1978, pp. 125–162.

Hampton, J. (1997). *The Authority of Reasons.* Cambridge, MA: Cambridge University Press.

Hobbes, T. (1651). *Leviathan.* Cambridge: Cambridge University Press (1991).

Hollis, M., and Sugden, R. (1993). Rationality in action. *Mind* 102, 405: 1–35.

Hume, D. (1740). *A Treatise of Human Nature.* Oxford: Oxford University Press (1978).

Kavka, G. (1983). The toxin puzzle. *Analysis* 43: 1.

Kreps, D. M., and R. Wilson. (1982). Reputation and imperfect information. *Journal of Economic Theory* 27: 253–279.

Lewis, D. K. (1985). Prisoner's dilemma is a Newcomb problem. In R. Campbell and L. Sowden, Eds., *Paradoxes of Rationality and Cooperation: Prisoner's Dilemma and Newcomb's Problem.* Vancouver: University of British Columbia Press, pp. 251–255. Originally published in *Philosophy and Public Affairs* 8(3): 235–240.

McClennen, E. (1989). *Rationality and Dynamic Choice: Foundational Explorations.* Cambridge: Cambridge University Press.

Nozick, R. (1969). Newcomb's problem and two principles of choice. In N. Rescher, Ed., *Essays in Honor of Carl G. Hempel.* Dordrecht: Reidel, pp. 114–146.

Nozick, R. (1993). *The Nature of Rationality.* Princeton: Princeton University Press.

Pettit, P., and R. Sugden. (1989). The backward induction paradox. *Journal of Philosophy* 86: 169–182.

Reny, P. J. (1992). Rationality in extensive-form games. *Journal of Economic Perspectives* 6: 103–118.

Rosenthal, R. (1982). Games of perfect information, predatory pricing, and the chain store paradox. *Journal of Economic Theory* 25: 92–100.

Savage, L. (1954). *The Foundations of Statistics.* New York: Wiley.

Selten, R. (1978). The chain store paradox. *Theory and Decision* 9: 127–159.

Shafir, E., and A. Tversky. (1993). Thinking through uncertainty: Nonconsequential reasoning and choice. *Cognitive Psychology.*

Von Neumann, J., and O. Morgenstern. (1947). *Theory of Games and Economic Behavior.* 2nd ed. Princeton: Princeton University Press.

Further Readings

Bratman, M. (1987). *Intentions, Plans and Practical Reason.* Cambridge, MA: Harvard University Press.

Davidson, D. (1980). *Essays on Actions and Events.* Oxford: Clarendon Press.

Davidson, D. (1982). Paradoxes of irrationality. In R. Wollheim, and J. Hopkins, Eds., *Philosophical Essays on Freud.* Cambridge: Cambridge University Press.

Dupuy, J.-P. (1992). Two temporalities, two rationalities: A new look at Newcomb's paradox. In P. Bourgine and B. Walliser, Eds., *Economics and Cognitive Science.* Pergamon Press.

Elster, J. (1979). *Ulysses and the Sirens.* Cambridge: Cambridge University Press.

Elster, J. (1986). *The Multiple Self.* Cambridge: Cambridge University Press.

Fischer, J. M., Ed. (1989). *God, Foreknowledge, and Freedom.* Stanford: Stanford University Press.

Frankfurt, H. (1971). Freedom of the will and the concept of a person. *Journal of Philosophy* 68: 5–20.

Gauthier, D. (1984). Deterrence, maximization and rationality. In D. MacLean, Ed., *The Security Gamble. Deterrence Dilemmas in the Nuclear Age.* Totowa, NJ: Rowman and Allanheld.

Gauthier, D., and R. Sugden, Eds. (1993). *Rationality, Justice and the Social Contract.* Hemel Hempstead, England: Harvester Wheatsheaf.

Hollis, M. (1987). *The Cunning of Reason.* Cambridge: Cambridge University Press.

Horwich, P. (1987). *Asymmetries in Time: Problems in the Philosophy of Science.* Cambridge, MA: MIT Press.

Hurley, S. (1989). *Natural Reasons.* Oxford: Oxford University Press.

Lewis, D. K. (1969). *Convention: A Philosophical Study.* Cambridge, MA: Harvard University Press.

Lewis, D. K. (1979). Counterfactual dependence and time's arrow. *Nous* 13: 455–476.

Luce, R. D., and H. Raiffa. (1957). *Games and Decisions.* New York: Wiley.

Parfit, D. (1984). *Reasons and Persons.* Oxford: Oxford University Press.

Quattrone, G. A., and A. Tversky. (1987). Self-deception and the voter's illusion. In J. Elster, Ed., *The Multiple Self.* Cambridge: Cambridge University Press.

Schelling, T. C. (1960). *The Strategy of Conflict.* Cambridge, MA: Harvard University Press.

Simon, H. A. (1982). *Models of Bounded Rationality.* Cambridge, MA: MIT Press.

Sugden, R. (1991). Rational choice: A survey of contributions from economics and philosophy. *Economic Journal* 101: 751–785.

Williams, B. (1981). Internal and external reasons. In *Moral Luck.* Cambridge: Cambridge University Press, pp. 101–113.

Rational Decision Making

Rational decision making is choosing among alternatives in a way that "properly" accords with the preferences and beliefs of an individual decision maker or those of a group making a joint decision. The subject has been developed in decision theory (Luce and Raiffa 1957; see RATIONAL CHOICE THEORY), decision analysis (Raiffa 1968), GAME THEORY (von Neumann and Morgenstern 1953), political theory (Muller 1989), psychology (Kahneman, Slovic, and TVERSKY 1982; see DECISION-MAKING), and economics (Debreu 1959; Henderson and Quandt 1980; see ECONOMICS AND COGNITIVE SCIENCE), in which it is the primary activity of homo economicus, "rational economic man." The term refers to a variety of notions, with each conception of alternatives and proper accord with preferences and beliefs yielding a "rationality" criterion. At its most abstract, the subject concerns unanalyzed alternatives (choices, decisions) and preferences reflecting the desirability of the alternatives and rationality criteria such as maximal desirability of chosen alternatives with respect to the preference ranking. More concretely, one views the alternatives as actions in the world, and determines preferences among alternative actions from preference rankings of possible states of the world and beliefs or probability judgments about what states obtain as outcomes of different actions, as in the maximal expected utility criterion of decision theory and economics. UTILITY THEORY and the FOUNDATIONS OF PROBABILITY theory provide a base for its developments. Somewhat unrelated, but common, senses of the term refer to making decisions through reasoning (Baron 1985), especially reasoning satisfying conditions of logical consistency and deductive completeness (see DEDUCTIVE REASONING; LOGIC) or probabilistic soundness (see PROBABILISTIC REASONING). The basic elements of the theory were set in place by Bernoulli (1738), Bentham (1823), Pareto (1927), Ramsey (1926), de Finetti (1937), VON NEUMANN and Morgenstern (1953), and Savage (1972). Texts by Raiffa (1968), Keeney and Raiffa (1976), and Jeffrey (1983) offer good introductions.

The theory of rational choice begins by considering a set of alternatives facing the decision maker(s). Analysts of particular decision situations normally consider only a restricted set of abstract alternatives that capture the important or interesting differences among the alternatives. This often proves necessary because, particularly in problems of what to do, the full range of possible actions exceeds comprehension. The field of decision analysis (Raiffa 1968) addresses how to make such modeling choices and provides useful techniques and guidelines. Recent work on BAYESIAN NETWORKS (Pearl 1988) provides additional modeling techniques. These models and their associated inference mechanisms form the basis for a wide variety of successful KNOWLEDGE-BASED SYSTEMS (Wellman, Breese, and Goldman 1992).

The theory next considers a binary relation of preference among these alternatives. The notation $x \precsim y$ means that alternative y is at least as desirable as alternative x, read as y is weakly preferred to x; "weakly" because $x \precsim y$ permits x and y to be equally desirable. Decision analysis also provides a number of techniques for assessing or identifying the preferences of decision makers. Preference assessment may lead to reconsideration of the model of alternatives when the alternatives aggregate together things differing along some dimension on which preference depends.

Decision theory requires the weak preference relation $\precsim$ to be a complete preorder, that is, reflexive ($x \precsim x$), transitive ($x \precsim y$ and $y \precsim z$ imply $x \precsim z$), and relating every pair of alternatives (either $x \precsim y$ or $y \precsim x$). These requirements provide a formalization in accord with ordinary intuitions about simple decision situations in which one can readily distinguish different amounts, more is better, and one can always tell which is more. Various theoretical arguments have also been made in support of these requirements; for example, if someone's preferences lack these properties, one may construct a wager against him he is sure to lose.

Given a complete preordering of alternatives, decision theory requires choosing maximally desirable alternatives, that is, alternatives x such that $y \precsim x$ for all alternatives y. There may be one, many, or no such maxima. Maximally preferred alternatives always exist within finite sets of alternatives. Preferences that linearly order the alternatives ensure that maxima are unique when they exist.

The rationality requirements of decision theory on preferences and choices constitute an ideal rarely observed but useful nonetheless (see Kahneman, Slovic, and Tversky 1982; DECISION MAKING, ECONOMICS AND COGNITIVE SCIENCE, JUDGMENT HEURISTICS). In practice, people apparently violate reflexivity (to the extent that they distinguish alternative statements of the same alternative), transitivity (comparisons based on aggregating subcomparisons may conflict), and completeness (having to adopt preferences among things never before considered). Indeed, human preferences change over time and through reasoning and action, which renders somewhat moot the usual requirements on instantaneous preferences. People also seem to not optimize their choices in the required way, more often seeming to choose alternatives that are not optimal but are nevertheless good enough. These "satisficing" (Simon 1955), rather than optimizing, decisions constitute a principal focus in the study of BOUNDED RATIONALITY, the rationality exhibited by agents of limited abilities (Horvitz 1987; Russell 1991; Simon 1982). Satisficing forms the basis of much of the study of PROBLEM SOLVING in artificial intelligence; indeed, NEWELL (1982: 102) identifies the method of problem solving via goals as the foundational (but weak) rationality criterion of the field ("If an agent has knowledge that one of its actions will lead to one of its goals, then the agent will select that action"). Such "heuristic" rationality lacks the coherence of the decision-theoretic notion because it downplays or ignores issues of comparison among alternative actions that all lead to a desired goal, as well as comparisons among independent goals. In spite of the failure of humans to live up to the requirements of ideal rationality, the ideal serves as a useful approximation, one that supports predictions, in economics and other fields, of surprisingly wide applicability (Becker 1976; Stigler and Becker 1977).

Though the notions of preference and optimal choice have qualitative foundations, most practical treatments of decision theory represent preference orders by means of numerical utility functions. We say that a function U that assigns numbers to alternatives represents the relation $\precsim$ just in case $U(x) \precsim U(y)$ whenever $x \precsim y$. Note that if a utility function represents a preference relation, then any monotone-increasing transform of the function represents the relation as well, and that such transformation does not change the set of maximally preferred alternatives. Such functions are called ordinal utility functions, as the numerical values only indicate order, not magnitude (so that $U(x) = 2 U(y)$ does not mean that x is twice as desirable as y).

To formalize choosing among actions that may yield different outcomes with differing likelihoods, the theory moves beyond maximization of preferability of abstract alternatives to the criterion of maximizing expected utility, which derives preferences among alternatives from preference orderings of the possible outcomes together with beliefs or expectations that indicate the probability of different consequences. Let Ω denote the set of possible outcomes or consequences of choices. The theory supposes that the beliefs of the agent determine a probability measure Pr, where $Pr(\omega|x)$ is the probability that outcome ω obtains as a result of taking action x. The theory further supposes a preference relation over outcomes. If we choose a numerical function U over outcomes to represent this preference relation, then the expected utility $\hat{U}(x)$ of alternative x denotes the total utility of the consequences of x, weighting the utility of each outcome by its probability, that is

$$\hat{U}(x) = \sum_{\omega \in \Omega} U(\omega) Pr(\omega|x).$$

Because the utilities of outcomes are added together in this definition, this utility function is called a cardinal utility function, indicating magnitude as well as order. We then define $x \precsim y$ to hold just in case $\hat{U}(x) \precsim \hat{U}(y)$. Constructing preferences over actions to represent comparisons of expected utility in this way transforms the abstract rational choice criterion into one of maximizing the expected utility of actions.

The identification of rational choice under UNCERTAINTY with maximization of expected utility also admits criticism (Machina 1987). Milnor (1954) examined a number of reasonable properties one might require of rational decisions, and proved no decision method satisfied all of them. In practice, the reasonability of the expected utility criterion depends critically on whether the modeler has incorporated all aspects of the decision into the utility function, for example, the decision maker's attitudes toward risk.

The theory of rational choice may be developed in axiomatic fashion from the axioms above, in which philosophical justifications are given for each of the axioms. The complementary "revealed preference" approach uses the axioms instead as an analytical tool for interpreting actions. This approach, pioneered by Ramsey (1926) and de Finetti (1937) and developed into a useful mathematical and practical method by von Neumann (von Neumann and Morgenstern 1953) and Savage (1972), uses real or hypothesized sets of actions (or only observed actions in the case of Davidson, Suppes, and Siegel 1957) to construct probability and utility functions that would give rise to the set of actions.

When decisions are to be made by a group rather than an individual, the above model is applied to describing both the group members and the group decision. The focus in group decision making is the process by which the beliefs and preferences of the group determine the beliefs and preferences of the group as a whole. Traditional methods for making these determinations, such as voting, suffer various problems, notably yielding intransitive group preferences. Arrow (1963) proved that there is no way, in general, to achieve group preferences satisfying the rationality criteria except by designating some group member as a "dictator," and using that member's preferences as those of the group. May (1954), Black (1963), and others proved good methods exist in a number of special cases (Sen 1977). When all preferences are well behaved and concern exchanges of economic goods in markets, the theory of general equilibrium (Arrow and Hahn 1971; Debreu 1959) proves the existence of optimal group decisions about allocations of these goods. Game theory considers more refined rationality criteria appropriate to multiagent settings in which decision makers interact. Artificial markets (Wellman 1993) and negotiation techniques based on game theory (Rosenschein and Zlotkin 1994) now form the basis for a number of techniques in MULTIAGENT SYSTEMS.

—Jon Doyle

References and Further Readings

Arrow, K. J. (1963). *Social Choice and Individual Values.* 2nd ed. New Haven: Yale University Press.

Arrow, K. J., and F. H. Hahn. (1971). *General Competitive Analysis.* Amsterdam: Elsevier.

Baron, J. (1985). *Rationality and Intelligence.* Cambridge: Cambridge University Press.

Becker, G. S. (1976). *The Economic Approach to Human Behavior.* Chicago: University of Chicago Press.

Bentham, J. (1823). *Principles of Morals and Legislation.* Oxford: Oxford University Press.

Bernoulli, D. (1738). Specimen theoriae novae de mensura sortis. *Comentarii academiae scientarium imperialis Petropolitanae,* vol. 5 for 1730 and 1731, pp. 175–192.

Black, D. (1963). *The Theory of Committees and Elections.* Cambridge: Cambridge University Press.

de Finetti, B. (1937). La prévision: Ses lois logiques, ses sources subjectives. *Annales de l'Institut Henri Poincaré* 7.

Davidson, D., P. Suppes, and S. Siegel. (1957). *Decision Making: An Experimental Approach.* Stanford, CA: Stanford University Press.

Debreu, G. (1959). *Theory of Value: An Axiomatic Analysis of Economic Equlibrium.* New York: Wiley.

Henderson, J. M., and R. E. Quandt. (1980). *Microeconomic Theory: A Mathematical Approach.* 3rd ed. New York: McGraw-Hill.

Horvitz, E. J. (1987). Reasoning about beliefs and actions under computational resource constraints. *Proceedings of the Third AAAI Workshop on Uncertainty in Artificial Intelligence.* Menlo Park, CA: AAAI Press.

Jeffrey, R. C. (1983). *The Logic of Decision.* 2nd ed. Chicago: University of Chicago Press.

Kahneman, D., P. Slovic, and A. Tversky, Eds. (1982). *Judgment under Uncertainty: Heuristics and Biases.* Cambridge: Cambridge University Press.

Keeney, R. L., and H. Raiffa. (1976). *Decisions with Multiple Objectives: Preferences and Value Tradeoffs.* New York: Wiley.

Luce, R. D., and H. Raiffa. (1957). *Games and Decisions.* New York: Wiley.

Machina, M. J. (1987). Choice under uncertainty: Problems solved and unsolved. *Journal of Economic Perspectives* 1 (1): 121–154.

May, K. O. (1954). Intransitivity, utility, and the aggregation of preference patterns. *Econometrica* 22: 1–13.

Milnor, J. (1954). Games against nature. In R. M. Thrall, C. H. Coombs, and R. L. Davis, Eds., *Decision Processes.* New York: Wiley, pp. 49–59.

Mueller, D. C. (1989). *Public Choice 2.* 2nd ed. Cambridge: Cambridge University Press.

Newell, A. (1982). The knowledge level. *Artificial Intelligence* 18 (1): 87–127.

Pareto, V. (1927). *Manuel d'economie politique,* deuxième édition. Paris: M. Giard.

Pearl, J. (1988). *Probabilistic Reasoning in Intelligent Systems: Networks of Plausible Inference.* San Mateo, CA: Morgan Kaufmann.

Raiffa, H. (1968). *Decision Analysis: Introductory Lectures on Choices Under Uncertainty.* Reading, MA: Addison-Wesley.

Ramsey, F. P. (1964). Truth and probability. In H. E. Kyburg, Jr. and H. E. Smokler, Eds., *Studies in Subjective Probability.* New York: Wiley. Originally published 1926.

Rosenschein, J. S., and G. Zlotkin. (1994). *Rules of Encounter: Designing Conventions for Automated Negotiation among Computers.* Cambridge, MA: MIT Press.

Russell, S. J. (1991). *Do the Right Thing: Studies in Limited Rationality.* Cambridge, MA: MIT Press.

Savage, L. J. (1972). *The Foundations of Statistics.* 2nd ed. New York: Dover Publications.

Sen, A. (1977). Social choice theory: A re-examination. *Econometrica* 45: 53–89.

Simon, H. A. (1955). A behavioral model of rational choice. *Quarterly Journal of Economics* 69: 99–118.

Simon, H. A. (1982). *Models of Bounded Rationality: Behavioral Economics and Business Organization,* vol. 2. Cambridge, MA: MIT Press.

Stigler, G. J., and G. S. Becker. (1977). De gustibus non est disputandum. *American Economic Review* 67: 76–90.

von Neumann, J., and O. Morgenstern. (1953). *Theory of Games and Economic Behavior.* 3rd ed. Princeton, NJ: Princeton University Press.

Wellman, M. P. (1993). A market-oriented programming environment and its application to distributed multicommodity flow problems. *Journal of Artificial Intelligence Research* 1: 1–23.

Wellman, M. P., J. S. Breese, and R. P. Goldman. (1992). From knowledge bases to decision models. *The Knowledge Engineering Review* 7(1): 35–53.

Rationalism vs. Empiricism

"Rationalism" and "empiricism" are best understood as names for two broad trends in philosophy rather than labels for specific articulated theories. "Sensationalism," "experientialism," and "empirical theory" are among other terms that have been used to denote the latter doctrine, while "intuitionalism," "intellectualism," and "transcendentalism" have had currency in alluding to the former. In the traditional pantheon of philosophers, the classic rationalists are René DESCARTES, Gottfried Wilhelm Leibniz, and Baruch Spinoza; the classic empiricists are John Locke, George Berkeley, and David HUME. Immanuel Kant's transcendental theses, although removed from empiricism, do not fit readily into the rationalist picture either. Theorists are usually said to be "rationalists" or "empiricists" in light of a discerned family resemblance between one of their positions and a position championed by members of one of the traditional schools (cf. KANT).

Roughly put, empiricism is the view that all knowledge of fact comes from experience. At birth the mind is a tabula rasa. Our senses not only provide the evidence available to justify beliefs, they are the initial source of the concepts constituting these thoughts. Innate biases and dispositions may influence the ideas experience leads us to acquire, but we do not come into the world equipped with anything deserving the title of an "idea." Some ideas, the simple ones, are found directly in experience; others are derived from these by abstraction, analogy, and definition.

According to the empiricists, there are also no a priori truths, except for those analytic statements (for example, "All bachelors are unmarried," or "Triangles have three sides"), which, being matters of meaning, can be depicted in terms of definitional, hence necessary, relations among ideas. The seemingly special status of mathematics might then be explained on the assumption that mathematical statements are analytic. Some prominent empiricists, notably John Stuart Mill (1956), argued even mathematics was empirically derived.

Knowledge of all matters of fact, however, rests on inductively gained experience. In particular, scientific knowledge is not based on a priori or necessary principles. Reason does not supply the ultimate foundation for science, nor can it enable us to achieve certainty in these areas. Reason can help to organize and see the implications of what sense offers, and logic puts constraints on appropriate patterns of reasoning, but reason on its own cannot provide the wherewithal for understanding nature.

Rationalism may be given an equally rough description in terms of its denial of these central empiricist tenets. For the rationalist, experience is not the source of all knowledge. Some concepts are neither derived nor derivable from sense experience. The mind comes equipped with a set of innate ideas. What's more, reason or intuition, when properly tapped, can provide true beliefs or principles, albeit not all or even most of those we entertain; determining the truth of mundane claims about the height of a tree or if the milk has gone bad require sense experience. Inductive exploration will also play a role in discovering empirical regularities theoretical science incorporates and seeks to explain.

Reason has a higher calling. It furnishes a priori principles that are not only true, but are necessary, and are recognizably so. These principles are not stipulative definitional truths; rather they delineate the real essences of the ideas of "God," "being," "triangle," and so on that they contain. In this way, they supply a bedrock of certainty upon which knowledge is built, and coherence with them is the sine qua non of acceptable hypotheses.

It is possible, then, to conceive of scientific theories along the lines of axiom systems in mathematics. The first principles (or axioms) of these systems of science are not established by the inductive amassing of evidence. They are intuited by reason as true and necessary. These principles provide the foundational certainty from which the rest of science can be seen to follow deductively.

The rationalist/empiricist distinction, as drawn above, is to be distinguished from the contrast between mentalistic versus behavioristic approaches to psychology and mind. Empiricists as well as rationalists were mentalists, and both placed heavy emphasis on the role of consciousness in cognition. None of these thinkers had qualms appealing to mental states, and none were committed to the view that human behavior was not mediated by and dependent upon such internal states. Descartes (*Discourse on the Method*, part 5, from Descartes 1984–85) perhaps stands out in his clear refusal to attribute CONSCIOUSNESS to animals and in his conviction that their behavior can be fully explained mechanistically without appeal to mental intermediaries. Hume, in his *Treatise of Human Nature* (1960: book I, sect. 16), forcefully argues that animals are endowed with thought and reason. Everyone agreed, however, that the coin of the mental was ideas, and the empiricists' ideas were no less

representational than those of the rationalists (cf. BEHAVIORISM and MENTAL REPRESENTATION).

Empiricists did stress and give wider scope to the role associative processes were seen to play in the acquisition and manipulation of ideas, and experienced similarity had a more prominent place in their theories. But it is a mistake to think they allowed for no other kinds of mental transitions and processing. In fact, Locke spends a chapter of his *Essay Concerning Human Understanding* (1975: book II, ch. 33) warning how too ready reliance on the happenstance of experiential co-occurrences will result in false beliefs.

At the same time, there is no reason to assume rationalists did not allow many transitions of thought and imagination were fueled by past associations or presently sensed similarities. For example, Descartes' influential theory of the emotions (*Passions of the Soul*, from Descartes 1984–85), has elements that are not only sensationalist but are behaviorist and associationist. It is also true, especially in his theory of vision (*Dioptrics*, from Descartes 1984-85), that Descartes talks of more intellectual-like reasoning and calculating that is neither conscious nor involves conscious ideas. But these processing claims are in tension with the standard interpretation of Descartes as the foremost champion of the view that *all* mental states are conscious.

Although the rationalist/empiricist dichotomy, loosely characterized, does have its uses in limited contexts, care must be taken employing it to make specific claims about specific historical figures. Further caution is warranted when their work is cited or used to support contemporary doctrines. For example, many seventeenth- and eighteenth-century arguments for innateness hinge on the claim that ideas such as "God" or "triangle" could not be acquired, because no actual instances of these sorts of concepts could possibly be found in experience. Current-day proponents of innate ideas, stressing inductive indeterminacy, extend the claim to ideas for which there clearly are observed cases. Similarly, rationalists often argued apprehension of certain principles, like the principles of noncontradiction and identity, must be a priori, because they are a prerequisite for having any thought at all. Current proponents of the INNATENESS OF LANGUAGE, for example, tend not to make comparable claims about the principles of universal grammar (cf. NATIVISM; NATIVISM, HISTORY OF; POVERTY OF THE STIMULUS ARGUMENTS).

The classic writers forged their theories in and against a background of assumptions about physics, mind, physiology, religion, and science in general that have been largely abandoned. Moreover, in the course of time, concepts and doctrines of consciousness, learning, innateness, mental states and processes versus nonmental states and processes, biological inheritance, and the like have come to be understood along new dimensions. This has led to further blurring the meaning and significance of the distinction between rationalist and empiricist positions.

In contemporary psychological literature, for instance, Hermann von HELMHOLTZ is frequently cited as the founding father of the cognitivist approach to perception. Since Helmholtz's (1950) unconscious inference model postulates mental representations and processes, his theory is said to stand in opposition to Gestalt, behaviorist, and Gibsonian positions. Yet Helmholtz's model is strikingly similar to the one Berkeley offers in his *New Theory of Vision* (from Berkeley 1948–57), and it explicitly mirrors Mill's account of inductive inference. But whereas the staunch empiricist Mill (1973) allows that certain visual inferences may be instinctive, Helmholtz claims (1950) his main result has been to show how a range of phenomena, usually thought innate, can be explained in terms of learning and psychological processing. So, for example, on the important issue of the fusion of binocular images, Helmholtz offers a cognitive account, in opposition to the purely physiological, nativist explanation given by Descartes and other theorists (cf. GIBSON; GESTALT PERCEPTION; *see also* PARSIMONY AND SIMPLICITY).

See also DOMAIN SPECIFICITY; LINGUISTIC UNIVERSALS AND UNIVERSAL GRAMMAR; MORAL PSYCHOLOGY

—*Robert Schwartz*

References

Berkeley, G. (1948–1957). *The Works of George Berkeley, Bishop of Cloyne*, vol. 1. A. A. Luce and T. E. Jessop, Eds. Edinburgh: Thomas Nelson.

Descartes, R. (1984–1985). *Philosophical Writings*. 2 vols. Translated by J. Cottingham, R. Stoothoff, and D. Murdoch. Cambridge: Cambridge University Press. Vol. 3, *The Correspondence*, trans. by C. S. M. Kenny and A. Kenny. Cambridge: Cambridge University Press (1991).

Helmholtz, H. (1950). *Treatise on Physiological Optics*. 3 vols. J. Southall, Ed. New York: Dover.

Hume, D. (1960). *Treatise of Human Nature*. L. A. Selby-Bigge, Ed. Oxford: Oxford University Press.

Locke, J. (1975). *An Essay Concerning Human Understanding*. P. H. Nidditch, Ed. Oxford: Oxford University Press.

Mill, J. S. (1956). *A System of Logic*. London: Longmans, Green and Co.

Mill, J. S. (1973). Bailey on Berkeley's theory of vision. In *Dissertations and Discussions*, vol. 2. New York: Haskell House, pp. 84–119.

Further Readings

Barbanell, E., and D. Garrett, Eds. (1997). *Encyclopedia of Empiricism*. Westport, CT: Greenwood Press.

Boring, E. G. (1950). *A History of Experimental Psychology*. 2nd ed. New York: Appleton-Century-Crofts.

Brown, S., Ed. (1996). *Routledge History of Philosophy*. Vol. 5, *British Philosophy and the Age of Enlightenment*. New York: Routledge.

Chomsky, N. (1966). *Cartesian Linguistics*. New York: Harper and Row.

Herrnstein, R., and E. G. Boring, Eds. (1968). *A Sourcebook in the History of Psychology*. Cambridge, MA: Harvard University Press.

James, W. (1950). *The Principles of Psychology*. 2 vols. New York: Dover.

Leibniz, G. W. (1981). *New Essays Concerning Human Understanding*. Translated by P. Remnant and J. Bennett, Ed. Cambridge: Cambridge University Press.

Parkinson, G. H. R., Ed. (1993). *Routledge History of Philosophy*. Vol. 4, *The Renaissance and 17th Century Rationalism*. New York: Routledge.

Piaget, J. (1970). *Genetic Epistemology*. New York: Norton.

Piattelli-Palmarini, M., Ed. (1980). *Language and Learning*. Cambridge, MA: Harvard University Press.

Schwartz, R. (1994). *Vision: Variations on Some Berkeleian Themes*. Oxford: Blackwell.

Smith, R. (1997). *The Human Sciences*. London: Fontana Press.

Stich, S., Ed. (1975). *Innate Ideas*. Berkeley: University of California Press.

Sully, J. (1878). The question of visual perception in Germany, pts. 1 and 2. *Mind* 9: 1–23, 167–195.

Rationality

See BOUNDED RATIONALITY; RATIONAL AGENCY; RATIONAL CHOICE THEORY; RATIONAL DECISION MAKING

Reading

At the close of the nineteenth century, the perceptual and cognitive processes involved in reading were central topics of theory and research (e.g., Cattell 1885; Pillsbury 1897). Yet, as learning theory came to dominate academic psychology, this interest waned. Across most of the twentieth century, reading was broadly viewed by research psychologists as the product of paired-associate learning and, thus, as largely understood at least in principle, despite the heated debate in the educational arena as to whether the effective stimulus in learning to read corresponded to letters or words (e.g., Chall 1967; Flesch 1955).

This attitude changed abruptly with the onset of the cognitive era. Text, after all, was language. If bottom-up learning theories were not adequate to explain the acquisition or comprehension of oral language (see LANGUAGE ACQUISITION), then neither, by extension, were they adequate to explain the acquisition or comprehension of written language (Smith 1971). Moreover, written as opposed to oral language had the amenably investigable property that its units were discrete, lending themselves to physical alteration, substitution, and rearrangement at every level, from letters to discourse structure. Thus, according to Besner and Humphreys (1991), research on reading has filled more pages in books and journals than any other topic in cognitive psychology. In consequence, few subdomains of cognitive psychology have seen as much progress—empirical, theoretical, and applied—as has the field of reading research.

During the 1970s and 1980s, working collaboratively with the fields of linguistic science and artificial intelligence, cognitive research on reading focused on two issues: how higher-order knowledge is organized and how, by virtue of that organization, the partial and temporally messy information of text might be restructured and implemented into coherent events and images.

The results were a wealth of empirical work demonstrating that readers can interpret and evaluate an author's message only to the extent that they possess and call forth the vocabulary, syntactic, rhetorical, topical, analytic, and social knowledge that the author has presumed, as well as a number of theories and models of the psychological structures and processes involved in bringing such knowledge to bear (for review, see Anderson and Pearson 1984; Sanford and

Garrod 1981). Alongside, text was shown to differ from normal oral discourse in language, content, and communicative modes and purposes. The implications were, first, that beyond learning to listen or speak, LITERACY demands more knowledge in depth, breadth, and kind and, second, that unlike learning to listen or speak, the processes of becoming literate require reflective access to such knowledge at every level. Of applied relevance, researchers also demonstrated that among younger and poorer readers the requisite knowledge, inferential capabilities, or comprehension monitoring tendencies were generally underdeveloped to a greater or lesser extent (for review, see Baker and Brown 1984), and instructional implications of this work quickly found its way into classroom materials and practice (see METACOGNITION).

An equally important outcome of this work was that it forced the field's awareness of its explanatory limitations. First, although this work helped make explicit the syntactic and semantic infrastructure on which text comprehension depends, it begged the question of how such knowledge might be accessed in process or acquired developmentally. Second, there was the issue of words. Much of the research of this era had been designed to elucidate how skillful readers might use the higher-order constraints of text to reduce or finesse the demands of word recognition while reading. Yet, as many times and as many ways as this question was empirically probed, the results contradicted the premise. Instead, skillful readers' recognition of printed words proved itself almost wholly indifferent to the type or strength of bias introduced by researchers; only among poor readers does the speed or accuracy of word recognition tend to be measurably influenced by context (Stanovich 1980). Furthermore, poorly developed word recognition skills were shown to account for much of the difference in good and poor readers' comprehension of text (Perfetti 1985).

The invention of parallel distributed processing models of perception and memory have been key in the theoretical reconciliation of the word recognition and comprehension research (see COGNITIVE MODELING, CONNECTIONIST). These computational models have demonstrated that many of the microphenomena of word recognition—including effects of word frequency, orthographic redundancy, spelling, sound irregularities (*aisle*) and inconsistencies (*head, bead*), and sensitivity to syllabic and onset-rime boundaries—reflect statistical properties of the language's orthographic and orthophonological structure and, as such, emerge through associative learning (Seidenberg and McClelland 1989; see VISUAL WORD RECOGNITION). More critically, perhaps, in positing such associative learning not just among letters but also between spellings and both phonology and meaning, the models provide means of understanding how, even as the print on the page is the raw data of reading, it might serve to activate and to reinforce and extend learning of the language and meaning on which text comprehension depends (Adams 1990).

With the help of a variety of new technologies, research has now affirmed that for skillful readers, regardless of the difficulty of the text, the basic dynamic of reading is line by line, left-to-right, and word by word. Further, during that fraction of a second while the eyes are paused on any given word of text, its spelling is registered with complete, letterwise precision even as it is instantly and automatically mapped to the speech patterns it represents (Rayner 1998; see also EYE MOVEMENTS AND VISUAL ATTENTION).

Although scientists are only beginning to understand the various roles of these spelling-to-speech translations, they are clearly of critical importance to the reading process. To the extent that knowledge of spelling-to-speech correspondences is underdeveloped (as evidenced, for example, by subnormal speed or accuracy in reading nonsense words), it is strongly and reliably associated with reading delay or disability. Moreover, given an alphabetic script such as English, research affirms that learning to recognize or spell an adequate number of words is essentially impossible except as children have internalized the spelling-to-speech correspondences of the language (Ehri 1992; Share and Stanovich 1995).

Although results of the 1992 and 1994 National Assessment of Educational Progress (NAEP) indicate that more than 40 percent of U.S. fourth graders are unable to read grade-appropriate text with minimally acceptable levels of understanding or fluency (Campbell, Donahue, Clyde, and Philips 1996), research indicates that, with the exception of no more than 1–3 percent of children, reading disability can be prevented through well-designed early instruction (Vellutino et al. 1996). As in method comparison studies of past decades (e.g., Bond and Dykstra 1967; Chall 1967), contemporary investigations (e.g., Foorman et al. 1998) affirm that initial reading instruction is most effective if it includes explicit, systematic attention to phonics as well as an active emphasis on practicing and using that knowledge both in isolation and in the context of meaningful reading and writing.

In addition, building on the seminal work of A. Liberman, Cooper, Shankweiler, and Studdert-Kennedy (1967) and I. Liberman, Shankweiler, Fischer, and Carter (1974), research has amply demonstrated that learning to read an alphabetic script depends critically on the relatively difficult insight that every word can be conceived as a sequence of phonemes (see PHONOLOGY). Indeed, poorly developed phonemic awareness has asserted itself as the core and causal factor underlying most cases of severe reading disability (Lyon 1995). Conversely, for normal as well as at-risk populations, activities designed to develop children's awareness of the phonemic structure of words have been shown to ease and accelerate both reading and writing growth (see Adams, Treiman, and Pressley 1997; Torgesen 1997). The relationship between phonemic awareness and learning to read is bidirectional such that some basic appreciation of the phonological structure of words appears necessary for grasping the alphabetic principle, while instruction and practice in decoding and spelling serves reciprocally to advance the child's phonemic sensitivity. In terms of cognition and metacognition, the important lesson of this work is that, no less than for higher-order dimensions of literacy growth, productive learning about decoding and spelling necessarily builds on prior knowledge and active understanding.

See also DYSLEXIA; WRITING SYSTEMS

—*Marilyn Adams*

References

Adams, M. J. (1990). *Beginning to Read: Thinking and Learning about Print.* Cambridge, MA: MIT Press.

Adams, M. J., R.Treiman, and M. Pressley. (1997). Reading, writing and literacy. In I. Sigel and A. Renninger, Eds., *Handbook of Child Psychology*, 5th ed., vol. 4, *Child Psychology in Practice.* New York: Wiley, pp. 275–357.

Anderson, R. C., and P. D. Pearson. (1984). A schema-theoretic view of basic processes in reading. In P. D. Pearson, Ed., *Handbook of Reading Research.* New York: Longman, pp. 255–292.

Baker, L., and A. L. Brown. (1984). Metacognitive skills and reading. In P. D. Pearson, R. Barr, M. Kamil, and P. Mosenthal, Eds., *Handbook of Reading Research,* vol. 1. New York: Longman, pp. 353–394.

Besner, D., and G. W. Humphreys. (1991). Introduction. In D. Besner and G. W. Humphreys, Eds., *Basic Processes in Reading: Visual Word Recognition.* Hillsdale, NJ: Erlbaum, 1–9.

Bond, G. L., and R. Dykstra. (1967). The cooperative research program in first-grade reading instruction. *Reading Research Quarterly* 2: 5–142.

Campbell, J. R., P. L. I. Donahue, M. R. Clyde, and G. W. Phillips. (1996). *NAEP 1994 Reading Report Card for the Nation and the States.* Washington, DC: National Center for Educational Statistics, US Department of Education.

Cattell, J. M. (1885). The inertia of the eye and brain. *Brain* 8: 295–312. Reprinted in A. T. Poffenberger, Ed., *James McKeen Cattell: Man of Science* (1947). York, PA: Science Press.

Chall, J. S. (1967). *Learning to Read: The Great Debate.* New York: McGraw-Hill.

Ehri, L. C. (1992). Reconceptualizing the development of sight word reading and its relationship to recoding. In P. B. Gough, L. C. Ehri, and R. Treiman, Eds., *Reading Acquisition.* Hillsdale, NJ: Erlbaum, pp.107–143.

Flesch, R. (1955). *Why Johnny Can't Read.* New York: Harper and Row.

Foorman, B., D. J. Francis, J. M. Fletcher, C. Schatschneider, and P. Mehta. (1998). The role of instruction in learning to read: Preventing reading failure in at-risk children. *Journal of Educational Psychology* to appear.

Liberman, A. M., F. Cooper, D. Shankweiler, and M. Studdert-Kennedy. (1967). Perception of the speech code. *Psychological Review* 74: 431–461.

Liberman, I. Y., D. Shankweiler, F. W. Fischer, and B. Carter. (1974). Reading and the awareness of linguistic segments. *Journal of Experimental Child Psychology* 18: 201–212.

(1995). Toward a definition of dyslexia. *Annals of Dyslexia* 45: 3–27.

Neisser, U. (1967). *Cognitive Psychology.* New York: Appleton-Century-Crofts.

Perfetti, C. A. (1985). *Reading Ability.* New York: Oxford University Press.

Pillsbury, W. B. (1897). A study in apperception. *American Journal of Psychology* 8: 315–393.

Rayner, K. (1998). Eye movements in reading and information processing: Twenty years of research. *Psychological Bulletin* to appear.

Sanford, A. J., and S. G. Garrod. (1981). *Understanding Written Language.* New York: Wiley.

Seidenberg, M. S., and J. L. McClelland. (1989). A distributed, developmental model of word recognition and naming. *Psychological Review* 96: 523–568.

Share, D., and K. Stanovich. (1995). Cognitive processes in early reading development: Accommodating individual differences into a mode of acquisition. *Issues in Education: Contributions from Educational Psychology* 1: 1–57.

Smith, F. (1971). *Understanding Reading.* New York: Holt, Rinehart and Winston.

Stanovich, K. E. (1980). Toward an interactive-compensatory model of individual differences in the development of reading fluency. *Reading Research Quarterly* 16:32–71.

Torgesen, J. K. (1997). The prevention and remediation of reading disabilities: Evaluating what we know from research. *Journal of Academic Language Therapy* 1: 11–47.

Vellutino, F. R., D. M. Scanlon, E. Sipay, S. Small, A. Pratt, R. Chen, and M. Denckla. (1996). Cognitive profiles of difficult-to-remediate and readily remediated poor readers: Early intervention as a vehicle for distinguishing between cognitive and experiential deficits as basic causes of specific reading disability. *Journal of Educational Psychology* 88: 601–638.

Further Readings

P. B. Gough, L. C. Ehri, and R. Treiman, Eds. (1992). *Reading Acquisition.* Hillsdale, NJ: Erlbaum, pp. 107–143.

Juel, C. (1994). *Learning to Read and Write in One Elementary School.* New York: Springer.

Just, M. A., and P. A. Carpenter. (1987). *The Psychology of Reading and Language Comprehension.* Boston: Allyn and Bacon.

National Research Council. (1998). *Preventing reading difficulties in young children.* Washington, DC: National Academy Press.

Olson, D. R. (1994). *The World on Paper.* New York: Cambridge University Press.

Plaut, D. C., J. L. McClelland, M. S. Seidenberg, and K. Patterson. (1996). Understanding normal and impaired word reading: Computational principles in quasi-regular domains. *Psychological Review* 103: 56–115.

Rack, J. P., M. J. Snowling, and R. K. Olson. (1992). The nonword reading deficit in developmental dyslexia: A review. *Reading Research Quarterly* 26: 28–53.

Rayner, K., and A. Pollatsek. (1989). *The Psychology of Reading.* Hillsdale, NJ: Erlbaum.

Shankweiler, D., S. Crain, L. Katz, A. E. Fowler, A. M. Liberman, S. A. Brady, R. Thornton, E. Lundquist, L. Dreyer, J. M. Fletcher, K. K. Stuebing, S. E. Shaywitz, and B. A. Shaywitz. (1995). Cognitive profiles of reading-disabled children: Comparison of language skills in phonology, morphology and syntax. *Psychological Science* 6: 149–156.

Treiman, R. (1993). *Beginning to Spell: A Study of First Grade Children.* New York: Oxford University Press.

Realism and Antirealism

Realism is a blend of metaphysics and epistemology. Metaphysically, realism claims that there is an observer-independent world; epistemologically, it claims that we can gain knowledge of that very world. In relation to science, realism asserts that, independently of our representations, the entities described by our scientific theories exist and that the theories themselves are objectively true (at least approximately). Opposed to scientific realism (hereafter just "realism") are a variety of antirealisms; notably positivism, empiricism, instrumentalism, and constructivism.

Twentieth-century positivism regarded realism as a pseudo-question external to science. Difficulties over the very possibility of a realist interpretation for the quantum theory of 1925–26 seemed to support this view (Fine 1996). The situation changed in the 1960s with the emergence of what came to be known as the "miracles" argument, namely, that unless the theoretical entities employed by scientific theories actually existed and the theories themselves were at least approximately true of the world at large, the evident success of science (in terms of its applications and predictions) would surely be a miracle (Putnam 1975; Smart 1963). During the next two decades versions of this argument became so fashionable that realism was often identified with science itself.

Despite the fashion, the argument is inconclusive because, at best, scientific success can show only that something is right about science. That could mean that science is actually getting at the truth, as the miracles argument urges, or it could just mean that science is developing reliable tools for organizing experience, perhaps using flawed representations of reality. Similar difficulties beset an influential "explanationist" variant of the argument (Boyd 1992). This version asks us to explain the evident success of science and argues that realism, with its emphasis on the truth of our theories, offers the best explanation. Among other problems, this version suffers from the defect that the conclusion in support of realism depends on the principle ("inference to the best explanation") to accept as true that which explains best (Lipton 1991). Antirealisms like instrumentalism and empiricism would deny the inference. (After all, the best may well be the best of a bad lot.) Thus the explanationist version of the "miracles" argument uses a principle of inference that begs a central question at issue between realism and antirealism—whether truth, or some other merit, attaches to a good theory (Fine 1996; Laudan 1981).

In addition to these logical difficulties, realism has a problem with the history of science, which shows our best theories repeatedly overthrown. Inductively, this may support pessimism about the stability of current science (Psillos 1996). It also has a problem with the underdetermination of theory by evidence, which suggests that theories may have empirical equivalents between which no evidence can decide (Earman 1993; Laudan and Leplin 1991). Both considerations tend to undermine claims for the reality of the objects of scientific investigation and the truth of scientific theories.

In response, some philosophers have suggested that realism confine itself to a doctrine about the independent existence of theoretical entities ("entity realism") without commitment to the truth of the theories employing them. There are several proposals of this sort concerning which entities to advance as real. We might promote only those entities that are used experimentally to generate new knowledge or, more generally, only those we regard as causal agents (Cartwright 1983; Hacking 1983). We might take only those that prove fruitful enough to survive scientific revolutions (McMullin 1987), or only those essential in specific cases of explanatory or predictive success (Kitcher 1993) or only those entities that stand out as supported by especially excellent scientific evidence (Newton-Smith 1989). Finally, we might just plead that surely *some* entities must be real, without specifying which ones (Devitt 1984). Unfortunately for entity realism, it is not clear that such criteria overcome the strategies that challenge realism in general. In particular these proposals do not seem to discriminate effectively between real entities and reliable

(or useful) constructs—and so between realism and instrumentalism (Fine 1986).

A number of fresh alternatives to realism have developed recently. Principal among them are Putnam's "internal realism" (1981, 1990), van Fraassen's "constructive empiricism" (1980), and what Fine calls the "natural ontological attitude," or NOA (1996). Internal realism is a perspectival position allowing that scientific claims are true from certain perspectives but denying that science tells the whole story, or even that there is a whole story to tell. There could be other versions of the truth—different stories about the world—each of which it may be proper to believe. Van Fraassen's constructive empiricism eschews belief in favor of what he calls commitment. In contrast with realism, constructive empiricism takes empirical adequacy (not truth) as the goal of science, and when it accepts a theory it accepts it only as empirically adequate. This involves commitment to working within the framework of the theory but not to believing in its literal truth. Fine's NOA is a minimal attitude that urges critical attention to local practice without imposing general interpretive agendas on science, such as goals for science as a whole or blanket empiricist limitations on knowledge. NOA regards truth as basic but, seeing science as open, it challenges general prescriptions for scientific truth, including the perspectivalism built into internal realism and the external-world correspondence built into realism itself. Despite their differences, these alternatives share with realism a basically positive attitude toward science. A contrary suspicion attaches to constructivism (Barnes, Bloor, and Henry 1996; Galison and Stump 1996; Latour 1987; Pickering 1984; Searle 1995).

Constructivism opposes realism's claim that in order to understand science we must take scientists to be exploring a world not of their own making. Inspired by developments in the history and sociology of science, it maintains instead that scientific knowledge is socially constituted and that "facts" are made by us. Constructivism emphasizes agency and (like NOA) sees unforced judgments throughout scientific activity. In their studies constructivists bracket the truth-claims of the activity under investigation and try to address scientific practice using little more than common sense psychology and an everyday pragmatism with respect to the familiar objects of experience. To the extent to which these studies succeed in understanding science they paint a picture quite different from realism's, a dynamic and open picture that challenges not only the arguments but also the intuitions on which scientific realism rests.

See also EPISTEMOLOGY AND COGNITION; NATURAL KINDS; RATIONALISM VS. EMPIRICISM

—*Arthur Fine*

References

Barnes, B., D. Bloor, and J. Henry. (1996). *Scientific Knowledge: A Sociological Analysis.* Chicago: University of Chicago Press.

Boyd, R. (1992). Constructivism, realism and philosophical method. In J. Earman, Ed., *Inference, Explanation and Other Frustrations.* Berkeley: University of California Press, pp. 131–198.

Cartwright, N. (1983). *How The Laws of Physics Lie.* New York: Clarendon Press.

Devitt, M. (1984). *Realism and Truth.* Princeton: Princeton University Press.

Earman, J. (1993). Underdetermination, realism and reason. *Midwest Studies in Philosophy* 18: 19–38.

Fine, A. (1986). Unnatural attitudes: Realist and instrumentalist attachments to science. *Mind* 95: 149–179.

Fine, A. (1996). *The Shaky Game: Einstein, Realism and the Quantum Theory.* 2nd ed. Chicago: University of Chicago Press.

Galison, P., and D. Stump, Eds. (1996). *The Disunity of Science: Boundaries, Contexts, and Power.* Stanford: Stanford University Press.

Hacking, I. (1983). *Representing and Intervening.* Cambridge: Cambridge University Press.

Kitcher, P. (1993). *The Advancement of Science.* Oxford: Oxford University Press.

Latour, B. (1987). *Science in Action.* Cambridge, MA: Harvard University Press.

Laudan, L. (1981). A confutation of convergent realism. *Philosophy of Science* 48: 19–49.

Laudan, L., and J. Leplin. (1991). Empirical equivalence and underdetermination. *Journal of Philosophy* 88: 449–472.

Lipton, P. (1991). *Inference to the Best Explanation.* London: Routledge.

McMullin, E. (1987). Explanatory success and the truth of theory. In N. Rescher, Ed., *Scientific Inquiry in Philosophical Perspective.* Lanham: University Press of America, pp. 51–73.

Newton-Smith, W. (1989). Modest realism. In A. Fine and J. Leplin, Eds., *PSA 1988,* vol. 2. E. Lansing, MI: Philosophy of Science Association, pp.179–189.

Pickering, A. (1984). *Constructing Quarks: A Sociological History of Particle Physics.* Chicago: University of Chicago Press.

Psillos, S. (1996). Scientific realism and the pessimistic induction. *Philosophy of Science* 63 Supplement: S306–S314.

Putnam, H. (1975). *Mathematics, Matter and Method,* vol. 1. Cambridge: Cambridge University Press.

Putnam, H. (1981). *Reason, Truth and History.* Cambridge: Cambridge University Press.

Putnam, H. (1990). *Realism with A Human Face.* Cambridge, MA: Harvard University Press.

Searle, J. (1995). *The Construction of Social Reality.* New York: Free Press.

Smart, J. C. C. (1963). *Philosophy and Scientific Realism.* London: Routledge and Kegan Paul.

van Fraassen, B. C. (1980). *The Scientific Image.* Oxford: Clarendon Press.

Further Readings

Blackburn, S. (1993). *Essays in Quasi-Realism.* Oxford: Oxford University Press.

Churchland, P. M., and C. A. Hooker, Eds. (1985). *Images of Science.* Chicago: University of Chicago Press.

Devitt, M. (1983). Realism and the renegade Putnam. *Nous* 17: 291–301.

Giere, R. (1987). *Explaining Science: A Cognitive Approach.* Chicago: University of Chicago Press.

Hollis, M., and S. Lukes, Eds. (1982). *Rationality and Relativism.* Oxford: Blackwell.

Kukla, A. (1996). Antirealist explanations of the success of science. *Philosophy of Science* 63 Supplement: S298–S305.

Leplin, J., Ed. (1984). *Scientific Realism.* Berkeley: University of California Press.

Leplin, J. (1997). *A Novel Defense of Scientific Realism.* New York: Oxford University Press.

Miller, R. W. (1987). *Fact and Method.* Princeton: Princeton University Press.

Morrison, M. (1988). Reduction and realism. In A. Fine and J. Leplin, Eds., *PSA* 1988, vol. 1. E. Lansing, MI: Philosophy of Science Association, pp. 286–293.

Papineau, D., Ed. (1996). *The Philosophy of Science.* Oxford: Oxford University Press.

Popper, K. (1972). Three views concerning human knowledge. Reprinted in *Conjectures and Refutations.* London: Routledge and Kegan Paul, pp. 97–119.

Rosen, G. (1994). What is constructive empiricism? *Philosophical Studies* 74: 143–178.

Rouse, J. (1996). *Engaging Science: How To Understand Its Practices Philosophically.* Ithaca, NY: Cornell University Press.

Reasoning

See CAUSAL REASONING; DEDUCTIVE REASONING; INDUCTION; PROBABILISTIC REASONING

Recognition

See FACE RECOGNITION; OBJECT RECOGNITION, ANIMAL STUDIES; OBJECT RECOGNITION, HUMAN NEUROPSYCHOLOGY; VISUAL OBJECT RECOGNITION, AI

Recording from Single Neurons

See SINGLE-NEURON RECORDING

Recurrent Networks

NEURAL NETWORKS are generally broken down into two broad categories: feedforward networks and recurrent networks. Roughly speaking, feedforward networks are networks without cycles (see PATTERN RECOGNITION AND FEEDFORWARD NETWORKS) and recurrent networks are networks with one or more cycles. The presence of cycles in a network leads naturally to an analysis of the network as a dynamic system, in which the state of the network at one moment in time depends on the state at the previous moment in time. In some cases, however, it is more natural to view the cycles as providing a specification of simultaneous constraints that the nodes of the network must satisfy, a point of view that need not involve any analysis of time-varying behavior. These two points of view can in principle be reconciled by thinking of the constraints as specifying the equilibrium states of a dynamic system.

Let us begin by considering recurrent networks which admit an analysis in terms of equilibrium states. These networks, which include *Hopfield networks* and *Boltzmann machines,* are generally specified as *undirected graphs,* that is, graphs in which the presence of a connection from node S_i to node S_j implies a connection from node S_j to node S_i (see figure 1). The graph may be completely connected or partially connected; we will consider some of the implications associated with particular choices of connectivity later in the article.

A Hopfield network is an undirected graph in which each node is binary (i.e., for each i, $S_i \in \{-1,1\}$), and each link is

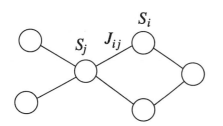

Figure 1. A generic undirected recurrent network, in which the presence of a connection from node S_i to node S_j implies a connection from node S_j to node S_i. The value of the weight J_{ij} is equal to J_{ji} by assumption.

labeled with a real-valued *weight* J_{ij}. Because the graph is undirected, J_{ij} and J_{ji} refer to the same link and thus are equal by assumption.

A Hopfield network also comes equipped with an *energy function E,* which can be viewed intuitively as a measure of the "consistency" of the nodes and the weights. The energy is defined as follows:

$$E = -\sum_{i<j} J_{ij} S_i S_j \tag{1}$$

Consider, for example, the case in which J_{ij} is positive. If S_i and S_j have the same value, then the energy is more negative (because of the minus sign), whereas if S_i and S_j have opposite values, then the energy is more positive. The opposite statements hold when J_{ij} is negative. Negative energy is "good," that is, it means that the nodes are more consistent with each other (with respect to the weights).

Let us define the "state" of the network to be an assignment of values to the nodes of the network. For Hopfield networks with N nodes this is simply a string of N bits.

Hopfield (1982) showed that the states of minimum energy are equilibrium states of a simple dynamic law known as the *perceptron* rule. In particular, suppose that at each moment in time a particular node i is chosen and that node updates its value as follows:

$$S_i = \begin{cases} 1 & \text{if } \sum_j J_{ij} S_j > 0 \\ -1 & \text{otherwise} \end{cases} \tag{2}$$

After a finite number of such updates the network will find itself in a state that is a local minimum of the energy E and it will no longer move from that state.

Hopfield networks can be utilized to perform a number of information-processing tasks. One such task is that of CONSTRAINT SATISFACTION. Here the weights J_{ij} are set, either by design or via a learning algorithm (see MACHINE LEARNING), to encode a particular set of desired constraints between nodes. Minimizing the energy corresponds to finding a state in which as many of the constraints are met as possible. Another task is *associative memory,* in which the minima of the energy function are viewed as memories to be retrieved. The updating of the system according to Eq. (2) corresponds to the "cleaning up" of corrupted memories. Finally, Hopfield networks can be used for optimization applications; in such applications the weights are chosen by design so that the energy E is equal to the quantity that it is desired to optimize.

The formulation of the Hopfield model in the early 1980s was followed by the development of the Boltzmann machine (Hinton and Sejnowski 1986), which is essentially a probabilistic version of the Hopfield network. The move to probabilities has turned out to be significant; it has led to the development of new algorithms for UNSUPERVISED LEARNING and SUPERVISED LEARNING, and to more efficient algorithms for Hopfield networks.

A Boltzmann machine is characterized by a probability distribution across the states of a Hopfield network. This distribution, known as the *Boltzmann distribution,* is the exponential of the negative of the energy of the state:

$$P(S_1, S_2, ..., S_N) = \frac{e^{-E/T}}{Z} \tag{3}$$

where Z is a normalizing constant (the sum across all states of the numerator), and T is a scaling constant. The Boltzmann distribution gives higher probability to states with lower energy, but does not rule out states with high energy. As T goes to zero, the lower energy states become the only ones with significant probability and the Boltzmann machine reduces to a Hopfield network.

There are three basic methods that have been used for calculating probabilities for Boltzmann machines: *exact calculation, Monte Carlo simulation,* and *mean field methods.*

Exact calculation methods are generally based on recursive procedures for transforming or eliminating nodes. One such method, known as decimation, is based on the fact that it is possible to remove, or "decimate," a node lying between a pair of other nodes, replacing the removed node with its weights by a single "effective" weight, while maintaining the same marginal probability on the remaining pair of nodes (Saul and Jordan 1994). For graphs with a chain-like or tree-like connectivity pattern, this procedure can be applied recursively to provide a general method for calculating probabilities under the Boltzmann distribution. There are interesting links between this procedure and exact algorithms for HIDDEN MARKOV MODELS and other more general probabilistic graphs known as BAYESIAN NETWORKS (Lauritzen 1996).

Monte Carlo simulation implements a stochastic search among states, biasing the search toward states of high probability (see also GREEDY LOCAL SEARCH). One simple Monte Carlo procedure is known as "Gibbs sampling" (Geman and Geman 1984). It turns out that Gibbs sampling for the Boltzmann machine is equivalent to the use of the perceptron rule [Eq. (2)] with a noisy threshold. Gibbs sampling was the method proposed in the original paper on the Boltzmann machine (Hinton and Sejnowski 1986). To speed the search, Hinton and Sejnowski also proposed the use of "simulated annealing," in which the temperature T is started at a high value and gradually decreased.

Finally, mean field methods take advantage of the fact that in networks that have dense connectivity each node has a value (under the Boltzmann distribution) that is well determined by its neighbors (by the law of large numbers). Thus it is possible to find and to exploit approximate deterministic

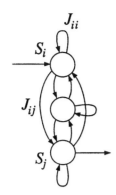

Figure 2. A generic recurrent network. The presence of cycles in the graph distinguishes these networks from the class of feedforward networks. Note that there is no requirement of reciprocity as in the Hopfield or Boltzmann networks.

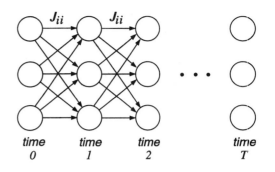

Figure 3. An "unrolled" recurrent network. The nodes S_i in the recurrent network in Figure 2 are copied in each of $T + 1$ time slices. These copies represent the time-varying activations $S_i[t]$. The weights in each slice are time-invariant; they are copies of the corresponding weights in the original network. Thus, for example, the weights between the topmost nodes in each slice are all equal to J_{ii}, the value of the weight from unit S_i to itself in the original network.

constraints between nodes. The resulting equations of constraint, known as "mean field equations," generally turn out to once again have the form of the perceptron update rule, although the sharp decision of Eq. (2) is replaced with a smoother nonlinear function (Peterson and Anderson 1987).

Mean field methods can also be utilized with decreasing T. If T is decreased to zero, this idea, referred to as "deterministic annealing," can be applied to the Hopfield network. In fact deterministic annealing has become the method of choice for the update of Hopfield networks, replacing the simple dynamics of Eq. (2).

General recurrent networks are usually specified by drawing a *directed graph* (see figure 2). In such graphs, arbitrary connectivity patterns are allowed; that is, there is no requirement that nodes are connected reciprocally. We associate a real-valued *weight* J_{ij} with the link from node j to node i, letting J_{ij} equal zero if there is no link.

At time t, the ith node in the network has an activation value $S_i[t]$, which can either be a discrete value or a continuous value. Generally the focus is on discrete-time systems (see also AUTOMATA), in which t is a discrete index, although continuous-time systems are also studied (see also CONTROL THEORY). The update rule defining the dynamics of the network is typically of the following form:

$$S_i[t + 1] = f\left(\sum_j J_{ij}S_j[t]\right), \qquad (3)$$

where the function f is generally taken to be a smooth nonlinear function.

General recurrent networks can show complex patterns of dynamic behavior (including limit cycles and chaotic patterns), and it is difficult to place conditions on the weights J_{ij} that guarantee particular kinds of desired behavior. Thus, researchers interested in time-varying behavior of recurrent networks have generally utilized learning algorithms as a method of "programming" the network by providing examples of desired behavior (Giles, Kuhn, and Williams 1994).

A general purpose learning algorithm for recurrent networks, known as *backpropagation-in-time,* can be obtained

by a construction that "unrolls" the recurrent network (Rumelhart et al. 1986). The unrolled network has $T + 1$ layers of N nodes each, obtained by copying the N of the recurrent network at every time step from $t = 0$ to $t = T$ (see figure 3). The connections in the unrolled network are feedforward connections that are copies of the recurrent connections in the original network. The result is an unrolled network that is a standard feedforward network. Applying the standard algorithm for feedforward networks, in particular backpropagation, yields the backpropagation-in-time algorithm.

Backpropagation-in-time and similar algorithms have a general difficulty in training networks to hold information over lengthy time intervals (Bengio, Simard, and Frasconi 1994). Essentially, gradient-based methods utilize the derivative of the state transition function of the dynamic system, and for systems that are able to hold information over lengthy intervals this derivative tends rapidly to zero. Many new ideas in recurrent network research, including the use of embedded memories and particular forms of prior knowledge, have arisen as researchers have tried to combat this problem (Frasconi et al. 1995; Omlin and Giles 1996).

Finally, there has been substantial work on the use of recurrent networks to represent finite automata and the problem of learning regular languages (Giles et al. 1992).

—Michael I. Jordan

References

Bengio, Y., P. Simard, and P. Frasconi. (1994). Learning long-term dependencies with gradient descent is difficult. *IEEE Transactions on Neural Networks* 5: 157–166.

Frasconi, P., M. Gori, M. Maggini, and G. Soda. (1995). Unified integration of explicit rules and learning by example in recurrent networks. *IEEE Transactions on Knowledge and Data Engineering* 7: 340–346.

Geman, S., and D. Geman. (1984). Stochastic relaxation, Gibbs distributions, and the Bayesian restoration of images. *IEEE Transactions on Pattern Analysis and Machine Intelligence* 6: 721–741.

Giles, C. L., G. M. Kuhn, and R. J. Williams. (1994). Dynamic recurrent neural networks: Theory and applications. *IEEE Transactions on Neural Networks* 5: 153–156.

Giles, C. L., C. B. Miller, D. Chen, H. H. Chen, G. Z. Sun, and Y. L. C. Lee. (1992). Learning and extracting finite state automata with second-order recurrent neural networks. *Neural Computation* 4: 393–401.

Hinton, G. E., and T. Sejnowski. (1986). Learning and relearning in Boltzmann machines. In D. E. Rumelhart and J. L. McClelland, Eds., *Parallel Distributed Processing*, vol. 1. Cambridge, MA: MIT Press, pp. 282–317.

Hopfield, J. J. (1982). Neural networks and physical systems with emergent collective computational abilities. *Proceedings of the National Academy of Sciences* 79: 2554–2558.

Lauritzen, S. L. (1996). *Graphical Models*. Oxford: Oxford University Press.

Omlin, C. W., and C. L. Giles. (1996). Extraction of rules from discrete-time recurrent neural networks. *Neural Networks* 9: 41–79.

Peterson, C., and J. R. Anderson. (1987). A mean field theory learning algorithm for neural networks. *Complex Systems* 1: 995–1019.

Rumelhart, D. E., G. E. Hinton, and R. J. Williams. (1986). Learning internal representations by error propagation. In D. E. Rumelhart and J. L. McClelland, Eds., *Parallel Distributed Processing*, vol. 1. Cambridge, MA: MIT Press.

Saul, L. K., and M. I. Jordan. (1994). Learning in Boltzmann trees. *Neural Computation* 6: 1174–1184.

Further Readings

Amit, D. (1989). *Modelling Brain Function*. Cambridge: Cambridge University Press.

Cohen, M., and S. Grossberg. (1983). Absolute stability of global pattern formation and parallel memory storage by competitive neural networks. *IEEE Transactions on Systems, Man, and Cybernetics* 13: 815–826.

Elman, J. (1990). Finding structure in time. *Cognitive Science* 14: 179–211.

Haykin, S. (1994). *Neural Networks: A Comprehensive Foundation*. New York: Macmillan.

Hertz, J., A. Krogh, and R. G. Palmer. (1991). *Introduction to the Theory of Neural Computation*. Redwood City, CA: Addison-Wesley.

Jensen, F. (1996). *An Introduction to Bayesian Networks*. London: UCL Press (also published by Springer-Verlag).

Jordan, M. I. (1997). Serial order: A parallel, distributed processing approach. In J. W. Donahoe and V. P. Dorsel, Eds., *Neural Network Models of Cognition: A Biobehavioral Approach*. Amsterdam: Elsevier.

Jordan, M. I., and C. Bishop. (1997). Neural networks. In A. B. Tucker, Ed., *CRC Handbook of Computer Science*. Boca Raton, FL: CRC Press.

Jordan, M. I., and D. E. Rumelhart. (1992). Forward models: Supervised learning with a distal teacher. *Cognitive Science* 16: 307–354.

Lang, K. J., A. H. Waibel, and G. E. Hinton. (1990). A time-delay neural network architecture for isolated word recognition. *Neural Networks* 3: 23–43.

Mozer, M. C. (1994). Neural net architectures for temporal sequence processing. In A. S. Weigend and N. A. Gershenfeld, Eds., *Time Series Prediction*. Redwood City, CA: Addison-Wesley, pp. 243–264.

Pearlmutter, B. A. (1989). Learning state space trajectories in recurrent neural networks. *Neural Computation* 1: 263–269.

Rabiner, L. R. (1989). A tutorial on Hidden Markov models and selected applications in speech recognition. *Proceedings of the IEEE* 77: 257–286.

Schmidhuber, J. (1992). Learning complex, extended sequences using the principle of history compression. *Neural Computation* 4: 234–242.

Smyth, P., D. Heckerman, and M. I. Jordan. (Forthcoming). Probabilistic independence networks for hidden Markov probability models. *Neural Computation* to appear.

Tsoi, A. C., and A. Back. (1994). Locally recurrent globally feed-forward networks: A critical review of architectures. *IEEE Transactions on Neural Networks* 5: 229-239.

Williams, R. J. (1989). A learning algorithm for continually running fully recurrent neural networks. *Neural Computation* 1: 270–280.

Reductionism

Reductionism is the position that holds that theories or things of one sort can exhaustively account for theories or things of another sort. So, for example, reductionism within the cognitive sciences holds that neuroscientific theories will explain the success of psychological theories and, therefore, will reveal that psychological states and processes are nothing but bodily states and processes.

Traditional reductionism within the philosophy of science (Nagel 1961/1979) especially emphasizes some theories' abilities to explain others. It focuses on theories' formal linguistic structures and endorses a model of EXPLANATION that requires that the reduced theory's laws follow deductively from the reducing theory's laws in combination with *bridge laws* that connect the two theories' predicates.

According to more ambitious reductionism, successful reductive explanation in *any* science allegedly reveals the in-principle dispensability of the reduced theory and its ontology. PHYSICALISM in the philosophy of mind anticipates a *comprehensive* reduction of just this kind for our best psychological theories. Both reductionism generally and psychology's reducibility in particular remain controversial.

Reductionistic analyses presuppose that a hierarchy of *analytical* (or *explanatory*) *levels* in science—encompassing the psychological and sociocultural sciences at its highest levels and the physical sciences at its lowest—duplicates a hierarchy of *organizational levels* in nature (Wimsatt 1976). Associated with each organizational level is a distinctive ontology and with each analytical level a distinctive set of theoretical concepts, explanatory principles, and investigative techniques. Traditional reductionism promotes a theoretical and ontological UNITY OF SCIENCE based on a series of reductive explanations of the theories at each level by the theories at the next lower level so that all theories in science, finally, are reducible to, which is to say, explained by, the theories of physics.

Bridge laws establish systematic connections between the predicates of the reduced and reducing theories. The more stringent the reductionism the more stringent the envisioned connections are. *Minimally,* bridge laws specify lower-level conditions sufficient for upper-level patterns. Such minimal bridge laws would be conditional in form; for example, if humans have a deficiency of noradrenaline in parts of their limbic systems, then they will experience depression. Under such circumstances reduction proves limited in scope, inasmuch as such bridge laws are domain specific. (Other conditions might suffice for depression as well.)

Reductionists are often more ambitious, seeking grounds not just for explaining the upper-level theory but also for claiming that its entities are "nothing but" configurations of lower-level entities. The reducing theory should replace the upper-level theory without explanatory or ontological loss. Because conditions sufficient for a reductive explanation do not guarantee these ontological consequences (Richardson 1979), reductionists seeking ontological economies (Causey 1977) in addition to explanatory consolidation argue that only *identities* between the theories' predicates will suffice as bridge principles. Such bridge laws amount to empirical hypotheses that initiate new lines of research. Consider, for example, the wealth of new hypotheses concerning the neural mechanisms constituting consciousness.

The identity theory of mind, which resolves the MIND-BODY PROBLEM by holding that mental states simply *are* brain states, is harmonious with ambitious reductionists' goals. The identity theory avoids the explanatory and metaphysical complexities that dualism introduces. It preserves MENTAL CAUSATION by identifying mental operations with the neural processes that are causally implicated in behavior.

The identity theory presumes many of the conditions necessary for reducing psychology to neuroscience; however, two controversies surround the presumption that all psychological states can be identified with neural ones. First, proponents of non-reductive theories of consciousness insist that no sort of physical information about the brain can explain how conscious mental states *feel*. The identity theory's defenders respond by showing how neurocomputational findings explain some intuitions about the similarity and relative intensity of QUALIA (Churchland 1989).

The second controversy concerns whether most *types* of states to which commonsense or FOLK PSYCHOLOGY appeals are readily identifiable with *types* of brain states. Most philosophers think not, citing numerous considerations to defend that conclusion. The critical question concerns what they make of that failure of systematic intertheoretic mapping.

Those who hold to ELIMINATIVE MATERIALISM exceed reductionists in their confidence in the explanatory sufficiency of neuroscience. They contend that this mapping failure impugns folk psychology, which—in the face of neuroscience's superior merits and promise—deserves eradication (Churchland 1989). Like traditional reductionists, eliminativists assume that one account of intertheoretic relations suffices to model not just interlevel relations but changes in theoretical commitments within particular levels too. Some question that assumption and whether theory eradication in science on the scale that eliminativists anticipate ever actually arises in interlevel contexts (McCauley 1986).

Accepting *token identities* of the mental with the physical, others interpret this failure of systematic mapping as support not for adopting a more radical eliminativism, but for repudiating psychology's reducibility. ANOMALOUS MONISM contends that *psycho-physical laws* are impossible, because evolving ideals of rationality partially control our use of intentional concepts. Fodor (1981) argues that PSY-CHOLOGICAL LAWS are not exceptionless and that the *multiple realizability* of psychological types is widespread, resulting in uninformative bridge principles with lengthy disjunctions of neural types that might realize some psychological type. Both considerations impede reduction and favor the AUTONOMY OF PSYCHOLOGY. Because psychological explanations rely on *intentional contents,* reductionism's requirements fail to guarantee their subsumption by neuroscience. Fodor claims that reducing psychology requires demonstrating that neural states instantiate a code but that this yields a neuroscience unamenable to further reduction.

Noting reductionism's restrictiveness in accounting for cross-scientific relations, opponents of the autonomy of psychology are untroubled by mapping failures. Paul Churchland stresses approximate reduction, where lower-level theories preserve an equipotent image of upper-level theories without comprehensive mapping. Patricia Churchland (1986) emphasizes how *coevolving* theories will often prove mutually instructive—yielding progressively better mappings.

Others have adopted even more pragmatic approaches, advocating *integrative models* of cross-scientific relations (Bechtel 1986). Examining issues of discovery, evidence, method, and more, they foresee many illuminating relationships (besides possible reductions) between psychological, neurocomputational, and neuroscientific models (McCauley 1996). Within some suitably restricted domains reductions of some psychological principles *are* possible (Bickle 1995), but Bechtel and Richardson (1993) argue that the chief goal of reductionistic research is the discovery and explication of the mechanisms underlying the functioning of complex systems. Integrative modelers pursue analyses showing how upper-level research often plays central roles in *justifying* lower-level proposals (McCauley 1996), motivating innovative research at intermediate levels (such as connectionist modeling), and stimulating research in what Hardcastle (1996) calls "bridge sciences" (such as event-related potential studies). Compared to standard reductionism, these integrative models examine a wider range of the cross-scientific relations that arise in the sort of interdisciplinary research characteristic of cognitive science.

—*Robert McCauley*

References

Bechtel, W., Ed. (1986). *Integrating Scientific Disciplines.* The Hague: Martinus Nijhoff.

Bechtel, W., and R. C. Richardson. (1993). *Discovering Complexity.* Princeton: Princeton University Press.

Bickle, J. (1995). Psychoneural reduction of the genuinely cognitive: Some accomplished results. *Philosophical Psychology* 8: 265–285.

Causey, R. (1977). *Unity of Science.* Dordrecht: Reidel.

Churchland, P. M. (1989). *A Neurocomputational Perspective.* Cambridge, MA: MIT Press.

Churchland, P. S. (1986). *Neurophilosophy.* Cambridge, MA: MIT Press.

Fodor, J. A. (1981). *Representations.* Cambridge, MA: MIT Press.

Hardcastle, V. G. (1996). *How to Build a Theory in Cognitive Science.* Albany: SUNY Press.

McCauley, R. N. (1986). Intertheoretic relations and the future of psychology. *Philosophy of Science* 53: 179–199.

McCauley, R. N. (1996). Explanatory pluralism and the coevolution of theories in science. In R. N. McCauley, Ed., *The Churchlands and Their Critics*. Oxford: Blackwell.

Nagel, E. (1961/1979). *The Structure of Science*. Indianapolis: Hackett.

Richardson, R. (1979). Functionalism and reductionism. *Philosophy of Science* 46: 533–558.

Wimsatt, W. (1976). Reductionism, levels of organization, and the mind-body problem. In G. Globus, G. Maxwell, and I. Savodnik, Eds., *Consciousness and the Brain*. New York: Plenum Press.

Further Readings

Bechtel, W. (1988). *Philosophy of Science: An Overview for Cognitive Science*. Hillsdale, NJ: Erlbaum.

Beckermann, A., H. Flohr, and J. Kim, Eds. (1992). *Emergence or Reduction? Essays on the Prospects of Nonreductive Physicalism*. New York: de Gruyter.

Bickle, J. (1995). Connectionism, reduction, and multiple realizability. *Behavior and Philosophy* 23: 29–39.

Bickle, J. (1998). *Psychoneural Reduction: The New Wave*. Cambridge, MA: MIT Press.

Burton, R. G. (1993). Reduction, elimination, and strategic interdependence. In R. G. Burton, Ed., *Natural and Artificial Minds*. Albany: SUNY Press.

Clark, A. (1980). *Psychological Models and Neural Mechanisms: An Examination of Reductionism in Psychology*. Oxford: Clarendon Press.

Churchland, P. M., and P. S. Churchland. (1990). Intertheoretic reduction: A neuroscientist's field guide. *Seminars in the Neurosciences* 2: 249–256.

Hardcastle, V. G. (1992). Reduction, explanatory extension, and the mind/brain sciences. *Philosophy of Science* 59: 408–428.

Hardcastle, V. G. (1996). Discovering the moment of consciousness? 1: Bridging techniques at work. *Philosophical Psychology* 9: 149–166.

Hooker, C. (1981). Towards a general theory of reduction. *Dialogue* 20: 38–59, 201–236, 496–529.

McCauley, R. N. (1993). Cross-scientific study and the complexity of psychology. In H. V. Rappard and L. P. Mos, Eds., *Annals of Theoretical Psychology*, vol. 9. New York: Plenum Press.

Putnam, H. (1973). Reductionism and the nature of psychology. *Cognition* 2: 131–46.

Richardson, R. C. (1980). Reductionist research programmes in psychology. *PSA 1980* 1: 171–183.

Schaffner, K. F. (1993). *Discovery and Explanation in Biology and Medicine*. Chicago: University of Chicago Press.

Schwartz, J. (1991). Reduction, elimination, and the mental. *Philosophy of Science* 58: 203–220.

Reference, Theories of

Referential relations hold between representations and the world; in particular, they hold between parts of sentences and the world and between parts of thoughts and the world (see LANGUAGE AND THOUGHT). The most striking example of such a relation is the *naming* relation, the sort that holds between "Babe Ruth" and the famous baseballer. However, it is usual to think of reference as covering a range of semantically significant relations; for example, between the word "dead" and deadness, and between the concept <bachelor> and all bachelors. Other expressions used for one or another of these relations include: "designate," "denote," "signify," "apply," "satisfy," "instantiate," "fall under," and "about."

Reference is important because it is thought to be the core of meaning and content. Thus, the fact that "Babe Ruth" refers to that famous baseballer is the core of its meaning and hence of its contribution to the meaning of any sentence—for example, "Babe Ruth is dead"—that contains it. And the fact that <bachelor> refers to all bachelors is the core of its content and hence of its contribution to the content of any thought—for example, <Babe Ruth is not a bachelor>—that contains it.

The central question about reference is: In virtue of what does a representation have its reference? Answering this requires a theory that explains the representation's relation to its referent. There has been a great surge of interest in theories of reference in the twentieth century.

Description theories are one sort. According to these theories, the reference of a representation is determined by certain descriptions associated with it by competent speakers; these descriptions *identify* the referent. The simplest form of description theory specifies a set of descriptions each of which is necessary and all of which are sufficient for reference determination (FREGE 1893; Russell 1912); for example, the reference of "adult," "unmarried," and "male" might be jointly sufficient and severally necessary for the reference of "bachelor." This theory calls to mind what is known in psychology as the "classical" theory of concepts. According to another form of description theory, the reference is whatever is picked out by (a weighted) *most* of certain descriptions associated with the representation. On this "cluster" theory, no one description is necessary for reference fixing (Searle 1958). Cluster theories call to mind theories of CONCEPTS known in psychology as "family resemblance," "prototype," and "exemplar."

Around 1970, several criticisms were made of description theories of proper names—for example, "Babe Ruth" (Kripke 1980; Donnellan 1972)—and natural-kind words—for example, "gold" and "tiger" (Kripke 1980; Putnam 1975). Perhaps the most important are the arguments from ignorance and error. Speakers who seem perfectly able to use a word to refer are too ignorant to provide descriptions adequate to identify the referent; worse, speakers are often so wrong about the referent that the descriptions they provide apply not to the referent but to other entities or to nothing at all. Sometimes the whole speech community is ignorant or wrong about the referent. In brief, description theories of these words seem to require too much knowledge, to place too great an epistemic burden on speakers.

This is not to say that description theories fail for all representations: they still seem plausible for "bachelor," for example. But even where they work, description theories have a problem: they are *essentially incomplete*. Thus, suppose that a theory claims that the reference of "bachelor" is determined by the reference of "adult," "unmarried," and "male." We then need to explain the reference of those words to complete the explanation of the reference of "bachelor." Description theories might be offered again. But then the explanation will still be incomplete. At some point we must offer a theory of reference that does not make the reference of one word parasitic on that of others. We need an "ultimate" explanation of reference that relates some words directly to the world. Description theories pass the referential buck. The buck must stop somewhere if there is to be any reference at all.

This deep problem for description theories is brought out by Hilary Putnam's slogan, "Meanings just ain't in the *head*," which he supported with his famous TWIN EARTH fantasy (1975: 227; see also Burge 1979). The association of descriptions with a representation is an inner state of the speaker. No such inner state can make the representation refer to a particular referent. For that we must look for some relation that language and mind have to things outside themselves—we must look for an external relation.

"Verificationist" theories of reference implicitly acknowledge this point, having a broader view than description theories of the required identification: speakers refer to whatever objects they would identify as the referents, whether by description *or by recognition*. Speakers recognize a referent by pointing it out in a crowd saying, for example, "That person." But these theories still seem to place too great an epistemic burden on speakers: we can but dimly call to mind the appearances of many objects we refer to.

Attempts to explain the external relation have appealed to one or more of three causal relations between representations and reality. First, there is the *historical* cause of a particular token, a causal chain going back to the dubbing of the token's referent. Theorists interested in this have emphasized the "reference borrowing" links in the chain: in acquiring a word or concept from others we borrow their capacity to refer, even if we are ignorant of the referent (Kripke 1980; Donnellan 1972; Putnam 1975; Devitt 1981). Second, there is the *reliable* cause of tokens of that type: a token refers to objects of a certain sort because tokens of that type are reliably correlated with the presence of those objects. The token "carries the information" that a certain situation holds in much the same way that tree rings carry information about the age of a tree (Dretske 1981; Fodor 1990). Third, there is the *teleological* cause or *function* of tokens of that type, where the function is explained along Darwinian lines: the function is what tokens of that type do that explains why they exist, what the type has been "selected for" (Millikan 1984; Papineau 1987; Neander 1995).

See also INDIVIDUALISM; MEANING; NATURAL KINDS; SEMANTICS; SENSE AND REFERENCE

—*Michael Devitt*

References

Burge, T. (1979). Individualism and the mental. In P. A. French, T. E. Uehling, Jr., and H. K. Wettstein, Eds., *Midwest Studies in Philosophy*, vol. 10: *Studies in the Philosophy of Mind*. Minneapolis: University of Minnesota Press, pp. 73–121.

Devitt, M. (1981). *Designation*. New York: Columbia University Press.

Devitt, M., and K. Sterelny. (1999). *Language and Reality: An Introduction to the Philosophy of Language*. 2nd ed. Cambridge, MA: MIT Press.

Donnellan, K. S. (1972). Proper names and identifying descriptions. In D. Davidson and G. Harman, Eds., *The Semantics of Natural Language*. Dordrecht: Reidel, pp. 356–379.

Dretske, F. I. (1981). *Knowledge and the Flow of Information*. Cambridge, MA: MIT Press.

Fodor, J. A. (1990). *A Theory of Content and Other Essays*. Cambridge, MA: MIT Press.

Frege, G. (1893). On sense and reference. In P. Geach and M. Black, Eds., *Translations from the Philosophical Writings of Gottlob Frege* (1952). Oxford: Blackwell.

Kripke, S. A. (1980). *Naming and Necessity*. Cambridge, MA: Harvard University Press.

Millikan, R. (1984). *Language, Thought, and Other Biological Categories*. Cambridge, MA: MIT Press.

Neander, K. (1995). Misrepresenting and malfunctioning. *Philosophical Studies* 79: 109–141.

Papineau, D. (1987). *Reality and Representation*. Oxford: Blackwell.

Putnam, H. (1975). *Mind, Language and Reality: Philosophical Papers,* vol. 2. Cambridge: Cambridge University Press.

Russell, B. (1912). *The Problems of Philosophy*. London: Oxford University Press, 1959.

Searle, J. R. (1958). Proper names. *Mind* 67: 166–173.

Further Readings

Chastain, C. (1975). Reference and context. In K. Gunderson, Ed., *Minnesota Studies in the Philosophy of Science.* 7, *Language, Mind and Knowledge.* Minneapolis: University of Minnesota Press, pp. 194–269.

Donnellan, K. S. (1966). Reference and definite descriptions. *Philosophical Review* 75: 281–304.

Dummett, M. (1973). Appendix: note on an attempted refutation of Frege. In *Frege: Philosophy of Language*. London: Duckworth, pp. 110–151.

Evans, G. (1973). The causal theory of names. *Proceedings of the Aristotelian Society* 47: 187–208.

Evans, G. (1982). *The varieties of reference*. Edited by J. McDowell. Oxford: Clarendon Press.

Field, H. (1973). Theory change and the indeterminacy of reference. *Journal of Philosophy* 70: 462–481.

Geach, P. (1962). *Reference and Generality*. Ithaca, NY: Cornell University Press.

Godfrey-Smith, P. (1992). Indication and adaptation. *Synthese* 92: 283–312.

Kaplan, D. (1989). Demonstratives: An essay on the semantics, logic, metaphysics, and epistemology of demonstratives and other indexicals. Afterthoughts. In J. Almog, J. Perry, and H. Wettstein, Eds., *Themes from Kaplan*. New York: Oxford University Press, pp. 481–614.

Kripke, S. A. (1979). Speaker's reference and semantic reference. In P. A. French, T. E. Uehling Jr., and H. K. Wettstein, Eds., *Contemporary Perspectives in the Philosophy of Language*. Minneapolis: University of Minnesota Press, pp. 6–27.

Mill, J. S. (1867). *A System of Logic*. London: Longmans.

Neale, S. (1990). *Descriptions*. Cambridge, MA: MIT Press.

Quine, W. V. (1960). *Word and Object*. Cambridge, MA: MIT Press.

Searle, J. R. (1983). *Intentionality: An Essay in the Philosophy of Mind*. Cambridge: Cambridge University Press.

Reinforcement Learning

Reinforcement learning is an approach to artificial intelligence that emphasizes learning by the individual from its interaction with its environment. This contrasts with classical approaches to artificial intelligence and MACHINE

LEARNING, which have downplayed learning from interaction, focusing instead on learning from a knowledgeable teacher, or on reasoning from a complete model of the environment. Modern reinforcement learning research is highly interdisciplinary; it includes researchers specializing in operations research, genetic algorithms, NEURAL NETWORKS, psychology, and control engineering.

Reinforcement learning is learning what to do—how to map situations to actions—so as to maximize a scalar reward signal. The learner is not told which action to take, as in most forms of machine learning, but instead must discover which actions yield the most reward by trying them. In the most interesting and challenging cases, actions may affect not only the immediate reward but also the next situation, and through that all subsequent rewards. These two characteristics—trial-and-error search and delayed reward—are the two most important distinguishing features of reinforcement learning.

One of the challenges that arises in reinforcement learning and not in other kinds of learning is the trade-off between exploration and exploitation. To obtain a lot of reward, a reinforcement learning agent must prefer actions that it has tried in the past and found to be effective in producing reward. But to discover which actions these are it has to select actions that it has not tried before. The agent has to *exploit* what it already knows in order to obtain reward, but it also has to *explore* in order to make better action selections in the future. The dilemma is that neither exploitation nor exploration can be pursued exclusively without failing at the task.

Modern reinforcement learning research uses the formal framework of *Markov decision processes* (MDPs). In this framework, the agent and environment interact in a sequence of discrete time steps, $t = 0, 1, 2, 3, \ldots$ On each step, the agent perceives the environment to be in a state, s_t, and selects an action, a_t. In response, the environment makes a stochastic transition to a new state, s_{t+1}, and stochastically emits a numerical reward, $r_{t+1} \in \Re$ (see figure 1). The agent seeks to maximize the reward it receives in the long run. For example, the most common objective is to choose each action a_t, so as to maximize the *expected discounted return:*

$$E\left\{ r_{t+1} + \gamma r_{t+2} + \gamma^2 r_{t+3} + \cdots \right\}$$

where γ is a discount-rate parameter, $0 \leq \gamma \leq 1$, akin to an interest rate in economics. This framework is intended to capture in a simple way essential features of the problem of

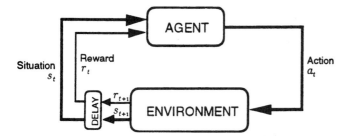

Figure 1. The Reinforcement learning framework.

learning from interaction and thus of the overall problem of artificial intelligence. It includes sensation and action, cause and effect, and an explicit goal involving affecting the environment. There is uncertainty both in the environment (because it is stochastic) and about the environment (because the environment's transition probabilities may not be fully known). Simple extensions of this problem include incomplete perception of the state of the environment and computational limitations. Most theoretical results about reinforcement learning apply to the special case in which the state and action spaces are finite, in which case the process is called a *finite MDP*.

Reinforcement learning methods attempt to improve the agent's decision-making policy over time. Formally, a policy is a mapping from states to actions, or to probability distributions over actions. The policy is stored in a relatively explicit fashion so that appropriate responses can be generated quickly in response to unexpected states. The policy is thus what is sometimes called a "universal plan" in artificial intelligence, a "control law" in CONTROL THEORY, or a set of "stimulus-response associations" in psychology. We can define the *value* of being in a state s under policy π as the expected discounted return starting in that state and following policy π. The function mapping all states to their values is called the state-value function for the policy:

$$V^\pi(s) = E_\pi\left\{ r_{t+1} + \gamma r_{t+2} + \gamma^2 r_{t+3} + \cdots \,\middle|\, s_t = s \right\}.$$

The values of states define a natural ordering on policies. Policy π is said to be better than or equal to policy π' iff $V^\pi(s) \geq V^{\pi'}(s)$ for all states s. For finite MDPs there are always one or more policies that are better than or equal to all others. These are the optimal policies, all of which share the same value function.

The simplest reinforcement learning algorithms apply directly to the agent's experience interacting with the environment, changing the policy in real time. For example, tabular one-step Q-learning, one of the simplest reinforcement learning algorithms, uses the experience of each state transition to update one element of a table. This table, denoted Q, has an entry, $Q(s,a)$, for each pair of state, s, and action, a. Upon the transition $s_t \to s_{t+1}$, having taken action and received reward r_{t+1}, this algorithm performs the update

$$Q(s_t, a_t) \leftarrow (1 - \alpha)Q(s_t, a_t)$$
$$+ \alpha[r_{t+1} + \gamma \max Q(s_{t+1}, a_t)]]$$

where α is a positive step-size parameter. Under appropriate conditions (ensuring sufficient exploration and reduction of α over time), this process converges such that the *greedy policy* with respect to Q is optimal. The greedy policy is to select in each state, s, the action, a, for which $Q(s,a)$ is largest. Thus, this algorithm provides a way of finding an optimal policy purely from experience, with no model of the environment's dynamics.

The algorithm described above is only the simplest of reinforcement learning methods. More sophisticated methods implement Q not as a table, but as a trainable parameterized function such as an artificial neural network. This enables generalization between states, which can greatly reduce learning time and memory requirements. Another common extension, *eligibility traces*, allows credit for a good state transition to spread more quickly to the states that preceded it, again resulting in faster learning. Continuous-time reinforcement learning problems require eligibility traces just as continuous-state or continuous-action problems require parameterized function approximators.

Reinforcement learning is also a promising approach to PLANNING and PROBLEM SOLVING. In this case, a model of the environment is used to simulate extensive interaction between it and the agent. This simulated experience is then processed by reinforcement learning methods just as if it had actually occurred. The result is a sort of "anytime planning," in which the agent's policy gradually improves over time and computational effort. Reinforcement learning methods appear most suited to planning problems that are too large or stochastic to be solved by conventional methods such as HEURISTIC SEARCH or DYNAMIC PROGRAMMING. This approach has already proved very effective in applications, having produced the best of all known methods for playing backgammon, dispatching elevators, assigning cellular radio channels, and scheduling space shuttle payload processing.

See also BEHAVIOR-BASED ROBOTICS; EVOLUTIONARY COMPUTATION; ROBOTICS AND LEARNING; SITUATEDNESS/EMBEDDEDNESS

—*Richard S. Sutton*

Further Readings

Bertsekas, D. P., and J. N. Tsitsiklis. (1996). *Neuro-Dynamic Programming*. Belmont, MA: Athena Scientific.

Kaelbling, L. P., Ed. (1996). Special issue on reinforcement learning. *Machine Learning* 22(1–3).

Kaelbling, L. P., M. L. Littman, and A. W. Moore. (1996). Reinforcement learning: A survey. *Journal of Artificial Intelligence Research* 4: 237–285.

Sutton, R. S., Ed. (1992). Special issue on reinforcement learning. *Machine Learning* 8.

Sutton, R. S., and A. G. Barto. (1998). *Reinforcement Learning: An Introduction*. Cambridge, MA: MIT Press.

Watkins, C. J. C. H., and P. Dayan. (1992). Q-learning. *Machine Learning* 8: 279–292.

Relational Grammar

Relational Grammar (RG) refers to a formal approach to SYNTAX that takes GRAMMATICAL RELATIONS like subject, direct object, and indirect object to be indispensable and primitive notions. According to Perlmutter (1980), they are indispensable for achieving three goals of linguistic theory:

1. to formulate linguistic universals
2. to characterize the class of grammatical constructions found in natural languages
3. to construct adequate and insightful grammars of individual languages

RG was motivated by syntactic work in a wide range of languages that revealed both language-particular and crosslinguistic generalizations involving subject and object. These included generalizations about morphological processes like agreement and case marking, semantic processes like the interpretation of anaphors, and grammatical processes like passive and relative clause formation. The earliest codified RG work (1974 lectures by David Perlmutter and Paul Postal; see Perlmutter and Postal 1983a, 1983b) argued that the relations subject, direct object, and indirect object were primitives because they could not be defined universally in terms of relations like linear order or dominance. These were the relations which formed the cornerstone of Transformational Grammar (TG), the prevailing theory of syntax in the early 1970s. The proposals of RG chiefly concern the relational structure of clauses.

Relational approaches to syntax were pursued in several forms during the mid-1970s, some a development of the ideas of Perlmutter and Postal, others a reaction to them (e.g., the papers in Cole and Sadock 1977). But the name "Relational Grammar" came to be associated with work that adheres to the program laid out by Perlmutter and Postal, work exemplified in Perlmutter 1983, Perlmutter and Rosen 1984, Postal and Joseph 1990; see Dubinsky and Rosen 1987 for a bibliography. RG, narrowly construed then, conceives of a clause as a network of grammatical relations. A clause might consist of a predicate, a subject, and a direct object. Under such a conception, two clauses that are superficially very different, perhaps because they are clauses from different languages, might in fact be structurally very similar. The fact that agreement, for example, is with the subject, whether the subject is clause-initial, clause-second, or clause-final, is directly statable and the parallelism between the two cases patent.

A crucial assumption of RG, inherited from TG, has been that the description of a clause refers not only to its superficial structure but also to a deeper structure and possibly to several intermediate levels of structure. In RG, these levels are called strata, and the RG position is that there is no one stratum at which all the properties associated with subject or object hold; rather these are apportioned at different strata. Relations in the initial stratum are linked to semantic role (e.g., agent, patient; Rosen 1984), whereas relations in the final stratum determine more superficial phenomena like agreement and word order. Clause pairs such as active/passive that express the same proposition in relationally different ways generally share the same initial stratum, accounting for their synonymy, but diverge in later strata (Perlmutter and Postal 1983a). The active sentence *the committee recommended us* has a single stratum, one in which *the committee* is subject and the pronoun *us* is direct object. The passive version, *we were recommended by the committee,* has, in addition, a second stratum in which *we* has been "advanced" to subject, and *the committee* "demoted" to an RG-specific relation called *chomeur* (= French "unemployed"). (This terminology reflects the relational hierarchy, a ranking of grammatical relations: subject > direct object > indirect object > other.) The diagrams in figure 1 represent these analyses. A and B are clausal nodes, and the grammatical relations borne by each element to the clause are organized into strata, represented by horizontal rows.

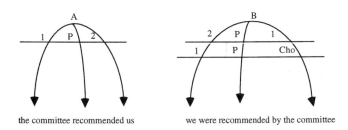

the committee recommended us   we were recommended by the committee

Figure 1. Active and Passive analyses.

Grammatical relations are represented by "1" = Subject, "2" = Direct Object, "Cho" = Chomeur, "P" = Predicate. Differences in word order and agreement between active and passive are due then to their different final strata. Universally, where grammatical relations determine word order, it is final stratum relations that are relevant. This generalization is deeply embedded in RG, which takes word order to be entirely irrelevant to nonfinal strata.

The demotion of the initial subject to chomeur in passive clauses reflects a universal principle of RG, the Stratal Uniqueness Law, which stipulates that a stratum may contain at most one subject, one direct object, and one indirect object. This law prevents the initial stratum subject in passive from persisting as subject when the direct object advances to subject. The fact that the chomeur in English passive is marked with *by* is, in contrast, a language-particular fact. RG has proposed an inventory of grammatical relations, and a set of principles ("laws") governing the well-formedness of networks (Perlmutter and Postal 1983b). The laws are linguistic universals (goal (1) above), and it is through the laws that RG proposes to characterize the class of grammatical constructions (goal (2)). Under certain conditions, the laws permit one nominal to assume the grammatical relation borne by another at a prior stratum, and they thereby define a typology of relation-changing constructions. Advancement to subject is seen in passive; advancement to direct object is also possible. In RG terms, *Every student gave the teacher a present* involves advancement of an indirect object, *the teacher,* to direct object. As direct object, it may advance further to subject in the passive version, *The teacher was given a present by every student.* The Stratal Uniqueness Law prevents the initial direct object from persisting as such when the indirect object advances to direct object. This explains why it cannot passivize: **A present was given the teacher by every student.* Also possible are demotions, as well as various kinds of clause merger (Davies and Rosen 1988). All these constructions are subject to the Stratal Uniqueness Law. The Stratal Uniqueness Law represents an empirically testable claim about syntactic organization and has not been uncontroversial (Perlmutter and Postal 1983b). Other important laws constrain the distribution of chomeurs and impose the requirement that the final stratum of every clause (but not necessarily any other stratum) have a subject (Perlmutter 1980; Perlmutter and Postal 1983b).

RG played an important part in the evolution of syntactic theory from the 1970s to the 1980s. During this period, languages other than English had significant impact on syntactic theorizing, leading to an increased appreciation of linguistic universals, and the need to distinguish more clearly between the universal and the language-particular. RG represents one early response to these issues, and it was extended in more formal work on Arc Pair Grammar (Johnson and Postal 1980). A number of ideas pioneered by RG were incorporated into other theories of the 1980s. The indispensability of grammatical relations has been a key assumption of LEXICAL FUNCTIONAL GRAMMAR, the disassociation of word order from more abstract syntactic representation was adopted in diverse guises by Lexical Functional Grammar and Generalized Phrase Structure Grammar, and the influential Unaccusative Hypothesis (Perlmutter 1978) was incorporated by Government Binding Theory (MINIMALISM). RG is currently pursued in Mapping Theory (Gerdts 1992), a relationally based typological approach to language difference.

See also ANAPHORA; COGNITIVE LINGUISTICS; GENERATIVE GRAMMAR; HEAD-DRIVEN PHRASE STRUCTURE GRAMMAR; MORPHOLOGY

—*Judith Aissen*

References

Cole, P., and J. Sadock, Eds. (1977). *Syntax and Semantics 8: Grammatical Relations.* New York: Academic Press.

Davies, W., and C. Rosen. (1988). Unions as multi-predicate clauses. *Language* 64: 52–88.

Dubinsky, S., and C. Rosen. (1987). *A Bibliography on Relational Grammar through May 1987 with Selected Titles on Lexical-Functional Grammar.* Bloomington, IN: Indiana University Linguistics Club.

Gerdts, D. (1992). Morphologically mediated relational profiles. *Proceedings of the Eighteenth Annual Meeting of the Berkeley Linguistics Society.* Berkeley, pp. 322–337.

Johnson, D., and P. Postal. (1980). *Arc Pair Grammar.* Princeton, NJ: Princeton University Press.

Perlmutter, D. (1978). Impersonal passives and the unaccusative hypothesis. *Proceedings of the Fourth Annual Meeting of the Berkeley Linguistics Society.* Berkeley, pp. 157–189.

Perlmutter, D. (1980). Relational grammar. In E. Moravcsik and J. Wirth, Eds., *Syntax and Semantics 13: Current Approaches to Syntax.* New York: Academic Press, pp. 195–229.

Perlmutter, D., Ed. (1983). *Studies in Relational Grammar* 1. Chicago: University of Chicago Press.

Perlmutter, D., and P. Postal. (1983a). Towards a universal characterization of passivization. In D. Perlmutter (1983), pp. 3–29.

Perlmutter, D., and P. Postal. (1983b). Some proposed laws of basic clause structure. In D. Perlmutter (1983), pp. 81–128.

Perlmutter, D., and C. Rosen, Eds. (1984). *Studies in Relational Grammar* 2. Chicago: University of Chicago Press.

Postal, P. and B. Joseph, Eds. (1990). *Studies in Relational Grammar* 3. Chicago: University of Chicago Press.

Rosen, C. (1984). The interface between semantic roles and initial grammatical relations. In D. Perlmutter and C. Rosen (1984), pp. 38–77.

Further Readings

Aissen, J., and D. Perlmutter. (1983). Clause reduction in Spanish. In D. Perlmutter (1983), pp. 360–403.

Blake, B. (1990). *Relational Grammar.* New York: Routledge.

Chung, S. (1976). An object creating rule in Bahasa Indonesian. *Linguistic Inquiry* 7: 41–87. Reprinted in D. Perlmutter (1983), pp. 219–271.

Davies, W. (1986). *Choctaw Verb Agreement and Universal Grammar.* Dordrecht: Reidel.

Dryer, M. (1986). Primary objects, secondary objects, and antidative. *Language* 62: 808–845.

Farrell, P., S. Marlett, and D. Perlmutter. (1991). Notions of subjecthood and switch-reference: Evidence from Seri. *Linguistic Inquiry* 22: 431–456.

Gibson, J., and E. Raposo. (1986). Clause union, the stratal uniqueness law and the chomeur relation. *Natural Language and Linguistic Theory* 4: 295–331.

Harris, A. (1981). *Georgian Syntax: A Study in Relational Grammar.* Cambridge: Cambridge University Press.

Perlmutter, D. (1983). Personal and impersonal constructions. *Natural Language and Linguistic Theory* 1: 141–200.

Postal, P. (1986). *Studies of Passive Clauses.* Albany: SUNY Press.

Postal, P. (1989). *Masked Inversion in French.* Chicago: University of Chicago Press.

Rosen, C. (1990). Rethinking Southern Tiwa: The geometry of a triple-agreement language. *Language* 66: 669–713.

Relativism

See CULTURAL RELATIVISM; ETHICS AND EVOLUTION; MORAL PSYCHOLOGY

Relevance and Relevance Theory

The notion of relevance has been used in many areas of cognitive science, including LOGIC, artificial intelligence and psychology of reasoning. This article focuses on the role of relevance in human communication, and presents a relevance-based theory of communication (Sperber and Wilson 1986/95) that has potential applications in broader domains.

The intuition that human communication is relevance-oriented is widely shared. Strawson (1964/1971: 92) put forward as a "general platitude" that he called the Principle of Relevance the claim that "stating is not a gratuitous and random human activity. We do not, except in social desperation, direct isolated and unconnected pieces of information at each other." However, recent approaches to PRAGMATICS have been sharply divided about how that intuition is to be explained. All current pragmatic treatments are influenced by the work of Paul GRICE (1967/1989), whose inferential approach to communication is fundamental.

Inferential communication succeeds when the communicator provides evidence of her intention to convey a certain thought, and the audience infers this intention from the evidence provided. Grice saw inferential intention-recognition as governed by a cooperative principle and maxims of quality, quantity, relation, and manner (truthfulness, informativeness, relevance, and clarity). He left the maxim of relation ("Be relevant") relatively undeveloped, and he acknowledged that its formulation concealed a number of problems that he found "exceedingly difficult" (Grice 1989: 46). Gazdar's comment (1979: 45), "That relevance is relevant to linguistic description is painfully apparent . . . . Equally apparent is the absence of any kind of formal treatment of the notion," reflects widespread skepticism about the possibility of progress in this area.

Theoretical accounts of relevance have taken two main forms. One links relevance to the notions of *topic, interest,* or *concern.* This approach was taken by Strawson (1964/1971: 92), whose Principle of Relevance was designed to capture the fact that we "intend in general to give or add information about what is a matter of standing or current interest or concern." Topic-based analyses have been proposed by Reinhart (1981) and Giora (1985), and criticized on the ground that the notion of topic is not only less clear but also less basic than the notion of relevance (Wilson 1998).

Another possibility is to link relevance to the notion of *required information,* following Grice's suggestion that a properly developed maxim of relevance might subsume his second Quantity maxim, "Do not make your contribution more informative than required." This approach is taken by Horn (1984), whose R-principle, "Make your contribution necessary; say no more than you must," is intended to subsume Grice's second Quantity maxim and his maxim of Relation. However, although the notions of information and degrees of informativeness are relatively easy to clarify, this approach sheds little light on what makes some information *required,* leaving the notion of relevance partially unexplained. (For discussion, see Carston 1998a.) Relevance theory (Sperber and Wilson 1986/1995) aims to remedy this defect by saying what makes information worth attending to, but without appealing to notions such as topic or interest.

Within relevance theory, *relevance* is treated as a property of inputs to cognitive processes and analyzed in terms of the notions of cognitive effect and processing effort. When an input (for example, an utterance) is processed in a context of available assumptions, it may yield some cognitive effect (for example, by modifying or reorganizing these assumptions). Other things being equal, the greater the cognitive effects, the greater the relevance of the input. However, the processing of the input, and the derivation of these effects, involves some mental effort. Other things being equal, the smaller the processing effort, the greater the relevance of the input.

On the basis of this definition, two general principles are proposed: the *cognitive principle* that human cognition tends to be geared to the maximization of relevance; and the *communicative principle* that every act of inferential communication communicates a presumption of its own optimal relevance (Sperber and Wilson 1986/1995, 1987). It follows from the cognitive principle of relevance that human attention and processing resources are allocated to information that seems relevant. It follows from the communicative principle of relevance (and the definition of optimal relevance; Sperber and Wilson 1986/1995: 266–278) that the speaker, by the very act of addressing someone, communicates that her utterance is the most relevant one compatible with her abilities and preferences, and is at least relevant enough to be worth the listener's processing effort.

Inferential comprehension starts with the recovery of a linguistically encoded logical form (see LOGICAL FORM IN LINGUISTICS); the goal of pragmatic theory is to explain how the hearer bridges the gap between the linguistically encoded logical form and the full intended interpretation of the utterance. The communicative principle of relevance motivates the following comprehension procedure, which, according to relevance theory, is automatically applied to the on-line processing of attended verbal inputs. The hearer takes the linguistically decoded logical form; following a path of least effort, he enriches it at the explicit level and complements it at the implicit level, until the resulting interpretation meets his expectations of relevance, at which point he stops. The mutual adjustment of explicit content and implicatures, constrained by expectations of relevance, is the central feature of relevance-theoretic pragmatics. (See Sperber and Wilson 1998.)

Relevance-theoretic pragmatics differs from other Gricean approaches in three main respects. It does not treat communication as necessarily cooperative in Grice's sense: for communication to be successful, the only goal that speaker and hearer need to share is that of understanding and being understood. It is not maxim-based: the communicative principle of relevance is not a maxim that speakers need to know, but a generalization about acts of inferential communication. It follows that deliberate maxim-violation, which is central to Gricean pragmatics, has no role in relevance-theoretic comprehension, and the examples that Griceans treat as involving maxim-violation must be reanalyzed.

The relevance-theoretic approach has potential applications in wider domains: for example, in the psychology of reasoning (Sperber, Cara, and Girotto 1995) and the analysis of autism (Happé 1993). For critique and discussion, see *Behavioral and Brain Sciences* (10.4: 1987).

See also IMPLICATURE; LANGUAGE AND COMMUNICATION; PRESUPPOSITION; SEMIOTICS AND COGNITION

—Deirdre Wilson

References

Carston, R. (1998). Informativeness, relevance and scalar implicature. In R. Carston and S. Uchida, Eds., *Relevance Theory: Applications and Implications.* Amsterdam: Benjamins, pp. 179–236.

Gazdar, G. (1979). *Pragmatics: Implicature, Presupposition and Logical Form.* New York: Academic Press.

Giora, R. (1985). Towards a theory of coherence. *Poetics Today* 6: 699–716.

Grice, H. P. (1967). *Logic and Conversation.* William James Lectures. Reprinted in H. P. Grice, *Studies in the Way of Words* (1989). Cambridge, MA: Harvard University Press, pp. 1–143.

Happé, F. (1993). Communicative competence and theory of mind in autism: A test of relevance theory. *Cognition* 48: 101–119.

Horn, L. (1984). A new taxonomy for pragmatic inference: Q-based and R-based implicature. In D. Schiffrin, Ed., *Meaning, Form and Use in Context (GURT 1984).* Washington: Georgetown University Press, pp. 11–42.

Reinhart, T. (1981). Pragmatics and linguistics: An analysis of sentence topics. *Philosophica* 27: 53–94.

Sperber, D., F. Cara, and V. Girotto. (1995). Relevance theory explains the selection task. *Cognition* 57: 31–95.

Sperber, D., and D. Wilson. (1986). *Relevance: Communication and Cognition.* Oxford: Blackwell. (2nd ed. 1995).

Sperber, D., and D. Wilson. (1987). Presumptions of relevance. *Behavioral and Brain Sciences* 10: 736–754.

Sperber, D., and D. Wilson. (1998). The mapping between the mental and the public lexicon. In P. Carruthers and J. Boucher, Eds., *Language and Thought.* Cambridge: Cambridge University Press, pp. 184–200.

Strawson, P. (1964). Identifying reference and truth-value. *Theoria* 30: 96–118. Reprinted in *Logico-Linguistic Papers* (1971). London, Methuen, pp. 75–95.

Wilson, D. (1998). Discourse, coherence and relevance: A reply to Rachel Giora. *Journal of Pragmatics* 29: 57–74.

Further Readings

Anderson, A., and N. Belnap. (1975). *Entailment.* Princeton: Princeton University Press.

Blakemore, D. (1992). *Understanding Utterances: An Introduction to Pragmatics.* Oxford: Blackwell.

Carston, R. (1998b). *Pragmatics and the Explicit-Implicit Distinction.* Ph.D. diss., University of London.

Dascal, M. (1979). Conversational relevance. In A. Margalit, Ed., *Meaning and Use.* Reidel: Dordrecht, pp. 72–96.

Evans, J. St. B. T. (1994). Relevance and reasoning. In S. Newstead and J. St. B. T. Evans, Eds., *Current Directions in Thinking and Reasoning.* Hillsdale, NJ: Erlbaum, pp. 177–201.

Greiner, R., and D. Subramanian, Eds. (1994). *Intelligent Relevance: Papers from the 1994 Fall Symposium.* Technical Report FS-94-02. Menlo Park, CA: AAAI Press.

Rouchota, V., and A. Jucker., Eds. (Forthcoming). *Current Issues in Relevance Theory.* Amsterdam: Benjamins.

Smith, N., and D. Wilson, Eds. (1992–93). Special Issue on Relevance Theory, vols. 1 and 2. *Lingua* 87: 1–2; *Lingua* 90: 1–2.

Sperber, D. (1994). Understanding verbal understanding. In J. Khalfa, Ed., *What is Intelligence?* Cambridge: Cambridge University Press, pp. 179–98.

Sperber, D., and D. Wilson. (1996). Fodor's frame problem and relevance theory. *Behavioral and Brain Sciences* 19: 530–532.

Wilson, D. (1994). Relevance and understanding. In G. Brown, K. Malmkjaer, A. Pollitt, and J. Williams, Eds., *Language and Understanding.* Cambridge: Cambridge University Press, pp. 35–58.

Religious Ideas and Practices

Religious ideas and the practices they inform show considerable variation across cultures. However, they do contain certain recurrent themes: gods that have minds and are alive but have no bodies; ancestors that, though dead, can still influence the living; and artifacts capable of revealing information about peoples' thoughts and actions. Accompanying such themes are ritual practices intended to get the gods to act, ancestors to bestow their blessings or curses, and carved blocks of wood to divine the future.

Anthropologists have typically attempted to account for the prevalence of such notions by postulating that they fill psychological and social needs, for example, social cohesion and personal integration. Symbolic anthropologists have emphasized the expressive role of religious ideas and practices in symbolizing social structure and have employed semiotic strategies in the explication of their meaning. Semiotics treats cultural symbols as surface phenomena that conceal hidden meanings requiring decoding in order to be understood. Only a few anthropologists have attempted to employ the resources of the cognitive sciences to explain the recurrence of religious ideas and practices.

Psychologists of religion have been less interested in religious ideas and practices and more interested in religious experience. Working primarily in the tradition of William JAMES (1902) they analyze extraordinary aspects of religious experience such as ecstatic states and altered states of consciousness and note, for example, that patients who have epileptic seizures in the left temporal lobe report extremely intense experiences of God's gaze.

Until recently neither anthropologists nor psychologists have explained how religious ideas and practices are related to garden variety cognition. The picture has now changed. Some anthropologists and psychologists have begun to employ the resources of the cognitive sciences to explain the prevalence of religious ideas and practices. The first anthropologist to approach religious ideas cognitively was Dan Sperber. In his ground-breaking work Sperber (1975) argued against the semiotic approach to religious ideas then fashionable in anthropology (cf. SEMIOTICS AND COGNITION). Whereas semioticians had searched for the hidden code, which, when specified, would, they thought, provide the interpretive key to symbolic discourse, Sperber demonstrated that symbolism in general and religious symbolism particularly could not be explained by appealing to a hidden code because the "meanings" of the symbols could not be mapped onto the putative underlying code. Symbolic "meanings" were too variable. In fact, symbolic anthropologists had long conceded the multivalence of symbolism. Turner (1969) had shown that the same religious symbol could be employed to represent many different sociocultural features. Sperber's critique of attributing meaning to symbolism in terms of an underlying code represented a major challenge to symbolists' arguments about the nature of religious ideas and practices. The symbolists' interpretations of symbolism were as symbolic as the symbols; symbolic interpretation extended symbolism rather than explicating it. Instead, Sperber argued that students of religion would do better by examining the *inferential processes* that religious people tacitly employ when they make their judgments about the world. Sperber further argued (1997) that, unlike *coevolutionary theories*, which overemphasize the supposed replication of religious ideas, an *epidemiological theory of beliefs* accounts for their cultural transmission by contagion. Sperber's goal was to develop a theory that showed how religious ideas spread and what selection forces were involved in their retention or elimination.

Pascal Boyer (1994) has furthered Sperber's claims by arguing that religious ideas can only spread if they attain a *cognitive equilibrium*. Religious ontological assumptions consist of a set of nonschematic or culturally transmitted assumptions and a set of schematic or standard commonsense assumptions. People make their inferences about the world in terms of an intuitive ontology in which categories such as person, animal, plant, and artificial object play a fundamental role. Such an intuitive ontology is common to all people (including religious ones) in all cultures. Religious ontologies differ from intuitive ontologies in very minor but significant ways by either violating one of the default assumptions of the intuitive ontology or by transferring one of these assumptions to another category. For example, if the default assumptions for "person" are intentional, biological, and physical, then the notion of a spirit violates only the ontology's physical properties. The other assumptions about persons remain in place. Or, if the

default assumption for an artifact is physical, then religious ideas involve the transfer of the property of intentionality to the category of artifact. For example, in some religions people transfer intentionality to artifacts and then regard them as knowing and thus revealing the future trajectory of the religious participant's life.

Lawson and McCauley (1990) focus more narrowly on the kinds of ideas presupposed in the practices that religious people perform. Specifically they have attempted to show that ordinary cognitive resources available for the *representation of action* are sufficient for the representation of religious ritual action by providing the framework for the representation of *agency*. For example a "transitive" action such as "Tom washes car" consists of an agent (with specific qualities) acting on a patient (with specific qualities). The representation of agents that populate religious systems (gods, ancestors, spirits, and their earthly stand-ins such as priests) differ from the representation of ordinary agents only in the special qualities they possess and in the inferences religious people make about their causal role in bringing about changes in states of affairs. Unlike ordinary causal sequences that can be driven back as far as one cares to go (back to the big bang if necessary), religious ritual actions presuppose that the causal sequence stops with the (cultural) postulation of superhuman agents (Spiro 1966). The buck stops with the gods. Lawson and McCauley also argue that where the agents are represented in the structural descriptions of religious ritual actions determines the types of rituals possible. Their theory enables them to predict the judgments that religious participants will make about matters such as their well-formedness, relative centrality, effectiveness, repeatability, substitutability, and reversibility, and a host of features about rituals concerning associated sensory stimulation, emotive responses, and mnemonic dynamics.

Very recently cognitive psychologists of religion have begun to work outside of the Jamesian tradition by focusing not on religious experience but on religious representations and have devised experiments to test the processing of religious ideas. Barrett and Keil (1996) have tested how people conceptualize nonnatural entities such as a god at various stages of cognitive development. Their results show that theological ideas such as God's omnipotence, omniscience, and omnipresence, which religious people themselves regard as essential truths, are not what are accessed when people are required to make on-line judgments about God's action in the world. Instead religious peoples' judgments are thoroughly anthropomorphic in nature.

See also COGNITIVE ANTHROPOLOGY; CULTURAL EVOLUTION; CULTURAL SYMBOLISM; MAGIC AND SUPERSTITION

—*E. Thomas Lawson*

References

Barrett, J. L., and F. C. Keil. (1996). Conceptualizing a non-natural entity: Anthropomorphism in god concepts. *Cognitive Psychology* 31: 219–247.

Boyer, P. (1994). *The Naturalness of Religious Ideas: A Cognitive Theory of Religion.* Berkeley: University of California Press.

James, W. (1902). *The Varieties of Religious Experience: A Study in Human Nature.* New York: Random House.

Lawson, E. T., and R. N. McCauley. (1990). *Rethinking Religion: Connecting Cognition and Culture*. Cambridge: Cambridge University Press.

Sperber, D. (1975). *Rethinking Symbolism*. Cambridge: Cambridge University Press.

Sperber, D. (1997). *Explaining Culture: A Naturalistic Approach*. Oxford: Blackwell.

Spiro, M. (1966). Religion: Problems of definition and explanation. In M. Banton, Ed., *Anthropological Approaches to the Study of Religion*. London: Tavistock, pp. 85–126.

Turner, V. (1969). *The Ritual Process: Structure and Anti-Structure*. Chicago: Aldine.

Representation

See DISTRIBUTED VS. LOCAL REPRESENTATION; KNOWLEDGE REPRESENTATION; MENTAL REPRESENTATION

Resolution

See LOGICAL REASONING SYSTEMS

Retardation

See MENTAL RETARDATION

Retina

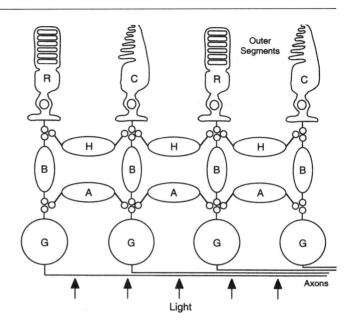

Figure 1. Schematic of retinal neurons and major connections. Light traverses the mostly transparent retina before being absorbed in the outer segments of the (R)od and (C)one photoreceptors (drawn schematically) where transduction takes place. (H)orizontal, (B)ipolar and (A)macrine cells further process visual signals. (G)anglion cells integrate information from bipolar and amacrine cells and send the resulting signals to the brain via long axons.

The retina is a sheet of brain tissue lining the rear of the eye. It transduces light imaged by the lens into electrical potentials, performs substantial processing on these signals, and transmits them to the brain. This initiates visual perception.

Less than half a millimeter thick, the retina consists of five major classes of neurons in three layers (see figure 1) as well as Müller glial cells. Rod and cone photoreceptor cells use an enzymatic amplification cascade to transduce light into graded electrical potentials. Rods (100 million per eye) mediate night vision and can reliably signal the absorption of an individual photon. Cones (5 million per eye) mediate daylight vision and adaptively adjust their sensitivity to register intensity over the extraordinary range of eight orders of magnitude. Rod and cone signals are transmitted to bipolar and horizontal cells which, along with amacrine cells, further process visual information with graded electrical potentials. Retinal ganglion cells integrate inputs from bipolar and amacrine cells and send the resulting visual signals as discrete action potentials (see NEURON) along 1.2 million nerve fibers to a number of targets in the brain.

Each of these major classes of neurons can be further divided into subclasses defined by distinctive morphology, connectivity, electrical responses to light, and biochemistry (see Rodieck 1988, 1998; Wässle and Boycott 1991). For example, there are four major subclasses of photoreceptors (rods and three types of cones) and at least nine types of ganglion cells. Though the major classes of neurons appear in all vertebrates, the characteristics of the subclasses vary considerably among species. Each known subclass is distributed across the retina, forming a mosaic that samples the visual world. Cones and many other neurons are concentrated in and near the fovea, the area of the retina corresponding to the center of gaze; here visual acuity is highest. Rods are absent in the fovea and concentrated in the peripheral retina.

Retinal ganglion cells provide visual information to the brain in signals that reflect spatial integration and parallel processing in the retina (see Rodieck 1973; Dowling 1987; Kuffler, Nichols, and Martin 1984; Davson 1972; Wandell 1995). A ganglion cell typically receives inputs over a roughly circular region of the visual field sampled by many photoreceptors. This region, the receptive field, usually consists of two concentric parts: a center region and a larger antagonistic surround region. In ON-center cells an increase in light intensity in the center increases the frequency of action potentials sent to the brain, while an increase in light intensity in the surround reduces action potential frequency. In OFF-center cells the effects of center and surround are reversed. This ON/OFF polarity is conferred by inputs from distinct types of bipolar cells which initiate the ON/OFF dichotomy (in photoreceptors the light response has a single polarity).

The ON and OFF pathways are examples of retinal subcircuits that carry different types of visual information. Likewise, rod and cone signals are processed by distinct types of bipolar and amacrine cells before being integrated in retinal ganglion cells. The subcircuits that give rise to other differences in the light responses of ganglion cells are less well understood. For example, some types of ganglion cells respond transiently at the onset or offset of a step of light while others respond for the duration of the step. Dif-

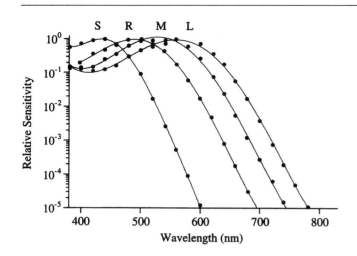

Figure 2. Photoreceptor spectral sensitivities. Points inidicate electrophysiologically measured relative spectral sensitivities of (R)ods and (L)ong, (M)iddle, and (S)hort wavelength-sensitive cones of the monkey, Macaca fascicularis, with peak sensitivities at about 500 nm, 561 nm, 531 nm, and 430 nm respectively. Human photoreceptors have very similar spectral sensitivities. Smooth curves are drawn through points to aid visualization. (Replotted from Baylor, Nunn, and Schnapf 1984, 1987.)

cone types has a characteristic spectral sensitivity endowed by its visual pigment. Quantum absorptions in the three types of cones (figure 2) provide the visual system with just three distinct components of information about the wavelength composition of light. Hence human color perception is limited to sensations that can be duplicated by the superposition of three primary lights.

Why is wavelength information so poorly represented? The answer may lie in a compromise between spatial and spectral resolution. Each point in the visual field is sampled by only one photoreceptor. Additional types of photoreceptors might improve spectral resolution, but only at the cost of spatial resolution within each spectral band. Such tradeoffs have undoubtedly had a significant impact on the evolution of retinal structure and function.

See also COLOR VISION; COLOR, NEUROPHYSIOLOGY OF; FEATURE DETECTORS; VISUAL CORTEX, CELL TYPES AND CONNECTIONS IN

—*E. J. Chichilnisky*

References

Baylor, D. A., B. J. Nunn, and J. L. Schnapf. (1984). The photocurrent, noise and spectral sensitivity of rods of the monkey *Macaca fascicularis. J. Physiol. (Lond.)* 357: 575–607.

Baylor, D. A., B. J. Nunn, and J. L. Schnapf. (1987). Spectral sensitivity of cones of the monkey *Macaca fascicularis. J. Physiol. (Lond.)* 390: 145–160.

Davson, H. (1972). *Physiology of the Eye.* New York: Academic Press.

Dowling, J. E. (1987). *The Retina: An Approachable Part of the Brain.* Cambridge, MA: Harvard University Press.

Kuffler, S. W., J. G. Nicholls, and A. R. Martin. (1984). *From Neuron to Brain.* Sunderland, MA: Sinauer.

Rodieck, R. W. (1973). *The Vertebrate Retina.* San Francisco: W. H. Freeman.

Rodieck, R. W. (1988). The primate retina. *Comparative Primate Biology* 4: 203–278.

Rodieck, R. W. (1998). *The First Steps in Seeing.* Sunderland, MA: Sinauer.

Wandell, B. A. (1995). *Foundations of Vision.* Sunderland, MA: Sinauer.

Wässle, H., and B. B. Boycott. (1991). Functional architecture of the mammalian retina. *Physiol. Rev.* 71: 447–480.

Further Readings

Spillman, L., and J. S. Werner, Eds. (1990). *Visual Perception: The Neurophysiological Foundations.* San Diego: Academic Press.

Robotics

See BEHAVIOR-BASED ROBOTICS; MANIPULATION AND GRASPING; MOBILE ROBOTS; ROBOTICS AND LEARNING

Robotics and Learning

Learning will play an increasingly important role in the design and implementation of autonomous robotic systems. Robots are notoriously difficult to program, because the

ferent types of ganglion cells also exhibit different spectral sensitivities determined by the relative strength of input from the three types of cones. As more subtle anatomical and physiological subdivisions of retinal neurons and their interconnections are elucidated (Rodieck 1988, 1998; Wässle and Boycott 1991), it is becoming clear that different visual messages are carried by a system of parallel retinal subcircuits. These messages are typically transmitted along different anatomical pathways to the brain where they may be locally processed in specific functional modules (see VISUAL PROCESSING STREAMS).

The operation of the retina limits visual performance. Spatial acuity is limited by the density of rods and cones and perhaps by spatial integration in the ganglion cells. Sensitivity to very dim lights is limited by the capacity of rods to faithfully signal absorption of single photons and by the capacity of subsquent circuits to transmit these signals uncorrupted by noise. Sensitivity to rapid variations in light intensity is limited by temporal integration in rods and cones (which occurs over intervals of about 300 msec and 50 msec respectively).

The operation of the rods and cones also establishes quantitative characteristics of color perception. Transduction in rods is initiated by a single visual pigment, rhodopsin. Rhodopsin has a characteristic probability of absorbing photons of different wavelength, giving the rod a characteristic spectral sensitivity (figure 2). However, once absorbed, all photons have the same effect on rhodopsin, so a rod cannot distinguish between one incident photon of 500-nm light and fifty-seven incident photons of 600-nm light. This property, called univariance, means that intensity and wavelength information are confounded in rod vision. Perceptual experience reflects this limitation: at night the world appears in shades of gray. Similarly, each of the three major correctness of their behavior depends on details of interaction with the environment, which are typically unknown to human engineers. In addition, truly flexible, robust robots will have to adapt to their specific and changing environmental conditions.

There are many opportunities for learning in a complex robotic system; the two most common are learning models and learning behavior. A robot may learn a model of its environment, in the form of a map, a kinematic or dynamical system, or an extended HIDDEN MARKOV MODEL. The model can then be used for planning, possibly using techniques of DYNAMIC PROGRAMMING. Another approach is to learn behavior, typically expressed as a mapping from perceptual input to effector outputs, directly.

A variety of MACHINE LEARNING algorithms exists, but they do not all apply well to robot learning, which is special for a number of reasons. Robots interact with their environments through physical sensors and effectors that always have some degree of noise; algorithms for robot learning must be particularly tolerant of noisy inputs and outputs. For learning to be effective, most robots must learn "on line"; that is, they learn while they are performing their task in the environment. This means that learning algorithms must be efficient and incremental (process data singly or in small batches rather than all at once) and that errors must be minimized throughout the life of the robot. Many robots are deployed in changing environments; this requires learning algorithms that can track a changing function. Finally, one of the most interesting special properties of robots is that they can often collect data actively, choosing to explore their environment in such a way as to make learning more efficient. This freedom to explore comes at the price of having to decide how to trade off gaining more information about the environment versus acting in the best possible way given the current information; this is often called the "exploration/exploitation dilemma."

Some of the most effective robot learning systems are built on SUPERVISED LEARNING, where there is a "teacher" that can supply a stream of desired outputs corresponding to the perceptual inputs of the robot. Pomerleau's ALVINN system (Pomerleau 1993) is an excellent example of supervised robot learning. A van learns to drive down a variety of roads at moderately high speeds based on visual input. The learning data is gathered with a human supervisor at the wheel, enabling the system to collect a series of input-output pairs, consisting of a computer-vision image and a desired steering angle. This data is used to train a neural network, which can then steer the car unaided.

Unfortunately, it is difficult to find such reliable supervisory information. Generally, humans are much better able to supply a "reinforcement" signal, which simply indicates when the robot is performing well or poorly. Techniques of REINFORCEMENT LEARNING can be used to learn behavior based on a reinforcement signal. This problem is much more difficult than supervised learning, because the robot is not told what outputs to generate for each input; this requires the robot to explore the space of possible actions and to be able to notice that an action taken much earlier may have been a contributing factor to current performance.

Because reinforcement learning is difficult, robot systems that make use of it must have a large amount of built-in structure. In BEHAVIOR-BASED ROBOTICS, for example, the robot may learn to switch between fixed behaviors or may learn a collection of specific behaviors given different reinforcement functions. Other robots learn a dynamical model of the world (Moore, Atkeson, and Schaal 1997) using supervised techniques, then use the model to generate actions using techniques of optimal control, which are appropriate for a restricted range of tasks.

There are still very few examples of real robotic systems that learn to behave, but this is a very active area of current research. The range of current robot learning applications and research is well documented in two collections of papers: a book edited by Connell and Mahadevan (1993) and a journal issue edited by Franklin, Mitchell, and Thrun (1996).

See also LEARNING; MOBILE ROBOTS; NEURAL NETWORKS

—*Leslie Pack Kaelbling*

References

Connell, J. H., and S. Mahadevan, Eds. (1993). *Robot Learning.* Dordrecht: Kluwer.

Franklin, J. A., T. M. Mitchell, and S. Thrun, Eds. (1996). *Machine Learning,* vol. 23, no. 2/3. Dordercht: Kluwer.

Moore, A. W., C. G. Atkeson, and S. A. Schaal. (1997). Locally weighted learning for control. *AI Review* 11: 75–113.

Pomerleau, D. A. (1993). *Neural Network Perception for Mobile Robot Guidance.* Boston: Kluwer.

Rules and Representations

Rules and representations is a label applied to the classical, computational approach in cognitive science, and more often to the general conception of cognition based on that approach.

The interdisciplinary field known as cognitive science grew up with the development of the modern digital computer. Researchers from such diverse fields as computer science, neurophysiology, psychology, linguistics, and philosophy were brought together by the conviction that the digital computer is the best model of cognition in general, and consequently of human cognition in particular. (This "classical" conception of cognition is now rivaled by connectionism, the other principal branch of contemporary cognitive science; see COGNITIVE MODELING, CONNECTIONIST.)

A distinctive feature of the modern digital computer is that its processes are determined by a program—a system of *rules* that govern transitions from one state to the next. (State transitions can be nondeterministic; for instance, the rules can determine the next state on the basis of both the current state and the outcome of consulting a random number table.) Computers process information represented in "data structures" or symbols, and it is these symbolic *representations* to which the rules apply. Thus, the classical conception of cognition gives a central and fundamental role to rules—specifically, rules for the manipulation and transformation of symbolic representations. The contents of the symbolic representations are the contents of thought.

The rules executed by a digital computer can be regarded in two ways. From one perspective the rules refer explicitly to the task domain. For instance, a set of rules might assign classes to classrooms on a university campus, taking into account such constraints as the location of each classroom, the number of seats in each classroom, the number of requested seats for each class, and the time of day each class will be offered. These rules must be precise, completely explicit, and exceptionless, so that a human being who had no idea what classes or classrooms are could still determine room assignments by following the rules. To do this, one would need only the ability to follow simple instructions and the ability to perform elementary logical and mathematical operations. Terms for classes, rooms, and the like could be replaced by nonsense syllables or schematic letters.

When rules about the task domain have been made precise, explicit, and exceptionless in this way, they can be viewed from a second perspective: not as having representational content, but as purely formal symbol-manipulating rules that determine processing on the basis of nothing other than the syntactic form of the representations. The elementary operations specified in such rules can then be mirrored by simple physical devices. Hence, such rules can be put in the form of a program that will run on a conventional computer. Both the rules constituting the program and the representations to which they apply thus have two complementary "guises." The rules are purely formal, applying to representations solely on the basis of their structural-syntactic features; but the representations, and hence the rules, are also appropriately interpretable as being about objects and facts in the problem domain—classes, classrooms, class times, and so on. It is because the rules have these two guises that the syntactic and the semantic aspects of symbolic representations hang together.

Classicism maintains that the rules that determine cognitive processes in cognitive systems also have these two guises (Haugeland 1981). On one hand they are interpretable as psychological laws governing transitions among mental states. But on the other hand they are purely formal, applying directly to the syntactic structure of symbolic representations. On this classicist picture, the brain is a "syntactic engine" in which the content-appropriate processing of mental representations is accomplished by means of the structure-sensitive processing of symbol-structures in accordance with formal-syntactic rules. A program that is intended to model a human cognitive capacity—say, visual perception or parsing sentences or getting about in crowded shopping areas—is a hypothesis about the states and processes that occur when a person exercises that capacity. The explanation of the capacity itself, according to classicism, is that a person has a (possibly hardwired) system of rules for performing the task, rules that constitute a program. (Frequently in classicist cognitive science, a program intended to model a cognitive capacity will involve *heuristic* rules; see HEURISTIC SEARCH. These do not guarantee a correct or optimal outcome in every case, but employ reasonable strategies that will yield solutions in a large range of cases.)

In connectionist models, representations are activation-states of nodes in a connectionist network. (Often the representations are *distributed* activation-patterns involving multiple nodes; and sometimes the representations are *fully* distributed, in the sense that the individual nodes within a distributed representation have no determinate representational content by themselves.) Whereas classicism is firmly committed to mental representations with language-like syntactic structure, connectionist representations are not inherently syntactic. It is sometimes assumed that connectionist representations cannot exhibit syntactic structure, and that lack of syntax therefore constitutes an essential difference between connectionism and classicism (e.g., Churchland 1995). On this view, connectionist models depart from the classical "rules and representations" conception of cognition because they eschew traditional symbolic, syntactically structured representations. But in fact some connectionist models do employ syntactically structured representations and exhibit structure-sensitive processing—although syntactic constituency in these models is not a simple part-whole relation. Examples of such models include Pollack (1990), Smolensky (1990), and Berg (1992). So connectionism need not eschew syntax—and arguably should not (Horgan and Tienson 1996).

In connectionist models, rules for processing representations are not explicitly represented. It is sometimes assumed that classicism is committed to explicitly represented rules, and that lack of such rules therefore constitutes an essential difference between classicism and connectionism (e.g., Hatfield 1991). But although programs are explicitly represented as stored "data structures" in the ubiquitous general-purpose computer, stored programs are not an essential feature of the classical point of view. In some computational devices—including, for example, many hand-held calculators—the rules are all hardwired into the system and are not explicitly represented. According to classicism, cognition must conform to representation-processing rules that constitute a computer program; but a cognitive system could conform to such rules simply by being hardwired to do so. For example, from the classical perspective it is plausible to regard some innate processes as hardwired.

Classicism is committed to *representation-level* rules—that is, programmable rules that apply directly to the formal structure of the representations themselves. But connectionism, at least insofar as it employs fully distributed representations in which local node-activations do not have representational content, is not committed to such representation-level rules as a feature of cognitive architecture. The rules governing a connectionist network are local and subrepresentational, applying within and between individual nodes in the network—not to the distributed representations. Although connectionist systems sometimes conform to emergent representational-level rules over and above these node-level rules, in general there is no guarantee that rule-describability of processing will "transfer upward" from the level of individual nodes to the level of distributed representations (Horgan and Tienson 1996: 63–67; Horgan 1997). In our view, it is neither necessary nor desirable for connectionist models of human cognition to conform to programmable representation-level rules; it is plausible that persistent problems within classicism—e.g., the FRAME PROBLEM—are a byproduct of classicism's commitment to such rules; and an appropriate nonclassical framework for cognitive science would be one in which the mathematics of dynamical systems theory replaces the classicist appeal to representation-level rules (Horgan and Tienson 1996).

See also COGNITIVE ARCHITECTURE; COMPUTATION; COMPUTATION AND THE BRAIN; COMPUTATIONAL THEORY OF MIND; DYNAMIC APPROACHES TO COGNITION

—*Terence Horgan and John Tienson*

References

Berg, G. (1992). A connectionist parser with recursive sentence structure and lexical disambiguation. In AAAI-92: *Proceedings of the Tenth National Conference on Artificial Intelligence.* Cambridge, MA: AAAI Press/MIT Press.

Churchland, P. (1995). *The Engine of Reason, the Seat of the Soul: A Philosophical Journey into the Brain.* Cambridge, MA: MIT Press.

Hatfield, G. (1991). Representation and rule-instantiation in connectionist systems. In T. Horgan and J. Tienson, Eds., *Connectionism and the Philosophy of Mind.* Kluwer.

Haugeland, J. (1981). Semantic engines: An introduction to mind design. In J. Haugeland, Ed., *Mind Design: Philosophy, Psychology, Artificial Intelligence.* Cambridge, MA: MIT Press.

Horgan, T. (1997). Modelling the noncomputational mind: Reply to Litch. *Philosophical Psychology* 10: 365–371.

Horgan, T., and J. Tienson. (1996). *Connectionism and the Philosophy of Psychology.* Cambridge, MA: MIT Press.

Pollack, J. (1990). Recursive distributed representations. *Artifical Intelligence* 46: 77–105.

Smolensky, P. (1990). Tensor product variable binding and the representation of symbolic structures in connectionist systems. *Artifical Intelligence* 46: 159–215.

Running Machines

See WALKING AND RUNNING MACHINES

Saccades

See EYE MOVEMENTS AND VISUAL ATTENTION; OCULOMOTOR CONTROL; READING

Sapir, Edward

Edward Sapir (1884–1939) was a leading figure in twentieth-century linguistics and anthropology. Educated at Columbia University (B.A. 1904, Ph.D. 1909) and initially a student of Germanic philology, he became attracted to the anthropology program then newly formed by Franz BOAS. Boas's project of studying the languages and cultures of North American Indians in their own right, rather than as evolutionary precursors or deficient versions of Europeans (as in some other approaches then current), became Sapir's own. Yet, his work grew to include linguistic topics worldwide, and his contributions in theory and analysis are among the foundations of modern linguistics.

Sapir's professional career began in fieldwork and museum administration. Director of the Anthropology section of the national museum of Canada (Ottawa) from 1910 to 1925, he organized anthropological and linguistic research on Canadian native populations. Moving to a university setting (University of Chicago, 1925–31; Yale 1931–39) provided him with students, new research opportunities, and more time for theoretical concerns in linguistics, cultural anthropology, and psychology.

Sapir's contribution to American Indian linguistics lies partly in his field research, documenting a wide range of languages in grammatical analyses, texts, and ethnography. The grammar of Southern Paiute (1930a), in particular, still stands as a model of linguistic analysis and description. He also undertook comparative and historical work, including a startling new classification of North American languages (1929a) that reduced the number of independent stocks from some 55, in Powell's classification, to 6. Most importantly, his historical and methodological discussions (e.g., 1916, 1931, 1936a, 1938a) showed how linguistic evidence could address questions in cultural history and how language change in "exotic" languages can shed light on Indo-European (and vice versa). Sapir saw language as a species-wide human creation, and he pursued that vision globally, supplementing his American work with studies in Indo-European, Semitic, and African linguistics, and a project for Sino-Tibetan.

As a linguistic theorist, Sapir is known for his demonstrations of "pattern" (systematicity) in language, for his process-oriented conception of grammar (an early, though discontinuous, precursor of GENERATIVE GRAMMAR), and for his interest in the psychology of language. His classic paper "Sound Patterns in Language" (1925) explored the principles of systematicity in a language's PHONOLOGY, where a psychological organization of sound relationships functioned to distinguish word meanings. Phonology's basic unit, the phoneme, was defined by its place in the system. Not merely the linguist's construct, it had a psychological reality for the language's speakers (Sapir 1933). Similarly, in *Language* (1921) and later works, Sapir discussed grammatical configurations and their associated "form-feeling"—grammar's subjective dimension (what we might now call linguistic intuition). Linguistic patterns, he suggested, revealed creative operations of the mind, despite the largely unconscious nature of grammatical rules. That creativity was also to be seen in poetry and in language change, explainable in part as a psychological reconfiguring of linguistic patterns.

Because Sapir always emphasized the ways linguistic forms are meaningful to their users, his work in SEMANTICS tended not to fall under a separate rubric (but see Sapir 1944). His discussions of the ways meanings are distributed, how they might be associated with a configuration of formal relations in MORPHOLOGY and SYNTAX, and how these configurations differ across languages, included statements later identified with the "Sapir-Whorf hypothesis" of LINGUISTIC RELATIVITY and determinism. The "hypothesis" that a particular language's structure influences its speakers' perception and cognition owes more to Sapir's student Benjamin Lee Whorf than to Sapir himself. Still, Sapir did maintain that a language's grammatical categories provide speakers with configurations of meaning that seem, to the speakers, to be located in the world rather than in language. He also argued that language influences what ideas are socially expressible, because communication depends on the available language and how it organizes meanings.

Sapir's linguistic psychology, with its emphasis on creativity and a level of mental patterning independent of actual behavior, contrasted sharply with the behaviorism of his Yale colleague Leonard BLOOMFIELD. Sapir was more interested in GESTALT PSYCHOLOGY and Jungian PSYCHOANALYSIS (CURRENT VIEWS), because they emphasized pattern and system in cognition and in personality organization. These interests also underlay Sapir's contributions in culture theory and cultural psychology.

Sapir shared with his fellow Boasians a view of culture as a system of configurations rather than a collection of traits. He differed from them, however, in emphasizing the role of individual psychology, experience, and creativity in shaping a personal world of meanings and actions. The "subjective side" of culture could be individually variable, therefore, even though the outward forms of behavior were shared. This distinction between collective and personal perspectives on culture posed methodological and epistemological problems that Sapir found especially interesting. His 1917 debate with Alfred Kroeber on the "superorganic" was the first of many discussions of these themes. Despite anthropologists' legitimate concern with abstracting cultural patterns from observable behavior, Sapir argued, they must not ignore the individual participant's life history and subjective experience.

In his later essays on culture and personality, Sapir again criticized approaches that failed to distinguish between collective and individual levels of analysis, and scholars who confused conventional behavior patterns with the personality patterns of actual individuals. Subjective experiences and meanings were to be carefully distinguished from the public symbols and social conventions prescribing the forms a person's behavior takes. Late in his life, influenced by his collaboration with psychotherapist Harry Stack Sullivan, Sapir began (1937, 1993) to explore the analysis of social interaction as the locus of cultural dynamics.

Sapir's conceptions of culture and of anthropological method were always influenced by his work in linguistics. Though better known today as linguist than as anthropologist, he saw these efforts as conjoined. Language was, for him, the cultural phenomenon par excellence. It offered the prime example of cultural difference and cultural systematicity, it provided the ethnographer with the terminological key to native concepts, and it suggested to its speakers the configurations of readily expressible ideas. Moving among linguistics, anthropology, psychology, and the humanities, Sapir's work transcended particular disciplines while contributing to their foundations.

—*Judith Irvine*

Works by Sapir

Sapir, E. (1911). The problem of noun incorporation in American languages. *American Anthropologist* 13: 250–282.

Sapir, E. (1916). Time perspective in aboriginal American culture: A study in method. *Canada Department of Mines, Geological Survey, Memoir* 90, *Anthropological Series* 13.

Sapir, E. (1917). Do we need a "superorganic"? *American Anthropologist* 19: 441–447.

Sapir, E. (1921). *Language: An Introduction to the Study of Speech.* New York: Harcourt, Brace, and Co.

Sapir, E. (1924). Culture, genuine and spurious. *American Journal of Sociology* 29:401–429.

Sapir, E. (1925). Sound patterns in language. *Language* 1: 37–51.

Sapir, E. (1927). Speech as a personality trait. *American Journal of Sociology* 32: 892–905.

Sapir, E. (1928). The unconscious patterning of behavior in society. In E. Dummett, Ed., *The Unconscious: A Symposium.* New York: A. A. Knopf, pp. 114–142.

Sapir, E. (1929a). Central and North American languages. *Encyclopaedia Britannica.* 14th ed. 5: 138–141.

Sapir, E. (1929b). The status of linguistics as a science. *Language* 5: 207–214.

Sapir, E. (1930a). Southern Paiute, a Shoshonean language. *Proceedings, American Academy of Arts and Sciences* 65(1): 1–296.

Sapir, E. (1930b). Totality. *Linguistic Society of America, Language Monographs* 6.

Sapir, E. (1931). The concept of phonetic law as tested in primitive languages by Leonard Bloomfield. In A. Rice, Ed., *Methods in Social Science: A Case Book.* Chicago: University of Chicago Press, pp. 297–306.

Sapir, E. (1932a). Cultural anthropology and psychiatry. *Journal of Abnormal and Social Psychology* 27: 229–242.

Sapir, E. (with M. Swadesh). (1932b). The expression of the ending-point relation in English, French, and German. In A. V. Morris, Ed., *Linguistic Society of America: Language Monographs* 10.

Sapir, E. (1933). La réalité psychologique des phonèmes. *Journal de Psychologie Normale et Pathologique* (Paris) 30: 247–265.

Sapir, E. (1936a). Internal linguistic evidence suggestive of the northern origin of the Navaho. *American Anthropologist* 38: 224–235.

Sapir, E. (1936b). Tibetan Influences on Tocharian. *Language* 12: 259–271.

Sapir, E. (1937). The contribution of psychiatry to an understanding of behavior in society. *American Journal of Sociology* 42: 862–870.

Sapir, E. (1938a). Glottalized continuants in Navaho, Nootka, and Kwakiutl (with a note on Indo-European). *Language* 14: 248–274.

Sapir, E. (1938b). Why cultural anthropology needs the psychiatrist. *Psychiatry* 1: 7–12.

Sapir, E. (1944). Grading, a study in semantics. *Philosophy of Science* 11: 93–116.

Sapir, E. (1947). The relation of American Indian linguistics to general linguistics. *Southwestern Journal of Anthropology* 3: 1–14.

Sapir, E. (1949). *Selected Writings of Edward Sapir in Language, Culture and Personality,* D. G. Mandelbaum, Ed. Berkeley and Los Angeles: University of California Press.

Sapir, E. (1989 et seq.). Collected Works of Edward Sapir. P. Sapir, Chief Ed.; W. Bright, R. Darnell, V. Golla, E. Hamp, R. Handler, and J. T. Irvine, Eds. Berlin: Mouton. 16 vols.

Sapir, E. (1993). *The Psychology of Culture: A Course of Lectures.* Reconstructed by J. T. Irvine, Ed. Berlin: Mouton.

Further Readings

Cowan, W., M. Foster, and K. Koerner, Eds. (1986). *New Perspectives in Language, Culture and Personality: Proceedings of the Edward Sapir Centenary Conference,* Ottawa, October, 1-3 1984. Amsterdam: Benjamins.

Darnell, R. (1990). *Edward Sapir: Linguist, Anthropologist, Humanist.* Berkeley and Los Angeles: University of California Press.

Darnell, R., and J. T. Irvine. (1997). Edward Sapir, 1884-1939. *National Academy of Sciences, Biographical Memoirs.* Washington, DC: National Academy Press.

Koerner, K., Ed. (1984). *Edward Sapir: Appraisals of His Life and Work.* Amsterdam: Benjamins.

Sapir-Whorf Hypothesis

See LINGUISTIC RELATIVITY HYPOTHESIS

Satisficing

See BOUNDED RATIONALITY; ECONOMICS AND COGNITIVE SCIENCE; HEURISTIC SEARCH

Saussure, Ferdinand de

Ferdinand de Saussure (1857–1913) is usually considered to be the father of modern linguistics. Born in Geneva into an illustrious family that included famous natural scientists, Saussure trained as a comparative philologist, studying (1876–78) in Leipzig, the main center of the Neogrammatical movement. There he gave precocious proof of his genius with a *Mémoire* (1879) containing insights that lie at the root of some of the most interesting twentieth-century developments in comparative philology. After a period of studying and teaching in Paris (1880–91), Saussure was called in 1891 to teach Sanskrit in Geneva. He published relatively little in his lifetime (see his *Recueil* 1922). Between 1907 and 1911, he taught three courses in general linguistics to small groups of students. After his death, two of his colleagues (Charles Bally and Albert Sechehaye, with the help of one of his students, Albert Riedlinger), on the basis of students' lecture notes and some of Saussure's own jottings, compiled a coherent *Cours de linguistique générale* (*CLG*; 1916). It proved to be perhaps the most influential text in linguistics, at least up to the publication of Noam Chomsky's work.

Before looking at some of Saussure's ideas, one needs to comment on the difficulties posed by their interpretation. As the text was not written by Saussure, the problem of establishing what certain passages of the *CLG* meant exactly and how far they represented the ideas of the "author" grew so complex that it became difficult to take a fresh look at questions without becoming embroiled in a specialized hermeneutic apparatus. The most useful contributions are Godel (1957), Engler (1967–74), De Mauro (1967), and the publication of sets of individual students' notes (see the volumes of the journal *Cahiers Ferdinand de Saussure*).

A further difficulty was added by the spread of postmodern attitudes (some claiming, ironically, a Saussurean inspiration) according to which it is impossible in this case, and anyway illegitimate in principle, to try to establish the correct meaning of a text, because texts are inevitably constructed by readers. "Semiological" readings of the *CLG* were proposed, which sometimes appeared more stimulating than convincing. To this we can finally add the fact that several linguistic movements refer to Saussure as the source of some of their insights, so that it has become difficult to separate Saussure's own ideas from those belonging to his followers (Lepschy 1982). We can quote the Genevan School of his immediate successors, the Danish Glossematic group of Louis Hjelmslev, some members of the Prague Circle (in particular Roman JAKOBSON and Nikolaj Sergeevic Trubeckoj), and many of the French trends that are loosely associated under the banner of "structuralism" or "post-structuralism," from Roland Barthes's semiology, to Jacques Lacan's brand of psychoanalysis, to Althusser's variety of Marxism, to Claude LÉVI-STRAUSS' structural anthropology, to Michel Foucault's cultural archaeology, to Jacques Derrida's deconstructionism. In the tradition of American linguistics, however, the influence of Saussure was limited from the start and further restricted by his being (misleadingly) associated with structural linguistics, which, in its post-Bloomfieldian incarnation, had next to nothing in common with Saussure.

Some of the main ideas that are central in the *CLG* are rooted in the debates current at the turn of the century concerning the nature of scientific explanation, the relation between natural sciences and the humanities (*Naturwissenschaften* vs. *Geisteswissenschaften*), the distinction between nomothetic and idiographic disciplines, and the place of linguistics within this intellectual map. The *CLG* introduced a series of dichotomies that are still, in one way or another, present in current research. The main ones are the following four.

1. Synchronic versus diachronic viewpoint: In the early twentieth century it was taken for granted that the scientific study of language had to be diachronic. Saussure's position was crucial in redressing the balance and in establishing synchronic study as a fully legitimate activity, indeed the one in which the most important insights of modern linguistics were to be obtained.
2. Syntagmatic versus associative (or, as it was later called, paradigmatic): Based on the psychological theories of the time, this was made into a basic distinction between two Cartesian axes: on the horizontal one the linear succession of units constituting the message, on the vertical one the set of items constituting the code.
3. *Langue* versus *parole*: The former refers to what is abstract (form), general, and social; the latter to the concrete (substance), specific, and individual speech acts.
4. Signifier versus signified: This is a more strictly semiotic dichotomy. The linguistic sign has two sides, expression and content, which do not exist without each other and yet can be separately analyzed; their relation is arbitrary, not in the traditional sense of a conventional relation between word and thing, as illustrated by the very existence of different languages, but in a deeper, more radical sense, referring to the split that runs through the very nature of language.

In the context of cognitive views as embodied in GENERATIVE GRAMMAR one can observe an analogy (which is obviously not an identity) between the langue/parole distinction and that of competence/performance, and a link between the notion of the arbitrary nature of the sign and that of the distance between surface and deep structures. An aspect that sets Saussure's views apart from those of contemporary linguistics is that whereas for him SYNTAX has a marginal and unclear status (linked mainly to the structure of individual acts of *parole*), nowadays it is thought to have a central and creative function.

See also BLOOMFIELD, LEONARD; SAPIR, EDWARD; SEMIOTICS AND COGNITION

—*Giulio Lepschy*

References

Godel, R. (1957). *Les Sources Manuscrites du Cours de Linguistique Générale de F. de Saussure*. Geneva and Paris: Droz-Minard.

Lepschy, G. (1982). *A Survey of Structural Linguistics*. New ed. London: Deutsch.

Saussure, F. de. (1879). *Mémoire sur le Système Primitif des Voyelles dans les Langues Indoeuropéennes*. Leipzig: Teubner.

Saussure, F. de. (1916). *Cours de Linguistique Générale*. Lausanne-Paris: Payot. (with De Mauro's notes, 1972).

Saussure, F. de. (1922). *Recueil des Publications Scientifiques*. Geneva: Sonor.

Saussure, F. de. (1959). *Course in General Linguistics*, trans. by W. Baskin. New York: Philosophical Library.

Saussure, F. de. (1967). *Corso di Linguistica Generale*. Italian translation and commentary by T. De Mauro. Bari: Laterza.

Saussure, F. de. (1967–74). *Cours de Linguistique Générale*. R. Engler, Ed. 4 vols. Wiesbaden: Harrassowitz.

Saussure, F. de. (1983). *Course in General Linguistics*, trans. by R. Harris. London: Duckworth.

Starobinski, J. (1971). *Les mots sous les mots. Les anagrammes de Ferdinand de Saussure*. Paris: Gallimard.

Scheduling

See CONSTRAINT SATISFACTION; PLANNING

Schemata

Schemata are the psychological constructs that are postulated to account for the molar forms of human generic knowledge. The term *frames*, as introduced by Marvin Minsky (1975), is essentially synonymous, except that Minsky used frame as both a psychological construct and as a construct in artificial intelligence. *Scripts* are the subclass of schemata that are used to account for generic (stereotyped) sequences of actions (Schank and Abelson 1977).

Although the term *schema* was used by the philosopher Immanuel KANT and the developmental psychologist Jean PIAGET, the direct line of intellectual descent for this construct in cognitive science is through the work of British psychologist Sir Frederic BARTLETT. Bartlett (1932) was investigating the recall of folktales and noticed that many of the errors that occurred in the recall protocols tended to make the recalls more conventional than the original text. In order to account for this class of memory errors, Bartlett proposed that human beings have substantial amounts of generic knowledge in the form of unconscious mental structures (schemata) and that these structures interact with incoming information to produce schematized (conventionalized) errors in recall. Bartlett's schema construct was not compatible with the world view that was dominant in psychology at the time (see BEHAVIORISM), and therefore the schema concept was not incorporated into mainstream MEMORY research in psychology (cf. Brewer and Nakamura 1984).

The schema construct was reintroduced into modern cognitive science through the work of the computer scientist Marvin Minsky (1975). Minsky was attempting to develop machines that would show humanlike intelligence. Minsky read Bartlett's book on memory (Bartlett 1932) and concluded that much of human intelligent behavior derived from the use of generic knowledge. This led Minsky to argue that in order to make machines intelligent it would be necessary for them to be provided with large amounts of knowledge. This proposal had an enormous influence on the development of the field of artificial intelligence (cf. Dyer, Cullingford, and Alvarado 1990; Maida 1990).

Minsky's more specific proposal was to introduce the construct of frames to represent knowledge of ordinary aspects of the world (e.g., rooms). Frames are knowledge structures that contain fixed structural information. They have slots that accept a range of values; each slot has a default value that is used if no value has been provided from the external world. For example, if a person or a machine is trying to represent a particular college classroom the generic classroom frame will contain the fixed information that the room will have walls, a ceiling, and a door. The frame will contain a slot for type of lighting. If no information is provided about this aspect of the world (e.g., if an individual has just glanced at a room without looking up to see the lights) then the frame provides a default value (in this case, that the lights are fluorescent). Thus the frame construct can be used to give an account for why someone walking into a room without a ceiling will be surprised and why an individual might recall that a particular classroom had fluorescent lights when it actually did not. Note that in this example there is a generic frame for classrooms in long-term memory, and to represent a specific classroom the generic frame is instantiated by a specific episodic representation. In general, Minsky's frames provided a much more structured account of KNOWLEDGE REPRESENTATION than previous proposals.

Work on frames in artificial intelligence has had a strong impact on psychological investigations of knowledge representation. Rumelhart (1980) developed a psychologically based theory of schemata derived from Minsky's work. (Psychologists working on these topics usually use the term *schema*, plural *schemata*, for these forms of knowledge representation.) In both psychology and artificial intelligence there has been much controversy over the relationship of schemata to other "simpler" forms of representation such as propositions, semantic nets, and CONCEPTS. In general, schema theorists (Minsky 1975; Rumelhart 1980) have made an ontological argument that there are molar phenomena (e.g., events, spatial scenes, discourse structure) in the (psychological?) world, and that schemata are the appropriate forms of knowledge representation for these molar phenomena (cf. Brewer and Nakamura 1984; Davis, Shrobe, and Szolovits 1993).

Schema theories have had a wide impact on empirical work in cognitive psychology. They provided an account for earlier work such as the finding of Bransford and Johnson (1972) that recall for an opaquely written passage is much improved when it is given with a schema-relevant title. They also generated much new research, such as the finding by Bower, Black, and Turner (1979) showing high rates of script-based intrusions in recall of script narratives, and the work of Brewer and Treyens (1981) showing schema-based intrusions in the recall of visual scenes (see Brewer and Nakamura 1984 for an extensive review of these empirical findings).

How are schema theories to be viewed within the overall study of knowledge representation in cognitive science? The original papers on frames and schemata invite the inference that schemalike representations will account for most of human and machine knowledge. Subsequent work has shown that although schema representations provide a powerful account for generic forms of knowledge, this type of representation is only a part of the total repertoire of human knowledge. It now seems clear (cf. Brewer 1987) that MENTAL MODELS (Johnson-Laird 1983), naive theories (Gopnik and Wellman 1992) and many other forms of representation (e.g., Schank 1982) are needed to give a comprehensive account of human and machine knowledge.

See also DOMAIN SPECIFICITY; FRAME-BASED SYSTEMS; FRAME PROBLEM; MENTAL REPRESENTATION

—*William F. Brewer*

References

Bartlett, F. C. (1932). *Remembering.* Cambridge: Cambridge University Press.

Bower, G. H., J. B. Black, and T. J. Turner. (1979). Scripts in memory for text. *Cognitive Psychology* 11: 177–220.

Bransford, J. D., and M. K. Johnson. (1972). Contextual prerequisites for understanding: Some investigations of comprehension and recall. *Journal of Verbal Learning and Verbal Behavior* 11: 717–726.

Brewer, W. F. (1987). Schemas versus mental models in human memory. In P. Morris, Ed., *Modelling Cognition.* Chichester, UK: Wiley, pp. 187–197.

Brewer, W. F., and G. V. Nakamura. (1984). The nature and functions of schemas. In R. S. Wyer, Jr. and T. K. Srull, Eds., *Handbook of Social Cognition,* vol. 1. Hillsdale, NJ: Erlbaum, pp. 119–160.

Brewer, W. F., and J. C. Treyens. (1981). Role of schemata in memory for places. *Cognitive Psychology* 13: 207–230.

Davis, R., H. Shrobe, and P. Szolovits. (1993). What is a knowledge representation? *AI Magazine* 14: 17–33.

Dyer, M., R. Cullingford, and S. Alvarado. (1990). Scripts. In S. C. Shapiro, Ed., *Encyclopedia of Artificial Intelligence,* vol. 2. New York: Wiley, pp. 980–994.

Gopnik, A., and H. M. Wellman. (1992). Why the child's theory of mind really *is* a theory. *Mind and Language* 7: 145–171.

Johnson-Laird, P. N. (1983). *Mental Models.* Cambridge, MA: Harvard University Press.

Maida, A. S. (1990). Frame theory. In S. C. Shapiro, Ed., *Encyclopedia of Artificial Intelligence,* vol. 1. New York: Wiley, pp. 302–312.

Minsky, M. (1975). A framework for representing knowledge. In P. H. Winston, Ed., *The Psychology of Computer Vision.* New York: McGraw-Hill, pp. 211–277.

Rumelhart, D. E. (1980). Schemata: The building blocks of cognition. In R. J. Spiro, B. C. Bruce, and W. F. Brewer, Eds., *Theoretical Issues in Reading Comprehension.* Hillsdale, NJ: Erlbaum, pp. 33–58.

Schank, R. C. (1982). *Dynamic Memory: A Theory of Reminding and Learning in Computers and People.* Cambridge: Cambridge University Press.

Schank, R. C., and R. P. Abelson. (1977). *Scripts, Plans, Goals and Understanding.* Hillsdale, NJ: Erlbaum.

Further Readings

Graesser, A. C., and G. V. Nakamura. (1982). The impact of a schema on comprehension and memory. In G. H. Bower, Ed., *The Psychology of Learning and Motivation,* vol. 16. New York: Academic Press, pp. 59–109.

Johnson-Laird, P. N., D. J. Herrmann, and R. Chaffin. (1984). Only connections: A critique of semantic networks. *Psychological Bulletin* 96: 292–315.

Mandler, J. M. (1984). *Stories, Scripts, and Scenes: Aspects of Schema Theory.* Hillsdale, NJ: Erlbaum.

Rumelhart, D. E., and D. A. Norman. (1988). Representation in memory. In R. C. Atkinson, R. J. Herrnstein, G. Lindzey, and R. D. Luce, Eds., *Stevens' Handbook of Experimental Psychology.* Vol. 2, *Learning and Cognition.* 2nd ed. New York: Wiley, pp. 511–587.

Rumelhart, D. E., and A. Ortony. (1977). The representation of knowledge in memory. In R. C. Anderson and R. J. Spiro, Eds., *Schooling and the Acquisition of Knowledge.* Hillsdale, NJ: Erlbaum, pp. 99–135.

Science, Philosophy of

See INTRODUCTION: PHILOSOPHY; REALISM AND ANTIREALISM; REDUCTIONISM; UNITY OF SCIENCE

Scientific Thinking and Its Development

Scientific thinking refers to the thought processes that are used in science, including the cognitive processes involved in theory generation, experiment design, hypothesis testing, data interpretation, and scientific discovery. Many of these aspects of scientific thinking involve cognitive processes that have been investigated in their own right, such as INDUCTION, DEDUCTIVE REASONING, CAUSAL REASONING, ANALOGY, EXPERTISE, and PROBLEM SOLVING. Research on scientific thinking uses many different methodologies such as analyzing historical records, conducting experiments on subjects that are given scientific problems, and building computer programs that make discoveries. Another focus of research on scientific reasoning has been its development. Research on children has been concerned with discovering how children design experiments and link theory and data, and with describing children's theories of the natural world and science. There has been a tremendous amount of research on scientific thinking over the past forty years. One way of classifying research in this area is in terms of experimental, computational, and real world investigations of scientific thinking. Other important areas not covered in this entry are historical and philosophical approaches to scientific thinking (see Nersessian 1992; Thagard 1992 for research in these areas).

The hallmark of experimental investigations of scientific thinking has been to take one aspect of scientific thinking that is thought to be important and investigate it in the laboratory. The three aspects of scientific thinking that have been most actively investigated are problem solving, hypothesis testing, and concept acquisition.

Scientific Thinking as Problem Solving

According to this view, scientific thinking can be characterized as a search in various problem spaces (Simon 1977). Simon has investigated a number of scientific discoveries by bringing subjects into the laboratory and getting them to rediscover a scientific concept (Qin and Simon 1990). He has then analyzed the verbal protocols that subjects generate and mapped out the types of problem spaces that the subjects search in (such as a space of possible mathematical functions when finding patterns in a set of numbers). In a similar vein, Klahr and Dunbar (1988) characterized scientific thinking as a search in two problem spaces, a hypothesis space and an experiment space. The goal of the researchers using this approach has been to identify the types of search strategies or heuristics that are used in scientific thinking.

Scientific Thinking as Hypothesis Testing

Many researchers have regarded hypothesis testing as a core attribute of scientific thinking. Much of this work has been concerned with Karl Popper's idea that the best way to test a hypothesis is to attempt to disconfirm it. Using this approach, researchers have found that subjects usually try to confirm their hypotheses rather than disconfirm their hypotheses. That is, subjects will conduct an experiment that will generate a result that is predicted by their hypothesis. This is known as confirmation bias. Many researchers have shown that it is very difficult to overcome this type of bias. Mynatt, Doherty, and Tweney (1977) devised a task in which subjects had to conduct experiments in an artificial universe and found that subjects attempt to confirm their hypotheses. Dunbar (1993) has found that although subjects do try to confirm hypotheses, their hypotheses will change in the face of inconsistent findings. Klayman has argued that people possess a positive test bias—people attempt to conduct experiments that will yield a result that is predicted by their current hypothesis, and that under certain circumstances, this is a good strategy to use (Klayman and Ha 1987). Summaries of work on hypothesis testing can be found in Tweney, Doherty, and Mynatt (1981) and Gorman (1992).

Scientific Thinking as Concept Discovery

Many researchers have noted that an important component of science is the generation of new CONCEPTS and modification of existing concepts. Starting with Bruner, Goodnow, and Austin (1956) researchers focused on the idea that scientists must formulate new concepts and theories. Whereas this work focused on strategies that are used to generate new concepts, later work focused on the ways that scientific concepts are represented and change with expertise (Chi, Felto-vitch, and Glaser 1981). There has also been a considerable amount of work on CONCEPTUAL CHANGE—the radical restructuring of concepts in COGNITIVE DEVELOPMENT and science (Brewer and Samarapungavan 1991; Wiser and Carey 1983). This research has uncovered the types of external events that precede conceptual change and the ways that scientific concepts change over time.

Experimental Approaches to the Development of Scientific Thinking

Many researchers have noted that children are like scientists; they have theories, conduct experiments, and revise their theories. Thus, although most researchers agree that scientists and adults have much more complex knowledge structures than children do, the developmental question has been whether there are differences between children's and adults' abilities to formulate theories and test hypotheses. Inhelder and PIAGET (1958) demonstrated that children of different ages have different abilities in testing hypotheses and interpreted their results in terms of Piaget's stage theory of cognitive development. Early research focused on different stages in the development of scientific thinking, but the idea of stages has largely disappeared from recent theorizing on this issue. Some researchers such as Deanna Kuhn (1989) have demonstrated differences in the ability of children to design experiments at different ages. Other researchers, such as Sodian, Zaitchik, and Carey (1991) have showed that even young children can design good experiments that test hypotheses. Klahr, Fay, and Dunbar (1993) have argued that when a scientific thinking task involves searching in one problem space, few if any developmental differences will be found, but if the task involves use of a number of problem spaces, then there will be developmental differences. Recent research, such as that of Schauble (1996), has tracked children's ability to test hypotheses over periods of time and found that children do change their experimentation strategies with experience. Research on children's theories of biological mechanisms reveals that preschoolers have coherent representations of many biological processes that, at certain levels, resemble those of adults (Wellman and Gelman 1997). Overall, recent research on the development of scientific reasoning indicates that, once amount of knowledge is held constant, there are few radical differences between children's and adults' abilities to form hypotheses, test hypotheses, and design experiments.

Computational Approaches

Computational approaches provide specific models of the cognitive processes underlying scientific thinking. Early computational work consisted of taking a scientific discovery and building computational models of the reasoning processes involved in the discovery. Langley et al. (1987) built a series of programs that simulated discoveries such as those of Copernicus and Stahl. These programs have various inductive reasoning algorithms built into them and, when given the data that the scientists used, were able to propose the same rules. Computational models since the mid 1980s have had more knowledge of scientific domains built into the programs. For example, Kulkarni and Simon (1990) built a program that represented knowledge of biology and experimental techniques. This program simulated Krebs's discovery of the urea cycle. The incorporation of scientific knowledge into the computer programs has resulted in a shift in emphasis from using programs to simulate discoveries to building programs that are used to help scientists make discoveries. A number of these computer programs have made novel discoveries. For example, Valdes-Perez (1994) has built systems for discoveries in chemistry, and Fajtlowicz has done this in mathematics (Erdos, Fajtlowicz, and Staton 1991). See Darden (1997) for a summary of work on computational models of scientific discovery.

Real-World Investigations of Science

Most psychological research on scientific thinking has been based on implicit assumptions and preconceptions about what is important in scientific thinking. Other than historical records and scientists' recollections, little is known about what scientists really do in their research. Thus we do not know how relevant the cognitive processes investigated by cognitive scientists are to real world science. Using techniques from verbal protocol analysis, Dunbar (1995, 1997) analyzed the "on-line" thinking of molecular biologists and immunologists at work in their laboratories. These data include important scientific discoveries that occurred "on-line." He found that more than 50 percent of the findings that the scientists obtained were unexpected and that much of the scientists' reasoning is concerned with interpreting these findings. As a consequence, scientists have developed specific strategies for dealing with unexpected findings that are very different from the strategies seen in the hypothesis testing literature. Dunbar has also found that scientists use analogies from related rather than unrelated domains in proposing new hypotheses. Furthermore the scientists distribute reasoning among members of a laboratory. For example, one scientist may add one fact to an induction, another scientist adds another fact, and yet a third scientist might make a generalization over the two facts. This type of research on real world science is now making it possible to see what aspects of scientific thinking are important. By fusing together findings from real world science with the results of the more standard experimental methods, it should be possible to build detailed models of scientific thinking that, when implemented, can be used by scientists to help make discoveries.

See also ANALOGY; NAIVE MATHEMATICS; NAIVE PHYSICS

—*Kevin Dunbar*

References

Brewer, W. F., and A. Samarapungavan. (1991). Children's theories vs. scientific theories: Differences in reasoning or differences in knowledge? In R. R. Hoffman and D. S. Palermo, Eds., *Cognition and the Symbolic Processes: Applied and Ecological Perspectives*. Hillsdale, NJ: Erlbaum, pp. 209–232.

Bruner, J. S., J. J. Goodnow, and G. A. Austin. (1956). *A Study of Thinking*. New York: NY Science Editions.

Chi, M. T. H., P. J. Feltovich, and R. Glaser. (1981). Categorization of physics problems by experts and novices. *Cognitive Science* 5: 121–152.

Darden, L. (1997). Recent work in computational scientific discovery. In *Proceedings of the Nineteenth Annual Conference of the Cognitive Science Society*. Stanford University, pp. 161–166.

Dunbar, K. (1993). Concept discovery in a scientific domain. *Cognitive Science* 17: 397–434.

Dunbar, K. (1995). How scientists really reason: Scientific reasoning in real-world laboratories. In R. J. Sternberg and J. Davidson, Eds., *Mechanisms of Insight*. Cambridge, MA: MIT Press.

Dunbar, K. (1997). How scientists think: Online creativity and conceptual change in science. In T. B. Ward, S. M. Smith, and S. Vaid, Eds., *Conceptual Structures and Processes: Emergence, Discovery and Change*. Washington, DC: APA Press.

Erdos, P., S. Fajtlowicz, and W. Staton. (1991). Degree sequences in the triangle-free graphs. *Discrete Mathematics* 92(91): 85–88.

Gorman, M. E. (1992). *Simulating Science*. Bloomington, IN: Indiana University Press.

Inhelder, B., and J. Piaget. (1958). *The Growth of Logical Thinking from Childhood to Adolescence*. New York: Basic Books.

Klahr, D., and K. Dunbar. (1988). Dual space search during scientific reasoning. *Cognitive Science* 12(1): 1–55.

Klahr, D., A. L. Fay, and K. Dunbar. (1993). Heuristics for scientific experimentation: A developmental study. *Cognitive Psychology* 24(1): 111–146.

Klayman, J., and Y. Ha. (1987). Confirmation, disconfirmation and information in hypothesis testing. *Psychological Review* 94: 211–228.

Kuhn, D. (1989). Children and adults as intuitive scientists. *Psychological Review* 96: 674–689.

Kulkarni, D., and H. A. Simon. (1990). The processes of scientific discovery: The strategy of experimentation. *Cognitive Science* 12: 139–176.

Langley, P., H. A. Simon, G. L. Bradshaw, and J. M. Zytkow. (1987). *Scientific Discovery: Computational Explorations of the Creative Processes*. Cambridge, MA: MIT Press.

Mynatt, C. R., M. E. Doherty, and R. D. Tweney. (1977). Confirmation bias in a simulated research environment: An experimental study of scientific inference. *Quarterly Journal of Experimental Psychology* 29: 85–95.

Nersessian, N. (1992). How do scientists think? In R. N. Giere, Ed., *Cognitive Models of Science: Minnesota Studies in the Philosophy of Science,* 15. Minneapolis: University of Minnesota Press, pp. 3–44.

Qin, Y., and H. A. Simon. (1990). Laboratory replication of scientific discovery processes. *Cognitive Science* 4: 281–312.

Simon, H. A. (1977). *Models of Discovery*. Dordrecht: Reidel.

Schauble, L. (1996). The development of scientific reasoning in knowledge-rich contexts. *Developmental Psychology* 32: 102–119.

Sodian, B., D. Zaitchik, and S. Carey. (1991). Young children's differentiation of hypothetical beliefs from evidence. *Child Development* 62: 753–766.

Thagard, P. (1992). *Conceptual Revolutions*. Princeton: Princeton University Press.

Tweney, R. D., M. E. Doherty, and C. A. Mynatt, Eds. (1981). *On Scientific Thinking*. New York: Columbia University Press.

Valdes-Perez, R. E. (1994). Conjecturing hidden entities via simplicity and conservation laws: Machine discovery in chemistry. *Artificial Intelligence* 65(2): 247–280.

Wason, P. C. (1960). On the failure to eliminate hypotheses in a conceptual task. *Quarterly Journal of Experimental Psychology* 12: 129–140.

Wellman, H. M., and S. A. Gelman. (1997). Acquisition of knowledge. In D. Kuhn and R. S. Siegler, Eds., *Handbook of Child Psychology*. Vol. 2, *Cognition, Perception and Language*. 5th ed. New York: Wiley.

Wiser, M., and S. Carey. (1983). When heat and temperature were one. In D. Gentner and A. Stevens, Eds., *Mental Models*. Hillsdale, NJ: Erlbaum, pp. 267–298.

Further Readings

Giere, R. N. (1992). Cognitive models of science. *Minnesota Studies in the Philosophy of Science* 15: 3–44.

Klahr, D. (1994). Searching for cognition in cognitive models of science. *Psycoloquy* 5(69). 94.5.69.

Shrager, J., and P. Langley. (1990). *Computational Models of Scientific Discovery and Theory Formation*. San Mateo, CA: Kaufmann.

Tweney, R. D., and S. Chitwood. (1995). Scientific reasoning. In S. E. Newstead and J. St. B. T. Evans, Eds., *Perspectives on Thinking and Reasoning: Essays in Honour of Peter Wason*. Hove, England: Erlbaum, pp. 241–260.

Valdes-Perez, R., and D. H. Sleeman, Eds. (1997). *Artificial Intelligence* 91(2), special issue on Scientific Discovery.

Scripts

See SCHEMATA

Search

See GREEDY LOCAL SEARCH; HEURISTIC SEARCH

Self

Questions about the self are typically posed as questions about persons or minds, about such self-reflexive capacities as SELF-KNOWLEDGE and self-reference, or about the semantics and pragmatics of "I." For example, we think of the self or person as something that endures through changes in its mental states; but what is it that makes us the same person now who we were ten years ago? Among those who reject the idea of a nonphysical substance or soul, the debate has focused on the relative importance of bodily continuity (especially continuity of the brain) and psychological continuity (Williams 1973; Parfit 1984). Because the focus on psychological continuity entails that there could in principle be more than one person in a single human body, the debate has clear implications for controversies in clinical psychology such as that surrounding multiple personality subjects (Hacking 1995). More recently the debate has expanded to include such normative issues as the nature of the justification of the sacrifices that we ordinarily make for our future selves (White 1991; Rovane 1997), raising the question whether personhood is a metaphysical or a normative concept.

Besides thinking of ourselves as enduring, we have the idea of ourselves as agents—as subjects of actions and not merely objects to which things happen. This raises the issue of whether we could make sense of agency, freedom, and responsibility if all our actions were causally determined or, indeed, whether we could do so even if they were uncaused and random. Compatibilists hold that free will is not a matter of our actions being uncaused but of their being caused in the right way—for example, by a process of deliberation that is uncoerced, uncompelled, and so forth (Ayer 1954). But this leaves open the question how we could be justified in allocating and accepting responsibility for actions that were determined to happen long before we were born (Strawson 1962; White 1991). Another issue that compatibilism leaves unresolved is over the nature of the experience that grounds our concepts of freedom and agency. This topic has been addressed extensively in the existentialist and phenomenological traditions and is currently under investigation in psychology (Heidegger 1962; Sartre 1956; Merleau-Ponty 1962; Neisser 1993: Introduction).

Our concept of the self, however, is not simply that of an enduring entity to which certain mental events and actions are ascribed. We normally assume that our knowledge of ourselves as subjects is nonobservational and noninferential and thus unlike our knowledge of ordinary physical objects. One reason is that our thoughts about ourselves as subjects (thoughts expressed in terms of "I") seem to enjoy an immunity to error that those regarding external objects lack. Although one might be mistaken about whether a body that one could observe was one's own, there is no possibility of losing track of oneself as a subject or of mistaking another subject for oneself or another mind for one's own (Shoemaker 1968). But though our knowledge of ourselves as subjects is apparently not a matter of external observation, it seems that anything to which we could have introspective access would be a mental state and not the enduring subject that has that state. David HUME (1888) concluded on this basis that we have no access to an enduring self and indeed that none exists, a position subsequently taken up by Ernst Mach (1939) and Moritz Schlick (1949).

Self-reference raises some of the same problems as self-knowledge and provides similar reasons for skepticism about the self. How does the term "I" refer? Evidently not through any associated linguistic descriptions, in that we can imagine experiencing amnesia while anesthetized in a sensory deprivation chamber and thinking "I won't let this happen again!" (Anscombe 1975). In such a situation we could not frame a description that would pick us out uniquely. Nor is it adequate to say simply that "I" refers demonstratively, because we normally perceive the object that we demonstrate. Anscombe (1975) has argued on the basis of considerations of this kind that "I" does not refer.

But neither the claim that "I" does not refer nor its denial answers the most basic question underlying the issues of self-reference and self-knowledge and the most basic question associated with the self—How *are* we given to ourselves when our access to ourselves is most immediate? One approach to this question is suggested by work in phenomenology and by contemporary psychologists influenced by James Jerome GIBSON (Heidegger 1962; Sartre 1956; Gibson 1986; Neisser 1988). These theorists hold that what we are given is a pragmatically structured world of opportunities and liabilities. These are perceived directly and immediately; they are not interpretations imposed on a neutral sensory field the perception of which is more direct or immediate. Gibson's term for what is given in such experiences is AFFORDANCES.

As both Sartre and Gibson make clear, in being given a world of human possibilities and things to be done—of doorways that we can walk through and streetcars we can catch if we hurry—we are given ourselves *implicitly*. A world of affordances is one in which we are necessarily implicated. To see the chair as something to sit on is to be given to ourselves (implicitly) as having a certain size, weight, and shape and a certain capacity for movement and action. And our perceiving the speeding car as a threat says as much about our vulnerabilities and liabilities to destruction as it does about automobiles (Warren and Whang 1987; Mark 1987).

The notion of a self implicit in our perceptual experience of the external world raises the question how such a self is related to our explicit conception of ourselves as objective entities. Strawson (1959) poses a similar question by asking how we can have a conception of an entity to which we ascribe both mental and physical properties. And the question how we can ascribe both mental and physical properties to ourselves raises many of the same issues as the question how we can ascribe the same mental properties to ourselves and to others. The problem is that our basis for the ascription of mental properties to others (observation of behavior) is so radically different from our basis for self-ascription that a commitment to the idea of meaning as use suggests that mental predicates must change their meanings from first-person to third-person contexts. This, in other words, is one version of the problem of other minds.

If views like those of Gibson and the phenomenologists that take the agential perspective as basic are correct, however, this way of posing the problem may exaggerate the asymmetries between ourselves and others. Recent research suggests that our capacity to engage in joint or complementary actions with others is in place at birth in the form of a capacity to engage in and recognize mimicry and slightly later in the ability to share affect in expressive exchanges (Meltzoff and Moore 1995; Stern 1985). This points to the possibility that our access to the other subjects' agential characteristics may be at least as direct as our access to their objective makeup. For example, just as we are given ourselves implicitly in the possibilities we see for individual action, the possibilities we see for acting jointly may give us an implicit other—a notion similar to Sartre's (1956: part III, chap. 1) understanding of Heidegger's "being-with." Alternatively, what we perceive most immediately may be a relation of INTERSUBJECTIVITY—"an appropriate match between the nature/direction/timing/intensities of two people's activities" (Neisser 1988: 41). If this general approach can be sustained, then the question how we can ascribe mental properties to an objectively characterized other is misleading. From the agential perspective the problem is rather one of acquiring a more objective conception both of one's partner and of oneself. And, as a large body of contemporary work in psychology suggests (Neisser 1993; Cicchetti and Beeghly 1990; Butterworth 1982), this reformulation may prove more tractable than the original problem.

See also ECOLOGICAL PSYCHOLOGY; IMITATION; SIMULATION VS. THEORY-THEORY; SITUATEDNESS/EMBEDDEDNESS

—*Stephen L. White*

References

Anscombe, G. E. M. (1975). The first person. In S. Guttenplan, Ed., *Mind and Language: Wolfson College Lectures*. New York: Oxford University Press.

Ayer, A. J. (1954). Freedom and necessity. In A. J. Ayer, Ed., *Philosophical Essays*. London: Macmillan.

Butterworth, G. E., Ed. (1982). *Infancy and Epistemology: An Evaluation of Piaget's Theory*. New York: St. Martin's Press.

Cicchetti, D., and M. Beeghly, Eds. (1990). *The Self in Transition: Infancy to Childhood*. Chicago: University of Chicago Press.

Gibson, J. J. (1986). *The Ecological Approach to Visual Perception*. Hillsdale, NJ: Erlbaum.

Hacking, I. (1995). *Rewriting the Soul: Multiple Personality and the Sciences of Memory*. Princeton: Princeton University Press.

Heidegger, M. (1962). *Being and Time*. New York: Harper and Row.

Hume, D. (1888). *A Treatise of Human Nature*. L. A. Selby-Bigge, Ed. Oxford: Clarendon Press.

Mach, E. (1939). *The Analysis of Sensations*. New York: Dover.

Mark, L. S. (1987). Eyeheight-scaled information about affordances: A study of sitting and stair climbing. *Journal of Experimental Psychology: Human Perception and Performance* 13: 361–370.

Meltzoff, A. N., and M. K. Moore. (1995). Infants' understanding of people and things: From body imitation to folk psychology. In J. L. Bermúdez, A. Marcel, and N. Eilan, Eds., *The Body and the Self*. Cambridge, MA: Bradford/MIT Press.

Merleau-Ponty, M. (1962). *Phenomenology of Perception*. London: Routledge and Kegan Paul.

Neisser, U. (1988). Five kinds of self-knowledge. *Philosophical Psychology* 1: 35–59.

Neisser, U., Ed. (1993). *The Perceived Self: Ecological and Interpersonal Sources of Self-Knowledge*. New York: Cambridge University Press.

Parfit, D. (1984). *Reasons and Persons*. New York: Oxford University Press.

Rovane, C. (1997). *The Bounds of Agency: An Essay in Revisionary Metaphysics*. Princeton: Princeton University Press.

Sartre, J.-P. (1956). *Being and Nothingness*. New York: Simon and Schuster.

Schlick, M. (1949). Meaning and verification. In H. Feigl and W. Sellars, Eds., *Readings in Philosophical Analysis*. New York: Appleton-Century-Crofts.

Shoemaker, S. (1968). Self-reference and self-awareness. *Journal of Philosophy* 65: 555–567.

Stern, D. N. (1985). *The Interpersonal World of the Infant*. New York: Basic Books.

Strawson, P. F. (1959). *Individuals*. Garden City, NY: Doubleday.

Strawson, P. F. (1962). Freedom and resentment. *Proceedings of the British Academy* 48: 1–25.

Warren, W. H., and S. Whang. (1987). Visual guidance of walking through apertures: Body-scaled information for affordances. *Journal of Experimental Psychology: Human Perception and Performance* 13: 371–383.

White, S. L. (1991). *The Unity of the Self*. Cambridge, MA: Bradford/MIT Press.

Williams, B. (1973). *Problems of the Self*. New York: Cambridge University Press.

Further Readings

Bermúdez, J. L., A. Marcel, and N. Eilan, Eds. (1995). *The Body and the Self*. Cambridge, MA: Bradford/MIT Press.

Campbell, J. (1994). *Past, Space, and Self*. Cambridge, MA: Bradford/MIT Press.

Cassam, Q., Ed. (1994). *Self-Knowledge.* New York: Oxford University Press.

Cassam, Q. (1997). *Self and World.* Oxford: Clarendon Press.

Dennett, D. C. (1992). The self as a center of narrative gravity. In F. Kessel, P. Cole, and D. Johnson, Eds., *Self and Consciousness: Multiple Perspectives.* Hillsdale, NJ: Erlbaum.

Eilan, N., R. McCarthy, and B. Brewer, Eds. (1993). *Spatial Representation.* Oxford: Blackwell.

Elster, J. (1986). *The Multiple Self.* New York: Cambridge University Press.

Evans, G. (1982). *The Varieties of Reference.* New York: Oxford University Press.

Gallagher, S., and J. Shear, Eds. (1997). Special issue: Models of the self. *Journal of Consciousness Studies* 4: 385–540.

Husserl, E. (1950). *Cartesian Meditations.* Dordrecht: Kluwer.

James, W. (1950). The consciousness of self. In *The Principles of Psychology.* New York: Dover.

Lewis, M., and J. Brooks-Gunn. (1979). *Social Cognition and the Acquisition of Self.* New York: Plenum.

Mead, G. H. (1934). *Mind, Self, and Society.* Chicago: University of Chicago Press.

Peacocke, C., Ed. (1994). *Objectivity, Simulation, and the Unity of Consciousness.* New York: Oxford University Press.

Radden, J. (1996). *Divided Minds and Successive Selves: Ethical Issues in Disorders of Identity and Personality.* Cambridge, MA: Bradford/MIT Press.

Sartre, J.-P. (1957). *The Transcendence of the Ego: An Existentialist Theory of Consciousness.* New York: Farrar, Straus, and Giroux.

Shoemaker, S. (1963). *Self-Knowledge and Self-Identity.* Ithaca: Cornell University Press.

Taylor, C. (1989). *Sources of the Self: The Making of the Modern Identity.* Cambridge, MA: Harvard University Press.

Tugendhat, E. (1986). *Self-Consciousness and Self-Determination.* Cambridge, MA: MIT Press.

Vygotsky, L. (1986). *Thought and Language.* Cambridge, MA: MIT Press.

Wilkes, K. (1988). *Real People: Personal Identity without Thought Experiments.* New York: Oxford University Press.

Wittgenstein, L. (1958). *The Blue and Brown Books.* Oxford: Blackwell.

Self-Knowledge

The beginning Socratic injunction "Know thyself" dates to the very beginning of the Western intellectual tradition, and self-knowledge in its many forms has been a central concern ever since. A wide variety of cognitive states fall under its conceptual umbrella. The sort of self-knowledge acquired through cognitive psychotherapy, for example, might include explicit beliefs about the motives of one's behavior couched in the concepts of folk psychological intentional discourse and available for application in the control or modification of future personal action. Alternatively, the Chomskyan self-knowledge that humans are alleged to have of the structure of their language processing systems is largely implicit, subpersonal, innate, and limited in application to the specific process of language-learning.

The types of self-knowledge vary along four main parameters:

- Content
- Manner or mode of representation
- Domain of application
- Means of acquisition

Although the four are importantly interdependent, each presents its own set of issues.

The content of self-knowledge essentially concerns what a cognitive agent knows about its own nature or organization. Though paradigm cases involve knowledge about one's psychological nature, any property or feature of the agent can be its object. One can have self-knowledge of the size, state, and orientation of one's body as well as of one's beliefs and emotions. Despite this breadth, it is the cases of metapsychological cognition that are of greatest interest; for it is they that provide the opportunity for radical increases in mental sophistication. It is virtually impossible to create a system with highly sophisticated mental abilities without building in a significant degree of metapsychological understanding. This point can be overlooked if one focuses exclusively on cases of explicit human self-knowledge of the sort that could be verbally reported. However, if one recognizes the wealth of implicit self-knowledge that must be implicitly embodied in the systems of self-monitoring and self-regulation required by any sophisticated cognitive agent, it becomes readily apparent that self-knowledge of one sort or another will be the pervasive and central feature of all but the most minimally minded systems. Even simple organisms and robots require some measure of self-knowledge to function as cognitive actors. Without knowledge of one's goals and abilities, it would be impossible to carry out multiple stage actions. And no learning would be possible in a system that totally lacked understanding of the function and organization of the processes to be modified. The requisite self-knowledge might all be implicitly embedded in the structure of the learning mechanisms, but that organization in itself counts as a form of self-knowledge insofar as it adaptively reflects the nature of the processes that are changed through learning.

Explicit human self-knowledge nonetheless remains of great interest to philosophers and psychologists. Adult humans have unique abilities to reason about their mental lives and generally reliable insight into their inferential processes, motives, and preferences. This enhances their ability to regulate their mental lives and to interact with others in social contexts. Empirical studies have nonetheless shown glaring gaps in human metacognitive powers; in specific test situations adult subjects show ignorance of the factors governing their choices, their sources of information, and the rules underlying their reasoning.

The degree to which explicit self-knowledge may be present in children or in nonhuman primates is controversial. Children under the age of three fail to distinguish between their own beliefs about a situation and those that an agent with different access would have; they seem unable to conceptualize their own view of reality as such, that is, as one among many possible views. Tests, especially those involving deceptions, on chimpanzees seem to show some grasp of explicit mental concepts, but only of the most limited sort. Other studies, such as those using mirror recognition tasks, give evidence that chimps and orangs have some type of self concept, but again of only a limited sort. Further research is needed to resolve these issues. In a surprising twist, the psychologist Alan Leslie has proposed that an inability to engage in METACOGNITION is the primary deficit in AUTISM and the source of most of the disabling symptoms associated with it.

Cases of self-knowledge vary not only in their objects but also in how they conceptualize or categorize their objects. Explicit human self-knowledge of the aims of one's behavior is likely to be conceptualized in the folk psychological notions of belief, desire, and intention, but such concepts are not likely to figure in the self-knowledge one's retrieval system has of the structure and organization of one's memory nor in a cat's knowledge of its current needs and goals. Indeed, there may be no public-language words or concepts that adequately capture the content of such implicit knowledge. But insofar as it partitions its pyschological objects in similarity classes and generates aptly matched responses, even such procedural self-knowledge must involve categorization or conceptualization.

Self-knowledge can be explicitly represented and stored as is likely the case with the propositional knowledge that humans have of their intentions and beliefs. The psychologist Philip Johnson-Laird has argued that the planning and control of intentional action requires a self model that explicitly represents one's goals, abilities, options, and current state. But significant self-knowledge can also be implicitly represented in the structure of a network or in the organization of a metacontrol system as is probably true of that embodied in many learning processes. The mechanism by which rats learn to avoid foods that have been followed by bouts of nausea several hours after feeding provides an apt example. One need not suppose that the rat has any explicit awareness of the processes that regulate its feeding behavior or taste sensations, yet its nervous system clearly carries information about those factors as shown by its ability to alter those mechanisms in just the way needed to produce the desired behavioral change.

Procedurally embodied self-knowledge will often be more limited in its scope of application; the metapsychological understanding carried in a learning process may have no impact outside the context of the specific modifications it is designed to produce. The rat can not reflect on the organization of its feeding mechanisms nor make open-ended use of that information, as one might if one had explicit propositional knowledge of them. The difference, however, is one of degree. Procedural self-knowledge can have a relatively broad range of application, and even explicit beliefs about one's mental state are limited in their impact to some degree by the larger context within which they occur.

Self-knowledge can arise in many ways. Traditional Cartesian mentalism treated the mind as fully transparent and open in all its significant properties to a faculty of conscious INTROSPECTION or reflection, which was conceived of by later empiricists as a form of inner perception. Though introspection is now regarded as fallible, incomplete, and theory-laden, it nonetheless remains a major source of self-knowledge. Though internal monitoring, like external monitoring through the senses, is subject to error, it still provides a regular ongoing supply of information about the current state and operation of at least some aspects of one's mind.

The development of self-knowledge depends on both cultural and biological sources. Some theorists argue that the child's mastery of mental concepts involves building a behaviorally based theory of mind; others see it more as a matter of projection from first person-based concepts. In either case, both innate information and culturally based learning will be involved. Children must acquire from their social context many of the concepts needed to categorize their mental states and processes, but folk psychology is likely also to embody an innate scheme of mental categories. Moreover, the neural mechanisms that underlie introspection probably depend on innate implicit self-knowledge in the same way that our perceptual processes depend on such knowledge about the environment.

Though self-knowledge has many obvious benefits, it may not always be adaptive. Ignorance of one's limitations may enhance one's ability to mobilize oneself to action, and a lack of self-knowledge may signal a happy freedom from narcissistic self-absorption. This creates a new puzzle about self-deception. The old puzzle was to explain how deceiving oneself was even possible, given the apparently self-defeating identity of deceiver and deceived. If self-deception is often adaptive, a new more normative problem arises. Must we abandon our intuition that self-deception in itself is a bad thing? Must we qualify the Socratic "Know thyself" with the proviso "but only when it's useful"?

See also EPISTEMOLOGY AND COGNITION; INNATENESS OF LANGUAGE; MENTAL MODELS; PRIMATE COGNITION; SELF

—*Robert van Gulick*

References

Beckoff, M., and D. Jameison. (1996). *Readings in Animal Cognition.* Cambridge, MA: MIT Press.

Bennett, J. (1988). Thoughtful brutes. *Proceedings and Addresses of the American Philosophical Association* 62: 196–211.

Chomsky, N. (1980). *Reflections on Language.* New York: Pantheon.

Garcia, J. A., and R. A. Koelling. (1967). A comparison of aversions caused by x-rays, toxins and drugs in rats. *Radiation Research Supplement* 7: 439–450.

Goldman, A. (1993). The psychology of folk psychology. *The Behavioral and Brain Sciences* 16: 15–28.

Gopnik, A. (1993). How we know our minds: The illusion of first-person knowledge of intentional states. *Behavioral and Brain Sciences* 16: 15–28.

Johnson, M., S. Hashtroudi, and D. Lindsay. (1993). Source monitoring. *Psychological Bulletin* 114: 3–28.

Johnson-Laird, P. (1983). *Mental Models.* Cambridge, MA: Harvard University Press.

Lyons, W. (1986). *The Disappearance of Introspection.* Cambridge, MA: MIT Press.

McLaughlin, B., and A. Rorty. (1988). *Perspectives on Self-Deception.* Berkeley: University of California Press.

Nisbet, R., and T. Wilson. (1977). Telling more than we can know: Verbal reports on mental processes. *Psychological Review* 84: 231–259.

Rorty, A. (1975). Adaptivity and self-knowledge. *Inquiry* 18: 1–22.

Wellman, H. (1990). *The Child's Theory of Mind.* Cambridge, MA: MIT Press.

Self-Organizing Systems

Self-organization refers to spontaneous ordering tendencies sometimes observed in certain classes of complex systems, both artificial and natural. Such systems have a large number of components that interact simultaneously in a sufficiently rich number of parallel ways; are at best only partially decomposable; are sensitive to initial conditions when they are in the chaotic regime; are constrained away from their most probable state; and exhibit nondeterministic bifurcations in their dynamic trajectories. Self-organization occurs in these systems when chance fluctuations are spontaneously amplified by nonlinear feedback. This sort of spontaneous ordering has been observed in computational systems that are programmed for nonlinear, parallel interactions under local constraints. Examples in nature range from dust devils and hurricanes to certain sorts of chemical and biological systems, such as Benard cells and chemical oscillators (see below). The topic of self-organization has also been explored under other rubrics, such as "emergent structuring," "self-assembly," "autocatalysis," and "autopoiesis." In each case, the contrast emphasized is between the additive building of structures from elemental building blocks in a decomposable or nearly decomposable system (in the sense defined by Simon 1962) by means of measured increments of force and the spontaneous emergence of nonadditive, nonlinear, highly integrated, highly interactive wholes in less decomposable systems.

Ilya Prigogine's model of dissipative structures, which obey the second law precisely by building structures that increase the entropy of their surroundings while decreasing it within their own boundaries, has facilitated both the recognition of self-organizing structures and their explanation (Prigogine 1973). The wider significance of Prigogine's work has been made known by Isabelle Stengers, Erik Jantsch, Jeffrey Wicken, and C. Dyke (Prigogine and Stengers 1984; Jantsch 1980; Wicken 1987; Dyke 1988). Stuart Kauffman has been prominent among those who have argued that the self-ordering properties of cellular AUTOMATA provide good dynamic models for self-organizing biological systems (Kauffman 1993). Cellular automata were originally developed by John VON NEUMANN and Warren McCULLOCH as tools for analyzing NEURAL NETWORKS.

The line between genuinely self-organizing systems and the self-ordering properties of a wider class of complex systems is difficult to draw. Those who stress the autocatalytic, self-promoting aspect of self-organizing systems, in which a reaction feeds on itself, and the far-from-thermodynamic-equilibrium locus of paradigmatic instances of it, may hesitate to recognize the self-assembly of microtubules, for example, as any more than a case of crystalline self-ordering. Similarly, a distinction might well be drawn between self-organizing systems generally and "autopoietic" systems, in the sense of Maturana and Varela's use of the term (Maturana and Varela 1980). The latter term connotes the kind of agency that appears when a complex dissipative system is coupled to its environment through autocatalytic feedback in such a way that it is capable of changing the parameters that govern its interactions with its surroundings. (Maturana and Varela suggest that the ability of some living things to represent their environment, and in some cases even themselves, to themselves is a function of self-organization, which creates a bond between self and environment that is more intimate than our philosophical tradition has hitherto allowed.)

One ought not, however, be too rigid about such definitional matters. Research into these issues is only in an early stage, and usage is in flux. Nonetheless, it is highly significant that the computational revolution has now given science mathematical tools to track and display the dynamics of systems that do not reduce either to ordered simplicity, as in classic mechanics, or to disordered complexity, as in statistical mechanics and thermodynamics. This allows the ordered complexity of phenomena that have hitherto remained beyond the reach of science itself, or that have been subjected to inappropriately reductionist forms of analysis, to be brought within the charmed circle of mathematized knowledge.

The best understood cases of natural self-organization occur in physical and chemical systems that are stabilized far from thermodynamic equilibrium. Benard cells are a classic example of self-organizing physical systems. A honeycomb of hexagonal cells forms at the bottom of the pan when a thin layer of oil is heated from below. This happens because the kinetic energy of the molecules becomes insufficient to dissipate the energy flux when it exceeds a certain threshold value. Macroscopic order then emerges in which billions of molecules move coherently in a convection stream, thereby more efficiently dissipating the energy gradient and increasing the entropy of the surroundings of the system. Increasing the gradient further can lead to a development of still more complex convection cells. Ultimately, however, excessive gradient will result in turbulence.

The Belouzov-Zhabotinskii, or BZ, reaction is a well-known example of self-organization in a chemical system. In a BZ reaction, citric acid, sulfuric acid, potassium bromate, and an iron salt, when combined in certain proportions, produce sudden and repeated alternations between blue and red states in stirred solutions. In thin layers, circular or spiral chemical waves of color can result. As in the case of Benard cells, increasing the gradient produces nondeterministic bifurcations and more complex patterns. But when the energy gradient (which in this case inheres in the chemical bonds between constituents) grows too steep, chaotic behavior results.

Chemical oscillators, such as the BZ reaction, may have implications for self-organization in biological systems, particularly in development. Alan TURING's paper on limit cycle solutions to reaction-diffusion equations has long been thought by some to model certain aspects of embryogenesis (Turing 1952). The life cycle of slime molds, a sort of colonial amoeba, also appears to embody a self-organizing pattern. It alternates between mere aggregation when food is plentiful and differentiation into a cellulose base and a fruiting body when it is scarce. The fruiting body eventually bursts, scattering spores that begin the cycle over again (Garfinkel 1987).

As these examples show, self-organization is potentially relevant to fundamental questions about EVOLUTION. One issue is whether life itself came into existence through a self-organizing process. Those who have used computers to explore the mathematically self-ordering properties of complex adaptive systems have studied this subject under the rubric of ARTIFICIAL LIFE. Those whose definition of life is less formal have looked for chemical conditions in the early history of the planet in which some form of prebiotic selection might have amplified the autocatalytic properties of self-organizing protocells into functional, adapted traits. Such studies begin with the plausible insight that life probably did not originate solely in the accidental assembly of nucleic acids, but in the coevolution of proteins and nucleic acids, with protein evolution perhaps playing the leading role. Sidney Fox's pioneering work on proteinoid microspheres reveals them to be spontaneously self-organized systems that might have provided the hydrophobic boundaries within which the subsequent coevolution of protein and nucleic acids can take place (Fox 1984). Harold Morowitz's and David Deamer's notion of abiotically forming vesicular amphiphile bilayers provides another possible such "cradle" for the emergence of life (Morowitz, Heinz, and Deamer 1988). Manfred Eigen's notion of hypercycles provides a model of how this interaction might have occurred. One can think of a hypercycle as a system of linked autocatalytic cycles, in which each member is catalyzed by at least one other member (Eigen and Schuster 1979.)

A second issue is the relationship between natural selection and self-organization once life is up and running. On the face of it, self-organization rivals natural selection as the basis of both individual development and of the larger contours of phylogenetic order. For the acquisition of functional traits by self-amplifying feedback is not the same thing as selection-by-consequences by means of a forcelike "selection pressure" that operates against an inertial, and indeed inert, dynamic background, which is how natural selection is usually conceived. The notion that self-organization and natural selection are rivals has been defended by several authors (Goodwin 1994; Oyama 1985; Salthe 1993). A more integrative, mutually reinforcing approach is, however, possible. Recognizing that when any system analogous to Boolean networks is set into motion it can be expected spontaneously to explore its space of future states and if mild "fitness" conditions are imposed it can be expected to reach peaks on "adaptive landscapes." Kauffman, Holland, and others who have studied genetic algorithms and EVOLUTIONARY COMPUTATION have suggested that "spontaneous order is available to natural selection for the further selective crafting of well-wrought designs" (Kauffman 1993: 1; Holland 1995). One might readily imagine, in accord with this suggestion, that natural selection has stabilized the self-organized life cycle of slime molds, and in the process has conferred an explicitly biological function on a spontaneously generated pattern. Kauffman himself argues that the regulatory systems of genetic networks, among whose many nodes much connectivity and parallel processing are at play, are self-organizing, functionally decomposable (see FUNCTIONAL DECOMPOSITION) systems that have been stabilized by natural selection in this way. Weber and Depew have argued that, considered as a natural phenomenon in its own right, natural selection emerges only in autocatalytic chemi-

cal systems that have managed to internalize information in macromolecules, the error rate of which provides the fuel of natural selection (Weber and Depew 1996). In this account, genes have the function of enhancing and stabilizing the coupling between organism and environment that self-organization first generates.

The human brain has about 10^{10} neurons, any of which can have up to 10^4 connections with other such neurons, stimulated and regulated by a large number of chemical neurotransmitters. This fact alone brings the study of cognitive and other psychological phenomena within hailing distance of the study of self-organizing complex systems. This distance has been reduced by those advocating DYNAMIC APPROACHES TO COGNITION, who recognize that learning is a process that occurs only in systems that are "environmentally embedded, corporeally embodied, and neurally entrained" by feedback (see Port and Van Gelder 1995; Smith and Thelen 1993; Kelso 1995; Cook and Murray 1995). If digital computationalism gives way to more dynamical studies of connectivity in neural networks, self-organization can be expected to play a more prominent role in both the ontogeny and phylogeny of mental functions. The purely adaptationist stories people like to tell about the Pleistocene origins of localized mental functions (Barkow, Cosmides, and Tooby 1992), as well as the inclination to model neurological development closely on Darwinian mechanisms (Edelman 1987), might then give way to a more nuanced view, in which neural organization is taken to be governed in part by self-organization working through intense feedback between organism and environment.

See also ADAPTATION AND ADAPTATIONISM; COMPUTATION AND THE BRAIN; EVOLUTIONARY PSYCHOLOGY

—*David Depew and Bruce Weber*

References

Barkow, J., L. Cosmides, and J. Toomy. (1992). *The Adapted Mind.* New York: Oxford University Press.

Cook, J., and J. D. Murray. (1995). Pattern formation, biological. In M. A. Arbib, Ed., *Handbook of Brain Theory and Neural Networks.* Cambridge, MA: MIT Press, pp. 705–710.

Dyke, C. (1988). *The Evolutionary Dynamics of Complex Systems.* Oxford: Oxford University Press.

Edelman, G. (1987). *Neural Darwinism.* New York: Basic Books.

Eigen, M., and P. Schuster. (1979). *The Hypercycle.* Berlin: Springer.

Fox, S. (1984). Proteinoid experiments and evolutionary theory. In M.-W. Ho and P. T. Saunders, Eds., *Beyond Neo-Darwinism.* London: Academic Press, pp. 15–60.

Garkinkel, A. (1987). The slime mold *Dictyostelium* as a model of self-organization in social systems. In F. E. Bates, Ed., *Self-Organizing Systems: The Emergence of Order.* New York: Plenum Press.

Goodwin, B. C. (1994). *How the Leopard Changed Its Spots: The Evolution of Complexity.* London: Weidenfeld and Nicolson.

Holland, J. A. (1995). *Hidden Order: How Adaptation Builds Complexity.* Reading, MA: Addison-Wesley.

Jantsch, E. (1980). *The Self-Organizing Universe.* Oxford: Pergamon Press.

Kauffman, S. A. (1993). *The Origins of Order: Self-Organization and Selection in Evolution.* New York: Oxford University Press.

Kelso, J. A. S. (1995). *Dynamic Patterns: The Self-Organization of Brain and Behavior*. Cambridge, MA: MIT Press/Bradford Books.

Maturana, J., and F. Varela. (1980). *Autopoiesis and Cognition: The Realization of the Living*. Dordrecht, Reidel.

Morowitz, H. J., B. Heinz, and D. W. Deamer. (1988). The chemical logic of a minimum protocell. *Origins of Life and Evolution of the Biosphere* 18: 281–287.

Oyama, S. (1985). *The Ontogeny of Information*. Cambridge: Cambridge University Press.

Port, R., and T. van Gelder. (1995). *Mind as Motion: Explorations of the Dynamics of Cognition*. Cambridge, MA: MIT Press.

Prigogine, I. (1973). Irreversibility as a symmetry breaking factor. *Nature* 248: 67–71.

Prigogine, I., and I. Stengers. (1984). *Order Out of Chaos: Man's New Dialogue with Nature*. New York: Bantam.

Salthe, S. N. (1993). *Development in Evolution: Complexity and Change in Biology*. Cambridge, MA: MIT Press.

Simon, H. A. (1962). The architecture of complexity. *Proceedings of the American Philosophical Society* 106: 467–482.

Smith, L. B., and E. Thelen. (1993). *A Dynamic Systems Approach to Development*. Cambridge, MA: MIT Press/Bradford Books.

Turing, A. M. (1952). The chemical basis of morphogenesis. *Philosophical Transactions of the Royal Society London. Series B. Biological Sciences* 237: 37–72.

Weber, B. H., and D. J. Depew. (1996). Natural selection and self-organization: Dynamical models as clues to a new evolutionary synthesis. *Biology and Philosophy* 11: 33–65.

Wicken, J. (1987). *Evolution, Information and Thermodynamics: Extending the Darwinian Program*. New York: Oxford University Press.

Further Readings

Bechtel, W., and R. C. Richardson. (1993). *Discovering Complexity: Decomposition and Localization as Strategies in Scientific Research*. Princeton, NJ: Princeton University Press.

Depew, D. J., and Weber, B. H. (1995). *Darwinism Evolving: Systems Dynamics and the Genealogy of Natural Selection*. Cambridge, MA: MIT Press/Bradford Books.

Godfrey-Smith, P. (1996). *Complexity and the Function of Mind in Nature*. Cambridge: Cambridge University Press.

Harrison, L. G. (1993). *Kinetic Theory of Living Pattern*. Cambridge: Cambridge University Press.

Juarrero, A. (Forthcoming). *Dynamics in Action: Intentional Behavior as a Complex System*. Cambridge, MA: MIT Press/Bradford Books.

Langton, C. G., Ed. (1995). *Artificial Life: An Overview*. Cambridge, MA: MIT Press/Bradford Books.

Mittenthal, J. E., and A. R. Baskin, Eds. (1992). *The Principles of Organization in Organisms*. Reading, MA: Addison-Wesley.

Morowitz, H. J., and J. L. Singer, Eds. (1995). *The Mind, The Brain, and Complex Adaptive Systems*. Reading, MA: Addison-Wesley.

Swenson, R., and M. T. Turvey. (1991). Thermodynamic reasons for perception-action cycles. *Ecological Psychology* 3: 317–348.

Stein, W., and F. J. Varela, Eds. (1993). *Thinking about Biology*. Reading, MA: Addison-Wesley.

Thelen, E., and B. D. Ulrich. (1991). Hidden skills: A dynamic systems analysis of treadmill stepping during the first year. *Monographs of the Society for Research in Child Development*, serial no. 223, 56 (1).

Ulanowics, R. E. (1997). *Ecology: The Ascendent Perspective*. New York: Columbia University Press.

Semantic Memory

See EPISODIC VS. SEMANTIC MEMORY

Semantic Networks

See FRAME-BASED SYSTEMS; SCHEMATA

Semantics

Semantics is the study of MEANING. It is not surprising that "semantics" can "mean" different things to different researchers within cognitive science. Notions relating to meaning have had long (and often contentious) histories within the disciplines that contribute to cognitive science, and there have been very diverse views concerning what questions are important, and for what purposes, and how they should be approached. And there are some deep foundational and methodological differences within and across disciplines that affect approaches to semantics. These have partly impeded but also stimulated cooperative discussion and fruitful cross-fertilization of ideas, and there has been great substantive progress in semantics, in the sister field of PRAGMATICS and at the SYNTAX-SEMANTICS INTERFACE in recent decades.

The logico-philosophical tradition divides semiotics (the study of signs, applicable to both natural and constructed languages) into syntax, semantics, and pragmatics (Morris 1938). On this view, SYNTAX concerns properties of expressions, such as well-formedness; semantics concerns relations between expressions and what they are "about" (typically "the world" or some model), such as reference; and pragmatics concerns relations between expressions and their uses in context, such as IMPLICATURE. Some approaches reject the characterization of semantics as dealing with relations between language and something external to language, especially between language and "the world" (see (1) and (2) below). And many approaches have challenged, in different ways, the autonomy of semantics from pragmatics implied by the traditional trichotomy. We return to some of these foundational issues below.

One of the basic issues that any theory of semantics must deal with is how we can understand the meanings of novel sentences. Syntax describes the recursive part-whole structure of sentences; semantics must account for how the meanings of smaller parts are combined to form the meanings of larger wholes (see COMPOSITIONALITY and LOGICAL FORM). There are many controversial issues surrounding the principle of compositionality, which contains several crucially theory-dependent terms: *The meaning of an expression is a function of the meanings of its parts and of how they are syntactically combined.* But most explicit semantic theories, especially formal semantics, accept it as a basic working principle. The extension of compositional semantics beyond the level of the sentence, to the interpretation of DISCOURSE, has been of increasing importance.

Another basic issue for semantic theory is the nature of the meanings of the smallest meaningful units of language, words or morphemes (or even smaller units if some morphemes are viewed as decomposable into submorphemic "features"). Lexical semantics has an even longer history than compositional semantics and is connected with the most fundamental problems in the philosophy of language and the psychology of CONCEPTS (see REFERENCE, THEORIES OF and LEXICON).

Crucial *interfaces* include the syntax-semantics interface and the interfaces of semantics with pragmatics, with encyclopedic and common-sense knowledge, and perhaps directly with PHONOLOGY (e.g., with respect to the semantic/pragmatic interpretation of PROSODY AND INTONATION). Other important areas of research concern acquisition, human semantic processing, and computational semantics.

Among the most important semantic properties of linguistic expressions that need to be accounted for, most semanticists would include the following:

Ambiguity: Having more than one meaning. Strongly compositional theories require all semantic ambiguity to reflect either *lexical* or *structural* (syntactic) AMBIGUITY.

Vagueness: A challenge for some theories of the nature of word meanings as well as to classical theories of concepts. Drawing the distinction between ambiguity and VAGUENESS is a classic problem (Quine 1960; Zwicky and Sadock 1975).

Anomaly: Some expressions, like the famous *Colorless green ideas sleep furiously* (Chomsky 1957), are judged to be *semantically anomalous* although syntactically well-formed. The lines between semantic and other sorts of anomaly are crucially theory-dependent and often debated.

Entailment: Sentence A *entails* sentence B if sentence B is true in every possible state of affairs in which sentence A is true. Entailment has always been a central semantic concern in LOGIC and the philosophy of language, and remains so in POSSIBLE WORLDS SEMANTICS. Cognitive semanticists replace concern with logical entailment by concern with human inference; formal semanticists see the relation of entailment to actual human inference as indirect. But most semanticists are concerned with some notion of entailment or inference, and many agree about the importance of revising (incrementally or radically) the formal logics invented by logicians to model the "natural logic(s)" implicit in the semantics of natural languages.

Presupposition: A precondition for the felicity or truth-valuedness of an expression in a context. PRESUPPOSITION research has been important in theorizing about the relation between (or possible integration of) semantics and pragmatics.

Context: Expressions are interpreted in the (linguistic) context of other expressions, and in the (nonlinguistic) context of an utterance situation in which the participants have various beliefs and intentions. Any approach to semantics has to take a stand on the relation of "semantics proper" to various aspects of context, including the treatment of INDEXICALS AND DEMONSTRATIVES (Kaplan 1977). One important trend in formal semantics has been the shift from "meanings as

truth conditions" to "meanings as functions from contexts to contexts" (with truth conditions as a corollary; Heim 1982); see CONTEXT AND POINT OF VIEW, SITUATEDNESS/EMBEDDEDNESS, DYNAMIC SEMANTICS.

Referential opacity: The construction exemplified in "Jones is seeking—" is *referentially opaque*, because the substitution of one coreferential expression for another in that context does not always preserve the truth-value of the whole. It may be true that Jones is seeking the president and false that Jones is seeking Mary's father even though the president is Mary's father. Frege's distinction between SENSE AND REFERENCE, Carnap's distinction between intension and extension, and Montague's intensional logic all treat the phenomenon of referential opacity, pervasive in PROPOSITIONAL ATTITUDE constructions.

Other issues important to semantics include ANAPHORA, negation and QUANTIFIERS, TENSE AND ASPECT, and modality; other issues important for semantics and pragmatics together include topic-FOCUS structure and the interpretation of questions, imperatives, and other speech acts.

Many foundational issues of semantics are relevant to cognitive science; some are particularly linguistic, others overlap heavily with issues in the philosophy of language and philosophy of mind. We mention a few central issues that divide different approaches to semantics.

1. The nonpsychologistic tradition of "objective" (though abstract) meanings (Frege 1892; Carnap 1956; Montague 1973) versus the psychologistic view of meanings "in the head" (Fodor 1975; Lakoff 1987; Jackendoff 1983; and all psychologists). Do expressions refer to objects or to concepts? Is semantics a branch of mathematics, or is it (as on the Chomskyan view of all of linguistics) a branch of psychology? Classical formal semanticists, who take the first disjunct in these choices, distinguish semantics from knowledge of semantics (Lewis 1975), making semantic competence interestingly different from syntactic competence. Jackendoff (1996), following Chomsky (1986) on "I-language" and "E-language," distinguishes "I-semantics" (internalized semantics, semantic competence) from "E-semantics" (an abstract relation external to language users), and characterizes his own Conceptual Semantics as well as COGNITIVE LINGUISTICS (Lakoff 1987) as studying the former whereas formal semantics studies the latter. Many today seek an integration of these two perspectives by studying mind-internal intuitions of mind-external relations such as reference and truth-conditions. See Putnam 1975 for an influential philosophical perspective.

2. Model-theoretic versus representational approaches. Many linguists think of semantics in terms of a "level of representation" of expressions analogous to a syntactic or phonological level. Psychologists generally think of semantics as relating expressions to concepts, regarding concepts as something like elements of a LANGUAGE OF THOUGHT. In AI, semantic interpretation is sometimes expressed in a language of KNOWLEDGE REPRESENTATION. A representational view of semantics is quite congenial to the popular COMPUTATIONAL THEORY OF MIND (Jackendoff 1983). The contrasting model-theoretic view sees semantic

interpretation relating expressions to elements of models (possibly MENTAL MODELS) defined in terms of constituents such as possible situations, entities, properties, truth-values, and so on. Intensional objects may be modeled, for instance, as functions from possible worlds or situations to extensions (see POSSIBLE WORLDS SEMANTICS). The question of the mental representation of such model-theoretic constructs is open (see Johnson-Laird 1983); the inclusion of Marrian "2½-D sketches" in Conceptual Structure in Jackendoff 1995 suggests the possibility of mixed approaches.

3. The issue of Natural Language Metaphysics (Bach 1986) or the "naive picture of the world" (Apresjan 1974) and its role in semantics. What presuppositions concerning the constitution and structure of the world as humans conceive it are built into human languages, and how, and which are universal? (See LINGUISTIC RELATIVITY HYPOTHESIS, NAIVE PHYSICS, FOLK BIOLOGY.) These questions may concern both semantic structure and semantic content, from the semantic difference between nouns and verbs to the content of color terms. Their investigation may challenge the lines between semantic knowledge and commonsense, encyclopedic, or other kinds of knowledge. Formal semantics, following the logical tradition, has employed relatively "austere" model structures; recent investigations, particularly into lexical semantics, tend to invite richer models.

4. The semantic atomism question: Are all meanings decomposable into combinations of "semantic atoms," "semantic primitives," or "atomic concepts" drawn from some fixed, universal, and presumably innate set? The affirmative view goes back at least to Leibniz (Kretzmann 1967), and is popular in cognitive science in spite of little progress on identification of a suitable set of primitives (see Wierzbicka's work, e.g., Wierzbicka 1985, for the most sustained attempt). A "yes" answer implies that lexical semantics will take the form of semantic decomposition; a "no" answer is compatible with various approaches to word meaning including the use of meaning postulates or a FUNCTIONAL ROLE SEMANTICS approach to word meaning.

5. The relation between meaning and use. The distinction between "sentence meaning," the literal meaning of a sentence abstracted away from any particular context, and "speaker's meaning," the intended interpretation of a particular utterance of a given sentence, presupposes a boundary between semantics and pragmatics, sometimes disputed. One traditionally influential approach (Austin 1962) is based on the identification of meaning and use.

See also SEMANTICS, ACQUISITION OF; WORD MEANING, ACQUISITION OF

—Barbara H. Partee

References

Apresjan, J. D. (1974). *Leksicheskaja Semantika* (Lexical semantics, 1992). Moscow: Nauka and Ann Arbor, MI: Karoma.

Austin, J. L. (1962). *How to Do Things with Words.* London: Oxford University Press.

Bach, E. (1986). Natural language metaphysics. In R. B. Marcus, G. J. W. Dorn, and P. Weingartner, Eds., *Logic, Methodology, and Philosophy of Science* 7. Amsterdam: Elsevier, pp. 573–595.

Carnap, R. (1956). *Meaning and Necessity.* 2nd ed. with supplements. Chicago: University of Chicago Press.

Chomsky, N. (1957). *Syntactic Structures.* The Hague: Mouton.

Chomsky, N. (1986). *Knowledge of Language: Its Nature, Origin, and Use.* New York: Praeger.

Fodor, J. A. (1975). *The Language of Thought.* New York: Thomas Y. Crowell.

Frege, G. (1892). *Über Sinn und Bedeutung* (On sense and reference). *Zeitschrift für Philosophie und philosophische Kritik* 100: 25–50. Reprinted in P. T. Geach and M. Black, Eds., *Translations from the Philosophical Writings of Gottlob Frege* (1952). Oxford: Blackwell, pp. 56–78.

Heim, I. (1982). *The Semantics of Definite and Indefinite NPs.* Ph.D. diss., University of Massachusetts, Amherst.

Jackendoff, R. (1983). *Semantics and Cognition.* Cambridge, MA: MIT Press.

Jackendoff, R. (1995). *Semantic Structures.* Cambridge, MA: MIT Press.

Jackendoff, R. (1996). Semantics and cognition. In S. Lappin, Ed., *The Handbook of Contemporary Semantic Theory.* Oxford: Blackwell, pp. 539–559.

Johnson-Laird, P. N. (1983). *Mental Models: Towards a Cognitive Science of Language, Inference, and Consciousness.* Cambridge, MA: Harvard University Press.

Kaplan, D. (1977). The logic of demonstratives. *Journal of Philosophical Logic* 8: 81–98.

Kretzmann, N. (1967). Semantics, history of. In P. Edwards, Ed. in chief, *The Encyclopedia of Philosophy,* vol. 7. New York: Macmillan, pp. 358–406.

Lakoff, G. (1987). *Women, Fire, and Dangerous Things.* Chicago: University of Chicago Press.

Lewis, D. (1975). Languages and language. In K. Gunderson, Ed., *Language, Mind, and Knowledge.* Minneapolis: University of Minnesota Press, pp. 3–35.

Montague, R. (1973). The proper treatment of quantification in ordinary English. In K. J. J. Hintikka, J. M. E. Moravcsik, and P. Suppes, Eds., *Approaches to Natural Language.* Dordrecht: Reidel, pp. 221–242. Reprinted in R. Montague, (1974). *Formal Philosophy: Selected Papers of Richard Montague,* R. Thomason, Ed. New Haven, CT: Yale University Press, pp. 247–270.

Morris, C. W. (1938). Foundation of the theory of signs. In O. Neurath, R. Carnap, and C. Morris, Eds., *International Encyclopaedia of Unified Science* 1, no. 2. Chicago: University of Chicago Press, pp. 1–59.

Putnam, H. (1975). The meaning of meaning. In K. Gunderson, Ed., *Language, Mind, and Knowledge.* Minnesota Studies in the Philosophy of Science. Minneapolis: University of Minnesota Press, pp. 131–193. Reprinted in H. Putnam, (1975). Mind, language, and reality. *Mind, language, and reality: Philosophical Papers*, vol. 2. Cambridge, MA: MIT Press, pp. 215–271.

Quine, W. V. O. (1960). *Word and Object.* Cambridge, MA: MIT Press.

Wierzbicka, A. (1985). *Lexicography and Conceptual Analysis.* Ann Arbor, MI: Karoma.

Zwicky, A., and J. M. Sadock. (1975). Ambiguity tests and how to fail them. In J. P. Kimball, Ed., *Syntax and Semantics* 4. New York: Academic Press, pp.1–36.

Further Readings

Bach, E. (1989). *Informal Lectures on Formal Semantics.* Albany: SUNY Press.

Chierchia, G., and S. McConnell-Ginet. (1990). *Meaning and Grammar: An Introduction to Semantics.* Cambridge, MA: MIT Press.

Cresswell, M. J. (1978). Semantic competence. In M. Guenthner-Reutter and F. Guenthner, Eds., *Meaning and Translation: Philosophical and Linguistic Approaches.* London: Duckworth.

Davidson, D. (1970). Semantics for natural languages. In B. Visentini et al., Eds., *Linguaggi nella Società e nella Tecnica.* Milan: Edizioni di Comunità.

Dowty, D. (1979). *Word Meaning and Montague Grammar.* Dordrecht: Reidel.

Dowty, D., R. Wall, and S. Peters. (1981). *Introduction to Montague Semantics.* Dordrecht: Reidel.

Fillmore, C. J. (1982). Frame semantics. In The Linguistic Society of Korea, Ed., *Linguistics in the Morning Calm.* Seoul: Hanshin Pub. Co., pp. 111–137.

Fodor, J. A. (1987). *Psychosemantics: The Problem of Meaning in the Philosophy of Mind.* Cambridge, MA: MIT Press.

Gamut, L. T. F. (1991). *Logic, Language, and Meaning.* Vol. 2: *Intensional Logic and Logical Grammar.* Chicago: University of Chicago Press.

Heim, I., and A. Kratzer. (1997). *Semantics in Generative Grammar.* Oxford: Blackwell.

Kamp, H. (1981). A theory of truth and semantic representation. In J. Groenendijk, T. Janssen, and M. Stokhof, Eds., *Formal Methods in the Study of Language: Proceedings of the Third Amsterdam Colloquium.* Amsterdam: Mathematical Centre Tracts, pp. 277–322. Reprinted in J. Groenendijk, T. M. V. Janssen, and M. Stokhof, Eds. *Truth, Interpretation, and Information* (1984). GRASS 2. Dordrecht: Foris.

Katz, J. J. (1981). *Language and Other Abstract Objects.* Totowa, NJ: Rowman and Littlefield.

Lappin, S., Ed. (1996). *The Handbook of Contemporary Semantic Theory.* Oxford: Blackwell.

Larson, R., and G. Segal. (1995). *Knowledge of Meaning: An Introduction to Semantic Theory.* Cambridge, MA: MIT Press.

Lewis, D. (1970). General semantics. *Synthese* 22: 18–67. Reprinted in D. Davidson and G. Harman, Eds., *Semantics of Natural Language* (1972). Dordrecht: Reidel, pp. 169–218.

Lyons, J. (1988). *Principles of Linguistic Semantics.* Cambridge: Cambridge University Press.

Partee, B. (1979). Semantics: Mathematics or psychology? In R. Bauerle, U. Egli, and A. von Stechow, Eds., *Semantics from Different Points of View.* Berlin: Springer, pp. 1–14.

Partee, B. (1995). Lexical semantics and compositionality. In D. Osherson, Gen. Ed., L. Gleitman, and M. Liberman, Eds., *Invitation to Cognitive Science.* Vol. 1, *Language.* 2nd ed. Cambridge, MA: MIT Press, pp. 311–360.

Partee, B. (1996). The development of formal semantics in linguistic theory. In S. Lappin, Ed., *The Handbook of Contemporary Semantic Theory.* Oxford: Blackwell, pp. 11–38.

Sgall, P., E. Hajičová, and J. Panevová. (1986). The Meaning of the Sentence in Its Semantic and Pragmatic Aspects. Prague: Academia; and Dordrecht: Reidel.

Stalnaker, R. (1978). Assertion. In P. Cole, Ed., *Syntax and Semantics.* Vol. 9, *Pragmatics.* New York: Academic Press, pp. 315–332.

Stechow, A. von, and D. Wunderlich, Eds. (1991). *Semantik/Semantics: An International Handbook of Contemporary Research.* Berlin: Mouton.

Talmy, L. (1991). Path to realization: A typology of event conflation. In *Buffalo Papers in Linguistics.* State University of New York at Buffalo, pp. 147–187.

Van Benthem, J., and A. ter Meulen, Eds. (1997). *Handbook of Logic and Language.* Amsterdam: Elsevier.

Semantics, Acquisition of

One area of research in the acquisition of semantics investigates children's use of logical connectives such as *and* and *or*, and QUANTIFIERS such as *every* and *some*. The main goal of this research is to determine the extent to which children assign a semantics to logical words that conforms to classical LOGIC. We will return to this topic. Another area of research investigates children's knowledge of semantic universals (see LINGUISTIC UNIVERSALS AND UNIVERSAL GRAMMAR). Semantic universals are often cast as constraints against certain linguistic forms or meanings. For example, a constraint on form prevents negative polarity items such as *any* from appearing in certain linguistic environments (the asterisk indicates deviance):

(1) * Every linguist fed any squirrel. Cf. No linguist fed any squirrel.

A second example is a constraint on meaning, called *closure.* Closure prevents pronouns from referring back to particular kinds of quantificational NPs that have appeared earlier in a discourse (e.g., Chierchia 1995). Thus, the pronoun *he* in (2) cannot be linked to the quantificational NP *every linguist*—the pronoun can refer to *Chomsky,* or it can refer to someone who is not mentioned in the DISCOURSE.

(2) Every linguist went to Chomsky's party. He was happy.

Suppose that children's grammars lack these constraints at some stage of development. If so, the language generated by their grammars would produce sentence forms that are illicit for adults, such as (1), and their grammars would permit illicit links between pronouns and quantificational NPs, as in (2). In the absence of systematically available negative semantic evidence (e.g., parental correction), it is difficult therefore to see how children could *learn* constraints. Embracing the conclusion of the argument from the-poverty-of-the-stimulus, we are led to consider an alternative source: innate specification (see POVERTY OF THE STIMULUS ARGUMENTS).

Among the hallmarks of innate specification are universality and the early emergence of a linguistic principle despite the absence of decisive evidence from experience (see INNATENESS OF LANGUAGE and NATIVISM). Research in the acquisition of semantics is directed at the early emergence hallmark of innateness. For example, 4- to 5-year-old children's understanding of negative polarity items was examined using an elicited production task (O'Leary and Crain 1994). One experimenter acted out stories with toys and props; a second experimenter manipulated a puppet, Kermit the Frog. Following each story, Kermit told the child what he thought happened in the story. The child's task was to decide whether or not Kermit "said the right thing" and, if not, to explain "what really happened." One of Kermit's (false) statements was (3).

(3) Only two squirrels got any food.

In light of what actually happened in the story, children consistently corrected Kermit's statement, producing sentences like "No, every squirrel got some food." Despite Kermit's own use of *any* in examples like this, children never (re)produced a negative polarity item. This is evidence of children's early mastery of the semantic constraint that regulates the appearance of these items.

Children's adherence to the closure constraint was examined by comparing their responses to discourse sequences like (2) and ones like (4) (Conway and Crain 1995; Conway 1997).

(4) A linguist wandered into Chomsky's kitchen. He cooked some pasta.

Example (4) shows that a pronoun can refer back to the indefinite NP *a linguist,* which appears earlier in the discourse. Using a comprehension task, it was found that 3- to 5-year-old children adhere to the closure constraint. They accepted coreference between pronouns and indefinite NPs in discourses like (4) but not between pronouns and other quantificational NPs (e.g., *every linguist*) in discourses like (2).

This brings us to the acquisition of logical reasoning. An extensive literature on this topic has led to the view that children's reasoning is not the same as that of adults. For example, studies of children's understanding of the universal quantifier, *every,* has resulted in the widespread belief that children younger than 7 lack adult-like competence. This belief is based in part on the finding that younger children reject sentences like (5) in circumstances with "extra squirrels", that is, ones that were not fed by a linguist (e.g., Bucci 1978; Inhelder and Piaget 1964).

(5) Every linguist fed a squirrel.

Children's nonadult responses have been interpreted as evidence that their grammars authorize nonadult domain restrictions for the universal quantifier, extending the domain of quantification beyond the boundary conditions established in the adult grammar (e.g., Barwise and Cooper 1981). By contrast, other research presented sentences like (5) in contexts that are arguably more felicitous, yielding consistent adult-like responses from children as young as 4 (Crain et al. 1996; Brooks and Braine 1996).

Studies of other logical words have led some researchers to conclude that children's logical reasoning does not conform to that of classical logic. A study by Neimark and Chapman (1975) found that children as old as 10 do not tolerate "*Some A are B*" as a description of a situation in which A and B are equivalent sets. Research findings have also led to the view that children lack the inclusive sense of *or* (see Braine and Rumain 1983). In making judgments about sentences with logical words, however, people are not only influenced by their semantic knowledge (the literal meanings of words) but also by the pragmatic norms they follow (how words are used in conversational contexts; see PRAGMATICS). For example, the statement "*Some boy is swimming*" is true in situations where every boy is swimming, but this fact is often difficult even for adults to see, because speakers tend to avoid using *some N* when the use of *every N* provides a more accurate description of the situation. Similarly, statements of the form *A or B* do not logically entail exclusivity, but this reading is often inferred (e.g., Chierchia and McConnell-Ginet 1990).

The presence of pragmatic implicatures masks the semantic contribution of logical words in ordinary circumstances, but these implicatures are canceled in certain contexts, such as when a speaker is making a bet or a prediction and, hence, does not know what the actual outcome will be. The conclusion that children's logical reasoning is not consistent with classical logic is based on research that has not systematically investigated children's use of logical expressions by manipulating the pragmatic context, so as to cancel the relevant implicatures (see IMPLICATURE). Therefore, it is premature to infer that children lack proper understanding of the truth conditions associated with logical words in standard logic. The critical investigations of children's logical reasoning are now underway (e.g., Chierchia et al. 1997). When the findings are in we will be in a better position to say how well the acquisition of semantics comports with conclusions based on linguistic research.

See also RADICAL INTERPRETATION; WORD MEANING, ACQUISITION OF

—Stephen Crain

References

Barwise, J., and R. Cooper. (1981). Generalized quantifiers and natural language. *Linguistics and Philosophy* 4: 159–219.

Braine, M. D. S., and B. Rumain. (1983). Logical reasoning. In J. Flavell and E. Markman, Eds. *Handbook of Child Psychology.* Vol. 3, *Cognitive development.* New York: Academic Press, pp. 263–339.

Brooks, P. J., and M. D. S. Braine. (1996). What do children know about the universal quantifiers *all* and *each*? *Cognition* 60: 235–268.

Bucci, W. (1978). The interpretation of universal affirmative propositions: A developmental study. *Cognition* 6: 55–57.

Chierchia, G. (1995). *Dynamics of Meaning: Anaphora, Presupposition and Syntactic Theory.* Chicago: University of Chicago Press.

Chierchia, G., S. Crain, M. T. Guasti, and R. Thornton. (1997). The emergence of logical form. Paper presented at the Twenty-first Annual Boston University Conference on Language Development, Boston, MA.

Chierchia, G., and S. McConnell-Ginet. (1990). *Meaning and Grammar: An Introduction to Semantics.* Cambridge, MA: MIT Press.

Conway, L. (1997). *Excavating Semantics.* Ph.D. diss., University of Connecticut.

Conway, L., and S. Crain. (1995). Dynamic acquisition. In D. MacLaughlin and S. McEwen, Eds., *Proceedings of the Boston University Conference on Child Language Development.* Somerville, MA: Cascadilla Press, pp. 180–191.

Crain, S., R. Thornton, C. Boster, L. Conway, D. Lillo-Martin, and E. Woodams. (1996). Quantification without qualification. *Language Acquisition* 3(2): 83–153.

Inhelder, B., and J. Piaget. (1964). *The early growth of logic in the child.* London: Routledge and Kegan Paul.

Neimark, E. D., and R. A. Chapman. (1975). Development of the comprehension of logical quantifiers. In R. J. Falmagne, Ed., *Reasoning: Representation and Process in Children and Adults.* Mahwah, NJ: Erlbaum.

O'Leary, C., and S. Crain. (1994). Negative polarity (a positive result) and positive polarity (a negative result). Paper presented at the Eighteenth Annual Boston University Conference on Language Development, Boston, MA.

Semantics-Syntax Interface

See SYNTAX-SEMANTICS INTERFACE

Semiotics and Cognition

Although the term "semiotics" has come into common usage only in this present century, the discipline of semiotics itself is much older and may be traced back to Greek philosophy. The first formulations of the notion of the so-called semiotic triangle may be found already in Aristotle, where three elements are seen as constitutive of signs: pragmata ("the things to which the sign refers"), the expressive element ("that which is in the voice"), and thoughts ("that which is in the mind"). This third element alludes to a level that we today would call the level of mental representations and, as such, is that aspect of the sign that is directly concerned with cognition. We could therefore say that semiotics is constitutively connected with cognition right from its historical roots.

In modern times, there seem to be two main directions in semiotic research projects: interpretative semiotics inspired by the work of Charles Sanders Peirce (1931–58), and structural semiotics, sometimes referred to as "semiology" following the terminology introduced by the Swiss linguist Ferdinand de SAUSSURE (1906–11). Their concerns with the issue of cognition and their possible connections with related works on contemporary cognitive science map onto different areas of interest, and I will discuss them separately.

It is certainly within Peircean semiotics that the most straightforward link between semiotic processes and processes of cognition can be found, so much so that this direction in semiotics is often referred to as cognitive semiotics. According to Peirce, KNOWLEDGE ACQUISITION and thought are never immediate, direct processes but are always mediated through signs, or interpretants, which are more developed signs and which thus allow the subject to know more than she knew before, in an endless process of interpretation known as unlimited semiosis. Interpretants, which are the central element in the sign process, are first of all mind-internal signs, that is to say mental representations. In this way, thought, signs, and cognition become one and the same thing. "All thought is in signs" (*Collected Papers* 5: 252), but because each interpretant sign adds something new to the process of thinking and knowing, cognition is strongly characterized as an inferential process.

Peirce's philosophy has strongly influenced Umberto Eco's semiotic theory of signs and interpretational processes (Eco 1976, 1984). Eco stresses in his theories the Peircean notion of semiosis as an inherently inferential process. Signs are not regulated by some kind of equivalence rule between expression and content but are always considered as inferential devices, even in cases where the inferential relation between the two has became so stabilized as to appear to be a purely automatized correlation. In this way, Eco, not unlike Peirce, considers that sign processes will always, and necessarily, imply the factual occurrence of some form of internal reasoning and inferencing process, so

making the sign process that is the object of study of his semiotics functionally indistinguishable from cognition.

The particular type of thought process involving inferences based on the interpretation of signs is referred to by Peirce as "abduction," which he distinguishes from INDUCTION and deduction on the basis of their fundamental logical forms. Abductive inference is considered as constituting the core of cognition itself, because it is the only type of inferential process that actually contributes to an increase in our knowledge of the object and, without deriving logical truths, only possible ones.

Abductive reasoning has recently received growing attention in cognitive circles, especially in relation to modeling in Artificial Intelligence (AI), where abduction is seen as a theory-forming or interpretative inference. In their textbook on AI, Charniak and McDermott (1985) claim that everyday reasoning as well as medical diagnosis, story understanding, and vision are all abductive processes. Many AI systems are presently being developed around various forms of abductive inference in order to model different areas of cognition (see Josephson and Josephson 1994), from perception to natural language understanding and even METAPHOR (Hobbs 1992) and translation (Hobbs and Kameyama 1990). In particular, abduction has been considered in relation to interpretation by both AI researchers (e.g., Hobbs et al. 1993) and by semioticians (Eco 1979, 1990). According to Eco (1979), no text can make all its premises explicit; in this sense, a text can be seen as a lazy machine asking the reader to fill in a whole series of gaps. In order to fully understand a text, the reader has to make a series of abductions (known as "inferential walks") on the basis of both her general knowledge of the world and specific textual scripts. Such an approach appears highly consistent with most of the cognitive work done in the field of READING comprehension of text (see among others Schank 1982; van Dijk and Kintsch 1983).

Turning now to the structuralist semiotic perspective developed along the lines of Saussure and Hjelmslev, one could say that this latter approach is far less interested in issues related to cognition. However, there is at least one area that brings to light some interesting similarities with work in cognitive science, and this is the study of narrative structure. Since the seminal work of Vladimir Propp (1928), structural semiotics has focused on the analysis of the structural properties of any kind of narrative text, developing a highly complex and articulated model to account for the different levels of structural organization (see Greimas 1970, 1983). This line of research could be compared to work done in the cognitive area on story grammar (Rumelhart 1975, 1980; Thorndyke 1977), which also aims to individuate an underlying structure in stories and to define the nature of concepts such as *state* and *event*, despite the fact that these two traditions seem, unfortunately, to ignore each other.

Finally, another line of research that also should be mentioned here in respect to the relationship between semiotics and cognition is that represented by some recent developments in what is usually referred to as dynamic semiotics or semio-cognitive morphodynamics (Petitot 1985, 1992; Brandt 1994, 1995). The basic hypothesis of these works is that there exist syntactico-semantic infrastructures of topological and dynamic nature that constitute universals underlying language, perception, and action. Such a line of thought is consistent with the basic tenets of much work being done in COGNITIVE LINGUISTICS today (see, for instance, Langacker 1987). Dynamic semiotics aims, however, not only to individuate the schematic structures that underlie meaning in different types of systems but also to model them through a qualitative mathematics based on the catastrophe theory developed by the French mathematician René Thom (1975), where states, events, acts, and processes are understood formally in terms of force topologies and where form is dynamically represented as based on opposing forces. Dynamic models can therefore be of help in reformulating the findings of structural semantics in dynamic terms, in a way that is very close to approaches used in more recent work in cognitive semantics, where the role and function of image schema and force-dynamic schema have been investigated (see Talmy 1988; Lakoff and Johnson 1980).

See also DYNAMIC APPROACHES TO COGNITION; FIGURATIVE LANGUAGE; MEANING; NATURAL LANGUAGE PROCESSING; SEMANTICS

—*Patrizia Violi*

References and Further Readings

Brandt, P. A. (1994). *Dynamique du sens.* Aarhus: Aarhus University Press.

Brandt, P. A. (1995). *Morphologies of Meaning.* Aarhus: Aarhus University Press.

Charniak, E., and D. McDermott. (1985). *Introduction to Artificial Intelligence.* Reading, MA: Addison-Wesley.

Eco, U. (1976). *A Theory of Semiotics.* Bloomington, IN: Indiana University Press.

Eco, U. (1979). *The Role of the Reader.* Bloomington, IN: Indiana University Press.

Eco, U. (1984). *Semiotics and the Philosophy of Language.* Bloomington, IN: Indiana University Press.

Eco, U. (1990). *The Limits of Interpretation.* Bloomington, IN: Indiana University Press.

Greimas, A. (1970). *Du Sens.* Paris: Seuil.

Greimas, A. (1983). *Du Sens 2.* Paris: Seuil.

Hobbs, J. (1992). Metaphor and abduction. In A. Ortony, J. Slack, and O. Stock, Eds., *Communication from an Artificial Intelligence Perspective: Theoretical and Applied Issues.* New York: Springer, pp. 35–58.

Hobbs, J., and M. Kameyama. (1990). Translation by abduction. In H. Karlgren, Ed., *Proceedings of the Thirteenth International Conference on Computational Linguistics.* Helsinki, pp. 155–161.

Hobbs, J., M. Stickel, D. Appelt, and P. Martin. (1993). Interpretation as abduction. *Artificial Intelligence Journal* 63(1–2): 69–142.

Josephson, J. R., and S. G. Josephson, Eds. (1994). *Abductive Inference: Computation, Philosophy, Technology.* Cambridge: Cambridge University Press.

Lakoff, G., and M. Johnson. (1980). *Metaphors We Live By.* Chicago: University of Chicago Press.

Langacker, R. (1987). *Foundations of Cognitive Grammar.* Stanford, CA: Stanford University Press.

Peirce, C. S. (1931–58). *Collected Papers.* Cambridge, MA: Harvard University Press.

Petitot, J. (1985). *Morphogenèse du Sens: Pour un Schématisme de la Structure.* Paris: P. U. F.

Petitot, J. (1992). *Physique du Sens.* Paris: Editions du CNRS.

Propp, V. (1928). *Morfologija skazki.* Leningrad.

Rumelhart, D. E. (1975). Notes on a schema for stories. In D. G. Bobrow and A. Collins, Eds., *Representation and Understanding: Studies in Cognitive Science.* New York: Academic Press.

Rumelhart, D. E. (1980). On evaluating story grammars. *Cognitive Science* 4: 313–316.

Saussure, F. de. (1906–11). *Cours de linguistique générale.* Lausanne-Paris: Payot.

Schank, R. (1982). *Reading and Understanding.* Hillsdale, NJ: Erlbaum.

Talmy, L. (1988). Force dynamics in language and cognition. *Cognitive Science* 12: 49–100.

Thom, R. (1975). *Structural Stability and Morphogenesis: An Outline of a General Theory of Models.* Amsterdam: Benjamins.

Thorndyke, P. W. (1977). Cognitive structures in comprehension and memory of narrative discourse. *Cognitive Psychology* 9: 77–110.

Van Dijk, T. A., and W. Kintsch. (1983). *Strategies in Discourse Comprehension.* New York: Academic Press.

Sensations

Sensations are mental states normally caused by the stimulation of sense organs. They are a varied lot. Even though philosophers have traditionally tended to give sensations a unified theoretical treatment, it is not obvious that this is either possible or desirable. Sensations are usually taken to be the paradigmatic bearers of qualitative appearance, but proprioceptive sensations do not seem to have a qualitative character at all. Furthermore, sensations' own nature as mental states is not readily apparent: sensations of hunger or pain appear to us as states of our bodies, and colors and visually presented shapes appear to us to be features of objects before the eyes. The differences among "bodily" and "distance" sensations are marked by common speech, which countenances, for example, "burning sensation," but rarely "visual sensation." The latter must rather be understood as a term of art used principally by philosophers and psychologists, to be justified by its theoretical utility.

Although it is plausible to say of sensations in this extended sense of the term that they are the sources, as well as the ultimate arbiters, of all claims about matters of fact (one form of a doctrine known as *empiricism*), they, unlike the items of the material world as scientifically understood, are qualitative in character and directly accessible only to the person who has them. This creates two closely related problems that have vexed philosophers from the seventeenth century until the present day. The first problem concerns how each of us may, beginning with our own sensations, obtain knowledge of the material world. The second problem is whether we can reconcile the private and qualitative nature of our sensations with our nature as material beings.

The first problem was widely discussed in the nineteenth and the first part of the twentieth century by philosophers as well as psychologists (Boring 1942), although it has more recently fallen into the background. Here is how it goes. Physics tells us that the world consists of elementary particles and fields. Our sensations inform us that the world contains not only strawberries, but also the colors, tastes, and smells of strawberries. Yet although the strawberry can be understood to be an assemblage of elementary particles, its red color, just like its characteristic smell and taste, is not reducible to physical properties (Hardin 1993). If colors and tastes have no place in the physical world, they must be sensations in our minds, perhaps generated by our brains, though not states of our brains, because our brains are themselves physical objects. But if the strawberry's color is a mental property, must not the shape that it delineates be likewise a mental property? Following this line of thought to its conclusion, Ernst Mach (1897) and some of the earlier positivists held that we are directly aware only of our sensations and can never be entitled to infer the existence of a world of matter that is distinct from those sensations. The world of perceivable physical objects, including our brains, must be understood to be a construction from actual and possible sensations. The unobservable entities of physics are to be regarded as convenient theoretical fictions that enable us economically to represent and predict our sensations.

One alternative to such a radical conclusion is to maintain that we can infer the existence and nature of a material world distinct from our sensations as the best explanation of their characteristics; some of our sensations, such as those of shape, resemble the properties of the objects that cause them, whereas others, such as smell or color, have causes but no counterparts in the external world (Russell 1914). However, it is not clear that an empiricism that uses sensations and the relationships among them as its basis can allow the required conceptions of cause, explanation, or resemblance, all of which require transcending that basis.

Another way to penetrate the epistemic wall of sensations is to deny that they are the direct objects of awareness, and thus the inescapable foundation of our knowledge of matters of fact. James J. GIBSON (1966), for example, effectively argues that our sensory awareness is in many cases best described as picking up unmediated information about the environment (see AFFORDANCES). Although Gibson does suggest how we might have direct access to some features of the physical world, he does not show how experiences that do have a qualitative character could arise simply by having perceptual systems extract information from the environment. Many instances of sensory apprehension seem to involve the awareness of something that cannot be identified with any item in the external world that acts upon the senses (Perkins 1983). How, for example, can a "direct contact" theory account for feeling a PHANTOM LIMB, or seeing a colored afterimage? It seems implausible to assert that in such cases one is either experiencing nothing at all, or else simply misperceiving some item that is outside of one's nervous system.

Our second principal problem is whether sensations can be identical to brain states (see PHYSICALISM), or functions of brain states (see FUNCTIONALISM), and thus find a place in the physical world after all, or whether a scientific psychology could make do without positing sensations (see ELIMINATIVE MATERIALISM). Either of these alternatives is consistent with a materialist view of the world. By contrast, mind-body dualists (see MIND-BODY PROBLEM) suppose that although sensations are caused by brain states, they are in no way reducible to them. This set of issues, nowadays known as the problem of QUALIA, has been of great interest to philosophers and to many psychologists during the second half of the twentieth century. A related question is whether any materialist solution to the problem of qualia must be confronted with an EXPLANATORY GAP. For even if it is in fact true that sensations are identical to brain states or functions, will it ever be possible for us to understand why this must be so? Perhaps our understanding can do no better than record de facto correlations between sensations and brain states. On the other hand, it has been argued that close attention to the character of explanations currently offered by PSYCHOPHYSICS will show that the gulf between sensory qualities and the functional organization of sensory systems is not as wide as has often been thought (Clark 1993). Finally, under what conditions would it make sense to ascribe sensations to machines, or extraterrestrial aliens (Lewis 1980), or closer to home, and perhaps more fruitfully, to other animals (Thompson 1995)?

—C. L. Hardin

References

Boring, E. G. (1942). *Sensation and Perception in the History of Experimental Psychology*. New York: Appleton-Century-Crofts.

Clark, A. (1993). *Sensory Qualities*. Oxford: Clarendon Press.

Gibson, J. J. (1966). *The Senses Considered as Perceptual Systems*. Boston: Houghton-Mifflin.

Hardin, C. L. (1993). *Color for Philosophers*. Enlarged ed. Indianapolis: Hackett.

Lewis, D. (1980). Mad pain and martian pain. In N. Block, Ed., *Readings in the Philosophy of Psychology*, vol. 1. Cambridge, MA: Harvard University Press.

Mach, E. (1897). *Contributions to the Analysis of the Sensations*. Translated by C. M. Williams. La Salle, IL: Open Court.

Perkins, M. (1983). *Sensing the World*. Indianapolis, IN: Hackett.

Russell, B. (1914). *Our Knowledge of the External World*. London: Allen and Unwin.

Thompson, E. (1995). *Colour Vision*. London and New York: Routledge.

Further Readings

Goodman, N. (1951). *The Structure of Appearance*. Cambridge MA: Harvard University Press.

Hacker, P. M. S. (1987). *Appearance and Reality*. Oxford: Blackwell.

Hirst, R. J. (1959). *The Problems of Perception*. London: Allen and Unwin.

Price, H. H. (1932). *Perception*. London: Methuen.

Savage, C. W. (1970). *The Measurement of Sensation*. Berkeley and Los Angeles: University of California Press.

Sense and Reference

The terms *sense* and *reference* in their technical meanings originate in the work of Gottlob FREGE, translating his "Sinn" and "Bedeutung" respectively (Frege 1967). According to Frege, every significant linguistic expression has both sense and reference, these being different kinds of semantic properties.

The reference of an expression is what it contributes to the truth or falsity of sentences in which it appears. Frege construed reference as a relation between the expression and some real object, the expression's *referent*. The referent of a singular term is what one would intuitively think the term stands for. The referent of both "Bill Clinton" and "The President of the United States in 1997" is the man, Bill Clinton. The referent of a sentence is its *truth value,* the True or the False, these being existent abstract objects. Predicative expressions refer to functions from objects to truth values. For example, the one-place predicate "runs" refers to a function that, given any object, x, as an argument, yields the value True if x runs and False if x does not run. In general, an n-place predicate refers to a function from ordered n-tuples to truth values. For example, the two-place predicate "likes" refers to a function from ordered pairs of objects, $<x, y>$ to truth values; True if x likes y, False if x does not like y.

Reference is *compositional* in that the reference of a complex expression is determined by the reference of its parts and their syntactic mode of combination. Consider, for example, "Bill Clinton likes Al Gore." The two names provide the pair $<Clinton, Gore>$, and this pair is the argument to the function referred to by "likes." The referent of the sentence is then the value of that function, given $<Clinton, Gore>$ as argument: True if Clinton likes Gore, False otherwise.

Frege applied a similar analysis to complex sentences built up from simpler ones. For example, a conjunction of the form "S1 and S2" has the value True, if S1 and S2 both have the value True, and False otherwise. So "and" refers to a function from pairs of truth values to truth values: it yields True given the pair $<True, True>$ and False given any other pair.

Because an expression's referent is what it contributes to determining the truth values of sentences, reference is governed by principle (P):

(P) Co-referring expressions may be inter-substituted in any sentence without altering the truth value of that sentence.

For example, given that "Hesperus" and "Phosphorus" refer to the same thing (Venus), these terms ought to be intersubstitutable in any sentence without altering its truth value. (P) appears to be correct for many cases. However, as will be seen in a moment, there are also apparent counterexamples, and it is partly to deal with these that Frege introduced the notion of sense.

An expression's sense is an aspect of its SEMANTICS that is not accounted for in terms of reference. The referential properties of "Hesperus is Hesperus" and "Hesperus is Phosphorus" are identical. But whereas the former is a tautology, the latter carries empirical information and so has different cognitive value. Frege invoked sense to account for this cognitive value.

The sense of an expression is a "mode of presentation" of its referent, a way in which the referent is presented to the mind. The senses of the significant expressions in a sentence compose to form the sense of the sentence, which Frege called a "thought" ("Gedanke"). Thoughts are the contents of PROPOSITIONAL ATTITUDES. If, for example, someone

believes that every even number is the sum of two primes, then they stand in a believing relation to the thought that every even number is the sum of two primes. If someone hopes that every even number is the sum of two primes, they stand in a hoping relation to the same thought.

In spite of their cognitive role, senses and thoughts are objective and mind-independent, in Frege's view: "When one apprehends . . . a thought one does not create it but only comes to stand in a certain relation . . . to what already existed beforehand" (1967: 30).

Because propositional attitudes are relations to thoughts, sentences ascribing propositional attitudes involve reference to thoughts. Notice that (P), above, appears to fail for (1) and (2), because one might be false while the other is true.

(1) Galileo believed that Hesperus is a planet.

(2) Galileo believed that Phosphorus is a planet.

Frege addressed this problem by proposing that in certain contexts (often called "referentially opaque contexts," after Whitehead and Russell 1925) words do not refer to their normal referents. Rather they refer to their normal senses. Thus (P) is preserved, because "Hesperus" and "Phosphorus" do not refer to the same thing in (1) and (2).

Sense also has a role in explaining reference. It is because an expression has its sense that it has its reference. Equally, a speaker's capacity to refer to or think about something is explained in terms of sense: a thinker thinks about a particular object by grasping a sense that presents that object (Evans 1982; Burge 1977; Dummett 1973).

It is sometimes thought that a further reason why Frege invoked senses was to account for the meaningfulness of expressions that lack a referent, such as "Vulcan" or "The largest prime." There is probably some truth in this, as Frege did allow that nonreferring expressions could have a sense. However, it is not clear that Frege should have allowed this, given the fundamental role of reference in his philosophy of language. (See Dummett 1973: 185; Evans 1982: chap. 1 for discussion.)

Frege's theories of sense and reference have been criticized in many ways. Most commentators have tended to propose modifications to the overall picture, rather than reject it outright. For example, it is a popular move to keep much of the account of reference in place, without insisting that truth values are objects or that predicates refer to functions. One replaces "refers to the True" by "is true," and replaces talk of predicates referring to functions by talk of predicates applying to objects under specified conditions, as in, for instance, "red" applies to any object x if and only if x is red (Davidson 1967; Evans 1982; McDowell 1977).

The account of sense is often criticized on the grounds that no one kind of thing can play all the roles that Frege assigned to sense. For example, it is often held that cognitive value does not determine reference, because two expressions might refer to different things, yet share the same cognitive value. For example "That man" might be used once to refer to Castor and then, on a separate occasion, to refer to Castor's identical twin, Pollux. The way in which the speaker thinks of Castor might be just the same as the way he thinks of Pollux, so the cognitive values of the expressions might be the same, although their referents differ (Burge 1977; Kaplan 1990; Perry 1990; for a defense of Frege, see Evans 1990).

Frege himself was primarily concerned with the development of symbolic LOGIC and semantics for formal languages of mathematics and science, rather than with a theory of natural language. Nevertheless, he provides a theory of content that can be applied to propositional attitudes and the other psychological states that are the subject matter of the cognitive sciences. Frege's work raises fundamental questions that lie at the heart of cognitive science and the philosophy thereof. Perhaps the most basic is whether the notion of content in cognitive science can be assimilated with either sense or reference or both (cf. PRAGMATICS; Segal 1995; Fodor 1994; Millikan 1997; Chomsky 1995).

See also INDEXICALS AND DEMONSTRATIVES; MEANING; NARROW CONTENT; REFERENCE, THEORIES OF

—*Gabriel Segal*

References

Burge, T. (1977). Belief *de re. The Journal of Philosophy* 74: 338–362.

Chomsky, N. (1995). Language and nature. *Mind* 104: 1–61.

Davidson, D. (1967). Truth and meaning. *Synthese* 17: 304–323.

Dummett, M. (1973). *Frege: Philosophy of Language.* London: Duckworth.

Evans, G. (1982). *The Varieties of Reference.* Oxford: Oxford University Press.

Evans, G. (1990). Understanding demonstratives. In P. Yourgrau, Ed., *Demonstratives.* Oxford: Oxford University Press.

Fodor, J. (1994). *The Elm and the Expert.* Cambridge, MA: MIT Press.

Frege, G. (1952/1892). On sense and reference. In P. Geach and M. Black, Eds., *Translations of the Philosophical Writings of Gottlob Frege.* Oxford: Blackwell.

Frege, G. (1967/1918). The thought: A logical enquiry. Translated by A. and M. Quinton; reprinted in P. F. Strawson, Ed., *Philosophical Logic.* Oxford: Oxford University Press.

Kaplan, D. (1990). Thoughts on demonstratives. In P. Yourgrau, Ed., *Demonstratives.* Oxford: Oxford University Press.

McDowell, J. (1977). The sense and reference of a proper name. *Mind* 86: 159–185.

Millikan, R. (1997). Images of identity: In search of modes of presentation. *Mind* 106: 499–519.

Perry, J. (1990). Frege on demonstratives. In P. Yourgrau, Ed., *Demonstratives.* Oxford: Oxford University Press.

Segal, G. (1995). Truth and Sense. In J. Biro and P. Kotatko, Eds., *Frege: Sense and Reference 100 Years On.* Dordrecht: Kluwer.

Whitehead, A. N., and B. Russell. (1925). *Principia Mathematica.* 2nd. ed. Cambridge: Cambridge University Press.

Further Readings

Burge, T. (1979). Sinning against Frege. *Philosophical Review* 58: 398–432.

Burge, T. (1986). Frege on Truth. In L. Haaparanta and J. Hintikka, Eds., *Frege Synthesised.* Dordrecht: Reidel.

Burge, T. (1992). Frege on knowing and the third realm. *Mind* 101: 633–650.

Dummett, M. (1981). *The Interpretation of Frege's Philosophy.* London: Duckworth.

Frege, G. (1980). *Philosophical and Mathematical Correspondence.* G. Gabriel, H. Hermes, et al., Eds. Oxford: Blackwell.

Frege, G. (1979). *Posthumous Writings.* H. Hermes, F. Kembertal, et al., Eds. Oxford: Blackwell.

Kripke, S. (1979). A puzzle about belief. In A. Margalit, Ed., *Meaning and Use.* Dordrecht: Reidel.

Kripke, S. (1980). *Naming and Necessity.* Cambridge, MA: Harvard University Press.

Larson, R., and G. Segal. (1995). *Knowledge of Meaning: An Introduction to Semantic Theory.* Cambridge, MA: MIT Press.

McDowell, J. (1984). De re senses. In C. Wright, Ed., *Frege: Tradition and Influence.* Oxford: Blackwell, pp. 98–109.

Millikan, R. (1984). *Language, Thought and Other Biological Categories.* Cambridge, MA: MIT Press.

Millikan, R. (1991). Perceptual content and the Fregean myth. *Mind* 100: 439–459.

Noonan, H. (1984). Fregean thoughts. In C. Wright, Ed., *Frege: Tradition and Influence.* Oxford: Blackwell, pp. 20–39.

Putnam, H. (1975). The meaning of "meaning." Reprinted in Putnam's *Philosophical Papers* 2, *Mind, Language and Reality.* Cambridge: Cambridge University Press.

Russell, B. (1905). On denoting. *Mind* 14: 479–493.

Salmon, N. (1986). *Frege's Puzzle.* Cambridge, MA: MIT Press.

Weiner, J. (1990). *Frege in Perspective.* Ithaca, NY: Cornell University Press.

Wright, C., Ed. (1984). *Frege: Tradition and Influence.* Oxford: Blackwell.

Sentence Processing

One of the reasons that reading a good novel or listening to an interesting lecture can be a pleasurable experience is because we are (blissfully) unaware of the cognitive work we do in understanding individual sentences and relating them to the discourse context. Research in sentence processing investigates the cognitive mechanism (or mechanisms) responsible for the real-time computation of the structural representation that underlies comprehension of visual or auditory language input. Sentence processing involves the rapid integration of various types of information (lexical, structural, discourse, etc.) and research in this area is necessarily interdisciplinary, drawing on work in theoretical linguistics, computer science, and experimental psychology (for reviews, see Mitchell 1994 and Fodor 1995)

A basic finding (that accords with our intuition) is that computation is "incremental." That is, we structure the words as they are perceived rather than store them as a list that is later combined when there is a pause in the input. Incremental structuring has the clear benefit of keeping short-term memory burdens to a minimum. For example, try to memorize a list of twelve random words versus a twelve-word sentence. Even a complex sentence such as "Not all of the targets were hit by some of the arrows" is easier to remember than a random array of words (e.g., "arrows by were of not of targets all the some hit the"), precisely because we can structure the sentence as we read or hear it (even in isolation, and despite the interpretive difficulties). But there is a potential cost to incremental processing if, as is quite common in human language, the input is ambiguous and processing must proceed in advance of relevant information. In fact, one of the most remarkable characteristics of the human sentence processing mechanism (commonly termed "the parser") is its ability to structure ambiguous input in an efficient manner.

One major focus of research in parsing theory, and one that serves as a good illustration of work in a wide-ranging, complex field, is the study of the incremental processing of temporarily ambiguous word sequences. A sequence is ambiguous if it is compatible with more than one well-formed structural representation. A temporary ambiguity is one that is resolved later on in the sentence. Consider the sentences in (1).

(1) a. Ian knew the schedule . . .
   b. Ian knew the schedule by heart.
   c. Ian knew the schedule was wrong.
   d. Ian knew that the schedule was wrong.

The sequence in (1a) is temporarily ambiguous—that is, the noun phrase *the schedule* after the verb may function either as the nominal object of the verb (as in (1b)), or as subject of a clause (e.g., *the schedule was wrong* in (1c,d)). Each function has a distinct structural representation. The ambiguity is due to the following properties of English: (i) verbs such as *know* may take either noun-phrase or clausal objects; and (ii) the word *that,* which can be an indicator of a clause, is not always obligatory (as a comparison of (1c) and (1d) illustrates). Given incremental processing, the sequence in (1a) presents the parser with a choice. It may either structure the phrase "the schedule" as the object of the verb or as the subject of a new clause. If it takes the first option, then the appearance of a verb (such as *was* in (1c)) will prove this choice to have been the wrong one. On the other hand, if it takes the clausal option, then the failure of a verb to appear (as in (1b)) may cause processing difficulty.

To investigate the parser's operations in ambiguities such as (1a), Rayner and Frazier (1987) used an eye-tracking technique to take precise recordings of subjects' eye movements as they read temporarily ambiguous sentences such as those above, with the (d) sentences serving as an unambiguous control. What they found was a significant slow down in reading rate ("fixation durations") after the noun phrase in the (c) sentences, compared to the (b) and (d) sentences. They interpreted this comparatively slow reading rate as evidence that the parser had incrementally structured the postverbal noun phrase as a direct object in the ambiguous (b) and (c) sentences, but they had to revise this analysis in the (c) sentences when the input after the noun phrase showed it to be incorrect. The comparison of reading times after the noun phrase in the (c) and (d) sentences is particularly informative. The presence of *that* in (1d), in conjunction with the following *the,* serves as an unambiguous indicator of a new clause. The fact that a slowdown in reading rate is only observed in the (c) sentences supports the hypothesis that this slowdown is due specifically to the parser's response to the ambiguity in (c) and not to the need to process a second clause in the sentence.

These results are consistent with the hypothesis that the parser operates in accord with a Minimal Attachment principle (Frazier and Fodor 1978). Minimal Attachment states that, when faced with an ambiguity, the parser structures (or,

attaches) new input to the current representation with the minimal amount of additional structure. A direct object attachment of a postverbal noun phrase is less complex than an attachment that would require the additional structure associated with a new clause. Therefore, it is the one pursued by the parser. Frazier and Fodor (1978) argued that Minimal Attachment follows from the temporal processing advantage enjoyed by minimal structures compared to their more complex competitors. Gorrell (1995) has argued that Minimal Attachment effects are due to the parser incrementally reflecting a central property of syntactic structure: economy of representations (Chomsky 1995). The preference for minimal structure has been demonstrated for numerous structural ambiguities in English, as well as German (Gorrell 1996), Italian (DeVincenzi 1991), and Japanese (Inoue and Fodor 1995).

But syntactic structure is just one factor in the processing of ambiguous sentences (clearly demonstrated in a seminal paper by Bever 1970). Work within the constraint-based framework, inspired, in part, by computational models adopting a connectionist architecture, has stressed the contribution of specific lexical information rather than more general structural preferences in sentence processing (e.g., MacDonald, Pearlmutter, and Seidenberg 1994). This interest in the contribution of specific lexical information to the resolution of structural ambiguities can be illustrated with a brief description of the experimental results reported by Osterhout, Holcomb, and Swinney (1994). They recorded event-related brain potentials (ERPs) elicited while subjects read sentences similar to those in (1). ERPs are measured voltage changes in an electroencephalogram that occur within a specified time after the presentation of a particular word or other input. The particular ERP of interest here is the P600, so called because it is a positive-going waveform that peaks approximately 600 milliseconds after the event of interest. The P600 has been associated with the processing of input that represents either a syntactic violation or a disconfirmation of a prior structural choice.

Although a first experiment replicated the major findings of Rayner and Frazier (1987), the results of a second experiment, in which verb preference (for either a noun phrase or clausal object) was manipulated, reveal the important role of lexical information in processing ambiguous input. In this experiment, temporarily ambiguous sentences containing verbs which prefer noun-phrase objects (e.g., *understand* in *The student understood the answer was easy*) were contrasted with sentences containing verbs that prefer clausal objects (e.g., *guess* in *The student guessed the answer was easy*). Osterhout, Holcomb, and Swinney (1994) found that the P600 was elicited as a function of verb type rather than as a function of comparative structural complexity. Demonstrations of the parser's incremental utilization of specific verb information, which typically occurs before potential objects in English, highlights the importance of studying the processing of verb-final clauses, a common property of many of the world's languages (Schriefers, Friederici, and Kuhn 1995; Mecklinger, Schriefers, Steinhauer, and Friederici 1995).

In addition to syntactic and lexical factors, work by Crain and Steedman (1985), St. John and McClelland

(1990), Altmann, Garnham, and Dennis (1992), and others have highlighted the important influence exerted by DIS-COURSE context on the process of resolving structural ambiguities. For example, consider the sentences in (2).

(2) a. The fireman told the woman that he had risked his life for many people in similar fires.
     b. The fireman told the woman that he had risked his life for to install a smoke detector.

In (2a), the phrase *that he had risked his life for many people in similar fires* is an assertion being told to some woman. In (2b), the phrase *that he had risked his life for* is a phrase specifying which woman was being addressed. As in (1), the sentences here display a temporary ambiguity between the two structures. Minimal Attachment predicts an initial preference for the assertion analysis in (2a). Altmann, Garnham, and Dennis (1992), using the eye-tracking technique, indeed found a reading-time advantage for sentences such as (2a) over (2b). But it is significant that they only found this in particular situations. That is, they found that the discourse context played an important role in determining how these sentences were read. Consider the fact that, if two women are mentioned in a conversation, then the use of distinguishing modification, as in (2b), would aid the listener in determining which woman was being referred to in a particular sentence. By testing sentences in contexts in which modification was useful in this way, Altmann, Garnham, and Dennis report that the initial reading time advantage for (2a) over (2b) disappeared. This indicates the rapid influence of discourse context on sentence processing.

Studies such as these indicate that sentence processing necessarily involves the efficient use of many different types of information. Exactly how these various information types interact in sentence processing is an important question in cognitive psychology. Sentence processing is center stage in the "modularity" debate—that is, the extent to which information processing is accomplished by specialized subprocessors or by more general mechanisms (Fodor 1983; Marslen-Wilson and Tyler 1987; Friederici 1990). In addition to lexical, structural, and discourse information, the role of prosodic factors is also an increasing focus of experimental research (Ferreira and Anes 1994; Warren 1996).

Another important research topic, inspired by the work of Baddeley and colleagues (Baddeley 1986), is the role of short-term memory in sentence processing. As noted, the limited capacity of short-term memory is one driving force in incremental processing, and many researchers accord it a significant role in the processing of ambiguous or complex sentences (Just and Carpenter 1992; Waters and Caplan 1996).

See also AMBIGUITY; CONNECTIONIST APPROACHES TO LANGUAGE; PROSODY AND INTONATION, PROCESSING ISSUES; PSYCHOLINGUISTICS

—*Paul Gorrell*

References

Altmann, G., A. Garnham, and Y. Dennis. (1992). Avoiding the garden-path: Eye movements in context. *Journal of Memory and Language* 31:685–712.

Baddeley, A. D. (1986). *Working Memory.* Oxford: Oxford University Press.

Bever, T. (1970). The cognitive basis for linguistic structures. In J. R. Hayes, Ed., *Cognition and the Development of Language.* New York: Wiley, pp. 279–352.

Chomsky, N. (1995). *The Minimalist Program.* Cambridge, MA: MIT Press.

Crain, S., and M. Steedman. (1985). On not being led up the garden path: The use of context by the psychological syntax processor. In D. R. Dowty, L. Karttunen, and A. Zwicky, Eds., *Natural Language Processing.* Cambridge: Cambridge University Press, pp. 320–358.

DeVincenzi, M. (1991). *Syntactic Parsing Strategies in Italian.* Dordrecht: Kluwer.

Ferreira, F., and M. Anes. (1994). Why study spoken language. In M. A. Gernsbacher, Ed., *Handbook of Psycholinguistics.* New York: Academic Press, pp. 33–56.

Fodor, J. A. (1983). *The Modularity of Mind.* Cambridge, MA: MIT Press.

Fodor, J. D. (1995). Comprehending sentence structure. In L. R. Gleitman and M. Liberman, Eds., *An Invitation to Cognitive Science,* vol. 1: *Language.* 2nd ed. Cambridge, MA: MIT Press, pp. 209–246.

Frazier, L., and J. D. Fodor. (1978). The sausage machine: A new two-stage parsing model. *Cognition* 6: 291–325.

Friederici, A. (1990). On the properties of cognitive modules. *Psychological Research* 52: 175–180.

Gorrell, P. (1995). *Syntax and Parsing.* Cambridge: Cambridge University Press.

Gorrell, P. (1996). Parsing theory and phrase-order variation in German V2 clauses. *Journal of Psycholinguistic Research* 25: 135–156.

Inoue, A., and J. D. Fodor. (1995). Information-paced parsing of Japanese. In R. Mazuka and N. Nagai, Eds., *Japanese Sentence Processing.* Hillsdale, NJ: Erlbaum.

Just, M., and P. Carpenter. (1992). A capacity theory of comprehension: Individual differences in working memory. *Psychological Review* 99: 122–149.

MacDonald, M., N. Pearlmutter, and M. Seidenberg. (1994). The lexical nature of syntactic ambiguity resolution. *Psychological Review* 101: 676–703.

Marslen-Wilson, W., and L. Tyler. (1987). Against modularity. In J. Garfield, Ed., *Modularity in Knowledge Representation and Natural-Language Processing.* Cambridge, MA: MIT Press, pp. 37–62.

Mecklinger, A., H. Schriefers, K. Steinhauer, and A. Friederici. (1995). Processing relative clauses varying on syntactic and semantic dimensions: An analysis with event related brain potentials. *Memory and Cognition* 23: 477–497.

Mitchell, D. (1994). Sentence parsing. In M. A. Gernsbacher, Ed., *Handbook of Psycholinguistics.* New York: Academic Press, pp. 375–409.

Osterhout, L., P. Holcomb, and D. Swinney. (1994). Brain potentials elicited by garden-path sentences: Evidence of the application of verb information during parsing. *Journal of Experimental Psychology: Learning, Memory, and Cognition* 20: 786–803.

Rayner, K., and L. Frazier. (1987). Parsing temporarily ambiguous complements. *The Quarterly Journal of Experimental Psychology* 39: 657–673.

Schriefers, H., A. Friederici, and K. Kuhn. (1995). The processing of locally ambiguous relative clauses in German. *Journal of Memory and Language* 34: 227–246.

St. John, M., and J. McClelland. (1990). Learning and applying contextual constraints in sentence comprehension. *Artificial Intelligence* 46: 217–257.

Warren, P. (1996). Prosody and parsing: An introduction. *Language and Cognitive Processes* 11: 1–16.

Waters, G. S., and D. Caplan. (1996), Processing resource capacity and the comprehension of garden path sentences. *Memory and Cognition* 24: 342–355.

Further Readings

Altmann, G. T. M., Ed. (1990). *Cognitive Models of Speech Processing: Psycholinguistics and Computational Perspectives.* Cambridge, MA: MIT Press.

Baddeley, A. D., and S. E. Gathercole. (1993). *Working Memory and Language.* Hillsdale, NJ: Erlbaum.

Balota, D. A., G. B. Flores d'Arcais, and K. Rayner, Eds. (1990). *Comprehension Processes in Reading.* Hillsdale, NJ: Erlbaum.

Carlson, G. N., and M. K. Tanenhaus, Eds. (1989). *Linguistic Structure in Language Processing.* Dordrecht: Kluwer.

Carpenter, P. A., A. Miyake, and M. A. Just. (1994). Working memory constraints in comprehension: Evidence from individual differences, aphasia and aging. In M. A. Gernsbacher, Ed., *Handbook of Psycholinguistics.* New York: Academic Press, pp. 375–409.

Clifton, C., L. Frazier, and K. Rayner, Eds. (1994). *Perspectives on Sentence Processing.* Hillsdale, NJ: Erlbaum.

Garfield, J. L., Ed. (1987). *Modularity in Knowledge Representation and Natural Language Understanding.* Cambridge, MA: MIT Press.

Garrett, M. (1990). Sentence processing. In D. N. Osherson and H. Lasnik, Eds., *Language: An Invitation to Cognitive Science,* vol. 1. 1st ed. Cambridge, MA: MIT Press, pp. 133–175.

Garman, M. (1990). Understanding utterances. In *Psycholinguistics.* Cambridge: Cambridge University Press.

Mitchell, D. (1994). Sentence parsing. In M. A. Gernsbacher, Ed., *Handbook of Psycholinguistics.* New York: Academic Press, pp. 375–409.

Sells, P., S. M. Shieber, and T. Wasow, Eds. (1991). *Foundational Issues in Natural Language Processing.* Cambridge, MA: MIT Press.

Simpson, G. B., Ed. (1991). *Understanding Word and Sentence.* Amsterdam: Elsevier.

Sexual Attraction, Evolutionary Psychology of

Evolutionary psychology is evolutionary biology applied to the brain's adaptations. An adaptation is a phenotypic feature, psychological or otherwise, whose ultimate cause is some type of historical Darwinian selection (Thornhill 1997). Genes, physiology, development, and environment are proximate causes of each adaptation. Because adaptations are the products of past selection, they exhibit functional or purposeful design. Evolutionary psychology's focus is on identifying and characterizing psychological adaptations, which are functionally designed for processing information about survival and reproductive success in human evolutionary history.

Humans make aesthetic judgments in numerous domains, and for theoretical and empirical reasons, these judgments are viewed as reflecting domain-specific psychological adaptations, not general-purpose ones (Thornhill 1998). Thus, it is proposed that there is special-purpose adaptation for assessing sexual attractiveness, and further,

that in this domain are numerous psychological adaptations, each functionally designed for assessing a component of attractiveness that corresponded to a marker of the reproductive value of an individual to the mate chooser during human evolutionary history. Aesthetic judgments in the domain of sexual attraction are sometimes sex specific because males and females, consistently throughout human evolutionary history, faced sex-specific adaptive problems in mate selection, and therefore have sex-specific psychological adaptation. For example, women value resources and status of potential mates more, and physical attractiveness and youth in a potential mate less, than men do (Symons 1979; Grammer 1993; Buss 1994).

Cross-cultural research has shown that although men place more value on physical attractiveness of a mate than women do, both sexes value it highly (Grammer 1993; Buss 1994; cf. HUMAN UNIVERSALS). Physical beauty is a health certification (Thornhill and Gangestad 1993; Symons 1995). In human evolutionary history, individuals who saw as sexually attractive body traits of health outreproduced other individuals because the formers' preferred mates survived better, had genetic health, and were better able to provide investment. Two important categories of physical beauty traits identified in recent research are the hormone markers and developmental stability/bilateral symmetry (Thornhill and Gangestad 1996), which are the focus of the rest of this article.

The adult human form is an array of sex-specific, sex hormone-mediated secondary sexual traits that signal health. These traits apparently evolved for the reason that health signalers outreproduced less healthy individuals, because the most healthy were preferred mates. Men's and women's faces differ in the size of the lower face. Largeness in the lower face is attractive in men's faces, whereas smallness is attractive in women's faces (Symons 1995; Thornhill and Gangestad 1996). High estrogen at puberty caps the growth of the adult female face. Testosterone facilitates the sex difference in muscle mass, body size, and athleticism, and largeness and athleticism are attractive in men. Estrogen facilitates the redistribution and increased deposition of fat on the bodies of females at adolescence, giving rise to the relatively small waist and large hips in women. Low waist-to-hip ratio in women connotes hormonal health, fertility, youth and relative freedom from a diversity of diseases (Singh 1993).

The hormone-facilitated facial features and the other hormone markers mentioned not only display information about an individual's hormonal health, but apparently also his/her immunocompetence, because both sex hormones are immunosuppressors (Thornhill and Gangestad 1993). Attractive expressions of secondary sexual traits require high hormone titers during their construction, and thus can be afforded only by immunocompetent individuals. Disease organisms are important in human attractiveness (reviewed in Thornhill and Møller 1997). For example, the value placed on physical attractiveness in choice of a long-term mate in each sex correlates positively with the prevalence of parasitic diseases across human societies (Gangestad and Buss 1993).

Developmental stability connotes developmental health in humans (Thornhill and Møller 1997). Developmental stability occurs when the adaptive developmental trajectory is achieved despite environmental and genetic perturbations during development. Developmental instability is most often measured as fluctuating asymmetry because fluctuating asymmetry is a highly sensitive measure of developmental disturbance. Fluctuating asymmetry is deviation from perfect bilateral symmetry in normally bilaterally symmetrical traits. These deviations are random in direction, typically small in any one trait, and found in every individual to some degree. Fluctuating asymmetry may be the best measure available of phenotypic and genetic quality of the individual. It reflects the individual's ability to resist environmental (e.g., parasites, low food quantity and quality, environmental toxins) and genetic perturbations during development, or an absence of genes that disrupt development (Møller and Swaddle 1997). Accordingly, low fluctuating asymmetry is associated in a wide range of species with rapid growth rate, reduced parasitism, longevity, fecundity, and sexual attractiveness (Møller and Swaddle 1997). It also shows significant heritability across species (Møller and Thornhill 1997).

Symmetry is a component of sexual attractiveness in humans. In both sexes, faces with high bilateral symmetry are more attractive than less symmetrical faces (e.g., Grammer and Thornhill 1994; review of studies in Møller and Thornhill 1998). Also, symmetry in body features such as fingers, elbows, ankles, and feet correlates with facial symmetry and attractiveness (Gangestad and Thornhill 1997). Interestingly, facial symmetry in each sex correlates with the sex-specific attractive expression of the facial secondary sex traits (e.g., symmetry positively correlates with lower face size in men and negatively with lower face size in women; Gangestad and Thornhill 1997). Moreover, women with symmetrical breasts report higher age-independent fertility (number of children) and earlier onset of child bearing, and breast-size symmetry positively affects women's attractiveness (Møller, Soler, and Thornhill 1995; Singh 1995; Manning et al. 1997).

Numerous studies show that nonfacial body symmetry of men positively correlates with their mating success. This pattern is not seen in women. Compared to men with high body fluctuating asymmetry, men with low asymmetry report having had more sex partners and more extra-pair-bond sex partners, are chosen as extra-pair partners more often by women in committed relationships, and begin sex earlier in their life history and in their romantic relationships (Thornhill and Gangestad 1994; Gangestad and Thornhill 1997). Also, the mates of symmetrical men show the most reported copulatory orgasms (Thornhill et al. 1995). The female copulatory orgasm seems to be a female choice adaptation. It increases sperm retention and may be involved in selective sperm retention (Baker and Bellis 1995). Also, it may affect selective bonding as a result of associated oxytocin (Thornhill et al. 1995). Finally, there is evidence that secondary sexual traits of the body in men such as musculature, athleticism, and body size correlate positively with their body symmetry (Gangestad and Thornhill 1997).

Social psychology had demonstrated earlier in research beginning in the 1960s the profound importance of physical attractiveness in human everyday life (e.g. Jackson 1992). Only relatively recently have evolutionary psychologists asked why the importance in the first place and what kinds of body features are expected to play central roles given the nature of the evolutionary process. Physical attractiveness signals the individual's ability to cope with stresses from reproductive hormones during puberty and adolescence, from disease organisms, and from the many environmental and genetic perturbations that throw off the development of bilateral symmetry. This is attractiveness described in terms of evolved human preferences. How these preferences interact with other criteria of sexual and romantic interest (e.g., status, age, need of investment) and through compromises or trade-off generate actual romantic choices is under investigation (Cunningham, Druen, and Barbee 1997; Gangestad and Thornhill 1997; Graziano et al. 1997).

See also ADAPTATION AND ADAPTATIONISM; DOMAIN-SPECIFICITY; EVOLUTION; EVOLUTIONARY PSYCHOLOGY

—*Randy Thornhill*

References

Baker, R. R. and M. A. Bellis. (1995). *Human Sperm Competition: Copulation, Masturbation and Infidelity*. London: Chapman and Hall.

Buss, D. (1994). *The Evolution of Desire: Strategies of Human Mating*. New York: Basic Books.

Cunningham, M. R., P. B. Druen, and A. P. Barbee. (1997). Angels, mentors, and friends: Trade-offs among evolutionary, social, and individual variables in physical appearance. In J. A. Simpson and D. T. Kenrick, Eds., *Evolutionary Social Psychology*. Mahwah, NJ: Erlbaum, pp. 109–140.

Gangestad, S. W., and D. M. Buss. (1993). Pathogen prevalence and human mate preference. *Ethology and Sociobiology* 14: 89–96.

Gangestad, S. W., and R. Thornhill. (1997). Human sexual selection and developmental stability. In J. A. Simpson and D. T. Kenrick, Eds., *Evolutionary Social Psychology*. Mahwah, NJ: Erlbaum, pp. 169–196.

Graziano, W. G., L. A. Jensen Campbell, M. Todd, and J. F. Finch. (1997). Interpersonal attraction from an evolutionary perspective: Women's reactions to dominant and prosocial men. In J. A. Simpson and D. T. Kenrick, Eds., *Evolutionary Social Psychology*. Mahwah, NJ: Erlbaum pp. 141–168.

Grammer, K. (1993). *Signale der Liebe: Die Biologischen Gesetze der Partnerschaft*. Berlin: Hoffman and Campe.

Grammer, K., and R. Thornhill. (1994). Human (*Homo sapiens*) facial attractiveness and sexual selection: The role of symmetry and averageness. *Journal of Comparative Psychology* 108: 233–242.

Jackson, L. A. (1992). *Physical Appearance and Gender*. Albany: SUNY Press.

Manning, J. T., D. Scutt, G. H. Whitehouse, and S. J. Leinster. (1997). Breast asymmetry and phenotypic quality in women. *Ethology and Sociobiology* 18: 223–236.

Møller, A. P., and J. P. Swaddle. (1997). *Asymmetry, Developmental Stability and Evolution*. Oxford: Oxford University Press.

Møller, A. P., and R. Thornhill. (1997). A meta-analysis of the heritability of developmental stability. *Journal of Evolutionary Biology* 10: 1–16.

Møller, A. P., and R. Thornhill. (1998). Bilateral symmetry and sexual selection: A meta-analysis. *American Naturalist* 151: 174–192.

Møller, A. P., M. Soler, and R. Thornhill. (1995). Breast asymmetry, sexual selection and human reproductive success. *Ethology and Sociobiology* 16: 207–219.

Singh, D. (1993). Adaptive significance of female physical attractiveness: Role of waist-to-hip ratio. *Journal of Personality and Social Psychology* 59.

Singh, D. (1995). Female health, attractiveness and desirability for relationships: Role of breast asymmetry and waist-to-hip ratio. *Ethology and Sociobiology* 16: 465–481.

Symons, D. (1979). *The Evolution of Human Sexuality.* Oxford: Oxford University Press.

Symons, D. (1995). Beauty is in the adaptations of the beholder: The evolutionary psychology of human female sexual attractiveness. In P. R. Abramson and S. D. Pinker, Eds., *Sexual Nature/Sexual Culture.* Chicago: University of Chicago Press, pp. 80–118.

Thornhill, R. (1997). The concept of an evolved adaptation. In G. R. Bock and G. Cardew, Eds., *Characterizing Human Psychological Adaptations.* CIBA Foundation Symposium. New York: Wiley, pp. 4–13.

Thornhill, R. (1998). Darwinian aesthetics. In C. Crawford and D. Krebs, Eds., *Handbook of Evolutionary Psychology: Ideas, Issues and Applications.* Hillsdale, NJ: Erlbaum.

Thornhill, R. and S. W. Gangestad. (1993). Human facial beauty: averageness, symmetry and parasite resistance. *Human Nature* 4: 237–269.

Thornhill, R., and S. W. Gangestad. (1996). The evolution of human sexuality. *Trends in Ecology and Evolution* 11: 98–102.

Thornhill, R., and S. W. Gangestad. (1994). Human fluctuating asymmetry and sexual behavior. *Psychological Science* 5: 297–302.

Thornhill, R., S. W. Gangestad, and R. Comer. (1995). Human female orgasm and mate fluctuating asymmetry. *Animal Behaviour* 50: 1601–1615.

Thornhill, R. and A. P. Møller. (1997). Developmental stability, disease and medicine. *Biological Reviews* 72: 497–548.

Further Readings

Folstad, I., and A. J. Karter. (1992). Parasites, bright males and the immunocompetence handicap. *American Naturalist* 139: 603–622.

Johnston, V. S. and M. Franklin. (1993). Is beauty in the eye of the beholder? *Ethology and Sociobiology* 14: 183–199.

Perrett, D. I., K. A. May, and S. Yoshikawa. (1994). Facial shape and judgments of female attractiveness. *Nature* 368: 239–242.

Shape Perception

This article concerns shape perception, so it is natural to consider what is meant by "shape." Most readers undoubtedly have an intuitive feel for the meaning of the term, sensing its relatedness to such concepts as form and structure. Nevertheless, a precise definition of shape has proved elusive. Instead, experimenters have adopted the working definition that shape is an aspect of a stimulus that remains invariant despite changes in size, position, and orientation. For example, 2-D visual stimuli have the same shape if there exists a transformation of spatial scale (e.g., magnification) or a rotation in the picture plane that renders them identical. Similarly, 3-D objects have the same shape if their volumes can be equated by size changes or a combination of rotations about three spatial axes.

Although our world is filled with objects and patterns, most studies of shape perception have used only 2-D stimuli. This emphasis reflects the belief that perception of 3-D form depends on the shape of 2-D regions in the retinal image. The fact that line drawings can evoke vivid percepts of 3-D form (see figure 1a) supports the idea that 2-D and 3-D shape perception are related, but how they are related is still debated (cf. Attneave 1954; GIBSON 1950; Hochberg 1964; Koffka 1935; MARR 1982). Furthermore, variables that affect LIGHTNESS PERCEPTION (e.g., shading) and DEPTH PERCEPTION (e.g., binocular disparity and relative motion) also affect form perception. How these variables interact with 2-D shape to yield a 3-D percept is not well understood.

In most viewing conditions, a pattern's shape is closely related to the spatial arrangement of its contours. Thus, shape perception depends in part on feature extraction processes that encode edges and elementary features in the retinal image, and on processes that group elements into higher-order units (see GESTALT PERCEPTION). In the latter case, we can perceive both the shape of the individual elements, as well as the global shape of the grouped elements (figure 1b). Despite the close connection between contours and shape, simultaneous presentation of contours is neither necessary nor sufficient for shape perception. It is not necessary because shape is perceived even when only isolated parts of contour are presented. For example, in anorthoscopic stimuli a visual pattern is moved behind a stationary slit in an opaque screen: although only a small dot or line is visible at any one time, observers often perceive the shape of the hidden pattern. Simultaneous presentation of contours is not sufficient for shape perception because observers do not necessarily attend to everything in the visual field. Although some attributes of an unattended object, such as its presence, location, and color, can be perceived, ATTENTION appears to be required for shape perception (Rock and Gutman 1981; Rock et al. 1992). Other top-down processes also affect shape perception, as is shown by ambiguous figures like the duck/rabbit pattern in figure 1c: The contours remain constant, but perceived shape depends on the interpretation of the figure. In some cases, the allocation of attention to particular stimulus features can bias the percept of ambiguous figures (Peterson and Gibson 1991).

Although clearly related to HIGH-LEVEL VISION phenomena such as OBJECT RECOGNITION, shape perception is better classified as an aspect of MID-LEVEL VISION because the perception of shape does not require recognition: One can perceive the shapes of novel stimuli that have no a priori meaning (figure 1d), and an observer can recognize objects based on surface properties like TEXTURE or color (Humphrey et al. 1994; see also SURFACE PERCEPTION). Nevertheless, shape provides important clues about an object's identity, as well as information that is critical to manipulating objects and determining their functional properties or AFFORDANCES (e.g., Can I stand on this object?). Thus, it is not surprising that visual mechanisms encode shape rapidly and accurately. For example, the response time needed to name line drawings of familiar objects, or to determine if two novel polygons have the same shape, is approximately 1 sec (Larsen 1985). Although these response times are short, they probably overestimate the time needed to perceive shape. For instance, observers can identify letters and line drawings of familiar objects presented for only 50 msec (Biederman and Ju 1988; Jolicoeur and Landau 1984). Other studies have shown that observers are exquisitely sensitive to shape differences that are much more subtle than those shown in figure 1e, even when the stimuli being compared differ substantially in size (De Valois et al. 1990; Regan and Hamstra 1992).

Further evidence of the versatility of shape perception comes from the fact that a stimulus need not be completely visible for observers to perceive shape accurately. In the everyday world, objects frequently occlude parts of neighboring objects, yet our visual systems are able to complete missing shape information (figure 1f). Although shape completion appears effortless and immediate, it is *not* instantaneous, and the way in which shapes are completed depends on factors such as stimulus regularity and symmetry (Sekuler 1994; Sekuler and Palmer 1992). A phenomenon related to visual completion is that of illusory contours, in which the percept of a shape is induced by other visible shapes (figure 1g; Kanizsa 1975).

At the beginning of this article we defined shape as that aspect of a stimulus that remained invariant despite changes in size and orientation. Thus, one might expect that per-

ceived shape would not depend on stimulus orientation or size. This suggestion seems intuitively obvious, and it is consistent with our experience in everyday tasks in which objects are recognized (in part on the basis of shape) despite substantial changes in retinal size and orientation. Nevertheless, there is ample evidence that our perception of shape is *not* invariant across spatial scales and orientations. For example, it is more difficult to recognize line drawings of familiar objects and abstract patterns presented in unfamiliar sizes or orientations (Edelman and Bülthoff 1992; Jolicoeur 1987; Rock, Schreiber, and Ro 1994; Tarr and Pinker 1989). Furthermore, it takes significantly more time to determine if two patterns have the same shape when they differ in size or orientation (Larsen 1985; Sekuler and Nash 1972). Finally, there are several demonstrations that phenomenological shape varies significantly with orientation. Mach's classic demonstration of the effect of orientation on the perceived shape of a square is shown in figure 1h. In Mach's words, "Two figures may be geometrically congruent, but physiologically quite different, . . . [these figures] could never be recognized as the same without mechanical and intellectual operations" (Mach 1959: 106; see also MENTAL ROTATION). These effects of size and orientation on shape perception have important implications for theories of object recognition. Specifically, they raise the possi-

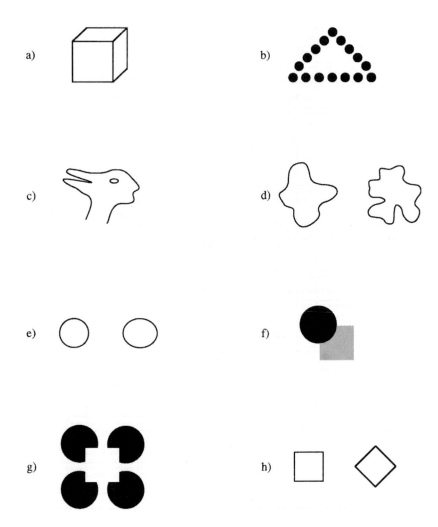

a)

b)

c)

d)

e)

f)

g)

h)

Figure 1. (a) Although this image is two-dimensional, observers perceive a three-dimensional cube. **(b).** Shape perception can occur after perceptual grouping. Observers can perceive both the global (triangle) and the local (circle) shapes. **(c).** Perceived shape is influenced by top-down processes. When one stimulus has multiple interpretations, perceived shape changes even with no stimulus change. This figure can be seen as a duck (facing left) or as a rabbit (facing right). When the percept changes, so does the interpretation of specific parts of the stimulus (e.g., what was a beak becomes ears). **(d).** We perceive shapes of unfamiliar figures that have no a priori meaning. Observers can discriminate these two shapes, although we have no memory association for either. **(e).** Quite small shape differences can be perceived. The length of this oval is just 20% longer than the diameter of the circle. Most observers can discriminate even more subtle differences in shape. **(f).** Shape perception proceeds even in the absence of complete stimulus information. This figure is consistent with both a circle partially occluding a square (in two depth planes), and a circle next to a notched square (in one or more depth planes). Most people perceive the former—filling in missing shape information. **(g).** We can perceive the shapes of completely invisible objects. In this example of an illusory figure, observers see a white square on top of four black circles. Although the edges of the square appear highly salient, they do not physically exist. **(h).** Mach's original demonstration that phenomenological shape can vary with orientation. The two stimuli have the same physical shape, but observers perceive the left shape as a square and the right as a diamond (if the reader tilts his or her head 45 degrees clockwise, the percepts reverse).

bility that an object is recognized by comparing it to multiple, viewpoint-dependent representations in long-term memory, rather than to a single, viewpoint-independent representation.

Relatively little is known about the physiological mechanisms underlying shape perception, but researchers have located neurons in the inferotemporal cortex (IT) that respond better to some shapes than to others, even when these shapes are not identified with specific previously learned objects. Whereas the primary VISUAL CORTEX initially codes basic features such as orientation, size, and color, area IT codes much more complex features such as particular shapes, or combinations of shapes and colors (Tanaka 1993). Neurons in area IT also have similar shape selectivity regardless of the cue that defines the shape (e.g., luminance-, texture-, or motion-defined shapes; Sary et al. 1995), the size and position of the shape (Ito et al. 1995; Logothetis, Pauls, and Poggio 1995), or the presence or absence of partially occluding contours (Kovacs, Vogels, and Orban 1995). These recent discoveries suggest that area IT plays a significant role in shape constancy and recognition, but other cortical areas may be involved in the use of shape to guide the manipulation of objects (Goodale and Milner 1992; see also VISUAL PROCESSING STREAMS). Additional physiological and psychophysical research in the next few years undoubtedly will increase our understanding of the physiological processes underlying shape perception.

See also ILLUSIONS; PICTORIAL ART AND VISION; SPATIAL PERCEPTION; TOP-DOWN PROCESSING IN VISION

—*Allison B. Sekuler and Patrick J. Bennett*

References

Attneave, F. (1954). Some informational aspects of visual perception. *Psychological Review* 61: 183–193.

Biederman, I., and G. Ju. (1988). Surface versus edge-based determinants of visual recognition. *Cognitive Psychology* 20: 38–64.

De Valois, K., V. Lakshminarayanan, R. Nygaard, S. Schlussel, and J. Sladky. (1990). Discrimination of relative spatial position. *Vision Research* 30: 1649–1660.

Edelman, S., and H. Bülthoff. (1992). Orientation dependence in the recognition of familiar and novel views of three-dimensional objects. *Vision Research* 32: 2385–2400.

Gibson, J. J. (1950). *Perception of the Visual World.* Boston, MA: Houghton-Mifflin.

Goodale, M., and A. Milner. (1992). Separate visual pathways for perception and action. *Trends in Neuroscience* 15: 20–25.

Hochberg, J. E. (1964). *Perception.* Englewood Cliffs, NJ: Prentice-Hall.

Humphrey, G., M. Goodale, L. Jakobson, and P. Servos. (1994). The role of surface information in object recognition: Studies of a visual form agnosic and normal subjects. *Perception* 23: 1457–1481.

Ito, M., H. Tamura, I. Fujita, and K. Tanaka. (1995). Size and position invariance of neuronal responses in monkey inferotemporal cortex. *Journal of Neurophysiology* 73: 218–226.

Jolicoeur, P. (1987). A size-congruency effect in memory for visual shape. *Memory and Cognition* 15: 531–543.

Jolicoeur, P., and M. Landau. (1984). Effects of orientation on the identification of simple visual patterns. *Canadian Journal of Psychology* 38: 80–93.

Kanizsa, G. (1975). Contours without gradients or cognitive contours? *Italian Journal of Psychology* 1: 93–112.

Koffka, K. (1935). *Principles of Gestalt Psychology.* New York: Harcourt, Brace, and World Inc.

Kovacs, G., R. Vogels, and G. Orban. (1995). Selectivity of macaque inferior temporal neurons for partially occluded shapes. *Journal of Neuroscience* 15: 1984–1997.

Larsen, A. (1985). Pattern matching: Effects of size ratio, angular difference in orientation and familiarity. *Perception and Psychophysics* 38: 63–68.

Logothetis, N., J. Pauls, and T. Poggio. (1995). Shape representation in the inferior temporal cortex of monkeys. *Current Biology* 5: 552–563.

Mach, E. (1959). *The Analysis of Sensations.* Translated by C. M. Williams. New York: Dover Publishers.

Marr, D. (1982). *Vision.* San Francisco, CA: W. H. Freeman.

Peterson, M. A., and B. S. Gibson. (1991). Directing spatial attention within an object: Altering the functional equivalence of shape descriptions. *Journal of Experimental Psychology: Human Perception and Performance* 17: 170–182.

Regan, D., and D. Hamstra. (1992). Shape discrimination and the judgement of perfect symmetry: Dissociation of shape from size. *Vision Research* 32: 1845–1864.

Rock, I., and D. Gutman. (1981). The effect of inattention on form perception. *Journal of Experimental Psychology: Human Perception and Performance* 7: 275–285.

Rock, I., C. Linnett, P. Grant, and A. Mack. (1992). Perception without attention: Results of a new method. *Cognitive Psychology* 24: 502–534.

Rock, I., C. Schreiber, and T. Ro. (1994). The dependence of two-dimensional shape perception on orientation. *Perception* 23: 1389–1506.

Sary, G., R. Vogels, G. Kovacs, and G. Orban. (1995). Responses of monkey inferior temporal neurons to luminance-, motion- and texture-defined gratings. *Journal of Neurophysiology* 73: 1341–1354.

Sekuler, A. (1994). Local and global minima in visual completion: Effects of symmetry and orientation. *Perception* 23: 529–545.

Sekuler, A., and S. Palmer. (1992). Perception of partly occluded objects: A microgenetic analysis. *Journal of Experimental Psychology: General* 121: 95–111.

Sekuler, R., and D. Nash. (1972). Speed of size scaling in human vision. *Psychonomic Science* 1972: 93–94.

Tanaka, K. (1993). Neuronal mechanisms of object recognition. *Science* 262: 685–688.

Tarr, M., and S. Pinker. (1989). Mental rotation and orientation-dependence in shape perception. *Cognitive Psychology* 21: 233–282.

Further Readings

Biederman, I. (1987). Recognition-by-components: A theory of human image understanding. *Psychological Review* 94: 115–147.

Cavanagh, P., and Y. Leclerc. (1989). Shape from shadows. *Journal of Experimental Psychology: Human Perception and Performance* 15: 3–27.

Jolicoeur, P. (1992). Identification of disoriented objects: A dual-systems theory. In G. Humphreys, Ed., *Understanding Vision: An Interdisciplinary Perspective.* Cambridge, MA: Blackwell, pp. 180–198.

Marr, D., and H. Nishihara. (1978). Representation and recognition of the spatial organization of three-dimensional shapes. *Proceedings of the Royal Society of London Series B Biological Sciences* 200: 269–294.

Rock, I. (1973). *Orientation and Form.* New York: Academic Press.

Rock, I. (1983). *The Logic of Perception*. Cambridge, MA: MIT Press.

Uttal, W. (1988). *On Seeing Forms*. Hillsdale, NJ: Erlbaum.

Zusne, L. (1970). Visual Perception of Form. New York: Academic Press.

Sight

See HIGH-LEVEL VISION; MID-LEVEL VISION; VISION AND LEARNING; VISUAL PROCESSING STREAMS

Sign Language and the Brain

Two prominent issues concerning brain organization in deaf users of SIGN LANGUAGES are whether deaf individuals show complementary HEMISPHERIC SPECIALIZATION for language and nonlanguage visuo-spatial skills, and whether classical language areas within the left hemisphere participate in sign-language processing. These questions are especially pertinent given that signed languages of the deaf make significant use of visuo-spatial mechanisms to convey linguistic information. Thus sign languages exhibit properties for which each of the cerebral hemispheres show specialization: visuo-spatial processing and language processing. Three sources of evidence have commonly been used to investigate brain organization in signers: behavioral studies using tachistoscopic visual half-field paradigms, studies of signers who have incurred focal brain damage, and, more recently, neural imaging studies of normal signing volunteers. Many of these studies have investigated American Sign Language (ASL), which is but one of the many naturally occurring signed languages of the world. These studies have provided insight into the determination of hemispheric specialization and the contribution of environmental and biological factors in the establishment of neural systems mediating human language.

The behavioral literature on cerebral lateralization for sign language is based largely upon tachistoscopic visual half-field studies. As a whole, these studies yield inconsistent and contradictory findings, ranging from reports of right-hemisphere dominance, left-hemisphere dominance, and no hemsipheric asymmetries for sign language processing in the deaf. Methodological factors such as variability in inclusion criteria for deaf subjects (e.g., etiology and degree of hearing loss), variability in language background and schooling (e.g., native signers, nonnative signers, oral schooling, sign-based schooling) and stimulus characteristics (e.g., manual-alphabet handshapes, static drawings of ASL signs and moving signs) contribute to the wide range of findings. Discussion here will be limited to studies using profoundly deaf, native signing adults as subjects. Poizner, Battison, and Lane (1979) compared the contribution of movement in sign language stimuli. They reported a left visual field (LVF) advantage for static signs and no hemispheric asymmetry for moving signs. In a study comparing depth of processing, Grossi et al. (1996) reported no hemisphere asymmetry for judgments of signs based on physical characteristics. However, a significant RVF advantage emerged when subjects were asked to make judgments of

handshapes that matched in morphological relationships to one another. Emmorey and Corina (1993) tested hemispheric specialization using a lexical decision paradigm for moving signs that varied in imagability. Deaf signers and hearing English speakers both showed a left-hemisphere advantage for abstract lexical items. English speakers exhibited no visual field effect for imageable words; however, deaf signers showed a significant right-hemisphere advantage for imageable signs. These studies suggest that hemispheric asymmetries are more likely to be elicited from moving sign stimuli as well as when deaf subjects are engaged in higher level lexical processing of sign stimuli. Under these constraints, patterns of left-hemisphere dominance for language may emerge.

In 1878, Hughlings Jackson wrote, "No doubt by disease of some part of his brain the deaf-mute might lose his natural system of signs" (p. 304). Since this time, roughly 25 individual case studies of signers with brain injury have been reported (see Corina 1998 for a recent review). However, many of the early case studies were compromised by a lack of understanding of the relationships among systems of communication used by deaf individuals. For example, several of the early studies compared disruptions of fingerspelling and only briefly mentioned or assessed sign-language use. More recently, well-documented case studies have begun to provide a clearer picture of the neural systems involved in sign-language processing. From these later studies, it becomes evident that right-handed deaf signers, like hearing persons, exhibit APHASIA when critical left-hemisphere areas are damaged (Poizner, Klima, and Bellugi 1987). Approximately one dozen case studies provide sufficient detail to implicate left-hemisphere structures in sign-language disturbances. A subset of cases provide neuroradiological or autopsy reports to confirm left-hemisphere involvement, and they provide compelling language assessment to implicate aphasic language disturbance. As well, five cases of signers with right-hemisphere pathology have been reported. All five of these signers showed moderate to severe degrees of nonlinguistic visuo-spatial impairment accompanied by relatively intact sign-language skills. In contrast, none of the left-hemisphere–damaged signers tested on nonlinguistic visuo-spatial tests were shown to have significant impairment. Taken together, these findings suggest that deaf signers show complementary specialization for language and nonlanguage skills. These studies demonstrate that the development of hemispheric specialization is not dependent upon exposure to oral/aural language.

Disruptions in sign-language ability following left-hemisphere damage are similar to those patterns found in hearing users of spoken languages. For example, execution of speech movements involves the cortical zone encompassing the lower posterior portion of the left frontal lobe (Goodglass 1993). Left-hemisphere posterior frontal regions also are implicated in sign-language production. A representative case is that of Poizner, Klima, and Bellugi's (1987) subject G. D., who had damage to Broadman's areas 44 and 45 of the left frontal lobe. This subject's signing was effortful and dysfluent, reduced largely to single-sign utterances, but her sign-language comprehension remained unimpaired. In hearing individuals, severe language comprehension deficits are associated with left-hemisphere posterior temporal lesions. Similar patterns have been observed in users of signed languages. For example, W. L., who suffered damage to the posterior temporal area, was globally aphasic for ASL (Corina et al. 1992). W. L. evidenced marked comprehension deficits and showed a gradation of impairment, with some difficulty in single-sign recognition, moderate impairment in following commands, and severe problems with complex ideational material. W. L.'s sign production remained moderately fluent, but he made numerous sign-language "phonemic" paraphasias. Phonemic paraphasias arise from substitutions or omissions of sublexical phonological components. In ASL, sublexical structure refers to the formational elements that comprise a sign form: handshape, location, movement, and orientation. A common form of sign paraphasic error involves the incorrect use of handshape for a given sign. Importantly, W. L. also showed intact production and comprehension of nonlinguistic pantomime. Thus, although profoundly aphasic for linguistic properties of ASL, W. L. was motorically facile and capable of producing and understanding nonlinguistic pantomime. Taken together, these findings provide evidence that language impairments following stroke in deaf signers follow the characteristic pattern of left frontal damage leading to nonfluent output with spared comprehension, whereas left posterior lesions yield fluent output with impaired language comprehension. Dissociation between nonlinguistic pantomime skills and language use further demonstrates that these impairments are aphasic in nature and do not reflect general problems in symbolic conceptualization or motor behavior.

Functional imaging techniques have been used to examine sign-language representation in the brain. Comparisons of sentence processing for written English and ASL reveal both commonalties and differences across hearing nonsigners and native users of sign language. A functional MAGNETIC RESONANCE IMAGING (fMRI) study by Neville et al. (1998) shows that when hearing or deaf subjects process their native languages (ASL or English), classical anterior and posterior language areas within the left hemisphere are recruited. This finding is consistent with data from studies of spoken- and sign-language aphasia. These results suggest that the early acquisition of a fully grammatical, natural language is important in the specialization of these systems. However, unlike patterns observed for English processing, when deaf and hearing native signers process sentences in ASL, robust activation is also observed in right hemisphere prefrontal regions and posterior and anterior parts of the superior temporal sulcus. These findings imply that the specific nature and structure of ASL results in the recruitment of the right hemisphere into the language system. Recent electrophysiological studies of neurologically intact native signers also indicate that both the left and right hemispheres are active during ASL sentence processing (Neville et al. 1997). These results suggest that activation within the right hemisphere may be specifically linked to the linguistic use of space. The degree of right-hemisphere activation observed in these studies is surprising given the lack of significant aphasic symptomology reported in right-hemisphere–damaged signers.

Taken together, studies of the neural basis of sign-language processing highlight the presence of strong biases that left inferior frontal and posterior temporal parietal regions of the left hemisphere are well suited to process a natural language independent of the form of the language, and they reveal that the specific structure and processing requirements of the language also, in part, determine the final form of the language systems of the brain.

See also AUDITION; INNATENESS OF LANGUAGE; LANGUAGE, NEURAL BASIS OF

—David P. Corina

References

Corina, D. P. (1998). The processing of sign language: evidence from aphasia. In H. Whitaker and B. Stemmer, Eds., *Handbook of Neurology.* San Diego, CA: Academic Press.

Corina, D. P., H. P. Poizner, T. Feinberg, D. Dowd, and L. O'Grady. (1992). Dissociation between linguistic and nonlinguistic gestural systems: A case for compositionality. *Brain and Language* 43: 414–447.

Emmorey, K., and D. Corina. (1993). Hemispheric specialization for ASL signs and English words: Differences between imageable and abstract forms. *Neuropsychologia* 31(7): 645–653.

Goodglass, H. (1993). *Understanding Aphasia.* San Diego, CA: Academic Press.

Grossi, G., C. Semenza, S. Corazza, and V. Volterra. (1996). Hemispheric specialization for sign language. *Neuropsychologia* 34(7): 737–740.

Jackson, J. H. (1878). On affections of speech from disease of the brain. *Brain* 1: 64. Reprint *Selected Writings of Hughlings Jackson.* J. Taylor, Ed. London. Vol. 2, 1932.

Neville, H. J., D. Bavelier, D. P. Corina, J. P. Rauschecker, A. Karni, A. Lalwani, A. Braun, V. P. Clark, P. Jezzard, and R. Turner. (1998). Cerebral organization for language in deaf and hearing subjects: Biological constraints and effects of experience. *Proceedings of the National Academy of Science* 95: 922–929.

Neville, H. J., S. A. Coffey, D. S. Lawson, A. Fischer, K. Emmorey, and U. Bellugi. (1997). Neural systems mediating American Sign Language: Effects of sensory experience and age of acquisition. *Brain and Language* 57(3): 285–308.

Poizner, H., R. Battison, and H. Lane. (1979). Cerebral asymmetry for American Sign Language: The effects of moving stimuli. *Brain and Language* 7(3): 351–362.

Poizner, H., E. S. Klima, and U. Bellugi. (1987) *What the Hands Reveal about the Brain.* Cambridge, MA: MIT Press.

Further Readings

Corina, D. P., M. Kritchevsky, and U. Bellugi. (1996). Visual language processing and unilateral neglect: Evidence from American Sign Language. *Cognitive Neuropsychology* 13(3): 321–351.

Corina, D. P. (1998). Aphasia in users of signed languages. In P. Coppens, Y. Lebrun, and A. Basso, Eds., *Aphasia in Atypical Populations.* Hillsdale, NJ: Erlbaum.

Corina, D. P., J. Vaid, and U. Bellugi. (1992). Linguistic basis of left hemisphere specialization. *Science* 225: 1258–1260.

Emmorey, K. (1996). The confluence of space and language in signed languages. In P. Bloom, M. Peterson, L. Nadel, and M.

Garrett, Eds., *Language and Space.* Cambridge, MA: MIT Press, pp. 171–209.

Hickok, G., U. Bellugi, and E. S. Klima. (1996). The neurobiology of sign language and its implications for the neural basis of language. *Nature* 381(6584): 699–702.

Kimura, D. (1981). Neural mechanisms in manual signing. *Sign Language Studies* 33: 291–312.

Kegl, J., and H. Poizner. (1991). The interplay between linguistic and spatial processing in a right-lesioned signer. *Journal of Clinical and Experimental Neuropsychology* 13: 38–39.

Neville, H. J. (1990). Intermodal competition and compensation in development: Evidence from studies of the visual system in congenitally deaf adults. *Annals of the New York Academy of Sciences* 608: 71–87.

Poizner, H., and J. Kegl. (1992). Neural basis of language and motor behavior: Perspectives from American Sign Language. *Aphasiology* 6(3): 219–256.

Soderfeldt, B., J. Ronnberg, and J. Risberg. (1994). Regional cerebral blood flow in sign language users. *Brain and Language* 46: 59–68.

Sign Languages

Sign languages (alternatively, signed languages) are human languages whose forms consist of sequences of movements and configurations of the hands and arms, face, and upper torso. Typically, sign languages are perceived through the visual mode. Sign languages thus contrast, of course, with spoken languages, whose forms consist of sounds produced by sequences of movements and configurations of the mouth and vocal tract. More informally, then, sign languages are visual-gestural languages, whereas spoken languages are auditory-vocal languages.

Most linguistic research has focused on spoken languages. Indeed, for many years all human languages were mistakenly believed to be spoken languages; signed languages (for example, those used by deaf people interacting with one another) were thought either to be pantomime or to be simple gestural codes representing the surrounding spoken language. However, recent linguistic work has shown these beliefs to be incorrect: natural signed languages show all the structural properties of other human languages yet have evolved independently of the spoken languages that surround them.

Signed languages typically appear as the primary communication systems of people for whom the use of spoken languages is blocked, either by deafness or muteness. The best-known sign languages are used by profoundly deaf people, but sign languages have also been noted (though less well studied) in non-deaf members of occupational or cultural groups where hearing or speaking is impossible (e.g., sawmill workers, monks taking vows of silence, cultures where speech is prohibited for long periods during mourning or surrounding puberty; Johnson 1978; Kendon 1988). Under any of these circumstances, sign languages appear to arise quite commonly: probably every known group of nonspeaking deaf people observed around the world uses some sign language, and even isolated deaf individuals have been observed to develop a sign language to communicate with hearing relatives and friends (Goldin-Meadow and Mylander 1984; Coppola et

al. 1997). Thus, although it is probably fair to say that the auditory-vocal (spoken) medium is biologically dominant for language in humans (in the sense that all groups for whom spoken language is viable seem to choose this medium), the visual-gestural (sign) medium is a robust, and therefore biologically normal, alternative.

One important distinction is between "natural sign languages" and "devised or derivative sign languages." Natural sign languages are those that have arisen spontaneously through time by unrestricted interactions among people who use them as a primary communication system. These are the sign languages on which most linguistic research has focused, because they offer the clearest evidence about the natural tendencies of humans to develop communicative structure in the visual-gestural mode. The natural sign languages of deaf communities are typically named by the region in which they have evolved—for example, American Sign Language (used in the United States and parts of Canada), British Sign Language (used in Great Britain), French Sign Language/Langue des Signes Française (used in France).

In contrast, devised or derivative sign languages (perhaps more properly termed "sign systems") are those that have been intentionally invented by some particular individuals (e.g., educators of deaf children), typically not the primary users of the language, and whose structures are often based directly on a spoken language. These devised systems are typically named by the spoken language on which they are based. One example is a set of sign systems devised by educators of the deaf in the 1970s to represent spoken English, known as Manually Coded English (similar but slightly different variants of MCE are called Signing Exact English, Seeing Essential English, and Linguistics of Visual English). Because these devised systems are invented by committees, rather than arising spontaneously among users, they do not offer the opportunity to observe the unfettered natural tendencies of humans to develop gestural languages. In fact, those sign systems studied by linguists have been found to violate the universal structural principles of both spoken and signed natural languages (even though the systems are intended to match a particular spoken language), probably because the inventors were unfamiliar with linguistic principles and performed their invention process outside of the implicit constraints and forces of the (natural) processing circumstances in which natural languages evolve. One interesting finding concerning these devised languages is that, presumably because of violating natural structural principles for human languages, children do not readily acquire these languages (Supalla 1986, 1990). Therefore use of these devised systems tends to be confined to the classrooms in which their use is required and does not spontaneously spread to a wider community or to broader employment in everyday communication.

As noted above, most research has focused on natural sign languages, asking whether natural sign languages are organized and learned in ways that are similar to or different from natural spoken languages. The largest amount of linguistic and psycholinguistic research on natural sign languages has been conducted on American Sign Language (Stokoe, Casterline, and Cronbach 1965; Klima and Bellugi

1979; Siple and Fischer 1990). More recent research has begun to investigate other natural sign languages, to compare unrelated sign languages to one another in an attempt to determine the universal properties and the range of language variation across sign languages, and to compare the outcome to that found in crosslinguistic research on spoken languages (Supalla 1997). Although our knowledge of American Sign Language is fairly detailed, our understanding of other signed languages and also of sign language universals is just beginning.

Like research on other languages, research on American Sign Language (ASL) focuses primarily on its structure, use, and acquisition among those signers for whom it is a native language, acquired from exposure in the home from earliest infancy. These are typically congenitally and profoundly deaf individuals whose parents are also deaf and who themselves acquired ASL early in life. (In contrast to spoken language communities, these native users are very rare and constitute only about 5 percent of the signing community.) Linguistic analyses of (natively acquired) ASL have revealed that it is a language with a quite different type of structure than that of English, but one that is found among other spoken languages (for example, it shares certain typological similarities with Navajo). Word structure in ASL is quite complex, particularly in verbs. Typical verbs are marked morphologically for agreement in person and number with both subject and object, and for temporal aspect and other grammatical features common to verbs in other languages. Verbs of motion are particularly complex, with stems involving morphemes for path, manner of motion, orientation, and classifier morphemes marking the semantic category or size and shape of both the moving object and a secondary object with respect to which the movement path occurs. As is common in spoken languages with complex MORPHOLOGY, word order in ASL is relatively free, with an unmarked SVO order but a number of ordering-changing syntactic structures commonly used (e.g., topicalization of the object, subject, or VP). Moved constituents are obligatorily marked by grammaticized facial expressions, which are produced throughout the signing of the words of that constituent. When verbs are marked for agreement and/or when discussing subjects and objects which have already been mentioned, both the subject and the object NP may be omitted from the sentence (i.e., the language permits null arguments). In short, the grammatical properties of ASL are unlike those of English, but are quite familiar to students of other languages of the world. This body of findings thus suggests that principles of word and sentence structure are, at least to some degree, common to both signed and spoken languages and are not inherently connected to the auditory-vocal mode.

Studies of the on-line processing of ASL by fluent adult signers, of the representation of ASL in the brain, and of the acquisition of ASL by native-speaking deaf children also show many similarities with the principles of processing, neurological organization, and acquisition of spoken languages of the world. For example, ASL is acquired on approximately the same timetable as spoken languages with similar TYPOLOGY. Acquisition begins with manual babbling appearing at around 10 months or earlier (Petitto and Marentette 1991); first signs appear at about one year of age; two-sign sentences appear during the second year; and each of these stages show structural characteristics like those of other languages (Meier and Newport 1990; Newport and Meier 1985). Adult signers process ASL using the same types of parsing strategies as those used in the processing of spoken languages (Emmorey 1991) and, like speakers of auditory-vocal languages, represent ASL in the left hemisphere of the brain (Poizner, Klima, and Bellugi 1987; Neville 1995).

As noted earlier, a highly unusual feature of signing communities is that native users are so rare; 95 percent or more of deaf signers are first exposed to their language beyond infancy and sometimes not until late childhood or even adulthood. These demographics result from the fact that most deaf children are born into hearing families and also from the fact that, until recently, hearing parents were often discouraged from learning sign language in the hopes that avoidance of sign language and therapeutic presentation of speech would result in improved spoken-language acquisition. Research does not suggest, however, that the avoidance of sign languages does improve speech abilities; in fact, much evidence suggests that, among the profoundly deaf, better speech, lipreading, and reading abilities are shown by native signers (Meadow 1966) and, more generally, that spoken language abilities depend much more on the ability to hear than on the availability (or avoidance) of signing (Jensema 1975; Quigley and Paul 1986). In recent years, it has therefore begun to be more common practice to encourage hearing parents of deaf children to learn to sign, and to expose deaf children to sign languages from early in life.

In the meantime, however, the presence of a large number of signers who have acquired their primary language beyond infancy has presented an unusual research opportunity: the study of the effects of age of exposure on the mastery of a primary language. A number of such studies have shown that there is a substantial effect of age on the acquisition of ASL: native and early ASL learners show much more fluency, consistency, and complexity in the grammatical structures of the language, and more extensive and rapid processing abilities, than those who have acquired ASL later in life (Emmorey 1991; Mayberry and Fischer 1989; Newport 1990). These effects persist even after as much as 50 years of daily use of ASL as a primary language (Newport 1990). Together with the work of Lenneberg (1967) and Curtiss (1977), and also comparable effects of age of exposure on the acquisition of English as a second language in hearing foreigners (Johnson and Newport 1989), these results provide important evidence of a critical, or sensitive, period for LANGUAGE ACQUISITION.

All of these findings on ASL suggest that the cognitive abilities supporting language and its acquisition in humans are not restricted or specialized to speech but rather permit the development of signed as well as spoken languages. One might ask, then, whether there are any effects of modality on language structure or acquisition. The answer to this question from the study of this one sign language appears to be no, but a more definitive answer awaits the results of research on a large number of unrelated sign languages. With further research we will be able to determine whether the universal similarities among spoken languages of the world, and also the range of differences and variation among them, are also characteristic of the signed languages of the world (Supalla 1997; Newport 1996).

See also EVOLUTION OF LANGUAGE; LANGUAGE AND COMMUNICATION; LANGUAGE VARIATION AND CHANGE; MODULARITY AND LANGUAGE; SIGN LANGUAGE AND THE BRAIN

—*Elissa L. Newport and Ted Supalla*

References

Coppola, M., A. Senghas, E. L. Newport, and T. Supalla. (1997). Evidence for verb agreement in the gesture systems of older Nicaraguan home signers. Boston University Conference on Language Development, Boston, MA.

Curtiss, S. (1977). *Genie: A Psycholinguistic Study of a Modern-Day "Wild Child"*. New York: Academic Press.

Emmorey, K. (1991). Repetition priming with aspect and agreement morphology in American Sign Language. *Journal of Psycholinguistic Research* 20: 365–388.

Goldin-Meadow, S., and C. Mylander. (1984). Gestural communication in deaf children: The effects and non-effects of parental input on early language development. *Monographs of the Society for Research in Child Development* 49 (3, Serial No. 207).

Jensema, C. (1975). *The Relationship Between Academic Achievement and the Demographic Characteristics of Hearing-Impaired Children And Youth*. Washington, DC: Gallaudet College, Office of Demographic Studies.

Johnson, J. S., and E. L. Newport. (1989). Critical period effects in second language learning: The influence of maturational state on the acquisition of English as a second language. *Cognitive Psychology* 21: 60–99.

Johnson, R. E. (1978). A comparison of the phonological structures of two northwest sawmill sign languages. *Communication and Cognition* 11: 105–132.

Kendon, A. (1988). *Sign Languages of Aboriginal Australia: Cultural, Semiotic and Communicative Perspectives*. Cambridge: Cambridge University Press.

Klima, E., and U. Bellugi. (1979). *The Signs of Language*. Cambridge, MA: Harvard University Press.

Lenneberg, E. H. (1967). *Biological Foundations of Language*. New York: Wiley.

Mayberry, R., and S. D. Fischer. (1989). Looking through phonological shape to lexical meaning: The bottleneck of non-native sign language processing. *Memory and Cognition* 17: 740–754.

Meadow, K. (1966). *The Effects of Early Manual Communication and Family Climate on the Deaf Child's Early Development*. Ph.D. diss., University of California, Berkeley.

Meier, R. P., and E. L. Newport. (1990). Out of the hands of babes: On a possible sign advantage in language acquisition. *Language* 66: 1–23.

Neville, H. (1995). Developmental specificity in neurocognitive development in humans. In M. Gazzaniga, Ed., *The Cognitive Neurosciences*. Cambridge, MA: MIT Press, pp. 219–231.

Newport, E. L., and R. P. Meier. (1985). The acquisition of American Sign Language. In D. I. Slobin, Ed., *The Cross-Linguistic Study of Language Acquisition*. Hillsdale, NJ: Erlbaum.

Newport, E. L. (1990). Maturational constraints on language learning. *Cognitive Science* 14: 11–28.

Newport, E. L. (1996). Sign language research in the Third Millennium. Plenary address presented at the Fifth International Conference on Theoretical Issues in Sign Language Research, Montreal, Quebec.

Petitto, L., and P. Marentette. (1991). Babbling in the manual mode: Evidence for the ontogeny of language. *Science* 251: 1493–1496.

Poizner, H., E. S. Klima, and U. Bellugi. (1987). *What the Hands Reveal about the Brain*. Cambridge, MA: MIT Press.

Quigley, S., and P. Paul. (1986). A perspective on academic achievement. In D. Luterman, Ed., *Deafness in Perspective*. San Diego, CA: College-Hill Press, pp. 55–86.

Siple, P., and S. D. Fischer, Eds. (1990). *Theoretical Issues in Sign Language Research*. Chicago: University of Chicago Press.

Stokoe, W. C., D. C. Casterline, and C. G. Cronbach. (1965). *A Dictionary of American Sign Language on Linguistic Principles*. Washington, DC: Gallaudet College Press.

Supalla, S. (1986). Manually Coded English: The modality question in signed language development. Master's thesis, University of Illinois.

Supalla, S. (1990). Manually Coded English: The modality question in signed language development. In P. Siple and S. D. Fischer, Eds., *Theoretical Issues in Sign Language Research*, vol. 2. Chicago: University of Chicago Press.

Supalla, T. (1997). An implicational hierarchy for verb agreement in American Sign Language. Unpublished manuscript, University of Rochester.

Signal Detection Theory

Signal detection theory (SDT) is a model of perceptual DECISION MAKING whose central tenet is that cognitive performance, limited by inherent variability, requires a decision process. Applying a statistical-decision approach developed in studying radar reception, W. P. Tanner and J. A. Swets proposed in 1954 a "decision-making theory of visual detection," showing how sensory and decision processes could be separated in the simplest perceptual task. Extensive early application to detection problems accounts for the name of the theory, but SDT is now used widely in cognitive science as a modeling tool and for analyzing discrimination and classification data (see PSYCHOPHYSICS).

In detection, an observer attempts to distinguish two stimuli, *noise (N)* and *signal plus noise (S + N)*. These stimuli evoke not single percepts, but trial-to-trial distributions of effects on some relevant decision axis, as in figure 1a. The observer's ability to tell the stimuli apart depends on the overlap between the distributions, quantified by d', the normalized difference between their means. The goal of identifying each stimulus as an example of N or $S + N$ as accurately as possible can be accomplished with a simple decision rule: Establish a *criterion* value of the decision axis and choose one response for points below it, the other for points above it. The placement of the criterion determines both the *hits* ("yes" responses to signals) and the *false alarms* ("yes" responses to noise). If the criterion is high (strict), the observer will make few false alarms, but also not that many hits. By adopting a lower (more lax) criterion (figure 1b), the number of hits is increased, but at the expense of also increasing the false alarm rate. This change in the decision strategy does not affect d', which is therefore a measure of *sensitivity* that is independent of *response bias*.

The statistic d' is calculated by assuming that the underlying distributions in the perceptual space are Gaussian and have equal variance. Both of these assumptions can be

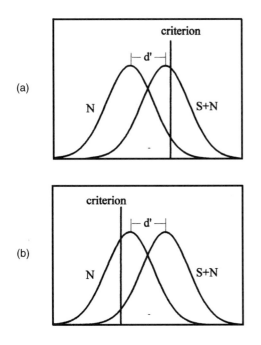

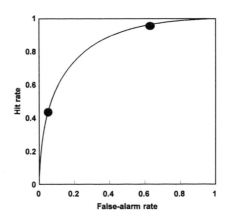

Figure 2. An ROC curve, the relation between hit and false-alarm rates, both of which increase as the criterion location moves (to the left, in figure 1).

Figure 1. Distributions assumed by SDT to result from N and $S + N$; the normalized difference between their means is d'. Criterion location is strict in (a), lax in (b), but d' is unchanged.

tested by varying the location of the criterion to construct an *ROC* (receiver operating characteristic) curve, the hit rate as a function of the false-alarm rate (figure 2). ROCs can be obtained by varying instructions to encourage criterion shifts; or more efficiently by using *confidence ratings,* interpreting each level of confidence as a different criterion location. Most data are consistent with the assumption of normality (Swets 1986) or the very similar predictions of logistic distributions, which arise from choice theory (Luce 1963). For data sets that reveal unequal variances, accuracy can be measured using the area under the ROC, a statistic that is nonparametric (makes no assumptions about the underlying distributions) when calculated from a full ROC rather than a single hit/false-alarm pair (Macmillan and Creelman 1996).

The source of the variability in the underlying distributions can be internal or external. When variability is external (as, for example, when a tone is presented in random noise), the statistics of the noise can be used to predict d' for *ideal observers* (Green and Swets 1966: chap. 6). Similarly, the decision rule adopted by the observer depends on experimental manipulations such as the frequency of the signal, and the optimal criterion location can be predicted using Bayes's rule. Ideal sensitivity and response bias are often not found, but in some detection and discrimination situations they provide a baseline against which observed performance may be measured. The stimulus noise is much harder to characterize in other perceptual situations, such as X-ray reading, where N is healthy tissue and $S + N$ diseased (Swensson and Judy 1981). Most of the many applications of SDT to memory invoke only internal variability. For example, in a recognition memory experiment (Snodgrass and Corwin 1988) the $S + N$ distribution arises from old

items and the N items from new ones. Klatzky and Erdelyi (1985) argued that the effect of hypnosis on recognition memory is to alter criterion rather than d', and that distinguishing these possibilities requires presenting both.

The examples so far use a one-interval experimental method for measuring discrimination: in a sequence of trials, N or $S + N$ is presented and the observer attempts to identify the stimulus, with or without a confidence rating. This paradigm has been widely used, but not exclusively: In *forced-choice* designs, each trial contains m intervals, one with $S + N$ and the rest with N, and the observer chooses the $S + N$ interval; in *same-different,* two stimuli are presented that may be the same (both $S + N$ or both N) or different (one of each); *oddity* is like forced-choice, except that the "odd" interval may contain either $S + N$ or both N; and so on. Workers in areas as diverse as SPEECH PERCEPTION and food evaluation have argued that such designs are preferable to the one-interval design in their fields.

In the absence of theory, it is difficult to compare performance across paradigms, but SDT permits the abstraction of the same statistic, d' or a derivative, from all (Macmillan and Creelman 1991). The basis of comparison is that d' can always be construed as a distance measure in a perceptual space that contains multiple distributions. For the one-interval design, this space is one-dimensional, as in figure 1, but for other designs each interval corresponds to a dimension. According to SDT, an unbiased observer with $d' = 2$ will be correct 93 percent of the time in two-alternative forced-choice but as low as 67 percent in same-different. Some tasks can be approached with more than one decision rule; for example, the optimal strategy in same-different is to make *independent observations* in the two intervals, whereas in the *differencing* model the effects of the two intervals are subtracted. By examining ROC curve shapes, Irwin and Francis (1995) concluded that the differencing model was correct for simple visual stimuli, the optimal model for complex ones.

Detection theory also provides a bridge between discrimination and other types of judgment, particularly identification (in which a distinct response is required for each of m stimuli) and classification (in which stimuli are sorted into subclasses). For sets of stimuli that differ along a single dimension, such as sounds differing only in loudness, SDT allows the estimation of d' for each pair of stimuli in both identification and discrimination. The two tasks are roughly equivalent when the range of stimuli is small, but increasingly discrepant as range increases. Durlach and Braida's (1969) theory of resolution describes both types of experiments and relates them quantitatively under the assumption that resolution is limited by both sensory and memory variance, the latter increasing with range.

For more complex stimulus sets, a multidimensional version of SDT is increasingly applied (Graham 1989; Ashby 1992). In natural extensions of the unidimensional model, each stimulus is assumed to give rise to a distribution in a multidimensional perceptual space, distances between stimuli reflect resolution, and the observer uses a decision boundary to divide the space into regions, one for each response. The more complex representation raises new issues about the perceptual interactions between dimensions, and about the form of the decision boundary; many of these concepts have been codified under the rubric of generalized recognition theory, or GRT (Ashby and Townsend 1986). Multidimensional SDT can be used to determine the optimal possible performance, given the MENTAL REPRESENTATION of the observer (Sperling and Dosher 1986). For example, Palmer (1995) accounted for the set-size effect in visual search without assuming any processing limitations, and Graham, Kramer, and Yager (1987) predicted performance in both uncertain detection (in which $S + N$ can take on one of several values) and summation (in which redundant information is available) for several models. In a more complex example of information integration, Sorkin, West, and Robinson (forthcoming) showed how a group decision can be predicted from individual inputs without assumptions about interaction among its members. In all of these cases, as for the complex designs described earlier, SDT provides a baseline analysis of the situation against which data can be compared before specific processing assumptions are invoked.

See also PATTERN RECOGNITION AND FEEDFORWARD NETWORKS; PROBABILITY, FOUNDATIONS OF; STATISTICAL TECHNIQUES IN NATURAL LANGUAGE PROCESSING

—*Neil Macmillan*

References

Ashby, F. G., Ed. (1992). *Multidimensional Models of Perception and Cognition.* Hillsdale, NJ: Erlbaum.

Ashby, F. G., and J. T. Townsend. (1986). Varieties of perceptual independence. *Psychological Review* 93: 154–179.

Durlach, N. I., and L. D. Braida. (1969). Intensity perception. 1. Preliminary theory of intensity resolution. *Journal of the Acoustical Society of America* 46: 372–383.

Graham, N., P. Kramer, and D. Yager. (1987). Signal-detection models for multidimensional stimuli: Probability distributions and combination rules. *Journal of Mathematical Psychology* 31: 366–409.

Graham, N. V. (1989). *Visual Pattern Analyzers.* New York: Oxford University Press.

Green, D. M., and J. A. Swets. (1966). *Signal Detection Theory and Psychophysics.* New York: Wiley.

Irwin, R. J., and M. A. Francis. (1995). Perception of simple and complex visual stimuli: Decision strategies and hemispheric differences in same-different judgments. *Perception* 24: 787–809.

Klatzky, R. L., and M. H. Erdelyi. (1985). The response criterion problem in tests of hypnosis and memory. *International Journal of Clinical and Experimental Hypnosis* 33: 246–257.

Luce, R. D. (1963). Detection and recognition. In R. D. Luce, R. R. Bush, and E. Galanter, Eds., *Handbook of Mathematical Psychology*, vol. 1. New York: Wiley, pp. 103–189.

Macmillan, N. A., and C. D. Creelman. (1991). *Detection Theory: A User's Guide.* New York: Cambridge University Press.

Macmillan, N. A., and C. D. Creelman. (1996). Triangles in ROC space: History and theory of "nonparametric" measures of sensitivity and response bias. *Psychonomic Bulletin and Review* 3: 164–170.

Palmer, J. (1995). Attention in visual search: Distinguishing four causes of a set-size effect. *Current Directions in Psychological Science* 4: 118–123.

Snodgrass, J. G., and J. Corwin. (1988). Pragmatics of measuring recognition memory: Applications to dementia and amnesia. *Journal of Experimental Psychology: General* 117: 34–50.

Sorkin, R. D., R. West, and D. E. Robinson. (Forthcoming). Group performance depends on majority rule. *Psychological Science* to appear.

Sperling, G. A., and B. A. Dosher. (1986). Strategy and optimization in human information processing. In K. Boff, L. Kaufman, and J. Thomas, Eds., *Handbook of Perception and Performance,* vol. 1. New York: Wiley, pp. 2–1 to 2–65.

Swensson, R. G., and P. F. Judy. (1981). Detection of noisy visual targets: Models for the effects of spatial uncertainty and signal-to-noise ratio. *Perception and Psychophysics* 29: 521–534.

Swets, J. A. (1986). Form of empirical ROCs in discrimination and diagnostic tasks. 99: 181–198.

Tanner, W. P., Jr., and J. A. Swets. (1954). A decision-making theory of visual detection. *Psychological Review* 61: 401–409.

Further Readings

Ashby, F. G., and W. T. Maddox. (1994). A response time theory of separability and integrality in speeded classification. *Journal of Mathematical Psychology* 38: 423–466.

Killeen, P. R. (1978). Superstition: A matter of bias, not detectability. *Science* 199: 88–90.

Kraemer, H. C. (1988). Assessment of 2 x 2 associations: Generalizations of signal-detection methodology. *American Statistician* 42: 37–49.

Macmillan, N. A., and C. D. Creelman. (1990). Response bias: Characteristics of detection theory, threshold theory and "nonparametric" measures. *Psychological Bulletin* 107: 401–413.

Maloney, L. T., and E. A. C. Thomas. (1991). Distributional assumptions and observed conservatism in the theory of signal detectability. *Journal of Mathematical Psychology* 35: 443–470.

Massaro, D. W., and D. Friedman. (1990). Models of integration given multiple sources of information. *Psychological Review* 97: 225–252.

McNicol, D. (1972). *A Primer of Signal Detection Theory.* London: Allen and Unwin.

Nosofsky, R. M. (1984). Choice, similarity and the context theory of classification. *Journal of Experimental Psychology: Learning, Memory and Cognition* 10: 104–114.

Nosofsky, R. M. (1986). Attention, similarity and the identification-categorization relationship. *Journal of Experimental Psychology: General* 115: 39–57.

Swets, J. A. (1986). Indices of discrimination or diagnostic accuracy: Their ROCs and implied models. *Psychological Bulletin* 99: 100–117.

Swets, J. A. (1996). *Signal Detection Theory and ROC Analysis in Psychology and Diagnostics: Collected Papers*. Mahwah, NJ: Erlbaum.

Similarity

An ability to assess similarity lies close to the core of cognition. In the time-honored tradition of legitimizing fields of psychology by citing William JAMES, "This sense of Sameness is the very keel and backbone of our thinking" (James 1890/1950: 459). An understanding of PROBLEM SOLVING, categorization, memory retrieval, inductive reasoning, and other cognitive processes requires that we understand how humans assess similarity. Four major psychological models of similarity are geometric, featural, alignment-based, and transformational.

Geometric models have been among the most influential approaches to analyzing similarity (Torgerson 1965), and are exemplified by multidimensional scaling (MDS) models (Nosofsky 1992; Shepard 1962). The input to MDS routines may be similarity judgments, confusion matrices (a table of how often each entity is confused with every other entity), probabilities of entities being grouped together, or any other measure of subjective similarity between all pairs of entities in a set. The output of an MDS routine is a geometric model of the entities' similarity, with each entity of the set represented as a point in N-dimensional space. The similarity of two entities i and j is taken to be inversely related to their distance, $D(i, j)$, which is computed by

$$D(i,j) = \left[\sum_{k=1}^{n} |X_{ik} - X_{jk}|^r \right]^{(1/r)}$$

where n is the number of dimensions, X_{ik} is the value of dimension k for entity i, and r is a parameter that allows different spatial metrics to be used. A Euclidean metric ($r = 2$) often provides good fits to human similarity judgments when the entities are holistically perceived or the underlying dimensions are psychologically fused, whereas a city-block metric ($r = 1$) often provides a better fit when entities are clearly divisible into separate dimensions (Garner 1974). Shepard (1987) has made a compelling case that cognitive assessments of similarity are related by an inverse exponential function to distance in MDS space.

Geometric models standardly assume minimality [$D(A, B) \geq D(A, A) = 0$], symmetry [$D(A, B) = D(B, A)$], and the triangle inequality [$D(A, B) + D(B, C) \geq D(A, C)$]. Amos TVERSKY (1977) criticized geometric models on the grounds that violations of all three assumptions are empirically observed. Minimality may be violated because not all identical objects seem equally similar; complex objects that are identical (e.g., twins) can be more similar to each other than simpler identical objects (e.g., two squares). Asymmetrical similarity occurs when an object with many features is judged as less similar to a sparser object than vice versa; for example, North Korea is judged to be more like China than China is to North Korea (Tversky 1977). The triangle inequality can be violated when A (e.g., "lamp") and B ("moon") share an identical feature (both provide light), and B ("moon") and C ("ball") share an identical feature, but A and C share no feature in common (Tversky and Gati 1982).

Although geometric models can be modified to correct these assumptions (Nosofsky 1991), Tversky suggested an alternative approach, the contrast model, wherein similarity is determined by matching features of compared entities, and integrating these features by the formula

$$S(A,B) = \theta f(A \cap B) - \alpha f(A - B) - \beta f(B - A).$$

The similarity of A to B, $S(A,B)$ is expressed as a linear combination of the measure of the common and distinctive features. The term $(A \cap B)$ represents the features that items A and B have in common. $(A - B)$ represents the features that A has but B does not. $(B - A)$ represents the features that B, but not A, possesses. The terms θ, α, and β reflect the weights given to the common and distinctive components, and the function f is often simply assumed to be additive. Other featural models calculate similarity by taking the ratio of common to distinctive features (Sjoberg 1972).

Neither geometric nor featural models of similarity are well suited for comparing things that are richly structured rather than just being a collection of coordinates or features. Often it is most efficient to represent things hierarchically (parts containing parts) and/or propositionally (relational predicates taking arguments). In such cases, comparing things involves not simply matching features, but determining which elements correspond to, or align with, one another. Matching features are aligned to the extent that they play similar roles within their entities. For example, a car with a green wheel and a truck with a green hood both share the feature *green,* but this matching feature may not increase their similarity much because the car's wheel does not correspond to the truck's hood. Drawing inspiration from work on analogical reasoning (Gentner 1983; Holyoak and Thagard 1989; see ANALOGY), in alignment-based models, matching features influence similarity more if they belong to parts that are placed in correspondence, and parts tend to be placed in correspondence if they have many features in common and if they are consistent with other emerging correspondences (Goldstone 1994; Markman and Gentner 1993).

A fourth approach to modeling similarity is based on transformational distance. The similarity of two entities is assumed to be inversely proportional to the number of operations required to transform one entity so as to be identical to the other (Hahn and Chater 1997; Imai 1977). For example, XXXXO requires only one transformation to become XXXOO (change an O to an X), but requires two transformations to become OOXXX (change an O to an X, and reverse string), and consequently is more similar to XXXOO.

Although testing between these four approaches to similarity is an ongoing topic of research, another major issue concerns the role of similarity in other cognitive processes. For example, although several models of categorization are completely similarity-based (see CONCEPTS and CATEGORIZATION), other researchers have argued that people's categorizations cannot be exhaustively explained by similarity but also depend on abstract, theoretical knowledge (Rips and Collins 1993; Murphy and Medin 1985). Likewise, Goodman (1972) raised philosophical objections to the explanatory role of similarity, arguing that "X is similar to Y . . ." is totally unconstrained until it is completed by "with respect to property Z," and that it is this latter clause that performs all of the explanatory work. However, other researchers have argued that even without the additional clause, similarity is constrained by perceptual processes, by the manner in which multiple properties are integrated together (Goldstone 1994), by the compared items themselves (Medin, Goldstone, and Gentner 1993), by default properties that are applied irrespective of context (Barsalou 1982), and by a natural tendency to perceive overall similarity across many properties rather than similarity with respect to a single property (Smith 1989).

Another caveat to the explanatory role of similarity is that similarity may not be a unitary phenomenon. Similarity assessments are influenced by context, perspective, choice alternatives, and expertise (Medin, Goldstone, and Gentner 1993; Tversky 1977). Different processes for assessing similarity are probably used for different tasks, domains, and stimuli. The choice of features, transformations, and structural descriptions used to describe entities will govern the predictions made by similarity models as much as do the model's mechanisms for comparing and integrating these representations. History has not supported a literal interpretation of Fred Attneave's (1950: 516) claim, "The question 'What makes things seem alike or seem different?' is one so fundamental to psychology that very few psychologists have been naive enough to ask it" in that the topic has inspired considerable research, but this research has vindicated Attneave at a deeper level by testifying to the importance and complexity of similarity.

See also GESTALT PERCEPTION; INDUCTION; METAPHOR

—*Robert Goldstone*

References

Barsalou, L. W. (1982). Context-dependent and context-independent information in concepts. *Memory and Cognition* 10: 82–93.

Attneave, F. (1950). Dimensions of similarity. *American Journal of Psychology* 63: 516–556.

Garner, W. R. (1974). *The Processing of Information and Structure.* New York: Wiley.

Gentner, D. (1983). Structure-mapping: A theoretical framework for analogy. *Cognitive Science* 7: 155–170.

Goldstone, R. L. (1994). Similarity, interactive activation, and mapping. *Journal of Experimental Psychology: Learning, Memory, and Cognition* 20: 3–28.

Goldstone, R. L. (1994). The role of similarity in categorization: Providing a groundwork. *Cognition* 52: 125–157.

Goodman, N. (1972). Seven strictures on similarity. In N. Goodman, Ed., *Problems and Projects.* New York: Bobbs-Merrill, pp. 23–32.

Hahn, U., and N. Chater. (1997). Concepts and similarity. In L. Lamberts and D. Shanks, Eds., *Knowledge, Concepts, and Categories.* Hove, UK: Psychology Press/MIT Press.

Holyoak, K. J., and P. Thagard. (1989). Analogical mapping by constraint satisfaction. *Cognitive Science* 13: 295–355.

Imai, S. (1977). Pattern similarity and cognitive transformations. *Acta Psychologica* 41: 433–447.

James, W. (1890/1950). *The Principles of Psychology.* Dover: New York. (Original work published 1890.)

Markman, A. B., and D. Gentner. (1993). Structural alignment during similarity comparisons. *Cognitive Psychology* 25: 431–467.

Medin, D. L., R. L. Goldstone, and D. Gentner. (1993). Respects for similarity. *Psychological Review* 100: 254–278.

Murphy, G. L., and D. L. Medin. (1985). The role of theories in conceptual coherence. *Psychological Review* 92: 289–316.

Nosofsky, R. M. (1991). Stimulus bias, asymmetric similarity, and classification. *Cognitive Psychology* 23: 94–140.

Nosofsky, R. M. (1992). Similarity scaling and cognitive process models. *Annual Review of Psychology* 43: 25–53.

Rips, L. J., and A. Collins. (1993). Categories and resemblance. *Journal of Experimental Psychology: General* 122: 468–486.

Shepard, R. N. (1962). The analysis of proximities: Multidimensional scaling with an unknown distance function. Part 1. *Psychometrika* 27: 125–140.

Shepard, R. N. (1987). Toward a universal law of generalization for psychological science. *Science* 237: 1317–1323.

Sjoberg, L. (1972). A cognitive theory of similarity. *Goteborg Psychological Reports* 2(10).

Smith, L. B. (1989). From global similarity to kinds of similarity: The construction of dimensions in development. In S. Vosniadu and A. Ortony, Eds., *Similarity and Analogical Reasoning.* Cambridge: Cambridge University Press, pp. 146–178.

Torgerson, W. S. (1965). Multidimensional scaling of similarity. *Psychometrika* 30: 379–393.

Tversky, A. (1977). Features of similarity. *Psychological Review* 84: 327–352.

Tversky, A., and I. Gati. (1982). Similarity, separability, and the triangle inequality. *Psychological Review* 89: 123–154.

Further Readings

Asbhy, F. G. (1992). *Multidimensional Models of Perception and Cognition.* Hillsdale, NJ: Erlbaum.

Ashby, F. G., and N. A. Perrin. (1988). Toward a unified theory of similarity and recognition. *Psychological Review* 95: 124–150.

Edelman, S. (Forthcoming). Representation is representation of similarity. *Behavioral and Brain Sciences* to appear.

French, R. (1995). *The Subtlety of Sameness.* Cambridge, MA: MIT Press.

Goldstone, R. L., D. L. Medin, and J. Halberstadt. (1997). Similarity in Context. *Memory and Cognition* 25: 237–255.

Hofstadter, D., and The Fluid Analogies Research Group. (1995). *Fluid Concepts and Creative Analogies.* New York: Basic Books.

Indurkhya, B. (1992). *Metaphor and Cognition.* Dordrecht: Kluwer.

Keil, F. C. (1989). *Concepts, Kinds and Development.* Cambridge, MA: MIT Press.

Krumhansl, C. L. (1978). Concerning the applicability of geometric models to simiarity data: The interrelationship between similarity and spatial density. *Psychological Review* 85: 450–463.

Lantermann, E. D., Ed. (1980). *Similarity and Choice.* New York: Burgess.

Link, S. W. (1992). *The Wave Theory of Difference and Similarity.* Newark, NJ: Erlbaum.

Melara, R. D. (1992). The concept of perceptual similarity: From psychophysics to cognitive psychology. In D. Algom, Ed., *Psychophysical Approaches to Cognition.* Amsterdam: North-Holland, pp. 303–388.

Ramscar, M., U. Hahn, E. Cambouropulos, and H. Pain, Eds. (1997). *Proceedings of the Interdisciplinary Workshop on Similarity and Categorization*. Edinburgh: Department of Artificial Intelligence, University of Edinburgh.

Sloman, S. A. (1996). The empirical case for two systems of reasoning. *Psychological Bulletin* 119: 3–22.

Vosniadu, S., and A. Ortony. (1989). *Similarity and Analogical Reasoning*. Cambridge: Cambridge University Press.

Simulation vs. Theory-Theory

The debate between the "simulation" theory and the "theory" theory, initiated in the late 1980s in philosophy of mind and developmental psychology, concerns the source of everyday human competence in predicting and explaining human behavior, including the capacity to ascribe mental states. Unlike earlier controversies concerning the role of empathetic understanding and historical reenactment in the human sciences, the current debate appeals to empirical findings, particularly experimental results concerning children's development of psychological competence.

Since the 1960s it has been widely assumed that the source of this competence is a body of implicit general knowledge or theory, commonly called FOLK PSYCHOLOGY by philosophers and THEORY OF MIND by psychologists, concerning the basic internal organization of the system that controls human behavior. The theory is either inherited as an innate module comparable to Noam Chomsky's language module (e.g., Jerry Fodor, Alan Leslie) or largely developed in childhood in a manner comparable to the development of scientific theories (e.g., Alison Gopnik, Josef Perner, and Henry Wellman). It is usually understood to consist in a body of lawlike generalizations, with PROPOSITIONAL ATTITUDES, especially beliefs and desires, thought to be the chief posits of the theory. Many but not all proponents of this view think that the theory must be measured against computational and/or neuroscientific accounts of the system that controls behavior. The chief disagreement among proponents of the theory theory is between those who think folk psychology likely to be largely vindicated by cognitive science and those who believe it has been or will be shown to be radically mistaken (see ELIMINATIVE MATERIALISM).

The simulation (or "mental simulation") theory, introduced in 1986 by Robert Gordon and Jane Heal and further developed by Alvin Goldman, Paul Harris, and others, is usually, though not always, taken to present a serious challenge to the very assumption that a theory underlies everyday psychological competence. According to this account, human beings are able to use the resources of their own minds to simulate the psychological etiology of the behavior of others, typically by making decisions within a "pretend" context. A common method is role-taking, or "putting oneself in the other's place." However, like the term *theory*, "simulation" has come to be used broadly and in a variety of ways. The term is often taken to cover reliance on a shared world of facts and emotive and motivational charges, where there is no need to put oneself in the other's place. (Gordon calls this the default mode of simulation.) Sometimes the term is taken to include automatic responses such as the subliminal mimicry of facial expressions and bodily move-

ments. Stephen Stich and Shaun Nichols, whose critical papers have clarified the issues and helped refine the theory, urge that the term be dropped in favor of a finer-grained terminology.

Simulation is often conceived in cognitive-scientific terms: one's own behavior control system is employed as a manipulable model of other such systems. The system is first taken off-line, so that the output is not actual behavior but only predictions or anticipations of behavior, and inputs and system parameters are accordingly not limited to those that would regulate one's own behavior. Many proponents hold that, because one human behavior control system is being used to model others, general information about such systems is unnecessary. The simulation is thus said to be process-driven rather than theory-driven (Goldman 1993).

Important differences exist among simulation theorists on several topics. According to Goldman and (less clearly) Harris, to ascribe mental states to others by simulation, one must already be able to ascribe mental states to oneself, and thus must already possess the relevant mental state concepts. Gordon holds a contrary view suggested by Kant and Quine: Only those who can simulate can understand an ascription of, for instance, belief—that *to S* it is the case that *p*. Although no simulation theorist claims that all our everyday explanations and predictions of the actions of other people are based on role-taking, Heal in particular has been a moderating influence, arguing for a hybrid simulation-and-theory account that reserves simulation primarily for items with rationally linked content, such as beliefs, desires, and actions.

Three main areas of empirical investigation have been thought especially relevant to the debate.

False belief. Taking into account another's ignorance or false belief when predicting or explaining his or her behavior requires imaginative modifications of one's own beliefs, according to the simulation theory. Thus the theory offers an explanation of the results of numerous experiments showing that younger children fail to take such factors into account. It would also explain the correlation, in AUTISM, of failure to take into account ignorance or false belief and failure to engage in spontaneous pretend-play, particularly role-play. Although these results can also be explained by certain versions of theory theory (and were so interpreted by the experimenters themselves), the simulation theory offers a new interpretation.

Priority of self- or other-ascription. A second area of developmental research asks whether children ascribe mental states to themselves before they ascribe them to others. Versions of the simulation theory committed to the view that we recognize our own mental states as such and make analogical inferences to others' mental states seem to require an affirmative answer to this question; other versions of the theory seem to require a negative answer. Some experiments suggest a negative answer, but debate continues on this question.

Cognitive impenetrability. Stich and Nichols suppose simulation to be "cognitively impenetrable" in that it operates independently of any general knowledge the simulator may have about human psychology. Yet they point to results suggesting that when subjects lack certain psychological information, they sometimes make incorrect predictions, and therefore must not be simulating. Because of problems of methodology and interpretation, as noted by a number of philosophers and psychologists, the cogency of this line of criticism is unclear.

The numerous other empirical questions of possible relevance to the debate include the following:

- Does brain imaging reveal that systems and processes employed in decision making are reemployed in the explanation and prediction of others' behavior?
- Does narrative (including film narrative) create emotional and motivational effects by the same processes that create them in real-life situations?

Some philosophers think the simulation theory may shed light on issues in traditional philosophy of mind and language concerning INTENTIONALITY, referential opacity (SENSE AND REFERENCE), broad and NARROW CONTENT, the nature of MENTAL CAUSATION, TWIN EARTH problems, the problem of other minds, and the peculiarities of SELF-KNOWLEDGE. Several philosophers have applied the theory to aesthetics, ethics, and philosophy of the social sciences. Success or failure of these efforts to answer philosophical problems may be considered empirical tests of the theory, in a suitably broad sense of "empirical."

—*Robert M. Gordon*

References

The following collections include most of the relevant papers by authors mentioned in the article:

Carruthers, P., and P. Smith, Eds. (1996). *Theories of Theories of Mind.* Cambridge: Cambridge University Press.

Davies, M., and T. Stone, Eds. (1995). *Folk Psychology: The Theory of Mind Debate.* Oxford: Blackwell. (The introductory chapter offers an excellent overview and analysis of the initial debate.)

Davies, M., and T. Stone, Eds. (1995). *Mental Simulation: Evaluations and Applications.* Oxford: Blackwell.

Further Readings

Fodor, J. A. (1987). *Psychosemantics.* Cambridge, MA: MIT Press.

Goldman, A. (1993). The psychology of folk psychology. *Behavioral and Brain Sciences* 16: 15–28.

Gopnik, A. (1993). How we know our minds: The illusion of first-person knowledge of intentionality. *Behavioral and Brain Sciences* 16: 1–14.

Gordon, R. M., and J. Barker. (1994). Autism and the "theory of mind" debate. In G. Graham and L. Stephens, Eds., *Philosophical Psychopathology: A Book of Readings.* Cambridge, MA: MIT Press, pp. 163–181.

Harris, P. (1989). *Children and Emotion.* Oxford: Blackwell.

Peacocke, C., Ed. (1994). *Objectivity, Simulation, and the Unity of Consciousness.* Oxford: Oxford University Press.

Perner, J. (1991). *Understanding the Representational Mind.* Cambridge, MA: MIT Press.

Wellman, H. M. (1990). *The Child's Theory of Mind.* Cambridge, MA: MIT Press.

Single-Neuron Recording

One of the most useful tools for the study of individual neurons in the nervous system is the microelectrode. A variety of specific techniques have evolved using this tool which enable investigators to determine how neurons act, how they communicate with each other, what kinds of NEUROTRANSMITTERS they use, what molecular mechanisms underlie their excitability, how they respond to sensory inputs, how they generate signals to activate muscles, and what the relationship is between their physiology and morphology.

In trying to understand the various uses to which microelectrodes have been put, the first distinction that needs to be made is between extracellular and intracellular recordings. In the case of extracellular recording, the tip of the microelectrode is not intended to enter the cell by penetrating its membrane; instead, electrical events are recorded in the immediate vicinity of each neuron. This method limits investigators mostly to the study of action potentials. A variety of electrode types have been developed for this kind of recording. These include fine-tipped glass pipettes filled with electrolytes and electrolytically sharpened metal wires coated with insulating material. Metal electrodes, especially those coated with a thin layer of molten glass except for the tip, are very strong and can penetrate without breaking even relatively tough tissue like dura. This makes it possible to record individual cells in alert animals, often for many hours, while they engage in various behavioral tasks. Using such methods, extensive sampling of neurons allows investigators to infer the functional characteristics of different brain structures. Such studies investigate how neurons respond to sensory inputs, how they discharge when various motor acts are executed, and even how higher-level mental events, such as ATTENTION, are represented at the neuronal level.

Intracellular recording methods enable investigators to study not only action potentials but also the graded potentials that reflect the excitatory and inhibitory inputs to the cell (excitatory and inhibitory postsynaptic potentials). Injection of current and pharmacological agents can provide information about the neurotransmitters and neuromodulators involved as well as the properties of the cell membrane at the molecular level.

Intracellular recording in the living organism is fraught with difficulties: the cells and axons are small and the movement artifact produced by heartbeat and breathing tends to dislodge the tip of the pipette from inside the cell. To combat this problem a variety of refinements have been made. Considerable improvement in recording stability can be realized in in vitro preparations: nerve tissue or individual cells are maintained outside of the body in an artificial medium, thereby eliminating movement due to heartbeat and breathing.

Three refinements in intracellular recording are noteworthy: *Voltage clamping* is a procedure that enables investigators to measure the flow of current across the membrane of single cells while the intracellular voltage is maintained at a constant value. This procedure has made a major contribution to our understanding of the mechanisms responsible for the electrical excitability of neurons. *Patch clamping* is also a technique for studying the flow of current through cell membranes. As in the case of voltage clamping, voltage across the membrane is typically controlled and the resultant current flow is measured. Mild suction is applied to the microelectrode when the tip comes in apposition with the cell membrane, which thereby creates a very tight and reliable connection. A variant of this technique, called *whole-cell clamping,* involves applying enough suction to rupture the cell membrane within the small opening of the pipette tip. Whole-cell clamping has the benefit of ease of fluid exchange. In general, these last two methods, compared with other intracellular recording approaches, can provide a more detailed description of the characteristics of membrane channel proteins; the experimenter has better control of the experimental situation and can study smaller cells than with previous methods.

To establish the relationship between function and morphology, investigators have carried out intracellular recordings using dye-filled glass pipettes; first, the response characteristics of the cell are studied, after which the dye is injected into the cell. Some dyes, such as Lucifer yellow, diffuse through the entire dendritic network of the cell so that subsequently, using a variety of anatomical procedures, the morphology of the cell can be disclosed in detail. Such studies have succeeded in establishing the functional characteristics of the major cell types identified in the mammalian RETINA, in the CEREBELLUM, and in several other neural structures.

Lastly, microelectrodes can also be used to eclectically stimulate various brain regions. When areas involved in the execution of motor acts are stimulated in alert animals with brief trains of 60- to 500-Hz pulses, the responses elicited provide important clues about the role these structures play in the control of eye, head, limb, and body movement.

See also CEREBRAL CORTEX; COMPUTING IN SINGLE NEURONS; ELECTROPHYSIOLOGY, ELECTRIC AND MAGNETIC EVOKED FIELDS; MAGNETIC RESONANCE IMAGING; NEURON; POSITRON EMISSION TOMOGRAPHY

—*Peter Schiller*

Further Readings

Articles in *Journal of Neuroscience Methods.*
Smith, T. G., Jr., Ed. (1985). Voltage and Patch Clamping with Microelectrodes. Bethesda, MD: American Physiological Society.

Situated Cognition and Learning

Situated cognition and learning is the study of cognition within its natural context. This perspective emphasizes that individual minds usually operate within environments that structure, direct, and support cognitive processes. "Context" can be defined as physical or task-based (including artifacts and external representations of information), environmental or ecological (such as workplace and marketplace), and social or interactional (as in educational instruction or clinical settings). This emphasis on the physical, environmental,

and social contexts for cognition was termed SITUATEDNESS/EMBEDDEDNESS by Lucy Suchman (1987).

As Roy Pea and John Seeley Brown (1987) note, "It may appear obvious that human minds develop in social situations, and that they use the tools and representational media that culture provides to support, extend, and reorganize mental functioning. But cognitive theories of knowledge representation and educational practice, in school and in the workplace, have not been sufficiently responsive to questions about these relationships." As evidence, Jean Lave (1988) cites laboratory studies of cognition that report extremely poor performance by adults on simple arithmetic problems. She argued that asking the same questions in the context of grocery shopping at a supermarket reveals people's competence, and the strategies (e.g., "get best price per unit") used to solve familiar problems. Ceci and Roazzi (1994) also demonstrate the importance of context by showing that child street vendors can solve sophisticated arithmetic problems only when posed as familiar vending decisions. But though related to the ECOLOGICAL PSYCHOLOGY movement, the situated perspective goes beyond arguing for realistic settings and problem content.

Instead, this situated cognition approach argues that the *nature* of cognitive processing is uniquely determined within its context, and that it cannot be studied in isolation without destroying its defining properties. Consider this example: Imagine the myriad devices and agents that play critical roles in cognition while flying a plane. Edwin Hutchins (1995a) conceptualizes this circumstance as a cognitive system extending beyond the physical boundary of the pilot's head, and *distributed* over the people and objects within the environment. The control panel on a 747 can be taken into a lab and studied; however, important features of its use by the pilot may only arise when she is functioning within a team of crew members, during a complete flight sequence, talking to flight controllers in her nonnative English, under darkness, in an airplane with a history of hydraulic indicator failures, for the second time. Hutchins (1995a) argues it is impossible to understand the cognition involved in flying a plane apart from this distributed system in which it is embedded.

Mind and environment interact not only in highly technical tasks, but also in everyday tasks where COGNITIVE ARTIFACTS represent needed information, support decisions, and potentially even interfere with performance (Norman 1987). For example, the mental artifact of the columnar format for arithmetic provides a structure to keep track of information when short-term memory would otherwise be overwhelmed. As Agre and Chapman (1987) suggest, the physical setting can greatly lighten the processing load of the thinker by providing external cues about what to do next and when goals are accomplished (such as giving feedback through elevator buttons that light up when activated). This relationship of cognition to environmental structure is also used in HUMAN-COMPUTER INTERACTION to design artifacts that can exploit cognitive processes while supporting difficult tasks (Winograd and Flores 1986).

The social environment also influences cognition through the presence of other minds to influence, assist, mislead, demonstrate, question, and raise other perspectives. The interactionist method (Cicourel 1987; Jordan and Henderson

1995) examines communication between participants as an externalized measure of cognition. The social context may also provide a method for LEARNING through the demonstration and assistance of others in a "socially constituted world" (Chaiklin and Lave 1993). For example, novices often learn through apprenticeships, where they spend many hours observing and interacting with more experienced team members as they learn to perform tasks on the job (Seifert and Hutchins 1992; Lave and Wenger 1991). Lev Semenovich VYGOTSKY's activity theory (c.f. Wertsch 1985) proposes that cognitive development even occurs through the witnessing of acts within a social context that are later internalized by the individual. For example, a child may first participate in a class where questions are asked and answered aloud during reading; later, the child may internalize these social interaction processes as the self-monitoring of comprehension during reading (Palincsar 1987).

This *social mediation* approach to the development of cognitive skills has had a tremendous impact on theories of learning and EDUCATION. For example, Tomasello, Kruger, and Ratner (1993) have theorized that underlying sociocognitive concepts and processes give rise to a developmental ordering of learning strategies, from imitative to instructed and finally to collaborative learning. Much recent work in education has focused on identifying the role of social interaction in classroom learning, and proposing ways of facilitating its effects (McDermott 1993; Brown 1989). The notion that a learner's progress can be understood only in the context of the social classroom directs educational interventions toward altering the social context (Cole 1991), rather than the individual. Many of these interventions are aimed at changing social context through new technology-based activities (Pea 1985; Tripp 1993; Wood 1995) that can expand the learning environment far beyond the time and space delimited by classroom walls.

The situated cognition perspective argues that our goal as cognitive scientists must be to understand the mind as it operates within a natural context. Our theories must account for "cognition in the wild" (Hutchins 1995b) because that is where cognition usually occurs, and where it demonstrates its true capabilities and limitations. The benefits of achieving this goal are not only theoretical, but may also provide many benefits for the structuring of cognition in our daily lives. As this example from Norman (1980) demonstrates, there is much at stake in this enterprise: "In March of 1977, two Boeing 747 airliners collided on a runway at Tenerife, in the Canary Islands, and the crash killed 582 people. What caused the accident? No single factor. The crash resulted from a complex interaction of events, including problems of attentional focus, the effects of expectation upon language understanding . . . a technically limited communication . . . the subtle effects of differences of social structure among the participants, the effects of stress, economic responsibilities and social and cultural factors upon decision making. All in all, it is a fascinating—if horrifying—story for Cognitive Science (pp. 4–5)."

See also DECISION MAKING; ECOLOGICAL VALIDITY; EXPERTISE

—*Colleen M. Seifert*

References

Agre, P., and D. Chapman. (1987). Pengi: An implementation of a theory of activity. In *The Proceedings of the Sixth National Conference on Artificial Intelligence,* American Association for Artificial Intelligence. Seattle: Kaufmann, pp. 268–272.

Brown, J. S. (1989). Situated cognition and the culture of learning. *Educational Researcher* 18(1): 32–42.

Ceci, S. J., and A. Roazzi. (1994). The effects of context on cognition: Postcards from Brazil. In R. J. Sternberg and R. K. Wagner, Eds., *Mind in Context.* New York: Cambridge University Press, pp. 74–101.

Chaiklin, S., and J. Lave. (1993). *Understanding Practice: Perspectives on Activity and Context.* New York: Cambridge University Press.

Cicourel, A. V. (1987). The interpenetration of communicative contexts: Examples from medical encounters. Special issue: Language and social interaction. *Social Psychology Quarterly* 50(2): 217–226.

Cole, M. (1991). A cultural theory of development: What does it imply about the application of scientific research? Special issue: Culture and learning. *Learning and Instruction* 1(3): 187–200.

Hutchins, E. (1995a). How a cockpit remembers its speeds. *Cognitive Science* 19(3): 265–288.

Hutchins, E. (1995b). *Cognition in the Wild.* Cambridge, MA: MIT Press.

Jordan, B., and A. Henderson. (1995). Interaction analysis: Foundations and practice. *Journal of the Learning Sciences* 4(1): 39–103.

Lave, J. (1988). *Cognition in Practice: Mind, Mathematics and Culture in Everyday Life.* Cambridge: Cambridge University Press.

Lave, J., and E. Wenger. (1991). *Situated Learning: Legitimate Peripheral Participation.* Cambridge: Cambridge University Press.

McDermott, R. P. (1993). The acquisition of a child by a learning disability. In S. Chaiklin and J. Lave, Eds., *Understanding Practice: Perspectives on Activity and Context.* New York: Cambridge University Press, pp. 179–211.

Norman, D. A. (1980). Twelve issues for Cognitive Science. *Cognitive Science* 4: 1–33.

Norman, D. A. (1987) *The Psychology of Everyday Things.* New York: Basic Books.

Palincsar, A. (1987). Reciprocal teaching: Can student discussion boost comprehension? *Instructor* 96(5): 56–58, 60.

Pea, R. (1985). Beyond amplification: Using computers to reorganize human mental functioning. *Educational Psychologist* 20: 167–182.

Pea, R., and J. Seeley Brown. (1987). Series foreword. In L. A. Suchman, Ed., *Plans and Situated Action.* New York: Cambridge University Press, pp. xiii–xiv.

Seifert, C. M., and E. Hutchins. (1992). Error as opportunity: Learning in a cooperative task. *Human-Computer Interaction* 7(4): 409–435.

Suchman, L. A. (1987). *Plans and Situated Action.* New York: Cambridge University Press.

Tomasello, M., A. C. Kruger, and H. H. Ratner. (1993). Cultural learning. *Behavioral and Brain Sciences* 16(3): 495–552.

Tripp, S. D. (1993). Theories, traditions and situated learning. *Educational Technology* 33(3): 71–77.

Wertsch, J. V. (1985). *Vygotsky and the Social Formation of Mind.* Cambridge, MA: Harvard University Press.

Winograd, T., and F. Flores. (1986). *Understanding Computers and Cognition: A New Foundation for Design.* Norwood, NJ: Ablex.

Wood, D. (1995). Theory, training and technology: Part 1. *Education and Training* 37(1): 12–16.

Further Readings

Button, G. (1993). *Technology in Working Order: Studies in Work, Interaction and Technology.* London: Rutledge.

Clancey, W. J. (1997). *Situated Cognition: On Human Knowledge and Computer Representations.* New York: Cambridge University Press.

Engestrom, Y., and D. Middleton. (1996). *Cognition and Communication at Work.* New York: Cambridge University Press.

Goodwin, C., and M. H. Goodwin. (1996). Seeing as situated activity: Formulating planes. In Y. Engestrom and D. Middleton, Eds., *Cognition and Communication at Work.* New York: Cambridge University Press, pp. 61–95.

Greeno, J. G. (1989). A perspective on thinking. *American Psychologist* 44 (2): 134–141.

Heath, C. C., and P. K. Luff. (1992). Crisis and control: Collaborative work in London underground control rooms. *Journal of Computer Supported Cooperative Work* 1 (10): 24–48.

Perrow, C. (1984). *Normal Accidents.* New York: Basic Books.

Resnick, L. B., J. M. Levine, and S. D. Teasley. (1991). *Perspectives on Socially-Shared Cognition.* Washington, DC: American Psychological Association.

Rogoff, B., and J. Lave. (1984). *Everyday Cognition: Its Development in Social Context.* Cambridge, MA: Harvard University Press.

Sternberg, R. J., and R. K. Wagner. (1994). *Mind in Context.* New York: Cambridge University Press.

Vera, J., and H. Simon. (1993). Situated action: A symbolic interpretation. *Cognitive Science* 17(1): 7–48.

Wertsch, J. V., and L. J. Rupert. (1993). The authority of cultural tools in a sociocultural approach to mediated agency. *Cognition and Instruction* 11 (3-4): 227–239.

Situatedness/Embeddedness

The situated movement—situated language, SITUATED COGNITION AND LEARNING, situated behavior—views intelligent human behavior as engaged, socially and materially embodied activity, arising within the specific concrete details of particular (natural) settings, rather than as an abstract, detached, general-purpose process of logical or formal ratiocination.

Situatedness arose in the 1980s as a reaction against the then-dominant classical view of mind. The classical approach, inherited from the logical and metamathematical traditions (dubbed "GOFAI" by Haugeland 1997, for "good old fashioned artificial intelligence"), views cognition as: *individual,* in the sense that the essential locus of intelligence is taken to be the solitary person; *rational,* in that deliberative, conceptual thought is viewed as the primary exemplar of cognition; *abstract,* in the sense that implementation and the nature of the physical environment are treated as of secondary importance (if relevant at all); *detached,* in the sense that thinking is treated separately from perception and action; and *general,* in the sense that cognitive science is taken to be a search for universal principles of general intellect, true of all individuals and applicable in all circumstances.

Situated approaches reject one or more of these assumptions, arguing instead that cognition (indeed all human activity) is: *social,* in the sense of being located in humanly constructed settings among human communities; *embodied,* in that material aspects of agents' bodies are taken to be both pragmatically and theoretically significant; *concrete,* in the sense that physical constraints of realization and circumstance are viewed as of the utmost importance; *located,* implying that context-dependence is a central and enabling feature of all human endeavor; *engaged,* in that ongoing interaction with the surrounding environment is recognized as primary; and *specific,* in that what people do is seen as varying, dramatically, depending on contingent facts about their particular circumstances.

Within these broad outlines, situated approaches vary widely, from incremental proposals incorporating a degree of context-dependence within largely classical frameworks to more radical suggestions with substantial methodological and metaphysical commitments.

Closest to traditional models are "situated language" proposals for treating INDEXICALS, tense, and other context-dependent linguistic constructs (Barwise and Perry 1983). Terms such as *here, I,* and *now* are used on different occasions, by different individuals, to refer to different people and places, in ways that depend systematically on the circumstances of use. Formally, treating such context-dependence requires a two-stage SEMANTICS, distinguishing the MEANING of a word or sentence (the stable "rule" or pattern that the child learns, such as that "I" is used to refer to the speaker) from the *interpretation* of any particular utterance. Thus when two people shout "I'm right! You're wrong!" their utterances are said to coincide in meaning, but to differ in interpretation. Similarly, "4:00 p.m." can be assigned a single, constant meaning, mapping utterance situations onto times, depending on the date and time zone.

This general strategy of treating meaning as a function from context to interpretation (λ context . interpretation) has been applied to other forms of circumstantially determined interpretation, including anaphora and ambiguity (Gawron and Peters 1991). Methodologically, it requires a shift in focus from sentence types to individual utterances, and a generalization of inference from truth-preservation to reference-preservation (e.g., to understand why tomorrow we use "yesterday" to refer to what today we refer to with "today"). Nevertheless, such treatments remain largely compatible with classical views of cognition as individualistic, deductive, even relatively abstract (see INDIVIDUALISM).

Many, however, feel that situated intuitions run deeper. A further step, embodied in research on COGNITIVE ARTIFACTS, recognizes that an agent's embedding situation is not only a semantical resource for determining REFERENCE, but also a material resource for simplifying thought itself. Agents need not remember what remains in their visual fields, nor measure what they can directly compare. More generally, as captured in Brooks's (1997) slogan that "the world is its own best model," it is more efficient for an agent to let the world do the computing, and determine the result by inspection, than to attempt to shoulder the full load deductively. Moreover (see, e.g., Kirsh 1995), if the world happens not to provide exactly what one wants, one can sometimes rearrange it a bit so that it does. Lave, Murtaugh, and de la Rocha (1984) cite a near-mythic example of someone who, when asked to make 3/4 of a recipe that called for 2/3 of a cup of cottage cheese, measured out 2/3 of a cup, smooshed it into a flattened circle, and cut away 1/4 of the resulting patty.

As these examples suggest, situated approaches tend to shift theoretical focus from abstract deduction onto concrete activity: cooking dinner, making one's way across a crowded subway platform, negotiating turn-taking in a conversation. Situated theorists take these activities not only to be nontrivial achievements, but also to be paradigmatic of human intelligence. With respect to action, furthermore, several writers advocate a shift in emphasis from (rational) advance planning to on-the-fly improvisation. Thus Brooks (1997), Agre and Chapman (1987), and Rosenschein (1995) argue that embodied agents can inventively exploit facts about their physical circumstances to avoid explicit representation and reasoning. Suchman (1987) claims that most human activity, rather than implementing preconceptualized plans, consists of incessant, creative, improvisational mobilization and appropriation of the vast array of resources that environments regularly make available. Not only do people rarely "figure it all out in advance," she argues, but their stories should be understood not as veridical reports of how activity comes to be, but as after-the-fact reconstructions whose role is to retrospectively render activity intelligible (and perhaps accountable).

These shifts in focus have substantial methodological implications. In part, they involve the rejection of long-standing Cartesian intuitions that although movement, sensation, and adaptive reaction to the physical world lie within the province of "mere brutes," high-level conceptualization is challenging and paradigmatic of what it is to be human. They also reflect a change in disciplinary affiliation, from LOGIC, mathematics, computer science, and (individual) psychology, toward sociology, anthropology, science studies, general epistemology, and philosophy of science. More concretely, they involve a shift in methods from *in vitro* toward *in vivo* studies, and from both statistical surveys and laboratory experiments toward "thick descriptions" of real people acting in real-life situations.

Such methodological and epistemological considerations lead to even more radical situated positions. In the situated language proposal discussed earlier, meanings were considered stable, but interpretation varied. But some writers argue that circumstance can affect *meaning,* too. Winograd (1985) argues that what *water* means in the question "Is there any water in the refrigerator?" depends on whether the questioner is thirsty, worried about humidity and condensation, or testing a child's understanding of the constitution of eggplants. Smith (1996: 328–329) considers a case where two friends, in late-night conversation, shape the meanings of their words (such as when describing a friend as "skewed"), rather in the way that blues players bend notes on a guitar. Such examples are theoretically challenging because they raise the ontological question of what properties such utterances designate. It is not obvious "bendable" predicates can be accommodated on the model of ambiguity, with contextual factors selecting from a fixed (pregiven) stock of external properties.

Pressed by such challenges, the strongest variants of situatedness bite the bullet and take ontology itself to be context-dependent. On such a view, not only is what we do, what we say, and how we get at the world viewed as dependent on facts about our circumstances, but also *how the world is*—the very objects and properties in the world we therein talk about and live in and get at—are also taken to depend on (interpretive) context (Cussins 1992; Smith 1996). Taken to its logical extreme, that is, situatedness leads to a view of an ontologically plastic (though perhaps still highly constrained) world that, in contrast with the naive realism implicit in the classical picture, is at least partially socially constructed. Not surprisingly, such views reflect back onto our understanding of the nature of science itself (see, e.g., Haraway 1991). This is situatedness with a vengeance.

At the broadest level, the basic tenet of the situated movement has been accepted. That language, cognition, and activity are fundamentally context-dependent is by now a theoretical truism. What remains a matter of debate is how far this situated intuition should be taken. Everyone agrees that language is indexical, a smaller number are prepared to dethrone ratiocination as the hallmark of the mental, and those who are prepared to take context-dependence through to metaphysics remain a distinct minority. How the issues are resolved may depend on the extent to which the various communities advocating a situated approach—linguistics, cognitive science, AI, sociology, philosophy, feminism, science studies, and so on—collaborate in following out the consequences of this transformation to our traditional self-conception.

See also ANIMAL NAVIGATION; ECOLOGICAL PSYCHOLOGY; FRAME PROBLEM; INTELLIGENT AGENT ARCHITECTURE; MOBILE ROBOTS; PLANNING

—*Brian Cantwell Smith*

References

Agre, P., and D. Chapman. (1987). Pengi: An implementation of a theory of activity. In *The Proceedings of the Sixth National Conference on Artificial Intelligence.* American Association for Artificial Intelligence. Seattle: Kaufmann, pp. 268–272.

Barwise, J., and J. Perry. (1983). *Situations and Attitudes.* Cambridge, MA: MIT Press.

Brooks, R. A. (1997). Intelligence without representation. *Artificial Intelligence* 47: 139–159 (1991). Revised version in J. Haugeland, Ed., *Mind Design* 2: *Philosophy, Psychology, Artificial Intelligence.* 2nd ed., revised and enlarged. Cambridge, MA: MIT Press, pp. 395–420.

Cussins, A. (1992). Content, embodiment and objectivity: The theory of cognitive trails. *Mind* 101: 651–688.

Gawron, M., and S. Peters. (1991). *Anaphora and Quantification in Situation Semantics* (CSLI Lecture Notes, No. 19). Stanford, CA: Center for the Study of Language and Information.

Haraway, D. (1991). Situated knowledges: The science question in feminism and the privilege of partial perspective. In *Simians, Cyborgs, and Women: The Reinvention of Nature.* New York: Routledge.

Haugeland, J. (1997). What is mind design? In J. Haugeland, Ed., *Mind Design* 2: *Philosophy, Psychology, Artificial Intelligence.* 2nd ed., revised and enlarged. Cambridge, MA: MIT Press, pp. 1–28.

Kirsh, D. (1995). The intelligent use of space. *Artificial Intelligence* 72: 1–52.

Lave, J., M. Murtaugh, and O. de la Rocha. (1984). The dialectic of arithmetic in grocery shopping. In B. Rogoff and J. Lave,

Eds., *Everyday Cognition: Its Development in Social Context.* Cambridge, MA: Harvard University Press, pp. 67–94.

Rosenschein, S., and L. Kaelbling. (1995). A situated view of representation and control. In P. A. Agre and S. Rosenschein, Eds., Special Issue on Computational Research on Interaction and Agency, *Artificial Intelligence* January/February 1995.

Smith, B. C. (1996). *On the Origin of Objects.* Cambridge, MA: MIT Press.

Suchman, L. A. (1987). *Plans and Situated Action.* New York: Cambridge University Press.

Winograd, T. (1985). Moving the semantic fulcrum. *Linguistics and Philosophy* 8(1): 91–104.

Further Readings

Agre, P. A. (1997). *Computation and Human Experience.* New York: Cambridge University Press.

Agre, P. A., and S. Rosenschein, Eds. (1995). Special Issue on Computational Research on Interaction and Agency, *Artificial Intelligence* January/February 1995.

Clancey, W. J. (1997). *Situated Cognition: On Human Knowledge and Computer Representations.* New York: Cambridge University Press.

Clark, A. (1997). *Being There: Putting Brain, Body and World Together Again.* Cambridge, MA: MIT Press.

Dreyfus, H. (1979). *What Computers Can't Do: A Critique of Artificial Reason.* New York: Harper and Row.

Hutchins, E. (1995). *Cognition in the Wild.* Cambridge, MA: MIT Press.

Latour, B. (1986). Visualization and cognition: Thinking with eyes and hands. *Knowledge and Society: Studies in the Sociology of Culture Past and Present* 6: 1–40.

Lave, J. (1988). *Cognition in Practice: Mind, Mathematics and Culture in Everyday Life.* New York: Cambridge University Press.

Lave, J., and E. Wenger. (1991). *Situated Learning: Legitimate Peripheral Participation.* New York: Cambridge University Press.

Norman, D. A. (1987). *The Psychology of Everyday Things.* New York: Basic Books.

Vera, J., and H. Simon. (1993). Situated action: A symbolic interpretation. With replies. *Cognitive Science* 17(1): 7–48.

Winograd, T., and F. Flores. (1986). *Understanding Computers and Cognition: A New Foundation for Design.* Norwood, NJ: Ablex.

Situation Calculus

The situation calculus is a language of predicate logic for representing and reasoning about *action* and *change*. This KNOWLEDGE REPRESENTATION language was originally developed by John McCarthy (McCarthy 1963; McCarthy and Hayes 1969) and is commonly used in artificial intelligence for purposes such as predicting the effects of actions on a system's state, PLANNING actions to achieve given goals (Green 1969), diagnosing what events might explain some observations, and analyzing the operation of programs that perform such tasks. Other formalisms used for the same purposes include modal logics such as dynamic logic and various logics for TEMPORAL REASONING (Goldblatt 1987), as well as the event calculus (Kowalski and Sergot 1986).

In the situation calculus, the initial situation of the world or system under consideration is represented by the constant S_0; this is simply understood as a situation where no actions of interest have yet occurred. The situation that results from an action a being performed in a situation s is represented by the term $do(a,s)$. For example, $do(pickup(Rob,Package_1),S_0)$ might represent the situation where the robot *Rob* has performed the action of picking up the object *Package₁* in the initial situation S_0; similarly, $do(goTo(Rob,MailRoom),do(pickup(Rob,Package_1),S_0))$ might represent the situation where *Rob* subsequently moved to the *MailRoom*. Thus, a situation is essentially a possible world history, viewed as a sequence of actions.

The situation calculus provides a way of specifying what the effects of an action are. For example, the axiom

$$\forall o \forall x \forall s (\neg Heavy(o, s) \rightarrow Holding(x, o, do(pickup(x, o), s)))$$

could be used to state that an agent x will be holding an object o in the situation that results from x performing the action of picking up o in situation s provided that o is not heavy. Note that relations whose truth value depends on the situation, such as *Heavy* and *Holding*, take a situation argument; such relations are called *fluents*. From the above axiom and the assumption $\neg\ Heavy(Package_1,S_0)$, that is, that *Package₁* is not heavy initially, one could conclude that $Holding(Rob,Package_1,do(pickup(Rob,Package_1),S_0))$, that is, that *Rob* would be holding *Package₁* after picking it up in the initial situation. One can also use the situation calculus to represent the preconditions of actions, that is, the conditions under which it is possible to perform the action. Note that a situation calculus model of a system is just a theory in classical first-order logic and thus an ordinary theorem proving system can be used to infer consequences from it. This may be an advantage over the alternative modal logic formalisms.

Some of the most problematic features of commonsense reasoning manifest themselves in reasoning about action. For instance, although it seems reasonable that a model of a system should include an effect axiom for every action affecting a fluent (actions typically affect very few fluents), one should not have to include an axiom for every fluent that remains unchanged by an action (e.g., that going to a location does not change the color of objects). Yet this is just what is required by a straightforward application of logic to such reasoning. Dealing with the resulting mass of axioms is error-prone and computationally costly. This problem of representing succinctly and computing effectively with the "invariants" of actions has been called the FRAME PROBLEM by McCarthy and Hayes (1969) and has been the subject of much recent research (Elkan 1992; Hanks and McDermott 1986; Pylyshyn 1987; Reiter 1991; Sandewall 1994; Shanahan 1997). It has been one of the major motivations for research on nonmonotonic logics where a conclusion may be invalidated by additional assumptions (Reiter 1987). A nonmonotonic logic might attempt to solve the frame problem by representing the "persistence" assumption that says that fluents remain unaffected by actions unless it is known to be otherwise.

Note that some approaches to reasoning about action or processes such as STRIPS-based planning (Fikes and Nilsson 1971) and most work in process control and software verification may use simple state database update techniques and avoid the frame problem because they assume that one always has complete information about the world state and the effects of actions. But this assumption is rarely justified for intelligent agents (e.g., a robot must acquire information about its environment through its sensors as it operates). This is where a logical approach, with its ability to represent incomplete information, becomes essential.

Another problem viewed as fundamental in the area is called the *ramification problem;* this concerns the effects of actions and how they could be represented so as to avoid having to explicitly mention all indirect effects (e.g., the robot going somewhere changes the location of the packages it is carrying). Finally, there is also the *qualification problem* (McCarthy 1977), that is, how to represent the preconditions of actions when there is in fact a very large number of things that could prevent an action from happening (e.g., the robot's being unable to pick up a package because it is glued to the floor).

The situation calculus continues to be at the center of much knowledge representation research. In recent years, it has been extended to model time and concurrent processes (Gelfond, Lifschitz, and Rabinov 1991; Pinto 1994; Reiter 1996), complex actions (Levesque et al. 1997; De Giacomo, Lespérance, and Levesque 1997), knowledge (Moore 1985), and other mental states. It is also at the core of a recently proposed framework for modeling and programming intelligent agents (Lespérance, Levesque, and Reiter 1999).

See also LOGIC; MODAL LOGIC; NONMONOTONIC LOGICS

—*Yves Lespérance*

References

De Giacomo, G., Y. Lespérance, and H. J. Levesque. (1997). Reasoning about concurrent execution, prioritized interrupts, and exogenous actions in the situation calculus. *Proceedings of the Fifteenth International Joint Conference on Artificial Intelligence,* Japan, pp. 1221–1226.

Elkan, C. (1992). Reasoning about action in first-order logic. *Proceedings of the Ninth Biennial Conference of the Canadian Society for Computational Studies of Intelligence.* San Mateo, CA: Kaufman, pp. 221–227.

Fikes, R. E., and N. J. Nilsson. (1971). STRIPS: A new approach to the application of theorem proving to problem solving. *Artificial Intelligence* 2: 189–208.

Gelfond, M., V. Lifschitz, and A. Rabinov. (1991). What are the limitations of the situation calculus? In R. Boyer, Ed., *Automated Reasoning: Essays in Honor of Woody Bledsoe.* Dordrecht: Kluwer, pp. 167–179.

Goldblatt, R. (1987). *Logics of Time and Computation.* 2nd ed. CSLI Lecture Notes No. 7, Center for the Study of Language and Information, Stanford University.

Green, C. C. (1969). Theorem proving by resolution as a basis for question-answering systems. In B. Meltzer and D. Michie, Eds., *Machine Intelligence* 4. Edinburgh: Edinburgh University Press, pp. 183–205.

Hanks, S., and D. McDermott. (1986). Default reasoning, nonmonotonic logics, and the frame problem. *Proceedings of the 5th National Conference on Artificial Intelligence.* Cambridge, MA: MIT Press, pp. 328–333.

Kowalski, R. A., and M. J. Sergot. (1986). A logic-based calculus of events. *New Generation Computing* 4: 67–95.

Lespérance, Y., H. J. Levesque, and R. Reiter. (1999). A situation calculus approach to modeling and programming agents. In A. Rao and M. Wooldridge, Eds., *Foundations and Theories of Rational Agency.* Dordrecht: Kluwer.

Levesque, H. J., R. Reiter, Y. Lespérance, F. Lin, and R. B. Scherl. (1997). GOLOG: A logic programming language for dynamic domains. *Journal of Logic Programming* 31: 59–84.

McCarthy, J. (1963). *Situations, Actions, and Causal Laws.* Memo 2, Stanford University Artificial Intelligence Project.

McCarthy, J. (1977). Epistemological problems of artificial intelligence. *Proceedings of the Fifth International Joint Conference on Artificial Intelligence:* 1038–1044.

McCarthy, J., and P. Hayes. (1969). Some philosophical problems from the standpoint of artificial intelligence. In B. Meltzer and D. Michie, Eds., *Machine Intelligence* 4. Edinburgh: Edinburgh University Press, pp. 463–502.

Moore, R. C. (1985). A formal theory of knowledge and action. In J. R. Hobbs and R. C. Moore, Eds., *Formal Theories of the Common Sense World.* Norwood, NJ: Ablex, pp. 319–358.

Pinto, J. (1994). *Temporal Reasoning in the Situation Calculus.* Ph.D. diss., Dept. of Computer Science, University of Toronto.

Pylyshyn, Z. W., Ed. (1987). *The Robot's Dilemma: The Frame Problem in Artificial Intelligence.* Norwood, NJ: Ablex.

Reiter, R. (1987). Nonmonotonic reasoning. *Annual Reviews of Computer Science* 2: 147–186.

Reiter, R. (1991). The frame problem in the situation calculus: A simple solution (sometimes) and a completeness result for goal regression. In V. Lifschitz, Ed., *Artificial Intelligence and Mathematical Theory of Computation: Papers in Honor of John McCarthy.* San Diego: Academic Press, pp. 359–380.

Reiter, R. (1996). Natural actions, concurrency and continuous time in the situation calculus. *In Principles of Knowledge Representation and Reasoning: Proceedings of the Fifth International Conference (KR'96).* Cambridge, MA, pp. 2–13.

Sandewall, E. (1994). *Features and Fluents: The Representation of Knowledge about Dynamical Systems,* vol. 1. New York: Oxford University Press.

Shanahan, M. (1997). *Solving the Frame Problem: A Mathematical Investigation of the Common Sense Law of Inertia.* Cambridge, MA: MIT Press.

Sleep

Sleep is a behavioral adaptation of vertebrate animals with much to teach the cognitive scientist about the relationship of mind to brain. In no other behavioral state are the differences from waking psychology so profound or so clearly tied to the underlying changes in neurophysiology. It is this psychophysiological concomitance that will be emphasized in the account given here of the natural history and neurobiology of sleep.

As a behavior, sleep is characterized by (1) a recumbent posture with varying degrees of relaxation of the skeletal musculature; (2) an increase in the threshold of response to sensory stimuli; and (3) a characteristic set of electrographic signs. From an evolutionary point of view sleep is clearly a strategy for energy conservation and for protection from predators since all animals sleep at times and in places that confer a benefit in one or both of these domains. Sleep is distinguished from simple rest, from torpor, and from anesthetic or traumatic unresponsiveness by its active and distinctive brain mechanisms of induction and maintenance, as well as by its ready reversibility.

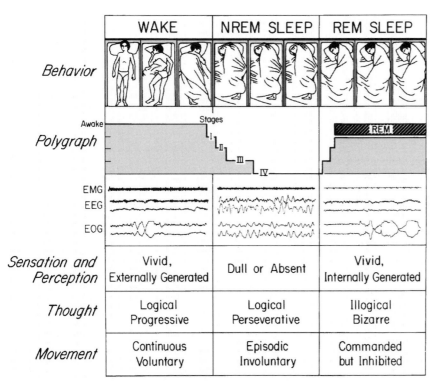

Figure 1. Sleep cycle schematic. The states of waking, NREM, and REM sleep have behavioral, polygraphic, and psychological manifestations that are depicted here. In the behavioral channel, posture shifts—detectable by time-lapse photography or video—can be seen to occur during waking and in concert with phase changes of the sleep cycle. Two different mechanisms account for sleep immobility: disfacilitation (during stages I–IV of NREM sleep) and inhibition (during REM sleep). In dreams, we imagine that we move, but we do not. The sequence of these stages is schematically represented in the polygraph channel and sample tracings are also shown. Three variables are used to distinguish these states: the electromyogram (EMG), which is highest in waking, intermediate in NREM sleep, and lowest in REM sleep; and the electroencephalogram (EEG) and electrooculogram (EOG), which are both activated in waking and REM sleep, and inactivated in NREM sleep. Each sample record is about 20 sec long. Other subjective and objective state variables are described in the three lower channels. (From J. A. Hobson and M. Steriade (1986), Neuronal basis of behavioral state control. In V. Mountcastle and F. E. Bloom, Eds., *Handbook of Physiology: The Nervous System.* Vol. 4, pp. 701–823.)

As a function of the circadian rhythm generated by the suprachiasmatic nucleus of the hypothalamus, all vertebrate animals show prominent rest-activity cycles with an endogenous period of about one day. Corresponding to the increased complexity of the supervening thalamocortical brain and the greater sophistication of their thermoregulatory capacity, the vertebrate mammals link active sleep control mechanisms in the lower brain stem to the circadian cycle. The result is a stereotyped sequence of events that is coordinated throughout the brain so as to alter every aspect of cognition in a dramatic and sometimes paradoxical fashion. The most surprising aspect of this automatic sequence of events is the regular recurrence of periods of brain activation and rapid eye movement (REM) in sleep that is associated in humans with hallucinoid DREAMING.

Waking, with all of its cognitive components, is an actively maintained brain state in which the thalamocortical circuitry is kept open and receptive to information from within and without by the depolarization of reticular thalamic neurons by cholinergic and aminergic modulatory elements of the brain stem. This activation, together with its specific neuromodulatory effects, renders the forebrain capable of sensation, perception, ATTENTION, orientation, emotion, and stimulus evaluation in terms of past experience, and deliberate action. Whenever the brain stem neuromodulatory influence declines to a critical level, the thalamocortical system tends to oscillate, producing its own endogenous rhythm of electroencephalographic (EEG) spindles and slow waves which are incompatible with waking conscious experience because the inputs to and outputs from the cortex are blocked and intracortical communication is preempted. Cognitive func-

tion is thus progressively obtunded as this progressive brain deactivation proceeds in nocturnal sleep. This is reflected by the shift from stage I to stage IV of so-called non-REM (NREM) sleep from the depths of which human subjects are very difficult to rouse. Even when verbally responsive they may then show marked sleep inertia with persistent slow waves in the EEG and an inability to perform even trivially simple cognitive tasks such as serial seven subtraction. This sleep inertia process is greatest in the first two NREM cycles of the night and is intensified in postdeprivation recovery sleep.

Recent POSITRON EMISSION TOMOGRAPHY (PET) studies of human NREM sleep have revealed decreased blood flow in the brain stem reticular formation, the subthalamus, and in frontal cortical regions denoting the massive deactivation of these structures in NREM sleep. Animal studies further confirm this deactivation process at the level of individual neurons, many of which decrease their rate of firing by as much as 50 percent. There is also a 50 percent decline in the output of the wake state neuromodulatory chemicals acetylcholine, norepinephrine, and serotonin. It is for all these reasons that the NREM sleeping brain is such a poor cognitive instrument and it is the carryover of these effects into subsequent waking that so severely impairs problem-solving behavior upon arousal from deep NREM sleep. That this cognitive impairment may nonetheless be beneficial is suggested by the finding that complex DECISION MAKING is more efficient during waking that follows nights with uninterrupted NREM sleep.

After sixty to seventy minutes of deep NREM sleep subjects show a reversal of these oscillatory EEG patterns and the brain spontaneously reactivates. Together with the EEG desynchronization is an activation of the upper brain's motor systems signaled by flurries of rapid saccadic movements of the eyes (the so-called REMs). However, the output of most of these signals in behavior is blocked by strong inhibition of final common path motor neurons. Postural tone is obliterated and signaled by the complete obliteration of electromyographic activity. Awakening subjects from REM sleep is much easier, they perform most tasks better, and they commonly give longer, more detailed dream reports than following NREM awakenings. Recent PET studies of human REM sleep indicate increased activation (compared even to waking) of the pontine brain stem, the basolateral forebrain, and especially the limbic subcortical and paralimbic cortical structures, while the more dorsofrontal cortical areas remain inactivated. This finding has a strong bearing on the strongly emotional character and the bizarreness of human dreaming because it indicates a bottom-up activation of the limbic brain with the release of emotions and related memories which must be integrated in conscious experience without the benefit of executive cortical guidance. Cellular-level studies in animals confirm the activation inferences of human PET studies for the pontine brain stem and other subcortical areas. In addition they describe a dissociation between cholinergic neuromodulation (which equals or exceeds that of waking) and noradrenergic and serotonergic neuromodulation which falls to near-zero levels.

These paradoxical findings show that the brain activation patterns of waking and REM sleep are actually quite different even though they are indistinguishable from an EEG point of view. They also shed light on the differences in cognition, especially the disorientation, the defective reasoning and judgment, and the poor memory during and after dreaming.

Subjects who are deprived of either NREM or REM sleep (or both) show progressively impaired cognitive capacities which may progress to psychotic disorganization if they can be kept awake despite the marked increase in their intrinsic drive to sleep. This finding indicates that sleep confers critical benefits to the brain and to cognitive capability. These benefits are yet to be fully elucidated but may relate to the dramatic alterations in neuromodulatory balance alluded to above. From a commonsense point of view, the hypothesis crying out for critical test is that sleep benefits cognition not only by cerebral energy conservation but also by a more specific and profound rest of the very chemical systems most critical to wake state cognition.

One of the most attractive hypotheses regarding the cognitive benefit of sleep is that it enhances LEARNING and MEMORY. Many experiments have shown increases in sleep to be associated with the mastery of learning tasks in both animal models and human subjects. Some of these increases are immediate while others are delayed. While most of these studies have emphasized REM sleep, others have presented evidence for a two-stage process with NREM sleep serving to iterate recently learned material followed by its consolidation in REM. This theory is congruent with the differential subjective experience of the two states of sleep: during NREM mental activity tends to be a perseverative and nonprogressive rumination regard-

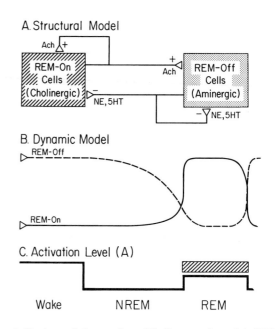

Figure 2. Reciprocal Interaction. (*A*) Structural model. REM-on cells of the pontine reticular formation are cholinoceptively excited and/or cholinergically excitatory (ACH+) at their synaptic endings (open boxes). Pontine REM-off cells are noradrenergically (NE) or serotonergically (5HT) inhibitory (–) at their synapses (filled boxes). (*B*) Dynamic model. During waking the pontine aminergic (filled box) system is tonically activated and inhibits the pontine cholinergic (open box) system. During NREM sleep aminergic inhibition gradually wanes and cholinergic excitation reciprocally waxes. At REM sleep onset aminergic inhibition is shut off and cholinergic excitation reaches its high point. (*C*) Activation level (A). As a consequence of the interplay of the neuronal systems shown in A and B, the net activation level of the brain (A) is at equally high levels in waking and REM sleep and at about half this peak level in NREM sleep.

ing recent events; in contrast, REM sleep mentation melds both recent and remote memories in bizarre scenarios that are often associated with strong, usually unpleasant, emotion, suggesting the possibility that emotional salience is a feature of the consolidation process. The specification of these hypotheses in cellular and molecular terms presents cognitive neuroscience with one of its central challenges. Because so much is known about the neuromodulatory underpinnings of the waking and NREM and REM sleeping states, a unique opportunity exists to unite neurobiological sleep research with classic experimental psychology, solving a central problem of both fields simultaneously.

That the cognitive and more general energetic benefits of sleep may have a unitary underlying mechanism is suggested by animal experiments which have consistently demonstrated reciprocal impairment (by deprivation) and enhancement (by normal or recovery sleep) of both thermoregulatory and cognitive functions. So critical is sleep to the life of the mind and the body that its loss is at first deleterious and later ultimately fatal to both.

— *J. Allan Hobson*

Further Readings

Braun, A. R., T. J. Balkin, N. J. Wesensten, R. E. Carson, M. Varga, P. Baldwin, S. Selbie, G. Belenky, and P. Herscovitch. (1997). Regional cerebral blood flow throughout the sleep-wake cycle. *Brain* 120: 1173–1197.

Hennevin, E., B. Hars, C. Maho, and C. Bloch. (1995). Processing of learned information in paradoxical sleep: Relevance for memory. *Behavioural Brain Research* 69: 125–135.

Hobson, J. A., R. W. McCarley, and P. W. Wyzinki. (1975). Sleep cycle oscillation: Reciprocal discharge by two brainstem neuronal groups. *Science* 189: 55–58.

Hobson, J. A., R. Lydic, and H. Baghdoyan. (1986). Evolving concepts of sleep cycle generation: From brain centers to neuronal populations. *Behav. Brain Sci.* 9: 371–448.

Hobson, J. A., and M. Steriade. (1986). The neuronal basis of behavioral state control. In F. E. Bloom, Ed., *Handbook of Physiology—The Nervous System,* vol. 4. Bethesda, MD: American Physiological Society, pp. 701–823.

Hobson, J. A., and R. Stickgold. (1995). Sleep, the beloved teacher. *Current Biology* 5: 35–36.

Maquet, P., J. M. Peters, J. Aerts, G. Delfiore, C. Degueldre, A. Luxen, and G. Franck. (1996). Functional neuroanatomy of human rapid-eye-movement sleep and dreaming. *Nature* 383: 163.

McCarley, R. W., and J. A. Hobson. (1975). Neuronal excitability modulations over the sleep cycle: A structured and mathematical model. *Science* 189: 58–60.

Nofzinger, E. A., M. A. Mintun, M. B. Wiseman, D. Kupfer, and A. Y. Moore. (1997). Forebrain activation in REM sleep: An FDG PET study. *Brain Res.* 770: 192–201.

Smith, C. (1996). Sleep states, memory processes, and synaptic plasticity. *Behavioural Brain Research* 78: 49–56.

Steriade, M., and R. W. McCarley. (1990). *Brainstem Control of Wakefulness and Sleep.* New York: Plenum Press.

Smell

The olfactory system is a phylogenetically ancient sensory system capable of detecting and discriminating among a vast number of different odorants. Olfaction is critical to the survival of a variety of lower animals ranging from insects to mammals, while in humans it has been considered less important than the other senses. Understanding how the olfactory system encodes and decodes information is not an easy task, given the lack of a clear physical energy continuum to characterize and control stimulus presentation, like wavelength for COLOR VISION (see VISUAL ANATOMY AND PHYSIOLOGY) or frequency for auditory pitch (see AUDITION and AUDITORY PHYSIOLOGY). The situation is made even more complex by the findings that similar chemical substances can sometimes have quite different odors and some substances with altogether different chemical formulas can smell alike.

The olfactory organ of vertebrates is a complex structure designed to collect odorant molecules and direct them to the sensory neurons. Although the chemoreceptive endings and neural projections of the olfactory nerve are primary to the sense of smell, other cranial nerves are involved, namely, the trigeminal, glossopharyngeal, and vagus. These accessory cranial nerves possess at least some chemoreceptive endings which line the nose, pharynx, and larynx, giving rise to the pungent or irritating quality often experienced as part of an odor sensation.

For much of the animal kingdom olfaction is basic to the maintenance of life, regulating reproductive physiology, food intake, and social behavior. In fact, the essence of ANIMAL COMMUNICATION is chemical, relying on odors produced by body glands, feces, and urine. For example, the male silk moth uses olfactory cues to find his mate, as does the adult salmon to return to the place where it was spawned. Many mammalian species, ranging from deer to cats and dogs, mark their territory with urine or other secretions. These chemical messages provide the animal sampling the scent mark with information regarding whether it came from a conspecific, if the depositor was male or female, dominant or submissive, and even its reproductive status.

There is also a dependency of reproductive and sexual behavior on olfactory cues. Introducing the odor of a male mouse or his urine can induce and accelerate the estrus cycle of a female. Moreover, appropriate odor cues from a female are important in attracting the male's interest during estrus and promoting copulation. In some species sexual dysfunction and even retarded development of the sex organs results when olfaction is compromised.

In humans, the sense of smell is considered less critical to survival than the other special senses, although the detection of stimuli such as smoke, gas, or decaying food prevents bodily harm. Instead, civilized society appears to emphasize the importance of olfaction on the quality of life. People attempt to modify attractiveness by adding perfumes to their bodies and incense to their homes. Consider the plethora of commercial products for use against "bad" odors. One instance in which smell plays a major role is in flavor perception and the recognition of tastes. Much of what people think they TASTE they actually smell and a large percentage of people coming to chemosensory clinics complaining of taste problems actually have smell dysfunction (consider what happens to food appreciation when a cold strikes). In fact, disorders of the sense of smell can often be profoundly distressing, as well as harbingers of more general disease states.

Although not as extensively documented as in animals, a relationship between olfaction and sex seems likely in humans. Olfactory acuity in women seems better at ovulation than during menstruation and there is evidence that olfactory cues (i.e., human pheromones) among women can synchronize the menstrual cycle and that odors serve as attractants to the opposite sex.

In vertebrates, olfactory receptor neurons (ORNs) differ in the number and profile of odorants to which they respond (see NEURON). For example, one electrophysiological study of single ORN responses to twenty different stimuli demonstrated that individual neurons responded to as few as two of the odorants within the panel. Furthermore, despite sampling over fifty neurons, each had a distinct odorant response profile. Thus, ORN responses define the range of odorants that can elicit a response in a given cell (termed its molecular receptive range [MRR], analogous to the spatial receptive field in the visual system). Emerging evidence further suggests that a cell's MRR may reflect interactions with particular ligand determinants (compounds with similar organization of carbon atoms or functional groups). Accordingly, if ORNs are to be classified as to type on the basis of their response to the odorant universe, then the number of such types must likely exceed fifty.

Recently, a large olfactory-specific gene family (numbering 500 to 1000 genes in humans) has been identified. The proteins encoded by these genes are expressed in ORNs and are considered to be putative odorant receptors (PORs) based on their structural and sequence homology with other known G protein–activating receptors (and G protein cascades have been implicated in the transduction of olfactory stimuli). At present, these PORs remain functionally anonymous. Nonetheless, the extremely large size of the gene family is considered strong evidence that these are odorant receptors, fulfilling the criterion of diversity to interact with an immense number of different odorants.

In other sensory systems (i.e., audition, vision, and somesthesis; see HAPTIC PERCEPTION), receptor cells encode specificity about the sensory stimulus by virtue of their exact placement in the receptor sheet. In contrast, the receptor sheet in olfaction does not form a spatial map about the environment. Instead, as previously noted, the responsivity of an ORN may result from the affinity of its receptor for a particular odorant ligand. So how is this molecular information mapped into the nervous system? Studies of the ensemble properties of the olfactory epithelium suggest that odorant quality information is encoded in large-scale spatial patterns of neural activity. That is, direct presentation of odorants to the exposed olfactory epithelium reveal intrinsic spatial differences in the sensitivity to different odorants across this neural tissue. The biological basis for these intrinsic patterns likely stems from the differential distribution of POR expression across the epithelium. Neurons expressing a particular POR are segregated to one of four broad nonoverlapping zones. Within a zone some PORs are dispersed throughout the anterior-posterior extent of the epithelium, while others are clustered in more limited areas.

Despite the fact that the vertebrate olfactory system does not process information about odors by virtue of a single type of ORN's placement in the receptor sheet, a degree of rhinotopy (analogous to retinotopy in the visual system) does exist in the organization of the central projection. The foundation for this rhinotopy lies in the topographical organization of bulbar glomeruli (neuropil structures comprised of ORN axon terminals and the distal dendrites of mitral, tufted, and periglomerular cells) in relation to the expression of POR type. An entire subset of ORNs expressing a particular POR send their axons to converge on a single glomerulus in the olfactory bulb. As a result, the odorant information contained in the large-scale differential activation of subsets of ORNs can be encoded by producing differential spatial patterns of activity across the glomerular layer of the olfactory bulb. This activity is further sharpened in the relay neurons of the bulb via complicated local circuits that act both locally and laterally on the signals impinging on the bulb.

Exactly how the aforementioned parameters of neural excitation lead to perception is unknown. However, recent work combining animal PSYCHOPHYSICS with neurophysiological techniques suggest a predictive relationship between the large-scale spatial patterning of neural excitation and odorant quality perception.

— *Steven Youngentob*

Further Readings

Adrian, E. D. (1950). Sensory discrimination with some recent evidence from the olfactory organ. *British Medical Bulletin* 6: 330–331.

Adrian, E. D. (1951). Olfactory discrimination. *Annals of Psychology* 50: 107–130.

Buck, L. B. (1992). The olfactory multigene family. *Current Opinions in Genetic Development* 2: 467–473.

Buck, L. B., and R. Axel. (1991). A novel multigene family may encode odorant receptors: A molecular basis for odor recognition. *Cell* 65: 175–187.

Cain, W. S. (1976). Olfaction and the common chemical sense: Some psychophysical contrasts. *Sensory Processes* 1: 57–67.

Doty, R. L., W. E. Brugger, P. C. Jurs, M. A. Orndorff, P. F. Snyder, and L. D. Lowry. (1978). Intranasal trigeminal stimulation from odorous volatiles: Psychometric responses from anosmic and normal humans. *Physiology and Behavior* 20: 175–187.

Doty, R. L., G. R. Huggins, P. J. Snyder, and L. D. Lowry. (1981). Endocrine, cardiovascular and psychological correlates of olfactory sensitivity changes during the human menstrual cycle. *Journal of Comparative and Physiological Psychology* 35: 45–60.

Engen, T. (1982). *The Perception of Odors.* New York: Academic Press.

Firestein, S., C. Picco, and A. Menini. (1993). The relation between stimulus and response in the olfactory receptor cells of tiger salamander. *Journal of Physiology (London)* 468: 1–10.

Gangestad, S. W., and R. Thornhill. (1998) Menstrual cycle variation in women's preference for the scent of symmetrical men. *Proceedings of the Royal Society of London, Series B: Biological Sciences.* 265: 927–933.

Gesteland, R. C., J. Y. Lettvin, and W. H. Pitts. (1965). Chemical transmission in the nose of the frog. *Journal of Physiology (London)* 181: 525–559.

Getchell, T. V., R. L. Doty, L. M. Bartoshuk, and J. B. Snow, Jr. (1991). *Smell and Taste in Health and Disease.* New York: Raven Press.

Hildebrand, J. G., and G. M. Shepherd. (1997). Mechanisms of olfactory discrimination: Converging evidence of common principles across phyla. *Annual Review of Neuroscience* 20: 595–631.

Kauer, J. S., and A. R. Cinelli. (1993). Are there structural and functional modules in the vertebrate olfactory bulb? *Microscopic Research Technology* 24: 157–167.

Kent, P. F., S. L. Youngentob, and P. R. Sheehe. (1995). Odorant-specific spatial patterns of mucosal activity predict spatial differences among odorants. *Journal of Neurophysiology* 74: 1777–1781.

Kubick, S., J. Strotmann, I. Andreini, and H. Breer. (1998). Subfamily of olfactory receptors characterized by unique structural features and expression patterns. *Journal of Neurochemistry* 69: 465–475.

MacKay-Sim, A., P. Shaman, and D. G. Moulton. (1982). Topographic coding of olfactory quality: Odorant specific patterns of epithelial responsivity in the salamander. *Journal of Neurophysiology* 48: 584–596.

McClintock, M. K. (1984). Estrous synchrony: Modulation of ovarian cycle length by female pheromones. *Physiology and Behavior* 32: 701–705

Mombaerts, P., F. Wang, C. Dulac, S. K. Chao, A. Nemes, M. Mendlesohn, J. Edmondson, and R. Axel. (1996). Visualizing an olfactory sensory map. *Cell* 87: 675–686.

Mori, K., and Y. Yoshihara. (1995). Molecular recognition and olfactory processing in the mammalian olfactory system. *Progress in Neurobiology* 45: 585–619.

Mozell, M. M., B. P. Smith, P. E. Smith, R. L. Sullivan, and P. Swender. (1969). Nasal chemoreception in flavor identification. *Archives of Otolaryngology* 90: 131–137.

Muller-Schwartze, D., and M. M. Mozell. (1977). *Chemical Signals in Vertebrates.* New York: Plenum Press.

Ressler, K. J., S. L. Sullivan, and L. B. Buck. (1993). A zonal organization of odorant receptor gene expression in the olfactory epithelium. *Cell* 73: 597–609.

Ressler, K. J., S. L. Sullivan, and L. B. Buck. (1994). Information coding in the olfactory system: Evidence for a stereotyped and highly organized epitope map in the olfactory bulb. *Cell* 79: 1245–1255.

Ronnet, G. V. (1995). The molecular basis of olfactory signal transduction. In R. L. Doty, Ed., *Handbook of Olfaction and Gustation.* New York: Marcel Decker, pp. 127–145.

Schoenfeld, T. A., A. N. Clancy, W. B. Forbes, and F. Macrides. (1994). The spatial organization of the peripheral olfactory system of the hamster. 1. Receptor neuron projections to the main olfactory bulb. *Brain Research Bulletin* 34: 183–210.

Shepherd, G. M. (1991). Computational structure of the olfactory system. In J. L. Davis and H. Eichenbaum, Eds., *Olfaction: A Model System for Computational Neuroscience.* Cambridge, MA: MIT Press, pp. 3–42.

Shepherd, G. M., and C. A. Greer. (1990). The olfactory bulb. In G. M. Shepherd, Ed., *Synaptic Organization of the Brain.* New York: Oxford University Press, pp. 133–169.

Stern, K., and M. K. McClintock. (1998). Regulation of ovulation by human pheromones. *Nature* 12: 177–179.

Strotmann, J., I. Wanner, J. Krieger, K. Raming, and H. Breer. (1992). Expression of odorant receptors in spatially restricted subsets of chemosensory neurons. *NeuroReport* 3: 1053–1056.

Strotmann, J., I. Wanner, T. Helfrich, A. Beck, and H. Breer. (1994). Rostro-caudal patterning of receptor expressing olfactory neurones in the rat nasal cavity. *Cell Tissue Research* 278: 11–20.

Vassar, R., S. K. Chao, R. Sitcheran, J. M. Nunez, L. B. Vosshall, and R. Axel. (1994). Topographic organization of sensory projections to the olfactory bulb. *Cell* 79: 981–989.

Whitten, W. K. (1956). Modification of the estrous cycle of the mouse by external stimuli associated with the male. *Journal of Endocrinology* 13: 399–404.

Wilson, E. O. (1970). Chemical communication within animal species. In E. Sondheimer and J. B. Simeone, Eds., *Chemical Ecology.* New York: Academic Press, pp. 133–156.

Yokoi, M., K. Mori, and S. Nakanishi. (1995). Refinement of odor molecule tuning by dendrodendritic synaptic inhibition in the bulb. *Proceedings of the National Academy of Science* 92: 3371–3375.

Youngentob, S. L., P. F. Kent, P. R. Sheehe, J. E. Schwob, and E. Tzoumaka. (1995). Mucosal inherent activity patterns in the rat: Evidence from voltage-sensitive dyes. *Journal of Neurophysiology* 73: 387–398.

Social Cognition

About the time that experimental psychology was trying to solve the problem of rat behavior, social psychology was trying to solve the problem of mind, and for several decades it stood virtually alone in its attempt to develop an experimental science of mental phenomena such as belief, judgment, inference, attitude, affect, and MOTIVATION (e.g., Allport 1954; Asch 1952; Heider 1958; Lewin 1951). Defined broadly, *social cognition* refers to those aspects of mental life that enable and are shaped by social experience, and in this sense, social cognition is among social psychology's perdurable concerns.

Although social psychology has been a cognitive science for the better part of a century, it was nonetheless profoundly influenced by the "cognitive revolution" that took place in its neighbor discipline during the 1960s and 1970s. Defined narrowly, *social cognition* refers to an intellectual movement (circa 1975) that borrowed the techniques, theories, and metaphors of the new cognitive psychology and brought them to bear on traditional social psychological problems, such as attitude structure and change (see COGNITIVE DISSONANCE), causal attribution (see ATTRIBUTION THEORY; CAUSAL REASONING), social inference (see JUDGMENT HEURISTICS), CATEGORIZATION and STEREOTYPING, SELF-KNOWLEDGE and self-deception (see SELF), and the like. The social cognition movement was characterized by (a) its allegiance to the information processing metaphor, which suggested that mental phenomena are properly explained by describing a sequence of hypothetical operations and structures that might produce them; (b) its emphasis on MENTAL REPRESENTATION with an attendant lack of emphasis on motivation, emotion, behavior, and social interaction; (c) its conviction that social cognition was a special case of cognition, and that theories of the former should thus be grounded in theories of the latter; and (d) its penchant for highly controlled experimental methods that maximized internal validity rather than ECOLOGICAL VALIDITY.

The movement was enormously influential, and in just a few years it came to dominate social psychology's intellectual landscape, giving rise to new journals, new societies, new graduate training programs, and new textbooks. Suddenly, social psychologists were theorizing about activation and inhibition, arguing about schemas and exemplars, manipulating cognitive load and search set size, and measuring interference effects and reaction times. The social cognition movement brought social psychology into the experimental mainstream, and for a while it looked as though other approaches within social psychology might soon be obsolete. But as enthusiasms often do, this one exceeded its warrant in at least two ways. First, the new experimental techniques did indeed provide more precise answers than social psychologists were used to receiving, but to smaller questions than social psychologists were used to asking. Cognitive psychology was able to set aside the problems of motivation, emotion, and action while concentrating on more tractable issues, but these problems were among social psychology's core concerns. To ignore them was to let the method pose the question rather than deliver the answer, and to many social psychologists, that seemed to be putting things back end first. Second, the social cognition movement was predicated on the assumption that social and nonsocial cognition are only superficially distinct, and that a single theory could thus explain both instances quite nicely. Alas, it is becoming increasingly clear that although all cognitive processes do share some basic, defining features, the mind is not an all-purpose information processing device that understands social objects in the same way that it understands tomatoes, giraffes, and nonsense syllables. Rather, it seems to be a family of highly specialized modules, many of which are dedicated explicitly to social tasks (see DOMAIN SPECIFICITY and MODULARITY OF MIND). The human brain is the evolutionary adaptation of an organism whose survival is largely dependent on its relations with others, and thus it is not surprising that special functions should develop to parse, understand, and remember the social world (see EVOLUTIONARY PSYCHOLOGY and MACHIAVELLIAN INTELLIGENCE HYPOTHESIS). In some ways, then, the social cognition movement's attempt to reduce social cognition to more general information-processing principles was a step in the wrong direction.

Like most intellectual movements, the social cognition movement's early excesses have been forgotten as its considerable wisdom has been incorporated into the mainstream. Indeed, the phrase *social cognition* no longer has much discriminating power because virtually all social psychologists are comfortable with the information-processing metaphor, fluent in its languages, and familiar with its techniques. The wall between social and cognitive psychology has never been thinner, and the two disciplines are distinguished more by topical emphasis and aesthetic sensibility than by theoretical orientation. Nonetheless, their separate histories allow each to play an important role for the other. Social psychology has always been driven by intellectual problems rather than by methodological innovations, which means that social psychologists have often had to look to their neighbors for new scientific tools and new conceptual metaphors. Cognitive psychologists have given both in abundance. On the other hand, social psychology's problem-focus has allowed it to maintain a steady orbit around a core set of issues and resist the faddish forces that remade experimental psychology several times in a single century. Social psychology is slow to respond to the zeitgeist and quick to retreat when the paradigm de jour threatens to ignore, set aside, or define away the problems that animate the discipline. As such, it serves as cognitive psychology's conscience, emphasizing the rich social context in which cognition evolved and occurs, keeping issues such as emotion and motivation on the table despite the daunting complexities they present, and insisting that cognition be thought of as a prelude to action and interaction rather than as an end unto itself.

Fiske and Taylor (1991) provide an excellent primer on social cognition; Higgins and Bargh (1987) and Fiske (1993) provide timely reviews of the field; Ostrom (1984) and Landman and Manis (1983) provide early analyses of the social cognition movement; and Devine, Hamilton, and Ostrom (1997) provide a useful retrospective. Extended treatments of most topics in social cognition can be found in Gilbert, Fiske, and Lindzey (1998).

See also ATTRIBUTION THEORY; CULTURAL CONSENSUS THEORY; EMOTIONS; MOTIVATION AND CULTURE; NAIVE SOCIOLOGY; SOCIAL COGNITION IN ANIMALS

—*Daniel Gilbert*

References

Allport, G. W. (1954). *The Nature of Prejudice.* New York: Addison Wesley.

Asch, S. E. (1952). *Social Psychology.* New York: Prentice Hall.

Devine, P. G., D. L. Hamilton, and T. M. Ostrom, Eds. (1997). *Social Cognition: Impact on Social Psychology.* New York: Academic Press.

Fiske, S. T. (1993). Social cognition and social perception. *Annual Review of Psychology* 44: 155–194.

Fiske, S. T., and S. E. Taylor. (1991). *Social Cognition.* 2nd ed. New York: McGraw Hill.

Gilbert, D. T., S. T. Fiske, and G. Lindzey, Eds. (1998). *The Handbook of Social Psychology.* 4th ed. New York: McGraw Hill.

Heider, F. (1958). *The Psychology of Interpersonal Relations.* New York: Wiley.

Higgins, E. T., and J. A. Bargh. (1987). Social cognition and social perception. *Annual Review of Psychology* 38: 369–425.

Landman, J., and M. Manis. (1983). Social cognition: Some historical and theoretical perspectives. In L. Berkowtiz, Ed., *Advances in Experimental Social Psychology,* vol. 16. New York: Academic Press.

Lewin, K. (1951). *Field Theory in Social Science.* New York: Harper.

Ostrom, T. M. (1984). The sovereignty of social cognition. In R. S. Wyer and T. K. Srull, Eds., *Handbook of Social Cognition,* vol. 1. Hillsdale, NJ: Erlbaum, pp. 1–38.

Social Cognition in Animals

Individuals in many animal species do not interact at random but have qualitatively different social relationships with different members of their group. The most stable, long-term bonds are typically found among matrilineal kin (paternity is generally unknown) and have their genesis in the close relationships formed between a mother and her offspring (Kummer 1971). For example, immature female African elephants interact at high rates with their mother and, through their mother, with their matrilineal aunts, siblings, and cousins. Matrilineal kin remain together throughout their lives, tolerating one another's proximity and cooperating to defend feeding areas against other matrilines (Moss 1988).

Old World monkeys, like the macaques of Asia or the baboons and vervet monkeys of Africa, are organized along similar lines but differ in the size of their social units. Groups of baboons may contain over one hundred individuals. Each group contains several matrilineal families. Immature animals acquire dominance ranks immediately below those of their mothers, and families are arranged in a linear rank order so that all members of family A rank above the members of family B, who rank above the members of family C, and so on. As in a Jane Austen novel, social interactions follow two general patterns. Most cooperative behavior (grooming, play, tolerance at feeding sites, and the formation of alliances) occurs among close kin, but cooperative behavior between the members of different matrilines can arise when a middle- or low-ranking individual attempts to groom, play, or form an alliance with the member of a higher-ranking family (for reviews, see Smuts et al. 1987).

The study of social cognition in animals attempts to identify the mechanisms that underlie these interactions. It is now clear that individuals in many species know a great deal about their own social relations. They recognize others as individuals, remember who has cooperated with them in the past, and adjust their future behavior accordingly. This is not surprising, given what is known about the learning and memory of animals in the laboratory, where they have been tested with objects. Social cognition in animals is most striking, however, when we consider what individuals know about the social relations of others in their group.

One hypothesis, derived from traditional learning theory, holds that animals develop their own social relationships and learn about the relationships of others through classical and operant CONDITIONING. Individuals recognize and respond differently to one another because of past experience, or because they have formed specific associations between particular individuals. A second view holds that social relationships in many species—particularly long-lived animals like elephants, parrots, dolphins, and primates—cannot be explained unless we assume that individuals differentiate among classes of relationships and make use of mental representations similar to our concepts of "kinship," "closely bonded," or "linear dominance hierarchy." These hypotheses have been tested most often on monkeys and apes.

In order to understand a dominance hierarchy or predict which individuals are likely to form alliances with each other, a monkey must step outside its own sphere of interactions and recognize the relationships that exist among others. Such knowledge can be obtained only by observing interactions in which one is not involved and making the appropriate inferences. There is, in fact, growing evidence that monkeys do possess knowledge of other animals' social relationships and that such knowledge affects their behavior. For example, in a test of individual recognition a juvenile vervet monkey's scream was played from a concealed loudspeaker to three adult females, one of whom was the juvenile's mother. As expected, the mother responded most strongly; however, even before this occurred the control females looked at the mother. Apparently, control females associated a particular scream with a particular juvenile and this juvenile with a particular adult female. They acted as if they recognized the kin relations that exist among others (Cheney and Seyfarth 1990).

Following aggression, a monkey may "reconcile" by engaging in friendly behavior with its former opponent. A fight may also cause a victim to "redirect" aggression and threaten a third, previously uninvolved individual. In both cases, individuals act as if they recognize their opponent's close kin. When animals reconcile they do so either with their former opponent or with one of their opponent's close matrilineal relatives; when they redirect aggression they do so most often against a close relative of their prior opponent (reviewed in Cheney and Seyfarth 1990; de Waal 1996).

Monkeys can also recognize the dominance ranks of others. When female vervet monkeys compete for grooming partners, competition is greatest for the highest-ranking female, next for the second-ranking female, and so on. When a high-ranking female approaches two lower-ranking individuals and interrupts their grooming, it is the lower-ranking of the two who is much more likely to move away (Cheney and Seyfarth 1990).

It is widely accepted, then, that nonhuman primates—and very likely many other animals—classify others according to their patterns of association and recognize the friendships and enmities that exist among individuals other than themselves. Humans, however, go further and classify different types of relationships into more abstract, superordinate categories like "friends," "family," and "enemies" that are independent of the particular individuals involved. Do social concepts of this sort exist in any animal species?

Dasser (1988) studied social knowledge in longtailed macaques that were members of a group of forty individuals living in a large outdoor enclosure. She trained three adult females to leave the group temporarily, enter a test room, and view slides of other group members. When shown two slides, one of a mother and her offspring and the other of two unrelated group members, subjects were rewarded for pressing a button below the mother-offspring slide. After training with five different slides of the same mother and her juvenile daughter, subjects were tested using fourteen novel slides of different mothers and offspring paired with fourteen novel unrelated alternatives. Mother-offspring pairs varied widely in their physical characteristics: they included mothers with infant daughters, mothers with juvenile sons, and mothers with adult daughters. Nonetheless, in all fourteen tests the subjects correctly selected the mother-offspring pair. They behaved as if they recognized a concept of "mother and offspring" that was independent of the particular individuals involved.

We have, as yet, no idea how monkeys might represent social relationships in their mind. They may use physical resemblance as a cue, because members of the same matriline often (but not always) look alike, or they may use rates of interaction. The latter seems unlikely, however, because kin do not always interact at higher rates than non-kin. Mothers and infants, for example, interact at high rates whereas mothers and older sons do not. Both were classified by Dasser's subjects as falling within the same category. Similarly, although bonds within matrilineal kin groups can be extremely variable (depending, for example, on the ages and sex of family members), monkeys nevertheless treat competitive interactions as pitting one family against another (Cheney and Seyfarth 1990).

In sum, monkeys seem to use a metric to classify social relationships that cannot be explained simply in terms of physical features or the number and type of interactions. To do this, they must compare relationships according to an underlying relation that has been abstracted from a series of interactions over time. Monkeys take note of the elements that make up a relationship (grooming, alliances, etc.), then make judgments of similarity or difference not by comparing specific elements but by comparing the different relationships that these elements instantiate. By this view, conditioning and the formation of mental representations are not *alternative* mechanisms underlying social cognition; instead, they interact, with the former helping to give rise to the latter (see also PRIMATE COGNITION).

The hypothesis that monkeys classify relationships into relatively abstract categories receives additional support from experiments indicating that vervet and diana monkeys classify vocalizations into categories according to their meaning. When asked to compare two vocalizations, vervets judge them to be similar or different not according to their acoustic properties, which are measurable and concrete, but according to their referents, which are more abstract (Seyfarth and Cheney 1992). Female diana monkeys give their characteristic leopard alarm when they hear either a leopard's growl, a male diana monkey's leopard alarm, which is acoustically different from their own, or the shriek of a duiker, a small antelope that is often hunted by leopards (Zuberbuhler, Noe, and Seyfarth 1997). These results suggest that, in the mind of a female diana monkey, some sort of MENTAL REPRESENTATION of a leopard serves as an intervening variable between hearing one type of call and producing another (see also ANIMAL COMMUNICATION).

It has been suggested that natural selection has acted with particular force in the domain of social interaction (Jolly 1966; Humphrey 1976), and that, as a result, the cognitive mechanisms that underlie social interactions are different from those that underlie, for example, foraging or ANIMAL NAVIGATION. The processing of knowledge about social relationships, it is argued, constitutes a mental module, much like the processing of language or music (Fodor 1983; Jackendoff 1987; Cheney and Seyfarth 1990; see also EVOLUTIONARY PSYCHOLOGY). Despite great theoretical interest, however (e.g., Byrne and Whiten 1988), this view is largely untested.

See also COGNITIVE ETHOLOGY; COMPARATIVE PSYCHOLOGY; DARWIN, CHARLES; EVOLUTION; INTENTIONALITY; MACHIAVELLIAN INTELLIGENCE HYPOTHESIS; SOCIAL COGNITION; SOCIAL PLAY BEHAVIOR; SOCIOBIOLOGY

—Dorothy Cheney and Robert Seyfarth

References

Byrne, R., and A. Whiten, Eds. (1988). *Machiavellian Intelligence.* Oxford: Oxford University Press.

Cheney, D. L., and R. M. Seyfarth. (1990). *How Monkeys See the World.* Chicago: University of Chicago Press.

Dasser, V. (1988). A social concept in Java monkeys. *Animal Behaviour* 36: 225–230.

de Waal, F. (1996). *Peacemaking Among Primates.* Cambridge, MA: Harvard University Press.

Fodor, J. A. (1983). *The Modularity of Mind.* Cambridge, MA: MIT Press.

Humphrey, N. K. (1976). The social function of intellect. In P. P. G. Bateson and R. A. Hinde, Eds., *Growing Points in Ethology.* Cambridge: Cambridge University Press, pp. 303–318.

Jackendoff, R. (1987). *Consciousness and the Computational Mind.* Cambridge, MA: MIT Press.

Jolly, A. (1966). Lemur social behavior and primate intelligence. *Science* 153: 501–506.

Kummer, H. (1971). *Primate Societies.* Chicago: Aldine.

Moss, C. J. (1988). *Elephant Memories.* Boston: Houghton Mifflin.

Seyfarth, R. M., and D. L. Cheney. (1992). Meaning and mind in monkeys. *Scientific American* 267: 122–129.

Smuts, B. B., D. L. Cheney, R. M. Seyfarth, R. W. Wrangham, and T. T. Struhsaker, Eds. (1987). *Primate Societies.* Chicago: University of Chicago Press.

Zuberbuhler, K., R. Noe, and R. M. Seyfarth. (1997). Diana monkey long distance calls: Messages for conspecifics and predators. *Animal Behaviour* 53:589–604.

Further Readings

Cheney, D. L., and R. M. Seyfarth. (1990). The representation of social relations by monkeys. *Cognition* 37: 167–196.

Essock-Vitale, S., and R. M. Seyfarth. (1987). Intelligence and social cognition. In B. Smuts, D. Cheney, R. Seyfarth, R. W. Wrangham, and T. Struhsaker, Eds., *Primate Societies.* Chicago: University of Chicago Press, pp. 452–461.

Seyfarth, R. M., and D. L. Cheney. (1994). The evolution of social cognition in primates. In L. Real, Ed., *Behavioral Mechanisms in Evolution and Ecology.* Chicago: University of Chicago Press, pp. 371–389.

Social Dominance

See DOMINANCE IN ANIMAL SOCIAL GROUPS

Social Intelligence

See MACHIAVELLIAN INTELLIGENCE HYPOTHESIS; SOCIAL COGNITION; SOCIAL COGNITION IN ANIMALS

Social Play Behavior

Recently, the scientific study of play behavior has undergone many significant changes. New data are forcing people to give up old ideas and set ways of thinking about this phenomenon. Most researchers recognize the importance of rigorous interdisciplinary collaboration in play research (Pelligrini 1995; Bekoff and Byers 1998; Burghardt 1999), and the interactions among those studying humans and non-humans are producing exciting new results. Currently, workers in many areas are conducting detailed theoretical, observational, and experimental analyses of play in mammals (including humans) and birds. (Using criteria that are employed to characterize play in mammals and birds, it appears that some reptiles might also play [Burghardt 1999].) They are concerned with such topics as evolution, ecology, development, social communication, individual well-being, neurobiology, LEARNING, and cognition (for references see Bekoff and Byers 1981, 1998; Fagen 1981; Smith 1982 and commentaries, 1984; Martin and Caro 1985; Burghardt 1999; Bekoff and Allen 1992, 1998; Allen and Bekoff 1994, 1997; Brown 1998; Pelligrini 1995; Sutton-Smith 1998).

Because social play (hereafter play) is a widespread phenomenon, especially among mammals, it offers the opportunity for comparative work on animal cognition, including such areas as intentionality, communication, and information sharing (Bateson 1956; Bekoff 1998; Bekoff and Allen 1992; Allen and Bekoff 1994, 1997). Through difficult to define and to study, play is generally recognized as a distinctive category of behavior. Difficulties with functional definitions led Bekoff and Byers (1981: 300–301; see also Martin and Caro 1985) to offer the following definition: "*Play* is all motor activity performed postnatally that *appears* [my emphasis] to be purposeless, in which motor patterns from other contexts may often be used in modified forms and altered temporal sequencing. If the activity is directed toward another living being it is called *social play*." This definition centers on the structure of play sequences— what individuals do when they play—and not on possible functions of play.

Why engage in social play? Despite physical risks (and perhaps other costs) associated with play, many individuals persistently seek it out. A major question centers on why play has evolved and what benefits outweigh the energy and risk costs of play. Play may serve a number of functions simultaneously (for example, socialization, exercise, practice, or cognitive development) and there are species, age, and sex differences. Functional (evolutionary) accounts are often tied to analyses of what individuals do when they play. Although many agree that play seems to have something to do with motor development, or with the development of cognitive skills that support motor performance, hard evidence is scant and opinions are divided. One important theme stemming from recent comparative research is that functional accounts of play resist being pigeonholed into simple and misleading summary statements. In the past, for example, play-fighting was considered important in learning fighting skills that would be used in adulthood or for physical training. Although in some species play may be important for the development of certain skills, in others this might not be the case. For example, play-fighting does not seem to be important in the development of motor training for fighting skills in some rats (Pellis and Pellis 1998), but others (Biben 1998; Heinrich and Smolker 1998; Miller and Byers 1998; Thompson 1998; Watson 1998) have shown that play may be important in the development of motor training, cognitive/motor training, or in the development of other social skills (social competence) in birds and mammals, including humans.

Questions dealing with the immediate causes and benefits of play also need more attention. Research on the neurobiology of play also centers on possible causes (Byers 1998). For example, it appears that dopamine, serotonin, and norepinephrine are important in the regulation of play, and that a lot of the brain is active during play (Siviy 1998). Based on these data, some have suggested that play may facilitate coping with environmental stressors and be important in coordinating an organism's response to stress. These data also provide the basis for more informed discussions of the role of play in learning and promoting creativity. Neurobiological data are also essential for assessing hypotheses about whether play is a pleasurable activity for nonhumans as it seems to be for humans, and there is some neurochemical evidence that suggests that it is. In light of these neurobiological data, scientists who study play might be less resistant to explanations that appeal to enjoyment as a motivator for the activity.

Communicative and cognitive aspects of play also are receiving attention. When individuals play they typically use action patterns that are also used in other contexts, such as predatory behavior, antipredatory behavior, and mating. These action patterns may not be intrinsically different across different contexts, or they may be hard to discriminate even for the participants. To solve the problems that might be caused by confusing play with mating or fighting, many species have evolved signals that function to establish and to maintain a play "mood." In most species in which play has been described, individuals have to communicate that "this is play, not fighting, mating, or preying," and there are data that show that certain signals are used to communicate "what follows is play" or "let's keep playing no matter what I just did or plan to do." For example, in infant coyotes, wolves, and domestic dogs, a behavior pattern called the "play bow" is not performed randomly, but rather immediately precedes or immediately follows behavior patterns that can be misinterpreted (for example, biting accompanied by vigorous side-to-side shaking of the head; Bekoff 1995). Suffice it to say, in most species in which play has been described, play-soliciting signals (or play markers) appear to foster some sort of cooperation between players so that each responds to the other in a way consistent with play and different from the responses the same actions would elicit in other contexts. There is little evidence that play signals are used to deceive others.

Bekoff and Allen (1998) point out that the strongly cooperative nature of much social play makes it a useful model for study of the communication of intention. For example, when two individuals engage in play-fighting, there is a risk of injury to each, especially if one switches from play-fighting to real fighting. Somehow, the playful and cooperative nature of the interaction is maintained, even though the motor acts themselves may closely resemble aggression. How do individuals "read" play intention in a conspecific? Cooperative social play may involve rapid exchange of information on intentions, desires, and beliefs. Discussions of self-handicapping (individuals do not bite or hit others as hard as they can) and role-reversals (dominant individuals allow subordinate individuals to dominate them) in play by individuals of many taxa can also inform cognitive inquiries. We can also ask what are the consequences of failure to play for individuals of species in which cooperative social play is a form a social cognitive training. By reviewing the lives of homicidal and antisocial personalities and the influence of diseases on early human behavior, Brown (1998) presents a set of interesting correlations showing that play in childhood is required for the social integration of humans. Data on nonhumans also support this idea.

The flexibility and versatility of play make it a good candidate for comparative and evolutionary cognitive studies. These data may provide important insights into what might be going on in an individual's mind.

See also ANIMAL COMMUNICATION; COGNITIVE ETHOLOGY; SOCIAL COGNITION IN ANIMALS

—*Marc Bekoff*

References

Allen, C., and M. Bekoff. (1994). Intentionality, social play and definition. *Biology and Philosophy* 9: 63–74.

Allen, C., and M. Bekoff. (1997). *Species of Mind: The Philosophy and Biology of Cognitive Ethology.* Cambridge, MA: MIT Press.

Bateson, G. (1956). The message "This is play." In B. Schaffner, Ed., *Group Processes: Transactions of the Second Conference.* New York: Josiah Macy Foundation, pp. 145–256.

Bekoff, M. (1995). Play signals as punctuation: The structure of social play in canids. *Behaviour* 132: 419–429.

Bekoff, M. (1998). Playing with play; what can we learn about evolution and cognition? In D. Cummins and C. Allen, Eds., *The Evolution of Mind.* New York: Oxford University Press.

Bekoff, M., and C. Allen. (1992). Intentional icons: Towards an evolutionary cognitive ethology. *Ethology* 91: 1–16.

Bekoff, M., and C. Allen. (1998). Intentional communication and social play: How and why animals negotiate and agree to play. In M. Bekoff and J. A. Byers, Eds., *Animal Play: Evolutionary, Comparative and Ecological Approaches.* New York: Cambridge University Press.

Bekoff, M., and J. A. Byers. (1981). A critical reanalysis of the ontogeny of mammalian social and locomotor play: An ethological hornet's nest. In K. Immelmann, G. W. Barlow, L. Petrinovich, and M. Main, Eds., *Behavioral Development, The Bielefeld Interdisciplinary Project.* New York: Cambridge University Press, pp. 296–337.

Bekoff, M., and J. A. Byers, Eds. (1998). *Animal Play: Evolutionary, Comparative and Ecological Approaches.* New York: Cambridge University Press.

Biben, M. (1998). Squirrel monkey playfighting: Making the case for a cognitive training hypothesis. In M. Bekoff and J. A. Byers, Eds., *Animal Play: Evolutionary, Comparative and Ecological Approaches.* New York: Cambridge University Press.

Brown, S. (1998). Play as an organizing principle: Clinical evidence and personal observations. In M. Bekoff and J. A. Byers, Eds., *Animal Play: Evolutionary, Comparative and Ecological Approaches.* New York: Cambridge University Press..

Burghardt, G. M. (1999). *The Genesis of Animal Play.* New York: Chapman and Hall.

Byers, J. A. (1998). Biological effects of locomotor play: Getting into shape, or something more specific. In M. Bekoff and J. A. Byers, Eds., *Animal Play: Evolutionary, Comparative and Ecological Approaches.* New York: Cambridge University Press.

Fagen, R. M. (1981). *Animal Play Behavior.* New York: Oxford University Press.

Heinrich, B., and R. Smolker. (1998). Play in common ravens (*Corvus corax*). In M. Bekoff and J. A. Byers, Eds., *Animal Play: Evolutionary, Comparative and Ecological Approaches.* New York: Cambridge University Press.

Martin, P., and T. M. Caro. (1985). On the functions of play and its role in behavioral development. *Advances in the Study of Behavior* 15: 59–103.

Miller, M. N., and J. A. Byers. (1998). Sparring as play in young pronghorn males. In M. Bekoff and J. A. Byers, Eds., *Animal Play: Evolutionary, Comparative and Ecological Approaches.* New York: Cambridge University Press.

Pelligrini, A. D., Ed. (1995). *The Future of Play Theory: A Multidisciplinary Inquiry into the Contributions of Brian Sutton-Smith.* Albany, New York: SUNY Press.

Pellis, S. M., and V. C. Pellis. (1998). The structure-function interface in the analysis of play fighting. In M. Bekoff and J. A. Byers, Eds., *Animal Play: Evolutionary, Comparative and Ecological Approaches.* New York: Cambridge University Press.

Siviy, S. M. (1998). Neurobiological substrates of play behavior: Glimpses into the structure and function of mammalian playfulness. In M. Bekoff and J. A. Byers, Eds., *Animal Play: Evolutionary, Comparative and Ecological Approaches.* New York: Cambridge University Press.

Smith, P. K. (1982). Does play matter? Function and evolutionary aspects of animal and human play. *The Behavioral and Brain Sciences* 5: 139–184 (with commentaries).

Smith, P. K., Ed. (1984). *Play in Animals and Humans.* New York: Blackwell.

Sutton-Smith, B. (1998). *The Ambiguity of Play.* Cambridge, MA: Harvard University Press.

Thompson, K. V. (1998). Self assessment in juvenile play. In M. Bekoff and J. A. Byers, Eds., *Animal Play: Evolutionary, Comparative and Ecological Approaches.* New York: Cambridge University Press.

Watson, D. M. (1998). Kangaroos at play: Play behaviour in the Macropodoidea. In M. Bekoff and J. A. Byers, Eds., *Animal Play: Evolutionary, Comparative and Ecological Approaches.* New York: Cambridge University Press.

Further Readings

Aldis, O. (1975). *Play Fighting.* New York: Academic Press.

Bekoff, M. (1972). The development of social interaction, play and metacommunication in mammals: An ethological perspective. *Quarterly Review of Biology* 47: 412–434.

Bekoff, M. (1975). The communication of play intention: Are play signals functional? *Semiotica* 15: 231–239.

Bekoff, M. (1977). Social communication in canids, evidence for the evolution of a stereotyped mammalian display. *Science* 197: 1097–1099.

Bekoff, M. (1978). Social play, structure, function and the evolution of a cooperative social behavior. In G. Burghardt and M. Bekoff, Eds., *The Development of Behavior: Comparative and Evolutionary Aspects.* New York: Garland, pp. 367–383.

Breuggeman, J. A. (1978). The function of adult play in free-ranging *Macaca mulatta.* In E. O. Smith (1978), pp. 169–191.

Burghardt, G. M. (1988). Precocity, play and the ectotherm-endotherm transition. In E. M. Blass, Ed., *Handbook of Behavioral Neurobiology,* vol. 9. New York: Plenum, pp. 107–148.

Burghardt, G. M. (1996). Play. In G. Greenberg and M. Haraway, Eds., *Encyclopedia of Comparative Psychology.* New York: Garland.

Costabile, A., P. K. Smith, L. Matheson, J. Aston, T. Hunter, and M. Bolton. (1991). Cross-national comparison of how children distinguish serious and playful fighting. *Developmental Psychology* 27: 881–887.

Dennett, D. C. (1983). Intentional systems in cognitive ethology, the "Panglossian paradigm" defended. *Behavioral and Brain Sciences* 6: 343–390.

Mitchell, R. W. (1990). A theory of play. In M. Bekoff and D. Jamieson, Eds., *Interpretation and Explanation in the Study of Animal Behavior.* Vol. 1, *Interpretation, Intentionality and Communication.* Boulder, CO: Westview Press, pp. 197–227.

Ortega, J. C., and M. Bekoff. (1987). Avian play: Comparative evolutionary and developmental trends. *Auk* 104: 338–341.

Rosenberg, A. (1990). Is there an evolutionary biology of play? In M. Bekoff and D. Jamieson, Eds., *Interpretation and Explanation in the Study of Animal Behavior.* Vol. 1, *Interpretation, Intentionality and Communication.* Boulder, CO: Westview Press, pp. 180–196.

Skutch, A. F. (1996). *The Minds of Birds.* College Station: Texas A & M University Press.

Smith, E. O., Ed. (1978). *Social Play in Primates.* New York: Academic Press.

Smith, P. K. (1994). Play training: An overview. In J. Hellendorn, R. van der Kooij, and B. Sutton-Smith, Eds., *Play and Intervention.* Albany, New York: SUNY Press.

Smith, P. K., and R. Vollstedt. (1985). Defining play: An empirical study of the relationship between play and various play criteria. *Child Development* 56: 1042–1050.

Symons, D. S. (1978). *Play and Aggression: A Study of Rhesus Monkeys.* New York: Columbia University Press.

Sociobiology

The term *sociobiology* (*behavioral ecology* and *evolutionary ecology* are synonyms) refers broadly to the application of the principles of Darwinian evolutionary theory to the study of behavior. It grew out of the integration of classical ethology (the naturalistic study of animal and human behavior), population ecology, and population genetics during the 1960s and early 1970s.

The fundamental breakthrough at the heart of sociobiology was provided by a solution to the problem of ALTRUISM. Ever since DARWIN, it had been recognized that altruistic behavior (such as alarm-calling) whereby an individual incurs a potentially life-threatening cost while others benefit creates an anomaly for Darwinian thinking. Any gene for such behavior would soon be eradicated from the population because its carriers would die prematurely, leaving few descendants, while "cheats" who exploited the behavior of the altruist would survive and leave many descendants. W. D. Hamilton provided the solution to this problem in a pair of seminal papers published in 1964. He realized that the anomaly evaporates when the unit of evolutionary accounting is the gene and not the individual: relatives share a proportion of their genes in common by virtue of the fact that they inherit them from the same common ancestor. A gene for altruism can thus evolve whenever the benefit to the altruist via its relatives is greater than the cost it bears through lost personal reproduction, even if the altruist dies in the process.

This observation is the basis of *kin selection theory* and provides the single most important theorem in sociobiology, known as *Hamilton's rule*. This in effect points out that the genetic fitness of a gene (loosely, the effectiveness with which it replicates itself in future generations) is made up of two components: the number of copies transmitted to the next generation through an individual carrier's own reproduction, and the number of copies of the same gene transmitted to the next generation through the additional reproduction achieved by his or her relatives as a direct result of that individual's actions. This combined measure is referred to as *inclusive fitness.*

The crucial assumption underlying this new perspective is that natural selection favors those behaviors that allow genetic fitness to be maximized (the so-called *selfish gene* perspective). However, the Darwinian formula for natural selection does not contain within it any explicit reference to DNA or genes (neither of which were known in the mid-nineteenth century). Rather, the modern theory of neo-Darwinism is built on the integration of Darwin's theory of natural selection with Mendel's theory of inheritance. Because Mendel's theory is concerned with the heritability of characters (or phenotypes) and not genes as such, it follows that anything that can faithfully copy itself is in principle a Darwinian entity and will evolve subject to the laws of natural selection. Learning and the transmission of cultural rules by imitation thus come under the remit of sociobiology as bona fide Darwinian processes.

It is important to appreciate that sociobiology makes no presuppositions about the genetic bases of behavior. The sociobiological perspective is concerned with functional explanations of behavior and centers on the question of whether an organism's behavior (or traits) are designed to maximize inclusive fitness. Although an intrinsically interesting question in itself, the issue of whether the mechanism of inheritance is genetic or learning is irrelevant to the sociobiological approach. Evolutionary theory assumes that organisms are locked into a perpetual scramble for representation in the next generation, but an important distinction thus has to be drawn between the processes involved at the level of the "gene" (the notional unit on which natural selection acts) and the behavioral mechanisms that implement these processes at the level of the individual. One of the central principles of evolutionary biology is that the "selfishness of genes" (the gene's imperative to replicate itself) may be expressed as cooperativeness at the level of the individual.

This important distinction lies at the root of many of the controversies that were generated by the emergence of sociobiology. Many critics assumed, for example, that sociobiology assumes that all behavior is genetically determined. However, such a view would be both biologically unrealistic and would miss the very insight that lies at the heart of Darwinian evolutionary theory. Nonetheless, the adoption of evolutionary ideas in disciplines outside of biology has sometimes resulted in views that approach a form of strict genetic determinism more strongly than is either justified or necessary.

These controversies aside, the extent to which evolutionary thinking revolutionized the understanding of animal behavior during the 1970s justifiably led to its being referred to as the *sociobiological revolution*. The explanatory power of its theories explained many previously puzzling phenomena, and their predictive power generated many new research programs in both the field and the laboratory. The sociobiological approach has widely been acknowledged as being especially successful in explaining foraging behavior, conflict resolution, mate choice patterns, and parental investment decisions in animals, as well as many aspects of communication and signaling.

The early success of the application of these ideas to the study of animal behavior inevitably raised the possibility of their being applied to human behavior. The early sociobiological discussions of human behavior were based on very limited empirical evidence, and were much criticized for their naivety as a result. However, since the mid-1980s, there has been a dramatic growth in the number of empirical studies. These included studies of both traditional societies, contemporary postindustrial Western societies, and historical societies, with the main focus being on mate choice, reproductive decisions, inheritance patterns, foraging strategies, and cultural evolution mechanisms (see Betzig, Mulder, and Turke 1988; Smith and Winterhalder 1992).

More recently, a second dimension has developed out of human sociobiology that focuses more on the cognitive mechanisms that underpin behavior. Because the sociobiological perspective was concerned exclusively with functional explanations of behavior (the purpose that behavior serves in the life history of the individual organism), little attention was given to the cognitive mechanisms underpinning these behavioral processes. A growing interest in these issues, informed by an evolutionary perspective, now makes it possible to distinguish two subdisciplines, at least in the context of research on humans: evolutionary anthropology (which focuses on the adaptiveness of individuals' behavioral decisions) and EVOLUTIONARY PSYCHOLOGY (which focuses on the cognitive mechanisms involved in the making of such decisions). The two subdisciplines are divided by the issue of whether contemporary human behavior is ever functionally adapted.

Evolutionary psychologists argue that because the cognitive mechanisms that guide behavior evolved during the Pleistocene and have been overtaken by rapid changes in culture and technology, the behavior they generate will commonly be nonadaptive: in effect, we operate with Stone Age minds in a Space Age environment. Instead, evolutionary psychologists typically focus on the design features of human cognition that give rise to universal patterns of behavior that are true of all humans (for some examples, see Barkow, Cosmides, and Tooby 1992). In contrast, evolutionary anthropologists argue that many aspects of behavior are still functionally adaptive, and most of their research is directed to empirical tests of the functional consequences of behavioral decisions. They focus on the adaptive flexibility of behavior at the level of the individual (for examples, see Betzig, Mulder, and Turke 1988; Smith and Winterhalder 1992).

Although it is no doubt true that cognition constrains behavior, it is a purely empirical question as to whether or not our cognitive mechanisms are sufficiently flexible to operate effectively in the modern world. The wealth of studies demonstrating that human and animal behavior is functionally adaptive despite radically changed environments undermines the strong version of the evolutionary psychologist's position, though there must surely be some aspects of behavior that are now maladaptive in this sense.

See also COGNITIVE ANTHROPOLOGY; CULTURAL EVOLUTION; ETHICS AND EVOLUTION; ETHOLOGY

—*R. I. M. Dunbar*

References

Barkow, J., L. Cosmides, and J. Tooby, Eds. (1992). *The Adapted Mind: Evolutionary Psychology and the Generation of Culture.* Oxford: Oxford University Press.

Betzig, L., M. Borgerhof Mulder, and P. Turke, Eds. (1988). *Human Reproductive Behaviour.* Cambridge: Cambridge University Press.

Buss, D. (1994). *The Evolution of Desire.* New York: Basic Books.

Daly, M., and M. Wilson. (1983). *Sex, Evolution and Behavior.* Belmont, CA: Wadsworth.

Daly, M., and M. Wilson. (1988). *Homicide.* New York: Aldine.

Dawkins, R. (1986). *The Selfish Gene.* 2nd ed. Oxford: Oxford University Press.

Dawkins, R. (1983). Universal Darwinism. In D. S. Bendall, Ed., *Evolution from Molecules to Men.* Cambridge: Cambridge University Press, pp. 403–425.

Dawkins, R. (1995). *River Out of Eden.* London: Weidenfield and Nicolson.

Dunbar, R. I. M., Ed. (1995). *Human Reproductive Decisions: Biological and Social Perspectives.* Basingstoke: Macmillan.

Hamilton, W. D. (1964). The genetical evolution of social behaviour, 1, 2. *Journal of Theoretical Biology* 7: 1–51.

Hughes, A. (1985). *Evolution and Human Kinship.* Oxford: Oxford University Press.

Ridley, M. (1993). *The Red Queen.* Harmondsworth: Penguin.

Smith, E. A., and B. Winterhalder, Eds. (1992). *Evolutionary Ecology and Human Behavior.* New York: Aldine.

Wright, R. (1995). *The Moral Animal.* London: Little Brown.

Sociolinguistics

See LANGUAGE AND COMMUNICATION; LANGUAGE AND CULTURE; LANGUAGE AND GENDER; PRAGMATICS

Sonar

See ECHOLOCATION

Spatial Perception

As we move through the world, new visual, auditory, vestibular, and somatosensory inputs are continuously presented to the brain. Given such constantly changing input, it is remarkable how easily we are able to keep track of where things are. We can reach for an object, or look at it, or even kick it without making a conscious effort to assess its location in space. Spatial perception is the faculty that allows us to do so. Sensory and motor information are used together to construct an internal representation of the space we perceive. The nature of this representation and the neural mechanisms underlying it have become a topic of great interest in cognitive neuroscience (Stein 1992; Milner and Goodale 1995). Both neuropsychological studies in humans and neurophysiological studies in nonhuman primates have yielded important insights into how the brain builds spatial representations (Colby 1998).

The dramatic impairments of spatial perception that result from damage to the parietal lobe indicate that this part of cortex plays a critical role in spatial functioning. The most striking of these deficits is the tendency to ignore or neglect objects in particular regions of space. A patient with hemineglect as a result of a right parietal lobe lesion may fail to notice objects on the left, including food on the left side of a plate or words on the left side of a page. Two aspects of neglect are particularly interesting with respect to spatial perception and representation.

First, neglect occurs in all sensory modalities (Bisiach and Vallar 1988). The multimodal nature of neglect indicates that what has been damaged is not simply a set of sensory maps but a high-level, supramodal representation of space. Second, neglect occurs with respect to a variety of spatial reference frames. A patient with right parietal damage is typically unaware of objects on the left side of space but left may be defined with respect to the body, or with respect to the line of sight, or with respect to the object to which the patient is attending. Moreover, these spatial impairments are dynamic, changing from moment to moment in accord with changes in body posture (Moscovitch and Behrmann 1994) and task demands (Behrmann and Tipper 1994). (See VISUAL NEGLECT and MODELING NEUROPSYCHOLOGICAL DEFICITS.)

The variety of deficits observed following parietal lobe damage in humans suggests that parietal cortex contains more than one kind of spatial representation. To understand more precisely how parietal cortex contributes to spatial perception and action, several groups of investigators have recorded from single neurons in alert monkeys trained to perform spatial tasks. Physiologists have sought to specify the sensory and motor conditions under that parietal neurons are activated, using tasks that typically require a hand or eye movement toward a visual target. This work in monkeys has provided direct evidence that parietal cortex contains multiple representations of space (Colby and Duhamel 1991, 1996). Parietal areas differ in their inputs, in the modalities and stimulus features represented, and in their outputs, projecting to separate regions of frontal cortex and subcortical structures, such as the superior colliculus. Of particular interest are parietal areas that contain bimodal somatosensory and visual neurons. These are obvious candidates for integrating information from different modalities into unified representations of space. The specific response properties in these areas and their projections to premotor cortex suggest that one function of parietal cortex is to perform the sensory-to-motor-coordinate transformations required for generating action. Parietal projections to posterior cingulate and parahippocampal cortex may also provide the sensory information essential to the construction of allocentric spatial maps in the HIPPOCAMPUS (O'Keefe and Nadel 1978). The emerging consensus is that neurons in separate areas within parietal cortex encode object location relative to a variety of reference frames (Arbib 1991; Colby and Duhamel 1991, 1996; Jeannerod et al. 1995; Rizzolatti, Fogassi, and Gallese 1997; Gross and Graziano 1995; Olson and Gettner 1995). (See MULTISENSORY INTEGRATION and VISUAL PROCESSING STREAMS.)

Contrasting types of spatial representations exist in two adjacent areas in monkey parietal cortex, the ventral intraparietal area (VIP) and the lateral intraparietal area (LIP). Area VIP, in the fundus of the sulcus, is distinguished from neighboring parietal areas by a preponderance of direction-selective visual neurons (Colby, Duhamel, and Goldberg 1993). In this respect, VIP neurons resemble those in other dorsal stream visual areas that process stimulus motion, especially areas MT and MST (see MOTION, PERCEPTION OF). An unexpected finding in VIP is that the majority of these visual neurons also respond to somatosensory stimuli, such as light touch (Colby and Duhamel 1991; Duhamel, Colby, and Goldberg 1998). These neurons are truly bimodal, in the sense that they can be driven equally well by either a visual or a somatosensory stimulus. Most VIP neurons have somatosensory receptive fields restricted to the head and face. The somatosensory and visual receptive fields of individual neurons match in location, in size, and even in their preferred direction of motion.

The observation of matching visual and somatosensory receptive fields raises the question of what happens to the relative locations of these fields in a single cell when the eyes move. If the visual receptive field were simply retinotopic, it would move when the eyes do. And if the somatosensory receptive field were purely somatotopic, it would be unchanged by eye position. There could not be a consistent correspondence in location if both receptive fields were defined solely with respect to the receptor surfaces. The answer is that some VIP visual receptive fields shift their location on the retina when the eyes move (Colby et al. 1993; Duhamel et al. 1997). A neuron that responds best to a visual stimulus approaching the mouth, and that has a somatosensory receptive field around the mouth, responds best to a stimulus moving on a trajectory toward the mouth regardless of where the monkey is fixating. This indicates that both the visual and somatosensory receptive fields are defined with respect to the skin surface. The receptive fields of these VIP neurons are head-centered: they respond to a certain portion of the skin surface and to the visual stimulus aligned with it, no matter what part of the retina is activated. In sum, these neurons encode bimodal sensory information in a head-centered representation of space. Similar neurons are found in the specific region of premotor cortex to which area VIP projects (Fogassi et al. 1992).

In contrast to area VIP, area LIP contains an eye-centered (oculocentric) representation of space. Neurons in area LIP have retinotopic receptive fields and are activated by sensory, motor, and cognitive events related to the receptive field (Andersen et al. 1990; Goldberg, Colby, and Duhamel 1990; Robinson, Goldberg, and Stanton 1978). Activity in LIP cannot be characterized as reflecting a simple sensory or motor signal. Rather, LIP neurons encode salient spatial locations; activity reflects the degree to which spatial attention has been allocated to the location of the receptive field (Colby, Duhamel, and Golberg 1995; Colby and Duhamel 1996).

Neural representations of space are maintained over time and the brain must solve the problem of updating them when a receptor surface is moved. Every time we move our eyes, each object in our surroundings activates a new set of retinal neurons. Despite this constant change, we experience the world as stable. This perceptual stability has long been understood to reflect the fact that what we perceive is not a direct impression of the external world but a construction, or internal representation, of it. It is this internal representation that is updated in conjunction with eye movements. Neurons in area LIP contribute to updating the internal image (Duhamel, Colby, and Goldberg 1992a). The experiment illustrated shows that an LIP neuron is activated when the monkey makes an eye movement that brings the receptive field to a screen location that previously contained a stimulus. The neuron's response is to the memory trace of the earlier stimulus: no stimulus was ever physically present in the receptive field, either before or after the saccade. The explanation for this surprising response is that the memory trace of the stimulus was updated, or remapped, at the time of the saccade. Nearly all LIP neurons show evidence of remapping the memory trace of a stimulus from the coordinates of the initial eye position to the coordinates of the final eye position.

The significance of this result is in what it tells us about spatial representation in area LIP. It shows that the internal image is dynamic and is always centered on the current position of the fovea. Instead of creating a spatial representation in purely retinotopic coordinates, tied solely to the specific neurons initially activated by the stimulus, area LIP

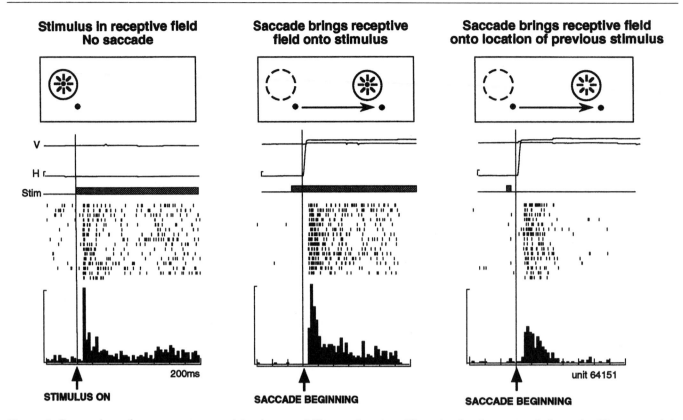

Figure 1. Remapping of memory trace activity in area LIP. Responses of one LIP neuron in three conditions. *Left:* during fixation, the neuron responds to the onset of a stimulus in the receptive field. *Center:* response following a saccade that moves the receptive field onto a stimulus. *Right:* response following a saccade that moves the receptive field onto a previously stimulated location. The stimulus is presented for only 50 msec and is extinguished before the saccade begins so that no stimulus is ever physically present in the receptive field. The response is to a memory trace that has been remapped from the coordinates of the initial eye position to those of the final eye position. (Modified from Duhamel et al. 1992a.)

constructs a representation in eye-centered coordinates. The distinction is a subtle one but very important for generating accurate spatial behavior. Maintaining visual information in eye-centered coordinates tells the monkey not just where the stimulus was on the retina when it first appeared but where it would be now, in relation to the current position of the fovea, if it were still visible. The result is that the monkey always has accurate spatial information with which it could program an eye movement toward a real or remembered target. Compared to a head-centered or world-centered representation, an eye-centered representation has the advantage that it is already in the coordinates of an effector system that could be used to acquire the target visually. Studies of patients indicate that the process of remapping and the construction of an eye-centered representation is selectively impaired by parietal lobe damage (Duhamel et al. 1992b; Heide et al. 1995). (See OCULOMOTOR CONTROL and AFFORDANCES.)

Our current understanding of the neural basis of spatial perception can be summarized as follows. First, parietal cortex contains multiple representations of space. These are instantiated in several discrete areas that have been defined on the basis of anatomical connections and neuronal response properties. Second, parietal neurons in each of these areas have complex response profiles, with sensitivity to multiple stimulus dimensions and, often, multiple stimulus modalities. Single neurons exhibit motor and cognitive activity in addition to sensory responses. Third, the spatial representation in each area can best be understood in terms of the effector system to which it is related: area VIP is most strongly connected to premotor regions controlling head movements, while area LIP projects to oculomotor structures. Finally, spatial representations in parietal cortex are dynamically updated in conjunction with self-generated movements. The primary insight gained from neuropsychological and neurophysiological studies of parietal cortex is that our unitary experience of space emerges from a diversity of spatial representations.

See also ANIMAL NAVIGATION; EYE MOVEMENTS AND VISUAL ATTENTION; HIGH-LEVEL VISION; MID-LEVEL VISION

—*Carol L. Colby*

References

Andersen, R. A., R. M. Bracewell, S. Barash, J. W. Gnadt, and L. Fogassi. (1990). Eye position effects on visual, memory and saccade-related activity in areas LIP and 7a of macaque. *J. Neurosci.* 10: 1176–1196.

Arbib, M. (1991). Interaction of multiple representations of space in the brain. In J. Paillard, Ed., *Brain and Space.* Oxford: Oxford University Press, pp. 379–403.

Behrmann, M., and S. P. Tipper. (1994). Object-based attentional mechanisms: Evidence from patients with unilateral neglect. In C. Umilta and M. Moscovitch, Eds., *Attention and Performance,* vol. 15. Cambridge, MA: MIT Press, pp. 351–375.

Bisiach, E., and G. Vallar. (1988). Hemineglect in humans. In F. Boller and J. Grafman, Eds., *Handbook of Neuropsychology,* vol. 1. Amsterdam: Elsevier, pp. 195–222.

Colby, C. L. (1998). Action-oriented spatial reference frames in cortex. *Neuron* 20: 1–10.

Colby, C. L., and J. -R. Duhamel. (1991). Heterogeneity of extrastriate visual areas and multiple parietal areas in the macaque monkey. *Neuropsychologia* 29: 517–537.

Colby, C. L., and J. -R. Duhamel. (1996). Spatial representations for action in parietal cortex. *Cogn. Brain Res.* 5: 105–115.

Colby, C. L., J. -R. Duhamel, and M. E. Goldberg. (1993). Ventral intraparietal area of the macaque: Anatomic location and visual response properties. *J. Neurophysiol.* 69: 902–91vt4.

Colby, C. L., J. -R. Duhamel, and M. E. Goldberg. (1995). Oculocentric spatial representation in parietal cortex. *Cereb. Cortex* 5: 470–481.

Colby, C. L., J. -R. Duhamel, and M. E. Goldberg. (1996). Visual, presaccadic and cognitive activation of single neurons in monkey lateral intraparietal area. *J. Neurophysiol.* 76: 2841–2852.

Duhamel, J. -R., F. Bremmer, S. BenHamed, and W. Graf. (1997). Spatial invariance of visual receptive fields in parietal cortex neurons. *Nature* 389: 845–848.

Duhamel, J. -R., C. L. Colby, and M. E. Goldberg. (1992a). The updating of the representation of visual space in parietal cortex by intended eye movements. *Science* 255: 90–92.

Duhamel, J. -R., C. L. Colby, and M. E. Goldberg. (1998). Ventral intraparietal area of the macaque: Convergent visual and somatic response properties. *J. Neurophysiol.* 79: 126–136.

Duhamel, J. -R., M. E. Goldberg, E. J. FitzGibbon, A. Sirigu, and J. Grafman. (1992b). Saccadic dysmetria in a patient with a right frontoparietal lesion: The importance of corollary discharge for accurate spatial behavior. *Brain* 115: 1387–1402.

Fogassi, L., V. Gallese, G. di Pelligrino, L. Fadiga, M. Gentilucci, G. Luppino, M. Matelli, A. Pedotti, and G. Rizzolatti. (1992). Space coding by premotor cortex. *Exp. Brain Res.* 89: 686–690.

Goldberg, M. E., C. L. Colby, and J. -R. Duhamel. (1990). The representation of visuomotor space in the parietal lobe of the monkey. *Cold Spring Harbor Symp. Quant. Biol.* 60: 729–739.

Gross, C. G., and M. S. A. Graziano. (1995). Multiple representations of space in the brain. *Neuroscientist* 1: 43–50.

Heide, W., M. Zimmermann, E. Blankenburg, and D. Kompf. (1995). Cortical control of double-step saccades: Implications for spatial orientation. *Ann. Neurol.* 38: 739–748.

Jeannerod, M., M. A. Rizzolatti, G. Arbib, and H. Sakata. (1995). Grasping objects: the cortical mechanisms of visuomotor transformation. *Trends Neurosci* 18: 314–320.

Milner, A. D., and M. A. Goodale. (1995). *The Visual Brain in Action.* Oxford: Oxford University Press.

Moscovitch, M., and M. Behrmann. (1994). Coding of spatial information in the somatosensory system: Evidence from patients with neglect following parietal lobe damage. *J. Cogn. Neurosci.* 6: 151–155.

O'Keefe, J., and L. Nadel. (1978). *The Hippocampus as a Cognitive Map.* Oxford: Clarendon Press.

Olson, C. R., and S. N. Gettner. (1995). Object-centered direction selectivity in the macaque supplementary eye field. *Science* 269: 985–988.

Rizzolatti, G., L. Fogassi, and V. Gallese. (1997). Parietal cortex: From sight to action. *Curr. Opin. Neurobiol.* 7: 562–567.

Robinson, D. L., M. E. Goldberg, and G. B. Stanton. (1978). Parietal association cortex in the primate: Sensory mechanisms and behavioral modulation. *J. Neurophysiol.* 41: 910–932.

Stein, J. F. (1992). The representation of egocentric space in the posterior parietal cortex. *Behav. Brain Sci.* 15: 691–700.

Further Readings

Andersen, R. A., L. H. Bradley, D. C. Snyder, and J. Xing. (1997). Multimodal representation of space in the posterior parietal cortex and its use in planning movements. *Annu. Rev. Neurosci.* 20: 303–330.

Behrmann, M., and S. P. Tipper. (1994). Object-based attentional mechanisms: Evidence from patients with unilateral neglect. In C. Umilta and M. Moscovitch, Eds., *Attention and Performance,* vol. 15. Cambridge, MA: MIT Press, pp. 351–375.

Bremmer, F., J.-R. Duhamel, B. S. Hamed, and W. Graf. (1997). The representation of movement in near extra-personal space in the macaque ventral intraparietal area (VIP). In P. Thier and O. Karnath, Eds., *Contribution of the Parietal Lobe to Orientation in Three-Dimensional Space.* Berlin: Springer, pp. 619–631.

Caminiti, R., S. Ferraina, and P. B. Johnson. (1996). The sources of visual information to the primate frontal lobe: A novel role for the superior parietal lobule. *Cerebral Cortex* 6: 319–328.

Farah, M. J., J. L. Brunn, A. B. Wong, M. A. Wallace, and P. A. Carpenter. (1990). Frames of reference for allocating attention to space. *Cogn. Neuropsych.* 28: 335–347.

Karnath, H. O., P. Schenkel, and B. Fischer. (1991). Trunk orientation as the determining factor of the 'contralateral' deficit in the neglect syndrome and as the physical anchor of the internal representation of body orientation in space. *Brain* 114: 1997–2014.

O'Keefe, J. (1993). Hippocampus, theta and spatial memory. *Curr. Opin. Neurobiol.* 3: 917–924.

Olson, C. R., and S. N. Gettner. (1996). Brain representation of object-centered space. *Curr. Opin. Neurobiol.* 6: 165–170.

Rizzolatti, G., L. Riggio, and B. M. Sheliga. (1994). Space and selective attention. In C. Umilta and M. Moscovitch, Eds., *Attention and Performance,* vol. 15. Cambridge, MA: MIT Press, pp. 231–265.

Sakata, H., M. Murata, A. Taira, and S. Mine. (1995). Neural mechanisms of visual guidance of hand action in the parietal cortex of the monkey. *Cerebral Cortex.* 5: 429–438.

Tipper, S. P., C. Lortie, and G. C. Baylis. (1992). Selective reaching: Evidence for action-centered attention. *J. Exp. Psychol. Hum. Percept. Perform.* 18: 891–905.

Speech Perception

The ability to comprehend spoken language derives from the operation of a highly complex set of perceptual, cognitive, and linguistic processes that permit the listener to recover the meaning of an utterance when listening to speech. The domain of speech perception concerns the earliest stages of this processing, during which the listener maps the time-varying acoustic signal of speech onto a set of discrete linguistic representations. These representations are typically (though not universally) construed in terms of sequences of phonetic segments—consonants and vowels—that form the words of the language. For example, the word *keep* is composed of three phonetic segments: an initial consonant (in phonetic notation, symbolized as /k/), a medial vowel (/i/), and a final consonant (/p/). Each phonetic segment can itself be described in terms of values on a small set of DISTINCTIVE FEATURES that recombine to form the set of segments in any given language. For example, at a featural level, the segment /k/ can be described as a voiceless stop consonant with a velar place of articulation; this segment contrasts minimally with /p/, which is also a voiceless stop consonant but has a labial place of articulation. Within this framework, the central issue in speech perception is how listeners are able to recover the phonetic structure—the sequences of featurally defined phonetic segments—when listening to speech, so that they can recognize the individual words that were produced and, ultimately, comprehend the meaning of the spoken utterance.

Mirroring the interdisciplinary nature of cognitive science itself, the study of speech perception has a long tradition of drawing from many diverse fields, most notably experimental psychology, linguistics, speech and hearing science, acoustics, and engineering. More than five decades of research from these disciplines have yielded a vast amount of information on the nature of the speech signal and the way in which listeners process it to derive the phonetic structure of the utterance.

One of the fundamental discoveries of this research is that there is not a simple one-to-one mapping between the phonetically relevant acoustic properties of speech and the phonetic structure of an utterance (though see Stevens and Blumstein 1981 for an alternative view). Many factors contribute to this complexity in mapping. One of the primary factors, called coarticulation, derives from the fact that when speakers talk, they do not produce the phonetic segments of a given word (such as *keep*) sequentially, one at a time (e.g., /k/, then /i/, then /p/; Liberman et al. 1967). Rather, phonetic segments are coarticulated, with the articulatory gestures for given segments overlapping in time; for example, the gestures for /i/ and even /p/ are in the process of being implemented during the ARTICULATION of /k/. Coarticulation allows speakers to produce sequences of segments rapidly, but it results in two major complications in the mapping between acoustic signal and phonetic structure. The first complication, called the *segmentation problem*, is that any given stretch of the acoustic signal contains, in parallel, information for more than one phonetic segment. Thus it is not possible to divide the acoustic signal into discrete "chunks" that correspond to individual phonetic segments. The second complication, called the *lack of invariance problem*, is that the precise form of a given acoustic property important for specifying a phonetic segment itself changes as a function of phonetic context (i.e., as a function of which segments precede and follow the target segment). So, for example, the form of critical acoustic information for /k/ is different when /k/ is followed by /i/ as in *keep* compared to when it is followed by /u/ as in *cool*. To complicate matters further, many factors other than coarticulation also alter the precise form of the acoustic properties specifying phonetic segments; among the most prominent of these are changes in speaker (Nearey 1989) and speaking rate (Miller 1981). Moreover, given the nature of the articulatory process, it is nearly always the case that phonetic contrasts are specified not by a single property of the acoustic signal but by multiple acoustic properties (Lisker 1986).

Given this considerable (though, importantly, highly systematic) complexity in the mapping between acoustic signal

and phonetic structure, the listener must have some means of "unpacking" the highly encoded, context-dependent speech signal. Indeed, there is now considerable evidence that listeners are exquisitely sensitive to such factors as acoustic-phonetic context, speaker, and speaking rate, and that they take into account the acoustic consequences of variation due to these factors when mapping the acoustic signal onto phonetic structure (for review, see Nygaard and Pisoni 1995). Just how this is accomplished, however, remains unknown, and current theoretical approaches are quite diverse (for review, see Remez 1994). One longstanding debate, for example, focuses on whether phonetic perception is accomplished by a modular, specialized, speech-specific mechanism that computes the intended phonetic gestures of the speaker and thereby recovers the phonetic structure of the utterance (Liberman and Mattingly 1985) or whether some form of general perceptual and/or cognitive processing is sufficient to accomplish the mapping from acoustic signal to phonetic structure, even given the complexity involved (Diehl and Kluender 1989; Pastore 1987; see also Fowler 1986).

Research on speech perception has not only revealed that the mapping between acoustic and phonetic levels is complex, but it has also shown that phonetic perception is itself influenced by input from higher-order linguistic levels, most notably information from the LEXICON. A classic example of this lexical influence is the finding that potentially ambiguous phonetic segments are typically identified so as to create real words of the language rather than nonwords (Ganong 1980). For example, a stimulus with acoustic information that is potentially ambiguous for stimulus-initial /b/ versus /p/ will be identified (under certain conditions) as /b/ in the context of -*eef* and as /p/ in the context of -*eace*, thus creating the real word *beef* (as opposed to *peef*) and the real word *peace* (as opposed to *beace*). Results such as these underscore the close tie between the processes underlying phonetic perception and those responsible for SPOKEN WORD RECOGNITION (lexical access). However, although the influence of lexical information on phonetic perception is well established, there is currently considerable controversy over the nature of this influence. One major alternative, in line with autonomous, modular models of perception, is that lexical factors operate independently of the initial acoustic-phonetic analysis to influence the final percept (e.g., Cutler et al. 1987). Another major alternative, in line with interactive approaches, is that lexical information plays a direct role in the initial acoustic-phonetic mapping per se (e.g., McClelland and Elman 1986). As in other domains of cognitive science, providing clear-cut empirical support for modular versus interactive models has proven to be extremely difficult (see Miller and Eimas 1995).

Finally, yet another major finding of research on speech perception is that the ability to map the acoustic signal onto linguistic representations has its origins in the perceptual processing of early infancy (see PHONOLOGY, ACQUISITION OF). It is now known that infants come to the task of speech perception with highly sophisticated abilities to process the speech signal (for review, see Jusczyk 1995). This includes the ability to distinguish nearly all (if not all) of the phonetic contrasts used in the world's languages and the ability to categorize variants of speech sounds in a linguistically relevant manner (Eimas et al. 1971). For example, young infants will spontaneously group together instances of a given vowel (e.g., /i/) that are produced by different speakers and hence are quite distinctive acoustically (Kuhl 1979). These initial abilities of the infant to perceive speech become tuned in accord with the sound structure of the native language over the course of development, such that infants gradually change from "language-general" to "language-specific" perceivers of speech. This attunement process begins very early—for example, within days of birth, infants show a preference for their native language (Mehler et al. 1988). It continues to unfold in a complex manner over the course of development, with major changes occurring during the first year of life (Best 1994; Jusczyk 1993; Kuhl 1993; Werker and Pegg 1992). Understanding the nature of the earliest abilities of infants to perceive speech, the way in which these abilities become tuned in the course of learning a particular language, and the role of this attunement process in the overall course of LANGUAGE ACQUISITION, remains a major challenge in the study of spoken-language processing.

See also AUDITION; MODULARITY AND LANGUAGE; PHONETICS; PHONOLOGICAL RULES AND PROCESSES; PHONOLOGY; PHONOLOGY, NEURAL BASIS OF

—*Joanne L. Miller*

References

Best, C. T. (1994). The emergence of native-language phonological influences in infants: A perceptual assimilation model. In J. C. Goodman and H. C. Nusbaum, Eds., *The Development of Speech Perception: The Transition from Speech Sounds to Spoken Words.* Cambridge, MA: MIT Press, pp. 167–224.

Cutler, A., J. Mehler, D. Norris, and J. Segui. (1987). Phoneme identification and the lexicon. *Cognitive Psychology* 19: 141–177.

Diehl, R. L., and K. R. Kluender. (1989). On the objects of speech perception. *Ecological Psychology* 1: 121–144.

Eimas, P. D., E. R. Siqueland, P. Jusczyk, and J. Vigorito. (1971). Speech perception in infants. *Science* 171: 303–306.

Fowler, C. A. (1986). An event approach to the study of speech perception from a direct-realist perspective. *Journal of Phonetics* 14: 3–28.

Ganong, W. F., III. (1980). Phonetic categorization in auditory word perception. *Journal of Experimental Psychology: Human Perception and Performance* 6: 110–125.

Jusczyk, P. W. (1993). From general to language-specific capacities: the WRAPSA model of how speech perception develops. *Journal of Phonetics* 21: 3–28.

Jusczyk, P. W. (1995). Language acquisition: Speech sounds and the beginning of phonology. In J. L. Miller and P. D. Eimas, Eds., *Speech, Language, and Communication.* San Diego, CA: Academic Press, pp. 263–301.

Kuhl, P. K. (1979). Speech perception in early infancy: Perceptual constancy for spectrally dissimilar vowel categories. *Journal of the Acoustical Society of America* 66: 1668–1679.

Kuhl, P. K. (1993). Innate predispositions and the effects of experience in speech perception: The native language magnet theory. In B. de Boysson-Bardies, S. de Schonen, P. Jusczyk, P. McNeilage, and J. Morton, Eds., *Developmental Neurocognition: Speech and Face Processing in the First Year of Life.* Dordrecht: Kluwer, pp. 259–274.

Liberman, A. M., F. S. Cooper, D. P. Shankweiler, and M. Studdert-Kennedy. (1967). Perception of the speech code. *Psychological Review* 74: 431–461.

Liberman, A. M., and I. G. Mattingly. (1985). The motor theory of speech perception revised. *Cognition* 21: 1–36.

Lisker, L. (1986). "Voicing" in English: A catalogue of acoustic features signaling /b/ versus /p/ in trochees. *Language and Speech* 29: 3–11.

McClelland, J. L., and J. L. Elman. (1986). The TRACE model of speech perception. *Cognitive Psychology* 18: 1–86.

Mehler, J., P. Jusczyk, G. Lambertz, N. Halsted, J. Bertoncini, and C. Amiel-Tison. (1988). A precursor of language acquisition in young infants. *Cognition* 29: 143–178.

Miller, J. L. (1981). Effects of speaking rate on segmental distinctions. In P. D. Eimas and J. L. Miller, Eds., *Perspectives on the Study of Speech.* Hillsdale, NJ: Erlbaum, pp. 39–74.

Miller, J. L., and P. D. Eimas. (1995). Speech perception: From signal to word. *Annual Review of Psychology* 46: 467–492.

Nearey, T. M. (1989). Static, dynamic, and relational properties in vowel perception. *Journal of the Acoustical Society of America* 85: 2088–2113.

Nygaard, L. C., and D. B. Pisoni. (1995). Speech perception: New directions in research and theory. In J. L. Miller and P. D. Eimas, Eds., *Speech, Language, and Communication.* San Diego, CA: Academic Press, pp. 63–96.

Pastore, R. E. (1987). Categorical perception: Some psychophysical models. In S. Harnad, Ed., *Categorical Perception: The Groundwork of Cognition.* Cambridge: Cambridge University Press, pp. 29–52.

Remez, R. E. (1994). A guide to research on the perception of speech. In M. A. Gernsbacher, Ed., *Handbook of Psycholinguistics.* San Diego, CA: Academic Press, pp. 145–172.

Stevens, K. N., and S. E. Blumstein. (1981). The search for invariant acoustic correlates of phonetic features. In P. D. Eimas and J. L. Miller, Eds., *Perspectives on the Study of Speech.* Hillsdale, NJ: Erlbaum, pp. 1–38.

Werker, J. F., and J. E. Pegg. (1992). Infant speech perception and phonological acquisition. In C. A. Ferguson, L. Menn, and C. Stoel-Gammon, Eds., *Phonological Development: Models, Research, Implications.* Timonium, MD: York Press, pp. 285–311.

Further Readings

Best, C. T., G. W. McRoberts, and N. M. Sithole. (1988). Examination of perceptual reorganization for nonnative speech contrasts: Zulu click discrimination by English-speaking adults and infants. *Journal of Experimental Psychology: Human Perception and Performance* 14: 345–360.

Connine, C. M., and C. Clifton, Jr. (1987). Interactive use of lexical information in speech perception. *Journal of Experimental Psychology: Human Perception and Performance* 13: 291–299.

Eimas, P. D. (1997). Infant speech perception: Processing characteristics, representational units, and the learning of words. In R. L. Goldstone, P. G. Schyns, and D. L. Medin, Eds., *The Psychology of Learning and Motivation,* vol. 36. San Diego, CA: Academic Press, pp. 127–169.

Eimas, P. D., and J. D. Corbit. (1973). Selective adaptation of linguistic feature detectors. *Cognitive Psychology* 4: 99–109.

Juscyzk, P. W. (1997). *The Discovery of Spoken Language.* Cambridge, MA: MIT Press.

Klatt, D. H. (1979). Speech perception: A model of acoustic-phonetic analysis and lexical access. *Journal of Phonetics* 7: 279–312.

Kuhl, P. K. (1991). Human adults and human infants show a "perceptual magnet effect" for the prototypes of speech categories, monkeys do not. *Perception and Psychophysics* 50: 93–107.

Kuhl, P. K., and A. N. Meltzoff. (1982). The bimodal perception of speech in infancy. *Science* 218: 1138–1141.

Kuhl, P. K., K. A. Williams, F. Lacerda, K. N. Stevens, and B. Lindblom. (1992). Linguistic experience alters phonetic perception in infants by 6 months of age. *Science* 255: 606–608.

Miller, J. L. (1994). On the internal structure of phonetic categories: a progress report. *Cognition* 50: 271–285.

Miller, J. L., and P. D. Eimas. (1983). Studies on the categorization of speech by infants. *Cognition* 13: 135–165.

Oden, G. C., and D. W. Massaro. (1978). Integration of featural information in speech perception. *Psychological Review* 85: 172–191.

Perkell, J. S., and D. H. Klatt, Eds. (1986). *Invariance and Variability in Speech Processes.* Hillsdale, NJ: Erlbaum.

Pisoni, D. B., and P. A. Luce. (1987). Acoustic-phonetic representations in word recognition. *Cognition* 25: 21–52.

Pitt, M. A., and A. G. Samuel. (1993). An empirical and meta-analytic evaluation of the phoneme identification task. *Journal of Experimental Psychology: Human Perception and Performance* 19: 699–725.

Remez, R. E., P. E. Rubin, S. M. Berns, J. S. Pardo, and J. M. Lang. (1994). On the perceptual organization of speech. *Psychological Review* 101: 129–156.

Samuel, A. G. (1981). Phonemic restoration: Insights from a new methodology. *Journal of Experimental Psychology: General* 110: 474–494.

Strange, W. (1989). Evolving theories of vowel perception. *Journal of the Acoustical Society of America* 85: 2081–2087.

Studdert-Kennedy, M., and D. Shankweiler. (1970). Hemispheric specialization for speech perception. *Journal of the Acoustical Society of America* 48: 579–594.

Summerfield, Q. (1987). Some preliminaries to a comprehensive account of audio-visual speech perception. In B. Dodd and R. Campbell, Eds., *Hearing by Eye: The Psychology of Lip-Reading.* Hillsdale, NJ: Erlbaum, pp. 3–51.

Sussman, H. M. (1989). Neural coding of relational invariance in speech: Human language analogs to the barn owl. *Psychological Review* 96: 631–642.

Werker, J. F., and R. C. Tees. (1984). Cross-language speech perception: Evidence for perceptual reorganization during the first year of life. *Infant Behavior and Development* 7: 49–63.

Speech Recognition in Machines

Over the past several decades, a need has arisen to enable humans to communicate with machines in order to control their actions or to obtain information. Initial attempts at providing human-machine communications led to the development of the keyboard, the mouse, the trackball, the touch-screen, and the joystick. However none of these communication devices provides the richness or the ease of use of speech, which has been the most natural form of communication between humans for tens of centuries. Hence a need has arisen to provide a voice interface between humans and machines. This need has been met, to a limited extent, by speech-processing systems that enable a machine to speak (speech synthesis systems) and that enable a machine to understand (speech recognition systems) human speech. We concentrate on speech recognition systems in this section.

Speech recognition by machine refers to the capability of a machine to convert human speech to a textual form, providing a transcription or interpretation of everything the human speaks while the machine is listening. This capability is required for tasks in which the human is controlling the actions of the machine using only limited speaking capability, such as while speaking simple commands or sequences of words from a limited vocabulary (e.g., digit sequences for a telephone number). In the more general case, usually referred to as *speech understanding,* the machine need only reliably recognize a limited subset of the user input speech—namely, the parts of the speech that specify enough about the action requested so that the machine can either respond appropriately or initiate some action in response to what was understood.

Speech recognition systems have been deployed in applications ranging from control of desktop computers, to telecommunication services, to business services.

The earliest approaches to speech recognition were based on finding speech sounds and providing appropriate labels to these sounds. This is the basis of the *acoustic-phonetic* approach (Hemdal and Hughes 1967), which postulates that there exist finite, distinctive phonetic units (phonemes) in spoken language and that these units are broadly characterized by a set of acoustic properties that are manifest in the speech signal over time. Even though the acoustic properties of phonetic units are highly variable, both with speakers and with neighboring sounds (the so-called coarticulation effect), it is assumed in the acoustic-phonetic approach that the rules governing the variability are straightforward and can be readily learned (by a machine).

The first step in the acoustic-phonetic approach is a spectral analysis of the speech combined with a feature detection that converts the spectral measurements to a set of features that describe the broad acoustic properties of the different phonetic units.

The next step is a segmentation and labeling phase in which the speech signal is segmented into stable acoustic regions, followed by attaching one or more phonetic labels to each segmented region, resulting in a phoneme lattice characterization of the speech. The last step in this approach attempts to determine a valid word (or string of words) from the phonetic label sequences produced by the segmentation to labeling. In the validation process, linguistic constraints on the task (i.e., the vocabulary, the syntax, and other semantic rules) are invoked in order to access the lexicon for word decoding based on the phoneme lattice. The acoustic-phonetic approach has not been widely used in most commercial applications.

The *pattern-matching approach* (Itakura 1975; Rabiner 1989; Rabiner and Juang 1993) involves two essential steps—namely, pattern training and pattern comparison. The essential feature of this approach is that it uses a well-formulated mathematical framework and establishes con-sistent speech-pattern representations, for reliable pattern comparison, from a set of labeled training samples via a formal training algorithm. A speech-pattern representation can be in the form of a speech template or a statistical model (e.g., a HIDDEN MARKOV MODEL or HMM) and can be applied to a sound (smaller than a word), a word, or a phrase. In the pattern-comparison stage

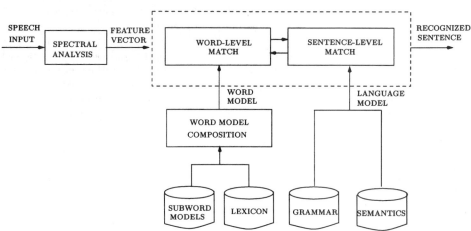

CONTINUOUS SENTENCE RECOGNIZER

of the approach, a direct comparison is made between the unknown speech (the speech to be recognized) with each possible pattern learned in the training stage in order to determine the identity of the unknown according to the goodness of match of the patterns. The pattern-matching approach has become the predominant method of speech recognition in the last decade.

The *artificial intelligence approach* (Lesser et al. 1975; Lippmann 1987) attempts to mechanize the recognition procedure according to the way a person applies intelligence in visualizing, analyzing, and characterizing speech based on a set of measured acoustic features. Among the techniques used within this class of methods are use of an expert system (e.g., a neural network) that integrates phonemic, lexical, syntactic, semantic, and even pragmatic knowledge for segmentation and labeling, and uses tools such as artificial NEURAL NETWORKS for learning the relationships among phonetic events. The focus in this approach has been mostly in the representation of knowledge and integration of knowledge sources. This method has not been used widely in commercial systems.

A block diagram of a complete system for *large vocabulary speech recognition* (Lee, Rabiner, and Pieraccini 1992; Jelinek 1985; Baker 1990) based on the pattern-matching approach is shown in Figure 1. The first step in the processing is spectral analysis to derive the feature vector used to characterize the spectral properties of the speech input. The second step in the recognizer is a combined word-level/sentence-level matching procedure. The way this is accomplished is as follows. Using a set of subword models (phoneme-like units) along with a word lexicon, a set of word models is created by concatenating each of the subword models as specified by the word lexicon. The word-level match procedure provides scores for individual words as specified by the sentence-level match procedure (which uses a word grammar—the syntax of the system) and the semantics (which specifies valid sentences in the task language). The final result is the sentence that provides the best match to the speech input according to the word vocabulary, task syntax, and task grammar.

Table 1 illustrates current capabilities in continuous speech recognition for three distinct and rather simple tasks—namely, database access (Resource Management), natural language queries (ATIS) for air-travel reservations, and read text from a set of business publications (NAB). The task syntax is the system grammar (or language model) and is realized as one of a finite-state word-pair grammar, a word-trigram grammar, or a five-gram word grammar. The systems all run in a speaker independent (SI) mode with either fluently read speech or naturally spoken dialogue.

It can be seen from Table 1 that for tasks with medium size vocabularies (1000–2500 words) and with language perplexities (average word-branching factors) significantly below that of natural language speech (perplexity of 100–200), word-error rates below 5 are easily obtainable with modern technology. Such systems could actually be utilized in limited (controlled) user environments and could be designed to work rather well. On the other hand, for more complex tasks like NAB with a 60,000-word vocabulary and perplexity comparable to that of natural-language speech, word-error rates exceed 10, thereby making these systems almost unusable in practical environments.

Table 1. Performance of continuous-speech recognition systems

Task	Syntax	Mode	Vocabulary	Word Error Rate
Resource Management (DARPA)	Finite State Grammar (Perplexity = 60)	SI Fluent Read Input	1000 Words	4.4%
Air Travel Information System (ATIS-DARPA)	Backoff Trigram (Perplexity = 18)	SI Natural Language	2500 Words	3.6%
North American Business (NAB) (DARPA)	Backoff 5-gram (Perplexity = 173)	SI Fluent Read Input	60000 Words	10.8%

Speech recognition has been successfully applied in a range of systems. We categorize these applications into five broad classes.

1. *Office or business system*   Typical applications include data entry onto forms, database management and control, keyboard enhancement, and dictation. Examples of voice-activated dictation machines include the IBM Via Voice system and the Dragon Dictate system.
2. *Manufacturing*   ASR is used to provide "eyes-free, hands-free" monitoring of manufacturing processes (e.g., parts inspection) for quality control.
3. *Telephone or telecommunications*   Applications include automation of operator-assisted services (the Voice Recognition Call Processing system by AT&T to automate operator service routing according to call types), inbound and outbound telemarketing, information services (the ANSER system by NTT for limited home-banking services, the stock-price quotation system by Bell Northern Research, Universal Card services by Conversant/AT&T for account information retrieval), voice dialing by name/number (AT&T VoiceLine, 800 Voice Calling services, Conversant FlexWord, etc.), directory-assistance call completion, catalog ordering, and telephone calling feature enhancements (AT&T VIP—Voice Interactive Phone for easy activation of advanced calling features such as call waiting, call forwarding, and so on by voice rather than by keying in the code sequences).
4. *Medical*   The application is primarily in voice creation and editing of specialized medical reports (e.g., Kurzweil's system).
5. *Other*   This category includes voice-controlled and -operated toys and games, aids for the handicapped, and voice control of nonessential functions in moving vehicles (such as climate control and the audio system).

For the most part, machines have been successful in recognizing carefully articulated and read speech. Spontaneous human conversation has proven to be much more difficult a task. Recent performance evaluations using speech recorded off a radio station, as well as from monitoring speech of family members talking over conventional telephone lines, shows word-error rates of from 27 to upwards of 50. These high word-error rates are an indication of how much more must be learned before machines are truly capable of recognizing human conversational speech.

See also NATURAL LANGUAGE GENERATION; NATURAL LANGUAGE PROCESSING; SPEECH PERCEPTION; SPEECH SYNTHESIS

—*Lawrence Rabiner*

References

Baker, J. M. (1990). Large vocabulary speech recognition prototype. *Proc. DARPA Speech and Natural Language Workshop*, pp. 414–415.

Hemdal, J. F., and G. W. Hughes. (1967). A feature based computer recognition program for the modeling of vowel perception. In W. Wathen-Dunn, Ed., *Models for the Perception of Speech and Visual Form*. Cambridge, MA: MIT Press.

Itakura, F. (1975). Minimum prediction residual principle applied to speech recognition. *IEEE Trans. Acoustics, Speech, and Signal Processing* ASSP-23: 57–72.

Jelinek, F. (1985). The development of an experimental discrete dictation recognizer. *IEEE Proceedings* 73(11): 1616–1624.

Lee, C. H., L. R. Rabiner, and R. Pieraccini. (1992). Speaker independent continuous speech recognition using continuous density hidden Markov models. In P. Laface and R. DeMori, Eds., *Proc. NATO-ASI, Speech Recognition and Understanding: Recent Advances, Trends and Applications*. Cetraro, Italy: Springer, pp. 135–163.

Lesser, V. R., R. D. Fennell, L. D. Erman, and D. R. Reddy. (1975). Organization of the Hearsay-II Speech Understanding System. *IEEE Trans. Acoustics, Speech, and Signal Processing* ASSP-23(1): 11–23.

Lippmann, R. (1987). An introduction to computing with neural networks. *IEEE ASSP Magazine* 4(2): 4–22.

Rabiner, L. R. (1989). A tutorial on hidden Markov models and selected applications in speech recognition. *Proc.* IEEE 77(2): 257–286.

Rabiner, L. R., and B. H. Juang. (1993). *Fundamentals of Speech Recognition*. Englewood Cliffs, NJ: Prentice-Hall.

Speech Synthesis

The history of "speaking machines" goes back at least to the work of Wolfgang von Kempelen in 1791, but until the advent of the digital computer all such devices required a human operator to "play" them, rather like a musical instrument. Perhaps the best known machine of this sort was Homer Dudley's VODER, which was demonstrated at the 1939 World's Fair.

Modern speech synthesis programs, of course, can produce speechlike output on the basis of symbolic input, with no further intervention. When the symbolic input to such a program is ordinary text, the program is often called a text-to-speech (TTS) system. Most TTS systems can be viewed as having two fairly distinct halves: a first stage that analyzes the text and transforms it into some form of annotated phonetic transcription, and a second stage, which is often thought of as synthesis proper, which produces a sound wave from the phonetic transcription.

Programs that generate their own sentences, for example, automated information systems, can produce synthesizer input directly and avoid the difficulties of textual analysis. There is, at the beginning of 1998, no standard format for synthesizer input, and most systems have their own ad hoc notations. There is a move toward the development of standardized speech markup languages, on the model of text markup languages like LaTex and HTML, but considerable work remains to be done.

Text analysis in TTS systems serves two primary purposes: (1) specifying the pronunciations of individual words and (2) gathering information to guide phrasing and placement of pitch accents (see PROSODY AND INTONATION).

Word pronunciations can be looked up in dictionaries, generated by spelling-to-sound rules, or produced through a combination of the two. The feasibility of relying on spelling-to-sound rules varies from language to language. Any language will need at least a small dictionary of exceptions. English spelling is sufficiently problematic that current practice is to have a dictionary with tens of thousands—or even hundreds of thousands—of entries, and to use rules only for words that do not occur in the dictionary and cannot be formed by regular morphological processes from words that do occur. Systems vary in the extent to which they use morphology. Some systems attempt to store all forms of all words that they may be called on to pronounce. The MITalk system had a dictionary of orthographic word fragments called "morphs" and applied rules to specify the ways in which their pronunciations were affected when they were combined into words.

The parsing and morphological analysis (see NATURAL LANGUAGE PROCESSING and MORPHOLOGY) techniques used in text processing for text-to-speech are similar to those used elsewhere in computational linguistics. One reason for parsing text in text-to-speech is that the part of speech assignment performed in the course of parsing can disambiguate homographs—forms like the verb *to lead* and the noun *lead,* or the present and past tenses of the verb *to read,* which are spelled the same but pronounced differently. The other main reason is that it is possible to formulate default rules for placement of pitch accents and phrase boundaries on the basis of syntax. On the basis of such rules, markers can be placed in the annotated phonetic output of the text analysis stage that instruct the synthesis component to vary vocal pitch and introduce correlates of phrasing, such as pauses and lengthening of sounds at the ends of phrases. Such default rules tend to yield the rather unnatural and mechanical effect generally associated with synthetic speech, and improving the quality of synthetic prosody is one of the major items on the research agenda for speech synthesis.

Synthesis proper can itself be broken into two stages, the first of which produces a numerical/physical description of a sound wave, and the second of which converts the description to sound. In some cases, the sound is stored in the computer as a digitized wave form, to be played out through a general purpose digital to analog converter, whereas in other cases, the numerical/physical description is fed to special purpose hardware, which plays the sound directly without storing a waveform.

Synthesizers can be distinguished in two primary ways according to the nature of the numerical/physical description they employ, and the manner in which they construct it. These distinctions are *acoustic vs. articulatory* and *stored unit vs. target interpolation.* The two distinctions are largely independent and any of the four possibilities they offer is in principle possible, but in practice articulatory synthesizers use target interpolation.

The acoustic vs. articulatory distinction depends on whether numerical/physical descriptions describe sounds or vocal tract shapes. In the acoustic case, converting the description to sound essentially means creating a sound that fits the description, and there are usually efficient algorithms to do the job. In the second case, the computation involves simulating the propagation of sound through a vocal tract of the given description. This requires a great deal more computation. Articulatory synthesis remains a research activity and is not used in practical applications. Formant synthesis, linear prediction synthesis, sinewave synthesis, and waveform concatenation are common forms of acoustic synthesis. The acoustic vs. articulatory distinction is to some extent blurred by systems such as YorkTalk that arrive at a (formant based) acoustic description by way of an intermediate articulatory feature level.

In target interpolation, descriptions of complete utterances are built up by establishing target values to be achieved during phonetic units (see PHONETICS) and then, as the term suggests, interpolating between the targets. The first synthesizers capable of producing intelligible renditions of a wide range of sentences, such as the JSRU synthesizer of John Holmes, Ignatius Mattingly, and John Shearme, and KlattTalk, were of this type, with formant values as targets.

The transitions between relatively stable regions of sound in natural speech are in fact very complex and difficult to model through interpolation. An alternative is to store the descriptions of whole stretches of speech, including the difficult transitions. This is the basis of *stored unit synthesis.* One popular unit is the diphone, which is essentially the transition between one stable region and the next. Many of the present generation of good quality commercial synthesizers use diphones. Other units in current use are demi syllables, syllables plus affixes, and units of varying length chosen on the spot from a large speech database to build a particular utterance.

Nearly all systems adopt the simplifying assumption that the aspects of speech dependent on the activity of the larynx —vocal pitch and much of what is often considered voice quality—can be modeled independently from the aspects dependent on mouth shape, which determine what phonemes, and hence what words are produced. In articulatory synthesis, this comes naturally in the form of separate modeling of separate articulators. In acoustic synthesis it is often done using Gunnar Fant's source-filter model of speech production, where the speech is modeled as the result of passing a sound corresponding to the larynx contribution through a filter corresponding to the mouth shape. Formant synthesis and linear prediction are based on the source filter model, but the more recently developed PSOLA and sinewave methods are not.

See also ARTICULATION; PHONOLOGY; LANGUAGE PRODUCTION; SPEECH RECOGNITION IN MACHINES; STATISTICAL TECHNIQUES IN NATURAL LANGUAGE PROCESSING

—*Stephen Isard*

References

Allen, J., S. Hunnicut, and D. H. Klatt. (1987). *From Text to Speech: The MITalk System.* Cambridge: Cambridge University Press.

Bailly, G., and C. Benoit, Eds. (1992). *Talking Machines, Theories, Models and Designs.* Amsterdam: Elsevier Science/North-Holland.

Dutoit, T. (1997). *An Introduction to Text-to-Speech Synthesis.* Dordrecht: Kluwer.

Holmes, J. N., I. G. Mattingly, and J. N. Shearme. (1964). Speech synthesis by rule. *Language and Speech* 7: 127–143.

Klatt, D. H. (1980). Software for a cascade/parallel formant synthesizer. *Journal of the Acoustical Society of America* 67: 971–995.

Klatt, D. H. (1987). Review of *Text-To-Speech Conversion for English. Journal of the Acoustical Society of America* 82: 737–793.

Linggard, R. (1985). *Electronic Synthesis of Speech.* Cambridge: Cambridge University Press.

O'Shaughnessy, D. (1987). *Speech Communication*. Reading, MA: Addison Wesley.

Sproat, R., Ed. (1998). *Multilingual Text-to-Speech Synthesis: The Bell Labs Approach*. Dordrecht: Kluwer.

van Santen, J. P. H., R. W. Sproat, J. P. Olive, and J. Hirschberg. (1996). *Progress in Speech Synthesis*. New York: Springer.

Witten, I. H. (1982). *Principles of Computer Speech*. New York: Academic Press.

Sperry, Roger Wolcott

Roger Wolcott Sperry (1913–1994), who received the Nobel Prize in Physiology and Medicine in 1981, made pathfinding contributions to the sciences of brain and mind through half a century. His experiments on nerve regeneration, on cortical mechanisms of perception and learning in split-brain cats and monkeys, and on hemispheric modes of consciousness in commissurotomy patients, display outstanding creativity and skill. The intrinsic factors of nerve net patterning and in psychological action and awareness that Sperry discovered are fundamental to cognitive science.

Mastery of his scientific vocation came quickly for Roger Sperry. While an english literature major at Oberlin, he chose a masters project with R. H. Stetson, an expert on timing in speech and music. Sperry's first paper on this myographic analysis of arm movements appeared in 1939. He proved that each time the subject repeated the same circle in space, electrical activity appeared in different muscles. The constancy of movement implied an internal image of the circular act. That year, with Paul Weiss at Chicago, Sperry published his Ph.D. abstract on the behavioral effects of surgical transposition of hindlimb muscles in rats. Within three years he had tested motor nerve regeneration in rats and monkeys, noting important species differences in motor plasticity. He also began experiments with newts that brought international renown, on growth of eye-to-brain connections after surgical rotations of the eyes (Evarts 1990). Results proved that chemical markers, previously envisaged by developmental studies of Ramon y CAJAL, Harrison, and Langley, were guiding prefunctional visual projections, even when rearranged eye-to-body relations produced totally nonfunctional reactions to stimuli (Hunt and Cowan 1990). This radically qualified prevailing theories of the construction of functional brain circuits by learning.

Experiments with optic nerve regeneration in fish after eye rotation uncovered a central patterning of movements that Sperry (1950) named "corollary discharge from efference." Independently, von Holst and Mittelstaedt in Germany had seen the same phenomenon, labeling it the "reafference principle." This proved a neural basis for the psychological fact that formulation of a motor purpose transforms processing of perceptual information. Sperry and the German scientists fully appreciated its importance in explaining the perceptual constancies, and the stability of the world seen by a moving eye. Current motor imagery theory identifies intrinsic processes defining the space-time frame for experience (Jeannerod 1994). Sperry's motor theory of perception made the same point.

In an influential paper, "Neurology and the Mind-Brain Problem," Sperry took the position that preoccupation with input to perception and cognition, disregarding constraints imposed by prewired motives or prospective MOTOR CONTROL, often leads psychology into arcane and unprofitable theorizing (Sperry 1952). His concept of biological determination of functional perceptual-motor systems met with resistance from the behaviorist psychology of his day. How he overcame this, and the strength of his evidence for chemical guidance of regenerating nerve fibers, has been reviewed recently (Evarts 1990; Levi-Montalcini 1990; Hunt and Cowan 1990). Now Sperry's principle of "chemo-affinity" as a constraining factor mapping both nerve cell interactions in the embryo and nerve tract regeneration in lower vertebrates (Sperry 1963) is beyond contention, despite powerful abstract theories developed to model order emerging in complex nonlinear dynamic systems of nerve cells, axonal and dendritic branches, and synapses, and evidence for selective retention of these elements under the validation of environmental input. Emergent order and selection create new functions, but these carry the imprint of the constraints of cell-to-cell communication set up prefunctionally in the embryo.

Surgical skills that he developed in operating on small fish enabled Sperry to attempt direct interference with corticocortical circuits in the cat by delicate subpial slicing of white matter to test various "field" theories of form perception. He proved that high-acuity vision of form must involve fiber loops leaving and returning to the cortex. Then, his interest in intrinsic whole-brain function in awareness led, by elegant logic, to division of the corpus callosum, the major axonal bridge between cortical circuits in the two cerebral hemispheres that mediate ideation and conscious guidance of purposes. Split-brain studies of cats and monkeys demonstrated that awareness and learning could be surgically bisected. They also showed that the aim of attention and voluntary responses around the subject's body, and their evolution in time, invoked a great array of structures, including undivided brain stem mechanisms (Sperry 1961).

Later, with the clinical application of commissurotomy to treat multifocal epilepsy, the split-brain approach was extended to human patients, opening the way to tests of active rational consciousnesses in left and right hemispheres, their convergent influence over acts and ideas of the whole person, and the role of language (Sperry, Gazzaniga, and Bogen 1969; Levy 1990). This research brought dramatic scientific confirmation of Sperry's theory of the causal potency of conscious ideas and beliefs. Commissurotomy research at CalTech boosted neuropsychological analysis of hemispheric differences, and, by clarifying the special modes of processing in isolated cortical territories, prompted the "cognitive revolution" of the 1960s (Sperry 1993).

In his scientific work Sperry had an idealist impulse that led him beyond searching for motive principles in awareness. In the 1960s, he formulated a philosophy of natural humanistic values, and enunciated ethical principles that recognize the innate causal power of human consciousness, for both good and ill (Sperry 1965, 1983). In the last ten years, 95 percent of his publications were on these more philosophical matters. Sperry claimed that his theory of "downward causation" or "macro-determinism" gave a new

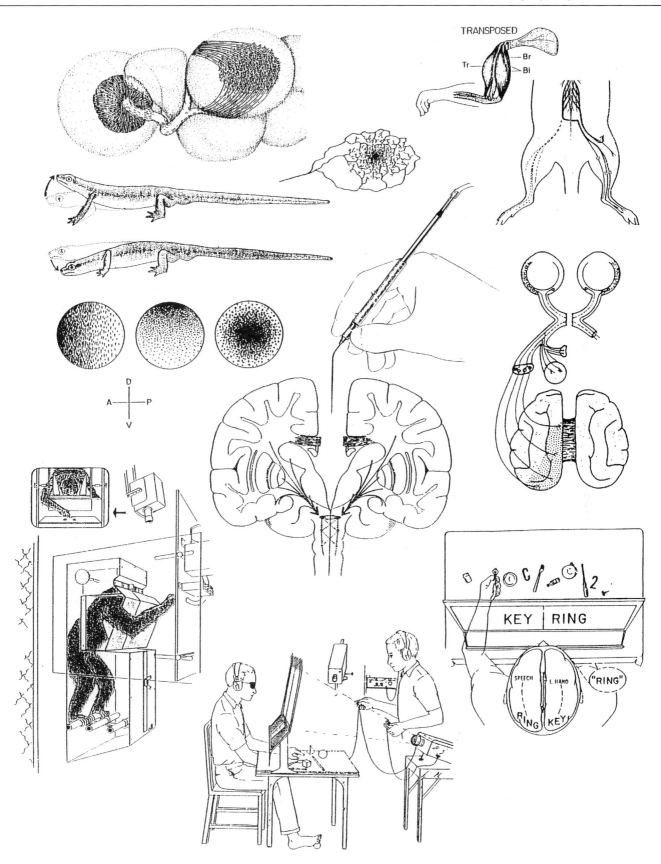

Figure 1. Selected drawings from articles by Roger Sperry, illustrating phases of his scientific career.

paradigm for resolving tensions between science and religion. At first, scientific colleagues thought he strayed from objectivity, but now it is clear that he foresaw the need for a larger perspective on brain activities at their highest level of organization, in human purposes, ideas, and beliefs. The foray into ethics and issues of values in policy and practice now seems prophetic. It is now far from strange to insist that a science of values is necessary.

Sperry's achievements depended on skills he showed in his earliest research—incisive anatomical logic, imagination for the inner dynamics of psychological action, and a gift for clear writing. Sperry's psychobiology was perfectly balanced between the hard anatomical and physiological facts of the brain in communication with the freely moving body, and an imaginative, creative psychology of the mind, with all of its ethical implications. This balance he described as a "monist" position, mind and matter as inseparable parts of natural psychological processes, and he worked tirelessly to explain his view of the continuity between everyday phenomena of consciousness and the matter of the brain that scientists observe.

See also EMERGENTISM; HEMISPHERIC SPECIALIZATION

—Colwyn Trevarthen

References

Evarts, E. V. (1990). Foreword: Coordination of movement as a key to higher brain function: Roger W. Sperry's contributions from 1939 to 1952. In C. Trevarthen, Ed., *Brain Circuits and Functions of the Mind: Essays in Honor of Roger W. Sperry.* New York: Cambridge University Press, pp. xiii–xxvi.

Hunt, R. K., and W. M. Cowan. (1990). The chemoaffinity hypothesis: An appreciation of Roger W. Sperry's contributions to developmental biology. In C. Trevarthen, Ed., *Brain Circuits and Functions of the Mind: Essays in Honor of Roger W. Sperry.* New York: Cambridge University Press, pp. 19–74.

Jeannerod, M. (1994). The representing brain: Neural correlates of motor intention and imagery. *Behavioral and Brain Sciences* 17: 187–245.

Levi-Montalcini, R. (1990). Ontogenesis of neural nets: the chemoaffinity theory, 1963–1983. In C. Trevarthen, Ed., *Brain Circuits and Functions of the Mind: Essays in Honor of Roger W. Sperry.* New York: Cambridge University Press, pp. 3–18.

Levy, J. (1990). Regulation and generation of perception in the asymmetric brain. In C. Trevarthen, Ed., *Brain Circuits and Functions of the Mind: Essays in Honor of Roger W. Sperry.* New York: Cambridge University Press, pp. 231–248.

Sperry, R. W. (1950). Neural basis of the spontaneous optokinetic response produced by visual inversion. *Journal of Comparative and Physiological Psychology* 43: 483–489.

Sperry, R. W. (1952). Neurology and the mind-brain problem. *American Scientist* 40: 291–312.

Sperry, R. W. (1961). Cerebral organization and behavior. *Science* 133: 1749–1757.

Sperry, R. W. (1963). Chemoaffinity in the orderly growth of nerve fiber patterns and connections. *Proceedings of the National Academy of Sciences* 50: 703–710.

Sperry, R. W. (1965). Mind, brain and humanist values. In J. R. Platt, Ed., *New Views on the Nature of Man.* Chicago: University of Chicago Press, pp. 71–92.

Sperry, R. W. (1983). *Science and Moral Priority.* New York: Columbia University Press.

Sperry, R. W. (1993). The impact and promise of the cognitive revolution. *American Psychologist* 48(3): 878–885.

Sperry, R. W., M. S. Gazzaniga, and J. E. Bogen. (1969). Interhemispheric relationships: The neocortical commissures; syndromes of hemisphere disconnection. In P. J. Vinken, and G. W. Bruyn, Eds., *Handbook of Clinical Neurology,* vol. 4. Amsterdam: North Holland, pp. 273–290.

Further Readings

Sperry, R. W. (1945). The problem of central nervous reorganization after nerve regeneration and muscle transposition. *Quarterly Review of Biology* 20: 311–369.

Sperry, R. W. (1958). Physiological plasticity and brain circuit theory. In H. F. Harlow and C. N. Woolsey, Eds., *Biological and Biochemical Bases of Behavior.* Madison: University of Wisconsin Press, pp. 401–421.

Sperry, R. W. (1959). The growth of nerve circuits. *Scientific American* 201: 68–75.

Sperry, R. W. (1964). Problems outstanding in the evolution of brain function: James Arthur lecture on the evolution of the human brain. In R. Duncan and M. Weston-Smith, Eds., *American Museum of Natural History and the Encyclopedia of Ignorance.* Oxford: Pergamon Press.

Sperry, R. W. (1964). The great cerebral commissure. *Scientific American* 210: 42–52.

Sperry, R. W. (1965). Embryogenesis of behavioral nerve nets. In R. L. Dehaan and H. Ursprung, Eds., *Organogenesis.* New York: Holt, Rinehart and Winston, pp. 161–185.

Sperry, R. W. (1968). Mental unity following surgical disconnection of the cerebral hemispheres. *The Harvey Lectures, 1966–1967.* (Series 62). New York: Academic Press, pp. 293–323.

Sperry, R. W. (1969). A modified concept of consciousness. *Psychological Reviews* 76: 532–536.

Sperry, R. W. (1970). Perception in absence of the neocortical commissures. *Research Publications of the Association for Research in Nervous and Mental Diseases* 48: 123–138.

Sperry, R. W. (1974). Lateral specialization in the surgically separated hemispheres. In F. Schmitt and F. Worden, Eds., *The Neurosciences. Third Study Program.* Cambridge, MA: MIT Press, pp. 5–19.

Sperry, R. W. (1974). Science and the problem of values. *Zygon* 9: 7–21.

Sperry, R. W. (1977). Forebrain commissurotomy and conscious awareness. *Journal of Medical Philosophy* 2(2): 101–126.

Sperry, R. W. (1982). Some effects of disconnecting the cerebral hemispheres. Nobel lecture. *Science* 217: 1223–1226.

Sperry, R. W. (1984). Consciousness, personal identity and the divided brain. *Neuropsychologia* 22(6): 661–673.

Sperry, R. W. (1987). Consciousness and causality. In R. L. Gregory, Ed., *Oxford Companion to the Mind.* Oxford: Oxford University Press, pp. 164–166.

Sperry, R. W. (1988). Psychology's mentalist paradigm and the religion/science tension. *American Psychologist* 43(8): 607–613.

Sperry, R. W. (1992). Paradigms of belief, theory and metatheory. *Zygon* 27: 245–259.

Spoken-Word Recognition

Listening to speech is a recognition process: SPEECH PERCEPTION identifies phonetic structure in the incoming speech signal, allowing the signal to be mapped onto representations of known words in the listener's LEXICON. Several facts about spoken-word recognition make it a challenging research area of PSYCHOLINGUISTICS. First, the process takes place in time—words are not heard all at once but from beginning to end. Second, words are rarely heard in isolation but rather within longer utterances, and there is no reliable equivalent in speech of the helpful white spaces that demarcate individual words in a printed text such as this article. Thus the process entails an operation of segmentation whereby continuous speech is effectively divided into the portions that correspond to individual words. Third, spoken words are not highly distinctive; language vocabularies of tens of thousands of words are constructed from a repertoire of on average only 30 to 40 phonemes (Maddieson 1984; see PHONOLOGY for further detail). As a consequence, words tend to resemble other words, and may have other words embedded within them (thus *steak* contains possible pronunciations of *stay* and *take* and *ache,* it resembles *state* and *snake* and *stack,* it occurs embedded within possible pronunciations of *mistake* or *first acre,* and so on). How do listeners know when to recognize *steak* and when not?

Methods for the laboratory study of spoken-word recognition are comprehensively reviewed by Grosjean and Frauenfelder (1996). This field of study is very active, but it began in earnest only in the 1970s; before then, models of word recognition such as Morton's (1969) *logogen* model were not specifically designed to deal with the characteristics of speech. Now, spoken-word recognition research is heavily model-driven, and the models differ, inter alia, as to which of the above challenges they primarily address. The first model specifically in this area was Marslen-Wilson and Welsh's (1978) *cohort* model; it focused on the temporal nature of spoken-word recognition and proposed that the initial portion of an incoming word would activate all known words beginning in that way, with this "cohort" of activated word candidates gradually being reduced as candidates incompatible with later-arriving portions of the word drop out. Thus /s/ could activate *sad, psychology, steak,* and so on; if the next phoneme were /t/, only words beginning with /st/ (*stay, steak, stupid,* etc.) would remain activated; and so on until only one word remained in the cohort. This could occur before the end of the word—thus *staple* could be identified by the /p/ because no other English words would remain in the cohort.

The *neighborhood activation model* (Luce, Pisoni, and Goldinger 1990) concentrates on similarities between words in the vocabulary and proposes that the probability of a word being recognized is a function of the word's frequency of occurrence (see VISUAL WORD RECOGNITION for more extensive discussion of this factor) and the number and frequency of similar words in the language; high-frequency words with few, low-frequency neighbors will be most easily recognized.

The currently most explicit models are TRACE (McClelland and Elman 1986) and SHORTLIST (Norris 1994), both implemented as connectionist networks (see COMPUTATIONAL PSYCHOLINGUISTICS; also Frauenfelder 1996). They both propose that the incoming signal activates potential candidate words that actively compete with one another by a process of interactive activation in which the more active a candidate word is, the more it may inhibit activation of its competitors. Activated and competing words need not be aligned with one another, and thus the competition process offers a potential solution to the segmentation problem; so although the recognition of *first acre* may involve competition from *stay, steak,* and *take,* this will eventually be overcome by joint inhibition from *first* and *acre.*

TRACE and SHORTLIST differ primarily in one other feature that is an important characteristic of most psycholinguistic processing models—namely, whether or not they allow unidirectional or bidirectional flow of information between levels of processing. TRACE is highly interactive. That is, it allows information to pass in both directions between the lexicon and prelexical (and in principle post lexical) processing levels. SHORTLIST allows information to flow from prelexical processing of the signal to the lexicon but not vice versa. In contrast to TRACE, SHORTLIST also has a two-stage architecture, in which initial word candidates are generated on the basis of bottom-up information alone, and competition occurs only between the members of this "shortlist." TRACE allows competition in principle within the entire vocabulary, which renders it less computationally tractable, whereas SHORTLIST's structure has the practical advantage of allowing simulations with a realistic vocabulary of tens of thousands of words.

All theoretical issues separating the models are still unresolved. There is abundant experimental evidence confirming the subjective impression that spoken-word recognition is extremely rapid and highly efficient (Marslen-Wilson 1987). Concurrent activation of candidate words is supported by a wide range of experimental findings from different experimental paradigms, and active competition between such simultaneously activated words—such that concurrent activation can produce inhibition—is also supported (McQueen et al. 1995). Many findings have been interpreted in terms of interaction between levels of processing (e.g., Pitt 1995; Samuel 1997; Tabossi 1988) but noninteractive models in general can account for these findings as well (Cutler et al. 1987; Massaro and Oden 1995). In some cases, apparent demonstrations of top-down information flow have proven to be spurious, arising instead from independent bottom-up processing (for example, Elman and McClelland 1988 reported an apparent effect of lexically determined compensation for coarticulation, but Pitt and McQueen 1998 showed that the finding was actually due to transitional probability effects and hence could be accounted for without postulating top-down lexical influences on prelexical processing).

Orthogonal to these principal questions of model architecture are further issues such as the nature of the primary prelexical unit of representation (Mehler, Dupoux, and Segui 1990; Pisoni and Luce 1987); the relative contribution to word activation of matching versus mismatching phonetic information (Connine et al. 1997); the phonological explicitness of lexical representations (Frauenfelder and Lahiri 1989); the processing of contextually induced phonological transformations such as *sweek girl* for *sweet girl* (Gaskell and Marslen-Wilson 1996); the role of prosodic structure in recognition (Cutler et al. 1997); and the role of word-internal morphological structure in recognition (Marslen-Wilson et al. 1994).

See also CONNECTIONIST APPROACHES TO LANGUAGE; LANGUAGE PROCESSING; PROSODY AND INTONATION, PROCESSING ISSUES

—*Anne Cutler*

References

Connine, C. M., D. Titone, T. Deelman, and D. Blasko. (1997). Similarity mapping in spoken word recognition. *Journal of Memory and Language* 13: 291–299.

Cutler, A., D. Dahan, and W. van Donselaar. (1997). Prosody in the comprehension of spoken language: A literature review. *Language and Speech* 40: 141–201.

Cutler, A., J. Mehler, D. G. Norris, and J. Segui. (1987). Phoneme identification and the lexicon. *Cognitive Psychology* 19: 141–177.

Elman, J. L. and J. L. McClelland. (1988). Cognitive penetration of the mechanisms of perception: Compensation for coarticulation of lexically restored phonemes. *Journal of Memory and Language* 27: 143–165.

Frauenfelder, U. H. (1996). Computational models of spoken word recognition. In T. Dijksta and K. de Smedt, Eds., *Computational Psycholinguistics.* London: Taylor and Francis, pp. 114–138.

Frauenfelder, U. H., and A. Lahiri. (1989). Understanding words and word recognition: Can phonology help? In W. D. Marslen-Wilson, Ed., *Lexical Representation and Process.* Cambridge, MA: MIT Press., pp. 319–341.

Gaskell, G. M., and W. M. Marslen-Wilson. (1996). Phonological variation and inference in lexical access. *Journal of Experimental Psychology: Human Perception and Peformance* 22: 144–156.

Grosjean, F., and U. H. Frauenfelder, Eds. (1996). Spoken word recognition paradigms. Special issue of *Language and Cognitive Processes* 11: 553–699.

Luce, P. A., D. B. Pisoni, and S. D. Goldinger. (1990). Similarity neighborhoods of spoken words. In G. T. M. Altmann, Ed., *Cognitive Models of Speech Processing.* Cambridge, MA: MIT Press, pp. 122–147.

Maddieson, I. (1984). *Patterns of Sounds.* Cambridge: Cambridge University Press.

Marslen-Wilson, W. D. (1987). Parallel processing in spoken word recognition. *Cognition* 25: 71–102.

Marslen-Wilson, W., L. K. Tyler, R. Waksler, and L. Older. (1994). Morphology and meaning in the English mental lexicon. *Psychological Review* 101: 3–33.

Marslen-Wilson, W. D., and A. Welsh. (1978). Processing interactions and lexical access during word recognition in continuous speech. *Cognitive Psychology* 10: 29–63.

Massaro, D. W., and G. C. Oden. (1995). Independence of lexical context and phonological information in speech perception. *Journal of Experimental Psychology: Learning, Memory, and Cognition* 2: 1053–1064.

McClelland, J. L., and J. L. Elman. (1986). The TRACE model of speech perception. *Cognitive Psychology* 18: 1–86.

McQueen, J. M., A. Cutler, T. Briscoe, and D. G. Norris. (1995). Models of continuous speech recognition and the contents of the vocabulary. *Language and Cognitive Processes* 10: 309–331.

Mehler, J., E. Dupoux, and J. Segui. (1990). Constraining models of lexical access: The onset of word recognition. In G. T. M. Altmann, Ed., *Cognitive Models of Speech Processing.* Cambridge, MA: MIT Press, pp. 236–262.

Morton, J. (1969). Interaction of information in word perception. *Psychological Review* 76: 165–178.

Norris, D. (1994). Shortlist: A connectionist model of continuous speech recognition. *Cognition* 52: 189–234.

Pisoni, D. B., and P. A. Luce. (1987). Acoustic-phonetic representations in word recognition. *Cognition* 25: 21–52.

Pitt, M. A. (1995). The locus of the lexical shift in phoneme identification. *Journal of Experimental Psychology: Learning, Memory, and Cognition* 21: 1037–1052.

Pitt, M. A., and J. M. McQueen. (1998). Is compensation for coarticulation mediated by the lexicon? *Journal of Memory and Language* 39: 347–370.

Samuel, A. G. (1997). Lexical activation produces potent phonetic percepts. *Cognitive Psychology* 32: 97–127.

Tabossi., P. (1988). Effects of context on the immediate interpretation of unambiguous nouns. *Journal of Experimental Psychology: Learning, Memory, and Cognition* 14: 153–162.

Further Readings

Cutler, A. (1995). Spoken word recognition and production. In J. L. Miller and P. D. Eimas, Eds., *Speech, Language, and Communication,* of E. C. Carterette and M. P. Friedman, Eds., *Handbook of Perception and Cognition,* vol. 11. New York: Academic Press, pp. 97–136.

Friederici, A., Ed. (1998). *Language Comprehension: A Biological Perspective.* Heidelberg: Springer.

Klatt, D. H. (1989). Review of selected models of speech perception. In W. D. Marslen-Wilson, Ed., *Lexical Representation and Process.* Cambridge, MA: MIT Press, pp. 169–226.

Massaro, D. W. (1989). Testing between the TRACE model and the fuzzy logical model of speech perception. *Cognitive Psychology* 21: 398–421.

Statistical Learning Theory

Statistical learning theory addresses a key question that arises when constructing predictive models from data—how to decide whether a particular model is adequate or whether a different model would produce better predictions. Whereas classical statistics typically assumes that the form of the correct model is known and the objective is to estimate the model parameters, statistical learning theory presumes that the correct form is completely unknown and the goal is to identify the best possible model from a set of competing models. The models need not have the same mathematical form and none of them need be correct. The theory provides a sound statistical basis for assessing model adequacy under these circumstances, which are precisely the circumstances encountered in MACHINE LEARNING, PATTERN RECOGNITION, and exploratory data analysis.

Estimating the performance of competing models is the central issue in statistical learning theory. Performance is measured through the use of *loss functions.* The loss $Q(\mathbf{z}, \alpha)$ between a data vector $\mathbf{z}$ and a specific model α (one with values assigned to all parameters) is a score that indicates how well α performs on $\mathbf{z}$, with lower scores indicating better performance. The squared-error function for regression models, the 0/1 loss function for classification models, and the negative log likelihood for other more general statistical models are all examples of loss functions. The choice of loss function depends on the nature of the modeling problem.

From the point of view of UTILITY THEORY, α is a decision variable, $\mathbf{z}$ is an outcome, and $Q(\mathbf{z}, \alpha)$ is the negative utility of the outcome given the decision. Hence, if the statistical properties of the data were already known, the optimum model would be the α that minimizes the expected loss $R(\alpha)$:

$$R(\alpha) = \underset{\mathbf{z}}{E} [Q(\mathbf{z}, \alpha)] = \int Q(\mathbf{z}, \alpha) dF(\mathbf{z}),$$

where $F(\mathbf{z})$ is the probability measure that defines the true statistical properties of the data. $R(\alpha)$ is also referred to as the *risk* of α. In learning situations, however, $F(\mathbf{z})$ is unknown and one must choose a model based on a set of observed data vectors $\mathbf{z}_i$, $i = 1, \ldots, l$, that are assumed to be random samples of $F(\mathbf{z})$. The average loss $R_{\text{emp}}(\alpha, l)$ on the observed data is used as an empirical estimate of the expected loss, where

$$R_{\text{emp}}(\alpha, l) = \frac{1}{l} \sum_{i=1}^{l} Q(\mathbf{z}_i, \alpha).$$

$R_{\text{emp}}(\alpha, l)$ is also referred to as the *empirical risk* of α.

The fundamental question in statistical learning theory is the following: under what conditions does minimizing $R_{\text{emp}}(\alpha, l)$ yield models that also minimize $R(\alpha)$, inasmuch as the latter is what we actually want to accomplish? This question is answered by considering the accuracy of the empirical loss estimate.

As in classical statistics, accuracy is expressed in terms of confidence regions; that is, how far can $R_{\text{emp}}(\alpha, l)$ be expected to deviate from $R(\alpha)$, and with what probability? One of the fundamental theorems of statistical learning theory shows that the size of the confidence region is governed by the maximum difference between the two losses over all models being considered:

$$\sup_{\alpha \in \Lambda} \left| R(\alpha) - R_{\text{emp}}(\alpha, l) \right|,$$

where Λ is a set of competing models. The maximum difference dominates because of the phenomenon of overfitting.

Overfitting occurs when the best model relative to the training data tends to perform significantly worse when applied to new data. This mathematically corresponds to a situation in which the average loss $R_{\text{emp}}(\alpha, l)$ substantially underestimates the expected loss $R(\alpha)$. Although there is always some probability that underestimation will occur for a fixed model α, both the probability and the degree of underestimation are increased by the fact that we explicitly search for the α that minimizes $R_{\text{emp}}(\alpha, l)$. This search biases the difference between $R(\alpha)$ and $R_{\text{emp}}(\alpha, l)$ toward the maximum difference among competing models. If the maximum difference does not converge to zero as the number of data vectors increases, then overfitting will occur with probability one.

The core results in statistical learning theory are a series of probability bounds developed by Vapnik and Chervonenkis (1971, 1981, 1991) that define small-sample confidence regions for the maximum difference between $R(\alpha)$ and $R_{\text{emp}}(\alpha, l)$. The confidence regions differ from those obtained in classical statistics in three respects. First, they do not assume that the models are correct. Second, they are based on small-sample statistics and are not asymptotic approximations. Third, a uniform method is used to take into account the degree to which overfitting can occur for a given set of competing models. This method is based on a measurement known as the Vapnik-Chervonenkis (VC) dimension.

Conceptually speaking, the VC dimension of a set of models is the maximum number of data vectors for which overfitting is virtually guaranteed in the sense that one can always find a specific model that fits the data exactly. For example, the VC dimension of the family of linear discriminant functions with n parametric terms is n, because n linear terms can be used to discriminate exactly n points in general position for any two-class labeling of the points. This conceptual definition of VC dimension accurately reflects the formal definition in the case of 0/1 loss functions, wherein $Q(\mathbf{z}, \alpha) = 0$ if α correctly predicts $\mathbf{z}$ and $Q(\mathbf{z}, \alpha) = 1$ otherwise. However, the formal definition is more general in that it considers arbitrary loss functions and does not require exact fits.

In the probability bounds obtained by Vapnik and Chervonenkis, the size of the confidence region is largely determined by the ratio of the VC dimension h to the number of data vectors l. For example, if $Q(\mathbf{z}, \alpha)$ is the 0/1 loss function used for classification models, then with probability at least $1 - \eta$,

$$R_{\text{emp}}(\alpha, l) - \frac{\sqrt{\varepsilon}}{2} \leq R(\alpha)$$

$$\leq R_{\text{emp}}(\alpha, l) + \frac{\varepsilon}{2} \left(1 + \sqrt{1 + \frac{4 R_{\text{emp}}(\alpha, l)}{\varepsilon}} \right)$$

where

$$\varepsilon = \frac{4h}{l} \left(\ln \frac{2l}{h} + 1 \right) - \frac{4}{l} \left(\ln \frac{\eta}{4} \right)$$

Note that the ratio of h over l is the dominant term in the definition of ε and, hence, in the size of the confidence region for $R(\alpha)$.

V. N. Vapnik (1982, 1995, 1998) has reported probability bounds for other families of loss functions that yield analogous confidence regions based on VC dimension. Bounds also exist for the special case in which the set of competing models is finite (continuous parameters typically imply an infinite number of specific models). These bounds avoid explicit calculation of VC dimension and are useful in validation-set methods. A remarkable property shared by all of the bounds is that they either make no assumptions at all or very weak assumptions about underlying probability distribution $F(\mathbf{z})$. In addition, they are valid for small sample sizes and they depend only on the VC dimension of the set of competing models Λ, or on its size, and on the properties of the loss function $Q(\mathbf{z}, \alpha)$. All bounds are independent of the mathematical forms of the models—the VC dimension and/or the number of specific models summarizes all relevant information. Thus, the bounds are equally

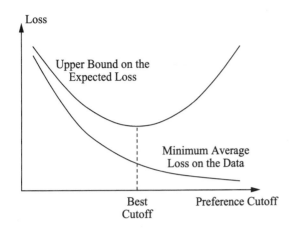

Figure 1. For each cutoff point in the model preference ordering, one selects the model that minimizes the average loss on the data from among those that occur before the cutoff. The most suitable model for the data is then the one with the smallest upper bound on the expected loss.

applicable to both nonlinear and nonparametric models, and to combinations of dissimilar model families. This includes NEURAL NETWORKS, DECISION TREES and rules, regression trees and rules, radial basis functions, BAYESIAN NETWORKS, and so on.

When using statistical learning theory to identify the best model from a set of competing models, the models must first be ordered according to preference. The most preferable model that best explains the data is then selected. The preference order corresponds to the notion of learning bias found in machine learning. No restrictions are placed on the order other than it must be fixed prior to model selection. The ordering itself is referred to as a *structure* and the process of selecting models is called *structural risk minimization.*

Structural risk minimization has two components: one is to determine a cutoff point in the preference ordering, the other is to select the best model from among those that occur before the cutoff. As the cutoff point is advanced through the ordering, both the subset of models that appear before the cutoff and the VC dimension of this subset steadily increase. With more models to choose from, the minimum average loss $R_{emp}(\alpha, l)$ for all models α before the cutoff tends to decrease. However, the size of the confidence region for $R(\alpha)$ tends to increase because the size is governed by the VC dimension. The cutoff point is selected by minimizing the upper bound on the confidence region for $R(\alpha)$, with the corresponding α chosen as the most suitable model given the available data. For example, for classification problems one would choose the cutoff and the associated model α so as to minimize the right hand side of the inequality presented above for a desired setting of the confidence parameter η.

The overall approach is illustrated by the graph in figure 1. The process balances the ability to find increasingly better fits to the data against the danger of overfitting and thereby selecting a poor model. The preference order provides the necessary structure in which to compare competing models. Judicious choice of the model order enables

one to avoid overfitting even in high-dimensional spaces. For example, Vapnik and others (Cortes and Vapnik 1995; Vapnik 1995, 1998) order models within parametric families according to the magnitudes of the parameters. Each preference cutoff then limits the parameter magnitudes, which in turn limits the VC dimension of the corresponding subset of models. Reliable models can thus be obtained using structural risk minimization even when the number of data samples is orders of magnitude less than the number of parameters.

See also PROBABILITY, FOUNDATIONS OF; PROBABILISTIC REASONING; STATISTICAL TECHNIQUES IN NATURAL LANGUAGE PROCESSING

—*Edwin P. D. Pednault*

References

Cortes, C., and V. N. Vapnik. (1995). Support vector machines. *Machine Learning* 20: 273–297.

Vapnik, V. N., and A. J. Chervonenkis. (1971). On the uniform convergence of relative frequencies of events to their probabilities. *Theory of Probability and Its Applications* 16: 264–280. Original work published 1968 as *Doklady Akademii Nauk USSR* 181(4).

Vapnik, V. N., and A. J. Chervonenkis. (1981). Necessary and sufficient conditions for the uniform convergence of means to their expectations. *Theory of Probability and Its Applications* 26: 532–553.

Vapnik, V. N., and A. J. Chervonenkis. (1991). The necessary and sufficient conditions for consistency of the method of empirical risk minimization. *Pattern Recognition and Image Analysis* 1: 284–305. Original work published as *Yearbook of the Academy of Sciences of the USSR on Recognition, Classification, and Forecasting* 2 (1989).

Vapnik, V. N. (1982). *Estimation of Dependencies Based on Empirical Data.* New York: Springer.

Vapnik, V. N. (1995). *The Nature of Statistical Learning Theory.* New York: Springer.

Vapnik, V. N. (1998). *Statistical Learning Theory.* New York: Wiley.

Further Readings

Biggs, N., and M. H. G. Anthony. (1992). *Computational Learning Theory: An Introduction.* Cambridge Tracts in Theoretical Computer Science, No. 30. London: Cambridge University Press.

Devroye, L., L. Gyorfi, and G. Lugosi. (1996). *A Probabilistic Theory of Pattern Recognition.* New York: Springer.

Dudley, R. M. (1984). A course on empirical processes. In R. M. Dudley, H. Kunita, and F. Ledrappier, Eds., *École d'Été de Probabilités de Sainte-Flour XII*–1982. Lecture Notes in Mathematics, vol. 1097. New York: Springer, pp. 1–142.

Kearns, M. J., and U. V. Vazirani. (1994). *An Introduction to Computational Learning Theory.* Cambridge, MA: MIT Press.

Parrondo, J. M. R., and C. Van den Broeck. (1993). Vapnik-Chervonenkis bounds for generalization. *Journal of Physics A* 26: 2211–2223.

Pollard, D. (1984). *Convergence of Stochastic Processes.* New York: Springer.

Pollard, D. (1990). *Empirical Processes: Theory and Applications.* NSF-CBMS Regional Conference Series in Probability and Statistics, vol. 2. Hayward, CA: Institute of Mathematical Statistics.

Shawe-Taylor, J. S., A. Macintyre, and M. Jerrum, Eds. (1998). Special Issue on the Vapnik-Chervonenkis Dimension. *Discrete Applied Mathematics* 86(1).

Vidyasagar, M. (1997). *A Theory of Learning and Generalization: With Applications to Neural Networks and Control Systems (Communications and Control Engineering).* New York: Springer.

Statistical Techniques in Natural Language Processing

Statistical natural language processing is concerned with the creation of computer programs that can perform language-processing tasks by virtue of information gathered from (typically large) corpora. Usually this information is in the form of statistics, but it may be distilled into other forms, such as DECISION TREES, dictionary entries, or various kinds of rules (see also NATURAL LANGUAGE PROCESSING). The techniques have been applied to (or have correlates in) areas as diverse as lexicography and document retrieval (Church and Mercer 1993). Here, however, we concentrate on subareas closer to cognitive science.

Most statistical language programs sacrifice depth or accuracy to breadth of coverage. That is, statistical NLP programs typically work on most everything one throws at them, but they do not provide very deep analyses and/or may make occasional mistakes. This has the salutary effect of making it easier to compare competing techniques since they will work on the same body of data (i.e., "everything"). They work as well as they do because one can get a great deal of leverage from relatively weak (and easily collected) pieces of information—combined with the fact that, at least at the shallower linguistic depths, computers seem better at collecting linguistic phenomena than people are at thinking them up.

Historically, the push behind statistical techniques came primarily from the speech community that discovered in the early 1970s that programs automatically trained from corpora worked better than their hand-tooled versions. These programs exploited the training properties of HIDDEN MARKOV MODELS (HMMs; Levinson, Rabiner, and Sondhi 1983). These models can be thought of as finite state machines in which the transitions between states have probabilities. There are well-understood mathematical techniques for training them—adjusting the probabilities to better fit the observed data. The "hidden" in their name comes from the fact that in such models one cannot know the sequence of states that produced the output (or, equivalently, accepted the input), but there are linear-time techniques for finding the most probable of such state sequences. The trick is then to identify states with the properties one wishes to infer (e.g., the word uttered).

These speech programs also typically incorporate language models, assignments of probabilities to all sequences of words in the language. The most popular such model is the simple but remarkably accurate trigram model (Jelenik 1985) in which the probability of the next word is conditioned on just the two previous words. The language model enables the speech recognizer to pick the best word in con-

text when the speech signal analysis by itself is insufficient (Church and Mercer 1993).

An early successful application of HMM technology to language tasks was the HMM "taggers," programs that try to assign the correct part of speech to each word in a text. For example, in *the can will rust* the program should identify *can* as a noun (not a modal verb) and *will* as a modal verb (not a noun). In these programs, the states of the HMM correspond to the parts of speech, so that finding the most probable sequence of states when the HMM is driven by the input gives us the desired tagging (Church 1988). Other schemes compile the statistics into rules (Brill 1995). Moderately well-crafted programs achieve about 96 percent accuracy. For comparison, human taggers are consistent with one another at a 98 percent level.

Moving up the linguistic food chain, statistical techniques are now being applied to wide-coverage syntactic parsing—determining the syntactic structure of a sentence. Such parsers are able to come up with at least a semi-reasonable structure for, say, every sentence on the front page of today's *New York Times*. In this area, statistical parsers rule the roost. One simple idea here is the probabilistic context-free grammar (PCFG; Charniak 1993). PCFGs are context-free grammars in which each rule is assigned a probability. Alternatively, they can be thought of as the context-free generalization of HMMs. PCFGs can be parsed using the standard techniques applied to their nonprobabilistic brethren, and the most probable parse for a sentence can be found in n-cubed time, where n is the length of the sentence.

Statistical parsing researchers have greatly benefited from moderate-size corpora of hand-parsed sentences, the most notable being the one-million-word Penn tree-bank (Marcus, Santorini, and Marcinkiewicz 1993). For example, one very simple technique for "learning" a PCFG grammar is to read it directly off the parse trees in the corpus. One estimates the rule probabilities by counting how often each rule is used and dividing this by the counts of productions for the same part of speech (Charniak 1996). Programs using this technique, or others using similar sources of information, parse at about a 75 percent level of accuracy. That is, 75 percent of the constituents produced are correct, where correct means that the constituent starts at the correct place, ends at the correct place, and has the right "label" (e.g., "noun phrase"). Researchers are exploring techniques that exploit more of the information in the hand-parsed corpora. One popular idea involves keeping track of the "head" of a constituent, the constituent's most important lexical item (e.g., the main noun in a noun phrase), and then conditioning probabilities on this head. These techniques are now achieving an 87 percent accuracy level (Charniak 1997; Collins 1997).

Statistical word-sense disambiguation is yet another thriving area. Here we can exploit the fact that very different senses of a word (e.g., river *bank* vs. savings *bank*) typically occur in texts concerning quite different topics, and this in turn is signaled by the occurrence of different content words in the surrounding text. So if we see "leaf" and "water" near "bank," *river bank* is a good guess. Thus, to a first approximation, statistical word-sense disambiguation programs work by taking a window of, say, the 100 words on either side of the ambiguous word and determining the probability of seeing these words if we assume that the ambiguous word is in one sense versus the other. Thus, to restate formally what we said informally about "bank," if the words in the window include "leaf" and "water" but do not include, say, "money" or "loan," then the probability of the words is higher under the *river bank* interpretation. The hard part in all of this is collecting the statistics needed without access to a large corpus in which the words are marked with their senses. Researchers have solved this in a variety of interesting ways: using extra sources of information such as bilingual corpora (Gale, Church, and Yarowsky 1992), looking for clusters in probability space that indicate an identifiable sense (Schütze 1992), or using dictionary definitions as key words to start the process (Yarowsky 1995).

One potential application of these ideas is MACHINE TRANSLATION. In preparation for such work, there is now an active research community looking at "parallel corpora"—articles and their translations side by side. One problem here is bringing the alignment down from the article level to the sentence level (Brown, Lai, and Mercer 1991) and another is creating bilingual lexica (Brown et al. 1993). Statistical techniques in both these areas (frequently done in parallel) are quite accurate.

See also COMPUTATIONAL LINGUISTICS; COMPUTATIONAL PSYCHOLINGUISTICS; NATURAL LANGUAGE GENERATION; SPEECH RECOGNITION; SPEECH SYNTHESIS

—*Eugene Charniak*

References

Brill, E. (1995). Unsupervised learning of disambiguation rules for part of speech tagging. *Proceedings of the Third Workshop on Very Large Corpora,* 1–13.

Brown, P., J. Lai, and R. Mercer. (1991). Aligning sentences in parallel corpora. *Proceedings of the Association for Computational Linguistics ACL:* 169–176.

Brown, P. F., S. A. Della Pietra, V. J. Della Pietra, and R. L. Mercer. (1993). The mathematics of statistical machine translation: Parameter estimation. *Computational Linguistics* 192: 263–312.

Charniak, E. (1993). *Statistical Language Learning.* Cambridge, MA: MIT Press.

Charniak, E. (1996). Tree-bank grammars. *Proceedings of the Thirteenth National Conference on Artificial Intelligence.* Menlo Park, CA: AAAI Press/MIT Press, pp. 1031–1036.

Charniak, E. (1997). Statistical parsing with a context-free grammar and word statistics. *Proceedings of the Fourteenth National Conference on Artificial Intelligence.* Menlo Park, CA: AAAI Press/MIT Press, pp. 598–603.

Church, K. W. (1988). A stochastic parts program and noun phrase parser for unrestricted text. *Second Conference on Applied Natural Language Processing* ACL, pp. 136–143.

Church, K. W., and R. L. Mercer. (1993). Introduction to the special issue on computational linguistics and large corpora. *Computational Linguistics* 19: 1–24.

Collins, M. J. (1997). Three generative lexicalised models for statistical parsing. *Proceedings of the Thirty-fifth Annual Meeting of the ACL,* pp. 16–23.

Gale, W. A., K. W. Church, and D. Yarowsky. (1992). A method for disambiguating word senses in a large corpus. *Computers and the Humanities.*

Jelinek, F. (1985). Self-organized language modeling for speech recognition. Yorktown Heights, NY: IBM T. J. Watson Research Center, Continuous Speech Recognition Group.

Levinson, S. E., L. R. Rabiner, and M. M. Sondhi. (1983). An introduction to the application of the theory of probabilistic functions of a Markov process to automatic speech recognition. *The Bell System Technical Journal* 62(4): 1035–1074.

Marcus, M. P., B. Santorini, and M. A. Marcinkiewicz. (1993). Building a large annotated corpus of English: The Penn treebank. *Computational Linguistics* 19: 313–330.

Schütze, H. (1992). Dimensions of meaning. *Proceedings of Supercomputing* 92.

Yarowsky, D. (1995) Unsupervised word-sense disambiguation rivaling supervised methods. *Proceedings of the Thirty-third Annual Meeting of the Association for Computational Linguistics.*

Further Readings

Brown, P .F., V. J. Della Pietra, P. V. DeSouza, J. C. Lai, and R. L. Mercer. (1992). Class-based *n*-gram models of natural language. *Computational Linguistics* 18(4): 467–479.

Caraballo, S., and E. Charniak. (Forthcoming). New figures of merit for best-first probabilistic chart parsing. *Computational Linguistics.*

Cardie, C. (1992). Corpus-based acquisition of relative pronoun disambiguation heuristics. *Proceedings of the Thirtieth Annual Meeting of the ACL,* pp. 216–223.

Francis, W. N., and H. Kucera. (1982). *Frequency Analysis of English Usage: Lexicon and Grammar.* Boston: Houghton Mifflin.

Goodman, J. (1996). Parsing algorithms and metrics. *Proceedings of the Thirty-fourth Annual Meeting of the ACL,* pp. 177–183.

Jelinek, F., and J. D. Lafferty. (1991). Computation of the probability of initial substring generation by stochastic context-free grammars. *Computational Linguistics* 17: 315–324.

Lappin, S., and H. J. Leass. (1994). An algorithm for pronominal anaphora resolution. *Computational Linguistics* 20: 535–561.

Lauer, M. (1995). Corpus statistics meet the noun compound: Some empirical results. *Proceedings the Thirty-third Annual Meeting of the ACL,* pp. 47–55.

Pereira, F., N. Tishby, and L. Lee. (1993). Distributional clustering of English words. *Proceedings of the Thirty-first Annual Meeting of the ACL.*

Riloff, E. (1996). Automatically generating extraction patterns from untagged text. *Proceedings of the Thirteenth National Conference on Artificial Intelligence.* Menlo Park, CA: AAAI Press/MIT Press, pp. 1044–1049.

Stereo and Motion Perception

Given several views of a scene, how does one recover its structure and, possibly, the pose of the cameras that have acquired the views? In the case of two views, this is known as the stereo problem; when there are more than two views, it is the discrete structure from motion (DSFM) problem. These are two of the subjects of COMPUTATIONAL VISION. Many applications of DSFM are found in robotics in general and in MOBILE ROBOTS in particular, as well as in VISUAL OBJECT RECOGNITION.

A general solution to the DSFM problem requires the availability of correspondences, based, for example, on TEXTURE, between some of the views. How to obtain those correspondences is itself a formidable problem that completely determines the solution to the DSFM problem.

Why is this a formidable task? Suppose that there are M views and the number of pixels per view is N. A correspondence is an M-tuple of features and there are N^M such tuples. If we take $N = 1$ million, $M = 10$, the number of possible tuples is 10^{60}!

To reduce this number, we must exploit the geometrical constraints that are induced by the fact that a camera is a projective engine. Projective geometry is a rich source of constraints on the number of possible correspondences and, as we will show, is a fundamental tool for determining the sort of geometrical structure that can be recovered from the views. DFSM can be thought of as a combination of a HEURISTIC SEARCH and CONSTRAINT SATISFACTION problem.

A camera is a projective engine because it can usually be accurately modeled as a pinhole camera. In the pinhole camera, an image is formed on the retinal plane by perspective projection with respect to the optical center (Faugeras 1993). Since this is a projective construction, it implies that the tools of projective geometry (Semple and Kneebone 1952) can immediately be brought to bear on the DSFM problem. In particular, projective geometry allows us to represent a camera by a matrix, called the perspective projection matrix.

Projective geometry is a rich source of constraints for the DSFM problem because M image points are the images of a single 3-D point, if and only if their image coordinates satisfy a number of polynomial constraints. The coefficients of those polynomials are functions of the (unknown) coefficients of the perspective projection matrices.

The simplest example occurs in the case of two views, that is, stereo, where the coordinates of two corresponding points satisfy a quadratic polynomial. This polynomial arises from the beautiful epipolar geometry of two views that is routinely used in common stereo programs (Grimson 1985).

The next example is the case of three views ($M = 3$), which offers an even richer geometry and algebra. The coordinates of three corresponding points satisfy four algebraically independent polynomials of degree 3, the trilinear constraints (Hartley 1997; Shashua 1995).

When does this process stop? There are two phenomena that take place. First, when $M = 4$ the constraints of degree 4 are algebraically dependent on the polynomials of degrees 2 and 3 obtained from subsets of 2 and 3 views of the M views (Faugeras and Mourrain 1995). Second, the case $M > 4$ does not bring in any new constraints. Since, moreover, the constraints of degree 3 imply all constraints of degree 2 (Heyden 1995), the geometrical constraints between $M > 3$ views are completely described by the trilinear constraints between all triples of views among the M.

In order to use the constraints to eliminate wrong correspondences or to reconstruct the scene, their coefficients have to be estimated. This can only be achieved if "correct" correspondences can be obtained. This sounds like a chicken-and-egg problem since correct correspondences are needed to estimate the constraints that will then be used to extract correct correspondences. RANSACK-like techniques (Fischler and Bolles 1981) can be used successfully to break that vicious circle and produce reliable estimates of the constraints (Zhang et al. 1995; Torr and Zissermann 1997).

The geometry of the M views being represented by the trilinear constraints, can we recover the perspective projection matrices of the cameras from them? There is no unique solution to this problem in the absence of further information; given all the trilinear constraints (in practice only a small subset of those are necessary), a four parameter family of perspective projection matrices of the M cameras can be computed. The four parameters correspond to the global scale of the scene and to the choice of a plane of reference (Luong and Viéville 1994).

Any element of this family of perspective projection matrices allows us to recover the projective structure of the scene (Faugeras 1992; Hartley and Gupta 1993). By projective structure we mean that the 3-D coordinates of the reconstructed points are defined up to an arbitrary projective transformation of the 3-D space, that is, up to fifteen parameters.

How can the Euclidean coordinates of the points be obtained? It is in general possible, even without any a priori information on the scene, thanks to the use of group invariance theory. The information contained in the perspective projection matrix of a camera can be decomposed into two parts, one that encodes the internal parameters of the camera, for instance its focal length, and the other that encodes its pose. In order to access the Euclidean coordinates of the scene it is only necessary to recover the internal parameters since the camera poses can be computed from them.

The internal parameters of the cameras can be recovered from feature correspondences in at least two cases: first, if the images were acquired by the same camera (Maybank and Faugeras 1992) with the same internal parameters; and second, if the internal parameters are different but satisfy some constraints which are true for most cameras (Heyden and Åström 1997). In both cases, a simple mathematical entity called the absolute conic, or umbilic, plays the role of a calibration grid. The difference between this conic and the usual calibration grids is that the umbilic is located in the plane at infinity, a plane that defines the affine geometry of three-space (it is invariant to affine transformations), and has only complex points. The umbilic defines the Euclidean geometry of three-space (it is invariant to Euclidean transformations). The process can be thought of as first recovering the projective, then affine, and finally Euclidean structure of the scene (Faugeras 1995). The scene is then defined up to an arbitrary rigid transformation and scaling of the 3-D space, that is, up to six parameters.

It is worth noting that this stratified way of solving the DSFM problem is a faint echo of the Erlangen program put forward by the two German mathematicians, Felix Klein and Herman Weyl, in 1872 in which they suggested the study of geometry from the viewpoint of invariance of geometrical figures to the action of groups of transformations (Mundy and Zisserman 1992).

See also MACHINE VISION; MOTION, PERCEPTION OF; STRUCTURE FROM VISUAL INFORMATION SOURCES

—*Olivier D. Faugeras*

References

Faugeras, O. (1992). What can be seen in three dimensions with an uncalibrated stereo rig. In G. Sandini, Ed., *Proceedings of the 2nd European Conference on Computer Vision.* Vol. 588, *Lecture Notes in Computer Science.* Santa Margherita Ligure, Italy: Springer, pp. 563–578.

Faugeras, O. (1993). *Three-Dimensional Computer Vision: A Geometric Viewpoint.* Cambridge, MA: MIT Press.

Faugeras, O. (1995). Stratification of 3-D vision: Projective, affine, and metric representations. *Journal of the Optical Society of America A.Optics and Image Science* 12(3): 465–484.

Faugeras, O., and B. Mourrain. (1995). About the correspondences of points between *n* images. In *Proceedings of the Workshop on the Representation of Visual Scenes.* Cambridge, MA: IEEE Computer Society.

Fischler, M., and R. Bolles. (1981). Random sample consensus: A paradigm for model fitting with applications to image analysis and automated cartography. *Communications of the ACM* 24: 381–385.

Grimson, W. (1985). Computational experiments with a feature based stereo algorithm. *IEEE Transactions on Pattern Analysis and Machine Intelligence* 7(1): 17–34.

Hartley, R. I. (1997). Lines and points in three views and the trifocal tensor. *The International Journal of Computer Vision* 22(2): 125–140.

Hartley, R. I., and R. Gupta. (1993). Computing matched-epipolar projections. In *Proceedings of the International Conference on Computer Vision and Pattern Recognition,* New York: IEEE Computer Society, pp. 549–555.

Heyden, A. (1995). *Geometry and Algebra of Multiple Projective Transformations.* Ph.D. diss., Lund University, Sweden.

Heyden, A., and K. Åström. (1997). Euclidean reconstruction from image sequences with varying and unknown focal length and principal point. In *Computer Vision and Pattern Recognition* IEEE Computer Society Press, pp. 438–443.

Luong, Q.-T., and T. Viéville. (1994). Canonic representations for the geometries of multiple projective views. In J.-O. Eklundh, Ed., *Proceedings of the 3rd European Conference on Computer Vision.* Vol. 1, *Lecture Notes in Computer Science.* Stockholm: Springer, pp. 589–599.

Maybank, S. J., and O. D. Faugeras. (1992). A theory of self-calibration of a moving camera. *The International Journal of Computer Vision* 8(2): 123–152.

Mundy, J. L., and A. Zisserman, Eds. (1992). *Geometric Invariance in Computer Vision.* Cambridge, MA: MIT Press.

Semple, J., and G. Kneebone. (1952/1979). *Algebraic Projective Geometry.* Oxford: Clarendon Press.

Shashua, A. (1995). Algebraic functions for recognition. *IEEE Transactions on Pattern Analysis and Machine Intelligence* 17(8): 779–789.

Torr, P., and A. Zissermann. (1997). Performance characterization of fundamental matrix estimation under image degradation. *Machine Vision and Applications* 9: 321–333.

Zhang, Z., R. Deriche, O. Faugeras, and Q.-T. Luong. (1995). A robust technique for matching two uncalibrated images through the recovery of the unknown epipolar geometry. *Artificial Intelligence Journal* 78: 87–119.

Stereotyping

Stereotyping is the process by which people use social categories (e.g., race, sex) in acquiring, processing, and recalling information about others. Stereotypes are the traits and roles associated with certain groups and may relate to the belief component of attitudes. By most historical accounts, Walter Lippmann introduced the term "stereotype" to behavioral scientists in 1922 to represent the typical picture that comes to mind when thinking about a particular social group.

Three general conceptual approaches have been applied historically to understand stereotyping (Ashmore and Del-Boca 1981). The *psychodynamic approach,* which has its origins in Freudian psychology, emphasizes the functions of stereotyping in satisfying personal needs (such as for esteem and status) and in operating as a defense mechanism (involving displacement and projection of negative feelings and characteristics). The *sociocultural approach* views stereotyping as an aspect of social learning in which stereotypes are acquired and transmitted along with other types of social "knowledge." At the societal level, stereotypes may help to rationalize and justify differential treatment of various social groups (such as limiting their rights). The *cognitive approach* describes stereotypes as mental representations and stereotyping in terms of information processing. This approach is derivative of the more general SOCIAL COGNITION framework. From this perspective, stereotyping is rooted in people's needs to simplify and organize social information. Although psychodynamic, sociocultural, and cognitive approaches are complementary rather than competing perspectives, the cognitive approach is the prevailing one in contemporary social psychology.

All of these perspectives view stereotyping as functional (Dovidio et al. 1996). Early accounts of stereotyping, influenced substantially by the psychodynamic approach, generally represented this process as functional but flawed. On the one hand, stereotyping was assumed to help manage the complexity of one's environment by simplifying the social world (see JUDGMENT HEURISTICS). On the other hand, stereotyping was considered a faulty process because (1) it was a rigid form of thinking that was highly resistant to change, and (2) it produced overgeneralizations that unfairly emphasized the influence of inborn and unalterable psychological characteristics relative to social or environmental influences. In line with the cognitive orientation that has characterized recent research on stereotyping, many current theorists have stressed the information-processing (e.g., simplification) function of stereotypes while deemphasizing any necessary objectionable aspects.

Needs to understand, to predict, and potentially to control one's environment lead to the development of social stereotypes (Mackie et al. 1996). Because of the complexity of the social environment and people's limited cognitive resources, people tend to categorize others into social groups. These categories are often based on readily apparent, salient similarities, such as physical characteristics associated with sex or race. However, the social context significantly influences which characteristics are the most relevant bases of categorization (Oakes, Haslam, and Turner 1994), even with minimal physical distinctiveness (e.g., first-year students vs. upper-class students). Once categorization occurs, members of the group are viewed as more similar to one another (the outgroup homogeneity effect) and as having common characteristics. Personal traits (dispositional attributions; see ATTRIBUTION THEORY) are often overemphasized in stereotypes because they offer more stable explanations for the group's behavior (which enhance feelings of predictability) than do situational or environmental attributions. Although not necessarily so, stereotypic characterizations of other groups also tend to be relatively negative. Perceiving members of other groups as possessing less favorable characteristics can increase personal feelings of regard as well as esteem for the group with which one identifies. Categorizing people into ingroups and outgroups typically initiates a process in which people attend to dimensions on which their group is superior and the other group is inferior (Tajfel 1981).

Once established, stereotypes operate as cognitive structures that influence how others are perceived and how information about others is stored and retrieved. These stereotyping processes operate in unconscious and unintentional ways, as well as consciously (Greenwald and Banaji 1995). Consistent with general principles of AUTOMATICITY, repetition during socialization or personal experience may make some social stereotypes so overlearned that they will automatically become activated when people are presented with a representative or symbol of that group. There are individual differences in attitudes that can influence the likelihood and strength of this effect (Lepore and Brown 1997), but often this effect occurs generally for people sharing common socialization experiences (Devine 1989). What distinguishes high and low prejudiced people is their difference in the likelihood of automatically activating stereotypes and their motivation to suppress these stereotypes when they are automatically activated. Nevertheless, attempts at suppressing automatically activated stereotypic thoughts, particularly for those who do not normally do so, can result in rebound effects in which stereotypical thoughts are even more prevalent than normally so (Macrae et al. 1994).

When stereotypes are activated, people are judged in terms of the group's standards. For example, an aggressive woman may be judged as more aggressive than an objectively comparable aggressive man because women are stereotyped as being less aggressive than men in general. Furthermore, behaviors that are consistent with a stereotype are assumed to reflect dispositional characteristics and traits, and are described in that way, more than those that are inconsistent. In addition, ambiguous behaviors by group members are interpreted in stereotype-consistent ways.

People not only tend to interpret the behaviors of others in ways consistent with stereotypes, but also, once interpreted in that way, people show a bias in the way that information is subsequently recalled. Stereotype-consistent information has a recall advantage: People recall information better and more readily when it is consistent with a preexisting stereotype than when it is inconsistent (Bodenhausen 1988). This recall advantage for consistent over inconsistent information may reflect how stereotypes facilitate retrieval of information rather than differences in how well the information is represented in MEMORY. Thus, this effect can be reversed or eliminated when recognition rather than recall measures are used (Stangor and McMillan 1992).

People also develop expectations about others substantially on the basis of their group membership and the associated stereotypes, although this effect may be undermined by providing information about the unique characteristics of a person (Fiske 1998). Stereotypes are particularly likely to influence expectations, inferences, and impressions when people are not motivated to attend to individuating information or are limited in their capacity to process information due to other demands on their attention and thoughts. Because stereotypes shape interpretations, influence how information is recalled, and guide expectations and inferences in systematic ways, they tend to be self-perpetuating. They also can produce self-fulfilling prophecies in social interaction, in which the stereotypes of the perceiver influence the interaction in ways that conform to stereotypical expectations (Jussim 1991). Stereotypes can also directly influence members of stereotyped groups. Under conditions that make stereotypes salient, such as aptitude testing situations or situations in which the group member has solo or token status, the performance of members of the stereotyped group may be adversely affected even though they do not personally endorse the stereotype (Steele and Aronson 1995).

Perhaps because of the functional properties of stereotyping, stereotypes are difficult to change or eliminate. Cognitive strategies focus on providing counterstereotypic or nonstereotypic information about group members to undermine or dilute stereotypic associations. This approach is more effective when stereotype-disconfirming information is dispersed among a broad range of group members rather than concentrated in one person or in a small number of group members (Weber and Crocker 1983). In the latter case, people are likely to maintain their overall stereotype of the group while subtyping, with a different stereotype, the set of group members who disconfirm the general group stereotype (e.g., black athletes; Hewstone 1994). Intergroup approaches to changing stereotypes focus on changing the social category representations on which the stereotypes are based (Gaertner et al. 1993). Decategorization approaches attempt to degrade group boundaries by drawing attention to the individualized or personalized characteristics of people originally perceived in terms of their group membership. Recategorization strategies involve redefining group boundaries either (1) to change the representations from separate groups to one group which reflects a common identity; or (2) to maintain the original group categories but simultaneously to emphasize connection to a larger entity through common goals and mutual interdependence (Hewstone and Brown 1986). Whereas the former approach may be more effective at changing attitudes and stereotypes of people immediately present in the situation, the latter approach may produce more generalized stereotype change because it maintains the associative links to group members not present in a contact situation. Producing significant and enduring stereotype change typically requires direct, sustained, and personal intergroup contact.

See also CATEGORIZATION; CONCEPTS; NAIVE SOCIOLOGY

—John F. Dovidio

References

Ashmore, R. D., and F. K. DelBoca. (1981). Conceptual approaches to stereotypes and stereotyping. In D. L. Hamilton, Ed., *Cognitive Processes in Stereotyping and Intergroup Behavior.* Hillsdale, NJ: Erlbaum, pp. 1–35.

Bodenhausen, G. V. (1988). Stereotypic biases in social decision making and memory: Testing process models of stereotype use. *Journal of Personality and Social Psychology* 55: 726–737.

Devine, P. G. (1989). Stereotypes and prejudice: Their automatic and controlled components. *Journal of Personality and Social Psychology* 56: 5–18.

Dovidio, J. F., J. C. Brigham, B. T. Johnson, and S. L. Gaertner. (1996). Stereotyping, prejudice, and discrimination: Another look. In N. Macrae, C. Stangor, and M. Hewstone, Eds., *Foundations of Stereotypes and Stereotyping.* New York: Guilford, pp. 276–322.

Fiske, S. T. (1998). Stereotyping, prejudice, and discrimination. In D. T. Gilbert, S. T. Fiske, and G. Lindzey, Eds., *The Handbook of Social Psychology.* 4th ed. New York: McGraw-Hill.

Gaertner, S. L., J. F. Dovidio, P. A. Anastasio, B. A. Bachman, and M. C. Rust. (1993). The common ingroup identity model: Recategorization and the reduction of intergroup bias. In W. Stroebe and M. Hewstone, Eds., *European Review of Social Psychology,* vol. 4. London: Wiley, pp. 1–26.

Greenwald, A. G., and M. R. Banaji. (1995). Implicit social cognition: Attitudes, self-esteem, and stereotypes. *Psychological Review* 102: 4–27.

Hamilton, D. L., and J. W. Sherman. (1994). Stereotypes. In R. S. Wyer, Jr. and T. K. Srull, Eds., *Handbook of Social Cognition* 2nd ed. Hillsdale, NJ: Erlbaum, pp. 1–68.

Hewstone, M. (1994). Revision and change of stereotypic beliefs: In search of the elusive subtyping model. In W. Stroebe and M. Hewstone, Eds., *European Review of Social Psychology,* vol. 5. London: Wiley, pp. 69–109.

Hewstone, M., and R. J. Brown. (1986). Contact is not enough: An intergroup perspective on the contact hypothesis. In M. Hewstone and R. Brown, Eds., *Contact and Conflict in Intergroup Encounters.* Oxford: Blackwell, pp. 1–44.

Jussim, L. (1991). Social perception and social reality: A reflection-construction model. *Psychological Review* 98: 54–73.

Lepore, L., and R. J. Brown. (1997). Category and stereotype activation: Is prejudice inevitable? *Journal of Personality and Social Psychology* 72: 275–287.

Lippmann, W. (1922). *Public Opinion.* New York: Harcourt-Brace.

Mackie, D. M., D. L. Hamilton, J. Susskind, and F. Rosselli. (1996). Social psychological foundations of stereotype formation. In N. Macrae, C. Stangor, and M. Hewstone, Eds., *Foundations of Stereotypes and Stereotyping.* New York: Guilford, pp. 41–78.

Macrae, C. N., G. V. Bodenhausen, A. B. Milne, and J. Jetten. (1994). Out of mind but back in sight: Stereotypes on the rebound. *Journal of Personality and Social Psychology* 67: 808–817.

Oakes, P. J., S. J. Haslam, and J. C. Turner, Eds. (1994). *Stereotyping and Social Reality.* Oxford: Blackwell.

Stangor, C., and D. McMillan. (1992). Memory for expectancy-congruent and expectancy-incongruent information: A review of the social and developmental literatures. *Psychological Bulletin* 111: 42–61.

Steele, C. M., and J. Aronson. (1995). Stereotype threat and intellectual test performance of African Americans. *Journal of Personality and Social Psychology* 69: 797–811.

Tajfel, H. (1981). Social stereotypes and social groups. In J. C. Turner and H. Giles, Eds., *Intergroup Behavior.* Chicago: University of Chicago Press, pp. 144–167.

Weber, R., and J. Crocker. (1983). Cognitive processes in the revision of stereotypical beliefs. *Journal of Personality and Social Psychology* 45: 961–977.

Further Readings

Basow, S. A. (1992). *Gender Stereotypes and Roles.* 3rd edition. Pacific Grove, CA: Brooks/Cole.

Higgins, E. T., and A. W. Kruglanski, Eds. (1996). *Social Psychology: Handbook of Basic Principles.* New York: Guilford.

Lee, Y., L. J. Jussim, and C. R. McCauley, Eds. (1995). *Stereotype Accuracy: Toward Appreciating Group Differences.* Washington, DC: American Psychological Association.

Leyens, J.-P., V. Yzerbyt, and G. Schadron. (1994). *Stereotypes and Social Cognition.* Thousand Oaks, CA: Sage.

Mackie, D. M., and D. L. Hamilton, Eds. (1993). *Affect, Cognition, and Stereotyping: Interactive Processes in Group Perception.* San Diego, CA: Academic Press.

Macrae, N., C. Stangor, and M. Hewstone, Eds. (1996). *Foundations of Stereotypes and Stereotyping.* New York: Guilford.

Spears, R., P. J. Oakes, N. Ellemers, and S. A. Haslam, Eds. (1997). *The Social Psychology of Stereotyping and Group Life.* Cambridge, MA: Blackwell.

Uleman, J. S., and J. A. Bargh, Eds. (1989). *Unintended Thought.* New York: Guilford.

Stress

Stress may be defined as a threat, real or implied, to the psychological or physiological integrity of an individual. Although stress can be assessed as subjective experience, it is the behavioral and physiological responses to stress that are the most closely linked to measurable health outcomes.

Stress involves a stressor and a stress response. Stressors include trauma or injury, physical exertion at the limit of the body's capacity, and environmental factors like noise, overcrowding, and excessive heat or cold. Major life events are stressful, as are daily hassles in the family and workplace. Social isolation is stressful, and supportive social contact reduces the physiological stress response.

Stress responses may be both behavioral and physiological. Behavioral responses to stress may avoid trouble, but they may also exacerbate the consequences of stress: for instance, confrontational behaviors that exacerbate the stress, as well as self-damaging behaviors like smoking, drinking, and driving an automobile recklessly. Physiological stress responses involve the activation of the autonomic nervous system and the hypothalamo-pituitary-adrenal (HPA) axis.

The brain and behavior play an important role in determining what is stressful. The brain interprets what is stressful on the basis of past experience of the individual, and then determines the behavioral response; and the brain regulates the physiological stress response. The brain is also a target of stress, which increases activity of systems that subserve fear (the AMYGDALA) and impairs systems that subserve declarative, episodic, spatial, and contextual MEMORY (the HIPPOCAMPUS; see also NEUROENDOCRINOLOGY).

Hans Selye described the "general adaptation syndrome" in response to stressors, which consists of the outpouring of catecholamines and cortisol as a common response to many noxious situations. There are two important features of the physiological stress response: (1) turning it on in amounts that are adequate to the challenge, and (2) turning it off when it is no longer needed. The physiological mediators of the stress response, namely, the catecholamines of the sympathetic nervous system and the glucocorticoids from the adrenal cortex, initiate cellular events that promote adaptive changes in cells and tissues throughout the body, which in turn protect the organism and promote survival.

The physiological systems that react to stress are important protectors of the body in the short run but cause damage and accelerate disease over long periods of time. Thus "good stress" involves the adaptive response to acute stress, and "bad stress" involves chronic stress, with sustained physiological responses that produce wear and tear on the body and brain over months and years. Stressful experiences can often be exhilarating to some individuals, whereas prolonged stress is generally not beneficial. "Bad stress" occurs when the stress response is stimulated frequently or when it does not shut off when not needed. The price of adapation, involving wear and tear on the body, has been called "allostatic load." *Allostasis,* meaning "achieving stability through change," describes the process of physiological adaptation, and *allostatic load* refers to a gradual process of wear and tear on the body. Examples of allostatic load include the exacerbation of atherosclerosis by psychosocial stress; stress-induced acceleration of abdominal obesity; hypertension and coronary heart disease resulting from job strain; bone calcium loss in depressive illness and as a result of intensive athletic training; and atrophy and damage to nerve cells in the hippocampus with accompanying memory impairment.

The vulnerability of many systems of the body to stress is influenced by experiences early in life. In animal models, unpredictable prenatal stress causes increased emotionality and increased reactivity of the HPA axis and autonomic nervous system, and these effects last throughout the lifespan. Postnatal handling in rats, a mild stress involving brief daily separation from the mother, counteracts the effects of prenatal stress and results in reduced emotionality and reduced reactivity of the HPA axis and autonomic nervous system, and these effects also last throughout the lifespan. The vulnerability of the hippocampus to age-related loss of function parallels these effects—prenatal stress increasing and postnatal handling decreasing the rate of brain aging.

Stress and stress-related disorders represent one of the most common complaints that physicians encounter, and these are estimated to cause a loss of $300 billion annually in lost productivity and medical expenses. Some examples show what stress means for health. Social conflict and the formation of hierarchies of dominance produce measurable effects in the body and brain: for example, changes in brain structure and function, and acceleration of coronary artery atherosclerosis. Stressful experiences and lack of social support have been reported to increase susceptibility to the common cold, and social support is a protective factor.

In Russia, there has been an increase of almost 40 percent in the mortality rate among men since the fall of communism. Less dramatic but still very meaningful are the gradients of health across socioeconomic status, as exemplified by the British civil service system. The lowest employment grades have increased overall mortality and increased rates of cardiovascular disease and abdominal obesity.

One of the most important aspects of stress related to disease is the sense of control. Learned helplessness is a condition that has been described in animals and humans and represents one type of coping mechanism. Less extreme, the lack of control on the job has been shown to have adverse health consequences, affecting rates of cardiovascular disease. Interventions that have increased the sense of control and reduced time pressures have increased physical and mental health.

Stress is a highly individualized experience: events that are stressful for one individual may not be stressful for others; and stress may be exhilarating and even beneficial in the short run. Individual differences in stress responses are traceable to life experiences during development and adult life, as well as to individual differences in physiological vulnerability based on genetic background and physical and mental health. Most individuals cope with stressful situations and adapt, as long as the stress does not continue for long periods. Nevertheless, prolonged stressful experiences and more subtle aspects of stress physiology captured under the term *allostatic load* do produce a gradual wear and tear on the body and brain that can accelerate the onset and severity of diseases.

See also CULTURAL VARIATION; EMOTION AND THE HUMAN BRAIN; EMOTIONS; PAIN

—*Bruce S. McEwen*

Further Readings

Adler, N. E., T. Boyce, M. A. Chesney, S. Cohen, S. Folkman, R. L. Kahn, and L. S. Syme. (1994). Socioeconomic status and health: The challenge of the gradient. *American Psychologist* 49: 15–24.

Bobak, M., and M. Marmot. (1996). East-West mortality divide and its potential explanations: Proposed research agenda. *BMJ* 312: 421–425.

Bosma, H., M. G. Marmot, H. Hemingway, A. C. Nicholson, E. Brunner, and S. S. Stansfield. (1997). Low job control and risk of coronary heart disease in Whitehall 2 (prospective cohort) study. *Brit. Med. J.* 314: 558–565.

Cohen, S., D. A. G. Tyrrell, and A. P. Smith. (1991). Psychological stress and susceptibility to the common cold. *N. Engl. J. Med.* 325: 606–612.

Cohen, S., W. J. Doyle, D. P. Skoner, B. S. Rabin, and J. M. J. Gwaltney. (1997). Social ties and susceptibility to the common cold. *J. Amer. Med. Assoc.* 277: 1940–1944.

Everson, S. A., J. W. Lynch, M. A. Chesney, G. A. Kaplan, D. E. Goldberg, S. B. Shade, R. D. Cohen, R. Salonen, and J. T. Salonen. (1997). Interaction of workplace demands and cardiovascular reactivity in progression of carotid atherosclerosis: Population based study. *Brit. Med. J.* 314: 553–558.

Gould, E., B. S. McEwen, P. Tanapat, L. A. M. Galea, and E. Fuchs. (1997). Neurogenesis in the dentate gyrus of the adult tree shrew is regulated by psychosocial stress and NMDA receptor activation. *J. Neurosci.* 17: 2492–2498.

Jayo, J. M., C. A. Lively, J. R. Kaplan, and S. B. Manuck. (1993). Effects of exercise and stress on body fat distribution in male cynomolgus monkeys. *Int. J. Obesity* 17: 597–604.

Lazarus, R. S., and S. Folkman. (1984). *Stress, Appraisal and Coping.* New York: Springer.

Magarinos, A. M., B. S. McEwen, G. Flugge, and E. Fuchs. (1996). Chronic psychosocial stress causes apical dendritic atrophy of hippocampal ca3 pyramidal neurons in subordinate tree shrews. *J. Neuro.* 16: 3534–3540.

Manuck, S. B., J. R. Kapley, M. R. Adams, and T. B. Clarkson. (1988). Studies of psychosocial influences on coronary artery atherosclerosis in cynomolgus monkey. *Health Psychol.* 7: 113–124.

Marmot, M., and T. Theorell. (1997). Social class and cardiovascular disease: The contribution of work. *International Journal of Health Services* 18: 659–674.

McEwen, B. S. (1998). Protective and damaging effects of stress mediators. *N. Engl. J. Med.* 238: 171–179.

McEwen, B. S., and E. Stellar. (1993). Stress and the individual: Mechanisms leading to disease. *Archives of Internal Medicine* 153: 2093–2101.

Melin, B., U. Lundberg, J. Soderlund, and M. Granqvist. (1997). Psychological and physiological stress reactions of male and female assembly workers: A comparison between two different forms of work organization. *Journal of Organizational Psychology.*

Pickering, T. G., R. B. Devereux, G. D. James, W. Gerin, P. Landsbergis, P. L. Schnall, and J. E. Schwartz. (1996). Environmental influences on blood pressure and the role of job strain. *Journal of Hypertension* 14: S179–S185.

Seligman, M. E. P. (1975). *Helplessness: On Depression, Development and Death.* San Francisco: W. H. Freeman.

Selye, H. (1956). *The Stress of Life.* New York: McGraw Hill.

Sterling, P., and J. Eyer. (1988). Allostasis: A new paradigm to explain arousal pathology. In S. Fisher and J. Reason, Eds., *Handbook of Life Stress, Cognition and Health.* New York: Wiley, pp. 629–649.

Weiner, H. (1992). *Perturbing the Organism: The Biology of Stressful Experiences.* Chicago: University of Chicago Press.

Stress, Linguistic

In pronouncing the word àutobìográphic, English speakers make the odd-numbered vowels more prominent than the even-numbered, with greatest prominence going on the last odd-numbered vowel. In the traditional terminology of phonetics, the odd-numbered vowels are said to be *stressed* and the even-numbered, *unstressed*. Stress is commonly—though not universally—implemented phonetically by an increase in the *pitch* (fundamental voice frequency) of the vowel. (For details of English stress, see Pierrehumbert 1980.)

In many languages, word stress is predictable. The principles and rules that make this possible are somewhat separate from the rest of the PHONOLOGY. This quasi-independence of the stress rules is reflected in the fact that when adding to its vocabulary a word from another language, the borrowing language often preserves the phonemes (sounds) of the original word but modifies its stress contour. For example, the Russian borrowing *babúshka* is stressed in English on the second syllable, whereas in Russian this word has initial stress (i.e., *bábushka*). Except for the stress, the sounds of the Russian word are (quite) faithfully reproduced in English. As there has been no concerted effort by the schools or media to instill a particular stress pattern, the most plausible explanation for the *babúshka* stress is that English speakers assign stress to this new word by analogy with such English words as *Aláska, fiásco.* Implicit in this explanation is the assumption that English speakers have knowledge of the English stress rules and make active use of this knowledge. Although little is known at present about how this knowledge is used by speakers in the production of utterances, a great deal has been learned in the last quarter century about the nature of this knowledge.

The fundamental insight into the nature of stress is due to Liberman 1975. It was he who suggested that stress reflects the grouping (chunking) of the vowels of the word—more exactly, of its stressable sounds—into subsequences called *feet*. Research since 1975 has shown that the construction of feet—and hence stress assignment—is governed by a small number of rules belonging to a few schemata that differ with respect to a handful of binary parameters. Because this perspective on stress is not widely known and may well fly in the face of common-sense views, the rest of this article presents a detailed illustration of how feet are employed to compute the stress of words. The discussion here adopts the formalism of Idsardi (1992), because it reflects most clearly the role of feet in the computation of stress. (For discussion of alternative approaches, see Halle and Vergnaud 1987; Idsardi 1992; Kenstowicz 1993; and Hayes 1995.)

We begin with the very simple stress system of colloquial Czech. In Czech, odd-numbered vowels are stressed, and main stress falls on the vowel of the word-initial syllable, as for example in *prábabìčkamì* in 'greatgrandmothers' (instrumental case) (Jakobson 1962). In most languages, vowels are stressable, but consonants are not. To reflect formally this difference between sounds that are and are not stressable, the Idsardi theory posits that metrical structure is computed on a separate plane onto which are projected all and only the stressable phonemes (usually the vowels) of the word. This is illustrated in (1) with the Czech word cited above.

(1)   * * * * * line 0
        | | | | |
        prábabìčkamì

In (1) each vowel projects an asterisk and the sequence of asterisks so generated is labeled *line 0*. Additional lines of asterisks are generated by devices explained below. The set of asterisk lines associated with a given word is its *metrical grid*.

The grouping of stressable elements into feet is notated here by means of parentheses: a left parenthesis groups into a foot the stressable elements on its right, whereas a right parenthesis groups the elements on its left (cf. below). The parentheses themselves are inserted by three types of rules.

The first of these is *iterative foot construction* (IFC) rules. An IFC rule inserts left or right parentheses into a sequence of asterisks beginning at either its left or its right edge and proceeding toward the opposite edge of the string, subject to the constraint that except for the initial parenthesis a substring of two or three asterisks must separate an inserted parenthesis from the nearest parenthesis on its left, where insertion is from left to right, and on its right, where insertion is from right to left. The Czech IFC rule is given in (2) and its effects are illustrated in (3).

(2) On line 0 insert left parentheses starting from the left edge at an interval of two asterisks

(3)   (* *(* * (* line 0
     | | | | |
    prábabìčkamì

What differentiates various IFC rules is the replacement of one or more of the three variables by its alternative (i.e., left by right or 2 by 3). The theory of metrical structure admits therefore exactly eight different IFC rules, of which a given language characteristically uses one. (For illustrations, see References.)

The second type are *head-marking* rules. In each foot, one of the elements—called the *head*—is specially marked (stressed). The head of a foot is either its left-most or its right-most element, and the head element of each foot is projected onto the next higher line in the grid, thereby signaling its marked (stressed) status. In Czech, line 0 feet are left-headed. This is illustrated in (4).

(4)   *   *   * line 1
   (* *(* *(* line 0
    | | | | |
    prábabìckamì

The third category are *edge-marking* rules. As noted above, the main stress in Czech words falls on the vowel of the initial syllable. In order to mark this vowel, the theory makes use of a second type of parenthesis insertion rule, Edge Marking, which in Czech has the form in (5).

(5) Insert a left parenthesis to the left of the left-most asterisk on line 1.

Like the IFC rule (2), the Edge Marking rule (5) has three binary variables. There exist therefore eight Edge Marking rules for languages to choose from.

The Edge Marking rule (5) creates a foot that includes all asterisks on line 1. Like all feet, those constructed by (5) have a head, which in Czech must evidently be the left-most asterisk. This is illustrated in (6).

(6)   *   line 2
   (* *   * line 1
   (* *(* *(* line 0
    | | | | |
    prábabìčkamì

It is worth noting that in (6) the height of the asterisk columns reflects the relative degree of prominence of the different vowels in the word.

The stress rules of Czech are summarized in (7).

(7) Line 0: i. IFC (2): Insert left parentheses starting from the left edge at an interval of 2 asterisks
       ii. Heads: left
  Line 1: iii. Edge Marking (5): Insert a left parenthesis to the left of the left-most asterisk on line 1
       iv. Heads: left
       v. Assign High pitch to vowel with line 1 asterisk

With one major addition detailed below, the machinery introduced above accounts correctly for the stress patterns of words of most (all?) languages. Two further examples are reviewed below.

Pintupi, an Australian language, differs from Czech in that the Pintupi IFC rule inserts Right rather than Left parentheses. The Pintupi word, like that of Czech, therefore has main stress on the initial vowel and secondary stresses on other odd-numbered vowels; Pintupi differs from Czech in that the word-final vowel is never stressed. This is illustrated in (8). (Capital letters represent retroflex consonants. For some additional discussion of Pintupi, see Kenstowicz 1994.)

(8)   *   line 2
   (* * *   line 1
)* *)* *)* *)* line 0
   | | | | | | |
   TiLiriŋulampatʲu
   'the fire for our benefit flared up'

To deal with our final example, that of Selkup, a language of Siberia, a third type of parenthesis insertion rule is needed. This rule inserts a left/right parenthesis to the left/right of asterisks projecting vowels of special syllables—for example, syllables with long vowels. In Selkup, stress falls on the last long vowel of the word, but in words without a long vowel, stress is on the initial vowel. This migration of the stress toward opposite ends of the word is accounted for by the rules in (9).

(9) Line 0: i. Long Syllable Marking: Insert left parenthesis to left of asterisks projecting long vowel
       ii. Edge Marking: Insert right parenthesis to the right of the right-most asterisk
       iii. Heads: left
  Line 1: iv. Edge Marking: Insert right parenthesis to the right of the right-most asterisk
       v. Heads: right
       vi. Assign High pitch to vowel with line 2 asterisk

As illustrated in (10a), these rules assign stress to the last long vowel, and, as shown in (10b), in words without a long vowel the rules assign stress to the word-initial syllable. In view of (9iv) and (vi), there is but one stress per word in Selkup.

(10) a.   * line 2
       *   *) line 1
     * (* *(*) line 0
     | | | |
     qumooqlilii
     'your two friends'

    b. * line 2
      *) line 1
    * * **) line 0
    | | | |
    qol'cImpatI
    'found'

Although Selkup stress is vastly different from that of both Czech and Pintupi, it is the result of the same rules (rule schemata) with different settings of the parameters. To explain this similarity, we hypothesize that the schemata are part of the innate cognitive capacities that normal children bring to the task of learning the language of their milieu. Because the rule schemata are part of the innate cognitive equipment of learners, the task of a child learning a language reduces to figuring out the setting of a dozen or so binary parameters. This hypothesis accounts for the speed and accuracy with which children normally accomplish this task. Finally, by positing that knowledge of rule schemata is part of the genetic endowment of humans, but not of other species, we explain also why language is a uniquely human trait.

See also DISTINCTIVE FEATURES; PHONOLOGICAL RULES AND PROCESSES; PHONOLOGY, ACQUISITION OF; PHONOLOGY, NEURAL BASIS OF; PROSODY AND INTONATION; PROSODY AND INTONATION, PROCESSING ISSUES

—*Morris Halle*

References

Halle, M., and J.-R. Vergnaud. (1987). *An Essay on Stress.* Cambridge, MA: MIT Press.

Hayes, B. (1995). *Metrical Stress Theory.* Chicago: University of Chicago Press.

Idsardi, W. J. (1992). *The Computation of Stress.* Ph.D. diss., MIT. Distributed by MIT Working Papers in Linguistics, Cambridge, MA.

Jakobson, R. (1962). Contributions to the study of Czech accent. In *Selected Writings* 1. S-Gravenhage: Mouton and Co., pp. 614–625.

Kenstowicz, M. (1994). Stress. In *Phonology in Generative Grammar.* Oxford: Blackwell, pp. 548–621.

Liberman, M. (1975). *The Intonational System of English.* Ph.D. diss., MIT.

Pierrehumbert, J. B. (1980). *The Phonology and Phonetics of English Intonation.* Ph.D. diss., MIT.

Structure from Visual Information Sources

Looking about, it is obvious to us that the surrounding world has many objects in it, each object with a particular identity and location in the environment. The primate nervous system effortlessly determines both the object structure and its location from multiple visual sources. The motion of the object, its reflectance and obscuring of light, and the fact that we view the object with two eyes are all combined to form its internal representation in our brain. These sources of visual information have been under intense scrutiny for more than a century beginning with the work of the physicist and physiologist HELMHOLTZ (Helmholtz 1962). However, it is only a relatively recent realization that there are substantial differences in how information from these sources is encoded by the primate brain to derive the shapes of objects. This development was driven by psychophysical, physiological, and anatomical determination of two VISUAL PROCESSING STREAMS in VISUAL CORTEX, one specialized for object shape and one for SPATIAL PERCEPTION. In the analysis of spatial environment, large portions of the visual field are typically analyzed through neurons leading to the parietal lobe. In contrast, the analysis of object shape requires fine details of each object integrated over space and time and occurs in the temporal cortex.

There are three major cues for the analysis of object shape. The most thoroughly studied is derived from motion. Fifteen years before any scientific publications, Ginger Rogers and Fred Astaire exploited the illusion of depth from motion in the black-and-white film *The Gay Divorcee* (1939). The shadow from a cardboard cutout of dancers rotating on a phonograph turntable fooled a gigolo into thinking the young couple was pirouetting behind closed doors. A number of papers by the gestalt psychologists (see GESTALT PERCEPTION) thoroughly explored the ability to extract 3-D shape-from-motion, typified by the work of Gibson (1966) and Wallach and O'Connell (1953). Subjects were only able to reconstruct the 3-D shape of a bent wire from its shadow when the wire was rotated. Further studies identified that 3-D structural cues such as length and angles between segments could be used to extract the 3-D shape, as reviewed by Ullman (1979). These studies provided a number of different explanations for the extraction of structure-from-motion, pitting purely motion cues against varying recognizable form cues. This bottom-up vs. top-down controversy was further examined using computer-generated displays in which the motion of each element could be individually controlled (Ullman 1979). These studies have shown that pure motion is sufficient to extract form information in both human and nonhuman primates (Siegel and Andersen 1988), although they do not explicitly exclude the possibility that form cues may supplement motion.

Another source of visual information arises from the horizontal separation between the two eyes (figure 1). The binocular depth effect is seen with old-style Wheatstone stereoscopes in which the scene leaps into depth when viewed with both eyes (Wade and Ono 1985). Sufficient information exists in the disparity of the two images on the RETINA to provide depth profiles. As in the study of structure-from-motion, the issue arises as to whether recognizable details are needed to extract structure-from-disparity. Julesz (1995) generated computer displays in which all the visual cues were removed except for disparity using stimuli that appeared to each eye as random visual noise. The fusion of the random dot stereograms demonstrated that depth could unambiguously be derived from the disparity of the retinal images.

The third major source of information about the shape of an object arises from the reflectance of light from its surface (see figure 1). Different surface characteristics provide shape information. Specular (shiny) highlights arise from shiny surfaces and may accentuate regions of high curvature while color may also help in determining object shape. A well-studied luminance cue is shape-from-shading in which light passes over an object and part of the object is illuminated while part remains in shadow. Unlike structure-from-motion and structure-from-disparity, a top-down assumption that the light source is above the object is needed to explain much of the psychophysical data.

An assumption, such as the invocation of a highly elevated light source in structure-from-shading, is called a constraint by those in COMPUTATIONAL NEUROSCIENCE.

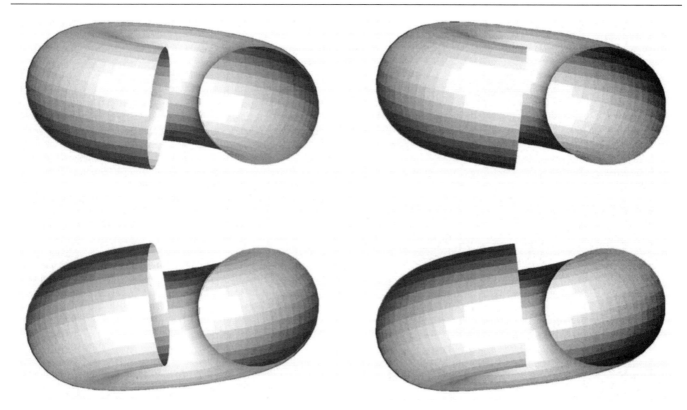

Figure 1. In both pairs of figures, the shape is easily determined from the shading cues, although the lower figure incorrectly appears to have a ball at one end. This is due to the expectation that all light sources are above. The pairs of figures may be fused by using a stereoviewer or free-fusing to provide unambiguous depth cues. In the upper pair, where the stereo and shape-from-shading cues agree, the right end of the tube is correctly seen as an opening. In the lower pair of figures, the disparity cues and the shape-from-shading cues are in opposition. Even with the presumably unambiguous disparity cues, the ball remains at the end of the tube. The shape-from-shading cues are dominant, suggesting that it is processed prior to disparity. Studies in which one type of shape cue is pitted against another are often used in psychophysical studies, with the actual physiological measurements lagging behind.

Constraints are often invoked in shape analysis because the raw measurements of motion, disparity, or luminance are insufficient to define objects in the world (MARR 1982; Poggio and Koch 1985). It arises because there are too many objects that can give rise to the measured motion, disparity, or shaded images. The constraints may be explicit or implicit in the theories, algorithms, or implementations (Marr 1982) that solve problems of shape recognition. For example, given a black-and-white photograph of an egg, most persons assume that the egg is lit from above and thus the egg's surface is perceived as convex. In fact, if the photograph is simply turned over, most observers will describe the surface as convex, their perception seemingly fixed on the idea that the light source is overhead (Ramachandran 1988). The rigidity of an object is often assumed in the analysis of structure-from-motion (Ullman 1979; Bennett and Hoffman 1985). It is still unknown how constraints are expressed in the brain and whether they are innate or develop through experience.

These assumptions combined with a geometrical description of the problem have led to a number of theorems that demonstrate the feasibility of obtaining information from the visual input. As a test of these theorems, algorithms are implemented on digital computers. These have been successful to some extent in that certain problems in MACHINE VISION, such as automobile part recognition, may be per-formed. However, the question as to whether the primate brain implements mathematically based approaches remains open.

Anatomical and physiological studies of the CEREBRAL CORTEX have been able to determine some of the actual processes and brain regions that are involved in shape recognition. Both hierarchical and parallel processes are involved in the representation of shape. The best-understood recognition process is the motion pathway that passes through striate cortex, to the middle temporal motion area (MT/V5). In MT/V5 there is a representation of the velocity of the image for different parts of the visual field (Albright, Desimone, and Gross 1984). This motion representation is further developed in the medial superior temporal area (MST) in which neurons are found that respond to environmental optic flow for spatial vision (Tanaka et al. 1986; Duffy and Wurtz 1991). Beyond MST, the motion signal passes to the parietal cortex (area 7a; Siegel and Read 1997) in which optic flow signals are further processed and combined with eye position information. Both 7a and MST project to the anterior polysensory temporal area (STPa) which has neurons that represent both flow and apparently 3-D shape (Bruce, Desimone, and Gross 1981; Anderson and Siegel submitted).

Running roughly in parallel to the processing of visual motion is the analysis of disparity cues. At each step from striate to MT/V5 to MST to 7a, neurons are found that are tuned to disparity (Poggio and Poggio 1984; Roy, Komatsu, and Wurtz 1992; Gnadt and Mays 1995). Little is known as to how binocular cues are used for shape representation.

A more temporal cortical stream represents shape using luminance and color cues. Neurons have been described that represent all sorts of luminance cues, such as orientation (Hubel and Wiesel 1977) and borders (von der Heydt, Peterhans, and Baumgartner 1984). Geometrical figures (Tanaka 1993), as well as shapes as complex as faces (Gross 1973), may be represented by temporal cortical neurons. Color analysis surely is used in object identification, although little formal work has been done. Surprisingly, the dependence of these neurons upon parameters of motion (Perrett et al. 1985) and disparity are as yet little explored. Such studies are crucial, as the psychophysical ability to describe shape (a putative temporal stream analysand) does not deteriorate when motion or disparity (a putative dorsal stream analysand) is the underlying representation.

In summary, the visual perception of 3-D structure utilizes motion, disparity, and luminance. Psychophysical studies have defined the limits of our ability, while computational studies have developed a formal framework to describe the perceptual process as well as to test hypotheses. Anatomical and physiological results have provided essential cues from functional systems.

See also HIGH-LEVEL VISION; MID-LEVEL VISION; MOTION, PERCEPTION OF; TOP-DOWN PROCESSING IN VISION

—*Ralph M. Siegel*

References

Albright T. D., R. Desimone, and C. G. Gross. (1984). Columnar organization of directionally selective cells in visual area MT of the macaque. *J. Neurophysiol.* 51: 16–31.

Anderson, K. A., and R. M. Siegel. (Submitted). Representation of three-dimensional structure-from-motion in STPa of the behaving monkey. *Cereb. Cortex.*

Bennett, B. M., and D. D. Hoffman. (1985). The computation of structure from fixed-axis motion: Nonrigid structures. *Biol. Cybern.* 51: 293–300.

Bruce, C., R. Desimone, and C. G. Gross. (1981). Visual properties of neurons in a polysensory area in superior temporal sulcus of the macaque. *J. Neurophysiol.* 46: 369–384.

Duffy, C. J., and R. H. Wurtz. (1991). Sensitivity of MST neurons to optic flow stimuli. 1. A continuum of response selectivity to large-field stimuli. *J. Neurophysiol.* 65:1329–1345.

Gibson, J. J. (1966). *The Senses Considered as Perceptual Systems.* Boston: Houghton Mifflin.

Gnadt, J. W., and L. E. Mays. (1995). Neurons in monkey parietal area LIP are tuned for eye-movement parameters in 3-D space. *J. Neurophysiol.* 73: 280–297.

Gross, C. G. (1973). Visual functions of inferotemporal cortex. In H. Autrum, R. Jung, W. R. Loewenstein, D. M. McKay, and H. L. Teuber, Eds., *Handbook of Sensory Physiology 7/3B.* Berlin: Springer, pp. 451–482.

Helmholtz, H. L. F. von. (1962). *Helmholtz's Treatise on Physiological Optics.* Translated by from the 3rd German ed., James P. C. Southall, Ed. New York: Dover Publications.

Hubel, D. H., and T. N. Wiesel. (1977). The Ferrier Lecture. Functional architecture of macaque monkey visual cortex. *Proc. R. Soc. Lond. B. Biol. Sci.* 198: 1–59.

Julesz, B. (1995). *Dialogues on Perception.* Cambridge, MA: MIT Press.

Marr, D. (1982). *Vision.* San Francisco: W. H. Freeman.

Perrett, D. I., P. A. Smith, A. J. Mistlin, A. J. Chitty, A. S. Head, D. D. Potter, R. Broennimann, A. D. Milner, and M. A. Jeeves. (1985). Visual analysis of body movements by neurones in the temporal cortex of the macaque monkey: A preliminary report. *Behav. Brain Res.* 16: 153–170.

Poggio, G. F., and T. Poggio. (1984). The analysis of stereopsis. *Ann. Rev. Neurosci.* 7: 379–412.

Poggio, T., and C. Koch. (1985). Ill-posed problems in early vision: From computational theory to analogue networks. *Proc. R. Soc. Lond. B. Biol. Sci.* 226: 303–323.

Ramachandran, V. S. (1988). Perceiving shape from shading. *Sci. Am.* 259(2): 76–83.

Roy, J. P., H. Komatsu, and R. H. Wurtz. (1992). Disparity sensitivity of neurons in monkey extrastriate area MST. *J. Neurosci.* 12: 2478–2492.

Siegel, R. M., and R. A. Andersen. (1988). Perception of three-dimensional structure from two-dimensional motion in monkey and man. *Nature* 331: 259–261.

Siegel, R. M., and H. L. Read. (1997). Analysis of optic flow in the monkey parietal area 7a. *Cereb. Cortex* 7: 327–346.

Tanaka, K. (1993). Neuronal mechanisms of object recognition. *Science* 262: 685–688.

Tanaka, K., K. Hikosaka, H. Saito, M. Yukie, Y. Fukada, and E. Iwai. (1986). Analysis of local and wide-field movements in the superior temporal visual areas of the macaque monkey. *J. Neurosci.* 6: 134–144.

Ullman, S. (1979). *The Interpretation of Visual Motion.* Cambridge, MA: MIT Press.

von der Heydt, R., E. Peterhans, and G. Baumgartner. (1984). Illusory contours and cortical neuron responses. *Science* 224: 1260–1262.

Wade, N. J., and H. Ono. (1985). The stereoscopic views of Wheatstone and Brewster. *Psychol. Res.* 47(3): 125–133.

Wallach, H., and D. N. O'Connell. (1953). The kinetic depth effect *J. Exp. Psychol.* 45: 205–217.

Superstition

See MAGIC AND SUPERSTITION; RELIGIOUS IDEAS AND PRACTICES

Supervenience

Supervenience is a determination relation, often thought to hold between physical characteristics and mental characteristics. In philosophy of mind, the concept of supervenience is sometimes employed as a way of articulating the metaphysical thesis of PHYSICALISM. The notion of supervenience, originally employed in ethics, was introduced into philosophy of mind by Donald Davidson (1970, 1973), who formulated the thesis that mental characteristics are supervenient on physical ones: "It is impossible for two events (objects, states) to agree in all their physical characteristics . . . and to differ in their psychological characteristics" (Davidson 1973: 716). This supervenience claim is weaker than certain other claims about physical-mental relations sometimes advocated in philosophy of mind—for instance, that mental characteristics are identical to, or are definable from, or are lawfully coextensive with, physical characteristics.

One commonly cited reason to favor physical/psychological supervenience over any of these stronger, more reductive, conceptions of the relation between the physical and the mental is that psychological characteristics allegedly are multiply realizable (i.e., multiply implementable) by physical ones. For instance, mental properties might get physically realized very differently in certain actual or possible nonhuman creatures (e.g., Martians) than in humans. Furthermore, for some species of actual or possible creatures (perhaps including humans), a given psychological characteristic might be physically multiply realizable within the species, or even in a single creature.

The physical characteristics that determine a given psychological characteristic M of a given creature (on a particular occasion when M is instantiated) are called the *supervenience base* for M (on that occasion). Typically the supervenience base will include not only the physical property P that physically realizes M in the creature with characteristic M, but also certain physical-structural characteristics of the creature in virtue of which the property P plays the causal role requisite for being a realization of M. For instance, the supervenience base for the property *wanting some ice cream* on a given occasion, will include not only the neurochemical property P that physically realizes this desire-property in a given person, but also various persisting structural features of the person's brain and body in virtue of which P plays a suitable desire-implementing causal role (e.g., the role of propelling the person's body toward a location where the person believes ice cream can be obtained).

Supervenience often figures in philosophical discussions of mental causation. It is sometimes suggested (e.g., Kim 1979, 1984) that causal efficacy and explanatory relevance are "transmitted" across levels of description, via supervenience connections, from physical characteristics to mental ones. The idea is that mental characteristics figure in "supervenient causation"—even though all human behavior, described as bodily motion, in principle is causally explainable in physico-chemical terms (see MENTAL CAUSATION).

A distinction is commonly made between intentional (representational) mental characteristics and qualitative (phenomenal) mental characteristics; and it is sometimes maintained that the former are supervenient on the physical in a way that the latter are not. (Intentional characteristics are the kind typically expressed by mentalistic locutions containing "that"-clauses, e.g., "believes that MIT is in Boston." Qualitative characteristics, or QUALIA, are the distinctive WHAT IT'S LIKE features of sensory experiences like seeing a bright red color patch, or smelling rotten eggs, or stubbing one's toe.) Intentional characteristics are widely thought to be *logically,* or *conceptually,* supervenient on physical characteristics (e.g., Chalmers 1996)—so that there is no "possible world" that is a perfect physical duplicate of the actual world, but differs from the actual world in the distribution of intentional mental properties. By contrast, it is sometimes claimed (e.g., Chalmers 1996) that qualia are not logically supervenient on the physical, because allegedly the following kinds of physical-duplicate worlds are conceptually coherent possibilities: (1) a physical-duplicate world in which color qualia are paired with the relevant neural states in the human visual cortex in ways that are systematically inverted relative to actual-world neural/qualia pairings (an "inverted qualia" world); and (2) a physical-duplicate world in which qualia are absent altogether (an "absent qualia" world).

Even if qualia are not logically supervenient on physical characteristics, they still might exhibit a weaker kind of dependence: *nomological* (i.e., lawful) supervenience. The nomological supervenience of qualia would mean there are fundamental laws of nature, over and above the basic laws of physics, linking certain physical (or perhaps certain functional) characteristics of certain physical systems (e.g., humans and other sentient creatures) with the concurrent presence of qualia—a view defended in Chalmers (1996). Arguably, such a position would be a version of naturalism about qualia, but not a version of physicalism. Issues of mental causation would arise for such a view, because it is sometimes maintained (e.g., Horgan 1987) that if qualia supervene on physical characteristics only nomically and not in a stronger way, then qualia are epiphenomenal—that is, they have no real causal efficacy or explanatory relevance vis-à-vis human behavior.

Supervenience issues also arise with respect to intentional mental characteristics. It is often claimed that for at least some intentional properties, the minimal supervenience base includes more than the intrinsic physical features of the person instantiating the property (at the time of instantiation); it also includes certain relational connections between the person and the wider environment. One very influential source for such claims is the TWIN EARTH thought experiment in Putnam (1975). An Earthling and a Twin Earthling who are just alike in all intrinsic physical respects could differ mentally: the Earthling is having a thought about water (viz., H_2O), whereas the Twin Earthling is having a thought about twater (viz., XYZ). The moral, apparently, is that the supervenience base for an intentional mental characteristic like *wanting some water* involves not merely the current intrinsic physical properties of the person who currently has this mental property, but also certain relational connections between the person and the person's physical—and/or social, and/or historical, and/or evolutionary—environment. Such mental properties are said to have *wide content,* because the supervenience base for such a property extends beyond the current intrinsic physical characteristics of the creature currently instantiating the property; wide-content characteristics, as the saying goes, are not supervenient upon "what's in the head." By contrast, intentional mental characteristics that do supervene upon a creature's current intrinsic physical characteristics are said to have NARROW CONTENT.

A variety of interrelated issues concerning wide and narrow content have received active discussion in recent philosophy, and have direct implications for the foundations of cognitive science. These include the following:

1. How should wide-content and narrow-content mental states (i.e., state-types) be characterized?
2. How pervasive is the phenomenon of wide content? Is it confined to beliefs and other mental states employing specific kinds of concepts (e.g., natural-kind concepts like "water" or "gold"), or is it much more widespread?

3. Do wide-content mental states have causal efficacy and explanatory relevance?
4. Should cognitive science concern itself with both wide-content and narrow-content psychological states, or should it rather focus on only one kind?
5. Is there really such a thing as narrow content at all?

Discussion of such questions has occurred in an intellectual climate where two broad currents of thought have been dominant. One approach assumes that most, or perhaps all, intentional mental states have both wide content and narrow content (e.g., Fodor 1980, 1987, 1991). A second approach eschews narrow content altogether, and construes mental intentionality as essentially a matter of suitable relational connections between intrinsic physical states of a creature and certain features of the creature's current environment and/or its evolutionary/developmental history (e.g., Dretske 1981, 1988; Millikan 1984; Fodor 1994). But some philosophers vigorously challenge both orientations—for instance, David Lewis (1994), whose dissident remarks are eminently sensible.

Two longer overview discussions of supervenience are Kim (1990) and Horgan (1993). Useful collections include Horgan (1984), Beckermann, Flohr, and Kim (1992), and Kim (1993).

See also EXPLANATORY GAP; FUNCTIONALISM; INTENTIONALITY; REDUCTIONISM

—*Terence Horgan*

References

Beckermann, A., H. Flohr, and J. Kim, Eds. (1992). *Emergence or Reduction? Essays on the Prospects of Nonreductive Physicalism.* Berlin: de Guyter.

Chalmers, D. (1996). *The Conscious Mind: In Search of a Fundamental Theory.* New York: Oxford University Press.

Davidson, D. (1970). Mental events. In L. Foster and J. W. Swanson, Eds., *Experience and Theory.* Amherst: University of Massachusetts Press.

Davidson, D. (1973). The material mind. In P. Suppes et al., Eds., *Logic, Methodology, and the Philosophy of Science.* Amsterdam: North-Holland.

Dretske, F. (1981). *Knowledge and the Flow of Information.* Cambridge, MA: MIT Press.

Dretske, F. (1988). *Explaining Behavior: Reasons in a World of Causes.* Cambridge, MA: MIT Press.

Fodor, J. (1980). Methodological solipsism considered as a research strategy in cognitive science. *Behavioral and Brain Sciences* 3: 63–109.

Fodor, J. (1987). *Psychosemantics: The Problem of Meaning in the Philosophy of Mind.* Cambridge, MA: MIT Press.

Fodor, J. (1991). *A Theory of Content and Other Essays.* Cambridge, MA: MIT Press.

Fodor, J. (1994). *The Elm and the Expert: Mentalese and Its Semantics.* Cambridge, MA: MIT Press.

Horgan, T., Ed. (1984). *The Concept of Supervenience in Contemporary Philosophy, Spindel Conference Supplement, Southern Journal of Philosophy* 22.

Horgan, T. (1987). Supervenient qualia. *Philosophical Review* 96: 491–520.

Horgan, T. (1993). From supervenience to superdupervenience: Meeting the demands of a material world. *Mind* 102: 555–586.

Kim, J. (1979). Causality, identity, and supervenience in the mind-body problem. In P. French, T. Uehling, and H. Wettstein, Eds., *Midwest Studies in Philosophy*, 4. Minneapolis: University of Minnesota Press.

Kim, J. (1984). Supervenience and supervenient causation. In Horgan (1984).

Kim, J. (1990). Supervenience as a philosophical concept. *Metaphilosophy* 21: 1–27.

Kim, J. (1993). *Supervenience and Mind: Selected Philosophical Essays.* Cambridge: Cambridge University Press.

Lewis, D. (1994). Reduction of mind. In S. Guttenplan, Ed., *A Companion to the Philosophy of Mind.* Cambridge, MA: Blackwell.

Millikan, R. (1984). *Language, Thought, and Other Biological Categories: New Foundations for Realism.* Cambridge, MA: MIT Press.

Moore, G. E. (1922). The conception of intrinsic value. In *Philosophical Studies.* New York: Harcourt, Brace, and Company.

Putnam, H. (1975). The meaning of "meaning." In K. Gunderson, Ed., *Language, Mind, and Knowledge, Minnesota Studies in the Philosophy of Science,* 7. Minneapolis: University of Minnesota Press.

Supervised Learning in Multilayer Neural Networks

Neural networks consist of simple processing units that interact via weighted connections. They are sometimes implemented in hardware but most research involves software simulations. They were originally inspired by ideas about how the brain computes, and understanding biological computation is still the major goal of many researchers in the field (Churchland and Sejnowski 1992). However, some biologically unrealistic neural networks are both computationally interesting and technologically useful (Bishop 1995).

A typical processing unit first computes a "total input," which is a weighted sum of the incoming activities from other units plus a bias. It then puts its total input through an activation function to determine the activity of the unit. The most common activation function is the logistic, $y = 1/1 + exp(-x)$. For deterministic analog units the activity that is communicated to other units is simply y. For binary stochastic units, y determines the probability that the activity of the unit is 1 rather than 0. For binary threshold units, the activity is 1 if the total input is positive and 0 otherwise. Sensory input to the network is typically handled by fixing the activities of some "input" units.

The most interesting property of NEURAL NETWORKS is their ability to learn from examples by adapting the weights on the connections. The most widely used learning algorithms are supervised: they assume that there is a set of training cases, each consisting of an input vector and a desired output or output vector. Learning involves sweeping through the training set many times, gradually adjusting the weights so that the actual output produced by the network gets closer to the desired output. The simplest neural network architecture consists of some input units with directed, weighted connections to an output unit. Such networks were extensively studied in the 1960s because there are very simple learning algorithms that are guaranteed to find the optimal weights when the output unit uses a linear or binary threshold activation function

(Widrow and Hoff 1960; Rosenblatt 1962). Unfortunately, such simple networks can only compute a very limited class of functions (Minsky and Papert 1969). They cannot, for example, compute the exclusive-or of two binary inputs.

The limitations of simple networks can be overcome by adding one or more intermediate, "hidden" layers of nonlinear units between the input and the output. The architecture remains feedforward, with each unit only receiving inputs from units in lower layers. With enough hidden units in a single layer, there exist weights that approximate arbitrarily closely any continuous, differentiable mapping from a compact input space to a compact output space. Finding the optimal weights is generally intractable, but gradient methods can be used to find sets of weights that work well for many practical tasks. Provided the hidden units use a nonlinearity with a well-behaved derivative, an algorithm called "back-propagation" (Rumelhart, Hinton, and Williams 1986) can be used to compute the derivatives, with respect to each weight in the network, of the error function. The standard error function is the squared difference between the actual and desired outputs, but cross-entropy error functions are more appropriate when the outputs represent class probabilities.

For each training case, the activities of the units are computed by a forward pass through the network. Then, starting with the output units, a backward pass through the network is used to compute the derivatives of the error function with respect to the total input received by each unit. This computation is a straightforward application of the chain rule and is as efficient as the forward pass. Given these derivatives, it is easy to compute the derivatives of the error function with respect to the weights.

There are many different ways of using the derivatives computed by backpropagation. In "on-line" learning, the weights are adjusted after each training case in proportion to the derivatives for that case. In "batch" learning, the derivatives are accumulated over the whole training set and then the weights are adjusted in the direction of steepest descent in the error function, or in some more sensible direction computed by a technique such as momentum, conjugate gradients, or delta-bar-delta. The simple on-line method is the most efficient for very large training sets in which the data are highly redundant, but batch conjugate gradient is faster and easier to use for small training sets. There are also constructive methods that add hidden units one at a time while keeping the incoming weights of earlier hidden units frozen (Fahlman and Lebiere 1990).

Feedforward neural networks that have one or more layers of logistic hidden units and are trained using backpropagation have worked very well for tasks such as discriminating similar phonemes (Lang, Waibel, and Hinton 1990) or recognizing handwritten digits (Le Cun et al. 1989; see also PATTERN RECOGNITION AND FEEDFORWARD NETWORKS). Performance is significantly improved if natural symmetries of the task are imposed on the network by forcing different weights to have the same values.

When training data are limited, a complicated network with a large number of weights is liable to overfit: it performs very well on the training data, but much less well on test data drawn from the same distribution. On the other hand, a simple network with few weights may perform poorly on both training and test data because it is unable to approximate the true function (Geman, Bienenstock, and Doursat 1992). Many different methods have been developed for optimizing the complexity of the network. If part of the training data is held out as a validation set, it is possible to try different numbers of hidden units and to pick the number that gives best performance on the validation set. The "early stopping" method, which is appropriate when computational resources are limited, stops the training of a complicated network as soon as its performance on the validation set starts to deteriorate. Another way of limiting the complexity of a network is to add a penalty to the error term. The simplest such penalty is the sum of the squares of the weights times a penalty coefficient, λ. This can be viewed in Bayesian terms as a zero-mean Gaussian prior which favors networks that have small weights. λ can be chosen using a validation set but this wastes training data and is awkward if different values of λ are required for the input-to-hidden and hidden-to-output weights. MacKay (1995) has developed Bayesian methods that estimate an appropriate λ without using a validation set.

Performance can almost always be improved by averaging the outputs of many different networks each of which overfits the data. Finding the appropriate weights to use when averaging the outputs can be viewed as a separate learning task (Wolpert 1992). The benefits of averaging increase as the networks' errors become less correlated so it helps to train networks on different subsets of the data (Breiman 1994). Training a net on data that earlier nets get wrong is an effective way of focusing computational resources on the difficult cases (Drucker, Schapire, and Simard 1993).

When fitting a network to data it is usual to search for a single good set of weights. The correct Bayesian method, by contrast, computes the posterior probability distribution over weight vectors and then combines the predictions made by all the different weight vectors in proportion to their posterior probabilities. MacKay's methods approximate the posterior by constructing a Gaussian distribution around each of a number of locally optimal weight vectors. Neal (1996) describes an efficient Monte Carlo method of approximating the full, multimodal posterior distribution. Rasmussen (1996) demonstrates that Neal's method gives better performance than many other neural network or statistical methods, but that it is no better than an equivalent statistical approach called Gaussian Processes.

Many varieties of feedforward net have been investigated. Radial basis function (RBF) networks use hidden units whose activations are a radially symmetrical function of the distance between the input vector and a mean vector associated with the unit (Broomhead and Lowe 1988). The usual function is a spherical Gaussian, but they can be generalized to have different variances on each input dimension or to have full covariance matrices. RBF networks can be fitted using the gradient computed by backpropagation. Alternatively, the means and variances of the hidden units can be set without reference to the desired outputs by fitting a mixture of Gaussian density models to the input vectors, or by simply using some of the training input vectors as means.

For tasks in which the data are expected to come from a number of different but unknown regimes, it is advantageous to use a "mixture of experts" architecture containing a different network for each regime and a "gating" network that decides on the probability of being in each regime (Jacobs et al. 1991). The whole system is trained to maximize the log probability of the correct answer under a mixture of Gaussian distributions, where each expert computes the input-dependent mean of a Gaussian and the gating network computes the input-dependent mixing proportion. Each expert can specialize on a specific regime because it only receives significant backpropagated gradients for cases where the gating network assigns it a significant mixing proportion. The gating network can discover the regimes because it receives backpropagated derivatives that encourage it to assign the expert that works best for each case. With a hierarchy of managers, this system is a soft version of decision trees (Jordan and Jacobs 1994).

See also COGNITIVE ARCHITECTURE; COGNITIVE MODELING, CONNECTIONIST; CONNECTIONIST APPROACHES TO LANGUAGE; RECURRENT NETWORKS; UNSUPERVISED LEARNING; VISION AND LEARNING

—*Geoffrey Hinton*

References

Bishop, C. M. (1995). *Neural Networks for Pattern Recognition.* Oxford: Oxford University Press.

Breiman, L. (1994). *Bagging Predictors.* Technical Report 421. Berkeley, CA: Department of Statistics, University of California.

Broomhead, D., and D. Lowe. (1988). Multivariable functional interpolation and adaptive networks. *Complex Systems* 2: 321–355.

Churchland, P. S., and T. J. Sejnowski. (1992). *The Computational Brain.* Cambridge, MA: MIT Press.

Drucker, H., R. Schapire, and P. Simard. (1993). Improving performance in neural networks using a boosting algorithm. In S. Hanson, J. Cowan, and C. Giles, Eds., *Neural Information Processing Systems,* vol. 5. San Mateo, CA: Kaufmann, pp. 42–49.

Fahlman, S. E., and C. Lebiere. (1990). The cascade-correlation learning architecture. In D. S. Touretzky, Ed., *Neural Information Processing Systems,* vol. 2. San Mateo, CA: Kaufmann, pp. 524–532.

Geman, S., E. Bienenstock, and R. Doursat. (1992). Neural networks and the bias/variance dilemma. *Neural Computation* 4: 1–58.

Jordan, M., and R. Jacobs. (1994). Hierarchical mixtures of experts and the EM algorithm. *Neural Computation* 6: 181–214.

Jacobs, R., M. I. Jordan, S. J. Nowlan, and G. E. Hinton. (1991). Adaptive mixtures of local experts. *Neural Computation* 3: 79–87.

Lang, K., A. Waibel, and G. E. Hinton. (1990). A time-delay neural network architecture for isolated word recognition. *Neural Networks* 3: 23–43.

Le Cun, Y., B. Boser, J. S. Denker, D. Henderson, R. E. Howard, W. Hubbard, and L. D. Jackel. (1989). Back-propagation applied to handwritten zipcode recognition. *Neural Computation* 1(4): 541–551.

MacKay, D. J. C. (1995). Probable networks and plausible predictions: A review of practical Bayesian methods for supervised neural networks. *Network: Computation in Neural Systems* 6: 469–505.

Minsky, M. L., and S. Papert. (1969). *Perceptrons.* Cambridge, MA: MIT Press.

Neal, R. M. (1996). *Bayesian Learning for Neural Networks.* New York: Springer.

Rasmussen, C. E. (1996). *Evaluation of Gaussian Processes and Other Methods for Non-linear Regression.* Ph.D. diss., University of Toronto.

Rosenblatt, F. (1962). *Principles of Neurodynamics.* New York: Spartan Books.

Rumelhart, D. E., G. E. Hinton, and R. J. Williams. (1986). Learning representations by back-propagating errors. *Nature* 323: 533–536.

Widrow, B., and M. E. Hoff. (1960). Adaptive switching circuits. In *IRE WESCON Convention Record,* part 4, pp. 96–104.

Wolpert, D. H. (1992). Stacked generalization. *Neural Networks* 5: 241–259.

Surface Perception

When we view a scene, the world seems to be filled with objects that have particular shapes, colors, and material properties. The primary source of information that we use to acquire information about our world is visual, which relies on the light reflected off of object surfaces to a point of observation. Thus, our knowledge of object structure—or any aspect of our visual world—is determined by the structure of the surfaces of objects, since it is here that light interacts with objects. Surface perception refers to our ability to use the images projected to our eyes to determine the color, shape, opacity, 3-D layout, and material properties of the objects in our environment. In this discussion, some of the basic problems studied in this domain are briefly introduced.

The problem of surface perception is to understand exactly how the visual system uses the structure in light to recover the 3-D structure of objects in the world. A solution to this problem requires that the visual system untangle the different causes that operate collectively to form the variations in luminance that project images to our eyes. The reason this problem is so hard is that there are a number of different ways that the same image could have been physically generated. Consider, for example, the problem of recovering the apparent lightness of a surface. The same shade of gray can be created by a dimly illuminated white surface, or a brightly illuminated black surface. Yet we seem to be remarkably good at untangling the contributions of illumination from the contributions of reflectance, and recovering the lightness of a surface. One of the major areas of research in surface perception is in LIGHTNESS PERCEPTION, which is one of the oldest areas of research in vision science. Yet even today, we are only beginning to understand how the photometric and geometric relationships in an image interact to determine the perceived lightness of a surface.

Another primary difficulty in recovering surface structure is in classifying the different types of luminance variations that arise in images. Consider the problem created by understanding the cause of a simple luminance discontinuity. Abrupt changes in luminance can be generated by occluding contours, shadows, or abrupt changes in the reflectance of a surface. An incorrect classification of luminance edges would lead to a variety of perceptual disasters. For example, consider a scene in which a face is brightly illuminated from the left, casting a strong shadow on the person's right cheek. If the boundary of this shadow is treated as an object boundary, the person's face would be split in pieces, and it would probably be impossible to recognize the underlying face. If the shadow boundary was interpreted as a change in the reflectance of the surface, the person's face would appear to have a large, dark stain. Both forms of misclassification would lead to distinct errors. In order to perceive the person's face as a homogeneously pigmented single object, the visual system must be capable of correctly classifying the shadow boundary as a shadow boundary, which can then provide information about the 3-D surface that generated the shadow.

A related problem arises when attempting to use luminance gradients ("shading") to determine perceived shape. The "shape from shading problem" refers to the difficulty in using luminance variations to reveal 3-D shape. However, the amount of light reflected off a 3-D surface to a point of observation depends on a number of variables, including the position and intensity of the light source, as well as the orientation and reflectance function of the surface. In order to use the luminance variations in an image to recover surface structure, the visual system must distinguish luminance variations due to changes in 3-D shape from changes in surface reflectance or changes in illumination. Virtually all models of this ability assume the existence of a single light source that has a known position, and further assume that the reflectance of a surface is known. The ability of our visual systems to recover shape from shading appears much more general than these models would suggest, but just how the visual system manages to use luminance gradients to infer 3-D shape in natural scenes remains largely unknown.

More generally, the visual system must be able to decompose a variation in luminance caused by intrinsic changes in surface properties (such as surface reflectance), from those caused by the variations that are extrinsic to a surface. There are two ways in which this decomposition seems to be accomplished. One method relies on image properties that provide a unique "signature" of their environmental cause to classify the causes of luminance variations. Such methods are usually described as "bottom-up" or data-driven processes, since they only depend on the form of the current input to the visual system. The other method is to use TOP-DOWN PROCESSING IN VISION to determine the causes of image structure, which relies on previously acquired information to classify ambiguous images. Both types of processes seem to operate when we view natural scenes in determining perceived surface structure.

One of the most challenging problems in the accurate recovery of surface structure is generated by the geometry of occlusion or camouflage. In cluttered scenes, many objects and surfaces are partially obscured by nearer, occluding surfaces, and some nearer surfaces are camouflaged by distant surfaces that have identical textural and reflectance properties. In order for the visual system to recover surface structure in these scenes, the visual system must be capable of distinguishing between those situations in which an object actually ends and those in which an object ends because it is partially occluded or obscured by a camouflaged background. Once it is determined that partial occlusion or camouflage is present, the visual system must

integrate the spatially separated scene fragments into a single surface. The perceptual interpolation of objects behind occluders is known as *amodal completion,* and was originally studied by workers in GESTALT PERCEPTION. A related phenomenon is the modal completion of surfaces and contours over image regions that are partially camouflaged by a more distant surface. Recent physiological work has demonstrated that there exist cells early in the cortical processing stream (V2) that respond to illusory contours, providing strong evidence that the interpolation of surface is truly a form of visual processing, and does not require more abstract "cognitive" processes to occur.

In summary, the problem of surface perception is difficult because the visual system is confronted with the problem of untangling the different physical causes of the images on our retinas, and filling in missing information when only portions of a surface are visible. Although much progress has been made in understanding how the visual system infers surface structure in some simplified images, much remains to be done before we have a full understanding of how our visual system works in the highly structured images created by natural scenes.

See also COMPUTATIONAL VISION; DEPTH PERCEPTION; MID-LEVEL VISION; STRUCTURE FROM VISUAL INFORMATION SOURCES; TEXTURE; TRANSPARENCY

—*Bart Anderson*

Further Readings

Adelson, E. H., and A. P. Pentland. (1996). The perception of shading and reflectance. In D. C. Knill and W. Richards, Eds. *Perception as Bayesian Inference.* New York: Cambridge University Press.

Anderson, B. L. (1997). A theory of illusory lightness and transparency in monocular and binocular images: The role of contour junctions. *Perception* 26: 419–453.

Anderson, B. L., and B. Julesz. (1995). A theoretical analysis of illusory contour formation in stereopsis. *Psychol. Rev.* 102: 705–743.

Barrow, H. G., and J. M. Tennenbaum. (1978). Recovering intrinsic scene characteristics from images. In A. R. Hanson and E. M. Riseman, Eds., *Computer Vision Systems,* pp. 3–26.

Cavanagh, P., and Y. Leclerc. (1989). Shape from shadows. *Journal of Experimental Psychology: Human Percption and Performance* 15: 3–27.

Gilchrist, A. L. (1977). Perceived lightness depends on perceived spatial arrangement. *Science* 185–187.

Gilchrist, A. L. (1994). *Lightness, Brightness, and Transparency.* Mawah, NJ: Erlbaum.

Metelli, F. (1974). The perception of transparency. *Scientific American* 230: 90–98.

Nakayama, K., Z. J. He, and S. Shimojo. (1995). Visual surface representation: A critical link between lower-level and higher-level vision. In S. M. Kosslyn and D. N. Osherson, Eds., *An Invitation to Cognitive Science: vol. 2, Visual Cognition.* Cambridge, MA: MIT Press.

Symbolism

See COGNITIVE MODELING, SYMBOLIC; CULTURAL SYMBOLISM

Synapse

See COMPUTATIONAL NEUROSCIENCE; NEURON

Syntax

Syntax is the study of the part of the human linguistic system that determines how sentences are put together out of words. Syntax interfaces with the semantic and phonological components, which interpret the representations ("sentences") provided by syntax. It has emerged in the last several decades that the system is largely universal across languages and language types, and therefore presumably innate, with narrow channels within which languages may differ from one another (Chomsky 1965; 1981b), a conclusion confirmed by studies of child language acquisition (Crain 1990 and numerous others).

The term *syntax* is also used to refer to the "structure" of sentences in a particular language. One aspect of the syntactic structure of sentences is the division of a sentence into phrases, and those phrases into further phrases, and so forth. The range of phrase types is quite specific and generally considered to be innately determined (and hence not learned) and so are the rules that determine how phrases are formed from words and other phrases. Essentially, the inventory of phrase types is derived from the inventory of the parts of speech, or lexical categories (noun, verb, etc.). First, any part of speech can be the "head" or nucleus of a phrase. Then, larger phrases are built from a head by combining it with another phrase in one of three ways: the added phrase can express an argument of the head; it can modify the head; or it can be a "specifier" of the head:

(1) a. argument: see + the boy   [V NP]$_{VP}$
    b. modification: see + clearly   [VP Adv]$_{VP}$
    c. specification: the + boys   [Article N]$_{NP}$

The structure of a phrase is indicated by surrounding the parts of the phrase with brackets labeled with the name of the phrase; hence the notation [V NP]$_{VP}$ asserts that a Verb Phrase (VP) can consist of a verb followed by a Noun Phrase (NP). The theory of phrase structure is sometimes called X-BAR THEORY, as the phrasal labels are alternatively written with a "bar" over the lexical category instead of a P after it: V' (for VP), N' (for NP), and so on.

Principles of this sort determine that every sentence has as part of its linguistic description a tree-like structure, which shows how the component phrases are related to each other by these three relations:

(2) a.

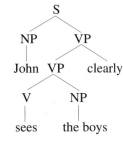

b. [[John]$_{NP}$[[sees]$_V$[[the]$_{Art}$[boys]$_N$]$_{NP}$]$_{VP}$[clearly]$_{Adv}$]$_{VP}$]$_S$

The two representations (a,b) are identical in their content—they both represent the phrase structure of the sentence *John sees the boys clearly*. The tree representation is often used because it is easier to read. "S" stands for *sentence*.

Ambiguity of phrasing arises when a single string of words can be associated with two different phrase structures according to the phrase definitions of a language; for example:

(3) a. John sees [the boys with the telescope]$_{NP}$
    b. John sees [the boys]$_{NP}$ with the telescope

In one structure, the boys have the telescope; in the other, John does.

Great uniformity is found in how the three relations in (1) are instantiated in languages. One dimension of variation is the position of the head in its phrase. In a language like English, the head uniformly precedes its arguments (except for the subject); in Japanese, the head uniformly follows its arguments:

(4) **English**   *Japanese*

VP: [V NP]$_{VP}$| read a book |[NP V]$_{VP}$| sakana o taberu
                                                    'fish eat'
PP: [P NP]$_{PP}$| to New York |[NP P]$_{PP}$| New York ni
                                                    'New York to'

We see here that in Japanese not only does the argument of the verb precede the verb, but the object of the preposition precedes the preposition (for which reason, it is called a *postposition*). Languages with postpositions instead of prepositions always show "object-verb" word order; because the verb and preposition are the heads of their respective phrases, this suggests that the head-order parameter is set once and for all for a given language, all phrases in that language taking the same value (Greenberg 1963).

Thus every language instantiates the "argument of" relation as a lexical item (the head) combined with a phrase (the argument), but languages differ in where the head stands in relation to the argument phrase. The rich concepts here—the notion "phrase," the notion "argument of," and so on—are innate; what must be learned is only the left-right order of head and argument. The ratio of learned things to innate things here is typical of syntax. The parameters of syntactic variation, of which head position is one, appear to be limited in number, and individually, limited in scope. The head parameter, for example, can only take "left" and "right" as values, meaning that there are only two types of languages in regard to head position.

Another aspect of the syntactic structure of a sentence is "movement" relations that hold between one syntactic position in a sentence and another. Among these are the relation of a question word in a question to the grammatical position in the sentence on which the question pivots:

(5) What$_i$ does John think that Bill wants t$_i$?

The position of the "trace" (t$_i$) is the "understood" position of the *wh*-word *what*—the question is about the "object" of

Bill's desires, so to speak. *What* is an "argument of" *wants* but does not appear in the correct position for such arguments; it has been "moved" to the front of the sentence. The relation between the moved *wh*-phrase and its understood position (marked by its trace, t_i) is called WH-MOVEMENT. (5) is understood to have a phrase-structure representation of the following form (its "d(eep) = structure") transformed into (5) by an operation moving the *wh*-word to the front:

(6) John does think that Bill wants what?

Wh-movement is an instance of what is called a "grammatical transformation."

Wh-movement is a relation of very particular character, as the following examples might suggest, if examined closely:

(7) a. What$_i$ does John think that Bill said that Mary would like t_i?
    b. *What$_i$ does John think that t_i would please Bill?
    c. *What$_i$ does John think t_i time it is?
    d. *What$_i$ does John wonder who has t_i?

The prefixed asterisk is used to mark ungrammatical strings of words, but strings that would correspond to reasonable questions, if they were grammatical. (7a) suggests that the relation may span perhaps an arbitrarily large amount of sentence structure. But the rest of the examples suggest sharp limitations on the relation. The movement relation has been studied in great detail in a number of languages and language families. A core set of restrictions on the relation, some of which are illustrated in (7), have been found to hold universally. For example, (7d) illustrates what has been called the "Empty Category Principle" (ECP; Chomsky 1981a).

The movement relation occurs in a number of sentence and clause types besides questions:

(8) a. [What a fool]$_i$ John turned   (exclamative)
       out to be t_i.
    b. The man who$_i$ Mary thinks   (relative clause)
       she met t_i.
    c. Happy$_i$ though Mary is t_i, she   (though-clause)
       is still insensitive to others.
    d. John$_i$ I think I saw t_i in the   (topicalized clause)
       store yesterday.
    e. John saw [more people]$_i$ than   (comparative clause)
       we thought he had seen t_i.

Exactly the same restrictions illustrated in (7) for questions hold for all these further types as well, suggesting the deep systematicity of the principles involved; for example, the ECP holds for comparative clauses, as the following shows:

(9) a. *John saw [more people]$_i$ that we thought that t_i were there.
    b. John saw [more people]$_i$ that we thought t_i were there.

The mental computation of the relation of a *wh*-word to its trace is easily detected by psycholinguistic testing of on-line real-time sentence comprehension, on which it imposes an extra processing load.

Languages can differ in some limited ways in this aspect of sentence structure—for example, in whether the *wh*-trace

relation is instantiated for a given sentence type in the language. Chinese, unlike English, does not use movement for questions; the *wh*-word stays in its "original" position (Huang 1982):

(10) Zhangsan xiangxin [shei mai-le shu]
     Zhangsan believes [who bought books]
     'Who does Zhangsan believe bought books?'

But if a language instantiates a sentence type with *wh*-movement, the movement will have the same very particular character it has in every other language that instantiates it.

The syntax of a language describes a set of forms (as in (3)) with which a sound and meaning can be associated, and so mediates between these two palpable aspects of a sentence. The interface of syntax to the sound and meaning components of the language system seems again largely universal. For example, languages typically have pronouns like the English reflexive and reciprocal pronouns (*himself, each other*) that require antecedents in the same utterance in which the pronouns themselves occur; such pronouns are called anaphors (see ANAPHORA):

(11) a. John likes himself.
     b. *Why did John succeed? Because himself is ambitious.
     c. Why did John succeed? Because he is ambitious.

A universal property of anaphors is that their antecedents cannot be contained in a phrase that does not contain the anaphor itself:

(12) a. [John's mother]$_{NP}$ likes herself.
     b.*[John's mother]$_{NP}$ likes himself.

In both cases, *John* is contained in the subject NP *John's mother*; in the first case, the antecedent is *John's mother,* and so the "containment condition" is satisfied; but in the second case, *John* is the antecedent, so the condition is violated. This "containment condition" (known as the "c-command condition") is a part of Binding Theory (see BINDING THEORY), which treats in a general way pronominal antecedence and its relation to syntactic structure.

Typically, the relation between anaphor and antecedent is governed by a locality condition—the anaphor and antecedent cannot be "too far apart;" in English, the pronoun cannot occur in an embedded clause that does not contain the antecedent:

(13) *John thinks that [Mary likes himself]$_S$

The English locality condition is not universal, however; languages differ in what "too far apart" means. In Icelandic, for example, the reflexive pronoun *sig* can be separated from its antecedent by a subjunctive clause boundary but not an indicative one:

(14) a. Jon$_i$ segir [að Maria elskar sig$_i$]$_{Subjunctive Clause}$
        'Jon says that Maria loves himself'
     b.*Jon$_i$ segir [að Maria elski sig$_i$]$_{Indicative Clause}$
     'Jon says that Maria loves himself'

The indices here indicate which NP is the antecedent of *sig*. Although the domain of anaphors is not fixed universally, there is only a small list of possible domains (Wexler and Manzini 1982). Although Icelandic differs from English in the details of the locality condition, it obeys the same containment condition mentioned earlier, as do all languages.

As with the case of phrase types, what is universal in the syntax of anaphors is considerable: the notion of anaphor, the necessity of antecedents for anaphors, the containment condition for anaphors, and the notion of locality condition. Beyond this, we see a slim range of linguistic variation: the identification of the domain of locality for anaphors. The language learner has simply to identify the anaphors in her language and identify the domain of locality in order for the full behavior of anaphors to be determined.

The syntactic system interfaces with lexical knowledge as well. The syntactic system of a language defines a set of general sentence patterns for that language, but any given lexical item will fit in only a subset of these. For example, the English VP could be described as a pattern of the following sort:

(15) V NP NP PP AP S AdvP

where only the head (V) is a necessary part of the phrase; but different verbs will in general match only limited subpatterns of this general pattern:

(16) a. think: [V S] "think that Bill was sick"
      b. persuade: [V NP S] "persuade him that Bill was sick"
                   [V NP PP] "persuade him of my good intentions"

These must be learned along with the verb's meaning and other properties (see WORD MEANING, ACQUISITION OF). It is an open but much pursued question how much of the syntactic parameterization of a language might be reducible to aspects of lexical learning (see SYNTAX, ACQUISITION OF). The principal obstacle to firm conclusions is that the LEXICON, or the human lexical ability, is comparatively less well understood than the syntactic system.

The most productive vein of research in syntax in recent years has been the comparison of closely related languages. The goal has been to discover the "minimum" differences between languages, as it stands to reason that these will correlate with the actual parameters of the syntactic system.

French and Italian are two closely related Romance languages with a signal difference in how the subject of the sentence is expressed. French, like English, requires a subject for every clause; but Italian permits the omission of subjects that are understood:

(17) a. Gianni credo che ha molto argento.   (Italian)
      b. *Jean pense que a beaucoup d'argent. (French)
      c. Jean pense qu'il a beaucoup d'argent. (French)
      d. John thinks that he has a lot of money. (English)
      e. *John thinks that has a lot of money.   (English)

By itself this difference between French and Italian might be of little general interest, but in fact it appears to correlate with other differences (Perlmutter 1978; Rizzi 1982). French is like English in blocking movement of the subject of embedded clauses when the "complementizer" *that* (*que* in French, *che* in Italian) is present, but Italian has no such restriction:

(18) a. Chi$_i$ credo che t$_i$ ha molto argento?   (Italian)
      b. *Qui$_i$ pense-tu que t$_i$ a beaucoup d'argent? (French)
      c. *Who do you think that has a lot of money? (English)

And Italian permits its subject to appear in postposed position, after the verb, but French, like English, excludes this:

(19) a. Credo che t$_i$ ha molto argento Sergio$_i$.   (Italian)
      b. *Je crois que t$_i$ a beaucoup d'argent Sergio$_i$.   (French)
      c. *I believe that t$_i$ has lots of money Sergio$_i$. (English)

In all three cases, Italian differs from English in permitting the trace of a moved or deleted subject in subject position under various circumstances. As there are other language pairs that differ in the same way, it is likely that these three differences between French and Italian are related and that in fact each is a manifestation of a single grammatical "parameter" set differently for French and Italian, a parameter governing the expression of the subject. Experiments in language acquisition have confirmed this view (Hyams 1986).

The mapping of the syntactic parameters through detailed study of language comparisons like the one just mentioned has been the principal goal of research in syntax in the 1980s and '90s. The general theory of syntax has been forced to become quite abstract in order to accommodate the parameterizations in a straightforward way, but the compensation has been a deeper understanding of what the range of possible human syntactic systems looks like.

—*Edwin Williams*

References

Chomsky, N. (1965). *Aspects of the Theory of Syntax.* Cambridge, MA: MIT Press.

Chomsky, N. (1981a). *Lectures on Government and Binding.* Dordrecht: Foris.

Chomsky, N. (1981b). Principles and parameters of linguistic theory. In N. Hornstein and D. Lightfoot, Eds., *Explanations in Linguistics.* Longmans, pp. 123–146.

Crain, S. (1990). Language learning in the absence of experience. *Brain and Behavioral Science* 14: 597–650.

Greenberg, J. (1963). *Universals of Language.* Cambridge, MA: MIT Press.

Huang, J. (1982). *Logical Relations in Chinese and the Theory of Grammar.* Ph.D. diss., MIT.

Hyams, N. (1986). *Language Acquisition and the Theory of Parameters.* Dordrecht: Reidel

Perlmutter, D. (1978). Impersonal passives and the unaccusative hypothesis. In J. Jaeger et al., Eds., *Proceedings of the Fourth Annual Meeting of the Berkeley Linguistics Society*, 1978: 157–189.

Rizzi, L. (1982). *Issues in Italian Syntax.* Dordrecht: Foris.

Wexler, K., and R. Manzini. (1982). Parameters and learnability in binding theory. In T. Roeper and E. Williams, Eds., *Parameter Setting.* Dordrecht: Reidel, pp. 41–89.

Syntax, Acquisition of

Probably there are very few fields in cognitive science that have shown as distinct a growth in the last decade as the field of SYNTAX acquisition. The increase in preciseness and knowledge has been extremely large, so large as to make the field hardly recognizable when compared to work of much more than a decade ago. In this short piece, I can hardly do more than to mention a few of the very active areas of research and some of the major results.

Inflectional and Clausal Development

At one time, it was thought by almost every approach to syntax acquisition (e.g., Wanner and Gleitman 1982) that a major reason that children's utterances (e.g., *me no going*) seemed to be different from adults' utterances (e.g., *I am not going*) is that children did not know the (morphophonological and/or morphosyntactic) properties of inflectional elements (e.g., English third singular *-s*), the case of pronouns, the existence of auxiliary verbs, and so on. It looked as if inflectional elements were omitted or that their properties were incorrectly known to the child. On the basis of extensive empirical research, the field has completely thrown over this idea, however. The main tool for this demonstration has been the correlation between word order and MORPHOLOGY in the optional infinitive stage of development (Wexler 1993; roughly up to 3;0, depending on the language). As Wexler showed, children in many languages often use nonfinite main verbs alongside finite main verbs, but they know the morphosyntactic and morphological properties of finiteness. One of the first examples was provided by Pierce (1992) concerning French. Finite and nonfinite verbs in French occur in different distributional positions—for example, French finite verbs precede negation *pas* and nonfinite verbs follow *pas*. Pierce determined the finiteness of the verb by morphological form and the word order by observing where the verb appeared with respect to *pas*. The following table from Wexler 1993, based in Pierce's data, shows the number of utterances with the relevant properties, from children around 2;0. Columns represent verb morphology, rows represent order of the verb and *pas*.

(1)	+finite	−finite
pas verb	11	77
verb *pas*	185	2

The stunning result is that despite the fact that children at this early age use very many nonfinite utterances (ungrammatical in matrix position) as well as finite utterances, they get the word-order facts correct. Even more stunning is the fact that, as Wexler (1993) showed, the correlation between morphology and word order holds over many different languages, despite very different constructions. Thus, Poeppel and Wexler (1993) showed that German children used nonfinite root verbs as well as finite ones, but they almost always placed the finite verbs in second position (correct for this V2 language) and the nonfinite ones in final position, again correct for German, an SOV language.

Wexler (1993) called the stage at which these root nonfinite forms occur the *optional infinitive* (OI) stage and showed that it occurred in many different languages. From the properties of the OI stage, it can be deduced that children at an extremely young age have learned the central parameter values of the clausal/inflectional syntax of their language. For example, the French children discussed above have learned that the finite verb raises around negation (to an inflectional position) whereas English-speaking children do not raise the verb (correct for their language). The German results show that German children know that German is a V2 language (there are many other related phenomena) and that German is an SOV language. Wexler (1996) hypothesized that *Very Early Parameter Setting* (VEPS) was true: namely, children have set the central clausal/inflectional parameters of their language correctly at an extremely early age, before 2;0, perhaps before they have entered the multiword utterance stage at about 1;6. Evidence to date suggests that VEPS is true.

Thus the learning of language-particular aspects of grammar (parameters) is extremely fast and might be mostly done (for central parameters) before children start speaking in more than single-word utterances. Thus crucial grammatical learning is a kind of perceptual learning, done without any kind of overt error made by the child, that can be corrected by an adult. At the moment, it can't be determined exactly how early children set parameters correctly because of a limitation of experimental method: the key instrument has been naturalistic production, and the data are extremely sparse before 1;6. The development of infant techniques in this field will be necessary to probe earlier.

Not only are the parameters set correctly (the morphosyntactic part), but for the most part, the morphophonological aspects of inflection are known. Thus Poeppel and Wexler (1993) showed that extremely young German children didn't make mistakes on (subject-verb) agreement: either a nonfinite verb was used or a correctly agreeing one. A further example is that children almost never use a third-singular verb in English with a first-person pronoun (*I likes candy*); there are almost no examples out of hundreds of possibilities (Harris and Wexler 1996). Children know that -s means third-person singular from an extremely early age. This contradicts earlier suggestions (Clahsen and Penke 1992) that children have a difficult time with agreement. The reason that this appeared to be so was that it wasn't understood that many of the child's forms are nonfinite forms.

One central mystery remains, alongside the discovery that children at the earliest observed ages know both the universal and language-particular aspects of clause structure, inflection, functional categories, and verb movement. This is the question of why they use optional infinitives at all. In his original paper, Wexler (1993) suggested that children had certain difficulties with *tense*. Other proposals have been made by Rizzi (1994), Hoekstra and Hyams (1995), Wexler (1996, 1997), and Schütze and Wexler (1996), among others. There is an intense debate as to the best model to explain the OI stage, a debate being carried out with a detail of syntactic and quantitative analysis of children's abilities that is truly astonishing compared to what was known only a decade ago. The rigorous theoretical analysis and detailed quantitative empirical study of early syntax has certainly pushed the field to a new level.

It is the foregoing work that has been primarily responsible for the fall from favor of the proposal by Radford (1990) that children do not have functional categories, for there is no reasonable way to account for the correlation between morphology and word order if children do not have functional categories. For balance, let me point out that at least Atkinson (1996) remains not completely convinced. I should also point out that there is now at least a beginning array of experimental results on comprehension confirming the general outlines of the OI stage (Schonenberger et al. 1995; Rice, Wexler, and Redmond 1998).

Null Subjects

An important early major result about the development of inflection within the principles-and-parameters approach was Hyams' (1986) discovery that English-speaking children very often use null subjects (e.g., *baking cookies*), despite the fact that English is not a null-subject language (unlike Italian, in which subjects are typically omitted from the sentence). Hyams suggested that these children had "mis-set" the null-subject parameter, so that English-speaking children thought that null subjects were grammatical, as in Italian. Since Hyams's work, it has been discovered that in every language that has been studied at early ages in this regard, children use null subjects.

Occasionally it has been suggested that the null subjects are the result of some kind of memory deficit (Bloom 1990) or production constraint (Gerken 1991). However, the empirical evidence is not consistent with this idea (Hyams and Wexler 1993; Bromberg and Wexler 1995). The weight of this evidence suggests that indeed children at an early age consider some null subjects to be grammatical even when their language isn't a null-subject language.

Thus one major part of Hyams's proposal is still considered to be correct—namely, that null subjects are grammatical for children. However, a second major part of Hyams's proposal does not now seem to be correct (as Hyams herself agrees: e.g., Sano and Hyams 1994). Namely, it does not appear that children have mis-set the null-subject parameter. Rather, null subjects appear to be the product of the OI stage. Children know that English, for example, is not null-subject in the Italian sense, but they produce null subjects because certain clauses (those missing tense, according to the hypothesis of Schütze and Wexler 1996) allow a null subject. Probably the strongest evidence for this position is the result of Roeper and Rohrbacher 1995 and Bromberg and Wexler 1995 that in *wh*-questions, children use null subjects only when the sentence is an OI, when tense is missing (e.g., *where going*, but not **where is going*). If English were truly an Italian-style null-subject language, null subjects would be grammatical even with a tensed verb. (Any suggestion that subjects are dropped because the first part of the sentence is "difficult," e.g., Bloom 1990, can't hold for the large numbers of *wh*-questions with null subjects, because the *wh*-form is at the beginning of the sentence.)

Italian children, on the other hand, will allow *wh*-questions with null subjects, because Italian *is* an Italian-style null-subject language. Thus the null-subject parameter is consistent with Wexler's (1996) VEPS: children have even set the null-subject parameter correctly at the earliest observed age.

Greatly simplifying the myriad structures studied, I have tried only to give enough detail to suggest the theoretical and empirical richness of this part of the field at the current moment and to suggest how this richness of detail represents something quite new in the study of linguistic development. There are an extremely large number of interrelated crosslinguistic and cross-construction generalizations that must be accounted for by any theory of linguistic development, and any theory that does not account for at least a large subset of these phenomena can hardly lay claim to being a serious contender for consideration. It is primarily for this reason that theories that involve only very general mechanisms of learning, and no linguistic details, are not seriously considered by the field: they seem to be nonstarters from the standpoint of empirical coverage. The primary task facing these "general learning mechanism/statistical procedures" theories is to make even a small dent in the empirical coverage that the major theories can already account for.

Development of Chains and Maturation

Is there any delay in knowledge of syntactic properties, or do the youngest children know *everything* about syntax? Borer and Wexler (1987; 1992) claimed that A-chains (argument-chains) are delayed in development, perhaps into the third or fourth year. A-chains involve movement of an argument to another A-position (argument-type position, not operator position). A primary example given by Borer and Wexler is the A-movement involved in the raising of an object into the subject position in the verbal passive construction (e.g., *the fox was kicked by the lion*, where *the fox* was raised from object position after *kicked* to subject position; see also GRAMMATICAL RELATIONS). Such passive constructions are known to be delayed in English-speaking children (2- and 3-year-old children do not correctly understand who kicked who in *the fox was kicked by the lion*). Borer and Wexler (1987) showed that *adjectival* passives (e.g., *the toy is broken*), which do not contain A-chains, were very early in English-speaking children, and they argued that the semantic and structural complexity of adjectival and verbal passives were about on a par. They thus suggested that it was the A-chain representation that was disallowed by children until a later age. Thus the children couldn't represent verbal passive constructions.

Furthermore, Borer and Wexler (1987) argued that the delay in A-chains was *maturational*; that A-chains were delayed because of biological development. Since then, the issue of maturation versus learning has been a hot topic of debate in LANGUAGE ACQUISITION. There are no other explanations of growth/change that have been suggested, except for learning and maturation. Borer and Wexler raised an objection to a learning analysis for a delayed construction like the passive, namely the *Triggering Problem*: If change occurs in grammar because of a reaction to an input trigger, why does this change often take years? A tip-off that maturation may in fact be on the right track can be found in the OI stage. Note that in that stage all the properties that we know must be learned—namely, the ones that differ from language to language—are learned extremely early (VEPS). It is the *universal* (apparently) property of finiteness of root clauses (morphology aside) that develops late. Thus a universal property is late, whereas an experience-dependent, learned property is early. This suggests maturation.

The topic of A-chains has recently been invigorated with a number of new constructions and languages studied (Babyonyshev et al. 1994, Snyder, Hyams, and Crisma 1995). One might expect that this topic will be a central one, as the development of complex syntax is investigated in the years to come.

See also BINDING THEORY; INNATENESS OF LANGUAGE; NATIVISM; PARAMETER-SETTING APPROACHES TO ACQUISITION, CREOLIZATION, AND DIACHRONY; SEMANTICS, ACQUISITION OF

—*Kenneth Wexler*

References

Atkinson, M. (1996). Now, hang on a minute: Some reflections on emerging orthodoxies. In H. Clahsen, Ed., *Generative Perspectives on Language Acquisition.* Amsterdam: Benjamin, pp. 451–485.

Babyonyshev, M., R. Fein, J. Ganger, D. Pesetsky, K. Wexler, and S. Avrutin. (1994). Maturation of syntax: New evidence from the acquisition of unaccusatives in Russian. Paper presented at the Nineteenth Annual Boston University Conference on Language Development.

Babyonyshev, M., R. Fein, J. Ganger, D. Pesetsky, and K. Wexler. (1998). The maturation of grammatical principles: Evidence from Russian unaccusatives. Unpublished ms, MIT and Microsoft Corporation, pp. 1–63.

Bloom, P. (1990). Subjectless sentences in child language. *Linguistic Inquiry* 21(4): 491–504.

Borer, H., and K. Wexler. (1987). The maturation of syntax. In T. Roeper and E. Williams, Eds., *Parameter Setting,* pp. 123–172.

Borer, H., and K. Wexler. (1992). Bi–unique relations and the maturation of grammatical principles. *Natural Language and Linguistic Theory* 10: 147–189.

Bromberg, H., and K. Wexler. (1995). Null subjects in child *wh*–questions. *MIT Working Papers in Linguistics* 26: 221–247.

Clahsen, H., and M. Penke. (1992). The acquisition of agreement morphology and its syntactic consequences. In J. Meisel, Ed., *The Acquisition of Verb Placement.* Dordrecht: Kluwer.

Gerken, L. (1991). The metrical basis for children's subjectless sentences. *Journal of Memory and Language* 30: 431–451.

Harris, A., and K. Wexler. (1996). The optional–infinitive stage in child English. In H. Clahsen, Ed., *Generative Perspectives on Language Acquisition.* Amsterdam: Benjamin, pp. 1–42.

Hoekstra, T., and N. Hyams. (1995). The syntax and interpretation of dropped categories in child language: A unified account. *Proceedings of the West Coast Conference on Formal Linguistics XIV.* Stanford, CA: CSLI Publications.

Hyams, N. (1986). *Language Acquisition and the Theory of Parameters.* Dordrecht: Reidel.

Hyams, N., and K. Wexler. (1993). On the grammatical basis of null subjects in child language. *Linguistic Theory* 24(3): 421–459.

Klima, E., and U. Bellugi. (1966). Syntactic regularities in the speech of children. In J. Lyons and R. Wales, Eds., *Psycholinguistic Papers.* Edinburgh: Edinburgh University Press, pp. 183–207.

Pierce, A. (1992). *Language Aquisition and Syntactic Theory: A Comparative Analysis of French and English Child Language.* Dordrecht: Kluwer.

Poeppel, D., and K. Wexler. (1993). The full competence hypothesis of clause structure in early German. *Language* 69: 1–33.

Radford, A. (1990). *Syntactic Theory and the Acquisition of English Syntax.* Oxford: Blackwell.

Rice, M., K. Wexler, and S. M. Redmond. (1998). Comprehension of an extended infinitive grammar: Evidence from English-speaking children with specific language impairment. Paper presented at Twenty-second Annual Boston University Conference on Language Development.

Rizzi, L. (1994). Some notes on linguistic theory and language development: The case of root infinitives. *Language Acquisition* 3(4): 371–393.

Roeper, T., and B. Rohrbacher. (1995). Null subjects in early child English and the theory of economy of projection. Unpublished ms, University of Massachusetts, Amherst, and the University of Pennsylvania.

Sano, T., and N. Hyams. (1994). Agreement, finiteness, and the development of null arguments. *Proceedings of NELS* 24: 1–16.

Schonenberger, M., A. Pierce, K. Wexler, and F. Wijnen. (1995). Accounts of root infinitives and the interpretation of root infinitives. *GenGenP* 3(2): 47–71.

Schütze, C., and K. Wexler. (1996). Subject case licensing and English root infinitives. *BUCLD 20 Proceedings,* pp. 670–681.

Snyder, W., N. Hyams, and P. Crisma. (1995). Romance auxiliary selection with reflexive clitics: Evidence for early knowledge of unaccusativity. *Proceedings of the Twenty-sixth Annual Child Language Research Forum.* Stanford, CA: Stanford Linguistics Association (SLA) and CSLI Publications, pp. 127–136.

Wexler, K. (1982). A principle theory for language acquisition. In E. Wanner and L. R. Gleitman, Eds., *Language Acquisition: The State of the Art.* Cambridge: Cambridge University Press, pp. 289–315.

Wexler, K. (1993). Optional infinitives, head movement, and the economy of derivations. In D. Lightfoot and N. Hornstein, Eds., *Verb Movement.* Cambridge: Cambridge University Press, pp. 305–350.

Wexler, K. (1996). The development of inflection in a biologically based theory of language acquisition. In M. L. Rice, Ed., *Toward a Genetics of Language.* Hillsdale, NJ: Erlbaum, pp. 113–144.

Wexler, K. (1997). D–Interpretability and interpretation in the OI stage. Presented at the Workshop on Interpretation of Root Infinitives and Bare Verbs, MIT, January 13,14.

Further Readings

Avrutin, S. (1994). *Psycholinguistic Investigations in the Theory of Reference.* Ph.D. diss., MIT.

Avrutin, S., and K. Wexler. (1995). Children's knowledge of subjunctive clauses. Unpublished ms, MIT.

Chien, Y. –C., and K. Wexler. (1990). Children's knowledge of locality conditions in binding as evidence for the modularity of syntax and pragmatics. *Language Acquisition* 1(3): 225–295.

Chomsky, N. (1995). *The Minimalist Program.* Cambridge, MA: MIT Press.

Crain, S., and C. McKee. (1985). Acquisition of structural restrictions on anaphora. *Proceedings of NELS* 16: 94–110.

Franks, S., and P. Connell. (1996). Knowledge of binding in normal and SLI children. *Journal of Child Language* 23(2): 431–464.

Grodzinsky, Y., and T. Reinhart. (1993). The innateness of binding and the development of coreference: a reply to Grimshaw and Rosen. *Linquistic Inquiry* 24(1): 69–103.

Hermon, G. (1992). Binding theory and parameter setting. *The Linguistic Review* 9(2): 145–181.

Jakubowicz, C. (1984). On markedness and binding principles. *Proceedings of NELS* 14.

Manzini, R., and K. Wexler. (1987). Parameters, binding theory and learnability. *Linguistic Inquiry* 18(3): 413–444.

McDaniel, D., H. S. Cairns, and J. R. Hsu. (1990). Binding principles in the grammars of young children. *Language Acquisition* 1(1): 121–138.

McDaniel, D., and T. L. Maxfield. (1992). Principle B and contrastive stress. *Language Acquisition* 2(4): 337–358.

Montalbetti, M., and K. Wexler (1985). Binding is linking. *Proceedings of the West Coast Conference on Formal Linguistics* 4. Stanford, CA: Stanford Linguistics Association, pp. 228–245.

Thornton, R., and K. Wexler. (Forthcoming). *VP Ellipsis and the Binding Theory in Child Grammars*. Cambridge, MA: MIT Press.

Wexler, K. (Forthcoming). Maturation and growth of grammar. In W. C. Ritchie and T. K. Bhatia, Eds., *Handbook of Language Acquisition*. New York: Academic Press.

Wexler, K., and Y. -C. Chien. (1985). The development of lexical anaphors and pronouns. *Papers and Reports on Child Language Development (PRCLD)*. Leland Stanford Junior University 24: 138–149.

Syntax-Semantics Interface

A commonplace observation about language is that it consists of the systematic association of sound patterns with meaning. SYNTAX studies the structure of well-formed phrases (spelled out as sound sequences); SEMANTICS deals with the way syntactic structures are interpreted. However, how to exactly slice the pie between these two disciplines and how to map one into the other is the subject of controversy. In fact, understanding how syntax and semantics interact (i.e., their interface) constitutes one of the most interesting and central questions in linguistics.

Traditionally, phenomena like word order, case marking, agreement, and the like are viewed as part of syntax, whereas things like the meaningfulness of a well-formed string are seen as part of semantics. Thus, for example, "I loves Lee" is ungrammatical because of lack of agreement between the subject and the verb, a phenomenon that pertains to syntax, whereas Chomky's famous "colorless green ideas sleep furiously" is held to be syntactically well-formed but semantically deviant. In fact, there are two aspects of the picture just sketched that one ought to keep apart. The first pertains to data, the second to theoretical explanation. We may be able on pretheoretical grounds to classify some linguistic data (i.e., some native speakers' intuitions) as "syntactic" and others as "semantic." But we cannot determine a priori whether a certain phenomenon is best explained in syntactic or semantics terms. So, for example, syntactic accounts of semantic deviance (in terms of mismatches of features) are possible. As are conceivable semantic accounts even of phenomena like agreement. To illustrate the latter case, one could maintain that a VP like "loves Lee" denotes a predicate that cannot be true of, say, the speaker. Hence, "loves Lee" predicated of the speaker results in something undefined. This account of the ungrammaticality of "I loves Lee" would qualify as semantic as it crucially uses notions like *truth* and *denotation,* which are the building

blocks of semantics. What is actually most likely is that agreement is ultimately a cluster of phenomena, whose optimal account will involve the interaction of both syntax and semantics (see Lapointe 1979). This is a simple illustration of how issues of interface arise and why they are so important. They concern both data and theory. It is not a matter of terminology but of which component is responsible for which phenomenon and how the modules of each component are set up, something that cannot be settled a priori once and for all (see MODULARITY AND LANGUAGE).

Perhaps the key issue at the interface of syntax and semantics concerns the nature of the mapping between the two, which has been at the center of much research within GENERATIVE GRAMMAR. An important approach, pursued especially within CATEGORIAL GRAMMAR and related lexicalist frameworks, has been dubbed by E. Bach the "rule-by-rule" hypothesis. It assumes that for each syntactic rule determining how two or more constituents are put together, there is a corresponding semantic rule determining how the respective meanings are to be composed. On this view, the interface task is to figure out which syntactic rules are mapped onto which semantic composition modes. A somewhat different line is pursued within transformational approaches to syntax such as the Government and Binding framework or the more recent Minimalist Program (see MINIMALISM). Within such approaches, there are no rules in the traditional sense but only very general schemata and principles that interact in yielding pairing of phonetic representations and logical forms. Logical forms (LFs) are syntactic representations where phenomena like scope and anaphoric links are unambiguously represented. For example, one possible LF for a sentence like (1a) would look roughly as (1b).

(1) a. An advisor was assigned to every student to help him out with his scheduling.
   b. [Every student$_i$] [an advisor was assigned to t$_i$ to help him$_i$ out with his$_i$ scheduling]
   c. Every student x is such that an advisor was assigned to x in order to help x with x's scheduling.

The way to understand a structure like (1b) is by interpreting the object "every student" (which has been moved from its surface position to the left periphery of the clause) as having wide scope over the subject "an advisor" and as binding the pronouns "him/his" in the adjunct (as per the informal paraphrase in (1c)). This interpretation is guaranteed by mapping structures such as (1b) into their meaning (i.e., their the truth-conditions or some other logically based representation of propositional content). The mapping usually employs three things: the lexical meaning of the words; a few universal semantic operations (like function application and abstraction); and a limited set of type-shifting or coercion mechanisms.

The lexical meaning of words is drawn from a restricted set of semantic types that correspond in systematic ways to syntactic categories. For example, the syntactic category "NP" encodes certain patterns of distribution (namely, the possibility of occurring in certain slots in the clause, like subject, object, prepositional object, etc.). The corresponding semantic type will be that of individuals (in the case of referential NPs like "Luciano Pavarotti") or generalized QUANTIFIERS (in case of quantificational NPs like "at most two tenors" or "every red cat"). Similarly for the other syntactic categories: VPs will denote functions from individuals into truth values, and so on. In interpreting complex structures, say, for example [$_S$ Pavarotti [$_{VP}$ sings well]], one first checks the semantic type of the meaning of the constituents. Generally, one finds a function and an argument that can be combined by functional application. If, however, types don't match, something will have to be done. One possibility is resorting to a limited set of mechanisms that make the types fit (type shifting or coercion). This procedure is known as "type-driven interpretation" (Klein and Sag 1985; see also Partee 1987).

To illustrate typeshifting further, consider an adverb like "for two hours," which normally combines felicitously only with atelic verb phrases (i.e. VPs that express an activity lacking an inherent end point or culmination; see Verkuyl 1993 or Moens 1987, among many others):

(2) a.   John pushed the cart for two hours.   [atelic]
    b. ?? John reached the summit for two hours. [telic]

Now certain telic eventualities can combine with such adverbs in spite of their telicity. They must, however, be reinterpreted iteratively, thereby becoming atelic:

(3) a. Yesterday John knocked at the door once.   [telic]
    b. Yesterday John knocked at the door for
       two hours.   [telic]

The idea here is that the type of adverbials "for two hours" and that of telic activities don't match. But, in certain cases, one can interpolate a functor ITERATE that turns a telic individuality into an atelic one:

(4) A. FOR TWO HOURS (KNOCK)→undefined
    B. FOR TWO HOURS (ITERATE(KNOCK))→
       defined

Pinango, Zurif, and Jackendoff (1997) argue that type shifting of this sort has consequences for real-time processing. Type shifting can also be implemented on the rule-by-rule approach. Both the rule-by-rule approach and the LF-based one are compositional (see COMPOSITIONALITY) and strive to understand the universal properties of the syntax-semantics mapping. The main differences between them are mostly traceable to the different conceptions of syntactic structure that they are tailored on.

Live issues at the syntax-semantic interface include the following: What are the universal rules of semantic composition? We mentioned above function application and abstraction; is this all there is? What kinds of type-shifting operations (besides aspect-related ones like ITERATE) are there? Is type shifting restricted to the LEXICON or is it also used in the compositional part of the semantics? What are the mappings from syntactic categories into semantic types? Is there any crosslinguistic variation in any of the above? What role does the syntax-semantics mapping play in acquisition? To illustrate the variation issue, consider for example the status of mass nouns in English versus Italian. The following paradigm is representative:

(5) a. Gold is rare
    b. *Oro e' raro
        'gold is rare'
    c. L'oro e' raro
        'the gold is rare'

In English, mass nouns like *gold* have the same syntactic distribution as proper names and can occur without a determiner in the canonical argumental positions (subject, object, object of preposition, etc.). In Italian (or French), mass nouns behave instead just like singular-count common nouns in that they can never occur in subject or object position without a determiner (see (5b–c)). This difference might be syntactic in nature (*gold* and *oro* belong to two different syntactic categories). Or, it is also conceivable that they belong to the same syntactic category (say, the category N) but their semantic type is different. In Romance, mass nouns are mapped into predicates (true of any portion of the relevant substance). As such, they are suited to restrict a determiner but not to occur bare in argument position. On the other hand, in English mass nouns might be names of substances, which would explain their proper noun-like behavior. This second approach is based on the assumption that there is a certain degree of variability across languages in the way items belonging to the same syntactic category are mapped into the corresponding meanings (Chierchia forthcoming, 1998).

From the above considerations, it should be clear why questions that arise at the syntax-semantics interface are fundamental. The empirical domains where one can hope to find answers to such questions are very broad. They range from the study of quantification and ANAPHORA, to TENSE AND ASPECT, to the study of THEMATIC ROLES, and much more.

See also COGNITIVE LINGUISTICS; LOGICAL FORM IN LINGUISTICS; MEANING; WORD MEANING, ACQUISITION OF

—*Gennaro Chierchia*

References

Chierchia, G. (1996). Reference to kinds across languages. *Natural Language Semantics.* (Forthcoming).

Chierchia, G. (1998). Plurality of mass nouns and the notion of 'semantic parameter.' In S. Rothstein, Ed., *Events and Grammar.* Dordrecht: Kluwer.

Klein, E., and I. Sag. (1985). Type-driven translation. *Linguistics and Philosophy* 8: 163–202.

Lapointe, S. (1979). *A Theory of Grammatical Agreement.* Ph.D. diss., University of Massachusetts, Amherst.

Moens, M. (1987). *Tense, Aspect and Temporal Reference.* Ph.D. diss., University of Edinburgh.

Partee, B. H. (1987). Noun phrase interpretation and type-shifting principles. In J. Groenendijk, D. de Jongh, and M. Stolehof, Eds., *Studies in Discourse Representation Theory and the Theory of Generalized Quantifiers.* Dordrecht: Foris.

Pinango, M., E. Zurif, and R. Jackendoff. (1997). *Real Time Processing Implications of Enriched Composition at the Syntax-Semantics Interface.* Unpublished ms, Brandeis University.

Verkuyl, H. (1993). *A Theory of Aspectuality.* Cambridge: Cambridge University Press.

Further Readings

Chierchia, G., and S. McConnell-Ginet. (1990). *Meaning and Grammar.* Cambridge, MA: MIT Press.

Chomsky, N. (1986). *Knowledge of Language.* New York: Prager.

Dowty, D., R. Wall, and S. Peters. (1981). *Introduction to Montague Semantics.* Dordrecht: Kluwer.

Dowty, D. (1979). *Word Meaning and Montague Grammar.* Dordrecht: D. Reidel.

Heim, I., and A. Kratzer. (1997). *Semantics in Generative Grammar.* Oxford: Blackwell.

Higginbotham, J. (1985). On semantics. *Linguistic Inquiry* 16: 547–593.

Jackendoff, R. (1972). *Semantic Interpretation in Generative Grammar.* Cambridge, MA: MIT Press.

Jackendoff, R. (1997). *The Architecture of the Language Faculty.* Cambridge, MA: MIT Press.

May, R. (1985). *Logical Form: Its Structure and Derivation.* Cambridge, MA: MIT Press.

Reinhart, T. (1990). *Anaphora and Semantic Interpretation.* 3rd ed. London: Routledge.

Systematicity

See CONNECTIONISM, PHILOSOPHICAL ISSUES; MENTAL REPRESENTATION

Taste

Taste, or gustation, in humans and other terrestrial mammals is an oral chemoreceptive, and also mechanoreceptive and thermoreceptive, sensory system. Gustatory receptor organs occur primarily in specialized epithelial structures, papillae, found in limited and species-characteristic regions of mammalian tongue and palate (Weijnen and Mendelson 1977; Finger and Silver 1987). The taste system normally responds during drinking, biting, licking, chewing, and swallowing.

Taste is a component of a cognitive system, *Flavor* (Gibson 1966; White 1996), which includes SMELL (especially retronasal olfaction), chemesthesis (common chemical sense), tactile (HAPTIC PERCEPTION) input from oral structures, proprioception from the temporomandibular joints, and, via bone conduction, auditory responses (AUDITION; McBride and MacFie 1990). Laboratory procedures (Cattalanotto et al. 1993) or respiratory disease (Doty 1995) can remove component sensory systems; smell is often a major factor.

Taste responses originate in epithelial-derived receptor cells which have a lifespan of a week or two, all spent within an intraoral cutaneous sensory structure called a taste bud. The receptor cells differentiate from precursor cells, move closer to the epithelial surface, contact one or more sensory neurons and other taste receptor cells, and often extend microvilli which are separated from the outside world only by the secretions of taste bud cells (Beidler 1971). The brief lifespan is presumably demanded by direct but indispensable interactions with the diverse and often intense chemical, thermal, and mechanical energy levels in the oral cavity.

No one biochemical or biophysical mechanism transduces all gustatory stimulus chemicals into biological events. Substantial differences between gustatory chemicals, and the requirement that responses be sensitive and selective over a million-fold concentration span, apparently underlie this diversity. Gustatory chemicals effective in humans range from hydrogen ions to relatively large and complex protein molecules, and encompass most classes and configurations of molecules (Pfaff 1985; Brand, et al. 1993; Beauchamp and Bartoshuk 1997).

Many different gustatory stimuli activate a single taste receptor cell or individual neurons of the afferent nerve that innervates that receptor cell (Simon and Roper 1993). However, there is disagreement concerning the implications of this breadth of responsiveness. The predominant view, known as the *basic tastes* model, proposes that only the most robust responses have a role in sensory processing, with the others filtered somewhere in the central nervous system. This conceptualization permits assignment of a receptor or neuron to one or two of the test stimuli, and categorization as a "N" best unit, "N" being the gustatory stimulus chemical that evoked the largest response. The theory asserts that direct linkages exist between the identified *best-stimulus,* the stimulated receptor cell or neuron, and a category of taste perception. However, no human gustatory SINGLE-NEURON RECORDINGS exist (Meiselman and Rivlin 1986; Halpern 1991). Most generalizations are made from laboratory rodents.

The *best-stimulus* and *best-response* outcomes provide neurophysiological support for the basic tastes model's claim that gustatory experience depends on four or five distinct, independent classes of "vertically integrated" taste stimuli, receptor cells, afferent neurons, and independent perceptual categories. The corresponding *basic or primary gustatory stimuli* and perceptual categories are commonly specified as an alkaloid derivative such as a quinine salt ∴ bitter, the metallic salt NaCl ∴ salty, an acid ∴ sour, a saccharide such as sucrose ∴ sweet, and monosodium glutamate plus a 5'-ribonucleotide ≈ umami.

Psychophysical evidence for the basic tastes model includes a single *basic taste* sufficing for human descriptions of aqueous solutions of pure chemicals, successful assignment of taste intensity into *basic tastes,* and inability to discriminate between a number of inorganic and organic acids, or between the sugars fructose, glucose, maltose, and sucrose (Bartoshuk, 1988). Further, in certain laboratory rodents in whom a pharmacological agent, amiloride, selectively blocks gustatory neural responses to small metallic salts, behavioral measures using the same agent show alteration of responses toward NaCl and KCl but not to sucrose.

Negating data for the basic tastes model include incompatibility with studies utilizing normal foods or many-component mixtures, inability to produce the range of human gustatory experiences by combining the primary or basic taste stimuli, discrimination between stimuli of a basic taste category, cross-adaptation failure within a basic taste, and frequent descriptions of many substances, including basic taste stimuli, using multiple basic taste terms and other words (side tastes).

An alternative theory is the *pattern* or *across fiber model,* utilized by a minority of investigators, which posits that relative responsiveness across an array of taste units with broadly overlapping but different sensitivity profiles is the initial sensory event. The number of gustatory response "types" is left unspecified at greater than four. Psychophysical supporting data include cross-adaptation between "basic taste" categories, inability to identify the components of natural and laboratory mixtures, characterization of some aqueous solutions as complex or "more-than-one," and the cited negating data for the basic tastes model. Furthermore, if oral application of amiloride, a pharmacological blocker of an epithelial sodium channel (see supporting data for the basic tastes model, above), is combined in laboratory rats with a procedure in which drinking of NaCl is followed by injection of a mild poison (conditioned taste aversion for NaCl induced by injection of LiCl), subsequent behavioral avoidance generalizes beyond NaCl drinking to nonsodium salts such as KCl and NH_4Cl, which humans and rats normally categorize as quite different from NaCl. On the other hand, all supporting observations for the basic tastes model represent serious difficulties for the pattern model of taste.

A union of the basic tastes and pattern models might be possible following classic "fusion" CONCEPTS, since CATE-GORIZATION neither precludes discrimination nor requires that processing reside primarily at the receptor level. Neither model addresses temporal aspects, although taste shows temporal integration over several seconds while stimulus durations of 50 msec are sufficient for taste PSYCHOPHYSICS.

Gustatory neuroanatomy is similar in all mammalian hindbrains. However, rostral organization in rhesus monkey and probably human differs dramatically from New World primates and most other mammals, with more direct brain stem connections and greater cortical representation (Getchell et al. 1991). The profound evolutionary implications remain unexplored.

Study of gustatory psychophysics as well as cognitive aspects offers many opportunities if investigations avoid excessive adherence to theoretical models. Taste is similar in outline to other perceptual systems, while also reflecting its unique role in adaptive behavior.

See also COLOR, NEUROPHYSIOLOGY OF; PAIN; QUALIA; SENSATIONS

—*Bruce Halpern*

References

Bartoshuk, L. M. (1988). Taste. In R. C. Atkinson, R. J. Herrnstein, G. Lindzey, and R. D. Luce, Eds., *Steven's Handbook of Experimental Psychology.* 2nd ed., vol. 1: *Perception and Motivation.* New York: Wiley, pp. 461–499.

Beauchamp, G. K., and L. M. Bartoshuk, Eds. (1997). *Tasting and Smelling. Handbook of Perception and Cognition.* 2nd ed. San Diego: Academic Press.

Beidler, L. M., Ed. (1971). *Handbook of Sensory Physiology.* Vol. 4, *Chemical Senses,* part 2. *Taste.* Berlin: Springer.

Brand, J. G., J. H. Teeter, R. H. Cagan, and M. R. Kare, Eds.. (1993). *Chemical Senses.* Vol. 1, *Receptor Events and Transduction in Taste and Olfaction.* New York: Marcel Dekker.

Cattalanotto, F. A., L. M. Bartoshuk, K. M. Östrom, J. F. Gent, and K. Fast. (1993). Effects of anesthesia of the facial nerve on taste. *Chemical Senses* 18: 461–470.

Doty, R. L., Ed. (1995). *Handbook of Olfaction and Gustation.* New York: Marcel Dekker.

Finger, T. E., and W. L. Silver, Eds. (1987). *Neurobiology of Taste and Smell.* New York: Wiley.

Getchell, T. V., R. L. Doty, L. M. Bartoshuk, and J. B. Snow, Jr., Eds. (1991). *Smell and Taste in Health and Disease.* New York: Raven Press.

Gibson, J. J. (1966). *The Senses Considered As Perceptual Systems.* Boston: Houghton Mifflin.

Halpern, B. P. (1991). More than meets the tongue: Temporal characteristics of taste intensity and quality. In H. T. Lawless and B. P. Klein, Eds., *Sensory Science Theory and Applications in Foods.* New York: Marcel Dekker, pp. 37–105.

McBride, R. L., and H. J. H. MacFie, Eds. (1990). *Psychological Basis of Sensory Evaluation.* London: Elsevier.

Meiselman, H. L., and R. S. Rivlin, Eds. (1986). *Clinical Measurement of Taste and Smell.* New York: Macmillan.

Pfaff, D. W., Ed. (1985). *Taste, Olfaction, and the Central Nervous System.* New York: Rockefeller University Press.

Simon, S. A., and S. D. Roper, Eds. (1993). *Mechanisms of Taste Transduction.* Boca Raton, FL: CRC Press.

Weijnen, J. A. W. M., and J. Mendelson, Eds. (1977). *Drinking Behavior: Oral Stimulation, Reinforcement, and Preference.* New York: Plenum Press.

White, B., Ed. (1996). Special issue on flavour perception. *Trends in Food Science and Technology* 7: 386–458.

Further Readings

Arnott, M. L., Ed. (1975). *Gastronomy: The Anthropology of Food and Food Habits.* The Hague: Mouton.

Beauchamp, G. K., K. Kurihara, Y. Ninomiya, T. Sato, and T. Yamamoto, Eds. (1994). Kirin international symposium on bitter taste. *Physiology and Behavior* 56: 1121–1266.

Bosma, J. F., Ed. (1973). *Fourth Symposium on Oral Sensation and Perception. Development in the Fetus and Infant.* Bethesda, MD: U.S. Department of Health, Education, and Welfare publication no. NIH-75–546.

Carterette, E. C., and M. P. Friedman, Eds. (1978). *Handbook of Perception,* vol. 6A, *Tasting and Smelling.* New York: Academic Press.

Collings, V. B. (1974). Human taste response as a function of locus of stimulation on the tongue and soft palate. *Perception and Psychophysics* 16: 169–174.

Delconte, J. D., S. T. Kelling, and B. P. Halpern. (1992). Speed and consistency of human decisions to swallow or spit sweet and sour solutions. *Experientia* 48: 1106–1109.

Faull, J. R., and B. P. Halpern. (1972). Taste stimuli: Time course of peripheral nerve responses and theoretical models. *Science* 178: 73–75.

Gay, W. I., Ed. (1973). *Methods of Animal Experimentation,* vol. 4. *Environment and the Special Senses.* New York: Academic Press.

Halpern, B. P. (1986). Constraints imposed on taste physiology by human taste reaction time data. *Neuroscience and Biobehavioral Reviews* 10: 135–151.

Halpern, B. P. (1998). Amiloride and vertebrate gustatory responses to NaCl. *Neuroscience and Biobehavioral Reviews* 23: 5–47.

Kawamura, Y., and M. R. Kare, Eds. (1987). *Umami: A Basic Taste.* New York: Marcel Dekker.

Kawamura, Y., K. Kurihara, S. Nicolaïdis, Y. Oomura, and M. J. Wayner, Eds. (1991). Umami: Proceedings of the second international symposium on umami. *Physiology and Behavior* 49: 831–1030.

Kurihara, K., N. Suzuki, and H. Ogawa, Eds. (1994). *Olfaction and Taste* 11. Tokyo: Springer.

Mathlouthi, M., J. A. Kanters, and G. G. Birch, Eds. (1993). *Sweet-taste Chemoreception.* London: Elsevier.

Seiden, A. M., Ed. (1997). *Taste and Smell Disorders.* New York: Thieme.

Weiffenbach, J. M., Ed. (1977). *Taste and Development. The Genesis of Sweet Preference.* Bethesda, MD: U.S. Department of Health, Education, and Welfare publication no. NIH-77–1068.

Technology and Human Evolution

Since the beginning of prehistoric archaeology, tools have been associated with prehistoric humans (called *Homo faber* by philosophers). The different stages of *Homo* have been related to their material culture, essentially lithic industries (assemblages of typical stone tools) that were the only artifacts to survive in number: *Homo habilis* is related with the Oldowan industry (from 1.9 million to 1.6 million years B.C.), *Homo erectus* with Acheulean (from 0.5 to 0.3 million years B.C., *Neandertal* with Mousterian (between 300,000 and 35,000 years B.C., *Homo sapiens* with Upper Paleolithic industries from (40,000 years B.C. on). Parallels were drawn between human evolution and CULTURAL EVOLUTION. But it was only in the 1960s that palaeontologists and prehistorians sought for theories relating technology and evolution. Sherwood Washburn (1960) proposed a model that related educated behavior to human evolution in a biocultural feedback system. In a quite different context, André Leroi-Gourhan (1964/1993) constructed a comprehensive theory of evolution that related the evolution of man and culture to the evolution of gesture/action and speech and to the exteriorization of physical and mental functions (by transfer of functions from mouth to hand and from hand to tools, and also from brain to books and to computer memory). In this theory, evolution, once the *Homo sapiens* stage is reached, is carried out through channels other than genetics: that is, the technological and the social realm. From the appearance of the first tool to the spread of *Homo sapiens,* there is a related evolution of *Homo* and technology. In the 1970s sociobiologists emphasized the relation between technology, as a learned behavior, and genetic evolution (E. O. Wilson 1975; see also SOCIOBIOLOGY). More recently a philosopher of science, Bernard Stiegler, proposed to see in this related evolution of man and its technology a phenomenon of epiphylogenesis as a new relation between the human organism and its environment: lithic technology and tools are preserved beyond the life of the individual who produced them and determine the relation of man with its environment, thus conditioning a part of the selection pressure (Stiegler 1992).

Research on prehistoric technology is becoming an important field within archaeological researches and a part of COGNITIVE ARCHAEOLOGY. It is based on flint-knapping experimentations, on refitting flint flakes, and on microwear and functional analysis of tools. It is a powerful approach to the cognitive abilities of prehistoric humans. The concept of *"chaînes opératoires"* (which presents technical productions as operational sequences of technical actions) introduced by Leroi-Gourhan (1964; Schlanger 1994) played a key role in its development, permitting the analysis of goals, intentions, realizations and their extent of variability, degree of anticipation and level of competence within a technological framework or technocomplex (Boëda 1994; Karlin and Julien 1994).

J. Pelegrin, whose conclusions are widely accepted, analyzes intellectual and physiological abilities of flint knappers in terms of knowledge and know-how. Knowledge includes concepts and mental representations of ideal tools and conceivable raw materials, and mental representations of a constellation of actions (gestures and results). Know-how includes the ability to imagine which actions are needed for a given task and to assess the results. It can be divided into an ideatory know-how, which critically assesses raw materials' potentials here and now and their consequences, and a sensorimotor know-how, which induces programming of knapping gestures and actions (Pelegrin 1990). This analytical framework has permitted the analysis of the "chaînes opératoires" characteristic of the main lithic industries, their increasing complexity and anticipatory strategies through time. Levels of complexity can be evidenced from the Oldowan to Upper Paleolithic industries according to number and variety of tasks and actions performed, from the intensity of preparation and rejuvenation of the core, from the degree of anticipation of the consequences of technical choices and gestures (Roche and Texier 1993). In the oldest lithic industries such as Oldowan, the ideational know-how is reduced to a simple repetition of elementary actions (Pelegrin 1990) but is associated with a motor know-how able to control the intensity and direction of hammer strokes. For Roche and Texier (1993), first bifaces (appearing in the late Oldowan) reflect an emerging concept poorly materialized by an insufficient sensorimotor know-how. The Acheulean bifaces already imply more complex conceptual and reflexive abilities: the final form of a biface is completely independent of the original raw material and includes a double symmetry; every flake removal results in modifying at the same time the edge contour and profile and the face thickness. Errors of judgment or poor sensorimotor control results in wasting raw material or even in rendering the core useless. For Pelegrin, technical aspects of hominization are achieved at this stage, even if numerous progressions are still to come.

A few British and American prehistorians and paleontologists interpret the same data in a quite different way and oppose what they call the "final object fallacy" (Wynn 1993). They privilege use upon conceptual creation in shaping the final product: polyhedrals and bolas (nearly perfect spheric stone balls) of the Oldowan are viewed as hammers that acquired their spheric shape through repeated use (Toth 1993); Mousterian sidescrapers as well acquire their shape through use (Dibble and Bar-Yosef 1995). However, Toth acknowledges that the double symmetry of later bifaces represent a conscious and planned shape (Toth and Schick 1993). At this stage, all agree that language is not necessary, but Toth and Schick consider that it could be incipient given the dominance of right-handed knappers. But most prehistorians advocate for language associated with Mousterian technology. All agree that the problem cannot be solved for the moment because there is no clear technological performance correlated with language (Ingold 1993; Wynn 1993).

Another problem has emerged with discoveries of remains from archaic *Homo sapiens* associated with Mousterian artifacts and technology, at the same time that remains from late Neandertals (Chatelperroniaa) were found with an early Upper Paleolithic industry (Hublin et al. 1996). Similarly, first bifaces appear in late Oldowan in *Homo habilis* context. Thus, it is no longer possible to equate technocomplexes and human species. However, technology is opening a new field of investigation about the cognitive abilities of prehistoric humans.

See also ARTIFACTS AND CIVILIZATION; COGNITIVE ANTHROPOLOGY; COGNITIVE ARCHAEOLOGY; CULTURAL EVOLUTION

—*Francoise Audouze*

References

Boëda, E. (1994). *Le concept Levallois: Variabilité des méthodes.* Paris: CNRS éditions, monographies du CRA no. 9.

Davidson, I., and W. Noble. (1993). Early stone industries and inferences regarding language and cognition. In K. R. Gibson and T. Ingold, Eds., *Tools, Language and Cognition in Human Evolution.* Cambridge: Cambridge University Press, pp. 363–388.

Dibble, H. L., and O. Bar-Yosef, Eds. (1995). *The Definition and Interpretation of Levallois Technology.* Madison: Prehistory Press, *Monographs in World Archaeology* no. 23.

Gibson, K. R., and T. Ingold, Eds. (1993). *Tools, Language and Cognition in Human Evolution.* Cambridge: Cambridge University Press.

Hublin, J.-J., F. Spoort, M. Braun, F. Zonneveld, and S. Condemi. (1996). A late Neanderthal associated with Upper Palaeolithic artefacts. *Nature* 381: 224–226.

Ingold, T. (1993). Epilogue—Technology, language, intelligence: A reconsideration of basic concepts. In K. R. Gibson and T. Ingold, Eds., *Tools, Language and Cognition in Human Evolution.* Cambridge: Cambridge University Press, pp. 449–472.

Karlin, C., and M. Julien. (1994). Prehistoric technology: A cognitive science? In C. Renfrew and E. B. W. Zubrow, Eds., *The Ancient Mind, Elements of Cognitive Archaeology.* Cambridge: Cambridge University Press, pp. 143–151.

Leroi-Gourhan, A. (1964). *Le Geste et la Parole,* vol. 1: *Technique et langage;* vol. 2: *La Mémoire et les Rythmes.* Paris: Albin Michel. (Translated as *Gesture and Speech* by A. Bostock Berger (1993). Cambridge, MA: MIT Press.)

Pelegrin, J. (1990). Prehistoric lithic technology, some aspects of research. *Archaeological Review from Cambridge* 9(1): 116–125.

Pelegrin, J. (1993). A framework for analysing prehistoric stone tool manufacture and a tentative application to some early stone age industries. In A. Berthelet and J. Chavaillon, Eds., *The Use of Tools by Human and Non-human Primates.* Symposia of the Fyssen Foundation no. 3. Oxford: Clarendon Press, pp. 302–314.

Roche, H., and P.-J. Texier. (1996). Evaluation of technical competence of *Homo erectus* in East Africa during the Middle Pleistocene. In J. R. F. Bower and S. Sartono, Eds., *Human Evolution in its Ecological Context.* Leiden: Royal Netherlands Academy of Arts and Science, pp. 153–167. (First volume of L. J. Slikkerveer, Ed., *Evolution and Ecology of* Homo erectus.)

Schlanger, N. (1994). Mindful technology: Unlashing the chaine opératoire for an archaeology of mind. In C. Renfrew and E. B. W. Zubrow, Eds., *The Ancient Mind, Elements of Cognitive Archaeology.* Cambridge: Cambridge University Press, pp. 143–151.

Stiegler, B. (1992). Leroi-Gourhan, part maudite de l'anthropologie. *Les Nouvelles de l'Archologie* 48/49: 23–30.

Toth, N. (1993). The Oldowan reassessed: A close look at early stone artifacts. In R. L. Ciochon and J. G. Fleagle, Eds., *The Human Evolution Source Book.* Englewood Cliffs, NJ: Prentice Hall, pp. 336–347.

Toth, N., and K. Schick. (1993). Early stone industries and inferences regarding language and cognition. In K. R. Gibson and T. Ingold, Eds., *Tools, Language and Cognition in Human Evolution.* Cambridge: Cambridge University Press, pp. 346–362.

Vandermeersch, B. (1990). Réflexions d'un anthropologue á propos de la transition Moustréien/Paléolithique supérieur. In C. Farizy, Ed., *Paléolithique moyen récent et Paléolithique supérieur ancien en Europe.* Nemours: APRAIF, pp. 21–24. (Mémoires du Muése de Préhistoire d'Ile-de-France, no. 3.)

Washburn, S. L. (1960). Tools and human evolution. *Scientific American* 203: 63–75.

Wilson, E. O. (1975). *Sociobiology: The New Synthesis.* Cambridge, MA: Harvard University Press.

Wynn, T. (1993). Layers of thinking in tool behavior. In K. R. Gibson and T. Ingold, Eds., *Tools, Language and Cognition in Human Evolution.* Cambridge: Cambridge University Press, pp. 389–406.

Further Readings

Berthelet, A., and J. Chavaillon, Eds. (1993). *The Use of Tools by Human and Non-human Primates.* Symposia of the Fyssen Foundation, no. 3. Oxford: Clarendon Press.

Gowlett, J. A. J. (1992). Early Human mental abilities. In S. Jones, R. Martin, and D. Pilbeam, Eds., *Human Evolution.* Cambridge: Cambridge University Press, pp. 341–345.

Mellars, P. (1973). Cognitive changes and the emergence of modern humans in Europe. *Cambridge Archaeological Journal* 1: 63–76.

Wynn, T. (1981). The intelligence of Oldowan hominids. *Journal of Human Evolution* 10(7): 529–541.

Temporal Reasoning

Temporal reasoning problems arise in many areas of artificial intelligence (AI), including planning, reasoning about physical systems, discourse analysis, and analysis of time-dependent data. Work in temporal reasoning can be classified in three general categories: algebraic systems, temporal logics, and logics of action. Although useful for many practical tasks, there is little evidence that any of these approaches accurately model human cognition about time. Less formal but more psychologically grounded approaches are discussed in some of the work in AI on plan recognition (Schmidt, Sridhaven, and Goodson 1978), work in linguistics on SEMANTICS and TENSE AND ASPECT (Jackendoff 1983), and the vast psychological literature on MEMORY.

Algebraic systems concentrate on the relationships between time points and/or time intervals, which are represented by named variables. A set of either quantitative or qualitative equations constrain the values that could be assigned to the temporal variables. These equations could take the form of a constraint satisfaction problem (CSP), a set of linear equations, or even a set of assertions in a restricted subset of first-order logic. The goal of the reasoning problem may be to determine consistency, to find a minimal labeling of the CSP, or to find consistent bindings for all the variables over some set of mathematical objects. In all of the algebraic systems described below, time itself is modeled as a continuous linear structure, although there has also been some investigation of discrete linear-time models (Dechter, Meiri, and Pearl 1991) and branching-time models (Ladkin, Angerm, and Rodriguez 1990).

The qualitative temporal algebra, originally devised by Allen (1983) and formalized as an algebra by Ladkin and Maddux (1994), takes time intervals to be primitive. There are thirteen primitive possible relationships between a pair of intervals: for example, before (<) meets (m) (the end of the first corresponds to the beginning of the second), overlaps (o), and so on. These primitive relationships can be combined to form 2^{13} complex relationships. For example, the constraint I_1 (< m >) I_2 means that I_1 is either before, meets, or is after I_2. Allen showed how a set of such constraints could be represented by a CSP, and how path-consistency could be used as an incomplete algorithm for computing a minimal set of constraints. The general problem of determining consistency is NP-complete (Vilain, Kautz, and van Beek 1989).

Quantitative algebras allow one to reason about durations of intervals and other metric information. The simple temporal constraint problems (STCSP) of Dechter, Meiri, and Pearl (1991) are a restricted form of linear equations. A time interval I is identified with the pair of its starting point I_s and ending point I_e. Difference equations allow one to place constraints on the relative ordering of points. For example, $I_e - J_s \in [-\infty, 0]$ means that I is before J, and $I_s - I_e \in [3, 5]$ means that the duration of I is between 3 and 5 units. Because they are just linear programs, STCSPs can be solved in polynomial time. General TCSPs allow the right-hand side of an equation to be a union of intervals, rather than a single interval, and solving them is NP-complete. However, TCSPs still cannot express certain complex constraints, such as that two intervals are disjoint but unordered (I (< >) J), which would involve four points ($I_e < J_s \lor J_e < I_s$).

Many researchers have explored tractable subsets of these algebras. A subset is specified by the form of the constraints allowed in the statement of the problem instance. Vilain, Kautz, and van Beek (1989) noted that the subset of Allen's algebra that can be exactly translated into equalities and inequalities over start and end points is polynomial. Nebel and Bürckert (1995) generalized this to relations that can be translated into "ord-Horn constraints," the largest tractable subclass that includes all the primitive relations. Koubarakis (1996) and Jonsson and Bäckström (1996) further showed that tractablity still holds if such constraints contain linear combinations of variables. However, none of these classes can express interval disjointed (< >), and in fact any tractable class that includes disjointedness cannot contain all of the primitive relations. Tractable classes including interval disjointedness include some of the "chordal graph" classes of Golumbic and Shamir (1993) and two of the algebras described in Drakengren and Jonsson (1997).

Temporal algebras say nothing about how time intervals or points are associated with events or propositions. In practice, some external mechanism (such as a planning system) generates interval and point tokens that are used to timestamp or index statements in a knowledge base. This external mechanism then computes some of the constraints between the temporal tokens that must hold according to the semantics of the knowledge base (for example, that a token associated with a proposition is disjoint from one associated with the negation of that proposition), and then asks the algebraic reasoning engine to compute consequences of those assertions.

By contrast, temporal logics (van Benthem 1983; Thayse 1989) directly represent the temporal relationships between propositions, and do away with any explicit tokens to represent time points or intervals. These are modal logics, which extend propositional or first-order logic with temporal operators. For example, propositional linear time temporal logic models time as a discrete sequence of states, and adds the modal operators next $\mathbf{O}$, always $\square$, eventually $\lozenge$, and until $\mathcal{U}$. For example, the formula $\square p \supset \mathbf{O} q$ means that whenever p holds, then q must hold in the next state.

The most successful applications of temporal logics have been in the area of program verification (Emerson 1990). One approach to this task exploits the fact that any formula in linear temporal logic can be converted into a kind of finite automata called a Büchi automata. The input language to the automata is sequences of states. The automata accepts exactly those sequences that are models of the corresponding temporal logic formula. In this application, the program to be verified is written as a finite automata, and properties one wishes to verify are written as formulas in temporal logic. The negation of the temporal logic formula is then converted to a Büchi automata, which is then intersected with the program automata. It is then easy to check whether the combined automata accepts any inputs; if it does not, then the program satisfies the desired properties. The worst-case complexity of this procedure is high, because the automata may be exponentially larger than the formula.

Although temporal logics are frequently used in the verification and temporal database communities, they are just beginning to find widespread use in AI, particularly in PLANNING. Applications include the specification and verification of real-time, reactive planners (Rosenschein and Kaelbling 1995; Williams and Nayak 1997), and specification of temporal-extended goals and search control rules (Bacchus and Kabanza 1996).

Finally, temporal reasoning is implicitly performed by all systems used to represent and reason about action and change, such as the SITUATION CALCULUS (McCarthy and Hayes 1969) or dynamic logic (Harel 1979). The situation calculus is simply a style of using first-order logic, in which the final argument to a predicate represents the state in which it holds. Actions are functions from state to state. Thus, the semantics for the situation calculus is based on a discrete, forward-branching model of time. The general approach can also be used to model continuous branching time (Reiter 1996). Successful planning systems have also been built (Blum and Furst 1995; Kautz and Selman 1996) that use a discrete linear model of time, where states are simply natural numbers used to index time-varying predicates.

See also CONSTRAINT SATISFACTION; KNOWLEDGE REPRESENTATION; MODAL LOGIC

—Henry Kautz

References

Allen, J. (1983). Maintaining knowledge about temporal intervals. *Comm. ACM* 26(11): 832–843.

Bacchus, F., and F. Kabanza. (1996). Planning for temporally extended goals. *Proc. AAAI-96* Portland, OR.

van Benthem, J. (1983). *The Logic of Time.* Dordrecht: Reidel.

Blum, A., and M. Furst. (1995). Fast planning through planning graph analysis. *Proc. IJCAI-95* Montreal, Canada.

Dechter, R., I. Meiri, and J. Pearl. (1991). Temporal constraint networks. *Artificial Intelligence* 49: 61–95.

Drakengren, T., and P. Jonsson. (1997). Towards a complete classification of tractablility in Allen's algebra. *Proc. IJCAI-97* Nagoya, Japan.

Emerson, E. A. (1990). Temporal and modal logic. In J. van Leeuwen, Ed., *Handbook of Theoretical Computer Science,* vol. B. Elsevier.

Golumbic, M., and R. Shamir. (1993). Complexity and algorithms for reasoning about time: A graph-theoretic approach. *J. ACM* 40(5): 1108–1133.

Harel, D. (1979). First-order dynamic logic. *Lecture Notes in Computer Science,* vol. 68. Berlin: Springer.

Jackendoff, R. (1983). *Semantics and Cognition.* Cambridge, MA: MIT Press.

Jonsson, P., and C. Bäckström. (1996). A linear-programming approach to temporal reasoning. *Proc. AAAI-96* Portland, OR.

Kautz, H., and B. Selman. (1996). Pushing the envelope: Planning, propositional logic, and stochastic search. *Proc. AAAI-96* Portland, OR.

Koubarakis, M. (1996). Tractable disjunctions of linear constraints. *Proc. Constraint Logic Programming* (*CLP*-96) Boston, MA.

Ladkin, P., F. Anger, and R. Rodriguez. (1990). Temporal reasoning with intervals in branching time. *TR-90028* International Computer Science Institute.

Ladkin, P., and Maddux, R. (1994). On binary constraint problems. *J. ACM* 41(3): 435–469.

McCarthy, J., and P. Hayes. (1969). Some philosophical problems from the standpoint of artificial intelligence. *Machine Intelligence* 4. Chichester: Ellis Horwood.

Nebel, B., and H. Bürkert. (1995). Reasoning about temporal relations: A maximal tractable subclass of Allen's interval algebra. *J. ACM* 42(1): 43–66.

Reiter, R. (1996). Natural actions, concurrency and continuous time in the situation calculus. *Proc. KR-96* Boston, MA.

Rosenschein, S., and L. Kaelbling. (1995). A situated view of representation and control. *Artificial Intelligence* 73(1): 149–174.

Schmidt, C. F., N. S. Sridharan, and J. L. Goodson. (1978). The plan recognition problem: An intersection of psychology and artificial intelligence. *Artificial Intelligence* 11: 45–83.

Thayse, A., Ed. (1989). *From Modal Logic to Deductive Databases.* Chichester: Wiley.

Vilain, M., H. Kautz, and P. van Beek. (1989). Constraint propagation algorithms for temporal reasoning: A revised report. In J. deKleer and D. Weld, Eds., *Readings in Qualitative Reasoning About Physical Systems.* Los Altos, CA: Kaufmann.

Williams, B., and P. Nayak. (1997). A reactive planner for a model-based executive. *Proc. IJCAI-97* Nagoya, Japan.

Tense and Aspect

With the exception of statements in textbooks in mathematics, almost everything that is expressed in natural languages involves time in some way. It is not easy to specify exactly what within the general realm of temporal reference should be subsumed under the headings *tense* and *aspect,* particularly because these terms have been used in widely divergent ways by different scholars in linguistics, logic and philosophy. Consider a declarative sentence such as (1) *The water was cold.* In its most common use, such a sentence "refers" to a definite time (point or period), although this time is not explicitly identified in the sentence itself. In English, the form of the verb tells us that the time is in the past—that is, prior to the time at which the sentence is uttered. Otherwise, one would have said (2) *The water is cold.* But in a language such as Mandarin Chinese, the sentence (3) *shuǐ hěn lěng* translates as both (1) and (2). Still, (3) shares with the English translations the property that it normally refers to a specific time when used. This kind of implicit time reference, then, is a universal property of human languages, which is independent of whether there is grammatical tense marking or not. Another universal property is the fundamentally deictic character of time reference—most spoken sentences refer to the time of speech, and even in those that do not, time reference usually takes the time of speech as the point of departure, one consequence being that the truth-value of a typical sentence in a natural language depends on when it is uttered. The study of tense in formal semantics focuses on these and similar phenomena, which are at least analytically distinct from the notion of *grammatical tense*—that is, the signaling of time reference by grammatical means such as verb inflection and auxiliaries. The *tense operators* of tense logic ("it has been the case that *p*", "it will be the case that *p*") as developed by Arthur Prior (Prior 1967) and reflected for example in Montague Grammar (Montague 1971) have only a partial overlap semantically and syntactically with the grammatical tenses of natural languages—they cannot for instance account for the implicit reference to a definite point in time characteristic of examples such as (1) or for the agreement-like character of the informationally redundant tense marker in a sentence such as (4) *It rained yesterday.*

The field of aspect displays a similar duality in that it may alternatively be seen as the ontology of those entities that are most intimately connected with time, such as events, processes, states, properties, and so on, or as the study of the grammatical phenomena that relate to such types of entities and their manifestation in time. With respect to the ontology of temporal entities, which is sometimes subsumed under labels such as *actionality* or *aktionsart,* the most well known taxonomy is that of Vendler (1967). Vendler distinguishes *states* (as exemplified by "love somebody"), *activities* ("run", "push a cart"), *accomplishments* ("draw a circle"), and *achievements* ("win a race"). These four categories may also be distinguished in terms of binary distinctions. States are opposed to the three others by lacking dynamicity. Activities are opposed to accomplishments and achievements by being atelic or unbounded—that is, unlike the latter, they do not have a well-defined endpoint or result-state. The difference between accomplishments and achievements may be described in terms of a distinction durative:punctual.

In the grammatical tradition, tense and aspect are usually seen as grammatical categories pertaining to the verb.

In actual grammatical systems, temporal and aspectual properties are commonly interwoven in the same forms, and many linguists nowadays talk of tense-aspect systems as integrated wholes. Tense-aspect markings arise through grammaticization processes out of phrasal constructions usually involving lexical morphemes. Future markers may, for example, develop out of constructions involving motion verbs such as *come* and *go*. Advanced stages of grammaticization lead to the rise of inflectional markings by the fusion of earlier free morphemes with the stem of the head word. The high degree of grammaticization of inflectional tense-aspect markers is reflected in their obligatory character and tendency to be used even if informationally redundant (see (4)).

Grammatical tense-aspect markings tend to fall into a relatively small number of crosslinguistic types characterized by their SEMANTICS and typical way of expression. A subset of those types are regularly expressed inflectionally, by affixes or stem alternations (e.g., "strong verbs" in Germanic languages). The tense-aspect markings most frequently found in inflectional systems are imperfective, perfective, past, and future markings. The opposition between imperfective and perfective forms the core of a large part, maybe the majority, of all inflectional tense-aspect systems. Perfective verb forms prototypically express completed events in the past, as in Mandarin Chinese *shé shǐ le* 'the snake died', where *le* is a perfective marker; imperfective forms prototypically express on-going activities or states that hold at the point of speech (but also habits), as in Modern Standard Arabic *yaktubu rasa:'ilan* 'he is writing a letter', where *yaktubu* is the imperfective form of the verb. The temporal reference properties may be overridden, however. Past markings may be applicable to all verb forms (as in English) or only to imperfective ones. Future markings are less often inflectional than the ones already discussed. Due to their special epistemological status, statements about the future tend to have modal nuances tinging the purely temporal character of grammatical futures.

Among tense-aspect markings that are usually expressed periphrastically (constructions involving more than one word) are progressives (a common diachronic source for imperfectives) as in English *I am singing,* and perfects (a common source for both pasts and perfectives), as in English *I have sung.* Progressives differ from imperfectives in having a narrower range of uses. The semantics of perfects is often described in terms of "current relevance" or in terms of an identity between "reference time" and "speech time" (in the terminology of Reichenbach 1947). Combinations of perfects and pasts yield pluperfects, used to express an event taking place before a reference time in the past.

Further types include habituals and generics, experientials (used to express that something took place at least once in the past), narratives (used to express that an event directly follows another in a narration), and markings of remoteness distinctions (e.g., hodiernal or "today" pasts versus hesternal or "yesterday" pasts).

See also INDEXICALS AND DEMONSTRATIVES; LOGIC; PRAGMATICS

—*Östen Dahl*

References

Montague, R. (1971). *Formal Philosophy,* Richmond H. Thomason, Ed. New Haven, CT: Yale University Press.
Prior, A. (1967). *Past, Present, and Future.* Oxford: Clarendon Press.
Reichenbach, H. (1947). *Elements of Symbolic Logic.* New York: Collier-Macmillan.
Vendler, Z. (1967). *Linguistics in Philosophy.* Ithaca, NY: Cornell University Press.

Further Readings

Bertinetto, P. M., V. Bianchi, Ö. Dahl, and M. Squartini, Eds. (1995). *Temporal Reference, Aspect and Actionality.* Vol. 2, *Typological Perspectives.* Torino: Rosenberg and Sellier.
Bertinetto, P. M., V. Bianchi, J. Higginbotham, and M. Squartini, Eds.. (1995). *Temporal Reference, Aspect and Actionality.* Vol. 1, *Semantic and Syntactic Perspectives.* Torino: Rosenberg and Sellier.
Binnick, R. I. (1991). *Time and the Verb: A Guide to Tense and Aspect.* Chicago: University of Chicago Press.
Bybee, J. L., R. Perkins, and W. Pagliuca. (1994). *The Evolution of Grammar: Tense, Aspect, and Modality in the Languages of the World.* Chicago: University of Chicago Press.
Comrie, B. (1976). *Aspect: An Introduction to the Study of Verbal Aspect and Related Problems.* Cambridge: Cambridge University Press.
Comrie, B. (1985). *Tense.* Cambridge: Cambridge University Press.
Contini-Morava, E. (1989). *Discourse Pragmatics and Semantic Categorization: The Case of Negation and Tense-Aspect with Special Reference to Swahili.* Berlin: Mouton.
Dahl, Ö. (1985). *Tense and Aspect Systems.* Oxford: Blackwell.
Dowty, D. (1979). *Word Meaning and Montague Grammar: The Semantics of Verbs and Times in Generative Semantics and in Montague's PTQ.* Dordrecht: Reidel.
Hopper, P., Ed. (1982). *Tense-aspect: Between Semantics and Pragmatics.* Amsterdam: Benjamins.
Klein, W. (1994). *Time in Language.* London: Routledge.
Partee, B. (1984). Nominal and temporal anaphora. *Linguistics and Philosophy* 7: 243–286.
Smith, C. (1991). *The Parameter of Aspect.* Dordrecht: Kluwer.
Tedeschi, P., and A. Zaenen, Eds. (1981). *Syntax and Semantics 14: Tense and Aspect.* New York: Academic Press.
Verkuyl, H. (1972). *On the Compositional Nature of Aspect.* Dordrecht: Reidel.

Teuber, Hans-Lukas

Hans-Lukas Teuber (1916–1977) was born in Berlin to Dr. Eugen Teuber, a psychologist, and Rose Knopf, a teacher. His father was the founder of the primate center on Tenerife in the Canary Islands, which later became famous as the site of Wolfgang's experiments on apes. After a classical education at the French College in Berlin, he studied biology and philosophy at the University of Basel.

In 1941, Teuber came to the Department of Psychology at Harvard University as a graduate student, and in the same year married Marianne Liepe, an art historian. She came to play a central and crucial role in the extended families that later made up his laboratory at New York University and his department at MIT.

Teuber's most important educational experiences in graduate school were probably the two years he spent away from Harvard in the U.S. Navy. In that period he began to work with the neurologist Morris B. Bender at the San Diego Naval Hospital on the effects of human brain lesions. This collaboration lasted more than fifteen years and produced a series of important neuropsychological articles, particularly on the effects of penetrating head wounds on visual and haptic function.

After returning to Harvard, he completed his doctoral dissertation in 1947 on a study of the effects of psychotherapy on teenagers at risk for delinquency. Teuber found that the experimental and control groups did not differ. This experience probably contributed to his lifelong skepticism of psychotherapists, as well as most other types of clinicians. In spite of this attitude, throughout his life Teuber spent an enormous amount of time counseling his colleagues, students, and research subjects with their personal problems.

In 1947, Teuber established his Psychophysiological Laboratory at the New York University-Bellevue Medical Center. Neuropsychological research on head-injured war veterans and other patients flourished there, as well as new lines of research on children and infrahuman animals. The work of Teuber and his colleagues in this period played a major role in the transformation of the study of human brain function from collecting case studies of florid neurological curios to a systematic experimental neuropsychology (e.g., Semmes et al. 1960; Teuber, Battersby, and Bender 1960). Among their major innovations were the use of matched control groups; the study of patients chosen on the basis of their brain damage and not their symptoms; follow up of patients beyond the stage of acute symptoms; use of nonverbal tests (he called them "monkified," as they were often derived from the animal laboratory); and, above all, the introduction of modern psychophysical methods with their rigor of instrumentation and statistical analysis.

Teuber came to the Massachusetts Institute of Technology in the fall of 1961 to organize a new department of psychology. Over the next decade this became a world center for the neuro- and cognitive sciences. Uniquely at the time, it brought together neuroanatomy, neurophysiology, neuropsychology, cognitive psychology, linguistics, COMPUTATIONAL NEUROSCIENCE, and philosophy into an interacting community and became a model for the establishment of similar neuroscience centers abound the world. Today the department continues to flourish as the Department of Brain and Cognitive Sciences.

Teuber was a charismatic teacher at every level. For a number of years he taught the introductory psychology course (twice a term for both terms) and it was taken by virtually every undergraduate at MIT. He was a brilliant speaker and particularly skilled at summing up conference proceedings. His theoretical and review papers helped to set the foundation for contemporary neuroscience (e.g. Teuber 1955, 1960, 1978).

Teuber's contributions extended far beyond the institutions he founded and the experimental and theoretical papers he wrote. He was a consummate organizer, synthesizer, and sponsor of research on the brain, as well as the mentor of many of today's leading brain researchers. His concern for others went beyond counseling and support. He resigned in protest as chair of the Advisory Committee to the Surgeon General of the U. S. Army over the use of psychedelic drugs on human subjects, he was instrumental in establishing the first MIT Review Committee on Human Subjects, and he was supportive of anti-Vietnam War activity at MIT. As he put it in a posthumously published address to the 21st International Psychology Congress (Teuber 1978), "our particular science is as central as physics, and ultimately more so. But it is also capable of as much abuse . . . All of us here will have to abide by a new kind of Hippocratic oath, never to do harm, always to heal rather than hinder, to make life richer, and to make it free."

See also LURIA, ALEXANDER ROMANOVICH; MARR, DAVID

— *Charles Gross*

References

Gross, C. (1994). Hans-Lukas Teuber: A tribute. *Cereb. Cor.* 5: 451–454.

Hecaen, H. (1979). H.-L. Teuber et la foundation de la neurologie experimentale. *Neuropsychologia* 17: 199–124.

Hurvich, L. M., D. Jameson, and W. A. Rosenblith. (1987). Hans-Lukas Teuber: A biographical memoir. *Biographical Memoirs, National Academy of Sciences* 57: 461–490.

Semmes, J., S. Weinstein, L. Ghent, and H.-L. Teuber. (1960). *Somatosensory Changes After Penetrating Brain Wounds in Man.* Cambridge, MA: Harvard University Press.

Teuber, H.-L. (1955). Physiological psychology. *Annual Review of Psychology* 6: 267–296.

Teuber, H.-L. (1960). Perception. In J. Field, H. W. Magain, and V. E. Hall, Eds., *Handbook of Physiology,* vol. 3. Washington, DC: American Physiological Society, pp. 1595–1688.

Teuber, H.-L. (1978). The brain and human behavior. In R. Held, H. W. Leibowitz, and H.-L. Teuber, Eds., *Handbook of Sensory Physiology,* vol. 7. New York: Springer, pp. 879–920.

Teuber, H.-L., W. S. Battersby, and M. Bender. (1960). *Visual Field Defects After Penetrating Missile Wounds of the Brain.* Cambridge, MA: Harvard University Press.

Texture

Visual texture is a perceptual property of image regions. In this respect texture is analogous to perceived brightness, COLOR, DEPTH, and MOTION. Just as we can describe a region of an image as bright or dark, red or green, near or far, or moving up or down, we can describe it as having a mottled, striped, or speckled texture. Note that none of these descriptions is redundant or inconsistent with any of the others; saying that a region is bright red, distant, and moving up does not in any way constrain its textural properties. In natural images visual texture frequently is related to qualities of surfaces indicating roughness or smoothness or other physical properties.

The English word *texture* derives from the Latin *texere,* meaning "to weave." "Texture" was first used to describe the character of a woven fabric as smooth, ribbed, twilled, and so forth. Similarly, in describing visual texture we refer to such properties of an image region as granularity, periodicity, orientation, and relative order or randomness.

Interest in the perception of visual texture has both applied and theoretical roots. Texture rendition is important for creation of natural-looking images. However, because of its high level of spatial detail, digital representation of image texture can also be expensive in terms of storage and transmission bandwidth. Therefore, it is useful to understand what characteristics of texture are perceptually important so that these can be represented efficiently. From the standpoint of understanding visual processes texture is also of interest because texture perception differs in some ways from more general visual perception.

The most basic manifestation of this difference can be seen in the fact that regions containing visually discriminable structure do not always form distinct textures. For example, as noted by Beck (1966; see also an example in Bergen 1991) a bipartite region containing upright T and L shapes appears as a uniformly textured area while a bipartite region containing upright and tilted T shapes (or tilted T and upright L shapes) shows a clear division into two visually distinct areas (see figure 1). This greater effectiveness of the orientation difference is not predicted by pattern discrimination properties: T, L, and tilted T shapes are all easily distinguishable when inspected as individual patterns within the texture image. This phenomenon is referred to variously as "texture segregation," "texture-based segmentation" or "pre-attentive," "instantaneous," or "effortless" texture discrimination. It can also be described as the tendency for some pairs of textured stimuli to induce the formation of an illusory contour between regions of different spatial structure (see SHAPE PERCEPTION, GESTALT PERCEPTION, SURFACE PERCEPTION). One of the major areas of activity in the study of texture perception has been to try to isolate the stimulus characteristics that support this phenomenon. Descriptions of these characteristics have included local features (e.g., Beck 1966, 1982; Julesz 1981), pixel statistics (e.g., Julesz 1962, 1975), and linear filters (e.g., Harvey and Gervais 1978, 1981; Richards and Polit 1974; Beck, Sutter and Ivry 1987; Bergen and Adelson 1988). For reviews of this work see Bergen (1991) and Graham (1991).

A rather ubiquitous idea found in this body of work is that texture segregation is based on a simplified analysis of spatial structure. According to this view, the reason that some texture pairs segregate and others do not is that the texture analysis process does not possess the powers of discrimination present in more sophisticated processes such as VISUAL OBJECT RECOGNITION, AI. Thus, the nonsegregating textures (such as those composed of the T and L shapes in the example) look the same to the (hypothetical) texture analysis process even though they look different to the (hypothetical) pattern discrimination process. Possible reasons that the visual system would perform such a simplified analysis involve issues of speed and complexity. It may be more important to have rapid (or "early") information about texture structure than to respond to all visible structure differences. This would be the case if texture-based segmentation has an orienting or ATTENTION control function. Alternatively, it may simply be too expensive of processing resources to make a more detailed analysis of texture structure. Texture stimuli have the inherent characteristic of spatial density as compared to the relative sparsity of other visual characteristics. Dense, more complex processing may not be a biologically feasible option.

Texture segregation is most strongly driven by simple differences in local spatial structure such as granularity (coarseness or spatial frequency content), orientation, and sign-of-contrast. These are also the kinds of spatial characteristics that most strongly determine the physiological responsiveness of cells in the early stages of mammalian VISUAL CORTEX (see also VISUAL ANATOMY AND PHYSIOLOGY). This coincidence raises the intriguing possibility that texture properties are actually computed at this rather early stage of visual processing. This possibility has been associated with all of the different styles of texture descriptions described earlier; at a qualitative level local feature extraction, analysis of image statistics, and analysis of spatial frequency content are all plausible (although crude) descriptions of early cortical processing.

The relationship between models of early visual processing (particularly those based on some understanding of mammalian cortex) and texture perception phenomena has been the basis for computational and psychophysical investigations. Examples include Caelli (1985), Turner (1986), Malik and Perona (1990), Bergen and Landy (1991), Chubb and Landy (1991), Graham (1991), and Landy and Bergen (1991). The underlying information representation in most of these studies is a collection of linear filters sensitive to different scales and orientations of spatial structure, possibly with a preceding static nonlinearity. These models (sometimes referred to as "energy models" or "filter models") provide a good description of texture phenomena for certain classes of stimuli. Heeger and Bergen have demonstrated that for textures of relatively "random" structure such models can be used as the basis for synthesis of textures that match a target texture in appearance. This procedure also demonstrates the limitations of this kind of representation: for textures with nonlocal or quasi-periodic structure, physiologically motivated filter models do not successfully capture texture structure. Promising extensions to this approach can be found in the work of Popat and Picard (1993) and De Bonet (1997), which uses more explicit spatial information to represent more coherent structure.

It is possible that the image characteristics that are commonly referred to as "texture" actually fall into two different

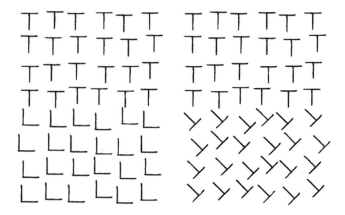

Figure 1.

categories: texture and pattern. In this case a representation comprising both components may be necessary to give a complete description. This may also mean that attempts to associate visual texture perception phenomena with the properties of visual brain components may succeed in the sense that aspects of texture perception can be related to individual or group properties of neurons, but fail in the sense that there is no single neural system displaying all of the properties of "texture".

See also COMPUTATIONAL VISION; HAPTIC PERCEPTION; MACHINE VISION; MARR, DAVID; MID-LEVEL VISION; PICTORIAL ART AND VISION

—*James R. Bergen*

References

Beck, J. (1966). Effect of orientation and of shape similarity on perceptual grouping. *Percept. Psychophysics* 1: 300–302.

Beck, J. (1982). Textural segmentation. In J. Beck, Ed., *Organization and representation in perception*. Mahwah, NJ: Erlbaum.

Beck, J., A. Sutter, and R. Ivry. (1987). Spatial frequency channels and perceptual grouping in texture segregation. *Computer Vis. Graphics Image Processing* 37: 299–325.

Bergen, J. R. (1991). Theories of visual texture perception. In D. Regan, Ed., *Spatial Vision*. London: Macmillan, pp. 114–133.

Bergen, J. R., and E. H. Adelson. (1988). Early vision and texture perception. *Nature* 333: 363–364.

Bergen, J. R., and M. S. Landy. (1991). Computational modeling of visual texture segregation. In M. S. Landy and J. A. Movshon, Eds., *Computational Models of Visual Processing*. Cambridge, MA: MIT Press, pp. 253–271.

Caelli, T. M. (1985). Three processing characteristics of visual texture segregation. *Spatial Vision* 1: 19–30.

Chubb, C., and M. S. Landy. (1991). Orthogonal distribution analysis: A new approach to the study of texture perception. In M. S. Landy and J. A. Movshon, Eds., *Computational Models of Visual Processing*. Cambridge, MA: MIT Press, pp. 291–301.

De Bonet, J. S. (1997). Multiresolution sampling procedure for analysis and synthesis of texture images. *Computer Graphics Proceedings, Annual Conference Series* 1997, ACM SIGGRAPH, pp. 361–368.

Graham, N. V. (1991). Complex channels, early local nonlinearities, and normalization in texture segregation. In M. S. Landy and J. A. Movshon, Eds., *Computational Models of Visual Processing*. Cambridge, MA: MIT Press, pp. 273–290.

Harvey, L. O., and M. J. Gervais. (1978). Visual texture perception and Fourier analysis. *Percept. Psychophysics* 24: 534–542.

Harvey, L. O., and M. J. Gervais. (1981). Internal representation of visual texture as the basis for the judgment of similarity. *F. Exp. Psychol. Hum. Percept.* 7: 741–753.

Julesz, B. (1962). Visual pattern discrimination. *IRE Trans. Information Theory* 8: 84–92.

Julesz, B. (1975). Experiments in the visual perception of texture. *Scient. Am.* 232: 34–43.

Julesz, B. (1981). Textons, the elements of texture perception and their interactions. *Nature* 290: 91–97.

Landy, M. S., and J. R. Bergen. (1991). Texture segregation and orientation gradient. *Vision Research* 31: 679–691.

Malik, J., and P. Perona. (1990). Preattentive texture discrimination with early vision mechanisms. *Journal of the Optical Society of America A* 7: 923–931.

Popat, K., and R. W. Picard. (1993). Novel cluster–based probability model for texture synthesis, classification, and compression.

Proceedings of SPIE Visual Communications and Image Processing: 756–768.

Richards, W., and A. Polit. (1974). Texture matching. *Kybernetik* 16: 155–162.

Turner, M. R. (1986). Texture discrimination by Gabor functions. *Biological Cybernetics* 55: 71–82.

Thalamus

The thalamus is a component of the brain of every mammal: it looks like a pair of small eggs, one underneath each of the cerebral hemispheres. Its volume is 2 percent and 4 percent of the volume of the cortex. It has a simple position in the overall architecture: virtually all information arriving at the CEREBRAL CORTEX comes from the thalamus, which receives it from subcortical structures. This architecture is shown in figure 1. In particular, all visual, auditory, tactile, and proprioceptive information passes through the thalamus on its way to cortex; all planning and motor information generated by the CEREBELLUM or by the BASAL GANGLIA is passed through the thalamus to cortex; and emotional or motivational data from the AMYGDALA and the mammilary body passes through the thalamus also. The main exceptions to this are (1) the direct pathway from the olfactory bulb to olfactory cortex; (2) a supplementary direct pathway from the amygdala to prefrontal cortex; and (3) diffuse neuromodulatory projections from various brain stem nuclei to cortex. These facts give rise to the classic view that the thalamus is a passive relay station which generates virtually all the information bearing input to the cortex. This view is strengthened by the simplicity of the internal connections in the thalamus: the pathways above are built from a homogeneous population of excitatory "relay" cells which give off almost no local collaterals in the thalamus, but synapse strongly on layer IV (and deep layer III) cortical neurons. Finally, this "feedforward" pathway is topographically organized, with various nuclei of the thalamus projecting to various areas of cortex and a "rod–to–column" pattern within each nucleus (Jones 1985: fig 3.20, 3.22, and p. 811).

BUT the above picture has omitted one fundamental fact: *all projections from thalamus to cortex are reciprocated by feedback projections from cortex to thalamus of the same or even larger size.* For instance, Sherman and Koch (1986) estimate that in cat there are roughly 10^6 fibers from the lateral geniculate nucleus in the thalamus to the VISUAL CORTEX, but 10^7 fibers in the reverse direction! As Jones says, "Can it be that such a highly organized and numerically dense projection has virtually no functional significance? One doubts it. The very anatomical precision speaks against it. Every dorsal thalamic nucleus receives fibers back from all cortical areas to which it projects; . . ." (Jones 1985: 819).

Feedback pathways are the hallmark of mammalian brains. Lower animals have brains which are, by and large, constructed on a feedforward, modular architecture. In the total reorganization that formed the mammalian telencephalon, two vast families of feedback pathways appear: the corticothalamic pathways just described and the corticocortical feedback pathways, by which virtually all nonlocal connections within the cortex (the myelinated tracts in the white matter connecting distinct cortical areas) are

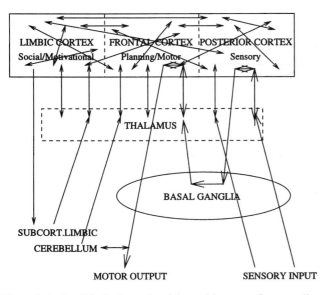

Figure 1. A simplified schematic of the architecture of mammalian brains, indicating the main connections of the thalamus.

reciprocated. This architecture is also indicated schematically in figure 1. From an information-processing point of view, modeling the role of these feedback pathways seems to be one of the first steps in making sense of cortical anatomy. And since the corticothalamic feedback is relatively simple, this would seem to be a prime target for models.

Perhaps the most accepted model for this feedback is that it is used to *gate* the information which reaches cortex, allowing the cortex to selectively attend to part of the data at a given time. Rather striking evidence for this was discovered by Singer and coworkers (Singer and Schmielau 1976; Singer 1977; Varela and Singer 1987): they found that cortical feedback was used to selectively enhance visual input from the two eyes at points where they were viewing a surface in the fixation plane. This highlights objects on the plane of fixation and suppresses objects which are nearer or farther. Subsequently Crick (1984) developed a specific mechanism for such gating, based on a small group of thalamic cells called the reticular nucleus. In his view, such thalamic gating might underlie the psychophysical results of Treisman (1980) implicating serial search in some visual tasks. The attention hypothesis has been used to explain effects in humans after thalamic strokes (Rafal and Posner 1987) and after direct electrode stimulation in the course of neurosurgery (Ojemann 1983). Very suggestive results on the enhancement and inhibition caused by coricothalamic feedback from S1 to VPM in rat have been discovered by Ghazanfar and Nicolelis (1997).

Does mere gating require such a massive backprojection? Beautiful evidence for a subtler role of corticothalamic feedback was discovered recently by Sillito and co-workers (1994). They found that cortical feedback caused thalamic relay cells responding to different parts of a coherent visual stimulus to synchronize. More precisely, an extended moving bar excites multiple thalamic relay cells whose receptive fields lie at different positions along the bar. When cortical

feedback was intact, the spike trains of these cells showed strong correlations which were absent if either the feedback was interrupted or if the stimulus was not coherent (e.g., being made up of two bars). This suggests that information can pass back and forth between thalamus and cortex and that important nonlocal patterns are recognized during this iterative operation. Further evidence is found in Nicolelis et al. (1995).

Several models for such iterative algorithms have been proposed. The earliest, to my knowledge, was the ALOPEX theory of Harth et al. (1987), described as follows: "A model is proposed in which the feedback pathways serve to modify afferent sensory stimuli in ways that enhance and complete sensory input patterns, suppress irrelevant features, and generate quasi-sensory patterns when afferent stimulation is weak or absent." I have elaborated this theory (see Mumford 1991–2, 1993), describing the role it imputes to the thalamus as that of an "active blackboard." The basic idea is that there are multiple cortical assemblies which respond to the presence of distinct nonlocal visual patterns; in a noisy ambiguous real-world stimulus, many of these will respond to varying degrees. These assemblies then compete to enhance the features they depend on while inhibiting their rival's features *via their feedback on both the thalamic relay cells and the thalamic inhibitory interneurons*. A related idea has been implemented in tracking algorithms in Isard and Blake (1996): their ALGORITHM infers multiple competing hypotheses which kill each other off as evidence accrues. One hopes that advances in recording techniques and the use of more realistic stimuli will enable tests of these hypotheses to be made in the coming decade.

See also AUDITORY ATTENTION; CONSCIOUSNESS, NEUROBIOLOGY OF; ECHOLOCATION; EMOTION AND THE ANIMAL BRAIN; LIMBIC SYSTEM; VISUAL ANATOMY AND PHYSIOLOGY

—*David Mumford*

References

Crick, F. (1984). Function of the thalamic reticular complex: The searchlight hypothesis. *Proc. Natl. Acad. Sci., USA* 81: 4586–4590.

Ghazanfar, A., and M. Nicolelis. (1997). Non-linear spatiotemporal computation of tactile information by thalamocortical ensembles. *J. Neurophys.* 78: 506–510.

Harth, E., K. P. Unnikrishnan, and A. S. Pandya. (1987). The inversion of sensory processing by feedback pathways: A model of visual cognitive functions. *Science* 1987: 184–187.

Isard, M., and A. Blake. (1996). Contour tracking by stochastic propagation of conditional density. *Proc Eur. Conf. Comp. Vision* 1: 343–356.

Jones, E. G. (1985). *The Thalamus*. New York: Plenum Press.

Mumford, D. (1991–2). On the computational architecture of the neocortex: 1. The role of the thalamo-cortical loop, 2. The role of the cortico-cortical loops. *Biol. Cybern.* 65: 135–145; 66: 241–251.

Mumford, D. (1993). Neuronal architectures for pattern-theoretic problems. In C. Koch, Ed., *Large Scale Neuronal Models of the Brain*. Cambridge, MA: MIT Press.

Nicolelis, M., L. Baccala, R. Lin, and J. Chapin. (1995). Sensorimotor encoding by synchronous neural ensemble activity at multiple levels of the somoatosensory system. *Science* 268: 1353–1358.

Ojemann, G. (1983). Brain organization for language from the perspective of electrical stimulation mapping. *Behav. Brain Sci.* 2: 189–206.

Rafal, R., and M. Posner. (1987). Deficits in human visual attention following thalamic lesions. *Proc. Natl. Acad. Sci. USA* 84: 7349–7353.

Sherman, M., and C. Koch. (1986). The control of retinogeniculate transmission in the mammalian LGN. *Exp. Brain Res.* 63: 1–20.

Sillito, A., H. Jones, G. Gerstein, and D. West. (1994). Feature-linked synchronization of thalamic relay cell firing induced by feedback from the visual cortex. *Nature* 369: 479–482.

Singer, W. (1977). Control of thalamic transmission by corticofugal and ascending reticular pathways in the visual system. *Physiol. Rev.* 57: 386–419.

Singer, W., and F. Schmielau. (1976). The effect of reticular stimulation on binocular inhibition in the cat LGN. *Exp Brain Res.* 14: 210–226.

Treisman, A., and G. Gelade. (1980). A feature integration theory of attention. *Cognitive Psychology* 12: 99–136.

Varela, F., and W. Singer. (1987). Neuronal dynamics in the visual corticothalamic pathway revealed through binocular rivalry. *Exp Brain Res.* 66: 10–20.

Thematic Roles

Grammatical studies, both traditional and contemporary, have recognized that formal distinctions, involving the case or syntactic position of the arguments of a verb or other part of speech, correlated significantly with intuitive semantic distinctions, involving the relations of those arguments to the action or state indicated by the verb. In simple English sentences with two or three nominal arguments, for example, where only syntactic position visibly distinguishes their relation to the verb, we can see that the first, subject position regularly belongs to the initiator of the action, or *agent;* that the direct object position regularly belongs to the recipient of the action, the *patient* or more generally the *theme;* and that the indirect-object position, if there is one, regularly belongs to the person or thing for the sake of which the action is done, or *goal* of the action:

(1) John hit Bill (≠ Bill hit John).

(2) The circuit controls the memory chip (≠ the memory chip controls the circuit).

(3) The girl gave the boy the dog (≠ the boy gave the girl the dog, the girl gave the dog the boy, etc.).

In languages with rich case systems, the cases will give information about the semantic relations of agent, patient, goal, and some others, including location and instrument. English, typically among languages with impoverished case systems, signals these relations through prepositions. The cases themselves also correlate with syntactic positions (e.g., with nominative as the case of the subject and accusative as the case of the direct object), so that the formal side comprises both syntactic and morphological elements; the relations between these elements are a subject of intense crosslinguistic study within linguistic theory (see GRAMMATICAL RELATIONS).

The semantic relations between a verbal form and its arguments, as in (1)–(3), were dubbed *thematic roles* Gruber (1965); the term *theta-roles* is also in common use, with the same meaning. The notion of a thematic role extends also to the *adjuncts* of the verbal form, elements that, like the goal, instrumental, and locative phrases in (4), are not obligatory but optional (as indicated by parentheses).

(4) I reproduced the picture (for my mother) (in the dining room) (with a pencil).

Following standard terminology, say that a verb *selects* an array of arguments and *permits* an array of adjuncts, each of which bears a given thematic role. The thematic roles of arguments must be syntactically realized: hence we do not have sentences like **John hit,* meaning that John hit someone. Conversely, and with greater generality, no thematic role can be distributed over more than one element, whether it be argument or adjunct; thus, for example, instrumental phrases cannot be repeated, as in (5).

(5) *The prisoner escaped with a bribe with a machine gun.

There is, then, for each simple clause a one-to-one correspondence between a certain set of theta-roles and their realization in certain syntactic positions, perhaps in construction with specific cases and/or prepositions (or postpositions). That human languages obey this correspondence principle is the *theta-criterion* in the sense of Chomsky 1981.

Assuming the theta-criterion and a preliminary grasp of the content of typical thematic roles, theoretical studies have endeavored to discover a full inventory of the thematic roles in principle admissible in human languages, and the syntactic or morphological conditions on the appearance of elements with those roles. Languages generally exhibit a hierarchy among thematic roles, realizing agents as subjects and themes as direct objects; for important surveys, see Rappaport and Levin 1988 and Jackendoff 1987. These studies have also shed light on the scope and limits of certain syntactic alternations. For instance, as observed Fillmore (1968), English and other languages have pairs such as (6)–(7).

(6) The bees swarmed in the garden.

(7) The garden swarmed with bees.

That such pairs should exist would follow if the verb *swarm* were specified for locative (*in the garden*) and instrumental (*with bees*) thematic roles, with either thematic element free to occupy the subject position. On the other hand, there are alternations that are not fully productive, as in (10)–(11) versus (8)–(9):

(8) I stuffed the pillow with feathers.

(9) I stuffed feathers into the pillow.

(10) I filled the pail with water.

(11) *I filled water into the pail.

The syntactic distribution shown may be predicted from the meaning of the verbs, in that *stuff,* but not *fill,* can take the direct object as its theme.

The subject position is crucially distinguished from others, in that it alone can be occupied by an expletive, as in (12)–(13):

(12) *It* is snowing.

(13) *There* are cats on the roof.

Furthermore, there are verbs whose sole argument may be argued to originate, not in the subject position but in the position of the direct object, the so-called *unaccusative* verbs. For these reasons, among others, it has been useful to distinguish the elements in close construction with the verb—the *internal* arguments—from the single element that will appear as the subject in a simple clause—the *external* argument (the terminology and much of the discussion is due to Williams 1980).

Besides the above and other syntactic studies, semantic research has considered the question how thematic roles contribute to meaning. On one view of the matter, discussed by Carlson (1984), Higginbotham (1989), and Parsons (1990), among others, thematic roles are relations between events or states and the things that participate in them. The semantics of (1), for instance, would then be expressed as (14).

(14) e is a hitting event and Agent (John, e) and Patient (Bill, e)

Alternatively, it has been suggested that the content of thematic roles is to be located in semantic postulates governing the verbs that assign them (see Dowty 1988).

See also SEMANTICS; SYNTAX; SYNTAX-SEMANTICS INTERFACE

—James Higginbotham

References

Carlson, G. (1984). Thematic roles and their role in semantic interpretation. *Linguistics* 22: 259–279.

Chomsky, N. (1981). *Lectures on Government and Binding.* Dordrecht: Foris.

Dowty, D. (1988). On the semantic content of the notion 'thematic role.' In G. Chierchia, B. Partee, and R. Turner, Eds., *Properties, Types and Meaning,* vol. 2, *Semantic Issues.* Dordrecht: Kluwer, pp. 69–130.

Fillmore, C. (1968). The case for Case. In E. Bach and R. T. Harms, Eds., *Universals in Linguistic Theory.* New York: Holt, Rinehart and Winston, pp.1–90.

Gruber, J. S. (1965). *Studies in Lexical Relations.* Ph.D. diss., MIT. Reprinted in *Lexical Structure in Syntax and Semantics* (1976). Amsterdam: North-Holland.

Higginbotham, J. (1989). Elucidations of meaning. *Linguistics and Philosophy* 12: 123–142. Reprinted in P. Ludlow, Ed., *Readings in the Philosophy of Language.* Cambridge, MA: MIT Press, pp. 157–178.

Jackendoff, R. (1987). The status of thematic relations in linguistic theory. *Linguistic Inquiry* 18: 369–411.

Rappaport, M., and B. Levin. (1988). What to do with theta-roles. In W. Wilkins, Ed., *Syntax and Semantics 21: Thematic Relations.* New York: Academic Press, pp. 7–36.

Parsons, T. (1990). *Events in the Semantics of English.* Cambridge, MA: MIT Press.

Williams, E. (1980). Predication. *Linguistic Inquiry* 11: 203–238.

Further Readings

Grimshaw, J. (1990). *Argument Structure.* Cambridge, MA: MIT Press.

Jackendoff, R. (1990). *Semantic Structures.* Cambridge, MA: MIT Press.

Levin, B. (1993). *English Verb Classes and their Alternations.* Chicago: University of Chicago Press.

Levin, B., and M. Rappaport Hovav. (1995). *Unaccusativity: At the Syntax-Lexical Semantics Interface.* Cambridge, MA: MIT Press.

Wilkins, W., Ed., *Syntax and Semantics 21: Thematic Relations.* New York: Academic Press.

Theorem Proving

See DEDUCTIVE REASONING; LOGIC; LOGICAL REASONING SYSTEMS

Theory of Mind

Understanding other people is one of the most fundamental human problems. We know much less, however, about our ability to understand other minds than about our ability to understand the physical world. The branch of cognitive science that concerns our understanding of the minds of ourselves and others has come to be called "theory of mind," though it should perhaps be called "theory of theory of mind." It involves psychological theorizing about our ordinary, intuitive, "folk" understanding of the mind.

A number of different disciplines have collaborated in this effort. Philosophers have debated the nature and origin of our understanding of the mind, our FOLK PSYCHOLOGY, at length. Comparative psychologists have explored the evolution of this capacity. One currently prevalent theory of the evolution of cognition suggests that the capacity to understand, and so manipulate, our conspecifics was the driving force behind the development of distinctively human intelligence (Byrne and Whiten 1988). There has also been extensive work on primates' ability to understand mental states. The most recent work suggests that these abilities are fragmentary, at best, compared to the abilities of humans (Povinelli 1996; Tomasello, Kruger, and Ratner. 1993; see PRIMATE COGNITION). Clinical psychologists have proposed that the disorder of AUTISM involves a deficit in "theory of mind" capacities. Social psychologists explore our understanding of aspects of the mind such as the stability of personality traits (Nisbett and Ross 1980). Anthropologists suggest that fundamental assumptions about the mind may differ across cultures (Shweder and Levine 1984).

The most extensive "theory of mind" research, however, has been developmental (see Astington, Harris, and Olson 1988; Perner 1991; Wellman 1990). Children seem to understand important aspects of the mind from a strikingly early age, possibly from birth, but this knowledge also undergoes extensive changes with development. Early research focused on the child's understanding of belief and reality, and on the period between three and five years of age. Several significant and correlated changes seem to take place at about this time. Wimmer and Perner (1983) found that children of this age had difficulty understanding the fact that beliefs could be false. In one experiment, for example, children saw a closed candy box. When they opened it, it turned out that there were pencils inside it, rather than the candy they had been expecting. The children were asked what another person would think was in the box at first, before they opened it. Three year-olds consistently said that the children would think that there were pencils in the box. They did not understand that the other person's belief could be false. Gopnik and Astington (1988) demonstrated that children make this same error when they are asked about their own immediately past false beliefs. Children say that they, too, thought that there were pencils in the box, just as they predict that the other person will think there are pencils there. Flavell and his colleagues showed that three year-olds have a similar problem understanding the distinction between appearance and reality. For example, children who were shown a sponge painted to look like a rock insisted that the object both really was a sponge and also looked like a sponge (Flavell, Green, and Flavell 1986). Finally, children at three also seem to have difficulty understanding the sources of their beliefs. In one experiment children learned about an object that was hidden under a tunnel by either seeing it, feeling it, or being told about it. Although children could identify the object, they could not identify how they came to know about the object (O'Neill and Gopnik 1991). These investigators suggested that these linked developments indicate a new understanding of the representational character of belief between the ages of three and five.

Some recent studies suggest that the first signs of this understanding of false belief may emerge when children place the problem in the context of their earlier understanding of desire or perception (Flavell et al. 1990; Moses 1993; Gopnik, Meltozoff, and Slaugnter 1994), or when they are confronted with counterevidence to their incorrect views (Mitchell and Lacohee 1991; Bartsch and Wellman 1989), and that they may demonstrate some implicit knowledge of belief before they make that knowledge explicit (Clements and Perner 1994). However, this very early understanding appears to be, at best, fragile and incomplete in comparison with the robust and coherent knowledge of belief demonstrated at four or five.

More recent studies have investigated both a wider range of ages and a wider range of mental states. There is extensive evidence that children understand important aspects of desire well before age three. These include the facts that desires can be unfulfilled, that desires determine emotions, and even that desires may differ in different people (Perner 1991; Wellman 1990; Wellman and Woolley 1990). Similarly, even two-and-a-half year olds seem to understand aspects of visual perception. They understand, for example, that two people may see different things if they are on opposite sides of a screen (Masangkay et al. 1974). Three-year-olds also seem to understand important aspects of pretense and imagination, and they can use this understanding to make a general distinction between mental and physical entities (Harris and Kavanaugh 1993; Wellman and Estes 1986; Woolley and Wellman 1990). For example, they understand that pre-

tending to be a rabbit is different from being one, or that an imagined toy is private and intangible while a real toy is not. Bartsch and Wellman (1995) have conducted extensive studies of early spontaneous conversations about mental states. They have demonstrated that children between eighteen months and three years of age do not just display these abilities in laboratory tasks, but they also spontaneously explain human action in these terms, and shift from desire to belief explanations.

As we study younger and younger infants it becomes more difficult to be certain that they are making genuinely mentalistic ascriptions to others. However, studies of nonverbal behavior suggest that even infants understand certain aspects of the mind. Studies of infant IMITATION (Meltzoff and Moore 1977) suggest that there are innate links between children's perception of the actions of others and their perception of their own internal kinesthetic states; newborns who see another person produce a particular gesture will produce that gesture themselves (Meltzoff and Gopnik 1993). Similarly, very young infants show special preferences for human faces and voices, and engage in complex nonverbal communicative interactions with others (Trevarthen 1979). By nine months infants begin to follow the gaze of others and to point objects out to them (Butterworth 1991). In the behavior known as "social referencing," infants who are faced with an ambiguous situation turn to check the adult's facial expression and regulate their actions in accordance with it (Campos and Sternberg 1980). These very early abilities suggest that there is a strong innate component to our "theory of mind."

However, other aspects of our understanding of the mind do not appear to be in place until well after five years of age. For example, although children understand EMOTIONS at a very early stage, they only understand the difference between real emotion and emotional expression at around six (Harris 1989). Similarly, understanding the inferential character of the mind appears to be quite difficult. Children who can understand simple cases of false belief still have difficulty when the questions involve multiple interpretations of ambiguous stimuli or more complex sources of information (Chandler and Helm 1984; Taylor 1988; Wimmer, Hogrefe and Sodian 1988). Finally, children appear to understand fundamental facts about conscious phenomenology, such as the existence of "the stream of consciousness," at a surprisingly late age. Six-year-olds, for example, reported that people could consciously decide to turn over in the midst of a deep dreamless sleep, or conversely, that a person who was awake but just sitting still doing nothing would have no thoughts or internal experience at all (Flavell, Green, and Flavell 1995).

As always in developmental psychology we have a better sense of when various developments take place than of the mechanisms that underlie these changes. Several different accounts of these underlying mechanisms have been proposed in the literature (see Carruthers and Smith 1995). Leslie (1994) and Baron-Cohen (1995) have suggested that the developments reflect the maturation of an innate theory of mind module, by analogy with similar modular theories of language and perception. In fact, in Leslie's view several different modules mature in succession. Harris (1991) has argued for a "simulation" theory of many theory of mind developments. On this view advances in the child's understanding of the mind reflect an increasing ability to simulate or imagine the experiences of others. Dunn suggests that socialization and social interaction may play a crucial role in children's development of a theory of mind (Dunn et al. 1991). In support of this view, there is evidence that younger siblings have a more advanced theory of mind than older siblings (Perner, Ruffman, and Leekam 1994) and that parent's conversations about mental states influence children's understanding of the mind (Dunn et al. 1991). Probably the most widely held view, however, is what has been called "the theory theory" (Perner 1991; Wellman 1990; Gopnik 1993; Flavell, Green, and Flavell 1995). Originally advanced in philosophy (see SIMULATION VS. THEORY-THEORY) this view also is part of a more general theoretical approach that explains children's COGNITIVE DEVELOPMENT by analogy to scientific theory change (Carey 1985; Gopnik and Meltzoff 1997; Wellman 1990). On this view children develop a succession of theories of the mind that they use to explain their experience and the behavior of themselves and others. Like scientific theories, these intuitive or naive theories postulate abstract coherent mental entities and laws, and they provide predictions, interpretations, and explanations. The theories change as children confront counterevidence, gather new data, and perform experiments. One consequence of this view is that the philosophical doctrine of first-person authority is incorrect; our knowledge of our minds is as theoretical as our knowledge of the minds of others. More broadly, the recent research suggests that empirical evidence from developmental psychology may be brought to bear on classic problems in the philosophy of mind.

See also CONCEPTUAL CHANGE; MACHIAVELLIAN INTELLIGENCE HYPOTHESIS; NATIVISM; PROPOSITIONAL ATTITUDES

—*Alison Gopnik*

References and Further Readings

Astington, P., L. Harris, and D. R. Olson, Eds. (1988). *Developing Theories of Mind*. Cambridge: Cambridge University Press.

Baron-Cohen, S. (1995). *Mindblindness*. Cambridge, MA: MIT Press.

Bartsch, K., and H. M. Wellman. (1989). Young children's attribution of action to beliefs and desires. *Child Development* 60(4): 946–964.

Bartsch, K., and H. M. Wellman. (1995). *Children Talk about the Mind*. New York: Oxford University Press.

Butterworth, G. (1991). The ontogeny and phylogeny of joint visual attention. In A. Whiten, Ed., *Natural Theories of Mind: Evolution, Development and Simulation of Everyday Mindreading*. Oxford: Blackwell, pp. 223–232.

Byrne, R., and A. Whiten, Eds. (1988). *Machiavellian Intelligence: Social Expertise and the Evolution of Intellect in Monkeys, Apes and Humans*. Oxford: Oxford University Press.

Campos, J. J., and C. R. Sternberg. (1980). Perception, appraisal and emotion: The onset of social referencing. In M. Lamb and L. Sherrod, Eds., *Infant Social Cognition*. Mahwah, NJ: Erlbaum, pp. 273–311.

Carey, S. (1985). *Conceptual Change in Childhood*. Cambridge, MA: MIT Press.

Carruthers, P., and P. Smith, Eds. (1995). *Theories of Theory of Mind*. Cambridge: Cambridge University Press.

Chandler, M. J., and D. Helm. (1984). Developmental changes in the contribution of shared experience to social role-taking competence. *International Journal of Behavioral Development* 7: 145–156.

Clements, W., and J. Perner. (1994). Implicit understanding of belief. *Cognitive Development* 9: 377–395.

Dunn, J., J. Brown, C. Slomkowski, C. Tesla, and L. Youngblade. (1991). Young children's understanding of other people's feelings and beliefs: Individual differences and their antecedents. *Child Development* 62: 1352–1366.

Flavell, J. H., E. R. Flavell, F. L. Green, and L. J. Moses. (1990). Young children's understanding of fact beliefs versus value beliefs. *Child Development* 61(4): 915–928.

Flavell, J. H., F. L. Green, and E. R. Flavell. (1986). Development of knowledge about the appearance-reality distinction. *Monographs of the Society for Research in Child Development* 51, no. 1.

Flavell, J. H., F. L. Green, and E. R. Flavell. (1995). Young children's knowledge about thinking. *Monographs of the Society for Research in Child Development*, serial no. 243.

Gopnik, A. (1993). How we know our minds: The illusion of first-person knowledge of intentionality. *Behavioral and Brain Sciences* 16: 1–14.

Gopnik, A., and J. W. Astington. (1988). Children's understanding of representational change and its relation to the understanding of false belief and the appearance-reality distinction. *Child Development* 59: 26–37.

Gopnik, A., and A. N. Meltzoff. (1997). *Words, Thoughts and Theories*. Cambridge, MA: MIT Press.

Gopnik, A., A. N. Meltzoff, and V. Slaughter. (1994). Changing your views: How understanding visual perception can lead to a new theory of the mind. In C. Lewis and P. Mitchell, Eds., *Origins of a Theory of Mind*. Mahwah, NJ: Erlbaum.

Harris, P. L. (1989). *Children and Emotion*. Oxford: Blackwell.

Harris, P. L. (1991). The work of the imagination. In A. Whiten, Ed., *Natural Theories of Mind: The Evolution, Development and Simulation of Second-Order Mental Representations*. Oxford: Blackwell.

Harris, P. L., and R. Kavanaugh. (1993). Young children's understanding of pretense. *Monographs of the Society for Research in Child Development* 58: 1.

Leslie, A. M. (1994). ToMM, To By, and agency: Core architecture and domain specificity. In L. Hirschfeld and S. Gelman, Eds., *Mapping the mind: Domain Specificity in Cognition and Culture*. New York: Cambridge University Press.

Masangkay, Z., K. McCluskey, C. McIntyre, J. Sims-Knight, B. Vaughan, and J. H. Flavell. (1974). The early development of inferences about the visual percepts of others. *Child Development* 45: 357–366.

Meltzoff, A. N., and A. Gopnik. (1993). The role of imitation in understanding persons and developing a theory of mind. In S. Baron-Cohen, H. Tager-Flusberg, and D. Cohen, Eds., *Understanding Other Minds: Perspectives from Autism*. Oxford: Oxford University Press, pp. 335–366.

Meltzoff, A. N., and M. K. Moore. (1977). Imitation of facial and manual gestures by human neonates. *Science* 198: 75–78.

Mitchell, P., and H. Lacohee. (1991). Children's early understanding of false belief. *Cognition* 39(2).

Moses, L. J. (1993). Young children's understanding of belief constraints on intention. *Cognitive Development*, pp. 1–27.

Nisbett, R., and L. Ross. (1980). *Human Inference: Strategies and Shortcomings of Social Judgment*. Englewood Cliffs, NJ: Prentice-Hall.

O'Neill, D. K., and A. Gopnik. (1991). Young children's ability to identify the sources of their beliefs. *Developmental Psychology* 27: 390–397.

Perner, J. (1991). *Understanding the Representational Mind*. Cambridge, MA: MIT Press.

Perner, J., T. Ruffman, and S. R. Leekam. (1994). Theory of mind is contagious: You catch it from your sibs. *Child Development* 65(5): 1228–1238.

Povinelli, D. (1996). What young chimpanzees know about seeing. *Monographs of the Society for Research in Child Development* 61(3).

Shweder, R., and R. Levine. (1984). *Culture Theory: Essays on Mind, Self and Emotion,* Cambridge: Cambridge University Press.

Taylor, M. (1988). The development of children's understanding of the seeing-knowing distinction. In J. W. Astington, P. L. Harris, and D. R. Olson, Eds., *Developing Theories of Mind*. Cambridge: Cambridge University Press.

Tomasello, M., A. Kruger, and H. Ratner. (1993). Cultural learning. *Behavioral and Brain Sciences* 495–552.

Trevarthen, C. (1979). Communication and cooperation in early infancy: A description of primary intersubjectivity. In M. Bullowa, Ed. *Before Speech: The Beginning of Interpersonal Communication*. New York: Cambridge University Press, pp. 231–347.

Wellman, H. (1990). *The Child's Theory of Mind*. Cambridge, MA: MIT Press.

Wellman, H. M. and K. Bartsch. (1988). Young children's reasoning about beliefs. *Cognition* 30: 239–277.

Wellman, H. M., and D. Estes. (1986). Early understanding of mental entities: A reexamination of childhood realism. *Child Development* 57: 910–923.

Wellman, H. M., and J. D. Woolley. (1990). From simple desires to ordinary beliefs: The early development of everyday psychology. *Cognition* (3): 245–275.

Wimmer, H., and J. Perner. (1983). Beliefs about beliefs: Representations and constraining function of wrong beliefs in young children's understanding of deception. *Cognition* 13: 103–128.

Wimmer, H., J. Hogrefe, and B. Sodian. (1988). A second stage in children's conception of mental life: Understanding informational access as origins of knowledge and belief. In J. Astington, P. Harris, and D. Olson, Eds. *Developing Theories of Mind*. Cambridge: Cambridge University Press.

Woolley, J., and H. M. Wellman. (1990). Young children's understanding of realities, non-realities and appearances. *Child Development* 61: 946–961.

Thought and Language

See LANGUAGE AND THOUGHT; LANGUAGE OF THOUGHT

Time in the Mind

Research on temporal perception goes back to the nineteenth century. In 1860, Karl Ernst von Baer introduced the notion of perceptual moment suggesting that different durations of the moments result in a different flow of subjective time. In 1865, Ernst Mach looked for Weber's law in temporal perception, and he observed that 30 ms is apparently the lowest limit for subjective durations. Then, in 1868 Frans Cornelis Donders presented the reaction time paradigm, which remains the basis for chronometric analyses of mental processes. In the same year, Karl von Vierordt investigated temporal integration using the paradigm of stimulus reproduction. These ideas embedded in the conceptual framework of PSYCHOPHYSICS as promoted by Gustav Theodor Fechner, set the stage for many decades, but then interest in temporal mechanisms of perception and cognition in general declined. Only recently has temporal perception become a central issue again, because cognitive processes cannot be understood without their temporal dynamics.

At least two independent temporal processing systems have been described that are basic for perceptual and cognitive processes and that are characterized by discrete time sampling. Both these systems are fundamental for the instantiation of perceptual acts, of cognitive processing, or of volitional MOTOR CONTROL. First, some observations on a high-frequency processing system generating discrete time quanta of 30 ms duration are mentioned. Then, a low-frequency processing system setting up functional states of approximately 3 seconds, which is believed to be the operative basis for what we refer to as "subjective present," is addressed. In between those two temporal processing levels additional timing mechanisms come into play that are fundamental for motor control, especially for the repeated initiation of movements.

Evidence for a high-frequency processing system derives from studies on temporal order threshold. If the temporal sequence of two stimuli has to be indicated, independent of sensory modality a threshold of approximately 30 ms is observed. Sensory data picked up within 30 ms are treated as cotemporal, that is, a relationship of separate stimuli with respect to the before-after dimension cannot be established (Pöppel 1997). Temporal order threshold being identical in different sensory modalities (Hirsh and Sherrick 1961), thus, also indicates a lower limit for event identification. Temporal order analysis of the speech signal seems to be the basis for phoneme identification, a disturbance of temporal acuity being associated with language disorders such as APHASIA and LANGUAGE IMPAIRMENT (Tallal, Miller, and Fitch 1993; see also DYSLEXIA).

Support for distinct processing stages comes from a variety of studies using qualitatively different paradigms. Under stationary experimental conditions response distributions of reaction times (Harter and White 1968) and of pursuit (Pöppel and Logothetis 1986) or saccadic eye movements (see EYE MOVEMENTS AND VISUAL ATTENTION and OCULOMOTOR CONTROL) show multimodal characteristics with a 30 ms separation of distinct response modes. These multimodalities can be explained on the basis of neuronal oscillations. After the transduction of a stimulus a relaxation oscillation with a period of 30 ms is initiated, which is triggered instantaneously by the stimulus. Such an oscillatory mechanism being under environmental stimulus control allows integration of information from different sensory modalities, that is, data from various sources can be collected within one period, which defines a basic system state (Pöppel 1997). Possibly, the separate response modes represent similar successive and discrete decision-making stages as are assumed in high-speed scanning of short-term memory.

Some neurophysiological observations support the notion of discrete temporal processing on the basis of system states implemented by oscillations. The auditory evoked potential (see ELECTROPHYSIOLOGY, ELECTRIC AND MAGNETIC EVOKED FIELDS) in the midlatency region shows an oscillatory component with a period of 30 ms. This component is a sensitive marker for the anesthetic state because it selectively disappears during general anesthesia. Oscillations with a period of 30 ms represent functional system states that are prerequisites for the establishment of events. If temporal coherence within a neuronal network as expressed by oscillations is removed as with general anesthetics conscious representation is interrupted (Schwender et al. 1994). Events cannot be implemented as functional "building blocks" of conscious activity.

A low-frequency mechanism, independent of a high-frequency mechanism implementing system states for event identification, binds successive events up to approximately 3 seconds into perceptual and action units (Fraisse 1984; Pöppel 1997). Support for such a binding operation comes from studies on spontaneous alteration rates of ambiguous figures (see ILLUSIONS). If stimuli can be perceived with two perspectives (like the Necker cube), there is an automatic shift of perceptual content after 3 seconds (Schleidt and Kien 1997; Gomez et al. 1995). Such a perceptual shift is true also for ambiguous auditory material like the phoneme sequence CU-BA-CU . . . where one hears either CUBA or BACU. The spontaneous alteration rate in the two modalities suggests that after an exhaust period of 3 seconds, attentional mechanisms (see ATTENTION and ATTENTION AND THE HUMAN BRAIN) are elicited that open sensory channels for new information; if the physical stimulus remains the same, the alternative interpretation of the stimulus will gain control. Metaphorically, the brain asks every 3 seconds "what is new?" and with unusual stimuli like the ambiguous material the temporal eigen-operations of the brain are unmasked.

Temporal integration up to 3 seconds is also observed in sensorimotor behavior. If a subject is requested to synchronize a regular sequence of auditory stimuli with finger taps, stimuli are anticipated by some tens of milliseconds. Stimulus anticipation with high temporal precision is, however, possible only up to interstimulus intervals of 3 seconds. If the next stimulus lies too far in the future, that is, more than 3 seconds, it is not possible to program an anticipatory movement that is precisely related to the stimulus (Mates et al. 1994).

Because the experiments referred to (and others) employ qualitatively different paradigms covering perceptual processes, cognitive evaluations, or movement control, it is proposed that temporal integration up to 3 seconds is a general principle of the neurocognitive machinery. This integration is automatic and presemantic, that is, the temporal limit is not determined by what is processed, but by intrinsic time constants. Because of the omnipresence of temporal integration, it can be used for a pragmatic definition of the subjective present, which is characterized phenomenally by a feeling of nowness, or one can relate temporal integration to singular single states of being conscious (see CONSCIOUSNESS and CONSCIOUSNESS, NEUROBIOLOGY OF).

Additionally, on a different timing level control of motor performance can be registered. Two categorically distinct speed modes with frequencies of 2 Hz and 5 Hz in the sequential initiation of motor behavior are most prominent and can be assessed in simple finger tapping tasks. Nevertheless, they represent basic temporal movement characteristics. Fast automatic movements in the maximum speed in finger tapping can be performed with interresponse intervals of 150 to 200 ms, representing a frequency of approximately 5 Hz. The speed in a personally chosen finger-tapping task is performed with interresponse intervals around 500 ms, representing a frequency of approximately 2 Hz (Fraisse 1982). These two different frequency modes are also seen in other movement tasks and are associated with distinct sensorimotor control processes, the 2-Hz movement being under voluntary control and allowing the collection of somatosensory information, the maximum speed 5-Hz performance requiring only coarse preattentive control (Kunesch et al. 1989). In sensorimotor synchronization where the frequency of a pacer signal has to be reproduced accurately by finger taps, the notion of the categorical difference of the two frequency modes is complemented. The subjective representation of every single finger tap is possible only when a subject is tapping to interstimulus intervals of above 300 ms (Peters 1989). The single taps cannot be temporally resolved in somatosensory perception with interstimulus intervals below 300 ms. This threshold of approximately 300 ms marks the categorical change in motor performance, dividing the aforementioned two motor control processes into automatized movement and voluntarily controlled behavior.

See also INTERSUBJECTIVITY; MOTOR LEARNING; TEMPORAL REASONING

—*Ernst Pöppel and Marc Wittmann*

References

Fraisse, P. (1982). Rhythm and tempo. In D. Deutsch, Ed., *The Psychology of Music*. New York: Academic Press, pp. 149–180.

Fraisse, P. (1984). Perception and estimation of time. *Annual Review of Psychology* 35: 1–36

Gomez, C., E. D. Argandona, R. G. Solier, J. C. Angulo, and M. Vazquez. (1995). Timing and competition in networks representing ambiguous figures. *Brain and Cognition* 29: 103–114.

Harter, M. R., and C. T. White. (1968). Periodicity within reaction time distributions and electromyograms. *Quarterly Journal of Experimental Psychology* 20: 157–166.

Hirsh, I. J., and C. E. Sherrick. (1961). Perceived order in different sense modalities. *Journal of Experimental Psychology* 62: 423–432.

Kunesch, E., F. Binkofski, and H.-J. Freund. (1989). Invariant temporal characteristics of manipulative hand movements. *Experimental Brain Research* 78: 539–546.

Mates, J., U. Müller, T. Radil, and E. Pöppel. (1994). Temporal integration in sensorimotor synchronization. *J. Cogn. Neuroscience* 6: 332–340.

Peters, M. (1989). The relationship between variability of intertap intervals. *Psychological Research* 51: 38–42.

Pöppel, E. (1997). A hierarchical model of temporal perception. *Trends in Cognitive Sciences* 1: 56–61.

Pöppel, E., and N. Logothetis. (1986). Neural oscillations in the brain. Discontinuous initiations of pursuit eye movements indicate a 30-Hz temporal framework for visual information processing. *Naturwissenschaften* 73: 267–268.

Schleidt, M., and J. Kien. (1997). Segmentation in behavior and what it can tell us about brain function. *Human Nature* 8: 77–111.

Schwender, D., C. Madler, S. Klasing, K. Peter, and E. Pöppel. (1994). Anaesthetic control of 40-Hz brain activity and implicit memory. *Consciousness and Cognition* 3: 129–147

Tallal, P., S. Miller, and R. Fitch. (1993). Neurobiological basis of speech: A case for the preeminence of temporal processing. In P. Tallal, A. Galaburda, R. Llinas, and C. von Euler, Eds., *Temporal Information Processing in the Nervous System. Special Reference to Dyslexia and Dysphasia.* New York: The New York Academy of Sciences, pp. 27–47.

Further Readings

Atmanspacher, H., and E. Ruhnau, Eds. (1997). *Time, Temporality, Now.* Berlin: Springer.

Block, R., Ed. (1990). *Cognitive Models of Psychological Time.* Hillsdale, NJ: Erlbaum.

Hazeltine, E., L. Helmuth, and R. Ivry. (1997). Neural mechanisms of timing. *Trends in Cognitive Sciences* 1: 163–169.

Nichelli, P. (1993). The neuropsychology of human temporal information processing. In F. Boiler and J. Grafman, Eds., *Handbook of Neuropsychology* 8. Amsterdam: Elsevier Science, pp. 337–369.

Pastor, M. A., and J. Artieda, Eds. (1996). *Time, Internal Clocks, and Movement.* Amsterdam: Elsevier Science.

Tone

One of the fundamental goals of phonological theory is to determine how, starting with a complete phonetic description of a language, we can establish a small number of discrete categories along the various dimensions in which speech sounds may vary (see PHONOLOGY and PHONETICS). These discrete categories along each phonetic dimension are the values assumed by DISTINCTIVE FEATURES, and in any given language they must be rich enough to distinguish utterances that differ with regard to their word choice or their grammatical information, but no richer; other phonetic detail is excluded from such a phonological description. *Pitch* is the name given to the frequency of pulsation of the vocal cords during speech; it describes a continuous variable, which can range from about 50 Hz, at the bottom of a man's range, to about 400 Hz, at the top of a woman's range. *Tone* refers to the small number of discrete categories necessary for analyzing pitch in a phonological fashion.

Tone is normally analyzed as a property not of individual segments (or sounds), but of syllables. From a descriptive point of view, the pitch of syllables may be either (roughly) constant throughout, or it may have a more complex, dynamic pitch—typically rising or falling. In the first case, such syllables are phonologically assigned a single "level" tone; in the second, in almost all cases, the syllable is analyzed as being assigned a sequence of more than one level tone, and it is this sequence of distinct tones that gives rise to the "dynamic" or "contour" pitch: a sequence of low tone plus high tone gives rise to a rising pitch, and so on. The number of distinct tonal levels (corresponding to different levels of pitch) varies from language to language, but two, three, and four levels of tone are not at all uncommon,

and a few languages with even more levels have been reported in the literature. In the neutral intonational pattern of English, a word with initial accent such as "wedding" has a high tone on the first syllable and a low tone on the second syllable, whereas a monosyllabic word such as "man" has a falling pitch, which is to say, the syllable is associated with a sequence of two tones, high and low, in that order.

The term *tone language* is traditionally used to refer to those languages that use differences in tone in order to distinguish between distinct lexical items (that is, distinct words; Pike 1948; Hyman 1978; McCawley 1978; Goldsmith 1994). Such systems may seem exotic from a European perspective, but tone languages are quite common around the world, including a large number of Asian languages (including notably the well-studied Sino-Tibetan languages; Yip 1995), most African languages (especially the well-studied Niger-Congo languages; Odden 1995), and many Mesoamerican languages, especially the Oto-Manguean languages. It is appropriate to bear in mind that in these languages, tone is just as often used to manifest grammatical categories as it is to mark lexical contrasts. For example, in many Bantu languages of Africa, the verb will consist of six or more syllables, composed of a polysyllabic stem with several prefixes. The first syllable of the stem is the lexical root, and its tone is a lexical (that is, idiosyncratic) property. The tones of the following syllables of the stem, however, will be determined by the tense of the sentence, and they are thus considered to express grammatical information.

Languages are often divided into three categories, from a prosodic point of view: tone languages, pitch-accent languages, and intonational languages, but the boundaries between these categories can be difficult to discern at times (see PROSODY AND INTONATION). Pitch-accent systems share in common with tone languages relatively strict principles determining the tone assigned to each syllable, and thus the pitch at which each syllable will be uttered, but rather than utilize tonal differences as such in the LEXICON, pitch-accent systems characteristically employ a single tonal melody (e.g., low-high-low, constant across the language), and assign it to an entire phonological word. However, such languages employ an assignment algorithm that recognizes that one syllable is prosodically special, the syllable that is called "accented." The accented syllable bears a special mark in the lexicon, and tone mapping will typically make that accented status be phonetically unique in some fashion, by making it the final high of the word, or the first high, or through some other means. The information that is thus transmitted by the pitch pattern is which syllable is accented, rather than what the tonal melody is. The location of the pitch accent will in some languages be predictable by simple rule, in others by complex rules involving the interaction of the morphemes involved, and in yet others be simply stipulated in the lexicon. Tokyo Japanese is a familiar example of a pitch-accent system. However, some systems exist (including other dialects of Japanese) that contain two distinct tonal patterns, and lexical items must be marked as to which tonal pattern is appropriate. Systems of this sort share functional characteristics with tone languages, and blur the boundary between tone languages and pitch-accent languages.

Intonational languages (a category that includes English) generally allow pragmatic factors to influence the tone and the pitch of an utterance to a greater degree than would a tone or pitch-accent language. Most intonational languages (French is an exception) share with pitch-accent systems the characteristic of marking exactly one syllable as accented, and using the location of that accented syllable in the algorithm that maps an intonational pattern to the phonological word. However, it is very difficult—indeed, at this point, it seems impossible—to draw a sharp boundary between those aspects of intonation that can be adequately handled with discrete linguistic categories and those that blend gradually into the noncategorical aspects of general communicative behavior. A consideration of the intonation of ironic, polite, or highly emotional speech quickly encounters this problem.

As these remarks suggest, one of the most important characteristics of tonal patterns in language is their considerable autonomy with respect to the other characteristics of spoken language, which are produced largely by the mouth and nose. This autonomy is manifested in several ways, including: (1) the numerical mismatch, or many-to-many relationship, found between tones and syllables; (2) the retention of a tone despite the synchronic or diachronic loss of a tone (so-called tonal stability); and (3) the existence of morphemes that consist solely of one or more tonal specifications (so-called floating tones). These observations are closely linked to the foundations of autosegmental phonology (Goldsmith 1990). In addition to the numerical mismatch between tones and syllables, tone languages often display a temporal mismatch between the tones and the syllables of a given morpheme. The consequence of this is that it is not at all uncommon to find in tone languages that a morpheme is underlyingly (or analytically) composed of both tones and syllables, and yet the tone(s) of the morpheme will be consistently realized on a different syllable, either earlier or later than the syllable(s) pertaining to that morpheme.

See also MORPHOLOGY; PROSODY AND INTONATION, PROCESSING ISSUES; STRESS, LINGUISTIC; TYPOLOGY

—*John Goldsmith*

References

Goldsmith, J. (1990). *Autosegmental and Metrical Phonology.* Oxford: Blackwell.

Goldsmith, J. (1994). Tone languages. *Encyclopedia of Language and Linguistics.* Pergamon Press, pp. 4626–4628.

Hyman, L. (1978). Tone and/or accent. In D. J. Napoli, Ed., *Elements of Tone, Stress, and Intonation.* Washington, DC: Georgetown University Press, pp. 1–20.

McCawley, J. (1978). What is a tone language? In V. A. Fromkin, Ed., *Tone: A Linguistic Survey.* New York: Academic Press, pp. 113–131.

Odden, D. (1995). Tone: African languages. In J. Goldsmith, Ed., *The Handbook of Phonological Theory.* Oxford: Blackwell, pp. 444–475.

Pike, K. (1948). *Tone Languages: A Technique for Determining the Number and Type of Pitch Contrasts in a Language, with Studies in Tonemic Substitution and Fusion.* University of Michigan Publications in Linguistics, no. 4. Ann Arbor: University of Michigan Press.

Yip, M. (1995). Tone in East Asian languages. In J. Goldsmith, Ed., *The Handbook of Phonological Theory.* Oxford: Blackwell, pp. 476–494.

Further Readings

Beckman, M., and J. Pierrehumbert. (1986). Intonation structure in Japanese and English. *Phonology Yearbook* 3: 255–309.

Bolinger, D. (1985). Two views of accent. *Journal of Linguistics* 21: 79–123.

Duanmu, S. (1996). Tone: An overview. *Glot International* 2: 3–10.

Fromkin, V., Ed. (1978). *Tone: A Linguistic Survey.* New York: Academic Press.

Hyman, L., and R. Schuh. (1974). Universals of tone rules: Evidence from West Africa. *Linguistic Inquiry* 5: 81–115.

Pulleyblank, D. (1986). *Tone in Lexical Phonology.* Dordrecht: Reidel.

van der Hulst, H., and N. Smith, Eds. (1988). *Autosegmental Studies on Pitch Accent.* Dordrecht: Foris.

Top-Down Processing in Vision

Perception represents the immediate present, what is happening around us as conveyed by the pattern of light falling on our RETINA. And yet the current pattern of light alone cannot explain the stable, rich experience we have of our surroundings. The problem is that each retinal image could have arisen from any of a vast number of possible 3-D scenes. That we rapidly perceive only one interpretation tells us that we see far more than the immediate information falling on our retina. The highly accurate guesses and inferences that we make rapidly and unconsciously are based on a wealth of knowledge of the world and our expectations for the particular scene we are seeing. The influences of these sources beyond the images on the retina are collectively known as top-down influences.

Both top-down analyses and the complementary bottom-up processes use local cues to assign depth to the regions of an image. They differ in the manner in which they resolve the ambiguity of the local cues. A bottom-up analysis, part of MID-LEVEL VISION and SURFACE PERCEPTION, makes direct links between local geometrical features and depth. For example, whenever one object partially covers another, the visible contours of the more distant object terminate at the outer boundary of the nearer one, forming what are called T-junctions. When a T-junction is encountered in an image, this logic can be reversed: the stem of the T is designated a contour of a more distant, partially hidden object and the top of the T is assigned to the outer boundary of a nearer object.

A top-down process, on the other hand, depends on the content of the image and its analysis by processes of HIGH-LEVEL VISION. Cues operate by suggesting objects—a nose contour might suggest a face, for example—and then stored information about that object's structure can be applied to the assignment of depth in the image. Other features in the image are then examined to verify or reject the postulated object. The cues used for the initial selection of potential objects are not limited to the current images but include pre-

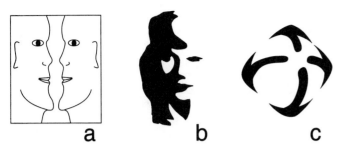

Figure 1.

ceding images as well as nonvisual sources which affect our expectations for the scene. The sources of object knowledge which are called upon may be built up over both evolutionary or individual time scales.

Our guesses for appropriate internal models are best when we know what to expect in a scene. Upon opening a door to a classroom, for example, we expect to see desks and a black or white board. If these elements are present in the scene, they are rapidly interpreted. Incongruent elements are seen less reliably, as Biederman (1981) showed when he reported increased errors in identifying fire hydrants presented in kitchens or sofas floating over city streets than when they were presented in their usual contexts. As Biederman's example demonstrates, top-down analyses work because there is a great deal of semantic redundancy in the content of a scene—noses are expected to be seen along with mouths, cars with roads, classrooms with desks, and sofas with coffee tables; moreover, noses, cars, and sofas have typical shapes so that once a few distinctive features have implied the presence of say, a car, the other expected features of a car can be verified or even just assumed to be present.

Textbook examples of top-down processing typically make use of images with two or more equally likely interpretations which are sometimes referred to as ILLUSIONS. A hint as to which interpretation to see may then trigger one or the other, as in the examples shown here. (a) Two faces, or one vase, or one face behind a vase (Costall 1980); (b) a man playing a saxophone seen in silhouette, or a woman's face in sharp shadow (Shepard 1990); and (c) a sphere in a four-point setting or a white angel (Tse 1998). In these instances, the 2-D positions of light and dark values are unchanged as we alternate our percepts, but new positions in depth are assigned to each point, some areas change from being dark shadow to dark pigment, and some regions change from being disconnected surfaces to continuous pieces.

Where do these new assignments come from when the 2-D pattern is the same in all cases? We cannot invoke a bottom-up analysis of the depth cues in the image since they would be inconclusive (insufficient to unambiguously assign depth). For some of the examples above we have to be told what to see before the image becomes organized as the intended 3-D object. On the other hand, some of us see some of the interpretations spontaneously, implying that some characteristic features in the image have suggested a familiar object (a nose outline or eye-like shape could suggest a face) and our visual system then matched a possible 3-D version of such an object to the image. In both cases,

our final perception is arrived at through the intermediate step of a guess or a suggestion of a possible object.

Once the presence of an object has been verified, our knowledge of that object can continue to constrain the interpretation of otherwise ambiguous dynamic changes to the object. For example, Chatterjee, Freyd, and Shiffrar (1996) have shown that the perception of ambiguous apparent motion involving human bodies usually avoids implausible paths where body parts would have to cross through each other.

Undoubtedly, the process of top-down matching of a candidate object to the image data occurs for natural images, not just the highly artificial ones shown in the figures above. Because of the extra information present in natural images, it is rare to have two alternative interpretations available. Nevertheless, the speed with which we organize and perceive the world around us arises to a great extent from the excellent (top-down), unconscious guesses we make based on sparse cues coming from either the actual or the expected content of the retinal image.

See also ATTENTION; DEPTH PERCEPTION; FACE RECOGNITION; FEATURE DETECTORS; GESTALT PERCEPTION

—*Patrick Cavanagh*

References

Biederman, I. (1981). On the semantics of a glance at a scene. In M. Kubovy and J. Pomerantz, Eds., *Perceptual Organization*. Hillsdale, NJ: Erlbaum, pp. 213–254.

Chatterjee, S. H., J. J. Freyd, and M. Shiffrar. (1996). Configural processing in the perception of apparent biological motion. *Journal of Experimental Psychology: Human Perception and Performance* 22: 916–929.

Costall, A. (1980). The three faces of Edgar Rubin. *Perception* 9: 115.

Shepard, R. (1990). *Mind Sights*. New York: W. H. Freeman.

Tse, P. (1998). Illusory volumes from conformation. *Perception* 27: 977–992.

Touch

See HAPTIC PERCEPTION

Transparency

The light projecting to a given point in the RETINA possesses but a single value of color and intensity. When *transparency* is perceived, however, this light is interpreted as being reflected off of two (or sometimes more) surfaces lying in different depth planes. Perceptual transparency is a type of SURFACE PERCEPTION and illustrates the visual system's remarkable ability to reconstruct the three spatial dimensions of the environment given a stimulus (i.e., the retinal images) with only two. There are an infinite number of possible environmental causes of any particular pattern of retinal stimulation. The perception of transparency relies, as does visual perception in general, upon *context* to determine the most likely interpretation. For example, whereas region *r'* in figure 1 (*left*) is usually interpreted in terms of the color

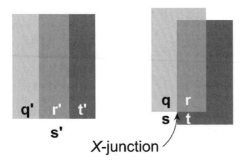

Figure 1.

of a single surface, region *r (right),* an identical shade of gray, is seen to arise from light reflected off of two surfaces. This difference in perceptual interpretation is due to the presence of a contextual cue known as an *X-junction.*

X-junctions are the single most important monocular cue for transparency. They are defined by the presence of four contiguous regions (*q,r,s,t*; see figure 1) of an image with a characteristic spatial arrangement. Psychophysical studies have shown that the intensity relationships between these four regions must lie within certain bounds for perceptual transparency to occur. When X-junctions elicit a perception of transparency, two regions (*q* and *s* in figure 1) are seen as differently colored parts of the unoccluded background and the other two regions (*r* and *t* in figure 1) appear to be viewed through a foreground transparent surface (the darker rectangle). Perceptual psychologists have developed several simple physical models to account for the perception of transparency (e.g., Beck et al. 1984; Matelli 1985). Though differing slightly in their details, the optical properties of *transmittance* and *reflectance* are generally invoked in these models.

Transmittance refers to the multiplicative attenuation of background intensity. One way to think of transmittance is to imagine that transparent surfaces are generally opaque but have holes (like a fine wire mesh) too small to resolve (Kersten 1991; Richards and Witkin 1979; Stoner and Albright 1996). Transmittance is then the proportion of the surface with holes. *Reflectance,* on the other hand, refers to the fraction of incident light reflected off of a surface. If the surface is a foreground transparent surface, this light adds to that reflected off of the background surface. X-junctions that elicit a sense of transparency are usually those in which the four sub-regions possess intensities consistent with physically realizable values of transmittance and reflectance, giving credence to the idea that the visual system possesses a tacit model of the physics of transparency. Given the relative rarity of transparent surfaces in natural scenes, however, it might seem puzzling that the visual system would devote neural machinery to its detection. An alternative possibility is that perceptual transparency depends upon mechanisms that typically process the more common visual phenomena of *shadows* and *opaque occlusion. Shadows* and *opaque occlusion* are ubiquitous in natural scenes and, moreover, can be thought of as defining limiting cases of perceptual transparency.

Objects that lie between a light source and another object cast shadows such that the intensities of the shadowed

regions appear multiplicatively diminished relative to the unshadowed regions. Shadows yield X-junctions that can be mimicked by a transparent surface possessing a transmittance less than one and having zero reflectance. Because the changes in intensities are purely multiplicative, the *contrast* (defined here as the intensity of one region divided by the intensity of another) between two adjacent regions in shadow should be the same as the contrast between spatially contiguous regions that lie out of shadow. Thus, if the X-junction in figure 1 were due to shadow-like transparency, the contrast between "unshadowed" regions *q* and *s* would be equal to that between their corresponding "shadowed" regions *r* and *t*.

Opaque occlusion, on the other hand, results in total contrast attenuation—regions *r* and *t* of figure 2 have identical intensities and hence no contrast exists between them. Opaque occlusion is associated with the presence of a contextual cue known as a *T-junction.* T-junctions are defined by the presence of three adjacent regions of differing intensity. In figure 2, these regions are *q, s,* and *r/t* (which form a single continuous region). The contrast reduction associated with opaque occlusion provides a very important cue for the depth ordering between surfaces. Indeed, the strength of the depth-ordering cue provided by transparent occlusion is directly proportional to the degree of contrast reduction with opaque occlusion providing the most potent cue. X-junctions associated with multiplicative transparency and T-junctions define two ends of a continuum within which perceptual transparency is most likely. Given this tight association between the stimulus conditions defining shadows, transparency, and opaque occlusion, it is tempting to speculate that transparency is detected by neural mechanisms that evolved to process shadows and opaque occlusion rather than transparency.

The neural mechanisms underlying the perception of transparency are only beginning to be understood. There are two important facets of this process. One is the detection of X-junctions suggestive of transparent overlap. As of this writing, no one has looked explicitly for neuronal responses to X-junctions. Baumann, van der Zwan, and Peterhans (1997) have, however, discovered neurons in area V2 of the macaque monkey that appear to encode the depth-ordering information implied by T-junctions. Whether, as the observations made above suggest, these neurons also respond selectively to X-junctions awaits an answer.

A second important facet of the neural processing of transparency is the existence of a multivalued representation

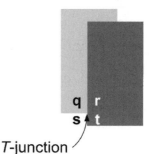

Figure 2.

of a particular surface property. For static displays there are at least two attributes that have multivalued perceptual representations—surface reflectance and depth. The neural correlates of these multivalued representations have yet to be identified. For dynamic stimuli, more than one motion may be seen to project upon the same point in the retinal images. It has been shown that the perception of "motion transparency" interacts with the perception of transparency of these other attributes. Thus, when overlapping gratings moving in different directions are superimposed ("plaid patterns") in a manner that produces X-junctions which elicit a percept of transparency in static images, a perception of motion transparency (also known as "motion noncoherency") results: the two gratings are seen to move independently (Stoner, Albright, and Ramachandran 1990). Conversely, when plaid patterns have X-junctions inconsistent with transparent overlap, motion transparency is unlikely to occur. Neural correlates for motion transparency have been located (Stoner and Albright 1992). When stimulated with perceptually transparent moving plaid patterns, each of the two gratings activates a separate population of directionally tuned neurons in area MT. Conversely, when stimulated with nontransparent stimuli, a single population of MT neurons, sensitive to the composite motion of the plaid pattern, is activated. A plausible neural substrate for this type of transparency, at least, therefore appears to have been identified.

See also COMPUTATIONAL VISION; DEPTH PERCEPTION; ILLUSIONS; LIGHTNESS PERCEPTION; MID-LEVEL VISION; PICTORIAL ART AND VISION

—*Gene R. Stoner*

References

Beck, J., K. Prazdny, and R. Ivry. (1984). The perception of transparency with achromatic colors. *Perception and Psychophysics* 35: 407–422.

Baumann R., R. van der Zwan, and E. Peterhans. (1997). Figure-ground segregation at contours: A neural mechanism in the visual cortex of the alert monkey. *Eur. J. Neurosci.* 9(6): 1290–1303.

Kersten, D. (1991). Transparency and the cooperative computation of scene attributes. In M. Landy and A. Movshon, Eds., *Computational Models of Visual Processing.* Cambridge, MA: MIT Press, pp. 209–228.

Matelli, F. (1985). Stimulation and perception of transparency. *Psychological Research* 7: 185–202.

Richards, W., and A. P. Witkin. (1979). *Efficient Computations and Representations of Visible Surfaces.* Tech. Rep. AFOSR-79-0020. Cambridge, MA: MIT.

Stoner, G. R., and T. D. Albright. (1992). Neural correlates of perceptual motion coherence. *Nature* 358: 412–414.

Stoner, G. R., and T. D. Albright. (1996). The interpretation of visual motion: Evidence for surface segmentation mechanisms. *Vision Research* 36: 1291–1310.

Stoner, G. R., T. D. Albright, and V. S. Ramachandran. (1990). Transparency and coherence in human motion perception. *Nature* 344: 153–155.

Further Readings

Anderson, B. L. (1997). A theory of illusory lightness and transparency in monocular and binocular images: The role of contour junctions. *Perception* 26(4): 419–453.

Gilchrist, A. L. (1994). *Lightness, Brightness, and Transparency.* Hillsdale, NJ: Erlbaum.

Kersten, D., H. H. Balthoff, B. L. Schwartz, and K. J. Kurtz. (1992). Interaction between transparency and structure from motion. *Neural Computation* 4: 573–589.

Masin, S. C. (1997). The luminance conditions of transparency. *Perception* 26(1): 39–50.

Nakayama, K., S. Shimojo, and V. S. Ramachandran. (1990). Transparency: Relation to depth, subjective contours, luminance, and neon color spreading. *Perception* 19(4): 497–513.

Snowden, R. J., S. Treue, R. G. Erickson, and R. A. Andersen. (1991). The response of area MT and V1 neurons to transparent motion. *J. Neurosci.* 11(9): 2768–2785.

Stoner, G. R., and T. D. Albright. (1993). Image segmentation cues in motion processing: Implications for modularity in vision. *Journal of Cognitive Neuroscience* 5: 129–149.

Trueswell, J. C., and M. M. Hayhoe. (1993). Surface segmentation mechanisms and motion perception. *Vision Res.* 33(3): 313–328.

Watanabe T., and P. Cavanagh. (1993). Surface decomposition accompanying the perception of transparency. *Spatial Vision* 7(2): 95–111.

Turing, Alan Mathison

Alan Mathison Turing (1912–1954), British mathematician and logician, was born in London and was educated at Sherborne School and King's College Cambridge. The originality and precocity of his mathematical thinking soon became apparent—not always to his advantage. A preference for supplementing theory with experiments (particularly of the kind that he could carry out himself) and an obsession with working everything out from first principles also developed during his school days. These traits distinguished him all his life. Thus he was elected a fellow of King's College Cambridge for a dissertation on the central limit theorem in probability theory. He had rediscovered this from scratch, being in ignorance of the previous work. His disinclination to build on the work of others sometimes slowed him down, but it preserved his forceful originality.

The contribution to LOGIC for which he is best known is his 1936–1937 paper. He set out to demonstrate rigorously what many already believed—that Hilbert's program, requiring a decision procedure to evaluate the truth or falsehood of any mathematical statement, was a logical impossibility.

Turing's search for a precise definition of "decision procedure" led him to devise and analyze the abstract notion of a computing machine. The invitation to Princeton that followed was prompted by his teacher M. H. A. Newman in a letter to Alonzo Church. With Stephen Kleene, Church had arrived at the same result as Turing by different means (see CHURCH-TURING THESIS). In fact the mathematical functions described in Gödel and Herbrand's system as general-recursive, in Church and Kleene's as lambda-definable, and in Turing's as computable all constitute identically the same class.

Soon after Turing returned to Cambridge from his two years in Princeton, World War II broke out. He wrote two further papers in mathematical logic but was mainly occupied with his work for the Foreign Office in the British cryptographic establishment at Bletchley Park. His major contribution to the breaking of the Enigma code made it possible routinely to read this German traffic, used widely in submarine warfare. He also made one of the important contributions in the breaking of Fish, the highest-level German cipher, and indirectly to the development for this work of the Colossus high-speed electronic computers (Good 1993).

At the end of the war Turing joined the National Physical Laboratory. In early 1946 he submitted initial design ideas for the NPL's groundbreaking "Automatic Computing Engine" ACE. He spent 1947 on leave of absence at King's College, during which he wrote on semigroups (published in 1950) and on "intelligent machinery" (published posthumously). Earlier in that same year Turing delivered a lecture to the London Mathematical Society. Taking the Pilot ACE as his point of departure, he formulated the main principles and future modes of application of practical embodiments of his Universal Turing Machine. These included their use to simulate human cognition. On the latter, his proposals were:

1. Programming can be done in symbolic logic and will then require the construction of appropriate interpreter/translator programs.
2. MACHINE LEARNING is needed so that computers can discover new knowledge inductively from experience as well as deductively.
3. Humanized interfaces are required to enable machines to adapt to people, so as to acquire knowledge tutorially.

These three points have been substantiated during the intervening fifty years. Their integration finds its most explicit expression in modern INDUCTIVE LOGIC PROGRAMMING, particularly in its applications to computer-assisted discovery of new CONCEPTS in the applied sciences.

Turing reinforced his second point in the final and rarely cited section of his *Mind* paper (1950) with calculations demonstrating the infeasibility of alternative means of equipping machines with the requisite knowledge. At least two attempts in the 1980s at general intelligent systems paid a price for neglecting his arguments, notably the CYC project of the MCC Corporation and the Fifth Generation project of the MITI department of the Japanese government (see Michie 1994). Both projects used explicit programming as their only KNOWLEDGE ACQUISITION tool.

Turing's celebrated 1950 paper in *Mind* described what became known as the "Turing test." Through a postulated imitation game, the intelligence of a machine is tested via its ability to sustain humanlike discourse. Several simple computer programs have since been able to deceive human observers into believing that a person and not a machine is "conversing" with them. This has accordingly led some to dismiss the Turing test as invalid. Closer reading of the paper shows that Turing was concerned with a machine's ability to *answer* questions, not to deflect them with counterquestions, as is done by the above-mentioned programs.

In the postwar period Turing also engaged in experimentation with CHESS mechanization. In the early 1950s he turned his attention to the mathematical description of the biological phenomena of morphogenesis. He was still working in this area in 1954, when he died just eleven days short of his forty-second birthday.

See also COMPUTATION; COMPUTATION AND THE BRAIN; COMPUTATIONAL THEORY OF MIND; FORMAL SYSTEMS, PROPERTIES OF; FUNCTIONALISM; GÖDEL'S THEOREMS

—*Donald Michie*

References

Carpenter, B. E., and R. W. Doran, Eds. (1986). *A. M. Turing's ACE Report of 1946 and Other Papers.* Vol. 10, the Charles Babbage Institute reprint series for the History of Computing, University of Minnesota. Cambridge, MA: MIT Press.

Good, I. J. (1993). Enigma and Fish. In F. H. Hinsley and A. Stripp, Eds., *Codebreakers: The Inside Story of Bletchley Park.* Oxford: Oxford University Press.

Michie, D. (1994). Consciousness as an engineering issue. Part 1. *J. Consc. Studies* 1(2): 182–195.

Turing, A. M. (1936–7). On computable numbers with an application to the Entscheidungsproblem. *Proc. Lond. Math. Soc.* 2(42): 230–265.

Turing, A. M. (1946). Proposal for Development in the Mathematical Division of an Automatic Computing Engine (ACE), Report to the Executive Committee of the National Physical Laboratory. Reprinted in B. E. Carpenter and R. W. Doran, *A. M. Turing's ACE Report of 1946 and Other Papers* (1986). Vol. 10, the Charles Babbage Institute reprint series for the History of Computing, University of Minnesota. Cambridge, MA: MIT Press.

Turing, A. M. (1947). Lecture to the London Mathematical Society. Reprinted in B. E. Carpenter and R. W. Doran, *A. M. Turing's ACE Report of 1946 and Other Papers* (1986). Vol. 10, the Charles Babbage Institute reprint series for the History of Computing, University of Minnesota. Cambridge, MA: MIT Press.

Turing, A. M. (1948). Intelligent Machinery, Report to the Executive Committee of the National Physical Laboratory. Reprinted in B. Meltzer and D. Michie, Eds., *Machine Intelligence 5.* Edinburgh: Edinburgh University Press, pp. 3–23.

Turing, A. M. (1950a). Computing machinery and intelligence. *Mind* 59: 433–460.

Turing, A. M. (1950b). The word problem in semi-groups with cancellation. *Ann. Math* 52: 491–505.

Further Readings

Britton, J. L., Ed. (1992). *Pure Mathematics.* Vol. 2, *Collected Works of A. M. Turing.* Amsterdam: North-Holland.

Gandy, R. O., and C. E. M. Yates, Eds. (1998). *Mathematical Logic.* Vol. 4, *Collected Works of A. M. Turing.* Amsterdam: North-Holland.

Herken, R., Ed. (1988). *The Universal Turing Machine: A Half-Century Survey.* Oxford: Oxford University Press.

Hodges, A. (1983). *Alan Turing: The Enigma.* London: Burnett Books Ltd, and Hutchinson Publishing Group.

Ince, D. C., Ed. (1992). *Mechanical Intelligence.* Vol. 1, *Collected Works of A. M. Turing.* Amsterdam: North-Holland.

Michie, D. (1982). Turing and the origins of the computer. In *Machine Intelligence and Related Topics.* New York: Gordon and Breach, pp. 28–37.

Millican, P., and A. Clark, Eds. (1996). *The Legacy of Alan Turing.* Vol. 1, *Machines and Thought.* Oxford: Clarendon Press.

Muggleton, S. (1994). Logic and learning: Turing's legacy. In K. Furukawa, D. Michie, and S. Muggleton, Eds., *Machine Intelligence* 13. Oxford: Clarendon Press, pp. 37–56.

Newman, M. H. A. (1955). A. M. Turing. *Biographical Memoirs of Fellows of the Royal Society* 1.

Robinson, J. A. (1994). Logic, computers, Turing and von Neumann. In K. Furukawa, D. Michie, and S. Muggleton, Eds., *Machine Intelligence* 13. Oxford: Clarendon Press, pp. 1–35.

Saunders, P. T., Ed. (1992). *Morphogenesis.* Vol. 3, *Collected Works of A. M. Turing.* Amsterdam: North-Holland.

Turing, S. (1959). *Alan M. Turing.* Cambridge: W. Heffer and Sons. (Biography by his mother.)

Turing Test

See CHINESE ROOM ARGUMENT; TURING, ALAN MATHISON

Turing's Thesis

See CHURCH-TURING THESIS

Tversky, Amos

Amos Tversky (1937–1996) was a cognitive and mathematical psychologist who was passionately committed to advancing knowledge of human judgment and DECISION MAKING, and the similarities between them. Tversky's contributions to these subjects, put forward with a research style that combined rigorous mathematical analysis with elegant empirical demonstrations and simple examples of irresistible force and clarity, had a profound influence on scholars in numerous disciplines. Indeed, one measure of Tversky's impact is how much his ideas have generated excitement and altered curricula in such varied fields as psychology, economics, law, medicine, political science, philosophy, and statistics.

Much of Tversky's research demonstrated that the thought processes governing people's judgments and choices are not as thorough or rigorous as people would like to believe, or that certain formal theories would have them believe. With his frequent collaborator Daniel Kahneman, Tversky identified a number of JUDGMENT HEURISTICS, or "rules of thumb," that people use to guide their judgments in numerous domains. Each heuristic consists of some "natural assessment," such as similarity, ease of retrieval from memory, or CAUSAL REASONING, that is coopted to tackle a difficult judgmental problem that people lack the cognitive mechanisms to solve readily with precision. Tversky and Kahneman likened heuristics to perceptual cues used to apprehend the world: both generally serve the individual well, but both can give rise to systematic error. The clarity of an object, for example, is one cue to its distance. The cue is generally helpful, because the closer something is, the more distinct it appears. On a hazy day, however, objects seem further away than they really are. Thus, the source of general accuracy, clarity, is also the very cause of predictable error.

Tversky and Kahneman identified several heuristics, such as availability, representativeness, and anchoring-and-adjustment. Most of their research, however, has focused on the first two. People employ the availability heuristic when they judge the size of a category or the probability of an event by the ease with which relevant instances can be brought to mind. The heuristic often yields accurate judgments: all else being equal, it is easier to think of examples from large categories than small ones. But extraneous factors can make examples from certain categories disproportionately easy (or difficult) to recall and thus render ease of generation misleading. Most people, for example, mistakenly assume that there are more English words that begin with "r" than words that have "r" in the third position. Availability is a poor guide in this context because it is so much easier to "find" words that begin with a particular letter than it is to find those that have the target letter anywhere else. The availability heuristic has been tied to people's distorted estimates of the likelihood of various health risks, and to the fact that collaborators often claim more credit for the success of a joint venture than there is credit to go around.

The representativeness heuristic consists of reducing complex judgments to relatively simple similarity assessments. It reflects people's unstated assumptions that outcomes typically resemble the processes that generated them, effects typically resemble their causes, and category members typically resemble their category prototypes. There is doubtless some truth to these assumptions (and hence some legitimacy to the use of representativeness), but just how much is impossible to say. What *is* clear is that these assumptions do not always hold, and where they break down can be found some telling judgmental errors. Tversky and Kahneman have shown, for example, that the representativeness heuristic plays a role in the "gambler's fallacy," in people's insensitivity to regression to the mean, in a misplaced faith in results based on small samples, and in the underutilization of "base rate" information or the prior probability of events.

The main thrust of Tversky and Kahneman's work on judgment—that people have cognitive capacity limitations and so must simplify some of the complex problems they confront—is fundamentally inconsistent with at least one widely touted model of human behavior, namely, the rational actor of economic theory. Economists contend that people are highly rational utility maximizers who compute any action's likely effect on their total wealth, and choose accordingly (see ECONOMICS AND COGNITIVE SCIENCE).

Tversky and Kahneman argued that people's choices—economic or otherwise—are often a good deal simpler. People typically do not monitor a prospect's likely effect on their final asset position. Rather, they pay attention to whether a given course of action might result in a gain or loss from the status quo (or some other salient reference point), and they are highly sensitive to how choices are presented or "framed." Tversky and Kahneman provided an account of these and other deviations from the standard normative model of expected UTILITY THEORY in a descriptive theory of decision making known as prospect theory.

Prospect theory captures several important elements of how people make decisions. One is the asymmetry between gains and losses. A loss of a given size generates more pain than an equally large gain yields pleasure. This asymmetry is what underlies many of the most powerful framing effects. Courses of action can sometimes be described either in the language of gains or losses, thereby invoking very different processes and producing markedly different decisions. For example, consumers are less likely to use credit cards if the difference between the cash and credit price is described as a "credit card surcharge" (a loss) rather than a "cash discount" (a foregone gain).

Prospect theory and the work it has inspired has driven a wedge between prescriptive and descriptive theories of choice. No single theory can be both prescriptively valid and descriptively accurate because the axioms of rational choice are normatively beyond dispute (see RATIONAL CHOICE THEORY), and yet the violations of these axioms are too reliable to be dismissed.

Among the topics that occupied Tversky's attention during the last years of his life was "support theory," a model of subjective probability based on the insight that people's probability judgments derive from descriptions of events, not from the events themselves. Support theory sheds light on a number of important phenomena, such as *subadditivity,* or the fact that the judged probability of an event increases when it is described in terms of its constituent elements. People judge it more likely, for example, that someone would die of "heart disease, cancer, or some other natural cause" than simply of "natural causes."

Nearly all of Tversky's research touched on the enduring question of the relative contribution of the heart and the mind to human irrationality. Cognitive scientists tend to approach this issue by emphasizing the mind and trying to determine how much of the fallibility of human reason can be explained in purely cognitive terms. Although Tversky would hardly deny that people's wants and passions often get the better of them (indeed, he did influential research on that topic too), much of his work demonstrates that many of our most egregious, most interesting, and most predictable mistakes are indeed entirely cognitive. His research makes it clear that many of our erroneous judgments and problematic decisions are the product, in his words, of "illusions, not delusions."

—Thomas Gilovich

References

Bell, D. E., H. Raiffa, and A. Tversky, Eds. (1988). *Decision Making: Descriptive, Normative, and Prescriptive Interactions.* New York: Cambridge University Press.

Gilovich, T., R. P. Vallone, and A. Tversky. (1985). The hot hand in basketball: On the misperception of random sequences. *Cognitive Psychology* 17: 295–314.

Griffin, D., and A. Tversky. (1992). The weighing of evidence and the determinants of confidence. *Cognitive Psychology* 24: 411–435.

Kahneman, K., and A. Tversky. (1972). Subjective probability: A judgment of representativeness. *Cognitive Psychology* 3: 430–454.

Kahneman, K., and A. Tversky. (1973). On the psychology of prediction. *Psychological Review* 80: 237–251.

Kahneman, K., and A. Tversky. (1979). Prospect theory: An analysis of decision under risk. *Econometrica* 47: 263–291.

Kahneman, D., and A. Tversky. (1996). On the reality of cognitive illusions. *Psychological Review* 103: 582–591.

Kahneman, D., P. Slovic, and A. Tversky, Eds. (1982). *Judgment under Uncertainty: Heuristics and Biases.* New York: Cambridge University Press.

Tversky, A. (1969). The intransitivity of preferences. *Psychological Review* 76: 31–48.

Tversky, A. (1972). Elimination by aspects: A theory of choice. *Psychological Review* 79: 281–299.

Tversky, A. (1977). Features of similarity. *Psychological Review* 84: 327–352.

Tversky, A., and D. Kahneman. (1973). Availability: A heuristic for judging frequency and probability. *Cognitive Psychology* 5: 207–232.

Tversky, A., and D. Kahneman. (1974). Judgment under uncertainty: Heuristics and biases. *Science* 185: 1124–1131.

Tversky, A., and D. Kahneman. (1981). The framing of decisions and the psychology of choice. *Science* 211: 453–458.

Tversky, A., and D. Kahneman. (1983). Extensional vs. intuitive reasoning: The conjunction fallacy in probability judgment. *Psychological Review* 91: 293–315.

Tversky, A., and D. Kahneman. (1992). Advances in prospect theory: Cumulative representation of uncertainty. *Journal of Risk and Uncertainty* 5: 297–323.

Tversky, A., and D. J. Koehler. (1994). Support theory: A nonextensional representation of subjective probability. *Psychological Review* 101: 547–567.

Tversky, A., and S. Sattath. (1979). Preference trees. *Psychological Review* 86: 542–573.

Tversky, A., S. Sattath, and P. Slovic. (1988). Contingent weighting in judgment and choice. *Psychological Review* 95: 371–384.

Twin Earth

Twin Earth thought experiments originate with Hilary Putnam 1975. Twin Earth features in the context of arguments about INDIVIDUALISM. Individualism is the thesis that psychological properties are essentially intrinsic, like being made of gold, as opposed to being partly relational, like being a planet. Anti-individualism is the denial of individualism. Examples like the following often motivate anti-individualism. Suppose that in 1750 there was a planet, Twin Earth, exactly like Earth in all respects except that where Earth had H_2O, Twin Earth had a chemically different compound, XYZ. XYZ is like water in macroscopic respects. Nobody on Earth or Twin Earth could have detected the difference between them in 1750. But a modern-day chemist could distinguish them in her laboratory. Now we consider an Earth person, Oscar, and his identical twin on Twin Earth, T-Oscar. Oscar and T-Oscar are molecule-for-molecule replicas, identical in all intrinsic, physical respects. (Pretend that humans are not made out of water). Each twin uses "water" to apply to his local wet substance. And, let us suppose, each twin utters the words "Water is good for plants."

An anti-individualist might argue along the following lines. First, XYZ is not water. Chemistry informs us that water is H_2O, and, by hypothesis, XYZ is not H_2O. Second, Oscar's word "water" refers to water (H_2O) and nothing else: if Oscar had been confronted with a glass of XYZ and said "That's water," he would have been wrong. But T-Oscar's word "water" refers to XYZ and nothing else: if T-Oscar had been confronted with a glass of XYZ and said "That's water," he would have been right, because he would have been speaking Twin English. Third, when each twin utters "Water is good for plants," the utterance expresses the contents of his belief. Both twins understand their words and both speak sincerely, so what they say is precisely what they believe. But what the twins say is different: Oscar says that water is good for plants, and that is what he believes. What T-Oscar says and believes is something we might put as "T-water is good for plants," where "T-water" is a non-technical word for XYZ.

Anti-individualists take the example to show that the contents of a person's beliefs are partly determined by his physical environment. Indeed, they are partly determined by factors that he does not know about, such as the underlying chemical constitution of water. Variant examples are designed to show that features of the social environment are also relevant. Here is one due to Tyler Burge (1979; adapted). Alf suffers from arthritis. One day, Alf wakes up with a pain in his thigh and comes to believe that his arthritis has spread. "Oh no! My arthritis has spread to my thigh," he mutters. He goes to his doctor who tells him that arthritis is, by definition, inflammation of the joints, and that therefore he cannot have arthritis in his thigh. Alf stands corrected and revises his belief.

We now turn to a new Twin Earth story. Again, Twin Earth is like Earth, barring one difference. Although the medical community on Earth applies "arthritis" only to inflammations of the joints, on Twin Earth they use it more generally, so that it would apply to the condition in Alf's thigh. Now T-Alf, Alf's twin, wakes up and mutters "Oh no! My arthritis has spread to my thigh."

Burge argues that while Alf believes he has arthritis in his thigh, T-Alf does not. T-Alf's word "arthritis" doesn't apply only to inflammations of the joints and hence does not express the concept of arthritis. Burge concludes that the contents of one's concepts are partly determined by the linguistic usage of those members of the community to whom one would (and should) defer. Recall that Alf accepts the doctor's assertion that by definition arthritis is a condition of the joints. It is in part because Alf is thus disposed to be corrected that his concept is a concept of arthritis and hence applies only to inflammations of the joints. T-Alf defers to different experts who use "arthritis" differently, and so has a different concept. This is so in spite of the exact similarity of the twins in all intrinsic respects.

Individualists have objected to the anti-individualist construal of the Twin Earth experiments and put forward counterarguments of their own. Responses to the Twin Earth examples have mainly been of two kinds.

The first kind of response concedes that, in the relevant cases, the twins' CONCEPTS refer to different things. For example Oscar's concept refers to water and T-Oscar's to T-water. But, it is argued, the essential psychological nature of a concept is not always given by what it refers to. Thus it is possible to hold that the twins' concepts are of exactly the same psychological type even though they refer to different things. This response needs to be supported by some method of individuating concepts that will generate the result that the twins' concepts are indeed of the same psychological type. (See Fodor 1987; Searle 1983; Loar 1988 for different attempts to do this.)

The second kind of response utilizes a distinction between commonsense intuition and science. It concedes that people have the intuition that the twins' concepts are different. But it holds that this is merely due to an unscien-

tific conception of psychological states. Thus, while there is an intuition that, for example, Oscar's concept applies to H_2O but not to XYZ, and T-Oscar's to XYZ and not to H_2O, this intuition is wrong. In fact, both Oscars' concepts applied both to H_2O and to XYZ, and were identical even in respect of what they referred to. A scientific psychology, not bound to preserve intuitions, would thus treat the twins as psychologically indistinguishable (Segal 1989, 1991; Crane 1991).

See also INDEXICALS AND DEMONSTRATIVES; NARROW CONTENT; REFERENCE, THEORIES OF

—Gabriel Segal

References

Burge, T. (1979). Individualism and the mental. In P. French, T. Uehling, and H. Wettstein, Eds., *Midwest Studies in Philosophy* 4. Minneapolis: University of Minnesota Press.

Crane, T. (1991). All the difference in the world. *The Philosophical Quarterly* 41: 1–26.

Fodor, J. (1987). *Psychosemantics: The Problem of Meaning in the Philosophy of Mind.* Cambridge, MA: MIT Press.

Loar, B. (1988). Social content and psychological content. In Grimm and Merrill (1988).

Putnam, H. (1975). The meaning of "meaning." In K. Gunderson, Ed., *Language, Mind and Knowledge: Minnesota Studies in the Philosophy of Science*, 7. Minneapolis: University of Minnesota Press.

Searle, J. (1983). *Intentionality: An Essay in the Philosophy of Mind.* Cambridge: Cambridge University Press.

Segal, G. (1989). Seeing what is not there. *The Philosophical Review* 98: 189–214.

Segal, G. (1991). Defence of a reasonable individualism. *Mind* 100: 485–493.

Further Readings

Bilgrami, A. (1992). *Belief and Meaning.* Oxford: Blackwell.

Burge, T. (1986). Individualism and psychology. *The Philosophical Review* 95: 3–46.

Burge, T. (1982). Other bodies. In A. Woodfield (1982), pp. 97–120.

Cummins, R. (1989). *Meaning and Mental Representation.* Cambridge, MA: MIT Press.

Davies, M. (1991). Individualism and perceptual content. *Mind* 100: 461–484.

Egan, F. (1991). Must psychology be individualistic? *The Philosophical Review* 100: 179–203.

Field, H. (1978). Logic, meaning and conceptual role. *The Journal of Philosophy* 74: 379–409.

Fodor, J. (1981). Methodological solipsism considered as a research strategy in cognitive science. In *Representations.* Cambridge, MA: MIT Press.

Fodor, J. (1987). *Psychosemantics: The Problem of Meaning in the Philosophy of Mind.* Cambridge, MA: MIT Press.

Fodor, J. (1994). *The Elm and the Expert.* Cambridge, MA: MIT Press.

Grimm, R. and D. Merrill, Eds. (1988). *Contents of Thought.* Tucson: University of Arizona Press.

Larson, R., and G. Segal. (1995). *Knowledge of Meaning: An Introduction to Semantic Theory.* Cambridge, MA: MIT Press.

McGinn, C. (1989). *Mental Content.* Oxford: Blackwell.

Patterson, S. (1991). Individualism and semantic development. *Philosophy of Science* 58: 15–35.

Wilson, R. (1994). Wide computationalism. *Mind* 103: 351–372.

Wilson, R. (1995). *Cartesian Psychology and Physical Minds.* Cambridge: Cambridge University Press.

Woodfield, A., Ed. (1982). *Thought and Object: Essays on Intentionality.* Oxford: Clarendon Press.

Typology

Typology is the systematic study of the ways in which languages are similar to and differ from one another. More specifically, the study of language universals concerns those properties that are common to all languages (see LINGUISTIC UNIVERSALS), whereas typology is concerned with the systematic variation across languages, although in practice both studies must be carried out simultaneously and are often subsumed under either the term *typology* or the term *language universals research.* As such, the subject matter of the typological approach to language does not differ from that of other approaches, such as GENERATIVE GRAMMAR (as illustrated in Haegeman 1997). Methodologically, however, the two approaches tend to differ in the extent to which each is data driven (typology) versus theory driven (generative grammar), although in recent years the two approaches have tended alternately to approach and recede from one another. Given the rate at which languages are dying out—an estimated 90 percent of the world's languages will be extinct or moribund by the end of the twenty-first century (Hale et al. 1992)—the data-driven typological approach assumes increased importance as much of the very data on which linguistic theorization is based is disappearing before us. Overviews of the field of typology are provided in Comrie (1989), Croft (1990), and Whaley (1997).

The relation between language universals and language typology can be seen in two parameters that are often used to distinguish different kinds of language universals. First, language universals can be absolute, that is, exceptionless, or tendencies, that is, occurring with a frequency that cannot plausibly be attributed to chance or other external factors (such as demographics). An example of an absolute universal is that all languages have consonants. (Examples will necessarily be somewhat banal, to avoid having to go into too much detail.) An example of a universal tendency is that nearly all languages have nasal consonants, although a few—3.2 percent of the languages in the sample used by Maddieson (1984: 60)—do not. In practice, it is often impossible to tell whether a universal is an absolute or rather a very strong tendency to which exceptions happen not to have been found. A second distinction is that between implicational and nonimplicational universals. The two universals previously cited are nonimplicational, inasmuch as each refers to only one linguistic property without relating it to other properties. An implicational universal, by contrast, has the structure "if p, then q," where p and q are two linguistic properties. An example of an absolute implicational universal is: If a language has distinct reflexive pronouns in the non-third person, then it also has distinct reflexive pronouns in the third person. "If p, then q" is to be interpreted strictly as material implication, that is, three possibilities are allowed: "p & q," "$\sim p$ & $\sim q$," "$\sim p$ & q," while one is disallowed: *"p & $\sim q$." Thus, in the example cited, there are languages like English with distinct reflexive pronouns in the non-third person (e.g., *me* versus *myself*) and in the third person (e.g., *him* versus *himself*), languages with no reflexive pronouns at all (e.g., Old English *me* "me, myself," *hine* "him, himself"), languages with reflexive pronouns only in the third person (e.g., French *me* "me, myself," but *le* "him," *se* "himself"), but no languages with distinct reflexives only in the non-third person. An example of an implicational tendency is that languages with verb-initial word order in the clause nearly always have prepositions ("if verb-initial, then prepositional"), although a handful of verb-initial languages have postpositions, such as Yagua, spoken in Peruvian Amazonia. Implicational universals provide a typology of languages by dividing languages into the three types allowed by the universal, plus, in the case of an implicational tendency, the rare fourth type.

Although typology has a history going back to the eighteenth century (Greenberg 1974), a major impetus to the modern study of typology was the volume Greenberg (1966b), in particular Greenberg's own contribution to that volume (Greenberg 1966a). In the early work inspired by Greenberg's model, the emphasis was primarily and explicitly on the empirical side of typological work, attempting to find out what nonimplicational universals could plausibly be put forward, and to find out what correlations among different linguistic features might plausibly serve as the basis of implicational universals. More recently—for a survey of recent approaches to typology and universals, Shibatani and Bynon (1995) may be consulted—the importance of explaining language universals has come increasingly to the fore (e.g., Butterworth, Comrie, and Dahl 1984; Hawkins 1988). A number of different kinds of explanations have been proposed.

As suggested also by generative grammar, some universals probably reflect innate properties of the human cognitive apparatus. For instance, it has been observed that syntactic properties are, with only a few exceptions that can probably be accounted for in other ways, "structure-dependent" (see SYNTAX). By this is meant that they require identification of elements of syntactic structure for their operation. In English, for instance, questions can be formed from corresponding statements by inverting the order of subject and auxiliary verb, as with *can the new professor speak Polish?* in relation to *the new professor can speak Polish.* A priori, a much simpler rule would be to invert the first two words of the sentence, or to put the words of the sentence in the inverse order, yet human languages invariably or almost invariably go for structure-dependent rules like the English rule just discussed, which involve sophisticated parsing of syntactic structure. Given that there is no aprioristic reason for this preference, it almost certainly reflects an innate constraint. (This leaves open, incidentally, whether the constraint relates specifically to the language faculty or whether it is a more general cognitive constraint. At least in this case, the linguistic constraint is probably a special case of the general pattern-seeking preference of human cognition, for which arbitrary strings are difficult to handle, while imposition of structure facilitates processing, as seen trivially in the breakdown of seven-digit telephone numbers into groups of three plus four.)

Processing considerations seem to be a major factor constraining cross-linguistic variation. An example from the early generative literature is the difficulty of processing self-embedded constructions, for instance where a relative clause is included internally within another relative clause, as in *the boy [that the man [that I saw] caught] took the apple,* although a slight change of construction to avoid the self-embedding produces a readily interpretable sentence: *the apple was taken by the boy [that was caught by the man [that was seen by me]].* A detailed theory relating word order universals (both absolute and tendencies) to processing constraints is developed by Hawkins (1994).

This leads into the area of functional motivations for language universals, including not only the needs of processing but also other considerations from SEMANTICS and PRAGMATICS. For instance, the universal stated above that "if a language has distinct reflexive pronouns in the non-third person, then it also has distinct reflexive pronouns in the third person" does not have any obvious formal explanation; this universal is no simpler in formal terms than its empirically incorrect opposite "if a language has distinct reflexive pronouns in the third person, then it also has distinct reflexive pronouns in the non-third person." But as soon as one starts thinking about the semantic function of pronouns, a plausible explanation emerges. First- and second-person pronouns are uniquely determined by the speech situation, with the speaker referred to in the first person and the hearer in the second person. They thus do not change within an utterance, and whether a language says *I hit myself* or *I hit me* does not affect the content, that is, marking reflexivity is in a sense redundant in the first and second persons. Third person pronouns can potentially refer to any other entity in the universe of DISCOURSE, so it is useful to have different forms that enable distinctions among potential referents to be maintained, as in the case of *he$_i$ hit himself$_i$* versus *he$_i$ hit him$_j$.* Quite generally, as predicted, pronoun systems tend to make more referential distinctions in the third person than in the other persons, as when English distinguishes gender in the third person singular *(he, she, it)* but not in the first person *(I)* or the second person *(you).* Comrie (1984) shows how certain language universals can plausibly be related to pragmatics, for instance universals of imperative formation to the pragmatic function of imperatives in encoding the speech act of directive (Searle 1969): because directives require that the addressee carry out a certain action, many languages have a constraint that only imperatives with the addressee as agent are possible, that is, they allow the equivalent of *eat the bread!* but not of *be eaten by the lion!;* no language shows the inverse pattern.

See also CULTURAL VARIATION; IMPLICATURE; PARAMETER-SETTING APPROACHES TO ACQUISITION, CREOLIZATION, AND DIACHRONY

—*Bernard Comrie*

References

Baker, M. (1987). *Incorporation.* Chicago: University of Chicago Press.

Butterworth, B., B. Comrie, and Ö. Dahl, Eds. (1984). *Explanations for Language Universals.* Berlin: Mouton.

Comrie, B. (1984). Form and function in explaining language universals. In B. Butterworth, B. Comrie, and Ö. Dahl, Eds., *Explanations for Language Universals.* Berlin: Mouton, pp. 87–103.

Comrie, B. (1989). *Language Universals and Linguistic Typology.* 2nd ed. Chicago: University of Chicago Press.

Croft, W. (1990). *Typology and Universals.* Cambridge: Cambridge University Press.

Greenberg, J. H., Ed. (1966a). *Universals of Language.* 2nd ed. Cambridge, MA: MIT Press.

Greenberg, J. H. (1966b). Some universals of grammar with particular reference to the order of meaningful elements. In J. H. Greenberg, Ed., *Universals of Language.* 2nd ed. Cambridge, MA: MIT Press.

Greenberg, J. H. (1974). *Language Typology: A Historical and Analytic Overview.* The Hague: Mouton.

Haegeman, L. (1997). *The New Comparative Syntax.* London: Longman.

Hale, K., M. Krauss, and L. J. Watahomijie. (1992). Endangered languages. *Language* 68: 1–42.

Hawkins, J. A., Ed. (1988). *Explaining Language Universals.* Oxford: Blackwell.

Hawkins, J. A. (1994). *A Performance Theory of Order and Constituency.* Cambridge: Cambridge University Press.

Maddieson, I. (1984). *Patterns of Sounds.* Cambridge: Cambridge University Press.

Searle, J. (1969). *Speech Acts: An Essay in the Philosophy of Language.* Cambridge: Cambridge University Press.

Shibatani, M., and T. Bynon, Eds. (1995). *Approaches to Language Typology.* Oxford: Oxford University Press.

Whaley, L. J. (1997). *Introduction to Typology: The Unity and Diversity of Language.* Thousand Oaks, CA: Sage Publications.

Further Readings

Bechert, J., G. Bernini, and C. Buridant, Eds. (1990). *Toward a Typology of European Languages.* Berlin: Mouton.

Bybee, J. (1985). *Morphology: A Study of the Relation between Meaning and Form.* Amsterdam: Benjamins.

Foley, W. A., and R. D. Van Valin, Jr. (1984). *Functional Syntax and Universal Grammar.* Cambridge: Cambridge University Press.

Givón, T. (1984–1990). *Syntax: A Functional-Typological Introduction.* 2 vols. Amsterdam: Benjamins.

Hawkins, J. A. (1986). *A Comparative Typology of English and German: Unifying the Contrasts.* Austin: University of Texas Press.

Hawkins, J. A., and H. Holmback, Eds. *Papers in Universal Grammar: Generative and Typological Approaches.* Amsterdam: North-Holland.

Keenan, E. L., and B. Comrie. (1977). Noun phrase accessibility and universal grammar. *Linguistic Inquiry* 8: 63–99.

Mallinson, G., and B. J. Blake. (1981). *Language Typology: Cross-Linguistic Studies in Syntax.* Amsterdam: North-Holland.

Nichols, J. (1986). Head-marking and dependent-marking grammar. *Language* 62: 56–119.

Ramat, P. (1987). *Linguistic Typology.* Berlin: Mouton.

Shopen, T., Ed. (1985). *Language Typology and Syntactic Description.* 3 vols. Cambridge: Cambridge University Press.

Uncertainty

Almost all information is subject to uncertainty. Uncertainty may arise from inaccurate or incomplete information (e.g., how large are the current U.S. petroleum reserves?), from linguistic imprecision (what exactly do we mean by "petroleum reserves"?), and from disagreement between information sources. We may even be uncertain about our degree of uncertainty. The representation of uncertainty is intrinsic to the representation of information, which is its dual.

Many schemes have been developed to formalize the notion of uncertainty and to mechanize reasoning under uncertainty within KNOWLEDGE-BASED SYSTEMS. Probability is, by far, the best-known and most widely used formalism. However, apparent limitations and difficulties in applying probability have spawned the development of a rich variety of alternatives. These include heuristic approximations to probability used in rule-based expert systems, such as certainty factors (Clancy and Shortliffe 1984); fuzzy set theory and FUZZY LOGIC (Zadeh 1984); interval representations, such as upper probabilities and Dempster-Shafer belief functions (Shafer 1976); NONMONOTONIC LOGICS and default reasoning (Ginsberg 1987); and qualitative versions of probability, such as the Spohn calculus and kappa-calculus. There has been controversy about the assumptions, appropriateness, and practicality of these various schemes, particularly about their use in representing and reasoning about uncertainty in databases and knowledge-based systems. It is useful to consider a variety of criteria, both theoretical and pragmatic, in comparing these schemes.

The first criterion concerns epistemology: What kinds of uncertainty does each scheme represent? Like most quantitative representations of uncertainty, probability expresses degree of belief that a proposition is true, or that an event will happen, by a cardinal number, between 0 and 1. Fuzzy set theory and fuzzy logic also represent degrees of belief or truth by a number between 0 and 1. Upper probabilities and Dempster-Shafer belief functions represent degrees of belief by a range of numbers between 0 and 1, allowing the expression of ambiguity or ignorance as the extent of the range. Qualitative representations of belief, such as nonmonotonic logic (Ginsberg 1987) and the kappa-calculus, often represent degrees of belief on an ordinal scale.

In the frequentist view, the probability of an event is the frequency of the event occurring in a large number of similar trials. For example, the probability of heads for a bent coin is the frequency of heads from a large number of tosses of that coin. Unfortunately, for most events, it is unclear what population of similar trials one should use. When estimating the probability that a chemical is carcinogenic, should you compare it with all known chemicals, only those tested for carcinogenicity, or only those chemicals with a similar molecular structure? Therefore, in practical reasoning, the personalist (also known as Bayesian or subjective) interpretation is often more useful: In this interpretation, the probability of an event is a person's degree of belief, given all the information currently known to that person. Different people may reasonably hold different probabilities, depending on what information they have.

It is important to be able to represent uncertain relationships between propositions as well as degrees of belief. A conditional probability distribution for proposition a given b, $P(a \mid b)$, expresses the belief in a given the state of b. Belief networks, also known as BAYESIAN NETWORKS (Pearl 1988), provide an intuitive graphical way to represent qualitative uncertain knowledge about conditional dependence, and independence, among propositions.

A common source of uncertainty is linguistic imprecision. We find it useful to say that a river is "wide," without explaining exactly what we mean. Even from the personalist view, an event or quantity must be well specified for a meaningful probability distribution to be assessable. It is therefore important to eliminate linguistic imprecision, by developing unambiguous definitions of quantities, as a first step to encoding uncertain knowledge as probabilities. Instead of asking for the probability that a river is "wide," one might ask for the probability that it is wider than, say, 50 meters. Without such precision, vagueness about meaning is confounded with uncertainty about value.

Fuzzy set theorists argue that, because imprecision is intrinsic in human language, we should represent this imprecision explicitly in any formalism. For example, the linguistic variable "wide river" may be represented by a fuzzy set with a membership function that associates degrees of membership with different widths. A river 5 meters wide has membership 0 in "wide river;" a river 100 meters wide has membership 1; and intermediate widths have intermediate degrees of membership.

A second criterion for comparison of schemes is descriptive validity: Does the scheme provide a good model of human reasoning under uncertainty? There has been extensive experimental research by behavioral decision theorists on human judgment under uncertainty, which documents systematic divergences between human judgment and the norms of probabilistic inference (Kahneman, Slovic, and Tversky 1982; see PROBABILISTIC REASONING, TVERSKY, and JUDGMENT HEURISTICS). People use mental heuristics that often provide a qualitative approximation to probabilistic reasoning, such as in explaining away (Wellman and Henrion 1993). But they also exhibit systematic biases. There has been little experimental research on the descriptive validity of nonprobabilistic schemes, although there is little reason to expect that any simple mathematical scheme will fare well as a descriptive model.

Poor descriptive validity is a deficiency in a psychological theory, but not necessarily in a scheme for automated reasoning. Indeed, if the automated scheme exactly duplicated human commonsense reasoning, there would be less justification for the automated systems. If we believe that the formal scheme is based on axioms of rationality, as is claimed for probabilistic reasoning, it may be preferable to our flawed human reasoning for complicated problems in defined domains. That is why we rely on statistical analysis rather than informal reasoning in science.

A third criterion is ease of knowledge engineering: Is it practical to express human knowledge in this formalism? Knowledge engineers use a variety of tools for eliciting numerical probabilities (Morgan and Henrion 1990) and structuring complex uncertain beliefs using *belief networks* (Pearl 1988) and influence diagrams (Howard and Matheson 1984). Fuzzy logic provides a variety of ways of eliciting fuzzy variables. Nonmonotonic logical and other qualitative representations appear easy for people to express uncertain knowledge, although there have been few practical large-scale systems.

A fourth criterion is ease of data mining: Is it practical to extract and represent knowledge from data using this scheme? Increasingly, knowledge-based systems are supplementing or replacing knowledge encoded from human experts with knowledge extracted by experts from large databases using a wide variety of statistical techniques. The probabilistic basis of statistics, and Bayesian techniques for combining judgmental and data-based knowledge, give probabilistic techniques a major advantage on this criterion.

A fifth criterion concerns the tractability of computation with large knowledge bases: Modular rule-based schemes, such as certainty factors and fuzzy logic rules, are efficient, with linear computation time. Exact probabilistic inference in belief networks is NP hard; that is, potentially intractable for very large belief networks. However, effective approximate methods exist, and probabilistic inference is practical for many real knowledge bases. Higher-order representations, such as Dempster-Shafer and interval probabilities, are intrinsically more complex computationally than conventional probabilistic representations.

A sixth criterion is the relation of the scheme to making decisions. In practice, uncertain inference becomes valuable primarily when it is used as the basis for important decisions. Subjective probability is embedded in decision theory and UTILITY THEORY, developed by VON NEUMANN and Morgenstern to provide a theory for RATIONAL DECISION MAKING. Utility theory provides a way to express attitudes to risk, especially risk aversion. There have been several attempts to develop fuzzy utilities, however decision theories for nonprobabilistic representations are less developed, and this is an important area for research.

Humans or machines can rarely be certain about anything, and so practical reasoning requires some scheme for representing uncertainty. We have a rich array of formalisms. Recent developments on knowledge engineering, and inference methods for probabilistic methods, notably Bayesian belief networks and influence diagrams, have resolved many of the apparent difficulties with probability, and have led to a resurgence of research on probabilistic methods, with many real world applications (Henrion, Breese, and Horvitz 1991). Fuzzy logic has also had notable success in applications to approximate control systems. However, each method has its merits and may be suitable for particular applications.

See also COMPUTATIONAL COMPLEXITY; EPISTEMOLOGY AND COGNITION; KNOWLEDGE REPRESENTATION; PROBABILITY, FOUNDATIONS OF

—*Max Henrion*

References

Clancy, W. J., and E. H. Shortliffe, Eds. (1984). *Readings in Medical Artificial Intelligence: The First Decade.* Reading, MA: Addison-Wesley.

Ginsberg, M. L., Ed. (1987). *Readings in Nonmonotonic Logic.* Los Altos, CA: Kaufman.

Henrion, M., J. S. Breese, and E. J. Horvitz. (1991). Decision analysis and expert systems. *Artificial Intelligence Magazine* 12(4): 64–91.

Horvitz, E. J., J. S. Breese, and M. Henrion. (1988). Decision theory in expert systems and artificial intelligence. *Intl. J. of Approximate Reasoning* 2: 247–302.

Howard, R. A., and J. E. Matheson. (1981). Influence diagrams. In Howard and Matheson (1984), pp. 719–762.

Howard, R. A., and J. E. Matheson, Eds. (1984). *Readings in the Principles and Applications of Decision Analysis.* Menlo Park, CA: Strategic Decisions Group.

Kahneman, D., P. Slovic, and A. Tversky. (1982). *Judgment under Uncertainty: Heuristics and Biases.* Cambridge: Cambridge University Press.

Morgan, M. G., and M. Henrion. (1990). *Uncertainty: A Guide to the Treatment of Uncertainty in Quantitative Policy and Risk Analysis.* New York: Cambridge University Press.

Pearl, J. (1988). *Probabilistic Reasoning in Intelligent Systems: Networks of Plausible Inference.* Los Angeles, CA: Kaufman.

Raiffa, H. (1968). *Decision Analysis: Introductory Lectures on Choice Under Uncertainty.* Reading, MA: Addison-Wesley.

Shafer, G. (1976). *A Mathematical Theory of Evidence.* Princeton, NJ: Princeton University Press.

Wellman, M., and M. Henrion. (1993). Explaining "explaining away". *IEEE Transactions on Pattern Analysis and Machine Intelligence* 15(3): 287–291.

Zadeh, L. A. (1984). The role of fuzzy logic in the management of uncertainty in expert systems. *Fuzzy Sets and Systems* 11: 199–227.

Further Readings

Heckerman, D. E., and E. J. Horvitz. (1988). The myth of modularity. In Lemmer and Kanal (1988), pp. 23–34.

Howard, R. A. (1988). Uncertainty about probability: A decision analysis perspective. *Risk Analysis* 8(1): 91–98.

Kanal, L. N., and J. Lemmer, Eds. (1986). Uncertainty in artificial intelligence. *Machine Intelligence and Pattern Recognition*, vol. 4. Amsterdam: Elsevier.

Kaufman, A. (1975). *Introduction to the Theory of Fuzzy Sets.* New York: Academic Press.

Lemmer, J. F., and L. N. Kanal, Eds. (1988). *Uncertainty in Artificial Intelligence* 2. Vol. 5, *Machine Intelligence and Pattern Recognition.* Amsterdam: Elsevier.

Henrion, M. (1987). Uncertainty in artificial intelligence: Is probability epistemologically and heuristically adequate? In J. Mumpower et al., Eds., *Expert Judgment and Expert Systems.* NATO. ISI Series F., vol. 35. Berlin: Springer, pp. 105–130.

Shachter, R. D., and D. Heckerman. (1987). Thinking backwards for knowledge acquisition. *Artif. Intell. Magazine* 8: 55–62.

Shortliffe, E. H., and B. G. Buchanan. (1975). A model of inexact reasoning in medicine. *Math. Biosciences* 23: 351–379.

Szolovits, P., and S. G. Pauker. (1984). Categorical and probabilistic reasoning in medical diagnosis. In Clancy and Shortliffe (1984), pp. 210–240.

Wallsten, T. S., D. V. Budescu, A. Rapaport, R. Zwick, and B. Forsyth. (1986). Measuring the vague meanings of probability terms. *J. Exp. Psych: General* 15(4): 348–365.

Unconscious

See CONSCIOUSNESS; FREUD, SIGMUND; PSYCHOANALYSIS, CONTEMPORARY VIEWS; PSYCHOANALYSIS, HISTORY OF

Understanding

See EXPLANATION; PSYCHOLINGUISTICS; SENTENCE PROCESSING

Unity of Science

The view that scientific knowledge should be integrated has a long history, with roots in Aristotle and the French Encyclopedists. Perhaps as a consequence of the ever increasing specialization in science, scientists have found it important to work in an interdisciplinary manner where they can draw upon the research skills and knowledge bases of scientists trained in other disciplines. Thus, attempts at integration at the level of individual laboratories, and at higher levels such as that of professional societies, have become relatively commonplace in modern science. Cognitive science itself represents one such integratory effort that began with collaborative conferences (the MIT Symposia on Information Theory in the 1950s) and collaborative research groups (the Center for Cognitive Studies at Harvard in the 1960s), and became institutionalized with funding by the Sloan Foundation in the 1970s and 1980s) and the founding of the Cognitive Science Society in 1978 (Bechtel, Abrahamsen, and Graham 1998).

The modern interest in unity of science stems largely from the work in the 1930s and 1940s of logical positivists of the Vienna Circle, especially the logician-philosopher Rudolf Carnap and the sociologist Otto Neurath. (Today the logical positivists have acquired the image of conservatives, but politically they were liberals and social democrats, and scientifically they advocated a pluralist and Enlightenment conception of science.) One of the driving concerns of Carnap and Neurath was epistemic. The nineteenth century witnessed the birth of many new scientific disciplines, especially in the life sciences and social sciences: cytology, physiological chemistry, psychology, anthropology, and so forth. These various disciplines employed different vocabularies and different methods of investigation, raising the question of whether they were generating real knowledge. One way Carnap and Neurath proposed to evaluate the epistemic status of those inquiries was in terms of their unity with other scientific pursuits, especially physics, which, despite the major controversies occurring within it in the wake of Einstein, was taken as a paragon of a scientific discipline. (One prominent forum for the positivists' proposals was the *Encyclopedia of Unified Science,* which Carnap and Neurath, in collaboration with the American pragmatist Charles Morris, began to edit in 1938.)

The tool for unifying other disciplines with physics was reduction of two different sorts. The first was reduction of theoretical claims of each science to a base class of sentences whose truth value could be directly determined through observation (Carnap 1928). Thus, all legitimate disciplines would be seen to have a similar base in that their theoretical claims were reducible, through logical analysis, to observations. Carnap initially proposed that the observational basis for all sciences lay in phenomenal reports, but eventually he followed Neurath in requiring only a reduction to observational reports of physical states (Carnap 1934). Such a reduction would show that all science relied on similar empirical foundations and tools of logic for securing their theoretical claims. The proponents of this approach never succeeded in developing an adequate logical analysis to ground theoretical claims in observation. The call for such reductions, however, had a significant influence in furthering the behaviorist movement in psychology, because it claimed to rely only on observations of behavior and laws relating such behaviors to stimuli or reinforcements.

The other sort of reduction Carnap and Neurath advanced was theory reduction, wherein theories of a higher-level science would be reduced to those of more basic sciences. (The best source for this view of reduction is Nagel 1961.) Such a reduction required both translation laws that connected the vocabulary of the higher-level science with that used in the more basic science (higher-level entities might, for example, be characterized in terms of their composition from lower-level entities) and derivations of the laws of the higher-level science from those of the more basic science under specified boundary conditions. It is important to note that success in developing such reductions was viewed not as eliminating the reduced theory but as providing epistemic support for it; thus, a reduction of PSYCHOLOGICAL LAWS to those of neuroscience in this view would provide support for the psychological laws. The theory reduction model has been seriously promoted as a framework for unifying psychology and neuroscience by such theorists as Patricia Churchland (1986); unlike the positivists, though, she focuses on the process of theory development, and proposes a coevolutionary research program in which both neuroscience and psychology will evolve until they are unified by a reduction (McCauley 1996). However, as with the attempt to reduce theoretical claims to observation claims, the attempt to reduce higher-level theories to lower-level ones has encountered serious objections. For further discussion, see REDUCTIONISM and Bechtel (1987).

A variation on the reductionist framework for unifying science that rejects the attempt to ground all theories in physics has emerged several times in the development of the study of cognition. This approach tries to show that a common theoretical framework applies at a number of levels of organization in nature, with the unification provided by this theoretical framework. Cybernetics (a theoretical framework emphasizing the role of feedback in maintaining stable states in complex systems; WIENER 1948) and General Systems Theory (von Bertalanffy 1951) both offered general frameworks that were intended to apply to biological and cognitive systems at a variety of different levels. One reason neither program endured was that at the time it was difficult to develop successful detailed empirical hypotheses about cognition within these frameworks; as a result, in the 1960s and 1970s most inquiries into cognition assumed some form of autonomy of the cognitive system from both the underlying neural structures and its situated context in the world. Today advocates of dynamical systems theory, though, have revitalized unificationist aspirations by offering the mathematical and geometrical models of dynamical systems as unifying frameworks (for applications to cognitive science, see Port and van Gelder 1995).

Another model of unification, developed by Lindley Darden and Nancy Maull (1987), rejects the insistence on a common theoretical framework. Darden and Maull propose instead that interfield theories, which establish connections between phenomena that have been studied in two or more fields of inquiry without making any one of them more basic, constitute the vehicle of unification. Such linkages constitute a discovery heuristic in that what is known about one set of phenomena can then suggest hypotheses about the other set of phenomena (Wimsatt 1976). The fruitfulness of such interfield theorizing can be seen within cognitive science. For example, Chomsky's initial proposals for transformational grammars in linguistics were intended to provide a finite characterization of the grammatically well-formed sentences in a language, not as models of language processing. But George Miller and other early cognitive psychologists attempted to employ them as process models in linguistics and to predict reaction times for processing sentences based on the number of transformations required to generate the sentence in Chomsky's grammar. This effort to forge an interfield connection, though initially promising, died when Chomsky revised his linguistic analysis in ways that no longer could account for such data (Reber 1987). Other attempts to develop interfield connections from linguistics to psychology have proven more successful (Abrahamsen 1987) and current efforts of cognitive grammarians to ground grammatical structures on general cognitive abilities (Langacker 1987) represent the attempt to develop connections in the opposite direction. Moreover, links between linguistics and neuropsychology prompted fruitful rethinking of the classical analysis of APHASIA as analyses in terms of syntax and semantics replaced those based on comprehension and production (Bradley, Garrett, and Zurif 1980).

So far discussion has focused on unification via theories, a natural consequence of the focus on theories in twentieth century philosophy of science. But increasingly theorists are recognizing other forms of unification in science, ones where research techniques and tools become the vehicle of integration. The development of cognitive neuroscience has been fostered in part by the integration of behavioral measures of cognitive psychology (e.g., reaction time studies and error analysis) with tools for studying brain activity (e.g., SINGLE-NEURON RECORDING and evoked potentials). In this light, the recent development of neuroimaging tools (POSITRON EMISSION TOMOGRAPHY and function MAGNETIC RESONANCE IMAGING) is particularly interesting. The resulting images, which indirectly measure neural activity, are interpreted functionally by applying the subtraction method developed by the nineteenth century Dutch psychologist Frans Cornelis Donders, so that images of the brain active in one task are subtracted from those of the brain active in another task, with the intent of revealing the brain structures responsible for the additional component of processing required in the second task (Posner and Raichle 1994).

Although the dreams of unity of science via reduction advanced by the positivists have generally not panned out, unification and integration, viewed in a more patchwork manner, are a routine part of modern science. Scientists regularly rely on phenomena studied in other disciplines to constrain their own studies or explain what seems inexplica-ble in their field alone. Tools and techniques are widely shared between related disciplines. The resulting picture is a network of local integration, not one of global unification.

See also BEHAVIORISM; COGNITIVE LINGUISTICS; DYNAMIC APPROACHES TO COGNITION; EXPLANATION

—*William Bechtel*

References

Abrahamsen, A. (1987). Bridging boundaries versus break boundaries. *Synthese* 72: 355–388.
Bechtel, W. (1987). *Philosophy of Science: An Overview for Cognitive Science.* Hillsdale, NJ: Erlbaum.
Bechtel, W., A. Abrahamsen, and G. Graham. (1998). The life of cognitive science. In W. Bechtel and G. Graham, Eds., *A Companion to Cognitive Science.* Oxford: Blackwell.
Bradley, D. C., M. F. Garrett, and E. B. Zurif. (1980). Syntactic deficits in Broca's aphasia. In D. Caplan, Ed., *Biological Studies of Mental Processes.* Cambridge, MA: MIT Press, pp. 269–286.
Carnap, R. (1928). *Der Logische Aufbau der Welt.* Berlin: Weltkreis.
Carnap, R. (1934). *The Unity of Science.* Translated by M. Black. London: K. Paul, Trench, Trubner & Co.
Churchland, P. S. (1986). *Neurophilosophy.* Cambridge, MA: MIT Press.
Darden, L., and N. Maull. (1987). Interfield theories. *Philosophy of Science* 43: 44–64.
Langacker, R. (1987). *Foundations of Cognitive Grammar.* Stanford: Stanford University Press.
McCauley, R. N. (1996). Explanatory pluralism and the co-evolution of theories of science. In R. N. McCauley, Ed., *The Churchlands and Their Critics.* Oxford: Blackwell, pp. 17–47.
Nagel, E. (1961). *The Structure of Science.* New York: Harcourt, Brace.
Port, R., and T. van Gelder. (1995). *Mind as Motion: Explorations in the Dynamics of Cognition.* Cambridge, MA: MIT Press.
Posner, M. I., and M. Raichle. (1994). *Images of Mind.* San Francisco, CA: Freeman.
Reber, A. S. (1987). The rise (and surprisingly rapid) fall of psycholinguistics. *Synthese* 72: 325–339.
von Bertalanffy, L. (1951). *General Systems Theory: A New Approach to Unity of Science.* Baltimore, MD: Johns Hopkins University Press.
Wiener, N. (1948). *Cybernetics: Or, Control and Communication in the Animal Machine.* New York: Wiley.
Wimsatt, W. C. (1976). Reductionism, levels of organization, and the mind-body problem. In G. Globus, G. Maxwell, and I. Savodnik, Eds., *Consciousness and the Brain: A Scientific and Philosophical Inquiry.* New York: Plenum, pp. 205–267.

Universal Grammar

See GENERATIVE GRAMMAR; LINGUISTIC UNIVERSALS AND UNIVERSAL GRAMMAR

Unsupervised Learning

Unsupervised learning studies how systems can learn to represent particular input patterns in a way that reflects the statistical structure of the overall collection of input patterns. By contrast with SUPERVISED LEARNING or REINFORCEMENT

LEARNING, there are no explicit target outputs or environmental evaluations associated with each input; rather, the unsupervised learner brings to bear prior biases as to what aspects of the structure of the input should be captured in the output.

Unsupervised learning is important because it is likely to be much more common in the brain than supervised learning. For instance there are around 10^8 photoreceptors in each eye whose activities are constantly changing with the visual world and which provide all the information that is available to indicate what objects there are in the world, how they are presented, what the lighting conditions are, and so forth. Developmental and adult plasticity are critical in animal vision (see VISION AND LEARNING)—indeed, structural and physiological properties of synapses in the neocortex are known to be substantially influenced by the patterns of activity in sensory neurons that occur. However, essentially none of the information about the contents of scenes is available during learning. This makes unsupervised methods essential, and, equally, allows them to be used as computational models for synaptic adaptation.

The only things that unsupervised learning methods have to work with are the observed input patterns $\mathbf{x}$ which are often assumed to be independent samples from an underlying unknown probability distribution $\mathcal{P}_I[\mathbf{x}]$, and some explicit or implicit a priori information as to what is important. One key notion is that input, such as the image of a scene, has distal independent *causes*, such as objects at given locations illuminated by particular lighting. Because it is on those independent causes that we normally must act, the best representation for an input is in their terms. Two classes of method have been suggested for unsupervised learning. Density estimation techniques explicitly build statistical models (such as BAYESIAN NETWORKS) of how underlying causes could create the input. Feature extraction techniques try to extract statistical regularities (or sometimes irregularities) directly from the inputs.

Unsupervised learning in general has a long and distinguished history. Some early influences were Horace Barlow (see Barlow 1989), who sought ways of characterizing neural codes; Donald MacKay (1956), who adopted a cybernetic-theoretic approach; and David MARR (1970), who made an early unsupervised learning postulate about the goal of learning in his model of the neocortex. The Hebb rule (HEBB 1949), which links statistical methods to neurophysiological experiments on plasticity, has also cast a long shadow. Geoffrey Hinton and Terrence Sejnowski, in inventing a model of learning called the Boltzmann machine (1986), imported many of the concepts from statistics that now dominate the density estimation methods (Grenander 1976–1981). Feature extraction methods have generally been less extensively explored.

Clustering provides a convenient example. Consider the case in which the inputs are the photoreceptor activities created by various images of an apple or an orange. In the space of all possible activities, these particular inputs form two clusters, with many fewer degrees of variation than 10^8, that is, lower *dimension*. One natural task for unsupervised learning is to find and characterize these separate, low dimensional clusters.

The larger class of unsupervised learning methods consists of maximum likelihood (ML) density estimation methods. All of these are based on building parameterized *models* $\mathcal{P}[\mathbf{x};\mathcal{G}]$ (with parameters $\mathcal{G}$) of the probability distribution $\mathcal{P}_I[\mathbf{x}]$, where the forms of the models (and possibly prior distributions over the parameters $\mathcal{G}$) are constrained by a priori information in the form of the representational goals. These are called *synthetic* or *generative* models, because, given a particular value of $\mathcal{G}$, they specify how to synthesize or generate samples $\mathbf{x}$ from $\mathcal{P}[\mathbf{x};\mathcal{G}]$, whose statistics should match $\mathcal{P}_I[\mathbf{x}]$. A typical model has the structure:

$$\mathcal{P}[\mathbf{x};\mathcal{G}] = \sum_{\mathbf{y}} \mathcal{P}[\mathbf{y};\mathcal{G}]\mathcal{P}[\mathbf{x}|\mathbf{y};\mathcal{G}]$$

where $\mathbf{y}$ represents all the potential causes of the input $\mathbf{x}$. The typical measure of the degree of mismatch is called the Kullback-Leibler divergence:

$$KL[\mathcal{P}_I[\mathbf{x}], \mathcal{P}[\mathbf{x};\mathcal{G}]] = \sum_{\mathbf{x}} \mathcal{P}_I[\mathbf{x}]\log\left[\frac{\mathcal{P}_I\mathbf{x}}{\mathcal{P}\mathbf{x};\mathcal{G}}\right] \geq 0$$

with equality if and only if $\mathcal{P}_I[\mathbf{x}] = \mathcal{P}[\mathbf{x}; G]$.

Given an input pattern $\mathbf{x}$, the most general output of this model is the posterior, *analytical,* or *recognition* distribution $\mathcal{P}[\mathbf{y} \mid \mathbf{x};\mathcal{G}]$, which recognizes which particular causes might underlie $\mathbf{x}$. This analytical distribution is the statistical inverse of the synthetic distribution.

A very simple model can be used in the example of clustering (Nowlan 1990). Consider the case in which there are two values for y (1 and 2), with $\mathcal{P}[y=1] = \pi$; $\mathcal{P}[y=2] = 1 - \pi$, where π is called a mixing proportion, and two different Gaussian distributions for the activities $\mathbf{x}$ of the photoreceptors depending on which y is chosen: $\mathcal{P}[\mathbf{x} \mid y=1] \sim N[\mu_1, \Sigma_1]$ and $\mathcal{P}[\mathbf{x} \mid y=2] \sim N[\mu_2, \Sigma_2]$ where μ are means and Σ are covariance matrices. Unsupervised learning of the means determines the locations of centers of the clusters, and of the mixing proportions and the covariances characterizes the size and (rather coarsely) the shape of the clusters. The posterior distribution $\mathcal{P}[y=1|\mathbf{x}; \pi, \mu, \Sigma]$ reports how likely it is that a new image $\mathbf{x}$ was generated from the first cluster, that is, that $y=1$ is the true hidden cause. Clustering can occur (with or) without any supervision information about the different classes. This model is called a *mixture of Gaussians*.

Maximum likelihood density estimation, and approximations to it, cover a very wide spectrum of the principles that have been suggested for unsupervised learning. This includes versions of the notion that the outputs should convey most of the information in the input; that they should be able to reconstruct the inputs well, perhaps subject to constraints such as being independent or sparse; and that they should report on the underlying causes of the input. Many different mechanisms apart from clustering have been suggested for each of these, including forms of Hebbian learning, the Boltzmann and Helmholtz machines, sparse coding, various other mixture models, and independent components analysis.

Density estimation is just a heuristic for learning good representations. It can be too stringent—making it necessary to build a model of all the irrelevant richness in sensory input. It can also be too lax—a look-up table that reported $\mathcal{P}_I[\mathbf{x}]$ for each $\mathbf{x}$ might be an excellent way of modeling the distribution, but provides no way to represent particular examples $\mathbf{x}$.

The smaller class of unsupervised learning methods seeks to discover how to represent the inputs $\mathbf{x}$ by defining some quality that good features have, and then searching for those features in the inputs. For instance, consider the case that the output $y(\mathbf{x}) = \mathbf{w} \cdot \mathbf{x}$ is a linear projection of the input onto a weight vector $\mathbf{w}$. The central limit theorem implies that most such linear projections will have Gaussian statistics. Therefore if one can find weights $\mathbf{w}$ such that the projection has a highly non-Gaussian (for instance, multimodal) distribution, then the output is likely to reflect some interesting aspect of the input. This is the intuition behind a statistical method called projection pursuit. It has been shown that projection pursuit can be implemented using a modified form of Hebbian learning (Intrator and Cooper 1992). Arranging that different outputs should represent different aspects of the input turns out to be surprisingly tricky.

Projection pursuit can also execute a form of clustering in the example. Consider projecting the photoreceptor activities onto the line joining the centers of the clusters. The distribution of all activities will be bimodal—one mode for each cluster—and therefore highly non-Gaussian. Note that this single projection does not itself characterize well the nature or shape of the clusters.

Another example of a heuristic underlying good features is that causes are often somewhat global. For instance, consider the visual input from an object observed in depth. Different parts of the object may share few features, except that they are at the same depth, that is, one aspect of the disparity in the information from the two eyes at the separate locations is similar. This is the global underlying feature. By maximizing the mutual information between different outputs that are calculated on the basis of the separate input, one can find this disparity. This technique was invented by Becker and Hinton (1992) and is called IMAX.

See also LEARNING; NEURAL PLASTICITY; SELF-ORGANIZING SYSTEMS; STATISTICAL TECHNIQUES IN NATURAL LANGUAGE PROCESSING

—*Peter Dayan*

References

Barlow, H. B. (1989). Unsupervised learning. *Neural Computation* 1: 295–311.

Becker, S., and G. E. Hinton. (1992). A self-organizing neural network that discovers surfaces in random-dot stereograms. *Nature* 355: 161–163.

Grenander, U. (1976–1981). *Lectures in Pattern Theory* 1, 2, and 3: *Pattern Analysis, Pattern Synthesis and Regular Structures.* Berlin: Springer.

Hebb, D. O. (1949) *The Organization of Behavior.* New York: Wiley.

Hinton, G. E., and T. J. Sejnowski. (1986). Learning and relearning in Boltzmann machines. In D. E. Rumelhart, J. L. McClelland, and the PDP Research Group, Eds., *Parallel Distributed Processing: Explorations in the Microstructure of Cognition.* Vol. 1, *Foundations.* Cambridge, MA: MIT Press, pp. 282–317.

Intrator, N., and L. N. Cooper. (1992). Objective function formulation of the BCM theory of visual cortical plasticity: Statistical connections, stability conditions. *Neural Networks* 5: 3–17.

MacKay, D. M. (1956). The epistemological problem for automata. In C. E. Shannon and J. McCarthy, Eds., *Automata Studies.* Princeton, NJ: Princeton University Press, pp. 235–251.

Marr, D. (1970). A theory for cerebral neocortex. *Proceedings of the Royal Society of London, Series B* 176: 161–234.

Nowlan, S. J. (1990). Maximum likelihood competitive learning. In D. S. Touretzky, Ed., *Advances in Neural Information Processing Systems*, 2. San Mateo, CA: Kaufmann.

Further Readings

Becker, S., and M. Plumbley. (1996). Unsupervised neural network learning procedures for feature extraction and classification. *International Journal of Applied Intelligence* 6: 185–203.

Dayan, P., G. E. Hinton, R. M. Neal, and R. S. Zemel. (1995). The Helmholtz machine. *Neural Computation* 7: 889–904.

Hinton, G. E. (1989). Connectionist learning procedures. *Artificial Intelligence* 40: 185–234.

Linsker, R. (1988). Self-organization in a perceptual network. *Computer* 21: 105–128.

Mumford, D. (1994). Neuronal architectures for pattern-theoretic problems. In C. Koch and J. Davis, Eds., *Large-Scale Theories of the Cortex.* Cambridge, MA: MIT Press, pp. 125–152.

Olshausen, B. A., and D. J. Field. (1996). Emergence of simple-cell receptive field properties by learning a sparse code for natural images. *Nature* 381: 607–609.

Utility Theory

The branch of decision theory concerned with measurement and representation of preferences is called utility theory. Utility theorists focus on accounts of preferences in RATIONAL DECISION MAKING, where an individual's preferences cohere with associated beliefs and actions. *Utility* refers to the scale on which preference is measured.

Identification of preference measurement as an issue is usually credited to Daniel Bernoulli (1954/1738), who exhibited a prospect (probability distribution over outcomes) that had infinite expected monetary value, but apparently not infinite utility. Bernoulli resolved the "St. Petersburg paradox" by suggesting that utility be logarithmic in monetary amounts, which in this case would yield a finite expected utility.

That utility could apply to all sorts of outcomes, not merely monetary rewards, was first argued forcefully by Jeremy Bentham (1823/1789), who proposed a system for tabulating "pleasures" and "pains" (positive and negative utility factors), which he called the "hedonic calculus" (regrettably, as critics henceforth have confounded the idea of universal preference measurement with hedonism). Bentham further argued that these values could be aggregated across society ("greatest good for the greatest number"), which became the core of an ethical doctrine known as utilitarianism (Albee 1901).

Although modern economists are quite reluctant to aggregate preferences across individuals, the concept of individual utility plays a foundational role in the standard neoclassical theory. Recognition of this role was the result of the so-called marginal utility revolution of the 1870s, in which Carl Menger, W. Stanley Jevons, Francis Ysidro Edgeworth, Léon Walras, and other leading "marginalists" demonstrated that values/prices could be founded on utility.

The standard theory of utility starts with a preference order, $\lesssim$, typically taken to be a complete preorder over the outcome space, ϑ. $y \lesssim x$ means that x is (weakly) preferred to y, and if in addition $\neg\,(x \lesssim y)$, x is strictly preferred. Granting certain topological assumptions, the preference order can be represented by a real-valued utility function, U: $\vartheta \to R$, in the sense that $U\,(y) \leq U\,(x)$ if and only if $y \lesssim x$. If U represents $\lesssim$, then so does $\varphi \circ U$, for any monotone function φ on the real numbers. Thus, utility is an ordinal scale (Krantz et al. 1971).

Under UNCERTAINTY, the relevant preference comparison is over prospects rather than outcomes. One can extend the utility-function representation to prospects by taking expectations with respect to the utility for constituent outcomes. Write $[F, p;\ F']$ to denote the prospect formed by combining prospects F and F' with probabilities p and $1 - p$, respectively. If $F(\omega)$ denotes the probability of outcome ω in prospect F, then

$$[F, p;\ F'](\omega) \equiv pF(\omega) + (1 - p)F'(\omega).$$

The *independence axiom* of utility theory states that if $F' \lesssim F''$, then for any prospect F and probability p,

$$[F', p;\ F] \lesssim [F'', p;\ F].$$

In other words, preference is decomposable according to the prospect's exclusive possibilities.

Given the properties of an order relation, the independence axiom, and an innocuous continuity condition, preference for a prospect can be reduced to the *expected* value of the outcomes in its probability distribution. The expected utility $\hat{U}$ of a prospect F is defined by

$$\hat{U}(F) \equiv E_F[U] = \sum_{\omega \,\in\, \vartheta} U(\omega)F(\omega)$$

For the continuous case, replace the sum by an appropriate integral and interpret F as a probability density function. Because expectation is generally not invariant with respect to monotone transformations, the measure of utility for the uncertain case must be cardinal rather than ordinal. As with preferences over outcomes, the utility function representation is not unique. If U is a utility function representation of $\lesssim$ and φ a positive linear (affine) function on the reals, then $\varphi \circ u$ also represents $\lesssim$.

Frank Plumpton Ramsey (1964/1926) was the first to derive expected utility from axioms on preferences and belief. The concept achieved prominence in the 1940s, when John VON NEUMANN and Oskar Morgenstern presented an axiomatization in their seminal volume on GAME THEORY (von Neumann and Morgenstern 1953). (Indeed, many still refer to "vN-M utility.") Savage (1972) presented what is now considered the definitive mathematical argument for expected utility from the Bayesian perspective.

Although it stands as the cornerstone of accepted decision theory, the doctrine is not without its critics. Allais (1953) presented a compelling early example in which most individuals would make choices violating the expectation principle. Some have accounted for this by expanding the outcome description to include determinants of regret (see Bell 1982), whereas others (particularly researchers in behavioral DECISION MAKING) have constructed alternate preference theories (Kahneman and TVERSKY's 1979 prospect theory) to account for this as well as other phenomena. Among those tracing the observed deviations to the premises, the independence axiom has been the greatest source of controversy. Although the dispute centers primarily around its descriptive validity, some also question its normative status. See Machina (1987, 1989) for a review of alternate approaches and discussion of descriptive and normative issues.

Behavioral models typically posit more about preferences than that they obey the expected utility axioms. One of the most important qualitative properties is risk aversion, the tendency to prefer the expected value of a prospect to the prospect itself. For scalar outcomes, the risk aversion function (Pratt 1964),

$$r(x) = \frac{-U''(x)}{U'(x)},$$

is the standard measure of this tendency. Properties of the risk aversion measure (e.g., is constant, proportional, or decreasing) correspond to analytical forms for utility functions (Keeney and Raiffa 1976), or stochastic dominance tests for decision making (Fishburn and Vickson 1978).

When outcomes are multiattribute (nonscalar), the outcome space is typically too large to consider specifying preferences without imposing some structure on the utility function. Independence concepts for preferences (Bacchus and Grove 1996; Gorman 1968; Keeney and Raiffa 1976)—analogous to those for probability—define conditions under which preferences for some attributes are invariant with respect to others. Such conditions lead to separability of the multiattribute utility function into a combination of subutility functions of lower dimensionality.

Modeling risk aversion, attribute independence, and other utility properties is part of the domain of decision analysis (Raiffa 1968; Watson and Buede 1987), the methodology of applied decision theory. Decision analysts typically construct preference models by asking decision makers to make hypothetical choices (presumably easier than the original decision), and combining these with analytical assumptions to constrain the form of a utility function.

Designers of artificial agents must also specify preferences for their artifacts. Until relatively recently, Artificial Intelligence PLANNING techniques have generally been limited to goal predicates, binary indicators of an outcome state's acceptability. Recently, however, decision-theoretic methods have become increasingly popular, and many developers encode utility functions in their systems. Some researchers have attempted to combine concepts from utility theory and KNOWLEDGE REPRESENTATION to develop flexible preference models suitable for artificial agents (Bacchus and Grove 1996; Haddawy and Hanks 1992; Wellman and Doyle 1991), but this work is still at an early stage of development.

See also BOUNDED RATIONALITY; ECONOMICS AND COGNITIVE SCIENCE; RATIONAL AGENCY; RATIONAL CHOICE THEORY

—*Michael P. Wellman*

References

Albee, E. (1901). *A History of English Utilitarianism.* London: Macmillan.

Allais, M. (1953). Le comportement de l'homme rationnel devant la risque: Critique des postulats et axiomes de l'école Americaine. *Econometrica* 21: 503–546.

Bacchus, F., and A. J. Grove. (1996). Utility independence in a qualitative decision theory. In *(KR-96), Proceedings of the Fifth International Conference on the Principles of Knowledge Representation and Reasoning.* Los Altos, CA: Morgan Kaufmann, pp. 542–552.

Bell, D. E. (1982). Regret in decision making under uncertainty. *Operations Research* 30: 961–981.

Bentham, J. (1823/1789). *Principles of Morals and Legislation.* Oxford: Oxford University Press. Original work published in 1789.

Bernoulli, D. (1954). Exposition of a new theory of the measurement of risk. *Econometrica* 22: 123–136. (Translation of *Specimen theoriae novae de mensura sortis* 1738.)

Debreu, G. (1959). *Theory of Value: An Axiomatic Analysis of Economic Equilibrium.* New York: Wiley.

Fishburn, P. C., and R. G. Vickson. (1978). Theoretical foundations of stochastic dominance. In G. A. Whitmore and M. C. Findlay, Eds., *Stochastic Dominance: An Approach to Decision Making Under Risk.* Lexington, MA: D. C. Heath and Company.

Gorman, W. M. (1968). The structure of utility functions. *Review of Economic Studies* 35: 367–390.

Haddawy, P., and S. Hanks. (1992). Representations for decision-theoretic planning: Utility functions for deadline goals. In *(KR-92) Proceedings of the Third International Conference on the Principles of Knowledge Representation and Reasoning.* San Mateo, CA: Morgan Kaufmann, pp. 71–82.

Kahneman, D., and A. Tversky. (1979). Prospect theory: An analysis of decision under risk. *Econometrica* 47: 263–291.

Keeney, R. L., and H. Raiffa. (1976). *Decisions with Multiple Objectives: Preferences and Value Tradeoffs.* New York: Wiley.

Krantz, D. H., R. D. Luce, P. Suppes, and A. Tversky. (1971). *Foundations of Measurement.* New York: Academic Press.

Machina, M. J. (1987). Choice under uncertainty: Problems solved and unsolved. *Journal of Economic Perspectives* 1: 121–154.

Machina, M. J. (1989). Dynamic consistency and non-expected utility models of choice under uncertainty. *Journal of Economic Literature* 27(4): 1622–1668.

Pratt, J. W. (1964). Risk aversion in the small and in the large. *Econometrica* 32: 122–136.

Raiffa, H. (1968). *Decision Analysis: Introductory Lectures on Choices Under Uncertainty.* Reading, MA: Addison-Wesley.

Ramsey, F. P. (1964/1926). Truth and probability. In H. E. Kyburg, Jr. and H. E. Smokler, Eds., *Studies in Subjective Probability.* New York: Wiley.

Savage, L. J. (1972). *The Foundations of Statistics.* 2nd ed. New York: Dover Publications.

von Neumann, J., and O. Morgenstern. (1953). *Theory of Games and Economic Behavior.* 3rd ed. Princeton, NJ: Princeton University Press.

Watson, S. R., and D. M. Buede. (1987). *Decision Synthesis: The Principles and Practice of Decision Analysis.* Cambridge: Cambridge University Press.

Wellman, M. P., and J. Doyle. (1991). Preferential semantics for goals. In *Proceedings of the National Conference on Artificial Intelligence.* Anaheim, CA: AAAI, pp. 698–703.

Vagueness

Vague expressions, such as "tall," "red," "bald," "heap," "tadpole," and "child," possess borderline cases where it is unclear whether or not the predicate applies. Some people are borderline tall: not clearly tall and not clearly not tall. It seems that the unclarity here is not merely epistemic. There need be no fact of the matter about which we are ignorant: the borderline predications are *indeterminate,* neither true nor false, and are exceptions to the principle of bivalence (which is a key feature of classical LOGIC). Relatedly, vague predicates lack well-defined extensions. On a scale of heights, there is no sharp division between the tall people and the rest. If candidates for satisfying some vague *F* are arranged with spatial closeness indicating similarity, no sharp line can be drawn round the cases to which *F* applies. Vague predicates are thus naturally described as having fuzzy boundaries: but according to classical SEMANTICS, all predicates have well-defined extensions, again suggesting that a departure from classical conceptions is needed to accommodate vagueness.

Vague predicates are also susceptible to sorites paradoxes. Intuitively, a hundredth of an inch cannot make a difference as to whether a person counts as tall: such tiny variations, which cannot be discriminated by the naked eye (or even by everyday measurements), are just too small to matter. This insensitivity to imperceptible differences gives the term its everyday utility and seems part of what it is for "tall" to be a *vague* height term lacking sharp boundaries— which suggests [S1] if *X* is tall, and *Y* is only a hundredth of an inch shorter than *X*, then *Y* is also tall. But imagine a line of men, starting with someone seven-foot tall, and each of the rest a hundredth of an inch shorter than the man in front of him. Repeated applications of [S1] as we move down the line imply that each man we encounter is tall, however far we continue. And this yields conclusions that are clearly false, for instance, that a man five feet high, reached after three thousand steps, still counts as tall. Similarly, there is the ancient example of the heap (Greek *soros,* hence the paradox's name). Plausibly, [S2] if *X* is a heap of sand, then the result *Y* of removing one grain will still be a heap. So take a heap and remove grains one by one; repeated applications of [S2] imply that even a solitary last grain must still count as a heap. Familiar ethical "slippery slope" arguments share the same sorites structure (see, e.g., Walton 1992 and Williams 1995).

Borderline-case vagueness must be distinguished from mere underspecificity (as in "*X* is an integer greater than thirty," which may be unhelpfully vague but has sharp boundaries). Nor is vagueness simple AMBIGUITY: "tadpole" has a univocal sense, though that sense does not determine a well-defined extension. Context-dependence is different again. Who counts as tall may vary with the intended comparison class; but fix on a definite context and "tall" will remain vague, with borderline cases and fuzzy boundaries.

A theory of vagueness must elucidate the logic and semantics of vagueness. The simplest approach argues that appearances are deceptive; we can retain classical logic and semantics for vague terms after all. On this *epistemic view* borderline case predications are either true or false, but we do not and cannot know which. The sorites paradox is avoided by denying principles like [S1]: there is a sharp divide between the tall men and the others in our series, though we are ignorant of where this boundary lies and so wrongly assume that it does not exist. For an ingenious defense of this initially surprising view, see Williamson (1994).

Competing theories reject classical logic and semantics. One option is to countenance nonclassical *degrees of truth,* introducing a whole spectrum of truth values from 0 to 1, with complete falsity as degree 0 and complete truth as degree 1 (see, e.g., Machina 1976). Borderline cases then each take some intermediate truth value, with "X is tall" gradually decreasing in truth value as we move down the sorites series. When Y is only a hundredth of an inch shorter than X, the claim "if X is tall, Y is also tall," which appears true, may actually be slightly less than completely true. Repeated application of the sorites principle [S1] then introduces an additional departure from the truth at each step, eventually reaching falsity.

The degree theory is typically associated with an infinite-valued logic or FUZZY LOGIC, and various versions have been proposed. It is normally assumed at least that, if V(P) is the value of P, then

$$V(\text{not-}P) = 1 - V(P)$$
$$V(P \ \& \ Q) = \text{minimum of } V(P), V(Q).$$

But suppose Tek is taller than Tom, and V(Tek is tall) is 0.5, V(Tom is tall) = 0.4. Then, by the standard rules, V(Tom is tall and Tek is not) = 0.4. Such a result is arguably implausible. If Tek is taller than Tom, then is it not entirely ruled out that Tom should be tall and Tek not—that is, should not V(Tom is tall and Tek is not) = 0? (see Chierchia and McConnell-Ginet 1990: Chapter 8, for more examples). However, not all degree theorists accept that the propositional connectives obey truth-functional rules (see Edgington 1997).

The other popular option is *supervaluationism.* The basic idea is to treat vagueness as a matter of semantic indecision, as if we have not settled which precise range of heights is to count as tall. A proposition involving "tall" is true (false) if it comes out true (false) on all the ways in which "tall" could be made precise (ways, that is, which preserve the truth-values of uncontentious cases of "X is tall"). A borderline case, "Tek is tall," will thus be neither true nor false, for it is true on some ways of making "tall" precise and false on others. But a classical tautology like "either Tek is tall or he is not tall" *will* still come out true because it remains true wherever a sharp boundary for "tall" is drawn. In this way, the supervaluationist adopts a nonclassical *semantics* while aiming to minimize divergence from classical *logic* (see Fine 1975). On any way of making "tall" totally precise, there will be some X who counts as tall when Y a hundredth

of an inch shorter does not, making [S1] false. So because [S1] is false on each precisification, [S1] counts as false *simpliciter.* But note, nobody counts as the last tall man on *every* precisification of "tall," so supervaluationism avoids commitment to a sharp boundary.

Both the supervaluationist and the degree theorist can naturally accommodate a range of linguistic phenomena. For example, both can give semantic treatments of comparatives. The degree theorist may say that "X is taller than Y" counts as true just if "X is tall" is true to a greater degree than "Y is tall." The supervaluationist may say that the comparative claim holds if the ways of making "tall" precise which make Y count as tall are a proper subset of those that make X count as tall. Likewise, both theorists can deal with various modifiers: for example "X is quite tall" is true if "X is tall" has a sufficiently (but not too) high degree of truth, or alternatively if "X is tall" is true on sufficiently many (but not too many) precisifications of "tall." (See Kamp 1975; Zadeh 1975.)

See also EXTENSIONALITY, THESIS OF; METAPHOR; META-PHOR AND CULTURE; RADICAL INTERPRETATION

—*Peter Smith and Rosanna Keefe*

References

Chierchia, G., and S. McConnell-Ginet. (1990). *Meaning and Grammar.* Cambridge, MA: MIT Press.

Edgington, D. (1997). Vagueness by degrees. In Keefe and Smith (1997a), pp. 294–316.

Fine, K. (1975). Vagueness, truth and logic. *Synthese* 30: 265–300. Reprinted in Keefe and Smith (1997a).

Kamp, J. A. W. (1975). Two theories about adjectives. In E. Keenan, Ed., *Formal Semantics of Natural Languages.* Cambridge: Cambridge University Press, pp. 123–155.

Keefe, R., and P. Smith. (1997a). *Vagueness: A Reader.* Cambridge, MA: MIT Press.

Machina, K. F. (1976). Truth, belief and vagueness. *Journal of Philosophical Logic* 5: 47–78. Reprinted in Keefe and Smith (1997a).

Walton, D. N. (1992). *Slippery Slope Arguments.* Oxford: Clarendon Press.

Williams, B. (1995). Which slopes are slippery? In *Making Sense of Humanity.* Cambridge: Cambridge University Press, pp. 213–223.

Williamson, T. (1994). *Vagueness.* London: Routledge.

Zadeh, L. A. (1975). Fuzzy logic and approximate reasoning. *Synthese* 30: 407–428.

Further Readings

Burns, L. C. (1991). *Vagueness: An Investigation into Natural Languages and the Sorites Paradox.* Dordrecht: Kluwer.

Keefe, R., and P. Smith. (1997b). Theories of vagueness. In Keefe and Smith (1997a), pp. 1–57.

Russell, B. (1923). Vagueness. *Australasian Journal of Philosophy and Psychology* 1: 84–92. Reprinted in Keefe and Smith (1997a).

Sainsbury, R. M. (1990). Concepts without boundaries. Inaugural lecture published by the King's College, London, Department of Philosophy. Reprinted in Keefe and Smith (1997a).

Tye, M. (1994). Sorites paradoxes and the semantics of vagueness. In J. E. Tomberlin, Ed., *Philosophical Perspectives,* 8: *Logic and Language.* Atascadero, CA: Ridgeview, pp. 189–206. Reprinted in Keefe and Smith (1997a).

Validity

See ECOLOGICAL VALIDITY; LOGIC

Vision

See COMPUTATIONAL VISION; MACHINE VISION; MID-LEVEL VISION; HIGH-LEVEL VISION

Vision and Learning

Learning is now perceived as the gateway to understanding the problem of INTELLIGENCE. Because seeing is a factor in intelligence, learning is also becoming a key to the study of artificial and biological vision. In the last few years both computer vision—which attempts to build machines that see—and visual neuroscience—which aims to understand how our visual system works—are undergoing fundamental changes in their approaches. Visual neuroscience is beginning to focus on the mechanisms that allow the CEREBRAL CORTEX to adapt its circuitry and learn a new task. Instead of building a hardwired machine or program to solve a specific visual task, computer vision is trying to develop systems that can be trained with examples of any of a number of visual tasks. The challenge is to develop machines that learn to perform visual tasks such as visual inspection and visual recognition from a set of training examples or even in an unsupervised way from visual experience.

This reflects an overall trend—to make intelligent systems that do not need to be fully and painfully programmed for specific tasks. In other words, computers will have to be much more like our brain, learning to see rather than being programmed to see. Biological visual systems are more robust and flexible than machine vision mainly because they continuously adapt and learn from experience. At stake are engineering as well as scientific issues. On the engineering side the possibility to build vision systems that can adapt to different tasks can have enormous impact in many areas such as automatic inspection, image processing, video editing, virtual reality, multimedia databases, computer graphics, and man-machine interfaces. On the biological side, our present understanding of how the cortex works may radically change if adaption and learning turn out to play a key role. Instead of the hardwired cortical structures implied by classical work, for instance by Harvard's David Hubel and Torsten Wiesel, we may be confronted with significant NEURAL PLASTICITY—that is, neuron properties and connectivities that change as a function of visual experience over time scales of a few minutes or seconds.

There are two main classes of learning techniques that are being applied to machine vision: *supervised* and *unsupervised* learning algorithms (see UNSUPERVISED LEARNING). Supervised learning—or *learning-from-examples*—refers to a system that is trained, instead of programmed, by a set of examples. The training thus can be considered as using input-output pairs. At run-time the trained system provides a correct output for a new input not contained in the training set. The underlying theory makes use of function approximation techniques, neural network architectures, and statistical methods. Systems have been developed that learn to recognize objects, in particular faces (see FACE RECOGNITION), systems that learn to find specific objects in cluttered scenes, software that learns to draw cartoon characters from an artist's drawings, and algorithms that learn to synthesize novel image sequences from a few real pictures and thereby promise to achieve extremely high compression in applications such as video conference and video e-mail. So far the most ambitious unsupervised learning techniques have been used only in simple, "toy" examples, but they represent the ultimate goal: learning to see, from experience, without a teacher.

In computer vision tasks (see COMPUTATIONAL VISION) the input to the supervised learning system is a digitized image or an image sequence and the output is a set of parameters estimated from the image. For instance, in the ALVIN system, developed by Dean Pomerleau (1993) at Carnegie Mellon University for the task of driving a car, the input is a series of images of the road and the output is degrees of steering. In recognition tasks the output parameters consist of a label identifying the object in the image (see VISUAL OBJECT RECOGNITION, AI).

The analysis problems of estimating object labels as well as other parameters from images is *the* problem of vision. It is the *inverse* of the classical problem of classical optics and modern computer graphics, where the question is how to synthesize images corresponding to given 3-D surfaces as a function of parameters such as direction of illuminant, position of the camera and material properties of the object. In the supervised learning framework it is natural to use a learning module to associate input parameters to output images. This module can then synthesize new images. Traditional 3-D computer graphics simulates the physics of the world by building 3-D models, transforming them in 3-D space, simulating their physical properties, and finally rendering them by simulating geometrical optics. The learning-from-examples paradigm suggests a rather different and unconventional approach: take several real images of a 3-D object and create new images by generalizing from those views, under the control of appropriate pose and expression parameters, assigned by the user during the training phase.

A large class of SUPERVISED LEARNING schemes suggests directly a view-based approach to computer vision and to computer graphics. Though it cannot be seen as a substitute for the more traditional approaches, the learning-from-examples approach to vision and graphics may represent an effective shortcut to several problems.

An obvious application of the supervised learning framework is recognition of 3-D objects. The idea is to train the learning module with a few views of the object to be recognized—in general, from different viewpoints and under different illuminations—and the corresponding label (as output), without any explicit 3-D model. This corresponds to a classification problem as opposed to the regression problem of estimating real-valued parameters associated with the image. An interesting demonstration of the power of this view-based paradigm is the development of several successful face recognition systems.

Even more difficult than recognizing an isolated specific object is detecting an object of a certain class in a cluttered image. Again, supervised learning systems have been developed that can be trained to detect faces, cars, and people in complex images.

The key problem for the practical use of most learning-from-examples schemes is often the insufficient size of the training set. Because input vectors typically have a high dimension (like the number of pixels in an image), the required number of training examples is very high. This is the so-called *curse of dimensionality*. The natural idea is to exploit prior information to generate additional *virtual* examples from a small set of real example images. For instance, knowledge of symmetry properties of a class of 3-D objects allows the synthesis of additional examples. More generally, it is possible to learn *legal* transformations typical for a certain class of objects from examples drawn from images of objects of the same class.

The example-based approach is successful in practical problems of object recognition, image analysis, and image synthesis. It is not surprising therefore to ask whether a similar approach may be used by our brain. Networks that learn from examples have an obvious appeal given our knowledge of neural mechanisms. Over the last four years psychophysical experiments have indeed supported the view-based schemes and physiological experiments have provided a suggestive glimpse on how neurons in the IT cortex may represent objects for recognition (Logothetis, Pauls, and Poggio 1995 and references therein). The experimental results seem to agree to a surprising extent with the view-based models.

See also HIGH-LEVEL VISION; PICTORIAL ART AND VISION; VISUAL NEGLECT; VISUAL OBJECT RECOGNITION, AI; VISUAL PROCESSING STREAMS; VISUAL WORD RECOGNITION

—*Tomaso Poggio*

References

Logothetis, N. K., J. Pauls, and T. Poggio. (1995). Shape representation in the inferior temporal cortex of monkeys. *Current Biology* 5(5): 552–563.

Pomerleau, D. A. (1993). *Neural Network Perception for Mobile Robot Guidance*. Dordrecht: Kluwer.

Further Readings

Beymer, D., and T. Poggio. (1996). Image representation for visual learning. *Science* 272: 1905–1909.

Murase, H., and S. K. Nayar. (1995). Visual learning and recognition of 3-D objects from appearance. *International Journal of Computer Vision* 14(1): 5–24.

Nayar, S. K., and T. Poggio, Eds. (1996). *Early Visual Learning*. Oxford: Oxford University Press.

Poggio, T., and D. Beymer. (1996). Learning to see. *IEEE Spectrum*: 60–69.

Poggio, T., and S. Edelman. (1990). A network that learns to recognize 3-D objects. *Nature* 343: 263–266.

Rowley, H. A., S. Baluja, and T. Kanade. (1995). Human face detection in visual scenes. *Technical report CMU-CS-95-158R*. School of Computer Science, CMU.

Turk, M., and A. Pentland. (1991). Face recognition using eigenfaces. *Proceedings CVPR*, Los Alamitos, CA: IEEE Computer Society Press, 586–591.

Visual Anatomy and Physiology

In primates visual processing is carried out in many different parts of the brain. Described here is the basic anatomy and physiology of the RETINA, the lateral geniculate nucleus of the THALAMUS, the striate cortex, higher cortical visual areas, the superior colliculus, and the accessory optic system (AOS).

The retina: Five major classes of neurons have been discerned in the primate retina: photoreceptors, horizontal cells, bipolar cells, amacrine cells, and ganglion cells. Several subclasses have been discerned within each of these cell types. The rod and cone photoreceptors subserve night and day vision. In humans and many primates three kinds of cones have been discerned that have maximum sensitivity for either short-(blue), medium-(green), or long-wavelength (red) light. All photoreceptors hyperpolarize to light, yield only graded potentials, and use the neurotransmitter glutamate. Bipolar cells form two major classes, the ON and OFF types, which by virtue of sign-inverting and sign-conserving synapses, respectively, depolarize and hyperpolarize to light. Several subclasses of ON and OFF bipolar cells have been identified. There are numerous classes of amacrine cells that use a variety of different neurotransmitters that include dopamine, acetylcholine, and serotonin. The ganglion cells are the output cells of the retina. Each ganglion cell is sensitive to a small area of the visual field, called the receptive field of the cell. Most commonly the shape of the receptive field is circular and consists of two regions, a central excitatory one which, when stimulated by light or dark spots (for the ON and OFF cells respectively), elicits a vigorous burst of action potentials in the cell, and a concentric inhibitory surround area produced largely by virtue of the horizontal cell network. As a result of this arrangement, responses arise predominantly when a local difference in luminance or chrominance is detected within the receptive field.

Two major classes of the primate ganglion cells are the midget and parasol cells. The midget ganglion cells, as their name implies, are quite small; in central retina their receptive field center is composed of but a single cone, rendering them thereby, in trichromatic primates, wavelength-selective. The parasol cells, by contrast, are much larger and receive input both in the center and surround of their receptive fields from several different cone types. As a result of convergent input from the receptors, the parasol cells are more sensitive to contrast but cannot provide information about differences in wavelength. Midget and parasol cells come in two subvarieties, the ON and the OFF. The ON cells are excited by light increment and the OFF cells are excited by light decrement. The midget system is believed to make a significant contribution to the processing of fine detail and color, and the parasol system to the processing of rapid motion and luminance changes. In central vision the midget cells outnumber the parasol cells ten to one. This ratio declines with increasing eccentricity; in the far periphery the two cells types are just about equally numerous. Another group of retinal ganglion cells receives convergent input from ON and OFF bipolar cells as a result of which they discharge to both light increment and light decrement.

Such cells make extensive projections to the superior colliculus.

The optic nerve consists of the axons of the retinal ganglion cell. In animals with lateral eyes, such as fish and amphibians, most of the axons in the optic nerve of each eye cross over at the optic chiasm to the contralateral hemisphere. In higher mammals with forward-looking eyes, only the axons of ganglion cells in the nasal hemiretinae cross over at the chiasm; the temporal hemiretinae project ipsilaterally. This arrangement makes it possible for corresponding points in the retinae of the two eyes to reach the same sites in cortex to realize binocular vision.

The retinal ganglion cell axons terminate in several central structures that include the lateral geniculate nucleus of the thalamus, the superior colliculus (called the optic tectum in reptiles and amphibians), and the terminal nuclei.

The lateral geniculate nucleus of the thalamus: The two lateral geniculate nuclei, one on each side of the brain, are laminated thalamic structures. Each receives input from the nasal hemiretina of one eye and the temporal hemiretina of the other, thereby representing the contralateral visual hemifield. In primates there are six layers for central vision, three of which receive input from one eye and three from the other. The midget retinal ganglion cells project to the top four parvocellular layers, whereas the parasol cells project to the bottom two magnocellular layers. The number of layers reduces to four for peripheral representation, two of which are parvocellular and two magnocellular. The interlaminar layers contain small cells innervated by several classes of small retinal ganglion cells. The retinal projections are orderly, thereby creating a neat topographic arrangement in the structure. The receptive field properties of single cells are quite similar to those seen in retinal ganglion cells. Their responses, however, can be modulated by the extensive inputs the lateral geniculate nucleus receives directly or indirectly from the cortex.

The striate cortex: The striate cortex is an expanse of cortical tissue that in higher mammals comprises a large portion of the occipital lobe. Transverse sections of this tissue, when stained with cresyl violet, reveal a distinct striation in layer 4, called the stripe of Gennary; this stripe is not evident in other cortical regions and thereby provides an easy anatomical delineation of the area. The striate cortex, often called V1 (for visual 1), spans a thickness of approximately 2 mm of gray matter; six major laminae have been discerned, some of which have subsequently been divided into several sublaminae. In primates the striate cortex is the major recipient zone of the input from the dorsal lateral geniculate nucleus of the thalamus; fibers terminate most profusely, but not exclusively, in layer 4c, which has two subdivisions, 4cα and 4cβ. The inputs to 4cα and 4cβ arise, respectively, from the magnocellular and parvocellular divisions of the lateral geniculate nucleus.

The visual field is represented in an orderly manner along the surface extent of the striate cortex with more space allocated for central than for peripheral vision. Each cell in the striate cortex is sensitive to a relatively small region of the visual field, the receptive field area of the cell. By virtue of elaborate excitatory and inhibitory connections, the input from the lateral geniculate nucleus is reorganized to yield six major changes in receptive field properties: (1) selectivity for the orientation of edges, (2) selectivity for the direction of stimulus movement, (3) selectivity for the spatial frequency of repetitive stimuli such as textures, (4) selectivity for color along several directions in color space in addition to the red/green and blue/yellow axes seen in the retinal ganglion cells and in the lateral geniculate nucleus, (5) sensitivity for both light increment (ON response) and light decrement (OFF response) in many cells, and (6) selectivity for binocular activation that gives rise to stereoscopic depth perception. Orientation-specific cells in the striate cortex appear to form several distinct classes that include the so-called simple and complex cells. The receptive fields of simple cells subdivide into spatially separate regions, within each of which responses are produced for either light increment (ON response) or light decrement (OFF response) but not both. Complex cells, which commonly receive input from both eyes, do not exhibit such subdivision; they typically respond to both light increment and decrement throughout their receptive fields. Furthermore, their receptive fields are larger than those of simple cells.

In addition to the laminar organization of the striate cortex, columnar organization has also been revealed, most notably for orientation specificity. Within each column cells have the same orientation. The columns form stripes along the cortical surface with neighboring columns showing progressive shifts in orientation preference. This arrangement, coupled with columnar organization for ocular dominance, is modular. Each module, sometimes called a "hypercolumn," measures approximately 1 mm by 1 mm with a depth of 2 mm; it is conceived to be a self-contained processing unit for a given location of the visual field within which the basic attributes believed to be necessary for the analysis of the visual scene are contained. These include a full representation of neurons for the local analysis of orientation, direction, spatial frequency, color, and depth. The columnar organization seen in the striate cortex is believed to optimize encoding and visual analysis.

Higher cortical areas: In the primate posterior cortex more than thirty distinct visual areas that make more than 300 interconnections have been identified. These include areas V2, V3, V4, the middle temporal (MT), the medial superior temporal (MST), the ventral interparietal (VIP), and the inferior temporal (IT) areas. Most of these areas are also modular, as is area V1. Physiological studies have shown that the modules perform a great variety of analyses. The receptive fields of single cells become larger in size the further the area is removed from V1; this goes along with a gradual loss in the topographic order with which the visual field is laid out in each area. The occipitoparietal areas are believed to play an important role in the analysis of spatial relationships and motion, whereas the occipito-temporal areas are believed to play a role in object recognition and color vision. Lesion studies suggest that there is considerable redundancy in processing as selective removal of single extrastriate areas such as V3, V4, and MT does not produce highly specific or long-lasting deficits in the analysis of basic visual capacities such as motion, color, shape, and depth. However, lesions of temporal cortex produce severe

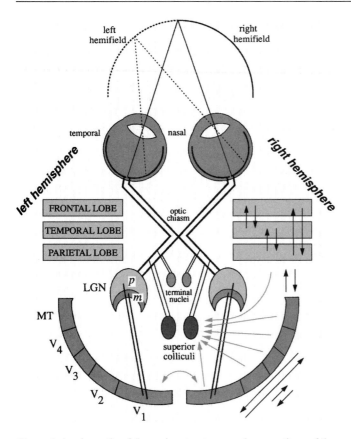

Figure 1. A schematic of the major structures and connections of the visual system as viewed from above. The temporal hemiretinae project ipsilaterally, whereas the projections from the nasal hemiretinae cross over at the optic chiasm to the contralateral hemisphere. As a consequence, corresponding retinal points in the two eyes project to the same hemisphere and to nearby regions within each target structure. Three retinal projections are depicted in the figure, which terminate in the lateral geniculate nuclei (LGN) of the thalamus, in the superior colliculi, and in the terminal nuclei. The magnocellular (*m*) and parvocellular (*p*) portions of the LGN project predominantly to primary visual cortex (V_1). The extrastriate areas shown are V_2, V_3, V_4, and MT. These areas are extensively interconnected, as indicated on the right. The temporal, parietal, and frontal lobes contain several additional visual areas that interconnect with each other as well as with the extrastriate areas. Most of these visual areas send projections to the superior colliculi as well as other subcortical visual centers.

deficits in object recognition and lesions of the parietal cortex, shorter-term deficits in spatial vision. At this stage of the research it is still not clearly understood why so many cortical visual areas have evolved in primates.

The superior colliculus: The superior colliculus, located on the roof of the midbrain, is a laminated structure. In the upper layers the visual field is represented in an orderly fashion. Most cells have relatively small receptive fields and give both ON and OFF responses to stimuli; little selectivity has been reported for color and shape. In some species, like the cat for example, cells having directionally selective attributes are common. In the primates so far studied the percentage of such cells in the superior colliculus is low.

In the deeper layers of the primate superior colliculus single cells that respond in association with eye movements are common. Each cell discharges optimally when an eye movement of a certain direction and amplitude is executed; each region in the colliculus represents different directions and amplitudes of eye movements arranged in an orderly fashion. Electrical stimulation elicits saccadic eye movements with very low currents. The superior colliculus plays a central role in the generation of saccadic eye movements. However, several other structures, including regions in the occipital and parietal lobes, the frontal eye fields, and the medial eye fields in the frontal lobe also contribute to eye movement generation. Electrical stimulation in these areas also produces eye movements. Removal of the superior colliculus causes moderate deficits in eye movements, most notable being the inability to execute saccades to visual targets with very short latencies (the so-called express saccades). After colliculus removal, electrical stimulation of the occipital and parietal lobes no longer produces eye movements, although stimulation-elicited eye movements from the frontal areas remain unaffected. Removal of the frontal eye fields and the medial eye fields produces only minor deficits in eye movements. However, when both the frontal eye fields and the superior colliculi are removed, visually guided saccadic eye movements can no longer be generated. These findings suggest that there are two major systems for saccadic eye movement control: the posterior, which involves the occipital and parietal lobes that pass through the colliculus to reach the brain stem, and the anterior, which involves the frontal lobe that reaches the brain stem directly.

The accessory optic system: The AOS, extensively studied in the rabbit, arises from a special class of ganglion cells, the cells of Dogiel, that are directionally selective and respond best to slow rates of movement. They project to the terminal nuclei which in turn project to the dorsal cap of Kooy of the inferior olive. The climbing fibers from the olive project to the flocculo-nodular lobe of the cerebellum from where the brain stem oculomotor centers are reached through the vestibular nuclei.

The prime function of the accessory optic system appears to be to stabilize the retinal image by counterrotating the eyes when either the organism or the visual field is set in motion at slow velocities. At higher velocities retinal slip is prevented by the vestibular system which also sends its signals to the brain stem for eye movement generation via the vestibular nuclei.

See also COLOR, NEUROPHYSIOLOGY OF; COLUMNS AND MODULES; EYE MOVEMENTS AND VISUAL ATTENTION; OCULOMOTOR CONTROL; VISUAL CORTEX, CELL TYPES AND CONNECTIONS IN; VISUAL PROCESSING STREAMS

—*Peter Schiller*

Further Readings

Rockland, K. S., J. H. Kaas, and A. Peters, Eds. (1997). Extrastriate Cortex. *Cerebral Cortex,* vol. 12, *Extrastriate Cortex.* New York: Plenum Press.

Schiller, P. H. (1986). The central visual system. *The 25th Jubilee Issue of Vision Research* 26: 1351–1386.

Spillman, L., and J. S. Werner, Eds. (1990). *Visual Perception, The Neurophysiological Foundations.* San Diego: Academic Press.

Visual Attention

See ATTENTION; ATTENTION IN THE HUMAN BRAIN; EYE-MOVEMENTS AND VISUAL ATTENTION

Visual Cortex, Cell Types and Connections in

Like all parts of the CEREBRAL CORTEX, the function of visual cortex is dependent on the organization of its connections, the types of synapses they form, and how postsynaptic neurons respond to and integrate synaptic inputs. The various neurons within the cerebral cortex can be classified based on differences in any of these traits and their unique relationships to cortical circuits.

Numerous neuronal types are found in visual cortex as well as other cortical areas. The actual categorization of individual cells is, of course, highly dependent on the definitions used to distinguish them. Among many possibilities, cells can be defined in terms of the functional influence of their synapses (excitatory or inhibitory, strong or weak); anatomical features (spiny or aspinous dendrites, spiny stellate or pyramidal dendritic morphology; see figure 1); laminar position (the cortical layer containing the cell body; see figure 1); intrinsic membrane properties (fast-spiking, regular-spiking, bursting; see figure 1); or patterns of connectivity. In the most clear-cut cases, many of these definitions generate the same groupings. Most notably, inhibitory and excitatory neurons compose two distinct groups on the basis of several features. They release different NEUROTRANSMITTERS and their synapses therefore have different functional influences (γ-aminobutyric acid, inhibitory vs. glutamate, excitatory). Inhibitory neurons also have aspinous dendrites and are fast-spiking compared to excitatory neurons which have spiny dendrites and are regular-spiking or bursting (see figure 1 and below).

Although inhibitory cells account for only about fifteen to twenty percent of visual cortical neurons, they are a highly diverse population. They have been distinguished experimentally based primarily on morphology. By such criteria more than a dozen different types of aspinous neurons can be identified. In a few cases, important functional implications can be inferred from the anatomy. For example, "chandelier" cells form inhibitory synapses onto the axon initial segments (where the axon leaves the cell body; see figure 1) of spiny neurons and can therefore veto their output. But most inhibitory connections probably have more subtle influences via connections onto dendrites, where they interact with nearby excitatory connections. A better understanding of the functional importance of most of the morphological distinctions awaits further study.

The great majority of visual cortical neurons (about 80–85 percent) are spiny and therefore excitatory. Outside of primary visual cortex (V1), virtually all of these have a pyramidal dendritic morphology (see figure 1). Such cells have a long apical dendrite extending from the cell body "up" toward more superficial layers (i.e., layer 1), as well as more numerous, shorter basal dendrites extending down-

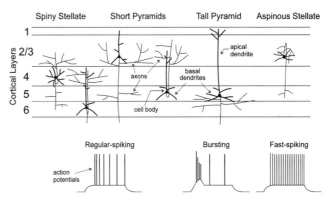

Spiny Stellate   Short Pyramids   Tall Pyramid   Aspinous Stellate

apical dendrite

axons   basal dendrites

cell body

Regular-spiking   Bursting   Fast-spiking

action potentials

Figure 1.

ward and obliquely. Thus, the top of the apical dendrite and bottoms of the most lateral basal dendrites define the corners of the "pyramid." Pyramidal neurons can be further distinguished by variations in their patterns of dendritic branching. Such differences are often correlated with different intrinsic physiological properties or patterns of connectivity. For example "tall" pyramids have long apical dendrites and often fire action potentials in bursts (see figure 1 and below). A second type of spiny neuron, the spiny stellate, is found in layer 4 of V1. These lack a prominent apical dendrite and instead have numerous shorter dendrites, extending obliquely upward as well as downward, to define a roughly spherical volume (see figure 1).

Cortical neurons also vary and can be classified according to intrinsic physiological differences. These differences are reflected in the patterns and shapes of action potentials that are generated on the injection of electrical current into the cell body (see figure 1). Inhibitory neurons fire high-frequency trains of brief action potentials. They are thus termed fast-spiking. Spiny neurons have broader, less brief action potentials and in most cases the firing rate decreases gradually with each spike. These are regular-spiking neurons. Bursting pyramidal neurons are rarer and fire action potentials in groups rather than singly. Bursting neurons are typically found in deep cortical layers and are also distinct from regular-spiking neurons in terms of both their dendritic morphology and axonal connections (see below).

A conspicuous feature of all cortical areas is their laminar organization. Layers are apparent in cross sections through the cortical sheet as regions with varying densities and sizes of neurons. The layers are numbered 1 to 6, with layer 1 located most superficially, at the outer surface, and layer 6 the deepest (see figure 1). Grouping of cortical neurons according to laminar position is straightforward and also useful since the most prominent feature of connectivity in visual cortex is its laminar organization. The laminar specificity of connections is a consequence of the laminar stratification of axonal arbors (see figure 1 and below). Thus, the laminar position of a neuron's cell body tends to be highly correlated with its connectivity. This is particularly true of aspinous, inhibitory neurons and spiny stellate neurons since their dendrites, which receive connections from the axons of other neurons, are usually confined to a single layer. But dendritic arbors of pyramidal neurons can span several layers, with apical dendritic branches also being highly stratified. Laminar specificity is a characteristic of both the corticocortical connections between the numerous visual cortical areas and local connections within a cortical area. And connections with subcortical structures also arise from and terminate in distinct cortical layers.

The laminar patterns of connections between visual cortical areas are closely correlated with hierarchical relationships between areas. At the bottom of the hierarchy is the primary visual area, V1. Virtually all of the visual information reaching the cortex is first channeled through this area, where it is processed before being sent on to higher areas. Corticocortical connections are made by pyramidal neurons and are therefore excitatory. Forward connections, from lower to higher areas in the hierarchy, originate in superficial layers (layers 2 and 3) and terminate in the middle layer (layer 4). (In the case of V1 the forward input to layer 4 originates from the THALAMUS.) Feedback connections originate from deep-layer (layer 5 or 6 or both) neurons, and the axons of these cells terminate in superficial and deep layers. The forward connections are strong and their organization has a dominant influence on the visual responses of recipient neurons (see SINGLE-NEURON RECORDING). Feedback connections, although generally more numerous, are functionally weaker and serve to modulate responses driven by the forward connections.

Local excitatory connections, intrinsic to a single visual cortical area, are also highly layer-specific and can be classified as forward, dominant and feedback, modulatory. This organization is most clear in V1, where the connections are understood in the greatest detail. As noted above, the dominant, forward input to a cortical area targets layer 4. Locally, these layer 4 neurons provide dominant, forward input via their axonal arbors to layers 2 and 3 (e.g., spiny stellates in layer 4 of V1, see figure 1). And these layer 2 and 3 neurons in turn provide the feedforward output to higher cortical areas (see above). Thus, there are two levels of local forward processing (layer 4 and layers 2 and 3). Each of these levels or layers also receives local, modulatory feedback from the axons of deep-layer cells (see figure 1). Layer 6 provides feedback to its partner, layer 4; and layer 5 to its partner, layers 2 and 3. The deep layers providing this feedback receive weaker forward input from the same sources as their partner plus from the partner itself (see figure 1). They therefore incorporate information about the input to and output from their partner and modulate the partner's activity with their feedback connections.

Visual cortical areas also interact extensively with subcortical areas, most notably the thalamus, superior colliculus, and visual claustrum. These connections are also layer-specific. Thalamic nuclei, including the lateral geniculate nucleus and pulvinar nucleus, are composed of anatomically and functionally distinct subdivisions, each of which connects to distinct visual cortical areas and layers (see VISUAL ANATOMY AND PHYSIOLOGY). Connections from visual cortex to subcortical targets originate from neurons in deep layers. Unlike corticocortical connections from deep layers, however, these do not necessarily constitute modulatory, feedback connections. They arise from populations of neurons different from those that make corticocortical or local

feedback connections and their input from superficial layers might be stronger. For example, in V1, connections from layer 5 to the superior colliculus or from layer 6 to the visual claustrum arise from neurons with longer apical dendrites ("tall" pyramids) and different intrinsic firing properties than those making corticocortical connections.

Since visual cortex offers many experimental advantages and has been more extensively studied than other cortical areas, it is understood in greater detail. It is expected, however, that many of the cell types and principles of connectivity that are revealed here will be applicable to the cerebral cortex as a whole.

See also COLUMNS AND MODULES; NEURON; OBJECT RECOGNITION, ANIMAL STUDIES; VISUAL NEGLECT; VISUAL PROCESSING STREAMS

—*Edward M. Callaway*

References

Callaway, E. M. (1998). Local circuits in primary visual cortex of the macaque monkey. *Annu. Rev. Neurosci.* 21: 47–74.

Connors, B. W., and M. J. Gutnick. (1990). Intrinsic firing patterns of diverse neocortical neurons. *Trends Neurosci.* 13: 99–104.

Felleman, D. J., and D. C. Van Essen. (1991). Distributed hierarchical processing in the primate cerebral cortex. *Cerebral Cortex* 1: 1–47.

Gilbert, C. D. (1983). Microcircuitry of the visual cortex. *Ann. Rev. Neurosci.* 6: 217–247.

Kasper, E. M., A. U. Larkman, J. Lubke, and C. Blakemore. (1994). Pyramidal neurons in layer 5 of the rat visual cortex. 1. Correlation among cell morphology, intrinsic electrophysiological properties, and axon targets. *J. Comp. Neurol.* 339: 459–474.

Katz, L. C. (1987). Local circuitry of identified projection neurons in cat visual cortex brain slices. *J. Neurosci.* 7: 1223–1249.

Lund, J. S. (1988). Anatomical organization of macaque monkey striate visual cortex. *Ann. Rev. Neurosci.* 11: 253–288.

Martin, K. A. C. (1984). Neuronal circuits in cat striate cortex. *Cereb. Cortex* 2: 241–284.

Salin, P. A., and J. Bullier. (1995). Corticocortical connections in the visual system: Structure and function. *Physiol. Rev.* 75: 107–154.

Valverde, F. (1985). The organizing principles of the primary visual cortex in the monkey. *Cereb. Cortex* 3: 207–257.

Further Readings

Anderson, J. C., R. J. Douglas, K. A. C. Martin, and J. C. Nelson. (1994). Map of the synapses formed with the dendrites of spiny stellate neurons of cat visual cortex. *J. Comp. Neurol.* 341: 25–38.

Bullier, J., J. M. Hupe, A. James, and P. Girard. (1996). Functional interactions between areas V1 and V2 in the monkey. *J. Physiol. (Paris)* 90: 217–220.

Callaway, E. M., and A. K. Wiser. (1996). Contributions of individual layer 2–5 spiny neurons to local circuits in macaque primary visual cortex. *Vis. Neurosci.* 13: 907–922.

Lund, J. S. (1987). Local circuit neurons of macaque monkey striate cortex: 1. Neurons of laminae 4C and 5A. *J. Comp. Neurol.* 257: 60–92.

Lund, J. S., M. J. Hawken, and A. J. Parker. (1988). Local circuit neurons of macaque monkey striate cortex: 2. Neurons of laminae 5B and 6. *J. Comp. Neurol.* 276: 1–29.

Lund, J. S., and T. Yoshioka. (1991). Local circuit neurons of macaque monkey striate cortex: Neurons of laminae 4B, 4A, and 3B. *J. Comp. Neurol.* 311: 234–258.

Martin, K. A. C., and D. Whitteridge. (1984). Form, function and intracortical projections of spiny neurons in the striate cortex of the cat. *J. Physiol.* 353: 463–504.

Rockland, K. S., and D. N. Pandya. (1979). Laminar origins and terminations of cortical connections of the occipital lobe in the rhesus monkey. *Brain Res.* 179: 3–20.

Stratford, K. J., K. Tarczy-Hornoch, K. A. C. Martin, N. J. Bannister, and J. J. Jack. (1996). Excitatory synaptic inputs to spiny stellate cells in cat visual cortex. *Nature* 382: 258–261.

Wiser, A. K., and E. M. Callaway. (1996). Contributions of individual layer 6 pyramidal neurons to local circuitry in macaque primary visual cortex. *J. Neurosci.* 16: 2724–2739.

Visual Information Sources

See STRUCTURE FROM VISUAL INFORMATION SOURCES

Visual Neglect

Visual neglect is a common neurological syndrome in which patients fail to acknowledge stimuli toward the side of space opposite to their unilateral lesion. This disability affects many aspects of their life. For example, after a right lesion, patients typically fail to eat the food located on the left side of their plate, or to shave or make up the left side of their face, and, in extreme cases, may no longer acknowledge the left side of their body as their own. In a common clinical test known as line cancellation, they fail to mark lines toward the left of the page (see figure 1A) despite often being able to detect isolated lines presented in their left visual field, demonstrating that they are not simply blind on that side.

This syndrome is observed primarily after unilateral lesions to the parieto-occipital junction, especially in the right hemisphere (Heilman, Watson, and Valenstein 1985; Bisiach 1996). Lesions to the right frontal cortex and to various subcortical sites can also trigger neglect-like symp-toms, although with subtle differences from parietal neglect (Heilman et al. 1985; Guariglia et al. 1993). Here we concentrate on parietal neglect, as it is the most common form, and can be related to recent data on the parietal lobe from nonhuman primates.

Two major accounts have been proposed for neglect. Some theories posit a deficit in directing attention toward contralesional events (Posner et al. 1984; Kinsbourne 1987; see ATTENTION and ATTENTION IN THE HUMAN BRAIN). For instance, right parietal patients—who suffer from left neglect—tend to have particular difficulty in detecting stimuli in the left hemifield if their attention has previously been drawn to the right side (Posner et al. 1984). By contrast, many "preattentive" aspects of vision appear to be spared on the affected side (Driver, Baylis, and Rafal 1992; McGlinchey-Berroth et al. 1996; Mattingley, Davis, and Driver 1997).

Other accounts argue that the patient's lesion simply disrupts the neuronal coding of contralesional space, at relatively high levels of representation (Bisiach and Luzzatti 1978; Bisiach, Luzzati, and Perani 1979; Rizzolatti and Berti 1990; Halligan and Marshall 1991; Karnath, Schenkel, and Fischer 1991). This perspective has drawn support from the finding that even mental IMAGERY can be impaired in some left-neglect patients (Bisiach and Luzzatti 1978), such that they fail to report what would appear on their left when retrieving from memory the view of a familiar visual scene.

The dichotomy between attentional and representational accounts has recently been challenged by several authors using neural network models in which attentional and representational functions are interwoven (Mozer and Behrmann 1990; Cohen et al. 1994; Pouget and Sejnowski 1997a). This work suggests a compromise view, whereby neglect results from damage to cortical areas that are located at the interface between sensory and motor systems, and which are responsible for both the representation of the position of objects and the selective control of spatial action, that is to say, "attention."

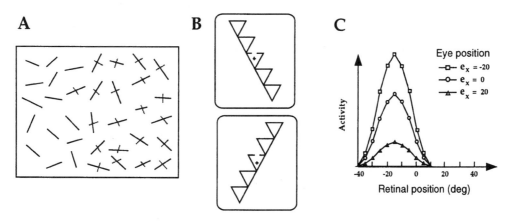

Figure 1. *A.* Left items neglected in a cancellation task. *B.* Visual displays from the Driver et al. (1994) experiment. The cross indicates the fixation point. Left-neglect patients performed better for the bottom configuration than the top one, even though the gap to be detected was at the same retinal location. This pattern is consistent with left object-centered neglect. *C.* Visual receptive field of a typical monkey parietal neuron, for three different eye positions. The retinotopic position of the receptive field is invariant across eye positions but the gain of the response changes. (Adapted from Andersen, Issick, and Siegel 1985.)

Frames of reference: In principle, "left" neglect might refer to the left of the visual field, or the left of the head, or the trunk, or even of the surrounding environment. To determine the frame of reference for hemineglect, one can test patients in various postures, so that a stimulus location changes in one frame of reference while remaining constant in the others. For instance, one might test a patient looking straight ahead vs. with the gaze deviated twenty degrees to the right, while keeping all stimuli at the same position with respect to the RETINA. If neglect were purely retinotopic, these conditions should not differ, whereas if it were head- or body-centered, performance should change accordingly. Such experiments have typically revealed that neglect affects a mixture of frames of reference concurrently, rather than just one single frame. Thus, the probability that a patient will neglect a particular visual stimulus is typically a function of its position in various egocentric frames of reference, such as eye-, head- or trunk-centered, as well as showing influences from cues in the environment, for example, as regards the gravitational upright (Bisiach, Capitani, and Porta 1985; Ladavas 1987; Ladavas, Pesce, and Provincial, 1989; Calvanio, Petrone, and Levine 1987; Farah et al. 1990; Karnath et al. 1991; Behrmann and Moscovitch 1994).

A few experiments suggest that visual neglect can also be "object-centered," that is, patients tend to neglect the left side of an object regardless of its position or orientation (Driver et al. 1994; Tipper and Behrmann 1996). For example, Driver et al. (1994) devised a situation in which left-neglect patients could detect a gap in part of a triangle when this gap was perceived to be on the right side of an object, but missed the same gap when it was seen as belonging to the left side, even though it still fell at the same location relative to the patient (figure 1B). Such results seem consistent with the existence of object-centered representations in the parietal cortex.

Many other studies claim to have found evidence for object-centered neglect (Driver and Halligan 1991; Arguin and Bub 1993; Halligan and Marshall 1994), but as pointed out by Driver et al. (1994), their results could be explained instead by what we will call *relative* neglect in strictly egocentric coordinates (see also Kinsbourne 1987; Mozer and Behrmann 1990; Desimone and Duncan 1995; and Pouget and Sejnowski 1997a for variations on this idea). When confronted with two competing objects, patients may neglect the one farther to the left even if both fall in the right hemispace egocentrically, and likewise for the subparts of a single object (Driver and Halligan 1991; Driver et al. 1992; Driver et al. 1994; Halligan and Marshall 1994). Thus, it appears that the *relative* position of objects or their subparts is just as important as their *absolute* position with respect to the patient. This phenomenon can be explained if the lesion induces a *gradient* of neglect with increasing severity in the egocentric contralesional direction (Kinsbourne 1987; Driver et al. 1994; Pouget and Sejnowski 1997a).

Neural basis: There have been several attempts to relate neglect to what is known of the response properties of parietal neurons from single-cell recordings in monkeys (Mozer and Behrmann 1990; Duhamel et al. 1992; Anderson 1996; Mozer, Halligan, and Marshall 1997; Pouget and Sejnowski 1997a; see also MODELING NEUROPSYCHOLOGICAL DEFICITS

and SPATIAL PERCEPTION). Such models generally rely on cells in the parietal cortex having retinotopic receptive fields, with each hemisphere tending to overrepresent the contralateral visual field (see, however, Duhamel et al. 1992 for a different approach). Consequently, a right lesion leads to a neuronal gradient in which the left side of the retina is less strongly represented than the right side, producing left neglect. In such models, there is no particular dividing midline such that any stimulus to the left of it is invariably neglected. Instead, neglect depends only on the *relative* position of competing stimuli, as discussed above, with objects or object parts that are farther toward the retinal left than their competitors being neglected. These models readily capture the behavior of patients in tasks such as line bisection, line cancellation, and in some of the paradigms discussed above that have revealed relative neglect.

Parietal neurons, however, do not simply respond to visual stimulation, but also integrate sensory responses with posture signals such as eye and head position. Andersen and colleagues have shown that the retinotopic receptive fields of parietal cells are *gain-modulated* by such posture signals (Andersen, Essick, and Siegel 1985; Andersen et al. 1997; see figure 1C for an example in which the visual receptive field of a cell is modulated by eye position). These response properties can be modeled as *basis functions* of the inputs, a type of function which is particularly well-suited to the computational demand of sensorimotor transformations (Pouget and Sejnowski 1997b).

A simulated unilateral lesion in such a basis-function representation produces an impairment that resembles clinical neglect, in that the deficit affects a mixture of egocentric frames of reference as found in patients (Pouget and Sejnowski 1997a). This approach can also be generalized to encompass object-centered neglect, as in the Driver et al. (1994) experiment depicted in figure 1B, by considering the perceived orientation of the object as providing a signal analogous to the posture signals integrated by the basis functions (Deneve and Pouget in press). This basis-function framework can explain why neglect may be influenced by stimulus position relative to the retina, head, body, other objects, and other parts of the same object, all at the same time, without requiring cells in the parietal cortex to have visual receptive fields explicitly defined in any single one of these frames of reference.

Neglect remains a fascinating but disabling disorder, which still poses a major challenge to rehabilitation. Its further study will hopefully lead to more effective treatments, as well as reveal more about how the brain represents space, and allows for selective spatial attention.

See also OBJECT RECOGNITION, HUMAN NEUROPSYCHOLOGY; PHANTOM LIMB; SELF; SELF-KNOWLEDGE

—*Alexandre Pouget and Jon Driver*

References and Further Readings

Anderson, B. (1996). A mathematical model of line bisection behaviour in neglect. *Brain* 119: 841–850.

Andersen, R. A., G. K. Essick, and R. M. Siegel. (1985). Encoding of spatial location by posterior parietal neurons. *Science* 230: 456–458.

Andersen, R. A., L. H. Snyder, D. C. Bradley, and J. Xing. (1997). Encoding of intention and spatial location in the posterior parietal cortex. *Ann. Rev. Neurosci.* 20: 303–330.

Arguin, M., and D. N. Bub. (1993). Evidence for an independent stimulus-centered reference frame from a case of visual hemineglect. *Cortex* 29: 349–357.

Behrmann, M., and M. Moscovitch. (1994). Object-centered neglect in patients with unilateral neglect: Effects of left-right coordinates of objects. *Journal of Cognitive Neuroscience* 6(2): 151–155.

Bisiach, E. (1996). Unilateral neglect and the structure of space representation. *Current Directions in Psychological Science* 5(2): 62–65.

Bisiach, E., E. Capitani, and E. Porta. (1985). Two basic properties of space representation in the brain: Evidence from unilateral neglect. *Journal of Neurology, Neurosurgery and Psychiatry* 48: 141–144.

Bisiach, E., and C. Luzzatti. (1978). Unilateral neglect of representational space. *Cortex* 14: 129–133.

Bisiach, E., C. Luzzatti, and D. Perani. (1979). Unilateral neglect, representational schema and consciousness. *Brain* 102: 609–618.

Calvanio, R., P. N. Petrone, and D. N. Levine. (1987). Left visual spatial neglect is both environment-centered and body-centered. *Neurology* 37: 1179–1181.

Cohen, J. D., M. J. Farah, R. D. Romero, and D. Servan-Schreiber. (1994). Mechanisms of spatial attention: The relation of macrostructure to microstructure in parietal neglect. *Journal of Cognitive Neuroscience* 6(4): 377–387.

Deneve, S., and A. Pouget. (Forthcoming). Neural basis of object-centered representations. In *Advances in Neural Information Processing Systems,* vol. 11. Cambridge, MA: MIT Press.

Desimone, R., and J. Duncan. (1995). Neural mechanisms of selective visual attention. *Ann. Rev. Neurosci.* 18: 193–222.

Driver, J., and P. W. Halligan. (1991). Can visual neglect operate in object-centered coordinates? An affirmative single case study. *Cognitive Neuropsychology* 8(6): 475–496.

Driver, J., G. C. Baylis, and R. D. Rafal. (1992). Preserved figure-ground segregation and symmetry perception in visual neglect. *Nature* 360: 73–75.

Driver, J., G. C. Baylis, S. J. Goodrich, and R. D. Rafal. (1994). Axis-based neglect of visual shapes. *Neuropsychologia* 32(11): 1353–1365.

Duhamel, J. R., M. E. Goldberg, E. J. Fitzgibbon, A. Sirigu, and J. Grafman. (1992). Saccadic dysmetria in a patient with a right frontoparietal lesion. The importance of corollary discharge for accurate spatial behaviour. *Brain* 115: 1387–1402.

Farah, M. J., J. L. Brunn, A. B. Wong, M. A. Wallace, and P. A. Carpenter. (1990). Frames of reference for allocating attention to space: Evidence from the neglect syndrome. *Neuropsychologia* 28(4): 335–347.

Guariglia, C., A. Padovani, P. Pantano, and L. Pizzamiglio. (1993). Unilateral neglect restricted to visual imagery. *Nature* 364: 235–237.

Halligan, P. W., and J. C. Marshall. (1991). Spatial compression in visual neglect: A case study. *Cortex* 27: 623–629.

Halligan, P. W., and J. C. Marshall. (1994). Figural perception and parsing in visuospatial neglect. *Neuroreport* 5: 537–539.

Heilman, K. M., R. T. Watson, and E. Valenstein. (1985). Neglect and related disorders. In K. M. Heilman and E. Valenstein, Eds., *Clinical Neuropsychology.* New York: Oxford University Press, pp. 243–294.

Karnath, H. O., P. Schenkel, and B. Fischer. (1991). Trunk orientation as the determining factor of the "contralateral" deficit in the neglect syndrome and as the physical anchor of the internal representation of body orientation in space. *Brain* 114: 1997–2014.

Kinsbourne, M. (1987). Mechanisms of unilateral neglect. In M. Jeannerod, Ed., *Neurophysiological and Neuropsychological Aspects of Spatial Neglect.* Amsterdam: North-Holland, pp. 69–86.

Ladavas, E. (1987). Is the hemispatial deficit produced by right parietal lobe damage associated with retinal or gravitational coordinates? *Brain* 110: 167–180.

Ladavas, E., M. D. Pesce, and L. Provinciali. (1989). Unilateral attention deficits and hemispheric asymmetries in the control of visual attention. *Neuropsychologia* 27(3): 353–366.

Mattingley, J. B., G. Davis, and J. Driver. (1997). Preattentive filling-in of visual surfaces in parietal extinction. *Science* 275: 671–674.

McGlinchey-Berroth, R, W. P. Milberg, M. Verfaellie, L. Grande, M. D'Esposito, and M. Alexandre. (1996). Semantic processing and orthographic specificity in hemispatial neglect. *Journal of Cognitive Neuroscience* 8: 291–304.

Mozer, M. C., and M. Behrmann. (1990). On the interaction of selective attention and lexical knowledge: A connectionist account of neglect dyslexia. *Journal of Cognitive Neuroscience* 2(2): 96–123.

Mozer, M. C., P. W. Halligan, and J. C. Marshall. (1997). The end of the line for a brain-damaged model of hemispatial neglect. *Journal of Cognitive Neuroscience* 9(2): 171–190.

Posner, M. I., J. A. Walker, F. J. Friedrich, and R. D. Rafal. (1984). Effects of parietal injury on covert orienting of visual attention. *Journal of Neuroscience* 4: 1863–1877.

Pouget, A., and T. J. Sejnowski. (1997a). Lesion in a basis function model of spatial representations: Comparison with hemineglect. In P. Thier and H. O. Karnath, Eds., *Parietal Lobe Contribution in Orientation in 3D Space.* Springer.

Pouget, A., and T. J. Sejnowski. (1997b). Spatial transformations in the parietal cortex using basis functions. *Journal of Cognitive Neuroscience* 9(2): 222–237.

Rizzolatti, G., and A. Berti. (1990). Neglect as a neural representation deficit. *Revue Neurologique* 146(10): 626–634.

Tipper, S. P., and M. Behrmann. (1996). Object-centered not scene-based visual neglect. *Journal of Experimental Psychology, Human Perception and Performance* 22(5): 1261–1278.

Visual Object Recognition, AI

Visual object recognition, a subdiscipline of machine vision, addresses the problem of finding and identifying objects in images. Research in this area primarily focuses on techniques that use models of specific objects, based on properties such as shape and appearance. Such techniques are referred to as *model-based recognition* methods, because of the strong reliance on prior models of specific objects. In contrast, human visual recognition is characterized by an ability to recognize novel objects for which the observer has no specific prior model. Such generic recognition involves the ability to perform CATEGORIZATION on the basis of abstract reasoning about objects, such as inferring their form from how they function. While there has been some study of generic object recognition in MACHINE VISION, the primary focus has been on model-based recognition.

Most approaches to model-based object recognition involve comparing an unknown image against stored object models, in order to determine whether any of the models are present in the image. Many techniques perform both recognition and localization, both identifying what objects are present in the image and recovering their locations in the image or in the world. Object recognition is often phrased as a search problem, involving several kinds of search, including search over possible locations of the object in the image, search over possible viewpoints of the observer with respect to the object, and search over possible object models. Not all recognition tasks involve all of these kinds of search. For example, recognizing faces in a database of mug shots need not involve search over possible viewpoints because the pictures are all frontal views.

A number of factors contribute to the difficulty of OBJECT RECOGNITION tasks. One factor is the complexity of the scene. This includes the number of objects in the image, the presence of objects that are touching and partly occluding one another, backgrounds that are highly textured or cluttered, and poor lighting conditions. Another factor is the generality of the object models. Objects that are composed of rigidly connected subparts, such as a pair of scissors, are harder to recognize than rigid objects such as a car. Nonrigid objects, such as a cat, are even more difficult to recognize. A third factor is the number of object models that a recognition system must consider. Many systems can only handle a small number of objects, in effect considering each model separately. A fourth factor is the complexity of the viewing transformation that maps the model coordinate frame to the image coordinate frame. For example, if an object can be viewed from an arbitrary 3-D position, then the different views of the object may look very different.

There is a trade-off in current approaches to object recognition: either it is possible to recognize objects from a small set of models appearing in complex scenes (with clutter and unknown viewpoints), or it is possible to recognize objects from a large set of models appearing in simple scenes (with a uniform background and known viewpoint). The remainder of this article will provide a brief overview of some of the major approaches used in object recognition. First, we consider search-based techniques, which operate by comparing local features of the model and image. These kinds of techniques are generally limited to a small set of object models, but handle complex images. Then we consider indexing approaches, which operate by computing a key which is used as an index into a large table or database of models. These techniques are generally limited to simple scenes.

Feature-based approaches to object recognition generally operate by recovering a correspondence between local attributes, or features, of an image and an object model. The features are usually geometrical, and are often based on detecting intensity edges in the image (places where there is a large change in image brightness). Brightness changes often correspond to the boundaries of objects or to surface markings on the objects. Local geometrical features can be simple, like corners, or involve more complex fitting of geometrical primitives, such as quadratic curves. The 2-D geometrical descriptions extracted from an image are compared with geometrical models, which may be either 2-D or 3-D.

Three major classes of feature-matching recognition methods can be identified, based on how the search for possible matches between model and image features is performed: (1) *correspondence methods* consider the space of possible corresponding features; (2) *transformation space methods* consider the space of possible transformations mapping the model to the image; and (3) *hypothesize and test* methods consider k-tuples of model and data features. A more detailed treatment of geometrical search methods can be found in Grimson (1990). In addition there are geometrical matching methods which make use of more global shape descriptors, such as entire silhouettes of objects (e.g., Kriegman and Ponce 1990).

Indexing-based approaches to object recognition are based on computing numerical descriptors of an image or portion of an image. These descriptors are then used as keys to index (or hash) into a table of object models. The most effective such methods are based on storing many 2-D views of each object. Such approaches are generally referred to as view-based because they explicitly store images or keys corresponding to each viewpoint from which an object could be seen. Another kind of indexing-based approach to recognition is based on computing *invariant descriptions* of objects that do not change as the viewpoint changes. The invariant properties of objects are generally geometrical. More information about invariant-based recognition methods can be found in Mundy and Zisserman (1992).

The most successful view-based approaches to object recognition are based on subspace techniques, which use principal components (or eigenvector) analysis to produce keys that form a concise description of a given set of images (e.g., Murase and Nayar, 1995). The main advantage of such methods is that they are useful for tasks in which there is a large database of objects to be searched. The main disadvantage is that in general they do not work well with occlusion or with complex scenes and cluttered backgrounds, because the measure of similarity is sensitive to such variation. A different view-based approach is taken in Huttenlocher, Klanderman, and Rucklidge (1993), which is based on computing distances between point sets using a measure of image similarity based on the Hausdorff distance. This similarity measure is designed to allow for partial occlusion and the presence of background clutter.

See also COMPUTATIONAL VISION; FACE RECOGNITION; FEATURE DETECTORS; HIGH-LEVEL VISION; STRUCTURE FROM VISUAL INFORMATION SOURCES; VISION AND LEARNING

—*Daniel P. Huttenlocher*

References

Grimson, W. E. L. (1990). *Object Recognition by Computer: The Role of Geometric Constraints.* Cambridge, MA: MIT Press.

Huttenlocher, D. P., G. A. Klanderman, and W. J. Rucklidge. (1993). Comparing images using the Hausdorff distance. *IEEE Transactions on Pattern Analysis and Machine Intelligence* 15(9): 850–863.

Kriegman, D. J., and J. Ponce. (1990). On recognizing and positioning curved 3-D objects from image contours. *IEEE Transactions on Pattern Analysis and Machine Intelligence* 12: 1127–1137.

Mundy, J. L., and A. Zisserman. (1992). *Geometric Invariants in Computer Vision.* Cambridge, MA: MIT Press.

Murase, H., and S. K. Nayar. (1995). Visual learning and recognition of 3-D objects from appearance. *International Journal of Computer Vision* 14: 5–24.

Visual Processing Streams

Vision, more than any other sense, provides us with information about the world beyond our bodies. The importance of vision in our daily lives, and the lives of our primate cousins, is reflected in the fact that we have large and highly mobile eyes. But our reliance on vision is also evident in the large amount of brain devoted to visual processing. It has been estimated, for example, that more than half of the CEREBRAL CORTEX in the macaque monkey is involved in processing visual signals.

Although the RETINA projects to a number of different nuclei in the primate brain, one of the most prominent projections is to the dorsal part of the lateral geniculate nucleus (LGNd), a multilayered structure in the THALAMUS. New projections arise from the LGNd and project in turn to an area in the occipital lobe of the cerebral cortex known variously as striate cortex, area 17, primary visual cortex, or V1. Beyond V1, visual information is conveyed to a bewildering number of extrastriate areas (for review, see Zeki 1993). Despite the complexity of the interconnections between these different areas, two broad "streams" of projections from V1 have been identified in the macaque monkey brain: a ventral stream projecting eventually to the inferotemporal cortex and a dorsal stream projecting to the posterior parietal cortex (Ungerleider and Mishkin 1982). Of course, these regions also receive differential inputs from a number of other subcortical visual structures, such as the superior colliculus (via the thalamus). Although some caution must be exercised in generalizing from monkey to human, it seems likely that the visual projections from primary VISUAL CORTEX to the temporal and parietal lobes in the human brain may involve a separation into ventral and dorsal streams similar to that seen in the monkey.

In 1982, Ungerleider and Mishkin argued that the two streams of visual processing play different but complementary roles in the processing of incoming visual information. According to their original account, the ventral stream plays a critical role in the identification and recognition of objects, while the dorsal stream mediates the localization of those same objects. Some have referred to this distinction in visual processing as one between object vision and spatial vision—"what" vs. "where." Support for this idea came from work with monkeys. Lesions of inferotemporal cortex in monkeys produced deficits in their ability to discriminate between objects on the basis of their visual features, but did not affect their performance on a spatially demanding "landmark" task. Conversely, lesions of the posterior parietal cortex produced deficits in performance on the landmark task but did not affect object discrimination learning. Although the evidence for the original Ungerleider and Mishkin proposal initially seemed quite compelling, recent findings from a broad range of studies in both humans and monkeys has forced a reinterpretation of the division of labor between the two streams (for review, see Jeannerod 1997; Milner and Goodale 1995).

Some of the most telling evidence against a simple "what" vs. "where" distinction has come from studies with neurologically damaged patients. It has been known for a long time that patients with damage to the human homologue of the dorsal stream have difficulty reaching in the correct direction to objects placed in different positions in the visual field contralateral to their lesion (even though they have no difficulty reaching out and grasping different parts of their own body indicated by the experimenter). Although this deficit in visually guided behavior, know clinically as optic ataxia, has often been interpreted as a failure of spatial vision, two other sets of observations in these patients suggest a rather different interpretation. First, patients with damage to this region of cortex often show an inability to rotate their hand or open their fingers properly to grasp an object placed in front of them, even when it is always placed in the same location. Second, these same patients are able to describe the orientation, size, shape, and even the relative spatial location of the very objects they are unable to grasp correctly (Perenin and Vighetto 1988). Clearly, this pattern of deficits and spared abilities cannot be explained by appealing to a general deficit in SPATIAL PERCEPTION.

Other patients, in whom the brain damage appears to involve ventral rather than dorsal stream structures, show the complementary pattern of deficits and spared visual abilities. Such patients have great difficulty recognizing common objects on the basis of their visual appearance (visual agnosia), but have no problem grasping objects placed in front of them or moving through the world without bumping into things. Consider, for example, patient D.F., a young woman who suffered damage to her ventral stream pathways as a result of anoxia from carbon monoxide poisoning. Even though D.F. is unable to indicate the size, shape, and orientation of an object, either verbally or manually, she shows normal preshaping and rotation of her hand when reaching out to grasp it (Goodale et al. 1991). Appealing to a general deficit in "object vision" does not help us to understand her problem. In her case, she is able to use visual information about the location, size, shape, and orientation of objects to control her grasping movements (and other visually guided movements) despite the fact that she is unable to perceive those same object features.

Goodale and Milner (1992) have suggested that one way to understand what is happening in these patients is to think about the dorsal stream not as a system for spatial vision per se, but rather as a system for the visual control of skilled action. To pick up a coffee cup, for example, not only must we have information about the spatial location of the cup with respect to our hand, but we must also have information about its size, shape, and orientation so that we can pick it up efficiently. The evidence from patients, and from studies with subjects with normal vision, suggests that the visual processing involved in the control of this kind of skilled behavior may take place quite independently of the visual processing mediating what we normally think of as visual perception. Indeed, Goodale and Milner have suggested that our visual experience of the world and the objects within it depends on visual processing in the ventral stream. In short, both streams process information about the orientation, size, and shape of objects, and about their spatial relations; both streams are also subject to modulation by ATTENTION. Each stream, however, deals with the incoming visual information in different ways. The ventral stream transforms visual information into perceptual representations that embody the enduring characteristics of objects and their spatial relations with each other. The visual transformations carried out in the dorsal stream, which utilize moment-to-moment information about the disposition of objects within egocentric frames of reference, mediate the control of goal-directed acts. Such a division of labor not only accounts for the behavioral dissociations observed in neurological patients with damage to different regions of the cerebral cortex but it is also supported by a wealth of anatomical, electrophysiological, and behavioral studies in the monkey (for review, see Milner and Goodale 1995).

Adaptive goal-directed behavior in humans and other primates depends on the integrated function of both these streams of visual processing. The execution of a goal-directed action might depend on dedicated control systems in the dorsal stream, but the selection of appropriate goal objects and the action to be performed depends on the perceptual machinery of the ventral stream. One of the important questions that remains to be answered is how the two streams interact both with each other and with other brain regions in the production of purposive behavior.

See also HIGH-LEVEL VISION; MID-LEVEL VISION; OBJECT RECOGNITION, ANIMAL STUDIES; OBJECT RECOGNITION, HUMAN NEUROPSYCHOLOGY; STRUCTURE FROM VISUAL INFORMATION SOURCES; TOP-DOWN PROCESSING IN VISION

—*Melvyn A. Goodale*

References

Goodale, M. A., and A. D. Milner. (1992). Separate visual pathways for perception and action. *Trends in Neurosciences* 15: 20–25.

Goodale, M. A., A. D. Milner, L. S. Jakobson, and D. P. Carey. (1991). A neurological dissociation between perceiving objects and grasping them. *Nature* 349: 154–156.

Jeannerod, M. (1997). *The Cognitive Neuroscience of Action.* Oxford: Blackwell.

Milner, A. D., and M. A. Goodale. (1995). *The Visual Brain in Action.* Oxford: Oxford University Press.

Perenin, M. -T., and A. Vighetto. (1988). Optic ataxia: A specific disruption in visuomotor mechanisms. 1. Different aspects of the deficit in reaching for objects. *Brain* 111: 643–674.

Ungerleider, L. G., and M. Mishkin. (1982). Two cortical visual systems. In D. J. Ingle, M. A. Goodale, and R. J. W. Mansfield, Eds., *Analysis of Visual Behavior.* Cambridge, MA: MIT Press, pp. 549–586.

Zeki, S. (1993). *A Vision of the Brain.* Oxford: Blackwell.

Further Readings

Andersen, R. A. (1987). Inferior parietal lobule function in spatial perception and visuomotor integration. In V. B. Mountcastle, F. Plum, and S. R. Geiger, Eds., *Handbook of Physiology,* sec. 1: *The Nervous System,* vol. 5: *Higher Functions of the Brain,* part 2. Bethesda, MD: American Physiological Association, pp. 483–518.

Baizer, J. S., R. Desimone, and L. G. Ungerleider. (1993). Comparison of subcortical connections of inferior temporal and posterior parietal cortex in monkeys. *Visual Neuroscience* 10: 59–72.

Duhamel, J. -R., C. L. Colby, and M. E. Goldberg. (1992). The updating of the representation of visual space in parietal cortex by intended eye movements. *Science* 255: 90–92.

Felleman, D. J., and D. C. Van Essen. (1991). Distributed hierarchical processing in the primate cerebral cortex. *Cerebral Cortex* 1: 1–47.

Ferrera, V. P., T. A. Nealey, and J. H. R. Maunsell. (1992). Mixed parvocellular and magnocellular geniculate signals in visual area V4. *Nature* 358: 756–758.

Fujita, I., K. Tanaka, M. Ito, and K. Cheng. (1992). Columns for visual features of objects in monkey inferotemporal cortex. *Nature* 343: 343–346.

Goodale, M. A. (1993). Visual pathways supporting perception and action in the primate cerebral cortex. *Current Opinion in Neurobiology* 3: 578–585.

Goodale, M. A., L. S. Jakobson, and J. M. Keillor. (1994). Differences in the visual control of pantomimed and natural grasping movements. *Neuropsychologia* 32: 1159–1178.

Goodale, M. A., J. P. Meenan, H. H. Bülthoff, D. A. Nicolle, K. S. Murphy, and C. I. Racicot. (1994). Separate neural pathways for the visual analysis of object shape in perception and prehension. *Current Biology* 4: 604–610.

Gross, C. G. (1973). Visual functions of inferotemporal cortex. In R. Jung, Ed., *Handbook of Sensory Physiology,* vol. 7, part 3B. Berlin: Springer, pp. 451–482.

Gross, C. G. (1991). Contribution of striate cortex and the superior colliculus to visual function in area MT, the superior temporal polysensory area and inferior temporal cortex. *Neuropsychologia* 29: 497–515.

Hyvärinen, J., and A. Poranen. (1974). Function of the parietal associative area 7 as revealed from cellular discharges in alert monkeys. *Brain* 97: 673–692.

Jakobson, L. S., Y. M. Archibald, D. P. Carey, and M. A. Goodale. (1991). A kinematic analysis of reaching and grasping movements in a patient recovering from optic ataxia. *Neuropsychologia* 29: 803–809.

Jeannerod, M. (1988). *The Neural and Behavioural Organization of Goal-Directed Movements.* Oxford: Oxford University Press.

Jeannerod M., M. A. Arbib, G. Rizzolatti, and H. Sakata. (1995). Grasping objects: The cortical mechanisms of visuomotor transformation. *Trends in Neurosciences* 18: 314–320.

Livingstone, M. S., and D. H. Hubel. (1988). Segregation of form, color, movement, and depth: Anatomy, physiology, and perception. *Science* 240: 740–749.

Milner, A. D., D. I. Perrett, R. S. Johnston, P. J. Benson, T. R. Jordan, D. W. Heeley, D. Bettucci, F. Mortara, R. Mutani, E. Terazzi, and D. L. W. Davidson. (1991). Perception and action in visual form agnosia. *Brain* 114: 405–428.

Mountcastle, V. B., J. C. Lynch, A. Georgopoulos, H. Sakata, and C. Acuna. (1975). Posterior parietal association cortex of the monkey: Command functions for operations within extrapersonal space. *Journal of Neurophysiology* 38: 871–908.

Mountcastle, V. B., B. C. Motter, M. A. Steinmetz, and C. J. Duffy. (1984). Looking and seeing: The visual functions of the parietal lobe. In G. Edelman, W. E. Gall, and W. M. Cowan, Eds., *Dynamic Aspects of Neocortical Function.* New York: Wiley, pp. 159–193.

Perrett, D. I., J. K. Hietanen, M. W. Oram, and P. J. Benson. (1992). Organisation and functions of cells responsive to faces in the temporal cortex. *Philosophical Transactions of the Royal Society of London. Series B, Biological Sciences* 335: 23–30.

Sakata, H., M. Taira, S. Mine, and A. Murata. (1992). Hand-movement–related neurons of the posterior parietal cortex of the monkey: Their role in visual guidance of hand movements. In R. Caminiti, P. B. Johnson, and Y. Burnod, Eds., *Control of Arm Movement in Space: Neurophysiological and Computational Approaches.* Berlin: Springer, pp. 185–198.

Snyder, L. H., A. P. Batista, and R. A. Andersen. (1997). Coding of intention in the posterior parietal cortex. *Nature* 386: 167–170.

Visual Word Recognition

The goal of research on visual word recognition is to understand the kinds of capacities that underlie the rapid and almost effortless comprehension of words in READING, how these capacities are acquired, and the impairments that occur developmentally and following brain injury (DYSLEXIA). Visual word recognition has also provided a domain in which to explore broader theoretical issues concerning knowledge representation, learning, perception, and memory; for example, it played a significant role in the development of both modular (MODULARITY OF MIND) and connectionist (COGNITIVE MODELING, CONNECTIONIST) approaches to cognition.

Studies of EYE MOVEMENTS in reading indicate that most words are fixated once for durations ranging from 50 to 250 ms. Short function words are sometimes skipped and longer words may be fixated more than once. Word recognition speeds vary depending on reading skill, the type of text, and how carefully it is being read; large increases in reading speed can only be achieved with significant loss of comprehension, as in skimming. The main bottleneck is perceptual: the perceptual span is approximately four letters to the left of fixation and fifteen to the right when reading from left-to-right (it is asymmetrical to the left in reading languages such as Hebrew). Letter identities can be determined only over a smaller range, approximately five to six letters; further from fixation only letter shape and length are perceived (Pollatsek and Rayner 1990).

A long-standing issue for reading researchers and educators is whether words are recognized on a visual basis or by first computing a phonological representation (see PHONOLOGY). Using visual information might seem to be more efficient because it involves a direct mapping from spelling to meaning; using phonology (translating from orthography to phonology to meaning) involves an extra step. However, a compelling body of research suggests that skilled readers compute phonological information as part of the recognition process (e.g., Van Orden 1987). Studies of learning to read have also highlighted the important role of phonological information (Wagner and Torgesen 1987). The quality of prereading children's knowledge of the structure of spoken language is a good predictor of later reading skill; children who are good readers are better able to translate from spelling to sound; and many dyslexic persons exhibit minor deviations in their representation of spoken language that disrupt reading acquisition (e.g., Bradley and Bryant 1983). Despite this evidence, reading education in most English-speaking countries attempts to discourage children from using phonological information on the mistaken view that it discourages reading efficiency. There is also strong evidence that learning to read an orthography has a reciprocal impact on phonological representation (Morais et al. 1986).

One barrier to using phonology in reading English and many other writing systems would seem to be the quasi-regular (Seidenberg and McClelland 1989) character of orthographic-phonological correspondences: most words can be pronounced "by rule" (e.g., *gave, mint*) but there are many exceptions that deviate from the rules in differing degrees (e.g., *have, pint*). This observation led to the development of "dual-route" models in which there are separate mechanisms for reading rule-governed words and exceptions (Coltheart 1978). Connectionist models provide an alternative approach in which a single network consisting of distributed representations of spelling, sound, and meaning is used for all words. Such networks can encode both "rule-governed" forms and "exceptions," while capturing the overlap between them. Whereas the older models involved parallel, independent visual and phonological recognition pathways, connectionist models permit continuous pooling of information from both sources until a word's meaning has been computed.

Research on WRITING SYSTEMS organized along different principles (see papers in Frost and Katz 1992) suggests that there may be more commonalities in how they are read than the differences among them might otherwise suggest. One major difference among writing systems is in how transparently they represent phonological information. For example, whereas the pronunciations of orthographic patterns in Finnish and Serbo-Croatian are highly predictable, many English words are irregularly pronounced, and the nonalphabetic Chinese writing system provides only partial cues to pronunciation. These differences have often led to suggestions that one or another writing system is optimal for learning to read. Writing systems exhibit trade-offs among other design features, however, that tend to level the playing field (Seidenberg 1992). For example, English has many irregularly pronounced words but they tend to be very short and to cluster among the highest-frequency words in the language; hence they are likely to be easy to learn and process. Serbo-Croatian is more transparent at the level of letters and phonemes but there are few monosyllabic words and there is also a complex system governing syllabic stress. The pronunciations of words in Hebrew can be reliably predicted from their spellings except that the vowels are normally omitted. Studies of reading acquisition in different writing systems do not suggest large differences in the average rate at which children learn to read.

A major unresolved issue concerns the role of subword units such as syllables and morphemes (see MORPHOLOGY) in word recognition. Does reading a word such as *farmer* involve parsing it into the morphemes [farm] + [er] or merely using orthographic and phonological information? Although several studies have provided evidence for lexical decomposition, the extent to which it occurs in reading is not known. Any decomposition scheme runs up against what to do with cases like *corner* or *display,* which appear to be morphologically complex but are not. Connectionist models have also begun to provide an alternative account in which morphological structure reflects an emergent, inter-level representation mediating correlations among orthography, phonology, SEMANTICS, and aspects of grammar.

Other research has addressed how readers determine the meanings of words and integrate them with the contexts in which they occur. Words in texts tend not to be very predictable, which makes using context to guess them an inefficient strategy. The computation of a word's meaning is nonetheless constrained by context, as is clearly the case for ambiguous words such as *rose* and *plane* but also relatively unambiguous words such as *cat*. For example, in a sentence about petting, the word *cat* may activate the feature <fur>; in a context about getting scratched, *cat* will activate <claws> (Merrill, Sperber, and MacCauley 1981).

Impairments in word recognition are characteristic of developmental dyslexia. Dyslexia is often associated with phonological impairments that interfere with learning the relationship between the written and spoken forms of language (Liberman and Shankweiler 1985). In other cases, dyslexic persons have normal phonology but are developmentally delayed: they read like much younger children. This delay may reflect impoverished experience or other deficits in perception or learning (Manis et al. 1996).

Dyslexia also occurs as a consequence of neuropathologic discorders such as Alzheimer's disease or herpes encephalitis. Three major subtypes have been identified: phonological dyslexia, in which the main impairment is in pronouncing novel letter strings such as *nust;* surface dyslexia, in which the main impairment is in reading irregularly pronounced words such as *pint;* and deep dyslexia, in which the patient makes semantic paraphasias such as pronouncing *sympathy* "orchestra" (Shallice 1988). Current research focuses on using computational models of normal word recognition to explain how these patterns of impairment could arise (see MODELING NEUROPSYCHOLOGICAL DEFICITS). For example, connectionist models of normal performance can be "lesioned" to create the reading impairments seen in several types of patients (Plaut et al. 1996). A growing body of neuroimaging evidence is beginning to clarify how the representations and processes specified in these models are realized in the brain.

See also CONNECTIONIST APPROACHES TO LANGUAGE; MAGNETIC RESONANCE IMAGING; POSITRON EMISSION TOMOGRAPHY; SPOKEN WORD RECOGNITION

—*Mark S. Seidenberg*

References

Bradley, L., and P. E. Bryant. (1983). Categorizing sounds and learning to read—a causal connection. *Nature* 301: 419–421.

Coltheart, M. (1978). Lexical access in simple reading tasks. In G. Underwood, Ed., *Strategies of Information Processing.* London: Academic Press.

Coltheart, M., B. Curtis, P. Atkins, and M. Haller. (1993). Models of reading aloud: Dual-route and parallel distributed processing approaches. *Psychological Review* 100: 589–608.

Frost, R., and L. Katz, Eds. (1992). *Orthography, Phonology, Morphology, and Meaning.* Amsterdam: North-Holland.

Liberman, I. Y., and D. Shankweiler. (1985). Phonology and the problem of learning to read and write. *Remedial and Special Education* 6: 8–17.

Manis, F., M. S. Seidenberg, L. Doi, C. McBride-Chang, and A. Petersen. (1996). On the basis of two subtypes of developmental dyslexia. *Cognition* 58: 157–195.

Merrill, E. C., R. D. Sperber, and C. McCauley. (1981). Differences in semantic encoding as a function of reading comprehension skill. *Memory and Cognition* 9: 618–624.

Morais, J., P. Bertelson, L. Cary, and J. Alegria. (1986). Literacy training and speech segmentation. *Cognition* 24: 45–64.

Plaut, D. C., J. L. McClelland, M. S. Seidenberg, and K. E. Patterson. (1996). Understanding normal and impaired word reading: Computational principles in quasiregular domains. *Psychological Review* 103: 56–115.

Pollatsek, S., and K. Rayner. (1990). Eye movements in reading: A tutorial review. In D. Balota, F. D'arcais, and K. Rayner, Eds., *Comprehension Processes in Reading.* Hillsdale, NJ: Erlbaum.

Seidenberg, M. S. (1992). Beyond orthographic depth: Equitable division of labor. In R. Frost and L. Katz, Eds., *Orthography, Phonology, Morphology, and Meaning.* Springer.

Seidenberg, M. S., and J. L. McClelland. (1989). A distributed, developmental model of visual word recognition and naming. *Psychological Review* 96: 523–568.

Shallice, T. (1988). *From Neuropsychology to Mental Structure.* Cambridge: Cambridge University Press.

Van Orden, G. C. (1987). A ROWS is a ROSE: Spelling, sound, and reading. *Memory and Cognition* 15: 181–198.

Wagner, R. K., and J. K. Torgesen. (1987). The nature of phonological processing and its causal role in the acquisition of reading skills. *Psychological Bulletin* 101: 192–212.

Further Readings

Coltheart, M., B. Curtis, P. Atkins, and M. Haller. (1993). Models of reading aloud: Dual-route and parallel distributed processing approaches. *Psychological Review* 100: 589–608.

Gough, P., L. Ehri, and R. Treiman, Eds. (1992). *Reading Acquisition.* Hillsdale, NJ: Erlbaum.

Harm, M., and M. S. Seidenberg. (Forthcoming). Phonology, reading acquisition, and dyslexia: Insights from connectionist models. *Psychological Review.*

Plaut, D. C., and T. Shallice. (1993). Deep dyslexia: A case study of connectionist neuropsychology. *Cognitive Neuropsychology* 10: 377–500.

Seidenberg, M. S. (1995). Visual word recognition: An overview. In J. L. Miller, and P. D. Eimas, Eds., *Speech, Language, and Communication.* San Diego: Academic Press.

Van Orden, G. C., B. F. Pennington, and G. O. Stone. (1990). Word identification in reading and the promise of a subsymbolic psycholinguistics. *Psychological Review* 97: 488–522.

von Neumann, John

John von Neumann was born in Hungary in 1903 and died in the United States in 1957. He was without doubt one of the great intellects of the century, and one of its most distinguished mathematicians. At the time of his death he was a member of the Institute for Advanced Study, at Princeton, New Jersey.

Von Neumann's scientific interests were very broad, ranging through mathematical logic, automata theory and computer science, pure mathematics—analysis, algebra and geometry, applied mathematics—hydrodynamics, meteorology, astrophysics, numerical computation, game theory, quantum and statistical mechanics, and finally to brain mechanisms and information processing. In addition von Neumann was heavily involved in the Manhattan Project both at the University of Chicago and at Los Alamos. After World War II he became a member of the Atomic Energy Commission, and of course he was a key figure in the early U.S. development of general purpose digital computers.

So far as the cognitive sciences are concerned, von Neumann's main contributions were somewhat indirect. Together with Oscar Morgenstern he developed a mathematical model for GAME THEORY that has many implications for human cognitive behavior. He also published two papers and one short monograph on AUTOMATA theory and related topics.

The first paper, published in the 1951 proceedings of the Hixon Symposium, was entitled "The General and Logical Theory of Automata." In it von Neumann introduced what are now known as cellular automata, and discussed in some detail the problem of designing a self-reproducing automaton. In some ways this is a remarkable paper in that it seems to anticipate the mechanism by which information is transmitted from DNA via messenger RNA to the ribosomal machinery underlying protein synthesis in all pro- and eukaryotes. Of more relevance for cognitive science was von Neumann's analysis of the logic of self-reproduction, which he showed to be closely related to Gödel's work on metamathematics and logic (see GÖDEL'S THEOREMS and SELF-ORGANIZING SYSTEMS). His starting point was McCULLOCH and PITTS's ground-breaking work on the mathematical representation of neurons and neural nets.

The McCulloch-Pitts neuron is an extremely simplified representation of the properties of real neurons. It was introduced in 1943, and was based simply on the existence of a threshold for the activation of a neuron. Let $u_i(t)$ denote the state of the ith neuron at time t. Suppose $u_i = 1$ if the neuron is active, 0 otherwise. Let $\varnothing[v]$ be the Heaviside step function, $= 1$ if $v \geq 0$, 0 if $v < 0$. Let time be measured in quantal units Δt, so that $u(t + \Delta t) = u(n\Delta t + \Delta t) = u(n + 1)$. Then the activation of a McCulloch-Pitts neuron can be expressed by the equation:

$$u_i(n + 1) = \varnothing[\Sigma_j w_{ij} u_j(n) - v_{TH}]$$

where w_{ij} is the strength or "weight" of the $(j \to i)$th connection, and where v_{TH} is the voltage threshold. Evidently activation occurs iff the total excitation $v = S_j w_{ij} u_j(n) - v_{TH}$ reaches or exceeds 0.

What McCulloch and Pitts discovered was that nets comprising their simplified neural units could represent the logical functions AND, OR, NOT and the quantifiers $\forall$ and $\exists$. These elements are sufficient to express most logical and mathematical concepts and formulas. Thus, in von Neumann's words, "anything that you can describe in words can also be done with the neuron method." However von Neumann also cautioned that "it does not follow that there is not a considerable problem left just in saying what you think is to be described." He conjectured that there exists a certain level of *complexity* associated with an automaton, below which its

description and embodiment in terms of McCulloch-Pitts nets is simpler than the original automaton, and above which it is more complicated. He suggested, for example, that "it is absolutely not clear a priori that there is any simpler description of what constitutes a visual analogy than a description of the visual brain." The implications of this work for an understanding of the nature of human perception, language, and cognition have never been analyzed in any detail.

In his second paper, "Probabilistic Logics and the Synthesis of Reliable Organisms from Unreliable Components," published in 1956 (but based on notes taken at a lecture von Neumann gave at CalTech in 1952), von Neumann took up another problem raised by McCulloch, of how to build *fault tolerant* automata.

Von Neumann solved the reliability problem in two different ways. His first solution was to make use of the error-correcting properties of majority logic elements. Such an element executes the logical function m(a,b,c) = (a AND b) OR (b AND c) OR (c AND a). The procedure is to triplicate each logical function to be executed, that is, execute each logical function three times in parallel, and then feed the outputs through majority logic elements.

Von Neumann's second solution to the reliability problem was to multiplex, that is, use N McCulloch-Pitts circuits to do the job of one. In such nets one bit of information (the choice between "1" and "0") is signaled not by the activation of one neuron, but instead by the synchronous activation of many neurons. Let Δ be a number between 0 and 1. Then "1" is signaled if ξ, the fraction of activated neurons involved in any job, exceeds Δ; otherwise "0" is signaled. Evidently a multiplexed net will function reliably only if is close to either 0 or 1. Von Neumann achieved this as follows. Consider nets made up entirely of NAND logic functions, as shown in figure 2.

Von Neumann subsequently proved that if circuits are built from such elements, then for N large, $\Delta = 0.07$ and the probability of an element malfunctioning, $\varepsilon < 0.0107$, the probability of circuit malfunction can be made to decrease with increasing N. With $\varepsilon = 0.005$, von Neumann showed that for logical computations of large depth the method of multiplexing is superior to majority logic decoding.

McCulloch was aware of the fact that the central nervous system (CNS) seems to function reliably in many cases, even in the presence of brain damage, or of fluctuations in baseline activity. It was therefore natural to look at how neural networks could be designed to achieve such performance.

Figure 1. McCulloch-Pitts neurons. Each unit is activated iff its total excitation reaches or exceeds 0. For example, the first unit is activated iff both the units x and y are activated, for only then does the total excitation, $(+1)x + (+1)y$ balance the threshold bias of -2 set by the threshold unit, t, whenever both x and y equal $+1$ (activated). The t-unit is always active. The numbers (± 1), etc. shown above are called "weights." Positive weights denote "excitatory" synapses, negative weights "inhibitory" ones. Similarly, open circles denote excitatory neurons; filled circles, inhibitory ones.

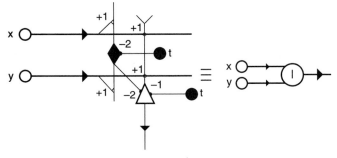

NOT (x and y) = x|y

Figure 2. NAND logic function implemented by a McCulloch-Pitts net comprising two units.

Von Neumann's work triggered a number of efforts to improve on his results, and led directly to the introduction of parallel distributed processing (Winograd and Cowan 1963), and indirectly to work on perceptrons and adalines, and associative memories.

Von Neumann's last publication in this area was the monograph "The Computer and the Brain," published posthumously in 1958, and based on his 1956 manuscript prepared for the Silliman Lectures at Yale University. In this monograph von Neumann outlined his view that computations in the brain are reliable but not precise, statistical and not deterministic, and essentially parallel rather than serial (see also COMPUTATION AND THE BRAIN). Had he lived he would have undoubtedly developed these themes into a detailed theory of brain-like computing. One can see in the many developments in artificial NEURAL NETWORKS since 1957 many echoes of von Neumann's ideas and insights.

See also ARTIFICIAL LIFE; COGNITIVE ARCHITECTURE; FORMAL SYSTEMS, PROPERTIES OF; RATIONAL CHOICE THEORY; WIENER

—*Jack D. Cowan*

References

McCulloch, W. S., and W. H. Pitts. (1943). A logical calculus of the ideas immanent in nervous activity. *Bul. Math. Biophys.* 5: 115–133.

Von Neumann, J. (1951). The general and logical theory of automata. In L. A. Jeffress, Ed., Cerebral Mechanisms in Behavior—*The Hixon Symposium,* September 1948, Pasadena, CA. New York: Wiley, pp. 1–31.

Von Neumann, J. (1956). Probabilistic logics and the synthesis of reliable organisms from unreliable components. In C. E. Shannon and J. McCarthy, Eds., *Automata Studies*. Princeton: Princeton University Press, pp. 43–98.

Von Neumann, J. (1958). *The Computer and the Brain, Silliman Lectures*. New Haven, CT: Yale University Press.

Von Neumann, J., and O. Morgenstern. (1944). *Theory of Games and Economic Behavior*. Princeton, NJ: Princeton University Press.

Winograd, S., and J. D. Cowan. (1963). *Reliable Computation in the Presence of Noise*. Cambridge, MA: MIT Press.

Vygotsky, Lev Semenovich

Lev Semenovich Vygotsky (1896–1934) grew up in Gomel', a provincial town in Belorussia. From 1913 to 1917 he studied history, philosophy, and law at universities in Moscow, and he returned to Gomel' from 1917 to 1924, where he taught literature and psychology at several schools and colleges. He also wrote extensively about language, pedagogy, drama, and poetry during this period.

After a brilliant presentation at a psychoneurological conference in 1924, Vygotsky was invited to join the staff of the Moscow Psychological Institute, and he continued to live and work primarily in Moscow until he died of tuberculosis in 1934. During the final decade of his life Vygotsky helped found several research and teaching institutions in the Soviet Union; he conducted extensive empirical studies on the history and ontogenesis of language and thought (Vygotsky 1987; Vygotsky and LURIA 1993); and he wrote about philosophy, pedagogy, and psychology (Vygotsky 1997), including the psychology of disabilities (Vygotsky 1993).

Throughout his career Vygotsky's fundamental concern was with how human mental functioning is shaped by its historical, cultural, and institutional context. The theoretical framework he developed for dealing with this problem can be summarized in a few basic themes. The first of these was his commitment to a genetic, or developmental, method. From this perspective mental functioning is understood by examining its origins and the transformations it undergoes in development. Vygotsky's formulation of this theme went well beyond the focus of contemporary accounts of child and lifespan psychology, seeking to address how mental functioning is shaped by phylogenetic, historical, and microgenetic, as well as ontogenetic, forces.

The second theme that runs throughout Vygotsky's writings is the claim that higher, uniquely human mental functioning in an individual has its origins in social processes and retains a "quasi-social" nature (Vygotsky 1981a). This claim led him to criticize psychological accounts that attempt to derive social from individual processes. In contrast to such approaches he argued that higher mental functions appear first on the social, or "intermental" plane— often in the form of joint, adult-child problem-solving activity—and only then emerge on the intramental, individual plane. The nature of intermental functioning and its role in shaping intramental processes has been the focus of recent research on the "zone of proximal development" (Vygotsky 1978) and related notions such as "scaffolding."

Vygotsky's claims about the social origins of individual mental functioning have some striking implications that run counter to widely held assumptions in psychology. Because he viewed terms such as "memory" and "thinking" as applying to social as well as individual processes, he argued for the need to identify an analytic unit that is not tied to the individual. His candidate for this unit was word meaning—a unit that mediates both intermental and intramental functioning. Furthermore, he argued that the particular form that mental processes take on the intramental plane derives largely from their intermental precursors. This points to the importance of examining linguistic and social interactional dimensions of intermental functioning as a means for understanding mental processes in the individual.

The third theme that runs throughout Vygotsky's writings is that higher mental processes are mediated by socioculturally evolved tools and signs (Vygotsky 1981b). Under the heading of mediation by signs, or semiotic mediation, Vygotsky included items such as maps, mathematical formulas, and charts, but he was particularly interested in human language. His claims about mediation lie at the center of his approach, something that is reflected in the analytic primacy he gave to this, over the two other themes. Vygotsky identified major turning points, or "revolutions" in development by the appearance of new forms of sign use, and he formulated intermental and intramental functioning in terms of semiotic mediation. The developmental relationship that he saw between these two planes existed precisely because language and other sign systems mediate both and hence serve to link them.

Vygotsky (1986) developed his theoretical claims in several empirical studies. For example, he conducted investigations on the emergence of abstract concepts and their relationship to language development, and he examined the relationship between external, social speech and inner speech in the individual. In the latter connection he analyzed a form of speech used by children in which they speak to themselves as they engage in problem-solving or fantasy play. Because such speech does not appear to take listeners into account, Piaget (1955) had labeled it "egocentric." Though not disputing many of Piaget's basic observations, Vygotsky disagreed with his interpretation. Instead of viewing such speech as a manifestation of children's egocentricity, a symptom that dies away with the increasing ability to understand others' perspectives, Vygotsky argued that egocentric speech plays an essential role in the transition from social speech to inner speech on the intramental plane. He concluded that instead of simply disappearing with age, this speech form "goes underground" to become inner speech, thereby shaping mental functioning in a uniquely human way.

See also COGNITIVE ARTIFACTS; COGNITIVE DEVELOPMENT; ECOLOGICAL VALIDITY; INDIVIDUALISM; MEMORY

—*James V. Wertsch*

References

Piaget, J. (1955). *The Language and Thought of the Child.* Translated by Marjorie Gabain. New York: World Publishing.

Vygotsky, L. S. (1978). *Mind in Society: The Development of Higher Psychological Processes.* In M. Cole, V. John-Steiner, S. Scribner, and E. Souberman, Eds. Cambridge, MA: Harvard University Press.

Vygotsky, L. S. (1981a). The development of higher forms of attention in childhood. In J. V. Wertsch, Ed., *The Concept of Activity in Soviet Psychology.* Armonk, NY: M. E. Sharpe, pp. 189–240.

Vygotsky, L. S. (1981b). The instrumental method in psychology. In J. V. Wertsch, Ed., *The Concept of Activity in Soviet Psychology.* Armonk, NY: M. E. Sharpe, pp.134–143.

Vygotsky, L. S. (1986). *Thought and Language.* Revised translation by A. Kozulin, Ed. Cambridge, MA: MIT Press.

Vygotsky, L. S. (1987). *The Collected Works of L. S. Vygotsky.* Vol. 1, *Problems of General Psychology.* Including the volume *Thinking and Speech.* Translated by N. Minick, Ed. New York: Plenum.

Vygotsky, L. S. (1993). *The Collected Works of L. S. Vygotsky.* Vol. 2, *The Fundamentals of Defectology (Abnormal Psychology and Learning Disabilities).* Translated with introduction by J. E. Knox and C. B. Stevens. New York: Plenum.

Vygotsky, L. S. (1997). *The Collected Works of L.S. Vygotsky.* Vol. 3, *Theory and History of Psychology,* Including the Chapter *Crisis in Psychology.* Translated by Rene Van Der Veer and Robert W. Rieber, Ed. New York: Plenum.

Vygotsky, L. S., and A. R. Luria. (1993). *Studies on the History of Behavior: Ape, Primitive, and Child.* Edited and translated by Victor I. Golod and Jane E. Knox, Eds. Hillsdale, NJ: Erlbaum.

Further Readings

Bruner, J. (1986). *Actual Minds, Possible Worlds.* Cambridge, MA: Harvard University Press.

Cole, M. (1996). *Cultural Psychology: A Once and Future Discipline.* Cambridge, MA: Harvard University Press.

Frawley, W. (1997). *Vygotsky and Cognitive Science: Language and the Unification of the Social and Computational Mind.* Cambridge, MA: Harvard University Press.

Rogoff, B. (1990). *Apprenticeship in Thinking: Cognitive Development in Social Context.* New York: Oxford University Press.

van der Veer, R., and J. Valsiner. (1991). *Understanding Vygotsky: A Quest for Synthesis.* Oxford: Blackwell.

Vygotsky, L. S. (1971). *The Psychology of Art.* Cambridge, MA: MIT Press.

Wertsch, J. V. (1985). *Vygotsky and the Social Formation of Mind.* Cambridge, MA: Harvard University Press.

Wertsch, J. V. (1991). *Voices of the Mind: A Sociocultural Approach to Mediated Action.* Cambridge, MA: Harvard University Press.

Wertsch, J. V. (1998). *Mind as Action.* New York: Oxford University Press.

Walking and Running Machines

Humans have built aircraft, submarines, and other machines that imitate or improve upon animal locomotion, but the design and construction of feasible walking and running machines remains a challenge. From a practical perspective, legged robots offer several potential advantages over wheeled vehicles. They can traverse rough terrain by stepping across or jumping over obstacles using isolated ground contacts rather than the continuous path of support required by wheels. This agility is important in difficult environments with few suitable footholds. Unlike wheeled vehicles, legged robots have an active suspension system that can decouple variations in the terrain from the motion of the body and provide a steady platform for a sensor or payload. From a scientific perspective, researchers would like to construct legged vehicles with the capabilities of animals to

Figure 1. The Adaptive Suspension Vehicle crossing uneven terrain. Photograph reprinted by permission of The Ohio State University.

better understand the principles of locomotion in biological systems. Over the past hundred years, researchers have combined innovative engineering with scientific observations of the agility and efficiency of legged animals to construct many types of legged mechanisms.

Walking and running machines are divided into two categories based on the stability of their motion: passively stable and dynamically stable. The vertical projection of the center of gravity of a *passively stable system* always remains within the convex region formed by the contact points of the feet on the ground. This region is called the *support polygon*. Statically stable machines can stop moving at any time in the locomotion cycle and maintain balance. They typically have four or six legs but may be bipeds with large feet. In contrast, *dynamically stable systems* utilize dynamic forces and feedback to maintain control and are stable in a limit cycle that repeats once each stride. Dynamically stable machines have been built with one, two, and four legs. Because dynamically stable systems are more difficult to design and analyze, the early development of legged robots focused on statically stable machines.

The earliest walking machines used gears to produce fixed patterns of leg motion for walking. The fixed patterns prevented these machines from responding in a flexible fashion to variations in terrain. Nevertheless, their construction initiated the study of leg mechanisms and gait patterns and they remain useful comparisons for the evaluation of current robots. A more agile walking machine was built in 1968 by Ralph Mosher at General Electric (Liston and Mosher 1968). An eleven-foot-tall, three-thousand-pound machine with twelve degrees of freedom, the walking truck was hydraulically powered and capable of climbing over obstacles, pushing large objects, and walking steadily at five miles per hour. The machine was controlled by a human driver who used his arms to control the front legs and his legs to control the rear

legs of the machine. Force feedback allowed the driver to sense the balance of the system, but the machine was difficult and tiring to control even after substantial training. Because the machine was human controlled, it was not an autonomous legged vehicle, but it provided a convincing demonstration of the agility possible with a mechanical legged system.

Digital computers provided the numerical computation necessary to develop automatically controlled walking robots in the 1970s. Computers were used to determine footholds that maintained stability, to solve the kinematic equations for positioning the legs, to provide feedback control based on the body orientation and leg positions, and to plan paths through the environment (see PLANNING). Several of these early machines were hexapods because six-leg designs allow walking with a stable, alternating tripod gait. The Ohio State University Hexapod was built in 1977 by Robert McGhee using electric drill motors (Bucket 1977; McGhee 1983). A second hexapod from OSU, the Adaptive Suspension Vehicle, was a three-ton vehicle with a human driver but automatic positioning of the legs under most terrain conditions (Song and Waldron 1989) as shown in figure 1. The first computer-controlled, self-contained walking robot was a hexapod, built by Sutherland in 1983 (Raibert and Sutherland 1983). The first commercially available legged robot was the ODEX 1 "Functionoid" built by Odetics in 1983 (Russell 1983).

Research in legged locomotion has proceeded primarily along two lines: leg design and control. Design considers the geometries of leg arrangements and mechanisms to increase motion, strength, speed, or reliability, decrease energy requirements or weight, or simplify control. For example, Shigeo Hirose's 1980 PV II quadruped used a pantograph leg mechanism that allowed actuators independently to control each degree of freedom in Cartesian space, considerably simplifying the kinematic equations (Hirose and Umetani

Figure 2. The planar biped running right to left, up and down a short flight of stairs. Photograph reprinted by permission of the MIT Leg Laboratory.

1980). The Ambler, a thirty-foot-tall, hexapod planetary explorer built at Carnegie Mellon University, used an orthogonal leg design to simplify the kinematic equations (Simmons et al. 1992). The design kept the outer segments of the legs vertical while positioning them with inner segments that rotated in a horizontal plane. Dante, also built at CMU, used sets of legs mounted on sliding frames. After one frame's legs lifted, the frame slid forward and then lowered the legs for the next step. In 1994, Dante II successfully descended into an active volcano in Alaska and analyzed high temperature gases (Wettergreen, Pangels, and Bares 1995).

Issues of control have been explored most often in bipedal walking and running robots. Computer-controlled bipeds that used large feet to allow static stability were built in 1972 (Kato and Tsuiki 1972). These were followed by quasi-static walkers that included a dynamic phase during which the machine fell forward onto the next stance foot (Kato et al. 1983). The first dynamically stable walking bipeds were designed by Miura and Shimoyama (1984). These machines used stiff legs that were raised by rotating the hip and produced motion that resembled walking on stilts.

In the early and mid-1980s, Raibert and colleagues at MIT and CMU designed dynamically stable running monopods, bipeds, and quadrupeds. These machines used springs in the legs to provide a passive rebound during the stance phase and hydraulic actuators to provide thrust and to control the leg angle (Raibert 1986). The control systems for these machines divided the complex system dynamics into three largely decoupled problems: hopping height, forward speed, and body attitude. Hopping height was maintained by extending the actuator in series with the leg spring. Body attitude was controlled by applying a torque at the hip while the foot was in contact with the ground. Forward running speed was controlled by positioning the foot at touchdown. A finite state machine determined the active control laws at any given moment. In addition to running, these machines also used a variety of gaits (Raibert, Chepponis, and Brown

1986), ran fast (Koechling and Raibert 1988), performed flips (Hodgins and Raibert 1990), and ran up and down stairs (Hodgins and Raibert 1991), as shown in figure 2.

Further exploration of control for legged robots has led to the discovery of an elegant class of legged robots with no computer control at all. Called *passive walkers,* these machines walk down an inclined slope but have no internal source of energy. The length of the legs and mass distribution are chosen so that the legs swing forward and the knees straighten for touchdown without actuation (McGeer 1990a, 1990b). Controllers for passive running have also been proposed (McGeer 1989; Ringrose 1997; Ahmadi and Buehler 1995). Recently, several researchers have begun to build a formal theoretical framework for analyzing the stability of dynamic running machines. This approach models dynamic robots as simpler systems such as spring/mass systems and then proves stability of the model given a particular set of control laws (Koditschek and Buehler 1991; Schwind and Koditschek 1997).

Although the dream of an artificial legged creature such as C-3PO from the movie *Star Wars* has not been realized, research into running and walking machines has furthered our understanding of legged locomotion in machines and animals. Researchers have explored a variety of geometries, mechanisms, control techniques, gaits, and motion styles for legged machines, and the resulting insights have enabled new applications and designs, as well as a growing theoretical foundation for legged locomotion and control.

See also BEHAVIOR-BASED ROBOTICS; CONTROL THEORY; MANIPULATION AND GRASPING; MOBILE ROBOTS; MOTOR CONTROL; ROBOTICS AND LEARNING

—*Gary Boone and Jessica Hodgins*

References

Ahmadi, M., and M. Buehler. (1995). A control strategy for stable passive running. *Proceedings of the International Conference on Intelligent Robots and Systems.* Los Alamitos, CA: IEEE Computer Society Press, pp. 152–157.

Bucket, J. R. (1977). *Design of an On-board Electronic Joint System for a Hexapod Vehicle.* Master's thesis, Ohio State University.

Hirose, S., and Y. Umetani. (1980). The basic motion regulation system for a quadruped walking machine. *American Society of Mechanical Engineers Paper 80-DET-34.*

Hodgins, J., and M. H. Raibert. (1990). Biped gymnastics. *International Journal of Robotics Research* 9: 115–132.

Hodgins, J., and M. H. Raibert. (1991). Adjusting step length for rough terrain locomotion. *IEEE Transactions on Robotics and Automation* 7: 289–298.

Kato, T., A. Takanishi, H. Jishikawa, and I. Kato. (1983). The realization of quasi-dynamic walking by the biped walking machine. In A. Morecki, G. Bianchi, and K. Kedzior, Eds. *Fourth Symposium on Theory and Practice of Robots and Manipulators.* Warsaw: Polish Scientific Publishers, pp. 341–351.

Kato, I., and H. Tsuiki. (1972). The hydraulically powered biped walking machine with a high carrying capacity. In *Fourth Symposium on External Extremities.* Dubrovnik: Yugoslav Committee for Electronics and Automation.

Koditschek, D. E., and M. Buehler. (1991). Analysis of a simplified hopping robot. *International Journal of Robotics Research* 10: 6.

Koechling, J., and M. Raibert. (1988). How fast can a legged robot run? In K. Youcef-Toumi and H. Kazerooni, Eds., *Symposium in Robotics, DSC,* vol. 1. New York: American Society of Mechanical Engineers.

Liston, R. A., and R. S. Mosher. (1968). A versatile walking truck. *Proceedings of the Transportation Engineering Conference.* London: Institution of Civil Engineers.

Miura, H., and I. Shimoyama. (1984). Dynamic walk of a biped. *International Journal of Robotics Research* 3.2: 60–74.

McGeer, T. (1989). Passive bipedal running. Centre for Systems Science, Simon Fraser University, Technical Report CSS-IS TR 89-02.

McGeer T. (1990a). Passive dynamic walking. *The International Journal of Robotics Research* 9: 62–82.

McGeer, T. (1990b). Passive walking with knees. *Proceedings of the 1990 IEEE Robotics and Automation Conference,* Cincinnati, OH, pp. 1640–1645.

McGhee, R. B. (1983). Vehicular legged locomotion. In G. N. Saridis, Ed., *Advances in Automation and Robotics.* JAI Press.

Raibert, M. H. (1986). *Legged Robots That Balance.* Cambridge, MA: MIT Press.

Raibert, M. H., M. Chepponis, and H. B. Brown, Jr. (1986). Running on four legs as though they were one. *IEEE J. Robotics and Automation* 2: 70–82.

Raibert, M. H., and I. E. Sutherland. (1983). Machines that walk. *Scientific American* 248(2): 44–53.

Ringrose, R. (1997). Self-stabilizing running. *Proceedings of the International Conference on Robotics and Automation,* Albuquerque, NM.

Russell, M. (1983). Odex 1: The first functionoid. *Robotics Age* 5(5): 12–18.

Schwind, W. J., and D. E. Koditschek. (1997). Characterization of monoped equilibrium gaits. *Proceedings of the 1997 International Conference on Robotics and Automation,* Albuquerque, NM, pp. 1986–1992.

Simmons, R., E. Krotkov, W. Whittaker, and B. Albrecht. (1992). Progress towards robotic exploration of extreme terrain. *Applied Intelligence: The International Journal of Artificial Intelligence, Neural Networks and Complex Problem-Solving Technologies* 2(2): 162–180.

Song, S. M., and K. J. Waldron. (1989). *Machines That Walk.* Cambridge, MA: MIT Press.

Wettergreen, D., H. Pangels, and J. Bares. (1995). Behavior-based gait execution for the Dante II walking robot. *Proceedings of the 1995 IEEE/RSJ International Conference on Intelligent Robots and Systems.* Los Alamitos, CA: IEEE Computer Society Press, 274–279.

Wh-Movement

A characteristic feature of natural languages is the fact that certain syntactic categories are systematically found "out of place." Normally, in English, a direct object follows the verb on which it depends (one says *I had seen it* rather than *I had it seen* or *It I had seen*). Nonetheless, if the object is interrogated, a *wh*-word (so called because most interrogative words in English begin with the letters *wh—who, what, which, when, where, why,* etc.) is used and "displaced" to first position in (root or subordinate) interrogative sentences (*What had you seen? I asked what you had seen*).

Such *wh*-movement is found in other contructions as well (relatives, exclamatives, concessives, etc.: *The film which you had seen . . . ; What a nice house you have! Whatever you do, . . .* , etc.) and is but an instance of a more general movement operation which "displaces" syntactic categories other than *wh*-phrases: for instance, nominal phrases and verbs (on the latter, see HEAD MOVEMENT).

After Chomsky 1977, 1986, 1995, and the references cited there, a better understanding is available of many of the properties of *wh*-movement; for example, (a) the nature of the position the *wh*-phrase moves to; (b) the rationale for such a movement; and (c) the conditions under which such movement is permitted or blocked.

Modern linguistic theory considers sentence structure as characterized by the alternation of a head (a syntactic atom such as a verb, noun, adjective, determiner, complementizer—that is, a subordinating conjunction—etc.) and a phrase (a larger syntactic unit built around a head), which can serve as a complement or as a specifier of another head (see X-BAR THEORY, Chomsky 1970; Kayne 1994). The simplified structure is thus:

(1) [Phrase *Complementizer* [Phrase *Agreement* [Phrase *Tense* [Phrase (subject) *Verb* Phrase (object)]]]]

(The phrase to the immediate left of each (italicized) head is its *specifier*).

An object *wh*-phrase is displaced from the complement position on the right of the verb to the specifier position on the left of the complementizer. This, for example, accounts for its occupying the first position of the (interrogative) sentence (as no other head precedes the complementizer), as well as for the fact that in certain languages the *wh*-phrase co-occurs with (and precedes) the complementizer itself (e.g., Middle English: *This bok which that I make mencioun of . . .*). In root interrogatives (in English and other languages), the finite verb (a head) is necessarily in second position, immediately after the *wh*-phrase (*What have you seen?*). This can be made sense of if it too is displaced to the complementizer head. The rationale for the movement of a wh-phrase appears to be related to the way a *wh*-phrase is interpreted. A question like *Which persons have you met?* means roughly "Tell me which is the value of *x*, where *x* ranges over the class of persons such that you have met *x*." In other terms, *which* is a sort of quantifier extracted from the object and binding a variable in the object position, much as in the (Polish) notation of standard predicate logic (see QUANTIFIERS). The displacement of a *wh*-phrase can thus be seen as a way of partially building in the syntax a representation of the LOGICAL FORM of the sentence, although not all languages displace their *wh*-phrases overtly in the syntax or have a special morphological way that distinguishes them from indefinite phrases (see Cheng 1991).

The displacement of *wh*-phrases is severely constrained. Although *wh*-movement gives the impression of taking place over an unbounded number of sentences (*How do you think that they said that they wanted to repair it?*, where *how* is moved from the sentence containing the verb *repair*), there is evidence that it proceeds stepwise through the specifier of each complementizer (at least in the case of phrases other than subjects and complements). This is shown by the fact that whenever the specifier of some intermediate complementizer is filled by another *wh*-phrase, such movement becomes impossible (**How do you wonder why he repaired it?*). Only subjects and complements can (marginally) skip over one such intermediate specifier (cf. *??Which one of his brothers did you wonder why they invited?*).

Such stepwise movement of *wh*-phrases is constrained in another fashion. In essence, it can apply only when the subordinate sentence is a complement of the next higher verb (for refinements, see Rizzi 1990 and Cinque 1990). As witnessed by the fact that they seem to involve a quantifier/variable interpretation, and that they are subject to the same constraints as overt *wh*-movement constructions, a number of other constructions have been analyzed as containing a covert type of *wh*-movement (see Chomsky 1977). These comprise comparative (*He buys more books than his father used to buy*), topicalized (*This film, I think that they saw*), "easy-to-please" (*John is easy for everybody to succeed in convincing*), and other constructions.

See also BINDING THEORY; GRAMMATICAL RELATIONS; SYNTAX; SYNTAX, ACQUISITION OF

—*Guglielmo Cinque*

References

Cheng, L. L. (1991). *On the Typology of Wh-Questions*. Ph.D. diss., MIT.

Chomsky, N. (1970). Remarks on nominalization. In R. A. Jacobs and P. Rosenbaum, Eds., *Readings in English Transformational Grammar.* Waltham, MA: Ginn and Co., pp.184–221.

Chomsky, N. (1977). On *wh*-movement. In P. Culicover, T. Wasow, and A. Akmajian, Eds., *Formal Syntax.* New York: Academic Press, pp. 71–132.

Chomsky, N. (1986). *Barriers.* Cambridge, MA: MIT Press.

Chomsky, N. (1995). *The Minimalist Program.* Cambridge, MA: MIT Press.

Cinque, G. (1990). *Types of A-bar Dependencies.* Cambridge, MA: MIT Press.

Jackendoff, R. (1977). *X-bar Syntax: A Study of Phrase Structure.* Cambridge, MA: MIT Press.

Kayne, R. (1994). *The Antisymmetry of Syntax.* Cambridge, MA: MIT Press.

Rizzi, L. (1990). *Relativized Minimality.* Cambridge, MA: MIT Press.

What-It's-Like

One of the most distinctive features of conscious mental states is that there is "something it is like" to have them. There is something it is like *for me* to smell a rose, daydream about my vacation, or stub my toe, but presumably *for the rose* there is nothing it is like to have an odor, and *for the table leg* there is nothing it is like to be kicked by my toe. Many philosophers feel that it is this feature of mentality, its subjectivity, that presents the most difficult challenge to a materialist theory of the mind.

There are two issues involved here. First, we want to know what distinguishes those states that there is something it is like to be in from those there is nothing it is like to be in; those states that have a subjective character from those that do not. Second, there is the more specific question concerning just what it is like to be in particular types of mental states. The qualitative character of smelling a rose is quite distinct from seeing it. What determines, for a state there is something it is like to be in, exactly what it is like?

Nagel (1974) poses the second question quite forcefully with the following example. Bats navigate by echolocation, a sensory system unlike any possessed by human beings. They emit high-pitched sounds and determine the spatial layout of their environment by the nature of the echoes they detect. To the question how this system performs its function of providing spatial information to the bat, a computational theory is the answer. If we can determine the function from sensory input to informational output, and see how the bat's neurophysiology implements that function, then the strictly computational question is answered. But there seems to be another question we want answered; namely, what is it like for the bat to perceive the world in this way? To this question, it does not seem as if the computational theory can provide even the beginning of an answer.

Another very influential thought experiment that illustrates the subjectivity of conscious mental states is Frank Jackson's (1982) story of Mary, the neuroscientist brought up in a black-and-white environment. Though she knows all there is to know about the physical mechanisms underlying color perception, it seems that she would not know what it is like to see red until she actually sees it for herself. Again, it seems as if one has to undergo conscious experiences to know what they are like. But why should that be?

Nagel's diagnosis of the problem is that conscious states essentially involve a "subjective point of view," whereas physicalist and computationalist theories involve adopting an objective point of view. Thus to know what it's like to have a certain conscious experience one must be capable of taking up the relevant point of view—that is, one must be capable of having this sort of experience. The puzzle for materialism is to explain just how the physical mechanisms underlying conscious experience could give rise to subjective points of view at all, and to particular facts concerning what it's like that are accessible only from certain points of view. How objectively describable physical processes result in subjective points of view is central to the problem known as the EXPLANATORY GAP.

Two of the most influential responses to the problem are the "knowledge how" strategy and the "indexical" strategy. The idea behind the first strategy (see Lewis 1990 and Nemirow 1990) is that knowledge of what it is like to have an experience is not factual knowledge, therefore not susceptible to explanation. Rather, to know what it's like to see red is to have the ability to recognize seeing red when it occurs. If this is right, then of course one has to actually undergo the relevant experience in order to manifest the ability. Many philosophers reject this solution, however. They do not find it plausible that knowing what it's like is merely "knowledge how," an ability, and not "knowledge that," factual knowledge. It seems clear to them that there is a fact involved here, and in certain cases, such as the bat's perception via echolocation, one that is inaccessible to us.

The idea behind the second strategy is to deflate the mystery by showing that the subjectivity of conscious experience is just another manifestation of the phenomenon of indexicality (see Lycan 1996; Rey 1996; Tye 1995). Though many people can describe me—my physical appearance, my behavior, and even many of my thoughts—they cannot do it in a first-person way. That is, they cannot capture what I am thinking or doing by saying "I am writing an essay"; only I can do that. So, in a sense, certain ways of thinking about me are inaccessible to them. Yet, no one finds this mysterious; it is just the way the "I"-concept works. Similarly, that there is a subjective point of view is not mysterious. What accounts for subjectivity is that the subject herself has a means of representing her own experience, that is, by the mere fact that it is her experience, inaccessible to others.

This solution has its problems as well (see Levine 1997). It is true that both phenomena, knowing what it's like and employing the first-person concept, involve adopting a perspective. But it is plausible that the first-person concept is purely a matter of perspective, and that is why it generates no mystery. When one considers what it is like to see red, however, it doesn't seem that one is merely apprehending from a different perspective the same fact as that which is captured by a graph of the spectral reflectance of the object observed; rather, it seems as if something completely new is revealed, a substantive fact that is not capturable in any way by a graph or verbal description.

How seriously one treats the problem of subjectivity in the end is largely a matter of one's attitude toward philosophical intuitions. Many philosophers (see Akins 1993; Churchland 1985; Dennett 1991) are willing to dismiss the intuitions driving the worries about what it's like in the hopes that enough scientific progress will render them impotent. Other philosophers continue to engage the problem directly, convinced that the intuitions Nagel and others express reveal a deep philosophical problem that demands a solution.

See also CONSCIOUSNESS; CONSCIOUSNESS, NEUROBIOLOGY OF; PHYSICALISM; QUALIA

—*Joseph Levine*

References

Akins, K. A. (1993). A bat without qualities? In M. Davies and G. W. Humphreys, Eds., *Consciousness: Psychological and Philosophical Essays.* Oxford: Blackwell.

Churchland, P. (1985). Reduction, qualia, and the direct introspection of brain states. *Journal of Philosophy* 82: 8–28.

Dennett, D. C. (1991). *Consciousness Explained.* Boston: Little, Brown.

Jackson, F. (1982). Epiphenomenal qualia. *Philosophical Quarterly* 32: 127–136.

Levine, J. (1997). Are qualia just representations? A critical notice of Michael Tye's ten problems of consciousness. *Mind and Language* 12(1): 101–113.

Lewis, D. (1990). What experience teaches. In W. Lycan, Ed., *Mind and Cognition.* Oxford: Blackwell.

Lycan, W. G. (1996). *Consciousness and Experience.* Cambridge, MA: Bradford Books/MIT Press.

Nagel, T. (1974). What is it like to be a bat? *The Philosophical Review* 82: 435–450.

Nemirow, L. (1990). Physicalism and the cognitive role of acquaintance. In W. Lycan, Ed., *Mind and Cognition.* Oxford: Blackwell.

Rey, G. (1996). *Contemporary Philosophy of Mind: A Renaissance of the Explanatory.* Oxford: Blackwell.

Tye, M. (1995). *Ten Problems of Consciousness: A Representational Theory of the Phenomenal Mind.* Cambridge, MA: Bradford Books/MIT Press.

Further Readings

Chalmers, D. (1996). *The Conscious Mind.* Oxford: Oxford University Press.

Flanagan, O. (1992). *Consciousness Reconsidered.* Cambridge, MA: Bradford Books/MIT Press.

Kirk, R. (1994). *Raw Feeling.* Oxford: Oxford University Press.

Levine, J. (1993). On leaving out what it's like. In M. Davies and G. Humphreys, Eds., *Consciousness: Psychological and Philosophical Essays.* Oxford: Blackwell, pp. 121–136.

McGinn, C. (1991). *The Problem of Consciousness.* Oxford: Blackwell.

Metzinger, T., Ed. (1995). *Conscious Experience.* Paderborn: Ferdinand Schöningh/ Imprint Academic.

Nagel, T. (1986). *The View from Nowhere.* New York: Oxford University Press.

Rosenthal, D. (1990). *A Theory of Consciousness.* Bielefeld: ZIF Report 40.

Shoemaker, S. (1996). *The First-Person Perspective and Other Essays.* Cambridge and New York: Cambridge University Press.

Whorfianism

See LINGUISTIC RELATIVITY HYPOTHESIS; SAPIR, EDWARD

Wiener, Norbert

Norbert Wiener (1894–1964) worked in pure mathematics, but also used mathematics to pioneer statistical communication theory, and in collaboration with engineers and neurobiologists originated and elaborated the field of "cybernetics" (the study of "control and communication in the animal and the machine"). Wiener's work in the 1940s, related to cybernetics, constitutes one of the roots of modern "cognitive science." After World War II, anticipating the social and philosophical significance of cybernetic technologies, Wiener developed an important prescient philosophy of technology incorporating humane values. Nearly all his work shows the mark of a highly original mind.

Son of a Russian Jewish immigrant professor of Slavic languages and literature at Harvard, Norbert Wiener was a child prodigy who received his doctorate in philosophy from Harvard at the age of eighteen. His postdoctoral mentors included Bertrand Russell and G. H. Hardy in Cambridge. From 1919 until his death he was a member of the faculty of mathematics (during the last five years a freewheeling "institute professor") at the Massachusetts Institute of Technology.

Within pure mathematics Wiener worked on potential theory, generalizations of harmonic analysis, proving Tauberian theorems, proving theorems concerning Fourier transforms in the complex plane, studies of chaos, ergodic theory, and other topics. One of Wiener's major mathematical innovations, developed when he was still in his twenties, was the invention of what has come to be known as the "Wiener process" or the "Wiener measure," extending the Lebesgue theory of measure, and combining it with probability theory to describe Brownian motion. This mathematical development, which offered a new way of thinking about many problems, has found subsequent application also in quantum field theory and other branches of science.

It was his collaboration in the early 1940s with the Mexican physiologist Arturo Rosenblueth, on the one hand, and with engineer Julian Bigelow, on the other, which led to the fundamental ideas of cybernetics. These fruitful collaborations were evidence of Wiener's capacity for bringing his own discipline to bear on other fields and transforming them. Application of sophisticated mathematics to wartime engineering problems led Wiener to create general statistical theories of communication, prediction, and filtering. "Information," rigorously defined, became a concept as precise as the concepts describing matter within the field of physics. Also, the concept of a "goal," and that of "feedback" of information indicating how far one is from reaching the goal, and the engineering task of building an automatic mechanism for computing a correction, and acting on the information so as to come closer to the goal, were part and parcel of the Wiener-Bigelow design work. Wiener's collaboration with Rosenblueth was based on the shared philosophical premise that the formal structures of mechanical or electrical systems are often isomorphic to the formal structures involving organisms, and can be described by mathematics. It led to joint work in analyzing human or animal heart flutter, heart fibrillations, muscle clonus, and detailed local electrical fluctuations in the central nervous system.

Wiener, Rosenblueth, and Bigelow presented a paradigm for a new, as yet unnamed area of interdisciplinary research in their 1943 article, "Behavior, Purpose, and Teleology." It dealt with the analysis of purposive action, whether in an animal or in a machine, although the notion of "purpose" had been largely excluded by the then-dominant behaviorist psychology. The ubiquitous process of achieving a "purpose" or goal, they suggested, entailed continuous or repeated negative feedback to guide action, and a circuit encompassing physical action as well as information. That feedback loop to implement purpose meant a circular causality, A effects B which in turn effects A, and so on, in contrast to traditional one-way cause-and-effect relations. When the war was over, Wiener made common cause with Warren McCulloch, Walter Pitts, and John VON NEUMANN, whose work on formal-logical modeling of the central nervous system and general-purpose computers suggested strong structural similarities between brains and computers. In a series of small conferences that became known as the Macy conferences on cybernetics, they discussed their ideas and presented them to an interdisciplinary group which included psychologists of diverse persuasions, psychiatrists, biologists, and anthropologists. A controversy at the meetings concerned the discrepant premises of the older GESTALT PSYCHOLOGY, on the one hand, and those of the emerging cognitive science (using electronic computer and information-processing models of the mind) on the other. Some of the group came to shift their research programs when they incorporated the new ideas into their own discipline. In 1948 Wiener presented his own synthesis of the new field, which had come to include what he learned from other Macy conferees, in a book titled *Cybernetics*. It brought the ideas to the attention of a large scientific audience worldwide.

After the war Wiener eschewed work likely to be useful to weapons development, and, using insights from cybernetics, turned his attention to topics such as analysis of electroencephalograms, and the principles of prosthetic devices for people who are blind, deaf, or have lost a limb. His criteria for sophisticated prosthetic devices have proved to be valid guiding principles for their design.

Wiener came to view the ideas of cybernetics as a theory of messages. He saw himself as an adherent of what he called the "Gibbsian point of view," the primacy of the contingent, not only within science but in life generally. Furthermore he took it upon himself to place engineering and technical innovation within a framework of ethics, using the legend of the golem as a metaphor. He described his outlook in various books for the general reader.

See also COMPUTATION AND THE BRAIN; COMPUTATIONAL THEORY OF MIND; INFORMATION THEORY; MARR

—*Steve J. Heims*

References and Further Readings

Gardner, H. (1985). *The Mind's New Science: A History of the Cognitive Revolution*. New York: Basic Books.

Heims, S. J. (1980). *John von Neumann and Norbert Wiener: From Mathematics to the Technologies of Life and Death*. Cambridge, MA: MIT Press.

Heims, S. J. (1991). *The Cybernetics Group*. Cambridge, MA: MIT Press.

Levinson, N., Ed. (1966). *Bulletin of the American Mathematical Society* 72, no. 1, part 2 (entirely devoted to Wiener's mathematics).

Masani, P. R. (1990). *Norbert Wiener 1894–1964*. Basel: Birkhäuser.

Rosenblueth, A., N. Wiener, and J. Bigelow. (1943). Behavior, purpose, and teleology. *Philosophy of Science* 10: 18–24.

Wiener, N. (1948). *Cybernetics, or Control and Communication in the Animal and the Machine.* Cambridge, MA: MIT Press.

Wiener, N. (1949). *Extrapolation, Interpolation, and Smoothing of Stationary Time Series with Engineering Applications.* Cambridge, MA: MIT Press.

Wiener, N. (1950). *The Human Use of Human Beings; Cybernetics and Society.* Boston: Houghton Mifflin.

Wiener, N. (1953). *Ex-Prodigy: My Childhood and Youth.* New York: Simon and Schuster.

Wiener, N. (1956). *I Am a Mathematician: The Later Life of a Prodigy.* New York: Doubleday.

Wiener, N. (1964). *God and Golem, Inc.: A Comment on Certain Points Where Cybernetics Impinges on Religion.* Cambridge, MA: MIT Press.

Wiener, N. (1976, 1979, 1981, 1985). *Norbert Wiener: Collected Works,* vols. 1–4. P. Masani, Ed. Cambridge, MA: MIT Press.

Word Meaning, Acquisition of

The acquisition of word meaning involves, at minimum, the process of mapping concepts onto sounds or signs. These mappings differ across languages—*siy* is the phonological string associated with the meaning "if" in French, "yes" in Spanish, and "apprehend visually" in English—and hence cannot be innate. Since antiquity, scholars interested in word learning have assumed that the source of information for acquiring the meaning of new words is the child's observation of the linguistic and extralinguistic contexts of their use. Recent theorizing, as we shall describe, contributes new insights and findings that argue that the process is dramatically more complex than thought in the past.

Children understand a few words starting at about 9 months, with first spoken words typically appearing at about 12–14 months. These milestones are identical for spoken and signed languages (Petitto 1992; see SIGN LANGUAGES and SIGN LANGUAGE AND THE BRAIN). The acquisition of new words is at first quite slow, averaging about 0.3 words per day, but this rate gradually increases, eventually to about 15 new words per day in the school years (Anglin 1993). Some children show a sudden spurt in vocabulary growth between about 20 to 30 months, and there is in general a high correlation between syntactic and lexical development (Fenson et al. 1994). The onset of SYNTAX also coincides with a change in the character of the vocabulary: Earliest words, even in very different linguistic communities, are mainly animal sounds, "routines" like *bye-bye,* and common nouns, with a relatively high proportion of object names. Verbs, adjectives, and function words are rare (compared to their proportions in maternal usage; Fenson et al. 1994; Gentner 1982).

The vocabulary of a monolingual high school graduate is in the neighborhood of 80,000 words (Miller 1996). This number is impressive—80,000 arbitrary sound/meaning pairings is a lot to learn and store in memory—but word learning is impressive for other reasons as well. Quine (1960) gives the example of hearing a word, "gavagai," in an unknown language under the most transparent of circumstances; let us say, only and always while viewing a rabbit. A first thought is that the listener would be warranted in supposing that this word means "rabbit." But Quine points

out that *gavagai* has a logical infinity of possible meanings, including rabbit tails or legs, rabbit shapes, colors, or motions, temporal rabbit-slices, and even undetached rabbit parts. Because all of these conjectures for the meaning are consistent with the listener's experience, how can he or she zoom in on the single interpretation "rabbit"? (See RADICAL INTERPRETATION.) In actual fact, real children are apparently faced with just this problem, yet they seem to converge just about unerringly on the adult interpretation—that the word refers to the whole animal. But so saying leaves the problem raised by Quine unanswered.

Matters get worse. Contrary to what is often assumed, words are typically not presented in such "transparent circumstances." Adult speech to young children even in middle-class American homes is frequently about the past or the future, when the word's referents often are not in view (Beckwith, Tinker, and Bloom 1989). In some cultures, there is no explicit labeling of objects, and yet children have no problem learning object names (Schieffelin 1985). Blind children, whose observational opportunities are limited compared to the normal case, acquire word meanings—even the meanings of color words and verbs of perception—at about the same rate as sighted children (Landau and Gleitman 1985). And philosophers such as Plato have noted the puzzles that arise for the learning of abstract terms, such as those for numbers or ideal geometrical forms. (Consider also terms that describe mental states, such as "idea" and "know.") In sum, the sorts of words that children must learn and the conditions under which they must learn them suggest that word learning cannot succeed solely by raw observation of the co-occurring world.

The solution to these puzzles must involve attributing certain powers to very young children. Some of these are conceptual. Surely children enter the language-learning situation equipped with natural ways of interpreting many things, properties, and events in the world around them. These "natural ways" include perceiving objects and even rabbits, but it is likely that they do not include perceiving undetached rabbit parts. In consequence, the task of early word learning ordinarily comes down to connecting these preexisting conceptions with phonetic sequences. In support of this, consider the speed and effectiveness of early word learning. Children grasp aspects of the meanings of new words with very few exposures, without training or feedback and without ostensive naming. This process has been dubbed "fast mapping" (Carey 1978). For instance, if a 3-year-old hears one object out of ten being referred to casually as "a koba," over a month later she will know that this object is a koba (Markson and Bloom 1997). Children under the age of two can fast map new nouns (Waxman and Markow 1995), and the meanings of these early acquired words seem to be the same as they are for adults (Huttenlocher and Smiley 1987). This suggests that word learning is indeed supported by a preexisting conceptual repertoire. This position is bolstered by research with prelinguistic infants that shows that they possess a rich understanding of objects, actions, and other ontological kinds (e.g., Spelke 1994).

But even if children have the required conceptual structure for word-meaning acquisition, making the mappings to the right phonetic sequences remains to be explained. For example, very often in the child's immediate environment "open" is uttered when nothing is opening, and often there is no utterance of "open" when something is saliently opening. How then do children make the connection between "open" and opening? Quite surprisingly, part of the solution is that even infants under two years of age will not passively associate all and only new sounds with all and only newly observed objects or actions. Rather, they regularly inspect the situation co-occurring with a new word to find out what the speaker intended to refer to when he or she used that word. For example, if 18-month-olds hear a novel word while they are playing with a novel toy, they will assume that the word names that toy only if the speaker is also attending to it: if the speaker is looking at a different object, children will spontaneously follow her line-of-regard and assume that the object she is looking at is the referent of the new word (Baldwin 1991). This pragmatic understanding might also underlie certain expectations about how the LEXICON works, such as the assumption that different words should not have the same meaning (Clark 1985; though see Woodward and Markman 1997 for a different perspective). And children's understanding of the actual meanings of many words—particularly for artifacts, such as "toy" or "clock," but also for certain collections such as "family" and "army"—might require an appreciation of the goals and motivations of others (Bloom 1996).

Finally, much of word learning results from the child's emerging appreciation of properties of language itself. As noted above, there is a strong relationship between the onset of syntax and the nature and development of word learning. In many regards (see SYNTAX, ACQUISITION OF), young children understand certain properties of language-specific grammar and balk when these are violated by adult speakers (Shipley, Smith, and Gleitman 1969). The ability to take into account more than one word in the adult sentence offers significant new clues to the word-learning child. One important cue comes from identification of a word's grammatical category, a process called "syntactic bootstrapping." For example, children who hear "This is ZAV" expect the word to refer to a specific individual, as with a proper name like "Fred" (Katz, Baker, and Macnamara 1974). Children who hear "a ZAV" expect it to refer to a kind of individual, such as "dog"; those who hear "some ZAV" expect it to refer to a substance name such as "water" (Brown 1957; Bloom and Kelemen 1995). And children hearing "John ZAVS Bill" expect the word to have a meaning similar to that of "hit," whereas those who hear "John and Bill ZAV" expect it to have a meaning similar to that of "stand" (Gleitman 1990; Naigles 1990)—that is, they can make inferences about the number and type of arguments that a new predicate encodes for. Ultimately, the view that structure can be informative for word learning is one that commits theorists to the view that there are links between syntax and semantics to which young learners are privy very early in their language development (e.g., Gleitman 1990; Pinker 1989).

This brings us back to a finding mentioned earlier—the large proportion of object names in children's very early vocabularies. One explanation that has been offered for this property of early lexicons is that object categories are conceptually simpler than categories such as parts and actions (Gentner 1982). Another proposed solution is that there are special default biases in word learning that guide children towards an object-kind interpretation of new words (Woodward and Markman 1997). A focus on syntactic development suggests a third possibility: no matter how conceptually sophisticated they are, learners who have no access to syntactic cues may be able to acquire only words whose referents are relatively "concrete," those whose referents can be directly observed in the extralinguistic environment. In support of this, Gillette et al. (1997) found that adults shown videotaped mother-child interactions with the audio turned off and with beeps used in place of words (that is, adults who were deprived of syntactic support) acquired only "concrete" terms, typically object names—just like presyntactic infants.

In sum, there are three recent discoveries that have increased our understanding of word learning. First, a range of ontological categories, including objects, are available to very young children. Second, in addition to being conceptual creatures like us, children are intentional creatures like us: far from being at the mercy of passive associations when words occur in extralinguistic contexts, they are sensitive to subtle cues to a speaker's referential intentions. Third, two findings about the form-meaning relations that children are acquiring may help explain how they perform their pyrotechnic learning feats—the increasing linguistic understanding of the SYNTAX-SEMANTICS INTERFACE; and the growing evidence that young children use cues at this level to constrain the interpretation of novel words.

See also LANGUAGE ACQUISITION; MEANING; NATIVISM; SEMANTICS, ACQUISITION OF

—Paul Bloom and Lila Gleitman

References

Anglin, J. (1993). Vocabulary development: A morphological analysis. *Monographs of the Society for Research in Child Development* 238: 1–166.

Baldwin, D. A. (1991). Infants' contribution to the achievement of joint reference. *Child Development* 62: 875–890.

Beckwith, R., E. Tinker, and L. Bloom. (1989). The acquisition of non-basic sentences. Paper presented at the Boston University Conference on Language Development.

Bloom, P. (1996). Intention, history, and artifact concepts. *Cognition* 60: 1–29.

Bloom, P., and D. Kelemen. (1995). Syntactic cues in the acquisition of collective nouns. *Cognition* 56: 1–30.

Brown, R. (1957). Linguistic determinism and the part of speech. *Journal of Abnormal and Social Psychology* 55: 1–5.

Carey, S. (1978). The child as word learner. In M. Halle, J. Bresnan, and A. Miller, Eds., *Linguistic Theory and Psychological Reality*. Cambridge, MA: MIT Press.

Clark, E. V. (1985). The principle of contrast: A constraint on language acquisition. In B. MacWhinney, Ed., *Mechanisms of Language Acquisition*. Hillsdale, NJ: Erlbaum, pp. 1–33.

Fenson, L., P. S. Dale, J. S. Reznick, E. Bates, D. J. Thal, and S.J. Pethick. (1994). Variability in early communicative development. *Monographs of the Society for Research in Child Development* 59: 1–173.

Gentner, D. (1982). Why nouns are learned before verbs: Linguistic relativity versus natural partitioning. In S. A. Kuczaj II, Ed., *Language Development*. Vol. 2, *Language, Thought, and Culture*. Hillsdale, NJ: Erlbaum, pp. 301–334.

Gleitman, L. R. (1990). The structural sources of word meaning. *Language Acquisition* 1: 3–55.

Gleitman, L. R., and J. Gillette. (1995). The role of syntax in verb learning. In P. Fletcher and B. MacWhinney, Eds., *The Handbook of Child Language.* Cambridge, MA: Blackwell, pp. 413–428.

Gillette, J., H. Gleitman, L. Gleitman, and A. Lederer. (1997). More surprises about word learning: The Human Simulation Paradigm. Unpublished ms, University of Pennsylvania.

Huttenlocher, J., and P. Smiley. (1987). Early word meanings: The case of object names. *Cognitive Psychology* 19: 63–89.

Katz, N., E. Baker, and J. T. Macnamara. (1974). What's in a name? A study of how children learn common and proper names. *Child Development* 45: 469–473.

Landau, B., and L. R. Gleitman. (1985). *Language and Experience.* Cambridge, MA: Harvard University Press.

Markman, E. M. (1990). Constraints children place on word meanings. *Cognitive Science* 14: 57–77.

Markson, L., and P. Bloom. (1997). Evidence against a dedicated system for word learning in children. *Nature* 385: 813–815.

Miller, G. A. (1996). *The Science of Words.* 2nd ed. New York: W. H. Freeman.

Naigles, L. (1990). Children use syntax to learn verb meanings. *Journal of Child Language* 17: 357–374.

Petitto, L. (1992). Modularity and constraints in early lexical acquisition: Evidence from children's early language and gesture. In M. R. Gunnar and M. Maratsos, Eds., *The Minnesota Symposia on Child Psychology,* vol. 25. Hillsdale, NJ: Erlbaum.

Pinker, S. (1989). *Learnability and Cognition.* Cambridge, MA: MIT Press.

Quine, W. V. O. (1960). *Word and Object.* Cambridge, MA: MIT Press.

Schieffelin, B. B. (1985). The acquisition of Kaluli. In D. I. Slobin, Ed., *The Crosslinguistic Study of Language Acquisition,* vol. 1, *The Data.* Hillsdale, NJ: Erlbaum.

Shipley, E., C. Smith, and L. R. Gleitman. (1969). A study in the acquisition of language: Free responses to commands. *Language* 45: 322–342.

Spelke, E. S. (1994). Initial knowledge: Six suggestions. *Cognition* 50: 431–445.

Waxman, S. R., and D. Markow. (1995). Words as an invitation to form categories: Evidence from 12- to 13-month-olds. *Cognitive Psychology* 29: 257–302.

Woodward, A. L., and E. M. Markman. (1997). Early word learning. In W. Damon, D. Kuhn, and R. Siegler, Eds., *Handbook of Child Psychology,* vol. 2, *Cognition, Perception, and Language.* New York: Wiley.

Further Readings

Bloom, P. (1996). Possible individuals in language and cognition. *Current Directions in Psychological Science* 5: 90–94.

Bloom, P. (1997). Intentionality and word learning. *Trends in Cognitive Sciences* 1: 9–12.

Clark, E. (1995). *The Lexicon in Acquisition.* Cambridge: Cambridge University Press.

Fisher, C., D. G. Hall, S. Rakowitz, and L. Gleitman. (1994). Why it is better to receive than to give: Syntactic and conceptual constraints on vocabulary growth. *Lingua* 92: 333–375.

Golinkoff, R. M., C. B. Mervis, and K. Hirsh-Pasek. (1994). Early object labels: The case for a developmental lexical principles framework. *Journal of Child Language* 21: 125–155.

Hall, D. G. (1994). How children learn common nouns and proper names. In J. Macnamara and G. Reyes, Eds., *The Logical Foundations of Cognition.* Oxford: Oxford University Press.

Macnamara, J. (1982). *Names for Things: A Study of Human Learning.* Cambridge, MA: MIT Press.

Markman, E. M. (1989). *Categorization and Naming in Children.* Cambridge, MA: MIT Press.

Oshima-Takane, Y. (1988). Children learn from speech not addressed to them: The case of personal pronouns. *Journal of Child Language* 15: 94–108.

Soja, N. N., S. Carey, and E. S. Spelke. (1992). Perception, ontology, and word meaning. *Cognition* 45: 101–107.

Tomasello, M., and M. Barton. (1994). Learning words in nonostensive contexts. *Developmental Psychology* 30: 639–650.

Word Recognition

See SPOKEN WORD RECOGNITION; VISUAL WORD RECOGNITION

Working Memory

Working memory is the cognitive system that allows us to keep active a limited amount of information (roughly, 7 ± 2 items) for a brief period of time (roughly, a few seconds). This system has been a major research topic since the advent of the cognitive revolution in the 1950s, and was earlier referred to as "short-term memory." It was then thought to have two functions: storing material that we have to recall in a few seconds, as when we rehearse a phone number until we dial it, and providing a gateway to long-term memory (e.g., Atkinson and Shiffrin 1968). While cognitive scientists continue to believe in the simple storage purpose, their belief in the gateway function has been somewhat undermined by the existence of neurological patients who are impaired in short-term memory tasks, but perform normally on long-term memory tasks (see, e.g., Shallice 1988). Rather, cognitive scientists now assume that the major function of the system in question is to temporarily store the outcomes of intermediate computations when PROBLEM SOLVING, and to perform further computations on these temporary outcomes (e.g., Baddeley 1986). For example, when mentally multiplying two-digit numbers like 38×19, we may first compute and store the partial product $8 \times 9 = 72$, later use this partial product in further computations, and subsequently drop it when it is no longer needed. Given this role, the system in question has been renamed "working memory," and is considered critical not only for analyzing MEMORY, but for understanding thought itself.

In what follows, first we review some basic characteristics of working memory, and then consider its role in higher-level cognition. We mention empirical evidence from various human studies, including cognitive-behavioral experiments, neuropsychological (patient) studies, and neuroimaging experiments (using POSITRON EMISSION TOMOGRAPHY or functional MAGNETIC RESONANCE IMAGING).

There appear to be different working memories for different kinds of materials, particularly different systems for verbal and spatial information. In a paradigm cognitive-behavioral experiment, subjects perform a working-memory task while concurrently performing a secondary task. Any secondary task usually causes some interference with a working-memory task, but verbal secondary tasks interfere more with verbal than with spatial working-memory tasks, whereas spatial secondary tasks interfere more with spatial than with verbal working-memory tasks (e.g., Brooks 1968). This pattern of *selective interference* supports the hypothesis of separate systems for verbal and spatial working memory. (These separate working-memory systems may be connected to separate verbal and spatial perceptual systems.)

The above results are bolstered by neuropsychological findings. There are pairs of neurological patients such that one is impaired on a standard measure of verbal working memory—digit span—but normal on a standard test of spatial working memory—Corsi blocks test—whereas the other patient shows the reverse pattern (see McCarthy and Warrington 1990). This *double-dissociation* between verbal and spatial working-memory tasks argues for two separate systems. Perhaps the most direct evidence for two systems comes from neuroimaging experiments. Subjects perform either a verbal recognition test—for example, remembering the names of four letters for 3 sec—or a spatial recognition test—for example, remembering the locations of three dots for 3 sec—while having their brains scanned. Different areas of the brain are activated in the two tasks, with almost all of the activations in the verbal task being in the left hemisphere, and most of the activations in the spatial task being in the right hemisphere (Smith, Jonides, and Koeppe 1996). (Other neuroimaging studies indicate that there might be separate working memories for spatial and visual-object information, just as the single-cell evidence shows for nonhuman primates—see WORKING MEMORY, NEURAL BASIS OF).

Within verbal and spatial working memory, there is evidence for a further subdivision, that between a passive storage process and an active rehearsal process. The evidence is strongest for the verbal system. In cognitive-behavioral studies, experimenters have argued that some effects reflect only a storage process, for example the *phonological similarity effect,* in which the short-term recall of words is poorer for phonologically similar than phonologically dissimilar ones (Conrad 1970) whereas other effects are due to rehearsal, for example, the *word-length effect,* in which the short-term recall of words declines with the time it takes to say the words (Baddeley, Thompson, and Buchanan 1975). Importantly, when subjects doing these tasks are prevented from rehearsing the words by having to articulate some irrelevant word or phrase, the word-length effect disappears but the phonological-similarity effect remains intact (Longoni, Richardson, and Aiello 1993). Presumably, the irrelevant articulation blocked rehearsal, but had no effect on the storage buffer. Further support for this interpretation comes from the study of a patient whose brain damage presumably disrupted only the rehearsal component. This patient shows a normal phonological-similarity effect, but no effect of word length or of irrelevant articulation (Basso et al. 1982).

There is converging evidence for the storage-rehearsal distinction from neuroimaging studies. Subjects are scanned while doing a short-term recognition task, which presumably involves storage plus rehearsal, or while doing a task that involves only articulation or rehearsal. Both tasks activate areas in the left-hemisphere frontal cortex that are known to be involved in the planning of speech, whereas only the memory task activates posterior-parietal regions thought to be involved in storage per se (Paulesu, Frith, and Frackowiak 1993; Awh et al. 1996). Recent neuroimaging experiments argue for a comparable storage-rehearsal distinction in spatial working memory, where spatial rehearsal appears to amount to selectively attending to particular locations (Awh and Jonides forthcoming).

Some of the best evidence for (verbal) working memory playing a role in higher-level cognition comes from cognitive-behavioral studies. One line of evidence is that there are substantial correlations between (1) a measure of a person's verbal working-memory capacity—the reading-span task—and (2) the person's performance on either a reasoning task—the Raven Progressive Matrices test—or language-understanding tasks (e.g., Carpenter, Just, and Shell 1990; Just and Carpenter 1992). A second piece of behavioral evidence is the finding that performing a working-memory task interferes with a concurrent reasoning task (solving syllogisms) more than does performing a non–working-memory task (Gilhooly et al. 1993). Again, there is converging evidence from recent neuroimaging experiments. When people engage in either a reasoning task (the Raven test again) or a complex-categorization task, many of the areas found active are those activated in standard working-memory studies (Prabhakaran et al. 1997; Smith, Patalano, and Jonides 1998).

Other persuasive evidence for working memory's role in higher-level cognition comes from computational research, specifically the use of symbolic models to simulate higher-cognitive processes. Simulations of this sort routinely give a major role to working-memory operations, and provide a detailed account of exactly how working memory can be used to regulate the flow of information processing during CATEGORIZATION, PLANNING, reasoning, PROBLEM SOLVING, and language understanding (e.g., Anderson 1983; Newell 1990; Carpenter et al. 1990).

See also AGING, MEMORY, AND THE BRAIN; EPISODIC VS. SEMANTIC MEMORY; IMPLICIT VS. EXPLICIT MEMORY; LANGUAGE PRODUCTION; MEMORY, HUMAN NEUROPSYCHOLOGY; PSYCHOLINGUISTICS

—Edward E. Smith

References

Anderson, J. R. (1983). *The Architecture of Cognition.* Cambridge, MA: Harvard University Press.

Atkinson, R. C., and R. M. Shiffrin. (1968). Human memory: A proposed system and its control processes. In K. W. Spence, and J. T. Spence, Eds., *The Psychology of Learning and Motivation: Advances in Research and Theory,* vol. 2. New York: Academic Press.

Awh, E., and J. Jonides. (1998). Spatial selective attention and spatial working memory. In R. Parasuraman, Ed., *The Attentive Brain.* Cambridge, MA: MIT Press, pp. 353–380.

Awh, E., J. Jonides, E. E. Smith, E. H. Schumacher, R. A. Koeppe, and S. Katz. (1996). Dissociation of storage and rehearsal in verbal working memory: Evidence from PET. *Psychological Science* 7: 25–31.

Baddeley, A. D. (1986). *Working Memory.* Oxford: Oxford University Press.

Baddeley, A. D., and G. J. Hitch. (1974). Working memory. In G. Bower, Ed., *Recent Advances in Learning and Motivation,* vol. 8. New York: Academic Press.

Baddeley, A. D., N. Thompson, and M. Buchanan. (1975). Word length and the structure of short-term memory. *Journal of Verbal Learning and Verbal Behavior* 14: 575–589.

Basso, A. H., H. Spinnler, G. Vallar, and E. Zanobia. (1982). Left hemisphere damage and selective impairment of auditory verbal short-term memory: A case study. *Neuropsychologica* 20: 263–274.

Brooks, L. R. (1968). Spatial and verbal components of the act of recall. *Canadian Journal of Psychology* 22: 349–368.

Carpenter, P. A., M. A. Just, and P. Shell. (1990). What one intelligence test measures: A theoretical account of the processing in the Raven Progressive Matrices Test. *Psychological Review* 97: 404–431.

Conrad, R. (1970). Short-term memory processes in the deaf. *British Journal of Psychology* 61: 179–195.

Gilhooly, K. J., R. H. Logie, N. E. Wetherick, and V. Wynn. (1993). Working memory and strategies in syllogistic-reasoning tasks. *Memory and Cognition* 21: 115–124.

Just, M. A., and P. A. Carpenter. (1992). A capacity theory of comprehension: Individual differences in working memory. *Psychological Review* 99: 122–149.

McCarthy, R. A., and E. K. Warrington. (1990). *Cognitive Neuropsychology: A Clinical Introduction.* San Diego: Academic Press.

Newell, A. (1990). *Unified Theories of Cognition.* Cambridge, MA: Harvard University Press.

Paulesu, E., C. D. Frith, and R. S. J. Frackowiak. (1993). The neural correlates of the verbal component of working memory. *Nature* 362: 342–344.

Prabhakaran, V., J. A. L. Smith, J. E. Desmond, G. H. Glover, and J. D. E. Gabrieli. (1997). Neural substrates of fluid reasoning: An fMRI study of neocortical activation during performance of the Ravens Progressive Matrices Test. *Cognitive Psychology* 33: 43–63.

Shallice, T. (1988). *From Neuropsychology to Mental Structure.* Cambridge: Cambridge University Press.

Smith, E. E., J. Jonides, and R. A. Koeppe. (1996). Dissociating verbal and spatial working memory using PET. *Cerebral Cortex* 6: 11–20.

Smith, E. E., A. Patalano, and J. Jonides. (1998). Alternative strategies of categorization. *Cognition* 65: 167–196.

Further Readings

Baddeley, A. D. (1992). Working memory. *Science* 255: 556–559.

Daneman, M., and P. A. Carpenter. (1980). Individual differences in working memory and reading. *Journal of Verbal Learning and Verbal Behavior* 19: 450–466.

Hitch, G. J. (1978). The role of short-term working memory in mental arithmetic. *Cognitive Psychology* 10: 302–323.

Jonides, J. (1995). Working memory and thinking. In E. E. Smith and D. Osherson, Eds., *Invitation to Cognitive Science,* vol. 3: *Thinking.* 2nd ed. Cambridge, MA: MIT Press.

Jonides, J., P. Reuter-Lorenz, E. E. Smith, E. Awh, L. Barnes, M. Drain, J. Glass, E. Lauber, A. Patalano, and E. Schumacher. (1996). Verbal and spatial working memory. In D. L. Medin, Ed., *The Psychology of Learning and Motivation* 35: 43–88.

Just, M. A., P. A. Carpenter, and T. A. Keller. (1996). The capacity theory of comprehension: New frontiers of evidence and arguments. *Psychological Review* 103: 773–780.

Kyllonen, P. C., and R. E. Christal. (1990). Reasoning ability is (little more than) working memory capacity?! *Intelligence* 14: 389–433.

Longoni, A. M., J. T. Richardson, and A. Aiello. (1993). Articulating rehearsal and phonological storage in working memory. *Memory and Cognition* 21: 11–22.

Martin, R. C. (1993). Short-term memory and sentence processing: Evidence from neuro-psychology. *Memory and Language* 21: 176–183.

Salthouse, T. A. (1990). Working memory as a processing resource in cognitive ageing. *Developmental Review* 10: 101–124.

Smith, E. E., and J. Jonides. (1997). Working memory: A view from neuroimaging. *Cognitive Psychology* 33: 5–42.

Vallar G., and T. Shallice, Eds.. (1990). *Neuropsychological Impairments of Short-Term Memory.* Cambridge: Cambridge University Press.

Waters, G. S., and D. Caplan. (1996). The capacity theory of sentence comprehension: Critique of Just and Carpenter (1992). *Psychological Review* 103: 761–772.

Working Memory, Neural Basis of

Working memory, as defined by cognitive psychologists, refers to "a system for the temporary holding and manipulation of information during the performance of a range of cognitive tasks such as comprehension, learning and reasoning" (Baddeley 1986). The adjective "working" is a critical part of the definition, emphasizing as it does the *processing* of information and not its particular content. Working memory is characterized by its limited storage capacity and rapid turnover and is differentiated from the larger capacity and archival memory system traditionally defined as long-term memory. The origin of the term "working memory" is difficult to trace. It was used by Miller, Galanter, and Pribram in their 1960 book, *Plans and the Structure of Behavior,* to describe the functions of the frontal lobe: "This most forward portion of the primate frontal lobe appears to us to serve as a "working memory" where plans . . . can be retained temporarily when they are being formed, or transformed, or executed." Metaphors for working memory include "blackboard of the mind" (Reddy 1980); "mental sketch-pad" (Baddeley 1986), and "on-line memory" (Goldman-Rakic 1987). When we listen to human speech, we are using working memory to hold the segments of sentences "on-line" millisecond by millisecond. We employ working memory to carry forward, in real time, the subject of a sentence and associate it with verbs and objects in order to comprehend the sense and meaning of sentences. When we perform a mental arithmetic problem, recall a phone number, plan a hand of bridge or a chess move, or follow a verbal instruction, we use working memory. In fact it is difficult to think of a cognitive function that does not engage the working-memory systems of the brain. A number of different models have been proposed regarding the functional architecture of human cognition (see WORKING MEMORY).

The study of short-term memory in nonhuman primates can be traced at least as far back as the seminal work of Jacobsen and Fulton which showed a dependence of delayed-response performance on the dorsolateral prefrontal areas of the primate frontal lobe (Jacobsen 1936). Delayed-response tasks are those in which a brief delay is introduced between the presentation of a stimulus (usually denoting either a location or the identity of an object) and the response that is required to indicate that the stimulus has

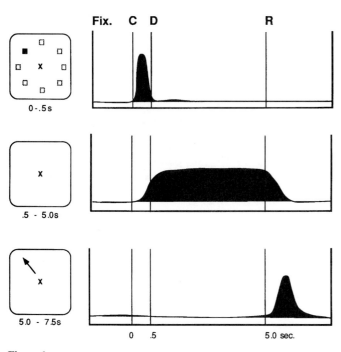

Figure 1.

their dorsolateral prefrontal cortices are unable to make correct choices but instead respond at random (Goldman-Rakic 1987; Fuster 1989). Physiological studies have revealed that the activity of prefrontal neurons correlates with events in the delayed-response tasks, that is, some neurons respond during the placement of the food stimulus, others respond during the delay period, and still other neurons respond at the time of the response (figure 1). Many neurons are combinatorial, having cue, delay, and response-related responses. The activity profiles of prefrontal neurons are thus strikingly related to the subfunctions of sensory registration, memory, and motor control, respectively. As the cue, delay, and response-related neurons are necessarily activated in sequence rather than simultaneously, these neurons mediate the real time events in working memory.

The neurons that respond in the delay period are of particular interest because they exhibit sustained activity for many seconds in the absence of any stimulus, a property that is not observed in primary sensory areas of the brain. Using an oculomotor paradigm which requires the monkey to fixate while small stimuli are presented in various locations in the visual field, it became possible to show that these prefrontal neurons have "memory fields," defined as maximal firing of a neuron to the representation of a target in one or a few locations of the visual field (Funahashi, Bruce, and Goldman-Rakic 1989). For example, a neuron's activity may rise sharply after a stimulus is presented briefly at its "preferred" (e.g., 270°) position, then remain tonically active during a 3 to 5 sec delay (in the absence of the stimulus), and then return to baseline activation abruptly at the end of delay when the response is initiated (as displayed in figure 2). Importantly, such activation occurs *every time* the animal has to remember the same location but not when the animal is remembering targets presented at other "nonpreferred" locations (e.g., 135°, 180°, 225°). An additional important feature of many prefrontal neurons is that while their rate of firing in the delay period is enhanced for one target location, it may be inhibited during the delay on trials with target stimuli of opponent polarity; such a pattern of activity indicates that some prefrontal neurons have "opponent memory fields." This functional distinction provides a valuable clue to how the neural circuitry subserving working memory might be organized. In particular, it points to the role of neural inhibition in sculpting the memory field of these neurons. Inhibition is provided by interneurons in the immediate vicinity of the pyramidal neurons which express memory fields and with the capacity to transmit the information to other areas of the brain. Finally, neuronal activity in the delay period appears essential to correct recall of the preceding stimulus; errors are invariably made on trials in which neurons with memory fields fail to maintain their activation during the delay period (Funahashi et al. 1989).

From CAJAL on, it has been appreciated that several types of interneurons populate the CEREBRAL CORTEX and interact with pyramidal cells. The overwhelming majority of interneurons utilize the inhibitory neurotransmitter, γ-aminobutyric acid (GABA), whereas pyramidal cells use the excitatory amino acid glutamate as their neurotransmitter. Recent evidence indicates that pyramidal-nonpyramidal interactions are critical to the formation of memory fields in

been recalled. It is important to point out, that, as studied in the 1930s and forward, delayed-response tasks were considered tests primarily of "immediate memory." This terminology denoted passive or short-term storage and did not embody the notion of processing or the linkage between storage and processing that are central concepts in the study of working memory (Baddeley 1986). For commonly used tasks of the delayed-response "family," little or no processing is in fact required. However, there is much evidence to indicate that the storage and processing functions within working memory are carried out by the same cells and circuits and that the study of the machinery for storage is an essential step in understanding the processes carried out by those cells and circuits.

Working memory is studied in humans mainly by the use of behavioral paradigms, most recently in conjunction with brain imaging. However, the physiological and circuit underpinnings of this process have come primarily from anatomical, physiological, and behavioral research in nonhuman primates. A cellular basis for working memory has emerged from the study of activity in single neurons recorded from the prefrontal cortex of monkeys that have been trained to perform delayed response tasks (Fuster and Alexander 1971; Kubota and Niki 1971; Goldman-Rakic, Lidow, and Gallager 1990). In the traditional type of spatial delayed-response task, a monkey observes an experimenter place a food morsel in one of two food wells, each of which is immediately covered by identical cards. A screen is lowered between the test tray to prevent the monkey from immediately displacing the card to reveal the hidden treat. After several seconds, the screen is raised and the animal is allowed to select one of the food wells. The imposed delay forces the monkey to base its choice on the memory of the location in which the food was placed before the delay, that is, the choice is memory-guided. Monkeys with lesions of

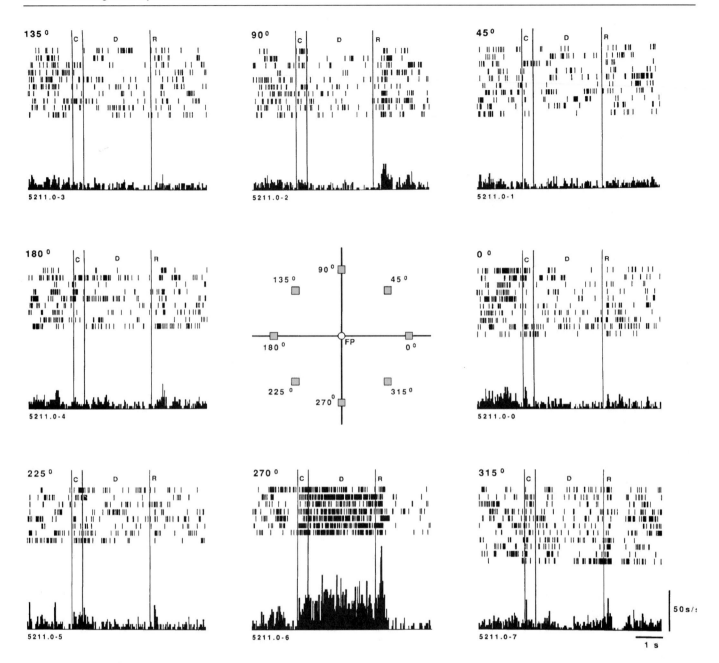

Figure 2.

prefrontal cortex just as they may play a role in establishing the orientation specificity of primary visual neurons. Wilson, O'Scalaidhe, and Goldman-Rakic (1994) have succeeded in classifying prefrontal neurons as interneurons or pyramidal neurons based on their firing rates *in vivo*, that is, as monkeys performed the oculomotor delayed response task. This study showed that interneurons, like pyramidal neurons, express directional preferences and the patterns of activity expressed by closely adjacent pyramidal and nonpyramidal neurons are often inverse, such that as a nonpyramidal neuron increases its rate of discharge, a nearby pyramidal neuron decreases its rate. Current studies are examining in more detail the nature of interactions between interneurons and pyramidal neurons engaged in the working

memory process. At present, it is clear that the mechanism of disinhibition is a process that plays a powerful role in the construction of a prefrontal neuron's memory field. Further, it is becoming clear that modulatory NEUROTRANSMITTERS such as dopamine and serotonin modulate the activity of and interactions between pyramidal and nonpyramidal cells.

Spatial and feature working memory mechanisms of prefrontal cortex are dissociable at the behavioral, cellular, and areal levels of functional architecture (figure 3). In nonhuman primates, lesions of the dorsolateral prefrontal cortex produce deficits on spatial working-memory tasks but not on object working-memory tasks while, conversely, lesions of the inferior convexity of the prefrontal cortex produce deficits on object-memory tasks but not on spatial tasks

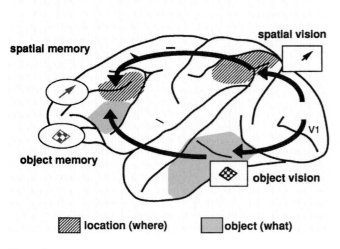

multiple memory domains

location (where)   object (what)

Figure 3.

(Goldman-Rakic 1987; Mishkin 1964). Consistent with lesion and behavior results, neurons located in dorsolateral prefrontal cortex (areas 46 and 8) code visual-spatial memoranda, while those that code simple, complex, or categorical features of stimuli are located in the inferior convexity (areas 12 and 45; Wilson, O'Scalaidhe, and Goldman-Rakic 1993; O'Scalaidhe, Wilson, and Goldman-Rakic 1997). Moreover, individual neurons that are engaged by the memory of an object rarely, if ever, code their peripheral location (Wilson et al. 1993). Physiologically guided injections of pathway tracers in the spatial and object-memory centers have shown them to be connected to the appropriate visual centers in the parietal (Cavada and Goldman-Rakic 1989) and temporal lobes, respectively (Webster, Bachevalier, and Ungerleider 1994; Bates et al. 1994).

Working memory is considered a major component of the machinery of executive function and it is not surprising that POSITRON EMISSION TOMOGRAPHY (PET) and functional MAGNETIC RESONANCE IMAGING (fMRI) studies in human subjects have focused on this function. Recent studies in healthy human subjects, for example, have shown that the middle frontal gyrus, the region corresponding to the dorsolateral areas studied in macaque monkeys, is activated when human subjects carry out analogous spatial working-memory tasks (McCarthy et al. 1994; Jonides et al. 1993). Inferior regions of the dorsolateral prefrontal cortex are activated for verbal and other nonspatial working-memory functions (e.g., Frith et al. 1991; Courtney et al. 1996; Demb et al. 1995). All of these results speak to the modular organization of working-memory systems in the prefrontal cortex, with each working-memory "domain" associated with an informationally constrained sensory-processing stream.

Working-memory capacity in human subjects can be assessed by numerous tasks designed by cognitive psychologists using visual or auditory stimuli and verbal, spatial, and object vision. Many of these tasks are formally similar to those used with nonhuman primates, assuring the generalizability of results from the nonhuman species to humans. fMRI and PET have been used to examine changes in blood flow or metabolic activity in the cerebral cortex of normal

human subjects performing a wide variety of working-memory tasks. The human prefrontal areas that are invariably activated under these behavioral conditions are dissociable from the areas activated by sensorimotor components of the tasks examined (Cohen et al. 1994; Courtney et al. 1996; Sweeney et al. 1996) as they are in nonhuman primates (for review, see Goldman-Rakic 1987; also Goldman et al. 1971).

Conversely, prefrontal areas display depressed blood flow or metabolism in patients with schizophrenia (e.g., Weinberger, Berman, and Zec 1986), depression (e.g., Buchsbaum, Debisi, and Holcomb 1984) and other conditions of impaired affect or cognition. As might be expected if working memory were essential to executive function, working-memory deficits and correlated prefrontal dysfunction have been demonstrated in schizophrenics (e.g., Weinberger et al. 1986; Fukushima et al. 1988; Park and Holzman 1992), in Parkinson patients (e.g., Gotham, Brown, and Marsden 1988; Levin, Labre, and Weiner 1989), and in age-related memory decline (e.g., Salthouse 1991)— neuropathological conditions in which impairments of higher cortical processing are expressed. Prefrontal cortical volume is reduced in schizophrenia, (e.g., Zipursky et al. 1992) and cellular changes (e.g., Benes et al. 1991; Selemon, Rajkowska, and Goldman-Rakic 1995) have also been observed in prefrontal areas in this disorder. On the strength of these and other findings, Goldman-Rakic has proposed that working memory dysfunction may be the core functional deficit underlying thought disorder in schizophrenia (Goldman-Rakic 1987, 1991). It has now become clear that schizophrenic patients are also impaired in tasks requiring working memory. Park and Holzman (1992) have demonstrated that patients with schizophrenia express delay-dependent errors on a modified spatial oculomotor delayed-response paradigm nearly identical to that used in the single-unit studies described above. Early evidence indicates that relatives of patients perform more poorly on spatial working-memory tasks than unrelated control subjects (Park, Holzman, and Goldman-Rakic 1995). Auditory working memory is also severely impaired in schizophrenic patients (Gold et al. 1997; Saykin et al. 1991). These and many other studies are laying the basis for a comprehensive analysis of psychiatric disorders in terms of working memory and the prefrontal mechanisms upon which it greatly depends.

See also IMPLICIT VS. EXPLICIT MEMORY; MEMORY; MEMORY, HUMAN NEUROPSYCHOLOGY; MEMORY STORAGE, MODULATION OF; VISUAL PROCESSING STREAMS

—*Patricia Goldman-Rakic*

References

Baddeley, A. (1986). *Working Memory*. London: Oxford University Press.

Bates, J. F., F. A. W. Wilson, S. P. O'Scalaidhe, and P. S. Goldman-Rakic. (1994). Area TE connections with inferior prefrontal regions responsive to complex objects and faces. *Soc. Neurosci. Abstr.* 20: 1054.

Benes, F. M., J. McSparren, E. D. Bird, J. P. San Giovanni, and S. L. Vincent. (1991). Deficits in small interneurons in prefrontal and cingulate cortices of schizophrenic and schizoaffective patients. *Arch. Gen. Psychiatry* 48: 996–1001.

Buchsbaum, M. S., L. E. DeLisi, and H. H. Holcomb. (1984). Anteroposterior gradients in cerebral glucose use in schizophrenia and affective disorders. *Arch. Gen. Psychiatry* 41: 1159–1166.

Cavada, C., and P. S. Goldman-Rakic. (1989). Posterior parietal cortex in rhesus monkey: 2. Evidence for segregated corticocortical networks linking sensory and limbic areas with the frontal lobe. *J. Comp. Neurol* 287: 422–445.

Cohen, J. D., S. D. Forman, T. S. Braver, B. J. Casey, D. Servan-Schreiber, and D. C. Noll. (1994). Activation of the prefrontal cortex in a nonspatial working memory task with functional MRI. *Hum. Brain Mapping* 1: 293–304.

Courtney, S. M., L. G. Ungerleider, K. Keil, and J. V. Haxby. (1996). Object and spatial visual working memory activate separate neural systems in human cortex. *Cereb. Cortex* 6: 39–49.

Demb, J. B., J. E. Desmond, A. D. Wagner, C. J. Vaidya, G. H. Glover, and J. D. E. Gabrieli. (1995). Semantic encoding and retrieval in the left inferior prefrontal cortex: A functional MRI study of task difficult and process specificity. *J. Neurosci.* 15: 5870–5878.

Frith, C. D., K. Friston, P. F. Liddle, and R. S. J. Frackowiak. (1991). Willed action and the prefrontal cortex in man. *Proc. R. Soc. Lond. B. Biol. Sci.* 244: 241–246.

Fukushima, J., K. Fukushima, T. Chiba, S. Tanaka, I. Yamashita, and M. Kato. (1988). Disturbances of voluntary control of saccadic eye movements in schizophrenic patients. *Biol. Psychiatry* 23: 670–677.

Funahashi, S., C. J. Bruce, and P. S. Goldman-Rakic. (1989). Mnemonic coding of visual space in the monkey's dorsolateral prefrontal cortex. *J. Neurophysiol* 61: 331–349.

Fuster, J. M. (1989). *The Prefrontal Cortex*. 2nd ed. New York: Raven Press.

Fuster, J. M., and G. E. Alexander. (1971). Neuron activity related to short-term memory. *Science* 173: 652–654.

Gold, J. M., C. Carpenter, C. Randolph, T. E. Goldberg, and D. R. Weinberger. (1997). Auditory working memory and Wisconsin Card Sorting Test performance in schizophrenia. *Arch. Gen. Psychiatry* 54: 159–165.

Goldman, P. S., H. E. Rosvold, B. Vest, and T. W. Galkin. (1971). Analysis of the delayed-alternation deficit produced by dorsolateral prefrontal lesions in the rhesus monkey. *J. Comp. Physiol. Psychol.* 77: 212–220.

Goldman-Rakic, P. S. (1987). Circuitry of the prefrontal cortex and the regulation of behavior by representational knowledge. In F. Plum and V. Mountcastle, Eds., *Handbook of Physiology*. Bethesda, MD: American Physiological Society, pp. 373–417.

Goldman-Rakic, P. S. (1991). Prefrontal cortical dysfunction in schizophrenia: The relevance of working memory. In B. J. Carroll and J. E. Barrett, Eds., *Psychopathology and the Brain*. New York: Raven Press, pp. 1–23.

Goldman-Rakic, P. S., M. S. Lidow, and D. W. Gallager. (1990). Overlap of dopaminergic, adrenergic, and serotonergic receptors and complementary of their subtypes in primate prefrontal cortex. *J. Neurosci.* 10: 2125–2138.

Gotham, A. M., R. G. Brown, and C. P. Marsden. (1988). "Frontal" cognitive function in patients with Parkinson's disease "on" and "off" levodopa. *Brain* 111: 299–321.

Jacobsen, C. F. (1936). Studies of cerebral function in primates. *Comp. Psychol. Mono.* 13: 1–68.

Jonides, J., E. E. Smith, R. A. Koeppe, E. Awh, S. Minoshima, and M. A. Mintun. (1993). Spatial working memory in humans as revealed by PET. *Nature* 363: 623–625.

Kubota, K., and H. Niki. (1971). Prefrontal cortical unit activity and delayed cortical unit activity and delayed alternation performance in monkeys. *J. Neurophysiol.* 34: 337–347.

Levin, B. E., M. M. Labre, and W. J. Weiner. (1989). Cognitive impairments associated with early Parkinson's disease. *Neurology* 39: 557–561.

McCarthy, G., A. M. Blamire, A. Puce, A. C. Nobre, G. Bloch, F. Hyder, P. S. Goldman-Rakic, and R. G. Shulman. (1994). Functional magnetic resonance imaging of human prefrontal cortex activation during a spatial working memory task. *Proc. Natl. Acad. Sci. USA* 91: 8690–8694.

Miller, G. A., E. H. Galanter, and K. H. Pribram. (1960). *Plans and Structure of Behavior*. New York: Holt.

Mishkin, M. (1964). Perseveration of central sets after frontal lesions in monkeys. In J. M. Warren and K. Akert, Eds., *The Frontal Granular Cortex and Behavior*. New York: McGraw-Hill, p. 219.

O'Scalaidhe, S. P., F. A. W. Wilson, and P. S. Goldman-Rakic. (1997). Area segregation of face-processing neurons in prefrontal cortex. *Science* 278: 1135–1138.

Park, S. and P. S. Holzman. (1992). Schizophrenics show spatial working memory deficits. *Arch. Gen. Psychiatry* 49: 975–982.

Park, S., P. S. Holzman, and P. S. Goldman-Rakic. (1995). Spatial working memory deficits in the relatives of schizophrenic patients. *Arch. Gen. Psychiatry* 52: 821–828.

Reddy, E. R. (1980). Machine models of speech perception. In R. A. Cole, Ed., *Perception and Production of Human Speech*. Hillsdale, NJ: Erlbaum pp. 215–242.

Salthouse, T. A. (1991). Mediation of adult age differences in cognition by reductions in working memory and speed of processing. *Psychological Sciences* 2: 170–183.

Saykin, A. J., R. C. Gur, R. E. Gur, P. D. Mozley, L. H. Mozley, S. M. Resnick, B. Kester, and P. Stafiniak. (1991). Neuropsychological function in schizophrenia: Selective impairment in memory and learning. *Arch. Gen. Psychiatry* 48: 618–624.

Selemon, L. D., G. Rajkowska, and P. S. Goldman-Rakic. (1995). Abnormally high neuronal density in two widespread areas of the schizophrenic cortex. A morphometric analysis of prefrontal area 9 and occipital area 17. *Arch. Gen. Psychiatry* 52: 805–818.

Sweeney, J. A., M. A. Mintun, B. S. Kwee, M. B. Wiseman, D. L. Brown, D. R. Rosenberg, and J. R. Carl. (1996). A positron emission tomography study of voluntary saccadic eye movements and spatial working memory. *J. Neurophysiol.* 75: 454–468.

Webster, M. J., J. Bachevalier, and L. G. Ungerleider. (1994). Connections of inferior temporal areas TEO and TE with parietal and frontal cortex in macaque monkeys. *Cereb. Cortex* 4: 470–483.

Weinberger, D. R., K. F. Berman, and R. F. Zec. (1986). Physiologic dysfunction of dorsolateral prefrontal cortex in schizophrenia. I: Regional cerebral blood flow (rCBF) evidence. *Arch. Gen. Psychiatry* 43: 114–125.

Wilson, F. A. W., S. P. O'Scalaidhe, and P. S. Goldman-Rakic. (1993). Dissociation of object and spatial processing domains in primate prefrontal cortex. *Science* 260: 1955–1958.

Wilson, F. A. W., S. P. O'Scalaidhe, and P. S. Goldman-Rakic. (1994). Functional synergism between putative γ-aminobutyrate-containing neurons and pyramidal neurons in prefrontal cortex. *Proc. Natl. Acad. Sci. USA* 91: 4009–4013.

Zipursky, R. B., K. O. Lim, E. V. Sullivan, B. W. Brown, and A. Pfefferbaum. (1992). Widespread cerebral gray matter volume deficits in schizophrenia. *Arch. Gen. Psychiatry* 42: 195–205.

Writing Systems

Writing systems entered the purview of cognitive science only recently. Twentieth-century linguistics was anxious to move away from prescription of "good usage" to scientific description of natural usage, so for many decades it focused almost exclusively on spoken language. Comprehensive psychological studies had to await the globalization of scholarship that has occurred since the 1970s; previously, the only Westerners knowledgeable about nonalphabetic writing systems were a handful of scholars with literary rather than cognitive-science training.

Nevertheless, there are several motives for cognitive scientists to investigate writing and writing systems. Whereas there are large controversies about how far spoken languages are products of nature rather than nurture, writing is one complex aspect of human behavior that is indisputably a cultural development rather than innate: it has come into existence recently (the earliest writing emerged in Mesopotamia perhaps five thousand years ago), and it is by no means universal either among individuals or among societies. The fundamental role of LITERACY training within all education systems means that psychologists who acquire new knowledge about reading and writing are assured of an audience. Many parents and teachers paid attention when it was reported that DYSLEXIA is rare among users of the nonalphabetic though complex Japanese script (Makita 1968).

Scientific analysis of writing requires a terminology to describe types of script; the following classification is based on Sampson 1987, which represents the relationships between script types as a tree diagram:

(1)

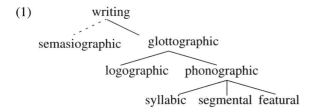

A fundamental distinction is between semasiographic and glottographic systems. *Semasiographic* systems are independent graphic languages not tied to any one spoken language; *glottographic* systems use visible marks to represent elements of a specific spoken language. Examples of semasiographic writing are the "language" of mathematics or the international system of road signs in which, for instance, triangle versus disc means warning versus command, and hollow red versus solid blue means negative versus positive. In theory one could imagine a script of this sort being expanded into a comprehensive system of communication; Otto Neurath's "Isotype" (Neurath 1936) was an attempt at such a system, although Isotype never came close to matching the expressivity of spoken languages. Archaeological evidence suggests that the earliest precursors of writing may have been semasiographic systems.

Glottographic scripts can be divided into *logographic* scripts, where the spoken elements represented by individual graphic symbols are meaningful units (words or "morphemes"), and *phonographic* scripts, where marks are assigned to the meaningless sounds from which words are built up. The leading example of logographic writing is Chinese script, in which words sounding identical will often be represented by entirely unrelated graphic characters.

Phonographic scripts in turn can be classified in terms of the "size" of the sound units symbolized. Alphabetic writing assigns a separate mark to each "phoneme" (consonant or vowel segment); but there are many *syllabic* scripts, in which for instance *pa, pe, po* would be represented by three individual and unrelated symbols. The remarkable Han'gŭl script of Korea is based on phonetic *features*: within the symbol for *t*, say, the fact of the tongue-tip touching the upper jaw and the fact of the soft palate being raised to block airflow through the nose are separately indicated.

These categories are ideal types; real scripts often mix the principles. (For an encyclopaedic survey of the world's scripts, see Daniels and Bright 1996.) English writing might be described as fundamentally phonemic but with elements of logography (to take one example among many, the spelling difference between *rain* and *reign* has nothing to do with pronunciation; it relates purely to word identity). Japanese writing is mixed in a more obvious way: it uses Chinese logographic script to represent the stems of "content words," such as nouns and verbs, and a visually distinct syllabic script for grammatical inflexions and particles.

The foregoing account of script types is not wholly uncontroversial. John DeFrancis (1989) has claimed that *all* writing systems are essentially phonographic. Against the reality of the semasiographic category he points out, correctly, that no semasiographic system with coverage as broad as a spoken language has ever existed. He adds that the crude semasiographic systems found in the archaeological record, although they may have been ancestral to writing, should not themselves be classed as writing; this seems to be a disagreement about definitions rather than facts. Some Central American peoples such as the Aztecs and Mixtecs used semasiographic systems that were far from crude and continued to do so for centuries after their neighbors developed glottographic writing (Boone and Mignolo 1994).

More surprisingly, DeFrancis argues that no true logographic scripts exist either: Chinese writing is based on pronunciation. This confuses historical origin with present-day reality. When Chinese script was developed, some three thousand years ago, its characters were based partly on the pronunciations of Chinese words at that period; it may well be true that no full-scale script could ever in practice be created without heavy use of a phonographic principle. But Chinese pronunciation has changed greatly over the millennia (and the script has evolved independently), with the consequence that Chinese writing now is far less phonographic than it once was. The suggestion that all scripts are necessarily phonographic is really untenable (Sampson 1994). Perhaps the clearest counterexample is the use of Chinese characters to write Japanese vocabulary. Japanese words are written with characters for Chinese words that mean the same, but (since the two languages are genetically unrelated) a graphic element that may still today give a hint about the pronunciation of the Chinese word will be totally uninformative about the pronunciation of the Japanese word.

Even the idea that English orthography is not perfectly phonographic has been challenged by one school, the generative phonologists. The usual explanation of (say) the odd spelling of *righteous* is that *gh* represented a velar fricative consonant (as in Scottish *loch*) that was pronounced in Middle English; the spelling became fixed and did not adapt when the fricative sound dropped out of the spoken language about five hundred years ago. But Chomsky and Halle (1968) argued that there is evidence from English sound patterns (for instance, the vowel alternation between *vice* and *vicious* versus lack of alternation between *right* and *righteous*) which implies that the fricative consonant remains a psychological reality with respect to the "underlying" word forms in which modern speakers mentally store their vocabulary. However, this concept of abstract phonology is no longer widely accepted.

Probably the liveliest current debate within the psychology of writing concerns the question how far a mature reader's ability to retrieve a meaningful word from a string of letters depends on an intermediate step of mentally converting the letters into a pronunciation. The question has obvious resonance with the debate in the teaching profession between "phonic" and "look-and-say" methods. The consensus view has been that pronunciation is often bypassed, particularly when reading common or irregularly spelled words. P. E. Bryant and Lynette Bradley (1980) showed that unskilled readers often cannot read words that they can spell correctly, when the spelling is regular but visually nondistinctive. But a minority of researchers (e.g., Lukatela and Turvey 1994) argue that phonetic mediation is essential in all word recognition.

In the last few years, research has begun to exploit new categories of data, including MAGNETIC RESONANCE IMAGING and POSITRON EMISSION TOMOGRAPHY, which are revealing correlations between the reading process and detailed neural activity. Findings to date are surveyed by Posner et al. (1996).

A very different area of intersection between writing systems and cognitive science concerns the question whether literacy changes the nature of mental life in societies that possess it. Learning to read and write undoubtedly affects awareness of the structure of language itself; for instance, although vowels and consonants seem natural units to users of alphabetic scripts, people who do not write alphabetically do not find it easy to segment speech into phonemes. But many scholars have claimed that literacy affects thought much more broadly.

Jack Goody and Ian Watt (1963) held that Western habits of thought, such as emphasis on logic, require not merely literacy but specifically phonographic script. However, although it is historically true that the Chinese were much less interested than the Greeks in logical issues, it is very hard to see how the special nature of Chinese writing can have been relevant to that fact. Many other writers do not claim that different script types have differential consequences for human thought, but they urge that the difference between possession and lack of writing has massive consequences for the intellectual life of societies and individuals.

Because professional academics live by the written word, this is a natural view for them to hold: at an earlier period, it ranked as an unquestioned though vague truism. More recently, scholars such as Walter Ong (1982) have tried to be more specific about the cognitive consequences of literacy. At the same time, several writers have argued that literacy is less significant than commonly supposed. Elizabeth Eisenstein (1979) claimed that systematic habits of mind that have been attributed to literacy arose only with the more recent invention of printing. Sylvia Scribner and Michael Cole (1981) investigated a Liberian tribe that uses a syllabic script that is learned informally, outside a school context, and they concluded that it is the formal schooling process itself that inculcates mental disciplines that have been taken for consequences of literacy. Several writers have suggested that literacy is less advantageous to individuals than it is to states that wish to control their subjects. David Olson (1994) offers a judicious survey of these issues.

See also EDUCATION; LANGUAGE AND CULTURE; LANGUAGE AND THOUGHT; NUMERACY AND CULTURE; READING

—*Geoffrey Sampson*

References

Boone, E. H., and W. D. Mignolo, Eds. (1994). *Writing Without Words.* Durham, NC: Duke University Press.

Bryant, P. E., and L. Bradley. (1980). Why children sometimes write words which they do not read. In Uta Frith, Ed., *Cognitive Processes in Spelling.* New York: Academic Press.

Chomsky, N., and M. Halle. (1968). *The Sound Pattern of English.* New York: Harper and Row.

Daniels, P. T., and W. Bright, Eds. (1996). *The World's Writing Systems.* Oxford: Oxford University Press.

DeFrancis, J. (1989). *Visible Speech: The Diverse Oneness of Writing Systems.* Honolulu: University of Hawaii Press.

Eisenstein, E. (1979). *The Printing Press as an Agent of Change*, 2 vols. Cambridge: Cambridge University Press.

Goody, J., and I. P. Watt. (1963). The consequences of literacy. *Comparative Studies in Society and History* 5: 304–345. Reprinted in J. Goody, Ed., *Literacy in Traditional Societies.* Cambridge: Cambridge University Press (1968).

Lukatela, G., and M. T. Turvey. (1994). Visual lexical access is initially phonological. *Journal of Experimental Psychology: General* 123: 107–128, 331–353.

Makita, K. (1968). The rarity of reading disability in Japanese children. *American Journal of Orthopsychiatry* 38: 599–614.

Neurath, O. (1936). *International Picture Language.* Cambridge: The Orthological Institute. Reprinted by Department of Typography and Graphic Communication, University of Reading (1980).

Olson, D. R. (1994). *The World on Paper.* Cambridge: Cambridge University Press.

Ong, W. J. (1982). *Orality and Literacy.* London: Methuen.

Posner, M. I., Y. G. Absullear, B. D. McCardliss, and S. C. Sereno. (1996). Anatomy, circuitry and plasticity of word reading. In J. Everatt, Ed., *Visual and Attentional Processes in Reading and Dyslexia.* New York: Routledge.

Sampson, G. R. (1987). *Writing Systems.* Rev. ed. London: Hutchinson.

Sampson, G. R. (1994). Chinese script and the diversity of writing systems. *Linguistics* 32: 117–132.

Scribner, S., and M. Cole. (1981). *The Psychology of Literacy.* Cambridge, MA: Harvard University Press.

Wundt, Wilhelm

Wilhelm Wundt (1832–1920) was born in Neckarau, Germany, the son of a Protestant minister. Despite a withdrawn adolescence, he was able to enter medical school first at Tübingen (1851), and then at Heidelberg (1852–56). After a semester's research on neuroscience in Berlin he returned to Heidelberg, where he taught physiology and acted as research assistant for Hermann HELMHOLTZ; here, independently of Helmholtz, he developed the notion that "unconscious inference" can determine perception (Richards 1980). In 1862 he wrote a book on perception that included a plan for a future science of psychology based on experiment, observation of behavior, and self-observation; this future psychology would include child psychology, animal psychology, and the study of linguistic, moral, and religious differences between ethnic groups (*Völkerpsychologie*). Such a science would be free of metaphysics and speculations based on introspection. Wundt distinguished between acceptable self-observation (e.g., "press a button when the identity of a word just briefly flashed before you comes clearly to mind") and unacceptable INTROSPECTION (e.g., "What do you think went on in your mind just before you pressed the button?"), a distinction stressed by Blumenthal (1980) and Danziger (1980).

From 1864 to 1868 Wundt served as a professor of both anthropology and medical psychology at Heidelberg and also, until 1869, as a representative, in the Baden legislature, of the city of Heidelberg. In 1872 he married Sophie Mau (1844–1912); they had three children. The first edition of his authoritative *Grundzüge der physiologischen Psychologie* appeared in 1874; the sixth and final edition would appear in 1908–11. Following a year at Zürich, in 1875 he moved to Leipzig with the title of professor of philosophy.

Wundt's famous Institute of Experimental Psychology, for which funding was first received in 1879, consisted initially of the use of a classroom on the third floor of a refectory building (destroyed by bombing in World War II), but in 1883 it was expanded to nine rooms (a floor plan is provided by Bringmann, Bringmann, and Ungerer 1980: 151). Further expansions took place in 1888, 1892, and 1897, when the institute moved to the top floor of a newly built building. Wundt (1910) himself chronicled these expansions and gave a floor plan of the 1897 laboratory. In 1881 he also founded a journal, *Philosophische Studien,* for the dissemination of the research from his Institute.

Students came there not only from Germany but also from North America, the United Kingdom, Russia, Japan, and other countries. For example, the American James McKeen Cattell (1860–1944) carried out research at Leipzig on word associations, introduced Wundt to the newly invented typewriter, and wrote letters home that give a good account of life and work in Wundt's laboratory (Sokal 1981). A full list of Wundt's Ph.D. students was provided by Tinker (1932), with more details on his thirty-three American students in particular being given by Benjamin et al. (1992). Between 1879 and 1920 Wundt published prolifically; a bibliography of his scientific writings was given by Titchener and Geissler (1908, with supplements continuing to 1922). Wundt's books included works on LOGIC and ethics as well as psychology, and his final years were devoted to his multivolume *Völkerpsychologie* (The Psychology of Peoples). It was in the first volume of this work that Wundt put forward an approach to PSYCHOLINGUISTICS that stressed

that a mental representation was psychologically prior to the formation of a sentence in the speaker's mind; variations in the use of grammar permitted the speaker to emphasize one or another aspect of the MENTAL REPRESENTATION (Blumenthal 1970).

Among Wundt's ideas that received extensive discussion at the turn of the century, we may note his hypothesis that all "feelings" have the tridimensional attributes of being pleasant/unpleasant, exciting/depressing, and strained/relaxed; and his belief that the frontal lobes mediated the process known since the eighteenth century as "apperception," namely, the identification and grouping by the brain of sense data so that the perceiver attained coherence in his or her interpretation of reality. In this latter opinion, he belonged to a tradition of German psychology inherited from Leibniz and KANT; and the first Ph.D. thesis awarded at Leipzig for an experiment in psychology, that of Max Friedrich (1883), attempted to measure apperception-time. Wundt also insisted that any system of psychology had to include a purposive element, that is, a component reflecting intentional, voluntary decision making. He argued that the laws of mental science differ from the laws of physical science particularly insofar as the former cannot be described without including variables concerned with "value" or "desirability." And he maintained that thinking can involve a "creative synthesis" such that genuinely new ideas can emerge from the mental fusion of two or more ideas; a combination of ideas is not necessarily a simple And-Sum. In these beliefs, he foreshadowed GESTALT PSYCHOLOGY.

Meischner and Eschler (1979: 110–112) provide a list of thirty honorary degrees and memberships of foreign societies awarded to Wundt between 1874 and 1918, as well as a photograph of his Leipzig home, where he died of natural causes.

See also JAMES, WILLIAM; LANGUAGE PRODUCTION; TIME IN THE MIND

—*David J. Murray*

References

Benjamin, L. T. Jr., M. Durkin, M. Link, M. Vestal, and J. Acord. (1992). Wundt's American doctoral students. *American Psychologist* 47: 123–131.

Blumenthal, A. L. (1970). Wilhelm Wundt the master psycholinguist, and his commentators. In A. L. Blumenthal, Ed., *Language and Psychology: Historical Aspects of Psycholinguistics.* New York: Wiley, pp. 9–78.

Blumenthal, A. L. (1980) Wilhelm Wundt—problems of interpretation. In W. G. Bringmann and R. D. Tweney, Eds., *Wundt Studies.* Toronto: C. J. Hogrefe, pp. 435–445.

Bringmann, W. G., M. J. Bringmann, and G. A. Ungerer. (1980). The establishment of Wundt's laboratory: An archival and documentary study. In W. G. Bringmann and R. D. Tweney, Eds., *Wundt Studies.* Toronto: C. J. Hogrefe, pp. 123–157.

Danziger, K. (1980). The history of introspection reconsidered. *Journal of the History of the Behavioral Sciences* 16: 242–262.

Friedrich, M. (1883). Über die Apperceptionsdauer bei einfachen und zusammengesetzten Vorstellungen. *Philosophische Studien* 1: 39–77. English summary by P. J. Behrens, The first dissertation in experimental psychology: Max Friedrich's study of apperception (1980). In W. G. Bringmann and R. D. Tweney, Eds., *Wundt Studies.* Toronto: C. J. Hogrefe, pp. 193–209.

Meischner, W., and E. Eschler. (1979). *Wilhelm Wundt.* Leipzig: Urania.

Richards, R. J. (1980). Wundt's early theories of unconscious inference and cognitive evolution in their relation to Darwinian biopsychology. In W. G. Bringmann and R. D. Tweney, Eds., *Wundt Studies.* Toronto: C. J. Hogrefe, pp. 42–70.

Sokal, M. M., Ed. (1980). *An Education in Psychology: James McKeen Cattell's Journal and Letters from Germany and England, 1880–1888.* Cambridge, MA: MIT Press.

Tinker, M. A. (1932). Wundt's doctoral students and their theses, 1875–1920. *American Journal of Psychology* 44: 630–637.

Titchener, E. B., and L. R. Geissler. (1908). A bibliography of the scientific writings of Wilhelm Wundt. *American Journal of Psychology* 19: 541–556; (1909) 20: 570; (1910) 21: 603–604; (1911) 22: 586–587; (1912) 23: 533; (1913) 24: 586; (1914) 25: 599; (1922) 33: 260–262.

Wundt, W. (1862). *Beiträge zur Theorie der Sinneswahrnehmung.* Leipzig: C. F. Winter. Introduction, "On the methods of psychology," trans. by T. Shipley, Ed., *Classics in Psychology.* New York: Philosophical Library, 1961, pp. 51–78.

Wundt, W. (1874). *Grundzüge der Physiologischen Psychologie.* Leipzig: W. Engelmann.

Wundt, W. (1910). Das Institut für experimentelle Psychologie zu Leipzig. *Psychologische Studien* 5: 279–293.

Wundt, W. (1900–1909). *Völkerpsychologie.* Leipzig: W. Engelmann.

Further Readings

Diamond, S. (1976). Wundt, Wilhelm. In C. C. Gillespie, Ed., *Dictionary of Scientific Biography.* New York: Scribner, pp. 526–529.

Murray, D. J. (1988). 1879 to about 1910: Wundt and his influence. In *A History of Western Psychology.* 2nd ed. Englewood Cliffs, NJ: Prentice-Hall, pp. 199–240.

Psychological Review. (1921). In Memory of Wilhelm Wundt: A symposium of reminiscences by seventeen of Wundt's American students. *Psychological Review* 28: 153–188.

Titchener, E. B. (1921). Wilhelm Wundt. *American Journal of Psychology* 32: 161–178.

X-Bar Theory

In generative SYNTAX (see GENERATIVE GRAMMAR), X-bar theory is the module of the grammar that regulates constituent structure. It aims at characterizing a possible syntactic configuration. In interaction with the other principles of the grammar, X-bar theory determines structural representations.

Syntactic structure is defined in terms of two principles: (i) constituents are endocentric, phrases are organized around a head (i.e. they are projections of heads); (ii) constituents are built up according to the schema (1).

(1)

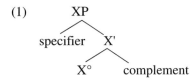

A head X° (a word, or a—possibly abstract—morpheme) combines with one maximal projection, its complement, to form the intermediate projection, $\overline{X}$ ("X-bar"), or X'. X' combines with another maximal projection, its spec(ifier) to

form the maximal projection, represented as XP, or as $\overline{\overline{X}}$ ("X-double bar") or as X". The variable X ranges over syntactic categories of two types: lexical categories N(oun), V(erb), A(djective), P(reposition); and functional categories such as I(inflection) or C(complementizer). Properties of the head percolate along the projection line: if the head is a V(erb), the projection will be a V(erb)P(phrase) (2a); a N(oun)head projects a N(oun)P(hrase) (2b), and so on. (2a) and (2b) are grammatical representations, but (2c) is ungrammatical:

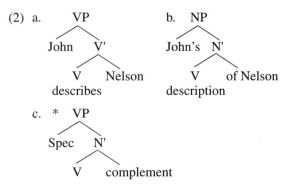

The X-bar format makes it possible to express crosscategorial generalizations. Thus, for instance, the selectional properties of the V *describe* in (2a) are parallel to those of the N *description* in (2b).

(1) is the format of X-bar theory adopted in the principles-and-parameters approach to syntax (see MINIMALISM). There are a number of variations to the implementation of the core idea. For instance, for some approaches, X-bar theory need not be committed to the strong claim (due to Stowell 1981) that all constituents are endocentric, only that this is the default option. LEXICAL FUNCTIONAL GRAMMAR respects X-bar theory but allows for a finite set of exocentric phrases with special properties (notably S in nonconfigurational languages). In some versions of X-bar theory, it is assumed that all syntactic structure is binary branching (Kayne 1984). Other versions allow multiple complements and multiple specifiers (see Carrier and Randall 1992, for example). There is also variation with respect to the number of bar levels (see Stuurman 1985 for discussion).

Originally, the X-bar format was mainly elaborated for the projection of lexical categories (see Jackendoff 1977: 53), functional categories (inflectional morphemes such as the tense and agreement morphemes of verbs, or function words such as determiners or conjunctions) being integrated within lexical projections, typically as their specifiers. The sentence was interpreted either as an exocentric category—that is, a category without a head or as a projection of the verb (Jackendoff 1977). In the principles-and-parameters approach (Stowell 1981 and Chomsky 1986), the X-bar format is extended to all syntactic categories, functional as well as lexical. A sentence is an extended projection of a verb (Grimshaw 1991): it is a projection of V augmented with projections of inflectional morphemes. The sentence is dominated by a projection of the functional category C(omplementizer), which encodes its illocutionary force. In embedded clauses like (3a), C is filled by the complementizer (the subordinating conjunctions *that, if, for*). C takes as its complement IP, a projection of the verbal inflection (tense, agreement morphemes; Van Riemsdijk and Williams 1986; Haegeman 1994 for introductions).

(3a)

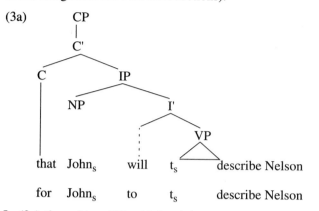

that John$_s$ will t$_s$ describe Nelson

for   John$_s$ to   t$_s$ describe Nelson

In (3a) the subject NP, which originates in the specifier of VP (2a) (McCloskey 1997 discusses the status of subject in generative syntax; see also GRAMMATICAL RELATIONS), moves to the specifier position of IP. Movement leaves a trace (ts). (3b) illustrates the X-bar format as applied to an interrogative root clause. See also HEAD MOVEMENT and WH-MOVEMENT.

(3b)

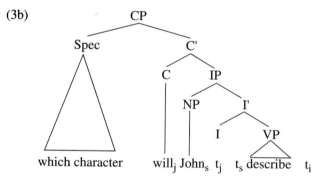

which character   will$_j$ John$_s$ t$_j$ t$_s$ describe   t$_i$

In (3b) the direct object, *which character*, has undergone *wh*-movement to the specifier of CP, and the auxiliary *will* has undergone head movement from I to C.

Abney (1987) shows that the projection of the noun (NP) must be reinterpreted as an extended projection of NP—that is, a projection of N augmented with functional projections, such as, among others, the projection of the D(eterminer), as shown in

(4)

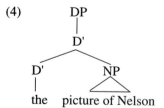

the   picture of Nelson

The X-bar format determines the hierarchical organization of structure but not the linear order of the constituents. English is an SVO language: in (5a) V precedes the direct object; West Flemish is an SOV language: in (5b) V follows the direct object. See also LINGUISTIC UNIVERSALS AND UNIVERSAL GRAMMAR.

(5) a. I think that John wants to buy this book.
   b. k peinzen da Valére wilt dienen boek kuopen.
      I think   that Valére wants that book buy

One option to account for the crosslinguistic variation is to postulate parametric variation in the base structure: whereas the underlying structure of the VP in (5a) is as in (6a), that of (5b) is as in (6b) (see Kayne 1984).

(6) a.   b.

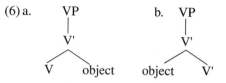

An alternative option is to maintain that the base structure is invariantly head-initial, hence, the direct object always originates to the right of the head, V. Crosslinguistic word-order variation as that in (5) is derived by additional movement rules. In OV languages (see (5b)), the object moves leftward to the specifier position of a functional projection dominating VP. The resulting representation (7) maps into an OV order.

(7)

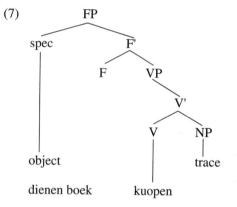

dienen boek   kuopen   trace

The mechanism of head movement, in conjunction with X-bar theory, accounts for the formation of complex verbs as found in POLYSYNTHETIC LANGUAGES (see Baker 1996).

The X-bar format is often claimed to find a predecessor in the superscripting convention of Harris (1951: chap. 6) whose aim was "to reduce the number of classes which we require when we state the composition of each utterance of the language" (1951: 262, in Stuurman 1985: 18). However, Stuurman (1985) has shown that structuralist superscripting is a lexical device and differs considerably from the generative X-bar format. The basis for the generative X-bar format was developed in Chomsky's (1970) "Remarks on Nominalization" whose aim was to capture crosscategorial generalizations without using transformations. X-bar theory is further elaborated by Emonds (1970) and Jackendoff (1974, 1977). Later developments concern the generalization to functional structure (Stowell 1981; Chomsky 1986), the binary branching format (Kayne 1984), the antisymmetry hypothesis (Kayne 1994), and the related universal base hypothesis (Kayne 1994).

Muysken (1981) interprets the concept of phrase-structure level in terms of a relational property expressed by two features [+projection], [+ maximal], where [–projection, –maximal] stands for X°, and [+projection, +maximal] stands for XP, the maximal projection. Intermediate projections are [+projection, –maximal]. Chomsky (1995), capitalizing on Muysken's proposal, explores ways of reducing the X-bar format via the concept of bare phrase structure, in which the levels of projection are derived notions and in which nonbranching projections are eliminated (Speas 1990 is a precursor for this view). Ongoing controversies concern the status of adjunction (May 1985; Kayne 1994), the status of intermediate projections (Chomsky 1995; Kayne 1994), and the status of multiple specifiers (Chomsky 1995). For the structure of nonconfigurational languages, see Hale (1983). For investigations of the application of the X-bar format to morphology, see, among others, Aronoff (1976).

In imposing restrictions on the format for phrase structure rules, the X-bar format restricts the expressive power of the technical devices available for natural language grammars. The X-bar format imposes that a constituent is a projection of a head and that the internal structure of constituents is invariant crosscategorially. Taken as part of Universal Grammar, this constrained view of the format of phrase structure contributes towards explaining the rapidity and uniformity of the acquisition of syntactic structures.

See also LANGUAGE ACQUISITION; MODULARITY AND LANGUAGE SYNTAX, ACQUISITION OF

—Liliane Haegeman

References

Abney, S. (1987). *The English Noun Phrase in its Sentential Aspect.* Ph.D. diss., MIT.

Aronoff, M. (1976). *Word Formation in Generative Grammar.* Cambridge, MA: MIT Press.

Baker, M. (1996). *The Polysynthesis Parameter.* Oxford: Oxford University Press.

Carrier, J., and J. H. Randall. (1992). The argument structure and syntactic structure of resultatives. *Linguistic Inquiry* 23: 173–234.

Chomsky, N. (1970). Remarks on nominalization. In R. Jacobs and P. Rosenbaum, Eds., *Readings in English Transformational Grammar.* Waltham, MA: Ginn, pp. 184–221. Also in N. Chomsky, *Studies on Semantics in Generative Grammar* (1972). The Hague: Mouton, pp. 11–61.

Chomsky, N. (1986). *Barriers.* Cambridge, MA: MIT Press.

Chomsky, N. (1995). Bare phrase structure. In G. Webelhuth, Ed., *Government and Binding Theory and the Minimalist Program.* Oxford: Blackwell, pp. 383–439.

Emonds, J. (1970). *Root and Structure Preserving transformations.* Ph.D. diss., MIT.

Grimshaw, J. (1991). *Extended Projections.* Unpublished manuscript, Brandeis University.

Haegeman, L. (1994). *Introduction to Government and Binding Theory.* Oxford: Blackwell.

Hale, K. (1983). Warlpiri and the grammar of nonconfigurational languages. *Natural Language and Linguistic Theory* 1: 1–43.

Harris, Z. (1951). *Methods in Structural Linguistics.* Chicago: University of Chicago Press.

Jackendoff, R. (1974). *Introduction to the X' Convention.* Mimeo, distributed by the Indiana University Linguistics Club, Bloomington, IN.

Jackendoff, R. (1977). *X' Syntax: A Study of Phrase Structure.* Cambridge, MA: MIT Press.

Kayne, R. (1984). *Connectedness and Binary Branching.* Dordrecht: Foris.

Kayne, R. (1994). *The Antisymmetry of Syntax.* Cambridge, MA: MIT Press.

May, R. (1985). *Logical Form.* Cambridge, MA: MIT Press.

McCloskey, J. (1997). Subjecthood and the subject position. In L. Haegeman, Ed., *Elements of Grammar.* Dordrecht: Kluwer.

Muysken, P. (1981). Parametrizing the notion head. *Journal of Linguistic Research* 2: 57–75.

Speas, M. (1990). *Phrase Structure in Natural Language.* Dordrecht: Foris.

Stowell, T. (1981). *Origins of Phrase Structure.* Ph.D. diss., MIT.

Stuurman, F. (1985). *X-Bar and X-Plain. A Study of X-Bar Theories of the Phrase Structure Component.* Dordrecht: Foris.

Van Riemsdijk, H., and E. Williams. (1986). *Introduction to the Theory of Grammar.* Cambridge: MIT Press.

Further Readings

Baker, M. (1988). *Incorporation: A Theory of Grammatical Function Changing.* Chicago: University of Chicago Press.

Emonds, J. (1976). *A Transformational Approach to English Syntax.* New York: Academic Press.

Emonds, J. (1985). *A Unified Theory of Syntactic Categories.* Dordrecht: Foris.

Fukui, N. (1986). *A Theory of Category Projection and its Applications.* Ph.D. diss., MIT.

Haegeman, L., Ed. (1997). *Elements of Grammar.* Dordrecht: Kluwer.

Hornstein, N. (1977). S and the X' convention. *Linguistic Analysis* 3: 137–176.

Koizumi, M. (1995). *Phrase Structure in Minimalist Syntax.* Ph.D. diss., MIT.

Koopman, H., and D. Sportiche. (1991). The position of subjects. *Lingua* 85: 211–258.

Koster, J. (1987). *Domains and Dynasties.* Dordrecht: Foris.

Kuroda, S. -Y. (1988). Whether we agree or not. *Linguisticae Investigationes* 12: 1–47.

Lasnik, H., and J. J. Kupin. (1977). A restrictive theory of transformational grammar. *Theoretical Linguistics* 4: 173–196.

Radford, A. (1988). *Transformational Grammar.* Cambridge: Cambridge University Press.

Selkirk, E. (1982). *The Syntax of Words.* Cambridge, MA: MIT Press.

Siegel, D. (1974). *Topics in English Morphology.* Cambridge, MA: MIT Press.

Speas, M. (1986). *Adjunctions and Projections in Syntax.* Ph.D. diss., MIT.

Sportiche, D. (1988). A theory of floating quantifiers and its corollaries for constituent structure. *Linguistic Inquiry* 19: 425–449.

Stowell, T. (1983). Subjects across categories. *The Linguistic Review* 2: 285–312.

Travis, L. (1984). *Parameters and Effects of Word Order Variation.* Ph.D. diss., MIT.

Williams, E. (1981). On the notions 'lexically related' and 'head of a word,' *Linguistic Inquiry* 2: 245–274.

Zwart, J.-W. (1997). The Germanic SOV languages and the Universal Base Hypothesis. In L. Haegeman, Ed., *The New Comparative Syntax.* London: Addison, Longman, and Wesley, pp. 246–267.

Contributors

Contributing Authors

Marilyn Adams
BBN Technologies and Harvard Graduate School of Education
READING
Karen Adolph
New York University
AFFORDANCES; PERCEPTUAL DEVELOPMENT
Cynthia Aguilar
Northwestern University
CATEGORIZATION
Judith Aissen
University of California, Santa Cruz
RELATIONAL GRAMMAR
Thomas D. Albright
Salk Institute
NEUROSCIENCES INTRODUCTION; MOTION, PERCEPTION OF
James Allen
University of Rochester
NATURAL LANGUAGE PROCESSING
Daniel Ames
University of California, Berkeley
ATTRIBUTION THEORY
Bart Anderson
Massachusetts Institute of Technology
SURFACE PERCEPTION
Stuart Anstis
University of California, San Diego
ILLUSIONS
Michael Arbib
University of Southern California
AUTOMATA
Mark Aronoff
SUNY, Stony Brook
MORPHOLOGY
Scott Atran
Centre de Recherche en Epistémologie Appliquée, Ecole Polytechnique, and University of Michigan
FOLK BIOLOGY
Terry Au
University of California, Los Angeles
LANGUAGE AND THOUGHT

Françoise Audouze
Centre National de la Recherche Scientifique, Centre de Recherches Archéologiques, Meudon
TECHNOLOGY AND HUMAN EVOLUTION
Kent Bach
San Francisco State University
GRICE, H. PAUL; MEANING
Alan Baddeley
University of Bristol
MEMORY
Jodie A. Baird
University of Oregon
METACOGNITION
Lynne Rudder Baker
University of Massachusetts, Amherst
FOLK PSYCHOLOGY
Mark Baker
Rutgers University
POLYSYNTHETIC LANGUAGES
Horace Barlow
University of Cambridge
CEREBRAL CORTEX; FEATURE DETECTORS
K. Jon Barwise
Indiana University
LOGIC
William H. Batchelder
University of California, Irvine
CULTURAL CONSENSUS THEORY
Elizabeth Bates
Center for Research in Language
BILINGUALISM AND THE BRAIN
William Bechtel
Washington University in St. Louis
UNITY OF SCIENCE
Marc Bekoff
University of Colorado, Boulder
DOMINANCE IN ANIMAL SOCIAL GROUPS; SOCIAL PLAY BEHAVIOR
Patrick J. Bennett
University of Toronto
SHAPE PERCEPTION

James R. Bergen
Sarnoff Corporation
TEXTURE

Stefano Bertolo
Massachusetts Institute of Technology
ACQUISITION, FORMAL THEORIES OF

Derek Bickerton
University of Hawaii
CREOLES

Christopher Bishop
Microsoft Research, Cambridge, U.K.
PATTERN RECOGNITION AND
FEED-FORWARD NETWORKS

Emilio Bizzi
Massachusetts Institute of Technology
MOTOR CONTROL

Ned Block
New York University
FUNCTIONAL ROLE SEMANTICS

Paul Bloom
University of Arizona
EVOLUTION OF LANGUAGE; LANGUAGE ACQUISITION;
WORD MEANING, ACQUISITION OF

Sheila Blumstein
Brown University
PHONOLOGY, NEURAL BASIS OF

Kathryn Bock
University of Illinois
LANGUAGE PRODUCTION

Margaret A. Boden
University of Sussex at Brighton
ARTIFICIAL LIFE

Gary Boone
Georgia Institute of Technology
WALKING AND RUNNING MACHINES

James Boster
University of Connecticut
CULTURAL VARIATION

Pascal Boyer
*Centre National de la Recherche Scientifique,
Lyon*
CULTURAL EVOLUTION; CULTURAL SYMBOLISM

David Brainard
University of California, Santa Barbara
COLOR VISION

Mary E. Brenner
University of California, Santa Barbara
NUMERACY AND CULTURE

William F. Brewer
University of Illinois
BARTLETT, FREDERIC CHARLES; SCHEMATA

Roger W. Brockett
Harvard University
CONTROL THEORY

Andrew Brook
Carleton University
KANT, IMMANUEL

Leslie Brothers
University of California, Los Angeles
EMOTION AND THE HUMAN BRAIN

Donald E. Brown
University of California, Santa Barbara
HUMAN UNIVERSALS

Edward M. Callaway
Salk Institute
VISUAL CORTEX, CELL TYPES AND CONNECTIONS IN

William H. Calvin
University of Washington, Seattle
COLUMNS AND MODULES

Murray Campbell
IBM T. J. Watson Research Center
GAME-PLAYING SYSTEMS

David N. Caplan
Massachusetts General Hospital
GRAMMAR, NEURAL BASIS OF

Francesco Cara
*Centre de Recherche en Epistémologie Appliquée, Ecole
Polytechnique*
COGNITIVE ERGONOMICS

Alfonso Caramazza
Harvard University
LEXICON, NEURAL BASIS OF

Ronald W. Casson
Oberlin College
COGNITIVE ANTHROPOLOGY

Patrick Cavanagh
Harvard University
PICTORIAL ART AND VISION; TOP-DOWN PROCESSING IN VISION

Eugene Charniak
Brown University
STATISTICAL TECHNIQUES IN NATURAL LANGUAGE PROCESSING

Peter Cheeseman
RIACS, NASA Ames Research Center
PROBABILITY, FOUNDATIONS OF

Dorothy Cheney
University of Pennsylvania
SOCIAL COGNITION IN ANIMALS

Patricia Cheng
University of California, Los Angeles
CAUSAL REASONING

Christopher Cherniak
University of Maryland
RATIONAL AGENCY

E. J. Chichilnisky
Salk Institute
RETINA

Gennaro Chierchia
University of Milan
LINGUISTICS AND LANGUAGE INTRODUCTION; SYNTAX-SEMANTICS
INTERFACE

Patricia S. Churchland
University of California, San Diego
COMPUTATION AND THE BRAIN

Guglielmo Cinque
University of Venice
WH-MOVEMENT

Herbert H. Clark
Stanford University
PSYCHOLINGUISTICS

G. N. Clements
Centre National de la Recherche Scientifique, Paris
PHONOLOGY

Carol Colby
University of Pittsburgh
SPATIAL PERCEPTION

Michael Cole
University of California, San Diego
ECOLOGICAL VALIDITY; LURIA, ALEXANDER ROMANOVICH

Bernard Comrie
*Max Planck Institute for Evolutionary Anthropology,
Leipzig*
TYPOLOGY

Eros Corazza
University of Nottingham
INDEXICALS AND DEMONSTRATIVES
David P. Corina
University of Washington
SIGN LANGUAGE AND THE BRAIN
Leda Cosmides
University of California, Santa Barbara
EVOLUTIONARY PSYCHOLOGY
Thomas M. Cover
Stanford University
INFORMATION THEORY
Jack Cowan
University of Chicago
VON NEUMANN, JOHN
Stephen Crain
University of Maryland
SEMANTICS, ACQUISITION OF
Tim Crane
University College London
AUTONOMY OF PSYCHOLOGY;
MIND-BODY PROBLEM
Max Cresswell
Victoria University of Wellington
MODAL LOGIC; POSSIBLE WORLDS SEMANTICS
Francis Crick
Salk Institute
CONSCIOUSNESS, NEUROBIOLOGY OF
Mihalyi Csikszentmihalyi
University of Chicago
CREATIVITY
Reagan Curtis
University of California, Santa Barbara
NUMERACY AND CULTURE
Anne Cutler
Max Planck Institute for Psycholinguistics
PROSODY AND INTONATION, PROCESSING ISSUES; SPOKEN WORD
RECOGNITION
Östen Dahl
Stockholm University
TENSE AND ASPECT
Mary Dalrymple
Xerox Palo Alto Research Center
LEXICAL FUNCTIONAL GRAMMAR
Donald Davidson
University of California, Berkeley
ANOMALOUS MONISM
Martin Davies
University of Oxford
CONSCIOUSNESS
Randall Davis
Massachusetts Institute of Technology
KNOWLEDGE-BASED SYSTEMS
Peter Dayan
University College London
UNSUPERVISED LEARNING
Rina Dechter
University of California, Irvine
CONSTRAINT SATISFACTION
Javier DeFelipe
Instituto Cajal (CSIC)
CAJAL, SANTIAGO RAMÓN Y
Michel DeGraff
Massachusetts Institute of Technology
PARAMETER-SETTING APPROACHES TO ACQUISITION,
CREOLIZATION, AND DIACHRONY

John Deigh
Northwestern University
MORAL PSYCHOLOGY
Daniel Dennett
Tufts University
INTENTIONAL STANCE
David J. Depew
University of Iowa
SELF-ORGANIZING SYSTEMS
Michael Devitt
University of Maryland
REFERENCE, THEORIES OF
Eric Dietrich
Binghamton University
ALGORITHM
Tom Dietterich
Oregon State University
MACHINE LEARNING
John F. Dovidio
Colgate University
STEREOTYPING
Jon Doyle
Massachusetts Institute of Technology
BOUNDED RATIONALITY; RATIONAL DECISION MAKING
Fred Dretske
Stanford University
INFORMATIONAL SEMANTICS
Jon Driver
University of London
VISUAL NEGLECT
Nina Dronkers
VA Northern California Health Care System and the University of California, Davis
LANGUAGE, NEURAL BASIS OF
Sascha du Lac
Salk Institute
MOTOR LEARNING
Robin Dunbar
University of Liverpool
COOPERATION AND COMPETITION; SOCIOBIOLOGY
Kevin Dunbar
McGill University
SCIENTIFIC THINKING AND ITS DEVELOPMENT
Susan Duncan
University of Chicago
LANGUAGE AND COMMUNICATION
John Duncan
MRC Cognition and Brain Sciences Unit, Cambridge, U.K.
ATTENTION
Jean-Pierre Dupuy
Centre de Recherche en Epistémologie Appliquée, Ecole Polytechnique and C.S.L.I., Stanford University
RATIONAL CHOICE THEORY
Howard Eichenbaum
Boston University
HIPPOCAMPUS
Marion Eppler
East Carolina University
AFFORDANCES; PERCEPTUAL DEVELOPMENT
K. Anders Ericsson
Florida State University
EXPERTISE
Martha Farah
University of Pennsylvania
MODELING NEUROPSYCHOLOGICAL DEFICITS; OBJECT
RECOGNITION, HUMAN NEUROPSYCHOLOGY

Olivier D. Faugeras
INRIA and Massachusetts Institute of Technology
STEREO AND MOTION PERCEPTION

Diego Fernandez-Duque
University of Oregon
ATTENTION IN THE HUMAN BRAIN

Arthur Fine
Northwestern University
REALISM AND ANTI-REALISM

Barbara Finlay
Cornell University
NEURAL DEVELOPMENT

Baruch Fischhoff
Carnegie Mellon University
JUDGMENT HEURISTICS

Malcolm R. Forster
University of Wisconsin, Madison
PARSIMONY AND SIMPLICITY

Lyn Frazier
University of Massachusetts, Amherst
MODULARITY AND LANGUAGE

Uta Frith
University College London
AUTISM

Albert M. Galaburda
Harvard Medical School; Beth Israel Deaconess Medical Center
DYSLEXIA; GESCHWIND, NORMAN

C. Randy Gallistel
University of California, Los Angeles
ANIMAL NAVIGATION

Sebastian Gardner
University of London
PSYCHOANALYSIS, CONTEMPORARY VIEWS

Michael S. Gazzaniga
Dartmouth College
HEMISPHERIC SPECIALIZATION

Susan A. Gelman
University of Michigan, Ann Arbor
DOMAIN-SPECIFICITY; ESSENTIALISM

Rochel Gelman
University of California, Los Angeles
COGNITIVE DEVELOPMENT; NAIVE MATHEMATICS

Dedre Gentner
Northwestern University
ANALOGY

Raymond W. Gibbs, Jr.
University of California, Santa Cruz
FIGURATIVE LANGUAGE

Eleanor J. Gibson
Cornell University
AFFORDANCES; PERCEPTUAL DEVELOPMENT

Charles Gilbert
Rockefeller University
NEURAL PLASTICITY

Daniel Gilbert
Harvard University
SOCIAL COGNITION

Alan Gilchrist
Rutgers University, Newark
LIGHTNESS PERCEPTION

Barbara Gillam
University of New South Wales
DEPTH PERCEPTION

Thomas Gilovich
Cornell University
TVERSKY, AMOS

Lila Gleitman
University of Pennsylvania
LANGUAGE ACQUISITION; WORD MEANING, ACQUISITION OF

Paul Glimcher
New York University
OCULOMOTOR CONTROL

Sam Glucksberg
Princeton University
METAPHOR

Fernand Gobet
University of Nottingham
CHESS, PSYCHOLOGY OF

Alvin Goldman
University of Arizona
EPISTEMOLOGY AND COGNITION; JUSTIFICATION

Patricia S. Goldman-Rakic
Yale University
WORKING MEMORY, NEURAL BASIS OF

John Goldsmith
University of Chicago
TONE

Robert Goldstone
Indiana University
SIMILARITY

Melvyn A. Goodale
University of Western Ontario
VISUAL PROCESSING STREAMS

Alison Gopnik
University of California, Berkeley
THEORY OF MIND

Robert M. Gordon
University of Missouri, St. Louis
SIMULATION VS. THEORY-THEORY

Paul Gorrell
Westat, Inc.
SENTENCE PROCESSING

Georgia M. Green
University of Illinois at Urbana-Champaign
HEAD-DRIVEN PHRASE STRUCTURE GRAMMAR

Richard Gregory
University of Bristol
HELMHOLTZ, HERMANN LUDWIG FERDINAND VON

Russell Greiner
University of Alberta
EXPLANATION-BASED LEARNING

Paul Griffiths
University of Sydney
ADAPTATION AND ADAPTATIONISM

Jane Grimshaw
Rutgers University
LEXICON

Jeroen Groenendijk
University of Amsterdam
DYNAMIC SEMANTICS

Charles Gross
Princeton University
CORTICAL LOCALIZATION, HISTORY OF; TEUBER, HANS-LUKAS

Rick Grush
University of Aarhus
COMPUTATION AND THE BRAIN

John Gumperz
University of California, Berkeley
CODESWITCHING

Liliane Haegeman
University of Geneva
X-BAR THEORY

Morris Halle
Massachusetts Institute of Technology
JAKOBSON, ROMAN; STRESS, LINGUISTIC

Bruce Halpern
Cornell University
TASTE

James A. Hampton
City University, London
CONCEPTS

C. L. Hardin
Syracuse University
SENSATIONS

Giyoo Hatano
Keio University
ANIMISM

Elvin Hatch
University of California, Santa Barbara
BOAS, FRANZ

Marc Hauser
Harvard University
ANIMAL COMMUNICATION; PRIMATE COGNITION

Patrick Hayes
University of West Florida
KNOWLEDGE REPRESENTATION

David Heckerman
Microsoft Research
BAYESIAN LEARNING

John Heil
Davidson College
MENTAL CAUSATION

Steve J. Heims
Gloucester, MA
WIENER, NORBERT

Marcel Hénaff
University of California, San Diego
LÉVI-STRAUSS, CLAUDE

Stewart Hendry
Johns Hopkins Medical School
PAIN

Max Henrion
Lumina Decision Sciences, Inc.
UNCERTAINTY

Arturo E. Hernandez
University of California, Santa Barbara
BILINGUALISM AND THE BRAIN

Jim Higginbotham
University of Oxford
THEMATIC ROLES

Ellen Hildreth
Wellesley College
COMPUTATIONAL VISION

Steven Hillyard
University of California, San Diego
ELECTROPHYSIOLOGY, ELECTRIC AND MAGNETIC EVOKED FIELDS

Geoffrey Hinton
University of Toronto
SUPERVISED LEARNING IN MULTILAYER NEURAL NETWORKS

Lawrence Hirschfeld
University of Michigan
CULTURE, COGNITION, AND EVOLUTION INTRODUCTION; NAIVE SOCIOLOGY

J. Allan Hobson
Harvard University
DREAMING; SLEEP

Jessica Hodgins
Georgia Institute of Technology
WALKING AND RUNNING MACHINES

James D. Hollan
University of California, San Diego
HUMAN-COMPUTER INTERACTION

Keith Holyoak
University of California, Los Angeles
PSYCHOLOGY INTRODUCTION

Jim Hopkins
King's College London
PSYCHOANALYSIS, HISTORY OF

Terence Horgan
University of Memphis
RULES AND REPRESENTATIONS; SUPERVENIENCE

Laurence Horn
Yale University
IMPLICATURE; PRAGMATICS

Steven Horst
Wesleyan University
COMPUTATIONAL THEORY OF MIND

Eduard Hovy
University of Southern California
MACHINE TRANSLATION; NATURAL LANGUAGE GENERATION

John Hummel
University of California, Los Angeles
BINDING PROBLEM

Edwin Hutchins
University of California, San Diego
COGNITIVE ARTIFACTS

Jeffrey J. Hutsler
Dartmouth College
HEMISPHERIC SPECIALIZATION

Daniel P. Huttenlocher
Cornell University
VISUAL OBJECT RECOGNITION, AI

Judith Irvine
Brandeis University
SAPIR, EDWARD

Stephen Isard
University of Edinburgh
SPEECH SYNTHESIS

Masao Ito
RIKEN Brain Science Institute
CEREBELLUM

Philip N. Johnson-Laird
Princeton University
MENTAL MODELS

Michael I. Jordan
University of California, Berkeley
COMPUTATIONAL INTELLIGENCE INTRODUCTION; NEURAL NETWORKS; RECURRENT NETWORKS

Aravind K. Joshi
University of Pennsylvania
COMPUTATIONAL LINGUISTICS

Leslie Pack Kaelbling
Brown University
DYNAMIC PROGRAMMING; ROBOTICS AND LEARNING

Annette Karmiloff-Smith
Institute of Child Health, University College London
MODULARITY OF MIND

Henry Kautz
AT&T Labs
TEMPORAL REASONING

Paul Kay
University of California, Berkeley
COLOR CATEGORIZATION

Micheal Kearns
AT&T Labs
COMPUTATIONAL LEARNING THEORY

Patricia A. Keating
University of California, Los Angeles
PHONETICS

Rosanna Keefe
University of Cambridge
VAGUENESS

Ed Keenan
University of California, Los Angeles
QUANTIFIERS

Frank C. Keil
Yale University
CONCEPTUAL CHANGE; NATIVISM

Michael Kenstowicz
Massachusetts Institute of Technology
PHONOLOGICAL RULES AND PROCESSES

Raymond D. Kent
University of Wisconsin
ARTICULATION

Samuel Jay Keyser
Massachusetts Institute of Technology
METER AND POETRY

Gerald D. Kidd, Jr.
Boston University
AUDITION

Jaegwon Kim
Brown University
PHYSICALISM

Robert Kirk
University of Nottingham
RADICAL INTERPRETATION

Patricia Kitcher
Columbia and University of California, San Diego
FREUD, SIGMUND

Roberta Klatzky
Carnegie Mellon University
HAPTIC PERCEPTION

Raymond M. Klein
Dalhousie University
BROADBENT, DONALD E.; HEBB, DONALD O.

Eric Knowles
University of California, Berkeley
ATTRIBUTION THEORY

Christof Koch
California Institute of Technology
COMPUTING IN SINGLE NEURONS; CONSCIOUSNESS, NEUROBIOLOGY OF

Daphne Koller
Stanford University
GAME THEORY

Richard E. Korf
University of California, Los Angeles
HEURISTIC SEARCH

Hilary Kornblith
University of Vermont
NATURAL KINDS

Stephen M. Kosslyn
Harvard University
IMAGERY

Robert Kowalski
Imperial College
LOGIC PROGRAMMING

Eileen Kowler
Rutgers University
EYE MOVEMENTS AND VISUAL ATTENTION

Manfred Krifka
University of Texas at Austin
COMPOSITIONALITY; FOCUS

Michael Kubovy
University of Virginia
GESTALT PSYCHOLOGY

D. Terence Langendoen
University of Arizona
BLOOMFIELD, LEONARD

Howard Lasnik
University of Connecticut
MINIMALISM

E. Thomas Lawson
Western Michigan University
RELIGIOUS IDEAS AND PRACTICES

Joseph LeDoux
New York University
EMOTION AND THE ANIMAL BRAIN

Barry B. Lee
Max Planck Institute for Biophysical Chemistry, Göttingen
COLOR, NEUROPHYSIOLOGY OF

Mark R. Lepper
Stanford University
DISSONANCE

Giulio Lepschy
University College London
SAUSSURE, FERDINAND DE

Yves Lesperance
York University
SITUATION CALCULUS

Jerome Lettvin
Massachusetts Institute of Technology
MCCULLOCH, WARREN S.; PITTS, WALTER

Hector Levesque
University of Toronto
COMPUTATIONAL COMPLEXITY

Janet Levin
University of Southern California
QUALIA

Joseph Levine
North Carolina State University
EXPLANATORY GAP; WHAT-IT'S-LIKE

Stephen C. Levinson
Max Planck Institute for Psycholinguistics, Nijmegen
LANGUAGE AND CULTURE

Richard L. Lewis
Ohio State University
COGNITIVE MODELING, SYMBOLIC

David Lightfoot
University of Maryland, College Park
LANGUAGE VARIATION AND CHANGE

Eric Lormand
University of Michigan
FRAME PROBLEM

Ronald Loui
Washington University in St. Louis
CASE-BASED REASONING AND ANALOGY

John A. Lucy
University of Chicago
LINGUISTIC RELATIVITY HYPOTHESIS

Peter Ludlow
SUNY Stony Brook
LINGUISTICS, PHILOSOPHICAL ISSUES

William Lycan
University of North Carolina
INTENTIONALITY; PSYCHOLOGICAL LAWS

William Lyons
Trinity College
JAMES, WILLIAM

Nicholas J. Mackintosh
University of Cambridge
CONDITIONING

Neil Macmillan
City University of New York
SIGNAL DETECTION THEORY

Jitendra Malik
University of California, Berkeley
MACHINE VISION

J. Christopher Maloney
University of Arizona
FUNCTIONALISM

Gary Marcus
New York University
POVERTY OF THE STIMULUS ARGUMENTS

Sandra L. Marcus
Boeing
KNOWLEDGE ACQUISITION

Hans J. Markowitsch
University of Bielefeld
LIMBIC SYSTEM

Peter Marler
University of California, Davis
ANIMAL COMMUNICATION; ETHOLOGY

Maja J. Matarić
University of Southern California
BEHAVIOR-BASED ROBOTICS

Robert C. May
University of California, Irvine
LOGICAL FORM IN LINGUISTICS

David McAllester
AT&T Labs
LOGICAL REASONING SYSTEMS

John McCarthy
University of Massachusetts, Amherst
DISTINCTIVE FEATURES

Robert McCauley
Emory University
REDUCTIONISM

James L. McClelland
Carnegie Mellon University
COGNITIVE MODELING, CONNECTIONIST

Sally McConnell-Ginet
Cornell University
LANGUAGE AND GENDER

Bruce S. McEwen
Rockefeller University
NEUROENDOCRINOLOGY; STRESS

James L. McGaugh
University of California, Irvine
MEMORY STORAGE, MODULATION OF

Brian P. McLaughlin
Rutgers University
EMERGENTISM; EPIPHENOMENALISM

Douglas L. Medin
Northwestern University
CATEGORIZATION

Andrew N. Meltzoff
University of Washington
IMITATION

Ronald Melzack
McGill University
PHANTOM LIMB

Carolyn Mervis
University of Louisville
MENTAL RETARDATION

Donald Michie
University of Edinburgh
TURING, ALAN MATHISON

Frank Middleton
VA Medical Center and SUNY Health Science Center, Syracuse
BASAL GANGLIA

Joanne L. Miller
Northeastern University
SPEECH PERCEPTION

Melanie Mitchell
Santa Fe Institute
EVOLUTIONARY COMPUTATION

Steven J. Mithen
University of Reading
COGNITIVE ARCHAEOLOGY

Leora Morgenstern
IBM T. J. Watson Research Center
NONMONOTONIC LOGICS

Michael W. Morris
Stanford University and University of California, Berkeley
ATTRIBUTION THEORY

Louis J. Moses
University of Oregon
METACOGNITION

Cynthia F. Moss
University of Maryland
ECHOLOCATION

Brad Motter
VA Medical Center, Syracuse
ATTENTION IN THE ANIMAL BRAIN

Stephen Muggleton
University of York
INDUCTIVE LOGIC PROGRAMMING

David Mumford
Brown University
THALAMUS

David J. Murray
Queen's University
WUNDT, WILHELM

Ken Nakayama
Harvard University
MID-LEVEL VISION

Bernhard Nebel
Albert-Ludwigs-Universität, Freiburg
FRAME-BASED SYSTEMS

Ulric Neisser
Cornell University
ECOLOGICAL PSYCHOLOGY

Carol Nemeroff
Arizona State University
MAGIC AND SUPERSTITION

Marina Nespor
University of Ferrara
PHONOLOGY, ACQUISITION OF

Helen J. Neville
University of Oregon
NEUROSCIENCES INTRODUCTION

Elissa L. Newport
University of Rochester
SIGN LANGUAGES

John K. Niederer
University of Chicago
NEURAL DEVELOPMENT

Dennis Norris
MRC Cognition and Brain Sciences Unit, Cambridge, U.K.
COMPUTATIONAL PSYCHOLINGUISTICS

Keith Oatley
University of Toronto
EMOTIONS

Yukari Okamoto
University of California, Santa Barbara
NUMERACY AND CULTURE

David Olson
University of Toronto
LITERACY

Daniel Osherson
Rice University
LEARNING SYSTEMS

John Palmer
University of Washington
PSYCHOPHYSICS

Stephen Palmer
University of California, Berkeley
GESTALT PERCEPTION

Barbara H. Partee
University of Massachusetts, Amherst
SEMANTICS

Judea Pearl
University of California, Los Angeles
BAYESIAN NETWORKS

Edwin P. D. Pednault
IBM T. J. Watson Research Center
STATISTICAL LEARNING THEORY

David Pesetsky
Massachusetts Institute of Technology
LINGUISTIC UNIVERSALS AND UNIVERSAL GRAMMAR

Mary A. Peterson
University of Arizona
HIGH-LEVEL VISION

Anne Pick
University of Minnesota
GIBSON, JAMES JEROME

Herbert Pick, Jr.
University of Minnesota
COGNITIVE MAPS; GIBSON, JAMES JEROME; HUMAN NAVIGATION

Janet Pierrehumbert
Northwestern University
PROSODY AND INTONATION

Ernst Pöppel
Ludwig-Maximilians-Universität, Munich
TIME IN THE MIND

Tomaso Poggio
Massachusetts Institute of Technology
VISION AND LEARNING

Jean Ponce
University of Illinois
MANIPULATION AND GRASPING

Michael I. Posner
University of Oregon
ATTENTION IN THE HUMAN BRAIN

Alexandre Pouget
University of Rochester
VISUAL NEGLECT

Dennis Proffitt
University of Virginia
NAIVE PHYSICS

Geoffrey K. Pullum
University of California, Santa Cruz
GENERATIVE GRAMMAR

James Pustejovsky
Brandeis University
COMPUTATIONAL LEXICONS

Naomi Quinn
Duke University
METAPHOR AND CULTURE

Carolyn S. Rabin
Rutgers University
IMAGERY

Lawrence Rabiner
AT&T Labs
SPEECH RECOGNITION IN MACHINES

Marcus Raichle
Washington University School of Medicine
POSITRON EMISSION TOMOGRAPHY

William Ramsey
University of Notre Dame
CONNECTIONISM, PHILOSOPHICAL ISSUES

Michael Ranney
University of California, Berkeley
EDUCATION

Peter Rapp
Mount Sinai School of Medicine
AGING, MEMORY, AND THE BRAIN

Josef Rauschecker
Georgetown University
AUDITORY PHYSIOLOGY

Gregg Recanzone
University of California, Davis
AUDITORY PLASTICITY

Tanya Reinhart
Tel Aviv University and University of Utrecht
ANAPHORA; BINDING THEORY

Daniel Reisberg
Reed College
LEARNING

Robert J. Richards
University of Chicago
DARWIN, CHARLES

Virginia M. Richards
University of Pennsylvania
AUDITION

Whitman A. Richards
Massachusetts Institute of Technology
MARR, DAVID

Robert C. Richardson
University of Cincinnati
FUNCTIONAL DECOMPOSITION

Lance J. Rips
Northwestern University
DEDUCTIVE REASONING

Carolyn A. Ristau
Barnard College of Columbia University
COGNITIVE ETHOLOGY

Craige Roberts
The Ohio State University
DISCOURSE; PRESUPPOSITION

Byron F. Robinson
University of Louisville
MENTAL RETARDATION

Kathleen Rockland
University of Iowa
GOLGI, CAMILLO

Hillary R. Rodman
Emory University
FACE RECOGNITION

Henry L. Roediger III
Washington University in St. Louis
EBBINGHAUS, HERMANN

Michael Rogan
Columbia University
EMOTION AND THE ANIMAL BRAIN

Edmund Rolls
University of Oxford
OBJECT RECOGNITION, ANIMAL STUDIES

A. Kimball Romney
University of California, Irvine
CULTURAL CONSENSUS THEORY

Stanley J. Rosenschein
Stanford University
INTELLIGENT AGENT ARCHITECTURE

David M. Rosenthal
City University of New York Graduate School
INTROSPECTION

Paul Rozin
University of Pennsylvania
MAGIC AND SUPERSTITION

Duane Rumbaugh
Georgia State University
PRIMATE LANGUAGE

Stuart Russell
University of California, Berkeley
COMPUTATIONAL INTELLIGENCE INTRODUCTION; METAREASONING

Timothy Salthouse
Georgia Institute of Technology
AGING AND COGNITION

Jerry Samet
Brandeis University
NATIVISM, HISTORY OF

Geoffrey Sampson
University of Sussex
WRITING SYSTEMS

David H. Sanford
Duke University
EXTENSIONALITY, THESIS OF

Sue Savage-Rumbaugh
Georgia State University
PRIMATE LANGUAGE

Daniel Schacter
Harvard University
IMPLICIT VS EXPLICIT MEMORY

Peter Schiller
Massachusetts Institute of Technology
SINGLE-NEURON RECORDING; VISUAL ANATOMY AND PHYSIOLOGY

Denise Schmandt-Besserat
The University of Texas, Austin
ARTIFACTS AND CIVILIZATION

Walter Schneider
University of Pittsburgh
AUTOMATICITY

Eric Schwartz
Boston University
COMPUTATIONAL NEUROANATOMY

Robert Schwartz
University of Wisconsin, Milwaukee
RATIONALISM VS. EMPIRICISM

John R. Searle
University of California, Berkeley
CHINESE ROOM ARGUMENT

Julie C. Sedivy
Brown University
AMBIGUITY

Gabriel Segal
King's College London
SENSE AND REFERENCE; TWIN EARTH

Mark S. Seidenberg
University of Southern California
VISUAL WORD RECOGNITION

Colleen Seifert
University of Michigan
SITUATED COGNITION AND LEARNING

Terrence J. Sejnowski
Salk Institute
COMPUTATIONAL NEUROSCIENCE

Allison B. Sekuler
University of Toronto
SHAPE PERCEPTION

Bart Selman
Cornell University
GREEDY LOCAL SEARCH

Robert Seyfarth
University of Pennsylvania
SOCIAL COGNITION IN ANIMALS

Eldar Shafir
Princeton University
DECISION MAKING; ECONOMICS AND COGNITIVE SCIENCE;
PROBABILISTIC REASONING

Patricia E. Sharp
Yale University
ANIMAL NAVIGATION, NEURAL NETWORKS

Gordon Shepherd
Yale University Medical School
NEURON

Todd Shimoda
University of California, Berkeley
EDUCATION

Peter Shizgal
Concordia University
MOTIVATION

Bradd Shore
Emory University
CULTURAL RELATIVISM

Tracey J. Shors
Rutgers University
LONG-TERM POTENTIATION

Thomas Shultz
McGill University
DISSONANCE

Richard A. Shweder
University of Chicago
CULTURAL PSYCHOLOGY

Wilfried Sieg
Carnegie Mellon University
CHURCH-TURING THESIS; FORMAL SYSTEMS, PROPERTIES OF;
GÖDEL'S THEOREMS

Ralph M. Siegel
Rutgers University, Newark
STRUCTURE FROM VISUAL INFORMATION SOURCES

Reid G. Simmons
Carnegie Mellon University
MOBILE ROBOTS

Herbert A. Simon
Carnegie Mellon University
NEWELL, ALLEN; PROBLEM SOLVING;
PRODUCTION SYSTEMS

Wolf Singer
Max Planck Institute for Brain Research
BINDING BY NEURAL SYNCHRONY

Steven Sloman
Brown University
COGNITIVE ARCHITECTURE

Barry Smith
State University of New York, Buffalo
BRENTANO, FRANZ

Brian Cantwell Smith
Indiana University
COMPUTATION; SITUATEDNESS/EMBEDDEDNESS

Edward E. Smith
University of Michigan
WORKING MEMORY

Peter Smith
University of Cambridge
VAGUENESS

Paul Smolensky
Johns Hopkins University
CONNECTIONIST APPROACHES TO LANGUAGE; OPTIMALITY THEORY

Padhraic Smyth
University of California, Irvine
HIDDEN MARKOV MODELS

Elizabeth Spelke
Massachusetts Institute of Technology
INFANT COGNITION

Dan Sperber
Centre de Recherche en Epistémologie Appliquée, Ecole Polytechnique
CULTURE, COGNITION, AND EVOLUTION INTRODUCTION; METAREPRESENTATION

Larry Squire
VA Medical Center and University of California, San Diego
MEMORY, HUMAN NEUROPSYCHOLOGY

Edward Stabler
University of California, Los Angeles
FORMAL GRAMMARS

Robert Stalnaker
Massachusetts Institute of Technology
LOGICAL OMNISCIENCE, PROBLEM OF; PROPOSITIONAL ATTITUDES

Terrence R. Stanford
Wake Forest University School of Medicine
MULTISENSORY INTEGRATION

Jason C. Stanley
Cornell University
FREGE, GOTTLOB; LOGICAL FORM, ORIGINS OF

Mark Steedman
University of Pennsylvania
CATEGORIAL GRAMMAR

Lisa Stefanacci
University of California, San Diego
AMYGDALA, PRIMATE

Barry E. Stein
Wake Forest University School of Medicine
MULTISENSORY INTEGRATION

Edward Stein
Yale University
ETHICS AND EVOLUTION

Kim Sterelny
Victoria University of Wellington
EVOLUTION; LANGUAGE OF THOUGHT

Robert J. Sternberg
Yale University
INTELLIGENCE

Stephen Stich
Rutgers University
ELIMINATIVE MATERIALISM

Petra Stoerig
Heinrich-Heine-Universität, Düsseldorf
BLINDSIGHT

Martin Stokhof
University of Amsterdam
DYNAMIC SEMANTICS

Gene R. Stoner
Salk Institute
TRANSPARENCY

Claudia Strauss
Duke University
MOTIVATION AND CULTURE

Peter L. Strick
VA Medical Center and SUNY Health Science Center at Syracuse
BASAL GANGLIA

Ted Supalla
University of Rochester
SIGN LANGUAGES

Richard S. Sutton
University of Massachusetts, Amherst
REINFORCEMENT LEARNING

David Swinney
University of California, San Diego
APHASIA

Paula Tallal
Rutgers University, Newark
LANGUAGE IMPAIRMENT, DEVELOPMENTAL

Michael K. Tanenhaus
University of Rochester
AMBIGUITY

Michael Tarr
Brown University
MENTAL ROTATION

Austin Tate
AIAI, University of Edinburgh
PLANNING

Richard Tees
University of British Columbia
PENFIELD, WILDER

Davida Teller
University of Washington
PSYCHOPHYSICS

Paul Thagard
University of Waterloo
EXPLANATION; INDUCTION

Joy Thomas
IBM T. J. Watson Research Center
INFORMATION THEORY

Richard F. Thompson
University of Southern California
CONDITIONING AND THE BRAIN; LASHLEY, KARL S.

Randy Thornhill
University of New Mexico
SEXUAL ATTRACTION, EVOLUTIONARY PSYCHOLOGY OF

John Tienson
University of Memphis
RULES AND REPRESENTATIONS

Michael Tomasello
Max Planck Institute for Evolutionary Anthropology
COMPARATIVE PSYCHOLOGY

John Tooby
University of California, Santa Barbara
EVOLUTIONARY PSYCHOLOGY

Michael Tooley
University of Colorado, Boulder
CAUSATION
Christina Toren
Brunel University
MALINOWSKI, BRONISLAW
Almeida Jacqueline Toribio
University of California, Santa Barbara
CODESWITCHING
Saul Traiger
Occidental College
HUME, DAVID
Lisa Travis
McGill University
HEAD MOVEMENT
Colwyn Trevarthen
University of Edinburgh
INTERSUBJECTIVITY; SPERRY, ROGER WOLCOTT
Endel Tulving
Rotman Research Institute of Baycrest Centre, Toronto
EPISODIC VS. SEMANTIC MEMORY
Kamil Ugurbil
University of Minnesota
MAGNETIC RESONANCE IMAGING
Paul Utgoff
University of Massachusetts, Amherst
DECISION TREES
Tim van Gelder
University of Melbourne
DISTRIBUTED VS. LOCAL REPRESENTATION; DYNAMIC APPROACHES
TO COGNITION
Robert van Gulick
Syracuse University
SELF-KNOWLEDGE
Karen van Hoek
University of Michigan
COGNITIVE LINGUISTICS
Kurt VanLehn
University of Pittsburgh
AI AND EDUCATION
J. William Vaughan
Wake Forest University School of Medicine
MULTISENSORY INTEGRATION
Patrizia Violi
University of Bologna
SEMIOTICS AND COGNITION
Barbara Von Eckardt
University of Nebraska, Lincoln
MENTAL REPRESENTATION
Jacques Vonèche
University of Geneva
PIAGET, JEAN
Chris Wallace
Monash University
MINIMUM DESCRIPTION LENGTH
Mark T. Wallace
Wake Forest University School of Medicine
MULTISENSORY INTEGRATION
Gregory Ward
Northwestern University
PRAGMATICS
Edward Wasserman
University of Iowa
BEHAVIORISM

Bruce H. Weber
California State University, Fullerton
SELF-ORGANIZING SYSTEMS
Michael P. Wellman
University of Michigan
MULTIAGENT SYSTEMS; UTILITY THEORY
James V. Wertsch
Washington University in St. Louis
VYGOTSKY, LEV SEMENOVICH
Kenneth Wexler
Massachusetts Institute of Technology
INNATENESS OF LANGUAGE; SYNTAX, ACQUISITION OF
Harry A. Whitaker
Northern Michigan University
BROCA, PAUL
Geoffrey M. White
University of Hawaii
ETHNOPSYCHOLOGY
Stephen White
Tufts University
NARROW CONTENT; SELF
Andrew Whiten
University of St. Andrews
MACHIAVELLIAN INTELLIGENCE HYPOTHESIS
George C. Williams
State University of New York, Stony Brook
ALTRUISM
Edwin Williams
Princeton University
SYNTAX
Deirdre Wilson
University College London
RELEVANCE AND RELEVANCE THEORY
Margaret D. Wilson
Princeton University (deceased)
DESCARTES, RENÉ
Robert A. Wilson
University of Illinois, Urbana-Champaign
PHILOSOPHY INTRODUCTION; INDIVIDUALISM
Marc Wittmann
Ludwig-Maximilians-Universität, Munich
TIME IN THE MIND
Marty G. Woldorff
*University of Texas Health Science Center at San Antonio and
Leibniz Institute for Neurobiology at Magdeburg*
AUDITORY ATTENTION
Ellen Woolford
University of Massachusetts, Amherst
GRAMMATICAL RELATIONS
Richard Wurtman
Massachusetts Institute of Technology
NEUROTRANSMITTERS
Steven L. Youngentob
SUNY Health Science Center at Syracuse
SMELL
Lofti Zadeh
University of California, Berkeley
FUZZY LOGIC
Thomas Ede Zimmermann
Universität Stuttgart
CONTEXT AND POINT OF VIEW
Stuart Zola
VA Medical Center, San Diego
MEMORY, ANIMAL STUDIES

Name Index

Subject Index

A

Aboutness, 1
Absolute conic, 803
Abstraction of numbers, 36
ABSTRIPS, 653
Accommodation, 227
Accurate understanding, 46
Acetylcholine, 605
A-chains, 822
Acheulean industry, 828
Acoustic vs. articulatory, 793
Acoustic-phonetic approach, 790
Acquisition, formal theories of, cvii, 1–3, 324, 342
  computational learning theory, 1
  language acquisition, 1
Acquisition of language, 3
Acquisition of phonology, 3
Acquisition of semantics, 3
Acquisition of syntax, 3
ACT*, 125
ACT-based computational models of cognition, 261
Action, 3
Activity theory, 126, 768
Adaptation, 18, 291, 647
Adaptation and adaptationism, xxxiv, xxxv, 3–4, 13, 39, 113, 151, 211, 219, 286, 293, 296, 383, 738, 752
  evolutionary psychology and, 3
Adaptation-level theory, 472
Adaptive consistency, 196
Affordance of falling, 633
Affordances, xlvi, xlviii, cxxiii, cxxviii, 4–6, 130, 255, 256, 346, 350, 416, 634, 679, 733, 746, 753, 786
Agency, 6
Aging and cognition, xlvii, xlviii, lxviii, 6–7, 9, 64, 120, 602
Aging and memory, 7
Aging, memory, and the brain, lxvi, lxvii, 7–9, 120, 279, 395, 522, 572, 602, 889
Agnosia, 615
Akaike's information criterion (AIC), 628
Algorithm, lxxiii, lxxv, xcii, xciv, 11–12, 117, 137, 155, 156, 163, 186, 195, 245, 246, 337, 357, 373, 406, 497, 539, 836
A-Life, 12, 37
Allostatic load, 807
ALOPEX, 836
Alpha-beta algorithm, 539
Altruism, cxiii, cxiv, 4, 12–14, 201, 219, 285, 297, 417, 783
Alvinn system, 724
Alzheimer's disease, 469, 606, 876
Ambiguity, c, ci, 14–15, 135, 231, 336, 514, 695, 740, 750, 861
Ambler, 881
American Association on Mental Retardation (AAMR), 530
American Psychological Association (APA), 530
American Sign Language, 669, 757, 758
Amodal completion, 817
Amygdala, 8, 184, 269, 270, 271, 493, 518, 522, 523, 602, 613, 806, 835
  primate, lxvi, lxvii, 15–17, 311, 618, 666

Analog retrieval by constraint satisfaction (ARCS), 19
Analogical constraint-mapping engine (ACME), 18
Analogical inference, 400
Analogy, xliv, xlv, xlvii, xlviii, 17–20, 29, 100, 105, 158, 301, 314, 399, 400, 409, 461, 526, 528, 537, 538, 730, 732, 763
  concepts, 17
  learning, 17
  mapping, 18
  mental models, 17
Anaphora, xcii, xciv, 20–22, 86, 232, 248, 360, 364, 487, 549, 622, 666, 718, 740, 819, 825
  binding and, 20
  covaluation and, 20
  procedural restrictions and, 21
  pronoun resolution procedures and, 20
  variable binding and, 21
Animal cognition, 22
Animal communication, xviii, cvi, cxiii, cxiv, 22–24, 33, 53, 133, 150, 254, 289, 415, 438, 478, 775, 780, 781
Animal navigation, xxxv, xl, 22, 24–26, 133, 136, 382, 460, 553, 567, 594, 770, 780, 786
  general abilities, 26
  neural networks, 26–28, 136, 382, 460, 594
Animal studies, 270, 308
Animism, xlvii, xlviii, cxxi, cxxii, 28–30, 648
  adults and, 29
  and naive biology, 28
Animistic thinking, 29
Anomalous dualism, 30
Anomalous monism, xxiv, xxv, 30–31, 65, 268, 276, 547, 561, 646, 684, 691, 699, 713
ANOVA model, 106
Anthropology, 31
Anthropomorphism, 28
Antirealism, 31
Anytime algorithms, 539
Aphasia, lxvii, lxviii, cvi, cvii, 31–32, 97, 203, 251, 330, 343, 354, 442, 447, 449, 469, 643, 756, 841, 857
  Broca's area and, 31
  connectionist/associationist approaches to, 31
  history of the field, 31
  link between types, 31
  use of behavioral techniques and, 32
Applied psychology, 96
Apraxia, 369
Arc consistency algorithm, 195
Arc pair grammar, 718
Archaeology, 32
Architecture, 33
Aristotle, xxxii, lii, lxxxi
Art, 33
Articulation, xci, xciv, 33–35, 235, 636, 639, 688, 788, 793
  methodologies for studying, 33
  as primary means of communication, 33
  serial order and, 33
  as suitable topic for cognitive science, 33
  theories of, 34
Articulatory implementation, 643
Articulatory phonological planning, 643
Artifacts, 35
  and civilization, cxxiv, 32, 35–37, 118, 127, 829

Artificial intelligence (AI), 37, 186, 294, 376
  approach, 791
  and education, xlvii, xlviii, 9–10, 37, 131, 432, 573
Artificial life, xxxiv, xxxv, lxxxiv, 12, 37–39, 75, 154, 295, 329, 471, 738, 878
  as a cognitive science, 38
  emergence and, 38
  as mathematical biology, 37
  methodology of, 38
  and self-organizing systems, 37
  technological applications of, 39
  theoretical focus of, 37
Artificial neural networks (ANNs), 157
Artificial scotoma, 600
Artificial vision systems, 613
Aspartic acid, 606
Aspect, 39
Asperger syndrome, 59
Associationist theory, 128
Associative learning, 460
Assumption of pure insertion, 657
ATN hold registers, 102
Attention, xxxv, xxxix, lxiv, lxv, 5, 7, 32, 39–41, 43, 50, 63, 68, 78, 85, 95, 124, 128, 130, 135, 167, 176, 192, 194, 249, 263, 269, 275, 307, 402, 420, 423, 448, 460, 474, 533, 546, 567, 619, 753, 766, 773, 834, 842, 845, 867, 869, 873
  human brain, and, 40
  neurobiology as active topic of current research, 40
  origins of information processing, 39
  selective activation of goals, 40
  selective perception in, 39
  setting and switching, 40
  study of, 40
Attention in the animal brain, xxxv, lxiv, lxv, 41–43, 45, 51, 194, 519
  capacity limitation in, 42
  dispersal of visual information, 42
  dorsal and ventral streams in, 42
  dynamic process of, 41
  early activation of, 43
  field of focal attention and, 42
Attention in the human brain, xxxv, lxiv, lxv, 43, 43–46, 51, 64, 96, 194, 264, 308, 565, 619, 842, 867, 869
  cognitive studies and, 44
  executive system in, 44
  imaging techniques and, 44
  PET studies and, 44
  voluntary control, 44
Attribution theory, cxxv, cxxviii, 46–48, 234, 777, 778, 805
Audition, xxxix, 48–50, 56, 58, 235, 254, 366, 368, 633, 691, 757, 775, 789, 826
  hearing range in humans, 48
  physiological process of, 48
  sound characteristics in, 48
  tonotopic organization of, 48
Auditory attention, lxiv, lxv, 41, 45, 50–52, 56, 58, 64, 263, 446, 836
  definition of, 50
  event-related potential studies of, 50–51
  neural mechanisms and, 50
  positron emission tomography studies and, 51
  selection theories of, 50